A MATTER OF
FACT

Acknowledgements

Special thanks are extended to
Congressman Sander Levin (D-Michigan) and
Eastern Michigan University Library
for providing access to U.S. Congressional hearings.

A MATTER OF FACT

Statements Containing Statistics on Current Social, Economic, and Political Issues

27

July-December 1997

Pierian Press
1997

ISBN 0-87650-376-8

The Pierian Press
P.O. Box 1808
Ann Arbor, MI 48106
(800) 678-2435
fax (734) 434-6409

INTRODUCTION

The selected full-text excerpts in *A Matter of Fact* encompass statistical statements related to current social, economic, political, health, and environmental public policy issues.

- Approximately 15 percent of the excerpts come from congressional hearings, where expert witnesses attempt to influence the perspectives of senators and representatives.

- Another 17 percent come from the *Congressional Record*, reflecting the statements of senators and representatives, which are constructed to influence colleagues or address the concerns of constituents back home.

- The remaining excerpts reflect the editorial content of sources designed to inform and influence the general public and/or special interest groups, who, in turn, elect public policy makers to support their values and objectives.

A Matter of Fact is designed for use on three levels:

- First, *A Matter of Fact* contains engaging information about the world and the human condition. Many people may benefit from browsing through the excerpts to gain a statistical perspective of the issues facing the United States and the world.

- Second, *A Matter of Fact* functions as a handy, current source of statistics and facts, much like an almanac. However, unlike an almanac or other statistical sources, *A Matter of Fact* presents the facts and statistics that have been selected by writers and speakers to influence others, in their own words. Writers of papers and speeches seeking brief, pertinent statements may wish to consult specific subject headings to find appropriate information (and arguments).

- Third, and most importantly, *A Matter of Fact* helps users locate sources containing the information they seek. The substantive, full-text statistical excerpts indicate the kind of related information likely to be found in the sources from which the excerpts are taken. *A Matter of Fact* entries always cite the source from which an excerpt is derived. Furthermore, if a statement included in a congressional hearing, periodical, or newspaper article is based on a book or recent study, the editors cite that book or study also. If the source is a resource available on the Internet, the editors provide the Uniform Resource Locators (URLs) that link to that resource. Thus, *A Matter of Fact* acts as a bibliography as well as a primary resource of facts that includes links to "virtual full text." (Readers should note that, occasionally, the focus of a particular entry may not match the primary focus of its source article. This can be determined in most cases by comparing the title of the article to the content of the excerpt.)

Content

This volume of *A Matter of Fact* provides excerpts from the *Congressional Record*, congressional hearings, the *Debates* of both the House of Commons and Senate of the Canadian Parliament, the *Debates* of the House of Commons of the British Parliament, numerous World Wide Web and gopher sites, and almost 400 newspapers and periodicals published and/or received during 1997. The statistical excerpts contained in *A Matter of Fact* generally reflect topics and subjects of high current, public policy interest. The contents of *A Matter of Fact* is governed by public policy issues facing the federal government, as well as by news coverage and recent scholarship.

Arrangement

Entries are grouped under Library of Congress subject headings, which are alphabetized as follows: 1) headings with no punctuation, 2) headings with subtopics set off by hyphens, and 3) inverted headings with commas. For example:

Education
Education--Finance
Education--United States
Education, Higher

Readers should be aware that in some subject headings geographic locations precede topics. For example:

Africa--Economic conditions
France--Religion

The editors recommend searching for specific topics of interest as well as for particular places.

Cross-References

Two types of cross-references are included in this volume. The first type includes cross-references to excerpts contained in this volume. These point to precise subject headings or to related topics. The second type is a cross-reference to excerpts that appear in volume twenty-six of *A Matter of Fact*. The latter cross-reference consists of the code "(v26)" following a subject heading. It is the policy of *A Matter of Fact* to provide cross-references to the most recent published volume.

Errors

The editors have encountered statistics and statements that may contain errors. Some excerpts contradict one another—for example, in volume one of *A Matter of Fact* conflicting dates were given for the construction of the first nuclear bomb and for the delivery dates of B-52 bombers. The editors have not resolved these discrepancies; however, the publication date of each article sometimes explains seemingly contradictory statements. The editors recognize that the content of *A Matter of Fact* is no more accurate than the sources cited.

Readers should use these statements with care and with critical skepticism, verifying facts and figures in alternative sources whenever possible (*A Matter of Fact* facilitates this cross-verification by frequently presenting two or more entries on the same subject from different sources) and checking the dates of sources to find which are the most current. Because the editors of *A Matter of Fact* excerpt statements as they are presented in their original sources, *A Matter of Fact* both encourages and aids critical reading and critical thinking, skills we should develop and apply to all sources at all times. Statistical statements are, obviously, only as accurate as the methods used to compile the statistics and subsequently interpret them. The editors of *A Matter of Fact* recommend that readers consult the sources cited for each entry in order to establish the original context as well as the perspectives of the author(s) and publication.

Sources

The newspapers and journals monitored for this volume represent, for the most part, major sources generally available in libraries. When initial publications were selected for this service, consideration was given to the accessibility of those sources. Increasingly, less-accessible sources have been introduced to *A Matter of Fact*, with the recognition that the full text excerpts can be used to gain perspectives of hard-to-locate sources, even when those sources can't be consulted directly. Nevertheless, the core of this publication—and one of its strengths—is the coverage of many sources that are readily available, many simply by entering the Uniform Resource Locators (URLs) attached to *A Matter of Fact* records.

A list of Internet sites monitored for this print volume follows the list of print sources covered. The list of print sources also provides URLs for periodicals that are available on the Internet. URLs that facilitate access to full-text resources on the Internet follow the records where they apply.

Abbreviations

The editors use standard abbreviations for countries, states, territories, provinces and measurements. The following abbreviations and acronyms are also used:

Admin.	Administration
AFDC	Aid to Families with Dependent Children
AFL-CIO	American Federation of Labor and Congress of Industrial Organizations
Approp.	Appropriation(s)
Assoc.	Association
Asst.	Assistant
CDC	Centers for Disease Control
CEO	Chief Executive Officer
CIA	Central Intelligence Agency
COO	Chief Operating Officer
Corp.	Corporation
Dept.	Department
Dev.	Development
Dir.	Director
Div.	Division
EC	European Community
EEC	European Economic Community
EPA	Environmental Protection Agency
EU	European Union
Exec.	Executive
FBI	Federal Bureau of Investigation
FDA	Food and Drug Administration
FY	Fiscal Year
GATT	General Agreement on Tariffs and Trade
GDP	Gross Domestic Product
GNP	Gross National Product
GOP	Grand Old Party
Gov.	Governor
GPO	Government Printing Office
HMO	Health Maintenance Organization(s)
ILO	International Labor Organization
Inc.	Incorporated
Inst.	Institute
IRS	Internal Revenue Service
MP	Member of Parliament
NAFTA	North American Free Trade Agreement
NATO	North Atlantic Treaty Organization
NASA	National Aeronautics and Space Administration
OECD	Organization for Economic Cooperation and Development
Org.	Organization(s)
PC	Personal Computer
Pres.	President
Rep.	Representative
Sec.	Secretary
Sen.	Senator
Sr.	Senior
UN	United Nations
UNICEF	United Nations Children's Fund
USDA	United States Department of Agriculture
WHO	World Health Organization

How to Use *A Matter of Fact*

Quickly locate facts on current topics.

For example:

Cross-reference

Facts

WEATHER (v26)
see also CLOUDINESS; LIGHTNING
According to the National Climatic Data Center, "so far this century, extreme weather events have increased by 20 percent. Annual precipitation is up 6 percent since 1900, and total winter precipitation is up 8 percent....Last winter, a couple of major blizzards buried California's Sierra Nevada, but a New Year's warm spell melted much of it, resulting in massive flooding in the Central Valley, causing 36 deaths and billions of dollars in damage....A Japanese government study predicts a 60 percent increase in the number of hurricanes hitting the eastern United States." (p40)
Rauber, Paul, "Heat Wave: Extreme Weather." Sierra v82 n5 Sep-Oct 1997. p40-41. (ISSN0161-7362)

Easily locate sources of further information.

See also this subject in volume 26 of AMOF

For example:

Subject

Sources

URLS

YOUTH--UNITED STATES--ALCOHOL USE (v26)
In the U.S., "two out of every three teenagers who drink report that they can buy their own alcoholic beverages....Junior and senior high school students drink 35 percent of all wine coolers and consume 1.1 billion cans of beer a year....Alcohol is a factor in the three leading causes of death for 15- to 24-year-olds: accidents, homicides, and suicides. In approximately 50 to 60 percent of youth suicides, alcohol is a factor....In 1995, there were 1,666 alcohol-related fatalities of children between the ages of 15 and 19....According to a WASHINGTON POST article from July 17, 1997, entitled, 'The Corner Store,' the District outranks every State with regard to deaths and diseases related to alcohol. In addition, according to Joye M. Carter, chief D.C. medical examiner, in 1993, 50 percent of the homicide victims had consumed alcohol." (pS10215)
Byrd, Robert C. (Sen.-W.Va.). "District of Columbia Appropriations Act, 1998." Congressional Record. Daily ed. v143 n133 30 Sep 1997. pS10211-10216. section/page-level access: <http://thomas.loc.gov/cgi-bin/query/R?r105:FLD001:S10215:> (ISSN0363-7239). (X1.1A.105/1).

Periodicals Covered by *A Matter of Fact*, Volume Twenty-Seven

ABA Journal
American Bar Association
750 N. Lake Shore Dr.
Chicago, IL 60611
http://www.abanet.org/

AFL-CIO News
America@Work
815 16th St., N.W.
Washington, DC 20006
http://www.aflcio.org/

APF Reporter
Alicia Patterson Foundation
101 Pennsylvania Ave., Ste. 1250
Washington, DC 20004
http://www.charm.net/~apfengel/home.html/

Abya Yala News
South and Meso American Indian Information Center
P.O. Box 28703
Oakland, CA 94604

Acres, U.S.A.
10008 E. 60th Terrace
Kansas City, MO 64133

Across the Board
Conference Board Inc.
845 Third Ave.
New York, NY 10022

Adolescence
Libra Publishers, Inc.
4901 Morena Blvd., Ste. 207
San Diego, CA 92117

Africa Recovery
Secretariat Rm. 931
United Nations
New York, NY 10017

Agricultural Outlook
U.S. Dept. of Agriculture
1301 New York Ave., N.W.
Washington, DC 20005-4789
http://www.econ.ag.gov/

Agricultural Research
U.S. Dept. of Agriculture
Rm. 318-A
Federal Building
Hyattsville, MD 20782
http://www.ars.usda.gov/

Alternative Agriculture News
Henry A. Wallace Institute for Alternative Agriculture
9200 Edmonston Rd.
Greenbelt, MD 20700

Alternatives: Social Transformation and Humane Governance
Lynee Rienner Publishers, Inc.
1800 30th St., Ste. 314
Boulder, CO 80301

America
America Press, Inc.
106 W. 56th St.
New York, NY 10019

American Demographics
108 N. Cayuga St.
Ithaca, NY 14850
http://www.demographics.com/

American Fire Journal
9072 Artesia Blvd., Ste. 7
Bellflower, CA 90706-6299

American Health
28 West 23rd St.
New York, NY 10010

American Journal of Alternative Agriculture
Henry A. Wallace Institute for Alternative Agriculture
9200 Edmonston Rd.
Greenbelt, MD 20700

American Journalism Review
College of Journalism
University of Maryland
College Park, MD 20742

American Rehabilitation
Mary E. Switzer Bldg., Rm. 3212
330 C St., S.W.
Washington, DC 20202

American Scholar
Phi Beta Kappa Society
1811 Q St., N.W.
Washington, DC 20009

American School Board Journal
National School Boards Association
1680 Duke St.
Alexandria, VA 22314

American Scientist
Sigma Xi, The Scientific Research Society
P.O. Box 13975
Research Triangle Park, NC 27709
http://www.amsci.org/amsci/

Amicus Journal
40 W. 20 St.
New York, NY 10011
http://www/nrdc.org/nrdc/

Anglican Digest
Society for Promoting and Encouraging the Arts and Knowledge
100 Skyline Dr.
Eureka Springs, AR 72632-9705

Animal Sheltering
(formerly Shelter Sense)
Humane Society of the U.S.
2100 L St., N.W.
Washington, DC 20037

Animals
350 S. Huntington Ave.
Boston, MA 02130

Ann Arbor News
340 E. Huron
Ann Arbor, MI 48104

Appalachia
Appalachian Regional Commission
1666 Connecticut Ave., N.W.
Washington, DC 20235

Aramco World
Aramco Services Company
9009 West Loop South
Houston, TX 77096

Arctic
Arctic Institute of North America
MLT 11th Floor
University of Calgary
2500 University Dr., N.W.
Calgary, AB T2N IN4
Canada

Armed Forces & Society
Transaction Periodicals Consortium
Rutgers State University
Department 3092
New Brunswick, NJ 08901-1265

Asia-Pacific Population & Policy
Asia-Pacific Population Research Reports
East-West Population Institute
Program on Population
Center for Cultural and Technical Interchange Between East and West, Inc.
1777 East-West Rd.
Honolulu, HI 96848
http://www.ewc.hawaii.edu/

BioScience
American Institute of Biological Sciences
1401 Wilson Blvd.
Arlington, VA 22209
http://www2.aibs.org/aibs/bioscience.html/

Boston Review
Boston Critic, Inc.
33 Harrison Ave.
Boston, MA 02111
http://polisci_mac_2.mit.edu/BostonReview/BostonReview.html/

Bulletin of Concerned Asian Scholars
3239 9th St.
Boulder, CO 80304-2112
http://csf.colorado.edu/bcas/bcashome.html/

Bulletin of the Atomic Scientists
Educational Foundation for Nuclear Science
6042 S. Kimbark Ave.
Chicago, IL 60637
http://neog.com/atomic/

Business and the Environment
Cutter Information Corporation
37 Broadway
Arlington, MA 02174-5539

California Community Care News
P.O. Box 163270
Sacramento, CA 95816-9270
http://members.aol.com/CRCAC/index.html/

California Journal
2101 K St.
Sacramento, CA 95816

California Lawyer
Daily Journal Corporation
915 E. First St.
Los Angeles, CA 90012

Canadian Geographic
Royal Canadian Geographical Society
39 McArthur Ave.
Vanier, ON K1L 8L7
Canada
http://www.cangeo.ca/

Canadian Parliamentary Debates
Canada Communications Group—Publishing
Public Works and Government Services Canada
Ottawa, ON K1A OS9
Canada
http://www.parl.gc.ca/

Capitalism, Nature, Socialism
Center for Political Ecology
P.O. Box 8467
Santa Cruz, CA 95061

Celebrate Life
American Life League, Inc.
P.O. Box 1350
Stafford, VA 22555

Center Focus
Center of Concern
3700 13th St., N.E.
Washington, DC 20017
http://www.coc.org/coc/

Center for Rural Affairs Newsletter
P.O. Box 405
Walthill, NE 68067

Change
Heldref Publications
1319 18th St., N.W.
Washington, DC 20036-1802

ChemEcology
Chemical Manufacturers Association
1300 Wilson Blvd.
Arlington, VA 22209

China Economic Review
Dept. of Economics
414 Uris Hall
Cornell University
Ithaca, NY 14853

China Review
The Great Britain-China Centre
15 Belgrave Sq.
London SW1X 8PS
England

Choices
UN Development Program
1 United Nations Plaza
New York, NY 10017

Christian Century
Christian Century Foundation
407 S. Dearborn St.
Chicago, IL 60605

The Christian Science Monitor
Christian Science Publishing Society
One Norway St.
Boston, MA 02115
http://csmonitor.com/

Christian Social Action
General Board of Church and Society
United Methodist Church
100 Maryland Ave., N.E.
Washington, DC 20002

Chronicles
Rockford Institute
934 North Main St.
Rockford, IL 61103

Church & State
Americans United for Separation of Church and State
1816 Jefferson Place, N.W.
Washington, DC 20036
http://www.netplexgroup.com/americansunited/

Citizen Airman
Headquarters Air Force Reserve
Office of Public Affairs
155 2nd St.
Robins AFB, GA 31098-1635

Clean Water Action News
1320 18th St., N.W.
Suite 300
Washington, DC 20036-1811

Clearing House
Heldref Publications
1319 18th St., N.W.
Washington, DC 20036-1802

Climate Alert
324 4th St., N.E.
Washington, DC 20016

Commonweal
Commonweal Publishing Co., Inc.
15 Dutch St.
New York, NY 10038

Community Change
Center for Community Change
1000 Wisconsin Ave., N.W.
Washington, DC 20007

Community Mental Health Journal
Human Sciences Press, Inc.
233 Spring Street
New York, NY 10013-1578

Community Service Newsletter
P.O. Box 243
Yellow Springs, OH 45387

Competitiveness Review
P.O. Box 1658
Indiana, PA 15705

Congressional Record
Government Printing Office
Washington, DC 20402
http://thomas.loc.gov/cgi-bin/query/

Criminal Law Forum
Rutgers University School of Law
5th & Penn Sts.
Camden, NJ 08102

Current History
Current History, Inc.
4225 Main St.
Philadelphia, PA 19127
http://www.currenthistory.com/

Currents in Theology and Mission
Lutheran School of Theology
1100 E. 55th St.
Chicago, IL 60615

DISAM Journal
Defense Institute of Security
Assistance Management
2335 7th St.
Wright-Patterson AFB, OH 45433-7803

DOE This Month
U.S. Dept. of Energy
U.S. Government Printing Office
Washington, DC 20402

Defense 97
American Forces Information
Service
1735 N. Lynn St., Rm. 210
Arlington, VA 22209-2086

Defense Monitor
Center for Defense Information
1500 Massachusetts Ave., N.W.
Washington, DC 20005

Detroit News and Free Press
615 W. Lafayette
Detroit, MI 48231
http://www.detnews.com/
http://www.freep.com/

Deutschland
Frankfurter Societaets-Druckerei
GmbH
Frankenalle 71-81
Postfach 100801
6000 Frankfurt a.M. 1, Germany
http://www.government.de/

Dispute Resolution Journal
Dispute Resolution Times
American Arbitration Association
140 W. 51 St.
New York, NY 10020

Dissent
Foundation for the Study of
Independent Social Ideas, Inc.
521 5th Ave., Ste. 1700
New York, NY 10017

Dollars and Sense
Economic Affairs Bureau, Inc.
38 Union Square, Rm. 14
Somerville, MA 02143
http://www.igc.apc.org/dollars/

EDF Letter
Environmental Defense Fund
257 Park Ave., S.
New York, NY 10010

ERS Information
U.S. Dept. of Agriculture
Rm. 228
1301 New York Ave., N.W.
Washington, DC 20005-4788
http://www.econ.ag.gov/

Earth Island Journal
300 Broadway #28
San Francisco, CA 94133
http://www.earthisland.org/ei/

Ecologist
Ecosystems Ltd.
Agriculture House
Bath Rd.
Sturminster Newton, Dorset DT10 1DU
England

Ecos
Commonwealth Scientific and
Industrial Research Organization
P.O. Box 89
E. Melbourne, Vic 3002 Australia
http://www.publish.csiro.au/

Endangered Species Bulletin
U.S. Dept. of the Interior
Fish and Wildlife Service
Washington, DC 20240
http://www.fws.gov/~r9endspp/endspp.html/

Endangered Species Update
School of Natural Resources and
Environment
University of Michigan
Ann Arbor, MI 48109-1115
http://www.umich.edu/~esupdate

Energy Studies Review
McMaster Institute for Energy
Studies
McMaster University
Hamilton, ON L8S 4M4
Canada

Engineer Update
CEPA-C
Washington, DC 20314-1000
http://www.hq.usace.army.mil/cepa/cepa.htm/

Environment
Heldref Publications
1319 18th St., N.W.
Washington, DC 20036-1802

Environment Watch: Western
Europe
Cutter Information Corporation
37 Broadway
Arlington, MA 02174-5539

Environmental Forum
Environmental Law Institute
1616 P St., N.W.
Washington, DC 20036

Environmental Health Monthly
Citizens Clearinghouse for
Hazardous Wastes, Inc.
P.O. Box 6806
Falls Church, VA 22040

Environmental Health Perspectives
U.S. National Institute of
Environmental Health Sciences
P.O. Box 12233
Research Triangle Park, NC 27709
http://ehpnet1.niehs.nih.gov/

Environmental Law
Northwestern School of Law
Lewis and Clark College
10015 S.W. Terwilliger Blvd.
Portland, OR 97219

Environmental Politics
Frank Cass and Co., Ltd.
Gainsborough House
11 Gainsborough Rd.
London E11 1RS
England

Environmental Values
White Horse Press
10 High St.
Knapwell, Cambridge CB3 8NR
England

European Security
Frank Cass & Co. Ltd.
Newbury House
900 Eastern Ave.
London IG2 7HH
England

Exceptional Children
Council for Exceptional Children
1920 Association Dr.
Reston, VA 22091-1589

EXTRA!
Extra! Update
Fairness and Accuracy in Reporting
(FAIR)
130 W. 25th St.
New York, NY 10001
http://www.fair.org/fair/

FBI Law Enforcement Bulletin
U.S. Federal Bureau of
Investigation
10th and Pennsylvania Ave., N.W.
Washington, DC 20535

Families in Society
11700 W. Lake Park Dr.
Milwaukee, WI 53224

Federal Election Commission
Record
U.S. Federal Election Commission
999 E St., N.W.
Washington, DC 20463
http://www.fec.gov/

Federal Probation
Probation Division
Administrative Office of the U.S.
Courts
Washington, DC 20544

Federal Reserve Bank of Atlanta
Economic Update
Federal Reserve Bank of Atlanta
Financial Update
Federal Reserve Bank of Atlanta
Regional Update
Public Affairs Dept.
Federal Reserve Bank of Atlanta
104 Marietta St., N.W.
Atlanta, GA 30303-2713
http://www.frbatlanta.org/

Federal Reserve Bank of Boston
New England Economic Review
Federal Reserve Bank of Boston
P.O. Box 2076
Boston, MA 02106-2076
http://www.std.com/frbbos/
economic/review.htm/

Federal Reserve Bank of Kansas
City Regional Economic Digest
Federal Reserve Bank of Kansas
City Fed Letter
Federal Reserve Bank of Kansas
City
925 Grand Blvd.
Kansas City, MO 64198-0001
http://www.kc.frb.org/

Federal Reserve Bank of
Minneapolis Fedgazette
Federal Reserve Bank of
Minneapolis
250 Marquette Ave.
Minneapolis, MN 55401-2171
http://woodrow.mpls.frb.fed.us/

Federal Reserve Bank of
Philadelphia Business Review
Dept. of Research and Statistics
10 Independence Mall
Philadelphia, PA 19106-1574
http://phil.frb.org/

Federal Reserve Bank of Richmond
Economic Quarterly
Federal Reserve Bank of Richmond
P.O. Box 27622
Richmond, VA 23261

Federal Reserve Bank of San
Francisco Economic Review
Federal Reserve Bank of
San Francisco
Public Information Dept.
P.O. Box 7702
San Francisco, CA 94120
http://www.frbsf.org/

Federal Reserve Bank of St. Louis
Review
Federal Reserve Bank of St. Louis
Public Information Dept.
P.O. Box 442
St. Louis, MO 63166
http://www.stls.frb.org/

Fellowship
Fellowship of Reconciliation
521 N. Broadway
Nyack, NY 10960
http://www.nonviolence.org/
~nvweb/for/

Fifth Estate
4632 Second Ave.
Detroit, MI 48201

Financial Counseling and Planning
Association for Financial Counseling
and Planning Education
1787 Neil Ave.
Columbus, OH 43210-1295

Florida Naturalist
Florida Audubon Society
460 S.R. 436, Ste. 200
Casselberry, FL 32707

Food First Backgrounder
Food First News and Views
Institute for Food and Development
398 60th St.
Oakland, CA 94618-1212

Food Review
U.S. Dept. of Agriculture, Rm. 228
1301 New York Ave., N.W.
Washington, DC 20005-4789

Ford Foundation Report
Ford Foundation
320 E. 43rd St.
New York, NY 10017
http://www.fordfound.org/

Forecast
American Demographics, Inc.
P.O. Box 68
Ithaca, NY 14851-0068
http://www.demographics.com/

Foreign Affairs
Council on Foreign Relations, Inc.
58 E. 68th St.
New York, NY 10021

Foreign Policy
Carnegie Endowment for
International Peace
2400 N St., N.W.
Washington, DC 20037-1153
http://www.foreignpolicy.com/

Forestry Research West
U.S. Dept. of Agriculture
Forest Service
240 West Prospect Rd.
Fort Collins, CO 80526

Free Inquiry
P.O. Box 5
Buffalo, NY 14215-0005

Freedom (Anarchists Fortnightly)
Freedom Press
84-B Whitechapel, High St.
London, E1 7QX
England
http://www.tao.ca/~freedom/

Freedom Network News
International Society for Individual
Liberty
1800 Market St.
San Francisco, CA 94102

Freedom Today
35 Westminister Bridge Rd.
London SE1 7JB
England

Geotimes
American Geological Institute
4220 King St.
Alexandria, VA 22302-1507
http://www.agiweb.org/agi/geotimes
.html/

Global Environmental Change
Report
Cutter Information Corporation
37 Broadway
Arlington, MA 02174-5539

Government Union Review
Public Services Research
Foundation
1761 Business Center Dr., Ste. 230
Reston, VA 22090-5333

Grist
Practice Program, National Park
Service
1849 C St., N.W.
Room 3643
Washington, DC 20240

Guild Practitioner
P.O. Box 673
Berkeley, CA 94701-0673

Hazardous Substances & Public Health
U.S. Agency for Toxic Substances and Disease Registry
1600 Clifton Rd., N.W.
Mailstop E33
Atlanta, GA 30333

Health Advocate
2639 S. LaCienega Blvd.
Los Angeles, CA 90034

Healthline
830 Menlo Ave., Ste. 100
Menlo Park, CA 94025
http://www.health-line.com/

High Country News
P.O. Box 1090
Paonia, CO 81428
http://www.hcn.org/

Home Education Magazine
P.O. Box 1083
Tonasket, WA 98855

Human Organization
Society for Applied Anthropology
Box 24083
Oklahoma City, OK 73124-0083

Human Quest
Churchman Co.
1074-23rd Ave., N.
St. Petersburg, FL 33704

Human Rights Quarterly
Johns Hopkins University Press
Journals Publishing Division
2715 N. Charles St.
Baltimore, MD 21218-4319

Hydrogen Today
American Hydrogen Association
216 S. Clark Dr., Ste. 103
Tempe, AZ 85281
http://www.getnet.com/charity/aha/

IDB
Inter-American Development Bank
1300 New York Ave., N.W.
Washington, DC 20577
http://www.iadb.org/

IFPRI Report
International Food Policy Research Institute
1200 17th St., N.W.
Washington, DC 20036
http://www.cgiar.org/fpri/

Imprint
National Student Nurses' Association, Inc.
555 W. 57th St.
New York, NY 10019

In These Times
Institute for Public Affairs
2040 N. Milwaukee Ave.
Chicago, IL 60647

Inner Voice
P.O. Box 11615
Eugene, OR 97440
http://www.afsee.org/

International Environmental Affairs
17 1/2 Lebanon
Hanover, NH 03755

International Journal
Canadian Institute of International Affairs
5 Devonshire Place
Toronto, ON M55 2VP
Canada

International Journal of Comparative and Applied Criminal Justice
Wichita State University
Dept. of Administration
Wichita, KS 67208

International Labour Review
ILO Publications
International Labour Office
Geneva 22 CH-1211
Switzerland
http://www.unicc.org/ilo/

Issues in Global Education
American Forum for Global Education
120 Wall St., Ste. 2600
New York, NY 10005

Jerusalem Report
Jerusalem Report Publications Ltd.
22 Rehov Rivlin
Jerusalem 91017
Israel
http://www.jreport.virtual.co.il/

Jewish Currents
Association for Promotion of Jewish Secularism, Inc.
22 E. 17th St., Rm. 601
New York, NY 10003

Journal of Aging Studies
University of Florida
P.O. Box 117330
Gainesville, FL 32611-7330

Journal of Communication
International Communication Association
8140 Burnet Rd.
P.O. Box 9589
Austin, TX 78766

Journal of Democracy
Johns Hopkins University Press
2715 N. Charles St.
Baltimore, MD 21218-4319

Journal of Education for Business
Heldref Publications
1319 18th St., N.W.
Washington, DC 20036-1802

Journal of Energy and Development
International Research Center for Energy and Economic Development
909 14th St., Ste. 201
Boulder, CO 80302

Journal of Environmental Sciences
Science Press
Beijing 100717
China

Journal of General Education
Penn State University Press
820 N. University Drive, Suite C
University Park, PA 16802-3801

Journal of Geography
National Council for Geographic Education
Indiana University of Pennsylvania
Indiana, PA 15705

Journal of Health Politics, Policy & Law
Duke University Press
6697 College Station
Durham, NC 27708

Journal of Interamerican Studies and World Affairs
North-South Center Press
University of Miami
1500 Monza Ave.
Coral Gables, FL 33146-3027

Journal of Peace Research
Sage Publications Ltd.
6 Bonhill St.
London EC2A 4PU
England

Journal of Pesticide Reform
Northwest Coalition for Alternatives to Pesticides
1249 Willamette St.
Eugene, OR 97440
http://www.efn.org/~ncap/

Journal of Public Administration
Education
Dept. of Public Administration
318 Blake Hall
University of Kansas
Lawrence, KS 66045

Journal of Third World Studies
P.O. Box 1232
Americus, GA 31709

Journal of Travel Research
Business Research Division
University of Colorado
Boulder, CO 80309-0420

Journal of Urban Affairs
Urban Affairs Association
Center for Urban and Economic
Research
University of Louisville
Louisville, KY 40292

Kerr Center Newsletter
P.O. Box 588, Hwy 271S
Poteau, OK 74953-0588

Kiwanis
Kiwanis International
3636 Woodview Trace
Indianapolis, IN 46268-3196

Labor Notes
7435 Michigan Ave.
Detroit, MI 48210

Land Stewardship Newsletter
The Land Stewardship Project
14758 Ostlund Trail North
Marine, MN 55047

Left Business Observer
250 W. 85th St.
New York, NY 10024-3217
http://www.panix.com/~dhenwood/
LBO_home.html/

Liberty
Liberty Foundation
1619 Lincoln St., 1st Fl.
Port Townsend, WA 98368

Library of Congress Information
Bulletin
Office of Public Affairs
101 Independence Ave., S.E.
Washington, DC 20540-1610
gopher://marvel.loc.gov/11/loc/
pubs/lcib/

Low Intensity Conflict & Law
Enforcement
Frank Cass & Co. Ltd.
900 Eastern Ave.
London IG2 7HH
England
http://www.frankcass.com/

Maclean's
Maclean Hunter Ltd.
Magazine Division
Maclean Hunter Bldg.
777 Bay St.
Toronto, ON M5W 1A7
Canada
http://www.canoe.ca/macleans/

Mankind Quarterly
Institute for the Study of Man Inc.
P.O. Box 34070, N.W.
Washington, DC 20043

Marine Corps Gazette
Marine Corps Association
P.O. Box 1775
Quantico, VA 22134

Maritime Newsletter
Room 510
815 16th St., N.W.
Washington, DC 20006

Middle East Policy
Middle East Policy Council
1730 M St., N.W., Ste. 512
Washington, DC 20036

Middle East Report
Middle East Research and
Information Project
1500 Massachusetts Ave., N.W.,
Ste. 119
Washington, DC 20005

Migration World
Center for Migration Studies
209 Flagg Place
Staten Island, NY 10304-1199

Modern Medicine
7500 Old Oak Blvd.
Cleveland, OH 44130
http://www.modernmedicine.com/

Monthly Energy Review
U.S. Energy Information
Administration
1000 Independence Ave., S.W.
Washington, DC 20585
http://www.eia.doe.gov/

Monthly Review
Monthly Review Foundation
122 W. 27th St.
New York, NY 10001

Mother Jones
Foundation for National Progress
1663 Mission St., 2nd Fl.
San Francisco, CA 94103
http://www.motherjones.com/

Municipal World
Municipal World Inc.
Box 399
St. Thomas, ON N5P 3V3
Canada
http://www.municipalworld.com/

NASSP Bulletin
National Association of Secondary
School Principals
1904 Association Dr.
Reston, VA 22091
http://www.nassp.org/

NATO Review
Atlantic Council of the United States
1616 H St., N.W.
Washington, DC 20006
http://www.nato.int/docu/review/

NCLC Energy & Utility Update
National Consumer Law Center,
Inc.
18 Tremont St.
Boston, MA 02108

NCMC Marine Bulletin
National Coalition for Marine
Conservation
3 West Market St.
Leesburg, VA 22075

NSTA Reports!
National Science Teachers
Association
1840 Wilson Blvd.
Arlington, VA 22201

Nation
The Nation Company, Inc.
72 5th Ave.
New York, NY 10011
http://www.TheNation.com/

Nature Conservancy
1815 N. Lynn St.
Arlington, VA 22209
http://www.tnc.org/

Naval War College Review
Code 32
Naval War College
686 Cushing Rd.
Newport, RI 02841-1207
http://www.usnwc.edu/nwc/press.
htm/

Networker
Alliance for the Wild Rockies
P.O. Box 8731
Missoula, MT 59807
http://www.wildrockies.org/awr/

New Leader
American Conference on
International Affairs, Inc.
275 Seventh Ave.
New York, NY 10001

New Left Review
6 Meard St.
London W1V 3HR
England

New Physician
American Medical Student Association
1902 Association Dr.
Reston, VA 22091

New Solutions
Oil, Chemical and Atomic Workers International Union, AFL-CIO
P.O. Box 281200
Lakewood, CO 80228-8200

New Statesman
Statesman and Nation Publishing Co. Ltd. and Contributors
Foundation House
Perseverance Works
38 Kingsland Rd.
London E28DQ
England

NewsNotes
Maryknoll Fathers and Brothers Justice and Peace Office
P.O. Box 29132
Washington, DC 20017

Nonviolent Activist
War Resisters League
339 Lafayette St.
New York, NY 10012
http://www.nonviolence.org/wrl/nva.htm/

Northwest Conservation
Northwest Ecosystem Alliance
P.O. Box 2813
Belsingham, WA 98227
http://www.pacificrim.net/~nwea/

Nursing Administration Quarterly
Aspen Publishers, Inc.
7201 Mckinney Circle
Frederick, MD 21701

Observer
Catholic Diocese of Rockford
921 W. State St.
Rockford, IL 61102

Pacific Affairs
University of British Columbia
Vancouver, BC V6T 1W5
Canada

Peace Review
Carfax Publishing Co.
P.O. Box 25
Abingdon, Oxfordshire OX14 3UE
England

Peace Watch
United States Institute of Peace
1550 M. St., N.W., Ste. 700
Washington, DC 20005-1708

Peacekeeping and International Relations
76 St. Clair Ave., W., Ste. 502
Toronto, ON M4V 1N2
Canada

Peacework
American Friends Service Committee
2161 Massachusetts Ave.
Cambridge, MA 02140
http://www.afsc.org/nero/nepq.htm/

The People
Socialist Labor Party of America
111 W. Evelyn Ave., Ste. 209
Sunnyvale, CA 94086-6140
gopher://gopher.slp.org:7019/

People's Medical Society Newsletter
People's Medical Society, Inc.
462 Walnut St.
Allentown, PA 18102

People's Tribune
League of Revolutionaries for a New America
P.O. Box 3524
Chicago, IL 60654
http://www.mcs.com/~jdav/league.html/

Perspectives in Health Promotion and Aging
National Eldercare Institute on Health Promotion
American Association of Retired Persons
601 E St., N.W., 5th floor-B
Washington, DC 20049

Photovoltaic Insider's Report
1011 W. Colorado Blvd.
Dallas, TX 75208

Planning
American Planning Association
1313 E. 60th St.
Chicago, IL 60637

Political Science Quarterly
Academy of Political Science
475 Riverside Dr., Ste. 1274
New York, NY 10115-1274
http://www.epn.org/psq.html/

Popline
Population Institute
110 Maryland Ave., N.W.
Washington, DC 20002-5626
http://www.populationinstitute.org/

Population and Development Review
Population Council
One Dag Hammarskjold Plaza
New York, NY 10017
http://www.popcouncil.org/pdr/

Population Bulletin
Population Reference Bureau
1875 Connecticut Ave., N.W., #520
Washington, DC 20009

Population Reports
Population Information Program
The Johns Hopkins School of Public Health
111 Market Place
Baltimore, MD 21202-4012

Population Today
Population Reference Bureau
1875 Connecticut Ave., N.W., #520
Washington, DC 20009
http://www.prb.org/prb/

Positive Alternatives
Center for Economic Conversion
222 View St., Ste. C
Mountain View, CA 94041-1344
http://www.conversion.org/

Proceedings
U.S. Naval Institute
2062 Generals Highway
Annapolis, MD 21401
http://www.usni.org/

Project Appraisal
BeechTree Publishing
10 Watford Close
Guildford, Surrey GU1 2EP
England

ProLife News
Alliance for Life, Canada
B1-90 Garry St.
Winnipeg, MB R3C 4H1
Canada

Psychiatric Services
American Psychiatric Association
1400 K St., N.W.
Washington, DC 20005

Public Manager
The Bureaucrat, Inc.
12007 Titian Way
Potomac, MD 20854

Public Perspective
Roper Center for Public Opinion Research
P.O. Box 440
Storrs, CT 06268-0440

Public Relations Quarterly
44 W. Market St.
Rhinebeck, NY 12572

Public Roads
U.S. Dept. of Transportation
Federal Highway Administration
400 7th St., S.W.
Washington, DC 20590
http://www.tfhrc.gov/

Reading Today
International Reading Association, Inc.
800 Barksdale Rd.
P.O. Box 8139
Newark, DE 19714-8139

Reason
Reason Foundation
3415 Sepulveda Blvd., Ste. 400
Los Angeles, CA 90034
http://www.reasonmag.com/reason/

Refugees
United Nations High Commissioner for Refugees
P.O. Box 2500
1211 Geneva 2 Depot
Switzerland
http://www.unhcr.ch/

Region
Federal Reserve Bank of Minneapolis
P.O. Box 291
Minneapolis, MN 55480-0291
http://woodrow.mpls.frb.fed.us/

Report from the Capital
Baptist Joint Committee
200 Maryland Ave., N.E.
Washington, DC 20002
http://www.erols.com/bjcpa/

Review
Fernand Braudel Center
Binghampton University
State University of New York
P.O. Box 6000
Binghampton, NY 13902-6000

Review for Religious
Missouri Province Educational Institute
3601 Lindell Blvd.
St. Louis, MO 63108

Review of Black Political Economy
Transaction Periodicals Consortium
Rutgers University
Department 3092
New Brunswick, NJ 08901-1265

Rolling Stone
1290 Ave. of the Americas
New York, NY 10104-0298

SIECUS Report
Sexuality Information and Education Council of the United States
130 W. 42nd St., Ste. 350
New York, NY 10036

Science and Public Policy
Beech Tree Publishing
10 Watford Close
Guildford, Surrey GU1 2EP
England

Security Dialogue
Sage Publications Ltd.
6 Bonhill St.
London EC2A 4PU
England

Security Letter
166 E. 96th St.
New York, NY 10128

Sierra
Sierra Club
730 Polk St.
San Francisco, CA 94109
http://www.sierraclub.org/

Social Forces
05 Manning Hall
University of North Carolina
Chapel Hill, NC 27599-3355
http://www.irss.unc.edu/sfhome.htm/

Social Justice
P.O. Box 40601
San Francisco, CA 94140

Social Security Bulletin
U.S. Social Security Administration
Office of Research and Statistics
Van Ness Center Bldg., Rm. 209
4301 Connecticut Ave., N.W.
Washington, DC 20008

Social Work
National Association of Social Workers
750 1st St., Ste. 700
Washington, DC 20002-4241
http://www.naswpress.org/

Society & Animals
White Horse Press
10 High Street
Knapwell, Cambridge CB3 8NR
England

Solar Industry Journal
777 N. Capitol St., N.E., #805
Washington, DC 20002

Solar Today
United States Section of the International Solar Energy Society
2400 Central Ave., #G-1
Boulder, CO 80301

Soldiers
U.S. Dept. of the Army
9325 Gunston Rd., Ste. S108
Fort Belvoir, VA 22060-5581
http://www.redstone.army.mil/soldiers/home.html/

Southern Exposure
Institute for Southern Studies
P.O. Box 531
Durham, NC 27702

Space and Security News
Institute for Space and Security Studies
5115 S. A1A Highway, Ste. 201
Melbourne Beach, FL 32951

State Education Leader
Education Commission of the States
707 17th St., Ste. 2700
Denver, CO 80202-3427

State Legislatures
States' Advocate
National Conference of State Legislatures
1560 Broadway, Ste. 700
Denver, CO 80202

Statistical Bulletin
Metropolitan Life Insurance Company
1 Madison Ave.
New York, NY 10010-3690
http://www.statbull.com/

Student Press Law Center Report
Student Press Law Center
1101 Wilson Blvd., Ste. 1910
Arlington, VA 22209
http://www.splc.org/

Studies in Conflict and Terrorism
Taylor & Francis Ltd.
4 John St.
London WC1N 2ET
England

Studies in Family Planning
Population Council
One Dag Hammarskjold Plaza
New York, NY 10017
http://www.popcouncil.org/sfp/

Surface Warfare
U.S. Dept. of the Navy
601 N. Fairfax St., Rm. 270
Alexandria, VA 22314-2007

Telos
Telos Press Ltd.
431 E. 12th St.
New York, NY 10009

Tennessee Agri Science
University of Tennessee Agricultural Experiment Station
Institute of Agriculture
P.O. Box 1071
Knoxville, TN 37901-1071
http://www.utk.edu/

Third Force
Center for Third World Organizing
1218 East 21st St.
Oakland, CA 94606

Toward Freedom
Toward Freedom, Inc.
209 College St.
Burlington, VT 05401
http://homepages.together.net/~tfmag/

UN Chronicle
United Nations
Rm. DC1-530
New York, NY 10017

U.S. Dept. of Agriculture Publications
Economic Research Service
1301 New York Ave., N.W.
Washington, DC 20005-4789

U.S. News & World Report
2400 N St., N.W.
Washington, DC 20037-1196
http://www.usnews.com/

University of Michigan News and Information Services
412 Maynard
Ann Arbor, MI 48109-1399

Urban Review
Human Sciences Press
233 Spring St.
New York, NY 10013-1578

WHO Fact Sheet
WHO Press
World Health Organization
Office of Information
1211 Geneva 27
Switzerland
http://www.who.ch/

Washington Weekly Report
UNA-USA Washington Office
1010 Vermont Ave., N.W., Ste. 904
Washington, DC 20005

Weekly Weather & Crop Bulletin
NOAA/NWS/NCEP
NOAA Science Center, Rm. 605
520 Auth Rd.
Camp Springs, MD 20746
http://www.usda.gov/oce/waob/jawf/

Wild Earth
Cenozoic Society, Inc.
P.O. Box 492
Canton, NY 13617

Windletter
American Wind Energy Association
122 C St., N.W., 4th Fl.
Washington, DC 20001

Windpower Monthly
P.O. Box 496007, Ste. 217
Redding, CA 96049
http://www.wpm.co.nz/

Witness
1249 Washington Blvd., Ste. 3115
Detroit, MI 48226-1822

World Affairs
American Peace Society
11319 18th St., N.W.
Washington, DC 20036-1802

World Health
World Health Report 1997
World Health Organization
Avenue Appia
1211 Geneva 27
Switzerland

World of Work
Bureau of Public Information
International Labor Organization
1828 L St., N.W., Ste. 801
Washington, DC 20036
http://www.ilo.org/

World Resource Review
Supcon International
1 Heritage Plaza
P.O. Box 5275
Woodridge, IL 60517-0275

World Rivers Review
International Rivers Network
1847 Berkeley Way
Berkeley, CA 94133-3312
http://www.irn.org/

World Watch
Worldwatch Institute
1776 Massachusetts Ave., N.W.
Washington, DC 20036
http://www.worldwatch.org/

Worldwatch Publications
Worldwatch Institute
1776 Massachusetts Ave., N.W.
Washington, DC 20036
http://www.worldwatch.org/

Yes! A Journal of Positive Futures
Positive Futures Network
P.O. Box 10818
Bainbridge Island, WA 98110
http://www.futurenet.org/

Your Health and Fitness
General Learning Corp.
Health Communications Group
60 Revere Dr.
Northbrook, IL 60062-1563

Internet Resources Covered by *A Matter of Fact*, Volume Twenty-Seven

Alabama Department of
Public Health
http://www.alapubhealth.org/

American Federation of Labor-Congress of Industrial Organizations
http://www.aflcio.org/

Arizona Department of Health Services
http://www.hs.state.az.us/

ABS Media Release
Australian Bureau of Statistics
http://www.statistics.gov.au/

California Department of Health Services
http://www.dhs.cahwnet.gov/

Eurostat (Europa)
European Commission
http://www.europa.eu.int/en/comm/eurostat/serven/home.htm/

Florida Department of Health
http://www.state.fl.us/

Gallup Organization
http://www.gallup.com/

German Federal Statistical Office
http://www.statistik.bund.de/presse/englisch/home.htm/

Great Britain
Parliament House of Commons Home Page
http://www.parliament.the stationery-office.co.uk/pa/cm/cmhome.htm/

Hawaii Department of Health
http://www.hawaii.gov/

Hong Kong Census and Statistics Department
http://www.info.gov.hk/

International Labour Organization
World Wide Web Server
http://www.unicc.org/ilo/

Ireland Central Statistics Office
http://www.cso.ie/

Maryland Department of Health and Mental Hygiene
Maryland Office of Public Relations
http://www.charm.net/~epi9/dhmtext.htm/

Massachusetts Department of Public Health
http://www.magnet.state.ma.us/

Michigan Department of Community Health
http://www.mdch.state.mi.us/

National Center for Health Statistics
http://www.cdc.gov/nchswww/nchshome.htm/

North Dakota Department of Health
http://www.health.state.nd.us/

Population Reference Bureau
http://www.prb.org/prb/

Singapore Department of Statistics
Ministry of Trade and Industry
http://www.singstat.gov.sg/

Statistics Iceland
http://eldur.stjr.is/

Statistics New Zealand
http://www.stats.govt.nz/

Tennessee Department of Health
http://170.142.16.205/

Texas Department of Health
http://www.tdh.texas.gov/

U.S. Administration on Aging
http://www.aoa.dhhs.gov/

U.S. Census Bureau
http://www.census.gov/

U.S. Department of Health and Human Services
http://www.hhs.gov/

U.S. Department of Justice
Bureau of Justice Statistics
gopher://www.ojp.usdoj.gov:70/00/bjs/

U.S. Department of Labor
Bureau of Labor Statistics
http://www.dol.gov/

U.S. Department of Transportation
http://www.dot.gov/

U.S. National Cancer Institute
http://rex.nci.nih.gov/

U.S. National Eye Institute
http://www.nei.nih.gov/

U.S. National Institutes of Health
http://www.nih.gov/

U.S. National Center for Education Statistics
http://www.ed.gov/

World Bank Home Page
http://www.worldbank.org/

World Health Organization
http://www.who.ch/

ABANDONED HOUSES--PENNSYLVANIA--PHILADELPHIA (v26)

ABDOMINAL DELIVERY

see CESAREAN SECTION

ABNORMALITIES, HUMAN--UNITED STATES (v26)

ABOLITION OF SLAVERY

see SLAVERY

ABORIGINES

see INDIGENOUS PEOPLES

ABORTION (v26)

see also BIRTH CONTROL

"Each year an estimated 36 million to 53 million abortions are performed worldwide....Of those, as many as 20 million are considered unsafe....In developing countries complications of unsafe abortion cause between 50,000 and 100,000 women's deaths annually....WHO estimates that the proportion of maternal mortality due to abortion complications ranges from 8% in Western Asia to 26% in South America, with a worldwide average of 13%...." (p4)

Salter, Cynthia/Johnston, Heidi Bart/Hengen, Nicolene. "Care for Postabortion Complications: Saving Women's Lives." Population Reports v25 n1 Sep 1997. p1-13,16-21,23,25-31.

ABORTION--AFRICA

In Kenya, "53% of septic abortion patients were under age 20....In two Nigerian studies adolescent girls represented 61% and 74% of septic abortion patients....In a Ugandan study almost 60% of deaths due to unsafe abortion occurred among women under age 20...." (p8)

"Care for Postabortion Complications: Saving Women's Lives: Unsafe Abortion Increasing among Young Women." Population Reports v25 n1 Sep 1997. p8.

ABORTION--AFRICA--MORTALITY

In Africa, "about one of every 150 abortions results in the woman's death....An estimated 3.7 million unsafe abortions are performed each year in sub-Saharan Africa, or 26 per 1,000 women, and about 23,000 African women die from complications....Abortion complications account for an estimated 13% of all maternal deaths in Africa....In Ethiopia a hospital-based study estimated that abortion complications accounted for nearly 40% of maternal deaths...." (p4-5)

Salter, Cynthia/Johnston, Heidi Bart/Hengen, Nicolene. "Care for Postabortion Complications: Saving Women's Lives." Population Reports v25 n1 Sep 1997. p1-13,16-21,23,25-31.

ABORTION--ASIA

"With the largest population of any region, Asia has the highest absolute number of unsafe abortions--about 9.2 million each year--although the estimated abortion rate is the lowest in the developing world, at 12 per 1,000 women. Nearly half the world's unsafe abortions take place in Asia, almost one-third in South Asia alone. Unsafe abortion accounts for 12% of all maternal deaths in Asia--40,000 deaths each year...." (p4)

Salter, Cynthia/Johnston, Heidi Bart/Hengen, Nicolene. "Care for Postabortion Complications: Saving Women's Lives." Population Reports v25 n1 Sep 1997. p1-13,16-21,23,25-31.

ABORTION--CHILE (v26)

ABORTION--DEVELOPING COUNTRIES

"In Latin America nearly one-third of women treated for abortion complications had undergone one or more previous abortions, a 4-country analysis of hospital records found....In Estonia more women being treated for postabortion complications had undergone a previous abortion (64%) than had ever used contraception (57%)....In Nigeria women seeking treatment for postabortion complications were more likely to have had a previous abortion than to have used contraception, according to a 3-year study at a university hospital. Only 5% had ever used contraception, while over twice as many--11%--reported a previous abortion...." (p13)

Salter, Cynthia/Johnston, Heidi Bart/Hengen, Nicolene. "Care for Postabortion Complications: Saving Women's Lives." Population Reports v25 n1 Sep 1997. p1-13,16-21,23,25-31.

ABORTION--GREAT BRITAIN--PUBLIC OPINION (v26)

ABORTION--HEALTH ASPECTS

"At least 75 million pregnancies each year (out of about 175 million) are unwanted; they result in 45 million abortions, 20 million of which are unsafe. 70,000 women die each year as a result of unsafe abortion, and an unknown number suffer infection and other health consequences." (p1)

"UNFPA Stresses Gender Equality, Maternal Health." Popline v19 May-Jun 1997. p1.

"Unsafe abortions cause 50,000 to 100,000 deaths each year....World Health Organization estimates that as many as 20 million abortions each year are unsafe and that 10% to 50% of women who undergo unsafe abortion need medical care for complications....In one country,...at 86 hospitals an estimated 28,000 women seek care for complications of unsafe or spontaneous abortion each month." (p1)

Salter, Cynthia/Johnston, Heidi Bart/Hengen, Nicolene. "Care for Postabortion Complications: Saving Women's Lives." Population Reports v25 n1 Sep 1997. p1-13,16-21,23,25-31.

"The number of worldwide published studies showing data on induced abortion and breast cancer incidence, has increased from 23 to 30, 24 of which (up from 18) reflect overall increased risk in the women who had chosen abortion. In terms of the magnitude of the increased risk, the average of all studies still centers around a highly significant 30% above the breast cancer risk of women who had not chosen abortion." (p3)

Brind, Joel. "Science Strikes Back." ProLife News v22 n9 Oct 1997. p3,11.

ABORTION--LATIN AMERICA

"According to a comprehensive study released last year by the Alan Guttmacher Institute, a New York-based reproductive research group, approximately 30 percent of all pregnancies in...[Latin America] end in abortion....The study finds that Latin American women are having an average of 1.2 abortions during their reproductive years....An estimated 800,000 Latin American women each year are hospitalized because of hemorrhages, infection or other complications of unsafe abortions, according to the study." (p6)

Constance, Paul. "The Region: Health: The Other Side of the Reproductive Revolution." IDB v24 n7 Jul 1997. p6-7. (ISSN0145-2274).

ABORTION--LATIN AMERICA--MORTALITY

"According to estimates from WHO and others, the highest rate of unsafe abortion is in Latin America, where an estimated 4.6 million unsafe abortions take place each year, or 40 per 1,000 women of reproductive age....Unsafe abortion is estimated to cause one-quarter of all maternal deaths in Latin America--6,000 deaths each year...." (p4)

Salter, Cynthia/Johnston, Heidi Bart/Hengen, Nicolene. "Care for Postabortion Complications: Saving Women's Lives." Population Reports v25 n1 Sep 1997. p1-13,16-21,23,25-31.

ABORTION--MICHIGAN (v26)

"There were 30,208 abortions performed in Michigan during 1996 and 31,091 abortions performed in 1995, a decrease of 2.8 percent. Abortions have decreased by 15.5 percent since 1993 and by 35.4 percent from 1988....Abortions to resident women under the age of 20 declined by 3.8 percent and for women between the ages of 20 through 24 abortions declined by 5.9 percent. There was a decrease of 2.6 percent in abortions performed to women between the ages of 30 and 39....Data from Michigan's 28 largest cities show an overall decline of 3.9 percent in the number of abortions performed. Of the women receiving abortions, 82.9 percent of them were not married, down from 83.7 percent in 1995 and from the 84.6 percent reported in 1994 which was the highest this percentage has ever been since reporting began in 1980."

Michigan. Dept. of Community Health. "Abortions Decrease 2.8% in Michigan." News Release 19 Jun 1997. document-level access: <http://www.mdch.state.mi.us/DCH/NewsRels/061997.htm>

ABORTION--NETHERLANDS--UNITED STATES (v26)

ABORTION--NIGERIA--GIRLS

"By the time they leave secondary school, 1 out of every 5 Nigerian girls has terminated an unwanted pregnancy....80 percent of patients in Nigerian hospitals with abortion-related complications are young girls." (p5)

"Providing Nigerian Youth with a Better Life, Future." SIECUS Report v25 n2 Dec 1996-Jan 1997. p5. (ISSN0091-3995).

ABORTION--RUSSIA (v26)

"The average Russian woman has four abortions in her life....According to Russian law, girls can have an abortion without parental consent after they reach 15. Abortions can be performed up to the 12th week of pregnancy...[in one particular St. Petersburg clinic], but other clinics perform them up to the sixth month....[One] clinic performs about 2,000 abortions a year, mostly for girls 12 to 18 years old." (p11)

Eskenazi, Jason. "Life and Death in St. Petersburg." APF Reporter v18 n3 1997. p11-14. (ISSN0913-4562).

Barbro Lenneer Axelson, who is an assistant professor of psychology at Gothenburg University in Sweden, and the Europe Region president of the International Planned Parenthood Federation, "asserts that the total number of abortions in Russia and other former Soviet republics is...9 million per year, 25,000 a day, 1,000 an hour. Axelson noted the official data reports that a 40-year-old Russian woman has a mean of four to five abortions in her background....[Axelson] said that 80 percent of Russian gynecologists are women, very badly paid and with a real shortage of economic and technical resources. 'Half of their time is occupied with abortions,' she pointed out." (p1)

"1,000 Abortions per Hour." Popline v19 Sep-Oct 1997. p1-2.

ABORTION--SOUTH AFRICA (v26)

ABORTION--UNITED STATES (v26)

The latest data "from the Guttmacher Institute, whose figures are relied upon by the [U.S.] Centers for Disease Control, indicates that 99 percent of all abortions are performed before 20 weeks of gestation; 90 percent are performed within the first 12 weeks; and less than 1 percent are performed after 20 weeks. Only four-hundredths of 1 percent performed after 20 weeks are performed during the third trimester. So this means there is a total of about 400 to 600 abortions performed annually during the third trimester of pregnancy. According to the Centers for Disease Control, 98.9 percent of all abortions are performed by the simple curettage procedure, which simply involves the scraping of the interior of the uterus." (pS4440)

Feinstein, Dianne (Sen.-Calif.). "Partial-Birth Abortion Ban Act of 1997." Congressional Record. Daily ed. v143 n63 14 May 1997. pS4431-4451. section/page-level access: <http://thomas.loc.gov/cgi-bin/query/R?r105:FLD001:S04439:> (ISSN0363-7239). (X1.1A.105/1).

ABORTION--UNITED STATES--CATHOLICS --ATTITUDES

In the 1996 U.S. presidential election, of those Catholics "who believed that abortion should be 'always legal' or 'mostly legal,' 68% and 55% respectively voted for [President] Clinton. But among those who believed abortion should be 'mostly illegal' or 'always illegal,' [presidential candidate Robert] Dole won the most votes: 48% and 57% respectively. Fifty-nine percent of all Catholic voters said in 1996 they believe abortion should be 'always legal' or 'mostly legal'; only 37% said it should be 'mostly illegal' or 'always illegal.'" (p48)

White, John Kenneth/D'Antonio, William. "The Catholic Vote in Election '96." Public Perspective v8 n4 Jun-Jul 1997. p45-48. (ISSN1050-5067).

ABORTION SERVICES--CRIMES AGAINST--UNITED STATES (v26)

"So far this year, 17 U.S. clinics have suffered arsons or bombings, triple the number of a year ago at this time. And in 1996, 27.6 percent of clinics that offer women the choice of abortion faced violent attacks that included death threats, stalkings, bombings, arsons, blockades, invasions and chemical attacks, all orchestrated to deny women their constitutional right to abortion." (p8 secE)

Dixson, J. B. "Accent: Anti-Choice Terrorist Groups Keep an Old Brand of Hatred Alive." Detroit News 1 Oct 1997. p8 secE.

ABSENCE, LEAVE OF

see LEAVE OF ABSENCE

ABSENCE FROM SCHOOL

see SCHOOL ATTENDANCE

ABSENTEE MOTHERS--UNITED STATES (v26)

ABSTINENCE, SEXUAL

see SEXUAL ABSTINENCE

ABUSE OF ANIMALS

see ANIMAL WELFARE

ABUSE OF CHILDREN

see CHILD ABUSE

ABUSE OF SUBSTANCES

see SUBSTANCE ABUSE

ABUSED AGED--UNITED STATES

In the U.S., "approximately 818,000 elderly individuals are victimized annually....Experts estimate that only 1 in 10 cases of elder abuse gets reported....In Tennessee, caseworkers with the Tennessee Department of Human Services receive approximately 400 new reports of adult abuse each month. The agency pursues about 3,200 cases per month. Thirty-five percent of the cases involve victims over the age of 80....A relatively recent study of various forms of elder abuse that occurred in Forsyth County, North Carolina, found financial abuse to be the most prevalent form, accounting for 46 percent of the total abuse cases." (p1)

Coker, Johnny/Little, Bobby/U.S. Dept. of Justice. Federal Bureau of Investigation. "Investing in the Future: Protecting the Elderly from Financial Abuse." FBI Law Enforcement Bulletin v66 n12 Dec 1997. p1-5. (ISSN0014-5688).

ABUSED CHILDREN

see also CHILD ABUSE; CHILD SEXUAL ABUSE; CRIME--UNITED STATES--ABUSED CHILDREN

ABUSED CHILDREN--MICHIGAN (v26)

ABUSED CHILDREN--UNITED STATES (v26)

ABUSED CHILDREN--UNITED STATES--MORTALITY

"Every day in America three children actually die of abuse and neglect at the hands of their parents or their caretakers. That is over 1,200 children every year. And almost half of these children are killed after...their tragic circumstances have already come to the attention of local child welfare agencies." (pS10262)

DeWine, Mike (Sen.-Ohio). "Another Tragedy." Congressional Record. Daily ed. v143 n134 1 Oct 1997. pS10262-10263. section/page-level access: <http://thomas.loc.gov/cgi-bin/query/R?r105:FLD001:S10262:> (ISSN0363-7239). (X1.1A.105/1).

ABUSED HANDICAPPED--CANADA (v26)

ABUSED WOMEN--CANADA

In Canada, "more than 100 women are victims of domestic homicide every year by an actual or former husband or common law partner. Approximately one-half of women 16 and over have been victims of violence as defined by the Canadian Criminal Code....Sixty per cent of women in Canada are afraid to walk alone in their neighbourhoods after dark....Violence costs the Canadian economy approximately $4 billion every year." (p1041)

Minna, Maria (MP-ON). "Statements by Members: Violence." Canada. Parliament. House of Commons. Debates. v135 n19 23 Oct 1997. p1041. section-level access: <http://www.parl.gc.ca/36/1/parlbus/chambus/house/debates/019_1997-10-23/han019-e.htm#LINK94> (ISSN0704-5603). (X3-361E).

ABUSED WOMEN--UNITED STATES (v26)

ABUSED WOMEN PRISONERS--UNITED STATES

In the U.S., "over half (53 percent) [of women prisoners] reported being physically abused before the age of fifteen (Crawford, 1988). A U.S. Department of Justice (1994) study found that more than 4 in every 10 women reported that they had been abused at least once before their current prison sentence. About 34 percent of female inmates reported being physically abused; 34 percent reported being sexually abused. Of those who were physically abused, about 32 percent said the abuse had occurred before age 18; 24 percent said the abuse occurred since age 18. Women in prison were at least three times more likely (then men in prison) to report any prior abuse, and women were six times more likely than men to report sexual abuse or abuse since age 18. About 50 percent of women in prison, who reported abuse, indicated that they had experienced abuse by an 'intimate,' while three percent of men reported that they had experienced abuse by an 'intimate.'" (p190-191)

Janeksela, Galan M. "Female Criminality: An Overview." International Journal of Comparative and Applied Criminal Justice v21 n2 Fall 1997. p181-205.

ACCIDENT INSURANCE

see INSURANCE, ACCIDENT

ACCIDENTS

see also AGRICULTURE--ACCIDENTS; AIRCRAFT ACCIDENTS; BASKETBALL--ACCIDENTS; BOATING ACCIDENTS; CYCLING ACCIDENTS; DEER--ACCIDENTS; DRINKING AND TRAFFIC ACCIDENTS; DROWNING VICTIMS; FIRES; FIREWORKS--ACCIDENTS; INDUSTRIAL ACCIDENTS; LOGGING, AERIAL--ACCIDENTS; PEDESTRIAN ACCIDENTS; PERSONAL WATERCRAFT--ACCIDENTS; SCHOOL BUS ACCIDENTS; SNOWMOBILE ACCIDENTS; TRAFFIC ACCIDENTS; TRUCK ACCIDENTS; UNITED STATES. ARMY--ACCIDENTS

ACCIDENTS--AUSTRALIA (v26)

ACCIDENTS--AUSTRALIA--MORTALITY

According to the Australian Bureau of Statistics, "over the last ten years the number of deaths from accidents decreased from 5,384 in 1987 to 4,696 in 1996 which was a 26 per cent decrease in the standardised death rate for all accidents. There was a 37 per cent fall in the death rate for motor vehicle traffic accidents and a 18 per cent decrease in the rate for accidental falls during this period."

Australian Bureau of Statistics. "Deaths from Diabetes and Senile Dementia Increase." Media Release 31 Oct 1997. document-level access: <http://www.abs.gov.au/websitedbs/d3110125.nsf/4a255eef008309e44a255eef00061e57/b963d1a23d007204ca25654000761a86?OpenDocument>

ACCIDENTS--UNITED STATES (v26)

In the U.S., "in 1995, 6 percent of all deaths, 8 percent of all hospital discharges, and 37 percent of all emergency department visits were injury-related....In 1992-94, three out of five injury hospitalizations among elderly persons 75 years of age and over were for fractures, and more than one-half of the fractures were to the hip. Hip fracture rates for elderly females were twice the rates for males. In 1993-94, three causes of injury morbidity--falls, being struck by or against something, and motor vehicle traffic-related injuries--accounted for nearly 1 in 5 emergency department visits."

U.S. Dept. of Health and Human Services. "Report on Nation's Health Documents Toll of Injuries in U.S.: Firearm Mortality Down 11%, Traffic Fatality...Up...." Press Release 24 Jul 1997. document-level access: <http://www.cdc.gov/nchswww/releases/97news/97news/hus96rel.htm>

In the U.S., of all ambulatory visits to a variety of health care settings, "there were an estimated 126.1 million injury-related visits in 1995, representing 14.7 percent of the total number of visits. Roughly 6 out of every 10 injury visits were made to physician offices, compared with 3 out of 10 to emergency departments and 1 out of 10 to outpatient departments. An estimated 48.2 ambulatory injury visits were made for every 100 persons during 1995. The rate for males was higher than for females (52.3 visits compared with 44.2 visits per 100 persons). Visits for intentional injuries accounted for 3 percent of the injury visits, with a rate of 14 visits per 1,000 persons. For persons between the ages of 18 and 64 years, at least 28 percent of the injury visits were related to the patient's employment. Unintentional falls was the stated cause of injury for 18 percent of all injury-related visits, followed by motor vehicle traffic accidents (10.4 percent)."

U.S. National Center for Health Statistics. "Monitoring Health Care in America: Spotlight on: Ambulatory Care in the U.S." Quarterly Fact Sheet Jun 1997. document-level access: <http://www.cdc.gov/nchswww/releases/97facts/97sheets/mhc0697.htm>

ACCIDENTS--UNITED STATES--COSTS (v26)

ACCIDENTS--UNITED STATES--MORTALITY (v26)

In the U.S., "age-adjusted firearm mortality, which increased 22 percent between 1985 and 1993, dropped 11 percent between 1993 and 1995. Meanwhile, age-adjusted motor vehicle fatality rates, which declined 15 percent between 1985 and 1993, increased 2 percent from 1993 to 1995....Motor vehicle traffic injuries, firearm injuries, and poisoning were the three leading causes of injury death in 1995, accounting for nearly two-thirds of all injury deaths. In 1994-95, unintentional injury death rates and suicide rates for persons 15-34 years were higher for American Indians than for other racial or ethnic groups. Homicide rates for ages 15-34 years were higher for black persons of the same age than for other groups."

U.S. Dept. of Health and Human Services. "Report on Nation's Health Documents Toll of Injuries in U.S.: Firearm Mortality Down 11%, Traffic Fatality...Up...." Press Release 24 Jul 1997. document-level access: <http://www.cdc.gov/nchswww/releases/97news/97news/hus96rel.htm>

"The National Safety Council estimates that there were 91,700 unintentional-injury deaths [in the U.S.] for 1996 and that this number represents a 2 percent decline from the 93,300 deaths occurring in 1995. Among the various age groups the largest decrease in these types of deaths occurred between the ages of 5 and 14 (8 percent) while persons age 75 and older had a 2 percent increase." (p19)

Yavarkovsky, Judith. "Statistical Information, Please." Statistical Bulletin v78 n4 Oct-Dec 1997. p19. (ISSN0790-8334).

ACCIDENTS, INDUSTRIAL

see INDUSTRIAL ACCIDENTS

ACCIDENTS, TRAFFIC

see TRAFFIC ACCIDENTS

ACCOUNTING

see also LAWYERS--UNITED STATES--ACCOUNTING

ACCOUNTING--AUSTRALIA

According to the Australian Bureau of Statistics, Australia's "8,389 accounting practices,...with a 19.6 per cent operating profit margin, experienced an almost 20 per cent boost in income and a 10 per cent increase in employment between June 1993 and June 1996....The 8,389 accounting practices generated $4,939 million in income during 1995-96 and employed 66,792 people at the end of June 1996. Since 1993 this represents an increase in income of about 20 per cent and an increase in employment of about 10 per cent. The three main sources of income for these practices were from taxation services ($1,575 million), general business and personal accounting services ($1,312 million) and auditing services ($896 million). The industry recorded an operating profit before tax of $829 million which represented an operating profit margin of 19.4 per cent, down slightly from the 20.5 per cent noted in June 1993."

Australian Bureau of Statistics. "Legal Profits Steady, Accounting Industry Grows." Media Release 10 Nov 1997. document-level access: <http://www.abs.gov.au/websitedbs/d3110125.nsf/4a255eef008309e44a255eef00061e57/4870c6ee56dae103ca25654b0004d5e2?OpenDocument>

ACCOUNTING--EMPLOYMENT--AUSTRALIA

According to the Australian Bureau of Statistics, "of the 66,792 people employed in the [accounting] industry, 36,694 were qualified accountants. Eighty-three per cent of employment was on a full-time basis, with 74 per cent of support staff working full-time. Females accounted for 79 per cent of the part-time employment."

Australian Bureau of Statistics. "Legal Profits Steady, Accounting Industry Grows." Media Release 10 Nov 1997. document-level access: <http://www.abs.gov.au/websitedbs/d3110125.nsf/4a255eef008309e44a255eef00061e57/4870c6ee56dae103ca25654b0004d5e2?OpenDocument>

ACCUMULATION, CAPITAL

see SAVING AND INVESTMENT

ACHES

see PAIN

ACHIEVEMENT TESTS

see also EDUCATIONAL TESTS AND MEASUREMENT; SCHOLASTIC ASSESSMENT TEST; TEST OF ACHIEVEMENT AND PROFICIENCY

According to the Third International Mathematics and Science Study "among the 41 countries whose students took the [science achievement] test, 16 had average national scores higher than the United States. These were significantly higher for nine nations, including the top scorers--Singapore, the Czech Republic, Japan, and Korea. The United States scored slightly above the international average; 15 countries scored significantly lower. Of our most direct economic competitors (the 'Group of Seven' or G-7 nations), only France ranked among this group....In the basic science areas (chemistry and physics), U.S. students scored only one or two percentage points above the international average....On average, U.S. students answered 58 percent of the items [in the earth-science categories] correctly, while the international average was 55 percent. Only four countries (Singapore, Slovenia, the Czech Republic, and Korea) scored significantly higher, with averages from 63 to 65 percent. Fourteen countries scored significantly lower, although none were G-7 countries." (p20)

Jakwerth, Pamela/Bianchi, Len/McKnight, Curtis C./Schmidt, William H. "Focus in School Science: An International Comparison." Geotimes v42 n7 Jul 1997. p19-22. (ISSN0016-8556).

ACID DEPOSITION--EUROPE (v26)

ACQUIRED IMMUNE DEFICIENCY SYNDROME

see AIDS (DISEASE)

ACTIONS AND DEFENSES--EMPLOYEES--UNITED STATES

In the U.S., "since passage of the 1991 Civil Rights Act, which made it easier for discrimination victims to get jury trials, employees have won more often. Between 1991 and 1995, when 47 percent of cases were decided by a jury rather than a judge, employees won 30 percent of the cases. Between 1978 and 1990, when just 24 percent of the cases went to a jury, the win rate for plaintiffs was 24.5 percent." (p69)

Saltzman, Amy. "U.S. News: News You Can Use: At Work & Home: Suppose They Sue?" U.S. News & World Report v123 n11 22 Sep 1997. p68-70. article-level access: <http://www.usnews.com/usnews/issue/970922/22DISC.HTM> (ISSN0041-5537).

ACTIONS AND DEFENSES--ILLINOIS--LAWYERS (v26)

ACTIONS AND DEFENSES--MICHIGAN--OAKLAND COUNTY

"Last year, 32,210 new cases were filed in [Michigan's] Oakland County Circuit Court with 10,674 involving domestic relations, said Court Administrator Judy Cunningham....Probate Court received 12,818 new cases in 1996, including the following juvenile cases: 241 child protection petitions, 2,292 delinquency hearings and 396 adoptions." (p5 secC)

Ilka, Douglas. "Suburban News: In Oakland County: Plan Pushes Family Cases through the Court Docket." Detroit News 10 Jul 1997. p5 secC.

ACTIONS AND DEFENSES--UNITED STATES (v26)

"During the past five years federal prosecutors [in the U.S.] won convictions in 26 percent of all the F.B.I. investigations they processed. (In 1996 the record was 28 percent.)...In that same year...59 percent of Drug Enforcement Administration matters ended with a conviction, 52 percent of those from the Bureau of Alcohol, Tobacco and Firearms and 41 percent of those from the Internal Revenue Service." (p12)

Burnham, David. "Articles: The FBI." Nation v265 n5 11 Aug 1997. p11-12,14-16,18-24. (ISSN0027-8378).

ACTIONS AND DEFENSES--UNITED STATES. DRUG ENFORCEMENT AGENCY--UNITED STATES. FEDERAL BUREAU OF INVESTIGATION

"Between 1992 and 1996, in cases where the principal charges were based on the [U.S.] government's two most frequently used drug laws, the D.E.A. got the green light from the prosecutors 81 percent of the time, compared with 75 percent for the F.B.I. The D.E.A.'s investigations led to prison sentences 54 percent of the time, the F.B.I.'s 49 percent. By another measure--how long it took attorneys to prosecute a matter--the D.E.A. also did better. Its median was 198 days, the F.B.I.'s 264....The median prison sentence of offenders investigated by these agencies was the same--sixty months." (p14)

Burnham, David. "Articles: The FBI." Nation v265 n5 11 Aug 1997. p11-12,14-16,18-24. (ISSN0027-8378).

ACTIONS AND DEFENSES--UNITED STATES. FEDERAL BUREAU OF INVESTIGATION

From 1992 to 1996, U.S. "federal prosecutors disposed, in one way or another, of 226,186 F.B.I. referrals. Only 57,871 of them--one-quarter--resulted in convictions; 67,710 of these referrals--about one-third of all they processed--assistant U.S. attorneys ruled legally insufficient. According to the department's data tapes, the prosecutors said they had rejected 25,599 of the matters because they were supported by 'weak or insufficient evidence.' Prosecutors declined an additional 28,680 on the grounds of lack of evidence that a federal offense had been committed or that criminal intent was involved. For 10,243 more, there was 'minimal federal interest.' Finally, 3,188 F.B.I. referrals were disposed of because there was 'no known suspect.'...During the five-year period in question,...19,419 were declined on the grounds that they had

been referred to 'other authorities' for prosecution; 13,294 because of a lack of prosecutorial or investigative resources; and 3,063 at the request of the Justice Department." (p12)
Burnham, David. "Articles: The FBI." Nation v265 n5 11 Aug 1997. p11-12,14-16,18-24. (ISSN0027-8378).

ACUTE CATARRHAL JAUNDICE
see HEPATITIS A

ADAPTIVE COLITIS
see IRRITABLE COLON

ADC PROGRAMS
see AID TO FAMILIES WITH DEPENDENT CHILDREN PROGRAMS

ADD (CHILD BEHAVIOR DISORDERS)
see ATTENTION-DEFICIT HYPERACTIVITY DISORDER

ADDICTION, SUBSTANCE
see SUBSTANCE ABUSE

ADDICTION TO ALCOHOL
see ALCOHOLISM

ADDICTION TO DRUGS
see DRUG ABUSE

ADMINISTRATION OF JUVENILE JUSTICE
see JUVENILE JUSTICE, ADMINISTRATION OF

ADOLESCENT PREGNANCY
see TEENAGE PREGNANCY

ADOPTION--NEW YORK (N.Y.)--AFRO-AMERICANS
"About 80 percent of all foster children waiting for adoption in New York City are black. Even though blacks adopt at four times the rate of whites, there are not enough black families available for the children." (p4)
Buckley, Gail Lumet. "Left, Right and Center." America v177 n8 27 Sep 1997. p4. (ISSN0002-7049).

ADOPTION--UNITED STATES (v26)

ADRENERGIC BETA BLOCKERS--UNITED STATES (v26)

ADULT EDUCATION--UNITED STATES (v26)

ADULTERY--AFRICA
According to a Demographic and Health Surveys study in Africa, "only 2 percent and 0.5 percent of wives in Central African Republic and Zimbabwe, respectively, reported having extramarital relations in the four-week period preceding the surveys, compared with 5 percent of the husbands in Ghana and Zimbabwe and 9 percent in Central African Republic. In Kenya, where a six-month reference period was used, 2 percent of wives and 16 percent of husbands reported having extramarital relations." (p110)
Ezeh, Alex Chika/Mboup, Gora. "Estimates and Explanations of Gender Differentials in Contraceptive Prevalence Rates." Studies in Family Planning v28 n2 Jun 1997. p104-121. (ISSN0039-3665).

ADULTERY--UNITED STATES--PUBLIC OPINION
According to a Gallup survey, "Americans are generally tolerant of adultery when a couple is separated, with only 38% saying it is always wrong in those circumstances. Almost half feel it is wrong only sometimes or not wrong at all....Four out of five think that having sexual relations with someone other than the marriage partner is always wrong, while another 11% think it is almost always wrong....73% say an affair between a college professor and his or her student is grounds for dismissal; only 23% say it is not....Only 32% think that an affair between coworkers of equal position in a work place is just cause for being fired....One occupation that the public holds accountable to its moral standards against adultery is the clergy, with 73% of Americans saying it is justifiable to dismiss a member of the clergy because of an extramarital affair. Just 21% disagree."
Saad, Lydia/Gallup Organization. "Most Americans Would Soften U.S. Military's Rules against Adultery." Press Release 13 Jun 1997. document-level access: <http://www.gallup.com/poll/news/970613.htm>

ADVERTISERS--UNITED STATES
"A survey of 55 members of the Society of American Business Editors and Writers at the society's 1992 conference revealed that advertiser pressure was common. Eighty percent reported that the pressure was a growing problem, and 45 percent knew of instances where news coverage was compromised by advertisers." (p11)
Soley, Lawrence. "Special Section: 'The Power of the Press Has a Price.'" Extra! v10 n4 Jul-Aug 1997. p11-13.

ADVERTISING
see also BILLBOARDS
"In a world where more than $1.4 trillion will be spent to market goods and services this year, more than 90 percent of the total is concentrated in 28 nations--most of them in Europe, the Pacific Rim, and North America. This set of countries accounts for about 17 percent of the world's population. Advertising spending per person ranges from a low of less than $1 in Laos to more than $2,100 for every man, woman, and child in Japan....About two-thirds of all media dollars spent around the world this year ($956 billion) will be spent to market consumer products and services. The rest ($478 billion) will be spent by businesses pitching their wares to other businesses....By itself, the United States accounts for over one-third of the planet's media spending--more than $479 billion, all told....AdWorld estimates that more than one-third of the world's total marketing expenditures ($508 billion) go for promotions rather than straightforward advertising." (p57-58)
Cassino, Kip D. "A World of Advertising." American Demographics v19 n11 Nov 1997. p57-60. article-level access: <http://www.demographics.com/publications/ad/97_ad/9711_ad/ad971131.htm> (ISSN0163-4089).

ADVERTISING--BIRTH CONTROL--KENYA (v26)

ADVERTISING--DAIRY PRODUCTS INDUSTRY --UNITED STATES (v26)

ADVERTISING--FOOD--UNITED STATES (v26)

ADVERTISING--MOTION PICTURES--UNITED STATES --PUBLIC OPINION (v26)

ADVERTISING--TOBACCO--CANADA (v26)

ADVERTISING--TOBACCO--CANADA--PUBLIC OPINION (v26)

ADVERTISING--UNITED STATES (v26)

ADVERTISING--UNITED STATES--PUBLIC OPINION (v26)

ADVERTISING--UNITED STATES--YOUTH (v26)

ADVERTISING--VIETNAM
"Vietnam's 71 million people own an estimated 7 million radios and 2.5 million TVs. Reported daily newspaper circulation is 1.2 million copies. But low levels of imports and one of the lowest per-capita incomes in the world means that marketing expenditures are concentrated in cities, where only one in five Vietnamese lives. No form of consumer media consistently reaches beyond the wealthiest one-fifth of the nation's population, which accounts for 44 percent of consumer spending. Outdoor advertising reaches the most Vietnamese--an estimated 14 million, followed by point-of-purchase materials, at 11 million." (p58)
Cassino, Kip D. "A World of Advertising." American Demographics v19 n11 Nov 1997. p57-60. article-level access: <http://www.demographics.com/publications/ad/97_ad/9711_ad/ad971131.htm> (ISSN0163-4089).

ADVERTISING--WORLD WIDE WEB (INFORMATION RETRIEVAL SYSTEM)
"Businesses will spend $446 million placing advertisements on the World Wide Web in 1997. That isn't much in the advertising world: spending on cable TV advertising is estimated at $9.2 billion this year, and newspaper ads are $43.4 billion. But

spending on Web ads is projected to increase more than 300 percent within two years, according to a new report, while overall ad spending increases about 6 percent a year....Global net-surfers will rack up 1.86 billion Internet sessions in 1997, according to Cowles/Simba [Information]. Multiplied by the number of stops and clicks in an average session, this means that users should view Web pages 14.9 billion times this year, and 'click-through' on advertisements that link to another Web site 594 million times." (p8)

"Web Advertising Poised for Takeoff." Forecast v17 n8 Aug 1997. p8. article-level access: <http://www.demographics.com/Publications/FC/97_fc/9708_fc/FC97085.htm> (ISSN0732-1597).

ADVERTISING, DIRECT-MAIL--UNITED STATES

"Christmas is the main reason why December is the number-one month for direct mail [in the U.S.]. Six of 11 direct-mail categories peak in December, according to The Kleid Company of New York City....Seventeen percent of business and finance mailings happen in December because budget years often start on January 1. Nineteen percent of 'home-interest' mailings happen in December because this category includes spring gardening and seed catalogs. Home-interest mailings also have peaks in June and September (12.5 percent each), when many gardeners are thinking about the fall growing season. Business and finance mailings go up in September (9 percent), for those organizations with a fiscal year starting September 1....Many people read books during their summer vacations, which may be why 16 percent of general reading mailings go out in June. Educational mail peaks in August (15 percent) because school starts in September. November is the top month for fund-raising appeals (22 percent), due to the December search for tax deductions." (p8)

"The Seasons of Direct Mail." Forecast v17 n9 Sep 1997. p8. article-level access: <http://www.demographics.com/Publications/FC/97_fc/9709_fc/FC97097.htm> (ISSN0732-1597).

"By year's end, each of us will have received, on average, 553 pieces of junk mail--a total of 4.5 million tons filling America's mailboxes annually. Though nearly half of it goes straight to the garbage, in the end U.S. consumers will have shelled out $244 billion this year in response to direct mail pitches, including $48 billion on catalog merchandise." (p40-41)

Headden, Susan. "Special Report: The Junk Mail Deluge." U.S. News & World Report v123 n22 8 Dec 1997. p40-44,48. article-level access: <http://www.usnews.com/usnews/issue/971208/8MAIL.HTM> (ISSN0041-5537).

ADVERTISING, TELEVISION

see TELEVISION ADVERTISING

AERIAL LOGGING

see LOGGING, AERIAL

AERONAUTICAL ACCIDENTS

see AIRCRAFT ACCIDENTS

AERONAUTICS

see also AIRPLANES; AIRPORTS

AERONAUTICS--ENVIRONMENTAL ASPECTS

"In 1992, 93 percent of aircraft fuel was burned in the Northern Hemisphere--70 percent of it between 60 and 30 degrees north latitude....Average cloudiness over the United States has increased 5 percent in the three decades since jet travel began to intensify." (p12)

Cowen, Robert C. "Science & Technology: Those Hazy Jet Trails May Heat Up the Debate about Global Warming." The Christian Science Monitor v89 n170 29 Jul 1997. p12. The Christian Science Monitor search engine: <http://www.csmonitor.com/plweb-cgi/iops1.pl> To retrieve this article, enter the following search: ED=19970729 AND warming. In the "retrieved list," click the title that matches this record. (ISSN0882-7729).

AERONAUTICS, COMMERCIAL

see also AIRLINES

"Air transport has undergone a dramatic expansion to meet the demands of an increasingly integrated planet. It accounts for an estimated 22 million jobs and $1 trillion in annual economic activity and grows at more than 6 percent each year. In the US, the Commerce Department estimates the industry accounts for $54 billion in direct output, making it one of the largest US industries." (p8)

Woodard, Colin. "Global Report: US-Europe for $296 Round-Trip: US Throttles Down Sky-High World Air Fares." The Christian Science Monitor v89 n248 19 Nov 1997. p1,8. The Christian Science Monitor search engine: <http://www.csmonitor.com/plweb-cgi/iops1.pl> To retrieve this article, enter the following search: ED=19971119 AND fares. In the "retrieved list," click the title that matches this record. (ISSN0882-7729).

AEROSPACE INDUSTRIES--EMPLOYMENT--GREAT BRITAIN

"There are more than 100,000 direct employees in the aerospace sector throughout Britain. In total, 500 establishments employ people directly in the aerospace sector....In Lancashire last year, 13,000 people, or 10 per cent of the county's total manufacturing work force, were employed directly by the industry in more than 40 different establishments. Lancashire also accounts for 13 per cent of the national total employment in the industry. In...[Chorley] alone in 1995, 400 people were working in the aerospace industry." (c849-850)

Hoyle, Lindsay (H.C.-Chorley). "European Fighter Aircraft." Great Britain. Parliament. House of Commons. Debates. 9 Jul 1997. c849-850. section-level access: <http://www.parliament.the-stationery-office.co.uk/pa/cm199798/cmhansrd/cm970709/debtext/70709-01.htm#70709-01_head0>

AEROSPACE INDUSTRIES--GREAT BRITAIN (v26)

AETA (PHILIPPINE PEOPLE)--MORTALITY (v26)

AETA (PHILIPPINE PEOPLE)--SOCIAL CONDITIONS (v26)

AFDC PROGRAMS

see AID TO FAMILIES WITH DEPENDENT CHILDREN PROGRAMS

AFFECTIVE DISORDERS (v26)

AFFIRMATIVE ACTION PROGRAMS--CANADA--PUBLIC OPINION (v26)

AFFIRMATIVE ACTION PROGRAMS--UNITED STATES (v26)

AFFIRMATIVE ACTION PROGRAMS--UNITED STATES --PUBLIC OPINION

In the U.S., "public opinion surveys repeatedly indicate large majorities [of Americans] in favor of eliminating or amending affirmative action. A 1995 poll by CNN/USA TODAY showed 83 percent in favor of change. Among African-American respondents, 23 percent said that 'on balance affirmative action has been bad for the country.'" (p5 secB)

Cantor, George. "Outlook: Racial Reconciliation: Michigan's Affirmative Reactions." Detroit News 22 Jun 1997. p5,8 secB.

AFFLUENCE

see WEALTH

AFGHAN REFUGEES

see REFUGEES, AFGHAN

AFGHANISTAN--SOCIAL CONDITIONS

Aabha Dixit, a research associate at the Delhi-based Institute for Defence Studies and Analyses, states that "'Afghanistan has lost 2 million martyrs to the cause of implementing the 'Sharia' [Islamic holy law].'...Since the beginning of the year more than 200,000 refugees have poured into Kabul to escape the fighting in the north, stretching to the limit the city's capacity to feed and provide basic necessities for them." (p7)

Zubrzycki, John. "Taliban Loses Ground, But Not Its Strict Ways." The Christian Science Monitor v89 n175 5 Aug 1997. p1,7. The Christian Science Monitor search engine: <http://www.csmonitor.com/plweb-cgi/iops1.pl> To retrieve this article, enter the following search: ED=19970805 AND ways. In the "retrieved list," click the title that matches this record. (ISSN0882-7729).

AFRICA--ECONOMIC CONDITIONS (v26)

"Last year Africa's economies grew by an average of 3.9 per cent, by far the highest during the decade....The growth rate for 1996 compares well with the 2.7 per cent recorded in 1995, and exceeds by a wide margin the annual average of 0.9 per cent over 1990-94. Eleven African countries saw their GDPs grow by 6 per cent or more in 1996. Only two had negative growth rates, compared with six in 1995 and an annual average of 16 over 1990-94." (p13)

"Africa Records Stronger Growth." Africa Recovery v11 n1 Jul 1997. p13.

According to UN Conference on Trade and Development estimates, African least developed countries "registered relatively strong GDP growth rate, averaging 4.6 per cent in 1996. This was down from 5.4 per cent in 1995, but still well above the 1990-94 average of 2.9 per cent." (p8)

"Agriculture in Africa: LDCs Must Give Higher Priority to Agriculture--UNCTAD." Africa Recovery v11 n2 Oct 1997. p8.

"The 1996 average rate of growth for the continent [of Africa] was 5 per cent....Ethiopia...has a growth rate of 12 per cent....Uganda...had a growth rate of nearly 10 per cent and has become a regional magnet for investment....Sub-Saharan Africa has a population of 600 million, which will double by 2025. Forty per cent of people live on less than $1 a day and the infant mortality rate is one in 10....In Mozambique, debt servicing accounts for one third of public expenditure, while education gets just 7.9 per cent and health a pitiful 3.3 per cent." (c136-137)

Vaz, Keith (H.C.-Leicester, East). "International Development." Great Britain. Parliament. House of Commons. Debates. 1 Jul 1997. c136-137. section-level access: <http://www.parliament.the-stationery-office.co.uk/pa/cm199798/cmhansrd/cm970701/debtext/70701-13.htm#70701-13_spnew0>

"The economies of many countries in Africa have been strengthened as a result of structural changes: The average rate of economic growth in Africa was 3.8 percent in 1995 and 5.4 percent in 1996, excluding Nigeria and South Africa. In 1995, United States exports to Africa totaled $5.4 billion." (p20)

Dinkins, David N. "Opinion/Essays: Many Favor African Trade Bill, But Will Congress Ever Vote?" The Christian Science Monitor v89 n248 19 Nov 1997. p20. The Christian Science Monitor search engine: <http://www.csmonitor.com/plweb-cgi/iops1.pl> To retrieve this article, enter the following search: ED=19971119 AND vote. In the "retrieved list," click the title that matches this record. (ISSN0882-7729).

Following the 1994 devaluation of the French African franc, "in Togo, the price of basic commodities (maize, rice, oil, and sugar) more than doubled, and the cost of pharmaceuticals rose by 70 percent or more. In Gabon, household spending rose by 60 percent, while in Chad gas prices shot up by 71 percent....In Chad, privatization of the national cotton company led to the closure of seven of its 12 ginning plants, leaving 1000 families without a breadwinner." (p20-21)

Onyango, William. "TF Reports: Africa: Losing Ground." Toward Freedom v46 n5 Sep-Oct 1997. p20-21. (ISSN0048-9898).

AFRICA--GEOGRAPHY

"Africa is the second largest continent in the world with a total area of 11,700,000 square miles....According to the 1990 World Almanac and Book of Facts, six countries can conveniently fit into Africa: namely: the United States (3,618,770 square miles); Argentina (1,065,189 square miles); China (3,705,390 sq. miles); Europe (1,905,000 sq. miles); India (1,266,000 sq. miles); and New Zealand (103,736 sq. miles)." (p15) "Nigeria, with a total area of 356,000 sq. mi. is the most populous country in Africa...." (p16)

Eleazu, Innocent. "ISIL International Report: Africa and Democratization in Nigeria." Freedom Network News n49 Sep 1997. p15-16.

AFRICA, NORTH--MIDDLE EAST--ECONOMIC CONDITIONS (v26)

AFRICA, NORTH--MIDDLE EAST--POPULATION (v26)

AFRICA, SOUTH

see SOUTH AFRICA

AFRICA, SUB-SAHARAN--SOCIAL CONDITIONS (v26)

AFRO-AMERICAN AGED--POPULATION (v26)

AFRO-AMERICAN BUSINESS ENTERPRISES (v26)

AFRO-AMERICAN CHILDREN

see also LEAD POISONING IN AFRO-AMERICAN CHILDREN

AFRO-AMERICAN CHILDREN--SOCIAL CONDITIONS

According to the U.S. "Bureau of the Census (Bennett, 1995), the living arrangements of African American children younger than 18 years have changed dramatically during the past 20 years. The number of children living in two-parent households has decreased from 85% in 1970 to 77% in 1980 and 71% in 1993 (Bennett, 1995)." (p342)

Cochran, Donna L. "Article: African American Fathers: A Decade Review of the Literature." Families in Society v78 n4 Jul-Aug 1997. p340-350. (ISSN1044-3894).

AFRO-AMERICAN COLLEGE STUDENTS (v26)

"According to a recent study by the Southern Education Foundation, the leading public universities in the South remain more than 80% white. In Mississippi, where college tuition costs represent about 40% of the annual income of an average black family, fewer African Americans earned bachelor's degrees in 1991 than in 1979 (Applebome, 1995...). Nationwide, the proportion of African Americans with a bachelor's degree in education decreased one percent between 1972 and 1992 (IBID...) and the production of African Americans with doctorates has been stagnant since the late 1970s." (p15-16)

Platt, Anthony M. "'The Land that Never Has Been Yet': U.S. Race Relations at the Crossroads." Social Justice v24 n1 Spr 1997. p7-23. (ISSN0094-7571).

AFRO-AMERICAN COLLEGE STUDENTS--MICHIGAN (v26)

AFRO-AMERICAN CONSUMERS (v26)

AFRO-AMERICAN FAMILIES

According to the U.S. Census Bureau's annual "report, only 46 percent of the country's 8.1 million black families were headed by married couples in 1996, the year studied by bureau statisticians. In recent years, that number has fluctuated just above the 50 percent mark, said Roderick Harrison, chief of the racial statistics branch of the Census Bureau. This is the first time it's gone below 50 percent, Harrison said." (p5 secA)

Eversley, Melanie. "Nation & World: Study Finds Drop in Black Families Led by Married Couples." Detroit Free Press 27 Jun 1997. p5 secA.

After 1960, the percentage of Afro-American children in central U.S. cities "living with two parents dropped sharply from 72% to 59% in 1970....By 1990 only 33% of black children in northern central cities were living with two parents." (p1223-1224)

Tolnay, Stewart E. "The Great Migration and Changes in the Northern Black Family, 1940 to 1990." Social Forces v75 n4 Jun 1997. p1213-1238. (ISSN0037-7732).

AFRO-AMERICAN FARMERS (v26)

AFRO-AMERICAN HIGH SCHOOL STUDENTS
see also ENTREPRENEURSHIP--AFRO-AMERICAN HIGH SCHOOL STUDENTS

AFRO-AMERICAN HIGH SCHOOL STUDENTS --CALIFORNIA--OAKLAND
In 1996, in Oakland, California schools, "black students had a grade-point average of 1.8 on a 4.0 scale, the lowest in the district. (The average GPA for white students was 2.12; for Asians, 3.0.) What's more, although black students made up just 53 percent of the district's 52,269 enrollment, 71 percent of the students in special education were black, as were 64 percent of those who were retained in grade and 80 percent of those who were suspended." (p30)
Marlowe, John. "Sounding Board: Beyond 'Ebonics'." American School Board Journal v184 n7 Jul 1997. p30-31,39. (ISSN0003-0953).

AFRO-AMERICAN LAW STUDENTS
A "study by educational researcher Linda Wightman carried the telltale title, 'The Threat to Diversity in Legal Education,' and muffled the negative evidence it found--21.9 percent of black law students entering schools [in the U.S.] in 1990-1991 failed to get a degree, compared with 9.7 percent of whites. Far from showing that blacks admitted under affirmative action did just as well as strongly credentialed blacks, Wightman found that blacks admitted under racial preferences were about three times more likely to drop out. And the affirmative-action group had a shockingly high attrition rate--43.2 percent either didn't finish law school or didn't pass the bar." (p22)
Leo, John. "On Society: Let's Attack Merit!" U.S. News & World Report v123 n20 24 Nov 1997. p22. article-level access: <http://www.usnews.com/usnews/issue/971124/24JOHN.HTM> (ISSN0041-5537).

AFRO-AMERICAN MEN
see also HOMICIDE--AFRO-AMERICAN MEN

AFRO-AMERICAN MEN--HEALTH AND HYGIENE
According to the Michigan Task Force on Improving African-American Male Health's "two-volume report, Challenge of a Lifetime, black men in Michigan...get lung cancer at a rate of 117 per 100,000--nearly double the overall state rate. [They] are diagnosed with prostate cancer at a frequency almost twice that of white men--83 per 100,000 to 47 per 100,000. [Black men] account for 7 percent of Michigan's 9.5 million residents, but 60 percent of its homicide victims. [They] get diabetes at a rate nearly twice that of white men--23 per 100,000 to 13 per 100,000. [They] get tuberculosis at a rate of 26 per 100,000, compared with 3 per 100,000 white men. [Black men] die at an average age of 64, compared with 74 for white men in Michigan." (p1,10 secA)
Cole, Kenneth. "Health Funding Angers Blacks." Detroit News 3 Nov 1997. p1,10 secA.

AFRO-AMERICAN MEN--MORTALITY
In the U.S., "the greatest cause of death for men younger than 25 years is murder. African American males between 20 and 24 years of age have the highest rate of death by gunfire--104 homicides by a firearm for every 100,000 persons. This rate is 10 times the rate for white males in the same age range (Bureau of the Census, 1992...)." (p372)
Kost, Kathleen A. "Article: The Effects of Support on the Economic Well-Being of Young Fathers." Families in Society v78 n4 Jul-Aug 1997. p370-382. (ISSN1044-3894).

AFRO-AMERICAN MEN--SOCIAL CONDITIONS
In the U.S. labor market, "black males earn on average 73% of the income earned by white males (Watson and Smitherman, 1996)." (p148) "The homicide rate for black males ages 15 to 24 is seven to eight times higher than that of white males in the same age group (Roper, 1991)....In most urban areas, 20 to 30% of black males drop out of school before graduation (Taylor-Gibbs, 1988). Black males are four times more likely than white males to be suspended or expelled from school, and nine times more likely to be placed in special education classes (Meier, Stewart, and England, 1989)....At colleges and universities throughout the U.S., fewer than 40% of those admitted to college graduate within six years....In 1995, one out of every three black males (versus one out of 10 white males) between the ages of 18 and 30 were either incarcerated or in some way ensnared by the criminal justice system (Noguera, 1995). In California, the percentage recently increased to 40% (SAN FRANCISCO EXAMINER, February 18, 1996)." (p149)
Noguera, Pedro A. "Reconsidering the 'Crisis' of the Black Male in America." Social Justice v24 n2 Sum 1997. p147-164. (ISSN0094-7571).

AFRO-AMERICAN POLITICIANS
"In 1972, there were 300 African-Americans elected to public office, nationwide; today, there are 7,000 in Federal, State, and local office. In 1972, there were 12 Members of Congress, and in 1997 there are 40 African-Americans in the U.S. Congress." (pE1873)
Visclosky, Peter J. (Rep.-Ind.). "Commemorating the 1972 National Black Political Convention's 25th Anniversary Celebration." Congressional Record. Daily ed. v143 n131 26 Sep 1997. pE1873. section/page-level access: <http://thomas.loc.gov/cqi-bin/query/R?r105:FLD001:E01873:> (ISSN0363-7239). (X1.1A.105/1).

"In 1995, when the new Republican majority [U.S.] Congress took over, they brought in sixty-five new pages, sixty-four of whom were white, the other an Asian-American. In previous recent sessions, fifteen to twenty had been Latino, African-American, or other minorities....From 1980 to 1992, only 2 of the 115 judges appointed to the U.S. Courts of Appeals were black, one of whom was Clarence Thomas." (p91)
Goldfield, Michael. "Race and Labor Organization in the United States." Monthly Review v49 n3 Jul-Aug 1997. p80-97. (ISSN0027-0520).

AFRO-AMERICAN POLITICIANS--WHITES--ATTITUDES
In the U.S., "according to a Gallup Poll, 93 percent of whites said they would vote for an African-American presidential candidate. That number is up from 77 percent a decade ago and up from 35 percent in 1958." (p2 secC)
Lewis, Shawn D./Brand-Williams, Oralandar. "The Metro: Special Report: Closing the Racial Gap: Level the Playing Field, African Americans Say." Detroit News 20 Jun 1997. p1-2 secC.

AFRO-AMERICAN PRISONERS
"A Washington-based advocacy group, known as the 'Sentencing Project,'...reported that...one-third, or 32.2 percent of young black men in the age group 20-29 is in prison, jail, probation, or on parole [in the U.S.]. In contrast, white males of the same age group are incarcerated at a rate that is only 6.7 percent. As the Nation experiences a slight overall decline in the crime rate, 5,300 black men of every 100,000 in the United States are in prison or jail. This compares to an overall rate of 500 per 100,000 for the general population, and is nearly five times the rate which black men were imprisoned in the apartheid era of South Africa. America is now the biggest incarcerator in the world and spends billions of dollars each year to incarcerate young people....The number of African-American males under criminal justice control is over 827,000. This figure exceeds the number of African-American males enrolled in higher education." (pH2389)
Stokes, Louis (Rep.-Ohio). "Juvenile Crime Control Act of 1997." Congressional Record. Daily ed. v143 n59 8 May 1997. pH2356-2398. section/page-level access: <http://

thomas.loc.gov/cgi-bin/query/R?r105:FLD001:H02389:> (ISSN0363-7239). (X1.1A.105/1).

"African Americans account for 37% of the prison population and 11.7% of the general population. 50% of low-income defendants go to prison, whereas only 25% of high-income defendants do. The rate of incarceration for African Americans in the northeast is fifteen times that of whites." (p6)

Suarez-Potts, Jamie. "The Labor of Prisoners." Peacework n275 Jun 1997. p5-7. (ISSN0748-0725).

"By the end of 1995, 1 in every 167 US residents was incarcerated. One out of every seven black men has been disenfranchised by felony convictions. African Americans were charged under California's 'three strikes' law at 17 times the rate of whites. Between 1986 and 1991, the number of African Americans in state prisons for drug offenses more than quintupled: 14,000 to 80,000." (p7)

Miller, Erin. "Drugs, AIDS, And Human Rights." Peacework n275 Jun 1997. p7-9. (ISSN0748-0725).

AFRO-AMERICAN PRISONERS--CALIFORNIA

"In 1992, African Americans made up the largest segment of California prison inmates (33.5%), followed by Latinos (33.1%), whites (28.9%), and 5.5% from other racial and ethnic groups (CDC, 1995). According to a new study by the Center for Juvenile and Criminal Justice, nearly two out of every five (39%) young African American men in their twenties (in contrast to five percent of young white men) are presently under some form of criminal justice control in California, representing an increase from 33% in 1990 (Schiraldi et al., 1996)." (p154)

Reed, Diane F./Reed, Edward L. "Children of Incarcerated Parents." Social Justice v24 n3 Fall 1997. p152-169. (ISSN0094-7571).

AFRO-AMERICAN SOLDIERS

"Between 1970 and 1990, blacks in the [U.S.] military almost doubled. Populations of color now comprise 42% of the Army, 32% of the Navy, and 25% of the Air Force. Of all women in the service, about one-third are black (Wood, 1996..., Graham, B., 1995..., NEW YORK TIMES, 1995...)." (p15)

Platt, Anthony M. "'The Land that Never Has Been Yet': U.S. Race Relations at the Crossroads." Social Justice v24 n1 Spr 1997. p7-23. (ISSN0094-7571).

AFRO-AMERICAN STUDENTS--CALIFORNIA--OAKLAND (v26)

AFRO-AMERICAN TEACHERS

In 1991, according to the National Education Association, the number of African American teachers "had dropped to 8 percent. The most recent projections estimate that by 2000 the proportion of African American teachers will be less than 5 percent...(King 1993...)." (p313)

Graybill, Susan W. "Questions of Race and Culture: How They Relate to the Classroom for African American Students." Clearing House v70 n6 Jul-Aug 1997. p311-318. (ISSN0009-8655).

AFRO-AMERICAN TEACHERS--MICHIGAN

In Michigan, in 1997, "black men make up only 2 percent of the state teaching force, Education Department statistics show. Of the 106,000 teachers in Michigan, about 2,200 are African-American men, according to the department. Their ranks are even thinner in the formative elementary grades where black men comprise less than 1 percent of all teachers. Of the 33,000 elementary teachers, only 236 are black males." (p1 secA)

"While black men make up 2 percent of the state teaching force, 17 percent of the state's public school students are black males. That amounts to about 140,000 students." (p11 secA)

Hornbeck, Mark. "News Special: Education: Only 2 Percent of Teachers in Michigan Are Black Males: Educators: Students...Role Models." Detroit News 14 Aug 1997. p1,11 secA.

AFRO-AMERICAN UNIVERSITIES AND COLLEGES

Enrollment in the U.S.'s "100 black colleges has increased by nearly 30 percent over the past two years, a rate of increase twice as fast as that for mainstream colleges. The number of students in black colleges has surged to 230,000 in 1994-95 compared with 179,000 a decade earlier." (p18)

Tyson, Ann Scott. "Black Support Wanes for Goal of Integration." The Christian Science Monitor v89 n162 17 Jul 1997. p1,18. The Christian Science Monitor search engine: <http://www.csmonitor.com/plweb-cgi/iops1.pl> To retrieve this article, enter the following search: ED=19970717 AND integration. In the "retrieved list," click the title that matches this record. (ISSN0882-7729).

AFRO-AMERICAN WOMEN

see also MARRIAGE--AFRO-AMERICAN WOMEN

AFRO-AMERICAN WOMEN--EMPLOYMENT--SOUTHERN STATES

In the U.S., "the majority of black women [in the South] still work in the least secure, poorest paid occupations: pink-collar, service and laborer jobs. In 1994, 50.8 percent of black women were employed in these jobs, a proportion virtually unchanged from 51.4 percent in 1975. Moreover, black women's largest gains in white-collar work have been at the bottom rung in the traditionally white female occupation of sales. Where 5.5 percent of all black women's work in 1975 was in sales, 1994 saw sales work make up more than 12 percent of jobs held by black women." (p9)

Eckman, Anne/Green, Jordan/Braasch, Peter/Schulman, David. "Job Equity in the Downsized South: A Special Report on Work in the 1990s." Southern Exposure v25 n3-4 Fall-Win 1997. p7-11. (ISSN0146-809X).

In the southern U.S., "black women's 1994 parity ratio for official and managerial positions was 0.28, meaning that their share of these jobs was about a quarter of what should be expected based on their share of the total workforce. For professional work, black women's parity ratio was 0.48 for the South, indicating that they held about half as many of these jobs as they would in a workplace with equitable job distribution." (p10)

Eckman, Anne/Green, Jordan. "Dislocation & Workforce Equity: The South at Work in the 1990s: Women Make Inroads into White-Collar Work." Southern Exposure: Institute for Southern Studies Report 1997. p10.

AFRO-AMERICAN YOUTH

see FIREARMS--AFRO-AMERICAN YOUTH

AFRO-AMERICANS

see also ADOPTION--NEW YORK (N.Y.)--AFRO-AMERICANS; AIDS (DISEASE)--AFRO-AMERICANS; COLLEGE APPLICATIONS--UNIVERSITY OF TEXAS--AFRO-AMERICANS; CONSUMER BEHAVIOR--AFRO-AMERICANS; DISCRIMINATION--AFRO-AMERICANS; EDUCATIONAL VOUCHERS--AFRO-AMERICANS; FATHERS--AFRO-AMERICANS; FINANCIAL SERVICES INDUSTRY--AFRO-AMERICANS; ILLEGITIMACY--AFRO-AMERICANS; INCOME--AFRO-AMERICANS; MASS MEDIA AND THE POOR--AFRO-AMERICANS; PAIN--AFRO-AMERICANS; QUALITY OF LIFE--AFRO-AMERICANS; SICKLE CELL ANEMIA--AFRO-AMERICANS; SINGLE FATHERS--AFRO-AMERICANS; SINGLE MOTHERS--AFRO-AMERICANS; SMOKING--AFRO-AMERICANS; UNEMPLOYMENT--AFRO-AMERICANS; UNITED STATES. ARMY--AFRO-AMERICANS; UNITED STATES. MARINE CORPS--AFRO-AMERICANS

"In 1996, 12.8 percent of the U.S. population, or 33.9 million people were African American, according to tabulations released...by the Commerce Department's Census Bureau....In 1996, there were 8.1 million African American families, 46 percent of whom were married-couple families. About 74 percent of all African Americans 25 years of age and older had at least a high school education; about 14 percent had at least a bachelor's degree. In 1995, African American families had a median income of $25,970. The income of 2.1 million African American families (26 percent) was below the poverty level."

U.S. Census Bureau. Economic and Statistics Administration. "African American Population Approaches 34 Million, Census Bureau Reports." Press Release 26 Jun 1997. document-level access: <http://www.census.gov/Press-Release/cb97-105.html>

AFRO-AMERICANS--ALABAMA (v26)

AFRO-AMERICANS--CIVIL RIGHTS--ATTITUDES

In the U.S., "a recent Gallup poll showed that black graduates freshly out of college remain deeply pessimistic about the possibility of more amicable race relations. In fact, 76 percent of them say race relations will remain contentious. By contrast, 56 percent of blacks without college degrees harbor such pessimism. Nearly half of white college graduates express similar pessimism." (p14 secA)

"The Road to Reconciliation." Detroit News 13 Jun 1997. p14 secA.

AFRO-AMERICANS--ECONOMIC CONDITIONS (v26)

"The annual income of the African-American community today stands at more than $400 billion. Unemployment among blacks is now at a 20-year low, and the number of African-American entrepreneurs has grown over the past three decades from around 45,000 to more than 621,000 today. When he first began publication of the list of America's top 100 black businesses, Earl Graves, publisher of BLACK ENTERPRISE magazine said their net sales were a little less than $500 million and they employed slightly more than 9,000 people. In the June [1997] issue of BLACK ENTERPRISE, the top 100 firms were listed as having sales of more than $14 billion and employing more than 55,000 people." (p14 secA)

Coleman, Trevor W. "Black Progress through Economic Power." Detroit Free Press 7 Aug 1997. p14 secA.

In the U.S., "the number of black-owned businesses grew by 46 percent to 620,912 in 1992 from 424,165 in 1987, according to Census Bureau surveys. Revenues during the same period rose by 63 percent to $32.2 billion from $19.8 billion. But in 1996, the median income of white households was $13,679 more than the median for black households, a difference that is slightly higher than it was 30 years ago. Although the share of blacks living in poverty has declined by nearly 11 points over the past 30 years, it still is close to 30 percent. The poverty rate for whites last year was 11.2 percent. A recent study by Congressional Quarterly in Washington shows that blacks' percentage of the workforce grew to 11.1 percent in 1994 from 10.2 percent in 1982. The study projects that blacks will represent 11.3 percent of the workforce by the year 2005. That's still below the 12.9 percent of the population that the Census Bureau projects that blacks will compose at the start of the new century." (p6 secA)

Bivins, Larry. "Blacks Say Economic Equality Is Next Frontier in Civil Rights." Detroit News 20 Oct 1997. p1,6 secA.

"African Americans number almost 30 million and comprise more than 12% of the U.S. population and 14% of its work force....The average income for African Americans in 1995 was $18,600, just 60% of Caucasian income." (p23) "Most (53%) still live in the South, where they earn low incomes. However, 75% are above the poverty level, and 13% have annual incomes of $50,000 or more....More than a third [of middle-class African Americans] (38%) work in white-collar jobs with slightly less (36%) working in blue collar jobs." (p24)

Morton, Linda P. "Targeting Minority Publics." Public Relations Quarterly v42 n2 Sum 1997. p23-28. (ISSN0033-3700).

A medical study released by the University of Michigan found that "African Americans in the study were 1.6 times more likely than whites not to have graduated from high school, and half as likely to have graduated from college. They were almost four times as likely to have an annual income less than $10,000 (21 percent vs. 6 percent) and were 1.4 times more likely to be in the $10,000 to $29,000 range. Whites were 2.5 times more likely to have incomes higher than $60,000 (41 percent vs. 16 percent)." (p3)

University of Michigan. News and Information Services. "U-M Study Links Everyday Discrimination to Higher Rates of Ill Health for African Americans." University of Michigan News Release 24 Sep 1997. p1-4.

AFRO-AMERICANS--EDUCATION (v26)

The U.S. Census Bureau's annual report "shows 74 percent of all black Americans at least 25 years old have a high school education, compared with 86 percent of white Americans. By comparison, 79.1 percent of whites at least 25 years old completed four years of high school in 1990, compared with 66.2 percent of blacks, according to the Census Bureau. About 14 percent of black Americans had a bachelor's degree last year, up from 11.3 percent in 1990, according to the Census Bureau." (p5 secA)

Eversley, Melanie. "Nation & World: Study Finds Drop in Black Families Led by Married Couples." Detroit Free Press 27 Jun 1997. p5 secA.

"In 1970, 56.2% of African Americans aged 25-29 were high school graduates compared to 77.8% of whites (U.S. Dept. of Education 1996...), but 1995 high school completion was at 86.5% for blacks and 87.4% for whites, both figures up from their 1970 levels and the black-white disparity much smaller. And college completion followed broadly in parallel, increasing by half among whites between 1970 and 1995 (from 17.3% to 26.0%), but more than doubling among African Americans (from 7.3% to 15.3%)." (p5)

Alexander, Karl L. "Public Schools and the Public Good." Social Forces v76 n1 Sep 1997. p1-30. (ISSN0037-7732).

AFRO-AMERICANS--EDUCATION (HIGHER) (v26)

AFRO-AMERICANS--EMPLOYMENT (v26)

"In 1995, African-Americans made up 19.4 percent of all enlisted [military] personnel, although only 11.4 percent of all officers....In the growing and important health care industry...African-Americans are concentrated in the lowest ranking occupations. While in 1994, they made up only 4.2 percent of doctors and 3.7 percent of dentists (a slight increase from 1983), they made up 9.3 percent of registered nurses, 18.7 percent of licensed practical nurses, and almost 30 percent of nurses aides, orderlies, and attendants. The same story can be told not only within but across various industries, with blacks in 1995 making up 24 percent of telephone operators, 29 percent of postal clerks, 29 percent of bus drivers, 34 percent of garbage collectors, and 28 percent of correctional officers in the nation's prisons, sadly one of the fastest growing of U.S. industries." (p87-89)

Goldfield, Michael. "Race and Labor Organization in the United States." Monthly Review v49 n3 Jul-Aug 1997. p80-97. (ISSN0027-0520).

AFRO-AMERICANS--EMPLOYMENT--SOUTHERN STATES

"African Americans' share of jobs in the [U.S.] South has increased by one-fifth, to 20 percent of all workers in 1994. African American women's participation in the southern labor market has increased from 7.0 percent in 1975 to 10.8 percent in 1994; African American men's participation has actually declined from 10.1 percent to 9.7 percent." (p9)

Eckman, Anne/Green, Jordan. "Dislocation & Workforce Equity:

The South at Work in the 1990s: Diversity and Continued Segregation." Southern Exposure: Institute for Southern Studies Report 1997. p9.

AFRO-AMERICANS--MICHIGAN--DETROIT (v26)

AFRO-AMERICANS--MORTALITY (v26)

AFRO-AMERICANS--OHIO--CLEVELAND (v26)

AFRO-AMERICANS--POPULATION (v26)

"Today African Americans make up 12 percent of the U.S. population. About half the black population is located in the South and half in large cities in the East, Midwest, and West (Baruth and Manning 1992...). According to the U.S. Department of Labor, over 86 percent live in urban areas where more than half the residents are black (Norton 1983...)." (p313)

Graybill, Susan W. "Questions of Race and Culture: How They Relate to the Classroom for African American Students." Clearing House v70 n6 Jul-Aug 1997. p311-318. (ISSN0009-8655).

"African Americans comprise 12.6 percent of the U.S. population. In a western Pennsylvania city, 28 percent of the total population consists of minority groups, predominantly African American. Approximately 14 percent of this city's minority population resides in one neighborhood of the city." (p47)

Resick, Lenore K./Taylor, Carol A./Caroll, Theresa L./ D'Antonio, Joyce A./de Chesnay, Mary. "Establishing a Nurse-Managed Wellness Clinic in a Predominantly Older African American Inner-City...Nursing Project." Nursing Administration Quarterly v21 n4 Sum 1997. p47-54. (ISSN0363-9568).

AFRO-AMERICANS--PUBLIC OPINION

According to a recent Gallup poll, in the U.S., "20 to 30 percent more whites than blacks believe blacks face equal opportunities in obtaining jobs, education, housing, as well as fair treatment in restaurants, shops, the workplace, and in the hands of police. Nearly twice as many whites as blacks polled say the quality of life for blacks has improved nationwide over the past 10 years. Collectively, whites also claim to harbor little prejudice against blacks, placing their level of bias at 2 on a scale of 10. On specific issues, most whites say they favor a racially mixed working environment (82 percent), would vote for a black presidential candidate (93 percent), approve of interracial marriage (61 percent), and would not object to sending their children to a school where the majority of students are black (59 percent)....Blacks polled--especially young black men--say they routinely experience prejudice day to day. Many say they have suffered discrimination in the previous month in the following areas: shopping (30 percent), dining out (21 percent), at work (21 percent), and with police (15 percent)." (p3)

Tyson, Ann Scott. "United States: Perception Gap Could Stymie Racial Initiatives." The Christian Science Monitor v89 n136 10 Jun 1997. p3. The Christian Science Monitor search engine: <http://www.csmonitor.com/plweb-cgi/iops1.pl> To retrieve this article, enter the following search: ED=19970610 AND initiatives. In the "retrieved list," click the title that matches this record. (ISSN0882-7729).

AFRO-AMERICANS--SOCIAL CONDITIONS (v26)

"African Americans, including Caribbean Americans, make up 12% of the U.S. population (U.S. Bureau of the Census, 1991). Nationally, African American families, which comprise more than 30 million people, have a combined annual income exceeding $300 billion....[There are] 400,000 African American-run churches and 100 African American colleges....Of the 2,855,691 children who were reported as abused or neglected in 1992, 27.4% were African American (Children's Defense Fund, 1995)." (p532)

Carter, Carolyn S. "Article: Using African-Centered Principles in Family-Preservation Services." Families in Society v78 n5 Sep-Oct 1997. p531-538. (ISSN1044-3894).

AGE--ASIAN AMERICANS

"In 1996, 30 percent of Asian Americans were under age 18, compared to less than 25 percent of whites. Nearly half (45 percent) of Asian Americans are ages 18 to 44 (the prime ages for immigration), compared with two-fifths (40 percent) of whites. By contrast, just 7 percent of Asians are ages 65 and older--less than half the elderly share of the white population." (p4)

Pollard, Kelvin M./De Vita, Carol J. "A Portrait of Asians and Pacific Islanders in the United States." Statistical Bulletin v78 n3 Jul-Sep 1997. p2-9. (ISSN0790-8334).

AGE-STRUCTURED POPULATIONS

"Between 1950 and 1996, the average number of births per woman worldwide declined from five to three, according to the Census Bureau. During the same period, average life expectancy at birth increased by 21 years in developing countries and by 8 years in industrial ones, according to the United Nations. One result is that the number of people aged 60 and older increased 125 percent in industrial countries, to 214 million in 1995; and 200 percent in less-developed countries, such as China, India, and Brazil, to reach 330 million....Between 1995 and 2025, the population aged 60 and older may increase 54 percent in industrial countries and 154 percent in developing countries. By 2050, developing countries could have more than four times as many elderly people as industrial countries do." (p3)

"The Age Wave Hits China." Forecast v17 n6 Jun 1997. p3. article-level access: <http://www.demographics.com/Publications/FC/97_fc/9706_fc/FC97062.htm> (ISSN0732-1597).

AGE-STRUCTURED POPULATIONS--DEVELOPING COUNTRIES

"Thirty-five percent of the population in developing countries is under age 15, compared with 20 percent in industrialized countries. In nearly all sub-Saharan African countries, close to half the population is under age 15." (p4)

Gelbard, Alene. "A Primer: Population 101." Population Today v25 n9 Sep 1997. p4-5. (ISSN0749-2448).

AGE-STRUCTURED POPULATIONS--IRELAND

According to Ireland's 1996 Census, "children aged from 0 to 14 make up 24% of the population in the State, down from 29% in 1986. In urban areas in 1996 the figure was 23%, and 25% for rural areas. The population aged 15 years and over increased by 10% between 1986 and 1996, due mainly to high birth rate in the late 1970s. The young dependency ratio, which is derived by expressing the population aged 0-14 as a percentage of the population of working age (15-64 years), peaked at over 50% in the 1970s. However, it has since been in decline and reached a low of 37% in 1996."

Ireland. Central Statistics Office. "1996 Census--Volume 2, Ages and Marital Status." Press Release 30 Oct 1997. document-level access: <http://www.cso.ie/pressreleases/prelcen96v2.html>

AGE-STRUCTURED POPULATIONS--UNITED STATES

In the U.S., "in 1996, more than one-third of Latinos were children under age 18, compared with nearly one-fourth of whites. Conversely, only 5 percent of Hispanics were elderly (65 years and older), compared with 14 percent of whites. About 59 percent of Latinos were in the working ages, compared with 62 percent of non-Hispanic whites. The age structure of African Americans is much closer to that of Latinos, with 34 percent children, 7 percent elderly, and 59 percent of working age. Among Latino groups, the proportion of children ranges from 19 percent among Cubans to 39 percent among Mexicans, while the proportion of elderly ranges from 4 percent among Mexicans,

Puerto Ricans, and Central and South Americans to 19 percent among Cubans...." (p17)

del Pinal, Jorge/Singer, Audrey. "Generations of Diversity: Latinos in the United States." Population Bulletin v52 n3 Oct 1997. p2-47. (ISSN0032-468X).

AGED

see also ABUSED AGED; AMBULATORY SURGERY--UNITED STATES--AGED; DEPRESSION, MENTAL--UNITED STATES--AGED; FOOD STAMPS--UNITED STATES--AGED; HANDICAPPED AGED; INCOME--UNITED STATES--AGED; INFLUENZA VACCINES--UNITED STATES--AGED; INTERNET (COMPUTER NETWORK)--UNITED STATES--AGED; LIVING ALONE--IRELAND--AGED; MEDICAID--AGED; POOR AGED; POPULATION FORECASTING--AGED; POPULATION FORECASTING--UNITED STATES--AGED; PUERTO RICAN AGED; SOCIAL GROUPS--CUBA--AGED; SOCIAL SECURITY--UNITED STATES--AGED

"By the year 2020 more than 1000 million of the people in the world will be over 60 years old, and more than two-thirds of them will be living in developing countries. In the early 1950s, average life expectancy at birth was 47 years worldwide. In 1995 it was more than 65 years, and in several countries it was almost 80." (p3)

Nakajima, Hiroshi. "Editorial: Towards a Healthy Old Age." World Health n4 Jul-Aug 1997. p3. (ISSN0043-8502).

"In 1995, UN estimates for the population aged 60 and over (almost one-tenth of the world's population) showed 302 million women and 247 million men. In the developed countries, women aged 60 and over represented over 20% of the total female population while the corresponding figure for men was only 16%. Projections suggest this divergence is accelerating at the global level, but is even more rapid in the developing world. This is largely explained by the fact that among people aged 80 years and over, the proportion of women is increasing faster than at lower ages. Today 61% of the world's women aged over 80 live in developed countries; by 2025, the majority of them will be living in developing countries." (p8-9)

Stuckelberger, Astrid. "Men and Women Age Differently." World Health n4 Jul-Aug 1997. p8-9. (ISSN0043-8502).

AGED--ARIZONA--SUICIDAL BEHAVIOR

Arizona's "senior suicide rate, at 29 per 100,000 in 1995, exceeded the suicide rates of all other age groups in Arizona. Also, suicide was the second leading cause of injury-related death among older Arizonans in 1995, following only falls....During the last comparable year, 1994, Arizona's rate of suicide for those 65 and older was 26.7 per 100,000, while the national rate was 19.9 per 100,000. Before 1990, Arizona's rate of senior suicide usually exceeded 31 per 100,000 and topped out at 34.2 per 100,000 in 1989. By comparison, the national senior suicide rate ranged from 18.6 to 21.8 per 100,000 during the late 1980s and early 1990s."

Arizona. Dept. of Health Services. "Mental Health Directory Targets Older Adults." News Release 16 Jan 1997. document-level access: <http://www.hs.state.az.us/news/news4.htm>

AGED--AUSTRALIA--POPULATION (v26)

AGED--CALIFORNIA--POPULATION (v26)

AGED--CARE (v26)

AGED--CARE--UNITED STATES

"The number of U.S. households that provide unpaid care to adults aged 50 and older more than tripled between 1987 and 1996, from 7 million to 22.4 million, according to the National Survey of Caregivers....Almost half of caregivers (48 percent) report spending 8 hours or less a week providing eldercare. A decade ago, just 28 percent of caregivers fell into this category. Thirty-eight percent of caregivers also pay for personal care or nursing services, compared with 22 percent in 1987....Those who provide financial help to their dependent spend a median of 3 percent of monthly income, compared with 7 percent in 1987." (p3)

"Eldercare: Less Time, More Money." Forecast v17 n7 Jul 1997. p3. article-level access: <http://www.demographics.com/Publications/FC/97_fc/9707_fc/FC97072.htm> (ISSN0732-1597).

AGED--CHINA--POPULATION (v26)

AGED--CUBA

Currently, over 12% of Cuba's "population (more than 1.3 million) are aged 60 years and over. Life expectancy for a child born today is 76 years, which is among the highest on the American continent. By the year 2020, one in every five Cubans will be an old person." (p28)

Vega, Enrique. "Cuba's 'Circulos de Abuelos.'" World Health n4 Jul-Aug 1997. p28. (ISSN0043-8502).

AGED--DISEASES--UNITED STATES

"Statistics show that approximately 80 percent of those 65 years of age and over are afflicted with one or more chronic diseases, compared with 40 percent of adults between 18 and 64 years of age." (p44) "The rate of hypertension in women is nearly twice that in men, and the rate of hypertension in blacks is higher than that of other races." (p45)

Weimer, Jon P./U.S. Dept. of Agriculture. Economic Research Service. "Nutrition: Many Elderly at Nutritional Risk." Food Review v20 n1 Jan-Apr 1997. p42-48. (ISSN1056-327X).

In the U.S., "only 20 to 30 percent of people over 70 have symptoms of heart disease; an additional 25 percent have heart disease but no symptoms....Only 10 percent of people over 65 ever develop dementia, and much of the cognitive decline that we associate with old age is due to treatable medical conditions and diseases such as depression, diabetes, and hypertension....In 1900, the average life span was 47. It has zoomed to 79 now, largely because of improved sanitation and nutrition and better medical care, which have effectively eliminated two major causes of death: childbirth and infectious diseases like smallpox and polio." (p68)

Shute, Nancy. "1997 Retirement Guide: A Study for the Ages." U.S. News & World Report v122 n22 9 Jun 1997. p66-70,72,76-78. article-level access: <http://www.usnews.com/usnews/issue/970609/9AGE.HTM> (ISSN0041-5537).

AGED--ECONOMIC CONDITIONS

"In the United States, the Congressional Budget Office estimates that under current law, the combined cost of Social Security retirement benefits and government spending on health care for the aged would increase from 10 percent of GDP now to 18 percent in 2030 and would go on rising after that. To pay for that 18 percent of GDP by raising taxes would require the equivalent of doubling the personal income tax or raising the payroll tax rate from 15 percent to more than 35 percent....While the United States will see the ratio of persons 65 and over to those aged 20 to 64 rise from 21 percent in 1990 to 36 percent in 2030, the change in Germany will be from 24 percent to 54 percent. The Organization for Economic Cooperation and Development projects that government retirement benefits (excluding health costs) will exceed 16 percent of the GDP of Germany, France, and Italy by 2030, compared with about 7 percent of GDP in the United States." (p24-25)

Feldstein, Martin. "Supporting Retirees I: The Case for Privatization." Foreign Affairs v76 n4 Jul-Aug 1997. p24-38. (ISSN0015-7120).

AGED--EMPLOYMENT--UNITED STATES (v26)

"The Bureau of Labor Statistics (BLS) confirms what most Americans already know--older, displaced workers face very difficult challenges when seeking new employment. For instance, in comparison with younger workers, older workers, those age 50 and above, have a higher unemployment rate--17 percent versus 12 percent--drop out of the labor force at higher rates after a lay-off--39 percent vs. 10 percent--suffer a longer period of unemployment between jobs--27.3 median weeks vs. 11.6 median weeks--and on average, take a 29.6 percent pay-cut in their median weekly earnings after they do finally secure a new job." (pE1772)

Smith, Christopher H. (Rep.-N.J.). "Displaced Older Workers Deserve Tax Relief." Congressional Record. Daily ed. v143 n124 17 Sep 1997. pE1772-1773. section/page-level access: <http://thomas.loc.gov/cgi-bin/query/R?r105:FLD001:E01772:> (ISSN0363-7239). (X1.1A.105/1).

"According to a recent Health and Retirement Survey sponsored by the National Institute of Aging, three-quarters of [U.S.] workers aged 51 to 61 said they would like to continue working beyond the traditional retirement age. But two-thirds of those surveyed said that they feared their employers wouldn't make it possible for them to continue working as long as they want.... In an analysis of data from a national survey taken in 1994,...[Joseph F. Quinn, a professor at Boston College and an authority on demographic trends among older Americans,] has determined that more than 40 percent of the men and women who quit full-time work moved to bridge jobs rather than directly out of the labor force. Many of these jobs were part-time--fewer than 1,600 hours a year--paid less than previous jobs and were less likely to include pension and health benefits." (p10 secF)

Teegardin, Carol. "Business Monday: Cover Story: Graying and Staying." Detroit Free Press 15 Dec 1997. p8-10 secF.

In the U.S., "the labor force participation rate for males aged 60-64 declined from 82.9 percent to 54.7 percent between 1957 and 1992. The decline for males aged 65-69 was from 52.6 percent to 25.9 percent." (p50)

Steuerle, C. Eugene/Bakija, Jon M. "Retooling Social Security for the 21st Century." Social Security Bulletin v60 n2 1997. p37-60. (ISSN0037-7910).

"Today, America's 55-to-64 year olds are considered a virtual trophy in the workplace--one that is having a beneficial impact on the overall economy....Over the past 2-1/2 years, more than a million seniors have traded their golf clubs and rose gardens for new careers. With the nation's jobless rate at an unusually low 4.9 percent--and expected to drop further today--they are helping to fill a growing labor gap in the United States at all levels." (p1) "After reaching a high of 5.1 percent in 1991, the unemployment rate for the 55-to-64 age group fell to 3 percent in June, according to the Labor Department. This year, older Americans are getting new jobs at an annual rate of 4.1 percent--more than double the 1.8 percent for the overall population. The older group of Americans makes up only 10 percent of the work force but they account for 22 percent of [the] nation's job growth since 1995. And older women are a big part of the story: 51 percent of them work, up from 43 percent in the last decade." (p9)

de Pommereau, Isabelle. "'Restless Retirees' Help Fill Labor Gap." The Christian Science Monitor v89 n241 7 Nov 1997. p1,9. The Christian Science Monitor search engine: <http://www.csmonitor.com/plweb-cgi/iops1.pl> To retrieve this article, enter the following search: ED=19971107 AND gap. In the "retrieved list," click the title that matches this record. (ISSN0882-7729).

In the U.S., "currently 79 percent of workers begin collecting Social Security benefits at age 62....[In 1997,] older Americans ages 55 to 64 are getting new jobs at an annual rate of 4.1 percent--more than double the 1.8 percent for the overall population. Among women ages 55 to 64, 51 percent work, up from 43 percent 10 years ago." (p10-11)

Gardner, Marilyn. "New Outlooks on Retirement: For More Americans, Retiring Includes Clocking in for Work." The Christian Science Monitor v89 n245 14 Nov 1997. p10-11. The Christian Science Monitor search engine: <http://www.csmonitor.com/plweb-cgi/iops1.pl> To retrieve this article, enter the following search: ED=19971114 AND work. In the "retrieved list," click the title that matches this record. (ISSN0882-7729).

AGED--FLORIDA--MIAMI

Miami, Florida, "has one of the nation's highest concentrations of senior citizens--30 percent of residents are older than 65....In Florida...1 in 5 residents is a senior...." (p4)

de Pommereau, Isabelle. "United States: Views from Miami Beach on Changes to Medicare." The Christian Science Monitor v89 n148 26 Jun 1997. p4. The Christian Science Monitor search engine: <http://www.csmonitor.com/plweb-cgi/iops1.pl> To retrieve this article, enter the following search: ED=19970626 AND medicare. In the "retrieved list," click the title that matches this record. (ISSN0882-7729).

AGED--HEALTH AND HYGIENE

In the U.S., "by the year 2000, the number of people aged 75 to 84 will increase by one-third, to 12.3 million people. People over 85, the fastest growing segment of our population, will grow 70 percent, to 4.9 million. One-third of U.S. health care spending today goes to people over age 65. These costs, left unabated, will grow exponentially. The rising aged population will tax Medicare, Medicaid and the health system overall....4 million Americans today have Alzheimer's disease, a degenerative disorder that can leave people unable to function on their own. By delaying the onset of Alzheimer's for 5 years, we can save $50 billion annually. Half of all people over age 65 have symptoms of arthritis. Osteoarthritis costs $8 billion annually. By delaying the onset by 5 years, we can save $4 billion. Hearing loss: 30 percent of adults age 65 to 75, and 40 percent of those over 75, have some degree of hearing impairment. Delaying the onset by just 5 years could save $15 billion annually." (pS4864)

Feinstein, Dianne (Sen.-Calif.). "Concurrent Resolution on the Budget." Congressional Record. Daily ed. v143 n68 21 May 1997. pS4851-4876. section/page-level access: <http://thomas.loc.gov/cgi-bin/query/R?r105:FLD001:S04864:> (ISSN0363-7239). (X1.1A.105/1).

AGED--HEALTH AND HYGIENE--JAPAN (v26)

AGED--HEALTH AND HYGIENE--UNITED STATES (v26)

AGED--INSTITUTIONAL CARE--JAPAN (v26)

AGED--IRELAND--POPULATION

According to Ireland's 1996 Census, "people aged 65 and over account for 11% of the total population in the State. However, there are more older people in rural areas than in urban locations. The 65+ age group account for 10% of the urban population (defined as all towns of 1,500 and over) but 13% of the rural population (the remainder). In the category of towns with a population of 1,500+, Kanturk in Co. Cork had the highest proportion of those aged 65+ with 22%."

Ireland. Central Statistics Office. "1996 Census--Volume 2, Ages and Marital Status." Press Release 30 Oct 1997. document-level access: <http://www.cso.ie/pressreleases/prelcen96v2.html>

AGED--ISRAEL--SEXUAL BEHAVIOR

"Pfeiffer and colleagues, who conducted the Duke Longitudinal Studies, found that more than 75 percent of men in their seventies [in Israel] engaged in coital activity at least once a month....33.4 percent of 80- to 90-year-olds report having sexual relations....A Consumer Union survey shows that 66 percent of men and 47 percent of women in their fifties masturbate with some regularity. The survey also shows that the percentage drops to 43 percent of men and 33 percent of women when they are 70 years of age or older." (p4-5)

Bronner, Gila. "Helping Health Care Professionals on Issues of Intimacy and Sexuality among the Aging." SIECUS Report v25 n5 Jun-Jul 1997. p4-7. (ISSN0091-3995).

AGED--JAMAICA

"Already in 1995 more than 9% of the population [in Jamaica] was aged 60 and over while less than 32% was aged under 15....The seniors in Jamaica (10% of the total population) constitute 23% of voters." (p27)

Eldemire, Denise. "Jamaica's 'Senior Citizens.'" World Health n4 Jul-Aug 1997. p27. (ISSN0043-8502).

AGED--JAPAN (v26)

"In Japan, between 1970 and 1994 the proportion of the population aged 65 and over doubled from 7% to 14%. Projections suggest that by 2020 more than 25% will be over 65, which will probably place Japan in the position of being the world's most aged country." (p20)

Gutman, Gloria M. "Healthy Population Ageing." World Health n4 Jul-Aug 1997. p20-21. (ISSN0043-8502).

AGED--LEBANON

"In 1970, the United Nations estimated the proportion of the population in Lebanon who were aged 60 and older at 7.4%, and in 1985 they estimated it at 7.8%. The figure for 1995 was 8.3%." (p36)

Sibai, Abla. "Ageing in Lebanon." World Health n4 Jul-Aug 1997. p36. (ISSN0043-8502).

AGED--MEDICAL CARE--UNITED STATES

In the U.S., "nearly two of three individuals who provide care to elderly family members are employed full or part time, and about half have reported that their caretaking duties have made them late for work, forced them to come home early or to take time off. These caregivers spend an average of 18 hours a week taking care of loved ones, grocery shopping, managing their medications, and helping with transportation and personal care. Many people needing care are chronically ill. More than one in five caregivers, or about 5 million households nationwide, take care of someone with Alzheimer's disease, confusion, dementia or forgetfulness....Currently, there are more than 33.5 million Americans who are 65 years of age and older. In...Pennsylvania, there are 2 million individuals 65 years of age and older. Many of these seniors live independent lives. However, nationwide approximately 3.9 million of our elderly citizens live with relatives other than their spouse and an additional 1.7 million seniors live in nursing homes." (pS6741)

Specter, Arlen (Sen.-Pa.). "Title II--Protection for Ancient Forests, Roadless Areas, Watershed Protection Areas, Special Areas, and Federal...." Congressional Record. Daily ed. v143 n93 27 Jun 1997. pS6735-6761. section/page-level access: <http://thomas.loc.gov/cgi-bin/query/R?r105:FLD001: S06741:> (ISSN0363-7239). (X1.1A.105/1).

"The elderly account for about 30 percent of all healthcare expenditures in the United States. They also use hospitals at nearly three times the rate of younger persons, average seven to eight medical visits per year, and occupy the majority of nursing residence beds." (p42)

Weimer, Jon P./U.S. Dept. of Agriculture. Economic Research Service. "Nutrition: Many Elderly at Nutritional Risk." Food Review v20 n1 Jan-Apr 1997. p42-48. (ISSN1056-327X).

AGED--MICHIGAN--DETROIT--POPULATION (v26)

AGED--NURSING HOME CARE--UNITED STATES --COSTS (v26)

AGED--POPULATION (v26)

AGED--RETIREMENT

see RETIREMENT

AGED--SWEDEN--SOCIAL CONDITIONS (v26)

AGED--UNITED STATES

In the U.S., "life expectancy for women is 79, for men it is 73. While the population of the United States has tripled since 1900, the number of people age 65 or older has increased 11 times, to more than 33 million Americans. By 2030, this group is projected to double in size to nearly 70 million....[A report issued by the Alliance for Aging Research entitled, 'Will You Still Treat Me When I'm 65?',] concluded that there are only 6,784 primary-care physicians certified in geriatrics. This number represents less than one percent of the total of 684,414 doctors in the United States. The report goes on to state that the United States should have at least 20,000 physicians with geriatric training to provide appropriate care for the current population, and as many as 36,000 geriatricians by the year 2030 when there will be close to 70 million older Americans." (pS5002)

Reid, Harry (Sen.-Nev.). "Statements on Introduced Bills and Joint Resolutions." Congressional Record. Daily ed. v143 n69 22 May 1997. pS5002-5013. section/page-level access: <http://thomas.loc.gov/cgi-bin/query/R?r105:FLD001:S05002:> (ISSN0363-7239). (X1.1A.105/1).

In the U.S., "72.3 percent of men survived from age 21 to age 65 in 1990, compared with just 53.9 percent in 1940; for women the figure rose from 60.6 percent to 83.6 percent....The average life expectancy of men at age 65 rose from 12.7 more years to 15.3 more years between 1940-90; the corresponding increase for women was from 14.7 years to 19.6 years. These figures are projected to rise to 17.2 years for men and 21.5 years for women by the year 2030....Between 1950-91, the share of men older than age 65 participating in the labor force declined sharply from 45.8 percent to just 15.8 percent. Among women, the share stayed low, falling from 9.7 percent to 8.6 percent....The average age at first receipt of Social Security benefits was 63.7 for men and 63.5 for women in 1991, compared with 68.7 and 68.0, respectively in 1950." (p40-41)

Steuerle, C. Eugene/Bakija, Jon M. "Retooling Social Security for the 21st Century." Social Security Bulletin v60 n2 1997. p37-60. (ISSN0037-7910).

AGED--UNITED STATES--ALCOHOL USE

A recent report, "Alcohol, Aging and Driving," by Patricia F. Waller, director of the University of Michigan Transportation Research Institute, says that "alcohol-related crashes for older drivers [in the U.S.] are rare--11 percent of drivers ages 65 to 74 and 5 percent of those 75 and older tested positive for alcohol in fatal crashes in 1994....The percentage of elderly drinkers who use alcohol heavily (19 percent of men, 10 percent of women) is just as high as that of any other age group of drinkers...." (p2)

University of Michigan. News and Information Services. "Alcohol Use for Older Drivers Could Be Higher in the Near Future, Says a U-M Researcher." University of Michigan News Release 29 May 1997. p1-2.

AGED--UNITED STATES--ATTITUDES

"The reasonable hope or strong certainty that social support will be available has a more beneficial effect on the mental and physical health of the elderly under economic stress than actually receiving help, according to a national study from the University of Michigan School of Public Health....The U-M findings are based on interviews with 947 persons aged 65 or older (average age was 74) from across the...[U.S.]." (p1) "The major economic stressors included having difficulty paying phone or utility bills, a loss of 20 percent or more of one's income, a problem with Social Security or retirement benefits, failing to qualify for money to pay for medical, food or housing expenses, and having been unable to pay for a major purchase. Sixteen percent of those in the study had encountered one of the economic stressors in the past year while 5 percent had encountered more than one....[According to Neal M. Krause, professor of health behavior and health education at the U-M School of Public Health,] 'the highest level of anticipated support reduced the noxious effects of economic stress on depression scores by approximately 77 percent.'" (p2)

University of Michigan. News and Information Services. "The Anticipation of Receiving Social Support...Reduces Stress in Elderly under...Stress...According to...U-M...." University of Michigan News Release 17 Dec 1997. p1-3.

AGED--UNITED STATES--ECONOMIC CONDITIONS (v26)

"According to 1995 estimates by the Bureau of Census, almost 11 percent of Americans over age 65 had incomes below the official Federal poverty levels, compared with, for example, a poverty rate of 8 percent for 'middle-aged' Americans (35-54 years of age)....Differences were even more pronounced for those 75 years of age and over. The overall poverty rate for this age group was 13 percent, but women in this age bracket had a poverty rate of almost 17 percent, versus 8 percent for men that age....About 33 percent of blacks over age 75 were in poverty, compared with 11 percent for whites and 27 percent for Hispanics....Many elderly live on fixed incomes (such as pensions), while retail food prices continue to rise. As a result, households headed by the elderly spend an average of about 15 percent of their incomes for food, compared with about 12 percent for all U.S. households." (p45-46)

Weimer, Jon P./U.S. Dept. of Agriculture. Economic Research Service. "Nutrition: Many Elderly at Nutritional Risk." Food Review v20 n1 Jan-Apr 1997. p42-48. (ISSN1056-327X).

U.S. "Census Bureau Data indicate that a higher percentage of those over 55 own vehicles, primary residences, investment real estate, and businesses than any other age group. Census Bureau data also show that only 10.1 percent of those 65 years to 75 years have incomes below the poverty line--compared with 21.8 percent under 18, and 18 percent of those 18 to 24." (p19)

Rueter, Ted. "Opinion/Essays: Senior Citizen Discounts Are Affirmative Action for the Wealthy." The Christian Science Monitor v89 n194 2 Sep 1997. p19. The Christian Science Monitor search engine: <http://www.csmonitor.com/plweb-cgi/iops1.pl> To retrieve this article, enter the following search: ED=19970902 AND wealthy. In the "retrieved list," click the title that matches this record. (ISSN0882-7729).

AGED--UNITED STATES--FAMILY RELATIONSHIPS (v26)

AGED--UNITED STATES--NUTRITION

"The Urban Institute recently estimated that as many as 4.9 million seniors--about 16 percent of the population aged 60 and older--are either hungry or malnourished [in the U.S.]. According to studies from the University of Florida, 89 percent of Meals on Wheels recipients are at moderate to high risk for malnutrition. Meals on Wheels and congregate meals help these Americans stay healthy. Yet, 41 percent of Meals on Wheels programs nationwide have waiting lists today....Today in America 4 million seniors live in poverty, and another 16 million are near poverty. Half of our senior citizens in this country live on incomes of $15,000 or less per year. As Mathematica Policy Research found last year, the senior nutrition programs are well targeted at poor elderly Americans. The average beneficiary of these programs is 77 years old, and 90 percent of beneficiaries live below 200 percent of poverty; about 40 percent have subpoverty incomes." (pH5685)

Sanders, Bernard (Rep.-Vt.). "Agriculture, Rural Development, Food and Drug Administration...Appropriations Act, 1998." Congressional Record. Daily ed. v143 n106 24 Jul 1997. pH5672-5732. section/page-level access: <http://thomas.loc.gov/cgi-bin/query/R?r105:FLD001:H05684:> (ISSN0363-7239). (X1.1A.105/1).

AGED--UNITED STATES--POPULATION (v26)

"The number of Americans age 60 or over has grown from about 5 million in 1900 to approximately 42 million in 1990--a figure that will more than double by the year 2030....The proportion of Americans over 60 years of age has also increased, from 6.4 to 18.4 percent of the U.S. population during 1900-90--a share that will expand to almost a quarter of the population by 2030." (p42)

Weimer, Jon P./U.S. Dept. of Agriculture. Economic Research Service. "Nutrition: Many Elderly at Nutritional Risk." Food Review v20 n1 Jan-Apr 1997. p42-48. (ISSN1056-327X).

According to the publication "A Profile of Older Americans, 1997," "the older population (persons 65 years or older) numbered 33.9 million in 1996. They represented 12.8% of the U.S. population, about one in every eight Americans. Over 2 million persons celebrated their 65th birthday in 1996 (5,570 per day). In 1996, there were 20.0 million older women and 13.9 million older men."

U.S. Administration on Aging. "AoA Announces Availability of 'A Profile of Older Americans, 1997.'" Press Release 3 Oct 1997. document-level access: <http://www.aoa.dhhs.gov/pr/profile97.html>

In the U.S., "the state with the largest proportion of elderly in 1995 was Florida (18.6 percent)....Alaska had only 5 percent of its total population in this age cohort in 1995....Only five states--Florida, Pennsylvania, Rhode Island, West Virginia and Iowa--in 1995 had elderly populations of 15 percent or higher." (p33)

Yavarkovsky, Judith. "Historical Perspectives." Statistical Bulletin v78 n4 Oct-Dec 1997. p33. (ISSN0790-8334).

AGED--UNITED STATES--SOCIAL CONDITIONS

"By age 65, 69 percent of Americans live with one or more chronic conditions. Those who make it to age 85 are more likely than the younger old to live alone: 29 percent of all men and 57 percent of all women aged 85-plus are on their own. Nearly half of people aged 85 and older require some assistance with at least one activity of daily living (ADL), such as bathing, dressing, getting in and out of a chair or a bed, or some Instrumental Activity of Daily Living (IADL), such as meal preparation, shopping, taking medications properly, paying bills, or using the telephone. This old-old age cohort will grow from 4.5 million today to 7 million by 2020, according to Census Bureau projections. In increments, the 85-plus population will grow 39 percent during the 1990s and 33 percent in the following decade....The number of available family and unrelated caregivers, primarily women aged 50 to 64, will shrink in proportion to the number of dependents with chronic conditions or disabilities, according to a study prepared for the Robert Wood Johnson Foundation by the Institute for Health & Aging at the University of California in San Francisco. In 1990, the ratio of potential caregivers aged 50 to 64 to persons aged 85 and older was 11 to 1. By the year 2010, it will be 10 to 1, and by 2030, 6 to 1." (p50)

Barton, Linda J. "A Shoulder to Lean On: Assisted Living in the U.S." American Demographics v19 n7 Jul 1997. p45-51. article-level access: <http://www.demographics.com/publications/ad/97_ad/9707_ad/ad970713.htm> (ISSN0163-4089).

AGED--UNITED STATES--SUICIDAL BEHAVIOR

In the U.S., "from 1980 to 1992, the suicide rate among persons age 65 and older increased nine percent, and most striking was a

35 percent rise in rates of suicide for men and women age 80 to 84. The suicide rate among males 85 years and older is six times the rate of the general population....Most older persons who are suicidal visit their primary care physician in the month before killing themselves, with nearly 40 percent making that visit in the week before committing suicide." (p6)

"Nearly 40 Percent of Older Suicide Victims Visit Doctor during Week before Killing Themselves." California Community Care News v9 n9 Sep 1997. p6,10.

AGED, ABUSED

see ABUSED AGED

AGED, HANDICAPPED

see HANDICAPPED AGED

AGED, POOR

see POOR AGED

AGED AUTOMOBILE DRIVERS--CONNECTICUT (v26)

AGED WOMEN

see also POOR AGED WOMEN

AGED WOMEN--UNITED STATES (v26)

In the U.S., "women comprise 60 percent of today's population aged 65 and over. By the year 2000, it is expected that there will be five women for every two men over the age of 75. Compared to men, elderly women are three times more likely to be widowed or living alone, spending more years and a larger portion of their lifetimes disabled or residing in a nursing facility."

U.S. Dept. of Health and Human Services. "Improving Women's Health." Fact Sheet 25 Oct 1997. document-level access: <http://www.hhs.gov/news/press/1997pres/971025c.html>

AGED WOMEN--UNITED STATES--SOCIAL CONDITIONS

According to the U.S. Census Bureau and the National Institute on Aging, "elderly women are more than three times as likely as men to be widowed. The poverty rate is higher for older women (15.7%) compared with elderly men (8.9%). Women (age 55 and older) make up an increasing share of the older workforce, from 23% in 1950 to 44% in 1993." (p11)

"Older Women: A Few Facts." California Community Care News v9 n11 Nov 1997. p11.

Although the majority of adult women in the U.S. "marry, 85 percent arrive at their final years alone--unmarried or widowed....In 1988, Social Security accounted for more than 90 percent of the total income for one-third of older women who are unmarried or widowed. And, according to the American Association of Retired Persons, of the 12 percent of elderly people who live in poverty, 74 percent are women." (p6 secB)

Heady, Christy. "Work & Money: Age-Old Question Even More Apt for Women." The Christian Science Monitor v90 n9 8 Dec 1997. p6 secB. The Christian Science Monitor search engine: <http://www.csmonitor.com/plweb-cgi/iops1.pl> To retrieve this article, enter the following search: ED=19971208 AND women. In the "retrieved list," click the title that matches this record. (ISSN0882-7729).

AGENT ORANGE

see TETRACHLORODIBENZODIOXIN

AGRICULTURAL ASSISTANCE, AMERICAN --DEVELOPING COUNTRIES (v26)

AGRICULTURAL BANKS

see BANKS AND BANKING

AGRICULTURAL CONSERVATION--UNITED STATES (v26)

AGRICULTURAL COOPERATIVE CREDIT ASSOCIATIONS --AFRICA

"Of the 86 farmers' organizations belonging to the International Federation of Agricultural Producers, 23 are from 19 countries in Africa. In Zimbabwe, 1.3 million households belong to the Zimbabwe Farmers Union (ZFU). With an average of six per family, the ZFU caters to almost 8 million people. In Senegal, the National Council for Rural Unity and Cooperation comprises nine farmers' associations with a combined membership of 3 million. According to the International Cooperative Alliance, the number of farmers' cooperatives in Africa is smaller than in other regions and accounts for just 6 per cent of the world total, but is still significant: 24,000 cooperative associations, with some 10.4 million members. In some countries, such as Morocco, one in five small-scale farmers belongs to a farmers' organization, most frequently a cooperative." (p19)

Tafirenyika, Masimba. "Agriculture in Africa: Farmers Organize to Promote Interests." Africa Recovery v11 n2 Oct 1997. p19.

AGRICULTURAL CREDIT--UNITED STATES (v26)

During 1996, the U.S. Farm Credit System's "earnings reached $1.2 billion. Total System capital increased to $10.6 billion at the end of 1996, which represented 14.1 percent of total assets. Total capital was 13.6 percent of total assets at yearend 1995....Nonperforming assets comprised only 1.6 percent of total loans and other property owned at the end of 1996, down from 2 percent a year earlier. Overall loan volume climbed by $2.6 billion during the year....With a 1 being the best rating, the percentage of System institutions rated 3, 4, or 5 dropped from 36 percent at the end of 1992 to only 5 percent on December 31, 1996." (p45)

Martin, Marsha Pyle (Chair and CEO, U.S. Farm Credit Administration). "Agriculture, Rural Development, Food and Drug Administration...Approp. for 1998 (Part 2)." Hearing. U.S. House. Committee on Appropriations. Washington, D.C. : GPO, 1997. (Y4.Ap6/1:Ag8/997/pt.2).

In the 1992 U.S. "Census, operators who were 35 or younger made up 11 percent of farm operators. Of these, 57 percent reported that they paid interest on farm debt, so about 6.3 percent were customers for farm lenders. At the end of 1992, the FCS [Farm Credit Service] had 31,735 loans outstanding to young farmers in a total portfolio of 609,030 loans, or about 5.2 percent of its loans." (p37-38)

U.S. Farm Credit Administration. "Agriculture, Rural Development, Food and Drug Administration...Approp. for 1998 (Part 2)." Hearing. U.S. House. Committee on Appropriations. Washington, D.C. : GPO, 1997. (Y4.Ap6/1:Ag8/997/pt.2).

In the U.S., "total farm loans outstanding increased from 1 percent in 1994 to 6.5 percent in 1996....Nonreal estate loans rose 6 percent in 1994, and 12 percent in 1995 and 1996. FCS [Farm Credit System] now accounts for almost 19 percent of all nonreal estate loans, its largest share of this market since 1984." (p20)

U.S. Dept. of Agriculture. Economic Research Service. "1996 Farm Income Estimates: Debt Repayment Ability Improves, With Higher Income Levels...Offsetting Larger Debt." Agricultural Income and Finance Situation and Outlook Report Sep 1997. p20-22.

AGRICULTURAL INCOME

see FARM INCOME

AGRICULTURAL LABORERS (v26)

see also MIGRANT LABOR; PESTICIDES--HEALTH ASPECTS--AGRICULTURAL LABORERS

AGRICULTURAL LABORERS--BRAZIL

In Brazil, "of the total number of landless or land poor agricultural workers only 17.4 percent are permanently employed. 20.5 percent can only find temporary employment, 5.8 percent are sharecroppers and another 4.9 percent rent small parcels of land for subsistence farming. Another 38 percent of rural workers own land, but most do not have enough land to produce for commercial purposes and thereby guarantee their tenure rights. Today, 13.4 percent of Brazil's rural workers are squatting on idle lands to claim land tenure rights in accord with the 1988 Federal Constitution." (p2)

"The Rural Poor." Food First Backgrounder v4 n3 Fall 1997. p2.

AGRICULTURAL LABORERS--CALIFORNIA--SOCIAL CONDITIONS

"In the early 1990's, 700 undocumented [farm] workers were discovered living in caves in California because of the lack of housing. Infant mortality rates are 25 percent higher among farm labor communities than the general population, and often children are forced into the fields as early as age 10." (p35)

Bautista, Liberato C. "Perspectives/UN: The US Government Must Fulfill Earth Summit Commitments." Christian Social Action v10 n8 Sep 1997. p34-35. (ISSN0897-0459).

AGRICULTURAL LABORERS--CHILDREN

According to International Labour Organization "estimates in a number of developing countries, the rate of economically active children between the ages 5 to 14 is 10% of the total economically active population. Seventy per cent of these working children are engaged in agriculture."

International Labour Organization. "ILO Warns on Farm Safety: Agriculture Mortality Rates Remain High: Pesticides Pose Major Health Risks to...Workforce." Press Release 22 Oct 1997. document-level access: <http://www.unicc.org/ilo/public/english/235press/pr/1997/23.htm>

AGRICULTURAL LABORERS--INDIA--KASHMIR, VALE OF (v26)

AGRICULTURAL LABORERS--TENNESSEE

In Tennessee, "the estimated number of workers employed during 1995 on a full-time, part-time, or migrant basis by agricultural, sawmill, and agri-processing operations equaled 61,476....This estimated level of agricultural employment in Tennessee included 15,484 full-time; 39,802 part-time; and 6,190 migrant workers. Full-time paid-labor represented 25% of all agricultural employees, but accounted for 73% of the total hours worked." (p6-7)

Pompelli, Greg/Danekas, Gene/Allen, Fred. "Ag Laborers--Who's Working Where and for What Wages?" Tennessee Agri Science n182 Spr 1997. p6-10.

In Tennessee, "the total earnings for agricultural workers exceeded $264 million in 1995--an average of $4,300 per worker....75% of the employees were part-time or migrant workers who, on average, were only employed about 30 days during the year. On average, full-time workers received annual earnings of $13,259." (p7)

Pompelli, Greg/Danekas, Gene/Allen, Fred. "Ag Laborers--Who's Working Where and for What Wages?" Tennessee Agri Science n182 Spr 1997. p6-10.

AGRICULTURAL LABORERS--UNITED STATES (v26)

In the U.S., "there has been a small, 34,000 worker, growth in agricultural employment since 1994, from 3,409,000 to 3,443,000....A more detailed listing of the published BLS [Bureau of Labor Statistics] household data reveals agricultural employment data included some agricultural service workers--198,000 in veterinary services, 803,000 in landscape and horticultural services, and 196,000 in other agricultural services--as well as 2,247,000 farm workers." (p467)

U.S. Dept. of Agriculture. "Agriculture, Rural Development, Food and Drug Administration...Approp. for 1998 (Part 4)." Hearing. U.S. House. Committee on Appropriations. Washington, D.C. : GPO, 1997. (ISBN0160551560). (Y4.Ap6/1:Ag8/997/pt.4).

AGRICULTURAL MACHINERY--UNITED STATES (v26)

AGRICULTURAL PESTS--CONTROL--ASIA (v26)

AGRICULTURAL POLLUTION--SWEDEN (v26)

AGRICULTURAL PROCESSING--UNITED STATES (v26)

AGRICULTURAL SUBSIDIES--CANADA--UNITED STATES (v26)

AGRICULTURAL SUBSIDIES--UNITED STATES

In the U.S., "data from the 1995 Farm Costs and Returns Survey show that government payments were 4 percent of gross cash income. The average participating farm received $8,225. Farms having sales over $250,000 received 31 percent of total payments and produced 47 percent of program commodities. Almost half of the payments accrued to farmers in the Corn Belt and northern Plains, where farms are predominantly cash grains. Government payments were 6-7 percent of gross cash income in these two regions. Another 17 percent of payments went to farmers in the Lake States." (p481-482)

U.S. Dept. of Agriculture. "Agriculture, Rural Development, Food and Drug Administration...Approp. for 1998 (Part 4)." Hearing. U.S. House. Committee on Appropriations. Washington, D.C. : GPO, 1997. (ISBN0160551560). (Y4.Ap6/1:Ag8/997/pt.4).

In 1996, the U.S. "Government spent $97 million on a variety of taxpayer-supported tobacco subsidies....In 1993, Federal taxpayers gave $65 million of Federal tax money to the growers and cultivators of tobacco. In 1994, the figure was $60 million. In 1995, $51 million....And it is estimated this year that we will spend $67 million to subsidize tobacco." (pS7902)

Durbin, Richard J. (Sen.-Ill.). "Agriculture, Rural Development, Food and Drug Administration...Appropriations Act, 1998." Congressional Record. Daily ed. v143 n105 23 Jul 1997. pS7898-7911. section/page-level access: <http://thomas.loc.gov/cgi-bin/query/R?r105:FLD001:S07902:> (ISSN0363-7239). (X1.1A.105/1).

"The U.S. Department of Agriculture estimates that between 1990 and 1995, farmers received 5 percent of their gross cash income via direct government payments....By forcing farmers to plant more for the world market and less for the government, policymakers hope to save the $9 billion taxpayers have spent annually on subsidy programs in recent years." (p10)

DeVore, Brian. "Freedom to Farm, Freedom to...?" Land Stewardship Letter v15 n3 Jun-Jul 1997. p1,10-12.

AGRICULTURE (v26)

see also ANIMAL INDUSTRY; AQUACULTURE; BURNING OF LAND; ENERGY CROPS; FARMERS; FARMS; FORESTS AND FORESTRY; GARDENING; HORTICULTURE; IRRIGATION FARMING; LIVESTOCK; NITROGEN IN AGRICULTURE; ORGANIC FARMING; OSTRICH FARMING; URBAN AGRICULTURE

AGRICULTURE--ACCIDENTS

"Workers in agriculture run at least twice the risk of dying on the job as workers in other sectors according to the Assistant Director General of the International Labour Office, Mr. Ali Taqi, who estimates that at least 170,000 agricultural workers are killed each year. In remarks prepared for an international meeting of farm safety and health experts...he said that millions more of the world's 1.3 billion agricultural workers are seriously injured in workplace accidents involving machinery, or poisoned by pesticides and other agrochemicals....In the US,...farmers and farm workers comprise only 3% of the workforce, but they account for nearly 8% of all work-related accidents. In Italy 9.7% of workers are in agricultural production, but they account for 28.7% of accidents."

International Labour Organization. "ILO Warns on Farm Safety: Agriculture Mortality Rates Remain High: Pesticides Pose Major Health Risks to...Workforce." Press Release 22 Oct 1997. document-level access: <http://www.unicc.org/ilo/public/english/235press/pr/1997/23.htm>

AGRICULTURE--AETA (PHILIPPINE PEOPLE) (v26)

AGRICULTURE--AFRICA

"Agriculture's impressive 5.2 per cent growth in 1996 was 'the major factor behind the strong economic recovery in...[sub-Saharan Africa],' said the UN Economic Commission for Africa (ECA) in its annual report on Africa's overall economic and social situation. The sector contributed significantly to the 3.9 per cent growth in the continent's gross domestic product (GDP)....African exporters of agricultural raw materials saw a 3 per cent decline in world prices, while those that exported cocoa, coffee and tea were hit by a 17 per cent decline....In Africa, overall agricultural production rose by an annual average of 2 per cent between 1965 and 1980, and has continued to climb about 1.8 per cent per year since then....With Africa's population growing rapidly (averaging 2.9 per cent a year), agricultural production, including of food, has declined steadily in per capita terms....According to the UN Conference on Trade and Development (UNCTAD), in its 'Trade and Development Report,' released in September 1997, the domestic terms of trade for agricultural products in 13 sub-Saharan African countries improved from the 1970s through the 1990s. The greatest gain came in the 1985-95 period, when the domestic value of agricultural products increased, in relation to manufactured goods, by 30.6 per cent." (p6-7)

Harsch, Ernest. "Agriculture in Africa: Africa Strives to Revitalize Agriculture." Africa Recovery v11 n2 Oct 1997. p6-9.

"In 12 African countries for which comparable budget data is available, agriculture's share of total budgetary expenditures fell from an average of 8.4 per cent during 1984-89 to 6.5 per cent during 1990-94....As a percentage of government spending on economic sectors, agriculture's overall share fell only slightly between the two periods, from 39.0 per cent to 38.8 per cent....For the three North African countries in the sample, agriculture's share increased from 36.5 per cent to 42.7 per cent, while for the nine countries in sub-Saharan Africa, it fell more clearly, from 39.9 per cent to 37.5 per cent." (p9)

Harsch, Ernest. "Agriculture in Africa: Africa Strives to Revitalize Agriculture." Africa Recovery v11 n2 Oct 1997. p6-9.

AGRICULTURE--AFRICA, NORTH--MIDDLE EAST --UNITED STATES (v26)

AGRICULTURE--ASIA--UNITED STATES

"Although Asia accounted for 46 percent of total U.S. agricultural exports in 1997 and as much as three-fourths of U.S. exports of some commodities, South Korea and Southeast Asia represent a far smaller portion of U.S. agricultural exports. Southeast Asia accounted for only 5 percent of U.S. agricultural exports in 1997, while South Korea accounted for 6 percent." (p8)

U.S. Dept. of Agriculture. "Regional Highlights." Outlook for U.S. Agricultural Exports 2 Dec 1997. p8,10.

"In 1997, Asia is the third largest source of U.S. [agricultural] imports, after Latin America and Western Europe. Imports from Asia have risen to $5.9 billion, 10 percent over 1996. U.S. exports to Asia, by far the United States' largest export market, have contracted 8 percent to $24.5 billion dollars....Agricultural trade with Asia is nearly a $19-billion surplus....Indonesia is the main source of agricultural imports, providing $1.4 billion in the first 11 months of 1997." (p1)

U.S. Dept. of Agriculture. Economic Research Service. "Agricultural Imports from Asia Expand, While Exports to Asia Contract." U.S. Agricultural Trade Update 23 Oct 1997. p1.

AGRICULTURE--ASIA, SOUTHEASTERN--UNITED STATES

In Southeast Asia, "imports from the U.S. totaled a record of almost $3.3 billion in 1996. Together the Philippines, Indonesia, Thailand, and Malaysia...increased imports of U.S. agricultural products at an annual rate of 17 percent from 1990 to 1996, and this growth accounted for 10 percent of the expansion of U.S. agricultural exports over this period." (p18)

Vocke, Gary/U.S. Dept. of Agriculture. Economic Research Service. "World Agriculture & Trade: Ag Trade Opportunities in Southeast Asia." Agricultural Outlook Nov 1997. p18-21.

AGRICULTURE--AUSTRALIA (v26)

"Preliminary estimates on the gross value of Australian agricultural production during 1996-97, released by the Australian Bureau of Statistics...show a decrease from 1995-96 of 0.8 per cent to $27,242.9m [million]....The statistics show falling average prices resulted in decreases in the value of barley, which fell 6.2 per cent to $1,197.4m and of sugar cane for crushing, which fell 7.0 per cent to $1,146.6m, despite increases in production for both of these commodities. Reductions in the area sown resulted in lower production and hence value, for many other crops, including oats, down 27.2 per cent to $210.6m and sorghum, down 45.2 per cent to $175.7m. Increases did occur, however, in the value of some crops such as wheat, up 10.1 per cent to a record $4,739.3m, cotton, up 9.2 per cent $1,106.7m and rice, up 32.7 per cent $299.8m. The gross value of all livestock slaughterings increased by 0.3 per cent to $6,210.4m, reflecting increases in the numbers of sheep and lambs, and poultry slaughtered during 1996-97."

Australian Bureau of Statistics. "Lower Prices Led to Reduction in Gross Value of Agricultural Production for 1996-97--ABS." Media Release 7 Oct 1997. document-level access: <http://www.abs.gov.au/websitedbs/d3110125.nsf/4a255eef008309e44a255eef00061e57/8f9c98c635cc911d4a256529000436f7?OpenDocument>

AGRICULTURE--AUSTRALIA--CHINA

In 1996, "Australia and New Zealand became China's second largest agricultural product suppliers, occupying 19 percent of the import market, only 2 percent behind the United States. Australia gained in all four types of commodity markets, with bulk goods gaining the most, from 4 percent in 1995 to nearly 20 percent in 1996, becoming one of the three dominant players in China's bulk goods import market (the other two were the United States and Canada, occupying 35 and 20 percent, respectively)." (p9)

Wang, Zhi/U.S. Dept. of Agriculture. Economic Research Service. "China's Agricultural Trade in 1996: Commodity Structure, Geographical Distribution, And Its Role in U.S...Trade." China: International Agriculture and Trade Reports Situation and Outlook Series Jun 1997. p6-15.

AGRICULTURE--BRAZIL (v26)

AGRICULTURE--CALIFORNIA

"For the last 50 years California has held the title as the Nation's No. 1 agricultural State....Agricultural exports account for over half of California's total agricultural products which brings $22 billion into the California economy every year....For some products, such as the sale of cotton...exports account for 75 percent of the $1 billion in total sales revenues. Agriculture provides 1 in every 10 jobs in the State....According to the California Department of Food and Agriculture's 1995 Crop Report, 'for every $1 billion in export sales, 27,000 jobs are created in the state'. By this approximation, agricultural exports helped the total California economy by creating 124,000 jobs, and these jobs, on average, pay more than non-export related jobs. In...Kern County's $350 million in exports sales creates almost 10,000 jobs, which does not include indirect economic benefits." (pE2018)

Thomas, William M. (Rep.-Calif.). "Agricultural Export

Benefit California." Congressional Record. Daily ed. v143 n142 21 Oct 1997. pE2018. section/page-level access: <http://thomas.loc.gov/cqi-bin/query/R?r105:FLD001:E02018:> (ISSN0363-7239). (X1.1A.105/1).

AGRICULTURE--CANADA (v26)

AGRICULTURE--CANADA--MEXICO--UNITED STATES

"During the 3 years since NAFTA's inception (1994-96), U.S. agricultural imports from Mexico grew 38 percent compared with the 3-year period preceding NAFTA (1991-93), while U.S. imports from Canada grew 46 percent. U.S. imports from all non-NAFTA source countries grew only 18 percent....In 1996, the U.S. imported more than $33 billion of agricultural products from more than 200 countries. Of this total, $6.8 billion, or 20 percent, came from Canada--the largest U.S. import source--and another $3.8 billion came from Mexico. Together, Canada and Mexico supplied 31 percent of U.S. agricultural imports in 1996." (p23)

Handy, Chuck/Ruppel, Fred/U.S. Dept. of Agriculture. Economic Research Service. "Special Article: NAFTA: Impacts on U.S. Consumers." Agricultural Outlook Sep 1997. p23.

"U.S. agricultural exports to Mexico and Canada increased from $8.87 billion in 1993 to $11.59 billion in 1996. During the same period, U.S. agricultural imports from the NAFTA partners grew from $7.33 billion to $10.55 billion....U.S. agricultural exports to Mexico plunged in 1995, offsetting the 22 percent growth in 1994. The Mexican economy began a strong recovery in 1996 and U.S. exports surged 55 percent...." (p2)

U.S. Dept. of Agriculture. Economic Research Service. "Foreword." NAFTA: International Agriculture and Trade Reports Situation and Outlook Series Sep 1997. p2.

AGRICULTURE--CANADA--UNITED STATES

"U.S. agricultural exports to Canada reached a record $6 billion in fiscal 1996. Growth was only 2 percent, much less than the previous year's 11 percent...." (p10)

Huang, Sophia Wu/U.S. Dept. of Agriculture. Economic Research Service. "U.S. Agricultural Exports to APEC Region at Another Record." APEC: International Agriculture and Trade Reports Situation and Outlook Series Aug 1997. p9-12.

"U.S. agricultural exports to Canada grew nearly 5 percent per year between 1993 and 1996, to a record $6.1 billion. Twelve commodities--corn, pork, cotton, orange juice, sugar and related products, hides and skins, beverages except juice, soybean meal, wine, peanuts, field seeds, and rice--as a group, increased $382 million, up 42 percent from 1993." (p5)

U.S. Dept. of Agriculture. Economic Research Service. "Executive Summary." NAFTA: International Agriculture and Trade Reports Situation and Outlook Series Sep 1997. p3-6.

"U.S. agricultural exports to Canada increased to a record $6.1 billion in 1996, accounting for a dominant 65-percent share of Canada's agricultural imports. Even in the mature Canadian market, U.S. agricultural exports have averaged 5.2 percent annual growth since 1993." (p4)

U.S. Dept. of Agriculture. Economic Research Service. "Executive Summary." NAFTA: International Agriculture and Trade Reports Situation and Outlook Series Sep 1997. p3-6.

"U.S. agricultural imports from Canada grew 13.7 percent per year from 1993 to 1996 to $6.8 billion. Twelve commodities--swine, pork, cocoa, potatoes, beef and veal, biscuits and wafers, cattle, oats, barley, sugar and related products, rapeseed, and beverages excluding fruit juices--as a group increased $1.1 billion." (p5)

U.S. Dept. of Agriculture. Economic Research Service. "Executive Summary." NAFTA: International Agriculture and Trade Reports Situation and Outlook Series Sep 1997. p3-6.

AGRICULTURE--CHINA (v26)

"In 1996, China's agricultural trade (exports and imports) reached US$20.3 billion, a decrease of nearly 10 percent from 1995. The decline stemmed from lower imports which fell 18.5 percent to US$9.7 billion. Exports increased 0.1 percent to $10.6 billion....In 1996, China shipped more than 65 percent of its agricultural exports to neighboring Asian markets. About half of China's agricultural imports came from the United States, Canada, and Australia. U.S. agricultural exports to China in 1996 declined from their 1995 peak but still remained above $2 billion....[1996] grain imports decreased by about 47 percent, with corn falling by more than 90 percent, followed by rice (54 percent), and wheat (29 percent). Cotton and vegetable oil imports also fell by 12 and 25 percent, respectively. On the export side, grain exports nearly doubled from 1995 (93 percent in quantity terms, 168 percent in value terms)....In calendar year 1996, net grain imports were 9.59 million metric tons (half the 1995 level), with more than 8 million metric tons wheat." (p6)

Wang, Zhi/U.S. Dept. of Agriculture. Economic Research Service. "China's Agricultural Trade in 1996: Commodity Structure, Geographical Distribution, And Its Role in U.S...Trade." China: International Agriculture and Trade Reports Situation and Outlook Series Jun 1997. p6-15.

"In terms of total agricultural trade, China shifted from a net importer in 1995 with a deficit of $1.3 billion to a net exporter in 1996 with a surplus of $0.9 billion....[China] has to feed 22 percent of the world's population with only 9 percent (Crook, 1993) of the world's arable land." (p7) "About 40 percent of China's agricultural exports were consumer-ready processed goods, while nearly 95 percent of its agricultural imports were bulk commodities and processed intermediates....The import share of bulk goods fell 6.8 percentage points in 1996, while the import share of processed intermediates increased by 6.3 percentage points. The reason for this change is that imports of bulk products fell dramatically compared with processed intermediates (29 over 6 percent)...." (p8)

Wang, Zhi/U.S. Dept. of Agriculture. Economic Research Service. "China's Agricultural Trade in 1996: Commodity Structure, Geographical Distribution, And Its Role in U.S...Trade." China: International Agriculture and Trade Reports Situation and Outlook Series Jun 1997. p6-15.

AGRICULTURE--CHINA--FINANCE

"Agricultural projects only constituted 2.2 and 2.4 percent of total FDI [foreign direct investment] projects in China in 1994 and 1995, respectively. The amount of pledged investment of those projects only accounted for 1.2 and 1.9 percent respectively, of the total pledged amount....From 1991 to 1995, the contracted funds to agriculture sectors were $4.82 billion, 4.2 times the amount pledged during the previous 12 years (1979-1990)....Guangdong, Fujian, and Shandong accounted for more than 70 percent of those pledged investments." (p14)

Wang, Zhi/U.S. Dept. of Agriculture. Economic Research Service. "China's Agricultural Trade in 1996: Commodity Structure, Geographical Distribution, And Its Role in U.S...Trade." China: International Agriculture and Trade Reports Situation and Outlook Series Jun 1997. p6-15.

AGRICULTURE--CHINA--UNITED STATES

"China only plays a moderate role in world agricultural trade, accounting for 2-3 percent of total world trade, despite the fact that its world market share increased over the past 10 years by about 1 percentage point....China is an important buyer of U.S. bulk commodities, although it absorbed less than 5 percent of total U.S. farm exports. In 1996, for instance, it was the world's largest buyer of U.S. cotton, taking 28 percent of total U.S. exports (the second largest buyer--Japan--took 11 percent). It was also the world's third largest buyer of U.S. wheat (7 percent) and the sixth largest buyer of U.S. soybeans

(6 percent). However, China is not a stable buyer of U.S. farm goods like Japan." (p12) "China imported nearly 20 million metric tons of grains in 1995....[China's] share in total U.S. grain exports fell from 7.7 to 2.3 percent, while its share in total U.S. cotton exports increased from 23 to 28 percent, and its share in total U.S. oilseeds exports increased from 4.6 to 6 percent." (p14)

Wang, Zhi/U.S. Dept. of Agriculture. Economic Research Service. "China's Agricultural Trade in 1996: Commodity Structure, Geographical Distribution, And Its Role in U.S...Trade." China: International Agriculture and Trade Reports Situation and Outlook Series Jun 1997. p6-15.

"In 1996, U.S. agricultural exports to China declined 21 percent from its 1995 peak because of sharply decreased grain sales (60 percent), but still reached $2.1 billion, much higher than 1994 ($1.1 billion)....Although the total U.S. agricultural exports to China declined in 1996, it still had an agricultural trade surplus with China close to US$ 1.5 billion. U.S. exports of consumer-ready products increased by 60 percent, despite declining sales in other commodity categories....Although U.S. sales of consumer-ready goods to China increased rapidly in recent years, it still accounted for less than 5 percent of U.S. farm products sold in China (its share doubled from 2.3 percent in 1995 to 4.6 percent in 1996). Bulk and semi-processed commodities still constituted more than 95 percent of U.S. agricultural exports to China....Labor-intensive consumer-oriented products constituted nearly 60 percent of U.S. agricultural imports from China. The share of such products was increasing as U.S. agricultural imports from China expanded at a rate of about 25 percent annually." (p11)

Wang, Zhi/U.S. Dept. of Agriculture. Economic Research Service. "China's Agricultural Trade in 1996: Commodity Structure, Geographical Distribution, And Its Role in U.S...Trade." China: International Agriculture and Trade Reports Situation and Outlook Series Jun 1997. p6-15.

AGRICULTURE--DEVELOPING COUNTRIES (v26)

AGRICULTURE--ECONOMIC ASPECTS--UNITED STATES (v26)

In the U.S. agricultural industry, "the $22.6-billion rise in final output far exceeded the $3.4-billion in out-of-pocket costs represented by intermediate consumption outlays, resulting in $19.1 billion more to be distributed among the providers of resources to the farm sector. As a consequence, hired workers received 6.1 percent more than in 1995 and lenders received an increase of 3.9 percent for their contributions to 1996 farm production. The earnings of non-operator landlords were up 19.3 percent, reflecting several factors. Holders of share-rent contracts benefitted from the additional $17 billion in crop production." (p4)

U.S. Dept. of Agriculture. Economic Research Service. "1996 Farm Income Estimates: Net Value-Added and Net Farm Income Attain New Highs in 1996." Agricultural Income and Finance Situation and Outlook Report Sep 1997. p4-13.

U.S. "final agricultural sector output, the value of the agricultural sector's output of commodities and services before expenses, rose $22.6 billion in 1996....Higher output, reduced by an increase in intermediate consumption outlays of $3.4 billion, accounts for most of the $19.1-billion jump in net value-added. The value of final 1996 crop output soared $17 billion, reflecting rebounds in acreage and yield for major crops, both of which had declined in 1995, following 1994's record harvest....Crop prices were much higher in the first half of 1996 relative to the same period in the prior year and tended to remain stable in the latter half of the year, despite the rebound in production...." (p5)

U.S. Dept. of Agriculture. Economic Research Service. "1996 Farm Income Estimates: Net Value-Added and Net Farm Income Attain New Highs in 1996." Agricultural Income and Finance Situation and Outlook Report Sep 1997. p4-13.

AGRICULTURE--EGYPT (v26)

AGRICULTURE--EGYPT--UNITED STATES (v26)

AGRICULTURE--EMPLOYMENT

"Though agriculture accounts on average for 9% of the workforce in most industrialized countries, almost one half of the world's total workforce remains involved in agricultural production, with the largest concentrations in developing countries. In Eastern Europe 20% of all workers are in agriculture and in Latin America 25%. About 63% of all workers in Africa and 62% of all workers in Asia are in agriculture, compared to only 5.2% in the European Union."

International Labour Organization. "ILO Warns on Farm Safety: Agriculture Mortality Rates Remain High: Pesticides Pose Major Health Risks to...Workforce." Press Release 22 Oct 1997. document-level access: <http://www.unicc.org/ilo/public/english/235press/pr/1997/23.htm>

AGRICULTURE--ENVIRONMENTAL ASPECTS (v26)

AGRICULTURE--EUROPE (v26)

"Real agricultural producer prices (output) in the EU were 2.7% down last year compared with 1995, according to a report...by Eurostat, Statistical Office of the European Communities in Luxembourg....Last year only Denmark registered an increase, albeit slight (0.1%). Biggest decrease by far was Finland's 14.8%, although less steep than the 26.1% fall in 1995, the year it joined the EU. Other notable falls were returned by Ireland (-6.5%), Luxembourg (-5.0%), Sweden (-4.6%), the United Kingdom and Spain (both -3.9%). Real prices for crop products were down by 3.9%, reversing the upward trend of the previous two years. Significant falls were seen for flowers etc. (-3.9%), fruit (-4.4%), cereals and rice (-4.7%), seeds (-5.8%) and especially root crops (-26.0%). The latter was due mainly to potato prices returning to a more usual level from 1995's exceptional high. There were rises for wine must and wine (3.1%) and olives and olive oil (17.4%)."

Eurostat. "EU Real Agricultural Prices 2.7% Down Last Year." Press Release 1 Aug 1997. document-level access: <http://europa.eu.int/en/comm/eurostat/compres/en/5597/6505597a.htm>

AGRICULTURE--EUROPE--RUSSIA (v26)

AGRICULTURE--FORMER SOVIET REPUBLICS (v26)

"In Estonia, production agriculture as a portion of GDP has dropped from 17.8 percent in 1989 to 6 percent 1996. In 1996, meat production in Estonia was 32 percent of its level in 1989. In Latvia, the portion of livestock production in total agricultural production (in current prices) fell from 66 percent in 1990 to 55 percent in 1995. This trend has been arrested in Lithuania in 1996, where agricultural production rose 15 percent." (p6) "Since 1991, agricultural production in Belarus has declined 21 percent, less than in most other NIS/B [Newly Independent States and Baltic] countries....Meat and milk production there have declined considerably faster than crop production, by 40 and 30 percent, respectively." (p7) "In Russia, the portion of livestock output in total agricultural production (in current prices) fell from 63 percent in 1990 to 48 percent in 1995." (p8)

Sedik, David J./U.S. Dept. of Agriculture. Economic Research Service. "Status of Agricultural Reforms in the NIS/B Countries in 1997." Newly Independent States and the Baltics: International Agriculture and Trade Reports Situation and Outlook Series May 1997. p4-9.

AGRICULTURE--FORMER SOVIET REPUBLICS --UNITED STATES (v26)

"U.S. agricultural exports to the NIS/B [Newly Independent States of the Soviet Union and the Baltics] region are forecast to rise over 10 percent from fiscal 1996 (October/September) to fiscal 1997, to just under $2 billion. While a marked recovery from the fiscal 1995 low of $1.2 billion, export value is still well below the 1989 peak when sales totaled more than $3 billion....U.S. agricultural exports, which made up over 80 percent of total U.S. exports to the region throughout the 1980's, now account for about a third of total sales. Poultry meat, the single largest U.S. export to the region (farm and non-farm exports included), accounting for more than one-half of total agricultural exports, has fueled this growth. The value of U.S. poultry meat shipments to the NIS/B countries almost doubled from fiscal 1995 to fiscal 1996, to nearly $1.0 billion, with Russia absorbing more than 85 percent." (p10)

Foster, Christian J./Liefert, Olga/Mitchell, Jay K./Hoskin, Roger L./U.S. Dept. of Agriculture. Economic Research Service. "NIS/B Farm Sector Continues Adjustment to Market Forces; U.S. Agricultural Exports to Region Post Recovery." Newly Independent States and the Baltics: International Agriculture and Trade Reports Situation and Outlook Series May 1997. p10,12-15,18,20,22-24.

AGRICULTURE--GEORGIA (REPUBLIC) (v26)

AGRICULTURE--HONG KONG

The value of Hong Kong's "1996 agricultural imports equaled $14.2 billion, 3 percent over 1995's $13.8 billion, while agricultural exports (including re-exports) reached $7.8 billion, compared with $7.5 billion in 1995. Agricultural re-exports again accounted for nearly 90 percent of all agricultural exports and amounted to $7 billion. The structure of Hong Kong's agricultural exports is dominated by consumer-ready goods (56 percent), while intermediate goods accounted for 35 percent. Bulk agricultural exports accounted for 9 percent of the total....In 1996, Hong Kong's agricultural trade accounted for 7 percent of all imports, and just 4 percent of total exports. Consumer-ready agricultural imports accounted for two-thirds of total trade with intermediate products making up 26 percent. Bulk goods accounted for 8 percent of total agricultural imports." (p44)

Whitton, Carolyn L./U.S. Dept. of Agriculture. Economic Research Service. "Hong Kong." China: International Agriculture and Trade Reports Situation and Outlook Series Jun 1997. p44-46.

AGRICULTURE--HONG KONG--UNITED STATES

"The United States accounted for 10 percent of Hong Kong's 1996 agricultural imports. Imports from the United States equaled $1.49 billion, less than 1 percent below the $1.5 billion imported from the United States in 1995, and the second largest of U.S. agricultural exports to Hong Kong since 1989. Hong Kong was the eighth largest market for U.S. agricultural exports in 1996. At $459 million, poultry and products again accounted for nearly one-third of U.S. agricultural shipments to the Territory...." (p45)

Whitton, Carolyn L./U.S. Dept. of Agriculture. Economic Research Service. "Hong Kong." China: International Agriculture and Trade Reports Situation and Outlook Series Jun 1997. p44-46.

AGRICULTURE--IDAHO

"Water is the absolute lifeblood of...[Idaho]. We have more than 15,000 farmers and more than 3 million irrigated acres....Nearly 40,000 individuals are employed in one way or another by agriculture....The Port of Lewiston and its two adjacent ports via the Snake and Columbia Rivers export 40 percent of America's grain exports to Asia." (pH3654)

Chenoweth, Helen (Rep.-Idaho). "American Heritage Rivers Initiative." Congressional Record. Daily ed. v143 n80 10 Jun 1997. pH3653-3656. section/page-level access: <http://thomas.loc.gov/cgi-bin/query/R?r105:FLD001:H03653:> (ISSN0363-7239). (X1.1A.105/1).

AGRICULTURE--INDIANA

"By some estimates, Indiana is losing more than 70,000 acres of prime farmland each year. Some groups calculate that, over the last decade, the United States has lost more than 10 million acres of farmland--an area almost half the size of Indiana....The loss of prime farmland eliminates a productive resource from future use. Almost 20% of the U.S. economy is linked to farm production....U.S. food production is important to international security. With just 4% of the world's population, the U.S. produces 20% of the world's field crops on 14% of the arable farmland. Yet China, for example, has 25% of the population and just 7% of the arable farmland." (pE1332)

Hamilton, Lee H. (Rep.-Ind.). "Farmland Preservation." Congressional Record. Daily ed. v143 n91 26 Jun 1997. pE1331-1332. section/page-level access: <http://thomas.loc.gov/cgi-bin/query/R?r105:FLD001:E01332:> (ISSN0363-7239). (X1.1A.105/1).

AGRICULTURE--ISRAEL--UNITED STATES (v26)

AGRICULTURE--KYRGYZSTAN

"Agriculture is important in the Kyrgyz economy as it accounts for about 30 percent of GDP and approximately one-third of employment. An additional 10 percent of the labor force is employed in agricultural-related industries, mostly agribusiness enterprises. Agribusiness enterprises add to the overall impact of agriculture to account for over 50 percent of GDP."

World Bank. "World Bank Promotes Rural Finance in Kyrgyz Republic: The Agriculture and Agribusiness Sectors." Press Release 5 Jun 1997. document-level access: <http://www.worldbank.org/html/extdr/extme/1376.htm>

AGRICULTURE--MEXICO--CHIAPAS (v26)

AGRICULTURE--MEXICO--UNITED STATES

"U.S. agricultural exports to Mexico surged $1.3 billion to a record $5 billion in fiscal 1996....High prices and sharp increases in import demand for many bulk commodities because of severe drought pushed U.S. bulk exports to Mexico to a record $2.8 billion....Sales in the consumer-ready product category...decreased nearly 7 percent to $1.1 billion." (p11)

Huang, Sophia Wu/U.S. Dept. of Agriculture. Economic Research Service. "U.S. Agricultural Exports to APEC Region at Another Record." APEC: International Agriculture and Trade Reports Situation and Outlook Series Aug 1997. p9-12.

"Of the U.S.'s two NAFTA trade partners, Mexico is the faster growing agricultural market, averaging nearly 15 percent growth per year since 1993, compared with about 12 percent for U.S. exports to the world. U.S. agricultural exports to Mexico climbed to $5.4 billion by 1996. The largest rates of NAFTA-specific gains in U.S. exports to Mexico have been for sorghum, cattle, beef, dairy products, apples, and pears. Analysis by ERS [Economic Research Service] indicated that U.S. exports of these products were 10-30 percent higher in 1996 than would have occurred without the agreement....U.S. imports of fresh vegetables from Mexico were about 5-10 percent higher in 1996 than they would have been without the agreement." (p22)

Raney, Terri/Shagam, Shayle/U.S. Dept. of Agriculture. Economic Research Service. "Special Article: NAFTA's Impact on U.S. Agriculture: The First 3 Years." Agricultural Outlook Sep 1997. p20-23.

"U.S. agricultural imports from Mexico increased 11.6 percent per year, on average, between 1993 and 1996, to $3.8 billion. Twelve commodities--coffee, tomatoes, beverages excluding fruit juices, melons, orange juice, onions, cucumbers, strawberries, grapes, biscuits and wafers, peppers, and molasses--as a group increased $1.1 billion." (p5)

U.S. Dept. of Agriculture. Economic Research Service. "Executive Summary." NAFTA: International Agriculture and

Trade Reports Situation and Outlook Series Sep 1997. p3-6.
"U.S. agricultural trade with the NAFTA partners is growing rapidly, with exports up 31 percent and imports up 44 percent since 1993....Since the NAFTA was implemented on January 1, 1994, U.S. agricultural exports to Mexico have increased by $1.8 billion, and the U.S. agricultural trade surplus with Mexico has grown by $800 million....Mexico is a rapidly growing market for U.S. agriculture, averaging 14.8 percent growth per year since 1993, compared with 12.4 percent average growth for U.S. exports....U.S. agricultural exports to Mexico dropped 22 percent in 1995...while Mexican exports to the United States grew 32 percent. The Mexican economy began a strong recovery in 1996, and U.S. agricultural exports to Mexico rebounded, increasing almost 55 percent...." (p3-4)

U.S. Dept. of Agriculture. Economic Research Service. "Executive Summary." NAFTA: International Agriculture and Trade Reports Situation and Outlook Series Sep 1997. p3-6.

AGRICULTURE--MICHIGAN (v26)

AGRICULTURE--NORTH AMERICA

"In the last 12 years, 600 CSA [Community Supported Agriculture] projects have been started in North America....A grower selling directly from his farm stand or in a city-operated Greenmarket can make about 30 percent more than one who sells to a wholesale distributor [according to reporter Molly O'Neil]." (unpaginated)

"New York Times Buys a Share of a CSA Project." Alternative Agriculture News v15 n8 Aug 1997. (ISSN8755-4941).

AGRICULTURE--NORTHERN IRELAND (v26)

AGRICULTURE--POLAND (v26)

AGRICULTURE--QUEBEC (PROVINCE) (v26)

AGRICULTURE--RESEARCH (v26)

"In developing countries, growth in public investments in agricultural research fell from 6.4 percent a year in 1971-81 to 3.8 percent in 1981-91, and in developed countries from 2.7 percent to 1.7 percent a year in the same period....Many studies report rates of return to agricultural research investments in excess of 20 percent per year." (p1)

Pardey, Philip G. "Commentary: Should Government Be Getting Out of Agricultural R&D?" IFPRI Report v19 n3 Oct 1997. p1,4.

AGRICULTURE--RUSSIA (v26)

AGRICULTURE--SAUDI ARABIA--UNITED STATES (v26)

AGRICULTURE--SWEDEN (v26)

AGRICULTURE--TANZANIA--DAR ES SALAAM (v26)

AGRICULTURE--TEXAS (v26)

AGRICULTURE--TURKEY

"In 1996, agricultural production accounted for approximately 14 percent of Turkey's GDP. Agriculture is the largest sector in terms of employment accounting for 42 percent compared to industry at 16 percent and services at 38 percent. Out of the 28 million hectares of arable land, 8.5 million hectares are classified as economically irrigable, of which 4.2 million hectares are presently irrigated. Irrigated land produces 34 percent of agricultural GDP (excluding livestock)."

World Bank. "World Bank Supports Community Participation in Improving Irrigation Systems in Turkey: Turkey's Irrigation Sector...." Press Release 14 Oct 1997. document-level access: <http://www.worldbank.org/html/extdr/extme/1504.htm>

AGRICULTURE--TURKEY--UNITED STATES (v26)

AGRICULTURE--UNITED ARAB EMIRATES (v26)

AGRICULTURE--UNITED STATES (v26)

The agriculture-food sector is the U.S.'s "largest industry, responsible for over 15 percent of the Gross Domestic Product. U.S. agricultural exports are projected to exceed agricultural imports by $30.5 billion in 1996. Employment in the U.S. food and fiber system represented 18 percent of all civilian jobs in the U.S. in 1995." (p552)

Knipling, Edward B. (Acting Administrator, U.S. Agricultural Research Service). "Agriculture, Rural Development, Food and Drug Administration...Approp. for 1998 (Part 4)." Hearing. U.S. House. Committee on Appropriations. Washington, D.C. : GPO, 1997. (ISBN0160551560). (Y4.Ap6/1:Ag8/997/pt.4).

In fiscal 1996, more than half of U.S. farm imports from the Association of Southeast Asia Nations "were rubber and allied products and tropical vegetable oils, with the former accounting for 94 percent and the latter 99 percent of U.S. imports in these categories. ASEAN supplied more than 10 percent of U.S. agricultural imports in fiscal 1996, slightly lower than the previous year. More than 70 percent of U.S. agricultural imports from Australia and New Zealand are animals and their products. Together with the tiny supplier of Papua New Guinea, the Oceania members of APEC [Asia-Pacific Economic Cooperation] provided 5 percent of total U.S. agricultural imports, slightly lower than the nearly 6 percent in fiscal 1995....East Asia and China supplied only 4 percent of total U.S. agricultural imports in fiscal 1996...." (p12)

Huang, Sophia Wu/U.S. Dept. of Agriculture. Economic Research Service. "U.S. Agricultural Exports to APEC Region at Another Record." APEC: International Agriculture and Trade Reports Situation and Outlook Series Aug 1997. p9-12.

In fiscal 1996, the emerging market of the Association of Southeast Asia Nations "grew rapidly (30 percent) to reach a record $3.3 billion, or 5.6 percent of total U.S. agricultural exports....With 10-percent growth, the huge East Asia market purchased a record $20 billion, or 33.5 percent, of total U.S. agricultural exports. Similarly, with 11-percent growth, the NAFTA market purchased $11 billion, or 17.6 percent, of total U.S. agricultural exports. U.S. agricultural exports to the region as a whole grew 10 percent in fiscal 1996, compared with 9 percent in the non-APEC [Asia-Pacific Economic Cooperation] region. Total U.S. agricultural exports to the region reached a record $37.6 billion or 61 percent of total U.S. agricultural exports in fiscal 1996...." (p9-10)

Huang, Sophia Wu/U.S. Dept. of Agriculture. Economic Research Service. "U.S. Agricultural Exports to APEC Region at Another Record." APEC: International Agriculture and Trade Reports Situation and Outlook Series Aug 1997. p9-12.

In the U.S., in 1990-1995, wheat exports by state trading enterprises of the Asia-Pacific Economic Cooperation "averaged 34 percent of the world market, while wheat imports by STEs averaged 21 percent. Rice trade under STEs in the APEC region is concentrated among major importing STEs, which accounted for 14 percent of the world rice market. Barley and corn ranked third and fourth in grain trade under STEs in the APEC region, with barley exports by STEs holding 36 percent of the world market during 1990-95." (p5)

U.S. Dept. of Agriculture. Economic Research Service. "Summary." APEC: International Agriculture and Trade Reports Situation and Outlook Series Aug 1997. p4-5.

U.S. agricultural exports to the Asia-Pacific Economic Cooperation "region reached a record $36.7 billion in fiscal 1996, up 10 percent from the year before. The region accounted for more than 60 percent of total U.S. agricultural exports....Mexico, the Association of Southeast Asian Nations (ASEAN), and Japan showed the biggest gains, while exports to China dropped from $2.4 billion in fiscal 1995 to $1.8 billion." (p4)

U.S. Dept. of Agriculture. Economic Research Service. "Summary." APEC: International Agriculture and Trade Reports Situation and Outlook Series Aug 1997. p4-5.

U.S. agricultural imports from the Asia-Pacific Economic Cooperation "region in fiscal 1996 grew 7.5 percent to a record

$17 billion....The region provided more than half of total U.S. agricultural imports, with Canada (20 percent) and Mexico (11 percent) the dominant suppliers. Imports from Canada surged 20 percent to a record $6.4 billion....U.S. farm imports from Mexico dropped 1 percent, to $3.7 billion, but they were still the second highest on record. A jump of 33 percent in fiscal 1995 was largely due to favorable terms of trade following the peso's devaluation against the dollar." (p12)

Huang, Sophia Wu/U.S. Dept. of Agriculture. Economic Research Service. "U.S. Agricultural Exports to APEC Region at Another Record." APEC: International Agriculture and Trade Reports Situation and Outlook Series Aug 1997. p9-12.

U.S. bulk commodity exports to the Asia-Pacific Economic Cooperation "region surged 22 percent to a record $16.5 billion in fiscal 1996....The region accounted for 58 percent of total value of U.S. bulk commodity exports, including 73 percent of coarse grains, 37 percent of wheat, and 56 percent of soybeans. A 42-percent jump in the value of U.S. soybean exports to the region led the growth....The increased export value of 29 percent for U.S. wheat and 37 percent for U.S. coarse grains was due to high grain prices, since the volume of U.S. wheat and coarse grain exports to the region declined 3 and 6 percent, respectively....U.S. cotton exports to the region dropped 9 percent to $2.4 billion because of an abundant world supply and high U.S. cotton prices. In fiscal 1996, the APEC region was the destination for 80 percent of total U.S. cotton exports...." (p9)

Huang, Sophia Wu/U.S. Dept. of Agriculture. Economic Research Service. "U.S. Agricultural Exports to APEC Region at Another Record." APEC: International Agriculture and Trade Reports Situation and Outlook Series Aug 1997. p9-12.

"Acres planted to major U.S. crops in 1996 were up 5.1 percent over 1995 and were at the highest in 10 years. Harvested acreage also rose (4.2 percent) and was also at its highest in 10 years. Farmers planted 11.6 percent more corn, 9.4 percent more wheat, and 2.6 percent more soybeans. At the same time, acres planted to cotton, rice, sorghum, and sugarbeets fell....The overall prices received index for crop was up 12.5 percent for 1996 over 1995." (p23)

U.S. Dept. of Agriculture. Economic Research Service. "1996 Cost of Production for Crops and Livestock: Although Input Expenses Rose in 1996,...Led to Higher Net Returns." Agricultural Income and Finance Situation and Outlook Report Sep 1997. p23-27.

"In 1996, bulk export growth accounted for much of the rise in U.S. agricultural exports. Even though export volume declined, higher grain and soybean prices boosted the export value to $28.1 billion. Corn export volume fell 13 percent, but increased prices raised the value 15 percent. Wheat shipments also declined, but export value surged 15 percent due to higher prices caused by tight supplies. Soybean volume, unlike grains, rose 12 percent to a record 25.6 million tons in 1996. Soybean exports to China, Mexico, and Indonesia were especially strong, setting records in 1996. At $286 per ton, soybean export prices were nearly 21 percent higher than in 1995, boosting the total value of soybean shipments 36 percent. While cotton exports declined 26 percent in both volume and value, exports to Canada and Mexico were a record 64,000 tons and 150,000 tons, respectively." (p6)

U.S. Dept. of Agriculture. Economic Research Service. "1996 Farm Income Estimates: Bulk Exports Led Growth in 1996." Agricultural Income and Finance Situation and Outlook Report Sep 1997. p6.

In the U.S., "although high-valued products (HVP) continued an 11-year upward trend, HVP exports increased only 5 percent in 1996, primarily due to the slowdown in beef exports and small horticultural export gains....Poultry meat exports jumped 23 percent to a record $2.5 billion. Shipments to Russia were a record 937,000 tons....U.S. pork exports also reached records, 306,000 tons and $1 billion in value. Exports of animal feeds and fodders advanced 5 percent to $2.6 billion in 1996. Sharply higher prices boosted the value of soybean meal exports 45 percent, its highest export value since 1988. U.S. horticultural product exports increased nearly 4 percent to about $9.9 billion, largely due to gains in wine and nuts." (p6)

U.S. Dept. of Agriculture. Economic Research Service. "1996 Farm Income Estimates: HVP Exports Advance for Eleventh Consecutive Year." Agricultural Income and Finance Situation and Outlook Report Sep 1997. p6.

In the U.S., in 1996, "corn and soybean sales were up an impressive $2.9 billion and $2.4 billion, respectively. Notable gains in sales were also achieved by wheat ($841 million), cotton ($610 million), greenhouse/nursery ($446 million), sorghum grain ($441 million), rice ($293 million), and potatoes ($235 million). Corn production, which typically represents close to one-fifth of crop sales value, contributed $6.1 billion to the rise in the value of crop production, as producers sold $3 billion more than in 1995 and added another $3.1 billion to year-end inventories for future sale. Soybeans also made a $2.9-billion contribution and, unlike corn, had almost no buildup in inventory." (p5-6)

U.S. Dept. of Agriculture. Economic Research Service. "1996 Farm Income Estimates: Net Value-Added and Net Farm Income Attain New Highs in 1996." Agricultural Income and Finance Situation and Outlook Report Sep 1997. p4-13.

"Fiscal 1998 U.S. agricultural exports are projected at $58.5 billion, up $2 billion from the 1997 forecast and second only to the 1996 record of $59.8 billion. At $38 billion, agricultural imports also are projected up $2 billion, so the agricultural trade surplus will remain unchanged from the 1997 forecast of $20.5 billion. The export value of both bulk and high-value products (HVP's) is expected to rise--HVP value is projected up $1.5 billion over fiscal 1997, and bulk exports are expected up $500 million." (p9)

Whitton, Carol/U.S. Dept. of Agriculture. Economic Research Service. "World Agriculture & Trade: U.S. Ag Exports in Fiscal '98 to Surpass '97." Agricultural Outlook Oct 1997. p9-11.

"From implementation of NAFTA through 1996, total U.S. agricultural trade has grown rapidly, rising from nearly $68 billion (exports $43 billion, imports $25 billion) to about $94 billion (exports $60 billion, imports $34 billion)....The share of trade with NAFTA partners has held steady at about 24 percent of total U.S. agricultural trade. During the 12 months prior to NAFTA's January 1, 1994 implementation, U.S. agricultural trade with Canada and Mexico totaled just over $16 billion (more than $9 billion in exports and $6 billion in imports). By the end of 1996, just 3 years after implementation, it had grown to over $22 billion (nearly $12 billion in exports and nearly $11 billion in imports)....U.S. agricultural exports to Mexico were about 3 percent higher in 1996 than they would have been without the reduction in trade barriers under NAFTA. U.S. agricultural exports to Canada were about 7 percent higher because of the free trade agreement....U.S. agricultural imports from Mexico were just over 3 percent higher in 1996 than they would have been without NAFTA, while imports from Canada were about 5 percent higher." (p20-21)

Raney, Terri/Shagam, Shayle/U.S. Dept. of Agriculture. Economic Research Service. "Special Article: NAFTA's Impact on U.S. Agriculture: The First 3 Years." Agricultural Outlook Sep 1997. p20-23.

"Despite the use of approximately 500 million kg [kilograms] of pesticides per year in US agriculture, approximately 37% of total potential crop production is lost to pest insects, weeds, and diseases....Currently, breeding crops for herbicide resistance dominates agricultural biotechnology, and in field trials of engineered organisms, more than 40% of test releases emphasize herbicide-tolerant crops (Paoletti and Pimentel 1996)....Pest insects destroy approximately 13% of potential crop production....Plant pathogens...destroy approximately 12% of all potential crop production....Today, 75-100% of agricultural crops contain some degree of host-plant resistance (Paoletti and Pimentel 1996)." (p712)

Pimentel, David. "Books: Biotechnology, Food, And the Environment." BioScience v47 n10 Nov 1997. p712-713. (ISSN0006-3568).

"American producers, who represent less than 3 percent of the total population, provide more than enough food and fiber to meet the needs of...[the U.S.], as well as many nations overseas....From 1910 to 1993 the number of American farms have declined from a little more than 6.4 million to less than 2.1 million, roughly a 70-percent decline and decrease. This decline is even greater in the year 1997. The decline in minority farmers is even sharper. In...North Carolina, there has been a 64-percent decline in minority farmers just over the last 15 years, from 6,996 farms in 1978 to 2,498 farms in 1992." (pH7611)

Clayton, Eva M. (Rep.-N.C.). "USDA Accountability and Equity Act of 1997." Congressional Record. Daily ed. v143 n128 23 Sep 1997. pH7610-7611. section/page-level access: <http://thomas.loc.gov/cgi-bin/query/R?r105:FLD001:H07610:> (ISSN0363-7239). (X1.1A.105/1).

In the U.S., "agriculture exports climbed again last year, fiscal year 1996, to $59.8 billion--up some $19 billion or close to 50 percent since 1990. In an average week this past year, U.S. producers, processors, and exporters shipped more than 1.1 billion dollars' worth of food and farm products to foreign markets, compared with about $775 million per week at the start of this decade. The overall export gains raised the fiscal year 1996 agricultural trade surplus to a new record of $27.4 billion. In the most recent comparisons among 11 major industries, agriculture ranked No. 1 as the leading positive contributor to the U.S. merchandise trade balance." (pH5718)

Fazio, Vic (Rep.-Calif.). "Agriculture, Rural Development, Food and Drug Administration...Appropriations Act, 1998." Congressional Record. Daily ed. v143 n106 24 Jul 1997. pH5672-5732. section/page-level access: <http://thomas.loc.gov/cgi-bin/query/R?r105:FLD001:H05718:> (ISSN0363-7239). (X1.1A.105/1).

In the U.S., "gross receipts for tobacco are around $4,000 per acre....For an acre of corn, you are lucky to bring out gross receipts of $300 to $400....For an acre of wheat, gross receipts of $200 or less....Data from the USDA indicate that net receipts from an acre of tobacco averaged between $450 and $1,100 per acre. According...[to another source,] farmers can get $1,844 in net profit from a net acre of tobacco compared to $100 for soybeans." (pS7903)

Durbin, Richard J. (Sen.-Ill.). "Agriculture, Rural Development, Food and Drug Administration...Appropriations Act, 1998." Congressional Record. Daily ed. v143 n105 23 Jul 1997. pS7898-7911. section/page-level access: <http://thomas.loc.gov/cgi-bin/query/R?r105:FLD001:S07902:> (ISSN0363-7239). (X1.1A.105/1).

U.S. "agricultural exports have exhibited a rather roller coaster ride, first declining from $43.8 billion to a low of $26 billion in 1986, and then rising to a record high of $60 billion in 1996, but at the same time agricultural imports have increased from $10.8 billion to approximately $30 billion in 1996, now equaling half of our exports." (pH5373)

Kaptur, Marcy (Rep.-Ohio). "Agriculture, Rural Development, Food and Drug Administration...Appropriations Act, 1998." Congressional Record. Daily ed. v143 n101 16 Jul 1997. pH5372-5382. section/page-level access: <http://thomas.loc.gov/cgi-bin/query/R?r105:FLD001:H05372:> (ISSN0363-7239). (X1.1A.105/1).

In 1995, "total U.S. planted acreage declined 1.7 percent. Crop prices received by farmers in 1995 rose an average of 6.7 percent, but average livestock prices declined 3.2 percent." (p11)

Peacock, Dave/U.S. Dept. of Agriculture. Economic Research Service. "Summary of Report: Farm Sector Financially Strong in 1995, Despite Drop in Farm Income." ERS Information Nov 1997. p11.

In the U.S., "for meat products, the farm value share dropped from 60 percent in 1973 to 35 percent in 1995; for poultry, from 59 to 42 percent; for fresh fruits, from 33 to 19 percent; and for fresh vegetables, from 35 to 23 percent." (p3)

Clauson, Annette/U.S. Dept. of Agriculture. Economic Research Service. "Food Prices: Economic Factors Holding Down Food Price Increases." Food Review v20 n2 May-Aug 1997. p2-4. (ISSN1056-327X).

"The top ten leading States accounted for 58 percent of total U.S. agricultural exports, the same as in 1995. A record 21 States exported more than $1 billion worth of agricultural commodities each. In 1996, the value of wheat and products exports jumped 35 percent to nearly $7.1 billion, feed grains and products rose 23 percent to $10.9 billion, and soybean and products increased 10 percent to $7.9 billion." (p8)

Greene, Joel/U.S. Dept. of Agriculture. Economic Research Service. "California Leading Exporter in Fiscal 1996." Foreign Agricultural Trade of the United States Jan-Mar 1997. p8-9.

"U.S. agricultural exports were a record $60.4 billion in 1996, 8 percent higher than in 1995. Strong prices for grains and soybeans boosted bulk exports 12 percent to $28.1 billion, the highest since 1981. High-value product (HVP) exports rose slower at 5 percent to reach a record $32.3 billion." (p2)

Greene, Joel/U.S. Dept. of Agriculture. Economic Research Service. "Agricultural Exports Surpass $60 Billion." Foreign Agricultural Trade of the United States Jan-Mar 1997. p2-3.

"U.S. agricultural imports totaled a record $33.3 billion in 1996. U.S. agricultural imports from the NAFTA partners grew from $7.3 billion in 1993 to $10.5 billion in 1996. U.S. agricultural imports from Mexico and Canada were about 3 and 5 percent higher, respectively, in 1996 than they would have been without the agreement." (p5)

U.S. Dept. of Agriculture. Economic Research Service. "Executive Summary." NAFTA: International Agriculture and Trade Reports Situation and Outlook Series Sep 1997. p3-6.

"Fiscal 1998 U.S. agricultural exports are projected at $58.5 billion, up $1.2 billion from the $57.3 billion shipped in fiscal year 1997....The anticipated export surplus of $20.5 billion is unchanged from August projections, but $1.0 billion less than the fiscal 1997 surplus." (p1)

U.S. Dept. of Agriculture. "Fiscal 1998 Agricultural Exports Forecast Unchanged at $58.5 Billion." Outlook for U.S. Agricultural Exports 2 Dec 1997. p1.

"The same 10 countries, accounting for $42.7 billion or 74 percent of 1997 U.S. agricultural exports, have been the top U.S. agricultural export markets for the last 3 fiscal years. The 10-percent gain in the leading market, Canada, was the largest growth among these 10 countries in 1997....U.S. agricultural imports in the last 3 fiscal years are also largely drawn from the same sources....The top 10 accounted for $26.1

billion or 73 percent of U.S. agricultural imports in 1997, with the largest percentage gains in Brazil (21%), Colombia (17%), New Zealand (15%), and Canada (12%)." (p1)
U.S. Dept. of Agriculture. Economic Research Service. "Little Change in Leading U.S. Agricultural Export and Import Markets in Fiscal 1997." U.S. Agricultural Trade Update 24 Nov 1997. p1.

"Total fiscal 1997 U.S. agricultural exports reached $57.4 billion, only 4 percent below 1996. Fiscal 1997 imports equalled $35.8 billion, up 10 percent from 1996. The 1997 agricultural export surplus, at $21.6 billion, is 21 percent less than in 1996." (p1)
U.S. Dept. of Agriculture. Economic Research Service. "Summary." U.S. Agricultural Trade Update 24 Nov 1997. p1.

"U.S. agricultural exports reached $4.4 billion in August 1997, 11 percent above July 1997 but 4 percent under August 1996. Cumulative exports for the first 11 months of fiscal year 1997 reached $52.9 billion, 5 percent below last year." (p1)
Whitton, Carol/U.S. Dept. of Agriculture. Economic Research Service. "Summary." U.S. Agricultural Trade Update 23 Oct 1997. p1.

U.S. agricultural exports for October through May 1997 "reached $40.3 billion, down 4 percent from the previous year. Imports were $3.2 billion in May, up 11 percent from a year ago." (p1)
U.S. Dept. of Agriculture. Economic Research Service. "Summary." U.S. Agricultural Trade Update 23 Jul 1997. p1.

AGRICULTURE--UNITED STATES--COSTS (v26)

AGRICULTURE--UNITED STATES--FINANCE (v26)

AGRICULTURE--WISCONSIN

"Wisconsin is home to 24,000 dairy farmers, 140 cheese processing plants and many other businesses associated with milk production and processing. Dairy contributes some $4 billion in income to Wisconsin's economy and provides 130,000 jobs. Wisconsin is also the fifth largest potato producing State with a large chip and french fry processing sector. Overall, Wisconsin ranks 10th in the Nation in farm numbers and 9th nationally with respect to market value of agricultural products sold." (pS9986)
Feingold, Russell D. (Sen.-Wis.). "The Nomination of Peter Scher to Be Special Trade Ambassador for Agriculture." Congressional Record. Daily ed. v143 n130 25 Sep 1997. pS9985-9986. section/page-level access: <http:// thomas.loc.gov/cgi-bin/query/R?r105:FLD001:S09985:> (ISSN0363-7239). (X1.1A.105/1).

AID TO FAMILIES WITH DEPENDENT CHILDREN PROGRAMS (v26)

AID TO FAMILIES WITH DEPENDENT CHILDREN PROGRAMS--UNITED STATES

In the U.S., "the average AFDC recipient was a 7 1/2-year-old child. Of the 13.8 million recipients, 9.5 million were children, according to 1995 federal data, the latest available. An average family on welfare consisted of a single mother and two children, who received $4,532 a year from AFDC and about $2,500 in food stamps. That left them more than $4,000 short of the poverty line....AFDC provided a family with three children just $2.78 a day more than a family with two children. Of the 4.3 million adults who received benefits in 1995, 3.8 million (88 percent) were women. About 9 percent of them had jobs and 70 percent had recent work experience. Low wages (40 percent of single mothers working full time earn wages below poverty), divorce and the need to escape domestic violence were among the factors that pushed these women onto welfare rolls. Forty-two percent of families on welfare received benefits for less than two years, but a significant proportion of families need help for five years or more." (p15)
"Corporate America's Welfare Windfall: What 'Welfare Queen?'" America@Work v2 n6 Jul 1997. p15. (ISSN1091-594X).

"For the United States as a whole, the average monthly payment per family from the [AFDC] program in 1993 was $381, but average payments per state ranged from a low of only $120 in Mississippi to a high of $748 in Alaska. Even within regions there was considerable variation: the average payment was $546 in New York but only $356 in neighboring New Jersey; Texas paid $159, while neighboring Oklahoma paid nearly twice as much, $297, and so on (U.S. Bureau of the Census 1995...)." (p697)
Anton, Thomas J. "New Federalism and Intergovernmental Fiscal Relationships: The Implications for Health Policy." Journal of Health Politics, Policy and Law v22 n3 Jun 1997. p691-720. (ISSN0361-6878).

AIDS (DISEASE) (v26)

see also HIV INFECTIONS

"AIDS killed an estimated 1.5 million people in 1996, according to the World Health Organization (WHO)....In America, each case of AIDS costs society about $100,000 in lifetime expenditures for medical care....An uninfected individual who has protected sex with an infected partner can reduce the probability that he or she will contract AIDS by about a factor of 10." (p364)
Pinkerton, Steven D./Abramson, Paul R. "Condoms and the Prevention of AIDS." American Scientist v85 n4 Jul-Aug 1997. p364-373. (ISSN0003-0996).

"The AIDS epidemic remains a massive and growing imposition on the lives of people in the developing world, where a UN report released last week estimates that 90 percent of the people with HIV or AIDS live....Of an estimated 30.6 million people living with HIV/AIDS today, two-thirds live in Sub-Saharan Africa. Sexually active adults are the most at risk, doctors say. An estimated 1 in 100 adults in the 15 to 49 age group have HIV. Even so, the UN estimates nearly 1.1 million children under the age of 15 are also living with AIDS. Some 16,000 people get the AIDS virus every day of the year, says the report. Only 1 in 10 are aware of their HIV status....In South Africa, for instance, 2.4 million citizens live with HIV, up by more than a third over 1996. In Zimbabwe, nearly 1 in 5 adults has the HIV virus." (p4)
Baldauf, Scott. "Mixed Global Progress against AIDS." The Christian Science Monitor v90 n4 1 Dec 1997. p4. The Christian Science Monitor search engine: <http:// www.csmonitor.com/plweb-cgi/iops1.pl> To retrieve this article, enter the following search: ED=19971201 AND global. In the "retrieved list," click the title that matches this record. (ISSN0882-7729).

"As of 25 November 1996, the cumulative number of cases of the acquired immunodeficiency syndrome (AIDS) ever reported to WHO was 1,544,067. This number, which includes both adults and children, represents a 20% rise from the 1,291,810 cases reported as of December 1995....It is estimated that around 8.4 million AIDS cases have occurred worldwide since the pandemic began." (p27)
"Health Briefs: Reported AIDS Cases Up 20%." World Health v50 n2 Mar-Apr 1997. p27. (ISSN0043-8502).

"Estimates concerning the AIDS epidemic, up to the end of 1996, were: 29 million people worldwide infected with HIV and 6.4 million deaths. About 90% of those now living with HIV/AIDS are in developing countries." (p20)
Shepard, Donald S. "The Cost of AIDS." World Health v50 n5 Sep-Oct 1997. p20-21. (ISSN0043-8502).

AIDS (DISEASE)--AFRO-AMERICANS

"About 30,700 Americans died of AIDS between January and September 1996, down from 37,900 during the same time period in 1995, the CDC said in July [1997]. Federal studies have shown HIV is spreading fastest among black people. According to the

CDC, black Americans make up 33 percent of the total AIDS cases but are 11 percent of the U.S. population." (p3 secB)

Wendland, Wendy. "Local News: Spread of HIV Still Troubling, Experts Say." Detroit Free Press 14 Oct 1997. p3 secB.

"Statistics released by the Centers for Disease Control show that in 1990, African Americans accounted for 31.2% of newly reported AIDS cases in America, though they only represented 12% of the general population. In 1993, African Americans accounted for 36% of all newly reported AIDS cases, three times their representation in the general population. In 1996, African Americans accounted for 41% of adults/adolescents in the United States with AIDS...." (p9)

"HIV/AIDS Update: Forty-One Percent of Reported AIDS Patients Are African American." Health Advocate n189 Sum 1997. p9.

AIDS (DISEASE)--AFRO-AMERICANS--HISPANIC AMERICANS

"Latinos and African Americans make up fully 60 percent of new AIDS cases in the United States. While the infection rate for gay white men has dropped dramatically, African Americans are infected at a rate of 92.6 for every 100,000 people, while the rate for Latinos stands at 46.2. The rate for whites, by comparison, is 15.4 out of every 100,000." (p9)

"Trendwatch: In Dying Color." Third Force v5 n3 Jul-Aug 1997. p9. (ISSN1067-3237).

AIDS (DISEASE)--AFRO-AMERICANS--HISPANIC AMERICANS--DRUG USE

According to the report, "Health Emergency 1997: The Spread of Drug-Related AIDS among African Americans and Latinos," "AIDS is now the leading cause of death among African American and Latino/a men and women between the ages of 25 and 44. Over half of these deaths are injection-related. Among persons who inject drugs, African Americans are four times as likely as whites to have AIDS. Among persons who inject drugs, Latinos are at least one and a half times as likely as whites to be diagnosed with AIDS." (p7)

Miller, Erin. "Drugs, AIDS, And Human Rights." Peacework n275 Jun 1997. p7-9. (ISSN0748-0725).

AIDS (DISEASE)--AFRO-AMERICANS--MICHIGAN

In 1997, "AIDS has surpassed homicide as the top killer of black men ages 25-44 in Michigan, according to state health statistics. Of the 8,590 AIDS cases reported in Michigan since 1981, 43 percent involved black men. Women make up about 15 percent of the total cases--and about two-thirds of those cases are black women. By contrast, African Americans make up just 13.9 percent of the state population....Among African-American men in Michigan, 47 percent were infected by sexual relations with other men, compared with 32 percent infected by drug abuse...." (p2 secD)

Brand-Williams, Oralandar. "The Metro: Special Report: Fighting AIDS: Black Churches Urged to Reach Out." Detroit News 30 May 1997. p1-2 secD.

AIDS (DISEASE)--ARGENTINA

In Argentina, "since 1992 and 1993--when 1,000 AIDS/HIV cases were reported in the country each year--the AIDS/HIV epidemic has increased significantly. In the first semester of 1996 alone, 10,793 cases were reported (equivalent to 312 AIDS cases per million inhabitants). In terms of the number of reported cases in the hemisphere, Argentina ranks fifth after the United States, Brazil, Mexico, and Canada. However, in terms of the number of cases per population, it...ranks third....While the majority of the cases at the beginning of the AIDS epidemic in the country were homosexual and bisexual men, by 1995 this category represented 26 percent of the total. Cases among hemophiliacs and blood transfusion recipients have decreased over time and in 1996 they represented only 1 percent of the total."

World Bank. "World Bank Loan Helps Argentina to Fight AIDS." Press Release 23 May 1997. document-level access: <http://www.worldbank.org/html/extdr/extme/1361.htm>

AIDS (DISEASE)--ARIZONA

"'In Arizona, preliminary figures show that AIDS deaths have declined...more than 70 percent--but these numbers are based on very incomplete data for the first six months of 1996,' cautioned Dr. Bob England, ADHS [Arizona Department of Health Services] state epidemiologist. Preliminary Arizona figures for the first six months of 1996 stand at 26 deaths, compared to 98 during the first half of 1995....[As of mid-1996,] in Arizona, there are 5,000 recorded cases of AIDS and an estimated 8,000 to 12,000 people living with HIV."

Arizona. Dept. of Health Services. "AIDS Deaths Declining in Arizona." News Release 3 Mar 1997. document-level access: <http://www.hs.state.az.us/news/aids97.htm>

AIDS (DISEASE)--AUSTRALIA--MORTALITY (v26)

According to the Australian Bureau of Statistics, in Australia, "in 1996 the number of AIDS related deaths decreased for the second consecutive year. There were 568 AIDS related deaths registered in 1996, a decrease on the 666 deaths registered in 1995 and 26 per cent lower than the 764 deaths recorded in 1994. Males comprised 96 per cent of total AIDS related deaths in 1996."

Australian Bureau of Statistics. "Deaths from Diabetes and Senile Dementia Increase." Media Release 31 Oct 1997. document-level access: <http://www.abs.gov.au/websitedbs/d3110125.nsf/4a255eef008309e44a255eef00061e57/b963d1a23d007204ca25654000761a86?OpenDocument>

AIDS (DISEASE)--BURMA

"In June 1994, Burma's health minister stated that 261 citizens suffered from full-blown AIDS and 20,000 were HIV+, but a report from the United Nations International Drug Control Programme documents much more alarming figures. The report states that 74.3% of all tested drug users, 9% of the prostitutes, .5% of blood donors and 14% of pregnant women in Burma were HIV+....This report still does not show how entrenched AIDS is throughout all of Burma. Most of those tested lived in towns and cities, while AIDS is more rampant in the rural areas of the less-developed north. In Hpakan in northern Kachim State, 91% of drug users were HIV+. Of 209 intravenous drug users tested in a jail in Bhamo, 96% carried the HIV virus. In the northeastern Shan State town of Lashio, often described as the drug capital of northern Burma, 40% of drug users were HIV+." (p96)

Flynn, Elizabeth. "Burma: An Activist's Guide to Instating Democracy." Guild Practitioner v54 n2 Spr 1997. p82-101. (ISSN0017-5390).

AIDS (DISEASE)--CANADA

"Federal health officials estimate that last year as many as 5,000 Canadians were infected with HIV--well above the 2,500 to 3,000 new cases recorded annually between 1989 and 1995....During the past three years, the numbers...[of AIDS and HIV cases] have plummeted--from more than 1,600 new AIDS cases and just over 1,000 deaths in 1994 to just under 800 new cases and only 271 deaths in 1996." (p72)

Nichols, Mark. "Health: Hope, Not Miracles." Maclean's v110 n38 22 Sep 1997. p72. (ISSN0024-9262).

"For the first time since the AIDS epidemic began, the number of deaths in Canada dropped sharply last year--by 20 per cent to 30 per cent from the annual averages in the previous three years. New AIDS cases diagnosed last year also declined by 20 per cent from 1995, according to statistics from the Laboratory Centre for Disease Control in Ottawa....The centre estimates there were 3,000 to 5,000 new HIV infections in 1996, compared with an

average of 2,500 annually from 1989 to 1994." (p67)
"Health Monitor: Mixed AIDS Results." Maclean's v110 n23 9 Jun 1997. p67. (ISSN0024-9262).

AIDS (DISEASE)--LATIN AMERICA (v26)

AIDS (DISEASE)--MICHIGAN (v26)

"About 69 percent of all Michigan residents who have AIDS live in six counties in southeast Michigan, said Loretta Davis-Satterla, administrator of the Detroit Health Department's HIV/AIDS programs....Those counties--Wayne, Oakland, Macomb, Monroe, St. Clair and Lapeer--have about 46 percent of the state's population. As of July [1997], Michigan had 8,429 AIDS cases....Drug use contributes to one-third of all new HIV cases in metro Detroit, and half of all AIDS-related deaths among black people, said...[Harry Simpson, executive director of Community Health Awareness Group,] who runs a needle exchange program in Detroit." (p3 secB)
Wendland, Wendy. "Local News: Spread of HIV Still Troubling, Experts Say." Detroit Free Press 14 Oct 1997. p3 secB.

AIDS (DISEASE)--MICHIGAN--DETROIT--DRUG USE (v26)

AIDS (DISEASE)--MICHIGAN--MORTALITY (v26)

In Michigan, "health officials were encouraged by the first decline in AIDS/HIV deaths during the first six months of 1996. Michigan's rate of 8.1 deaths per 100,000 population is well below the national average of 15.4 per 100,000." (p1 secC)
Cain, Charlie. "Metro: Special Report: Health Snapshot: Michigan Gaining Ground in the Fight against Diseases." Detroit News 17 Jul 1997. p1-2 secC.

AIDS (DISEASE)--NEW YORK (N.Y.) (v26)

"More than 2% of the adult and adolescent population in LES [New York City's Lower East Side] zip codes has been diagnosed and reported as having AIDS (New York City Department of Health, Office of AIDS Surveillance, 1996). It is estimated that more than 1 in 10 adults and adolescents are infected with HIV (Edgar, 1994; Fleming, 1993; New York City Human Services Administration, 1990), 40%-50% of IDUs [injection-drug users] (Friedman et al., 1993), and a self-reported 11% of non-IDU sexual partners of IDUs (Krauss, Tross, & Silvert, 1994)." (p580)
Krauss, Beatrice J. "Article: HIV Education for Teens and Preteens in a High-Seroprevalence Inner-City Neighborhood." Families in Society v78 n6 Nov-Dec 1997. p579-591. (ISSN1044-3894).

According to a 1992 U.S. congressional report, "only 3% of the nation's teens lived in New York City, yet more than 20% of adolescent AIDS cases (occurring between the ages of 13 and 21) in the United States had been reported in New York City, making it the city with the largest adolescent AIDS caseload (AIDS Surveillance Update, 1988-1995). Also alarming in New York City was the situation of African-American and Hispanic women between the ages of 25 and 34, for whom AIDS had become the leading cause of mortality; undoubtedly, many of these women had been infected during adolescence....The ratio of seropositivity of males to females between the ages of 13 and 21 was 3 to 1 (AIDS Surveillance Update, 1988-1995)...." (p150)
Elbaz, Gilbert. "Adolescent Activism for Postmodern HIV/AIDS Education: A New Social Movement." Urban Review v29 n3 Sep 1997. p145-174. (ISSN0042-0972).

AIDS (DISEASE)--NEW YORK (N.Y.)--MEN --MORTALITY (v26)

AIDS (DISEASE)--PHILIPPINES--YOUTH --ATTITUDES (v26)

AIDS (DISEASE)--UGANDA (v26)

AIDS (DISEASE)--UNITED STATES (v26)

"An estimated 650,000 to 900,000 Americans are believed to be living with HIV, the virus that causes AIDS. Since the AIDS epidemic began in 1981, more than 600,000 Americans have been diagnosed with AIDS and more than 370,000 men, women, and children have lost their lives to this disease....CDC recently reported that in 1996, for the first time in the history of the AIDS epidemic, the number of Americans diagnosed with AIDS declined, falling by 6 percent for Americans over 12 between 1995 and 1996. In addition, CDC has reported that HIV/AIDS mortality declined 26 percent between 1995 and 1996, falling from the leading cause of death among 25-44 year olds to the second leading cause of death in that age group."
U.S. Dept. of Health and Human Services. "Clinton Administration Record on HIV/AIDS." Fact Sheet 29 Sep 1997. document-level access: <http://www.hhs.gov/news/press/1997pres/970929b.html>

In the U.S., "while the overall number of AIDS cases reported last year continued the downward trend that began in 1993, the trend is most pronounced in non-Latino whites, whose AIDS rate per 100,000 people has dropped almost in half from 25 in 1993 to 13.5 in 1996. During that same time period, the rate for African Americans has only dropped from 125 to just under 90....In 1993, African Americans were five times more likely than non-Latino whites to contract AIDS. By 1996, African Americans were almost seven times more likely than whites to contract AIDS." (p9)
"HIV/AIDS Update: Forty-One Percent of Reported AIDS Patients Are African American." Health Advocate n189 Sum 1997. p9.

"In a review of available data, Pennbridge et al. (1992a...) report that the number of US adolescents actually diagnosed with AIDS is small--representing less than one-half percent of all cases. However, in 1991, adults aged 20 to 29 comprised 20 percent of all AIDS cases....Centers for Disease Control and Prevention (CDC) data for 1993 shows that while men aged 20 to 29 comprised 18% of male AIDS cases, women in this age range comprised 23% of female cases (CDC 1994...)....CDC data reported in Pennbridge et al. (1992...) show that 13 in 1000 males and 6 in 1000 females between the ages of 15 and 24 are infected with HIV. Data from studies of runaway and homeless youths in New York City show that youths between 16 and 20 years of age are at a particularly high risk for HIV infection, with a seroprevalence rate of 53 per 1000." (p311-312)
Sobo, Elisa J./Zimet, Gregory D./Zimmerman, Teena/Cecil, Heather. "Doubting the Experts: AIDS Misconceptions among Runaway Adolescents." Human Organization v56 n3 Fall 1997. p311-320. (ISSN0018-7259).

In the U.S., "AIDS deaths declined 13% during the first six months of 1996, compared to the first six months of 1995....People living with AIDS have increased 10 percent since mid-1995. As of mid-1996, an estimated 223,000 people were living with AIDS....'It can cost up to $18,000 per year to treat someone with HIV disease,'...[said Christopher Brown, chief of the Arizona Dept. of Health Services Office of HIV/STD Services]."
Arizona. Dept. of Health Services. "AIDS Deaths Declining in Arizona." News Release 3 Mar 1997. document-level access: <http://www.hs.state.az.us/news/aids97.htm>

"In 1996, for the first time in the history of the HIV/AIDS epidemic, the number of Americans diagnosed with AIDS declined, according to a new report released...by the Centers for Disease Control and Prevention (CDC). The incidence of AIDS among people over age 12 declined 6% between 1995 and 1996, from 60,620 cases to 56,730 cases, says the report in the CDC 'Morbidity and Mortality Weekly Report.'...While the incidence (new AIDS diagnoses) declined 15% among white gay and bisexual men, the incidence of AIDS among heterosexuals continued to rise, increasing 11% among men and 7% among women. AIDS incidence declined or leveled in all racial and ethnic groups with the largest drop (-13%) occurring among whites, followed by Hispanics (-5%) and African Americans (0%). There was a significant decline in AIDS incidence among gay and bisexual men who also inject drugs (-17% among whites and -13% among African Americans)....CDC reports that the number of people living with AIDS (also known as AIDS prevalence) increased 11% between 1995 and 1996. As of December 1996, there were 235,470 Americans reported to be living with AIDS."

U.S. Dept. of Health and Human Services. "CDC Reports First-Ever Decline in AIDS Diagnoses Treatment and Prevention Advances Spur New Trend." Press Release 18 Sep 1997. document-level access: <http://www.hhs.gov/news/press/1997pres/970918.html>

According to a Gallup poll, "a decade ago, over two-thirds of all Americans identified AIDS as 'the most urgent health problem facing this country at the present time.' Five years ago, 41% cited AIDS and another 30% cited the costs of health care as the most urgent health problems. Today, just 29% say AIDS is the most urgent health problem, with 15% mentioning cancer, and another 15% mentioning health care costs....In October, 1987, 42% expressed some degree of concern about getting AIDS, compared with 30% who feel that way today....Today, just over half of all Americans feel the government is not doing enough about the problem, virtually identical to the sentiment expressed ten years ago. And today just under half say that people with the AIDS virus should be made to carry a card indicating they have AIDS, while in 1987 just over half felt that way....The public is somewhat less critical of those who get AIDS than it was a decade ago, but 31% of Americans still believe that AIDS is a punishment for a decline in moral standards (compared with 43% who felt that way ten years ago), and 40% say that the victims of AIDS are themselves to blame for getting the disease (compared with 51% who felt that way in 1987)."

Moore, David W./Gallup Organization. "AIDS Issue Fades among Americans." Press Release 17 Oct 1997. document-level access: <http://www.gallup.com/poll/news/971017.html>

According to the "Morbidity and Mortality Weeky Report," published by the U.S. Centers for Disease Control and Prevention in September 1997, "the incidence, or new cases, of AIDS among people over age 12 declined by 6 percent between 1995 and 1996, from 60,620 cases to 56,730 cases....Significant declines in new AIDS diagnoses were found among white gay and bisexual men--15 percent between 1995 and 1996--and among both white and African-American gay and bisexual intravenous drug users, who had declines of 17 percent and 13 percent, respectively. Incidence of AIDS among heterosexuals continued to rise, increasing 11 percent among men and 7 percent among women....Incidence of AIDS decreased by 8 percent among men but increased by 2 percent among women. AIDS incidence declined or leveled off in all racial and ethnic groups and in all regions of the country. The largest drop (13 percent) occurred among whites, followed by Hispanics (5 percent)....By region, the largest decline was in the West (12 percent), followed by the Midwest (10 percent), the Northeast (8 percent), and the South (1 percent)." (p1481)

"News & Notes: Number of New AIDS Cases in U.S. Declines for First Time since AIDS/HIV Epidemic Began." Psychiatric Services v48 n11 Nov 1997. p1481. (ISSN1075-2730).

In the U.S., "during the 1980s, the top 25 counties with the greatest increase in the number of AIDS cases were mostly rural, with an average population of 73,000, according to a study by Nina Siu-Ngan Lam and Kam-biu Liu, geographers at Louisiana State University in Baton Rouge. Between 1990 and 1992, the number of cases diagnosed increased just 8 percent in large cities--and 21 percent in rural communities." (p53) "There are still far fewer cases in rural areas--4,605 in 1996, compared with 56,556 in large metropolitan areas....In a study published in the STATISTICAL BULLETIN earlier this year, New York City Department of Health epidemiologist E. James Fordyce charted the migration of AIDS patients diagnosed in New York City between 1990 and 1995. One in 10 of those who left the city returned to Puerto Rico; a quarter went to Southern states. In all, he found that among those who left New York, nearly three times more died in states that were largely rural than in states with more urban populations." (p54)

Brownlee, Shannon/McDonald, Marci/Ackerman, Elise. "U.S. News: AIDS Comes to Small-Town America." U.S. News & World Report v123 n18 10 Nov 1997. p52-55. article-level access: <http://www.usnews.com/usnews/issue/971110/10AIDS.HTM> (ISSN0041-5537).

AIDS (DISEASE)--UNITED STATES--DRUG USE (v26)

AIDS (DISEASE)--UNITED STATES--FINANCE

In the U.S., "overall funding for AIDS-related programs increased by 55 percent in the first four years of the Clinton Administration, with funding for AIDS care under the HHS [U.S. Dept. of Health and Human Services] Health Resources and Services Administration-administered Ryan White CARE Act increasing by 158 percent and assistance for the purchase of AIDS drugs nearly tripling....Altogether, discretionary AIDS-related spending by HHS in FY 1997 will total $3.2 billion, an increase of 55 percent from FY 1993. An additional $2.8 billion is expected to be expended in FY 1997 for AIDS care under Medicare and Medicaid. It is estimated that more than 50 percent of Americans living with AIDS rely on Medicaid for their health care coverage."

U.S. Dept. of Health and Human Services. "Clinton Administration Record on HIV/AIDS." Fact Sheet 29 Sep 1997. document-level access: <http://www.hhs.gov/news/press/1997pres/970929b.html>

AIDS (DISEASE)--UNITED STATES--MINORITIES (v26)

AIDS (DISEASE)--UNITED STATES--MINORITY WOMEN

"African American and Latina women are 25% of the U.S. population, whereas 77% of women with AIDS are members of these two ethnic groups. Their rates of HIV/AIDS are 16 and 7 times higher, respectively, than that for White women (U.S. Department of Health and Human Services, 1995). More than 80% of youth orphaned by HIV/AIDS in New York City are also children of women of color (Michaels & Levine, 1993). Of the 5,734 cases of pediatric AIDS reported to the Centers for Disease Control (1994) as of June 1994, 55.8% were Black children, 24.3% were Hispanic, and 18% were White (others were Asian/Pacific Islanders or American Indian/Alaska natives)." (p491)

Burnette, Denise. "Article: Grandparents Raising Grandchildren in the Inner City." Families in Society v78 n5 Sep-Oct 1997. p489-499. (ISSN1044-3894).

AIDS (DISEASE)--UNITED STATES--MINORITY YOUTH

In the U.S., "African-American and Hispanic youth aged 13 to 19 account for 65 percent of teenage AIDS cases and 70 percent of HIV-infected teenagers in the United States. AIDS is the fourth leading cause of death in African-American females aged 15 to 24. It is the fifth leading cause of death among their male peers. Latino adolescents comprise 18 percent of reported AIDS cases among youth aged 13 to 19; 21 percent of AIDS cases among affected Latino adolescents are among females. Among Asian/Pacific Islander and Native-American adolescents, AIDS is the sixth leading cause of death." (p15)

"Fact Sheet: Sexuality and Underserved Youth in Communities of Color." SIECUS Report v25 n5 Jun-Jul 1997. p15-16. (ISSN0091-3995).

AIDS (DISEASE)--UNITED STATES--MORTALITY (v26)

The CDC's 1996 Vital Statistics Report "shows the national age-adjusted death rate from HIV/AIDS [in the U.S.] dropped an estimated 26 percent between 1995 and 1996, from 15.6 deaths per 100,000 population in 1995 to 11.6 in 1996. HIV infection, previously the leading cause of death for those 25-44, now ranks second behind accidents and adverse effects and just ahead of cancer....HIV/AIDS mortality had increased an average of 16 percent per year between 1987 and 1994, before leveling off in 1995."

U.S. National Center for Health Statistics. "Vital Statistics Report Shows Significant Gains in Health." News Release 11 Sep 1996. document-level access: <http://www.cdc.gov/nchswww/releases/97news/97news/mortgain.htm>

AIDS (DISEASE)--UNITED STATES--PHYSICIANS --ATTITUDES (v26)

AIDS (DISEASE)--UNITED STATES--PREGNANT WOMEN

In the U.S., "a 1994 national study has shown that perinatal HIV transmission can be greatly reduced when AZT is given to HIV-infected pregnant women in their second and third trimesters, and to their infants during and after delivery. The rate of perinatal transmission without treatment is as high as three out of 12 babies; with treatment, the rate can drop to one out of 12, with no increased incidence of birth defects....Perinatal transmission is the most common cause of HIV infection in children up to age 13. The average life expectancy for an HIV-infected infant is five to 10 years, and the average cost of care or a child with HIV is estimated at $418,863. DOH [Hawaii Dept. of Health] estimates that there are approximately 12 pregnant women in Hawai'i each year who are HIV positive. Nationally, women account for 15 percent of all cumulative reported cases of AIDS, up from 10 percent in 1990. Twenty percent of the new cases of AIDS reported in 1996 were teen and adult women, with an increasing number infected through heterosexual contact. In the United States, AIDS is the third leading cause of death among women age 25 to 44 years and the seventh leading cause of death among children age one to four."

Hawaii. Dept. of Health. "Helping Mothers-To-Be Stop the Spread of the AIDS Virus." Press Release 1997. document-level access: <http://www.hawaii.gov/health/press/prmomhiv.htm>

AIDS (DISEASE)--UNITED STATES--PUBLIC OPINION

According to a Gallup poll, "in 1987, 43% of Americans said they avoided associating with people who might have AIDS, while only 15% do that today. Similarly, 28% used to avoid public rest rooms to lessen their chances of getting AIDS, compared with just 12% today. Many Americans are still concerned about the blood supply in hospitals, with 33% saying they would avoid elective surgery that would require blood transfusions. Ten years ago, 42% expressed a similar sentiment. One of the most drastic steps to avoid AIDS--isolating people with AIDS from the rest of society--was supported by 21% of Americans in 1987, but by just 7% today."

Moore, David W./Gallup Organization. "AIDS Issue Fades among Americans." Press Release 17 Oct 1997. document-level access: <http://www.gallup.com/poll/news/971017.html>

AIDS (DISEASE)--UNITED STATES--YOUNG ADULTS --ATTITUDES

In the U.S., "in a survey conducted jointly by Yale University and the cable station MTV, 87 percent of those responding said they do not consider themselves at any risk for catching HIV--this despite the fact that one-fifth said that a friend or acquaintance died of AIDS. And only half of sexually active respondents reported that they used condoms the last time they had sex....The Yale/MTV study was conducted among a sample of 770 people nationwide, ages 12 to 34. A majority of respondents thought the media could do a better job at spreading the word about the danger." (p1 secF)

Hodges, Michael H. "Accent: Young People Think They Won't Contract AIDS, Study Says." Detroit News 18 Dec 1997. p1 secF.

AIDS (DISEASE)--UNITED STATES--YOUTH (v26)

"A 1992 congressional committee--with the self-explanatory title 'A Decade of Denial'--concluded in a report that the number of teenagers with AIDS [in the U.S.] had increased by more than 70% in the past two years and that AIDS was the sixth leading cause of death among people 15 to 24 (Select Committee on Children, Youth, and Families, 1992)....The 1992 congressional report revealed that adolescent research programs received less than 5% of the AIDS budget...." (p150)

Elbaz, Gilbert. "Adolescent Activism for Postmodern HIV/AIDS Education: A New Social Movement." Urban Review v29 n3 Sep 1997. p145-174. (ISSN0042-0972).

AIDS (DISEASE)--UNITED STATES--YOUTH --ATTITUDES

In the U.S., "the number of AIDS cases reported for persons under the age of 25 almost tripled from 1992 to 1993 (Centers for Disease Control, 1993). Of all AIDS cases reported in the U.S., one in five was probably contracted during adolescence (Alan Guttmacher Institute, 1994)....[In 1988,] Pleck, Sonenstein, and Ku (1993) report that the degree of worry about AIDS and perceived likelihood of getting AIDS declined over time for sexually active males aged 15-22." (p991)

Bailey, C. Everett/Piercy, Fred P. "Enhancing Ethical Decision Making in Sexuality and AIDS Education." Adolescence v32 n128 Win 1997. p989-998. (ISSN0001-8449).

AIDS (DISEASE) IN CHILDREN

"More than 40 million children in 23 foreign countries will have lost one or both parents to AIDS by the year 2010, a mounting epidemic creating a generation of vulnerable children, a new report...predicts. The impact is so severe that one-third of the population in some nations will be children under age 15 who have lost one or both parents to AIDS, according to a preliminary report from the United States Agency for International Development." (p1 secA) "The countries studied include 19 African and four non-African nations where the level of HIV infection was at or near 5 percent of the population....UNICEF statistics show that 400,000 children under age 15 became infected with HIV worldwide in 1996, and more than 90 percent of them lived in developing countries." (p6 secA)

Anstett, Patricia. "A FREE PRESS Campaign: Children First: Health: AIDS Orphan Epidemic Looms." Detroit Free Press 20 Nov 1997. p1,6 secA.

"At least 1,000 children a day are contracting AIDS, reports the UN, which also warns of severe increases in infant mortality due to the disease unless immediate steps are taken. There were some 400,000 new AIDS cases involving children under age 18 last year, and some 350,000 children died of the disease, the Geneva-based group UNAIDS stated." (p73)

Cohn, Alvin W. "Juvenile Focus." Federal Probation v61 n3 Sep 1997. p71-73. (ISSN0014-9128).

AIDS (DISEASE) IN CHILDREN--DEVELOPING COUNTRIES (v26)

AIDS (DISEASE) IN CHILDREN--UNITED STATES (v26)

AIDS (DISEASE) IN INFANTS--UNITED STATES (v26)

AIR--POLLUTION (v26)

Since the 1992 Earth Summit in Rio de Janeiro, "the level of greenhouse gas emissions worldwide has risen by 2 percent each year. In the United States alone, emissions of greenhouse gases have grown by as much as 13 percent over the last decade, according to the Worldwatch Institute." (p16) "Between 1990 and 1994, carbon emissions from the developing world grew rapidly: Brazil's carbon emission levels rose 16 percent; India's, 24 percent; South Korea's, 44 percent. China, the world's second-largest producer of greenhouse gases after the United States, has registered a 13 percent rate of growth in the same period." (p17)

Lynch, Colum. "Stormy Weather." Amicus Journal v19 n4 Win 1998. p15-19. (ISSN0276-7201).

"According to the Environmental Protection Agency (EPA), indoor air can be up to 40 times more polluted than outdoor air....According to the [U.S.] Centers for Disease Control, allergies and aggravated respiratory problems are caused by particulates (35 percent of the time), Bioaerosols (34 percent) and VOCs [Volatile Organic Compounds] (31 percent). Particulates in a home come from dirt, dust and pollen. The most common Bioaerosols are animal microorganisms such as dust mites, mold spores, bacteria and germs from sneezes and coughs. VOCs are fumes off-gassed from the artificial products in homes (carpeting, furniture, insulation, composites and other products, household chemicals, cooking, grease and wood smoke, combustion gases, etc.). Particulates from dust, insecticide, smog, fumes and even cooking and wood smoke can be as small as 0.0001 microns....VOCs are even smaller. VOCs, various household odors and gas molecules can be as small as 0.000001 microns." (p29 secD)

Haege, Glenn. "Homestyle: The Handyman: Air Purifiers Make Our Homes Safer Places to Live and Breathe." Detroit News 25 Oct 1997. p29 secD.

The United Nations Framework Convention on Climate Change allows "nations that have emissions reduction commitments to implement policies and measures jointly with other parties. This approach...[is] known as joint implementation...." (p15) "By June 1996, 12 countries had incorporated joint implementation into their formal national climate action plans. The United States alone had approved 24 pilot projects by April 1997....40 percent of these projects involve carbon storage in forests, 28 percent supply-side and end-use energy efficiency improvements, 16 percent renewable energy technologies, 8 percent fuel switching, and 8 percent measures to capture methane....Under the FCCC the only nations with specific emission reduction commitments are the...24 nations that belonged to the Organisation for Economic Cooperation and Development (OECD) in 1992, six countries from the former Soviet Union, and five other East European nations. These nations have informally committed themselves to lowering their net emissions of greenhouse gases to 1990 levels by the year 2000." (p17)

Harvey, L. D. Danny/Bush, Elizabeth J. "Joint Implementation: An Effective Strategy for Combating Global Warming?" Environment v39 n8 Oct 1997. p14-20,36-44. (ISSN0013-9157).

The Northern Hemisphere "with a little more than 20 percent of the global population, accounts for about 75 percent of the world's energy use, emission of two-thirds of greenhouse gases, and 90 percent of CFCs [chlorofluorocarbons], which damage the earth's ozone layer. The US, Russia, Germany, France, and the United Kingdom are responsible for 85 percent of the global arms trade." (p19)

Bandarage, Asoka. "Opinion/Essays: Economic Inequality, Not Overpopulation, Is the Key Issue." The Christian Science Monitor v89 n159 14 Jul 1997. p19. The Christian Science Monitor search engine: <http://www.csmonitor.com/plweb-cgi/iops1.pl> To retrieve this article, enter the following search: ED=19970714 AND issue. In the "retrieved list," click the title that matches this record. (ISSN0882-7729).

"The typical efficiency of an American coal-fired power plant is 36 percent. This means a third of the energy value in coal is transformed into kilowatts, the rest lost as waste heat; that is a stark way of stating just how far even the sophisticated United States must go to improve energy use. But in China, thermal efficiency of power plants may be as low as 6 percent, meaning six times as much coal burned per kilowatt, and hence six times the greenhouse gases....1 Chinese death in 8 is linked to air pollution; in some cities it reaches 10 times the World Health Organization danger level. A joint study by the WHO and the World Resources Institute estimates that, at current rates of fossil-fuel increase, by the year 2020 there will be 700,000 premature deaths from greenhouse-related pollutants annually, with the most fatalities in the developing world." (p62)

Easterbrook, Gregg/Palmer, Brian. "Culture & Ideas: Greenhouse Common Sense." U.S. News & World Report v123 n21 1 Dec 1997. p58-62. article-level access: <http://www.usnews.com/usnews/issue/971201/1GLOB.HTM> (ISSN0041-5537).

"By the World Bank's own estimates, air pollution causes at least 4 million new cases of chronic bronchitis and contributes to a half million premature deaths each year. In many developing countries, air pollution costs run to as much as 2.5 percent of the annual GDP, and in China they are estimated to be 5 percent. In Shanghai alone, the health costs have reached an estimated $3.5 billion per year." (p28)

Flavin, Christopher. "Banking against Warming." World Watch v10 n6 Nov-Dec 1997. p25-35. (ISSN0896-0615).

AIR--POLLUTION--CHINA (v26)

"Fossil fuel combustion in China now produces close to 20 million metric tons of sulfur dioxide and about 15 million metric tons of particulates a year. Monitoring shows the long-term averages of both pollutants to be multiples of the maximum limits recommended by the World Health Organization (WHO).... WHO has established a limit of no more than 40-60 micrograms per cubic meter of sulfur dioxide as the annual mean. But even the cleanest suburbs of Beijing average 80 micrograms per cubic meter a year. In the city's most polluted neighborhoods, the annual mean is double that value. Still, these levels are low when compared to annual means of more than 400 micrograms per cubic meter in Taiyuan and Lanzhou and more than 300 micrograms in Linfeng, Chongqing (Sichuan), and Guiyang (Guizhou)....At least 200 million Chinese are exposed to annual particulate concentrations of more than 300 micrograms per cubic meter; at least 20 million are exposed to twice that level. With the spread of new industries across the country, between 100 million and 200 million rural inhabitants may already be breathing air nearly as polluted as that in the cities." (p9)

Smil, Vaclav. "China Shoulders the Cost of Environmental Change." Environment v39 n6 Jul-Aug 1997. p6-9,33-37. (ISSN0013-9157).

"China already generates at least 18 percent of the world's ozone-depleting substances, and is the second-biggest producer of greenhouse gases...." (p11) "'China is one of the most polluted countries in the world,' reports the World Bank, which estimates that air and water pollution alone costs China about 8 percent of its G.D.P. every year in damage to life, health and property....Air pollution alone kills up to 289,000 people a year." (p14)

Riskin, Carl. "Articles: China: Behind the Silk Curtain: We Need Summitry beyond Sanctimony." Nation v265 n15 10 Nov 1997. p11-12,14,17. (ISSN0027-8378).

AIR--POLLUTION--CHINA--UNITED STATES

"The United States, with 22 percent of global emissions, is the world's largest emitter of greenhouse gases. And today the industrial world comprises nearly three-quarters of all of the global emissions....China is currently the world's second largest emitter, and it is expected to displace the United States as the largest emitter by the year 2015. Over the next few decades, 90 percent of the world's population growth will take place in the developing world. Given the projected economic and population growth statistics of China and other quickly developing countries such as India, Mexico and Brazil, the developing world will exceed the industrialized world in emissions by the year 2035." (pS10873-10874)

Kerry, John F. (Sen.-Mass.). "Global Warming." Congressional Record. Daily ed. v143 n142 21 Oct 1997. pS10871-10876. section/page-level access: <http://thomas.loc.gov/cqi-bin/query/R?r105:FLD001:S10871:> (ISSN0363-7239). (X1.1A.105/1).

AIR--POLLUTION--CZECH REPUBLIC (v26)

AIR--POLLUTION--EUROPE

In 1997, "about 20% of Europe's ecosystems are still above their critical loads for acidification, and about 33% are above their critical loads for eutrophication....Ozone pollution in 1995 exceeded the EU threshold for the protection of vegetation (a daily average of 65 micrograms/m3 [micrograms per cubic meter]) for more than 150 days of the year over 27% of the EU area, in some cases by a factor of three." (p9)

"Energy, Atmosphere, And Transport: Air Quality Improving Too Slowly to Meet Targets, EEA Says." Environment Watch: Western Europe v6 n12 20 Jun 1997. p8-9. (ISSN1066-6001).

AIR--POLLUTION--HEALTH ASPECTS--UNITED STATES (v26)

In the U.S., "when the EPA proposed the new [clean air] standards in November [1996], it cited 271 health studies. Among them were 70 studies linking ozone to respiratory problems, especially in children and elderly people, and 46 studies that found particulates cause coughing, chest pain and up to 15,000 premature deaths each year." (p1 sec B)

Magner, Mike. "Business: Clearing the Air." Ann Arbor News 13 Jul 1997. p1,4 secB.

AIR--POLLUTION--LAW AND LEGISLATION --TAXATION (v26)

AIR--POLLUTION--MICHIGAN

According to the Clean Air Coalition of Southeast Michigan, "if southeast Michigan reduced its driving by 20 percent, it would eliminate more than 100 tons of ozone-forming pollutants from the air....Emissions from cars, lawn mowers, refueling and maintenance activities are the main ingredients for almost 50 percent of the region's ozone-forming pollutants, according to Chuck Hersey of the Clean Air Coalition of Southeast Michigan." (p8 secD)

"MetroLife: Environment: Hot Topic: Take Action against Ozone Today." Detroit News 24 Jun 1997. p8 secD.

AIR--POLLUTION--NETHERLANDS

In the Netherlands, in 1996, carbon dioxide "emissions rose by 0.5%, well below the 3.3% economic growth rate....Emissions are currently 8% above 1990 levels, while the target for 2000 is a 3% cut from 1990....Emissions of sulfur dioxide, nitrogen oxides, volatile organic compounds, and particulates have dropped by 44%, 22%, 43%, and 52%, respectively, since 1990....Ammonia emissions from agriculture have fallen by 37% between 1990 and 1996, while phosphorus emissions have gone down by 16%. The amount of pesticides used has dropped by 75% since 1988...." (p17)

"General Policy: Dutch Waste Production Grows, Industrial Emissions Drop." Environment Watch: Western Europe v6 n18 19 Sep 1997. p17. (ISSN1066-6001).

AIR--POLLUTION--POLAND (v26)

AIR--POLLUTION--UNITED STATES (v26)

"Harvard School of Public Health studies indicate that 60,000 Americans die prematurely each year from respiratory and cardiovascular illnesses linked to air pollution....Late last winter, the Environmental Protection Agency (EPA) announced that 300 additional areas have unsafe air and proposed stronger standards for smog and 'finer particulate' pollution." (p42)

Buell, John W. "Books: Sky's the Limit." Boston Review v22 n6 Dec 1997-Jan 1998. p42-43. (ISSN0734-2306).

"More than 43 million people in the United States live in areas that fail to meet EPA's air quality standards for carbon monoxide. We have 13 million people in nonattainment areas for nitrogen oxide....In...California, nearly 26 million people live in a nonattainment area for one or more pollutants, out of a state of nearly 32 million people....According to the EPA, the current annual average concentrations of fine particulate matter in southeast Los Angeles County may be responsible for up to 3,000 deaths annually, and more than 52,000 incidences of respiratory symptoms including 1,000 hospital admissions. Young children constitute the largest group at high risk from exposure to air pollutants. They breathe 50 percent more air by body weight than the average adult. In California alone there are over 6 million children under the age of 14 and approximately 90 percent of them live in areas that fail to meet State and Federal standards....Studies show health effects ranging from 20 to 60 percent losses of lung capacity." (pS5259)

Boxer, Barbara (Sen.-Calif.). "Statements on Introduced Bills and Joint Resolutions." Congressional Record. Daily ed. v143 n74 3 Jun 1997. pS5253-5264. section/page-level access: <http://thomas.loc.gov/cgi-bin/query/R?r105:FLD001:S05259:> (ISSN0363-7239). (X1.1A.105/1).

In the U.S., "the Emissions Efficiency Index has been in a free fall for 71 percent of the S&P [Standard & Poor's Corporation] 500 companies covered. The index, compiled by the Investor Responsibility Research Center in Washington, D.C., is calculated by dividing pounds of emissions as reported on each year's Toxics Release Inventory by annual corporate revenues. Leading the decline over the five-year period 1988-93 was the specialty chemical industry, down 58 percent. Glass and metal containers was close behind at 51 percent and drug manufacturing was off 49 percent. The metals industry continued to head the benchmark three-year average emissions index, with a high of 14.38 pounds per $1,000 in revenue. Chemicals was second at 7.37, and all other industries were under 4." (p14)

Dujack, Stephen R. "Notice & Comment: S&P Index Plunges; Entire Nation Cheers." Environmental Forum v14 n3 May-Jun 1997. p14. (ISSN0731-5732).

"Ozone, a powerful respiratory irritant found in most of the...[U.S.'s] urban areas during summer months, is estimated to kill several thousand Americans annually through its contribution to lung disease, says Ronald H. White, deputy director of national programs for the American Lung Association in Washington, DC. According to the EPA, ozone is linked to approximately 10,000-15,000 hospital admissions and 30,000-50,000 emergency room visits annually in 13 metropolitan areas. Ozone forms when hydrocarbons and nitrogen oxides (NOx), two important constituents of automobile exhaust, react in the presence of sunlight. Cars are responsible for about one-third of the smog in the Los Angeles Basin, says Carl Moyer, chief scientist at Acurex Environmental Corporation in Mountain View, California." (p582-583)

Holzman, David/U.S. National Institute of Environmental Health Sciences. "Focus: A Driving Force." Environmental Health Perspectives v105 n6 Jun 1997. p582-587. article-level access: <http://ehpnet1.niehs.nih.gov/docs/1997/105-6/focus-abs.html>

In the U.S., "the measured pollutants have decreased nationally by almost 30 percent, even as population has increased by 28 percent, and vehicle miles by 116 percent....The current standard for ozone is no more than 0.12 parts per million (ppm) during the highest-level hour each day." (p29) For particulates, the current PM10, or particles 10 microns wide or smaller "standard allows an annual average concentration of 50 micrograms per cubic meter of air, and a maximum of 150 such micrograms in a 24-hour period....PM2.5 particles are the most likely to lodge deeply in the lungs...." (p30)

Fumento, Michael. "Polluted Science." Reason v29 n4 Aug-Sep 1997. p28-42. (ISSN0048-6906).

In the U.S., "forty percent of smog is caused by emissions from automobiles and other vehicles, and 67 percent of the carbon monoxide results from the combustion of transportation fuels....The level of carbon dioxide and other greenhouse gases in the atmosphere has risen significantly. A key contributor to this increase has been the combustion of transportation fuels, which contribute 33 percent of the CO2 [carbon dioxide] released in the U.S. on an annual basis." (p28-29)

Hinman, Norman D. "The Benefits of Biofuels." Solar Today v11 n4 Jul-Aug 1997. p28-30. (ISSN1042-0630).

According to James Laurin of the LOS ANGELES DAILY NEWS, "'the Environmental Protection Agency figures that based on the amount of charcoal sold nationwide, backyard cook-outs create less than 15,000 tons of volatile organic chemical pollution annually--vs. some 23 million tons from industry as a whole. As for those big-league burger broilers, they produce just 4 percent (or half a ton) of southern California's daily airborne particulates--while the region receives a combined 79 tons of the stuff each day from construction and demolition projects, diesel trucks and farming operations.'" (p2)

Featheringill, Linda. "Industry Is Worst Polluter." The People v107 n8 Nov 1997. p2. (ISSN0199-350X).

AIR--POLLUTION--UNITED STATES--INFANTS --MORTALITY

"High levels of industrial soot and dust appear to increase the risk of babies dying, according to a new study of the relationship between air quality and infant mortality in the United States. Researchers at the Environmental Protection Agency and the Centers for Disease Control and Prevention studied 4 million infants born between 1989 and 1991 in 86 metropolitan areas....They found a 10-percent increased risk of mortality among full-term infants living in cities with high levels of pollution, known as particulate matter, even after other infant death risk factors were taken into account. The study also found a 26-percent increased risk for Sudden Infant Death Syndrome, or SIDS, after the other risk factors were considered, in cities with high exposure compared to those with low exposure." (p5 secA)

Zagaroli, Lisa. "Nation World: Pollution Tied to Infant Deaths." Detroit News 13 Jun 1997. p5 secA.

AIR--POLLUTION--UNITED STATES--MORTALITY

In the U.S., "in December 1993, Douglas Dockery and other Harvard School of Public Health researchers released the Harvard 'Six City' study, which tracked the health of more than 8,000 people for fourteen to sixteen years; it showed that fine particles [in the air] increased the risk of premature death for residents of the most polluted city by 26 percent over that for residents of the least polluted city. Two years later, the American Cancer Society Study, which tracked about 500,000 people in 151 cities, reported that people living in areas most polluted with fine particles had a 17 percent greater risk of mortality than those in areas with the lowest levels. And in 1996, the NRDC [Natural Resources Defense Council] report 'Breath Taking' applied these findings to 239 cities, and found that approximately 64,000 people may die prematurely from heart or lung disease every year due to particulate pollution." (p30)

Skelton, Renee. "Clearing the Air: An Epidemiologist Takes on the Worst Air Pollution Problems of Our Time." Amicus Journal v19 n2 Sum 1997. p27-30. (ISSN0276-7201).

"Air pollution kills from 50,000 to 100,000 people yearly in the United States alone...concludes Curtis Moore, an expert on pollution control technology with the...American Lung Association....Fine particulates, caused by combustion, as well as ozone, are what make air pollution so dangerous to human health, he says. In fact, such air pollution is second only to tobacco as a cause of lung disease in America. And...one-third to 35% or even 40% of these deadly pollutants are caused by fuel combustion in conventional power plants, he says. Much of the remainder is from car exhaust and factories." (p29) "The EPA, under administrator Carol Browner, estimates that its new standards on smog and soot would prevent 15,000 premature deaths--especially of children and the elderly--and would eliminate 250,000 annual cases of serious respiratory problems in children." (p31)

Davidson, Ros. "US News: Scientific Evidence Overwhelming: Renewables Can Make the Difference." Windpower Monthly v13 n7 Jul 1997. p29,31. (ISSN0109-7318).

AIR--POLLUTION--VIETNAM (v26)

AIR BAG RESTRAINT SYSTEMS (v26)

AIR BAG RESTRAINT SYSTEMS--UNITED STATES (v26)

In the U.S., "the mandate requiring air bags was supported by government claims that they would save more than 90,000 lives per decade. The current...claim is that they have saved 1,700 lives from 1986 to 1996, less than 2 percent of the original claim, and an even smaller percent of the 400,000 traffic deaths that occurred during the same period. The three best technical studies consistently find that air bags reduce the risk of death in a crash by 9 percent for drivers wearing their safety belts....Even for those driving without safety belts,...air bags reduce fatality risk by only 13 percent....There are already 62 known deaths caused by air bags in crashes that, without the air bag, were unlikely to injure." (p11 secA)

Evans, Leonard. "Other Voices: Air Bags: Even the Smartest Technology Is a Dumb, Dangerous Mandate." Detroit Free Press 16 Jun 1997. p11 secA.

In the U.S., the National Highway Traffic Safety Administration "changed its regulations on air bags to allow automakers to reduce the inflation-power of air bags by 20 to 35 percent. Air bags have killed 67 people, mostly children and small women, but saved an estimated 1,900 since 1986." (p1 secB) "Currently, the government requires an air bag to protect just average-size males who aren't wearing seat belts in 30-mph [miles per hour] collisions." (p3 secB)

Knox, Noelle. "Business: Second Generation Air Bags: Slower Air Bags Start Showing Up on Vehicles." Detroit News 18 Jun 1997. p1,3 secB.

AIR BAG RESTRAINT SYSTEMS--UNITED STATES --CHILDREN--MORTALITY

In the U.S., "since 1993, 49 children--ranging in age from 3 weeks to 9 years--have been killed by rapidly deploying air bags, according to the National Highway Traffic Safety Administration. That's more than half of the 87 people who've been killed by air bags this decade....[Researchers at the Insurance Institute for Highway Safety in Arlington, Virginia] found that air bags do work for older children and adults. Their fatalities were 18 percent fewer than expected in frontal crashes of cars with dual air bags. Passenger-side air bags have killed only three people 10 or older this decade, according to NHTSA. Meanwhile, air bags overall have saved 2,620 lives through Oct 15, [1997,] the agency estimated." (p1 secB)

Cole, Kenneth. "Business: Side Air Bags Take Large Toll on Youths." Detroit News 5 Nov 1997. p1 secB.

AIR BAG RESTRAINT SYSTEMS--UNITED STATES --MORTALITY

In the U.S., "in 1996, 27 people--including 22 children--were killed by air bags, according to federal safety data." (p1 secA) "In all, 67 people are known to have been killed by air bags, most of them because they were not belted or were not in the proper child restraint....So far in 1997, air bag fatality rates--as a percentage of air bags on the road--are the lowest for any year since 1993, when air bags were in less than 10 percent of U.S. autos." (p14 secA)

Fix, Janet L. "Air Bag Death Rate Plummets This Year." Detroit Free Press 12 Jun 1997. p1,14 secA.

In the U.S., "while air bags have been blamed for the deaths of 76 children and adults--most of them small and unbelted--they also have been credited with saving more than 2,000 lives....As many as 400 people a year could die in accidents who otherwise would have lived if their air bags had been working, according to a study requested by TRW, a major air bag supplier. That estimate is based on NHTSA's [National Highway Traffic Safety Administration] estimate that 3,000 lives a year would be saved by air bags once all vehicles are equipped with air bags." (p6 secE)

Fix, Janet L. "Business: Carmakers Ready Kits to Disable 1 Million Air Bags." Detroit Free Press 25 Jul 1997. p1,6 secE.

AIR BAG RESTRAINT SYSTEMS--UNITED STATES --PUBLIC OPINION (v26)

Currently, the U.S. National Highway Traffic Safety Administration agency gives permission to have air bags disabled "only to consumers who have a medical condition that makes an air bag hazardous, or must carry infants in rear-facing seats in the front seat. So far, NHTSA has granted 3,237 vehicle owners permission for these reasons. Through July 11, 5,518 people, without medical reasons, have written NHTSA asking to have their air bag disabled. About half of the 24,773 who have called NHTSA's hotline have indicated a desire to have an air bag disabled." (p1,6 secE)

Fix, Janet L. "Business: Carmakers Ready Kits to Disable 1 Million Air Bags." Detroit Free Press 25 Jul 1997. p1,6 secE.

AIR BASES--FLORIDA

Just south of Crestview, Florida, Elgin Air Force Base's "464,000 acres--more than 700 square miles--span three counties....State roads bisect the base, and administrative offices, living quarters and recreational facilities for many of Elgin's 15,000 employees and their families claim a chunk of real estate on the base's southeastern flank." (p12)

Biondo, Brenda. "In Defense of the Longleaf Pine." Nature Conservancy v47 n4 Sep-Oct 1997. p10-17. (ISSN0028-5200).

AIR SHOWS--UNITED STATES--COSTS

"In a typical year, the U.S. Government helps promote U.S. weaponry at over half a dozen major international air shows. Costs to U.S. taxpayers include revenues foregone from leasing fees that are no longer charged to U.S. manufacturers to display U.S. Government-owned weaponry. These waived fees alone can cost taxpayers $5-10 million per show. These weapons exhibitions are called training missions so the costs of getting U.S. equipment and personnel to them don't have to be reported to Congress. The flight of a B-2 bomber to the Paris Air Show involved at least a 24-hour round-trip at $14,166 per hour to operate the plan....The cost to U.S. taxpayers for these shows in 1995 was $27 million." (pE1923)

Furse, Elizabeth (Rep.-Oreg.). "Equity for Immigrants Act." Congressional Record. Daily ed. v143 n135 2 Oct 1997. pE1922-1923. section/page-level access: <http://thomas.loc.gov/cgi-bin/query/R?r105:FLD001:E01922:> (ISSN0363-7239). (X1.1A.105/1).

AIR TRANSPORT

see AERONAUTICS, COMMERCIAL

AIR TRAVEL (v26)

AIR TRAVEL--MICHIGAN--PUBLIC OPINION (v26)

AIR TRAVEL--UNITED STATES (v26)

AIR TRAVEL--UNITED STATES--FINANCE (v26)

AIRCRAFT ACCIDENTS--UNITED STATES (v26)

"In 1996, there were 287 runway incursions in the US. More than half were caused by pilots failing to do things like stop short of an active runway. More than 70 percent of the pilot deviations involved general-aviation aircraft, the smaller, noncommercial planes." (p4)

Marks, Alexandra. "United States: Jammed US Runways Increase Close Calls." The Christian Science Monitor v90 n17 18 Dec 1997. p1,4. The Christian Science Monitor search engine: <http://www.csmonitor.com/plweb-cgi/iops1.pl> To retrieve this article, enter the following search: ED=19971218 AND calls. In the "retrieved list," click the title that matches this record. (ISSN0882-7729).

AIRLINES--ISRAEL

In Israel, figures for the first four months of 1997 "show a 2.5-percent drop in the number of passengers flying in and out of Ben-Gurion. Between 1995 and 1996, the number of passengers on scheduled airlines was up almost 4 percent, due to a 17-percent drop in charters." (p38)

Sher, Hanan. "Special Report: Tourism: Losing Altitude?" Jerusalem Report v8 n5 10 Jul 1997. p36,38. (ISSN0792-6049).

AIRLINES--UNITED STATES (v26)

AIRLINES--UNITED STATES--SAFETY MEASURES

"The Air Travelers Association, a recently formed Washington lobby group for airline passengers,...issues an Airline Safety Report Card. It ranks 260 airlines worldwide, including 29 US airlines....The Report Card includes airline-safety ratings of 0 to 100 for the fatal accident history, with corresponding grades of A to F for the passenger airlines. All US-owned airlines received an A, except for ValuJet, which received an F....The fatal accidents category...gives the same weight to an accident in which one person dies as it does to a crash that kills 100 people....The Report Card uses an index of one accident per 1 million flights as the criterion for receiving an A. Delta Airlines...got an A for having two fatal accidents for 9,372,000 flights in the 10-year-period. US Airways had six fatal accidents for 9,496,000 flights and also received an A....[Arnold Barnett is a statistics professor at the Massachusetts Institute of Technology in Cambridge. According to his] latest risk calculations, using data from August 1987 to August 1997, 'If a person took a flight every single day, including Saturdays, Sundays, and holidays, he could go 21,000 years before succumbing to a fatal crash.'..." (p3)

Bowers, Faye. "United States: Airline-Safety Report Card: Most Carriers Make Grade." The Christian Science Monitor v89 n186 20 Aug 1997. p3. The Christian Science Monitor search engine: <http://www.csmonitor.com/plweb-cgi/iops1.pl> To retrieve this article, enter the following search: ED=19970820 AND grade. In the "retrieved list," click the title that matches this record. (ISSN0882-7729).

AIRPLANE ACCIDENTS

see AIRCRAFT ACCIDENTS

AIRPLANES--ENVIRONMENTAL ASPECTS

"British Airways estimates that the air travel industry burns 170 million metric tons of fuel each year. For every kilogram (2.2 pounds) of fuel burned, 1.5 kilos (3.3 pounds) of water vapor are produced. Every year, therefore, aircraft produce 255 million metric tons of vapor, much of it injected into the dry upper troposphere and the even drier stratosphere....Researchers from NASA's Langley Research Center presented evidence that contrails [or 'condensation trails'] are contributing to global warming and causing local effects over areas with heavy air traffic. In April 1996, they found contrails over New York during 40 percent of the month. Above Arizona, contrails appeared during 30 percent of the month." (p36)

Scanlon, Jim. "Contrail Cover-Up: Behind the Contrail Curtain." Earth Island Journal v12 n3 Sum 1997. p36. (ISSN1041-0406).

"With 10,000 large commercial aircraft flying today and the number expected to double by the year 2020, contrails (short for 'condensation trails') pose a growing environmental threat....One of the world's most traveled routes, the North Atlantic Flight Corridor (NAFC), lies between 45 and 65 degrees north latitude and runs almost entirely over water. In 1990, between 700 and 800 aircraft traveled this route between the US and Europe each day--amounting to more than 200,000 flights per year....By 1996, NASA scientists using GOES-8 satellite measurements reported that 'in certain heavy air traffic corridors, cloud cover has increased by as much as 20 percent.' In its May 1996 study, 'Atmospheric Effects of Aviation,' NASA estimated that subsonic flights in the NAFC had increased atmospheric soot by 10 percent, sulfur oxides (SOx) by nearly 10 percent and nitrogen oxides (NOx) from 10 to 100 percent. The world's aircraft currently produce about 3 percent of the carbon dioxide (CO2) gases attributed to human activity. During takeoff, a jumbo jet can devour 2 million liters (528,344 gallons) of air per second. In the first five minutes of flight, a commercial airliner can burn as much oxygen as 49,000 acres of forest produce in a day....Boeing 747 averages 32 minutes taxiing, taking off and landing. During this time, it can generate 190 pounds of NOx--equal to the amount produced by driving a car 53,500 miles....In 1996, aircraft generated nearly half the NOx found in the mid-latitudes of the Northern Hemisphere between 26,000 and 40,000 feet, according to estimates cited by Ulrich Schumann of the DLR Institute in Oberpfaffenhofen, Germany." (p34)

Smith, Gar. "Contrail Cover-Up: Oil Spills in the Sky." Earth Island Journal v12 n3 Sum 1997. p34-35. (ISSN1041-0406).

AIRPLANES--ENVIRONMENTAL ASPECTS--UNITED STATES (v26)

AIRPLANES--EUROPE--FUEL CONSUMPTION

"Further evidence of the rapid growth in air travel has been provided by a 5.3% jump in consumption of kerosene and other jet fuels within the EU last year, a bigger increase than for any other category of oil product. Figures published by Eurostat, the EU's statistical office, show an accelerating expansion of jet fuel deliveries after growth of 4.1% in 1995....Demand soared by no less than 32.5% in Finland, while Ireland and Belgium recorded increases of 19.1% and 17.8% respectively." (p13)

"Energy, Atmosphere, And Transport: In Brief...: Jet Fuel Use Jumps in EU." Environment Watch: Western Europe v6 n17 5 Sep 1997. p13. (ISSN1066-6001).

AIRPLANES--FUEL CONSUMPTION

"Transatlantic jets burn between 2.5 and 3 tons of fuel per hour....According to Department of Transportation figures, flying a Boeing 747-400 from Washington, DC to San Francisco burns 17,232 gallons of jet fuel. (Fuel efficiency: 6.7 mpg [miles per gallon])." (p34) "The EDF [Environmental Defense Fund] estimates that, in 1990, civil aviation consumed 133 million tons of fuel and generated 422 million tons of CO2 [carbon dioxide]. According to a 1996 analysis by Boeing researcher Steven L. Baughcum, in 1990, airline and cargo flights burned more than 10 billion tons of jet fuel and generated 125.6 million tons of NOx [nitrogen oxides]. Baughcum estimated that military aircraft consumed 912 million tons of fuel and produced 21.4 million tons of NOx. The global total for 1990 came to 14.8 billion tons burned, which produced 160 million tons of NOx and 124.5 million tons of CO2." (p35)

Smith, Gar. "Contrail Cover-Up: Oil Spills in the Sky." Earth Island Journal v12 n3 Sum 1997. p34-35. (ISSN1041-0406).

AIRPLANES, COMPANY--UNITED STATES

Should "corporate jets pay their fair share of the $6 billion annual cost of keeping America's air routes safe? Private planes--about 40 percent of them business planes--use well over 20 percent of the capacity of the nation's rickety air-traffic-control system (ATC). But all these planes pay only about 3 percent of the expenses, via a tax on aviation fuel. The rest comes from airline passengers, through a 10 percent tax on tickets." (p49)

Glassman, James K. "Commentary: Corporate Welfare in the Sky." U.S. News & World Report v123 n4 28 Jul 1997. p49. article-level access: <http://www.usnews.com/usnews/issue/970728/28GLAS.HTM> (ISSN0041-5537).

AIRPORTS

see also AIR BASES

AIRPORTS--ASIA (v26)

AIRPORTS--CANADA (v26)

AIRPORTS--JAPAN--KASAOKA

In Kasaoka, Japan, "a $4.96-billion agricultural airport, completed in 1991, lies all but unused. In 1995, 4 metric tons of agricultural goods passed through the facility, less than 1 percent of target goals. Five more such airports are under construction at a cost of $79 million." (p7)

Hasegawa, Miharu. "International: A Lineup of White Elephants." The Christian Science Monitor v89 n148 26 Jun 1997. p7. The Christian Science Monitor search engine: <http://www.csmonitor.com/plweb-cgi/iops1.pl> To retrieve this article, enter the following search: ED=19970626 AND elephants. In the "retrieved list," click the title that matches this record. (ISSN0882-7729).

AIRPORTS--MASSACHUSETTS--BOSTON (v26)

AIRPORTS--MICHIGAN

In Michigan, Willow Run Airport's busiest hours are between 2 and 4 o'clock in "the morning. That's when its 21 air cargo carriers make many of their small- to medium-size deliveries of auto parts and other manufactured goods--an estimated 22,500 tons this year. That's up from 19,600 tons in 1996. The airport on the Wayne-Washtenaw county border and its tenants employ 2,500 people with an annual payroll of $77 million, in an operation that Wayne County Economic Development Director Dewey Henry compares to an auto assembly plant. More than 500 planes are based at the airport, which, like [Detroit] Metro Airport, is owned and operated by the county." (p7 secF)

Fricker, Dan. "Business Monday: Cover Story: The Second Flight: Willow Run Airport." Detroit Free Press 29 Sep 1997. p6-8 secF.

AIRPORTS--MICHIGAN--OAKLAND COUNTY

Oakland County International Airport is Michigan's "second-busiest airport. [It is] the fourth-busiest in the Great Lakes area. [It is] the nation's fifth-busiest reliever airport, which is the FAA [Federal Aviation Administration] designation for an airport that serves as an alternate for business, corporate and other general aviation. [It is] among the world's top 30 in number of takeoffs and landings. Although the airport in Waterford Township has no scheduled commercial service, an estimated 500,000 passengers use it annually. Sports teams and entertainers appearing at the Silverdome, Palace of Auburn Hills and Pine Knob fly chartered Boeing 727s into Oakland International....Daily takeoffs and landings are projected to rise to about 1,100 in 2010 from about 1,000 today. The number of jet and turbo-prop aircraft at the airport also is expected to rise from today's 180." (p9 secF)

Fricker, Dan. "Business Monday: Cover Story: The Second Flight: Oakland County International Airport." Detroit Free Press 29 Sep 1997. p9 secF.

AIRPORTS--MICHIGAN--OAKLAND COUNTY

"In the year since the Customs presence has been established at Oakland County [Michigan], international flights have increased fivefold, from 700 before the office opened to 3,500. The international passengers are almost exclusively executives from 462 foreign-owned businesses located in Oakland County. Oakland International serves private pilots and businesses, but no commercial airlines....Only a fraction of the airport's 350,000 annual takeoffs and landings are international. The rest are corporate planes, charter flights, freight deliveries and private planes. The constant comings and goings rank Oakland International among the world's 30 busiest airports. The airport also is home to 150 corporations and businesses who have aircraft based there, and hundreds more private pilots." (p6 secB)

McDiarmid, Hugh, Jr. "Local News: Airport Is Soaring to New Heights." Detroit Free Press 21 Jul 1997. p1,6 secB.

AIRPORTS--NEW YORK (N.Y.)

At New York City's "Kennedy Airport, an estimated $3M [million] to $5M of goods are stolen within the facilities per year....$88B [billion] of high value assets pass through the port, according to Robert Caron of the Port Authority police." (unpaginated)

"Cargo Security: Many Ports Reporting Less Theft: But Ground Transport Still Vulnerable." Security Letter v27 n19 1 Nov 1997. (ISSN0363-4922).

AIRPORTS--SECURITY MEASURES--MICHIGAN --DETROIT (v26)

AIRPORTS--SWITZERLAND

Over the first half of 1997, Zurich's Kloten airport "experienced an 8% rise in takeoffs and landings. In the area around the airport, NOx [nitrogen oxides] levels are 30% above the maximum concentration allowed on average over the year....In line with existing fees on noise, the NOx charges are based on engine type, with the different types divided into five categories. The newest aircraft (category 5) receive a 5% reduction on landing charges. For other planes, fees range from 5% of the regular charge for category 4 to 40% for category 1 engines, the oldest and dirtiest. According to airport management estimates, approximately half the planes landing at Kloten fall into category 5. Some 17% fall into category 4. Around 30% are in category 3, on which a 10% surcharge is levied." (p7)

"Energy, Atmosphere, And Transport: Swiss Airport to Levy NOX Emissions Charges." Environment Watch: Western Europe v6 n17 5 Sep 1997. p7. (ISSN1066-6001).

AIRPORTS--TEXAS

In Texas, "Dallas Fort Worth and Love Field airports are only 8 miles apart. Only 2 nautical miles separate the approach patterns between DFW and Love Field. The runways at Love Field point into Dallas Forth Worth's most heavily used arrival routes....The approach procedures into Love Field are more circuitous in order to facilitate a more direct approach into Dallas Fort Worth....The Federal Aviation Administration's data shows that Dallas Forth Worth totaled almost 900,000 operations in 1995, making it the second most active U.S. airport. Analysts at the Federal Aviation Administration believe that this will increase to over 1.2 million operations per year by 2010, an increase of almost 40 percent. Love Field, on the other hand, experienced about 208,700 operations in 1995 and is expected to grow by about 5.9 percent by 2010." (pH8751)

Oberstar, James L. (Rep.-Minn.). "Conference Report on H.R. 2169, Department of Transportation...Appropriations Act, 1998." Congressional Record. Daily ed. v143 n140 9 Oct 1997. pH8741-8752. section/page-level access: <http://thomas.loc.gov/cgi-bin/query/R?r105:FLD001:H08751:> (ISSN0363-7239). (X1.1A.105/1).

AK-47 RIFLE

"The most notorious assault rifle is the AK-47, also known by its inventor's name, Kalashnikov. Manufactured in the former Soviet Union and in nine other countries, more than 70 million Kalashnikovs have been produced in some 100 different versions since 1947; most of these are still in use by the armies of 78 countries and countless guerrilla groups the world over....According to the Bonn International Center for Conversion (BICC), the standard black-market price for an AK-47 is about $200, but it is far lower in areas where the rifle is abundant." (p19-20)

Renner, Michael. "Small Arms, Big Impact: The Next Challenge of Disarmament." Worldwatch Paper n137 Oct 1997. p5-77.

ALABAMA--ARIZONA--POPULATION (v26)

ALABAMA--EMPLOYMENT--MANUFACTURES (v26)

ALAMEDA (CALIF.) (v26)

ALASKA

"Alaska encompasses 586,412 square miles. It is one-fifth the size of the contiguous United States; 120 times larger than the State of Rhode Island; and larger than the three largest States in the union combined. If a map of Alaska were superimposed on a map of the lower 48 States, Alaska would touch South Carolina, Mexico, California and the United States-Canadian border. In short, Alaska has 1 million acres of land for every day of the year....Though Alaska contains 586,412 square miles, it only has 12,200 miles of roads." (pS5367)

Murkowski, Frank H. (Sen.-Alaska). "Statements on Introduced Bills and Joint Resolutions." Congressional Record. Daily ed. v143 n76 5 Jun 1997. pS5342-5368. section/page-level access: <http://thomas.loc.gov/cgi-bin/query/R?r105:FLD001:S05367:> (ISSN0363-7239). (X1.1A.105/1).

ALASKA--ECONOMIC CONDITIONS

"Annual increases in employment opportunities (2.1 percent annually from 1985 to 1994) are higher in southeast Alaska than in much of the rest of the country (1.5 percent annual growth), as is population growth (1.6 percent in southeast Alaska compared to 1 percent nationally). Real average earnings per job, however, have declined at a rate of 1.5 percent annually since 1985...." (p6)

Richardson, Sherri/U.S. Dept. of Agriculture. Forest Service. "Tongass Management Plan: Research Played a Key Role." Forestry Research West Sep 1997. p3-7. (ISSN0195-5861).

ALBANIA--ECONOMIC CONDITIONS

In Albania, starting in 1992, "an estimated 60% of the population invested approximately $1.5 billion in...[pyramid schemes], sometimes by selling their property, livestock or family heirlooms." (p12) "The six major pyramid schemes gradually engaged in an interest war, which peaked in December 1996 and January 1997 with interest rates as high as 80%." (p13)

Abrahams, Fred. "The Albanian House of Cards." Dollars and Sense n212 Jul-Aug 1997. p11-13. (ISSN0012-5245).

"Albania is a small, mountainous nation in the Balkan peninsula of southeastern Europe with a population of approximately 3.25 million people....Gross domestic product is below $400 U.S. dollars per year, unemployment stands at 18 percent, and private ownership of vehicles was banned until 1991...." (p64)

Germain, John T. "Albania 1997: Operation SILVER WAKE." Marine Corps Gazette v81 n9 Sep 1997. p64-66. (ISSN0025-3170).

ALBANIA--RELIGION

"Before 1967, when Communist dictator Enver Hoxja banned all religions in Albania, the country was 70 percent Muslim, 20 percent Catholic, and 10 percent Greek Orthodox. But since 1991, 58 religious groups and sects have registered at the Department of Religions in the Ministry of Culture." (p7)

Kociu, Uliana. "International: Albania in Passage: A Rush to Reach Ex-Atheist People." The Christian Science Monitor v89 n148 26 Jun 1997. p7. The Christian Science Monitor search engine: <http://www.csmonitor.com/plweb-cgi/iops1.pl> To retrieve this article, enter the following search: ED=19970626 AND people. In the "retrieved list," click the title that matches this record. (ISSN0882-7729).

ALBERTA--ECONOMIC CONDITIONS (v26)

"Alberta's economy is expected to grow by 4.3 per cent this year, well ahead of the 3.4-per-cent national average....Over the past three years of a determined austerity drive, it has eliminated the provincial deficit and amassed budgetary surpluses totalling $4.6 billion. This year's surplus alone is expected to pass the $1-billion mark." (p20)

Eisler, Dale. "Canada: Letter from Brooks, Alta.: Boom Times Are Back." Maclean's v110 n41 13 Oct 1997. p20. (ISSN0024-9262).

ALBERTA--POPULATION (v26)

ALCOHOL--PHYSIOLOGICAL EFFECT--UNITED STATES (v26)

ALCOHOL AS FUEL--UNITED STATES--COSTS (v26)

ALCOHOL FUEL INDUSTRY--MINNESOTA

In the U.S., "farmer-owned coops are now the leading producers of ethanol. They make up 60 percent of the ethanol facilities around the country. By year's end, nine plants will be in operation in Minnesota, producing 126 million gallons annually and creating 500 new jobs. Overall, ethanol contributes between $109 and $260 million yearly to the State's economy. Currently, 71 percent of the gas sold in Minnesota contains ethanol. By the end of the year, 100 percent of the gas sold in Minnesota will be blended with ethanol." (pS6697)

Wellstone, Paul D. (Sen.-Minn.). "Revenue Reconciliation Act of 1997." Congressional Record. Daily ed. v143 n93 27 Jun 1997. pS6670-6720. section/page-level access: <http://thomas.loc.gov/cgi-bin/query/R?r105:FLD001:S06697:> (ISSN0363-7239). (X1.1A.105/1).

ALCOHOL FUEL INDUSTRY--TAXATION--UNITED STATES

"The American taxpayers have subsidized the ethanol industry, with guaranteed loans and tax credits, for more than 20 years. Since 1980, government subsidies for ethanol have totaled more than $10 billion....Current law provides tax credits for ethanol producers which are estimated to cost the Treasury $770 million a year in lost revenue, and the Congressional Research Service estimates that loss may increase to $1 billion by the year 2000." (pS6689)

McCain, John (Sen.-Ariz.). "Revenue Reconciliation Act of 1997." Congressional Record. Daily ed. v143 n93 27 Jun 1997. pS6670-6720. section/page-level access: <http://thomas.loc.gov/cgi-bin/query/R?r105:FLD001:S06689:> (ISSN0363-7239). (X1.1A.105/1).

ALCOHOL FUEL INDUSTRY--UNITED STATES (v26)

"A recent study conducted by the Midwest Governors' Conference concluded that the ethanol program produces a net savings to the [U.S.] Federal budget of more than $3.6 billion, adds over $450 million to State tax receipts each year, increases total U.S. employment by 195,200 jobs, and boosts net farm income by more than $4.5 billion annually. The Federal Government gains $1.30 for each gallon of ethanol sold in America--more than double the 54-cent-per-gallon cost of the incentive....Ethanol-blended fuels reduce emissions of carbon monoxide, nitrogen oxides, and air toxics. Also, ethanol reduces the demand for imported gasoline and imported oxygenates by more than 90,000 barrels per day." (pS7302)

Durbin, Richard J. (Sen.-Ill.). "Statements on Introduced Bills and Joint Resolutions." Congressional Record. Daily ed. v143 n98 11 Jul 1997. pS7302-7303. section/page-level access: <http://thomas.loc.gov/cgi-bin/query/R?r105:FLD001:S07302:> (ISSN0363-7239). (X1.1A.105/1).

"As a result of progressive policymakers, ethanol is now produced in 53 plants in 19 [U.S.] States. The production of fuel ethanol results in more than 55,000 high-wage jobs, generates greater than $2.1 billion in household income, and adds more than $7.2 billion to the economy every year. Farmers will receive an additional $2.2 billion each year because of ethanol production. Moreover, nearly all new expansion in the ethanol industry has been completed by farmer-owned cooperatives. The Department of Agriculture estimates that a 100 million gallon ethanol plant will add 2,250 jobs to a community--enhancing rural development and expansion." (pS6690)

Johnson, Tim (Sen.-S.Dak.). "Revenue Reconciliation Act of 1997." Congressional Record. Daily ed. v143 n93 27 Jun 1997. pS6670-6720. section/page-level access: <http://thomas.loc.gov/cgi-bin/query/R?r105:FLD001:S06690:> (ISSN0363-7239). (X1.1A.105/1).

In the U.S., "ethanol producers currently get a tax break of 54 cents a gallon to help make the [corn-based] fuel more competitive with gasoline. Corn is not only the largest crop in Michigan, accounting for nearly 20 percent of the state's agricultural production, it also is a key ingredient in the auto industry's plan to build cleaner-burning cars and trucks....Currently, there are fewer than 50 ethanol fueling stations nationwide, and none in Michigan....Since 1990, the auto industry has sold 23,000 vehicles that can run on gasoline or ethanol." (p1 secB)

Knox, Noelle. "Business: Plan Would End Tax Cut for Ethanol." Detroit News 12 Jun 1997. p1 secB.

ALCOHOLIC BEVERAGE INDUSTRY--LICENSES

see LICENSE SYSTEM

ALCOHOLIC BEVERAGES--AUSTRALIA (v26)

ALCOHOLIC BEVERAGES--CANADA (v26)

ALCOHOLIC BEVERAGES--CANADA--PUBLIC OPINION (v26)

ALCOHOLIC BEVERAGES--CHINA (v26)

ALCOHOLIC BEVERAGES--GREAT BRITAIN

In May 1997, British officials appointed a special team to look into the problem of alcopops, alcoholic beverages that are packaged to look like soda pop and appeal to young people. "It found that alcopops with names such as Hooch (4.7 percent alcohol), Thickhead (4.9 percent), and Thunderbird (13.1 percent) were being sold in ever-increasing quantities....In less than two years, British sales have rocketed to $575 million. There are about 100 different brands of alcopops, accounting for 10 percent of the alcoholic-beverage market, according to industry figures....Zenith International, a market-research company, forecasts that alcopop sales in Britain will reach 1.3 billion [pounds sterling] ($2.1 billion) by 2000, if current consumption trends continue." (p14)

MacLeod, Alexander. "Global Report: Countries Put Cork in Marketing to Teens: Sweet Drinks That Lure Kids Pack a Surprise--Alcohol." The Christian Science Monitor v89 n181 13 Aug 1997. p1,14. The Christian Science Monitor search engine: <http://www.csmonitor.com/plweb-cgi/iops1.pl> To retrieve this article, enter the following search: ED=19970813 AND alcohol. In the "retrieved list," click the title that matches this record. (ISSN0882-7729).

ALCOHOLIC BEVERAGES--UNITED STATES (v26)

ALCOHOLIC BEVERAGES--UNITED STATES--PUBLIC OPINION

According to the Gallup Organization, "the percentage of Americans who say they drink alcoholic beverages--as opposed to being total abstainers--varies slightly from year to year, but has generally hovered around the 60% level for the past decade. In June of this year, 61% of Americans said that they 'use alcoholic beverages.' A substantial plurality of America's drinkers, now 45%, continue to cite beer as the alcoholic beverage they drink most often; however, a third of the public, 32%, now prefers wine. This is the highest figure for wine consumption recorded by Gallup in the last several years, and is five percentage points higher than a year ago. Only 18% cite liquor as their favorite beverage. Beer is the overwhelming first alcoholic beverage choice for men, preferred over wine by a 63% to 16% margin. Women, in stark contrast, prefer wine over beer by a 48% to 27% margin."

McAneny, Leslie/Gallup Organization. "Drinking a Cause of Family Problems for Three out of Ten Americans." Press Release 27 Sep 1997. document-level access: <http://www.gallup.com/poll/news/970927b.html>

ALCOHOLISM (v26)

see also AGED--UNITED STATES--ALCOHOL USE; COLLEGE STUDENTS--UNITED STATES--ALCOHOL USE; YOUTH--GREAT BRITAIN--ALCOHOL USE; YOUTH--UNITED STATES--ALCOHOL USE

ALCOHOLISM--CANADA (v26)

ALCOHOLISM--GREAT BRITAIN--MORTALITY (v26)

ALCOHOLISM--RUSSIA

In Russia, "seventy-one per cent of adult males drink, consuming an average of a shot of vodka daily for a staggering total of 13.6 litres of pure alcohol a year. (Women down a mere 1.5 litres yearly.) From 1990 to 1995, there was a five-fold increase in the number of people seeking treatment for alcoholism." (p14)

"Opening Notes: Death at an Earlier Age." Maclean's v110 n22 2 Jun 1997. p14. (ISSN0024-9262).

ALCOHOLISM--SOUTH AFRICA (v26)

ALCOHOLISM--UNITED STATES

"'About 14 million Americans--almost 10 percent of adults--meet diagnostic criteria for alcohol abuse and alcoholism,' writes...[U.S. Dept. of Health and Human Services Secretary, Donna E. Shalala, in the foreward of the 'Ninth Special Report to the U.S. Congress on Alcohol and Health']....The rate of alcohol abuse and alcoholism among men is almost three times that for women....As many as 44 percent of more than 40,000 traffic crash fatalities each year involve alcohol and, although such crashes are decreasing, young drivers continue to be over-represented in drinking driving deaths. Liver cirrhosis, on the decline since 1973, remains the 11th leading cause of death, and heavy drinking contributes to other leading killers: heart disease, stroke, and certain cancers."

U.S. National Institutes of Health. "Ninth Special Report on Alcohol and Health Marks Research Gains." News Advisory 18 Jul 1997. document-level access: <http://www.nih.gov/news/pr/jul97/niaaa-18.htm>

"Almost one third of Americans now report that drinking has been a source of trouble in their family, up seven points from last year and now at the highest rate recorded since Gallup began asking the question in 1950. At the same time, the number of adults who say that they, personally, sometimes drink more than they should has fallen from a high of 32% in 1985 to only 22% today....Slightly fewer Americans this year than in the 1996 survey admit to sometimes drinking more than they should--22%, compared with 25%. However, when asked if 'drinking has ever been a cause of trouble in your family,'...30% said yes--the highest percentage ever recorded, and 7 points higher than last year. In the current survey, men and women indicate similar levels of drinking as a cause of family problems: 27% of men and 32% of women admit to family difficulties attributable to alcohol....Only 24% of easterners cite family problems due to drinking, compared with 37% of westerners."

McAneny, Leslie/Gallup Organization. "Drinking a Cause of Family Problems for Three out of Ten Americans." Press Release 27 Sep 1997. document-level access: <http://www.gallup.com/poll/news/970927b.html>

"The most recent calculations by the Centers for Disease Control and Prevention place the number of alcohol-related deaths in the United States each year at 108,000....Alcohol not only kills, it wounds. 'In 1990,' reports the U.S. Substance Abuse and Mental Health Services Administration (SAMHSA), 'alcohol-related crashes resulted in 22,084 fatalities and 1.9 million nonfatal injuries.' Accidents are only the beginning. Alcohol-induced liver diseases kill 20,000 yearly. In 1993, some 708,255 patients were treated for alcoholism, and alcohol addiction was the fourth-leading cause of hospital stays for men ages 16 to 44, requiring a total of more than 1 million days of hospital care, compared with 741,000 for heart disease. The National Institute on Alcohol Abuse and Alcoholism reports that 13.8 million adults 'met standard diagnostic criteria for alcohol abuse or dependence during 1992.' In addition, says the NIAAA, '30 percent of suicides, 50 percent of homicides, and 30 percent of accidental deaths are associated with alcohol abuse.' Two thirds of all violent crimes are committed by perpetrators using alcohol, and 1 in 500 babies is afflicted with fetal alcohol syndrome....Enoch Gordis, director of the NIAAA, puts the total cost of alcohol misuse at about $100 billion a year." (p57)

Glassman, James K. "Commentary: Next Target: Liquor Companies?" U.S. News & World Report v123 n1 7 Jul 1997. p57. article-level access: <http://www.usnews.com/usnews/issue/970707/7GLAS.HTM> (ISSN0041-5537).

"There are 40 million problem drinkers in the United States--people whose drinking causes economic, physical, or family harm but who are not technically alcoholic (defined as being physiologically dependent on alcohol)." (p57) "Misuse of alcohol costs the nation dearly--$100 billion a year in quantifiable costs, in addition to untold emotional pain. Yet the bulk of these costs are incurred not by alcoholics but by problem drinkers, who are four times more numerous than alcoholics, are more active in society, and usually reject abstinence as a solution. Alcohol figures in 41 percent of traffic crash fatalities and is a factor in 50 percent of homicides, 30 percent of suicides, and 30 percent of accidental deaths....According to a 1996 report by the University of Connecticut's Alcohol Research Center, 20 percent of American adults are problem drinkers, compared with 5 percent who are alcohol dependent." (p58)

Shute, Nancy/Tangley, Laura. "Culture & Ideas: The Drinking Dilemma." U.S. News & World Report v123 n9 8 Sep 1997. p54-55,57-62,64,65. article-level access: <http://www.usnews.com/usnews/issue/970908/8DRIN.HTM> (ISSN0041-5537).

ALCOHOLISM--UNITED STATES--MORTALITY

"In a recent article in SCIENTIFIC AMERICAN, December 1996, it was reported that excessive alcohol consumption is estimated to cause more than 100,000 deaths in the United States each year. Of these deaths, 24 percent are due to drunken driving, 11 percent are homicides, and 8 percent are suicides. Alcohol contributes to cancers of the esophagus, larynx, and oral cavity, which account for 17 percent of the deaths. Strokes related to alcohol use account for another nine percent of deaths. Alcohol causes several other ailments such as cirrhosis of the liver. These ailments account for 18 percent of the deaths." (pS8823)

Wellstone, Paul D. (Sen.-Minn.). "Statements on Introduced Bills and Joint Resolutions." Congressional Record. Daily ed. v143 n115 4 Sep 1997. pS8823-8831. section/page-level access: <http://thomas.loc.gov/cgi-bin/query/R?r105:FLD001:S08823:> (ISSN0363-7239). (X1.1A.105/1).

ALCOHOLISM AND CRIME--MEXICO--RUSSIA (v26)

ALCOHOLISM AND CRIME--UNITED STATES

"Alcohol abuse is involved in 50 percent of the arrests made in the United States. Alcohol plays a role in at least 41 percent of all murders and 34 percent of all rapes. According to the Department of Justice, about one-third of the nation's prison inmates drank heavily before committing the crimes that landed them in jail." (p9)

Warburton, Robert. "'Lock 'Em Up and Leave 'Em There!" Christian Social Action v10 n9 Oct 1997. p8-10. (ISSN0897-0459).

"In 1987, 64 percent of all reported child abuse and neglect cases in the city of New York were related to alcohol and other drug abuse. With respect to domestic violence, a study of over 2,000 American couples demonstrated that rates of domestic violence were almost 15 times higher in households where husbands were often drunk as compared to those households in which they were never drunk. And, alcohol has been shown to be present in over 50 percent of all incidents of domestic violence. In addition, substance use itself may result from direct experience with interpersonal violence, as demonstrated by a study of 472 women. This study showed that 87 percent of alcoholic women had been physically or sexually abused as children as compared to 59 percent of the nonalcoholic women in the study. We know that over 40 percent of motor vehicle crash fatalities are alcohol-related, and that many of the alcohol drinkers involved in these crashes have had long standing problems with alcohol abuse. It is estimated that over 25 percent of emergency department visits may be alcohol related, and that alcohol and other drug use accounts for at least 40 percent of hospital admissions." (pS8824)

Wellstone, Paul D. (Sen.-Minn.). "Statements on Introduced Bills and Joint Resolutions." Congressional Record. Daily ed. v143 n115 4 Sep 1997. pS8823-8831. section/page-level access: <http://thomas.loc.gov/cgi-bin/query/R?r105:FLD001:S08823:> (ISSN0363-7239). (X1.1A.105/1).

ALCOHOLISM AND TRAFFIC ACCIDENTS

see DRINKING AND TRAFFIC ACCIDENTS

ALGERIA--ECONOMIC CONDITIONS

Algeria's "oil-and-gas revenues hit $13 billion last year. Exports are expected to grow 5 to 7 percent by 2000....Unemployment rates hover at 30 percent, and are closer to 70 percent for those under 30 years old....[In 1996,] only 110,000 new housing units were built when 300,000 were necessary. To catch up, the government would need to build 800,000 a year for the next five years...." (p6)

Peterson, Scott. "International: Peace in Algeria May Get Boost from New Oil Deals with US." The Christian Science Monitor v89 n160 15 Jul 1997. p6. The Christian Science Monitor search engine: <http://www.csmonitor.com/plweb-cgi/iops1.pl> To retrieve this article, enter the following search: ED=19970715 AND boost. In the "retrieved list," click the title that matches this record. (ISSN0882-7729).

ALGERIA--SOCIAL CONDITIONS

In Algeria, the Islamic Salvation Front "has unleashed a campaign of terror that has killed over 50,000 residents, and has targeted foreigners, those who attended French schools, feminists, and gays....Since January 1992 several hundred women have been assassinated by the fundamentalists for not wearing a head scarf, for wearing Western clothing--such as jeans--for working alongside men, or for living without a male guardian in their own apartments." (p93)

Afary, Janet. "The War against Feminism in the Name of the Almighty: Making Sense of Gender and Muslim Fundamentalism." New Left Review n224 Jul-Aug 1997. p89-110. (ISSN0028-6060).

"According to the human-rights activist Abdenour Ali Yahia, Algeria has 35,000 political prisoners, 100,000 have died since 1992 and thousands more have 'disappeared'....Already 400,000 people have left the country since 1992: Britain alone has 4,000 Algerians seeking asylum status." (p34)

Evans, Martin. "Boiling Under." New Statesman 30 May 1997. p34-35. (ISSN0028-6842).

ALIEN LABOR--CANADA (v26)

ALIEN LABOR--ISRAEL (v26)

ALIENS, ILLEGAL

see ILLEGAL ALIENS

ALLEGIANCE--CANADA--PUBLIC OPINION (v26)

ALLERGIC RHINITIS

see HAY FEVER

ALLERGY

see also ASTHMA

ALLERGY--UNITED STATES

In the U.S., "it is estimated that approximately 2 million school days are missed by children annually because of allergies....A 1989 Gallup Poll of allergy sufferers found that use of nonprescription allergy medications resulted in a 25 percent loss of work productivity....This loss of productivity translated into a loss of nearly $4 billion by American businesses. When considered in light of the approximately $1.39 billion spent for nonprescription medications, the costs of allergic rhinitis are immense. This Gallup survey also found that 62 percent of allergy sufferers who reported using nonprescription medications did not take the medications at times because of side effects. In addition, 29 percent of the users of nonprescription medications reported that it was always or usually true that they would prefer to suffer with symptoms than with the side effects of these medications." (p6-7)

Philpot, Edward. "Allergy: Allergic Rhinitis: What Are the Costs?" Healthline v16 n11 Nov 1997. p6-7. (ISSN0736-7929).

ALLIANCES (v26)

ALLIANCES--UNITED STATES (v26)

ALMOND INDUSTRY--CALIFORNIA

"California expects 680 million pounds (shelled basis) of almonds to be harvested this year, 33 percent higher than last season's crop. Although the July forecast was 4 percent lower than the May forecast, production is expected to be the second only to the record 1994 crop of 735 million pounds. The crop has a bearing acreage of 420,000 acres, up from 405,000 acres in 1996....Stocks at the end of the 1996/97 marketing year (June 30) totaled 66.6 million pounds, among the lowest in recent years. Domestic almond demand declined last year to 128 million pounds or .48 pounds per capita....The season-average grower price was $2.06 per pound, compared with 1995's record high of $2.48." (p32)

U.S. Dept. of Agriculture. Economic Research Service. "Tree Nut Outlook." Fruit and Tree Nuts Situation and Outlook Report Aug 1997. p32-33.

ALMOND INDUSTRY--UNITED STATES (v26)

"Almonds represented more than $1 billion (including prepared and preserved almonds) or 71 percent of all U.S. tree nut exports in 1996....Seventy percent of almond exports enter Western European markets, with Germany being the major buyer....Asia is the second most important market with 23 percent of the total. Japan typically purchases about one-half of U.S. almond exports to Asia....U.S. exports to Western Europe during 1996 jumped 36 percent from the prior year....The Almond Board of California estimates U.S. domestic consumption of almonds by the following categories, in order of importance: candy (32 percent), cereal (10), snack nuts (10), ice cream (7), food service (7), in-shell (7), cookie and granola (3), baking (2), and all other uses (22 percent)." (p38)

Johnson, Doyle C./U.S. Dept. of Agriculture. Economic Research Service. "Special Article: United States Is World Leader in Tree Nut Production and Trade." Fruit and Tree Nuts Situation and Outlook Report Aug 1997. p35-39.

ALMS AND ALMSGIVING

see CHARITIES

ALTERNATE ENERGY SOURCES

see RENEWABLE ENERGY SOURCES

ALTERNATIVE DEFENSE

see CIVILIAN-BASED DEFENSE

ALTERNATIVE FUEL

see AUTOMOBILES--MICHIGAN--MOTORS--ALTERNATE FUELS; AUTOMOBILES--UNITED STATES--MOTORS--ALTERNATE FUELS

ALTERNATIVE MEDICINE (v26)

ALTERNATIVE MEDICINE--CANADA

An Angus Reid Group national poll released on Sept. 1, 1997 in Canada "found that 42 per cent of adults use treatments such as chiropractic, herbology, acupuncture and homeopathy--nearly twice as many as five years ago....Some 91 per cent of the non-conventional therapy users visit a family doctor as well--most seeing the physician for acute illnesses and the other therapists for chronic conditions or to supplement standard treatment." (p70)

Elash, Anita/Pirisi, Angela. "Health: Freedom of Choice." Maclean's v110 n40 6 Oct 1997. p70. (ISSN0024-9262).

ALTERNATIVE MEDICINE--UNITED STATES (v26)

ALTERNATIVE WORK SCHEDULES

see HOURS OF LABOR

ALTERNATIVES TO IMPRISONMENT

see PAROLE

ALUMINUM--RECYCLING--EUROPE

"The recycling rate for used aluminum beverage cans in western Europe rose to at least 37% last year from 35% in 1995, according to the European Aluminium Association (EAA) and Aluminium Can Recycling Europe (ACRE). Despite the relatively small increase, ACRE predicts that the rate will exceed 50% by 2000 due to increasing public awareness and continued expansion of collection infrastructure....Sweden again achieved the highest recycling rate for aluminum cans last year, at 91%....The biggest recycling increases came in Finland, which has reached a rate of 80% despite having set up the collection infrastructure only within the last two years, and in Germany, where the rate rose to 81% from 70% in 1995. Germany also achieved an 81% rate for steel cans, with five regional states reaching levels of over 90%, according to APEAL, the Association of European Producers of Steel for Packaging." (p3-4)

"Western European Aluminum Can Recycling Rate Shows Modest Rise." Environment Watch: Western Europe v6 n17 5 Sep 1997. p3-4. (ISSN1066-6001).

ALUMINUM CANS--UNITED STATES (v26)

ALZHEIMER'S DISEASE--TREATMENT--UNITED STATES (v26)

ALZHEIMER'S DISEASE--UNITED STATES (v26)

"Alzheimer's disease has a high prevalence, affecting 4 million Americans....With the aging of the U.S. population, it is projected to affect more than 10 million individuals by 2040....The economic burden of Alzheimer's disease is enormous: estimates of the total direct and indirect costs resulting from the disorder are between $40 and $70 billion annually....One study estimated that the annual cost of caring for a patient with Alzheimer's disease averaged about $47,000 per year (in 1990 dollars) whether the patient lives at home or in a nursing home...." (p1440)

Neumann, Peter J./Hermann, Richard C./Berenbaum, Pamela A./Weinstein, Milton C. "Methods of Cost-Effectiveness Analysis in the Assessment of New Drugs for Alzheimer's Disease." Psychiatric Services v48 n11 Nov 1997. p1440-1444. (ISSN1075-2730).

ALZHEIMER'S DISEASE--UNITED STATES--COSTS (v26)

AMBASSADOR BRIDGE (DETROIT, MICH. AND WINDSOR, ONT.)

The Ambassador Bridge is one of the U.S.'s busiest border crossings. "According to Patrick Reed, [U.S.] supervisory Customs inspector, the bridge averages 200 trucks an hour. Last year, nearly five million vehicles entered the United States at the bridge." (p2 secB)

Dixon, Jennifer. "Local News: Cities and Counties: Detroit: Project Uses Art as a Bridge." Detroit Free Press 13 Jun 1997. p2 secB.

AMBULATORY MEDICAL CARE--UNITED STATES (v26)

In 1994, in the U.S., "the leading ambulatory procedures were extraction of lens, performed almost 2 million times, endoscopy of large intestine with or without biopsy (1.8 million) and insertion of prosthetic lens (1.6 million). Endoscopy of small intestine with or without biopsy was also done more than a million times. Next in frequency were excision or destruction of lesion or tissue of skin and subcutaneous tissue (892,000) and cystoscopy with or without biopsy (774,000). Five additional ambulatory procedures were performed more than 500,000 times: dilation and curettage of uterus (593,000); myringotomy with insertion of tube (575,000); operations on muscle, tendon, fascia and bursa (569,000); arthroscopy of knee (563,000); and arteriography and angiocardiography using contrast material (511,000)....Cataract was the most frequent first-listed diagnosis of patients with ambulatory surgery....At 1.8 million, cataract accounted for almost 10 percent of the diagnoses of ambulatory surgical patients. Almost 800,000 patients had malignant neoplasms as a first-listed diagnosis. Rheumatism (excluding back); otitis media and Eustachian tube disorders; and benign neoplasm of colon were diagnoses for more than half a million ambulatory patients." (p20)

Hall, Margaret Jean/Kozak, Lola Jean/Gillum, Brenda S. "National Survey of Ambulatory Surgery: 1994." Statistical Bulletin v78 n3 Jul-Sep 1997. p18-27. (ISSN0790-8334).

AMBULATORY SURGERY--UNITED STATES

In the U.S., "in 1994 there were 1,069.1 ambulatory [surgical] procedures per 10,000 population while the rate was 1,572.2 per 10,000 population for inpatient procedures....More than half of the ambulatory procedures were in three major categories: operations on the digestive system; the eye; and the musculoskeletal system. In contrast, more than two-thirds of inpatient procedures fell into four major categories of miscellaneous diagnostic and therapeutic procedures; obstetrical procedures; operations on the digestive system; and operations on the cardiovascular system." (p19)

Hall, Margaret Jean/Kozak, Lola Jean/Gillum, Brenda S. "National Survey of Ambulatory Surgery: 1994." Statistical Bulletin v78 n3 Jul-Sep 1997. p18-27. (ISSN0790-8334).

In the U.S., in 1994, "more than half (54 percent) of ambulatory procedures among men were operations on the eye, digestive system and musculoskeletal system....These procedures accounted for only 25 percent of inpatient procedures among men." (p22) "For women, operations on the eye, digestive system and genital organs made up the majority (51 percent) of ambulatory procedures but only 21 percent of inpatient procedures." (p23)

Hall, Margaret Jean/Kozak, Lola Jean/Gillum, Brenda S. "National Survey of Ambulatory Surgery: 1994." Statistical Bulletin v78 n3 Jul-Sep 1997. p18-27. (ISSN0790-8334).

AMBULATORY SURGERY--UNITED STATES--AGED

In 1994, in the U.S., "operations on the eye and the digestive system together accounted for 62 percent of ambulatory procedures on persons 65 years of age and over. These categories made up only 17 percent of inpatient procedures for the elderly. Operations on the eye accounted for 38 percent of ambulatory procedures, but only 1 percent of inpatient procedures on persons 65 years and over." (p25) "The two leading ambulatory procedures for persons 65 and over were extraction of lens and insertion of prosthetic lens. As with patients aged 15 to 44 and 45 to 64, endoscopies of large and small intestine were also frequent ambulatory procedures." (p27)

Hall, Margaret Jean/Kozak, Lola Jean/Gillum, Brenda S. "National Survey of Ambulatory Surgery: 1994." Statistical Bulletin v78 n3 Jul-Sep 1997. p18-27. (ISSN0790-8334).

AMBULATORY SURGERY--UNITED STATES--WOMEN

In 1994, U.S. "women had significantly more ambulatory surgery procedures than men (15.6 vs. 12.1 million) and a higher rate (1,173.8 vs. 958.3 per 10,000 population). Women also had a larger number of inpatient procedures (24.8 vs. 15.9 million) and a higher rate (1,866.3 vs. 1,261.2 per 10,000 population). Under age 15, men had a higher rate of ambulatory surgery procedures per 1,000 population than women, but women's rate was higher for ages 15-24, 25-34, 35-44 and 45-54...." (p20)

Hall, Margaret Jean/Kozak, Lola Jean/Gillum, Brenda S. "National Survey of Ambulatory Surgery: 1994." Statistical Bulletin v78 n3 Jul-Sep 1997. p18-27. (ISSN0790-8334).

AMBULATORY SURGICAL CENTERS

see SURGICAL CLINICS

AMERASIAN CHILDREN--JAPAN--PHILIPPINES (v26)

AMERICAN BISON (v26)

AMERICAN BISON--MONTANA

In the winter of 1996, "almost 1,100 bison were sent to slaughterhouses or shot by the Montana Department of Livestock after they left...[Yellowstone National Park] in search of food....A harsh winter added to the deaths, dropping the herd to 2,200 animals from 3,500 the previous fall." (p2)

Matthews, Mark. "Activists 'Shepherd' Wayward Bison." High Country News v29 n24 22 Dec 1997. p2. (ISSN0191-5657).

AMERICAN BISON--YELLOWSTONE NATIONAL PARK (v26)

"The Greater Yellowstone Ecosystem is home to America's last wild buffalo herd, some 3500 strong in the fall of 1996....Over 1100 [wild buffalo] were gunned down by Montana Department of Livestock shooters as they ranged into mostly National Forest land outside Yellowstone Park boundaries in search of food. About 1000 were left living and breathing." (p14)

Kelly, Steve. "Member Group News: Billboard Creates Furor, Increases Public Awareness." Networker v9 n2 Sum 1997. p14.

AMERICAN BISON--YELLOWSTONE NATIONAL PARK --MORTALITY

In the winter of 1996-1997, of Yellowstone National Park's "estimated 3500 Bison, over 1100 were shipped to slaughter by the National Park Service or blown away by shooters of the Montana Departments of Livestock or Fish, Game, and Parks. Another estimated 1400 were winter-killed by April." (p6) "On the west border of Yellowstone, the wild Bison that couldn't be corralled (90% of them) were...shot by sharpshooters of Montana's Department of Livestock....On the west border, the Montana DOL shot another 200....By the third week of January, the number of Bison killed by humans exceeded the previous late twentieth century record of 569 (for the winter of 1988-89)....By the end of February, 1000 of Yellowstone's estimated 3500 Bison had been shot by government sharpshooters or shipped to the slaughterhouse....An aerial survey conducted on February 21 counted 1720 Bison left, meaning another 800 had starved to death...." (p8) "By the end of March, we had lost more than 2500 of the estimated 3500 Yellowstone Bison." (p9)

Peacock, Doug. "Viewpoints: Field Report: Yellowstone Bison Slaughter." Wild Earth v7 n2 Sum 1997. p6-11. (ISSN1055-1166).

AMERICAN DOLLAR

see DOLLAR, AMERICAN

AMERICAN ECONOMIC ASSISTANCE

see ECONOMIC ASSISTANCE, AMERICAN

AMERICAN GINSENG INDUSTRY (v26)

AMERICAN JEWS

see JEWS, AMERICAN

AMERICAN MILITARY ASSISTANCE

see MILITARY ASSISTANCE, AMERICAN

AMERICAN MILITARY BASES

see MILITARY BASES, AMERICAN

AMERICAN TRYPANOSOMIOSIS

see CHAGAS' DISEASE

AMERICANS (v26)

AMERICORPS

In 1996, "more than 25,000 AmeriCorps members served across the United States. AmeriCorps members assisted more than 11.5 million people, collected almost 1 million pounds of food, and distributed 5,000 pounds of clothes. Participants in the AmeriCorps program ran violence-prevention after school programs for nearly 50,000 youth and developed and distributed almost 40,000 packets of information on drug abuse, health care, and street safety. AmeriCorps volunteers immunized almost 65,000 children and adults, cleaned up over 3,000 neighborhoods, rehabilitated nearly 5,000 housing units, [and] tutored over 500,000 children....The AmeriCorps Service Program leveraged almost 700,000 hours of service by unstipened volunteers last year." (pH5333)

Vento, Bruce F. (Rep.-Minn.). "Departments of Veterans Affairs and Housing and Urban Development...Appropriations Act, 1998." Congressional Record. Daily ed. v143 n101 16 Jul 1997. pH5309-5371. section/page-level access: <http://thomas.loc.gov/cgi-bin/query/R?r105:FLD001:H05333:> (ISSN0363-7239). (X1.1A.105/1).

AMHERST (N.Y.)--BUFFALO (N.Y.)--ECONOMIC CONDITIONS

"More than 78% of persons 16 years of age and older in Amherst [New York] work in managerial, professional, or technical occupations, compared with 55% of those employed in Buffalo [New York]. As a consequence, the average family income in Amherst is $52,330, compared with $22,787 in Buffalo....The average income of African American families [in Buffalo] is $19,509 and that of Hispanic families only $16,573." (p371)

Kost, Kathleen A. "Article: The Effects of Support on the Economic Well-Being of Young Fathers." Families in Society v78 n4 Jul-Aug 1997. p370-382. (ISSN1044-3894).

AMPHETAMINES

see METHAMPHETAMINE

AMUSEMENTS

see CASINOS

ANATOMICAL GIFTS

see DONATION OF ORGANS, TISSUES, ETC.

ANEMIA, DREPANOCYTIC
see SICKLE CELL ANEMIA
ANESTHESIA, PERIDURAL
see PERIDURAL ANESTHESIA
ANGINA PECTORIS--UNITED STATES (v26)
ANGIOPLASTY--UNITED STATES
In the U.S., "two new studies show that balloon angioplasty results in a lower complication rate--2.9 percent vs. 9.3 percent--when performed by a physician who does 70 or more a year....[Michigan] state laws require physicians do more than 75 angioplasties a year....Nationwide, according to one of the new studies, fewer than half of the nation's doctors meet that standard." (p7 secC)
Bondi, Nicole. "MetroLife: Health Care: Michigan Heart Surgeons Provide Edge of Experience." Detroit News 13 Jun 1997. p7 secC.
ANGLICAN COMMUNION--CANADA (v26)
ANGLICANS--AUSTRALIA
"The 1996 national census results had shown Anglican numbers [in Australia] falling by 116,000 in the past five years. The Anglican proportion of the population has now slipped to an all-time low of 21 percent." (p20)
"Too Many Eucharists?" Anglican Digest v39 n6 1997. p20. (ISSN0003-3278).
ANIMAL BITES
see BITES AND STINGS
ANIMAL FEEDS
see FEEDS
ANIMAL HUSBANDRY
see LIVESTOCK
ANIMAL INDUSTRY
see also CATTLE TRADE; HIDES AND SKINS INDUSTRY; HORSE INDUSTRY; IVORY INDUSTRY; LIVESTOCK; POULTRY INDUSTRY; TURKEY INDUSTRY
ANIMAL INDUSTRY--EUROPE
In the EU, in 1996, "real prices for animals and animal products fell by 1.5%, continuing the downward trend of several years. Calves fell by 14.3% and cattle excluding calves by 15.0%--the BSE [bovine spongiform encephalopathy] effect. In contrast, prices for sheep and lambs were up by 11.0%, pigs by 8.4% and poultry by 4.7%. Milk's decline continued (-2.7%). But egg prices, up sharply by 17.9%, contrasted with big 1994 and 1995 falls."
Eurostat. "EU Real Agricultural Prices 2.7% Down Last Year." Press Release 1 Aug 1997. document-level access: <http://europa.eu.int/en/comm/eurostat/compres/en/5597/6505597a.htm>
ANIMAL INDUSTRY--RUSSIA (v26)
ANIMAL INDUSTRY--UNITED STATES (v26)
In the U.S., "the total value of livestock production in 1996 was $4.4 billion higher than the previous year, the first increase in 3 years....Substantial increases in the sales of hogs, poultry, and dairy products more than offset a $4-billion decline in cattle production....Total cattle receipts in 1996 declined from 1995 to $2.9 billion in decreased value of sales and $1.1 billion from a reduction in the herd (inventory adjustment)." (p5)
U.S. Dept. of Agriculture. Economic Research Service. "1996 Farm Income Estimates: Net Value-Added and Net Farm Income Attain New Highs in 1996." Agricultural Income and Finance Situation and Outlook Report Sep 1997. p4-13.
According to the 1992 Farm Costs and Returns Survey conducted by USDA, "the cost per hundredweight (cwt) gained was $69.02 for a hog operation producing fewer than 500 head, while the cost for an operation of 3,000 head or more was $46.43. A 1993 survey on milk production indicates that the cost of producing milk on smaller operations was also higher: $18.96 per cwt of milk sold for dairy operations with fewer than 60 milk cows, and $12.56 per cwt for operations with 300 or more milk cows." (p4)
Clauson, Annette/U.S. Dept. of Agriculture. Economic Research Service. "Food Prices: Economic Factors Holding Down Food Price Increases." Food Review v20 n2 May-Aug 1997. p2-4. (ISSN1056-327X).
U.S. "exports of animal feeds and fodders advanced 5 percent to $2.6 billion in 1996, mainly because of higher prices for corn gluten products. The export value of corn gluten products rose 9 percent to $945 million, but volume fell 17 percent to 5.8 million tons. The European Union (EU-15) was the leading market for corn gluten products with an 87-percent share of U.S. export volume." (p2)
Greene, Joel/U.S. Dept. of Agriculture. Economic Research Service. "Agricultural Exports Surpass $60 Billion." Foreign Agricultural Trade of the United States Jan-Mar 1997. p2-3.
ANIMAL INDUSTRY--UNITED STATES--MINORITIES (v26)
ANIMAL SHELTERS--EMPLOYMENT--UNITED STATES
In the U.S., "studies done by the National Animal Control Association (NACA) and regional organizations have shown that the average ratio of field animal control officers to residents is approximately one to 16,000 to 18,000....The Society of Animal Welfare Administrators recently did an internal survey of its members throughout the nation and found the average salary for animal control officers to be just above $23,600. The Florida Animal Control Association's (FACA) comprehensive 1996 survey reflects the fact that there are variations from region to region, as the average yearly salary of animal control officers in the state is $19,910." (p23)
"Answers to Common Questions: The Shelter Advisor." Animal Sheltering v20 n5 Sep-Oct 1997. p23. (ISSN0734-3078).
ANIMAL SHELTERS--MICHIGAN (v26)
ANIMAL WELFARE--CALIFORNIA (v26)
ANIMAL WELFARE--MASSACHUSETTS
"Between 1975 and 1996, there were approximately 80,000 complaints of abuse and neglect investigated by the MSPCA [Massachusetts Society for the Prevention of Cruelty to Animals]....From 1980 to 1984, the MSPCA investigated 17,480 complaints of abuse and neglect. From 1985 to 1989, the number of these cases jumped to 20,698, or a 12.7% increase over the prior five-year period. And from 1990 to 1994, the number reached 27,587, or a 33.2% increase over the prior five-year period....From 1975 to 1985, there were 148 prosecuted cruelty cases, compared to 120 cases between 1986 and 1996, representing approximately 20% fewer cases. These 268 prosecuted cases represent .3% of all cases of neglect and abuse that were investigated by the MSPCA during the time frame of this study....The vast majority of victims were dogs and cats (84.7%) in prosecuted cases. Dogs (57.8%) were the most commonly abused animals, followed by cats (26.9%), and other animals (e.g., birds, wildlife, horses, farm animals--15.3%). The vast majority of animal victims were owned (89.1%) rather than stray or wild. Most complainants (i.e., reporters of crime) were owners (48.5%), followed by anonymous or unknown complainants (24.6%), strangers (23.9%), and intimates/housemates (3%). Of the complainants who were not anonymous, females filed complaints in 41.8% of the incidents, male/female couples 36.6% of the time, and males in 21.6% of the cases." (p197-198)
Arluke, Arnold/Luke, Carter. "Physical Cruelty toward Animals in Massachusetts, 1975-1996." Society & Animals v5 n3 1997. p195-204. (ISSN1063-1119).
ANIMAL WELFARE--UNITED STATES (v26)
ANIMAL WELFARE--UNITED STATES--PUBLIC OPINION
"A December 1996 survey of 1,008 American households conducted by Penn & Schoen, Inc. for The Humane Society of the United

States found that 42% of respondents believed animal cruelty to be moderately to extremely serious as a problem in this country, compared with 61% responding in this way to 'environmental issues' and 78% to 'child abuse.' Of those surveyed, 71% supported making animal abuse a felony and 81% felt that the enforcement of animal cruelty laws should be strengthened." (p188)

Arluke, Arnold/Lockwood, Randall. "Guest Editors' Introduction: Understanding Cruelty to Animals." Society & Animals v5 n3 1997. p183-193. (ISSN1063-1119).

ANIMAL WELFARE--UNITED STATES--SOCIETIES, ETC.

In the U.S., "the Humane Society estimates that up to 60 percent of the animals brought into animal shelters must be killed because no one wants them. The good news is that up to 35 percent will find new homes." (p22)

Hasenauer, Heike. "Pets: Know before You Buy." Soldiers v52 n12 Dec 1997. p20-22. (ISSN0093-8440).

ANIMALS

see AMERICAN BISON; ANTELOPES; BEARS; CROCODILES; DEER; DOGFIGHTING; DOGS; ELEPHANTS; ELK; FERRET; GRASSLAND ANIMALS; GRIZZLY BEAR; LIONS; LYNX; MARMOTS; NITROGEN IN ANIMAL NUTRITION; OSTRICH FARMING; TIGERS; WOLVES

ANIMALS, PROTECTION OF

see ANIMAL WELFARE; WILDLIFE CONSERVATION

ANOREXIA NERVOSA--UNITED STATES (v26)

"Seven million girls and women in the United States currently suffer from serious eating disorders, according to the National Association of Anorexia Nervosa and Associated Disorders. Of those, 30 percent will have continuing difficulties, and 5 to 6 percent eventually will die of the illness, most from either suicide or heart failure. Although researchers cannot be sure if deaths from anorexia and bulimia are increasing, they believe the incidence of eating disorders is rising, particularly among men, who now account for roughly 1 million victims, and among preadolescent girls and boys." (p67-68)

Streisand, Betsy. "Culture & Ideas: Overcoming Anorexia." U.S. News & World Report v123 n12 29 Sep 1997. p67-69. article-level access: <http://www.usnews.com/usnews/issue/970929/29THIN.HTM> (ISSN0041-5537).

ANOREXIA NERVOSA--UNITED STATES--YOUNG WOMEN

In the U.S., "a 1991 congressional study indicates that five in every 1,000 adolescent and young adult women are anorexic (Costello & Stone, 1994; Renzetti & Curran, 1989). An estimated 9% of anorexics die prematurely, either from suicide or starvation, and fewer than half of the anorexics are able to recover fully." (p716)

Kaplan, Elaine Bell. "Women's Perceptions of the Adolescent Experience." Adolescence v32 n127 Fall 1997. p715-734. (ISSN0001-8449).

ANTARCTICA--ENVIRONMENTAL ASPECTS

"The South Pole stands 2,800 meters above sea level, but 2,722 of those meters are made of ice. Furthermore, about 50 percent of the coastline of the continent consists of floating extensions of this ice sheet--ice shelves that breed most of the icebergs calving from the continent....The sea ice on the Southern Ocean undergoes an annual change from a minimum area of about 4 million square kilometers in February to a maximum of 19 million square kilometers in September--one of the greatest seasonal changes of surface characteristics on earth. Sea ice stretches as much as 2,200 kilometers from the coast into the Weddell Sea during winter. But between the longitudes of 120 [degrees] E [East] and 135 [degrees], the winter ice edge may extend only 300 kilometers offshore." (p426)

Nicol, Stephen/Allison, Ian. "The Frozen Skin of the Southern Ocean." American Scientist v85 n5 Sep-Oct 1997. p426-439. (ISSN0003-0996).

ANTELOPES--HART MOUNTAIN (OR.)

The size of the antelope fawn herd in the Hart Mountain National Antelope Refuge in Oregon "has dropped from 1,900 to 1,300 since 1990....The size of...[the herd that ranges between Hart Mountain and the Sheldon National Wildlife Refuge in northern Nevada, and east to the Malheur Wildlife Refuge,] has fallen from 7,200 to 5,300 since 1990, according to state and federal wildlife tallies....Biologists believe a survival rate of 25 to 30 fawns per 100 does is needed to assure the survival of the herd. At Hart Mountain, fawn survival rates fluctuated from 14 to 44 fawns per 100 does between 1991 and 1994, then dropped to an all-time low of 0.8 per 100 does in 1995....[In 1995,] when the refuge recorded its record-low survival, only eight of an estimated 1,700 fawns survived....The Oregon Department of Fish and Wildlife had done a predator-control experiment on BLM [Bureau of Land Management] land north of the refuge....With predator control, survival rates increased from 14 to 80 fawns per 100 does." (p11)

Durbin, Kathie. "Do Coyotes Need 'Control' on the Refuge?" High Country News v29 n22 24 Nov 1997. p11. (ISSN0191-5657).

ANTI-POVERTY PROGRAMS

see ECONOMIC ASSISTANCE, DOMESTIC

ANTIBIOTICS--UNITED STATES

"Dr. Ralph Gonzales, from the University of Colorado Health Sciences Center in Denver, and his colleagues found that in 50 percent to 70 percent of the cases in which patients sought medical attention at their physicians' offices for colds, upper respiratory tract infections or bronchitis, the physicians prescribed antibiotic drugs. Office visits for these three ailments resulted in approximately 12 million antibiotic prescriptions in 1992, or about one in five of all antibiotic prescriptions given to adults, the study said." (p8)

Humphrey, Dana. "Monitor: Research: Drug Overuse." New Physician v46 n8 Nov 1997. p8. (ISSN0028-6451).

ANTICHOLESTEREMIC AGENTS--UNITED STATES (v26)

ANTIDOTES--HOSPITALS--COLORADO--MONTANA --NEBRASKA (v26)

ANTISEMITISM--CANADA (v26)

ANTISLAVERY

see SLAVERY

ANTS, FIRE

see FIRE ANTS

AORTO-CORONARY BYPASS

see CORONARY ARTERY BYPASS

APOPLEXY

see CEREBROVASCULAR DISEASE

APPAREL

see CLOTHING AND DRESS

APPENDECTOMY--UNITED STATES (v26)

APPLE INDUSTRY--EUROPE

"Apples are the most widely grown of the fruit crops in the European Union (the EU 12 as of 1994) with some 320,000 hectares under cultivation, producing in the region of 8 million tons per annum valued at approximately 2500 million ecu [European currency units] (Confcooperative, 1994). The EU provides approximately 20% of world production, of around 40 million tons (O'Rourke, 1994)." (p2)

Quin, F. S./Abin, A./McGregor, M. J. "Technology Assessment: A Framework for Identifying the Social, Environmental and Economic Impacts of a New...Project." Project Appraisal v12 n1 Mar 1997. p2-10. (ISSN0268-8867).

APPLE INDUSTRY--JAPAN

"In 1995/96, Japan produced 963,300 metric tons of apples, making it the world's twelfth largest producer....From 1990 to 1995, Japan's apple production declined 9 percent. Imports and exports both account for 1 percent or less of consumption....Japan's processing sector used 17 percent of the apple crop in the 1995/96 marketing season....Fuji is...[Japan's] most important apple with 52 percent of production in 1995/96....Tsugaru apples accounted for 15 percent of production in 1995/96. Japanese Red Delicious apples accounted for about 2 percent of production. Red Delicious acreage has been decreasing, with a 20-percent decline in production from 1994/95 to 1995/96." (p43-44)

Krissoff, Barry/Calvin, Linda/Gray, Denice/U.S. Dept. of Agriculture. Economic Research Service. "Special Article: Barriers to Trade in Global Apple Markets." Fruit and Tree Nuts Situation and Outlook Report Aug 1997. p42-51.

APPLE INDUSTRY--JAPAN--UNITED STATES

"During the 1994/95 season, the first year of apple trade with Japan, U.S. exports to Japan totaled 8,497 metric tons....Although U.S. apples accounted for 95 percent of imports, total imports were only 1 percent of Japanese consumption. U.S. exports declined in the 1995/96 season to 843 metric tons, shipped from December through April. Through March of the 1996/97 season, exports totaled only 106 metric tons. Acres enrolled in the Japanese apple export program totaled 2,406 in the 1994/95 season (with 2,508 in buffer zones), 2,123 in 1995/96, and 739 in 1996/97." (p44)

Krissoff, Barry/Calvin, Linda/Gray, Denice/U.S. Dept. of Agriculture. Economic Research Service. "Special Article: Barriers to Trade in Global Apple Markets." Fruit and Tree Nuts Situation and Outlook Report Aug 1997. p42-51.

APPLE INDUSTRY--KOREA (SOUTH)

"In 1995/96, South Korea produced 715,982 metric tons of apples, up 16 percent from the previous year because of high yields. Apple production area declined from 50,000 hectares in 1994/95 to an estimated 44,000 in 1995/96....Fuji is the most important variety of apple produced in Korea with 77 percent of total production in 1992. Tsugaru and Jonagold account for 12 and 1 percent of production. Most apples are consumed fresh with only about 20 percent going into the processing sector....In 1994, [apple] exports totaled 2,293 metric tons and in 1995 they rose to 5,315 metric tons. Taiwan is South Korea's primary export market with 43 percent of total exports in 1995." (p46)

Krissoff, Barry/Calvin, Linda/Gray, Denice/U.S. Dept. of Agriculture. Economic Research Service. "Special Article: Barriers to Trade in Global Apple Markets." Fruit and Tree Nuts Situation and Outlook Report Aug 1997. p42-51.

APPLE INDUSTRY--MEXICO

"Mexican commercial apple production totaled 387,000 metric tons in 1995/96, down 12 percent from the previous year....In Chihuahua, Mexico's most important apple producing state, about 60 percent of production is Golden Delicious and about 40 percent is Red Delicious....Mexico imported 80,000 metric tons of apples in 1995/96, accounting for 18 percent of fresh consumption. In 1993/94, that figure was 28 percent but it fell to 17 percent in 1994/95 during the peso crisis." (p46)

Krissoff, Barry/Calvin, Linda/Gray, Denice/U.S. Dept. of Agriculture. Economic Research Service. "Special Article: Barriers to Trade in Global Apple Markets." Fruit and Tree Nuts Situation and Outlook Report Aug 1997. p42-51.

APPLE INDUSTRY--MEXICO--UNITED STATES (v26)

APPLE INDUSTRY--UNITED STATES (v26)

"According to the U.S. Apple Association (formerly known as International Apple Institute), U.S. apple stocks on July 1, 1997, were up 35 percent from a year ago and 46 percent above the 5-year average (1992-96). Washington-grown apples make up 92 percent of the total stocks, and are mostly for fresh use. Apple stocks consist mostly of Red Delicious (70 percent), Golden Delicious (16 percent), and Granny Smith (5 percent)." (p7)

U.S. Dept. of Agriculture. Economic Research Service. "Noncitrus Fruit Outlook." Fruit and Tree Nuts Situation and Outlook Report Aug 1997. p7-26.

"Apples are the third most valuable fruit crop grown in the United States, behind grapes and oranges. In 1996, the value of the commercial apple crop was $1.7 billion. Production has grown from an annual average of 6.5 billion pounds in 1970-75 to 10.4 billion pounds in 1990-96. In 1994, production reached a record 11.6 billion pounds. Apple production is spread across many States, but Washington, Michigan, New York, and California dominate, typically accounting for 75 percent of total production. In 1996, 61 percent of commercial apple production went to the fresh market....In the 1995/96 marketing season (August 1995-July 1996), Washington accounted for 67 percent of the U.S. fresh apple supply." (p42-43)

Krissoff, Barry/Calvin, Linda/Gray, Denice/U.S. Dept. of Agriculture. Economic Research Service. "Special Article: Barriers to Trade in Global Apple Markets." Fruit and Tree Nuts Situation and Outlook Report Aug 1997. p42-51.

"The U.S. Apple Association estimates Red Delicious production at 42 percent of the 1996 U.S. crop. Golden Delicious is the second most popular, with 14 percent of production. Granny Smith, Rome, and McIntosh comprise approximately 7, 6, and 5 percent of the market, respectively. These varietal shares have been rather stable over the 1990s. In contrast, Fuji and Gala apple production have increased rapidly, each growing from less than 2 percent of the market in the early 1990s to over 5 and 3 percent, respectively, in 1996....Americans consumed over 5 billion pounds of fresh apples in 1995/96, averaging 19 pounds per person. This level of per capita consumption is equal to the average of the previous 10 years." (p43)

Krissoff, Barry/Calvin, Linda/Gray, Denice/U.S. Dept. of Agriculture. Economic Research Service. "Special Article: Barriers to Trade in Global Apple Markets." Fruit and Tree Nuts Situation and Outlook Report Aug 1997. p42-51.

"U.S. fresh apple exports from August 1996 to May 1997 totaled 1.29 billion pounds, up 21 percent from a year earlier....Canada, Mexico, and Asian countries, particularly Taiwan, Indonesia, and Hong Kong, will continue to be top markets for U.S. apples. These countries made up 13 percent, 12 percent, 20 percent, 8 percent, and 7 percent, respectively, of the cumulative export volume thus far for the 1996/97 season. The European Union and Brazil will continue to be important markets, representing 5 percent and 3 percent of the total export volume....U.S. fresh apple shipments to Brazil have risen from 847,000 pounds in 1991/92 to 29.1 million pounds in 1995/96." (p7-8)

U.S. Dept. of Agriculture. Economic Research Service. "Noncitrus Fruit Outlook." Fruit and Tree Nuts Situation and Outlook Report Aug 1997. p7-26.

In the U.S., "the 1996 season-average grower price for fresh-market apples declined 13 percent, dropping the total 1996 crop value 5 percent to $1.67 billion. While grower prices for processing apples rose in 1996, the quantity of processing apples declined 12 percent, also contributing to the decline in the total crop value. The 1996/97 season-average all-apple grower price (August-July) was 16.2 cents a pound, down from 17 cents the previous year, but up 8 percent from the 1990-1995 average. Fresh-market grower prices averaged 20.9 cents per pound in 1996, down from 24 cents in 1995. Grower prices for processing apples averaged 8.8 cents per pound in 1996, compared with 8.0 cents a year earlier." (p7)

U.S. Dept. of Agriculture. Economic Research Service. "Noncitrus Fruit Outlook." Fruit and Tree Nuts Situation and Outlook Report Aug 1997. p7-26.

APPLE INDUSTRY--WASHINGTON (STATE) (v26)

APPLICATIONS FOR COLLEGE

see COLLEGE APPLICATIONS

APRICOT INDUSTRY--UNITED STATES

In the U.S., "fresh use of the 1996 apricot crop declined 18 percent while processing use was up 51 percent. The season-average grower price for processing apricots increased from 0.14 cents a pound ($287 per ton) in 1995 to 0.16 cents a pound ($314 per ton) last year. Prices paid by processors for apricots to be frozen and dried each rose 1 percent in 1996 from a year earlier while prices paid by canneries were up 10 percent. The decline in fresh-market production and the strong demand from canneries supported grower prices for fresh-market apricots last year, with the season-average at 0.59 cents a pound ($1,180 per ton), up from 0.45 cents ($900 per ton) in 1995." (p15)

U.S. Dept. of Agriculture. Economic Research Service. "Noncitrus Fruit Outlook." Fruit and Tree Nuts Situation and Outlook Report Aug 1997. p7-26.

AQUACULTURE (v26)

AQUACULTURE--CHINA (v26)

AQUACULTURE--UNITED STATES

"Fish and shellfish are now farmed in every state and U.S. territory, and aquaculture is the fastest growing segment of U.S. agriculture. Production has increased 24% by weight and 60% in market value over the last decade....About 25% of all fish consumed by humans worldwide is now farmed." (p7)

Goldburg, Rebecca J. "Old MacDonald Had a Fish." EDF Letter v28 n4 Sep 1997. p7. (ISSN0163-2566).

AQUACULTURE--VIETNAM (v26)

AQUATIC BIRDS

see WATER BIRDS

ARAB PALESTINIANS

see PALESTINIAN ARABS

ARAL SEA (UZBEKISTAN AND KAZAKHSTAN)

"With an area of about 1.5 million square kilometers...and a population of about 32 million, population density in the [Aral Sea] basin varies from less than 10 persons per square kilometer in the desert plains to more than 300 in the valleys and foothills of the eastern and southern mountains." (p208) "About 7.5 million hectares (ha) of farmland are currently irrigated within the five Central Asian states [of Kazakhstan, Kyrgyzstan, Tajikstan, Turkmenistan, and Uzbekistan] sharing the Aral Basin; the livelihood of 35 million people, of which 20 million are in Uzbekistan, is dependent primarily on an economy based on irrigated agriculture. Cotton accounts for up to 50 percent and 35 percent of the agriculture water use in the Amu Darya and Syr Darya basins, respectively. Uzbekistan is the largest consumer of water for irrigation. Between 1965 and 1990, irrigated area in Uzbekistan grew from 2.7 million to 4.2 million ha, more than three times the irrigated area of the next largest irrigator, Turkmenistan." (p209)

Elhance, Arun P. "Conflict and Cooperation over Water in the Aral Sea Basin." Studies in Conflict & Terrorism v20 n2 Apr-Jun 1997. p207-218. (ISSN1057-610X).

ARAL SEA (UZBEKISTAN AND KAZAKHSTAN) --ENVIRONMENTAL ASPECTS

The Aral Sea "has been shrinking at an alarming rate: its level has fallen by more than 14 m [meters] over the last three decades, its area has shrunk by more than 40 percent, and its volume by 60 percent....Twenty of the 24 native species of fish in the Aral Sea have already vanished; the number of animal species in the surrounding area has dropped from 173 to 38, some of which are now on the endangered list." (p210)

Elhance, Arun P. "Conflict and Cooperation over Water in the Aral Sea Basin." Studies in Conflict & Terrorism v20 n2 Apr-Jun 1997. p207-218. (ISSN1057-610X).

ARAUCANIANS INDIANS

see MAPUCHE INDIANS

ARBITRATION, INTERNATIONAL

The American Arbitration Association's International Center for Dispute Resolution Services in New York City "has received cases from parties that have originated in 47 countries....The center administered over 300 cases in its first full year and is expected to surpass 400 in its second year. About 20% of the cases involve parties from Latin America and the Caribbean, 25% from Canada, 40% from Europe, 10% from Asia and 5% from the Middle East. Up to 10% of the cases attempt mediation first, with an astounding 90% resulting in a settlement." (p20)

Martinez, Luis. "AAA International Center at One Year: Foreign Caseloads Soar." Dispute Resolution Times Sum 1997. p20.

ARBITRATION AND AWARD--UNITED STATES

"Case filings with the American Arbitration Association showed a robust 13% growth last year, increasing from 62,459 cases in 1995 to 70,516 cases in 1996. Of the cases filed last year, 68,346 were arbitrations and 2,170 were mediations, according to a report from the AAA's Case Administration Department....No-fault cases, which originate from states with no-fault insurance law such as New York, New Jersey and Minnesota, constituted the bulk of the 1996 case filings (42%). No-fault cases rose 36%, increasing from 22,048 in 1995 to 29,896 in 1996....There were 15,617 labor cases filed with the AAA last year, compared with 14,768 cases in 1995. Construction case filings increased from 3,991 in 1995 to 4,114 in 1996. There were 581 cases filed with the Association's Large, Complex Case Program (LCCP) in 1996, with claims totaling $1.2 billion. Cases filed with the LCCP primarily involve claims in excess of $1 million...." (p5)

"AAA Reports Jump in Case Filings Last Year." Dispute Resolution Times Sum 1997. p5.

"Results of a recent survey of the top 1,000 corporations in America show that the vast majority use alternative means of dispute resolution and that they are likely to continue using ADR processes in the future....General counsel, deputy counsel and chief litigators for 528 corporations responded, with the smallest company in the group reporting sales of more than $1 billion." (p1) "Eighty-eight percent of the respondents have used mediation in the last three years, while 79% have used arbitration, according to the study....More than 84% said they were likely or very likely to use mediation in the future, while 69% indicated that they would use arbitration in the future....Nearly 90% of the companies viewed mediation as a cost-saving measure; 54% said cost pressures affected their decision to use ADR....Eighty-one percent of the respondents said their companies use mediation because it provides 'a more satisfactory process' than litigation; 66% said it provides more 'satisfactory settlements'; and 59% said it 'preserves good relationships.'...Forty-one percent reported using mediation-arbitration or med-arb, while 23% used mini-trial. Only 21% said they used fact-finding and 11% used peer review. Fifty-five respondents said they have an ombudsperson on staff, and 185 use an in-house grievance procedure....Among the respondents, there was a group of more than 60 corporations that consistently tried to use ADR....Sixty percent have used mediation in personal-injury disputes but only a third have used arbitration; 40% have used mediation in product-liability cases but only 24% have used arbitration." (p18)

"Nationwide Survey: Top Companies Favor ADR Use." Dispute Resolution Times Sum 1997. p1,18.

ARCTIC OCEAN (v26)
ARGENTINA--COMMERCE--BRAZIL (v26)
ARGENTINA--ECONOMIC CONDITIONS
In Argentina, "18% of the capital in the [banking] system, over $7.5 billion, flowed out during the first four months of 1995. Economic growth plummeted. An economy that had expanded by 7% during 1994 (including 6.2% in the last quarter of the year) contracted sharply in each of the last three quarters of 1995 (-4.6%, -8.1%, and -7.7%, respectively). For the full 1995 year, the economy shrank -4.4% (Republica Argentina, 1995...EIU, 1996b). In this environment, unemployment, which had reached historic levels even during the years of miracle growth, jumped from 10.8% in May 1994, to 12.2% in October 1994, and to 18.6% in May 1995. Although the rate of unemployment did fall to 17.1% by May of 1996, most of this decline was due to workers dropping out of the job market rather than to any gains in employment (Microseminarios, 1996a)." (p98)
Starr, Pamela K. "Government Coalitions and the Viability of Currency Boards: Argentina under the Cavallo Plan." Journal of Interamerican Studies & World Affairs v39 n2 Sum 1997. p83-133. (ISSN0022-1937).
ARGENTINA--ECONOMIC CONDITIONS--PUBLIC OPINION
"A Gallup Poll conducted in September 1993 indicated that the main preoccupation of a large plurality (41%) of Argentines were the low salaries. A second poll, taken a year later (1994), revealed that, while 5 out of 10 Argentines believed that maintaining fiscal and monetary stability was still one of the main problems facing the government, it was no longer viewed as a top priority. When asked to name the single most important problem facing the government, respondents mentioned a number of other issues--corruption, the welfare of pensioners, low pay, and unemployment--more often than preserving economic stability." (p111)
Starr, Pamela K. "Government Coalitions and the Viability of Currency Boards: Argentina under the Cavallo Plan." Journal of Interamerican Studies & World Affairs v39 n2 Sum 1997. p83-133. (ISSN0022-1937).
ARMAMENTS
see MILITARY WEAPONS
ARMED FORCES (v26)
see CANADA--ARMED FORCES; CHILD CARE--UNITED STATES--ARMED FORCES; CHINA--ARMED FORCES; COLOMBIA--ARMED FORCES; FRANCE--ARMED FORCES; GERMANY--ARMED FORCES; MICHIGAN--ARMED FORCES; NORTH ATLANTIC TREATY ORGANIZATION--ARMED FORCES; PERSIAN GULF REGION--ARMED FORCES; RUSSIA--ARMED FORCES; SEXUAL HARASSMENT--UNITED STATES--ARMED FORCES; SEXUAL HARASSMENT OF WOMEN--UNITED STATES--ARMED FORCES; SOUTH ASIA--ARMED FORCES; SWEDEN--ARMED FORCES; TANKS (MILITARY SCIENCE)--UNITED STATES--ARMED FORCES; UNITED NATIONS--ARMED FORCES; UNITED STATES--ARMED FORCES; VETERANS
ARMENIA--ECONOMIC CONDITIONS
"Armenia's GDP increased by 5 percent in 1994 and a further 7 percent in 1995. Exports increased by 22 percent in 1995, and the inflation rate dropped to 32 percent, the second-lowest in the Commonwealth of Independent States. The energy sector improved dramatically, up 32 percent from the first quarter of 1995 through the first quarter of 1996....An estimated 80 percent or more of Armenians remain poverty-stricken. Whereas the poorest fifth of the population earned 16 percent of what the wealthiest fifth made in 1991, by 1995 the poorest 20 percent were earning only 4 percent of the top bracket's income." (p89)
Bremmer, Ian/Welt, Cory. "Armenia's New Autocrats." Journal of Democracy v8 n3 Jul 1997. p77-91. (ISSN1045-5736).
"Armenia is a country of 3.7 million people situated on a crossroads between Europe, the former Soviet Union, and the Middle East....Policies of fiscal and monetary restraint, launched in the Spring of 1994 and supported since end-1994 by inflows of external financing from the IMF [International Monetary Fund] and the World Bank, helped bring down the budget defect to 8.8 percent of GDP in 1996, a sixth of the 1993 figure. Annual inflation fell to under 8 percent in 1996--one of the lowest rates in the Former Soviet Union. After years of collapse, GDP grew by 5.4 percent in 1994, by nearly 7 percent in 1995 and by 5.8 percent in 1996."
World Bank. "World Bank Assists in Armenia's Economic Reform Program: Background." Press Release 26 Aug 1997. document-level access: <http://www.worldbank.org/html/extdr/extme/1451.htm>
ARMENIA (REPUBLIC)--ECONOMIC CONDITIONS (v26)
ARMENIANS--EMIGRATION AND IMMIGRATION
"Since 1991, nearly 700,000 Armenians--a staggering 18 percent of the population--have gone to seek better opportunities in Russia and the West. More than a third of these emigrants were middle class (more than twice their percentage in the population at large); three-quarters were city dwellers; and half had university or professional educations." (p87)
Bremmer, Ian/Welt, Cory. "Armenia's New Autocrats." Journal of Democracy v8 n3 Jul 1997. p77-91. (ISSN1045-5736).
ARMORED CARS (TANKS)
see TANKS (MILITARY SCIENCE)
ARMS CONTROL--BELARUS--KAZAKHSTAN--UKRAINE
As a result of the Cooperative Threat Reduction program, "Belarus, Kazakstan and Ukraine transferred over 3,300 strategic warheads to Russia for dismantlement. All SS-24 and SS-19 intercontinental ballistic missiles in Ukraine have been deactivated. Kazakstan removed all its 100+ SS-18 ICBMs, and Belarus withdrew 63 of its 81 SS-25 mobile ICBMs and launchers. Russia removed over 1,200 deployed strategic warheads. Through Project Sapphire, Kazakstan transferred 600 kilograms of weapons-usable uranium to the United States for secure storage. In addition, about 12,000 former Soviet weapon scientists and engineers have or soon will have new jobs on peaceful, civilian research projects." (p44) "Prior to January 1993, when [U.S.] President Clinton took office, only $26 million had been obligated. By March 1996, obligations for specific projects had reached over $1 billion." (p45)
Smith, Harold P., Jr. "Cooperative Threat Reduction: Defense by Other Means." Defense 97 n3 1997. p42-47.
ARMS CONTROL--CROATIA
In Croatia, "the removal of heavy weaponry took place during an intense thirty day period lasting from 21 May-20 June 1996, when UN forces supervised the demilitarization of 16,000 Serb troops, as well as the withdrawal of approximately 120 tanks, 20 armoured personnel carriers, 41 self-propelled anti-tank guns, 120 artillery pieces, 140 mortars and 50 anti-aircraft guns back to the Federal Republic of Yugoslavia." (p14) "According to UN sources, the weapons turned in [as a result of the buy-back scheme] included 1,883 rifles, 277 nondisposable anti-tank rocket launchers, 3,545 disposable rocket launchers, 6,873 grenades and over 286,000 rounds of ammunition." (p15)
Marnika, Maurice. "UNTAES: Demilitarization and Hopes for Future Peace." Peacekeeping & International Relations v26 n3 May-Jun 1997. p14-15. (ISSN1187-3485).
ARMS INDUSTRY
see WEAPONS INDUSTRY
ARMS SALES
see DEFENSE INDUSTRIES

ARMS TRANSFERS

"The value of all arms transfer agreements worldwide (to both developed and developing nations) in 1996 was $31.8 billion....In 1996, the United States led in arms transfer agreements worldwide, making agreements valued at nearly $11.3 billion, or 35.5 percent of all such agreements, up from $9.2 billion in 1995. The United Kingdom ranked second with $4.8 billion in agreements, or 15.1 percent of all such agreements globally, up from $1 billion in 1995. Russian arms transfer agreements worldwide dropped notably from $8.4 billion in 1995 to $4.6 billion in 1996. The United States, the United Kingdom and Russia collectively made agreements in 1996 valued at $20.7 billion, 65.1 percent of all international arms transfer agreements made by all suppliers...." (p46)

Grimmett, Richard F. "Conventional Arms Transfers to Developing Nations, 1989-1996." DISAM Journal v20 n1 Fall 1997. p44-69.

ARMS TRANSFERS--CHINA--DEVELOPING COUNTRIES

"The value of China's arms transfer agreements with developing nations peaked in 1990 at $2.6 billion. After 1990, the value of China's arms transfer agreements with developing nations have averaged about $550 million annually. In 1996, the value of China's arms transfer agreements with developing nations was $500 million...." (p49)

Grimmett, Richard F. "Conventional Arms Transfers to Developing Nations, 1989-1996." DISAM Journal v20 n1 Fall 1997. p44-69.

ARMS TRANSFERS--DEVELOPING COUNTRIES --RUSSIA

"The total value of Russia's arms agreements with developing nations fell from $5.6 billion in 1995, to $3.9 billion in 1996, placing it second in such agreements with the developing world. Russia's share of all developing world arms transfer agreements decreased..., falling from 32.5 percent in 1995, to 20.1 percent in 1996...." (p48) Russia's "arms agreements values ranged from a high of $12.6 billion in 1990 to a low of $1.4 billion in 1993 (in constant 1996 dollars)." (p49)

Grimmett, Richard F. "Conventional Arms Transfers to Developing Nations, 1989-1996." DISAM Journal v20 n1 Fall 1997. p44-69.

ARMS TRANSFERS--DEVELOPING COUNTRIES --UNITED STATES

"In 1996, the total value, in real terms, of U.S. arms transfer agreements with developing nations increased notably to $7.3 billion from $4.1 billion in 1995....The U.S. share of the value of all such agreements was 37.6 percent in 1996, an increase from 23.7 percent in 1995...." (p48)

Grimmett, Richard F. "Conventional Arms Transfers to Developing Nations, 1989-1996." DISAM Journal v20 n1 Fall 1997. p44-69.

During the period 1989-1996, conventional U.S. "arms transfers to developing nations have comprised 67.5 percent of the value of all international arms transfers....Arms transfer agreements, which represent orders for future delivery, have shifted slightly from the developing nations. But the portion of agreements with developing countries still constituted 63.2 percent of all agreements globally from 1993-1996. In 1996, arms transfer agreements comprised 61 percent of the value of all such agreements globally. In the period from 1993-1996, deliveries of conventional arms to developing nations represented 70.9 percent of the value of all international arms deliveries. In 1996, arms deliveries to developing nations constituted over 73.9 percent of the value of all such arms deliveries worldwide." (p44)

Grimmett, Richard F. "Conventional Arms Transfers to Developing Nations, 1989-1996." DISAM Journal v20 n1 Fall 1997. p44-69.

ARMS TRANSFERS--MIDDLE EAST

"The Near East continues to be the largest developing world arms market. In 1989-1992 it accounted for 45.9 percent of the total value of all developing nations arms transfer agreements ($52.4 billion in current dollars). During 1993-1996, the region accounted for 57.4 percent of all such agreements (nearly $48 billion in current dollars). The United States has dominated arms transfer agreements with the Near East during the 1993-1996 time period with 52 percent of their total value (about $25 billion in current dollars). France was second during 1993-1996 with 27.9 percent ($13.4 billion in current dollars). In 1989-1992, the United States accounted for 59 percent of arms agreements with this region, while Russia held 10.7 percent." (p51)

Grimmett, Richard F. "Conventional Arms Transfers to Developing Nations, 1989-1996." DISAM Journal v20 n1 Fall 1997. p44-69.

ARMY POSTS

see MILITARY BASES

ARSON--MICHIGAN--DETROIT

"A few Michigan counties recorded 200 percent increases, going from zero to two arsons between 1995 and 1996. But the percentage rise in arson in Wayne County is particularly revealing. Per the Michigan State Police Uniform Crime Report, arson in the county jumped from 1,422 in 1995 to 2,111 in 1996, a 48.5 percent increase....In 1994,...the FBI recorded 845 arsons in Detroit. That number accelerated to 1,151 in 1995. Preliminary data show the number of incidents had risen to 1,811 by 1996, more than double the 1994 figure." (p10 secA)

Johnson, Bill. "Editorial Notebook: For Detroit Residents, Every Night Has Become Devil's Night." Detroit News 1 Aug 1997. p10 secA.

In 1997, "there was more fire but apparently less arson in Detroit [Michigan] this Halloween. Mayor Dennis Archer announced...that the number of fires from Wednesday to Friday jumped to 168, 16 more than last year. However, suspicious blazes dropped to 75 from 85, down 12 percent....Detroit recorded 354 fires over the Halloween period in 1994, Archer's first year as mayor....[In 1997,] Angels' Night--Thursday--saw the most fires with 66. There were 56 on Wednesday and 46 on Halloween Friday." (p3 secB)

Harmon, Brian. "Metro & State News: In Detroit: Halloween Arsons Fall from '96." Detroit News 2 Nov 1997. p3 secB.

In Detroit, Michigan, during the 1997 Halloween period, "although there were several arson-related arrests and some curfew violators, the total number was down from last year, when 142 blazes were called in during the period. That was significantly better than 1985 when the Halloween Eve arson blitz peaked at 297. It decreased annually until 1994's sharp increase, Mayor [Dennis] Archer's first year in office. That year, there were 182 Devil's Night fires, the most since 215 in 1986....Federal Bureau of Investigation and Michigan State Police crime statistics show substantial increases in arsons in Detroit during 1995 and 1996. Arsons more than doubled--from 845 in 1994 to 1,811 in 1996." (p8 secB)

"More Smoke than Fire." Detroit News 2 Nov 1997. p8 secB.

ARSON--UNITED STATES

In the U.S., "arsonists are responsible for over 500,000 fires every year. Arson is the No. 1 cause of all fires. Even though it is the leading cause of fire, only 15 percent of arson cases result in arrests with juveniles accounting for 55 percent of arrests, and only 2 percent result in convictions. It is the second leading cause of fire deaths in residences and the leading cause of dollar loss due to fire. In 1994, the most recent year for which comprehensive data is available, the total number of arson fires in the United States was estimated at 548,500--accounting for an estimated 560 fire deaths, 3,440 fire injuries, and $3.6 billion in property damage." (pS10064)

Hollings, Ernest F. (Sen.-S.C.). "Statements on Introduced Bills and Joint Resolutions." Congressional Record. Daily ed. v143 n131 26 Sep 1997. pS10055-10067. section/page-level access: <http://thomas.loc.gov/cqi-bin/query/R?r105:FLD001:S10064:> (ISSN0363-7239). (X1.1A.105/1).

ARSON--UNITED STATES--MORTALITY (v26)

ARSON--UNITED STATES--YOUTH

"According to the Federal Bureau of Investigation (FBI), a staggering 52 percent of US arson arrests in 1995 were youths under age 18....A third of all people arrested for arson in 1995 were under 15 years old, and playing with fire is also the leading cause of death among preschoolers....Approximately $2 billion in property damage is caused by arson each year....Some experts say that juvenile arson statistics could even be higher because 80 to 85 percent of suspicious fires are never solved. From 1986 to 1995, the net changes in arson arrests were a 40 percent increase for juveniles and a 15 percent decrease for adults, according to the NFPA [National Fire Protection Association]." (p1,9)

Holmstrom, David. "Alarms Ring over Juvenile Fire Setting." The Christian Science Monitor v89 n248 19 Nov 1997. p1,9. The Christian Science Monitor search engine: <http://www.csmonitor.com/plweb-cgi/iops1.pl> To retrieve this article, enter the following search: ED=19971119 AND setting. In the "retrieved list," click the title that matches this record. (ISSN0882-7729).

ARTIFICIAL FOODS--EUROPE--PUBLIC OPINION (v26)

ARTIFICIAL SATELLITES IN TELECOMMUNICATION --SWEDEN (v26)

ARTISTS--UNITED STATES (v26)

ARTS--CANADA

"The cultural sector represents a significant part of the Canadian economy. The cultural sector contributes $25 billion to Canada's gross domestic product. This means 900,000 jobs or 6.9 per cent of total employment. "Last year Canadians spent over $2.9 billion on arts events and products. For every dollar that the federal government has invested in the arts industry ten dollars of economic activity has been generated, an excellent rate of return." (p15)

Bulte, Sarmite (MP-ON). "Speech from the Throne." Canada. Parliament. House of Commons. Debates. v135 n2 23 Sep 1997. p13-18. section-level access: <http://www.parl.gc.ca/36/1/parlbus/chambus/house/debates/002_1997-09-23/han002-e.htm#LINKT7> (ISSN0704-5603). (X3-361E).

ARTS--EMPLOYMENT--SWEDEN (v26)

ARTS--FRANCE--UNITED STATES--PUBLIC OPINION (v26)

ARTS--MARYLAND (v26)

ARTS--MICHIGAN--FINANCE (v26)

ARTS--RHODE ISLAND

"The Rhode Island State Council on the Arts supports many arts organizations, social service organizations conducting arts programs, and arts educators. One of the Rhode Island Council's funding categories, which supports 26 of the State's largest arts organizations, is known as general operating support. In 1995-96, the council's grants in this category totaled $355,000, with an average grant size of $10,000. For this investment of $355,000, the State of Rhode Island saw an enormous return. The 26 general operating support organizations directly contributed more than $24 million into the Rhode Island economy. More than 1.1 million people attended these organizations' programs last year, further spurring the economy. Using modest Department of Commerce multipliers, these figures suggest that the activities of the general operating support organizations alone contributed a total of more than $97 million to Rhode Island's economy last year." (pS9400)

Reed, Jack (Sen.-R.I.). "Department of the Interior and Related Agencies Appropriations Act, 1998." Congressional Record. Daily ed. v143 n123 16 Sep 1997. pS9386-9406. section/page-level access: <http://thomas.loc.gov/cgi-bin/query/R?r105:FLD001:S09399:> (ISSN0363-7239). (X1.1A.105/1).

ARTS--SWEDEN (v26)

ARTS--SWEDEN--FINANCE (v26)

ARTS--UNITED STATES

Before the National Endowment for the Arts, "there were 58 orchestras in the...[U.S.]. Today there are more than 1,000. Before the NEA there were 37 professional dance companies. Now there are 300. Before the NEA, only 1 million people went to the theater in this country every year. Today more than 55 million do." (pH5147)

Nadler, Jerrold (Rep.-N.Y.). "Personal Explanation." Congressional Record. Daily ed. v143 n98 11 Jul 1997. pH5138-5168. section/page-level access: <http://thomas.loc.gov/cgi-bin/query/R?r105:FLD001:H05147:> (ISSN0363-7239). (X1.1A.105/1).

ARTS--UNITED STATES--FINANCE (v26)

"In the State of Mississippi, with a per capita income of about $18,000 per person, they received about 25 cents per person from the NEA [National Endowment for the Arts] last year, while the State of New York, which has a per capita income of $29,000 per person, received $1 per person from the National Endowment for the Arts. After looking more closely at the per capita numbers, the NEA used very selective funding. The Midwestern State of Iowa, with a per capita income of $22,000, received 20 cents per person, while the State of Maryland, with a higher per capita income of $27,000, received more than twice the per capita expenditure than the State of Iowa--Maryland received 45 cents per person....If you break that down by the number of direct grants from the National Endowment for the Arts, you find that almost 1,300 direct grants went to congressional districts represented by Democrats, while only 408 went to congressional districts represented by Republicans. When the funding is broken down per district, on average, about $223,000 was sent to districts represented by Democrats, and on average, about $60,000--almost one-fourth--went to congressional districts represented by Republicans." (pS9310)

Hutchinson, Tim (Sen.-Ark.). "Department of the Interior and Related Agencies Appropriations Act, 1998." Congressional Record. Daily ed. v143 n122 15 Sep 1997. pS9303-9332. section/page-level access: <http://thomas.loc.gov/cgi-bin/query/R?r105:FLD001:S09310:> (ISSN0363-7239). (X1.1A.105/1).

In the U.S., "of all the urban economic development programs, arts funding has proven to be among the most important...[to] our cities. An investment equal to 38 cents per American, one one-hundredth of 1 percent of our total Federal budget, stimulates 18 times that amount from other sources. Nationally, nonprofit arts generate $37 billion in economic activity, support 1.3 million jobs, and return $3.4 billion in Federal income taxes." (pH5149)

Johnson, Nancy L. (Rep.-Conn.). "Personal Explanation." Congressional Record. Daily ed. v143 n98 11 Jul 1997. pH5138-5168. section/page-level access: <http://thomas.loc.gov/cgi-bin/query/R?r105:FLD001:H05148:> (ISSN0363-7239). (X1.1A.105/1).

In the U.S., "private funding of the arts has been rising consistently since 1965. It is estimated that individuals alone will donate nearly $1 billion to the arts and humanities this year. That is the estimate of the House Committee on Education and the Workforce, Subcommittee on Oversight and Investigations.

Overall giving to the arts in 1996 totaled almost $10 billion, up from $6.5 billion in 1991, dwarfing the NEA's [National Endowment for the Arts] Federal subsidy. This 40-percent increase in private giving occurred during the same period that the NEA budget was reduced by 40 percent from approximately $170 million to $99.5 million." (pS9326)

Ashcroft, John (Sen.-Mo.). "Department of the Interior and Related Agencies Appropriations Act, 1998." Congressional Record. Daily ed. v143 n122 15 Sep 1997. pS9303-9332. section/page-level access: <http://thomas.loc.gov/cgi-bin/query/R?r105:FLD001:S09325:> (ISSN0363-7239). (X1.1A.105/1).

ASIA--COMMERCE--EUROPE (v26)

ASIA--COMMERCE--UNITED STATES

"According to Standard & Poor's, a rating service, Western [U.S.] states make up 7 out of the top 10 exporters to Asia on a per capita basis....The Port of Los Angeles's top five trading partners are all Asian countries--representing more than $52 billion a year in commerce." (p9)

Scherer, Ron/Wood, Daniel B. "How Asia's Woes Hurt US Companies." The Christian Science Monitor v90 n16 17 Dec 1997. p1,9. The Christian Science Monitor search engine: <http://www.csmonitor.com/plweb-cgi/iops1.pl> To retrieve this article, enter the following search: ED=19971217 AND companies. In the "retrieved list," click the title that matches this record. (ISSN0882-7729).

ASIA--ECONOMIC CONDITIONS (v26)

"Between 1965 and 1990, capital per worker grew at an annual rate of more than 8 percent in Taiwan and South Korea, nearly 8 percent in Japan, and more than 6 percent in Thailand....This was two to three times faster than the growth of capital per worker in the U.S." (p3)

Mason, Andrew. "Population and the Asian Economic Miracle." Asia-Pacific Population & Policy n43 Oct 1997. p1-4. (ISSN0891-6683).

"Today, Asia--from Pakistan east through Japan--has 3.1 billion people, more than half the world total. Excluding Japan, the economy of this region grew by some 8 percent a year from 1991 to 1996, much faster than the growth achieved earlier by either Western Europe or North America. Economic growth in Asia is led by China, where per capita income climbed by nearly four fifths between 1990 and 1996." (p12)

Brown, Lester R. "The Agricultural Link: How Environmental Deterioration Could Disrupt Economic Progress." Worldwatch Paper n136 Aug 1997. p5-73.

ASIA--ECONOMIC CONDITIONS--POPULATION (v26)

ASIA--UNITED STATES--ARMED FORCES --APPROPRIATIONS AND EXPENDITURES (v26)

ASIA, CENTRAL--POPULATION

The World Bank estimated the total mid-1994 population of the five Central Asian states of Kazakhstan, Kyrgyzstan, Tajikistan, Turkmenistan, and Uzbekistan "to be about 54 million. If the present trends in population growth continue, by the year 2025 the combined population of the five countries is expected to rise to 86 million, before stabilizing at about 128 million at some later date." (p209)

Elhance, Arun P. "Conflict and Cooperation over Water in the Aral Sea Basin." Studies in Conflict & Terrorism v20 n2 Apr-Jun 1997. p207-218. (ISSN1057-610X).

ASIA, SOUTHEASTERN--ECONOMIC CONDITIONS --SOCIAL CONDITIONS (v26)

ASIAN AMERICAN BUSINESS ENTERPRISES (v26)

ASIAN AMERICAN FAMILIES (v26)

ASIAN AMERICANS (v26)

see also AGE--ASIAN AMERICANS; HOUSEHOLDS--ASIAN AMERICANS; POPULATION FORECASTING--ASIAN AMERICANS; POPULATION GEOGRAPHY--ASIAN AMERICANS

"Comprising nearly 10 million, or 3.7 percent of the U.S. population, Asian Pacific Americans rank among the highest in our educational institutions, hold high political office and log advances in entrepreneurship. According to the U.S. Census Bureau, in 1994, nearly 90 percent of Asian Pacific Islander men and 80 percent of Asian Pacific Islander women aged 25 years and older had at least a high school diploma. In addition, an estimated 46 percent of men and 37 percent of women had at least a bachelor's degree. Median income of Asian and Pacific Islander households in 1995 was $40,614. Business ownership figures show that the number of businesses owned by Asian and Pacific Islanders increased 56 percent between 1987 and 1992, from 386,291 to 603,439." (pH3149)

Mink, Patsy T. (Rep.-Hawaii). "In Honor of Asian Pacific American Heritage Month." Congressional Record. Daily ed. v143 n68 21 May 1997. pH3149-3151. section/page-level access: <http://thomas.loc.gov/cgi-bin/query/R?r105:FLD001:H03149:> (ISSN0363-7239). (X1.1A.105/1).

ASIAN AMERICANS--ECONOMIC CONDITIONS (v26)

Asian Americans "are the wealthiest of all minorities, averaging annual incomes of $38,500 in 1995 compared to $31,000 for Caucasians. They are the only minority to earn more than Caucasians. According to TIME more than 32% of Asian Americans have family incomes exceeding $50,000 compared to only 29% of Caucasian families. In 1992, Asian Americans spent $120 billion. Only 11% of Asian American families live in poverty.... Most [Asian Americans] are married, and both husband and wife work. Almost three-quarters of Asian Americans are employed with 80% of those employed working in white collar jobs." (p24-25)

Morton, Linda P. "Targeting Minority Publics." Public Relations Quarterly v42 n2 Sum 1997. p23-28. (ISSN0033-3700).

In 1995, median income for Asian and Pacific Islander "households was about 9 percent higher than for white households--$40,600 compared with $37,200....The 1995 earnings of white men...were about 12 percent greater than for Asian men, while the earnings for white and Asian women were nearly identical....Despite their higher median income, however, API families were nearly twice as likely as whites to live in poverty...." (p8) "The difference in the poverty level was greatest for married-couple families (10.7 percent for Asians, 3.8 percent for whites). Nearly one in seven Asian Americans (14.6 percent) lived below the poverty level, compared with about one in 11 whites (8.5 percent)....Nearly one in five [Asian and Pacific Islander children] were poor in 1995--almost twice the rate for whites." (p9)

Pollard, Kelvin M./De Vita, Carol J. "A Portrait of Asians and Pacific Islanders in the United States." Statistical Bulletin v78 n3 Jul-Sep 1997. p2-9. (ISSN0790-8334).

ASIAN AMERICANS--EDUCATION

In the U.S., "42 percent of all API [Asian and Pacific Islander] adults had at least a bachelor's degree in 1996, compared with 26 percent of their white counterparts....Among young adults (ages 25 to 34), the differences were even more striking--49 percent of young Asian Americans had at least a bachelor's degree, compared with 31 percent of young whites....One in 10 API adults has less than a 9th grade education and one in six lacks a high school diploma. Comparable ratios for non-Hispanic white adults are one in 20 and one in seven, respectively." (p7)

Pollard, Kelvin M./De Vita, Carol J. "A Portrait of Asians and Pacific Islanders in the United States." Statistical Bulletin v78 n3 Jul-Sep 1997. p2-9. (ISSN0790-8334).

ASIAN AMERICANS--EDUCATION (HIGHER) (v26)

ASIAN AMERICANS--EMPLOYMENT (v26)

"Two-thirds of Asian Americans were in the civilian labor force in 1996, with men more likely to be in the labor force than women (74 percent versus 59 percent). Asians and whites also had similar rates of unemployment in 1996--about 5 percent for each group. Roughly one-third of Asians held managerial and professional jobs...." (p7-8)

Pollard, Kelvin M./De Vita, Carol J. "A Portrait of Asians and Pacific Islanders in the United States." Statistical Bulletin v78 n3 Jul-Sep 1997. p2-9. (ISSN0790-8334).

ASIAN AMERICANS--HOUSING (v26)

ASIAN AMERICANS--LANGUAGES (v26)

ASIAN AMERICANS--POPULATION (v26)

In the 1990 U.S. "census (the most recent year for which data on specific API [Asian and Pacific Islanders] groups are available), 76 percent of Asians and Pacific Islanders were from one of five ethnic origins: Chinese, Filipino, Japanese, Asian Indian and Korean....Groups from other Asian origins (such as Vietnamese and Cambodian) accounted for an additional 19 percent; Pacific Islanders (e.g., native Hawaiians and Samoans) comprise 5 percent." (p2) "Between 1980 and 1996, the API population more than doubled--rising from 3.8 million persons in 1980 to 9.7 million in 1996....Whereas Asians and Pacific Islanders were less than 2 percent of the U.S. population in 1980, by 1996 they accounted for nearly 4 percent of all Americans." (p3)

Pollard, Kelvin M./De Vita, Carol J. "A Portrait of Asians and Pacific Islanders in the United States." Statistical Bulletin v78 n3 Jul-Sep 1997. p2-9. (ISSN0790-8334).

ASIAN PACIFIC ECONOMIC COOPERATION (v26)

ASIANS--EMIGRATION AND IMMIGRATION--BRITISH COLUMBIA--VANCOUVER

In Vancouver, British Columbia, "in less than 15 years, the Asian population in the metropolitan area exploded from 3 percent to more than 25 percent. Today, more than 350,000 Asian immigrants live in Vancouver, three-quarters of them from Hong Kong." (p1 secA) "'In recent years, Asians--particularly Hong Kong Chinese--have accounted for half of all home buyers in Vancouver. And for homes that cost $1 million, ($730,000 U.S.), they are 75 to 80 percent of the buyers,' said Wyng Chow, a reporter for the VANCOUVER SUN who examined land registrations." (p6 secA) "According to statistics gathered by the British Columbia provincial government, the annual number of immigrants to the Vancouver area from Hong Kong has slipped from 16,159 in 1994 to 12,180 in 1996." (p7 secA)

Volgenau, Gerry. "Vancouver Losing Its Asians." Detroit Free Press 2 Jun 1997. p1,6-7 secA.

ASPARAGUS--CHILE--UNITED STATES (v26)

ASPARAGUS--LATIN AMERICA--UNITED STATES (v26)

ASPARAGUS--MICHIGAN--WASHINGTON (STATE) (v26)

ASPARAGUS--PERU--UNITED STATES (v26)

ASPARAGUS--TAXATION--MEXICO--UNITED STATES (v26)

ASPARAGUS--UNITED STATES (v26)

"In 1997, U.S. asparagus production was 198 million pounds, 21 percent below the record 250 million in 1989. About 61 percent of U.S. asparagus production was marketed in fresh form in 1997, compared with only 37 percent from 1975 to 1979...." (p20) "In 1997, Washington accounted for 42 percent of total production, compared with California's 41 percent. Michigan's share was 13 percent. New Jersey, Illinois, Indiana, Maryland, Minnesota, and Oregon combined accounted for 4 percent of production." (p21)

Calvin, Linda/Cook, Roberta/U.S. Dept. of Agriculture. Economic Research Service. "Special Article: The U.S. Asparagus Industry in a Global Environment: A Commodity Highlight." Vegetables and Specialties Situation and Outlook Report Nov 1997. p20-26.

ASPHALT-RUBBER (v26)

ASSAULT, CRIMINAL

see RAPE

ASSAULT RIFLES

see also AK-47 RIFLE

Among assault rifles "are the U.S.-made M-16, of which 8 million copies have been turned out, the German G-3 (7 million), the Belgian-designed FN-FAL (5 to 7 million), and the Israeli Uzi machine pistol (10 million)....More than 100 million military-style rifles are thought to exist worldwide." (p20)

Renner, Michael. "Small Arms, Big Impact: The Next Challenge of Disarmament." Worldwatch Paper n137 Oct 1997. p5-77.

ASSEMBLY INDUSTRY, OFFSHORE

see OFFSHORE ASSEMBLY INDUSTRY

ASSISTED SUICIDE--MICHIGAN--PUBLIC OPINION

"An EPIC/MRA-Lansing poll showed that a large majority--some 66 percent--of Michigan adults believe terminally ill, mentally competent adults 'definitely should' or 'probably should' have the option of physician aid in dying. Some 63 percent of Catholics felt the same way." (p7 secB)

Pierce, Edward C. "Comment: Aid in Dying a Better Way to End Suffering." Detroit News 29 Jun 1997. p7 secB.

ASSOCIATIONS, INSTITUTIONS, ETC.

see CHARITIES

ASSOCIATIONS, INSTITUTIONS, ETC.--UNITED STATES (v26)

ASTEROIDS

"Current scientific theory holds that asteroids are construction debris left over from the solar system's formation more than 4.5 billion years ago....Carbonaceous asteroids are thought to be about 75 percent of all asteroids." (p3)

Spotts, Peter N. "United States: Waltzing 'Mathilde': Asteroid Offers Insight into Space Mysteries." The Christian Science Monitor v89 n148 26 Jun 1997. p3. The Christian Science Monitor search engine: <http://www.csmonitor.com/plweb-cgi/iops1.pl> To retrieve this article, enter the following search: ED=19970626 AND mysteries. In the "retrieved list," click the title that matches this record. (ISSN0882-7729).

ASTEROIDS--UNITED STATES

A few years ago, when the U.S. Congress "mandated a study of an early [asteroid] warning system--dubbed 'Safeguard'--the system was expected to cost some $50 million. But the NASA team now says it could map the sky for about $1 million with a Near Earth Asteroid Tracking (NEAT) system....In early tests on an Air Force telescope on Mt. Haleakala in Hawaii, NEAT has identified 10,185 asteroids--55 percent of which were previously unknown....So far, NEAT and other early-warning systems have targeted 99 potentially dangerous objects--rocks that are one kilometer across or larger and will get within 5 million miles of Earth." (p3)

Cowen, Robert C. "United States: Falling Space Rocks: Asteroid Trackers Build a Better Warning System." The Christian Science Monitor v89 n180 12 Aug 1997. p3. The Christian Science Monitor search engine: <http://www.csmonitor.com/plweb-cgi/iops1.pl> To retrieve this article, enter the following search: ED=19970812 AND system. In the "retrieved list," click the title that matches this record. (ISSN0882-7729).

ASTHMA--CANADA (v26)

ASTHMA--NEW YORK (N.Y.) (v26)

ASTHMA--UNITED STATES (v26)

"In the United States alone, 14.6 million people--4.8 million of whom are children--have asthma....Between 1982 and 1992, asthma increased 40 percent in the United States." (p8 secF)

Anstett, Patricia. "Body & Mind: Cover Story: Programs Aim

to Beat Asthma." Detroit Free Press 28 Oct 1997. p8 secF.
"The US National Institute of Allergy and Infectious Diseases suggests that 'allergies affect as many as 40 to 50 million people in the US'--one in five people. The number of children diagnosed with allergic dermatitis in the US has increased from three per cent in the 1960s to ten per cent in the 1990s....The most thoroughly documented rise in incidence is in asthma. Its prevalence in the United States rose by 30 per cent from 1980 to 1987. From 1990 to 1992, the number of people in the country who said they had asthma increased from 10.4 million to 12.4 million. Asthma is far more common in African-American children than in white children (26 per cent more prevalent). From 1980 to 1987, asthma deaths in the US increased by 30 per cent." (p107)

Cone, Richard A./Martin, Emily. "Corporeal Flows: The Immune System, Global Economies of Food and Implications for Health." Ecologist v27 n3 May-Jun 1997. p107-111. (ISSN0261-3131).

In the U.S., "about 4.8 million people under the age of 18 have asthma, and its prevalence has risen in all age groups. Between 1980 and '93, asthma mortality rose 118% in patients younger than 25--from 1.7 to 3.7 per million population. Blacks, especially those aged 15 to 24, have the highest risk of any group. Hospitalizations for asthma increased 28% from 1980 to '93 in all patients younger than 25." (p44)

"Meeting News: How to Identify, Help Younger Patients Who Are at Risk for Asthma Death." Modern Medicine v65 n8 Aug 1997. p44. (ISSN0026-8070).

ASTHMA--UNITED STATES--COSTS (v26)

ASTHMA--UNITED STATES--MORTALITY (v26)

ASTHMA IN CHILDREN--MICHIGAN--DETROIT

In Michigan, "studies show that 15 to 20 percent of Detroit elementary schoolchildren have asthma, three times the national average. One local study of third-graders found a 17-percent rate in Detroit, compared with 9.5 percent in Southfield, said Jim Moore, a program director for the American Lung Association of Michigan, a major group involved in asthma education." (p8 secF)

Anstett, Patricia. "Body & Mind: Cover Story: Programs Aim to Beat Asthma." Detroit Free Press 28 Oct 1997. p8 secF.

ASTHMA IN CHILDREN--UNITED STATES (v26)

In the U.S., "asthma is the fastest-growing chronic illness among school-aged children, affecting nearly 5 million younger than 18. In 1996, there were 15 asthma-related deaths of people ages 10-19 in Michigan, according to information from the Michigan Department of Community Health. Ten of those deaths occurred in southeastern Michigan. Across the country, more than $1.9 billion a year is spent on treating school-aged children with asthma, according to information from the Centers for Disease Control and Prevention in Atlanta. More than 10 million school days are lost each year to asthma-related illnesses." (p1 secE)

Lopez, Manny. "Metro: News Special: Health: School Repairs Cause Attacks, Asthmatics Say." Detroit News 13 Nov 1997. p1,4 secE.

ASYLUM, RIGHT OF--EUROPE (v26)

ASYLUM, RIGHT OF--UNITED STATES

In the U.S., "during the 1980s, 97% of all political asylum claims filed by Salvadoran and Guatemalan nationals were denied at a time when nearly 50% of all Nicaraguan asylum claims were approved. In 1990, 250,000 Salvadoran and Guatemalan refugees benefited from the court case brought by a number of churches and religious organizations against the US Department of Justice." (p7) "The political asylum cases for these 250,000 refugees have been pending for years." (p8)

"Permanent Residency--A Right for Salvadorans and Guatemalans." Peacework n280 Dec 1997. p7-8. (ISSN0748-0725).

ATHABASCA (ALBERTA)--ENVIRONMENTAL ASPECTS

"Most visitors to Athabasca, a small town of just 2,000 people in the Canadian province of Alberta, perceive the countryside around it as wilderness or relatively unspoiled nature. Like the rest of the northern half of the province, the region is a mix of farmland, bogs, fens, streams, rivers and marshes and of boreal forest--spruce, pine, balsam fir, tamarack, birch and aspen trees--which covers 43 per cent of Alberta....Unlike temperate regions, vegetation in the boreal forest is slow to regenerate; the growing season is 50-100 days; the topsoil is thin; the forest is covered with snow for half the year; and the mean average temperature is 1.6 [degrees Celcius]. On average, an aspen tree takes eight years to reach a height of four metres, 70 to 80 years to reach a size suitable for logging." (p64)

Sherman, Joan. "Some Consequences of Cheap Trees and Cheap Talk: Pulp Mills and Logging in Northern Alberta." Ecologist v27 n2 Mar-Apr 1997. p64-68. (ISSN0261-3131).

ATHEROSCLEROSIS--UNITED STATES (v26)

ATHLETES, WOMEN

see WOMEN ATHLETES

ATLANTA (GA.)--ECONOMIC CONDITIONS

In Atlanta, Georgia, "unemployment is at 3.5 percent, one of the nation's lowest rates, and jobs are being created faster in Atlanta than in any other city, according to a recent Manpower survey. Convention bookings are up 14 percent from 1995. More than 7 million tourists visit yearly." (p3)

Nifong, Christina. "United States: Atlanta Crafts Olympic Legacy." The Christian Science Monitor v89 n162 17 Jul 1997. p3. The Christian Science Monitor search engine: <http://www.csmonitor.com/plweb-cgi/iops1.pl> To retrieve this article, enter the following search: ED=19970717 AND legacy. In the "retrieved list," click the title that matches this record. (ISSN0882-7729).

ATMOSPHERIC GREENHOUSE EFFECT

see GREENHOUSE EFFECT, ATMOSPHERIC

ATMOSPHERIC OZONE

see also OZONE LAYER DEPLETION

ATMOSPHERIC OZONE--CALIFORNIA--REDLANDS

"For 65 days last year, the city of Redlands [in California] violated permissible limits of ozone--a slight improvement on its 98 days of violation in 1994....Ozone may not exceed an average of .1 parts per million over a workday. Ozone levels in Redlands are sometimes double the EPA limit of .12 ppm per hour...." (p28)

Weston, Harold. "Lay of the Land: Bad-Air Days." Sierra v82 n5 Sep-Oct 1997. p28. (ISSN0161-7362).

ATMOSPHERIC OZONE--REDUCTION (v26)

ATMs

see AUTOMATED TELLERS

ATOLLS

see CORAL REEFS AND ISLANDS

ATOMIC ENERGY

see NUCLEAR ENERGY

ATOMIC POWER PLANTS

see NUCLEAR POWER PLANTS

ATOMIC WEAPONS

see NUCLEAR WEAPONS

ATRAZINE--WISCONSIN (v26)

ATTENDANCE, COLLEGE

see COLLEGE ATTENDANCE

ATTENTION-DEFICIT HYPERACTIVITY DISORDER --TREATMENT--UNITED STATES

In the U.S., "the prescription of stimulant drugs is the most common treatment for children with ADHD [attention-deficit hyperactivity disorder]. A school-age population in excess of 600,000 receive medication for behavior management (Barkley, 1990)." (p857) "The three most commonly prescribed stimulants are d-amphetamine (Dexedrine), methylphenidate (Ritalin), and pemoline (Cylert) (Barkley, 1990)....In reviewing fourteen studies of the use of Ritalin with ADHD children, Barkley (1990) found improvement in 77% of the cases, with 23% unchanged or worsened. Fifteen studies of amphetamines indicated that 74% showed improvement, with 26% unchanged or worsened. A newer drug, Cylert, produced similar results in two studies. The placebo treatments in eleven studies accounted for improvement in 39-50% (Barkley, 1990)....In seventeen studies reviewed, 83.6% of children were unaffected by medication in academic achievement testing (Barkley, 1990)." (p858) "Seventy-nine to ninety percent of the studies reviewed by Barkley (1990) reported irritability and weight loss in clients and negative mood changes, such as sadness and crying." (p859)

Ballard, Shirley/Bolan, Morna/Burton, Michael/Snyder, Sherry/Pasterczyk-Seabolt, Claire/Martin, Don. "The Neurological Basis of Attention Deficit Hyperactivity Disorder." Adolescence v32 n128 Win 1997. p855-862. (ISSN0001-8449).

ATTENTION-DEFICIT HYPERACTIVITY DISORDER --UNITED STATES (v26)

Attention-deficit hyperactivity disorder "is found in 3-6% of the child population in the United States, or nearly 2 million children (Dulcan & Popper, 1991). Recent estimates indicate that close to 40% of children referred to mental health clinics show symptoms of ADHD. It is more likely to occur in males than females, with ratios as high as 9:1 in clinic populations." (p855)

Ballard, Shirley/Bolan, Morna/Burton, Michael/Snyder, Sherry/Pasterczyk-Seabolt, Claire/Martin, Don. "The Neurological Basis of Attention Deficit Hyperactivity Disorder." Adolescence v32 n128 Win 1997. p855-862. (ISSN0001-8449).

In the U.S., "in 1993, nearly 2 million children and adolescents were diagnosed or being treated for ADHD [Attention-Deficit/Hyperactivity Disorder]." (p11) "The male to female ratio for ADHD is approximately 6 to 1. Nearly 80 percent of children and adolescents with ADHD experience problems related to the areas of impulsivity, hyperactivity, inattention, and rewards....Well-controlled prospective studies of children with ADHD find that at least 70 percent continue to meet the full diagnostic criteria for the disorder into adolescence....Compared to other young adults, they engage in activities that result in more school suspension (14 percent vs. 2 percent), have more adversarial contacts with law enforcement agencies (19:3), and are more likely to be admitted into juvenile justice facilities (5:1)....50 percent of those with ADHD evaluated in clinics progress to a level of aggressive behavior defined by most law enforcement agencies as deliquency." (p12)

Goldstein, Sam. "Attention-Deficit/Hyperactivity Disorder: Implications for the Criminal Justice System." FBI Law Enforcement Bulletin v66 n6 Jun 1997. p11-16. (ISSN0014-5688).

In the U.S., "researchers consistently report an overlap of ADHD [Attention-Deficit/Hyperactivity Disorder] and addictive disorders beginning in adolescence and continuing into early adulthood affecting at least 10 to 20 percent of the adult population with ADHD....Studies have found that nearly 40 percent of all cocaine and opiate abusers meet the diagnostic criteria for ADHD....One study, published in 1989, followed 103 males in New York State who had been diagnosed with ADHD at ages ranging from 6 to 12. When this group reached 16 to 23 years, the team conducted followup interviews with the subjects and their parents. The researchers then compared the subjects' arrest records with a control group of 100 individuals in the same age range. The researchers found that significantly higher percentages of individuals with ADHD had been arrested (39 percent vs. 20 percent), convicted of a crime (28:11), and incarcerated (9:1)." (p13)

Goldstein, Sam. "Attention-Deficit/Hyperactivity Disorder: Implications for the Criminal Justice System." FBI Law Enforcement Bulletin v66 n6 Jun 1997. p11-16. (ISSN0014-5688).

ATTENTION-DEFICIT HYPERACTIVITY DISORDER --UNITED STATES--SUBSTANCE USE

In the U.S., "a prevalence rate of approximately 25 percent has been found for ADHD [attention-deficit hyperactivity disorder] among adults in substance abuse treatment....In a sample of 298 adult cocaine abusers, Rounsaville and associates found that 35 percent had a history of childhood ADHD that was not entirely accounted for by sociopathy; however, none of the adults were reported to have ADHD." (p1378)

Milin, Robert/Loh, Elliot/Chow, Joy/Wilson, Allan. "Alcohol & Drug Abuse: Assessment of Symptoms of Attention-Deficit Hyperactivity Disorder in Adults with...Disorders." Psychiatric Services v48 n11 Nov 1997. p1378-1380,1395. (ISSN1075-2730).

ATTORNEYS

see LAWYERS

AU PAIRS--EUROPE--UNITED STATES

The U.S. "Congress authorized the au pair program in 1986 and put it under the control of the U.S. Information Agency (USIA). Some 11,000 au pairs between the ages of 18 and 26 arrive in the United States each year for a 12-month, live-in experience with an American family. The only cultural requirement is six credit hours of study at an American college....European norms for child-care work are different from those of the U.S. au pair program. Many European countries don't allow au pairs to work more than 25 hours a week, but in the United States, au pairs may work up to 45 hours a week....Nannies who reside in this country typically earn about $21,000 per year, whereas the total cost of an au pair typically comes to less than $12,000 a year....An estimated 60,000 families have hired European au pairs during the program's existence." (p11 secA)

Cohen, Warren. "Other Voices: A Free Press Campaign: Children First: Au Pair: More Regulation Might...Saved Matthew--And...Woodward." Detroit Free Press 10 Nov 1997. p11 secA.

AUSTRALIA--ECONOMIC CONDITIONS (v26)

AUSTRALIA--EMIGRATION AND IMMIGRATION (v26)

According to the Australian Bureau of Statistics, "for the second year in a row, New Zealanders were the largest group of permanent arrivals with 13,070 arrivals, 7 per cent more than last year. The number of people coming from the United Kingdom, the second largest group, fell by 14 per cent to 9,680. Over the last 10 years, an average of 40 per cent of Australia's settlers have come from Asian regions. Over the same period, the Asian born component of Australia's resident population has grown from 3 per cent to 5 per cent. In 1996-97, permanent arrivals from Asian regions numbered 32,100, a decline of 19 per cent on the previous year. There were 3,600 permanent departures of Asian born people, resulting in a net gain of 28,500 people."

Australian Bureau of Statistics. "Migration Levels Fall, But New Zealanders Defy Trend." Media Release 22 Aug 1997. document-level access: <http://www.abs.gov.au/websitedbs/d3110125.nsf/4a255eef008309e44a255eef00061e57/656a1ecfb5bb60fd4a2564fb00060a42?OpenDocument>

Australian Bureau of Statistics figures "show that in 1996-97 Australia welcomed 85,760 permanent arrivals. This was a decline of 14 per cent on the previous 12 months when there were 99,140 permanent arrivals, but only 2 per cent less than in 1994-95. When the 29,860 permanent departures for 1996-97 were taken into account, Australia experienced a net permanent gain of 55,900 people, compared to 70,470 in the previous year....In 1996-97, the net gain of permanent and long term arrivals over departures was 94,400, 14 per cent less than in 1995-96 (109,700). This net gain was the result of 261,000 permanent and long term arrivals and 166,600 permanent and long term departures."

Australian Bureau of Statistics. "Migration Levels Fall, But New Zealanders Defy Trend." Media Release 22 Aug 1997. document-level access: <http://www.abs.gov.au/websitedbs/d3110125.nsf/4a255eef008309e44a255eef00061e57/656a1ecfb5bb60fd4a2564fb00060a42?OpenDocument>

AUSTRALIA--EMPLOYMENT (v26)

According to the publication, "Labour Force Experience, Australia, February 1997," by the Australian Bureau of Statistics, "of the 12,739,300 civilians aged 15 to 69 years old, in the 12 months to February: 77 per cent (9,866,100) were in the labour force at some time during the year with 56 per cent (7,170,300) working or looking for work for the full 52 weeks. 72 per cent (9,186,600 people) worked at some time during the year, with 48 per cent (6,082,100) working for all 52 weeks....15 per cent (1,926,500) looked for work at some time during the year. Of these, 276,900 looked for work for 52 weeks with the largest proportion spending between 4 and 13 weeks looking for work (32 per cent or 613,400 people)....Of the 1,926,500 persons who looked for work at some time during the year 64 per cent of females and 62 per cent of males were aged 15-34 years. Of the persons who looked for work at some time during the year, 16 per cent of males and 13 per cent of females looked for...[work] for the whole 52 weeks."

Australian Bureau of Statistics. "Female Labour Force Participation Continues to Rise." Media Release 1 Aug 1997. document-level access: <http://www.abs.gov.au/websitedbs/d3110125.nsf/4a255eef008309e44a255eef00061e57/654318539623b1e54a2564e5007fa39d?OpenDocument>

AUSTRALIA--ENVIRONMENTAL ASPECTS--PUBLIC OPINION (v26)

AUSTRALIA--HEALTH AND HYGIENE

In Australia, "final results of the 1995 National Health Survey showed that 83 per cent considered themselves to be in good, very good or excellent health. Despite this, 83 per cent of people in this age group reported having one or more long-term medical condition. The conditions most commonly reported were long or short sight (51 per cent), arthritis (19 per cent), hayfever (16 per cent) and hypertension (13 per cent). Long term conditions most common among children (less than 15) were respiratory conditions, particularly asthma and hayfever. Across all age groups, 18 per cent reported a medical condition due to an accident or exposure. Seventy per cent of males and 80 per cent of females...reported taking action for their health in the previous two weeks. Almost 70 per cent used medication, 23 per cent consulted a doctor, 6 per cent consulted a dentist and 10 per cent consulted another health professional."

Australian Bureau of Statistics. "ABS Health Report on Australia." Media Release 28 Aug 1997. document-level access: <http://www.abs.gov.au/websitedbs/d3110125.nsf/4a255eef008309e44a255eef00061e57/7ad11af58d37387a4a25650100031cfd?OpenDocument>

AUSTRALIA--LANGUAGES (v26)

AUSTRALIA--POPULATION (v26)

AUSTRALIA CAPITAL TERRITORY--EMPLOYMENT

According to the publication, "Australian Capital Territory in Focus, 1997," by the Australian Bureau of Statistics, "in 1996-97 about 26 per cent of ACT people were employed in the Government administration and defence industry. Retailing (13.3 per cent), property and business services (12.1 per cent), education (8.8 per cent) and health and community services (8.1 per cent) were the other major employment industries. At 30 June 1996 Canberra and Queanbeyan accounted for 69.5 per cent of the labour force in the Australian Capital Region."

Australian Bureau of Statistics. "ABS Focus on the National Capital." Media Release 24 Sep 1997. document-level access: <http://www.abs.gov.au/websitedbs/d3110125.nsf/4a255eef008309e44a255eef00061e57/f5e5faf940e2901c4a25651c00019bcc?OpenDocument>

AUSTRALIA CAPITAL TERRITORY--SOCIAL CONDITIONS

According to the publication, "Australian Capital Territory in Focus, 1997," by the Australian Bureau of Statistics, "life expectancy at birth is 81.5 years for females and 76.7 for males, the highest for all States and Territories in Australia....In 1996 high school and college retention rates at 91.9 per cent were much higher than the national average of 71.3 per cent. Crime rose 18.5 per cent between 1994-95 and 1995-96. Burglary, fraud and other offences of theft accounted for 65.3 per cent of offences. Just over one-quarter (25.7 per cent) of ACT people were born overseas, nearly half of them in Europe and the former USSR and one-fifth from Asia. Some 86 per cent of people aged 15 years and over reported their health was either good, very good or excellent."

Australian Bureau of Statistics. "ABS Focus on the National Capital." Media Release 24 Sep 1997. document-level access: <http://www.abs.gov.au/websitedbs/d3110125.nsf/4a255eef008309e44a255eef00061e57/f5e5faf940e2901c4a25651c00019bcc?OpenDocument>

AUTISM--UNITED STATES

"Autism is not rare. It affects 400,000 people in the United States. One in 500 children born today will be autistic. Though 5 percent will make strides with early intervention, 95 percent of those affected will never marry, have a meaningful job, or live on their own. More than half will never learn to speak. Autism affects more people than multiple sclerosis, cystic fibrosis, and childhood cancer combined, yet autism still receives less than 5 percent of the research funding of these other diseases. Autism costs America over $20 billion dollars each year, yet just last year the NIH [National Institutes of Health] spent only $31 per child on autism research, significantly less than what is spent on other diseases which affect fewer individuals." (pE1123)

Rothman, Steven R. (Rep.-N.J.). "Support for Autism Funding." Congressional Record. Daily ed. v143 n76 5 Jun 1997. pE1123-1124. section/page-level access: <http://thomas.loc.gov/cgi-bin/query/R?r105:FLD001:E01123:> (ISSN0363-7239). (X1.1A.105/1).

AUTOMATED TELLERS--CALIFORNIA (v26)

AUTOMATED TELLERS--UNITED STATES

In the U.S., a survey by the Public Interest Research Group found that 45 percent of automated teller machines "assess surcharges of 25 cents to $2.50 per transaction. Banks that impose a surcharge--about 59 percent--charged $1 per transaction; about 31 percent charged $1.50. The average fee is $1.15, the study found. Aggressive competition for these fees has fueled a huge increase to about 140,000 U.S. machines in 1996 from 94,822 in 1993, according to Mentis Corp., a research firm in Durham, N.C. The number is expected to exceed 220,000 in the year 2000....In 1993, less than 20 percent of ATMs were owned by nonfinancial institutions, said Beth Phillips, Mentis' senior projects manager. Three years later, that figure had risen to 25 percent....[Automated teller machine] transactions are expected to decline about 25 percent per-terminal annually." (p1-2 secB)

Serju-Harris, Tricia. "Business: Savvy Business Owners Offer In-House Cash Source: But Too Many ATMs May Cut Profits, Use." Detroit News 14 Oct 1997. p1-2 secB.

AUTOMATED TELLERS--UNITED STATES--COSTS

A recent U.S. General Accounting Office report found that "in just over a year, the number of ATMs [automated teller machines] that double charge consumers has risen 320 percent since the end of 1995. That means that consumers have less and less of a choice when they need to use an ATM. The GAO study also reveals that 54 percent of the ATMs in the United States are now double-charging....Until April...[1996], most consumers paid a fee, usually about $1, to their own bank each time they used another bank's ATM. This fee was intended to cover the cost of the transaction. Now, in addition to that fee, the ATM operator may charge these consumers a second fee. This second fee can run as high as $3 per transaction....Recent estimates show that the average consumer is paying a whopping $155 per year to use automated teller machines or ATMs....A transaction conducted at an ATM costs about 25 cents while the same transaction conducted by a teller in a bank branch costs well over a dollar....A recent study by the U.S. Public Interest Research Group (U.S. PIRG) reported that banks will profit $1.9 billion from ATM surcharges alone this year." (pS5531)

D'Amato, Alfonse M. (Sen.-N.Y.). "Statements on Introduced Bills and Joint Resolutions." Congressional Record. Daily ed. v143 n81 11 Jun 1997. pS5508-5541. section/page-level access: <http://thomas.loc.gov/cgi-bin/query/R?r105:FLD001:S05531:> (ISSN0363-7239). (X1.1A.105/1).

AUTOMATIC DATA PROCESSORS

see COMPUTERS

AUTOMOBILE ACCIDENTS

see TRAFFIC ACCIDENTS

AUTOMOBILE AIR BAG RESTRAINT SYSTEMS

see AIR BAG RESTRAINT SYSTEMS

AUTOMOBILE CHILD RESTRAINT SYSTEMS

see CHILD RESTRAINT SYSTEMS IN AUTOMOBILES

AUTOMOBILE DRIVERS--MENTAL HEALTH--UNITED STATES (v26)

AUTOMOBILE DRIVERS' LICENSES--MICHIGAN (v26)

AUTOMOBILE DRIVERS' TESTS--MICHIGAN

"Michigan examiners flunked more than 1,000 new drivers who took road tests in the first month after the exams became mandatory in April [1997]. The failure rate amounted to 15 percent of those taking the test....Under the new system, all new drivers must pass the road tests offered by private examiners. Of the 1,042 who failed the test in April, 61 percent slipped up on the basic control portion, including such things as parallel parking and backing up. Others missed the mark on driving tests taken on streets and highways." (p3 secC)

"Briefly: Lansing: 15% of Tested Drivers Fail April Road Exams." Detroit News 17 Jun 1997. p3 secC.

AUTOMOBILE DRIVING--AUSTRALIA--GREAT BRITAIN (v26)

AUTOMOBILE DRIVING--NORTHWEST, PACIFIC (v26)

AUTOMOBILE DRIVING--UNITED STATES

"In a recent member survey by the American Automobile Association Potomac office, motorists named aggressive driving as their top concern on the roads. Drivers fear the aggressive driver (44 percent) more than the drunk driver (31 percent). Ninety percent say they witnessed aggressive driving behavior within the last year, and half said they had seen an extreme example in the past week....Almost two out of three people in the survey admitted to driving aggressively in the last year....Reported incidents of aggressive driving have increased by 7 percent every year since 1990, according to the American Automobile Association Foundation for Traffic Safety. The group studied 10,037 separate incidents reported in police records and newspaper articles between Jan. 1, 1990, and Sept. 1, 1996....The National Highway Traffic Safety Administration (NHTSA) reports 41,901 people died and more than 3 million more were injured in police-reported crashes in 1996." (p28)

Goehring, Jan. "Taming the Road Warrior." State Legislatures v23 n10 Dec 1997. p28-29. (ISSN0147-6041).

AUTOMOBILE INDUSTRY AND TRADE (v26)

"Nissan, the most productive automaker...[according to a] Harbour [and Associates Inc.] report, has the worst profit per vehicle of any of the six automakers in the study. In 1996, Nissan lost $332 after taxes on each vehicle it sold. Toyota made $540 on each vehicle and Honda made $90. Chrysler made about 12 times that--$1,076 after taxes on each vehicle. Ford made $534 and GM [General Motors], which four years ago was losing nearly $200 on each vehicle it sold, pocketed $242 per vehicle. 'It's because of product mix,' said Jim Harbour, chairman of the Troy-based manufacturing consulting firm. 'The Big Three are selling high-profit trucks and sport-utility vehicles that the Japanese don't have yet.'" (p3 secE)

Konrad, Rachel. "Business: Harbour Report: Japanese Hold Edge on Big 3." Detroit Free Press 12 Jun 1997. p1,3 secE.

AUTOMOBILE INDUSTRY AND TRADE--ASIA (v26)

AUTOMOBILE INDUSTRY AND TRADE--AUSTRALIA

According to "Motor Vehicles in Australia, 1997," by the Australian Bureau of Statistics, "in 1995-96, there were 302,551 passenger vehicles manufactured in Australia. The value of vehicles imported into Australia in 1995-96 was $6,200 million, comprising 8 per cent of total imports. By contrast, exports amounted to $686 million or just 0.9 per cent of total exports. Total motor vehicle retailing and services employed over 215,000 persons in 1991-92, paying out $3,630 million in wages and salaries, recording almost $43,700 million in turnover and operating from 37,672 establishments."

Australian Bureau of Statistics. "Motor Vehicle Related Statistics--New ABS Compendium." Media Release 27 Jun 1997. document-level access: <http://www.abs.gov.au/websitedbs/d3110125.nsf/4a255eef008309e44a255eef00061e57/abae37bef5c8b3874a2564c200793fda?OpenDocument>

AUTOMOBILE INDUSTRY AND TRADE--ENVIRONMENTAL ASPECTS (v26)

AUTOMOBILE INDUSTRY AND TRADE--ENVIRONMENTAL ASPECTS--NETHERLANDS

"The recovery surcharge paid by buyers of new cars in The Netherlands will be cut from currently 250 guilders (US $125) to 150 guilders ($75) from 1 January 1998 onward....Revenue from the surcharge has enabled the industry to set up a national network of 275 certified car dismantling companies that accept end-of-life vehicles free of charge and dispose of them in an environmentally sound way. With some 90% of all end-of-life cars in the country currently covered, industry now feels able to lower the surcharge....Companies have to pay a fee of 5 guilders (US $2.50) per standard frame or 0.17 guilders ($0.08) per kilogram of plastic delivered." (p6)

"In Brief...: Dutch Car Industry Cuts Recovery Fee; Charge for Plastic Frames Becomes Mandatory." Environment Watch: Western Europe v6 n17 5 Sep 1997. p6. (ISSN1066-6001).

AUTOMOBILE INDUSTRY AND TRADE--EUROPE (v26)

AUTOMOBILE INDUSTRY AND TRADE--JAPAN (v26)

AUTOMOBILE INDUSTRY AND TRADE--JAPAN--KOREA (SOUTH)--UNITED STATES

"U.S. automakers sold 4,400 vehicles in South Korea last year, less than 0.3 percent of the market. Sales in the first half of this year, however, were up almost 70 percent at 2,275. In

Japan, imports from Detroit's auto companies totaled 52,559 in the first half of the year, down almost 14 percent from the same period in 1996." (p1 secB)

Knox, Noelle. "Business: Automakers Upset over Increased Tax on Imported Goods." Detroit News 31 Jul 1997. p1 secB.

AUTOMOBILE INDUSTRY AND TRADE--JAPAN --UNITED STATES (v26)

AUTOMOBILE INDUSTRY AND TRADE--LABOR PRODUCTIVITY--JAPAN--UNITED STATES

"The gap is narrowing, but Japan still takes the lead over U.S. automakers when it comes to assembly line productivity. On average, it takes fewer than three workers to build a vehicle at the most efficient Japanese auto plants. All Detroit automakers need more. Nissan Motor Corp. has the most productive plant for the fourth straight year according to a yearly report...from Harbour and Associates Inc. Nissan's plant in Smyrna, Tenn., uses 2.23 workers to build one vehicle. Calculated another way, it takes Nissan workers 17.84 hours. American Honda averages 2.51 workers, or 20.08 hours, for one vehicle and Toyota Motor Manufacturing USA averages 2.67 workers, or 21.36 hours. At the other end of the productivity spectrum is General Motors Corp., which averages 3.47 workers or 27.76 hours per vehicle." (p1 secE) "Ford Motor Co., which uses 3.09 workers, or 24.72 hours, per vehicle, was the top domestic finisher. Chrysler Corp. was No. 2, with 3.29 workers, or 26.32 hours, per vehicle." (p3 secE)

Konrad, Rachel. "Business: Harbour Report: Japanese Hold Edge on Big 3." Detroit Free Press 12 Jun 1997. p1,3 secE.

AUTOMOBILE INDUSTRY AND TRADE--LATIN AMERICA (v26)

AUTOMOBILE INDUSTRY AND TRADE--UNITED STATES (v26)

In the U.S., "total retail spending on [automobile] service and repair increased 72 percent in constant 1996 dollars between 1980 and 1996, to an estimated $96.8 billion. Sales of retail replacement parts declined 13 percent, to an estimated $56.9 billion in 1996. Replacement glass is a much smaller segment of the auto-repair market, but its sales grew at a fast clip, also. Glass sales increased 59 percent, from $1.7 billion in 1980 to an estimated $2.7 billion in 1996....Tires are the largest aftermarket sales category after 'other' parts, with 1995 sales of $17.7 billion. That reflects a 3 percent decline in constant dollars from 1993. Steeper drops occurred in exhaust system parts and heating and cooling parts. Both fell 10 percent, to $2.1 billion and $2.3 billion, respectively." (p58)

Wellner, Alison Stein. "Keeping Old Cars on the Road." American Demographics v19 n7 Jul 1997. p53-55,57-58. article-level access: <http://www.demographics.com/publications/ad/97_ad/9707_ad/ad970715.htm> (ISSN0163-4089).

In the U.S., the aftermarket auto parts "industry as a whole only experienced a 3 percent increase in sales between 1994 and 1995 to $188 billion, while in other recent years, one-year growth has been as high as 10 percent....The Automotive Parts and Accessories Association (APAA) reports that long-lasting parts have cut into sales in certain segments of the replacement-part market, such as exhaust system parts, engine hard parts, and general service parts. Although sales of replacement parts totaled more than $76 billion in 1995, they increased less than 1 percent from the previous year....Americans spent $54.5 billion in automobile repair shops in 1994, a 10 percent increase from the previous year, according to the parts association. That figure does not include spending on repairs done at gasoline stations. About three-fourths of the 12,000 independent service repair shops belonging to the Automotive Service Association (ASA), had a one-year sales increase in 1996, says Monica Buchholz, the association's vice president of communication. Eighty-five percent expect increased sales in 1997." (p54)

Wellner, Alison Stein. "Keeping Old Cars on the Road." American Demographics v19 n7 Jul 1997. p53-55,57-58. article-level access: <http://www.demographics.com/publications/ad/97_ad/9707_ad/ad970715.htm> (ISSN0163-4089).

"Nearly 80,000 Americans work for 275 Japanese-owned auto suppliers operating in the United States, the University of Michigan estimates. Of those plants, 12.3 percent are unionized." (p12 secA)

Howes, Daniel/Phillips, Dave. "The Shrinking UAW: Membership: One-Time Symbol of Labor Strength Being Outmanned." Detroit News and Free Press 13 Jul 1997. p12 secA.

In the U.S., in 1997, "Lexus is getting a 40 percent jump in sales....Cadillac sales are up 6.3 percent so far this year. Mercedes-Benz sales have risen 23.5 percent in North America....For the first time, the German firm expects to sell 100,000 cars on this side of the Atlantic. Prices run $30,000 to $133,000. BMW, another German maker of luxury cars, broke the 100,000 sales mark in North America for the first time last year." (p9)

Francis, David R. "'Wealth Effect' Buoys Sales of Yachts and BMWs." The Christian Science Monitor v89 n186 20 Aug 1997. p9. The Christian Science Monitor search engine: <http://www.csmonitor.com/plweb-cgi/iops1.pl> To retrieve this article, enter the following search: ED=19970820 AND yachts. In the "retrieved list," click the title that matches this record. (ISSN0882-7729).

AUTOMOBILE LICENSE PLATES--OHIO (v26)

AUTOMOBILE MECHANICS--UNITED STATES

In the U.S., "federal labor officials estimate a shortage of more than 60,000 qualified mechanics...[in 1997,] with as many as 2,000 more jobs going unmet in following years. That's despite estimates that 126,000 more auto technicians will be employed six years from now than there were in 1994. Michigan is expected to see an average of 1,080 auto repair jobs come open each year through 2005." (p3 secB)

Taylor, April. "Inside Business: Contest Recruits Auto Students." Detroit News 17 Jun 1997. p3 secB.

AUTOMOBILE PARKING

see also SHOPPING CENTER PARKING FACILITIES

AUTOMOBILE PARKING--IOWA--IOWA CITY

"In 1983, Iowa City established six neighborhood commercial districts within two miles of downtown, each covering seven acres and serving residents within a one-mile radius....In 1995, after studying parking within the six districts, the city reduced parking requirements there by one third. Within each district, banks, offices, groceries, and other stores must provide one parking space for every 300 square feet of business use; outside the districts, the requirement is one parking space for each 200 square feet. 'It's not a drastic reduction,'...[Jeffrey Davidson, American Institute of Certified Planners--who is both the city's assistant planning director and the director of the Johnson County Council of Governments] says. 'But it's enough to reflect that five to 20 percent of [people who visit the districts] will walk or bike there...'....Elsewhere, the city's minimum of one space per 200 feet of office or retail use is among the highest in the nation." (p14)

Wormser, Lisa. "Planning Practice: Don't Even Think of Parking Here." Planning v63 n6 Jun 1997. p10-15. (ISSN0001-2610).

"Iowa City's population of 60,000 includes 20,000 University of Iowa students. Every five years the city takes a hard look at its downtown parking supply. Exactly 9,592 spaces are available downtown, but commercial parking lots are not allowed there. Instead, the city provides 733 metered spaces and 870 unmetered spaces on the street and 2,453 off-street spaces in municipal lots and structures. The university provides 2,125 spaces. Private spaces--mostly for retail, apartment, and office buildings--number 3,411. Overall, non-university parking has increased by about 11 percent downtown since 1988." (p13)

Wormser, Lisa. "Planning Practice: Don't Even Think of Parking Here." Planning v63 n6 Jun 1997. p10-15. (ISSN0001-2610).

AUTOMOBILE PARKING--UNITED STATES

Richard Willson and the Washington based COMSIS Corporation, say each unused parking space in the U.S., "wastes $600 to $900 a year in land development costs; vacant spaces in parking structures cost more....A 1995 survey conducted by the city of Olympia, Washington, found that over half the city's commercial sites were devoted to parking and driveways. In auto-dependent Texas and California, office and shopping developments typically have nearly twice the parking they need,...and in Seattle, there are 36 percent more spaces than cars to fill them." (p12) Seventy-four communities in the Midwest "exceed local demand by 16 to 63 percent--with retail having the lowest discrepancy and multifamily housing the highest." (p13)

Wormser, Lisa. "Planning Practice: Don't Even Think of Parking Here." Planning v63 n6 Jun 1997. p10-15. (ISSN0001-2610).

AUTOMOBILE SAFETY BELTS

see AUTOMOBILES--SEAT BELTS

AUTOMOBILE SUPPLIES INDUSTRY--UNITED STATES (v26)

AUTOMOBILE THEFT

see also THEFT FROM MOTOR VEHICLES

AUTOMOBILE THEFT--MICHIGAN

According to an insurance trade group report issued in October 1997, "the number of vehicles stolen in Michigan last year--62,930--was the highest since 1991....That's well below the peak in 1986, when thieves made off with more than 72,000 vehicles....Michigan motorists pay an average of about $150 a year to cover theft and fraud losses, according to the insurance association. Last year the value of vehicles stolen in Michigan was more than $455 million." (p2 secB)

Laitner, Bill. "Cities & Counties: Car Crooks Thrived in '96: Detroit Thefts Pushed Up State's Rate." Detroit Free Press 14 Oct 1997. p2 secB.

AUTOMOBILE THEFT--MICHIGAN--DETROIT

In Michigan, from 1996 to 1997, Wayne County's automobile "theft rate jumped 13.4 percent, with most of that rise blamed on thefts in Detroit,...[Michigan Association of Insurance Agents] spokesman Gary Mitchell said. 'If you took away the auto theft in Detroit, auto theft in the rest of Wayne County would have increased just 0.7 percent last year, and that includes Highland Park and Hamtramck,' Mitchell said....Auto thefts were down 4.4 percent in Macomb County and 7.5 percent in Oakland County." (p2 secB)

Laitner, Bill. "Cities & Counties: Car Crooks Thrived in '96: Detroit Thefts Pushed Up State's Rate." Detroit Free Press 14 Oct 1997. p2 secB.

THE DETROIT NEWS "reported that auto thefts increased 9 percent last year in Michigan, following nine consecutive years of decline. The rate of increase in Detroit...was almost double the state average....According to THE [DETROIT] NEWS' report, 62,930 vehicles, valued at some $455 million, were stolen statewide last year, the highest number since 1991. More than half of all cars and trucks stolen, 34,265, were taken in Detroit. The Detroit number represents an increase of 17 percent over the previous year. And for the first eight months of 1997, car thefts in the Motor City were up another 1 percent. Oakland County's auto theft rate, by comparison, fell by 7.4 percent, down nearly 25 percent since 1990. Macomb County's rate dropped 4.4 percent, down 45 percent during the same period." (p8 secA)

"The Price of Auto Theft." Detroit News 21 Oct 1997. p8 secA.

AUTOMOBILE THEFT--MICHIGAN--MACOMB COUNTY (v26)

AUTOMOBILE TRAVEL--CALIFORNIA--LOS ANGELES (v26)

AUTOMOBILE TRAVEL--MICHIGAN (v26)

AUTOMOBILE TRAVEL--UNITED STATES

"Two-thirds of American adults took a leisure trip of 100 or more miles one way by car last year. Men are slightly more likely than women to hit the open road, at 70 percent and 62 percent, respectively. Almost three in four married people took a car trip for fun in 1996....Those who aren't married are less likely to take road trips, at 56 percent. Whites take road trips at an average pace, 68 percent, but non-whites travel at the same lower-than-average rate as unmarried people, 56 percent....Six in ten adults aged 18 to 24 went on a leisure car trip in the past year, and the share rises to about eight in ten adults aged 55 to 64. However, only about half of seniors aged 65 and older made a lengthy car trip for leisure in the past year....Nine percent of those who took no road trips in 1996 list other reasons that prevent them from hitting the road, such as car problems or small children at home. An additional 15 percent have no problems with road trips; they just don't want to take them. The youngest and oldest adults are most content to stay put. Twenty-one percent of those aged 18 to 24 and 25 percent of those aged 65 and older say they didn't want to go anywhere, compared with 15 percent of all nonroadtrippers." (p44)

Fisher, Christy. "The Not-So-Great American Road Trip." American Demographics v19 n5 May 1997. p42-48. article-level access: <http://www.demographics.com/Publications/AD/97_ad/9705_ad/AD970531.htm> (ISSN0163-4089).

In the U.S., "less than one-third of households with incomes below $15,000 took a road trip last year, compared with eight in ten households with incomes of $40,000 or more....Seven in ten adults who work full-time or part-time took a road trip in the previous year, compared with 57 percent of retirees and 53 percent of adults who do not work--mostly homemakers and students. Money is clearly one of the biggest deterrents to the one-third of adults who don't take road trips, mentioned by 25 percent. But it's not the biggest obstacle. Twenty-seven percent of those who don't take trips say they don't have time. Younger adults are more likely to say they are pressed for time. More than half of adults aged 18 to 24 say they are too busy to get away, but only 6 percent of those aged 65 and older say time is a problem." (p44)

Fisher, Christy. "The Not-So-Great American Road Trip." American Demographics v19 n5 May 1997. p42-48. article-level access: <http://www.demographics.com/Publications/AD/97_ad/9705_ad/AD970531.htm> (ISSN0163-4089).

AUTOMOBILE TRAVEL--UNITED STATES--EMPLOYEES (v26)

AUTOMOBILE TRAVEL--UNITED STATES--PUBLIC OPINION

A 1997 survey, conducted for AMERICAN DEMOGRAPHICS by Market Facts, found that "when asked what bothers car leisure travelers the most about road trips, 11 percent say nothing--they enjoy the experience without reservations....An overwhelming three in four grievances regarding road trips revolve around driving. Twenty-two percent are irritated by traffic and other drivers, closely followed by 21 percent who are bothered by the driving process itself. Eighteen percent are annoyed by the length of time spent in the car, while 12 percent are concerned about road conditions and safety. Only 16 percent find fault with roadside hospitality services...." (p43)

Fisher, Christy. "The Not-So-Great American Road Trip."

American Demographics v19 n5 May 1997. p42-48. article-level access: <http://www.demographics.com/Publications/AD/97_ad/9705_ad/AD970531.htm> (ISSN0163-4089).

In the U.S., "the people most likely to take road trips are also most likely to have no complaints about them. Twenty-three percent of car travelers aged 55 to 64 say they like road trips and can think of nothing that bothers them about the experience. Fourteen percent of those aged 65 and older are also completely satisfied with the experience. Car travel enjoyment is significantly higher among retirees and those who do not work, at 17 percent each, than among those who work full-time or part-time, at 10 percent and 2 percent, respectively." (p44) "Only 7 percent of car travelers with kids at home report having a trouble-free time on the road. Although just 3 percent of respondents specifically mention children as the primary source of annoyance on a road trip....Younger travelers are more irritated by the length of time spent in the car and the driving process itself. Thirty-two percent of travelers aged 18 to 24 are impatient with the length of time spent in the car, but only about 10 percent of travelers 55 and older consider it a problem. Driving also bothers 25 percent of 18-to-34-year-old car travelers, compared with only 16 percent of travelers aged 55 and older." (p45)

Fisher, Christy. "The Not-So-Great American Road Trip." American Demographics v19 n5 May 1997. p42-48. article-level access: <http://www.demographics.com/Publications/AD/97_ad/9705_ad/AD970531.htm> (ISSN0163-4089).

AUTOMOBILES (v26)

see also LIMOUSINES

"The motor car is one of the main users of oil. Over the last ten years, 132 million cars have come onto the world's roads. OECD countries currently have car ownership rates of 494 vehicles per 1,000 people, non-OECD countries 23 per 1,000....Recent indications are that by the year 2006 there will [be] one billion vehicles worldwide. Car ownership in the Asia-Pacific region is set to rocket from 25 million in 1995 to 70 million by the year 2010, fueling a demand for oil faster than anywhere else in the world." (p99)

Rowell, Andrew. "Crude Operators: The Future of the Oil Industry." Ecologist v27 n3 May-Jun 1997. p99-100,102,105-106. (ISSN0261-3131).

AUTOMOBILES--AUSTRALIA

According to "Motor Vehicles in Australia, 1997," by the Australian Bureau of Statistics, "in the 12 months to 30 September 1995, the [automobile] fleet travelled an estimated total of 164,988 million kilometres with the petrol powered vehicles consuming an estimated 15,180 million litres of fuel. Male drivers/riders accounted for just under 70 per cent of the total distance travelled."

Australian Bureau of Statistics. "Motor Vehicle Related Statistics--New ABS Compendium." Media Release 27 Jun 1997. document-level access: <http://www.abs.gov.au/websitedbs/d3110125.nsf/4a255eef008309e44a255eef00061e57/abae37bef5c8b3874a2564c200793fda?OpenDocument>

AUTOMOBILES--BRAZIL (v26)

AUTOMOBILES--BRAZIL--SAO PAULO (v26)

AUTOMOBILES--CHINA (v26)

AUTOMOBILES--ENVIRONMENTAL ASPECTS (v26)

AUTOMOBILES--ENVIRONMENTAL ASPECTS--CHINA --INDIA (v26)

AUTOMOBILES--ENVIRONMENTAL ASPECTS--GREAT BRITAIN (v26)

AUTOMOBILES--ENVIRONMENTAL ASPECTS--UNITED STATES (v26)

AUTOMOBILES--FIRES AND FIRE PREVENTION --MICHIGAN--DETROIT (v26)

AUTOMOBILES--IRELAND

According to Ireland's Central Statistics Office, "Meath (78%) had the highest number of households with the use of at least one car in 1991, followed by Fingal in North County Dublin (77%) and Dun Laoghaire--Rathdown (76%). Less than half the households in Dublin city (44.5%) and in Limerick city (46.2%) had a car. Almost three quarters of rural households had at least one car in 1991, compared with six out of every ten urban households, underscoring the importance of a car in rural areas. Households where the head was a higher professional had the highest car ownership (92.2%) of all socio-economic groups, followed by employers and managers (91.3%). Half the households where the head was an unskilled manual worker had a car. The trend in car ownership was up steadily between 1986 and 1991. In 1986 only 56.8% of urban households had a car compared with 71.8% for rural households. This had risen to 59.5% and 74.6%, respectively, by 1991."

Ireland. Central Statistics Office. "Census 1991--Volume 11: Travel to Work, School and College." Press Release 10 Jul 1997. document-level access: <http://www.cso.ie/pressreleases/prelcentrav.html>

AUTOMOBILES--MICHIGAN--MOTORS--ALTERNATE FUELS

In Michigan, "of the 241 state vehicles that run on power sources other than gasoline, 114--or 47 percent--are electric Cushman carts, similar to golf carts....The U.S. Energy Department says the carts are not what Congress had in mind when it passed the Energy Policy Act of 1992 to get states to help boost the market for alternative-fuel cars....Michigan met this year's 10-percent requirement largely because Congress amended the law to give states credit for alternative-fuel vehicles already purchased. Next year, states will be required to guarantee 15 percent of their new vehicles run on alternative fuels. By 2001, it rises to 75 percent." (p4 secA)

Cole, Kenneth. "State Says Carts Count in Mandate." Detroit News 11 Nov 1997. p4 secA.

AUTOMOBILES--MICHIGAN--SEAT BELTS

"About 71 percent of Michigan drivers wear their seat belts....Last year, 1,025 people died in Michigan in car crashes, 56 of them were unbelted." (p1 secB)

Knox, Noelle. "The Metro: Push On for Tougher Seat Belt Laws." Detroit News 29 Jun 1997. p1 secB.

According to Anne Readett, public information specialist for the Office of Highway Safety Planning for the Michigan State Police, "70.8 percent of Michigan drivers wore their [seat] belts in 1996. In 1997, that number has dipped slightly to 70.1 percent. Wayne County has the lowest rate in the state, at 63 percent. At 75.6 percent, seat belt usage is highest in Oakland, Washtenaw, Kalamazoo and Ingham counties. Using a seat belt reduces the risk of fatal injury to front seat passengers by 45 percent, and of moderate to critical injury by 50 percent, Readett said." (p8 secC)

Greenwood, Tom. "Wayne: MetroLife: Commuting: Don't Become a Statistic; Wear Your Seat Belt." Detroit News 10 Dec 1997. p8 secC.

In Michigan, "a new survey shows that seat belt use is leveling off among state drivers after rising annually for nearly a decade. A University of Michigan study conducted in September [1997] shows use has dipped to 70.1 from 70.8 percent last year....State drivers have been required to wear seat belts since 1985. The law requires all front-seat passengers to buckle up, regardless of age, and infants under 1 year old must be strapped in an approved safety seat. Compliance rates had been rising steadily since 1988, officials said. Police have been issuing $50 seat belt tickets to drivers pulled over for a primary traffic offense like speeding." (p3 secC)

Garrett, Craig. "City & Suburban News: In Michigan: Seat Belt Use Dips despite Enforcement and Education." Detroit News 6 Oct 1997. p3 secC.

In an annual study of about 10,300 drivers and front-seat passengers in Michigan's 28 most populous counties, David W. Eby of the University of Michigan Transportation Research Institute "and colleague Michelle L. Hopp found that the rate of safety belt use has held steady at about 70 percent for all drivers of passenger cars, sport-utility vehicles (SUVs) and vans/minivans, while the rate for pickup truck drivers improved from less than 48 percent in 1996 to more than 56 percent in 1997. In addition, the percentage of drivers under age 30 who wear safety belts increased from about 59 percent in 1996 to nearly 65 percent this year. The largest percentage increase for young motorists was reported for drivers of vans/minivans (from less than 52 percent in 1996 to about 79 percent in 1997) and pickup trucks (from 42.5 percent last year to more than 51 percent this year)." (p1) "According to the study, about three-fourths of women driving passenger cars, SUVs and vans/minivans wear their safety belts, while less than two-thirds of men in those vehicles buckle up. For drivers of pickup trucks, the rates are about 65 percent for women and 54 percent for men. The most notable gender difference, Eby says, is in the 16- to 29-year-old age group, where the estimated belt-use rate is 12.9 percentage points higher for females (72.6 percent) than for males (59.7)." (p2)

University of Michigan. News and Information Services. "Safety Belt Use Is on the Rise for those Michigan Drivers Least Likely to Buckle Up, A U-M Study Shows." University of Michigan News Release 15 Dec 1997. p1-2.

AUTOMOBILES--PRICES--UNITED STATES (v26)

In the U.S., "the average price of a new car this year is up less than 1 percent, the lowest in several years....Overall auto rebates are up 30 percent over last year, and although the average price of a new car is $21,000, car buyers are able to pay off their purchase faster. The average-priced vehicle was paid off with 26.2 weeks of pay during the first quarter this year, down from 27.5 weeks a year ago, according to a survey by Comerica Bank." (p6 secA)

Fix, Janet L. "A Golden Age for Making Money Rolls On: Prices: Whatever Happened to Inflation?: Not since the Mid-1960s...This Low." Detroit Free Press 17 Jul 1997. p1,6 secA.

AUTOMOBILES--RECYCLING--MICHIGAN--DETROIT

"Coming soon to a Metro Detroit highway: a smoother ride, thanks to 15 tons of recycled car parts under your wheels....Every year, some 11 million cars in the United States are scrapped, with steel companies utilizing about 75 percent of the car. The remaining 25 percent--some 4.5 million tons--ends up in landfills....New roads are typically 94-percent gravel and stone and 6-percent asphalt, or the hot tar hydrocarbon 'glue' that keeps the road together. Under the process tested at U-D [University of Detroit Mercy], researchers will mix 30-percent heavy automotive residue, which is rubber, plastics, glass and dirt (found in the car) with the gravel and 6-percent light 'ASR,' which is foam, fabrics, padding and plastic, with the asphalt....The car-part payment is $47.95 a ton, or about 20 percent higher than the conventional pavement, $40.20." (p4 secA)

Shepardson, David. "Road to Repair: Research: New Pavement Uses Recycled Automobile Parts." Detroit News 16 Sep 1997. p4 secA.

AUTOMOBILES--RECYCLING--UNITED STATES (v26)

AUTOMOBILES--RUSSIA

"Whenever per-capita income in a country reaches around $6,000 a year, car sales rise steeply. At $5,300, Russia's per-capita income is slightly lower, but still follows the pattern....Officials here project an increase of 10,000 privately owned autos a year. And in the nation's capital, Moscow, the 3 million private cars clogging the streets will rise another million by 2005, according to officials at City Hall....With nearly twice as many cars on the road today as when the Soviet era ended in 1991, reported accidents have increased by 50 percent." (p7)

Colin, Molly. "International: Car Culture in Russia Shifts into High Gear." The Christian Science Monitor v90 n24 30 Dec 1997. p7. The Christian Science Monitor search engine: <http://www.csmonitor.com/plweb-cgi/iops1.pl> To retrieve this article, enter the following search: ED=19971230 AND gear. In the "retrieved list," click the title that matches this record. (ISSN0882-7729).

AUTOMOBILES--SWEDEN (v26)

AUTOMOBILES--UNITED STATES

In the U.S., "the price of new vehicles is soaring. The average retail price of a 1997 vehicle was almost $22,000, up 7.3 percent from 1996, according to the National Automobile Dealers Association. In 1992, a new car would have cost closer to $17,000....More than three in ten new vehicles are leased, says Donna Reichle, media relations manager for the National Automobile Dealers Association....About 3 million leased cars will be returned to dealers in 1997, and 'consumers are just snapping them up,' Reichle says....Borrowing heavily to finance a new car may be impossible for many Americans, who are already loaded with consumer debt. In November 1996, U.S. consumer debt totaled more than $1.19 trillion, according to the Federal Reserve. The Consumer Federation of America estimates average household consumer debt at $6,000." (p53-54)

Wellner, Alison Stein. "Keeping Old Cars on the Road." American Demographics v19 n7 Jul 1997. p53-55,57-58. article-level access: <http://www.demographics.com/publications/ad/97_ad/9707_ad/ad970715.htm> (ISSN0163-4089).

AUTOMOBILES--UNITED STATES--COST OF OPERATION (v26)

"U.S. households spend an average of $653 a year on vehicle maintenance, whether they do it themselves, pay a professional, or a combination of the two. All told, U.S. consumers spent an estimated $196 billion in 1996 on gasoline, tires, replacement parts, touch-up paint, and the like. Their spending in the automotive aftermarket has more than doubled, from $88 billion in 1980....The median age of the U.S. vehicle fleet is almost eight years....In 1995, there were 193 million vehicles registered in the U.S. That represents an all-time record, and up more than 4.7 million vehicles from the year before." (p53)

Wellner, Alison Stein. "Keeping Old Cars on the Road." American Demographics v19 n7 Jul 1997. p53-55,57-58. article-level access: <http://www.demographics.com/publications/ad/97_ad/9707_ad/ad970715.htm> (ISSN0163-4089).

AUTOMOBILES--UNITED STATES--DESIGN AND CONSTRUCTION--MORTALITY (v26)

AUTOMOBILES--UNITED STATES--FUEL CONSUMPTION (v26)

"In 1996, the United States' automobiles, minivans, and sport utility vehicles burned 15 quadrillion British thermal units (quads) of gasoline, two-thirds of the nation's petroleum consumption. Total U.S. energy use was nearly 90 quads that year. Half of the United States' petroleum comes from abroad, and the cost of importing oil is $100,000 every minute, says Jason Mark, a transportation analyst with the Union of Concerned Scientists' Berkeley, California, office....Fuel accounts for only 15% of the cost of car ownership." (p582)

Holzman, David/U.S. National Institute of Environmental Health Sciences. "Focus: A Driving Force." Environmental Health Perspectives v105 n6 Jun 1997. p582-587. article-level access: <http://ehpnet1.niehs.nih.gov/docs/1997/105-6/focus-abs.html>

"Although U.S. vehicle fuel economy increased by 8 percent between 1988 and 1994, U.S. households consumed more fuel in 1994 than in preceding years because they drove more miles. This result is from the 1994 Residential Transportation Energy Consumption Survey, a national sample survey representing the characteristics of the 84.9 million households nationwide that owned or had access to vehicles....Older vehicles represent a smaller share of the vehicle stock, down to 13 percent in 1994 from 23 percent in 1991, and they tend to be driven fewer miles than the new vehicles replacing them....Passenger cars, at a 68-percent share in 1994, continued to dominate the fleet, but to a lesser extent than in 1988, when their share was 74 percent. In contrast, growth in the share of minivans and sport-utility vehicles between 1988 and 1994 was dramatic, rising from 5 percent of the total vehicle stock in 1988 to 11 percent in 1994." (unpaginated)

U.S. Dept. of Energy. Energy Information Administration. "Energy Plug: Household Vehicles Energy Consumption 1994." Monthly Energy Review Aug 1997. (ISSN0095-7356).

AUTOMOBILES--UNITED STATES--FUEL CONSUMPTION --LAW AND LEGISLATION (v26)

The U.S. "Congress sets the fuel-efficiency standards for cars, known as corporate average fuel economy or CAFE standards. Passenger cars produced by automakers currently must average 27.5 miles per gallon on the highway. But CAFE standards for trucks don't have to be approved by Congress, according to...[Richard Klimisch, a chemist and vice president of engineering affairs for the American Automobile Manufacturers Association]. Light trucks--those most popular among buyers now as pickups, minivans and sport-utility vehicles--must average 20.7 miles per gallon. Almost half the vehicles sold in the United States now are classified as trucks....Minivans with six-cylinder engines get about 24 miles per gallon on the highway; full-size pickups with small V8 engines get about 18 or 19 miles per gallon--less if they have four-wheel drive or bigger engines." (p8 secA)

Craig, Charlotte W./Konrad, Rachel. "Big 3 Feel Heat of Global Warming." Detroit Free Press 12 Dec 1997. p1,8 secA.

AUTOMOBILES--UNITED STATES--MAINTENANCE AND REPAIR

In the U.S., "one-fourth of car-owning women aged 18 and older bought a part or accessory in the past year that was installed by someone else in their household....Eleven percent of male car owners who bought a part had it installed by another household member....More than six in ten women car owners have shopped for auto parts in the past year, and they are just as likely to handle the installation themselves as to ask another household member, at 28 percent versus 25 percent. Women are less likely than men to buy motor oil--50 percent, compared with 64 percent of men. Female car owners are also less likely than men to buy several other auto-maintenance necessities, but not by much. Thirty-six percent buy anti-freeze, compared with 44 percent of men; 22 percent purchase batteries, as do 28 percent of men; and 17 percent buy spark plugs, versus 29 percent of men." (p57-58)

Wellner, Alison Stein. "Keeping Old Cars on the Road." American Demographics v19 n7 Jul 1997. p53-55,57-58. article-level access: <http://www.demographics.com/publications/ad/97_ad/9707_ad/ad970715.htm> (ISSN0163-4089).

AUTOMOBILES--UNITED STATES--MOTORS --ALTERNATE FUELS (v26)

When 1997 ends, U.S. "federal agencies will have fallen 17 percent short of their four-year mandate to buy about 34,500 vehicles that run on alternatives to gasoline, according to Energy Department estimates." (p1 secA) "The Energy Policy Act of 1992 prescribed specific purchasing goals for U.S. and state governments. The federal target is limited to the country's 125 cities with populations of at least 250,000, including Detroit. The U.S. government had to ensure a certain number of the new vehicles it purchased for its agencies in those cities ran on alternative fuels. Federal agencies usually buy about 20,000 new vehicles for use in those cities each year. From 1993 to today, the U.S. government had to buy roughly 34,500 alternative-fuel vehicles....[Lee Slezac, manager of federal fleet alternative-fuel vehicle programs,] said it only bought 28,000, and just 22,000 of those are in use. That's less than one of every 10 U.S. government vehicles subject to the 1992 energy act, which doesn't apply to heavy trucks or law enforcement autos." (p4 secA)

Cole, Kenneth. "Feds Drag Feet on Alternative Fuel." Detroit News 11 Nov 1997. p1,4 secA.

"An estimated 385,744 alternative fueled vehicles are currently in use in the United States, according to ALTERNATIVES TO TRADITIONAL TRANSPORTATION FUELS 1995, a December 1996 publication of the Energy Information Administration. These include 273,000 vehicles that run on liquid petroleum gases, 81,000 that run on compressed natural gas, 26,000 that run on 85% alcohol, and 3,900 electric vehicles (EVs)." (p582)

Holzman, David/U.S. National Institute of Environmental Health Sciences. "Focus: A Driving Force." Environmental Health Perspectives v105 n6 Jun 1997. p582-587. article-level access: <http://ehpnet1.niehs.nih.gov/docs/1997/105-6/focus-abs.html>

AUTOMOBILES--UNITED STATES--SEAT BELTS (v26)

"Injuries and fatalities involving people who fail to buckle up cost Americans $14.3 billion a year in higher medical and insurance costs and taxes....Nationwide, only 68 percent of people on the road wear seat belts. President [Bill] Clinton has vowed to boost that figure to 85 percent by 2000, an increase the administration says will save 4,200 lives and $6.7 billion in medical costs." (p2 secB)

"Inside Business: Unused Belts Costly to Society." Detroit News 26 Nov 1997. p2 secB.

"According to the National Safety Council, 9,800 car occupants more than four years old were saved by seat belts [in the U.S.] in 1995. Another 9,000 could have been saved had they been wearing their belts." (p1)

"Prevention Takes Practice." People's Medical Society Newsletter v16 n6 Dec 1997. p1,6. (ISSN0736-4873).

AUTOMOBILES--UNITED STATES--SEAT BELTS --LAW AND LEGISLATION (v26)

AUTOMOBILES, ELECTRIC (v26)

AUTOMOBILES, THEFT FROM

see THEFT FROM MOTOR VEHICLES

AUTONOMY--SCOTLAND--PUBLIC OPINION (v26)

AUTOPSY--UNITED STATES (v26)

AVIATION ACCIDENTS

see AIRCRAFT ACCIDENTS

AVIATION INDUSTRY

see AIRLINES

AVOCADO INDUSTRY--CALIFORNIA (v26)

"In the U.S. over 90 percent of all avocado trees are in California, with roughly half of U.S. production located in San Diego County....California yields are...about 5 metric tons per hectare." (p22) "Total California shipments from November 1996 to March 1, 1997 were up 12 percent from the previous year, with prices down 3 percent. For the Hass variety, shipments were up 10 percent and prices down 5 percent." (p23)

Plunkett, Daniel/U.S. Dept. of Agriculture. Economic Research Service. "World Agriculture & Trade: U.S. & Mexican Avocado Sectors: A Comparison." Agricultural

Outlook Jun 1997. p22-23.

AVOCADO INDUSTRY--CHILE--UNITED STATES

"The U.S. imported 25,000 tons of fresh avocados worth $23 million from all sources during calendar 1996, about 15 percent of domestic demand. In the past few years, Chile has been supplying about two-thirds of U.S. avocado imports, mainly during September-December. During the 1990's, Chile exported an average 13,000 tons of fresh avocados to the U.S., with 40 percent entering during November and December. Chilean avocados face a U.S. tariff of 12.9 cents per kilogram, as opposed to the 7.9 cents/kg tariff for Mexico...." (p23)

Plunkett, Daniel/U.S. Dept. of Agriculture. Economic Research Service. "World Agriculture & Trade: U.S. & Mexican Avocado Sectors: A Comparison." Agricultural Outlook Jun 1997. p22-23.

AVOCADO INDUSTRY--FLORIDA (v26)

AVOCADO INDUSTRY--MEXICO--UNITED STATES

"Mexico is the world's largest avocado producer and second-largest exporter, accounting for about 67 percent of global production and 24 percent of world trade in 1995/96. Mexico currently exports about 7 percent of total production, mainly to Europe, Canada, and Japan. The U.S. is the second-largest producer of avocados (about 15 percent of world production) and the sixth-largest exporter (5 percent of global trade). The U.S. exports about 5 to 7 percent of production, with the EU, Japan, and Canada the most important markets. Mexican per capita consumption is about 7 kilograms per person, compared with U.S. consumption of less than 1 kilogram....Mexico produces mainly the Hass variety, with over 85 percent grown in the state of Michoacan near Mexico City....At a national level, Mexican yields are typically 7 to 9 metric tons per hectare, although a mature orchard with 8-year-old trees generally averages 15 tons per hectare." (p22)

Plunkett, Daniel/U.S. Dept. of Agriculture. Economic Research Service. "World Agriculture & Trade: U.S. & Mexican Avocado Sectors: A Comparison." Agricultural Outlook Jun 1997. p22-23.

AVOCADO INDUSTRY--UNITED STATES (v26)

AWARD AND ARBITRATION

see ARBITRATION AND AWARD

BABIES

see INFANTS

BABIES, TEST TUBE

see FERTILIZATION IN VITRO, HUMAN

BABY BOOM GENERATION--UNITED STATES --ATTITUDES (v26)

BABY BUST GENERATION

see GENERATION X

BABY FOODS INDUSTRY--UNITED STATES

"In the United States, retail sales of baby food exceeded $1.2 billion in 1995. Fruits and juices accounted for 40 percent of these sales....Meats and combination meals were second with slightly more than 27 percent of baby food sales, followed by vegetables with nearly 14 percent, desserts with slightly more than 10 percent, and infant cereals with more than 8 percent. Supermarkets are the primary retail outlet for baby foods in the United States (supermarkets are large grocery stores offering a variety of food and nonfood products with annual sales of $2 million or more). About 60 percent of baby food fruits and juices are sold in supermarkets. Another 25 percent of baby food fruit and juice sales occur in grocery stores (foodstores with less than $2 million in sales, excluding club stores, specialty foodstores, and drug stores). Grocery stores and supermarkets account for about 90 percent of retail sales of baby food fruits and juices. Sales for other baby food product categories range from 59 to 64 percent sold in supermarkets and 24 to 25 percent sold in grocery stores. Desserts have the smallest share of baby food sales in supermarkets and grocery stores--59 percent and 24 percent, respectively." (p14)

Harris, J. Michael/U.S. Dept. of Agriculture. Economic Research Service. "Food Prices: Consumers Pay a Premium for Organic Baby Foods." Food Review v20 n2 May-Aug 1997. p13-16. (ISSN1056-327X).

BACKACHE--UNITED STATES (v26)

BAGELS--UNITED STATES (v26)

BAHAI FAITH (v26)

BAHIA (BRAZIL : STATE)--ECONOMIC CONDITIONS --SOCIAL CONDITIONS (v26)

BAHRAIN--ECONOMIC CONDITIONS

"THE ECONOMIST recently estimated that unemployment rates may be as high as 30 percent [in Bahrain]--almost exclusively among Shi'a young men....The number of offshore banking units operating in Bahrain has dropped from a high of 75 to today's 46....Bahrain's Labor Minister, 'Abd al-Nabi al-Shu'ala, in a recent speech, said that between 4,500 and 6,500 Bahrainis enter the workforce each year. At the same time, he acknowledged, his Labor Ministry every month issues 2,450 new work permits and renews 3,450 permits for expatriate workers, who still constitute two-thirds of the total workforce." (p35)

Stork, Joe. "Update: Bahrain's Crisis Worsens." Middle East Report v27 n3 Jul-Sep 1997. p33-35. (ISSN0899-2851).

BAIKAL, LAKE (RUSSIA) (v26)

BALAENOPTERA ACUTOROSTRATA--NORWAY

International Whaling Commission "scientists say the minke whale stock consists of about 900,000 worldwide, including some 118,000 in Norwegian waters, enough for a limited hunt....During the three-month whaling season that ended July 31, Norwegians grilled, pan-fried, and stewed the meat from 503 minke whales, about 100 more than last year....Only 32 boats took part in the minke whale hunt this year, their crews selling meat ashore for $3.2 million. By weight, this meat equaled only 6 percent of Norway's yearly consumption of moose." (p8)

Gibbs, Walter. "Why Norway Puts Whale on Menu." The Christian Science Monitor v89 n179 11 Aug 1997. p8. The Christian Science Monitor search engine: <http://www.csmonitor.com/plweb-cgi/iops1.pl> To retrieve this article, enter the following search: ED=19970811 AND menu. In the "retrieved list," click the title that matches this record. (ISSN0882-7729).

BALANCE OF TRADE--AFRICA--CARIBBEAN AREA --EUROPE--PACIFIC AREA (v26)

BALANCE OF TRADE--CANADA--MEXICO--UNITED STATES (v26)

BALANCE OF TRADE--CHILE--UNITED STATES (v26)

BALANCE OF TRADE--CHINA--UNITED STATES

"America's trade deficit with China continues to grow. According to recent Commerce Department figures, it totaled $21.2 billion for the first six months of 1997. This marked a $5.6 billion increase over last year, making China's trade surplus the second largest, next to Japan's." (p4)

"Economic: Chinese Deficit." Maritime Newsletter v29 n9 Sep 1997. p4. (ISSN0161-9373).

BALANCE OF TRADE--CHINA--UNITED STATES --PUBLIC OPINION (v26)

BALANCE OF TRADE--DEVELOPING COUNTRIES --EUROPE (v26)

BALANCE OF TRADE--EUROPE (v26)

BALANCE OF TRADE--EUROPE--FORMER SOVIET REPUBLICS (v26)

BALANCE OF TRADE--EUROPE--NORTH AMERICA (v26)

BALANCE OF TRADE--EUROPE--SOUTH AMERICA (v26)

BALANCE OF TRADE--ISRAEL--UNITED STATES (v26)
BALANCE OF TRADE--SOUTH AFRICA--SWITZERLAND (v26)
BALANCE OF TRADE--UNITED STATES (v26)

In the U.S., "June's trade deficit was $15 billion....The Department of Commerce estimates that the cumulative deficit for the first half of 1997 was $96.7 billion, an increase of 7 percent from the year before." (p4)

"Economic: Trade Deficit." Maritime Newsletter v29 n9 Sep 1997. p4. (ISSN0161-9373).

BALANCE OF TRADE--UNITED STATES--PUBLIC OPINION (v26)
BALDNESS--UNITED STATES

In the U.S., "a growing number of the nation's 40 million balding men and 20 million balding women are turning to drugs, hairpieces, and surgical procedures to alleviate their hair loss, in the process creating a $1.5 billion-a-year industry. Americans now spend 1 1/2 times as much money on products intended to help them keep or replenish their hair as they do on razors that remove it." (p44)

Fischer, David. "Business & Technology: The Bald Truth." U.S. News & World Report v123 n5 4 Aug 1997. p44-50. article-level access: <http://www.usnews.com/usnews/issue/970804/4HAIR.HTM> (ISSN0041-5537).

BALDNESS--UNITED STATES--MEN

"FORTUNE magazine says American men spend $9.5 billion a year on beauty products and treatment, including remedies for hair loss. A 1992 research report by Old Dominion University in Norfolk, Va., found that 85 percent of 145 balding men were self-conscious, felt helpess, and envied men with full heads of hair." (p13)

Holmstrom, David. "For the Fashion-Conscious Man, Bald Is Beautiful." The Christian Science Monitor v89 n228 21 Oct 1997. p13. The Christian Science Monitor search engine: <http://www.csmonitor.com/plweb-cgi/iops1.pl> To retrieve this article, enter the following search: ED=19971021 AND beautiful. In the "retrieved list," click the title that matches this record. (ISSN0882-7729).

BALLISTIC MISSILES

"Duncan Lennox, editor of JANE'S STRATEGIC WEAPONS SYSTEMS, estimates that 13,450 ballistic missiles are in service with thirty-four countries, and that thirty new types of ballistic missiles are in development. Short-range ballistic missiles are being augmented by medium-range (500-2,000 kilometer) missiles that promise greater accuracy, lethality, and sophistication. Currently, eighteen short-range ballistic missile types with ranges of 70-480 kilometers and ten intermediate-range ballistic missiles (or IRBMs, of 600-4,000 kilometer range) are in service--excluding French, British, and U.S. systems but including Chinese ones. Six developing countries are working on eleven follow-on short-range ballistic missiles with 100-350 kilometer ranges. Eleven countries are developing, or have the capability to develop, fifteen types of IRBMs (including Spain, France, and Japan)." (p55)

Ritcheson, Philip L. "Proliferation: Scope, Prospects, And Implications." Naval War College Review v50 n3 Sum 1997. p50-64. (ISSN0028-1484).

BAMBOO--CHINA (v26)
BANANA TRADE--CARIBBEAN AREA (v26)
BANANA TRADE--CARIBBEAN AREA--FRANCE --GREAT BRITAIN

"Bananas are one of the principal agricultural exports from the DOM [France's Departements d'Outre-Mer], accounting for 60% of the export revenue of Guadeloupe and 49% of that of Martinique (Nurse and Sandiford, 1995...). Costs of production are high, at some 0.555 ECU/kg [European currency units per kilogram], and export sales are sustained only because France has had a policy of reserving up to two-thirds of its market for DOM bananas and one-third for bananas from the African ACP [Africa-Caribbean-Pacific group of countries] (Pedler, 1995...). In 1992, France obtained 37% of its bananas from Martinique and 22% from Guadeloupe....In 1992, the principal banana exporters from the ACP Caribbean to the European Union were, in descending order: St. Lucia (29% of the ACP Caribbean total), Jamaica (17%), St. Vincent (17%), Dominica (13%), the Dominican Republic (9%), Suriname (7%), Belize (7%), and Grenada (1%) (ECommission, 1995...)....In 1992, the UK obtained 20% of its bananas from St. Lucia, 14% from Jamaica, 10% from St. Vincent, and 8% from Dominica (Stevens, 1996)." (p7-8)

Sutton, Paul. "The Banana Regime of the European Union, The Caribbean, And Latin America." Journal of Interamerican Studies & World Affairs v39 n2 Sum 1997. p5-36. (ISSN0022-1937).

BANANA TRADE--EUROPE

"The European Union is the largest importer of bananas, consuming nearly 40 per cent of all traded bananas. Former Eastern Germans eat the most, consuming about 25 kilogrammes of the fruit per capita each year. Swedes come second with 16.5 kilogrammes. North Americans...eat 13 kilogrammes per capita per year, twice as much as apples. Europe grows less than 20 per cent of the bananas it consumes. Latin American countries supply 60 percent of the European Union market, led by Ecuador (the world's largest exporter), Costa Rica, Colombia, Panama, Honduras, Nicaragua, Guatemala, and Venezuela." (p117)

Sexton, Sarah. "Report: Going Bananas." Ecologist v27 n3 May-Jun 1997. p117-118. (ISSN0261-3131).

Within the European Union, "in 1992, the highest consumption [of bananas] was in Germany, at 14.9 kg per capita, as against 8.2 kg in the UK and 8.5 kg in France; the overall average for the EU was 9.3 kg (Nurse and Sandiford, 1995...). At the same time, Germany also had the lowest prices: in August 1991 bananas cost US$ 1.3 a kilo in Germany compared to US$ 2.07 in the UK." (p12)

Sutton, Paul. "The Banana Regime of the European Union, The Caribbean, And Latin America." Journal of Interamerican Studies & World Affairs v39 n2 Sum 1997. p5-36. (ISSN0022-1937).

BANANA TRADE--EUROPE--LATIN AMERICA

"Latin America dominates the world trade in bananas; in 1990, it accounted for 75% of the world's exports....The major players in the banana trade are United Brands (Chiquita), with 35% of the world market, Standard Fruit (Dole), with 20%, and Del Monte with 15% (Nurse and Sandiford, 1995...). The 'big 5' exporters to the EU were (1) Ecuador, responsible for 28% of the bananas imported by the EU in 1992, followed by (2) Colombia with 22%, (3) Panama with 20%, (4) Costa Rica with 19%, and (5) Honduras with 8% (ECommission, 1995...). Bananas account for 36% of all export revenue in Honduras, 29% in Panama, 20% in Costa Rica, 14% in Ecuador, and 5% in Colombia (Nurse and Sandiford, 1995...)....In 1992, Germany imported 27% of its bananas from Ecuador, 17% from Panama, 17% from Colombia, 16% from Costa Rica, and 6% from Honduras (Stevens, 1996)....In 1992, 28% of...bananas [to Belgium, the Netherlands, and Luxembourg] came from Panama, 25% from Colombia, 15% from Costa Rica, 11% from Ecuador, and 7% from Honduras (Stevens, 1996)." (p9)

Sutton, Paul. "The Banana Regime of the European Union, The Caribbean, And Latin America." Journal of Interamerican Studies & World Affairs v39 n2 Sum 1997. p5-36. (ISSN0022-1937).

BANANA TRADE--HAWAII

Banana "production in Hawaii, the only place in the United States that produces bananas, stayed level with the previous year's utilized production at 13 million pounds, less than 1 percent of domestic supply. Banana acreage increased in 1996 to

1,040 acres....Hawaiian banana growers received an average of 40 cents a pound for a total crop value of $5.2 million in 1996, the same as 1995. Locally grown bananas accounted for about 44 percent of Hawaiian banana consumption." (p23-24)

U.S. Dept. of Agriculture. Economic Research Service. "Noncitrus Fruit Outlook." Fruit and Tree Nuts Situation and Outlook Report Aug 1997. p7-26.

BANANA TRADE--UNITED STATES

U.S. "banana consumption reached a record 28.2 pounds per person in 1996, up 3 percent from the previous year. Bananas continued to be the most popular fresh-market fruit consumed in the United States, followed by apples and oranges. Contributing to high banana consumption were record imports totaling 7.5 billion pounds. Retail prices for bananas averaged 50 cents a pound in 1996, about the same as a year earlier....Costa Rica continues to provide the largest share of fresh bananas for the U.S. market, accounting for 26 percent of total imports. Ecuador remains the second largest source. However, its share fell in 1996 to 22 percent, down from 25 percent in 1995. Honduras became the third largest banana supplier to the United States as imports from Colombia, previously the third most important source, declined for the third consecutive year." (p23)

U.S. Dept. of Agriculture. Economic Research Service. "Noncitrus Fruit Outlook." Fruit and Tree Nuts Situation and Outlook Report Aug 1997. p7-26.

BANGLADESH--ECONOMIC CONDITIONS

In Bangladesh, "the external current account deficit declined from more than 5 percent of GDP in FY96 to less than 3 percent in FY97. This was the result of a healthy 14 percent export growth and a significant rebound in remittances....A marginal increase in revenue and a marginal decline in expenditure led to a drop in the fiscal deficit from 5.7 percent of GDP in FY96 to 5.3 percent in FY97. In addition, net domestic financing declined from 2.2 percent of GDP to 1.9 percent....GDP growth at 5.7 percent in FY97 was the highest since the beginning of the 1990s, mostly to be attributed to a bumper harvest. At the same time, the rate of industrial growth at about 3.6 percent, however, was one of the lowest."

World Bank. "Accelerating Reforms and Exploiting Investment Opportunities Can Spur Growth and Reduce Poverty in Bangladesh." Press Release 21 Oct 1997. document-level access: <http://www.worldbank.org/html/extdr/extme/1508.htm>

BANGLADESH--SOCIAL CONDITIONS (v26)

In Bangladesh, "there has been a dramatic reduction in the infant mortality rate from 116 per 1000 births in 1988 to 75 in 1995. This has been accompanied by an increase in life expectancy at birth--from 55 to 59 years in the same period. Much of the progress at the aggregate level was propelled by the rapid growth of the immunization programme, which covered less than 3% of all children in the late 1970s and over 80% in the mid-1990s." (p28)

Sen, Binayak/Acharya, Shambhu. "Health and Poverty in Bangladesh." World Health v50 n5 Sep-Oct 1997. p28-29. (ISSN0043-8502).

BANK FRAUD--MICHIGAN

In the U.S., according to a study of FBI data conducted by Syracuse University's Transactional Records Access Clearinghouse, "of 168 bank fraud cases FBI agents developed in Michigan's eastern district, only 12.5 percent--21 cases--resulted in convictions. That compares to 15 percent nationally....Nationally, fewer than one out of seven of the FBI's bank fraud cases ended in convictions....Bank fraud represented 22.6 percent of all the cases that Detroit-based FBI agents developed last year." (p1 secA)

Bivins, Larry. "White Collar Crime Ties Up FBI." Detroit News 8 Aug 1997. p1,6 secA.

BANK INVESTMENTS--EUROPE (v26)

BANK LOANS--UNITED STATES

In the U.S., "banks and assets of less than $500 million held nearly 60 percent of all business loans under $100,000 even though they controlled only 18 percent of banking assets as of June 1996." (p19) "A recent analysis by the Federal Reserve found that banks provided a little over 60 percent of small business credit outstanding in 1993....Sixty-three percent of the business loans held by banks with less than $100 million in assets (about 85 percent of Ninth District banks at the time) were for under $100,000. In contrast, 62 percent of loans held by banks with assets greater than $1 billion were for over $1 million....Banks [in the Ninth District] with assets of less than $500 million held 80 percent of all business loans under $100,000 despite controlling only 47 percent of district assets." (p20) "A survey of senior lending officers of larger banks by the Federal Reserve in early 1997 found that a little over 70 percent of respondents used a scoring system when making small business loans, with banks over $15 billion in assets most likely to use scoring." (p22) "The amount of very small business loans (under $100,000) made by banks with assets over $5 billion increased by 16 percent from June 1995 to June 1996....At the same time, other small business lending did not increase and loans for over $1 million increased by a little less than 3.5 percent. In contrast, large banks saw a huge increase in loans over $1 million and only a 4 percent increase in loans for under $100,000 from June 1994 to June 1995 when credit scoring was much less common." (p23)

Feldman, Ron/Federal Reserve Bank of Minneapolis. "Small Business Loans, Small Banks and a Big Change in Technology Called Credit Scoring." Region v11 n3 Sep 1997. p18-24. (ISSN1045-3369).

BANK MERGERS--UNITED STATES (v26)

BANK ROBBERIES--CALIFORNIA--FLORIDA --ILLINOIS--NEW YORK (v26)

BANK ROBBERIES--ILLINOIS--CHICAGO (v26)

BANK ROBBERIES--MICHIGAN (v26)

BANK ROBBERIES--MICHIGAN--DETROIT (v26)

BANK ROBBERIES--UNITED STATES (v26)

In the U.S., according to the FBI's Bank Crime Statistics report for 1996, "robberies grew to 8,046 incidents last year....Bank burglaries, trending down for years to their lowest level in a generation in '95, took a 24% increase in '96....Loot taken in 7,704 of the 8,383 violations increased by 30% over the previous year. Recovery was only 17.5%." (unpaginated) "Bank crime incidents in residential areas grew from 395 to 542, a jump of 37%....A surge in the number of employees injured was noted from 115 in '95 to 160 last year. Guard injuries grew to 20 from 9. And law enforcement injuries rose to 14 from 10." (unpaginated)

"Reported Bank Crimes Move Up, Reversing a Trend of Several Years." Security Letter v27 n17 1 Oct 1997. (ISSN0363-4922).

BANKRUPTCY--CANADA (v26)

BANKRUPTCY--CANADA--COLLEGE GRADUATES (v26)

BANKRUPTCY--MARYLAND (v26)

BANKRUPTCY--MICHIGAN (v26)

BANKRUPTCY--UNITED STATES (v26)

In the U.S., "the Bankruptcy Code makes virtually no attempt to calibrate the level of bankruptcy protection to the level of each debtor's need. Rather, it allows a debtor to discharge debts even if the debtor can repay those debts. Currently, about 70 percent of bankruptcy filers use chapter 7, which has no provision for debt repayment even if the filer can repay. Only 30 percent use chapter 13, which sets up repayment plans." (pE1824)

Boucher, Rick (Rep.-Va.). "The Responsible Borrower Protection Bankruptcy Act." Congressional Record. Daily ed. v143 n128 23 Sep 1997. pE1824. section/page-level access: <http://thomas.loc.gov/cgi-bin/query/R?r105:FLD001:E01824:> (ISSN0363-7239). (X1.1A.105/1).

BANKS AND BANKING--BULGARIA

"Due to an overt banking crisis in 1996 and early 1997 [in Bulgaria], the overall size of the banking system had shrunk dramatically by March 1997, not only in terms of the number of banks, but also in terms of deposits, which decreased from the equivalent of US$7.4 billion at end-1995 to US$1.8 billion. This decrease was partly the result of withdrawals totaling US$900 million, which accounted for 40 percent of foreign currency deposits...."

World Bank. "World Bank Supports Enterprise and Banking Reforms in Bulgaria: Bulgaria's Enterprise and Financial...Background." Press Release 30 Oct 1997. document-level access: <http://www.worldbank.org/html/extdr/extme/1519.htm>

BANKS AND BANKING--CANADA (v26)

BANKS AND BANKING--EUROPE

"The principal tests each European nation must pass in order to be admitted to the System of Central Banks are that its deficit cannot be more than 3 per cent of its GDP, and its debt cannot be more than 60 per cent of its GDP. The only country now certain to meet the standards is the Grand Duchy of Luxembourg, whose population is 415,870, and whose territory is about 32 miles square." (p9)

Brockway, George P. "The Dismal Science: Why Germans Are Drinking Less Beer." New Leader v80 n10 2 Jun 1997. p9-10. (ISSN0028-6044).

BANKS AND BANKING--FRANCE--GREAT BRITAIN --JAPAN--UNITED STATES (v26)

BANKS AND BANKING--HISPANIC AMERICANS (v26)

BANKS AND BANKING--UNITED STATES (v26)

The Export-Import Bank is an independent "Federal agency established to provide export financing for U.S. businesses. The Bank has a dual purpose: to neutralize aggressive financing by foreign export credit agencies, and to furnish prudent export credit financing when private financing is unavailable or insufficient to complete the deal. It does this through a variety of loan, guarantee, and insurance programs. Since its founding, Eximbank has supported more than $300 billion in U.S. exports, almost $100 billion in this decade alone. The Bank currently supports about $15 billion in U.S. exports annually. More than 80 percent of Eximbank's transactions are for exports from small businesses, a dramatic increase from just a few years ago. Most of Eximbank's activities are directed at supporting U.S. exports to emerging market economies....More than 40 percent of U.S. exports, worth about $180 billion, go to developing countries, and the amount is rising. The World Bank estimates that by the year 2010, these countries will consume 40 percent of all goods and services produced worldwide." (pH8193-8194)

Leach, James A. (Rep.-Iowa). "Personal Explanation." Congressional Record. Daily ed. v143 n133 30 Sep 1997. pH8188-8200. section/page-level access: <http://thomas.loc.gov/cqi-bin/query/R?r105:FLD001:H08193:> (ISSN0363-7239). (X1.1A.105/1).

The Export-Import Bank is an independent federal agency established to provide export financing for U.S. businesses. "Eximbank's financial statements show that the Bank has paid $3.8 billion in claims from 1980-94. These dollars paid off commercial banks who couldn't collect from foreign borrowers. American taxpayers took the hit....The Eximbank is a prime example of corporate welfare. The majority of Eximbank subsidies go to Fortune 500 companies that could easily afford financing from commercial banks: Boeing--over $2 billion worth of loan guarantees; McDonnell Douglas--$647 million; Westinghouse Electric--$492 million; General Electric--$381 million; and AT&T--$371 million." (pH8195)

Smith, Nick (Rep.-Mich.). "Personal Explanation." Congressional Record. Daily ed. v143 n133 30 Sep 1997. pH8188-8200. section/page-level access: <http://thomas.loc.gov/cqi-bin/query/R?r105:FLD001:H08194:> (ISSN0363-7239). (X1.1A.105/1).

"From 1991 to 1996, the number of banks and thrifts with offices in the Sixth Federal Reserve District states [in the southeastern U.S.] declined by nearly 20 percent, from 1,677 to 1,345....During the same period, the percentage of the average Sixth District states' deposits held by the three largest depository institutions, or the three-firm ratio, increased by nearly 20 percent--from 35 percent to 42 percent." (p2)

Woosley, Lynn. "Consolidation Concentrates Bank Markets in Sixth District." Federal Reserve Bank of Atlanta Financial Update v10 n4 Oct-Dec 1997. p2-3.

"The number of commercial banks operating in the United States and its territories declined from 12,204 in 1991 to 9,755 in 1996. During the same period, the number of thrifts in the United States fell from 2,909 to 1,398." (p2)

Woosley, Lynn. "Consolidation Concentrates Bank Markets in Sixth District." Federal Reserve Bank of Atlanta Financial Update v10 n4 Oct-Dec 1997. p2-3.

"Cardholders for Visa U.S.A. made 878 million transactions worth a total of $39.7 billion in the first six months of 1997, up from 500 million transactions worth $21.1 billion a year earlier....The number of checks written in the U.S. grew at an annual rate of 8 percent in the 1970s, 6 percent in the 1980s and 3.6 percent in the early 1990s. But check volume will increase only 2 percent each year through 2005, according to projections published in 'The Green Sheet.'...Only 1.04 percent of checks written in the United States are dishonored, and nearly half of those are ultimately recovered, says ['The Green Sheet' editor, Paul] Green....Green estimates that Americans will write 65.4 billion checks in 1997, moving $51.8 trillion around the U.S. economy. Payments by individuals to businesses are the type of transaction most likely to migrate from paper checks to debit cards, and these account for 48 percent of all checks written. Business-to-business payments are a candidate for replacement with other electronic payment systems, and these account for 23 percent of checks. Business payments to individuals represent the next largest category of checks written, at 16 percent." (p3)

"Will the Check Get Lost?" Forecast v17 n12 Dec 1997. p3. article-level access: <http://www.demographics.com/publications/fc/97_fc/9712_fc/f971203.htm> (ISSN0732-1597).

In the U.S., "the share of industry assets controlled by multiple bank holding companies has increased rapidly since 1980, when just 16 multi-state holding companies held 4 percent of industry assets....By the middle of 1995, 250 multi-state holding companies held approximately 75 percent of industry assets (Ludwig, 1996)." (p31)

Neely, Michelle Clark/Wheelock, David C. "Why Does Bank Performance Vary across States?" Review v79 n2 Mar-Apr 1997. p27-40. (ISSN0147-9032).

In the U.S., between 1980 and 1995, "the after-tax earnings of commercial banks ranged from a low of $2.7 billion (in 1987) to a record $48.3 billion (in 1995), while return on average assets (ROA) ranged from 0.09 percent (in 1987) to 1.17 percent (in 1993)....At least 10 [bank] failures occurred every year. There were more than 100 failures in eight of those years and more than 200 failures in three years (1987, 1988, and 1989)....Four states--Delaware, Idaho, Nevada, and South Carolina--had just one bank failure each between 1980 and 1995. Two states, however, had more than 100 failures over the same period: Oklahoma (117 failures) and Texas (525 failures)....The rate of annual average bank failures ranged from 0.02 percent (in Wisconsin) to 4 percent (in Alaska and Connecticut) between 1980 and 1995....State-level commercial bank ROA...ranged from a low of -4.10 percent in Alaska in 1987 to 4.33 percent in Nevada in 1994." (p28)

Neely, Michelle Clark/Wheelock, David C. "Why Does Bank Performance Vary across States?" Review v79 n2 Mar-Apr 1997. p27-40. (ISSN0147-9032).

BANKS AND BANKING--UNITED STATES--PUBLIC OPINION (v26)

"In the spring of 1995, the National Federation of Independent Business (NFIB) surveyed over 3,600 member firms [in the U.S.] concerning their experience with credit and financial institutions during the previous three years....Asked whether their primary financial institution is a reliable source of credit, 49 percent of sampled rural firms rated their lender good, compared with 37 percent of the urban firms. Only 9 percent of rural firms, and 13 percent of urban respondents, failed to eventually obtain a loan the last time they tried to obtain credit....A plurality of 41 percent of the rural firms reported that bank loans were their primary source of working capital, with 32 percent depending on retained earnings. At 35 percent, retained earnings was the most common source for urban firms, with 31 percent depending on banks as the primary source." (p479-480)

U.S. Dept. of Agriculture. "Agriculture, Rural Development, Food and Drug Administration...Approp. for 1998 (Part 4)." Hearing. U.S. House. Committee on Appropriations. Washington, D.C. : GPO, 1997. (ISBN0160551560). (Y4.Ap6/1:Ag8/997/pt.4).

BARBECUE COOKERY--UNITED STATES

In the U.S., "Fourth of July weekend will be one of the hottest barbecuing occasions of the summer; 81 percent of Americans are expected to fire up their grills, according to the GrillWatch survey from Weber-Stephens Products Co., makers of Weber grills. The survey also says that 81 percent of Americans like to add flavor to food on the grill with barbecue sauce, followed by marinades (74 percent) and spice rubs (34 percent)." (p1 secD)

Selasky, Susan. "Food: The Perfect Barbecue Sauce?: It Depends on Where You Live." Detroit Free Press 2 Jul 1997. p1,3 secD.

BARBIERO FEVER

see CHAGAS' DISEASE

BARLEY INDUSTRY (v26)

"All barley ranks third in grain trade under STEs [state trading enterprises] in the APEC [Asia-Pacific Economic Cooperation] region, with a total of $1 billion. Canada and Australia are two major barley exporters, with a world market share of nearly 20 percent and 16 percent, respectively, in quantity terms in 1990-95....The CWB [Canadian Wheat Board] markets almost 100 percent of Canada's barley exports...." (p31)

Langley, Suchada/U.S. Dept. of Agriculture. Economic Research Service. "State Trading Enterprises in the APEC Region: Grain Markets." APEC: International Agriculture and Trade Reports Situation and Outlook Series Aug 1997. p29-32.

BARLEY INDUSTRY--CANADA--UNITED STATES (v26)

BARLEY INDUSTRY--CHINA

"For 1996, USDA estimates that farmers [in China] sowed 1.3 million hectares of land to barley and harvested a 4-million-ton crop. Barley imports rose in 1996/97 to an estimated 2 million tons, up from the 1.4 million tons of imports in 1995/96....In calendar year 1996, China imported 1.3 million tons of barley, the same as in 1995....USDA estimates that about 40 percent of total barley supply is used to brew beer and 20 percent is used for animal feed. The remaining 40 percent is used for human consumption and for other uses." (p30) China's "beer production for 1996 reached 16.3 million tons, up 5.6 percent from 1995....In 1995 annual urban per capita beer consumption totaled 5.8 kilograms." (p31)

Crook, Frederick W./U.S. Dept. of Agriculture. Economic Research Service. "Good Grain Crop Projected for 1997." China: International Agriculture and Trade Reports Situation and Outlook Series Jun 1997. p26-31.

BARLEY INDUSTRY--UNITED STATES (v26)

"U.S. farmers planted barley on 7.17 million acres and produced about 397 million bushels in 1996. Area planted and production were 7 and 10 percent above 1995, respectively....Rising input prices increased 1996 total economic costs 8.2 percent. With an average 1996 yield of 54.5 bushels per planted acre, barley growers would have covered all cash costs at $2.14 per bushel, and total economic costs at $3.72 per bushel. At the average 1996 harvest period price of $2.97 per bushel, only those growers with yields of 68.2 bushels or more and costs near the national average would have covered total economic costs." (p24)

U.S. Dept. of Agriculture. Economic Research Service. "1996 Cost of Production for Crops and Livestock: Although Input Expenses Rose in 1996,...Led to Higher Net Returns." Agricultural Income and Finance Situation and Outlook Report Sep 1997. p23-27.

BASEBALL--UNITED STATES (v26)

BASES, MILITARY

see MILITARY BASES

BASIC RIGHTS

see HUMAN RIGHTS

BASKETBALL--ACCIDENTS--UNITED STATES

In the U.S., "basketball injuries alone sent more than 690,000 people to hospital emergency rooms in 1995, according to the U.S. Consumer Product Safety Commission....The National Athletic Trainers Association (NATA) shows the average school's basketball team can expect two serious injuries every year. (The study defines a serious injury as one that sidelines an athlete for at least a week.)" (p22)

Jones, Rebecca. "Playing It Safe." American School Board Journal v184 n8 Aug 1997. p22-24. (ISSN0003-0953).

BASKETBALL--UNITED STATES

In the U.S., "in 1996, 10.5 million [basketball] players--23 percent of the total 45.6 million--said they played most often at home. This compares to 6.8 million--19 percent of the total 35.7 million--in 1987. Some 27 percent--12.3 million--said they played most often at the school gym in 1996, down from 36 percent, or 12.9 million, in 1987." (p5 secF)

"Body & Mind: Rec Notes: More Players Shooting Hoops at Home." Detroit Free Press 16 Dec 1997. p5 secF.

BASTARDY

see ILLEGITIMACY

BATHING CUSTOMS--UNITED STATES

In 1995, 23 percent of U.S. "women responding to a Roper Starch Worldwide survey had taken a bath in the past day, up from 17 percent in 1995. Sixty-two percent of women use bath and shower-care products at least occasionally, according to a 1996 Simmons Market Research Bureau survey. Americans bought an estimated $921 million worth of bath and shower-care products in 1996, according to Packaged Facts of New York City." (p35)

Crispell, Diane. "Kaleidoscope: Stress Reduction with Rubber Duckies." American Demographics v19 n6 Jun 1997. p35. article-level access: <http://www.demographics.com/publications/ad/97_ad/9706_ad/ad970618.htm>

(ISSN0163-4089).

BATHROOMS--UNITED STATES (v26)

BATTERED AGED

see ABUSED AGED

BATTERED CHILDREN

see ABUSED CHILDREN

BATTERED WOMEN

see ABUSED WOMEN; ABUSED WOMEN PRISONERS

BATTERIES--RECYCLING--UNITED STATES (v26)

BBQ

see BARBECUE COOKERY

BEACHES--ENVIRONMENTAL ASPECTS--UNITED STATES

"According to a recent report by the Natural Resources Defense Council, coastal nonpoint source pollution is now the leading cause of beach closings...[in the U.S.]. In fact, over half of the beach closings and advisories last year for which there was a determined cause, 893 of 1,627 closings and advisories were caused by nonpoint source pollution." (pH7893)

Pallone, Frank, Jr. (Rep.-N.J.). "Departments of Commerce, Justice, And State, The Judiciary...Appropriations Act, 1998." Congressional Record. Daily ed. v143 n130 25 Sep 1997. pH7890-7907. section/page-level access: <http://thomas.loc.gov/cgi-bin/query/R?r105:FLD001:H07893:> (ISSN0363-7239). (X1.1A.105/1).

BEACHES--MICHIGAN

In Michigan, "about 24,000 fewer cars--an estimated 84,000 fewer people--came to...[Metropolitan Beach] this year in August compared with 1996. The drop in attendance for the year was about 54,000 cars. Attributing the drop to beach closings alone is difficult, but records show a general pattern that more people come to the park in years following summers where bacteria wasn't a problem. For instance, 1994--when bacteria counts closed the beach for most of the summer--was followed by a drop in some 40,000 cars the next year. The relatively bacteria-free summer 1995 was followed by an increase of some 20,000 cars in 1996." (p1 secC)

Savitskie, Jeffrey. "Metro: Metro Beach Attendance Slumps." Detroit News 6 Oct 1997. p1-2 secC.

BEACHES--UNITED STATES

"The United States has 650 public beaches to choose from. Together they are the most-visited leisure destination on the planet--180 million pilgrimages last year." (p1)

Wood, Daniel B. "United States: National Report: Surf Monitor: A Guide to America's Best Sand, Sun, And Solitude." The Christian Science Monitor v89 n161 16 Jul 1997. p1,4. The Christian Science Monitor search engine: <http://www.csmonitor.com/plweb-cgi/iops1.pl> To retrieve this article, enter the following search: ED=19970716 AND solitude. In the "retrieved list," click the title that matches this record. (ISSN0882-7729).

BEAN CURD

see TOFU

BEAN INDUSTRY--CHINA

China's "dry pea and bean exports rose from 799,000 tons in 1993 to 1.5 million in 1994, fell to 1 million in 1995 and decreased to 576,000 tons in 1996....According to SSB's [State Statistical Bureau] A STATISTICAL SURVEY OF CHINA, 1997, area sown to beans (soybeans and dry peas and beans) fell from 11.2 million hectares in 1995 to 10.6 million in 1996, a decrease of 600,000 hectares....In 1995, broad bean area totaled 963,000 hectares and output totalled 4.9 million tons. Sichuan province produced 3.3 million tons, accounting for two-thirds of total output....From 1991 through 1995, broad bean exports averaged 322,000 tons a year. But in 1996 exports dropped to 93,000 tons....In 1995, kidney bean area was 1.6 million hectares with output at 496,000 tons. Henan province is the largest producer with 145,000 tons....China exported an average 330,000 tons of kidney beans from 1991-95. In 1996, kidney bean exports dropped to 270,000 tons....In 1995, area sown to meng beans totalled 1.4 million hectares and ouput reached 594,000 tons. Henan is China's largest producer of meng beans with 108,000 tons....From 1991 to 1995, China exported an average of 118,000 tons of meng beans a year. For 1996, meng bean exports dropped to 81,000 tons." (p31)

Crook, Frederick W./U.S. Dept. of Agriculture. Economic Research Service. "Good Grain Crop Projected for 1997." China: International Agriculture and Trade Reports Situation and Outlook Series Jun 1997. p26-31.

BEAN INDUSTRY--UNITED STATES (v26)

"The U.S. is the fifth-largest producer of dry edible beans in the world--following India, China, Brazil, and Mexico. In 1997, U.S. dry bean growers will produce an estimated 29 million cwt [hundredweight]--7 percent more than a year earlier and 3 percent above the annual average for the 1990's. Acreage and yields have been trending higher over time, and both rose in 1997....In 1996, U.S. dry bean exports were valued at $202 million (imports were $28 million)....Over the past 5 years, an average of 18 percent of U.S. dry bean supplies has been exported, and estimates suggest that this could rise to nearly 20 percent in 1997. An export share of production of 18 percent is relatively high compared with other sectors of the vegetable industry, such as fresh vegetables (8 percent), frozen vegetables (7 percent), and canned vegetables (6 percent). Colored beans, such as pintos and kidneys, accounted for 64 percent of U.S. dry bean export value in 1996....U.S. per capita consumption of dry beans has risen to an estimated 7.8 pounds in 1997." (p3-4)

Plummer, Charles/Lucier, Gary/U.S. Dept. of Agriculture. Economic Research Service. "Commodity Briefs: Specialty Crops: Dry Bean Production Up as Demand Grows Steadily." Agricultural Outlook Oct 1997. p3-4.

In the U.S., "dry edible bean harvested area was up 2 percent in 1997 from last year's 1.7 million acres due to higher prices for some bean classes and lower prices for competing crops. Acreage was up or unchanged in 14 of the 17 major States this year. Excessive rains and flooding in early July in the Red River Valley of North Dakota and Minnesota caused about 100,000 acres of dry beans to be abandoned." (p14)

U.S. Dept. of Agriculture. Economic Research Service. "Pulses." Vegetables and Specialties Situation and Outlook Report Nov 1997. p14.

In the U.S., "per capita use of dry edible beans totaled 7.5 pounds in 1996, down 4 percent from a year earlier but 1 percent above the average of the 1990's. Most of the decline came in navy beans as domestic use dropped to 1.2 pounds per person. Pinto beans accounted for 47 percent of the dry bean market at 3.5 pounds per person (up 6 percent from a year earlier), followed by navy beans with 16 percent at 1.2 pounds per person. Red kidney beans (0.6 pounds) and Great Northern beans (0.5 pounds) are the next most widely used dry bean classes." (p5)

U.S. Dept. of Agriculture. Economic Research Service. "Summary." Vegetables and Specialties Situation and Outlook Yearbook Jul 1997. p3-5.

BEARS

see also GRIZZLY BEAR

BEARS--SOUTH AMERICA

Bernie Peyton, an eminent biologist who led a four-year, 60-person survey of the Andean bear "calculates some 18,000 to 65,000 bears surviving over the whole of its South American range. The new numbers are a leap from popular statistics, which have declared there to be as few as 2,000 bears." (p10)

"But in many places, Peyton found the niche missing its bears. In Machu Picchu National Park, a park he judged to be nearly 100 percent suitable for bears, he found a lowly third of it occupied. As he and others looked elsewhere, the Machu Picchu scenario would be echoed up and down the Andean cordilleras, accounting for population estimates as low as 2,000 bears in the wild." (p13)

Stolzenburg, William. "Andean Ambassador." Nature Conservancy v47 n4 Jul-Aug 1997. p10-15. (ISSN0028-5200).

In South America, there are "58 national parks, reserves or sanctuaries with Andean bears. Among them are several stretching more than 475,000 acres, big enough to house what biologists refer to as a viable population--that is, one unlikely to disappear by the bad luck of nature's inevitable cataclysmic plague, drought or storm....In Venezuela, the government park agency INPARQUES has tripled the extent of their national park system to accommodate the bears. In 1993 and 1994, the Ecuadoran government doubled a 5,000-acre refuge of prime bear habitat and, in Bolivia, the country's biggest bear area was more than doubled in 1988 when the 1.6-million-acre Carrasco National Park was added to the border of Amboro National Park....Ninety-five percent of the bear's habitat remains outside the official protection of parks; and the remaining 5 percent carries no guarantee of sanctuary." (p15)

Stolzenburg, William. "Andean Ambassador." Nature Conservancy v47 n4 Jul-Aug 1997. p10-15. (ISSN0028-5200).

BEARS--UNITED STATES (v26)

BEAUTY AIDS

see COSMETICS INDUSTRY

BEDOUINS--ISRAEL--SOCIAL CONDITIONS (v26)

BEE CULTURE--ARIZONA--EQUIPMENT AND SUPPLIES (v26)

BEEF INDUSTRY--CANADA

Canadian beef "inventories stood at 12.8 million head on January 1, 1997. Inventories in western Canada declined 4 percent while eastern Canadian inventories were only down 2 percent. As the liquidation continues, slaughter through the beginning of May is about 10 percent above 1996." (unpaginated)

U.S. Dept. of Agriculture. Economic Research Service. "Higher Exports to Mexico and Korea Unlikely to Offset Declines to Japan and Canada." Livestock, Dairy and Poultry Situation and Outlook Series 16 May 1997.

BEEF INDUSTRY--RUSSIA (v26)

BEEF INDUSTRY--UNITED STATES (v26)

"Some of the larger beef processing plants in the United States that prepare ground beef for fast-food establishments and retailers handle up to 250,000 pounds a day, or about 65 million pounds a year, assuming the plant operates 5 days a week, year round." (p35) "In the United States, if 25 percent of the 7 billion pounds of ground beef consumed in 1995 was irradiated and this treatment successfully prevented 25 percent of the ground-beef-caused salmonellosis and E. coli O157:H7 disease, $56.4 million to $137.7 million in medical costs and productivity losses would have been saved. Irradiating 25 percent of the U.S. ground beef supply is estimated to cost the industry $28.3 million per year." (p36)

Morrison, Rosanna Mentzer/Buzby, Jean C./Lin, C. -T. Jordan/ U.S. Dept. of Agriculture. Economic Research Service. "Food Safety: Irradiating Ground Beef to Enhance Food Safety." Food Review v20 n1 Jan-Apr 1997. p33-37. (ISSN1056-327X).

In the U.S., "boxed beef production, particularly in the large plants that now account for most cattle slaughter, has grown dramatically, from 7.9 percent of large plant output in 1963 to 21.3 percent in 1972 and 67.2 percent in 1992....Boxed beef accounted for more than two-thirds of the output in large plants, but less than 15 percent of output in plants with fewer than 400 employees, as smaller cattle slaughterhouses continued to ship whole carcasses and ground beef products." (p23)

MacDonald, James M./Ollinger, Michael/U.S. Dept. of Agriculture. Economic Research Service. "Market Trends: U.S. Meat Slaughter Consolidating Rapidly." Food Review v20 n2 May-Aug 1997. p22-27. (ISSN1056-327X).

"U.S. beef export volume advanced 3 percent to a record 611,000 tons, however, lower export prices dropped export value 8 percent to $2.4 billion....During the first half of 1996, U.S. beef exports were advancing at a strong 22-percent pace until an E. coli outbreak in Japan depressed import demand for beef. During the last half of 1996, total beef export shipments were 13 percent lower than the latter half of 1995. Most of the decline was to Japan where shipments went from a 29-percent gain during the first 6 months of 1996 to a 21-percent fall during the last 6 months. After double-digit growth the past 4 years, beef shipments to Japan rose just 1 percent to nearly 337,000 tons, and export value dropped 11 percent to $1.5 billion due to lower prices." (p2) "Mexico was the exception as beef exports rose 90 percent to $163 million, and volume jumped 100 percent to 59,000 tons." (p3)

Greene, Joel/U.S. Dept. of Agriculture. Economic Research Service. "Agricultural Exports Surpass $60 Billion." Foreign Agricultural Trade of the United States Jan-Mar 1997. p2-3.

"U.S. beef export volume advanced 3 percent to a record 611,000 tons, however, lower export prices dropped export value 8 percent to $2.4 billion....During the first half of 1996, U.S. beef exports were advancing at a strong 22-percent pace until an E. coli outbreak in Japan depressed import demand for beef. During the last half of 1996, total beef export shipments were 13 percent lower than the latter half of 1995. Most of the decline was to Japan where shipments went from a 29-percent gain during the first 6 months of 1996 to a 21-percent fall during the last 6 months. After double-digit growth the past 4 years, beef shipments to Japan rose just 1 percent to nearly 337,000 tons, and export value dropped 11 percent to $1.5 billion due to lower prices." (p2) "Mexico was the exception as beef exports rose 90 percent to $163 million, and volume jumped 100 percent to 59,000 tons." (p3)

Greene, Joel/U.S. Dept. of Agriculture. Economic Research Service. "Agricultural Exports Surpass $60 Billion." Foreign Agricultural Trade of the United States Jan-Mar 1997. p2-3.

In 1996, U.S. "beef imports remained nearly the same as a year ago at 708,000 tons. However, the value of beef was down 7 percent because of lower prices....The unit import value for beef dropped 7 percent from $2,046 per ton in 1995 to $1,894 per ton [in] 1996....Canada supplied 33 percent of beef imports with 234,000 tons, while Australia and New Zealand supplied 50 percent with 350,000 tons." (p6)

Gehlhar, Mark/U.S. Dept. of Agriculture. Economic Research Service. "Imports Advance 12 Percent in 1996." Foreign Agricultural Trade of the United States Jan-Mar 1997. p6-7.

BEEKEEPERS--UNITED STATES (v26)

BEEPERS (PAGERS)--UNITED STATES

"Since 1992, the use of pagers has doubled in the US. Forty million Americans own a pager today and 60 million are expected to have one by 2002, according to a survey by the biggest pager manufacturer, Motorola. Today 14 percent of teenagers own a beeper, compared with 7 percent two years ago." (p5)

de Pommereau, Isabelle. "United States: Beeper Culture: Tech-Hip Teens Tell '007s' '121.'" The Christian Science Monitor v89 n230 23 Oct 1997. p1,5. The Christian Science Monitor search engine: <http://www.csmonitor.com/plweb-cgi/iops1.pl> To retrieve this article, enter the following search: ED=19971023 AND beeper. In the "retrieved list,"

click the title that matches this record. (ISSN0882-7729).

BEES (v26)

BEES--EFFECT OF INSECTICIDES ON--UNITED STATES (v26)

BEES--NEBRASKA (v26)

BEES--UNITED STATES (v26)

BEHAVIOR, CONSUMER

see CONSUMER BEHAVIOR

BEHAVIOR, SEXUAL

see SEXUAL BEHAVIOR

BEHAVIOR, SUICIDAL

see SUICIDE

BEIJING (CHINA) (v26)

BELL PEPPER INDUSTRY--UNITED STATES (v26)

BELTS, AUTOMOBILE SEAT

see AUTOMOBILES--SEAT BELTS

BELUGA (WHALE)

see WHITE WHALE

BENEVOLENCE--UNITED STATES--PUBLIC OPINION (v26)

BENEVOLENT INSTITUTIONS

see CHARITIES; SOCIAL SERVICE

BERRY INDUSTRY

see BLUEBERRY INDUSTRY; CRANBERRY INDUSTRY; STRAWBERRY INDUSTRY; WAGES--STRAWBERRY INDUSTRY

BETTING

see GAMBLING

BEVERAGE INDUSTRY

see also ALCOHOLIC BEVERAGES; COFFEE INDUSTRY; FRUIT JUICE INDUSTRY; GRAPE JUICE INDUSTRY; GRAPEFRUIT JUICE INDUSTRY; MILK CONSUMPTION; ORANGE JUICE INDUSTRY; TEA TRADE; WINE INDUSTRY

BEVERAGE INDUSTRY--UNITED STATES

U.S. "beverage imports showed consistent growth throughout 1996 with a 21-percent increase to $2.9 billion for the year....Wine imports were $1.4 billion, up 24 percent....Beer imports reached $1.3 billion, a 12-percent increase. Beer imports from Mexico, increasing 29 percent to $307 million, gained the most among all suppliers." (p6)

Gehlhar, Mark/U.S. Dept. of Agriculture. Economic Research Service. "Imports Advance 12 Percent in 1996." Foreign Agricultural Trade of the United States Jan-Mar 1997. p6-7.

BEVERAGES--AUSTRALIA (v26)

BEVERAGES--UNITED STATES (v26)

BIAS, JOB

see DISCRIMINATION IN EMPLOYMENT

BIAS CRIMES

see HATE CRIMES

BICYCLE INDUSTRY (v26)

BIG BROTHERS/BIG SISTERS PROGRAM--UNITED STATES (v26)

BILINGUAL EDUCATION

see EDUCATION, BILINGUAL

BILINGUALISM--CANADA (v26)

BILLBOARDS--MICHIGAN (v26)

BILLBOARDS--MICHIGAN--PUBLIC OPINION (v26)

BILLBOARDS--UNITED STATES

"According to Scenic America, driving on a [U.S.] federal-aid highway you can expect to see at least 47 billboards an hour. Further, billboards are going up about 10 times faster (5,000 to 15,000 annually) than they are coming down....Florida has the most billboards of any state (more than 20,000)....South Carolina has the most billboard structures per 10 miles of federal-aid highway (25.3)...." (p13)

"Stateline: Oh Beautiful for Bigger Billboards." State Legislatures v23 n7 Jul-Aug 1997. p13. (ISSN0147-6041).

BILLIONAIRES--UNITED STATES

In 1996, "the richest American, Microsoft billionaire Bill Gates, more than doubled his net worth, from $18.5 billion to $39.8 billion. It would take the median U.S. household earning $35,500 some 600,000 years to make as much as Gates did last year. Today, the United States has 170 billionaires by FORBES's count, up from 135 last year...." (p7)

Sklar, Holly/Collins, Chuck. "Editorials: Forbes 400 World Series." Nation v265 n12 20 Oct 1997. p6-7. (ISSN0027-8378).

BIO-BIO RIVER (CHILE)

The Biobio river "originates in the lakes of Icalma and Galletue high in the Andes and runs all the way to the sea. Over 400 km [kilometers] long, it contains an estimated 15,000 waterways." (p25) "One million people depend upon the water of the Biobio and almost 500,000 drink directly out of it." (p26)

Jana, Dario. "Environment: In Chile's Upper Biobio: The Battle against the...Dam...Attacks on...the Environment Continue." Abya Yala News v10 n4 Fall 1997. p25-29. (ISSN1056-5876).

BIOLOGICAL DIVERSITY (v26)

BIOLOGICAL DIVERSITY--ALABAMA

The 29th largest state "of the United States, Alabama is the nation's fourth-richest kingdom of plant and animal species; in species per square mile, only Florida can match it. Its waterways hold half of all species of turtles found in North America, six out of 10 species of freshwater mussel. Since 1991, three new kinds of fish have been described from Alabama waters. Only two years ago, a near-barren patch of rock--within 50 miles of the state's largest city--presented eight undescribed species of flowering plants." (p8)

Stolzenburg, William. "Ecology Forum: Sweet Home Alabama." Nature Conservancy v47 n4 Sep-Oct 1997. p8-9. (ISSN0028-5200).

BIOLOGICAL DIVERSITY--ALABAMA--CAHABA RIVER

"Running 200 undammed miles, the Cahaba is Alabama's longest remaining free-flowing river, bearing unusual diversities of mussels, crayfish and snails. Its 131 species of fish total more than any river its size in North America." (p9)

Stolzenburg, William. "Ecology Forum: Sweet Home Alabama." Nature Conservancy v47 n4 Sep-Oct 1997. p8-9. (ISSN0028-5200).

BIOLOGICAL DIVERSITY--ARGENTINA--PARANA RIVER

The middle Parana River "is Argentina's equivalent of the Pantanal wetlands, with an extraordinary biodiversity, which includes 250 bird species, 200 kinds of mammals, and nearly 400 reptile and amphibian species. The alluvial valley is home to more than 300 fish species." (p10)

Cappato, Jorge. "Argentina's Parana Medio Dam is Resurrected." World Rivers Review v12 n3 Jun 1997. p10-11. (ISSN0890-6211).

BIOLOGICAL DIVERSITY--ASIA

"The Asia-Pacific region covers almost half the earth's surface and has almost...[a] quarter of [the] world's total land area and a third of the agricultural land. It is also home to half of the planet's population and supplies approximately 40 per cent of the inland and marine fish catch." (p162)

Park, Jacob. "APEC and ASEAN: The Future of Asian Environmental Regionalism." Environmental Politics v6 n3 Aut 1997. p162-167. (ISSN0964-4016).

BIOLOGICAL DIVERSITY--CHILE

"While 18 percent of Chile's land--14.43 million hectares--is set aside in national reserves, environmentalists say many critical biodiversity zones fall outside the protected areas....More than 80 percent of Chile's natural reserves are in the extreme south, while the greatest biodiversity is in the south-central part of the country....Of Chile's 642 species of mammals, birds, reptiles, amphibians and freshwater fish, experts say 243 will be at risk if conservation measures are not taken. Of the country's 5,500 plant species, 14 percent exist only in Chile." (p7)

"Chile: U.S. Millionaire Buys Land." NewsNotes v22 n6 Nov-Dec 1997. p7. (ISSN1064-1556).

BIOLOGICAL DIVERSITY--COSTA RICA

Wedged between Costa Rica's "380-mile Pacific coastline and 133-mile Caribbean seaboard are rain forests, cloud forests, tropical jungles, swamps, savannas, peninsulas, mangroves, bays, marshes, caves, capes, lakes, lagoons, islands, and beaches galore. Mountains reaching 12,500 feet rip across its interior. Nine of these 'cordilleras' are active volcanoes with hissing fumaroles and boiling mud pots....More than 200 species of mammals, 380 classes of reptiles and amphibians, 9,000 flowering plant genera, 35,000 insect types, 1,500 kinds of fish, and 850 varieties of birds--one-tenth of the world's total--populate this tiny isthmus....With more than 1,000 strains, the orchid claims the title of national flower, and that suits some 400 species of butterflies just fine. All this is packed into less than 20,000 square miles--just three one-hundredths of Earth's surface (about the size of West Virginia). Yet 5 percent of the planet's animal and plant classifications thrive in this land." (p29)

Drake, Nicholas. "Kiwanis Nation: Costa Rica's Pacific Passion." Kiwanis v82 n8 Sep 1997. p28-31,33. (ISSN0162-5276).

BIOLOGICAL DIVERSITY--FLORIDA

The Elgin Air Force Base in the Florida Panhandle "contains more than 90 rare or imperiled species, including the Okaloosa darter, Florida bog frog, Florida black bear, Florida pine snake, Bachman's warbler, gopher tortoise and a salamander new to science. Among the 1,200 plant species on the base are the imperiled bogbutton, toothed savory, pond spicebush, naked-stemmed panic grass and white-topped pitcher plant." (p14)

Biondo, Brenda. "In Defense of the Longleaf Pine." Nature Conservancy v47 n4 Sep-Oct 1997. p10-17. (ISSN0028-5200).

BIOLOGICAL DIVERSITY--INDONESIA (v26)

BIOLOGICAL DIVERSITY--NEW ZEALAND

A "report, called the 'State of New Zealand's Environment 1997' highlights the decline of biodiversity as the most pressing issue currently facing this so-called natural paradise. It claims that at least 800 species are currently threatened with extinction--including the national icon, the kiwi. Of the original 93 kinds of birds known to have evolved and existed only in New Zealand, 43 have become extinct, with another 37 now on the edge of extinction. The report notes that nearly 85 percent of the country's lowland forests and wetlands have vanished over the 800 years since the country was settled....The remaining 4.2 million acres of forest are under threat from browsing creatures such as possums, which are estimated to number around 70 million. Human newcomers and their accompanying pests have wiped out 32 percent of the country's land and freshwater birds, 18 percent of seabirds, and at least a dozen invertebrates, such as snails and insects, the report says. More than 1,000 of New Zealand's known animals, plants, and fungi are currently threatened by a dozen introduced mammals and numerous exotic plants." (p7)

Cohen, David. "International: New Zealand's Eco-Myth." The Christian Science Monitor v89 n241 7 Nov 1997. p7. The Christian Science Monitor search engine: <http://www.csmonitor.com/plweb-cgi/iops1.pl> To retrieve this article, enter the following search: ED=19971107 AND myth. In the "retrieved list," click the title that matches this record. (ISSN0882-7729).

BIOLOGICAL DIVERSITY--SWEDEN

"Fewer plant species live along the banks of Swedish rivers dammed for hydroelectric power than alongside neighboring free-flowing rivers, reports SCIENCE magazine (May 2, 1997)....Ecologist Christer Nilsson and colleagues at Umea University in Sweden studied the vegetation at almost 90 sites alongside hydroelectric power schemes....The team found about one-third fewer species around storage reservoirs than at comparable undisturbed sites; the index of species richness was half as great for these sites. At impoundment sites, the richness index was comparable to that at control sites, but 15 percent fewer species were crammed into a much narrower band of habitat than in natural rivers." (p13)

"News Briefs: Biodiversity: Sweden." World Rivers Review v12 n3 Jun 1997. p13. (ISSN0890-6211).

BIOLOGICAL DIVERSITY--UNITED STATES

In the U.S., "estimates are that invasive foreign plants are spreading at a rate of 4,600 acres a day. The problem is widespread: 61 percent of national-park supervisors reported problems with foreign plants last year, and 12 percent of Nature Conservancy land stewards--overseeing more than 1,500 private preserves--said invasive foreign plants now pose the most dangerous threat to the ecological health of their preserves....A study released...by the Arlington, Va.-based Nature Conservancy found that invasive foreign plants and nonnative animals contributed to the decline of 42 percent of 958 threatened or endangered species. For 18 percent of species on the list, invaders were 'the major cause of endangerment.' Of the roughly 4,000 nonindigenous plants in North America, several hundred are seen as potential pests, and 50 are considered particularly dangerous." (p3)

Richey, Warren. "United States: Leafy Invaders Creep into US Soil and Sink Tough Roots." The Christian Science Monitor v89 n224 15 Oct 1997. p3-4. The Christian Science Monitor search engine: <http://www.csmonitor.com/plweb-cgi/iops1.pl> To retrieve this article, enter the following search: ED=19971015 AND roots. In the "retrieved list," click the title that matches this record. (ISSN0882-7729).

BIOLOGICAL DIVERSITY CONSERVATION--AFRICA, SUB-SAHARAN (v26)

BIOMASS CROPS

see ENERGY CROPS

BIOMASS ENERGY--UNITED STATES

"Municipal solid waste, which is produced at the rate of one ton per year for every man, woman and child in the United States, is also a source of cellulosic biomass. Sixty-one percent of this material is biomass in the form of paper, yard trimmings and demolition wood, and represents a large current biomass source....More than 35 million acres (14 million hectares) of land are currently available for energy crop production....Today, most U.S. ethanol production is based in the large grain growing states of the Midwest, where about 300 million bushels of corn were used in 1993 to produce about 1.2 billion gallons (4.5 billion liters) of ethanol....Currently, ethanol from corn is blended with gasoline at 10 percent ethanol and 90 percent gasoline to produce the fuel product known as gasohol. Gasohol represents 8 percent of the light duty transportation fuel market. The product has been found to be very effective in reducing CO [carbon] levels in urban air." (p29) "Over the last decade, the [U.S. Department of Energy ethanol research and development] program has succeeded in reducing the predicted cost of biomass-derived ethanol from $3.60/gal [gallon] ($0.95/liter) to $1.22/gal ($0.34/liter). The cost of $1.22 presumes a feedstock cost of $42/dry ton which accounts for $0.46/gal....At zero cost for feedstock, the predicted cost of ethanol would be $0.86/gal ($0.23/liter), which is well below the current price at the blending terminal of around $1.20/gal ($0.32/liter)." (p30)

Hinman, Norman D. "The Benefits of Biofuels." Solar Today v11 n4 Jul-Aug 1997. p28-30. (ISSN1042-0630).

BIOMASS STOVES

"Worldwide, nearly 3 billion people cook their meals over open fires or on simple metal canisters that utilize biomass fuels such as wood, charcoal, dung, and crop residues. In terms of energy use, these cooking systems are very inefficient, often delivering as little as 10 to 20 percent of the potential heat to the cooking pots." (p13)

"The Virtues of Mundane Science: Improving Cookstoves." Environment v39 n6 Jul-Aug 1997. p13. (ISSN0013-9157).

Biomass "stove programs have led to the dissemination of more than 120 million stoves in China (reaching a remarkable 60 to 70 percent of all households), several million stoves each in India, Sri Lanka, and Bangladesh, and hundreds of thousands in a number of African nations, including almost 1 million in Kenya, where more than 50 percent of urban households and 10 percent of all households, use improved stoves. But steady and sufficient funding for such projects has been difficult to obtain: Fewer than 200 projects have been undertaken during the last decade, most with budgets of only thousands or tens of thousands of dollars." (p13)

Kammen, Daniel M./Dove, Michael R. "The Virtues of Mundane Science." Environment v39 n6 Jul-Aug 1997. p10-15,38-41. (ISSN0013-9157).

BIOTECHNOLOGY--RESEARCH--JAPAN--UNITED STATES

"In 1993, the Japanese government spent...US$1 billion for biotechnology, compared to nearly US$4 billion by the US....In the US 47.8% of gross expenditures on R&D [research & development] are by the government, according to the OECD (Organization for Economic Cooperation and Development) the figure for Japan is...21.5%." (p152)

Callan, Benedicte. "Biotechnology Strategy: Why Production Technology Is Not a Measure of Competitiveness in the Biotechnologies." Science and Public Policy v24 n3 Jun 1997. p146-160. (ISSN0302-3427).

BIOTECHNOLOGY INDUSTRIES--EUROPE--UNITED STATES

"There are some 1,800 biotechnological companies world wide, two thirds of which, including the 10 largest, are in the United States. There are 500 in Europe. The stock market valuation of biotechnology companies is in excess of 70,000 million [pounds sterling], despite aggregate reserves being less than 15,000 million [pounds sterling]....It is estimated that currently there are 27,000 jobs in European biotechnology companies with direct applications of techniques, and some 200,000 in biotechnology and related activities. In the United States, however, 5,000 billion [pounds sterling] has been invested in biotechnology. Forty new drug products and vaccines are in use because of that and 300 more are currently in clinical trials to treat Alzheimer's, heart disease, multiple sclerosis, AIDS and obesity." (c1246)

Gibson, Ian (H.C.-Norwich, North). "The Future of Biotechnology." Great Britain. Parliament. House of Commons. Debates. 11 Jul 1997. c1246. section-level access: <http://www.parliament.the-stationery-office.co.uk/pa/cm199798/cmhansrd/cm970711/debtext/70711-19.htm#70711-19_head0>

BIOTECHNOLOGY INDUSTRIES--UNITED STATES (v26)

For small U.S. "companies, biotechnology expenditures tend to be high, averaging about US$30 million for a public firm in 1993. Only 18% of these firms have revenues from products to offset their expenses. As a result, the median survival index for public firms is a short 25 months...." (p150)

Callan, Benedicte. "Biotechnology Strategy: Why Production Technology Is Not a Measure of Competitiveness in the Biotechnologies." Science and Public Policy v24 n3 Jun 1997. p146-160. (ISSN0302-3427).

BIOTIC COMMUNITIES--ECONOMIC ASPECTS

"Robert Costanza of the University of Maryland's Institute for Ecological Economics and colleagues from around the world synthesized the findings of more than 100 studies to compute the average per-hectare value of each of 17 services that ecosystems provide. The result: nature provides about $33 trillion in services each year, compared with $25 trillion for the global GNP." (p9) "The current value of all services and biomes were found to be in the range of $16 trillion to $54 trillion per year. The report was published in the May 15, 1997 issue of the journal NATURE." (p10)

Abramovitz, Janet N. "Environmental Intelligence: Report Turns 'Economy-Versus-Environment' Argument on Its Head." World Watch v10 n5 Sep-Oct 1997. p9-10. (ISSN0896-0615).

BIRACIAL DATING

see INTERRACIAL DATING

BIRD WATCHING--UNITED STATES

In the U.S., "bird-watching has soared in popularity. The activity drew about 54 million participants in 1994-95, up from 21 million in 1982-83, according to a pair of recreational surveys by the federal government. By the mid-'90s birders outnumbered golfers by almost a 2-to-1 ratio and downhill skiers by 3-to-1....At the 550,000-strong Audubon Society, which seeks to preserve and restore natural ecosystems for birds and other wildlife, the median member age is 44, the median household income $56,300. At the American Birding Association, a 20,000-member, Colorado Springs-based group, the typical John Q. Birder is pushing 53, holds a postgraduate degree and enjoys a family income of $60,000." (p86)

Holt, Nancy D. "Out of the Office: Birding Takes Off." ABA Journal v83 Oct 1997. p86-87. (ISSN0747-0088).

"In 1996, nearly 63 million Americans spent $31 billion observing, feeding, and photographing wildlife of all kinds, according to a new study by the US Fish and Wildlife Service, to be released later this month. While 3 million hunters shoot ducks and other migratory birds, some 14.3 million people prefer to watch or feed them." (p15)

Chaddock, Gail Russell. "Habitat: Glamour Duck Achieves Stardom on Wildlife Stamp." The Christian Science Monitor v89 n243 12 Nov 1997. p15. The Christian Science Monitor search engine: <http://www.csmonitor.com/plweb-cgi/iops1.pl> To retrieve this article, enter the following search: ED=19971112 AND stamp. In the "retrieved list," click the title that matches this record. (ISSN0882-7729).

BIRDS

see also CANADA GOOSE; GOSHAWK; SONGBIRDS; SPOTTED OWL; WATER BIRDS

BIRDS--COLLISIONS WITH AIRPLANES

see AIRCRAFT ACCIDENTS

BIRDS--FLORIDA--FLORIDA KEYS

The Florida Keys "now have nine species of breeding seabirds, 19 species of other aquatic birds and only 35 land birds (seven of which are West Indian). The bird fauna of the Florida Keys is changing rapidly, with more than 20 species colonizing recently and a few disappearing." (p8)

Hoffman, Wayne. "America's Tropics: Examining the Keys' Ever-Changing Bird Life." Florida Naturalist v70 n2 Sum 1997. p8-9. (ISSN0015-4172).

BIRDS--GREAT BRITAIN

Birds in Great Britain "are laying their eggs earlier as a result of warmer spring temperatures, according to a report in the 7 August [1997] issue of NATURE....Humphrey Crick and colleagues of the British Trust for Ornithology (Norfolk, UK) analyzed more than 74,000 records of the date of the first egg laid in a given nest for some 225 species, collected by birdwatchers across the country over the past 25 years. The scientists found significant trends toward earlier laying dates for 20 species, with the laying date advancing by an average of almost 9 days, and ranging between 4 and 17 days." (p5-6)

"Science Update: Birds Laying Eggs Earlier." Global Environmental Change Report v9 n15 8 Aug 1997. p5-6. (ISSN1049-9083).

BIRDS--WYOMING

The U.S. Fish and Wildlife Service "estimates that more than 2 million birds die annually from contact with contaminated oil evaporation ponds, or pits, a byproduct of fossil-fuel drilling....The FWS and US Environmental Protection Agency pinpointed 200 illegal oil pits and broken lines as well as oil leaks into sensitive riparian areas used by breeding birds [in Wyoming]. At one location, 98 percent of the existing pits were out of compliance....The 213 wells identified by the FWS represent less than 2 percent of the state's oil field portfolio." (p3)

Wilkinson, Todd. "United States: Government, Industry Flock Together for Bird Conservationism." The Christian Science Monitor v89 n131 3 Jun 1997. p3. The Christian Science Monitor search engine: <http://www.csmonitor.com/plweb-cgi/iops1.pl> To retrieve this article, enter the following search: ED=19970603 AND conservationism. In the "retrieved list," click the title that matches this record. (ISSN0882-7729).

BIRDS, PROTECTION OF--WESTERN HEMISPHERE (v26)

BIRTH

see CHILDBIRTH; LABOR (OBSTETRICS); MULTIPLE BIRTH

BIRTH CONTROL (v26)

see also ABORTION; CHILDLESSNESS; CONTRACEPTION

"In the 1990s, 95 percent of the world's population lives in countries with government or private support for family planning....According to one estimate, these programs accounted for 43 percent of the fertility reduction in less industrialized countries between 1960 and 1990." (p36)

Riley, Nancy E. "Gender, Power, And Population Change." Population Bulletin v52 n1 May 1997. p2-46. (ISSN0032-468X).

A recent survey in Kenya "found that 91% of providers reported that women treated after unsafe abortions do not routinely receive family planning information in their facilities, even though 86% thought that women should receive family planning information....Observations in two major Egyptian hospitals in 1994 found that fewer than 3% of women treated for postabortion complications were counseled about family planning....At one Turkish government hospital only 14% of women reported receiving family planning counseling and information...." (p12-13)

Salter, Cynthia/Johnston, Heidi Bart/Hengen, Nicolene. "Care for Postabortion Complications: Saving Women's Lives." Population Reports v25 n1 Sep 1997. p1-13,16-21,23,25-31.

BIRTH CONTROL--AFRICA (v26)

BIRTH CONTROL--AFRICA--ASIA--LATIN AMERICA

According to the report, "Monitoring Family Planning Programs 1996," "in Africa, only 17 percent of married, reproductive-age women use a modern form of contraception, ranging from 11 percent in sub-Saharan Africa to 36 percent in North Africa. Contraceptive prevalence is significantly higher in Asia and Latin America, ranging from a low of 34 percent in South Central Asia to 53 percent in Latin America and a high of 78 percent in East Asia....The ratio of married women ages 15-44 per family planning staff member ranges from a high of 111,235 in the Ivory Coast to a low of 109 in Vietnam. Although the highest ratios of women per provider are found in Africa, several Latin American and Asian countries also have high ratios: of the 38 countries that have more than 1,000 women per staff member, 16 are in Africa, 12 in Latin America, and 10 in Asia." (p5)

"Data Sheet Charts Family Planning Progress." Population Today v25 n6 Jun 1997. p5. (ISSN0749-2448).

BIRTH CONTROL--CHINA--MEXICO (v26)

BIRTH CONTROL--DEVELOPING COUNTRIES (v26)

"Access to contraceptives is still inadequate in 50 of the 88 developing countries examined in a recent study by Population Action International (PAI)....The study, 'Contraceptive Choice: Worldwide Access to Family Planning,' ranked each country's access to five modern contraceptive methods: condoms, oral contraceptives, intrauterine devices (IUDs), female voluntary sterilization, and vasectomy, which together represent 98 percent of all modern methods in use in developing countries. For each country, the study rated contraceptive access on a scale from 1 to 100. Scores ranged from 0 (inaccessible to any of the population) to 20 (easy access by at least 80 percent of the population) for each of the five methods....Hong Kong, Singapore, South Korea, Taiwan, and Tunisia all earned the maximum 100 points....China and India, the two most populous countries, scored 93.6 and 79.8 points, respectively. Overall, both the 'very good' and 'good' categories contained 19 countries each....African countries, which accounted for 70 percent (21 out of 31) of the countries ranked as poor or very poor, lagged far behind developing countries in Latin America and Asia. In Mali, Mauritania, Chad, and the Congo, couples have virtually no access to any modern contraceptive method. These 50 countries contain approximately 10 percent of the world's women of childbearing age. The percentage of couples using family planning in developing countries has increased from less than 10 percent in the 1960s to more than 55 percent in the 1990s." (p7)

Mitchell, Jennifer. "Environmental Intelligence: Many Who Want Contraceptives Still Can't Get Them." World Watch v10 n4 Jul-Aug 1997. p7. (ISSN0896-0615).

BIRTH CONTROL--DEVELOPING COUNTRIES--UNITED STATES--APPROPRIATIONS AND EXPENDITURES (v26)

BIRTH CONTROL--EGYPT (v26)

BIRTH CONTROL--HUNGARY--KOREA (SOUTH) --TURKEY (v26)

BIRTH CONTROL--IRAN--SHIRAZ

A study in Shiraz, Iran "showed that 80 percent of married women of reproductive age (15 to 49 years) were practicing family planning. Pills and female sterilization were the most common modern methods....In 1996, women in Shiraz had higher rates of contraceptive use and lower fertility than women in urban areas in Turkey and Egypt a few years earlier." (p5)

Roudi, Farzaneh. "Surprising Decline in Iran's Growth Rates." Population Today v25 n11 Nov 1997. p4-5. (ISSN0749-2448).

BIRTH CONTROL--SOUTH AMERICA (v26)

BIRTH CONTROL PILLS

see ORAL CONTRACEPTIVES

BIRTH WEIGHT--UNITED STATES--MEN (v26)

BIRTH WEIGHT, LOW--MICHIGAN (v26)

BIRTH WEIGHT, LOW--UNITED STATES (v26)

In the U.S., "the low birthweight rate was 7.3 percent for 1995, the same level reported for 1994--and the highest reported since 1976. Low birthweight increased among white mothers from 6.1 to 6.2 percent. Although the rate of low birthweight is still more than twice as high among black women (13.1 percent), the rate of low birthweight for black infants has been dropping since 1992."

U.S. National Center for Health Statistics. "1995 Birth

Statistics Released." Fact Sheet 10 Jun 1997. document-level access: <http://www.cdc.gov/nchswww/releases/97facts/97sheets/95natrel.htm>

BISON, AMERICAN

see AMERICAN BISON

BITES AND STINGS--UNITED STATES

According to THE JOURNAL OF THE AMERICAN ACADEMY OF DERMATOLOGY, in an article entitled "Dog, Cat and Human Bites," "injuries inflicted by the mouth are caused most often by dogs: 1.6 million bites a year. The No. 2 'mammalian bite' is that of cats, harming perhaps 400,000 people a year. Human bites seem less frequent; some studies show as few as 72,000 a year." (p8)

Kulman, Linda. "Outlook: Bites: Dogs, Cats, And Tyson." U.S. News & World Report v123 n2 14 Jul 1997. p8. article-level access: <http://www.usnews.com/usnews/issue/970714/14OUT.HTM> (ISSN0041-5537).

BLACK MARKET

"The worldwide market for illegally traded plants and animals last year reached an estimated $10 to $20 billion, with reptiles making up a considerable part of that....The wildlife trade watchdog organization TRAFFIC USA reports that around 125,000 rattlesnakes are caught and killed annually in the United States for their meat, skins, gall bladders (to be used in traditional Asian medicines), or to be sold as souvenirs." (p25)

Youth, Howard. "Neglected Elders." World Watch v10 n5 Sep-Oct 1997. p22-29. (ISSN0896-0615).

BLACK MARKET--CIGARETTES

"WHO estimates that about one-third of the cigarettes produced in 1994 were moved from the legal market into the smuggling economy--a 300 percent increase since 1989. Cigarette smuggling is now thought to be costing governments some $16.2 billion annually." (p24)

McGinn, Anne Platt. "The Nicotine Cartel." World Watch v10 n4 Jul-Aug 1997. p18-27. (ISSN0896-0615).

BLACK MARKET--COLOMBIA

"The Colombian government has estimated the annual income of the CGN [Coordinadora Nacional Guerrillera, or the Colombian Guerrilla movement]--i.e., its revenues on investments and income flows--for 1994 at almost $600 million (Colombia/Advisory Office, 1994). In global terms, this figure approximated 0.52% of Colombia's gross domestic product (GDP) for 1995. According to the balance sheet prepared by the Inter-Institutional Committee for the study of Subversives (a group formed by the government to follow guerrilla finances), the CGN received more than 485 billion pesos ($600 million at an exchange rate of 700 pesos per US dollar) during 1994, of which it spent about $65 million. This means that its profits totaled $535 million, far exceeding that received by the country's most profitable, and legal, company: the National Coffee fund, which earned just 365 billion pesos (about $521 million) in 1994. This is also twice the amount earned by ECOPETROL (Colombia Petroleum Enterprise), Colombia's second-ranking industry, which earned 216 billion pesos, or about $309 million (FBIS-LAT, 1995...)." (p45)

Richani, Nazih. "The Political Economy of Violence: The War-System in Colombia." Journal of Interamerican Studies & World Affairs v39 n2 Sum 1997. p37-81. (ISSN0022-1937).

BLACKS--LATIN AMERICA (v26)

BLIND (v26)

BLIND--EDUCATION--CHINA

"China has 8.77 million blind or visually impaired people, a fifth of the world's blind population....Of these 8.77 million, 16% completed only primary school, 4% junior high, 0.9% senior high and only 0.2% higher education. In total only 21% of the total blind population have received some form of formal education. It is calculated that only 100,000 of the blind population can read braille." (p22)

Jianmin, Song/Shuping, Wo. "Politics and Society: China Braille Press." China Review n8 Aut-Win 1997. p22-24. (ISSN1359-5091).

BLIND--EMPLOYMENT--CHINA

In China, "1.4 million blind people now work in various enterprises....The greatest source of employment is in the massage clinics, of which there are over 800 in China employing 10,000 blind doctors and therapists." (p22)

Jianmin, Song/Shuping, Wo. "Politics and Society: China Braille Press." China Review n8 Aut-Win 1997. p22-24. (ISSN1359-5091).

BLIND--UNITED STATES--COSTS (v26)

BLOOD ALCOHOL--LAW AND LEGISLATION--UNITED STATES (v26)

BLOOD BANKS--RISK MANAGEMENT--UNITED STATES (v26)

BLOOD PRESSURE

"According to a new meta-analysis of English-language articles published prior to 1995, potassium supplementation does indeed lower diastolic and systolic BP [blood pressure] significantly....This meta-analysis, which was conducted by Paul K. Whelton, MD, MSc [Master of Science], and colleagues, examined the results of 33 randomized, controlled studies in which potassium supplementation was the only difference between the intervention and control groups. The trials involved a total of 2,609 patients. Twenty-one of the studies involved hypertensive patients, and 12 involved normotensives. Most of the trials were based on a potassium intake of roughly 2,300 mg/day [milligrams per day] (60 mmol [millimoles]), which is about the amount that most Americans consume in their usual diet....Potassium intake produced a mean 3.11-mm Hg decrease in systolic BP and a mean 1.97-mm Hg decrease in diastolic BP. Potassium supplementation was most effective in blacks and in patients who were consuming a high amount of sodium." (p12)

"Clinical News: Study Backs Argument That Potassium Supplementation Is Beneficial for Reducing Blood Pressure." Modern Medicine v65 n7 Jul 1997. p12. (ISSN0026-8070).

BLOOD PRESSURE, HIGH

see HYPERTENSION

BLUE COLLAR WORKERS--SOUTHERN STATES

"Job losses for black and white men in the [U.S.] South have been most strongly felt in blue-collar skilled crafts and semi-skilled operative positions which accounted for 46.7 percent of the male workforce in 1975 and now accounts for 37.7 percent of men's work, a 19.3 percent loss. In 1975, 14.5 percent of black men held skilled crafts positions and 23.4 percent of white men held skilled crafts positions. By 1994, 13.0 percent of black men held skilled positions while 18.0 percent of white men held skilled positions. Black men's rate of job loss in this category was 10.3 percent while white men's rate of job loss was 23.1 percent." (p18)

Eckman, Anne/Green, Jordan. "Dislocation & Workforce Equity: The South at Work in the 1990s: Job Losses for Both Black and White Men." Southern Exposure: Institute for Southern Studies Report 1997. p18.

BLUE-GRAY GNATCATCHER--ENVIRONMENTAL ASPECTS --CALIFORNIA

In 1991, in Southern California, "conservationists had petitioned the U.S. Fish and Wildlife Service (USFWS) to add the California gnatcatcher to the federal endangered species list. The gnatcatcher is a tiny bluish-gray songbird whose call sounds like the soft mew of a kitten. It depends on coastal sage scrub habitat for survival. The trouble is, all but between 10 percent and 20 percent of the unique mix of sagebrush and chaparral that once ranged from Ventura County to San Diego has been destroyed; the remaining 250,000 acres are highly fragmented, and much is degraded. USFWS surveys indicate gnatcatcher populations have declined dramatically in the last 20 years." (p19)

Holing, Dwight. "The Coastal Sage Scrub Solution." Nature Conservancy v47 n4 Jul-Aug 1997. p16-24. (ISSN0028-5200).

BLUEBERRY INDUSTRY--NEW JERSEY

According to North American Blueberry Council "estimates, U.S. blueberries for fresh use will likely be up 6 percent from a year ago in 1997, attributed mainly to the increase in New Jersey's production. New Jersey is the largest source of fresh blueberries, providing about one-third of fresh-market use during 1994-96. Fresh-market production in the State is expected to reach 26 million pounds in 1997, 13 percent above a year ago and New Jersey's share of U.S. fresh-market use will rise to 41 percent." (p20-21)

U.S. Dept. of Agriculture. Economic Research Service. "Noncitrus Fruit Outlook." Fruit and Tree Nuts Situation and Outlook Report Aug 1997. p7-26.

BLUEBERRY INDUSTRY--UNITED STATES (v26)

"Despite reduced supplies (including imports and beginning stocks) last year, strong demand from key export markets raised U.S. frozen blueberry exports 49 percent above a year earlier in 1996. U.S. shipments of frozen blueberries to Canada were up 134 percent and accounted for nearly 50 percent of all frozen exports. Frozen exports to other major markets also rose sharply, including those to Japan (up 132 percent), the United Kingdom (up 83 percent), France (387 percent), and Italy (up 25 percent). Exports to Germany and to the Netherlands, also major destinations for U.S. frozen blueberries, declined 13 and 58 percent, respectively. U.S. fresh blueberry exports were down 19 percent, to 7.3 million pounds in 1996. A surge in fresh exports to Germany and the United Kingdom were offset by declines to Canada (down 36 percent), the largest U.S. market, and to other major markets such as the Netherlands (down 13 percent), Switzerland (down 38 percent), and Italy (down 28 percent)." (p22)

U.S. Dept. of Agriculture. Economic Research Service. "Noncitrus Fruit Outlook." Fruit and Tree Nuts Situation and Outlook Report Aug 1997. p7-26.

"Fresh-market production makes up about 47 percent of all cultivated blueberries in the United States." (p20) "Cumulative imports of frozen blueberries during January-May 1997 totaled 11.6 million pounds, up 85 percent from the same period last year. At the same time, U.S. imports of fresh blueberries totaled 2.2 million pounds, up 29 percent. The increase in total imports (frozen and fresh) during the first 5 months of 1997 may be attributed to the small 1996 U.S. blueberry crop. Fresh use and processing use of domestic production fell 17 percent and 25 percent, respectively....Canada is also a major supplier of fresh blueberries to the United States, accounting for about 87 percent of the fresh volume imported in 1996." (p21-22)

U.S. Dept. of Agriculture. Economic Research Service. "Noncitrus Fruit Outlook." Fruit and Tree Nuts Situation and Outlook Report Aug 1997. p7-26.

BLUEFIN TUNA FISHERIES (v26)

BLUEFIN TUNA FISHERIES--ATLANTIC OCEAN

In the Atlantic Ocean, bluefin tuna discards "have averaged 125 tons annually over the past several years. In 1995 (latest data), 142 tons or an estimated 1,349 giant tunas were discarded....The US delegation to ICCAT [International Commission for the Conservation of Atlantic Tunas] justified a 134 ton increase in the allowable catch of western Atlantic bluefin in 1997 and '98...." (p9)

"Ocean Wildlife Campaign: NCMC, OWC Demand US Reduce Bluefin Discards." NCMC Marine Bulletin n79 Spr-Sum 1997. p9.

BLUEFIN TUNA FISHERIES--UNITED STATES

In the U.S., the catch of bluefin tuna "in the west is only about 6% of the total Atlantic catch....Catches amounting to between 10-20% of the US quota, or 0.007% of the Atlantic-wide catch, are contributing to overfishing an Atlantic-wide stock." (p3)

"Stock Answers: The Secret Is Asking the Right Questions." NCMC Marine Bulletin n79 Spr-Sum 1997. p3.

BLUEWATER BRIDGE (PORT HURON, MICH. AND SARNIA, ONT.)

On the Blue Water Bridge, which connects Michigan and Ontario, "traffic exceeds what it was built for. In 1938, they had about 1,000 vehicles a day. In 1992, they had 17,000....In peak summer months, 8,000 to 11,000 cars and 2,500 trucks cross daily from Canada to Michigan over the Blue Water Bridge, with about the same number heading into Canada, [U.S. Customs port director Russ] Day said....In 1990, 352,000 trucks crossed west into Michigan. In 1997, truck traffic is heading for 650,000, Day said." (p3 secB)

Blanchard, Rick. "Michigan: Blue Water Bridge II to Open as Original Closes for Repairs." Detroit News 6 Jul 1997. p3 secB.

BOATING ACCIDENTS--MICHIGAN (v26)

"The number of reported boating crashes more than doubled in Washtenaw County [Michigan] last summer, while the statewide total declined 17 percent. It was the first decline in boating crashes statewide in four years. According to an analysis of state figures by the Michigan Association of Insurance Agents, the 122 percent increase in boating crashes in Washtenaw County from 1995 to 1996 was the largest in the state. But the numbers--20 crashes up from nine the year before--are not high. St. Clair County, with 75 crashes, and Macomb County, with 50, recorded the highest number of crashes....[According to Lieutenant Lyle Belknap, boating and law administrator for the Michigan Department of Natural Resources,] there were 20 fatal boating accidents last summer in Michigan, where more than one million boats cruise both inland lakes and the Great Lakes. And 80 percent of the fatalities occur because people don't wear life jackets...." (p3 secC)

Hall, Sheri. "Ann Arbor Report: Number of Reported Boat Crashes Jumps in Washtenaw County." Ann Arbor News 26 Jun 1997. p3 secC.

"The number of boating accidents across Michigan fell 17 percent last year, the first such drop in four years. In the tri-county Detroit area, accident tallies fell even more--46 percent in Wayne County, 39 percent in Macomb County and 32 percent in Oakland County." (p1 secB)

Laitner, Bill. "Local News: Local Dateline: Metro Area: Boat Mishaps Fall across State." Detroit Free Press 20 Jun 1997. p1 secB.

BOATING ACCIDENTS--MICHIGAN, LAKE

"According to July 1996 Census Bureau statistics, the population of counties bordering Lake Michigan in Indiana and Illinois is 6.4 million people....On an average day in the summer, there are roughly 2,000 boats in the water along the 70 miles of shoreline from Gary to Waukegan. This tremendously heavily traffic gives rise to an average of 10 to 20 Coast Guard search and rescue boat missions a day within 3 to 5 miles of the Waukegan/Gary shoreline....The increased risk to boaters due to this situation was brought to light by a recent Chicago SUN TIMES article which reported that almost seven times more people have died in the lake waters near the Gary to Waukegan shoreline or connecting rivers in the past year than that in the previous year. Twenty-six people have died since October 1, 1996, compared to just four during the previous fiscal year....Nine of these deaths were the result of plane crashes, 11 deaths involved boating

incidents, and 2 people died in jet skiing accidents." (pE2040)
Blagojevich, Rod R. (Rep.-Ill.). "Improve the Safety of Boaters in Southern Lake Michigan." Congressional Record. Daily ed. v143 n142 21 Oct 1997. pE2039-2040. section/page-level access: <http://thomas.loc.gov/cqi-bin/query/R?r105:FLD001:E02039:> (ISSN0363-7239). (X1.1A.105/1).

BOATS AND BOATING
see also PERSONAL WATERCRAFT

BOATS AND BOATING--MICHIGAN--MACOMB COUNTY
"The number of registered boats in Michigan more than 26 feet long--the size of craft usually docked at marinas--jumped to 39,250 in 1996 from 34,700 in 1990, the Michigan Secretary of State reports. Meanwhile, the total number of registered boats in Macomb County, where there are almost no sizable inland lakes, is up to 54,000 from 50,600 during the same period." (p1-2 secC)
Puls, Mark. "Metro: Lake St. Clair Marinas Enjoying Wave of Prosperity." Detroit News 28 Jul 1997. p1-2 secC.

BOATS AND BOATING--REGISTRATION AND TRANSFER --MICHIGAN (v26)

BODY IMAGE IN ADOLESCENCE--UNITED STATES
A study of teenagers in the U.S. found that "for females, 26.0% reported themselves to be overweight compared with 4.7% classified as overweight based on BMI [body mass index]-weight status. Of the females who considered themselves to be overweight, 84.8% would not be so classified using BMI-weight status....For males, 92.2% were classified as normal or underweight compared with 88.9% reporting that they were not overweight. Of the males who considered themselves overweight, 63.1% would not be so classified using BMI-weight status....Females were more than twice (2.8) as likely as males to perceive themselves as overweight." (p868)
Pritchard, Mary E./King, Sondra L./Czajka-Narins, Dorice M. "Adolescent Body Mass Indices and Self-Perception." Adolescence v32 n128 Win 1997. p863-880. (ISSN0001-8449).

BODY WEIGHT
see also BIRTH WEIGHT, LOW

BODY WEIGHT--AUSTRALIA
According to the 1995 Australian National Health Survey, "based on self-reported height and weight, Body Mass Index (BMI) was calculated for people aged 15 or more. Around 55 per cent of men and women rated in the acceptable weight range for their height. A higher proportion of males (40 per cent) than females (28 per cent) were recorded as being overweight or obese. When asked to assess their own weight, 58 per cent of females assessed their weight as acceptable, 39 per cent as overweight and 6 per cent as underweight. Almost 40 per cent of young women (aged 15-24) considered themselves to be in a higher weight category than indicated by their BMI."
Australian Bureau of Statistics. "ABS Health Report on Australia." Media Release 28 Aug 1997. document-level access: <http://www.abs.gov.au/websitedbs/d3110125.nsf/4a255eef008309e44a255eef00061e57/7ad11af58d37387a4a25650100031cfd?OpenDocument>

BODY WEIGHT--RUSSIA (v26)

BODY WEIGHT--UNITED STATES
In the U.S., between 1988 and 1994, "33% of adult men, 36% of women, 12% of teens, and 14% of children were too heavy....Children and adolescents were categorized as being overweight when their body-mass index (BMI) was at or above the sex- and age-specific 95th percentile. The limit for adults was a BMI of at least 27.8 for men and at least 27.3 for women." (p36-37)
"Abstracts: Primary Care: CDC Reports that Americans Keep Putting On the Weight." Modern Medicine v65 n6 Jun 1997. p36-37. (ISSN0026-8070).

BODY WEIGHT--UNITED STATES--WOMEN
"A 1995 analysis of the Harvard Nurses' Health Study, which tracked 115,195 [U.S.] women for 16 years, showed that the lowest mortality rate for middle-aged women is for those who weigh at least 15% less than the U.S. average for women their age or those who haven't gained more than about 20 pounds since age 18. For example, the healthiest 5'5" women in this study weighed less than 120 pounds; weighing between 120 and 149 increased the risk of early death 20%. Yet by our 40s, more than 37% of women are obese." (p37)
Reichman, Judith. "Office Visit: Fighting Fat after 40." American Health v16 n6 Jul-Aug 1997. p37. (ISSN0730-7004).

BOEING 747 (JET TRANSPORTS) (v26)

BOILWORM, OLD WORLD
see HELICOVERPA ARMIGERA

BOLIVIA
Most of Bolivia "lies at elevations of 10,000 feet or more above sea level, making communications, transportation, agriculture, and even the efficient operation of automobiles a challenge....Bolivia is about the size of Arkansas, Louisiana, Texas, and Oklahoma combined. About half its area is taken up by the Altiplano plateau, home to two-thirds of the country's 7.8 million people. At the western end of the Altiplano is Lake Titicaca, the highest navigable lake in the world; at the plateau's center is La Paz, at 12,000 feet the highest capital city in the world." (p7)
Weber, Elizabeth. "Spotlight: Bolivia." Population Today v25 n10 Oct 1997. p7. (ISSN0749-2448).

BOLIVIA--SOCIAL CONDITIONS
"Bolivia's population is projected to reach 13.2 million by 2025. Infant and child mortality are high--71 of every 1,000 babies born do not live to see their first birthdays, and 116 do not live to age five. Child mortality is especially high between the ages of one and three years because many children become malnourished after they are weaned. Maternal mortality is also high, with 650 deaths for every 100,000 births." (p7)
Weber, Elizabeth. "Spotlight: Bolivia." Population Today v25 n10 Oct 1997. p7. (ISSN0749-2448).

BONDS--UNITED STATES
In the U.S., "with about $61.3 billion raised by mid-year, corporations are on pace to issue more in junk bonds this year than any other year in history--and almost three times the amount issued each year between 1986 and 1989....So far this year, almost $9 billion of plungers' dollars have found their way into mutual funds that invest exclusively in high-yield bonds....Historically, C-level-rated and nonrated issues make up about 10% of annual junk issuance, however, some estimates put this year's total at almost twice that percentage." (p2)
Wirth, Gregg. "One Man's Treasure: The Renaissance of Junk." Left Business Observer n79 29 Sep 1997. p2,7. (ISSN1042-0134).

BONES--DISEASES
see OSTEOPOROSIS

BONN (GERMANY)--EMPLOYMENT
In Bonn, Germany, "only 15% of the city's jobs are in industry." (p9) According to Hermann Tengler, "'between 1991 and 1996 we have seen 15,000 new jobs in the region, a growth of some 7%.'" (p10) According to Martin Hennicke, "the job growth rate in this area has been above average, some 14% since 1991....[Bonn is] a communications centre, with more than 500 businesses in the computer, multimedia, and telecommunications fields already employing 18,000 in the...area." (p11)
Schayan, Janet. "The New Bonn: The Federal City, Centre for Science and Communication." Deutschland n5 Oct 1997. p6-11. article-level access: <http://www.bundesregierung.de/.bin/lay/ausland/magazines/deutschland/d970501.html>

(ISSN0945-6791).

BONUS SYSTEM--MICHIGAN--CIVIL SERVICE (v26)

BOOBY TRAPS (MILITARY SCIENCE)

see MINES (MILITARY EXPLOSIVES)

BOOKS AND READING--GERMANY

A survey by the Bertelsmann Foundation states that, in Germany, "only 3% of the 2,300 people over the age of 14 interviewed had a 'very close attachment' to books; over the past year, one in three of all those questioned had not read a book at all. Some 57% take up a book once a week or less." (p60)

"Kulter the Arts: Books." Deutschland n6 Dec 1997. p60. (ISSN0945-6791).

BOOKS AND READING--SWEDEN (v26)

BOOKS AND READING--UNITED STATES (v26)

"According to statistics from a 1996 survey, 57 percent of children ages 3 to 5 in the United States were read aloud to by a family member every day during the week preceding the survey. This represents a slight increase from the 53 percent figure reported in 1993....More than 77 percent of children whose mothers were college graduates were read aloud to every day. In comparison, daily reading occurred with 62 percent of children whose mothers had some college experience, with 49 percent of children whose mothers had completed high school but had no education beyond that, and with just 37 percent whose mothers had not completed high school....Sixty-four percent of white children, 44 percent of black children, and 39 percent of Hispanic children were read to every day in 1996." (p25)

"News of the Profession: Parents & Reading: Reading to Young Children: Statistics to Consider." Reading Today v15 n3 Dec 1997-Jan 1998. p25. (ISSN0737-4208).

BOOKSELLERS AND BOOKSELLING--SWEDEN (v26)

BOOKSTORES--UNITED STATES

"The American Booksellers Association reports that in fiscal year 1994-95, nearly 200 independent bookstores in the US closed shop, up 21.6 percent from a year earlier. And the market share of bookselling by independents has dropped from 32 percent in 1991 to 18 percent in 1996." (p9)

Holmstrom, David. "Business & Money: Workplace: Survival Is in the Margins for Small Booksellers." The Christian Science Monitor v89 n219 7 Oct 1997. p9. The Christian Science Monitor search engine: <http://www.csmonitor.com/plweb-cgi/iops1.pl> To retrieve this article, enter the following search: ED=19971007 AND booksellers. In the "retrieved list," click the title that matches this record. (ISSN0882-7729).

BOOTS AND SHOES

see SHOES

BORAGINACEAE--OREGON (v26)

BORDER DISPUTES

see BOUNDARY DISPUTES

BORDER PATROLS--MEXICO--UNITED STATES

"According to a report by the University of Houston, '1,185 people had drowned, died of exposure or dehydration, or been hit by automobiles while...trying to cross the [U.S.-Mexican] border away from designated checkpoints' over the past four years. (THE SEATTLE TIMES, Aug 24.)....The Border Patrol is bringing in 230 more agents to patrol the Rio Grande River west and northwest of Brownsville, Texas...." (p8)

Turner, Charles. "Immigrants Risk Injury, Death at U.S. Border." The People v107 n7 Oct 1997. p8. (ISSN0199-350X).

BORDERS

see BOUNDARIES

BORROWING

see BANK LOANS; CREDIT CARDS; LOANS; LOANS, PERSONAL; STUDENT LOAN FUNDS

BOSNIA AND HERCEGOVINA--HISTORY--CIVIL WAR (v26)

BOSNIA AND HERCEGOVINA--SOCIAL CONDITIONS

"Ninety-six percent of international funds have gone to Bosnia, and a mere 1.3 percent have gone to Srpska,...[says Dusan Strbac, a Bosnian Serb and former career diplomat]. About a third of Srpska's population is refugees, and of those about 100,000 are still without homes, living in schools, factories, and other shelters." (p14)

"Short Takes: Is War Inevitable in Bosnia?" Peace Watch v3 n4 Jun 1997. p14. (ISSN1080-9864).

BOSTON (MASS.)--APPROPRIATIONS AND EXPENDITURES (v26)

BOTSWANA--ECONOMIC CONDITIONS

"In the early 1990s, Botswana's external debt represented less than 20 percent of GNP....As of 1993, Botswana had foreign exchange reserves equal to approximately 30 months' worth of imports. Botswana's per capita GNP grew at an average annual rate of 7 percent in real terms between 1965 and 1994." (p47)

U.S. Congressional Budget Office. "The Challenge of Development: Illustrations from Eight Countries." The Role of Foreign Aid in Development May 1997. p39-56.

BOUNDARIES--CANADA--UNITED STATES

"In 1996 alone, over 116 million people entered the United States by land from Canada. Similarly, over 52 million Canadian residents and United States permanent residents entered Canada last year....[A] new provision would require a stop on the U.S. side to record the exit of each person in every car. That's more than 140,000 every day; 6,000 every hour; 100 every minute....In 1993, nearly 9 million people traveled over the Ambassador Bridge..., 6.4 million traveled through the Detroit-Windsor tunnel, and approximately 6.1 million crossed the Blue Water Bridge in Port Huron." (pS10252)

Abraham, Spencer (Sen.-Mich.). "Section 110 of the Illegal Immigration Reform and Immigrant Responsibility Act." Congressional Record. Daily ed. v143 n134 1 Oct 1997. pS10251-10252. section/page-level access: <http://thomas.loc.gov/cqi-bin/query/R?r105:FLD001:S10252:> (ISSN0363-7239). (X1.1A.105/1).

BOUNDARY DISPUTES--WESTERN SAHARA

The Polisario Front "has fought hard against Moroccan troops for Western Sahara's independence. But its forces control less than one-third of the territory, which has been cut off by a 700-mile-long sand barrier built by Morocco. On its side of this berm--guarded by 150,000 troops and lined with minefields and barbed wire--Morocco controls one of the world's largest reserves of phosphate, used for making fertilizers and other chemicals....In 1991, Morocco transferred 40,000 people who it claimed were Saharawis--though they had no identity papers--into the territory....Some 150,000 more names were also submitted by Morocco." (p7)

Peterson, Scott. "International: James Baker Steps Into a N. African Sandstorm." The Christian Science Monitor v89 n185 19 Aug 1997. p7. The Christian Science Monitor search engine: <http://www.csmonitor.com/plweb-cgi/iops1.pl> To retrieve this article, enter the following search: ED=19970819 AND sandstorm. In the "retrieved list," click the title that matches this record. (ISSN0882-7729).

BOUNDARY PATROLS

see BORDER PATROLS

BOVINE SPONGIFORM ENCEPHALOPATHY (v26)

BOVINE SPONGIFORM ENCEPHALOPATHY--GREAT BRITAIN (v26)

BOWLING--UNITED STATES

In the U.S., there "has been a decline of 40 percent, between 1980 and 1993, in league bowling....During the same period the number of solitary bowlers has increased by 10 percent." (p21)

Vogl, A. J. "Soul Searching: Looking for Meaning in the Workplace." Across the Board v34 n9 Oct 1997. p16-23. (ISSN0147-1554).

BOY PREFERENCES OF PARENTS

see SEX OF CHILDREN, PARENTAL PREFERENCES FOR

BOY SCOUTS--UNITED STATES--ATTITUDES (v26)

BOYS AS SOLDIERS--RWANDA (v26)

BRAILLE--MICHIGAN (v26)

BRAIN--DISEASES

see CEREBROVASCULAR DISEASE

BRAND NAME PRODUCTS--CHINA--PUBLIC OPINION

"As in 1994, of the 20 most widely recognized foreign (or foreign-derived) brands in China, fully half are Japanese. Seven are American, two are German, and one is Dutch....At the very top (among non-Chinese brands), the five leaders now consist of three brands with U.S. origins (Coca Cola, Beijing Jeep, Head and Shoulders), one German joint venture subsidiary (Volkswagen's Santana), and Japan's Panasonic. Each of these is recognized by at least two-thirds of all Chinese adults nationwide (Coca Cola 81%, Beijing Jeep 77%, Santana 76%, Head and Shoulders 72%, Panasonic 70%). In contrast, Gallup's 1994 survey found that four of the top five leaders in foreign brand awareness were of Japanese origin, with only one non-Japanese mark (Coca Cola) attaining this select group. The overall foreign leader at that time, Hitachi, was recognized by 65% nationwide--a level which if gained today would place it only seventh among all foreign brands (Hitachi's 1997 score: 67%)."

Gallup Organization. "1997 Survey: The People's Republic of China: Consumer Attitudes & Lifestyle Trends." Press Release 27 Oct 1997. document-level access: <http://www.gallup.com/poll/special/china/chinarel.html>

BRAND NAME PRODUCTS--UNITED STATES --TEENAGERS--ATTITUDES

According to the Zandl Group of New York City, the "top-ten list of coolest teen apparel and footwear brands for fall [in the U.S.] is dominated by high-visibility, high-priced brands. Seventy-three percent of teens say that Nike is cool. Sixty-seven percent say the same of Tommy Hilfiger, 59 percent of Calvin Klein, and 50 percent of Oakley." (p38)

Heubusch, Kevin. "Kaleidoscope: Teens Warm Up to Value." American Demographics v19 n11 Nov 1997. p38. article-level access: <http://www.demographics.com/publications/ad/97_ad/9711_ad/ad971115.htm> (ISSN0163-4089).

BRAZIL--ECONOMIC CONDITIONS (v26)

Brazil "is now in its third year of a reform process that succeeded in reducing inflation from 5,000 percent in 1994 to 11 percent in 1996." (p8) "The current account deficit increased from balance in 1993 to 3.3 percent of GDP in 1997...." (p9)

Drosdoff, Daniel. "The Region: Reform: Same Tune, Different Steps." IDB v24 n9-10 Sep-Oct 1997. p8-9. (ISSN0145-2274).

The U.S. economy is "more than 10 times larger than that of Brazil....Three years ago, Brazil's annual inflation exceeded 7,000 percent; today it is less than 10 percent....Privatization and infrastructure development are proceeding, and there has been an explosion of foreign direct investment to Brazil, expanding from $2 billion in 1993 to $9 billion last year and a projected $15 billion this year." (p19)

Hakim, Peter. "Opinion/Essays: Brazil and the US: Key Partners." The Christian Science Monitor v89 n149 27 Jun 1997. p19. The Christian Science Monitor search engine: <http://www.csmonitor.com/plweb-cgi/iops1.pl> To retrieve this article, enter the following search: ED=19970627 AND partners. In the "retrieved list," click the title that matches this record. (ISSN0882-7729).

BRAZIL--EMPLOYMENT (v26)

BRAZIL--MANUFACTURES (v26)

BRAZIL--SOCIAL CONDITIONS

"According to a 1996 United Nations study, 46 percent of...[Brazil's] northeastern population is poor, compared with 20 percent of the south. And while Brazil's overall illiteracy rate is about 17 percent, the northeast's is 37.6 percent, according to the Brazilian Institute of Geography and Statistics. Small farmers own just 14 percent of land holdings in the region, says Osmil Galindo, a researcher at the Joaquim Nabuco government research foundation in Recife....[The city of] Canudos lies 252 miles north of Salvador. Fifty-two percent of the 15,000 residents can't read, half have no sewage link, and 30 percent lack running water, according to city hall." (p11)

Epstein, Jack. "Centennial of a War Stirs a Nation." The Christian Science Monitor v89 n216 2 Oct 1997. p10-11. The Christian Science Monitor search engine: <http://www.csmonitor.com/plweb-cgi/iops1.pl> To retrieve this article, enter the following search: ED=19971002 AND nation. In the "retrieved list," click the title that matches this record. (ISSN0882-7729).

BREADSTUFFS

see GRAIN

BREAKFAST PROGRAMS, SCHOOL

see SCHOOL BREAKFAST PROGRAMS

BREAST--AUSTRALIA--EXAMINATION (v26)

BREAST--CANCER

Breast cancer "is the number one cancer for women in the United States, having killed more than 44,000 women in 1996. Worldwide, it accounts for 19 per cent of all female cancers, and its incidence has risen by 26 per cent since 1980." (p37)

"From Silent Spring to Vocal Vanguard." UN Chronicle v34 n3 1997. p35-38. (ISSN0251-7329).

BREAST--CANCER--CANADA (v26)

"Breast cancer remains a major health problem for women in Canada. We estimate that approximately 18,400 new breast cancer cases will be diagnosed this year and that 5,100 women will die of this disease.... "In 1992 Health Canada launched a five year $25 million initiative on breast cancer, a collaboration among breast cancer survivors, health care professionals, NGOs [non-governmental organizations], provincial authorities, researchers and support groups." (p324)

Augustine, Jean (MP-ON). "Statements by Members: Breast Cancer." Canada. Parliament. House of Commons. Debates. v135 n8 1 Oct 1997. p324. section-level access: <http://www.parl.gc.ca/36/1/parlbus/chambus/house/debates/008_1997-10-01/han008-e.htm#LINK11> (ISSN0704-5603). (X3-361E).

"In 1960, one in twenty Canadian women developed breast cancer; it is now one in nine....Breast cancer kills approximately one million women world wide each year, including about 7,000 in Canada in 1997. It is the single most frequent cause of death among middle-aged women." (p7)

LeBow, Barbara. "The ABC Link." ProLife News v22 n8 Sep 1997. p7.

BREAST--CANCER--CANADA--MORTALITY

In Canada, "over 5,000 women...died of breast cancer in 1997.... "Breast cancer takes one life every two hours in this country. These statistics are alarming and discouraging for the 18,600 women who are diagnosed each year." (p325)

Meredith, Val (MP-BC). "Statements by Members: Breast Cancer." Canada. Parliament. House of Commons. Debates. v135 n8 1 Oct 1997. p325. section-level access: <http://www.parl.gc.ca/36/1/parlbus/chambus/house/debates/008_1997-10-01/han008-e.htm#LINK23> (ISSN0704-5603). (X3-361E).

BREAST--CANCER--CANADA--UNITED STATES (v26)

BREAST--CANCER--EUROPE--UNITED STATES --MORTALITY (v26)

BREAST--CANCER--GREAT BRITAIN (v26)

BREAST--CANCER--MICHIGAN

According to a Michigan state health report, "the breast cancer incidence rate rose slightly in 1995 after three years of decline, also credited to early screening. There were 6,170 cases reported in 1995, compared with 6,044 in 1994." (p13 secA)

Schulz, Karen. "Cancer Diagnoses Fall; Cancer Deaths Up Slightly." Ypsilanti Press 22 Nov 1997. p1,13 secA.

BREAST--CANCER--NEW JERSEY (v26)

BREAST--CANCER--NORTHEASTERN STATES

"Scientists at the National Cancer Institute (NCI) have discovered that women living in a broad stretch of the metropolitan northeastern United States are slightly more likely to die from breast cancer than women in other parts of the Northeast....'The breast cancer mortality rate along a section of the East Coast stretching from New York City to Philadelphia is 7.4 percent higher than the rest of the Northeast,' said Martin Kulldorff, Ph.D., who led the study....Previous studies have shown that the northeastern United States (including Conn., Del., Md., Maine, Mass., N.H., N.J., N.Y., Pa., R.I., Vt. and D.C.) has about a 16 percent higher breast cancer mortality rate than the rest of the country....During the five years (1988-1992) covered by the analysis, 24,044 women in the New York/ Philadelphia region died of breast cancer. This was about 200 more deaths per year than researchers would have expected to find if this area had the same breast cancer mortality rate as the rest of the 11-state northeastern region of the U.S."

U.S. National Institutes of Health. "New Statistical Methodology Suggests Elevated Breast Cancer Mortality in Large Parts of Northeastern United States." News Release 15 Jul 1997. document-level access: <http://www.nih.gov/news/pr/jul97/nci-15.htm>

BREAST--CANCER--TREATMENT--MICHIGAN --COSTS

U.S. federal funds for breast cancer "exceeded $600 billion this year, up from $90 billion in 1990. The U-M [University of Michigan] has 27 grants, worth about $8 million, for breast cancer research. St. Joseph [Hospital] recently received $1 million for breast cancer studies over the next five years....Stem cell transplants are the most aggressive and expensive treatments for breast cancer, costing between $80,000 and $150,000....In August [1997], Blue Cross & Blue Shield of Michigan agreed to pay for stem cell transplants for breast cancer, following a 1995 class-action lawsuit from more than 100 patients." (p6 secA)

Wahlberg, David. "Fighting Breast Cancer: New Strategies: A Tough Fight." Ypsilanti Press 16 Nov 1997. p1,6-7 secA.

BREAST--CANCER--TREATMENT--UNITED STATES (v26)

BREAST--CANCER--UNITED STATES (v26)

Breast cancer accounts for "3 percent [of the deaths among American women]....By age 35, a woman has 1 chance in 622 of developing breast cancer. The risk rises to 1 in 93 by age 45, 1 in 33 by age 55 and 1 in 17 by age 65. The 'one woman in eight' figure now frequently heard refers to the lifetime risk of breast cancer for a woman who lives beyond the age of 85....The five-year survival rate for women with localized breast cancer is now 97 percent (up from 72 percent in the 1940s). Even if the cancer has spread to tissues surrounding the breast, 76 percent of the women will be alive five years later. Over all, including cases diagnosed in an advanced stage, 65 percent of women with breast cancer will survive for 10 years and 56 percent for 15 years." (p2 secF)

Brody, Jane. "Connection: Focus on Breast Cancer Leading Women to Neglect Other Serious Health Issues." Ann Arbor News 12 Oct 1997. p2 secF.

In the U.S., "only 10 percent to 15 percent of breast cancers are familial and not all of those are hereditary....As for the 85 percent of cases without a family history, there are several well-established risk factors....The risk...increases if menarche comes at an early age or menopause starts late--both lengthen the exposure of breast tissue to high doses of growth-stimulating estrogens. A woman who started to menstruate before age 14 has a risk that is 30 percent higher than a woman who reached menarche at 16....Likewise, a woman who enters menopause at age 55 or later has a risk 50 percent higher than that for a woman whose menopause begins earlier. Another risk factor is having a first baby late in life or having no biological children, which one study suggests could account for almost 30 percent of breast cancer cases in this country." (p2 secF)

Brody, Jane. "Connection: Focus on Breast Cancer Leading Women to Neglect Other Serious Health Issues." Ann Arbor News 12 Oct 1997. p2 secF.

"An estimated 2.6 million women in the United States are living with breast cancer. Currently, there are 1.8 million women in this country who have been diagnosed with breast cancer and 1 million more who do not yet know that they have the disease. It was estimated that in 1996, 184,300 new cases of breast cancer would be diagnosed and 44,300 women would die from the disease. Breast cancer costs this country more than $6 billion each year in medical expenses and lost productivity....The death rate from breast cancer has not been reduced in more than 50 years. One out of four women with breast cancer dies within the first 5 years; 40 percent die within 10 years of diagnosis. Furthermore, the incidence of breast cancer among American women is rising each year. One out of eight women in the United States will develop breast cancer in her lifetime--a risk that was 1 in 14 in 1960. For women ages 30 to 34, the incidence rate tripled between 1973 and 1987; the rate quadrupled for women ages 35 to 39 during the same period." (pH8982)

Jackson-Lee, Sheila (Rep.-Tex.). "Breast Cancer Legislation." Congressional Record. Daily ed. v143 n143 22 Oct 1997. pH8982-8984. section/page-level access: <http://thomas.loc.gov/cgi-bin/query/R?r105:FLD001:H08982:> (ISSN0363-7239). (X1.1A.105/1).

"Breast cancer is the most common cancer among women, after skin cancer. In 1996, 184,300 new cases were diagnosed and 44,300 women died [in the U.S.]. Breast cancer is the second leading cause of cancer deaths among women, after lung cancer. Breast cancer is the leading cause of cancer death in women between ages 40 and 55. Most women diagnosed with breast cancer are over age 50. For women age 40 to 44, the incidence rate is 125.4 per 100,000 women; for women ages 50 to 54, it jumps to 232.7 per 100,000." (pS4242)

Feinstein, Dianne (Sen.-Calif.). "Statements on Introduced Bills and Joint Resolutions." Congressional Record. Daily ed. v143 n59 8 May 1997. pS4217-4246. section/page-level access: <http://thomas.loc.gov/cgi-bin/query/R?r105:FLD001:S04242:> (ISSN0363-7239). (X1.1A.105/1).

In the U.S., "in the 1950's, 1 in 20 women developed breast cancer. Today, the incidence is one in eight, and growing. It kills 46,000 women a year. Every 12 minutes an American woman dies of breast cancer. It is the leading cause of cancer death for women between the ages of 35 and 52, and it is the second leading cause of death in all women. So, today, 1.8 million women in America are diagnosed with breast cancer, and 1 million women, in addition to that, don't know they have breast cancer. This year, 184,300 new breast cancer cases will be diagnosed, and 17,100 of those in California." (pS7661)

Feinstein, Dianne (Sen.-Calif.). "Treasury and General Government Appropriations Act, 1998." Congressional Record. Daily ed. v143 n102 17 Jul 1997. pS7659-7663. section/page-level access: <http://thomas.loc.gov/cgi-bin/query/

R?r105:FLD001:S07661:> (ISSN0363-7239). (X1.1A.105/1).

Esther John, a breast cancer epidemiologist in Union City, California, "studied 4,881 white women [in the U.S.], including 133 who had breast cancer. She reported that women in the South have a 41-percent lower risk of dying of breast cancer, compared to cold-belt states like Michigan. Women with the lowest risk lived 20 or more years in areas with high exposure to sunlight. But as little as one hour a day of sunlight might be sufficient to improve breast cancer outcomes, she said." (p1 secA)

Anstett, Patricia. "Breast Cancer Risks Updated: Extra Pounds, Lack of Sun Tied to Disease." Detroit Free Press 3 Nov 1997. p1,8 secA.

"Breast cancer is the most frequently diagnosed non-skin cancer in women in the United States. It is second only to lung cancer in cancer-related deaths....About 80 percent of breast cancers occur in women age 50 or older. The risk is especially high in women over age 60. Breast cancer is uncommon under age 40. Present rates project that each year, out of 100,000 women: in their 30s, 43 women will be diagnosed with breast cancer and 8 will die of the disease; in their 40s, 163 women will be diagnosed with breast cancer and 29 will die of the disease; in their 50s, 263 women will be diagnosed with breast cancer and 59 will die of the disease; in their 60s, 374 women will be diagnosed with breast cancer and 91 will die of it."

U.S. Dept. of Health and Human Services. "Breast Cancer and Mammography." Fact Sheet 25 Oct 1997. document-level access: <http://www.hhs.gov/news/press/1997pres/971025a.html>

In the U.S., "the lifetime risk of developing breast cancer today is one in every eight women, up from one in every 13 women just two decades ago. Although death rates from breast cancer have been declining in recent years, breast cancer accounts for 31 percent of all cancers among women. Approximately 180,000 new cases of breast cancer will be diagnosed in 1997, and about 44,000 women are expected to die from breast cancer. Epidemiologic studies estimate that breast cancer will be diagnosed in 1.5 million American women in this decade and that breast cancer will claim nearly half a million lives."

U.S. Dept. of Health and Human Services. "Breast Cancer: New Efforts Underway." Fact Sheet 25 Oct 1997. document-level access: <http://www.hhs.gov/news/press/1997pres/971025.html>

In the U.S., "the lifetime risk of developing breast cancer today is one in every eight women, up from one in every 20 women just two decades ago....Breast cancer accounts for 31 percent of all cancers among women. Approximately 180,200 new cases of breast cancer will be diagnosed in 1997....Epidemiologic studies estimate that breast cancer will be diagnosed in 1.5 million American women in this decade....Between 1982 and 1987, breast cancer incidence (rate of new cases) for women increased about 4 percent per year, but recently has leveled off."

U.S. Dept. of Health and Human Services. "Breast Cancer: New Efforts Underway." Fact Sheet 11 Jun 1997. document-level access: <http://www.hhs.gov/news/press/1997pres/970611.html>

"Currently, there are 2.6 million women living with breast cancer in...[the U.S.]. This year, more than 180,000 new cases of invasive breast cancer will be diagnosed and approximately 44,000 women will die from the disease. In fact, breast cancer is the leading cause of death for American women between the ages of 40 and 55. Other than skin cancer, breast cancer is the most frequently occurring cancer in women, costing the U.S. $6 billion annually in medical costs and lost productivity." (p28)

Smith, Kathleen T. "Issues: Breast Cancer Legislation: A Review of Federal and State Initiatives." Imprint v44 n5 Nov-Dec 1997. p28,30,32. (ISSN0019-3038).

"In 1997, there will be an estimated 180,200 new cases of invasive breast cancer among women in the United States, and an estimated 44,190 women will die from the disease. Breast cancer mortality rates vary widely from state to state. Hawaii's rate is 32 percent lower than the national age-adjusted average of 26.4 per 100,000 women, and Washington D.C.'s rate is 28 percent higher."

U.S. National Institutes of Health. "New Statistical Methodology Suggests Elevated Breast Cancer Mortality in Large Parts of Northeastern United States." News Release 15 Jul 1997. document-level access: <http://www.nih.gov/news/pr/jul97/nci-15.htm>

In the U.S., "breast cancer is the most frequently diagnosed cancer in women and the second leading cause of cancer deaths among women (after lung cancer). In 1995 the age-adjusted death rate for breast cancer for black females was 34 percent higher than for white females. Between 1990 and 1995 breast cancer death rates for black females were relatively stable while those for white females decreased 10 percent."

U.S. Dept. of Health and Human Services. "Report on Nation's Health Documents Toll of Injuries in U.S.: Firearm Mortality Down 11%, Traffic Fatality...Up...." Press Release 24 Jul 1997. document-level access: <http://www.cdc.gov/nchswww/releases/97news/97news/hus96rel.htm>

BREAST--CANCER--UNITED STATES--FINANCE

U.S. Dept. of Health and Human Services "discretionary funding for breast cancer research, prevention and treatment has increased from approximately $274 million in FY 1993 to an estimated $513 million in FY 1997. As the Centers for Disease Control and Prevention (CDC) have worked to increase access for all women to mammography screening and follow up services, the resources devoted to breast cancer services have increased from an estimated $42 million in FY 1993, to $81 million in FY 1997....The Clinton Administration has invested in breast cancer research at the National Institutes of Health by increasing funding from $229 million in FY 1993, to $401 million in FY 1997, and a President's budget request of $408 million in FY 1998."

U.S. Dept. of Health and Human Services. "Breast Cancer: New Efforts Underway." Fact Sheet 25 Oct 1997. document-level access: <http://www.hhs.gov/news/press/1997pres/971025.html>

BREAST--CANCER--UNITED STATES--MORTALITY

Death rates from breast cancer in the U.S. "are highest among older, black, and low-income women. With proper screening and treatment, however, the chances of surviving breast cancer are improving. Breast cancer mortality trends among both black and white women have improved markedly in the United States since the 1980s. Between 1982 and 1987, breast cancer incidence for women increased about 4 percent per year, but recently has leveled off. The death rate for women with breast cancer declined 6.3 percent between 1991 and 1995. The death rate for women with breast cancer declined 6.3 percent between 1991 and 1995. The greatest reductions in death rates were among younger women (9.3 percent) and white women (6.6 percent), with more modest reductions among African Americans (1.6 percent) and women age 65 and older (2.8 percent). During the most recent 5-year period, death rates among white women declined for all decades of age from 30 to 79 years. Among black women, rates were down for all decades of age from 30 to 69 years. Among both groups, the greatest improvements in mortality were seen in the younger age groups. For women aged 30 to 39 years, rates dropped about 13 percent about whites and 5 percent among blacks. For women aged 40 to 49 years, rates dropped 9 percent among whites and 2 percent among blacks."

U.S. Dept. of Health and Human Services. "Breast Cancer: New Efforts Underway." Fact Sheet 25 Oct 1997. document-level access: <http://www.hhs.gov/news/press/1997pres/971025.html>

In the U.S., in 1997, "about 44,000 women are expected to die from breast cancer....[In this decade,] breast cancer will claim nearly half a million lives....During the last 20 years, death rates from breast cancer for women over 65 increased by 35 percent for black women and 11 percent for white women. Mortality rates vary widely among racial and ethnic groups in the United States. Hispanic, Chinese, Filipino and Japanese women have annual rates at or below 15 per 100,000 women, while black, white and Native Hawaiian women have rates above 25 per 100,000 women....The death rate for women with breast cancer declined 6.3 percent between 1991 and 1995. The greatest reductions in death rates were among younger women (9.3 percent) and white women (6.6 percent), with more modest reductions among African Americans (1.6 percent)...."

U.S. Dept. of Health and Human Services. "Breast Cancer: New Efforts Underway." Fact Sheet 11 Jun 1997. document-level access: <http://www.hhs.gov/news/press/1997pres/970611.html>

BREAST--CANCER--UNITED STATES--PREVENTION (v26)
BREAST--RADIOGRAPHY--UNITED STATES (v26)

"An estimated 180,000 American women will be diagnosed with breast cancer in 1997, and 44,000 will die from it. More than 80 percent of the deaths are to women aged 50 or older. Doctors estimate that breast-cancer deaths could be cut by 30 percent if every older woman got regular screenings, including a mammogram every year. But just over one-third of women aged 50 to 64 got a mammogram in 1992, according to the National Center for Health Statistics (NCHS)....Only 19 percent of uninsured women aged 50 to 64 got a mammogram in 1992. Even among older women, virtually all of whom are covered by Medicare, the share was just 33 percent among 65-to-69-year-olds, 30 percent for those aged 70 to 74, and 24 percent for those aged 75 to 79." (p17)

Edmondson, Brad. "New Frontiers: Missing Mammograms." American Demographics v19 n5 May 1997. p16-17. article-level access: <http://www.demographics.com/Publications/AD/97_ad/9705_ad/AD97054.htm> (ISSN0163-4089).

"A study by the Centers for Disease Control found that only 41 percent of [American] women age 40 to 49 reported having a recent mammogram. Only half of women aged 50 to 64 had a recent mammogram. And only 39 percent of women over age 65 reported a recent mammogram....A survey by the Jacob Institute of Women's Health likewise found that 56 percent of women in their 40's and 47 percent of women in...[their] 50's were meeting the ACS [American Cancer Society] screening guideline. After lack of a family history, the cost of a mammogram was the principal reason for not having a mammogram. The lack of insurance coverage, the CDC study found, is an important factor in determining which women follow the recommended guidelines. Among commercially insured women, more than half were following the guidelines. However, for women in government insurance programs, between 58 percent and 66 percent were not following the guidelines. For women with no insurance of any kind, 84 percent were not in compliance with the guidelines. The cost of a mammogram also varies widely, depending on the radiologist's technique, the location, the interpretation needed. One unofficial estimate of cost is that a mammogram ranges from $75.00 to $200.00 per visit." (pS4243)

Feinstein, Dianne (Sen.-Calif.). "Statements on Introduced Bills and Joint Resolutions." Congressional Record. Daily ed. v143 n59 8 May 1997. pS4217-4246. section/page-level access: <http://thomas.loc.gov/cgi-bin/query/R?r105:FLD001:S04243:> (ISSN0363-7239). (X1.1A.105/1).

"Breast cancer is the most commonly diagnosed cancer and the second leading cause of cancer deaths among American women....For women age 50-69, having regular mammograms can reduce the chance of death from breast cancer by one third or more. Despite these numbers, 40 percent of women age 50 and older have reported not having a mammogram in the past two years, while 54 percent of women age 65 and older have a mammogram every two years."

U.S. Dept. of Health and Human Services. "Breast Cancer: New Efforts Underway." Fact Sheet 11 Jun 1997. document-level access: <http://www.hhs.gov/news/press/1997pres/970611.html>

In the U.S., "about 50 percent of women whose breast cancer is detected by mammography would not have died from the cancer even if they had waited until a lump could be felt because the tumors are slow-growing and easy to treat....About 25 percent of breast tumors are missed in women in their 40s compared to 10 percent for women in their 50s. Also, between 5 percent and 10 percent of mammograms are abnormal."

U.S. Dept. of Health and Human Services. "Breast Cancer and Mammography." Fact Sheet 25 Oct 1997. document-level access: <http://www.hhs.gov/news/press/1997pres/971025a.html>

In the U.S., "a woman who has annual mammograms from ages 40 to 49 has about a 30 percent risk of undergoing additional diagnostic tests. The use of mammography screening in younger women has produced a significant increase in the diagnosis of ductal carcinoma in situ (DCIS), a precancerous condition in which abnormal cells are confined to mammary ducts. Many, if not most, DCIS lesions will never progress to invasive tumors if left untreated, yet 40 percent of women with this diagnosis are treated with breast removal....Radiation from mammograms is thought to cause breast cancer in one of every 10,000 women who get annual mammograms from ages 40 to 49." (p5)

"The Mammography Controversy." People's Medical Society Newsletter v16 n3 Jun 1997. p4-5. (ISSN0736-4873).

In the U.S., "over the past three years, the quality of mammography has improved dramatically. Almost all of the nation's 10,000 mammography facilities have been inspected and accredited. Prior to 1992, only about 46 percent of facilities were accredited and many facilities were never inspected....Physicians who interpret mammograms must now have 60 hours training in mammography, technologists must keep their skills current by doing an average of 200 mammograms every two years, and medical physicists who survey mammography equipment and facilities must meet initial and ongoing training requirements....Annual inspections to date show that overall the nation's mammography facilities have a very good record of complying with standards. The first year's inspections in 1996 showed that 80 percent of the facilities had either no violations or minor ones, and that only two percent had violations serious enough to warrant a warning letter from the FDA. The second year's inspections have shown further improvement. So far, less than one percent of facilities have been found to have serious problems."

U.S. Dept. of Health and Human Services. "FDA Issues Final Standards for Mammography Facilities." Press Release 27 Oct 1997. document-level access: <http://www.hhs.gov/news/press/1997pres/971027b.html>

BREAST--RADIOGRAPHY--UNITED STATES--PUBLIC OPINION

"A February 1997 CBS poll found that 71 percent of [American] women think early detection of breast cancer significantly increases a woman's chances of surviving. 85 percent believe mammograms are safe and 88 percent trust the accuracy of mammograms. Between 1987 and 1992, the National Health Interview survey found that there was at least a two-fold increase in the percentage of women of all ages who had a recent mammogram." (pS4243)

Feinstein, Dianne (Sen.-Calif.). "Statements on Introduced Bills and Joint Resolutions." Congressional Record. Daily ed. v143 n59 8 May 1997. pS4217-4246. section/page-level access: <http://thomas.loc.gov/cgi-bin/query/R?r105:FLD001:S04242:> (ISSN0363-7239). (X1.1A.105/1).

BREMERTON (WASH.) (v26)

BRIBERY--UNITED STATES (v26)

BRIDGES

see also AMBASSADOR BRIDGE; BLUE WATER BRIDGE; MACKINAC BRIDGE; RAINBOW BRIDGE

BRIDGES--UNITED STATES

In the U.S., "the National Bridge Inventory contains about 570,000 highway bridges. If we exclude culverts and tunnels for the moment, the inventory still includes about 470,000 bridges....There are about 110,000 structurally deficient bridges in the inventory. While steel bridges represent about 40 percent of the overall bridge total, they include about 60 percent of the structurally deficient bridges. Reinforced concrete bridges fare well in the comparison of proportions, and only a relatively small proportion of the prestressed concrete bridges are structurally deficient. Timber bridges, while representing only 9 percent of the entire number of bridges, represent 20 percent of the structurally deficient bridges. About half of the nation's timber bridges are classified as structurally deficient." (p16-17) "Today, about 187,000 bridges are classified as deficient." (p18)

Chase, Steven B./Washer, Glenn/U.S. Dept. of Transportation. Federal Highway Administration. "Nondestructive Evaluation for Bridge Management in the Next Century." Public Roads v61 n1 Jul-Aug 1997. p16-25. (ISSN0033-3735).

BRIDGES--UNITED STATES--FINANCE (v26)

BRIDGES--UNITED STATES--MAINTENANCE AND REPAIR (v26)

BRIDGES, TOLL

see TOLL BRIDGES

BRITISH--HONG KONG (v26)

BRITISH COLUMBIA--POPULATION (v26)

BROADCAST JOURNALISM--MICHIGAN--DETROIT

In Detroit, Michigan, television is now "the main source of news for 63 percent of the area's residents, according to a DETROIT NEWS survey that asked 799 people about TV news and its impact on viewers. In comparison, daily newspapers were named as the main source by 16 percent and radio by 12 percent....African Americans are more likely to name television as a chief source of news. Some 83 percent of African Americans surveyed named TV, compared with 62 percent of whites....Young adults are the group most dependent on local TV news for information. Some 71 percent of those surveyed in the 18-36 age category said it was their main source, compared with 58 percent in the 37-56 age group." (p1 secE)

Kiska, Tim. "Accent: Crime Time Live: Viewers Speak Out: Television Has Become the Main Source of News for Most in Metro Detroit." Detroit News 18 Jun 1997. p1,5 secE.

BROADCAST JOURNALISM--MICHIGAN--PUBLIC OPINION

In Michigan, a DETROIT NEWS survey of 799 viewers found that "two-thirds think local television news spends too much time on crime and disaster stories....The older one gets, the more likely he or she is to dislike the violent content of the news. Some 58 percent of those in the 18-36 age group objected, and 74 percent in the 57-plus age group. Seventy percent of females complain about violent coverage, compared with 61 percent of males....Only about 2 percent of viewers stopped watching because of excessive crime coverage." (p1 secB)

Kiska, Tim. "Accent: Crime Time Live: Viewers Speak Out: Scenes of Violence." Detroit News 16 Jun 1997. p1,6 secB.

BROADCAST JOURNALISM--UNITED STATES--PUBLIC OPINION

"According to a recent poll by the Pew Research Center, only 26 percent of US viewers enjoy watching network news, down sharply from 42 percent a decade ago....Only seven percent actually look forward to reading their daily paper. Favorable ratings for network news have fallen steadily, from 27 percent five years ago to 15 percent....Only 40 percent say they watch network news regularly, compared with 60 percent in 1993." (p12)

"Notebook: The Audience Isn't Listening." Toward Freedom v46 n4 Aug 1997. p12. (ISSN0048-9898).

BROCCOLI--UNITED STATES (v26)

BROCCOLI INDUSTRY--GUATEMALA--MEXICO --UNITED STATES (v26)

BROILERS (POULTRY)--RUSSIA--UNITED STATES (v26)

BROMOMETHANE (v26)

"Methyl bromide is a highly-toxic, colourless, odourless chemical....Soil fumigation accounts for 71 per cent of worldwide sales of methyl bromide. Five crops account for over half [of] methyl bromide's use worldwide to fumigate soil: tomatoes, strawberries, peppers, ornamental flowers and tobacco. The chemical is also used before planting grapes, almonds, melons, forest tree seedlings and walnuts....Industrialized nations currently account for more than 80 per cent of global methyl bromide consumption, although the proportion is gradually shifting towards less regulated Third World markets....Nearly half of all reported illnesses due to methyl bromide occur as a result of accidental drift from agricultural fields and fumigated structures." (p90) "Global methyl bromide sales increased by more than 50 per cent from 1984 to 1992, growing from roughly 45,000 tonnes to more than 75,000 tonnes....In Zimbabwe, it is used on 98 per cent of the tobacco seedbed area; tobacco accounts for about 25 per cent of the country's export earnings. Dead Sea Bromine and Great Lakes Chemicals have helped ensure that the use of methyl bromide for soil fumigation in China has grown from roughly 40,000 pounds in 1991 to more than 700,000 pounds in 1995--a nearly 18-fold increase." (p97)

Karliner, Joshua/Morales, Alba/O'Rourke, Dara. "The Barons of Bromide: The Corporate Forces behind Toxic Poisoning & Ozone Depletion." Ecologist v27 n3 May-Jun 1997. p90-98. (ISSN0261-3131).

BROMOMETHANE--CALIFORNIA

"The use of methyl bromide in California has risen rapidly in recent years. It jumped from 49 types of applications in 1971 to 109 uses in 1992....The strawberry industry is California's largest user of pesticides. Strawberries consume more than 25 times as much pesticide as lettuce and 50 times more than grapes. Strawberry fields are covered with pesticides at the average rate of about 300 pounds per acre. Half of this volume consists of methyl bromide....Overall, between 1982 and 1993, California physicians reported 454 cases of methyl bromide poisoning. Of these illnesses, 282 occurred due to agricultural applications and 172 in structural fumigations. At least 19 deaths were attributed to residential methyl bromide fumigation in California during the same period." (p91)

Karliner, Joshua/Morales, Alba/O'Rourke, Dara. "The Barons of Bromide: The Corporate Forces behind Toxic Poisoning & Ozone Depletion: Poisoning in California." Ecologist v27 n3 May-Jun 1997. p90-98. (ISSN0261-3131).

BROMOMETHANE--UNITED STATES

"The United States is by far the largest producer and consumer of the chemical [bromomethane], accounting for approximately 40 per cent of global consumption. US agribusiness and small growers consumed 43.5 million pounds of methyl bromide in 1994. The states of Florida and California are the largest users of the chemical in the country; Florida accounts for almost 40 per cent of pre-plant uses, California 36 per cent." (p90) "TriCal Corporation...conducts 60 per cent of its business with methyl bromide and is the largest methyl bromide application company in California." (p91)

Karliner, Joshua/Morales, Alba/O'Rourke, Dara. "The Barons of Bromide: The Corporate Forces behind Toxic Poisoning & Ozone Depletion." Ecologist v27 n3 May-Jun 1997. p90-98. (ISSN0261-3131).

BRONCHIAL ASTHMA

see ASTHMA

BRUCELLOSIS--MEDITERRANEAN REGION--MIDDLE EAST

"In Mediterranean and Middle East countries the annual incidence of brucellosis in people varies from less than 1 up to 78 cases per 100,000; however, over 550 cases have been reported from confined endemic areas where no animal control measures are applied. Up to 77 cases per 100,000 people have been reported from certain communities of south European countries in which animal control measures are mandatory. Reported cases largely underestimate the size of the problem. From a recent survey in a randomly selected human population of a country of the Arabic Peninsula, serological evidence of exposure to 'Brucella' has been found to be close to 20%, with more than 2% of these having active disease." (p3)

World Health Organization. "Brucellosis." WHO Fact Sheet n173 Jul 1997. p1-3. document-level access: <http://www.who.ch/programmes/inf/facts/fact173.htm>

BUDDHISM--UNITED STATES

In the U.S., "within the past decade, the number of English language Buddhist teaching centers coast to coast has grown from 429 to more than 1,166. Sociologists estimate that the number of informal sitting groups has grown to three to five times that. The overall statistics are still small compared with mainstream American religions. Sociologists estimate that from 600,000 to 1 million Americans of Jewish and Christian background utilize Buddhist practices." (p9)

Wood, Daniel B. "Religion: Buddhist Practices Make Inroads in the US." The Christian Science Monitor v89 n237 3 Nov 1997. p9. The Christian Science Monitor search engine: <http://www.csmonitor.com/plweb-cgi/iops1.pl> To retrieve this article, enter the following search: ED=19971103 AND buddhist. In the "retrieved list," click the title that matches this record. (ISSN0882-7729).

BUDGET--CANADA (v26)

BUDGET--UNITED STATES

In the U.S., "the revenue to the Federal Government has grown by an average 7.3 percent....Over the last 5 years the average growth was 7.3. Over the last 10 years it was 6.2, and over the last 17 years it was 6.8." (pH4328)

Neumann, Mark W. (Rep.-Wis.). "The Economy." Congressional Record. Daily ed. v143 n90 24 Jun 1997. pH4320-4328. section/page-level access: <http://thomas.loc.gov/cgi-bin/query/R?r105:FLD001:H04327:> (ISSN0363-7239). (X1.1A.105/1).

"In Texas, where the state budget surplus has reached $1 billion, taxpayers can expect a cut in property taxes and teachers can expect a 6.5 percent pay raise. In California, taxpayers will likely see a $2.3 billion surplus spent on everything from aging highways and schools to relief for bankrupt cities and counties....In Alaska, where tax revenues this year are 104 percent larger than the entire state budget, citizens can expect a whopping check in the mail....Last year, states squirreled away a total $20 billion in reserve funds. Twenty-four states had more than 5 percent of their budgets in some form of reserve. This year, state revenue projections are all running much higher than expected." (p4)

Baldauf, Scott. "United States: States Weigh Whether to Save or Spend Surpluses." The Christian Science Monitor v89 n143 19 Jun 1997. p4. The Christian Science Monitor search engine: <http://www.csmonitor.com/plweb-cgi/iops1.pl> To retrieve this article, enter the following search: ED=19970619 AND surpluses. In the "retrieved list," click the title that matches this record. (ISSN0882-7729).

BUDGET--UNITED STATES--PUBLIC OPINION (v26)

BUDGET DEFICITS--CANADA (v26)

"In 1992 Statistics Canada issued a report which stated that the debt in this country, some 50 percent, was created by high interest rates; 44 percent of the debt from tax breaks and only 6 percent by government programs. Of that 6 percent only half of that is from social programs." (p257)

Nystrom, Lorne (MP-SK). "Government Orders: Supply." Canada. Parliament. House of Commons. Debates. v135 n7 30 Sep 1997. p247-281. section-level access: <http://www.parl.gc.ca/36/1/parlbus/chambus/house/debates/007_1997-09-30/han007-e.htm#LINK45> (ISSN0704-5603). (X3-361E).

Canada "has reduced the deficit from $42 billion to under $14 billion. This is a remarkable drop, over $28 billion in four years, or a reduction of over 70 percent." (p17)

Drouin, Claude (MP-PQ). "Speech from the Throne." Canada. Parliament. House of Commons. Debates. v135 n2 23 Sep 1997. p13-18. section-level access: <http://www.parl.gc.ca/36/1/parlbus/chambus/house/debates/002_1997-09-23/han002-e.htm#LINKT10> (ISSN0704-5603). (X3-361E).

BUDGET DEFICITS--HONDURAS (v26)

BUDGET DEFICITS--RUSSIA

In Russia, "the federal budget deficit increased by 0.6 per cent of GDP in February from January 1997, while the deficit of the consolidated budget rose from 3.3 per cent of GDP in 1995, to 4.2 per cent in 1996. But according to the International Monetary Fund (IMF), the deficit is in fact much greater and stood at 7 per cent of GDP in 1996." (p27)

"News Section: Russian Wage Arrears Reach Astronomical Proportions." World of Work n21 Sep-Oct 1997. p27. (ISSN1020-0029).

BUDGET DEFICITS--UNITED STATES (v26)

In the U.S., "in fiscal year 1992, the deficit was at $290 billion. And it has come down in each succeeding year, to $255 billion in 1993, $203 billion in 1994, $164 billion in 1995, and to $107 billion in the last fiscal year, the year that ended this past September 30....As a percent of the gross domestic product, the deficit has declined in a most impressive way, from 4.9 percent in 1992 to 1.4 percent for the fiscal year that ended this past September 30....It declined from 4.9 percent in 1992 to 4.1 percent in 1993 to 3.1 percent in 1994 to 2.3 percent in 1995 to 1.4 percent in the fiscal year ending September 30, and it is now anticipated that the deficit as a percent of gross domestic product will be less than 1 percent for the current fiscal year, the lowest percentage since 1974....In fact, just comparing the United States with the other major industrial countries,...we see that our deficit as a share of GDP is 1.4 percent. Japan is at 3.1 percent, Germany at 3.5 percent, Canada at 4.2 percent, France at 5 percent, the United Kingdom at 5.1 percent, and Italy at 7.2 percent." (pS4726)

Sarbanes, Paul S. (Sen.-Md.). "Concurrent Resolution on the Budget." Congressional Record. Daily ed. v143 n67 20 May 1997. pS4725-4745. section/page-level access: <http://thomas.loc.gov/cgi-bin/query/R?r105:FLD001:S04726:> (ISSN0363-7239). (X1.1A.105/1).

In the U.S., "the deficit under President Carter was $73.8 billion when he left office. Under President Reagan it ballooned to $221 billion, and reached $290 under President Bush. When President Clinton took office, he inherited a $290 billion deficit. The national family was in debt $4.4 trillion.

Under President Clinton's leadership, however, the deficit has been reduced to $67 billion, the lowest nominal level since 1981. During the Bush administration, private sector growth averaged 1.3 percent annually, but under President Clinton, growth has averaged 3.5% per year. Furthermore, last year's deficit was 1.4 percent of the size of our economy, well below the deficits of other major economies, and the smallest level since 1974. This year, it will fall to about 1 percent of the economy." (pS5046)

Moseley-Braun, Carol (Sen.-Ill.). "Concurrent Resolution on the Budget." Congressional Record. Daily ed. v143 n70 23 May 1997. pS5023-5066. section/page-level access: <http://thomas.loc.gov/cgi-bin/query/R?r105:FLD001:S05046:> (ISSN0363-7239). (X1.1A.105/1).

BUDGET DEFICITS--WALES (v26)

BUFFALO (N.Y.)--SOCIAL CONDITIONS

In 1992, Buffalo, New York's "rate of 96.6 adolescent pregnancies per 1,000 adolescent females exceeded the New York City rate of 72.32. Its poverty rate of 25.9% in 1990 was higher than Chicago's 21.6%, Los Angeles' 18.9%, and Washington, D.C.'s 16% (Keller, 1995)." (p370)

Kost, Kathleen A. "Article: The Effects of Support on the Economic Well-Being of Young Fathers." Families in Society v78 n4 Jul-Aug 1997. p370-382. (ISSN1044-3894).

BUILDING INDUSTRY

see CONSTRUCTION INDUSTRY

BUILDINGS (v26)

see CASINOS; CHURCH BUILDINGS; LIBRARY OF CONGRESS THOMAS JEFFERSON BUILDING (WASHINGTON, D.C.); OFFICE BUILDINGS; OKLAHOMA CITY FEDERAL BUILDING BOMBING, OKLAHOMA CITY, OKLA., 1995; SCHOOL BUILDINGS

BULGARIA--ECONOMIC CONDITIONS (v26)

In Bulgaria, "since 1990, declining or stagnant output in the state-owned enterprise (SOE) sector has resulted in large losses, reaching about 27 percent of GDP in 1993, falling to 12 percent in 1995, and then increasing again to about 19 percent during the first nine months of 1996. In order to reverse these losses, the government's reform program aims at accelerating privatization and at imposing financial discipline in the state enterprise sector. So far, the privatization effort has resulted in the sale of about 18 percent of aggregate long-term SOE assets, of which about 8 percent have been sold through cash privatization, about 9 percent through mass privatization, and 1 percent through a combination of the two methods."

World Bank. "World Bank Supports Enterprise and Banking Reforms in Bulgaria: Bulgaria's Enterprise and Financial...Background." Press Release 30 Oct 1997. document-level access: <http://www.worldbank.org/html/extdr/extme/1519.htm>

BULLET WOUNDS

see GUNSHOT WOUNDS

BULLETS--UNITED STATES (v26)

BUREAUCRATS

see CIVIL SERVICE

BURGLAR ALARMS--MICHIGAN--DETROIT (v26)

BURGLARS--UNITED STATES--ATTITUDES

In a survey of felony convicts in U.S. "state prisons, 73 percent of the convicts who had committed a burglary or violent crime agreed 'one reason burglars avoid houses when people are at home is that they fear being shot.' Another study found that over 90 percent of burglars said that they would not even attempt a burglary in a house that they thought might be occupied....A 1996 study of 310 armed robbers, by Athena Research in Seattle, reported that many robbers are afraid of armed victims more than anything else." (p36)

Kopel, David. "Vital Signs: Crime: Burglary and the Armed Homestead." Chronicles v22 n1 Jan 1998. p36-38. (ISSN0887-5731).

BURGLARY--CANADA--UNITED STATES

"Only 13 percent of residential burglaries in the United States are attempted against occupied homes....In Canada,...a Toronto study found that 48 percent of burglaries were against occupied homes, and 21 percent involved a confrontation with the victim. In Edmonton, about half of all burglaries are 'hot' [burglaries in which the victim is present during the burglary]." (p36)

Kopel, David. "Vital Signs: Crime: Burglary and the Armed Homestead." Chronicles v22 n1 Jan 1998. p36-38. (ISSN0887-5731).

BURGLARY--UNITED STATES (v26)

BURMA--ECONOMIC CONDITIONS

According to Burma's State Law and Order Restoration Council, the Burmese "government approved more than $6 billion in foreign investment since 1992. Yet, only one-third of the approved investments were implemented....Statistics indicate anywhere between 39 and 50 percent of the government's national budget is spent on the military." (p19)

Brandon, John J. "Opinion/Essays: New Name, Same Regime." The Christian Science Monitor v90 n11 10 Dec 1997. p19. The Christian Science Monitor search engine: <http://www.csmonitor.com/plweb-cgi/iops1.pl> To retrieve this article, enter the following search: ED=19971210 AND regime. In the "retrieved list," click the title that matches this record. (ISSN0882-7729).

BURMA--SOCIAL CONDITIONS (v26)

BURNING OF LAND--IDAHO--WASHINGTON

"Farmers have been burning harvested land in eastern Washington and northern Idaho to rejuvenate soil and eliminate weeds and pests for more than a century. But burning bluegrass--after the seed harvest--became a yearly practice only in 1963, when Washington farmers torched 16,000 acres. Bluegrass seed has since become a $130 million crop and in 1993, farmers in both states burned an all-time-high of 100,000 acres of bluegrass, including 40,000 acres within a 40-mile radius of Spokane....The Washington Department of Ecology monitors all crop burning, but it is unregulated across the state line in Idaho--some six miles away--where 40,000 acres are planted in bluegrass....Farmers have...cut the burning by two-thirds, torching just 20,000 acres this fall." (p4)

Phillips, Sara. "Western Roundup: Idaho Chokes Spokane." High Country News v29 n24 22 Dec 1997. p4. (ISSN0191-5657).

BURNS AND SCALDS

"Every year in Australia, 100,000 victims--many of them children--are burned badly enough to require medical attention....About 2 million people in the United States suffer burns each year, including 300,000 serious injuries, 50,000 hospitalizations, and 5,500 fatalities. One-half of these victims are children." (p28) "'The incidence of burns--about 300 burns requiring hospitalization per million people--is surprisingly constant around the world,' says Basil Pruitt, MD, president of the International Society for Burn Injuries....House fires cause many burns. Annually in the US, 47,000 kids--more than one-half age four or younger--are injured in such fires....Since 1994, nine Australian children have died from burns that began with cigarette lighter play....In the US in 1993, children (mostly preschoolers) started 100,000 fires that resulted in more than 400 deaths and 3,100 burn injuries. Recently, the US Consumer Products Safety Commission recalled 200,000 cigarette lighters, because their truck-like shape made them look like toys to children....A study this past year in Chicago found that only 14 percent of housing units with young children had adequate covers for radiators and their attendant pipes. In 1993, nearly 2,000 US children were treated for burns from home or apartment steam or hot water heat radiators." (p29)

Turbak, Gary. "Children: The Agony of Burns." Kiwanis v82 n9 Oct 1997. p28-31. (ISSN0162-5276).

BURNS AND SCALDS IN CHILDREN--AUSTRALIA --UNITED STATES

"Each year in the US, more than 35,000 children--most of them age five and younger--are treated for scalds. In Australia, 1,800 kids with scalds (many under age three) are admitted annually to hospitals, and about 20 percent of them require skin grafts." (p29) Gary Stocco, vice-president of the U.S. National Burn Victim Foundation says, "'kids with 80 or 90 percent of their bodies burned can survive.'" (p30)

Turbak, Gary. "Children: The Agony of Burns." Kiwanis v82 n9 Oct 1997. p28-31. (ISSN0162-5276).

BUS LINES--TECHNOLOGICAL INNOVATIONS --MARYLAND--MISSOURI

Transit "systems that allow authorities to pinpoint the location of buses on computerized maps have created more efficient fleets. In Baltimore [Maryland],...a November 1995 study reported a 23-percent improvement in on-time buses equipped with the form of ITS [Intelligent Transportation Systems] known as automatic vehicle location....A 1995 study reported that automatic vehicle location systems made the Kansas City, Mo., fleet efficient enough that seven fewer buses were needed. The city's transit authority saved $500,000." (p28)

Koklanaris, Maria/U.S. Dept. of Transportation. Federal Highway Administration. "Intelligent Transportation Systems: ITS Is Already Paying Dividends." Public Roads v61 n2 Sep-Oct 1997. p26-29. (ISSN0033-3735).

BUSES, SCHOOL

see SCHOOL BUSES

BUSINESS

see also ACCOUNTING; ADVERTISING; FAMILY-OWNED BUSINESS ENTERPRISES; HISPANIC AMERICAN BUSINESS ENTERPRISES; INTERNATIONAL BUSINESS ENTERPRISES; MINORITY BUSINESS ENTERPRISES; REAL ESTATE BUSINESS; SMALL BUSINESS; WEALTH; WOMEN IN BUSINESS; WOMEN-OWNED BUSINESS ENTERPRISES

BUSINESS--GOVERNMENT POLICY

see INDUSTRIAL POLICY

BUSINESS AIRPLANES

see AIRPLANES, COMPANY

BUSINESS DISTRICTS, ROADSIDE

see COMMERCIAL STRIPS

BUSINESS ENTERPRISES

see also CORPORATIONS; FAMILY-OWNED BUSINESS ENTERPRISES; HISPANIC AMERICAN BUSINESS ENTERPRISES; INTERNATIONAL BUSINESS ENTERPRISES; MINORITY BUSINESS ENTERPRISES; REAL ESTATE BUSINESS; SMALL BUSINESS; TELEPHONE COMPANIES; WOMEN IN BUSINESS; WOMEN-OWNED BUSINESS ENTERPRISES

"From 1980 to 1993, the Fortune 500 companies had sales increase 140%, assets increase 230%, and CEO compensation increase 610%. And they eliminated 4.4 million jobs. These companies control 25% of the world's output and 70% of the world's trade. Yet they provide jobs to only 1/20th of 1% of the world's people." (p3)

Bowman, Robert M. "How Can We Make a Difference?" Space and Security News v14 n2 Aug 1997. p2-5. (ISSN1071-2569).

BUSINESS ENTERPRISES--ACCOUNTING

see ACCOUNTING

BUSINESS ENTERPRISES--ALABAMA

In Alabama, "Jefferson county was home to 17,834 businesses with employees, the most of any county in the state in 1995, according to new tabulations released...on the Internet by the Commerce Department's Census Bureau....Mobile County was second with 9,269 businesses, followed by Madison County with 6,584, Montgomery County with 6,015 and Tuscaloosa County with 3,671. The numbers of employees in each of the five counties were as follows: Jefferson (361,636), Mobile (149,274), Madison (116,332), Montgomery (100,707) and Tuscaloosa (59,308)....The number of businesses in the state totaled 96,053 in 1995, an increase of 1,834 from 1994. Payroll for the state went up 6.7 percent, from $32.3 billion in 1994 to $34.5 billion in 1995, while the number of employees grew from 1,478,717 in 1994 to 1,553,309 in 1995. The services sector employed the largest portion of the state's private-sector work force (29.3 percent), with an average annual payroll per employee of $21,840."

U.S. Dept. of Commerce. Economic & Statistics Administration. "Jefferson Leads Alabama's Counties in Number of Businesses, Census Bureau Reports." Census Bureau Press Release 16 Oct 1997. document-level access: <http://www.census.gov/Press-Release/al95cbp.html>

BUSINESS ENTERPRISES--ALASKA

In Alaska, "Anchorage Burough was home to 7,568 businesses with employees, the most of any burough in the state in 1995, according to new tabulations released...on the Internet by the Commerce Department's Census Bureau....Fairbanks North Star Burough was second with 2,091 businesses, followed by Kenai Peninsula Burough with 1,599, Matanuska-Susitna Burough with 1,091 and Juneau Burough with 1,050. The numbers of employees in each of the five buroughs were as follows: Anchorage (98,302), Fairbanks North Star (19,460), Kenai Peninsula (10,166), Matanuska-Susitna (7,227) and Juneau (9,124)....The number of businesses in the state totaled 17,264 in 1995, an increase of 348 from 1994. Payroll for the state went up 3.7 percent, from $5.7 billion in 1994 to $6.0 billion in 1995, while the number of employees grew from 178,529 in 1994 to 181,975 in 1995. The services sector employed the largest portion of the state's private-sector work force (32.3 percent), with an average annual payroll per employee of $28,984."

U.S. Dept. of Commerce. Economic & Statistics Administration. "Anchorage Leads Alaska's Buroughs in Number of Businesses, Census Bureau Reports." Census Bureau Press Release 23 Oct 1997. document-level access: <http://www.census.gov/Press-Release/ak95cbp.html>

BUSINESS ENTERPRISES--ARIZONA

In Arizona, "Maricopa County was home to 61,372 businesses with employees, the most of any county in the state in 1995, according to new tabulations released...on the Internet by the Commerce Department's Census Bureau....Pima County was second with 17,167 businesses, followed by Yavapai County with 3,743, Coconino County with 3,383 and Mohave County with 2,998. The numbers of employees in each of the five counties were as follows: Maricopa (1,035,214), Pima (247,225), Yavapai (32,441), Coconino (33,647) and Mohave (28,679)....The number of businesses in the state totaled 99,583 in 1995, an increase of 2,576 from 1994. Payroll for the state went up 10.3 percent, from $33.1 billion in 1994 to $36.5 billion in 1995, while the number of employees grew from 1,414,980 in 1994 to 1,507,132 in 1995. The services sector employed the largest portion of the state's private-sector work force (34.4 percent), with an average annual payroll per employee of $22,491."

U.S. Dept. of Commerce. Economic & Statistics Administration. "Maricopa Leads Arizona's Counties in Number of Businesses, Census Bureau Reports." Census Bureau Press Release 22 Oct 1997. document-level access: <http://www.census.gov/Press-Release/az95cbp.html>

BUSINESS ENTERPRISES--ARKANSAS

In Arkansas, "Pulaski County was home to 11,748 businesses with employees, the most of any county in the state in 1995, according to new tabulations released...on the Internet by the Commerce Department's Census Bureau....Washington County was second with 3,711 businesses, followed by Sebastian County with 3,377, Benton County with 3,063 and Garland County with 2,406. The numbers of employees in each of the five counties were as follows: Pulaski (207,814), Washington (59,189), Sebastian (67,654), Benton (53,135) and Garland (27,139)....The number of businesses in the state totaled 60,231 in 1995, an increase of 1,210 from 1994. Payroll for the state went up 8.3 percent, from $16.8 billion in 1994 to $18.2 billion in 1995, while the number of employees grew from 842,709 in 1994 to 891,175 in 1995. The manufacturing sector employed the largest portion of the state's private-sector work force (28.1 percent), with an average annual payroll per employee of $23,330."

U.S. Dept. of Commerce. Economic & Statistics Administration. "Pulaski Leads Arkansas' Counties in Number of Businesses, Census Bureau Reports." Census Bureau Press Release 21 Oct 1997. document-level access: <http://www.census.gov/Press-Release/ar95cbp.html>

BUSINESS ENTERPRISES--AUSTRALIAN CAPITAL TERRITORY

According to the publication, "Australian Capital Territory in Focus, 1997," by the Australian Bureau of Statistics, as of "June 1996, there were just over 13,000 businesses employing wage and salary earners in the ACT. Just under 66 per cent of these businesses were small businesses employing less than five people, 17.5 per cent employing 5-9 people and 8.1 per cent employing 10-19 people. Another 14,000 businesses employing wage and salary earners are located in the Australian Capital Region (ACR). Just over 60 per cent of the 27,000 businesses in the ACR were small businesses of which the highest numbers were in agriculture, forestry and fishing, retail trade, property and business services and construction."

Australian Bureau of Statistics. "ABS Focus on the National Capital." Media Release 24 Sep 1997. document-level access: <http://www.abs.gov.au/websitedbs/d3110125.nsf/4a255eef008309e44a255eef00061e57/f5e5faf940e2901c4a25651c00019bcc?OpenDocument>

BUSINESS ENTERPRISES--CALIFORNIA

In California, "Los Angeles County was home to 214,320 businesses with employees, the most of any county in the state in 1995, according to new tabulations released...on the Internet by the Commerce Department's Census Bureau....Orange County was second with 70,783 businesses, followed by San Diego County with 60,243, Santa Clara County with 40,442 and Alameda County with 33,460. The numbers of employees in each of the five counties were as follows: Los Angeles (3,494,193), Orange (1,151,819), San Diego (844,451), Santa Clara (800,482) and Alameda (525,644)....The number of businesses in the state totaled 740,583 in 1995, an increase of 5,013 from 1994. Payroll for the state went up 6.8 percent, from $301.4 billion in 1994 to $321.8 billion in 1995, while the number of employees grew from 10,624,807 in 1994 to 10,959,318 in 1995. The services sector employed the largest portion of the state's private-sector work force (36.7 percent), with an average annual payroll per employee of $28,785."

U.S. Dept. of Commerce. Economic & Statistics Administration. "Los Angeles Leads California's Counties in Number of Businesses, Census Bureau Reports." Census Bureau Press Release 23 Oct 1997. document-level access: <http://www.census.gov/Press-Release/ca95cbp.html>

"California is creating 2,000 jobs a month in computer services: the equivalent of opening a major car plant every month....In 1995 California had almost 500 multimedia firms, compared with fewer than 100 in New York and about 60 in Texas....For every job in aerospace lost since 1994, two have been created in the motion picture industry." (p28-29)

Leadbeater, Charles. "A Slice of the Silicon Pie." New Statesman 23 May 1997. p28-29. (ISSN0028-6842).

BUSINESS ENTERPRISES--CALIFORNIA--SILICON VALLEY

"Last year venture capitalists invested more than $2 billion in small companies [in Silicon Valley]. The Valley is home to six thousand hi-tech companies and a fifth of these have grown at more than 20 per cent a year for the past four years. At the last count there were 355 Internet hosts (computers permanently connected to the Internet) per 1,000 people in Silicon Valley, a far higher ratio than elsewhere in the US." (p28)

Leadbeater, Charles. "A Slice of the Silicon Pie." New Statesman 23 May 1997. p28-29. (ISSN0028-6842).

BUSINESS ENTERPRISES--CANADA (v26)

BUSINESS ENTERPRISES--COLORADO

In Colorado, "Denver County was home to 20,793 businesses with employees, the most of any county in the state in 1995, according to new tabulations released...on the Internet by the Commerce Department's Census Bureau....Arapahoe County was second with 14,664 businesses, followed by Jefferson County with 13,565, El Paso County with 11,826 and Boulder County with 9,588. The numbers of employees in each of the five counties were as follows: Denver (361,212), Arapahoe (225,174), Jefferson (151,938), El Paso (165,390) and Boulder (127,691)....The number of businesses in the state totaled 118,192 in 1995, an increase of 4,123 from 1994. Payroll for the state went up 9.4 percent, from $37.0 billion in 1994 to $40.4 billion in 1995, while the number of employees grew from 1,480,796 in 1994 to 1,558,141 in 1995. The services sector employed the largest portion of the state's private-sector work force (35.7 percent), with an average annual payroll per employee of $24,465."

U.S. Dept. of Commerce. Economic & Statistics Administration. "Denver Leads Colorado's Counties in Number of Businesses, Census Bureau Reports." Census Bureau Press Release 22 Oct 1997. document-level access: <http://www.census.gov/Press-Release/co95cbp.html>

BUSINESS ENTERPRISES--CONNECTICUT

In Connecticut, "Fairfield County was home to 27,650 businesses with employees, the most of any county in the state in 1995, according to new tabulations released...on the Internet by the Commerce Department's Census Bureau....Hartford County was second with 23,161 businesses, followed by New Haven County with 20,851, New London County with 5,811 and Litchfield County with 5,047. The numbers of employees in each of the five counties were as follows: Fairfield (399,276), Hartford (440,154), New Haven (314,290), New London (98,665) and Litchfield (55,185)....The number of businesses in the state totaled 91,189 in 1995, an increase of 400 from 1994. Payroll for the state went up 7.1 percent, from $44.0 billion in 1994 to $47.1 billion in 1995, while the number of employees grew 1,385,484 in 1994 to 1,415,400 in 1995. The services sector employed the largest portion of the state's private-sector work force (34.9 percent), with an average annual payroll per employee of $28,793."

U.S. Dept. of Commerce. Economic & Statistics Administration. "Fairfield Leads Connecticut's Counties in Number of Businesses, Census Bureau Reports." Census Bureau Press Release 16 Oct 1997. document-level access: <http://www.census.gov/Press-Release/ct95cbp.html>

BUSINESS ENTERPRISES--DELAWARE

In Delaware, "New Castle County was home to 14,096 businesses with employees, the most of the state's three counties in 1995, according to new tabulations released...on the Internet by the

Commerce Department's Census Bureau....Sussex County was second with 4,166 businesses, followed by Kent County with 2,729. The numbers of employees in each county were as follows: New Castle (242,619), Sussex (43,811) and Kent (38,068)....The number of businesses in the state totaled 20,991 in 1995, an increase of 512 from 1994. Payroll for the state went up 7.9 percent, from $8.7 billion in 1994 to $9.4 billion in 1995, while the number of employees grew from 306,846 in 1994 to 324,498 in 1995. The services sector employed the largest portion of the state's private-sector work force (30.5 percent), with an average annual payroll per employee of $23,815."

U.S. Dept. of Commerce. Economic & Statistics Administration. "New Castle Leads Delaware's Counties in Number of Businesses, Census Bureau Reports." Census Bureau Press Release 20 Oct 1997. document-level access: <http://www.census.gov/Press-Release/de95cbp.html>

BUSINESS ENTERPRISES--DISTRICT OF COLUMBIA

"The District of Columbia had 19,451 businesses with employees in 1995 according to new tabulations released...on the Internet by the Commerce Department's Census Bureau....The 19,451 businesses in the District in 1995, was an increase of 136 from 1994. Payroll for the District went up 5.5 percent, from $13.9 billion in 1994 to $14.6 billion in 1995, while the number of employees increased from 411,489 in 1994 to 413,757 in 1995. The services sector employed the largest portion of the District's private-sector work force (69.6 percent), with an average annual payroll per employee of $35,792."

U.S. Dept. of Commerce. Economic & Statistics Administration. "Census Bureau Releases Business, Employment, and Payroll Figures for the District of Columbia." Census Bureau Press Release 20 Oct 1997. document-level access: <http://www.census.gov/Press-Release/dc95cbp.html>

BUSINESS ENTERPRISES--EMPLOYMENT--EUROPE (v26)

BUSINESS ENTERPRISES--EMPLOYMENT--EUROPE, CENTRAL--EUROPE, EASTERN (v26)

BUSINESS ENTERPRISES--EUROPE, CENTRAL --EUROPE, EASTERN (v26)

BUSINESS ENTERPRISES--FLORIDA

In Florida, "Dade County was home to 66,011 businesses with employees, the most of any county in the state in 1995, according to new tabulations released...on the Internet by the Commerce Department's Census Bureau....Broward County was second with 46,105 businesses, followed by Palm Beach County with 32,701, Pinellas County with 25,605 and Hillsborough County with 24,734. The numbers of employees in each of the five counties were as follows: Dade (804,923), Broward (526,178), Palm Beach (379,154), Pinellas (350,105) and Hillsborough (431,933)....The number of businesses in the state totaled 398,232 in 1995, an increase of 5,470 from 1994. Payroll for the state went up 7.6 percent, from $110.8 billion in 1994 to $119.3 billion in 1995, while the number of employees grew from 4,984,065 in 1994 to 5,208,285 in 1995. The services sector employed the largest portion of the state's private-sector work force (39.5 percent), with an average annual payroll per employee of $23,175."

U.S. Dept. of Commerce. Economic & Statistics Administration. "Dade Leads Florida's Counties in Number of Businesses, Census Bureau Reports." Census Bureau Press Release 20 Oct 1997. document-level access: <http://www.census.gov/Press-Release/fl95cbp.html>

BUSINESS ENTERPRISES--GEORGIA

In Georgia, "Fulton County was home to 28,205 businesses with employees, the most of any county in the state in 1995, according to new tabulations released...on the Internet by the Commerce Department's Census Bureau....De Kalb County was second with 17,530 businesses, followed by Cobb County with 15,586, Gwinnett County with 13,468 and Chatham County with 6,221. The numbers of employees in each of the five counties were as follows: Fulton (603,247), De Kalb (312,011), Cobb (237,631), Gwinnett (208,860) and Chatham (96,308)....The number of businesses in the state totaled 179,006 in 1995, an increase of 5,690 from 1994. Payroll for the state went up 9.1 percent, from $67.5 billion in 1994 to $73.6 billion in 1995, while the number of employees grew from 2,754,041 in 1994 to 2,920,361 in 1995. The services sector employed the largest portion of the state's private-sector work force (30.6 percent), with an average annual payroll per employee of $24,720."

U.S. Dept. of Commerce. Economic & Statistics Administration. "Fulton Leads Georgia's Counties in Number of Businesses, Census Bureau Reports." Census Bureau Press Release 20 Oct 1997. document-level access: <http://www.census.gov/Press-Release/ga95cbp.html>

BUSINESS ENTERPRISES--GERMANY (v26)

"When the Berliner Innovations und Grunderzentrum (BIG) was established in November 1983 with funding from the Berlin Senate and the EU, it was the first [technology and business incubation] centre of its kind [in Germany]....There are now 200 of these technology and business incubation centres in the Federal Republic of Germany. By the year 2000, say the experts, there will be 270 of these centres whose aim is to provide favourable conditions for enterprising pioneers to transform innovative ideas into profitable products." (p25) "In technology and business incubation centres, the proportion of start-ups abandoned or forced into bankruptcy is only 6%." (p28) "Since 1983, estimates Bernd Gross...[the chief executive of the Association of German Technology and Business Incubation Centres,] almost 7,000 firms have been created in technology and business incubation centres. In turn, these have created 50,000 to 60,000 jobs--not including, suppliers and co-operating firms." (p29)

"Technologie Zentren in Deutschland." Deutschland n5 Oct 1997. p24-30. (ISSN0945-6791).

In the first half of 1997 in the Federal Republic of Germany, while "the absolute number of [business] transactions rose by only a moderate 2.6% to 874, the number of big deals increased dramatically. Sales of businesses with a turnover of more than 100 million marks were up by 42%. The number of companies sold with sales of more than a billion marks rose from 12 to 34." (p19)

Noack, Hans-Christoph. "New Markets, New Strategies:...German Business...Globalization...1997--The Year of Major Transactions." Deutschland n6 Dec 1997. p18-21. (ISSN0945-6791).

BUSINESS ENTERPRISES--HAWAII

In Hawaii, "Honolulu County was home to 21,004 businesses with employees, the most of any county in the state in 1995, according to new tabulations released...on the Internet by the Commerce Department's Census Bureau....Hawaii County was second with 3,649 businesses and Maui County was third with 3,639. The numbers of employees in each of the three counties were as follows: Honolulu (322,339), Hawaii (37,217) and Maui (46,141)....The number of businesses in the state totaled 29,942 in 1995, a decrease of 53 from 1994. Payroll for the state went up 1.4 percent, from $10.6 billion in 1994 to $10.7 billion in 1995, while the number of employees dropped from 425,987 in 1994 to 423,822 in 1995. The services sector employed the largest portion of the state's private-sector work force (38.7 percent), with an average annual payroll per employee of $25,293."

U.S. Dept. of Commerce. Economic & Statistics Administration. "Honolulu Leads Hawaii's Counties in Number of Businesses, Census Bureau Reports." Census Bureau Press Release 23 Oct 1997. document-level access: <http://

www.census.gov/Press-Release/hi95cbp.html>

BUSINESS ENTERPRISES--IDAHO

In Idaho, "Ada County was home to 8,389 businesses with employees, the most of any county in the state in 1995, according to new tabulations released...on the Internet by the Commerce Department's Census Bureau....Kootenai County was second with 3,142 businesses, followed by Canyon County with 2,455, Bonneville County with 2,340 and Twin Falls County with 1,969. The numbers of employees in each of the five counties were as follows: Ada (126,168), Kootenai (29,777), Canyon (32,144), Bonneville (27,903) and Twin Falls (23,014)....The number of businesses in the state totaled 32,972 in 1995, an increase of 1,090 from 1994. Payroll for the state went up 6.4 percent, from $7.9 billion in 1994 to $8.4 billion in 1995, while the number of employees grew from 368,120 in 1994 to 379,161 in 1995. The services sector employed the largest portion of the state's private-sector work force (28.2 percent), with an average annual payroll per employee of $19,464."

U.S. Dept. of Commerce. Economic & Statistics Administration. "Ada Leads Idaho's Counties in Number of Businesses, Census Bureau Reports." Census Bureau Press Release 22 Oct 1997. document-level access: <http://www.census.gov/Press-Release/id95cbp.html>

BUSINESS ENTERPRISES--ILLINOIS

In Illinois, "Cook County was home to 124,980 businesses with employees, the most of any county in the state in 1995, according to new tabulations released...on the Internet by the Commerce Department's Census Bureau....Du Page County was second with 29,412 businesses, followed by Lake County with 15,967, Kane County with 9,317 and Will County with 7,841. The numbers of employees in each of the five counties were as follows: Cook (2,374,539), Du Page (508,351), Lake (261,383), Kane (152,648) and Will (109,546)....The number of businesses in the state totaled 293,694 in 1995, an increase of 5,005 from 1994. Payroll for the state went up 6.9 percent, from $134.6 billion in 1994 to $143.9 billion in 1995, while the number of employees grew from 4,802,306 in 1994 to 4,950,462 in 1995. The services sector employed the largest portion of the state's private-sector work force (33.4 percent), with an average annual payroll per employee of $25,873."

U.S. Dept. of Commerce. Economic & Statistics Administration. "Cook Leads Illinois' Counties in Number of Businesses, Census Bureau Reports." Census Bureau Press Release 16 Oct 1997. document-level access: <http://www.census.gov/Press-Release/il95cbp.html>

BUSINESS ENTERPRISES--INDIANA

In Indiana, "Marion County was home to 23,910 businesses with employees, the most of any county in the state in 1995, according to new tabulations released...on the Internet by the Commerce Department's Census Bureau....Lake County was second with 9,958 businesses, followed by Allen County with 8,557, St. Joseph County with 6,611 and Vanderburgh County with 5,196. The numbers of employees in each of the five counties were as follows: Marion (500,953), Lake (167,675), Allen (166,194), St. Joseph (117,353) and Vanderburgh (102,461)....The number of businesses in the state totaled 141,253 in 1995, an increase of 2,554 from 1994. Payroll for the state went up 6.5 percent, from $55.9 billion in 1994 to $59.6 billion in 1995, while the number of employees grew from 2,315,241 in 1994 to 2,403,189 in 1995. The manufacturing sector employed the largest portion of the state's private-sector work force (28.0 percent), with an average annual payroll per employee of $34,241."

U.S. Dept. of Commerce. Economic & Statistics Administration. "Marion Leads Indiana's Counties in Number of Businesses, Census Bureau Reports." Census Bureau Press Release 16 Oct 1997. document-level access: <http://www.census.gov/Press-Release/in95cbp.html>

BUSINESS ENTERPRISES--IOWA

In Iowa, "Polk County was home to 11,008 businesses with employees, the most of any county in the state in 1995, according to new tabulations released...on the Internet by the Commerce Department's Census Bureau....Linn County was second with 5,081 businesses, followed by Scott County with 4,369, Black Hawk County with 3,134 and Woodbury County with 2,842. The numbers of employees in each of the five counties were as follows: Polk (221, 914), Linn (98,757), Scott (70,022), Black Hawk (54,088) and Woodbury (45,325)....The number of businesses in the state totaled 78,464 in 1995, an increase of 700 from 1994. Payroll for the state went up 7.7 percent, from $23.3 billion in 1994 to $25.1 billion in 1995, while the number of employees grew from 1,089,774 in 1994 to 1,138,402 in 1995. The services sector employed the largest portion of the state's private-sector work force (31.4 percent), with an average annual payroll per employee of $18,700."

U.S. Dept. of Commerce. Economic & Statistics Administration. "Polk Leads Iowa's Counties in Number of Businesses, Census Bureau Reports." Census Bureau Press Release 16 Oct 1997. document-level access: <http://www.census.gov/Press-Release/ia95cbp.html>

BUSINESS ENTERPRISES--KANSAS

In Kansas, "Johnson County was home to 13,622 businesses with employees, the most of any county in the state in 1995, according to new tabulations released...on the Internet by the Commerce Department's Census Bureau....Sedgwick County was second with 11,453 businesses, followed by Shawnee County with 4,529, Wyandotte County with 3,123 and Douglas County with 2,334. The numbers of employees in each of the five counties were as follows: Johnson (218,049), Sedgwick (203,765), Shawnee (75,290), Wyandotte (63,518) and Douglas (30,088)....The number of businesses in the state totaled 70,894 in 1995, an increase of 1,072 from 1994. Payroll for the state went up 7.7 percent, from $21.2 billion in 1994 to $22.8 billion in 1995, while the number of employees grew from 954,488 in 1994 to 982,066 in 1995. The services sector employed the largest portion of the state's private-sector work force (31.2 percent), with an average annual payroll per employee of $20,484."

U.S. Dept. of Commerce. Economic & Statistics Administration. "Johnson Leads Kansas' Counties in Number of Businesses, Census Bureau Reports." Census Bureau Press Release 16 Oct 1997. document-level access: <http://www.census.gov/Press-Release/ks95cbp.html>

BUSINESS ENTERPRISES--KENTUCKY

In Kentucky, "Jefferson County was home to 19,102 businesses with employees, the most of any county in the state in 1995, according to new tabulations released...on the Internet by the Commerce Department's Census Bureau....Fayette County was second with 7,454 businesses, followed by Kenton County with 3,073, Warren County with 2,365 and Daviess County with 2,335. The numbers of employees in each of the five counties were as follows: Jefferson (377,188), Fayette (132,372), Kenton (55,238), Warren (37,550) and Daviess (37,253)....The number of businesses in the state totaled 85,123 in 1995, an increase of 960 from 1994. Payroll for the state went up 6.3 percent, from $28.3 billion in 1994 to $30.1 billion in 1995, while the number of employees grew from 1,292,731 in 1994 to 1,347,087 in 1995. The services sector employed the largest portion of the state's private-sector work force (29.5 percent), with an average annual payroll per employee of $19,851."

U.S. Dept. of Commerce. Economic & Statistics Administration. "Jefferson Leads Kentucky's Counties in Number of Businesses, Census Bureau Reports." Census Bureau Press Release 16 Oct 1997. document-level access: <http://

www.census.gov/Press-Release/ky95cbp.html>

BUSINESS ENTERPRISES--LATIN AMERICA (v26)

BUSINESS ENTERPRISES--LOUISIANA

In Louisiana, "Jefferson Parish was home to 12,694 businesses with employees, the most of any parish in the state in 1995, according to new tabulations released...on the Internet by the Commerce Department's Census Bureau....East Baton Rouge Parish was second with 10,869 businesses, followed by Orleans Parish with 10,862, Caddo Parish with 6,292 and Lafayette Parish with 5,963. The numbers of employees in each of the five parishes were as follows: Jefferson (196,152), East Baton Rouge (189,080), Orleans (209,110), Caddo (105,946) and Lafayette (84,937)....The number of businesses in the state totaled 96,063 in 1995, an increase of 925 from 1994. Payroll for the state went up 6.5 percent, from $31.6 billion in 1994 to $33.6 billion in 1995, while the number of employees grew from 1,425,286 in 1994 to 1,452,355 in 1995. The services sector employed the largest portion of the state's private-sector work force (36.1 percent), with an average annual payroll per employee of $21,224."

U.S. Dept. of Commerce. Economic & Statistics Administration. "Jefferson Leads Louisiana's Parishes in Number of Businesses, Census Bureau Reports." Census Bureau Press Release 21 Oct 1997. document-level access: <http://www.census.gov/Press-Release/la95cbp.html>

BUSINESS ENTERPRISES--MAINE

In Maine, "Cumberland County was home to 9,181 businesses with employees, the most of any county in the state in 1995, according to new tabulations released...on the Internet by the Commerce Department's Census Bureau....York County was second with 4,512 businesses, followed by Penobscot County with 3,958, Kennebec County with 3,150 and Androscoggin County with 2,659. The numbers of employees in each of the five counties were as follows: Cumberland (128,876), York (41,673), Penobscot (52,579), Kennebec (40,299) and Androscoggin (39,431)....The number of businesses in the state totaled 36,298 in 1995, an increase of 708 from 1994. Payroll for the state went up 5.2 percent, from $9.3 billion in 1994 to $9.8 billion in 1995, while the number of employees grew from 419,774 in 1994 to 432,290 in 1995. The services sector employed the largest portion of the state's private-sector work force (33.6 percent), with an average annual payroll per employee of $20,993."

U.S. Dept. of Commerce. Economic & Statistics Administration. "Cumberland Leads Maine's Counties in Number of Businesses, Census Bureau Reports." Census Bureau Press Release 16 Oct 1997. document-level access: <http://www.census.gov/Press-Release/me95cbp.html>

BUSINESS ENTERPRISES--MARYLAND

In Maryland, "Montgomery County was home to 23,494 businesses with employees, the most of any county in the state in 1995, according to new tabulations released...on the Internet by the Commerce Department's Census Bureau....Baltimore County was second with 19,198 businesses, followed by Baltimore (city) with 14,231, Prince George's County with 13,789 and Anne Arundel County with 11,420. The independent city of Baltimore is treated as a county for this report. The numbers of employees in each of the five counties were as follows: Montgomery (342,624), Baltimore (300,961), Baltimore (city) (295,031), Prince George's (233,595) and Anne Arundel (155,704)....The number of businesses in the state totaled 122,350 in 1995, an increase of 1,972 from 1994. Payroll for the state went up 6.6 percent, from $46.1 billion in 1994 to $49.1 billion in 1995, while the number of employees grew from 1,752,262 in 1994 to 1,820,731 in 1995. The services sector employed the largest portion of the state's private-sector work force (39.0 percent), with an average annual payroll per employee of $27,160."

U.S. Dept. of Commerce. Economic & Statistics Administration. "Montgomery Leads Maryland's Counties in Number of Businesses, Census Bureau Reports." Census Bureau Press Release 20 Oct 1997. document-level access: <http://www.census.gov/Press-Release/md95cbp.html>

BUSINESS ENTERPRISES--MASSACHUSETTS

In Massachusetts, "Middlesex County was home to 39,745 businesses with employees, the most of any county in the state in 1995, according to new tabulations released...on the Internet by the Commerce Department's Census Bureau....Suffolk County was second with 19,136 businesses, followed by Norfolk County with 18,041, Essex County with 16,763 and Worcester County with 16,387. The numbers of employees in each of the five counties were as follows: Middlesex (734,997), Suffolk (511,455), Norfolk (292,097), Essex (251,278) and Worcester (270,856)....The number of businesses in the state totaled 160,350 in 1995, an increase of 2,278 from 1994. Payroll for the state went up 7.9 percent, from $77.3 billion in 1994 to $83.4 billion in 1995, while the number of employees grew from 2,660,831 in 1994 to 2,735,963 in 1995. The services sector employed the largest portion of the state's private-sector work force (40.9 percent), with an average annual payroll per employee of $28,722."

U.S. Dept. of Commerce. Economic & Statistics Administration. "Middlesex Leads Massachusetts' Counties in Number of Businesses, Census Bureau Reports." Census Bureau Press Release 16 Oct 1997. document-level access: <http://www.census.gov/Press-Release/ma95cbp.html>

BUSINESS ENTERPRISES--MICHIGAN

In Michigan, "Oakland County was home to 40,440 businesses with employees, the most of any county in the state in 1995, according to new tabulations released...on the Internet by the Commerce Department's Census Bureau....Wayne County was second with 35,234 businesses, followed by Macomb County with 17,909, Kent County with 14,618 and Genesee County with 9,067. The numbers of employees in each of the five counties were as follows: Oakland (665,004), Wayne (727,006), Macomb (316,640), Kent (303,241) and Genesee (154,427)....The number of businesess in the state totaled 226,973 in 1995, an increase of 4,284 from 1994. Payroll for the state went up 7.8 percent, from $99.5 billion in 1994 to $107.3 billion in 1995, while the number of employees grew from 3,542,398 in 1994 to 3,704,315 in 1995. The services sector employed the largest portion of the state's private-sector work force (32.0 percent), with an average annual payroll per employee of $24,678."

U.S. Dept. of Commerce. Economic & Statistics Administration. "Oakland Leads Michigan's Counties in Number of Businesses, Census Bureau Reports." Census Bureau Press Release 16 Oct 1997. document-level access: <http://www.census.gov/Press-Release/mi95cbp.html>

BUSINESS ENTERPRISES--MICHIGAN--DETROIT (v26)

BUSINESS ENTERPRISES--MINNESOTA

In Minnesota, "Hennepin County was home to 36,725 businesses with employees, the most of any county in the state in 1995, according to new tabulations released...on the Internet by the Commerce Department's Census Bureau....Ramsey County was second with 12,926 businesses, followed by Dakota County with 7,106, Anoka County with 5,456 and St. Louis County with 5,374. The numbers of employees in each of the five counties were as follows: Hennepin (765,277), Ramsey (279,169), Dakota (117,207), Anoka (80,651) and St. Louis (71,110)....The number of businesses in the state totaled 125,927 in 1995, an increase of 2,485 from 1994. Payroll for the state went up 8.6 percent, from $50.4 billion in 1994 to $54.8 billion in 1995, while the number of employees grew from 1,995,417 in 1994 to 2,072,503 in 1995. The services sector employed the largest portion of the state's private-sector work force (34.8 percent), with an average annual payroll per employee of $22,833."

U.S. Dept. of Commerce. Economic & Statistics Administration. "Hennepin Leads Minnesota's Counties in Number of Businesses, Census Bureau Reports." Census Bureau Press Release 16 Oct 1997. document-level access: <http://www.census.gov/Press-Release/mn95cbp.html>

BUSINESS ENTERPRISES--MISSISSIPPI

In Mississippi, "Hinds County was home to 6,870 businesses with employees, the most of any county in the state in 1995, according to new tabulations released...on the Internet by the Commerce Department's Census Bureau....Harrison County was second with 4,212 businesses, followed by Forrest County with 2,259, Lee County with 2,203 and Jackson County with 2,151. The numbers of employees in each of the five counties were as follows: Hinds (128,653), Harrison (65,058), Forrest (32,395), Lee (45,317) and Jackson (41,166)....The number of businesses in the state totaled 57,095 in 1995, an increase of 945 from 1994. Payroll for the state went up 6.1 percent, from $16.4 billion in 1994 to $17.4 billion in 1995, while the number of employees grew from 834,922 in 1994 to 871,814 in 1995. The services sector employed the largest portion of the state's private-sector work force (29.9 percent), with an average annual payroll per employee of $19,175."

U.S. Dept. of Commerce. Economic & Statistics Administration. "Hinds Leads Mississippi's Counties in Number of Businesses, Census Bureau Reports." Census Bureau Press Release 16 Oct 1997. document-level access: <http://www.census.gov/Press-Release/ms95cbp.html>

BUSINESS ENTERPRISES--MISSOURI

In Missouri, "St. Louis county was home to 29,630 businesses with employees, the most of any county in the state in 1995, according to new tabulations released...on the Internet by the Commerce Department's Census Bureau....Jackson County was second with 17,831 businesses, followed by St. Louis (city) with 10,665, Greene County with 7,269 and St. Charles County with 5,306. The independent city of St. Louis is treated as a county for this report. The numbers of employees in each of the five counties were as follows: St. Louis (528,032), Jackson (336,450), St. Louis (city) (284,665), Greene (119,485) and St. Charles (68,426)....The number of businesses in the state totaled 139,980 in 1995, an increase of 1,706 from 1994. Payroll for the state went up 6.3 percent, from $50.2 billion in 1994 to $53.3 billion in 1995, while the number of employees grew from 2,101,239 in 1994 to 2,169,026 in 1995. The services sector employed the largest portion of the state's private-sector work force (33.6 percent), with an average annual payroll per employee of $22,289."

U.S. Dept. of Commerce. Economic & Statistics Administration. "St. Louis Leads Missouri's Counties in Number of Businesses, Census Bureau Reports." Census Bureau Press Release 16 Oct 1997. document-level access: <http://www.census.gov/Press-Release/mo95cbp.html>

BUSINESS ENTERPRISES--MONTANA

In Montana, "Yellowstone County was home to 4,479 businesses with employees, the most of any county in the state in 1995, according to new tabulations released...on the Internet by the Commerce Department's Census Bureau....Missoula County was second with 3,219 businesses, followed by Flathead County with 2,829, Gallatin County with 2,677 and Cascade County with 2,460. The numbers of employees in each of the five counties were as follows: Yellowstone (51,765), Missoula (34,242), Flathead (23,259), Gallatin (22,544) and Cascade (25,574)....The number of businesses in the state totaled 29,109 in 1995, an increase of 751 from 1994. Payroll for the state went up 5.3 percent, from $4.8 billion in 1994 to $5.1 billion in 1995, while the number of employees grew from 249,601 in 1994 to 260,973 in 1995. The services sector employed the largest portion of the state's private-sector work force (35.2 percent), with an average annual payroll per employee of $17,999."

U.S. Dept. of Commerce. Economic & Statistics Administration. "Yellowstone Leads Montana's Counties in Number of Businesses, Census Bureau Reports." Census Bureau Press Release 22 Oct 1997. document-level access: <http://www.census.gov/Press-Release/mt95cbp.html>

BUSINESS ENTERPRISES--NEBRASKA

In Nebraska, "Douglas County was home to 13,377 businesses with employees, the most of any county in the state in 1995, according to new tabulations released...on the Internet by the Commerce Department's Census Bureau....Lancaster County was second with 6,403 businesses, followed by Hall County with 1,831, Sarpy County with 1,819 and Madison County with 1,226. The numbers of employees in each of the five counties were as follows: Douglas (275,647), Lancaster (108,537), Hall (26,424), Sarpy (22,680) and Madison (17,907)....The number of businesses in the state totaled 47,128 in 1995, an increase of 488 from 1994. Payroll for the state went up 7.3 percent, from $13.5 billion in 1994 to $14.5 billion in 1995, while the number of employees grew from 648,374 in 1994 to 674,779 in 1995. The services sector employed the largest portion of the state's private-sector work force (33.9 percent), with an average annual payroll per employee of $20,184."

U.S. Dept. of Commerce. Economic & Statistics Administration. "Douglas Leads Nebraska's Counties in Number of Businesses, Census Bureau Reports." Census Bureau Press Release 16 Oct 1997. document-level access: <http://www.census.gov/Press-Release/ne95cbp.html>

BUSINESS ENTERPRISES--NEVADA

In Nevada, "Clark County was home to 21,289 businesses with employees, the most of any county in the state in 1995, according to new tabulations released...on the Internet by the Commerce Department's Census Bureau....Washoe County was second with 9,729 businesses, followed by Carson City (city) with 1,817, Douglas County with 1,166 and Elko County with 873. The independent city of Carson City is treated as a county for this report. The numbers of employees in each of the five counties were as follows: Clark (449,215), Washoe (144,052), Carson City (city) (19,085), Douglas (17,716) and Elko (14,536)....The number of businesses in the state totaled 37,219 in 1995, an increase of 1,576 from 1994. Payroll for the state went up 9.9 percent, from $15.0 billion in 1994 to $16.5 billion in 1995, while the number of employees grew from 627,510 in 1994 to 672,260 in 1995. The services sector employed the largest portion of the state's private-sector work force (50.4 percent), with an average annual payroll per employee of $23,951."

U.S. Dept. of Commerce. Economic & Statistics Administration. "Clark Leads Nevada's Counties in Number of Businesses, Census Bureau Reports." Census Bureau Press Release 22 Oct 1997. document-level access: <http://www.census.gov/Press-Release/nv95cbp.html>

BUSINESS ENTERPRISES--NEW HAMPSHIRE

In New Hampshire, "Hillsborough County was home to 10,050 businesses with employees, the most of any county in the state in 1995, according to new tabulations released...on the Internet by the Commerce Department's Census Bureau....Rockingham County was second with 8,343 businesses, followed by Merrimack County with 3,747, Grafton County with 2,749 and Strafford County with 2,305. The numbers of employees in each of the five counties were as follows: Hillsborough (155,400), Rockingham (103,207), Merrimack (48,823), Grafton (39,744) and Strafford (34,542)....The number of businesses in the state totaled 34,647 in 1995, an increase of 782 from 1994. Payroll for the state went up 8.1 percent, from $10.9 billion in 1994 to $11.8 billion in 1995, while the number of employees grew from 445,551 in 1994 to 464,122 in 1995. The services sector employed the largest portion of the state's private-sector work force (33.8 percent), with an average annual payroll per employee of $24,440."

U.S. Dept. of Commerce. Economic & Statistics Administration. "Hillsborough Leads New Hampshire's Counties in Number of Businesses, Census Bureau Reports." Census Bureau Press Release 16 Oct 1997. document-level access: <http://www.census.gov/Press-Release/nh95cbp.html>

BUSINESS ENTERPRISES--NEW JERSEY

In New Jersey, "Bergen County was home to 32,034 businesses with employees, the most of any county in the state in 1995, according to new tabulations released...on the Internet by the Commerce Department's Census Bureau....Essex County was second with 19,635 businesses, followed by Middlesex County with 18,178, Monmouth County with 17,362 and Morris County with 15,992. The numbers of employees in each of the five counties were as follows: Bergen (424,051), Essex (333,646), Middlesex (333,722), Monmouth (187,447) and Morris (239,512)....The number of businesses in the state totaled 220,991 in 1995, an increase of 3,485 from 1994. Payroll for the state went up 5.0 percent, from $97.9 billion in 1994 to $102.8 billion in 1995, while the number of employees grew from 3,124,672 in 1994 to 3,184,458 in 1995. The services sector employed the largest portion of the state's private-sector work force (34.5 percent), with an average annual payroll per employee of $29,267."

U.S. Dept. of Commerce. Economic & Statistics Administration. "Bergen Leads New Jersey's Counties in Number of Businesses, Census Bureau Reports." Census Bureau Press Release 16 Oct 1997. document-level access: <http://www.census.gov/Press-Release/nj95cbp.html>

BUSINESS ENTERPRISES--NEW MEXICO

In New Mexico, "Bernalillo County was home to 15,001 businesses with employees, the most of any county in the state in 1995, according to new tabulations released...on the Internet by the Commerce Department's Census Bureau....Santa Fe County was second with 4,210 businesses, followed by Dona Ana County with 3,071, San Juan County with 2,253 and Lea County with 1,501. The numbers of employees in each of the five counties were as follows: Bernalillo (239,130), Santa Fe (39,564), Dona Ana (32,071), San Juan (30,045) and Lea (15,628)....The number of businesses in the state totaled 40,631 in 1995, an increase of 630 from 1994. Payroll for the state went up 7.0 percent, from $10.3 billion in 1994 to $11.0 billion in 1995, while the number of employees grew from 488,802 in 1994 to 506,634 in 1995. The services sector employed the largest portion of the state's private-sector work force (36.7 percent), with an average annual payroll per employee of $22,678."

U.S. Dept. of Commerce. Economic & Statistics Administration. "Bernalillo Leads New Mexico's Counties in Number of Businesses, Census Bureau Reports." Census Bureau Press Release 23 Oct 1997. document-level access: <http://www.census.gov/Press-Release/nm95cbp.html>

BUSINESS ENTERPRISES--NEW YORK (STATE)

In New York, "New York County (the Manhattan portion of New York City) was home to 99,779 businesses with employees, the most of any county in the state in 1995, according to new tabulations released...on the Internet by the Commerce Department's Census Bureau....Nassau County was second with 46,240 businesses, followed by Suffolk County with 39,270, Kings County with 34,154 and Queens County with 33,947. Like New York County, above, Kings County and Queens County are parts of New York City (Brooklyn and Queens portions, respectively). The numbers of employees in each of the five counties were as follows: New York (1,819,293), Nassau (522,215), Suffolk (460,288), Kings (403,635) and Queens (421,561)....The number of businesses in the state totaled 467,262 in 1995, an increase of 4,870 from 1994. Payroll for the state went up 6.7 percent, from $211.1 billion in 1994 to $225.2 billion in 1995, while the number of employees grew from 6,664,883 in 1994 to 6,782,174 in 1995. The services sector employed the largest portion of the state's private-sector work force (40.4 percent), with an average annual payroll per employee of $29,208."

U.S. Dept. of Commerce. Economic & Statistics Administration. "New York County Leads All Counties in New York State in Number of Businesses, Census Bureau Reports." Census Bureau Press Release 16 Oct 1997. document-level access: <http://www.census.gov/Press-Release/ny95cbp.html>

BUSINESS ENTERPRISES--NEW YORK (STATE)--NEW YORK

In Harlem, New York, "African-Americans own some 158 of the 322 businesses between Fifth Avenue and Frederick Douglass Boulevard." (p401) "One million square feet of commercial space lies vacant while as much as 70% of Harlem's residents shop elsewhere for gifts, clothes, furniture, and electrical appliances." (p402)

Stamato, Linda. "Commerce and Conflict Resolution in Harlem." Peace Review v9 n3 Sep 1997. p399-404. (ISSN1040-2659).

BUSINESS ENTERPRISES--NEW ZEALAND

In New Zealand, between 1995 and 1996, "the construction industry and personal and other services industry shared the highest percentage growth of 12.2 per cent ($1,264 million and $200 million respectively). Total income within the property and business services industry increased by 11.7 per cent ($1,638 million) and accommodation, cafes and restaurants increased by 10.8 per cent ($421 million). The smallest percentage increase in total income was recorded in retail trade at 0.8 per cent ($240 million)....The finance and insurance industry showed the largest value increase of $1,010 million (19.2 per cent). Property and business services industry net profit rose by $950 million (38.9 per cent)."

Statistics New Zealand. "Annual Enterprise Survey--1996 Financial Year." Press Release 28 Nov 1997. document-level access: <http://www.stats.govt.nz/statsweb.nsf/52518ce3e01f62f4cc256388000c48c0/d46d5cccc861efd74c25655d000cae1d?OpenDocument>

BUSINESS ENTERPRISES--NORTH CAROLINA

In North Carolina, "Mecklenburg County was home to 20,929 businesses with employees, the most of any county in the state in 1995, according to new tabulations released...on the Internet by the Commerce Department's Census Bureau....Wake County was second with 16,497 businesses, followed by Guilford County with 12,739, Forsyth County with 7,914 and Buncombe County with 5,671. The numbers of employees in each of the five counties were as follows: Mecklenburg (414,113), Wake (255,873), Guilford (235,023), Forsyth (159,791) and Buncombe (86,069)....The number of businesses in the state totaled 181,972 in 1995, an increase of 5,169 from 1994. Payroll for the state went up 8.3 percent, from $64.8 billion in 1994 to $70.2 billion in 1995, while the number of employees grew from 2,854,742 in 1994 to 2,992,175 in 1995. The manufacturing sector employed the largest portion of the state's private-sector work force (29.1 percent), with an average annual payroll per employee of $26,867."

U.S. Dept. of Commerce. Economic & Statistics Administration. "Mecklenburg Leads North Carolina's Counties in Number of Businesses, Census Bureau Reports." Census Bureau Press Release 20 Oct 1997. document-level access: <http://www.census.gov/Press-Release/nc95cbp.html>

BUSINESS ENTERPRISES--NORTH DAKOTA

In North Dakota, "Cass County was home to 4,056 businesses with employees, the most of any county in the state in 1995, according to new tabulations released...on the Internet by the Commerce Department's Census Bureau....Burleigh County was second with 2,178 businesses, followed by Grand Forks County with 1,789, Ward County with 1,696 and Williams County with 864. The numbers of employees in each of the five counties were as follows: Cass (64,576), Burleigh (29,796), Grand Forks (25,630), Ward (19,982) and Williams (6,760)....The number of businesses in the state totaled 20,269 in 1995, an increase of 140 from 1994. Payroll for the state went up 7.3 percent, from $4.2 billion in 1994 to $4.5 billion in 1995, while the number of employees grew from 220,712 in 1994 to 230,090 in 1995. The services sector employed the largest portion of the state's private-sector work force (35.8 percent), with an average annual payroll per employee of $17,505."

U.S. Dept. of Commerce. Economic & Statistics Administration. "Cass Leads North Dakota's Counties in Number of Businesses, Census Bureau Reports." Census Bureau Press Release 16 Oct 1997. document-level access: <http://www.census.gov/Press-Release/nd95cbp.html>

BUSINESS ENTERPRISES--OHIO

In Ohio, "Cuyahoga County was home to 38,190 businesses with employees, the most of any county in the state in 1995, according to new tabulations released...on the Internet by the Commerce Department's Census Bureau....Franklin County was second with 26,702 businesses, followed by Hamilton County with 25,577, Summit County with 13,870 and Montgomery County with 13,650. The numbers of employees in each of the five counties were as follows: Cuyahoga (709,226), Franklin (539,282), Hamilton (522,152), Summit (243,766) and Montgomery (282,871)....The number of businesses in the state totaled 263,739 in 1995, an increase of 2,964 from 1994. Payroll for the state went up 6.6 percent, from $110.6 billion in 1994 to $117.9 billion in 1995, while the number of employees grew from 4,385,611 in 1994 to 4,550,590 in 1995. The services sector employed the largest portion of the state's private-sector work force (31.6 percent), with an average annual payroll per employee of $22,394."

U.S. Dept. of Commerce. Economic & Statistics Administration. "Cuyahoga Leads Ohio's Counties in Number of Businesses, Census Bureau Reports." Census Bureau Press Release 16 Oct 1997. document-level access: <http://www.census.gov/Press-Release/oh95cbp.html>

BUSINESS ENTERPRISES--OKLAHOMA

In Oklahoma, "Oklahoma County was home to 20,580 businesses with employees, the most of any county in the state in 1995, according to new tabulations released...on the Internet by the Commerce Department's Census Bureau....Tulsa County was second with 17,508 businesses, followed by Cleveland County with 3,624, Comanche County with 2,097 and Garfield County with 1,694. The numbers of employees in each of the five counties were as follows: Oklahoma (313,106), Tulsa (273,399), Cleveland (38,646), Comanche (26,485) and Garfield (19,872)....The number of businesses in the state totaled 81,395 in 1995, an increase of 876 from 1994. Payroll for the state went up 4.6 percent, from $22.0 billion in 1994 to $23.0 billion in 1995, while the number of employees grew from 1,024,904 in 1994 to 1,055,227 in 1995. The services sector employed the largest portion of the state's private-sector work force (33.7 percent), with an average annual payroll per employee of $19,488."

U.S. Dept. of Commerce. Economic & Statistics Administration. "Oklahoma Leads Oklahoma's Counties in Number of Businesses, Census Bureau Reports." Census Bureau Press Release 21 Oct 1997. document-level access: <http://www.census.gov/Press-Release/ok95cbp.html>

BUSINESS ENTERPRISES--OREGON

In Oregon, "Multnomah County was home to 22,627 businesses with employees, the most of any county in the state in 1995, according to new tabulations released...on the Internet by the Commerce Department's Census Bureau....Washington County was second with 11,110 businesses, followed by Lane County with 9,170, Clackamas County with 8,409 and Marion County with 6,840. The numbers of employees in each of the five counties were as follows: Multnomah (367,961), Washington (156,073), Lane (106,351), Clackamas (106,947) and Marion (84,783)....The number of businesses in the state totaled 93,468 in 1995, an increase of 2,000 from 1994. Payroll for the state went up 9.9 percent, from $27.1 billion in 1994 to $29.8 billion in 1995, while the number of employees grew from 1,129,493 in 1994 to 1,185,415 in 1995. The services sector employed the largest portion of the state's private-sector work force (31.2 percent), with an average annual payroll per employee of $22,466."

U.S. Dept. of Commerce. Economic & Statistics Administration. "Multnomah Leads Oregon's Counties in Number of Businesses, Census Bureau Reports." Census Bureau Press Release 23 Oct 1997. document-level access: <http://www.census.gov/Press-Release/or95cbp.html>

BUSINESS ENTERPRISES--PENNSYLVANIA

In Pennsylvania, "Allegheny County was home to 34,506 businesses with employees, the most of any county in the state in 1995, according to new tabulations released...on the Internet by the Commerce Department's Census Bureau....Philadelphia County was second with 26,239 businesses, followed by Montgomery County with 25,391, Bucks County with 15,934 and Delaware County with 13,225. The numbers of employees in each of the five counties were as follows: Allegheny (654,009), Philadelphia (594,043), Montgomery (451,540), Bucks (211,829) and Delaware (204,898)....The number of businesses in the state totaled 283,998 in 1995, an increase of 2,085 from 1994. Payroll for the state went up 5.8 percent, from $116.8 billion in 1994 to $123.5 billion in 1995, while the number of employees grew from 4,583,555 in 1994 to 4,702,892 in 1995. The services sector employed the largest portion of the state's private-sector work force (36.1 percent), with an average annual payroll per employee of $24,773."

U.S. Dept. of Commerce. Economic & Statistics Administration. "Allegheny Leads Pennsylvania's Counties in Number of Businesses, Census Bureau Reports." Census Bureau Press Release 16 Oct 1997. document-level access: <http://www.census.gov/Press-Release/pa95cbp.html>

BUSINESS ENTERPRISES--PUERTO RICO

In Puerto Rico, "San Juan Municipio was home to 12,563 businesses with employees, the most of any municipio in the commonwealth in 1995, according to new tabulations released...on the Internet by the Commerce Department's Census Bureau....Bayamon Municipio was second with 2,877 businesses, followed by Ponce Municipio with 2,166, Caguas Municipio with 1,855 and Mayaguez Municipio with 1,589. The numbers of employees in each of the five municipios were as follows: San Juan (224,629), Bayamon (36,794), Ponce (37,732), Caguas (28,044) and Mayaguez (31,325)....The number of businesses in the commonwealth totaled 38,832 in 1995, an increase of 1,042 from 1994. Payroll for the commonwealth went up 8.6 percent, from $9.0 billion in 1994 to $9.7 billion in 1995, while the number of employees grew from 597,389 in 1994 to 617,986 in 1995. The manufacturing sector employed the largest portion of the commonwealth's private-sector work force (25.3 percent), with an average annual payroll per employee of $19,460."

U.S. Dept. of Commerce. Economic & Statistics Administration. "San Juan Leads Puerto Rico's Municipios in Number of Businesses, Census Bureau Reports." Census Bureau Press Release 23 Oct 1997. document-level access: <http://www.census.gov/Press-Release/pr95cbp.html>

BUSINESS ENTERPRISES--QUEBEC (PROVINCE) (v26)

BUSINESS ENTERPRISES--RHODE ISLAND

In Rhode Island, "Providence County was home to 16,276 businesses with employees, the most of any county in the state in 1995, according to new tabulations released...on the Internet by the Commerce Department's Census Bureau....Kent County was second with 4,762 businesses, followed by Washington County with 3,158, Newport County with 2,520 and Bristol County with 1,050. The numbers of employees in each of the five counties were as follows: Providence (248,929), Kent (63,863), Washington (31,008), Newport (23,468) and Bristol (12,327)....The number of businesses in the state totaled 27,766 in 1995, an increase of 299 from 1994. Payroll for the state went up 5.0 percent, from $9.0 billion in 1994 to $9.5 billion in 1995, while the number of employees grew from 370,342 in 1994 to 379,595 in 1995. The services sector employed the largest portion of the state's private-sector work force (37.8 percent), with an average annual payroll per employee of $23,948."

U.S. Dept. of Commerce. Economic & Statistics Administration. "Providence Leads Rhode Island's Counties in Number of Businesses, Census Bureau Reports." Census Bureau Press Release 16 Oct 1997. document-level access: <http://www.census.gov/Press-Release/ri95cbp.html>

BUSINESS ENTERPRISES--SOUTH CAROLINA

In South Carolina, "Greenville County was home to 10,748 businesses with employees, the most of any county in the state in 1995, according to new tabulations released...on the Internet by the Commerce Department's Census Bureau....Charleston County was second with 9,414 businesses, followed by Richland County with 8,565, Horry County with 6,271 and Spartanburg County with 5,645. The numbers of employees in each of the five counties were as follows: Greenville (221,686), Charleston (140,536), Richland (147,809), Horry (68,314) and Spartanburg (109,827)....The number of businesses in the state totaled 87,990 in 1995, an increase of 2,061 from 1994. Payroll for the state went up 7.1 percent, from $29.2 billion in 1994 to $31.3 billion in 1995, while the number of employees grew from 1,347,896 in 1994 to 1,395,070 in 1995. The services sector employed the largest portion of the state's private-sector work force (28.9 percent), with an average annual payroll per employee of $20,939."

U.S. Dept. of Commerce. Economic & Statistics Administration. "Greenville Leads South Carolina's Counties in Number of Businesses, Census Bureau Reports." Census Bureau Press Release 20 Oct 1997. document-level access: <http://www.census.gov/Press-Release/sc95cbp.html>

BUSINESS ENTERPRISES--SOUTH DAKOTA

In South Dakota, "Minnehaha County was home to 4,862 businesses with employees, the most of any county in the state in 1995, according to new tabulations released...on the Internet by the Commerce Department's Census Bureau....Pennington County was second with 3,056 businesses, followed by Brown County with 1,332, Codington County with 912 and Lawrence County with 815. The numbers of employees in each of the five counties were as follows: Minnehaha (84,431), Pennington (37,007), Brown (16,159), Codington (12,111) and Lawrence (8,903)....The number of businesses in the state totaled 22,708 in 1995, an increase of 331 from 1994. Payroll for the state went up 10.1 percent, from $4.7 billion in 1994 to $5.1 billion in 1995, while the number of employees grew from 256,070 in 1994 to 268,483 in 1995. The services sector employed the largest portion of the state's private-sector work force (33.1 percent), with an average annual payroll per employee of $18,156."

U.S. Dept. of Commerce. Economic & Statistics Administration. "Minnehaha Leads South Dakota's Counties in Number of Businesses, Census Bureau Reports." Census Bureau Press Release 16 Oct 1997. document-level access: <http://www.census.gov/Press-Release/sd95cbp.html>

BUSINESS ENTERPRISES--TENNESSEE

In Tennessee, "Shelby County was home to 20,766 businesses with employees, the most of any county in the state in 1995, according to new tabulations released...on the Internet by the Commerce Department's Census Bureau....Davidson County was second with 18,717 businesses, followed by Knox County with 10,916, Hamilton County with 8,741 and Sullivan County with 3,621. The numbers of employees in each of the five counties were as follows: Shelby (406,899), Davidson (371,515), Knox (175,189), Hamilton (152,426) and Sullivan (67,742)....The number of businesses in the state totaled 124,814 in 1995, an increase of 2,799 from 1994. Payroll for the state went up 8.4 percent, from $47.1 billion in 1994 to $51.1 billion in 1995, while the number of employees grew from 2,041,973 in 1994 to 2,153,264 in 1995. The services sector employed the largest portion of the state's private-sector work force (31.0 percent), with an average annual payroll per employee of $23,137."

U.S. Dept. of Commerce. Economic & Statistics Administration. "Shelby Leads Tennessee's Counties in Number of Businesses, Census Bureau Reports." Census Bureau Press Release 16 Oct 1997. document-level access: <http://www.census.gov/Press-Release/tn95cbp.html>

BUSINESS ENTERPRISES--TEXAS

In Texas, "Harris County was home to 80,034 businesses with employees, the most of any county in the state in 1995, according to new tabulations released...on the Internet by the Commerce Department's Census Bureau....Dallas County was second with 63,586 businesses, followed by Tarrant County with 30,368, Bexar County with 28,091 and Travis County with 20,537. The numbers of employees in each of the five counties were as follows: Harris (1,475,299), Dallas (1,256,339), Tarrant (514,017), Bexar (479,745) and Travis (336,854)....The number of businesses in the state totaled 438,262 in 1995, an increase of 8,291 from 1994. Payroll for the state went up 8.7 percent, from $160.9 billion in 1994 to $174.9 billion in 1995, while the number of employees grew from 6,453,230 in 1994 to 6,786,893 in 1995. The services sector employed the largest portion of the state's private-sector work force (34.1 percent), with an average annual payroll per employee of $23,970."

U.S. Dept. of Commerce. Economic & Statistics Administration. "Harris Leads Texas' Counties in Number of Businesses, Census Bureau Reports." Census Bureau Press Release 21 Oct 1997. document-level access: <http://www.census.gov/Press-Release/tx95cbp.html>

BUSINESS ENTERPRISES--UNITED STATES (v26)

BUSINESS ENTERPRISES--UTAH

In Utah, "Salt Lake County was home to 22,507 businesses with employees, the most of any county in the state in 1995, according to new tabulations released...on the Internet by the Commerce Department's Census Bureau....Utah County was second with 5,665 businesses, followed by Weber County with 3,564, Davis County with 3,504 and Washington County with 1,846. The numbers of employees in each of the five counties were as follows: Salt Lake (408,445), Utah (106,584), Weber (60,353), Davis (44,817) and Washington (20,516)....The number of businesses in the state totaled 45,882 in 1995, an increase of 2,143 from 1994. Payroll for the state went up 11.0 percent, from $15.3 billion in 1994 to $17.0 billion in 1995, while the number of employees grew from 699,654 in 1994 to 744,430 in 1995. The services sector employed the largest portion of the state's private-sector work force (34.3 percent), with an average annual payroll per employee of $21,611."

U.S. Dept. of Commerce. Economic & Statistics Administration. "Salt Lake Leads Utah's Counties in Number of Businesses, Census Bureau Reports." Census Bureau Press Release 22 Oct 1997. document-level access: <http://www.census.gov/Press-Release/ut95cbp.html>

BUSINESS ENTERPRISES--VERMONT

In Vermont, "Chittenden County was home to 5,059 businesses with employees, the most of any county in the state in 1995, according to new tabulations released...on the Internet by the Commerce Department's Census Bureau....Rutland County was second with 2,289 businesses, followed by Washington County with 2,192, Windsor County with 2,045 and Windham County with 1,791. The numbers of employees in each of the five counties were as follows: Chittenden (72,237), Rutland (24,630), Washington (21,916), Windsor (17,318) and Windham (21,946)....The number of businesses in the state totaled 20,542 in 1995, an increase of 221 from 1994. Payroll for the state went up 6.4 percent, from $4.7 billion in 1994 to $5.0 billion in 1995, while the number of employees grew from 218,783 in 1994 to 224,327 in 1995. The services sector employed the largest portion of the state's private-sector work force (34.5 percent), with an average annual payroll per employee of $19,736."

U.S. Dept. of Commerce. Economic & Statistics Administration. "Chittenden Leads Vermont's Counties in Number of Businesses, Census Bureau Reports." Census Bureau Press Release 16 Oct 1997. document-level access: <http://www.census.gov/Press-Release/vt95cbp.html>

BUSINESS ENTERPRISES--VIRGINIA

In Virginia, "Fairfax County was home to 23,464 businesses with employees, the most of any county in the state in 1995, according to new tabulations released...on the Internet by the Commerce Department's Census Bureau....Virginia Beach (city) was second with 9,491 businesses, followed by Richmond (city) with 8,470, Henrico County with 5,805 and Norfolk (city) with 5,559. The independent cities in Virginia are treated as counties for this report. The numbers of employees in each of the five counties were as follows: Fairfax (372,035), Virginia Beach (city) (119,643), Richmond (city) (179,412), Henrico (102,505) and Norfolk (112,562)....The number of businesses in the state totaled 162,378 in 1995, an increase of 3,352 from 1994. Payroll for the state went up 6.8 percent, from $59.3 billion in 1994 to $63.3 billion in 1995, while the number of employees grew from 2,393,128 in 1994 to 2,481,306 in 1995. The services sector employed the largest portion of the state's private-sector work force (36.1 percent), with an average annual payroll per employee of $26,514."

U.S. Dept. of Commerce. Economic & Statistics Administration. "Fairfax Leads Virginia's Counties in Number of Businesses, Census Bureau Reports." Census Bureau Press Release 20 Oct 1997. document-level access: <http://www.census.gov/Press-Release/va95cbp.html>

BUSINESS ENTERPRISES--WASHINGTON

In Washington, "King County was home to 56,521 businesses with employees, the most of any county in the state in 1995, according to new tabulations released...on the Internet by the Commerce Department's Census Bureau....Pierce County was second with 14,316 businesses, followed by Snohomish County with 12,745, Spokane County with 11,260 and Clark County with 6,815. The numbers of employees in each of the five counties were as follows: King (862,946), Pierce (178,569), Snohomish (160,468), Spokane (154,255) and Clark (83,711)....The number of businesses in the state totaled 151,925 in 1995, an increase of 2,309 from 1994. Payroll for the state went up 7.4 percent, from $49.8 billion in 1994 to $53.5 billion in 1995, while the number of employees grew from 1,895,158 in 1994 to 1,948,923 in 1995. The services sector employed the largest portion of the state's private-sector work force (33.0 percent), with an average annual payroll per employee of $26,372."

U.S. Dept. of Commerce. Economic & Statistics Administration. "King Leads Washington's Counties in Number of Businesses, Census Bureau Reports." Census Bureau Press Release 23 Oct 1997. document-level access: <http://www.census.gov/Press-Release/wa95cbp.html>

BUSINESS ENTERPRISES--WEST VIRGINIA

In West Virginia, "Kanawha County was home to 5,847 businesses with employees, the most of any county in the state in 1995, according to new tabulations released...on the Internet by the Commerce Department's Census Bureau....Cabell County was second with 2,644 businesses, followed by Wood County with 2,301, Monongalia County with 1,967 and Raleigh County with 1,950. The numbers of employees in each of the five counties were [as] follows: Kanawha (88,894), Cabell (40,251), Wood (36,237), Monongalia (28,427) and Raleigh (22,213)....The number of businesses in the state totaled 40,599 in 1995, an increase of 368 from 1994. Payroll for the state went up 4.8 percent, from $11.4 billion in 1994 to $11.9 billion in 1995, while the number of employees grew from 510,890 in 1994 to 530,596 in 1995. The services sector employed the largest portion of the state's private-sector work force (33.3 percent), with an average annual payroll per employee of $19,817."

U.S. Dept. of Commerce. Economic & Statistics Administration. "Kanawha Leads West Virginia's Counties in Number of Businesses, Census Bureau Reports." Census Bureau Press Release 20 Oct 1997. document-level access: <http://www.census.gov/Press-Release/wv95cbp.html>

BUSINESS ENTERPRISES--WISCONSIN

In Wisconsin, "Milwaukee County was home to 22,057 businesses with employees, the most of any county in the state in 1995, according to new tabulations released...on the Internet by the Commerce Department's Census Bureau....Dane County was second with 11,413 businesses, followed by Waukesha County with 11,398, Brown County with 5,671 and Racine County with 4,141. The numbers of employees in each of the five counties were as follows: Milwaukee (474,292), Dane (198,563), Waukesha (191,297), Brown (107,195) and Racine (73,331)....The number of businesses in the state totaled 133,238 in 1995, an increase of 1,624 from 1994. Payroll for the state went up 6.2 percent, from $50.5 billion in 1994 to $53.7 billion in 1995, while the number of employees grew from 2,100,173 in 1994 to 2,186,060 in 1995. The services sector employed the largest portion of the state's private-sector work force (29.3 percent), with an average annual payroll per employee of $21,015."

U.S. Dept. of Commerce. Economic & Statistics Administration. "Milwaukee Leads Wisconsin's Counties in Number of Businesses, Census Bureau Reports." Census Bureau Press Release 16 Oct 1997. document-level access: <http://www.census.gov/Press-Release/wi95cbp.html>

BUSINESS ENTERPRISES--WYOMING

In Wyoming, "Natrona County was home to 2,545 businesses with employees, the most of any county in the state in 1995, according to new tabulations released...on the Internet by the Commerce Department's Census Bureau....Laramie County was second with 2,111 businesses, followed by Teton County with 1,452, Fremont County with 1,212 and Park County with 1,162. The numbers of employees in each of the five counties were as follows: Natrona (23,306), Laramie (24,689), Teton (11,678), Fremont (9,378) and Park (8,443)....The number of businesses in the state totaled 17,133 in 1995, an increase of 385 from 1994. Payroll for the state went up 3.6 percent, from $3.3 billion in 1994 to $3.5 billion in 1995, while the number of employees grew from 154,354 in 1994 to 157,472 in 1995. The services sector employed the largest portion of the state's private-sector work force (32.6 percent), with an average annual payroll per employee of $18,228."

U.S. Dept. of Commerce. Economic & Statistics Administration. "Natrona Leads Wyoming's Counties in Number of Businesses, Census Bureau Reports." Census Bureau Press Release 22 Oct 1997. document-level access: <http://www.census.gov/Press-Release/wy95cbp.html>

BUSINESS ENTERPRISES, HISPANIC AMERICAN
see HISPANIC AMERICAN BUSINESS ENTERPRISES

BUSINESS ENTERPRISES, HOME
see HOME-BASED BUSINESSES

BUSINESS ENTERPRISES, INTERNATIONAL
see INTERNATIONAL BUSINESS ENTERPRISES

BUSINESS ENTERPRISES, MINORITY
see MINORITY BUSINESS ENTERPRISES

BUSINESS EXECUTIVES
see EXECUTIVES

BUSINESS SCHOOLS--UNITED STATES

In the U.S., a recent Graduate Management Admission Council "survey of its member business schools found that 61 percent have seen an increase in applications this year. And more than 1 in 5 report jumps of 20 percent or more. At Indiana University in Bloomington, applications are up 26 percent this year....International students provided a boost for many schools; 78 percent reported an increase in international applications, according to the GMAC survey. Nearly half of Indiana University's increase in applicants this year came from foreign students. The top three countries: India, South Korea, and China. And at the University of Virginia's Darden School, foreign students make up 21 percent of this year's incoming class, versus 12 percent a year ago." (p9)

Coolidge, Shelley Donald. "Business & Money: Workplace: MBA Becomes Ticket to Tomorrow." The Christian Science Monitor v89 n199 9 Sep 1997. p9. The Christian Science Monitor search engine: <http://www.csmonitor.com/plweb-cgi/iops1.pl> To retrieve this article, enter the following search: ED=19970909 AND tomorrow. In the "retrieved list," click the title that matches this record. (ISSN0882-7729).

BUSINESSMEN
see CANADA--ECONOMIC CONDITIONS--BUSINESSMEN--ATTITUDES

BUSINESSWOMEN
see WOMEN IN BUSINESS

BUTTERFLY, MONARCH
see MONARCH BUTTERFLY

BUYER BEHAVIOR
see CONSUMER BEHAVIOR

BYPASS SURGERY, CORONARY
see CORONARY ARTERY BYPASS

C SECTION
see CESAREAN SECTION

CABLE TELEVISION (v26)

CABLE TELEVISION--UNITED STATES (v26)

CABS
see TAXICABS

CAIMAN--SOUTH AMERICA

A study of South America's caimans, published in the conservation journal ORYX, found that "more than half the animals sampled in the caiman survey had startlingly high levels of lead in their tissues....Over the course of the survey, which was conducted between 1985 and early 1992, black caimans completely disappeared from 41 of the 47 areas studied, while common caimans vanished from 4 of 39 sites, and declined in many more." (p26)

Youth, Howard. "Neglected Elders." World Watch v10 n5 Sep-Oct 1997. p22-29. (ISSN0896-0615).

CAIRO (EGYPT)--ECONOMIC CONDITIONS (v26)

CAIRO (EGYPT)--ENVIRONMENTAL ASPECTS --PUBLIC OPINION (v26)

CALCIUM IN HUMAN NUTRITION

"Females between the ages of 9 and 18 should consider raising their intake of calcium to 1,300 milligrams per day in order to increase bone density and prevent osteoporosis, says a new report. The [U.S.] Institute of Medicine report also recommends that adults ages 19 to 50 increase their calcium intake from 800 mg daily to 1,000 mg daily. Adults 51 and over should now aim to consume 1,200 mg daily, up from 800 mg. The report...is the first in a series on Dietary Reference Intakes, which will update and expand the Recommended Daily Allowances (RDAs) for nutrients. The RDA for calcium last changed in 1989." (p1 secF)

Pipp, Tracy L. "Accent: Health: RDA Overhaul Starts Off by Urging Higher Calcium Intake." Detroit News 14 Aug 1997. p1 secF.

CALCIUM IN HUMAN NUTRITION--UNITED STATES --CHILDREN (v26)

CALCIUM IN HUMAN NUTRITION--UNITED STATES --TEENAGERS

"Bones grow and incorporate calcium most rapidly during the teen years, and establish approximately 90 percent of adult bone mass by age 17....Six out of ten teen boys and eight out of ten teen girls [in the U.S.] don't get enough calcium in their diets at a critical time when nearly half of all bone is formed. Most teens are getting only about 800 mg [milligrams] of the 1,300 mg required each day, setting the stage for osteoporosis....One-half of women will have an osteoporosis-related fracture at age 50 or older, and doctors believe that inadequate calcium consumption during the teen years is largely to blame. Recent NICHD [National Institute of Child Health and Human Development] research indicates that supplementing the diets of teenage girls with an extra 350 mg of calcium per day produced a 14 percent increase in bone density."

U.S. Dept. of Health and Human Services. "Secretary Shalala Announces Partnership to Increase Teen Calcium Consumption." Press Release 12 Nov 1997. document-level access: <http://www.hhs.gov/news/press/1997pres/971112.html>

CALGARY (ALTA.)--ECONOMIC CONDITIONS (v26)

CALIFORNIA--APPROPRIATIONS AND EXPENDITURES (v26)

"California had the largest amount of state revenues in 1996, collecting $123 billion. Forty-seven percent or $58 billion of these revenues were from taxes, 23 percent from intergovernmental aid and 20 percent from insurance trust revenue. Expenditures for California reached $113 billion in 1996, with education ($35 billion) and public welfare ($29 billion) accounting for more than 55 percent of the total."

U.S. Dept. of Commerce. Economic and Statistics Administration. "Nearly One-Third of 1996 State Expenditures Spent on Education, According to Census Bureau Data for 50 States." Census Bureau Press Release 15 Sep 1997. document-level access: <http://www.census.gov/Press-Release/cb97-146.html>

CALIFORNIA--POLITICS AND GOVERNMENT

"In the two elections leading up to 1996, the [California] Assembly turnover rate increased to 36 percent, and the share of incumbents seeking re-election dropped to 67 percent." (p19)

"As of June [1997], according to the Assembly Rules Committee, 73 percent of current Assembly staff had been on the job for three years or less, and 45 percent had been employed for one year or less. In 1990, before term limits, only 23 percent had worked there less than a year. In 1990, there were more than 200 Assembly employees who had over 10 years' experience. Now there are only about 100 with 10 years' experience." (p21)

Hayward, Steven. "Same as the Old Boss?" Reason v29 n7 Dec 1997. p16-22. (ISSN0048-6906).

CALIFORNIA--POPULATION (v26)

CALIFORNIA--PUBLIC OPINION

"A LOS ANGELES TIMES poll taken in October [1997] revealed that 46 percent of those asked [about the future] believe that...[Californians are] headed in the right direction. Forty percent thought otherwise....Five years ago only 12 percent expressed an optimistic view and 82 percent felt we were sliding downhill....Breaking the TIMES poll down, only 28 percent of the blacks and 38 percent of the Latinos questioned felt optimistic about the state's future. Similarly, analyzing it along economic lines, the majority of those who expressed optimism (58 percent) earned over $60,000 a year, compared to only 33 percent of those making under $20,000 a year." (p10-11)

Martinez, Al. "Can We All Get Along?" California Journal v29 n1 Jan 1998. p6-11. (ISSN0008-1205).

CALL GIRLS

see PROSTITUTION

CAMERAS--UNITED STATES

In the U.S., the number of single-use "cameras sold has increased more than 1,800 percent since their introduction in 1988, to more than 54 million units in 1995. Annual increases continue to exceed 20 percent....From unit sales to film processing, they generated over $1 billion of the $13 billion market in 1995....An estimated 65.5 million units were sold in 1996. The number may climb to 76 million units in 1997." (p6)

Heubusch, Kevin. "Tomorrow's Markets: Look at the Birdie." American Demographics v19 n7 Jul 1997. p4,6-10. article-level access: <http://www.demographics.com/publications/ad/97_ad/9707_ad/ad97072.htm> (ISSN0163-4089).

CAMPAIGN FUNDS

see also POLITICAL ACTION COMMITTEES

CAMPAIGN FUNDS--CALIFORNIA

"It was at a Buddhist Temple in Hacienda Heights [California] that [U.S.] Vice President Al Gore raised $140,000 for the Democratic Party. Among the $5,000 donors were Buddhist nuns who had taken a vow of poverty....Yogesh Gandhi of Walnut Creek [California], who only weeks before telling the IRS he had no U.S. holdings, donated $50,000 to the Democratic National Committee....Republicans identified three California subsidiaries of the Lippo Group, a massive Indonesian bank with close ties to China, who allegedly funneled over $100,000 to Democrats despite never turning a profit. The companies, all based in Los Angeles, contributed at least $20,500 to California candidates. Recipients included former state Treasurer Kathleen Brown ($7,000), former Lieutenant Governor Leo McCarthy ($4,500) and current Lieutenant Governor Gray Davis ($3,000)." (p44)

Sandalow, Marc. "Washington Notes: Perspective: Gold Rush." California Journal v28 n9 Sep 1997. p44. (ISSN0008-1205).

CAMPAIGN FUNDS--CANADA

"Any given year between 1983 and 1990, 40% of the 500 biggest corporations in Canada and 35% of the 155 biggest financial institutions in Canada made a financial contribution to a federal political party. "Between 1974 and 1990, less than 2% of voters saw fit to contribute to a federal political organization in any one of those years." (p751)

Dalphond-Guiral, Madeleine (MP-PQ). "Government Orders: Supply." Canada. Parliament. House of Commons. Debates. v135 n14 9 Oct 1997. p736-761. section-level access: <http://www.parl.gc.ca/36/1/parlbus/chambus/house/debates/014_1997-10-09/han014-e.htm#LINKT89> (ISSN0704-5603). (X3-361E).

CAMPAIGN FUNDS--FLORIDA (v26)

CAMPAIGN FUNDS--INDIANS OF NORTH AMERICA

In the U.S., "according to the Center for Responsive Politics, national donations from the 184 tribes with gambling interests shot from $117,871 in 1992 to $1.7 million in 1996. They spent an additional $2.3 million in disclosed fees to lobbyists. Last year, the Mashantucket Pequot, who run the world's most profitable casino in Ledyard, Conn., were among the Democrats' largest contributors, giving $319,625." (p59)

Barnes, Julian E. "U.S. News: Lobbies with Wolves." U.S. News & World Report v123 n18 10 Nov 1997. p59. article-level access: <http://www.usnews.com/usnews/issue/971110/10CASI.HTM> (ISSN0041-5537).

CAMPAIGN FUNDS--INDIANS OF NORTH AMERICA --CALIFORNIA

"By spending $4 million on lobbying and political donations since 1994, the [American] Indian lobby has emerged as one of the most powerful in...[California]." (p6,8) "Indians gave to Democratic gubernatorial candidate Kathleen Brown, and they also poured a huge sum of money--$843,000--into the campaign of [Attorney General Dan] Lungren's opponent, Tom Umberg....The Rumsey Rancheria, which operates a large casino on the western edge of the Sacramento Valley...made front page news when it handed out $100,000 to the Sacramento Symphony." (p9) Senator Richard Polanco "received $34,200 in contributions from gaming Indians....[Republican Assemblyman Jim Battin] received $45,700 in contributions from gaming Indians in 1996...." (p10)

Ainsworth, Bill. "Betting on Politics." California Journal v28 n8 Aug 1997. p6-10. (ISSN0008-1205).

CAMPAIGN FUNDS--UNITED STATES (v26)

In the U.S., "the costs of running for office are exploding. The average Senate race in 1996 cost $3.6 million. Twenty years ago, the average Senate race cost just $609,100. The cost of a race for the House of Representatives has increased sixfold over the last 20 years, from $99 million in 1976 to $626 million in 1996. Spending on Federal election campaigns increased to an estimated $2.7 billion in the most recent election cycle, a threefold increase over campaign spending just 20 years ago, even after adjusting for inflation....The money is increasingly coming through channels designed to skirt the Federal Election Campaign Act. The use of soft money...has skyrocketed in the last 4 years. In the 1995-96 cycle, the two major parties spent $263 million in soft money, compared with $81 million in the 1993-94 cycle. That's an increase of 224 percent." (pS8933)

Dorgan, Byron L. (Sen.-N.Dak.). "McCain-Feingold Campaign Finance Reform Legislation." Congressional Record. Daily ed. v143 n117 8 Sep 1997. pS8933. section/page-level access: <http://thomas.loc.gov/cgi-bin/query/R?r105:FLD001:S08933:> (ISSN0363-7239). (X1.1A.105/1).

In the U.S., "total congressional campaign spending has exploded in the last 20 years. We spent $115 million on Federal campaigns in the 1975-76 election cycle. Ten years later, in the 1985-86, we spent $450 million. In the last cycle, 1995-96,...we spent $765 million on Federal campaigns. Each election cycle shatters another spending record; 1996 was no exception. Spending in Federal campaigns increased 73 percent over the previous Presidential cycle....To put that in perspective, during the same period, wages rose 13 percent, college tuition rose 17 percent, but Federal campaign spending rose 73 percent. The average cost of winning a Senate seat in 1996 was $4.5 million. To raise that much money, a Senator has to raise $14,000 a week, every week, for 6 years....The average cost of winning a House seat in 1996 was $660,000. To raise that much money, Members in the House had to raise $6,000 a week, every week, for 2 years." (pS9998)

Daschle, Thomas A. (Sen.-S.Dak.). "Bipartisan Campaign Reform Act of 1997." Congressional Record. Daily ed. v143 n131 26 Sep 1997. pS9994-10026. section/page-level access: <http://thomas.loc.gov/cqi-bin/query/R?r105:FLD001:S09997:> (ISSN0363-7239). (X1.1A.105/1).

In the U.S., "Democratic and Republican national committees collected a combined total of more than $35 million in soft money donations during the first half of 1997 according to mid-year disclosure reports filed with the FEC [Federal Election Commission]. The three national Republican committees--the Republican National Committee, National Republican Senatorial Committee and National Republican Congressional Committee--raised $21.7 million in soft money between January 1 and June 30. The three national Democratic committees--the Democratic National Committee, Democratic Senatorial Campaign Committee and Democratic Congressional Campaign Committee--took in $13.7 million in soft money during the same period....The Republican committees raised more than $59 million [in 'hard dollars'] while the Democratic committees took in $35.1 million....Republicans reported 87 percent of contributions from individuals, while the Democrats showed 66 percent of contributions from individuals." (p3)

"Statistics: National Party Committees Increase Soft Money." Federal Election Commission Record v23 n11 Nov 1997. p3.

"Between January 1, 1995, and November 6, 1996, [U.S.] President Bill Clinton invited 477 friends and supporters to fly with him on Air Force One. According to the White House, of these guests, 56 were major contributors--that is, either personally or through affiliated organizations, they gave at least $5,000 to the Democratic National Committee or raised at least $25,000 for the Clinton-Gore campaign." (p9)

Bleifuss, Joel. "In Short: The Jet-Set Cabinet." In These Times v21 n16 30 Jun 1997. p9. (ISSN0160-5992).

In the U.S., during last year's presidential "election campaign, the top 25 weapons exporters contributed $10.8 million, according to a study by the World Policy Institute. This marks a 56 percent increase in political action committee (PAC) and soft money contributions over the previous peak of $6.9 million during the 1991-92 election cycle." (p16)

Honey, Martha. "Weapons: Guns 'R' Us." In These Times v21 n19 11 Aug 1997. p14-17. (ISSN0160-5992).

The 1995-1996 U.S. "election cycle represented a quantum leap in our capital-intensive politics, with the national Democratic Party increasing its take of soft money a whopping 242 percent in comparison to 1992, for a total of $123.9 million--nearly equaling the $138 million raked in by the 'party of privilege.'...A new study by the U.S. Public Interest Research Group calculates that raising the current cap of $1,000 per election to $2,500 would allow fat cats to flood the system with $318 million in new hard money, or $56 million more than the current soft-money system allows. And soft money is only a small part of the problem, constituting one-eighth of the more than $2 billion spent in 1995-96 on federal elections alone." (p12)

Ireland, Doug. "View Point: Campaign Finance Deform." In These Times v21 n24 2 Nov 1997. p12. (ISSN0160-5992).

In the U.S., "a 1996 study by the Center for Public Integrity found that between 1991 and 1995, gambling contributions to federal politicians and soft money accounts amounted to $4.5 million....The industry ponied up nearly $5 million for the 1996 election alone, a sum evenly distributed between Democrats and Republicans....A MOTHER JONES investigation has found that over the past five years the gambling industry has spent more than $100 million in political contributions and lobbying fees to influence state governments." (p35)

Koughan, Martin. "Easy Money." Mother Jones v22 n4 Jul-Aug 1997. p32-37. article-level access: <http://www.motherjones.com/coinop_congress/easymoney/koughan.html> (ISSN0362-8841).

In the U.S., "from a tolerable $45 million in 1987-88, soft money [campaign contributions] climbed to $80 million in 1991-92 and hit a phenomenal $271.5 million in the race between Clinton and Bob Dole, according to Colby College political scientist Anthony Corrado. The number of checks accepted by the two major parties quintupled from roughly 8,000 in the 1991-92 election cycle to over 40,000 in 1995-96--not counting those made out to state organizations." (p3)

Mollison, Andrew. "Washington-USA: Peddling Political Access." New Leader v80 n16 6 Oct 1997. p3. (ISSN0028-6044).

CAMPAIGN FUNDS--UNITED STATES--CORPORATIONS (v26)

CAMPAIGN FUNDS--UNITED STATES--PUBLIC OPINION (v26)

"Ninety-two percent of Americans think that too much money is spent on campaigns; 89 percent want fundamental change in the campaign finance system; 85 percent believe special interests have more influence than the voters; 69 percent believe that public officials are indifferent to their views, their concerns, their needs; 51 percent believe that quite a few Government officials are corrupt....In 1996, voter turnout was below 50 percent, which is the lowest since the early 1920's." (pS10453)

Reed, Jack (Sen.-R.I.). "Campaign Finance Reform." Congressional Record. Daily ed. v143 n138 7 Oct 1997. pS10450-10456. section/page-level access: <http://thomas.loc.gov/cgi-bin/query/R?r105:FLD001:S10452:> (ISSN0363-7239). (X1.1A.105/1).

According to a recent Gallup poll, "by a 63% to 24% margin, Americans support new restrictions on large 'soft money' donations to the political parties....Seven in ten Americans also favor new restrictions on labor union leaders' ability to spend members' dues for political purposes....The public is deeply cynical about the influence of money in the political process, with 77% saying that special interests, rather than the best interests of the country, carry more weight with lawmakers. In addition, 59% think elections are for sale to the candidate with the most money, rather than decided on the basis of who is the better candidate....Three out of five respondents, 59%, say that special interests will always find a way to maintain their power in Washington regardless of what new laws are passed. And despite the extensive amount of coverage given this year to alleged 1996 campaign fundraising abuses, the public is about evenly divided, 46% to 50%, as to whether the problems are much worse today than in the past, or just the same as always."

Saad, Lydia/Gallup Organization. "Americans Not Holding Their Breath on Campaign Finance Reform." Press Release 11 Oct 1997. document-level access: <http://www.gallup.com/poll/news/971011.html>

CAMPAIGN FUNDS--UNITED STATES. CONGRESS (v26)

U.S. "congressional candidates in 1996 raised nearly $800 million....The 2,605 candidates vying for seats in the U.S. House and Senate raised $790.5 million, a 20 percent increase over 1992, and spent $765.3 million, which was a 12 percent increase. The fundraising also was ahead of 1994 election cycle financial activity, with increases of 7 percent in money raised and 5 percent in expenditures. The jump in fundraising and spending is due to House candidates, who raised $505.4 million of the total and spent $477.8 million. Among these candidates, Republicans outdid their Democratic counterparts with a 32 percent increase in financial activity over the previous election cycle. The Democrats mustered only an 8 percent increase in receipts and a 4 percent increase in expenditures compared with the 1994 election cycle." (p9)

"Statistics: Congressional, PAC Fundraising and Expenditures Continue Strong Showings in 1996 Election Cycle." Federal Election Commission Record v23 n6 Jun 1997. p9-10.

"By most estimates, the minimum cost of a successful campaign for US Senate is about $10 million, and most House candidates must raise about $500,000 to survive the primary alone....According to the Center for Responsive Politics, personal spending on Senate races rose from $13 million in 1986 to $64 million in 1994. In the most recent elections, 93 congressional candidates and 54 would-be senators spent more than $100,000 in personal funds." (p4)

Walker, Sam. "Golden Age for the Millionaire Politician." The Christian Science Monitor v89 n177 7 Aug 1997. p4. The Christian Science Monitor search engine: <http://www.csmonitor.com/plweb-cgi/iops1.pl> To retrieve this article, enter the following search: ED=19970807 AND politician. In the "retrieved list," click the title that matches this record. (ISSN0882-7729).

CAMPAIGN FUNDS--UNITED STATES. SENATE (v26)

CAMPING--UNITED STATES

"This summer 6.5 million campers will descend on the 8,500 camps in the US. The number of campers has been rising between 7 and 10 percent a year since 1993, according to the American Camping Association (AMA), as more working parents search for supervised summer activities for their children." (p13)

Coolidge, Shelley Donald. "Reports from the Bug-Juice Brigade." The Christian Science Monitor v89 n140 16 Jun 1997. p13. The Christian Science Monitor search engine: <http://www.csmonitor.com/plweb-cgi/iops1.pl> To retrieve this article, enter the following search: ED=19970616 AND brigade. In the "retrieved list," click the title that matches this record. (ISSN0882-7729).

CAMPUS VIOLENCE--UNITED STATES (v26)

CAMPYLOBACTER INFECTIONS--UNITED STATES

"Microbial pathogens in food cause between 6.5 million and 33 million cases of human illness and up to 9,000 deaths each year in the United States....'Campylobacter' is the most common cause of foodborne diarrheal illness in the U.S. Sources of 'Campylobacter' include raw and undercooked poultry, raw milk, and polluted water. Up to $5.6 billion in human illness costs could be saved each year in the United States by reducing 'Campylobacter' in food. Out of an estimated 2,628 to 9,575 patients diagnosed with Guillain-Barre syndrome (GBS) in the United States each year, 526 to 3,830 (20-40 percent) are triggered by 'Campylobacter' infection....Two percent die from the illness, and up to 65 percent of patients with GBS report neurological pain." (p9)

U.S. Dept. of Agriculture. Economic Research Service. "ERS Summary of Report: Savings from Reducing 'Campylobacter' in Food Could Total up to $5.6 Billion per Year." ERS Information Sep 1997. p9.

CAMPYLOBACTER INFECTIONS--UNITED STATES --COSTS

"A new report by USDA's Economic Research Service, 'Estimated Annual Costs of Campylobacter-Associated Guillain-Barre Syndrome,' estimates: the annual U.S. cost of 'Campylobacter'-associated GBS: $0.2 to $1.8 billion (1995 dollars); the annual U.S. cost from 'Campylobacter' infections of $1.5-$8.0 billion (total annual costs of 'Campylobacter'-associated GBS plus costs of campylobacteriosis ($1.3-$6.2 billion))....Assuming that 55-70 percent of all 'Campylobacter' infections are attributable to foodborne sources, costs of foodborne campylobacteriosis ($0.7-$4.3 billion) and associated GBS ($0.1-$1.3 billion) equal $0.8-$5.6 billion each year." (p9)

U.S. Dept. of Agriculture. Economic Research Service. "ERS Summary of Report: Savings from Reducing 'Campylobacter' in Food Could Total up to $5.6 Billion per Year." ERS Information Sep 1997. p9.

CANADA--APPROPRIATIONS AND EXPENDITURES (v26)

"Preliminary estimates from the Canadian Institute for Health Information indicate that health-care spending dropped one-fifth of a percentage point between 1995 and 1996--or $77 million--even though the population grew by about 1.4 per cent and the inflation rate was two per cent. Provincial spending on universities fell an estimated eight per cent between 1995-1996 and 1996-1997. And the federal human resources department estimates that welfare spending declined 4.7 per cent between 1994-1995 and 1995-1996. Since then, every province has made further cuts to welfare rates or services, such as Manitoba's 10-percent paring of payments to employable singles and childless couples in May, 1996....Between 1990-1991 and 1995-1996, welfare spending went up an estimated 59 per cent--to $13.7 billion....Provincial health-care expenditures between 1990 and 1996 were up only 15.4 per cent--when an increase of almost 25 per cent was required to keep pace with population growth and inflation." (p21)

Janigan, Mary. "Cover: Election '97: Dustup over Dollars." Maclean's v110 n20 19 May 1997. p20-22. (ISSN0024-9262).

CANADA--ARMED FORCES (v26)

CANADA--ARMED FORCES--WOMEN

"In 1989, the Department of National Defence was ordered by the Canadian Human Rights Commission to enrol more women in the next ten years. At the time, only 9.9 per cent of the members of our armed forces were women. "Today, eight years later, their numbers have remained virtually the same, with women accounting for a mere 10.7 per cent of the Canadian Armed Forces." (p20)

Venne, Pierrette (MP-PQ). "Statements by Members: National Defence." Canada. Parliament. House of Commons. Debates. v135 n3 24 Sep 1997. p20. section-level access: <http://www.parl.gc.ca/36/1/parlbus/chambus/house/debates/003_1997-09-24/han003-e.htm#LINK9> (ISSN0704-5603). (X3-361E).

CANADA--BOUNDARIES--UNITED STATES

"Last year more than 116 million people entered the United States by land from Canada. Of these, more than 76 million were Canadian or American permanent residents who would be subject to entry controls. More than 52 million returning Canadian residents and American permanent residents entered Canada by land from the United States that same year. That's more than 140,000 every day; 6,000 every hour; 100 every minute....In 1993 alone, 8,801,389 vehicles crossed the Ambassador Bridge [which links Detroit and Windsor]. On average, more than 1,000 vehicles used the bridge every hour." (p13 secA)

Abraham, Spencer. "Comment: Section 110 Hurts U.S.-Canada Trade." Detroit News 6 Nov 1997. p13 secA.

CANADA--COMMERCE (v26)

"Canada is now the most trade intensive country in the G7 [Group of Seven]. One in three jobs is devoted to export sales of goods and services. In manufacturing alone, 60 per cent of output is exported." (p10178)

Torsney, Paddy (MP-ON). "Statements by Members: Trade." Canada. Parliament. House of Commons. Debates. v134 n163 24 Apr 1997. p10178. page-level access: <http://www.parl.gc.ca/hansard/163_97-04-24/163SM1E.html#10178> section-level access: <http://www.parl.gc.ca/hansard/163_97-04-24/163SM1E.html#TRADE> (ISSN0704-5603). (X3-352E).

"One out of three Canadian jobs is directly tied to trade. Forty per cent of our GDP is directly tied to exports and trade, which is one of the highest, if not the highest, percentages of any western economic base. "Canadian sales abroad come to more than a quarter of a trillion dollars. Every $1 billion of trade in merchandise creates or sustains 11,000 jobs for Canadian workers.... "Currently only 10 percent of Canada's small and medium size firms directly export.... "While Canada is very much an exporting nation, we have not become a nation of exporters. Fifty large corporations account for over 50 percent of Canada's trade." (p61)

Marchi, Sergio (MP-ON). "Government Orders: Speech from the Throne." Canada. Parliament. House of Commons. Debates. v135 n4 25 Sep 1997. p60-92. section-level access: <http://

www.parl.gc.ca/36/1/parlbus/chambus/house/debates/004_1997-09-25/han004-e.htm#LINK56> (ISSN0704-5603). (X3-361E).

CANADA--COMMERCE--HONG KONG (v26)

CANADA--COMMERCE--MEXICO--UNITED STATES

"The United States increased its agricultural exports to Mexico and Canada by $2.7 billion dollars between 1993 and 1996....U.S. agricultural imports from Mexico and Canada have shown a steady upward trend throughout the 1993 to 1996 period, increasing by $3.2 billion. The net trade surplus was almost $2 billion in 1994 with a negative balance in 1995 and a rebound in 1996 to $1 billion. Overall, the U.S. had a cumulative net trade balance of $2.9 billion over the 3 years. Agricultural exports to Mexico and Canada have increased from $8.87 billion to $11.59 billion in 1996. U.S. imports expanded from $7.33 billion to $10.55 billion. Our analysis shows that total U.S. agricultural exports to Mexico and Canada in 1996 were about 3 and 7 percent higher, respectively, as a result of NAFTA. Similarly U.S. agricultural imports from Mexico and Canada were about 7 and 5 percent higher, respectively." (p467)

U.S. Dept. of Agriculture. "Agriculture, Rural Development, Food and Drug Administration...Approp. for 1998 (Part 4)." Hearing. U.S. House. Committee on Appropriations. Washington, D.C. : GPO, 1997. (ISBN0160551560). (Y4.Ap6/1:Ag8/997/pt.4).

"During 1993-96, U.S. agricultural exports to Mexico and Canada rose from $8.9 billion to $11.6 billion. U.S. agricultural imports from the two NAFTA partners grew from $7.3 billion to $10.5 billion. Analysis by the Economic Research Service finds that NAFTA is responsible for a little more than 20 percent of the increase in U.S. agricultural exports to Mexico and Canada since the agreement began. Slightly less than 20 percent of the increase in U.S. agricultural imports from the two countries can be attributed to NAFTA. Mexico is a rapidly growing market for U.S. agriculture, averaging 14.8 percent growth per year since 1993, compared with 12.4 percent average growth for all U.S. agricultural exports. In the mature Canadian market, U.S. agricultural exports have grown an average 5.2 percent a year since 1993." (p6)

U.S. Dept. of Agriculture. Economic Research Service. "Highlights from...NAFTA: International Agriculture and Trade Report." ERS Information Oct 1997. p6.

CANADA--COMMERCE--PUBLIC OPINION (v26)

CANADA--COMMERCE--UNITED STATES (v26)

CANADA--ECONOMIC CONDITIONS (v26)

"Since the beginning of this decade 320,000 more Canadians are unemployed. The average family income has dropped by $3,000 and 52,000 more Canadians every year are declaring bankruptcy, and child poverty increased by 25%." (p880)

McDonough, Alexa (MP-NS). "Government Orders: Supply." Canada. Parliament. House of Commons. Debates. v135 n17 21 Oct 1997. p879-911. section-level access: <http://www.parl.gc.ca/36/1/parlbus/chambus/house/debates/017_1997-10-21/han017-e.htm#LINKT5> (ISSN0704-5603). (X3-361E).

In Canada, in 1990, "the bank rate was 13%. Today in 1997 I believe the bank rate is 3.75%. In 1990...the prime rate was 14%. Today the prime rate is a mere 5.25%. Best of all, in 1990...the five year mortgage rate was 13%. Today in 1997...the five year mortgage rate is a mere 6.75%." (p945)

Bryden, John (MP-ON). "Government Orders: Supply." Canada. Parliament. House of Commons. Debates. v135 n17 21 Oct 1997. p925-953. section-level access: <http://www.parl.gc.ca/36/1/parlbus/chambus/house/debates/017_1997-10-21/han017-e.htm#LINK229> (ISSN0704-5603). (X3-361E).

In 1997, in Canada, "the unemployment rate in April was 9.6 per cent, compared with 11.9 per cent in late 1992. Over the same five-year period, the expanding economy created a million new jobs, bringing the employment total to 13.8 million. Compare that with the number of personal bankruptcies. For a while after the last recession, it drifted steadily downward, bottoming out at 53,802 in 1994. Then it took off, hitting 65,432 in 1995 and 79,631 in 1996. Another 14,055 Canadians filed for bankruptcy in the first two months of 1997, 11 per cent more than in the same period a year earlier." (p47)

Laver, Ross. "Personal Business: The Insolvency Crisis." Maclean's v110 n20 19 May 1997. p47. (ISSN0024-9262).

In Canada, "between the fiscal years 1990-1991 and 1997-1998, the total value of federal transfer payments--tax points and cash--has fallen $1.36 billion, or 5.2 per cent. Because the value of the tax points has gone up, the value of the cash transfer declined even further: it plummeted $3.9 billion--or 23.7 per cent. During that same period, Canada's population has grown by more than 10 per cent. And inflation has taken its toll: it takes $1.13 to exercise the same purchasing power that a dollar wielded in 1990." (p21)

Janigan, Mary. "Cover: Election '97: Dustup over Dollars." Maclean's v110 n20 19 May 1997. p20-22. (ISSN0024-9262).

CANADA--ECONOMIC CONDITIONS--BUSINESSMEN --ATTITUDES (v26)

CANADA--ECONOMIC CONDITIONS--PUBLIC OPINION (v26)

CANADA--ECONOMIC CONDITIONS--SOCIAL CONDITIONS (v26)

CANADA--EMIGRATION AND IMMIGRATION--FINANCE (v26)

CANADA--EMIGRATION AND IMMIGRATION--PUBLIC OPINION (v26)

CANADA--EMPLOYMENT (v26)

"During the last 46 months the Canadian economy has created 975,000 new jobs. The level of unemployment went down from 11.5 per cent to 9 per cent...." (p25)

Chretien, Jean (MP-PQ). "Oral Question Period: Employment." Canada. Parliament. House of Commons. Debates. v135 n3 24 Sep 1997. p25-26. section-level access: <http://www.parl.gc.ca/36/1/parlbus/chambus/house/debates/003_1997-09-24/han003-e.htm#LINK58> (ISSN0704-5603). (X3-361E).

CANADA--HISTORY

According to a "survey, in every province except Quebec, more Canadians thought Neil Armstrong was the first Canadian in space rather than Marc Garneau. Only 28 per cent of Quebec youth could name John A. Macdonald as our first prime minister, although 78 per cent of them could name Wilfrid Laurier as the first Francophone prime minister." (p42)

Chretien, Jean (MP-PQ). "Government Orders: Speech from the Throne." Canada. Parliament. House of Commons. Debates. v135 n3 24 Sep 1997. p31-55. section-level access: <http://www.parl.gc.ca/36/1/parlbus/chambus/house/debates/003_1997-09-24/han003-e.htm#LINKT32> (ISSN0704-5603). (X3-361E).

CANADA--LANGUAGES (v26)

CANADA--POLITICS AND GOVERNMENT (v26)

CANADA--PUBLIC OPINION (v26)

CANADA--SEXUAL BEHAVIOR--PUBLIC OPINION (v26)

CANADA--SOCIAL CONDITIONS--PUBLIC OPINION (v26)

CANADA--UNITED STATES--EMPLOYMENT (v26)

CANADA GOOSE

The snow goose "population has skyrocketed over the past 30 years, up from 750,000 in 1969 to almost 3 million today....A study by the Arctic Goose Habitat Working Group, a volunteer committee of biologists and representatives from conservation groups, found the snow goose population growing at 5 percent a year....The U.S. Fish and Wildlife Service, which sets hunting regulations,...[has increased] bag limits to 10 snow geese per person, per day, up from five. The group is also proposing to expand the current 107-day hunting season to 365 days." (p5)

Phillips, Sara. "Hotline: Nation: Serious Trouble for Snow

Geese." High Country News v29 n21 10 Nov 1997. p5. (ISSN0191-5657).

CANADA GOOSE--CANADA--MIDDLE WEST

In Canada, the goose "population is ballooning, with perhaps 1 million birds continentwide, wildlife officials say. There are between 300,000 and 400,000 Canada geese in southern Ontario, according to the Canadian Wildlife Service (CWS)....Mass culling of Canada geese is...a fact in parts of the Midwest. Michigan has applied for permission to kill 3,000 and relocate 12,000, according to Anne Frisch, national director of the Coalition to Protect Canada Geese, a US animal-rights group. Minneapolis is seeking a permit to kill 2,000 geese." (p11)

Clayton, Mark. "Habitat: No Giggles When Gaggles of Geese Goop Up Your Town." The Christian Science Monitor v89 n140 16 Jun 1997. p11. The Christian Science Monitor search engine: <http://www.csmonitor.com/plweb-cgi/iops1.pl> To retrieve this article, enter the following search: ED=19970616 AND town. In the "retrieved list," click the title that matches this record. (ISSN0882-7729).

CANADIAN PERIODICALS (v26)

CANADIANS--HONG KONG (v26)

CANADIANS--PUBLIC OPINION (v26)

CANCER (v26)

see also BREAST--CANCER; CERVIX UTERI--CANCER; COLON (ANATOMY)--CANCER; ESOPHAGUS--CANCER; LIVER--CANCER; LUNGS--CANCER; OVARIES--CANCER; PROSTATE--CANCER; SKIN--CANCER; THYROID GLAND--CANCER; UTERUS--CANCER

"Ten million people in the world developed cancer last year. And seven million died from it....In the first sweeping report on diet and cancer since the 1980s, medical experts and nutritionists from around the world concluded that between 30 and 40 percent of all cancers could be avoided by changing lifestyles and eating habits....[Dr. Walter Willett, of the Harvard School of Public Health,] and 14 other experts spent three years reviewing 4,500 scientific studies from around the world on nutrition and cancer to come up with the 650-page report and their recommendations." (p5 secA)

Schulte, Brigid. "Nation & World: Lifestyle, Food Tied to Cancer in Report." Detroit Free Press 1 Oct 1997. p5-6 secA.

"In 2020, at least 15 million people worldwide will develop cancer, compared to about 10 million cases annually now. The doubling of new cases will occur in developing countries, with about 40% increase in industrialized countries...." (p2)

According to the WORLD HEALTH REPORT 1997, "the eight most common cancers worldwide in terms of incidence are also the eight which cause most deaths. These are cancers of the lung, stomach, breast, colon/rectum, mouth, liver, cervix, and oesophagus. Together they accounted for about 60% of the 6.3 million cancer deaths and 10.3 million cancer cases in 1996." (p4)

World Health Organization. "World Health Report 1997." Press Release 5 May 1997. p1-7. document-level access: <http://www.who.ch/whr/1997/presse.htm>

CANCER--AFRO-AMERICANS--MORTALITY (v26)

CANCER--AUSTRALIA--MORTALITY

According to the Australian Bureau of Statistics, in Australia, "in 1996, the major cancer deaths in males were cancer of the trachea, bronchus and lung (24 per cent of total male cancer deaths), prostate cancer (14 per cent) and colon cancer (9.5 per cent). For females breast cancer accounted for 17 per cent of total female cancer deaths, while cancer of the trachea, bronchus and lung (14 per cent) and colon cancer (11 per cent) were the other leading cancers."

Australian Bureau of Statistics. "Deaths from Diabetes and Senile Dementia Increase." Media Release 31 Oct 1997. document-level access: <http://www.abs.gov.au/websitedbs/d3110125.nsf/4a255eef008309e44a255eef00061e57/b963d1a23d007204ca25654000761a86?OpenDocument>

CANCER--BRITISH COLUMBIA (v26)

CANCER--GREAT BRITAIN--WOMEN--PREVENTION (v26)

CANCER--MICHIGAN

A Michigan state health report "shows that 40,082 cases of invasive cancer were diagnosed in 1995, the most recent year available. That's down 4 percent from 41,762 new cases in 1994. According to the report, 19,442 people died of cancer in 1995, just 32 more than in the previous year." (p1 secA)

Schulz, Karen. "Cancer Diagnoses Fall; Cancer Deaths Up Slightly." Ypsilanti Press 22 Nov 1997. p1,13 secA.

According to a Michigan state health report, "there were 493 cases of breast cancer in Washtenaw County and 209 cases in Livingston County between 1993 and 1995. There were 347 cases of lung cancer in Washtenaw County and 152 cases in Livingston County from 1993-95. There were 215 cases of colon...[cancer] in Washtenaw County and 93 cases in Livingston County from 1993-95." (p13 secA)

Schulz, Karen. "Cancer Diagnoses Fall; Cancer Deaths Up Slightly." Ypsilanti Press 22 Nov 1997. p1,13 secA.

CANCER--MICHIGAN--MORTALITY

The second "Critical Health Indicators" report was compiled by the Michigan Department of Community Health in July 1997. It found that "more than 19,400 Michigan residents died of various forms of cancer in 1995, but the death rate is edging downward. In 1991, it was 139.5 per 100,000 population and the latest numbers show the rate at 133.1 per 100,000." (p2 secC)

Cain, Charlie. "Metro: Special Report: Health Snapshot: Michigan Gaining Ground in the Fight against Diseases." Detroit News 17 Jul 1997. p1-2 secC.

CANCER--MORTALITY (v26)

CANCER--UNITED STATES (v26)

In the U.S., "according to the National Cancer Institute, all cancers increased by 19% in men and by 12% in women during the 12-year period ending in 1991 and by 13% in boys and by 10% in girls (see EHM [ENVIRONMENTAL HEALTH MONTHLY], April, 1995). Since 1970, deaths from all forms of cancer have increased 6% from 189.6 to 200.9 per 100,000." (unpaginated)

"Abstract: Editorial: Cancer Undefeated." Environmental Health Monthly v10 n1-2 Oct-Nov 1997.

"In 1950, 25 percent of adults in the US could expect to get cancer during their lifetimes; today about 40 percent of us (38.3 percent of women, 48.2 percent of men) can expect to get cancer. Among Americans age 35 to 64, cancer is the number one killer." (p56)

Montague, Peter. "In Review: LIVING DOWNSTREAM: AN ECOLOGIST LOOKS AT CANCER AND THE ENVIRONMENT: By Sandra Steingraber." Yes! A Journal of Positive Futures n4 Win 1997-1998. p56-57. (ISSN1089-6651).

CANCER--UNITED STATES--MEN--MORTALITY (v26)

CANCER--UNITED STATES--MORTALITY (v26)

CANCER--UNITED STATES--WHITES--MORTALITY (v26)

CANCER--UNITED STATES--WOMEN--MORTALITY (v26)

CANNABIS

see MARIJUANA

CANNED ASPARAGUS--UNITED STATES (v26)

CANNED FRUIT INDUSTRY--UNITED STATES

In the U.S., "total canned fruit consumption in 1996 was 18.6 pounds (fresh-weight equivalent) per person. Per capita use of canned fruit rose 6 percent in 1996." (p2)

U.S. Dept. of Agriculture. Economic Research Service. "Summary." Fruit and Tree Nuts Situation and Outlook Report Oct 1997. p2-3.

CANNED VEGETABLES INDUSTRY--UNITED STATES

In 1997, "in the United States, which accounts for a little more than a third of the world [canned tomato] crop, contract production was down 11 percent to about 10.0 million short tons. Reduced area in California accounted for most of the decline, with the California Processing Tomato Advisory Board reporting that 9.3 million short tons were processed this season. Another 0.6 million tons were expected to be produced in other States." (p9)

U.S. Dept. of Agriculture. Economic Research Service. "Processing Vegetables." Vegetables and Specialties Situation and Outlook Report Nov 1997. p9-10.

In the U.S., "total supplies of canned vegetables (excluding tomatoes) for 1996 were down 1 percent from a year earlier to 12.6 billion pounds. Frozen vegetable supplies (excluding potatoes) were also down slightly to 10.9 billion pounds--but it was the second largest supply on record after 1995. With canned vegetable supplies in generally tighter supply than frozen in 1996, canned retail prices averaged 5 percent above a year earlier, while frozen vegetables increased 2 percent. During the first half of 1997, retail prices for canned vegetables again increased 5 percent, while frozen vegetables averaged 3 percent above a year ago." (p3)

U.S. Dept. of Agriculture. Economic Research Service. "Summary." Vegetables and Specialties Situation and Outlook Yearbook Jul 1997. p3-5.

CANTON (MICH.) (v26)

CAPACITY AND DISABILITY--UNITED STATES

Complaints about violations of the Americans with Disabilities Act Accessibility Guidelines are grouped into three categories. "73% of complaints to date involve...[failure to remove barriers]....[Discriminatory policies] account for 17% of complaints to date....[Lack of auxiliary aids] constitute 10% of complaints." (unpaginated)

"Management: Latest ADA Changes Demand 'Accessibility,' Rapid Response, Says Consultant." Security Letter v27 n15 2 Sep 1997. (ISSN0363-4922).

CAPITAL ACCUMULATION

see SAVING AND INVESTMENT

CAPITAL GAINS--UNITED STATES (v26)

In the U.S., "since 1987, the highest capital-gains tax rate for individuals has been 28 percent....According to a new study from the nonpartisan Congressional Budget Office, more than one-half of capital gains (excluding taxes on the sale of homes) were made by the 1 percent of taxpayers--those who make $200,000 or more....Federal revenue from capital gains taxes was $42.7 billion in 1995." (p4)

Francis, David R. "United States: Briefing: Capital-Gains Tax Cut: Congress to Taxpayers: Keep More of the Change." The Christian Science Monitor v89 n146 24 Jun 1997. p4. The Christian Science Monitor search engine: <http://www.csmonitor.com/plweb-cgi/iops1.pl> To retrieve this article, enter the following search: ED=19970624 AND change. In the "retrieved list," click the title that matches this record. (ISSN0882-7729).

CAPITAL GAINS TAX--UNITED STATES (v26)

CAPITAL PUNISHMENT--CALIFORNIA--PUBLIC OPINION

"An overwhelming 83 percent of Californians favored the death penalty in the mid-1980s. But this figure has gradually decreased over the past five years, with 74 percent in support in March 1997, according to a poll conducted by the Field Institute. Statewide, 36 percent agreed with the ABA'S [American Bar Association's] call for a moratorium; 42 percent think many criminal defendants who face the death penalty are represented by inadequately paid or incompetent lawyers." (p17)

Roemer, John. "California: ESQ.: Rethinking the Death Penalty." California Lawyer v17 n6 Jun 1997. p17-18. (ISSN0279-4063).

CAPITAL PUNISHMENT--UNITED STATES (v26)

"Florida, with 349 inmates on death row, ranks third in the nation, behind only Texas, with 394, and California, with 470. California courts sentenced 39 murderers to death in 1996, down from a peak of 42 in 1992. Last year there were 45 executions nationwide, down from a high of 56 in 1995." (p17)

Roemer, John. "California: ESQ.: Rethinking the Death Penalty." California Lawyer v17 n6 Jun 1997. p17-18. (ISSN0279-4063).

"Since a 1976 Supreme Court decision that revived the use of capital punishment, 398 persons have been executed in the United States. About 3,000 persons are currently on 'death row': sentenced to death but awaiting court appeals. Roughly 40 are women. Because of the seriousness and irreversibility of the punishment, most states require immediate review of all death sentences. In 1996, 45 persons were executed. Forty persons were executed in the first half of 1997, the fastest rate since the 1950s....[The U.S. spends] about $10 billion per year to implement the death penalty. The cost of the death penalty per executed prisoner in Texas is $2.3 million--three times the cost to put someone in maximum security for 40 years." (pE1717)

Hamilton, Lee H. (Rep.-Ind.). "The Death Penalty." Congressional Record. Daily ed. v143 n119 10 Sep 1997. pE1717-1718. section/page-level access: <http://thomas.loc.gov/cgi-bin/query/R?r105:FLD001:E01717:> (ISSN0363-7239). (X1.1A.105/1).

CAPITAL PUNISHMENT--UNITED STATES--PUBLIC OPINION

In the U.S., "support for the death penalty has hovered around the 70 percent level for most of the last decade....[A 1997 TIME/CNN poll] says nearly three-fourths of the [American] public is in favor of capital punishment....Eight southern states account for three-quarters of all the executions in the country...." (p1 secE)

Dickerson, Brian. "Sunday Voices: Conversations: James Brenner." Detroit Free Press 22 Jun 1997. p1 secE.

CAPITALISM--RUSSIA--PUBLIC OPINION

"A study of the Moscow elite in June 1991 by Judith Kullberg, an American political scientist, confirmed that the conversion to capitalism was widespread within the top layer of Soviet society. Of the sample of the elite studied, 77% supported capitalism, 12% democratic socialism, and 10% held a 'Communist or Nationalist' position....In May 1991 the Times-Mirror Center for the People and the Press, an American survey research firm, conducted a large-scale public opinion survey in European Russia. It found that...only 10% favored the pre-reform system. But 36% in the public opinion survey favored democratic socialism and another 23% favored the Swedish model of social democracy. Only 17% wanted 'capitalism such as found in the United States or Germany' (14% had no opinion). Thus, a large majority (69%) of the public apparently wanted some kind of socialism or social democracy, and few wanted Western-style capitalism." (p26)

Kotz, David/Weir, Fred. "Why Did the USSR Fall?: The Party Elite, Not the Masses, Wanted Capitalism." Dollars and Sense n212 Jul-Aug 1997. p22-26. (ISSN0012-5245).

CAPITALISTS AND FINANCIERS

see BILLIONAIRES; MILLIONAIRES; STOCKHOLDERS

CAPITALISTS AND FINANCIERS--UNITED STATES --POLITICS AND GOVERNMENT--ATTITUDES (v26)

CAR POOLS--CALIFORNIA (v26)

CAR SAFETY SEATS

see CHILD RESTRAINT SYSTEMS IN AUTOMOBILES

CAR THEFT

see AUTOMOBILE THEFT

CARBON

"The world's soils and organic matter such as peat store about two-thirds of carbon released annually, and now forests are believed to trap a large portion of another 20 percent. Environmentalists are recommending better forest management, reduced deforestation and planting of new trees. It is estimated that the earth's soils, forests and other vegetation could trap enough carbon between 1995 and 2050 to offset 12 to 15 percent of fossil fuel emissions." (p4)

"Eco-Update: News from around the World: Plant Trees." Acres, U.S.A. v27 n10 Oct 1997. p4. (ISSN1076-4968).

CARBON DIOXIDE (v26)

see also GREENHOUSE EFFECT, ATMOSPHERIC

"Currently, the industrialized countries (including the former Soviet Union) emit about 4 billion tons of carbon [dioxide] per year as a result of burning fossil fuels. The developing countries emit about 2 billion tons of carbon per year." (p40)

Harvey, L. D. Danny/Bush, Elizabeth J. "Joint Implementation: An Effective Strategy for Combating Global Warming?" Environment v39 n8 Oct 1997. p14-20,36-44. (ISSN0013-9157).

"In 1996 the EU accounted for 6% of the global population but 14.7% of CO2 [carbon dioxide] emissions, while the 5.5% of the global population living in the US, Canada, and Australia generated 28.4% of total emissions....India and China--together accounting for 37.8% of the world's population--produced 17.2% of global CO2 emissions." (p7)

"EU CO2 Emissions Set to Rise Substantially, Survey Shows." Environment Watch: Western Europe v6 n15 1 Aug 1997. p7. (ISSN1066-6001).

Increases from major EU carbon dioxide "emitters ranged from 8.4% in Belgium to 41% in Denmark....UK emissions...went up 3% between 1995 and 1996....Outside the EU...emissions grew rapidly over the 1990-1996 period, despite a 31% drop in emissions from the former Soviet republics and Central and Eastern Europe in the early 1990s. While global CO2 [carbon dioxide] emissions rose by 6.4%, emissions went up by 8.4% in the US, by 14.3% in Japan, and by 10.7% in New Zealand. Emissions from developing countries rose by 32%, bringing the developing country share of the global total from 29% to just under 36%. The tiger economies of the Asia/Pacific region are responsible for 37% of the increase there, while the largest overall rise at 41% is attributed to the Middle East." (p7)

"EU CO2 Emissions Set to Rise Substantially, Survey Shows." Environment Watch: Western Europe v6 n15 1 Aug 1997. p7. (ISSN1066-6001).

"Based on measurements taken throughout the world, scientists have estimated that about 1,500 Gt.C [gigaton carbon] (approximately 1.5 trillion tons) currently reside in the soil....An article that appeared in...[a] recent issue of RADIOCARBON, stated that between 0.5 and 0.7 Gt.C may be going into soil--a figure that may account for between 45 percent and 65 percent of the lost carbon dioxide." (p8)

Childress, Janice O. "News Notes: Missing Carbon May Be 'Soilbound.'" Geotimes v42 n9 Sep 1997. p7-8. (ISSN0016-8556).

"In 1996, the 5.5% of the world's population residing in the US, Canada, and Australia was responsible for 28.4% of global CO2 [carbon dioxide] emissions....The 6% residing in the EU's 15 member countries generated 14.7% of global CO2 emissions, while the 9% living in the whole of Europe were responsible for 19.6% of global emissions....India and China--with 37.8% of global population between them--generated only 17.2% of the world's CO2 emissions in 1996." (p2)

"Focus Report: Latest Emissions Estimates Bode Poorly for Future Reductions." Global Environmental Change Report v9 n14 25 Jul 1997. p1-3. (ISSN1049-9083).

"Within the OECD (excluding Mexico, Korea, Hungary, and Poland), CO2 [carbon dioxide] emissions now account for more than half of the global total (50.25% in 1996 compared to 49.2% in 1990). Emissions from developing countries rose 32% between 1990 and 1996, bringing the developing nation contribution to global emissions to just under 36% in 1996, compared to 29% in 1990....The rapidly growing economies of the AsiaPacific Rim nations contributed to a 37% rise in that region, although the largest overall rise (41%) is attributed to the Middle East." (p2)

"Focus Report: Latest Emissions Estimates Bode Poorly for Future Reductions." Global Environmental Change Report v9 n14 25 Jul 1997. p1-3. (ISSN1049-9083).

Global emissions of carbon dioxide "from fossil fuel combustion rose some 6.4% between 1990 and 1996, according to the latest survey conducted by the World Energy Council (WEC--London, UK). In 1990, global energy-related carbon emissions totaled 6.12 billion metric tons of carbon (GtC), while in 1996 the total rose to 6.513 GtC--an increase of 394 million metric tons of carbon. Between 1990 and 1996, total OECD emissions rose by 7.8%, and EU emissions topped 1990 levels for the first time....Over the 1990-1996 time period, increases among significant emitters in the EU ranged from 8.4% in Belgium to...41% in Denmark...." (p1) "Of the larger emitters, Japan's rise was the greatest (14.3%), followed by Australia (9.5%), the US (8.4%), and Canada (5.5%). With a drop in emissions of 1.2% between 1990 and 1996, Switzerland was one of the few industrial nations outside of the EU and Eastern Europe to show a decline." (p2)

"Focus Report: Latest Emissions Estimates Bode Poorly for Future Reductions." Global Environmental Change Report v9 n14 25 Jul 1997. p1-3. (ISSN1049-9083).

Globally, carbon dioxide "emissions from natural gas increased 15% between 1990 and 1996, compared to a 5.7% rise for oil and less than 3% for coal. This increase is most evident within the OECD nations, where emissions from natural gas rose by more than 23% over the 1990-1996 time period." (p2)

"Focus Report: Latest Emissions Estimates Bode Poorly for Future Reductions." Global Environmental Change Report v9 n14 25 Jul 1997. p1-3. (ISSN1049-9083).

"The U.S. is responsible for approximately 22 percent of all global emissions....The Energy Information Administration estimates that U.S. emissions will actually increase by 15 percent by the year 2000. At the same time, a study completed by 2000 top atmospheric scientists warns that the Earth's average temperature will likely increase by 2 to 6 degrees F [fahrenheit] over the next century accompanied by a rise in sea level of 1 to 3 feet....China and India currently have annual emission levels of 0.7 and 0.3 tons of CO2 [carbon dioxide] per person, respectively, compared to the U.S. figure of over 5 tons of CO2 per person." (p12)

Hochanadel, Joel R. "The View from Washington: Climate Change Alert." Solar Today v11 n5 Sep-Oct 1997. p12,14. (ISSN1042-0630).

"About 48,000 tons of anthropogenic (human-produced) carbon dioxide (CO2) are emitted every minute. Since the start of the Industrial Revolution, 850 billion tons of CO2 has been emitted due to the burning of fossil fuels....To stabilize CO2 in the atmosphere at 1990 levels, global emissions would have to be reduced by 60% compared to 1990 levels." (p3)

"A Few Basic Facts about Global Climate Change." Windletter v24 n10 Oct 1997. p3. (ISSN0747-5500).

"Global emissions of carbon--which in the atmosphere forms

carbon dioxide (CO2), the greenhouse gas responsible for an estimated 64 percent of the warming now under way--reached a record high of 6.2 billion tons in 1996, and have now increased nearly fourfold since 1950." (p6) "Between 1990 and 1996, worldwide emissions of carbon from the burning of fossil fuels rose 5 percent, or the equivalent of 300 million tons each year." (p11)

Flavin, Christopher/Dunn, Seth. "Rising Sun, Gathering Winds: Policies to Stabilize the Climate and Strengthen Economies." Worldwatch Paper n138 Nov 1997. p5-84.

"Industrial countries are responsible for 76 percent of the world's cumulative carbon emissions since 1950." (p12) "Among the leading emitters are the United States, Australia, and Japan, whose carbon emissions in 1996 were 8.8, 9.6, and 12.5 percent above 1990 levels." (p13)

Flavin, Christopher/Dunn, Seth. "Rising Sun, Gathering Winds: Policies to Stabilize the Climate and Strengthen Economies." Worldwatch Paper n138 Nov 1997. p5-84.

CARBON DIOXIDE--CHINA (v26)

CARBON DIOXIDE--DEVELOPING COUNTRIES (v26)

CARBON DIOXIDE--ENVIRONMENTAL ASPECTS

Carbon dioxide accounts "for 60 percent of the enhanced greenhouse effect. Fuel burning, agriculture, automobile exhaust, and other human emissions contribute an estimated 22 billion metric tons of carbon dioxide each year, and have caused an unprecedented 10 percent increase in atmospheric levels of the gas in the last 20 years....The US and the six other industrial nations of the Group of Seven...account for 38 percent of greenhouse gas production...." (p19)

Fornos, Werner. "Opinion/Essays: Global Warming and Population Growth: Inseparable." The Christian Science Monitor v89 n145 23 Jun 1997. p19. The Christian Science Monitor search engine: <http://www.csmonitor.com/plweb-cgi/iops1.pl> To retrieve this article, enter the following search: ED=19970623 AND inseparable. In the "retrieved list," click the title that matches this record. (ISSN0882-7729).

CARBON DIOXIDE--EUROPE

Data "from Eurostat--Statistical Office of the European Communities in Luxembourg--show 1995 EU emissions of carbon dioxide due to fuel combustion still below 1990 for the fourth year running, but 1.7% up on 1994. The 1994 total had been 2997 million tonnes, 2.9% below the 3088 million recorded in 1990. In 1995 it was back to 3048 million, only 1.3% below 1990....The trend in Germany--by far the EU's largest producer of CO2 emissions--is still down, despite a 1.7% rise in industrial production in 1995. It had a 0.6% fall between '94 and '95, and now accounts for just under 28% of EU emissions compared to 30.8% in 1990. There was a similar trend in the UK (-1%), second largest source of EU emissions. This decreased its share of the total to 17.5% from 18.4% in 1990. Luxembourg recorded the biggest fall in 1995--18.7% due to the closure of blast furnaces in the iron and steel industry. Next came Denmark (-4.5%) and Finland (-4.4%), but they are relatively minor sources of emissions."

Eurostat. "EU CO2 Emissions Rise by 1.7% in 1995." Press Release 27 Nov 1997. document-level access: <http://europa.eu.int/en/comm/eurostat/compres/en/8097/6808097a.htm>

"Carbon emissions in the United Kingdom fell roughly 2.0 percent between 1990 and 1996, while those in France declined 1.1 percent and Germany's dropped by 7.6 percent." (p14) "Together, the 15 countries of the European Union (EU) have held their carbon emissions to just 1 percent above the 1990 level in 1996...." (p15)

Flavin, Christopher/Dunn, Seth. "Rising Sun, Gathering Winds: Policies to Stabilize the Climate and Strengthen Economies." Worldwatch Paper n138 Nov 1997. p5-84.

CARBON DIOXIDE--GERMANY (v26)

CARBON DIOXIDE--JAPAN

Japan recently released figures showing that total carbon dioxide "emissions in 1995 amounted to 1,218 million metric tons (Mt)--an increase of 8.3% over 1990 levels. The energy industry is the primary source of emissions with 359 Mt (up 6% from 1990), followed by industry and construction with 346 Mt (up 2.1%); transportation at 242 Mt (up 16.7%); domestic, tertiary, and agriculture at 177 Mt (up 11.9%); cement and other industrial processes with 61 Mt (up 4.2); and incineration of wastes at 19 Mt (up 46.1%). Japan also reported a total sink of 95 Mt from reforestation." (p4)

"Policy and Economics: Japan's CO2 Emissions Up Substantially." Global Environmental Change Report v9 n11 13 Jun 1997. p4-5. (ISSN1049-9083).

CARBON DIOXIDE--JAPAN--UNITED STATES (v26)

CARBON DIOXIDE--NEW ZEALAND

New Zealand's carbon dioxide "emissions rose by 11.2% between 1990 and 1996, according to ENERGY GREENHOUSE GAS EMISSIONS 1990-1996, released by Energy Minister Max Bradford on 16 July [1997]. The report shows that total CO2 emissions were 25.5 million metric tons (Mt) in 1990, and grew to 28.3 Mt in 1996." (p3)

"Policy and Economics: New Zealand CO2 Emissions Up 11.2%." Global Environmental Change Report v9 n14 25 Jul 1997. p3. (ISSN1049-9083).

CARBON DIOXIDE--UNITED STATES

"Undersecretary of State for Global Affairs Tim Wirth has testified, 'the U.S. produces about 20 percent of the world's carbon emissions and has only four percent of the world's population.'" (p44) "According to OECD figures, in 1990 the U.S. produced over 26 percent of the world's goods and services, while producing only about 20 percent of its carbon emissions." (p45)

Jasinowski, Jerry. "The Forum: Potentially Hundreds of Thousands of Jobs." Environmental Forum v14 n6 Nov-Dec 1997. p44-45. (ISSN0731-5732).

"Cars account for nearly 20% of CO2 [carbon dioxide] emissions in the United States and 15% of emissions worldwide, says James Ohi, team leader for light duty vehicle research and development at the National Renewable Energy Laboratory in Golden, Colorado. The United States contributes a total of 23% of the world's burden of CO2, and CO2 accounts for about 60-70% of greenhouse gas emissions." (p583)

Holzman, David/U.S. National Institute of Environmental Health Sciences. "Focus: A Driving Force." Environmental Health Perspectives v105 n6 Jun 1997. p582-587. article-level access: <http://ehpnet1.niehs.nih.gov/docs/1997/105-6/focus-abs.html>

"The United States is the world leader in CO2 [carbon dioxide] emissions. With only 5% of the world population, the U.S. is responsible for 23% of global CO2 emissions....Every 10,000 MW [megawatts] of wind installed can reduce CO2 emissions by about 21 million metric tons (MMT) if it replaces generation from the average U.S. fuel mix....If the U.S. increases its wind power capacity to 30,000 MW...by the year 2010, national CO2 emissions could be reduced by 100 MMT annually." (p3)

"A Few Basic Facts about Global Climate Change." Windletter v24 n10 Oct 1997. p3. (ISSN0747-5500).

CARCINOMA

see CANCER

CARDAMOM INDUSTRY--GUATEMALA (v26)

CARDIAC DISEASES

see HEART--DISEASES

CARDIAC FAILURE
see HEART FAILURE
CARDIAC RESUSCITATION--NURSING HOME CARE --UNITED STATES (v26)
CARDIOVASCULAR SYSTEM
see also HEART
CARDIOVASCULAR SYSTEM--DISEASES

According to the WORLD HEALTH REPORT 1997, "heart attacks, stroke and other circulatory diseases together kill more than 15 million people a year, or 30% of the annual total of deaths from all causes. Many of these deaths are both premature--occurring in people under 65 years--and preventable. Circulatory diseases are emerging rapidly as a major public health concern in most developing countries, where they now account for about 25% of all deaths, compared to about half of all deaths in developed countries....High blood pressure is a leading risk factor for heart disease and stroke, and affects about 20% of adults in most countries." (p6)

World Health Organization. "World Health Report 1997." Press Release 5 May 1997. p1-7. document-level access: <http://www.who.ch/whr/1997/presse.htm>

CARDIOVASCULAR SYSTEM--DISEASES--AUSTRALIA

"One in five Australian adults (2.8 million people) reported that they had a cardiovascular condition (such as hypertension, heart disease, stroke, etc.), according to...[the publication 'National Health Survey: Cardiovascular and Related Conditions, Australia, 1995,'] by the Australian Bureau of Statistics....The most common cardiovascular condition was hypertension which was reported by 14 per cent of the adult population. Heart disease was reported by 4 per cent of adults, almost half a million people (493,500). The prevalence of cardiovascular conditions increased with age from 4 per cent for 18-24 year olds to 61 per cent for those aged 75 years and over. Cardiovascular conditions overall were more prevalent among women (23 per cent) than among men (19 per cent) and this was partly explained by the higher proportion of women reporting hypertension. However, a higher proportion of men (4 per cent) than women (3 per cent) reported heart disease. This latter difference was most marked among those aged 65-74 years, where 17 per cent of men compared with 9 per cent of women in this age group reported heart disease."

Australian Bureau of Statistics. "One in Five Adults Have a Cardiovascular Condition." Media Release 11 Nov 1997. document-level access: <http://www.abs.gov.au/websitedbs/d3110125.nsf/4a255eef008309e44a255eef00061e57/463a3a34c19dc7e8ca25654b007f12be?OpenDocument>

CARDIOVASCULAR SYSTEM--DISEASES--CHILDREN (v26)
CARDIOVASCULAR SYSTEM--DISEASES--CHINA (v26)
CARDIOVASCULAR SYSTEM--DISEASES--MICHIGAN --MORTALITY

The second "Critical Health Indicators" report was compiled by the Michigan Department of Community Health in July 1997. It found that "about a third of Michigan deaths are caused by heart diseases, the No. 1 killer in the state. But the death rate has declined for the last 10 years. The death rate today is 151 per 100,000 population, down from 260.4 per 100,000 in 1970." (p2 secC)

Cain, Charlie. "Metro: Special Report: Health Snapshot: Michigan Gaining Ground in the Fight against Diseases." Detroit News 17 Jul 1997. p1-2 secC.

CARDIOVASCULAR SYSTEM--DISEASES--MORTALITY (v26)
CARDIOVASCULAR SYSTEM--DISEASES--UNITED STATES (v26)

In the U.S., "cardiovascular disease is the nation's No.1 killer, claiming about 954,000 lives annually, the American Heart Association estimates. More than 57 million people have heart disease. Within six years of a heart attack, 23 percent of men and 31 percent of women will have another." (p8 secF)

Emmons, Mark. "Body & Mind: Cover Story: Getting Heart-Healthy." Detroit Free Press 22 Jul 1997. p6-8 secF.

CARDIOVASCULAR SYSTEM--DISEASES--UNITED STATES--COSTS (v26)
CARDIOVASCULAR SYSTEM--DISEASES--UNITED STATES--MORTALITY (v26)
CARDS, CREDIT
see CREDIT CARDS
CARE OF CHILDREN
see CHILD CARE
CAREGIVERS--EMPLOYMENT (v26)
CARIBBEAN AREA--COMMERCE--UNITED STATES (v26)
CARIBBEAN AREA--ECONOMIC CONDITIONS (v26)
CARIBBEAN AREA--LATIN AMERICA--ECONOMIC CONDITIONS (v26)

"Countries in the Latin American and Caribbean region registered an average growth in the region of some 3.5 per cent (1.5 per cent per capita) for 1996, and average inflation fell to 20 per cent. More than half the countries registered single-digit price increases or very little more....The increase in the volume of exports was almost three times the growth of the gross domestic product (GDP)....Average regional inflation continued to fall in 1996--to 20 per cent--the lowest rate since the beginning of the 1970s." (p42)

"Positive Outlook for Economy in Latin America and Caribbean." UN Chronicle v34 n1 1997. p42. (ISSN0251-7329).

CARNIVAL--NORTH AMERICA (v26)
CARPET AND RUG INDUSTRY
see RUG AND CARPET INDUSTRY
CARROT INDUSTRY--UNITED STATES

In the U.S. carrot industry, "although imports and exports have both been trending higher in the 1990's, import growth has been stronger (up 82 percent since 1990 versus 32 percent for exports). Much of the import growth reflects a combination of rising demand for fresh-cut product and the 1994/95 peso devaluation which caused imports from Mexico to jump 300 percent between 1994 and 1995. Imports of fresh-market carrots account for 8 percent of U.S. supply, up from 5 percent in 1990....Ninety percent of U.S. fresh carrot exports go to three countries--Canada, the United Arab Emirates (UAE), and Japan. Shipments to Canada account for 84 percent of exports and help make the U.S. the world's fourth-leading exporter of fresh carrots. The Netherlands is first, followed by Italy and Belgium-Luxembourg. Exports now account for 7 percent of U.S. supply and are valued at $44 million." (p13)

Lucier, Gary/U.S. Dept. of Agriculture. Economic Research Service. "Commodity Spotlight: What's Up, Doc?--Carrots!" Agricultural Outlook Nov 1997. p11-13.

In the U.S., "in the 1990's, per capita use of fresh-market carrots has averaged 25 percent above the average of the 1980's, while use of carrots for freezing is up 30 percent during the same period....According to the Census of Agriculture, carrots were produced on 2,039 farms in 1992--up 29 percent from the previous Census in 1987. California accounts for 73 percent of the fresh-market carrot crop, followed by Colorado and Michigan with about 5 percent each (USDA statistics include baby carrots and other fresh-cut products in fresh-market output). On the processing side (canned, frozen, juice, dehydrated), Washington state produces about a third of the U.S. crop, followed by California with 25 percent and Wisconsin with 13 percent. Fresh-market carrots account for 70 percent of total U.S. carrot output." (p11)

Lucier, Gary/U.S. Dept. of Agriculture. Economic Research

Service. "Commodity Spotlight: What's Up, Doc?--Carrots!" Agricultural Outlook Nov 1997. p11-13.

In the U.S., in terms of domestic use, carrots are now the seventh-largest fresh vegetable (including melons) and third among frozen vegetables. Use of fresh-market carrots totaled 10.2 pounds per person in 1996--up 23 percent since 1990, the highest per capita use since the 1940's and the third largest on record. Per capita use of carrots for freezing between 1990 and 1996 rose 22 percent to 2.8 pounds--tied for the highest on record." (p12)

Lucier, Gary/U.S. Dept. of Agriculture. Economic Research Service. "Commodity Spotlight: What's Up, Doc?--Carrots!" Agricultural Outlook Nov 1997. p11-13.

CARS

see AUTOMOBILES

CARTS, SHOPPING

see SHOPPING CARTS

CASIGURAN (PHILIPPINES)--POPULATION (v26)

CASINOS

"As of 1993, there were 1,478 legal casinos in 86 countries (Bain 1994). Of these, North America (583) and Europe (555) represent 39.4% and 37.6% of the total, respectively, followed by Central and South America (121), Africa (93), the Caribbean (83), Asia (32), and Oceania (11)." (p52)

Lee, Choong-Ki/Kwon, Kyung-Sang. "The Economic Impact of the Casino Industry in South Korea." Journal of Travel Research v36 n1 Sum 1997. p52-58. (ISSN0047-2875).

CASINOS--AUSTRALIA (v26)

CASINOS--EMPLOYMENT--AUSTRALIA (v26)

CASINOS--KOREA (SOUTH)

"Today, 13 casinos are operating at international tourist hotels around...[South Korea]....In 1988 there were more than 343,000 foreign visitors to Korean casinos....Attendance increased at an average annual rate of 19% through 1992....In 1994 more than one-half million tourists (626,000) visited Korean casinos, accounting for 17.5% of the total foreign visitors to Korea and 30.7% of the pleasure tourists....An on-site survey was conducted with 571 respondents at 10 casino hotels in five different regions....The survey results show that the Japanese represented almost 70% of the Korean casino market, followed by the Taiwanese (16%), Americans (5%), Hong Kong Chinese (4%), and Mainland Chinese (3%). Of the total number of respondents, 80% were found to be repeat visitors, while 20% were first-time visitors. Males accounted for 90% of respondents. Those visitors who were 31 to 50 years old represented more than 70% of all respondents. In terms of occupation, business owners accounted for 42% of the sample, followed by businessmen/ managers (27%). Pleasure travelers represented 66% of the foreign visitors patronizing casinos, followed by those who were conducting business (18%), attending conventions (5%), and visiting friends and relatives (5%). Thirty-six percent of visitors stated that the decision to visit a casino was their own, while 34% cited that the visit was recommended by friends and relatives. Other reasons included the advice of travel agents (20%), junket representatives (5%), and advertisements (3%)." (p53)

Lee, Choong-Ki/Kwon, Kyung-Sang. "The Economic Impact of the Casino Industry in South Korea." Journal of Travel Research v36 n1 Sum 1997. p52-58. (ISSN0047-2875).

CASINOS--MEXICO

"Secretary of Tourism Silvia Hernandez has--at times--made the legalization of casinos in Mexico the centerpiece of her plan to bring in hundreds of millions of dollars in foreign investment by building up to 10 'Integral Tourism Centers.'...Though no one yet knows what the final plan will look like, one Tourism Ministry report estimated the centers would cost between $250 million and $400 million apiece....The Tourism Ministry estimates that 10.5 percent of US gamblers would be attracted to Mexico if it built casinos now." (p11)

Stoll, Michael. "Mexico Debates Pros, Cons of Legalization." The Christian Science Monitor v89 n153 3 Jul 1997. p11. The Christian Science Monitor search engine: <http:// www.csmonitor.com/plweb-cgi/iops1.pl> To retrieve this article, enter the following search: ED=19970703 AND legalization. In the "retrieved list," click the title that matches this record. (ISSN0882-7729).

CASINOS--NEVADA--LAS VEGAS

"About 30 million people visited...[Las Vegas in 1996]--the percentage of tourists under the age of 21 was only 11 percent....If state regulators catch minors at gaming tables,...a casino faces a $10,000 fine....The presence of children has also been a boon to the city's gambling industry, which accounts for 40 percent of Nevada's gross state product." (p18)

Walker, Sam. "The Las Vegas Divide: Rethinking a City's Family-Friendly Facade." The Christian Science Monitor v89 n130 2 Jun 1997. p1,18. The Christian Science Monitor search engine: <http://www.csmonitor.com/plweb-cgi/iops1.pl> To retrieve this article, enter the following search: ED=19970602 AND facade. In the "retrieved list," click the title that matches this record. (ISSN0882-7729).

CASINOS--TAXATION--MICHIGAN

Michigan's Proposal E, which is the state's ballot issue that approved casino gambling in Detroit, "set forth a tax rate of 18 percent on gross revenue, plus a 1.25 percent 'municipal services tax' to offset police, fire and other protection....The state Gaming Control Board, as well as Republicans in the state Legislature..., are proposing an increase to 21 percent in order to defray 'regulatory costs' to the state. (The city gets 55 percent of casino tax revenue; the state gets 45 percent, most of which would go to the school aid fund.) That's more than double the state tax on Indian reservation casinos, which pay no federal or other taxes. And while Indiana, Illinois and Windsor levy a 20 percent tax, New Jersey and Nevada charge far less." (p8 secA)

"Comment: Uncompetitive Casinos?" Detroit News 17 Jun 1997. p8 secA.

CASINOS--UNITED STATES--ECONOMIC CONDITIONS --PUBLIC OPINION

In the U.S., "states and localities collected an estimated $16 billion in gambling privilege taxes in 1995. Nevada raises 40 percent of its state tax revenue from Las Vegas casinos....Most Americans have a positive attitude toward gambling's impact on local economies. Nearly two-thirds of adults say that casinos create a lot of jobs and tax revenues, according to [a] Roper [survey]. Sixty-five percent agree that state-sponsored gambling stimulates local economies, and half say it provides revenue for education and senior citizens. A pragmatic 62 percent of respondents say that people will gamble whether gambling is legal or not, so the state may as well get a piece of the action, according to a 1996 Gallup/CNBC poll." (p37)

Heubusch, Kevin. "Taking Chances on Casinos." American Demographics v19 n5 May 1997. p34-40. article-level access: <http://www.demographics.com/Publications/AD/97_ad/ 9705_ad/AD970530.htm> (ISSN0163-4089).

CATARACT (v26)

CATARACT--UNITED STATES (v26)

CATFISH FISHERIES (v26)

CATFISH FISHERIES--UNITED STATES (v26)

In the U.S., "in the first 8 months of 1997, catfish deliveries to processing plants totaled 355 million pounds, 12 percent higher than in the same period in 1996. This will be the third consecutive year of higher sales following a decline of approximately 20 million pounds in 1994." (unpaginated)

Harvey, Dave/U.S. Dept. of Agriculture. Economic Research Service. "Catfish Production at New High." Aquaculture Outlook 3 Oct 1997.

In the U.S., "over the first 8 months of 1997, processors sold 179 million pounds of catfish products, 11 percent more than in the same period in 1996....At the end of August, processors reported holding 9.7 million pounds of finished products in inventory, 1 percent less than a year earlier....The weighted average price for fresh and frozen catfish products over the first 8 months of 1997 was $2.38 per pound, down 4 percent from the same period in 1996....For frozen catfish products, sales of filleted and other products rose, while sales of whole catfish fell 2 percent." (unpaginated)

Harvey, Dave/U.S. Dept. of Agriculture. Economic Research Service. "Processor Sales Higher." Aquaculture Outlook 3 Oct 1997.

CATHOLIC CHURCH--CLERGY

According to the STATISTICAL YEARBOOK OF THE CHURCH, "the world had 404,750 religious and diocesan priests at the end of 1995, an increase of 289 over the previous year. That's one for every 2,500 lay Catholics....[The U.S. has] a priest for every 1,117 lay Catholics. In Brazil they have one priest for every 8,708 Catholics....In Mexico there are 6,804 Catholics per priest. In the Philippines, its 8,823 Catholics per priest....There are 980 Catholics per priest...[in Italy]." (p30)

Phelps, Owen, Jr. "Forum: Owen on the Road: You're One in a Billion, Dear Reader." Observer v62 n21 3 Oct 1997. p30. (ISSN0029-7712).

CATHOLIC CHURCH--PHILIPPINES (v26)

CATHOLIC CHURCH--UNITED STATES--FINANCE (v26)

CATHOLIC SCHOOLS--MICHIGAN (v26)

"In the Archdiocese of Detroit, which stretches from Port Huron south to the Ohio state line, [catholic school] tuition averages $1,700 a year for elementary schools and $3,318 for secondary schools--well below the $5,878 per-pupil state aid grant the average public school receives....Prior to 1950, lay teachers comprised just 5 percent of teachers in the Detroit archdiocese. Today, they make up about 90 percent....The average Michigan public school teacher earned $47,430 in 1995-96, more than double the $20,716 earned by the average U.S. Catholic school elementary teacher that year." (p6 secA)

Crumm, David/Van Moorlehem, Tracy. "Bishops Looking for Ways to Improve Catholic Schools." Detroit Free Press 12 Nov 1997. p1,6 secA.

CATHOLIC SCHOOLS--MICHIGAN--DETROIT (v26)

CATHOLIC SCHOOLS--NEW YORK (N.Y.)

"A 1990 Rand Corp. comparison of schools in New York City...found that the Catholic schools graduated 95 percent of their students annually, while the comparable public schools graduated slightly more than 50 percent....The Rand Corp. report also showed that the Catholic school students out-performed their counterparts in the public schools and--again, this is in New York City--on the SAT [Scholastic Assessment Test] exam by an average of 160 points. A study released earlier this year by Derek Neal of the University of Chicago found that low-income Catholic school students were twice as likely to graduate from college as their public school counterparts." (pS9923)

Lieberman, Joseph I. (Sen.-Conn.). "District of Columbia Appropriations Act, 1998." Congressional Record. Daily ed. v143 n130 25 Sep 1997. pS9914-9925. section/page-level access: <http://thomas.loc.gov/cgi-bin/query/R?r105:FLD001:S09921:> (ISSN0363-7239). (X1.1A.105/1).

CATHOLIC SCHOOLS--UNITED STATES (v26)

In the U.S., "enrollment in Catholic schools has risen every school year since 1992-93, reaching 2.9 million nationally in 1996-97....[There are] 155,000 teachers in Catholic schools around the country." (p1 secA)

Crumm, David/Van Moorlehem, Tracy. "Bishops Looking for Ways to Improve Catholic Schools." Detroit Free Press 12Nov 1997. p1,6 secA.

CATHOLIC SCHOOLS--UNITED STATES--FINANCE (v26)

CATHOLIC WOMEN

see VOTING--UNITED STATES--CATHOLIC WOMEN

CATHOLICS

see also ABORTION--UNITED STATES--CATHOLICS; DISCRIMINATION IN EMPLOYMENT--IRELAND--CATHOLICS; VOTING--UNITED STATES--CATHOLICS

According to the STATISTICAL YEARBOOK OF THE CHURCH, the U.S. has "57 million [Catholic church] members. Ahead of us: the Philippines with 58.7 million, Mexico with 86.3 million, and Brazil with...134.8 million Catholics. Behind us: Italy with 55.6 million Catholics." (p30)

Phelps, Owen, Jr. "Forum: Owen on the Road: You're One in a Billion, Dear Reader." Observer v62 n21 3 Oct 1997. p30. (ISSN0029-7712).

CATHOLICS--CHINA--UNITED STATES

Since 1991, "Chinese bishops have sent 47 priests, seminarians and sisters [to China] to study on scholarships provided by 15 U.S. seminaries and houses of formation....[There are] 60,000 Chinese Catholics in the United States....We have 98 parishes that minister especially to the Chinese, with 88 priests and 80 sisters dedicated to that service...." (p19)

Cummins, John S. "The Church in China: Three Pastoral Concerns." America v177 n2 19 Jul 1997. p18-19. (ISSN0002-7049).

CATHOLICS--FRANCE

"The number of churchgoing Catholics has declined in France, from 24 per cent in 1974 to 17 per cent in the mid-'90s....The actual number of self-professed Catholics in France, whose total population is 58 milliòn, has remained more or less constant (86.5 per cent in 1974, 80 per cent in the '90s)." (p6)

Valls-Russell, Janice. "While Admiring John Paul II French Catholicism Loosens Its Collar." New Leader v80 n14 8 Sep 1997. p6-8. (ISSN0028-6044).

CATHOLICS--HISPANIC AMERICANS

"In a 15-year period beginning in 1972, approximately one out of ten Hispanic Catholics [in the U.S.] had left the church and either become Protestants or renounced all religious affiliation....In the early 1970's, 78 percent of Americans of Hispanic origin were Catholic....By the middle 1990's that proportion had fallen to 67 percent....The equivalent of one out of seven Hispanics has left Catholicism in a little less than a quarter of a century. The annual loss is approximately one half of one percent....Eighty-five percent of Hispanics were raised Catholic, which suggests that they had Catholic parents. Only 67 percent are Catholics now, which means that a fifth of those who were raised Catholics are no longer such." (12-13)

Greeley, Andrew M. "Defection among Hispanics (Updated)." America v177 n8 27 Sep 1997. p12-13. (ISSN0002-7049).

CATHOLICS--MICHIGAN--OAKLAND COUNTY (v26)

CATHOLICS--UNITED STATES

"The number of U.S. Catholics grew by nearly a million last year, but there were 974 fewer priests and 1,481 fewer nuns, according to figures in the 1997 Official Catholic Directory....The number of Catholic educational institutions also rose at all levels--including 145 more diocesan or parish elementary schools." (p21)

"Nation: Update: Directory Shows: More Catholics, Fewer Religious." Observer v62 n15 20 Jun 1997. p21. (ISSN0029-7712).

CATHOLICS--UNITED STATES--ATTITUDES (v26)
CATHOLICS--UNITED STATES--CHARITIES (v26)
CATS--DISEASES

A 1990 study found the rate of chronic kidney disease "to be as high as 7.7 percent in cats over 10 years of age and 15.3 percent in cats over 15." (p25) "Up to 75 percent of the kidney function can be destroyed before the cat begins to show significant symptoms." (p26) "Dialysis is rarely available and is expensive--about $750 to $1,000 a week. Only four veterinary hospitals in the United States offer the procedure...." (p28)

Swift, W. Bradford. "Kidney Disease and Your Cat." Animals v130 n4 Jul-Aug 1997. p24-29. (ISSN0030-6835).

CATTLE

see also DAIRY CATTLE; GRAZING

CATTLE TRADE--AUSTRALIA (v26)
CATTLE TRADE--AUSTRALIA--NEW ZEALAND --UNITED STATES

In April and May 1997, U.S. beef "imports from Australia jumped 25 percent above January-March imports and 60 percent above imports for the same period in 1996....April-May imports [from New Zealand] were 13 percent above a year earlier and January-May imports were up 4 percent." (unpaginated)

U.S. Dept. of Agriculture. Economic Research Service. "Beef Imports Up on Shipments from Oceania." Livestock, Dairy and Poultry Situation and Outlook Series 15 Aug 1997.

CATTLE TRADE--CANADA--UNITED STATES

"According to the U.S. Department of Commerce, imports of cattle weighing over 320 kilograms (primarily for slaughter) from Canada were down 21 percent through May. Through August 2, USDA's APHIS [Animal and Plant Health Inspection Service] reports feeder cattle imports, from Canada into the western United States, were down almost 6 percent while slaughter cattle imports were 20 percent lower. Total imports of cattle from Canada were 19 percent lower during the same period." (unpaginated)

U.S. Dept. of Agriculture. Economic Research Service. "Cattle Imports from Canada Lower." Livestock, Dairy and Poultry Situation and Outlook Series 15 Aug 1997.

CATTLE TRADE--HAWAII

"Hawaii cattle sales plummeted from $29.2 million in 1992 to $14.6 million in 1995, and since the 1980s, the percentage of beef eaten on the islands that comes from Hawaiian ranches has dropped from 30 to 5 percent....The cost of transporting a cow 3,000 miles across the Pacific equals about half of the value of the animal." (p5)

Engel, Robin. "Is Hawaii's Cowboy Legacy on the Brink of Extinction?" The Christian Science Monitor v90 n24 30 Dec 1997. p5. The Christian Science Monitor search engine: <http://www.csmonitor.com/plweb-cgi/iops1.pl> To retrieve this article, enter the following search: ED=19971230 AND extinction. In the "retrieved list," click the title that matches this record. (ISSN0882-7729).

CATTLE TRADE--UNITED STATES (v26)

In the U.S., "cattle and calves remained the top-ranked commodity in generation of cash receipts...for 1996 comprising 15 percent of all commodities, even though their value of sales fell by $2.9 billion or 8.4 percent. Following trend, the sales value of cattle and calves has declined by $8.2 billion, or 21 percent, since 1993 due to lower prices...." (p9)

U.S. Dept. of Agriculture. Economic Research Service. "1996 Farm Income Estimates: Net Value-Added and Net Farm Income Attain New Highs in 1996." Agricultural Income and Finance Situation and Outlook Report Sep 1997. p4-13.

In the U.S., "expenditures for cattle and calves in 1996 were down $3.9 billion (32 percent) from the previous peak in 1993. As in 1994, both total liveweight and average value per cwt [hundredweight] were down in 1996. In 1995, total liveweight rose 5 percent, but the average value fell 14 percent. In 1996, the average value fell another 9.4 percent in response to record high prices for grain and continuing low beef prices (consistent with increased beef production due to unusually high slaughter rates)." (p11)

U.S. Dept. of Agriculture. Economic Research Service. "1996 Farm Income Estimates: Net Value-Added and Net Farm Income Attain New Highs in 1996." Agricultural Income and Finance Situation and Outlook Report Sep 1997. p4-13.

In the U.S., "by 1992, 13 large slaughter plants, owned by four different firms, accounted for more than half of all steer and heifer slaughter in the United States (the leading firms also operate a dozen smaller plants in dispersed locations)....Each is designed to slaughter 4,000 to 5,000 cattle a day, in two 8-hour shifts....Each large plant provides employment for between 1,500 and 2,500 workers, who receive compensation, including fringe benefits, averaging $12 to $15 an hour....Today, there are a little over 200 large feedlots (those selling more than 16,000 head of cattle a year) that together sell over 13 million steers and heifers--or more than half of the total slaughter." (p26)

U.S. Dept. of Agriculture. Economic Research Service. "The Cattle Industry Today." Food Review v20 n2 May-Aug 1997. p26. (ISSN1056-327X).

An article in the KERR CENTER FOR SUSTAINABLE AGRICULTURE NEWSLETTER "stated, '50% of the beef cows in the United States were in herds of less than 100 cows in 1995...'....Standardized Performance Analysis (SPA) has shown the economic disadvantage of owning less than 100 cows. Data consisting of 200,000 cows from 20 different states has shown a net return of a negative $38.02/cow in herds with less than 50 cows and a net return of only $28.21/cow in herds of 50 to 99 cows." (p5)

Lathrop, Will. "Follow-Up on 'Future of the Beef Industry.'" Kerr Center Newsletter v23 n3 1997. p5.

In the U.S., in 1997, "first-half commercial cattle slaughter was down nearly 2 percent from a year earlier....Total cow slaughter was down nearly 8 percent, with beef cow slaughter down 12 percent and dairy cow slaughter down 3 percent....Calf slaughter in first-half 1997 was down 8 percent from a year earlier."

U.S. Dept. of Agriculture. Economic Research Service. "Cattle Herd Liquidation Ends, Inventory Slide Continues." Livestock, Dairy and Poultry Situation and Outlook Series 17 Jul 1997.

The U.S. "midyear Cattle report indicated that the number of cattle and calves on farms and ranches was 108.8 million head, down 2 percent from a year earlier and the lowest for this date since 1992's 107.2 million head. The total cow inventory was down 2 percent, with beef cow numbers down 3 percent and dairy cows continuing the recent decline of 1 percent per year. Beef replacement heifers were down 4 percent while dairy replacement heifers were down 3 percent....Other heifers were up 1 percent." (unpaginated)

U.S. Dept. of Agriculture. Economic Research Service. "Inventory Decline Continues." Livestock, Dairy and Poultry Situation and Outlook Series 15 Aug 1997.

U.S. "first-half commercial cattle slaughter was down nearly 2 percent from a year earlier....Total cow slaughter was down nearly 8 percent, with beef cow slaughter down 12 percent and dairy cow slaughter down 3 percent." (unpaginated)

U.S. Dept. of Agriculture. Economic Research Service. "Inventory Decline Continues." Livestock, Dairy and Poultry Situation and Outlook Series 15 Aug 1997.

CELLULAR RADIO--CANADA--UNITED STATES (v26)

CELLULAR RADIO--UNITED STATES (v26)

CELLULAR RADIO--UNITED STATES--PUBLIC OPINION

In the U.S., "thirty-two percent of 55-to-64-year-olds believe cellular phones are a necessity, while only 19 to 22 percent of other age groups feel as strong a need to have a cell phone. Seven in ten 25-to-34-year-olds say a cell phone is a convenience. About six in ten 18-to-24-year-olds and 35-to-54-year-olds agree....Only about two in ten people aged 55 or older say it's a status symbol. And just 11 percent of 25-to-34-year-olds say cell phones give them status, followed by 15 percent of 45-to-54-year-olds and 18 percent of those aged 18 to 24 and 35 to 44." (p32)

Kate, Nancy Ten. "Kaleidoscope: Cell Phone Attitudes." American Demographics v19 n6 Jun 1997. p32. article-level access: <http://www.demographics.com/publications/ad/97_ad/9706_ad/ad970613.htm> (ISSN0163-4089).

CEMENT INDUSTRIES--CHINA (v26)

CEMENT INDUSTRIES--ENVIRONMENTAL ASPECTS

Global carbon dioxide "emissions from cement manufacture may be considerably higher than previously thought, and could be responsible for 10% of global CO2 emissions by the year 2000, according to calculations by Joseph Davidovits of the Geopolymer Institute (Saint-Quentin, France)....His estimate suggests that current world production of 1.4 billion metric tons of cement each year contributes some 7% of global CO2 emissions." (p7)

"Industry Watch: CO2 Emissions from Concrete Addressed." Global Environmental Change Report v9 n15 8 Aug 1997. p7. (ISSN1049-9083).

CEMETERIES--VIRGINIA--ARLINGTON (v26)

CENTRAL AMERICA--POPULATION (v26)

CENTRAL ASIA

see ASIA, CENTRAL

CENTRAL NERVOUS SYSTEM

see also SPINAL CORD

CENTRAL NERVOUS SYSTEM--DISEASES--FLORIDA

In Florida, "in 1995 a record 199 cases [of meningococcal disease] were reported, of which 185 were confirmed....Since 1987 the annual number of confirmed cases has ranged between 91 and 185. Of the cases reported in 1995, 84 were meningitis alone, 46 were bacteremia alone, 46 were both, and 7 were combinations of otitis media, pneumonia, meningitis, cellulitis, epiglottitis, or arthritis with meningitis or septicemia....Fifty-three cases were in children aged 5 or less. Rates were 60% higher in non-whites than in whites....The counties with the most cases were Hillsborough (32), Dade (22), Palm Beach (15), and Duval (14). There was at least one case in 34 of the counties. Seven were imported from outside the United States. Nine of the cases were reported to be part of an outbreak, while 170 were apparently sporadic because they did not have direct contact with another case. Twelve of the 66 children under age 5 were reported to have attended day-care."

Florida. Dept. of Health. "Meningococcal Disease in Florida, 1995." EPI Update 20 Jun 1997. article-level access: <http://www.state.fl.us/health/public_html/epi/eu970619.htm>

CENTRAL VALLEY (CALIF. : VALLEY)

In California, "in the Central Valley, 90 percent of the riparian forests and 95 percent of wetlands have been lost and fish and wildlife resources have been devastated. The winter-run Chinook salmon has been listed as an endangered species, plummeting from 117,000 to fewer than 200 between 1969 and 1991; populations of migrating birds and waterfowl have been reduced to less than 5 percent of what they were forty years ago; and salmon spawning habitat has been reduced from 6,000 miles to less than 300." (p50)

"NRDC: On the Agenda: Searching for Solutions: NRDC's Work to Protect California's Water Resources." Amicus Journal v19 n2 Sum 1997. p50-51. (ISSN0276-7201).

CEREALS

see GRAIN

CEREBROVASCULAR DISEASE--MORTALITY (v26)

CEREBROVASCULAR DISEASE--NORWAY (v26)

CEREBROVASCULAR DISEASE--OHIO--CINCINNATI (v26)

CEREBROVASCULAR DISEASE--UNITED STATES (v26)

"Cerebrovascular disease, or stroke, continues to be the third leading cause of death in the United States, behind diseases of the heart and cancer. In 1995 it was the cause of almost one in every 15 U.S. deaths for a total of 157,991. Each year approximately half a million people suffer a new or recurrent stroke in this country and currently almost four million Americans are stroke survivors. According to the American Heart Association, on average, a stroke occurs every 60 seconds in the United States and someone dies from one every 3.4 minutes." (p9)

Mushinski, Margaret. "Variations in Average Charges for Strokes and TIAs: United States, 1995." Statistical Bulletin v78 n4 Oct-Dec 1997. p9-18. (ISSN0790-8334).

CEREBROVASCULAR DISEASE--UNITED STATES --COSTS (v26)

"Costs associated with the care of stroke patients have been estimated to be between $25 and $30 billion a year in the United States....The costs are reported the highest among subarachnoid hemorrhage patients (around $2,200 per day) while less than half this among those with a TIA [transient ischemic attack], approximately $1,050 a day." (p11-12)

Mushinski, Margaret. "Variations in Average Charges for Strokes and TIAs: United States, 1995." Statistical Bulletin v78 n4 Oct-Dec 1997. p9-18. (ISSN0790-8334).

According to a MetLife study in the U.S., in 1995, "stroke patients remained in the hospital for an average of 6.0 days. These confinements ranged from 8.1 days in New Jersey to 5.2 days in Oregon. The per diem charge averaged $1,829, with Arizona reporting the highest ($3,254, 78 percent above the average) and Ohio the lowest ($1,110, 39 percent below the nation) and around one-third that of Arizona. Per diem charges in excess of $2,600 were also reported in California and Connecticut, whereas those in New Jersey and Tennessee were less than $1,225, some 36 and 34 percent, respectively, below the average." (p15)

Mushinski, Margaret. "Variations in Average Charges for Strokes and TIAs: United States, 1995." Statistical Bulletin v78 n4 Oct-Dec 1997. p9-18. (ISSN0790-8334).

CEREBROVASCULAR DISEASE--UNITED STATES --MORTALITY (v26)

In the U.S., "stroke deaths occur proportionately more among women than men (61 and 39 percent, respectively, in 1995), although incidence is about 19 percent higher among men than women. Death rates are higher among non-Hispanic blacks of both sexes than their white counterparts, and in any given year, around 28 percent of strokes occur among persons under 65 years of age. Incidence and mortality rates increase with age and for persons over 55, stroke incidence more than doubles with each succeeding decade. In 1995 the age-adjusted death rate from cerebrovascular disease was 26.7 per 100,000 resident population, 24.8 for women and 28.9 for men...." (p9)

Mushinski, Margaret. "Variations in Average Charges for Strokes and TIAs: United States, 1995." Statistical Bulletin v78 n4 Oct-Dec 1997. p9-18. (ISSN0790-8334).

CEREMONIES

see MANNERS AND CUSTOMS

CERVIX UTERI--CANCER

"Eighty per cent of [cervical cancer] cases occur in developing countries, where it is often the most common cancer in women....The sexually-transmitted human papilloma virus is found in more than 95% of cases; it is necessary but probably not sufficient cause of the disease. A vaccine against the virus is being developed. Survival depends on the stage of the disease at diagnosis, with 90% of localized cases surviving five years compared to less than 10% with distant spread." (p5)

World Health Organization. "World Health Report 1997." Press Release 5 May 1997. p1-7. document-level access: <http://www.who.ch/whr/1997/presse.htm>

Worldwide, cervical cancer "is the second most common cancer problem in women, with half a million new cases each year. It kills more than 300,000 women every year. In more than 9 out of 10 cases, cervical cancer is caused by the human papilloma virus (HPV) which is transmitted sexually and has various types." (p27)

"Health Briefs: Cervical Cancer and the Human Papilloma Virus." World Health v50 n2 Mar-Apr 1997. p27. (ISSN0043-8502).

CERVIX UTERI--CANCER--UNITED STATES

In the U.S., "cervical infections with oncogenic types of human papillomavirus are associated with at least 80 percent of invasicocervical cancer cases; and women with human papillomavirus infection of the cervix are ten times more likely to develop invasive cervical cancer than are women without such infection. Approximately 4,900 American women will die from cervical cancer in 1996, and approximately 16,000 new cases of cervical cancer are diagnosed each year, making cervical cancer the third most common reproductive tract cancer in women and the seventh most common type of cancer overall in women." (p5)

The Committee on Prevention and Control of STDs. Institute of Medicine. "The Hidden Epidemic: Confronting Sexually Transmitted Diseases." SIECUS Report v25 n3 Feb-Mar 1997. p4-14. (ISSN0091-3995).

CESAREAN SECTION--UNITED STATES

In the U.S., "the cesarean birth rate declined 8 percent between 1991 and 1995, to 20.8 per 100 births for a total of 806,722 cesarean births in 1995....Non-Hispanic white women experienced the greatest decline in the cesarean rate at 9 percent, compared with less than 1 percent for non-Hispanic blacks and 6 percent for Hispanics. Hispanic women have the lowest overall cesarean birth rate, at 20.2, compared with 21.8 for non-Hispanic blacks and 21.0 for non-Hispanic whites." (p40)

Miller, Berna. "Kaleidoscope: Hold the Scalpel." American Demographics v19 n11 Nov 1997. p40. article-level access: <http://www.demographics.com/publications/ad/97_ad/9711_ad/ad971119.htm> (ISSN0163-4089).

"From 1991 to 1995 the total cesarean rate for the United States declined 8 percent and the vaginal births after cesarean (VBAC) rate increased 29 percent." (p24) "The cesarean section rate for stimulated births was lower than the national objective of 15.0 from 1993 to 1995." (p25)

Mathews, T. J. "Trends in Stimulation and Induction of Labor 1989-1995." Statistical Bulletin v78 n4 Oct-Dec 1997. p20-26. (ISSN0790-8334).

CFCs

see CHLOROFLUOROCARBONS

CHAGAS' DISEASE

"Chagas' disease is caused by a parasite transmitted to humans by a household bug found primarily in South and Central America. At least 16 million people are infected with the parasite--about one-third of whom develop a chronic form of the disease. Chagas' disease can severely damage the digestive tracts and nervous and cardiac systems of its victims. It is the leading cause of cardiac deaths among young adults in areas of South America." (p9)

Olshansky, S. Jay/Carnes, Bruce/Rogers, Richard G./Smith, Len. "Infectious Diseases--New and Ancient Threats to World Health." Population Bulletin v52 n2 Jul 1997. p2-46. (ISSN0032-468X).

CHAGAS' DISEASE--BRAZIL (v26)

CHAGAS' DISEASE--LATIN AMERICA (v26)

CHAIN RESTAURANTS (v26)

CHAIN RESTAURANTS--UNITED STATES (v26)

CHANCE, GAMES OF

see GAMBLING

CHARGE CARDS

see CREDIT CARDS

CHARITABLE USES, TRUSTS, AND FOUNDATIONS

see also CORPORATIONS--CHARITABLE CONTRIBUTIONS

CHARITABLE USES, TRUSTS, AND FOUNDATIONS --CANADA (v26)

CHARITABLE USES, TRUSTS, AND FOUNDATIONS --MICHIGAN

In Michigan, "Dexter is one of several area school districts that receives financial support from an education foundation, a non-profit group that solicits donations to pay for programs which might otherwise miss the district's budget....More than 200 of Michigan's 555 school districts have the foundations, which solicit money to pay for things like classroom projects, scholarships, computers, field trips, foreign language instruction and academic competitions. And while the average foundation gives about $60,000, some foundations...are able to raise more. The Grand Rapids-area Forest Hills Educational Foundation...gave $100,000 to a school, and other foundations have endowment funds. 'Michigan has more foundations from a percentage of its schools than any other state,' said Dan McCormick, president of Williamston-based McCormick Group-Educational Foundation Consultants....The Ann Arbor Public Schools Educational Foundation raises about $50,000 a year, using the money toward an endowment fund and grants to teachers." (p1 secA) In 1996, Chelsea's education foundation "raised almost $26,000. Ypsilanti's Education Foundation has been around since the late 1980s. Its annual fund--raiser...earns about $1,500....The Foundation for Saline Area Schools distributes about $10,000 a year." (p10 secA)

Schulz, Karen/Hollander, Sarah. "Foundations Ease Pinch for Schools: Groups Raise Donations." Ypsilanti Press 7 Dec 1997. p1,10 secA.

CHARITABLE USES, TRUSTS, AND FOUNDATIONS --UNITED STATES (v26)

CHARITIES

see also FOOD RELIEF; SOCIAL WORKERS

CHARITIES--CANADA (v26)

CHARITIES--MICHIGAN

"Michiganders claimed $2.7 billion in charitable deductions on their taxes in 1995, an increase of almost 4 percent over the previous year....The wealthy in Michigan gave on average $5,455 to charity in 1995--placing them seventh to last in the nation....In Michigan, nearly 84 percent of the people claiming charitable tax deductions made less than $100,000 a year; their average donation was $1,680, slightly above the national average for their income bracket, according to the IRS data. For total money given to charity by all Michiganders--$2.7 billion--the state ranks eighth in the nation." (p3 secB)

Young, Alison. "Local News: Michiganders Donating More to Charity." Detroit Free Press 25 Jul 1997. p3 secB.

CHARITIES--MICHIGAN--DETROIT--FINANCE

In Detroit, Michigan, "the Rosa and Raymond Parks Institute for Self-Development spent slightly more than one-third of its $164,445 in revenues last year on its annual Pathways to Freedom tour, according to the group's federal tax statement and a financial report by its accountant. The rest of the money, according to the 1996 documents, was used for 'management and general expenses'--including $72,344 for unspecified 'outside services.'...Charities generally spend roughly 75 percent of their annual budgets on programs, services and gifts, according to...[Dan Langan of the National Charities Information Bureau], with the rest of the money going toward administration and fund-raising costs. In 1996, 27 percent of the Parks Institute's expenses of $220,957 went toward 'program services,' its IRS tax-exempt filing shows. In 1995, according to the group's audit, it spent $33,155 on the tour--66 percent of that year's overall expenses. The institute, which received $151,406 in public support last year, ended 1996 with a $56,512 deficit on paper because spending exceeded revenues." (p1 secA) "The Pathways to Freedom tour cost $55,091 in 1996, according to the organization's figures. Management and administrative expenses were $161,866." (p4 secA)

Josar, David. "Expenses Eat Up Parks Funds." Detroit News 15 Sep 1997. p1,4 secA.

CHARITIES--UNITED STATES

"Last year, churches collected $71 billion of the $150.7 billion in charitable donations made in the United States, said Charles Stephens, at Indiana University's Center for Philanthropy in Indianapolis. The center has forecast that U.S. charitable giving will top $160 billion for 1997, meaning that the churches' traditional 45- to 47-percent portion will come to more than $75 billion." (p1 secA)

Heinlein, Gary. "For Churches, Christmas Time Is Good for Bottom Line." Detroit News and Free Press 14 Dec 1997. p1,13 secA.

In 1996, "Americans gave $151 billion to charities. And most of it came from individuals, who put a $121 billion price tag on generosity, far more than the $30 billion from corporations, foundations, and the like. The total represents about 2 percent of the nation's household income, roughly equal to levels of the past few decades." (p1 secB) "'Some 25,000 new charities spring up annually,' [says Daniel Borochoff, president of the American Institute of Philanthropy]....While two-thirds of US households contribute to charities financially, about 93 million Americans are citizen volunteers, reckons Independent Sector in Washington." (p5 secB)

Halverson, Guy. "Work & Money: Charitable Gifts, And Causes, Grow." The Christian Science Monitor v90 n14 11 Dec 1997. p1,5 secB. The Christian Science Monitor search engine: <http://www.csmonitor.com/plweb-cgi/iops1.pl> To retrieve this article, enter the following search: ED=19971211 AND grow. In the "retrieved list," click the title that matches this record. (ISSN0882-7729).

CHARTER SCHOOLS--MICHIGAN (v26)

CHARTER SCHOOLS--UNITED STATES

"Since the first one in 1991, some 750 charter schools have opened [in the U.S.], and lawmakers expect to approve at least $80 million to start more. In Arizona, some 30,000 students, or about 5 percent, now attend charter schools. By next year, that number should jump to 40,000 or 50,000, state officials say. Florida aims to be the first state with public school choice in every district." (p9)

Chaddock, Gail Russell. "Learning: Charter Schools Face Tough Test: Accountability." The Christian Science Monitor v89 n242 10 Nov 1997. p9. The Christian Science Monitor search engine: <http://www.csmonitor.com/plweb-cgi/iops1.pl> To retrieve this article, enter the following search: ED=19971110 AND accountability. In the "retrieved list," click the title that matches this record. (ISSN0882-7729).

In the U.S., according to Bruce Mano, a researcher at the Hudson Institute in Washington, "there are only 700...[charter schools] in a nation that has 80,000 public schools....Half the children in the nation's charter schools are from ethnic minorities; in conventional public schools, one-third of the children are minorities....Charters on average receive only 80 percent of the funding the conventional public school receives, and few have enough money to run a bus service." (p4)

Baldauf, Scott. "United States: 15 Years of School Reform: New Ideas, Modest Results." The Christian Science Monitor v89 n194 2 Sep 1997. p1,4. The Christian Science Monitor search engine: <http://www.csmonitor.com/plweb-cgi/iops1.pl> To retrieve this article, enter the following search: ED=19970902 AND results. In the "retrieved list," click the title that matches this record. (ISSN0882-7729).

CHECK CASHING SERVICES--UNITED STATES (v26)

In the U.S., "the number of check-cashing outlets has more than tripled since the late 1980s to an estimated 5,500. Conservative estimates are that these institutions cashed 128 million checks (totaling $38 billion) in 1990, taking in an estimated $700 million in fees. The nation's leading publicly traded chain of check cashers, ACE Cash Express, has expanded to more than 680 outlets with an infusion of capital from American Express." (p15)

"The New Loan Sharks: The Poverty Industry." Dollars and Sense n212 Jul-Aug 1997. p15. (ISSN0012-5245).

CHECKS--UNITED STATES

"Each year, about 60 billion checks are collected in the United States. Paper checks account for about 80 percent of noncash transaction volume." (p27)

Stavins, Joanna. "A Comparison of Social Costs and Benefits of Paper Check Presentment and ECP with Truncation." Federal Reserve Bank of Boston New England Economic Review Jul-Aug 1997. p27-44. (ISSN0028-4726).

"A majority of the checks in the United States are presented in time for payment the next business day. According to a recent survey by the American Bankers Association (1994), over 80 percent of local checks are presented within one business day, while only about half of nonlocal checks are presented within one business day....Over 90 percent of the dollar volume of checks cleared through the Federal Reserve are presented within one business day." (p4)

Lacker, Jeffrey M. "The Check Float Puzzle." Federal Reserve Bank of Richmond Economic Quarterly v83 n3 Sum 1997. p1-25. (ISSN1069-7225).

In the U.S., "nearly 63 billion checks were written in 1995 according to one estimate, representing 78.6 percent of all noncash payments (Committee on Payment and Settlement Systems of the central banks of the Group of Ten countries 1995).... The per capita number of checks written grew at an average The annual rate of 1.3 percent from 1991 to 1995." (p1)

Lacker, Jeffrey M. "The Check Float Puzzle." Federal Reserve Bank of Richmond Economic Quarterly v83 n3 Sum 1997. p1-25. (ISSN1069-7225).

CHECKS--UNITED STATES--COSTS

In the U.S., the checking system "consumes a billion pounds of paper a year. It steals away perhaps as much as 1 percent of the nation's annual production....Sixty-three billion times a year--2,000 times a second--Americans sign a check to pay for something....The government's...[mandate to eliminate most of its paper checks by 1 January 1999] means that millions of government checks going to contractors, Social Security retirees, and welfare recipients will land electronically in their banking accounts. (Tax refunds are exempted.) The savings look huge. The federal government spends an average 44 cents to print and send a paper check; an electronic deposit costs only 2 cents. The US Treasury Department says it sees $500 million in savings on postage and handling during the first five years." (p9)

Belsie, Laurent. "Business & Money: Consumer: 'The Check's in the Mail': A Costly Way to Pay Your Bills." The Christian Science Monitor v89 n158 11 Jul 1997. p9. The Christian Science Monitor search engine: <http://www.csmonitor.com/plweb-cgi/iops1.pl> To retrieve this article, enter the following search: ED=19970711 AND bills. In the "retrieved list," click the title that matches this record. (ISSN0882-7729).

CHEESE INDUSTRY--UNITED STATES (v26)

CHEMICAL DEPENDENCY

see SUBSTANCE ABUSE

CHEMICAL FERTILIZERS

see FERTILIZERS

CHEMICAL INDUSTRY--ENVIRONMENTAL ASPECTS --BELGIUM (v26)

CHEMICAL MILLING--FINLAND--SWEDEN (v26)

CHEMICAL POLLUTION

see POLLUTION

CHEMICAL WEAPONS

"The United States, which has started to destroy its chemical weapons, has a stockpile of about 30,000 tons. Russia has declared 40,000 tons." (p35) "In testimony before the Senate Committee on Intelligence last February, CIA Director George Tenet said that some 20 countries, among them Iran, Iraq, and Syria, have or are actively developing chemical and biological weapons." (p36) "Since the end of the Gulf War, U.N. specialists have destroyed more than 480,000 litres of Iraq's chemical agents and 1.8 million litres of precursor chemicals." (p37)

Hogendoorn, E. J. "A Chemical Weapons Atlas." Bulletin of the Atomic Scientists v53 n5 Sep-Oct 1997. p35-39. (ISSN0096-3402).

CHEMICAL WEAPONS DISPOSAL--UNITED STATES

Since the U.S. Congress passed the Marine Protection Research and Sanctuaries Act of 1972, "the U.S. Army has accumulated nearly 400,000 chemical weapons at eight sites across the country and has spent much time and money developing plans to dispose of them....[A 1993] ACDA [U.S. Arms Control and Disarmament Agency] study puts the cost of the current U.S. disposal program at between $8.5 and $9.5 billion...." (p43)

Chepesiuk, Ron. "A Sea of Trouble?" Bulletin of the Atomic Scientists v53 n5 Sep-Oct 1997. p40-44. (ISSN0096-3402).

CHEMICALS--UNITED STATES--PHYSIOLOGICAL EFFECT (v26)

CHERNOBYL NUCLEAR ACCIDENT, CHERNOBYL', UKRAINE, 1986

"Nuclear powerplants account for 33-43 percent of Ukraine's electric power generation. Since the Chernobyl disaster, new reactors have come on line, construction of two new reactors has continued and two reactors at the damaged Chernobyl complex still generate 5 percent of Ukraine's electricity. The hastily built cement sarcophagus covering the remains of reactor No. 4 is leaking radiation....Radiation levels near the sarcophagus are 1,000 times normal and pose a life-threatening danger to employees. Although 176 towns and villages near Chernobyl were evacuated, many people still live on contaminated land. Preschool children in contaminated areas suffer from respiratory distress (69.5 percent), thyroid problems (65 percent) and neuropsychic disorders (30 percent)." (p29)

Center for Safe Energy. "Nuclear Amnesia: Chernobyl...There Is No End to It." Earth Island Journal v12 n3 Sum 1997. p29. (ISSN1041-0406).

CHERNOBYL NUCLEAR ACCIDENT, CHERNOBYL', UKRAINE, 1986--HEALTH ASPECTS

"Thyroid cancer is caused by iodine-131, which comprised 10 to 15 percent of Chernobyl's fallout. Today, the rate of thyroid cancer is 10 times higher than that any scientist anticipated after the meltdown. The UN estimates the number of thyroid cancers among children in Belarus--where 70 percent of the fallout landed--at 285 times the pre-Chernobyl number. In 1995, the BRITISH MEDICAL JOURNAL reported that the rate of thyroid cancer in Ukraine and Belarus is 200 times higher than normal. The British Imperial Cancer Research Fund found a 500 percent increase in thyroid cancers among Ukrainian children between 1986 and 1993." (p28)

LaForge, John M. "Nuclear Amnesia: Chernobyl: A Global Tragedy." Earth Island Journal v12 n3 Sum 1997. p28-29. (ISSN1041-0406).

CHERRY INDUSTRY--UNITED STATES (v26)

"Between 1990 and 1996, the U.S. exported about 35 percent of its fresh-use [sweet cherry] supply, compared with 25 percent in 1985-89 and 14 percent in 1980-84. Japan is the largest market for U.S. fresh sweet cherries, importing an average of 56 percent of U.S. export volume over the last 3 years. Canada, the European Union, Taiwan, and Hong Kong are also important export markets for fresh cherries. During January-May 1997, sweet cherry exports were up 27 percent from the same time a year ago." (p7)

Plummer, Charles/Perez, Agnes/Haley, Steve/U.S. Dept. of Agriculture. Economic Research Service. "Commodity Briefs: Specialty Crops: Exports Bolster Sweet Cherry Prices." Agricultural Outlook Aug 1997. p6-7.

"In 1997, 44 percent of the U.S. sweet cherry crop is expected to be produced in Washington, 23 percent in Oregon, 18 percent in California, 13 percent in Michigan, and the remaining 2 percent in Idaho, Montana, New York, Pennsylvania, and Utah. Michigan ranks first in tart cherry production, supplying nearly three-quarters of the nation's output last year. New York, Utah, and Washington follow with 6 percent each, and Colorado, Oregon, Pennsylvania, and Wisconsin account for the remainder. About half of the U.S. sweet cherry crop is marketed for fresh use, while almost all tart cherries are processed....Nearly 70 percent of processed sweet cherries produced domestically are brined and used in candies, ice cream, and fruit cakes....Nearly two-thirds of the volume of processed tart cherries is frozen, and about one-third canned." (p6)

Plummer, Charles/Perez, Agnes/Haley, Steve/U.S. Dept. of Agriculture. Economic Research Service. "Commodity Briefs: Specialty Crops: Exports Bolster Sweet Cherry Prices." Agricultural Outlook Aug 1997. p6-7.

"On average, Americans consume less than 1.5 pounds of fresh and processed cherries per year....Since 1987, per capita consumption of fresh sweet cherries has ranged from a high of 0.7 pounds in 1987 to a low of 0.3 pounds in 1995....The season-average grower price for sweet cherries reached a record $1.12 per pound in 1995, over one and a half times the 1994 level...." (p6)

Plummer, Charles/Perez, Agnes/Haley, Steve/U.S. Dept. of Agriculture. Economic Research Service. "Commodity Briefs: Specialty Crops: Exports Bolster Sweet Cherry Prices." Agricultural Outlook Aug 1997. p6-7.

"About half of the U.S. sweet cherry crop is marketed for fresh use....The season-average grower price for sweet cherries reached a record in 1995 at $1.12 per pound ($2,240 per ton), nearly twice the average in 1994. Fresh use supplies declined 35 percent in 1995 and the share of exports rose from 33 percent in 1994 to 43 percent....Between 1990 and 1996, the United States exported about 35 percent of its fresh-use supply, compared with 25 percent in 1985-89 and 14 percent in 1980-84. Japan is the largest market for U.S. sweet cherries, with an average of 56 percent of U.S. export volume over the past 3

years." (p16-17)
U.S. Dept. of Agriculture. Economic Research Service. "Noncitrus Fruit Outlook." Fruit and Tree Nuts Situation and Outlook Report Aug 1997. p7-26.

In the U.S., "as of May 30, 1997, stocks of frozen tart cherries were running 2 percent higher than a year ago. Last year, the decline in production reduced processing use 17 percent from a year earlier to 256.1 million pounds, with all processing categories (canned, frozen, and other) down from the previous year....Frozen tart cherry supplies fell 6 percent to 180.7 million pounds in 1996 and processors paid 15.2 cents per pound for these cherries, up from 5.5 cents in 1995. Nearly 1 percent of the U.S. tart cherry crop is for fresh use. In 1996, fresh use fell 7 percent from a year earlier to 2.5 million pounds. Tart cherry growers received an average of 48.1 cents a pound for fresh-market cherries in 1996, up from 44.4 cents in 1995." (p17)
U.S. Dept. of Agriculture. Economic Research Service. "Noncitrus Fruit Outlook." Fruit and Tree Nuts Situation and Outlook Report Aug 1997. p7-26.

CHIAPAS (MEXICO)--SOCIAL CONDITIONS (v26)

CHIAPAS HIGHLANDS (MEXICO) (v26)

CHICKEN INDUSTRY

see also POULTRY INDUSTRY; TURKEY INDUSTRY

CHICKEN INDUSTRY--TENNESSEE

"Tennessee broiler production has grown 75% during the past ten years....The total production value jumped 25% from $186 million in 1995 to $232.2 million in 1996 (USDA 1997)." (p20)
Grizzle, Judith M./Saxton, Arnold M. "Using Soft Red Winter Wheat in Broiler Diets." Tennessee Agri Science n182 Spr 1997. p20-23.

CHICKEN INDUSTRY--UNITED STATES (v26)

Over the first half of 1997, total U.S. "broiler exports have been 2.2 billion pounds, 2.6 percent above the same period in 1996....In the six largest Asian markets (Hong Kong, Japan, China, Singapore, Korea, and Taiwan) U.S. broiler exports fell 19 percent in the first half of 1997....Over the first half of 1997, six countries in...[Eastern Europe and the Newly Independent States of the Soviet Union] were among the top 20 export markets (Russia, Latvia, Poland, Estonia, Ukraine, and Azerbaijan). They accounted for 1.2 billion (55 percent) of the 2.2 billion pounds of broiler exports or about 9 percent of total U.S. broiler production in first-half 1997." (unpaginated)
U.S. Dept. of Agriculture. Economic Research Service. "Lower Broiler Export Growth Expected." Livestock, Dairy and Poultry Situation and Outlook Series 17 Sep 1997.

CHIEF EXECUTIVE OFFICERS--SALARIES, ETC. --MICHIGAN (v26)

CHIEF EXECUTIVE OFFICERS--SALARIES, ETC. --MICHIGAN--ATTITUDES (v26)

CHIEF EXECUTIVE OFFICERS--SALARIES, ETC. --UNITED STATES (v26)

"The $39.8 million John Welch, CEO of General Electric, took in last year would take the average worker 1,612 years to earn. Apple Computer CEO Gilbert Amelio's pay package of $23.3 million equals the combined average earnings of 945 workers. And the staggering $141.3 million Lawrence Coss, CEO of Greentree Financial, pulled in amounts to $67,929 per hour (or $1,132 per minute)....According to BUSINESS WEEK, [U.S.] CEO pay packages skyrocketed another 54 percent last year--to an average $5.8 million in salary, bonuses and stock option grants. That's more than 200 times the average worker's pay (which increased only 3 percent last year)." (p18) "A survey conducted by the Mellman Group and Peter D. Hart Research Associates for the AFL-CIO last year,...revealed that 58 percent of respondents were extremely or very angry that 'the average CEO makes more than 100 times what the average worker makes.'" (p19)
"Executive Paywatch: Why America's CEOs Are Running for Cover." America@Work v2 n5 May-Jun 1997. p18-19. (ISSN1091-594X).

CHIEF JUSTICES

see JUDGES

CHILD ABUSE (v26)

see also ABUSED CHILDREN; CHILD SEXUAL ABUSE

CHILD ABUSE--CALIFORNIA

In its "annual 'Children's Budget,' the prestigious Children's Advocacy Institute reported that, at 75 per 1,000 children, 'California has the highest rate of reported abuse among the 10 largest states--almost 50 percent above New York, its nearest competitor.' Each year, the institute noted, the number of child abuse reports in California increases--up to nearly 700,000 in 1994, a 394 percent increase over the previous 15 years....According to a January 1996 report by the Legislative Analyst's Office on child abuse and neglect in California, half of the children in foster care in 1994-95 'had been removed from their homes due to general or severe neglect.' And, the analyst noted, 'while physical and sexual abuse comprise nearly half of the types of child abuse/neglect reports received,' sexual and physical abuse was involved in less than one-fourth of the children placed in foster care." (p12-13)
Bathen, Sigrid. "California's Lost Children." California Journal v28 n12 Dec 1997. p8-15. (ISSN0008-1205).

CHILD ABUSE--MICHIGAN (v26)

Richard Bearup, the Michigan Ombudsman for Children, said "about 65 percent of the cases investigated by his office are about CPS [Children's Protective Services]....Some 544 CPS caseworkers statewide investigated 58,655 complaints in the 1995-96 fiscal year that ended last Sept. 30. Bearup says there's simply...no way they can comply with all 364 rules and 1,150 pages of child welfare regulations in every case." (p1 secA)
Oppat, Susan L. "State Looks at Handling of Abuse Complaints." Ann Arbor News 10 Jun 1997. p1,12 secA.

CHILD ABUSE--UNITED STATES (v26)

"The Third National Incidence Study (NIS) of Child Abuse and Neglect estimates that child abuse and neglect nearly doubled in the United States between 1986 and 1993. The report estimates that the number of abused and neglected children grew from 1.4 million in 1986, when the last NIS report was conducted, to over 2.8 million in 1993. During the same period, the number of children who were seriously injured quadrupled from about 143,000 to nearly 570,000."
U.S. Dept. of Health and Human Services. "State Child Welfare Demonstrations." Fact Sheet 18 Jul 1997. document-level access: <http://www.hhs.gov/news/press/1997pres/970718b.html>

In the U.S., "child-maltreatment incident reports increased by 50% between 1988 and 1993, totaling more than 2.9 million reports in 1993 (McCurdy & Daro, 1994)....The National Committee to Prevent Child Abuse's recent survey of public child welfare agencies indicates that as many as 80% of child-maltreatment cases are associated with alcohol and other drug problems (McCurdy & Daro, 1994)." (p393)
Akin, Becci A./Gregoire, Thomas K. "Article: Parents' Views on Child Welfare's Response to Addiction." Families in Society v78 n4 Jul-Aug 1997. p393-404. (ISSN1044-3894).

CHILD ABUSE VICTIMS

see ABUSED CHILDREN

CHILD AND PARENT

see PARENT AND CHILD

CHILD BIRTH

see CHILDBIRTH

CHILD CARE--AFRO-AMERICANS (v26)
CHILD CARE--AUSTRALIA (v26)
CHILD CARE--CANADA (v26)
CHILD CARE--CANADA--PUBLIC OPINION (v26)
CHILD CARE--ILLINOIS--FINANCE (v26)
CHILD CARE--NEW YORK (N.Y.)--COSTS (v26)
CHILD CARE--SWEDEN (v26)
CHILD CARE--UNITED STATES (v26)

In the U.S., "since 1990, the costs of child care have risen about 6 percent annually. This is almost triple the annual increase in the cost of living. At the same time, there are strong indicators that the quality of child care has significantly decreased during the same period of time....A recent nationwide study found that 40-percent of the child care provided to infants in child care centers was potentially injurious. Fifteen percent of center-based child care providers for all pre-schoolers are so bad that a child's health and safety are threatened; 70-percent are mediocre--not hurting or helping children; and 15-percent actively promote a child's development." (pS11043)

Jeffords, James M. (Sen.-Vt.). "Senate Resolution 139--To Designate National Child Care Professional's Day." Congressional Record. Daily ed. v143 n144 23 Oct 1997. pS11043-11044. section/page-level access: <http://thomas.loc.gov/cgi-bin/query/R?r105:FLD001:S11043:> (ISSN0363-7239). (X1.1A.105/1).

In the U.S., "4.6 million infants, toddlers, and preschool children from every income group spend part of their day in licensed day care....In a query of all 50 states and the District of Columbia concerning deaths in child-care facilities, U.S. NEWS [& WORLD REPORT] tallied 76 deaths in 1996....The data are sketchy, since many states do not report the causes of these deaths....In Texas, a state that has recently revamped its reporting system and does collect detailed data, 22 day-care deaths and 134 serious injuries were recorded in fiscal 1996. If the deaths recorded in Texas and Massachusetts (which also collects detailed data) were projected per capita on the national population, day-care deaths would number between 240 and 320 a year. As a comparison, in 1995, 2,260 American kids between ages 1 and 4 died in all accidents, including 825 in motor vehicle collisions." (p34)

Pope, Victoria/Loftus, Margaret/Sieder, Jill Jordan/Knight, Zachary. "Special Report: Day-Care Dangers." U.S. News & World Report v123 n5 4 Aug 1997. p30-31,34-37. article-level access: <http://www.usnews.com/usnews/issue/970804/4CARE.HTM> (ISSN0041-5537).

CHILD CARE--UNITED STATES--ARMED FORCES (v26)

The U.S. "Pentagon spends $273 million a year on child care; combined with parents' investment, it costs about $6,800 a year for each child-care slot. That's well above the $3,700 national average for day care and roughly comparable to the $6,300 to $8,500 average for high-quality care. Even that investment fails to provide for 130,000 military children, whose parents must make other arrangements." (p41)

Auster, Bruce B. "U.S. News: The Clintons' Day-Care Model: The Pentagon." U.S. News & World Report v123 n16 27 Oct 1997. p41. article-level access: <http://www.usnews.com/usnews/issue/971027/27CARE.HTM> (ISSN0041-5537).

CHILD CARE--UNITED STATES--COSTS

In the US., "since 1990, the costs of child care have risen about 6 percent annually. This is almost triple the annual increase in the cost of living. At the same time, there are strong indicators that the quality of child care has significantly decreased during that same period of time....For a 3- to 4-year-old, which is the least expensive age group, the national average for center-based child care is $4,600 a year. The average cost for high quality care...is between $8,500 and $9,100 a year. A family normally spends about 20 percent of its income on housing and 10 percent on food. The costs of child care for a low- or middle-income family can rival the cost of housing and be double the cost of food." (pS6548)

Jeffords, James M. (Sen.-Vt.). "Jeffords (And Others) Amendment No. 555." Congressional Record. Daily ed. v143 n91 26 Jun 1997. pS6544-6551. section/page-level access: <http://thomas.loc.gov/cgi-bin/query/R?r105:FLD001:S06548:> (ISSN0363-7239). (X1.1A.105/1).

CHILD CARE--UNITED STATES--FATHERS

In the U.S., "among the 6.3 million married-couple families with preschoolers whose mothers worked in the fall of 1993, 25 percent of the fathers provided care. That figure is down from 30 percent in 1991, according to a report released...by the Commerce Department's Census Bureau. The report, 'My Daddy Takes Care of Me! Fathers as Care Providers,'...also found that the proportion of fathers who were primary care providers--those who cared for preschoolers during more of the mothers' working hours than any other care provider--was 19 percent in 1993, compared with 22 percent in 1991....Poor fathers were almost twice as likely as non-poor fathers to care for their preschoolers, 43 percent and 24 percent, respectively....Among families with only one preschooler, 23 percent of fathers were care providers compared with 33 percent of fathers in families with two or more preschoolers."

U.S. Dept. of Commerce. Economic & Statistics Administration. "Economic Conditions Can Influence Married Fathers' Caring for Preschoolers, Census Bureau Reports." Census Bureau Press Release 8 Oct 1997. document-level access: <http://www.census.gov/Press-Release/cb97-165.html>

In the U.S., "among the 6.3 million married-couple families with preschoolers whose mothers worked in the fall of 1993, 25 percent of the fathers provided some of the child care. That figure is down from 30 percent in 1991, according to a newly released Census Bureau report." (p2)

"24-Hour Economy Changing How We Work and Live." Population Today v25 n12 Dec 1997. p1-2. (ISSN0749-2448).

CHILD CARE--UNITED STATES--PUBLIC OPINION (v26)

"In 1995, in one of the largest studies of child care ever conducted, trained observers concluded that 2 in 5 [U.S.] children in 225 infant-toddler rooms received poor-quality care--care so bad that it was judged to jeopardize the child's health, safety, and learning. Yet not one of the parents with a child in a lousy day-care center gave their infant-toddler room a poor rating, and almost 9 in 10 of those parents felt their kids enjoyed high-quality care." (p10)

Whitman, David. "One Week: Waiting for Mary Poppins." U.S. News & World Report v123 n20 24 Nov 1997. p10. article-level access: <http://www.usnews.com/usnews/issue/971124/24WEEK.HTM> (ISSN0041-5537).

CHILD CARE WORKERS

see also AU PAIRS

CHILD CARE WORKERS--SALARIES, ETC. --MINNESOTA

"In Minnesota child care centers, the average hourly wage for a child care provider is $8.72; for an assistant teacher is $6.66; and for an aide is $5.69. Minnesota family child care providers, who are never covered by the Fair Labor Standards Act, have an average hourly wage of $2.79, and make $7,800 a year for a 60-hour work week....In the meantime, in Minnesota, there are 8,960 children on the waiting list for child care." (pS7716)

Wellstone, Paul D. (Sen.-Minn.). "Statements on Introduced Bills and Joint Resolutions." Congressional Record. Daily ed. v143 n102 17 Jul 1997. pS7710-7732. section/page-level access: <http://thomas.loc.gov/cgi-bin/query/R?r105:FLD001:S07715:> (ISSN0363-7239). (X1.1A.105/1).

CHILD CARE WORKERS--SALARIES, ETC.--UNITED STATES

In the U.S., "since the 1970's there has been a decline in child care teacher salaries. In 1990, teachers in child care centers earned an average of $11,500 a year. Assistant teachers, the largest growing segment of child care professionals, were paid 10- to 20-percent less than child care teachers. The 1990 annual income of regulated family child care providers was $10,944 which translates to about $4 an hour. Nonregulated family child care, generally comprised of providers taking care of a smaller number of children, earned an average of $4,275 a year--substantially less than minimum wage." (pS11043)

Jeffords, James M. (Sen.-Vt.). "Senate Resolution 139--To Designate National Child Care Professional's Day." Congressional Record. Daily ed. v143 n144 23 Oct 1997. pS11043-11044. section/page-level access: <http://thomas.loc.gov/cgi-bin/query/R?r105:FLD001:S11043:> (ISSN0363-7239). (X1.1A.105/1).

CHILD CARE WORKERS--SALARIES, ETC. --WISCONSIN (v26)

CHILD CARE WORKERS--SWEDEN (v26)

CHILD CARE WORKERS--UNITED STATES

In the U.S., "child care workers have the following statistics: 97 percent are female; 33 percent are women of color; 41 percent have children; 10 percent are single parents; only 18 percent of child care centers offer their workers health coverage....Child care teaching staff earn $6.89 an hour and $12,000 a year. Family child care providers earn $9,500, and unregulated providers, $5,100. Although they are better educated than the average worker, child care workers earn one-third of the average male salary and one-half of the average female salary. It is no surprise that one-third of them leave their centers every year." (pS7715-7716)

Wellstone, Paul D. (Sen.-Minn.). "Statements on Introduced Bills and Joint Resolutions." Congressional Record. Daily ed. v143 n102 17 Jul 1997. pS7710-7732. section/page-level access: <http://thomas.loc.gov/cgi-bin/query/R?r105:FLD001:S07715:> (ISSN0363-7239). (X1.1A.105/1).

CHILD CUSTODY

see CUSTODY OF CHILDREN

CHILD HEALTH SERVICES

see IMMUNIZATION OF CHILDREN

CHILD LABOR

see CHILDREN--EMPLOYMENT

CHILD MENTAL HEALTH--UNITED STATES

In the U.S., "only one-third of the children who need psychiatric care receive it (United States Congress, 1986; 1991). Prevalence rates for child mental illness are estimated at 12% (Gould, Wunsch-Hitzig, & Dohrenwend, 1981) (United States Congress, 1986, 1991). However, in some populations, such as inner city children exposed to high levels of psychosocial adversity, the rate is estimated to be as high as 22% (Costello, 1989). Zahner and colleagues (1991), in their study of inner city school children, found that almost 40% of these children were at risk for psychiatric disorder, and only 11% of these (at risk) children had utilized mental health services." (p199-200)

Armbruster, Paula/Gerstein, Stephanie H./Fallon, Theodore. "Bridging the Gap between Service Need and Service Utilization: A School-Based Mental Health Program." Community Mental Health Journal v33 n3 Jun 1997. p199-211. (ISSN0010-3853).

CHILD PLACING

see FOSTER HOME CARE

CHILD RESTRAINT SYSTEMS IN AUTOMOBILES --MICHIGAN

"About a quarter of young children riding in motor vehicles on Michigan roads are not fastened in child safety seats and of those who are, nearly 90 percent are improperly secured, according to a University of Michigan study....In their study of more than 1,200 children under age 4 riding in passenger cars, pickup trucks, sport utility vehicles, and vans and minivans,...[David W. Eby of the U-M Transportation Research Institute] and colleagues Lidia P. Kostyniuk and Carl Christoff found that child safety seat use is higher in vehicles driven by women (75 percent vs. 67 percent) and in which the driver wears a safety belt (81 percent vs. 52 percent)....Eby found that about two-thirds of the drivers in the study's sub-sample made at least one mistake in placing the child safety seat in the vehicle and about three-fourths made at least one error in placing the child in the safety seat itself." (p1)

University of Michigan. News and Information Services. "A Fourth of Young Children Are Not Placed in Child Safety Car Seats...Most...Incorrectly Secured, Say U-M Researchers." University of Michigan News Release 27 Oct 1997. p1-2.

CHILD SEXUAL ABUSE--CANADA (v26)

CHILD SEXUAL ABUSE--GREAT BRITAIN (v26)

CHILD SEXUAL ABUSE--UNITED STATES

"A recent Gallup Poll estimates that approximately 1.3 million children [in the U.S.] are sexually abused each year--about 10 times the number of cases actually reported....Convicted child molesters victimize an average of 91 children, according to statistics provided by the National Children's Advocacy Center in Huntsville, Ala. The National Coalition Against Pornography gave a higher estimate, saying a pedophile will typically sexually abuse 380 children in their lifetime." (p1 secD)

Harmon, Brian. "Metro: News Special: Public Safety: Pedophiles Can Hide under Many Guises." Detroit News 18 Nov 1997. p1,4 secD.

CHILD SUPPORT--UNITED STATES

"In a December 1994 report entitled 'Child Support Enforcement, Families Could Benefit from Stronger Enforcement Programs,' the [U.S.] General Accounting Office (GAO) stated that greater Federal leadership coupled with equally intensive state efforts could better position the national child support enforcement program to serve the families that depend on it....It also stated that the child support enforcement caseload grew 180 percent between 1980 and 1992. Another study cited by GAO estimated that the gap between total child support that should be paid nationwide and total child support paid as $34 billion in 1990....United States Bureau of the Census data quoted in the report shows that there were 9.8 million custodial mothers aged 18 years and older in 1990, or 39 percent more than in 1989 and that 62 percent of all custodial mothers in the United States did not receive child support in 1989." (p728) "The average amount of restitution ordered is approximately $33,500....In FY 1993, court-ordered restitution was $25,000; in FY 1994, it increased to $183,504; and, in FY 1995 totaled $1,246,344--a 579 percent increase over FY 1994." (p729)

U.S. Dept. of Justice. "Departments of Commerce, Justice, And State, The Judiciary...Approp. for 1998 (Part 2)." Hearing. U.S. House. Committee on Appropriations. Washington, D.C. : GPO, 1997. (ISBN0160549094). (Y4.Ap6/1:C73/2/997/pt.2).

In the U.S., child support "collections have risen from $1 billion a year to more than $11 billion in 1995; and in that same year, more than 5 million parents were located and paternity was established for over 600,000 children. But that is not good enough. Of the 9.9 million female-headed families in 1991 eligible for child support, only 56 percent had child support orders. That means that 4.5 million families did not even have an order to enforce. Those with child support orders were not always much better off. Only about half of those due money from a noncustodial parent actually received 100 percent of their court-ordered child support payments." (pH8084)

Levin, Sander M. (Rep.-Mich.). "Child Support Incentive Act of 1997." Congressional Record. Daily ed. v143 n132 29 Sep 1997. pH8081-8084. section/page-level access: <http://thomas.loc.gov/cgi-bin/query/R?r105:FLD001:H08084:> (ISSN0363-7239). (X1.1A.105/1).

In the U.S., "in 1996, the federal-state child support enforcement system collected a record $12 billion from non-custodial parents, up 50 percent from $8 billion in FY 1992. The federal government also collected a record of over $1 billion in delinquent child support by intercepting income tax refunds on non-paying parents for tax year 1995. Preliminary data for paternity establishment show an estimated 800,000 in FY 1996, up from 515,857 in FY 1992."

U.S. Dept. of Health and Human Services. "HHS Invests in America's Children." Fact Sheet 23 Jul 1997. document-level access: <http://www.hhs.gov/news/press/1997pres/970917.html>

CHILD SUPPORT--UNITED STATES--SINGLE-PARENT FAMILY (v26)

CHILD WELFARE

see also CHILD ABUSE; FOSTER HOME CARE

CHILD WELFARE--MICHIGAN

Between July 1996 and June 1997, the office of Richard Bearup, Michigan's ombudsman for children, "received 564 complaints involving 1,445 children from 71 of Michigan's 83 counties. After preliminary investigations, the 14-person staff opened 254 full-scale investigations involving 625 children. Over that time, 44 percent of the investigations involved complaints about Child Protective Services, a division of the FIA [Family Independence Agency]. Twenty-eight percent involved children of divorce, 27 percent involved reports of domestic violence and 24 percent involved substance abuse. The office said the issues often overlap. Nine of the ombudsman's investigations involved a child's death, and about 22 percent involved the police." (p3 secB)

Kresnak, Jack. "Local News: A Free Press Campaign: Children First: FIA Told How It Can Keep Kids Safer." Detroit Free Press 11 Dec 1997. p1,3 secB.

CHILD WELFARE--MICHIGAN--APPROPRIATIONS AND EXPENDITURES (v26)

CHILD WELFARE--NEW YORK (N.Y.) --APPROPRIATIONS AND EXPENDITURES (v26)

CHILD WELFARE WORKERS--MICHIGAN

Michigan governor John Engler committed to an additional 125 Child Protective Services caseworkers "for the 1997 fiscal year....Wayne County...was allocated an additional 30 workers and has gone from 141 to 171 caseworkers. Statewide, the official statistic covers child welfare workers, a category that includes several other positions besides CPS workers. Those numbers also have increased: from 1,442 in September '96 to 1,518 in October '97." (p10 secA)

"In Our Opinion: A Free Press Campaign: Children First: Abuse & Neglect:...Protective Services Gets...Improvements." Detroit Free Press 31 Oct 1997. p10 secA.

CHILDBIRTH

see also LABOR (OBSTETRICS); MULTIPLE BIRTH

CHILDBIRTH--AFRICA (v26)

CHILDBIRTH--BOLIVIA

Forty-seven "percent of Bolivian women who give birth never receive prenatal care. 57 percent of births take place in homes, usually without the assistance of a health worker....100 out of 1,000 newlyborn babies in rural Bolivia die." (p10)

Valente, Thomas W./Saba, Walter P. "Reproductive Health Is in Your Hands: The National Media Campaign in Bolivia." SIECUS Report v25 n2 Dec 1996-Jan 1997. p10-11,13. (ISSN0091-3995).

CHILDBIRTH--BURKINA FASO--NOUNA--MORTALITY (v26)

CHILDBIRTH--CALIFORNIA--HISPANIC AMERICANS

"The Hispanic share of all births in California...more than doubled between 1975 and 1995--from 20 percent to 46 percent--in part because of the fourfold growth in the number of Hispanic women of childbearing age in California during that period. Women born in Mexico contributed 27 percent of all California births in 1992, compared with only 7 percent in 1970. More babies were born to Hispanic women of all origins than to white women in California, even though there were twice as many non-Hispanic whites of childbearing age. In 1992, women born in Mexico accounted for 61 percent of Hispanic women giving birth in California." (p27)

del Pinal, Jorge/Singer, Audrey. "Generations of Diversity: Latinos in the United States." Population Bulletin v52 n3 Oct 1997. p2-47. (ISSN0032-468X).

CHILDBIRTH--CANADA

According to a paper based on records of childbirths in British Columbia in 1994 and released in Statistics Canada's HEALTH REPORTS, "while cesarean sections occurred in 21.5 per cent of deliveries to women who were having their first child in their 20s, the rate was 34.7 per cent in women older than 35. While 6.2 per cent of babies born to women in their 20s had a risky birth weight below 2,500 grams, the percentage was 9.1 in women older than 35. And premature birth occurred in 6.6 per cent of pregnancies in women in their 20s, compared with 10.5 per cent in older women....The number of cases of genetic defects was .32 per cent in women older than 35, compared with .13 per cent in women aged 30-34, and .08 per cent in women in their 20s." (p8)

LeBow, Barbara. "Happenings around the World: Risks of Late Motherhood." Prolife News v22 n10 Nov-Dec 1997. p8.

CHILDBIRTH--COMPLICATIONS--DEVELOPING COUNTRIES

Every day, "more than 31,000 children under the age of 5 die in developing countries. By helping women space their children at least 2 years apart, at least one in four of these infant deaths can be prevented. Every year 585,000 women, one woman for every minute of every day, dies of causes related to pregnancy and childbirth....99 percent of these women live in developing countries. The fact is that 25 percent of these deaths can be prevented by allowing women the simple means to delay motherhood." (pH8507)

Frelinghuysen, Rodney P. (Rep.-N.J.). "Motion to Instruct Conferees on H.R. 2159, Foreign Operations, Export Financing...Appropriations Act, 1998." Congressional Record. Daily ed. v143 n138 7 Oct 1997. pH8502-8512. section/page-level access: <http://thomas.loc.gov/cgi-bin/query/R?r105:FLD001:H08507:> (ISSN0363-7239). (X1.1A.105/1).

CHILDBIRTH--DEVELOPING COUNTRIES--MORTALITY (v26)

CHILDBIRTH--EDUCATION--UNITED STATES

According to the U.S. National Center for Health Statistics, "for women ages 30 to 34 years, birth rates were highest for college graduates, at 124 births per 1,000 women, followed by women with a grade school education at 107 per 1,000 women. Rates for women in other educational groups were much lower: 54 to 70 per 1,000....In 1994, the probability of first births to childless female college graduates ages 30 to 34 years was 107 births per 1,000 women compared with 64 to 73 births per 1,000 for their less-educated peers." (p8)

"News and Resources: Delayed Childbearing Continuing, NCHS Reports." Population Today v25 n6 Jun 1997. p8.

(ISSN0749-2448).

CHILDBIRTH--GHANA

"According to the 1993 Demographic and Health Survey for Ghana, 56% of all married women want to have children, as against 34% who either do not want to have any more or have been sterilized. This marks a significant change as compared with 65% and 23% respectively in 1988. The survey also found that, especially in the northern parts of the country, women prefer to have a large family, averaging 6.4 children. For elderly women in Ghana, the mean ideal family size is 5.5." (p22) "In Ghana, seven births in every 10 take place at home under the supervision of trained or untrained traditional birth attendants (TBAs)." (p23)

Nyinah, Stella. "Cultural Practices in Ghana." World Health v50 n2 Mar-Apr 1997. p22-23. (ISSN0043-8502).

CHILDBIRTH--HEALTH ASPECTS--UNITED STATES (v26)

CHILDBIRTH--IRELAND

Figures released by Ireland's "Central Statistics Office show that the number of births in 1996 was 50,400--an increase of 1,900 on 1995 but still 24,000 below the 1980 peak. The trend towards smaller families is evident from the decrease of about 18,000 (from 34,400 in 1980 to 16,300 in 1996) in the number of births to mothers with at least two previous children. Nearly one in every four births in 1996 was outside marriage, this proportion has increased almost fivefold since 1980. In just under 2,600 of these extra-marital births, the mother was a teenager."

Ireland. Central Statistics Office. "Births, Marriages and Deaths in 1996." Press Release 22 May 1997. document-level access: <http://www.cso.ie/pressreleases/vstats1996.html>

CHILDBIRTH--MORTALITY

"About 600,000 women a year die while giving birth. Many of them are teenagers....Of those 600,000 women, 140,000 bleed to death....About 75,000 women die from the results of self-inflicted abortions....About 75,000 women die from convulsions due to eclampsia, which is a complication of pregnancy, and 100,000 from blood poisoning. About 40,000 go into obstructed labour, which goes on for days and days...." (c147)

Tonge, Jenny (H.C.-Richmond Park). "International Development." Great Britain. Parliament. House of Commons. Debates. 1 Jul 1997. c147. section-level access: <http://www.parliament.the-stationery-office.co.uk/pa/cm199798/cmhansrd/cm970701/debtext/70701-16.htm#70701-16_spnew0>

CHILDBIRTH--NEW ZEALAND

In New Zealand, "the number of live births registered in the 1997 September year was 57,323, just 52 or 0.1 per cent fewer than the previous September year....The number of nuptial births (children born to legally married couples) increased marginally by 27 or 0.1 per cent to 33,430 in the 1997 September year. Ex-nuptial births (children born to women not legally married) decreased by 79 or 0.3 per cent from 23,972 to 23,893, reversing a previous upward trend."

Statistics New Zealand. "Vital Statistics--Year Ended September 1997." Press Release 17 Nov 1997. document-level access: <http://www.stats.govt.nz/statsweb.nsf/52518ce3e01f62f4cc256388000c48c0/daf24c21850f74d84c2565510081d8b3?OpenDocument>

CHILDBIRTH--THAILAND

"Among women in refugee camps in Thailand, birthrates were much lower among lowland Laotians than among the Hmong....Only 3% of Hmong women were using contraception compared with 42% of the lowland Lao. On average, Hmong women wanted 6.2 children compared with 3.4 children among the lowland Lao...." (p9)

Gardner, Robert/Blackburn, Richard. "People Who Move: New Reproductive Health Focus." Population Reports v24 n3 Nov 1996. p1-27.

CHILDBIRTH--UNITED STATES

"Births in the United States declined in 1995 for the fifth consecutive year, to 3,899,589, 1 percent lower than 1994 and 6 percent lower than in 1990. The 1995 birth rate (14.8 births per 1,000 population) was down 3 percent from 1994 and 11 percent from 1990. Similarly, the fertility rate dropped 2 percent to 65.6 births per 1,000 women aged 15-44."

U.S. National Center for Health Statistics. "1995 Birth Statistics Released." Fact Sheet 10 Jun 1997. document-level access: <http://www.cdc.gov/nchswww/releases/97facts/97sheets/95natrel.htm>

In the U.S., "ten percent of births between 1990 and 1995 were unwanted by the mother at the time of conception, compared with 12 percent between 1984-88. For black women, the decrease in unwanted births between these two periods was particularly large--from 29 to 21 percent....Medicaid was used to help pay for about one out of three deliveries in 1991-95 (34 percent). Among unmarried mothers and teenage mothers, two-thirds (68-69 percent) were paid for, at least partly, by Medicaid, compared with 20 percent of births to married mothers."

U.S. National Center for Health Statistics. "New Report Documents Trends in Childbearing, Reproductive Health." Fact Sheet 5 Jun 1997. document-level access: <http://www.cdc.gov/nchswww/releases/97facts/97sheets/nsfgfact.htm>

In the U.S., "the rate of cesarean deliveries declined for the sixth consecutive year, to 20.8 percent in 1995 compared with 22.8 percent in 1989, a drop of 9 percent. At the same time vaginal births after previous cesarean deliveries increased 46 percent during this same time period....The birth rate for women aged 40-44 years rose 20 percent between 1990 and 1995, and increased 74 percent during 1981-95. The rising birth rate along with the increasing number of women in this age group has meant that there were more babies born in 1995 to mothers in their forties than in any year since 1966."

U.S. National Center for Health Statistics. "1995 Birth Statistics Released." Fact Sheet 10 Jun 1997. document-level access: <http://www.cdc.gov/nchswww/releases/97facts/97sheets/95natrel.htm>

"Between 1985 and 1994, the proportion of births that were to [U.S.] women in their 20s decreased from 62 percent to 53 percent, and the proportion to women aged 30 to 44 increased from 25 percent to 34 percent. The birth rate increased for all age groups, but the fastest increases were to women aged 30 to 39. Births to teenagers (aged 15 to 19) were 13 percent of all births in both years. The share of births to women with a high school education (measured as 12 years of formal education) declined sharply from 1985 to 1994, from 43 percent to 35 percent of all births. Births to high school dropouts increased from 21 percent to 23 percent, and births to women with a 4-year college degree increased from 17 percent to 20 percent. Women with some college experience were the only group whose birth rate decreased, and it was a sharp decrease--from 65.7 live births per 1,000 women with 13 to 15 years of education in 1985, to 48.4 births in 1994." (p8)

"Motherhood: Squeezed in the Middle." Forecast v17 n6 Jun 1997. p8. article-level access: <http://www.demographics.com/Publications/FC/97_fc/9706_fc/FC97067.htm> (ISSN0732-1597).

"Provisional reports to the National Center for Health Statistics produced an estimate of 3,899,000 live births in the U.S. in 1996, a number almost identical to the 3,892,000 babies born in 1995. Births have slowly declined since their peak of 4,158,000 in 1990, as baby-boomer mothers are being replaced by a much smaller cohort of women....The number of births in the U.S. will fluctuate within a range of 350,000 between 1990 and 2010." (p1) "The share of births for Hispanic women increased from 15 percent in 1990 to 17 percent in 1995, the latest year for which such statistics are available. The share of births to non-Hispanic black women increased from 15 to 16 percent. Only 61 percent of births were to non-Hispanic white women in 1995, compared with 64 percent in 1990." (p2)

"No More Baby Booms." Forecast v17 n9 Sep 1997. p1-2. article-level access: <http://www.demographics.com/Publications/FC/97_fc/9709_fc/FC97091.htm> (ISSN0732-1597).

According to the CDC's 1996 Vital Statistic Report, in the U.S., "the proportion of mothers beginning care in the first trimester (82 percent) improved again in 1996 (from 81 percent in 1995). Early care improved among white (84 percent), black (71 percent), and Hispanic mothers (72 percent) in 1996. The cesarean delivery rate declined for the seventh consecutive year (20.6 percent for 1996)....The percent of babies born [with] low birthweight increased slightly from 7.3 in 1995 to 7.4 in 1996, the highest level reported in more than two decades."

U.S. Dept. of Health and Human Services. "Vital Statistics Report Shows Significant Gains in Health." Press Release 11 Sep 1997. document-level access: <http://www.hhs.gov/news/press/1997pres/970911a.html>

In the U.S., "in 1995, 90 percent of all live births were attended by doctors of medicine (MD's). Doctors of osteopathy (DO's) attended nearly 4 percent and certified nurse-midwives (CNM's) attended nearly 6 percent....The successive single year increases for DO's between 1993 to 1994 and 1994 to 1995 were 11 and 10 percent, respectively. The overall percent increases from 1989 to 1995 for DO's and CNM's were 62 and 58, while for MD's the increase was 47 percent." (p23)

Mathews, T. J. "Trends in Stimulation and Induction of Labor 1989-1995." Statistical Bulletin v78 n4 Oct-Dec 1997. p20-26. (ISSN0790-8334).

CHILDBIRTH--UNITED STATES--MORTALITY

"In 1900, some 600 women died in childbirth in the United States for every 100,000 live births....But by 1970, 21.5 women died in childbirth for every 100,000 live births. Today, that number has dropped to less than 10." (pS4525)

Moseley-Braun, Carol (Sen.-Ill.). "Partial-Birth Abortion Ban Act of 1997." Congressional Record. Daily ed. v143 n64 15 May 1997. pS4517-4575. section/page-level access: <http://thomas.loc.gov/cgi-bin/query/R?r105:FLD001:S04525> (ISSN0363-7239). (X1.1A.105/1).

CHILDHOOD LEAD POISONING

see LEAD POISONING IN CHILDREN

CHILDLESSNESS--IRELAND

In Ireland, according to the 1996 Census, "28% of wives (this includes women in cohabiting couples) in the 25 to 34 age group had no children in 1996, compared with 20% in 1991 and 16% in 1986....Households made up of both married and cohabiting couples with no children was the fastest-growing category of family household in the five-year intercensal period. This type of household went from 125,400 to 152,500--a rise of 22%. Almost a third of all families in Donabate in Fingal (North Co. Dublin) had no children when the Census was carried out in April 1996. For the State as a whole 22% of families had no children. The Fingal town was closely followed by Skibbereen, Co. Cork, where 31% of families had no children. In Maynooth, Co. Kildare (note that this is a university town), Dunshaughlin, Co. Meath, and Carrick-on-Shannon, Co. Leitrim, 30% of families had no children. At the other end of the scale Portmarnock, in Co. Dublin, emerged as the town with the highest proportion of families with children at 89%, followed by Rathcoole, Co. Dublin, at 88%. There were 17,045 households comprised of cohabiting couples with no children in April 1996, when the Census was conducted. This Census was the first time that a question on cohabitation was asked. Just over 70% or 12,139 of these couples lived in Leinster with more than half the total in Dublin County and County Borough."

Ireland. Central Statistics Office. "1996 Census--Volume 3, Household Composition and Family Unit." Press Release 27 Nov 1997. document-level access: <http://www.cso.ie/pressreleases/prelcen96v3.html>

CHILDREN

see also ABUSED CHILDREN; AFRO-AMERICAN CHILDREN; AGRICULTURAL LABORERS--CHILDREN; AID TO FAMILIES WITH DEPENDENT CHILDREN PROGRAMS; AIDS (DISEASE) IN CHILDREN; AIR BAG RESTRAINT SYSTEMS--UNITED STATES--CHILDREN; ASTHMA IN CHILDREN; BODY IMAGE IN ADOLESCENCE; BURNS AND SCALDS IN CHILDREN; CRIME--UNITED STATES--CHILDREN; DRUGS--UNITED STATES--TESTING--CHILDREN; FIREARMS--UNITED STATES--CHILDREN; FOOD HABITS--UNITED STATES--CHILDREN; FOSTER CHILDREN; FRUIT JUICE INDUSTRY--UNITED STATES--CHILDREN; HOMELESS CHILDREN; IMMUNIZATION OF CHILDREN; INFANTS; INSURANCE, HEALTH--FLORIDA--CHILDREN; INSURANCE, HEALTH--UNITED STATES--CHILDREN; LEAD POISONING IN CHILDREN; LEISURE--CHILDREN; LITERACY--UNITED STATES--CHILDREN; MALNUTRITION IN CHILDREN; OBESITY IN CHILDREN; POOR CHILDREN; POST-TRAUMATIC STRESS DISORDER--UNITED STATES--CHILDREN; PRESCHOOL CHILDREN; RUG AND CARPET INDUSTRY--EMPLOYMENT--INDIA--CHILDREN; RUG AND CARPET INDUSTRY--EMPLOYMENT--SOUTH ASIA--CHILDREN; SCHOOL CHILDREN; SEX OF CHILDREN, PARENTAL PREFERENCES FOR; SHOPPING CARTS--WOUNDS AND INJURIES--UNITED STATES--CHILDREN; SILK INDUSTRY--EMPLOYMENT--INDIA--CHILDREN; SILVER INDUSTRY--EMPLOYMENT--INDIA--CHILDREN; SOCIAL SECURITY--UNITED STATES--CHILDREN; SOCIAL SECURITY--UNITED STATES--HANDICAPPED CHILDREN; TEENAGERS; TOBACCO INDUSTRY--EMPLOYMENT--INDIA--CHILDREN; TRAFFIC ACCIDENTS--UNITED STATES--CHILDREN; VACCINATION OF CHILDREN; VISION DISORDERS IN CHILDREN; WOMEN, INFANTS, AND CHILDREN PROGRAM; YOUTH

CHILDREN--ABUSE OF

see CHILD ABUSE

CHILDREN--AFRICA, SUB-SAHARAN--SOCIAL CONDITIONS (v26)

CHILDREN--ARIZONA--MORTALITY

"The deaths of at least 270 Arizona children could have been prevented last year through the use of common safety practices, according to a report released...by the Arizona Child Fatality Review Team....The report said 28 percent of the deaths could have been prevented through the use of seat belts, locked storage of guns, secure pool fences, smoke detectors, bicycle helmets and other safety precautions, including closer parental supervision. It added that when newborns younger than 28 days are excluded from the count, the proportion of preventable death rises to nearly 42 percent....The leading causes of preventable death were motor vehicle crashes with 121 deaths, drowning and other unintentional injuries with 72 deaths, violence-related incidents with 38 deaths, untreated perinatal or medical disorders with 21 deaths, and Sudden Infant Death Syndrome with 13 deaths."

Arizona. Dept. of Health Services. "Hundreds of Child Deaths Preventable, Report Finds." Press Release 13 Nov 1997. document-level access: <http://www.hs.state.az.us/news/news81.htm>

CHILDREN--CARE AND HYGIENE

see CHILD CARE

CHILDREN--DEVELOPING COUNTRIES--MORTALITY

"Between 1960 and 1995, child mortality dropped by 32 percent in sub-Saharan Africa, according to the Population Reference Bureau, but by 70 percent or more in several other developing regions including the Middle East and North Africa....In sub-Saharan Africa, 256 children under five died for every 1,000 live births in 1960, compared with 175 in 1995. In the Middle East and North Africa, 244 children under five died for every 1,000 live births in 1960, compared with 60 in 1995." (p4)

"Child Mortality Decreasing." Popline v19 Sep-Oct 1997. p4.

In developing countries, "some progress has been made in reducing mortality among children under age five--death rates in this age group declined globally by 40 percent between 1970 and 1995, from 134 to 80 deaths per 1,000 live births....In 1997, more than 20 countries--primarily in sub-Saharan Africa--still had infant mortality rates greater than 100 infant deaths per 1,000 live births. Infant mortality rates were 195 in Sierra Leone, 163 in Afghanistan, and 134 in Mali and Malawi, for example. Most infant deaths occur within the first weeks of life. WHO estimates that about 5 million infants died in their first month of life in 1995--about 36 per 1,000 live births." (p6)

Olshansky, S. Jay/Carnes, Bruce/Rogers, Richard G./Smith, Len. "Infectious Diseases--New and Ancient Threats to World Health." Population Bulletin v52 n2 Jul 1997. p2-46. (ISSN0032-468X).

CHILDREN--DISEASES--MORTALITY (v26)

"Seven out of 10 childhood deaths in developing countries can be attributed to just five main causes, or a combination of them: pneumonia, diarrhoea, measles, malaria and malnutrition. Around the world, three out of every four children who seek health care are suffering from at least one of these conditions." (p1) "Acute respiratory infection (ARI) is the leading cause of death in children under five, killing over two million children annually. Up to 40% of children seen in health clinics are suffering from ARI....Over 2 million children die each year in developing countries from diarrhoeal diseases." (p2) "Despite the major impact made on...[measles] by successful immunization programmes, measles infects over 40 million children and kills over 800,000 under-fives each year. That translates to 2,000 deaths of young children every day from measles....Nearly 600,000 children die of malaria each year, most of them in sub-Saharan Africa." (p3)

World Health Organization. "Reducing Mortality from Major Childhood Killer Diseases." WHO Fact Sheet n178 Sep 1997. p1-6. document-level access: <http://www.who.ch/programmes/inf/facts/fact178.htm>

"More than 11 million children die each year before reaching the age of five; of them, 70%, or around 8 million children, die from one or more of five causes: pneumonia, diarrhoea, measles, malaria and malnutrition." (p1) "In 1995, pneumonia, diarrhoea, malaria and measles caused one half of all deaths of children under five. Many of these children also suffered from malnutrition, a causative or contributory factor in an estimated 54% of child deaths...." (p2)

World Health Organization. "11 Million Child Deaths per Year: Many Can Be Prevented." WHO Press n64 8 Sep 1997. p1-2. document-level access: <http://www.who.ch/press/1997/pr97-64.html>

CHILDREN--DISEASES--UNITED STATES

In the U.S., among children "in 1996, three diseases reached the elimination targets; there were no reported cases of tetanus among children under 15 years of age or of poliomyelitis due to wild polio virus and, with 725 cases of mumps in 1996, surpassed by more than half the reduction goal set for mumps of 1,600. Reported levels of disease were at or near record lows and close to the 1996 elimination targets for diphtheria (4 cases), 'Haemophilus influenzae' invasive disease among children under 5 years of age (165 cases), rubella (196 cases) and measles (443 cases)."

U.S. Dept. of Health and Human Services. "Nation Reaches 1996 Immunization Goals with Highest-Ever Coverage Levels." Press Release 23 Jul 1997. document-level access: <http://www.hhs.gov/news/press/1997pres/970723a.html>

CHILDREN--EDUCATION

see EDUCATION

CHILDREN--EMPLOYMENT (v26)

"According to the International Labour Organisation (ILO), in developing countries as many as 250 million children between the ages of five and fourteen are engaged in some kind of economic activity. At least half are employed full-time. Between 15 and 20 per cent are under the age of ten....The ILO claims that the biggest problem is in Asia, which has an estimated 153 million child workers. Africa comes second with 80 million child labourers. There are an estimated 17.8 million child labourers in Latin America....Turkey has 24 million child labourers, while Thailand has more than 16 million." (p412)

Cooper, James. "Child Labour." International Journal v52 n3 Sum 1997. p411-430. (ISSN0020-7020).

International Programme on the Elimination of Child Labour "programmes fall into two categories: 'action programmes,' dealing with specific issues, and 'mini programmes' (US$3,000 at the most)....By the end of January 1997, IPEC had undertaken 555 action programmes and 280 mini programmes in 19 countries....Some 77 per cent of IPEC programmes focus on forms of child labour in the 'intolerable' category....Most of the programmes targeting the 'intolerable' forms of child labour are geared either to prevention (41 per cent) or to withdrawal from work and provision of alternatives (40 per cent)." (p251)

"Perspectives: Child Labour: How the Challenge Is Being Met." International Labour Review v136 n2 Sum 1997. p233-257. (ISSN0020-7780).

According to a recent International Labour Organization study, "some 250 million children aged 5-14 are working. About half, or 120 million, work full-time, while the remaining children struggle to combine work with schooling or other non-economic activities....The figure of 250 million working children is considered to be an under-estimate. It does not include those who work in regular non-economic activities, such as providing full-time domestic service in the homes of their own parents or guardians. The number of such children is relatively large (about 15-20 percent of the total population of the same age group). While current data shows that boys outnumber girls who work by three to two, statistical surveys often underestimate the number of girls who work by failing to include unpaid economic activity in and around the house, including household enterprises....Many children work long hours for low pay. In some countries, up to 80 percent of working children work seven days a week."

International Labour Organization. "Oslo Conference to Seek Global Strategy for Combating Child Labour: Conference...Focus...'...Child Labour.'" Press Release 27 Oct 1997. document-level access: <http://www.unicc.org/ilo/public/english/235press/pr/1997/25.htm>

CHILDREN--EMPLOYMENT--ASIA (v26)

CHILDREN--EMPLOYMENT--BRAZIL

"A 1994 study by the Brazilian Institute for Geography and Statistics found that approximately two million, or 14.3 percent, of children between 10 and 13 years of age are working. Separate studies reveal that there are more than 200,000 child prostitutes (some as young as six years old) on the streets throughout Brazil." (p8)

Lantos, Tom (Rep.-Calif.)/Porter, John Edward (Rep.-Ill.). "Brazil: Congressional Human Rights Caucus Letter." NewsNotes v22 n6 Nov-Dec 1997. p8. (ISSN1064-1556).

CHILDREN--EMPLOYMENT--DEVELOPING COUNTRIES (v26)

Child labour is most prevalent in the developing regions "because that is where 87 per cent of the world's children under 18 live (UNICEF, 1997...)." (p242) The International Labour Organization's "Bureau of Statistics now estimates that 'in the developing countries alone, there are at least 120 million children between the ages of five and 14 who are fully at work, and more than twice as many (or about 250 million) if those for whom work is a secondary activity are included' (ILO, 1996...). Asia has the largest absolute number of child workers--with an estimated 61 per cent of the world total, as against 7 per cent for Latin America. But Africa has the highest incidence, now estimated at around 40 per cent of all children between five and 14." (p243)

"Perspectives: Child Labour: How the Challenge Is Being Met." International Labour Review v136 n2 Sum 1997. p233-257. (ISSN0020-7780).

CHILDREN--EMPLOYMENT--GREAT BRITAIN --UNITED STATES

"In June 1996, a British House of Commons report estimated that 1.5 million children under the age of 16 were working illegally in Britain, often in dangerous conditions....In the United States, where the number of those between the ages of 12 and 17 who work is close to 5.5 million, or 27 per cent of children in this age group, prosecutions are rare." (p413)

Cooper, James. "Child Labour." International Journal v52 n3 Sum 1997. p411-430. (ISSN0020-7020).

CHILDREN--EMPLOYMENT--INDIA

"In India, there are an estimated fifteen million bonded child laborers, and possibly more. The debt that binds them to their employer is usually incurred by a parent, and ranges on average from 500 rupees to 7,500 rupees, depending on the industry and the age and skill of the child....As much as 85 percent of Indian bonded child labor is in agriculture." (p572-573)

Tucker, Lee. "Child Slaves in Modern India: The Bonded Labor Problem." Human Rights Quarterly v19 n3 Aug 1997. p572-629. (ISSN0275-0392).

CHILDREN--EMPLOYMENT--KENYA (v26)

CHILDREN--EMPLOYMENT--LATIN AMERICA (v26)

"A report prepared by the ILO [International Labour Organization] for the Cartagena Meeting estimated that no less than 15 million children work in Latin America, with approximately half of these child workers between the ages of six and 14 years old....Available statistics show that between 20 and 25 per cent of children between the ages of six and 14 are currently working in Latin America, a labour force representing on average just under 5 per cent of the economically active population in the region....According to the report, almost 60 per cent of the child labour force is concentrated in the agricultural sector. Children from rural areas, and girls in particular, usually begin working between the ages of five and seven....Hundreds of thousands of girls, approximately 10 per cent of the child labour force according to the report work long days as domestic workers in an environment where beatings, insults and sexual harassment are all too common." (p26)

"News Section: Most Intolerable Forms of Child Labour Targeted at the Cartagena Meeting." World of Work n21 Sep-Oct 1997. p25-26. (ISSN1020-0029).

CHILDREN--EMPLOYMENT--LAW AND LEGISLATION --INDIA

In India, "at the national level, from 1990 to 1993, 537 inspections were carried out under the Child Labour Act. These inspections turned up 1,203 violations. Inexplicably, only seven prosecutions were launched. At the state level, the years 1990 to 1993 produced 60,717 inspections in which 5,060 violations of the Act were detected; 772 of these 5,060 violations resulted in convictions. At the state level during the 1993 to 1994 year, the latest period for which data are available, 1,596 cases were filed against employers....Most offenders receive fines of five dollars or less--just a few hundred rupees, as opposed to the 10,000 to 20,000 fine stipulated by the [Child Labour] Act itself." (p624-625)

Tucker, Lee. "Child Slaves in Modern India: The Bonded Labor Problem." Human Rights Quarterly v19 n3 Aug 1997. p572-629. (ISSN0275-0392).

CHILDREN--EMPLOYMENT--PAKISTAN (v26)

CHILDREN--EMPLOYMENT--PAKISTAN--SIALKOT (v26)

CHILDREN--EMPLOYMENT--SOUTH ASIA

"Millions of children are enslaved throughout the world--15 million are in India alone....[In Pakistan,] it is not uncommon for children to work 14 to 18 hours a day, seven days a week....In Bangladesh, according to UNICEF [United Nations Children's Fund], under foreign pressure, the garment industry in 1993 released about 50,000 child laborers, mostly girls." (p10)

Barry, Skip. "Taking Aim at Child Slavery." Dollars and Sense n212 Jul-Aug 1997. p10. (ISSN0012-5245).

CHILDREN--EMPLOYMENT--TANZANIA (v26)

CHILDREN--EMPLOYMENT--TURKEY

According to "Child Labour in Turkey," an International Labor Organization report, "of the total number of persons employed in Turkey in 1994, one in 20--or about 4 million--are children between the ages of six and 14. Seventy-two per cent of these children worked and also attended schools, while 28 per cent worked but did not attend school. Among these child labourers, about 26 per cent worked in the agricultural, industrial, trade and service sectors, while about 74 per cent worked in domestic labour." (p11)

International Labor Organization. "Turkey: 'The Extent of the Child Labour Problem in the Country Should Not Be Underestimated.'" World of Work n20 Jun 1997. p11. (ISSN1020-0029).

CHILDREN--ERITREA--MORTALITY

In Eritrea, "mortality among children under age 5 from 1981 to 1985 was 185 deaths per 1,000 live births, compared with the rate of 136 deaths per 1,000 live births for 1991 to 1995. Child mortality also has declined substantially, but the current rate indicates that nearly one in seven children born in Eritrea dies before his or her fifth birthday." (p7)

"Spotlight: Eritrea." Population Today v25 n12 Dec 1997. p7. (ISSN0749-2448).

CHILDREN--GREAT BRITAIN--SOCIAL CONDITIONS (v26)

CHILDREN--HEALTH AND HYGIENE--UNITED STATES

"An American child drops out of school every 8 seconds; an American child is reported neglected or abused every 10 seconds, is arrested every 15 seconds, is born with a low birthweight every 2 minutes, born into poverty every 34 seconds...an American child is killed by gunfire every hour and a half and commits suicide every 4 hours. The costs to our society of these children who are being raised without adequate supervision, without adequate input, are simply enormous. BUSINESS WEEK estimated, in a study that it released recently, that we are spending $425 billion a year annually on crime in the United States. The total annual economic cost to society of drug abuse is $67 billion." (pS4953)

Kerry, John F. (Sen.-Mass.). "Concurrent Resolution on the Budget." Congressional Record. Daily ed. v143 n69 22 May 1997. pS4944-4994. section/page-level access: <http://

thomas.loc.gov/cgi-bin/query/R?r105:FLD001:S04952:> (ISSN0363-7239). (X1.1A.105/1).

The U.S. has "an infant mortality rate of 9.8 per 1,000 live births...compared with Canada's 7.2 per 1,000 live births. The U.S. rate of immunization for common childhood illnesses does not reach 60 percent while Canada's is 85 percent. Yet, the United States still spends over 50 percent more per capita for health care than Canada....The 17 percent of the population without insurance can seldom afford the out-of-pocket expenses of immunizations, well-child examinations, and screening procedures that have been traditionally performed in the private physician's office." (p20-21)

Carter, Michael A. "The Promise of Nurse Practitioners." Nursing Administration Quarterly v21 n4 Sum 1997. p19-24. (ISSN0363-9568).

CHILDREN--HEALTH AND HYGIENE--UNITED STATES --PUBLIC OPINION

In the U.S., "more than nine in ten parents with family incomes over $50,000 say their children are in excellent or very good health, compared with 78 percent of those with incomes below $25,000. White parents are more likely than black parents to report good health among their children--88 percent compared with 72 percent of blacks....For children aged 5 and under, 90 percent of the parents say they were in excellent or good health. This compares with 84 percent for 6-to-12-year-olds and 82 percent for 13-to-17-year-olds." (p29-30)

Stoneman, Bill. "Kaleidoscope: Risky Behavior and Children's Health." American Demographics v19 n7 Jul 1997. p29-30. article-level access: <http://www.demographics.com/publications/ad/97_ad/9707_ad/ad970721.htm> (ISSN0163-4089).

CHILDREN--IRAQ--MORTALITY (v26)

CHILDREN--MEDICAL CARE--UNITED STATES

"More than 1.3 million U.S. children did not receive necessary medical treatment in 1993 and another 2.7 million received care late due to concern over the high cost of medical services, a new report from the National Center for Health Statistics finds. In addition, more than 4.2 million children 17 years or younger were unable to receive needed dental care that year and more than 800,000 went without prescription medicine and eyeglasses." (p8)

"News and Resources: Many U.S. Children Lack Access to Health Care." Population Today v25 n10 Oct 1997. p8. (ISSN0749-2448).

CHILDREN--MEXICO--SOCIAL CONDITIONS (v26)

CHILDREN--MICHIGAN--DETROIT--SOCIAL CONDITIONS (v26)

CHILDREN--MICHIGAN--MORTALITY (v26)

CHILDREN--MICHIGAN--SOCIAL CONDITIONS (v26)

CHILDREN--PARENTAL SEX PREFERENCES

see SEX OF CHILDREN, PARENTAL PREFERENCES FOR

CHILDREN--PROTECTION

see CHILD WELFARE

CHILDREN--PUBLIC OPINION

According to an international Gallup poll, "approximately nine out of ten adults in Hungary, India and Taiwan agree with the statement that having children is necessary for fulfillment. The number agreeing is closer to eight in ten in Iceland, Thailand, Lithuania, and Singapore. Seven in ten feel this way in Guatemala, France and Colombia, with agreement closer to 60% in Mexico, Spain, Canada and Great Britain. The two countries where less than a majority of residents say having children is necessary for their personal fulfillment are Germany and the U.S. This statement is agreed with by only 49% of Germans and 46% of Americans."

Gallup Organization. "Global Study of Family Values: An International Gallup Poll: Family Values Differ Sharply around the World." Press Release 7 Nov 1997. document-level access: <http://www.gallup.com/poll/special/family.html>

CHILDREN--RWANDA--SOCIAL CONDITIONS

"The genocide of 1994--in which some 800,000 Rwandans died--left an estimated 400,000 children separated from their parents. While thousands have been reunited with their families, nearly 200,000 are still undocumented, and more than 8,000 remain crammed into orphanages and centers. Many of these children watched as their parents were slaughtered by immediate neighbors. UNICEF says two-thirds of the children have seen someone killed, and 80 percent have lost at least one family member....An estimated 85,000 Rwandan adolescents are caring for their younger sisters and brothers." (p18)

Kazickas, Jurate. "Opinion/Essays: Has the World Forgotten These Children?: Central Africa's Lost and Orphaned." The Christian Science Monitor v89 n241 7 Nov 1997. p18. The Christian Science Monitor search engine: <http://www.csmonitor.com/plweb-cgi/iops1.pl> To retrieve this article, enter the following search: ED=19971107 AND orphaned. In the "retrieved list," click the title that matches this record. (ISSN0882-7729).

CHILDREN--SOCIAL CONDITIONS (v26)

CHILDREN--TOBACCO USE

In Kenya, "a 1989 survey found that about 40 percent of primary school children are smokers. In Hong Kong, children as young as 7 are addicted. And in China, a 1988 survey of elementary school children in Beijing found that nearly half of them had tried smoking between ages 5 and 9, and that 28 percent of the boys and 3 percent of the girls had smoked during the past month. Assuming current trends continue, about 800 million of the world's 2 billion children are destined to become smokers, according to WHO, and tobacco will eventually kill at least one-third of them." (p24-25)

McGinn, Anne Platt. "The Nicotine Cartel." World Watch v10 n4 Jul-Aug 1997. p18-27. (ISSN0896-0615).

CHILDREN--UNITED STATES (v26)

CHILDREN--UNITED STATES--BOOKS AND READING (v26)

CHILDREN--UNITED STATES--COSTS (v26)

"According to the U.S. Department of Agriculture, the estimated cost for a husband-wife family earning less than $33,700 per year (lowest income) to raise an only child to age 18 in 1995 dollars is $132,544. This figure rises to $180,197 for families earning between $33,700 and $56,700 (middle income) and for families with incomes higher than $56,700 a year (highest income) the cost becomes $262,669." (p19)

Yavarkovsky, Judith. "Statistical Information, Please." Statistical Bulletin v78 n4 Oct-Dec 1997. p19. (ISSN0790-8334).

CHILDREN--UNITED STATES--MORTALITY (v26)

According to the 1997 KIDS COUNT DATA BOOK, issued by the Annie E. Casey Foundation, in the U.S., "the rate of infant deaths declined by 25 percent between 1985 and 1994, dropping from 10.6 deaths per 1,000 live births in 1985 to 8.0 in 1994....The child death rate (deaths from all causes for children 14 and younger) improved 15 percent nationwide between 1985 and 1994. All but seven states and the District of Columbia showed improvement in this area." (p3)

"Report Gauges U.S. Child Welfare." Population Today v25 n6 Jun 1997. p3. (ISSN0749-2448).

CHILDREN--UNITED STATES--POPULATION (v26)

CHILDREN--UNITED STATES--PUBLIC OPINION

In the U.S., "only 37 percent of the public think today's children aged 6 to 12 will make the world a better place when they're grown. Only 12 percent say children treat people with respect....[According to a Public Agenda survey,] only 22 percent of the public think parents who are good role models are 'very common.' Half of adults say parents spoil their children. Half also say parents fail to discipline their children....According to a survey by the Washington, D.C.-based Pew Research Center For The People & The Press, a 56 percent majority of women think today's mothers are doing a worse job of mothering than their own mothers did." (p12) "Just 32 percent of 12-to-17-year-olds surveyed by Public Agenda say parents who don't know how to communicate with kids are very common, compared with 51 percent of adults. Only 11 percent of kids think parents who value their jobs more than time with children are very common, versus 27 percent of adults who feel this way about mothers and 35 percent who feel this way about fathers." (p16)

Russell, Cheryl. "Trend Cop: What's Wrong with Kids?" American Demographics v19 n11 Nov 1997. p12,14-16. article-level access: <http://www.demographics.com/publications/ad/97_ad/9711_ad/ad97114.htm> (ISSN0163-4089).

CHILDREN--UNITED STATES--SEXUAL BEHAVIOR (v26)

CHILDREN--UNITED STATES--SOCIAL CONDITIONS (v26)

In the U.S., "the National Incidence Studies of Missing, Abducted, Runaway and Throwaway Children reports between 3,200 and 4,600 short-term, non-family abductions annually. Of that number, it is estimated that 70 percent of those child victims are sexually assaulted. The 1995 UCR [Uniform Crime Reports] states that approximately 1,265 children under the age of 18 were murdered. The National Crime Information Center has on file approximately 71,000 missing children, all potential victims of sexual abuse or exploitation." (p1159)

U.S. Dept. of Justice. "Departments of Commerce, Justice, And State, The Judiciary...Approp. for 1998 (Part 2)." Hearing. U.S. House. Committee on Appropriations. Washington, D.C. : GPO, 1997. (ISBN0160549094). (Y4.Ap6/1:C73/2/997/pt.2).

"In 1960 children accounted for 36% of all Americans; in 1990 they were 26%, and by 2010 only 23% of the population will be children (U.S. Department of Commerce, Bureau of the Census, No. 1018, 1989)....Between 1970 and 1990, the proportion of mothers with children under age six who were working or looking for work rose from 32 to 58%. In 1990, over 74% of women with children between the ages of 6 to 13 were working or looking for work (Cherlin, 1988). Children today are the poorest Americans; one in five lives in a family below the poverty level (U.S. Department of Commerce, Bureau of the Census, No. 169, 1989). Thirty-two million Americans, including 8.3 million children under age 18, have no form of health insurance coverage (National Commission on Children, 1991)....Since 1981, there has been an 80% rise in the proportion of children receiving psychological assistance annually (Zill & Schoenborn, 1990)." (p429-430)

Chung, Woo Sik/Pardeck, John T. "Explorations in a Proposed National Policy for Children and Families." Adolescence v32 n126 Sum 1997. p429-436. (ISSN0001-8449).

In the U.S., "there are more than 500,000 children in foster care. In Missouri, there are 10,361 children in the foster care system. Since 1975, the number of reported incidents of abuse and neglect has increased from less than 10,000 to 52,964 in 1995, an all-time high...." (pS9653)

Bond, Christopher S. (Sen.-Mo.). "Statements on Introduced Bills and Joint Resolutions." Congressional Record. Daily ed. v143 n125 18 Sep 1997. pS9637-9659. section/page-level access: <http://thomas.loc.gov/cgi-bin/query/R?r105:FLD001:S09653:> (ISSN0363-7239). (X1.1A.105/1).

"Following are some social and economic indicators for the...48.3 million [children], or 7 in 10, who lived with two parents....For children living with both parents: 1994 median family income was $46,195. Eleven percent were poor. More than 8 out of 10 lived with at least one sibling. Eighty-six percent had at least one parent with a high school diploma; 29 percent had at least one parent with a bachelor's degree or more. Eighty-five percent had at least one parent who was working. Less than 3 out of 10 lived in rental housing."

U.S. Census Bureau. Economic and Statistics Administration. "Census Facts for Father's Day." Fact Sheet 9 Jun 1997. document-level access: <http://www.census.gov/Press-Release/fs97-06.html>

In the U.S., "according to the Department of Health and Human Services, an incredible 1.2 million children are now taken from their parents by the government every year--either temporarily or permanently. In 90%+ of the cases, parents whose children are taken are never convicted or even charged with any offenses....There are thousands of cases in which children in government 'care' are beaten, raped, and even contract sexually-transmitted diseases." (p11)

Wollstein, Jarret B. "A Liberty Charter to Stop Violent Government Attacks on Our Lives and Property." Freedom Network News n49 Sep 1997. p11-12.

According to the 1997 KIDS COUNT DATA BOOK, issued by the Annie E. Casey Foundation, in the U.S., "forty-one percent of fourth graders scored below the basic reading level in 1994 and 38 percent scored below the basic math level in 1996. In addition, 40 percent of the nation's three- to five-year-olds were not enrolled in nursery school or kindergarten in 1993, despite evidence that preschool helps prepare children for school....In 1994, 15 percent of our nation's children were living with parents who were high school dropouts. Additionally, 9.8 percent were living in a neighborhood where more than one-quarter of 16- to 19-year-olds were high school dropouts in 1990." (p3)

"Report Gauges U.S. Child Welfare." Population Today v25 n6 Jun 1997. p3. (ISSN0749-2448).

CHILDREN--VACCINATION

see VACCINATION OF CHILDREN

CHILDREN, AFRO-AMERICAN

see AFRO-AMERICAN CHILDREN

CHILDREN, FOSTER

see FOSTER CHILDREN

CHILDREN, HOMELESS

see HOMELESS CHILDREN

CHILDREN, POOR

see POOR CHILDREN

CHILDREN, PRESCHOOL

see PRESCHOOL CHILDREN

CHILDREN, SCHOOL

see SCHOOL CHILDREN

CHILDREN AND WAR (v26)

"According to the most recent annual human rights report of the U.S. State Department, 'an estimated quarter of a million children, even as young as age 5, have been conscripted to serve as soldiers in dozens of armed conflicts around the world....'" (p1) In Afghanistan, "the proportion of soldiers who are children is believed to have risen in recent years from roughly 30 to at least 45 per cent. Agencies such as UNICEF estimate that more than 200,000 children have been recruited into armies over the past decade....Of the approximately 60,000 personnel in the Salvadoran military ex-soldiers estimate that about 80%, 48,000, were under 18 years of age." (p2) "In late 1996 children below 18 years of age were reportedly participating in 33 ongoing or recently ended conflicts, according to Radda Barnen. In 26 of the conflicts, almost 80%, the children involved were under 15, the current minimum age limit stipulated in international law for participation in hostilities." (p3)

"The Invisible Soldiers: Child Combatants." Defense Monitor v26 n4 Jul 1997. p1-7. (ISSN0195-6450).

"An estimated quarter of a million children are soldiers, and children under 18 years of age were among the combatants in 33 current or recent conflicts. Child combatants under 15 years of age fought in 26 of these conflicts. Project Ploughshares, a Canadian research group, reports that children participated in fighting in more than 80 percent of the countries at war in 1995." (p12)

Renner, Michael. "Small Arms, Big Impact: The Next Challenge of Disarmament." Worldwatch Paper n137 Oct 1997. p5-77.

CHILDREN AND WAR--RWANDA (v26)

CHILDREN OF MINORITIES--MASSACHUSETTS --BOSTON--SOCIAL CONDITIONS (v26)

CHILDREN OF MINORITIES--UNITED STATES --POPULATION (v26)

CHILDREN OF PRISONERS--UNITED STATES

"Most of the information known about children of people in the criminal justice system is obtained from surveys of incarcerated populations, the majority of whom--78% of women and 64% of men--are parents (USDJ [United States Department of Justice], 1994). A 1991 study of state prison inmates found that 67% of the women and 56% of the men surveyed were parents of over 826,000 children under 18 years of age (USDJ, 1993). A 1989 survey of 5,675 women incarcerated in 424 local jails showed that 68% had a child or children under 18 (USDJ, 1992). Six to nine percent of incarcerated women are pregnant when they enter prison (USDJ, 1994; Bloom and Steinhart, 1993), and about 15% have had a baby within the previous year (McCall et al., 1985). A 1991 National Council on Crime and Delinquency survey of mothers in jails and prisons in eight states and the District of Columbia found that 439 respondents had an average of 2.6 children each (Bloom and Steinhart, 1993)....All told, about 10 million children in the U.S. are affected by current or past parental involvement with the criminal justice system." (p155)

Reed, Diane F./Reed, Edward L. "Children of Incarcerated Parents." Social Justice v24 n3 Fall 1997. p152-169. (ISSN0094-7571).

"Of the approximately 1.5 million children of U.S. prisoners, about 1.2 million, or 87%, of children of male inmates are in the care of their biological mothers (USDJ [United States Department of Justice], 1993), while only about 20%, or 29,000 children, of incarcerated mothers are in the care of their biological fathers (USDJ, 1993; American Correctional Association, 1990). This leaves over a quarter of a million children of incarcerated parents in the care of grandparents, other relatives, friends, or foster care....Studies of prison and jail inmates have found that about 70% of female inmates with children under age 18 had lived with their children prior to incarceration, compared to about 50% of males (USDJ, 1993; 1992). A 1991 survey of mothers in jails and prisons in eight states and the District of Columbia found that 17% of children whose mothers were incarcerated were living with their fathers, nearly half (47%) with their grandparents, 22% with relatives or friends, and about 7% had been placed in foster care (Bloom and Steinhart, 1993). The 1989 national 'Women in Jail' study reported that half the minor children of incarcerated women were living with their grandparents, 23.5% were in their father's care, and 27% were living with other relatives or friends. About eight percent were in foster or other institutional care (USDJ, 1992)." (p156)

Reed, Diane F./Reed, Edward L. "Children of Incarcerated Parents." Social Justice v24 n3 Fall 1997. p152-169. (ISSN0094-7571).

In the U.S., "the most recent survey of state prison inmates revealed that while most parents of minor children had some form of contact, 28% of mothers and 40% of fathers reported never having called or received a telephone call from their children, 21% of mothers and 32% of fathers never sent or received any mail from their children, and fully 52% of mothers and 55% of fathers were never once visited by their children (USDJ [United States Department of Justice], 1994). Bloom and Steinhart (1993) found similarly disturbing trends in the frequency of visits from children during the mother's incarceration. Over half (54%) of the 439 mothers in that study reported that their children had never visited them in jail or prison. Seventeen percent were visited by their children once a month, 12% every four to six months, and seven percent once a year or less. Only 10% saw their children once or more a week." (p158)

Reed, Diane F./Reed, Edward L. "Children of Incarcerated Parents." Social Justice v24 n3 Fall 1997. p152-169. (ISSN0094-7571).

CHILDREN'S DAY CARE CENTERS

see DAY CARE CENTERS

CHILE--ECONOMIC CONDITIONS (v26)

Chile's "growth rate, which last year reached 7 percent, is the highest in Latin America. In 1996, inflation fell, real wages rose 4.5 percent, and the country's savings rate now stands at 30 percent." (p8)

Drosdoff, Daniel. "The Region: Reform: Same Tune, Different Steps." IDB v24 n9-10 Sep-Oct 1997. p8-9. (ISSN0145-2274).

"In nearly every year from 1986 through estimates for 1996,...[Chile] has enjoyed higher real growth than any other country in the region and has the most dynamic export sector....In the period 1975 through 1993, the number of exporters grew from roughly 500 to 5,500, the number of products exported increased from about 500 to approximately 3,500, and the number of countries to which Chile exported went from 50 to more than 130....By 1995, total savings (as a percent of GDP) had reached 25% of GDP...." (p180)

Whitney, Peter. "Review Essay: Economics of Modern Latin America: Books to Explain the Present and Bury the Past." Journal of Interamerican Studies & World Affairs v39 n2 Sum 1997. p159-185. (ISSN0022-1937).

CHILE--UNITED STATES--ECONOMIC CONDITIONS

"Chile's private savings rate is 26 percent of GDP, compared with 4 percent in the United States. The infusion of capital into the private sector has contributed in large part to Chile's phenomenal 7 percent annual economic growth rate over the past 10 years, double...[the U.S.'s]....[In Chile,] the average rate of return on investment has been more than 14 percent per year....The typical retiree is receiving a benefit equal to nearly 80 percent of his average annual income over the last 10 years of his working life, almost double the US replacement value." (p5)

Tanner, Michael D. "Mini-Forum: Social Security Reform: A New Social Security System for the New Century." Public Manager v26 n2 Sum 1997. p3-6. (ISSN1061-7639).

CHILE PEPPER INDUSTRY--NEW MEXICO

"Chile pepper production in New Mexico, the largest producing State, increased 30 percent in 1996 compared with the weather-reduced output of 1995. The value of the State's crop increased 46 percent to $65 million. Although much smaller than New Mexico's industry, California and Texas are also important producers of chile peppers. Per capita use of chile peppers was estimated at 6.4 pounds per person (fresh-weight basis) in 1996." (p5)

U.S. Dept. of Agriculture. Economic Research Service. "Summary." Vegetables and Specialties Situation and Outlook Yearbook Jul 1997. p3-5.

CHINA--ARMED FORCES

"China already has the world's largest military at 2.9 million and is taking steps to enhance its force projection capabilities, including the acquisition of a blue water navy and a 21st century air force....While China's official military budget is roughly $8 billion, Beijing effectively conceals military spending through off-budget funding and revenue. Reliable estimates place China's military spending from 4 to 10 times the official budget. Russia alone, has made over $7 billion in arm sales to China since 1990, and hundreds, perhaps thousands, of underemployed Russian nuclear engineers have been hired by China in the last several years....The People's Liberation Army of China, has 20,000 companies, business enterprises, that funnel revenue into the military's coffers." (pS7052)

Ashcroft, John (Sen.-Mo.). "Chinese Military Expansion and United States National Security." Congressional Record. Daily ed. v143 n96 9 Jul 1997. pS7052-7091. section/page-level access: <http://thomas.loc.gov/cgi-bin/query/R?r105:FLD001:S07052:> (ISSN0363-7239). (X1.1A.105/1).

"China is a member of the exclusive nuclear club, possessing the world's third-largest nuclear arsenal. It also maintains the world's largest standing army, with 3 million soldiers....Using the official exchange rate of 8.29 renminbi to the dollar, China's announced defense budget for the 1996-1997 fiscal year stands at $9.72 billion. The actual amount devoted to military spending is generally estimated to be at least four to five times greater than an official defense budget; this means that China's total military spending for the 1996-1997 fiscal year is between $38.6 billion and $48.25 billion....As much as 30 percent of China's military expenditures are used to subsidize inefficient military industrial enterprises...." (p247)

Kim, Samuel S. "China as a Great Power." Current History v96 n611 Sep 1997. p246-251. (ISSN0011-3530).

CHINA--ARMED FORCES--APPROPRIATIONS AND EXPENDITURES (v26)

"China continues to claim that its defense expenditure is but a fraction of Western estimates. In 1997 this amounted to $9.7 billion, although most credible Western estimates place it at four or five times this figure. It is hardly believable that the PLA [People's Liberation Army] could maintain a force of 2.9 million under arms (and a nearly 1 million strong paramilitary People's Armed Police and a 1.2 million reserve force), while financing an across-the-board modernization program (including expensive arms purchases from Russia and other countries) on $9.7 billion." (p243)

Shambaugh, David. "The United States and China: Cooperation or Confrontation?" Current History v96 n611 Sep 1997. p241-245. (ISSN0011-3530).

CHINA--COMMERCE (v26)

"China's exports only grew by 1.5 percent to $151 billion in 1996. Imports grew by 5.1 percent and reached $139 billion in 1996....Although exports grew slower than imports, China still ran a $12.3 billion foreign trade surplus in 1996, which was the third consecutive year for China to have an external trade surplus. China's foreign exchange reserves reached $105 billion at the end of 1996, $31.4 billion more than at the beginning of the year." (p3)

Diao, Xinshen/U.S. Dept. of Agriculture. Economic Research Service. "China Controlled Inflation in 1996." China: International Agriculture and Trade Reports Situation and Outlook Series Jun 1997. p3-5.

CHINA--COMMERCE--EUROPE--UNITED STATES

"As Sino-Hong Kong trade slipped in 1996, the United States became China's second largest trade partner. In 1996, Sino-U.S. trade reached $63.5 billion according to U.S. Census trade statistics, while the U.S. trade deficit with China widened to 1995's $40 billion. While EU-bound China exports rose by 3.6 percent from 1995 to $19.83 billion, imports from the EU fell by 6.5 percent to $19.87 billion in 1996. By reducing its imports, China balanced its trade with the EU in 1996. In 1995, China had a $2-billion trade deficit with the EU." (p4)

Diao, Xinshen/U.S. Dept. of Agriculture. Economic Research Service. "China Controlled Inflation in 1996." China: International Agriculture and Trade Reports Situation and Outlook Series Jun 1997. p3-5.

CHINA--COMMERCE--HONG KONG

"In the second quarter of 1997, 48% of Hong Kong's total exports to the mainland of China were for outward processing; the figure was 72% for domestic exports and 45% for re-exports, according to statistics released...by the Census and Statistics Department. On the other hand, 80% of Hong Kong's imports from the mainland of China were related to outward processing. Over the same period, 87% of Hong Kong's re-exports of mainland origin to other places were produced through outward processing in the mainland of China. The corresponding proportions for exports to the mainland in the second quarter of 1996 were 48% for total exports, 72% for domestic exports and 45% for re-exports; whilst proportions for imports from the mainland and re-exports of mainland origin to other places were 80% and 85% respectively. In the first half of 1997, 48% of Hong Kong's total exports to the mainland were for outward processing; the figure was 72% for domestic exports and 45% for re-exports. On the other hand, 78% of Hong Kong's imports from the mainland were related to outward processing."

Hong Kong. Census and Statistics Department. "Statistics on Trade Involving Outward Processing in China." Press Release 11 Nov 1997. document-level access: <http://www.info.gov.hk/censtatd/hkstat/press/t72q97.htm>

"As of 1995, China's transhipment of goods through Hong Kong amounted to some 37% each way. China enjoyed a surplus in its visible trade with Hong Kong of about USD [U.S. dollars] 9 billion. Hong Kong's contribution to utilization of contracted foreign capital in China was also substantial, as more than half of the total foreign investment in China came from Hong Kong and an estimated 20% of total foreign loans derived from Hong Kong either as direct lender or centre of syndication....A total of 3 million workers in Guangdong, a Chinese province adjacent to Hong Kong, are working for Hong Kong employers. This figure exceeds the total labour force in Hong Kong....A recent estimate revealed that 40% of Hong Kong's investment in China actually comes from China-controlled enterprises in the territory." (p235)

Kuan, Hsin-Chi. "Does Hong Kong Have a Future?" Security Dialogue v28 n2 Jun 1997. p233-236. (ISSN0967-0106).

CHINA--COMMERCE--JAPAN

In 1996, "Japan remained China's largest trade partner for the fourth consecutive year. Sino-Japan bilateral trade volume hit a record $60 billion, or 20.7 percent of China's external trade in 1996. China shipped $30.9 billion worth of commodities to Japan in 1996, up 8.4 percent from 1995, while its imports from Japan amounted to $29.2 billion, almost the same as in 1995." (p4)

Diao, Xinshen/U.S. Dept. of Agriculture. Economic Research Service. "China Controlled Inflation in 1996." China: International Agriculture and Trade Reports Situation and Outlook Series Jun 1997. p3-5.

CHINA--COMMERCE--RUSSIA

"By 1993 Russia had become China's seventh largest trading partner and enjoyed a two to one trade surplus....After the successes of 1993, trade between the two countries fell away. In 1993 it amounted to US $7.7 billion, but in 1995 it billion...." (p18)

Ferdinand, Peter. "Politics and Society: China and Russia: A Strategic Partnership?" China Review n8 Aut-Win 1997. p16-21. (ISSN1359-5091).

CHINA--COMMERCE--UNITED STATES

"Since economic reforms were initiated in the early 1980s, China's agricultural imports and exports increased rapidly from $8.7 billion in 1986 to $24 billion in 1995. U.S. agricultural exports to China rose from $.06 to $2.6 billion during this same time period. In 1996, U.S. exports were $2.1 billion and imports $600 million....Corn imports, which had increased to 4.3 million tons in 1994/95, fell to 50,000 tons in 1996/97." (p473)

U.S. Dept. of Agriculture. "Agriculture, Rural Development, Food and Drug Administration...Approp. for 1998 (Part 4)." Hearing. U.S. House. Committee on Appropriations. Washington, D.C. : GPO, 1997. (ISBN0160551560). (Y4.Ap6/1:Ag8/997/pt.4).

U.S. exports to China "declined 25 percent to $1.8 billion in fiscal 1996....The volume of U.S. exports to China in fiscal 1996 declined 39 percent for wheat (from 3.8 to 2.3 billion tons) and 63 percent for corn (from 4 to 1.5 billion tons)....Bulk commodities accounted for 81 percent of China's purchases of U.S. agricultural products in fiscal 1996; intermediate and consumer-ready products accounted for 14 and 5 percent, respectively." (p10)

Huang, Sophia Wu/U.S. Dept. of Agriculture. Economic Research Service. "U.S. Agricultural Exports to APEC Region at Another Record." APEC: International Agriculture and Trade Reports Situation and Outlook Series Aug 1997. p9-12.

"China's economy is smaller than California's and consumes only 1.8 percent of U.S. exports....In 1991, the U.S. trade deficit with China was less than $13 billion. This year, it's expected to top $50 billion." (p14 secA)

Murray, Michael J. "China Doesn't Deserve Most Favored Nation Status." Ann Arbor News 12 Jun 1997. p14 secA.

"The United States ran a $39.5 billion trade deficit with China in 1996, buying five times as much from China as it sold to China....American exports were static at a mere $11.8 billion. This amounted to barely two percent of our total exports." (p48)

Hawkins, William R. "Vital Signs: Foreign Affairs: Declaring China 'Normal.'" Chronicles v21 n8 Aug 1997. p47-48. (ISSN0887-5731).

"Less than 2 percent of United States exports went to China last year. America sold more goods and services individually to Belgium, Brazil, and Singapore than to the People's Republic of China. Meanwhile, the United States took more than 30 percent of China's exports creating a $39.5 billion merchandise trade deficit. This represents a threefold increase since 1990. A 200-percent increase in just 6 years!...The Commerce Department reported that our trade gap is widening--fully 41 percent higher in the first 4 months of this year than in 1996." (pS6072)

Ashcroft, John (Sen.-Mo.). "Communist China: America's Most Favored Nation." Congressional Record. Daily ed. v143 n88-89 23 Jun 1997. pS6072-6074. section/page-level access: <http://thomas.loc.gov/cgi-bin/query/R?r105:FLD001:S06072:> (ISSN0363-7239). (X1.1A.105/1).

U.S. "exports to China increased 13 percent last year to almost $12 billion, and goods shipped from Michigan rose 51 percent to $211 million. But imports soared, leaving the United States with a $39.5-billion trade deficit." (p3 secB)

Knox, Noelle. "Inside Business: U.S. Keeps Trade Open with China." Detroit News 25 Jun 1997. p3 secB.

CHINA--ECONOMIC CONDITIONS (v26)

"Based on the purchasing power parity, China's labor productivity is about one tenth that of the US in 1993-94." (p148) "In most market economies ('steady state'), state owned enterprises account for 5% to 15% of GNP and 10% to 20% of investment..., while in China the corresponding figures are 30% to 40% and 55% to 65%, respectively....China's government budgetary expenditure/GDP ratio remained above 25% from the 1950s to the 1970s. It dropped to around 20% in the 1980s, and below 20% in the early 1990s. It is expected to go up after the tax reform in 1994 when the ratio dropped to about 15%." (p149) "According to the purchasing power parity, China's export-GDP ratio is still less than 5%, which is below that of the US (about 7%) and Japan (about 10%)....From 1978 to 1995, the labor force grew at about 3% annually, which is about twice as high as the population growth rate....In recent years...China's education expenditure/GDP is around 3%, which is lower than the average of developing countries (around 4%)....In recent years,...[the national savings rate] increased to around 35%-40% (World Bank, 1994)." (p150)

Li, Shuhe. "The Search for Determinants of Catching Up: Theory, The East Asian Experience and the Chinese Case." China Economic Review v8 n2 Fall 1997. p137-155. (ISSN1043-951X).

China's "Gross Domestic Product (GDP) increased by 9.7 percent in 1996....The officially announced inflation rate (measured by retail prices) was 6.1 percent in 1996....By mid-1996, the growth in the retail price index, the most often quoted number for inflation, dropped from double-digit levels to 7.1 percent....In 1996, its fixed investment with respect to GDP was about 35 percent, while the world average rate was around 20 percent....In 1996, China's urban and rural resident domestic savings deposits increased by 30 percent, equivalent to 13 percent of gross domestic products....Growth of government revenues was faster than the growth of the expenditures by 2 percentage points in 1996....The government deficit was 54.8 billion renminbi (RMB) yuan in 1996, smaller than in 1995. The U.S. dollar/RMB exchange rate in 1996 was 8.3 which was the same as the previous year." (p3-4)

Diao, Xinshen/U.S. Dept. of Agriculture. Economic Research Service. "China Controlled Inflation in 1996." China: International Agriculture and Trade Reports Situation and Outlook Series Jun 1997. p3-5.

"Deregulation and the marketization of the Chinese economy has led to unprecedented improvements in the living standards--and purchasing power--of ordinary Chinese. In the past 15 years, China's per capita GDP has more than tripled, from $889 to $2,923, and is forecast to be $4,190 in 2000. Not uncoincidentally, China's demand for United States exports has increased in similarly substantial leaps. United States goods and services exports destined for China have increased from $3.7 million in 1980 to $11.1 billion in 1995. China is now America's fifth largest trading partner." (pS10893)

Lieberman, Joseph I. (Sen.-Conn.). "Statements on Introduced Bills and Joint Resolutions." Congressional Record. Daily ed. v143 n142 21 Oct 1997. pS10882-10897. section/page-level access: <http://thomas.loc.gov/cgi-bin/query/R?r105:FLD001:S10892:> (ISSN0363-7239). (X1.1A.105/1).

"China's external debt stands at about $120 billion and is still growing. While China has had the fastest-growing economy in the world--its total output quadrupled between 1978 and 1995--its external trade dependence, defined as the sum of imports and exports as a percentage of GNP, rose dramatically during the same period, from less than 10 percent to more than 56 percent (Beijing's foreign trade increased more than 13 times during the same period, from $21 billion to $280 billion)....China registered a $39.5 billion surplus in its bilateral trade with the United States in 1996...." (p247)

Kim, Samuel S. "China as a Great Power." Current History v96 n611 Sep 1997. p246-251. (ISSN0011-3530).

In China, "G.D.P. per capita has increased by an average of about 6.8 percent per year from 1978 to 1995--bringing a doubling every ten years....With 1.23 billion people, China has a labor surplus economy....September's issue of the Beijing magazine LIAOWANG ('Outlook') reported that more than 10 million urban workers have been laid off on partial wages or none at all, and many retired workers are not getting their pensions on time." (p12) "The government controlled more than one-third of China's G.D.P. back in the seventies but has allowed its share to fall to less than 11 percent now (in the United States, about a third of G.D.P. is spent by governments at all levels)." (p14)

Riskin, Carl. "Articles: China: Behind the Silk Curtain: We Need Summitry beyond Sanctimony." Nation v265 n15 10 Nov 1997. p11-12,14,17. (ISSN0027-8378).

"China's drive to replace Marxism with free markets has barely touched huge swaths of the economy. State-owned companies still employ roughly 2 out of every 3 urban workers and are managed by party apparatchiks rather than the business-savvy entrepreneurs who run the best private firms. China's curious hybrid of socialist and capitalist economics has created some schizophrenic statistics: The economy has been growing at about 10 percent annually for nearly two decades, but state firms are running into the red faster than ever. While China now has 1 million millionaires, half a billion peasants still earn less than $1 per day. The fledgling private sector is expanding, but as many as 30 million laborers laid off by the state still can't find jobs...." (p9)

Platt, Kevin. "International: China Begins to Feel Economic Shock Waves." The Christian Science Monitor v90 n6 3 Dec 1997. p9. The Christian Science Monitor search engine: <http://www.csmonitor.com/plweb-cgi/iops1.pl> To retrieve this article, enter the following search: ED=19971203 AND waves. In the "retrieved list," click the title that matches this record. (ISSN0882-7729).

"More than 70 percent of China's annual imports and exports, which now total more than $300 billion, go through Hong Kong. Last year, foreign direct investment into China was $42 billion, but 60 percent of that came from Hong Kong companies. Over 70 large Chinese corporations now have regional headquarters in Hong Kong; and Chinese companies have invested well over $30 billion in the territory." (p19)

Greenberg, Gary. "Opinion/Essays: Hong Kong's Role as China's Wall Street." The Christian Science Monitor v89 n179 11 Aug 1997. p19. The Christian Science Monitor search engine: <http://www.csmonitor.com/plweb-cgi/iops1.pl> To retrieve this article, enter the following search: ED=19970811 AND street. In the "retrieved list," click the title that matches this record. (ISSN0882-7729).

"One hundred million unemployed Chinese crowd their cities, looking for work at less than a dollar a day." (p1) "Economist Philip Braverman says a Chinese trade official recently told him that when 100 million unemployed Chinese in the cities find work, 100 million in the countryside will take their place." (p8)

Francis, David R. "Global Report: Falling Prices: Cheap Labor Ripples through Global Economy." The Christian Science Monitor v89 n186 20 Aug 1997. p1,8. The Christian Science Monitor search engine: <http://www.csmonitor.com/plweb-cgi/iops1.pl> To retrieve this article, enter the following search: ED=19970820 AND economy. In the "retrieved list," click the title that matches this record. (ISSN0882-7729).

CHINA--EMIGRATION AND IMMIGRATION

"By 1995, sixty thousand Qingtian Chinese had left their native country and were dispersed to 50 different countries, with 80% being in Europe. These massive population movements took place from Qingtian country, which in 1987 had only 480,000 inhabitants, and from a small number of villages primarily in the southeastern part of the county. By comparison, the number of emigrants from neighbouring Wencheng county, with a population in 1994 of 370,000, was only 5,577 by 1984 with migration from only a few villages to 27 different countries." (p27)

Thuno, Mette. "Society: Far Away from Home." China Review n7 Sum 1997. p24-27. (ISSN1359-5091).

CHINA--EMPLOYMENT--RURAL CONDITIONS (v26)

CHINA--ENVIRONMENTAL ASPECTS (v26)

CHINA--EUROPE--POPULATION (v26)

CHINA--INDIA--ECONOMIC CONDITIONS

In terms of population, "China leads with 1.2 billion, and India is second with 929 million (1995 figures)....China's economic growth rate in 1995 was 8.9 percent....[According to a World Bank report, India's] 'growth accelerated to 5 percent in 1992-94, 6 percent in 1994-95, and an estimated 7 percent in 1995-96.'...Foreign direct investment in...[China] grew from $2.3 billion in 1987 to $37 billion in 1995. In 1995-96, India's foreign direct investment was only $2 billion." (p19)

Newsom, David D. "Opinion/Essays: Democratic India versus Disciplined China." The Christian Science Monitor v89 n156 9 Jul 1997. p19. The Christian Science Monitor search engine: <http://www.csmonitor.com/plweb-cgi/iops1.pl> To retrieve this article, enter the following search: ED=19970709 AND china. In the "retrieved list," click the title that matches this record. (ISSN0882-7729).

CHINA--POLITICS AND GOVERNMENT--UNITED STATES--PUBLIC OPINION

According to a Gallup poll in the U.S., "only 26% agree that China's government is becoming more democratic and allowing more freedoms for its citizens. Just 34% say that China's economy is becoming more like the kind of free market system found in the U.S. and other Western nations. There is no clear-cut majority opinion when Americans are asked whether China's wealth and economic power makes it more of a threat to the U.S. or more of an opportunity for the U.S. About 45% choose each of these alternatives. A majority of Americans, 54%, say that the Chinese government attempted to influence the outcome of the U.S. elections last year by donating money to the Democratic party. Twenty eight percent say that China did not, while 18% say they are unsure."

Newport, Frank/Gallup Organization. "Americans Support Linking U.S.-China Relations to Human Rights." Press Release 31 Oct 1997. document-level access: <http://www.gallup.com/poll/news/971031.html>

CHINA--POPULATION (v26)

CHINA--RELIGION

Luo Guanzong, chairman of the government's Three-Self Patriotic Movement of Protestant Churches in China, tells foreign journalists, 'there are over 12,000 churches nationwide'--14 times more than when Mao Zedong's regime took over in 1949. The state has approved 70,000 places of worship, including 10,000 Buddhist temples, 30,000 mosques, and 1,000 Taoist temples, according to the Religious Affairs Bureau (RAB), the government body that oversees China's five recognized faiths--Islam, Buddhism, Taoism, Catholicism, and Protestantism. In all, the RAB says, more than 100 million people ascribe to state-authorized religions." (p41)

Palmer, Brian. "World Report: Caesar vs. Christ in China." U.S. News & World Report v123 n5 4 Aug 1997. p41-42. article-level access: <http://www.usnews.com/usnews/issue/970804/4CHUR.HTM> (ISSN0041-5537).

CHINA--UNITED STATES--FOREIGN RELATIONS--PUBLIC OPINION

In a U.S. Gallup poll, "a little more than half of those polled--

55%--say that there should be a link between U.S.-China trade policy and human rights in China, but more than a third--36%--say that there should not....72% of those polled say that the U.S. taking a strong stand on China's sale of nuclear weapons internationally is more important than maintaining good relations with China. 65% say that taking a stance against China's forceful take over of Taiwan is more important than maintaining good relations. 59% say that taking a stance on human rights is more important. 51% say that taking a stance of treatment of Christians within China is more important. 37% say that taking a stand on the status of Tibet is more important (although almost one out of five don't have an opinion on this issue either way...)."

Newport, Frank/Gallup Organization. "Americans Support Linking U.S.-China Relations to Human Rights." Press Release 31 Oct 1997. document-level access: <http://www.gallup.com/poll/news/971031.html>

CHINESE--NEW YORK (N.Y.) (v26)

CHINESE LANGUAGE--CANADA

"Chinese has become the third-most-spoken language in Canada after English and French, according to statistics from the 1996 census released [in December 1997]....The census found that between 1991 and 1996, the number of people who reported Chinese as their mother tongue increased by 42 percent to 736,000 people, representing 2.6 percent of Canada's 28 million population. This is a big jump since 1971 when Chinese speakers were only 0.4 percent of the population." (p1) In Toronto, "the Chinese-speaking population, according to the latest census, is 294,872." (p8)

Langan, Fred. "Canada's Chinese Speakers on a Roll as Numbers Rise." The Christian Science Monitor v90 n16 17 Dec 1997. p1,8. The Christian Science Monitor search engine: <http://www.csmonitor.com/plweb-cgi/iops1.pl> To retrieve this article, enter the following search: ED=19971217 AND rise. In the "retrieved list," click the title that matches this record. (ISSN0882-7729).

CHINOOK SALMON--SNAKE RIVER (WYO.-WASH.)

Rob Jones, a regional spokesman for the National Marine Fisheries Service, says that in 1990, "only 78 adult fall chinook [salmon] made it past the uppermost dam on the lower Snake River. Last year, 639 fall chinook made the passage, and this year, he says, the number should be higher. NMFS projected that 58,000 spring chinook would come into the upper Columbia this year, but data suggest that the actual number will be closer to 100,000." (p413)

Di Silvestro, Roger. "Steelhead Trout: Factors in Protection." BioScience v47 n7 Jul-Aug 1997. p409-414. (ISSN0006-3568).

CHLAMYDIA--UNITED STATES (v26)

CHLAMYDIA INFECTIONS--UNITED STATES

In the U.S., "an estimated 4 million new [chlamydia] infections [occur]...every year. In fact, in 1995, the first year that it was nationally reportable, chlamydia led the list of infections reported to the National Notifiable Disease Surveillance System (NNDSS)....Approximately 75 percent of infected women and up to half of infected men have no symptoms or such mild ones that they will not likely seek treatment." (p18)

DeLisle, Susan. "Preserving Reproductive Choice: Preventing STD-Related Infertility in Women." SIECUS Report v25 n3 Feb-Mar 1997. p18-21. (ISSN0091-3995).

CHLAMYDIA INFECTIONS--UNITED STATES--WOMEN

"Of the estimated 2.6 million American women with chlamydia, 20 to 40 percent of those with untreated infections will develop pelvic inflammatory disease (PID)....In one study, 50 percent of women seeking infertility treatment and with confirmed tubal occlusion reported no history of PID yet showed serological evidence of prior genital chlamydia infection....Up to 50 percent of infants born to mothers with active chlamydial infection contract congenital eye infections, while almost one in five develop neonatal pneumonia." (p18)

DeLisle, Susan. "Preserving Reproductive Choice: Preventing STD-Related Infertility in Women." SIECUS Report v25 n3 Feb-Mar 1997. p18-21. (ISSN0091-3995).

CHLOROFLUOROCARBONS--CANADA--UNITED STATES

The illegal international trade of chlorofluorocarbons "has been estimated to be worth $300 million (U.S.) a year. Lawmakers in the U.S. unintentionally stimulated the black market by slapping a $6.25 (U.S.) surcharge on every pound of CFCs sold, making cheaper, smuggled CFCs a valuable commodity....A cylinder containing 30 pounds of CFCs would now fetch about $620 in the U.S. In Canada, one Toronto distributor says a cylinder of the same size has jumped in price from $85 to $295 in the past two years....It takes one to two pounds of CFCs to fill an automobile air conditioner, so that 85 tons would fill the air conditioners in 85,000 cars and trucks. Given the current price spread, 85 tons purchased in Canada would be worth up to $1.8 million more in the U.S." (p42) "Ten years ago, Canada's annual consumption of CFCs was about 20,000 tonnes, roughly two percent of the world's total. Today, it is close to zero....The last year [CFC] imports were allowed was 1995 and even then the total amount that companies were allowed to bring into the country was 5,000 tonnes, the estimated annual demand." (p44)

Smith, Michael/Vincent, Mary. "Tanking a Killer Coolant." Canadian Geographic v117 n5 Sep-Oct 1997. p40-44. (ISSN0008-3658).

CHLOROFLUOROCARBONS--EUROPE

"The European Commission's antifraud unit (UCLAF) said that Dutch customs officers had recently seized over 150 tons of CFCs [chlorofluorocarbons] in the port of Rotterdam, and German police had arrested a German suspected of masterminding the imports. The suspect had brought in a total of 630 tons of CFCs and 365 tons of halons between early 1996 and the spring of this year through Rotterdam, Hamburg, and Antwerp, Belgium, according to Bernard Cardot of UCLAF." (p3)

"Policy and Economics: EU Uncovers Major CFC Smuggling Operation." Global Environmental Change Report v9 n15 8 Aug 1997. p3. (ISSN1049-9083).

CHLOROFLUOROCARBONS--RUSSIA

"Russia currently accounts for 48% of global CFC [chlorofluorocarbon] production capacity. UN figures indicate that Russia produced about 18,000 metric tons of CFCs in 1996." (p5)

"Policy and Economics: Funds Needed to Help Russia Phase Out CFCs." Global Environmental Change Report v9 n12 27 Jun 1997. p5. (ISSN1049-9083).

CHLOROFLUOROCARBONS--UNITED STATES (v26)

"In the U.S., the automobile air-conditioner repair industry has seen a thirty-fold increase in CFC [chlorofluorocarbons]-12 prices, from $0.665 per pound before 1990 to $20.00 in July 1996, due to the accelerating excise tax that was imposed upon CFCs....The cost of retrofitting older cars with new equipment that can operate with CFC substitutes is estimated to be between $300 and $1,000 for each vehicle. However, this cost decreases dramatically, to only $100 to $150, for cars that were built more recently." (p221)

Papasavva, Stella/Moomaw, William R. "Adverse Implications of the Montreal Protocol Grace Period for Developing Countries." International Environmental Affairs v9 n3 Sum 1997. p219-231. (ISSN1041-4665).

CHOCOLATE--UNITED STATES (v26)

CHOCOLATE INDUSTRY (v26)

CHOCOLATE INDUSTRY--ASIA (v26)
CHOICE OF SCHOOL
see SCHOOL CHOICE
CHOLERA--PACIFIC AREA (v26)
CHOLERA--PERU--COSTS
"When cholera broke out in Peru in 1991, over US$ 700 million were lost in fish and fishery products exports. In the three months following the start of the epidemic, US$ 70 million were lost due to closure of food service establishments and a decrease in tourism. The global value of international trade in agricultural products and commodities was estimated at US$ 381 billion in 1993." (p2)
World Health Organization. "Foodborne Diseases--Possibly 350 Times More Frequent than Reported." WHO Press n58 13 Aug 1997. p1-4. document-level access: <http://www.who.ch/press/1997/pr97-58.html>
CHOLESTEROL--UNITED STATES (v26)
CHOLESTEROL--UNITED STATES--YOUTH (v26)
CHRISTIAN SCHOOLS
see CHURCH SCHOOLS
CHRISTIANITY--HONG KONG (v26)
CHRISTIANITY--SWEDEN (v26)
CHRISTIANITY AND POLITICS--UNITED STATES (v26)
CHRISTIANS
see also CATHOLICS; EPISCOPALIANS; LUTHERAN CHURCH; PROTESTANTS; RELIGIOUSNESS
CHRISTIANS--CHINA
The China Christian Council estimates that "about 12 million Protestant Christians...worship in 12,000 church buildings and 25,000 home meeting points. The CCC also oversees the printing and distribution of more than 3 million Bibles per year....The August [1997] CCC figures range from a low estimate of 9.2 million to a high of 13.3 million Protestants. Counterestimates by those who do not accept CCC authority range from 40 to 80 million for both Catholics and Protestants....An August READER'S DIGEST article titled 'The Global War on Christians' claims that 'many of China's estimated 40 million Christians still worship in fear....'" (p833)
Martin, Ann/Byler, Myrrl. "The Christian Century: What's Happening to Christians in China?" Christian Century v114 n26 24 Sep 1997. p832-833,835-839. (ISSN0009-5281).
CHRISTIANS--INDIA
In India, "Christians make up only 2 percent of a population of 950 million....The country's 13 million Catholics have had a high profile because of the elite schools and clinics run by their missionaries." (p14)
Zubrzycki, John. "India Unites to Honor Nun's Deeds." The Christian Science Monitor v89 n199 9 Sep 1997. p1,14. The Christian Science Monitor search engine: <http://www.csmonitor.com/plweb-cgi/iops1.pl> To retrieve this article, enter the following search: ED=19970909 AND deeds. In the "retrieved list," click the title that matches this record. (ISSN0882-7729).
CHRISTIANS--SOUTH AFRICA (v26)
CHRISTIANS--UNITED STATES
"Now numbering about 4 million--out of approximately 300 million worldwide--Orthodox Christians in America cite the religion's tradition and ceremonial beauty as a reason for its swift, silent growth across the United States. It has increased over the past five years at the rate of some 50 new parishes per day nationwide, according to estimates by the National Council of Churches (NCC) in New York....At St. Mary of Egypt Orthodox Church in Norcross, Ga.,...one-third of the congregation's 450 members are converts. Sixty percent of the priests in the Antiochean Archdiocese in Spokane, Wash., are converts." (p12)
Kurop, Marcia. "Religion: Orthodoxy's Modern Appeal." The Christian Science Monitor v89 n169 28 Jul 1997. p12. The Christian Science Monitor search engine: <http://www.csmonitor.com/plweb-cgi/iops1.pl> To retrieve this article, enter the following search: ED=19970728 AND appeal. In the "retrieved list," click the title that matches this record. (ISSN0882-7729).
CHRISTMAS--UNITED STATES
In the U.S., "just 3 percent of people aged 18 to 24 think about [Christmas] shopping more than six months in advance. By the time we hit 65, 18 percent of us are thinking of Santa in June....One-third of young adults bought an unplanned gift because they unexpectedly saw something they liked, more than double the proportion of 55-to-64-year-olds who did so....On the day before the holiday, just 15 percent of people with incomes of $15,000 or less finish shopping, compared with 30 percent of people with incomes of $65,000-plus who may be less concerned with breaking the Christmas Club budget. Seventeen percent of this affluent group also splurged last year for express delivery....The $46 billion catalog industry grows increasingly popular in our convenience-craving society. Catalogs accounted for 7.4 percent of general merchandise, apparel, and furniture sales in 1995, up from 4.7 percent in 1985, reports Everen Securities, a Chicago firm that monitors catalog stocks." (p44)
Speer, Tibbett L. "Stretching the Holiday Season." American Demographics v19 n11 Nov 1997. p42-49. article-level access: <http://www.demographics.com/publications/ad/97_ad/9711_ad/ad971128.htm> (ISSN0163-4089).
In the U.S., "one in four men wait until one to three weeks before the holidays to start shopping. Another 6 percent start less than one week in advance. A noticeable but smaller share of women start shopping within three weeks of the holidays, too, 15 percent. But this equals the share of women who start shopping in July. Only 9 percent of men start this soon....Twenty-four percent finish shopping on the eve of the holiday. A woeful 8 percent finish 'on the day or later.'...Twenty-one percent of women put things off until the last minute or later." (p44)
Speer, Tibbett L. "Stretching the Holiday Season." American Demographics v19 n11 Nov 1997. p42-49. article-level access: <http://www.demographics.com/publications/ad/97_ad/9711_ad/ad971128.htm> (ISSN0163-4089).
"Most Americans--70 percent--say they would welcome less Christmas spending and gift-giving...." (p1) "Half of all Americans carried debts from last Christmas into 1997. Of those, 28 percent were still paying off 1996 holiday bills in October, according to a national survey....And the annual holiday splurge creates a huge trash heap of wrapping paper, trees, boxes, and food, some 5 million extra tons between Thanksgiving and New Year's Day, says Bob Lilienfeld of the 'Use Less Stuff' report in Ann Arbor, Mich." (p9)
Tyson, Ann Scott. "Fewer Neckties: Christmas without Shopping." The Christian Science Monitor v90 n12 11 Dec 1997. p1,9. The Christian Science Monitor search engine: <http://www.csmonitor.com/plweb-cgi/iops1.pl> To retrieve this article, enter the following search: ED=19971211 AND shopping. In the "retrieved list," click the title that matches this record. (ISSN0882-7729).
CHURCH ATTENDANCE--UNITED STATES (v26)
CHURCH BUILDINGS--FIRES AND FIRE PREVENTION --UNITED STATES
"Since June of 1996, at the direction of the President and the Attorney General, efforts have been directed to establish the National Church Arson Task Force (NCATF) to address the recent rash of fires across the...[U.S.], at many predominately black churches, as well as coordinating the investigation and prosecution of arsonists, dissemination of information to the

public and developing initiatives to help mitigate losses, heal communities and strengthen prevention efforts. Thus far, approximately 328 incidents of fire at houses of worship occurring since January of 1995 have been reported to the Task Force. Almost half of the 328 fires have been at African-American churches; of the fires at African-American churches, approximately 80 percent have been in the South. Since 1995, arrests, both local and federal, of 143 suspects have been made in connection with 107 fires at churches and other houses of worship." (p479)

U.S. Dept. of Justice. "Departments of Commerce, Justice, And State, The Judiciary...Approp. for 1998 (Part 2)." Hearing. U.S. House. Committee on Appropriations. Washington, D.C. : GPO, 1997. (ISBN0160549094). (Y4.Ap6/1:C73/2/997/pt.2).

As a result of the joint efforts of the National Church Arson Task Force and the U.S. Dept. of Treasury and Justice, "199 suspects have been arrested in connection with 150 of the task force's 429 investigations of arsons, bombings or attempted bombings of houses of worship across the country between January 1, 1995, and May 27 of this year. The 35 percent arrest rate is double the 16 percent rate of arrest for arsons in general and slightly higher than the arrest rate the task force reported in January. A total of 110 defendants have been convicted in federal and state courts in connection with fires at 77 houses of worship since January 1995. The task force's June report, released at a news conference, indicates that 17 new arson investigations were launched in March, 21 in April and 12 in May. The 199 persons who have been arrested include 160 whites, 34 African-Americans and five Hispanics. Eighty-three juveniles were among the total arrested....Fourteen of the 25 defendants found guilty of federal offenses have been convicted of civil rights violations in cases in which there was evidence of racial motivation." (p584)

"News: Report Issued on Church Burnings." Christian Century v114 n19 18 Jun 1997. p584-585. (ISSN0009-5281).

In the U.S., "fewer than 20 of the 73 fires at black churches that the AP [Associated Press] counted since 1995 can be blamed on 'racism.' Five states have suffered more fires at white churches than at black churches, and in only 12 to 18 fires is there any evidence of racial motivations. In nine fires at black churches, black suspects have been named, while in six other church burnings, white churches were also targets of the arsonists. USA TODAY found that 64 black churches in Southern states had been burned since January 1, 1995. Of these, eight were torched by black suspects and one by a racially harmonious trio of two whites and one black. Only three cases involved whites who might have had racial motives." (p16)

Francis, Samuel. "Views: Witchfinder: The Strange Career of Morris Dees." Chronicles v21 n11 Nov 1997. p14-17. (ISSN0887-5731).

In the U.S., the National Church Arson Task Force "found no evidence that racism had motivated more than a small minority of arsonists, and found that only two or three out of 199 suspects so far arrested for church arson have had ties to white supremacist groups....The Atlanta-based Center for Democratic Renewal (CDR), has admitted that white churches were burning at five times the rate of black churches. According to the National Council of Churches (NCC), which was the CDR's chief partner in pushing church burnings as a media event, 20 percent of America's churches are black." (p47)

Tooley, Mark. "Religion: Church Arson Mania." Chronicles v21 n11 Nov 1997. p47. (ISSN0887-5731).

Fires at Afro-American "churches have dropped by 44 percent this year, even though the number of church arsons overall has risen. The National Church Arson Task Force has reported 82 church burnings in the first six months of 1997, including 19 at black churches. The task force investigated 68 incidents from the same period last year, 34 at black churches....The task force has investigated 429 cases since January 1955, with 35 percent of them solved....The National Council of Churches has raised $8.5 million for the burned churches, and has awarded $4.7 million in grants so far to 90 churches, most predominantly black and located in the Southeast." (p10 secA)

"In Our Opinion: Church Fires: Nation Must Do More than Rebuild the Structures." Detroit Free Press 16 Jun 1997. p10 secA.

In the U.S., a "report by the National Church Arson Task Force said federal and state authorities have arrested 199 suspects in 150 arsons, bombings or attempted bombings of mostly black churches between Jan. 1, 1995, and May 27 of this year." (p1) "35 percent of the arson cases have been solved, more than double the rate of arrests for arson across the country. Of 199 people arrested in 150 cases, about 75 percent have been charged. Suspects in 14 of 25 federal cases were charged with hate crimes. Sixty-eight percent of suspects in attacks on black churches are white, while 89 percent of suspects in attacks on nonblack churches are also white." (p9 secA)

Slevin, Peter/Cannon, Angie. "Torch of Church Fires Not Racism, Panel Says." Detroit Free Press 9 Jun 1997. p1,9 secA.

CHURCH BUILDINGS--GREAT BRITAIN--MAINTENANCE AND REPAIR (v26)

CHURCH EMPLOYEES--SWEDEN (v26)

CHURCH MEMBERSHIP--UNITED STATES

Thomas Reeves, a professor of history at the University of Wisconsin-Parkside said that U.S. Protestant Churches have "lost 20-30 percent of their members since the 1960s and other related signs of problems in these churches include: The United Methodists are losing 1,000 members a week; the United Church of Christ loses 40 churches a year; and, Presbyterian Church membership has declined from 4.2 million to 2.5 million in a single generation." (p28)

"Forum: At Annual Presbytery Meeting: Author Tells Priests What Doesn't Work in Other Churches." Observer v62 n20 19 Sep 1997. p28. (ISSN0029-7712).

CHURCH OF SWEDEN (v26)

CHURCH SCHOOLS--MICHIGAN--DETROIT

In Metro Detroit, enrollment in Islamic schools "has more than doubled to more than 1,100 in five years, amounting to 5 percent of the total enrollment in Islamic schools nationwide." (p1 secA) "The number enrolled is small compared to the number of students at Catholic schools in Metro Detroit--54,115 in 1996, said Tawnya Bender of the Detroit Archdiocese." (p6 secA)

Shepardson, David. "News Special: Education: Faith, Values Drive Growth of Islamic Schools: New Academy Opens as Local Enrollment Booms." Detroit News 15 Sep 1997. p1,6 secA.

CHURCH WORK--COLORADO--DENVER

A study in Denver, Colorado, suggests that church-based community outreach activities "are now widespread: 60 to 75 percent of the 80 African-American churches surveyed there provide at least one community service. Of 333 identified programs, nearly half (148) were targeted to adults and families and commonly involved the distribution of food and clothing. The many programs for children (160) involved youth activities, tutoring services, scholarship assistance, drug and alcohol education, and before-school and after-school childcare. Community development activities (59) included church-sponsored voter registration drives and candidate forums as well as the operation of credit unions and housing development." (p30)

Cisneros, Henry G. "Higher Ground: Faith Communities and Community Building." Christian Social Action v10 n10 Nov

1997. p29-33. (ISSN0897-0459).

CIGAR HABIT--MASSACHUSETTS--YOUTH

"The Massachusetts Department of Public Health surveyed 7,000 students in grades 6 to 12. Here, 5% of the 6th graders, 14% of the 7th and 8th graders, and 28% of the high-schoolers said that they had smoked a cigar during the previous year; 2, 8, and 15%, respectively, said that they had smoked a cigar during the previous month." (p48)

"Abstracts: Primary Care: Cigar Smoking Is Becoming a Fad among Teens." Modern Medicine v65 n8 Aug 1997. p48. (ISSN0026-8070).

CIGAR HABIT--NEW YORK (STATE)--YOUTH

"The Roswell Park Cancer Institute surveyed more than 11,000 9th-grade students in two New York counties. In Erie County, nearly 13% of the students surveyed (20% of the boys and 6% of the girls) said they had smoked a cigar during the previous month. In Chautauqua County,...nearly 15% of those surveyed said they had smoked a cigar during the previous month (24% of the boys and 5% of the girls)." (p48)

"Abstracts: Primary Care: Cigar Smoking Is Becoming a Fad among Teens." Modern Medicine v65 n8 Aug 1997. p48. (ISSN0026-8070).

CIGAR HABIT--UNITED STATES--YOUTH

In the U.S., "the Robert Wood Johnson Foundation's national survey was completed by more than 16,000 students aged 14 to 19. Some 37% of the males and 16% of the females said that they had smoked a cigar during the previous year. Extrapolating these findings, the CDC estimates that 6 million U.S. children in this age group had smoked a cigar in the previous year....54% of the cigarette smokers (74% of the males and 34% of the females) said they had smoked a cigar during the previous year, compared with just 14% of non-cigarette smokers (20% of the males and 8% of the females)." (p48)

"Abstracts: Primary Care: Cigar Smoking Is Becoming a Fad among Teens." Modern Medicine v65 n8 Aug 1997. p48. (ISSN0026-8070).

CIGAR INDUSTRY--CUBA--UNITED STATES (v26)

CIGAR INDUSTRY--UNITED STATES (v26)

"Total U.S. cigar leaf production gained 7 percent in 1996/97, reaching 20.9 million pounds....Total cigar leaf imports advanced 11 percent. About 100 million pounds were used domestically for cigar and loose leaf chewing tobacco production. For 1996/97, imports accounted for about 75 percent of total domestic use, slightly more than last year....During October 1996-June 1997, manufacturers used 47.3 million pounds of imported cigar tobacco, compared with 55.4 million pounds during the same period the previous year." (p24)

U.S. Dept. of Agriculture. Economic Research Service. "Cigar Tobacco." Tobacco Situation and Outlook Report Sep 1997. p24.

CIGARETTE HABIT (v26)

CIGARETTE HABIT--AFRICA (v26)

CIGARETTE HABIT--DEVELOPING COUNTRIES

"In the mid-1970s, 41 percent of the world's cigarettes were consumed in developing countries. But that proportion jumped to 61 percent a decade later and is expected to hit 70 percent by the year 2000." (p23)

McGinn, Anne Platt. "The Nicotine Cartel." World Watch v10 n4 Jul-Aug 1997. p18-27. (ISSN0896-0615).

CIGARETTE HABIT--POLAND (v26)

CIGARETTE INDUSTRY--DEVELOPING COUNTRIES (v26)

CIGARETTE INDUSTRY--RUSSIA

In Russia, "since 1986, cigarette production and imports increased by 40%, from 215 thousand million in 1986 to about 300 thousand million in 1995." (p2) "In 1995, 26 factories located in Russia manufactured 140 thousand million cigarettes and papirossi--a uniquely Russian smoking product. The rest of the demand--more than 50%--was met by imports. Today, Russia is importing about 150 thousand million cigarettes a year." (p3)

World Health Organization. "Tobacco Epidemic in the Russian Federation Kills 750 People Every Single Day." WHO Fact Sheet v6 n157 May 1997. p1-3. document-level access: <http://www.who.ch/programmes/inf/facts/fact157.htm>

CIGARETTE INDUSTRY--UNITED STATES (v26)

CIGARETTE TAX (v26)

CIGARETTE TAX--MICHIGAN (v26)

CIGARETTE TAX--UNITED STATES (v26)

"According to American Economics Group, Inc., nearly 662,402 [U.S.] citizens are employed in the production, manufacturing, and marketing of tobacco. If enacted, the 43-cent excise tax on tobacco products would abolish 43,000 jobs nationwide, and North Carolina alone would lose 17,849 jobs. Furthermore, any increase in the cigarette excise tax will fall disproportionally on lower- and middle-income consumers--the citizens least able to pay it. Those earning less than $30,000 annually already pay 5 times more in excise taxes than those earning $60,000 or more. Those families earning less than $30,000 pay a staggering 47 percent of all tobacco excise taxes, yet these families earn only 16 percent of national family income." (pS4787-4788)

Helms, Jesse (Sen.-N.C.). "Concurrent Resolution on the Budget." Congressional Record. Daily ed. v143 n68 21 May 1997. pS4782-4849. section/page-level access: <http://thomas.loc.gov/cgi-bin/query/R?r105:FLD001:S04787:> (ISSN0363-7239). (X1.1A.105/1).

"When Michigan hiked its cigarette excise tax by 50 cents to 75 cents per pack in 1994, taxable cigarette sales plunged 21 percent. But, sales in neighboring Indiana rose 8.5 percent. California, Massachusetts, Michigan, and New York, with combined populations of 65.4 million and an average cigarette excise tax of 55 cents per pack, reported fewer taxable cigarette sales than the states of Indiana, Kentucky, Missouri, New Hampshire, North Carolina, Tennessee and Virginia, which host half the population and average excise taxes of just 12 cents. New Hampshire sold twice as many packs of cigarettes as Massachusetts, even though the rate of smoking in both states is nearly identical. The difference: Massachusetts has a 76-cent per-pack excise tax, while New Hampshire's excise tax is just 25 cents per pack." (p1 secB)

Kristof, Kathy. "Business: Cigarette Taxes Force Smokers to Cross Borders in Search of Deals." Detroit News 22 Jul 1997. p1 secB.

In the U.S., "cross-border cigarette shopping soared 395 percent between 1980 and 1994 as the state-by-state disparity in cigarette excise taxes widened, according to the Tax Foundation, a Washington, D.C.-based tax research organization. Full-scale cigarette smuggling--the type done for profit with semi-trucks--rose a tidy 253 percent during the same period, according to the tax research group." (p1 secB)

Kristof, Kathy. "Business: Cigarette Taxes Force Smokers to Cross Borders in Search of Deals." Detroit News 22 Jul 1997. p1 secB.

The U.S. "Congress approved a budget package that will raise the federal excise tax by 10 cents a pack [on cigarettes] in 2000 and another 5 cents in 2002....The current federal tax [on cigarettes] is 24 cents, and state taxes range from 2.5 cents to more than 80 cents a pack. For the average pack of cigarettes, the total tax represents about a third of the price....In 1990, reports Harvard economist W. Kip Viscusi, smokers represented 19 percent of Americans earning $50,000 or more a year and about 32 percent of those earning less than $10,000. Tobacco taxes consumed 0.4 percent of the median income for smokers in the first group, compared to 5.1 percent for smokers in the second group--nearly 13 times as much." (p21)

Sullum, Jacob. "Data: Vice Charge." Reason v29 n6 Nov 1997. p21. (ISSN0048-6906).

CIGARETTES

see BLACK MARKET--CIGARETTES

CINEMAS

see MOTION PICTURE THEATERS

CIRCUIT COURTS--WASHINGTON (D.C.) (v26)

CIRCUIT COURTS--WEST (U.S.)

In the U.S., the ninth circuit court "outstrips the other circuits in all measures of size, both physically and legally. The ninth circuit encompasses a land mass the size of Western Europe. Its nine States and two territories--Alaska, Arizona, California, Hawaii, Idaho, Montana, Nevada, Oregon, Washington, Guam, and the Northern Mariana Islands--stretch from the Arctic Circle south to the United States-Mexico border and west across the international dateline. It has a population of nearly 50 million people, about 1 in 5 Americans, and is expected to grow by 43 percent over just the next 13 years. Second, the ninth's caseload is the largest. More than 8,500 appeals were filed last year, and that number is expected to jump by nearly 700 percent in the next 25 years, making the ninth less than a model of fair and speedy justice. In fact, of the 11 regional circuits and the District of Columbia circuit, it ranks next-to-worst in the duration of pending appeals--an average of 429 days, usually more for criminal cases, compared to the national average of 315 days." (pS8048)

Burns, Conrad R. (Sen.-Mont.). "Departments of Commerce, Justice, And State, The Judiciary...Appropriations Act, 1998." Congressional Record. Daily ed. v143 n106 24 Jul 1997. pS8041-8087. section/page-level access: <http://thomas.loc.gov/cgi-bin/query/R?r105:FLD001:S08047:> (ISSN0363-7239). (X1.1A.105/1).

CIRCULATORY SYSTEM

see CARDIOVASCULAR SYSTEM

CITIES AND TOWNS (v26)

see also URBANIZATION

CITIES AND TOWNS--CANADA--POPULATION

"From 1991 to 1996, metropolitan areas across Canada witnessed a boom on the so-called urban fringes. Kanata, outside Ottawa, grew by 10,600 people, a 28-per-cent increase. Similar growth rates occurred around Toronto and Vancouver, and Foothills, outside Calgary, grew by 26 per cent....In Calgary, city planners estimate that the metro area will soar by 500,000 people by 2024--and that fully 98 per cent of that growth will occur in new suburbs." (p18)

Chidley, Joe/Steele, Scott/Anthony, Lorrayne/Eisler, Dale/Vase, Bageshree. "Cover: The New Burbs." Maclean's v110 n29 21 Jul 1997. p16-21. (ISSN0024-9262).

CITIES AND TOWNS--GERMANY (v26)

CITIES AND TOWNS--GERMANY--ECONOMIC CONDITIONS (v26)

CITIES AND TOWNS--HISPANIC AMERICANS

In the U.S., "about 90 percent of Latinos lived in metropolitan areas in 1990, compared with 76 percent of non-Hispanics. Nearly one-half lived in the six metropolitan areas with 1 million or more Latino residents in 1996: Los Angeles, New York, Miami, San Francisco, Chicago, and Houston....About 6.1 million Latinos--more than one-fifth of all Latinos--lived in the Los Angeles metropolitan area in 1996. Latinos have a high profile in Los Angeles and Miami, where they are about 40 percent of the population, but these two areas are home to very different Hispanic populations....Nearly 80 percent of Los Angeles's 1996 Latino population was Mexican....Central and South Americans comprised another 17 percent of Los Angeles's Hispanic population in 1996....In 1995, Miami was the intended residence for three-fourths of the U.S. immigrants from Cuba, according to Immigration and Naturalization Service (INS) records." (p11-12)

del Pinal, Jorge/Singer, Audrey. "Generations of Diversity: Latinos in the United States." Population Bulletin v52 n3 Oct 1997. p2-47. (ISSN0032-468X).

CITIES AND TOWNS--IRELAND--POPULATION

A Central Statistics Office of Ireland "publication reveals the Swords, in Fingal (North County Dublin), was the fastest growing town between 1991 and 1996 when its population increased by one quarter (26%) from 17,705 in 1991 to 22,314 in 1996, a rise of 4,609 people. The percentage increase for this Fingal town compares with an overall rise in the State's population in the same five-year period of 2.8%. The city with the highest growth was Galway. It had a population (including its suburbs) of 57,363 in 1996, which is 6,510 higher than the last census in 1991--an increase of 12.8%. Other large towns which experienced rapid growth...include Tralee where the population went from 17,862 in 1991 to 19,950 in 1996, an 11.7% increase, and Ennis where the population rose from 16,058 in 1991 to 17,726 in 1996, a 10.4% increase. Dublin County Borough and its suburbs had a population of 952,692 in 1996, up 23,602 from the 1991 census figure."

Ireland. Central Statistics Office. "1996 Census--Volume 1--Population Classified by Area." Press Release 15 Aug 1997. document-level access: <http://www.cso.ie/pressreleases/prelc96v1.html>

CITIES AND TOWNS--MEXICO

"Over 10 percent of Mexico's population of approximately 95 million lives within 25 miles of the United States." (p4) "A cabinet-level official in the administration of Baja California Norte governor Ernesto Ruffo Appel confirms that over 1 million of Tijuana's nearly 2.5 million residents live in...[carboard and scrap metal houses, in makeshift tents, in caves and in lean-tos thatched with newspaper and cactus]." (p5)

Stout, Robert Joe. "Caught in the Middle." Christian Social Action v10 n9 Oct 1997. p4-6. (ISSN0897-0459).

CITIES AND TOWNS--SOUTH AMERICA

"Between 1975 and 1995, urban populations in South America increased by approximately 300%. The continent has 41 large cities (defined by the World Resources Institute as having populations over 750,000), and four of them--Sao Paulo, Buenos Aires, Rio de Janeiro, and Lima--rank among the world's 25 largest cities." (p795)

Joyce, Stephanie/U.S. National Institute of Environmental Health Sciences. "Focus: Growing Pains in South America." Environmental Health Perspectives v105 n8 Aug 1997. p794-799.

CITIES AND TOWNS--UNITED STATES (v26)

CITIES AND TOWNS--UNITED STATES--ECONOMIC CONDITIONS

"Median household income in central cities is 11 percent below that of the U.S. overall, while poverty levels are 37 percent greater, suggesting there are also high levels of inequality within central cities. Likewise, within these areas home ownership rates are 23 percent below that of the nation overall. Futhermore, while blacks comprise just 12 percent of the U.S. population, they make up nearly 22 percent of the population residing in central cities." (p61-62)

Leigh, Nancey Green/Gradeck, Robert. "Urban Neighborhood Demographics Associated with...Properties...Redevelopment Implications." Review of Black Political Economy v25 n1 Sum 1996. p61-81. (ISSN0034-6446).

CITIES AND TOWNS--UNITED STATES--POPULATION

"Between 1990 and 1996, Henderson, Nev.'s population grew by 88.4 percent, making it the fastest growing U.S. city with more than 100,000 people in 1996, according to new population estimates released...by the Commerce Department's Census Bureau....'Henderson's 1996 population was 122,339, up by over 57,000 since 1990,' said Greg Harper, a Census Bureau statistician....Ten cities had populations of more than 1 million in 1996. Both Phoenix, Ariz. and San Antonio, Texas reached the 1 million mark during the April 1990 to July 1996 period. By 1996, Phoenix had become the seventh most populous city, climbing from ninth in 1990. San Antonio, in the meantime, rose from 10th to eighth place. Detroit, which was ranked seventh in 1990, fell to 10th in 1996, while Dallas dropped from eighth to ninth."

U.S. Dept. of Commerce. Economic & Statistics Administration. "Henderson, Nev. Is Nation's Fastest Growing Large City, Census Bureau Says." Census Bureau Press Release 18 Nov 1997. document-level access: <http://www.census.gov/Press-Release/cb97-185.html>

The U.S. Department of Agriculture's Economic Research Service reported in 1996 "that the population of non-metropolitan places (places with a population of less than 100,000 and with no city of over 50,000) rose by 5.1 percent between 1990 and mid-1995....Half of those 2.6 million additional people migrated from metro areas. During the same period, metro growth was 5.8 percent." (p5)

Jossi, Frank. "Small Town Survival Strategies." Planning v63 n10 Oct 1997. p4-8. (ISSN0001-2610).

"In 1990, just over 30% of the total U.S. population lived in central cities, down less than 1% since 1970. And well over half of African Americans lived in central cities in 1990, down just 1.5% since 1970." (p6)

Alexander, Karl L. "Public Schools and the Public Good." Social Forces v76 n1 Sep 1997. p1-30. (ISSN0037-7732).

CITIES AND TOWNS--UNITED STATES--PUBLIC OPINION

"For the first time in six years, more elected [U.S.] officials say conditions [of city affairs] improved in the previous year than say they worsened....Forty-six percent say unfunded mandates worsened, compared with 7 percent who say they improved. At the same time, overall fiscal affairs were seen as improving by 46 percent, and getting worse by 17 percent....Officials saying the 'prospects of a young person finding a job and beginning a career in your town' were split nearly equally. Half said the prospects are good or great, and half said they are poor or fair." (p32)

Stoneman, Bill. "Kaleidoscope: Cities Get a Break." American Demographics v19 n7 Jul 1997. p32. article-level access: <http://www.demographics.com/publications/ad/97_ad/9707_ad/ad970725.htm> (ISSN0163-4089).

CITIES AND TOWNS, MOVEMENT TO

see RURAL-URBAN MIGRATION

CITRUS FRUIT INDUSTRY

see GRAPEFRUIT INDUSTRY; ORANGE INDUSTRY

CITY CRIME

see CRIME

CITY TRANSIT

see LOCAL TRANSIT

CIVIL ACTIONS

see ACTIONS AND DEFENSES

CIVIL AERONAUTICS

see AERONAUTICS, COMMERCIAL

CIVIL DISORDERS

see RIOTS

CIVIL RIGHTS

see AFRO-AMERICANS--CIVIL RIGHTS

CIVIL RIGHTS (INTERNATIONAL LAW)

see HUMAN RIGHTS

CIVIL SERVICE

see also AFRO-AMERICAN POLITICIANS; HISPANIC AMERICAN POLITICIANS; WOMEN IN POLITICS

CIVIL SERVICE--BRAZIL

In Brazil, "between 1988 and 1995, the number of federal employees fell from 700,000 to 576,000 as a result of attrition, retirement and a hiring freeze from 1990 to 1993....Nearly 90 percent of all public workers are currently vested....In 1988, salaries for these employees accounted for 3.9 percent of GDP, while in 1995 that figure had risen to 6.7 percent. The federal budget for personnel in 1996 was equivalent to 47.5 percent of total revenues, or 62 percent of discretionary/nonentitlement spending....Although public employees make up less than 6 percent of the total workforce, the average state-level expenditures for public workers is 74 percent of revenue." (p1)

McQuerry, Elizabeth. "International Focus: Brazil: Shifting from Vast Bureaucracy to Managerial State." Federal Reserve Bank of Atlanta Economics Update v10 n3 Jul-Sep 1997. p1,6. (ISSN0899-6563).

CIVIL SERVICE--CANADA (v26)

In Canada, "70 per cent of all public service executives will be eligible for retirement within the next eight years. In 1996, only 1 per cent of staff were under the age of 25, compared to 15 per cent in 1976." (p10142)

Fillion, Gilbert (MP-PQ). "Routine Proceedings: Committees of the House: Government Operations." Canada. Parliament. House of Commons. Debates. v134 n163 24 Apr 1997. p10142. page-level access: <http://www.parl.gc.ca/hansard/163_97-04-24/163RP1E.html#10142> section-level access: <http://www.parl.gc.ca/hansard/163_97-04-24/163RP1E.html#GOVERNMENTOPERATIONS> (ISSN0704-5603). (X3-352E).

CIVIL SERVICE--CANADA--LANGUAGES (v26)

CIVIL SERVICE--EUROPE, EASTERN--WOMEN

"From 1987 to 1994 the percentage of women in parliament decreased from 28 percent to 6 percent in Albania, from 34 percent to 4 percent in Romania, and from 21 percent to 11 percent in Hungary. Parliament was 33 percent female in the Soviet Union, but in many of the newly independent states the figure is now under 3 percent. The same downward trend is apparent for women in top ministerial posts: representation in Albania, Romania, and Hungary declined from 6 percent, 12 percent, and 4 percent, respectively, to zero." (p4)

Hunt, Swanee. "Women's Vital Voices: The Costs of Exclusion in Eastern Europe." Foreign Affairs v76 n4 Jul-Aug 1997. p2-7. (ISSN0015-7120).

CIVIL SERVICE--MICHIGAN (v26)

CIVIL WAR

see RUSSIA--HISTORY--CIVIL WAR; SRI LANKA--HISTORY--CIVIL WAR; URABA (COLOMBIA)--HISTORY--CIVIL WAR

CIVILIAN-BASED DEFENSE--MARYLAND--BALTIMORE

Oleoresin capsicum "spray successfully incapacitated 156 out of 174 (90%) agitated or violent personal confrontations in the Baltimore police research project. Persons on drugs or mentally disturbed may respond differently to OC. In 18 encounters, subjects were not fully subdued. Of these, seven may have been on drugs or mentally disturbed, suggesting lesser effects from OC." (unpaginated) "Side effects from use of the spray were few. Among officers, 21 reported minor injuries in using OC none of which required lost work days. Among suspects, 14 were injured, none requiring hospital treatment." (unpaginated)

"Pepper or Spice?: Non-Violent Weapon Evaluated Positively in Baltimore Police Study." Security Letter v27 n18 16 Oct 1997. (ISSN0363-4922).

CIVILIANS, EVACUATION OF

see EVACUATION OF CIVILIANS

CLASSROOMS--CALIFORNIA

Class-size cuts have "changed the look and feel of California's schools, where nearly an eighth of the nation's students are enrolled. In slightly over a year, the state has created at least 17,000 new classes and over half of the state's 1.9 million eligible students have been placed in classes of no more than 20 students. (In recent years California has had classes averaging 30 students.)...The state's teachers' unions have been silenced by surveys showing that over 90 percent of their members believe the class cuts have improved instruction....But there is one catch: Reducing class size is expensive. California is spending $2.5 billion over two years to cut class size, and the annual cost of sustaining the reform will start at about $1.5 billion (a 7.5 percent increase in state-level education spending) and rise steadily as new teachers climb salary ladders. To reduce the average class size by 10 students nationally would cost on the order of $85 billion for teachers alone." (p24)

Toch, Thomas/Streisand, Betsy/Butler, Steven. "U.S. News: Does Class Size Matter?" U.S. News & World Report v123 n14 13 Oct 1997. p22-25,28-29. article-level access: <http://www.usnews.com/usnews/issue/971013/13SIZE.HTM> (ISSN0041-5537).

CLEANING--UNITED STATES--EQUIPMENT AND SUPPLIES (v26)

CLEARCUTTING--ASIA (v26)

CLERGY

see also CATHOLIC CHURCH--CLERGY

CLERGY--EMPLOYMENT--UNITED STATES (v26)

CLERGY--UNITED STATES

In the U.S., "national leaders of the Catholic Church say the average age of seminary students rose to 32 in 1993, from 25 in 1966. Even greater is the change in the United Methodist church, where the average age of new clergy--men and women--has risen from 27 to 42 in the last quarter-century." (p1 secC) "The portion of United Methodist churches supplied with second-career clergy has grown from 20 percent to 25 percent in 10 years....In the Catholic church, an influx of older men to the priesthood hasn't offset the reduced numbers of seminarians. A Georgetown University study shows that 2,393 parishes nationwide lack priests now, compared with 702 in that predicament 30 years ago." (p7 secC)

Heinlein, Gary. "Metro: Special Report: More Joining Clergy in Mid-Life." Detroit News 18 Sep 1997. p1,7 secC.

CLERGY--UNITED STATES--FAMILY RELATIONSHIPS --ATTITUDES (v26)

CLERGY--UNITED STATES--YOUTH--ATTITUDES

In the U.S., "in a recent survey of several thousand young people more than 90 percent of them had a favorable attitude about priests and sisters. Over six percent of these young people are going into, or are seriously considering, a Church vocation." (p19)

Heinz, Martin. "Vocations: From the Front Lines of Vocations: You Can Win with God." Observer v62 n20 19 Sep 1997. p19. (ISSN0029-7712).

CLERKS--PROMOTIONS--WISCONSIN--WHITEWATER (v26)

CLERKS--SALARIES, ETC.--WISCONSIN --WHITEWATER (v26)

CLERKS--WISCONSIN--WHITEWATER (v26)

CLEVELAND (OHIO)--SOCIAL CONDITIONS

Cleveland's unemployment rate "is more than 10 percent, double the national average. Downtown unemployment rose just 4.8 percent to 137,000 between 1989 and 1996. The proportion of residents in poverty rose to nearly 30 percent in 1994 from 22 percent in 1980. The most basic measure of a city's well-being, population, declined from 751,000 in 1970 to 506,000 in 1990 and has continued to dwindle in recent years, according to Census estimates." (p14 secA)

"Comment: The Cleveland 'Model.'" Detroit News 31 Jul 1997. p14 secA.

CLIENTS, ADVERTISING

see ADVERTISERS

CLIMATIC CHANGES (v26)

see also GLOBAL TEMPERATURE CHANGE; GLOBAL WARMING

CLIMATIC CHANGES--ENVIRONMENTAL ASPECTS

As a result of global climate changes, "sea level is expected to rise between 15 and 95 centimeters over the next century as oceans expand and ice melts." (p12) "Midwinter temperatures have risen 4 to 5 [degrees Celsius] on the western Antarctic Peninsula over the past five decades. University of Montana ecologist William Fraser has studied the Adelie penguins for 22 years, has seen their population drop 40 percent, and thinks that warmth could be causing changes that make it hard for penguins to find food and breed....A Dutch study suggests that major vegetation changes will take place by 2050 in 24 percent of the world's parks and protected areas....Ecologists at the University of Vienna have found that plants have been 'climbing' the Alps as fast as 3.7 meters per decade over the past 90 years [as a result of warmer temperatures]." (p13)

O'Meara, Molly. "The Risks of Disrupting Climate." World Watch v10 n6 Nov-Dec 1997. p10-24. (ISSN0896-0615).

CLIMATIC CHANGES--UNITED STATES--PUBLIC OPINION

Surveys in the U.S. show that "while 83 percent of U.S. voters support higher fuel efficiency standards, only 23 percent support taxes on energy....66 percent of U.S. voters believe that 'reducing pollution is a more effective way to prevent global climate change than energy conservation,' whereas most analysts would say just the reverse." (p13) "Eighty-three percent of the survey respondents agreed that 'you can already notice the effects of global climate change on the weather around here.'" (p16) "When asked about the consequences of the greenhouse effect,...46 percent of those surveyed said, 'It will be hotter.' The next most common response was 'flooding' (24 percent), followed by the statements that climate change would 'destroy (the) ozone layer' (21 percent) and that there would be 'more cancer' (19 percent). Regarding the causes of the greenhouse effect, 35 percent said that it was cars and industry, 28 percent simply 'emissions,' and 27 percent spray bottles or chlorofluorocarbons; only 8 percent said that it was fossil fuels and another 8 percent carbon dioxide." (p20-21)

Kempton, Willett. "How the Public Views Climate Change." Environment v39 n9 Nov 1997. p12-21. (ISSN0013-9157).

CLOTHING, PROTECTIVE

see PROTECTIVE CLOTHING

CLOTHING AND DRESS

see also SKIRTS; WORK CLOTHES

CLOTHING AND DRESS--UNITED STATES

In an August 1996, Roper Starch Worldwide poll, in the U.S., "three-quarters of men report wearing jeans regularly, up from two-thirds in 1990. Sixty-nine percent said they routinely don T-shirts, up from 62% in 1990. Forty percent of men own a leather jacket, but only 12% report that they wear it often. When asked what they look best in, jeans and sport shirts top the list....Fifty-five percent of women say they wear jeans regularly, up from 49% in 1990....Although 56% of women report owning a suit with a skirt, only 16% wear it regularly. The same percent of men report owning a conservative business suit, but fewer than two in ten say they routinely wear it....Just 17% of men own a tuxedo, but only 2% wear it regularly." (p58)

Bowman, Karlyn H. "American Fashion Embraces the Casual and Comfortable." Public Perspective v8 n5 Aug-Sep 1997. p58-60.

(ISSN1050-5067).

CLOTHING FACTORIES--UNITED STATES (v26)

CLOTHING TRADE--ASIA (v26)

CLOTHING TRADE--EMPLOYMENT (v26)

CLOTHING TRADE--UNITED STATES (v26)

CLOUDINESS--EUROPE--UNITED STATES

"Weather records show that cloudiness has been increasing in some areas of the United States, by about 5 percent since jet travel mushroomed several decades ago. Over Europe, the increase in cloudiness has been only 0.5 to 2.0 percent...." (p4)

"Eco-Update: News from around the World: Jets Alter Climate?" Acres, U.S.A. v27 n11 Nov 1997. p4. (ISSN1076-4968).

CO-OPS

see COOPERATIVE SOCIETIES

COACHES (ATHLETICS)--MICHIGAN--AFRO-AMERICANS (v26)

COACHES (ATHLETICS)--SALARIES, ETC. --MICHIGAN (v26)

COAL-FIRED FURNACES--CHINA (v26)

COAL MINES AND MINING--JAPAN

"There were 370,000 Japanese coal workers in 1971; by 1989 the number had dropped to around 9,000....In 1992, the government announced that it would end all coal subsidies by 2001....Just two coal pits remain in Japan." (p7)

Barr, Cameron W. "Pink Slips Come with a Big Heart in Japan Layoffs." The Christian Science Monitor v89 n139 13 Jun 1997. p1,7. The Christian Science Monitor search engine: <http://www.csmonitor.com/plweb-cgi/iops1.pl> To retrieve this article, enter the following search: ED=19970613 AND layoffs. In the "retrieved list," click the title that matches this record. (ISSN0882-7729).

COAL TRADE (v26)

COAL TRADE--ALBERTA (v26)

COAL TRADE--BRITISH COLUMBIA (v26)

COAL TRADE--CANADA (v26)

COAL TRADE--CHINA (v26)

COAL TRADE--CHINA--INDIA

Between 1990 and 1996, "coal and oil use rose dramatically in developing nations--25% and 33.7%, respectively....Emissions from coal burning in China grew by 56% between 1990 and 1996, while emissions from oil use in India grew 74% over the same time period." (p2)

"Focus Report: Latest Emissions Estimates Bode Poorly for Future Reductions." Global Environmental Change Report v9 n14 25 Jul 1997. p1-3. (ISSN1049-9083).

COAL TRADE--NEW ZEALAND

In New Zealand, "a total of 876 thousand tonnes of coal was sold in the September 1997 quarter--the highest level of coal sales for a September quarter since the records began in 1981, said Deputy Government Statistician Ian Ewing when releasing the latest energy statistics. Coal sales in the September 1997 quarter increased by 13.1 per cent when compared to the September 1996 quarter, mainly due to higher thermal electricity generation. The coal types which contributed to the increase were sub-bituminous, up by 28.1 per cent and lignite, up 9.0 per cent. Due to lower exports, bituminous coal sales decreased 9.3 per cent. For the year ended September 1997 coal sales increased by 16.6 per cent to 3.9 million tonnes."

Statistics New Zealand. "New Zealand Energy Statistics--September 1997 Quarter." Press Release 2 Dec 1997. document-level access: <http://www.stats.govt.nz/statsweb.nsf/52518ce3e01f62f4cc256388000c48c0/8f5cccf6df0814734c25656000831341?OpenDocument>

COAL TRADE--UNITED STATES (v26)

In the U.S., "coal production in April 1997 totaled 86 million short tons, 3 percent lower than the 89 million short tons produced in April 1996. Coal production during the first 4 months of 1997 totaled 350 million short tons, 1 percent higher than production during the first 4 months of 1996. Electric utility coal consumption in February 1997 totaled 68 million short tons, 2 percent lower than the consumption level in February 1996." (p85)

U.S. Dept. of Energy. Energy Information Administration. "Coal." Monthly Energy Review May 1997. p85-92. (ISSN0095-7356).

U.S. "coal production in July 1997 totaled 90 million short tons, 1 percent higher than the 89 million short tons produced in July 1996. Coal production during the first 7 months of 1997 totaled 628 million short tons, 3 percent higher than production during the first 7 months of 1996." (p85)

U.S. Dept. of Energy. Energy Information Administration. "Coal." Monthly Energy Review Aug 1997. p85-92. (ISSN0095-7356).

U.S. "electric utility coal consumption during the first 4 months of 1997 totaled 283 million short tons, 2 percent higher than the 277 million short tons consumed during the first 4 months of 1996....Coal exports in April 1997 totaled 7 million short tons, 9 percent lower than exports in April 1996. Coal imports in April 1997 totaled 528 thousand short tons, 207 percent higher than imports in April 1996." (p85)

U.S. Dept. of Energy. Energy Information Administration. "Coal." Monthly Energy Review Jul 1997. p85-92. (ISSN0095-7356).

COAL TRADE--WYOMING

Wyoming "supplies about 25 percent of the nation's coal and 5 percent of its natural gas....91 percent of Wyoming's coal is shipped out of state. In 1996, that figured out to about 255 million tons of coal hauled out of Wyoming by rail. Even at a conservative delivered price of $25 per ton, and deducting a statewide average coal price at the mine of a little more than $6 per ton, the railroads collected about $4.8 billion hauling Wyoming's coal out of the state." (p15)

Jackson, Hugh. "Taxing the Wrong Side of the Tracks." High Country News v29 n13 7 Jul 1997. p15. (ISSN0191-5657).

COASTS--CALIFORNIA--POPULATION (v26)

COASTS--UNITED STATES--POPULATION (v26)

COATS ISLAND (N.W.T.)

Coats Island, at the north end of Hudson Bay "is 130 km [kilometers] long and comprises 5600 km2 [square kilometers] of mainly lowland tundra, reaching a maximum elevation of 185 m [meters] above sea level (asl). Less than 5% of the island is more than 100 m asl." (p101)

Gaston, Anthony J./Ouellet, Henri. "Birds and Mammals of Coats Island, N.W.T." Arctic v50 n2 Jun 1997. p101-118. (ISSN0004-0843).

COCA INDUSTRY--COLOMBIA

In Colombia, coca "can earn up to $10,000 an acre; corn, perhaps $200....Coca crops have...increased sharply in Colombia, from 39,700 acres at the end of 1993 to over 125,000 acres two years later." (p15) "Between 1993 and 1996 alone, Colombia's drug lords increased their holdings by almost two and a half million acres, giving them a total of up to four million acres and presence in 400 municipalities, according to INCORA [Colombian Institute of Agricultural Reform]." (p16)

Chepesiuk, Ron. "TF Reports: Americas: Spoils of the Drug War." Toward Freedom v46 n4 Aug 1997. p14-16. (ISSN0048-9898).

COCA INDUSTRY--LATIN AMERICA

"Colombia is now only the third largest cultivator of coca.

Peru and Bolivia account for about 65 and 20 per cent of the world's coca production, respectively. In Peru, Bolivia and Colombia an estimated one million people grow coca leaves and process and export cocaine products....The US Government estimates that in Peru as many as 60,000 families depend on coca growing for their livelihood. An academician in Peru estimates that in the Huallaga Valley alone, 100,000 families earned their living through coca production in the 1980s....According to the March 1995 'International Narcotics Control Strategy Report,' Peru grows 108,600 hectares of coca per year; Bolivia 48,100; and Colombia 38,000." (p468)

Van de Velde, James R. "Issues of Law Intensity Conflict and Law Enforcement: The Growth of Criminal...Drug Trafficking." Low Intensity Conflict & Law Enforcement v5 n3 Win 1996. p466-483. (ISSN0966-2847).

COCAINE HABIT--UNITED STATES

"In 1996, according to the US Department of Health and Human Services, the United States had 2.6 million occasional users--people using cocaine fewer than 12 times a year. An estimated 608,000 cocaine users ingest the drug more than 51 days a year. The National Clearing House for Alcohol and Drug Information says that a staggering 41,000 people try cocaine for the first time each month in the United States." (p13)

Holmstrom, David. "Justice: Chances Are, There's a Trace of Cocaine in Your Wallet." The Christian Science Monitor v90 n5 2 Dec 1997. p13. The Christian Science Monitor search engine: <http://www.csmonitor.com/plweb-cgi/iops1.pl> To retrieve this article, enter the following search: ED=19971202 AND wallet. In the "retrieved list," click the title that matches this record. (ISSN0882-7729).

COCAINE INDUSTRY--BOLIVIA--COLOMBIA--PERU --UNITED STATES (v26)

COCAINE INDUSTRY--COLOMBIA--MEXICO--UNITED STATES (v26)

COCAINE INDUSTRY--COLOMBIA--UNITED STATES (v26)

COCAINE INDUSTRY--LATIN AMERICA

"In Bolivia an estimated 350,000 to 400,000 people (5 to 6 per cent of the population; 10 to 14 per cent of the labor force) are employed direct in the cocaine industry. Over 80 per cent of the cocaine produced in Latin America is consumed in the US--the single largest market in the world. (As a comparison, 172,000 are employed in the legal drug business in the US producing shipments valued at $39 billion. Only 32,000 are employed in the American tobacco industry producing shipments valued at $17 billion.)...'The International Narcotics Control Strategy Report' of April 1993, published by the US Office of National Drug Control Policy, estimates that over 1,100 metric tons of cocaine were produced in Central and South America for shipment world-wide; 400 metric tons were successfully smuggled into the US; 100 metric tons were seized in the USA by the authorities (therefore approximately 300 metric tons were probably consumed in the US); 100 metric tons were consumed by Europeans and 200 were seized by Latin American governments." (p468-469)

Van de Velde, James R. "Issues of Law Intensity Conflict and Law Enforcement: The Growth of Criminal...Drug Trafficking." Low Intensity Conflict & Law Enforcement v5 n3 Win 1996. p466-483. (ISSN0966-2847).

COCAINE INDUSTRY--MEXICO

"Mexican drug trafficking groups smuggle approximately 70 to 80 per cent of the cocaine that enters the US across the 2,000-mile US-Mexico border, accounting for a total of 200-400 tons of cocaine annually....The DEA estimates the total income generated by Mexico's drug trade to have been around $7 billion in 1995. As of 1985, 25 per cent of the cocaine successfully smuggled into the US was transshipped through Mexico; by 1989 the figure was 40 to 50 per cent, and today the figure is 70 to 80 per cent." (p474)

Van de Velde, James R. "Issues of Law Intensity Conflict and Law Enforcement: The Growth of Criminal...Drug Trafficking." Low Intensity Conflict & Law Enforcement v5 n3 Win 1996. p466-483. (ISSN0966-2847).

COCOA TRADE--UNITED STATES

In 1996, U.S. "cocoa imports reached a record 847,000 tons, surpassing the previous record in 1993 of 801,000 tons. The value of cocoa was up 26 percent, reaching $1.4 billion...." (p7)

Gehlhar, Mark/U.S. Dept. of Agriculture. Economic Research Service. "Imports Advance 12 Percent in 1996." Foreign Agricultural Trade of the United States Jan-Mar 1997. p6-7.

CODLING MOTH--UNITED STATES (v26)

COFFEE HABIT--UNITED STATES (v26)

COFFEE INDUSTRY--EL SALVADOR--MEXICO (v26)

COFFEE INDUSTRY--ENVIRONMENTAL ASPECTS --MEXICO (v26)

COFFEE INDUSTRY--UNITED STATES (v26)

In 1996, U.S. "coffee imports increased slightly, from 989,000 tons to 1.1 million tons, however, the import value dropped 15 percent due to lower world prices. The coffee import unit value dropped from $3,300 per ton in 1995 to $2,483 per ton in 1996....The U.S. increased coffee imports from Mexico by 30 percent, while imports from Brazil fell 17 percent." (p6)

Gehlhar, Mark/U.S. Dept. of Agriculture. Economic Research Service. "Imports Advance 12 Percent in 1996." Foreign Agricultural Trade of the United States Jan-Mar 1997. p6-7.

COINS, RUSSIAN

see KOPECK

COLLEGE APPLICATIONS--UNIVERSITY OF TEXAS --AFRO-AMERICANS--HISPANIC AMERICANS

At the University of Texas, Austin, "law school applications fell by 42 percent for blacks this year, and undergraduate applications by 26 percent. The comparable numbers for Hispanics were 26 percent and 32 percent." (p15 secA)

Raspberry, William. "Comment: Students' Group Softens Impact of Hopwood Case." Detroit News 5 Nov 1997. p15 secA.

COLLEGE ATTENDANCE--MICHIGAN

"While the bulk of growth is concentrated among midsize universities, the echo has 11 of Michigan's 15 public universities showing at least some enrollment increases this year, preliminary counts show. Statewide enrollment is up 1.4 percent this year and 6 percent over the decade....'We are expecting a 1.5-percent increase in freshman statewide in each of the next five years,' said Courtney McAnuff, a vice-president at Eastern Michigan University....At Michigan State [University], preliminary estimates indicate 42,603 students enrolled--a jump of 2.5 percent for the state's largest student body....Last year, Wayne [State University] had its biggest freshman class in 15 years with 1,970 students. This year it's about 1,920...." (p1 secC)

Hoover, Rusty. "Metro: News Special: Education: Baby Boomers' Children Fuel Growth." Detroit News 13 Oct 1997. p1 secC.

In Michigan, "three universities--Grand Valley, Saginaw Valley and Oakland--lead the state in percentage gains within the past year and over the past decade. Those same universities can claim 70 percent of the enrollment growth over the past decade among Michigan's 15 public universities." (p1 secC) "Grand Valley in western Michigan has 75 percent more students than a decade ago, while Saginaw Valley is up 30.5 percent. Oakland has increased by nearly 15 percent in the same period....75

percent of classes at Grand Valley have 30 or fewer students and 90 percent are below 40." (p2 secC)

Hoover, Rusty. "Metro: News Special: Education: Midsize Colleges Grow Up." Detroit News 13 Oct 1997. p1-2 secC.

COLLEGE COSTS

see also STUDENT LOAN FUNDS

Worldwide, the 11 mega-universities, which are unitary institutions with one campus and hundreds of faculty to teach at least 100,000 students each, "enroll, between them, some 2.8 million students. Their budgets aggregate to a bit less than $1 billion--that's under $350 per student." (p14)

Daniel, John S. "Why Universities Need Technology Strategies." Change v29 n4 Jul-Aug 1997. p10-17. (ISSN0009-1383).

COLLEGE COSTS--CANADA--LAW STUDENTS

"A survey conducted in 1995 by a three-member student committee at the University of Toronto found that 37 per cent of [Canadian] law students brought debt with them into law school--compared with just 19 per cent two years earlier. According to the survey, the average law student planned to go $18,000 deeper into the red before finishing their course work and heading out to article." (p17)

Dwyer, Victor. "Cover: Privilege and Pressure." Maclean's v110 n40 6 Oct 1997. p16-20. (ISSN0024-9262).

COLLEGE COSTS--FLORIDA (v26)

COLLEGE COSTS--ILLINOIS (v26)

COLLEGE COSTS--UNITED STATES (v26)

"According to the College Board, average tuition at private four-year institutions [in the U.S.] increased between 1987 and 1996 by 36 percent in constant dollars and a full 89 percent in current dollars. For public four-year institutions, the increases over that period were 60 percent and 122 percent, respectively." (p4)

Kramer, Martin. "Forum: Tuition Tax Benefits: Winners and Losers." Change v29 n4 Jul-Aug 1997. p4,51. (ISSN0009-1383).

"In 1991, the average student at the average U.S. college paid $3,100 for an education that cost $10,600 to produce--thus receiving a subsidy of $7,500....There's little difference, on average, between public and private schools--average subsidies were $7,800 and $7,200, respectively." (p34) "In 1991, the 10 percent of U.S. schools with the largest student subsidies gave the average student a subsidy worth $21,000 a year; those with the smallest subsidies gave $1,500." (p35)

Winston, Gordon C. "Why Can't College Be More Like a Firm?" Change v29 n5 Sep-Oct 1997. p32-38. (ISSN0009-1383).

Figures from USA TODAY, "show that for a U.S. family the cost of sending a child to college--tuition, room, and board--is approaching 15 percent of the median family income. That's up from 9 percent of median family income 15 years ago. Moreover, 15 percent of income is the cost of sending your offspring to a public university. If you pick a private university, the figure is nearly 40 percent of median family income--up from just over 20 percent in the same 15-year period." (p12-13) "In the United States, there are 3,500 colleges and universities enrolling 14 million students, with an annual expenditure on higher education of around $175 billion. That's an average cost of $12,500 per student." (p14)

Daniel, John S. "Why Universities Need Technology Strategies." Change v29 n4 Jul-Aug 1997. p10-17. (ISSN0009-1383).

According to the U.S. General Accounting Office, "tuition at a 4-year university rose 234 percent between 1980-94. During this same period, median household income rose 84 percent and the consumer price index rose a mere 74 percent. The College Board reports that tuition costs for the 1996-97 school year will rise 5 percent while average room and board costs will rise between 4 to 6 percent....In 1995, $50 billion in financial aid was available to students from Federal, State, and institutional sources. This was $3 billion higher than the previous year. A majority of this increase has come in the form of loans, which now make up the largest portion of the total Federal-aid package at 57 percent. Grants, which a decade ago made up 49 percent of assistance, have been reduced to 42 percent." (pS6697)

McConnell, Mitch (Sen.-Ky.). "Revenue Reconciliation Act of 1997." Congressional Record. Daily ed. v143 n93 27 Jun 1997. pS6670-6720. section/page-level access: <http://thomas.loc.gov/cgi-bin/query/R?r105:FLD001:S06697:> (ISSN0363-7239). (X1.1A.105/1).

In the U.S., "the College Board reports that tuition at 4-year private institutions has risen by 89 percent over the past 15 years while median family income has risen by only 5 percent. Students are responding by borrowing at record levels--in fact, student borrowing under Title IV since 1990 exceeds student borrowing in the 1960's, 1970's, and 1980's combined. Between 1993 and 1995, graduate and professional student borrowing increased by over 74 percent." (pS10807)

Jeffords, James M. (Sen.-Vt.). "Statements on Introduced Bills and Joint Resolutions." Congressional Record. Daily ed. v143 n140 9 Oct 1997. pS10788-10808. section/page-level access: <http://thomas.loc.gov/cgi-bin/query/R?r105:FLD001:S10807:> (ISSN0363-7239). (X1.1A.105/1).

In the U.S., "the College Board found that four year public colleges and universities boosted undergraduate tuition in 1996 by an average of 6%. However, this is below the double digit increases in tuition costs which occurred annually between 1991 and 1993. For 1996-97, in state tuition and fees, not counting room and board, averaged $2,811 at public four-year colleges and $12,823 at private schools. The amount of aid from federal, state, and school sources was up 4% from 1994-95....A report from the General Accounting Office showed that college tuition on average jumped 234% between the 1980-81 and 1994-95 school years (Meckler, 1996)....Between 1992 and 1994, borrowing under federal student-loan programs rose 57% to $23.1 billion." (p26)

Todd, Kelly J./DeVaney, Sharon A. "Financial Planning for Retirement by Parents of College Students." Financial Counseling and Planning v8 n1 1997. p25-32. (ISSN1052-3073).

In the U.S., a study by "Lee, Hanna and Sirigar (1997) found that only 28% of parents with children under 18 listed saving for college as an important goal. An International Association of Financial Planning (IAFP) survey of 550 parents who have children under 18 living at home and with household incomes of at least $30,000 found that less than half of parents with a financial plan were saving for college (IAFP PLANNING MATTERS, 1996). While 83% said they had a financial plan, only 44% of those said they were saving for children's college education....A survey by Fidelity Investments found that almost half of parents with children in college expected the total costs to be less than $25,000, far less than the $44,740 to $94,400 they are likely to pay (O'Connell, 1996)." (p27)

Todd, Kelly J./DeVaney, Sharon A. "Financial Planning for Retirement by Parents of College Students." Financial Counseling and Planning v8 n1 1997. p25-32. (ISSN1052-3073).

In the U.S., "back in 1980, a student could expect to pay, on average, about $6,000 for tuition at a private research university such as Stanford or Yale. By 1994, tuition at such schools had reached a whopping $19,500. But even at public universities and small, nonresearch-oriented colleges, tuition costs had jumped proportionately--up an average of 225 percent--a far steeper increase than the U.S. median household income or the Consumer Price Index during the same period, reports the National Science Foundation (NSF)....In 1994 the average tuition at public research universities was roughly 14 percent higher than at public doctoral institutions and 27 percent to 30 percent higher than at comprehensive institutions and four-year colleges." (p10)

Childress, Janice O. "News Notes: Do Research Costs Drive Up Tuition?" Geotimes v42 n11 Nov 1997. p10-11. (ISSN0016-8556).

"From 1961-62 to 1991-92, the college enrollment rate of Americans between the ages of 18 and 24 more than doubled, from 24 percent to 53 percent....Between 1965-94, tuition and fees grew by 70 percent or more, depending on the type of institution, according to the US Department of Education's National Center for Education Statistics....The average annual tuition bill took about 10 percent of median family income in 1994 compared with 6 percent in 1976....Average annual tuition (excluding other expenses) in 1992 was $3,517...." (p18)

Tregarthen, Suzanne. "Opinion/Essays: Think College Is out of Reach? Think Again." The Christian Science Monitor v89 n178 8 Aug 1997. p18. The Christian Science Monitor search engine: <http://www.csmonitor.com/plweb-cgi/iops1.pl> To retrieve this article, enter the following search: ED=19970808 AND college. In the "retrieved list," click the title that matches this record. (ISSN0882-7729).

"According to the Council for Aid to Education, a subsidiary of the Rand Corp., if tuition rises in the next 20 years as it has in the past 20, 6.7 million students (or half those expected to want it) will be 'priced out' of higher education [in the U.S.]....In the academic year 1976-77, the number of high school graduates peaked in the United States, falling by almost 22 percent by 1991-92. Yet despite the rise in tuition and the falloff in the college-age population, the number of full-time students went up approximately 25 percent....The real costs of higher education per student grew about 40 percent." (p80)

Caplan, Lincoln. "Best Colleges 1998: Contemporary Calculus." U.S. News & World Report v123 n8 1 Sep 1997. p80-82. article-level access: <http://www.usnews.com/usnews/issue/970901/1OPEN.HTM> (ISSN0041-5537).

"From 1974 to 1994, the average cost of four years of tuition, room, board, and fees at public universities [in the U.S.] rose from $11,032 to $25,785. Private school costs went from $25,514 to $64,410....So far this decade, students have borrowed at least $140 billion--more than total student borrowing over the past three decades combined. Since 1977, median student loan debt has leapt from $2,000 to about $15,000....In the only national survey on...[the question of parental contribution], taken in 1991, just 26 percent of student borrowers said their parents paid for more than one fifth of college costs. Studies have shown that typical parents pick up about 10 percent of their kids' student loans." (p38-39)

Shenk, Joshua Wolf. "U.S. News: In Debt All the Way up to Their Nose Rings." U.S. News & World Report v122 n22 9 Jun 1997. p38-39. article-level access: <http://www.usnews.com/usnews/issue/970609/9DEBT.HTM> (ISSN0041-5537).

COLLEGE COUNSELING

see COUNSELING IN HIGHER EDUCATION

COLLEGE FACULTY

see COLLEGE TEACHERS

COLLEGE FRATERNITIES

see GREEK LETTER SOCIETIES

COLLEGE FRESHMEN--UNITED STATES--ATTITUDES

According to a study of U.S. college freshmen conducted by the University of California at Los Angeles Graduate School of Education and Information Studies, "the top goal of today's students is to be 'very well-off financially.' Less than one-third think keeping up with political issues is important....One in four has divorced or separated parents. One in 10 students reports being 'frequently depressed,' and close to 30 percent often feel 'overwhelmed by all I have to do.'...Two-thirds believe now, as before, that individuals can change society, and volunteerism is almost at a 72 percent rate. Support for legalized marijuana rose from 19.4 percent in 1968 to a 52.9 percent high during the 1970s, but today only 33 percent would legalize marijuana. Eighteen percent of the students report that they were 'conservatives' in 1970 while 22.7 percent profess such a political ideology in 1996." (p73)

Cohn, Alvin W. "Juvenile Focus." Federal Probation v61 n3 Sep 1997. p71-73. (ISSN0014-9128).

COLLEGE GRADUATES--EMPLOYMENT--MICHIGAN --DETROIT

"Michigan ranks 38th out of the 50 states in the percentage of adults with college degrees and the Detroit metropolitan area ranks 22nd out of the 24 metropolitan areas with populations of two million or more, according to the data compiled by...[Wayne State University's] Center for Urban Studies....Of the 54 common occupations in Michigan paying at least $33,000 per year--10 percent more than the median income of $30,000--31 require a degree. Most of the remaining 23 jobs require post-high school technical training...." (p1 secA)

Walsh-Sarnecki, Peggy. "Michigan Low on College Grad List." Detroit Free Press 4 Aug 1997. p1,7 secA.

COLLEGE GRADUATES--EMPLOYMENT--UNITED STATES (v26)

COLLEGE GRADUATES--PENNSYLVANIA--ECONOMIC CONDITIONS

The Pennsylvania Independent College and University Research Center surveyed "11,000 baccalaureate graduates from the class of 1990 at 46 independent colleges in Pennsylvania, the group found that 84 percent are employed full-time....Based on a 61 percent response rate, young people said their average college loan was $11,000, of which 44 percent was still owed in 1996....Members of the class of 1990 report earning an average of $38,000 at their full-time employment and exercising significant supervisory responsibility on the job....More than half reported owning their own home (51 percent) and performing volunteer service (54 percent) in 1995." (p19)

Mitchell, Brian C. "Opinion/Essays: And Now for the Good News about Higher Education." The Christian Science Monitor v89 n160 15 Jul 1997. p19. The Christian Science Monitor search engine: <http://www.csmonitor.com/plweb-cgi/iops1.pl> To retrieve this article, enter the following search: ED=19970715 AND education. In the "retrieved list," click the title that matches this record. (ISSN0882-7729).

COLLEGE GRADUATES--UNITED STATES (v26)

COLLEGE GRADUATES--UNITED STATES--ECONOMIC CONDITIONS

In the U.S., "more than six in ten black and Hispanic college students take out loans to pay for school, compared with 48 percent of non-Hispanic white students....In June 1994, only 37 percent of those who received a bachelor's degree in 1993 were still carrying undergraduate debt....In 1994, 56 percent of employed borrowers and 54 percent of non-borrowers said their current job was closely related to their undergraduate degree....The share of students who considered graduate school but then decided against applying was 75 percent among borrowers and 71 percent for non-borrowers. But only 10 percent of the borrowers who decided against graduate school said the primary reason was too much undergraduate debt." (p7)

"Demographics of Student Debtors." Forecast v17 n11 Nov 1997. p7. article-level access: <http://www.demographics.com/publications/fc/97_fc/9711_fc/

fc97116.htm> (ISSN0732-1597).

In the U.S., according to a survey by Phoenix Life, "only 20 percent of parents now supporting college-age kids say they will continue after graduation. That's down from 28 percent last year. Only 62 percent plan to help their children buy a car, down from 67 percent last year. Only 27 percent plan to help with a home, a drop from 33 percent last year....While 90 percent of graduates understand the importance of saving, only 9 percent understand compound interest....Only 45 percent understand the concept of a budget. And while 60 percent of college graduates have credit cards, only 29 percent understand the credit system." (p8)

Halverson, Guy. "Business & Money: Personal Finance: Your Money: Grads: Do as Your Parents Didn't." The Christian Science Monitor v89 n130 2 Jun 1997. p8. The Christian Science Monitor search engine: <http://www.csmonitor.com/plweb-cgi/iops1.pl> To retrieve this article, enter the following search: ED=19970602 AND parents. In the "retrieved list," click the title that matches this record. (ISSN0882-7729).

COLLEGE PRESIDENTS--SALARIES, ETC.--MICHIGAN (v26)

COLLEGE PRESIDENTS--UNITED STATES--ATTITUDES (v26)

COLLEGE SORORITIES

see GREEK LETTER SOCIETIES

COLLEGE SPORTS--UNITED STATES--WOMEN

In the U.S., "today, more than 100,000 women participate in intercollegiate athletics, a fourfold increase since 1971, according to the US Department of Education. In 1995, women were 37 percent of college student athletes compared with 15 percent in 1972. But, says a 'Report Card,' released...by the Women's Sports Foundation, the majority of colleges are allocating resources and opportunities 'at a roughly 2 to 1 ratio between male athletes and female athletes.'" (p7)

Wood, Daniel B. "United States: Desperately Seeking Gender Balance." The Christian Science Monitor v89 n151 1 Jul 1997. p7. The Christian Science Monitor search engine: <http://www.csmonitor.com/plweb-cgi/iops1.pl> To retrieve this article, enter the following search: ED=19970701 AND balance. In the "retrieved list," click the title that matches this record. (ISSN0882-7729).

COLLEGE STUDENT NEWSPAPERS AND PERIODICALS --UNITED STATES (v26)

COLLEGE STUDENTS

see also AFRO-AMERICAN COLLEGE STUDENTS; JOURNALISTS--UNITED STATES--COLLEGE STUDENTS

COLLEGE STUDENTS--CANADA--ECONOMIC CONDITIONS

"Recently the Canadian Federation of Students produced a major report called the 'Blueprint for Access.' In that document they pointed out that the average debt load will be $25,000 for students by June 1998. That is up from $13,000 in 1993 when the Liberals took office.... "In 1995-96 more than 7,800 students who received Canada student loans declared bankruptcy.... "Tuition fees in Canada have reached a national average of $3,100 which surpasses the average of publicly funded institutions in the United States." (p647)

Davies, Libby (MP-BC). "Adjournment Proceedings: Post-Secondary Education." Canada. Parliament. House of Commons. Debates. v135 n12 7 Oct 1997. p647-648. section-level access: <http://www.parl.gc.ca/36/1/parlbus/chambus/house/debates/012_1997-10-07/han012-e.htm#LINK245> (ISSN0704-5603). (X3-361E).

COLLEGE STUDENTS--EMPLOYMENT--UNITED STATES (v26)

COLLEGE STUDENTS--GERMANY

In Germany, "1996 saw 268,000 [college] freshmen which represented an increase of 1.5% over the previous year. Of that number, 186,000 chose to study at university or another academic institution, 81,000 went to the Fachhochschule [a system of specialized universities], and 4,000 to study at arts colleges. Today, almost half the student population are women, and this trend is increasing....In the 1950s only 4% of students came from what might be called working-class families; today that figure is 19%." (p26) "The majority of students can be found studying law, economics, and social sciences (546,400 registered students in the 1995/1996 winter semester), engineering (418,000), and linguistics, languages, and the humanities (404,700). Mathematics and the natural sciences come in fourth on the student's popularity ladder (280,800)....The average age of university graduates is 27.5, significantly older than in other countries. For example, first degrees are taken in Great Britain at an average age of just under 23, in the United States that age is 24, and 26 in France." (p28)

Schayan, Janet. "Universities: Studying in Germany." Deutschland n3 Jun 1997. p24-30. article-level access: <http://www.bundesregierung.de/.bin/lay/ausland/edu/edu.html> (ISSN0945-6791).

COLLEGE STUDENTS--MICHIGAN--ECONOMIC CONDITIONS

In Michigan, "undergraduate students who attend schools that hold [tuition] increases to the state rate of inflation can qualify for a tax break. Students can deduct 4 percent of their tuition or $250, whichever is less, from state income-tax bills. The state's inflation rate for last year was certified at 3 percent. The tuition tax credit, in its third year, cost the state $13.3 million in lost taxes last year and $8 million in 1995." (p1 secC)

Hoover, Rusty. "The Metro: Michigan Universities Ease Tuition Increases." Detroit News 20 Jun 1997. p1 secC.

COLLEGE STUDENTS--SOCIAL NETWORKS--UNITED STATES (v26)

COLLEGE STUDENTS--UNITED STATES (v26)

"In October 1995, 10 million U.S. families had dependent members aged 18 to 24, according to a Census Bureau survey. In 40 percent of these families, at least one young-adult dependent was a full-time college student, up from 35 percent in 1984....The young-adult population of the U.S. declined by more than 4 million during this period. So the sheer number of families with dependents aged 18 to 24 attending college full-time dropped from 4.4 million to 4 million." (p39)

Crispell, Diane. "Kaleidoscope: Depending on College." American Demographics v19 n11 Nov 1997. p39. article-level access: <http://www.demographics.com/publications/ad/97_ad/9711_ad/ad971117.htm> (ISSN0163-4089).

In the U.S., "nearly one-third of college freshmen will not enroll for the following year of study, according to POSTSECONDARY EDUCATION OPPORTUNITY. Persistence rates, also known as retention rates, for all college freshmen have been declining slightly since 1983, from 68 percent to a little less than 67 percent in 1997. About 70 percent of this decrease has occurred in the last five years. The decrease in retention means that about 21,000 college students who started their freshman year in 1996 are not back as sophomores this fall....College freshmen who were in the top 10 percent of their high school graduating class have the highest persistence rate, 91 percent in 1997. In contrast, just 54 percent of those who started at a college with an 'open door' policy of admissions went back the next year." (p41)

Cravatta, Matthew. "Kaleidoscope: Hanging On to Students." American Demographics v19 n11 Nov 1997. p41. article-level access: <http://www.demographics.com/publications/ad/97_ad/9711_ad/ad971121.htm> (ISSN0163-4089).

In the U.S., "just over 43 percent of persons aged 18 to 21 were enrolled in college in October 1995. The same was true for 23 percent of 22 to 24 year-olds, 11 percent of 25-29 year-olds, 6 percent of 30-34 year-olds, and 2 percent of those aged 35 or more. This added up to 14.7 million college students. Six million college students, or 41 percent, were 25 years old and over; of this number, 2.7 million, or 18 percent of all college students, were aged 35 or older. About 1.7 million students in the 35 plus age group were undergrads. More than half of college students (54 percent) were women. Women constituted an even larger share (58 percent) of students 25 and over. A total of 12 million persons were undergrads: of these, 8.1 million were enrolled in 4-year colleges and 3.9 million attended 2-year colleges. Among those in 4-year colleges or universities, 3 in 4 attended a public school."

U.S. Dept. of Commerce. Economic and Statistics Administration. "Census Back to School Facts." Census Bureau Fact Sheet 18 Aug 1997. document-level access: <http://www.census.gov/Press-Release/fs97-08.html>

"Americans aged 18 to 24 are 55 percent of all college students, and their numbers are projected to increase 23 percent between 1995 and 2007, according to the National Center for Education Statistics. While the number of adults aged 25 to 44 is projected to decline, total college enrollment increases 16 percent in the NCES's middle-series projections, from 13.9 million to 16.1 million, as a higher percentage of adults in all age groups attend college. The number of adults aged 25 to 29 will decrease 10 percent between 1995 and 2002, then increase 10 percent between 2002 and 2007. Yet enrollment in this age group is projected to increase 11 percent over the 12-year period. Men and women aged 30 to 34 may decline 19 percent, but their enrollment could decline only 4 percent....In 1995, 56 percent of all college students were full-time; in 2007, 59 percent may be full-time. The reason is the baby boomlet. While 77 percent of college students aged 18 to 24 are enrolled full-time, 71 percent of those aged 25 and older attend part-time." (p8)

"New Growth for Colleges." Forecast v17 n10 Oct 1997. p8. article-level access: <http://www.demographics.com/publications/fc/97_fc/9710_fc/fc97107.htm> (ISSN0732-1597).

COLLEGE STUDENTS--UNITED STATES--ALCOHOL USE

"A recent study by the Center on Addiction and Substance Abuse at Columbia University in New York reported that alcohol is a factor in 28 percent of dropouts and 40 percent of all academic problems. It also reported that, over a two-week span, 42 percent of all students get involved in 'binge drinking.'" (p11)

Clayton, Mark. "Learning: Colleges Turn to Peer Pressure to Curb Drinking." The Christian Science Monitor v89 n232 27 Oct 1997. p11. The Christian Science Monitor search engine: <http://www.csmonitor.com/plweb-cgi/iops1.pl> To retrieve this article, enter the following search: ED=19971027 AND drinking. In the "retrieved list," click the title that matches this record. (ISSN0882-7729).

U.S. "college students spend $5.5 billion on alcohol each year--more than on books, soda, coffee, juice, and milk combined." (p1) "According to a 1995 nationwide survey of college students, 44 percent admitted to drinking in binges (meaning that men drink five or more drinks at a setting, and women drink four or more). Members of fraternities and sororities are among the most likely to binge, at 86 percent and 80 percent, respectively, according to the Harvard University study." (p18)

Baldauf, Scott. "More Colleges Struggle to Cap Beer Culture." The Christian Science Monitor v89 n216 2 Oct 1997. p1,18. The Christian Science Monitor search engine: <http://www.csmonitor.com/plweb-cgi/iops1.pl> To retrieve this article, enter the following search: ED=19971002 AND culture. In the "retrieved list," click the title that matches this record. (ISSN0882-7729).

In the U.S., "a 1995 Harvard School of Public Health survey of 17,000 students at 140 colleges found that 86 percent of frat-house residents engaged in binge drinking--defined as five or more drinks in a row, one or more times in a two-week period--compared with 45 percent of non-Greek men. Similarly, 80 percent of sorority-house residents binged--defined for women as four or more drinks--compared with only 35 percent of non-Greek women." (p96-97)

Lord, Lewis. "Best Colleges 1998: From Party Hearty to Party Hardly?" U.S. News & World Report v123 n8 1 Sep 1997. p96-97. article-level access: <http://www.usnews.com/usnews/issue/970901/1FRAT.HTM> (ISSN0041-5537).

COLLEGE STUDENTS--UNITED STATES--ATTITUDES (v26)

COLLEGE STUDENTS--UNITED STATES--ECONOMIC CONDITIONS (v26)

COLLEGE STUDENTS, FOREIGN--GERMANY

"Germany has the third highest number of students from other countries, behind the United States and France. Of 140,000 students with non-German passports only 80,000 are considered as foreigners, whereas the vast majority of the remaining 60,000 are, for educational purposes, considered German due to their residence status....3,300 Indonesians studied in Germany in 1975, 1,000 more than today, even though twice as many Indonesians are now studying outside Indonesia....11.4% of US students who study abroad...[studied] in Germany in 1980, while today that figure is just 7.3%." (p29)

Schayan, Janet. "Universities: Studying in Germany." Deutschland n3 Jun 1997. p24-30. article-level access: <http://www.bundesregierung.de/.bin/lay/ausland/edu/edu.html> (ISSN0945-6791).

COLLEGE TEACHERS--SALARIES, ETC.--UNITED STATES (v26)

COLLEGE TEACHERS--TENURE--UNITED STATES (v26)

"Approximately 90% of all 4-year institutions in the United States have tenure systems, and 66% of all professors nationwide are estimated to be tenured (Mooney, 1993)....In the last decade, universities terminated only about 12 people per year for just cause (Painton, 1990)." (p349)

Premeaux, Shane R./Mondy, R. Wayne. "Tenure: Tenured versus Nontenured Faculty Perspectives." Journal of Education for Business v72 n6 Jul-Aug 1997. p349-353. (ISSN0883-2323).

COLLEGES, BUSINESS

see BUSINESS SCHOOLS

COLLISIONS, AIRCRAFT

see AIRCRAFT ACCIDENTS

COLLISIONS, AUTOMOBILE

see TRAFFIC ACCIDENTS

COLOMBIA--ARMED FORCES

"Among the Latin American countries, the size of Colombia's military forces (140,000) is second only to those of Brazil. Meanwhile, the number of persons employed in the country's defense and security agencies has increased from 165,000 (in 1985) to more than 303,000 in 1995 (Colombia/Comision de Racionalizacion, 1996...Colombia/Dept. of Treasury, 1994)....[Between 1991 and 1994,] the salaries of generals went up by 407.7%, while salaries of lieutenants increased by 200%." (p50) "In 1996, the military forces obtained about $400 million in redeemable security bonds (with no interest), to which the military attributed their successes, at least in part, against the guerrillas for that year (El Tiempo, 1997)." (p51)

Richani, Nazih. "The Political Economy of Violence: The War-System in Colombia." Journal of Interamerican Studies & World Affairs v39 n2 Sum 1997. p37-81. (ISSN0022-1937).

COLOMBIA--ARMED FORCES--APPROPRIATIONS AND EXPENDITURES

In Colombia, "the defense budget experienced a significant increase in recent years: rising from 2.2% of the gross domestic product (GDP) in 1980 up to 2.9% in 1994 (Leal Buitrago, 1994...); if one adds to this sum the service paid on the military debt, then the total allocated for defense in 1995 came to 3.6% of GDP--which places Colombia fifth in the Hemisphere (after the United States, Brazil, Argentina and Cuba) in absolute amounts allotted for that purpose (SIPRI, 1993). In general terms, the defense expenditures for 1993 were 2.5 times higher than those for 1990; however, the figures for 1990 were already double those of 1980 (Americas Watch, 1994...)." (p50)

Richani, Nazih. "The Political Economy of Violence: The War-System in Colombia." Journal of Interamerican Studies & World Affairs v39 n2 Sum 1997. p37-81. (ISSN0022-1937).

COLON (ANATOMY)--CANCER--MICHIGAN (v26)

COLON (ANATOMY)--CANCER--TESTING

The fecal blood test for colon cancer "'misses some early cancers, and it reduces mortality only about 15 to 30%, but it does detect some early cancers and large adenomas, and it definitely saves some lives,' [says David F. Ransohoff, MD]....'A work-up after a positive fecal test may detect cancer in 5 to 10% of patients, and half of those cancers may be in the early stages....'" (p10)

"Clinical News: Colonoscopy Recommended after Positive Fecal Blood Test, Says ACP." Modern Medicine v65 n7 Jul 1997. p10. (ISSN0026-8070).

COLON (ANATOMY)--CANCER--UNITED STATES (v26)

COLON, IRRITABLE

see IRRITABLE COLON

COLUMBUS (IND.)--EMPLOYMENT (v26)

COMFORT, STANDARD OF

see COST AND STANDARD OF LIVING

COMMERCE (v26)

see also ASIA--COMMERCE; BLACK MARKET; BUSINESS; CANADA--COMMERCE; CHINA--COMMERCE; CZECH REPUBLIC--COMMERCE; DEVELOPING COUNTRIES--COMMERCE; EUROPE--COMMERCE; FRANCE--COMMERCE; HONG KONG--COMMERCE; HOUSTON (TEX.)--COMMERCE; HUNGARY--COMMERCE; ICELAND--COMMERCE; INTERNATIONAL TRADE; IRELAND--COMMERCE; LATIN AMERICA--COMMERCE; MEXICO--COMMERCE; NOGALES (MEXICO)--COMMERCE; PERSIAN GULF REGION--COMMERCE; RUSSIA--COMMERCE; SAUDI ARABIA--COMMERCE; SINGAPORE--COMMERCE; SOUTH ASIA--COMMERCE; UKRAINE--COMMERCE; UNITED STATES--COMMERCE; UZBEKISTAN--COMMERCE; WHOLESALE TRADE

"Between 1950 and 1990, world trade increased 11-fold to about $3.5 trillion (in 1990 $), over twice as fast as the world product, which increased a little less than five times over the same period....The turnover of each of the world's largest 100 corporations exceeded the individual GDP of more than half the world's nation-states." (p62)

Ekins, Paul. "The Future of the World Trade Organization: Proposals for Fair and Environmentally Sustainable Trade." Democracy & Nature v3 n3 1997. p57-89.

"The World Trade Organization reports that global trade for 1996 was about $5.1 trillion. This 4 percent increase was, however, five times less than the increase recorded for 1995. THIS WEEK IN GERMANY reports that export earnings for European Union nations only increased by 4 percent--compared to 8 percent in 1995." (p16)

"The Global Marketplace: World Trade Ain't Working." Earth Island Journal v12 n3 Sum 1997. p16. (ISSN1041-0406).

COMMERCIAL AERONAUTICS

see AERONAUTICS, COMMERCIAL

COMMERCIAL CREDIT--UNITED STATES--WOMEN (v26)

COMMERCIAL FISHING

see FISHERIES

COMMERCIAL PRODUCTS--SAFETY MEASURES

see PRODUCT SAFETY

COMMERCIAL STRIPS--UNITED STATES

In the U.S., "more than 56,000 businesses operate within one-quarter mile of an interstate highway interchange. These businesses employed 1.8 million Americans and generated sales of $111 billion in 1996....Interstate businesses in the U.S. include 28,100 restaurants, 13,200 gas stations, 10,200 hotels and motels, 1,100 truck stops, and 3,500 other establishments. The number-one product in this market--gasoline--should also post the fastest rate of sales growth in the next four years, according to forecasts produced by Thomas Corsi and colleagues at the University of Maryland for the NATSO Foundation, a research group for the travel plaza and truck-stop industry." (p3)

"The Gas/Food/Lodging Forecast." Forecast v17 n9 Sep 1997. p3. article-level access: <http://www.demographics.com/Publications/FC/97_fc/9709_fc/FC97092.htm> (ISSN0732-1597).

COMMERCIALS, TELEVISION

see TELEVISION ADVERTISING

COMMODITY EXCHANGES--UNITED STATES (v26)

"Since 1980 the volume of contracts traded on the U.S. commodity markets grew from 83 million to over 495 million in fiscal 1996, an increase of over 412 million contracts or more than a five-fold increase in total volume. During that same period, the number of designated contracts rose from 80 to over 500. Currently, we have over 157 futures and option contracts trading on U.S. futures exchanges....Although the breadth and scope of the markets which the [Commodity Futures Trading Administration] Commission regulates has grown roughly 500 percent since 1980, the Commission's staffing level grew from 459 full time equivalent staff-years in 1980 to 541 in 1996, an increase of only 82 staff years or 18 percent. To fund this operation, the Commission's budget grew from 17 million to 54 million dollars, an increase of 37 million dollars over the 1980-96 period." (p112)

U.S. Farm Credit Administration. "Agriculture, Rural Development, Food and Drug Administration...Approp. for 1998 (Part 2)." Hearing. U.S. House. Committee on Appropriations. Washington, D.C. : GPO, 1997. (Y4.Ap6/1:Ag8/997/pt.2).

The Commodity Futures Trading Commission "supervises all trading of futures and option contracts on eleven U.S. futures exchanges....Exchange futures and option trading has more than doubled in the last decade (from 216 million to 495 million contracts)--an increase of 131%. This growth is expected to continue with a volume of 562 million contracts projected for 1998 (an increase of 160% over 1986)." (p165)

Born, Brooksley (Chair, Commodity Futures Trading Commission). "Agriculture, Rural Development, Food and Drug Administration...Approp. for 1998 (Part 2)." Hearing. U.S. House. Committee on Appropriations. Washington, D.C. : GPO, 1997. (Y4.Ap6/1:Ag8/997/pt.2).

COMMUNICABLE DISEASES (v26)

see also FOODBORNE DISEASES; SEXUALLY TRANSMITTED DISEASES

"Greater population density contributes to the spread of disease, a new report by the Population Reference Bureau (PRB) stresses. The number of people living in cities of one million or more is expected to grow from 927 million in 1995 to 1.7 billion by 2015....More than 28 new disease-causing microbes have been identified since 1973, the study notes....IPDs [infectious and parasitic diseases] are a leading cause of death worldwide. More than 17 million people died from these diseases in 1995--accounting for more than one-fourth of all deaths. About 97 percent of deaths from these diseases occur in low-income countries, many of which have high fertility rates and soaring urbanization....IPDs also exact enormous financial costs. In the United States alone, their annual cost--including the direct cost of medical treatment and prevention combined with the indirect costs of lost productivity--is estimated to be some $120 billion." (p1) "The United States records 600,000 cases of pneumonia each year, resulting in 25,000 to 50,000 deaths, and between 10,000 and 40,000 deaths due to influenza. The new states of the former Soviet Union experienced an epidemic of diphtheria in recent years with more than 40,000 cases reported in 1994." (p4)

"Urbanization Spurs Return of Diseases." Popline v19 Sep-Oct 1997. p1,4.

"More than 28 new disease-causing microbes have been identified since 1973....IPDs [infectious and parasitic diseases] are a leading cause of death worldwide. More than 17 million people died from these diseases in 1995--accounting for more than one-fourth of all deaths. About 97 percent of deaths from these diseases occur in low-income countries....In the United States alone, the annual cost of IPDs (including the direct cost of medical treatment and prevention combined with the indirect costs of lost productivity) is estimated to be some $120 billion....The United States records 600,000 cases of pneumonia each year, resulting in 25,000 to 50,000 deaths, and between 10,000 and 40,000 deaths due to influenza. The new states of the former Soviet Union experienced an epidemic of diphtheria in 1990, with more than 40,000 cases reported in 1994."

Population Reference Bureau. "Infectious and Parasitic Diseases Continue to Threaten World Health, Report Finds." Press Release 4 Aug 1997. document-level access: <http://www.prb.org/media/pressrel.htm>

COMMUNICABLE DISEASES--VACCINATION

see VACCINATION OF CHILDREN

COMMUNICATION AND TRAFFIC

see also AERONAUTICS; BUS LINES; TAXICABS

COMMUNICATION AND TRAFFIC--UNITED STATES

In the U.S., "three decades ago, there were 5.5 automobile-related deaths for every 100 million miles driven. Today, that number is 1.7, the lowest ever in the United States. (Sweden's is 1.3, Britain's 1.4). And there's been a 90-percent reduction in the fatality rate since statistics were first kept back in the 1920s....Miles traveled have increased by 35 percent in the past decade, while miles of road have barely increased at all. The Federal Highway Administration estimates that almost 70 percent of today's urban freeways are clogged during rush hour, compared to 55 percent in 1983. And in the past decade, the number of cars on the road has grown faster (17 percent) than the number of people in the United States (10 percent)." (p1 secE)

Hazleton, Lesley. "Stop: Hell on Wheels." Detroit Free Press 30 Oct 1997. p1-2 secE.

COMMUNISM--FRANCE (v26)

COMMUNIST COUNTRIES--POLITICS AND GOVERNMENT --PUBLIC OPINION (v26)

COMMUNITIES, BIOTIC

see BIOTIC COMMUNITIES

COMMUNITIES, RELIGIOUS

see RELIGIOUS COMMUNITIES

COMMUNITY COLLEGES--UNITED STATES

Of the U.S.'s "1,200 two-year colleges with 5.5 million students, 660 are in rural areas and enroll some 1.5 million students. About 150 of the rural colleges are located in economically distressed communities." (p19)

Higuera, Jonathan J. "Going Home, Staying Home." Ford Foundation Report v28 n2 Spr 1997. p19-22. (ISSN1063-7281).

COMMUNITY DEVELOPMENT--AUSTRALIA

"During 1995-96, Australia's community service organisations spent a total of $9,705 million on provision of community service and related activities, according to preliminary figures released...by the Australian Bureau of Statistics (ABS). The publication 'Community Services, Australia 1995-96'...reveals that $8,946 million was spent on direct community service provision and a further $759 million was spent on community service related activities. The major areas of expenditure on direct community service provision were residential care and accommodation support ($5,062 million), personal and social support ($1,526 million) and child care ($1,043 million). 'Not for profit' organisations accounted for 51 per cent ($4,520 million) of all expenditure on direct community service provision while Government organisations accounted for 29 per cent ($2,585 million)."

Australian Bureau of Statistics. "Australia's Community Services Expenditure, 1995-96." Media Release 4 Aug 1997. document-level access: <http://www.abs.gov.au/websitedbs/d3110125.nsf/4a255eef008309e44a255eef00061e57/e8c69115a7ccd72d4a2564e8007fb98f?OpenDocument>

COMMUNITY DEVELOPMENT, URBAN--UNITED STATES (v26)

COMMUNITY DEVELOPMENT CORPORATIONS--UNITED STATES (v26)

COMMUNITY HEALTH SERVICES--UNITED STATES

In the U.S., "today, more than eight million people are served by 685 health centers nationwide, and 42 percent of those patients are children....The number of uninsured patients seen at health centers rose 46 percent between 1990 and 1996. The centers encourage people to use preventive services so that serious health conditions can be averted or resolved early and quickly....Current data show 63 percent of women using the centers have up-to-date mammograms and 88 percent have current pap smears."

U.S. Dept. of Health and Human Services. "HHS Expands Access to Health Care with $18.2 Million for New Health Centers and Voucher Programs." Press Release 6 Oct 1997. document-level access: <http://www.hhs.gov/news/press/1997pres/971006.html>

COMMUNITY LEADERSHIP--THAILAND--BANGKOK (v26)

COMMUTING--IRELAND

In Ireland, the Central Statistics Office report, "'Census 1991, Volume 11, Travel to Work, School and College,' reveals that driving a car to work has been the main mode of transport in each of the census years of 1981, 1986 and 1991. More than one third (38.9%) of commuters used this means of transport in 1991, compared with 37.2% in 1986 and 36% in 1981....The use of buses and trains, taken together, has declined from 11% in 1981 to 9.4% in 1991. Bus use dropped steadily between 1981 and 1991 while there was a moderate increase in train use. Some 7.7% of workers used the bus in 1991 compared with 9.7% in 1981. However, train use (which includes the DART) went from 1.3% in 1981 to 1.7% in 1991. The numbers walking or riding a motorcycle to work have also fallen steadily. Walking, as a mode of commuting, accounted for 13.4% in 1981, but this was down to 11.1% in 1991."

Ireland. Central Statistics Office. "Census 1991--Volume 11: Travel to Work, School and College." Press Release 10 Jul 1997. document-level access: <http://www.cso.ie/pressreleases/prelcentrav.html>

COMMUTING--IRELAND--WOMEN

According to Ireland's Central Statistics Office, "the percentage of women driving to work has increased between 1981 and 1991 from 22.3% to 34.7% while the male percentage remained static at around 41%. The average distance travelled to work by women has gone up between 1981 and 1991. Women in rural areas travelled an average of more than 6.5 miles in 1981, but this had gone up to more than 7 miles in 1991. Their urban counterparts travelled more than 3 miles in 1981 and just under 4 miles in 1991."

Ireland. Central Statistics Office. "Census 1991--Volume 11: Travel to Work, School and College." Press Release 10 Jul 1997. document-level access: <http://www.cso.ie/pressreleases/prelcentrav.html>

COMMUTING--MICHIGAN--DETROIT

In the Detroit metropolitan area, "four out of 10 employed Macomb County residents now travel to another county to work, according to the most recent U.S. Census statistics. Almost one in three of Oakland County's employed work elsewhere in the region; 23 percent of Wayne County's workers cross county lines for jobs." (p7 secA)

French, Ron/Daugherty, Jane/Kiska, Tim. "Archer Landslide: THE DETROIT NEWS WWJ 950 Exit Poll: Suburbs Back Archer and Rebirth of Detroit." Detroit News 5 Nov 1997. p1,7 secA.

COMMUTING--UNITED STATES

"A 1996 report conducted by the Eno Transportation Foundation entitled 'Commuting in America II,' found that today, the dominant commuting flow pattern is suburban, with 50 percent of the Nation's commuters living in the suburbs and over 41 percent of all jobs located there, up from 37 percent in 1980. Suburban areas are now the main destination of work trips. The report also found there was a substantial increase in reverse commuting, central city to suburbs, commuting rose from 9 percent share of growth over the decade from 1970 to 1980 to 12 percent from 1980 to 1990." (pS10525)

Lautenberg, Frank R. (Sen.-N.J.). "Intermodal Surface Transportation Efficiency Act of 1997--Motion to Proceed." Congressional Record. Daily ed. v143 n139 8 Oct 1997. pS10522-10536. section/page-level access: <http://thomas.loc.gov/cgi-bin/query/R?r105:FLD001:S10525:> (ISSN0363-7239). (X1.1A.105/1).

COMPACT DISC INDUSTRY--UNITED STATES (v26)

COMPANIES

see BUSINESS ENTERPRISES

COMPANIES, TELEPHONE

see TELEPHONE COMPANIES

COMPANY AIRCRAFT

see AIRPLANES, COMPANY

COMPENSATION

see PENSIONS

COMPENSATION (LAW)--UNITED STATES

In the U.S., a recent in-depth study "on punitive damages was published last year by Theodore Eisenberg, a professor of bankruptcy, civil rights and empirical studies at Cornell Law School. It was based on data gathered by the National Center for State Courts from all of about 6,000 tort trials in 45 large counties during the course of one year. Eisenberg found that juries sided with the plaintiffs in 2,849 cases but awarded punitive damages only 177 times, or just 6 percent of the time. The statistical mean punitive award of $534,000 that plaintiffs received was just 38 percent higher than the mean compensatory damages award of $386,000." (p69) A "study of 1,000 lawsuits in San Francisco Superior Court found that businesses and government defendants face punitive damages in one-third of all lawsuits against them....Cases in which punitive damages were sought took 21 months to resolve, 40 percent longer than the 15 months it took to resolve cases without punitive claims, the study reported." (p70)

Thompson, Mark. "Tort Law: Applying the Brakes to Punitives." ABA Journal v83 Sep 1997. p68-72. (ISSN0747-0088).

COMPREHENSIVE HEALTH CARE DELIVERY ORGANIZATIONS

see HEALTH MAINTENANCE ORGANIZATIONS

COMPULSIVE GAMBLING--UNITED STATES (v26)

COMPUTER GAMES--UNITED STATES--EMPLOYEES

"According to a 1995 study conducted by Coleman & Associates, Inc. a Teaneck, N.J.-based high-tech market-research firm, 44 percent of the U.S. population play games on their PCs. And among adult game players who were asked when they had their most recent experience playing a game, 23 percent reported that they'd last done so while at work....DVD Software, an Irvine, Calif.-based firm that sells a popular program called 'Antigame,' claims that games cost American corporations and governments an estimated $50 billion per year in lost productivity." (p18)

Stuller, Jay. "Games Workers Play." Across the Board v34 n7 Jul-Aug 1997. p16-22. (ISSN0147-1554).

COMPUTER NETWORKS

see INTERNET (COMPUTER NETWORK)

COMPUTER SERVICE INDUSTRY--AUSTRALIA

"Data released by the Australian Bureau of Statistics...showed that, at the end of June 1996, there were 9,679 businesses in the computing services industry, which was almost double the 4,894 businesses in the industry at the end June 1993. The ABS publication 'Computing Services Industry, Australia 1995-96'...stated that businesses in the industry generated $8,088 million in income in 1995-96. The main single source of this income was from software consultancy services ($2,099 million), which represented 26 per cent of total income of the industry. The other major source of income was the sale of computer and communication hardware, which accounted [for] 13 per cent ($1,048 million) of total income. Although the majority of indicators showed growth in the industry, the operating profit margin declined from 9.3 per cent in 1992-93 to 5.7 per cent in 1995-96."

Australian Bureau of Statistics. "Computing Services Industry Doubles, Profits Fall--ABS Survey Results." Media Release 15 Oct 1997. document-level access: <http://www.abs.gov.au/websitedbs/d3110125.nsf/4a255eef008309e44a255eef00061e57/6512ebe586ae1ac5ca2565380002179d?OpenDocument>

COMPUTER SERVICE INDUSTRY--EMPLOYMENT --AUSTRALIA

According to the Australian Bureau of Statistics, "there were 55,046 people employed in the [computing services] industry at the end of June 1996, of which 27,797 employees were computer and technical staff. Since June 1993, employment in the industry rose from 30,056. This represented an 87 per cent rise in full-time employment and a 71 per cent rise in part-time employment. At the end of June 1996, 88 per cent of businesses in the industry employed less than 5 people. These businesses accounted for 27 per cent (15,006) of people employed in the industry and generated 14 per cent ($1,157 million) of total income. There were 51 businesses in the industry with employment of over 100 people, accounting for 42 per cent of employment and contributing 59 per cent of total income."

Australian Bureau of Statistics. "Computing Services Industry Doubles, Profits Fall--ABS Survey Results." Media Release 15 Oct 1997. document-level access: <http://www.abs.gov.au/websitedbs/d3110125.nsf/4a255eef008309e44a255eef00061e57/6512ebe586ae1ac5ca2565380002179d?OpenDocument>

COMPUTER SOFTWARE--UNITED STATES (v26)

COMPUTER SOFTWARE INDUSTRY

Internet Web Site commercial software packages can "cost from $500 to upwards of $15,000....Web sites will spend $47 million on analysis software this year, according to the International Data Corporation, a figure that will rise to $100 million a year by 2001." (p36)

Kirsner, Scott. "Web of Confusion." American Journalism Review v19 n6 Jul-Aug 1997. p34-39. (ISSN1067-8654).

COMPUTER SOFTWARE INDUSTRY--CROATIA --HUNGARY

The Business Software Alliance "estimates that in Hungary alone about three-quarters of all software in use is pirated....In Croatia,...where the BSA recently set up an office, use of illicit software is estimated at about 94 percent." (p20)

Horvath, John. "MediaReports: Cyberspace: Leveling Effects." Toward Freedom v46 n7 Dec 1997-Jan 1998. p20-21. (ISSN0048-9898).

COMPUTER SOFTWARE INDUSTRY--UNITED STATES (v26)

COMPUTERS (v26)

"On 29 November 1995, the MITRE Corporation began an assessment of the effects of the year 2000 on software applications. A team of MITRE analysts studied nine command-and-control systems and two automated information systems and analyzed more than 5.4 million lines of code. MITRE found that between 1% and 5% of the code would be affected by the year change, and determined that correcting the command-and-control systems would require from 8 to 71 staff years per million lines of code and cost $1.00 to $8.52 for each line. The automated information systems code would require 9 to 16 staff years per million lines of code to correct and cost $0.75 to $1.70 for each line." (p70)

"Experts estimate that the global cost of conversion to 2000 compliance will be $300 to $600 billion. Some estimate that testing will account for 50% to 70% of the time and resources required to solve the problem. The estimated U.S. government cost alone is $30 billion." (p72)

Gutsch, Barbara J. "Countdown to 2000." Proceedings v123 n9 Sep 1997. p69-73. (ISSN0041-798X).

COMPUTERS--AFRO-AMERICANS (v26)

COMPUTERS--AUSTRALIA

In Australia, "of the estimated 4 million home computer users only 300,000 (7.5 per cent) accessed the Internet, 200,000 (5 per cent) used electronic mail, and 100,000 (2.5 per cent) accessed other online services/databases according to the survey Household Use of Information Technology released...by the Australian Bureau of Statistics. The highest proportion of home computer users were the 5-17 year olds (41 per cent), followed by the 18-24 year olds (29 per cent), 25-39 year olds (23 per cent), 40-54 year olds (25 per cent), and persons 55 years and over, (7 per cent)....Two million (31 per cent) Australian households frequently used a computer. A further 3 per cent of households (nearly 190,000) had a computer, but did not use it frequently. These 2 million households used 2.6 million computers. Nearly 1.6 million households used 1 computer, and only 0.4 million households used 2 or more computers. Over 0.5 million households had a modem, and nearly 1 million households had CD-ROM equipment."

Australian Bureau of Statistics. "Take-Up Rate for Modem and Internet Use Low." Media Release 14 Nov 1997. document-level access: <http://www.abs.gov.au/websitedbs/d3110125.nsf/4a255eef008309e44a255eef00061e57/a183eeba1ad8e68cca25654f0004efc9?OpenDocument>

COMPUTERS--ECONOMIC ASPECTS--UNITED STATES

According to Daniel E. Sichel's book, THE COMPUTER REVOLUTION: AN ECONOMIC PERSPECTIVE, in the U.S., "private consultants estimate...that a $2,500 PC costs a typical big business from $6,000 to $13,000 a year in...secondary expenditures....For the first half of 1997, just a hair over 1% of GDP was devoted to business investment in computers; in 1996, they accounted for only 2% of the value of all capital equipment...." (p4) "Sichel estimates that computers contributed just 5% to total U.S. economic growth between 1970 and 1992. Other forms of capital investment contributed nearly seven times as much." (p5)

"Where's the Payoff?: Daniel E. Sichel, THE COMPUTER REVOLUTION: AN ECONOMIC PERSPECTIVE." Left Business Observer n79 29 Sep 1997. p4-5. (ISSN1042-0134).

COMPUTERS--EDUCATION--UNITED STATES

"Believing computers enhance education, [U.S.] schools have added between 300,000 and 400,000 of them every year for the past decade, according to the Office of Technology Assessment. The average number of students per computer has fallen dramatically over the past 10 years from 125 in 1983 to nine in 1995. States vary: Kentucky has eight students per computer; New Hampshire has 22....About 75 percent of public schools have computers...[that are linked to the Internet]....Only 40 percent of schools have computers with telecommunication capabilities in the classrooms. Thirty-five percent of public schools have access to the Internet, but only 3 percent of instructional rooms (classrooms, labs and media centers) are connected....There is a huge gap in the availablility of the Internet between schools with large proportions of students from low-income families: 31 percent compared with 62 percent of schools with relatively few low-income students." (p7)

"Statestats: The Newest Way to Learn." State Legislatures v23 n6 Jun 1997. p7. (ISSN0147-6041).

COMPUTERS--GREAT BRITAIN

"One-third of British homes already have a personal computer, compared with 28 percent in the United States, and 20 percent in Germany, according to a report by Italian-based Olivetti personal computers. Britain also has proportionately more schools with computers than any other nation, and more pupils with access to them. Secondary schools have an average of 85 computers each--1 for every 8.5 pupils. This is double the provision in Germany, and better than Japan, France, and Italy. Currently, however, only 6,000 schools in Britain are connected to the Internet, and surveys have shown that more than a third of the country's 500,000 teachers are uncomfortable using computers." (p1,7)

MacLeod, Alexander. "International: Wiring Schools to Net Alarms British Teachers." The Christian Science Monitor v89 n225 16 Oct 1997. p1,7. The Christian Science Monitor search engine: <http://www.csmonitor.com/plweb-cgi/iops1.pl> To retrieve this article, enter the following search: ED=19971016 AND teachers. In the "retrieved list," click the title that matches this record. (ISSN0882-7729).

COMPUTERS--INDIA

"India's annual software exports are now running at $1.1 billion, up from just $100 million at the beginning of the decade. Although this constitutes just a fraction of the $250 billion global software market, that figure is growing at about 50 percent a year....India has only about one computer for every 1,000 people, a low figure." (p18)

Zubrzycki, John. "Mastering Software Helps India Youths Snag Foreign Jobs." The Christian Science Monitor v89 n244 13 Nov 1997. p1,18. The Christian Science Monitor search engine: <http://www.csmonitor.com/plweb-cgi/iops1.pl> To retrieve this article, enter the following search: ED=19971113 AND jobs. In the "retrieved list," click the title that matches this record. (ISSN0882-7729).

COMPUTERS--UNITED STATES (v26)

A 1996 study by the U.S. government's "General Accounting Office estimated that in 1995 alone, the 2 million computers on the 10,000 networks of the Defense Department were broken into as many as 250,000 times. The likely number for 1996 is twice that many: a half-million break-ins. The success rate for hackers is high--nearly two-thirds of attempts succeed--while less than 1 percent of attacks are detected." (p72)

Jefferson, Jon. "Cyber Law: Deleting Cybercrooks." ABA Journal v83 Oct 1997. p68-72,74. (ISSN0747-0088).

In the U.S., "the share of households with personal computers and modems may increase from 16 percent in 1995 to 42 percent in 2000, as the share of household PCs that have modems may increase from 41 percent to 94 percent....The number of Internet host sites has increased from 1.3 million in January 1993 to 12.9 million in July 1996, and it is estimated at 16.1 million in January 1997." (p8)

"Web Advertising Poised for Takeoff." Forecast v17 n8 Aug 1997. p8. article-level access: <http://www.demographics.com/Publications/FC/97_fc/9708_fc/FC97085.htm> (ISSN0732-1597).

COMPUTERS--UNITED STATES--HIGH SCHOOL STUDENTS (v26)

COMPUTERS--UNITED STATES--SCHOOLS (v26)

"Some 6.3 million computers were available to students in 1996-97, a 23.5 percent increase for the year and a 186 percent jump over the 2.2 million machines in the schools in 1991-92, according to statistics compiled by Market Data Retrieval of Shelton, Conn. The ratio of students per computer declined from 36.5 a decade ago to 19.3 five years ago, and 7.3 in the last school year....Schools with less than 5 percent minorities have a ratio of 6.6 students per computer; those where more than half the students are minorities have a ratio of 8.4 students per computer....The percentage of schools with Internet access went from 32 percent in 1995-96 to 70 percent last year. In affluent neighborhoods, the figure is 78 percent, compared with 69 percent for blue-collar neighborhoods and 66 percent in rural areas." (pA12)

"E-Wire: The Boom Goes On--And So Do the Inequities." American School Board Journal Sep 1997. pA12,A14. (ISSN0003-0953).

According to "Computers and Classrooms: The Status of Technology in U.S. Schools," a recent report by the Educational Testing Service, "in schools with 90% or more minority students, the ratio is about 30 students per multimedia computer. At schools with minority enrollments between 24% and 49%, the ratio is 22-to-1. While about three-quarters of schools with smaller percentages of poor students have Internet access, the percentage drops to slightly more than half of schools with high levels of poor students." (p4)

Ziebarth, Todd. "Will Computers Close the Equity Gap--Or Widen It?" State Education Leader v15 n3 Fall 1997. p4. (ISSN0736-7511).

COMPUTERS--UNITED STATES--TEENAGERS

In the U.S., a 1997 NEWSWEEK poll revealed that "89 percent of teens use computers at least several times a week....61 percent surf the Internet. Boys are more likely than girls to have online experience (66 percent to 56 percent), and teens from wealthier families are more likely to have online experience than teens from lower-income families." (p6)

"News of the Profession: Parents & Reading: Teens and Technology." Reading Today v15 n1 Aug-Sep 1997. p6. (ISSN0737-4208).

COMPUTERS--UNITED STATES--YOUTH (v26)

COMPUTERS--UNIVERSITY OF MICHIGAN (v26)

CONCEPTION--PREVENTION

see CONTRACEPTION

CONCERTS--INSURANCE--UNITED STATES (v26)

CONDOMS--PHILIPPINES--PROSTITUTES--YOUNG MEN (v26)

CONDOMS--PHILIPPINES--YOUNG ADULTS (v26)

CONDOMS--PHILIPPINES--YOUNG MEN--ATTITUDES (v26)

CONDOMS--UNITED STATES--YOUTH

"In 1991, New York City schools became the first in the...[U.S.] to hand out condoms....[Recently,] a total of 7,119 students from 12 randomly selected New York high schools were surveyed, as were 5,738 students from 10 high schools in Chicago, which does not have a condom-giveaway program. Virtually equal numbers of students in both cities admitted to sexual activity: 59.7 percent in New York and 60.1 percent in Chicago, according to the study. But researchers noted that 60.8 percent of New York students said they used a condom during their most recent sexual intercourse, compared with 55.5 percent of Chicago students." (p9)

"Before the Board: Condoms Don't Mean More Sex, Study Says." American School Board Journal v184 n12 Dec 1997. p9. (ISSN0003-0953).

CONFECTIONERY--UNITED STATES (v26)

CONFLICT MANAGEMENT

see also MEDIATION

CONFLICT MANAGEMENT--UNITED STATES

The vast majority of U.S. corporations participating in a recent alternative dispute resolution "survey said they have used alternative means of dispute resolution in the last three years....Eighty-eight percent of the respondents have used mediation in the last three years, while 79% have used arbitration....More than 84% said they were likely or very likely to use mediation in the future, while 69% indicated that they would use arbitration in the future. Forty-one percent reported using mediation-arbitration or med-arb; 23% used minitrial; 21% said they used fact-finding; and only 11% used peer review. Fifty-five respondents said they have an ombudsperson on staff, and 185 use an in-house grievance procedure (as distinguished from grievance procedures that might exist in collective bargaining agreements). Almost 90% of the companies viewed mediation as a cost-saving measure; 54% said cost pressures affected their decision to use ADR....Eighty-one percent of the respondents said their companies use mediation because it provides 'a more satisfactory process' than litigation; 66% said it provides more 'satisfactory settlements'; and 59% said it 'preserves good relationships.'" (p7)

"ADR News: Extensive Study Reveals: Big Corporations Often Use ADR." Dispute Resolution Journal v52 n3 Sum 1997. p7.

CONGENITAL HEART DISEASE--UNITED STATES (v26)

CONGESTIVE HEART FAILURE--UNITED STATES (v26)

In the U.S., "half of the men diagnosed with heart failure die within 1.7 years, and half of the women within 3.2 years....In the United States,...[congestive heart failure] is the chief cause of some 40,000 deaths every year and is a contributing factor in an additional 225,000 deaths....An estimated 4.8 million Americans have congestive heart failure, and about 400,000 new cases are recorded every year in the United States....In the United States, congestive heart failure is the leading cause of hospitalization among people age 65 and older. The condition led to 822,000 hospitalizations in 1992, up from 377,000 in 1979." (p8)

"Heart Disease: Congestive Heart Failure." Healthline v16 n9 Sep 1997. p8-9. (ISSN0736-7929).

CONGRESSIONAL MEDAL OF HONOR

see MEDAL OF HONOR

CONJUGAL VIOLENCE--COLOMBIA--NORTH AMERICA

In a recent Gallup poll, "as many as one-fifth of American women, and substantial numbers of women in three other nations in this hemisphere, report having been physically abused at some point in their lives by their spouses or companions....A total of 22% of women in the U.S., a projected 30 million, say they have been physically abused by their husbands or partners. The percentages reported in the other three nations are Colombia, 17%, Canada, 9%, and Mexico, 6%....Some men in each nation also report physical abuse by their spouses or companions, generally a third the number of women. In the U.S., the number of men who report having been abused is 8%....About one in five U.S. residents who report having been abused say that it occurred within the past year."

Gallup, George, Jr./Gallup Organization. "Many Women Cite Spousal Abuse; Job Performance Affected." Press Release 25 Oct 1997. document-level access: <http://www.gallup.com/poll/news/971025.html>

CONJUGAL VIOLENCE--MICHIGAN (v26)

CONJUGAL VIOLENCE--UNITED STATES (v26)

In the U.S., "recent statistics show that 29 percent of all violence against women by a single offender is committed by an intimate--a husband, ex-husband, boyfriend or ex-boyfriend. Estimates of assaults on women by partners or cohabitants range from 1.8 million to almost 4 million per year."

U.S. Dept. of Health and Human Services. "Improving Women's Health." Fact Sheet 25 Oct 1997. document-level access: <http://www.hhs.gov/news/press/1997pres/971025c.html>

In a recent Gallup poll, "53% of the total sample of Americans say they personally know of...a situation or situations [in which women have been physically abused by their husbands or boyfriends]. The picture in the U.S. has not improved over the last three years--49% in a June 1994 Gallup survey said they knew of such incidents. All persons who said they have been abused and currently have a job outside the home were asked this question: 'Has this physical abuse by your spouse or companion caused you to perform less effectively at your job, or to miss days of work, or both?' The findings indicate that between one-third and one-half of Americans (men and women combined) who have been abused and who are employed outside the home have experienced negative consequences related to their work--in terms of being less effective, missing days of work, or both."

Gallup, George, Jr./Gallup Organization. "Many Women Cite Spousal Abuse; Job Performance Affected." Press Release 25 Oct 1997. document-level access: <http://www.gallup.com/poll/news/971025.html>

CONSERVATION OF ENERGY

see FORCE AND ENERGY

CONSERVATION OF ENERGY RESOURCES

see ENERGY CONSERVATION

CONSERVATION OF HABITAT

see HABITAT CONSERVATION

CONSERVATION OF NATURAL RESOURCES

see also ENERGY CONSERVATION; NATIONAL PARKS AND RESERVES; RECYCLING (WASTE, ETC.)

CONSERVATION OF NATURAL RESOURCES--GEORGIA

In 1996, Conservation Reserve Program "contracts expired on 260,000 acres, or 4 percent of Georgia's total farmland. Contracts on approximately 176,000 additional acres in Georgia will expire from the CRP in 1997, followed by about 160,000 acres in 1998....Georgia, the state with the largest number of program acres in the Southeast, had approximately 706,500 acres enrolled in CRP at the end of 1996; 91 percent of that acreage was planted in trees....In Georgia, about 47 percent of the state's acreage enrolled in the CRP at the end of 1996 will not qualify under the new, stricter criteria, according to the University of Georgia." (p8)

"Georgia Landowners Face Decision on Conservation Reserve Program Acreage." Federal Reserve Bank of Atlanta Regional Update v10 n3 Jul-Sep 1997. p1,8-9.

CONSERVATION OF NATURAL RESOURCES--UNITED STATES

In the U.S., "the 36 million acres enrolled in the original CRP [Conservation Reserve Program] represented approximately 8 percent of the nation's farmland, based on 1992 census data....By the end of 1997, original CRP contracts will expire on 21 million acres nationwide, about 58 percent of the original CRP contracts, according to the USDA." (p1) "Nationally only 2.5 million acres, or 6.8 percent, of the total CRP lands were planted in trees as of 1996, according to the USDA....While contracts on approximately 21 million acres expire in 1997, only 16 million acres will be accepted into the program this year." (p8)

"Georgia Landowners Face Decision on Conservation Reserve Program Acreage." Federal Reserve Bank of Atlanta Regional Update v10 n3 Jul-Sep 1997. p1,8-9.

CONSERVATION OF PLANT GENETIC RESOURCES

see GERMPLASM RESOURCES, PLANT

CONSERVATION OF WILDLIFE

see WILDLIFE CONSERVATION

CONSTRUCTION CONTRACTS--UNITED STATES --FINANCE (v26)

CONSTRUCTION INDUSTRY--BRAZIL (v26)

CONSTRUCTION INDUSTRY--HONG KONG

In Hong Kong, "the gross value of construction work, in nominal terms, performed by main contractors amounted to $31.8 billion in the second quarter of 1997, according to the preliminary results of the Quarterly Survey of Construction Output released...by the Census and Statistics Department. This represented an increase of 15.4% over the same quarter last year....The gross value of construction work, measured at constant (1990) market prices, performed in the second quarter of 1997 increased by 6.2% over the same quarter last year. The gross value of construction work, in nominal terms, performed at private sector sites totalled $13.0 billion, representing a notable increase of 32% over the same quarter last year. When measured at constant (1990) market prices, it was up by 17.8%. The gross value of construction work, in nominal terms, performed at public sector sites amounted to $10.9 billion, representing a slight decrease of 2.3% over the same quarter last year. When measured at constant (1990) market prices, it was down by 8%."

Hong Kong. Census and Statistics Department. "Construction Output Statistics for 1997 2nd Quarter." Press Release 3 Oct 1997. document-level access: <http://www.info.gov.hk/censtatd/hkstat/press/bu12q97.htm>

CONSTRUCTION INDUSTRY--MICHIGAN

"A report by the Southeast Michigan Council of Governments shows that residential construction in southeast Michigan reached its highest level this decade during 1996. More than 23,000 residential building permits were issued in the council's seven-county region. Almost 80 percent were for single-family homes....Oakland County accounted for a third of the building permits, but Macomb Township led the region's municipalities in total units authorized with 1,346. Neighboring Shelby Township ranked second, with 1,183 permits." (p1,4 secB)

McDiarmid, Hugh, Jr. "Local News: Macomb Boom Leads Region's Home Growth." Detroit Free Press 24 Jul 1997. p1,4 secB.

CONSTRUCTION INDUSTRY--MIDDLE WEST

According to the Kansas City Fed's Second Quarter 1997 REGIONAL ECONOMIC DIGEST, in the Middle West, "construction employment rose 2.9 percent in the first quarter and was up 5.7 percent from a year ago....The total value of construction contracts rose 5.2 percent above the previous quarter but was 4.9 percent below the previous year....The value of construction contracts in the...[U.S.] dropped 3.0 percent in the first quarter but was

1.3 percent higher than a year ago." (unpaginated)

"Regional Economy Enjoys Solid Growth in First Quarter." Federal Reserve Bank of Kansas City Fed Letter Aug 1997.

According to the Kansas City Fed's Third Quarter 1997 REGIONAL ECONOMIC DIGEST, the total value of construction contracts in the Tenth Federal Reserve District, which includes Colorado, Kansas, Missouri, Nebraska, New Mexico, Oklahoma and Wyoming, "was up 16.3 percent from the previous quarter but was 9.6 percent below the previous year's level. Construction employment slipped 1.8 percent in the second quarter but was 2.7 percent above a year ago. Nationally, the total value of construction contracts rose 26.5 percent in the quarter but was 1.7 percent below year-ago levels." (unpaginated)

"Regional Economy Continued to Expand in Second Quarter of '97." Federal Reserve Bank of Kansas City Fed Letter Oct 1997.

CONSTRUCTION INDUSTRY--RECYCLING--FINLAND (v26)

CONSUMER ADVERTISING

see ADVERTISING

CONSUMER BEHAVIOR--AFRO-AMERICANS

In the U.S., "the buying power of blacks is growing almost two and a half times as fast as inflation, and it currently stands at $469 billion....One-third of black buying power is in California, Texas, New York, and Illinois. The ten states with the largest concentrations of black consumers claim 61 percent of the national market." (p1) "Seventeen states had less than $1 billion in black spending power in 1997. Eight of these are in the West (Alaska, Hawaii, Idaho, Montana, New Mexico, Oregon, Utah, and Wyoming); four are in the Midwest (Iowa, Nebraska, North Dakota, and South Dakota); four are in the Northeast (Maine, New Hampshire, Vermont, and Rhode Island); and only one is in the South (West Virginia)." (p2) "Blacks account for 12 percent of Americans and 8.2 percent of U.S. consumer power." (p3)

"Minority Markets Take the Lead." Forecast v17 n8 Aug 1997. p1-3. article-level access: <http://www.demographics.com/Publications/FC/97_fc/9708_fc/FC97081.htm> (ISSN0732-1597).

CONSUMER BEHAVIOR--CHINA

According to a Gallup survey, "when Chinese consumers are asked whether they 'usually prefer to buy foreign-made products' or 'usually prefer to buy products made in this country', only 22% opt for the former description, while 73% say they typically prefer to purchase Chinese-made goods. And even among the most affluent segment of Chinese consumers--those with annual household incomes nearly at least three times the national average (i.e., RMB [renminbi] 30,000/$3,610 or more per year)--no more than 37% say they have a general preference for foreign products....While one in four Chinese is unable to offer an evaluation of Japanese goods, nearly two-thirds call Japanese products either 'good' (29%), 'very good' (24%), or 'excellent' (12%) in quality--very few rate them either 'fair' (7%) or 'poor' (2%). High ratings are also given to U.S.-made products: 21% 'good', 14% 'very good' and 5% 'excellent'; only 9% 'fair' and just 1% 'poor' (50% 'don't know'). In comparison, 34% rate Chinese manufactures as being of good quality, while 18% call them 'very good' and 9% 'excellent'. But Chinese 'negatives' are relatively high as well: 30% of all Chinese rate Chinese manufactures as typically being of 'fair' quality, and 4% call them 'poor'."

Gallup Organization. "1997 Survey: The People's Republic of China: Consumer Attitudes & Lifestyle Trends." Press Release 27 Oct 1997. document-level access: <http://www.gallup.com/poll/special/china/chinarel.html>

CONSUMER BEHAVIOR--HISPANIC AMERICANS

In the U.S., "the Hispanic market is growing at three times the rate of inflation in the 1990s, and it will reach $348 billion this year....Almost one-third of Hispanic buying power (32 percent) is in California, with another 15 percent in Texas, 10 percent in Florida, and 10 percent in New York." (p1) "Twenty-one states had less than $1 billion in Hispanic buying power in 1997. Seven of these are in the South (Alabama, Arkansas, Kentucky, Mississippi, South Carolina, Tennessee, and West Virginia); five are in the Northeast (Delaware, Maine, New Hampshire, Rhode Island, and Vermont); five are in the Midwest (Iowa, Minnesota, Nebraska, North Dakota, and South Dakota); and four are in the West (Alaska, Idaho, Montana, and Wyoming)." (p2) "Hispanics are a little more than 10 percent of Americans and 6.1 percent of the U.S. market." (p3)

"Minority Markets Take the Lead." Forecast v17 n8 Aug 1997. p1-3. article-level access: <http://www.demographics.com/Publications/FC/97_fc/9708_fc/FC97081.htm> (ISSN0732-1597).

CONSUMER BEHAVIOR--UNITED STATES (v26)

In the U.S., "middle-aged households have the most money, so they outspend everyone else. The 45-to-54 age group, which is now filling with boomers, spends more than any other--17 percent more than the average household on a per-capita basis. Ranking second are householders aged 55 to 64, who spend 15 percent more than average per capita, according to the Bureau of Labor Statistics' 1995 Consumer Expenditure Survey....Householders aged 65 to 74 spend an average amount per person. In contrast, householders aged 25 to 34 spend 13 percent less than average. Households headed by people aged 35 to 44 and those aged 75 or older spend about the same amount per person--just slightly below the average mark....Householders aged 55 to 64 spend the most per capita on women's clothing, for example, 56 percent more than the average household....Householders aged 65 to 74 spend an average amount per person in restaurants--which is 9 percent more than householders aged 25 to 34 spend. Younger householders spend an average amount per capita on clothing and related accessories and services, while those aged 65 to 74 spend 14 percent less than average....In the important category of women's apparel, the older age group spends 11 percent more than average, while the younger age group spends 23 percent less than average." (p14-15)

Russell, Cheryl. "Trend Cop: The Ungraying of America." American Demographics v19 n7 Jul 1997. p12,14-15. article-level access: <http://www.demographics.com/publications/ad/97_ad/9707_ad/ad97073.htm> (ISSN0163-4089).

CONSUMER DEMAND

see CONSUMPTION (ECONOMICS)

CONSUMER PRICE INDEXES--BRAZIL (v26)

CONSUMER PRICE INDEXES--GERMANY (v26)

CONSUMER PRICE INDEXES--NEW YORK (N.Y.)

Of the 25 largest U.S. "metros, the cost of living is significantly below average in only 2, and above average in all the rest, according to the ACCRA Cost of Living Index for the third quarter of 1996....The national cost-of-living average is 100....[New York City] is the most expensive place to live in the U.S. ACCRA found that it costs 2.3 times the national average to live in Manhattan. This is primarily due to extremely high housing (index of 465.5) and health-care costs (206.9). It also costs a lot to buy groceries in Manhattan (144.6), as well as miscellaneous goods and services (132.2)." (p30)

Miller, Berna. "Kaleidoscope: Beating the High Cost of Living." American Demographics v19 n6 Jun 1997. p30. article-level access: <http://www.demographics.com/publications/ad/97_ad/9706_ad/ad97069.htm> (ISSN0163-4089).

CONSUMER PRICE INDEXES--NEW ZEALAND

In New Zealand, "the Consumers Price Index rose by 0.5 per cent in the September 1997 quarter, said Deputy Government Statistician Ian Ewing. This follows an increase of 0.1 per cent in the June quarter and a decrease of 0.3 per cent in the March quarter. The Consumers Price Index for the September 1997 quarter was 1.0 per cent higher than in the September 1996 quarter. Housing costs contributed the most to the increase in the September quarter, recording a rise of 1.4 per cent....Tobacco and alcohol prices had the next most significant increase, rising by 1.5 per cent in the September 1997 quarter....The costs of operating a household increased 0.6 percent, with price increases being recorded for household insurance and electricity."

Statistics New Zealand. "Consumers Price Index--September 1997 Quarter." Press Release 15 Oct 1997. document-level access: <http://www.stats.govt.nz/statsweb.nsf/52518ce3e01f62f4cc256388000c48c0/6eedf72fbc497e864c25653000794740?OpenDocument>

CONSUMER PRICE INDEXES--UNITED STATES (v26)

In the U.S., "the Consumer Price Index (CPI) for food in 1998 is forecast to rise 2.5-3 percent, below the 3.3-percent increase in 1996 but close to the 2.8-percent rise forecast for 1997. The at-home component of the CPI, which increased 3.7 percent in 1996, is forecast to increase 2.5 percent in 1997 and 2.5-3 percent in 1998. The away-from-home component of the CPI, which increased 2.5 percent in 1996, is expected to increase 2.9 percent in 1997 and 2.5-3 percent in 1998....The CPI for food remained relatively flat during the first 8 months of 1997, with month-to-month increases of only 0.1 percent in both January and March, 0.3 percent in July, and 0.4 percent in August....For the first 8 months of 1997, the price index for all food increased 3 percent. The all-food index is forecast to increase 2.5 percent in the remaining 4 months of 1997, for an annual increase of 2.8 percent." (p220)

Clauson, Annette/U.S. Dept. of Agriculture. Economic Research Service. "Food & Marketing: Food Prices to Maintain Slow Rise in 1998." Agricultural Outlook Oct 1997. p22-25.

According to U.S. Consumer Price Indexes for selected items between 1984 and 1994, "the price of cereals increased by 34.8 percent, the price of sirloin steaks increased by 37.5 percent, the price of coffee increased by 40.4 percent, the price of housing increased by 44.8 percent, the price of transportation increased by 34.3 percent, the price of energy by 4.6 percent, medical care increased by 111 percent, and the price of college tuition increased by 149 percent." (pH2725)

Castle, Michael N. (Rep.-Del.). "1997 Emergency Supplemental Appropriations Act for Recovery from Natural Disasters, And...Peacekeeping...In Bosnia." Congressional Record. Daily ed. v143 n64 15 May 1997. pH2697-2775. section/page-level access: <http://thomas.loc.gov/cgi-bin/query/R?r105:FLD001:H02725:> (ISSN0363-7239). (X1.1A.105/1).

In the U.S., in 1990, "the Consumer Price Index (CPI) fell from 5.4 per cent to 3.0 per cent. Since 1992, employment has increased by over 4 million a year, and the CPI has...fallen to 1.4 per cent." (p12)

Brockway, George P. "The Dismal Science: Madness Is Not Statesmanship." New Leader v80 n13 11 Aug 1997. p11-12. (ISSN0028-6044).

CONSUMER PROTECTION

see FOOD ADULTERATION AND INSPECTION

CONSUMPTION (ECONOMICS) (v26)

CONSUMPTION (ECONOMICS)--SINGAPORE (v26)

CONSUMPTION (ECONOMICS)--UNITED STATES

"With less than 5 percent of the world's population, the United States tears through about 25 percent of the planet's resources....According to Northwest Environment Watch, if everyone on the globe exhausted resources at the U.S. rate--about 120 pounds a day per capita--we'd need three more Earths to meet the demand and nine additional atmospheres to absorb the resulting greenhouse gases....Per capita consumption has risen 45 percent, but quality of life, as reported by the Index of Social Health, has plummeted 52 percent since the 1970s." (p20)

Shurgot, Mara. "Hearth & Home: The Goods Life: How Much Stuff Is Enough?" Sierra v82 n4 Jul-Aug 1997. p20-21. (ISSN0161-7362).

"As much as 93 per cent of materials bought and 'consumed' do not end up in finished products, according to a recent study by the United States National Academy of Engineers. Some 80 per cent of goods are discarded after a single use and many others do not last as long as they should. By one industry estimate, 99 per cent of the original materials used in the production of goods made in the United States are thrown away within six weeks of sale." (p31)

"Assessment: Civilization under Seige." UN Chronicle v34 n3 1997. p30-34. (ISSN0251-7329).

CONSUMPTION OF ELECTRIC POWER

see ELECTRIC POWER CONSUMPTION

CONSUMPTION OF ENERGY

see ENERGY CONSUMPTION

CONSUMPTION OF FOOD

see FOOD CONSUMPTION

CONSUMPTION OF FUEL

see AIRPLANES--FUEL CONSUMPTION; AUTOMOBILES--UNITED STATES--FUEL CONSUMPTION

CONSUMPTION OF MILK

see MILK CONSUMPTION

CONTAGIOUS DISEASES

see COMMUNICABLE DISEASES

CONTAMINANTS, AIR

see AIR--POLLUTION

CONTAMINATION OF ENVIRONMENT

see POLLUTION

CONTINUING EDUCATION--GREAT BRITAIN (v26)

CONTRACEPTION (v26)

see also BIRTH CONTROL

Worldwide, "120-150 million women who want to limit or space their pregnancies are still without the means to do so effectively. Altogether 350 million couples lack information about and access to a range of contraceptive services." (p1)

"UNFPA Stresses Gender Equality, Maternal Health." Popline v19 May-Jun 1997. p1.

CONTRACEPTION--AFRICA

In a Demographic and Health Surveys study of Central African Republic, Ghana, Haiti, Kenya, and Zimbabwe, the data found that "more than 90 percent of all male and female respondents know at least one method of contraception, except Central African Republic, where only 76 percent of the women know any method....Men are more likely than women to report ever use of contraceptives. The gap ranges from five percentage points in Ghana to 25 percentage points in Kenya. For three of these five countries, the gap is about 20 percentage points or more." (p106)

Ezeh, Alex Chika/Mboup, Gora. "Estimates and Explanations of Gender Differentials in Contraceptive Prevalence Rates." Studies in Family Planning v28 n2 Jun 1997. p104-121. (ISSN0039-3665).

CONTRACEPTION--BANGLADESH

In Bangladesh, "forty-nine percent of married women report that they or their husbands are using a contraceptive method, compared with only 8 percent of women in 1975, according to the latest Demographic and Health Survey for Bangladesh, conducted by Macro International, Inc....Fertility rates have fallen from 6.3 children per woman in the late 1970s, to 4.8 in the late

1980s, to 3.3 today....Oral contraceptives, used by 20.8 percent of married women, remain by far the most popular method of family planning accounting for half of all modern contraceptive use. Pill use among currently married women has increased by 20 percent since 1993-94. Other methods used are female sterilization (used by 8 percent of married women), injectables (6 percent), the rhythm method (5 percent), and condoms (4 percent)....The proportion of women using withdrawal, the IUD [intrauterine device], or whose husbands are sterilized is each 2 percent or less....One in three married women ages 15-19 is now using a family planning method, especially the pill, as opposed to 25 percent in 1993-94. Contraceptive use is the highest among married women in their 30s, almost two-thirds of whom are using a method." (p2)

"Contraceptive Use Rises in Bangladesh." Popline v19 Sep-Oct 1997. p2.

CONTRACEPTION--BOLIVIA

The Johns Hopkins University Population Communication Services surveyed 2,256 men and women between the ages 15 and 49 in seven urban areas in Bolivia. "The survey covered current use rates of both modern and traditional contraceptive methods. The intrauterine device (IUD) was the most prevalent modern method, used by 10.3 percent of women in the survey, followed by condoms, the pill, and female sterilization. The rhythm method was the most prevalent traditional method, used by 16.5 percent of women in the sample. A total of 30.9 percent of women in the sample used modern methods and 22.1 percent used traditional methods (also including withdrawal and periodic abstinence). Of the 16.5 percent of women who said they currently used the rhythm method, 39 percent could not identify the 'dangerous time' in the menstrual cycle for risking pregnancy." (p11)

Valente, Thomas W./Saba, Walter P. "Reproductive Health Is in Your Hands: The National Media Campaign in Bolivia." SIECUS Report v25 n2 Dec 1996-Jan 1997. p10-11,13. (ISSN0091-3995).

CONTRACEPTION--CHINA

According to a study on the use of Norplant as a contraceptive method that was conducted in four counties in Hebei and Shandong Provinces, China, "the contraceptive prevalence rate among married women of reproductive age in these counties was very high (87 percent) in 1992." (p123) "Eighty percent of [the Norplant acceptors] were between 30 and 39 years old and had two children, with an average age of 33 and parity of 1.9. Most of the Norplant acceptors reported the IUD [intrauterine device] (43 percent) or barrier methods (24 percent) as the last contraceptive method they had used before accepting Norplant." (p124) "Side effects from Norplant use were fairly common. About 49 percent of users reported experiencing at least one side effect in the first six-month use interval; the proportion of users with recorded side effects declined with duration of use; nevertheless, 23 percent of the users reported experiencing at least one side effect in the second year of use. The most common side effect among users was menstrual disorders (reported by 31 percent in the first six months), followed by headache, vertigo, and nausea (reported by 5 percent in the first six months)....Only three pregnancies resulting from method failure were observed among the 1,550 Norplant acceptors....The gross cumulative pregnancy rate [of Norplant] resulting from method failure is 0.0 percent at month six and remained at 0.2 percent at months 12 and 24...." (p127)

Ping, Tu/Shuhua, Qui/Huimin, Fang/Smith, Herbert L. "Reports: Acceptance, Efficacy, And Side Effects of Norplant Implants in Four Counties in North China." Studies in Family Planning v28 n2 Jun 1997. p122-131. (ISSN0039-3665).

CONTRACEPTION--COMPLICATIONS--TURKEY --ISTANBUL (v26)

CONTRACEPTION--DEVELOPING COUNTRIES (v26)

CONTRACEPTION--EUROPE, WESTERN

According to Barbro Lenneer Axelson, who is an assistant professor of psychology at Gothenburg University in Sweden, and the Europe Region president of the International Planned Parenthood Federation, in most western European countries, "contraceptive use is as high as 80-90 percent, but in others use is less than 60 percent. 'The pill and IUD [intrauterine device] dominate in stable relationships,' she noted. 'The use of the condom is regrettably much lower compared with Japan,' Axelson pointed out. 'It is used by some 50 percent of teenage boys, compared with 25 percent of adult men, most often in so-called serial monogamy relationships before marriage.'" (p1)

"1,000 Abortions per Hour." Popline v19 Sep-Oct 1997. p1-2.

CONTRACEPTION--GHANA

Between 1988 and 1993, according to Demographic and Health Surveys, "in Ghana, contraceptive prevalence increased by 54 and 57 percent among all women and currently married women, respectively, and by 61 percent for husbands (GSS and IRD, 1989; GSS and MI, 1994). The results show that overall, CPR [contraceptive prevalence rate] estimates calculated from surveys of men are about six to 25 percentage points higher than those from surveys of women." (p106) "In Ghana, 7 percent and 9 percent of wives and husbands, respectively, reported current practice of periodic abstinence at the time of the survey. Also, about 30 percent of husbands and wives had accurate knowledge of the ovulatory cycle." (p112)

Ezeh, Alex Chika/Mboup, Gora. "Estimates and Explanations of Gender Differentials in Contraceptive Prevalence Rates." Studies in Family Planning v28 n2 Jun 1997. p104-121. (ISSN0039-3665).

CONTRACEPTION--GUATEMALA

According to Guatemala's most recent Demographic and Health Survey, "contraceptive use among married women increased from 23 percent in 1987 to 32 percent in 1995....Contraceptive use in countries bordering Guatemala is: 65 percent in Mexico; 53 percent in El Salvador, and 47 percent in Belize and Honduras. Female sterilization is the contraceptive method chosen by almost half (15 percent) of family planning users in Guatemala, while relatively few use the pill (4 percent) or the IUD [intrauterine device] (3 percent)." (p3)

"Education Is Fertility Factor in Guatemala." Popline v19 Sep-Oct 1997. p3.

CONTRACEPTION--INDIA

In India, "contraceptive prevalence has risen substantially, from 13 percent of married women using contraception in 1970 to 41 percent in 1993. But nearly 35 million married Indian women have an unmet need for family planning....The 1992-93 National Family Health Survey found nearly universal knowledge of family planning, with 96 percent of married women ages 13-49 having heard of at least one modern method, and almost 41 percent, about 70 million women, using contraception. Eighty-nine percent of married women who practice family planning in India rely upon modern contraceptive methods....Nearly 67 percent of married women who use contraception, about 47 million women, had been sterilized compared with a world average of only 30 percent. A small proportion of users rely on birth spacing methods, primarily available through the private sector: the condom, 6 percent; IUD [intrauterine device], 5 percent, and the pill, 3 percent....Nearly half of the married women with some primary schooling use contraception compared with one third of illiterate women....Higher prevalence rates (48 to 63 percent) are found among small minority religions (Jains, Sikhs, Buddhists and Christians) than among Hindus (42 percent) and the lowest use (28 percent) is found among Muslims. Fifty-one percent of urban married women use contraceptives, compared with only 37 percent of rural married women." (p3)

"25 Million Births in India Each Year." Popline v19 Jul-Aug 1997. p3.

CONTRACEPTION--LATIN AMERICA

According to the United Nations Population Fund's "1997 State of the World's Population Report, the percentage of women in Latin America who would like to control their fertility but are unable to because they lack effective contraceptives ranges from a low of 17 in Colombia to a high of 43 in Bolivia. In other Latin American countries, an average of around 25 percent of women claim to have an 'unmet need' for effective contraception." (p6)

Constance, Paul. "The Region: Health: The Other Side of the Reproductive Revolution." IDB v24 n7 Jul 1997. p6-7. (ISSN0145-2274).

CONTRACEPTION--NEPAL

"The percentage of Nepalese women who want to stop childbearing has increased substantially, from 40 percent in 1981 to 59 percent in 1996. Only 4 percent of married woman in Nepal had ever used contraception in 1976, compared with 27 percent in 1991 and 35 percent in 1996. In 1996, contraceptive prevalence among married women was 29 percent, with the majority using modern methods. But one in three Nepalese women still has an unmet need for family planning." (p4)

"Fertility Is Declining in Nepal." Popline v19 Sep-Oct 1997. p4.

In Nepal, "contraceptive use has nearly doubled in the past decade to 29 percent of married women. The most popular methods of contraception are female sterilization (12 percent), male sterilization (5 percent), and injectables (5 percent). Although 75 percent of all currently married women know about condoms, only 2 percent reported that their partners use them." (p7)

Rauniyar, Durga S. "Spotlight: Nepal." Population Today v25 n6 Jun 1997. p7. (ISSN0749-2448).

CONTRACEPTION--NETHERLANDS (v26)

CONTRACEPTION--NETHERLANDS--YOUTH (v26)

CONTRACEPTION--RUSSIA (v26)

CONTRACEPTION--TURKEY (v26)

CONTRACEPTION--TURKEY--ISTANBUL (v26)

CONTRACEPTION--TURKEY--ISTANBUL--WOMEN --ATTITUDES (v26)

CONTRACEPTION--UNITED STATES (v26)

In the U.S., according to the CDC's "National Survey of Family Growth," "the leading method of contraception remains female sterilization (10.7 million women), followed by the oral contraceptive pill (10.4 million), the male condom (7.9 million), and male sterilization (4.2 million). New contraceptive methods were used by small proportions of women in 1995, such as hormonal injectables (used by 2 percent of women), hormonal implants (1 percent), and female condoms (less than 1 percent). Condom use among never-married women tripled between 1982 and 1995, from 4 to 14 percent. Condom use at first intercourse increased from 18 percent in the 1970's to 36 percent in the late 1980's and 54 percent in the 1990's."

U.S. National Center for Health Statistics. "New Report Documents Trends in Childbearing, Reproductive Health." Fact Sheet 5 Jun 1997. document-level access: <http://www.cdc.gov/nchswww/releases/97facts/97sheets/nsfgfact.htm>

According to an Alan Guttmacher Institute report, in the U.S., "only 40 percent of young women go to a doctor or clinic for contraceptive services within the first year after they begin having intercourse....In 1994, federal and state tax revenues provided $715 million for contraceptive services and supplies to millions of poor women and teenagers, helping to prevent at least 1.5 million unintended pregnancies that would have occurred otherwise. The Guttmacher report claims that every dollar spent for contraceptive services saved $3 in public funds that would have been needed for prenatal and newborn medical care alone." (p1)

"60% of U.S. Pregnancies Unintended." Popline v19 Jul-Aug 1997. p1.

CONTRACEPTION--UNITED STATES--WOMEN (v26)

CONTRACEPTION--UNITED STATES--YOUTH

In 1997, a study of 235 U.S. teenagers found that "frequency of use for specific methods of birth control for the 97 adolescents who had been sexually active in the last 6 months was as follows: 66% (64) were using the male condom (although not consistently); 20% (19) were using oral contraceptives; 3% (3) were using either Norplant, an IUD [intrauterine device], or the sponge; 9% (9) used 'nothing'; and 2% (2) indicated a category labeled 'other' (e.g., withdrawal). No one was using Depo-Provera or the diaphragm....Consistent with earlier studies (Creatsas, 1993; Galavotti et al., 1995; Grimley et al., 1993), sexually active adolescents did not perceive any contraceptive methods other than the male condom or the pill as being very acceptable." (p774-775)

Grimley, Diane M./Lee, Patricia A. "Condom and Other Contraceptive Use among a Random Sample of Female Adolescents: A Snapshot in Time." Adolescence v32 n128 Win 1997. p771-779. (ISSN0001-8449).

Youths in the U.S. "are the most educated about sexual reproduction, contraception, and STDs [sexually transmitted diseases] (90% of those between the ages of 12 and 25 know the primary causes of AIDS transmission and 86% are aware that condoms reduce the risk of AIDS), yet the majority have not changed their sexual practices and frequently engage in unprotected sexual behavior (Select Committee on Children, Youth, and Families, 1991). Despite the increased availability of contraception to teenagers, the percentage of girls using contraception rose slightly, from 24% in 1982 to 32% in 1988....Although data show an increase in condom use, in 1988 4 in 10 unmarried males aged 17-19 used no contraceptive method or an ineffective one at first intercourse (Miller & Moore, 1990)." (p991)

Bailey, C. Everett/Piercy, Fred P. "Enhancing Ethical Decision Making in Sexuality and AIDS Education." Adolescence v32 n128 Win 1997. p989-998. (ISSN0001-8449).

"Fifty-four percent of African-American and Latino youth aged 15 to 19 use contraception at first intercourse compared to 69 percent of their Caucasian peers. The 1995 'Youth Risk Behavior Surveillance' reported that 45.6 percent of sexually active teenagers in grades nine through 12 had not used condoms during their latest sexual intercourse. The report found that 66.4 percent of African-American male teenagers reported condom usage as compared to 52 percent of Caucasian teenagers and 44.4 percent of Latino teenagers." (p15-16)

"Fact Sheet: Sexuality and Underserved Youth in Communities of Color." SIECUS Report v25 n5 Jun-Jul 1997. p15-16. (ISSN0091-3995).

CONTRACTING OUT--UNITED STATES (v26)

CONTRACTS, AGRICULTURAL--UNITED STATES (v26)

CONTRACTS, RESEARCH AND DEVELOPMENT

see RESEARCH AND DEVELOPMENT CONTRACTS

CONVERSION OF MILITARY BASES

see MILITARY BASE CONVERSION

CONVERSION OF SALINE WATERS

see SALINE WATER CONVERSION

CONVERSION OF WASTE PRODUCTS

see RECYCLING (WASTE, ETC.)

CONVICT LABOR--UNITED STATES (v26)

In the U.S., "from 1980 to 1994, the value of goods produced by prisoners rose from $392 million to $1.31 billion....The average wage for prison labor in this country is between $0.23 and $1.23 per hour. The total burdened cost to the company (all the expenses involved in production factored in with the worker's wage) is usually $6.01 per hour." (p6)

Suarez-Potts, Jamie. "The Labor of Prisoners." Peacework n275 Jun 1997. p5-7. (ISSN0748-0725).

CONVICTS

see PRISONERS

COOKERY--UNITED STATES--NEWSPAPER EDITORS --ATTITUDES (v26)

COOKERY--UNITED STATES--PUBLIC OPINION (v26)

COOKERY, BARBECUE

see BARBECUE COOKERY

COOPERATIVE CREDIT ASSOCIATIONS, AGRICULTURAL

see AGRICULTURAL COOPERATIVE CREDIT ASSOCIATIONS

COOPERATIVE SOCIETIES--CANADA

"Some 17 of the top 500 revenue producing companies in Canada are registered as co-ops. In 1995, 617,000 people belonged to agricultural co-ops alone.... "These 617,000 people in agricultural co-ops generated $16 billion in sales and handled 40% of total farm cash receipts in the areas of grains, oilseeds, dairy products, eggs and poultry, livestock, fruits and vegetables." (p978)

Solomon, John (MP-SK). "Government Orders: Canada Co-Operatives Act." Canada. Parliament. House of Commons. Debates. v135 n18 22 Oct 1997. p976-997. section-level access: <http://www.parl.gc.ca/36/1/parlbus/chambus/house/debates/018_1997-10-22/han018-e.htm#LINKT24> (ISSN0704-5603). (X3-361E).

"Today the biggest non-financial co-operatives in Canada in terms of revenues are agricultural co-operatives. In 1996 eight of them had revenues greater than $1 billion. It has been estimated that co-operatives account for 47% of the market share for poultry, 57% for milk and 59% for grains.... "Over all Canada's 10,000 co-ops employ about 136,000 people, with total assets of more than $155 billion." (p977)

Vanclief, Lyle (MP-ON). "Government Orders: Canada Co-Operatives Act." Canada. Parliament. House of Commons. Debates. v135 n18 22 Oct 1997. p976-997. section-level access: <http://www.parl.gc.ca/36/1/parlbus/chambus/house/debates/018_1997-10-22/han018-e.htm#LINKT22> (ISSN0704-5603). (X3-361E).

COOPERATIVE SOCIETIES--ITALY--UNITED STATES (v26)

COPYRIGHT--UNITED STATES (v26)

In the U.S., "the copyright industries had over $53 billion in foreign sales in 1995, surpassing every other export industry except automobiles and agriculture....The copyright industries employ nearly 6 million people in the United States, or about 4.8 percent of our work force. But despite the tremendous contribution these businesses make to our economy, we still lose more than $15 billion each year due to foreign copyright piracy, according to some estimates." (pS8586)

Kohl, Herb (Sen.-Wis.). "The Ronald H. Brown Federal Building Designation Act of 1997." Congressional Record. Daily ed. v143 n111 31 Jul 1997. pS8571-8590. section/page-level access: <http://thomas.loc.gov/cgi-bin/query/R?r105:FLD001:S08586:> (ISSN0363-7239). (X1.1A.105/1).

COPYRIGHT INFRINGEMENT--CANADA (v26)

COPYRIGHT INFRINGEMENT--UNITED STATES --COSTS

"Copyright industries represent nearly 6% of the U.S. gross domestic product, and nearly 5% of U.S. employment. Yet American companies lose $18-20 billion every year due to international piracy of copyrighted works. The film industry alone estimates its annual losses due to counterfeiting in excess of $2.3 billion....The recording industry estimates that it looses more than $1.2 billion each year due to piracy, with seizures of bootleg CDs up some 1,300 percent in 1995." (pS8583)

Hatch, Orrin G. (Sen.-Utah). "The Ronald H. Brown Federal Building Designation Act of 1997." Congressional Record. Daily ed. v143 n111 31 Jul 1997. pS8571-8590. section/page-level access: <http://thomas.loc.gov/cgi-bin/query/R?r105:FLD001:S08582:> (ISSN0363-7239). (X1.1A.105/1).

CORAL REEFS AND ISLANDS (v26)

CORAL REEFS AND ISLANDS--ENVIRONMENTAL ASPECTS

Reefs surrounding the South Pacific island of Palau "nurture nine species of seagrass, more than 300 species of coral, and 2000 varieties of fish. The Great Barrier Reef of Australia boasts 400 species of coral, providing habitat for more than 1500 species of fish, 4000 different kinds of mollusc, and 400 species of sponge....The world's 600,000 square kilometers of reef provide habitat for more than 1 million species of plant and animal....Ten percent of reefs are already degraded beyond recognition, and 30% are in critical condition." (p554)

According to Terence Hughes, a marine ecologist with James Cook University in Townsville, "Jamaica's coral cover--the amount of healthy coral in coastal waters--dropped from 52% in 1980 to just 3% in 1993....A survey of 735 reefs carried out in 1991 found that 70% of the coral cover on those reefs was in fair to poor condition, with less than 50% live coral cover. Only 5% of the cover remained in excellent condition." (p555)

Hinrichsen, Don. "Features: Coral Reefs in Crisis." BioScience v47 n9 Oct 1997. p554-558. (ISSN0006-3568).

CORAL REEFS AND ISLANDS--FLORIDA (v26)

CORN EARWORM

see HELICOVERPA ARMIGERA

CORN INDUSTRY (v26)

"At just over 4 tons per hectare, the 1995 world corn yield is the highest of all the cereals, well above the 2.5 tons for wheat and rice. The prospect for raising it any further rests largely with the United States and China, the countries that account for two fifths and one fifth, respectively, of the world harvest....The U.S. corn yield of 7.9 tons per hectare in 1995 is the highest of any cereal in a major producing country." (p14) "Argentina, where the 1995 corn yield was 4.3 tons per hectare, may have the largest unrealized potential for raising corn yields of any country....In Brazil,...the corn yield per hectare is only one third that of the United States...." (p15)

Brown, Lester R. "Can We Raise Grain Yields Fast Enough?" World Watch v10 n4 Jul-Aug 1997. p8-17. (ISSN0896-0615).

CORN INDUSTRY--ASIA--UNITED STATES (v26)

CORN INDUSTRY--CHINA (v26)

"China's 1997/98 corn production has been reduced by drought and high temperatures in many major growing areas. China is forecast to produce 110 million tons of corn, nearly 14 percent less than a year ago. Because China is the world's second-largest corn producer, a drop of this magnitude can dominate the year-to-year change in world production. China plays a key role in world corn markets as both exporter and importer. For example, in 1993/94 China exported nearly 12 million tons of corn, but imported 4 million the next year. In 1996/97, China produced a bin-buster corn crop of 127 million tons, boosted exports, and built huge stocks. China's corn supplies in 1997/98 are projected at 151 million tons, down from last year but higher than any other year." (p6)

Allen, Ed/U.S. Dept. of Agriculture. Economic Research Service. "Commodity Spotlight: Reduced Foreign Production Boosts U.S. Export Prospects." Agricultural Outlook Oct 1997. p6.

In China, "corn yields are projected at 5.19 metric tons per hectare, down from the record 1996/97 yield of 5.2 tons per hectare which is projected to make a crop of 122 million tons, more than 5 million less than last year....Corn imports are projected to rise from 1.5 million tons in 1995/96 to 8.9 million tons by 2005/06. Corn exports fell from more than 12 million tons in 1992/93 to an estimated 230,000 tons in 1995/96. China's corn exports are projected to decrease from 2.5 million tons in 1996/97 to 285,000 tons by 2005/06....Corn output in 1996 was a record 127 million tons, up 13 percent from the 1995 crop. Area increased 7.5 percent to 24.5 million hectares....In 1993/94, China exported 11.8 million tons of corn with no imports. In 1994/95...China's corn trade shifted dramatically, with exports of 1.4 million tons but imports of 4.3 million tons. In 1995/96, China exported 227,000 tons while imports fell to 1.5 million tons. In 1996/97, corn exports are projected to increase to 2.5 million tons and imports to fall to 50,000 tons." (p29)

Crook, Frederick W./U.S. Dept. of Agriculture. Economic Research Service. "Good Grain Crop Projected for 1997." China: International Agriculture and Trade Reports Situation and Outlook Series Jun 1997. p26-31.

CORN INDUSTRY--MEXICO--UNITED STATES (v26)

"According to the National Chamber of Sugar and Alcohol Industries in Mexico City, soft drink bottlers--one of the largest consumers of cane sugar--have used 350,000 tons of corn syrup this year, which accounts for about a quarter of the industry's total demand for sweeteners. Ninety percent of the corn syrup was imported from the United States....Before NAFTA, U.S. manufacturers paid a 15 percent tariff on corn syrup exports. But under NAFTA, that rate declined to 9.5 percent and was scheduled for elimination over a 15-year period." (p11)

Bigler, Ron. "Trade: NAFTA Sours Mexican Sugar." In These Times v22 n1 14 Dec 1997. p11. (ISSN0160-5992).

CORN INDUSTRY--TURKEY--UNITED STATES (v26)

CORN INDUSTRY--UNITED STATES (v26)

In the U.S., "the average corn yield improved in 1996 to about 5 percent above the previous 5-year average. Despite higher yields, corn prices remained near $3.00 per bushel at harvest. This combination of relatively high prices and yields pushed the value of corn at harvest to a record high of $389 per acre. Average returns above cash costs, at $166 per acre, were also the highest reported by USDA since the costs and returns series began in 1975." (p23)

U.S. Dept. of Agriculture. Economic Research Service. "1996 Cost of Production for Crops and Livestock: Although Input Expenses Rose in 1996,...Led to Higher Net Returns." Agricultural Income and Finance Situation and Outlook Report Sep 1997. p23-27.

In the U.S., "domestic demand for corn is expected to be strong over the next year, with use projected at 7.3 billion bushels, about 100 million bushels above the 1994/95 record and topping 1996/97 by more than 300 million. Feed and residual use of corn is projected to increase 5 percent to 5.55 billion bushels....Food, seed, and industrial (FSI) use of corn is also projected to rise 5 percent in 1997/98 to 1.78 billion bushels....Although corn for ethanol use is forecast to increase 11 percent to 485 million bushels, it will not rebound to the peak level of 533 million reached in 1994/95." (p6-7)

Riley, Pete/U.S. Dept. of Agriculture. Economic Research Service. "Commodity Spotlight: Corn Output Stable, Demand Prospects Strong." Agricultural Outlook Oct 1997. p5-8.

In the U.S., "with much larger carryin stocks, corn supplies in 1997/98 are expected to increase 5 percent. Corn production is forecast at 9.268 billion bushels, based on crop conditions as of September 1....Farmers planted more than 80.2 million acres of corn this spring, up more than 700,000 acres from the previous year. The sharp gains of 1996, when corn plantings rose more than 8 million acres, were sustained on a national level, although with small shifts in the state pattern....The average corn yield is forecast at 125.2 bushels per acre, compared with the long-term trend of about 128 bushels and just below the 1996 yield of 127.1 bushels." (p5)

Riley, Pete/U.S. Dept. of Agriculture. Economic Research Service. "Commodity Spotlight: Corn Output Stable, Demand Prospects Strong." Agricultural Outlook Oct 1997. p5-8.

U.S. corn plantings "increased in 1997, to an estimated 80.2 million acres, up 1 percent from last year and the highest planted corn acreage since 1985. Corn acres harvested for grain are expected to increase to an estimated 74 million, also up 1 percent from 1996." (p2) "Among Corn Belt states, Ohio showed the largest increase in 1997 corn acreage--700,000 acres--as farmers returned to normal planting levels....In both Iowa and Minnesota, corn plantings declined by an estimated 500,000 acres in 1997, and by lesser amounts in several southern states as farmers shifted from corn to soybeans....At the end of June, USDA reported that 74 percent of the nation's corn crop was in good or excellent condition." (p3)

Simone, Mark/U.S. Dept. of Agriculture. Economic Research Service. "Commodity Briefs: Field Crops: Sharp Rise in U.S. Soybean Acreage Planted for 1997." Agricultural Outlook Aug 1997. p2-4.

In the U.S., "to pupate from caterpillars into adult moths, fall army-worms and southwestern corn borers must go on a 10- to 20-day feeding binge. Their fare is the stalks, leaves, husks, and ears of corn plants. Unchecked, they can cause losses of 30-plus percent. But now scientists may have a way to turn the tables on the pests: genetically engineer the plants so they churn out a rare natural enzyme that curbs the caterpillars' destructive appetite--so much so, they'd grow to less than half their normal size and weight....Lab and field studies suggest this could mean fewer than 50 percent of the pests survive to adulthood." (p19)

Suszkiw, Jan/U.S. Dept. of Agriculture. Agricultural Research Service. "'Mir1' Gene Stalls Corn Pests." Agricultural Research v45 n6 Jun 1997. p19. (ISSN0002-161X).

U.S. "corn exports were 3.1 million tons in May [1997], a 38-percent decrease from a year ago. Cumulative corn exports were 34 million tons, down 15 percent from 1996. Corn exports to Japan remained stronger, with a year-to-date total of 10.8 million tons, a 3-percent increase from 1996. Cumulative shipments to Mexico fell from 4.4 million tons in 1996 to 2.1 million tons in 1997. Canada nearly doubled its imports of U.S. corn from 333,000 tons in 1996 to 634,000 tons in 1997. The cumulative value of corn shipments was $4.6 billion, down 24 percent from a year earlier." (p1)

U.S. Dept. of Agriculture. Economic Research Service. "Exports." U.S. Agricultural Trade Update 23 Jul 1997. p1.

U.S. corn shipments "continued less than fiscal 1996 as March 1997 shipments of 4.2 million tons dropped 22 percent from March 1996. Year-to-date shipments of 27.3 million tons fell 9 percent." (unpaginated)

Whitton, Carol/U.S. Dept. of Agriculture. Economic Research Service. "Exports." U.S. Agricultural Trade Update 23 May 1997.

In the U.S., in November 1997, harvest of the "corn crop was winding down, with 95 percent (%) of the crop out of the field. This compares with 93% harvested at this time in 1996 and the 5-year average of 90%....In Michigan, growers harvested 18% of their State's crop during the week [of November 17-23], catching up to only 3 percentage points behind the average." (p6)

U.S. Dept. of Agriculture. Dept. of Commerce. "National Agricultural Summary: Corn." Weekly Weather and Crop

Bulletin 25 Nov 1997. p6. (ISSN0043-1974).

CORN INDUSTRY--UNITED STATES--PRICES

In the U.S., "the season-average price of corn received by farmers is forecast at $2.45-$2.85 per bushel in 1997/98. The midpoint of the forecast is slightly below the 1996/97 price of $2.70, despite a tighter outlook. This is because the 1996/97 average was pulled up by very high prices at the onset of the marketing year, before supplies were replenished. While down from the 1995/96 record of $3.24 per bushel, corn prices will still be relatively strong compared with the $2.30 average of the 1990/91-1994/95 period." (p8)

Riley, Pete/U.S. Dept. of Agriculture. Economic Research Service. "Commodity Spotlight: Corn Output Stable, Demand Prospects Strong." Agricultural Outlook Oct 1997. p5-8.

CORNEA--TRANSPLANTATION--UNITED STATES (v26)

CORONARY ARTERY BYPASS--UNITED STATES

"Each year, about 300,000 Americans undergo heart bypass surgery....In traditional bypass surgery--a technique first done 40 years ago--doctors make an 8-inch incision and use an electrical saw to cut through the breastbone to expose the heart....Complications occur 1 percent to 4 percent of the time...." (p7 secA)

Anstett, Patricia. "Second Front Page: Tools Make Heart Surgery Safer, Cheaper." Detroit Free Press 20 Sep 1997. p3,7 secA.

CORONARY HEART DISEASE

see also CARDIOVASCULAR SYSTEM--DISEASES; MYOCARDIAL INFARCTION

CORONARY HEART DISEASE--UNITED STATES (v26)

CORONARY HEART DISEASE--UNITED STATES --MORTALITY (v26)

CORPORATE DOWNSIZING

see DOWNSIZING OF ORGANIZATIONS

CORPORATIONS (v26)

see also BUSINESS ENTERPRISES; COOPERATIVE SOCIETIES; INTERNATIONAL BUSINESS ENTERPRISES; STOCKHOLDERS

"Of the world's 100 largest economies, 50 are corporations...not nations. The Fortune 500 firms employ 1/20th of 1 percent of the world's population, yet control 70 percent of world trade." (p29) "The Worldwatch Institue reported in VITAL SIGNS 1996 that in 1995 the global economy grew by 3.7 percent." (p30)

Artaza-Regan, Maria Paz. "In the Name of Economic Well-Being." Christian Social Action v10 n6 Jun 1997. p29-32. (ISSN0897-0459).

CORPORATIONS--CHARITABLE CONTRIBUTIONS --HONG KONG--TAIWAN (v26)

CORPORATIONS--CHARITABLE CONTRIBUTIONS --UNITED STATES (v26)

CORPORATIONS--CHARITABLE CONTRIBUTIONS --UNITED STATES--PUBLIC OPINION

"Three in four Americans (76 percent) say that when price and quality are equal, they would be likely to switch brands or retailers who are associated with a good cause, according to a Roper survey for Cone Communications. In 1993, only 66 percent said they would switch to a cause-related product, and 62 percent would switch retailers....In 1993, 58 percent of respondents to the Cone survey said that they suspected cause-related marketing efforts were 'just for show.' In 1996, only 21 percent were as suspicious....One in three Americans frequently buys products because a company donates money to a cause the consumer believes in, according to a Roper survey for the Pearlman Group. Another 37 percent do so occasionally. And 57 percent of Americans frequently or occasionally refuse to buy 'quality' products because they don't like the company that makes them....More than half of those surveyed by Cone (59 percent) want companies to get involved in improving the quality of life on a local level, up 4 points from 1993. Half of Americans say they want businesses to improve the quality of local public schools, up 14 points." (p9)

"Cause Marketing Is Mainstream." Forecast v17 n9 Sep 1997. p9. article-level access: <http://www.demographics.com/Publications/FC/97_fc/9709_fc/FC97098.htm> (ISSN0732-1597).

CORPORATIONS--DATA PROCESSING (v26)

CORPORATIONS--ENVIRONMENTAL ASPECTS

"According to Riva Krut, president of Benchmark Environmental Consulting, 38 of the largest 100 companies in the world have environmental policies and/or environmental reports....Benchmark's preliminary data by region reveals that US-based firms lead the Global 100, with nearly 67% with environmental policies or reports. Thirty-four percent of European firms offer this information, while nearly 24% of the Asian firms do....On the industry sector basis, Benchmark has found that the Global 100's chemical companies have the highest levels of environmental policies and reporting (76.9%) followed by the automotive, heavy manufacturing, electronics, and retail sector." (p3)

"Focus Report: Corporate Environmental Reports: Relevant and Required?" Business and the Environment v8 n9 Sep 1997. p2-4. (ISSN1052-7206).

CORPORATIONS--ENVIRONMENTAL ASPECTS --MICHIGAN (v26)

CORPORATIONS--ENVIRONMENTAL ASPECTS--SOUTH AFRICA--PUBLIC OPINION

"The July 1997 issue of the EAGLE BULLETIN reported on the results of a recent national survey conducted by South Africa's Human Sciences Research Council (HSRC). Nearly 75% of the 2,241 respondents thought that companies should inform the public about their environmental impact. However, 33% indicated radio as the preferred communication medium. Another 17% wanted to see pamphlets, 16% chose television, 11% wanted public meetings, and only 3% chose environmental reports. Only 10% of the respondents said they received environmental information from companies; 77% said they did not. 41% said the information provided by companies was not reliable, 21% thought it was reliable, and 38% were unsure." (p4)

"Focus Report: Corporate Environmental Reports: Relevant and Required?" Business and the Environment v8 n9 Sep 1997. p2-4. (ISSN1052-7206).

CORPORATIONS--GERMANY--UNITED STATES (v26)

CORPORATIONS--RESEARCH--UNITED STATES (v26)

CORPORATIONS--SALARIES, ETC.--UNITED STATES

In the U.S., "while average wages for all workers rose 3% in 1996, the average CEO salary and bonus rose 39% to $2.3 million--and that is without stock options. Benefitting even more than average were the top managers of the 30 U.S. corporations that laid off the most people last year, according to a new study, 'Executive Excess: CEOs Gain from Massive Downsizing,' by the Institute for Policy Studies and United for a Fair Economy. The axmen who laid off between 2,800 and 49,000 workers last year upped their own compensation by 67%....[In 1996], the top 365 U.S. firms avoided paying $514 million with salary deductions for their top two employees alone." (p9)

Collins, Chuck. "Making Sense: Let's Close the CEO Salary Loophole." Dollars and Sense n212 Jul-Aug 1997. p9. (ISSN0012-5245).

CORPORATIONS--TAXATION (v26)

CORPORATIONS--TAXATION--CANADA (v26)

CORPORATIONS--TAXATION--NEBRASKA (v26)

CORPORATIONS--UNITED STATES (v26)

CORPORATIONS--UNITED STATES--ECONOMIC CONDITIONS

"While the world's top 200 corporations control more than 25 percent of the planet's economic activity, they employ only 18.8 million workers--less than three quarters of 1 percent of the global workforce." (p16) "The sales of the top 200 are twice as large as the personal incomes of four-fifths of humanity, and corporate earnings are larger than the economies of 182 of the world's 191 countries." (p17)

"The Global Marketplace: Growing Corps Kills Economies." Earth Island Journal v12 n3 Sum 1997. p16-17. (ISSN1041-0406).

CORPORATIONS--UNITED STATES--FINANCE

"According to the U.S. Department of Commerce, the return on nonfinancial corporate assets was 6.7 percent in 1995. From this, corporations paid 2.2 percent in taxes, leaving an after-tax rate of return of just 4.5 percent. As modest as this was, it represented a substantial rise from recent years. It was 2.25 times higher than the 2 percent after-tax return U.S. corporations earned in 1980, and more than one-third higher than the 3.3 percent rate in 1990. But the rate of return in 1995 was still well below that of the 1960s, when corporations routinely earned between 5 percent and 7 percent after taxes." (p10 secA)

Bartlett, Bruce. "Bartlett's Notations: Market Trends Bolster Profits and Individuals." Detroit News 27 Oct 1997. p10 secA.

CORPORATIONS--UNITED STATES--PUBLIC OPINION (v26)

CORPORATIONS, INTERNATIONAL

see INTERNATIONAL BUSINESS ENTERPRISES

CORRECTIONS--CALIFORNIA (v26)

CORRUPT PRACTICES IN POLITICS

see POLITICAL CORRUPTION

COSMETICS--MICROBIOLOGY--UNITED STATES (v26)

COSMETICS--UNITED STATES (v26)

COSMETICS INDUSTRY

see also PERFUMES INDUSTRY

COSMETICS INDUSTRY--UNITED STATES (v26)

According to the U.S. Food and Drug Administration, "the number of cosmetic ingredients in the industry's own inventory is over 7,500. The industry has been adding new ingredients at a rate of 1,000 per year for the last few years. Virtually none of these ingredients have been properly tested for safety. The industry's safety review process has reviewed only 450 of the most commonly used cosmetic ingredients. That is about 20 a year." (pS08862)

Kennedy, Edward M. (Sen.-Mass.). "Food and Drug Administration Modernization and Accountability Act of 1997--Motion to Proceed." Congressional Record. Daily ed. v143 n116 5 Sep 1997. pS8851-8869. section/page-level access: <http://thomas.loc.gov/cgi-bin/query/R?r105:FLD001:S08862:> (ISSN0363-7239). (X1.1A.105/1).

COST AND STANDARD OF LIVING

see also CONSUMER PRICE INDEXES; FOOD CONSUMPTION

COST AND STANDARD OF LIVING--MICHIGAN --OAKLAND COUNTY

"Oakland University and the American Chamber of Commerce Researchers Association announced that the cost of living in Oakland County [Michigan] is 13.4-percent higher than the national average. The county is the eighth most expensive place to live in the United States, according to the quarterly survey." (p1 secF) "People who shop...[in Oakland County] pay about 11 percent more than the national average for groceries. Health care--including the cost of a physical checkup, teeth cleaning and an overnight stay at a hospital--costs nearly 19 percent more than average....Homes are 37.5 percent more expensive than the national average." (p2 secF)

Konrad, Rachel. "Business: Oakland County Life Is Costly." Detroit Free Press 5 Jun 1997. p1-2 secF.

COST OF LIVING INDEXES

see CONSUMER PRICE INDEXES

COST OF MEDICAL CARE

see MEDICAL CARE, COST OF

COSTA RICA--SOCIAL CONDITIONS

In Costa Rica, "infant mortality is low, 12.4 deaths per 1000 live births, and longevity is high, an average of 78 years. A public network of urban and rural health centres and hospitals, built over decades, serve the 3.5 million citizens." (p10) "According to a World Bank report, progressive health policies have increased the income of the poorest 10% of the population by more than 65%. With per capita income of about US$2000, Costa Rica is considered a lower-middle income country....About 86% of the population is now covered [by Social Security]....While wealthier cantons show crude death rates below 10 per 1000, the poorest canton in the Huetar Atlantica region has a crude death rate of 40 per 1000." (p11)

Salas, Alvaro/Miranda, Guido. "Costa Rica Reforms 'Model' Health Care System." World Health v50 n5 Sep-Oct 1997. p10-11. (ISSN0043-8502).

COTE D'IVOIRE--ECONOMIC CONDITIONS

"The average urban dweller in Cote d'Ivoire consumes roughly twice as much as the typical rural resident. Mean per capita consumption for the 5,374 urban households is estimated at 273,803 francs of the Communaute Financiere Africaine (CFAF), compared with 164,619 CFAF for the 7,349 rural households. Urban per capita labor income is also much larger than rural: 228,210 CFAF in the urban and 136,750 CFAF in the rural sector. For Cote d'Ivoire as a whole, per capita consumption is estimated at 210,737 CFAF and per capita labor income at 175,381 CFAF. Within both sectors, per capita consumption is about 20 percent greater than per capita labor income." (p527)

Stecklov, Guy. "Intergenerational Resource Flows in Cote d'Ivoire: Empirical Analysis of Aggregate Flows." Population and Development Review v23 n3 Sep 1997. p525-553. (ISSN0098-7921).

COTTON BALING--UNITED STATES

"Cotton bales weighing about 500 pounds are held together by six or eight restraining ties made of either wire or steel straps. Occasionally, one or more of the ties that encircle the cotton bale breaks. About 2 percent of the cotton bales produced in the United States experience breakage of one or more ties. This means that each year, about 400,000 bales require repair, at a cost of $4 to $14 million, estimates agricultural engineer W. Stanley Anthony, who is in the ARS [Agricultural Research Service] Cotton Ginning Research Unit at Stoneville, Mississippi....Repair costs range from $10 to $35 per bale, depending on the availability of a press. Currently, the only equipment that can be used for rebanding costs over $300,000." (p20)

Cooke, Linda/U.S. Dept. of Agriculture. Agricultural Research Service. "Mending the Ties That Bind." Agricultural Research v45 n7 Jul 1997. p20. (ISSN0002-161X).

COTTON TRADE

"Grown in more than ninety countries, cotton is a cash crop worth more than US$20 billion annually." (p28) "A recently harvested crop of engineered cotton produced a cloth that held 12 percent more heat than ordinary cotton cloth and retained heat 9 percent longer at body temperature." (p29)

Frazer, Lance. "Planting Plants as Plants." Kiwanis v82 n10 Nov-Dec 1997. p28-31. (ISSN0162-5276).

COTTON TRADE--ALABAMA (v26)

COTTON TRADE--CHINA

"Over the last 3 years, estimates of China's cotton stocks have increased strongly. From an ending stock-to-use ratio of 29 percent in 1993/94, the ratio has risen to 42, 64, and finally, 76 percent in 1996/97....As cotton supply has grown over the last 2 years, yarn mills have gradually decreased their cotton stocks from 2-3 months of consumption to a reported 1-2 months at most....Cotton consumption is expected to rise in 1997/98 from an estimated 4.4 million metric tons in 1996/97. On a marketing year (August/July) basis through April 1997 (the most recent data available), monthly yarn output (including cotton yarn, synthetic yarn, and blended yarn) rose 7.8 percent compared with the same period the previous year." (p42)

Colby, Hunter/U.S. Dept. of Agriculture. Economic Research Service. "China's Cotton Imports Rise despite High Stocks." China: International Agriculture and Trade Reports Situation and Outlook Series Jun 1997. p41-43.

COTTON TRADE--GEORGIA (v26)

COTTON TRADE--LOUISIANA (v26)

COTTON TRADE--UNITED STATES (v26)

"U.S. farmers planted an estimated 14.4 million acres of upland cotton in 1996 (down 14 percent from 1995) and harvested 12.6 million acres (down 20 percent). However, higher yields led to about a 6-percent increase in 1996 cotton lint production....The Southern Plains (particularly Texas) have continued to have weather-related problems which resulted in the abandonment of about 30 percent of the 1996 planted acreage but only a 2-percent reduction in production." (p24)

U.S. Dept. of Agriculture. Economic Research Service. "1996 Cost of Production for Crops and Livestock: Although Input Expenses Rose in 1996,...Led to Higher Net Returns." Agricultural Income and Finance Situation and Outlook Report Sep 1997. p23-27.

In the U.S., "cotton sales for 1996 were up by $610 million, equivalent to 7 percent of the total increase in the value of crop sales. Cotton acreage was down in 1996, but yields were up 30 percent, leading to increased production. Prices did not fall dramatically in the face of the rebound in production, the result being a 9-percent rise in cotton sales....Given that acres planted were down almost 14 percent, producers experienced a considerable improvement in their returns." (p8)

U.S. Dept. of Agriculture. Economic Research Service. "1996 Farm Income Estimates: Net Value-Added and Net Farm Income Attain New Highs in 1996." Agricultural Income and Finance Situation and Outlook Report Sep 1997. p4-13.

In the U.S., "as of the end of June, 56 percent of the 1997 [cotton crop] area was rated 'good' or 'excellent,' compared with 59 percent a year ago. At the same time, only 13 percent was 'poor' or 'very poor' so far this year, compared with 17 percent in 1996....With 1997/98 harvested acreage estimated at about 13.3 million acres, and a national average yield of 670 pounds, U.S. cotton production in 1997 would reach 18.5 million 480-pound bales. Final 1996 production was more than 18.9 million bales." (p2)

Meyer, Leslie/U.S. Dept. of Agriculture. Economic Research Service. "Commodity Briefs: Field Crops: Early Outlook Points to Smaller Cotton Crop." Agricultural Outlook Jul 1997. p2-3.

In the U.S., in 1996, "cotton exports declined 26 percent in both volume and value to 1.5 million tons and $2.7 billion, respectively....Exports to Canada and Mexico were a record 64,000 tons and 150,000 tons, respectively, a combined increase of 30 percent." (p2)

Greene, Joel/U.S. Dept. of Agriculture. Economic Research Service. "Agricultural Exports Surpass $60 Billion." Foreign Agricultural Trade of the United States Jan-Mar 1997. p2-3.

U.S. cotton "imports went from 4,000 tons in 1995 to a record 174,000 tons in 1996. However, much of the import activity occurred in the third quarter which accounted for 70 percent of the yearly total....The NIS [Newly Independent States of the Soviet Union] supplied 48 percent of the total in 1996." (p6)

Gehlhar, Mark/U.S. Dept. of Agriculture. Economic Research Service. "Imports Advance 12 Percent in 1996." Foreign Agricultural Trade of the United States Jan-Mar 1997. p6-7.

"The 1996/97 U.S. cottonseed crop was produced on a planted area of 14.634 million acres, of which 12.868 million were harvested. Cotton lint production amounted to 18.942 million 480-pound bales while cottonseed production was 7.144 million short tons--for a national average ratio of 1.57152 pounds of seed per pound of lint. The 1996 outturn was 4.3 percent above a year earlier and, when combined with 517,000 tons of beginning stocks, resulted in a 3.5-percent increase in total supply to 7.661 million short tons." (p9)

U.S. Dept. of Agriculture. Economic Research Service. "Situation for Other U.S. Oil Crops." Oil Crops Situation and Outlook Series Oct 1997. p9.

"Fiscal 1997 U.S. cotton exports fell 4 percent to 1.57 million tons from 1.64 million in 1996. But the decline in value of cotton exports was greater, 9 percent, to $2.7 billion." (p1)

U.S. Dept. of Agriculture. Economic Research Service. "Exports." U.S. Agricultural Trade Update 24 Nov 1997. p1.

U.S. "cotton exports were 137,000 tons in May [1997], up 83 percent from May 1996. Cumulative cotton exports were 1.2 million tons, down from 1.5 million tons in 1996....The October to May value for cotton exports was $2 billion, down 24 percent from a year ago." (p1)

U.S. Dept. of Agriculture. Economic Research Service. "Exports." U.S. Agricultural Trade Update 23 Jul 1997. p1.

In the U.S., in August 1997, "eighty-eight percent of the national cotton acreage was setting bolls, behind 94% in 1996 but ahead of the average of 87%. Bolls were opening on 7% of the acreage, behind both 1996 and the average." (p14)

U.S. Dept. of Commerce./Dept. of Agriculture. "National Agricultural Summary: August 4-10, 1997: Highlights." Weekly Weather and Crop Bulletin v84 n32 12 Aug 1997. p14. (ISSN0043-1974).

COTTON TRADE--UZBEKISTAN

"Uzbek cotton exports have been near 1 million tons in recent years and are projected at 930,000 tons for 1996/97, a 17-percent drop from pre-reform 1991....Uzbekistan exports are second only to the United States and in recent years have been about 15 percent of world trade....Russia, the second largest market for Uzbek cotton after Italy last year, is projected to import 200,000 tons for 1996/97....Uzbekistan accounts for 70 percent of NIS/B [Newly Independent States of the Soviet Union and the Baltics] cotton production...." (p24)

Foster, Christian J./Liefert, Olga/Mitchell, Jay K./Hoskin, Roger L./U.S. Dept. of Agriculture. Economic Research Service. "NIS/B Farm Sector Continues Adjustment to Market Forces; U.S. Agricultural Exports to Region Post Recovery." Newly Independent States and the Baltics: International Agriculture and Trade Reports Situation and Outlook Series May 1997. p10,12-15,18,20,22-24.

COUNSELING IN HIGHER EDUCATION--UNITED STATES

The counseling center at the University of Pennsylvania, "which was swamped by phone calls and consultations, assisted roughly 10 percent of the student body last year, or about 2,500 students....According to a recent study at the University of Pittsburgh, 75 percent of college counseling services have seen a rise in the number of students with serious psychological needs....Despite its enrollment of just 3,000 students, Colgate [University in Hamilton, N.Y.,] has a drug and alcohol awareness group, a sexual-crisis resource center (including a 24-hour hotline), and a new women's center....[The Reverend Nancy Devries, who has served as university chaplain at Colgate for nine years] estimates that in the past few years she has consulted with 50 percent more students than in the past." (p12)

Paul, Noel Christian. "Learning: College Students Seek More Counsel." The Christian Science Monitor v89 n180 12 Aug 1997. p12. The Christian Science Monitor search engine: <http://www.csmonitor.com/plweb-cgi/iops1.pl> To retrieve this article, enter the following search: ED=19970812 AND counsel. In the "retrieved list," click the title that matches this record. (ISSN0882-7729).

COUNTERFEITS AND COUNTERFEITING--LATIN AMERICA--UNITED STATES--COSTS

Counterfeiting "costs the US movie industry nearly $70 million annually in Mexico alone and well over $2 billion worldwide....Antipiracy forces will take any good news they can get as they fight against the knockoff movies, musical recordings, books, video games, and software packages that cost United States industries an estimated $15 billion a year....Noting that more than half--some surveys indicate more than two-thirds--of all copies of software currently in use in Latin America were illegally made, the BSA [Business Software Alliance] said the legitimate software industry still accounted for nearly 115,000 jobs and more than $1 billion in tax revenues across Latin America in 1996. Those numbers are projected to rise to 219,000 jobs and nearly $4 billion in tax revenues by 2000." (p6)

LaFranchi, Howard. "International: Mexico's Video Pirates Can't Get You 'Hercules'--Just Yet." The Christian Science Monitor v89 n159 14 Jul 1997. p6. The Christian Science Monitor search engine: <http://www.csmonitor.com/plweb-cgi/iops1.pl> To retrieve this article, enter the following search: ED=19970714 AND hercules. In the "retrieved list," click the title that matches this record. (ISSN0882-7729).

COUNTRY-CITY MIGRATION

see RURAL-URBAN MIGRATION

COUNTRY MUSIC (v26)

COUNTRY MUSIC--UNITED STATES

In the U.S., "in 1993, country music held 18.7 percent of the record buying market. But for the first half of 1997, that figure dipped to 12.4 percent, down from 14.7 percent for the same period a year ago. Ticket sales for country concert tours have also slumped, and the number of country radio stations hovers at 2,285, down from its peak of 2,427 in 1994....Country record sales climbed from $447 million in 1989 to $1.8 billion in 1996." (p75)

Geier, Thom. "Culture & Ideas: Country's Riding in the Saddle, But Not So High." U.S. News & World Report v123 n19 17 Nov 1997. p75. article-level access: <http://www.usnews.com/usnews/issue/971117/17COUN.HTM> (ISSN0041-5537).

COUPONS, FOOD

see FOOD STAMPS

COURT CALENDARS--UNITED STATES

In the U.S., "a 1996 Judicial Council survey of county courts shows that 64 percent of superior courts reported more criminal trials and pretrial appearances because of the three strikes law. Forty percent said they were holding longer criminal trials, and 38 percent reported a backlog of criminal cases." (p41,90)

Mackey, Aurora. "Postcard from Hollister: Ronald George Brings His Goodwill Tour to Small-Town California." California Lawyer v17 n7 Jul 1997. p38-41,90. (ISSN0279-4063).

COURTS

see also JUDGES

COURTS--AUSTRALIA

Data in the publication "Australian Criminal Courts, 1995," by the Australian Bureau of Statistics, show that "during 1995 there were 17,295 defendants who had criminal cases finalised in the Supreme and Intermediate courts, representing a national rate of 126.2 defendants finalised per 100,000 persons aged 17 years and over in Australia during 1995. Of the 17,295 defendants with criminal cases finalised during 1995, the majority (14,408 or 83 per cent) resulted in the defendants being proven guilty or proven not guilty. A further 333 defendants (2 per cent) had their cases transferred to another court level while the remaining 2,554 defendants finalised (15 per cent) involved the defendant absconding or their case being withdrawn. Of the 14,408 defendants that were finalised as a result of the charges being adjudicated, 89 per cent had at least one charge with a proven outcome (guilty verdict or guilty plea) whereas 11 per cent were acquitted. Where information was available about the process of determining whether or not the defendant was guilty, the data showed that three-quarters of these defendants (74 per cent) pleaded guilty, while one in every four (26 per cent) went through trial and the court decided whether or not the defendant was guilty."

Australian Bureau of Statistics. "Statistical Look at Australia's Criminal Courts." Media Release 28 Aug 1997. document-level access: <http://www.abs.gov.au/websitedbs/d3110125.nsf/4a255eef008309e44a255eef00061e57/d4de87cb9c1f6bf34a25650100151fa2?OpenDocument>

COURTS--CALIFORNIA--OFFICIALS AND EMPLOYEES

The California "Supreme Court employs a permanent in-house staff of 67 attorneys (by far the largest such contingent in the nation) who do virtually all of the research and a great deal of the writing for its seven justices." (p43) "The seven justices, burdened with some 6,800 new filings during the past fiscal year...and a rigid 90-day deadline for issuing decisions following oral arguments, must rely heavily on staff attorneys to get the work done....A central staff of 29 attorneys...prepares memorandums for the court's consideration...accompanied by a recommendation on whether or not to hear the case. Some memos are only two or three pages; others run 50 pages or more....It is from these staff summaries...that the justices decide which 5 percent or so of the appeals to undertake each year....Last fiscal year the court's central legal staff, 15 attorneys on the criminal side and 14 on the civil side, processed more than 4,600 petitions for review and 1,800 original proceedings." (p44)

Goldberg, Dick. "Special Supreme Court Report: The Shadow Court." California Lawyer v17 n7 Jul 1997. p42-47. (ISSN0279-4063).

COURTS--GERMANY

Between 1951 and 1996, the Federal Constitutional Court in Karlsruhe, Germany, "received a total of 107,890...complaints [of unconstitutionality], of which only 2.73% were successful. By comparison, there were just 114 institutional disputes; the court had to mediate between the federation and the Lander on 31 occasions; abstract compatibility reviews were requested 128 times; and there were 2,998 submissions by judges." (p26)

Fromme, Friedrich Karl. "Its Decision Is Final: The Federal Constitutional Court." Deutschland n6 Dec 1997. p24-30. article-level access: <http://www.government.de/ausland/index_e.html> (ISSN0945-6791).

COURTS--UNITED STATES (v26)

COURTS--UNITED STATES--TEENAGERS (v26)

COURTS, CIRCUIT
see CIRCUIT COURTS

CRANBERRY INDUSTRY--CANADA
"Traditionally, British Columbia dominated Canadian [cranberry] production, accounting for 98 percent of bearing acres in 1994. Between 1994 and 1997, Canadian bearing acres in cranberry production increased 42 percent to 3,761 acres, and Quebec became a significant production area with 20 percent of total acreage, leaving British Columbia with only 78 percent....British Columbia production for 1996 was 399,500 barrels, compared with 73,934 barrels in Quebec. In 1997 production area in Quebec is 702 acres, up 29 percent from 1996, with an additional 598 planted, nonbearing acres....Cranberry production is increasing in Newfoundland, Prince Edward Island, Nova Scotia, New Brunswick, and Ontario. Production in these provinces rose from 45 bearing acres in 1994 to 118 bearing acres in 1997." (p10)
Calvin, Linda/U.S. Dept. of Agriculture. Economic Research Service. "Commodity Spotlight: Cranberry Supply Expands in Response to Higher Demand." Agricultural Outlook Nov 1997. p8-10.

CRANBERRY INDUSTRY--CANADA--UNITED STATES
"Canada has been the primary source of U.S. cranberry imports. In calendar-year 1996, fresh imports from Canada totaled 424,437 barrels, over 99 percent of all U.S. fresh cranberry imports and 78 percent of total Canadian cranberry production....The U.S. imports only a small amount of frozen cranberries--13,058 barrels in calendar year 1996. Canada has been the traditional source, accounting for at least 95 percent of all frozen imports from 1992 to 1995....[In 1996,] as imports of Canadian frozen cranberries fell 11 percent, Estonia captured 52 percent of U.S. imports, leaving Canada with only 40 percent, with the remaining 8 percent split between Sweden and Russia....From 1993 to 1996, 43 percent of concentrate imports came from Sweden, 24 percent from Finland, 15 percent from the Netherlands, 8 percent from Austria, 4 percent from Germany, 3 percent from Russia, and 2 percent from Chile." (p10)
Calvin, Linda/U.S. Dept. of Agriculture. Economic Research Service. "Commodity Spotlight: Cranberry Supply Expands in Response to Higher Demand." Agricultural Outlook Nov 1997. p8-10.

CRANBERRY INDUSTRY--UNITED STATES (v26)
"In 1996, Americans consumed the fresh-weight equivalent of 1.6 pounds of cranberries per person....The 1996 U.S. cranberry crop totaled 4.67 million barrels (100 pounds), close to the record of 4.68 million in 1994, and up 11 percent from the short 1995 crop. Despite the rebound in production in 1996, the average grower price was a record $62.50 per barrel, up 17 percent from 1995, bringing the farm value of the 1996 crop to $292 million....The 1997 cranberry crop is forecast to reach a record 5.04 million barrels....In 1996, Wisconsin accounted for 42 percent of production and Massachusetts for 37 percent....New Jersey, Oregon, and Washington are the other major cranberry producing states, with 10, 7, and 4 percent of production." (p8)
Calvin, Linda/U.S. Dept. of Agriculture. Economic Research Service. "Commodity Spotlight: Cranberry Supply Expands in Response to Higher Demand." Agricultural Outlook Nov 1997. p8-10.

CRASHES, AIRPLANE
see AIRCRAFT ACCIDENTS

CRAYFISH INDUSTRY--CHINA--LOUISIANA
"During the past five years, Louisiana crawfish producers have forfeited 80 percent of their market share of processed crawfish tail meat to Chinese imports, resulting in a loss of about $40 million to the state's economy, according to Louisiana Department of Agriculture and Forestry's Roy Johnson, director of market development and trade. One-quarter of the state's processing plants have gone out of business, and 3,000 workers have lost their jobs....While Louisiana producers typically sell crawfish tail meat at between $4.50 and $7 per pound, depending on the season, prices for tail meat imported from China were as low as $2.38 per pound in 1994, hovering more typically around $3 per pound." (p1) "Figures filed in the antidumping petition show that Louisiana tail meat sales dropped 70 percent over a three-year period. Between 1993 and 1996, U.S. tail meat shipments dropped 63 percent in value. Revenue to the state's processing industries collapsed from $21.8 million to $4.9 million." (p8)
Grissom, Harriette. "Chinese Crawfish Reduce Louisiana Market Share." Federal Reserve Bank of Atlanta Regional Update v10 n2 Apr-Jun 1997. p1,8.

CRAYFISH INDUSTRY--CHINA--UNITED STATES
"Chinese crawfish exports, most of which are shipped to the United States, reached 2.8 million pounds in 1995--up from a mere 72,000 pounds in 1991. The value of Chinese imports, worth only $238,000 in 1991, climbed to $9,066,000 in 1995. Chinese crawfish tail meat now supplies more than 80 percent of U.S. markets, according to...[Louisiana Department of Agriculture and Forestry's Ray Johnson, director of market development and trade]." (p8)
Grissom, Harriette. "Chinese Crawfish Reduce Louisiana Market Share." Federal Reserve Bank of Atlanta Regional Update v10 n2 Apr-Jun 1997. p1,8.

CRAYFISH INDUSTRY--UNITED STATES (v26)
In the U.S., "over the first half of 1997, crawfish meat imports totaled about 590,000 pounds, up 328 percent from first-half 1996....In 1996 almost all the crawfish imports occurred in the second half of the year and imports for all of 1996 totaled 2.8 million pounds....Exports [to the Scandinavian countries] totaled 5.7 million pounds and were valued at $10.1 million. While this is more than double the value of exports in first-half 1996, it still is well below the $13.2 million shipped in first-half 1994....Domestic production of crawfish (basically Louisiana) in 1996 was 44.4 million pounds liveweight, down 20 percent from the previous year." (unpaginated)
Harvey, Dave/U.S. Dept. of Agriculture. Economic Research Service. "Crawfish Imports and Exports Up." Aquaculture Outlook 3 Oct 1997.

CREDIT--UNITED STATES (v26)

CREDIT, AGRICULTURAL
see AGRICULTURAL CREDIT

CREDIT CARDS--PENNSYLVANIA
In Pennsylvania, "the Federal Reserve's November 1996 Senior Loan Officer Opinion Survey of Bank Lending Practices reported that 97 percent of the responding banks that use credit scoring in their credit card lending operations use it for approving card applications and 82 percent use it to determine from whom to solicit applications. About 20 percent said they used scoring for either setting terms or adjusting terms on their credit cards." (p6)
Mester, Loretta J. "What's the Point of Credit Scoring?" Federal Reserve Bank of Philadelphia Business Review Sep-Oct 1997. p3-16. (ISSN0007-7011).

CREDIT CARDS--UNITED STATES (v26)
"Most Americans own at least one credit card. And of the seven in ten who do, an amazing 34 percent do not know the interest rate of the credit card they use most often, according to a new survey." (p31) "The top-three reasons given for rising debt are that people are living beyond their means (26 percent), credit cards are easily obtained (17 percent), and incomes aren't keeping up with expenses (17 percent)." (p32)
Kate, Nancy Ten. "Kaleidoscope: Debt Perception." American

Demographics v19 n5 May 1997. p31-32. article-level access: <http://www.demographics.com/Publications/AD/97_ad/9705_ad/AD970519.htm> (ISSN0163-4089).

In the U.S., "data from the Bank for International Settlements indicate that the number of credit cards in circulation increased 34 percent between 1988 and 1994, and the number of credit card transactions increased 55 percent. The data also show that the value of credit card transactions increased 98 percent during the same period. The higher number of cards and their use increased the size of credit card debt, so that total consumer revolving credit outstanding grew from $175 billion to $339 billion." (p3)

Yoo, Peter S. "Charging Up a Mountain of Debt: Accounting for the Growth of Credit Card Debt." Review v79 n2 Mar-Apr 1997. p3-13. (ISSN0147-9032).

In the U.S., credit card delinquency "is defined as debt 90 days or more past due or in nonaccrual status....Serious credit card delinquencies fell slightly in total to $4.42B [billion] in the most recent qtr [quarter]. But expressed as a percentage of card debt outstanding, the decline was to 1.95% from 2%....Just 50 banks control 36.4% of the card market and account for 55.2% of serious delinquencies." (unpaginated)

"Banking: Credit Card Delinquencies High, But Only Serious for a Few Banks." Security Letter v27 n17 1 Oct 1997. (ISSN0363-4922).

"American consumers have loaded their debt levels to a record $1.16 trillion....According to a new study by the American Bankers Association, two-thirds of consumers start their holiday shopping without a budget, but a quarter say they'll spend at least $700. Studies also show that Americans spend about $100 more and take two to three months longer to pay off holiday debt than they expect." (p1 secB) "A record $4.45 billion of credit-card debt is more than 90 days past due from a 1.95 percent of card owners....Among student-loan borrowers, 20 percent had at least four cards. The average undergraduate carried $2,226 of credit-card debt in 1996. Industry spokesmen say the focus on delinquencies ignores the fact that 98 percent of credit-card owners pay their bills on time." (p4-5 secB)

Evarts, Eric C. "Work & Money: Don't Get 'Malled' This Christmas." The Christian Science Monitor v90 n4 1 Dec 1997. p1,4-5 secB. The Christian Science Monitor search engine: <http://www.csmonitor.com/plweb-cgi/iops1.pl> To retrieve this article, enter the following search: ED=19971201 AND christmas. In the "retrieved list," click the title that matches this record. (ISSN0882-7729).

"Between 1990 and 1995, the average outstanding credit card balance of [U.S.] households headed by someone under 25 grew from $885 to $1,721. Carrying plastic is the norm for young people--65 percent of college students have cards, for example--and they are more prone than those in other age groups to get in over their heads. Of the debtors seeking professional help at the National Consumer Counseling Service, more than half are between 18 and 32." (p38)

Shenk, Joshua Wolf. "U.S. News: In Debt All the Way up to Their Nose Rings." U.S. News & World Report v122 n22 9 Jun 1997. p38-39. article-level access: <http://www.usnews.com/usnews/issue/970609/9DEBT.HTM> (ISSN0041-5537).

CREDIT UNIONS--AFRICA (v26)

CREMATION--UNITED STATES (v26)

CRIB DEATH

see SUDDEN INFANT DEATH SYNDROME

CRICKET--SOUTH AFRICA (v26)

CRIME

see also ABORTION SERVICES--CRIMES AGAINST; ALCOHOLISM AND CRIME; BURGLARY; DRUG ABUSE AND CRIME; FIREARMS--UNITED STATES--CRIME; HATE CRIMES; JOURNALISTS--CRIMES AGAINST; RECIDIVISM; SENTENCES (CRIMINAL PROCEDURE); TEENAGE MOTHERS--CRIMES AGAINST; VICTIMS OF CRIMES; VIOLENT CRIMES; WHITE COLLAR CRIMES

CRIME--CALIFORNIA--SAN DIEGO

According to Alan Bersin, the U.S. Attorney in San Diego, "'the crime rate...[in San Diego] is down by more than 32 percent.'...'According to FBI statistics, San Diego now has the lowest crime rate among the 70 largest U.S. cities.'" (p36) "Selective prosecution, plea bargains, and a 'fast-track' program dispose of approximately 80 percent of felony cases preindictment, according to Bersin." (p37) "In 1993, before Bersin took over, the U.S. Attorney's office in San Diego prosecuted 4,021 misdemeanors and 1,249 felonies. In 1996 the breakdown was 183 misdemeanors and 2,504 felonies." (p39)

Canlen, Brae. "Immigration Law: The Border Honcho." California Lawyer v17 n8 Aug 1997. p34-39,80-82. (ISSN0279-4063).

CRIME--CALIFORNIA--SAN DIEGO--ILLEGAL ALIENS

"During the past two years the U.S. Attorney's office [in San Diego, Calif.] charged more than 2,930 illegal immigrants with felonies--double the combined total of the previous ten years." (p36) "In 1996 only 21 percent of the felony cases filed by [U.S. Attorney Alan] Bersin's office were drug related. Sixty-three percent of his caseload that year dealt with immigrant smugglers or immigration violators with criminal backgrounds." (p80)

Canlen, Brae. "Immigration Law: The Border Honcho." California Lawyer v17 n8 Aug 1997. p34-39,80-82. (ISSN0279-4063).

CRIME--CANADA (v26)

CRIME--CANADA--CHILDREN (v26)

CRIME--COLOMBIA (v26)

CRIME--COLOMBIA--COSTS (v26)

CRIME--ECONOMIC ASPECTS--COLOMBIA

In Colombia, "in 1993, it was estimated that the proceeds from robberies of public service enterprises, kidnappings, and homicides in the course of robbery constituted 2.2% of the GDP....In 1993, this sum was slightly less than the amount that the government spent for education (2.62% of GDP), but was more than it spent for health care and services (1.2% of GDP) when social security and child care are omitted from the tally (Bonilla Castro, 1995...)....The total income from all criminal activity (robberies, kidnapping for ransom, the narcotraffic), excluding contraband, comes close to $3 billion a year. This figure constitutes more than 7% of the GDP and is equivalent to the total annual sales of the 14 largest industrial enterprises in the country (Rubio, 1995...). The population of those engaged in some form of criminal activity has been estimated to encompass about 100,000 persons; if one assumes an average of 4 persons per family, then it would appear that some 400,000 individuals must benefit from, or subsist on, income derived from criminal acts. Furthermore, this figure does not include the estimated 100,000 peasants engaged in cultivating illicit crops." (p61)

Richani, Nazih. "The Political Economy of Violence: The War-System in Colombia." Journal of Interamerican Studies & World Affairs v39 n2 Sum 1997. p37-81. (ISSN0022-1937).

CRIME--GREAT BRITAIN--LONDON (v26)

CRIME--INDIANS OF NORTH AMERICA

According to the U.S. "Justice Department, violent crime nationwide has declined significantly between 1992 and 1996. The overall violent crime rate has dropped about 17 percent, and homicides are down 22 percent....In the same period of time, homicides in Indian country rose...87 percent....The Indian

Health Service tells us that the homicide rate among Indians is the highest among any ethnic group in the country--2 1/2 times the rate among white Americans....The FBI reports a dramatic increase in violent crime attributable to gangs in Indian country, nearly doubling between 1994 and 1997. The BIA's [Bureau of Indian Affairs] law enforcement division identified 181 active gangs on or near Indian reservations in 1994. By 1997, that estimate had risen to 375 gangs with approximately 4,650 gang members. The Navajo Nation alone reports at least 75 active gangs....There is a small reservation just east of the Phoenix area that has 19 active gangs on it. These are among Indian kids. On the Menominee reservation in Wisconsin, there was a 293 percent increase in the number of juveniles arrested between 1990 and 1994." (pS9563)

Kyl, Jon (Sen.-Ariz.). "Department of the Interior and Related Agencies Appropriations Act, 1998." Congressional Record. Daily ed. v143 n125 18 Sep 1997. pS9553-9574. section/page-level access: <http://thomas.loc.gov/cgi-bin/query/R?r105:FLD001:S09563:> (ISSN0363-7239). (X1.1A.105/1).

CRIME--JAPAN--ALIENS (v26)

CRIME--JOURNALISTS

"In 1996, a record number of journalists were jailed: 185 journalists in 24 countries. While jailings of journalists are up, murders are down. In 1995, 57 reporters were killed. In 1996, there were 27." (p10 secA)

"In Our Opinion: Jailed Journalists." Detroit Free Press 17 Jul 1997. p10 secA.

CRIME--KOREA (SOUTH)

In Korea, "in 1993, a total number of 287,451 crimes were reported, compared to 258,176 in 1992 and 242,332 in 1989....Of 287,451 crimes reported, 185,929 were property crimes while 197,763 were personal crimes. Among personal crimes, assaults accounted for almost 93%, followed by rape (3.6%) and robbery (1.5%)....The victimization rate per 1,000 population for burglary, robbery, personal theft, and assaults were 74.07, 37.54, 96.1, and 19.02 respectively. The victimization rates for robbery, theft, and assault were 2.3, 10.8, and 1.4 respectively for women, while those for males were 5.2, 8.4, and 2.3 respectively." (p318)

Lee, Yoon Ho. "Explaining Korean Women's Fear of Crime." International Journal of Comparative and Applied Criminal Justice v21 n2 Fall 1997. p317-329.

CRIME--KOREA (SOUTH)--PUBLIC OPINION

"According to the Social Indicators in Korea which has been annually published by the Korean National Statistical Office (1993), 53.6% of women surveyed compared to 48.0% of male respondents expressed their apprehensions about criminal offenses. In addition, only 35.5% of males but 60.9% of females indicated they were afraid to walk alone at night." (p318)

Lee, Yoon Ho. "Explaining Korean Women's Fear of Crime." International Journal of Comparative and Applied Criminal Justice v21 n2 Fall 1997. p317-329.

CRIME--MARYLAND--BALTIMORE

"According to the BALTIMORE COMPREHENSIVE COMMUNITIES PROGRAM SUMMARY written by Michael Sarbanes and distributed by the Mayor's Coordinating Council on Criminal Justice, violent crime in Boyd-Booth [a Baltimore neighborhood] decreased by 52% over the past three years, total crime dropped by 40% between 1994 and 1995, and drug arrests decreased by 80% from 1993 to 1995." (p12-13)

Mitten, Lauren. "The Little Neighborhood That Could--And Did." Community Service Newsletter v45 n3 Jul-Sep 1997. p12-13. (ISSN0277-6189).

CRIME--MASSACHUSETTS--BOSTON (v26)

"The homicide rate in Boston for people under 24 dropped more than 70 percent in 1996 compared with 1995, and juvenile arrests for assaults with a gun have dropped 81 percent since 1993. Boston's overall homicide rate dropped to a 30-year low last year, robberies to a 26-year low and assaults with weapons to a 10-year low....[Strike force leader Lt. Gary French] estimated the number of 14- to 24-year-olds involved in gang activity to be about 1,500, but only about 400 of those were aggressive and violent." (p4 secA)

Kresnak, Jack. "Children First: Team Effort Pays." Detroit Free Press 8 Jul 1997. p1,4 secA.

CRIME--MASSACHUSETTS--BOSTON--YOUTH (v26)

CRIME--MEXICO--MEXICO CITY

Mexico City "averages five murders and 218 violent robberies a day. An estimated 60,000 cars were stolen last year, most sold in Central America. Mexico City has 1 police officer for every 150 residents--but 8 out of every 10 residents don't trust the police, according to surveys." (p6)

LaFranchi, Howard. "International: Mexico City: A Pinata Full of Big Troubles--And Many Delights." The Christian Science Monitor v89 n50 30 Jun 1997. p6. The Christian Science Monitor search engine: <http://www.csmonitor.com/plweb-cgi/iops1.pl> To retrieve this article, enter the following search: ED=19970630 AND delights. In the "retrieved list," click the title that matches this record. (ISSN0882-7729).

CRIME--MICHIGAN (v26)

Michigan Governor "John Engler announced that the number of crimes reported in the state had decreased 1.8 percent in 1996--the fifth consecutive year of declines....The total number of violent crimes decreased 8.1 percent last year, according to preliminary statistics from the state police. Murders hit the lowest point since 1969 with a 10.7-percent decline. Rapes were down 9.2 percent; robberies 6.2 percent; and aggravated assaults 8.7 percent." (p3 secC)

Cohen, Jodi S. "City & Suburban News: In Taylor: Crimes in State Down Nearly 2%." Detroit News 25 Jul 1997. p3 secC.

CRIME--MICHIGAN--DETROIT (v26)

In 1996, Detroit, Michigan, "ranked eighth in the nation in per-capita rates of murder and arson, but topped the United States with almost 3.5 auto thefts for every 1,000 people....Homicides in Detroit went down by about 10 percent, compared to 13 percent for other major U.S. cities. Robbery was down 6 percent in Detroit, compared to the 11-percent drop in its group. Arson grew dramatically in Detroit. The FBI numbers show an increase of more than 57 percent from 1995 to 1996, with 1,811 deliberate fires reported last year." (p2 secA)

Newman, Heather/McConnell, Darci. "Fewer Killings in Detroit, But Other Crime Rises." Detroit Free Press 2 Jun 1997. p2 secA.

In 1997, "the FBI reported Detroit's homicide rate dropped for the third consecutive year. Murders dropped from 475 in 1995 to 428 in 1996--the lowest since 1960. The violent crime index also dropped to 2,318 violent crimes per 100,000 people from 2,407 in 1995. The city also has cut the number of carjackings by 35 percent since the formation of the Detroit police carjacking unit in October 1995....Robberies also have fallen...from 10,076 in 1995 to 9,504 in 1996." (p8 secA)

"Election '97: Detroit's Future:...Voter Priorities: THE DETROIT NEWS WWJ 950 Exit Poll:...Issues for City...: Crime." Detroit News 5 Nov 1997. p8 secA.

In southeast Detroit, Michigan, "in terms of crime, the 4th Precinct falls somewhere near the middle of the 13 precincts. In 1996, there were 25 murders, 611 robberies and 1,816 burglaries. The precinct with the lowest crime rate, the 1st (Clinton) Precinct, which covers downtown, had six murders, 205 robberies and 176 burglaries last year. The highest crime area was within the 9th (Gratiot) Precinct on the east side, which last year reported 70 murders, 1,569 robberies and 4,724 burglaries." (p4 secD)

Woolley, Wayne. "The Metro: Special Report: Public Safety: Protesters Seeking New Police Station." Detroit News 24 Jun 1997. p1,4 secD.

CRIME--MICHIGAN--UNIVERSITIES AND COLLEGES (v26)

CRIME--MICHIGAN--WARREN (v26)

CRIME--MICHIGAN--WASHTENAW COUNTY (v26)

CRIME--MICHIGAN--YOUTH

In the U.S., a "report, issued by the National Institutes of Health and coordinated by the American Sociological Association, showed juveniles in Michigan were arrested 36 percent more frequently for violent crimes in 1994 than they were a decade earlier. That's still almost half the national rate, where juvenile violent crime arrests jumped by 70 percent. Counter to the trend, however, Michigan's rate of juvenile violent crimes fell 15 percent between 1994 and 1995, compared with a 2.6-percent decline nationwide." (p5 secA)

Potts, Laura A. "Nation & World: Teens March toward Wild Side." Detroit News 1 Jul 1997. p5 secA.

CRIME--MICHIGAN--YOUTH--COSTS (v26)

CRIME--NEW YORK (N.Y.) (v26)

"In 1994, crime in New York City declined 12% in the major index categories as opposed to a 2% national drop-off. In the first six months of 1995, the city's crime rate declined 16% compared to the same period in 1994, as opposed to 1% in the nation as a whole. The New York decreases for 1995 and 1996 accounted for over 60% of the national decline in crime. Over the last three years, the overall crime rate in the city's seven major categories has plummeted a whopping 38%....Overall crime dropped about 16% for the first four months of 1997 compared to the same period in 1996." (p3)

Silverman, Eli B. "Crime in America: Crime in New York: A Success Story." Public Perspective v8 n4 Jun-Jul 1997. p3-5. (ISSN1050-5067).

CRIME--TEXAS--HOUSTON (v26)

CRIME--UNITED STATES (v26)

A multistate study of felony prisoners in the U.S. "found that 62 percent of burglars had also perpetrated robberies. (A burglary is an entry into a building to commit a felony, and does not necessarily involve a confrontation; a robbery is the taking of property from a victim through force or the threat of force.)...In 30 percent of the cases in which a burglar does confront a victim, the victim is assaulted or threatened. In ten percent of these cases, the assaults turn into rapes." (p37)

Kopel, David. "Vital Signs: Crime: Burglary and the Armed Homestead." Chronicles v22 n1 Jan 1998. p36-38. (ISSN0887-5731).

"The FBI's annual Uniform Crime Report tracked eight categories of crime in 1996 in the 213 U.S. cities with populations of more than 100,000--homicide, rape, robbery, aggravated assault, burglary, larceny, auto theft and arson. Nationally, violent crimes reported to police dropped by a record 7 percent as overall serious crime declined for a fifth consecutive year. Preliminary figures show that the violent crimes of homicide, rape, robbery and aggravated assault together had the largest one-year decline in the 35 years since the FBI began reporting year-to-year comparisons in 1961. Murder dropped by 11 percent and aggravated assault by 6 percent--both records." (p2 secA)

Newman, Heather/McConnell, Darci. "Fewer Killings in Detroit, But Other Crime Rises." Detroit Free Press 2 Jun 1997. p2 secA.

"According to a study cited by the Independent Insurance Agents of America, about 80 percent of crimes at [U.S.] shopping centers happen...[in parking lots]. One in five automobile-crash claims comes from accidents in parking lots, reports the Insurance Institute for Highway Safety." (p1 secA)

Martindale, Mike/Garrett, Craig/Pardo, Steve. "Malls Fight Traffic Congestion, Crime: Security Measures Range from Videos to Cops on Horseback." Detroit News 9 Dec 1997. p1-2 secA.

According to the FBI, in the U.S., "overall violent crime--homicide, robbery, aggravated assault, and rape--fell 7 percent. Homicide dropped by 11 percent. Since 1993, total crime has fallen in seventeen of the country's twenty-five largest cities: by 36 percent in New York, by 25 percent in Los Angeles, by 20 percent in Boston and San Francisco, by 14 percent in Denver. In Hartford, Connecticut, crime fell by 20 percent in just one year, from 1995 to 1996, and has hit a ten-year low." (p85)

Tomasky, Michael. "Arguments: The Left and Crime." Dissent v44 n4 Fall 1997. p85-90. (ISSN0012-3846).

According to the U.S. Bureau of Justice Statistics, "property crime was down more than 8 percent last year and was 17 percent lower than in 1993. Certain personal crimes were down dramatically during the 1993-1996 period: rape, including attempted rape, fell 44 percent, other sexual assaults dropped 37 percent and aggravated assault declined 27 percent. Some property crimes also fell substantially during the 1993-1996 period: household burglary down 19 percent, motor vehicle theft 29 percent and personal theft (pocket picking, purse snatching and attempted purse snatching), down 35 percent....There were an estimated 27.4 million completed or attempted household property crimes during 1996 (a rate of 266 per 1,000 households), compared to 29.5 million during 1995 (a rate of 291 such crimes per 1,000 households)."

U.S. Dept. of Justice. Bureau of Justice Statistics. "Violent Victimizations Fell 10 Percent Last Year: Property Crimes Declined 8 Percent." Press Release 15 Nov 1997. document-level access: <http://www.ojp.usdoj.gov/pub/bjs/press/cv96.pr>

U.S. "law enforcement agencies reported a 4-percent decrease in serious crime during the first 6 months of 1997 when compared to figures reported during the same time period of the previous year, according to preliminary Uniform Crime Reporting Program figures released...by the Federal Bureau of Investigation....Violent crime decreased 5 percent and property crime fell 4 percent during the first half of 1997. In the category of violent crime, murder and robbery both dropped 9 percent; aggravated assault fell 3 percent; and forcible rape declined 2 percent. Among the property crimes, arson decreased 9 percent; motor vehicle theft and burglary both dropped 5 percent; and larceny-theft declined 4 percent."

U.S. Dept. of Justice. Federal Bureau of Investigation. "UCR Preliminary Release--January through June 1997." Press Release 23 Nov 1997. document-level access: <http://www.fbi.gov/pressrel/ucr/ucrnov.htm>

In the U.S., "some communities have shown modest increases in serious crime over the past year. Five largest increases among major urban areas: Raleigh, up 13.1%; Las Vegas, 8.4%; Portland, OR, 8.3%; Orlando, 7.2%; and Little Rock, 4.9%. Five large cities with the greatest decrease in the past year: Corpus Christi, down 19.8%; Long Beach, 18.9%; Boston, 18.8%; Atlanta, 16.2%; and Wash., DC, 14.2%." (unpaginated)

"Serious Crime Continues Its Decline in All Categories during First Half of Year: Patterns Vary." Security Letter v27 n21 1 Dec 1997. (ISSN0363-4922).

In the U.S., in 1996, "total property crime decreased 3%; less frequent violent crime declined 7%....Among the largest 25 cities for the years 1993-96, the five largest declines were: New York 31.6%; San Diego 27.8%; Los Angeles 24.6%; Boston, 19.5%; and San Francisco 19.3%." (unpaginated)

"Violent Crime in U.S. Declines by 7%, Highest Drop since

'61." Security Letter v27 n11 2 Jun 1997. (ISSN0363-4922).

CRIME--UNITED STATES--ABUSED CHILDREN

A study on the effects of child abuse conducted by Cathy Spatz Widom, entitled "The Cycle of Violence," found that, in the U.S., "those who had been abused or neglected were 53 percent more likely to be arrested as juveniles; 38 percent more likely to be arrested as adults; 38 percent more likely to be arrested for a violent crime; and 77 percent more likely to be arrested if they were females. The study further showed that abuse and neglect cases were more likely to average nearly 1 year younger at first arrest, commit twice as many offenses, and were arrested 89 percent more frequently. A more troubling conclusion was that a child who is neglected is just as likely as a child who is abused to be arrested for a violent crime." (p5-6)

Briscoe, Judy. "Breaking the Cycle of Violence: A Rational Approach to At-Risk Youth." Federal Probation v61 n3 Sep 1997. p3-13. (ISSN0014-9128).

CRIME--UNITED STATES--COSTS (v26)

CRIME--UNITED STATES--ILLEGAL ALIENS

The U.S. General Accounting Office spot checked released criminal illegal aliens "from 7/96 through 3/97 to determine if they committed further crimes. A group of 6,000 aliens was found to have totally avoided the IHP [Institutional Hearing Program] screen. Of 1,899 analyzed, 635 were defined as having committed aggravated felonies leading to conviction. After release, 148 of the 635 were re-arrested, and 31 of the 635 were re-arrested more than once. GAO determined that the costs of additional prison time that could have been avoided reached nearly $63M [million] for those who were released before INS [Immigration & Naturalization Service] completed the IHP process." (unpaginated)

"Criminal Justice: INS Criticized for Failure to Identify, Deport Illegal Jailed Aliens." Security Letter v27 n16 15 Sep 1997. (ISSN0363-4922).

CRIME--UNITED STATES--IMMIGRANTS

In the U.S., "the Clinton Administration is seeking to strip the citizenship of nearly 5,000 immigrants who were wrongly naturalized in an immigration drive in 1996. An audit had found that of 1.1 million people who were granted citizenship in 1996, 16,400 of the new citizens had a record of at least one felony arrest. The audit also found 4,946 cases in which a criminal arrest should have disqualified an applicant or in which an applicant lied about his or her criminal history." (p12)

"Dateline Migration: National: U.S. Is Seeking to Strip 5,000 of Citizenship." Migration World v25 n4 1997. p12. (ISSN1058-5095).

CRIME--UNITED STATES--UNIVERSITIES AND COLLEGES (v26)

In the U.S., "between 1992 and 1994, campus arrests for weapons possessions rose from 1,760 to 1,960; drug arrests rose from 4,010 to 7,230; and liquor law violation arrests rose from 18,310 to 20,430....About one in four colleges (26 percent) reported any occurrence of violent crime in 1994, up slightly from 24 percent in 1992. Eighteen percent reported aggravated assaults, 12 percent reported robberies, and 9 percent reported forcible sex offenses, which include forcible rape." (p30-31)

Klein, Matthew. "Kaleidoscope: Colleges: Still Safer." American Demographics v19 n7 Jul 1997. p30-31. article-level access: <http://www.demographics.com/publications/ad/97_ad/9707_ad/ad970723.htm> (ISSN0163-4089).

CRIME--UNITED STATES--YOUTH (v26)

In the U.S., "a Gallup Poll conducted in 1994 shows that the average adult believes juveniles commit 43 percent of violent crimes, nearly three times the number reported by the FBI. In 1995, for instance, 16.5 percent of those arrested for violent crimes were 13 through 17 years old, according to the FBI. And, although teen crime had increased during the mid-1980s and early 1990s, the trend began a reversal in 1995 with the first decrease in juvenile arrests for violent offenses in nearly a decade, down 3 percent from arrests the year before." (p64)

Gibeaut, John. "Juvenile Justice: Who's Raising the Kids?" ABA Journal v83 Aug 1997. p62-67. (ISSN0747-0088).

In the U.S., "youths account for 14% of the arrests for murder and nonnegligent manslaughter; for rape, 15%; larceny/theft, 30%; and motor vehicle theft, 43%. In 1990, 15.6% of the nation's crimes were perpetrated by 14- to 17-year-olds (United States Department of Education, 1993)." (p885)

Dondero, Grace M. "Mentors: Beacons of Hope." Adolescence v32 n128 Win 1997. p881-886. (ISSN0001-8449).

In the U.S., "arrest rates for juveniles have more than tripled in the last decade. The average stay in youth correction facilities is about 1 year for crimes against persons, 248 days for drug offenses, and 17 days for weapons crimes. The total number of juveniles arrested that are under the age of 18 rose 20.1 percent between 1991 and 1995." (pH7130)

Schaffer, Bob (Rep.-Colo.). "Departments of Labor, Health and Human Services, And Education...Appropriations Act, 1998." Congressional Record. Daily ed. v143 n119 10 Sep 1997. pH7129-7169. section/page-level access: <http://thomas.loc.gov/cgi-bin/query/R?r105:FLD001:H07130:> (ISSN0363-7239). (X1.1A.105/1).

In the U.S., in September 1997, a report released by Fight Crime: Invest in Kids, a youth advocacy group made up of police chiefs, prosecutors, and crime survivors found that "nearly half of all violent juvenile crime on school days occurs from 2 to 8 p.m., not late at night....According to the report, just one-seventh of violent crime--murders, rapes, robberies and aggravated assaults--committed by those under 18 occurs between 11 p.m. and 7 a.m., when curfews typically are in effect....Violent juvenile crime triples from 3 to 4 p.m., the hour immediately after school, compared with 1 to 2 p.m., when school is still in session....The new report focuses on school days, when 57 percent of violent juvenile crime is committed." (p17 secA)

Cannon, Angie. "Nation & World: Children First: A Free Press Campaign: After-School Hours Are Prime for Youth Crime, Report Says." Detroit Free Press 11 Sep 1997. p17 secA.

CRIME AND ALCOHOLISM

see ALCOHOLISM AND CRIME

CRIME AND DRUG ABUSE

see DRUG ABUSE AND CRIME

CRIME LABORATORIES--UNITED STATES

Eleven months into the O.J. Simpson murder trial, the U.S. "National Institute of Justice announced grants of up to $150,000 to individuals or organizations willing to develop guidelines for death investigations and for the training of death investigators. Number of crime labs accredited by the American Society of Crime Lab Directors/Laboratory Accreditation Board: 1995: 22, 1996: 36, 1997 (as of August): 25, with 34 more pending. (Accrediation is voluntary, except in New York State. Only 35 to 40 percent of the nation's forensic labs have ASCLD/LAB accreditation.) Forensic Lab Improvement Program grants offered by the National Institute of Justice to expand and improve DNA [Deoxyribo-nucleic Acid] testing at state and local crime labs that offer DNA testing: 1995: 46 applications received, 1996: 62 applications received." (p35)

Canlen, Brae. "I'm O.J.--You're O.J.: How the O.J. Simpson Case Has Affected the Legal System." California Lawyer v17 n10 Oct 1997. p28-35,77. (ISSN0279-4063).

CRIME PREVENTION--MICHIGAN--DETROIT

In June 1997, the Clinton administration announced a $270-

million grant for some of the 3,400 U.S. housing organizations for "continuing and expanding anti-crime efforts such as the one-strike-and-you're-out policy and Operation Safe Home....In three years, the initiatives have led to 12,000 arrests and the seizure of $22 million in drugs nationwide. U.S. Housing and Urban Development officials say Detroit has been allocated more than $5.6 million in grants for its anti-crime efforts so far....But 148 people have been denied admission to Detroit's public housing units since the one-strike policy began last year, and there have been about 70 arrests on drug charges." (p14 secA)

"In Our Opinion: Public Housing." Detroit Free Press 13 Jun 1997. p14 secA.

CRIME SYNDICATES

see GANGS

CRIME VICTIMS

see VICTIMS OF CRIMES

CRIMES, VIOLENT

see VIOLENT CRIMES

CRIMINAL ASSAULT

see RAPE

CRIMINAL JUSTICE, ADMINISTRATION OF

see also JUVENILE JUSTICE, ADMINISTRATION OF; POLICE; PRISONS

CRIMINAL JUSTICE, ADMINISTRATION OF--VERMONT

According to John Perry, director of planning for the Vermont Department of Corrections, the victim-offender mediation "program handles about 20 percent of the caseload now, he says, but the goal is 50 percent....So far, according to state correctional figures, the approach appears to be working. Of the 497 people who had completed the program as of June 1 [1997], about 82 percent completed their sentences without further court intervention. And a follow-up study of 154 participants showed a recidivism rate of 8.2 percent after six months, about 3 percent less than the recidivism rate for offenders placed on conventional probation. Meanwhile, the percentage of violent offenders in the state's prison system has grown from about 42 percent before the program began to about 75 percent today, correctional officials estimate. The rest of the country's violent offender population grew by only 3 percent during the same period." (p20)

Hansen, Mark. "News: Repairing the Damage." ABA Journal v83 Sep 1997. p20. (ISSN0747-0088).

CRIMINAL REGISTERS--UNITED STATES (v26)

CRIMINALS

see also BURGLARS; DELINQUENT GIRLS; FEMALE OFFENDERS; FUGITIVES FROM JUSTICE; GANGS; JUVENILE DELINQUENTS

CRIMINALS--UNITED STATES (v26)

"Almost 3.9 million adult men and women were on probation or parole at the end of 1996, an increase of about 128,000 during the year, the [U.S.] Justice Department reported....The number of offenders being supervised in the community on probation or parole increased 3.4 percent during 1996, compared to the 3.3 percent annual average since 1990. The total number of adults under correctional supervision--incarcerated or in the community--reached a new high of 5.5 million at the end of 1996. As of last December 31, 2.8 percent of the U.S. adult population, or about one in every 35 adults, were incarcerated or on probation or parole."

U.S. Dept. of Justice. "Nation's Probation and Parole Population Reached Almost 3.9 Million Last Year." Press Release 14 Aug 1997. document-level access: <http://www.ojp.usdoj.gov/pub/bjs/press/papp96.pr>

"At the end of 1996 just over a third of [U.S.] probationers (765,700) and nearly half of parolees (297,000) were black, while two-thirds of probationers (1,417,700) and half of parolees (345,400) were white. Persons of other races accounted for about 1 percent of each population (29,900 probationers and 8,200 parolees.) Hispanics, who may be of any race, comprised 15 percent of probationers (271,000) and 20 percent of parolees (108,400)."

U.S. Dept. of Justice. "Nation's Probation and Parole Population Reached Almost 3.9 Million Last Year." Press Release 14 Aug 1997. document-level access: <http://www.ojp.usdoj.gov/pub/bjs/press/papp96.pr>

At the end of 1996, "Texas had the largest number of adults on probation and parole with more than 538,000 under supervision, followed by California with 389,000. At the end of 1996, 3.9 percent of all adults in Texas were on probation or parole. Fourteen states reported that fewer than 1 percent of their adult populations were on probation or parole. West Virginia had the lowest probation and parole supervision rate (466 offenders per 100,000 adults), followed by North Dakota (553), Kentucky (560) and Mississippi (587). Five states reported increases of at least 10 percent in their probation populations during 1996, led by Virginia (up 22.1 percent) and Alabama (up 16.0 percent). Eight states reported increases of at least 10 percent in their parole populations, led by New Hampshire (up 35.8 percent) and Alaska (up 20.5 percent)."

U.S. Dept. of Justice. "Nation's Probation and Parole Population Reached Almost 3.9 Million Last Year." Press Release 14 Aug 1997. document-level access: <http://www.ojp.usdoj.gov/pub/bjs/press/papp96.pr>

CRIMINALS--WASHINGTON--SEATTLE--PUBLIC OPINION

In a study of residents of Seattle, Washington conducted by Jacqueline Helfgott of the Dept. of Criminal Justice at Seattle University, "the respondents reported that the bases for objection to having an ex-offender [released from a correctional facility] as a neighbor...were fear for personal safety (44.8 percent), the personal view that rehabilitation doesn't work and that the person will reoffend (21.2 percent), personal preference (17.2 percent), fear for community safety (13.1 percent), past experience (2.2 percent), and news coverage on crime (1.5 percent). In response to the question, 'You may be aware that in Washington State there is a Community Protection Act, a component of which requires sex offender registration and community notification if a sex offender moves into your neighborhood. If this issue were to be on a future ballot, would you be inclined to vote for or against the Act?,' the majority of the respondents (94.2 percent...) said they would be inclined to vote for the Act, with 74.6 percent...reporting that they would like the Act to be expanded to include other types of offenders such as murderers (97.2 percent), other violent offenders (80.4 percent), drug offenders (73.4 percent), arsonists (71.5 percent), and property offenders (57.5 percent)." (p19)

Helfgott, Jacqueline. "Ex-Offender Needs versus Community Opportunity in Seattle, Washington." Federal Probation v61 n2 Jun 1997. p12-24. (ISSN0014-9128).

CRISIS INTERVENTION (PSYCHIATRY)--UNITED STATES--YOUTH (v26)

CROCODILES

"Of the approximate 21 distinct species of crocodilians in the world, about 17 are threatened with extinction....Nests in the wild are sometimes raided by animals and eggs often suffer a mortality rate of up to 40 percent. Normally about 90 percent of all newborn crocodilians are devoured during the first two months of life by wading birds, big fish and other predators....Saltwater and freshwater crocodiles in Australia are marketed commercially from farms, and it is currently over a

$5 million-per-year industry." (p16) "In Papau, New Guinea, crocodile management consists of village farms (up to 300 crocodiles), small-business farms (up to 1,000 animals), and large-business farms (1,000 to 25,000 or more reptiles)." (p17)

Saunders, Melvin D. "Finding Opportunity in Diversity...: Raising Exotic Livestock." Acres, U.S.A. v27 n9 Sep 1997. p16-17. (ISSN1076-4968).

CROCODILES--AUSTRALIA

In Australia, "traps account for 70 percent of the crocodiles...[Tom Nichols and Nevelle Haskins, rangers with the Parks & Wildlife Commission of the Northern Territory] catch. The other 30 percent are caught in open waters. In 1996, they caught 120. Most go to crocodile farms where they are placed in a breeding program." (p10)

Freeman, Melanie Stetson. "Caution: Crocs on Board." The Christian Science Monitor v89 n177 7 Aug 1997. p10-11. The Christian Science Monitor search engine: <http://www.csmonitor.com/plweb-cgi/iops1.pl> To retrieve this article, enter the following search: ED=19970807 AND board. In the "retrieved list," click the title that matches this record. (ISSN0882-7729).

CROCODILES--ZIMBABWE

Zimbabwe's "50,000-strong wild crocodiles are now thriving, and the captive crocodile population is now about three times the size of the wild population. The [Nile crocodile ranching] program has been a definite success, generating $2.8 million in 1994 alone." (p28)

Youth, Howard. "Neglected Elders." World Watch v10 n5 Sep-Oct 1997. p22-29. (ISSN0896-0615).

CROP INSURANCE--UNITED STATES

"Crop insurance is an essential part of the producer 'safety net' envisioned by the...[U.S. government's] agricultural policy. There were some 89,000 tobacco growers with crop insurance policies in 1996, of which 69,000 actually planted the crop for the year. More than 550,000 acres were insured with liability exceeding $1.15 billion. Tobacco producers paid more than $20 million in premiums to insure their crops in recognition of the need to provide for their own risk management at a time when the Government is providing fewer and fewer farm subsidies. Tobacco growers in three States (North Carolina, South Carolina, and Virginia) received $77.8 million in indemnities for losses due to back-to-back hurricanes that hit the East Coast last year." (pS7908)

Glickman, Dan (Secretary, U.S. Dept. of Agriculture). "Agriculture, Rural Development, Food and Drug Administration...Appropriations Act, 1998." Congressional Record. Daily ed. v143 n105 23 Jul 1997. pS7898-7911. section/page-level access: <http://thomas.loc.gov/cgi-bin/query/R?r105:FLD001:S07908:> (ISSN0363-7239). (X1.1A.105/1).

CROPS--FERTILIZERS

see FERTILIZERS

CROSS-COUNTRY SKIING--MICHIGAN

"Great Lakes Nordic Ski Council (GLNSC), an association of 11 Michigan nordic ski areas and two in Ontario, offers more than 1,750 kilometers of groomed trails....[Michigan] has 52 nordic ski areas, more than any state in the region. We lead the nation in sales of nordic skis, accounting for nearly 15 percent of sales." (p7 secF)

Huyser-Honig, Joan. "Connection: Travel: Michigan a Hot Spot for Nordic Skiing." Ann Arbor News 7 Dec 1997. p7 secF.

CROSS-COUNTRY SKIING--UNITED STATES

Nordic skiing "is the most gender-balanced of all snow sports: 51 percent of U.S. nordic skiers are women, compared to 39 percent of alpine (downhill) skiers and 27 percent of snowboarders. Almost a quarter of the nation's nordic skiers live in Wisconsin, Illinois, Indiana, Ohio or Michigan." (p7 secF)

Huyser-Honig, Joan. "Connection: Travel: Michigan a Hot Spot for Nordic Skiing." Ann Arbor News 7 Dec 1997. p7 secF.

CRUELTY TO ANIMALS

see ANIMAL WELFARE

CRUELTY TO CHILDREN

see CHILD ABUSE

CRUISE SHIPS--RECYCLING (WASTE, ETC.) (v26)

CRUISES

see OCEAN TRAVEL

CRUZ-CHAGAS DISEASE

see CHAGAS' DISEASE

CUBA--ECONOMIC CONDITIONS (v26)

"The average worker in Cuba makes about 240 pesos a month (the equivalent of $10)....Three avocados cost 24 pesos, or 10 percent of an average monthly wage." (p12) In July 1997, "a new rent law went into effect requiring anyone who rents to pay a $100 or $200 monthly tax (depending on the location) for each room rented....The Cuban economy grew by...7 percent in both 1995 and 1996....Today, 24 Cuban pesos will buy $1, a significant improvement over the 1995 rate of 35 to 1." (p13)

Bleifuss, Joel. "The First Stone: 90 Miles Away." In These Times v21 n19 11 Aug 1997. p12-13. (ISSN0160-5992).

"For the first half of 1996, Minister Carlos Lage (vice president of the Council of the State, secretary of the Executive Committee of the Council of Ministers, and considered Cuba's 'economic czar') recognized that Cuba's financial situation remained negative and reported a decrease of 7 percent in export prices together with a rise of 13 percent in import costs. Cuba's 1995 GDP of 13,125 million pesos, if translated into U.S. dollars at free market rates, would be equivalent to a pitiful US$596.5 million. To put this into context, sales of chopped bag lettuce in the United States in 1996 amounted to over $1 billion, twice Cuba's reported GDP!" (p55)

Werlau, Maria C. "Foreign Investment in Cuba: The Limits of Commercial Engagement." World Affairs v160 n2 Fall 1997. p51-69. (ISSN0043-8200).

CUBA--RELIGION

"It's estimated that 1 million of the 11 million Cubans are actively related to some religious movement, including Santeria (or 'the way of the saints'). In addition, a recent poll found that at least 74 percent of the population claim some belief in 'a higher power'...." (p580)

Wall, James M. "Cuba's Religion Factor: Diplomatic Dance." Christian Century v114 n19 18 Jun 1997. p579-580. (ISSN0009-5281).

CUBA--SOCIAL CONDITIONS (v26)

CUBAN AMERICANS

"About one-half of the Cubans in the 1990 census had entered the United States before 1980....Less than one-fifth of the 1990 Cuban population entered between 1980 and 1990....Hispanics of Cuban descent numbered 1,053,000 in 1990; by 1996 they numbered 1,127,000, about 4 percent of U.S. Hispanics." (p8)

del Pinal, Jorge/Singer, Audrey. "Generations of Diversity: Latinos in the United States." Population Bulletin v52 n3 Oct 1997. p2-47. (ISSN0032-468X).

CUBAN AMERICANS--EMPLOYMENT

"Cuban American males are almost equally divided among three areas of employment: technicians, sales and administrative support positions (25%), operators, fabricators, and laborers (23%), managerial and professional positions (21%). Of the remaining minority 15% work in precision production, craft and repair and 12% work in service occupations. The largest percentage (49%) of Cuban American females work in technical, sales or administrative support. Another 27% hold managerial and professional positions, 13% work in service occupations, and

10% work as operators, fabricators, and laborers." (p26)
"Targeting Minority Publics: Employment of Hispanic Americans by Country of Origin." Public Relations Quarterly v42 n2 Sum 1997. p26. (ISSN0033-3700).

CUCUMBER INDUSTRY--UNITED STATES (v26)

CULTS--UNITED STATES--JEWS

In the 4 April 1997 N.Y. JEWISH WEEK, Arnold Markowitz, director of the Cult Hotline and Clinic, said "that 'Jews are disproportionately involved in destructive cults across the...[U.S.]. About 15 to 17 percent of the estimated 6 million cult members in the country are Jewish.' Because Jews constitute only 2.3% (5.9 million) of the total U.S. population, this figure...means that 1 in 6 Jews is a member of a cult!" (p46)
Katz, Lyber. "Around the World: At Home." Jewish Currents v51 n6 Jun 1997. p45-46. (ISSN0021-0639).

CULTURAL ANTHROPOLOGY
see ETHNOLOGY

CULTURAL DIVERSITY POLICY
see MULTICULTURALISM

CULTURE, POPULAR
see POPULAR CULTURE

CUMMINS RIVER VALLEY (B.C.)

"Located 140 kilometers north of Golden, British Columbia, the Cummins River Valley is one of the few remaining BC interior rain forests. The 6400 hectare upper portion of the valley, with spectacular twin lakes and waterfalls received protected status in March, 1995." (p17)
"Canadian Wildlands: Rocky Mountain Rainforest Protected." Networker v9 n2 Sum 1997. p17.

CURFEW--UNITED STATES--YOUTH

A survey "published in the AMERICAN JOURNAL OF POLICE found that 93 of the nation's 200 largest cities had curfews in January 1990. The number surged to 146 by the spring of 1995." (p64) Monrovia, California Mayor Robert T. Bartlett says the curfew "ordinance has reduced truancy by 44 percent. He also claims that since the ordinance was enacted, daytime burglaries have decreased by 61 percent and vandalism has decreased by 49 percent. But like District of Columbia officials, Bartlett was unable to say what percentage of those crimes occurred during curfew hours or how many were committed by truants." (p66)
Gibeaut, John. "Juvenile Justice: Who's Raising the Kids?" ABA Journal v83 Aug 1997. p62-67. (ISSN0747-0088).

CURRENCY
see MONEY

CURRENCY EXCHANGE
see FOREIGN EXCHANGE

CURRICULA
see HIGH SCHOOLS--UNITED STATES--CURRICULA

CUSTODY OF CHILDREN--CANADA (v26)

CUSTOMS, SOCIAL
see MANNERS AND CUSTOMS

CUSTOMS ADMINISTRATION--CANADA--OFFICIALS AND EMPLOYEES (v26)

CUT FLOWERS--UNITED STATES

"Over 3 billion stems of cut flowers are imported annually [to the U.S.] from 45 countries, though most are from Latin America (primarily Colombia, Ecuador, Mexico, and Costa Rica) and from Europe (primarily the Netherlands, which resells from a number of countries)....About 78 percent of the cut flowers for the U.S. market pass through Miami, most from Colombia....On an average day, 30,000 boxes of flowers arrive at Miami's airport." (p9)
Johnson, Doyle. "Commodity Spotlight: 'Green' Industry Grower Receipts to Exceed $11 Billion." Agricultural Outlook Jul 1997. p9-10.

CYCLING--DENMARK--COPENHAGEN (v26)

CYCLING ACCIDENTS--UNITED STATES (v26)

CYPRUS--ARMED FORCES (v26)

CZECH REPUBLIC--COMMERCE

In the Czech Republic, "between 1993-96 foreign trade expanded vigorously with imports growing by 26% annually and exports by 15%. This turned a surplus of 0.30 billion ECU [European currency units] in 1993 into a deficit of -4.6 bn last year, representing almost 12% of GDP. The deficit with the EU was -2.77 bn. Between 1995-96 imports grew by 13.3% to 21.88 bn ECU and exports by 4.1% to 17.24 bn. Imports from EU were 8.6% up and exports to EU -0.5% down. The EU's share of total trade with the country rose from 42% in 1993 to 58.5% in 1996. Eight percentage points of this was due to the accession of Austria, Finland and Sweden. Germany accounted in 1996 for 29.8% of the Czech Republic's total world imports (up 6.7% over '95) and 36.0% of exports (down -0.3%). This left a deficit of -0.33 bn. Next biggest EU partner was Austria: 5.8% of imports (down -5.7%) and 6.5% of exports (up 2.3%), with a deficit of -0.14bn. Russia accounted for 7.4% of imports and 3.2% of exports. Between 1995-96 these were up by 13.0% (imports) and 13.2% (exports), with a deficit of -1.07 bn ECU. USA had shares of 3.4% (imports) and 2.1% (exports) with 1995-96 rises of 13.7% and 15.6% respectively, with a deficit of -0.37 bn."
Eurostat. "Around 60% of Czech & Hungarian Trade with EU: Rapid Expansion Highlighted." Press Release 16 Oct 1997. document-level access: <http://europa.eu.int/en/comm/eurostat/compres/en/7197/6607197a.htm>

CZECH REPUBLIC--ECONOMIC CONDITIONS

Prague "now draws nearly 100 million tourists...each year....With growth last year of 4.4 percent, a private sector accounting for 70 percent of gross domestic product (GDP), a retail/consumer boom, and the only reform government in the region still in place after the transition from Communism in 1989, the Czech Republic is understandably a favorite of Western journalists, businesspeople, and visitors....Many Czech products are uncompetitive, which largely explains the country's sizable balance of trade/current account deficit (7 percent of GDP). This lack of strong corporate governance also explains both the Czech Republic's remarkably low employment rate of 3.3 percent (almost 0 percent in Prague), and the economic retrenchment the country now faces....Czech growth will likely slow to 2 to 3 percent, with uncertain social implications and reduced import levels." (p18)
Randolph, R. Sean. "Opinion/Essays: Hungarians, Czechs, Poles Race to Join EU." The Christian Science Monitor v89 n180 12 Aug 1997. p18. The Christian Science Monitor search engine: <http://www.csmonitor.com/plweb-cgi/iops1.pl> To retrieve this article, enter the following search: ED=19970812 AND hungarians. In the "retrieved list," click the title that matches this record. (ISSN0882-7729).

CZECH REPUBLIC--POLITICS AND GOVERNMENT (v26)

DAIRY CATTLE--WISCONSIN (v26)

DAIRY FARMS--UNITED STATES (v26)

DAIRY PRODUCTS INDUSTRY
see also MILK CONSUMPTION

DAIRY PRODUCTS INDUSTRY--AUSTRALIA (v26)

DAIRY PRODUCTS INDUSTRY--CANADA (v26)

DAIRY PRODUCTS INDUSTRY--CANADA--UNITED STATES (v26)

DAIRY PRODUCTS INDUSTRY--INDIA (v26)

DAIRY PRODUCTS INDUSTRY--UNITED STATES (v26)

In 1997, "August 1 stocks of American cheese varieties amounted to 469 million pounds, 18 percent higher than a year earlier, far outweighing the small decline in holdings of other cheese varieties....Manufacturers' stocks of nonfat dry milk on August

1 were 159 million pounds, more than double those of a year earlier. Commercial stocks of butter on August 1 were 62 million pounds, nearly twice the level reported for a year earlier." (p2)

Miller, Jim/U.S. Dept. of Agriculture. Economic Research Service. "Commodity Briefs: Livestock, Dairy & Poultry: Large Stocks Limit Dairy Price Recovery." Agricultural Outlook Oct 1997. p2-3.

In the U.S., "dairy cooperatives and private companies supply milk and manufactured dairy products....About 86 percent of the milk sold to plants and dealers in 1994 was handled by cooperatives, up from 76 percent in 1973. There are two major types of dairy cooperatives: bargaining-only and manufacturing/processing. In 1992, about 68 percent of dairy cooperatives could be considered bargaining-only." (p7)

Manchester, Alden/U.S. Dept. of Agriculture. Economic Research Service. "Summary of Report: Dramatic Changes in Dairy Industry over Last 50 years." ERS Information Nov 1997. p7-8.

In the U.S., "farms with 100 cows were considered large in 1950. Today, there are many dairy farms with 5,000 cows....Over half of the milk delivered in 1950 was to the home in quart bottles. Today, that share is 2 percent, with most milk sold through supermarkets in gallon jugs." (p7)

Manchester, Alden/U.S. Dept. of Agriculture. Economic Research Service. "Summary of Report: Dramatic Changes in Dairy Industry over Last 50 years." ERS Information Nov 1997. p7-8.

Bonuses in fiscal 1997 from the U.S. Dairy Export Incentive Program "of $121 million facilitated sales of 140,324 metric tons of anhydrous milk fat, butter, butter oil, cheddar cheese, mozzarella cheese, nonfat dry milk, processed American cheese, and whole milk powder. The DEIP is off to a strong start in fiscal 1998 as of December 1, as bonuses valued at $33.5 million assisted 38,484 metric tons of dairy product sales, chiefly to African and Middle Eastern countries." (p11)

U.S. Dept. of Agriculture. "U.S. Agricultural Export Programs." Outlook for U.S. Agricultural Exports 2 Dec 1997. p11-12.

DAM SAFETY--UNITED STATES (v26)

DAMS (v26)

DAMS--CHILE

In Chile, the 450 megawatt Pangue Dam, "the first of six planned for the Biobio, began operation in 1997....The dam was built with the help of a US$150 million loan from the International Finance Committee (IFC), the [World] Bank's private sector arm....The 155-meter-high, US$500 million Ralco Dam is projected to generate 570 MW of electricity at full capacity. The project would displace 600 people, 400 of them Pehuenche." (p9)

Brown, Aleta. "Background on the Biobio Dams." World Rivers Review v12 n3 Jun 1997. p9. (ISSN0890-6211).

DAMS--EARTHQUAKE EFFECTS

"There is evidence linking earth tremors and reservoir operation for more than 70 dams....Most of the strongest cases of RIS [reservoir-induced seismicity] have been observed for dams over 100 metres high--but dams just half this height are also believed to have induced quakes....For most well-studied cases of RIS, the intensity of seismic activity increased within around 25 kilometers of the reservoir as it was filled." (p7)

McCully, Patrick. "About Reservoir-Induced Seismicity." World Rivers Review v12 n3 Jun 1997. p7. (ISSN0890-6211).

DAMS--EARTHQUAKE EFFECTS--INDIA

In India, "a strong earthquake hit the Narmada Valley on May 22, [1997,] killing around 50 people and injuring 1,000 in the city of Jabalpur in the state of Madhya Pradesh. The epicenter of the magnitude 6.0 earthquake is believed to have been about 20-40 kilometers from Bargi Dam, which completed filling in 1990....Some seismologists...believe that the devastating magnitude 6.4 earthquake which struck Killari, Maharashtra in 1993, killing 10,000 people, was induced by a nearby reservoir." (p7)

McCully, Patrick. "Earthquake Hits Narmada Valley." World Rivers Review v12 n3 Jun 1997. p7. (ISSN0890-6211).

DAMS--HEALTH ASPECTS--LATIN AMERICA

"The more than 100 dams on the rivers of the La Plata Basin are spreading diseases which had previously been under control in the region....Some 50 million people are affected directly or indirectly by these dams' diseases. The region includes nearly one-sixth of the population of South America." (p12)

"News Briefs: Updates: Latin America." World Rivers Review v12 n3 Jun 1997. p12. (ISSN0890-6211).

DAMS--SOUTH AFRICA

In South Africa, the Mohale Dam, the second dam in the massive Lesotho Highlands Water Project, "will displace about 300 households (1,500-2,000 people), according to the World Bank, only 70 of which are moving voluntarily. The reservoir will inundate 1,300 hectares of the Highlands' best arable land and 1,600 hectares of grazing land. At least 300 households will be affected by the loss of communal lands." (p4)

Pottinger, Lori. "Lesotho Villagers Sue Dam Authorities." World Rivers Review v12 n3 Jun 1997. p4. (ISSN0890-6211).

DAMS--UNITED STATES

In the U.S., "there are more than 75,000 dams taller than six feet. Reservoirs behind dams cover 3 percent of the United States and can store 60 percent of the combined annual flow of the nation's rivers." (p2)

Rasmussen, Matt. "Editor's Note: Paying a Heavy Price." Inner Voice v9 n5 Sep-Oct 1997. p2.

"Currently, the United States--with some 74,000 dams, most of which are relatively small--has perhaps the most active dam-removal movement....More than 500 of the 50-year licenses given by the US Federal Energy Regulatory Commission (FERC) to private hydrodam operators are expiring between 1989 and 2004....FERC announced in late 1994 that it has authority to order owners of the more than 1,800 dams under its jurisdiction to decommission dams which fail to win new licenses....The average age of dams in the US is now around 40 years....A 1994 survey showed at least 1,800 non-federal dams were still unsafe." (p8)

McCully, Patrick. "Taking Down Bad Dams." World Rivers Review v12 n4 Aug 1997. p8,14. (ISSN0890-6211).

DANE COUNTY (WIS.)--POPULATION (v26)

DATING (SOCIAL CUSTOMS)--UNITED STATES --ATTITUDES

"It's Just Lunch! Inc., a Chicago-based executive dating service that arranges blind lunch dates for busy professionals, found the following differences between men and women: Sixty-two percent of women say it takes at least one hour to decide if a man is worth going out with a second time. Fifty-six percent of men say it takes them 15 minutes or less. Consistent with men's quick assessment of first dates is the following: The vast majority (86 percent) of men will call a woman for a second date within 24 hours of their first date if he's interested. In other words, women: If he hasn't called you within 24 hours, you have less than a 1-in-7 chance that you'll hear from him again....Ninety percent of women list income of their date as an important dating criteria, but only 51 percent of men say the same." (p1 secE)

"Accent: Relationships: Men and Women Have Totally Different Views after First Date." Detroit News 26 Sep 1997. p1 secE.

DATING, BIRACIAL

see INTERRACIAL DATING

DATING VIOLENCE--UNITED STATES--YOUTH (v26)

DAY CARE CENTERS--ACCREDITATION--UNITED STATES (v26)

DAY CARE CENTERS--HEALTH ASPECTS--CANADA --UNITED STATES (v26)

DAY CARE CENTERS--UNITED STATES (v26)

In the U.S., "a 1995 study of day care in four states found that 40 percent provided 'less than minimal care.' Dropping a child off at a relative's house is no guarantee either. Nearly 70 percent of the 226 informal day-care arrangements studied by the Families and Work Institute in New York in 1994 were deemed 'potentially harmful to children's growth.'" (p4)

Baldauf, Scott. "United States: Parents Get an Online Peek at Tots." The Christian Science Monitor v89 n158 11 Jul 1997. p1,4. The Christian Science Monitor search engine: <http://www.csmonitor.com/plweb-cgi/iops1.pl> To retrieve this article, enter the following search: ED=19970711 AND tots. In the "retrieved list," click the title that matches this record. (ISSN0882-7729).

DAY SURGERY

see AMBULATORY SURGERY

DDT (INSECTICIDE)--MEXICO--VERACRUZ --SAFETY MEASURES (v26)

DEAF-SIGN LANGUAGE

see SIGN LANGUAGE

DEATH

see DROWNING VICTIMS; MORTALITY

DEATH--UNITED STATES (v26)

DEATH, MERCY

see EUTHANASIA

DEATH-DUTIES

see INHERITANCE AND TRANSFER TAX

DEATH PENALTY

see CAPITAL PUNISHMENT

DEBIT CARDS--UNITED STATES (v26)

DEBT

see also BANKRUPTCY

DEBT--CANADA (v26)

DEBT--UNITED STATES

In the U.S., "the use of general purpose credit cards jumped from 56 percent of all families in 1989 to about 66 percent in 1995. About 52 percent always paid off their balances, 20 percent paid off sometimes, while 28 percent hardly ever paid them off....In 1995, 41 percent of families had a mortgage or home equity debt; 47 percent had an installment debt; 48 percent, credit card debt; and six percent with an investment real estate debt."

U.S. Dept. of Commerce. Economic & Statistics Administration. "New Statistical Abstract Highlights Household Lifestyles." Census Bureau Press Release 4 Dec 1997. document-level access: <http://www.census.gov/Press-Release/cb97-199.html>

"Spurred by credit card debt, bankruptcy claims in the United States have escalated by more than 20 percent over the past 5 years, increasing from 971,000 in 1992 to 1.2 million in 1996. This has translated into expanding caseloads for U.S. bankruptcy courts and placed a substantial added burden upon bankruptcy judges and staff. The district of Maryland is among those jurisdictions affected most severely by the rise in bankruptcy filings, experiencing a staggering 35.8 percent jump in the last year, and an astounding 544 percent increase over the 12-year period beginning December 31, 1984, and ending December 31, 1996." (pH5854)

Hoyer, Steny H. (Rep.-Md.). "Bankruptcy Judgeship Act of 1997." Congressional Record. Daily ed. v143 n108 28 Jul 1997. pH5848-5854. section/page-level access: <http://thomas.loc.gov/cgi-bin/query/R?r105:FLD001:H05854:> (ISSN0363-7239). (X1.1A.105/1).

DEBTS, EXTERNAL--DEVELOPING COUNTRIES

In 1996 the International Monetary Fund "and the World Bank designated 41 of their member states as 'heavily indebted poor countries' (HIPCS) whose debt was not likely ever to be repaid in full. The total external debt of these countries, mostly public or official rather than private, rose from $55 billion in 1980 to $183 billion only a decade later and to $215 billion by 1995, a sum more than twice their export earnings. Of the 41, 32 are from sub-Saharan Africa....All but 6 fall into the United Nations Development Program's lowest human development category....Average gross domestic product growth between 1985 and 1990 was 2.2 percent and fell to only 1 percent between 1990 and 1995. In 1993, 32 of them had gross national product per capita figures of $695 or less, debt to export ratios higher than 220 percent, and/or debt to GNP ratios of more than 80 percent. Over half often have annual debt service due of more than 20 percent of government revenue." (p395)

Callaghy, Thomas M. "Globalization and Marginalization: Debt and the International Underclass." Current History v96 n613 Nov 1997. p392-396. (ISSN0011-3530).

DEBTS, PUBLIC--CANADA (v26)

"A couple of years ago a study by Statistics Canada showed that 50% of the debt was caused by high interest rates. Only 6% of the debt was caused by government programs. The other 44% was caused by tax expenditures and tax loopholes, and the failure to have a fair tax system in Canada." (p882)

Nystrom, Lorne (MP-SK). "Government Orders: Supply." Canada. Parliament. House of Commons. Debates. v135 n17 21 Oct 1997. p879-911. section-level access: <http://www.parl.gc.ca/36/1/parlbus/chambus/house/debates/017_1997-10-21/han017-e.htm#LINKT8> (ISSN0704-5603). (X3-361E).

DEBTS, PUBLIC--DEVELOPING COUNTRIES (v26)

DEBTS, PUBLIC--EUROPE (v26)

A survey on the structure of government debt in EU Member States in 1991-1996 by Eurostat, Statistical Office of the European Communities in Luxembourg found that "as a general rule, central government is responsible for over 75% of government debt. Over 95%: Greece, Ireland, Italy, Portugal and the UK; 90%-95%: Belgium, Denmark, Austria, Finland (since 1994) and Sweden; 75%-90%: Germany, Spain, France and the Netherlands....Social security funds account for a minute--in some case negligible--share of government debt: under 1% since 1994 for all Member States except France. France had 4% of debt imputable to social security funds in 1995. Medium-/long-term indebtedness covers over 87% of government debt in Germany, Denmark, Ireland, Luxembourg, the Netherlands, Norway, Austria and Finland. For the others, medium-/long-term financial instruments account for under 82%, despite a marked increase since 1991. In seven of these countries short-term government debt in 1996 ranged from 18% in Belgium to 28% in Portugal. Only France with 36% had a higher rate."

Eurostat. "Survey Sheds Light on Structure of Government Debt." Press Release 25 Nov 1997. document-level access: <http://europa.eu.int/en/comm/eurostat/compres/en/7897/6207897a.htm>

In the European Union, "long-term bond issues accounted for 46%-71% of government debt in 14 countries in 1996. Exceptions were Denmark (91%) and Finland (80%)....Bills and short-term bonds--generally the second largest source of public financing--accounted for the following percentages in 1993-96: 19%-29%: Spain, France, Greece, Italy and Sweden; 8%-18%: Belgium, Denmark, Norway, Portugal and Finland; under 6%: Germany, Ireland, the Netherlands, Austria and the UK....If Member States were to be classified by proportion of loans in government debt, the result would be: under 10%: Denmark, Italy, Portugal and the UK; 10%-30%: Belgium, Spain, France, Finland and Sweden; over 30%: Germany, Greece, Ireland, Luxembourg, the Netherlands, Norway and Austria."

Eurostat. "Survey Sheds Light on Structure of Government Debt." Press Release 25 Nov 1997. document-level access: <http://europa.eu.int/en/comm/eurostat/compres/en/7897/6207897a.htm>

DEBTS, PUBLIC--GERMANY (v26)

DEBTS, PUBLIC--MASSACHUSETTS--BOSTON (v26)

DEBTS, PUBLIC--MEXICO (v26)

DEBTS, PUBLIC--MICHIGAN

Since 1991, the Michigan "government's direct debt has increased 60 percent, from $1.88 billion to $3.02 billion....According to Moody's Investors Service, Michigan's debt to personal income in 1997 equals 1.5 percent, ranking...35th among the 50 states." (p11 secA)

Khouri, Nick. "Comment: Michigan's Debt Load Is Worth Cost to Taxpayers." Detroit News 8 Aug 1997. p11 secA.

DEBTS, PUBLIC--UNITED STATES (v26)

"The amount of debt facing...[the U.S.] today is $5.3 trillion....Take the amount of debt and divide by the number of people in the United States of America. What one would find...is that the amount of money that the Federal Government has borrowed on behalf of the American people is the same as $20,000 for every man, woman and child in the United States of America." (pH5291)

Neumann, Mark W. (Rep.-Wis.). "Economic Situation Facing the Nation." Congressional Record. Daily ed. v143 n100 15 Jul 1997. pH5290-5295. section/page-level access: <http://thomas.loc.gov/cgi-bin/query/R?r105:FLD001:H05290:> (ISSN0363-7239). (X1.1A.105/1).

DEER--ACCIDENTS--MICHIGAN

"Car-deer crashes cost Michigan drivers $100 million yearly and jumped 9.7 percent to 68,233 in 1996, with 2,221 injuries and six deaths. They're up 43 percent over the last four years." (p1 secC) "Some 15 percent of all reported car accidents in Michigan involve a deer, said...[Jerry Basch, of the community traffic safety division of the Automobile Association of America, the state's largest insurance company,] and repairs cost on average...about $1,600 in each car-deer crash. More than half of all crashes in 1996 happened in southern Michigan, with 321 in Wayne [County]; 1,500 in Oakland; 1,455 in Washtenaw, and 599 in Macomb." (p2 secC)

Shepardson, David. "Metro: News Special: Reflector System Reduces Car-Deer Accidents in State: Wall of Light from Headlamps...Deer." Detroit News 12 Nov 1997. p1-2 secC.

DEFECTIVE VISION

see VISION DISORDERS

DEFENSE (LAW)

see ACTIONS AND DEFENSES

DEFENSE, SOCIAL

see CIVILIAN-BASED DEFENSE

DEFENSE INDUSTRIES (v26)

see also WEAPONS INDUSTRY

"The United States spends almost seven times as much as France on military R&D [research & development] and France is the second biggest spender. The United States spends 10 times as much as Britain, the third largest spender. According to official statistics on military R&D reported in SIPRI YEARBOOK 1997, global expenditures on military R&D are less than half of what they were during the height of the Cold War--about $58 billion in 1997 dollars....$38 billion of that total is attributable to the United States; $51 billion to the NATO nations, which include the United States....The Russian R&D budget appears to be 10 times smaller in real terms than was its Soviet counterpart in the late 1980s....When it comes to military technology, the entire developing world (excluding China) spends less than four percent of the world's R&D total, much of which is accounted for by India's $680 million R&D budget." (p4)

Arnett, Eric. "Guest Opinion: And Still Champion." Bulletin of the Atomic Scientists v53 n4 Jul-Aug 1997. p4. (ISSN0096-3402).

"The global weapons trade has declined dramatically over the past decade, from an estimated $80 billion in 1987 to about $30 billion annually throughout the first half of the 1990s." (p4)
"In the past five years, 60-70% of all arms transfers (measured in dollar volume) have gone to poorer countries, with the vast majority going to non-democratic or repressive governments." (p6)

Lumpe, Lora. "The Arms Market Today: Dangerous Competition, Diminishing Returns." Peacework n276 Jul-Aug 1997. p4-7. (ISSN0748-0725).

DEFENSE INDUSTRIES--ARGENTINA

Under Argentina's President Raul Alfonsin, "the armed forces' share of public expenditures plummeted from 32.3 percent in 1982 to 18.4 percent in 1990." (p464) "Economic adjustment and neo-liberal restructuring have caused the government to contain defense spending, privatize military industries, [and] reduce force levels (from 95,000 men in 1989 to 65,000 in 1993).... Military expenditures fell from 2.6 percent of GNP in 1989 to 1.7 percent in 1993." (p465)

Hunter, Wendy. "Continuity or Change? Civil-Military Relations in Democratic Argentina, Chile, And Peru." Political Science Quarterly v112 n3 Fall 1997. p453-475. (ISSN0032-3195).

DEFENSE INDUSTRIES--ASIA (v26)

DEFENSE INDUSTRIES--EUROPE--UNITED STATES (v26)

DEFENSE INDUSTRIES--GREAT BRITAIN (v26)

DEFENSE INDUSTRIES--INDIA--RUSSIA (v26)

DEFENSE INDUSTRIES--INDONESIA--UNITED STATES

"Non-democratic governments received 84 percent--nearly $50 billion--of the $59.1 of American weapons that were transferred to developing countries through foreign aid or Pentagon administered corporate sales during the past 5 years. Developing countries received 67 percent of the $88.5 billion total of U.S. arms transfers during the past 5 years. Perhaps Indonesia provides the best example of what we ought not to be doing. The Indonesian Armed Forces have become a military mafia, receiving $1.6 billion every year in United States backed loans from the World Bank--equal to that country's entire reported military budget. Yet it is no secret that the Indonesian military under-reports its military expenditures by somewhere between 25 and 50 percent." (pH3625)

Kennedy, Joseph P., II (Rep.-Mass.). "Foreign Relations Authorization Act, Fiscal Years 1998 and 1999." Congressional Record. Daily ed. v143 n80 10 Jun 1997. pH3591-3632. section/page-level access: <http://thomas.loc.gov/cgi-bin/query/R?r105:FLD001:H03625:> (ISSN0363-7239). (X1.1A.105/1).

DEFENSE INDUSTRIES--MIDDLE EAST

"Some 42 percent of the world's arms sales are made to the Middle East, most of it top-dollar US hardware. Already the Earth's most militarized region, planned Gulf purchases of $75 billion in the next five years ensure it will retain this status." (p13-14)

"Notebook: Buying Spree." Toward Freedom v46 n5 Sep-Oct 1997. p13-14. (ISSN0048-9898).

DEFENSE INDUSTRIES--PERSIAN GULF REGION

"According to Dr. al-Rubi of Kuwait, over $82 million has been spent on security by the Gulf states since the 1991 [Persian Gulf] war....Kuwaiti economic expert Jasim al-Sudan states that the money the GCC [Gulf Cooperation Council] states spend on one soldier or defense job (an average of $60,000 per year) could create five civilian jobs." (p6)

Al-Shayeji, Abdullah. "Dangerous Perceptions: Gulf Views of the U.S. Role in the Region." Middle East Policy v5 n3 Sep 1997. p1-13. (ISSN1061-1924).

"In 1995, every Gulf state except Iran devoted more of its GDP to military expenditures than the world average of 4.2 percent....According to the US Arms Control and Disarmament Agency (ACDA), during the period 1992 to 1994 the Middle East as a whole imported $34 billion in arms, 43 percent of the world's total; the eight Gulf states account for more than 70 percent of the Middle East imports." (p12) The Stockholm International Peace Research Institute "calculates that from 1991 to 1995 Saudi Arabia imported $7.1 billion in arms, ranking third in the world behind Turkey and Egypt for that period." (p13)

Gause, F. Gregory. "Arms Supplies and Military Spending in the Gulf." Middle East Report v27 n3 Jul-Sep 1997. p12-14. (ISSN0899-2851).

DEFENSE INDUSTRIES--PERSIAN GULF REGION --UNITED STATES

"Graham Fuller and Ian Lessor, in a recent article in FOREIGN AFFAIRS, contend that the annual cost of American military activity in the Gulf could be as high as $60 billion per year, about one-fifth of the total US defense budget....According to the ACDA [U.S. Arms Control and Disarmament Agency], during the period 1992 to 1994 the US was the source of over 50 percent of the arms sold in the Middle East as a whole, and approximately 43 percent of the arms sold in the Gulf." (p13)

Gause, F. Gregory. "Arms Supplies and Military Spending in the Gulf." Middle East Report v27 n3 Jul-Sep 1997. p12-14. (ISSN0899-2851).

DEFENSE INDUSTRIES--RUSSIA (v26)

DEFENSE INDUSTRIES--RUSSIA--UNITED STATES (v26)

DEFENSE INDUSTRIES--SOUTH ASIA

"While military spending as a proportion of gross domestic product (GDP) has declined in every region of the world since 1985, in South Asia it has increased by 12 per cent. The region spent $14 billion on defence in 1994, and the figure is rising every year." (p25)

"Notebook: Guns, Or Better?" Choices v6 n4 Oct 1997. p25.

DEFENSE INDUSTRIES--UNITED STATES (v26)

"U.S. weapons are currently being used in 39 of the world's current 42 ethnic and territorial conflicts. In the past 4 years, 85 percent of U.S. arms sales to the Third World have gone to undemocratic governments. The United States is responsible for 44 percent of all weapons deliveries in the world....A total of 453 American soldiers have been killed by armies strengthened by our own weapons and military training....In fiscal year 1994 $7 billion of taxpayer money went to subsidize U.S. arms exports. In fiscal year 1995, that figure jumped to $7.6 billion. After agricultural price supports, this represents the largest subsidy program for business in the entire Federal budget....Our Government employs nearly 6,500 full time personnel to promote and service foreign arms sales by U.S. companies. U.S. subsidies for arms transfers are scheduled to increase. The international market for U.S. arms is estimated to be around $12 to $16 billion per year. Therefore, our foreign customers aren't even paying for the weapons that they get. And more than half of U.S. weapons sales will be paid for by the U.S. taxpayers. In 1995, subsidies for arms exports accounted for over 50 percent of U.S. bilateral aid and more than 39 percent of total U.S. foreign aid." (pH3620)

McKinney, Cynthia A. (Rep.-Ga.). "Foreign Relations Authorization Act, Fiscal Years 1998 and 1999." Congressional Record. Daily ed. v143 n80 10 Jun 1997. pH3591-3632. section/page-level access: <http://thomas.loc.gov/cgi-bin/query/R?r105:FLD001:H03620:> (ISSN0363-7239). (X1.1A.105/1).

The U.S. "is the world's largest arms dealer, employing nearly 6,500 full-time personnel to promote foreign arms sales by U.S. companies. For the sixth consecutive year, the United States led the world in arms deliveries in 1996. We are militarizing foreign aid. In 1995, subsidies for arms exports accounted for over 50 percent of U.S. bilateral aid. Major weapons manufacturing firms buy influence by contributing to congressional candidates--$14.8 million between 1990 and 1994....The U.S. Government ranks first in the world in subsidizing arms exports. Meanwhile we spend only $150 million a year to help U.S. firms get a foothold in the expanding international market for environmental technologies. That market is expected to reach $190 to $240 billion by the end of this decade. This is at a time that by DOD's [Dept. of Defense's] own reckoning, the international arms market will likely continue to shrink from its current level of $32 billion." (pE1922)

Furse, Elizabeth (Rep.-Oreg.). "Equity for Immigrants Act." Congressional Record. Daily ed. v143 n135 2 Oct 1997. pE1922-1923. section/page-level access: <http://thomas.loc.gov/cgi-bin/query/R?r105:FLD001:E01922:> (ISSN0363-7239). (X1.1A.105/1).

"In 1995 the United States exported $16 billion of newly manufactured arms, more than all other countries of the world combined....The United States has exported an estimated $7 billion of surplus arms since 1990, including nearly 4,000 tanks, 125 attack helicopters, over 500 bombers, and more than 200,000 pistols and rifles....According to one study, the American public paid out an estimated $7.6 billion to underwrite weapons exports in 1995, while new sales contracts signed that year were valued at $8.2 billion." (p4-5)

Lumpe, Lora. "The Arms Market Today: Dangerous Competition, Diminishing Returns." Peacework n276 Jul-Aug 1997. p4-7. (ISSN0748-0725).

A U.S. "aircraft carrier spends approximately $855,000 maintaining three NSSMS [NATO Sea Sparrow Missile Systems]....With ESSM [Evolved Sea Sparrow Missile] CMP [Capability Modernization Program] incorporation, maintenance costs are reduced 65 percent to $255,000....An estimated savings of $10 million is expected with the incorporation of the ESSM CMP....These cost reductions do not reflect the 40-50 percent proposed decrease in manning and a 40 percent training pipeline reduction." (p25)

"A New Life for NATO Sea Sparrow." Surface Warfare v22 n5 Sep-Oct 1997. p24-25. (ISSN0145-1073).

DEFICITS, BUDGET

see BUDGET DEFICITS

DEFICITS, TRADE

see BALANCE OF TRADE

DEFORESTATION (v26)

DEFORESTATION--BRAZIL

"Brazil now ranks No. 1 in deforestation, according to the Washington-based World Wildlife Fund. Brazil's National Space Research Institute estimates fires have jumped more than a quarter during May to October [1997] compared with last year's burning season. But that information has touched off a raging debate about whether the surge in burnings actually means accelerated destruction of the Amazon. 'We're finding that 94 percent of these burnings are repeat clearings of already deforested areas, while only 6 percent are in new areas,' says Eduardo Martins, president of IBAMA, Brazil's environmental protection agency." (p1) "Brazil's Institute for Environmental Research in the Amazon (IPAM), associated with the Woods Hole Research Center in Massachusetts, estimates that about 70 percent of the fires this year occurred on already deforested lands....[The World Wildlife Fund] miffed Brazilian officials recently when it issued the report finding that, at 15,000 square kilometers a year (5,776 square miles, based on 1994 figures), Brazil is No. 1 in the world in deforestation." (p8)

LaFranchi, Howard. "Is Burning of Amazon All Smoke?" The Christian Science Monitor v89 n247 18 Nov 1997. p1,8. The Christian Science Monitor search engine: <http://www.csmonitor.com/plweb-cgi/iops1.pl> To retrieve this article, enter the following search: ED=19971118 AND smoke. In the "retrieved list," click the title that matches this record. (ISSN0882-7729).

DEFORESTATION--CENTRAL AMERICA

"A study included in 'Toward a Green Central America: Integrating Conservation and Development,' a collection of articles published by the Panos Institute in London in 1992, estimated that three-fourths of Central America was covered with forests in 1950. By 1990, the forested area was only one-third. Only 173,000 acres a year were being replanted with trees and half of them died due to lack of proper care, the study showed. Between 1990 and 1995, in the combined area of Central America and Mexico, tree loss is estimated at about 1 million hectares (roughly 2.5 million acres) a year, or 1.2 percent a year....'We are losing 40,000 to 50,000 hectares every year' of trees, says Roman Cabrera, a federal forester." (p12)

Press, Bob. "Habitat: Logging and Clearing Continues in Central America." The Christian Science Monitor v89 n151 1 July 1997. p12. The Christian Science Monitor search engine: <http://www.csmonitor.com/plweb-cgi/iops1.pl> To retrieve this article, enter the following search: ED=19970701 AND america. In the "retrieved list," click the title that matches this record. (ISSN0882-7729).

DEFORESTATION--CHINA

A Chinese study "estimated that China has lost approximately 290 million hectares of forest since the beginning of the country's history. Roughly 50 percent of this loss can be attributed to the conversion of forestland to farmland, settlements, and transportation networks, the unavoidable consequences of an ancient civilization's growth. The other half of the loss represents the costs of excessive logging." (p34) "According to figures compiled by the Chinese Ministry of Forestry, 25 out of the 131 state forestry bureaus in the most important timber production zones had exhausted their reserves by 1990. Only 40 of these bureaus post figures showing that they can harvest up to the year 2000. By 2000, almost 70 percent of China's state forestry bureaus will basically have no mature trees left to fell....The official figure for the average amount of wood growing in forest plantings--28.27 cubic meters per hectare--makes it quite clear that the new plantings (whose growing stock may be yielding the statistical wood surplus) cannot hope to replace the felled mature forests, which had a growing stock of at least 70 to 80 cubic meters per hectare, for many decades." (p35)

Smil, Vaclav. "China Shoulders the Cost of Environmental Change." Environment v39 n6 Jul-Aug 1997. p6-9,33-37. (ISSN0013-9157).

DEFORESTATION--CHINA--COSTS

In China, "in terms of the loss of future timber supplies alone,...overcutting would cost between 13 billion and 26 billion yuan a year....Chinese foresters have estimated the combined ecosystem benefits of mature forests to be between 8 and 25 times the profit from harvested timber sales....A detailed study of the Changbaishan natural reserve in Jilin concluded that to replace the forest's water storage capacity with a reservoir, control soil erosion by terracing the slopes, and use pesticides rather than forest-sheltered birds to control insects the cost would be about 49,000 yuan (in 1990 monies) per hectare, more than 20 times the value of sustainably harvested timber from the same area." (p35-36)

Smil, Vaclav. "China Shoulders the Cost of Environmental Change." Environment v39 n6 Jul-Aug 1997. p6-9,33-37. (ISSN0013-9157).

DEFORESTATION--LATIN AMERICA

"Between 1960 and 1990, Latin America lost nearly 18% of its forest cover, mostly to agricultural production. Nearly 200 million hectares are now cultivated...." (p794)

Joyce, Stephanie/U.S. National Institute of Environmental Health Sciences. "Focus: Growing Pains in South America." Environmental Health Perspectives v105 n8 Aug 1997. p794-799.

DEFORESTATION--VIETNAM

The rate of deforestation in Vietnam is "estimated on average to be 350,000 hectares (ha) per year....Of the 19 million ha of land currently classified as forest land in Vietnam, some 13 million ha are largely depleted former forests--only 1 million ha contain medium to rich quality forests containing a wealth of plant species and highest avian and primate diversity in mainland Southeast Asia."

World Bank. "Protecting Forests in Vietnam." Press Release 31 Oct 1997. document-level access: <http://www.worldbank.org/html/extdr/extme/1524.htm>

DEGRADATION, ENVIRONMENTAL

see ENVIRONMENTAL DEGRADATION

DEGRADATION, LAND

see LAND DEGRADATION

DEGREES, ACADEMIC--UNITED STATES --HANDICAPPED (v26)

DEGREES, ACADEMIC--UNITED STATES--WOMEN (v26)

DEJECTION

see DEPRESSION, MENTAL

DELINQUENCY

see CRIME

DELINQUENT GIRLS--UNITED STATES

"In 1993, U.S. law enforcement agencies made an estimated 570,100 arrests involving females under the age of 18. Between 1989 and 1993, the number of arrests involving female juveniles increased by 23 percent compared with an 11 percent increase in arrests from male juveniles....The female proportion of all juvenile arrests grew from 21 percent to 24 percent between 1983 and 1993. Females were responsible for 17 percent of the growth in juvenile arrests for Violent Crime Index offenses between 1989 and 1993. Juvenile courts in the United States handled an estimated 1,489,700 delinquency cases in 1993, 20 percent of which involved females. Between 1989 and 1993, the number of juvenile court cases involving females charged with delinquency offenses increased by 31 percent, while the number of cases involving males increased by 21 percent." (p184)

Janeksela, Galan M. "Female Criminality: An Overview." International Journal of Comparative and Applied Criminal Justice v21 n2 Fall 1997. p181-205.

DELINQUENT WOMEN

see FEMALE OFFENDERS

DELINQUENTS

see CRIMINALS

DELINQUENTS, JUVENILE

see JUVENILE DELINQUENTS

DELIRIUM--UNITED STATES--AGED (v26)

DEMENTIA--UNITED STATES (v26)

DEMOCRACY (v26)
see also LIBERTY
"According to the most recent survey by Freedom House, 118 countries qualify as electoral democracies. Only 79 of these countries, however, are rated by Freedom House as 'free'--that is, as liberal democracies. Some 39 countries with elected governments are judged only 'partly free,' including such important countries as Russia, India, Ukraine, Turkey, Brazil, Pakistan, and Colombia." (p7)
Huntington, Samuel P. "After the Twenty Years: The Future of the Third Wave." Journal of Democracy v8 n4 Oct 1997. p3-12. (ISSN1045-5736).
"Now, 0.5% of the world's population casts more than 25% of General Assembly votes, in direct contradiction to democracy if individuals are taken as subjects. The General Assembly would become more democratic if the voting power of member states varied according to their population size." (p334) "According to the 1995 Freedom House Report, 117 of 191 states can be considered democratic, at least in formal structures, with 54% of the world's population living under democratic regimes." (p335)
Bienen, Derk/Rittberger, Volker/Wagner, Wolfgang. "Individuals and States as Democratic Subjects." Peace Review v9 n3 Sep 1997. p329-336. (ISSN1040-2659).

DEMOCRACY--KOREA (SOUTH)--PUBLIC OPINION
"Beginning in 1991, when the first democratic government of Korea was three years old, four national-sample surveys asked respondents to express on a 10-point scale the extent to which they thought their country should be democratized. A score of 1 on this scale indicated that 'complete dictatorship' was the state that the respondent desired, while a score of 10 indicated a wish to see the triumph of 'complete democracy.'...In 1991, when a question soliciting the desired level of democracy was asked for the first time, responses averaged 6.3 on the 10-point scale, indicating support for a partially democratic system. In 1994, when a second democratic election brought to power civilian president Kim Young Sam, the mean rating jumped to 8.6. For the next two years, however, desire for democracy remained at that level." (p113-114) "All in all, more than a third (35 percent) of the Korean people fall outside the category of unconditional or unwavering democrats, those who always prefer a democratic polity to a dictatorship. They are conditional or 'fair-weather' democrats (17 percent), the indifferent (10 percent), or the uninformed (8 percent)." (p119)
Shin, Doh Chull/Shyu, Huoyan. "Public Opinion in New Democracies: Political Ambivalence in South Korea and Taiwan." Journal of Democracy v8 n3 Jul 1997. p109-124. (ISSN1045-5736).

DEMOCRACY--LATIN AMERICA--PUBLIC OPINION (v26)
A 1996 survey of 17 Latin American countries "showed that even in countries where a strong majority prefers democracy, a significant minority would choose an authoritarian regime under certain circumstances. That minority is 26 percent of the population in Paraguay, 24 percent in Brazil, 23 percent in Chile and Mexico and 21 percent in Guatemala. According to Latinobarometro, Costa Rica and Uruguay stand out as the countries where democracy enjoys the highest level of support--80 percent. With one exception, at least 50 percent of citizens in every other surveyed country also prefer democracy. In Honduras, only 42 percent of those surveyed favor democracy, while close to 30 percent said they do not care what kind of government they have and 14 percent said an authoritarian regime could sometimes be preferable....In all but two of the surveyed countries, less than 34 percent of respondents answered 'yes' when asked if they were satisfied with democracy as it functions in their own country. Only in Costa Rica (51 percent) and Uruguay (52 percent), did more than half answer yes." (p9)
Silva, Samuel. "Figuratively Speaking: Opinion Polls: A Verdict on Democracy." IDB v24 n6 Jun 1997. p9. (ISSN0145-2274).
According to a 1996 Latinobarometro survey of 17 Latin American countries, "support for democracy is highest in Costa Rica, Uruguay, Panama, and Argentina, where it ranges from 80 down to 71 percent. By comparison, the figure for Spain today...is 81 percent. In Portugal and Greece, the other two Southern European countries that inaugurated the 'third wave' of democratization, the current levels of support for democracy are 61 and 87 percent, respectively....In the remaining 13 Latin American countries surveyed, support for democracy runs between 50 percent and 70 percent, except for Honduras, where it stands at only 42 percent. Support for authoritarianism is very low--only 16 percent on average. The highest preference for authoritarianism--23 percent--is found in Chile and Ecuador. In Portugal and Greece, the comparable figures are 9 and 5 percent, respectively." (p132)
Lagos, Marta. "Public Opinion in New Democracies: Latin America's Smiling Mask." Journal of Democracy v8 n3 Jul 1997. p125-138. (ISSN1045-5736).

DEMOCRACY--PUBLIC OPINION
When the percentage of South Koreans "unconditionally supportive of democracy is compared against such democratic supporters in ten influential new democracies in other regions, Korea (65 percent) ranks eighth, ahead of Brazil (50 percent), Russia (50 percent), and Chile (54 percent). In the extent of preference for authoritarian rule, however, Korea (17 percent) ranks near the top of the list, behind only Russia (27 percent), Brazil (24 percent), and Chile (19 percent)." (p119,121)
Shin, Doh Chull/Shyu, Huoyan. "Public Opinion in New Democracies: Political Ambivalence in South Korea and Taiwan." Journal of Democracy v8 n3 Jul 1997. p109-124. (ISSN1045-5736).

DEMOCRACY--SOUTH AMERICA--PUBLIC OPINION (v26)

DEMOCRACY--TAIWAN--PUBLIC OPINION
In Taiwan, "the percentage favoring more democracy rose during the first three years of democratic rule and then leveled off, going from 50 percent in 1991 to 60 percent in 1992 and 66 percent in 1993. In that year, constitutional reforms formally ended the one-party dictatorship and instituted a multiparty representative democracy. By 1995...the relative number of democratic reformers had leveled off a bit to 61 percent, indicating that further growth is hard to attain in the short run." (p114-115)
Shin, Doh Chull/Shyu, Huoyan. "Public Opinion in New Democracies: Political Ambivalence in South Korea and Taiwan." Journal of Democracy v8 n3 Jul 1997. p109-124. (ISSN1045-5736).

DENGUE--COSTA RICA (v26)

DENGUE--LATIN AMERICA (v26)

DENGUE--PACIFIC AREA (v26)

DENMARK--EMPLOYMENT (v26)

DENMARK--UNITED STATES--ECONOMIC CONDITIONS (v26)

DENMARK. NAVY (v26)

DENOMINATIONAL SCHOOLS
see CHURCH SCHOOLS

DENTAL HYGIENISTS--MICHIGAN
In Michigan, "the average starting salary for a dental hygienist is $34,500, according to Dale Harrison, department head for Allied Dental Program....Harrison says that 6,425 dental hygienists were employed in Michigan in 1994, and about 270 positions are expected to open annually, a 26-percent growth rate by 2005....Ferris State University's dental hygiene program is the largest of 11 in the state, with 60 slots available each

year." (p3 secF)

Corcoran, Megan E. "Strategies: Careers: Outlook Good for Dental Hygienists." Detroit News 1 Dec 1997. p3 secF.

DEPARTMENT PROMOTIONS

see PROMOTIONS

DEPLETION OF FORESTS

see DEFORESTATION

DEPLETION OF OZONE LAYER

see OZONE LAYER DEPLETION

DEPOSIT BANKING--UNITED STATES (v26)

DEPRESSION, MENTAL--UNITED STATES (v26)

DEPRESSION, MENTAL--UNITED STATES--AGED

In the U.S., "as many as nine out of 10 older persons who have depression do not get treatment for this disorder....Of the 33 million Americans age 65 and older, a reported five million suffer from serious and persistent symptoms of depression. Another one million suffer from major, or clinical, depression." (p6)

"Nearly 40 Percent of Older Suicide Victims Visit Doctor during Week before Killing Themselves." California Community Care News v9 n9 Sep 1997. p6,10.

DEPRESSION, MENTAL--UNITED STATES--COSTS (v26)

DEPRESSION, SEASONAL

see SEASONAL AFFECTIVE DISORDER

DERIVATIVE SECURITIES (v26)

DERMATOPHYTES--UNITED STATES (v26)

DERRICKS, OIL

see OIL WELL DRILLING RIGS

DESERTIFICATION (v26)

DESERTIFICATION--CHINA (v26)

DETERMINATION (PERSONALITY TRAIT)--MICHIGAN (v26)

DETROIT (MICH.)--ECONOMIC CONDITIONS (v26)

DETROIT (MICH.)--EMPLOYMENT (v26)

"In 1990, only 18% of jobs in the metropolitan area were located in the city of Detroit, whereas 56% of the area's jobs were located there in 1960. The city continues to lose workers, suffering a 22% decline in the number of jobs from 1980 to 1990. Commuting between suburbs is now the most common pattern in the Detroit metropolitan area; 7 out of 10 metropolitan residents who commute neither live nor work in the city of Detroit (Southeast Michigan Council of Governments, 1994)." (p125)

Turner, Susan C. "Barriers to a Better Break: Employer Discrimination and Spatial Mismatch in Metropolitan Detroit." Journal of Urban Affairs v19 n2 1997. p123-141. (ISSN0735-2166).

DETROIT (MICH.)--POPULATION

"Detroit's population continued to drop in 1996--though by smaller rates than the early 1990s--while the metro area continued to grow, the Southeast Michigan Council of Governments reported....Some areas registered eye-popping increases: 32 percent in Novi, 50 percent in Macomb Township and 69.5 percent in Lenox Township....But in Detroit, the population in 1996 fell to an estimated 985,074--15,000 below the million mark." (p1 secA) "The region's fastest-growing county was Livingston, which grew nearly 20 percent from 1990 to 1996....Oakland County was second in metro-area gain at 8.4 percent." (p2 secA)

Gerritt, Jeff. "'Area Is Pushing Out Farther and Farther.'" Detroit Free Press 12 Aug 1997. p1-2 secA.

"Detroit's population dipped by 27,702 to 1,000,272 from 1990 to 1996, according to figures the Census Bureau released....But that 2.7-percent decline is a trickle compared to the 14.6 percent of residents who moved out of Detroit between 1980 and 1990. Detroit also dropped to the 10th largest city in the nation from seventh in 1990 and fifth in 1970. The city's population is half the Census Bureau estimate of two million in 1955." (p1 secA)

Eversley, Melanie. "Latest Census Count Shows Exodus Slowing." Detroit Free Press 19 Nov 1997. p1,10 secA.

Detroit's "population in 1996 was 1,000,272, according to U.S. Census figures....That's a 2.7-percent decline from the beginning of the decade, and pulls Detroit from the nation's seventh-largest city to 10th....If Detroit loses just 273 more residents in the 2000 census count, it would be stripped of...[its 1.5-percent commuter income] taxing authority, which raises about $100 million annually." (p1 secA)

Cain, Charlie/Hornbeck, Mark. "Detroit's Population Drops: If Residents Fall below 1 Million, 1.5-Percent Tax Paid by Suburbanites...Become Illegal." Detroit News 19 Nov 1997. p1 secA.

DEVELOPING COUNTRIES--COMMERCE

"In 1990, manufactured products exported by the newly industrialized countries of Southeast Asia to the developed countries still represented only 1.61% of the latter's GNP. In France, commercial exchanges with newly industrialized countries account for about 1% of the current unemployment rate. But this tendency is likely to grow. Between 1970 and 1990, the share emerging countries had in the stock exchanges of advanced countries went from .7% to 6.44%." (p128)

Benoist, Alain de. "Confronting Globalization." Telos n108 Sum 1996. p117-137.

The share of least-developed countries in world trade "has been reduced to a minuscule 0.3 percent in the 1990s....90 percent of the global foreign direct investment is received by the industrial triad and China. For a third of the developing countries, the ratio of such investments to gross domestic product has actually fallen over the past decade." (p13)

Nadkarni, Avadhoot. "Globalization: The Excluded and the Marginalized." Center Focus n137 Sep 1997. p13-14.

DEVELOPING COUNTRIES--ECONOMIC CONDITIONS (v26)

DEVELOPING COUNTRIES--ECONOMIC CONDITIONS --SOCIAL CONDITIONS (v26)

DEVELOPING COUNTRIES--HEALTH AND HYGIENE

"An estimated 840 million developing-country residents are classified as malnourished, about 20 percent of the population. More than half of the children in South Asia--which includes India, Bangladesh, and Pakistan--are underweight for their age. One-fourth or more of the children are seriously underweight in Africa, the Middle East, and East and Southeast Asia. Less than half of the sub-Saharan African population and less than two-thirds of the Southeast Asian population have access to safe water for drinking and bathing....An estimated 80 percent of developing-country residents have access to health services; in the least developed countries, such as Bangladesh, Haiti, Somalia, and the Democratic Republic of Congo (formerly Zaire), only 50 percent have access to health services." (p5-6)

Olshansky, S. Jay/Carnes, Bruce/Rogers, Richard G./Smith, Len. "Infectious Diseases--New and Ancient Threats to World Health." Population Bulletin v52 n2 Jul 1997. p2-46. (ISSN0032-468X).

DEVELOPING COUNTRIES--MANUFACTURES (v26)

DEVELOPING COUNTRIES--POPULATION

"In 1997, the world's developing countries accounted for 98 percent of world population increase....World population now stands at 5.8 billion, 4.7 of whom live in the developing countries. By the century's end, world population will likely total 6.1 billion. And, by 2025, today's developing countries are projected to total about 6.8 billion while the developed countries remain at 1.2, the same as today."

Population Reference Bureau. "Developing Nations Account for 98 Percent of World Population Growth." Press Release 1997. document-level access: <http://www.prb.org/media/pressrel.htm>

DEVELOPING COUNTRIES--SOCIAL CONDITIONS (v26)

"The United Nations Development Programme estimates that 'more than one billion people in developing countries lack access to basic health and education, safe drinking water and adequate nutrition. And one person in three lives in poverty.' An estimated 100 million are homeless. More than 800 million are too poor to afford an adequate diet." (p32)

Macdougall, A. Kent. "Pandemic Immiseration." Monthly Review v49 n2 Jun 1997. p31-34. (ISSN0027-0520).

DIABETES (v26)

According to the WORLD HEALTH REPORT 1997, "the projected rise in the number of diabetes sufferers from about 135 million now to almost 300 million by the year 2025 is due to population aging, unhealthy diets, obesity and a sedentary lifestyle. Developing countries will bear the brunt of the diabetes epidemic in the 21st century. Up to 90% of all cases of diabetes worldwide are non-insulin-dependent." (p6)

World Health Organization. "World Health Report 1997." Press Release 5 May 1997. p1-7. document-level access: <http://www.who.ch/whr/1997/presse.htm>

"Recently compiled data show that approximately 135 million people suffer from diabetes mellitus worldwide, and that this number will rise to 300 million by the year 2025....There are basically two forms of diabetes: the insulin-dependent (IDDM) and non-insulin dependent (NIDDM) forms....NIDDM is much more common and accounts for about 90% of all diabetes cases worldwide." (p1) "The price of insulin (without syringes and necessary equipment for monitoring blood glucose levels) varies widely from country to country, ranging from less than US$3 to US$22 a vial. The mean cost of a vial of insulin is lowest in the Middle East (US$2.70) and Southeast Asia (US$2.80) with Africa (US$9.20) and South and Central America (US$12.20) in the middle range. However, in many African countries the cost of a vial of insulin may be the equivalent of a month's salary....Findings, consistent from study to study, make it possible to suggest that, after 15 years of diabetes, approximately 2% of people become blind while about 10% develop severe visual handicap." (p2)

World Health Organization. "Diabetes Mellitus." WHO Fact Sheet n138 Sep 1997. p1-3. document-level access: <http://www.who.ch/programmes/inf/facts/fact138.htm>

DIABETES--AUSTRALIA

"Over 430,000 Australians (2.4 per cent of the population) reported they had been diagnosed with diabetes mellitus at some time during their lives, according to...[the publication, 'National Health Survey: Diabetes, Australia, 1995,'] by the Australian Bureau of Statistics....One in three people with diabetes mellitus did not know what type of diabetes they had. Among those who knew their diabetes type, 63 per cent reported having non-insulin dependent diabetes mellitus....Diabetes mellitus prevalence increases with age from 0.1 per cent for people aged under 15 to 8.9 per cent for people aged 75 and over. Among people aged 15 years and over who reported both their height and weight, 37 per cent of those with diabetes mellitus were overweight (compared with 25 per cent of those without diabetes) and a further 21 per cent were obese (compared with 8 per cent of those without diabetes)."

Australian Bureau of Statistics. "Over 430,000 Diagnosed with Diabetes." Media Release 22 Oct 1997. document-level access: <http://www.abs.gov.au/websitedbs/d3110125.nsf/4a255eef008309e44a255eef00061e57/fef945c208a9f6acca256530008277cd?OpenDocument>

DIABETES--TREATMENT--UNITED STATES--COSTS (v26)

DIABETES--UNITED STATES (v26)

"Between the ages of 65 and 74, nearly 17 percent of the U.S. white population, 25 percent of African-Americans, and more than 33 percent of Hispanic-Americans have diabetes. Each year we are spending $1.5 billion on diabetic amputations. Within 3 years of a major amputation 30 to 50 percent of diabetic patients will die...." (pH5896)

Duncan, John J., Jr. (Rep.-Tenn.). "Calling on HCFA to Stop Restricting Use of Multidex by Denying Reimbursement When It Is Used." Congressional Record. Daily ed. v143 n108 28 Jul 1997. pH5895-5896. section/page-level access: <http://thomas.loc.gov/cgi-bin/query/R?r105:FLD001:H05895:> (ISSN0363-7239). (X1.1A.105/1).

"Diabetes can't be cured, but it can be controlled. The problem is, about 6 million Americans have the disease and don't know....The Centers for Disease Control and Prevention announced recently a six-fold increase in diabetes diagnoses from 1958 to 1997. It estimates 15.7 million people have the disease. Diabetes symptoms include thirst, frequent urination, itchy skin, blurred vision or unexplained weight loss...." (p8 secC)

Bondi, Nicole. "MetroLife: U.S. Cases of Diabetes Soar." Detroit News 10 Nov 1997. p8 secC.

"More Americans than ever before are suffering from diabetes, with the number of new cases averaging 798,000 each year, HHS' [U.S. Dept. of Health and Human Services] Centers for Disease Control and Prevention reported....In 1997, 15.7 million people in the United States have diabetes, nearly 6 percent of the U.S. population....CDC reports that the prevalence of diabetes among African-Americans rose 33 percent from 1980 to 1994, compared with 11 percent for white Americans....Among Americans aged 65 and older, 6.3 million persons (18.4 percent of this age group) have diabetes; among those aged 20 and older, 15.6 million (8.2 percent of all Americans 20 and over) have the disease. Prevalence of the disease by ethnic group includes: Non-Hispanic whites: 11.3 million (7.8 percent of those aged 20 and older); Non-Hispanic African-Americans: 2.3 million (10.8 percent); Mexican Americans: 1.2 million (10.6 percent); Other Hispanic/Latino Americans: on average, almost twice as likely to have diabetes as non-Hispanic whites of similar age....American Indians: Rates vary among tribes and communities, ranging from 5 percent to 50 percent for diagnosed diabetes....Of the 15.7 million total, 10.3 million are diagnosed and 5.4 million are undiagnosed."

U.S. Dept. of Health and Human Services. "Diabetes at Highest Levels Ever in the U.S.: Minority Populations Especially Affected." Press Release 30 Oct 1997. document-level access: <http://www.hhs.gov/news/press/1997pres/971030.html>

"More than half of lower limb amputations in the United States are among people with diabetes. Diabetes is the seventh leading cause of death in the United States. This disease also takes a high financial toll on the United States, costing more than $92 billion in medical expenses, disability, and lost wages each year, according to the estimate of the American Diabetes Association. Type 2 diabetes, which accounts for more than 90 percent of all cases of diabetes, is associated with older age, race, ethnicity, and a family history of diabetes....Type 1 diabetes, formerly known as Insulin-Dependent or Juvenile Onset Diabetes, occurs when the body does not produce any insulin, most often occurring in children and young adults. It accounts for 5 to 10 percent of diabetes."

U.S. Dept. of Health and Human Services. "Diabetes at Highest Levels Ever in the U.S.: Minority Populations Especially Affected." Press Release 30 Oct 1997. document-level access: <http://www.hhs.gov/news/press/1997pres/971030.html>

DIABETES--UNITED STATES--COSTS (v26)

DIABETES--UNITED STATES--MINORITIES (v26)

DIABETES--UNITED STATES--MORTALITY (v26)
DIABETES--UNITED STATES--PREVENTION (v26)
DIAMOND INDUSTRY AND TRADE--CANADA (v26)
DIAMOND INDUSTRY AND TRADE--NORTHWEST TERRITORIES (v26)
DIAMOND MINES AND MINING--SOUTH AFRICA

"In 1995, there were 51 registered operating diamond mines and concession holders in South Africa. Nineteen produced diamonds from kimberlite; 19 recovered stones from marine deposits; and 13 worked alluvial sources. In addition, there were at least 500 small-scale diggers, located mainly in the Northern Cape, Free State, and Northwest provinces, who produced small quantities of diamonds from alluvial deposits. De Beers [Mining Company] operated 17 mines and sea concession areas in the country in 1995 and accounted for 93 percent of the 9.69 million carats of diamonds produced....Of the 19 kimberlite (pipe and fissure) mines operated in 1995, five produced more than 100,000 carats while the remainder produced less than 50,000 carats. The Venetia Mine, which lies 80 kilometers west of Messina in the Northern Province, is currently South Africa's largest diamond producer....The mine produced 4.35 million carats in 1995. It exploits the two largest of a cluster of 12 kimberlite pipes. The two pipes yield an average 135 carats of diamond per hundred tons (cpht) of ore and have sufficient reserves to sustain present production rates for more than 20 years." (p15-16) "In 1995, only three of South Africa's alluvial diamond mines produced more than 100,000 carats; the remaining 10 each recovered less than 50,000 carats....At least one of... [Lichtenburg field's] potholes (Cowper's) yielded more than 1 million carats of diamonds." (p17) "Marine diamond mining off the west coast of South Africa is still in its infancy. In 1995, the total production of all concession holders was just less than 100,000 carats." (p18)

Wilson, Mike G. C. "Diamonds through the Decades: A Review of South African Production." Geotimes v42 n7 Jul 1997. p14-18. (ISSN0016-8556).

DIET (v26)
DIET--AFRICA--EUROPE (v26)
DIET--UNITED STATES--PUBLIC OPINION (v26)
DIET AND DISEASE
see NUTRITIONALLY INDUCED DISEASES
DIET IN DISEASE--AUSTRALIA (v26)
DIET IN DISEASE--UNITED STATES (v26)
DIETING FOR WEIGHT LOSS
see REDUCING DIETS
DINNERS AND DINING--UNITED STATES (v26)
DIOCESAN SCHOOLS
see CHURCH SCHOOLS
DIOXIN (HERBICIDE CONTAINMENT)
see TETRACHLORODIBENZODIOXIN
DIOXINS--UNITED STATES (v26)
DIPHTHERIA (v26)
DIPHTHERIA--FORMER SOVIET REPUBLICS (v26)

"An epidemic of diphtheria began in Russia in 1990 and spread to 12 of the 13 newly independent states (NIS) within just four years. The annual number of diphtheria cases in the NIS rose from 839 in 1989 to 47,802 in 1994." (p20)

Olshansky, S. Jay/Carnes, Bruce/Rogers, Richard G./Smith, Len. "Infectious Diseases--New and Ancient Threats to World Health." Population Bulletin v52 n2 Jul 1997. p2-46. (ISSN0032-468X).

DIRECT-MAIL ADVERTISING
see ADVERTISING, DIRECT-MAIL
DISABILITY (LAW)
see CAPACITY AND DISABILITY
DISABILITY INSURANCE
see INSURANCE, DISABILITY
DISABILITY RETIREMENT--CHILE (v26)
DISABLED
see HANDICAPPED
DISASTER RELIEF
see FOOD RELIEF
DISASTER RELIEF--UNITED STATES --APPROPRIATIONS AND EXPENDITURES (v26)
DISCIPLINE OF CHILDREN--UNITED STATES --PUBLIC OPINION (v26)
DISCRIMINATION
see also SEGREGATION
DISCRIMINATION--AFRO-AMERICANS

"As part of the settlement of a civil rights lawsuit, the Maryland State Police tracked the race of drivers stopped since January 1995. Statistics released last November showed that 73 percent of drivers who were stopped and searched on Interstate 95 between Baltimore and Delaware were African-American. A corresponding American Civil Liberties Union study concluded that only 14 percent of drivers on the highway were black. And in central Florida, black drivers on the Florida Turnpike were 6.5 times more likely to be searched than white drivers, according to an analysis by the ORLANDO SENTINEL, which studied more than 3,800 traffic stops between January 1996 and April 1997." (p49) "Searches that followed traffic stops in Maryland came up empty about 70 percent of the time, says Jonathan Guy, an attorney with Swidler & Berlin in Washington D.C., who worked pro bono with the ACLU on the case that resulted in the settlement and study." (p50)

Higgins, Michael. "Cover Story/Civil Rights: Looking the Part." ABA Journal v83 Nov 1997. p48-50,52. (ISSN0747-0088).

According to a study released by the University of Michigan, "African Americans were twice as likely as whites to report having had two major discriminatory experiences in their lifetime (22.1 percent vs. 9.8 percent) and seven times more likely to report three major discriminatory experiences (11.5 percent vs. 1.6 percent)....Like major discriminatory experiences, African Americans experienced more everyday discrimination. For instance, 10.4 percent of African Americans said they were treated less courteously than others compared with 3.2 percent of whites. Also 17 percent of African Americans said they were treated as if they were not smart compared with just 3.9 percent of whites, and 24.6 percent of Blacks said they were treated as if they were inferior compared with 9 percent of whites." (p2-3)

University of Michigan. News and Information Services. "U-M Study Links Everyday Discrimination to Higher Rates of Ill Health for African Americans." University of Michigan News Release 24 Sep 1997. p1-4.

DISCRIMINATION, RACE
see RACE DISCRIMINATION
DISCRIMINATION IN EDUCATION--CALIFORNIA

Eighty "percent of the voters in...[California's] Prop. 209 election [which bars racial preferences in college admissions and government jobs and contracts] agreed that 'discrimination is still common in society today.'" (p5 secB) "The University of California-Berkeley had a...two-track admissions program, but weighted far more heavily toward race and ethnicity. The average Scholastic Achievement Test (SAT) score for entering black freshmen in 1994 was 994; for whites 1256....According to statistics gathered by the WALL STREET JOURNAL, admissions of black and Hispanic students at UC-San Diego and UC-Riverside have increased as minority applications drop at Berkeley and the University of California at Los Angeles. At Riverside, they

were up 24 percent and at San Diego by 30 percent." (p8 secB)
Cantor, George. "Outlook: Racial Reconciliation: Michigan's Affirmative Reactions." Detroit News 22 Jun 1997. p5,8 secB.

DISCRIMINATION IN EDUCATION--CALIFORNIA --MINORITIES (v26)

DISCRIMINATION IN EDUCATION--DEVELOPING COUNTRIES (v26)

DISCRIMINATION IN EMPLOYMENT

see also AFFIRMATIVE ACTION PROGRAMS; EQUAL PAY FOR EQUAL WORK

DISCRIMINATION IN EMPLOYMENT--GREAT BRITAIN

In Britain, according to Baroness Blackstone, "'since January of this year, the Equal Opportunities Commission has a target to move from the current staff ratio of 80 per cent women: 20 per cent men to one of 70:30. It will reassess this target after two years. As ethnic minorities represent 5 percent of its staff, the Commission has set no target in this regard.'...The EOC, according to its 1996 annual report, did not have a single ethnic minority male on its workforce." (p24)
"Civil Rights: EOC May Take On More Men." Freedom Today v22 n4 Aug 1997. p24.

In Britain, the Commission for Racial Equality "recommended in 1994 that all ethnic monitoring systems should include an Irish category. But by 31 December 1996, Irish people were almost extinct in its own organisation, being reduced from an endangered species of three in 1994 to just one Irish female out of 203 staff. Thanks to the CRE, we know that as many as 11.5 per cent of the population of Greater London were either born in Ireland or were children of Irish people, and that 4.6 per cent of the total population of Great Britain are Irish....By 1993, two thirds of CRE staff were from ethnic minorities. The organisation had even dropped a temporarily introduced racial target of 50 per cent whites across all grades as either undesirable, unachievable or politically incorrect....In December 1994,...the CRE 1993 Annual Report revealed that only five of its 32 typists were white. The 1996 Annual Report shows just 2.5 white secretarial and typing grades out of 23.5." (p23)
"Civil Rights: Anti-Irish Bias at the CRE Too?" Freedom Today v22 n4 Aug 1997. p23-24.

DISCRIMINATION IN EMPLOYMENT--INDIA --KURUMPATTI

A study of silkworm rearing conducted in Kurumpatti, India, in 1993-1994, found that "disinfecting the tray was considered a 'woman's job' and 92 per cent of the women were involved in it....Disinfecting of the rearing house was considered a male activity and 91 per cent of men were responsible for it. Application of bed disinfectants was performed by both men and women, (42 per cent of men and 58 per cent of women)....Marketing of cocoons was considered a predominantly male activity. Nearly three quarters (72 per cent) of all marketing was done by men. Similarly the purchasing of disinfectants (86 per cent) and trays/nets (92 per cent) was considered a male domain. The renting of the chandrikes (bamboo mountages on which silkworms are placed when they are just about to spin their cocoons) was shared by men and women (38 per cent men, 62 per cent women)...." (p50)
Inbanathan, Anand/Vijayalakshmi, V. "Women, Sericulture and Development: A Case in South India." Journal of Third World Studies v14 n1 Spr 1997. p37-63. (ISSN8755-3449).

DISCRIMINATION IN EMPLOYMENT--IRELAND --CATHOLICS

"Job discrimination against Catholics in the north of Ireland is the status quo....Out of the 87,000 children below the poverty line, 58,000, or 66 percent, are Catholic. In Northern Ireland, over 42 percent of Catholic men are unemployed compared to 25 percent of their Protestant colleagues. According to the most recent Labor Force Survey, 55 percent of the unemployed are Catholics, even though they comprise 38 percent of the population over the age of 16." (pH3617)
Smith, Christopher H. (Rep.-N.J.). "Foreign Relations Authorization Act, Fiscal Years 1998 and 1999." Congressional Record. Daily ed. v143 n80 10 Jun 1997. pH3591-3632. section/page-level access: <http://thomas.loc.gov/cgi-bin/query/R?r105:FLD001:H03617:> (ISSN0363-7239). (X1.1A.105/1).

DISCRIMINATION IN EMPLOYMENT--UNITED STATES (v26)

"Last year, 23,152 suits alleging race, sex, disability, or age discrimination were filed in [U.S.] federal courts, more than double the 1992 total of 10,771. But given the number of employed Americans, currently at a record 129.7 million (11 million more than in 1992), the number of people who actually take legal action is minuscule. Last year 77,990 people filed complaints with the Equal Employment Opportunity Commission, the first step in pursuing a lawsuit--a rate of less than six claims per 10,000 workers annually." (p69)
Saltzman, Amy. "U.S. News: News You Can Use: At Work & Home: Suppose They Sue?" U.S. News & World Report v123 n11 22 Sep 1997. p68-70. article-level access: <http://www.usnews.com/usnews/issue/970922/22DISC.HTM> (ISSN0041-5537).

DISCRIMINATION IN EMPLOYMENT--UNITED STATES --GAYS

In the U.S., "a collection of nearly two dozen studies shows that as many as 46 percent of gay and lesbian workers have experienced significant discrimination in the workplace. The fear in which these workers live was clear from a survey of 1,400 gay men and lesbians in Philadelphia. Seventy-six percent of the men and 81 percent of the women told those conducting the survey that they hide their orientation at work out of concern for their job security. This result, although unfortunate, is not surprising in light of a University of Maryland study that found gay men's income to be 11 to 27 percent lower than that of heterosexual men, thanks to the effects of discrimination." (pS5460)
Lieberman, Joseph I. (Sen.-Conn.). "Statements on Introduced Bills and Joint Resolutions." Congressional Record. Daily ed. v143 n80 10 Jun 1997. pS5444-5464. section/page-level access: <http://thomas.loc.gov/cgi-bin/query/R?r105:FLD001:S05460:> (ISSN0363-7239). (X1.1A.105/1).

DISCRIMINATION IN EMPLOYMENT--UNITED STATES --PUBLIC OPINION (v26)

In the U.S., according to a Gallop poll released 10 June 1997, "most whites say blacks are not discriminated against, 79%...[believe] blacks have as good a chance as whites of getting jobs. Only 46% of blacks say their chances are as good as whites." (p336)
Everist, Norma Cook. "The Burning of Black Churches and the Ecclesiology of American Civil Religion." Currents v24 n4 Aug 1997. p336-347.

DISCRIMINATION IN EMPLOYMENT--WOMEN (v26)

DISEASES (v26)

see also AGED--DISEASES; CARDIOVASCULAR SYSTEM--DISEASES; CATS--DISEASES; CENTRAL NERVOUS SYSTEM--DISEASES; CHILDREN--DISEASES; COMMUNICABLE DISEASES; ENVIRONMENTALLY INDUCED DISEASES; FISHES--DISEASES; FOODBORNE DISEASES; GLOBAL WARMING--DISEASES; HEART--DISEASES; INTESTINES--DISEASES; IODINE DEFICIENCY DISEASES; NUTRITIONALLY INDUCED DISEASES; SEXUALLY TRANSMITTED DISEASES; THYROID GLAND--DISEASES; specific diseases, e.g., CANCER

"The World Health Organization (WHO) estimates that respiratory diseases, such as pneumonia and influenza, account for nearly 9 percent of all deaths worldwide--about 4.3 million in 1995.

These two diseases alone claim anywhere from 35,000 to 90,000 lives annually in the United States, where they were the sixth-ranked cause of death in 1994. Diarrheal diseases, which include cholera and typhus as well as gastroenteritis, cause about 6 percent of all deaths throughout the world. TB and measles--two infectious diseases that usually can be prevented or treated--are responsible for an estimated 6 percent of deaths worldwide. Another 7 percent of deaths are attributed to other infectious and parasitic diseases, including malaria, dengue hemorrhagic fever, neonatal tetanus, whooping cough, schistosomiasis, AIDS, and syphilis...." (p5)

Olshansky, S. Jay/Carnes, Bruce/Rogers, Richard G./Smith, Len. "Infectious Diseases--New and Ancient Threats to World Health." Population Bulletin v52 n2 Jul 1997. p2-46. (ISSN0032-468X).

"More than 28 new disease-causing microbes have been identified since 1973....IPDs [infectious and parasitic diseases] are a leading cause of death worldwide. More than 17 million people died from these diseases in 1995--accounting for more than one-fourth of all deaths. About 97 percent of deaths from these diseases occur in low-income countries." (p2)

"Infectious Diseases Continue to Threaten World Health." Population Today v25 n7-8 Jul-Aug 1997. p1-2. (ISSN0749-2448).

"More than 28 new disease-causing microbes have been identified since 1973....More than 17 million people died from...[infectious and parasitic] diseases in 1995--accounting for more than one-fourth of all deaths. About 97 percent of deaths from these diseases occur in low-income countries....In the United States alone, the annual cost of IPDs (including the direct cost of medical treatment and prevention combined with the indirect costs of lost productivity) is estimated to be some $120 billion....The United States records 600,000 cases of pneumonia each year, resulting in 25,000 to 50,000 deaths, and between 10,000 and 40,000 deaths due to influenza. The new states of the former Soviet Union experienced an epidemic of diphtheria in 1990, with more than 40,000 cases reported in 1994."

Population Reference Bureau. "Infectious and Parasitic Diseases Continue to Threaten World Health, Report Finds." Press Release 1997. document-level access: <http://www.prb.org/media/pressrel.htm>

DISEASES--AFRICA--COSTS (v26)

DISEASES--AFRICA--MORTALITY

Infectious and parasitic diseases "are responsible for more than half of the deaths in sub-Saharan Africa, which has the youngest age structure of all the major world regions. An estimated 1 million children die of malaria annually in Africa, and millions more fall prey to diarrheal diseases, TB, measles, hepatitis, tetanus, cholera, and other IPDs." (p7)

Olshansky, S. Jay/Carnes, Bruce/Rogers, Richard G./Smith, Len. "Infectious Diseases--New and Ancient Threats to World Health." Population Bulletin v52 n2 Jul 1997. p2-46. (ISSN0032-468X).

DISEASES--ASIA

"In China, exposure to the Hantaan virus causes 100,000 cases of Korean hemorrhagic fever annually....Each year in Asia, 7,000 people die of Japanese encephalitis, a mosquito-borne disease. More than 30,000 Asians are infected with the disease." (p30)

Olshansky, S. Jay/Carnes, Bruce/Rogers, Richard G./Smith, Len. "Infectious Diseases--New and Ancient Threats to World Health." Population Bulletin v52 n2 Jul 1997. p2-46. (ISSN0032-468X).

DISEASES--AUSTRALIA--MORTALITY (v26)

DISEASES--BRAZIL (v26)

DISEASES--BRAZIL--MORTALITY (v26)

DISEASES--DEVELOPING COUNTRIES

"More than 17 million people died from IPDs [infectious and parasitic diseases] in 1995--accounting for more than one-fourth of all deaths....IPDs exact their heaviest toll in developing countries, where about three-fourths of the world's population lives. About 79 percent of all deaths each year occur in developing countries--a percentage commensurate with their share of total population. However, an estimated 97 percent of deaths from IPDs are in developing countries, with a disproportionately high share in the poorest countries. India and countries in Africa and the Middle East account for 44 percent of all deaths, but more than three-fourths of IPD deaths...." (p5)

Olshansky, S. Jay/Carnes, Bruce/Rogers, Richard G./Smith, Len. "Infectious Diseases--New and Ancient Threats to World Health." Population Bulletin v52 n2 Jul 1997. p2-46. (ISSN0032-468X).

DISEASES--LATIN AMERICA (v26)

DISEASES--MICHIGAN--MORTALITY (v26)

DISEASES--MORTALITY (v26)

Infectious and parasitic diseases "contributed to the loss of more than 265 million person years of life in 1990, according to estimates from the Global Burden of Disease project sponsored by WHO, the World Bank, and the Harvard School of Public Health. If a person is expected to live until age 80, but dies of an infectious disease at age 10, he or she will have lost 70 person years of life. Three-quarters of all years of life lost to IPDs are the result of just four diseases--diarrheal diseases, measles, TB, and malaria." (p7)

Olshansky, S. Jay/Carnes, Bruce/Rogers, Richard G./Smith, Len. "Infectious Diseases--New and Ancient Threats to World Health." Population Bulletin v52 n2 Jul 1997. p2-46. (ISSN0032-468X).

DISEASES--UNITED STATES (v26)

"Millions of Americans have serious, debilitating illnesses for which there is no treatment or cure. There are 3,000 to 4,000 genetic diseases alone. Cancer kills half a million Americans per year. Diabetes afflicts 15 million Americans a year, half of whom do not even know they have it. Fifteen thousand American children die every year." (pS9843)

Feinstein, Dianne (Sen.-Calif.). "Food and Drug Administration Modernization and Accountability Act of 1997." Congressional Record. Daily ed. v143 n129 24 Sep 1997. pS9811-9847. section/page-level access: <http://thomas.loc.gov/cgi-bin/query/R?r105:FLD001:S09843:> (ISSN0363-7239). (X1.1A.105/1).

In the U.S., "AIDS has surpassed accidents as the leading killer of young adults. It is now the leading cause of death among Americans age 25 to 44....[According to TIME magazine,] asthma rates jumped 58 percent, from 1982 to 1992 for children, and asthma is the leading cause of school absences from chronic conditions. 40,000 infants die each year from devastating diseases, and 20 million Americans have rare diseases for which there are few effective treatments. Seven to ten percent of children are learning disabled. The rate of low birth-weight among African-American children is 13 percent, compared to 6.2 percent for white Americans." (pS4864)

Feinstein, Dianne (Sen.-Calif.). "Concurrent Resolution on the Budget." Congressional Record. Daily ed. v143 n68 21 May 1997. pS4851-4876. section/page-level access: <http://thomas.loc.gov/cgi-bin/query/R?r105:FLD001:S04864:> (ISSN0363-7239). (X1.1A.105/1).

"Last year the amount of money spent on prostate cancer research in the United States was $80 million, for breast cancer it was $550 million and for AIDS $1.6 billion. In the United States, approximately 41,000 die annually of prostate cancer, which is just about the same number as those dying of breast cancer. The recent number who die of AIDS is slightly higher at 51,000." (p9)

Amiel, Barbara. "Column: How Gender Politics Threatens Freedom." Maclean's v110 n40 6 Oct 1997. p9. (ISSN0024-9262).

"In the United States alone, the annual cost of IPDs [infectious and parasitic diseases] (including the direct cost of medical treatment and prevention combined with the indirect costs of lost productivity) is estimated to be some $120 billion....The United States records 600,000 cases of pneumonia each year, resulting in 25,000 to 50,000 deaths, and between 10,000 and 40,000 deaths due to influenza, mainly among older Americans." (p2)

"Infectious Diseases Continue to Threaten World Health." Population Today v25 n7-8 Jul-Aug 1997. p1-2. (ISSN0749-2448).

DISEASES--UNITED STATES--MORTALITY (v26)

"One study of U.S. death statistics found that fewer than half of the deaths directly attributable to infectious diseases were labeled with the subcategory of ICD's [International Classification of Diseases] code for an infectious disease.... When U.S. deaths from these diseases were included in a more comprehensive IPD [infectious and parasitic diseases] category, death rates from infectious diseases rose by 58 percent (from 41 to 65 per 100,000) between 1980 and 1992. Infectious and parasitic diseases were listed as an underlying or contributing cause of death for 375,000 people in the United States in 1992, 17 percent of all deaths that year." (p7-8)

Olshansky, S. Jay/Carnes, Bruce/Rogers, Richard G./Smith, Len. "Infectious Diseases--New and Ancient Threats to World Health." Population Bulletin v52 n2 Jul 1997. p2-46. (ISSN0032-468X).

DISEASES--VIETNAM (v26)

DISEASES, MENTAL

see MENTAL ILLNESS

DISORDERS, VISION

see VISION DISORDERS

DISPLACED HOMEMAKERS--MICHIGAN (v26)

DISPLACED HOMEMAKERS--UNITED STATES

"One of every six American women is a displaced homemaker. In 1990, there were 17.8 million displaced homemakers in the United States. In...Florida, there were over 1.1 million displaced homemakers in 1990--a 55-percent increase since 1980." (pH5533)

Bilirakis, Michael (Rep.-Fla.). "Carl D. Perkins Vocational-Technical Education Act Amendments of 1997." Congressional Record. Daily ed. v143 n104 22 Jul 1997. pH5526-5544. section/page-level access: <http://thomas.loc.gov/cgi-bin/query/R?r105:FLD001:H05532:> (ISSN0363-7239). (X1.1A.105/1).

DISPOSAL OF CHEMICAL WEAPONS

see CHEMICAL WEAPONS DISPOSAL

DISPOSAL OF REFUSE

see REFUSE AND REFUSE DISPOSAL

DISPUTE SETTLEMENT

see CONFLICT MANAGEMENT

DISPUTES, LABOR

see LABOR DISPUTES

DISTRIBUTION OF INCOME

see INCOME DISTRIBUTION

DISTRICT OF COLUMBIA--SOCIAL CONDITIONS

The District of Columbia's "population is only 543,000, down 10 per cent since 1990. This year, its public schools did not open until Sept. 22, three weeks late, because inspectors found 11,000 fire-code violations, including leaky roofs in 43 schools. The city spends $13,300 a year per pupil--20 per cent above the national average--but many schools are decrepit and students have the lowest test scores of any urban area in the country....The capital still has one of the worst homicide rates (393 murders last year)--and one of the poorest records of solving them." (p33)

Phillips, Andrew. "World: United States: A Blight at the Center of Power." Maclean's v110 n41 13 Oct 1997. p32-33. (ISSN0024-9262).

DIVERSITY, BIOLOGICAL

see BIOLOGICAL DIVERSITY

DIVERSITY IN THE WORKPLACE (v26)

DIVORCE--ASIA, SOUTHEASTERN--MUSLIMS (v26)

DIVORCE--AUSTRALIA

According to "Marriages and Divorces, Australia," by the Australian Bureau of Statistics, "the number of divorces granted in 1996 was 52,500 compared with 39,400 in 1986. Over the last 20 years, the divorced population has increased four times from 233,400 people in 1976 to 942,000 in 1996. About 8 percent of all marriages are likely to end in divorce within five years of marriage, 19 percent within ten years, 32 percent within twenty years and 39 percent within thirty years. The median age at divorce was 40.2 years for men and 37.4 years for women. This was 2.7 years higher than in 1986, for both men and women. Over the last 20 years the median duration of marriage for parties divorcing ranged between 10 and 11 years (11.0 years in 1996). The median duration of marriage to the time the parties separated was 7.6 years in both 1996 and 1986."

Australian Bureau of Statistics. "Australians Marry Less and Later but Divorce More." Media Release 30 Jul 1997. document-level access: <http://www.abs.gov.au/websitedbs/d3110125.nsf/4a255eef008309e44a255eef00061e57/4b6e63a715002b084a2564e3007937fe?OpenDocument>

DIVORCE--CANADA

In 1997, "the Vanier Institute advised Canadians that the divorce rate in Canada had...reached 50 percent and that 75 percent of common law relationships break down within the first five years. Sixty per cent of these relationships involve children. When they break down, 85 percent of the families are mother led." (p217)

Szabo, Paul (MP-ON). "Routine Proceedings: Divorce Act." Canada. Parliament. House of Commons. Debates. v135 n6 29 Sep 1997. p217. section-level access: <http://www.parl.gc.ca/36/1/parlbus/chambus/house/debates/006_1997-09-29/han006-e.htm#LINKT51> (ISSN0704-5603). (X3-361E).

DIVORCE--CHILE

In Chile, divorce is illegal. "Today about 6,000 marriages are annulled each year, a number experts consider only the tip of an iceberg of separations. Though separation statistics are hard to come by, family experts note that courts for juvenile matters receive more than 40,000 cases involving child support, tuition, and visitation demands each year. That number suggests a high level of separation in a country of 13 million people.... In Chile, more than 2 of every 5 children are born out of wedlock....Chile is about 75 percent Catholic, but one recent poll showed that almost 80 percent of Chilean Catholics favor a divorce law." (p6)

LaFranchi, Howard. "International: Chile May Allow Divorce to Snip Those Ties That Bind." The Christian Science Monitor v90 n24 30 Dec 1997. p6. The Christian Science Monitor search engine: <http://www.csmonitor.com/plweb-cgi/iops1.pl> To retrieve this article, enter the following search: ED=19971230 AND bind. In the "retrieved list," click the title that matches this record. (ISSN0882-7729).

DIVORCE--GREAT BRITAIN

"First-time marriage in Britain is at its lowest since 1889. Our divorce rate went up sixfold between 1961 and 1991. Two in five marriages fail; most in the first ten years. Children suffer, so do their divorced parents, and the whole business costs 4 billion [pounds sterling] a year....This year's [divorce] figure...[is] 165,000....Even among long-married couples, 15 per cent cite their church-decreed promises as a reason for staying together." (p7)

Riddell, Mary. "Fancy a Curry Tonight, Darling, Or a Wedding?" New Statesman v126 n4321 14 Feb 1997. p7. (ISSN0028-6842).

DIVORCE--LAW AND LEGISLATION--IRELAND (v26)

DIVORCE--UNITED STATES (v26)

In the U.S., "the national divorce rate in 1991 was 4.7 percent. In New England it was only 3 percent; in the Middle Atlantic, 3.2 percent; East North Central, 4.4 percent and West North Central, 4.4 percent....New York had the lowest rate in the nation, 3.1 percent....The divorce rate...[in Alabama] is 6.5 percent. Oklahoma has a 7.8 percent divorce rate, the highest in the nation. The East South Central states (6.1 percent) and West South Central (6.5 percent) have more than double the New England rate." (p815)

Marty, Martin E. "M.E.M.O: Data on Denial." Christian Century v114 n25 10 Sep 1997. p815. (ISSN0009-5281).

"In a 1993 article co-written by [Judith] Wallerstein and Nicholas Zill, they report that among 18- to 22-year-olds from disrupted families [in the U.S.], 25 percent had dropped out of high school, 40 percent had received psychological help, 65 percent had poor relationships with their fathers, and 30 percent had poor relationships with their mothers. Members of a comparable group who had not experienced parental divorce were half as likely to have had those problems." (p71-72)

Cohn, Alvin W. "Juvenile Focus." Federal Probation v61 n3 Sep 1997. p71-73. (ISSN0014-9128).

DIVORCE--UNITED STATES--PHYSICANS (v26)

DNA FINGERPRINTING--UNITED STATES

In the U.S., "tucked into a report last year from the nonprofit Institute for Law and Justice is a finding that FBI tests of DNA [deoxyribonucleic acid] submitted by state and local law enforcement agencies exonerated 23 percent of suspects and proved inconclusive for another 16 percent....[Jane Siegel, executive director of the Innocent Project at the Cardozo School of Law], says DNA has exonerated 42 convicted people since the late 1980s, mostly in sex crimes cases. And 31 of those were handled in part by the project." (p21)

Carter, Terry. "News: Numbers Tell the Story." ABA Journal v83 Oct 1997. p20-21. (ISSN0747-0088).

DOCTOR-ASSISTED SUICIDE

see ASSISTED SUICIDE

DOCTOR OF PHILOSOPHY DEGREE--EMPLOYMENT --UNITED STATES

In the U.S., "Ph.D.s' unemployment rates are significantly lower than average, at 1.6 percent in 1993, compared with 7 percent for all U.S. workers aged 16 and older....And at a median salary of $53,200 in 1995, doctorates are much better off than their bachelor's degree counterparts, who earned a median $35,700." (p34-35)

Stoneman, Bill. "Kaleidoscope: Whining by Winners." American Demographics v19 n11 Nov 1997. p34-35. article-level access: <http://www.demographics.com/publications/ad/97_ad/9711_ad/ad971110.htm> (ISSN0163-4089).

DOCTORS

see PHYSICIANS

DOGFIGHTING--UNITED STATES

The sport of dog fighting "is increasing around the country; experts conservatively estimate some 10,000 people now fight dogs in the United States, and California is one of the hot spots." (p47) "The Humane Society of the United States estimates that 30 to 40 percent of fought dogs die from injuries, which can include punctured organs, shock, dehydration, and blood loss....Organizing or participating in a dog fight is a felony in 44 states, including California...(it's a misdemeanor in the remaining 6)." (p83) Admission fees to dog matches range "from $50 to $500 or more. Winners can take home $40,000, and side bets can be thousands of dollars. (In one Arkansas case police confiscated $500,000 from 250 people.)" (p84)

Davis, Susan E. "Blood Sport: Dog Fighting Is Big Business in California, And Just About Impossible to Stop." California Lawyer v17 n11 Nov 1997. p44-47,83-87. (ISSN0279-4063).

DOGS

see also PIT BULL TERRIERS

DOGS--UNITED STATES--POLITICS AND GOVERNMENT

In the U.S., "federal agencies use at least 2,987 dogs: The military employs some 1,600 for bomb detection, narcotics control, and scouting; the U.S. Customs Service fields 450 at airports and on the border; the Secret Service admits to 35 dogs; the CIA has a seven-dog Canine Corps; and the Agriculture Department runs a 50-dog Beagle Brigade to check for foods that could carry plant and animal diseases." (p42)

Kaplan, David E. "U.S. News: Bomb-Sniffing Tests Provoke a Dogfight." U.S. News & World Report v123 n20 24 Nov 1997. p42. article-level access: <http://www.usnews.com/usnews/issue/971124/24DOG.HTM> (ISSN0041-5537).

DOLLAR, AMERICAN (v26)

According to estimates of the U.S. "General Accounting Office and the Federal Reserve, replacing the $1 bill with a coin saves the Government $2.28 billion during the first 5 years it circulates....A public opinion poll conducted in May 1997 reveals that 58 percent of the American public favors replacing the $1 bill with a coin when informed that such a change would save the Government $456 million annually....A $1 coin lasts about 30 years while costing about 8 cents. A $1 bill is significantly more expensive, as it lasts only 1 year and 1 month at a cost of 4 cents per bill....The private sector will save money. A $1 coin is easier to process than a $1 bill. Paper money received on buses must be hand-straightened at a cost of over $20 per 1,000, or about 2 cents for each dollar. Coins can be processed for less than one-tenth of the cost. The change to a $1 coin is estimated to save the mass transit industry $124 million annually." (pS7768)

Grams, Rod (Sen.-Minn.). "Statements on Introduced Bills and Joint Resolutions." Congressional Record. Daily ed. v143 n103 21 Jul 1997. pS7768-7776. section/page-level access: <http://thomas.loc.gov/cgi-bin/query/R?r105:FLD001:S07768:> (ISSN0363-7239). (X1.1A.105/1).

DOLLAR, AMERICAN--VALUATION (v26)

DOLPHINS--MORTALITY (v26)

DOMESTIC ECONOMIC ASSISTANCE

see ECONOMIC ASSISTANCE, DOMESTIC

DOMESTIC PRODUCT, GROSS

see GROSS DOMESTIC PRODUCT

DOMESTIC VIOLENCE

see FAMILY VIOLENCE

DOMESTICS--CHILDREN (v26)

DOMESTICS--DEVELOPING COUNTRIES--CHILDREN (v26)

DONATION OF ORGANS, TISSUES, ETC.--MICHIGAN (v26)

"Each year in Michigan, about 150 people die waiting for an organ, according to the Transplantation Society. As of Sept. 1, [1997,] there were 1,587 people waiting for kidneys, 70 waiting for hearts, one for a heart and lungs, 120 for lungs, 243 for livers, 96 for a pancreas and 258 for corneas, according to the society." (p2 secB)

Wendland, Wendy. "Cities & Counties: Heart-To-Heart Meeting:

Donor's Mom, Recipient Share Hugs and Tears." Detroit Free Press 11 Sep 1997. p2 secB.

DONATION OF ORGANS, TISSUES, ETC.--UNITED STATES

"More than 50,000 Americans are waiting for organ transplants and hundreds of thousands more need tissue transplants. Every year, thousands die needlessly due to lack of donors. In 1996 alone, 3,916 people on the transplant waiting list died because no organs were available for them. Nearly one-fifth of all heart and liver transplant candidates die while waiting for organs. Every 18 minutes another person is added to the waiting list for organs. Each day, eight people die because an organ was not available." (pS8962)

Durbin, Richard J. (Sen.-Ill.). "Departments of Labor, Health and Human Services, And Education...Appropriations Act, 1998." Congressional Record. Daily ed. v143 n118 9 Sep 1997. pS8958-8971. section/page-level access: <http://thomas.loc.gov/cgi-bin/query/R?r105:FLD001:S08961:> (ISSN0363-7239). (X1.1A.105/1).

DONATIONS

see CHARITABLE USES, TRUSTS, AND FOUNDATIONS

DONATIONS OF ORGANS, TISSUES, ETC.--CANADA (v26)

DONATIONS OF ORGANS, TISSUES, ETC.--QUEBEC (PROVINCE) (v26)

DOWN'S SYNDROME--CANADA

"Of 22,000 women who received prenatal diagnosis in one 1990 study in Canada, 88 percent of those who found they were carrying a child with Down Syndrome aborted the fetus. Other studies have put the rate of Down Syndrome abortions at about 90 percent, some even higher." (p13)

Carlson, Tucker/O'Brien, Denis. "Eugenics for Jesus' Brothers?" Celebrate Life v19 n4 Jul-Aug 1997. p12-13. (ISSN0733-1231).

DOWNSIZING OF ORGANIZATIONS--UNITED STATES

"Recent research by management experts finds that major job cuts by companies--the downsizing trend so dominant in the 1990s--bears little relation to intelligent cost-saving....Some 63 percent of firms eliminating jobs last year were also hiring in other parts of the company, according to a 1996 survey of 1,441 companies by the American Management Association in New York. In those companies reporting job cuts, 7.1 percent of the work force was hit. But the net job loss added up to a mere 0.7 percent. Less than half the companies surveyed said operating profits rose after downsizing; only a third claimed greater productivity; and three quarters reported a drop in morale among surviving employees." (p9)

Francis, David R. "Business and Money: Economic Scene: Downsizing: A Fad that Spins Wheels." The Christian Science Monitor v89 n137 11 Jun 1997. p9. The Christian Science Monitor search engine: <http://www.csmonitor.com/plweb-cgi/iops1.pl> To retrieve this article, enter the following search: ED=19970611 AND wheels. In the "retrieved list," click the title that matches this record. (ISSN0882-7729).

DRACUNCULIASIS (v26)

DRESS

see CLOTHING AND DRESS

DRILLING, OIL WELL

see OIL WELL DRILLING RIGS

DRILLING PLATFORMS--NORTH SEA

"In the British North Sea, some 155 structures (along with thousands of miles of pipeline) will have to be removed. Some of these rigs are larger than a 30-storey building, and the economic costs--let alone the environmental ones--of their disposal are high. In the case of the North Sea alone, the removal of all 155 structures will cost an estimated 4.4 billion [pounds sterling] to 5.5 billion [pounds sterling]...." (p101)

"Crude Operators: The Future of the Oil Industry: The Ecological Impacts of the Oil Industry." Ecologist v27 n3 May-Jun 1997. p101. (ISSN0261-3131).

DRILLING RIGS

see OIL WELL DRILLING RIGS

DRINK INDUSTRY

see BEVERAGE INDUSTRY

DRINKING AND TRAFFIC ACCIDENTS--BRITISH COLUMBIA--ONTARIO--MORTALITY (v26)

DRINKING AND TRAFFIC ACCIDENTS--CANADA (v26)

DRINKING AND TRAFFIC ACCIDENTS--LAW AND LEGISLATION--UNITED STATES--YOUTH--MORTALITY (v26)

DRINKING AND TRAFFIC ACCIDENTS--MICHIGAN (v26)

"In their study of more than 700 drivers treated for automobile crash injuries at hospital emergency rooms in Michigan, researchers at the U-M [University of Michigan] Transportation Research Institute (UMTRI) found that more than 15 percent of motorists had been drinking, while less than 8 percent tested positive for drugs. Another 6 percent had both been drinking and using drugs....According to the study, drunk drivers are more likely to suffer fatal and serious injuries (55 percent), engage in hazardous actions leading to a crash (96 percent), and sustain more severe vehicular damage (65 percent) than those drivers who have not been drinking, regardless of illicit drug use....About two-thirds of the crashes of drunk drivers involve a single-vehicle collision occurring at night, with nearly half taking place on weekends....The study found that a third of the drivers in the sample had a history of alcohol abuse, while about 14 percent had a record of drug abuse. About half of each of these groups were alcohol- and drug-free at the time of their crash injuries." (p1-2)

University of Michigan. News and Information Services. "Alcohol Plays a Greater Role in Car Crashes than Do Illicit Drugs, A U-M Study Reveals." University of Michigan News Release 18 Nov 1997. p1-2.

DRINKING AND TRAFFIC ACCIDENTS--MICHIGAN--WASHTENAW COUNTY (v26)

DRINKING AND TRAFFIC ACCIDENTS--UNITED STATES (v26)

DRINKING AND TRAFFIC ACCIDENTS--UNITED STATES--COSTS (v26)

DRINKING AND TRAFFIC ACCIDENTS--UNITED STATES--MORTALITY (v26)

DRINKING PROBLEM

see ALCOHOLISM

DRINKING WATER--CONTAMINATION--UNITED STATES (v26)

DRINKING WATER--EUROPE

"Modeling indicates that groundwater across 22% of Europe's agricultural area has nitrate concentrations that exceed the maximum concentration of 50 milligrams per liter (mg/l) for nitrates in drinking water and in surface waters used for drinking water set by the EU, according to the European Environment Agency's 1995 publication EUROPE'S ENVIRONMENT. Moreover, in 87% of the area, nitrate concentrations are higher than the recommended 25 mg/l 'guide level' set for drinking water." (p13)

"Water Management: Commission Lambastes Governments over EU Nitrates Law." Environment Watch: Western Europe v6 n20 17 Oct 1997. p12-14. (ISSN1066-6001).

DRINKING WATER--HEALTH ASPECTS--UNITED STATES

"Microorganisms in tap water--giardia and cryptosporidium, to name two--cause 900,000 illnesses in...[the U.S.] each year; 900 of those illnesses will prove fatal, according to some scientists' estimates....Trihalomethanes and halocetic acid...are two...families of byproducts [used to cleanse drinking water] which scientists estimate are linked to more than 10,700 rectal and bladder cancers per year." (p6)

"NRDC News: Water: Raise Your (Water) Glasses." Amicus Journal v19 n4 Win 1998. p6. (ISSN0276-7201).

"In 1990, the U.S. Environmental Protection Agency (EPA) released results from a nationwide survey of drinking water wells conducted over a 5-year period. The survey showed that while at least half of the Nation's drinking water wells contained detectable amounts of nitrates, only about 1.2 percent of community water systems and 2.4 percent of private rural wells contained nitrates at levels higher than EPA's recognized safe level of 10 milligrams per liter. The Environmental Working Group, a public-interest group, estimated that 2 million people drank water from community water systems that violated the EPA nitrate standard at least once between 1986 and 1995, and that an additional 3.8 million people drank water from private wells with nitrate levels above the 10 milligram per liter standard." (p38)

Crutchfield, Stephen R./Cooper, Joseph/U.S. Dept. of Agriculture. Economic Research Service. "Food Safety: Valuing Risk Reduction: The Example of Nitrates in Drinking Water." Food Review v20 n1 Jan-Apr 1997. p38-39,41. (ISSN1056-327X).

"The drinking water of 4.3 million Americans last year had concentrations of pesticides exceeding new federal standards of acceptable risk, according to a study by the Environmental Working Group....The worst example was Williamsburg, Ohio, where unsafe levels of 10 toxic chemicals were found in a glassful." (p13)

"News Briefs: Troubled Waters: US." World Rivers Review v12 n5 Oct 1997. p13. (ISSN0890-6211).

DRINKING WATER--OREGON

"In 1996, floods and landslides exacerbated by decades of logging forced over 200,000 Oregon residents to boil their drinking water....Streams draining Forest Service lands provide drinking water to two-thirds of Oregonians and 70 communities in Washington." (p5)

Schussman, Alan. "Hotline: Oregon: Coalition Says: Stop Logging Watersheds." High Country News v29 n13 7 Jul 1997. p5. (ISSN0191-5657).

DRINKING WATER--UNITED STATES (v26)

DRIVING, AUTOMOBILE

see AUTOMOBILE DRIVING

DRIVING TESTS, AUTOMOBILE

see AUTOMOBILE DRIVERS' TESTS

DRIVING UNDER THE INFLUENCE

see DRUNK DRIVING

DROPOUTS

see also HIGH SCHOOL DROPOUTS

DROPOUTS--UNITED STATES

In the U.S., "from 1981 to 1991 the overall dropout rate decreased from 13.9% to 12.5%. However, while the rates for white (8.9%) and black (13.6%) youths improved, the rate for Hispanics increased from 33.2% to 35.3% (United States Department of Education, 1993)." (p885)

Dondero, Grace M. "Mentors: Beacons of Hope." Adolescence v32 n128 Win 1997. p881-886. (ISSN0001-8449).

DROPOUTS, HIGH SCHOOL

see HIGH SCHOOL DROPOUTS

DROWNING--MISSISSIPPI--SARDIS LAKE (v26)

DROWNING VICTIMS--UNITED STATES

In the U.S., "national statistics indicate that children ages 1 to 4 have the highest drowning rate. Seventy percent of preschoolers who drown are in the care of one or both parents when the drowning occurs, and 75 percent of those parents report they were away from their child less than five minutes." (p10)

Marsicano, Judy. "Corps Helps with 'Safe Kids' Program." Engineer Update v21 n10 Oct 1997. p10. (ISSN0733-8163).

DRUG ABUSE

see also AIDS (DISEASE)--AFRO-AMERICANS--HISPANIC AMERICANS--DRUG USE; HIV INFECTIONS--MARYLAND--DRUG USE; HIV INFECTIONS--UNITED STATES--DRUG USE; TEENAGERS--MICHIGAN--ANN ARBOR--DRUG USE; TEENAGERS--UNITED STATES--DRUG USE; YOUTH--RUSSIA--DRUG USE; YOUTH--UNITED STATES--DRUG USE

DRUG ABUSE--GREAT BRITAIN

In Great Britain, "national surveys indicate that roughly 1 in 4 people aged 16 to 29 has used illegal drugs. Home Secretary Jack Straw, who is responsible for law and order, has suggested that heroin alone accounts for 1.3 billon [pounds sterling] ($2.1 billion) of property crimes. 'One out of 5 people arrested by police is using heroin,' Mr. Straw said in a public statement. A Home Office health survey of 1,100 addicts revealed that they had committed a total of 70,000 crimes to finance their habit....The Home Office says statistics show that two-thirds of people under 25 want the use of marijuana to be legalized." (p6)

MacLeod, Alexander. "International: Britain Girds to Attack Old Problem: Drug Abuse." The Christian Science Monitor v89 n196 4 Sep 1997. p6. The Christian Science Monitor search engine: <http://www.csmonitor.com/plweb-cgi/iops1.pl> To retrieve this article, enter the following search: ED=19970904 AND abuse. In the "retrieved list," click the title that matches this record. (ISSN0882-7729).

DRUG ABUSE--GREAT BRITAIN--PUBLIC OPINION (v26)

DRUG ABUSE--LAW AND LEGISLATION--UNITED STATES

In the U.S., most drug-court approaches "involve setting up a special court to handle drug-possession cases involving nonviolent offenders. Prosecutors agree to drop the charges if the defendant, usually an addict, successfully completes a one-year, drug-treatment program....The number of drug-court participants re-arrested within one year was only 12 percent in Ventura, Calif., 25 percent in Austin, Texas, and 29 percent in Seattle. That is markedly better than the recidivism rate for similar offenders who did not go to drug court, which was 32 percent in Ventura, 59 percent in Austin and 44 percent in Seattle....About 43 percent of defendants do make it through...[the program, Los Angeles Municipal Judge Stephen] Marcus says. And of the court's 120 graduates since 1995, less than 10 percent have been re-arrested on any felony charge....The recidivism rate for most drug addicts is about 70 percent...." (p25)

Higgins, Michael. "News: Drug War on the Cheap." ABA Journal v83 Aug 1997. p24-25. (ISSN0747-0088).

DRUG ABUSE--MEXICO--UNITED STATES

"An estimated 72 million Americans--34 percent of the total U.S. population--age 12 and older have used illegal drugs at one time or another. In Mexico, only 3.9 percent of that population has done the same. Approximately 12.8 million Americans say they use illegal drugs currently and 22.7 million report having used narcotics at least once in 1995. Domestic production in states like California, Kentucky, and Tennessee may account for as much as one-half of U.S. marijuana consumption....In 1991, over one-third of the Mexican students who tried drugs such as cocaine, crack, and heroin first did so while in the United States....A 1993 survey showed that 1.6 million Mexicans had tried an illegal drug at least once. However, only 319,000 people said that they used narcotics during 1993 itself. Although cocaine use has risen slightly (.3 percent of the population in 1993 up from .14 in 1988), heroin and hallucinogen use is almost nonexistent in a population of 95 million." (p146-147)

Baer, M. Delal. "Dispatch: Misreading Mexico." Foreign Policy n108 Fall 1997. p138-150. (ISSN0015-7228).

DRUG ABUSE--NEW YORK (N.Y.)

"Half a million New Yorkers are believed to be drug addicted. Some 70 to 80 percent of people arrested every year test positive for drug use. The cost to the city--in terms of crime, corrections, and treatment--is an estimated $20 billion annually....During the past four years, special units were set up in two areas with the most severe drug problems. The result was more than 100,000 drug arrests in 1996, a record high, and drug seizures were up more than 50 percent." (p3)

Marks, Alexandra. "United States: Mayor Who Quashed Crime Tries Hand at Curbing Drugs." The Christian Science Monitor v89 n236 31 Oct 1997. p3. The Christian Science Monitor search engine: <http://www.csmonitor.com/plweb-cgi/iops1.pl> To retrieve this article, enter the following search: ED=19971031 AND drugs. In the "retrieved list," click the title that matches this record. (ISSN0882-7729).

DRUG ABUSE--PREVENTION--UNITED STATES

In the U.S., "drug-prevention programs--following certain accepted principles--dramatically reduce the number of children who fall prey to smoking, drinking, and illicit drug use. One such program has reduced such behavior by 50 to 75 percent among seventh-graders." (p1) "Federal funding for drug-free school programs dropped from $623 million in 1992 to $466 million last year....According to...[a] Drug Strategies report, [the] Life Skills [program] reduced smoking, drinking, and marijuana use by 50 to 75 percent among seventh-grade participants. When the students were in high school, their use of the substances was 44 percent less than students who hadn't had the training." (p7)

Richey, Warren. "Best Weapon in War on Drugs: Sixth Grade." The Christian Science Monitor v89 n143 19 Jun 1997. p1,7. The Christian Science Monitor search engine: <http://www.csmonitor.com/plweb-cgi/iops1.pl> To retrieve this article, enter the following search: ED=19970619 AND grade. In the "retrieved list," click the title that matches this record. (ISSN0882-7729).

DRUG ABUSE--THAILAND (v26)

DRUG ABUSE--TREATMENT--UNITED STATES --PRISONERS

In the U.S., "comprehensive treatment of drug-addicted prison inmates, when coupled with post-release aftercare, reduces the probability of their being rearrested by 57 percent and reduces the likelihood they will return to drug use by 37 percent. In a study just published in the JOURNAL OF DRUG ISSUES, researchers at the University of Delaware's Center for Drug and Alcohol Studies found that within 18 months after release from prison, 54 percent of untreated drug-addicted inmates were rearrested and 84 percent were back using drugs. By comparison, of the individuals receiving drug abuse treatment during their prison stay and in aftercare programs, only 23 percent had been rearrested and 53 percent had used drugs again....At the 18-month followup, 77 percent of those who had received all three stages of treatment were arrest-free and 47 percent were drug-free. Of those individuals who had received only the work-release and aftercare stage, 57 percent were arrest-free and 31 percent were drug-free. Of the individuals who had received no treatment, only 46 percent were arrest-free and 16 percent were drug-free at 18 months."

U.S. National Institutes of Health. "Later Criminal Behavior and Drug Use Dramatically Reduced by Drug Treatment Beginning in Prison." News Release 18 Jul 1997. document-level access: <http://www.nih.gov/news/pr/jul97/nida-18.htm>

DRUG ABUSE--UNITED STATES (v26)

"The Office of National Drug Control Policy reports that approximately 12,800,000 Americans use illegal drugs. Illegal drug use occurs among members of every ethnic and socioeconomic group in the United States. And 10.9 percent of all children between 12 and 17 use illegal drugs and 1 child in 4 claims to have been offered illegal drugs in the last year. Drug-related illness, death and crime cost the United States approximately $67 billion each year, including costs for lost productivity, premature death, and incarceration." (pS8020)

Hutchison, Kay Bailey (Sen.-Tex.). "Departments of Commerce, Justice, And State, The Judiciary...Appropriations Act, 1998." Congressional Record. Daily ed. v143 n106 24 Jul 1997. pS8007-8040. section/page-level access: <http://thomas.loc.gov/cgi-bin/query/R?r105:FLD001:S08019:> (ISSN0363-7239). (X1.1A.105/1).

In the U.S., a report released by the nation's drug czar showed "the number of Americans who used drugs in 1995 fell by 50 percent from 1979's peak of 25 million drug users. And the number of regular drug users is down by half to 6 percent of the population from 12 percent over the past 15 years....In 1995, 10.9 percent of youths ages 12-17 years reported taking drugs in the past month, compared to 5.3 percent in 1992." (p5 secA)

Potts, Laura A. "Nation World: Youth Drug Abuse Rising, Report Shows." Detroit News 25 Jun 1997. p5 secA.

DRUG ABUSE--UNITED STATES--COSTS (v26)

DRUG ABUSE--UNITED STATES--HOSPITALS (v26)

DRUG ABUSE AND CRIME--AFRO-AMERICANS (v26)

DRUG ABUSE AND CRIME--CANADA (v26)

DRUG ABUSE AND CRIME--GREAT BRITAIN (v26)

"Some 50 per cent of property crimes in...[Great Britain] are related to substance misuse....More than half the criminal cases in London's magistrates courts are drink or drug-related, and 20 per cent of people who are arrested in police stations test positive for drugs....There are more than 130 prisons, and 150,000 people pass through our prison system each year. Some 25 per cent of receptions are on drugs at the point at which they enter the prison system." (c495)

Malins, Humfrey (H.C.-Woking). "Prisons (Drug and Alcohol Abuse)." Great Britain. Parliament. House of Commons. Debates. 16 Jul 1997. c495. section-level access: <http://www.parliament.the-stationery-office.co.uk/pa/cm199798/cmhansrd/cm970716/debtext/70716-47.htm#70716-47_head0>

DRUG ABUSE AND CRIME--STUDY AND TEACHING --NEW YORK--BROOKLYN

"Begun in 58 schools with a $1.2 million federal grant in 1990, Project Legal Lives reaches about 10,000 children in...[Brooklyn,] New York....Some 500 attorneys--armed with a curriculum called 'Choices' and in partnership with teachers in 330 classrooms--teach children about the law in a bid to keep them on its right side....Emulated in 14 cities, Project Legal Lives was incorporated in 1995 into the US Education Act as a drug and crime prevention program for which district attorneys can get federal grants. Administrators estimate it costs about $130 per child, paid in part by private donations....Since 1991,...[Charles Hynes, the Kings County district attorney who founded the program, says] murders in Brooklyn have dropped by nearly two-thirds, from 800 a year, including 129 involving children 17 or younger." (p13)

Katz, Nancie L. "Learning: Violence Prevention: Lawyers Give Children a Lesson in Judgment." The Christian Science Monitor v89 n189 25 Aug 1997. p13. The Christian Science Monitor search engine: <http://www.csmonitor.com/plweb-cgi/iops1.pl> To retrieve this article, enter the following search: ED=19970825 AND judgment. In the "retrieved list," click the title that matches this record. (ISSN0882-7729).

DRUG ENFORCEMENT
see NARCOTICS, CONTROL OF

DRUG INDUSTRY
see PHARMACEUTICAL INDUSTRY

DRUG TRAFFIC (v26)
see also COCAINE HABIT; HEROIN INDUSTRY; MARIJUANA

"Drugs account for 20 per cent of Colombia's foreign exchange, worth about the same as the country's largest legal export--coffee. Over $US300 million a month or $3.5 billion a year go to the Colombian drug cartels from the US illicit drug market. Perhaps 3-8 per cent or more of the Colombian GDP is related to drug production and trafficking. In Peru, drugs account for 30 per cent of its foreign exchange and 50 per cent in Bolivia. Drug money may account for 25 per cent of Pakistan's GNP. Over one billion dollars a year is suspected to be shipped to the Italian Mafia from heroin proceeds alone. The Mafia controls 40 per cent of the internal drug trade in the US." (p467)

Van de Velde, James R. "Issues of Law Intensity Conflict and Law Enforcement: The Growth of Criminal...Drug Trafficking." Low Intensity Conflict & Law Enforcement v5 n3 Win 1996. p466-483. (ISSN0966-2847).

DRUG TRAFFIC--FLORIDA

"Illegal drug activities continue to plague the State of Florida. In 1994, more than $5 billion in funds from cocaine traffic were laundered through south Florida and the I-4 corridor [Interstate 4 which runs from Daytona Beach to Tampa Bay]. Over 23 metric tons of cocaine were seized during that same time period. Over 250 organized drug trafficking groups have been identified as operating between south Florida and the I-4 corridor....Seized assets from drug traffickers in this area during 1996 included over $425 million in currency and property." (pS7608)

Graham, Bob (Sen.-Fla.). "Statements on Introduced Bills and Joint Resolutions." Congressional Record. Daily ed. v143 n101 16 Jul 1997. pS7603-7608. section/page-level access: <http://thomas.loc.gov/cgi-bin/query/R?r105:FLD001:S07608:> (ISSN0363-7239). (X1.1A.105/1).

DRUG TRAFFIC--FORMER SOVIET REPUBLICS

"The former Soviet Union (FSU) is the third largest drug producing and trafficking region in the world today behind the cocaine industry in the Andean Ridge (Peru, Colombia and Bolivia) and the opium refineries of Myanmar....There are 2.4 million acres, over 100 square miles, of wild marijuana in the country. The amount of marijuana in the FSU is 25 times greater than the amount cultivated in the rest of the world put together. The Chu Valley of Kazakhstan grows over 60,000 square miles of wild hemp, marijuana and poppies. In Uzbekistan alone, there has been a ten-fold increase in the quantity of poppies sown since 1991. A hectare of opium offers a Central Asian farmer 20 to 35 times more than legitimate crops." (p478)

Van de Velde, James R. "Issues of Law Intensity Conflict and Law Enforcement: The Growth of Criminal...Drug Trafficking." Low Intensity Conflict & Law Enforcement v5 n3 Win 1996. p466-483. (ISSN0966-2847).

DRUG TRAFFIC--LAW AND LEGISLATION--SINGAPORE

"Singapore--a tiny island nation of 3 million perched at the southern tip of the Asian continent--prides itself on its strict drug laws, which include a mandatory death sentence for anyone caught with as little as half an ounce of heroin....On September 27, 1996, six people were hanged in one morning. Four had been hanged the previous Friday, all for drug trafficking. According to Amnesty International, 1995...was a busy year at the gallows in Singapore, when more than fifty people were hanged, the majority for drug offenses." (p11,13)

Bernstein, Dennis/Kean, Leslie. "Articles: Singapore's Blood Money: Hanging Drug Couriers but Investing with Their Suppliers." Nation v265 n12 20 Oct 1997. p11,13,15-16. (ISSN0027-8378).

DRUG TRAFFIC--LAW AND LEGISLATION--UNITED STATES (v26)

DRUG TRAFFIC--MEXICO (v26)

DRUG TRAFFIC--MEXICO--UNITED STATES (v26)

"Mexico is the primary transit country for cocaine entering the United States from South America, as well as a major source country for heroin, marijuana and more recently, methamphetamine. The amount of cocaine seized and the number of drug-related arrests in Mexico have declined significantly since 1992. In addition, U.S. funding for counter narcotics efforts in the transit zone and Mexico has declined from approximately $1 billion in Fiscal Year 1992 to about $570 million in FY 1995. Estimates indicate that up to 70 percent of the more than 300 tons of cocaine entering the United States in 1994 came through Mexico. In March 1996, the State Department reported that Mexico supplied up to 80 percent of the foreign-grown marijuana consumed in the United States and from 20 to 30 percent of the heroin....[A General Accounting Office report entitled 'Border Patrol, Revised Strategy Is Showing Some Positive Results,' December 1994] highlights the fact that between FY 1990 and FY 1993, the number of Border Patrol drug seizures along the Southwest Border alone rose from around 4,200 to 6,400, an increase of over 50 percent. The amount of cocaine seized nearly doubled in the same period of time from about 14,000 pounds to about 27,000 pounds....The United States Attorneys continued to direct substantial resources to the prosecution of non-OCDETF narcotics cases during 1996. These cases represented 23.5 percent of all criminal cases filed during the year, up from 22.9 percent in 1995. A total of 8,992 cases were filed, up from 8,434 cases filed in 1995, an increase of 16.2 percent. During 1996, 16,837 defendants were charged, up from 15,767 in 1995, an increase of 6.8 percent." (p722-723)

U.S. Dept. of Justice. "Departments of Commerce, Justice, And State, The Judiciary...Approp. for 1998 (Part 2)." Hearing. U.S. House. Committee on Appropriations. Washington, D.C. : GPO, 1997. (ISBN0160549094). (Y4.Ap6/1:C73/2/997/pt.2).

Mexico "is the source of between 20 and 30 percent of the heroin, 70 percent of the marijuana, and 50 to 70 percent of the cocaine shipped into the United States. If the flow of drugs is going to stop, the front line of that war will be along our Nation's border with Mexico. The United States-Mexico border is 2,000 miles long, and Texas has 1,200 miles of that border....Texas has 1.7 agents for every 1 of our 1,254 miles....New Mexico and Arizona do not fare much better. California has 16.3 agents for every one mile of the border." (pS8020)

Hutchison, Kay Bailey (Sen.-Tex.). "Departments of Commerce, Justice, And State, The Judiciary...Appropriations Act, 1998." Congressional Record. Daily ed. v143 n106 24 Jul 1997. pS8007-8040. section/page-level access: <http://thomas.loc.gov/cgi-bin/query/R?r105:FLD001:S08019:> (ISSN0363-7239). (X1.1A.105/1).

DRUG TRAFFIC--MYANMAR

"Myanmar is the largest source of illicit opium and heroin accounting for 60 per cent of the heroin on American streets....[There] has been an increase in opium production from approximately 1,000 tons in 1988 to 2,550 tons in 1994--an increase greater than 250 per cent in six years." (p476)

Van de Velde, James R. "Issues of Law Intensity Conflict and Law Enforcement: The Growth of Criminal...Drug Trafficking." Low Intensity Conflict & Law Enforcement v5 n3 Win 1996. p466-483. (ISSN0966-2847).

DRUG TRAFFIC--NORTHERN IRELAND (v26)

DRUG TRAFFIC--UNITED STATES

"Today, approximately 12,800,000 Americans use illegal drugs, including 1,500,000 cocaine users, 600,000 heroin addicts, and 9,800,000 smokers of marijuana....The human and economic costs are enormous: Drug related illness, death, and crime cost the United States approximately $67 billion in 1996, including costs for lost productivity, premature death, and incarceration. This is an enormously lucrative business--drug trafficking generates estimated revenues of $400 billion annually. The United States has spent more than $25 billion for foreign interdictions and source country counter narcotics programs since 1981...." (pS6760)

Dodd, Christopher J. (Sen.-Conn.). "Title II--Protection for Ancient Forests, Roadless Areas, Watershed Protection Areas, Special Areas, and Federal...." Congressional Record. Daily ed. v143 n93 27 Jun 1997. pS6735-6761. section/page-level access: <http://thomas.loc.gov/cgi-bin/query/R?r105:FLD001:S06760:> (ISSN0363-7239). (X1.1A.105/1).

In 1996, the U.S. Air Force's airborne warning and control system "provided information that led to four cocaine interdictions worth $945 million--about 35 percent of all cocaine intercepted coming into the US....The AWACS...play an important role, intercepting about 15 percent of all illegal drugs entering the US....In 1994, the White House slashed the interdiction budget by more than $300 million--a 28.5 percent cut....This year the Department of Defense will spend $957.5 million for interdiction efforts, up $100 million from 1996 expenditures." (p18)

Bowers, Faye. "Fingering Smugglers from Four Miles Up." The Christian Science Monitor v89 n141 17 Jun 1997. p1,18. The Christian Science Monitor search engine: <http://www.csmonitor.com/plweb-cgi/iops1.pl> To retrieve this article, enter the following search: ED=19970617 AND smugglers. In the "retrieved list," click the title that matches this record. (ISSN0882-7729).

DRUG TRAFFIC--UNITED STATES--SCHOOLS

In the U.S., "forty-one percent of the high schoolers interviewed last summer said they witnessed drug deals on school grounds, compared to only 25 percent who claimed they saw deals in their neighborhoods, according to the study released in September by Columbia's National Center on Addiction and Substance Abuse in New York. School officials, however, saw much less: Only 12 percent of the 789 high school teachers questioned said they witnessed drug deals at school....Middle school students in the survey reported fewer drug transactions: 18 percent had witnessed drug deals at school, and 12 percent had seen drug deals in their neighborhood....Three-fourths of high school students and nearly half of middle school students said drugs are kept, used, or sold on school grounds." (p12-13)

"Before the Board: Drug Deals Common in Schools." American School Board Journal v184 n11 Nov 1997. p12-13. (ISSN0003-0953).

DRUGS

see also MEDICINE; METHAMPHETAMINE

DRUGS--CANADA (v26)

DRUGS--GERMANY--UNITED STATES (v26)

DRUGS--GREAT BRITAIN--MORTALITY (v26)

DRUGS--GREAT BRITAIN--UNITED STATES (v26)

DRUGS--JAPAN--UNITED STATES (v26)

DRUGS--LAW AND LEGISLATION (v26)

DRUGS--LAW AND LEGISLATION--EUROPE--UNITED STATES

In 1996, the U.S. Food and Drug Administration compared "all new drugs that were approved...by both the FDA and the new centralized drug approval process of the European Union. There were 15 of such drugs, and their median time for FDA review and marketing approval was 5.8 months. The median time for review by the Committee for Proprietary Medicinal Products and final EU authorization for a company to sell those 15 common drugs in Europe was 12.2 months. In four instances, the EU authorization came first--in one case, just three days ahead of FDA. In 11 instances, the drugs were first approved in the U.S." (p493)

Friedman, Michael A. (Deputy Commissioner for Operations, U.S. Food and Drug Administration). "Agriculture, Rural Development, Food and Drug Administration...Approp. for 1998 (Part 2)." Hearing. U.S. House. Committee on Appropriations. Washington, D.C. : GPO, 1997. (Y4.Ap6/1:Ag8/997/pt.2).

DRUGS--LAW AND LEGISLATION--UNITED STATES (v26)

All the drugs approved by the U.S. Food and Drug Administration "are important, but none are as meaningful in bringing new hope to patients as new molecular entities (NMEs). These are products that include active ingredients never before marketed in this country....FDA approved 53 NMEs submitted by the pharmaceutical industry, nearly twice as many as the year before." (p490) In the 1960s, "the average annual total of NMEs in that decade was 13.7. In the 1970s, the corresponding figure went up to 17.3. In the 1980s, the average was 21.7 NMEs, and in the first half of this decade, the average was 25.6 NMEs. That's less than one-half of the 53 NME approvals last year. Last year's approvals also were much faster than in the past. In the late 1980s, median times to NME approval approached 30 months. The median time to approval for the 53 drugs approved in calendar year 1996 was 14.3 months....Several of the NMEs approved last year, including two drugs for cancer and three for HIV, were approved in six months or less....Twelve of the NMEs, including three protease inhibitors, were developed--from the first commercial Investigational New Drug submission to marketing approval--in less than six years." (p491)

Friedman, Michael A. (Deputy Commissioner for Operations, U.S. Food and Drug Administration). "Agriculture, Rural Development, Food and Drug Administration...Approp. for 1998 (Part 2)." Hearing. U.S. House. Committee on Appropriations. Washington, D.C. : GPO, 1997. (Y4.Ap6/1:Ag8/997/pt.2).

In 1996, the median time for the U.S. Food and Drug Administration's approval of new drugs was "14.3 months; 10 percent faster than in the year before; and...nearly twice as fast as in the late 1980s....In the first year of PDUFA [Prescription Drug User Fee Act], we approved 70 new products in a median time of 24.1 months. Last year, we approved 131 new products, including the NMEs [new molecular entities], in a median time of 15.4 months....Another outstanding achievement last year was the approval of the 118 efficacy supplements...." (p314)

Friedman, Michael A. (Deputy Commissioner for Operations, U.S. Food and Drug Administration). "Agriculture, Rural Development, Food and Drug Administration...Approp. for 1998 (Part 2)." Hearing. U.S. House. Committee on Appropriations. Washington, D.C. : GPO, 1997. (Y4.Ap6/1:Ag8/997/pt.2).

In the U.S., "all drugs approved by FDA are important, but none are as meaningful in bringing new hope to patients as new molecular entities, or NMEs....In calendar year 1996, we approved 53 NMEs, nearly twice as many as the year before. These approvals were also done much more quickly. The median time to approve of these 53 was only 14.3 months, less than half the time it took as recently as the late 1980s. Further, several of the NMEs approved last year, including two drugs for cancer and three for HIV, were approved in six months or less. Finally, the total number of new drugs and biological products approved in the last calendar year was 139--a 63 percent increase over the previous year. New Drug Applications accounted for 131 of these products, and their median time to approval was 15.4 months, seven percent faster than the 16.5 months the year before." (p462)

U.S. Food and Drug Administration. "Agriculture, Rural Development, Food and Drug Administration...Approp. for 1998 (Part 2)." Hearing. U.S. House. Committee on Appropriations. Washington, D.C. : GPO, 1997. (Y4.Ap6/1:Ag8/997/pt.2).

DRUGS--PRESCRIBING--MICHIGAN

"From 1990 through 1995 in Michigan, the number of prescriptions for morphine, the most powerful pain reliever available, increased by more than 75 percent, from 393,000 to 691,000, according to the state Office of Health Services, which monitors such prescriptions. Prescriptions for another pain reliever, fentanyl, nearly doubled, to 32,000 in 1995 from 17,000 in 1991." (p6 secA)

"Pain--And Fear of Pain." Detroit News 30 Jun 1997. p6 secA.

DRUGS--UNITED STATES--TESTING--CHILDREN

"Despite evidence that drugs affect children differently than adults, 80 percent of all drugs marketed in the United States have not been labeled for use by infants, children, and adolescents. Only forty-two percent of drugs that are widely used in pediatric populations have been tested on children. Many drugs commonly given to children under the age of six including Prozac, Zoloft, Ritalin, and drugs for asthma, allergic reactions, and ear infections are inadequately tested and labeled for use by children. These drugs, taken together, are given to over five million children each year. Less than half of the drugs used in the treatment of HIV infections carry any safety or effectiveness information for children. Of those that do, the data is often incomplete. Safety and effectiveness information is especially sparse for the over seven million children under the age of two. The percentage of drugs being tested on children decreased by over one-third between 1991 and 1996."

U.S. Dept. of Health and Human Services. "President Clinton Announces New Measures to Increase Availability of Information...Medications Used to Treat Children." Fact Sheet 13 Aug 1997. document-level access: <http://www.hhs.gov/news/press/1997pres/970813.html>

DRUGS, NONPRESCRIPTION--UNITED STATES (v26)

DRUNK DRIVING--MICHIGAN (v26)

"Officials blame the deadly mixture of alcohol and autos for 36 percent of...[Michigan's] traffic fatalities last year. That is down from a staggering 57 percent in 1980, but the ad campaigns and billboards don't seem to be reaching persistent drinkers. The average motorist arrested last year for driving while intoxicated (DWI) had a blood alcohol level of 0.16, far above the legal limit of 0.10." (p1 secA)

Knox, Noelle. "State Looks to Toughen Laws to Keep Drunken Driving Down: Experts Say Counseling, Education Are Needed, Too." Detroit News 25 Sep 1997. p1,12 secA.

DRUNK DRIVING--UNITED STATES

In the U.S., "in 1992, more people were arrested for DWI [driving while intoxicated]--1.6 million--than for any other reported criminal activity including larceny or theft, or for drug abuse violations....A shocking number of DWI convictions are repeat offenders. When the National Highway Traffic and Safety Administration studied this issue, it found that about one-third of all drivers arrested or convicted of DWI each year are repeat DWI offenders. One study in California demonstrated the extent of this problem over the long term. It found that 44 percent of all drivers convicted of DWI in California in 1980 were convicted again of DWI within the next 10 years....The danger of these repeat offenders is illustrated by the fact that drivers with prior DWI convictions are over-represented in fatal crashes. These drivers have a 4.1 times greater risk of being in a fatal crash, as do intoxicated drivers without a prior DWI, and the risk of a particular driver being involved in a fatal crash increases with each DWI arrest." (pS4009)

Lautenberg, Frank R. (Sen.-N.J.). "Statements on Introduced Bills and Joint Resolutions." Congressional Record. Daily ed. v143 n57 6 May 1997. pS3998-4010. section/page-level access: <http://thomas.loc.gov/cgi-bin/query/R?r105:FLD001:S04009:> (ISSN0363-7239). (X1.1A.105/1).

DRUNKEN DRIVERS

see DRINKING AND TRAFFIC ACCIDENTS

DRUNKENNESS

see ALCOHOLISM

DUAL DIAGNOSIS--TREATMENT--UNITED STATES --YOUTH (v26)

DUNGEONS

see PRISONS

DWARFISM--UNITED STATES (v26)

DWELLINGS

see also PUBLIC HOUSING; RENTAL HOUSING

DWELLINGS--ENERGY CONSUMPTION--GREAT BRITAIN (v26)

DWELLINGS--IRELAND

According to Ireland's 1991 Census, "nearly four out of five private dwellings in the State were owner occupied in 1991. While solid fuel continues to be the main fuel used to heat private dwellings in winter time, its importance declined from 70 per cent in 1981 to 62 per cent in 1991."

Ireland. Central Statistics Office. "Census 91--Volume 10: Housing." Press Release 27 Feb 1997. document-level access: <http://www.cso.ie/pressreleases/prel91hous.html>

DWELLINGS--MICHIGAN

Washtenaw County, Michigan "expanded its new housing stock by 33.2 percent last year--the highest rate of growth in southeast Michigan--with Pittsfield Township gaining more than 1,000 new dwelling units in one year, according to figures released by the Southeast Michigan Council of Governments. Livingston County's 22.6 percent increase in new homes was the second highest for 1996 in the seven-county region. Municipalities in Washtenaw County authorized 2,702 new dwellings last year, up 33.2 percent from 2,029 in 1995, rebounding from a slump in that year when home building dropped 2.4 percent from 1994. Pittsfield Township, which has made the top 10 list in the seven-county southeast Michigan for the past several years, jumped to the No. 3 spot with 1,028 new units, including 590 single-family, 428 multifamily and 10 two-family dwellings....Livingston County saw 1,968 housing starts, up 22.6 percent." (p3 secC)

Pyen, Chong W. "Local: Ann Arbor Report: Washtenaw Leads in New Home Building." Ann Arbor News 17 Jun 1997. p3 secC.

DWELLINGS--SWEDEN (v26)

DWELLINGS--UNITED STATES

"Of the nearly 1.5 million new homes built in the United States last year, the vast majority used traditional wood-frame construction. Nearly 1.2 million of those were single-family homes (the remainder were apartments), each of which claimed an average of 40 to 50 trees. That works out to about 50 million trees cut down to satiate the nation's demand for new wooden houses." (p16)

Rasmussen, Matt. "A Growing Demand: The Straw Alternative." Inner Voice v9 n6 Nov-Dec 1997. p16-18.

DWELLINGS--UNITED STATES--COSTS

In the U.S., "in inflation-adjusted dollars, the nation-wide median price of an existing house was $51,000 in 1970 and $84,000 in 1990....[In Michigan,] the median price of an existing house in 1970 was $55,000 (in 1990 dollars). The corresponding figure in 1990 was $61,000, an increase of about 11 percent in 20 years." (p240) In California, "the median price of an existing house nearly tripled, from $73,000 in 1970 to $196,000 in 1990." (p241)

Gersmehl, Philip J. "Putting Information in Perspective: A Mapping Activity to Help Students Understand the California Dilemma." Journal of Geography v96 n5 Sep-Oct 1997. p235-242. (ISSN0022-1341).

DWELLINGS--UNITED STATES--REMODELING --COSTS

According to REMODELING magazine, the average cost of upgrading a bathroom in 1996, in the U.S., "was $8,423. Replacing 10 3-by-5-foot windows was $6,112, and just adding a 16-by-20-foot pressure-treated pine deck was $6,172. Adding a 16-by-25-foot family room was $31,846." (p33 secD)

Haege, Glenn. "Homestyle: The Handyman: Realize Quality Doesn't Come Cheap in Any Remodeling Project." Detroit News 21 Jun 1997. p33 secD.

According to the U.S. "National Association of Home Builders, average home buyers spend $6,500 decorating and furnishing their home in the first year. This year, all...[homebuyers] together will spend $125 billion on home repair and improvements in the United States. Maintenance and repair will amount to $45.3 billion; home improvements and upgrades will account for the other $80 billion....American Express says the total is really $135.4 billion." (p33 secD)

Haege, Glenn. "Homestyle: The Handyman: Realize Quality Doesn't Come Cheap in Any Remodeling Project." Detroit News 21 Jun 1997. p33 secD.

D.W.I. (DRUNK DRIVING)

see DRUNK DRIVING

E. COLI (BACTERIA)

see ESCHERICHIA COLI INFECTIONS

EARTH--CORE (v26)

EARTH SCIENCES

see also GEOGRAPHY; GEOLOGY

EARTH SCIENCES--STUDY AND TEACHING--UNITED STATES--WOMEN

In the U.S., "between 1980 and 1996, the percentage of doctoral degrees earned by women in the geosciences doubled and the percentage for Master's degrees went from 20 percent to 30 percent. The American Geological Institute (AGI) reported that in 1980, barely one in 10 of the doctoral degrees in geosciences went to women. By 1996, the percentage had increased to nearly 22 percent. Master's degrees earned by women geoscientists in 1980 were 20 percent of the total; by 1996, that number had grown to nearly 31 percent. Undergraduate degrees for women in the geosciences went from 25 percent of the total to 36 percent. Enrollment of women in college geoscience classes rose from 15 percent in the 1980s to 45 percent today." (p5)

Cullicott, Catherine E./Tarrant, Christi A. "Comment: Something to Celebrate: Women in Geoscience Make Progress." Geotimes v42 n12 Dec 1997. p5. (ISSN0016-8556).

EARTHQUAKES (v26)

see also DAMS--EARTHQUAKE EFFECTS; INSURANCE, EARTHQUAKE

EARTHQUAKES--CALIFORNIA (v26)

Run by the California Institute of Technology in Pasadena, the US Geological Survey, and California's Division of Mines and Geology, "the TriNet consortium is replacing 300 old seismometers with 200 smaller, more capable digital devices. So far, 50 of the new detectors have been installed,...[Dr. Hiroo Kanamori, director of the Seismology Laboratory at Cal Tech] says." (p13)

Spotts, Peter N. "Science & Technology: Electronic Moles Map Route for Rapid Response When Earth Moves." The Christian Science Monitor v89 n180 12 Aug 1997. p13. The Christian Science Monitor search engine: <http://www.csmonitor.com/plweb-cgi/iops1.pl> To retrieve this article, enter the following search: ED=19970812 AND moves. In the "retrieved list," click the title that matches this record. (ISSN0882-7729).

EASEMENTS

see SERVITUDES

EAST (MIDDLE EAST)

see MIDDLE EAST

EAST ASIA--ECONOMIC CONDITIONS

In East Asia, "export growth rose just 5 percent last year, about one quarter of the rate in 1994 and 1995. Average economic growth across the region slipped from 9 percent in 1995 to 7 percent in 1996." (p9)

Tyson, James L. "Business & Money: Mutual Funds: Asia's Tigers Declawed, For Now." The Christian Science Monitor v89 n187 21 Aug 1997. p9. The Christian Science Monitor search engine: <http://www.csmonitor.com/plweb-cgi/iops1.pl> To retrieve this article, enter the following search: ED=19970821 AND tigers. In the "retrieved list," click the title that matches this record. (ISSN0882-7729).

EATING DISORDERS

see ANOREXIA NERVOSA

EATING DISORDERS--UNITED STATES (v26)

ECOLOGICAL COMMUNITIES

see BIOTIC COMMUNITIES

ECOLOGY (v26)

ECOLOGY, KELP BED

see KELP BED ECOLOGY

ECONOMIC ASSISTANCE (v26)

The European Union's contributions to humanitarian relief "quadrupled in 1991 to $900 million while the number of NGOs [non-governmental organizations] increased from around 9,000 organizations in 1981 to more than 16,000 in 1990. According to the US Mission to the UN, the total 'global emergency aid' for 1995 was $7.1 Billion including $2 Billion from private sources." (p3)

"Getting the Military out of Humanitarian Relief." Defense Monitor v26 n6 Oct 1997. p1-7. (ISSN0195-6450).

"In the early 1990s, official development assistance, or ODA, from the United States for all purposes averaged around $10.9 billion annually, or roughly 0.2 percent of gross national product, and less than 1 percent of the Federal budget. In 1993, US ODA was $38 per US citizen (World Resources Institute 1996...). For comparison, in 1993 Italy's ODA was $53 per Italian; Austria's was $69 per Austrian; Canada's was $82 per person; France's was $138 per person; and Denmark's was $259 per person. In these cases, ODA was a higher percentage of gross national product than in the United States, and in Denmark ODA was 1.0 percent of GNP." (p579)

Cohen, Joel E. "Why Should More United States Tax Money Be Used to Pay for Development Assistance in Poor Countries?" Population and Development Review v23 n3 Sep 1997. p579-584. (ISSN0098-7921).

"Approximately 70 countries are receiving foreign aid this year. Some of them have been for more than 50 years, especially in Latin America where technical assistance started earlier than elsewhere. Other long-term recipients are in the Middle East and South Asia, notably Israel and Egypt, which get more than any other countries. Israel has achieved middle-income status with a gross national product per capita of $14,000. Egypt is still mired in poverty with a GNP per capita of $710." (p19)

Holt, Pat M. "Opinion/Essays: Like Welfare, Foreign Aid Shouldn't Go On Endlessly." The Christian Science Monitor v89 n133 5 Jun 1997. p19. The Christian Science Monitor search engine: <http://www.csmonitor.com/plweb-cgi/iops1.pl> To retrieve this article, enter the following search: ED=19970605 AND endlessly. In the "retrieved list,"

click the title that matches this record. (ISSN0882-7729).

ECONOMIC ASSISTANCE--AFGHANISTAN

In the last few years, the United Nations High Commissioner for Refugees "has helped more than 28,000 families rebuild their homes [in Afghanistan]. The agency has financed reconstruction of 230 primary schools and 58 clinics, rehabilitated more than 60 potable water and 160 irrigation schemes and completed around 140 road and bridge repair projects. More than 100 skills training and income generating projects have been launched. Two pilot lending programs for women were started in the northern part of the country...." (p12-13)

Damato, Zivan. "The Long Way Home." Refugees v2 n108 1997. p11-13. (ISSN0252-791X).

ECONOMIC ASSISTANCE--ASIA--UNITED STATES

South Korea "has been promised a $55 billion package of credits from the International Monetary Fund (IMF), plus at least $5 billion directly from the U.S. Treasury. The rescue effort follows substantial bailouts for Thailand, Indonesia and the Philippines, bringing total commitments to more than $160 billion...." (p16 secA)

"Why Bail Out Asia?" Detroit News 11 Dec 1997. p16 secA.

ECONOMIC ASSISTANCE--CARIBBEAN AREA--LATIN AMERICA--INDIGENOUS PEOPLES

"Six countries have pledged a total of $20 million toward an eventual $100 million fund to finance development projects benefitting indigenous peoples [in Latin America and the Caribbean]....The pledges were made by Bolivia, for $5 million; Spain, $5 million; Chile, $5 million; Mexico, $2 million; France, $2 million; and Guatemala, $1 million." (p5)

"The Region: Pledges Made to Indigenous Fund." IDB v24 n7 Jul 1997. p5. (ISSN0145-2274).

ECONOMIC ASSISTANCE--DEVELOPING COUNTRIES (v26)

ECONOMIC ASSISTANCE--PUBLIC OPINION (v26)

ECONOMIC ASSISTANCE--REFUGEES (v26)

ECONOMIC ASSISTANCE, AMERICAN (v26)

ECONOMIC ASSISTANCE, AMERICAN--AFRICA

"US Ambassador to the UN Bill Richardson told AFRICA RECOVERY, 65 per cent of the debates in the Security Council focus on Africa--and usually its crises....The US has provided over $10 mn [million] over the past five years to strengthen the OAU's [Organization of African Unity's] conflict management centre...." (p5)

Novicki, Margaret A. "U.S. Highlights Africa's Achievements." Africa Recovery v11 n2 Oct 1997. p5.

ECONOMIC ASSISTANCE, AMERICAN--EGYPT --ISRAEL (v26)

ECONOMIC ASSISTANCE, AMERICAN--FORMER SOVIET REPUBLICS

"From 1991 through 1995 the United States obligated about $8.7 billion in assistance to the former Soviet successor states (of which about $4 billion went to Russia), and about $11 billion in credits (again, about $4 billion to Russia)....During the...years of 1992 and 1993, the United States gave about two-thirds of its economic assistance to Russia, and one-third to Ukraine and the other states, more or less in line with the relative size of the countries' populations. By 1995 and 1996 this ratio was reversed, with about one-third going to Russia and two-thirds to the others....In 1997 the administration has requested an increase to a total of $900 million for all the successor states, of which $240 million is earmarked for Russia." (p309)

Garthoff, Raymond L. "The United States and the New Russia: The First Five Years." Current History v96 n612 Oct 1997. p305-312. (ISSN0011-3530).

ECONOMIC ASSISTANCE, AMERICAN--HAITI--PERU (v26)

ECONOMIC ASSISTANCE, AMERICAN--ISRAEL (v26)

The U.S. provides "more than $8 billion annually to Israel (more than $3 billion in foreign aid; some $2 billion in loan guarantees; $1 billion in tax-free charitable contributions; and $2 billion in investment and tourism)." (p16)

Khalidi, Rashid. "Middle East: A Flawed Peace." In These Times v21 n16 30 Jun 1997. p14-16. (ISSN0160-5992).

ECONOMIC ASSISTANCE, AMERICAN--JORDAN

"On paper, the figures of increasing US aid look impressive: Jordan is receiving nearly 20 times what it did last year. It is the sixth-largest recipient of non-food US Agency for International Development money in the world, and $637 million in official debts has been forgiven. Jordan is tied with Thailand for the largest US-financed military training program in the world, for 200 military personnel. Last year, it received used US military hardware valued at $100 million--including 18 helicopters, 50 tanks, 250 trucks, and a C-130 transport plane--and the US is providing $175 million financing for the delivery of 16 F-16 jet fighters....US assistance totals just $126 million this year--a tiny fraction of the annual peace dividend paid out to Israel and Egypt." (p8)

Peterson, Scott. "International: Key Peace Player Jordan Feels Slighted by US." The Christian Science Monitor v89 n227 20 Oct 1997. p1,8. The Christian Science Monitor search engine: <http://www.csmonitor.com/plweb-cgi/iops1.pl> To retrieve this article, enter the following search: ED=19971020 AND jordan. In the "retrieved list," click the title that matches this record. (ISSN0882-7729).

ECONOMIC ASSISTANCE, AMERICAN--LATIN AMERICA

Latin America's "share of U.S. foreign aid spending never exceeded 25 percent of the bilateral aid budget....Since 1979, Latin American countries have received about 13 percent of U.S. bilateral assitance." (p11)

U.S. Congressional Budget Office. "The Flow of Foreign Aid and Private Capital to Developing Countries." The Role of Foreign Aid in Development May 1997. p7-19.

ECONOMIC ASSISTANCE, AMERICAN--PALESTINIANS

"To help create a 'civil society' in Palestinian-controlled areas, the American government has launched a 'democracy and governance program' with $15.3 million in spending. Some $700,000 will go to an 'Arab Thought Forum' for setting up public discussion groups and a citizens' rights center....A $1.1 million grant will go to a US Republican-led institute to help private activists cooperate with the Palestinian Authority." (p6)

"International: US Doubts Its Role as Main Donor to Palestinians: US Taxpayers Help Launch a Democracy." The Christian Science Monitor v89 n142 18 Jun 1997. p6. The Christian Science Monitor search engine: <http://www.csmonitor.com/plweb-cgi/iops1.pl> To retrieve this article, enter the following search: ED=19970618 AND democracy. In the "retrieved list," click the title that matches this record. (ISSN0882-7729).

ECONOMIC ASSISTANCE, AMERICAN--PUBLIC OPINION

In the U.S., in the Program on International Policy Attitudes's "January 1995 poll an overwhelming 77% rejected the argument that 'We should only make commitments to send aid to parts of the world where we have security interests,' while 76% agreed that 'We should send aid to starving people irrespective of whether it will promote the national interest.'...In PIPA's July 1994 poll, 84% said that 'sometimes the US should be willing to make some sacrifices if this will help the world as a whole.'" (p3) "In the January 1995 poll, 63% agreed that the US should give some foreign aid because 'in the long run, helping Third World countries develop is in the economic interest of the

US.'...In a March 1993 poll by Intercultural Communication, Inc., 67% disagreed with the idea that it was 'against our interests to help developing countries because they will compete with us economically and politically.'" (p4)

Kull, Steven. "Americans Have Not Turned Isolationist." Public Perspective v8 n5 Aug-Sep 1997. p1-4. (ISSN1050-5067).

ECONOMIC ASSISTANCE, BRITISH--DEVELOPING COUNTRIES (v26)

ECONOMIC ASSISTANCE, CANADIAN (v26)

ECONOMIC ASSISTANCE, CANADIAN--DEVELOPING COUNTRIES (v26)

ECONOMIC ASSISTANCE, DOMESTIC--CANADA --INDIGENOUS PEOPLES (v26)

ECONOMIC ASSISTANCE, DOMESTIC--CHECHNYA --RUSSIA

According to Russian President Boris Yeltsin, "more than $100 million of Russian aid destined for reconstruction projects in war-shattered Chechnya has disappeared this year....[President] Yeltsin said that while Moscow had allocated $138 million to Chechnya this year, only $21 million had reached the National Bank of Chechnya." (p6)

Ford, Peter. "International: The Lost $100 Million: Yeltsin Admits Aid Misses Chechnya." The Christian Science Monitor v89 n185 19 Aug 1997. p6. The Christian Science Monitor search engine: <http://www.csmonitor.com/plweb-cgi/iops1.pl> To retrieve this article, enter the following search: ED=19970819 AND chechnya. In the "retrieved list," click the title that matches this record. (ISSN0882-7729).

ECONOMIC ASSISTANCE, DOMESTIC--MASSACHUSETTS (v26)

ECONOMIC ASSISTANCE, DOMESTIC--MICHIGAN

Like Michigan "as a whole, Wayne and Oakland counties got less federal money in 1996 than they did the previous year--but Macomb County got 14 percent more. Among Michigan's 83 counties, Wayne and Macomb ranked 19th and 22nd, respectively, in per capita federal spending, Oakland County, the state's second largest county with 1.1 million residents, ranked 71st....Statewide, one of the biggest financial hits was a $77.4 million, or 71 percent, decrease in money received from the Commerce Department, compared to a national drop of 37 percent....[Michigan gained] 79 percent more from the Justice Department in 1996 than it received in the previous year, compared to a national average increase of 35 percent. Other pluses and minuses shown in the report include: a $2.5 million increase from the Agricultural Department....A $6.3-million decrease, or 46 percent cut by the Energy Department....A 114-percent increase, or $411,809 more from the Department of Education....A 33-percent decrease, or $10.9 million less from the National Aeronautics and Space Administration." (p1 secC)

Bivins, Larry. "Metro: Feds Cut Funding to State." Detroit News 12 Dec 1997. p1 secC.

ECONOMIC ASSISTANCE, DOMESTIC--NORTHERN IRELAND (v26)

ECONOMIC ASSISTANCE, DOMESTIC--UNITED STATES (v26)

In the U.S., the Emergency Food and Shelter Program is a public/private partnership that "began in 1983, $1.6 billion has been appropriated to the FEMA [Federal Emergency Management Agency] EFS program. In 1995, prior to the devastating rescissions bill, the funding for this program annually was $130 million. Since the rescissions bill, the funding has been level at a less than adequate $100 million....Specifically reviewing EFS/FEMA in fiscal year 1996, the National Board accomplished the following with an appropriation of $100 million: provided over 82.6 million meals at an average meal cost of 47 cents; provided more than 3.8 million nights of shelter at an average cost of $5.93 per night; paid over 177,000 utility bills allowing families to remain in their homes; directly funded more [than] 10,300 charitable organizations and governmental agencies in over 2,400 jurisdictions in all 50 States, the District of Columbia, Puerto Rico, and the U.S. territories." (pH5346)

Vento, Bruce F. (Rep.-Minn.). "Departments of Veterans Affairs and Housing and Urban Development...Appropriations Act, 1998." Congressional Record. Daily ed. v143 n101 16 Jul 1997. pH5309-5371. section/page-level access: <http://thomas.loc.gov/cgi-bin/query/R?r105:FLD001:H05342:> (ISSN0363-7239). (X1.1A.105/1).

In the U.S., "as late as 1991, 74 percent of FEMA's [Federal Emergency Management Agency] budget was related to defense issues, and much of what it did was classified. Today, only 11 percent of its $320 million operational budget is defense-related." (p5 secB)

Ryan, Richard A. "Outlook: Politics of Disaster Relief." Detroit News 13 Jul 1997. p5,8 secB.

ECONOMIC ASSISTANCE, JAPANESE (v26)

ECONOMIC DEVELOPMENT (v26)

see COMMUNITY DEVELOPMENT; INFRASTRUCTURE (ECONOMICS); RESEARCH AND DEVELOPMENT CONTRACTS; WATER RESOURCES DEVELOPMENT

ECONOMIC FORECASTING (v26)

New estimates from Nariman Behravesh, chief global forecaster for Standard & Poor's Denver Research Institute have "reduced Japan's expected 1998 growth from 2.7 percent to 0.7 percent, Thailand's from 4.8 percent to minus 0.7 percent, Indonesia's from 6.3 percent to 2.2 percent, and Brazil's from 4.4 percent to 1.8 percent....Yet Behravesh doesn't expect the world economy to slump. He's cut his 1998 forecast for global growth only slightly, from 2.9 percent to 2.5 percent." (p11 secA)

Samuelson, Robert. "Comment: Asian Crises Threaten Domino Effect." Detroit News 21 Nov 1997. p11 secA.

"Growth of world gross domestic product (GDP) is now projected at 2.8 percent in 1998, down from 3.1 percent in 1997. Developed country GDP growth is expected to slow to 2.4 percent from 2.7 percent in 1997, while developing countries slide to 4.5 percent GDP growth from 5.2 percent. The U.S. GDP is forecast to drop to 2.5 percent growth from 3.8 percent in 1997....The European Union's GDP growth is projected to rise to 2.7 percent from 2.4 percent in 1997. GDP growth in Japan also is expected to rise, but at...1.6 percent in 1998. Growth of GDP in Canada and Mexico likely will slow to 2.8 percent and 5 percent, respectively, from 3.6 percent and 7 percent, respectively in 1997....The Middle East is expected to remain unchanged at 3.5 percent GDP growth....Thailand's growth is forecast...at only 1 percent in 1998, and South Korea's growth is expected to slow to 2.7 percent, from 4.9 percent in 1997....GDP growth in Latin America will slump to 3.5 percent, from 4.5 percent this year. GDP growth in Africa also is projected down to only 3.1 percent." (p7-8)

U.S. Dept. of Agriculture. "Economic Outlook." Outlook for U.S. Agricultural Exports 2 Dec 1997. p7-8.

ECONOMIC FORECASTING--AFRICA--FORMER SOVIET REPUBLICS (v26)

ECONOMIC FORECASTING--ASIA

"By 2025, Asia will likely reassume its place at the center of the world economy. Asia may account for 55 to 60 percent of world income in the year 2025, with the West's share falling from around 45 percent today to between 20 and 30 percent. Standards of living will still be much higher in the West, but average per capita income in Asia will probably increase to around one-third of the U.S. level, compared with a meager 13 percent today." (p46)

Radelet, Steven/Sachs, Jeffrey. "Asia's Reemergence." Foreign Affairs v76 n6 Nov-Dec 1997. p44-59.

(ISSN0015-7120).

ECONOMIC FORECASTING--CHINA

"According to the World Bank's purchasing power party (PPP) estimates, China, with a 1994 GDP of just under $3 trillion, has become the second-largest economy in the world, after the United States. If we accept the projections of a 1995 Rand study, China's GDP will reach $11.3 trillion by the year 2010 (in 1994 PPP dollars) compared to $10.7 trillion for the United States, $4.5 trillion for Japan, $3.7 trillion for India, and $2 trillion for a unified Korea." (p247)

Kim, Samuel S. "China as a Great Power." Current History v96 n611 Sep 1997. p246-251. (ISSN0011-3530).

ECONOMIC FORECASTING--EUROPE (v26)

ECONOMIC FORECASTING--FRANCE--GERMANY --GREAT BRITAIN--ITALY (v26)

ECONOMIC FORECASTING--HONG KONG (v26)

ECONOMIC FORECASTING--JAPAN (v26)

ECONOMIC FORECASTING--MICHIGAN

Joan P. Crary and University of Michigan "economists George A. Fulton and Saul H. Hymans predict increases of about 52,000 jobs [in Michigan] in each of the next two years, down from the 59,000 job additions reported for 1997. This translates into moderate employment growth of 1.2 percent for both 1998 and 1999, down slightly from the 1.4 percent rate of the current year. Unemployment...will drift upward...from the current rate of about 4 percent to an average of 4.3 percent in 1998 and 4.5 percent in 1999." (p1) "In addition to moderate overall job growth, the U-M forecast indicates that growth in personal income will hold fairly steady at 4.8 percent in 1998 and 4.7 percent in 1999, after rising 4.6 percent this year....The growth in real disposable income, or consumer purchasing power, will increase from a current rate of 1.3 percent to 2.5 percent next year before dropping slightly to 2.3 percent in 1999." (p2)

University of Michigan. News and Information Services. "Michigan's Economy Will Continue to Expand, But at a Slower Rate, In 1998-99, Say U-M Researchers." University of Michigan News Release 21 Nov 1997. p1-2.

ECONOMIC FORECASTING--UNITED STATES (v26)

The U.S. economy should grow "by 2.6 percent in 1998 and 2.1 percent in 1999, significantly less than the 3.7 percent growth rate this year, according to analysis performed by U-M [University of Michigan] economics professor Saul Hymans and researchers Joan Crary and Janet Wolfe. Steady but slightly lower economic growth also is expected to keep: The unemployment rate under 5 percent during the next year, but above 5 percent by late 1999. U.S. auto and truck sales relatively steady. U-M projects Americans will buy 15.1 million cars and trucks in 1998 and 15 million in 1999. Household purchasing power up, increasing 3.3 percent in 1998 and 3 percent in 1999....Housing starts...are projected to slip from 1.46 million units in 1997 to 1.39 million in 1998 and 1.35 million in 1999. Business capital spending also is expected to slow from a growth rate of 12.3 percent in 1997 to 6 percent in 1998 and to 3.2 percent in 1999. The federal budget deficit of $22.6 billion in fiscal 1997 will fall to $21.6 billion in fiscal 1998, before increasing again to $48.4 billion in 1999 and $69.6 billion in 2000." (p1,8 secE)

Brennan, Mike. "Business: Confidence in Economy Is Soaring: U-M Survey Index Highest in 32 Years." Detroit Free Press 21 Nov 1997. p1,8 secE.

"In their U.S. economic forecast for 1998-99,...[Professor] Saul H. Hymans and researchers Joan P. Crary and Janet C. Wolfe of the U-M [University of Michigan] Department of Economics predict that the economy will grow by 2.6 percent in 1998 and 2.1 percent in 1999, slowing from the torrid 3.7 percent growth rate of the current year." (p1) "Real disposable income, or household purchasing power, will increase 3.3 percent in 1998 and 3 percent in 1999....Business capital spending will slow from a growth rate of 12.3 percent in 1997 to 6 percent in 1998 and to 3.2 percent in 1999. The federal deficit of $49 billion in 1997 will fall to $22 billion in fiscal 1998 before increasing again to $48 billion in 1999." (p2)

University of Michigan. News and Information Services. "The American Economy Will Remain Strong Through 1999, Despite Slightly Rising Inflation...Say U-M Economists." University of Michigan News Release 20 Nov 1997. p1-2.

ECONOMIC FORECASTING--UNITED STATES--PUBLIC OPINION

"A September 1996 Gallup/BAN Poll shows that 58 percent of future middle-agers [in the U.S.] believe they will make more money than they did in 1996....Men (48 percent) appear more confident about a larger paycheck than women (39 percent)....Although 18-to-34-year-olds are hopeful they will be able to save any of the extra money they are projecting to take in, 27 percent of respondents plan to apply for an automobile loan. Another 5 percent plan to purchase a house." (p30)

Cravatta, Matthew. "Kaleidoscope: Financial Futures." American Demographics v19 n6 Jun 1997. p30-31. article-level access: <http://www.demographics.com/publications/ad/97_ad/9706_ad/ad970610.htm> (ISSN0163-4089).

ECONOMIC HISTORY (v26)

see also QUALITY OF LIFE

"Turnover in global foreign exchange markets is estimated to have risen from $188 billion in 1986 to $1.2 trillion in 1995--an increase almost three times as fast as the increase in trade. Foreign direct investment by the advanced industrial countries has risen nearly as fast (by a factor of five between the mid-1980s and the mid-1990s), and cross-border transactions in bonds and equities in nearly all the Group of Seven economies have risen tenfold over this period....One indication is the increase in private capital flows, from 0.5 percent of developing country GDP in 1983-1989 to more than 3.5 percent in 1994-1996." (p377)

Eichengreen, Barry. "The Tyranny of the Financial Markets." Current History v96 n613 Nov 1997. p377-382. (ISSN0011-3530).

"All other things being equal, growth rates tend to fall gradually (over decades) as developing countries close the income gap with the United States (at around $27,000 per capita). A country at one-fourth the U.S. income level experiences a growth rate roughly 2.8 percentage points above the U.S. rate. If the United States manages per capita growth of about 2.0 percent per year, a country at $7,000 per capita (such as Thailand) could have per capita growth around 4.8 percent per year, equivalent to aggregate GDP growth of 6.5 percent to 7.0 percent per year. When the income gap narrows to around half the U.S. level, growth diminishes by about 1.4 percent per year, so a country at around $13,500 might be expected to have a per capita growth rate near 3.4 percent per year." (p49)

Radelet, Steven/Sachs, Jeffrey. "Asia's Reemergence." Foreign Affairs v76 n6 Nov-Dec 1997. p44-59. (ISSN0015-7120).

ECONOMIC INFRASTRUCTURE

see INFRASTRUCTURE (ECONOMICS)

ECTOPIC PREGNANCY--UNITED STATES

"Ectopic pregnancy usually results from partial tubal blockage associated with PID [pelvic inflammatory disease]. [In the U.S.,] in 1992, the estimated number of ectopic pregnancies was 108,800, or one in 50 pregnancies. In the same year, approximately 9 percent of all pregnancy-related deaths were a result of ectopic pregnancy, making ectopic pregnancy one of the leading and most preventable causes of maternal death during pregnancy." (p5)

The Committee on Prevention and Control of STDs. Institute of Medicine. "The Hidden Epidemic: Confronting Sexually Transmitted Diseases." SIECUS Report v25 n3 Feb-Mar 1997. p4-14. (ISSN0091-3995).

ECUADOR--ECONOMIC CONDITIONS

According to Ecuadorian "government estimates, 47 percent of the population lived at or below the official poverty line in 1975; by 1995, that figure climbed to 67 percent....Up to 60 percent of the [oil] revenues remaining in the country have gone to pay interest on the foreign debt." (p10)

Fieweger, Mary Ellen. "Development Struggle: The Copper Concession." Toward Freedom v46 n5 Sep-Oct 1997. p9-11. (ISSN0048-9898).

EDUCATION (v26)

see also AFRO-AMERICANS--EDUCATION; ASIAN AMERICANS--EDUCATION; BLIND--EDUCATION; CHILDBIRTH--EDUCATION; COMPUTERS--EDUCATION; DISCRIMINATION IN EDUCATION; FEDERAL AID TO EDUCATION; GIRLS--EDUCATION; FERTILITY, HUMAN--EDUCATION; FOREIGN STUDY; HANDICAPPED--EDUCATION; HIGH SCHOOL STUDENTS--EDUCATION; HISPANIC AMERICANS--EDUCATION; IMMIGRANTS--EDUCATION; INDIANS OF NORTH AMERICA--EDUCATION; MARRIAGE--EDUCATION; MINORITIES--EDUCATION; NURSES--EDUCATION; POOR--EDUCATION; PRISONERS--EDUCATION; RUSSIA--ARMED FORCES--EDUCATION; SPECIAL EDUCATION; UNITED STATES--MANUFACTURES--EDUCATION; UNITED STATES. ARMY--EDUCATION; VOCATIONAL EDUCATION; WAGES--EFFECT OF EDUCATION ON; WOMEN--EDUCATION

According to the "1997 Report on the World Social Situation," "enrolment in primary and secondary schools has risen since 1960 from an estimated 250 million children to more than 1 billion. The enrolment in higher education more than doubled in the past 20 years, from 28 million students in 1970 to more than 60 million today. The number of literate adults has almost tripled, from approximately 1 billion in 1960 to more than 2.7 billion. However, despite enormous efforts to eradicate adult illiteracy, the absolute number of illiterate adults has increased from 877 million in 1980 to 885 million in 1995, the majority of which (872 million) live in developing countries." (p33)

"...But Severe Poverty Afflicts a Quarter of the World." UN Chronicle v34 n1 1997. p33. (ISSN0251-7329).

EDUCATION--ALBERTA

In 1994, Alberta "reduced the number of elected school boards from 181 to 66. The province's 530,000 students are served by 42 public school boards, 21 separate boards (for publicly funded denominational schools), and three francophone boards for French-speaking schools. The province provides all education funding--more than $2.6 billion in 1996-97--under a block grant system to the districts. Almost half of the money is derived from general revenues; the balance comes from residential ($661 million) and nonresidential ($665 million) property taxes levied by the province. Some $38 million in funding was also provided in 1996-97 for independent schools, home schoolers, and early childhood services that are privately operated. Per-pupil funding in independent schools is about one-third of that in public schools." (p29)

Pierce, Marie. "Report from the North." American School Board Journal v184 n9 Sep 1997. p29-30. (ISSN0003-0953).

EDUCATION--ARGENTINA (v26)

EDUCATION--ASIA

"In South Korea, the proportion of the school-age population enrolled in school increased from 54 percent in 1950 to 97 percent in 1990. In Indonesia over the same period, the increase was from 21 percent to 81 percent." (p3)

Mason, Andrew. "Population and the Asian Economic Miracle." Asia-Pacific Population & Policy n43 Oct 1997. p1-4. (ISSN0891-6683).

EDUCATION--AUSTRALIA (v26)

EDUCATION--BRITISH COLUMBIA

In December 1996, British Columbia's "75 public school districts were restructured into 59 districts serving 583,000 students....Independent schools receive public funds up to 50 percent of the per-pupil funding level for public schools, depending on the degree of compliance with provincial requirements regarding curriculum, teacher certification, and facilities." (p29)

Pierce, Marie. "Report from the North." American School Board Journal v184 n9 Sep 1997. p29-30. (ISSN0003-0953).

EDUCATION--CHINA (v26)

EDUCATION--ECONOMIC ASPECTS--UNITED STATES (v26)

EDUCATION--EMPLOYMENT (v26)

EDUCATION--EMPLOYMENT--QUEBEC (PROVINCE) --DURHAM (v26)

EDUCATION--EMPLOYMENT--UNITED STATES (v26)

EDUCATION--FEDERAL AID

see FEDERAL AID TO EDUCATION

EDUCATION--FINANCE (v26)

EDUCATION--FORMER SOVIET REPUBLICS--ISRAEL --TEENAGE IMMIGRANTS--ATTITUDES (v26)

EDUCATION--GREAT BRITAIN (v26)

In Britain, "National Opinion Polls carried out a survey for Microsoft electronic publishers on 900 pupils aged between eight and 16, to find out their level of knowledge....Almost 20 per cent had no idea that the Statue of Liberty was in the United States, nor that the pyramids were in Egypt. On being asked to identify Germany on a map of Europe, 58 per cent failed. Asked to find Edinburgh on a map, 72 per cent failed, whereas in Scottish schools the failure rate dropped to 62 per cent." (p18)

McWhirter, Norris. "News and Comment: Lest We Forget...: Moronification Rules, OK?" Freedom Today v22 n4 Aug 1997. p18.

EDUCATION--GREAT BRITAIN--FINANCE (v26)

EDUCATION--INDIA (v26)

"As of 1990, India earmarked 3.6 percent of its GNP to education, and this percentage was slated to go up to 6 percent by 1997....India spends less than half of its educational budget on primary education, choosing instead to subsidize secondary and university education. As a result, according to MIT [Massachusetts Institute of Technology] Professor Myron Weiner, 'India rank[s] second among the twenty-one largest developing countries in the proportion of its young people going on for higher education, but rank[s] fifteenth in overall literacy and twelfth in the percentage attending primary school.'" (p577)

Tucker, Lee. "Child Slaves in Modern India: The Bonded Labor Problem." Human Rights Quarterly v19 n3 Aug 1997. p572-629. (ISSN0275-0392).

"An estimated 33 million of...[India's] 105 million 6-10 year olds are not in school. In 1991, adult literacy rates for Indian women (34 percent) and for men (64 percent) were almost identical to those for Sub-Saharan Africa and far behind those in China--85 percent for women, 96 for men. Female literacy rates, on the other hand, rose twice as fast as those for men during the 40 years since 1950-51, when only 9 percent of all Indian women could read and write."

World Bank. "India Shows Mixed Progress in the War against Poverty." Press Release 26 Aug 1997. document-level access: <http://www.worldbank.org/html/extdr/extme/1449.htm>

EDUCATION--LATIN AMERICA (v26)

EDUCATION--MANITOBA

"The provincial government has delayed proposals to restructure schools in Manitoba, where 1995-96 figures show 56 school boards served 191,000 public school students and one francophone board served 4,000 students....About three-fourths of the province's portion comes from general revenues, and the balance--about $200 million in 1994-95--comes from the provincial Educational Support Levy on property. School boards levied some $310 million on property that year, and $24.5 million in provincial funding went to 55 independent schools." (p29)

Pierce, Marie. "Report from the North." American School Board Journal v184 n9 Sep 1997. p29-30. (ISSN0003-0953).

EDUCATION--MANITOBA--FINANCE (v26)

EDUCATION--MASSACHUSETTS--BOSTON--FINANCE (v26)

EDUCATION--MEXICO

"Today only 70 percent of Mexican children complete elementary education, while just 45 percent complete secondary level, according to...[an INEGI, the country's national statistics institute,] study. In Chiapas, in Mexico's far south, 27 percent of school-age children (6-14) don't go to school....In northern states, the average educational level is 10th grade, while the average in some southern states falls below Grade 4." (p6)

LaFranchi, Howard. "In Land of TVs, A Fair Tries to Boost Literacy." The Christian Science Monitor v89 n139 13 Jun 1997. p6. The Christian Science Monitor search engine: <http://www.csmonitor.com/plweb-cgi/iops1.pl> To retrieve this article, enter the following search: ED=19970613 AND literacy. In the "retrieved list," click the title that matches this record. (ISSN0882-7729).

EDUCATION--MICHIGAN (v26)

"Michigan's school readiness program serves about 15 percent of the state's approximately 145,000 4-year-olds, says Lindy Buch, early childhood education consultant for the state Department of Education....The number of 4-year-olds participating in the state program has grown from fewer than 700 in 1985 to 21,077 last year. Additionally, the funding has doubled to $3,000 per child since the program began in 1985. The program is budgeted to serve 21,644 children at $3,100 per child for the coming school year." (p4 secF)

"Children First: A Free Press Campaign: Early Years: Ready for School." Detroit Free Press 3 Aug 1997. p4 secF.

EDUCATION--NEW YORK (N.Y.)--FINANCE (v26)

EDUCATION--NORTHWEST TERRITORIES--YUKON

"About 16,000 students attend public schools in the Northwest Territories. There are three private schools, all in the capital of Yellowknife, with a total enrollment of 25 students. Private schools receive 40 percent of the per-pupil allocation received by public schools....Yellowknife has two DEAs [District Education Authorities], one public and one denominational. Both have powers similar to school boards, and both obtain 25 percent of their funding from local property taxes and the balance from the territorial government....There are no school boards in the Yukon. Each of the 29 schools enrolling a total of 6,000 students has a school advisory council to provide local input and direction." (p30)

Pierce, Marie. "Report from the North." American School Board Journal v184 n9 Sep 1997. p29-30. (ISSN0003-0953).

EDUCATION--PAKISTAN

In Northern Pakistan, "the most recent statistics indicate a literacy rate of around 15 percent, and 3 percent for females....The percentage of school-age children in school (participation rate) at the primary level is estimated to be 74 percent for boys and 35 percent for girls....Nearly 58 percent of teachers in primary and middle schools in the Northern Areas lack appropriate teaching credentials and have limited academic training....More than 30 percent of schools in AJK [Azad Jammu and Kashmir] are classified as 'shelterless' or 'dangerous.'"

World Bank. "Education Project to Improve School Quality and Access in Northern Pakistan's...Mountain Regions: Education...." Press Release 31 Oct 1997. document-level access: <http://www.worldbank.org/html/extdr/extme/1521.htm>

EDUCATION--QUEBEC (PROVINCE)

Quebec "has announced its intentions to reduce the number of school boards (from 158 to 70) and to seek a bilateral constitutional amendment allowing the government to move from denominational to linguistic-based school systems. The province now has 137 Roman Catholic, 18 Protestant, and three special-status First Nation boards serving the Canadian version of Native Americans. There are 1.3 million students in publicly funded schools....The province provides about 84 percent of school board revenues....Independent schools receive about 55 percent of their revenues from the province." (p30)

Pierce, Marie. "Report from the North." American School Board Journal v184 n9 Sep 1997. p29-30. (ISSN0003-0953).

EDUCATION--SASKATCHEWAN

In Saskatchewan, "there are 89 public, 21 Roman Catholic separate, eight francophone, and six joint school boards that serve both Catholic and public schools at the secondary level. Another 49 independent schools enroll some 3,000 students. The province provides about 40 percent of school boards' operating revenues. About $525 million are generated through locally determined levies." (p30)

Pierce, Marie. "Report from the North." American School Board Journal v184 n9 Sep 1997. p29-30. (ISSN0003-0953).

EDUCATION--TEXAS--SAN ANTONIO

In San Antonio, Texas "nearly 3,000 of the corporate-sponsored scholarships [from the nonprofit Education Partnership scholarship program] have been awarded since 1989, when the San Antonio-based initiative began. Sixty percent of the recipients are the first in their families to graduate from high school or attend college. Dropout rates for seniors have fallen 10 percent, and the percentage of students who graduate with B averages and good attendance has jumped from 19 percent in 1989 to 50 percent last year." (p13)

Baldauf, Scott. "Holding Power: Schools Try Tuning into Latino Ways." The Christian Science Monitor v89 n186 20 Aug 1997. p1,13. The Christian Science Monitor search engine: <http://www.csmonitor.com/plweb-cgi/iops1.pl> To retrieve this article, enter the following search: ED=19970820 AND ways. In the "retrieved list," click the title that matches this record. (ISSN0882-7729).

EDUCATION--UNITED STATES (v26)

According to the U.S. Census Bureau, "82 percent of all adults ages 25 and over have completed high school and 24 percent had completed a bachelor's degree or more. 82 percent of women 25 years and over had earned a high school diploma and 21 percent completed a bachelor's degree or more. Annual average earnings in 1995 for persons 18 years and over with a bachelor's degree as their highest degree were $36,980."

U.S. Dept. of Commerce. Economic and Statistics Administration. "Nearly Nine in 10 Young Adults Graduate from High School, Census Bureau Reports." Census Bureau Press Release 29 Jul 1997. document-level access: <http://www.census.gov/Press-Release/cb97-122.html>

"Although reading is the foundation for virtually all other learning in our country, it is estimated that 40 percent of America's fourth graders cannot read at a basic level. Likewise, nearly 40 percent of eighth graders in our country are not achieving at a basic level, and 76 percent are not achieving at a proficient level. According to a recently released Third

International Math and Science Study, 55 percent of U.S. eighth graders score below the international average in math." (pS8943)

Dorgan, Byron L. (Sen.-N.Dak.). "National Testing." Congressional Record. Daily ed. v143 n118 9 Sep 1997. pS8942-8945. section/page-level access: <http://thomas.loc.gov/cgi-bin/query/R?r105:FLD001:S08942:> (ISSN0363-7239). (X1.1A.105/1).

"In America today there are approximately 3 million teachers....We have about 111,000 private and public schools. We have 51 million students in secondary and elementary education....The student/teacher ratio is 1 to 17 and the average salary for the teacher ranges from about $21,000 to $38,000. The United States spends $286 billion on secondary and elementary education. Among the top 12 countries in the world in terms of education spending, Hong Kong, Japan, Britain, Sweden, and so forth, we rank No. 2. We spend approximately $6,000 per student in Washington, D.C. It is $10,000 in Utah." (pH7193)

Kingston, Jack (Rep.-Ga.). "More on Campaign Finance Reform and Education." Congressional Record. Daily ed. v143 n119 10 Sep 1997. pH7192-7198. section/page-level access: <http://thomas.loc.gov/cgi-bin/query/R?r105:FLD001:H07192:> (ISSN0363-7239). (X1.1A.105/1).

Based on a recent U.S. study, the percentage of the Even Start educational program "children rated average or above in their class by their current grade school teacher: 65 percent on overall academic performance, 77 percent on motivation to learn, 82 percent on support from parents, 87 percent on relations with other children, 88 percent on attendance, 82 percent on classroom behavior, 71 percent on self-confidence, 74 percent on probable success in school. After participating in high quality Even Start family literacy programs, we have some good statistics about the adults, the parents who are participating: 62 percent of those parents...received their GED [general equivalency diploma] or some other high school equivalency certificate; 50 percent obtained a job or a better job; 40 percent are enrolled in some form of higher education or training; 45 percent reduced the amount of public assistance they received because of their improved employment; 3 percent no longer receive any public assistance." (pH2248)

Goodling, William F. (Rep.-Pa.). "A Successful Educational Program." Congressional Record. Daily ed. v143 n57 6 May 1997. pH2247-2248. section/page-level access: <http://thomas.loc.gov/cgi-bin/query/R?r105:FLD001:H02247:> (ISSN0363-7239). (X1.1A.105/1).

In the U.S., "high school completion rates--now roughly 90 percent--and college graduation rates are the highest in history. One in four adult Americans has at least a bachelor's degree--the highest percentage in the world (and the percentage keeps getting higher). A larger percentage of 22-year-olds receive degrees in math, science or engineering in the United States than in any of the nation's major economic competitors. Although SAT [Scholastic Assessment Test] verbal scores declined over the years 1975 to 1990, the decline occurred chiefly because a larger percentage of lower-ranking students (those from the bottom half of their school classes) began taking the test. If the same population that took the SATs in 1975 had taken them this year, the average score would be significantly higher than it was then--and higher than it was in 1990. Because of reforms instituted in the 1980s, more American high school students than ever before are taking four years of English and at least three years of math and science. Far more are taking and passing Advanced Placement examinations (98,000 in 1978 and 535,000 in 1996)." (p2 secB)

Schrag, Peter. "Outlook: Commentary: Schools Disprove Myth of Failure." Detroit News 16 Nov 1997. p1-2 secB.

"A report from the Federal Interagency Forum on Childhood Family Statistics gives a statistical overview of the...[U.S.'s] young people. According to 'America's Children: Key National Indicators of Well-Being,' the percentage of high school graduates between 25 and 29 years old who earned a bachelor's or more advanced degree rose to 31 percent in 1996 from 22 percent in 1971. In 1996, 34 percent of white, 17 percent of black, and 16 percent of Hispanic high school graduates in this age group had a bachelor's degree or higher, and an additional 10 percent of white and 8 percent of both black and Hispanic high school graduates had an associate's degree but not a bachelor's. The high school completion rate for blacks increased substantially between 1989 and 1995, from 75 percent to 85 percent. For whites the rate rose from 88 percent to 90 percent, and for Hispanics from 57 percent to 63 percent....In 1995, only 7 percent of all 18- to 24-year-olds not enrolled in high school had earned a GED [General Equivalency Diploma] or alternative credential. The number of school-age children speaking English almost doubled between 1979 and 1995, from 1.25 million to 2.44 million." (p4)

"News Bits & Bulletins." NSTA Reports! v9 n2 Oct-Nov 1997. p4-6.

In the U.S., "among whites aged 25 to 29, median years of schooling increased from 10.7 in 1940 to 12.3 in 1960 to 13.0 in 1993 (U.S. Dept. of Education 1994...), or from high school dropout to high school graduate to some college education. And the majority-minority schooling gap (at the median) virtually closed over this same period, dropping from 3.6 in 1940 (10.7 vs. 7.1) to .1 years in 1993 (13.0 vs. 12.9)." (p4)

Alexander, Karl L. "Public Schools and the Public Good." Social Forces v76 n1 Sep 1997. p1-30. (ISSN0037-7732).

In the U.S., "per pupil expenditures at the pre-college level increased 2.5 fold between 1965 and 1995, from $2,600 to $6,300 (U.S. Dept. Of Education 1996...). Pupil-teacher ratios at the elementary level have declined from 28.4 in 1960 to 18.8 in 1993 (U.S. Dept. of Education 1996...)." (p11)

Alexander, Karl L. "Public Schools and the Public Good." Social Forces v76 n1 Sep 1997. p1-30. (ISSN0037-7732).

In the U.S., "federal officials predict that public and private school enrollment will hit a high of 52.2 million students this fall, about 800,000 greater than last year. Education Secretary Richard Riley has estimated that in the next decade, the nation will have to build 6,000 additional schools and hire 2 million more teachers. Enrollment is expected to peak at 54.3 million in 2007, according to a recent Department of Education report." (p12)

Hardy, Alexandara. "Back to School: As the Doors Swing Open, Schools Scramble for Teachers." The Christian Science Monitor v89 n194 2 Sep 1997. p12-13. The Christian Science Monitor search engine: <http://www.csmonitor.com/plweb-cgi/iops1.pl> To retrieve this article, enter the following search: ED=19970902 AND teachers. In the "retrieved list," click the title that matches this record. (ISSN0882-7729).

EDUCATION--UNITED STATES--COSTS (v26)

The U.S. "Congressional Research Service recently reported that for 1993, the last year for which data are available, the Federal Government provided a tax subsidy of $16.5 billion for the outgoing and capital costs of elementary and secondary education. The report indicated the Federal Government had tax expenditures of $1.4 billion for tax exempt bonds used for school construction, $6.1 billion for the exclusion of the portion of property tax payments from Federal taxation that go directly for education, and $9 billion for the exclusion of the portion of other State and local taxes that go directly for education." (pH7215)

Porter, John Edward (Rep.-Ill.). "Departments of Labor,

Health and Human Services, And Education...Appropriations Act, 1998." Congressional Record. Daily ed. v143 n120 11 Sep 1997. pH7206-7247. section/page-level access: <http://thomas.loc.gov/cgi-bin/query/R?r105:FLD001:H07214:> (ISSN0363-7239). (X1.1A.105/1).

In the U.S., "private expenditures for education in 1994 were $101.8 billion, 11.1 percent of all private social welfare expenditures. Of this amount, $59.7 billion was spent on higher education, $21.2 billion on elementary and secondary education, and $15.5 billion on commercial and vocational schools. Outlays for education have declined from 15.6 percent of total private-sector spending in 1972 to 11.1 percent in 1994." (p54)

"Private Social Welfare Expenditures, 1972-94." Social Security Bulletin v60 n1 1997. p54-60. (ISSN0037-7910).

EDUCATION--UNITED STATES--EXPERIMENTAL METHODS (v26)

EDUCATION--UNITED STATES--FATHERS

A new U.S. Department of Education report "says a father's involvement is crucial to student achievement, regardless of whether he lives with his children....In two-parent households where both parents were highly involved, 51 percent of the children got mostly A's. When only the father was highly involved, 48 percent of the kids got mostly A's. When only the mother was highly involved, 44 percent got mostly A's. When involvement was low for both parents, only 27 percent of the children got mostly A's." (p9)

"Before the Board: Dad's Role Is Key." American School Board Journal v184 n12 Dec 1997. p9. (ISSN0003-0953).

EDUCATION--UNITED STATES--FINANCE

"The U.S. average per-pupil expenditure is $6,327--a modest increase from last year's $6,098. Alaska has the highest per-pupil expenditure ($10,393), followed closely by New Jersey ($10,133). The two lowest are Utah ($4,086) and Arizona ($4,387)....On average, 6.9 percent comes from the federal government, 48.9 percent from state coffers, and 44.2 percent from local revenues." (pA25)

"Education Vital Signs: State of the States." American School Board Journal v184 n12 Dec 1997. pA24-A25. (ISSN0003-0953).

"New Jersey, New York, Alaska and Connecticut led all states in the amount of money they spent per student on elementary and secondary education in 1994, according to a new 50-state tabulation released...by the Commerce Department's Census Bureau. New Jersey spent the most on each student, spending $8,902, followed by New York, $8,162; Alaska, $7,890; and Connecticut, $7,629. The national average was $5,363. States spending the least per student were: Alabama, $3,777; Idaho, $3,602; Mississippi, $3,423; and Utah, $3,280."

U.S. Dept. of Commerce. Economic & Statistics Administration. "New Jersey Spent Most Educating Students in 1994, Census Bureau Says in New State-By-State Report." Census Bureau Press Release 18 Sep 1997. document-level access: <http://www.census.gov/Press-Release/cb97-151.html>

In the U.S., "a study by the Economic Policy Institute finds that per-pupil spending has grown only 0.7 percent after inflation between 1991 and 1996. And much of that extra spending--about 37 percent--went to special education, that is, to helping students with learning problems and other disabilities....Spending on 'regular' education fell by 2 percent in the 1990s." (p20)

"The Monitor's View: Throwing $$ at Schools?" The Christian Science Monitor v90 n18 19 Dec 1997. p20. The Christian Science Monitor search engine: <http://www.csmonitor.com/plweb-cgi/iops1.pl> To retrieve this article, enter the following search: ED=19971219 AND schools. In the "retrieved list," click the title that matches this record.

(ISSN0882-7729).

EDUCATION--UNITED STATES--FINANCE--PUBLIC OPINION

In the U.S., "with over 750 education programs run by more than three dozen different government agencies, voters are generally supportive of Republicans who have undertaken a one-year study to identify and eliminate ineffective, overlapping, and wasteful programs. Overall, 56% support such an effort (39% strongly) while 29% say Republicans are simply trying to cut education. Not surprisingly, men (61%) are more likely to support this approach than women (51%) although majority support among females is an important factor for lawmakers to consider....82% of Republicans are supportive compared to 56% of ticket-splitters and 34% of Democrats. However, the group most likely to say this approach represents a cut in education spending--women ages 18-34 (39%)--is just as likely to support the Republican initiative as older women (18-34, 52%; 60+, 50%). Further, support increases with likelihood of voting. Sixty-one percent of those who say they vote in all elections support this approach. Additionally, a majority (55%) of those who vote in most elections are supportive. Among those who vote in half of all elections or less, just 46% favor the approach while 35% call it an attempt to cut education funding." (p50)

Ferguson, Gary A. "Consensus in Education Reform?: Searching for Consensus in Education Reform." Public Perspective v8 n4 Jun-Jul 1997. p49-52. (ISSN1050-5067).

EDUCATION--UNITED STATES--MORTALITY (v26)

EDUCATION--UNITED STATES--PUBLIC OPINION (v26)

A Gallup poll released in August 1997, in the U.S., "found that 49 percent of the respondents favor government payment of all or part of tuition at private schools, including those that are church-affiliated, and 48 percent do not....According to a poll taken in June of this year, 57 percent of blacks favored tuition vouchers and 38 percent did not." (p3)

"Editorial: School Vouchers, Good Policy." America v177 n8 27 Sep 1997. p3. (ISSN0002-7049).

According to a Phi Delta Kappa/Gallup Poll, in the U.S., "half of the poll's respondents (48 percent) say the current emphasis on achievement testing is appropriate, and 28 percent say there is not enough emphasis. Only 20 percent believe the public schools are testing kids too much." (pA18) "Three-quarters of Americans favor having kids start school at age 5 or even younger if it would help prepare them to learn. Forty-six percent of Americans give their local public schools a grade of A or a B, and 56 percent of public school parents give their children's schools those marks. A majority of those surveyed (60 percent) says that a C is the lowest grade their child could bring home on a report card without causing them to be worried their child was doing poorly in school. Fifty-seven percent of public school parents say they would be more likely to side with the school than with their child if a teacher or principal reported the child misbehaving in school." (pA19)

"Education Vital Signs: Common Measures." American School Board Journal v184 n12 Dec 1997. pA18-A23. (ISSN0003-0953).

"According to the annual Phi Delta Kappa/Gallup Poll of the Public's Attitudes Toward the Public Schools released in early September [1997], the percentage of Americans who oppose allowing 'parents to choose a private school to attend at public expense' has declined. Forty-four percent of poll respondents favored the idea while 52 percent were opposed. This is significantly different than the results of the same survey done in 1993, when only 24 percent of respondents favored public funding of private school education while 74 percent opposed it....When people were asked in this study whether academic achievement in local public schools would improve, get worse, or remain the same after students left to go to private schools, 70 percent said achievement would 'remain about the same.' Seventeen percent thought improvements would be made while 11 percent believed achievement would actually get worse....When poll respondents were asked if they thought private schools should be required by the government to accept students that they might now reject, 78 percent thought the schools should be required to do so, while only 18 percent did not." (p18)

"People & Events: Voucher Support Grows, But Americans Still Harbor Reservations." Church & State v50 n9 Oct 1997. p18. (ISSN0009-6334).

According to surveys conducted by Public Agenda, a New York-based nonprofit organization, "three in five Americans say public schools don't focus enough on reading, writing and math, but only 19 percent of education professors felt it 'absolutely essential' that their teaching graduates emphasize 'correct spelling, grammar and punctuation in their teaching.' Similarly, 86 percent of the...[professors] said it was more important that kids 'struggle with the process of trying to find the right answers' than with 'knowing the right answers.'...Four out of five said the public's view of learning is 'outmoded and mistaken.'" (p14 secA)

"Outmoded and Mistaken?" Detroit News 5 Nov 1997. p14 secA.

A national survey conducted by American Viewpoint in February 1997 "found registered voters nearly unanimous (93%) in their desire for better teaching of basic subjects, involving parents more, and putting additional dollars directly into the classroom....In response to the American Viewpoint question, 'Should the federal government be involved in establishing a national test for reading and math,' 49% are in favor and 47% are opposed." (p49) "Sixty-four percent of respondents...said we should spend federal education funds on incentive packages--including monetary bonuses or other recognition--for teachers, administrators, and schools that achieve significant improvements in student academic performance. Agreement on this proposal cuts across party and income lines, and is equal among men and women. Only those age 60 and older are more likely to disagree with allowing federal funds to be used for such incentive packages." (p50)

Ferguson, Gary A. "Consensus in Education Reform?: Searching for Consensus in Education Reform." Public Perspective v8 n4 Jun-Jul 1997. p49-52. (ISSN1050-5067).

In the U.S., "November 1996 post-election research revealed that 31% of all 1996 voters said the first or second priority they would like the new Congress to address is education reform. Education reform is of particular concern to younger voters and, more interestingly, cuts across party lines. That is, education is the first priority for 18% of all Republicans age 18-29, for 23% of Independents in the same age group, and 27% of all young Democrats." (p51)

Ferguson, Gary A. "Consensus in Education Reform?: Searching for Consensus in Education Reform." Public Perspective v8 n4 Jun-Jul 1997. p49-52. (ISSN1050-5067).

In the U.S., according to an NBC News/WALL STREET JOURNAL poll conducted March 6-10, 1997 "58% said fundamental changes are needed in our education system while 36% believed that 'just some' changes are needed....86% believe our public schools would improve if students were required to pass standardized tests before moving to the next grade...." (p49) The "poll found support for the belief that the primary responsibility for improving the quality of education rests with local school boards (47%) rather than state government (25%) or the federal government (13%)...." (p50)

Ferguson, Gary A. "Consensus in Education Reform?: Searching for Consensus in Education Reform." Public Perspective v8 n4 Jun-Jul 1997. p49-52. (ISSN1050-5067).

According to a U.S. Gallup poll, "two-thirds of the public favors the proposal for placing a computer with access to the Internet in every public school classroom, and 57 percent supports Clinton's voluntary national tests of student achievement in reading and math....And when Gallup pollsters asked if people favored a standardized national test (leaving Clinton's name off the proposal), support jumped to 67 percent." (p12)

Chaddock, Gail Russell. "Learning: National Aims, Local Schools." The Christian Science Monitor v89 n208 22 Sep 1997. p1,12. The Christian Science Monitor search engine: <http://www.csmonitor.com/plweb-cgi/iops1.pl> To retrieve this article, enter the following search: ED=19970922 AND schools. In the "retrieved list," click the title that matches this record. (ISSN0882-7729).

EDUCATION--UNITED STATES--YOUTH--ATTITUDES (v26)

EDUCATION--VIETNAM (v26)

EDUCATION--WALES (v26)

EDUCATION--WASHINGTON (D.C.)

"In 1996, 12 percent of the classrooms in the District of Columbia did not have textbooks at the beginning of the year and 20 percent lacked adequate supplies. The D.C. public school system spends more money per pupil than any other district in America, and yet 65 percent of all D.C. public school-children test below their grade level. And 56 percent who take the Armed Forces qualification test...fail....The system has 1 administrator for every 16 teachers while the national average is 1 administrator for every 42 teachers....Two-thirds of the teachers report that violent student behavior is a serious obstacle to teaching. And 16 percent of students report carrying a weapon to school. Over 1 in 10 avoid school because they fear for their safety." (pS9915)

Coats, Dan (Sen.-Ind.). "District of Columbia Appropriations Act, 1998." Congressional Record. Daily ed. v143 n130 25 Sep 1997. pS9914-9925. section/page-level access: <http://thomas.loc.gov/cgi-bin/query/R?r105:FLD001:S09914:> (ISSN0363-7239). (X1.1A.105/1).

EDUCATION, BILINGUAL--CALIFORNIA

"California, with its burgeoning immigrant population, leads the country in students who are not proficient in English at 25 percent, compared with 6.7 percent of students nationally....At last count, about 1.3 million children in California--twice as many students as 10 years ago--attended some type of bilingual class....Only about 6 percent of children in bilingual classes in California are well prepared to move into English-speaking classes each year....And while bilingual education alone can't be blamed, Latino children have the lowest test scores of any ethnic group in California and--at 40 percent--the highest dropout rate." (p36)

Streisand, Betsy. "U.S. News: Is It Hasta La Vista for Bilingual Ed?" U.S. News & World Report v123 n20 24 Nov 1997. p36,38. article-level access: <http://www.usnews.com/usnews/issue/971124/24BILI.HTM> (ISSN0041-5537).

EDUCATION, BILINGUAL--UNITED STATES

"2.8 million elementary and secondary students in the U.S. are limited-English proficient (LEP)....Less than 1 in 5 teachers who currently serve LEP students are certified to teach LEP students." (p13)

"Dateline Migration: National: Bilingual Education in the U.S." Migration World v25 n4 1997. p13. (ISSN1058-5095).

In the U.S., "between $6 billion and $12 billion per year is spent on 2.6 million students in bilingual education. About $4 billion to $5 billion is spent in California, where the number of LEP [limited English proficient] students has doubled in 10 years." (p4)

Wood, Daniel B. "United States: California's Latino Divide

over Bilingual Education." The Christian Science Monitor v89 n251 24 Nov 1997. p4. The Christian Science Monitor search engine: <http://www.csmonitor.com/plweb-cgi/iops1.pl> To retrieve this article, enter the following search: ED=19971124 AND education. In the "retrieved list," click the title that matches this record. (ISSN0882-7729).

EDUCATION, HIGHER

see also COUNSELING IN HIGHER EDUCATION; MINORITIES--EDUCATION (HIGHER)

EDUCATION, HIGHER--ECONOMIC ASPECTS

see also COLLEGE COSTS

EDUCATION, HIGHER--ECONOMIC ASPECTS--UNITED STATES

In the U.S., "of the 7.2 million full-time students in higher education in 1994, almost half (3.5 million) attended four-year public schools, about a quarter (1.9 million) attended two-year public schools, and about a quarter (1.8 million) attended private schools, including research universities....[Michael McPherson and Morton Schapiro, authors of THE STUDENT AID GAME, divided U.S. college students for the years 1980 and 1994] into six income groups, ranging from 'lower' (with household income in those years under $10,000 in 1980 and $20,000 in 1994), through 'middle' ($15,000 to $30,000 in '80 and $30,000 to $60,000 in '94) and 'upper' ($50,000 to $100,000 and $100,000 to $200,000, respectively), to 'richest' (above $100,000 and above $200,000). Among students from upper-income families, 41 percent attended a university, public or private; among students from the richest families, it was 47 percent. For those from lower-income families, by contrast, only 13.5 percent did. The figures were effectively reversed for two-year public community colleges, with 47.3 percent of the lower-income students attending, compared with only 13.9 percent of the upper and 8.6 percent of the richest." (p80-81)

Caplan, Lincoln. "Best Colleges 1998: Contemporary Calculus." U.S. News & World Report v123 n8 1 Sep 1997. p80-82. article-level access: <http://www.usnews.com/usnews/issue/970901/1OPEN.HTM> (ISSN0041-5537).

EDUCATION, HIGHER--EMPLOYMENT--GERMANY (v26)

EDUCATION, HIGHER--EMPLOYMENT--GREAT LAKES REGION (v26)

EDUCATION, HIGHER--EMPLOYMENT--UNITED STATES

"Two-thirds of students awarded baccalaureate degrees in 1992-93 (67 percent) were employed full-time and not enrolled in school in April 1994, according to the first wave of a 12-year longitudinal study. Another 9 percent were out of school and in the labor force part-time, 12 percent were both enrolled and employed, and 6 percent were going to school full-time. Only 6 percent of the class of 1993 were neither employed nor enrolled a year after they graduated from college....Seventy-two percent of four-year college grads with a grade point average (GPA) of less than 3.0 were employed full-time, and only 13 percent were still in school. Yet only 61 percent of grads with a GPA of 3.5 and higher were employed full-time, and 24 percent were enrolled in college." (p5)

"Watching the Class of 1993." Forecast v17 n8 Aug 1997. p5. article-level access: <http://www.demographics.com/Publications/FC/97_fc/9708_fc/FC97083.htm> (ISSN0732-1597).

EDUCATION, HIGHER--GERMANY

"The highest academic degree awarded by German universities is the Doctorate, of which some 20,000 are granted annually. The wide range of degree programs on offer--some 200--constantly attracts more young people. The Federal Statistics Office counted 1,827,000 students for the winter semester 1996/1997. The downside of that is that there are two students for each place available. The number of students has doubled just since 1970. The number of those beginning to study as a proportion of the general population has...grown from 4% in the 1950s to some 36% today." (p26)

Schayan, Janet. "Universities: Studying in Germany." Deutschland n3 Jun 1997. p24-30. article-level access: <http://www.bundesregierung.de/.bin/lay/ausland/edu/edu.html> (ISSN0945-6791).

EDUCATION, HIGHER--GREAT BRITAIN

Great Britain has "182 higher education institutions, 1.6 million students, and an annual expenditure of some $16 billion. That's around $10,000 per student." (p14)

Daniel, John S. "Why Universities Need Technology Strategies." Change v29 n4 Jul-Aug 1997. p10-17. (ISSN0009-1383).

EDUCATION, HIGHER--HISPANIC AMERICANS

U.S.-born Hispanics "are more likely than other Hispanics to have completed at least four years of college--12 percent versus 8 percent in 1996--although the difference is smaller....Nearly 28 percent of the U.S.-born Latinos from a Central or South American heritage had completed college, compared with about 12 percent of those born abroad. Similarly, 28 percent of U.S.-born Cubans had completed college, compared with 17 percent of foreign-born Cubans." (p33)

del Pinal, Jorge/Singer, Audrey. "Generations of Diversity: Latinos in the United States." Population Bulletin v52 n3 Oct 1997. p2-47. (ISSN0032-468X).

EDUCATION, HIGHER--SWEDEN (v26)

EDUCATION, HIGHER--UNITED STATES (v26)

"According to the U.S. NEWS & WORLD REPORT'S 1998 AMERICA'S BEST COLLEGES guide, 23 percent of Americans over the age of 25 hold college degrees. That's more than twice the figure from 25 years ago, when only 11 percent were college graduates....Between 1983-1984 and 1994-1995, the number of master's degrees awarded in the United States rose from 284,000 to 405,000, and the number of doctorates awarded rose from 33,000 to 43,000." (p7)

"Fact and Fiction." Reading Today v15 n2 Oct-Nov 1997. p7. (ISSN0737-4208).

"Twenty-three percent of the total population age 25 and older had a bachelor's degree or higher in 1995 as compared with 19 percent in 1985 and only around 14 percent in 1975. Men with college degrees increased 48 percent between 1975 and 1995, whereas women experienced a 91 percent increase over the 20-year period. Twenty-seven percent of white men and 21 percent of white women had degrees in 1995....[The percentage of Afro-Americans with degrees] more than doubled between 1975 and 1995, rising from slightly over 6 percent to more than 13 percent....From 1975 to 1995, the percent of Hispanic men with bachelor's degrees rose 22 percent, from slightly over 8 percent to around 10 percent." (p33)

Yavarkovsky, Judith. "Historical Perspectives: College Graduates Age 25 and Older, By Sex and Race: United States, 1975, 1985 and 1995." Statistical Bulletin v78 n3 Jul-Sep 1997. p33. (ISSN0790-8334).

In the U.S., "5 out of 11 college students are over the age of 24, boosting overall enrollment from 12 million to 20 million students....[According to Glenn Jones, founder of the Jones Education Company,] 'There are 100 million adults learning in the US alone, but college systems can only serve 15 million of them.'...Nearly 79 percent of the high school class of 1998 intend to go to college, only about 61 percent actually enroll, and only 28 percent actually graduate from college." (p12)

Baldauf, Scott. "Learning: Cyber Classes Offer New Route to College Degrees." The Christian Science Monitor v89 n135 9 Jun 1997. p12. The Christian Science Monitor search engine:

<http://www.csmonitor.com/plweb-cgi/iops1.pl> To retrieve this article, enter the following search: ED=19970609 AND degrees. In the "retrieved list," click the title that matches this record. (ISSN0882-7729).

EDUCATION, HIGHER--UNITED STATES--FINANCE (v26)

EDUCATION, HIGHER--UNITED STATES--PUBLIC OPINION (v26)

EDUCATION, HUMANISTIC--UNITED STATES --PUBLIC OPINION (v26)

EDUCATION, PRESCHOOL--UNITED STATES (v26)

EDUCATION, PRESCHOOL--UNITED STATES --FINANCE

"According to data compiled by the Rand Corp., while 90 percent of human brain growth occurs by the age of 3, [U.S.] public spending on children in that age range equals only 8 percent of spending on all children....A look at the current Department of Education budget shows the stark funding disparity against early childhood education. Of $29.4 billion in current estimated education expenditures, only $1.5 billion or 5 percent is spent on children from birth to age 5. A new commitment to quality child care is a necessary response to the fact that children between the ages of zero and 3 are spending more time in care away from their homes. Almost 60 percent of women in the work force have children under the age of 3 requiring care. Many of these working families will not be able to find quality child care for their young children." (pS4952)

Kohl, Herb (Sen.-Wis.). "Concurrent Resolution on the Budget." Congressional Record. Daily ed. v143 n69 22 May 1997. pS4944-4994. section/page-level access: <http://thomas.loc.gov/cgi-bin/query/R?r105:FLD001:S04952:> (ISSN0363-7239). (X1.1A.105/1).

EDUCATION, SPECIAL

see SPECIAL EDUCATION

EDUCATION, VOCATIONAL

see VOCATIONAL EDUCATION

EDUCATIONAL CHANGE--MICHIGAN--DETROIT --PUBLIC OPINION (v26)

EDUCATIONAL DISCRIMINATION

see DISCRIMINATION IN EDUCATION

EDUCATIONAL LAW AND LEGISLATION--ONTARIO (v26)

EDUCATIONAL TECHNOLOGY--UNITED STATES

According to "Computers and Classrooms: The Status of Technology in U.S. Schools," a report from the Educational Testing Service, "about one-third of U.S. schools have videodisc technology, ranging from a high of 95 percent in Florida to a low of 10 percent in Mississippi. Also, less than 20 percent of U.S. schools have access to satellite technology, ranging from a high of 50 percent in Missouri to a low of 1 percent in Hawaii....About 40 percent of fourth-grade teachers use computers to teach reading, U.S. history/social studies, and geography, the report says. About one-third of eighth-grade teachers use computers to teach U.S. history/social studies and geography, but only 17 percent use them for reading." (pA22-A23)

"Education Vital Signs: Common Measures." American School Board Journal v184 n12 Dec 1997. pA18-A23. (ISSN0003-0953).

As of 1994, U.S. Senator Carl Levin said, "only 10 percent of Michigan teachers had at least nine hours of training in education technology. Kentucky and Washington led with 28 percent; the U.S. average was 15; Ohio and Oklahoma were last, at 8. Citing 1997 reports from Quality Education Data, a Denver research firm, Levin said: Florida and Wyoming had the fewest students per computer, at 5.9 each; the U.S. average was 10. In Michigan, the student-to-computer ratio is 11 to one. Nationwide, an average of 38 percent of schools have local area networks; in Michigan it's 31 percent. Colorado, Utah and North Carolina led with 57 percent each. Sixty percent of Michigan schools have Internet access, compared to the U.S. average of 64. Delaware, Hawaii, New Mexico and South Carolina led with a full 100 percent." (p3 secD)

Weeks, George. "City & Suburban News: Carl Levin Travels Michigan to Push Computer Access for Schools, Libraries." Detroit News 14 Oct 1997. p3 secD.

EDUCATIONAL TECHNOLOGY--UNITED STATES --COSTS

In the U.S., "truckloads of computers are being delivered to schools, adding approximately 300,000 to 400,000 computers annually to the estimated 4.4 million already in classrooms....Recent reports indicate that America's schools spent between $3.5 and $4.3 billion in 1995-96 on educational technology, or about 1.2% of K-12 expenditures. According to a 1997 study by the Educational Research Service (ERS)..., spending on instructional technology has nearly doubled in the past six years, from $2.1 billion in 1991-92 to about $4.3 billion in 1996-97. A Quality Education Data...survey projects K-12 technology spending to reach $5.2 billion in 1997-98." (p5)

Fulton, Mary. "Technology's Financial Crunch." State Education Leader v15 n3 Fall 1997. p5-6. (ISSN0736-7511).

EDUCATIONAL TESTS AND MEASUREMENTS (v26)

see also ACHIEVEMENT TESTS

"In 1995, researchers tested more than 500,000 students in about 50 countries, focusing on grades four, eight, and 12....Twenty-six nations were included in the fourth-grade report. Twelve scored significantly lower than the United States in math, six scored about equal, and seven--Singapore, Korea, Japan, Hong Kong, the Netherlands, the Czech Republic and Austria--scored significantly higher. One, Korea, scored significantly higher in science. The United States outperformed such nations as England, Canada, and Singapore in science, and such countries as England, Norway, and New Zealand in math. If the researchers were to conduct a 'talent search' of the top 10 percent of fourth-graders from the 26 nations, 16 percent of U.S. science students and 9 percent of the math students would qualify, said NCES [National Center for Educational Statistics] Commissioner Pascal D. Forgione Jr." (p12)

Hardy, Lawrence. "News Analysis: A Strong Showing for U.S. Students." American School Board Journal v184 n8 Aug 1997. p12-13. (ISSN0003-0953).

EDUCATIONAL TESTS AND MEASUREMENTS --CALIFORNIA--LOS ANGELES--MINORITIES

In the 100 schools in the Los Angeles Unified School District "with the lowest test scores, white students account for only 1.6 percent, according to a recent LOS ANGELES TIMES survey of the district's 100 'lowest performing' schools. Latinos accounted for 72.3 percent, blacks 23.2 percent and Asian/Pacific Islanders 9 percent....[The TIMES survey] found that more than 42 percent of the students in those schools came from families on welfare, compared to 30 percent in a sampling of 465 other schools in the district." (p33)

Bathen, Sigrid. "Los Angeles Unified School District." California Journal v29 n1 Jan 1998. p32-38. (ISSN0008-1205).

EDUCATIONAL TESTS AND MEASUREMENTS --MASSACHUSETTS--BOSTON (v26)

EDUCATIONAL TESTS AND MEASUREMENTS--MICHIGAN (v26)

In the Van Buren Public Schools district in Michigan, "from 1992 to 1995, the number of fourth-grade students achieving satisfactory scores on the Michigan Education Assessment Program tests increased by 56 percent in math and 41 percent in reading. For fifth-grade science, the percentage of satisfactory scores rose 9 percent. Scores for 1996 and 1997 are not comparable to the earlier scores because the MEAP test changed substantially."

(p1 secC)

Kauth-Karjala, Marjorie. "Local: Superintendant Answers Critics' Contentions." Ann Arbor News 16 Jun 1997. p1-2 secC.

In 1997, "the average score for the 66,628 Michigan students who took the ACT [American College Test]--the college entrance exam taken by most state students--was 21.3 out of 36. The 959,301 students who took the test nationally scored an average of 21....In Michigan, 56 percent of students who took the ACT had a college-prep curriculum, which includes four years of English and three years each of math, science and social studies. Nationally, 61 percent took the college-prep curriculum....About 23.5 percent of test takers identified themselves as minorities, an all-time high. Scores of those students increased slightly, up 0.1 to 19.9 for Mexican-American/Chicanos, 22.5 for Asian/ Pacific Islanders and 20.1 for Puerto Rican, Cuban and other Hispanics. American Indians' scores rose 0.2 to 20.4. Black students' scores remained the same, at 17.9. White students scored an average 22.8, up 0.1." (p5 secB)

Walsh-Sarnecki, Peggy. "Local News: State Teens Exceed U.S. Average on Exam." Detroit Free Press 14 Aug 1997. p5 secB.

The findings from the second annual round of the High School Proficiency Test (HSPT) were released on June 5, 1997. In Michigan, "statewide scores on the controversial exams, given in January and February to the graduating class of '98, show an improvement of 5.2 percentage points in math, 6.5 in science and less than a point in reading. Math is the only category in which a majority of Michigan's high school juniors got a score described as 'proficient.' Among the 110,000 juniors who took the challenging test, fewer than one-third mastered the writing test--a 4-percentage point dip from last year's scores." (p1 secA)

Hornbeck, Mark. "Math, Reading and Science Proficiency Tests Improve: Writing Skills Get Worse; Some Say It's Too Tough." Detroit News 5 Jun 1997. p1 secA.

EDUCATIONAL TESTS AND MEASUREMENTS--UNITED STATES (v26)

According to the National Assessment of Educational Progress, in the U.S., "only 6 percent of 17-year-olds 'can synthesize and learn from specialized reading materials,' according to the 1996 report. That percentage has stayed relatively the same for the past 25 years. Less than half (39 percent) of 17-year-olds 'can find, understand, summarize, and explain relatively complicated information'--a percentage that has also remained stagnant over the past 25 years....Only 2 percent of 11th-graders 'can write effective responses containing supportive details and discussion.' That figure has hovered around 2 percent since 1984. The percentage of students who 'can write complete responses containing sufficient information' has actually declined since 1984--from 39 percent to 31 percent, according to the report....In math, 67 percent mastered the upper-level skills, and in science, 60 percent of 17-year-old students were able to master the upper-level skills." (pA21)

"Education Vital Signs: Common Measures." American School Board Journal v184 n12 Dec 1997. pA18-A23. (ISSN0003-0953).

The National Assessment of Educational Progress 1996 Science Report Card for the Nation and the States, released by the U.S. Department of Education's National Center for Education Statistics, "gathered detailed information about what our nation's fourth, eighth, and 12th graders know and can do in science....In 19 of the 44 jurisdictions, the average score for eighth graders was higher than the national average of 148, while 11 jurisdictions performed at or around the national average; 14 performed below 148....In the grade four floating pencil task, just over 25 percent of the students could distinguish salt water from fresh water and give a totally complete explanation. Another 45 percent gave a partial answer; In a grade 8 salt solution task, about 40 percent of students carried out the measurement completely and successfully, and another 37 percent carried it out, but had less than complete level of performance; 12th graders were asked to separate five components in a mixture and explain how they did it. About one fourth of the 12th graders were able to give a complete response explaining the steps that led to the separation of all components in the mixture. Another 32 percent described how to separate 3 of the 5 components."

U.S. National Center for Education Statistics. "Latest Science Assessment Emphasizes 'Hands On' Experiments." News Release 2 May 1997. document-level access: <http://www.ed.gov/PressReleases/05-1997/science9.html>

EDUCATIONAL TESTS AND MEASUREMENTS--UNITED STATES--GIRLS (v26)

EDUCATIONAL TESTS AND MEASUREMENTS--UNITED STATES--TEACHERS--ATTITUDES (v26)

EDUCATIONAL VOUCHERS--AFRO-AMERICANS --ATTITUDES (v26)

In the U.S., a poll taken in March 1997 "by the Joint Center for Political and Economic Studies found that 57.3 percent of blacks now support the idea of school vouchers, a jump of 10 points in just one year. The poll also revealed stark divisions within the black community. While 86.5 percent of African-Americans from ages 26 to 35--the prime ages of early child-rearing--supported vouchers, only 19 percent of those older than 65 did." (p11)

Muwakkil, Salim. "Color Blind: School Choice: Do Vouchers Help or Harm Black Children?" In These Times v22 n3 11 Jan 1998. p11-12. (ISSN0160-5992).

EDUCATIONAL VOUCHERS--UNITED STATES--PUBLIC OPINION (v26)

EEL FISHERIES--CANADA--MAINE (v26)

EEL FISHERIES--MAINE (v26)

EGG TRADE (v26)

EGG TRADE--UNITED STATES (v26)

EGGPLANT INDUSTRY--MEXICO--UNITED STATES (v26)

EGGS AS FOOD--UNITED STATES (v26)

In the U.S., "according to the Menu Census survey, 5 percent of the households surveyed in 1992-95 ate raw or near-raw eggs at least once a year. Most of the times that those foods were eaten (about 40 percent) occurred between July and September, while April-June was the least likely season of the year such foods were consumed. The Menu Census survey also indicates that frosting accounted for 53 percent of the times that raw or near-raw eggs were used as ingredients....Salad dressing was the next most popular use (18 percent). The data suggest the typical consumer of raw or near-raw eggs tended to be a 15- to 24-year-old white male who lived in the West. He came from a household earning an annual income of $15,000-$24,999 or $50,000 and above....In...[the Food Safety Survey], 53 percent of the respondents said they had ever eaten a food containing raw eggs, such as homemade cookie batter and homemade ice cream. Of those, 27 percent mentioned cookie batter as a specific raw egg food...." (p29)

Lin, C. -T. Jordan/Morales, Roberta A./Ralston, Katherine/ U.S. Dept. of Agriculture. Economic Research Service. "Food Safety: Raw and Undercooked Eggs: A Danger of Salmonellosis." Food Review v20 n1 Jan-Apr 1997. p27-32. (ISSN1056-327X).

In the U.S., according to the 1996-1997 Food Consumption and Preparation Diary "survey, 27 percent of all egg dishes consumed were undercooked--described as either 'runny yolk,' 'runny,' or 'runny white.' Each person on average consumed undercooked eggs

20 times a year. Eggs fried 'over easy' and 'sunny side up' accounted for almost half (49 percent) of the undercooked eggs eaten....Eggs fried 'over easy' and 'sunny side up' accounted for over one-quarter (27 percent) of all eggs consumed by households participating in the FCPD survey, and nearly half of these dishes were described as 'runny,' 'runny yolk,' or 'runny white.' Scrambled eggs and omelets accounted for only 29 percent of undercooked eggs....Based on the combined data of the CSFII [Continuing Survey of Food Intakes by Individuals] and the FCPD survey, teenage boys and adult men (13-64 years old) and elderly women (over 65 years) had the highest frequencies of consuming undercooked egg dishes, at 23 and 21 times per year, respectively...." (p30-31)

Lin, C. -T. Jordan/Morales, Roberta A./Ralston, Katherine/ U.S. Dept. of Agriculture. Economic Research Service. "Food Safety: Raw and Undercooked Eggs: A Danger of Salmonellosis." Food Review v20 n1 Jan-Apr 1997. p27-32. (ISSN1056-327X).

EGYPT (v26)

EGYPT--ECONOMIC CONDITIONS (v26)

"Egypt's GNP grew at an average annual rate of 5.6 percent between 1974 and 1993....The country's external debt...grew from about 30 percent of GNP in 1974, peaked at 170 percent in 1988, then fell back to a little more than 100 percent by 1994....As a proportion of gross domestic product, manufacturing has declined from 18 percent in 1974 to 15 percent in 1995...." (p51) "Since 1988, Egypt's "GNP has fallen by 0.2 percent a year." (p52)

U.S. Congressional Budget Office. "The Challenge of Development: Illustrations from Eight Countries." The Role of Foreign Aid in Development May 1997. p39-56.

"Egypt has reaped real dividends of economic reform: Its foreign currency reserves, $600 million not so long ago, have risen to $19 billion. Inflation has fallen from 22 percent in 1990 to 7 percent. And the budget deficit, once 16 or 17 percent of gross national product, has shrunk to 1 percent." (p40)

Ajami, Fouad. "Commentary: The Region Left Behind." U.S. News & World Report v123 n4 28 Jul 1997. p40. article-level access: <http://www.usnews.com/usnews/issue/970728/28FOUA.HTM> (ISSN0041-5537).

EGYPT--ISRAEL--ARMED FORCES--APPROPRIATIONS AND EXPENDITURES (v26)

EGYPT--SOCIAL CONDITIONS

"Egypt is the Middle East's most populous nation. Two in five Egyptians live in cities. Slightly more than half cannot read or write. One in 13 owns a radio, and 1 in 45 has a television--fed by the world through five satellite receivers. The nation circulates more than 2.2 million newspapers daily, to be read by 27 million of Egypt's 56 million people. In this nation, point-of-purchase and cinema advertising join outdoor advertising in reaching beyond the wealthiest 20 percent of the total population, which, however, accounts for 52 percent of Egypt's total consumer buying power...." (p59)

Cassino, Kip D. "A World of Advertising." American Demographics v19 n11 Nov 1997. p57-60. article-level access: <http://www.demographics.com/publications/ad/97_ad/9711_ad/ad971131.htm> (ISSN0163-4089).

EL PETEN (GUATAMALA)--ENVIRONMENTAL CONDITIONS

"Thirty years ago there were 16,000 people living in El Peten [Guatemala]. Today there are 360,000, and the annual population growth is a shocking 15-20 percent. With perhaps 50,000 migrants arriving each year, all seizing free stands of jungle, the rain forest is vanishing at a staggering rate. More than 40 percent of unprotected forests in the region have been 'severely degraded,' according to government estimates. Even the 1.6 million hectares of ostensibly protected jungle is under threat." (p10)

Woodard, Colin. "Reports: Guatemala: After the Killing." Bulletin of the Atomic Scientists v53 n4 Jul-Aug 1997. p9-11. (ISSN0096-3402).

EL SALVADOR--ECONOMIC CONDITIONS (v26)

ELDERLY PERSONS

see AGED

ELECTION CONTRIBUTIONS

see CAMPAIGN FUNDS

ELECTIONS

see also TRADE-UNIONS--UNITED STATES--ELECTION

ELECTIONS--AFRICA (v26)

ELECTIONS--ALBANIA

In Albania, "more than 10 parties have applied to get candidates on the ballots being printed...by the Organization for Security and Cooperation in Europe (OSCE), which will monitor the [parliamentary] election....Party candidates receiving more than 2 percent of the vote will win seats in the parliament....Armed soldiers will watch over international observers on election day. All told, more than 6,500 European soldiers have come to Albania, a measure that seems to have restored law and order in some areas." (p6)

Potter, Beth. "International: Albania in Passage: A Nation's Climb from Mob Rule to Ballot Box." The Christian Science Monitor v89 n148 26 Jun 1997. p6. The Christian Science Monitor search engine: <http://www.csmonitor.com/plweb-cgi/iops1.pl> To retrieve this article, enter the following search: ED=19970626 AND box. In the "retrieved list," click the title that matches this record. (ISSN0882-7729).

ELECTIONS--BOSNIA AND HERCEGOVINA

"More than 75 percent of Bosnians went to the polls [during September's municipal elections]....Of the 2.5 million registered voters--nearly half of whom are refugees--89 percent chose to vote for governments in their prewar municipalities. Thousands even crossed borderlines to vote in person." (p7)

Hockenos, Paul. "Bosnia: A Glimmer of Hope." In These Times v21 n24 2 Nov 1997. p7. (ISSN0160-5992).

During the September 1996 elections held in Bosnia and Herzegovina, over 1,200 Organization for Security and Cooperation in Europe "supervisors helped the commissions of every polling station and counting center in Bosnia and Herzegovina, and over 800 observers monitored the electoral process." (p360) "Of the roughly 120,000 refugees who were supposed to cross the boundary between the two 'entities' to vote in their home areas, only 15,000 did so on election day...." (p362)

Koenig-Archibugi, Mathias. "International Electoral Assistance." Peace Review v9 n3 Sep 1997. p357-364. (ISSN1040-2659).

ELECTIONS--FRANCE

In France's June 1, 1997 "legislative elections, the Socialist Party and its coalition partners, including the Communist Party and the Greens, formed a government under the leadership of Socialist Prime Minister Lionel Jospin....The [French] left won 315 seats out of 577, including 245 for the Socialist Party, 39 for the Communists, seven for the Greens (their first seats ever) and 24 for other left-of-center candidates. The right lost more than 200 of its 477 seats." (p6) "The new government reflects a new diversity on the French left. It includes two Communist ministers, one Green and one dissident Socialist. It features eight women out of 24, including three in top-ranking positions." (p7)

Cohen, James. "In Short: The French Left Rises Again." In These Times v21 n16 30 Jun 1997. p6-7. (ISSN0160-5992).

ELECTIONS--IRAN

Iran's President Mohammad Khatami "was one of four candidates--

out of 238--who were hand-picked by the Council of Guardians and allowed to run for election....Of 33 million eligible voters, 29 million (88 per cent) voted, an unprecedented number in Iranian elections. 20 million votes (70 per cent) went to Khatami, who did equally well in cities and in villages." (p108)

Afary, Janet. "The War against Feminism in the Name of the Almighty: Making Sense of Gender and Muslim Fundamentalism." New Left Review n224 Jul-Aug 1997. p89-110. (ISSN0028-6060).

ELECTIONS--UNITED STATES (v26)

In the U.S., according to the Voter News Service "exit poll, non-Hispanic white voters favored [Bob] Dole (46 percent) [in the 1996 presidential election] over [Bill] Clinton (43 percent). The president won because of overwhelming support among blacks (84 percent) and Latinos (72 percent)." (p43)

Pitney, John J., Jr. "Special Book Section: All Things Dull and Ugly." Reason v29 n7 Dec 1997. p42-45. (ISSN0048-6906).

ELECTRIC LIGHTING--MEXICO

The ILUMEX project is an end-use energy efficiency project in Mexico. "Since 1990...the national utility has been promoting the use of compact fluorescent lights (CFLs) through a series of small-scale projects. CFLs use 75 percent less energy and last 10 to 13 times longer than incandescent bulbs....Organizers hope to eventually distribute 1.7 million CFLs throughout the cities of Monterrey and Guadalajara....ILUMEX will directly reduce carbon dioxide emissions by 700,000 metric tons over the project's lifespan....Estimates show the project costing a total of $23 million. Currently, the Mexican government has allocated $10 million to meet expenses. The Global Environment Facility ($10 million) and Norway ($3 million) have contributed the extra funds." (p20)

"The ILUMEX Project." Environment v39 n8 Oct 1997. p20. (ISSN0013-9157).

ELECTRIC POWER--CANADA (v26)

ELECTRIC POWER--CHINA

"Thermal stations generate about 82 percent of China's electrical power. Hydroelectric stations, some very large and many small local stations, generate 17 percent of the power. Nuclear power stations now generate about 1 percent of China's electrical power output." (p16)

Crook, Frederick W./U.S. Dept. of Agriculture. Economic Research Service. "Input Supplies Adequate for 1997." China: International Agriculture and Trade Reports Situation and Outlook Series Jun 1997. p16-18.

"By the end of 1996, China's electric power industry ranked third in the world in installed electrical generating capacity (236,000 MW [megawatts]) and second in output (1750 billion kWh [kilowatt hours]). More than 80% of this amount of power stems from burning fossil fuel....With CNY 800 million ($100 million) allocated from the state economic and trade commission, wind turbines with capacities totalling 83 MW from Denmark, Germany and the United States have been installed this year in four major wind plants: Dabancheng in Xinjiang Uygur Autonomous Region, Huiteng Xile in Inner Mongolia, Kuocangshan in Zhejiang Province and Zhangjiakou in Hebei Province." (p31)

Dan, Zhang. "News from China: China Eases the Way for Steady Progress." Windpower Monthly v13 n11 Nov 1997. p30-31. (ISSN0109-7318).

ELECTRIC POWER--DEVELOPING COUNTRIES (v26)

ELECTRIC POWER--ENVIRONMENTAL ASPECTS --EUROPE

In 1995, "EU-wide, the biggest emissions rise was the 2.9% resulting from electricity generation; thermal power stations are responsible for over 30% of total emissions. This reversed the 1990-94 trend when such emissions fell by 6%. The '95 rise was due to ever-increasing electricity demand--up 12.9% on 1990--and despite an increase in supplies from hydro and nuclear sources. In particular, demand by the Households and Tertiary sector, which consumes some 55% of electricity, has risen by 17.5% since 1990."

Eurostat. "EU CO2 Emissions Rise by 1.7% in 1995." Press Release 27 Nov 1997. document-level access: <http://europa.eu.int/en/comm/eurostat/compres/en/8097/6808097a.htm>

ELECTRIC POWER--EUROPE

In Europe, "where conventional electricity generation plants waste the heat produced in the generation process, typically converting only 30%-40% of the fuel used into useful energy, CHP [combined heat and power generation] plants recover the heat for industrial or residential use and so achieve efficiency rates of 85%-90%....Use of CHP currently varies widely in the EU...generating 40% of electricity in The Netherlands but only 1% in Ireland (1994 figures)." (p17)

"Energy, Atmosphere, And Transport: Doubling of EU's CHP Proposed under Climate Strategy." Environment Watch: Western Europe v6 n21 7 Nov 1997. p16-17. (ISSN1066-6001).

ELECTRIC POWER--GREECE

"By the end of 1993, the mainland (interconnected) power system of the Greek Public Power Corporation (GPPC), essentially the sole producer and distributor of electricity in Greece, consisted of 32 thermal and 43 hydroelectric units located in West Macedonia, southern, and central Greece. The thermal-generating units account for 90 percent of the total generation of electricity, of which 78 percent is generated by lignite-burning plants....In 1991 the economically recoverable lignite reserves were estimated to be 4,000 million tons (550 million tons of oil equivalent)....Hydroelectric production, with an installed capacity of approximately 30 percent of the total capacity of the system, accounts for only 8 percent of the total generation of electricity in 1993. It has been estimated that the hydropower potential may reach 20 million megawatt-hours (MWh) per year while the wind potential is estimated to exceed 5 million MWh annually in mainland Greece and the Aegean islands." (p194-195)

Vassos, Spyros/Vlachou, Andriana. "Evaluating the Impact of Carbon Taxes on the Electricity Supply Industry." Journal of Energy and Development v21 n2 Spr 1996. p189-215. (ISSN0361-4476).

ELECTRIC POWER--INDONESIA (v26)

ELECTRIC POWER--NEW ZEALAND

In New Zealand, "electricity generation in the September 1997 quarter increased by 2.4 per cent to 9,523 gigawatt hours when compared with the same quarter of the previous year. Due to low hydro lake levels, thermal generation increased 9.3 per cent, while hydro generation decreased by 1.3 per cent to 5,957 gigawatt hours. Over the year to September 1997, electricity generation rose 0.7 per cent on the September 1996 year, with thermal generation increasing from 24 per cent of total electricity generation to 33 per cent. Between the June and September 1997 quarters, the electricity price index rose 0.8 per cent for household consumers and decreased 0.3 per cent for commercial consumers."

Statistics New Zealand. "New Zealand Energy Statistics--September 1997 Quarter." Press Release 2 Dec 1997. document-level access: <http://www.stats.govt.nz/statsweb.nsf/52518ce3e01f62f4cc256388000c48c0/8f5cccf6df0814734c25656000831341?OpenDocument>

ELECTRIC POWER--UNITED STATES (v26)

In the U.S., "coal produces 55% of our electricity....Nuclear is in second place with 22% of our electrical generation....Hydropower produces 10%....Natural Gas produces 10% of electricity generation." (pS11011)

Murkowski, Frank H. (Sen.-Alaska). "The Global Climate Treaty." Congressional Record. Daily ed. v143 n144 23 Oct 1997. pS11007-11011. section/page-level access: <http://thomas.loc.gov/cgi-bin/query/R?r105:FLD001:S11010:> (ISSN0363-7239). (X1.1A.105/1).

U.S. "electric utility sales of electricity to all ultimate consumers in the United States in May 1997 were 235 billion kilowatthours, 1 percent lower than sales during May 1996. Sales to industrial consumers totaled 86 billion kilowatthours in May 1997, 1 percent above the level 1 year earlier. Sales to residential consumers during May 1997 were 70 billion kilowatthours, 5 percent below the level of sales during the previous year. Commercial sales were 70 billion kilowatthours, 1 percent below the level of commercial sales during the previous year. In May 1997, other sales totaled 8 billion kilowatthours, 4 percent lower than the May 1996 level." (p93)

U.S. Dept. of Energy. Energy Information Administration. "Electricity." Monthly Energy Review Aug 1997. p93-102. (ISSN0095-7356).

ELECTRIC POWER CONSUMPTION--UNITED STATES (v26)

U.S. "electric utility consumption of coal during May 1997 was 68 million short tons, 1 percent higher than consumption in May 1996. Petroleum consumption (excluding petroleum coke) during May 1997 was 7 million barrels, 8 percent above the level of consumption in May 1996." (p93)

U.S. Dept. of Energy. Energy Information Administration. "Electricity." Monthly Energy Review Aug 1997. p93-102. (ISSN0095-7356).

ELECTRIC POWER PLANTS

see also NUCLEAR POWER PLANTS

ELECTRIC POWER PLANTS--ENVIRONMENTAL ASPECTS --UNITED STATES (v26)

"More than 55 percent of the electricity generated in the United States comes from coal-fired plants, and 80 percent of those plants have at least one boiler that does not have to meet current air standards...says the Environmental Information Center, a nonprofit advocacy group in Washington. 'These outdated plants generate more than 70 percent of our total nitrogen oxide emissions,' says EIC's Will Callaway." (p18)

Marks, Alexandra. "Will 'Greensneakers' Prevail?: Nation Holds Its Breath over Clean-Air Rules." The Christian Science Monitor v89 n138 12 Jun 1997. p1,18. The Christian Science Monitor search engine: <http://www.csmonitor.com/plweb-cgi/iops1.pl> To retrieve this article, enter the following search: ED=19970612 AND rules. In the "retrieved list," click the title that matches this record. (ISSN0882-7729).

ELECTRIC SHOCK THERAPY

see ELECTROCONVULSIVE THERAPY

ELECTRIC UTILITIES--CALIFORNIA

"More than 100 companies are registered to sell electricity in the US $20 billion California household retail market....Renewable electricity accounts for about 9% of California's household retail electricity market." (p7)

"Industry Watch: Coalition Launches Renewable Energy Ecolabel." Global Environmental Change Report v9 n19 10 Oct 1997. p6-7. (ISSN1049-9083).

ELECTRIC UTILITIES--ENVIRONMENTAL ASPECTS --UNITED STATES (v26)

ELECTRIC UTILITIES--EUROPE--COSTS (v26)

ELECTRIC UTILITIES--MICHIGAN--DETROIT

In Michigan, in nearly all communities except Detroit and Wyandotte, "Detroit Edison Co. provides power for both streetlights and homes and businesses....Warren, Detroit's largest suburb, pays Detroit Edison $2.4 million a year to power the city's 11,522 streetlights, according to a spokesman for Mayor Mark Steenbergh. In Wyandotte, with a population of 32,000, a power plant owned by the city provides electricity to homes and businesses and also to streetlights." (p8 secA)

"Detroit's Streetlighting System: Municipal Utilities: Few Cities Use Their Own Power." Detroit News 13 Oct 1997. p8 secA.

ELECTRIC UTILITIES--NEW HAMPSHIRE--POOR --COSTS

"Of the 50,000 households in New Hampshire, the average non-heating PSNH (Public Service New Hampshire) customer pays approximately 2.5 per cent of income towards the electric bill and the average heating customer on the PSNH system pays approximately 5 per cent....[The Community Action Agency] broke down the percentage of income going towards electricity into three categories: customers whose incomes were between 0% and 49% of the federal poverty level, customers whose incomes were between 50% and 100% of the federal poverty level, and customers whose incomes were between 100% and 150% of the federal poverty level. Non-heating low income PSNH customers paid 23.4%, 7.8%, and 4.7% of their incomes for electricity, respectively, while heating low income customers paid 47.4%, 15.8%, and 9.5% of their incomes for electricity, respectively." (p6)

"Electricity Developments: New Hampshire Public Service Commission Orders...Program...Consumer Protections." NCLC Energy & Utility Update v15 n2 Apr 1997. p5-8. (ISSN1070-9312).

ELECTRIC UTILITIES--SOUTH AFRICA (v26)

ELECTRIC UTILITIES--UNITED STATES (v26)

"Sales of electricity to all ultimate consumers in the United States in February 1997 were 249 billion kilowatthours, 2 percent lower than sales during February 1996. Sales to residential consumers during February 1997 were 90 billion kilowatthours, 6 percent below the level of sales during the previous year. Sales to industrial consumers totaled 81 billion kilowatthours in February 1997, less than 1 percent above the level 1 year earlier. Commercial sales were 69 billion kilowatthours, 1 percent below the level of commercial sales during the previous year. In February 1997, other sales totaled 8 billion kilowatthours, 5 percent lower than the February 1996 level." (p93)

U.S. Dept. of Energy. Energy Information Administration. "Electricity." Monthly Energy Review May 1997. p93-102. (ISSN0095-7356).

In the U.S., "during February 1997, electric utilties generated 234 billion kilowatthours of electricity, 5 percent less than in February 1996. Coal-fired generation totaled 135 billion kilowatthours, 2 percent lower than the February 1996 level. Nuclear generation totaled 51 billion kilowatthours, 9 percent lower than the level 1 year earlier. Hydroelectric generation totaled 30 billion kilowatthours, slightly lower than the February 1996 level. Natural gas-fired generation was 13 billion kilowatthours, 1 percent higher than the February 1996 level. Petroleum-fired generation totaled 5 billion kilowatthours, 44 percent below the level 1 year earlier." (p93)

U.S. Dept. of Energy. Energy Information Administration. "Electricity." Monthly Energy Review May 1997. p93-102. (ISSN0095-7356).

In the U.S., "during May 1997, electric utilities generated 243 billion kilowatthours of electricity, 3 percent less than in May 1996. Coal-fired generation totaled 136 billion kilowatthours, 1 percent higher than the May 1996 level. Nuclear generation totaled 47 billion kilowatthours, 15 percent lower than the level 1 year earlier. Hydroelectric generation totaled 33 billion kilowatthours, 3 percent more than the May 1996 level. Natural gas-fired generation was 22 billion kilowatthours, 13 percent lower than the May 1996 level. Petroleum-fired generation totaled 4 billion kilowatthours, 12 percent above the level 1 year earlier." (p93)

U.S. Dept. of Energy. Energy Information Administration. "Electricity." Monthly Energy Review Aug 1997. p93-102. (ISSN0095-7356).

U.S. "electric utility consumption of coal during February 1997 was 68 million short tons, 2 percent below consumption in February 1996. Petroleum consumption (excluding petroleum coke) during February 1997 was 7 million barrels, 48 percent below the level of consumption in February 1996." (p93)

U.S. Dept. of Energy. Energy Information Administration. "Electricity." Monthly Energy Review May 1997. p93-102. (ISSN0095-7356).

ELECTRIC UTILITIES--UNITED STATES--COSTS

"The average price of electricity sold to all ultimate consumers in the United States in February 1997 was 6.64 cents per kilowatthour, less than 1 percent higher than the February 1996 mean price. The price of electricity sold to residential consumers in February 1997 averaged 8.01 cents per kilowatthour, 2 percent higher than the February 1996 price. The price of electricity sold to commercial consumers averaged 7.43 cents per kilowatthour in February 1997, 1 percent higher than the February 1996 price." (p109)

U.S. Dept. of Energy. Energy Information Administration. "Energy Prices." Monthly Energy Review May 1997. p109-128. (ISSN0095-7356).

In the U.S., "on average, consumers in the Northeast spend $1,840 a year on electricity....The average consumer in the Northeast pays electricity rates that are almost 40 percent higher than consumers in the rest of the country." (p19)

Michael, William J. "Opinion/Essays: Electric Industry: Let the Competition Begin." The Christian Science Monitor v89 n179 11 Aug 1997. p19. The Christian Science Monitor search engine: <http://www.csmonitor.com/plweb-cgi/iops1.pl> To retrieve this article, enter the following search: ED=19970811 AND begin. In the "retrieved list," click the title that matches this record. (ISSN0882-7729).

ELECTRIC VEHICLES--UNITED STATES

"In 1912, there were 50,000 electric vehicles (EVs) in this country. Soon overtaken by the gasoline-powered car, EVs are back on the road today thanks to federal clean air standards and a California state mandate that requires that 10 percent of all cars sold in the state by 2003 be electric. EVs are powered by batteries, which can net the car from sixty to ninety miles on a single charge. It now takes several hours to recharge an EV battery, which owners can do at home or, by year's end, at more than 200 public charging stations." (p52)

"NRDC: Living Green: Cars for the Planet?" Amicus Journal v19 n2 Sum 1997. p52. (ISSN0276-7201).

ELECTROCONVULSIVE THERAPY--UNITED STATES

"A recent nationwide survey of psychiatrists in 317 [U.S.] cities found utilization rates of ECT [electroconvulsive therapy] to vary widely....Psychiatrists in a third of the cities reported no use of ECT. Use in the remaining cities varied from .4 to 81.2 patients treated per 10,000 population....More than 80 percent of patients receiving ECT in the United States are diagnosed as having affective disorders...." (p1537-1538)

Rosenbach, Margo L./Hermann, Richard C./Dorwart, Robert A. "Use of Electroconvulsive Therapy in the Medicare Population between 1987 and 1992." Psychiatric Services v48 n12 Dec 1997. p1537-1542. (ISSN1075-2730).

In the U.S., "between 1987 and 1992 the number of Medicare enrollees receiving ECT [electroconvulsive therapy] treatment increased nationally by 30 percent, from 12,000 to 15,560 patients. This represents a 20 percent increase in the rate per 10,000 Medicare beneficiaries, from 4.2 to 5.1. However, in relation to the number of mental health service users, the rate of use actually declined from 185.9 to 126.6 per 10,000 patients....Medicare-allowed charges for ECT services grew from $6.8 million in 1987 to $9.4 million in 1992, an increase of 38 percent. When adjusted for inflation, this increase represents a real growth of 12 percent. Average ECT expenditures per user increased from $565 to $603 (7 percent), but when adjusted for inflation, average expenditures actually fell by 14 percent....The proportion of patients receiving outpatient ECT, either alone or in combination with inpatient treatment, increased from 20 percent to 24 percent." (p1539) "Eighty percent of Medicare beneficiaries receiving ECT in 1992 had a primary diagnosis of an affective disorder....Another 9 percent were diagnosed as having schizophrenia." (p1540)

Rosenbach, Margo L./Hermann, Richard C./Dorwart, Robert A. "Use of Electroconvulsive Therapy in the Medicare Population between 1987 and 1992." Psychiatric Services v48 n12 Dec 1997. p1537-1542. (ISSN1075-2730).

ELECTRONIC BRAINS

see COMPUTERS

ELECTRONIC COMPUTERS

see COMPUTERS

ELECTRONIC FILING SYSTEMS--TAXATION--UNITED STATES (v26)

ELECTRONIC INDUSTRIES--SWEDEN (v26)

ELEMENTARY SCHOOL STUDENTS

see SCHOOL CHILDREN

ELEPHANTS--AFRICA (v26)

"Poachers killed more than 80 percent of elephants in Kenya and Tanzania in 15 years. Kenya's elephant population dropped from 130,000 in 1973 to 20,000 in 1988. By 1989, more than 70,000 elephants were being killed each year....CITES [Convention on International Trade in Endangered Species] put elephants on Appendix I of the endangered species list in October 1989, a move that outlawed all international trade in the animal's ivory, hides, and meat....Ivory prices plummeted and elephant populations are recovering, now estimated at about 600,000 across 37 African nations." (p6 secA)

Tucker, Neely. "Nation & World: A Thundering Showdown." Detroit Free Press 17 Jun 1997. p5-6 secA.

"Today censuses estimate that 500,000 elephants roam African forests and savannahs, but accuracy varies by as much as 50,000, as herds migrate across borders and countries count at different times. Field experts say it will take 50 years for populations to recover, not the eight that have elapsed since the [1989 elephant trade] ban." (p18)

Spence, Betty. "Opinion/Essays: Elephants and the Ivory Trade." The Christian Science Monitor v89 n139 13 Jun 1997. p18. The Christian Science Monitor search engine: <http://www.csmonitor.com/plweb-cgi/iops1.pl> To retrieve this article, enter the following search: ED=19970613 AND trade. In the "retrieved list," click the title that matches this record. (ISSN0882-7729).

ELEPHANTS--ASIA

"With a total wild population of 35,000 to 50,000, the Asian elephant (Elephas maximus) numbers less than one-tenth of its African counterpart. Although the Asian elephant did not suffer the ravages of excess poaching that reduced African elephant numbers by half in the 1980s, the erosion of its habitat over the past century has fragmented populations to the point that fewer than ten populations comprising more than 1,000 individuals are left throughout the species' range, greatly diminishing long-term viability." (pE1136)

Hemley, Ginette (Director, International Wildlife Policy). "Regarding the Asian Elephant Conservation Act."

Congressional Record. Daily ed. v143 n76 5 Jun 1997. pE1135-1137. section/page-level access: <http://thomas.loc.gov/cgi-bin/query/R?r105:FLD001:E01136:> (ISSN0363-7239). (X1.1A.105/1).

ELEPHANTS--KENYA

"A recent government survey of one region in Kenya found that 97 percent of peasant farmers 'strongly dislike' elephants. Since banning hunting in 1976, Kenya's elephant population has plunged from well more than 100,000 to 26,000, despite the ban and the putative protection of Kenya's famous national parks. Between 30 percent and 50 percent of its other wildlife has also disappeared since the ban." (p4 secB)

Sugg, Ike C. "Outlook: Commentary: You Can Put a Price Tag on Saving Africa's Elephants." Detroit News 6 Jul 1997. p4 secB.

ELEPHANTS--PROTECTION--AFRICA--COSTS (v26)

ELEPHANTS--ZIMBABWE

Since 1975, "Zimbabwe's elephants have increased by about 50 percent, from fewer than 45,000 to more than 65,000 today. During that same period, the amount of land in Zimbabwe managed for wildlife nearly doubled, from 12 percent to well more than 22 percent of the country. That increase represents more than 39,000 square kilometers, and it occurred entirely on private and communal land." (p4 secB)

Sugg, Ike C. "Outlook: Commentary: You Can Put a Price Tag on Saving Africa's Elephants." Detroit News 6 Jul 1997. p4 secB.

Of the 65,000 elephants in Zimbabwe, "the Inter Press Service (IPS) reports that each elephant consumes 300 pounds of food per day and millions of litres of water collectively in the drought-prone Southern African region. Nearly every day the region's press carries stories of people maimed or trampled to death by these animals." (p5)

"The Short Run: Wildlife Preservation: Too Much of a Good Thing?" Dollars and Sense n212 Jul-Aug 1997. p5. (ISSN0012-5245).

ELK--WYOMING

Today, the National Elk Refuge in Wyoming "has grown to 25,000 acres....Last winter, more than 11,000 elk ate 2,349 tons of alfalfa on the refuge. The feed cost the U.S. Fish and Wildlife Service and the Wyoming Game and Fish Department $323,000. The state of Wyoming also feeds elk at 22 feedgrounds in western Wyoming....Last year, more than 800,000 people visited the National Elk Refuge." (p12)

Bama, Lynne. "Jackson Hole Tries 'Unnatural' Elk Management." High Country News v29 n17 15 Sep 1997. p12. (ISSN0191-5657).

EMBARGO

"According to the U.S. Department of Agriculture, the five countries currently under total U.S. trade embargoes--Iran, Iraq, Libya, Cuba, and North Korea--will together account for roughly 11 percent of the world's wheat export market this year. This means that 11 percent of the world wheat market is off-limits to U.S. farmers....A number of studies have concluded that sanctions, both unilateral and multilateral, have worked less than half the time since the early 1970's. One of the most thorough and credible of these studies, from the Institute for International Economics, found that unilateral and multilateral sanctions together have succeeded less than 20 percent of the time since 1990." (pE2080)

Hamilton, Lee H. (Rep.-Ind.). "Introduction of the Sanctions Reform Act, H.R. 2708." Congressional Record. Daily ed. v143 n145 24 Oct 1997. pE2080-2081. section/page-level access: <http://thomas.loc.gov/cgi-bin/query/R?r105:FLD001:E02080:> (ISSN0363-7239). (X1.1A.105/1).

EMBASSY BUILDINGS--FRANCE--UNITED STATES (v26)

EMERGENCIES

see ACCIDENTS

EMERGENCY MEDICAL TECHNICIANS--UNITED STATES

"In 1997, the U.S. and its provinces have more than 805,000 EMTs [emergency medical technicians] and paramedics, according to Dennis Hitchens of the Florida EMS (Emergency Medical Services) Clearinghouse in Tallahassee, Florida. Fewer than two in ten held paying jobs in emergency services in 1994." (p22) "With 233 EMTs per 100,000 population, New York lags behind many other states in the ratio of these volunteers to residents. Minnesota has the largest concentration, with 835 EMTs per 100,000 residents. Alaska ranks second, with 725 EMTs per 100,000 population. In contrast, Hawaii has only 37 EMTs for every 100,000 residents." (p26)

Kate, Nancy Ten. "Exceptional Americans: Neighbors to the Rescue." American Demographics v19 n7 Jul 1997. p22,24-27. article-level access: <http://www.demographics.com/publications/ad/97_ad/9707_ad/ad97077.htm> (ISSN0163-4089).

EMERGENCY ROOMS

see HOSPITALS--EMERGENCY SERVICE

EMIGRANTS

see IMMIGRANTS

EMIGRATION AND IMMIGRATION (v26)

see also ARMENIANS--EMIGRATION AND IMMIGRATION; ASIANS--EMIGRATION AND IMMIGRATION; AUSTRALIA--EMIGRATION AND IMMIGRATION; CHINA--EMIGRATION AND IMMIGRATION; EUROPE--EMIGRATION AND IMMIGRATION; JEWS--EMIGRATION AND IMMIGRATION; NEW ZEALAND--EMIGRATION AND IMMIGRATION; RURAL-URBAN MIGRATION; UNITED STATES--EMIGRATION AND IMMIGRATION; UNITED STATES. DEPT. OF JUSTICE--EMIGRATION AND IMMIGRATION

"An estimated 2 to 4 million people migrate internationally each year....An estimated 125 million people or more, about one in every 50 people, are living outside their country of birth. In addition, some 18 million people, almost all in developing countries, have fled their home countries. About 15 million are formally recognized as refugees. An estimated 20 million more are considered to be internally displaced persons: they have fled their homes but remain within their own countries...." (p3)

Gardner, Robert/Blackburn, Richard. "People Who Move: New Reproductive Health Focus." Population Reports v24 n3 Nov 1996. p1-27.

The report "World Population Monitoring, 1997: International Migration and Development," "attributed 45 per cent of the overall population growth in the more developed regions of the world from 1990 to 1995 to net international migration. At the same time, international migration lowered by 3 per cent the overall growth rate of the population in the less developed regions. The number of international migrants worldwide rose from 75 million in 1965 to 120 million in 1990. Despite this accelerating growth, by 1990 international migrants accounted for just 2.3 per cent of the total population of the world. According to a related report..., while the proportion of international migrants among the total population of developing countries remained low (1.6 per cent of the total), international migrants constituted 4.1 per cent of the developed countries' population....By 1990, [the report]...said, Europe and Northern America were host to 25 million and 24 million international migrants, respectively; in the developing world, Asia hosted the largest number of migrants in the world--43 million in 1990." (p71)

"Your Papers, Please: International Migration: What Prompts It? What Problems Arise?" UN Chronicle v34 n3 1997. p71.

(ISSN0251-7329).

EMIGRATION AND IMMIGRATION LAW--UNITED STATES (v26)

EMPLOYEE FRINGE BENEFITS

see PENSIONS; SOCIAL SECURITY

EMPLOYEE FRINGE BENEFITS--MICHIGAN--CIVIL SERVICE--COSTS (v26)

EMPLOYEE FRINGE BENEFITS--UNITED STATES (v26)

EMPLOYEE OWNERSHIP--UNITED STATES

"Workers' direct ownership of shares in their company--amounts to some 8 per cent of total share ownership in the United States. The best-known example is the large private airline, United Airlines, 51 per cent of whose shares have recently been acquired by its workforce. But in fact United Airlines, with its 75,000 employees, comes only sixth in the list of the hundred largest US companies of this type. Some 15 million workers and more than 10,000 companies participate in such schemes in the United States, where legislation encourages them by making corporate donations tax-deductible for the purposes of employee share ownership." (p99)

Fazio, Hugo/Riesco, Manuel. "The Chilean Pension Fund Associations." New Left Review n223 May-Jun 1997. p90-100. (ISSN0028-6060).

EMPLOYEE PROMOTIONS

see PROMOTIONS

EMPLOYEES

see also ACTIONS AND DEFENSES--EMPLOYEES--UNITED STATES; AGRICULTURAL LABORERS; BLUE COLLAR WORKERS; CHILD CARE WORKERS; CHILD WELFARE WORKERS; COMPUTER GAMES--UNITED STATES--EMPLOYEES; CONVICT LABOR; COURTS--CALIFORNIA--OFFICIALS AND EMPLOYEES; HOME LABOR; HOURS OF LABOR; INTERNET (COMPUTER NETWORK)--UNITED STATES--EMPLOYEES; MENTAL HEALTH PERSONNEL; MIGRANT LABOR; SOCIAL WORKERS; UNITED STATES--OFFICIALS AND EMPLOYEES; UNITED STATES. NATIONAL AERONAUTICS AND SPACE ADMINISTRATION--EMPLOYEES

EMPLOYEES--ACCIDENTS

see INDUSTRIAL ACCIDENTS

EMPLOYEES--AUSTRALIA

In November 1996, "75 per cent of Australia's 6,857,400 employees had been with their current employer for one year or more. Of these, almost all (93 per cent) had experienced some change in their work in the previous 12 months, according to figures released...by the Australian Bureau of Statistics in the publication 'Career Experience, Australia, November 1996.' The most common changes reported were: more responsibility (37 per cent), new, different or extra duties (34 per cent) and changed hours (18 per cent). Other changes surveyed were: changed location (9 per cent), transferred (8 per cent) and promoted (7 per cent)."

Australian Bureau of Statistics. "Australia's Employment Experience--ABS." Media Release 27 Jun 1997. document-level access: <http://www.abs.gov.au/websitedbs/d3110125.nsf/4a255eef008309e44a255eef00061e57/aa9c2c6faed989664a2564c200798129?OpenDocument>

EMPLOYEES--DISMISSAL OF--BRAZIL (v26)

EMPLOYEES--RELOCATION--UNITED STATES --COSTS (v26)

EMPLOYEES--TENNESSEE

In Tennessee, in 1995, "full-time employees provided 96% of the paid-labor for sawmills, 79% of the paid-labor for agri-processors, and 61% of the paid-labor for farming operations. Part-time employees supplied 4% of the paid-labor for sawmills, 11% of the paid-labor for agri-processors, and 27% of the paid-labor for farming operations. Migrant employees provided almost none of the paid-labor for sawmills, 10% of the paid-labor for agri-processing firms, and 12% of the paid-labor for farming operations in Tennessee." (p7)

Pompelli, Greg/Danekas, Gene/Allen, Fred. "Ag Laborers--Who's Working Where and for What Wages?" Tennessee Agri Science n182 Spr 1997. p6-10.

EMPLOYEES--TRAINING OF--UNITED STATES

Eighty-eight "percent of US manufacturers report a shortage of qualified workers in at least one job category, says a recent survey of 4,500 companies by the National Association of Manufacturers (NAM)....About half of manufacturers spend at least 2 percent of payroll to train hourly workers, up threefold from 1991. Moreover, the portion of employees in formal training has swelled from 5 percent in 1987 to 16 percent today, says the American Society for Training and Development in Alexandria, Va." (p3 secB)

Tyson, James L. "Work & Money: Tight-Labor Economy Boosts Training." The Christian Science Monitor v90 n4 1 Dec 1997. p3 secB. The Christian Science Monitor search engine: <http://www.csmonitor.com/plweb-cgi/iops1.pl> To retrieve this article, enter the following search: ED=19971201 AND training. In the "retrieved list," click the title that matches this record. (ISSN0882-7729).

EMPLOYEES--TRAINING OF--UNITED STATES --COSTS (v26)

EMPLOYEES--UNITED STATES (v26)

EMPLOYEES--UNITED STATES--ATTITUDES (v26)

EMPLOYMENT

see also EMPLOYMENT, under specific topics, e.g., AGRICULTURE--EMPLOYMENT

EMPLOYMENT (ECONOMIC THEORY)

see also DISCRIMINATION IN EMPLOYMENT; UNEMPLOYMENT

The United States provides "jobs for 73.5 percent of the working-age population....[The number is] 69 percent in Australia, 67.8 percent in the UK, and 67.7 percent in Canada. On the other side, it is true that some European welfare states have still much lower employment/population ratios: 55.7 percent in Belgium, 59.5 percent in France, 64.3 percent in the Netherlands, 65.1 percent in Germany....The European group also includes Sweden, with an employment level of 71.1 percent; Denmark, which at 73.4 percent practically equals the U.S. record; and Norway, which at 74 percent is even ahead of the United States in terms of employment....Iceland...manages to employ 81 percent of its working-age population." (p9)

Scharpf, Fritz W. "New Democracy Forum: Can a 'Third Way' Work?: European Distinctions." Boston Review v22 n3-4 Sum 1997. p9-11. (ISSN0734-2306).

"Forty per cent of the labour force in Japan is self-employed, part-time or temporary, and the proportion is similar in the United Kingdom. Part-time employment has increased very rapidly since the early 1980s in France, Germany and the United Kingdom; in France temporary employment grew from 3 to 10 per cent of total employment in 1980-93." (p27)

Carnoy, Martin/Castells, Manuel/Benner, Chris. "Labour Markets and Employment Practices in the Age of Flexibility: A Case Study of Silicon Valley." International Labour Review v136 n1 Spr 1997. p27-48. (ISSN0020-7780).

EMPLOYMENT, PART-TIME

see PART-TIME EMPLOYMENT

EMPLOYMENT, TEMPORARY

see TEMPORARY EMPLOYMENT

EMPLOYMENT AGENCIES--UNITED STATES (v26)

EMPLOYMENT CREATION

see JOB CREATION

Using 1994 data, Global Biodiversity Assessment "analysts estimated that at least 5,400 species of animals and 26,000 species of plants are threatened globally. In the same vein, the 1996 IUCN [International Union for Conservation of Nature and Natural Resources] Red List classifies 5,205 animals as threatened. Using the most recent information, we can say that at least 11 percent of all bird species are currently threatened, along with 25 percent of mammal species, 34 percent of fish species, 25 percent of amphibian species, and 11 percent of plant species....The current rate at which closed tropical forests are being lost (approximately 10 million hectares per year, or slightly less than 1 percent) implies that the equilibrium number of species in those forests is falling 0.16 to 0.32 percent per year. If the current rate of loss continues for another 30 years, the equilibrium number of species would decline 5 to 10 percent." (p19-20)

Reid, Walter V. "Strategies for Conserving Biodiversity." Environment v39 n7 Sep 1997. p16-20,39-43. (ISSN0013-9157).

"Worldwide, at least 21 reptile species have completely vanished within the last 400 years....The 1996 World Conservation Union's (IUCN) 'Red List of Threatened Animals' reports that 20 percent of reptiles for which there 'is adequate information to assign a conservation status' are threatened with extinction: 3 percent of these are 'critically endangered;' 5 percent 'endangered;' and 12 percent 'vulnerable.'" (p22) "The scientists who compiled the Red List were only able to fully assess three of the six reptile orders: the crocodilians, the testudines (turtles, tortoises, and terrapins), and the lizard-like tuataras, each of which ranked high in the number of threatened species--43 percent, 38 percent, and 50 percent, respectively." (p24)

Youth, Howard. "Neglected Elders." World Watch v10 n5 Sep-Oct 1997. p22-29. (ISSN0896-0615).

ENDANGERED SPECIES--ALABAMA

Among Alabama's "remaining 3,800 species of plants and animals, more than one of every four are considered in danger of extinction." (p8) "Like many tropical systems of developing nations, the fauna is in an imperiled state, with 10 percent, 65 percent, 69 percent and 43 percent of Alabama's fishes, gill-breathing snails, mussels and turtles, respectively, considered either extinct, endangered, threatened or of special concern." (p9)

Stolzenburg, William. "Ecology Forum: Sweet Home Alabama." Nature Conservancy v47 n4 Sep-Oct 1997. p8-9. (ISSN0028-5200).

ENDANGERED SPECIES--ALABAMA--MOBILE RIVER BASIN

In Alabama, "the Mobile River Basin...once supported close to 270 kinds of fish and mussels, 77 of them found nowhere else. Its 120 species of aquatic snails were considered the most diverse assemblage in the world." (p8) "The Mobile River Basin has hosted the presumed extinction of 54 species of mussels and snails since European settlement and, over the last century, almost 50 percent of all extinctions within the continental United States." (p9)

Stolzenburg, William. "Ecology Forum: Sweet Home Alabama." Nature Conservancy v47 n4 Sep-Oct 1997. p8-9. (ISSN0028-5200).

The Galapagos "Islands--13 major ones and 115 smaller ones, 500 miles off the coast of Ecuador--are the prickly tips of underwater volcanoes that broke the surface some 5 million years ago." (p12) "Ninety-five percent of the Galapogos' reptiles, half of the birds and 42 percent of the plants are found nowhere else in the world." (p15) "'The Galapagos still have about 95 percent of their native (species of) flora and fauna,' says Thomas Fritts, a wildlife biologist with the National Museum of Natural History in Washington....Four of the 15 subspecies of Galapagos tortoises are gone, and a fifth is hanging on the flickering hopes of the aging Lonesome George. Three of seven species of rice rat have disappeared since the black rat of sailing ships scampered ashore. Seven of the 24 native animal species represented by bones and historical accounts on Isla Floreana have disappeared since humans arrived, reports paleontologist David Steadman of the University of Florida." (p16)

Stolzenburg, William. "Collision at the Galapagos." Nature Conservancy v46 n6 Nov-Dec 1996. p10-16. (ISSN0028-5200).

In the U.S., "every two years the Fish and Wildlife Service submits a report to Congress about the status of threatened and endangered species. Back in the early 1970s, the report described only 12 percent of the species as having 'uncertain population trends,' meaning no one knew what was happening to them. The latest count showed that 44 percent were in the unknown column." (p5)

Margolis, Jon. "Washington Watch: Feds Learn that a Man's Ranch Is His Castle." High Country News v29 n10 26 May 1997. p5. (ISSN0191-5657).

"Poland has cut its energy supports by $3 billion annually, which contributed to a decline in coal use of more than 30 percent between 1987 and 1994....Russia...has slashed fossil fuel subsidies by more than half since 1990, and in the six years since, its carbon emissions have dropped more than 30 percent." (p26)

Flavin, Christopher/Dunn, Seth. "Rising Sun, Gathering Winds: Policies to Stabilize the Climate and Strengthen Economies." Worldwatch Paper n138 Nov 1997. p5-84.

ENERGY CONSERVATION--UNITED STATES

"The US Environmental Protection Agency (EPA) recently announced the latest addition to its Energy Star programs--'Energy Star Small Business.' EPA has so far signed up 100 small businesses in 25 states and the District of Columbia to participate in the new program....EPA suggests that partners in the new program can potentially save 30%-50% on their energy bills by implementing efficiency improvements...." (p13)

"Regulatory and Policy Trends: US 'Energy Star' Program Continues to Expand." Business and the Environment v8 n8 Aug 1997. p13-14. (ISSN1052-7206).

"Each year U.S. businesses spend $100 billion operating commercial and industrial buildings. By using energy-efficient technologies and practices, they can reduce their energy use by an average of 35 percent, achieving savings of around $35 billion and substantial pollution reduction....A typical business that upgrades its lighting can expect to reduce costs between 25 to 45 cents per square foot....As of May 1997, more than 2,300 companies, nonprofit groups, academic institutions, and state and local governments had signed up to participate in the Energy Star Buildings and Green Lights Programs. Together, they committed to upgrading more than 6 billion square feet of building space. One and a half billion square feet of that space has already been redone. Cumulatively, these participants have already saved more than $600 million on their electric bills and eliminated 10.5 billion pounds of carbon dioxide as well as significant quantities of nitrogen oxide, sulfur dioxide, particulates, and heavy metals from the air....By purchasing an Energy Star home, which must be at least 30 percent more efficient than it would have to be to satisfy the national Model Energy Code, consumers will realize an average monthly savings of $50. And while a conventional computer, monitor, printer, fax machine, and large copier cost about $350 annually to operate, similar equipment that meets the Energy Star criteria costs only about $150--a savings of nearly 60 percent....Energy Star-compliant monitors now represent 93 percent of the U.S. market, printers 98 percent." (p28)

Dolin, Eric Jay. "EPA's Energy Efficiency Programs." Environment v39 n7 Sep 1997. p28-29. (ISSN0013-9157).

"The U.S. 'Green Lights' lighting efficiency program, which since 1989 has committed participants to upgrade the lighting on at least 90 percent of their floor space for which such improvements are cost-effective. The program now has 2,300 participants covering one in every 14 buildings, averages lighting energy savings of 48 percent, and in 1996 is estimated to have removed the annual equivalent of the carbon emissions of 400,000 cars." (p41)

Flavin, Christopher/Dunn, Seth. "Rising Sun, Gathering Winds: Policies to Stabilize the Climate and Strengthen Economies." Worldwatch Paper n138 Nov 1997. p5-84.

ENERGY CONSUMPTION (v26)

see also ELECTRIC POWER CONSUMPTION; TRANSPORTATION--ENERGY CONSUMPTION

"Most of the energy, water and transport services we pay for are wasted before we are able to use them. Only 3 per cent of the energy from a nuclear- or coal-fired power station becomes light in an incandescent lamp (about 70 per cent of the original fuel energy is wasted before it reaches the lamp which, in turn, converts only 10 per cent of the remainder into light). Some 80 to 85 per cent of the energy generated by burning petrol is wasted in the car's engine and drive-train before it gets to the wheels." (p31)

"Assessment: Civilization under Seige." UN Chronicle v34 n3 1997. p30-34. (ISSN0251-7329).

ENERGY CONSUMPTION--BELGIUM (v26)

ENERGY CONSUMPTION--CANADA (v26)

ENERGY CONSUMPTION--CHINA (v26)

ENERGY CONSUMPTION--DEVELOPING COUNTRIES (v26)

Biomass "fuels comprise 40 to 60 percent of total energy consumption, both industrial and domestic, in many developing nations. Household cooking alone accounts for more than 60 percent of total energy use in sub-Saharan Africa (exceeding 80 percent in several countries). Further, some poor families spend 20 percent or more of their disposable income on wood and charcoal or devote upwards of 25 percent of their household labor to collecting wood. Inefficient combustion of these traditional fuels results in high concentrations of pollutants that cause acute respiratory infections. These infections, in turn, are the most pervasive cause of chronic illness in developing nations and the culprit in an estimated 4.3 million deaths per year." (p12-13)

Kammen, Daniel M./Dove, Michael R. "The Virtues of Mundane Science." Environment v39 n6 Jul-Aug 1997. p10-15,38-41. (ISSN0013-9157).

ENERGY CONSUMPTION--ENVIRONMENTAL ASPECTS --SLOVENIA (v26)

ENERGY CONSUMPTION--EUROPE (v26)

"Energy consumption in the EU jumped 3.6% last year, growing more than twice as fast as the economy in general, according to provisional data from Eurostat, the Union's statistics office....Gross inland energy consumption rose last year in all EU member states except Italy (-0.7%), Spain (-3.8%), and Portugal (-3.6%). The biggest rises were in the Nordic countries, with consumption up 13.8% in Denmark, 12.6% in Sweden, and 10.3% in Finland....Crude oil comprises 43% of the EU's total energy consumption, followed by natural gas at 22%, nuclear energy at 16%, and hard coal at 13%." (p9)

"Energy, Atmosphere, And Transport: In Brief...: EU Energy Consumption Outstrips Economic Growth." Environment Watch: Western Europe v6 n14 18 Jul 1997. p9. (ISSN1066-6001).

"Energy consumption in the EU jumped 3.6% last year, growing more than twice as fast as the economy in general, according to provisional data from Eurostat, the Union's statistics office....Gross inland energy consumption rose last year in all EU member states except Italy (-0.7%), Spain (-3.8%), and Portugal (-3.6%). The biggest rises were in the Nordic countries, with consumption up 13.8% in Denmark, 12.6% in Sweden, and 10.3% in Finland, according to a report in...ENVIRONMENT WATCH: WESTERN EUROPE." (p4)

"Policy and Economics: EU Energy Consumption Outstrips Economic Growth." Global Environmental Change Report v9 n14 25 Jul 1997. p4. (ISSN1049-9083).

ENERGY CONSUMPTION--EUROPE--FORMER SOVIET REPUBLICS (v26)

ENERGY CONSUMPTION--GREAT BRITAIN

"Chancellor (Finance Minister) Gordon Brown announced two energy tax cuts likely to stimulate energy consumption and jeopardize Britain's ability to deliver on its target of reducing CO2 [carbon dioxide] emissions by 20% from 1990 by 2010. A levy on gas supplies was removed altogether, a change that will lower gas bills by around 2% from next April. [The] Labour [government] also made good on its pledge to cut value-added tax (VAT) on domestic fuel from 8% to 5%. VAT on energy-saving products is left at 17.5%, pending the outcome of a review by the Treasury (Finance Ministry) promised before the end of this year....The increase rate for fuel taxes will go from 5% to 6% above the level of inflation....The Treasury calculates that the transport measures will prevent emissions of 2.5 million tons of carbon by 2010. Research suggests, however, that UK drivers are willing to pay at least double the current price of gasoline before abandoning their cars, and recent government statistics show levels of road traffic rose by nearly 3% in 1996 compared with 1995, bringing total growth since 1986 to 36%." (p9)

"Energy, Atmosphere, And Transport: Few Immediate Green Measures in UK Budget." Environment Watch: Western Europe v6 n14 18 Jul 1997. p9. (ISSN1066-6001).

ENERGY CONSUMPTION--INDONESIA

"At present only 70% of Indonesia's 62,000 villages have

electricity. Indonesia's demand for energy has grown by 10% yearly over the last decade, a higher rate than the 2% annual growth of world energy consumption, said [director general for electricity, Endro Utomo] Notodisuryo. But the proportion of renewable energy in the total energy supply is still insignificant, at less than 0.1%." (p8)

"Wind Wire: Indonesia: To the Rescue." Windpower Monthly v13 n11 Nov 1997. p8,10. (ISSN0109-7318).

ENERGY CONSUMPTION--TURKEY

In Turkey, there "has been an increase in total energy consumption from 5.43 million tons of oil equivalent (toe) in 1963 to 43.69 million toe in 1992....The average share of transportation [energy] demand of 21.47 percent was lower than the OECD average of 28 percent in 1992, while the average share of the residential sector of 35.73 percent was higher than the OECD average of 19 percent because of the substantial use of noncommercial fuels in the Turkish residential sector." (p174)

Erdogan, Meftun/Dahl, Carol. "Energy Demand in Turkey." Journal of Energy and Development v21 n2 Spr 1996. p173-188. (ISSN0361-4476).

ENERGY CONSUMPTION--UNITED STATES (v26)

"A Department of Transportation study of the 50 largest urban areas in the United States suggests that nearly 4 billion gallons of gasoline a year are wasted due to traffic congestion--approximately 94 million barrels of oil....The annual economic loss to businesses in the United States caused by traffic congestion is estimated at $40 billion by the Federal Transit Administration....Public transportation is a lifeline for millions of Americans and deserves substantial funding for that reason alone. However, it deserves even greater funding when one considers that public transportation saves 1.5 billion gallons of fuel consumption annually in the United States and that each commuter who switches from driving alone to using public transportation saves 200 gallons of gasoline per year, according to government and private studies." (pS4680)

Specter, Arlen (Sen.-Pa.). "Statements on Introduced Bills and Joint Resolutions." Congressional Record. Daily ed. v143 n66 19 May 1997. pS4677-4682. section/page-level access: <http://thomas.loc.gov/cgi-bin/query/R?r105:FLD001:S04680:> (ISSN0363-7239). (X1.1A.105/1).

"U.S. total energy consumption in April 1997 was 7.3 quadrillion Btu [British thermal units]....Residential and commercial sector consumption was 2.5 quadrillion Btu in April 1997, up 2 percent from the April 1996 level. The sector accounted for 35 percent of April 1997 total consumption, about the same share as in April 1996....Transportation sector consumption of energy was 2.1 quadrillion Btu in April 1997, up 3 percent from the April 1996 level. The sector accounted for 28 percent of April 1997 total consumption, about the same share as in April 1996. Electric utility consumption of energy totaled 2.4 quadrillion Btu in April 1997, up 2 percent from the April 1996 level." (p23)

U.S. Dept. of Energy. Energy Information Administration. "Energy Consumption." Monthly Energy Review Jul 1997. p23-39. (ISSN0095-7356).

"U.S. total energy consumption in February 1997 was 7.5 quadrillion Btu [British thermal units]. Petroleum products accounted for 36 percent of the energy consumed in February 1997, while natural gas accounted for 31 percent, and coal accounted for 21 percent. Residential and commercial sector consumption was 3.1 quadrillion Btu in February 1997, down 6 percent from the February 1996 level. The sector accounted for 41 percent of February 1997 total consumption, down 1 percentage point from its 42-percent share in February 1996. Industrial sector consumption was 2.6 quadrillion Btu in February 1997, down 1 percent from the February 1996 level. The industrial sector accounted for 35 percent of February 1997 total consumption...." (p23)

U.S. Dept. of Energy. Energy Information Administration. "Energy Consumption." Monthly Energy Review May 1997. p23-39. (ISSN0095-7356).

"US total energy consumption in May 1997 was 7.1 quadrillion Btu [British thermal units]. Petroleum products accounted for 42 percent of the energy consumed in May 1997, while natural gas accounted for 23 percent, and coal accounted for 22 percent. Residential and commercial sector consumption was 2.3 quadrillion Btu in May 1997, down 3 percent from the May 1996 level....Industrial sector consumption was 2.8 quadrillion Btu in May 1997, up 2 percent from the May 1996 level....Transportation sector consumption of energy was 2.1 quadrillion Btu in May 1997, up 1 percent from the May 1996 level." (p23)

U.S. Dept. of Energy. Energy Information Administration. "Energy Consumption." Monthly Energy Review Aug 1997. p23-39. (ISSN0095-7356).

In the U.S., "energy consumption during February 1997 totaled 7.5 quadrillion Btu [British thermal units], 4.0 percent below the level of consumption during February 1996. Consumption of petroleum products decreased 4.4 percent, consumption of natural gas was down 3.5 percent, and consumption of coal fell 2.2 percent. Consumption of all other forms of energy combined decreased 6.7 percent from the level 1 year earlier." (p1)

U.S. Dept. of Energy. Energy Information Administration. "Energy Overview." Monthly Energy Review May 1997. p1-21. (ISSN0095-7356).

ENERGY CONSUMPTION--UNITED STATES--PUBLIC OPINION

"In 1997, 5 percent of Americans say a potential energy shortage is one of the top two or three things they are most concerned about, according to Roper Starch Worldwide. That's down from 46 percent in 1974, when energy supplies were short and prices high....In December 1994, 58 percent of U.S. adults said a shortage of energy supplies would be a serious problem 25 to 50 years down the road. That share is down from a peak of 68 percent in 1980, but it represents a substantial increase from 50 percent in 1984." (p6) "The average U.S. household used about 36 million British Thermal Units (BTUs) of electricity in 1995, but may consume almost 40 million BTUs in 2015." (p10)

Dortch, Shannon. "Tomorrow's Markets: America at the Plug." American Demographics v19 n11 Nov 1997. p6,8-11. article-level access: <http://www.demographics.com/publications/ad/97_ad/9711_ad/ad97113.htm> (ISSN0163-4089).

ENERGY CROPS--IOWA

Ed Woolsey, project manager for the Iowa switchgrass project, "points out that Iowa, with a population of only 2.7 million, spends over $5 billion annually on energy--and that number is rising. 'Iowa imports 96 percent of all raw feedstocks used for energy production,' he says....The Chariton Valley RC&D, representing a consortium of public and private partners, will grow switchgrass on 40,000 acres (16,000 hectares) of marginal cropland as energy feedstocks for 35 MW [megawatts] of cofired power. A 735-MW power plant operated by IES Utilities will be modified to accept the switchgrass, which will most likely be chopped and blown pneumatically into the boiler along with pulverized coal....Of the 735 MW, the goal is to cofire 5 percent switchgrass (the product of 40,000 acres [16,000 hectares]). In addition to the planned cofiring, project partners are looking at an option for 6 MW of capacity from switchgrass gasification with the possibility of using the resulting product gas in fuel cells." (p17-18)

Moon, Susan. "Sowing Seed, Planting Trees, Producing Power." Solar Today v11 n4 Jul-Aug 1997. p16-19. (ISSN1042-0630).

ENERGY CROPS--MINNESOTA

The Minnesota Valley Alfalfa Producers "project will produce 700,000 tons of alfalfa annually. Multiply that times $125 a ton and it brings $87.5 million into the rural community....Farmers in Minnesota have been growing alfalfa successfully for over a hundred years. They now produce about 5.5 million tons annually, most of which is used for livestock feed....Growing alfalfa offers the environmental advantage of offsetting the carbon dioxide production that results from using a fossil fuel....The MnVAP cooperative is an established commercial enterprise with 50,000 tons of product signed up and another 50,000 ready to come on line. The co-op is now processing and marketing alfalfa pellets made from the whole plant. The city of Granite Falls, Minnesota, donated 100 acres (40 hectares) of land for the power project and provided a loan guarantee. And the Minnesota State Legislature appropriated $200,000 to assist MnVAP in developing alfalfa production and processing capabilities." (p17)

Moon, Susan. "Sowing Seed, Planting Trees, Producing Power." Solar Today v11 n4 Jul-Aug 1997. p16-19. (ISSN1042-0630).

ENERGY CROPS--NEW YORK (STATE)

"A major goal for the Salix Consortium [led by the Niagara Mohawk Power Corporation] is to deliver willow feedstock at less than $2.00 per million Btu [British thermal units], without subsidies, by the year 2001. The first development site, New York State Electric & Gas Corporation's 108-MW Greenidge Station, has been converted to accept biomass fuels and is now using wood residues for 8 to 10 MW [megawatts] of its output. This will be followed by Niagara Mohawk's 600-MW Dunkirk Steam Station, with an anticipated 10 to 20 MW of biomass capacity from conversion of one 100-MW boiler (and probably two eventually)." (p19)

Moon, Susan. "Sowing Seed, Planting Trees, Producing Power." Solar Today v11 n4 Jul-Aug 1997. p16-19. (ISSN1042-0630).

ENERGY DEVELOPMENT (v26)

see also WATER RESOURCES DEVELOPMENT

ENERGY DEVELOPMENT--UTAH--SALT LAKE CITY

The Utah Department of Natural Resources's "new headquarters in Salt Lake City is designed to cost half as much to light, heat and cool as a typical office building, saving taxpayers about $50,000 per year in energy bills. And at a price tag of almost $10 million, the DNR project cost only about $300,000 more than what a conventional building would have cost." (p24) "Based on the modeling, designers expect the new office building to use about 43 percent of the energy predicted for a reference design that meets current energy codes....Lighting use will be cut in half and the cooling load should be almost 90 percent less compared with a conventional building....The heating load is about 10 percent greater in the DNR headquarters than it would be in a typical office....[Jim] Wingerden [a DNR energy engineer,] calculates that a building designed to the baseline (code) specifications would generate energy bills of about $100,000 annually. He expects the DNR building to require about half of that, which means an annual savings of $50,000....Because personnel costs are by far the largest expenditure associated with the building (accounting for $320 million out of $345 million over a 30-year life cycle), even a small increase in productivity can mean huge savings. With this in mind, the Utah DNR expects to save taxpayers close to $18 million over 30 years on its new building." (p26)

Miller, Burke. "Daylighting on the Cutting Edge in Utah." Solar Today v11 n4 Jul-Aug 1997. p24-27. (ISSN1042-0630).

ENERGY INDUSTRIES (v26)

see also COAL MINES AND MINING; ELECTRIC UTILITIES; GAS INDUSTRY; NUCLEAR ENERGY; PETROLEUM INDUSTRY AND TRADE; WIND POWER

ENERGY INDUSTRIES--AUSTRALIA (v26)

ENERGY INDUSTRIES--CANADA (v26)

ENERGY INDUSTRIES--DENMARK (v26)

ENERGY INDUSTRIES--UNITED STATES (v26)

In the U.S., "energy production during February 1997 totaled 5.4 quadrillion Btu [British thermal units] a 1.9-percent decrease from the level of production during February 1996. Coal production increased 1.2 percent, natural gas production decreased 2.9 percent, and production of crude oil and natural gas plant liquids decreased 2.1 percent. All other forms of energy production combined were down 6.3 percent from the level of production during February 1996." (p1)

U.S. Dept. of Energy. Energy Information Administration. "Energy Overview." Monthly Energy Review May 1997. p1-21. (ISSN0095-7356).

ENERGY SOURCES, RENEWABLE

see RENEWABLE ENERGY SOURCES

ENERGY TAX (v26)

ENGINEERING--GREAT BRITAIN (v26)

ENGINEERING--SWEDEN (v26)

ENGINEERING STUDENTS--PURDUE UNIVERSITY --WOMEN

"Female students accounted for 23 percent of the undergraduate engineering degrees awarded by Purdue [University] in 1995-96. As the time neared to confer degrees after the 1997 summer session, that figure approached 25 percent, up from 19 percent in 1993." (p9)

Lyon, Betsey. "Working to Encourage Women in Science." ChemEcology v26 n6 Sep 1997. p8-9. (ISSN0738-7776).

ENGINEERS--GREAT BRITAIN (v26)

ENGINEERS--ISRAEL (v26)

ENGLISH LANGUAGE (v26)

ENGLISH LANGUAGE--AUSTRALIA--PUBLIC OPINION (v26)

ENGLISH LANGUAGE--STUDY AND TEACHING--CITY UNIVERSITY OF NEW YORK

In the City University of New York (CUNY) community-college system, "students born outside the United States rose to more than 53 percent from about 46 percent between 1992 and 1996....More than half of CUNY community college students report annual household incomes of $20,000 or less....English is a second or third language for 56 percent of CUNY community-college students." (p12)

Siegel, Laura A. "Learning: Immigrants' English Gets Put to the Test." The Christian Science Monitor v89 n145 23 Jun 1997. p12. The Christian Science Monitor search engine: <http://www.csmonitor.com/plweb-cgi/iops1.pl> To retrieve this article, enter the following search: ED=19970623 AND test. In the "retrieved list," click the title that matches this record. (ISSN0882-7729).

ENROLLMENT, SCHOOL

see SCHOOL ENROLLMENT

ENTERPRISES

see BUSINESS ENTERPRISES

ENTITLEMENT SPENDING--UNITED STATES (v26)

ENTREPRENEURSHIP--AFRO-AMERICAN HIGH SCHOOL STUDENTS--ATTITUDES

"In a recent survey conducted by Gallup (1996) on black [American] high-school students' attitudes and knowledge with respect to entrepreneurship, the following provocative results were revealed....75% of black high school students rated their knowledge of entrepreneurship as fair to very poor....The average score of black high-school youth on basic entrepreneurship knowledge was 38%....84% of black high-school youth believe that there should be more entrepreneurship education in the schools....75% of black high school youth want to start a business of their own....80% of black youth believe it is very important for entrepreneurs to give something back to the community beyond providing jobs." (p206)

Kourilsky, Marilyn L./Esfandiari, Mahtash. "Entrepreneurship Education and Lower Socioeconomic Black Youth: An Empirical Investigation." Urban Review v29 n3 Sep 1997. p205-215. (ISSN0042-0972).

ENTREPRENEURSHIP--EUROPE, CENTRAL--EUROPE, EASTERN (v26)

ENTREPRENEURSHIP--GEORGIA--ATLANTA--AFRO-AMERICANS (v26)

ENVIRONMENTAL ACTION

see GREEN MOVEMENT

ENVIRONMENTAL ASPECTS

see AERONAUTICS--ENVIRONMENTAL ASPECTS; AIRPLANES--ENVIRONMENTAL ASPECTS; ANTARCTICA--ENVIRONMENTAL ASPECTS; ARAL SEA (UZBEKISTAN AND KAZAKHSTAN)--ENVIRONMENTAL ASPECTS; ATHABASCA (ALBERTA)--ENVIRONMENTAL ASPECTS; AUTOMOBILE INDUSTRY AND TRADE--ENVIRONMENTAL ASPECTS; BEACHES--ENVIRONMENTAL ASPECTS; BLUE-GRAY GNATCATCHER--ENVIRONMENTAL ASPECTS; CARBON DIOXIDE--ENVIRONMENTAL ASPECTS; CEMENT INDUSTRIES--ENVIRONMENTAL ASPECTS; CLIMATIC CHANGES; CORAL REEFS AND ISLANDS--ENVIRONMENTAL ASPECTS; CORPORATIONS--ENVIRONMENTAL ASPECTS; ELECTRIC POWER--ENVIRONMENTAL ASPECTS; ELECTRIC POWER PLANTS--ENVIRONMENTAL ASPECTS; EVERGLADES (FLA.)--ENVIRONMENTAL ASPECTS; FLORIDA KEYS (FLA.)--ENVIRONMENTAL ASPECTS; GOLF COURSES--ENVIRONMENTAL ASPECTS; INDIAN RESERVATIONS--ENVIRONMENTAL ASPECTS; LAND USE--ENVIRONMENTAL ASPECTS; LOCAL TRANSIT--ENVIRONMENTAL ASPECTS; MILITARY BASES, AMERICAN--ENVIRONMENTAL ASPECTS; NATIONAL PARKS AND RESERVES--ENVIRONMENTAL ASPECTS; OIL INDUSTRIES--ENVIRONMENTAL ASPECTS; PERSIAN GULF WAR, 1991--ENVIRONMENTAL ASPECTS; PERSONAL WATERCRAFT--ENVIRONMENTAL ASPECTS; PETROLEUM INDUSTRY AND TRADE--ENVIRONMENTAL ASPECTS; POLITICAL PARTIES--ENVIRONMENTAL ASPECTS; REFUSE AND REFUSE DISPOSAL--ENVIRONMENTAL ASPECTS; RIVERS--ENVIRONMENTAL ASPECTS; ROADS--ENVIRONMENTAL ASPECTS; STEEL INDUSTRY AND TRADE--ENVIRONMENTAL ASPECTS; SWINE--ENVIRONMENTAL ASPECTS; TONGASS NATIONAL FOREST (ALASKA)--ENVIRONMENTAL ASPECTS; TRANSPORTATION--ENVIRONMENTAL ASPECTS; UNITED STATES--ENVIRONMENTAL ASPECTS

ENVIRONMENTAL DEGRADATION (v26)

see also LAND DEGRADATION

"Current extinction rates are 100-1000 times higher than prehuman levels, and the expected extinction of currently threatened species could increase this rate by a factor of 10 (Pimm et al. 1995)....The spread of Polynesians across the Pacific Islands during the past 1000-4000 years resulted in the extinction of approximately 2000 bird species (Pimm et al. 1995, Steadman 1995)--15% of the world's avian diversity....European settlement in the Hawaiian Islands eliminated 84 plant species, almost 10% of the native flora of the islands, and an additional 133 plant species are threatened with extinction (Sohmer 1994)....The fynbos vegetation of South Africa has lost 36 species, and an additional 618 species are threatened with extinction (Pimm et al. 1995)." (p45)

Chapin, F. Stuart, III/Sala, Osvaldo E. "Ecosystem Consequences of Changing Biodiversity." BioScience v48 n1 Jan 1998. p45-52. (ISSN0006-3568).

Research sponsored by the U.S. "National Science Foundation concluded that the annual value of services provided by nature worldwide averaged some \$33 trillion--nearly twice the global gross national product of \$18 billion....Carbon dioxide in the atmosphere (the prime 'greenhouse gas' suspected of causing global warming) has increased 30 percent since the Industrial Revolution. Sixty-six percent of marine fisheries are overexploited or have reached the limit of the exploitation. Species are going extinct at least 10 times faster than in the millennia before modern-day humans." (p11)

Knickerbocker, Brad. "Conversations with Outstanding Americans: Jane Lubchenco." The Christian Science Monitor v89 n183 15 Aug 1997. p10-12. The Christian Science Monitor search engine: <http://www.csmonitor.com/plweb-cgi/iops1.pl> To retrieve this article, enter the following search: ED=19970815 AND lubchenco. In the "retrieved list," click the title that matches this record. (ISSN0882-7729).

Since 1992, "the world's population has increased by 450 million; deforestation has continued at a rate of more than 27 million acres per year. Over the next century, with polar ice melting, the oceans are expected to rise between two and three feet. In his speech to the General Assembly...,President Clinton said that island nations like the Maldives would disappear from the map while 9,000 square miles of Florida, Louisiana, and other US coastal areas would be flooded. An estimated 60 percent of the world's people live within 60 miles of the sea, and many of the largest cities are practically at sea level. The prospect is so frightening that 160 governments have signed a treaty seeking reductions of CO2 [carbon dioxide] emissions, with the level to be set at a conference in Kyoto, Japan, this December....The Europeans have pledged a reduction by 2010 of 15 percent from the level of 1990. And Britain, Germany, Austria, and Denmark have set a target of 25 percent....Water use has been growing at twice the 400 percent rate of population increase in this century." (p19)

Hottelet, Richard C. "Opinion/Essays: The Great Global Dilemma." The Christian Science Monitor v89 n152 2 Jul 1997. p19. The Christian Science Monitor search engine: <http://www.csmonitor.com/plweb-cgi/iops1.pl> To retrieve this article, enter the following search: ED=19970702 AND dilemma. In the "retrieved list," click the title that matches this record. (ISSN0882-7729).

ENVIRONMENTAL DEGRADATION--ASIA

Asia "has already lost 68 per cent of its original wildlife habitat and over 600 animal and 5,000 plant species are considered to be rare or threatened. More than 85 per cent of Asia's 170 million hectares of wetlands are either moderately or severely threatened." (p163-164)

Park, Jacob. "APEC and ASEAN: The Future of Asian Environmental Regionalism." Environmental Politics v6 n3 Aut 1997. p162-167. (ISSN0964-4016).

ENVIRONMENTAL DEGRADATION--AUSTRALIA (v26)

ENVIRONMENTAL DEGRADATION--CANADA

Canada's "wetlands have been reduced by 70 per cent to 80 per cent in some parts of Canada. Old growth forests are down by 85 per cent to 90 per cent in some areas. Tall grass prairie has diminished by 99 per cent since the earliest settlements." (p10195)

Knutson, Gar (MP-ON). "Government Orders: Canada Endangered Species Protection Act." Canada. Parliament. House of Commons. Debates. v134 n163 24 Apr 1997. p10191-10206. page-level access: <http://www.parl.gc.ca/hansard/163_97-04-24/163PB1E.html#10194> section-level access: <http://www.parl.gc.ca/hansard/163_97-04-24/163PB1E.html#CANADAENDANGEREDSPECIESPROTECTIONACT> (ISSN0704-5603). (X3-352E).

ENVIRONMENTAL DEGRADATION--CHINA--COSTS

"The economic burden of environmental pollution and ecosystem degradation in China was no less than 5 percent of the country's GDP in the early 1990s. The most likely conservative estimate falls somewhere in the range of 6 to 8 percent....These burdens greatly surpass China's recent spending on environmental protection. During the 1980s and early 1990s, annual investment in this area equalled just 0.56 to 0.81 percent of GDP. Only in 1996 did officials promise to raise spending on environmental protection to just more than 1 percent by the year 2000....The World Bank's latest study argues that China's actual per capita gross domestic product in 1995 was about $2,000. This rate implies a purchasing power parity rate roughly four times the official exchange rate. Using this conversion, the annual economic burden of air and water pollution would amount to about $50 billion...." (p36)

Smil, Vaclav. "China Shoulders the Cost of Environmental Change." Environment v39 n6 Jul-Aug 1997. p6-9,33-37. (ISSN0013-9157).

ENVIRONMENTAL DEGRADATION--ERITREA

"From 11 percent forest cover in 1952,...[Eritrea] was reduced by 1996 to less than half a percent....With up to 13 tons of topsoil stripped off every acre of land in the highlands, much of Eritrea is under attack by...the desert." (p16) "The central government has supervised the planting of 35 million seedlings across the country since 1991, while local communities have put in close to 3 million." (p17)

Hinrichsen, Don. "International Notebook: Building (And Greening) from Scratch." Amicus Journal v19 n3 Fall 1997. p16-19. (ISSN0276-7201).

ENVIRONMENTAL DEGRADATION--FINLAND--COSTS

In Finland, "during the period from 1989 to 1994, more than 250 environmental accidents were recorded, resulting in a total loss of 22 million Finnish marks (US $4.3 million). Some 50% of these accidents occurred during industrial operations, while 20% occurred during transports of hazardous chemicals. In 34 cases during the five-year period, the guilty party was not found or the company was unable to meet its financial obligations. As a result, state authorities had to bear cleanup costs of more than 4.5 million marks ($0.9 million)." (p18)

"News Briefs: Finland Proposes Mandatory Liability Insurance." Environment Watch: Western Europe v6 n12 20 Jun 1997. p18. (ISSN1066-6001).

ENVIRONMENTAL DEGRADATION--GREAT BRITAIN

At the Town and Country Planning Summer School at Lancaster in 1993, Sir Richard Body claimed that in the last 25 years, in Great Britain, damage to the rural environment included "130,000 miles of hedgerows ripped up. 40% of our ancient woodlands gone. Seven million acres of pastureland ploughed up. Over 95% of our wetlands drained. 875 miles of stone wall destroyed. 95% of the downlands of southern England gone. 180,000 acres of moorland ploughed up." (p4)

Ward, Colin. "Features: Anarchist Notebook: Re-Settling Rural England." Freedom (Anarchist Fortnightly) v58 n17 6 Sep 1997. p4. (ISSN0016-0504).

ENVIRONMENTAL IMPACT ANALYSIS (v26)

ENVIRONMENTAL IMPACT CHARGES--CZECH REPUBLIC (v26)

ENVIRONMENTAL LAW--COMPLIANCE COSTS--UNITED STATES (v26)

ENVIRONMENTAL LAW--UNITED STATES--PUBLIC OPINION (v26)

ENVIRONMENTAL MONITORING--TAXATION (v26)

ENVIRONMENTAL POLICY--EMPLOYMENT

The OECD says that a large number of jobs "have been created by environmental policies. Employment directly or indirectly related to environmental policies is estimated at 1%-3% of the work force in OECD countries. In Germany, for example, the figure is put at 2.4%, or 956,000 jobs, and in the US, 3%, or 4 million jobs. 'Eco-industries' on their own produce a turnover of some US $250 billion each year and are growing at a rate of 5% each year, the OECD says." (p16)

"Regulatory and Policy Trends: OECD Report Says Environment Policy Is a 'Net Creator of Jobs.'" Business and the Environment v8 n6 Jun 1997. p16. (ISSN1052-7206).

ENVIRONMENTAL POLICY--FINANCE

The annual agreed contributions to the Ozone Fund, which is a multilateral fund for the Implementation of the Montreal Protocol on Substances that Deplete the Ozone Layer, "climbed from $53.31 million in 1991 to $151.67 million in 1996.... Although most industrialized countries were rather slow to pay their share, 88 percent of all pledged contributions for the period 1991 to 1995 have been received by now....The total of all agreed contributions (including 1996) now stands at $687.70 million, of which $444.20 million had actually been paid by 10 May 1996....All developing countries consuming more than 300 grams ODS [ozone-depleting substances] per capita and year must contribute to the Fund. This applied in 1995 to only five parties: Cyprus, Kuwait, Lebanon, Slovenia, and the United Arab Emirates." (p186) "The most critical contributors, however, are the so-called countries with economies in transition (CEIT), that is, the former group of socialist countries. Seventy-six percent of all outstanding contributions for the period 1991-1994 are attributed to countries in transition; 61 percent if 1995 is included." (p187) In May 1996, "the Russian Federation owed $54.81 million (100 percent of total 1991-1996 contributions), and the Ukraine owed $12.84 million (93.9 percent)." (p188)

Biermann, Frank. "Articles: Financing Environmental Policies in the South: Experiences from the Multilateral Ozone Fund." International Environmental Affairs v9 n3 Sum 1997. p179-218. (ISSN1041-4665).

ENVIRONMENTAL POLICY--TAXATION (v26)

ENVIRONMENTAL POLICY--UNITED STATES--PUBLIC OPINION (v26)

ENVIRONMENTAL POLLUTION

see POLLUTION

ENVIRONMENTAL PROTECTION

see also CONSERVATION OF NATURAL RESOURCES; HABITAT CONSERVATION; WILDLIFE CONSERVATION

"Solar cells are now providing environmentally benign electricity to more than 400,000 homes in the developing world. But the solar alternative still only accounts for one watt out of every four thousand watts--less than 0.0003 (or 0.03 percent)--of the world's total installed electric capacity....According to the U.S. Department of Agriculture,...[pesticide-free organic farming] accounts for less than 0.001 (or 0.1 percent) of food produced in the United States, where it has its strongest foothold....According to biologists, the rate at which species are continuing to vanish exceeds natural extinction rates by 100 to 1,000 times." (p3)

Ayres, Ed. "Note from a Worldwatcher: Fighting Brushfires." World Watch v10 n4 Jul-Aug 1997. p3. (ISSN0896-0615).

ENVIRONMENTAL PROTECTION--ARIZONA

In May 1997, residents of Pima County, Arizona, voted "yes" to "the Sonoran Desert Open Space and Historic Preservation Bond. Their support directed $36.3 million in general obligation bonds to protect the desert surrounding Tucson....In and around Phoenix,...in Maricopa County, Sonoran Desert disappears under the assault of bulldozers and asphalt at a rate of an acre per hour; and between 1995 and 1996, the state recorded a 2.9 percent increase in residents." (p7)

Green, Martha Hodgkins. "Sightings: Gimme Space: Sonorous Voice Raised in the Sonoran Desert." Nature Conservancy v47 n4 Sep-Oct 1997. p7. (ISSN0028-5200).

ENVIRONMENTAL PROTECTION--AUSTRALIA--COSTS (v26)

ENVIRONMENTAL PROTECTION--BRITISH COLUMBIA

The Muskwa-Kechica region in British Columbia "comprises 50 undisturbed watersheds and is bigger than the province of Nova Scotia, encompassing 4.4 million hectares (10.8 million acres)....The core of the protected [wilderness] area [in the Muskwa-Kechica region] totals nearly 3 million acres and is surrounded by an 8 million acre contiguous buffer, or 'special management area.'...The Muskwa-Kechica package of protected areas and special management zones brings the total amount of B.C.'s protected lands to just under 11 percent of the total land mass of the province." (p18)

Scott, Joe. "News from the North: Northern Rockies Agreement Protects Massive B.C. Wilderness." Northwest Conservation n32 Nov 1997. p18.

ENVIRONMENTAL PROTECTION--CZECH REPUBLIC (v26)

ENVIRONMENTAL PROTECTION--EMPLOYMENT --UNITED STATES (v26)

ENVIRONMENTAL PROTECTION--NETHERLANDS

In the Netherlands, the National Environmental Policy Plans and covenants "demand reductions in emissions of sulfur dioxide, ammonia, volatile organic chemicals, and nitrogen oxide on the order of 70 to 90 percent by the year 2010....Eleven industrial sectors representing some 1,200 companies, have signed voluntary emissions reduction agreements with the government. This coverage accounts for some 90 percent of industrial pollution in the Netherlands." (p33)

Beardsley, Dan/Davies, Terry/Hersh, Robert. "Improving Environmental Management: What Works What Doesn't." Environment v39 n7 Sep 1997. p6-9,28-35. (ISSN0013-9157).

ENVIRONMENTAL PROTECTION--NEW JERSEY

New Jersey's pollution prevention "program has set a 50 percent reduction over five years in the 'use, discharge, and generation of hazardous substances' as its goal." (p30) "In terms of environmental benefits, the Department of Environmental Protection estimates that New Jersey facilities will use approximately 24 million pounds less of hazardous substances per year. At present, annual statewide usage of hazardous substances totals 4 to 5 billion pounds. Projections for nonproduct (waste) output show a reduction of 13 million pounds per year compared with a baseline of about 320 million pounds." (p32)

Beardsley, Dan/Davies, Terry/Hersh, Robert. "Improving Environmental Management: What Works What Doesn't." Environment v39 n7 Sep 1997. p6-9,28-35. (ISSN0013-9157).

ENVIRONMENTAL PROTECTION--TAXATION--UNITED STATES (v26)

ENVIRONMENTAL PROTECTION--UNITED STATES (v26)

Environmental "compliance costs continue to grow, now accounting for almost 2.5 percent of the United States' total gross national product." (p7) "States carry out about 85 percent of the enforcement actions in environmental protection and most of the permitting functions....Twenty-five states have undergone formal processes for comparing risks among environmental problem areas." (p30) "According to the Department of Environmental Protection's own report, preparing a pollution prevention plan costs a facility on average about $26,000. For facilities that estimated the amount of time spent by all personnel involved, the average number of workdays was 60.7. In terms of benefits to these 42 facilities, '29 (69 percent) predicted net cost savings as a result of pollution prevention techniques identified through the planning process.' The agency estimates a total net benefit to the facilities of about $6.3 million per year. Put another way, the preliminary analysis 'shows that for every dollar spent on the entire process...facilities project net savings of $5 to $8.'" (p31)

Beardsley, Dan/Davies, Terry/Hersh, Robert. "Improving Environmental Management: What Works What Doesn't." Environment v39 n7 Sep 1997. p6-9,28-35. (ISSN0013-9157).

The U.S. Environmental Protection Agency "sponsors a number of innovative environmental management programs....A recent agency compilation listed 51 separate 'reinvention' projects. Twelve of these programs adopted the 'flexibility for results' approach, 15 were described as 'partnerships,' 7 were devoted to facilitating compliance, and 17 aimed to 'cut red tape.'" (p30)

"EPA and Management Innovations." Environment v39 n7 Sep 1997. p30. (ISSN0013-9157).

The U.S. spends "nearly $150 billion per year (around 2.4 percent of gross national product) on environmental protection...." (p11) "Ford's bumper recycling program...[has] 400 dismantlers across the country helping to recycle approximately 1.5 million pounds of plastic per year that would otherwise have ended up in landfills....In 1995...the five largest manufacturers of rechargeable nickel-cadmium batteries formed the RBRC [Rechargeable Battery Recycling Corporation] to handle the collection and recycling of such batteries throughout the United States. This corporation collected more than 15 percent of the available batteries in its first year and has set a goal of collecting 100 percent of such batteries (and recycling 70 percent of them) by the year 2000....Xerox Corporation's asset recycle management program...aims at attaining 'waste free' factories by 1998 and developing waste-free products....Under this program...the company achieved a 60 percent return for copier cartridges in 1995." (p15)

Davis, Gary A./Wilt, Catherine A./Barkenbus, Jack N. "Extended Product Responsibility: A Tool for a Sustainable Economy." Environment v39 n7 Sep 1997. p10-15,36-38. (ISSN0013-9157).

In the U.S., the Clinton "administration has nearly doubled (to 643) the number of chemicals that companies must report annually under the Toxics Release Inventory program. It has increased by 30 percent (to more [than] 31,000) the number of industrial facilities required to make such information public, and it proposed putting pollution information on several key industries--oil products, steel and other metals, autos, and paper--on the Web....Clinton administration officials point to the record of the Toxics Release Inventory (TRI) program as proof that making more information available to the public helps reduce pollution. Since the TRI program began in 1988, says [EPA administrator Carol] Browner, 'industrial facilities required to report their toxic releases have reduced their emissions by 46 percent.'" (p4)

Knickerbocker, Brad. "United States: Debate over How to Punish Repentant Polluters." The Christian Science Monitor v89 n216 2 Oct 1997. p4. The Christian Science Monitor search engine: <http://www.csmonitor.com/plweb-cgi/iops1.pl> To retrieve this article, enter the following search: ED=19971002 AND polluters. In the "retrieved list," click the title that matches this record. (ISSN0882-7729).

ENVIRONMENTAL PROTECTION--VENEZUELA (v26)

ENVIRONMENTAL PROTECTION--WASHINGTON--PUGET SOUND--PUBLIC OPINION

"According to a recent survey by LGDinsight, many Puget Sound citizens would support measures to restore the region's salmon and their habitat. 60 percent of the 275 voters polled in King, Snohomish, Skagit and Whatcom counties support establishing healthy stream reserves on public and private lands in order to protect wild salmon and trout. Nearly 70 percent believe we need to make changes in the way we develop land in and around our communities to restore wild salmon and trout habitat." (p20)

Barnett, Emily. "Poll Shows Demand for Stream Protection: Puget Sound Citizens Say YES! to Salmon." Northwest

Conservation Sum 1997. p20.

ENVIRONMENTALLY INDUCED DISEASES

"About 25 percent of the global burden of disease and injury is linked to environmental decline, according to a recent U.N. World Health Organization report....Diarrheal diseases like cholera kill 3 million people every year; 90 percent of that toll results from contaminated water. Malaria claims 1.5 to 2.7 million lives a year, and 90 percent of these deaths can be linked to environmental trends as well--but usually through a complex of natural and social pressures....Acute respiratory infections like pneumonia are 60 percent driven by environmental factors, primarily the burning of wood, coal, or other smoky fuels in the home. Of the 3 million deaths a year caused by air pollution, 2.8 million are from indoor air pollution." (p7)

Chandra, Candace/Bright, Chris. "Environmental Intelligence: Sick Planet, Sick People." World Watch v10 n6 Nov-Dec 1997. p7. (ISSN0896-0615).

EPHEDRINE--HEALTH ASPECTS--UNITED STATES

In the U.S., "more than 900 injuries and 40 deaths related to ephedrine--also called Ma huang or herbal ecstasy--have been reported to the Food and Drug Administration, spokesman Arthur Whitmore said. Problems range from dizziness and tremors to heart attacks or strokes....Ephedrine, available over the counter, is a central nervous system stimulant used in diet pills and food supplements. Medically, it's used in decongestants and asthma medicines to help people breathe easier. But it's also touted by herbal experts as an appetite suppressant and energy booster....In Michigan, possessing more than 10 grams is a felony, punishable by up to two years in jail or a $2,000 fine." (p1,6 secC)

Bondi, Nicole. "Metro: News Special: Health: Mom Wages War on Ephedrine." Detroit News 2 Dec 1997. p1,6 secC.

EPIDEMIC HEPATITIS

see HEPATITIS A

EPIDURAL ANESTHESIA

see PERIDURAL ANESTHESIA

EPILEPSY

"The prevalence of a disorder is the proportion of a population with that disorder at a given point in time. The mean prevalence of active epilepsy (i.e. continuing seizures or the need for treatment) from many studies around the world is approximately 7 per 1,000 of the general population. Thus, 40 million people in the world have epilepsy at any one time." (p1) "The lifetime prevalence of epilepsy, i.e. the number of people presently in the world who have epilepsy now or have had it in the past (e.g. childhood) or will get it in the future (e.g. old age), rises to approximately 100 million people. The incidence of a disorder is the number of new cases at a given time, usually one year. Studies in developed countries suggest an annual incidence of epilepsy of approximately 50 per 100,000 of the general population. However, studies in developing countries suggest this figure is nearly 100 per 100,000...." (p2)

World Health Organization. "Epilepsy: Aetiology, Epidemiology and Prognosis." WHO Fact Sheet n165 Jun 1997. p1-4. document-level access: <http://www.who.ch/programmes/inf/facts/fact165.htm>

EPILEPSY--CHINA--GERMANY--PUBLIC OPINION

"There is a marked social stigma and discrimination attached to epilepsy, and it is not exclusive to the developing world. Epilepsy often diminishes the prospect of marriage, especially for women. In China, a survey of public awareness in 1992 revealed that 72% of parents objected to their children marrying someone with epilepsy....A survey carried out in Germany in 1996 revealed that 20% of respondents believed that epilepsy was a form of mental disease, 21% objected to their child marrying someone with epilepsy." (p2)

World Health Organization. "Epilepsy: Social Consequences and Economic Aspects." WHO Fact Sheet n166 Jun 1997. p1-4. document-level access: <http://www.who.ch/programmes/inf/facts/fact166.htm>

EPILEPSY--GREAT BRITAIN--COSTS

"In the UK, the total annual cost in 1993 of established epilepsy, based on a sample of 1,628 patients, was 1,930,000 [pounds sterling]. Indirect costs due to premature mortality and especially morbidity accounted for almost 70% of the total. The cost of active epilepsy per patient was 4,167 [pounds sterling] per annum and of inactive epilepsy--1,630 [pounds sterling] per annum." (p3)

World Health Organization. "Epilepsy: Social Consequences and Economic Aspects." WHO Fact Sheet n166 Jun 1997. p1-4. document-level access: <http://www.who.ch/programmes/inf/facts/fact166.htm>

EPILEPSY--INDONESIA--COSTS

"In Indonesia, where an estimated 1,260,000 people have epilepsy, the cost per patient per year in 1993 was US$487 of which 40% were indirect costs. Of the medical costs, medication amounted to 50% because of relatively little in-patient care. The cost of drugs varied 10-fold, but with some newer drugs the variation can be 100-fold." (p4)

World Health Organization. "Epilepsy: Social Consequences and Economic Aspects." WHO Fact Sheet n166 Jun 1997. p1-4. document-level access: <http://www.who.ch/programmes/inf/facts/fact166.htm>

EPILEPSY--TREATMENT

"Recent studies in both developed and developing countries have shown that up to 70% of newly diagnosed children and adults with epilepsy can be successfully treated (complete control of seizures for several years) with anti-epileptic drugs. After two to five years of successful treatment drugs can be withdrawn in about 70% of children and 60% of adults without relapses. Up to 30% of patients may not respond to drug therapy....For economic and social reasons, three out of four people in the world with epilepsy do not receive treatment at all, and most of these who do not receive treatment are in developing countries." (p3-4)

World Health Organization. "Epilepsy: Aetiology, Epidemiology and Prognosis." WHO Fact Sheet n165 Jun 1997. p1-4. document-level access: <http://www.who.ch/programmes/inf/facts/fact165.htm>

EPILEPSY--UNITED STATES

An "estimated 2.5 million people in the United States...suffer from repeated [epileptic] seizures....Overall, anti-epilepsy medications successfully control seizures in about 7 out of 10 patients with epilepsy." (p8) "About half of the 30 percent of patients whose seizures cannot be controlled with medication may be candidates for epilepsy surgery. In the United States alone, more than 100,000 epilepsy sufferers might benefit from the surgery. Yet only 3,000 epilepsy surgeries are performed in this country each year." (p9)

Benbadis, Selim R. "Neurology: The Management of Epilepsy." Healthline v16 n6 Jun 1997. p8-9. (ISSN0736-7929).

EPILEPTICS--EMPLOYMENT

"Unemployment and underemployment exist worldwide, but more so with people with epilepsy....A survey carried out in China showed that 31% of respondents believed that people with epilepsy should not be employed....Nearly a quarter of Nepalese people with epilepsy took the view, in recent research, that they were not able to work....Data from the United States, Italy and Germany indicate that, of people with epilepsy of working age, from 40% to 60% are employed (although often in jobs below their potential), 15% to 20% are unemployed and about 20% retire

early." (p3)
World Health Organization. "Epilepsy: Social Consequences and Economic Aspects." WHO Fact Sheet n166 Jun 1997. p1-4. document-level access: <http://www.who.ch/programmes/inf/facts/fact166.htm>

EPISCOPALIANS--UNITED STATES
"According to the Rev. J. Hugh Magers, National Director of Stewardship, the body of the Episcopal Church in the U.S. lines up roughly as follows: About 55% of us are known as traditionalists....Evangelicals make up about 10% of the national congregation." (p5) "About 5% of us are deemed to be Anglo-Catholic....Another 10% may fall under the title of rationalists....Perhaps 15% of Episcopalians are found to be charismatics....Outreach is the major concern of the 5% who identify themselves as social activists." (p6)
Foster, Mary D. B. "Color Me Episcopalian." Anglican Digest v39 n5 1997. p5-7. (ISSN0003-3278).

EQUAL EMPLOYMENT OPPORTUNITY
see AFFIRMATIVE ACTION PROGRAMS; DISCRIMINATION IN EMPLOYMENT

EQUAL PAY FOR EQUAL WORK--UNITED STATES (v26)
Th U.S. "Bureau of Labor Statistics reports that the median weekly paycheck for women has fallen to 75 percent of men's. Women's earnings had risen from 62 percent of men's in 1979 to a high of 77 percent in 1993." (p4)
"News Watch." Labor Notes n224 Nov 1997. p4. (ISSN0275-4452).

ERITREA--HEALTH AND HYGIENE
In Eritrea, "about 30 percent of 1-year-olds were fully immunized by their first birthday, compared to 19 percent of 2-year-olds....Nearly four out of 10 children under age 3 were judged chronically malnourished....About 41 percent of women with a recent birth showed signs of chronic energy deficiency, a type of malnutrition....Just half of Eritrean women received prenatal care for births during the three years before the survey. Women received delivery assistance from a medical professional for only 21 percent of recent births." (p7)
"Spotlight: Eritrea." Population Today v25 n12 Dec 1997. p7. (ISSN0749-2448).

ERITREA--SOCIAL CONDITIONS
"Most of Eritrea's people (95 percent) make their living as subsistence agriculturists--highland farmers or lowland nomads....Eritrea's population is about half Muslim and half Christian. Many of the 340,000 Eritrean refugees who remain in Sudan are active in Islamic rebel groups seeking to destabilize the Eritrean government." (p7)
"Spotlight: Eritrea." Population Today v25 n12 Dec 1997. p7. (ISSN0749-2448).

EROSION, SOIL
see SOIL EROSION

ERRORS, MEDICAL
see MEDICAL ERRORS

ESCHERICHIA COLI--UNITED STATES
"The Centers for Disease Control (CDC) estimates that 20,000 cases of E. coli infection are reported each year [in the U.S.]. Approximately 75% of these are attributed to eating contaminated meat, and even though outbreaks traced to plant foods seem to be increasing, the numbers continue to be comparatively low....In about five percent of the cases...especially the elderly, people with compromised immune systems, and kids...who are under the age of five, the infection can lead to hemolytic uremic syndrome in which red blood cells are destroyed and kidneys fail." (p19)
Abrams-McHenry, Maribeth. "E. Coli: New Concerns." Vegetarian Voice v22 n2 Sum 1997. p18-21. (ISSN0271-1591).

ESCHERICHIA COLI INFECTIONS--UNITED STATES
"According to the American Gastroenterological Association, between 10,000 and 20,000 cases of E. coli O157:H7 disease occur each year in the United States. The disease usually produces a mild gastrointestinal illness that occurs 3 to 5 days after eating contaminated food....Approximately 16 percent of the annual cases of E. coli O157:H7 disease develop hemorrhagic colitis, mostly young children. Less than 5 percent of E. coli O157:H7 disease cases develop hemolytic uremic syndrome." (p34) "The U.S. Centers for Disease Control and Prevention (CDC) estimates that 49 percent of the annual cases of E. coli P0157:H7 disease (4,900 to 9,800) are due to consumption of insufficiently cooked ground beef. USDA's Economic Research Service (ERS) estimates that these cases result in $196 million to $441 million, respectively, in annual medical costs and productivity losses." (p35)
Morrison, Rosanna Mentzer/Buzby, Jean C./Lin, C. -T. Jordan/U.S. Dept. of Agriculture. Economic Research Service. "Food Safety: Irradiating Ground Beef to Enhance Food Safety." Food Review v20 n1 Jan-Apr 1997. p33-37. (ISSN1056-327X).

ESOPHAGUS--CANCER
"Smoking accounts for 45% of [oesophageal cancer] cases in men worldwide, but only 11% of female cases. About 85% of cases are in developing countries. About 75% of patients die within a year of diagnosis: only 5-10% survive for five years." (p5)
World Health Organization. "World Health Report 1997." Press Release 5 May 1997. p1-7. document-level access: <http://www.who.ch/whr/1997/presse.htm>

ESPIONAGE, AMERICAN (v26)

ESTATE TAX
see INHERITANCE AND TRANSFER TAX

ESTROGEN--THERAPEUTIC USE--UNITED STATES (v26)
In the U.S., "at age 50, a white woman has a 9 percent risk of developing breast cancer over the next 30 years. HRT [hormone replacement therapy] increases that risk by approximately a third, or 3 percentage points, to about 12 percent. However, the same woman faces a 46 percent risk of developing heart disease. HRT cuts it 12 percentage points to 34 percent....As for osteoporosis, one-quarter of white women over 45 have detectable bone-thinning, and by age 75, the figure is 90 percent. In a study of women over age 50, HRT reduced hip fracture risk from 15 to 12 percent." (p22) "Researchers from the National Institute on Aging who followed 472 post-menopausal women for 16 years found that, compared with those who had used estrogen, those who had never taken it were more than twice as likely to develop Alzheimer's. A similar study in New York showed that women taking estrogen had a 2.7 percent risk of being diagnosed with Alzheimer's; among those not taking the hormone, the risk was 8.4 percent....After 50, 6 percent of white women develop colon cancer; new research shows that HRT cuts this risk to just 3 percent....While HRT increases risk of developing breast cancer, it also reduces risk of dying from it by a whopping 22 percent. These findings come from American Cancer Society researchers who followed 422,000 post-menopausal women for nine years." (p23)
Castleman, Michael. "Well Being: Hormonious Heart." Mother Jones v22 n4 Jul-Aug 1997. p21-23. article-level access: <http://www.motherjones.com/mother_jones/JA97/wellbeing.html> (ISSN0362-8841).

ETHIC, WORK
see WORK ETHIC

ETHICS
see LAWYERS--UNITED STATES--ETHICS

ETHNIC DIVERSITY POLICY
see MULTICULTURALISM

ETHNIC MINORITIES
see MINORITIES

ETHNOLOGY

see also INDIGENOUS PEOPLES; MANNERS AND CUSTOMS; RACE RELATIONS

"Of the world's 6,000 distinct human cultures, some 3,000 are believed to be headed for extinction. Many of the remaining 3,000 are being weakened by the homogenizing influences of global media and commerce." (p4)

Ayres, Ed. "Note from a Worldwatcher: Outcompeting Ourselves." World Watch v10 n5 Sep-Oct 1997. p3-4. (ISSN0896-0615).

ETHNOLOGY--CALIFORNIA (v26)

"Despite measures to keep foreigners out, a quarter of California's population, eight million, are foreign born, mostly from Latin America (51 percent) and Asia (33 percent). More than 80 languages are spoken in the state. By the year 2010, according to one estimate, the white population will be California's new minority." (p8)

Martinez, Al. "Can We All Get Along?" California Journal v29 n1 Jan 1998. p6-11. (ISSN0008-1205).

ETHNOLOGY--CALIFORNIA--LOS ANGELES

"In the 1980s alone, Greater Los Angeles grew by three million people--enough to populate a city the size of Chicago. By the mid-'80s, 78 languages were being spoken at Hollywood High School....'The Ethnic Quilt,' published by California State University, Northridge, identifies 34 ethnic populations in Greater L.A...." (p10)

Olney, Warren. "Which Way, L. A.?" California Journal v28 n7 Jul 1997. p8-11. (ISSN0008-1205).

ETHNOLOGY--CALIFORNIA--ORANGE COUNTY

In 1980, Orange County's "population was 78 percent white, 15 percent Latino, 5 percent Asian and 1 percent African-American. By 1990, it was 65 percent white, 23 percent Latino, 10 percent Asian and 2 percent black....Its student population of some 28,000 is roughly 50 percent white, 34 percent Latino, 11 percent Asian, 2 percent black...." (p39)

Jeffe, Sherry Bebitch. "Perspective: Southern Exposure." California Journal v29 n1 Jan 1998. p39. (ISSN0008-1205).

ETHNOLOGY--FLORIDA--DADE COUNTY

According to the 1970 census figures: of the total Dade County, Florida "population of 1,268,000 people, 62 percent were Anglo (non-Hispanic white); 15 percent African American; and 23 percent Latinos/Hispanics. By 1995, the total population had changed dramatically. Out of 2,057,000 people, now 25 percent were non-Hispanic white (Anglo); 21 percent African American; and 55 percent Latinos/Hispanics....In 1973, of a total of 16,537 employees, 55 percent were non-Hispanic white (Anglo); 32 percent were African American; and 10 percent were Latinos/ Hispanics....In 1997 the number of County employees had grown to 24,472 of which 27 percent were non-Hispanic white (Anglo); 36 percent were African American; and thirty-six percent were Hispanic." (p60)

Ojeda, J. A., Jr. "Managing/Valuing Diversity: Managing Diversity's Impact in Metropolitan Dade County." Public Manager v26 n3 Fall 1997. p59-61. (ISSN1061-7639).

ETHNOLOGY--GREAT BRITAIN (v26)

ETHNOLOGY--GUYANA

"East Indians and Africans account for approximately 51 percent and 31 percent respectively of the total population [of Guyana]. Mixed-Africans account for an additional 12 percent, and Amerindians, Chinese, and Europeans for the remaining 6 percent." (p114-115)

Singh, Chaitram. "Changing the Basis of Civilian Control over the Military in Guyana." Journal of Third World Studies v14 n2 Fall 1997. p113-131. (ISSN8755-3449).

ETHNOLOGY--HISPANIC AMERICANS

In the U.S., "Central and South Americans have the largest percentage of recent immigrants. Nearly one-half (48 percent) of the 2.4 million Hispanics of Central and South American origin counted in the 1990 census entered the United States in the previous decade....By 1996, the number of Hispanics of Central and South American origin had reached 4.1 million and made up 14 percent of U.S. Latinos....More than two-thirds (68 percent) of Central and South American Hispanics in the 1990 census identified themselves with one of five countries: El Salvador, Colombia, Guatemala, Nicaragua, and Ecuador. Another 800,000 Hispanics traced their origins to Peru, Honduras, Argentina, or another Spanish-speaking country in Central and South America." (p7-8)

del Pinal, Jorge/Singer, Audrey. "Generations of Diversity: Latinos in the United States." Population Bulletin v52 n3 Oct 1997. p2-47. (ISSN0032-468X).

ETHNOLOGY--LAOS

"Roughly half of Laos's population of four million is ethnic Lao....An estimated 20 percent are Lao Tai....Mon-Khmer people...constitute another 15 to 20 percent of Laos's population." (p36)

Forbes, Andrew. "The Crescent in Laos: Islam in Vientiane." Aramco World v48 n3 May-Jun 1997. p36-38. (ISSN1044-1891).

ETHNOLOGY--MOLDOVA

"Ethnic Russians comprise just 25% of Transdniestria's population....Ethnic Moldovans may make up over 40% of the populace....Ethnic Ukrainians...[are] 28% of the PMR [Transdniestrian Moldovan Republic]...." (p50)

Meier, Andrew. "Independence Free Fall: The Collapse of Moldova's Industrial Engine." APF Reporter v18 n3 1997. p45-52. (ISSN0913-4562).

ETHNOLOGY--SRI LANKA (v26)

ETHNOLOGY--UNITED STATES (v26)

"There are 24.6 million people living in the U.S. who were born in another country, according to the 1996 Current Population Survey. That is 9.3 percent of the population, the highest share since 1940....Americans are 6.7 million, or 27 percent of all foreign-born. Mexicans are young, with 30 percent under age 25. Almost half have not completed high school, compared with 16 percent of natives. And 35 percent of the Mexican-born live in poverty, compared with 22 percent of all foreign-born and 13 percent of all Americans." (p33)

Miller, Berna. "Kaleidoscope: Foreign-Born Diversity." American Demographics v19 n7 Jul 1997. p33. article-level access: <http://www.demographics.com/publications/ad/97_ad/9707_ad/ad970727.htm> (ISSN0163-4089).

"According to AMERICAN DEMOGRAPHICS magazine, the number of people who check off the census' 'other' box in the race category has increased 45 percent since the 1980 census. The Census Bureau estimates that such people number 9.8 million, or one in every 25 Americans. Under the category of race in the U.S. Census, there are five choices: American Indian or Alaskan Native, Asian or Pacific Islander, Black, white and other. Ethnicity is a separate category, with only two choices: Hispanic and not of Hispanic origin. Most of the 9.8 million who feel they do not belong in any of the four official categories for race are officially Hispanic, but for the Census Bureau, 'Hispanic' refers to only ethnic origin: you can be Hispanic and be any race. It's an additional 400,000 people who are not Hispanic who are among those agitating for more census choices." (p28-29)

Kobylarz, Xenia P. "(Multi)culture: Common Census: The Movement for a New Multi-Racial Category." Third Force v5 n5 Nov-Dec 1997. p28-31. (ISSN1067-3237).

"In 1990, the U.S. Census Bureau offered Americans the choice of 16 racial categories. The main groupings were white and black, which 92 percent of the population chose....Some 9.8 million

Americans, or 4 percent of the total population, chose 'Other' rather than one of the established monoracial categories--compared with fewer than 1 million in 1970." (p13)

"Dateline Migration: National: The Place of Race in the Census." Migration World v25 n4 1997. p13. (ISSN1058-5095).

In the U.S., "since 1990, the number of interracial children has quadrupled--now reaching the two million mark. Millions of other Americans are viewed as members of one race but see themselves as members of another. The 1990 Census allowed these Americans to select the marginalizing label of 'other.'...About 9.8 million, 4% of the total population, chose this designation rather than be defined according to the established mono-racial categories." (p39)

Etzioni, Amitai. "New Issues: Rethinking Race." Public Perspective v8 n4 Jun-Jul 1997. p39-41. (ISSN1050-5067).

ETHNOLOGY--UNITED STATES--FINANCE (v26)

EUROPE--COMMERCE (v26)

According to Eurostat, Statistical Office of the European Communities in Luxembourg, in the first quarter of 1997, "extra-EU exports and imports rose by 9.9% and 8.4% respectively. This compares with growth of 4% (exports) and 6.3% (imports) in the first quarter last year. But intra-EU trade was up by only 1.6% compared to 4.3% in Q1 '96....Growth in extra-EU exports was particularly strong in Ireland (17.5%), the United Kingdom (26.2%) and Belgium-Luxembourg (16.5%). But there were falls in Denmark (-3.8%), Spain (-1.8%) and Portugal (-2.9%). On the import side, the United Kingdom (16.3%), Finland (9.4%), Denmark (9.4%) and France (12.1%) had above average rises. As in Q1 '96, Germany registered the biggest extra-EU surplus (6.5 bn [billion]) followed by Italy (3.6 bn) and Sweden (3.1 bn). Largest deficits were the Netherlands' -7.2 bn, the UK's -4.1 bn and Spain's -1.6 bn. In the case of the Netherlands this has to be seen in the context of its intra-EU surplus and transit role in EU trade."

Eurostat. "'Dynamic' EU Trade with Rest-Of-World." Press Release 31 Jul 1997. document-level access: <http://europa.eu.int/en/comm/eurostat/compres/en/5497/6605497a.htm>

EUROPE--COMMERCE--JAPAN

"The EU's trade deficit with Japan has fallen for the fourth year running, Eurostat--Statistical Office of the European Communities in Luxembourg--reports....It was down to 16.8 bn [billion] ECU [European currency units] last year from 21.4 bn in 1995. Imports from Japan fell by 3.3% to 52.5 bn. Exports rose by 8.4% to 35.6 bn. This resulted import/export cover ratio of 68%--30 points up on the lowest level in 1992. In 1996, Japan was the EU's third largest trading partner after the USA and Switzerland, accounting for 7.3% of total value of extra-EU trade....Germany and the UK accounted for most EU trade with Japan: 30% and 18% respectively last year. The UK recorded the largest deficit (5.9 bn), followed by the Netherlands (4.6 bn) and Germany (4.4 bn)--a reversal of the second position in 1995. In the case of the UK and Germany deficits were down by 1.2 bn and 1.5 bn respectively...[in] 1995...."

Eurostat. "EU Trade Deficit with Japan Falls Again." Press Release 25 Nov 1997. document-level access: <http://europa.eu.int/en/comm/eurostat/compres/en/7997/6207997a.htm>

EUROPE--COMMERCE--JAPAN--UNITED STATES (v26)

EUROPE--COMMERCE--MEDITERRANEAN REGION (v26)

EUROPE--COMMERCE--NORTH AMERICA (v26)

EUROPE--COMMERCE--PERSIAN GULF REGION

"More than 22 percent of Europe's oil imports come from...[the Persian Gulf] region....The six members of the GCC [Gulf Cooperation Council] account for 40 percent of the total trade of the European Union with the Arab countries. The GCC is the sixth largest client of the European Union....Europe is the second foreign investor in the [Gulf] region, and it is a region which receives the greatest volume of Arab foreign investment." (p9-10)

Magro, Herve. "Symposium--The Challenge in the Gulf: Building a Bridge from Containment to Stability." Middle East Policy v5 n2 May 1997. p1-21. (ISSN1061-1924).

EUROPE--COMMERCE--SOUTH AMERICA (v26)

EUROPE--ECONOMIC CONDITIONS (v26)

"From 1985 to 1995, trade among EU member countries increased by about 50 percent in volume....Between 1979 and 1990 the GDP of the EU rose by 2.2 percent per annum, compared with 2.6 percent growth in the United States, a world average of 2.7 percent and 4.1 percent in Japan. In the last decade, manufacturing productivity growth in the EU has averaged 2.5 percent per annum--one percentage point per annum below the US and two points below Japan." (p34)

Heidensohn, Klaus/Hibbert, Edgar P. "A Sectoral Analysis of Europe's International Competitiveness." Competitiveness Review v7 n2 1997. p25-37. (ISSN1059-5422).

"All EU member-nations have adopted inflation-fighting monetary policies and tight fiscal policies in an attempt to meet the convergence criteria [for the European Monetary Union]. These actions have resulted in average GDP growth rates of less than 2% in 1996, while the average unemployment rate in Europe was 11% at the beginning of 1997. Britain represents the low end of this unemployment rate spectrum at 6%, with Germany at 12.2% and France at 12.7%." (p11)

Isenberg, Dorene. "Economy in Review: The European Monetary Union: Greenspan's Federal Reserve Writ Large." Dollars and Sense n214 Nov-Dec 1997. p11-14,39. (ISSN0012-5245).

"There are now more than 18 million officially unemployed people in the European Union....Seventeen percent of the present population of the EU live below the official poverty line (defined as an income less than 50 percent of the average in a person's country of residence)....The highest level of official poverty, after Portugal, is in Great Britain, where 22 percent of the population (over 14 million people) live below the poverty line...." (p98)

Judt, Tony. "The Social Question Redivivus." Foreign Affairs v76 n5 Sep-Oct 1997. p95-117. (ISSN0015-7120).

EUROPE--EMIGRATION AND IMMIGRATION (v26)

"In 1995 immigration contributed a post-war high of nearly 80% of EU population growth. Although it fell last year, it still formed three-quarters. In Germany (population: over 82 million, the EU's largest), total population increase last year was 210,200 but net migration was 303,200; the deficit was caused by a negative natural increase (fewer live births than deaths) of -93,000. Comparative figures for Italy (population: over 57 m, the EU's fourth largest) were 131,400, 150,300 and -18,900. Eurostat says that without net migration the German and Italian populations 'would be in decline'. Greece (natural increase 1,000, net migration 18,900) and Sweden (1,200 and 5,800) 'are in similar situations'. Neighbours France and the UK have similar total populations of between 58 and 59 million (with Germany and Italy, the EU's largest)--but a different pattern of growth. France's population was up by 238,000 last year, a natural rise of 198,000 with net migration of 40,000. But the UK's growth of 179,400 was more or less evenly balanced between natural increase (94,400) and net migration (85,000). A recent feature of Ireland and Spain is that they are attracting fairly significant net migration: 8,300 and 41,700 respectively last year."

Eurostat. "EU Women Average 1.44 Babies." Press Release 1 Aug 1997. document-level access: <http://europa.eu.int/en/comm/eurostat/compres/en/5697/6305697a.htm>

EUROPE--EMPLOYMENT (v26)

In the EU, in 1991, there was a "prevalence of a high proportion of temporary employment among young workers: 27.5 per cent of those between 14 and 24 years old are employed under fixed-term contracts with no prospect of permanent employment. This is three times the average proportion of temporary to total employment...(9.3 per cent)....On average, the rate of part-time employment is slightly lower among young workers than it is for the EU's total working population (13.9 versus 15 per cent)...." (p59)

DeGrip, Andries/Hoevenberg, Jeroen/Willems, Ed. "Atypical Employment in the European Union." International Labour Review v136 n1 Spr 1997. p49-71. (ISSN0020-7780).

"The 1996 European Labour Force Survey indicated 149.3 million people in the EU with a job, according to a report...by Eurostat, Statistical Office of the European Communities in Luxembourg. This was an EU employment rate of 49.4% in the survey week in spring last year....Highest employment rate was Denmark's 60.7%, lowest Spain's 37.9%. 16.3% (24.3 m [million]) of those with jobs said they worked part-time; 80.6% of these were women; 16.6 m part-timers said they were not available for full-time work; 83.0% of these were women. EU-wide, 31.5% of female employment is part-time; highest is the Netherlands' 68.3% followed by the UK's 44.8%. Nearly two million unemployed women said they were looking for a part-time job. Of the 124.8 m people with a full-time job, only a third were women. 14.1% of employees had a 'contract of limited duration'. This ranged from 2.6% in Luxembourg to 33.6% in Spain. The EU figure for the under-25s was 35.1% (75.4% in Spain)."

Eurostat. "149.3 Million in the EU with a Job." Press Release 22 Jul 1997. document-level access: <http://europa.eu.int/en/comm/eurostat/compres/en/5397/6305397a.htm>

EUROPE--JAPAN--UNITED STATES--ECONOMIC CONDITIONS (v26)

EUROPE--LANGUAGES (v26)

EUROPE--NORTH AMERICA--MANUFACTURES (v26)

EUROPE--POPULATION (v26)

In 1996, "the EU population rose by an estimated 1,037,600 (nearly 0.3%) to 373,691,200. The natural increase (live births minus deaths) was 309,900; the balance of 727,700 was net migration into the EU....World population growth last year was almost 81 million. The EU contributed only 1.3% of this, although it has 6.4% of total world population. India accounted for nearly 21% of the rise, China nearly 15%. Share of the USA, Japan and other more developed countries was 2.9%."

Eurostat. "EU Women Average 1.44 Babies." Press Release 1 Aug 1997. document-level access: <http://europa.eu.int/en/comm/eurostat/compres/en/5697/6305697a.htm>

EUROPE--UNITED STATES--ECONOMIC CONDITIONS

"The European Union's GDP was $8.4 trillion in 1996, compared with $7.2 trillion for the United States." (p86) "The European Union also has a larger volume of global trade. EU external trade totaled $1.9 trillion in 1996, compared with $1.7 trillion for the United States....The share of exports and imports in total output is now about 23 percent in both the EU and the United States. This ratio has doubled for the United States over the past 25 years while rising only modestly in Europe, but it is also likely to remain broadly similar." (p87)

Bergsten, C. Fred. "The Dollar and the Euro." Foreign Affairs v76 n4 Jul-Aug 1997. p83-95. (ISSN0015-7120).

"The global economic roles of the European Union and the United States are nearly identical. The EU accounts for about 31 percent of world output and 20 percent of world trade. The United States provides about 27 percent of global production and 18 percent of world trade. The dollar's 40 to 60 percent share of world finance far exceeds the economic weight of the United States. This total also exceeds the share of 10 to 40 percent for the European national currencies combined. The dollar's market share is three to five times that of the deutsche mark, the only European currency now used globally." (p83-84)

Bergsten, C. Fred. "The Dollar and the Euro." Foreign Affairs v76 n4 Jul-Aug 1997. p83-95. (ISSN0015-7120).

EUROPE--UNITED STATES--EMPLOYMENT (v26)

EUROPEAN UNION--GERMANY--PUBLIC OPINION (v26)

EUTHANASIA--BRITISH COLUMBIA--PUBLIC OPINION

The Euthanasia Prevention Coalition British Columbia "commissioned a June [1997] poll on euthanasia. It discovered that 81 per cent of the 603 people surveyed want the government to guarantee pain relief and other care to alleviate suffering among the dying. Seventy-one per cent said 'people who want to commit suicide should be helped with their problems, not helped to die by means of assisted suicide.'...Those favoring legalization usually had reservations about the abuses that could occur, with 76 per cent of those favoring legalization being concerned that, if euthanasia is allowed, people in a temporary state of depression might ask to have their lives ended." (p9-10)

LeBow, Barbara. "Happenings around the World: British Columbians Reject Euthanasia." Prolife News v22 n10 Nov-Dec 1997. p9-10.

EUTHANASIA--NETHERLANDS (v26)

A new "report finds that in the Netherlands there are about 135,000 deaths each year, of which more than 96 percent occur from natural causes. Medical actions to terminate life caused 3.4 percent of the deaths, of which 2.4 percent involved euthanasia and 0.3 percent assisted suicide. (In euthanasia, the physician administers the lethal act; in assisted suicide, the patient does.) Those two causes were responsible for roughly 3,600 deaths. Doctors received almost 10,000 requests for euthanasia and assisted suicide, so it is clear that requests are refused far more often than they are granted....In 53 percent of the cases, euthanasia has been discussed with the patient, though the discussion has not yet led to an explicit request. In 79 percent of the cases, the patients were not competent any longer to discuss euthanasia. In most of the cases, the family of the patient had asked for a hastening of death. In 91 percent of those cases, life was shortened by a few hours or days at most." (p7 secA)

Barnard, Herbert. "Comment: Dutch Euthanasia Policy Avoids the Slippery Slope." Detroit News 30 Jun 1997. p7 secA.

EUTHANASIA--SWITZERLAND

The Swiss Society for Humane Dying, also referred to as EXIT, is "a 65,000-member, private, nonprofit organization serving the German-speaking part of Switzerland....About 300 doctors are...EXIT members....EXIT...insists that the client be at least 18 years old, mentally competent, a resident of Switzerland, and suffering from unbearable health problems....EXIT reports that the number of members who request assisted suicide is increasing--on average, 100 to 120 patients per year...." (p23)

Kerckhoff, Richard K. "Last Word: This Way Out." Toward Freedom v46 n5 Sep-Oct 1997. p23. (ISSN0048-9898).

EUTHANASIA--UNITED STATES

Oregon voters "seem to be very closely split on the assisted suicide issue. A 1994 ballot initiative allowing doctors to prescribe drugs that patients with an estimated six months or less to live could use to end their lives was approved by just 51 percent." (p51) "It is widely recognized that physician-assisted suicide occurs across the United States, even though the practice is banned by statute in 35 states and criminalized by common law in nine others." (p52)

Lowe, Alexandra Dylan. "Cover Story/Individual Rights:

Facing the Final Exit." ABA Journal v83 Sep 1997. p48-52. (ISSN0747-0088).

"Since Oregon's 'Measure 16' passed three years ago, not a single bill allowing physician-assisted suicide has passed in the more than 20 states where such bills have been introduced....Thirty-five states now have laws outlawing physician-assisted suicide or euthanasia....Seven percent of Oregon physicians surveyed by the NEW ENGLAND JOURNAL OF MEDICINE had written prescriptions for a lethal dose of medication." (p4)

Knickerbocker, Brad. "United States: Oregon Revisits Assisted-Suicide Debate." The Christian Science Monitor v89 n185 19 Aug 1997. p1,4. The Christian Science Monitor search engine: <http://www.csmonitor.com/plweb-cgi/iops1.pl> To retrieve this article, enter the following search: ED=19970819 AND debate. In the "retrieved list," click the title that matches this record. (ISSN0882-7729).

In the U.S., "when put to a vote, a 'right to die' law has been defeated every time except in Oregon, where it passed by 51 percent. Some 59 percent of senior citizens were opposed in a recent Gallop poll." (p18)

Marquand, Robert. "Court's Moral Stamp: Ruling Banning Assisted Suicide Will Slow, But Not End, Right-To-Die Trend." The Christian Science Monitor v89 n149 27 Jun 1997. p1,18. The Christian Science Monitor search engine: <http://www.csmonitor.com/plweb-cgi/iops1.pl> To retrieve this article, enter the following search: ED=19970627 AND trend. In the "retrieved list," click the title that matches this record. (ISSN0882-7729).

EUTHANASIA--UNITED STATES--AGED--ATTITUDES (v26)

EUTHANASIA--UNITED STATES--PUBLIC OPINION

According to a new survey by RxRemedy of Westport, Connecticut, "among Americans aged 55 to 64, 65 to 79, and 80 and older, 65 percent either agree or strongly agree that 'people should have the legal right to commit suicide with a physician's assistance if they have a terminal disease, such as cancer.' Across all of these age groups, 57 to 60 percent agree that 'fear of legal repercussions would deter me from assisting someone in committing suicide.' Fifty-seven percent of the RxRemedy sample agrees that 'more attention to pain control would virtually or totally eliminate the need for euthanasia.'" (p29)

Edmondson, Brad. "Kaleidoscope: Control in the End." American Demographics v19 n5 May 1997. p29. article-level access: <http://www.demographics.com/Publications/AD/97_ad/9705_ad/AD970514.htm> (ISSN0163-4089).

"A recent national poll found 57 percent of Americans think assisted suicide should be legal. Fifty-three percent in 1973 believed doctors should be allowed to end a patient's life if the patient requested it; by 1996, it jumped to 75 percent." (p9 secA)

French, Ron. "Nation World: Reaction: Court's Focus on Suicide Issue Forces Doctors to Address It, Too." Detroit News 27 Jun 1997. p9 secA.

EVACUATION OF CIVILIANS--IRAQ--KURDS

"Last fall, the US evacuated its Kurdish employees from the north [of Iraq], along with their families, a total of 2,150 persons. Shortly thereafter, a group of 600 CIA-backed Iraqi dissidents followed. Most were resettled in the US following a transitional stay in Guam. In December [1996], the US military evacuated what promised to be the last group of Kurds, primarily employees of US-funded nongovernmental organizations (the 'principals') and their families, a total of 3,779 persons...." (p44)

Hiltermann, Joost R. "The Demise of Operation Provide Comfort." Middle East Report v27 n2 Spr 1997. p44-45. (ISSN0899-2851).

EVACUATION OF CIVILIANS--SIERRA LEONE

"More than 2,250 people were evacuated in May and June [1997] from Sierra Leone by Sailors from USS [United States Naval Vessel] Kearsarge (LHD 3) [multipurpose amphibous assault ship] and embarked elements of the 22nd Marine Expeditionary Unit (Special Operations Capable). Among the evacuees were people of 21 nationalities, including 38 Americans, 200 British citizens and several hundred children." (p42)

"Sitrep: Kearsarge/22nd MEU Conduct Third Evacuation." Surface Warfare v22 n4 Jul-Aug 1997. p42. (ISSN0145-1073).

EVERGLADES (FLA.)--ENVIRONMENTAL ASPECTS --COSTS

In the U.S., the cost of the Florida "Everglades restoration [project] rockets toward $5 billion....Last November, the sugar industry spent $22.7 million to defeat a statewide referendum that sought to levy a penny-a-pound tax on raw Florida sugar over the next 25 years. It would have raised $900 million for Everglades restoration projects, including efforts to eliminate fertilizer runoff from sugar fields and to restore the natural flow of water to the Everglades' 'river of grass.'...Today, after decades of flood control, farming, and urban sprawl, the population of wading birds is down 95 percent, and saltwater from the Atlantic Ocean is seeping into water wells....Sugar farmers have already pledged to contribute $232 million over 20 years to the cleanup." (p3)

Richey, Warren. "United States: Saving Everglades: Who Should Pay?" The Christian Science Monitor v89 n181 13 Aug 1997. p3-4. The Christian Science Monitor search engine: <http://www.csmonitor.com/plweb-cgi/iops1.pl> To retrieve this article, enter the following search: ED=19970813 AND pay. In the "retrieved list," click the title that matches this record. (ISSN0882-7729).

EX-CONVICTS--EMPLOYMENT--MICHIGAN (v26)

EXCHANGES, COMMODITY

see COMMODITY EXCHANGES

EXECUTIVES

see also CHIEF EXECUTIVE OFFICERS; WOMEN EXECUTIVES

EXECUTIVES--SALARIES, ETC.--MICHIGAN (v26)

In Michigan, "nine chief executives sit on their own compensation committees, down from 14 last year and 18 in 1995....Directors of 20 companies--compared to 38 last year and 25 in 1995--maintain business relationships with the companies they are elected by shareholders to oversee....Nine companies rewarded executives with substantially higher pay--and sometimes bonuses--despite sagging financials and poor share performance. In 1995, seven companies made similar awards, compared to a dozen in 1994....10 companies buy services--such as aircraft charters, or lease building space--from outside companies affiliated with senior executives or their relatives." (p2 secB)

Howes, Daniel/Smith, Joel J. "Serving the Shareholders 1997: More Companies Link Execs' Pay to Performance: Questionable Practices Still Persist." Detroit News 28 Nov 1997. p2,6 secB.

EXECUTIVES--SALARIES, ETC.--UNITED STATES

In the U.S., in 1996, Chief Executive Officer "pay increased 20 percent while workers' wages rose just 3.3 percent." (p6)

"While hundreds of thousands of workers were laid off in 1995, the CEOs of the 20 companies with the largest announced layoffs saw their salaries and bonuses actually increase by 25 percent. The average salary and compensation package for CEOs of large corporations is nearly $4 million according to BUSINESS WEEK....The AFL-CIO computes that CEO pay is now 212 times greater than the average worker's pay, up from 44 times in 1965." (p7)

Mattern, Douglas. "Globalized Corporate Capitalism: 'It's

the Economy, Stupid!'" Human Quest v211 n5 Sep-Oct 1997. p6-7. (ISSN0897-8786).

EXECUTIVES--UNITED STATES

Companies across the U.S. "say they plan to hire middle managers and other professionals at the fastest rate in more than 15 years, according to a recent survey....The hiring binge poses one drawback. It is largely targeted at the country's 40 million managerial and professional workers, the best-paid and best-educated third of the work force." (p1) "Staff cuts through June [1997] fell 28 percent below the average of the same period during the prior four years, according to a recent survey by Challenger, Gray & Christmas, a Chicago outplacement firm....Some 52 percent of executives plan rapid expansions in the ranks of middle-to-upper management and professional staffs by 1998, according to a nationwide survey of more than 4,800 executives by MRI." (p9)

Tyson, James L. "Business & Money: Workplace: Even 'White Collar' Jobs Bounce Back." The Christian Science Monitor v89 n175 5 Aug 1997. p1,9. The Christian Science Monitor search engine: <http://www.csmonitor.com/plweb-cgi/iops1.pl> To retrieve this article, enter the following search: ED=19970805 AND back. In the "retrieved list," click the title that matches this record. (ISSN0882-7729).

EXECUTIVES--UNITED STATES--ATTITUDES

In the U.S., "a 1996 Deloitte & Touche survey cites an overwhelming majority of Fortune 1000 senior executives (84 percent) who maintain that 'companies make good profits in part because they treat their employees well.' A sizable majority (67 percent) claim their companies are 'making more of an effort to balance the needs of their employees with those of their customers and investors' than they did five years ago." (p62)

Yankelovich, Daniel/Fenichell, Stephen. "The Workin' Life: Got to Give to Get." Mother Jones v22 n4 Jul-Aug 1997. p60-63. article-level access: <http://www.motherjones.com/mother_jones/JA97/yankelovich.html> (ISSN0362-8841).

EXERCISE

see also PHYSICAL FITNESS

EXERCISE--CANADA (v26)

EXERCISE--UNITED STATES (v26)

An annual study by the U.S. Centers for Disease Control "shows that the share of adults who exercise was stable between 1985 and 1994. About 19 percent participated in regular sustained activity in 1994, and 11 percent participated in regular vigorous activity. Thirty-one percent were sedentary." (p41)

Dortch, Shannon. "America Weighs In." American Demographics v19 n6 Jun 1997. p38-43,45. article-level access: <http://www.demographics.com/publications/ad/97_ad/9706_ad/ad970629.htm> (ISSN0163-4089).

"About one-third of Americans report having no leisure-time physical activities, according to an analysis of the 1994 Behavioral Risk Factor Surveillance System. Inactivity peaks in January and February, when 35 percent of adults are inactive, and is lowest in June at 25 percent. Women are more likely than men to be inactive. And Southerners are significantly more likely than Northerners to be inactive in April, June, July, August, October, and November." (p6)

"Sitting around down South." Forecast v17 n6 Jun 1997. p6. article-level access: <http://www.demographics.com/Publications/FC/97_fc/9706_fc/FC97065.htm> (ISSN0732-1597).

The Centers for Disease Control and Prevention "estimates that lack of regular exercise kills as many as 250,000 Americans each year--about 12 percent of the total who die. People who don't exercise have twice as great a risk of coronary heart disease as those who exercise regularly. Middle-aged women are more likely to die of heart disease than breast cancer by a factor of more than 2 to 1." (p96)

Rosellini, Lynn. "1997 Health Guide: How Far Should You Go to Stay Fit?" U.S. News & World Report v123 n18 10 Nov 1997. p95-96. article-level access: <http://www.usnews.com/usnews/issue/971110/10HEAR.HTM> (ISSN0041-5537).

EXHAUSTION

see FATIGUE

EXOTIC SPECIES--UNITED STATES

"Of the roughly 4,000 exotic plants and 2,300 exotic animals in the United States, only about 15 percent are considered 'harmful,' according to a 1993 U.S. Office of Technology Assessment report. However, this small percentage can have a big impact: From 1906 to 1991, a scant 79 exotic species exacted about $97 billion in damages." (p19)

Flack, Stephanie/Furlow, Elaine. "America's Least Wanted: The Dirty Dozen." Nature Conservancy v46 n6 Nov-Dec 1996. p17-23. (ISSN0028-5200).

EXPECTANT MOTHERS

see PREGNANT WOMEN

EXPORT ASSEMBLY INDUSTRY

see OFFSHORE ASSEMBLY INDUSTRY

EXPORTS (v26)

EXPORTS--AFRICA

Africa's "export receipts increased by 8.7 per cent in 1996, spurred by a 4 per cent rise in output volume and a 4.7 per cent increase in world market prices for its commodities. The rise in commodity prices also translated into a 4.6 per cent improvement in Africa's terms of trade....[Oil exporting countries's] export receipts increased by 23.3 per cent and their terms of trade improved by 18.9 per cent....Non-oil exporting countries experienced a 5 per cent decline in export earnings." (p13)

"Africa Records Stronger Growth." Africa Recovery v11 n1 Jul 1997. p13.

EXPORTS--AFRICA, SUB-SAHARAN (v26)

EXPORTS--ALABAMA (v26)

EXPORTS--AUSTRALIA (v26)

EXPORTS--CALIFORNIA

"In fiscal 1996, the value of California's estimated exports rose to $7.3 billion, a 4-percent gain over 1995. California's horticultural exports dominated its export mix, with fruit, vegetable, and tree nut exports totaling $4.6 billion. This accounted for 63 percent of California's farm exports and was 55 percent of total U.S. fruit, vegetable, and tree nut exports. California was also the leading exporter of seeds at $157 million...." (p8)

Greene, Joel/U.S. Dept. of Agriculture. Economic Research Service. "California Leading Exporter in Fiscal 1996." Foreign Agricultural Trade of the United States Jan-Mar 1997. p8-9.

"Four of California's top six export partners are Asian Pacific Rim economies (Japan, South Korea, Taiwan and Singapore). The fastest growing export markets between 1990 and 1995 were Malaysia (growth of 216.7 per cent) and Hong Kong (up 123.5 per cent)." (p29)

Leadbeater, Charles. "A Slice of the Silicon Pie." New Statesman 23 May 1997. p28-29. (ISSN0028-6842).

EXPORTS--CANADA (v26)

EXPORTS--CANADA--FRANCE--UNITED STATES (v26)

EXPORTS--CHINA--UNITED STATES (v26)

"Total US exports of goods to China in 1996 amounted to approximately $12 billion, or about 2 percent of US exports overall....US exports so far this year have decreased about 7 percent." (p19)

Hennig, Jutta. "Opinion/Essays: Why Give China (M)ore (F)or (N)othing?" The Christian Science Monitor v89 n144 20 Jun

1997. p19. The Christian Science Monitor search engine: <http://www.csmonitor.com/plweb-cgi/iops1.pl> To retrieve this article, enter the following search: ED=19970620 AND nothing. In the "retrieved list," click the title that matches this record. (ISSN0882-7729).

EXPORTS--EGYPT (v26)

EXPORTS--EMPLOYMENT--UNITED STATES (v26)

EXPORTS--EUROPE--FORMER SOVIET REPUBLICS (v26)

EXPORTS--EUROPE--SOUTH AMERICA (v26)

EXPORTS--GEORGIA (v26)

EXPORTS--GERMANY (v26)

EXPORTS--HONDURAS (v26)

EXPORTS--HONG KONG

"According to the statistics released by the Census and Statistics Department..., re-exports accounted for 86% of the value of total exports and 40% of the total value of external trade of Hong Kong in the first half of 1997, affirming the importance of re-export trade in the territory. In the same period of 1996, the corresponding shares were 85% and 40% respectively. The mainland of China (the Mainland) remained the largest partner for Hong Kong's re-export trade. As a source, re-exports originating in the Mainland accounted for 57% of Hong Kong's re-export value in the first half of 1997. As a destination, the Mainland's share was 36%....Other main origins of Hong Kong's re-exports in the first half of 1997 included Japan (accounting for 11%), Taiwan (6.9%), the United States (5.4%) and South Korea (3.4%). The other main destinations included the United States (accounting for 20%), Japan (6.5%), Germany (3.7%) and the United Kingdom (2.8%)."

Hong Kong. Census and Statistics Department. "Analysis of Re-Export Trade Statistics in First Half of 1997." Press Release 21 Aug 1997. document-level access: <http://www.info.gov.hk/censtatd/hkstat/press/t61h97.htm>

"In the third quarter of 1997, domestic exports classified to the four major industries of textiles; wearing apparel; machinery, equipment, apparatus, parts and components; and consumer electrical and electronic products; together accounted for 72% of Hong Kong's total domestic exports of manufactured goods, according to statistics released...by the Census and Statistics Department. In the third quarter of 1997, domestic exports classified to the machinery, equipment, apparatus, parts and components industry increased by 18% over a year earlier to $10.3 billion. Domestic exports classified to the textiles industry increased by 8% to $14.8 billion; and those to the wearing apparel industry increased by 1% to $11.2 billion....Domestic exports classified to the consumer electrical and electronic products industry decreased by 9% to $6.0 billion."

Hong Kong. Census and Statistics Department. "Domestic Export Statistics Classified by Industrial Origin." Press Release 14 Nov 1997. document-level access: <http://www.info.gov.hk/censtatd/hkstat/press/t33q97.htm>

EXPORTS--ILLINOIS

In 1996, exports from Illinois "rose 16 percent to nearly $4 billion as its feed grain exports increased to $1.6 billion and soybeans rose to about $1.4 billion. Illinois exports of livestock products jumped 70 percent to $251 million." (p8)

Greene, Joel/U.S. Dept. of Agriculture. Economic Research Service. "California Leading Exporter in Fiscal 1996." Foreign Agricultural Trade of the United States Jan-Mar 1997. p8-9.

EXPORTS--IOWA

"Estimated exports for Iowa rose 16 percent to nearly $4.7 billion in fiscal 1996. Iowa was the leading exporter of feed grains and soybeans at $2 billion and $1.5 billion, respectively. This was a combined increase of 21 percent. Iowa's exports were also boosted by livestock exports of $611 million, up 10 percent." (p8)

Greene, Joel/U.S. Dept. of Agriculture. Economic Research Service. "California Leading Exporter in Fiscal 1996." Foreign Agricultural Trade of the United States Jan-Mar 1997. p8-9.

EXPORTS--JORDAN--MICHIGAN

"Michigan exports to Jordan jumped 75 percent between 1992 and 1994, up to more than $5.9 million, the last year for which exact numbers are available. The state's exports to Jordan are now believed to be worth about $10 million." (p3 secD)

Shepardson, David. "City & Suburban News: In Detroit: Jordanian Prince's Visit to Open Business Expo." Detroit News 26 Jun 1997. p3 secD.

EXPORTS--KANSAS

In 1996, "estimated exports for Kansas were more than $3.1 billion. Wheat was the leading export from Kansas, but the value of wheat exports dropped 5 percent to $860 million....Kansas was the leading exporter of hides and skins at $289 million and the second in livestock and products at $789 million." (p8)

Greene, Joel/U.S. Dept. of Agriculture. Economic Research Service. "California Leading Exporter in Fiscal 1996." Foreign Agricultural Trade of the United States Jan-Mar 1997. p8-9.

EXPORTS--LATIN AMERICA--UNITED STATES (v26)

In fiscal 1997, exports to Latin America (excluding Mexico) "have increased to $3.7 billion, up 3 percent from 1996. The largest export gains are in soybeans and soybean meal, which to date are up $101 and $81 million, respectively....Already trade with Venezuela, Argentina, the Caribbean, Central America, Ecuador, and Chile exceeds $100 million each and is up 6-27 percent." (p8)

U.S. Dept. of Agriculture. "Regional Highlights." Outlook for U.S. Agricultural Exports 28 Aug 1997. p8.

EXPORTS--MEXICO--UNITED STATES (v26)

U.S. export performance with Mexico has been strong, "with exports increasing nearly 15 percent per year, on average, between 1993 and 1996, to a record $5.4 billion. Twelve commodities having the fastest growth--corn, soybeans, wheat, field seeds, vegetable oils, cotton, sugar and related products, barley, pulses, beef and veal, rice, and soybeans--as a group increased $2 billion, more than 150 percent." (p5)

U.S. Dept. of Agriculture. Economic Research Service. "Executive Summary." NAFTA: International Agriculture and Trade Reports Situation and Outlook Series Sep 1997. p3-6.

EXPORTS--MICHIGAN--DETROIT

"Metro Detroit lost its No. 1 ranking among U.S. metropolitan areas in production of goods for overseas customers last year, but remains a strong player in the nation's export market. Figures released...by the U.S. Department of Commerce showed Metro Detroit fell to third in 1996 in total exports. Led by shipments of automotive goods and industrial machinery, Metro Detroit exported $27.5 billion in 1996, slightly behind San Jose, Calif., and New York City. Metro Detroit exported $27.3 billion in 1995. Ranked by growth in the dollar value of exports since 1993, however, Detroit was second to San Jose with an increase of $10.8 billion during the four-year period....In 1996, Michigan had six metro areas in the top 100 export regions in the country. They are Detroit, 3rd; Grand Rapids/Muskegon/Holland, 43rd; Flint, 73rd; Ann Arbor, 74th; Saginaw/Bay City/Midland, 77th; and Kalamazoo/Battle Creek, 93rd." (p1 secB)

Smith, Joel J. "Business: Auto and Machinery Sales Keep Detroit among Top Exporters." Detroit News 1 Oct 1997. p1 secB.

EXPORTS--MICHIGAN--OAKLAND COUNTY

Oakland County, Michigan "exported 1.75 billion in goods and services to Mexico in 1995, according to the most recent county figures. It also leads the state in foreign trade, accounting for 35 percent of Michigan's exports....600 of the county's 2,700 manufacturing companies export...." (p1 secB)

Durfee, Doug. "The Metro: Patterson Leads Hopeful Mexico Trade Mission." Detroit News 8 Jun 1997. p1 secB.

EXPORTS--MINNESOTA

In 1996, "Minnesota exports exceeded $3 billion, a 25-percent gain. Exports of Minnesota feed grains jumped 36 percent to nearly $1.1 billion. Wheat and soybean exports also were strong, rising to $315 million and $854 million, respectively." (p8)

Greene, Joel/U.S. Dept. of Agriculture. Economic Research Service. "California Leading Exporter in Fiscal 1996." Foreign Agricultural Trade of the United States Jan-Mar 1997. p8-9.

EXPORTS--MISSOURI

"Missouri alone serves over 100 different countries around the world with our exports. In 1995, our exports exceeded $5.5 billion. Not only does Missouri export electronics, machinery, and chemicals, but Missouri is one of the largest exporters in the country of agricultural products. In overall agricultural exports, Missouri is ranked 15th among all 50 States in the value of its agricultural exports. Missouri is the sixth largest soybean producer and eighth largest feed corn producer in the country. Missouri ranks 6th in rice production and 13th in wheat production." (pS11030)

Bond, Christopher S. (Sen.-Mo.). "ISTEA." Congressional Record. Daily ed. v143 n144 23 Oct 1997. pS11029-11032. section/page-level access: <http://thomas.loc.gov/cgi-bin/query/R?r105:FLD001:S11029:> (ISSN0363-7239). (X1.1A.105/1).

EXPORTS--NEBRASKA

In 1996, "Nebraska's exports rose to $3.5 billion, a 10-percent increase. Nebraska led the United States in exports of livestock products at $834 million, feeds and fodders at $226 million, and fats and oils at $119 million." (p8)

Greene, Joel/U.S. Dept. of Agriculture. Economic Research Service. "California Leading Exporter in Fiscal 1996." Foreign Agricultural Trade of the United States Jan-Mar 1997. p8-9.

EXPORTS--OREGON

"Oregon's exports nearly doubled in...[the past seven years], from $5 billion in 1989 to $9.8 billion last year, nearly twice the rate of overall economic growth. Electronics exports in the state grew exponentially, from $336 million to $2.1 billion." (p18)

Sneider, Daniel. "Mile-High Economic Summit: The G-7: In New West, Disk Drives Replace the Cattle Drives." The Christian Science Monitor v89 n142 18 Jun 1997. p1,18. The Christian Science Monitor search engine: <http://www.csmonitor.com/plweb-cgi/iops1.pl> To retrieve this article, enter the following search: ED=19970618 AND drives. In the "retrieved list," click the title that matches this record. (ISSN0882-7729).

EXPORTS--PAKISTAN (v26)

EXPORTS--PERSIAN GULF REGION--UNITED STATES

"In the mid-1990s, U.S. annual exports in commercial goods and services to the GCC [Gulf Cooperation Council] region averaged $12 billion and imports approximately $13 billion. Based on U.S. Department of Commerce figures that one billion dollars of exports equals 20,000 American jobs, such exports supported more than 260,000 U.S. jobs and were the primary source of livelihood for nearly 1.2 million Americans...." (p36)

Anthony, John Duke. "The U.S.-GCC Relationship: A Glass Half-Empty or Half-Full?" Middle East Policy v5 n2 May 1997. p22-41. (ISSN1061-1924).

EXPORTS--SINGAPORE (v26)

EXPORTS--SWEDEN (v26)

EXPORTS--TEXAS

In Texas, in 1996, "exports rose to $3.6 billion. Texas was the leading cotton exporter at $760 million, but the estimate was nearly $120 million less than in 1995...." (p8)

Greene, Joel/U.S. Dept. of Agriculture. Economic Research Service. "California Leading Exporter in Fiscal 1996." Foreign Agricultural Trade of the United States Jan-Mar 1997. p8-9.

EXPORTS--UNITED STATES (v26)

"At $7.2 billion, Japan is by far the largest export market for U.S. processed foods, accounting for 24 percent of the total in 1996. More than 60 percent ($4.5 billion) of exports to Japan was meat and fish. NAFTA partners Canada and Mexico were second and third at $4.5 billion and $2 billion, a combined 22 percent of total U.S. processed food trade. Others in the top 10 included three Asia Pacific Rim nations (South Korea, Hong Kong, and Taiwan), three western European nations (Netherlands, United Kingdom, and Germany), and Russia. Russia recorded the largest export growth rate of any major market, as exports reached $1.3 billion, a 32-percent increase over 1995." (p12)

Ruppel, Fred J./Handy, Charles R./Malanoski, Margaret A./U.S. Dept. of Agriculture. Economic Research Service. "World Agriculture & Trade: U.S. Processed Food Trade Continues to Expand." Agricultural Outlook Jul 1997. p11-13.

"U.S. exports increased 50 percent since 1991 without fast track [authority for the President]. Today, exports are 30 percent higher than in 1993. According to trade data released by the International Monetary Fund, United States exports to Brazil, South America's richest market, grew 56 percent from 1994 to 1995. During that same period, the European Union's exports to Brazil grew only 8 percent, while Japan's exports grew only 18 percent." (pS10460)

Feinstein, Dianne (Sen.-Calif.). "Bosnia and NATO Enlargement." Congressional Record. Daily ed. v143 n138 7 Oct 1997. pS10456-10462. section/page-level access: <http://thomas.loc.gov/cgi-bin/query/R?r105:FLD001:S10460:> (ISSN0363-7239). (X1.1A.105/1).

In the U.S., in 1996, "even though bulk export volume declined 6 percent to 119 million tons, higher grain and soybean prices boosted export value 12 percent to $28.1 billion. Wheat shipments declined 4 percent to 30.9 million tons, but export value surged 15 percent to $6.3 billion due to higher prices caused by tight supplies. Likewise, corn exports fell 13 percent to 52.2 million tons as prices raised the export value 15 percent to $8.4 billion." (p2)

Greene, Joel/U.S. Dept. of Agriculture. Economic Research Service. "Agricultural Exports Surpass $60 Billion." Foreign Agricultural Trade of the United States Jan-Mar 1997. p2-3.

In the U.S., "over the first 4 months of 1997, broiler exports totaled 1.4 billion pounds, down 2 percent from the same period in 1996....Exports to Russia, the largest market for U.S. broiler products, have continued to expand, totaling 647 million pounds over the first 4 months, up 13 percent." (p3)

U.S. Dept. of Agriculture. Economic Research Service. "Broiler Exports Fall." Livestock, Dairy and Poultry Situation and Outlook Series 17 Jul 1997. p3.

Year-to-date U.S. "poultry meat exports of $491 million continue at a record pace and account for more than 70 percent of U.S. agricultural exports to Russia. U.S. exports to the other NIS [Newly Independent States] republics have dropped 31 percent in fiscal 1997...." (p8)

U.S. Dept. of Agriculture. Economic Research Service.

"Regional Highlights." Outlook for U.S. Agricultural Exports 29 May 1997. p6-8.

In the U.S., "at $31.2 billion, high value product (HVP) exports are up 6 percent in 1997....HVP export value now exceeds bulk export value by nearly $10 billion for the year." (p1)

Whitton, Carol/U.S. Dept. of Agriculture. Economic Research Service. "Exports." U.S. Agricultural Trade Update 23 Oct 1997. p1.

In the U.S., "the cumulative value of bulk commodity exports is $21.7 billion, 17 percent below fiscal 1996....Exports of wheat to date are $3.6 billion, 42 percent below 1996, while corn exports, at $5.7 billion, are down 28 percent....In August, exports of wheat and corn rose, reaching $504 million and $420 million, respectively....Soybean exports have risen to $6.6 billion in the year-to-date, an 11-percent gain. August exports jumped 57 percent from July....Cotton exports in August 1997 declined from July to $167 million....Cumulative exports are 11 percent below 1996 at $2.6 billion." (p1)

Whitton, Carol/U.S. Dept. of Agriculture. Economic Research Service. "Exports." U.S. Agricultural Trade Update 23 Oct 1997. p1.

In the U.S., "the total value of fiscal 1997 bulk exports (wheat, rice, feed grains, soybeans, tobacco, and cotton) was $23.3 billion, 17 percent below a year ago. The value of bulk exports remained below that of high-value product exports, which continued to increase. Bulk export quantity also declined by 11 percent." (p1)

U.S. Dept. of Agriculture. Economic Research Service. "Exports." U.S. Agricultural Trade Update 24 Nov 1997. p1.

The top seven U.S. exporting "states were unchanged from fiscal 1995, with California the leading exporter at $7.3 billion. Iowa was second, followed by Illinois, Texas, Nebraska, Kansas, Minnesota, Indiana, Washington, and North Dakota....The top ten leading States accounted for 58 percent of total U.S. agricultural exports, the same as in 1995. A record 21 States exported more than $1 billion worth of agricultural commodities." (unpaginated)

Whitton, Carol/U.S. Dept. of Agriculture. Economic Research Service. "FY 1996 State Export Estimates." U.S. Agricultural Trade Update 23 May 1997.

Through July 1997, U.S. "vegetables and preparations exports reached $3.5 billion, up 10 percent, with most of the gains in value occuring in tomato and lettuce exports. Poultry meat exports rose to $2.1 billion compared with $1.9 billion last year. Tobacco exports are up 19 percent to $1.4 billion in 1997, and seed exports have risen 22 percent to $788 million." (unpaginated)

Whitton, Carol/U.S. Dept. of Agriculture. Economic Research Service. "Exports." U.S. Agricultural Trade Update 23 Sep 1997.

EXPORTS--UNITED STATES--WESTERN HEMISPHERE (v26)

EXTENDED CARE FACILITIES

see LONG-TERM CARE FACILITIES

EXTERNAL DEBTS

see DEBTS, EXTERNAL

EXTERNAL TRADE

see INTERNATIONAL TRADE

EXTINCTION (BIOLOGY)--ALABAMA (v26)

EXTINCTION (BIOLOGY)--CALIFORNIA (v26)

EXTINCTION (BIOLOGY)--HAWAII (v26)

EXTINCTION (BIOLOGY)--UNITED STATES (v26)

EXTRA-MARITAL SEX

see ADULTERY

EXTRAUTERINE PREGNANCY

see ECTOPIC PREGNANCY

EYEGLASSES--UNITED STATES--BABY BOOM GENERATION (v26)

FACTORY AND TRADE WASTE

see HAZARDOUS WASTES

FACTORY AND TRADE WASTE--CHINA--NANJING CITY (v26)

FACULTY (EDUCATION)

see COLLEGE TEACHERS

FAILURES OF SAVINGS AND LOANS

see SAVINGS AND LOAN ASSOCIATION FAILURES

FAIR EMPLOYMENT PRACTICE

see DISCRIMINATION IN EMPLOYMENT

FAMILIES, AFRO-AMERICAN

see AFRO-AMERICAN FAMILIES

FAMILY

see also AFRO-AMERICAN FAMILIES; CHILDREN; DIVORCE; FATHERS; HISPANIC AMERICAN FAMILIES; HOUSEHOLDS; PARENT AND CHILD; SINGLE-PARENT FAMILY; UNMARRIED COUPLES

FAMILY--AUSTRALIA (v26)

"In June 1997, 84 percent of Australia's 2.5 million families with dependants had one or more family members in employment, according to the report 'Labour Force Status and Other Characteristics of Families' released...by the Australian Bureau of Statistics (ABS). The ABS report showed that there were five million families in Australia made up of two or more related people usually living in the same household. There were over four million couple families (83 per cent of all families) and just under half of these had dependants (children under 15 years of age plus other family members aged 15-24 who were full-time students). For couple families with dependants: one or both partners were employed in 91 per cent of these families; 9 per cent had neither parent employed, and in most of these families, one or both parents were unemployed; the husband was unemployed in 5 per cent of these families, half of whom had been looking for work for 30 weeks or more; the wife was unemployed in 3 per cent of these families."

Australian Bureau of Statistics. "Australia's Families and the Workforce--ABS." Media Release 30 Sep 1997. document-level access: <http://www.abs.gov.au/websitedbs/d3110125.nsf/4a255eef008309e44a255eef00061e57/ed1997d7b1f812a84a25652100810827?OpenDocument>

FAMILY--CANADA (v26)

FAMILY--CANADA--ECONOMIC CONDITIONS (v26)

FAMILY--EUROPE (v26)

FAMILY--GREAT BRITAIN (v26)

FAMILY--QUEBEC (PROVINCE) (v26)

FAMILY--UNITED STATES (v26)

In the U.S., "the percentage of Hispanic children living with both parents fell from 78 percent in 1970 to 63 percent between 1970 and 1995. During the same period, the percentage of children living with both parents slipped from nearly 90 percent to 76 percent among whites, and from 59 percent to 33 percent among African American children." (p30)

del Pinal, Jorge/Singer, Audrey. "Generations of Diversity: Latinos in the United States." Population Bulletin v52 n3 Oct 1997. p2-47. (ISSN0032-468X).

FAMILY--UNITED STATES--ECONOMIC CONDITIONS

In the U.S., "in 1995, about 4.0 million families lived below the poverty level despite having at least one family member in the labor market for 27 weeks or more, little changed from the 1994 total. The poverty rate for families, defined as the ratio of poor families with workers to all families with workers, was 7.0 percent in 1995. Families maintained by women had over four times the poverty rate, and families maintained by men had over twice the poverty rate than that of married-couple families.

Families with children under age 18 that were maintained by a woman who was the only labor force member had the highest poverty rate--25.2 percent--while similar families headed by men had a 15 percent rate of poverty. Over five times as many poor families were maintained by women, than were maintained by men....Married-couple families had the lowest rate of poverty. For married couples with one member in the workforce, the poverty rate was 10.5 percent if the husband worked, and 6.8 percent if the wife worked. Poverty was rare (1.7 percent) among married-couple families in which two or more members were in the workforce."

Hale, Thomas W./U.S. Dept. of Labor. Bureau of Labor Statistics. "A Profile of the Working Poor, 1995." Press Release Aug 1997. document-level access: <http://stats.bls.gov/cpswp96.htm>

FAMILY--UNITED STATES--SOCIAL CONDITIONS

"The Census Bureau's report 'Household and Family Characteristics: March 1995,' found that married families made up 70.0 percent of America's households. That's down from 81.2 percent in 1970. Still, last year there was a 4-percent reduction in out-of-wedlock births, according to the federal Centers for Disease Control and Prevention. This slowed a 16-year rise in the number of unwed women choosing to become mothers....During the past 30 years, the rise in violent crime has paralleled the rise in families abandoned by fathers. But even in high-crime, core-city neighborhoods, well over 90 percent of children from homes with dads manage to avoid delinquency." (p6 secB)

"The Metro: Dad's Back." Detroit News 15 Jun 1997. p6 secB.

FAMILY INCOME

see INCOME

FAMILY LEAVE

see PARENTAL LEAVE

FAMILY-OWNED BUSINESS ENTERPRISES--UNITED STATES--SUCCESSION

University of Connecticut associate business professor Karen File and consultant Russ Prince, of Prince and Associates, conducted a study of 800 U.S. "heirs of recently failed family businesses [and] found the death or disability of the founding family member often destroyed the business. Before the crisis that precipitated the failure of the business, the firms surveyed experienced significant revenue growth. In the five years preceding the failure, 91.3 percent of these firms had average annual revenue growth exceeding 5 percent....About 46 percent of them had more than 100 employees, about 47 percent employed 51 to 100 workers and just 7 percent had 50 or less employees. In most instances, the transition and ultimate business collapse was precipitated by the founder's death (47.7 percent) or unexpected disability (29.8 percent). Only in a relatively few instances was business failure an outcome of an orderly transition process between founder and heir (16.4 percent) or a situation in which the heirs forced the founder to retire (6.1 percent)." (p8 secF)

Seebacher, Noreen. "Strategies: Small Business: Experience Lets Children Decide Whether to Follow in Your Footsteps." Detroit News 11 Aug 1997. p8-9 secF.

FAMILY PLANNING

see BIRTH CONTROL

FAMILY SIZE

see also CHILDLESSNESS

FAMILY SIZE--PUBLIC OPINION

"The Gallup International Poll records a wide range of opinions about the ideal family size....The preference for larger numbers of children is particularly evident in Iceland, Guatemala and Taiwan, where the mean number is close to 3. Also on the high side are the U.S., France, Singapore, Mexico and Canada, where the mean number ranges from over 2.4 to 2.6. In Thailand, Great Britain and Colombia, the average is slightly lower, ranging from 2.2 to 2.4. Only in Germany, Spain and urban India is the mean number close to the population replacement rate, ranging from 2.0 to 2.1."

Gallup Organization. "Global Study of Family Values: An International Gallup Poll: Family Values Differ Sharply around the World." Press Release 7 Nov 1997. document-level access: <http://www.gallup.com/poll/special/family.html>

FAMILY VIOLENCE

see also CHILD ABUSE; CONJUGAL VIOLENCE

FAMILY VIOLENCE--GUAM

"In Guam, police officers have responded to 5,969 family violence offenses from 1993 through 1995. During that same time period, the Child Protective Services received 5,881 referrals, and in 1996 they have reviewed over 3,000 of these referrals. In 1995, the Guam Attorney General's Office prosecuted 106 criminal felony cases and 248 criminal misdemeanor cases; while from January through June, 1996, they prosecuted 50 criminal felonies and 248 criminal misdemeanor cases." (pE1957)

Underwood, Robert A. (Del.-Guam). "Guam Battles Family Violence." Congressional Record. Daily ed. v143 n138 7 Oct 1997. pE1957. section/page-level access: <http://thomas.loc.gov/cgi-bin/query/R?r105:FLD001:E01957:> (ISSN0363-7239). (X1.1A.105/1).

FAMILY VIOLENCE--MEXICO--WOMEN--ATTITUDES

In a study of Mexican women ages 25-31 and 40-49 conducted in 1992, "approximately 19% of the respondents report having been hit by their husbands, with 6.4% hit frequently and 12.5% hit a few times at most. Conversely, the vast majority of wives (81%) claim to have never been hit....Among those claiming never to have been hit, approximately 39% indicate that their spouse has the last word [in family decisions], 14% claim that they themselves have the last word, and 47% claim that decision making is shared equally by both spouses. These figures depart from those for wives who report infrequent violence. Of this group, 59% indicate that their spouses have the last word, 12% claim that they have the last word, and 29% claim that decision making is shared. Wives who claim to be hit frequently have an equal probability of falling in the various response categories for say in decisions--37% of frequently hit wives say that their husband has the last word, 30% indicate that they themselves have the last word, and 33% say both spouses have the last word." (p1303-1304)

Oropesa, R. S. "Development and Marital Power in Mexico." Social Forces v75 n4 Jun 1997. p1291-1317. (ISSN0037-7732).

FAMILY VIOLENCE--UNITED STATES (v26)

In the U.S., "about 1.8 million females are victims of severe domestic violence each year. But so are 2.1 million men (men sometimes hurt other men in the home). Most violent situations involve both parties. Researcher Murray Straus, analyzing several studies, concludes that 25 to 30 percent of violent clashes between partners are the result only of attacks by women." (p15 secA)

Charen, Mona. "Comment: Feminist Prejudices Cloud Spousal Abuse." Detroit News 14 Aug 1997. p15 secA.

A hospital study by the U.S. Dept. of Justice, "showed that approximately 243,000 people (17 percent) were treated for injuries inflicted by someone with whom they had an intimate relationship--a spouse, former spouse, boyfriend, girlfriend or former boyfriend or girlfriend. This was four times higher than the estimates of the number of such crime victims treated in hospital emergency rooms as measured by BJS's [Bureau of Justice Statistics] National Crime Victimization Survey, one of the nation's principal sources of crime victim data....Children younger than 12 years old represented about 5 percent of all patients treated for violence-related injuries."

U.S. Dept. of Justice. "1.4 Million People Treated in Hospital Emergency Rooms for Violence-Related Injuries." Press Release 24 Aug 1997. document-level access: <http://www.ojp.usdoj.gov/pub/bjs/press/vrithed.pr>

In the U.S., the National Coalition Against Domestic Violence's "figures indicate that 95 percent of adult physical abuse victims are women. There are at least 4 million reported incidents of domestic violence against women every year and, on average, 10 women a day are killed by their batterers. Compounding the problem is the fact that 70 percent of men who abuse their female partners also abuse their children. Each year some 3 million children in the United States are victims of child abuse and neglect, the NCADV reports, and as many as 1,500 children die each year as a result." (p34)

Hasenauer, Heike. "Taking On Domestic Violence." Soldiers v52 n10 Oct 1997. p34-36. (ISSN0093-8440).

FAMILY VIOLENCE--UNITED STATES. ARMY

"Since 1993, 208 [U.S. Army] soldiers have been court-martialed for domestic violence,...[Jonnelle Davidson, an Army Community Service program analyst] said. Bob Anthony, deputy clerk of court of the Army Judiciary, which includes the Court of Military Review, said that in 1996 military courts tried 38 soldiers on domestic violence charges." (p36)

Hasenauer, Heike. "Taking on Domestic Violence: Compensating the Victims." Soldiers v52 n10 Oct 1997. p36. (ISSN0093-8440).

The U.S. "Army received 9,409 reports of spouse abuse in fiscal year 1996, said Delores Johnson, manager of the Army Community and Family Support Center's Family Advocacy Program in Alexandria, Va. Of those, 6,346 reports were substantiated--and of 7,500 reports of child abuse, 3,246 were substantiated." (p35)

Hasenauer, Heike. "Taking on Domestic Violence: Domestic Violence Snapshot." Soldiers v52 n10 Oct 1997. p35. (ISSN0093-8440).

FAMINE RELIEF

see FOOD RELIEF

FAMINE VICTIMS

see VICTIMS OF FAMINE

FAMINES--KENYA (v26)

FARM ANIMALS

see LIVESTOCK

FARM CORPORATIONS--UNITED STATES (v26)

FARM CREDIT

see AGRICULTURAL CREDIT

FARM INCOME--CANADA (v26)

FARM INCOME--MICHIGAN (v26)

FARM INCOME--UNITED STATES (v26)

"Data on farm revenues and expenses have been collected through USDA's annual Farm Costs and Returns survey and reported every year since 1984....Results for 1995 show that 16-20 percent of farms were large enough that, relying solely on farm income, a family of four would have income above the official poverty threshold. If 'adequate' income is the ability to cover average household expenditures, data show that 7-9 percent of farms generated sufficient income to cover expenditures for at least one household, if farming was the only source of earnings. The average farm with 'adequate' income had sales of more than $200,000 and assets valued at $800,000 to $1,300,000....On average, farm households are on par with other households in the United States--both earning approximately $45,000. In 1995, about three-fourths of all farm households had total household incomes above the poverty level for a family of four....Because almost three-quarters of farms have gross sales less than $50,000--small farms typically lose money--most farm households rely on off-farm income sources for family income." (p446)

U.S. Dept. of Agriculture. "Agriculture, Rural Development, Food and Drug Administration...Approp. for 1998 (Part 4)." Hearing. U.S. House. Committee on Appropriations. Washington, D.C. : GPO, 1997. (ISBN0160551560). (Y4.Ap6/1:Ag8/997/pt.4).

In the U.S., "net value-added and net farm income reached record levels in 1996, rising substantially from 1995....Net value-added for 1996 was $19.1 billion more than in 1995, up 25 percent, and $9.5 billion greater than its previous high in 1994....Net farm income, which jumped $15.4 billion from 1995 to 1996, is that portion of net value-added earned by farm operators (defined as those individuals and entities who share in the risks of production)....Net cash income rose by $8.8 billion, a 17.1-percent increase from 1995 to 1996...." (p4)

U.S. Dept. of Agriculture. Economic Research Service. "1996 Farm Income Estimates: Net Value-Added and Net Farm Income Attain New Highs in 1996." Agricultural Income and Finance Situation and Outlook Report Sep 1997. p4-13.

According to "Structural and Financial Characteristics of U.S. Farms, 1994: 19th Annual Family Farm Report to the Congress," "more than 2 million U.S. farms produced agricultural commodities that generated an average of $74,000 in gross value of sales per farm in 1994. Still, 73 percent of farms had gross value of sales under $50,000 (noncommercial farms), although they accounted for just 11 percent of total U.S. farm sales. Gross cash farm income (adjusted to exclude the share of production accruing to landlords and contractors) averaged near $69,000. However, gross cash farm income for the Nation's largest farms (sales $1 million or more) averaged almost $2 million, so that less than 1 percent of farms accounted for 23 percent of gross cash farm income. Commodity sales accounted for 84 percent of total gross cash farm income, with government payments adding 5 percent and other farm income 11 percent....Net cash farm income averaged $11,696 for farms nationwide, but ranged from negative for farms with sales under $50,000 to over $380,000 for farms with sales of $1 million or more." (p7)

U.S. Dept. of Agriculture. Economic Research Service. "ERS Summary of Report: The 19th Annual Family Farm Report: From Acres Farmed to Business Goals." ERS Information Sep 1997. p7-8.

In the U.S., in 1994, "more than a third of farms received income from government payments, averaging $9,306 per receiving farm. Almost two-thirds of commercial farms (gross value of sales $50,000 or more) compared with one-fourth of noncommercial farms received government payments. However, government payments accounted for less than 3 percent of gross cash farm income for commercial farms compared with 41 percent for noncommercial farms." (p8)

U.S. Dept. of Agriculture. Economic Research Service. "ERS Summary of Report: The 19th Annual Family Farm Report: From Acres Farmed to Business Goals." ERS Information Sep 1997. p7-8.

FARM LABOR

see AGRICULTURAL LABORERS

FARM OWNERSHIP--UNITED STATES

According to "Structural and Financial Characteristics of U.S. Farms, 1994: 19th Annual Family Farm Report to the Congress," "more than 90 percent of farm businesses were legally organized as individual operations, while 6 percent of farms were partnerships and 4 percent were corporations (most of which were family-owned). Farms organized as individual operations averaged more than $50,000 in gross value sales and had farm assets that averaged more than $350,000." (p7)

U.S. Dept. of Agriculture. Economic Research Service. "ERS Summary of Report: The 19th Annual Family Farm Report: From Acres Farmed to Business Goals." ERS Information Sep 1997. p7-8.

FARM OWNERSHIP--ZIMBABWE

"One-third of Zimbabwe, including more than 50 percent of the nation's farmland, is owned by 4,500 white commercial farmers--17 years after independence....Though they make up less than one-tenth of 1 percent of the population, white farmers control the land, produce 12 percent of the nation's gross domestic product and earn 45 percent of its foreign currency. Meanwhile, they pay black farm-workers about $50 per month....Since independence, the government has bought up or foreclosed 1,953 white-owned farms, some 7.7 million acres of real estate. It has resettled about 60,000 black families on that territory--far short of the 152,000 families they claimed would be settled by 1983....At one point, 23 of 48 estates taken over went to government officers." (p1,8 secA)

Tucker, Neely. "White Zimbabweans Fear for Their Land." Detroit Free Press 17 Nov 1997. p1,8 secA.

FARM SUBSIDIES

see AGRICULTURAL SUBSIDIES

FARMERS--CHINA

"According to Tian (1993), 99.6 percent of the laborers [in China] who worked outside of agriculture had either farmed their land only during peak seasons or had arranged other family members to take care of the land. Only .4 per cent of the workers who left agriculture had given back the land to the villages. Among households who were willing to leave agriculture, 91 per cent of them did not want to return the land to local authorities." (p111)

Yang, Dennis Tao. "China's Land Arrangements and Rural Labor Mobility." China Economic Review v8 n2 Fall 1997. p101-115. (ISSN1043-951X).

FARMERS--UNITED STATES (v26)

see also INCOME--UNITED STATES--FARMERS

"The median age of the American dairy farmer is 58 years according to the USDA. VETERINARY ECONOMICS, June 1997 reports that 34 percent of all agricultural asset owners are older than 65 and, as a result, 75 percent of all farm and ranch assets will be changing hands in the next 20 years." (p31)

Sheaffer, C. Edgar. "The Natural Vet: Holistic Livestock Healthcare: Holistic Methods Progressing in Europe...: Homeopathy for...Cure." Acres, U.S.A. v27 n10 Oct 1997. p31. (ISSN1076-4968).

FARMERS--UNITED STATES--ATTITUDES (v26)

FARMERS--UNITED STATES--ECONOMIC CONDITIONS --ATTITUDES (v26)

FARMERS' COOPERATIVES

see AGRICULTURAL COOPERATIVE CREDIT ASSOCIATIONS

FARMING

see AGRICULTURE

FARMING, OSTRICH

see OSTRICH FARMING

FARMS--ARMENIA--GEORGIA (REPUBLIC)

"Armenian agriculture was decollectivized in 1991, and now all but 20 percent of arable land has been distributed to private farms. In Georgia, private farms hold only 49 percent of cultivated land....The typical farm size in Armenia and Georgia is about 1.5 and 0.75 hectares, respectively....These farms tend to market 30 to 40 percent of their main products, mostly directly to consumers." (p5)

Sedik, David J./U.S. Dept. of Agriculture. Economic Research Service. "Status of Agricultural Reforms in the NIS/B Countries in 1997." Newly Independent States and the Baltics: International Agriculture and Trade Reports Situation and Outlook Series May 1997. p4-9.

FARMS--AUSTRALIA--ECONOMIC CONDITIONS (v26)

FARMS--FORMER SOVIET REPUBLICS

"In Moldova, private farms and household plots occupied only 18 percent of agricultural land in 1996. In Ukraine, private farms comprise a mere 2 percent of total agricultural land. Private subsidiary plots occupy another 16 percent of agricultural land....In Russia, 96 percent of potatoes, 89 percent of vegetables, 55 percent of pork, and 45 percent of beef are now produced either on private plots or farms...." (p8-9)

Sedik, David J./U.S. Dept. of Agriculture. Economic Research Service. "Status of Agricultural Reforms in the NIS/B Countries in 1997." Newly Independent States and the Baltics: International Agriculture and Trade Reports Situation and Outlook Series May 1997. p4-9.

FARMS--INDIANS OF NORTH AMERICA

"In 1992, American Indians operated 8,346 of the nation's 1.9 million farms. Of these 8,346 farms, 2,977 had sales of $10,000 or more that year. While the total number of farms in the United States declined by 162,459 between 1987 and 1992, the number operated by American Indians climbed by 1,212."

U.S. Dept. of Commerce. Economic & Statistics Administration. "Census Facts for Native American Month." Census Bureau Fact Sheet 31 Oct 1997. document-level access: <http://www.census.gov/Press-Release/fs97-11.html>

FARMS--MICHIGAN (v26)

FARMS--MINNESOTA--ECONOMIC CONDITIONS

"An analysis of the financial records of more than 400 farms in southeast Minnesota between 1991 and 1995 shows that on average 28 percent of their net income was made up of crop subsidy payments....A financial analysis of 418 farms from southeast Minnesota that are enrolled in the Farm Business Management Education program showed alfalfa hay had on average a net annual income per acre of $121 between 1991 and 1995, as compared to $17 for corn during that same period." (p10)

DeVore, Brian. "Freedom to Farm, Freedom To...?" Land Stewardship Letter v15 n3 Jun-Jul 1997. p1,10-12.

FARMS--OKLAHOMA (v26)

FARMS--UKRAINE

In Ukraine, "while officials boast that as of January 1, 1997, 75 percent of state farms and 99 percent of collective farms have been reformed or privatized, much of the transformation is in name only....While the number of private farms grew notably from 2,000 in 1990 to 32,000 in 1995, it has not increased significantly during the last 2 years. In fact as of January 1, 1997, there were 35,400 private farms, up less than 2 percent from 1996. Private farms occupy 835,000 hectares of land, or only about 2 percent of total agricultural land." (p33)

"Household plots...play a crucial role in Ukraine's agriculture. In 1990 they accounted for only 6 percent of total agricultural land yet produced about 26 percent of total value of output. As of July 1, 1996, land holding and production by household plots had increased significantly to 12 percent and 47 percent, respectively. Data from 1996 show that household plots proved particularly important in a few key crops, as they produced 95 percent of the total volume of potatoes, 82 percent of vegetables, 51 percent of milk, and 59 percent of eggs...." (p34)

Bjornlund, Britta S./U.S. Dept. of Agriculture. Economic Research Service. "Ukrainian Land Reform and Farm Privatization: Still a Long Road Ahead." Newly Independent States and the Baltics: International Agriculture and Trade Reports Situation and Outlook Series May 1997. p32-34.

FARMS--UNITED STATES (v26)

In the U.S., "the land mass that encompasses the 48 contiguous states totals 1.9 billion acres....According to USDA statistics, the United States--excluding Alaska--has 423 million acres of cropland....[The] grand total of prime farmland--232 million acres--is barely more than 1 out of every 2 acres of U.S. cropland, again excluding Alaska." (p2)

Jawson, Michael D./U.S. Dept. of Agriculture. Agricultural Research Service. "Forum: Making More Cropland by Tinkering with Plants." Agricultural Research v45 n8 Aug 1997. p2. (ISSN0002-161X).

According to "Change in U.S. Livestock Production, 1969-92," a new report from USDA's Economic Research Service, "farm numbers declined 30 percent from 1969 to 1992, but hog and dairy operations were down 70 percent, farms producing eggs dropped 85 percent, and broiler operations declined 35 percent. Operations feeding cattle declined 40 percent from 1978 to 1992." (p10)

U.S. Dept. of Agriculture. Economic Research Service. "ERS Summary of Report: Economic Forces Suggest Continued Change in Livestock Production, But Differ by Area." ERS Information Sep 1997. p10.

In the U.S., agriculture "credit conditions in the seven states of the Tenth Federal Reserve District improved greatly in the first quarter of 1997, according to a survey of 344 agricultural bankers in the district....Ranchland values rose 3.4 percent, reflecting, in part, higher feeder cattle prices. Nonirrigated cropland value rose 2.3 percent, while irrigated cropland value rose 1.4 percent. Compared with a year ago, all three land classes recorded strong increases. During the past year, ranchland values jumped 7.8 percent, nonirrigated cropland values rose 7.0 percent, and irrigated cropland values were up 6.4 percent....Interest rates averaged 9.4 percent on farm real estate loans, 9.9 percent on feeder cattle loans, 9.9 percent on intermediate loans, and 10.0 percent on farm operating loans." (unpaginated)

"Farm Credit Conditions Strengthen in First Quarter." Federal Reserve Bank of Kansas City Fed Letter Jul 1997.

In the Tenth District, which includes Colorado, Kansas, Missouri, Oklahoma, Nebraska, New Mexico, and Wyoming, "ranchland values gained the most, rising 1.3 percent from the previous quarter, with all states showing gains. Over the past year, district ranchland values have risen 8.2%....Cropland values rose most noticeably in Missouri, gaining 2 percent, somewhat higher than the 1.3 percent increase in Kansas." (p6)

McDaniel, Kendall/Lamb, Russell. "Survey of Agricultural Credit Conditions." Federal Reserve Bank of Kansas City Regional Economic Digest v8 n3 Fall 1997. p6-8. (ISSN1049-5339).

In the U.S., "the number of farms (any establishment from which $1,000 or more agricultural products were sold or would normally be sold during the year) fell from 2.8 million in 1974 to 2.1 million in 1996, while the average farm size increased from 384 to 469 acres." (p4)

Clauson, Annette/U.S. Dept. of Agriculture. Economic Research Service. "Food Prices: Economic Factors Holding Down Food Price Increases." Food Review v20 n2 May-Aug 1997. p2-4. (ISSN1056-327X).

In the U.S., "there were 6.8 million farms in 1935; there are 2 million today. And less than a third of profit-making farms--many of which are big commercial operations--own 70 percent of farmed land and grow most of the nation's agricultural products." (p4)

Nifong, Christina. "United States: Pooling Ideas to Rescue Family Farms." The Christian Science Monitor v89 n232 27 Oct 1997. p4. The Christian Science Monitor search engine: <http://www.csmonitor.com/plweb-cgi/iops1.pl> To retrieve this article, enter the following search: ED=19971027 AND farms. In the "retrieved list," click the title that matches this record. (ISSN0882-7729).

FARMS--UNITED STATES--ECONOMIC CONDITIONS (v26)

In the U.S., "total farm business debt rose by almost $6 billion during 1996, reaching nearly $157 billion, its highest level since 1986 (USDA)....It follows increases of $4 billion in 1995, almost $5 billion in 1994, and about $3 billion in 1993....Farm debt has risen almost $17.5 billion since 1992....The 1996 net cash income gain of nearly $9 billion was not materially reduced by the interest expense rise of about $0.5 billion. Although rising in the middle of the year, average annual interest rates on new bank loans decreased from 9.5 percent in 1995 to 8.4 percent in 1996....Debt repayment capacity utilization fell from about 56 percent in 1995 to less than 49 percent in 1996, as the relatively high 1996 net income more than compensated for rising debt and interest expense." (p20)

U.S. Dept. of Agriculture. Economic Research Service. "1996 Farm Income Estimates: Debt Repayment Ability Improves, With Higher Income Levels...Offsetting Larger Debt." Agricultural Income and Finance Situation and Outlook Report Sep 1997. p20-22.

FARMS--UNITED STATES--FOREIGN OWNERSHIP (v26)

FARMS--UNITED STATES--FUEL CONSUMPTION (v26)

FARMS--VALUATION--CHINA--HEBEI (PROVINCE)

"Putterman (1993) estimated the scarcity value of land using a sample of 250 households in the Dahe township in the Hebei province [of China]. He defined the explicit cost of land to farmers as the sum of agricultural tax, collective obligations, and the opportunity cost of fulfilling quota procurement with low crop prices. The explicit cost to farmers amounted to an average of 1,272 Yuan per hectare. On the other hand, the estimated (implicit) average marginal product of land was about 3,548 Yuan per hectare. This implies that farmers in the Dahe township obtained approximately 2,276 Yuan of land rent per hectare in 1985, or 64 percent of the total unit land value." (p111)

Yang, Dennis Tao. "China's Land Arrangements and Rural Labor Mobility." China Economic Review v8 n2 Fall 1997. p101-115. (ISSN1043-951X).

FARMS--VALUATION--UNITED STATES--ECONOMIC CONDITIONS

According to the Federal Reserve Bank of Kansas City's Third Quarter 1997 REGIONAL ECONOMIC DIGEST, during the past year in the Tenth Federal Reserve District, which includes Colorado, Kansas, Missouri, Nebraska, New Mexico, Oklahoma and Wyoming, "ranchland values rose 8.2 percent, reflecting a rebound in feeder cattle prices....Cropland values rose 2 percent in Missouri and 1.3 percent in Kansas." (unpaginated)

"Farm Credit Conditions Improved in Second Quarter of '97." Federal Reserve Bank of Kansas City Fed Letter Oct 1997.

FAST FOOD RESTAURANTS--UNITED STATES (v26)

In the U.S., in 1995, "fast foods were by far the most common source of meals away from home, accounting for 43 percent of all meals away from home....Fast-food places were particularly popular among adults age 18-39, accounting for more than half of all away-from-home meals....Fast-food establishments increase in popularity as a source of away-from-home snacks as children age, accounting for 18 percent of away-from-home snacks eaten by children age 6-11, 20 percent for adolescent males, and 28 percent for adolescent females....Fast-food outlets accounted for 10 percent of all eating occasions, and provided 14 percent of total dietary calories and 41 percent of the away-from-home calories." (p34-35)

Lin, Biing-Hwan/Frazao, Elizabeth/U.S. Dept. of Agriculture. Economic Research Service. "Nutrition: Nutritional Quality of Foods at and away from Home." Food Review v20 n2 May-Aug 1997. p33-40. (ISSN1056-327X).

FATHERS
see also CHILD CARE--UNITED STATES--FATHERS; EDUCATION--UNITED STATES--FATHERS
FATHERS--AFRO-AMERICANS
According to a study on African American husbands and fathers conducted by P. Bowman in 1993, "single fathers (42%) were more likely to be unemployed than were married fathers (25%)." (p345) "Most married fathers (60%) worried at least 'a little' about their families' economic hardships. A large percentage of married men felt they had done 'very well' (77%) in their role as father. Very little difference was found between married (57%) and unmarried (52%) fathers who described themselves as being 'very satisfied' with their family life." (p346)
Cochran, Donna L. "Article: African American Fathers: A Decade Review of the Literature." Families in Society v78 n4 Jul-Aug 1997. p340-350. (ISSN1044-3894).
FATHERS--UNITED STATES (v26)
FATHERS--UNITED STATES--ECONOMIC CONDITIONS (v26)
FATIGUE--UNITED STATES
In the U.S., "THE ANNALS OF INTERNAL MEDICINE learned from a recent study that 24 percent of the persons surveyed complained of fatigue that lasted longer than two weeks. Moreover, the journal notes, fatigue is among the five most frequent causes of medical consultations." (p38)
Rakstis, Ted J. "Workaholism: An Entrepreneurial Ill." Kiwanis v82 n8 Sep 1997. p38-41,48. (ISSN0162-5276).
FATIGUE--UNITED STATES--CANCER--PATIENTS (v26)
FATNESS
see OBESITY
FAYETTEVILLE (ARK.)--ECONOMIC CONDITIONS (v26)
FEDERAL AID
see also ECONOMIC ASSISTANCE, DOMESTIC
FEDERAL AID TO EDUCATION--UNITED STATES (v26)
In the U.S., "in the decade between 1986 and 1996, the amount of Federal dollars invested in Pell grants fell by 16 percent. For work-study programs, Federal aid deceased 32 percent; for Perkins loans, funding decreased by 17 percent; and for the Federal SEOG [Supplemental Educational Opportunity Grants] program, funding fell by 33 percent." (pH8058)
McGovern, James P. (Rep.-Mass.). "Making College Affordable for All." Congressional Record. Daily ed. v143 n132 29 Sep 1997. pH8058. section/page-level access: <http://thomas.loc.gov/cgi-bin/query/R?r105:FLD001:H08058:> (ISSN0363-7239). (X1.1A.105/1).
FEDERAL AID TO RESEARCH (v26)
FEDERAL AID TO RESEARCH--UNITED STATES
In a memo to the U.S. Congress that was prepared in March 1997, "the President's Office of Management and Budget (OMB) targeted 254 programs and projects for elimination. Roughly half of these programs are of interest to biologists, including grant money for aquaculture, crop disease research, water quality, and alternative forestry products....In dollar amounts, the biology-related programs on OMB's...[list for elimination accounted] for roughly $210 million of $3.4 billion in savings....According to an April [1997] analysis by the American Association for the Advancement of Science (AAAS), 60% of R&D [research and development] conducted at colleges and universities is funded by the federal government. The President's FY 1998 budget calls for a 0.2% decrease in such support. Overall, AAAS projects that federal R&D spending will decline by 14% over the next five years." (p416)
Baker, Beth. "Washington Watch: OMB Hit List." BioScience v47 n7 Jul-Aug 1997. p416. (ISSN0006-3568).
FEDERAL AID TO RESEARCH--UNITED STATES --UNIVERSITIES AND COLLEGES (v26)
FEDERAL FUNDS MARKET (UNITED STATES) (v26)
FEEDS--UNITED STATES--COSTS (v26)
In the U.S., "estimated expenditures for feed were $25.2 billion in 1996, up $1.4 billion (5.9 percent) from a revised estimate of $23.8 billion in 1995. Feed costs in 1995 were $1.2 billion (5.3 percent) more than in 1994. This makes 1996 the fifth straight year that feed expenses have risen significantly, and the fourth straight year that their rise has been the largest increase among production expenses." (p9)
U.S. Dept. of Agriculture. Economic Research Service. "1996 Farm Income Estimates: Net Value-Added and Net Farm Income Attain New Highs in 1996." Agricultural Income and Finance Situation and Outlook Report Sep 1997. p4-13.
FELONIES
see CRIME
FEMALE GENERATIVE ORGANS
see GENERATIVE ORGANS, FEMALE
FEMALE OFFENDERS
see also DELINQUENT GIRLS
FEMALE OFFENDERS--UNITED STATES
"Women represent a growing percentage of the probation and parole populations...[in the U.S.]. There were 515,600 women on probation (21 percent of all probationers) and 79,300 on parole (11 percent of all parolees) in 1996, up from 18 percent and 8 percent respectively in 1990."
U.S. Dept. of Justice. "Nation's Probation and Parole Population Reached Almost 3.9 Million Last Year." Press Release 14 Aug 1997. document-level access: <http://www.ojp.usdoj.gov/pub/bjs/press/papp96.pr>
FEMINISM--UNITED STATES--PUBLIC OPINION (v26)
FERRET--UNITED STATES
"Only about 100 wild ferrets live in isolated prairie dog towns in a few Western [U.S.] states after six years of transplanting captive ferrets and hoping they would breed. In Wyoming, the 224 animals released over four years cost $5,000 apiece, not including the cost of radio collars and the salaries of wildlife biologists who monitored them. Only a handful of the ferrets' offspring have survived....Captive-bred ferrets are especially vulnerable to predators in the wild and only about 30 percent survive." (p4)
Matthews, Mark. "Western Roundup: Completing a Prairie Ecosystem." High Country News v29 n23 8 Dec 1997. p4. (ISSN0191-5657).
FERTILITY, HUMAN (v26)
"While world population remains on course to exceed six billion before the end of the century, countries that have experienced significant fertility declines in recent years include: Bangladesh, from 6.2 children per woman to 3.4; India, from 4.5 to 3.4; Pakistan, from 6.5 to 5.5; Turkey, from 4.1 to 2.7; Myanmar, from 4.9 to 3.6; Syria, from 7.4 to 4.7; Kenya, from 7.5 to 5.4; and Cote d'Ivoire, from 7.4 to 5.7. Africa, where women average 5.7 children, had the highest fertility rate of any region from 1990-1995." (p3)
"Fertility Declines Reported." Popline v19 May-Jun 1997. p3.
"U.S. figures for 1994 show that women born in Mexico had the highest fertility rate of any major immigrant group--147 births per 1,000 women ages 15 to 44. Women born elsewhere in Latin America had a fertility rate of 82. In contrast, women born in Europe had 53 births per 1,000, women in Asia had 58 births per 1,000, and women born in the United States had 62 births per 1,000." (p27)
del Pinal, Jorge/Singer, Audrey. "Generations of Diversity: Latinos in the United States." Population Bulletin v52 n3 Oct 1997. p2-47. (ISSN0032-468X).
FERTILITY, HUMAN--AUSTRALIA
According to the report, "Demography SA, 1995," by the

Australian Bureau of Statistics, "in 1995 there were 19,336 births registered in South Australia, a drop of 2.3 per cent in ten years, although the total fertility rate in South Australia has remained steady over the last ten years at 1.7 children per woman. Ex-nuptial births represented 27.4 per cent of all births registered in South Australia compared with only 14.5 per cent in 1985 (2,865)."

Australian Bureau of Statistics. "South Australians--Living Longer." Media Release 11 Jun 1997. document-level access: <http://www.abs.gov.au/websitedbs/d3110125.nsf/4a255eef008309e44a255eef00061e57/6d35166d881934c74a2564b30004f29d?OpenDocument>

FERTILITY, HUMAN--BOLIVIA

"The 1994 Demographic and Health Survey found that only 45 percent of pregnancies were wanted [in Bolivia] even though knowledge and use of contraceptives had increased dramatically over the previous five years. The average Bolivian woman gives birth to 4.8 children, but the number is as high as seven in rural areas. However, the average woman reports that she would like to have 2.5 children. Overall, 42 percent of women at risk for pregnancy now use some method of contraception, and 18 percent of them use a modern method, which includes pills, IUDs [intrauterine devices], and condoms." (p7)

Weber, Elizabeth. "Spotlight: Bolivia." Population Today v25 n10 Oct 1997. p7. (ISSN0749-2448).

FERTILITY, HUMAN--BRAZIL--EGYPT (v26)

FERTILITY, HUMAN--DEVELOPING COUNTRIES (v26)

"Fertility is now estimated to have declined in Bangladesh from 6.2 children per woman from 1980 to 1985 to 3.4 from 1990 to 1995, in India from 4.5 to 3.4, in Pakistan from 6.5 to 5.5, in Turkey from 4.1 to 2.7, in Myanmar from 4.9 to 3.6, in Syria from 7.4 to 4.7, in Kenya from 7.5 to 5.4, and in Cote d'Ivoire from 7.4 to 5.7. Globally, fertility in Africa is estimated to be 5.7 children per woman from 1990 to 1995, instead of 5.8 as projected two years ago." (p72)

"Population 2050: 9.4 Billion." UN Chronicle v34 n3 1997. p72. (ISSN0251-7329).

FERTILITY, HUMAN--DEVELOPING COUNTRIES --PUBLIC OPINION (v26)

FERTILITY, HUMAN--EDUCATION--BRAZIL --GUATEMALA

In Brazil, "women with no formal schooling have an average of 6.7 children while those with secondary or higher schooling have only 3.2 children on average. In Guatemala, where few women stay in school beyond the primary level, the TFR [total fertility rate] drops from 6.9 for women with no education to 5.4 for women who have attended a few years of school...." (p20)

Riley, Nancy E. "Gender, Power, And Population Change." Population Bulletin v52 n1 May 1997. p2-46. (ISSN0032-468X).

FERTILITY, HUMAN--EDUCATION--UNITED STATES (v26)

FERTILITY, HUMAN--EGYPT (v26)

FERTILITY, HUMAN--EUROPE

A report "by Eurostat, Statistical Office of the European Communities in Luxembourg, says the EU's total fertility rate has stopped declining. It reached 1.44 babies per woman after years of decline due mainly to postponed motherhood and increasing childlessness. This follows a post-war record low of 1.43 babies per woman in 1995....The EU 1.44 fertility rate is similar to Japan's 1.41 and that of other developed countries, although the US rate is considerably higher at 2.06. In most less well developed countries it is well above 3; for example, in India it is 3.37. Inside EU, [the] highest fertility rate in 1996 was Ireland's 1.91, lowest Spain's 1.15. Elsewhere the picture remained one of comparative highs in Scandinavian countries, the UK and France and lows in Germany and southern Member States. When the average fertility rate from 1991 to 1995 (EU=1.48) is compared to 1996 (EU=1.44), the only significant changes were in Sweden (down from 1.96 to 1.61), Spain (down from 1.26 to 1.15) and Luxembourg (up from 1.67 to 1.76)."

Eurostat. "EU Women Average 1.44 Babies." Press Release 1 Aug 1997. document-level access: <http://europa.eu.int/en/comm/eurostat/compres/en/5697/6305697a.htm>

FERTILITY, HUMAN--GUATEMALA

"Nearly a quarter of the married women in Guatemala, where the population of 11.2 million is estimated to double in only 23 years, want to space or limit their births but are not using contraception. Guatemalan women average 5.1 children, one of the highest fertility levels in Latin America, according to the country's most recent Demographic and Health Survey. Fertility was substantially lower among more educated women, the survey found. Women with at least some secondary education average two or three children, compared with an average of seven for women with no formal education. Those with secondary education have 2.7 children and women with higher education have 1.8." (p3)

"Education Is Fertility Factor in Guatemala." Popline v19 Sep-Oct 1997. p3.

FERTILITY, HUMAN--HISPANIC AMERICANS

In the U.S., for 1990 and 1995, "the total fertility rate (TFR)--a hypothetical measure of the total number of births women would have given current birth rates--was three children per woman for Hispanics and was below two for all non-Hispanics." (p26) "In 1995, the TFR ranged from 3.3 for Mexicans to 1.7 for Cubans....Among women with less than nine years of education, the TFRs were above 4.0 children per woman for black and Hispanic women and about 1.9 children among white women in 1994....Women with exactly 12 years of school had TFRs ranging from 3.8 for Hispanics to 2.4 for whites." (p27)

del Pinal, Jorge/Singer, Audrey. "Generations of Diversity: Latinos in the United States." Population Bulletin v52 n3 Oct 1997. p2-47. (ISSN0032-468X).

In the U.S., "births to Hispanics contributed nearly two-thirds of the increase in the Hispanic population during 1995....The total fertility rate (TFR) averaged three children per woman for Hispanics and was below two for all non-Hispanics. (The TFR is a hypothetical measure of the total number of births women would have given current birth rates. A TFR of 2.1 children per woman is required for a generation to replace itself, after allowing for deaths.)"

Population Reference Bureau. "Diverse Hispanic Population to Become Largest U.S. Minority." Press Release 1997. document-level access: <http://www.prb.org/media/pressrel.htm>

FERTILITY, HUMAN--INDIA (v26)

"The 25 million babies estimated to be born in India this year are nearly as many as those expected to be born in all of Sub-Saharan Africa, the world's fastest growing region, and more than the 21 million expected in China, the world's most populous country. Since the mid-1960s, India's total fertility rate has declined by 42 percent....Total fertility rate (TFR) in India has declined from 5.7 children per woman in the mid-1960s to 3.3 children in 1997, two-thirds of the distance to replacement fertility of just over two children per woman....With a TFR of 5.2, [the state of] Uttar Pradesh stands out as having especially high fertility, nearly 50 percent above the national average." (p3)

"25 Million Births in India Each Year." Popline v19 Jul-Aug 1997. p3.

FERTILITY, HUMAN--IRAN

"A study by Marie Ladier-Fouladi of the Institut National d'Etudes Demographiques (INED) in Paris, published in 1996 in the French journal POPULATION, estimated that Iran's total fertility rate (TFR) dropped from an average of 6.2 children per woman in 1986 to 3.5 children per woman in 1993. Based on analyses of sample surveys, the Iranian government's health ministry reported that the TFR dropped from 5.0 in 1991 to 3.3 in 1995." (p4)

Roudi, Farzaneh. "Surprising Decline in Iran's Growth Rates." Population Today v25 n11 Nov 1997. p4-5. (ISSN0749-2448).

FERTILITY, HUMAN--IRAN--SHIRAZ

"A 1996 study in the city of Shiraz, Iran's fifth largest urban area with a population of 1.2 million, found a sharp decline in fertility. The study's authors estimate that fertility declined 60 percent in a 20-year period, from a TFR [total fertility rate] of 4.9 children per woman in 1976, to 4.7 in 1986, to 2.2 in 1996. They report that the 1996 TFR for illiterate and rural-born women was 3.5 children per woman, 1.1 for economically active women, and 1.2 for university-educated women." (p5)

Roudi, Farzaneh. "Surprising Decline in Iran's Growth Rates." Population Today v25 n11 Nov 1997. p4-5. (ISSN0749-2448).

FERTILITY, HUMAN--ISRAEL (v26)

FERTILITY, HUMAN--ITALY (v26)

FERTILITY, HUMAN--KOREA--TAIWAN--PUBLIC OPINION (v26)

FERTILITY, HUMAN--LATIN AMERICA (v26)

FERTILITY, HUMAN--LATIN AMERICA--POPULATION (v26)

FERTILITY, HUMAN--MALI

"The sub-Saharan, West African country of Mali continues to have one of the highest fertility rates on the continent, despite a slight decline from an average of 7.1 children per woman to 6.7 between 1987 and 1995-96. According to the second Demographic and Health survey carried out in the country, factors contributing to high fertility in Mali include: Only 5 percent of women in union use a modern method of contraception; for 26 percent of births, the interval between births is less than two years, which may affect the health of the mother and child. By the age of 16, half of the women are married or have become sexually active." (p2)

"23% of Children in Mali Too Thin." Popline v19 Sep-Oct 1997. p2.

FERTILITY, HUMAN--MAURITIUS

The Indian Ocean island nation of Mauritius, located east of Madagascar, "has Africa's highest population density (about 1,450 people per square mile) and one of the world's fastest fertility declines....Today, about 75 percent of married women use a contraceptive method; overall, about 50 percent of married women use a modern method, mainly oral contraceptives, condoms, and injectables." (p7)

Lutz, Wolfgang. "Spotlight: Mauritius." Population Today v25 n11 Nov 1997. p7. (ISSN0749-2448).

FERTILITY, HUMAN--MIDDLE EAST

According to data from the United Nations Population Division, in Iraq, "women average 5.7 children and the population of 21.2 million is projected to double in only 25 years....In Libya,...women average 6.4 children and the population of 5.6 million is projected to double in only 19 years....Governments view the birth rates as stable in...Saudi Arabia (6.4 children per woman, 19.5 million people and projected to double in 23 years)...[and in] Syria (4.7 children per woman, 15 million people and projected to double in 25 years)...." (p4)

"85 Nations Believe Birth Rates Too High." Popline v19 Sep-Oct 1997. p4.

FERTILITY, HUMAN--NEPAL

"Fertlity in Nepal has declined steadily from six births per woman in the mid-1970s to 4.6 births per woman in the mid-1990s....One in four women age 15-19 is already a mother or pregnant with her first child....The [most recent Nepal Family Health] survey shows that at current fertility levels, a woman will have, on average, almost 60 percent more births than she wants." (p4)

"Fertility Is Declining in Nepal." Popline v19 Sep-Oct 1997. p4.

FERTILITY, HUMAN--NEW ZEALAND (v26)

FERTILITY, HUMAN--OMAN (v26)

FERTILITY, HUMAN--UGANDA (v26)

FERTILITY, HUMAN--UNITED STATES (v26)

In the U.S., "just less than 3.9 million babies were born in 1995, the fifth straight year in which births declined. The crude birth rate declined 3 percent to 14.8 births per 1,000 women, the lowest birth rate since 1987. The fertility rate--the birth rate for women of childbearing age in a given year--also declined 2 percent, to 65.6 births per 1,000 women aged 15 to 44....The teenage birth rate declined 4 percent from 1994 to 1995, to 56.8 per 1,000 for women aged 15 to 19." (p40)

Miller, Berna. "Kaleidoscope: The Echo Bust Continues." American Demographics v19 n11 Nov 1997. p40. article-level access: <http://www.demographics.com/publications/ad/97_ad/9711_ad/ad971118.htm> (ISSN0163-4089).

In the U.S., "in 1960, a typical woman of child-bearing age gave birth to 3.6 children. That rate has fallen to 2.0 today and is expected to fall to 1.9 by 2020. Since a country needs a fertility rate of 2.1 just to replace the existing population, the United States is already in a negative population growth position." (p15 secA)

Bartlett, Bruce. "Comment: There's No 'Free Lunch' with Social Security." Detroit News 3 Dec 1997. p15 secA.

According to the CDC's 'National Survey of Family Growth,' in the U.S., "about 6.1 million women had impaired fecundity in 1995, compared with 4.9 million in 1988. Some of this increase is due to the aging of the baby boom generation. The percent with impaired fecundity was 8.4 in 1988 and 10.2 in 1995. Approximately 2 percent of women (1.2 million) had an infertility visit in the past year, and another 13 percent (7.6 million) reported an infertility visit at some point earlier in their lives."

U.S. National Center for Health Statistics. "New Report Documents Trends in Childbearing, Reproductive Health." Fact Sheet 5 Jun 1997. document-level access: <http://www.cdc.gov/nchswww/releases/97facts/97sheets/nsfgfact.htm>

"In the United States in 1995, there were 110 live births per 1,000 women ages 20-24. In 1955, there were 242 live births to women in the same age range. By 1995, fertility rates for women ages 25-29 were slightly higher than those for women 20-24, reflecting a trend toward delayed childbearing."

Population Reference Bureau. "Today's U.S. Population: Details and Definitions." Press Release 1997. document-level access: <http://www.prb.org/media/pressrel.htm>

FERTILIZATION IN VITRO, HUMAN--CANADA (v26)

FERTILIZATION IN VITRO, HUMAN--MASSACHUSETTS--BOSTON--PUBLIC OPINION

"Neumann and Johannesson (1994) reported that survey respondents in the Boston, Massachusetts area would pay $17,730 on average for IVF [in vitro fertilization] if they were infertile and the procedure had a 10 percent chance of success. Respondents stated that they would pay $865--far above the actuarially fair value--for a lifetime insurance policy which gave them access to a 10 percent chance at the procedure. Neumann and Johannesson also found that individuals were willing to pay substantial amounts so that others would have access to the procedure. Among 231 respondents of all ages in their study, average willingness to pay was $32 per year in taxes for a hypothetical public program that would provide twelve hundred couples per

year in Massachusetts a 10 percent chance at IVF." (p1224-1225)
Neumann, Peter J. "Should Health Insurance Cover IVF?: Issues and Options." Journal of Health Politics, Policy and Law v22 n5 Oct 1997. p1215-1239. (ISSN0361-6878).

FERTILIZATION IN VITRO, HUMAN--UNITED STATES

"Only about 3 percent (or fewer than 50,000) of Americans who seek treatment for infertility each year receive IVF [in vitro fertilization]. Collins et al. (1995) estimated that even if utilization rose 300 percent as a result of adding IVF services to a typical employer health plan, average premiums per employee would only rise about $9 per year. Another group previously estimated that in 1990, IVF would have added under a dollar to annual premiums, as opposed to over $7 for chiropractic services and $26 for alcoholic and psychiatric services (Resolve 1991)....Facilities performing IVF generally charge between $8,000 to $10,000 for a complete cycle, including the costs for initial consultations, laboratory tests, prescription drugs, ultrasound, egg retrieval, gamete culturing, embryo transfer, and related physician services (Neumann et al. 1994; Collins et al. 1995). When longer-term costs are included, such as those associated with medical complications and multiple births (which are much more likely with in vitro fertilization compared to natural childbirth), costs per cycle are approximately $10,500 (Neumann et al. 1994)." (p1220-1221) "The cost per IVF delivery--the cost of a single cycle divided by the probability of achieving a successful birth on that cycle--has been estimated to vary from $66,667 on the first cycle to $114,286 on the sixth cycle (Neumann et al. 1994)....For couples with a diagnosis of tubal disease, costs per delivery vary from $50,000 on the first cycle to $73,000 on the sixth; however, for an older population with male factor infertility, costs rise from $160,000 on the first cycle to as much as $800,000 on the sixth." (p1222)
Neumann, Peter J. "Should Health Insurance Cover IVF?: Issues and Options." Journal of Health Politics, Policy and Law v22 n5 Oct 1997. p1215-1239. (ISSN0361-6878).

"Some 1.5 to 2 million Americans seek treatment for fertility problems annually (Chandra and Mosher 1994)." (p1216) "In 1985 in the United States, 7,500 IVF [in vitro fertilization] cycles were initiated and there were 1,200 deliveries; by 1993, the number had risen to 50,800 cycles and 8,700 deliveries (American Society for Reproductive Medicine 1995). Over three hundred facilities in the United States now perform the procedure, with the largest facilities conducting over 1,000 procedures annually (American Fertility Society 1994)....Most Americans' health insurance does not cover IVF. One study estimated that IVF is routinely covered by only 14 percent of large group plans, 16 percent of preferred provider organizations, and 17 percent of point-of-service networks and health maintenance organizations (Alan Guttmacher Institute 1993). Another study concluded that 30 to 40 percent of IVF services are covered partially or completely by insurance, and for those covered, insurance pays approximately 50 percent of the costs (Collins et al. 1995)." (p1217-1218) "One study estimated that adding IVF services to a typical employer's health plan in 1995 would add only $3.14 per year to an employee's annual premium (Collins et al. 1995)." (p1219)
Neumann, Peter J. "Should Health Insurance Cover IVF?: Issues and Options." Journal of Health Politics, Policy and Law v22 n5 Oct 1997. p1215-1239. (ISSN0361-6878).

FERTILIZERS (v26)

FERTILIZERS--CHINA

"Investment in chemical fertilizer plants boosted China's production to 28.4 million tons in 1996 (nutrient-weight basis), an increase of 11.3 percent over 1995....Plans called for chemical fertilizer imports in 1996 of about 27 million tons (product-weight basis)....According to State Statistics Bureau estimates, farmers applied 38.5 million tons of chemical fertilizers in 1996 (nutrient-weight basis), an increase of 6.5 percent over 1995." (p16)
Crook, Frederick W./U.S. Dept. of Agriculture. Economic Research Service. "Input Supplies Adequate for 1997." China: International Agriculture and Trade Reports Situation and Outlook Series Jun 1997. p16-18.

According to a Chinese Ministry of Agriculture survey, from 1994 to 1996, "19 of 25 provinces added subsidies to their fixed-quota grain purchase price and added subsidies for chemical fertilizers as well....The average support for chemical fertilizers ranged from 100 to 640 kilograms of chemical fertilizer per ton of grain sold under the fixed quota purchase system. Chemical fertilizers applied increased from 33.1 million tons on a nutrient-weight basis in 1994 to 35.9 million tons in 1995 and 38.2 million tons in 1996, an 8.1 percent and 6.5 percent increase, respectively. Chemical pesticide production increased from 268,000 tons in 1994 to 360,000 tons in 1995 and 427,000 tons in 1996...." (p22)
Crook, Frederick W./U.S. Dept. of Agriculture. Economic Research Service. "Current Agricultural Policies Highlight Concerns about Food Security." China: International Agriculture and Trade Reports Situation and Outlook Series Jun 1997. p19-25.

In China, "imports of chemical fertilizers increased dramatically; from 10.2 million tons in 1993 to 12.7 million in 1994, to 19.9 million in 1995, and 18.6 million tons in 1996. In 1996, China imported 6 million tons of urea (2.76 million tons nutrient-weight basis); 3.4 million tons of potassium chloride (2.04 million tons nutrient-weight basis); 420,000 tons of potassium sulphate; 7.2 million tons of compound fertilizers (4.6 million tons nutrient-weight basis); and 1.49 million tons of other chemical fertilizers not specified." (p23-24)
Crook, Frederick W./U.S. Dept. of Agriculture. Economic Research Service. "Current Agricultural Policies Highlight Concerns about Food Security." China: International Agriculture and Trade Reports Situation and Outlook Series Jun 1997. p19-25.

FERTILIZERS--DEVELOPING COUNTRIES (v26)

FETAL ALCOHOL SYNDROME--CANADA (v26)

FETAL ALCOHOL SYNDROME--NORTH DAKOTA (v26)

FETICIDE

see ABORTION

FEUDAL TENURE

see LAND TENURE

FIBER IN HUMAN NUTRITION--FINLAND--UNITED STATES (v26)

FIBER IN HUMAN NUTRITION--UNITED STATES --CHILDREN (v26)

FIELD BURNING

see BURNING OF LAND

FIGHTER PLANES (v26)

FIGHTER PLANES--CHINA (v26)

FIGHTER PLANES--IRAN (v26)

FIGHTER PLANES--IRAQ (v26)

FIGHTER PLANES--KOREA (NORTH) (v26)

FIGHTER PLANES--RUSSIA (v26)

FILBERT INDUSTRY--UNITED STATES

"The 1996 U.S. hazelnut crop was produced in an 'off-year' with output totaling only 19,000 tons (in-shell basis), compared with the large crop of 39,000 tons in 1995. Nearly all U.S. hazelnut production occurs in Oregon. The grower price for the 1996/97 marketing year averaged $859 per ton. In spite of a large supply during the 1995/96 season, the grower price averaged $913 per ton, the highest since 1987 due to strong domestic demand." (p32)

U.S. Dept. of Agriculture. Economic Research Service. "Tree Nut Outlook." Fruit and Tree Nuts Situation and Outlook Report Aug 1997. p32-33.

FILIPINO AMERICANS (v26)

FILLS (EARTHWORK)--UNITED STATES (v26)

FILM INDUSTRY

see MOTION PICTURE INDUSTRY

FILMS

see MOTION PICTURES

FINANCE

see also AGRICULTURE--CHINA--FINANCE; ARTS--UNITED STATES--FINANCE; BANKS AND BANKING; BREAST--CANCER--UNITED STATES--FINANCE; CHARITIES--MICHIGAN--DETROIT--FINANCE; CORPORATIONS--UNITED STATES--FINANCE; DEBT; EDUCATION--UNITED STATES--FINANCE; EDUCATION, PRESCHOOL--UNITED STATES--FINANCE; ENVIRONMENTAL POLICY--FINANCE; HEAD START PROGRAMS--UNITED STATES--FINANCE; HOME OWNERSHIP--UNITED STATES--FINANCE; INCOME; INFLATION (FINANCE); INSURANCE; INSURANCE, HEALTH--UNITED STATES--CHILDREN--FINANCE; INVESTMENTS; LOANS; LONG-TERM CARE FACILITIES--UNITED STATES--FINANCE; MEDICAL CARE--FORMER SOVIET REPUBLICS--FINANCE; MEDICAL CARE--TURKEY--FINANCE; MEDICAL CARE--VENEZUELA--FINANCE; MONEY; PRIVATE SCHOOLS--UNITED STATES--FINANCE; PROFIT; RENEWABLE ENERGY SOURCES--UNITED STATES--FINANCE; ROADS--FINANCE; ROADS--UNITED STATES--FINANCE; SCIENCE--STUDY AND TEACHING--UNITED STATES--FINANCE; TRANSPORTATION--EUROPE--FINANCE; TRANSPORTATION--UNITED STATES--FINANCE; UNITED NATIONS--FINANCE; UNITED NATIONS--UNITED STATES--FINANCE; UNIVERSITIES AND COLLEGES--MICHIGAN--FINANCE; UNIVERSITY OF MICHIGAN--RESEARCH--FINANCE; WEALTH; WILDLIFE CONSERVATION--FINANCE

FINANCE, PERSONAL

see INSURANCE

FINANCIAL ACCOUNTING

see ACCOUNTING

FINANCIAL INSTITUTIONS

see BANKS AND BANKING

FINANCIAL PLANNERS--UNITED STATES

In general, in the U.S., "financial planners are compensated in three ways--fee only, commission only, or a combination of fee and commission....Peggy Ruhlin, 1996-97 president of the International Association for Financial Planning,...[supplied] the percentage of planners in each category. The numbers look like this: Fee only: 20 percent to 25 percent; Commission only: 10 percent to 15 percent; Fee and commission: 60 percent to 70 percent." (p8 secF)

Haas, Donald Ray. "Strategies: Opposites Attack: Donald 'The Stingray' Haas: Integrity, Not Method of Payment, Is the Issue." Detroit News 1 Dec 1997. p8,10 secF.

FINANCIAL SERVICES INDUSTRY

see also SECURITIES INDUSTRY

FINANCIAL SERVICES INDUSTRY--AFRO-AMERICANS

In the U.S., "four percent of officials and managers in financial services are black, compared with 5.5 percent in all businesses, according to the federal Equal Employment Opportunity Commission. And of the thousands of stockbrokers in the United States, only 600 are black, estimates Tony Chapelle, publisher of SECURITIES PRO, a New York-based newsletter that reports on blacks in the financial industry." (p9)

Coolidge, Shelley Donald. "A Deficit of Diversity on Wall Street." The Christian Science Monitor v89 n141 17 Jun 1997. p1,9. The Christian Science Monitor search engine: <http://www.csmonitor.com/plweb-cgi/iops1.pl> To retrieve this article, enter the following search: ED=19970617 AND street. In the "retrieved list," click the title that matches this record. (ISSN0882-7729).

FINE ARTS

see ARTS

FINGERPRINTS--UNITED STATES--PUBLIC OPINION (v26)

FINGERPRINTS--UNITED STATES. FEDERAL BUREAU OF INVESTIGATION

"The FBI's Criminal Justice Information Services (CJIS) Division serves as the...[U.S.'s] centralized repository and clearinghouse for fingerprint records." (p1222) "The CJIS Division maintains a repository containing approximately 87,000,000 civil fingerprint cards, representing more than 39,000,000 individuals, including military personnel, applicants for federal employment, and other non-criminal justice purposes. Also, this repository retains over 130,000,000 fingerprint cards with related criminal history records information on more than 35,000,000 individuals represented in the criminal file. Currently, the FBI processes fingerprint cards through its Identification Automated System (IDAS), which is a semi-automated system requiring a high degree of manual intervention. IDAS, operational since June 1989, was designed to support average daily receipts and throughput of 31,000 fingerprint cards, with infrequent 'spikes' in receipts of up to 37,500 submissions. However, the FBI now averages over 57,000 fingerprint card submissions daily. The criminal file continues to grow, with approximately 5,000 new individuals added per day. Besides criminal submissions from law enforcement agencies, requests are received through law enforcement and other authorized entities for such purposes as handgun purchases, banking institution employees, child care providers and numerous others. During 1996, the FBI received approximately 11,243,500 fingerprint cards. Of this number, more than 5,535,000 criminal fingerprint cards were received, of which approximately 3,140,000 identifications were matched with existing records. Over 5,708,000 civil fingerprint cards were received in 1996." (p1223)

U.S. Dept. of Justice. "Departments of Commerce, Justice, And State, The Judiciary...Approp. for 1998 (Part 2)." Hearing. U.S. House. Committee on Appropriations. Washington, D.C. : GPO, 1997. (ISBN0160549094). (Y4.Ap6/1:C73/2/997/pt.2).

FIRE ANTS--SOUTHERN STATES

"Over the last 76 years, imported fire ants have infested over 275 million acres in 13 Southern [U.S.] States. The fire ant affects both urban and rural areas with damage estimates in the billions of dollars annually. In Texas, fire ant damage is estimated at $300 million annually, and the cattle industry alone suffers annual losses of $67 million. Further, it is estimated that the State of Georgia loses $46 million annually, with Louisiana and Alabama incurring annual damages of $23.8 and $16 million respectively. Mississippi has estimated losses of $12.3 million. Homeowners in the State of Arkansas spend approximately $106 million each year to combat fire ant infestation." (pS5929)

Gramm, Phil (Sen.-Tex.). "Statements on Introduced Bills and Joint Resolutions." Congressional Record. Daily ed. v143 n85 18 Jun 1997. pS5927-5935. section/page-level access: <http://thomas.loc.gov/cgi-bin/query/R?r105:FLD001:S05929:> (ISSN0363-7239). (X1.1A.105/1).

FIRE DETECTORS--AUSTRALIA (v26)

FIRE FIGHTERS

see also WAGES--FIRE FIGHTERS

FIRE FIGHTERS--CALIFORNIA--LA MESA (v26)

FIRE FIGHTERS--CALIFORNIA--LIVERMORE (v26)

FIRE FIGHTERS--MICHIGAN--BRIGHTON

In Michigan, calls to volunteers and paid-on-call firefighters "in Brighton alone have risen by more than 180 percent in the last 10 years, said Fire Chief Larry Lane, and that trend looks like it will continue. 'We responded to 464 runs last year,' he said. 'At the present pace, we should hit about 525 calls this year.'...The City of Brighton Fire Department has 35 paid-on-call firefighters, 70 percent of whom are under 25. Another 12 members are part of the junior department--young people age 15-18 who respond to calls, but cannot go into life-threatening conditions. Recruits often work more than 200 hours on training to earn their Firefighter I designation from the state before they can even go into the field to fight fires." (p5 secD)

Kirkbride, Rob. "Local: Volunteer Firefighter Shortage Growing." Ann Arbor News 15 Jun 1997. p5 secD.

FIREARMS

see also AK-47 RIFLE; ASSAULT RIFLES

"Assault rifles and other small arms, the hundreds of millions of these low-tech, inexpensive, sturdy, and easy-to-use weapons now spread around the world are the tools for most of the killing in contemporary conflicts--causing as much as 90 percent of the deaths." (p5) "There may be about 500 million military-style firearms, in addition to many hundreds of millions of guns designed for police forces or for civilian use." (p6) "Worldwide, perhaps $3 billion worth of small arms and light weapons are being shipped across international borders each year...; that would be equivalent to about one eighth of all international arms sales....For just $50 million--roughly the cost of a single modern jet fighter--one can equip a small army with some 200,000 assault rifles at today's 'fire-sale' prices." (p11)

Renner, Michael. "Small Arms, Big Impact: The Next Challenge of Disarmament." Worldwatch Paper n137 Oct 1997. p5-77.

FIREARMS--AFRO-AMERICAN YOUTH--MORTALITY

"Among African-American teenage males, 60% of deaths result from firearm injury compared with 23% of white teenage males. Among African-American teenage females it is 22% compared with 10% of white female teenagers (Fingerhut, 1993). The number of African-American males aged 15-19 who died from gunshot wounds in 1990 was nearly five times higher than the number who died from AIDS, sickle-cell disease, and all other natural causes combined (Fingerhut, 1993; Kellerman, 1994)....Firearm homicide for African-American males 15-19 years of age was 11 times the rate among white males, 105.3 compared with 9.7 per 100,000 population. The rate for African-American females was five times the rate for white females, 10.4 compared with 2.0 per 100,000 population (Fingerhut, 1993)." (p508-509)

Page, Randy M./Hammermeister, Jon. "Weapon-Carrying and Youth Violence." Adolescence v32 n127 Fall 1997. p505-513. (ISSN0001-8449).

FIREARMS--AUSTRALIA--MORTALITY (v26)

FIREARMS--BRAZIL--MORTALITY

According to a "U.N. survey, Brazil has by far the highest number of firearm homicides--41,000 per year--and places a close second to South Africa in the rate of killings per total population. The murder rate in Sao Paulo has reached one per hour, and 90 percent of all killings are committed with firearms. There are an estimated 18.5 million firearms in the country, only one third of which are registered." (p22)

Renner, Michael. "Small Arms, Big Impact: The Next Challenge of Disarmament." Worldwatch Paper n137 Oct 1997. p5-77.

FIREARMS--ILLINOIS--MISSISSIPPI (v26)

FIREARMS--LAW AND LEGISLATION--UNITED STATES

"In its first analysis of a subset of the estimated 250,000 illegal firearm sales blocked by the Brady Act since it took effect in February of 1994, the [U.S.] Justice Department's Bureau of Justice Statistics (BJS) announced...that an estimated 173,000 illegal handgun sales were blocked by Brady background checks. Approximately 70,000 of the illegal handgun sales were blocked in 1996, BJS reported....A previous BJS statistical report, 'Presale Firearms Checks,' estimated that 6,600 firearms applications were rejected each month, totaling more than 250,000 illegal firearms--including rifles and other long guns in addition to handguns--blocked between the establishment of Brady background checks and June 1997."

U.S. Dept. of Justice. "Brady Act Background Checks Prevent 173,000 Illegal Handgun Purchases since February 1994 Implementation." Press Release 4 Sep 1997. document-level access: <http://www.ojp.usdoj.gov/pub/bjs/press/phc96.pr>

Since 1994, 14 U.S. "states have adopted right-to-carry laws, which allow citizens to carry guns in public, often after passing licensing requirements. Currently, law-abiding residents of 31 states, home to 127 million Americans, can legally carry firearms for self-protection after securing a permit. (Vermont residents don't even need a permit, as the state doesn't regulate gun ownership.) In 1987 Florida became one of the first states to liberalize its law....A decade later, Florida's handgun homicide rate has dropped by 41 percent, compared to a 24 percent increase nationally, according to FBI data." (p15)

Lynch, Michael W. "Data: Clash and Carry." Reason v29 n7 Dec 1997. p15. (ISSN0048-6906).

FIREARMS--LAW AND LEGISLATION--UNITED STATES--MORTALITY (v26)

FIREARMS--MANITOBA--WINNIPEG (v26)

FIREARMS--MARYLAND--BALTIMORE

"The FBI recently reported 1996 was the fifth consecutive year that overall serious crime declined in the United States. While the city of Baltimore also showed a decline in the crime index total--the sum of aggravated assaults, auto thefts, burglaries, larcenies-thefts, murders, rapes, and robberies--from 94,855 in 1995 to 85,982 in 1996, the city's homicide rate remained practically the same: 328 in 1996 compared with 325 in 1995. Homicides by guns totaled 264 in 1995 and 267 in 1996....The Bureau of Alcohol, Tobacco, and Firearms revealed that handguns accounted for 82% of all firearms used in a crime and recovered by Baltimore police from April 1, 1993 to March 31, 1994. More than 45% of the guns traced in the study were tracked to seven gun dealers....In Baltimore, 31 of 1993's homicide victims were under 18." (p20)

Obuszewski, Max. "Challenging the Violence Epidemic in Baltimore." Peacework n276 Jul-Aug 1997. p20-21. (ISSN0748-0725).

FIREARMS--MEXICO (v26)

FIREARMS--MICHIGAN--DETROIT (v26)

FIREARMS--MICHIGAN--DETROIT--YOUTH--MORTALITY (v26)

FIREARMS--SOUTH AFRICA

"Every day, 30 South Africans are shot dead, a rate of 11,000 each year. Faced with a murder rate six times that of the US, South Africa is increasingly worried that a runaway gun culture is partly to blame. One in 12 South Africans is now legally licensed to both own and carry a firearm, with handguns by far the most common category among the 4.1 million legally held weapons." (p1) "Recently, Safety and Security Minister Sydney Mufamadi revealed that in the first six months of this year alone, firearms were used in 25,783 robberies, 5,127 murders, and 10,050 attempted murders....Figures released by the police show that nearly 1 in 4 of the firearms stolen since the beginning of the year were taken from a police officer. During the same period, 208 officers were murdered, most of them shot. In the US, with seven times the population, 55 officers were shot dead in 1996." (p7)

O'Loughlin, Ed. "Trigger-Happy South Africa Aims to Curb a Love of Guns." The Christian Science Monitor v90 n20 23 Dec 1997. p1,7. The Christian Science Monitor search engine: <http://www.csmonitor.com/plweb-cgi/iops1.pl> To retrieve this article, enter the following search: ED=19971223 AND guns. In the "retrieved list," click the title that matches this record. (ISSN0882-7729).

FIREARMS--UNITED STATES (v26)

"Every day in the United States there are 733 shootings (Cotton, 1992). It is estimated that 66.7 million handguns and 200 million firearms of all kinds are in circulation (Larson, 1994). About one-half of all households own at least one firearm and one-quarter own a handgun (Reiss & Roth, 1993)." (p507)

Page, Randy M./Hammermeister, Jon. "Weapon-Carrying and Youth Violence." Adolescence v32 n127 Fall 1997. p505-513. (ISSN0001-8449).

In the U.S., "since September 1994, licensed firearms dealers have reported 23,775 guns stolen, lost, or missing to the BATF [Bureau of Alcohol, Tobacco and Firearms]. Up to 32 percent of firearms used in the commission of a crime are obtained by the criminal directly by theft." (pH7477)

Roukema, Marge (Rep.-N.J.). "Treasury, Postal Service, And General Government Appropriations Act, 1998." Congressional Record. Daily ed. v143 n124 17 Sep 1997. pH7456-7480. section/page-level access: <http://thomas.loc.gov/cgi-bin/query/R?r105:FLD001:H07477:> (ISSN0363-7239). (X1.1A.105/1).

"There are enough guns in private hands to provide every adult in America with one, according to a survey recently released by the Police Foundation....Of the 192 million privately owned firearms in the United States, 65 million are handguns, 70 million are rifles, and 49 million are shotguns." (p6)

U.S. Dept. of Justice. Federal Bureau of Investigation. "Bulletin Reports: Gun Ownership Survey." FBI Law Enforcement Bulletin v66 n9 Sep 1997. p6. (ISSN0014-5688).

According to the U.S. "Bureau of Justice Statistics bulletin, 'Presale Firearm Checks' by Don Manson and Gene Lauver, presale background checks on potential handgun buyers required by the Brady Handgun Violence Act have stymied more than 186,000 illegal over-the-counter gun sales during the first 28 months. Of the 9 million applications to purchase firearms submitted from March 1, 1994, through June 30, 1996, an estimated 186,000 were rejected, an average of 6,600 per month. Over 70 percent of the individuals rejected were convicted or indicted felons." (p6)

U.S. Dept. of Justice. Federal Bureau of Investigation. "Bulletin Reports: Presale Firearm Checks." FBI Law Enforcement Bulletin v66 n9 Sep 1997. p6. (ISSN0014-5688).

"In 1993, 35,595 people were killed by guns in the United States....A 1993 study by the National Association of Children's Hospitals and Related Institutions determined that it costs, on average, $14,000 to treat a child struck by gunfire....The study indicated that 5356 people under age 19 were killed by guns in 1991, about 15 per day." (p20)

Obuszewski, Max. "Challenging the Violence Epidemic in Baltimore." Peacework n276 Jul-Aug 1997. p20-21. (ISSN0748-0725).

"Altogether last year, dealers throughout the United States obtained background checks for almost 2.6 million handgun purchase applications. Of these, 2.7 percent were rejected following checks by state or local law enforcement officials. Approximately 47,000 handgun sales were denied because the applicants had been indicted for felony offenses or had felony convictions; 4,200 were fugitives from justice; 3,900 were prohibited because of state laws; 2,700 were the subjects of restraining orders; and 1,000 had mental disabilities....When doing background checks either following the Brady Act procedures or under state laws, 49 states searched criminal history files, 45 checked for fugitives, 32 checked restraining order files and 16 checked for a mental disability."

U.S. Dept. of Justice. "Brady Act Background Checks Prevent 173,000 Illegal Handgun Purchases since February 1994 Implementation." Press Release 4 Sep 1997. document-level access: <http://www.ojp.usdoj.gov/pub/bjs/press/phc96.pr>

Over 200 million "guns are in Amercia, more than one for each adult. But due to multiple gun ownership, only about 25% of the population (42% male; 9% female) own guns....The primary reasons for owning and possessing guns are: self-defense (74.4%) and target/sport shooting (10.8%), followed by job-related (4.7%)." (p2-3)

"Research: Comprehensive Gun Study Shows Little Use by Security Practitioners." Security Letter v27 n12 16 Jun 1997. p2-3. (ISSN0363-4922).

"Junk guns" "are cheaply made pistols that can be purchased in gun shops for less than $100 [in the U.S.]....On America's streets, gun-control activists say, 7 of 10 guns confiscated at crime scenes today are junk guns....80 percent...are made by a half dozen firms in southern California." (p3)

Wood, Daniel B. "United States: California Targets Junk-Gun Sales and Producers." The Christian Science Monitor v89 n198 8 Sep 1997. p3. The Christian Science Monitor search engine: <http://www.csmonitor.com/plweb-cgi/iops1.pl> To retrieve this article, enter the following search: ED=19970908 AND producers. In the "retrieved list," click the title that matches this record. (ISSN0882-7729).

"There are a quarter of a million federally licensed firearms dealers in the...[U.S.]--20 times the number of McDonald's restaurants. Estimates of private firearm ownership in the United States run from 192 million in a recent Justice Department study, to 230 million according to the U.S. National Rifle Association, to a figure of 250 million put forward by the Federal Bureau of Investigation (FBI). At the high end of that range, this would mean one firearm for every American, from infant to senior citizen. Aside from illegal transactions, legitimate domestic production adds some 3-6 million firearms annually to the stockpile, and imports up to another 1 million....But about half a million firearms are reported stolen in non-commercial thefts alone each year." (p21)

Renner, Michael. "Small Arms, Big Impact: The Next Challenge of Disarmament." Worldwatch Paper n137 Oct 1997. p5-77.

FIREARMS--UNITED STATES--CHILDREN--MORTALITY

"American children aged 14 and younger are 16 times more likely to be killed by firearms than are children in 25 other industrialized nations averaged together, according to the Centers for Disease Control and Prevention....The murder rate for American kids under age 14 is five times the average rate for the other countries....The risk that an American aged 15 to 19 will die from a firearm injury more than doubled between 1985 and 1994." (p30)

Klein, Matthew. "Kaleidoscope: Kids and Guns: All-American." American Demographics v19 n7 Jul 1997. p30. article-level access: <http://www.demographics.com/publications/ad/97_ad/9707_ad/ad970722.htm> (ISSN0163-4089).

In the U.S., "a child is killed by firearms every 92 minutes--5,751 deaths in 1993....A gun in the home is forty-three times more likely to be used in a homicide, suicide, or accidental shooting than for self-defense. A child growing up in America is fifteen times more likely to be killed by gunfire than a child growing up in Northern Ireland. Between 1979 and 1991, nearly 50,000 children were killed by firearms--a total equivalent to the number of American casualties in the Vietnam War." (p24)

"News: Too Young to Die." Fellowship v63 n9-10 Sep-Oct 1997. p24. (ISSN0014-9810).

A 1991 U.S. National Safety Council figures shows "that handgun accidents killed 10 to 15 children under the age of 6....A child under the age of 6 is 25 times more likely to drown in an unattended swimming pool or bathtub than to be killed in a handgun accident." (p66)

Funk, T. Markus. "Straight Shooters." Reason v29 n4 Aug-Sep 1997. p65-68. (ISSN0048-6906).

FIREARMS--UNITED STATES--CRIME

In the U.S., "fewer than 150,000 police officers are ever on duty at a given time in a country of over 3 million square miles and more than 260 million people. Estimates indicate that a 12-year-old child has an 83 percent chance of being the victim of a violent crime in his or her lifetime, but Department of Justice statistics reveal that for all crimes of violence, the police respond to 911 calls within five minutes only 28 percent of the time....The threat of victimization is...the main reason that nearly 50 percent of American homes have guns....Although there are only about 1.7 million annual arrests for violent crime and burglary...there are at least 2.2 million defensive uses of a firearm by civilians each year (most involving incidents in which a gun is not actually fired)." (p66)

Funk, T. Markus. "Straight Shooters." Reason v29 n4 Aug-Sep 1997. p65-68. (ISSN0048-6906).

FIREARMS--UNITED STATES--HIGH SCHOOL STUDENTS

"According to the 1990 Youth Risk Behavior Survey, 1 in 20 senior high school students [in the U.S.] carried a firearm, usually a handgun, and 1 in 5 carried a weapon of some type during the 30 days preceding the survey (Centers for Disease Control, 1991). A survey of 10 inner-city high schools in four states found that 35% of male and 11% of female students reported carrying a gun (Sheley, McGee, & Wright, 1992). A study of rural school students in southeast Texas found that 6% of male students had taken guns to school, and almost 2% reported that they did so almost every day. In addition, 42.3% of those surveyed said they could get a gun if they wanted one (Kissell, 1993). More than one-third (34%) of urban high school students in Seattle reported having easy access to handguns, while 11.4% of males and 1.5% of females reported owning a handgun. One-third of those who owned handguns reported that they had fired at someone. Further, almost 10% of female students reported a firearm homicide or suicide among family members or close friends (Callahan & Rivara, 1992). Another study from the southeast U.S. found that 9% of urban and suburban youth owned a handgun (Larson, 1994)." (p505-506)

Page, Randy M./Hammermeister, Jon. "Weapon-Carrying and Youth Violence." Adolescence v32 n127 Fall 1997. p505-513. (ISSN0001-8449).

FIREARMS--UNITED STATES--MORTALITY (v26)

"Gun-related homicides, suicides, and accidental shootings account for approximately 38,000 deaths a year in the United States (Buchsbaum, 1994); approximately 60% of all homicide victims in the United States are killed with firearms. Handguns account for 80% of homicides committed with firearms, although they comprise only about one-third of all firearms owned (Roth, 1994). For the first time in many decades, the number of firearm-related deaths surpassed that of motor-vehicle-related deaths in seven states (California, Louisiana, Maryland, Nevada, New York, Texas, and Virginia) and the District of Columbia (Centers for Disease Control, 1994)." (p507)

Page, Randy M./Hammermeister, Jon. "Weapon-Carrying and Youth Violence." Adolescence v32 n127 Fall 1997. p505-513. (ISSN0001-8449).

In the 1994 book LETHAL PASSAGE, E. Larson noted that "'over the last two years firearms killed almost 70,000 Americans, more than the total of U.S. soldiers killed in the entire Vietnam War. Every year handguns alone account for 22,000 deaths. In Los Angeles County, 8,050 people were killed or wounded in 1991, according to a report in the LOS ANGELES TIMES--thirteen times the number of U.S. forces killed in the Persian Gulf war. Every day, the handguns of America kill sixty-four people; twenty-five of the dead are victims of homicide; most of the rest shoot themselves." (p508)

Page, Randy M./Hammermeister, Jon. "Weapon-Carrying and Youth Violence." Adolescence v32 n127 Fall 1997. p505-513. (ISSN0001-8449).

"Every 2 minutes, someone in the United States is shot. Every 14 minutes, someone dies from a gunshot wound. In 1994 alone, over 15,000 people in our country were killed by handguns. Compare that to countries like Canada, where 90 people were killed by handguns that year, or Great Britain, which had 68 handgun fatalities....The Federal Centers for Disease Control and Prevention estimate that by the year 2003, gunfire will have surpassed auto accidents as the leading cause of injury-related deaths in the United States. In fact, this is already the case in seven States." (pS5810)

Lautenberg, Frank R. (Sen.-N.J.). "Statements on Introduced Bills and Joint Resolutions." Congressional Record. Daily ed. v143 n84 17 Jun 1997. pS5791-5875. section/page-level access: <http://thomas.loc.gov/cgi-bin/query/R?r105:FLD001:S05809:> (ISSN0363-7239). (X1.1A.105/1).

FIREARMS--UNITED STATES--YOUTH

In the U.S., "a poll of students in grades six through twelve conducted by Louis Harris for the Harvard School of Public Health in 1993 found that 59% said they could get a handgun if they wanted one, and 21% said they could get one within the hour. More than 60% of urban youth reported that they could get a handgun, and 58% of suburban youth also claimed that they could (Larson, 1994). Fifteen percent of students reported carrying a handgun in the past month, 11% said that they had been shot at, 9% said that they had fired a gun at someone, and 4% said they had carried a gun to school in the past year (Drevitch, 1994; Hull, 1993)." (p506)

Page, Randy M./Hammermeister, Jon. "Weapon-Carrying and Youth Violence." Adolescence v32 n127 Fall 1997. p505-513. (ISSN0001-8449).

"The National Crime Prevention Council reported the following: [in the U.S.,] every day 15 children under the age of 19 are killed by gunfire and many more are injured. Homicide is the second leading cause of death for youths ages 10 to 19. Most of these offenses are committed with firearms--especially handguns. Youths between 10 and 19 years old commit suicide using handguns every 6 hours. Firearms kill more people between the ages of 15 and 24 than all natural causes combined. An estimated 1.2 million elementary-aged children who return to an empty house after school have access to guns." (p5)

Briscoe, Judy. "Breaking the Cycle of Violence: A Rational Approach to At-Risk Youth." Federal Probation v61 n3 Sep 1997. p3-13. (ISSN0014-9128).

"Almost half of the guns recovered at crime scenes in America's largest cities, a Bureau of Alcohol Tobacco and Firearms study found, were possessed by offenders under age 25; and 13 percent by teenagers under 18. Nationally, FBI data show, homicides by juveniles with handguns increased four-fold between 1984 and 1994, while non-gun homicides remained the same. Put another way, the entire growth in the juvenile homicide rate during the 10-year period was handgun-related. In 1990, one in 20 teenage students reported carrying a firearm during the previous 30 days. Teenage boys are now more likely to die from gunshot wounds than all natural causes combined." (p19)

Schiraldi, Vincent. "Opinion/Essays: Youthful Arms Race: Lawmakers Don't Get It." The Christian Science Monitor v89 n203 15 Sep 1997. p19. The Christian Science Monitor search engine: <http://www.csmonitor.com/plweb-cgi/iops1.pl> To retrieve this article, enter the following search: ED=19970915 AND lawmakers. In the "retrieved list," click the title that matches this record. (ISSN0882-7729).

FIREARMS--UNITED STATES--YOUTH--MORTALITY (v26)

In the U.S., "among teenagers 15-19 years of age and young adults 20-24 years of age, 1 of every 4 deaths is by a firearm. One of every 8 deaths in children 10-14 is by a firearm....In 1990, 82% of all homicide victims aged 15-19 (91% and 77% African-American and white males, respectively) and 76% of victims aged 20-24 (87% and 71% among African-American and white males, respectively) were killed with guns." (p508)

Page, Randy M./Hammermeister, Jon. "Weapon-Carrying and Youth Violence." Adolescence v32 n127 Fall 1997. p505-513. (ISSN0001-8449).

FIREARMS--VIRGINIA (v26)

FIREARMS INDUSTRY AND TRADE--UNITED STATES (v26)

FIREARMS THEFT--UNITED STATES

In the U.S., "reports indicate almost half a million guns are stolen each year. As of March 1995, there were over 2 million reports in the stolen gun file of the FBI's National Crime Information Center including 7,700 reports of stolen machine guns and submachine guns. In a 5 year period between 1987 and 1992, the National Crime Victimization Survey notes that there were over 300,000 incidents of guns stolen from private citizens. Studies conducted by the Bureau of Alcohol, Tobacco and Firearms note that felons steal firearms to avoid background checks. A 1991 Bureau of Justice Statistics survey of State prison inmates notes that almost 10 percent had stolen a handgun, and over 10 percent of all inmates had traded or sold a stolen firearm....A Justice Department study of juvenile inmates in four States shows that over 50 percent of those inmates had stolen a gun. In...Colorado, the Colorado Bureau of Investigation receives over 500 reports of stolen guns each month. As of this month, the Bureau has a total of 34,825 firearms on its unrecovered firearms list." (pS6993)

Campbell, Ben Nighthorse (Sen.-Colo.). "Statements on Introduced Bills and Joint Resolutions." Congressional Record. Daily ed. v143 n95 8 Jul 1997. pS6990-7012. section/page-level access: <http://thomas.loc.gov/cgi-bin/query/R?r105:FLD001:S06993:> (ISSN0363-7239). (X1.1A.105/1).

In the U.S., "studies have found that between 10 and 32 percent of guns used in the commission of a crime are obtained as a direct result of theft, while an approximately equal number of guns used during a criminal act were stolen before being used in a crime....During the 1992 Los Angeles riots, 19 gun stores were looted and robbed of about 4,000 guns. One pawnshop lost 970 guns, while another outlet was robbed of 1,150 guns. An ATF [Bureau of Alcohol, Tobacco and Firearms] report reveals that these guns continue to be recovered on the street." (pS5809)

Lautenberg, Frank R. (Sen.-N.J.). "Statements on Introduced Bills and Joint Resolutions." Congressional Record. Daily ed. v143 n84 17 Jun 1997. pS5791-5875. section/page-level access: <http://thomas.loc.gov/cgi-bin/query/R?r105:FLD001:S05809:> (ISSN0363-7239). (X1.1A.105/1).

In the U.S., "many crimes are committed using stolen guns. Research suggests about half a million firearms are stolen a year. While that pales in comparison with the 192 million privately owned guns nationwide, stolen guns by definition pass into the hands of criminals and are more likely to be used in the commission of another crime. Surveys show that somewhere between 10 and 32 percent of the guns used in crime were obtained 'directly' through theft, while an approximately equal number of other guns used in crime were stolen somewhere along the line....Weapons bought at legitimate retail dealers account for somewhere between 17 and 27 percent of the guns used in crime....The government's National Crime Victimization Survey reveals that about 80 percent of the guns stolen yearly come from private homes. Since the average gun-owning household has 4.5 firearms, guns can be among the most valuable types of loot burglars take away. At least 7,000 guns a year also are pilfered from automobiles." (p34)

Witkin, Gordon. "U.S. News: Handgun Stealing Made Real Easy." U.S. News & World Report v122 n22 9 Jun 1997. p34,36. article-level access: <http://www.usnews.com/usnews/issue/970609/9GUNS.HTM> (ISSN0041-5537).

FIREFIGHTERS

see FIRE FIGHTERS

FIRES

see also ARSON; CHURCH BUILDINGS--FIRES AND FIRE PREVENTION; FOREST FIRES; POLYVINYL CHLORIDE--FIRES AND FIRE PREVENTION--UNITED STATES

FIRES--ALABAMA--MORTALITY

"Alabama had the second highest fatality rate from unintentional injury due to fire and flames among all 50 states in 1993, according to the National Safety Council. While more than half of all unintentional injury fatalities to Alabamians involve motor vehicle accidents, deaths from fire and flames were second only to Mississippi's in 1993....There were 138 deaths to Alabamians from fire and flames in 1995, exceeding the 130 deaths in 1993. The fire and flame death rate was 3.2 per 100,000 in 1993 and 3.4 in 1995."

Alabama. Dept. of Public Health. "Alabama Has Second Highest Fire Fatality Rate in Nation." News Release 10 Feb 1997. document-level access: <http://www.alapubhealth.org/Press/pr021097b.htm>

FIRES--CANADA (v26)

FIRES--ENVIRONMENTAL ASPECTS--AUSTRALIA --KAKADU (v26)

FIRES--GREAT BRITAIN (v26)

FIRES--MARYLAND--MORTALITY

"The number of fire related fatalities reached an all time low in Maryland last year, according to the Maryland Department of Health and Mental Hygiene's (DHMH) Office of the Chief Medical Examiner. The number of fire deaths in 1996 fell nearly 30 percent from the previous year, for a total of 67. The decrease shows significant improvement from 1994 when fire deaths reached 119. Although the total number of fatalities has fallen, children and the elderly accounted for a disproportionate number of deaths in 1996. One third of fire victims were under age 21, and 25 percent of those killed were age 60 or older....According to the Maryland Fire Incident Reporting System, nearly 49 percent of fatalities occurred in homes without an operational smoke detector."

Maryland. Office of Public Relations. "Maryland Fire Deaths Reach All-Time Low in 1996." Press Release 30 Jul 1997. document-level access: <http://www.charm.net/~epi9/pr1847.htm>

FIRES--MICHIGAN (v26)

FIRES--UNITED STATES (v26)

FIRES--WASHINGTON (STATE)

The Washington Department of Natural Resources "has been fighting wildfires since the early 1900's. According to a DNR Forest Fire Study, in the past 25 years, the department has fought 28,000-plus wildfires involving more than 370,000 acres of Washington forest land. In recent years, firefighting budgets have decreased and the intensity of fires has increased, with the terrible fire season of 1994 breaking the record at 79,000 acres burned in Washington." (pS8597)

Murray, Patty (Sen.-Wash.). "Workplace Religious Freedom Act." Congressional Record. Daily ed. v143 n111 31 Jul 1997. pS8590-8607. section/page-level access: <http://thomas.loc.gov/cgi-bin/query/R?r105:FLD001:S08597:> (ISSN0363-7239). (X1.1A.105/1).

FIREWORKS--ACCIDENTS--UNITED STATES

"In 1996, close to 7,600 people nationwide were injured by fireworks, according to the U.S. Consumer Product Safety Commission. That's down from 13,200 injuries in 1994 and 11,313 in 1995. But injuries from illegal M80s and M100s account for more injuries than ever, commission reports show....Despite the warnings, Americans continue their love affair with fireworks. Sales have quadrupled since 1976, according to the National Council on Fireworks Safety." (p4 secB)

Mishra, Raja. "Local News: Fireworks Still Entice despite Dangers." Detroit Free Press 1 Jul 1997. p1,4 secB.

"According to the Centers for Disease Control, every year over 13,000 people are treated in [U.S.] emergency rooms because of severe injuries from malfunction or careless use of fireworks. Over 40 percent of those injured from fireworks are children under age 15. Males are injured three times as frequently as females....Even sparklers can cause injury. These seemingly harmless fireworks can burn at more than 1000 degrees and can ignite a participant's or observer's clothing."

North Dakota. Dept. of Health. "Fireworks Safety." Press Release 27 Jun 1997. document-level access: <http://www.health.state.nd.us/n970627a.htm>

FIRMS

see BUSINESS ENTERPRISES

FISH AS FOOD--UNITED STATES (v26)

FISHERIES (v26)

see also BLUEFIN TUNA FISHERIES; CATFISH FISHERIES; CRAYFISH INDUSTRY; SALMON FISHING; SHELLFISH TRADE; SHRIMP FISHERIES; SWORDFISH; SWORDFISH FISHING; TROUT INDUSTRY

"Thirteen of the world's 15 major fishing regions have seen a decline in total catch, putting an estimated 100,000 fishers out of work and threatening the food supply of millions in developing countries." (p1) In the Black Sea, "twenty of 26 commercial fish species have vanished since 1970, while the anchovy harvest fell by more than 95 percent....The Rome-based United Nations Food and Agriculture Organization reports that 60 percent of the world's top 200 marine-fish resources are highly exploited or in decline." (p10) "Researchers are discovering that fishing directly affects a wide range of nontarget species....Nearly 30 million tons of this dead or dying 'by-catch' is thrown overboard by fishing boats every year--a quantity equal to a third of the world's total catch." (p11)

Woodard, Colin. "Global Report: Lifeless Areas Spread: Troubles Bubble under the Sea." The Christian Science Monitor v89 n200 10 Sep 1997. p1,10-11. The Christian Science Monitor search engine: <http://www.csmonitor.com/plweb-cgi/iops1.pl> To retrieve this article, enter the following search: ED=19970910 AND sea. In the "retrieved list," click the title that matches this record. (ISSN0882-7729).

FISHERIES--BANGLADESH (v26)

FISHERIES--BERING SEA (v26)

FISHERIES--BRITISH COLUMBIA

The Canadian "federal department of fisheries and oceans estimates that the B.C. [British Columbia] sport salmon fishery is worth $600 million a year, the commercial fishery $400 million. And a report prepared for the federal and provincial fisheries departments last year found that a sports-caught chinook is worth more than $670 to the provincial economy compared with only $26 for the very same fish harvested commercially. In addition, angling generated nearly six times as many jobs as commercial fishing....Each year, the federal fisheries department issues about 400,000 saltwater fishing licences in British Columbia, with between 80,000 and 100,000 going to non-residents. Revenues from licence fees usually average about $7 million, compared with about $11 million for commercial licences. But the big money comes from the spinoffs generated by sports anglers--some of whom pay up to $1,000 a day to fish at exclusive remote fly-in lodges--including travel, accommodation and guiding." (p19)

Steele, Scott. "Cover: A Haul of Hard Cash." Maclean's v110 n31 4 Aug 1997. p19. (ISSN0024-9262).

FISHERIES--CANADA (v26)

FISHERIES--EMPLOYMENT--ASIA--CHILDREN (v26)

FISHERIES--ENVIRONMENTAL ASPECTS (v26)

FISHERIES--EUROPE (v26)

FISHERIES--HURON, LAKE (MICH. AND ONT.)

Between Michigan and Ontario, on Lake Huron, "anglers caught 11.14 chinook salmon per 100 angling hours as part of an 18.34 overall catch rate, based on nine index ports. That compares to 5.2 chinook and 12.5 for all trout and salmon at Lake Michigan index ports....[For Lake Huron,] catch rates were up from last year for chinook (11.14 up from 7.45 in 1996) and for late trout--5.71, up from 4.08 in 1996. Catch rates for coho salmon were up marginally (.24; .18 in '96) but were down for rainbow trout (1.04; 1.28 in '96) and brown trout (.21; .43 in '96). The overall catch rate (18.34) improved from 13.42 in 1996." (p3 secC)

Gwizdz, Bob. "Venture Outdoors: Lake Huron's Catch Rates Improve, Making '97 a 'Super' Year for Anglers." Ann Arbor News 13 Dec 1997. p3 secC.

FISHERIES--MICHIGAN, LAKE

For Lake Michigan in 1997, "the coho harvest was up 24 percent while the catch rate increased 15 percent. The chinook harvest was up 12 percent, while the catch rate was up 7 percent. The brown trout harvest increased 52 percent, while the catch rate was up 43 percent. The laker harvest increased 15 percent, while the catch rate was unchanged. And the steelhead harvest was down 24 percent, with the catch rate down 30 percent." (p2 secC)

"Venture Outdoors: Lake Michigan Has One of Its Best Fishing Seasons Ever in '97." Ann Arbor News 29 Nov 1997. p2 secC.

FISHERIES--NORTHERN IRELAND (v26)

FISHERIES--UNITED STATES (v26)

"The United States and its insular areas have more than 95,000 miles of coastline and the offshore U.S. Exclusive Economic Zone (EEZ) encompasses more than 3.4 million square miles, nearly equal to the land area of the United States. Over the last 30 years the coastal area populations have increased from 80 to over 110 million and is projected to reach 127 million by 2010....Since 1977 total fish harvest from the EEZ increased more than 325 percent to a peak of 6.65 billion pounds annually in 1986-88, but has subsequently declined--only 6.32 in 1993. Alaska pollock and Gulf of Mexico shrimp were the leading fisheries in 1993. Imported seafood comprised 57 percent of U.S. consumption during 1996, a 3 percent increase from 1995." (pS9893)

Kerry, John F. (Sen.-Mass.). "Statements on Introduced Bills and Joint Resolutions." Congressional Record. Daily ed. v143 n129 24 Sep 1997. pS9887-9897. section/page-level access: <http://thomas.loc.gov/cgi-bin/query/R?r105:FLD001:S09892:> (ISSN0363-7239). (X1.1A.105/1).

FISHES

see also CHINOOK SALMON; MARLIN; SALMON FISHING;

SHARKS; SWORDFISH; WHALES; WHITE WHALE

FISHES--DISEASES--MICHIGAN, LAKE

In Michigan, research biologist Jory Jonas says the percentage of fish in Department of Natural Resources sampling this spring that was suffering from bacterial kidney disease "was 'significantly higher than last year.' Jonas has divided...[Lake Michigan] into four districts. The district south of Holland showed 40 percent of the chinooks and 60 percent of the lake trout sampled suffered from BKD. The mid-lake destrict, Holland to Pentwater, was worse: a whopping 84 percent of the chinooks and 79 percent of the lakers had BKD. The districts north of Pentwater were better. Overall, 12 percent of the chinooks and 37 percent of the lakers had BKD." (p1 secC)

Gwizdz, Bob. "Venture Outdoors: Lake Michigan Salmon Harvest Is Back Up, But for How Long?" Ann Arbor News 20 Sep 1997. p1 secC.

FISHING INDUSTRY

see FISHERIES

FLAGS--UNITED STATES

In the U.S., "about 40 percent of the flags manufactured for the DVA [Department of Veterans Affairs] are made under a set-aside contract awarded to nonprofit organizations sponsored by the National Industries for the Severely Handicapped. One of those organizations, North Bay Industries, near San Francisco, Calif, produces about 500 flags a day. The company's annual output accounts for about 12 percent of the flags ordered by the DVA. Bill Teresky, NBI's director of manufacturing, said about 70 percent of his workers are developmentally disabled or in physical rehabilitation....The DVA estimates that more than half a million veterans will die in 1997. About 80 percent of their families will request a burial flag. Interment flags, which cost about $25 to make, are free for honorably discharged veterans." (p36,38)

Moore, Alan/U.S. Army. "Old Glory: Making Old Glory." Soldiers v52 n6 Jun 1997. p36,38. (ISSN0093-8440).

FLEXIBLE WORK HOURS

see HOURS OF LABOR, FLEXIBLE

FLOODS--KOREA (NORTH) (v26)

FLOODS--SIERRA NEVADA (CALIF. AND NEV.)

On the western side of the Sierra Nevada, the 1997 New Year's "floodwaters covered 250 square miles and destroyed or damaged at least 16,000 homes, killed eight people and caused an estimated $1.6 billion in damage in California. Flooding on the eastern side of the Sierra Nevada was not as severe, but rising rivers shut down casinos in Reno, flooded the state capital and caused one death in Nevada." (p8)

Christensen, Jon. "Ecology Forum: A Flood of Lessons." Nature Conservancy v47 n4 Jul-Aug 1997. p8-9. (ISSN0028-5200).

FLORA

see PLANTS

FLORICULTURE

see also CUT FLOWERS; ROSES

FLORICULTURE--CHINA

In China, "the export of flowers (shrubs, nursery stock plants, and foliage) rose from $6.5 million in the mid-1980s to $44 million in the mid-1990s, more than a 6-fold increase. Imports of these materials increased even more rapidly, from $627,000 in the mid-1980s, to $12 million in 1995...." (p49)

Crook, Frederick W./U.S. Dept. of Agriculture. Economic Research Service. "Introduction to China's Horticultural Economy." China: International Agriculture and Trade Reports Situation and Outlook Series Jun 1997. p47-51.

FLORICULTURE--UNITED STATES

In the U.S., "preliminary estimates for grower cash receipts in the floriculture production sector in 1996 is $4 billion, up 3 percent over 1995. The 1997 outlook is for an additional increase of 2 percent." (p9) "Last year consumers spent about $8.2 billion on cut flowers and cut greens ($31 per capita), a 9-percent increase over 1995. Cut flower and cut greens expenditures this year are anticipated to rise 6 percent. Expenditures for potted plants (flowering and foliage) in 1996, on the other hand, were up only 2 percent from the prior year, to $7 billion ($26 per capita)....U.S. consumers will spend almost $16 billion on floriculture products in 1997, or $59 per capita, which ranks the U.S. as 12th highest in the world in per capita expenditures on indoor flowers/plants." (p10)

Johnson, Doyle. "Commodity Spotlight: 'Green' Industry Grower Receipts to Exceed $11 Billion." Agricultural Outlook Jul 1997. p9-10.

"Grower cash receipts for U.S. floriculture and environmental horticulture crops reached $10.9 billion in 1996, up 5 percent from a year earlier. Value of production has grown an average of 5 percent a year since 1989. The value of environmental horticulture production rose 6 percent annually to $6.9 billion last year....In the floriculture sector, value of bedding and garden plants increased from $1.1 billion in 1989 to $1.8 billion in 1996. Potted plants (flowering and foliage varieties used indoors) registered small gains, increasing from $1.4 billion to $1.6 billion. Cut flowers and cut cultivated greens were valued at $642 million in 1996, down from $671 million in 1989....Compared with a year earlier, the total value of floriculture crops (cut flowers, cut greens, potted plants, and bedding plants) increased 3 percent in 1996. The value of cut flowers increased 5 percent and cut greens jumped 7 percent. Value of potted flowering plants rose 1 percent and potted foliage plants 2 percent. Bedding plant value advanced 4 percent, while outdoor landscaping plants, including nursery stock and sod, increased 6 percent. Ten States account for more than two-thirds of U.S. output. The most important States (and their percent of U.S. receipts) are California (20), Florida (11), North Carolina and Texas (8 each), Ohio and Oregon (5 each), and Michigan, Pennsylvania, Oklahoma, and New York (2-4 each)....Growth in expenditures has averaged 5 percent a year since 1989....Expenditures for cut flowers and cut greens increased $100 million from 1995 to $6.5 billion ($26.80 per capita)." (p5)

Johnson, Doyle/U.S. Dept. of Agriculture. Economic Research Service. "Summary of Report: Floriculture and Environmental Horticulture Cash Receipts Up 5 Percent in 1996." ERS Information Nov 1997. p5-6.

FLORIDA--EMPLOYMENT--MANUFACTURES (v26)

FLORIDA KEYS (FLA.)

"The Florida Keys are a chain of islands largely built upon the remains of ancient reef systems, stretching 200 miles from north of Key Largo all the way down to the Dry Tortugas. The Florida Keys miss the tropics by only 30 miles and temperatures never have been below 40 degrees Fahrenheit there." (p16)

Kruer, Curtis. "America's Tropics: FAS Restoration: Florida Audubon Spearheading Restoration in the Florida Keys." Florida Naturalist v70 n2 Sum 1997. p16-17. (ISSN0015-4172).

FLORIDA KEYS (FLA.)--ENVIRONMENTAL ASPECTS

In the Florida Keys, forests "may support up to 100 species of woody plants in a single stand, in contrast to northern Florida forests, which may support a few dozen." (p6) "The White-crowned Pigeons have been documented feeding on at least 38 plant species and probably use many more throughout the year....More than 70 percent of the woody plants in the Keys produce fleshy fruits that are eaten by birds and mammals....Through a separate mapping study, it was estimated that by 1991, there had been a loss of 41 percent of upland forested area from the northernmost Keys in Biscayne Bay to Long Key in the Middle Keys. The Keys, along Highway 1 where most development has occurred, lost 66 percent of their forested area on the average, and more than 75 percent on some Keys. Prior to settlement, most of the Keys had continuous coverage of hammock forest. Today, the remaining forested area is divided into more than 1,000 fragments of varying size and ecological integrity." (p7)

Sawicki, Richard. "America's Tropics: Tropical Flyways and the White-Crowned Pigeons." Florida Naturalist v70 n2 Sum 1997. p6-7. (ISSN0015-4172).

FLORISTS--UNITED STATES (v26)

FLOYD COUNTY (KY.)--SOCIAL CONDITIONS (v26)

FLU

see INFLUENZA

FLUORIDES

"Fluoride inhibits an estimated 100 different enzyme systems in human soft tissues." (p44) "Mottling of teeth occurs in 10-40% of children raised on fluoridated water at one ppm [parts per million]....Drs. Alfred Taylor and Nell Taylor of the University of Texas...found that fluoride in the drinking water at levels of one half to one ppm increased tumor growth in cancer prone mice by 15-20%....Fluoridated toothpastes contain 1000 ppm fluoride. The consumption of a seven ounce family sized tube contains enough fluoride to kill a small child of 20 lbs. In the typical fluoride treatments received at the dental office, a gel (10,000 to 50,000 ppm) is left on the child's teeth for several minutes...." (p45)

Bass, Charles. "Health & Healing: The Case against Fluoride." Acres, U.S.A. v27 n7 Jul 1997. p44-45. (ISSN1076-4968).

FLUOROCARBONS INDUSTRY

see CHLOROFLUOROCARBONS

FOLIC ACID IN HUMAN NUTRITION--UNITED STATES

"Folate--which includes folic acid and its several food forms--is one of three B vitamins the body needs to convert the amino acid homocysteine to an innocuous relative....[In the U.S.,] researchers estimate that high homocysteine increases the odds for coronary artery disease by 60 percent in men and by 80 percent in women, based on studies prior to 1995. And the odds for cerebrovascular disease increases by 50 percent in both genders by these estimates....The risk of coronary artery disease may drop by 3 to 5 percent when grain products are fortified [with folic acid] at the regulated level." (p16) "In setting the fortification regulation, FDA adopted the conservative level of 0.43 to 1.4 milligrams of folic acid per pound of product. In scientific measure, 'that's about 140 micrograms of folic acid per 100 grams of flour,' says FDA food chemist Jeanne Rader....At the mandated level, a little more than half the elderly population would get the desired 400 mcg of folate daily, compared to a third without fortification. And the percentage of elderly with high homocysteine would drop from 26 to 21." (p17)

McBride, Judy/U.S. Dept. of Agriculture. Agricultural Research Service. "Foods to Be Fortified with Folic Acid." Agricultural Research v45 n6 Jun 1997. p16-17. (ISSN0002-161X).

FOLIC ACID IN HUMAN NUTRITION--UNITED STATES --WOMEN

In the U.S., "in 1992, the Public Health Service recommended that all women of childbearing age consume 400 micrograms (mcg) of folic acid daily to reduce risk. That 400 millionths of a gram could spare many of the 2,500 infants born in the United States with neural tube defects each year....According to FDA estimates, the benefits of reducing neural tube defects outweigh the costs of fortification by at least 24 to 1." (p16)

McBride, Judy/U.S. Dept. of Agriculture. Agricultural Research Service. "Foods to Be Fortified with Folic Acid." Agricultural Research v45 n6 Jun 1997. p16-17. (ISSN0002-161X).

Gallup Organization "researchers polled a representative sample of 2,001 U.S. women between the ages of 18 and 45....In 1997, 66% of women had heard or read about folic acid, compared with 52% in 1995....The percentage of women who knew that folic acid helps avert birth defects such as spina bifida and anencephaly rose from 5% in 1995 to 11% in '97. Only 2% of respondents in 1995 said they knew that folic acid should be taken regularly before pregnancy. This percentage jumped to 5% this year....30% of women who were not pregnant at the time of the survey said they took a daily multivitamin supplement that contained folic acid. This was an increase of 5% over the 1995 responses." (p39)

"Abstracts: Primary Care: More American Women Know about the Importance of Folic Acid." Modern Medicine v65 n10 Oct 1997. p39,43. (ISSN0026-8070).

FOLKWAYS

see MANNERS AND CUSTOMS

FOOD (v26)

see also BABY FOODS INDUSTRY; BEVERAGE INDUSTRY; EGGS AS FOOD; FAST FOOD RESTAURANTS; GRAIN; NATURAL FOODS INDUSTRY; SNACK FOOD INDUSTRY

FOOD--BIOTECHNOLOGY--UNITED STATES--PUBLIC OPINION (v26)

FOOD--CALIFORNIA--NEW YORK (N.Y.) (v26)

FOOD--CENTRAL AMERICA (v26)

FOOD--CHOLESTEROL CONTENT--UNITED STATES --CHILDREN (v26)

FOOD--DEVELOPING COUNTRIES--PRESERVATION (v26)

FOOD--FAT CONTENT--UNITED STATES--CHILDREN (v26)

FOOD--UNITED STATES--PUBLIC OPINION (v26)

FOOD, COST OF

see COST AND STANDARD OF LIVING

FOOD ADULTERATION AND INSPECTION--GREAT BRITAIN (v26)

FOOD ADULTERATION AND INSPECTION--UNITED STATES

U.S. "federal guidelines allow 3 percent soybean product in the hamburger. Any junk food operation is able to get 16 hamburgers (sometimes 20) out of a pound of meat. Some 16 to 20 pounds of ice are added to each 100 pounds of meat. This is absorbed quickly. The meat swells. Soy is added, as are additives and all the 400 to 600 ppm [parts per million] of dissolved solids in tap water. By the time the stuff is ready for the grill, 100 pounds has been transformed into 124 pounds." (p2)

"Opinion: The Truth about E. Coli." Acres, U.S.A. v27 n10 Oct 1997. p2-3. (ISSN1076-4968).

"According to published studies, a typical food product is handled an average of 33 times before it is ever touched by a consumer in the supermarket....According to USDA's Food Safety and Inspection Service (FSIS), 0.2 percent of hogs, 1.7 percent of calves, and 0.4 percent of chickens and turkeys were 'condemned' or otherwise rejected at slaughter in 1993 and could not be used for human food." (p4)

Kantor, Linda Scott/Lipton, Kathryn/Manchester, Alden/Oliveira, Victor/U.S. Dept. of Agriculture. Economic Research Service. "Food Loss: Estimating and Addressing America's Food Losses." Food Review v20 n1 Jan-Apr 1997. p2-12. (ISSN1056-327X).

FOOD ALLERGY--CANADA (v26)

FOOD ASSISTANCE PROGRAMS

see FOOD RELIEF

FOOD CONSUMPTION (v26)

see also MILK CONSUMPTION

"Rich people consume roughly four times as much grain as poor people do. In a country like India, only some 200 kilograms of grain are available per person, so nearly all of them must be consumed directly just to satisfy basic caloric needs. The average American, in contrast, uses roughly 800 kilograms of grain a year, most of them consumed indirectly in the form of beef, pork, poultry, eggs, milk, cheese, yogurt, and ice cream....A kilogram of beef added in the feedlot requires roughly 7 kilograms of grain; a kilogram of pork needs 4 kilograms; a kilogram of eggs, roughly 3 kilograms; a kilogram of poultry, just over 2 kilograms; and a kilogram of fish produced in a pond, just under 2 kilograms." (p10)

Brown, Lester R. "The Agricultural Link: How Environmental Deterioration Could Disrupt Economic Progress." Worldwatch Paper n136 Aug 1997. p5-73.

FOOD CONSUMPTION--RUSSIA (v26)

FOOD CONSUMPTION--UNITED STATES (v26)

According to new USDA Economic Research Service "estimates, about 96 billion pounds of food, or 27 percent of the 356 billion pounds of the edible food available for human consumption in the United States, were lost to human use at these three marketing stages in 1995....Fresh fruits and vegetables, fluid milk, grain products, and sweeteners (mostly sugar and high-fructose corn syrup) accounted for two-thirds of these losses....On average, each American consumes about 3 pounds of food each day. If even 5 percent of the 96 billion pounds were recovered, that quantity would represent the equivalent of a day's food for each of 4 million people. Recovery rates of 10 percent and 25 percent would provide enough food for the equivalent of 8 million and 20 million people, respectively." (p3)

Kantor, Linda Scott/Lipton, Kathryn/Manchester, Alden/ Oliveira, Victor/U.S. Dept. of Agriculture. Economic Research Service. "Food Loss: Estimating and Addressing America's Food Losses." Food Review v20 n1 Jan-Apr 1997. p2-12. (ISSN1056-327X).

FOOD HABITS (v26)

FOOD HABITS--CANADA

"Statistics Canada reports that the average person's consumption of red meat has declined nearly 10 per cent over the past two decades....During the same period, the intake of cheese--most of it high-fat cheddar--has more than doubled. Canadians drink less milk now and have largely switched to skim, one and two per cent, but they consume 50 per cent more cream than they did two decades ago." (p51)

Driedger, Sharon Doyle. "Cover: Eating Right." Maclean's v110 n43 27 Oct 1997. p50-51. (ISSN0024-9262).

FOOD HABITS--ECONOMIC ASPECTS

"In the U.S., we spend only 11 percent of disposable income on food compared to 15-20 percent in other affluent countries in Europe and in Japan, 35-40 percent in developing countries such as Mexico and Thailand, and more than 50 percent in the lowest income countries such as India and other southeast Asia countries." (p582)

Robinson, B. H. (Administrator, Cooperative State Research, Education, And Extension Service). "Agriculture, Rural Development, Food and Drug Administration...Approp. for 1998 (Part 4)." Hearing. U.S. House. Committee on Appropriations. Washington, D.C. : GPO, 1997. (ISBN0160551560). (Y4.Ap6/1:Ag8/997/pt.4).

FOOD HABITS--ECONOMIC ASPECTS--MICHIGAN

"Americans waste 27 percent of all their food, according to a recent U.S. Department of Agriculture study. That adds up to 96 billion pounds of food wasted each year; Michigan's share of that, based on population, is 3.5 billion pounds....For the average household, that translates to about $600 a year. The percentage wasted is even higher among single people, experts say." (p1 secC) Figures "suggest consumers waste $240 million of Michigan's $807 million dairy output, as much as $220 million of the state's $1.5 billion livestock production, and about $20 million of Michigan's $68-million egg production is disposed." (p2 secC)

Puls, Mark. "Metro: News Special: Michiganians Waste Millions on Discarded Food Each Year." Detroit News 3 Nov 1997. p1-2 secC.

FOOD HABITS--ECONOMIC ASPECTS--UNITED STATES

"In 1992 (USDA's most recently published survey data), households in the poorest 20 percent of the Nation's income distribution (household income averaging $6,669) spent $1,249 per person on food, compared with $1,997 for the wealthiest 20 percent (household income averaging $77,311). The survey also revealed that higher income households spent more money and a larger share of their food budget on food away from home: 24 percent for the lowest income households, compared with 40 percent for the highest income households....The CES [Consumer Expenditure Survey] data reveal that the highest income group bought $48 worth of fish and seafood per person per year, while the lowest income group spent $26." (p10)

Kaufman, Phil/Lutz, Steven M./U.S. Dept. of Agriculture. Economic Research Service. "Food Prices: Competing Forces Affect Food Prices for Low-Income Households." Food Review v20 n2 May-Aug 1997. p8-12. (ISSN1056-327X).

FOOD HABITS--EGYPT (v26)

FOOD HABITS--ETHIOPIA (v26)

FOOD HABITS--IRELAND

"Buying food eats up nearly a third of the weekly spending of the poorest households in...[Ireland] compared with just over a fifth for the average household, a report released...by the Central Statistics Office (CSO) reveals....The CSO survey shows that the poorest 10% of rural households spend 30 [pounds sterling] a week on food out of a weekly expenditure of just 93 [pounds sterling]. This compares with all rural households where the weekly food bill is more than double that at 72 [pounds sterling] out of a total weekly spend of 283 [pounds sterling]. In urban areas, the poorest 10% of households spend 24 [pounds sterling] a week on food out of total expenditure of 83 [pounds sterling] a week. In the case of all urban households the weekly food bill comes to 70 [pounds sterling] out of a total of 328 [pounds sterling]. However, it should be noted that the lowest income households were smaller, having only 1.2 people, compared with the highest income households which had 4.8 people in rural areas and 4.1 people in urban areas."

Ireland. Central Statistics Office. "Household Budget Survey 1994-95--Volume 2: Detailed Results for Urban and Rural Households." Press Release 1 Dec 1997. document-level access: <http://www.cso.ie/pressreleases/prelhbsv2.html>

FOOD HABITS--RUSSIA (v26)

FOOD HABITS--UNITED STATES (v26)

In the U.S., "average annual per-capita consumption of beef fell 14 percent between 1980-84 and 1990-94, to 63 pounds per person. As Americans heeded medical advice to cut back on dietary fat from red meat, their chicken consumption jumped 37 percent, to 46 pounds each....The average American ate 121 pounds of fresh fruit per year in 1990-94, up 12 percent from ten years earlier. Fresh vegetable consumption rose 14 percent, to 169 pounds each....The average American consumed almost twice as much cheese in 1990-94 as 20 years earlier, at 25.7 pounds....Per-capita consumption of nondiet soft drinks increased 13 percent between 1990 and 1994, to 40 gallons a year. That equates to 645 8-ounce servings a year, or just less than 2 soft drinks a day. In 1990, carbonated soft drinks accounted for 21 percent of the refined sugar consumed by the average U.S. resident." (p42)

Dortch, Shannon. "America Weighs In." American Demographics v19 n6 Jun 1997. p38-43,45. article-level access: <http://www.demographics.com/publications/ad/97_ad/9706_ad/ad970629.htm> (ISSN0163-4089).

In the U.S., "households with children aged 6 to 12 are 79 percent more likely than expected to buy...'good for you' foods, according to ACNielsen. Households with teenagers aged 13 to 17 are also heavily into granola bars and such; they're 74 percent more likely than expected to buy them. The healthy-bar craze hasn't crossed generational lines, though. Singles and childfree couples aged 55-plus are 67 percent and 48 percent, respectively, less likely than expected to buy them." (p30)

Mogelonsky, Marcia. "Kaleidoscope: Checkout Line: Hippies' Legacy." American Demographics v19 n7 Jul 1997. p30. article-level access: <http://www.demographics.com/publications/ad/97_ad/9707_ad/ad970733.htm> (ISSN0163-4089).

"During 1995, Americans ate an average of 2.7 meals and 1.6 snacks each day....The number of meals eaten by Americans exhibits a U-shape pattern (drops and then increases) with respect to age, declining from 2.9 meals a day among preschoolers (age 2-5) to 2.5 meals among adolescent females, and then rising to 2.7 meals among adults age 40 and older. Preschoolers also snacked most frequently, averaging 2.1 snacks a day. Seniors age 60 and older snacked least frequently with 1.4 snacks consumed by senior males and 1.2 snacks by senior females. On average, Americans ate out more than once for every four meals (29 percent) and more than once for every five snacks (22 percent) during 1995." (p33-34)

Lin, Biing-Hwan/Frazao, Elizabeth/U.S. Dept. of Agriculture. Economic Research Service. "Nutrition: Nutritional Quality of Foods at and away from Home." Food Review v20 n2 May-Aug 1997. p33-40. (ISSN1056-327X).

"On any given day, only 1 in 10 Americans reports eating a dark green or deep yellow vegetable. That's compared to 1 out of 4 that indulges in a basket of French fries....In 1977, 40 percent of the calories consumed came from fat. Today, only 33 percent do. But 1 in 3 Americans is now overweight, according to the USDA, as opposed [to] 20 years ago, when only 1 in 5 was tipping over the scales....Consumption of savory, salty snacks like pretzels, potato chips, popcorn, and corn chips soared more than 200 percent in the last 20 years....'50 percent of the time potato chips are eaten, they're eaten with meals,' says James Shufelt, president of the Snack Food Association, a Washington-based trade group that represents more than 700 snack-food manufacturers....Surveys today show only 7 percent of all Americans consider themselves 'truly natural' in their eating habits, but 25 percent of all shoppers report buying natural or organic foods at the supermarket once a week. And more than 75 percent of all senior supermarket managers see 'organic' as a coming trend." (p8)

Marks, Alexandra. "Pass the Soba?: America's Changing Dinner Plate." The Christian Science Monitor v89 n178 8 Aug 1997. p1,8. The Christian Science Monitor search engine: <http://www.csmonitor.com/plweb-cgi/iops1.pl> To retrieve this article, enter the following search: ED=19970808 AND plate. In the "retrieved list," click the title that matches this record. (ISSN0882-7729).

In the U.S., "nationally recognized food surveys like the Nationwide Food Consumption Survey and the National Health and Nutrition Survey indicate that fat consumption is actually between 37 and 38 percent of calories." (p10) "In 1980, Americans were consuming 2000 calories per day. By 1990 that figure had increased to 2200 calories per day, a jump of ten percent!" (p11)

Raymond, Jennifer. "Another Fad Diet Crumbles Upon Examination: Caution: Approaching the Zone." Vegetarian Voice v22 n3 Aut 1997. p10-13. (ISSN0271-1591).

FOOD HABITS--UNITED STATES--CHILDREN (v26)

"American children are getting 40 percent of their calories from extra fat and added sugars and are routinely failing to meet national dietary recommendations, according to an analysis reported by National Cancer Institute (NCI) researchers. Only 1 percent of children between 2 and 19 years old met all the Food Pyramid recommendations for grains, vegetables, fruits, meats, and dairy foods. Sixteen percent of children met none of the recommendations. Those children who met the recommendations had the highest levels of fiber and lowest amount of added sugars in their diet, but their fat intakes were still not as low as recommended (30 percent or less of total calories should be from fat)."

U.S. National Cancer Institute. "U.S. Children Failing to Meet National Dietary Recommendations: Extra Fat and Added Sugar Are Main Culprits." Press Release 2 Sep 1997. document-level access: <http://rex.nci.nih.gov/massmedia/pressreleases/childrendiet.html>

FOOD HABITS--UNITED STATES--YOUTH (v26)

"A recent survey by the USDA, 'What We Eat in America,' conducted by the Beltsville Human Nutrition Research Center in Beltsville, Maryland, has identified changes in food consumption by children when compared to data collected in 1977-78. Milk consumption by children and teenagers dropped, and low-fat and skim milk is now consumed more frequently than whole milk among school-age children. The proportion of these children drinking low- or non-fat milk has doubled since the late 1970s, and consumption of soft drinks has markedly increased. Fruit consumption decline with age for children and teenagers, with fewer than half of teenagers in the U.S. consuming a serving of fruit or fruit juice daily. On any given day, nearly two-thirds of the school-age children now consume food or drink provided outside the home. Food outside the home provided about 25 percent of the total calories for grade school-age children and 33 percent for teenagers." (p65-66)

U.S. Dept. of Agriculture. "Agriculture, Rural Development, Food and Drug Administration...Approp. for 1998 (Part 4)." Hearing. U.S. House. Committee on Appropriations. Washington, D.C. : GPO, 1997. (ISBN0160551560). (Y4.Ap6/1:Ag8/997/pt.4).

FOOD HANDLING--UNITED STATES--NEWSPAPER EDITORS--ATTITUDES (v26)

FOOD HANDLING--UNITED STATES--PUBLIC OPINION (v26)

FOOD INDUSTRY AND TRADE (v26)

see also BABY FOODS INDUSTRY; DAIRY PRODUCTS INDUSTRY; FAST FOOD RESTAURANTS; GROCERY TRADE; MEAT INDUSTRY AND TRADE; NATURAL FOODS INDUSTRY; SNACK FOOD INDUSTRY; SUGAR TRADE; WAGES--FOOD INDUSTRY AND TRADE

"Processed food products 'account for nearly two-thirds of total world food and agricultural trade'. As of the mid-1990s, an estimated 80 per cent of food consumed in developed countries is processed by the food industries. Purchases of processed food make up as much as 70 per cent of household expenditure on food. The amount of fresh fruit and vegetables in the US diet has been steadily decreasing. Between 1960 and 1981, per capita consumption of fresh potatoes declined by half, while frozen potatoes increased nearly seven-fold. Per capita consumption of fresh vegetables stayed constant, while frozen vegetables nearly doubled." (p109)

Cone, Richard A./Martin, Emily. "Corporeal Flows: The Immune System, Global Economies of Food and Implications for Health." Ecologist v27 n3 May-Jun 1997. p107-111. (ISSN0261-3131).

"World production of beef from 1990 to 1996 was essentially unchanged. Pork production, led by growth in China, increased by 15 percent during this period. Meanwhile, poultry production jumped by some 32 percent. And egg production, climbing almost as fast, rose by 25 percent." (p12)

Brown, Lester R. "The Agricultural Link: How Environmental Deterioration Could Disrupt Economic Progress." Worldwatch Paper n136 Aug 1997. p5-73.

FOOD INDUSTRY AND TRADE--ASIA

"In India, where the economy has expanded 6 percent a year during the mid-1990s, the broiler industry is growing by 15 percent annually. Egg consumption is rising at 3 percent a year....The broiler industry in Indonesia, a country of 200 million people, is doubling every five years....Japan imports close to two thirds of the beef it consumes....And China and Japan are two of the world's three leading poultry importers, along with Russia." (p13)

Brown, Lester R. "The Agricultural Link: How Environmental Deterioration Could Disrupt Economic Progress." Worldwatch Paper n136 Aug 1997. p5-73.

FOOD INDUSTRY AND TRADE--EMPLOYMENT--UNITED STATES (v26)

In the U.S., "in 1996, 13.5 million people were employed in the farm industry sector beyond the farm. Food industry employment increased almost 1.5 percent in 1996, a smaller rate of increase than the nearly 3-percent rise recorded in 1995. Food-service establishments employed the single largest share at 56 percent. About 25 percent of the food-sector work force was employed by food stores, 12 percent by food manufacturing firms, and 7 percent by wholesalers. Employment in the food manufacturing sector dropped by about 1.5 percent, reflecting higher labor productivity and increased use of labor-saving technology, which continued to dampen hiring rates." (p15)

Elitzak, Howard/U.S. Dept. of Agriculture. Economic Research Service. "Food & Marketing: Marketing Costs for Food Rose Slightly in 1996." Agricultural Outlook Aug 1997. p15-16.

FOOD INDUSTRY AND TRADE--EUROPE--UNITED STATES (v26)

FOOD INDUSTRY AND TRADE--RUSSIA (v26)

FOOD INDUSTRY AND TRADE--RUSSIA--UNITED STATES (v26)

FOOD INDUSTRY AND TRADE--UNITED STATES (v26)

The Asia-Pacific Economic Cooperation "region is a $20-billion market for U.S. exports of processed foods that has increased more than 50 percent since 1990....The region is the destination for two-thirds of total U.S. processed food exports, with Japan, Canada, South Korea, and Mexico the major destinations and the principal growth markets in the 1990s....Most of the increase in U.S. processed food exports in 1990-96 was accounted for by meat products ($3.7 billion, a 79-percent increase), although exports of dairy products, baked goods, and beverages all doubled." (p26)

Bolling, Chris/Handy, Charles/Neff, Steve/U.S. Dept. of Agriculture. Economic Research Service. "Trade Environment in APEC: U.S. Direct Investment in the APEC Food Processing Sector." APEC: International Agriculture and Trade Reports Situation and Outlook Series Aug 1997. p26-28.

"Total U.S. trade in processed foods and beverages continued to expand in calendar year 1996 to a record $58 billion. Exports reached $30.1 billion, about 3 percent higher than in 1995, while imports rose 11 percent to $27.8 billion. As a result, the 1996 trade surplus, while well below 1995's record $4.4 billion, was still the third largest on record. Relatively slow export growth for processed foods--3 percent compared with a 9-percent annual average for the previous 3 years--coincided with a slowdown in global meat consumption....The value of U.S. processed food exports grew only $726 million during 1996, well below the $2.1-billion annual average increase for the previous 5 years. Of the 10 major processed food groups, meat product exports (including poultry) remain the largest, accounting for nearly 30 percent of total U.S. export value of processed foods." (p11)

Ruppel, Fred J./Handy, Charles R./Malanoski, Margaret A./ U.S. Dept. of Agriculture. Economic Research Service. "World Agriculture & Trade: U.S. Processed Food Trade Continues to Expand." Agricultural Outlook Jul 1997. p11-13.

"U.S. consumers spent $547 billion on food in 1996 (excluding imports and seafood), $17 billion more than in 1995. For every dollar spent, 23 cents covered the farm value of food purchases, and the rest was marketing costs....A sharp 8-percent increase in farm value--reflecting higher prices for pork, eggs, dairy products, and cereal--accounted for a larger-than-usual portion of the increase in consumer food costs....The marketing bill rose only about 2 percent to $424 billion in 1996, following a nearly 4-percent increase in 1995. The rise in food marketing costs in 1996 was lower than the overall 2.9-percent rate of inflation, and substantially below the average annual increase of about 4.5 percent during the last decade." (p15)

Elitzak, Howard/U.S. Dept. of Agriculture. Economic Research Service. "Food & Marketing: Marketing Costs for Food Rose Slightly in 1996." Agricultural Outlook Aug 1997. p15-16.

In the U.S., "labor costs (wages and salaries, and employee benefits such as group health insurance) comprise 38 percent of total consumer food expenditures, and make up the largest component of the marketing bill. Labor costs grew about 5 percent to more than $206 billion in 1996, but at a marginally slower pace than the annual average rise during the last 10 years." (p15) "Packaging costs, nearly 9 percent of food expenditures and the second-largest component of marketing costs, dropped 2 percent to nearly $47 billion, restraining aggregate food marketing costs in 1996. The price of paperboard, which accounts for about 40 percent of food industry packaging costs, plummeted over 7 percent in 1996, following a record 16-percent rise the previous year....Energy costs, comprising 3.5 percent of food expenditures, rose nearly 4 percent last year, despite a 2-percent drop in the price of electricity. Higher energy costs were largely the result of a 4-percent rise in the price of natural gas and increased volume of marketing services....Transportation costs rose 2.5 percent, about the same as in 1995, as a result of higher trucking rates which climbed by more than 2 percent....Advertising expenses, which account for about 4 percent of food expenditures, rose 4 percent to nearly $21 billion in 1996, slightly faster than in 1995." (p16)

Elitzak, Howard/U.S. Dept. of Agriculture. Economic Research Service. "Food & Marketing: Marketing Costs for Food Rose Slightly in 1996." Agricultural Outlook Aug 1997. p15-16.

"About 20 percent of the weight of a fresh apple is lost when it is processed into applesauce....An estimated 5.4 billion pounds of food, less than 2 percent of edible food supplies, was discarded at the retail level in 1995....Nearly half of these retail losses came from fluid milk and other dairy products and fresh fruits and vegetables....Losses of processed fruit and vegetables, including fruit juices (on a fresh-fruit equivalent basis), were estimated at 521 million pounds, or almost 10 percent of total retail food losses in 1995." (p5)

Kantor, Linda Scott/Lipton, Kathryn/Manchester, Alden/ Oliveira, Victor/U.S. Dept. of Agriculture. Economic Research Service. "Food Loss: Estimating and Addressing America's Food Losses." Food Review v20 n1 Jan-Apr 1997. p2-12. (ISSN1056-327X).

"More than 16,000 new food products--including new sizes, packaging, flavors, and brands of existing products--were placed on U.S. grocery store shelves in 1995, more than double the fewer than 8,000 introduced in 1988. Although ERS [USDA Economic Research Service] does not know the success rate for such products, industry experts estimate that more than 90 percent of new food products are removed from the market." (p5-6)

Kantor, Linda Scott/Lipton, Kathryn/Manchester, Alden/ Oliveira, Victor/U.S. Dept. of Agriculture. Economic Research Service. "Food Loss: Estimating and Addressing America's Food Losses." Food Review v20 n1 Jan-Apr 1997. p2-12. (ISSN1056-327X).

In the U.S., "in 1995, 11.0 percent of household disposable personal income went to pay for food (6.7 percent for food at home, 4.3 percent for food away from home), down from 12-13 percent in the 1980's and 13-14 percent in the 1970's....In 1995, Americans spent about 26 percent of their disposable personal income on housing (including supplies, fuel, and furniture), 16 percent on medical care and drugs, 10 percent on transportation (including cars and gasoline), and 4.5 percent on savings....The farm value share of the amount spent on food has continued to shrink, falling from an average of 36 cents for every food dollar in 1974 to only 22 cents in 1995." (p3)

Clauson, Annette/U.S. Dept. of Agriculture. Economic Research Service. "Food Prices: Economic Factors Holding Down Food Price Increases." Food Review v20 n2 May-Aug 1997. p2-4. (ISSN1056-327X).

"The United States produces more than 6 billion pounds of turkey a year, or almost 300 million turkeys!...As of September 1 [1997], there were 884 million bushels of corn stored on and off the farm in this country." (p2)

"Editorial: Cooperation vs. Competition." People's Tribune v24 n11 Nov 1997. p2. (ISSN1081-4787).

FOOD INDUSTRY AND TRADE--UNITED STATES --TRANSPORTATION (v26)

FOOD POISONING--UNITED STATES

According to the U.S. "Centers for Disease Control and Prevention, 7 million illnesses and 7,000 deaths occur from food poisoning annually in the United States. Of these, 5 million illnesses and 4,000 deaths come from contaminated meat and poultry....The CDC estimates that up to 9,800 E. coli cases and 120,000 salmonella cases a year occur when people don't sufficiently cook ground beef containing bacteria." (p8 secA)

Mishra, Raja. "School Lunch Favorites Get Scrutiny in Ark. Plant." Detroit Free Press 8 Sep 1997. p1,8 secA.

FOOD PRICES--BULGARIA (v26)

FOOD PRICES--UNITED STATES (v26)

In the U.S., "retail food prices, as measured by the Consumer Price Index (CPI), increased 3.3 percent in 1996, slightly above the 2.9-percent increase in the CPI for all goods and services. Americans spent $691 billion for food in 1996 and another $92 billion for alcoholic beverages. In 1996, 46 percent of U.S. food spending went for away-from-home meals and snacks, up from 34 percent in 1970 and 39 percent in 1980. The percentage of disposable personal income spent on food declined from 13.8 percent in 1970 to 10.9 percent in 1996." (p5)

U.S. Dept. of Agriculture. Economic Research Service. "Summary of Report: Food Consumption Scorecard Mixed on U.S. Adherence to Dietary Recommendations." ERS Information Oct 1997. p5.

In the U.S., "overall food prices rose a modest 3.3 percent in 1996, continuing the fairly stable trend of 3-percent annual increases since 1992...." (p2) "Costs for labor, packaging, transportation, advertising, and other miscellaneous costs accounted for 37 cents, 8 cents, 4.5 cents, 4 cents, and 4.5 cents of every food dollar in 1995." (p4)

Clauson, Annette/U.S. Dept. of Agriculture. Economic Research Service. "Food Prices: Economic Factors Holding Down Food Price Increases." Food Review v20 n2 May-Aug 1997. p2-4. (ISSN1056-327X).

FOOD PROCESSING BY-PRODUCTS INDUSTRY--UNITED STATES (v26)

FOOD RELIEF (v26)

see also FOOD STAMPS

The International Fund for Agricultural Development's "annual investments in new projects exceed $435 million....'So far, over 100 million rural poor families (a total of more than 450 million persons) have benefited from the hundreds of projects financed by IFAD in 105 countries,' [says IFAD's Taysir Mustafa]." (p21)

Sedge, Michael H. "International: Feeding the World, Forever." Kiwanis v82 n10 Nov-Dec 1997. p20-23,39. (ISSN0162-5276).

FOOD RELIEF--AFRICA

"Food aid needs for 65 developing countries are estimated at 9 million tons for 1996/97, 35 percent below the estimate needs for 1995/96....[Sub-Saharan Africa's] needs in 1996/97 are estimated to fall 40 percent to 3.4 million tons. Grain production is up significantly in Southern Africa due to expanded plantings and favorable weather; as a result, 1996/97 food aid needs are estimated at just over 400,000 tons, compared with 1995/96 receipts of about 800,000 tons." (p458)

U.S. Dept. of Agriculture. "Agriculture, Rural Development, Food and Drug Administration...Approp. for 1998 (Part 4)." Hearing. U.S. House. Committee on Appropriations. Washington, D.C. : GPO, 1997. (ISBN0160551560). (Y4.Ap6/1:Ag8/997/pt.4).

FOOD RELIEF--ANGOLA (v26)

FOOD RELIEF--DEVELOPING COUNTRIES (v26)

FOOD RELIEF--KOREA (NORTH) (v26)

FOOD RELIEF--MICHIGAN

"Since food banks began collecting more than 20 years ago, the number in Michigan has actually decreased from 15 to 12. But there's evidence the number of hungry people has increased." (p1 secD) "One person in 10 will need help with food at least once this year, according to the Food Bank Council of Michigan....[Operation Get Down, a non-profit grass-roots community-based agency on Detroit's east side,] says more people are asking for help; so does the Macomb County Food Program, which distributes food to 27 pantries across the county on a monthly basis." (p6 secD)

Lewis, Shawn D. "Metro: News Special: Food Banks Find Growing Ranks of Hungry." Detroit News 9 Dec 1997. p1,6 secD.

FOOD RELIEF--RUSSIA--UNITED STATES (v26)

FOOD RELIEF--UNITED STATES (v26)

"The Food Stamp Program is the largest of USDA's food-assistance programs, accounting for almost two-thirds of total food-assistance expenditures....From fiscal 1989 through fiscal 1994, average monthly participation rose from less than 19 million to 27.5 million due to rising poverty rates, the economic recession, and declining median family incomes." (p463) "In 1994, about 71 percent of all eligible persons, and 69 percent of all eligible households participated in the Food Stamp

Program. These participating households received 81 percent of total potential food stamp benefits. Each school day in fiscal year 1996, about 58 percent of all children in the participating schools and resident childcare institutions, participated in the School Lunch Program. An estimated 80 percent of the WIC eligible population would participate if the program was fully funded." (p464)

U.S. Dept. of Agriculture. "Agriculture, Rural Development, Food and Drug Administration...Approp. for 1998 (Part 4)." Hearing. U.S. House. Committee on Appropriations. Washington, D.C. : GPO, 1997. (ISBN0160551560). (Y4.Ap6/1:Ag8/997/pt.4).

"Between 20 and 30 million Americans suffer from hunger, including 1 of every 12 pre-teen children, according to studies by the Congressional Hunger Center and the Food Research and Action Center. Nearly 26 million Americans rely on food banks for emergency food assistance every year. In...New Jersey, more than 500,000 people depend on food stamps to get by each month. Eleven percent of New Jersey children live below the poverty level and almost 300,000 under the age [of] 12 are hungry or at the risk of hunger." (pE1829)

Roukema, Marge (Rep.-N.J.). "In Recognition of the Food Bank of New Jersey." Congressional Record. Daily ed. v143 n128 23 Sep 1997. pE1828-1829. section/page-level access: <http://thomas.loc.gov/cgi-bin/query/R?r105:FLD001:E01828:> (ISSN0363-7239). (X1.1A.105/1).

In 1997, "requests for food assistance increased 20 percent in Detroit...a figure on par with other cities. The increase is the largest since 1992, when requests for food jumped 18 percent....[Nationally,] requests for emergency food assistance were up an average of 16 percent; 86 percent of the cities surveyed reported requests were up, and 92 percent of the cities expected requests for emergency food assistance to increase next year. 22 percent of families' requests for food went unmet and, on average, 19 percent of individuals' requests went unmet." (p2 secA)

Robles, Jennifer Juarez/Eversley, Melanie/Pickler, Nedra. "Many Left Out of Economy's Boom." Detroit Free Press 16 Dec 1997. p1-2 secA.

"In 1995, 36.4 million people in this country were living in poverty (annual income of less than $15,569 for a family of four). According to USDA food consumption data for the early 1990's, almost 12 percent of U.S. households with annual incomes below the poverty line reported that they sometimes or often did not get enough to eat. USDA spent almost $38 billion providing food assistance to an estimated 45 million people--about 1 in every 6 Americans--at some time during 1996. In addition, an estimated 150,000 nonprofit organizations, including food banks and neighborhood charity outlets, provided more than 10 percent of the U.S. population with a portion of their nutritional needs....Even with the extensive network of Federal and private food-assistance programs, almost 20 percent of requests for emergency food assistance went unmet in 1995, according to the U.S. Conference of Mayors." (p8)

Kantor, Linda Scott/Lipton, Kathryn/Manchester, Alden/Oliveira, Victor/U.S. Dept. of Agriculture. Economic Research Service. "Food Loss: Estimating and Addressing America's Food Losses." Food Review v20 n1 Jan-Apr 1997. p2-12. (ISSN1056-327X).

In the U.S., the Child and Adult Care Food Program "served 1.5 million meals in fiscal 1996, a 2 percent increase over the previous year. Expenditures totaled $1.5 billion in fiscal 1996, an increase of 5 percent over fiscal 1995. The childcare portion of the program, which provides meals and snacks to children in non-profit childcare centers and family and group daycare homes, accounted for over 98 percent of total program costs in fiscal 1996, while the adult care portion of the program, which provides meals to the elderly and functionally impaired adults in adult daycare settings, accounted for the remaining 2 percent." (p51)

Oliveira, Victor/U.S. Dept. of Agriculture. Economic Research Service. "Food Assistance: Food-Assistance Spending Held Steady in 1996." Food Review v20 n1 Jan-Apr 1997. p49-56. (ISSN1056-327X).

The USDA's domestic food assistance "programs, which served an estimated 1 in 6 Americans in fiscal 1996, provide a nutritional safety net to people in need. Spending on these programs accounted for about 70 percent of USDA's total budget....Federal outlays for USDA's food-assistance programs totaled $38 billion in fiscal 1996....This was an increase of less than 1 percent from fiscal 1995, the smallest 1-year increase since 1982." (p49)

Oliveira, Victor/U.S. Dept. of Agriculture. Economic Research Service. "Food Assistance: Food-Assistance Spending Held Steady in 1996." Food Review v20 n1 Jan-Apr 1997. p49-56. (ISSN1056-327X).

The U.S. "fiscal 1998 appropriation for Title I and Food for Progress (FFP) programs funded with Title I funds totaled $244.5 million, a slight increase of $3.8 million from the 1997 level. Appropriations for Title II remained at $837 million, and those for Title III totaled $30 million, a $500,000-increase from 1997. For fiscal 1998, Title I programs are planned with 16 countries, with allocations totaling about $165 million. These funds are estimated to provide about 755,000 tons of commodity assistance. Under the Title I-funded FFP program, programs are planned with 5 countries, with allocations totaling about $69 million, providing an estimated 224,000 tons of commodity assistance. Title I and FFP programs are estimated to provide roughly 1 million tons of commodity assistance to 21 countries." (p11-12)

U.S. Dept. of Agriculture. "U.S. Agricultural Export Programs." Outlook for U.S. Agricultural Exports 2 Dec 1997. p11-12.

"According to the United States Conference of Mayors...about 19 percent of requests for emergency food went unfulfilled in the past year." (p1) "Catholic Charities USA reports that between 1995 and 1996 demand for emergency food increased by more than 14 percent, from 4.9 million people served in 1995 to 5.6 million in 1996....California is spending $35 million of state money to buy federal food stamps for legal immigrant children and some elderly immigrants, though 178,000 legal immigrants are still unserved, according to California Food Policy Advocates in San Francisco....Of the billion pounds of food a year that go through food pantries, USDA commodities account for about 10 percent." (p14)

Feldmann, Linda. "Amid US Prosperity, Hunger Grows." The Christian Science Monitor v90 n14 11 Dec 1997. p1,14. The Christian Science Monitor search engine: <http://www.csmonitor.com/plweb-cgi/iops1.pl> To retrieve this article, enter the following search: ED=19971211 AND grows. In the "retrieved list," click the title that matches this record. (ISSN0882-7729).

According to a report released in December 1997 by the U.S. Conference of Mayors, in the U.S., "over the last year, 'emergency food assistance requests increased in 24 of 29 cities surveyed.' According to the report, 'About one-fifth of emergency food help demands is estimated to have gone unfulfilled,' and '17 of the cities saw shelter requests rise, while the number of emergency shelter beds among all the cities decreased an average of 3 percent.'...Food banks in one of the 'richest' areas of the country, California's Silicon Valley, experiencing 25 to 50 percent increases in demand over last year, were finding corporate and other donations drying up....According to information available from Second Harvest, the nation's largest system of food banks, 'hunger afflicts 30 million people in the United States, including 13 million children.'" (p4)

Boettcher, Ken. "An Ugly Dichotomy." The People v107 n10 Jan 1998. p4. (ISSN0199-350X).

FOOD RELIEF--UNITED STATES--AGED (v26)

FOOD RELIEF--UNITED STATES--ARMED FORCES (v26)

FOOD SPOILAGE--UNITED STATES

"From foods forgotten and spoiled in the refrigerator to the uneaten vegetables tossed in the garbage, consumer and foodservice food waste is the single largest source of food loss in the marketing chain. Estimated at 91 billion pounds, this food loss accounted for 26 percent of the edible food available for human consumption in 1995. Fresh fruits and vegetables accounted for 19 percent of consumer and foodservice food losses, with an estimated 18 billion pounds discarded annually. An additional 16 billion pounds of fluid milk--the equivalent of one-third of an 8-ounce glass per person per day--and 14 billion pounds of grain products were also lost. Together these foods accounted for more than half of total estimated consumer and foodservice food losses in 1995...." (p6-7)

Kantor, Linda Scott/Lipton, Kathryn/Manchester, Alden/ Oliveira, Victor/U.S. Dept. of Agriculture. Economic Research Service. "Food Loss: Estimating and Addressing America's Food Losses." Food Review v20 n1 Jan-Apr 1997. p2-12. (ISSN1056-327X).

FOOD STAMP FRAUD--UNITED STATES--PRISONERS (v26)

FOOD STAMPS--COLORADO--IOWA

"The Cooperative Extension System, in at least 35 [U.S.] States, is conducting nutrition education programs for Food Stamp recipients under the Family Nutrition Program funded by the Food Stamp Program. In Fiscal Year 1996, the Federal dollars awarded were over $36 million....Colorado FNP graduates report that they are able to extend their food stamps by an average of 6.39 days, and have an average savings of $85.82 on their monthly grocery bills; 96 percent of FNP graduates demonstrated positive change in their eating habits. Of the 381 food stamp participants in Iowa's FNP from Jan-Mar 1996, 50 percent reported that they were better able to meet family nutritional needs and to budget food dollars to last all month; 71 percent increased their skills in setting up a spending plan; and 70 percent were able to control impulse buying." (p289)

U.S. Dept. of Agriculture. "Agriculture, Rural Development, Food and Drug Administration...Approp. for 1998 (Part 4)." Hearing. U.S. House. Committee on Appropriations. Washington, D.C. : GPO, 1997. (ISBN0160551560). (Y4.Ap6/1:Ag8/997/pt.4).

FOOD STAMPS--UNITED STATES (v26)

"The Food Stamp Program, the single largest Federal food-assistance program with 64 percent of all USDA food-assistance expenditures, is the primary source of nutrition assistance for low-income Americans (certain legal immigrants may also qualify for food stamps). Expenditures for the Food Stamp Program totaled $24.3 billion in fiscal 1996, a decrease of 1 percent from fiscal 1995." (p49) "An average of 25.5 million people per month, or about 1 in every 10 Americans, received food stamps in fiscal 1996. This was down more than 1 million people from fiscal 1995, which in turn was 0.8 million people less than in fiscal 1994 when food stamp participation peaked....The Food Stamp Program provided an average $73.26 worth of food per month to each participant in fiscal 1996, up from $71.27 in fiscal 1995." (p50)

Oliveira, Victor/U.S. Dept. of Agriculture. Economic Research Service. "Food Assistance: Food-Assistance Spending Held Steady in 1996." Food Review v20 n1 Jan-Apr 1997. p49-56. (ISSN1056-327X).

In the U.S., "according to Congressional Budget Office figures, almost 1.5 million people have lost food-stamp benefits over the past several months--two-thirds of them legal immigrants. The savings to taxpayers, says the CBO, will be at least $2.1 billion per year. Of noncitizens who were getting food stamps, about 10 percent (100,000 people) live in Texas." (p3)

Bryce, Robert. "United States: Food Pantries Stretch to Fill 'Safety Net' Role." The Christian Science Monitor v89 n199 9 Sep 1997. p3. The Christian Science Monitor search engine: <http://www.csmonitor.com/plweb-cgi/iops1.pl> To retrieve this article, enter the following search: ED=19970909 AND role. In the "retrieved list," click the title that matches this record. (ISSN0882-7729).

FOOD STAMPS--UNITED STATES--AGED

In the U.S., "in 1995, the Food Stamp Program served approximately 2 million people ages 60 or over each month--about 7 percent of all food stamp participants. Only 35 percent of elderly Americans who were eligible for food stamps actually applied for and received them in January 1994, compared with 71 percent of the 38 million people in the United States eligible for benefits. Elderly persons who received food stamps tended to live alone--76 percent of all food stamp households with elderly members were single-person households." (p46)

Weimer, Jon P./U.S. Dept. of Agriculture. Economic Research Service. "Nutrition: Many Elderly at Nutritional Risk." Food Review v20 n1 Jan-Apr 1997. p42-48. (ISSN1056-327X).

FOOD SUPPLY (v26)

see also AGRICULTURE; FAMINES; FOOD CONSUMPTION

FOOD SUPPLY--AFRICA (v26)

FOOD SUPPLY--DEVELOPING COUNTRIES (v26)

FOOD SUPPLY--KOREA (NORTH) (v26)

FOOD SUPPLY--RWANDA (v26)

FOOD SUPPLY--UNITED STATES

"Americans spend a smaller share of their disposable income on food than citizens of any other country and choose from an average of 50,000 different food products on a typical outing to the supermarket. In 1994, the food supply provided an estimated 3,800 calories per person per day, enough to supply every American with more than one and a half times their average daily energy needs." (p2)

Kantor, Linda Scott/Lipton, Kathryn/Manchester, Alden/ Oliveira, Victor/U.S. Dept. of Agriculture. Economic Research Service. "Food Loss: Estimating and Addressing America's Food Losses." Food Review v20 n1 Jan-Apr 1997. p2-12. (ISSN1056-327X).

FOODBORNE DISEASES--CANADA--UNITED STATES

"In both the United States and Canada, salmonellosis cases seem to have reached a plateau of about 40,000 and 9,000 each year....The United States commitment to epidemiological surveillance was reinforced by the presidential proposal for the 1998 budget to allocate US$43 million for a programme to detect foodborne outbreaks before they become widespread. This will help to reduce morbidity and mortality due to foodborne diseases, estimated at 6.5-33 million people and 9,000 deaths annually." (p3)

World Health Organization. "Foodborne Diseases--Possibly 350 Times More Frequent than Reported." WHO Press n58 13 Aug 1997. p1-4. document-level access: <http://www.who.ch/press/1997/pr97-58.html>

FOODBORNE DISEASES--EUROPE

Food poisoning "outbreaks rose from 594 in 1990 to 732 in 1992....In Germany, about 1,000 cases of salmonellosis were linked to the consumption of paprika and paprika-powdered potato chips which makes it the largest documented outbreak from contaminated spices. Powdered infant formula was responsible for 48 known cases of salmonellosis in infants under seven months from 14 regions in Spain in 1994....In Scotland, there was a large meatborne 'Escherichia coli' O157 outbreak with 396 cases and 11 deaths at the end of last year." (p2)

World Health Organization. "Foodborne Diseases--Possibly 350 Times More Frequent than Reported." WHO Press n58 13 Aug 1997. p1-4. document-level access: <http://www.who.ch/press/1997/pr97-58.html>

FOODBORNE DISEASES--JAPAN--UNITED STATES (v26)

FOODBORNE DISEASES--UNITED STATES (v26)

"According to estimates based largely on data collected by CDC from local and state health departments, millions of people become sick from contaminated food each year, and several thousand die. CDC estimates that for every reported case of Salmonella, the foodborne pathogens for which surveillance information is most complete, between 50 and 100 cases are undetected....The limited data from the latest CDC Morbidity and Mortality Weekly Report, or MMWR, Surveillance for Foodborne-Disease Outbreaks-United States, 1988-1992, reported a total of 2,423 outbreaks of foodborne disease which caused 77,373 persons to become ill." (p429) "A more recent report, 'Foodborne Pathogens: Risks and Consequences', published by the Council for Agricultural Science and Technology, a private non-profit organization, estimated that as many as 9,000 deaths and 6.5 to 33 million illnesses in the United States each year are food-related." (p430)

U.S. Food and Drug Administration. "Agriculture, Rural Development, Food and Drug Administration...Approp. for 1998 (Part 2)." Hearing. U.S. House. Committee on Appropriations. Washington, D.C. : GPO, 1997. (Y4.Ap6/1:Ag8/997/pt.2).

In the U.S., "E.coli and Salmonella are two of the most prominent bacteria associated with serious foodborne illnesses. Campylobacter causes an estimated two million cases of illness each year. Another 800 Americans become seriously ill each year from Listeria monocytogenes. The Centers for Disease Control estimate that foodborne pathogens cause millions of illnesses and contribute to thousands of deaths annually. Medical costs and productivity losses total from $5 to $13 billion per year." (p550)

Knipling, Edward B. (Acting Administrator, U.S. Agricultural Research Service). "Agriculture, Rural Development, Food and Drug Administration...Approp. for 1998 (Part 4)." Hearing. U.S. House. Committee on Appropriations. Washington, D.C. : GPO, 1997. (ISBN0160551560). (Y4.Ap6/1:Ag8/997/pt.4).

In the U.S., "of all the hazards associated with foods, microbial hazards account for 90 percent of the confirmed foodborne outbreaks and cases. The Council for Agricultural Science and Technology--a private, nonprofit scientific organization--estimated in its 1994 report entitled, 'Foodborne Pathogens: Risks and Consequences,' that between 6.5 and 33 million illnesses and up to 9,000 deaths occur each year in the United States, because of microbial contamination of food. Hospital stays associated with microbial foodborne illnesses are estimated to cost society more than $3 billion a year. The estimated total costs of foodborne illness are at least $5.6 billion." (p524)

U.S. Food and Drug Administration. "Agriculture, Rural Development, Food and Drug Administration...Approp. for 1998 (Part 2)." Hearing. U.S. House. Committee on Appropriations. Washington, D.C. : GPO, 1997. (Y4.Ap6/1:Ag8/997/pt.2).

The U.S. Centers for Disease Control and Prevention "estimates based largely on data collected from local and state health departments, show that millions of people become sick from contaminated food each year, and several thousand die. Further, for every reported case of Salmonella--the foodborne pathogens for which surveillance information is most complete--between 50 and 100 cases are undetected. Estimates provided by several studies conducted over the past 10 years indicate that between 6.5 million and 33 million cases of foodborne illness and as many as 9,000 deaths occur each year." (p387)

U.S. Food and Drug Administration. "Agriculture, Rural Development, Food and Drug Administration...Approp. for 1998 (Part 2)." Hearing. U.S. House. Committee on Appropriations. Washington, D.C. : GPO, 1997. (Y4.Ap6/1:Ag8/997/pt.2).

"Each year up to 81 million Americans suffer a foodborne illness; 9,100 die. The cost to the nation is anywhere from $5.6 billion to more than $22 billion per year in medical treatment and lost wages....About 70 percent of outbreaks of food-borne illness are traced back to meat and poultry products, according to the USDA, which regulates animal foods production and processing. Eighty percent of illnesses and 75 percent of deaths from meat and poultry products are caused by two pathogens--salmonella and campylobacter." (p72) "The CDC estimates there are 2 million to 4 million salmonella cases in the United States annually, and perhaps 200,000 of those people are sick enough to see doctors. About 6 percent of serious infections invade the bloodstream. An estimated 1,000 to 2,000 people die of salmonella yearly." (p73)

Spake, Amanda. "Culture & Ideas: O Is for Outbreak." U.S. News & World Report v123 n20 24 Nov 1997. p70-73,75,77,79,83-84. article-level access: <http://www.usnews.com/usnews/issue/971124/24FOOD.HTM> (ISSN0041-5537).

"The Centers for Disease Control and Prevention in Atlanta estimates there may be as many as 80 million incidences of food-borne illness each year in the United States, and about 9,000 deaths....Salmonella accounts for 4 million cases, of which 500 to 1,000 are fatal. Campylobacter, which causes acute gastroenteritis, afflicts between 4 million and 6 million people annually, killing about 100. E. coli...causes up to 250 fatalities and triggers serious illness in up to 20,000 people annually." (p23)

Satchell, Michael/Hedges, Stephen J./Kulman, Linda. "U.S. News: The Next Bad Beef Scandal?" U.S. News & World Report v123 n8 1 Sep 1997. p22-24. article-level access: <http://www.usnews.com/usnews/issue/970901/1FEED.HTM> (ISSN0041-5537).

FORCE AND ENERGY

see BIOMASS ENERGY; NUCLEAR ENERGY; RENEWABLE ENERGY SOURCES; SOLAR ENERGY

FORCE AND ENERGY--SLOVENIA (v26)

FORCE AND ENERGY--UNITED STATES--FINANCE (v26)

FORECASTING--PSYCHICS--SPECIALISTS (v26)

FORECASTING, ECONOMIC

see ECONOMIC FORECASTING

FORECASTING, POPULATION

see POPULATION FORECASTING

FOREIGN AFFAIRS

see INTERNATIONAL RELATIONS

FOREIGN AID PROGRAM

see ECONOMIC ASSISTANCE

FOREIGN-BORN POPULATION

see IMMIGRANTS

FOREIGN COLLEGE STUDENTS

see STUDENTS, FOREIGN COLLEGE

FOREIGN COMMERCE

see INTERNATIONAL TRADE

FOREIGN DEBTS

see DEBTS, EXTERNAL

FOREIGN EXCHANGE

Foreign exchange "daily turnover has climbed from around $10 billion a day in the early 1970s to around $50 billion of the 1980s and to the astronomical $1 trillion a day in the 1990s. The ratio of foreign-exchange turnover to world trade has climbed from 10:1 in the early 1980s to more than 60:1 today. The most recent estimates of turnover from the Bank of International Settlements suggest a climb to more than $1.2 trillion a day. Against this, the entire foreign reserves of the OECD are a mere $650 billion." (p276)

Goldblatt, David/Held, David/McGrew, Anthony/Perraton, Jonathan. "Economic Globalization and the Nation-State: Shifting Balances of Power." Alternatives: Social Transformation and Human Governance v22 n3 Jul-Sep 1997. p269-285. (ISSN0304-3754).

FOREIGN INVESTMENTS

see INVESTMENTS, FOREIGN

FOREIGN STUDENTS

see STUDENTS, FOREIGN

FOREIGN STUDY--MICHIGAN STATE UNIVERSITY

The number of Michigan State University "students studying abroad has increased 45 percent over the last three academic years. Nearly 1,100 MSU students took classes in foreign countries in 1996-97, more than any other campus in America. Spartans were studying in 40 countries on six continents....By the year 2006, the school wants 40 percent of its graduating seniors to have some type of study abroad experience. That's compared with about 17 percent now....Most of MSU's 95 programs are two- to seven-week excursions led by MSU professors....Most of MSU's shorter trips cost around $2,000, not including airfare and spending money. The average semester program costs about $3,800, with Nepal as the cheapest destination at $2,370 and China the most expensive at $5,676." (p7 secC)

Schulz, Todd. "MSU at Helm for Student Travel Abroad." Detroit News 21 Nov 1997. p7 secC.

FORENSIC LABORATORIES

see CRIME LABORATORIES

FOREST DEPLETION

see DEFORESTATION

FOREST FIRES--NORTHWEST TERRITORIES

"In 1994, forest fires swept through the boreal forest in the Northwest Territories, affecting three million hectares--three times the annual average. A year later, fires forced the evacuation of about 900 people from Fort Norman and Norman Wells, through which Exxon's oil passes on its journey south via the Norman Wells pipeline." (p39)

Grescoe, Taras. "Special Report: Temperature Rising." Canadian Geographic v117 n6 Nov-Dec 1997. p36-44. (ISSN0008-3658).

FOREST FIRES--SPAIN

Spain "has an appalling record of forest fires, which between 1975 and 1992 affected 16 per cent of its national wooded area and as much as 52 per cent of the regional wooded area in Extremadura, 46 per cent in Galicia, 38 per cent in Valencia and 33 per cent in Asturias. In Spain as a whole, 40 per cent of these fires are known to have been started intentionally, while the cause of a further 40 per cent remains unknown (Instituto Nacional de Estadistica, 1995...)." (p171-172)

Holliday, Ian. "Living on the Edge: Spanish Greens in the Mid-1990s." Environmental Politics v6 n3 Aut 1997. p168-175. (ISSN0964-4016).

FOREST PRODUCTS INDUSTRY (v26)

FOREST PRODUCTS INDUSTRY--AMAZON RIVER VALLEY (v26)

FOREST PRODUCTS INDUSTRY--ASIA (v26)

FOREST PRODUCTS INDUSTRY--CANADA (v26)

FOREST PRODUCTS INDUSTRY--UNITED STATES (v26)

FOREST ROADS--UNITED STATES

"The U.S. Forest Service oversees a staggering 380,000 miles of logging roads in the country's national forests--a road network more than eight times larger than the entire interstate highway system." (p12) "Highway 20 effectively divides the North Cascades in two, disrupting wildlife migration patterns and creating an insurmountable obstacle for many species in the region. If not for Highway 20, the North Cascades would be the largest contiguous roadless area in the lower 48 states." (p13)

Friedman, Greg. "The End of the Road?: The Bad, The Ugly and the Awful Reasons We Don't Need Any More Roads." Northwest Conservation Sum 1997. p12-13.

In the U.S. "our national forests are...choked with almost 380,000 miles of road--many times more than the entire interstate highway system....In 1998, the public will pay an additional $80 million for road maintenance and more than half that again to directly build or rebuild logging roads....The three major storms of 1995 and 1996 actually cost us taxpayers over $45 million just in repairs to roads on Southwest Washington's Gifford Pinchot National Forest....One study found that about 70 percent of the 422 landslides that occured during a 1996 storm in Idaho started at roads." (p3)

Friedman, Mitch. "A Word in Edgewise: Road Subsidies: The Big Blowout Sale." Northwest Conservation Sum 1997. p3.

FORESTS AND FORESTRY (v26)

see also FUEL CROPS; LOOMIS STATE FOREST (WASH.); LUMBER TRADE; NORTHERN FOREST; PRIMATES--BRAZIL--ATLANTIC FOREST; TIMBER; TONGASS NATIONAL FOREST (ALASKA)

FORESTS AND FORESTRY--BRITISH COLUMBIA (v26)

FORESTS AND FORESTRY--CAMBODIA (v26)

FORESTS AND FORESTRY--CANADA (v26)

FORESTS AND FORESTRY--CHILE (v26)

FORESTS AND FORESTRY--EMPLOYMENT--CANADA (v26)

FORESTS AND FORESTRY--ENVIRONMENTAL ASPECTS (v26)

FORESTS AND FORESTRY--GOVERNMENT OWNERSHIP --CANADA (v26)

FORESTS AND FORESTRY--LOUISIANA

Forestry in Louisiana "employs some 8,000 in harvesting and transplanting trees and another 26,000 in forest products manufacturing jobs and some 113,000 Louisianans own forestland." (pH4679)

McCrery, Jim (Rep.-La.). "Taxpayer Relief Act of 1997." Congressional Record. Daily ed. v143 n91 26 Jun 1997. pH4668-4816. section/page-level access: <http://thomas.loc.gov/cgi-bin/query/R?r105:FLD001:H04679:> (ISSN0363-7239). (X1.1A.105/1).

FORESTS AND FORESTRY--MEXICO--OAXACA (v26)

FORESTS AND FORESTRY--TENNESSEE (v26)

FORESTS AND FORESTRY--UNITED STATES (v26)

FORESTS AND FORESTRY--VIETNAM (v26)

FORTUNES

see INCOME; WEALTH

FOSSIL FUELS

see also GASOLINE; PETROLEUM AS FUEL

"Ninety percent of the world's population uses a small fraction of the fossil fuel per person in comparison to the U.S. where five percent of the population uses twenty five percent of [the] world's oil production....Every year 100 million more persons seek respect and the good life that requires energy-intensive food production, manufacturing and transportation....One hundred gallons of oil can be converted to durable recyclable goods such as TVs, CDs, carpeting, clothing, and piping products that generate $3,500 in sales compared to $100 for fuel sales." (p21)

McAlister, Roy E. "Is the World Running Out of Oil?" Hydrogen Today v8 n2 1997. p21.

FOSTER CHILDREN--ILLINOIS--NEW YORK (STATE)

"Between 1986 and 1992, the number of children in New York City's 'approved relative homes' increased from less than 100 to more than 24,000, while children in the Illinois 'home-of-relative' program increased from 3,700 to more than 16,000 children (Testa, Shook, Cohen, & Woods, 1996). At present, 59% of children in out-of-home placements in Illinois and more than 40% of children in out-of-home placements in Illinois and more than 40% of children in state custody in New York and California are placed with relatives (Bonecutter & Gleeson, 1997)." (p492)

Burnette, Denise. "Article: Grandparents Raising Grandchildren in the Inner City." Families in Society v78 n5 Sep-Oct 1997. p489-499. (ISSN1044-3894).

FOSTER CHILDREN--UNITED STATES (v26)

In the U.S., "at the end of 1996, over 525,000 children were in foster homes. Over a year's time, it is estimated that over 650,000 children will spend some time in foster homes..., 25 percent of the children in the foster care system at any one given point in time will languish in foster care longer than 4 years....Ten percent will be in foster care longer than 7 years." (pS10262)

DeWine, Mike (Sen.-Ohio). "Another Tragedy." Congressional Record. Daily ed. v143 n134 1 Oct 1997. pS10262-10263. section/page-level access: <http://thomas.loc.gov/cqi-bin/query/R?r105:FLD001:S10262:> (ISSN0363-7239). (X1.1A.105/1).

"The national foster care caseload grew from 340,000 cases in 1988 to 460,000 cases in 1996, an increase of 40 percent. The cost of the foster care program, both in maintenance payments and administrative costs, has grown from $800 million in 1988 to $3.7 billion in 1996, an increase of 462 percent in federal expenditures."

U.S. Dept. of Health and Human Services. "State Child Welfare Demonstrations." Fact Sheet 18 Jul 1997. document-level access: <http://www.hhs.gov/news/press/1997pres/970718b.html>

"Although the substitute-care child population in the United States decreased from 502,000 in 1977 to 276,000 in 1985, by the end of the states' fiscal year 1995 the foster care population had an average daily census of 483,000, and the system was estimated to have served an annual total of 710,000 children and adolescents (Tatara, 1997)." (p453)

Traglia, James J./Pecora, Peter J./Paddock, Glen B./Wilson, Linda. "Article: Outcome-Oriented Case Planning in Family Foster Care." Families in Society v78 n5 Sep-Oct 1997. p453-462. (ISSN1044-3894).

"The 1990 United States Census indicated that 4.3 million children live with relatives and 878,000 children live away from their parents with grandparents (Child Welfare League of America, 1994). According to the American Public Welfare Association (1993), 276,000 children were in placement in 1985; in 1992, 442,000 children were in placement outside the home. The American Public Welfare Association projected that 500,000 children would be in out-of-home care in 1995. The Child Welfare League of America (1994) suggested that five major factors contribute to the rise in out-of-home placements: substance abuse, HIV/AIDS, physical and mental illness, homelessness, and poverty." (p502) "In 1991, it was estimated that 600,000 children were living apart from their family (Barthel, 1992). Tatara (1989) estimated that 200,000 new out-of-home placements occurred each year in the United States." (p503)

Davidson, Beverly. "Article: Service Needs of Relative Caregivers: A Qualitative Analysis." Families in Society v78 n5 Sep-Oct 1997. p502-510. (ISSN1044-3894).

"The number of children entering foster care in the United States is increasing at an alarming rate: approximately 23% from 1985 to 1988. In 1990, it was estimated that the population of children in foster care would increase 73.4% by 1995, and this estimate was validated (U.S. House of Representatives, 1990)....Estimates suggested that more than a half million children would be kinship-care arrangements by 1995 (Center for the Study of Social Policy, 1990)....As of several years ago, approximately 1.3 million children lived with relatives in homes where their parents were absent, including 0.77 million children who received Aid to Families with Dependent Children (AFDC)--10% of the AFDC rolls (National Commission on Family Foster Care, 1991)." (p480)

Scannapieco, Maria/Hegar, Rebecca L./McAlpine, Catherine. "Article: Kinship Care and Foster Care: A Comparison of Characteristics and Outcomes." Families in Society v78 n5 Sep-Oct 1997. p480-488. (ISSN1044-3894).

"Of the approximately 500,000 children in foster care in...[the U.S.] about 53,000 are eligible for adoption but remain in temporary homes....Adoption rates of eligible children in California...are about 35 percent; in Texas, 29 percent; and in New York, 25 percent....1 in 10 foster children remains in the system for more than seven years." (p20)

"The Monitor's View: A Family for Every Child." The Christian Science Monitor v89 n184 18 Aug 1997. p20. The Christian Science Monitor search engine: <http://www.csmonitor.com/plweb-cgi/iops1.pl> To retrieve this article, enter the following search: ED=19970818 AND child. In the "retrieved list," click the title that matches this record. (ISSN0882-7729).

FOSTER CHILDREN--WEST VIRGINIA (v26)

FOSTER HOME CARE

see also ADOPTION

FOSTER HOME CARE--UNITED STATES (v26)

In the U.S., "the number of children in foster care--either abandoned or taken from parents--climbed to 494,000 at the end of 1995, a nearly 80-percent increase over the previous decade. With about 17,000 foster children placed in permanent adoptive homes each year, the number left behind in foster care continues to grow, as does their wait for adoption." (p5 secA)

Thomma, Steven/Eversley, Melanie. "Nation & World: A Free Press Campaign: Children First: Adoption: Congress OKs Adoption Bill." Detroit Free Press 14 Nov 1997. p5 secA.

In 1997, Michigan's "36.6-percent adoption rate ranked 19th among the 50 states and the District of Columbia. Only 2,189 of the 5,979 children waiting to be placed in permanent homes were adopted." (p1 secA) In the U.S., "one out of 10 foster care children, 53,642, remained in the system at the end of 1996. The federal government will spend about $12 billion this fiscal year to care for 650,000 foster children. About 15,000 children will leave the system this year because they have reacheo the 18 year age limit." (p8 secA)

Bivins, Larry. "Thousands Languish in Foster Care." Detroit News 8 Aug 1997. p1,8 secA.

In the U.S., "the foster care caseload has grown from 340,000 cases in 1988 to 500,000 cases in 1996, an increase of 47 percent. The cost of the federal foster care program, both in maintenance payments and administrative and training costs, has grown from $891 million in 1988 to $3.7 billion in 1996, an increase of 315 percent."

U.S. Dept. of Health and Human Services. "HHS Invests in America's Children." Fact Sheet 23 Jul 1997. document-level access: <http://www.hhs.gov/news/press/1997pres/970917.html>

In the U.S., "between 1985 and 1990, the number of foster homes decreased by 27% while the number of children in out-of-home placement increased by 47%. The National Foster Parent Association (1991) estimates that 29% of all foster families leave the system each year." (p502)

Davidson, Beverly. "Article: Service Needs of Relative Caregivers: A Qualitative Analysis." Families in Society v78 n5 Sep-Oct 1997. p502-510. (ISSN1044-3894).

In the U.S., "the foster care system served 276,300 children in 1985, 407,000 in 1990, and an estimated 553,600 in 1995 (U.S. Department of Health and Human Services, 1996)....It is estimated that 15 percent of child welfare workers have BSWs [Bachelor of Social Work] and that 13 percent have MSWs [Master of Social Work] (Lieberman, Hornby, & Russell, 1988)....About 75 percent of cases in public child welfare were handled by staff that were untrained." (p398)

Litzelfelner, Pat/Petr, Christopher G. "Case Advocacy in Child Welfare." Social Work v42 n4 Jul 1997. p392-402. (ISSN0037-8046).

FOSTER HOME CARE--WASHINGTON (D.C.) (v26)

FOUNDATIONS (ENDOWMENTS)

see CHARITABLE USES, TRUSTS, AND FOUNDATIONS

FRANCE--ARMED FORCES--WOMEN

In 1997, "women make up only 7.5 percent of the French military and 4 percent of its officers. In a recent survey, some 80 percent of women in the military say that relations with men are good." (p10)

Chaddock, Gail Russell. "Global Report: Europe's Quiet Approach: Sex Issues in US Military Puzzle, Fascinate the World: France." The Christian Science Monitor v89 n142 18 Jun 1997. p10-11. The Christian Science Monitor search engine: <http://www.csmonitor.com/plweb-cgi/iops1.pl> To retrieve this article, enter the following search: ED=19970618 AND france. In the "retrieved list," click the title that matches this record. (ISSN0882-7729).

FRANCE--COMMERCE--PERSIAN GULF REGION

"For France, trade with...[the Persian Gulf] region represents 2.5-3 percent of our total trade. In the Gulf area, Saudi Arabia is our first client and first supplier; the United Arab Emirates is our second client; Iran our third client and our second supplier, and Kuwait is our third supplier." (p10)

Magro, Herve. "Symposium--The Challenge in the Gulf: Building a Bridge from Containment to Stability." Middle East Policy v5 n2 May 1997. p1-21. (ISSN1061-1924).

FRANCE--ECONOMIC CONDITIONS (v26)

FRANCE--POPULATION

"According to a census taken in 1990, there were at that time in France only 614,000 officially registered Algerians, 572,000 Moroccans, 206,000 Tunisians, 43,000 Senegalese, 37,000 immigrants from Mali, 22,000 from Zaire, and 18,000 from Cameroon. These figures might seem insignificant in a country of close to 60 million inhabitants. But this ignores the fact that many more foreign immigrants have gone unregistered, so that the real number may well be two to three times as high....No fewer than five million persons--more, that is, than the entire population of Norway or Finland--now live in 1,100 so-called 'sensitive' quarters, which are constantly on the verge of erupting into violence. Of these, almost one-third (1.5 million) now live like tightly packed sardines in 130 highly volatile 'cites' (collective housing lots) or 'zones de non droit' (lawless zones)...." (p17)

Cate, Curtis. "Views: The Revolt of the French Masses." Chronicles v21 n7 Jul 1997. p15-19. (ISSN0887-5731).

FRANCE--RELIGION--PUBLIC OPINION

An opinion poll released during Pope John Paul II's three day visit to France in August 1997 "showed that although three-quarters of French 18-to-30-year-olds resent his conservatism on issues like AIDS and abortion, 34 per cent said religion means a lot to them. One-fifth of those polled linked religious practice to membership in a given church, while 65 per cent saw no need to do so. Three-quarters of the respondents thought religion can be both a divisive factor and an active force against poverty and social discrimination, especially in the case of the Catholic Church." (p6)

Valls-Russell, Janice. "While Admiring John Paul II French Catholicism Loosens Its Collar." New Leader v80 n14 8 Sep 1997. p6-8. (ISSN0028-6044).

FRANCHISES (RETAIL TRADE)--UNITED STATES (v26)

"More than 40 percent of all retail dollars are spent in the 600,000 franchises currently operating in the United States. For decades, franchisees operated at the pleasure of their corporate parents, who wielded close to total power by virtue of ironclad contracts. These pacts were offered on a take-it-or-leave-it basis to franchisees but were heavily skewed to the interest of franchisers....Lately franchisees have been fighting back and coming up victorious in court....Last year...a class of some 2,500 [franchise] dealers of Meineke Discount Muffler Shops, Inc. won a $347 million judgment in North Carolina after alleging that payments to an advertising fund had been fraudulently handled." (p45-46) "In 1994 a group of 42 Carvel Corp. franchisees filed suit in New York when the parent company began selling its ice cream cakes in supermarkets within their territories....Membership in the Chicago-based American Franchisee Association...has risen from 4,000 in 1993 to 7,500....AAFD [American Association of Franchisees and Dealers] expects to have 25,000 members within three years." (p47)

Gomes, Lee. "Business Litigation: Mac Attack." California Lawyer v17 n8 Aug 1997. p45-47. (ISSN0279-4063).

FRANKFURTERS--UNITED STATES (v26)

FRATERNITIES

see GREEK LETTER SOCIETIES

FRAUD, BANK

see BANK FRAUD

FREEDOM

see LIBERTY

FREEDOM OF THE PRESS (v26)

FREELANCERS

see SELF-EMPLOYED

FRENCH LANGUAGE--QUEBEC--CHICOUTIMI

In Chicoutimi, Quebec, "ninety-eight percent of the 60,000 residents of the city, located 130 miles north of Quebec City, are of French heritage. More than 1,000 students a year come to study [French] at its many language schools." (p9)

Langan, Fred. "Global Report: Why an American Professor Bids Quebec Separatists 'Adieu.'" The Christian Science Monitor v90 n11 10 Dec 1997. p9. The Christian Science Monitor search engine: <http://www.csmonitor.com/plweb-cgi/iops1.pl> To retrieve this article, enter the following search: ED=19971210 AND adieu. In the "retrieved list," click the title that matches this record. (ISSN0882-7729).

FRESHMEN, COLLEGE

see COLLEGE FRESHMEN

FROGS

"From the rain forest of Puerto Rico, 12 of 18 endemic amphibians are recently extinct or disappearing; missing since 1990 from the Monteverde Cloud Forest of Costa Rica is the golden toad....Frog numbers are falling in 140 countries, with the counting far from done." (p25)

Stolzenburg, William. "The Naked Frog." Nature Conservancy v47 n4 Sep-Oct 1997. p24-27. (ISSN0028-5200).

FROGS--UNITED STATES

"James Petranka of the University of North Carolina estimates that clearcutting in national forests in western North Carolina subtracts nearly 14 million salamanders annually...." (p25) "Five years ago in the Laramie Basin of Wyoming,...[the Nature Conservancy] helped the U.S. Fish and Wildlife Service purchase a lake...harboring the last 200 or fewer Wyoming toads known....The 1994 spring census turned up two toads. They became two of an emergency breeding colony of 12 captive toads, whose progeny have since rebuilt the wild population to a tentative 90 individuals--none of which have yet reproduced. In the [Nature] Conservancy's Aravaipa Canyon Preserve of southern Arizona,...freelance biologist Jay Schnell's 20-year streamside census has fallen from 48 frogs per kilometer to three." (p26) "Two years ago,...[in Arizona,] the Ramsey Canyon frogs crashed. A tenuous population of 60 fell to a dire group of 16....'This year there are at least 36 adults in the pond and creek,'...[Rena Ann Abolt, an ecologist based at the Ramsey Canyon Preserve,] says." (p27)

Stolzenburg, William. "The Naked Frog." Nature Conservancy v47 n4 Sep-Oct 1997. p24-27. (ISSN0028-5200).

FROZEN VEGETABLES--UNITED STATES--PUBLIC OPINION (v26)

FRUIT JUICE INDUSTRY

see also GRAPE JUICE INDUSTRY; GRAPEFRUIT JUICE INDUSTRY; ORANGE JUICE INDUSTRY

FRUIT JUICE INDUSTRY--UNITED STATES

U.S. "fruit juice imports were up 45 percent in 1996, reaching $913 million. Increased fruit juice imports were led by orange juice which jumped 73 percent to $274 million, while volume was up 55 percent to 10.7 million hectoliters. Fourth-quarter 1996 was particularly strong for orange juice imports....Brazil was the leading source, at $183 million, supplying 67 percent of total U.S. orange juice imports. Apple juice reached $357 million, a 28-percent increase over 1995. Volume was up 12 percent while the import unit value for apple juice jumped 14 percent....For the year, Argentina was the leading source for apple juice, supplying $101 million, surpassing Germany which supplied $80 million. Eastern and Western Europe supplied 41 percent of total apple juice imports." (p6)

Gehlhar, Mark/U.S. Dept. of Agriculture. Economic Research Service. "Imports Advance 12 Percent in 1996." Foreign Agricultural Trade of the United States Jan-Mar 1997. p6-7.

"Americans consumed 8.6 gallons of juice per person in 1996/97, down fractionally from 1995/96. On a fresh weight basis, juices accounted for 47 percent of total fruit consumed. Consumption of total noncitrus juices rose less than 1 percent from a year ago. Apple juice consumption increased 6 percent largely due to the big 1996 crop in Washington. Apple juice accounted for about two-thirds of noncitrus juice consumption in 1996/97. Grape juice consumption fell 17 percent in 1996 because of a smaller quantity of grapes processed to juice....Citrus juice consumption was fairly steady in 1996/97 because a decline in grapefruit and lemon juice was offset by a 3-percent increase in orange juice. Domestic consumption of orange juice totalled 1.4 billion gallons in 1996/97....Grapefruit juice consumption fell 21 percent in 1996/97, despite a large crop." (p3)

U.S. Dept. of Agriculture. Economic Research Service. "Summary." Fruit and Tree Nuts Situation and Outlook Report Oct 1997. p2-3.

FRUIT JUICE INDUSTRY--UNITED STATES --CHILDREN

"In the United States, children 5 years of age and younger consume an average of nine gallons of juice per year per child....Some children in this country drink as much as 30 ounces of juice--25 percent to 60 percent of their total calorie intake--in a single day." (p14)

"Juicy Truths about Fruit Juice." Your Health and Fitness v19 n3 Sum 1997. p14.

FRUIT TRADE

see also APPLE INDUSTRY; APRICOT INDUSTRY; AVOCADO INDUSTRY; BANANA TRADE; BLUEBERRY INDUSTRY; CANNED FRUIT INDUSTRY; CHERRY INDUSTRY; CRANBERRY INDUSTRY; GRAPE INDUSTRY; GRAPEFRUIT INDUSTRY; KIWIFRUIT INDUSTRY; MANGO INDUSTRY; MELON INDUSTRY; ORANGE INDUSTRY; PAPAYA INDUSTRY; PEACH INDUSTRY; PEAR INDUSTRY; PINEAPPLE INDUSTRY; RAISIN INDUSTRY; STRAWBERRY INDUSTRY

FRUIT TRADE--CHILE--UNITED STATES (v26)

FRUIT TRADE--CHINA

In China "orchard area rose from 1.8 million hectares in 1980 to 8.1 million hectares in 1995, an increase of 350 percent....Fruit production increased dramatically from 6.8 million tons in 1980 to 46.5 million tons in 1996, a 583-percent increase. The United States produces more citrus and grapes than China, but China is a large producer of many varieties of fruit, and total output is nearly 70 percent larger than that of the United States....China's fruit exports from the mid-1980s to the mid-1990s continued at about 375,000 tons per year....The value of fruit exports in the same period decreased slightly from about $270 million a year to $200 million. China's fruit imports were $32 million in 1994." (p48)

Crook, Frederick W./U.S. Dept. of Agriculture. Economic Research Service. "Introduction to China's Horticultural Economy." China: International Agriculture and Trade Reports Situation and Outlook Series Jun 1997. p47-51.

FRUIT TRADE--MEXICO--UNITED STATES (v26)

FRUIT TRADE--UNITED STATES (v26)

"U.S. fruit and nut receipts in 1996 rose 6 percent over 1995, with a 7-percent increase in noncitrus fruit receipts and less than 1 percent increase in citrus receipts....Receipts to the United States' second most important fruit commodity, apples, increased 17 percent to $1.8 billion in 1996, the highest in the past 5 years....U.S. orange receipts rose 5 percent in 1996 to $1.8 billion, setting a record for the 5-year period." (p8)

U.S. Dept. of Agriculture. Economic Research Service. "1996 Farm Income Estimates: Net Value-Added and Net Farm Income Attain New Highs in 1996." Agricultural Income and Finance Situation and Outlook Report Sep 1997. p4-13.

"During 1996, U.S. growers produced 5.54 million tons of grapes valued at $2.2 billion, about 20 percent of the total farm value of fruit and nut production and about 11 percent of fruit, nut, and vegetable production. Orange production ranked second, with a value of $1.9 billion, followed by apples, valued at $1.8 billion." (p7)

Pollack, Susan/Perez, Agnes/U.S. Dept. of Agriculture. Economic Research Service. "Commodity Spotlight: Prospects Favorable for U.S. Grape Industry." Agricultural Outlook Jun 1997. p7-10.

In the U.S., "in 1996, per capita consumption of all fruit grew to 287.5 pounds (fresh-weight equivalent). U.S. fresh fruit consumption averaged 119.2 pounds for citrus and 168.3 pounds for noncitrus fruit....Overall fresh noncitrus per capita consumption rose less than 1 percent in 1996, after having fallen in 1995. Since 1990, per capita consumption of fresh noncitrus fruit has been growing at an average of 1 percent annually....In 1996, fresh cherry consumption grew 41 percent and plums/prunes grew 50 percent from a year earlier, because of increased utilized production. Papaya consumption grew 49 percent, mangos increased 20 percent, and avocados increased 17 percent....Fresh citrus consumption increased 11 percent in the 1996/97 marketing year." (p2)

U.S. Dept. of Agriculture. Economic Research Service. "Summary." Fruit and Tree Nuts Situation and Outlook Report Oct 1997. p2-3.

In the U.S., "the Consumer Price Index (CPI) for fresh fruits averaged 3 percent above a year ago during the first 6 months of

1997....This year's retail prices for fresh Valencia oranges averaged 60.7 cents a pound in July, compared with 60.4 cents in July 1996. July retail prices for Thompson Seedless grapes and peaches were 10 percent and 22 percent lower than a year ago, respectively....The Consumer Price Index for processed fruit averaged 4 percent higher from January to June 1997, due mostly to higher prices for orange juice. The CPI for frozen fruit and juice averaged 6 percent higher than a year ago in 1996. For the first 6 months of 1997, the CPI for frozen fruit and juice advanced 4 percent from the same period in 1996. Despite the forecast of increased orange juice supplies in 1996/97, retail prices for FCOJ [frozen concentrate orange juice] averaged 6 percent higher during the first half of 1997. The CPI for canned and dried fruit averaged 4 percent higher." (p5-6)

U.S. Dept. of Agriculture. Economic Research Service. "Fruit Price Outlook." Fruit and Tree Nuts Situation and Outlook Report Aug 1997. p5-6.

In the U.S., "the value of fruit production rose for the twelfth consecutive year to $9.7 billion in 1996. The noncitrus fruit crop value was up 4 percent over the previous year, and the citrus crop value rose 10 percent. While the value of production rose from the previous year, the quantity declined slightly (less than 1 percent)." (p2)

U.S. Dept. of Agriculture. Economic Research Service. "Summary." Fruit and Tree Nuts Situation and Outlook Report Oct 1997. p2-3.

FUEL

see also ALCOHOL FUEL INDUSTRY; AUTOMOBILES--MICHIGAN--MOTORS--ALTERNATE FUELS; AUTOMOBILES--UNITED STATES--MOTORS--ALTERNATE FUELS; BIOMASS ENERGY; FOSSIL FUELS; PETROLEUM AS FUEL

"Ethanol is a good substitute for gasoline in spark-ignition engines (Marrow et al. 1987, Parisi 1983); methanol can also be used as a substitute for gasoline....Existing vehicles cannot run on 100% ethanol or methanol fuel unless engines are modified substantially....Gasoline and biofuel mixtures in a proportion of 85% and 15%, respectively, can be used with only minor adjustments to the engine." (p587)

Giampietro, Mario/Ulgiati, Sergio/Pimentel, David. "Feasibility of Large-Scale Biofuel Production." BioScience v47 n9 Oct 1997. p587-600. (ISSN0006-3568).

FUEL--EUROPE (v26)

FUEL--UNITED STATES (v26)

FUEL CONSUMPTION

see AIRPLANES--EUROPE--FUEL CONSUMPTION; AIRPLANES--FUEL CONSUMPTION; AUTOMOBILES--UNITED STATES--FUEL CONSUMPTION; ENERGY CONSUMPTION

FUEL CROPS

see ENERGY CROPS

FUEL OIL

see PETROLEUM AS FUEL

FUEL SWITCHING--CALIFORNIA--SAN DIEGO (v26)

FUEL TRADE

see ALCOHOL FUEL INDUSTRY; COAL TRADE

FUGITIVES FROM JUSTICE--MICHIGAN

In Michigan, "more than 31,000 people have either been convicted of a felony or have had felony warrants issued against them, and yet they still are walking the streets throughout the state....Police officials say that of the 31,822 persons being sought on local, county, state and federal felony warrants, 274 are wanted for murder, 397 for rape, 226 for robbery and 97 for kidnapping. More than 650 are Department of Corrections escapees. Wayne County, where most crimes occur, has more than half of the people on the outstanding felony warrant list with 17,256. Oakland County has 2,345 wanted people; Macomb has 1,365." (p10 secA)

"The Fugitives." Detroit News 15 Aug 1997. p10 secA.

FUGITIVES FROM JUSTICE--UNITED STATES (v26)

FUJIAN PROVINCE (CHINA)--ECONOMIC CONDITIONS

As of 1990, county GDP per capita in China's Fujian province "ranged from a low of 515 yuan in Anxi to a high of 7271 yuan in Xiamen. Collectively, the four poorest counties reported GDP per capita of 653 yuan, while the four richest reported 4725 yuan--a relative gap of 1:7.2. The absolute gap between the two groups exceeded 4000 yuan (of 1990)--an amount many times larger than the GDP per capita reported by the poor group....Half the counties of Fujian reported GDP per capita in the 800-1400 yuan range....The poorest county (Anxi) had a population of 880,000 in mid 1990; the richest (Xiamen) had 600,000. More generally, at the lower end of the income distribution, counties with 20 percent of Fujian's population accounted for about 9.7 percent of provincial GDP, while at the upper end, counties with 20 percent of population accounted for about 43 percent of GDP." (p122)

Lyons, Thomas P. "Development in Fujian: A County-Level Perspective." China Economic Review v8 n2 Fall 1997. p117-136. (ISSN1043-951X).

FUMIGATION--UNITED STATES

"About 85 percent of the structural fumigations in the U.S. use sulfuryl fluoride. Total use is estimated at between 3 and 4 million pounds annually in the U.S. In California over 1,700,000 pounds were used in 1995, the last year for which data are available." (p17) "In laboratory tests, exposure to 4507 parts per million (ppm) sulfuryl fluoride (17.5 milligrams per liter (mg/l) of air) for one hour caused death....Sulfuryl fluoride has adversely affected reproduction in laboratory animals....In a single generation study, the number of fetal resorptions (fetuses that died, and then were absorbed into mother's body) increased about 30 percent at all exposures tested." (p18)

Cox, Caroline. "Fumigant Factsheet: Sulfuryl Fluoride." Journal of Pesticide Reform v17 n2 Sum 1997. p17-20. (ISSN0893-357X).

FUNERAL HOMES--UNITED STATES (v26)

FUNERAL RITES AND CEREMONIES--UNITED STATES --COSTS (v26)

FUNGAL TOXINS

see MYCOTOXINS

FUR TRADE--MICHIGAN (v26)

GAMBLERS--UNITED STATES

In the U.S., "among those with incomes below $15,000 in 1996, only one in ten visited a casino in the previous year. For those with incomes of $75,000 or more, the share was one in three." (p37) "Three in four casino patrons say they go primarily to win 'a really large amount of money,' according to a Roper survey. Entertainment and recreation follow money, cited as an important reason for 57 percent of patrons." (p38)

Heubusch, Kevin. "Taking Chances on Casinos." American Demographics v19 n5 May 1997. p34-40. article-level access: <http://www.demographics.com/Publications/AD/97_ad/9705_ad/AD970530.htm> (ISSN0163-4089).

GAMBLING (v26)

see also CASINOS; INDIANS OF NORTH AMERICA--GAMBLING; INTERNET (COMPUTER NETWORK)--GAMBLING; LOTTERIES; SLOT MACHINES

GAMBLING--AUSTRALIA (v26)

GAMBLING--CANADA (v26)

GAMBLING--EMPLOYMENT--MISSISSIPPI--TUNICA

"Gaming has brought more than $2 billion in investments to Tunica, [Mississippi]....In five years, 11,500 casino jobs have come to a county of 8,500 residents. Unemployment has shrunk from 14.3 percent in 1992 to 7.2 percent today, and 55 percent fewer people are receiving payments from the Aid to Families with Dependent Children program. The number of payments is down from 1,618 in 1992 to 726 in 1997. Food-stamp distribution during the 1996 fiscal year was about one-fifth of what it was before casinos, falling to $59,385 worth of food stamps. Child-support payments have nearly doubled to $80,157....Entry-level casino positions in the county start at $6 an hour, plus benefits....[Bill] McNeece, a labor analyst for the Mississippi Employment Security Commission, estimates 30 percent of Tunica's labor force of 5,800 is working in casinos. Another 15 percent are in spinoff businesses." (p8 secA)

DeHaven, Judy. "Casinos Rebuild Economy, Hope in the Poorest County in Nation." Detroit News 7 Jul 1997. p1,8 secA.

GAMBLING--MICHIGAN

In 1997, a survey by Western Michigan University "asked 3,942 Michigan adults over 18 about their gambling habits. Researchers found that 5.2 percent of state residents have a history of gambling problems, including 3.4 percent who still have problems with gambling....The study estimated that Michigan has 232,000 compulsive gamblers--nearly equivalent to the populations of Flint and Kalamazoo. Of those considered compulsive gamblers, 88,000 are 'pathological gamblers,' whose addiction is so serious that the American Psychiatric Association considers it an impulse control disorder....Wayne County has the largest share of problem gamblers. About 8 percent of Wayne County residents have a history of compulsive gambling, with almost 5 percent suffering current problems." (p1 secC)

French, Ron. "Metro: Special Report: Wagering Wisely: Detroit Casinos Expected to Raise Gambling Woes." Detroit News 11 Jul 1997. p1-2 secC.

In Michigan, a survey by Western Michigan University found that "85 percent of residents have gambled at some point in their lives; 77 percent had gambled in the past year. Young people have higher rates of gambling problems....[A] survey found 6.3 percent of residents ages 18-29 were compulsive gamblers; the next-highest age group was ages 30-49, in which 3.2 percent had gambling problems. The lottery appears to attract fewer compulsive gamblers than most other forms of betting. Of lottery players, 5 percent were judged to be problem gamblers; compared to 7.7 percent who favor casinos, nearly 9 percent of sporting event gamblers and almost 15 percent of those who wager on horse and dog racing." (p2 secC)

French, Ron. "Metro: Special Report: Wagering Wisely: Detroit Casinos Expected to Raise Gambling Woes." Detroit News 11 Jul 1997. p1-2 secC.

"A new survey of 600 Michigan voters shows that more and more state residents are gambling, and those who go to casinos tend to be white, middle-aged, middle class. Men and women gamble in about equal numbers....The survey was conducted by Marketing Resource Group Inc. of Lansing [in March 1997]....The margin of error is 4.1 percentage points. The survey shows that 73 percent of the state's voters have gambled at least once, and 57 percent gambled in the last year. The company has been asking questions about gambling for the last five years. Since then, the number of people in Michigan who say they've been inside a casino has grown from 30 percent in 1993 to 47 percent in March [1997]. That's higher than the national average, which is about 31 percent, said Tom Shields, an MRG partner." (p1 secA)

Lam, Tina. "Gamblers' Poll Belies Image of Casino Goers." Detroit News and Free Press 28 Jun 1997. p1-2 secA.

GAMBLING--NEW JERSEY--ATLANTIC CITY (v26)

GAMBLING--UNITED STATES (v26)

"Fifty-six percent of Americans gambled at least once in 1996, according to Roper Starch Worldwide Inc. of New York City....Americans spent $44.4 billion on wagers in 1995, according to research by Christiansen/Cummings Associates, Inc. in INTERNATIONAL GAMING & WAGERING BUSINESS magazine. That's more than three times the combined amount they spent on box-office movies and theme parks." (p35)

Heubusch, Kevin. "Taking Chances on Casinos." American Demographics v19 n5 May 1997. p34-40. article-level access: <http://www.demographics.com/Publications/AD/97_ad/9705_ad/AD970530.htm> (ISSN0163-4089).

"Just over half of Americans gambled at least once in 1995 (56 percent). The most popular gamble was on a state lottery (45 percent), followed by a visit to a casino (20 percent). The overall share of risk-takers is virtually the same as in 1988, when 54 percent of adults made a wager....Bingo parlors and race tracks saw little change in attendance between 1988 and 1996, according to [a] Roper [survey]. The share of people who reported playing lotteries grew by only 3 percentage points over the same eight years; most state lotteries were already in place by the late 1980s. But the share of adults who visited a casino in the previous year rose from 12 to 20 percent between 1988 and 1996....Casinos now account for 41 percent of all money spent on wagers, according to Christiansen/Cummings." (p37)

Heubusch, Kevin. "Taking Chances on Casinos." American Demographics v19 n5 May 1997. p34-40. article-level access: <http://www.demographics.com/Publications/AD/97_ad/9705_ad/AD970530.htm> (ISSN0163-4089).

A U.S. Congressional Research Service report "showed that since the Indian Gaming Regulatory Act was passed in 1988, the Secretary of the Interior has approved over 180 tribal-State gambling compacts. As of June...[1997], 24 States now have gambling on Indian reservations within their borders....145 Indian tribes currently have one or more casinos on their lands....John Kindt, a professor of commerce and legal policy at the University of Illinois, has concluded that for every $1 in tax revenue that gambling raises, it creates $3 in costs to handle such expenses as economic disruption, compulsive gambling, and crime." (pS9555)

Enzi, Michael B. (Rep.-Wyo.). "Department of the Interior and Related Agencies Appropriations Act, 1998." Congressional Record. Daily ed. v143 n125 18 Sep 1997. pS9553-9574. section/page-level access: <http://thomas.loc.gov/cgi-bin/query/R?r105:FLD001:S09555:> (ISSN0363-7239). (X1.1A.105/1).

In the U.S., "there are only 8 [Indian] tribes out of 121 casinos that are making money. The Nation at this moment is spending about $40 billion in gaming. Of that amount, $3 billion is being spent in Indian country, but the profits of less than 10 percent go to the Indians at this time." (pS9560)

Inouye, Daniel K. (Sen.-Hawaii). "Department of the Interior and Related Agencies Appropriations Act, 1998." Congressional Record. Daily ed. v143 n125 18 Sep 1997. pS9553-9574. section/page-level access: <http://thomas.loc.gov/cgi-bin/query/R?r105:FLD001:S09560:> (ISSN0363-7239). (X1.1A.105/1).

In 1996, "Americans sank more than $550 billion in legal wagers into casinos, racetracks, lotteries, and other gambling operations....In 1978, only two states had casinos; now 27 states do, though some have been mired in legal disputes. In the past five years, the number of Americans visiting casinos has doubled. As a result of casino gambling, Las Vegas is now the fastest-growing city in America, boasting 11 of the 12 largest hotels in the world. Another $6 billion worth of facilities are slated to open within the next two years--including a $1.3 billion Italianate casino, Bellagio, that will feature $50 million in original paintings by masters such as Picasso, Manet, and Renoir." (p32) "37 states and the District of Columbia sponsor lotteries, which bring in more than $30 billion each year....The states spent $382 million on lottery advertising and promotional expenditures in fiscal 1995." (p35)

Koughan, Martin. "Easy Money." Mother Jones v22 n4 Jul-Aug 1997. p32-37. article-level access: <http://www.motherjones.com/coinop_congress/easymoney/koughan.html> (ISSN0362-8841).

In the U.S., according to a June 1997 report by the WEFA Group, "between 1991 and 1996, legalized gambling was responsible for a net increase of more than 22,000 jobs, which produced a $619 million net increase in wages and salaries." (p26) "Americans paid 154 million visits to casinos in 1995...." (p28) "'The American Insurance Institute estimated that 40 percent of all white-collar crime had its roots in gambling'....[According to Robert Goodman, author of THE LUCK BUSINESS, 'problem gamblers' comprise] 'between 1.5 and 6.5 percent of the adult population.'...With casino games, between 85 and 95 percent of the money wagered is returned to bettors in the form of winnings." (p29)

Detlefsen, Robert. "Wagers of Sin: The Not-So-Secret Agenda of America's Anti-Gambling Guru." Reason v29 n7 Dec 1997. p24-30. (ISSN0048-6906).

GAMBLING--UNITED STATES--PUBLIC OPINION

In the U.S., "twenty-seven percent of adults say gambling is immoral, according to a 1996 Gallup Organization poll, although the share is down from 32 percent in 1992....Among people who did not gamble in the previous year, 25 percent say they didn't gamble because of moral or religious objections, according to a 1993 Roper survey. The reasons most people give for not gambling are that they don't want to spend the money (35 percent) and they don't have the money to spend (33 percent)....Forty-two percent of Americans agree that allowing more casinos to open 'threatens our values,' according to a 1996 Roper survey. Forty-one percent say that casinos disrupt the quality of life in the surrounding area. Two-thirds of people agree that legalized gambling encourages the people who can least afford...to squander their money, according to the Gallup Organization. Sixty-one percent say that legalized gambling can make a compulsive gambler out of a person who would never gamble illegally." (p36)

Heubusch, Kevin. "Taking Chances on Casinos." American Demographics v19 n5 May 1997. p34-40. article-level access: <http://www.demographics.com/Publications/AD/97_ad/9705_ad/AD970530.htm> (ISSN0163-4089).

GAMES OF CHANCE

see GAMBLING

GANGES RIVER (INDIA AND BANGLADESH) (v26)

GANGS

see also JUVENILE DELINQUENTS

GANGS--QUEBEC (PROVINCE) (v26)

GANGS--UNITED STATES (v26)

"As of 1994, there were more than 4,880 established gangs identified in the United States....According to a 1992 survey by the Justice Department's Office of Juvenile Justice and Delinquency, 77 percent of all gang members come from broken homes. In addition, 61 percent come from low-income families, while 26 percent have family members with arrest records." (p50) "All four branches of the [U.S.] military have reported gang activity of some sort at over 50 posts and bases worldwide within the past 5 years." (p51)

Coursey, Guy R. "Coping with the Threat of Gangs." Marine Corps Gazette v81 n9 Sep 1997. p50-52. (ISSN0025-3170).

A U.S. survey of law-enforcement agencies "found that numbers of youth gangs and gang members were higher than previously thought, and that gangs had spread into new localities, especially smaller cities and rural counties. The survey, conducted in 1995 by the government-funded National Youth Gang Center, reported a total of 23,388 youth gangs and 664,906 members. By comparison, a 1991 law-enforcement survey estimated fewer than 5,000 gangs with about 250,000 members." (p4)

Sneider, Daniel. "United States: When Does the 'Gang' Label Fit Teens?" The Christian Science Monitor v89 n154 7 Jul 1997. p4. The Christian Science Monitor search engine: <http://www.csmonitor.com/plweb-cgi/iops1.pl> To retrieve this article, enter the following search: ED=19970707 AND teens. In the "retrieved list," click the title that matches this record. (ISSN0882-7729).

GANGS--UTAH--SALT LAKE CITY (v26)

GANGS--WINNIPEG (v26)

GAOLS

see PRISONS

GARBAGE

see REFUSE AND REFUSE DISPOSAL

GARDENING--GREAT BRITAIN (v26)

GARDENING--UNITED STATES--COSTS

"Americans spent $22.5 billion to make their gardens grow in 1996, almost double the $12 billion they spent in 1985, according to a Gallup Poll taken for the National Gardening Association....Last year, Americans aged 30-49 spent $10.1 billion on gardens, about 45 percent of the industry's U.S. total." (p1 secD)

Cohen, Jodi S. "Metro: Special Report: Boomer Trends: Gardening Grows as Americans Age." Detroit News 9 Jul 1997. p1-2 secD.

GARMENTS

see CLOTHING AND DRESS

GAS, NATURAL

see NATURAL GAS

GAS INDUSTRY--NEW ZEALAND

In New Zealand, "gas production for the September 1997 year rose by 7.8 per cent or 16,456 terajoules when compared to the September 1996 year. At 226,458 terajoules, gas production is at the highest level for a September year since the series began in 1972. The amount of refined petrol produced in the September 1997 quarter increased by 26.9 per cent when compared to the previous September quarter....Between the September 1996 and 1997 quarters refining of Regular (91 octane) petrol increased 60.2 per cent while refining of Premium (96 octane) petrol decreased by 23.8 per cent, continuing its downward trend. Over the year to September 1997 petrol refining increased by 9.3 per cent when compared to the previous September year. Premium production at 388 thousand tonnes was at its lowest level for a September year since the series began in 1981 while Regular production was at its highest at 1,044 thousand tonnes."

Statistics New Zealand. "New Zealand Energy Statistics--September 1997 Quarter." Press Release 2 Dec 1997. document-level access: <http://www.stats.govt.nz/statsweb.nsf/52518ce3e01f62f4cc256388000c48c0/8f5cccf6df0814734c25656000831341?OpenDocument>

GAS INDUSTRY--UNITED STATES (v26)

"Total dry natural gas production in the United States during July 1997 was forecast as 1.6 trillion cubic feet, 1 percent higher than production during the previous July. Dry natural gas production during the first 7 months of 1997 was an estimated 11.0 trillion cubic feet, the same as production during the first 7 months of 1996." (p71)

U.S. Dept. of Energy. Energy Information Administration. "Natural Gas." Monthly Energy Review Aug 1997. p71-79. (ISSN0095-7356).

U.S. "dry natural gas production during the first half of 1997 was an estimated 9.4 trillion cubic feet, slightly lower than production during the first half of 1996....Imports of natural gas in April 1997 were estimated as 253 billion cubic feet, 16

percent higher than imports in the previous April." (p71)
U.S. Dept. of Energy. Energy Information Administration. "Natural Gas." Monthly Energy Review Jul 1997. p71-79. (ISSN0095-7356).

GASES, GREENHOUSE
see GREENHOUSE GASES

GASOLINE
see also AIRPLANES--EUROPE--FUEL CONSUMPTION; AIRPLANES--FUEL CONSUMPTION; AUTOMOBILES--UNITED STATES--FUEL CONSUMPTION; FARMS--UNITED STATES--FUEL CONSUMPTION

GASOLINE--CANADA--ADDITIVES (v26)

GASOLINE--EUROPE
In the European Union, "demand for gasoline recorded a small fall of 0.2% after dropping by 1.4% in 1995....The market share of unleaded gasoline rose to an EU average of 71.6% from 67.2%. Unleaded already accounts for 100% of the gasoline market in Denmark, Austria, Finland, and Sweden, while in Germany and The Netherlands it took over 90% and in Luxembourg over 80%....Less than 40% of gasoline sold in Spain and Greece was unleaded, and less than 50% in Italy and Portugal." (p13)
"Energy, Atmosphere, And Transport: In Brief...: Jet Fuel Use Jumps in EU." Environment Watch: Western Europe v6 n17 5 Sep 1997. p13. (ISSN1066-6001).

GASOLINE--TAXATION (v26)

GASOLINE--TAXATION--MALAYSIA (v26)

GASOLINE--TAXATION--MICHIGAN (v26)

GASOLINE--TAXATION--MICHIGAN--PUBLIC OPINION (v26)

GASOLINE--TAXATION--SOUTH CAROLINA (v26)

GASOLINE--TAXATION--UNITED STATES
"'Since 1965, in real terms, the amount of federal gas tax paid by American households has actually declined by 41 percent from 1965 until 1995,' said Dr. T. R. Lakshmanan, Director of BTS [U.S. Bureau of Transportation Statistics]. In current dollars, federal motor fuel taxes increased from 4 cents in 1965 to 18.4 cents per gallon in 1995."
U.S. Dept. of Transportation. "Household Expenditures for Federal Gas Taxes Declined over 30 Years." Press Release 25 Aug 1997. document-level access: <http://www.dot.gov/affairs/dot12797.htm>

GASOLINE--UNITED STATES
In the U.S., "the average price, excluding taxes, of aviation gasoline sold to end users in February 1997 was $1.15 per gallon, 1 percent higher than the previous month's price and 14 percent higher than the February 1996 price. The average price, excluding taxes, of kerosene-type jet fuel sold to end users in February 1997 was 71 cents per gallon, 4 percent lower than the previous month's price but 25 percent higher than the February 1996 average price." (p109)
U.S. Dept. of Energy. Energy Information Administration. "Energy Prices." Monthly Energy Review May 1997. p109-128. (ISSN0095-7356).
In the U.S., "the national city average retail price of unleaded regular gasoline at all types of stations was $1.24 per gallon in March 1997, 6 percent higher than the price in March 1996. The price of unleaded premium gasoline averaged $1.42 per gallon in March 1997, 5 percent higher than the price in March 1996." (p109)
U.S. Dept. of Energy. Energy Information Administration. "Energy Prices." Monthly Energy Review May 1997. p109-128. (ISSN0095-7356).
U.S. "motor gasoline supplied during April 1997 averaged 8.0 million barrels per day, 2 percent higher than the previous month's rate and 1 percent higher than the April 1996 rate. Total motor gasoline stocks were 194 million barrels at the end of April 1997, 6 million barrels below the stock level in the previous month and 9 million barrels below the level 1 year earlier." (p41)
U.S. Dept. of Energy. Energy Information Administration. "Petroleum." Monthly Energy Review May 1997. p41-70. (ISSN0095-7356).
U.S. "motor gasoline supplied during July 1997 averaged 8.5 million barrels per day, 3 percent higher than the previous month's rate and 4 percent higher than the July 1996 rate. Total motor gasoline stocks were 191 million barrels at the end of July 1997, 14 million barrels below the stock level in the previous month and 11 million barrels below the level 1 year earlier." (p41)
U.S. Dept. of Energy. Energy Information Administration. "Petroleum." Monthly Energy Review Aug 1997. p41-70. (ISSN0095-7356).
U.S. "motor gasoline supplied during June 1997 averaged 8.2 million barrels per day, 1 percent higher than both the previous month's rate and the June 1996 rate. Total motor gasoline stocks were 204 million barrels at the end of June 1997, 2 million barrels above the stock level in the previous month but 1 million barrels below the level 1 year earlier." (p41)
U.S. Dept. of Energy. Energy Information Administration. "Petroleum." Monthly Energy Review Jul 1997. p41-70. (ISSN0095-7356).

GASOLINE CONSUMPTION OF AUTOMOBILES
see AUTOMOBILES--FUEL CONSUMPTION

GAY YOUTH--UNITED STATES--SOCIAL CONDITIONS (v26)

GAYS
see also DISCRIMINATION IN EMPLOYMENT--UNITED STATES--GAYS; HATE CRIMES--MICHIGAN--DETROIT--GAYS

GAYS--CRIMES AGAINST--MICHIGAN--DETROIT (v26)

GAYS--CRIMES AGAINST--UNITED STATES (v26)

GAYS--EMPLOYMENT--UNITED STATES--PUBLIC OPINION (v26)

GAYS--UNITED STATES--PUBLIC OPINION (v26)

GAYS--UNITED STATES--SOCIAL WORKERS --ATTITUDES
In the U.S., in 1994, a study was conducted to determine the nature of heterosexual social workers's attitudes toward gay men and lesbians. "According to norms established by Hudson and Ricketts (1980), slightly more than one-quarter (26.7 percent) of the respondents were high-grade nonhomophobic, 62.0 percent were low-grade nonhomophobic, 10.7 percent were low-grade homophobic, and only one respondent (0.5 percent) was high-grade homophobic." (p323)
Berkman, Cathy S./Zinberg, Gail. "Homophobia and Heterosexism in Social Workers." Social Work v42 n4 Jul 1997. p319-332. (ISSN0037-8046).

GDP
see GROSS DOMESTIC PRODUCT

GENERATION X--UNITED STATES
In the U.S., "a Generation X child of the 1980s faced twice the risk of parental divorce as a child of the mid-1960s and three times the risk of a child of the 1950s. Through the 1980s, approximately five thousand children under age eighteen committed suicide, the largest number and proportion ever recorded for that age bracket. Through the 1970s, the number of 'latchkey' children under age fourteen left alone after school roughly doubled. A third more Generation X youth are in jail compared to Baby Boomers. In 1990, Generation Xers became the majority of the U.S. prison population. A dramatic subset of this 1990 data shows that one in four black men between the ages of twenty and twenty-nine was in jail, on probation, or on parole." (p399)
Marshall, Gary S. "Theory and Generation X." Journal of

Public Administration Education v3 n3 Sep 1997. p397-403.
In the U.S., "some 60 percent of [Generation] X-ers surveyed say they are actively saving for retirement. X-ers now make up one fifth of all U.S. investors and the share is likely to grow. The cohort has a combined buying power of $125 billion a year...." (p68) "Of the 67 percent of X-ers between 25 and 34 who don't have college degrees, the average income is only slightly less than $24,000 a year....Nearly 80 percent of X-ers are employed full time: 5 percent are unemployed; the remaining 15 percent are either employed part time or nonworking students. Those between 25 and 34 who have college degrees and full-time careers earn an average income of $34,000 a year. When asked whether becoming wealthy was 'very much a part' of the American dream, X-ers in one poll were nearly 10 percent more likely to agree than [baby] boomers." (p76) A "report by IBM found that 1 in 5 small businesses today is owned by someone under 35, and in a recent Yankelovich poll, 40 percent of X-ers selected 'owning your own business' as a sign of success, compared with fewer than a third of boomers and a quarter of matures." (p77)

Zevin, Dan/Edy, Carolyn. "Special Report: Boom Time for Gen X?" U.S. News & World Report v123 n15 20 Oct 1997. p68-70,72,74,76-77. article-level access: <http://www.usnews.com/usnews/issue/971020/dwintro.HTM> (ISSN0041-5537).

GENERATIVE ORGANS, FEMALE--MUTILATION (v26)

"Earlier this year, a new U.S. law took effect that criminalizes female genital mutilation (FGM)--the practice of cutting off part or all of a girl's genitalia (also known as female circumcision)....At least two dozen other countries, including 19 in Africa, have issued official statements or enacted laws against FGM....Girls between the ages of four and eight typically undergo the procedure, but it may be carried out on infants, adolescents, or after the birth of a woman's first child. According to the UNFPA [United Nations Fund for Population Activities] and UNICEF, as many as 85 million to 115 million women worldwide have undergone FGM, with 2 million girls newly operated on each year. There are at least three types of genital mutilation procedures." (p4) "The CDC now estimates that more than 150,000 girls currently residing in the U.S. have either experienced FGM or risk having the operation this year." (p5)

Chalkley, Kate. "Female Genital Mutilation: New Laws, Programs Try to End Practice." Population Today v25 n10 Oct 1997. p4-5. (ISSN0749-2448).

GENERATIVE ORGANS, FEMALE--MUTILATION --AFRICA

"Demographic and Health Surveys (DHS) find as many as 89 percent of women in northern Sudan and 95 percent in Eritrea have undergone FGM--suggesting that in some areas the practice is nearly universal....In Egypt, new and unexpected DHS results show that up to 97 percent of ever-married women have undergone FGM. A majority of women (82 percent) told interviewers in 1995 that they believe FGM should continue. Three-quarters said that husbands prefer their wives to be circumcised and 72 percent reported that female circumcision is an important religious tradition. A small share of the women could identify the operation's negative consequences, such as reduced sexual satisfaction (29 percent), the risk of death (24 percent), and the greater risk of problems in childbirth (5 percent)." (p4)

Chalkley, Kate. "Female Genital Mutilation: New Laws, Programs Try to End Practice." Population Today v25 n10 Oct 1997. p4-5. (ISSN0749-2448).

GENETIC FINGERPRINTING

see DNA FINGERPRINTING

GEOGRAPHICAL BOUNDARIES

see BOUNDARIES

GEOGRAPHICAL NAMES

see NAMES, GEOGRAPHICAL

GEOGRAPHY--STUDY AND TEACHING--UNITED STATES

"Schwendeman's DIRECTORY OF COLLEGE GEOGRAPHY OF THE UNITED STATES reported that 605 colleges or universities listed undergraduate geography courses among their course offerings in 1994. Over 22 percent, or 136, of these institutions from 40 [U.S.] states offered home state geography courses. In 1994, home state courses enrolled 10,662 students. This represents the second highest enrollment among all geography courses offered (Walker 1995)." (p264)

Brady, Scott A. "Some Ideas for Teaching the Home State Geography Course." Journal of Geography v96 n5 Sep-Oct 1997. p264-267. (ISSN0022-1341).

GEOGRAPHY OF POPULATION

see POPULATION GEOGRAPHY

GEOLOGISTS--SALARIES, ETC.--UNITED STATES (v26)

GEOLOGY--RESEARCH

The International Geological Correlation Program's 1996 report, issued by IGCP Secretary Vladislav Babuska of the United Nations Educational, Scientific, and Cultural Organization "lists 44 active projects; 10 were newly approved by the IGCP Scientific Board and 15 were slated for termination....Since 1990, the funding available for IGCP has averaged about $320,000 per year ($5,000 to $10,000 per project). IUGS [International Union of Geological Sciences] has traditionally provided about 42 percent of that amount." (p27)

Reinemund, John. "International Geoscience: International Geological Correlation Program (IGCP)." Geotimes v42 n8 Aug 1997. p27. (ISSN0016-8556).

GEORGIA PINE

see LONGLEAF PINE

GEOTHERMAL RESOURCES (v26)

GEOTHERMAL RESOURCES--UNITED STATES (v26)

GERIATRICS--UNITED STATES (v26)

GERMANY--ARMED FORCES--APPROPRIATIONS AND EXPENDITURES

The German Ministry of Defense has had "drastic cuts since the end of the Cold War. While the last defense budget of the Cold War, submitted in 1989, allocated DM [Deutsche Mark] 51 billion, the 1997 budget was reduced to DM 46.3 billion....With the 1995 defense budget accounting for only 1.7 per cent of its GDP, Germany ranks third lowest (together with Belgium) among its European NATO allies...." (p22)

Peters, Susanne. "Germany's Security Policy after Unification: Taking the Wrong Models." European Security v6 n1 Spr 1997. p18-47. (ISSN0966-2839).

GERMANY--CLIMATE

"The average temperature in Germany is 8.5 degrees Celsius (around 50 degrees Fahrenheit), the sun shines for 1,630 hours a year, and there is frost on ninety days of the year....According to figures kept for a number of years by the German Weather Service in Offenbach, the Black Forest and the Bavarian Alps sustain more precipitation annually than any other part of the country, around 2,000 millimetres. The driest areas of the country are to be found in parts of Thuringia across to Halle and Rhine-Hesse, where precipitation amounts to some 500 mm per year....The island of Rugen enjoys the most sun during the year, where it shines for a total of 1,800 hours. The warmest city in Germany is Freiburg im Breisgau, with an average temperature of 10.7 degrees Celsius from 1961 to 1990. At 6.1 degrees Celsius and 5.9 degrees Celsius respectively, Obertsdorf and Braunlage in Harz are, on average, the coldest places in the Federal Republic. The sun shines for exactly 1,806 hours a year at the sunniest place in Germany, Cape Arcona on Rugen, and the one place with the most precipitation is Obertsdorf in Allgau, 1,831 mm per year." (p39)

"Meteorology: Where Is It Warmest, Where Coldest, And Where Does It Rain the Most in Germany?" Deutschland n3 Jun 1997. p39. (ISSN0945-6791).

GERMANY--COMMERCE (v26)

GERMANY--COMMERCE--SOUTH AMERICA (v26)

GERMANY--ECONOMIC CONDITIONS (v26)

In Germany, "levels of corporate taxation have fallen from 34% to 19% between 1980 and 1994....The number of public-sector workers fell between 1991 and 1994 from 28.5 per 1,000 residents to 24 in the federal states, and from 19.2 per 1,000 to 13.5 in towns....The pension received by an average earner who paid contributions for 45 years rose from 1,942 to 1,975 marks per month in west Germany. That same figure in east Germany rose from 1,598 to 1,683 marks per month." (p13)

"Nachrichten News: Social Policy." Deutschland n5 Oct 1997. p13. (ISSN0945-6791).

According to Theo Sommer, one of Germany's foremost authorities on international relations and strategic issues, Germany's "federal budget deficit grew from DM [deutschmark] 19.2 billion ($33.2 billion) in 1989 to 70 billion ($121 billion) in 1997....Where there were only 20,000 private businesses in the old East Germany, there are now a half-million....Among eastern Germany's most troubling economic problems, he said, is the 18.3 percent unemployment rate. Mr. Sommer noted that the problem with the financial aid package for the east was that 'only one-third of the massive financial transfers went into investment. The remainder served as a 'social mollifier,' cushioning the shock of unemployment and boosting pensions, wages and salaries to 85 percent of the West German level.'" (p348)

Manus, Susan. "Perspectives on German Reunification: Theo Sommer Shares International Expertise." Library of Congress Information Bulletin v56 n16 Nov 1997. p348-349. (ISSN0041-7904).

In Germany, "at current prices, the gross domestic product and the gross national product rose by 3.7% and 3.6%, respectively, in the second quarter of 1997 from the corresponding period of the previous year. The national income (DM [deutschemark] 681 bn [billion]) was 3.7% higher than a year earlier. Gross compensation of employees, which accounted for over 67% of national income, grew by 0.7%, while income from entrepreneurial activity and property was up 10.5%. The disposable income of households was up 2.5%."

Germany. Federal Statistical Office. "Detailed Version: 2.9% Economic Growth in the Second Quarter of 1997." Press Release 10 Sep 1997. document-level access: <http://www.statistik-bund.de/presse/englisch/pm/p7267121.htm>

GERMANY--EMPLOYMENT (v26)

"In the second quarter of 1997, the number of persons engaged in economic activity in Germany declined by 536,000 (-1.6%) from a year earlier. In the former territory of the Federal Republic, the number of persons engaged in economic activity was down 356,000 (-1.3%), while it was down 180,000 (-2.9%) in the new Lander and Berlin-East. The average number of unemployed persons registered in Germany in the second quarter of 1997 increased by 402,000 (+10.3%). Overall labour productivity (gross domestic product per person engaged in economic activity at 1991 prices) went up 4.5% in Germany (western part: +4.3%, eastern part: +5.1%). Unit labour costs, i.e. gross compensation of employees per person engaged divided by labour productivity, were 1.8% lower in the second quarter of 1997 compared with a year earlier."

Germany. Federal Statistical Office. "Detailed Version: 2.9% Economic Growth in the Second Quarter of 1997." Press Release 10 Sep 1997. document-level access: <http://www.statistik-bund.de/presse/englisch/pm/p7267121.htm>

GERMANY--EMPLOYMENT--MANUFACTURES (v26)

GERMANY--NEWSPAPERS (v26)

GERMANY--PUBLIC OPINION

In two Allensbach Institute for Opinion Research "surveys of easterners and westerners [in Germany], the institute has found that more than 70 percent of each group said they 'got along well' with those from 'the other side.'...An Allensbach survey taken in March found 39 percent of east Germans aged 16 through 29 identify themselves simply as 'German,' whereas 56 percent saw themselves as 'east Germans.' For the next age group surveyed (30 through 44), the split was 19 percent to 76 percent. Attitudes on reunification itself show an interesting east/west split. The number of west Germans who regard unity as 'an occasion for happiness' fell since 1990 to only 37 percent earlier this year, compared with 40 percent who see unity as an 'occasion for concern.' For east Germans, 'happiness' beat out 'concern' 55 to 25 percent--despite high proportions (nearly half) of them who in other Allensbach surveys have called the period of communist rule a 'good time.'" (p8)

Walker, Ruth. "International: Once Divided, Young Germans Reflect on Meaning of Unity." The Christian Science Monitor v89 n218 6 Oct 1997. p8. The Christian Science Monitor search engine: <http://www.csmonitor.com/plweb-cgi/iops1.pl> To retrieve this article, enter the following search: ED=19971006 AND unity. In the "retrieved list," click the title that matches this record. (ISSN0882-7729).

GERMPLASM RESOURCES, PLANT

The combined world market of industries that to some extent use plant genetic resources "for pharmaceuticals, agro-chemicals and seeds exceeds $250 billion per annum (Putterman, 1994). Approximately half of these source species are derived from tropical regions. Only approximately 5,000 flowering plant species, i.e. 2% of the estimated total of 250,000, have been screened for alkaloid content. These have yielded about 120 therapeutic agents from approximately 90 plants...." (p163)

Zamora, Carlos/Thomas, Sandra M. "User/Supplier Relationship: Ownership of Plant Genetic Resources: Screening and Industrial Utilisation." Science and Public Policy v24 n3 Jun 1997. p161-172. (ISSN0302-3427).

GIFTS--TAXATION--DEDUCTIONS--UNITED STATES (v26)

GIRL PREFERENCES OF PARENTS

see SEX OF CHILDREN, PARENTAL PREFERENCES FOR

GIRLS

see also ABORTION--NIGERIA--GIRLS; DELINQUENT GIRLS; SMOKING--UNITED STATES--GIRLS

GIRLS--EDUCATION--CHINA

In China, "70 percent of school-age drop-outs are girls. Official statistics do not adequately reflect the lower school attendance of Chinese girls. Girls make up nearly half (47 percent) of children enrolled in primary school in China, but they also comprise about three-fourths of the children who are enrolled in school but seldom attend." (p10)

Riley, Nancy E. "Gender, Power, And Population Change." Population Bulletin v52 n1 May 1997. p2-46. (ISSN0032-468X).

GIRLS--HEALTH AND HYGIENE--UNITED STATES

In the U.S., "thirty percent [of girls] smoke cigarettes by 10th grade. By the time they are high school seniors, two-thirds have had sex and 50 percent say they have drunk alcohol in the last month. One in five has been sexually abused. Often the abuse occurred because the girls didn't understand the consequences of situations that left them vulnerable to violence and date rape. One in four is depressed--twice as often as boys." (p6 secF)

Anstett, Patricia. "Body & Mind: Cover Story: An Unkind

World for Girls." Detroit Free Press 16 Dec 1997. p6-8 secF.

GIRLS--MENTAL HEALTH--UNITED STATES

In the U.S. "one in seven older girls reported low self-confidence. But while self-confidence improves as boys age, it worsens among girls. Among girls, 39 percent of older girls expressed feelings scored as highly confident, compared to 44 percent of younger girls. In contrast, 55 percent of older boys expressed highly self-confident feelings. One in four girls reported feeling depressed in the past two weeks--a 50-percent higher rate than boys. Asked whom they turned to when depressed, one in four replied, 'Nobody.' Ten percent of girls, compared to 7.2 percent of boys, said they had considered suicide though they did not attempt it, according to a large study published Sept. 10 in the Journal of the American Medical Association." (p6 secF)

Anstett, Patricia. "Body & Mind: Cover Story: An Unkind World for Girls." Detroit Free Press 16 Dec 1997. p6-8 secF.

GIRLS--NIGERIA--SEXUAL BEHAVIOR

A study in Benin City, Nigeria, "showed that 55 percent of the secondary school girls had sexual intercourse before age 16. A more recent study showed that the mean age of initiation of sexual intercourse is 13 years." (p7)

"Facts about Adolescent Reproductive Health in Nigeria." SIECUS Report v25 n2 Dec 1996-Jan 1997. p7. (ISSN0091-3995).

GIRLS--UNITED STATES--DRUG USE (v26)

GIRLS--UNITED STATES--SUBSTANCE USE

According to a report by the U.S. Substance Abuse and Mental Health Services Administration "in the early 1960's, among girls, about 7 percent of the new users of alcohol were between the ages of 10-14. By the early 1990's, that percent had increased to 31 percent of new users of alcohol. Likewise, among girls reporting their first use of marijuana in the early 60's only 5 percent were 10-14 years olds; in the early 90's it has risen to 24 percent."

U.S. Dept. of Health and Human Services. "New National Study on Substance Use among Women in the United States Released." Press Release 22 Sep 1997. document-level access: <http://www.hhs.gov/news/press/1997pres/970922.html>

GLACIERS--EUROPE--UNITED STATES

Mauri Pelto is director of the North Cascade Glacier Climate Project (Nichols College, Dudley, Massachusetts). His "data show that in the North Cascades of Washington State, the number of glaciers in retreat, advancing, or stationary were approximately equal in 1967, but that 47 glaciers were in retreat in 1995, with none advancing or stationary....In Italy 48 glaciers were advancing and 32 were stationary while only 28 were retreating in 1975, whereas 126 glaciers were in retreat, 10 were stationary, and only 6 were advancing in 1994....In 1975 in Switzerland, 44 glaciers were advancing, 12 were stationary, and 54 were retreating. As of 1993, 6 were advancing, none were stationary, and 73 were retreating." (p6-7)

"Science Update: Alpine Glaciers Continue to Retreat." Global Environmental Change Report v9 n18 26 Sep 1997. p6-7. (ISSN1049-9083).

GLAUCOMA (v26)

GLOBAL CLIMATIC CHANGES

see CLIMATIC CHANGES

GLOBAL TEMPERATURE CHANGES

"According to satellite measurements, global temperature has actually cooled by 0.09 degrees Celsius since 1979. Those who allege global warming point to ground-based thermometers, which show an increase of .54 degrees Celsius between 1881 and 1993." (p44)

Jasinowski, Jerry. "The Forum: Potentially Hundreds of Thousands of Jobs." Environmental Forum v14 n6 Nov-Dec 1997. p44-45. (ISSN0731-5732).

GLOBAL WARMING (v26)

The Intergovernmental Panel on Climate Change predicted in 1995 "an increase in global warming in the range of 1 [degree Celsius] to 3.5 [degrees] by the year 2100, with a best estimate being 2 [degrees]....World temperatures, as measured by several groups, have risen by about 0.5 [degrees] in the past century....In Canada they have risen, on a spatially uneven basis, by just over 1 [degree] in the past century....Most affected has been the Mackenzie Basin, the upper reaches of which have seen a century-long warming of 1.5 [degrees]." (p46)

Hare, F. Kenneth. "Special Report: Clearing the Air." Canadian Geographic v117 n6 Nov-Dec 1997. p45-46. (ISSN0008-3658).

"There has been a very slight warming of Earth's atmosphere in this century (although...satellite and balloon data show no net temperature rise in the last 19 years)....[In 1990, the Intergovernmental Panel on Climate Change] predicted a 6-degree (Fahrenheit) rise by 2100. The prediction is now down to a 3 1/2-degree rise, a 40 percent drop. And there is a huge range of uncertainty: the lower-end estimate is less than 2 degrees." (p11 secA)

Krauthammer, Charles. "Comment: Global Warming Fears Have Come Full Circle." Detroit News 9 Dec 1997. p11 secA.

"The world is currently heating up faster than at any time in the last 10,000 years. Every climate model predicts rates of global warming between 10 and 100 times faster than at any moment since human beings began to walk the earth. These models are based on indications that human activity has increased atmospheric greenhouse gases by 90 parts per million (ppm). Gases found trapped deep in Antarctic ice 15,000 years ago indicate that increases in greenhouse gases of 100ppm were sufficient to raise global temperature by three degrees Centigrade....The ten hottest years in human history have all been recorded since the beginning of the 1980s. Norwegian scientists reported in September 1993 that the polar ice cap is melting at a rate 10 per cent faster than it can be replaced. A year later, researchers at the British Antarctic Survey (BAS) reported 'the greening of Antarctica'--a 'rapid increase' in the continent's only two flowering plants at sites 600 miles apart, with one flowering grass 25 times more common than it was 30 years ago. According to BAS, Antarctic summer temperatures now persist 50 per cent longer than they did during the 1970s." (p2)

Edwards, David. "Editorial: Hot Air: Global Warming and the Political Economy of Threats." Ecologist v27 n1 Jan-Feb 1997. p2-4. (ISSN0261-3131).

"A 5 degree rise in average water temperatures would devastate many trout populations; an EPA study last year concluded that 24 states could lose 50 to 100 percent of their cold-water fish populations." (p38) "University of California researchers estimate that global warming could render 20 to 50 percent of the state's natural areas unsuitable for their current species." (p39)

Rauber, Paul. "Heat Wave: Vanishing Habitat." Sierra v82 n5 Sep-Oct 1997. p38-39. (ISSN0161-7362).

"Given the right conditions, fast-growing trees like spruce can move up to 100 yards a year. For most species, however, progress is measured in feet per decade. A shift of 40 miles north (or 60 yards in altitude) has already been necessary to compensate for the one-degree rise in temperature. On the West Coast, Edith's checkerspot butterfly has shifted its range 100 miles to the north, and entire populations of sea life in Monterey Bay have moved north in response to a water temperature 4 degrees warmer than it was 60 years ago." (p38) "With a doubling of atmospheric CO_2 [carbon dioxide], the ranges of birch, hemlock, and beech trees could also shift 300 to 600 miles to the north....Migrating red-winged blackbirds now arrive in Michigan 21 days earlier than they did in 1960....Spruce forests are already advancing into what is now tundra; a doubling of CO2 is expected to reduce the tundra's size by 30 percent." (p39)

Rauber, Paul. "Heat Wave: Vanishing Habitat." Sierra v82 n5 Sep-Oct 1997. p38-39. (ISSN0161-7362).

"The greater the concentration of CO2 [carbon dioxide] in the atmosphere, the hotter it gets. Before the Industrial Revolution, the atmosphere contained about 280 parts per million of CO2. Today, that figure is 360 ppm. The Intergovernmental Panel on Climate Change (IPCC), an assembly of the top climatologists on the planet, estimates that by the end of the next century, the CO2 level will be somewhere between 480 and 800 ppm....1996 was...among the warmest years, and 1991 to 1995 was the warmest five-year period in recorded history. Human activity has increased the earth's average temperature by one degree this century. The IPCC predicts a further increase of 2 to 6 degrees over the next century." (p36)

Rauber, Paul. "Heat Wave: Heat." Sierra v82 n5 Sep-Oct 1997. p36. (ISSN0161-7362).

GLOBAL WARMING--DISEASES

"Global warming in the range of 6 to 10 degrees would unleash malaria-carrying mosquitoes on 60 percent of the globe....At present, malaria kills about 2 million people annually....Scientists in New Zealand have already linked outbreaks of dengue in the South Pacific to global warming. A hot summer in 1995 led to 140,000 cases of dengue fever from Argentina to Texas." (p37)

Rauber, Paul. "Heat Wave: Disease." Sierra v82 n5 Sep-Oct 1997. p37. (ISSN0161-7362).

GLOBAL WARMING--LAW AND LEGISLATION--UNITED STATES

"Although there are dissenters, many scientists predict that, unless waste gases from burning coal, oil and natural gas--primary sources of energy in modern economies--are kept from trapping heat in the atmosphere, levels of carbon dioxide would be about twice as much as before the Industrial Age began in the late 18th Century. If that happens, scientists told the delegates in Kyoto that the Earth's average surface temperature will rise by 2 to 6 degrees Fahrenheit by 2100. (By comparison, the world is now 5 to 9 degrees warmer than in the depths of the last Ice Age.) To combat this, the Kyoto accord calls for the United States to reduce the emission of greenhouse gases to 7 percent below 1990 levels--a significant cut since we are currently 8 or 9 percent above 1990 emission levels....Cars and trucks make about 25 percent of all the carbon dioxide created in America...." (p8 secE)

Konrad, Rachel/Craig, Charlotte W./Solomon, Deborah. "Business: Global Warming Plan a Blow to Michigan." Detroit Free Press 12 Dec 1997. p1,8 secE.

GLOBAL WARMING--UNITED STATES--PUBLIC OPINION

"A recent survey of 27,000 people in 24 countries by Environics International, a Toronto-based research firm, shows that Americans are much more likely than people in other countries to feel that 'we should not take major action to reduce human impacts on climate until we know more, because of the great economic costs involved.'...This doesn't mean that Americans would not be willing to help out in reducing global warming. In fact, nearly three-quarters of those polled say they'd pay 5 cents more for a gallon of gasoline, if that's what it took. Sixty percent would pay as much as a quarter more per gallon, according to a recent poll by the Pew Research Center for the People and the Press." (p9)

Knickerbocker, Brad. "Should US Pay Bulk of Global Warming Tab?" The Christian Science Monitor v90 n3 28 Nov 1997. p1,9. The Christian Science Monitor search engine: <http://www.csmonitor.com/plweb-cgi/iops1.pl> To retrieve this article, enter the following search: ED=19971128 AND tab. In the "retrieved list," click the title that matches this record. (ISSN0882-7729).

GOAT INDUSTRY--UNITED STATES (v26)

GOLD (v26)

GOLD MINES AND MINING--NEVADA

"For the fifth year in a row, Nevada's mines have collectively topped the 6 million ounce mark in gold production. In 1996, there was a total of 7.08 million ounces of gold produced in Nevada. The state's rich landscape has made Nevada the largest gold producer in the...[U.S.] with 66.5 percent of all production. In addition, it now accounts for 10 percent of all the gold in the world. The most recent information from the State of Nevada indicates that direct mining employment in Nevada exceeds 13,000 jobs. The average annual pay for these jobs, the highest of any sector in the state, is about $46,000, compared to the average salary in Nevada of about $26,000 per year. In addition to the direct employment in mining, there are an estimated 36,000 jobs in the state related to providing goods and services needed by the industry." (pS9586-9587)

Bryan, Richard H. (Sen.-Nev.). "Department of the Interior and Related Agencies Appropriations Act, 1998." Congressional Record. Daily ed. v143 n125 18 Sep 1997. pS9575-9600. section/page-level access: <http://thomas.loc.gov/cgi-bin/query/R?r105:FLD001:S09586:> (ISSN0363-7239). (X1.1A.105/1).

GOLD MINES AND MINING--SOUTH AFRICA

South Africa "holds 40 percent of the world's [gold] reserves. Since gold was first discovered there in 1886, 47,000 tons have been mined, or half its reserves." (p6)

Matloff, Judith. "International: Falling Prices Land Hard on S. African Gold Miners." The Christian Science Monitor v89 n173 1 Aug 1997. p6. The Christian Science Monitor search engine: <http://www.csmonitor.com/plweb-cgi/iops1.pl> To retrieve this article, enter the following search: ED=19970801 AND miners. In the "retrieved list," click the title that matches this record. (ISSN0882-7729).

GOLD STANDARD--UNITED STATES (v26)

GOLF--CANADA

"According to a survey last winter by SCORE magazine and ComQuest Research of Toronto, 25 per cent of Canadians over age 18 played at least one round of golf in 1996, up from 18 per cent in 1990. By all accounts, that makes Canadians the world's most avid golfers. In the United States, by comparison, only 16 per cent of the adult population teed up last year. The ComQuest findings were supported by another study released in April by the Royal Canadian Golf Association. It concluded that nearly a million Canadians have taken up the sport in the past seven years." (p34)

Fennell, Tom. "Business: Green Dreams." Maclean's v110 n28 14 Jul 1997. p34-35. (ISSN0024-9262).

GOLF--UNITED STATES

Seventy "percent of all rounds of golf played in the US take place on daily-fee courses open to the public. And although golfers have slightly higher median incomes than most Americans, surveys show that 40 percent describe themselves as blue-collar workers." (p7)

Walker, Sam. "A Golf Revolution?: America's Melting Pot Moves to the Public Links." The Christian Science Monitor v89 n143 19 Jun 1997. p1,7. The Christian Science Monitor search engine: <http://www.csmonitor.com/plweb-cgi/iops1.pl> To retrieve this article, enter the following search: ED=19970619 AND links. In the "retrieved list,"

click the title that matches this record. (ISSN0882-7729).

GOLF COURSES--ASIA (v26)

GOLF COURSES--ENVIRONMENTAL ASPECTS--UNITED STATES

In the U.S., "as much as nine million pounds of pesticides are used every year on the nation's 15,700 golf courses....On average, about 6.5 pounds of pesticides are applied per acre to U.S. golf courses each year (compared to 1.5 pounds per acre to agricultural lands)....A 1996 study published in Environmental Science and Technology showed that as much as three percent of the 'dislodgeable' turf residues (the portion of the herbicide that does not adhere to the turf) of the herbicides 2,4-D and dicamba that were sprayed on grass were later found in carpet dust [of homes built near golf courses], ready to be taken up on the hands of infants and children playing on the floor....In 1994, Dr. Burton Kross and colleagues released a study, commissioned by the Golf Course Superintendents Association of America, of 618 of its members who died between 1970 and 1992. They found that 'golf course superintendents died from cancer more often than the general public.'...In 1995, at a golf course near Pensacola, Florida, approximately 1,000 grackles were killed or sickened from chlorpyrifos mixed with bird food as a bait for crickets and moles." (p15)

Marquardt, Sandra. "News from Around: Golf's Green Handicap." Journal of Pesticide Reform v17 n2 Sum 1997. p15-16. (ISSN0893-357X).

GONORRHEA--UNITED STATES (v26)

GORONGOSA NATIONAL PARK (MOZAMBIQUE) (v26)

GOSHAWK--UNITED STATES

In the U.S., "three goshawk subspecies occur in the 11 western states: the Queen Charlotte (AK, WA), the Apache (AZ, NM) and northern (all western states.) Goshawks in the lower 48 states have declined because of the logging of old growth forests, especially ponderosa pine." (p9)

"Endangered Species Update: Goshawks: Ruling May Result in Endangered Species Act Protection for the Goshawk." Networker v9 n2 Sum 1997. p9.

GOVERNMENT ASSISTANCE

see ECONOMIC ASSISTANCE, DOMESTIC

GOVERNMENT DEBTS

see DEBTS, PUBLIC

GOVERNMENT EMPLOYEES

see CIVIL SERVICE

GOVERNMENT HOUSING

see PUBLIC HOUSING

GOVERNMENT SPENDING POLICY (v26)

GOVERNMENT SPENDING POLICY--CANADA (v26)

GOVERNMENT SPENDING POLICY--GREAT BRITAIN --BUCKINGHAMSHIRE (v26)

GOVERNMENT SPENDING POLICY--GREAT BRITAIN --HOUNSLOW (v26)

GOVERNMENT SPENDING POLICY--LATIN AMERICA

According to the report, "Economic and Social Progress in Latin America," "Latin America's public sector typically spends about a quarter of a country's gross domestic product, compared with 50 percent in a typical advanced industrialized country. However, despite the steady pace of privatizations, Latin American countries still typically spend 6 percent of their GDP on public investment. In industrialized countries, where the private sector plays a more important investment role, the corresponding figure is less than 2 percent of GDP....[Social security] accounts for roughly 15 percent of GDP in an advanced industrial country compared with only 2.5 percent of GDP for the typical Latin American country." (p11)

"Figuratively Speaking: Public Spending: Government Getting Leaner." IDB v24 n9-10 Sep-Oct 1997. p11. (ISSN0145-2274).

GOVERNMENT SPENDING POLICY--UNITED STATES (v26)

Current U.S. "international affairs spending ($18.78 billion in fiscal 1998 dollars) is 25 percent below the annual average of the past 20 years ($24.97 billion), and 30 percent below the level of a decade ago ($26.68 billion)....Our international affairs dollars are important investments in American economic and security interests. For example, trade promotion activities generate $15 billion to $20 billion in exports each year and support more than 300,000 American jobs." (p19)

Biden, Joseph R., Jr. (Sen.-Del.). "Opinion/Essays: Maintain America's Investment in Diplomacy." The Christian Science Monitor v89 n134 6 Jun 1997. p19. The Christian Science Monitor search engine: <http://www.csmonitor.com/plweb-cgi/iops1.pl> To retrieve this article, enter the following search: ED=19970606 AND diplomacy. In the "retrieved list," click the title that matches this record. (ISSN0882-7729).

GOVERNMENT SPENDING POLICY--UNITED STATES --PUBLIC OPINION (v26)

GRADE LABELING

see LABELS

GRADING AND MARKING (STUDENTS)--EUROPE (v26)

GRADING AND MARKING (STUDENTS)--MICHIGAN --DETROIT (v26)

GRADING AND MARKING (STUDENTS)--UNITED STATES (v26)

In the U.S., "a recent report by the College Board found that since 1987, the proportion of SAT [Scholastic Assessment Test] test takers with A+, A, and A- averages has risen 'from 28 percent to a record 37 percent, while their SAT scores have fallen an average of 13 points on verbal and one point on math.' This year, the grade-point average of test takers was 3.22, compared to 3.07 in 1987." (p28) In 1994, "in schools where more than 75 percent of the students received lunch subsidies, 23 percent reported getting mostly A's in English, and 38 percent received mostly B's. Twenty-eight percent received mostly A's in math, and 32 percent got mostly B's." (p29)

Hardy, Lawrence. "Grade Inflation." American School Board Journal v184 n12 Dec 1997. p28-30. (ISSN0003-0953).

Eighty percent "of Princeton students 'earn' A's and B's, while at Stanford only 8% of students get C's and D's and none get F's. Similarly, the mean grade at Harvard is now better than a B+, up from a B- twenty-five years ago. Additionally, Yale recently graduated 50% of its seniors with honors (Alexander, 1993)." (p196)

Browne, M. Neil/Hoag, John H./Myers, Melanie L./Hiers, Wesley J. "Student Evaluation of Teaching as if Critical Thinking Really Mattered." Journal of General Education v46 n3 1997. p192-206.

In the U.S., "this year, 37 percent of the graduating seniors who took the SAT [Scholastic Assessment Test] college aptitude test boasted A-plus, A, or A-minus GPAs [grade point averages]. A decade ago, only 28 percent of the seniors had such high grades....Of the graduating seniors taking the ACT [American College Test] last year, 32 percent had GPAs of 3.5 or higher--equaling a B-plus or above--on a 4.0 scale, twice as many as in 1970." (p12)

Marshall, Jon. "Learning: Seniors Boast Higher Grades, So-So SAT Scores." The Christian Science Monitor v89 n198 8 Sep 1997. p12. The Christian Science Monitor search engine: <http://www.csmonitor.com/plweb-cgi/iops1.pl> To retrieve this article, enter the following search: ED=19970908 AND scores. In the "retrieved list," click the title that matches this record. (ISSN0882-7729).

GRADUATE STUDENTS--UNITED STATES (v26)

GRADUATE TEACHING ASSISTANTS--UNITED STATES (v26)

GRADUATES, COLLEGE
see COLLEGE GRADUATES
GRADUATES, HIGH SCHOOL
see HIGH SCHOOL GRADUATES
GRAIN TRADE (v26)
see also BARLEY INDUSTRY; CORN INDUSTRY; RICE TRADE; SORGHUM INDUSTRY; WHEAT TRADE

"World coarse grain production in 1997/98 is forecast at 882 million tons, down 2 percent from a year earlier, but larger carryin stocks have left world supplies unchanged. As a result, coarse grain prices are expected to be generally stable. World coarse grain trade in 1997/98 is expected to exceed 91 million tons, virtually unchanged from the previous year." (p6)

Allen, Ed/U.S. Dept. of Agriculture. Economic Research Service. "Commodity Spotlight: Reduced Foreign Production Boosts U.S. Export Prospects." Agricultural Outlook Oct 1997. p6.

"After climbing at more than two percent a year from 1950 to 1990, the rise in world grainland productivity has fallen to scarcely one percent a year during the nineties, well below the growth of world population....The United States, in 1996, returned to production the last of the cropland that had been idled under commodity programs for much of the last half century. Meanwhile, world carryover stocks of grain were drawn down to just 51 days of consumption, the lowest on record." (p1)

Worldwatch Institute. "Can Scientists Restore the Rapid Rise in Cropland Productivity?" News Release 25 Jun 1997. p1-4.

"Each year, as population continues to expand, the world's farmers must stretch their production capacity to feed an additional 80 million people....The world's farmers responded heroically to past increases in demand, nearly tripling the grain harvest from 630 million tons in 1950 to 1.8 billion tons in 1990....Between 1950 and 1990, the yield per hectare grew at 2.1 percent per year." (p8) "In contrast,...the rise between 1990 and 1995 averaged only 1 percent a year." (p10)

Brown, Lester R. "Can We Raise Grain Yields Fast Enough?" World Watch v10 n4 Jul-Aug 1997. p8-17. (ISSN0896-0615).

World "rice production, which was modernized later than wheat and corn, achieved an annual increase in productivity of 2.1 percent per year between 1960 and 1990, but has dropped to 1.0 percent per year since 1990. Wheat yields grew between 1960 and 1990 at an average of 2.6 percent per year, then slowed to 0.1 percent during the 1990s. (If the former Soviet Union is excluded from the global trend after 1990, wheat yields increase by 1.0 percent.) Corn averaged 2.6 percent from 1950 to 1980, then fell to 1.3 percent in the 1980s. The rise in corn yields accelerated slightly during the first half of the 1990s, reaching 1.7 percent, largely because of a belated surge in yields in both China and Brazil." (p15-16)

Brown, Lester R. "Can We Raise Grain Yields Fast Enough?" World Watch v10 n4 Jul-Aug 1997. p8-17. (ISSN0896-0615).

"Among the world's top seven grain exporters, which includes nations as diverse as Canada and Vietnam, exports of grain nutrients range from 12 percent to 66 percent of domestic production....10 percent of the world's grain nutrients flow across borders in grain...." (p19)

Gardner, Gary. "Recycling Organic Waste: From Urban Pollutant to Farm Resource." Worldwatch Paper n135 Aug 1997. p5-59.

"From 1950 to 1990, the world grain harvest increased from 631 million tons to 1.78 billion tons, nearly tripling....After expanding at close to 3 percent a year from 1950 to 1990, the harvest increased only 1 percent annually between 1990 and 1996. Signs of slower growth were already evident in the late 1980s as the growth in grain production fell below that of population, dropping the harvest per person from the all-time high of 342 kilograms in 1984 to 335 kilograms in 1990, a fall of 2 percent. By 1996, the harvest per person had fallen to 321 kilograms, declining an additional 4 percent." (p15) "As of 1997, the world consumes 5 million tons of grain a day. Thus, rebuilding the grain stocks from the 57 days of carryover for 1997 to 70 days will require an increase in production over consumption of 65 million tons....After dropping to a recent low of $3.97 per bushel in 1993, the price [of wheat] increased in each of the next three years, reaching $5.54 per bushel in 1996, a rise of 39 percent." (p16-17)

Brown, Lester R. "The Agricultural Link: How Environmental Deterioration Could Disrupt Economic Progress." Worldwatch Paper n136 Aug 1997. p5-73.

"In 1996 world carryover stocks of grain, perhaps the most sensitive indicator of food security, dropped to the lowest level on record--a mere 52 days of consumption. Even with the exceptional harvest of 1996, stocks were rebuilt to only 57 days of consumption, far below the 70 days needed to provide a minimal buffer against a poor harvest." (p8) "Wheat traded at over $7 a bushel, more than double the price in early 1995. In mid-July, corn traded at an all-time high of $5.54 a bushel, also double the level of a year earlier." (p9)

Brown, Lester R. "The Agricultural Link: How Environmental Deterioration Could Disrupt Economic Progress." Worldwatch Paper n136 Aug 1997. p5-73.

GRAIN TRADE--AFRICA (v26)
GRAIN TRADE--AFRICA--UNITED STATES

Sub-Saharan African nations "use 97 percent of the grain they grow for food. (By contrast, direct human consumption of grain in the United States accounts for only 28 percent of the total grain flows...)....Sub-Saharan Africa...feeds only 2 percent of its grain to animals, but in the United States, 41 percent of grain nutrients go to animal consumption." (p18)

Gardner, Gary. "Recycling Organic Waste: From Urban Pollutant to Farm Resource." Worldwatch Paper n135 Aug 1997. p5-59.

GRAIN TRADE--AFRICA, NORTH--MIDDLE EAST --UNITED STATES (v26)
GRAIN TRADE--ASIA (v26)

"Asia's grain imports have increased from some 6 million tons in 1950 to more than 90 million tons in 1995. Some Asian countries, including Japan, South Korea, and Taiwan, now import more than 70 percent of the grain they consume." (p14)

Brown, Lester R. "The Agricultural Link: How Environmental Deterioration Could Disrupt Economic Progress." Worldwatch Paper n136 Aug 1997. p5-73.

GRAIN TRADE--AUSTRALIA (v26)
GRAIN TRADE--CANADA

The Canadian "Atlantic coast ports decreased from 552,000 tonnes [of grain] in 1987 to 73,000 tonnes today....The ports along the St. Lawrence have had an even bigger decrease. In 1987 they handled 11.8 million tonnes of grain. Today they are only handling about 4.4 million tonnes." (p794) "Thunder Bay has done a little better. It has actually increased from 1.1 million tonnes to 1.4 million tonnes....Churchill...used to handle about half a million tonnes or better of grain in 1987. In 1996 they were down to 227,000 tonnes....That has increased to about 400,000 tonnes." (p795)

Hoeppner, Jake E. (MP-MB). "Government Orders: Canada Marine Act." Canada. Parliament. House of Commons. Debates. v135 n15 10 Oct 1997. p788-797. section-level access: <http://www.parl.gc.ca/36/1/parlbus/chambus/house/debates/015_1997-10-10/han015-e.htm#LINK196> (ISSN0704-5603). (X3-361E).

GRAIN TRADE--CHINA (v26)

In 1995-1996, "on the export side, [China's] bulk export share was generally below 3 percent of the world market (most years less than 2 percent except 1991-1994), while its grain exports had taken nearly 4 percent of the world market in 1993 and 1994, when China was a net grain exporter. On the import side, China is a big buyer of grains in the world market, but the amount it bought fluctuated significantly from year to year. In 1995, it bought more than 8 percent of total world grain exports (in value terms)." (p12)

Wang, Zhi/U.S. Dept. of Agriculture. Economic Research Service. "China's Agricultural Trade in 1996: Commodity Structure, Geographical Distribution, And Its Role in U.S...Trade." China: International Agriculture and Trade Reports Situation and Outlook Series Jun 1997. p6-15.

In China, cultivated grain area "dropped steadily from 99.5 million hectares in 1979 to 94.3 million in 1996. Sown area decreased from 148.4 million hectares in 1979 to 143.6 million in 1985, but increased since then. There was a slight dip in sown area in 1993 but then rose to 152.2 million hectares in 1996. China's multiple cropping ratio decreased slightly in the early 1980s but increased in the late 1980s and early 1990s. The ratio increased from 1.562 in 1994 to a record 1.61 in 1996....Provincial leaders used various measures to boost grain sown area by 517,000 hectares in 1995 and 2.3 million hectares in 1996....Grain self-sufficient provinces in 1995 increased the area sown by 250,000 hectares....Grain deficit provinces in 1995 increased area sown to grain crops by only 57,000 hectares." (p21)

Crook, Frederick W./U.S. Dept. of Agriculture. Economic Research Service. "Current Agricultural Policies Highlight Concerns about Food Security." China: International Agriculture and Trade Reports Situation and Outlook Series Jun 1997. p19-25.

From 1990 to 1996, "China's grain consumption increased by some 40 million tons, with more than 30 million tons of this growth consumed as feed. Between 1978, when economic reforms were adopted in China, and 1997, the grain used to feed livestock, poultry, and fish increased from less than 20 million tons to more than 100 million." (p12)

Brown, Lester R. "The Agricultural Link: How Environmental Deterioration Could Disrupt Economic Progress." Worldwatch Paper n136 Aug 1997. p5-73.

GRAIN TRADE--CHINA--INDONESIA (v26)

GRAIN TRADE--FORMER SOVIET REPUBLICS

In the Newly Independent States of the Soviet Union and the Baltics, grain "production stabilized at around 125 million tons in 1995 and 1996....Total 1997 NIS/B grain production (including pulses, buckwheat, and miscellaneous) was forecast in May 1997 to rise 6 percent to 132 million tons....Following price reforms, faster growth in wheat prices relative to coarse grains has led to an increase in the share of wheat in total NIS/B grain area from 43 percent in 1993/94 to 51 percent in 1996/97, and a forecast 52 percent in 1997/98....Total NIS/B grain area...decreased more than 10 percent from 1992 to 1996...." (p20)

Foster, Christian J./Liefert, Olga/Mitchell, Jay K./Hoskin, Roger L./U.S. Dept. of Agriculture. Economic Research Service. "NIS/B Farm Sector Continues Adjustment to Market Forces; U.S. Agricultural Exports to Region Post Recovery." Newly Independent States and the Baltics: International Agriculture and Trade Reports Situation and Outlook Series May 1997. p10,12-15,18,20,22-24.

Net grain imports by the Newly Independent States of the Soviet Union and the Baltic "countries are estimated down from about 5.5 million tons in 1995/96 (July/June) to below 4 million tons in 1996/97, and are unlikely to change significantly in 1997/98....Net wheat imports from the world market fell to a record low of under 3 million tons estimated for 1996/97 in the wake of a strong Russian harvest and higher wheat production in most other countries as well....[Ukranian] net coarse grain imports, which have averaged less than 1 million tons over the past 3 years, are unlikely to change significantly in 1997/98....In the grain-deficit countries of the Caucasus and Central Asia, import demand (most of which is satisfied by wheat purchases outside the NIS/B region) is likely to remain stable in 1997/98 at around 1.5 and 3 million tons, respectively....U.S. wheat exports to the NIS/B region, which have found niches in the Uzbek and Russian Far Eastern markets, increased from about 0.7 million tons in 1994/95 to around 0.9 million in 1995/96." (p18)

Foster, Christian J./Liefert, Olga/Mitchell, Jay K./Hoskin, Roger L./U.S. Dept. of Agriculture. Economic Research Service. "NIS/B Farm Sector Continues Adjustment to Market Forces; U.S. Agricultural Exports to Region Post Recovery." Newly Independent States and the Baltics: International Agriculture and Trade Reports Situation and Outlook Series May 1997. p10,12-15,18,20,22-24.

GRAIN TRADE--INDIA--UNITED STATES (v26)

GRAIN TRADE--RUSSIA (v26)

GRAIN TRADE--SAUDI ARABIA--UNITED STATES (v26)

GRAIN TRADE--TAIWAN

"Currently, Taiwan produces only about 5 percent of its coarse grain requirements and less than 1 percent of its soybean needs....Corn is the dominant feed grain, and most corn--95 percent--is imported....By the early 1990's, Taiwan's corn imports surpassed 5 million tons, hitting a record 6.3 million in the 1994/95 marketing year. The U.S. is the leading supplier of coarse grain (mostly corn) and soybeans to Taiwan, with market shares of over 90 percent for both commodities. In 1996, the U.S. exported 5.8 million tons of coarse grain and 2.6 million tons of soybeans to Taiwan, each accounting for about a tenth of total U.S. exports of those commodities. U.S. corn exports to Taiwan have averaged 212 million bushels per year in the 1990's, reaching 234 million bushels for the 1995/96 marketing year." (p3-4) "USDA is projecting Taiwan's 1997/98 corn imports at 4.5 million tons, the lowest since 1988/89, and down 22 percent from the 1993-95 average of 5.8 million tons." (p5)

Southard, Leland/Riley, Pete/U.S. Dept. of Agriculture. Economic Research Service. "Commodity Briefs: Livestock, Dairy & Poultry: Hog Disease in Taiwan Affects U.S. Pork & Corn Exports." Agricultural Outlook Jun 1997. p3-5.

GRAIN TRADE--UNITED STATES (v26)

"U.S. coarse grain exports are forecast at nearly 58 million tons, with the U.S. global market share rebounding to about 63 percent. U.S. exports of corn in 1997/98 are forecast at 51.5 million tons, up 13 percent from a year earlier. Corn supplies are forecast up 5 percent, mostly because of increased carryover stocks, leaving competitively priced U.S. corn readily available for export." (p6)

Allen, Ed/U.S. Dept. of Agriculture. Economic Research Service. "Commodity Spotlight: Reduced Foreign Production Boosts U.S. Export Prospects." Agricultural Outlook Oct 1997. p6.

In 1997, "U.S. wheat exports equalled 24.5 million tons and $4.1 billion, a 27-percent drop in quantity and down 40 percent in value from the high levels of 1996. U.S. corn exports also declined sharply from 1996, and at 46.6 million tons and $6.1 billion, dropped 11 percent and 27 percent, respectively. U.S. exports of rice fell 9 percent in quantity and 4 percent in value to 2.6 million tons and $959 million." (p1)

U.S. Dept. of Agriculture. Economic Research Service. "Exports." U.S. Agricultural Trade Update 24 Nov 1997. p1.

In September 1997, "spring wheat harvest reached 84% complete, 2 points ahead of harvest in 1996 and 18 points ahead of average....Barley was 88% harvested, 2 points ahead of last year and 10 points ahead of normal. Oat harvest was in its final stages as harvest reached 96% complete, 1 point behind 1996 but 4 points ahead of average." (p16)

U.S. Dept. of Commerce. Dept. of Agriculture. "National Agricultural Summary: September 1-7, 1997: Highlights." Weekly Weather and Crop Bulletin v84 n36 9 Sep 1997. p16. (ISSN0043-1974).

In the U.S., in August 1997, "spring wheat harvest advanced to 41% complete, behind 49% in 1996 but ahead of the average of 39%. Barley harvest reached 50% complete, 1 percentage point behind 1996 but equal to the average....Nationally, oat harvest was 78% complete, compared with 79% in 1996 and 76% for the average." (p10)

U.S. Dept. of Commerce. Dept. of Agriculture. "National Agricultural Summary: August 25-31, 1997: Highlights." Weekly Weather and Crop Bulletin v84 n35 3 Sep 1997. p10. (ISSN0043-1974).

In the U.S., in May 1997, "83% of the spring wheat crop was planted, well ahead of the 65% planted a year ago and equal to the average....Eighty-three percent of the barley crop was planted, also well ahead of 1996 and just 1 point behind the average....Oat planting progressed to 93% complete, ahead of both the 80% planted in 1996 and the average of 89%." (p10)

U.S. Dept. of Commerce. Dept. of Agriculture. "National Agricultural Summary: May 19-25, 1997: Highlights." Weekly Weather and Crop Bulletin v84 n21 28 May 1997. p10. (ISSN0043-1974).

GRANDPARENTS AS PARENTS--UNITED STATES (v26)

In the U.S., "in 1996, about 4 million children (6 percent) lived in a grandparent's home, nearly double the 2.3 million (4 percent) who did so in 1980. Of the children living in a grandparent's home in 1996, more than one-third (1.4 million) had neither parent present. Another 1.9 million lived with their mother, but not their father, in their grandparent's home....Of the 2.4 million families maintained by grandparents who had one or more of their grandchildren living with them in 1996, nearly half (48 percent) were families with both grandparents present and statistically the same percentage (46 percent) were maintained by grandmothers with no grandfather present."

U.S. Dept. of Commerce. Economic and Statistics Administration. "Census Facts for Grandparent's Day." Census Bureau Fact Sheet 2 Sep 1997. document-level access: <http://www.census.gov/Press-Release/fs97-09.html>

"According to 1990 census data, 3.2 million children (5% of all children younger than 18 years) lived with a grandparent or other relative, a significant increase from the 2 million in 1980 (U.S. Bureau of the Census, 1991). By 1994, this number had risen to 3.7 million, with 36% of these children living in homes where neither parent was present (Saluter, 1996)." (p489)
"Studies of kinship foster care families suggest that 50% to 60% of kin caregivers are grandmothers, followed by aunts, then siblings, uncles, and grandfathers (Dubowitz, 1990, Thorton, 1991). Census data likewise indicate that 60% of grandparent caregivers are women (Chalfie, 1994)." (p490)

Burnette, Denise. "Article: Grandparents Raising Grandchildren in the Inner City." Families in Society v78 n5 Sep-Oct 1997. p489-499. (ISSN1044-3894).

"Data from the U.S. Bureau of the Census (1993) indicate that 60% of today's grandparent caregivers are grandmothers, three quarters are married, and a similar proportion are between 45 and 64 years of age. Although 68% of these caregivers are White and 29% are African American, midlife and older African Americans are nearly twice as likely as are same-age Whites to be grandparent caregivers (9% vs. 5%). Ten percent of caregivers are of Hispanic origin, 1% are American Indian, and 2% are Asian/Pacific Islanders (Chalfie, 1994)....Fifty-eight percent did not graduate from high school, and another 26% obtained a high school diploma but no further schooling. In part as a result of lack of education, grandparent-headed households are the most impoverished of all types of nontraditional households--with a median income half that of traditional households with children ($18,000 vs. $36,204). Twenty-seven percent of midlife and older grandparent caregivers live at or below the poverty level, and another 14% are near-poor with incomes between 100% and 149% of the threshold." (p493)

Burnette, Denise. "Article: Grandparents Raising Grandchildren in the Inner City." Families in Society v78 n5 Sep-Oct 1997. p489-499. (ISSN1044-3894).

GRAPE INDUSTRY--AUSTRALIA (v26)

GRAPE INDUSTRY--CALIFORNIA (v26)

"In 1996, growers in California received $718 per ton for fresh grapes, compared with $410 for grapes used for wine and $231 for those used for raisins. In 1996, 64 percent of the California grapes sold fresh were table varieties and 31 percent were raisin varieties." (p7)

Pollack, Susan/Perez, Agnes/U.S. Dept. of Agriculture. Economic Research Service. "Commodity Spotlight: Prospects Favorable for U.S. Grape Industry." Agricultural Outlook Jun 1997. p7-10.

"In California, the largest agricultural state, with crop revenues of $14 billion in 1996, the value of the total grape harvest reached a record $2 billion. California typically produces more than 95 percent of the grapes crushed for U.S. wine....California prices for wine-type grapes averaged $590 per metric ton in 1996, 26 percent higher than 1995....In California, wineries paid growers $1,260 per metric ton on average for these four varieties in 1996, compared with $390 for other wine-type varieties." (p12)

Love, John/U.S. Dept. of Agriculture. Economic Research Service. "Commodity Spotlight: The U.S. Wine Market Uncorked." Agricultural Outlook Aug 1997. p12-14.

GRAPE INDUSTRY--CALIFORNIA--NEW YORK (STATE)--WASHINGTON (STATE)

"USDA's National Agricultural Statistics Service surveys grape production in 13 states, but nearly 90 percent of the U.S. grape crop is produced in California. New York and Washington are the next-largest producers, each harvesting about 3 percent of all domestic grapes." (p7) "Last year, grape production totaled 144,000 tons in Washington, down 44 percent from the state's 1995 crop. In contrast, New York's output of 189,000 tons was up 14 percent from the previous year." (p8)

Pollack, Susan/Perez, Agnes/U.S. Dept. of Agriculture. Economic Research Service. "Commodity Spotlight: Prospects Favorable for U.S. Grape Industry." Agricultural Outlook Jun 1997. p7-10.

GRAPE INDUSTRY--MEXICO--UNITED STATES (v26)

GRAPE INDUSTRY--NEW YORK (STATE)--WASHINGTON (STATE) (v26)

GRAPE INDUSTRY--PRICES--UNITED STATES

"Reduced production, coupled with increased domestic and export demand in 1995 and 1996, helped strengthen fresh grape prices to growers, with the U.S. average rising from $581 per ton in 1994 to $620 in 1995, reaching a record $727 in 1996. Prior to 1996, the highest price growers had received for fresh-market grapes was $678 in 1992. Production of processing grapes also declined in 1996, leading to grower prices 16 percent higher than in 1995, with the season average reaching $348 per ton, the highest on record. Strong demand for U.S. wines also supported grape prices as an 8-percent decline in California's wine-type grape output led to some diversion of raisin, table, and juice-type grapes." (p7-8)

Pollack, Susan/Perez, Agnes/U.S. Dept. of Agriculture. Economic Research Service. "Commodity Spotlight: Prospects Favorable for U.S. Grape Industry." Agricultural Outlook Jun 1997. p7-10.

GRAPE INDUSTRY--UNITED STATES (v26)

In the U.S., "nearly 55 percent of the 1996 grape crop was used for wine....The U.S. agricultural sector contributes 10 percent of the world's grape output, the third largest after Italy and France. In 1996, grapes ranked number 15 according to each commodity's contribution to U.S. agricultural cash receipts, ahead of apples and oranges, but also ahead of such crops as rice or barley....Total U.S. grape receipts were up a total of 14 percent, with wine receipts reflecting a 24-percent increase in 1996, raisin varieties a 10-percent increase, and fresh table grapes a 5-percent increase over 1995....Prices to growers for grapes increased 17 percent for fresh use and 16 percent for processing uses." (p8)

U.S. Dept. of Agriculture. Economic Research Service. "1996 Farm Income Estimates: Net Value-Added and Net Farm Income Attain New Highs in 1996." Agricultural Income and Finance Situation and Outlook Report Sep 1997. p4-13.

"The U.S. is one of the world's leading grape producers, accounting for 10 percent of the world's grape output--third largest after Italy and France....About 85 percent of domestic grape production is processed, nearly two-thirds of which is used in manufacturing wine. More than a quarter is dried for raisin production, while less than 10 percent is used for juice....Less than 1 percent of processed grape output is canned....U.S. grape production used for fresh and processing markets in 1996 was 5.53 million tons, down 6 percent from 1995 and down 8 percent from the record 1992 crop....U.S. fresh-market grape production declined nearly 2 percent from 1995's record output of 852,900 tons." (p7)

Pollack, Susan/Perez, Agnes/U.S. Dept. of Agriculture. Economic Research Service. "Commodity Spotlight: Prospects Favorable for U.S. Grape Industry." Agricultural Outlook Jun 1997. p7-10.

In the U.S., grape "consumption more than doubled from 3.61 pounds per person in the marketing year 1975/76 to a record high of 7.94 pounds in 1989/90....In 1995/96 a 5-percent increase in fresh grape production outweighed continued growth in exports, increasing available domestic table-grape supplies by 4 percent from the previous year. Fresh grape consumption recovered nearly 3 percent that season, and following a similar recovery in 1994/95, brought consumption to 7.52 pounds per person....U.S. consumption of raisins, on the other hand, has remained relatively stable in the 1990's at 8-9 pounds per person (fresh-weight equivalent)." (p8)

Pollack, Susan/Perez, Agnes/U.S. Dept. of Agriculture. Economic Research Service. "Commodity Spotlight: Prospects Favorable for U.S. Grape Industry." Agricultural Outlook Jun 1997. p7-10.

The U.S. "export share of domestic grape supplies has risen...from an average of 9 percent in the 1970's to 12 percent in the 1980's and 17 percent in the 1990's. U.S. grape exports (both fresh and processed) increased 18 percent in value between 1990 and 1996, with last year's total reaching $208.6 million, accounting for 9 percent of the value of domestic production....U.S. imports of fresh table grapes rose 8 percent between 1994 and 1995, but tighter supplies of Chilean grapes and a decline in Mexican production held growth to 3 percent between 1995 and 1996....Shipments to Canada, the major U.S. market, fell an average of 6 percent per year between 1990 and 1996....While shipments to Hong Kong, the second-largest U.S. grape export market in 1996, are only 44 percent of the amount sent to Canada, the Hong Kong market has been growing at 13 percent yearly and is expected to continue to grow. Taiwan and the Philippines, ranked third and fourth in 1996 among U.S. grape export markets, have shown average annual growth rates of 6 percent and 29 percent since 1990 and are expected to continue strong." (p8-9)

Pollack, Susan/Perez, Agnes/U.S. Dept. of Agriculture. Economic Research Service. "Commodity Spotlight: Prospects Favorable for U.S. Grape Industry." Agricultural Outlook Jun 1997. p7-10.

U.S. "wine processors used 50 percent more raisin-type grapes and 3 percent more table-type grapes in 1996 than the previous year, although total grape use for wine rose only 1 percent. Despite increased use for wine, the smaller 1996 U.S. grape crop reduced total processing use of grapes to 4.69 million tons, 7 percent below the previous year and the lowest since 1987. Although grape use for canning rose 3 percent from 1995, use of grapes for juice (including small quantities used for processing jams, jellies, etc.) declined 27 percent, and grapes used for raisins fell 17 percent." (p8)

Pollack, Susan/Perez, Agnes/U.S. Dept. of Agriculture. Economic Research Service. "Commodity Spotlight: Prospects Favorable for U.S. Grape Industry." Agricultural Outlook Jun 1997. p7-10.

"Fresh use and processing use of the 1996 U.S. grape crop declined 10 percent and 6 percent, respectively, from a year earlier, reflecting below-average production compared with 1990-95....Fresh use amounted to 1.5 billion pounds and processing use totaled 9.5 billion pounds. Reduced production caused 1996 grower prices to rise sharply to the highest levels on record for fresh-market grapes and all processing use grape categories. Grower prices for fresh-market grapes averaged 36.2 cents a pound ($725 per ton) in 1996, up 17 percent from a year earlier, while grower prices for processing use grapes averaged 18.7 cents a pound ($374 per ton), up 25 percent." (p10)

U.S. Dept. of Agriculture. Economic Research Service. "Noncitrus Fruit Outlook." Fruit and Tree Nuts Situation and Outlook Report Aug 1997. p7-26.

"The United States produces about 10 percent of the world's grape output, the third largest after Italy and France....The export share of domestic grape supplies has risen, from an average of 9 percent in the 1970's to 12 percent in the 1980's and 17 percent in the 1990's....The volume of fresh-market grapes imported during the 1996/97 marketing season (May 1996-April 1997) was 6 percent lower than the previous season....Although lower, imports still constitute about one-third of U.S. fresh-market grape supplies. Over three-fourths of U.S. fresh grape imports come from Chile, and enter the country between January and May....Chilean shipments totaled 590.1 million pounds during 1996/97, down 2 percent from a year earlier. At the same time Mexican shipments totaled 132.2 million pounds, down 26 percent. Small quantities of fresh grapes were also shipped to the United States from Italy, Peru, and Brazil in 1996/97." (p10)

U.S. Dept. of Agriculture. Economic Research Service. "Noncitrus Fruit Outlook." Fruit and Tree Nuts Situation and Outlook Report Aug 1997. p7-26.

"The processing sector captures about 86 percent of all utilized grapes produced in the United States. Wine is the largest category, making up 64 percent of all domestic grapes processed in 1996. This is followed by dried grapes with 28 percent, juice with 8 percent (which also happens to include minute quantities for other processed uses such as jam, jellies, etc.), and canned grapes with less than 1 percent....In 1996, grape growers received 13.4 cents more per pound for fresh-market grapes than for grapes sold to wineries and 24.7 cents per pound more than for grapes sold to raisin processors. In the same year, 63 percent of California's fresh-market grapes were table varieties, 31 percent were raisin varieties, and the remainder were wine varieties." (p9-10)

U.S. Dept. of Agriculture. Economic Research Service. "Noncitrus Fruit Outlook." Fruit and Tree Nuts Situation and Outlook Report Aug 1997. p7-26.

"U.S. fresh grape exports in 1996/97 (May 1996-April 1997) totaled 457.1 million pounds, down 9 percent from the previous season. The three major markets were Canada, Hong Kong, and Mexico. Canada remained the major destination, receiving 41 percent of U.S. fresh grape exports in 1996/97, but the growth was in shipments to Hong Kong (up 21 percent from a year ago) and other Asian countries such as South Korea (up 295 percent), Taiwan (up 25 percent), and the Philippines (up 22 percent). Fresh grape shipments to Canada and Mexico declined 17 percent and 28 percent, respectively." (p10-11)

U.S. Dept. of Agriculture. Economic Research Service. "Noncitrus Fruit Outlook." Fruit and Tree Nuts Situation and Outlook Report Aug 1997. p7-26.

GRAPE JUICE INDUSTRY--UNITED STATES

"U.S. grape juice consumption is generally up in the 1990's--consumption rose from 2.51 pounds per person (fresh-weight equivalent) in 1990/91 to 4.1 pounds in 1995/96." (p8) "Grape juice imports soared between 1995 and 1996--rising by over 150 percent....During the 1990's, grape juice exports increased at an annual rate of 6 percent in value and 4 percent in volume....Japan is the second-largest market for U.S. grape juice exports....U.S. grape juice exports to Japan in 1996 about equaled the amount shipped in 1990. Korean demand for U.S. grape juice, on the other hand, has grown rapidly in the 1990's, accounting for 20 percent of shipments in 1996." (p10)

Pollack, Susan/Perez, Agnes/U.S. Dept. of Agriculture. Economic Research Service. "Commodity Spotlight: Prospects Favorable for U.S. Grape Industry." Agricultural Outlook Jun 1997. p7-10.

"During 1996, U.S. grape juice imports totaled 4.95 billion pounds (fresh-weight equivalent) while exports totaled 1.75 billion pounds. Around 75 percent of the imports last year came from Argentina, followed by nearly 12 percent from Chile and 11 percent combined from Mexico and Brazil. Grape juice imports rose 153 percent from a year earlier in 1996....Despite a decline in domestic grape juice supplies, U.S. grape juice exports rose 13 percent from a year earlier in 1996. Exports rose mainly to the Republic of Korea (up 189 percent), United Kingdom (up 145 percent), the Philippines (up 34 percent), Japan (up 15 percent), and Taiwan (up 8 percent). Exports to Canada, still the largest market, declined 6 percent while exports to Hong Kong fell 23 percent." (p11)

U.S. Dept. of Agriculture. Economic Research Service. "Noncitrus Fruit Outlook." Fruit and Tree Nuts Situation and Outlook Report Aug 1997. p7-26.

GRAPEFRUIT INDUSTRY--UNITED STATES (v26)

"Grower prices for fresh-market grapefruit in Florida averaged about 4 percent lower from October through May than the previous year....[U.S.] fresh grapefruit consumption is expected to increase 1 percent from a year ago, but drop 3 percent lower than the 3 previous years....Retail prices are averaging 6 percent above last year and 12 percent above 1994/95, ranging from $0.496 to $0.775 per pound....Fresh grapefruit exports fell 4 percent from September through May 1996/97 from a year earlier. Exports fell 10 percent to Japan, which accounted for 45 percent of the export market in 1996/97. Exports to the European Union fell 2 percent during this time, but exports to the United Kingdom and Germany rose....In 1996/97, grapefruit exports accounted for 42 percent of fresh supply." (p30) "The on-tree equivalent price received by growers for 1996/97 averaged minus $1.554 per 85-pound box. Prices this year were the lowest in the nineties, ranging from minus $0.56 to minus $2.36." (p31)

U.S. Dept. of Agriculture. Economic Research Service. "Citrus Fruit Outlook." Fruit and Tree Nuts Situation and Outlook Report Aug 1997. p27-31.

GRAPEFRUIT JUICE INDUSTRY--UNITED STATES

In the U.S., "an estimated 1.6 million short tons of grapefruit went into processing this year, the second largest amount in at least 10 years. Grapefruit juice yields are also up this year, at 1.20 gallons per box (40-degree Brix)." (p30) "Florida juice processors packed 30 million 40-degree Brix gallons of concentrated grapefruit juice this year, up 12 percent from 1995/96, but 4 percent below 1994/95. While production is high, juice movement has been slower than the previous 2 years, raising grapefruit stocks 17 percent from last year. White grapefruit juice accounted for about 70 percent of stocks at the end of July...." (p31)

U.S. Dept. of Agriculture. Economic Research Service. "Citrus Fruit Outlook." Fruit and Tree Nuts Situation and Outlook Report Aug 1997. p27-31.

GRASSHOPPERS

"A typical grasshopper has a gut capacity of approximately one-third of its body volume, and the food takes approximately five hours to pass through." (p38) "At optimal temperatures and on high-quality food,...[chewing herbivores, the orthopoteroids, such as grasshoppers and stick insects,] spend 5-10% of their time feeding." (p39) "Among the generalist grasshoppers, each individual tends to mix its foods, and some aposematic species, which advertise their chemical defenses, forage on as many as 20 different hosts in the course of a day." (p41)

Bernays, Elizabeth A. "Evolution of Feeding Behavior in Insect Herbivores." BioScience v48 n1 Jan 1998. p35-44. (ISSN0006-3568).

GRASSLAND ANIMALS--NORTH DAKOTA

In North Dakota, tallgrass prairies support "40 neotropical migratory birds, 12 species of waterfowl, 30 State-classified rare species, such federally-listed species as the western prairie fringed orchid ('Platanthera praeclara'), and another estimated 300 plant and 1,500 insect species. Forty-two species of plants and insects of the tallgrass prairie are designated as sensitive species by the U.S. Forest Service." (p10)

Kreil, Karen. "North Dakota's Tallgrass Prairie." Endangered Species Bulletin v22 n4 Jul-Aug 1997. p10-11.

GRASSLANDS--INDIANA

"In Indiana, over 7 million acres (2.8 million hectares) of tallgrass prairie stretched across the State prior to the arrival of the first settlers 200 years ago. Today, less than 1,000 acres (400 ha) remain, and these are in scattered patches....The largest unfragmented grassland remaining in Indiana occurs on Jefferson Proving Ground (JPG), a 55,000-acre (22,250-ha) Army ammunition testing facility that closed in 1995. JPG contains approximately 5,000 acres (2,020 ha) of grassland, in patches ranging from 10 to 500 acres (4 to 200 ha) in size." (p18-19)

Pruitt, Lori. "From Bombs to Bird Songs." Endangered Species Bulletin v22 n4 Jul-Aug 1997. p18-19.

GRAZING--UNITED STATES (v26)

GRAZING FEES--WEST (U.S.) (v26)

GREAT BARRIER REEF (QLD.) (v26)

GREAT BRITAIN--ECONOMIC CONDITIONS (v26)

In Great Britain, "between the late 1970s and the early 1990s, the nonemployment rate for the least-educated working-age men tripled to reach 33 percent, the pay of the worst-paid tenth of wage earners fell by 28 percent relative to the best paid, and the level of state pensions fell by more than 25 percent compared to average earnings....Between 1985 and 1988, an increase in output of 4.7 percent per year in the United Kingdom translated into employment growth of 2 percent per year; from 1990 to 1992 employment declined by 3 percent per year in response to a 1.4 percent annual decline in output." (p4)

Glyn, Andrew. "New Democracy Forum: Egalitarianism in a Global Economy." Boston Review v22 n6 Dec 1997-Jan 1998. p4-8. (ISSN0734-2306).

In the United Kingdom, "between 1979 and 1994 the real incomes of the bottom tenth of the income distribution (after housing costs) fell by 13 per cent, while those of the top tenth rose by 65 per cent....Between 1985 and 1995 the personal tax burden on the top tenth of the income distribution declined from 42 to 38 per cent of income, while for the bottom decile it increased from 22 to 25 per cent....The number of people dependent on the main means-tested benefit (supplementary benefit or, as it later became known, income support) grew from 4.4 million in 1979 to 9.8 million--or one-sixth of the population--in 1995....Expenditure on means-tested benefits rose from 17 to 30 per cent of total social security expenditure." (p268)

Beattie, Roger A. "Books: Reviews: Britain Divided: The Growth of Social Exclusion in the 1980s and 1990s." International Labour Review v136 n2 Sum 1997. p267-271. (ISSN0020-7780).

GREAT BRITAIN--ECONOMIC CONDITIONS--PUBLIC OPINION

According to last year's edition of the British Social Attitudes Survey, "most people say they want more spending on health, education and social benefits even if it means they have to pay more tax. Over 60% favoured 'tax and spend'; only 5% favoured reduction of taxes. A large proportion of people in Britain believed that 'government should redistribute income from the better-off to the less well-off': 43% of those in the South of England, 48% of those in Wales and the Midlands, 51% of those in London, 60% of those in Scotland, and 61% of those in the North. Most people believed 'ordinary people do not get their fair share of the nation's wealth': 59% in the South, rising to 70% in Scotland. Unemployment should be given a higher priority than inflation, according to 65% in the South, rising to 77% in Scotland. An emphatic majority believed that 'big business benefits owners at the expense of workers': 56% in the South, rising to 66% in Scotland." (p4)

Rai, Milan. "Features: Above the Parapets: New Labour Did Not Win." Freedom (Anarchist Fortnightly) v58 n12 21 Jun 1997. p4. (ISSN0016-0504).

GREAT BRITAIN--EMPLOYMENT (v26)

GREAT BRITAIN--EMPLOYMENT--MANUFACTURES (v26)

GREAT BRITAIN--HEALTH AND HYGIENE (v26)

GREAT BRITAIN--OFFICIALS AND EMPLOYEES (v26)

GREAT BRITAIN--POLITICS AND GOVERNMENT (v26)

GREAT BRITAIN--RELIGION

In England, "Church of England membership is only 40 percent of what it was in the 1930's, and the number of Sunday worshipers has dropped from 1.6 million in 1968 to 1.1 million in 1992 (DAILY TELEGRAPH, October 30, 1996). Over the last 25 years, 350 Anglican churches have closed for good (out of 16,000), although there has actually been a slight increase in the number of Roman Catholic churches over the same period (four in 1994-95, to bring the figure to 3,760)." (p39)

Turner, Derek. "Correspondence: Letter from London: Allah in Piccadilly." Chronicles v21 n8 Aug 1997. p38-39. (ISSN0887-5731).

GREAT BRITAIN--SOCIAL CONDITIONS (v26)

GREAT LAKES (v26)

see also BOATING ACCIDENTS--MICHIGAN, LAKE; FISHERIES--HURON, LAKE (MICH. AND ONT.); FISHES--DISEASES--MICHIGAN, LAKE; FISHERIES--MICHIGAN, LAKE; SALMON FISHING--MICHIGAN, LAKE

Twenty "percent of the world's fresh water exists in the Great Lakes basin. They contain 95 percent of the fresh water surface in the United States." (pH3875) "Right now, the Great Lakes are suffering a plague...in that zebra mussels, an invasive species who originated in the Caspian Sea, have become predominant across the Great Lakes basin. Damage attributable to zebra mussels during the 1990's is estimated to be as high as $5 billion." (pH3876)

Rivers, Lynn N. (Rep.-Mich.). "National Sea Grant College Program Reauthorization Act of 1997." Congressional Record. Daily ed. v143 n85 18 Jun 1997. pH3871-3889. section/page-level access: <http://thomas.loc.gov/cgi-bin/query/R?r105:FLD001:H03875:> (ISSN0363-7239). (X1.1A.105/1).

The Laurentian Great Lakes "is the largest freshwater system in the world, containing some 23,000 km3 [cubic kilometers] of water and representing approximately 18% of the world's surface freshwater supply (Botts and Krushelniski, 1987; Botkin and Keller, 1995). The Great Lakes-St. Lawrence River watershed is home to more than 39 million people, who have a wide variety of uses for the waters. Approximately 220 million tons (200 million metric tonnes) of international and interlake cargo are transported through the Great Lakes-St. Lawrence Seaway each year (US Army Corps of Engineers, 1991). Iron ore, coal, limestone, and grain accounted for 85% of all shipments across the lakes and in 1990, the commercial fleet on the lakes numbered 185 vessels (117 Canadian and 68 US registry) (Waxmonsky, 1992)." (p1) "Although commercial fishing has declined on the lakes, the Ontario waters of Lake Erie, for example, still produced 35.5 million tons (32.2 million metric tonnes) of fish (primarily smelt, walleye, white and yellow perch) worth Cdn$27.5 million in 1994 (Ontario Ministry of Natural Resources, 1995)....Slightly more than 100,000 residential (i.e., riparian) properties and 40 Native North American communities line the shores (International Joint Commission, 1993a)." (p2)

Irvine, Kim N./Taylor, S. W./Leonard, M. "Impacts of Alternative Great Lakes Regulation Plans on Hydropower Production." Energy Studies Review v8 n1 1996. p1-15. (ISSN0843-4379).

GREAT PLAINS (v26)

GREAT SMOKEY MOUNTAINS NATIONAL PARK (N.C. AND TENN.) (v26)

GREECE--ECONOMIC CONDITIONS

"Over the past 10 years, real GDP growth in Greece averaged only 1.6 percent, lagging behind the European Union's (E.U.'s) average of 2.2 percent. At 140 percent of GDP, Greece's national debt is the highest of all E.U. members, while its GDP per capita is the E.U.'s lowest. Inflation, at almost 11 percent, is also well above the E.U. average....Greece continues to rely heavily on E.U. aid, which accounts for 6 percent of GDP. Like many European countries, Greece is plagued by high unemployment, estimated at 10 percent in recent years." (p7)

Lim, Aun Ling. "Spotlight: Greece." Population Today v25 n7-8 Jul-Aug 1997. p7. (ISSN0749-2448).

GREECE--PUBLIC OPINION (v26)

GREECE--SOCIAL CONDITIONS

In Greece, "the total fertility rate, or number of lifetime births per woman, has been falling steadily for 10 years and is now well below replacement level at 1.4....An estimated 18 percent of the population will be over age 65 by the year 2000; by 2030, almost a quarter of the population will be over 65." (p7)

Lim, Aun Ling. "Spotlight: Greece." Population Today v25 n7-8 Jul-Aug 1997. p7. (ISSN0749-2448).

GREEK LETTER SOCIETIES--UNITED STATES

In the U.S., "after rising sharply for two decades, membership in Greek [college] organizations has leveled off, even though total college enrollment keeps rising. In the 1996-97 school year, barely 6 percent of the 12.5 million undergraduates at four-year colleges were in the Greek system: 400,000 men and just over 300,000 women. Fraternities in particular have suffered. Since 1990, for instance, the University of Texas-Austin has seen a 29 percent drop in fraternity recruits. Nationally, the average fraternity chapter shrank from 51 members in 1989 to 38 in 1996." (p96)

Lord, Lewis. "Best Colleges 1998: From Party Hearty to Party Hardly?" U.S. News & World Report v123 n8 1 Sep 1997. p96-97. article-level access: <http://www.usnews.com/usnews/issue/970901/1FRAT.HTM> (ISSN0041-5537).

GREEN MARKETING--AUSTRIA--PUBLIC OPINION (v26)

GREEN MOVEMENT--UNITED STATES

"John O'Connor, head of the former National Toxics Coalition, estimates that at any given moment there are likely to be around 10,000 toxics/environmental justice groups in the U.S. Lois Gibbs believes that this number is low; she points out that there are 7,332 local groups on the mailing list of the Citizens' Clearinghouse on Hazardous Waste alone." (p71)

Epstein, Barbara. "The Environmental Justice/Toxics Movement: Politics of Race and Gender." Capitalism, Nature, Socialism v8 n3 Sep 1997. p63-87. (ISSN1045-5752).

GREEN MOVEMENT--UNITED STATES. CONGRESS

In the U.S., in the 1996 election, "many of the Congress' worst anti-environmentalists were defeated, bringing a net environmental gain in the House of 22 seats, according to Clean Water Action's (CWA) analysis. 21 of 22 House incumbents who lost in 1996 had voted earlier to gut the Clean Water Act, and averaged only 22 percent on CWA's 'Clean Water Congressional Scorecard.' Incumbents who retired in 1996 averaged only slightly better, at just 36 percent." (p4)

"National Campaign Report: Congress Now Greener?" Clean Water Action News v24 n1 1997. p4,10.

GREENHOUSE EFFECT, ATMOSPHERIC

"Eighty to eighty-five percent of emissions that cause global warming are supposed to be CO2 [carbon monoxide]....96.9 percent of the CO2 emissions on this Earth come from natural causes....The rest of the world contributes 3.1 percent. The U.S. contribution is less than 1 percent, .6 percent." (pS8143)

Sessions, Jeff (Sen.-Ala.). "Global Warming." Congressional Record. Daily ed. v143 n107 25 Jul 1997. pS8143-8144. section/page-level access: <http://thomas.loc.gov/cgi-bin/query/R?r105:FLD001:S08143:> (ISSN0363-7239). (X1.1A.105/1).

GREENHOUSE GASES

Hydrofluorocarbons "used as alternatives to ozone-depleting substances in refrigerants and cleaning and foaming agents, have between 1,300 and 24,000 times the warming effect of CO2 [carbon dioxide] and are projected to quadruple in use by 2050. PFCs [perfluorocarbons], emitted from aluminum smelting and used in semiconductor manufacturing, have a warming effect between 6,500 and 9,200 times that of CO2 and generally remain in the atmosphere for several thousand years....HFC and PFC emissions are projected to increase by 430 percent by 2020." (p59)

Flavin, Christopher/Dunn, Seth. "Rising Sun, Gathering Winds: Policies to Stabilize the Climate and Strengthen Economies." Worldwatch Paper n138 Nov 1997. p5-84.

GREENHOUSE GASES--AUSTRALIA (v26)

GREENHOUSE GASES--CANADA

"Canadians--by heating their homes, running their appliances, and driving their cars--generate 5.4 tonnes of greenhouse gases per capita each year. Add emissions from industry and energy production and that number jumps to 21 tonnes per capita, putting us second only to the United States among developed countries. And those emissions are expected to increase by 8.2 percent by the year 2000." (p43)

Grescoe, Taras. "Special Report: Temperature Rising." Canadian Geographic v117 n6 Nov-Dec 1997. p36-44. (ISSN0008-3658).

"Canada's greenhouse gas emissions increased 9.2% from 1990 to 1995, according to a new report from Environment Canada. TRENDS IN CANADA'S GREENHOUSE GAS EMISSIONS (1990-1995) states that Canada's 1995 emissions of greenhouse gases were about 619 million metric tons (Mt) of CO2 [carbon dioxide] equivalent--about 2% of total global emissions. CO2 comprised the bulk of the emissions (81%), followed by methane (13%) and nitrous oxide (5%)....The transportation sector accounted for the largest share of emissions, at 27% of the total. CO2 emissions...increased at a slower rate (7.8% from 1990 to 1995) than emissions of methane and nitrous oxide, which increased by 16.4% and 22.2%, respectively....The growth in energy use--9.2% from 1990 to 1995--exactly matches the growth in emissions, while population grew by 6.5% and gross domestic product grew by 8.2% over the same time period." (p4)

"Policy and Economics: Canada's Emissions Up 9.2%." Global Environmental Change Report v9 n12 27 Jun 1997. p4. (ISSN1049-9083).

In Canada, "emissions associated with energy use accounted for 89% of the country's greenhouse gas (GHG) emissions in 1995....Canada's GHG emissions increased by about 9% between 1990 and 1995...." (p3)

"Policy and Economics: Warming Will Impact Canada's Environment and Economy." Global Environmental Change Report v9 n14 25 Jul 1997. p3. (ISSN1049-9083).

GREENHOUSE GASES--CHINA

"Runaway fires in coal fields in northern China could be contributing up to 3% of worldwide CO2 [carbon dioxide] emissions, according to a report in the 9 August issue of NEW SCIENTIST....The fires, some of which have been burning for years or decades, are consuming as much as 200 million metric tons of coal every year." (p4)

"Policy and Economics: Coal Fires Add to Greenhouse Problem." Global Environmental Change Report v9 n17 12 Sep 1997. p4. (ISSN1049-9083).

GREENHOUSE GASES--ONTARIO--TORONTO

"Toronto, Ontario, is the first city in North America to report that it has stabilized its greenhouse gas (GHG) emissions at 1990 levels, according to a report in the newsletter ENVIROLINE (vol. 8...). In 1990, Toronto's GHG emissions totaled 7.7 million metric tons of CO2 [carbon dioxide]-equivalent, but by 1995 emissions had fallen to 7.5 million metric tons." (p3)

"Policy and Economics: Toronto Stabilizes Emissions." Global Environmental Change Report v9 n13 11 Jul 1997. p3. (ISSN1049-9083).

GREENHOUSE GASES--UNITED STATES

"With only four percent of the world's population, the United States accounts for 23 percent of the world's greenhouse gas emissions. And within transportation, cars and other light vehicles account for 53 percent of these emissions; freight trucks, 20 percent; and aviation 10 percent."

U.S. Dept. of Transportation. "Transportation Secretary Slater Says New American Travel Survey Results Underscore Need for Investment...." Press Release 10 Nov 1997. document-level access: <http://www.dot.gov/affairs/dot18597.htm>

GREETING CARDS--UNITED STATES (v26)

GRIZZLY BEAR--ALBERTA--BANFF NATIONAL PARK (v26)

GRIZZLY BEAR--UNITED STATES (v26)

The grizzly "bear's future depends on its achieving and maintaining a 'viable population,' which Alaska bear biologist John Schoen estimated could be anywhere from 'hundreds up to thousands.' A group of Canadian bear experts puts the number at 3,700, which is more than 10 times the number of grizzlies in Yellowstone [National Park]....Grizzlies are now confined to 1 or 2 percent of their habitat in the lower 48 [U.S.] states and will never be permitted to recover their losses." (p16)

Olsen, Lance. "Saying Goodbye to the Bear." High Country News v29 n22 24 Nov 1997. p16. (ISSN0191-5657).

GRIZZLY BEAR--YELLOWSTONE NATIONAL PARK (v26)

GROCERY TRADE--UNITED STATES (v26)

"Loyalty programs are currently offered by about 45 percent of grocery retailers across the...[U.S.], according to the Washington, D.C.-based Food Marketing Institute (FMI). And only 35 percent of U.S. households belong to one or more supermarket loyalty programs, according to ACNielsen....The major reason consumers give for joining frequent-shopper programs is to take advantage of member specials (75 percent); 19 percent sign up because membership is required for check writing, according to ACNielsen. Those who join the programs use them--75 percent of members show their cards on every shopping trip." (p36)

Mogelonsky, Marcia. "Kaleidoscope: Checkout Line: Supermarket Loyalty." American Demographics v19 n11 Nov 1997. p36. article-level access: <http://www.demographics.com/publications/ad/97_ad/9711_ad/ad971123.htm> (ISSN0163-4089).

In the U.S., "a typical supermarket may offer more than 25,000 food items, differentiated not only by product category, but also by brand, flavor, and package size. Nationwide, more than 200,000 grocery items (excluding fresh meat and poultry, and produce) are offered by food stores at any given time." (p8)

Kaufman, Phil/Lutz, Steven M./U.S. Dept. of Agriculture. Economic Research Service. "Food Prices: Competing Forces Affect Food Prices for Low-Income Households." Food Review v20 n2 May-Aug 1997. p8-12. (ISSN1056-327X).

GROSS DOMESTIC PRODUCT (v26)

"In 1995 Trinidad and Tobago had a per capita GDP (at purchasing power parity) of $8,610; St. Kitts and Nevis, $9,410; Barbados, $10,620; Malta, $11,570; Cyprus, $14,060; and Singapore, $22,770. These countries have far surpassed Puerto Rico's per capita GDP of $7,670, while Puerto Rico has overtaken no one during the last quarter-century." (p111)

Martinez, Ruben Berrios. "Puerto Rico's Decolonization." Foreign Affairs v76 n6 Nov-Dec 1997. p100-114. (ISSN0015-7120).

GROSS DOMESTIC PRODUCT--CUBA (v26)

GROSS DOMESTIC PRODUCT--EUROPE (v26)

"EU GDP in real terms rose strongly by 1.4% in the second quarter [1997] compared with the first quarter, according to revised estimates...from Eurostat, Statistical Office of the European Communities in Luxembourg. This compares with 0.2% growth in Q1....GDP increased by 2.7% between Q2 '96 and Q2 '97 and by 2.1% in first half this year compared with same period last year....Among Member States with available data, Finland (2.8%), the Netherlands (2.1%), Germany (1.8%) and Italy (1.6%) enjoyed growth between Q1 and Q2 after the falls recorded in Q1. In Denmark (1.4%) and France (1.0%) there was acceleration. UK (1.0%) and Spain (0.9%) recorded similar figures to the previous quarter. Only Sweden took a fall, of -0.1%."

Eurostat. "EU GDP Up Strongly by 1.4%." Press Release 17 Nov 1997. document-level access: <http://europa.eu.int/en/comm/eurostat/compres/en/7797/6207797a.htm>

GROSS DOMESTIC PRODUCT--EUROPE--JAPAN --UNITED STATES (v26)

GROSS DOMESTIC PRODUCT--GERMANY

"As reported by the Federal Statistical Office, the German gross domestic product rose a real 2.4% in the third quarter of 1997 compared with the third quarter of 1996, following a 3.0% increase in the second and a 1.0% increase in the first quarter of 1997. Seasonal and calendar adjusted (Deutsche Bundesbank procedure), the gross domestic product was up 1% in the third quarter of 1997 from the previous quarter. In the second quarter, the increase from the preceding quarter was 1% too, while in the first quarter the relevant increase was 0.5%."

Germany. Federal Statistical Office. "Concise Version: German Economy Expands 2.4% in the Third Quarter of 1997." Press Release 4 Dec 1997. document-level access: <http://www.statistik-bund.de/presse/englisch/pm/p7358121.htm>

"As reported by the Federal Statistical Office, the German gross domestic product rose a real 2.9% in the second quarter of 1997 from a year earlier. That rise was considerably higher than the increase recorded for the first quarter (+1.1%)....In the new Lander and Berlin-East, the gross domestic product rose a real 2.1% in the second quarter of 1997 compared with the corresponding period of 1996 (after an increase of 1.5% in the first quarter of 1997). In the former territory of the Federal Republic, the economic output was up 2.9% (after an increase of 1.1% in the first quarter of 1997)."

Germany. Federal Statistical Office. "Detailed Version: 2.9% Economic Growth in the Second Quarter of 1997." Press Release 10 Sep 1997. document-level access: <http://www.statistik-bund.de/presse/englisch/pm/p7267121.htm>

GROSS DOMESTIC PRODUCT--HONG KONG

In Hong Kong, "Gross Domestic Product (GDP) grew by 6.4% in real terms in the second quarter of 1997 over a year earlier, further up from the 6.1% increase in the first quarter....Amongst the major GDP components, private consumption expenditure rose strongly by 8.7% in real terms in the second quarter of 1997 over a year earlier....Government consumption expenditure had a 5.8% increase in real terms. On investment spending, gross domestic fixed capital formation recorded a large year-on-year increase of 16.2% in real terms in the second quarter of 1997."

Hong Kong. Census and Statistics Department. "Estimates of Gross Domestic Product for Second Quarter of 1997." Press Release 3 Nov 1997. document-level access: <http://www.info.gov.hk/censtatd/hkstat/press/gdp12q97.htm>

GROSS DOMESTIC PRODUCT--TAXATION--UNITED STATES (v26)

GROSS NATIONAL PRODUCT (v26)

GROSS NATIONAL PRODUCT--DEVELOPING COUNTRIES (v26)

GROUP HOMES--CALIFORNIA (v26)

GROUP MEDICAL PRACTICE, PREPAID

see HEALTH MAINTENANCE ORGANIZATIONS

GROUP PARENTS

see CHILD CARE WORKERS

GUATEMALA--ECONOMIC CONDITIONS--SOCIAL CONDITIONS (v26)

GUERRILLAS--COLOMBIA

The guerrilla movement in Colombia is led by the Colombian Armed Forces (FARC). "They number approximately 13,000 armed guerrillas and several hundred thousand civilian activists, overwhelmingly peasants. The other three guerrilla groups are much smaller and number about 4,000 armed fighters. Informed observers estimate that the guerrillas have a presence in half of the 1,000 municipalities in the country and are strongly established in the principal productive areas, including the coffee, banana and petroleum regions....The FARC and its allies in the ELN (National Liberation Army) organized in the Simon

Bolivar Guerrilla Coordinating Movement is in daily combat with the military in 15 of the 32 departments (provinces) of the country. Over the past six years the FARC has increased its number of military fronts from 10 to 105. The guerrillas, armed with automatic rifles, grenade launchers and rockets, are attacking military garrisons and airbases; so far, the government concedes that almost 500 soldiers have been killed or wounded....To counteract peasant organization, over 100 paramilitary groups with over 2,000 members have been formed and financed by the military and the landowners." (p32-33)

Petras, James. "Latin America: The Resurgence of the Left." New Left Review n223 May-Jun 1997. p17-47. (ISSN0028-6060).

GUIDANCE IN HIGHER EDUCATION

see COUNSELING IN HIGHER EDUCATION

GULF WAR, 1991

see PERSIAN GULF WAR, 1991

GUN CONTROL--LAW AND LEGISLATION

see FIREARMS--LAW AND LEGISLATION

GUN CONTROL--UNITED STATES (v26)

GUNS

see FIREARMS

GUNSHOT WOUNDS--UNITED STATES (v26)

GUNSHOT WOUNDS--UNITED STATES--COSTS

In the U.S., "the cost of firearm shootings, through violent attacks, accidents, or intentional self-infliction, is estimated at $19 billion nationwide for medical care, long-term disability, and premature death (New York Academy of Medicine, 1994). The average cost per firearm fatality is $373,000, and 40% of spinal injuries in inner-city areas are the result of gunshot injuries (Cotton, 1992). A study of one urban area hospital revealed that 86% of the costs of firearm injuries are paid by taxes (Cotton, 1992)." (p508)

Page, Randy M./Hammermeister, Jon. "Weapon-Carrying and Youth Violence." Adolescence v32 n127 Fall 1997. p505-513. (ISSN0001-8449).

According to the U.S. "Bureau of Alcohol, Tobacco and Firearms, nearly 2,000 M-1 garand rifles and M1911 pistols were traced to crime scenes in 1995 and 1996. In New York, 71 of these so-called curios and relics were linked to crimes committed during the past 2 years....According to a May 1997 Violence Policy Center study, firearm injuries cost society approximately $20.4 billion in 1990. Of that figure, at least $17.4 billion represents the value of lost productivity due to premature deaths. According to the Center to Prevent Handgun Violence, direct healthcare expenditures for firearm-related injuries in the United States in 1995 was $4 billion." (pH7471)

McCarthy, Carolyn (Rep.-N.Y.). "Treasury, Postal Service, And General Government Appropriations Act, 1998." Congressional Record. Daily ed. v143 n124 17 Sep 1997. pH7456-7480. section/page-level access: <http://thomas.loc.gov/cgi-bin/query/R?r105:FLD001:H07471:> (ISSN0363-7239). (X1.1A.105/1).

GYNECOLOGY--DIAGNOSIS--INDIA--KARNATAKA

In 1994, a study on gynecological morbidity was conducted in a district of the state of Karnataka, South India. The study found that "a total of 152 women reported 226 gynecological complaints to the social worker who interviewed them....Fewer than one-fourth (23 percent) of the women complained of excessive weakness....The major gynecological complaints mentioned were vaginal discharge with bad odor or itching or irritation (22 percent), lower abdominal pain or vaginal discharge with fever (16 percent), and menstrual bleeding disorders or painful menstruation or spotting (15 percent)." (p97) "About two-thirds of the women reported one or more menstrual problems. The problems reported included irregular periods (9 percent), long or short menstrual cycles (9 percent), long or short periods (20 percent), profuse discharge (15 percent), and passing of clots (8 percent). More than one-half of the women reported painful menstruation (dysmenorrhea)." (p98) "By clinical criteria, 36 percent of the women studied were diagnosed as having...[reproductive tract infections]. The laboratory tests revealed evidence of reproductive tract infections in 56 percent of cases....Approximately one-fourth of the women had clinical evidence of PID [pelvic inflammatory disease], cervical ectopy, and fistula....Evidence of STD infections was found in 10 percent of the women studied...." (p102)

Bhatia, Jagdish C./Cleland, John/Bhagavan, Leela/Rao, N. S. N. "Levels and Determinants of Gynecological Morbidity in a District of South India." Studies in Family Planning v28 n2 Jun 1997. p95-103. (ISSN0039-3665).

GYPSIES--EUROPE--SOCIAL CONDITIONS

In the Czech Republic, "up to 5,000 Gypsies plan to emigrate to Canada....The Gypsies are believed to have arrived in Europe from India and the Middle East some 700 years ago....Gypsy advocate groups estimate that between 150,000 to 300,000 Gypsies live in the Czech Republic, and more than 20 million live throughout Europe....While the overall unemployment rate in the Czech Republic is 3 percent, it is conservatively estimated at 30 percent for Gypsies. In Slovakia, Gypsies are 30 times more likely to drop out of high school." (p7)

Drew, Kevin. "International: Czechs Feel New Pressure over Their 'Mistreatment' of Gypsies." The Christian Science Monitor v89 n184 18 Aug 1997. p7. The Christian Science Monitor search engine: <http://www.csmonitor.com/plweb-cgi/iops1.pl> To retrieve this article, enter the following search: ED=19970818 AND gypsies. In the "retrieved list," click the title that matches this record. (ISSN0882-7729).

HABITAT CONSERVATION--UNITED STATES

"Between 1982 and 1992, the U.S. Fish and Wildlife Service approved just 14 HCPs [Habitat Conservation Plans] throughout the country....Today, nearly 19 million acres are 'protected' under HCPs for the benefit of hundreds of species, both listed and unlisted." (p10)

Larmer, Paul. "Vanishing Habitat: Habitat Conservation Plans: Who Wins and Who Loses when Uncle Sam Cuts Deals with...Species?" High Country News v29 n14 4 Aug 1997. p10-11. (ISSN0191-5657).

In the U.S., though Habitat Conservation Plans "were authorized by law in 1982, only 14 of them existed before 1993. Now there are 211 in full effect and another 200 in the works." (p10)

Margolis, Jon. "Critics Say 'No Surprises' Means No Protection." High Country News v29 n14 4 Aug 1997. p10-13. (ISSN0191-5657).

HABITAT FOR HUMANITY

"Habitat for Humanity has built homes in 1,366 cities in all 50 states, and 53 other countries....Michigan has more affiliates than any other state, with chapters in 80 cities and six more prospects pending." (p1 secA)

Oppat, Susan L. "Rally Caps Home Blitz." Ypsilanti Press 29 Jun 1997. p1,11 secA.

HAIR

see also BALDNESS

HAIR--CARE AND HYGIENE--MICHIGAN

In Michigan, in response to a DETROIT NEWS survey regarding hair care, many respondents "said they spend 10 minutes or less shampooing, conditioning, drying and styling (37.5 percent), and another 37.5 percent said they spend between 10 and 20 minutes on their hair each day. Twelve and a half percent said it takes them 20 to 30 minutes to get their hair looking just right. And another 12.5 percent said they spend more than 30 minutes on their mane...." (p1 secE)

Pipp, Tracy L. "Accent: Survey of the Week: Simplicity Comes Out Ahead When Readers Take Care of Their Hair." Detroit News 6 Aug 1997. p1 secE.

HAIRCUTTING--GREAT BRITAIN

"We have approximately 110,000 hairdressers in...[Great Britain], but just 13,000 of them are registered. The industry has a turnover of 2.5 billion [pounds sterling] a year, but it is largely unregulated." (c629) "The Hairdressing Council receives more than 3,000 complaints a year, but it cannot act if the hairdressers are not registered." (c630)

Mitchell, Austin (H.C.-Great Grimsby). "Hairdressers Registration (Amendment)." Great Britain. Parliament. House of Commons. Debates. 7 Jul 1997. c629-630. section-level access: <http://www.parliament.the-stationery-office.co.uk/pa/cm199798/cmhansrd/cm970707/debtext/70707-10.htm#70707-10_spnew6>

HAITI--ECONOMIC CONDITIONS (v26)

HAITI--SOCIAL CONDITIONS (v26)

HALOGEN INCANDESCENT LAMPS--UNITED STATES (v26)

HAND WASHING--UNITED STATES (v26)

HANDICAPPED

see also NURSING HOMES--UNITED STATES--HANDICAPPED; SOCIAL SECURITY--UNITED STATES--HANDICAPPED CHILDREN

HANDICAPPED--EDUCATION--UNITED STATES

In the U.S., "rehabilitation programs are focusing most of their energies on training and placing [handicapped] people in private-sector jobs....Between 1991 and 1995, 2.6 million disabled individuals were eligible for involvement in one of these federally funded programs, according to an analysis by the U.S. General Accounting Office (GAO). The median age of participants is 34. Three-fourths (73 percent) of participants in state vocational rehabilitation programs are severely disabled; 60 percent are male. Nearly half (43 percent) do not have a high school degree, while 17 percent have completed one or more years of college. Nearly one-third of participants dropped out of their programs before obtaining employment, 31 percent were still receiving services at the time of the GAO analysis, and 37 percent were considered rehabilitated....One in ten obtained unpaid employment or became a homemaker. The average starting salary for a program graduate is $10,000, according to the GAO." (p40)

Mergenhagen, Paula. "From Sheltered Workshops to Competitive Employment." American Demographics v19 n7 Jul 1997. p40. article-level access: <http://www.demographics.com/publications/ad/97_ad/9707_ad/ad970711.htm> (ISSN0163-4089).

In the U.S., the Individuals With Disabilities Education Act "serves 5.4 million children with disabilities from birth through age 21. Every State in the Nation offers public education and early intervention services to children with disabilities. Fewer than 6,000 children with disabilities are living in institutional settings away from their families today, compared to 95,000 children in 1969. This transformation represents a major accomplishment in keeping families together, and it also reflects a significant reduction in the cost to the Government and taxpayers of paying for institutional care, which averages $50,000 a year for each child....The number of students with disabilities completing high school with a diploma or certificate increased from 55 percent in 1984 to 64 percent in 1992. Some 44 percent of all people with disabilities have some college education today, compared to only 29 percent in 1986. This dramatic increase demonstrates the success of the equal access provisions of IDEA; 47 percent of people without disabilities have some college education, so the gap has almost closed. For young people with disabilities, as for so many others, education leads to economic success; 57 percent of people with disabilities are competitively employed within 5 years of leaving school today, compared to an employment rate of only 33 percent for older people with disabilities who have not benefited from IDEA." (pS4318)

Kennedy, Edward M. (Sen.-Mass.). "Individuals with Disabilities Education Act Amendments of 1997." Congressional Record. Daily ed. v143 n61 12 May 1997. pS4311-4319. section/page-level access: <http://thomas.loc.gov/cgi-bin/query/R?r105:FLD001:S04319:> (ISSN0363-7239). (X1.1A.105/1).

HANDICAPPED--EMPLOYMENT--UNITED STATES (v26)

"Currently half of the 29 million disabled Americans aged 21 to 64 are working. The participation rate is lower, at one-fourth, for those who are severely disabled. Altogether, the disabled account for 14 percent of the employed population." (p37)

Mergenhagen, Paula. "Enabling Disabled Workers." American Demographics v19 n7 Jul 1997. p36-42. article-level access: <http://www.demographics.com/publications/ad/97_ad/9707_ad/ad970710.htm> (ISSN0163-4089).

"In 1994, more than 29 million Americans aged 21 to 64 had a physical disability, meaning that they reported a substantial impairment in a major life activity (seeing, hearing, speaking, walking, climbing stairs, and lifting and carrying), according to the Census Bureau's Survey of Income and Program Participation (SIPP). Nearly half of these people were severely disabled....52 percent of all disabled people aged 21 to 64 had a job in 1994, the same proportion as in 1991. The share of severely disabled people with a job increased from 23 percent to 26 percent over the time period. These shares are much lower than for the nondisabled population aged 21 to 64, 82 percent of whom were working in 1994....One in five mildly disabled and one in four severely disabled workers are aged 55 and older, compared with one in ten nondisabled employees, according to the 1991-92 SIPP. Almost half of nondisabled workers are under age 35, compared with 30 percent of mildly disabled and 28 percent of severely disabled workers." (p38)

Mergenhagen, Paula. "Enabling Disabled Workers." American Demographics v19 n7 Jul 1997. p36-42. article-level access: <http://www.demographics.com/publications/ad/97_ad/9707_ad/ad970710.htm> (ISSN0163-4089).

"Twelve percent of Americans aged 25 to 64 have some type of disability, and 64 percent of that group have one serious enough to require assistance with daily activities like walking, bathing, shopping, or using the telephone, according to the Census Bureau's March 1996 Current Population Survey....Almost three in ten 25-to-64-year-olds with a disability are working, 18 percent of them full time....Thirteen percent of disabled Americans aged 25 to 64 with less than 12 years of education are employed. The rate almost quadruples (46 percent) for their counterparts with 16 or more years of schooling." (p31)

Klein, Matthew. "Kaleidoscope: Disabled and Working." American Demographics v19 n5 May 1997. p31. article-level access: <http://www.demographics.com/Publications/AD/97_ad/9705_ad/AD970518.htm> (ISSN0163-4089).

In the U.S., "between 1986 and 1995, the percentage of companies that have hired people with disabilities edged up from 62 percent to 64 percent, according to surveys by Louis Harris and Associates, Inc. for the National Organization on Disability. The trend did not hold for businesses of all sizes, however. The share rose from 63 percent to 71 percent for medium-sized companies and from 69 percent to 74 percent for large companies. But in small companies, it fell from 54 percent to 48 percent." (p39)

Mergenhagen, Paula. "Enabling Disabled Workers." American

Demographics v19 n7 Jul 1997. p36-42. article-level access: <http://www.demographics.com/publications/ad/97_ad/9707_ad/ad970710.htm> (ISSN0163-4089).

In the U.S., "the median age of the disabled population aged 18 to 64 is 42, compared with 36 for the general population, finds an analysis of 1990 SIPP [Survey of Income and Program Participation] data by Michele Adler of the Department of Health and Human Services....Only 18 percent of individuals with mental retardation/developmental disabilities were working in 1990, as were 23 percent of the mentally ill. About one-third of those with cancer, spinal-cord injuries, heart and respiratory diseases, and arthritis had jobs. Almost half of those with bad backs and visual impairments were employed, as were nearly two-thirds of those with hearing impairments....The average monthly earnings of severely disabled workers in 1991-92 were $1,400, compared with $1,800 for the mildly disabled and $2,000 for the nondisabled....While only 15 percent of nondisabled workers have less than 12 years of schooling, 21 percent of mildly disabled and 29 percent of severely disabled workers did not complete high school. Forty-eight percent of nondisabled workers have at least some college, but this is true for just 40 percent of the mildly disabled and 34 percent of the severely disabled." (p38-39)

Mergenhagen, Paula. "Enabling Disabled Workers." American Demographics v19 n7 Jul 1997. p36-42. article-level access: <http://www.demographics.com/publications/ad/97_ad/9707_ad/ad970710.htm> (ISSN0163-4089).

In the U.S., "of the 113.8 million employed people who were 21 to 64 years old at the time of the [1991-1992 Census Bureau] survey, 11.7 million had a 'non-severe' disability and 3.7 million had a severe disability. The employment rate for those 21 to 64 years old was 82.1 percent for those with no disability, 76.9 percent for those with non-severe disabilities and 26.1 percent for those with severe disabilities." (p5 secF)

Novoselick, Paul. "Connection: Dealing with Disability: One in 10 Americans Say They Have a Severe Disability, Census Reports." Ann Arbor News 19 Oct 1997. p5 secF.

In the U.S., "from 1988 through 1992 vocational rehabilitation has placed 5,000 people with disabilities in self-employment, which represents only 2.7 percent of those placements, and while 5,000 is a large number, the 1990 census stated that over 12 percent of working age people with disabilities are self-employed." (pH2803)

Hill, Rick (Rep.-Mont.). "Employment, Training, And Literacy Enhancement Act of 1997." Congressional Record. Daily ed. v143 n65 16 May 1997. pH2797-2851. section/page-level access: <http://thomas.loc.gov/cgi-bin/query/R?r105:FLD001:H02803:> (ISSN0363-7239). (X1.1A.105/1).

According to the U.S. Social Security Administration, of the entire New Beneficiary Survey "population of 137,144 persons, almost one-fourth (22.2 percent) report working in some job since they were entitled to DI [Disability Insurance] benefits in 1981. Females (21.0 percent) are just as likely to have been employed as are males (22.8 percent), and a similar proportion of whites and blacks (22.0 percent and 20.6 percent, respectively) reported working at a job sometime in the 10-year NBS-NBF [New Beneficiary Followup] period." (p4) "Slightly more than one-fourth of both males and females worked for sometime within 1 to 3 of the reporting years, or in all 9 years of the period." (p5)

Schechter, Evan S. "Work While Receiving Disability Insurance Benefits: Additional Findings from the New Beneficiary Followup Survey." Social Security Bulletin v60 n1 1997. p3-17. (ISSN0037-7910).

HANDICAPPED--EMPLOYMENT--UNITED STATES --ATTITUDES

"Peter Blanck, a University of Iowa professor of law, has been tracking a group of mentally disabled workers and their employers for a number of years. In a 1990 study, he reports that virtually all (96 percent) of the employers surveyed were very satisfied with the work attendance of the mentally disabled employees, and six in ten were very satisfied with their productivity and initiative. Two-thirds of employers in the study were also very satisfied with the interactions of mentally disabled workers with coworkers, but nearly as many (60 percent) expressed one common fear of employers; they were less than very satisfied with the customer-related interactions of these employees." (p39)

Mergenhagen, Paula. "Enabling Disabled Workers." American Demographics v19 n7 Jul 1997. p36-42. article-level access: <http://www.demographics.com/publications/ad/97_ad/9707_ad/ad970710.htm> (ISSN0163-4089).

HANDICAPPED--INSTITUTIONAL CARE--UNITED STATES--COSTS

In 1974, the year before the enactment of the Individuals With Disabilities Education Act, "there were 70,655 children and youth with disabilities living in...[U.S.] institutions. By 1994, 20 years later, as a result of IDEA, the number had fallen to 4,001, less than 6 percent of what it was 20 years earlier. In 1994, the average State institution cost was $82,256 per person in an institution, with 66,654 fewer children institutionalized than in 1974. Because the States were footing the bill, the savings to the States is $5.46 billion per year that the States do not have to come up with for institutionalized care." (pS4309)

Harkin, Tom (Sen.-Iowa). "Individuals with Disabilities Education Act Amendments of 1997." Congressional Record. Daily ed. v143 n61 12 May 1997. pS4295-4311. section/page-level access: <http://thomas.loc.gov/cgi-bin/query/R?r105:FLD001:S04309:> (ISSN0363-7239). (X1.1A.105/1).

HANDICAPPED--UNITED STATES (v26)

The "Americans with Disabilities 1994-95" federal "report said that about 54 million Americans--about one in five--reported some level of disability, and 26 million Americans--that's one in 10--described their disability as severe. The statistics showed an increase from Census Bureau figures taken in 1991-92. At that time, the bureau found 49 million Americans with disabilities and 24 million with severe disabilities....[According to the U.S. Census Bureau,] among Americans 80 years old and older, 71.5 percent had a disability and 53.5 percent had a severe disability." (p5 secF)

Novoselick, Paul. "Connection: Dealing with Disability: One in 10 Americans Say They Have a Severe Disability, Census Reports." Ann Arbor News 19 Oct 1997. p5 secF.

"Between October 1994 and January 1995, approximately 54 million Americans (1 in 5) reported some level of disability and 26 million (1 in 10) described their disability as severe, according to a new report released...by the Commerce Department's Census Bureau. Data collected three years earlier (1991-92) showed nearly 49 million people with a disability, 24 million of whom said their disability was severe....Among the 202.4 million people age 15 years and older, 33.2 million had at least some difficulty with one or more functional activities. Eight million people age 15 years and older had difficulty with one or more activities of daily living. Twelve million people age 15 years and older had difficulty doing one or more of the following activities: going outside the home alone to shop or visit a doctor, doing light housework, preparing meals, keeping track of money and bills and using a telephone."

U.S. Dept. of Commerce. Economic and Statistics Administration. "One in 10 Americans Reported a Severe Disability in 1994-95, Census Bureau Reports." Census Bureau

Press Release 16 Sep 1997. document-level access: <http://www.census.gov/Press-Release/cb97-148.html>

According to a report by the U.S. Census Bureau, "of the 113.8 million employed people age 21 to 64 years old, 11.7 million had a non-severe disability and 3.7 million had a severe disability. The employment rate for persons 21 to 64 years of age was 82.1 percent for those with no disability, 76.9 percent for those with a non-severe disability and 26.1 for those with a severe disability. Of the 9.3 million people providing assistance to those with a severe disability, 2.6 million were spouses, 1.7 million were daughters, 1.2 million were sons and 800,000 were parents. Among persons 80 years old and over, 71.5 percent had a disability and 53.5 percent had a severe disability. Despite the high rate of disability in this age group, only 34.1 percent required personal assistance."

U.S. Dept. of Commerce. Economic and Statistics Administration. "One in 10 Americans Reported a Severe Disability in 1994-95, Census Bureau Reports." Census Bureau Press Release 16 Sep 1997. document-level access: <http://www.census.gov/Press-Release/cb97-148.html>

HANDICAPPED AGED--UNITED STATES (v26)

"Researchers at Duke University estimate that 1.2 million fewer people [in the U.S.] age 65 and older were disabled in 1994 than would have been expected if the age-specific chronic disability rates observed in 1982 had persisted. The number of older people with functional problems stood at 7.1 million in 1994--not the 8.3 million who would have been disabled if health had not improved since 1982. This is a 63-percent reduction in the increase in the number of chronically disabled people that had been projected from the 1982 rates; while an increase of 1.9 million had been expected, an increase of only 700,000 was actually observed....Based on the 1982 rates, 24.9 percent of older people were expected to be chronically disabled in 1994; instead, the observed proportion was only 21.3 percent. This reduction of 3.6 percentage points--or 1.2 million fewer disabled older persons--represents a relative decline of some 14.5 percent in the rates." (p3)

"Chronic Disability Declines Dramatically among U.S. Elderly." Population Today v25 n9 Sep 1997. p3. (ISSN0749-2448).

HANDICAPPED CHILDREN--UNITED STATES (v26)

HANDICAPPED STUDENTS--UNITED STATES (v26)

HANSEN'S DISEASE

see LEPROSY

HARASSMENT OF WOMEN, SEXUAL

see SEXUAL HARASSMENT OF WOMEN

HARLEM (N.Y.)--SOCIAL CONDITIONS (v26)

HARVARD UNIVERSITY

see LAW STUDENTS--HARVARD UNIVERSITY

HATE CRIMES--MICHIGAN (v26)

HATE CRIMES--MICHIGAN--DETROIT--GAYS

"Anti-gay violence is increasing in Metro Detroit and other major cities that have concentrations of gays and lesbians, according to a report by the Triangle Foundation, a gay rights group in Detroit. Sixty-nine people were killed or hurt in 127 anti-gay incidents in Metro Detroit last year, the foundation reports. Firearms were used most often, followed by knives, then bats, clubs, lead pipes or other objects....The foundation estimates that only 26 percent of all hate crimes in Metro Detroit are reported to police." (p1 secC)

Lynch, Kevin. "Metro: Gay Man Battles Bashing." Detroit News 13 Oct 1997. p1-2 secC.

HATE CRIMES--UNITED STATES

According to U.S. "Justice Department statistics, 8,759 hate crimes were reported in 1996, compared with 7,947 reported in the previous year. Race was a factor in 63 percent of all reported hate crimes, followed by religion (13.9 percent), sexual orientation (12 percent), and ethnic origin (11 percent)." (p10 secA)

"In Our Opinion: Hate Crimes: A Troubling Trend Demands Tougher Federal Laws." Detroit Free Press 14 Nov 1997. p10 secA.

In the U.S., "the FBI counted 9,759 [hate crimes] last year, well behind the 1.6 million violent crimes reported nationwide....Of those reported last year, race was a factor in 63 percent, followed by religion (13.9 percent), sexual orientation (12 percent), and ethnic origin (11 percent), according to the Justice Department." (p12)

Chaddock, Gail Russell. "Taking Steps to Curb Hate Crimes." The Christian Science Monitor v90 n1 25 Nov 1997. p12. The Christian Science Monitor search engine: <http://www.csmonitor.com/plweb-cgi/iops1.pl> To retrieve this article, enter the following search: ED=19971125 AND crimes. In the "retrieved list," click the title that matches this record. (ISSN0882-7729).

HATE CRIMES--UNITED STATES--JEWS (v26)

HAWAII--ECONOMIC CONDITIONS

"Since 1991, Hawaii has grown less than any other state in the country, and last year income here rose only 1.7 percent....Bankruptcies have skyrocketed from fewer than 1,000 per year in the '80s to 3,083 in 1996--the fastest rate of increase in the US. Home foreclosures are also at record levels. 'Before, I saw people with $15,000 or $20,000 in debts on a credit card. Now they are coming in with $50,000 and $60,000 in debt--and a lot of them are homeowners," says Dawn Smith, a bankruptcy attorney...." (p3)

Salkever, Alex. "United States: An Ill Wind Whips Economy in America's Paradise Islands." The Christian Science Monitor v89 n231 24 Oct 1997. p3. The Christian Science Monitor search engine: <http://www.csmonitor.com/plweb-cgi/iops1.pl> To retrieve this article, enter the following search: ED=19971024 AND islands. In the "retrieved list," click the title that matches this record. (ISSN0882-7729).

Hawaii's "economy has been stagnant for the past six years. Its unemployment rate has risen from 2.6 percent in 1991 to 6.1 percent, fifth worst in the nation. For three straight years, Hawaii has led the nation in an annual cost-of-doing-business survey by Regional Financial Associates, and last year it ranked fourth highest in the rate of business failures. Even the $11.6 billion tourism industry has suffered, with more than half of the state's 770 hotels currently operating in the red....Last year, the Aloha State (pop. 1.2 million) saw a net loss of about 13,000 residents." (p46)

Ito, Timothy M. "Business & Technology: Down and Out in Waikiki." U.S. News & World Report v123 n14 13 Oct 1997. p46-47. article-level access: <http://www.usnews.com/usnews/issue/971013/13HAWI.HTM> (ISSN0041-5537).

HAY FEVER--UNITED STATES

"One to two out of every 10 Americans suffer from allergic rhinitis, making it the most common allergy problem in the country....The condition consistently ranks among the top 10 reasons for physician visits in the United States. It is the third most common reason why patients ages 25 to 44 visit a physician, after pregnancy and physicals. And it is the eighth most common reason for return physician visits." (p6)

Philpot, Edward. "Allergy: Allergic Rhinitis: What Are the Costs?" Healthline v16 n11 Nov 1997. p6-7. (ISSN0736-7929).

HAY FEVER--UNITED STATES--COSTS

"According to a 1993 study, physician visits for allergic rhinitis alone add up to $1.13 billion per year [in the U.S.], not counting costs for allergy shots or other treatments. The estimated total direct cost of allergic rhinitis is $3.4 billion per year, according to the same study. In arriving at this number, the authors considered the results of several earlier studies. Notably, a 1990 study estimated the direct annual cost (including prescription medications, diagnostic laboratory tests, and physician visits) at $1.16 billion. Based on average annual growth in medication and physician-related expenditures, the direct annual cost of allergic rhinitis was estimated to be $1.41 billion in 1993 dollars....In the 1993 study, 45 percent of allergy sufferers who used medications purchased prescription medications, for an approximate cost of $907 million per year, or $56 per patient. The remaining patients used nonprescription medications, at an estimated cost of $1.39 billion yearly. From these two studies, it could be estimated that direct costs of allergy medications alone easily ran from $1.41 to $3.4 billion in the United States in 1993...." (p6)

Philpot, Edward. "Allergy: Allergic Rhinitis: What Are the Costs?" Healthline v16 n11 Nov 1997. p6-7. (ISSN0736-7929).

HAY TRADE--UNITED STATES (v26)
HAZARDOUS WASTE SITES--MICHIGAN (v26)
HAZARDOUS WASTE SITES--UNITED STATES (v26)
HAZARDOUS WASTE SITES--UNITED STATES --MINORITIES (v26)
HAZARDOUS WASTES

see also CHEMICAL WEAPONS DISPOSAL; MEDICAL WASTES; POLLUTION

HAZARDOUS WASTES--AUSTRALIA (v26)
HAZARDOUS WASTES--EUROPE

According to the report "Recovery of WEEE: Economic and Environmental Impacts--Final Report," waste electrical and electronic equipment "accounts for less than 1% by weight of the total solid waste stream in the EU, although it makes up about 4% of municipal solid waste. WEEE is...expected to grow at an average of 3%-5% per year." (p16)

"Regulatory and Policy Trends: Commission to Develop EU Legislation on Electronics Waste." Business and the Environment v8 n8 Aug 1997. p15-16. (ISSN1052-7206).

HAZARDOUS WASTES--THAILAND (v26)
HAZARDOUS WASTES--UNITED STATES

"Sixty percent of both the total US black and Hispanic populations live in communities with one or more uncontrollable toxic waste sites; In Los Angeles, the higher the concentration of Hispanics in an area, the higher the concentration of uncontrolled waste sites in that area." (p34)

Schut, Michael. "The Great Economy/The Big Economy." Christian Social Action v10 n6 Jun 1997. p33-38. (ISSN0897-0459).

HEAD START PROGRAMS--MICHIGAN (v26)
HEAD START PROGRAMS--UNITED STATES (v26)
HEAD START PROGRAMS--UNITED STATES--FINANCE

In the U.S., "under the Clinton Administration, funding for Head Start has grown $1.8 billion, from $2.2 billion in FY 1992 to nearly $4 billion in FY 1997, an increase of more than 80 percent. These additional funds have enabled Head Start to serve 180,000 more children and their families, enhance the quality of Head Start services, launch a new initiative to serve infants and toddlers, and improve program research....President Clinton's FY 1998 budget plan includes $4.3 billion for the Head Start program, $324 million more than in 1997, to ensure that Head Start stays on track to reach this goal. The additional funds will allow Head Start to serve an additional 36,000 new children and their families, bringing total enrollment to an estimated 836,000."

U.S. Dept. of Health and Human Services. "HHS Invests in America's Children." Fact Sheet 23 Jul 1997. document-level access: <http://www.hhs.gov/news/press/1997pres/970917.html>

HEADACHE

see MIGRAINE

HEALING SYSTEMS

see ALTERNATIVE MEDICINE

HEALTH

see also DIET; EXERCISE

"Mental health problems constitute 8.1 percent of the total health burden, which is more than cancer (5.8 percent), heart diseases (4.4 percent), or cerebrovascular diseases (3.2 percent). For people aged 15 to 44, the health burden of mental disorders reaches 15.1 percent for women and 16.1 percent for men....As a group, behavior-related problems such as unintentional injury, violence, sexually transmitted diseases and AIDS, diarrheal diseases, and malnutrition constitute 34 per cent of the global health burden." (p1090)

Wig, Narendra N. "Book Reviews: World Mental Health: Problems and Priorities in Low-Income Countries." Psychiatric Services v48 n8 Aug 1997. p1089-1090. (ISSN1075-2730).

"THE WORLD HEALTH REPORT 1997 describes some of the hazards of living longer, as follows: Of more than 15 million deaths from circulatory diseases in 1996, 7.2 million were caused by coronary heart disease, 4.6 million by stroke, 500,000 by rheumatic fever and rheumatic heart disease, and 3 million by other forms of heart disease. An estimated 691 million people have high blood pressure....Tobacco causes 3 million deaths a year. Smoking accounts for one in seven cancer deaths....More than 50 million people suffer from different types of epilepsy, 29 million have dementia, and 45 million are affected by schizophrenia. Rheumatoid arthritis is estimated to affect 165 million people." (p37)

"Facts and Figures: Health Expectancy Is More Important than Life Expectancy." World Health n4 Jul-Aug 1997. p37. (ISSN0043-8502).

HEALTH BEHAVIOR--UNITED STATES (v26)
HEALTH BEHAVIOR IN CHILDREN--UNITED STATES (v26)
HEALTH CARE

see MEDICAL CARE

HEALTH CARE COSTS

see MEDICAL CARE, COST OF

HEALTH CARE PERSONNEL

see MEDICAL PERSONNEL

HEALTH CARE TECHNOLOGY

see MEDICAL TECHNOLOGY

HEALTH CLUBS

see PHYSICAL FITNESS CENTERS

HEALTH FACILITIES

see HOSPITALS

HEALTH FOODS INDUSTRY

see NATURAL FOODS INDUSTRY

HEALTH INSURANCE

see INSURANCE, HEALTH

HEALTH MAINTENANCE ORGANIZATIONS--MICHIGAN

The Health Maintenance Organization industry "provides health care for about 2.2 million Michiganders. In 1990, 15 percent of Michiganders were insured through HMOs. In 1995, 22 percent were enrolled....Michigan is in the process of transferring its Medicaid population to HMOs. This means southeast Michigan and Genesee County alone will have up to 475,000 new HMO enrollees in the next year." (p10 secF)

Mishra, Raja. "Body & Mind: Cover Story: Keeping HMOs in Balance." Detroit Free Press 10 Jun 1997. p8,10 secF.

Allan Baumgarten, a health care finance and policy analyst from Minneapolis, researched "21 of the 24 HMOs [health maintenance organizations] operating in Michigan last year. His study, the Michigan Managed Care Review, found that HMO profit margins were less than 1 percent, membership increased slightly and out-of-state competitors are becoming more aggressive. The forecast for 1997 is more of the same....The study also revealed that the medical loss ratios of the state's HMOs increased 2 percentage points to nearly 91 percent. That means the HMOs are spending a greater portion of their premium dollars on medical care, rather than on administrative costs....Baumgarten's study found the cost of an HMO premium in Michigan declined 2.3 percent last year, to $130 from $133 in 1995." (p1 secB)

Raphael, Steve. "Business: HMO Subscribers May Soon Pay More for Less Care." Detroit News 16 Jul 1997. p1 secB.

HEALTH MAINTENANCE ORGANIZATIONS--UNITED STATES--RURAL HOSPITALS (v26)

HEALTH OF WORKERS

see INDUSTRIAL HYGIENE

HEALTH TESTING, MULTIPHASIC

see MULTIPHASIC HEALTH TESTING

HEART--DISEASES

see also CONGESTIVE HEART FAILURE

HEART--DISEASES--AFRO-AMERICANS (v26)

HEART--DISEASES--TREATMENT--UNITED STATES (v26)

HEART--DISEASES--UNITED STATES (v26)

"About 20 million Americans of all ages live with the ramifications of heart disease. Of this group, nearly 13.7 million, including about 7 million under age 60, live with the effects of heart attack and about 5 million suffer from congestive heart failure, the leading cause of hospitalization for Americans age 65 and older. Heart defects are the most common birth defect, the major cause of birth defects-related infant deaths and a considerable cause of childhood disability. The prevalence of heart disease is rising rapidly, with a tremendous economic toll on the economy of the United States. For example, in 1994 there were 4.7 million cardiovascular operations and procedures, compared to 1.2 million in 1979--a fourfold increase. It is estimated that heart attack, stroke and other cardiovascular diseases will cost this nation $259 billion in medical expenses and lost output in 1997." (pS8696)

Christmas, Charles. "Departments of Labor, Health and Human Services, And Education...Appropriations Act, 1998." Congressional Record. Daily ed. v143 n114 3 Sep 1997. pS8693-8710. section/page-level access: <http://thomas.loc.gov/cgi-bin/query/R?r105:FLD001:S08696:> (ISSN0363-7239). (X1.1A.105/1).

"Cardiovasular disease continues to be the No. 1 cause of death in the United States and in Michigan. It also is a source of significant disability and economic loss, reaching into the billions of dollars in Michigan alone....An elevated blood cholesterol level (above 150) may be the single most important risk factor for heart disease....Statin drugs, designed to modify cholesterol and its components, are highly effective in combating heart disease. Depending on the drug and its dosage, cholesterol reductions average 22 to 42 percent, whereas the 'bad' cholesterol, called LDL, is typically decreased by 27 to 55 percent." (p3 secF)

Franklin, Barry. "Body & Mind: Good for You: Experts Discuss Paths to Fighting Heart Disease." Detroit Free Press 4 Nov 1997. p3 secF.

HEART--TRANSPLANTATION--MICHIGAN

"The average wait for a heart in Michigan is 200 days, although some people may get a heart in less than a week, and some may wait more than a year for a match. In 1994, 108 patients died while waiting for an organ transplant, according to the Transplantation Society of Michigan." (p1 secB) As of 22 October 1997, "3,886 people...[in the U.S.] were registered for heart transplants and waiting for donor hearts to become available, with 68 of them in Michigan, according to the United Network for Organ Sharing. In 1996, 2,342 were performed nationally, UNOS said." (p2 secB)

Van Dine, Lynn. "Discovery: Patients Take Heart." Detroit News 17 Nov 1997. p1-2 secB.

HEART--TRANSPLANTATION--UNITED STATES (v26)

HEART BYPASS SURGERY

see CORONARY ARTERY BYPASS

HEART FAILURE

see also CONGESTIVE HEART FAILURE; MYOCARDIAL INFARCTION

HEART FAILURE--UNITED STATES (v26)

"'Heart failure has been increasing in the United States in recent years, the only cardiovascular disorder to do so,' said NHLBI [National Heart, Lung, and Blood Institute] Director Dr. Claude Lenfant. 'There are now about 400,000 new cases annually.'...Heart failure affects about 4.8 million Americans--3.4 million age 60 or older. It causes about 875,000 hospitalizations a year and is the most common diagnosis for hospital admissions in those age 65 or older. Half of those with heart failure die within 5 years of diagnosis."

U.S. National Institutes of Health. "Hypertension Therapy Prevents Heart Failure among Elderly." News Release 15 Jul 1997. document-level access: <http://www.nih.gov/news/pr/jul97/nhlbi-15.htm>

HEART VALVES

see MITRAL VALVE

HEATING--GREAT BRITAIN (v26)

HEATING--GREAT BRITAIN--COSTS (v26)

HEATSTROKE--ARIZONA--GRAND CANYON

"In 1996, Grand Canyon rangers responded to more than 400 emergencies, 200 of them clearly heat related. Four visitors, including two children, died of heatstroke or dehydration. The number of heat-related incidents has increased about 10 percent each year for the past five years." (p61) "Last year 297 people died in America's national parks." (p62)

Danyliw, Norie Quintos/Loftus, Margaret. "U.S. News: News You Can Use: Travel: Stupid Park Tricks." U.S. News & World Report v122 n25 30 Jun 1997. p61-64. article-level access: <http://www.usnews.com/usnews/issue/970630/30PARK.HTM> (ISSN0041-5537).

HEBREW DAY SCHOOLS

see JEWISH DAY SCHOOLS

HELICOPTERS, MILITARY

see MILITARY HELICOPTERS

HELICOVERPA ARMIGERA--UNITED STATES

"Earworms cost U.S. growers more than $100 million annually. Increasing maysin concentrations in corn silks could reduce insecticide used on sweet corn by up to 85 percent. Commercial growers sometimes have to apply insecticides 30 times a season to keep earworms out of sweet corn. Adult earworms lay their eggs directly on the silk of growing corn, where the larvae hatch about 3 days later. The newly hatched larvae eat their way through the silk, then feed on kernels, before dropping to the soil to mature. After 12 days, new adults emerge from the soil and fly away in search of fresh food." (p18)

Cooke, Linda/U.S. Dept. of Agriculture. Agricultural Research Service. "Maysin: A Natural Insecticide from Corn Silk." Agricultural Research v45 n6 Jun 1997. p18. (ISSN0002-161X).

HELMINTHS (v26)

HEMOCHROMATOSIS--UNITED STATES (v26)

HEMOPHILIA--GREAT BRITAIN (v26)

HEPATITIS A--MICHIGAN (v26)

As of the second week of September 1997, "Detroit had 211

confirmed hepatitis A cases, up from 104 at the same time last year. Elsewhere in Wayne County, the confirmed cases almost doubled, with 65 reported through mid-September, compared to 49 reported for all of 1996. In Michigan, the number of confirmed hepatitis A cases through the third week of September was 943. Last year, there were 501 cases in the state. In 1995, there were 364." (p1,6 secB)

Wendland, Wendy. "Local News: Hepatitis Increase Puzzles Officials." Detroit Free Press 29 Sep 1997. p1,6 secB.

HEPATITIS A--UNITED STATES (v26)

HEPATITIS A--VACCINATION

"The old hepatitis A vaccine was immune globulin. It was 80 percent effective and had to be repeated every three months. The new one came out two years ago,...says [Dr. Jeffrey Band, director of the Beaumont Interhealth Service in Royal Oak, Michigan]. It's safe for adults and kids and is 95 percent effective for six to 12 months. If you get a second shot after six months, you are protected for life, he says." (p1 secH)

Volgenau, Gerry. "Travel: New Vaccines Fight Hepatitis, Typhoid." Detroit Free Press 7 Dec 1997. p1 secH.

HEPATITIS C

The Hepatitis C virus "has been identified as the most common cause of post-transfusion hepatitis worldwide, accounting for approximately 90% of this disease in Japan, USA and Western Europe....WHO has recently published the first global estimate of HCV prevalence, which suggests that up to 3% of the world's population has been infected with HCV. There may be more than 170 million chronic carriers at risk of developing liver cirrhosis and/or liver cancer." (p1) "It is estimated today that about 80% of acutely infected patients progress to chronic hepatitis, that about 20% of these chronic infections develop cirrhosis, and that 1% to 5% of cirrhotic individuals will develop hepatocellular carcinoma (cancer of the liver) during the next 10 years. Hepatitis C exacerbates the severity of underlying liver disease when it coexists with other hepatic conditions. About 40% to 60% of alcoholics with cirrhosis are infected with HCV, whereas only 5% to 20% of alcoholics without liver pathology have anti-HCV antibodies." (p2)

World Health Organization. "Hepatitis C." WHO Fact Sheet n164 Jun 1997. p1-3. document-level access: <http://www.who.ch/programmes/inf/facts/fact164.htm>

HEPATITIS C--UNITED STATES (v26)

The Hepatitis C virus "causes approximately 150,000 cases of acute viral hepatitis each year in the United States. Recovery from infection is rare and between 70 and 90 percent of infected persons become chronic carriers of the virus. According to the Centers for Disease Control and Prevention, chronic liver disease due to HCV causes between 8,000 and 10,000 deaths and leads to about 1,000 liver transplants each year in the United States."

U.S. National Institutes of Health. "Researchers Clone Infectious Hepatitis C Virus." News Release 24 Jul 1997. document-level access: <http://www.nih.gov/news/pr/jul97/niaid-24.htm>

HERBICIDES--UNITED STATES (v26)

HEROIN--UNITED STATES

In the U.S., "during 1995, the nationwide average purity for retail heroin from all sources was 39.7 percent, much higher than the average of 7 percent a decade ago, and considerably higher than the 26.6 percent recorded in 1991....The 1995 National Household Survey on Drug Abuse estimated that 1.4 million people have smoked heroin in their lifetime. This estimate was nearly double the 1994 estimate. Although the change was statistically significant only for the 35 and older age group, estimates for other age groups were also higher in 1995 than in 1994, including youths age 12-17." (p1387)

U.S. Dept. of Justice. "Departments of Commerce, Justice, And State, The Judiciary...Approp. for 1998 (Part 2)." Hearing. U.S. House. Committee on Appropriations. Washington, D.C. : GPO, 1997. (ISBN0160549094). (Y4.Ap6/1:C73/2/997/pt.2).

HEROIN HABIT--AUSTRALIA

In Australia, "statistics show that the number of deaths from heroin overdoses has increased by 700 percent in the past 20 years, with about 550 dying a year. At least 100,000 Australians use heroin." (p7)

Coatney, Caryn. "Aussies Nix Plan for Heroin Users." The Christian Science Monitor v89 n186 20 Aug 1997. p7. The Christian Science Monitor search engine: <http://www.csmonitor.com/plweb-cgi/iops1.pl> To retrieve this article, enter the following search: ED=19970820 AND users. In the "retrieved list," click the title that matches this record. (ISSN0882-7729).

HEROIN HABIT--UNITED STATES (v26)

HEROIN HABIT--WASHINGTON (STATE)--KING COUNTY (v26)

HEROIN INDUSTRY

"The output of illicit opium world-wide exceeded 4,000 metric tons in 1993. This was twice the 1986 output. The purity of heroin in the US has soared from 7 per cent in the mid 1980s to 39.7 per cent in 1994. Estimates of annual retail sales of heroin in the US range from $4 to $10 billion, and rough estimates put the number of heroin addicts in the US at 600,000. Myanmar produces over 2,300 metric tons of heroin a year, the world's largest producer....62 per cent of all heroin smuggled into the US now comes from Colombia. In 1989 the figure was 4 per cent." (p469) "There are approximately 323,000 heroin users in the US and 1.84 million lifetime heroin users." (p470)

Van de Velde, James R. "Issues of Law Intensity Conflict and Law Enforcement: The Growth of Criminal...Drug Trafficking." Low Intensity Conflict & Law Enforcement v5 n3 Win 1996. p466-483. (ISSN0966-2847).

HEROIN INDUSTRY--ASIA

"The southern Chinese province of Yunnan which shares a 1,000-km border with Myanmar is now a smuggling point for half of the heroin from the Golden Triangle. More than 14,000 drugs-related arrests were made in Yunnan in 1991. In 1990, 1.45 tons of heroin were seized in Yunnan China, more than five times the amount seized in 1989....Royal Hong Kong Police intelligence estimates report...the Chinese Triads' total heroin profits to be $2-4 billion per year." (p477) "In 1977 southeast Asian heroin accounted for 9 per cent of all US heroin; by 1991 it rose to 58 per cent. Today it is around 44 per cent with a purity of 34.4 per cent." (p478)

Van de Velde, James R. "Issues of Law Intensity Conflict and Law Enforcement: The Growth of Criminal...Drug Trafficking." Low Intensity Conflict & Law Enforcement v5 n3 Win 1996. p466-483. (ISSN0966-2847).

HEROIN INDUSTRY--COLOMBIA

"Street-level purity for Colombian heroin averages over 60 per cent while the overall average from all the producing regions is 40 per cent....Just ten years ago the average street purity was 7 per cent and in 1991 stood at 26 per cent. The 1994 National Narcotics Intelligence Consumers Committee (NNICC) report on pricing figures was published in August 1995; it showed that Colombian heroin retail prices per kilogram were $15,000 to $80,000 less than the most expensive southeast Asian product and that the maximum price of Colombian heroin was less than the maximum prices of either southwest Asian or Mexican heroin." (p370)

Chappell, J. L. "The Colombian Heroin Threat: Demand and Supply." Low Intensity Conflict & Law Enforcement v5 n3 Win

1996. p366-376. (ISSN0966-2847).

HEROIN INDUSTRY--MEXICO

Mexico is "a leading supplier of heroin for the US. The State Department estimated that total Mexican poppy cultivation in 1994 was 12,415 hectares, net cultivation was 5,795 hectares, and net production of opium gum was 60 metric tons. Approximately 17 per cent of the heroin available in the US market is of Mexican origin." (p474)

Van de Velde, James R. "Issues of Law Intensity Conflict and Law Enforcement: The Growth of Criminal...Drug Trafficking." Low Intensity Conflict & Law Enforcement v5 n3 Win 1996. p466-483. (ISSN0966-2847).

HERPES SIMPLEX VIRUS--UNITED STATES

In the U.S., "the incidence of herpes simplex virus type 2 (HSV-2) has risen substantially since the late 1970s, according to a study in the Oct. 15 edition of THE NEW ENGLAND JOURNAL OF MEDICINE. The researchers say that roughly one in five Americans aged 12 and older (about 45 million Americans) are seropositive....The largest [increases] were seen in white teen-agers, whose seroprevalence jumped from 0.96 to 4.5%, and in whites in their 20s, whose rates rose from 7.7 to 14.7%. The age-adjusted rate among all whites in NHANES III [the 1988 to 1994 National Health and Nutrition Examination Survey] was 16.5%." (p25)

"Clinical News: Study Says 45 Million Americans Carry the Herpes Simplex 2 Virus." Modern Medicine v65 n12 Dec 1997. p25. (ISSN0026-8070).

According to a study published "in the NEW ENGLAND JOURNAL OF MEDICINE, since the late 1970s, the proportion of Americans infected with the herpes simplex type 2 virus (HSV-2) has increased by almost one third. Today, 45 million people over the age of 12 carry it--about 1 in 5....One in five white women is infected, versus one in seven white men. One in two black women has the virus, compared with one in three black men....Studies have shown that 2 out of 3 people with the virus don't know they are infected and potentially contagious." (p78)

Carpenter, Betsy. "1997 Health Guide: The Other Epidemic." U.S. News & World Report v123 n18 10 Nov 1997. p78-80,82. article-level access: <http://www.usnews.com/usnews/issue/971110/10HERP.HTM> (ISSN0041-5537).

HIDES AND SKINS INDUSTRY--UNITED STATES

"The United States is the world's leading producer and exporter of cattle hides. U.S. exporters had 44 percent of the import market in East Asia, and 13 percent in Southeast Asia in 1995 (United Nations, 1997)....The U.S. shares in 1990 were 29 percent in East Asia and only 2 percent in Southeast Asia." (p24)

Vocke, Gary/U.S. Dept. of Agriculture. Economic Research Service. "Special Article: Emerging Import Markets in Asia." APEC: International Agriculture and Trade Reports Situation and Outlook Series Aug 1997. p13-25.

In 1996, U.S. exports of hides and skins to China, the Association of Southeast Asia Nations, "and Mexico increased $73.3 million to about $270 million, but exports to East Asia dropped $195 million to $1.1 billion. In fiscal 1996, 88 percent of total U.S. hides and skins exports went to the APEC [Asia-Pacific Economic Cooperation] region." (p9)

Huang, Sophia Wu/U.S. Dept. of Agriculture. Economic Research Service. "U.S. Agricultural Exports to APEC Region at Another Record." APEC: International Agriculture and Trade Reports Situation and Outlook Series Aug 1997. p9-12.

HIGH BLOOD PRESSURE

see HYPERTENSION

HIGH SCHOOL DROPOUTS--HISPANIC AMERICANS

In the U.S., "the dropout rate for Latino students has remained higher than rates experienced by their black and white peers since the early 1970s. Federal statistics show the percentage of young Latino adults without high school certification has fluctuated around one-third, and that Latinos often quit school at earlier ages than black or white dropouts....According to the education department, immigrants who come to the United States seeking employment without a high school education and never enroll in U.S. schools traditionally have been counted as dropouts. This inflates the Latino dropout rate. The Latino droupout rate of 30 percent in 1995 includes such young immigrants. The dropout rate for Latino immigrants ages 16-24 was 46 percent. The comparable rate for Latinos born in the United States was 18 percent." (p10 secA)

Lewis, Shawn D. "Hispanic Heritage Month: Power Presence Action: Education: Dropout Rates Remain High for U.S. Latinos." Detroit News 29 Sep 1997. p10 secA.

"Hispanics have the highest dropout rates of any racial and ethnic group [in the U.S.]. The 174,000 Hispanic youths who dropped out of school in 1995 constituted 29 percent of high school dropouts that year....The dropout rate for Hispanic 16- and 17-year-olds declined between 1980 and 1995, from 17 percent to 11 percent. The rate fell from 9 percent to 5 percent for white youths over the same period." (p34)

del Pinal, Jorge/Singer, Audrey. "Generations of Diversity: Latinos in the United States." Population Bulletin v52 n3 Oct 1997. p2-47. (ISSN0032-468X).

"The dropout rate for Hispanic students...[in the U.S.] is 30 percent--nearly three times the rate for whites and twice the rate for blacks....Forty-three percent of Hispanic dropouts are foreign born, and many of them don't get special language help....Most Hispanic dropouts were born here and speak English fluently. The greater problem--particularly among poor Hispanics, where the dropout rate is close to 41 percent--may be handicaps to learning in any language. One third of Hispanic children live in poverty...." (p64)

Headden, Susan. "Culture & Ideas: The Hispanic Dropout Mystery." U.S. News & World Report v123 n15 20 Oct 1997. p64-65. article-level access: <http://www.usnews.com/usnews/issue/971020/20HISP.HTM> (ISSN0041-5537).

HIGH SCHOOL DROPOUTS--MICHIGAN (v26)

HIGH SCHOOL DROPOUTS--MICHIGAN--DETROIT

The Michigan governor's annual report card showed that the high school dropout rate "climbed to 7.7 percent in 1995-96 from 5.2 percent in 1994-95....In the Metro Detroit area, the rate fell slightly in Macomb and Oakland [Counties] but rose dramatically in Wayne [County], driven largely by Detroit, where the state report shows the rate increasing to 24.8 percent from 13.8 percent. At the same time, the statewide graduation rate--the percentage of ninth-graders who complete their senior year--tumbled to 73.1 percent from 81.4 percent." (p1 secA) Figures show "an increase in the dropout rate in Wayne County to 20.7 percent in 1995-96 from 8.7 percent in 1994-95....In Macomb, the dropout rate dipped to 3 percent from 3.5 percent....In Oakland, the rate fell to 3 percent from 3.6 percent." (p12 secA)

Hornbeck, Mark/Naylor, Janet. "State's Dropout Rates Surge." Detroit News and Free Press 3 Aug 1997. p1,12 secA.

HIGH SCHOOL DROPOUTS--UNITED STATES

The U.S. Department of Education's "National Center for Education Statistics found that nearly one-third of Hispanics ages 16 to 24 were dropouts in 1995--a rate that has held steady for more than 20 years." (p10) "The dropout rate for black Americans ages 16 to 24 has fallen and is approaching the rate for whites, the center says in its yearly report on dropouts....Overall, 12 percent of young adults were not enrolled in high school and had not finished it in October 1995. That's nearly 4 million people out of 32.4 million. The rate

has eased down from nearly 15 percent in 1972." (p12)
"Before the Board: No Drop in Hispanic Dropout Rate." American School Board Journal v184 n10 Oct 1997. p10,12. (ISSN0003-0953).

In the U.S., "during the year beginning October 1994, 5 percent of all high school students in 10th, 11th and 12th grades dropped out of school. The dropout pool (persons not enrolled and not high school graduates) of young adults 18 to 24 years old totaled 3.5 million in October 1995--14 percent of this age group."
U.S. Dept. of Commerce. Economic and Statistics Administration. "Census Back to School Facts." Census Bureau Fact Sheet 18 Aug 1997. document-level access: <http://www.census.gov/Press-Release/fs97-08.html>

In the U.S., in the 1930s, "public school dropout rates were as high as 75 percent. (By the early '50s they had dropped to a still very high 43 percent.) Today the graduation rate, when you add in people who complete general equivalency diplomas or go to night school, hovers around 90 percent." (p23)
Lynn, Barry W. "Perspective: Fit and Fifty: AU's First Five Decades." Church & State v50 n10 Nov 1997. p23. (ISSN0009-6334).

HIGH SCHOOL GRADUATES--ASIAN AMERICANS (v26)

HIGH SCHOOL GRADUATES--CALIFORNIA (v26)

HIGH SCHOOL GRADUATES--HISPANIC AMERICANS

"About 70 percent of Latinos born in the United States had completed high school in 1996, compared with just 42 percent of those born abroad. In every national origin group, those born outside the United States were much less likely to have at least a high school education. The difference is greatest among Mexicans--67 percent of U.S.-born Mexicans had completed high school in 1996 compared with only 29 percent of those born outside the United States....Similarly, more than one-half (54 percent) of foreign-born Mexicans had less than a ninth-grade education compared with 16 percent of those born here. Cubans and Central and South Americans born in the United States have high school completion rates similar to whites, at 86 percent and 85 percent, respectively, while only about 60 percent of their foreign-born counterparts had completed high school." (p33)
del Pinal, Jorge/Singer, Audrey. "Generations of Diversity: Latinos in the United States." Population Bulletin v52 n3 Oct 1997. p2-47. (ISSN0032-468X).

HIGH SCHOOL GRADUATES--UNITED STATES

In the U.S., "eighty-seven percent of young adults age 25 to 29 had received high school diplomas in March 1996, according to tabulations released...on the Internet by the Commerce Department's Census Bureau....82 percent of all adults ages 25 and over have completed high school and 24 percent had completed a bachelor's degree or more. 82 percent of women 25 years and over had earned a high school diploma and 21 percent completed a bachelor's degree or more. Annual average earnings in 1995 for persons 18 years and over with a bachelor's degree as their highest degree were $36,980. 89 percent of the employed civilian labor force ages 25 and over had a high school degree or more."
U.S. Dept. of Commerce. Economic and Statistics Administration. "Nearly Nine in 10 Young Adults Graduate from High School, Census Bureau Reports." Census Bureau Press Release 29 Jul 1997. document-level access: <http://www.census.gov/Press-Release/cb97-122.html>

HIGH SCHOOL STUDENTS

see also AFRO-AMERICAN HIGH SCHOOL STUDENTS; ENTREPRENEURSHIP--AFRO-AMERICAN HIGH SCHOOL STUDENTS; FIREARMS--UNITED STATES--HIGH SCHOOL STUDENTS; JOURNALISTS--UNITED STATES--HIGH SCHOOL STUDENTS; VOLUNTARISM--UNITED STATES--HIGH SCHOOL STUDENTS

HIGH SCHOOL STUDENTS--EDUCATION--UNITED STATES

"Only 4 percent of high school graduates in Mississippi take the SAT [Scholastic Assessment Test], while in Connecticut, 79 percent of high school graduates take the college entrance exam....Connecticut's high school completion rate--the percentage of 18 to 24-year-olds who have completed high school--is 95 percent, compared to Mississippi's 84 percent....Nationwide, an average of 85.3 percent of people between 18 and 24 years old have completed high school. The percentage is highest in North Dakota (96.6 percent), Connecticut (94.7), and Nebraska (94.5). The lowest performing states are California (78.9), Texas (79.5), and Georgia (80.3)." (pA25)
"Education Vital Signs: State of the States." American School Board Journal v184 n12 Dec 1997. pA24-A25. (ISSN0003-0953).

HIGH SCHOOL STUDENTS--EDUCATION--UNITED STATES--ATTITUDES (v26)

HIGH SCHOOL STUDENTS--MICHIGAN--DETROIT (v26)

HIGH SCHOOL STUDENTS--UNITED STATES

In the U.S., "by 1995, about 15 million students were enrolled in high school, roughly 300,000 more than in 1994. Eight percent of high school students attended private schools, down from 10 percent in 1963. One-third (33 percent) of 15-to-17 year-olds were enrolled below the appropriate grade level for their age in October 1995, up from 23 percent in 1980. Of enrolled 16 year olds, 60 percent were in their junior year of high school but 27 percent were in their sophomore year and 5 percent were freshmen. On the other hand, 7 percent were above the appropriate grade level: they were seniors. (Fewer than 1 percent were in their first year of college.) The percentages for freshmen and seniors were not statistically different."
U.S. Dept. of Commerce. Economic and Statistics Administration. "Census Back to School Facts." Census Bureau Fact Sheet 18 Aug 1997. document-level access: <http://www.census.gov/Press-Release/fs97-08.html>

U.S. Secretary of Education Richard Riley "projected a 13 percent increase in high school students over the next decade (a jump of 1.7 million)....More students will...need more teachers--at least another 150,000 high school instructors over the same decade....The nation's bill to fix up old and inadequate school buildings is estimated at $112 billion, and 6,000 new schools are needed." (p20)
"The Monitor's View: Widen the School Doors." The Christian Science Monitor v89 n189 25 Aug 1997. p20. The Christian Science Monitor search engine: <http://www.csmonitor.com/plweb-cgi/iops1.pl> To retrieve this article, enter the following search: ED=19970825 AND doors. In the "retrieved list," click the title that matches this record. (ISSN0882-7729).

HIGH SCHOOL STUDENTS--UNITED STATES--ATTITUDES (v26)

HIGH SCHOOL STUDENTS--UNITED STATES--TOBACCO USE--ATTITUDES (v26)

HIGH SCHOOLS--UNITED STATES--CURRICULA

"Between 1980 and 1990, 42 states [in the U.S.] raised their high school graduation requirements along the lines of the recommendations of the [Excellence] Commission (ETS [Educational Testing Service] 1990), which mandated 4 years of English, 3 years of math, 3 years of science, 3 years of social studies, and a half year of computer science for all high school graduates, along with 2 years of foreign language for the college bound. Around the time of the Commission's work, just

13% of high school graduates met the New Basics targets. A decade later the figure was 47%, and the upgrading has been broad based: completion among whites went from 14% in 1982 to 49% in 1992; among blacks, from 11% to 44%; among youths with high school dropout parents, from 10% to 45%; and among youths with college graduate parents, from 20% to 49% (all figures from U.S. Dept. of Education 1994...)." (p11-12)

Alexander, Karl L. "Public Schools and the Public Good." Social Forces v76 n1 Sep 1997. p1-30. (ISSN0037-7732).

"In California, Florida, Missouri, and Pennsylvania...Clune and White (1992) document large increases in higher-level or advanced course taking [in high school], and much the same is reflected in national data: geometry, up from 48% completion in 1982 to 70% in 1992; trigonometry, up from 12% to 21%; calculus from 4% to 10%; chemistry from 32% to 56%; and, physics from 14% to 25% (U.S. Dept. of Education 1995...). Along the same lines, the College Board (1996) recently reported an increase in honors-level course work comparing 1996 SAT-takers [Scholastic Assessment Test] against their counterparts from 1987: in English, 38% in 1996 versus 28% in 1987; in math, 29% versus 22%; and, in the natural sciences, 29% versus 19%." (p12)

Alexander, Karl L. "Public Schools and the Public Good." Social Forces v76 n1 Sep 1997. p1-30. (ISSN0037-7732).

HIGH TECHNOLOGY--UNITED STATES

In the U.S., "the number of high tech jobs increased 6 percent from 1993 to 1995. In Oregon alone over 10,000 new jobs were created from 1990 to 1995; provide the greatest number of high-paying and high-skilled jobs to Americans. Nationally, high technology companies provide over 4 million jobs and provide an average wage of about $47,000, well above the national median. In Oregon high technology workers were paid an average of $46,319 in 1995, 84 percent more than the average wage of all private sector workers in the State; and contribute to improving the balance of trade in relation to our major competitors. Nationally, U.S. exports exceeded $140 billion--about one-fourth of all U.S. exports, in 1995. In Oregon, high technology companies account for 46 percent of all State exports, for a total of $4.3 billion in sales." (pH7907)

Blumenauer, Earl (Rep.-Oreg.). "Departments of Commerce, Justice, And State, The Judiciary...Appropriations Act, 1998." Congressional Record. Daily ed. v143 n130 25 Sep 1997. pH7890-7907. section/page-level access: <http://thomas.loc.gov/cgi-bin/query/R?r105:FLD001:H07907:> (ISSN0363-7239). (X1.1A.105/1).

HIGH TECHNOLOGY INDUSTRIES

see also BIOTECHNOLOGY INDUSTRIES

HIGH TECHNOLOGY INDUSTRIES--CALIFORNIA --SILICON VALLEY--MINORITIES

In Silicon Valley, California, within "the high tech work force, Asian immigrants make up 30 percent of skilled production workers, 47 percent of semi-skilled workers and 41 percent of unskilled workers....Latinos constitute 18 percent of skilled workers, 21 percent of semiskilled workers and 36 percent of unskilled workers. African-Americans constitute less than 7.5 percent of the electronics work force in any category." (p19)

Bacon, David. "Toxic Technology." In These Times v21 n25-26 23 Nov 1997. p18-20. (ISSN0160-5992).

HIGH TECHNOLOGY INDUSTRIES--MONTANA (v26)

HIGHER EDUCATION

see EDUCATION, HIGHER

HIGHER EDUCATION COUNSELING

see COUNSELING IN HIGHER EDUCATION

HIGHWAY ACCIDENTS

see TRAFFIC ACCIDENTS

HIGHWAY BRIDGES

see BRIDGES

HIGHWAY BUSINESS DISTRICTS

see COMMERCIAL STRIPS

HIGHWAYS

see ROADS

HILLBILLY MUSIC

see COUNTRY MUSIC

HISPANIC AMERICAN BUSINESS ENTERPRISES

"The number of Hispanic-owned businesses in the United States increased 76 percent between 1987 and 1992, from 489,973 to 862,605. This compared to a rate increase of 26 percent for all U.S. firms, from 13.7 million in 1987 to 17.3 million in 1992. Receipts for Hispanic-owned firms increased 134 percent during the five-year span, from $32.8 billion to $76.8 billion. In comparison, receipts for all U.S. firms grew by 67 percent, from $2 trillion to $3.3 trillion. About two-thirds (68 percent) of firms owned by Hispanics in 1992 were located in either California, Texas or Florida. New Mexico, however, had the highest concentration of such firms, with 20 percent of its businesses Hispanic-owned."

U.S. Dept. of Commerce. Economic and Statistics Administration. "Census Facts for Hispanic Heritage Month." Census Bureau Fact Sheet 11 Sep 1997. document-level access: <http://www.census.gov/Press-Release/fs97-10.html>

HISPANIC AMERICAN FAMILIES

In the U.S., "as of March 1995, 54 percent of Hispanic men and 57 percent of women aged 15 and over were married. Nearly two-thirds (63 percent) of Hispanic children under 18 years old lived with both parents while 28 percent lived with their mother only, 4 percent with their father only and 4 percent with neither parent. In 1996, married couples made up 68 percent of Hispanic families; another 26 percent were made up of a woman with no husband present. The typical Hispanic family consisted of 3.95 people compared with an average of 3.2 people in all families. About two-thirds of Hispanic families (64 percent or 4 million) included children. Families with children had an average of 2.2 children and more than a quarter (29 percent) of these families had three or more children."

U.S. Dept. of Commerce. Economic and Statistics Administration. "Census Facts for Hispanic Heritage Month." Census Bureau Fact Sheet 11 Sep 1997. document-level access: <http://www.census.gov/Press-Release/fs97-10.html>

HISPANIC AMERICAN POLITICIANS

"The number of Latinos holding public office throughout the United States stood at 5,459 in 1994, slightly more than 1 percent of all elected officials. Since 1984, however, the number has increased 48 percent. In 1994, about 84 percent of all Latino elected officials were in four states: Texas, Illinois, California, and New Mexico. Arizona, Colorado, New York, Florida, Illinois, and New Jersey also elected notable numbers of Hispanics. Women claimed about 40 percent of the offices held by Hispanics, while women hold 24 percent of all elected offices." (p43)

del Pinal, Jorge/Singer, Audrey. "Generations of Diversity: Latinos in the United States." Population Bulletin v52 n3 Oct 1997. p2-47. (ISSN0032-468X).

HISPANIC AMERICAN WOMEN (v26)

HISPANIC AMERICAN WOMEN--MEDICAL CARE (v26)

HISPANIC AMERICANS (v26)

see also AIDS (DISEASE)--AFRO-AMERICANS--HISPANIC AMERICANS; CATHOLICS--HISPANIC AMERICANS; CHILDBIRTH--CALIFORNIA--HISPANIC AMERICANS; CITIES AND TOWNS--HISPANIC AMERICANS; COLLEGE APPLICATIONS--UNIVERSITY OF TEXAS--AFRO-AMERICANS--HISPANIC AMERICANS; CONSUMER BEHAVIOR--HISPANIC AMERICANS; EDUCATION, HIGHER--HISPANIC AMERICANS; ETHNOLOGY--HISPANIC AMERICANS; FERTILITY, HUMAN--

HISPANIC AMERICAS; HIGH SCHOOL DROPOUTS--HISPANIC AMERICANS; HIGH SCHOOL GRADUATES--HISPANIC AMERICANS; HOME OWNERSHIP--HISPANIC AMERICANS; HOUSEHOLDS--HISPANIC AMERICANS; INCOME--HISPANIC AMERICANS; INTERRACIAL MARRIAGE--HISPANIC AMERICANS; NATURALIZATION--HISPANIC AMERICANS; PENSIONS--HISPANIC AMERICANS; POOR--HISPANIC AMERICANS; POPULATION FORECASTING--HISPANIC AMERICANS; POPULATION GEOGRAPHY--UNITED STATES--HISPANIC AMERICANS; UNITED STATES. CONGRESS--HISPANIC AMERICANS; VOTING--HISPANIC AMERICANS

"Almost two-thirds (64 percent) of Hispanic Americans trace their roots back to Mexico, compared with 15 percent to Central and South America, 10 percent to Puerto Rico, 5 percent to Cuba, and 6 percent to other places. More than three-fourths of the Hispanic population lives in the 20 largest Hispanic markets, according to Strategy Research. More than one-third live in just three markets: Los Angeles (with 6.3 million Hispanic residents), New York (3.6 million), and Miami (1.4 million)." (p1-2)

"Spanish Unites Hispanic Americans." Forecast v17 n12 Dec 1997. p1-2. article-level access: <http://www.demographics.com/publications/fc/97_fc/9712_fc/f971201.htm> (ISSN0732-1597).

"More than two-thirds of the Latinos residing in the United States are immigrants or the children of immigrants. In 1996, more than one-third of Hispanics were first-generation Americans (foreign-born of foreign-born parents) and one-third were second-generation Americans (U.S.-born with at least one foreign-born parent). Less than one-third of Hispanics were third generation or higher (U.S.-born of U.S.-born parents)...." (p6)

del Pinal, Jorge/Singer, Audrey. "Generations of Diversity: Latinos in the United States." Population Bulletin v52 n3 Oct 1997. p2-47. (ISSN0032-468X).

HISPANIC AMERICANS--ALABAMA (v26)

HISPANIC AMERICANS--ARIZONA--PHOENIX

In Phoenix, Arizona, Hispanics "spend an estimated $5 billion annually and are forming businesses at a faster rate than in the rest of the US. From 1987 to 1992, the number of Hispanic businesses in Arizona grew by 81 percent. They now account for 7 percent of all businesses in the state, says the US Census Bureau....About 50 Latino-owned restaurants have opened in the past few years, reports THE ARIZONA REPUBLIC....There currently are no Hispanics on the Phoenix City Council, only one-eighth of Arizona's US congressional delegation is Hispanic, and only five of Arizona's 25 largest publicly traded companies have Hispanics in senior management." (p4)

Carlile, William H. "All Anglo No More, A Latin Phoenix Rises." The Christian Science Monitor v89 n176 6 Aug 1997. p1,4. The Christian Science Monitor search engine: <http://www.csmonitor.com/plweb-cgi/iops1.pl> To retrieve this article, enter the following search: ED=19970806 AND rises. In the "retrieved list," click the title that matches this record. (ISSN0882-7729).

HISPANIC AMERICANS--CALIFORNIA--POPULATION (v26)

HISPANIC AMERICANS--CALIFORNIA--LOS ANGELES --SOCIAL CONDITIONS (v26)

HISPANIC AMERICANS--ECONOMIC CONDITIONS

In the U.S., "the 1995 income level of Hispanic households ($22,860) was not statistically different from that of African American households ($22,393). The median income of non-Hispanic White households was $37,178. The 1995 Hispanic poverty rate of 30.3 percent was not significantly different from that of African Americans but higher than the 8.5 percent for non-Hispanic Whites."

U.S. Dept. of Commerce. Economic and Statistics Administration. "Census Facts for Hispanic Heritage Month." Census Bureau Fact Sheet 11 Sep 1997. document-level access: <http://www.census.gov/Press-Release/fs97-10.html>

"There are an estimated 22 million Latinos in the United States (Castex, 1994). The median income for Latino families is $23,884, compared to $39,239 for non-Latino white families (Institute for Puerto Rican Policy, 1993). All Latino groups have incomes below the national median (Holmes, 1996); Puerto Rican families have the lowest income of any group ($20,654), followed by Mexican families ($23,018). Cuban families have the highest median income of any Latino group ($30,095). Puerto Rican families have the highest percentage of people living below the poverty rate (39.4 percent), followed by Mexican families (29.5 percent), Central or South American families (24.6 percent), other Latino families (20.6 percent), and Cuban families (18.0 percent). These rates are in sharp contrast with the poverty rate of 9.4 percent for non-Latino white families (Institute for Puerto Rican Policy, 1993)." (p446)

Delgado, Melvin. "Role of Latina-Owned Beauty Parlors in a Latino Community." Social Work v42 n5 Sep 1997. p445-453. (ISSN0037-8046).

HISPANIC AMERICANS--EDUCATION

"In March 1996, 53 percent of the...Hispanics [in the U.S.] aged 25 and over had at least a high school diploma and 9 percent had earned at least a bachelor's degree. The proportion of high school graduates is up 7 percentage points since 1983. An estimated 54,000 Hispanics aged 25 and over had PhDs while 71,000 had professional degrees, such as an M.D. or J.D., in March 1996. (These two totals are not statistically different from one another.) During the year beginning October 1994, 12 percent of Hispanic high school students in 10th, 11th, and 12th grades dropped out of school. One quarter (25 percent) of Hispanics aged 18 to 21 were attending college in October 1995."

U.S. Dept. of Commerce. Economic and Statistics Administration. "Census Facts for Hispanic Heritage Month." Census Bureau Fact Sheet 11 Sep 1997. document-level access: <http://www.census.gov/Press-Release/fs97-10.html>

In the U.S., "in 1996, little more than one-half (53 percent) of Hispanics ages 25 or older had completed high school, and less than 10 percent had at least a bachelor's degree....Nearly 85 percent of non-Hispanic adults were high school graduates, and nearly 25 percent were college graduates....Nearly one-third (30 percent) of Latinos had less than a ninth-grade education in 1996, compared with only about 5 percent of whites and 10 percent of blacks. One-tenth of Hispanic adults had less than a fifth-grade education....More than one-third (36 percent) of Mexicans ages 25 or older had less than a ninth-grade education, compared with 18 percent of Other Hispanics and 19 percent of Cubans. Just less than one-half (47 percent) of Mexicans had completed high school in 1996, compared with about two-thirds of Other Hispanics and Cubans. Only about 7 percent of Mexicans had a bachelor's degree or higher, compared with about 19 percent of Cubans and 13 percent of Other Hispanics." (p31)

del Pinal, Jorge/Singer, Audrey. "Generations of Diversity: Latinos in the United States." Population Bulletin v52 n3 Oct 1997. p2-47. (ISSN0032-468X).

In the U.S., "Latinos have the lowest rates of high school and college graduation of any major population group. In 1996, slightly more than one-half (53 percent) of Hispanics ages 25 or older had completed high school, and less than 10 percent had at least a bachelor's degree. Nearly 85 percent of non-Hispanic adults were high school graduates, and nearly 25 percent were college graduates....Nearly one-third (30 percent) of Latinos had less than a ninth-grade education in 1996, compared with only about 5 percent of whites and 10 percent of blacks....About 55 percent of Latinos who graduated from high school in 1994 enrolled in college the next fall."

Population Reference Bureau. "Diverse Hispanic Population to Become Largest U.S. Minority." Press Release 1997. document-level access: <http://www.prb.org/media/pressrel.htm>

HISPANIC AMERICANS--EDUCATION--MICHIGAN

"In Michigan, 60 percent of Latinos have graduated from high school, compared to 49.8 percent nationwide, according to 1990 U.S. Census Bureau figures. Nearly 11.6 percent of Latinos in Michigan have earned bachelor's degrees or higher, compared to 9.2 percent nationwide. In 1970, only 30 percent of Latinos nationwide 25 years and older had completed high school. In 1980, 1 of 13 completed four years or more of college." (p1 secA)

Lewis, Shawn D. "Hispanic Heritage Month: Power Presence Action: More Hispanics in Michigan Head to College." Detroit News 29 Sep 1997. p1,10 secA.

HISPANIC AMERICANS--EDUCATION--NEW YORK (N.Y.) (v26)

HISPANIC AMERICANS--EMPLOYMENT

In the U.S., "in March 1994, employed Hispanic men, aged 16 and over, most commonly worked as operators, fabricators or laborers or in precision production, craft and repair jobs (30 percent and 19 percent, respectively). Their female counterparts most frequently worked in technical, sales or administrative support occupations or in service jobs (39 percent and 28 percent, respectively). Among Hispanic groups, the March 1994 unemployment rate ranged from 7 percent for Cubans to an apparent high of 14 percent for Puerto Ricans. Overall, 11 percent of Hispanics and 6 percent of non-Hispanic Whites were unemployed."

U.S. Dept. of Commerce. Economic and Statistics Administration. "Census Facts for Hispanic Heritage Month." Census Bureau Fact Sheet 11 Sep 1997. document-level access: <http://www.census.gov/Press-Release/fs97-10.html>

HISPANIC AMERICANS--MICHIGAN

According to the U.S. Census Bureau, in Grand Rapids, Michigan, "in 1970, there were 4,441 people of Spanish or Hispanic descent. By 1990, that number had increased to 8,447. By 1996, according to a Grand Valley State University study, the number of Hispanics rose to nearly 12,000--a 41-percent increase in six years. Meanwhile, the city's overall population grew 31 percent from 1990-96. In Ottawa County, where Holland is located, the Hispanic population grew 42 percent during this decade compared with the county's overall growth of 18 percent." (p1-2 secC)

Cardenas, Edward L. "Metro: Special Report: Diversity: Michigan Sees Hispanic Boom." Detroit News 22 Sep 1997. p1-2 secC.

HISPANIC AMERICANS--NEW YORK (N.Y.) --POPULATION

"The New York and northern New Jersey metropolitan area is about 17 percent Hispanic. Puerto Ricans are the largest single Hispanic group, making up about 6 percent of the metropolitan areas's 20 million residents in 1996. They account for more than one-third of the metropolitan area's 3.3 million Hispanics. Many immigrated from Puerto Rico in the 1950s and 1960s. Central and South Americans, dominated by Colombians, Ecuadorians, and Salvadorans, make up 6 percent of New York's Latinos. The Other Hispanics group, which consists primarily of Dominicans, is the second largest Hispanic ethnic group in New York. Dominicans, along with Cubans and smaller Hispanic groups, made up 5 percent of New York's population in 1996." (p13)

del Pinal, Jorge/Singer, Audrey. "Generations of Diversity: Latinos in the United States." Population Bulletin v52 n3 Oct 1997. p2-47. (ISSN0032-468X).

HISPANIC AMERICANS--POPULATION

"The proportion of Hispanics in the U.S. population increased 53 percent during the 1980's and is expected to increase 36 percent in the 1990's. Today, people of Hispanic origin account for 10 percent of the U.S. population--up from 6 percent in 1980. The Census Bureau estimates that by the year 2020, Hispanics will account for about 15 percent of the U.S. population." (p4)

Plummer, Charles/Lucier, Gary/U.S. Dept. of Agriculture. Economic Research Service. "Commodity Briefs: Specialty Crops: Dry Bean Production Up as Demand Grows Steadily." Agricultural Outlook Oct 1997. p3-4.

"On June 1, 1997, there were an estimated 29.2 million Hispanics in the United States, comprising 10.9 percent of the total population. Since July 1, 1990, the Hispanic population has grown 29 percent, while the non-Hispanic White population has increased 3 percent. (These totals do not include persons living in Puerto Rico, whose estimated population on July 1, 1996 was 3.8 million.) In 1995, 74 percent of the nation's Hispanics resided in either California, Texas, New York, Florida or Illinois."

U.S. Dept. of Commerce. Economic and Statistics Administration. "Census Facts for Hispanic Heritage Month." Census Bureau Fact Sheet 11 Sep 1997. document-level access: <http://www.census.gov/Press-Release/fs97-10.html>

"The United States has the world's fifth-largest Hispanic population in 1998. It will have the second-largest by 2025, according to Strategy Research's annual report. The firm estimates the U.S. population of Hispanic origin at 30.5 million in 1998, which is slightly larger than the Census Bureau estimate of 29.1 million due to differing immigration assumptions." (p1)

"Spanish Unites Hispanic Americans." Forecast v17 n12 Dec 1997. p1-2. article-level access: <http://www.demographics.com/publications/fc/97_fc/9712_fc/f971201.htm> (ISSN0732-1597).

"Central Americans, South Americans, and Dominicans are lumped together by the Census Bureau under the title 'Other' Hispanics. About one-half of all Central Americans live in California (637,656), especially Los Angeles County (453,048). About three-fourths of all Dominicans live in New York City (357,868). South Americans also prefer New York (279,101), but also live in California (182,384), Florida (170,531) and New Jersey (126,286)....The 'Other' Hispanic population is essentially bicoastal, with about 90 percent of the population living along the northeastern seaboard, Florida, or California." (p141) "The Puerto Rican, Cuban, and 'Other' Hispanic population is primarily eastern. In 1990, the East had 25 counties greater than 5 percent Hispanic, compared to zero in 1960. The same is true of Florida, which in 1960 was overwhelmingly Anglo, but in 1990 had 15 counties greater than 5 percent Hispanic, including Dade County, the only county east of the Mississippi greater than 50 percent Hispanic. The Midwestern cluster of counties centered around Chicago is primarily Mexican (612,442 or about 70 percent of the Illinois Hispanic population)....In 1990, there were 34 counties with a Hispanic population greater than 5 percent [in the Northwest]." (p142)

Haverluk, Terrence. "The Changing Geography of U.S. Hispanics, 1850-1990." Journal of Geography v96 n3 May-Jun 1997. p134-145. (ISSN0022-1341).

"The U.S. Hispanic population has increased from four million in 1960, to 32 million in 1997, and the United States is now the fifth largest Spanish speaking country in the world after Mexico, Spain, Argentina, and Colombia (U.S. Department of Commerce 1993)." (p134) "According to the 1990 census, there were 2.6 million Puerto Ricans in the United States, (triple the number from 1960) 70 percent of whom lived in megalopolis."

(p139) "Between 1959 and 1994, approximately 715,000 Cubans successfully relocated to the United States (WASHINGTON POST 1994), most to Florida." (p141)

Haverluk, Terrence. "The Changing Geography of U.S. Hispanics, 1850-1990." Journal of Geography v96 n3 May-Jun 1997. p134-145. (ISSN0022-1341).

"The number of Hispanics increased by 53 percent between 1980 and 1990, and another 27 percent between 1990 and 1996. The non-Hispanic population grew by 7 percent during the 1980s, and 4 percent between 1990 and 1996....Hispanics made up 11 percent of the U.S. population in 1996....Hispanics accounted for about 35 percent of the national population growth between 1980 and 1990, and they are projected to furnish more than one-half of the national population growth between 2020 and 2050." (p15)

del Pinal, Jorge/Singer, Audrey. "Generations of Diversity: Latinos in the United States." Population Bulletin v52 n3 Oct 1997. p2-47. (ISSN0032-468X).

"In 1970, U.S. Hispanics numbered about 9 million, roughly 4 percent of the national population. The number of Hispanics increased by 53 percent between 1980 and 1990, and another 27 percent between 1990 and 1996....In 1970, nearly 16 percent of all Hispanics were of Puerto Rican descent. In 1996, the Puerto Rican share was down to 11 percent. At the same time, the Mexican share rose from 50 percent to 64 percent, and the Central and South American-origin share rose from 8 percent to 14 percent."

Population Reference Bureau. "Diverse Hispanic Population to Become Largest U.S. Minority." Press Release 1997. document-level access: <http://www.prb.org/media/pressrel.htm>

"In 1996, 11 percent of the U.S. population was Hispanic. A question on Spanish (or Hispanic) origin was first asked in the 1970 Census, when 4.5 percent of the population said they were Hispanic. In 1994, New Mexico's population had the highest percentage of Hispanics--39 percent."

Population Reference Bureau. "Today's U.S. Population: Details and Definitions." Press Release 1997. document-level access: <http://www.prb.org/media/pressrel.htm>

"The Hispanic American population is predicted to grow to 30 million by the year 2000 and 41.2 million by 2020. This population is about 75% (13 million) Mexicans who live mostly in southwestern states, with the remaining 25%: Cubans (1 million) who live primarily in Florida; Puerto Ricans (2.5 million) who live mainly in New York, New Jersey and Chicago; and others (2.2 million) who primarily come from Central and South America. In 1990, Hispanics lived primarily in California, Texas, New York, Florida, and Illinois." (p25)

Morton, Linda P. "Targeting Minority Publics." Public Relations Quarterly v42 n2 Sum 1997. p23-28. (ISSN0033-3700).

HISPANIC AMERICANS--SOCIAL CONDITIONS

"Strategy Research estimates that the median income of an Hispanic [American] household will be $31,600 in 1998. Cuban Americans have the highest median income, at $37,000; Puerto Ricans have the lowest, at $25,000....In 1998, an estimated 7 percent of main income earners in Hispanic households will not have a primary school education, about 60 percent will be high school graduates, and 14 percent will hold college degrees. Just 44 percent of U.S. Hispanic households own their dwellings, compared with a national homeownership rate of 65 percent. Forty-five percent of Hispanics are registered to vote, but voter registration ranges from 86 percent among Puerto Ricans to 29 percent for Central Americans. Among registered voters, 60 percent of all Hispanics are Democrats--but the Democratic share ranges from 86 percent among Dominicans to 23 percent among Cubans." (p2)

"Spanish Unites Hispanic Americans." Forecast v17 n12 Dec 1997. p1-2. article-level access: <http://www.demographics.com/publications/fc/97_fc/9712_fc/f971201.htm> (ISSN0732-1597).

HISPANIC AMERICANS--TEXAS

"In Texas, the Tejano Homeland has expanded northward and westward--in 1960 Texas had 17 counties greater than 50 percent Hispanic, in 1990 there were 34 counties greater than 50 percent Hispanic....In 1990, these counties had a population of 2.2 million and is one reason that Texas overtook New York to become the second largest state in 1994." (p142)

Haverluk, Terrence. "The Changing Geography of U.S. Hispanics, 1850-1990." Journal of Geography v96 n3 May-Jun 1997. p134-145. (ISSN0022-1341).

HISPANIC AMERICANS--TEXAS--POPULATION

In Texas, "Hispanics--predominately Mexicans--make up more than one-quarter of the population of the Houston metropolitan area. In 1996, Mexican Americans accounted for 23 percent of that area's 4.3 million residents; Central and South Americans made up another 4 percent. Texas, like portions of other south-western states, was once part of Mexico and has a large Mexican American community....The 1990 census showed Hispanics made up 48 percent of the residents in San Antonio, 70 percent in El Paso, and more than 80 percent in the border cities of Brownsville, Laredo, and McAllen." (p12)

del Pinal, Jorge/Singer, Audrey. "Generations of Diversity: Latinos in the United States." Population Bulletin v52 n3 Oct 1997. p2-47. (ISSN0032-468X).

HISPANIC AMERICANS--WEST (U.S.)

"In California and Nevada, almost every county has seen sharp rises in the percentage of Hispanics since 1960, yet only one county, Imperial, along the Mexican border is greater than 50 percent Hispanic. Even though the western Hispanic population is not as dominant as it once was, 66 percent of all Hispanics live in the West and it is America's most ethnically diverse region." (p142)

Haverluk, Terrence. "The Changing Geography of U.S. Hispanics, 1850-1990." Journal of Geography v96 n3 May-Jun 1997. p134-145. (ISSN0022-1341).

HIV INFECTIONS (v26)

see also AIDS (DISEASE)

"In 1996, 22.6 million pepole were infected with HIV, according to WHO figures. The epidemic is growing by more than 3 million cases a year. Predictions of the pandemic suggest that by the year 2000 between 40 and 110 million people will be infected with the virus." (p367) "Drug therapies [for HIV] are very expensive, costing from $10,000 to $20,000 per year. Therefore, they are out of reach of the 90 percent of the world's HIV-infected people, who live in developing countries." (p373)

Pinkerton, Steven D./Abramson, Paul R. "Condoms and the Prevention of AIDS." American Scientist v85 n4 Jul-Aug 1997. p364-373. (ISSN0003-0996).

"According to UNAIDS, the new AIDS program run by the United Nations, 28 million people are now infected with HIV worldwide. Every year, 3 million more become infected. These figures represent 8,500 new cases a day....More than 90 percent of HIV-infected people live in the developing world far from our sophisticated medical systems." (p11)

Farthing, Charles. "Perspectives: A Necessary Risk." New Physician v46 n9 Dec 1997. p11-13. (ISSN0028-6451).

"According to WHO, an estimated 24 million adults worldwide are infected with...[HIV], more than 4.5 million of whom have developed AIDS. By 2000, WHO estimates that more than 26 million adults will be living with HIV throughout the world....In Zimbabwe, where an estimated 900,000 people were infected with HIV in 1994, some scientists have projected that AIDS may reduce life expectancy at birth from its 1997 level of

51 years to 33 years by 2010. If HIV and AIDS were eliminated, Zimbabwe's life expectancy would be expected to rise to 69.9 years in 2010--a level approaching that of many developed nations today." (p19-20)

Olshansky, S. Jay/Carnes, Bruce/Rogers, Richard G./Smith, Len. "Infectious Diseases--New and Ancient Threats to World Health." Population Bulletin v52 n2 Jul 1997. p2-46. (ISSN0032-468X).

HIV INFECTIONS--AFRICA (v26)

In Africa, genital ulcer disease may increase the risk of transmission of HIV infection "per exposure by a factor of ten to 50 for male-to-female transmission and by a factor of 50 to 300 for female-to-male transmission....A large prospective, randomized controlled trial in Tanzania found that the incidence of HIV infection was 42 percent lower in communities with improved management of STDs [sexually transmitted diseases] after two years compared with control communities....N.J. Robinson and colleagues predicted that a 50 percent reduction in the duration of STDs in Uganda could decrease HIV transmission by 43 percent....It is estimated that successfully treating or preventing 100 cases of syphilis among high-risk groups for STDs would prevent 1,200 HIV infections that are ordinarily linked to those 100 syphilis infections during a ten-year period." (p7)

The Committee on Prevention and Control of STDs. Institute of Medicine. "The Hidden Epidemic: Confronting Sexually Transmitted Diseases." SIECUS Report v25 n3 Feb-Mar 1997. p4-14. (ISSN0091-3995).

HIV INFECTIONS--ASIA (v26)

HIV INFECTIONS--CHILDREN (v26)

HIV INFECTIONS--DEVELOPING COUNTRIES

The report, "Confronting AIDS: Public Priorities in a Global Epidemic," "says that 23 million people worldwide are now infected with HIV and that 8,500 people are newly infected each day. Two decades after the first appearance of the human immunodeficiency virus, 6 million people have died from AIDS, and new evidence suggests that while Sub-Saharan Africa has most people infected--14 million--the virus may be on the verge of exploding in other regions such as Central and Eastern Europe....In 30 developing countries, and in large areas of China and India, HIV has infected less than 5 percent of people who engage in very high risk behavior....Twenty-one countries have 'generalized' epidemics in which 5 percent or more of women attending maternity clinics are infected."

World Bank. "Confronting the Spread of AIDS." Press Release 3 Nov 1997. document-level access: <http://www.worldbank.org/html/extdr/extme/1513.htm>

HIV INFECTIONS--DEVELOPING COUNTRIES--COSTS

In a study of 5 countries, Cote d'Ivoire, the United Republic of Tanzania, Thailand, Brazil and Mexico, "the resulting annual per capita expenditures for the total population on HIV-related prevention and treatment ranged from $1.48 in Mexico to $8.69 in Sao Paulo, Brazil. The simple average across the five countries was $4.36. As Sao Paulo had the highest per capita GDP among all five areas ($5600), its high absolute expenditures per person were understandable. Because the state spent so much on health care overall, however, Sao Paulo actually devoted the lowest share of its health expenditures to HIV-related illness (1.4%) among all five countries. The United Republic of Tanzania, the poorest of the five, devoted 13.7% of its health expenditure to HIV....Of Tanzania's AIDS expenditures, 85% were directed to prevention, supported largely by international donor contributions. The share of health expenditures devoted to HIV/AIDS was 1.5% in Thailand, 1.8% in Mexico and 6.7% in Cote d'Ivoire. The simple average was 5.0%." (p20-21)

Shepard, Donald S. "The Cost of AIDS." World Health v50 n5 Sep-Oct 1997. p20-21. (ISSN0043-8502).

HIV INFECTIONS--MARYLAND--DRUG USE

In "Maryland, injection drug use is the major mode of transmission for HIV/AIDS. Baltimore city's needle exchange program has been associated with a 40 percent reduction in new cases of HIV, and evaluation of the program has demonstrated that needle exchange did not increase drug use. In fact, a bill was approved to continue the program by an overwhelming vote in the Maryland State Legislature earlier this year. It passed by a vote of 113 to 23 in the house of delegates and by a vote of 30 to 17 in the State senate. Nationally, 66 percent of all AIDS cases among women and more than half of AIDS cases in children are related to injection drug use." (pH7224)

Morella, Constance A. (Rep.-Md.). "Departments of Labor, Health and Human Services, And Education...Appropriations Act, 1998." Congressional Record. Daily ed. v143 n120 11 Sep 1997. pH7206-7247. section/page-level access: <http://thomas.loc.gov/cgi-bin/query/R?r105:FLD001:H07224:> (ISSN0363-7239). (X1.1A.105/1).

HIV INFECTIONS--PROSTITUTES (v26)

HIV INFECTIONS--THAILAND (v26)

HIV INFECTIONS--UGANDA--KAMPALA--PREGNANT WOMEN (v26)

HIV INFECTIONS--UNITED STATES

"People with an active syphilis, genital herpes, or chancroid infection, or who have chlamydia, gonorrhea, or trichomoniasis are 3 to 5 times more likely to contract HIV than other people. More than half (54 percent) of American adults under 65 do not know that STDs [sexually transmitted diseases] increase susceptibility to HIV." (p22)

"Fact Sheet: Sexually Transmitted Diseases in the United States." SIECUS Report v25 n3 Feb-Mar 1997. p22-24. (ISSN0091-3995).

HIV INFECTIONS--UNITED STATES--DRUG USE (v26)

In the U.S., "in 1995, a panel of the National Research Council and the Institute of Medicine reported that between 1981 and 1993 the proportion of AIDS cases resulting from injection drug use rose from 12 to 28 percent. They concluded that 'the HIV epidemic in this country is now clearly driven by infections occurring in the population of injection drug users, their sexual partners, and their offspring.' One-third of all reported cases of AIDS in adults can be traced directly or indirectly to injection drug use. Over half of the children with AIDS got it from others who were injection drug users." (pH7219)

Ganske, Greg (Rep.-Iowa). "Departments of Labor, Health and Human Services, And Education...Appropriations Act, 1998." Congressional Record. Daily ed. v143 n120 11 Sep 1997. pH7206-7247. section/page-level access: <http://thomas.loc.gov/cgi-bin/query/R?r105:FLD001:H07219> (ISSN0363-7239). (X1.1A.105/1).

HIV INFECTIONS--UNITED STATES. MARINE CORPS (v26)

HMOS

see HEALTH MAINTENANCE ORGANIZATIONS

HOGS

see SWINE

HOLIDAYS (v26)

see also CHRISTMAS

HOLIDAYS--UNITED STATES

"Most Americans (93 percent of adults) celebrate one December holiday or another, according to a survey conducted for AMERICAN DEMOGRAPHICS by Maritz Marketing Research. Christmas dominates the season, attracting 98 percent of the celebrants. Two percent each celebrate Hanukkah and Kwanzaa." (p43) "While 98 percent of those aged 45 to 54 celebrate a December holiday, just 88 percent of those aged 65 and older make the effort....Just 5 percent of people aged 35 to 44 say they buy nothing special for the holidays, compared with 19 percent of those aged 65 and older." (p44)

Speer, Tibbett L. "Stretching the Holiday Season." American Demographics v19 n11 Nov 1997. p42-49. article-level access: <http://www.demographics.com/publications/ad/97_ad/9711_ad/ad971128.htm> (ISSN0163-4089).

HOME ACCIDENTS--AUSTRALIA--CHILDREN --PREVENTION (v26)

HOME ACCIDENTS--AUSTRALIA--PREVENTION (v26)

HOME-BASED BUSINESSES--UNITED STATES (v26)

HOME BUILDING INDUSTRY

see CONSTRUCTION INDUSTRY

HOME ECONOMICS--UNITED STATES (v26)

HOME ECONOMICS--UNITED STATES--WOMEN --ATTITUDES (v26)

HOME LABOR

see also TELECOMMUTING

HOME LABOR--UNITED STATES

"Today, 31 percent of Americans have a designated room in their home used specifically as an office away from the office, according to the Wirthlin Worldwide Home Office Trends study conducted in late 1996....Still, 89 percent of study respondents say they need a home office primarily to conduct 'personal business' like paying bills. Nearly half of those surveyed use the office to finish homework assignments (49 percent)....An equal share (47 percent) use the home office to finish uncompleted work from their day job. A smaller percentage use it to conduct home-based businesses (31 percent) or do work for an outside employer (27 percent)." (p35)

Cravatta, Matthew J. "Kaleidoscope: Everybody's Doing Homework." American Demographics v19 n7 Jul 1997. p35. article-level access: <http://www.demographics.com/publications/ad/97_ad/9707_ad/ad970731.htm> (ISSN0163-4089).

HOME OWNERSHIP

see also FARM OWNERSHIP

HOME OWNERSHIP--HISPANIC AMERICANS

In the U.S., the Southwest Initiative, a project started by the National Council of La Raza in 1993, "is supported by several banks and foundations, including the Ford Foundation, which recently granted it an additional $1 million. The Southwest Initiative provides grants and technical assistance to 25 Latino-run community development corporations (CDCs)....To date the CDCs have built more than 600 housing units and helped more than 500 families become new homeowners. NCLR's research on home ownership among Latinos led to a partnership with the Federal National Mortgage Association (Fannie Mae) that enabled CDCs to extend $10 million in mortgage credit to Latino households in Arizona....According to NCLR president Raul Yzaguirre, the [Home-To-Own] program has helped more than 230 low-income families obtain mortgages in Arizona and has accounted for a full percentage point increase in Hispanic home ownership in Phoenix." (p32)

Cabral, Elena. "Briefly Noted: Home Loans for Low-Income Families." Ford Foundation Report v28 n2 Spr 1997. p32. (ISSN1063-7281).

HOME OWNERSHIP--AUSTRALIA

According to the Australian Bureau of Statistics, "in 1995-96, almost 1.1 million households were recent home purchasers. A majority of these (61 per cent) were changeover buyers and they purchased more expensive homes than first home buyers ($162,000 compared with $121,000). They faced lower housing costs as they generally borrowed less. Over 70 per cent of recent home buyers bought established homes which were less expensive ($131,000 compared with $159,000) but also, on average, slightly smaller (3.0 bedrooms compared with 3.3)."

Australian Bureau of Statistics. "Australia's Housing Costs--ABS." Media Release 29 Oct 1997. document-level access: <http://www.abs.gov.au/websitedbs/d3110125.nsf/4a255eef008309e44a255eef00061e57/0a5297cfa5c18ad7ca25653e007aa13e?OpenDocument>

HOME OWNERSHIP--MICHIGAN

U.S. "Vice-President Al Gore and other Clinton administration officials announced...that a record 66 percent--or 67.6 million--families in the United States are homeowners. The old record was set in 1980. Homeownership in Michigan regularly hovers above the national average, and the third quarter numbers continue that trend. Census Bureau data shows a 73.7-percent homeownership rate for Michigan compared to 73.3 percent last year, while Metro Detroit's rate was unchanged at 71.3 percent." (p1 secB)

Stertz, Bradley A. "Business: U.S. Homeowners Hit Record 67.6 Million." Detroit News 24 Oct 1997. p1 secB.

HOME OWNERSHIP--UNITED STATES (v26)

In the U.S., "in 1996, the homeownership rate for married couple families was 83 percent for native-born citizens, 78 percent for foreign-born citizens and 42 percent for non-citizens. The homeownership rate for native-born and foreign-born citizens was highest among 55-64 year-olds (82 percent and 79 percent) and lowest for the age group 35 years old and under (41 percent and 39 percent)."

U.S. Dept. of Commerce. Economic and Statistics Administration. "Foreign-Born Citizens as Likely to Own Homes as Native-Born Census Bureau Finds." Census Bureau Press Release 11 Sep 1997. document-level access: <http://www.census.gov/Press-Release/cb97-145.html>

HOME OWNERSHIP--UNITED STATES--FINANCE

In the U.S., the national rate of home ownership "now is 65.4 percent; among households under age 35, it's 58.8 percent....The FHA [Federal Housing Administration] limits the size of the mortgages it underwrites to $157,000 in the nation's most expensive markets, like New York and San Francisco; the limit is as low as $78,000 in other areas....FHA loans also have down payment requirements as low as 3 percent, which may sound great to newlyweds who don't receive enough in cash gifts to make a 10 or 20 percent down payment. Down payments of less than 20 percent, though, generally require private mortgage insurance, which can add $30 to $50 a month to mortgage payments....Interest rates are set by the individual banks, rather than by the FHA, and those rates may range from 3 percent to 5.25 percent, depending on the balance." (p15)

Decker, Jonathan P. "Getting Married? Uncle Sam Has a House for You." The Christian Science Monitor v89 n146 24 Jun 1997. p15. The Christian Science Monitor search engine: <http://www.csmonitor.com/plweb-cgi/iops1.pl> To retrieve this article, enter the following search: ED=19970621 AND house. In the "retrieved list," click the title that matches this record. (ISSN0882-7729).

HOME OWNERSHIP--UNITED STATES--IMMIGRANTS

"The homeownership rate for foreign-born citizens was virtually the same last year--about 67 percent--as for persons born in the United States, according to a first-time report released...by the Commerce Department's Census Bureau. The report shows that 33 percent of non-citizens owned their own homes....Foreign-born citizens of Hispanic origin were more likely to own a home than native-born citizens of Hispanic origin in 1996 (57 percent versus 48 percent). Foreign-born citizens who entered this country before 1970 had a higher rate of homeownership, (77 percent), compared with...foreign-born citizens who entered in 1970 or later, (57 percent)."

U.S. Dept. of Commerce. Economic and Statistics Administration. "Foreign-Born Citizens as Likely to Own

Homes as Native-Born Census Bureau Finds." Census Bureau Press Release 11 Sep 1997. document-level access: <http://www.census.gov/Press-Release/cb97-145.html>

"The number of foreign-born Americans who own homes grew by an estimated 1.4 million between 1980 and 1995....Between 1980 and 1995, immigrants formed 3.1 million new households, accounting for 18 percent of the nation's total household growth....By the time immigrants become citizens, 67 percent own homes, which is equal to the share of native-born citizens who own homes....In 1990, 42 percent of the recently arrived group had formed households, and of these, 47 percent were homeowners." (p9)

"Newest Americans Head for Homes." Forecast v17 n11 Nov 1997. p9. article-level access: <http://www.demographics.com/publications/fc/97_fc/9711_fc/fc97118.htm> (ISSN0732-1597).

HOME REMODELING

see DWELLINGS--UNITED STATES--REMODELING

HOME SCHOOLING--MICHIGAN (v26)

HOME SCHOOLING--UNITED STATES (v26)

HOME SCHOOLING--UNITED STATES--PERFORMANCE (v26)

HOME SCHOOLING--UNITED STATES--SCHOOL ADMINISTRATORS--ATTITUDES (v26)

HOMELESS CHILDREN (v26)

HOMELESS CHILDREN--MEXICO--MEXICO CITY (v26)

HOMELESS CHILDREN--MICHIGAN--DETROIT

"Children have become the fastest-growing segment of Detroit's homeless population over the past 10 years....'On any given day, there are approximately 10,000 homeless people in the area, and 800 to 1,300 of them are children,' said Gregory Murray at the Detroit Department of Senior Citizens and Homeless Coordination." (p1 secA)

Bivins, Larry/Schabath, Gene. "Detroit's Homeless Rate Soars: Welfare Reform Gets Blame for 20% Jump in People on Street." Detroit News 15 Dec 1997. p1,4 secA.

HOMELESS CHILDREN--PHILIPPINES

In the Philippines, there are "1.5 million street children....More than 100 million children live on the streets, UNICEF estimates....Only some 5 to 10 percent of street children actually sleep on the street....Most of the Philippines' 60,000 to 100,000 child prostitutes are street children, according to UNICEF." (p19)

Walsh, Catherine. "Street Children around the World." America v177 n8 27 Sep 1997. p18-20. (ISSN0002-7049).

HOMELESS PERSON SHELTERS

see SHELTERS FOR THE HOMELESS

HOMELESS PERSONS--MASSACHUSETTS--BOSTON--MINORITIES (v26)

HOMELESS PERSONS--MENTAL HEALTH--UNITED STATES--ATTITUDES (v26)

HOMELESS PERSONS--MICHIGAN--DETROIT

"Homelessness in Detroit grew 20 percent over...[1997]....About 2,000 people are sleeping in the city's 27 emergency shelters, an increase of about 400, the study by the U.S. Conference of Mayors noted....Requests for emergency shelter by homeless people rose more in Detroit than in any of the 29 cities surveyed except San Antonio." (p1 secA)

Bivins, Larry/Schabath, Gene. "Detroit's Homeless Rate Soars: Welfare Reform Gets Blame for 20% Jump in People on Street." Detroit News 15 Dec 1997. p1,4 secA.

"The U.S. Conference of Mayors reported a 20 percent increase in Detroit's homeless population during the past year....Detroit was one of 29 cities surveyed for hunger and homelessness by the conference. Detroit's 27 emergency shelters counted 2,000 temporary residents, an increase of 400, the biggest increase in the study. By comparison, census takers counted 1,141 in emergency shelters and 170 visible Detroit street people in 1990. The conference report also said children have become the fastest growing segment of Detroit's homeless population during the past 10 years....75 percent of Detroit's homeless were substance abusers...." (p18 secA)

"Understanding Homelessness." Detroit News 18 Dec 1997. p18 secA.

HOMELESS PERSONS--MICHIGAN--WASHTENAW COUNTY

"It's estimated by various sources that the number of homeless people in Washtenaw County [Michigan] ranges anywhere from 1,000 to 1,500 over the course of a year. Washtenaw County Administrator Robert Guenzel says the figure he finds most reliable is the estimate that at any given time, there are up to 200 adults homeless and needing shelter in the county....The Shelter Association of Washtenaw County, a private, non-profit agency that runs the county's three, permanent homeless shelters, receives 40 percent of its annual $722,000 funding through the city of Ann Arbor and Washtenaw County." (p8 secA)

Stewart, Will. "Faces of the Homeless: Issue Has Deep Roots Locally: As Stakes Rise, Public Debate Increases." Ypsilanti Press 29 Jun 1997. p1,8 secA.

HOMELESS PERSONS--NEW YORK (N.Y.) (v26)

HOMELESS PERSONS--UNITED STATES (v26)

"In its annual survey, the U.S. Conference of Mayors found that 20 percent of all requests for emergency shelter went unmet because of a lack of resources. Emergency shelter requests increased in the 29-city survey by an average of 5 percent, with the requests for assistance from homeless families increasing by 7 percent. On average, people remain homeless for 6 months in the survey cities. The No. 1 reason...is the lack of affordable housing." (pH5367)

Vento, Bruce F. (Rep.-Minn.). "Departments of Veterans Affairs and Housing and Urban Development...Appropriations Act, 1998." Congressional Record. Daily ed. v143 n101 16 Jul 1997. pH5309-5371. section/page-level access: <http://thomas.loc.gov/cgi-bin/query/R?r105:FLD001:H05367:> (ISSN0363-7239). (X1.1A.105/1).

A US Conference of Mayors survey "reports that requests for shelter by families increased by 5 percent over last year, compared with a 3 percent rise in requests by individual men and women. Families with children are estimated to be 36 percent of the homeless population--and the fastest-growing group of homeless nationwide. The survey also reports that 88 percent of the cities queried regularly turn away homeless families because of a lack of resources." (p14)

Nifong, Christina. "Ranks of Homeless Include More Families." The Christian Science Monitor v90 n14 15 Dec 1997. p14. The Christian Science Monitor search engine: <http://www.csmonitor.com/plweb-cgi/iops1.pl> To retrieve this article, enter the following search: ED=19971215 AND families. In the "retrieved list," click the title that matches this record. (ISSN0882-7729).

In 1996, "38 percent of homeless Americans were families, up from 23 percent in the mid-1980s, according to Mary Ann Gleason, executive director of the National Coalition for the Homeless in Washington. Children account for 27 percent of the homeless." (p12)

Gardner, Marilyn. "Community: Shelter Festivities Bring Holiday Smiles to Children." The Christian Science Monitor v90 n16 17 Dec 1997. p12. The Christian Science Monitor search engine: <http://www.csmonitor.com/plweb-cgi/iops1.pl> To retrieve this article, enter the following search: ED=19971217 AND children. In the "retrieved list," click the title that matches this record. (ISSN0882-7729).

HOMELESS YOUTH--MAINE--NEW HAMPSHIRE (v26)

HOMELESS YOUTH--NEW ENGLAND (v26)

HOMELESSNESS--UNITED STATES

"In San Antonio, 35 percent more people requested emergency shelter this year than last year. That increase led the nation; Detroit was second with a 20-percent rise....Detroit also registered the second-highest wait for public housing-- 36 months. Alexandria, Va., had the longest wait at 54 months....59 percent of the cities surveyed said they experienced an increase in requests for emergency shelter; shelter requests were up an average of 3 percent. Single men make up an average of 47 percent of homeless people, while families comprise 36 percent. Single women make up 14 percent and unaccompanied minors make up 4 percent. Children were about a quarter of the homeless population. Substance abusers made up 43 percent." (p2 secA)

Robles, Jennifer Juarez/Eversley, Melanie/Pickler, Nedra. "Many Left Out of Economy's Boom." Detroit Free Press 16 Dec 1997. p1-2 secA.

In the U.S., "on any given night, experts say, there are now at least 60,000 more homeless people than in recent years--a 10 to 15 percent increase." (p1) "Between 2 million and 3 million people are without shelter at least once over the year, advocates say." (p5)

Wood, Daniel B. "Beyond Beds: Innovations for Helping Homeless." The Christian Science Monitor v90 n3 28 Nov 1997. p1,5. The Christian Science Monitor search engine: <http://www.csmonitor.com/plweb-cgi/iops1.pl> To retrieve this article, enter the following search: ED=19971128 AND homeless. In the "retrieved list," click the title that matches this record. (ISSN0882-7729).

HOMEMAKERS, DISPLACED

see DISPLACED HOMEMAKERS

HOMES

see DWELLINGS

HOMEWORK (v26)

HOMEWORK--UNITED STATES

According to the Monitoring the Future study, in the U.S., "in 1976, 67 percent of the seniors reported spending 1-9 hours per week [doing homework], while in 1995, 66 percent of the seniors spent that amount of time doing homework. The proportion of seniors who reported spending 10 or more hours per week on homework was 23 percent in 1976 and 24 percent in 1995. In 1976, 10 percent of the seniors reported they spent no time doing homework and in 1995 that figure remained at 10 percent. Expressed as a measurement of central tendency, the mean number of hours per week that seniors in 1976 spent on homework was 6.5, or slightly more than one hour and 15 minutes per school day. By 1995, the mean had risen to 6.8 hours, or about an hour and 20 minutes per school day." (p95-96)

Freedman-Doan, Peter/Libsch, Margaret. "Features: Student Reports of Time Spent on Homework: Results from 20 Years of National Samples." NASSP Bulletin v81 n591 Oct 1997. p95-98. (ISSN0192-6365).

In the U.S., "according to statistics gathered for the 1997 Phi Delta Kappa/Gallup poll of education, 56 percent of parents reported spending three or more hours per week during the school year helping their oldest child with his or her homework. This represented a huge increase from 1986, when only 21 percent of parents showed that level of involvement." (p7)

"Fact and Fiction." Reading Today v15 n3 Dec 1997-Jan 1998. p7. (ISSN0737-4208).

HOMICIDE

see also EUTHANASIA; MURDER; SUICIDE

HOMICIDE--AETA (PHILIPPINE PEOPLE) (v26)

HOMICIDE--AFRO-AMERICAN MEN (v26)

HOMICIDE--BRAZIL--SAO PAULO

"In Sao Paulo, a city of 11 million inhabitants, 1,470 homicides-- 1 out of 3 killings--were committed by the police in 1992, according to an April report by Human Rights Watch/Americas.... 1 out of 4 city residents said they fear the police more than criminals, according to a recent poll by the Sao Paulo-based firm Datafolha....While there has been a dramatic decrease in people killed by Sao Paulo police--183 killings in 1996--it is still high when compared with other large cities. In New York, police are responsible for about 20 deaths annually. In Rio de Janeiro, a 240-man swat team trained to fight drug traffickers has killed 699 people in the past 29 months. Some 61 percent of the victims showed signs of being summarily executed, according to a recent investigation by the Rio daily, O DIA." (p7)

Epstein, Jack. "Brazil Hopes to Throw the Book at Cop Abuses." The Christian Science Monitor v89 n170 29 Jul 1997. p1,7. The Christian Science Monitor search engine: <http://www.csmonitor.com/plweb-cgi/iops1.pl> To retrieve this article, enter the following search: ED=19970729 AND abuses. In the "retrieved list," click the title that matches this record. (ISSN0882-7729).

HOMICIDE--JAMAICA (v26)

HOMICIDE--LOUISIANA--NEW ORLEANS--AFRO-AMERICANS (v26)

HOMICIDE--MEXICO

"Mexico has a murder rate as high as 19.7 per 100,000 inhabitants, which is far higher than that of most countries. However, Mexico's rate has remained relatively constant since 1970 while the U.S. rate, for example, has climbed from 4.5 to 9.5 per 100,000 inhabitants since 1960. In absolute terms, the United States registered 23,440 homicides in 1990 while the per annum average in Mexico in recent years is approximately 16,000 with half of the deaths involving premeditated murders and the other half consisting of involuntary manslaughter cases. On average, almost a fifth of the inmates in Mexican prisons are serving time for homicide. The same proportion applies to Mexico City prisoners, where 931 men and 50 women were serving murder sentences with similar numbers of men and women being held while awaiting trial for the same crime." (p331-332)

Azaola, Elena. "Women Serving Time for Homicide in Mexico City." International Journal of Comparative and Applied Criminal Justice v21 n2 Fall 1997. p331-340.

HOMICIDE--NEW YORK (N.Y.)

In 1994, in New York City, there was nearly a "50% drop in the homicide rate. The 985 homicides in 1996 represent the first time that homicides have dropped below 1,000 since 1968....April 1997 recorded 45 murders, the lowest incidence since November 1966, the last month to have fewer than 50 killings." (p3)

Silverman, Eli B. "Crime in America: Crime in New York: A Success Story." Public Perspective v8 n4 Jun-Jul 1997. p3-5. (ISSN1050-5067).

HOMICIDE--UNITED STATES (v26)

In the U.S., "of all homicides, more than 50 percent of the victims knew their assailants; 47 percent of homicides are caused by arguments, whereas ony 15 percent occur during the commission of another crime (Prothrow-Stith, 1990). Studies of victims reveal that alcohol was present in approximately 50 percent of the cases (FBI, 1981). The risk of becoming a victim of a nonfatal violent assault in the United States was three times greater for persons from families with incomes below $7,500 than those with incomes above $50,000 (Bureau of Justice Statistics, 1992)....Firearms are used in almost 70 percent of all homicides (FBI, 1994)." (p10)

Waters, Robert L./Cressy, Jeffrey/Adkins, Rodney H. "Spinal Cord Injuries Due to Violence." American Rehabilitation v22 n3 Aut 1996. p10-15. (ISSN0362-4048).

In the U.S., "most investigators agree that the first 48 to 72 hours are critical to solving a homicide case....Research has shown that in 66 percent of solved murder cases, police take a suspect into custody within 24 hours. If the case is not solved within 48 hours, the chances of it ever being solved fall markedly." (p4)

Regini, Charles L./U.S. Dept. of Justice. Federal Bureau of Investigation. "The Cold Case Concept." FBI Law Enforcement Bulletin v66 n8 Aug 1997. p1-6. (ISSN0014-5688).

"One study showed that roughly 90 percent of murderers [in the U.S.] have prior adult criminal records, with an average criminal career of six or more years that includes four major felony arrests....Domestic homicides, which accounted for roughly 12 percent of all U.S. homicides in 1994, do not happen without warning. Ninety percent of the time, the police had been called to the residence at least once in the two years prior; in 54 percent of the cases they had been called five or more times." (p67)

Funk, T. Markus. "Straight Shooters." Reason v29 n4 Aug-Sep 1997. p65-68. (ISSN0048-6906).

HOMICIDE--UNITED STATES--YOUTH (v26)

HOMICIDE--WASHINGTON (D.C.)

"In 1985, 21 percent of Washington [D.C.'s] homicides were drug-related; by 1988, that amount has risen to 80 percent." (p2)

"At the end of 1991, only 54 percent of the homicides that occurred in Washington that year had been solved." (p3)

Regini, Charles L./U.S. Dept. of Justice. Federal Bureau of Investigation. "The Cold Case Concept." FBI Law Enforcement Bulletin v66 n8 Aug 1997. p1-6. (ISSN0014-5688).

HOMOSEXUALITY--UNITED STATES--PUBLIC OPINION

"According to the latest Gallup poll, some six in ten Americans (59%) believe homosexuality is morally wrong and a majority (52%) say it should not be considered an acceptable alternative lifestyle. There are also signs that Americans are growing weary of the visibility of homosexuality on TV, with 46% now saying there are too many gay characters and situations on network television, up from 37% who felt this way in 1995. Today one-third feel there is the right amount of homosexual content on TV while only 9% feel there is too little....Roughly half of women and young adults consider...[homosexuality] wrong compared to about two-thirds of men and adults 50 and older....Half of all women (49%) think homosexuality should be considered acceptable by society compared to only 35% of men. Similarly half of adults aged 18-49 think it should be acceptable compared to only 30% of those aged 50 and older."

Saad, Lydia/Gallup Organization. "Majority of Americans Not Fazed by Ellen's Coming Out Episode." Press Release 29 Apr 1997. document-level access: <http://www.gallup.com/poll/news/970429~1.htm>

HOMOSEXUALS

see GAYS

HONDURAS--ARMED FORCES (v26)

HONDURAS--ECONOMIC CONDITIONS (v26)

HONG KONG--COMMERCE

"Hong Kong's 1996 total merchandise imports reached $198 billion, up slightly from $193 billion in 1995, and total exports (including re-exports) climbed to $181 billion from 1995's $174 billion. Re-exports accounted for $153 billion or 85 percent of exports. Thirty-seven percent of Hong Kong's total imports came from China, and a little more than one-third of Hong Kong's re-exports went back to China, about the same share as in 1995." (p44)

Whitton, Carolyn L./U.S. Dept. of Agriculture. Economic Research Service. "Hong Kong." China: International Agriculture and Trade Reports Situation and Outlook Series Jun 1997. p44-46.

"In 1995, Japan was the largest source of Hong Kong's factor income inflow, accounting for 28.7% (or $111.2 billion) of the total. In the second position was the British Virgin Islands which accounted for 13.8% (or $53.3 billion) of the total inflow, reflecting the dominant practice for investors to set up holding companies in tax havens. China and the United Kingdom were the third and fourth largest sources of external factor income, accounting for 6.7% (or $25.9 billion) and 6.4% (or $24.6 billion) of the total respectively. Japan also ranked on top of the list of countries earning factor income from Hong Kong, accounting for 26.3% (or $98.3 billion) of Hong Kong's total factor income outflow; followed by the United Kingdom, accounting for 9.0% (or $33.8 billion). The USA and the British Virgin Islands came third and fourth, accounting for 8.0% (or $29.7 billion) and 7.5% (or $28.1 billion) of the total outflow respectively."

Hong Kong. Census and Statistics Department. "Estimates of Hong Kong's Gross National Product for 1995." Press Release 27 May 1997. document-level access: <http://www.info.gov.hk/censtatd/hkstat/press/gnp195.htm>

In Hong Kong, "as to external trade in goods, re-exports registered a year-on-year growth rate of 7.3% in real terms in the second quarter of 1997, while domestic exports decreased marginally by 0.1% in real terms. Taken together, total exports of goods increased by 6.2% in real terms....Imports of goods recorded a 6.9% growth in real terms. Exports of services increased only modestly by 2.0% in real terms in the second quarter of 1997 over a year earlier, amidst a decline in tourist receipts over the same period. Concurrently, imports of services declined by 1.2% in real terms, partly due to a slower growth in spending on overseas trips by Hong Kong residents."

Hong Kong. Census and Statistics Department. "Estimates of Gross Domestic Product for Second Quarter of 1997." Press Release 3 Nov 1997. document-level access: <http://www.info.gov.hk/censtatd/hkstat/press/gdp12q97.htm>

HONG KONG--COMMERCE--TRANSPORTATION

"The value of Hong Kong's external trade by ocean accounted for 47% of Hong Kong's total value of external trade in the first half of 1997, according to statistics released by the Census and Statistics Department....Another 25% was transported by land, another 21% by air and the remaining 6.0% included shipment by river, postal parcels and accompanied goods of passengers travelling on various means of transport. Shipment by ocean amounted to $682.6 billion in the first half of 1997, representing an increase of 1.2% over that in the same period in 1996. Shipment by land went up 3.6% to $361.9 billion in the first half of 1997 while that by air rose by 9.7% to $307.5 billion."

Hong Kong. Census and Statistics Department. "Analysis of External Trade Statistics by Mode of Transport." Press Release 26 Aug 1997. document-level access: <http://www.info.gov.hk/censtatd/hkstat/press/t51h97.htm>

HONG KONG--COMMERCE--UNITED STATES (v26)

"The United States remained the largest destination for Hong Kong's total exports (comprising domestic exports and re-exports) by ocean, accounting for a share of 31% in value terms in the first half of 1997. The value of total exports by ocean to the United States went up by 6.3% in the first half of 1997 over a year earlier....In the first half of 1997, the value of total exports by air to the United States accounted for 26% of the value of Hong Kong's total exports by air and increased by 14% over the same period in 1996."

Hong Kong. Census and Statistics Department. "Analysis of

External Trade Statistics by Mode of Transport." Press Release 26 Aug 1997. document-level access: <http://www.info.gov.hk/censtatd/hkstat/press/t51h97.htm>

HONG KONG--ECONOMIC CONDITIONS (v26)

"Hong Kong's 1996 Gross Domestic Product (GDP) is estimated to have reached nominal $155 billion, a real rate of growth of 4.7 percent over 1995, the same as 1995's expansion over 1994....Population continued to expand at an average annual rate of 1.9 percent to exceed 6.3 million people. Real per capita GDP growth slowed from 1995's 3.1 percent to 2.1 percent in 1996. But at 6.5 percent, inflation, represented by the consumer price index, declined from 1995....In 1996, agricultural production again accounted for only 0.2 percent of Hong Kong's total GDP." (p44)

Whitton, Carolyn L./U.S. Dept. of Agriculture. Economic Research Service. "Hong Kong." China: International Agriculture and Trade Reports Situation and Outlook Series Jun 1997. p44-46.

In Hong Kong, "there are thousands of automobiles on this island of 6.31 million people that carry a price tag in excess of $100,000. The tax on a new car is 120 percent of the purchase price....Restaurants often charge $25 for breakfast, $50 for lunch and $100 for dinner....[The rich and the poor] both pay a flat income tax of 15 percent. There are no taxes on property, dividends or capital gains. Corporations pay a flat 17-percent tax." (p1 secC)

Smith, Joel J. "Business: Hong Kong Opens Borders: Michigan Companies Tout Entry to Orient." Detroit News 12 Oct 1997. p1-2 secC.

"The preliminary estimate of Hong Kong's GNP in 1995, at constant market prices, was 5.2% above that in 1994. During the same period, the growth rate of Gross Domestic Product (GDP) at constant prices was 4.7%....When measured at current market prices, Hong Kong's GNP in 1995 was estimated to be $1,097.9 billion. Its difference from the estimated GDP for 1995 ($1,084.6 billion) represents net factor income inflow into Hong Kong ($13.3 billion). With reference to the estimated mid-year population of Hong Kong in 1995, per capita GNP in 1995 was $178,344, representing an increase of 5.7% over 1994 in nominal terms."

Hong Kong. Census and Statistics Department. "Estimates of Hong Kong's Gross National Product for 1995." Press Release 27 May 1997. document-level access: <http://www.info.gov.hk/censtatd/hkstat/press/gnp195.htm>

HONG KONG--EMPLOYMENT

In Hong Kong, "taking all the major sectors surveyed together, there were around 54,100 vacancies [in employment] in June 1997, up 13.8% from the number recorded in June 1996. In terms of the number of persons engaged, the wholesale, retail and import/export trades, restaurants and hotels sector was the largest, employing 1,029,600 persons in June 1997. This was followed by the financing, insurance, real estate and business services sector, with an employment of 414,600; the manufacturing sector, 315,400; the community, social and personal services sector, 313,800; and the transport, storage and communications sector, 181,800. Also, there were 81,700 manual workers at construction sites."

Hong Kong. Census and Statistics Department. "Employment and Vacancy Statistics for June." Press Release 13 Oct 1997. document-level access: <http://www.info.gov.hk/censtatd/hkstat/press/1b20697.htm>

In Hong Kong, "the seasonally adjusted unemployment rate for the period July-September 1997 was 2.2%, and the underemployment rate was 1.0%, according to the latest labour force statistics released...by the Census and Statistics Department. For the period August-October 1997, the provisional seasonally adjusted unemployment rate was marginally higher, at 2.3%, while the provisional underemployment rate remained unchanged at 1.0%....In the three months ending September 1997, total employment showed a notable increase of 4.3% over a year earlier, while total labour supply grew by 3.8%. During the period July-September 1997, the number of unemployed persons was estimated at 69,700, and the number of underemployed persons was estimated at 33,100."

Hong Kong. Census and Statistics Department. "Unemployment and Underemployment Statistics." Press Release 17 Nov 1997. document-level access: <http://www.info.gov.hk/censtatd/hkstat/press/1b10997.htm>

HONG KONG--POPULATION

"The estimated mid-1997 population of Hong Kong was 6,502,100, according to figures released...by the Census and Statistics Department. There was an increase of 191,100 persons as compared with the mid-1996 population estimate, representing a growth rate of 3 per cent."

Hong Kong. Census and Statistics Department. "Estimated Population of Hong Kong." Press Release 18 Sep 1997. document-level access: <http://www.info.gov.hk/censtatd/hkstat/press/endjun97.htm>

HORSE INDUSTRY--MICHIGAN

"Michigan's horse population fell by nearly one-fifth in the last 12 years, and experts expect that decline to continue as farm land is gobbled up by development and Detroit-area casinos lure gamblers from race tracks. The state's horse population is 130,000, down from 160,000 in 1984. In tricounty Metro Detroit, which still accounts for more than 10 percent of the statewide total, the 13,700-member herd is down dramatically--nearly 22 percent....All together, the value of Michigan horses tops $400 million....Oakland, with 7,000, has more horses than the other 82 counties....The breeds used for horse racing are those that experienced the greatest decline in population since 1991. Today's standard-bred population of 12,000 is down 30 percent since 1991. Thoroughbred horses now number 7,600 in Michigan, down 20 percent from five years earlier." (p1 secA)

Cain, Charlie. "Metro: Horse Population Declines." Detroit News 30 Sep 1997. p1,4 secC.

HORSE INDUSTRY--TURKMENISTAN

Bazarbay Meredov, deputy chief of the Atlaree, the Turkmen State Horse Company, "notes, there are 3100 Akhal Tekes [horses], with 110 registered stallions and 300 one-year-olds. There are 15 new private stud farms, and each has between 20 and 80 Akhal Tekes." (p17)

Maslow, Jonathan. "The Golden Horses of Turkmenistan." Aramco World v48 n3 May-Jun 1997. p10-13,15-17,19. (ISSN1044-1891).

HORSE INDUSTRY--UNITED STATES (v26)

HORTICULTURE

see also CUT FLOWERS; ROSES

HORTICULTURE--ASIA--UNITED STATES

"Asia accounted for 35 percent of the expansion of U.S. horticultural exports in the 1990s....The top ranked U.S. horticultural exports are citrus, apples, frozen potatoes (mostly french fries), and almonds. These items accounted for about 30 percent of U.S. horticultural exports to Asia." (p23)

Vocke, Gary/U.S. Dept. of Agriculture. Economic Research Service. "Special Article: Emerging Import Markets in Asia." APEC: International Agriculture and Trade Reports Situation and Outlook Series Aug 1997. p13-25.

"U.S. horticultural exports to Asia averaged $3.2 billion during 1994 to 1996, while exports to other countries averaged $5.5 billion....The 1994-96 share of U.S. horticultural exports to Asia averaged 37 percent, growing from 31 percent in 1990. Although Southeast Asia is a relatively minor market for U.S.

horticultural exporters, the region's share has increased from 3 percent in 1990 to 4.6 percent in 1996. Asia averaged a 12-percent share of total U.S. horticultural imports from 1994 to 1996....Southeast Asia's share of the U.S. [import] market, at 5 percent in 1996, has fared similarly with the rest of Asia." (p7)

U.S. Dept. of Agriculture. Economic Research Service. "Fresh-Market Vegetables." Vegetables and Specialties Situation and Outlook Report Nov 1997. p5-8.

HORTICULTURE--COLOMBIA--UNITED STATES

"Colombian fresh-cut flowers have been the greatest beneficiary of the ATPA [Andean Trade Preference Act]. In 1992, Colombia exported $87.7 million worth of fresh-cut flowers to the United States. By 1995, Colombian exports increased to over $374.4 million. This represents a 427-percent increase over that 3-year period. Domestic growers of roses and carnations have been particularly hard-hit. In 1996, Colombia exported approximately 1.7 billion roses and carnations to the United States. Colombia now controls more than 50 percent of the United States market for roses and 80 percent of the carnation market. Overall, Colombian flowers account for about 65 percent of the United States fresh-cut flower market. The preferential treatment accorded Colombian fresh-cut flowers under the ATPA has had a direct and dire impact on the United States flower industry--approximately 58 percent of which is located in California." (pS7868)

Boxer, Barbara (Sen.-Calif.). "Statements on Introduced Bills and Joint Resolutions." Congressional Record. Daily ed. v143 n104 22 Jul 1997. pS7863-7869. section/page-level access: <http://thomas.loc.gov/cgi-bin/query/R?r105:FLD001:S07868:> (ISSN0363-7239). (X1.1A.105/1).

HORTICULTURE--UNITED STATES

"The U.S. leads the world in the production and marketing of flowers, cut foliage, potted plants, bedding plants and other nursery crops, and turfgrass--known collectively as the 'green' industry. U.S. growers' cash receipts for these products are projected to reach $11.3 billion in 1997, an increase of more than 8 percent over last year. U.S. consumers, businesses, and institutions are expected to spend an estimated $53 billion for these products, including the value of closely associated accessories and services, in 1997....Grower receipts for 1996 in the environmental horticulture production sector are estimated at $6.9 billion, a 6-percent increase over the previous year, with expectations of a further increase of 7 percent in 1997....Since 1994, the value of imports [of floral and potted plants] at port of entry has increased about $100 million every year, driven primarily by cut flowers. Imports of floral and potted plant products reached $700 million in 1996. Other imported greenhouse and nursery products added about $250 million in value in 1996. For 1997, the total import value of all floriculture and environmental horticulture products is expected easily to exceed $1 billion." (p9)

Johnson, Doyle. "Commodity Spotlight: 'Green' Industry Grower Receipts to Exceed $11 Billion." Agricultural Outlook Jul 1997. p9-10.

In 1996, "U.S. horticultural product exports increased nearly 4 percent to about $9.9 billion, largely due to gains in wine and nut exports....Wine exports expanded 37 percent to $302 million, and nut exports rose 15 percent to $1.6 billion. Wine exports to the EU-15 jumped 54 percent to $144 million....Exports to Canada also advanced 33 percent to $67 million. The value of almond exports surpassed $1 billion, a 30-percent increase over 1995....Almond volume only advanced 10 percent to 276,000 tons." (p3)

Greene, Joel/U.S. Dept. of Agriculture. Economic Research Service. "Agricultural Exports Surpass $60 Billion." Foreign Agricultural Trade of the United States Jan-Mar 1997. p2-3.

HOSPICE CARE--UNITED STATES

In the U.S., "there are 2,800 hospice programs in all 50 States and in 1995 they cared for more than 390,000 patients. One out of every three people who died from cancer or AIDS were cared for by hospice....With 28 percent of all Medicare costs now going toward the care of people in their last year of life, and almost 50 percent of those costs spent during the last 2 months of life, cost-effective alternatives are needed. Studies show hospices reduce Medicare spending. A 1995 Lewin study showed that for every dollar Medicare spent on hospice, it saved $1.52 in Medicare part A and part B expenditures. Similarly, a 1989 study commissioned by the Health Care Financing Administration showed savings of $1.26 for every Medicare dollar spent on hospice." (pS4320)

Breaux, John B. (Sen.-La.). "Statements on Introduced Bills and Joint Resolutions." Congressional Record. Daily ed. v143 n61 12 May 1997. pS4320-4322. section/page-level access: <http://thomas.loc.gov/cgi-bin/query/R?r105:FLD001:S04320:> (ISSN0363-7239). (X1.1A.105/1).

HOSPICES (TERMINAL CARE)--GREAT BRITAIN --NETHERLANDS (v26)

HOSPICES (TERMINAL CARE)--UNITED STATES (v26)

HOSPITALITY INDUSTRY

see also HOTELS

HOSPITALITY INDUSTRY--AUSTRALIA (v26)

According to the report, "Accommodation Industry, Australia 1995-96," by the Australian Bureau of Statistics, "in 1995-96 the Australian accommodation industry recorded a 7.8 per cent operating profit margin, after experiencing an 8.4 per cent operating loss in 1991-92. The industry's pre tax profit in the 1995-96 financial year was $401 million....Hotels operated by the 5,288 businesses in the industry recorded an operating profit margin of 4.4 per cent, compared to 14.8 per cent for motels and guest houses and 15.8 per cent for caravan parks. The relatively low profit margin for hotels was mainly attributable to those hotels with star grading of 4 or 5 (which recorded an operating profit margin of 2.9 per cent) and/or those with more than 100 rooms (3.8 per cent). Accommodation industry businesses generated $5,259 million in income in 1995-96, of which 62 per cent ($3,253 million) was from the provision of accommodation. A further 26 per cent of income was generated from meal and liquor sales."

Australian Bureau of Statistics. "Accommodation Industry Profits Rise--ABS Survey Results." Media Release 10 Nov 1997. document-level access: <http://www.abs.gov.au/websitedbs/d3110125.nsf/4a255eef008309e44a255eef00061e57/c3dfdc043673f69cca25654b000531de?OpenDocument>

HOSPITALITY INDUSTRY--EMPLOYMENT--AUSTRALIA

According to the report, "Accommodation Industry, Australia 1995-96," by the Australian Bureau of Statistics, "there were 81,086 people employed in the [hospitality] industry at the end of June 1996, an increase of 9 per cent since 30 June 1992. Full-time employment rose 14 per cent and part-time employment rose 3 per cent. At the end of June 1996, 90 per cent of businesses in the industry employed fewer than 20 people. These businesses accounted for 31 per cent (25,525) of people employed in the industry and 53 per cent ($213 million) of the industry's operating profit before tax. In contrast, businesses employing more than 100 people accounted for 2 per cent of all businesses in the industry, but accounted for 49 per cent (39,459) of industry employment and 21 per cent ($84.3 million) of operating profit before tax."

Australian Bureau of Statistics. "Accommodation Industry Profits Rise--ABS Survey Results." Media Release 10 Nov 1997. document-level access: <http://www.abs.gov.au/

websitedbs/d3110125.nsf/4a255eef008309e44a255eef00061e57/c3dfdc043673f69cca25654b000531de?OpenDocument>

HOSPITALS--AUSTRALIA (v26)

In 1995-1996, the Australian Bureau of Statistics "found that for every four days of hospitalisation, one day was provided by private hospitals and the other three by public hospitals. Revenue generated by private hospitals amounted to $3,183 million in 1995-96, or 0.7 per cent of Australia's gross national product. The publication 'Private Hospitals, Australia'...states that the number of free-standing day hospitals run by private operators has almost doubled, from 72 in 1991-92 to 140 in 1995-96....[Private acute and psychiatric hospitals] have increased from 319 in 1991-92 to 323 in 1995-96. However, in the same period the number of day hospital facilities (day surgery theatres and endoscopy rooms) operating within these hospitals has increased from 125 to 156."

Australian Bureau of Statistics. "Strong Growth for Day Hospitals in the Private Sector--ABS." Media Release 5 Nov 1997. document-level access: <http://www.abs.gov.au/websitedbs/d3110125.nsf/4a255eef008309e44a255eef00061e57/b8cdcb1b3381ce28ca256545007fc903?OpenDocument>

HOSPITALS--BRITISH COLUMBIA--WAITING LISTS (v26)

HOSPITALS--CANADA--WAITING LISTS (v26)

HOSPITALS--EUROPE (v26)

HOSPITALS--GREAT BRITAIN--WAITING LISTS (v26)

In Great Britain, "at the end of March 1979, there were 185,195 patients waiting more than a year for treatment at national health service hospitals--an increase of 24 per cent over the previous year. The final figure for the end of March 1997 is 31,208. This represents an increase of 580 per cent over the previous year." (c745)

Milburn, Alan (H.C.-Darlington). "Waiting Times." Great Britain. Parliament. House of Commons. Debates. 22 Jul 1997. c745. section-level access: <http://www.parliament.the-stationery-office.co.uk/pa/cm199798/cmhansrd/cm970722/70722-03.htm#70722-03_sbhd2>

HOSPITALS--MASSACHUSETTS--BOSTON (v26)

HOSPITALS--MICHIGAN (v26)

HOSPITALS--MICHIGAN--DETROIT (v26)

HOSPITALS--NORTHERN IRELAND (v26)

HOSPITALS--UNITED STATES (v26)

HOSPITALS--UNITED STATES--ADMINISTRATION --COSTS

In the U.S., "a recent study published in the NEW ENGLAND JOURNAL OF MEDICINE shows an increase in hospital administrative costs in 1994 as compared to 1990. Overall, administration accounted for an average of 26 percent of total hospital costs in 1994 (as compared to 24.8 percent in 1990). Administrative costs...varied by type of hospital, from 24.3 percent at short-term general hospitals to 37.5 percent at psychiatric hospitals....From 1990 to 1994, hospital administrative costs increased by 2.2 percentage points, to 34.0 percent, for for-profit hospitals; by 1.2 percentage points, to 24.5 percent, for private, non-profit hospitals; and by 0.6 percentage points, to 22.9 percent, for public hospitals....In 1994, administration accounted for 37.5 percent of total costs at psychiatric hospitals (44.4 percent at for-profits) and 33.0 percent at rehabilitation hospitals (37.7 percent at for-profits)." (p12)

Woolhandler, Steffie/Himmelstein, David U. "Around the Nation: Study Finds Highest Administrative Costs at For-Profit Hospitals." Health Advocate n188 Spr 1997. p12.

HOSPITALS--UNITED STATES--EMERGENCY SERVICE (v26)

HOSPITALS--UNITED STATES--EMERGENCY SERVICE --AGED (v26)

HOSPITALS--UNITED STATES--EMERGENCY SERVICE --YOUTH

In the U.S., "hospital emergency room reports show a total of 6,500 teens nationwide were treated for any kind of marijuana or hashish effects in 1995--less than 0.1 percent of the 10 million teenage ER visits, and only one-fourth the number of teens treated for adverse affects from aspirin or Tylenol (Drug Abuse Warning Network, Annual Emer-gency Department Data, 1994). Further, four-fifths of these 6,500 'marijuana' treatments involved youths who had also ingested more dangerous drugs, such as alcohol. Only 1,300 teen emergency cases involved marijuana alone, the same number attributed to the allergy medication Benadryl." (p20)

Males, Mike. "Pot Boiler: Why Are Media Enlisting in the Government's Crusade against Marijuana?" Extra! v10 n4 Jul-Aug 1997. p20-21.

HOSPITALS--UNITED STATES--MORTALITY

"Dr. William Jarvis, chief of investigation and prevention for the [U.S.] Centers for Disease Control and Prevention's Hospital Infections Program, estimates that at least 80,000 patients die each year from infections they acquire after entering the hospital. That makes hospital infections the nation's fourth most common cause of death, accounting for more mortalities than car accidents and homicides combined. Jarvis believes that about 5 to 10 percent of patients--from 1.75 million to 3.5 million people annually--contract infections while hospitalized, a rate experts estimate has probably increased at least 50 percent in the last decade." (p28)

Leslie, Jacques. "Unsanitary Behavior." Mother Jones v22 n4 Jul-Aug 1997. p28-30. (ISSN0362-8841).

HOTELS--AUSTRALIA (v26)

HOTELS--CALIFORNIA

"According to the Tourism Industry Development Council, a housekeeper starts at $11.59 an hour in a union hotel in San Francisco, where the union has organized 83 percent of the industry, but at only $7.85 an hour in Los Angeles, where 50 percent of the industry is unionized....[San Francisco's] unionized hotels contribute cash: 15 cents an employee-hour to a new childcare fund. Starting later this year, the fund will reimburse employees $100 to $200 a month for childcare." (p20)

Seymour, Chris. "Corporate America: Low-Wage Innovations." In These Times v21 n19 11 Aug 1997. p18-20. (ISSN0160-5992).

HOTELS--EUROPE (v26)

HOTELS--ISRAEL

"Five years ago, there were 10 Israeli chains with 40 hotels, and five international chains with 11 hotels. This year, 14 Israeli chains have 61 hotels, and 14 international chains have 57 hotels....Today, half of Israel's 23,000 hotel rooms belong to international chains....'There are two major trends at work,' says Avi Rosental, chairman of the Israel Hotel Association. 'In the past six months, there's been a 15-percent drop in incoming tourism, while simultaneously, international chains are coming into the market.'" (p40) "Last year, there was a 6-percent drop in hotel occupancy among tourists, but Israeli hotel occupancy rose by 11 percent. Of last year's 16.2 million bed-nights in Israel's hotels, 7.2 million were domestic....[Avi Cassouto, general manager of Days Inn, Israel,] says that more than 85 percent of incoming tourism comes via travel agents, who prefer chains, which provide special packages." (p42)

Sugarman, Margo Lipschitz. "Special Report: Tourism: Chain Reaction." Jerusalem Report v8 n5 10 Jul 1997. p40,42. (ISSN0792-6049).

HOTELS--MEXICO

"The Mexican lodging industry grew from 5,310 properties with 262,475 rooms in 1983 to 7,984 facilities with 333,547 rooms in 1990. Of those 333,547 rooms, 28% were categorized as rooms in grand tourism and five- and four-star establishments; 36% of the

rooms were in three-, two-, and one-star properties; and 36% were located in budget/economy or no-classification accommodations....The number of lodging rooms at the end of 1994 was 374,107 (Secretaria de Turismo 1992-93, 1993-94)." (p46)
Casado, Matt A. "Mexico's 1989-94 Tourism Plan: Implications of Internal Political and Economic Instability." Journal of Travel Research v36 n1 Sum 1997. p44-51. (ISSN0047-2875).

HOTELS--RATES--MICHIGAN--DETROIT

"Though prices for U.S. hotel rooms are up an average of 20 percent to 25 percent in two years, room rates in Detroit are pretty good,...[a] New York-based Zagat Survey reported.... In pricing, not only were Detroit's prices slightly below the average of the 32 major cities of Zagat's list, its hotels' average 19-percent rate of increase in the last two years was below the average of 24 percent. According to Zagat, the average price of a hotel room in Detroit this year is $144.19. This compares to $187.85 in New York, the most expensive, and $105.15 in Las Vegas, the least expensive." (p3 secE)
Volgenau, Gerry. "Business: Detroit's Best Hotels Not among Top Ones." Detroit Free Press 10 Jul 1997. p3 secE.

HOTELS--RATES--UNITED STATES

In the U.S., "prices for a double room [in a hotel] have jumped by 24 percent in the past two years, according to a recent nationwide Zagat survey of 12,300 frequent travelers....The average room price this year is $187.85 in Miami, up 40 percent; $153.36 in Orlando, up 32 percent; $155.05 in Fort Lauderdale, up 41 percent. In Detroit, the rate is $144.19, up 19 percent." (p1 secG)
Volgenau, Gerry. "Travel: Hotel Rates Elevate to Penthouse Level." Detroit Free Press 12 Oct 1997. p1 secG.

HOTELS--UNITED STATES

"More than two-thirds of leisure car travelers [in the U.S.] checked in at paid accommodations for at least one night last year--at a hotel, motel, or bed-and-breakfast inn....Nearly three-fourths of car travelers with household incomes of $50,000 or more stay in paid accommodations, versus half of those with incomes below $15,000. Income levels also explain why seven in ten car travelers with college or postgraduate educations stay at a hotel, motel, or inn, compared with 64 percent of car travelers who have no college education." (p46) "For those who don't use paid accommodations, the two biggest reasons that would change their minds are if hotels and the like were convenient to their destination or it was cheaper. Thirty-one percent say they would stay the night if there were no restrictions on animals, and 16 percent would prefer that there were restrictions on children or young adults. Fifteen percent say none of these factors would influence them to stay in paid accommodations." (p47)
Fisher, Christy. "The Not-So-Great American Road Trip." American Demographics v19 n5 May 1997. p42-48. article-level access: <http://www.demographics.com/Publications/AD/97_ad/9705_ad/AD970531.htm> (ISSN0163-4089).

"The priciest hotel stay among major U.S. cities can be had in New York City, where a double room for one night runs an average of $188, according to a new Zagat Survey. Miami is close behind, at $186....The average double room in Miami increased 40 percent in price between 1995 and 1997, compared with a 16 percent increase in the Big Apple, and a 24 percent rise on average for the 32 most-expensive cities....Fort Lauderdale is the 14th most expensive place to stay, with an average per-night cost of $155....The average price of a hotel room in Honolulu rose 7 percent between 1995 and 1997, to $149." (p34)
Klein, Matthew. "Kaleidoscope: High-Priced Digs." American Demographics v19 n11 Nov 1997. p34. article-level access: <http://www.demographics.com/publications/ad/97_ad/9711_ad/ad97118.htm> (ISSN0163-4089).

HOTLINES (COUNSELING)--MICHIGAN

Over the past year, Project Life, a hotline for people considering suicide or abortion that was organized a year ago by the Roman Catholic Archdiocese of Detroit, Michigan, "received calls from 140 people considering suicide. Of the 140 callers, 25 were within six months of death and were offered palliative care by Angela Hospice in Livonia, Michigan. The other 115 callers had chronic pain or disabilities and were helped...." (p2)
"ProLife Efforts Paying Off." ProLife News v22 n9 Oct 1997. p2.

HOURS OF LABOR

see also HOLIDAYS; LEAVE OF ABSENCE; OVERTIME

HOURS OF LABOR--GREECE

Amongst the small European "countries, Greece, with 4.5 million days not worked each year, holds fourth place in western Europe. According to this measure, it has headed the list in Europe since 1985. In the early 1990s, industrial action in Greece alone accounted for 43 per cent of days not worked in Europe." (p79-80)
Aligisakis, Maximos. "Labour Disputes in Western Europe: Typology and Tendencies." International Labour Review v136 n1 Spr 1997. p73-94. (ISSN0020-7780).

HOURS OF LABOR--ITALY

Italy had "over 13 million days not worked per year (average for the 1970-93 period)....Italian workers were responsible for 35 per cent of the total days not worked in Europe, but accounted for more than half of all European workers on strike....A substantial decrease was observed over the years: the number of days not worked fell from approximately 20 million in the 1970s to under 4 million in the early 1990s." (p79)
Aligisakis, Maximos. "Labour Disputes in Western Europe: Typology and Tendencies." International Labour Review v136 n1 Spr 1997. p73-94. (ISSN0020-7780).

HOURS OF LABOR--MOROCCO--ZIMBABWE--CHILDREN (v26)

HOURS OF LABOR--NEW ZEALAND

"Employees worked an average of 38.6 hours per week in August 1997, latest figures from Statistics New Zealand show. This is the lowest level since August 1992 when the average was 38.4 hours. Over the year to August 1997, average weekly hours worked decreased by 0.5 per cent."
Statistics New Zealand. "Quarterly Employment Survey--August 1997 Quarter." Press Release 19 Nov 1997. document-level access: <http://www.stats.govt.nz/statsweb.nsf/52518ce3e01f62f4cc256388000c48c0/643ce4a7904078754c25655300718c6c?OpenDocument>

HOURS OF LABOR--TEACHERS

"Data published by the Organization for Economic Cooperation and Development indicate that in 1992 the average amount of time per year public school teachers at the primary level spent teaching (excluding other school responsibilities) in 15 countries (mostly European) was 858 hours. The range ran from a low of 624 hours in Sweden to a high of 1,093 hours in the United States." (p9)
"News of the Profession: Teacher Workload." Reading Today v15 n3 Dec 1997-Jan 1998. p9. (ISSN0737-4208).

HOURS OF LABOR--UNITED STATES (v26)

"The United States Department of Labor cites surveys which show a link between factors such as absenteeism or unproductive time at work with the fact that workers have children. One survey showed that about 57 per cent of women and 33 per cent of men spent unproductive time at work because of child-care concerns." (p123)
"Perspectives." International Labour Review v136 n1 Spr 1997. p109-128. (ISSN0020-7780).

"Nearly one-half of all American businesses have slashed their payrolls in the past ten years, according to the United States Department of Labor. In the typical company, one employee is now doing the work of one-and-one-third persons--for the same pay with less time off....'Experts believe that burnout-related absenteeism, tardiness, low productivity, and job turnover cost American companies $75 billion to $160 billion annually,' AMERICAN HEALTH magazine reports. 'Work time has increased by 158 hours a year--nearly a whole month--since 1969....'...In 58 percent of today's marriages, AMERICAN HEALTH adds, both spouses work." (p38)

Rakstis, Ted J. "Workaholism: An Entrepreneurial Ill." Kiwanis v82 n8 Sep 1997. p38-41,48. (ISSN0162-5276).

Harriet Presser, director of the University of Maryland's Center on Population, Gender, and Social Inequality, "found that less than one-third of all employed Americans ages 18 and older in 1991 regularly worked a standard workweek--daytime employment, 35 to 40 hours per week, Monday through Friday....About one-fourth of dual-earner couples work split shifts--one spouse working during the daytime, the other working evenings, nights, or weekends. The share is higher (about one-third) among couples with preschool-age children....More than half of those who worked nonstandard hours said they did so because their jobs required it, she found." (p1) "Fully 52 percent of the survey respondents said that they worked nonstandard hours because their jobs required it....Only 5 percent of people working nonstandard hours did so to meet child-care responsibilities." (p2)

"24-Hour Economy Changing How We Work and Live." Population Today v25 n12 Dec 1997. p1-2. (ISSN0749-2448).

"According to a new U.S. NEWS/Bozell Worldwide poll conducted by KRC Research and Consulting, 49 percent of Americans say society puts too much emphasis on work and not enough on leisure. That's a big change from 11 years ago. In a study conducted by the Opinion Research Corp. in 1986, just 28 percent felt that way." (p79) "According to the U.S. NEWS/Bozell poll, 60 percent of respondents, including 62 percent of the managers surveyed, say shorter work hours would give employees an incentive to be more productive on the job and would have little impact on the country's overall standard of living." (p81)

Saltzman, Amy. "1998 Career Guide: News You Can Use: When Less Is More." U.S. News & World Report v123 n16 27 Oct 1997. p78-82,84. article-level access: <http://www.usnews.com/usnews/issue/971027/27WORK.HTM> (ISSN0041-5537).

HOURS OF LABOR--UNITED STATES--TEACHERS

"In addition to spending an average of 33 hours per week at school to conduct classes, prepare lessons, attend staff meetings, and fulfill a variety of other school-related responsibilities, the average full-time public school teacher in the United States worked an average of 12 additional hours per week before and after school and on weekends during the 1993-1994 school year, according to statistics released by the U.S. National Center for Education Statistics." (p9)

"News of the Profession: Teacher Workload." Reading Today v15 n3 Dec 1997-Jan 1998. p9. (ISSN0737-4208).

HOURS OF LABOR--UNITED STATES--WOMEN (v26)

HOURS OF LABOR, FLEXIBLE--CALIFORNIA --SILICON VALLEY

In California, "between 219,600 and 325,660 people in Silicon Valley are engaged in some form of flexible employment....If the upper boundary is correct: flexible employment accounted for about 40 per cent of total employment in Santa Clara County in 1995; flexible employment is growing five times as fast as overall employment....If the lower boundary is more accurate: flexible employment accounted for about 27 per cent of total employment in Santa Clara County in 1995; flexible employment is growing two and a half times as fast as overall employment; growth in flexible employment has accounted for approximately 55 per cent of the net job growth in the county in the past 10 years....More than half of all growth in employment in Santa Clara County in the past ten years can be accounted for by the rise in flexible employment." (p37-38)

Carnoy, Martin/Castells, Manuel/Benner, Chris. "Labour Markets and Employment Practices in the Age of Flexibility: A Case Study of Silicon Valley." International Labour Review v136 n1 Spr 1997. p27-48. (ISSN0020-7780).

HOUSE CONSTRUCTION--SWEDEN--COSTS (v26)

HOUSE PARENTS

see CHILD CARE WORKERS

HOUSEHOLD APPLIANCES--UNITED STATES (v26)

HOUSEHOLD EXPENSES

see COST AND STANDARD OF LIVING

HOUSEHOLD INCOME

see INCOME

HOUSEHOLD MOVING

see MOVING, HOUSEHOLD

HOUSEHOLD SURVEYS--UNITED STATES (v26)

HOUSEHOLD VIOLENCE

see FAMILY VIOLENCE

HOUSEHOLDS

see also COST AND STANDARD OF LIVING; LIVING ALONE

"Average household size among the 111 reporting countries or areas ranged from 7 persons in Algeria to 2.1 persons in Sweden, the...[UN's 'Demographic Yearbook 1995'] indicates. Among the 25 largest countries in the world, the largest average household size was in India--5.5 persons per household--and the smallest was in the United States, the Russian Federation and France, which had 2.6 per household." (p77)

"The Chronicle Library Shelf: Demographic Yearbook 1995." UN Chronicle v34 n3 1997. p77. (ISSN0251-7329).

HOUSEHOLDS--ALABAMA (v26)

HOUSEHOLDS--ALASKA--NEVADA

"Household growth between 1990 and 1996 was fastest in Nevada, at 32 percent, according to recent Census Bureau estimates....Wyoming and Alaska saw the biggest declines, at 26 percent and 25 percent, respectively. Alaska didn't lose out altogether, though. It ranked tenth among states for total household growth between 1990 and 1996, partly because it ranked first for growth among householders aged 55 to 64, at 37 percent, followed by Nevada at 29 percent. It ranked second for growth among householders aged 65 and older (40 percent), after first-place Nevada (43 percent)." (p34)

Cravatta, Matthew. "Kaleidoscope: Where Households Are Booming." American Demographics v19 n11 Nov 1997. p34. article-level access: <http://www.demographics.com/publications/ad/97_ad/9711_ad/ad97119.htm> (ISSN0163-4089).

HOUSEHOLDS--ASIAN AMERICANS

In the U.S., "of the 2.8 million Asian and Pacific Islander households in 1996, 77 percent were families, compared with 69 percent of white households....Nearly 40 percent of API households consisted of a married couple with children, compared with about 26 percent of white households. The share of single mothers with children, however, was about the same for Asians and whites--around 5 percent....About one in six API households has five or more persons, compared with one in 12 white households....In 1996 only 17 percent of API households were comprised of an adult living alone versus 26 percent of white households." (p6-7)

Pollard, Kelvin M./De Vita, Carol J. "A Portrait of Asians and Pacific Islanders in the United States." Statistical Bulletin v78 n3 Jul-Sep 1997. p2-9. (ISSN0790-8334).

HOUSEHOLDS--CARIBBEAN AREA--LATIN AMERICA --WOMEN

"Data compiled by the Population Council show a rise in female-headed households in 18 out of 26 censuses and surveys reviewed globally. Tabulations by the U.N. Economic Commission for Latin America and the Caribbean (ECLAC) find this trend in 8 out of 13 countries in the region. Another new phenomenon in some countries is households maintained by wives. Two Argentine researchers, Rosa Geldstein and Nena Delpino, report that the number of households maintained by women in Buenos Aires rose from 19 percent in 1980 to 27 percent in 1992--one in every 3.7 households. Almost one-half of these female heads of household were wives who became main earners." (p43,45)

Buvinic, Mayra. "Women in Poverty: A New Global Underclass." Foreign Policy n108 Fall 1997. p38-53. (ISSN0015-7228).

HOUSEHOLDS--CHINA (v26)

HOUSEHOLDS--EUROPE (v26)

HOUSEHOLDS--HISPANIC AMERICANS

In the U.S., "in 1996, 79 percent of Latino households were composed of families, compared with less than 70 percent of white and black households....About three-fourths of the households in each Hispanic ethnic group are made up of families. The percentages ranged from 84 percent of Mexican households to 73 percent of households of Other Hispanics. The share of family households headed by a married couple in 1996 ranged from about one-half among Puerto Rican families to three-fourths among Cuban families. The percentage of families maintained by women ranged from 19 percent among Cuban families to 42 percent among Puerto Rican families." (p30)

del Pinal, Jorge/Singer, Audrey. "Generations of Diversity: Latinos in the United States." Population Bulletin v52 n3 Oct 1997. p2-47. (ISSN0032-468X).

HOUSEHOLDS--IRELAND

According to Ireland's 1991 Census, "during the 1986-1991 period the average number of persons per private household fell from 3.54 to 3.34. Average household size in rural areas was 3.46 compared with 3.26 in urban areas. The proportion of the population in private households with a density of 2 or more persons per room fell from 37 per cent in 1926 to 2 per cent in 1991. 97 per cent of rural private households had a piped water supply in 1991 compared with 58 per cent twenty years earlier."

Ireland. Central Statistics Office. "Census 91--Volume 10: Housing." Press Release 27 Feb 1997. document-level access: <http://www.cso.ie/pressreleases/prel91hous.html>

According to Ireland's 1996 Census, "the average size of private households in permanent housing units in the State fell from 3.34 in 1995 to 3.14 in 1996, which is a continuation of a long-term decline. The report shows that the average size in 1946 was 4.16. The Census 96 volume also details how the smallest households are to be found in Dublin County Borough with an average of 2.67 people. The largest households were enumerated in South Dublin with an average size of 3.50. The total number of private households is up from 1.029 million to 1.123 million between 1991 and 1996--a rise of 94,000 or 9%. The average number of children per family has fallen from 2.2 in 1981 to 1.8 in 1996. Households composed of one person increased by 17% (+34,274) since 1991. Almost a third of these were in Dublin County and County Borough with 78,913. One-person households represent 22% of the total number in the State. South Dublin had the lowest percentage at 12%."

Ireland. Central Statistics Office. "1996 Census--Volume 3, Household Composition and Family Unit." Press Release 27 Nov 1997. document-level access: <http://www.cso.ie/pressreleases/prelcen96v3.html>

HOUSEHOLDS--JAPAN--AGED (v26)

HOUSEHOLDS--MASSACHUSETTS--BOSTON--CHILDREN (v26)

HOUSEHOLDS--MICHIGAN--LIVINGSTON COUNTY --WASHTENAW COUNTY (v26)

HOUSEHOLDS--SWEDEN (v26)

HOUSEHOLDS--UNITED STATES (v26)

"There were 29.2 million households maintained by women with no husband present in 1996, according to tabulations released...by the [U.S.] Commerce Department's Census Bureau....Married couples with their own children under age 18 accounted for 25 percent of all households. The average number of people per household was 2.65. Thirty-two percent of all family groups with children were single-parent situations. People living alone made up 25 percent of all households."

U.S. Census Bureau. Economic and Statistics Administration. "Three in Ten Households Were Maintained by Women in 1996." Press Release 1 Jul 1997. document-level access: <http://www.census.gov/Press-Release/cb97-110.html>

HOUSEHOLDS--UNITED STATES--AGED (v26)

HOUSEHOLDS--UNITED STATES--ECONOMIC CONDITIONS (v26)

HOUSEHOLDS--UNITED STATES--INDIGENOUS PEOPLES

"Between 1997 and 2010, the number of American Indian, Eskimo and Aleut households in the United States is projected to climb from 713,397 to 906,036. In 1997, 75 percent of the nation's American Indian, Eskimo and Aleut households were made up of families. Of these family households, 65 percent consisted of married couples, 27 percent were maintained by women with no husband present, and 9 percent were maintained by men with no wife present."

U.S. Dept. of Commerce. Economic & Statistics Administration. "Census Facts for Native American Month." Census Bureau Fact Sheet 31 Oct 1997. document-level access: <http://www.census.gov/Press-Release/fs97-11.html>

HOUSEHOLDS--UNITED STATES--SINGLE PEOPLE (v26)

HOUSEHOLDS--UNITED STATES--SINGLE WOMEN (v26)

HOUSEHUSBANDS--UNITED STATES (v26)

HOUSING

see also HOMELESSNESS; OFFSHORE ASSEMBLY INDUSTRY--HOUSING--MEXICO; POOR--HOUSING--TEXAS--HOUSTON; PUBLIC HOUSING; RENTAL HOUSING; SUPPLEMENTAL SECURITY INCOME PROGRAM--HOUSING

HOUSING--ALABAMA (v26)

HOUSING--AUSTRALIA

According to the Australian Bureau of Statistics, "in 1995-96, 70 per cent of the 6.9 million households in Australia were owner-occupied and 28 per cent were renting. Of those who owned their home, 60 per cent owned it outright and the remainder were paying off a mortgage or loan secured against the property. For many households, housing costs are the largest regular item of expenditure. This is particularly true for households paying off a mortgage (28 per cent of households) and households paying rent to private landlords (20 per cent) and even for government tenants (6 per cent)....The separate house is the most popular dwelling in Australia, making up 79 per cent of all homes. Flats, units or apartments followed with 12 per cent and semi-detached, row or terrace houses comprised another 8 per cent."

Australian Bureau of Statistics. "Australia's Housing Costs--ABS." Media Release 29 Oct 1997. document-level access: <http://www.abs.gov.au/websitedbs/d3110125.nsf/4a255eef008309e44a255eef00061e57/0a5297cfa5c18ad7ca25653e007aa13e?OpenDocument>

HOUSING--AUSTRALIA--COSTS

According to the Australian Bureau of Statistics, "in 1995-96, households paying off a mortgage had average housing costs (i.e. mortgage and rates payments) of $203 per week, which consumed

19 per cent of their income. Private renters paid an average of $148 per week or 20 per cent of their income, while public renters paid an average of only $62 per week or 17 per cent of their income. Housing costs of outright owners, (property rates), were significantly lower at $21 per week, representing, on average, only 3 percent of their income. Survey results show that housing costs are strongly related to life-cycle stages, such as young singles, young marrieds, families with children and the retired. Costs are high for young singles living alone (on average $136 per week) and young couples ($198 per week). The cost for couples with children declines as the children get older. Couples whose eldest child is 15 to 24 paid $107 per week and couples with non dependants paid $73. Couples 65 and over paid the least amount, on average $23 per week."

Australian Bureau of Statistics. "Australia's Housing Costs--ABS." Media Release 29 Oct 1997. document-level access: <http://www.abs.gov.au/websitedbs/d3110125.nsf/4a255eef008309e44a255eef00061e57/0a5297cfa5c18ad7ca25653e007aa13e?OpenDocument>

HOUSING--CALIFORNIA--LOS ANGELES COUNTY

The Los Angeles-Long Beach, Calif. Metropolitan Area "had 3,276,000 housing units in 1995, of which 2,948,000 were occupied (47 percent by owners and 53 percent by renters). Single-family homes, at 58 percent of all occupied units, represented the predominant housing type in the area. The median age of homes in Los Angeles city was 38 years, compared with 34 years for the remaining area. Homes in the area had a median of 2.2 bedrooms. Occupied homes in the area had a median of 2.5 persons per unit and a median of 4.9 rooms per unit."

U.S. Dept. of Commerce./U.S. Dept. of Housing and Urban Development. "Twenty-Two Percent of the Los Angeles-Long Beach Metropolitan Area's Households Give High Marks to...Neighborhood...." Census Bureau Press Release 22 Oct 1997. document-level access: <http://www.census.gov/Press-Release/cb97h11.html>

HOUSING--CALIFORNIA--LOS ANGELES COUNTY --COSTS

In the Los Angeles-Long Beach, Calif. Metropolian Area, in 1995, "the median monthly housing costs for owners was $943 and for renters was $654. Monthly housing costs include mortgage payments or contract rent, utilities, fuels, insurance, real estate taxes (for owners) and other housing-related expenditures. Monthly housing costs that were $1,000 or more accounted for 48 percent of the owners and 13 percent of the renters....Owners had monthly housing costs that represented a median of 23 percent of their current income; for renters, it was 36 percent."

U.S. Dept. of Commerce./U.S. Dept. of Housing and Urban Development. "Twenty-Two Percent of the Los Angeles-Long Beach Metropolitan Area's Households Give High Marks to...Neighborhood...." Census Bureau Press Release 22 Oct 1997. document-level access: <http://www.census.gov/Press-Release/cb97h11.html>

HOUSING--CALIFORNIA--LOS ANGELES COUNTY --PUBLIC OPINION

"About 22 percent of households in the Los Angeles-Long Beach, Calif. Metropolitan Area rated their neighborhood a perfect 10 and about 27 percent said their home was 'the best place to live,' according to a new report released...by the Commerce Department's Census Bureau and the Department of Housing and Urban Development (HUD). In the report, 'American Housing Survey for the Los Angeles-Long Beach Metropolitan Area in 1995,'...respondents were asked to rate their neighborhood and their house or apartment as a place to live based on scales of 1 to 10, where 10 is the best and 1 is the worst. Of the households in these neighborhoods, 16 percent reported problems with crime, 9 percent reported problems with traffic and 4 percent experienced problems with litter or housing deterioration."

U.S. Dept. of Commerce./U.S. Dept. of Housing and Urban Development. "Twenty-Two Percent of the Los Angeles-Long Beach Metropolitan Area's Households Give High Marks to...Neighborhood...." Census Bureau Press Release 22 Oct 1997. document-level access: <http://www.census.gov/Press-Release/cb97h11.html>

HOUSING--CALIFORNIA--SAN FRANCISCO

"Housing in San Francisco is scarce and exorbitantly expensive. Rents have reached an astronomic $1,200 for the average one-bedroom apartment, according to the non-profit Tenants Union, and vacancies have shrunk to a near-invisible 0.1 percent....An estimated 100,000 city residents (including as many as 12,000 homeless people) lack affordable housing." (p6)

Cook, Christopher D. "In Short: Affordable Housing--Who Needs It?" In These Times v21 n17 14 Jul 1997. p6-7. (ISSN0160-5992).

HOUSING--CALIFORNIA--SAN JOSE--COSTS (v26)

HOUSING--COLORADO--DENVER

The Denver, Colo. Metropolitan Area "had 774,000 housing units in 1995, of which 726,000 were occupied (65 percent by owners and 35 percent by renters). Single-family homes, at 73 percent of all occupied units, represented the predominant housing type in the area. The median age of homes in Denver city was 39 years, compared with 19 years for the remaining area. Homes in the area had a median of 2.7 bedrooms. Occupied homes in the area had a median of 2.2 persons per unit and a median of 6.0 rooms per unit."

U.S. Dept. of Commerce./U.S. Dept. of Housing and Urban Development. "Twenty-Nine Percent of the Denver Metropolitan Area's Households Give High Marks to Their Neighborhood...." Census Bureau Press Release 28 Oct 1997. document-level access: <http://www.census.gov/Press-Release/cb97h15.html>

HOUSING--COLORADO--DENVER--COSTS

In 1995, in the Denver, Colo. Metropolitan Area, "the median monthly housing costs for owners was $763 and for renters was $539. Monthly housing costs include mortgage payments or contract rent, utilities, fuels, insurance, real estate taxes (for owners) and other housing-related expenditures. Monthly housing costs that were $1,000 or more accounted for 30 percent of the owners and 7 percent of the renters....Owners had monthly housing costs that represented a median of 20 percent of their current income; for renters, it was 27 percent."

U.S. Dept. of Commerce./U.S. Dept. of Housing and Urban Development. "Twenty-Nine Percent of the Denver Metropolitan Area's Households Give High Marks to Their Neighborhood...." Census Bureau Press Release 28 Oct 1997. document-level access: <http://www.census.gov/Press-Release/cb97h15.html>

HOUSING--COLORADO--DENVER--PUBLIC OPINION

"About 29 percent of households in the Denver, Colo. Metropolitan Area rated their neighborhood a perfect 10 and about 31 percent said their home was 'the best place to live,' according to a new report jointly released...by the Commerce Department's Census Bureau and the Department of Housing and Urban Development (HUD). In the report, 'American Housing Survey for the Denver Metropolitan Area in 1995,'...respondents were asked to rate their neighborhood and their house or apartment as a place to live based on scales of 1 to 10, where 10 is the best and 1 is the worst. Of the households in these neighborhoods, 10 percent reported problems with crime, a comparable proportion reported problems with traffic and 4 percent experienced problems with litter or housing deterioration."

U.S. Dept. of Commerce./U.S. Dept. of Housing and Urban

Development. "Twenty-Nine Percent of the Denver Metropolitan Area's Households Give High Marks to Their Neighborhood...." Census Bureau Press Release 28 Oct 1997. document-level access: <http://www.census.gov/Press-Release/cb97h15.html>

HOUSING--FLORIDA (v26)

The Miami-Fort Lauderdale, Fla. Metropolitan Area "had 1,484,000 housing units in 1995, of which 1,245,000 were occupied (62 percent by owners and 38 percent by renters). Single-family homes, at 59 percent of all occupied units, represented the predominant housing type in the area. The median age of homes in Miami city was 35 years, compared with 21 years for the remaining area. Homes in the area had a median of 2.3 bedrooms. Occupied homes in the area had a median of 2.3 persons per unit and a median of 4.9 rooms per unit."

U.S. Dept. of Commerce./U.S. Dept. of Housing and Urban Development. "Thirty-One Percent of the Miami-Fort Lauderdale Metropolitan Area's Households Give High Marks to...Neighborhood...." Census Bureau Press Release 20 Oct 1997. document-level access: <http://www.census.gov/Press-Release/cb97h01.html>

HOUSING--FLORIDA--COSTS

In the Miami-Fort Lauderdale, Fla. Metropolitan Area, in 1995, "the median monthly housing costs for owners was $729 and for renters was $609. Monthly housing costs include mortgage payments or contract rent, utilities, fuels, insurance, real estate taxes (for owners) and other housing-related expenditures. Monthly housing costs that were $1,000 or more accounted for 29 percent of the owners and 7 percent of the renters....Owners had monthly housing costs that represented a median of 24 percent of their current income; for renters, it was 35 percent."

U.S. Dept. of Commerce./U.S. Dept. of Housing and Urban Development. "Thirty-One Percent of the Miami-Fort Lauderdale Metropolitan Area's Households Give High Marks to...Neighborhood...." Census Bureau Press Release 20 Oct 1997. document-level access: <http://www.census.gov/Press-Release/cb97h01.html>

HOUSING--FLORIDA--PUBLIC OPINION

"About 31 percent of households in the Miami-Fort Lauderdale, Fla. Metropolitan Area rated their neighborhood a perfect 10 and about 36 percent said their home was 'the best place to live,' according to a new report released...by the Commerce Department's Census Bureau and the Department of Housing and Urban Development (HUD). In the report, 'American Housing Survey for the Miami-Ft. Lauderdale Metropolitan Area in 1995,'...respondents were asked to rate their neighborhood and their house or apartment as a place to live based on scales of 1 to 10, where 10 is the best and 1 is the worst. Of the households in these neighborhoods, 10 percent reported problems with crime, 7 percent reported problems with traffic and 5 percent experienced problems with litter or housing deterioration."

U.S. Dept. of Commerce./U.S. Dept. of Housing and Urban Development. "Thirty-One Percent of the Miami-Fort Lauderdale Metropolitan Area's Households Give High Marks to...Neighborhood...." Census Bureau Press Release 20 Oct 1997. document-level access: <http://www.census.gov/Press-Release/cb97h01.html>

HOUSING--FRANCE (v26)

HOUSING--GEORGIA (v26)

HOUSING--GREAT BRITAIN (v26)

"The latest Welsh House Condition Survey was conducted in 1993. From this, it is estimated that 151,200 occupied first homes, 13.4 per cent of the total, in Wales were unfit....The 1991 English House Condition Survey identified 7.6 per cent of all dwellings in England as being unfit. The Northern Ireland 1991 survey identified 8.8 per cent of dwellings as unfit. In Scotland in 1991, 4.7 per cent of the stock was assessed as being Below Tolerable Standard." (c160)

Griffiths, Win (H.C.-Bridgend). "Written Answers to Questions: Poor Housing Conditions." Great Britain. Parliament. House of Commons. Debates. 15 Jul 1997. c160. section-level access: <http://www.parliament.the-stationery-office.co.uk/pa/cm199798/cmhansrd/cm970715/debtext/70715w20.htm#70715w20.html_sbhd1>

HOUSING--ILLINOIS--CHICAGO

The Chicago, Ill. Metropolitan Area "had 2,987,000 housing units in 1995, of which 2,789,000 were occupied (64 percent by owners and 36 percent by renters). Single-family homes, at 58 percent of all occupied units, represented the predominant housing type in the area. The median age of homes in Chicago city was 51 years, compared with 27 years for the remaining area. Homes in the area had a median of 2.6 bedrooms. Occupied homes in the area had a median of 2.4 persons per unit and a median of 5.6 rooms per unit."

U.S. Dept. of Commerce./U.S. Dept. of Housing and Urban Development. "Thirty-One Percent of the Chicago Metropolitan Area's Households Give High Marks to Their Neighborhood...." Census Bureau Press Release 20 Oct 1997. document-level access: <http://www.census.gov/Press-Release/cb97h02.html>

HOUSING--ILLINOIS--CHICAGO--COSTS

In the Chicago, Ill. Metropolitan Area, in 1995, "the median monthly housing costs for owners was $850 and for renters was $584. Monthly housing costs include mortgage payments or contract rent, utilities, fuels, insurance, real estate taxes (for owners) and other housing-related expenditures. Monthly housing costs that were $1,000 or more accounted for 42 percent of the owners and 7 percent of the renters....Owners had monthly housing costs that represented a median of 21 percent of their current income; for renters, it was 29 percent."

U.S. Dept. of Commerce./U.S. Dept. of Housing and Urban Development. "Thirty-One Percent of the Chicago Metropolitan Area's Households Give High Marks to Their Neighborhood...." Census Bureau Press Release 20 Oct 1997. document-level access: <http://www.census.gov/Press-Release/cb97h02.html>

HOUSING--ILLINOIS--CHICAGO--PUBLIC OPINION

"About 31 percent of households in the Chicago, Ill. Metropolitan Area rated their neighborhood a perfect 10 and about 35 percent said their home was 'the best place to live,' according to a new report released...by the Commerce Department's Census Bureau and the Department of Housing and Urban Development (HUD). In the report, 'American Housing Survey for the Chicago Metropolitan Area in 1995,'...respondents were asked to rate their neighborhood and their house or apartment as a place to live based on scales of 1 to 10, where 10 is the best and 1 is the worst. Of the households in these neighborhoods, 12 percent reported problems with crime, 7 percent reported problems with traffic and 4 percent experienced problems with litter or housing deterioration."

U.S. Dept. of Commerce./U.S. Dept. of Housing and Urban Development. "Thirty-One Percent of the Chicago Metropolitan Area's Households Give High Marks to Their Neighborhood...." Census Bureau Press Release 20 Oct 1997. document-level access: <http://www.census.gov/Press-Release/cb97h02.html>

HOUSING--IRELAND--COSTS

"The weekly expenditure on housing in the Dublin area is twice that in rural areas and small towns [in Ireland]. Dublin households allocate 42 [pounds sterling] a week to housing while in rural areas and towns with a population under 1,500 it is 21 [pounds sterling], and 13 [pounds sterling] a week for rural farm households. Housing accounts for 36 [pounds sterling] of the weekly budget in towns with a population of 10,000 or more and 30 [pounds sterling] a week in towns with between 1,500 and 10,000 people living in them, according to the 1994-95 [Household Budget] survey."

Ireland. Central Statistics Office. "Household Budget Survey 1994-95--Volume 2: Detailed Results for Urban and Rural Households." Press Release 1 Dec 1997. document-level access: <http://www.cso.ie/pressreleases/prelhbsv2.html>

HOUSING--ISRAEL--MODI'IN (v26)

HOUSING--JERUSALEM--PALESTINIAN ARABS

"In the past three and a half years, Jerusalem municipality policy has destroyed 291 Palestinian homes." (p12) "The Israelis have subsidized 60,000 apartments in East Jerusalem for Israelis, and only 5,000 for Palestinians." (p13)

Hoffman, Gene Knudsen. "An Enemy Is One Whose Story We Have Not Heard." Fellowship v63 n5-6 May-Jun 1997. p12-15. (ISSN0014-9810).

HOUSING--KANSAS--MISSOURI--KANSAS CITY

The Kansas City, Mo.-Kan. Metropolitan Area "had 715,500 housing units in 1995, of which 659,000 were occupied (67 percent by owners and 33 percent by renters). Single-family homes, at 81 percent of all occupied units, represented the predominant housing type in the area. The median age of homes in the city of Kansas City, Mo. was 37 years, compared with 23 years for the remaining area. Homes in the area had a median of 2.8 bedrooms. Occupied homes in the area had a median of 2.2 persons per unit and a median of 5.8 rooms per unit."

U.S. Dept. of Commerce./U.S. Dept. of Housing and Urban Development. "Thirty-Two Percent of the Kansas City Metropolitan Area's Households Give High Marks to Their Neighborhood...." Census Bureau Press Release 28 Oct 1997. document-level access: <http://www.census.gov/Press-Release/cb97h13.html>

HOUSING--LOUISIANA (v26)

HOUSING--LOUISIANA--NEW ORLEANS

The New Orleans, La. Metropolitan Area "had 548,000 housing units in 1995, of which 485,000 were occupied (62 percent by owners and 38 percent by renters). Single-family homes, at 73 percent of all occupied units, represented the predominant housing type in the area. The median age of homes in New Orleans city was 42 years, compared with 22 years for the remaining area. Homes in the area had a median of 2.7 bedrooms. Occupied homes in the area had a median of 2.3 persons per unit and a median of 5.5 rooms per unit."

U.S. Dept. of Commerce./U.S. Dept. of Housing and Urban Development. "Thirty-Four Percent of the New Orleans Metropolitan Area's Households Give High Marks to Their Neighborhood...." Census Bureau Press Release 22 Oct 1997. document-level access: <http://www.census.gov/Press-Release/cb97h07.html>

HOUSING--LOUISIANA--NEW ORLEANS--COSTS

In 1995, in the New Orleans, La. Metropolitan Area, "the median monthly housing costs for owners was $404 and for renters was $441. Monthly housing costs include mortgage payments or contract rent, utilities, fuels, insurance, real estate taxes (for owners) and other housing-related expenditures. Monthly housing costs that were $1,000 or more accounted for 11 percent of the owners and 3 percent of the renters....Owners had monthly housing costs that represented a median of 15 percent of their current income; for renters, it was 28 percent."

U.S. Dept. of Commerce./U.S. Dept. of Housing and Urban Development. "Thirty-Four Percent of the New Orleans Metropolitan Area's Households Give High Marks to Their Neighborhood...." Census Bureau Press Release 22 Oct 1997. document-level access: <http://www.census.gov/Press-Release/cb97h07.html>

HOUSING--LOUISIANA--NEW ORLEANS--PUBLIC OPINION

"About 34 percent of households in the New Orleans, La. Metropolitan Area rated their neighborhood a perfect 10 and a comparable proportion said their home was 'the best place to live,' according to a new report released...by the Commerce Department's Census Bureau and the Department of Housing and Urban Development (HUD). In the report, 'American Housing Survey for the New Orleans Metropolitan Area in 1995,'... respondents were asked to rate their neighborhood and their house or apartment as a place to live based on scales of 1 to 10, where 10 is the best and 1 is the worst. Of the households in these neighborhoods, 14 percent reported problems with crime, 7 percent reported problems with traffic and a comparable proportion experienced problems with litter or housing deterioration."

U.S. Dept. of Commerce./U.S. Dept. of Housing and Urban Development. "Thirty-Four Percent of the New Orleans Metropolitan Area's Households Give High Marks to Their Neighborhood...." Census Bureau Press Release 22 Oct 1997. document-level access: <http://www.census.gov/Press-Release/cb97h07.html>

HOUSING--MASSACHUSETTS--BOSTON (v26)

HOUSING--MICHIGAN (v26)

HOUSING--MICHIGAN--ANN ARBOR--PUBLIC OPINION (v26)

HOUSING--MICHIGAN--DETROIT

The Detroit, Mich. Metropolitan Area "had 1,803,000 housing units in 1995, of which 1,681,000 were occupied (71 percent by owners and 29 percent by renters). Single-family homes, at 79 percent of all occupied units, represented the predominant housing type in the area. The median age of homes in Detroit city was 49 years, compared with 31 years for the remaining area. Homes in the area had a median of 2.8 bedrooms. Occupied homes in the area had a median of 2.3 persons per unit and a median of 5.6 rooms per unit."

U.S. Dept. of Commerce./U.S. Dept. of Housing and Urban Development. "Thirty-Seven Percent of the Detroit Metropolitan Area's Households Give High Marks to Their Neighborhood...." Census Bureau Press Release 22 Oct 1997. document-level access: <http://www.census.gov/Press-Release/cb97h10.html>

HOUSING--MICHIGAN--DETROIT--COSTS

In 1995, in the Detroit, Mich. Metropolitan Area, "the median monthly housing costs for owners was $551 and for renters was $508. Monthly housing costs include mortgage payments or contract rent, utilities, fuels, insurance, real estate taxes (for owners) and other housing-related expenditures. Monthly housing costs that were $1,000 or more accounted for 20 percent of the owners and 4 percent of the renters....Owners had monthly housing costs that represented a median of 16 percent of their current income; for renters, it was 27 percent."

U.S. Dept. of Commerce./U.S. Dept. of Housing and Urban Development. "Thirty-Seven Percent of the Detroit Metropolitan Area's Households Give High Marks to Their Neighborhood...." Census Bureau Press Release 22 Oct 1997. document-level access: <http://www.census.gov/Press-Release/cb97h10.html>

HOUSING--MICHIGAN--DETROIT--PUBLIC OPINION

"About 37 percent of households in the Detroit, Mich. Metropolitan Area rated their neighborhood a perfect 10 and a comparable proportion said their home was 'the best place to live,' according to a new report released...by the Commerce Department's Census Bureau and the Department of Housing and Urban Development (HUD). In the report, 'American Housing Survey for the Detroit Metropolitan Area in 1995,'...respondents were asked to rate their neighborhood and their house or apartment as a place to live based on scales of 1 to 10, where 10 is the best and 1 is the worst. Of the households in these neighborhoods, 9 percent reported problems with crime, a comparable proportion reported problems with traffic and 5 percent experienced problems with litter or housing deterioration."

U.S. Dept. of Commerce./U.S. Dept. of Housing and Urban Development. "Thirty-Seven Percent of the Detroit Metropolitan Area's Households Give High Marks to Their Neighborhood...." Census Bureau Press Release 22 Oct 1997. document-level access: <http://www.census.gov/Press-Release/cb97h10.html>

HOUSING--MISSISSIPPI (v26)

HOUSING--MISSOURI--KANSAS CITY--COSTS

In the Kansas City, Mo.-Kan. Metropolitan Area in 1995, "the median monthly costs for owners was $565 and for renters was $481. Monthly housing costs include mortgage payments or contract rent, utilities, fuels, insurance, real estate taxes (for owners) and other housing-related expenditures. Monthly housing costs that were $1,000 or more accounted for 18 percent of the owners and 3 percent of the renters....Owners had monthly housing costs that represented a median of 17 percent of their current income; for renters, it was 26 percent."

U.S. Dept. of Commerce./U.S. Dept. of Housing and Urban Development. "Thirty-Two Percent of the Kansas City Metropolitan Area's Households Give High Marks to Their Neighborhood...." Census Bureau Press Release 28 Oct 1997. document-level access: <http://www.census.gov/Press-Release/cb97h13.html>

HOUSING--MISSOURI--KANSAS CITY--PUBLIC OPINION

"About 32 percent of households in the Kansas City, Mo.-Kan. Metropolitan Area rated their neighborhood a perfect 10 and a comparable proportion said their home was 'the best place to live,' according to a new report jointly released...by the Commerce Department's Census Bureau and the Department of Housing and Urban Development (HUD). In the report, 'American Housing Survey for the Kansas City Metropolitan Area in 1995,'...respondents were asked to rate their neighborhood and their house or apartment as a place to live based on scales of 1 to 10, where 10 is the best and 1 is the worst. Of the households in these neighborhoods, 9 percent reported problems with crime and comparable proportions reported problems with traffic and litter or housing deterioration."

U.S. Dept. of Commerce./U.S. Dept. of Housing and Urban Development. "Thirty-Two Percent of the Kansas City Metropolitan Area's Households Give High Marks to Their Neighborhood...." Census Bureau Press Release 28 Oct 1997. document-level access: <http://www.census.gov/Press-Release/cb97h13.html>

HOUSING--NEW JERSEY

The Northern N.J. Metropolitan Area "had 2,442,200 housing units in 1995, of which 2,202,500 were occupied (62 percent by owners and 38 percent by renters). Single-family homes, at 61 percent of all occupied units, represented the predominant housing type in the area. The median age of homes in Newark city was 53 years, compared with 39 years for the remaining area. Homes in the area had a median of 2.6 bedrooms. Occupied homes in the area had a median of 2.4 persons per unit and a median of 5.6 rooms per unit."

U.S. Dept. of Commerce./U.S. Dept. of Housing and Urban Development. "Thirty-Two Percent of the Northern New Jersey Metropolitan Area's Households Give High Marks to Their Neighborhood...." Census Bureau Press Release 20 Oct 1997. document-level access: <http://www.census.gov/Press-Release/cb97h04.html>

HOUSING--NEW JERSEY--COSTS

In the Northern N.J. Metropolitan Area, in 1995, "the median monthly housing costs for owners was $976 and for renters was $669. Monthly housing costs include mortgage payments or contract rent, utilities, fuels, insurance, real estate taxes (for owners) and other housing-related expenditures. Monthly housing costs that were $1,000 or more accounted for 49 percent of the owners and 11 percent of the renters....Owners had monthly housing costs that represented a median of 23 percent of their current income; for renters, it was 31 percent."

U.S. Dept. of Commerce./U.S. Dept. of Housing and Urban Development. "Thirty-Two Percent of the Northern New Jersey Metropolitan Area's Households Give High Marks to Their Neighborhood...." Census Bureau Press Release 20 Oct 1997. document-level access: <http://www.census.gov/Press-Release/cb97h04.html>

HOUSING--NEW JERSEY--PUBLIC OPINION

"About 32 percent of households in the Northern N.J. Metropolitan Area rated their neighborhood a perfect 10 and a comparable proportion said their home was 'the best place to live,' according to a new report released...by the Commerce Department's Census Bureau and the Department of Housing and Urban Development (HUD). In the report, 'American Housing Survey for the Northern NJ Metropolitan Area in 1995,'... respondents were asked to rate their neighborhood and their house or apartment as a place to live based on scales of 1 to 10, where 10 is the best and 1 is the worst. Of the households in these neighborhoods, 5 percent reported problems with crime, a comparable proportion reported problems with traffic and 3 percent experienced problems with litter or housing deterioration."

U.S. Dept. of Commerce./U.S. Dept. of Housing and Urban Development. "Thirty-Two Percent of the Northern New Jersey Metropolitan Area's Households Give High Marks to Their Neighborhood...." Census Bureau Press Release 20 Oct 1997. document-level access: <http://www.census.gov/Press-Release/cb97h04.html>

HOUSING--NEW YORK (N.Y.) (v26)

The New York-Nassau-Suffolk-Orange, N.Y. Metropolitan Area "had 4,577,300 housing units in 1995, of which 4,207,900 were occupied (45 percent by owners and 55 percent by renters). Multi-family homes, at 67 percent of all occupied units, represented the predominant housing type in the area. The median age of homes in New York City was 56 years, compared with 38 years for the remaining area. Homes in the area had a median of 2.1 bedrooms. Occupied homes in the area had a median of 2.3 persons per unit and a median of 4.6 rooms per unit."

U.S. Dept. of Commerce./U.S. Dept. of Housing and Urban Development. "Twenty-One Percent of the New York-Nassau-Suffolk-Orange Metropolitan...Households Give High Marks...Neighborhood...." Census Bureau Press Release 20 Oct 1997. document-level access: <http://www.census.gov/Press-Release/cb97h03.html>

HOUSING--NEW YORK (N.Y.)--COSTS (v26)

In 1995, in the New York-Nassau-Suffolk-Orange, N.Y. Metropolitan Area, "the median monthly housing costs for owners was $931 and for renters was $650. Monthly housing costs include mortgage payments or contract rent, utilities, fuels, insurance, real estate taxes (for owners) and other housing-related expenditures. Monthly housing costs that were $1,000 or more accounted for 46 percent of the owners and 16 percent of the renters....Owners had monthly housing costs that represented a median of 22 percent of their current income; for renters, it was 32 percent."

U.S. Dept. of Commerce./U.S. Dept. of Housing and Urban

Development. "Twenty-One Percent of the New York-Nassau-Suffolk-Orange Metropolitan...Households Give High Marks...Neighborhood...." Census Bureau Press Release 20 Oct 1997. document-level access: <http://www.census.gov/Press-Release/cb97h03.html>

HOUSING--NEW YORK (N.Y.)--PUBLIC OPINION

"About 21 percent of households in the New York-Nassau-Suffolk-Orange, N.Y. Metropolitan Area rated their neighborhood a perfect 10 and about 26 percent said their home was 'the best place to live,' according to a new report released...by the Commerce Department's Census Bureau and the Department of Housing and Urban Development (HUD). In the report, 'American Housing Survey for the New York-Nassau-Suffolk-Orange Metropolitan Area in 1995,'...respondents were asked to rate their neighborhood and their house or apartment as a place to live based on scales of 1 to 10, where 10 is the best and 1 is the worst. Of the households in these neighborhoods, 14 percent reported problems with crime, 8 percent reported problems with traffic and a comparable proportion experienced problems with litter or housing deterioration."

U.S. Dept. of Commerce./U.S. Dept. of Housing and Urban Development. "Twenty-One Percent of the New York-Nassau-Suffolk-Orange Metropolitan...Households Give High Marks...Neighborhood...." Census Bureau Press Release 20 Oct 1997. document-level access: <http://www.census.gov/Press-Release/cb97h03.html>

HOUSING--NORTH CAROLINA--CHARLOTTE

The Charlotte, N.C.-S.C. Metropolitan Area "had 539,000 housing units in 1995, of which 503,000 were occupied (67 percent by owners and 33 percent by renters). Single-family homes, at 80 percent of all occupied units, represented the predominant housing type in the area. The median age of homes in Charlotte city was 19 years, compared with 21 years for the remaining area. Homes in the area had a median of 2.7 bedrooms. Occupied homes in the area had a median of 2.3 persons per unit and a median of 5.4 rooms per unit."

U.S. Dept. of Commerce./U.S. Dept. of Housing and Urban Development. "Forty Percent of the Charlotte Metropolitan Area's Households Give High Marks to Their Neighborhood, Census...Says." Census Bureau Press Release 20 Oct 1997. document-level access: <http://www.census.gov/Press-Release/cb97h05.html>

HOUSING--NORTH CAROLINA--CHARLOTTE--COSTS

In 1995, in the Charlotte, N.C.-S.C. Metropolitan Area, "the median monthly housing costs for owners was $532 and for renters was $489. Monthly housing costs include mortgage payments or contract rent, utilities, fuels, insurance, real estate taxes (for owners) and other housing-related expenditures. Monthly housing costs that were $1,000 or more accounted for 17 percent of the owners and 3 percent of the renters....Owners had monthly housing costs that represented a median of 17 percent of their current income; for renters, it was 25 percent."

U.S. Dept. of Commerce./U.S. Dept. of Housing and Urban Development. "Forty Percent of the Charlotte Metropolitan Area's Households Give High Marks to Their Neighborhood, Census...Says." Census Bureau Press Release 20 Oct 1997. document-level access: <http://www.census.gov/Press-Release/cb97h05.html>

HOUSING--NORTH CAROLINA--CHARLOTTE--PUBLIC OPINION

"About 40 percent of households in the Charlotte, N.C.-S.C. Metropolitan Area rated their neighborhood a perfect 10 and a comparable proportion said their home was 'the best place to live,' according to a new report jointly released...by the Commerce Department's Census Bureau and the Department of Housing and Urban Development (HUD). In the report, 'American Housing Survey for the Charlotte Metropolitan Area in 1995,'...respondents were asked to rate their neighborhood and their house or apartment as a place to live based on scales of 1 to 10, where 10 is the best and 1 is the worst. Of the households in these neighborhoods, 7 percent reported problems with crime, a comparable proportion reported problems with traffic and 3 percent experienced problems with litter or housing deterioration."

U.S. Dept. of Commerce./U.S. Dept. of Housing and Urban Development. "Forty Percent of the Charlotte Metropolitan Area's Households Give High Marks to Their Neighborhood, Census...Says." Census Bureau Press Release 20 Oct 1997. document-level access: <http://www.census.gov/Press-Release/cb97h05.html>

HOUSING--OHIO--COLUMBUS

"About 32 percent of households in the Columbus, Ohio Metropolitan Area rated their neighborhood a perfect 10 and a comparable proportion said their home was 'the best place to live,' according to a new report jointly released...by the Commerce Department's Census Bureau and the Department of Housing and Urban Development (HUD). In the report, 'American Housing Survey for the Columbus Metropolitan Area in 1995,'...respondents were asked to rate their neighborhood and their house or apartment as a place to live based on scales of 1 to 10, where 10 is the best and 1 is the worst. Of the households in these neighborhoods, 9 percent reported problems with crime, 10 percent reported problems with traffic and 4 percent experienced problems with litter or housing deterioration."

U.S. Dept. of Commerce./U.S. Dept. of Housing and Urban Development. "Thirty-Two Percent of the Columbus Metropolitan Area's Households Give High Marks to Their Neighborhood...." Census Bureau Press Release 20 Oct 1997. document-level access: <http://www.census.gov/Press-Release/cb97h06.html>

The Columbus, Ohio Metropolitan Area "had 605,000 housing units in 1995, of which 556,000 were occupied (63 percent by owners and 37 percent by renters). Single-family homes, at 81 percent of all occupied units, represented the predominant housing type in the area. The median age of homes in Columbus city was 23 years, compared with 25 years for the remaining area. Homes in the area had a median of 2.7 bedrooms. Occupied homes in the area had a median of 2.2 persons per unit and a median of 5.7 rooms per unit."

U.S. Dept. of Commerce./U.S. Dept. of Housing and Urban Development. "Thirty-Two Percent of the Columbus Metropolitan Area's Households Give High Marks to Their Neighborhood...." Census Bureau Press Release 20 Oct 1997. document-level access: <http://www.census.gov/Press-Release/cb97h06.html>

HOUSING--OHIO--COLUMBUS--COSTS

In 1995, in the Columbus, Ohio Metropolitan Area, "the median monthly housing costs for owners was $654 and for renters was $484. Monthly housing costs include mortgage payments or contract rent, utilities, fuels, insurance, real estate taxes (for owners) and other housing-related expenditures. Monthly housing costs that were $1,000 or more accounted for 23 percent of the owners and 2 percent of the renters....Owners had monthly housing costs that represented a median of 18 percent of their current income; for renters, it was 26 percent."

U.S. Dept. of Commerce./U.S. Dept. of Housing and Urban Development. "Thirty-Two Percent of the Columbus Metropolitan Area's Households Give High Marks to Their Neighborhood...." Census Bureau Press Release 20 Oct 1997. document-level access: <http://www.census.gov/Press-Release/cb97h06.html>

HOUSING--OREGON--PORTLAND

The Portland, Ore. Metropolitan Area "had 703,000 housing units in 1995, of which 655,000 were occupied (65 percent by owners and 35 percent by renters). Single-family homes, at 78 percent of all occupied units, represented the predominant housing type in the area. The median age of homes in Portland city was 45 years, compared with 20 years for the remaining area. Homes in the area had a median of 2.7 bedrooms. Occupied homes in the area had a median of 2.2 persons per unit and a median of 5.8 rooms per unit."

U.S. Dept. of Commerce./U.S. Dept. of Housing and Urban Development. "Twenty-Nine Percent of the Portland Metropolitan Area's Households Give High Marks to Their Neighborhood...." Census Bureau Press Release 22 Oct 1997. document-level access: <http://www.census.gov/Press-Release/cb97h09.html>

HOUSING--OREGON--PORTLAND--COSTS

In 1995, in the Portland, Ore. Metropolitan Area, "the median monthly housing costs for owners was $704 and for renters $566. Monthly housing costs include mortgage payments or contract rent, utilities, fuels, insurance, real estate taxes (for owners) and other housing-related expenditures. Monthly housing costs that were $1,000 or more accounted for 26 percent of the owners and 6 percent of the renters....Owners had monthly housing costs that represented a median of 19 percent of their current income; for renters, it was 28 percent."

U.S. Dept. of Commerce./U.S. Dept. of Housing and Urban Development. "Twenty-Nine Percent of the Portland Metropolitan Area's Households Give High Marks to Their Neighborhood...." Census Bureau Press Release 22 Oct 1997. document-level access: <http://www.census.gov/Press-Release/cb97h09.html>

HOUSING--OREGON--PORTLAND--PUBLIC OPINION

"About 29 percent of households in the Portland, Ore. Metropolitan Area rated their neighborhood a perfect 10 and about 31 percent said their home was 'the best place to live,' according to a new report released...by the Commerce Department's Census Bureau and the Department of Housing and Urban Development (HUD). In the report, 'American Housing Survey for the Portland Metropolitan Area in 1995,'... respondents were asked to rate their neighborhood and their house or apartment as a place to live based on scales of 1 to 10, where 10 is the best and 1 is the worst. Of the households in these neighborhoods, 10 percent reported problems with crime, 14 percent reported problems with traffic and 5 percent experienced problems with litter or housing deterioration."

U.S. Dept. of Commerce./U.S. Dept. of Housing and Urban Development. "Twenty-Nine Percent of the Portland Metropolitan Area's Households Give High Marks to Their Neighborhood...." Census Bureau Press Release 22 Oct 1997. document-level access: <http://www.census.gov/Press-Release/cb97h09.html>

HOUSING--PENNSYLVANIA--PHILADELPHIA

The Philadelphia, Pa. Metropolitan Area "had 1,986,600 housing units in 1995, of which 1,820,600 were occupied (69 percent by owners and 31 percent by renters). Single-family homes, at 76 percent of all occupied units, represented the predominant housing type in the area. The median age of homes in Philadelphia city was 60 years, compared with 32 years for the remaining area. Homes in the area had a median of 2.8 bedrooms. Occupied homes in the area had a median of 2.3 persons per unit and a median of 6.0 rooms per unit."

U.S. Dept. of Commerce./U.S. Dept. of Housing and Urban Development. "Thirty-Four Percent of the Philadelphia Metropolitan Area's Households Give High Marks to Their Neighborhood...." Census Bureau Press Release 28 Oct 1997. document-level access: <http://www.census.gov/Press-Release/cb97h14.html>

HOUSING--PENNSYLVANIA--PHILADELPHIA--COSTS

In 1995, in the Philadelphia, Pennsylvania Metropolitan Area, "the median monthly housing costs for owners was $673 and for renters was $578. Monthly housing costs include mortgage payments or contract rent, utilities, fuels, insurance, real estate taxes (for owners) and other housing-related expenditures. Monthly housing costs that were $1,000 or more accounted for 31 percent of the owners and 7 percent of the renters....Owners had monthly housing costs that represented a median of 22 percent of their current income; for renters, it was 31 percent."

U.S. Dept. of Commerce./U.S. Dept. of Housing and Urban Development. "Thirty-Four Percent of the Philadelphia Metropolitan Area's Households Give High Marks to Their Neighborhood...." Census Bureau Press Release 28 Oct 1997. document-level access: <http://www.census.gov/Press-Release/cb97h14.html>

HOUSING--PENNSYLVANIA--PHILADELPHIA --PUBLIC OPINION

"About 34 percent of households in the Philadelphia, Pa. Metropolitan Area rated their neighborhood a perfect 10 and about 37 percent said their home was 'the best place to live,' according to a new report released...by the Commerce Department's Census Bureau and the Department of Housing and Urban Development (HUD). In the report, 'American Housing Survey for the Philadelphia Metropolitan Area in 1995,'... respondents were asked to rate their neighborhood and their house or apartment as a place to live based on scales of 1 to 10, where 10 is the best and 1 is the worst. Of the households in these neighborhoods, 9 percent reported problems with crime, a comparable proportion reported problems with traffic and 6 percent experienced problems with litter or housing deterioration."

U.S. Dept. of Commerce./U.S. Dept. of Housing and Urban Development. "Thirty-Four Percent of the Philadelphia Metropolitan Area's Households Give High Marks to Their Neighborhood...." Census Bureau Press Release 28 Oct 1997. document-level access: <http://www.census.gov/Press-Release/cb97h14.html>

HOUSING--PENNSYLVANIA--PITTSBURGH

The Pittsburgh, Pa. Metropolitan Area "had 1,052,000 housing units in 1995, of which 970,000 were occupied (72 percent by owners and 28 percent by renters). Single-family homes, at 81 percent of all occupied units, represented the predominant housing type in the area. The median age of homes in Pittsburgh city was 55 years, compared with 39 years for the remaining area. Homes in the area had a median of 2.7 bedrooms. Occupied homes in the area had a median of 2.2 persons per unit and a median of 5.8 rooms per unit."

U.S. Dept. of Commerce./U.S. Dept. of Housing and Urban Development. "Forty Percent of the Pittsburgh Metropolitan Area's Households Give High Marks to Their Neighborhood...." Census Bureau Press Release 22 Oct 1997. document-level access: <http://www.census.gov/Press-Release/cb97h08.html>

HOUSING--PENNSYLVANIA--PITTSBURGH--COSTS

In 1995, in the Pittsburgh, Pa. Metropolitan Area, "the median monthly housing costs for owners was $416 which was not statistically different than the $417 for renters. Monthly housing costs include mortgage payments or contract rent, utilities, fuels, insurance, real estate taxes (for owners) and other housing-related expenditures. Monthly housing costs that were $1,000 or more accounted for 13 percent of the owners and 2 percent of the renters....Owners had monthly housing costs that represented a median of 18 percent of their current income; for renters, it was 27 percent."

U.S. Dept. of Commerce./U.S. Dept. of Housing and Urban Development. "Forty Percent of the Pittsburgh Metropolitan Area's Households Give High Marks to Their Neighborhood...." Census Bureau Press Release 22 Oct 1997. document-level access: <http://www.census.gov/Press-Release/cb97h08.html>

HOUSING--PENNSYLVANIA--PITTSBURGH--PUBLIC OPINION

"About 40 percent of households in the Pittsburgh, Pa. Metropolitan Area rated their neighborhood a perfect 10 and a comparable proportion said their home was 'the best place to live,' according to a new report released...by the Commerce Department's Census Bureau and the Department of Housing and Urban Development (HUD). In the report, 'American Housing Survey for the Pittsburgh Metropolitan Area in 1995,'...respondents were asked to rate their neighborhood and their house or apartment as a place to live based on scales of 1 to 10, where 10 is the best and 1 is the worst. Of the households in these neighborhoods, 5 percent reported problems with crime, 6 percent reported problems with traffic and 4 percent experienced problems with litter or housing deterioration."

U.S. Dept. of Commerce./U.S. Dept. of Housing and Urban Development. "Forty Percent of the Pittsburgh Metropolitan Area's Households Give High Marks to Their Neighborhood...." Census Bureau Press Release 22 Oct 1997. document-level access: <http://www.census.gov/Press-Release/cb97h08.html>

HOUSING--SCOTLAND (v26)

HOUSING--SWEDEN (v26)

HOUSING--SWEDEN--COSTS (v26)

HOUSING--TEXAS--SAN ANTONIO

The San Antonio, Texas Metropolitan Area "had 539,000 housing units in 1995, of which 485,000 were occupied (62 percent by owners and 38 percent by renters). Single-family homes, at 76 percent of all occupied units, represented the predominant housing type in the area. The median age of homes in San Antonio city was 22 years, compared with 18 years for the remaining area. Homes in the area had a median of 2.7 bedrooms. Occupied homes in the area had a median of 2.4 persons per unit and a median of 5.4 rooms per unit."

U.S. Dept. of Commerce./U.S. Dept. of Housing and Urban Development. "Thirty-Five Percent of the San Antonio Metropolitan Area's Households Give High Marks to Their Neighborhood...." Census Bureau Press Release 28 Oct 1997. document-level access: <http://www.census.gov/Press-Release/cb97h12.html>

HOUSING--TEXAS--SAN ANTONIO--COSTS

In the San Antonio, Texas Metropolitan Area, in 1995, "the median monthly housing costs for owners was $507 and for renters was $475. Monthly housing costs include mortgage payments or contract rent, utilities, fuels, insurance, real estate taxes (for owners) and other housing-related expenditures. Monthly housing costs that were $1,000 or more accounted for 15 percent of the owners and 4 percent of the renters....Owners had monthly housing costs that represented a median of 18 percent of their current income; for renters, it was 27 percent."

U.S. Dept. of Commerce./U.S. Dept. of Housing and Urban Development. "Thirty-Five Percent of the San Antonio Metropolitan Area's Households Give High Marks to Their Neighborhood...." Census Bureau Press Release 28 Oct 1997. document-level access: <http://www.census.gov/Press-Release/cb97h12.html>

HOUSING--TEXAS--SAN ANTONIO--PUBLIC OPINION

"About 35 percent of households in the San Antonio, Texas Metropolitan Area rated their neighborhood a perfect 10 and a comparable proportion said their home was 'the best place to live,' according to a new report released...by the Commerce Department's Census Bureau and the Department of Housing and Urban Development (HUD). In the report, 'American Housing Survey for the San Antonio Metropolitan Area in 1995,'...respondents were asked to rate their neighborhood and their house or apartment as a place to live based on scales of 1 to 10, where 10 is the best and 1 is the worst. Of the households in these neighborhoods, 11 percent reported problems with crime, 7 percent reported problems with traffic and a comparable proportion experienced problems with litter or housing deterioration."

U.S. Dept. of Commerce./U.S. Dept. of Housing and Urban Development. "Thirty-Five Percent of the San Antonio Metropolitan Area's Households Give High Marks to Their Neighborhood...." Census Bureau Press Release 28 Oct 1997. document-level access: <http://www.census.gov/Press-Release/cb97h12.html>

HOUSING--THAILAND--BANGKOK (v26)

HOUSING--UNITED STATES (v26)

"Between 1990 and 1996, Nevada had a 31.9 percent growth in the number of housing units, according to new state housing unit estimates released...by the Commerce Department's Census Bureau. Idaho had the second highest growth (15.5 percent), followed by Georgia (14.1 percent), Utah (14.0 percent) and Arizona (13.9 percent). For 1996 alone, California had the most housing units with 11,811,000, followed by Texas with 7,468,000. Wyoming had the fewest with 209,000. In another finding of these new estimates, Utah had the highest average of persons per household (3.06), while the District of Columbia had the lowest (2.24)."

U.S. Census Bureau. Economic and Statistics Administration. "Nevada Leads All States in Housing Unit Growth from 1990-1996, According to State-By-State Census Bureau Report." Press Release 7 Jul 1997. document-level access: <http://www.census.gov/Press-Release/cb97-112.html>

In the U.S., in 1995, "65 percent of the occupied housing units were owned or being bought compared with 35 percent that were being rented. 5.8 million total units were constructed between 1991 and 1995. Most of the new housing construction (units built between 1991 and 1995) took place in the South (2.6 million), followed by the West and the Midwest (both 1.3 million) and the Northeast (600,000)."

U.S. Census Bureau. Economic and Statistics Administration. "Median Value of Nation's Homes Hits $92,500 Mark, Census Bureau Reports." Press Release 23 Jun 1997. document-level access: <http://www.census.gov/Press-Release/cb97-104.html>

HOUSING--UNITED STATES--POLICE

The new "Officer Next Door" program, administered by the U.S. Department of Housing and Urban Development, "makes federally foreclosed residential properties in urban areas available to qualified law-enforcement personnel at 50 percent of their appraised value. Since its inception in May [1997], the program has attracted nearly 12,000 inquiries--about a third of them from officers in departments in greater Los Angeles....The total number of officers who have closed on a house is just under 400, HUD officials say." (p3)

Blair, James. "United States: For More Cops, Home Is Where the Beat Is." The Christian Science Monitor v90 n21 24 Dec 1997. p3. The Christian Science Monitor search engine: <http://www.csmonitor.com/plweb-cgi/iops1.pl> To retrieve this article, enter the following search: ED=19971224 AND beat. In the "retrieved list," click the title that matches this record. (ISSN0882-7729).

HOUSING--UNITED STATES--SINGLE MOTHERS (v26)

HOUSING--VALUATION--UNITED STATES

"The median value of owner-occupied homes in the...[U.S.] in 1995 was $92,500, according to a report released...by the Commerce Department's Census Bureau and the Department of Housing and Urban Development. The median value of the 63.5 million owner-occupied units varied greatly by region: from $140,300 in the West and $118,900 in the Northeast to $80,100 in the Midwest and $76,000 in the South."

U.S. Census Bureau. Economic and Statistics Administration. "Median Value of Nation's Homes Hits $92,500 Mark, Census Bureau Reports." Press Release 23 Jun 1997. document-level access: <http://www.census.gov/Press-Release/cb97-104.html>

HOUSING--WALES (v26)

HOUSING, RURAL--SCOTLAND (v26)

HOUSING, SINGLE FAMILY--UNITED STATES (v26)

HOUSING PROJECTS, GOVERNMENT

see PUBLIC HOUSING

HOUSING STARTS--UNITED STATES (v26)

HOUSING SUBSIDIES--GREAT BRITAIN (v26)

HOUSING SUBSIDIES--SWEDEN (v26)

HOUSING SUBSIDIES--UNITED STATES (v26)

HOUSTON (TEX.)--COMMERCE--JAPAN

Houston, Texas "is the fourth largest city in the...[U.S.] and is a huge market which is currently unserved by nonstop service to Japan. The addition of nonstop air service will result in substantial economic benefit to Houston as it would increase annual output by over $800 million, provide over 5,600 new jobs, and increase incomes in Houston by $170 million....Two hundred seventy-three Houston firms currently trade goods and services with Japan. Nearly 540 other Houston companies do business with East Asia as a whole, including Japan. Japanese companies have almost 90 subsidiaries in Houston as well as the largest concentration of Japanese specialty chemical companies outside of Japan....Houston is the Nation's second leading city for international business." (pH7716)

Green, Gene (Rep.-Tex.). "Houston Needs Nonstop Service to Tokyo." Congressional Record. Daily ed. v143 n128 23 Sep 1997. pH7716-7717. section/page-level access: <http://thomas.loc.gov/cgi-bin/query/R?r105:FLD001:H07716:> (ISSN0363-7239). (X1.1A.105/1).

HOUSTON (TEX.)--POPULATION

"The total population of Houston, TX, is over 1.8 million with 26.7 percent African-Americans, 4 percent American Indian, 3.9 percent Asian, 26.8 percent Hispanic, and 42.2 percent white. Those residents of Houston who live in poverty number over 370,000 families." (pH2808)

Jackson-Lee, Sheila (Rep.-Tex.). "Employment, Training, And Literacy Enhancement Act of 1997." Congressional Record. Daily ed. v143 n65 16 May 1997. pH2797-2851. section/page-level access: <http://thomas.loc.gov/cgi-bin/query/R?r105:FLD001:H02807:> (ISSN0363-7239). (X1.1A.105/1).

HUMAN BEHAVIOR--UNITED STATES--PUBLIC OPINION (v26)

HUMAN FERTILITY

see FERTILITY, HUMAN

HUMAN IN VITRO FERTILIZATION

see FERTILIZATION IN VITRO, HUMAN

HUMAN MALES

see MEN

HUMAN POPULATION

see POPULATION

HUMAN REPRODUCTION

see also FERTILITY, HUMAN

HUMAN REPRODUCTION--HEALTH ASPECTS --DEVELOPING COUNTRIES--WOMEN

"In developing countries each year an estimated 585,000 women die from complications of pregnancy, childbirth, and unsafe abortion--about one every minute....Pregnancy-related complications cause one-quarter to one-half of deaths among women of reproductive age in developing countries compared with less than 1% in the US....On average, in developing countries a pregnancy is 18 times more likely to end in the woman's death than in developed countries....In some developing regions a woman's risk of dying due to maternal causes over the course of her life is as much as 300 times greater than the risk faced by the average woman in a developed country....For example, a woman in Eastern Africa faces the highest risk of maternal death--1 in 12--compared with only 1 in 3,700 for a woman in North America...." (p3)

Salter, Cynthia/Johnston, Heidi Bart/Hengen, Nicolene. "Care for Postabortion Complications: Saving Women's Lives." Population Reports v25 n1 Sep 1997. p1-13,16-21,23,25-31.

HUMAN RIGHTS (v26)

HUMAN RIGHTS--AFRICA--ASIA--LATIN AMERICA (v26)

HUMAN RIGHTS--ALABAMA

"The exercise of discretion by individual F.B.I. agents often produces widely disparate outcomes, as shown by a comparison of civil rights matters referred by agents from 1992 to 1996 in Alabama's three judicial districts. In Montgomery, civil rights referrals made up 23 percent of all bureau referrals, while in Mobile and Birmingham they made up 7 and 9 percent. When looked at in relation to population, the pattern is a bit different. Birmingham, with the largest population, had 88 referrals per million people while Mobile had 137 and Montgomery 168." (p20)

Burnham, David. "Articles: The FBI." Nation v265 n5 11 Aug 1997. p11-12,14-16,18-24. (ISSN0027-8378).

HUMAN RIGHTS--ECONOMIC CONDITIONS (v26)

HUMAN RIGHTS--FORMER YUGOSLAVIA--KOSOVA (v26)

HUMAN RIGHTS--SOUTH AFRICA

In August 1997, "the 17 members of South Africa's Truth and Reconciliation Commission (TRC) began the last stage of their work: reviewing the 8,000 applications for amnesty from those who have confessed violations of human rights....In the first phase of its work, the commission heard more than 10,000 testimonies from victims and their relatives....Commission supporters insist that the membership of seven blacks, two coloreds, two Indians, and six whites, including a member of an ultra-nationalist Afrikaner group, ensures fair judgments." (p19)

Newsom, David D. "Opinion/Essays: A Crucial Few Weeks for South Africa's Truth Seekers." The Christian Science Monitor v89 n181 13 Aug 1997. p19. The Christian Science Monitor search engine: <http://www.csmonitor.com/plweb-cgi/iops1.pl> To retrieve this article, enter the following search: ED=19970813 AND seekers. In the "retrieved list," click the title that matches this record. (ISSN0882-7729).

HUMAN RIGHTS--TIBET

"Human rights groups estimate that nearly one-fifth of Tibet's 6 million population, about 1.2 million, has died as a direct result of China's policies. Tens of thousands have gone to labor camps and more than 6,000 monasteries have been destroyed." (p10)

Wood, Daniel B. "Film Diplomacy: Hollywood's Newest Star: Tibet." The Christian Science Monitor v89 n236 31 Oct 1997. p1,10-11. The Christian Science Monitor search engine: <http://www.csmonitor.com/plweb-cgi/iops1.pl> To retrieve this article, enter the following search: ED=19971031 AND tibet. In the "retrieved list," click the title that matches this record. (ISSN0882-7729).

HUMAN RIGHTS--TURKEY (v26)

HUMAN RIGHTS--UNITED STATES

"In 1996, according to a report by the [U.S.] Justice

Department's civil rights division, 11,721 people came to the federal government with complaints that their civil rights had been violated....After preliminary screening, the F.B.I. investigated 2,619 of the matters, most of which were then referred to prosecutors. Criminal charges were brought in seventy-nine cases. (According to the department data tapes, the two largest categories of civil rights convictions included seventeen under the law reserved for brutal law-enforcement officers and an additional forty-three under a broad conspiracy law.) Justice Department records show that the 1996 pattern--in which the prosecutors filed charges in less than 1 percent of all complaints and less than 4 percent of all referrals sent [to] them by the F.B.I.--has pretty much repeated itself for the past twenty years." (p20)

Burnham, David. "Articles: The FBI." Nation v265 n5 11 Aug 1997. p11-12,14-16,18-24. (ISSN0027-8378).

HUMAN RIGHTS--UNITED STATES. DEPT. OF JUSTICE

The Civil Rights Prosecution "Section is responsible for the investigation and prosecution of violations of [U.S.] federal criminal civil rights statutes which were designed to protect personal liberties...." (p478) "During fiscal year 1996, the Section received over 10,000 complaints alleging criminal interference with civil rights, approximately 2,600 requiring investigation by the Federal Bureau of Investigation. A substantial majority of the complaints involved allegations of official misconduct, especially allegations of physical abuse by law enforcement officers. This year, 70 new investigations were presented to the grand jury and 79 cases were filed charging 128 defendants. Trials were conducted in 22 cases resulting in the conviction of 22 defendants and the acquittal of 14. In addition, guilty pleas from 85 defendants, in conjunction with trial convictions, resulted in a success rate of 87%." (p479)

U.S. Dept. of Justice. "Departments of Commerce, Justice, And State, The Judiciary...Approp. for 1998 (Part 2)." Hearing. U.S. House. Committee on Appropriations. Washington, D.C. : GPO, 1997. (ISBN0160549094). (Y4.Ap6/1:C73/2/997/pt.2).

The U.S. Federal Appellate program has primary responsibility for handling the Civil Rights "Division's work before the U.S. Supreme Court and the courts of appeals, for giving legal advice to federal agencies and other organizations within the Department and the Division, and for resolving appeals of decisions rendered by the Division's Office of Redress Administration....The Appellate Section's caseload and productivity has been increasing steadily over the past few years. In fiscal year 1995, we produced 112 briefs and other papers of substance for filing in the courts of appeals and the Supreme Court, a significant increase over 83 such filings in fiscal year 1994, 78 in fiscal year 1993, and 68 in fiscal year 1985. In fiscal year 1996, we filed 124 briefs and other substantive papers involving civil rights matters in the courts of appeals and the Supreme Court--more than in any year in the last 10 years. In addition, Civil Rights Division attorneys participated in 29 oral arguments before the courts of appeals....Of 46 decisions on the merits this fiscal year, we have won full or partial victories in 31 (67%)." (p477)

U.S. Dept. of Justice. "Departments of Commerce, Justice, And State, The Judiciary...Approp. for 1998 (Part 2)." Hearing. U.S. House. Committee on Appropriations. Washington, D.C. : GPO, 1997. (ISBN0160549094). (Y4.Ap6/1:C73/2/997/pt.2).

HUMAN SERVICES--CANADA--FINANCE (v26)

HUMANE SOCIETIES

see ANIMAL WELFARE--UNITED STATES--SOCIETIES, ETC.

HUMANE TREATMENT OF ANIMALS

see ANIMAL WELFARE

HUMANITARIANISM--CANADA--PUBLIC OPINION (v26)

HUMBOLDT AWARD--GERMANY

"So far, 19 Nobel Prize winners from the United States alone have come to Germany as a result of the...[Humboldt Award], ten of whom received their Swedish laurels subsequent to their participation in the program. A total of more than 1,800 American academics have worked together with German researchers within the framework of the program over the past 25 years. As of 1996, 2,244 academics from 41 countries had been honoured with the award." (p34)

"North America: Culture/Science: Atlantic Bridge for Scientists: 25 Years of Humboldt Research Awards." Deutschland n5 Oct 1997. p34. (ISSN0945-6791).

HUNGARY--COMMERCE

"Between 1990-96 Hungarian world imports rose by 11.1% a year--twice as fast as exports (5.4%). Deterioration in the balance of trade--down 3.2 bn [billion] ECU [European currency units] 1990-96 to -2.4 bn--can be attributed largely to energy products (-0.6 bn) and industrial products (-2.5 bn). Between 1995-96 imports grew by 8.0% to 12.77 bn and exports by 5.3% to 10.35 bn. EU trade rose by 4.9% (imports) and 5.2% (exports). Between 1990-96 the EU's share of Hungarian world imports rose from 31% to almost 60% and of exports from 32% to nearly 63%. As in the case of the Czech Republic, this 'exceptional expansion', as Eurostat describes it, was due to both increased trade with longer-standing Member States and 1995 enlargement. Germany accounted in 1996 for 23.6% of total Hungarian imports (up 8.5% over '95) and 29.0% of exports (up 6.6%). This left a zero balance. Next biggest EU partner was Austria: 9.5% of imports (down -4.9%) and 10.6% of exports (up 10.3%), with a deficit of -0.11 bn. Russia accounted for 12.5% of imports and 5.9% of exports. Between 1995-96 imports rose by 13.2% and exports were down -2.8%, with a deficit of -0.98 bn ECU. USA had a share of 3.5% of both imports and exports with 1995-96 rises of 21.7% and 15.7% respectively, with a deficit of -0.08 bn."

Eurostat. "Around 60% of Czech & Hungarian Trade with EU: Rapid Expansion Highlighted." Press Release 16 Oct 1997. document-level access: <http://europa.eu.int/en/comm/eurostat/compres/en/7197/6607197a.htm>

HUNGARY--ECONOMIC CONDITIONS (v26)

HUNGER (v26)

"The unequal distribution of food within and among countries means that 840 million people worldwide, including 200 million children, will go hungry today. Poverty, natural disasters, political violence, and geopolitical factors prevent at least one-seventh of the world from getting enough to eat....Earth produces enough food for the nearly 6 billion people alive today. In fact, if everyone adopted a vegetarian diet and no food were wasted, current production would theoretically feed 10 billion people, more than the projected population for the year 2050....Some 43 percent of the population in sub-Saharan Africa and 22 percent of the population in South Asia are malnourished, according to the UN Food and Agriculture Organization (FAO)....In 1969-1970, more than one-third of the developing-world population--about 918 million people--were classified as 'food-energy deficient.' By 1990, the number had fallen to 840 million, or one in five people in the developing world."

Population Reference Bureau. "Can We Feed the Future World Population?" Press Release 1997. document-level access: <http://www.prb.org/media/pressrel.htm>

HUNGER--BRAZIL

In 1997, "two out of every three [Brazilians are malnourished]. There are 16 million abandoned children. Out of every ten children who die, seven are killed by hunger. Brazil is fourth in the world in food exports, fifth in area, and sixth in hunger." (p138)

Stallabrass, Julian. "Sebastiao Salgado and Fine Art Photojournalism." New Left Review n223 May-Jun 1997. p131-160. (ISSN0028-6060).

HUNGER--MEXICO

In Mexico, as a result of the December 1994 peso devaluation, "worker buying power from 1982 to 1994 has been estimated as dropping between 65-70% (McDonald 1996...). As a consequence, there has been a significant decrease in the consumption of all staples, including a drop in the average consumption of milk by 35% and meat by as much as 60% (Munoz Rios 1997). Malnutrition now effects 50% of the population (SIGLO 21 1996...)....The top 40% of Mexicans based on income consume 64% of the country's milk, while the bottom 30% account for only 8.7% of total milk consumption annually (Adorno Jimenez 1994)." (p324)

McDonald, James H. "Privatizing the Private Family Farmer: NAFTA and the Transformation of the Mexican Dairy Sector." Human Organization v56 n3 Fall 1997. p321-332. (ISSN0018-7259).

HUNGER--UNITED STATES

Hunger is widespread and increasing in the United States "where, according to Congressional testimony, the hungry increased to 30 million in 1995 from 20 million in 1985. By the government's own estimate, 36 million Americans lived in poverty in 1995." (p33)

Macdougall, A. Kent. "Pandemic Immiseration." Monthly Review v49 n2 Jun 1997. p31-34. (ISSN0027-0520).

HUNTERS--MICHIGAN

"Nationally, the percentage of Americans who hunt is in decline. It is now below 6 percent. In Michigan, the number of hunting licenses sold has been steadily declining. Between 1991 and 1996 (the last year for which complete stats are available), resident and non-resident firearms deer licenses declined by 127,103, or nearly 18 percent...." (p7 secA)

McDiarmid, Hugh. "Taking Aim: A Countdown to Deer Season: Antihunters Gain Ground vs. Thrill-Seeking Killers." Detroit Free Press 13 Nov 1997. p1,7 secA.

HUNTING--GREAT BRITAIN (v26)

In Great Britain, "fourteen thousand acres of woodland are owned or managed by hunts, and 95 per cent of hunts undertake conservation work--the maintenance of bridle ways, gates and so forth--while 1.4 million carcases are disposed of each year, either free of charge or at minimum cost....There are 385 registered packs of hounds and 228,000 participants in registered packs and clubs. The 1997 update of the Cobham report estimated direct employment at 15,300 and direct expenditure at 176 million [pounds sterling], with a turnover of 122 million [pounds sterling] involving 9,700 separate businesses. Five thousand pubs are patronised for hunt meets and other fixtures....Seventy per cent of all woodland planting on English and Welsh farms is for sporting purposes....Last year, 3.3 million people went fishing and more than 700,000 shot game and wild fowl." (c311-312)

Spring, Richard (H.C.-Bury St. Edwards). "Rural Policies." Great Britain. Parliament. House of Commons. Debates. 16 Jul 1997. c311-312. section-level access: <http://www.parliament.the-stationery-office.co.uk/pa/cm199798/cmhansrd/cm970716/debtext/70716-02.htm#70716-02_spnew1>

HUNTING--MICHIGAN (v26)

In 1997, "hunters in Michigan killed 282,000 deer during the 16-day firearms season, about 6 percent fewer than in 1996, the DNR [Department of Natural Resources] estimated....The harvest--the seventh best in state history--was significantly below the record firearms kill of 334,940 in 1989....Hunters killed 26,000 bucks and 10,000 antlerless deer in the Upper Peninsula, a significant decline from last year's total of 52,890. The northern Lower Peninsula kill was down, too--106,000 (77,350 bucks and 38,975 antlerless deer), down from 116,325 last year. In southern Michigan, hunters killed 140,000 deer--72,000 bucks and 68,000 antlerless animals--up from 130,104 (74,360 and 55,744, respectively) last year. The total harvest was slightly below the DNR's preseason estimate that hunters would kill about 290,000 deer this firearms season." (p7 secA)

Gwizdz, Bob. "State: Firearm Deer Kill Down 6% in 1997." Ann Arbor News 6 Dec 1997. p7 secA.

In Michigan, in 1997, "Department of Natural Resources biologists expect hunters to kill 450,000 whitetails over the three months of deer hunting, with the bulk of them taken during the gun season....Although the herd is down approximately 11 percent from last year--the DNR guesstimated the herd at 1.8 million on Oct. 1 [1997]--wildlife officials expect hunters to kill almost as many whitetails as last year, when they took 456,000. But the makeup of the harvest should be different. The DNR expects hunters to kill about 30,000 fewer bucks and about that many more does than last year." (p3 secC)

Gwizdz, Bob. "Venture Outdoors: DNR Expects Fewer Bucks, More Does to Be Taken." Ann Arbor News 8 Nov 1997. p3 secC.

In Michigan, "competition for food results in undersized deer with spindly antlers. And though whitetails don't develop fully until they are 5 1/2 years old, about 70 percent of Michigan bucks are killed at 1 1/2....It is estimated that of all the free-roaming deer killed in the United States, one in 100,000 is a record buck. On game ranches, 25 percent to 50 percent of the bucks have record racks." (p8 secA)

Sharp, Eric. "Taking Aim: A Countdown to Deer Season: For Big Fee, Hunters Can Bag Trophy Buck." Detroit Free Press 13 Nov 1997. p1,8 secA.

In Michigan, "sales of resident deer-hunting licenses have fallen by 20,000 in the past five years and officials are predicting further declines this year. As Michigan's archery season for deer opens...[on Oct 1, 1997], the state's deer herd remains at a near-record 1.8 million animals." (p1 secA) "Hunters will be allowed to shoot more female deer, take part in longer seasons in some areas and try a special December firearms season--the first such season in memory. About 450,000 deer are expected to be killed." (p9 secA)

Pearce, Jeremy. "Fewer Hunters, More Deer Could Cost State Millions." Detroit News 1 Oct 1997. p1,9 secA.

In Michigan, "an estimated 750,000 hunters--the most on record--will head into the trees for two weeks of backwoods bonding....During the season, hunters will pour $500 million into the state's economy....The state's herd is at an all-time high of 1.8 million, up from only 800,000 in 1963. The main reason for the increase is improved habitat....The state will pocket $16.6 million in license fees. Nationwide, the 11 million, big-game hunters spent about $16.9 billion in 1996." (p3)

Bachus, Richard C. "United States: Deer Season Means Big Bucks, Long Traditions in Michigan." The Christian Science Monitor v89 n245 14 Nov 1997. p3. The Christian Science Monitor search engine: <http://www.csmonitor.com/plweb-cgi/iops1.pl> To retrieve this article, enter the following search: ED=19971114 AND michigan. In the "retrieved list," click the title that matches this record. (ISSN0882-7729).

HUNTING--TENNESSEE (v26)

HUNTING LEASES--TENNESSEE (v26)

HUNTINGTON'S CHOREA (v26)

HYDROELECTRIC POWER PLANTS--NEPAL (v26)

HYGIENE, INDUSTRIAL

see INDUSTRIAL HYGIENE

HYPERACTIVE CHILD SYNDROME
see ATTENTION-DEFICIT HYPERACTIVITY DISORDER

HYPERTENSION--UNITED STATES (v26)

"Treatment with a low-dose diuretic cuts by half the chance that an older person with high systolic blood pressure will develop heart failure, according to results from a [U.S.] National Institutes of Health (NIH) trial. Those who had already had a heart attack experienced an even greater benefit--their chance of developing heart failure dropped by 80 percent....[According to Dr. Richard J. Hodes, Director of the National Institute on Aging,] 'isolated systolic hypertension is the most common form of high blood pressure among people age 60 and older. It is a major risk factor for heart disease and stroke, the number one and number three killers of Americans today.' In isolated systolic hypertension (ISH), the systolic blood pressure is high (140 or greater millimeters of mercury, or mmHg) but the diastolic is normal (less than 90 mmHg). Millions of Americans over age 60 have ISH and more than 3 million have the degree of ISH treated in SHEP [Systolic Hypertension in the Elderly Program]--a systolic of 160-219 mmHg and a normal diastolic."

U.S. National Institutes of Health. "Hypertension Therapy Prevents Heart Failure among Elderly." News Release 15 Jul 1997. document-level access: <http://www.nih.gov/news/pr/jul97/nhlbi-15.htm>

HYPERTENSION--UNITED STATES--MEN (v26)

HYPOTHERMIA--UNITED STATES (v26)

ICE CREAM, ICES, ETC.

"Americans are the ice-cream-eating-est people in the world. In 1994, each person in the United States consumed 16.1 pounds of the sweet stuff....Vanilla is the most popular flavor. One out of 4 ice creams sold is vanilla. One of the major ingredients in ice cream is air. In fact, 10 to 25 percent air is desirable....The world's largest ice cream bar was made in Kalisz, Poland. The giant bar weighed 19,357 pounds and took 11 days to make in September 1994." (p17)

Mayr, Diane. "The Home Forum: I Scream, You Scream, Here's a Few Facts about Ice Cream." The Christian Science Monitor v89 n152 2 Jul 1997. p17. The Christian Science Monitor search engine: <http://www.csmonitor.com/plweb-cgi/iops1.pl> To retrieve this article, enter the following search: ED=19970702 AND cream. In the "retrieved list," click the title that matches this record. (ISSN0882-7729).

ICE SPORTS
see WINTER SPORTS

ICELAND--COMMERCE

In Iceland, "the value of exported goods January-August 1997 was 85,600 million ISK [krona] while the value of imports amounted to almost 84,100 million. Thus, there was a trade surplus of almost 1,600 million as compared with a trade surplus of 4,100 million January-August 1996, at constant rates of exchange. In January-August 1997 the value of exports was 5% higher than in the same period the year before, at constant rates of exchange....Marine products constituted 73% of all exports, their value being 1% higher than the year before. The value of exported manufactured goods was 12% higher than in January-August 1996, the value of aluminium increased by 9% and the value of ferro-silicon increased by 26%. The total value of imports in January-August 1997 was 9% higher than in the same period the year before, at constant exchange rates."

Statistics Iceland. "Iceland's Balance of Trade in January-August 1997." Press Release 8 Oct 1997. document-level access: <http://eldur.stjr.is/statice/news/trade.htm>

ICES
see ICE CREAM, ICES, ETC.

ILLEGAL ALIENS--MEXICO--UNITED STATES

"The Binational Center for Human Rights in Tijuana estimates that 75 percent of those who attempt to cross into the United States are robbed, beaten, exhorted or raped." (p4) "Since the mid-'70s, the Border Patrol has been dumping illegal entrants back across the border (over 1 million apprehensions during each of the last two fiscal years)." (p5) "Health official [Jose] Cortes estimates that more than 3.5 million Mexican adults, caught between poverty conditions in Mexico and legal restrictions in the United States, are struggling to survive on the border until they can squeeze into the United States." (p6)

Stout, Robert Joe. "Caught in the Middle." Christian Social Action v10 n9 Oct 1997. p4-6. (ISSN0897-0459).

ILLEGAL ALIENS--UNITED STATES (v26)

"The Southwest Border States--California, Arizona, New Mexico, and Texas--contain the principal corridors into the United States for illegal immigrants. The five districts located directly on the border adjacent to Mexico--Southern California, Arizona, New Mexico, Western Texas and Southern Texas--account for more than 80 percent of illegal entries into this country....In FY 1995, 15 Special Assistant United States Attorney positions were detailed from the DOJ [Department of Justice] for Operation Gatekeeper, to address the increase in immigration prosecutions which resulted from higher illegal entries in the Southwest Border States. As a result of these Special Assistant United States Attorney placements during 1995, more than 1,000 previously deported aliens were prosecuted for illegal reentry after deportation. This is seven times the number of cases prosecuted in 1992. The number of felony smuggling cases has more than doubled in FY 1995 to a total of 60 indictments in the first 9 months of 1995, compared to 24 cases in all of 1994 and 33 in 1993." (p724) "During FY 1996, the five United States Attorneys' offices along the border filed 3,089 cases against 3,461 defendants. This is an increase of 242.1 percent over cases filed in FY 1994, and an increase of 231.5 percent in defendants. Cases terminated increased by 188.7 percent during the same period to 2,746. The defendants terminated increased by 174.7 percent to 3,079." (p725)

U.S. Dept. of Justice. "Departments of Commerce, Justice, And State, The Judiciary...Approp. for 1998 (Part 2)." Hearing. U.S. House. Committee on Appropriations. Washington, D.C. : GPO, 1997. (ISBN0160549094). (Y4.Ap6/1:C73/2/997/pt.2).

U.S. "Immigration and Naturalization Service (INS) enforcement measures are disproportionately concentrated on the U.S.-Mexico border. According to the Urban Institute, only four out of ten individuals who are in the country illegally entered by crossing the southern border; the rest entered with legal visas that later expired. Yet 85 percent of all border enforcement resources are concentrated on the southern border. The enforcement of immigration law is selectively applied to people of Mexican origin or descent. Mexican nationals represent only 39 percent of the undocumented immigrants in the United States, but 90 percent of those arrested for illegal entry by the INS. In a 1994 study by the University of Arizona, 18 percent of the people surveyed at random in South Tucson reported mistreatment by immigration authorities. Of these, 60 percent were native-born U.S. citizens." (p15)

"Militarization of the U.S.-Mexico Border." NewsNotes v22 n4 Jul-Aug 1997. p15. (ISSN1064-1556).

The U.S. Immigration and Naturalization Service "estimated an average annual growth [of undocumented immigrants] of 275,000 per year between 1992 and 1996, yielding an estimated total of 5 million undocumented migrants in October 1996. Mexico was the source for more than one-half of the unauthorized migrants. The INS estimated that there were about 2.7 million Mexicans living in the United States illegally in 1996....In September 1997, the Mexico-United States Binational Commission estimated a similar figure--about 2.4 million undocumented Mexicans residing in the United States during roughly the same period. About 60 percent of all undocumented migrants come from clandestine border crossings; the other 40 percent involve people who are here legally but overstay or otherwise violate the terms of their visas." (p20)

del Pinal, Jorge/Singer, Audrey. "Generations of Diversity: Latinos in the United States." Population Bulletin v52 n3 Oct 1997. p2-47. (ISSN0032-468X).

"Eighty-five thousand [illegal aliens] were caught last year [trying to enter the U.S.]. Somewhere between 85,000 and 500,000 more got through, Border Patrol officials estimate." (p1) "Border Patrol agents...say they have cut arrests along the San Diego County border in half--from 18,847 to 9,130--over the past year....A satellite operation to San Diego's Operation Gatekeeper opened this month in El Centro, adding 133 agents to the 180 that already patrol the 72-mile border of Imperial County." (p18)

Wood, Daniel B. "Illegals Find Backyard Gate to the US." The Christian Science Monitor v89 n239 5 Nov 1997. p1,18. The Christian Science Monitor search engine: <http://www.csmonitor.com/plweb-cgi/iops1.pl> To retrieve this article, enter the following search: ED=19971105 AND backyard. In the "retrieved list," click the title that matches this record. (ISSN0882-7729).

ILLEGAL CONTRACTS--RUSSIA--MORTALITY (v26)

ILLEGITIMACY--AFRO-AMERICANS

Currently, in the U.S., "68% of all Black births are out of wedlock--the highest proportion ever recorded (Angel & Angel, 1993)....If current trends continue more than 85% of Black children will spend some portion of their childhood without their father (Angel & Angel, 1993)." (p564-565) "Black children born to unmarried couples increased from 38% in 1970 to more than 68% in 1991 (U.S. Bureau of the Census, 1994)." (p566)

Hamer, Jennifer F. "Article: The Fathers of 'Fatherless' Black Children." Families in Society v78 n6 Nov-Dec 1997. p564-578. (ISSN1044-3894).

ILLEGITIMACY--DENMARK--SWEDEN--UNITED STATES

"In 1993, 47% of all live births in Denmark were to unmarried mothers. The analogous figures in Sweden and the U.S. were 50% and 31% respectively (U.S. Bureau of the Census 1996)." (p6-7)

Coney, Nancy S./Mackey, Wade C. "Fatherhood as a Deterrent against Female Promiscuity: A Time to Refurbish the Electra Complex." Mankind Quarterly v38 n1-2 Fall-Win 1997. p3-23. (ISSN0001-3455).

ILLEGITIMACY--PUBLIC OPINION

"The International Gallup Poll finds substantial variation around the world in the percent of citizens in the sixteen countries surveyed who condone having children outside of marriage. The most liberal countries on this issue--with 90% or more of adults saying it is morally acceptable--are Germany, France and Iceland....The United States stands out as the country most evenly divided over the morality of out-of-wedlock births, with 47% saying it is wrong and 50% saying it is not wrong....Less than 20% of young adults in...[Canada, Great Britain, and Spain] consider it wrong, compared with nearly half of adults aged 55 and older."

Gallup Organization. "Global Study of Family Values: An International Gallup Poll: Family Values Differ Sharply around the World." Press Release 7 Nov 1997. document-level access: <http://www.gallup.com/poll/special/family.html>

ILLEGITIMACY--UNITED STATES (v26)

ILLICIT DRUG TRADE

see DRUG TRAFFIC

ILLINOIS--POPULATION

"The population of Illinois did not grow in the 1980s. It is projected to grow 6 percent in the 1990s and 5 percent in each of the next two decades, according to new county-level projections of the state....Thirty-eight of the state's 102 counties may lose population in the next three decades, while 8 are projected to grow at an average annual rate of 1 percent or more....Illinois's population is projected to grow from 11.8 million in 1995 to 13.3 million in 2020. Hispanics will account for 55 percent of that growth. The projections assume that about 1 million people will move to Illinois every year, and about 1 million will move out." (p3)

"Land of Lincoln and Latinos." Forecast v17 n10 Oct 1997. p3. article-level access: <http://www.demographics.com/publications/fc/97_fc/9710_fc/fc97102.htm> (ISSN0732-1597).

ILLITERACY

see LITERACY

ILLNESS

see DISEASES

IMMIGRANTS

see also CRIME--UNITED STATES--IMMIGRANTS; HOME OWNERSHIP--UNITED STATES--IMMIGRANTS; POPULATION FORECASTING--UNITED STATES--IMMIGRANTS; UNEMPLOYMENT--AUSTRALIA--IMMIGRANTS

IMMIGRANTS--CANADA (v26)

IMMIGRANTS--CANADA--HONG KONG (v26)

IMMIGRANTS--CENTRAL AMERICA--UNITED STATES

"More than 1 million immigrants from Central America were admitted [to the U.S.] between 1820 and 1995, but more than two-thirds of them entered after 1980." (p24) "El Salvador is the leading source of both legal and illegal immigration from Central America. More than 340,000 immigrants came from El Salvador between 1981 and 1995. An estimated 335,000 undocumented Salvadorans lived in the United States in 1996. Many of the illegal immigrants sought political asylum, but few received it. Guatemala contributed 134,000 immigrants admitted between 1985 and 1995, and ranks just after El Salvador." (p25)

del Pinal, Jorge/Singer, Audrey. "Generations of Diversity: Latinos in the United States." Population Bulletin v52 n3 Oct 1997. p2-47. (ISSN0032-468X).

IMMIGRANTS--CUBA--UNITED STATES

"Cuba has been the major source of political refugees from this hemisphere, contributing more than 92 percent of the 597,000 refugees and asylees from the Americas who were granted permanent residency status [in the U.S.] between 1946 and 1995. The majority of Cuban immigrants entered the United States before 1982; about 30 percent before 1965, and 58 percent between 1965 and 1981. A new wave of Cubans came in 1980, when more than 125,000 Cubans arrived in Miami from Cuba's Mariel Harbor. This mass departure contributed 86 percent of that decade's Cuban immigrants." (p24)

del Pinal, Jorge/Singer, Audrey. "Generations of Diversity: Latinos in the United States." Population Bulletin v52 n3 Oct 1997. p2-47. (ISSN0032-468X).

IMMIGRANTS--DOMINICAN REPUBLIC--UNITED STATES

"More than 240,000 Dominicans were admitted [to the U.S.] during the 1960s and 1970s. The flow has accelerated, swelling to 252,000 during the 1980s and 219,000 between 1991 and 1995. The Dominican Republic, a country of only 8 million inhabitants, was the fourth largest source of U.S. immigrants in 1995, after Mexico, the Philippines, and China. In addition, an estimated 50,000 unauthorized Dominicans were living in the United States in 1996." (p24)

del Pinal, Jorge/Singer, Audrey. "Generations of Diversity:

Latinos in the United States." Population Bulletin v52 n3 Oct 1997. p2-47. (ISSN0032-468X).

IMMIGRANTS--EDUCATION--AUSTRALIA

According to the report, "Labor Force Status and Other Characteristics of Migrants," by the Australian Bureau of Statistics, "the proportion of migrants who had arrived in Australia [after 1970] with post-school qualifications was 49 per cent. The majority (55 per cent) of these migrants had those qualifications was 49 per cent. The majority (55 per cent) of these migrants had those qualifications recognised in Australia. Some 56 per cent of bachelor degrees were recognised, while 52 per cent of skilled and basic vocational qualifications were recognised. Of 221,800 migrants who obtained post-school qualifications after arrival, 44 per cent obtained a skilled or basic vocational qualification and 30 per cent obtained a bachelor degree or higher."

Australian Bureau of Statistics. "Migrants Have Higher Unemployment Rate." Media Release 11 Jun 1997. document-level access: <http://www.abs.gov.au/websitedbs/d3110125.nsf/4a255eef008309e44a255eef00061e57/67dbd33c47ca98f04a2564b3000526f7?OpenDocument>

IMMIGRANTS--EMPLOYMENT

"In Canada, a traditional immigration country, the number of temporary worker visas issued quadrupled during the last decade. The average annual inflow of temporary workers into Canada was two and one half times larger than the number of permanent immigrants, with 234,000 temporary workers compared to 114,000 immigrant workers. In the United States, another large immigration country, the number of non-immigrant work visas grew by 4 per cent annually, from 340,000 in 1990 to 413,000 in 1995....France has about 100,000 permanent immigrants, of whom 80,000 are from outside the EU: temporary workers included about 11,000 seasonal workers from Morocco and Poland. Germany has about 150,000 seasonal workers and another 100,000 foreign guest and contract workers. A middle-income country such as Mexico admits more than 70,000 workers from Central America each year for seasonal work in agriculture." (p21) "The number of migrant workers in the Republic of Korea...has trebled in recent years, from around 44,000 in 1992 to 136,000 in 1996....In the Czech Republic there were 14,500 foreign work-permit holders in mid-1992, nearly 32,900 in 1994 and 67,300, in addition to 67,000 Slovaks, in 1996." (p22)

"Migrants Facing Risks of Abuse and Exploitation." World of Work n20 Jun 1997. p20-22. (ISSN1020-0029).

IMMIGRANTS--EMPLOYMENT--AUSTRALIA

According to the report, "Labour Force Status and Other Characteristics of Migrants," by the Australian Bureau of Statistics, "the labour force participation rate for migrants [who arrived after 1970] was 68.0 per cent, compared with 58.0 per cent for all persons born outside Australia and 65.1 per cent for persons born in Australia. The participation rates for male and female migrants were 81.2 per cent and 55.4 per cent respectively. Almost three quarters (71 per cent) of migrants who were employed in November 1996 had a job before they migrated. Of this group, 46 per cent remained in the same occupation. The most common occupations for employed migrants were: professionals (19 per cent), tradespersons and related workers (16 per cent), intermediate clerical, sales and service workers (14 per cent), and intermediate production and transport workers (12 per cent)."

Australian Bureau of Statistics. "Migrants Have Higher Unemployment Rate." Media Release 11 Jun 1997. document-level access: <http://www.abs.gov.au/websitedbs/d3110125.nsf/4a255eef008309e44a255eef00061e57/67dbd33c47ca98f04a2564b3000526f7?OpenDocument>

IMMIGRANTS--EMPLOYMENT--NEW YORK (N.Y.) (v26)

IMMIGRANTS--EUROPE

"Throughout the 1980s and 1990s, only about 3 percent of all European Union...inhabitants were non-EU nationals. In France...the percentage of foreigners has been about 6.5 percent since 1970...." (p330)

Soguk, Nevzat. "Predicaments of Territorial Democracy and Statecraft in Europe: How...Movements." Alternatives: Social Transformation and Human Governance v22 n3 Jul-Sep 1997. p313-352. (ISSN0304-3754).

IMMIGRANTS--EUROPE--UNITED STATES (v26)

IMMIGRANTS--EUROPE--UNITED STATES--ECONOMIC CONDITIONS (v26)

IMMIGRANTS--FRANCE (v26)

"At present, some 1.6 million non-European foreigners live legally in France, with the number of illegal immigrants variously estimated at between 100,000 and 300,000....Estimates of the number [of immigrants] affected [by a government plan to revoke two anti-immigration laws enacted by the former center-right administration] vary between 10,000 and 40,000." (p9)

"Dateline Migration: International: French Socialists Ease Up on Immigrant Crackdown." Migration World v25 n4 1997. p9. (ISSN1058-5095).

IMMIGRANTS--GERMANY

"Today one person in 12 living in Germany is a foreigner....One in five new babies born there is not German. The largest group of foreigners, about 2 million, are ethnic Turks." (p8)

"Dateline Migration: International: Redefining German Citizenship." Migration World v25 n4 1997. p8. (ISSN1058-5095).

IMMIGRANTS--GHANA

According to Robert Lee, a dentist in Accra, Ghana's capital, "during the past 40 years...50 Africans have set up shop [in Ghana]. Half are women....In recent years, Ghana has again begun attracting African-Americans. Some 200 live here, mostly investors and retirees, according to the African-American association in Accra." (p7)

Ludden, Jennifer. "International: Black American Couple Finds Home in Ghana." The Christian Science Monitor v89 n177 7 Aug 1997. p7. The Christian Science Monitor search engine: <http://www.csmonitor.com/plweb-cgi/iops1.pl> To retrieve this article, enter the following search: ED=19970807 AND ghana. In the "retrieved list," click the title that matches this record. (ISSN0882-7729).

IMMIGRANTS--GREECE

"The OECD reports that some estimates put the total of foreigners (both legal and illegal) in Greece at 4 to 5 percent of the population. About 1 in 12 workers is a foreigner and most foreign workers work illegally. Undocumented workers earn about half the rate of Greek citizens, but about three to six times more than they could earn in their home countries....Albanians made up more than 95 percent of the illegal immigrants deported from Greece between 1991 and 1994." (p7)

Lim, Aun Ling. "Spotlight: Greece." Population Today v25 n7-8 Jul-Aug 1997. p7. (ISSN0749-2448).

IMMIGRANTS--IRELAND--DUBLIN

In Dublin, Ireland, there has been a large "illegal influx in the last two years of more than 3,000 foreigners....More than 50 refugees are arriving every week, a rate expected to double in coming months. Five years ago the rate was less than one a month." (p9)

"Dateline Migration: International: Dublin's Rare Quandary: Immigrants." Migration World v25 n4 1997. p9. (ISSN1058-5095).

IMMIGRANTS--ITALY (v26)

IMMIGRANTS--KOREA (SOUTH)--UNITED STATES

In the U.S., "the number of Korean immigrants has increased from 70,000 in 1990 to 799,000 in 1992 (U.S. Bureau of the Census, 1992). It is estimated that there are between 800,000 and 900,000 Korean-Americans with more than 90% foreign-born (Awanohara, 1991). About 30,000 South Koreans who are predominantly well-educated are settling in U.S. cities each year (Awanohara, 1991). It seems that Korean immigrants are attracted to self-employment, and it is estimated that perhaps as many as 80% (about 1,300) of all green grocers in the New York tri-state area (New York, New Jersey, and Connecticut), are owned by Koreans. In Los Angeles, which has the largest Korean population outside of Seoul, 40% of Korean men owned their own businesses in 1989 (Awanohara, 1991)." (p625-626)

Chung, Woo Sik/Pardeck, John T. "Treating Powerless Minorities through an Ecosystem Approach." Adolescence v32 n127 Fall 1997. p625-634. (ISSN0001-8449).

IMMIGRANTS--MEXICO--UNITED STATES

"Nearly 5.4 million Mexicans immigrated to the United States between 1820 and 1995. Only Germany (7.1 million), and Ireland (5.4 million) sent more immigrants during that 176-year period. Mexico ranked fourth among sending nations between 1921 and 1940, third between 1941 and 1960, and first after 1960. In 1995, more than 90,000 immigrants were admitted from Mexico, about 40,000 more than the Philippines, the second-ranked country of origin for U.S. immigrants." (p21)

del Pinal, Jorge/Singer, Audrey. "Generations of Diversity: Latinos in the United States." Population Bulletin v52 n3 Oct 1997. p2-47. (ISSN0032-468X).

IMMIGRANTS--MICHIGAN (v26)

IMMIGRANTS--NEW YORK (N.Y.) (v26)

New York City "currently absorbs about 22,000 Dominicans a year, according to an analysis of 1990-94 immigration data by the Department of City Planning....The average annual flow of immigrants from former Soviet republics to the city increased from 1,300 a year in 1982-89 to 13,300 a year in 1990-94, vaulting the region from 12th to 2nd place among immigrant source countries....Most immigrants to New York City are young adults, with a median age of 27. Two-thirds settle in Brooklyn or Queens. Former Soviet immigrants are older than average, with a median age of 36. Immigrants from China--the third-largest source country in the 1990s, with an average of 12,000 new arrivals a year--are also older (median age 32). Dominicans are one of the youngest groups (median age 23)....The fourth-largest source country, Jamaica, sent an average of 9,000 a year in the 1980s, but only 6,600 in the 1990s. The fifth-largest, Guyana, sent 6,700 a year in the 1980s and 6,200 in the 1990s." (p16-17)

Edmondson, Brad. "New Frontiers: The Newest New Yorkers." American Demographics v19 n7 Jul 1997. p16-17. article-level access: <http://www.demographics.com/publications/ad/97_ad/9707_ad/ad97074.htm> (ISSN0163-4089).

"According to recent census data, nearly 20 percent of New York State residents are immigrants, and nearly 50 percent of New York City inhabitants are either immigrants or first generation. The city has maintained its population base and its housing stock through the influx of over 100,000 legal immigrants per year....Experts estimate that New York City is home to around 400,000 out-of-status individuals, mainly visa overstayers. Approximately 40,000 per year have come to the city in the past." (p17)

Shaw, Karen. "New York City Mayor Rudolph Giuliani Campaigns for Immigrants." Migration World v25 n4 1997. p15-17. (ISSN1058-5095).

IMMIGRANTS--OMAN (v26)

IMMIGRANTS--QUEBEC (PROVINCE)--PUBLIC OPINION (v26)

IMMIGRANTS--SOUTH AMERICA--UNITED STATES

"More than 1.5 million South Americans were admitted [to the U.S.] from 1820 to 1995, and about 49 percent of them entered after 1980....Between 1985 and 1995, more than 440,000 South Americans (excluding Guyanese and Brazilians) were admitted. Colombia sent the most immigrants of any country in South America--more than 361,000 since 1932. More than 192,000 Ecuadorians and 147,000 Argentineans gained admission from 1932 to 1995....The INS [Immigration and Naturalization Service] estimated that 65,000 Colombians, 55,000 Ecuadorians, and 30,000 Peruvians were living illegally in the United States in 1996." (p25)

del Pinal, Jorge/Singer, Audrey. "Generations of Diversity: Latinos in the United States." Population Bulletin v52 n3 Oct 1997. p2-47. (ISSN0032-468X).

IMMIGRANTS--UNITED STATES (v26)

"In 1995, the U.S. took in about 720,000 legal immigrants. Most (64%) were admitted because they are immediate family members of U.S. citizens. The second-largest group (16%) was composed of refugees and asylum-seekers fleeing persecution in their homelands and seeking freedom in our country. A relatively small number (12%) were admitted because they possess special professional skills and high education which would significantly contribute to our economy and society. The smallest category (7%) included people admitted to bring about greater geographic diversity in the immigrant pool. Most were from Western European countries." (pE1337)

Hamilton, Lee H. (Rep.-Ind.). "Immigration." Congressional Record. Daily ed. v143 n93 27 Jun 1997. pE1337. section/page-level access: <http://thomas.loc.gov/cgi-bin/query/R?r105:FLD001:E01337:> (ISSN0363-7239). (X1.1A.105/1).

"About 915,900 people legally immigrated to the United States in 1996, up from 720,461 in 1995. According to the U.S. Census Bureau, 24.5 million people--nearly one of every 10 people living in the United States today--was born in another country." (p11)

"Dateline Migration: National: Legal Immigration Up 27 Percent in U.S." Migration World v25 n4 1997. p11. (ISSN1058-5095).

"Last year almost 1.2 million people came to the United States to live, to cities large and small, to suburbs and to rural areas. The 916,000 legal arrivals were joined by an estimated 275,000 illegal immigrants, the Immigration and Naturalization Service says. The largest numbers of legal settlers went initially to six states--California, New York, Florida, Texas, New Jersey, and Illinois....The foreign-born population of the U.S. today is just over nine percent, the highest proportion in more than 50 years....Legal immigration last year jumped 27 percent from 1995." (p4)

Andrews, James H. "The Newest Americans." Planning v63 n9 Sep 1997. p4-9. (ISSN0001-2610).

"According to the U.S. Immigration and Naturalization Service (INS), 911,000 legal immigrants entered the U.S. in 1996. 198,000 received refugee status. 595,000 were admitted under family reunification guidelines, and 118,000 for their job skills. The INS estimates that an estimated 250,000 additional people entered the country without proper documentation. About 37 percent of 1996's legal immigrants came from Asia. This includes immigrants from Vietnam, China, Pakistan and India. Slightly less than one-third--32 percent--came from the Caribbean, Central America and Mexico. Mexico is the single largest home nation for U.S. immigrants: 163,572 legal immigrants--and about 50,000 undocumented immigrants--came to

the U.S. from Mexico last year. About 18 percent of legal U.S. immigrants came from Europe." (p8)
Colatosti, Camille. "The Flight into America." Witness v80 n12 Dec 1997. p8-12. (ISSN0197-8896).

IMMIGRANTS--UNITED STATES--LANGUAGES (v26)

IMMIGRANTS--UNITED STATES--SOCIAL CONDITIONS (v26)

IMMIGRATION
see EMIGRATION AND IMMIGRATION

IMMUNIZATION
see also HEPATITIS A--VACCINATION; INFLUENZA VACCINES; TYPHOID VACCINE; VACCINATION

IMMUNIZATION OF CHILDREN (v26)

IMMUNIZATION OF CHILDREN--COSTS (v26)

IMMUNIZATION OF CHILDREN--MICHIGAN (v26)
The second "Critical Health Indicators" report was compiled by the Michigan Department of Community Health in July 1997. It found that "in 1991, just 41 percent of Michigan 2-year-olds were up-to-date in immunization for chicken pox, diphtheria, hepatitis B, measles, mumps, whooping cough, polio, rubella and tetanus. Today the number of kids immunized has risen to 74 percent, on a par with the national average." (p2 secC)
Cain, Charlie. "Metro: Special Report: Health Snapshot: Michigan Gaining Ground in the Fight against Diseases." Detroit News 17 Jul 1997. p1-2 secC.

IMMUNIZATION OF CHILDREN--MICHIGAN--DETROIT (v26)
The U.S. "Centers for Disease Control and Prevention reported that 76 percent of Michigan children were properly immunized in 1996. In 1994, the number was 51 percent, the lowest rate in the nation. The 15-percent increase from 1995 moves Michigan up to 38th among states. The state ranked 47th in 1995. The numbers in Detroit improved dramatically, too. In 1991, only 29 percent of Detroit children were immunized. That jumped to 65 percent in 1996." (p1 secB)
Mishra, Raja. "Local News: Children First: Immunization Score Rises." Detroit Free Press 24 Jul 1997. p1 secB.

IMMUNIZATION OF CHILDREN--UNITED STATES (v26)
"According to the Centers for Disease Control, 76% of two-year-olds in the U.S. received their vaccines on schedule in 1995. This reflects a one percent increase in the number of toddlers receiving vaccines the previous year. The CDC's goal is for more than 90% of two-year-olds to receive their vaccines by the year 2000." (p13)
"Around the Nation: Increased Child Immunizations." Health Advocate n188 Spr 1997. p13.

IMPAIRED VISION
see VISION DISORDERS

IMPORTS--AFRICA--CARIBBEAN AREA--EUROPE --PACIFIC AREA (v26)

IMPORTS--CANADA--UNITED STATES (v26)

IMPORTS--EUROPE--FORMER SOVIET REPUBLICS (v26)

IMPORTS--EUROPE--SOUTH AMERICA (v26)

IMPORTS--GERMANY (v26)

IMPORTS--HONG KONG
"Japan was the largest supplier of Hong Kong's imports by ocean, accounting for a share of 22% in the first half of 1997. The value, however, decreased by 0.8% over the same period in 1996. The value of seaborne imports from Taiwan and South Korea also decreased, by 6.3% and 2.5% respectively in the first half of 1997. Comparing the first half of 1997 with the same period in 1996, the value of seaborne imports from the Mainland and the United States increased by 5.1% and 1.6% respectively."
Hong Kong. Census and Statistics Department. "Analysis of External Trade Statistics by Mode of Transport." Press Release 26 Aug 1997. document-level access: <http://www.info.gov.hk/censtatd/hkstat/press/t51h97.htm>

IMPORTS--UNITED STATES (v26)
"The 11-percent growth in U.S. processed food purchases in 1996 was the strongest in recent years. A 2-percent increase in U.S. real per capita disposable income, following 1995's 2.6-percent rise, boosted consumer spending. In addition, the value of the dollar, weighted by countries' share of U.S. exports, rose approximately 7 percent during 1996, effectively reducing prices of foreign goods for U.S. consumers. Most of the 10 processed food groups registered double-digit import growth, led by sugar and confections at 30 percent, grain mill products at 23 percent, and fats and oils at 21 percent....Among the larger industries, cane sugar imports surged 58 percent to nearly $1.2 billion, becoming a 'billion-dollar' import industry for the first time as U.S. sugar production fell significantly from 1995." (p12)
Ruppel, Fred J./Handy, Charles R./Malanoski, Margaret A./ U.S. Dept. of Agriculture. Economic Research Service. "World Agriculture & Trade: U.S. Processed Food Trade Continues to Expand." Agricultural Outlook Jul 1997. p11-13.
"U.S. agricultural imports in fiscal year 1998 are projected at $38 billion, up 6 percent from fiscal 1997....Red meat imports...are expected to reach $2.8 billion, an increase of 8 percent from 1997....Horticultural imports for fiscal 1998 are expected to reach $14.4 billion, up 13 percent over fiscal 1997....Total vegetable imports for 1998 are projected at $4.1 billion, up from $3.6 billion in 1997. The forecast for wine and malt beverages was revised upward by $200 million to $3.5 billion in 1998. Sugar imports for fiscal 1998 are projected to fall from 2.9 million tons in 1997 to 2.5 million tons in 1998." (p12)
U.S. Dept. of Agriculture. "Import Highlights." Outlook for U.S. Agricultural Exports 2 Dec 1997. p12.
U.S. "fiscal 1997 imports were up 10 percent to $35.8 billion and are again a record. Coffee was by far the largest single import product, reaching $3.7 billion for the fiscal year, a 29-percent increase from 1996....Except for imports of rubber, which declined 8 percent this year, all the other major imports rose." (p1)
U.S. Dept. of Agriculture. Economic Research Service. "Imports." U.S. Agricultural Trade Update 24 Nov 1997. p1.

IMPOVERISHED PEOPLE
see POOR

IMPRISONMENT--UNITED STATES (v26)

INCANDESCENT LAMPS (v26)

INCAPACITY (LAW)
see CAPACITY AND DISABILITY

INCARCERATED PERSONS
see PRISONERS

INCOME (v26)
see also FARM INCOME; RETIREMENT INCOME; SUPPLEMENTAL SECURITY INCOME PROGRAM; WAGES
"Between 1960 and '91, the income share of the richest 20 percent of the global population increased from 70.2 percent to 85 percent, while the share of the poorest 20 percent declined from 2.3 percent to 1.4 percent. Seventy percent of the world's absolutely poor are now women." (p19)
Bandarage, Asoka. "Opinion/Essays: Economic Inequality, Not Overpopulation, Is the Key Issue." The Christian Science Monitor v89 n159 14 Jul 1997. p19. The Christian Science Monitor search engine: <http://www.csmonitor.com/plweb-cgi/iops1.pl> To retrieve this article, enter the following search: ED=19970714 AND issue. In the "retrieved list," click the title that matches this record. (ISSN0882-7729).

INCOME--AFRO-AMERICANS
"According to a recent [U.S.] Census Bureau report, African Americans had per capita income of nearly $11,000 in 1995,

compared to $18,000 for whites, or a total annual income of $363 billion." (p11 secA)

Malveaux, Julianne. "Other Voices: Blacks Should Flex Their Economic Muscles." Detroit Free Press 16 Jul 1997. p11 secA.

For the past 30 years in the U.S., "the median income for black families has remained stuck at 59 percent of the median income for whites....Married African Americans today earn 84 percent as much as white couples. That's up from 68 percent in 1967. Married black couples where both partners work now earn 86 percent as much as similar white couples. The problem is that married couples are now just 45 percent of all black families--down from two-thirds in 1967." (p5 secB)

Brownstein, Ronald. "Outlook: Battle to Eliminate Poverty Must Focus on Fatherless Families." Detroit News 12 Oct 1997. p5 secB.

INCOME--AGED (v26)

INCOME--ALABAMA (v26)

INCOME--ALASKA (v26)

INCOME--AUSTRALIA

In Australia, "in 1995-96 the average weekly income received by couple families was $868, by one-parent families $433 and by single persons $370, according to results from the latest household survey of income released...by the Australian Bureau of Statistics....Young couples under 35 with no dependent children received an average of $1092 a week....The average income of couples with young children, eldest under 5, was $925 per week. Income rises again as the children grow older. Couples with older children, eldest 15 to 24, had an average income of $1080 a week....Lone parents aged between 25 and 34 received an average weekly income of $394. For lone parents over 45, the average was $524. The level of income received by couple families is at its peak when they are between 45 and 54 years, at $1077 a week....Couples aged 55 to 64 received an average income of $703 and for those over 65 the average income fell to $429 a week."

Australian Bureau of Statistics. "Income Survey." Media Release 1 Aug 1997. document-level access: <http://www.abs.gov.au/websitedbs/d3110125.nsf/4a255eef008309e44a255eef00061e57/eefd91df6dbfd24f4a2564e5007f7b13?OpenDocument>

INCOME--AUSTRALIA--SINGLE PEOPLE

According to the Australian Bureau of Statistics, "young, independent single persons aged under 25 had an average weekly income of $313. This rose to $495 for single persons aged between 25 and 34, reflecting their higher employment rates and higher salaries....Single persons aged 45 to 54 had an average income of $442 per week and those over 65 an average of $226."

Australian Bureau of Statistics. "Income Survey." Media Release 1 Aug 1997. document-level access: <http://www.abs.gov.au/websitedbs/d3110125.nsf/4a255eef008309e44a255eef00061e57/eefd91df6dbfd24f4a2564e5007f7b13?OpenDocument>

INCOME--BRAZIL (v26)

INCOME--CALIFORNIA--SAN FRANCISCO BAY AREA --MINORITIES (v26)

INCOME--CANADA (v26)

INCOME--CANADA--WOMEN (v26)

INCOME--CANADA--UNITED STATES

"In the United States over the last 10 years there has been an 11 per cent increase in real incomes. In the corresponding period in Canada there has been a 1.3 per cent decrease in real incomes." (p107)

Thompson, Greg (MP-NB). "Government Orders: Speech from the Throne." Canada. Parliament. House of Commons. Debates. v135 n4 25 Sep 1997. p106-132. section-level access: <http://www.parl.gc.ca/36/1/parlbus/chambus/house/debates/004_1997-09-25/han004-e.htm#LINK221> (ISSN0704-5603). (X3-361E).

INCOME--CHINA

In China, "nationwide, the mean reported total annual household income has risen to RMB [renminbi] 10,400 (US$ 1,250)--a sharp 75% gain over the mean income of RMB 5,960 ($680) found by Gallup's 1994 survey. Similarly, median income levels have risen from RMB 4,380 ($500) to RMB 8,000 ($960) over this same three year period....The median income level of urban residents (RMB 10,000/$1,200) remains considerably higher than that in rural China (RMB 6,000/$720). Simply put, the most typical rural household has an income which is 60% of that reported by the most typical urban family. Median income levels in major cities are higher still--from twice to 2.6 times the national average. Income levels reported by respondents in Guangzhou, Shanghai, and Beijing have now reached RMB 21,600, 20,000, and 16,000 respectively ($2,600, $2,410, and $1,920)."

Gallup Organization. "1997 Survey: The People's Republic of China: Consumer Attitudes & Lifestyle Trends." Press Release 27 Oct 1997. document-level access: <http://www.gallup.com/poll/special/china/chinarel.html>

INCOME--CUBA

In Cuba, workers are "reported to be receiving an average monthly salary of $202.5 pesos (US$9.20). This--the average wage for all Cuban workers, including joint ventures--translates into US$2.19 per week, equal to US$0.44 a day or 5.5 cents an hour, which could be the lowest in the world. Economists in Cuba have estimated that to buy goods at free market rates workers on the average peso salary ($202.5 pesos) have to labor 116 hours to purchase 1 kilogram of powdered milk, 70 hours for 1 kilogram of chicken, 13 hours for one lightbulb, and 500 to 1,700 hours for a pair of shoes." (p60)

Werlau, Maria C. "Foreign Investment in Cuba: The Limits of Commercial Engagement." World Affairs v160 n2 Fall 1997. p51-69. (ISSN0043-8200).

INCOME--EFFECT OF EDUCATION ON--UNITED STATES (v26)

INCOME--EFFECT OF EDUCATION ON--UNITED STATES--WOMEN (v26)

INCOME--HISPANIC AMERICANS

In the U.S., "in 1979, the median income of Hispanic family households was about $29,200 (in 1995 dollars), compared with $42,800 for white families and $23,800 for black families. In 1995, however, the Hispanics' median family income was $24,600, lower than the 1979 figure, and further below that of non-Hispanic whites ($45,000). And for the first time since 1972, Hispanic family incomes slipped below that of African Americans ($26,000)....Nearly one-fifth of Hispanic family households had incomes of $50,000 or more in 1995, about the same percentage as African American family households....The percentage was higher for Cuban families--close to one-third had incomes of $50,000 or more--but still well below the share of white families in the higher income group (44 percent)." (p38)

del Pinal, Jorge/Singer, Audrey. "Generations of Diversity: Latinos in the United States." Population Bulletin v52 n3 Oct 1997. p2-47. (ISSN0032-468X).

In the U.S., "in 1979, the median income of Hispanic family households was about $29,200 (in 1995 dollars), compared with $42,800 for white families and $23,800 for black families. In 1995...the Hispanics' median family income was $24,600, lower than the 1979 figure and further below that of non-Hispanic whites ($45,000). And for the first time since 1972, Hispanic family income has slipped below that of African Americans ($26,000)."

Population Reference Bureau. "Diverse Hispanic Population to Become Largest U.S. Minority." Press Release 1997. document-level access: <http://www.prb.org/media/pressrel.htm>

INCOME--ILLINOIS (v26)

INCOME--INDIA

In India, "'whatever income goes into the hands of women, almost 98 per cent is spent for the family--for food, clothes, for the children's education, for shelter,' [Ela Bhatt, founder of the Self Employed Women's Association of India,]...says. In the case of a typical man, studies in India show that only 50 to 60 per cent of his earnings go for the family, and the rest he spends on himself. If he has bad habits, alcohol consumption, for instance, or gambling, then 90 per cent will be wasted." (p13)

Helmore, Kristin. "Ela Bhatt: Warrior for Women: A Voice for the Poor." Choices v6 n4 Oct 1997. p10-13.

INCOME--JAPAN--AGED (v26)

INCOME--LATIN AMERICA--SOCIAL CONDITIONS (v26)

INCOME--MEXICO

An Instituto Nacional de Estadistica Geografia e Informatica survey in Mexico "indicates that every decile of the Mexican population, except for the richest, lost relative income between 1984 and 1994. The poorest ten percent lost the most relative income, 22.3 percent, while coincidentally the richest ten percent increased their share of national personal income by exactly the same amount." (p29) "The poorest ten percent suffered the steepest decline in absolute income--23 percent. The second to the eighth deciles each suffered declines from 12 to 16 percent. The next to the richest suffered the least loss--5 percent. Meanwhile, the absolute income of the richest ten percent increased by 20.8 percent." (p31)

Russell, James W. "Mexico's Rising Inequality." Monthly Review v49 n7 Dec 1997. p28-33. (ISSN0027-0520).

INCOME--MICHIGAN

Macomb County, Michigan "ranked first in per-person income growth this decade among comparable counties across the nation studied by University of Michigan researchers. Macomb County's per-person income grew 21.2 percent from 1990 to 1994, their study found. Oakland County, which paid for the research, was relegated to second place. Its income growth was 19.3 percent." (p1 secA)

Ackerman, Jennifer/Heinlein, Gary/Puls, Mark. "Macomb 1st in Income Growth." Detroit News 15 Jul 1997. p1,4 secA.

INCOME--MICHIGAN--ANN ARBOR (v26)

INCOME--MICHIGAN--OAKLAND COUNTY

Oakland County, Michigan "is the second wealthiest county in the United States with a population of more than 1 million. Earlier this decade, it surpassed...New York County in personal income rank....It has five communities with median household incomes of more than $100,000: Bloomfield Hills ($162,000), Orchard Lake ($121,000), Bingham Farms and Franklin ($114,000) and Bloomfield Township ($102,000)....In a study of the 28 fastest growing suburban counties in the nation, Oakland ranks second in income growth during the 1990s, according to Jeff Kaczmarek, the county's director of community and economic development." (p1 secD)

Pepper, Jon. "Business: Sorry, But Barney's Reason for Closing Its Somerset Store is a Bunch of Blarney." Detroit News 22 Jun 1997. p1 secD.

INCOME--MIDDLE EAST

"Saudi Arabia's per capita income has shrunk from a peak of $20,000 to a maximum of $7,000....In...Iran, revolution and war have taken a peak per capita income of about $11,000 and reduced it to between $2,000 and $3,000. Iraq's per capita income peaked at $14,000. The Iraqi government cut it by 60 percent long before any sanctions were ever imposed, and it is now probably below $1,000." (p8)

Cordesman, Anthony H. "Symposium--The Challenge in the Gulf: Building a Bridge from Containment to Stability." Middle East Policy v5 n2 May 1997. p1-21. (ISSN1061-1924).

INCOME--MIDDLE WEST

According to the Kansas City Fed's Second Quarter 1997 REGIONAL ECONOMIC DIGEST, "real personal income in the [Middle West] district grew 1.0 percent in the fourth quarter of 1996, the most recent quarter for which data are available, and was up 4.0 percent from a year ago....The...[U.S.'s] income increased 0.8 percent in the quarter and was up 3.3 percent from a year ago." (unpaginated)

"Regional Economy Enjoys Solid Growth in First Quarter." Federal Reserve Bank of Kansas City Fed Letter Aug 1997.

According to the Kansas City's Fed's Third Quarter 1997 REGIONAL ECONOMIC DIGEST, real personal income in the Tenth Federal Reserve District, which includes Colorado, Kansas, Missouri, Nebraska, New Mexico, Oklahoma and Wyoming, "grew 1.2 percent in the first quarter of 1997, the most recent quarter for which data are available. Income was up 3.8 percent from a year ago. The nation's income rose 1.3 percent in the quarter and 4.0 percent for the year." (unpaginated)

"Regional Economy Continued to Expand in Second Quarter of '97." Federal Reserve Bank of Kansas City Fed Letter Oct 1997.

INCOME--NETHERLANDS--AGED WOMEN (v26)

INCOME--NEW YORK (N.Y.) (v26)

INCOME--NEW YORK (N.Y.)--TEXAS--STARR COUNTY

"New York City ranked as the highest-paid per-capita U.S. county in 1994, at $53,190, or 245 percent of the national average. Meanwhile, Starr County, Texas placed last, at $6,583 per capita, only 30 percent of the average for the country as a whole." (p31)

Klein, Matthew. "Kaleidoscope: Site to See: Who Gets Paid." American Demographics v19 n6 Jun 1997. p31. article-level access: <http://www.demographics.com/publications/ad/97_ad/9706_ad/ad970624.htm> (ISSN0163-4089).

INCOME--RUSSIA (v26)

INCOME--SINGAPORE (v26)

INCOME--SWEDEN--AGED WOMEN (v26)

INCOME--UNITED STATES (v26)

"Between 1984 and 1989, the average annual change in real disposable income in the U.S. was $137 billion. Over the same time, real consumer expenditures also grew $137 billion per year. Between 1992 and 1996, real disposable income grew an average of $117 billion per year. Concurrently, real consumer spending grew $114 billion per year." (p20)

Kacapyr, Elia. "Current Conditions: Disposable Dollars Determine Spending." American Demographics v19 n6 Jun 1997. p18,20. article-level access: <http://www.demographics.com/publications/ad/97_ad/9706_ad/ad97065.htm> (ISSN0163-4089).

In the U.S., "the South was the only region to experience a significant year-to-year change in real median household income between 1995 and 1996. Real median household income increased there from $31,856 in 1995 to $32,422 in 1996. By comparison, the median household income in 1996 was $37,406 in the Northeast, $37,125 in the West and $36,579 in the Midwest. (The differences between the median household incomes of the Northeast, Midwest and West were not statistically significant.)...Households maintained by persons of Hispanic origin experienced a 5.8 percent increase in real median household income (to $24,906) offsetting the drop observed in 1995. The percentage changes in household income of White ($37,161), African American ($23,482) and Asian and Pacific Islander households ($43,276) were not statistically different from 1995. Real per capita income increased significantly between 1995 and 1996, for Whites (1.8 percent to $19,181),

African Americans (5.2 percent to $11,899) and Hispanics (4.9 percent to $10,048). The 1996 per capita income of Asians and Pacific Islanders ($17,921) was statistically unchanged."

U.S. Dept. of Commerce. Economic & Statistics Administration. "Income Improves, Poverty Levels Stabilize, Health Insurance Coverage Slips, Census Bureau Reports." Census Bureau Press Release 29 Sep 1997. document-level access: <http://www.census.gov/Press-Release/cb97-162.html>

"The bottom 20 percent of income earners in America in 1975 were earning $18,947, on average. In 1985, they were earning $18,816....And in the year 1995, 20 years later, they were earning $19,070, which was an increase of about $110 or so over 20 years. The next 20 percent of income earners went from a $30,701 average in 1975, to $32,415 in 1985, to $32,895 in 1995. So they had about a $380 gross increase, on average, in 10 years; and they had a $2,000 increase before that. When you factor in inflation, it is a loss....The only people in America who grew in that period of time were the top 20 percent of income earners. And they grew more than 100 percent." (pS6407)

Kerry, John F. (Sen.-Mass.). "Balanced Budget Act of 1997--Extraneous Material." Congressional Record. Daily ed. v143 n91 26 Jun 1997. pS6401-6437. section/page-level access: <http://thomas.loc.gov/cgi-bin/query/R?r105:FLD001:S06406:> (ISSN0363-7239). (X1.1A.105/1).

"The Census Bureau released data for 1996 on the incomes and poverty status of Americans. Median household income was up 1.2 percent to $35,492....Real (inflation-adjusted) median household income is still 2.7 percent below its 1989 level of $36,575 (in 1996 dollars). Virtually all of the growth in income between 1995 and 1996 was in one region of the country: the South. Income levels essentially were unchanged in the Northeast and West and actually fell slightly in the Midwest." (p8 secA)

Bartlett, Bruce. "Bartlett's Notations: New 'Prosperity' Data Actually Cause for Alarm." Detroit News 6 Oct 1997. p8 secA.

"Median household income in the U.S. increased 1.2 percent between 1995 and 1996, after adjusting for inflation....Household income rose last year to $35,492, edging back toward the 1989 peak of $36,575 (in 1996 dollars)....Median household income increased 1.8 percent in the South, to $32,422, which is still below the rest of the country. It was $37,406 in the Northeast last year, $37,125 in the West, and $36,579 in the Midwest....Between 1993 and 1996, incomes rose fastest in South Carolina (up 23 percent to $34,665), Kentucky (up 22 percent, to $32,413), and other states in the Mississippi and Ohio Valleys. During the same period, incomes declined fastest in New Mexico (down 14 percent, to $25,086), Hawaii (down 10 percent, to $41,772), and other states in New England and the West." (p1)

"Income Is Rising. So Is Poverty." Forecast v17 n11 Nov 1997. p1-2. article-level access: <http://www.demographics.com/publications/fc/97_fc/9711_fc/fc97111.htm> (ISSN0732-1597).

In 1995, "the Federal Reserve Board published a study that said the U.S. wealth and income gap is wider than that in any other industrial country. In 1980 the average CEO made 42 times as much money as her or his average employee. Today it is about 200 times as much. The productivity of U.S. workers has increased by 25 percent since 1980. Executive compensation has increased by 360 percent since 1980, while wages have declined by about 12 percent." (p8)

Acuff, Stewart. "Labor's New 'Culture of Organizing.'" Nonviolent Activist v14 n6 Nov-Dec 1997. p8-9. (ISSN8755-7428).

In the U.S., "the richest 1 percent of the population enjoys a total income equal to that of the combined earnings of the bottom 40 percent....Through the 1990s so far, the real earnings of those without a college degree have fallen by 5 percent. For those with a college degree, earnings have remained the same....Over the last 20 years, the incomes of the poorest 20 percent of the population have dropped by 17 percent, but the richest 1 percent has raked in a 91 percent gain in income, after taxes." (p8)

Rodwan, John G., Jr. "Guess Who Is Losing the Numbers Game?: Guess Who Can Win It?: The Resurgence of the Working Class." People's Tribune v24 n9 Sep 1997. p8. (ISSN1081-4787).

INCOME--UNITED STATES--AGED (v26)

According to the publication "A Profile of Older Americans, 1997," "the median income of older persons in 1996 was $16,684 for males and $9,626 for females. After adjusting for inflation, these figures represented a decrease of -1.7% in 'real' income from 1995 for men and -0.1% for women. The major source of income for older couples and individuals in 1996 was Social Security (reported by 92% of older persons), income from property (reported by 66%), public and private pensions (reported by 32%), earnings (reported by 16%), and public assistance (reported by 5%)."

U.S. Administration on Aging. "AoA Announces Availability of 'A Profile of Older Americans, 1997.'" Press Release 3 Oct 1997. document-level access: <http://www.aoa.dhhs.gov/pr/profile97.html>

INCOME--UNITED STATES--AGED WOMEN (v26)

INCOME--UNITED STATES--FARMERS

"Using data from the 1995 Farm Costs and Returns Survey (FCRS),...AGRICULTURAL INCOME AND FINANCE estimated that the average [U.S.] farm operator household income was $44,392 compared with $44,938 for the average U.S. household, as estimated by the Current Population Survey (CPS)....According to data from the FCRS, about 68 percent of operator households have income below the U.S. average, compared with just over 60 percent of all U.S. households....Median income for all U.S. households was $34,076, compared with $30,698 for farm operator households....Median income for all non-metro households is $27,776....Fewer than 50 percent of operator households by category have income below the non-metro median mark...." (p13)

U.S. Dept. of Agriculture. Economic Research Service. "Farm Operator Household Income Is on Par with the Average U.S. Household." Agricultural Income and Finance Situation and Outlook Series Jun 1997. p13.

INCOME--UNITED STATES--IMMIGRANTS (v26)

INCOME--UNITED STATES--MINORITIES

"The Census Bureau released data for 1996 on the incomes and poverty status of Americans....Among racial groups, virtually all of the growth in income was confined to Hispanics, who saw a 5.8 percent rise in their median household incomes to $23,906. The average income for Hispanics is now above that of blacks, who averaged $23,482 in 1996. Whites, blacks and Asians saw practically no rise in income between 1995 and 1996." (p8 secA)

Bartlett, Bruce. "Bartlett's Notations: New 'Prosperity' Data Actually Cause for Alarm." Detroit News 6 Oct 1997. p8 secA.

INCOME--UNITED STATES--STUDENTS--ATTITUDES (v26)

INCOME--UNITED STATES--WOMEN (v26)

"The Census Bureau released data for 1996 on the incomes and poverty status of Americans....Women's earnings as a share of men's rose to an all-time high of 74 percent. However, this gain was achieved almost entirely by a decline from $32,426 in 1995 to $32,144 in 1996 in earnings for men working full-time, year-round....Men's earnings have fallen steadily since 1986 and are now 11 percent lower. Although women's earnings as a share of men's have risen 10 percent since 1986, their actual earnings are only 2 percent higher." (p8 secA)

Bartlett, Bruce. "Bartlett's Notations: New 'Prosperity'

Data Actually Cause for Alarm." Detroit News 6 Oct 1997. p8 secA.

In the U.S., "average incomes for all women were 54% of men's in 1996,...a lot better than 1980s 39%....For women who work outside the home, their incomes were 62% of men's in 1996, up from 47% in 1980 and 38% in 1970; for those who work a full schedule, their incomes were 74% of men's, up from the 60% average that prevailed through most of the 1970s....Men's real incomes in 1996 were 5% below 1989 levels, while women's were 5% above." (p7)

"Income News." Left Business Observer n80 17 Nov 1997. p2,7. (ISSN1042-0134).

In the U.S., "in dual-income families, 22 percent of wives out-earn their husbands, up from 18 percent in 1987, according to the US Bureau of Labor Statistics. And that's up from 4.4 percent in 1970....A 1996 survey by New York-based Catalyst found that 75 percent of senior-level women executives are the primary breadwinners of their families." (p8)

Coolidge, Shelley Donald. "Business & Money: Workplace: Two Jobs, Dueling Incomes." The Christian Science Monitor v89 n160 15 Jul 1997. p1,8. The Christian Science Monitor search engine: <http://www.csmonitor.com/plweb-cgi/iops1.pl> To retrieve this article, enter the following search: ED=19970715 AND incomes. In the "retrieved list," click the title that matches this record. (ISSN0882-7729).

INCOME DISTRIBUTION (v26)

INCOME DISTRIBUTION--CANADA (v26)

INCOME DISTRIBUTION--GREAT BRITAIN (v26)

INCOME DISTRIBUTION--IRELAND

In Ireland, "in urban areas the richest 10% of households have a disposable income 10 times that of the lowest income groups. However, the highest income households are 3.6 times larger than the lowest income ones. Allowing for this means that the average disposable income per head of the highest income households is 3 times that of the lowest. Similarly, in rural areas the disposable income per head of the richest households is 3 times that of the poorest."

Ireland. Central Statistics Office. "Household Budget Survey 1994-95--Volume 2: Detailed Results for Urban and Rural Households." Press Release 1 Dec 1997. document-level access: <http://www.cso.ie/pressreleases/prelhbsv2.html>

INCOME DISTRIBUTION--ISRAEL--POPULATION (v26)

INCOME DISTRIBUTION--LATIN AMERICA (v26)

INCOME DISTRIBUTION--MEXICO (v26)

INCOME DISTRIBUTION--MICHIGAN--DETROIT

In Detroit, "the mayor's salary...has risen about 179 percent since 1977, or about 5.26 percent a year. The pay of [the city] council has risen more than 4 percent a year....Last year's increase in the private sector was 3.5 percent, the highest in a decade." (p10 secA)

"Buffering the City's Politicians." Detroit News 15 Dec 1997. p10 secA.

"The 1990 census reported that the typical white household in the Detroit...[suburban area] had an income of $46,100, while the typical black household's income was $26,900. This racial discrepancy is getting larger: In 1980, black households in Detroit had incomes that were 65% those of whites in contrast to 58% in 1990. In Detroit, black poverty increased from 26% to 38% of all households; among whites it climbed from 6% to 8%. Eleven percent of white children were in poverty, while 44% of black children were impoverished (1990 census)." (p125)

Turner, Susan C. "Barriers to a Better Break: Employer Discrimination and Spatial Mismatch in Metropolitan Detroit." Journal of Urban Affairs v19 n2 1997. p123-141. (ISSN0735-2166).

INCOME DISTRIBUTION--MOROCCO (v26)

INCOME DISTRIBUTION--RUSSIA (v26)

INCOME DISTRIBUTION--RUSSIA--MOSCOW

"In 1996, 5 percent of the Russian population living in Moscow generated 35 percent of Russia's GDP and controlled 70 to 80 percent of its capital. In contrast to the rich in Moscow, in 1995 as much as 35 percent of the Russian population was below the poverty level. By 1997 that had fallen to 22 percent, but at the same time the average income of the richest 10 percent of the population was 13 times that of the poorest 10 percent....It was nonetheless an improvement over 1996, when the income of the richest 10 percent was 16 times higher." (p316)

Goldman, Marshall I. "Russia's Reform Effort: Is There Growth at the End of the Tunnel?" Current History v96 n612 Oct 1997. p313-318. (ISSN0011-3530).

INCOME DISTRIBUTION--UNITED STATES (v26)

"Fully 70 percent of the nation's wealth is now in the hands of the richest 10 percent of Americans. Between 1980 and 1995, corporate profits rose 145 percent and CEO pay skyrocketed 499 percent. By contrast, real average wages fell 9 percent between 1979 and 1994." (p10)

Kameras, David. "The Top 10 Myths about the Economy." America@Work v2 n5 May-Jun 1997. p10-12. (ISSN1091-594X).

In the U.S., "households in the top one-fifth of the income distribution received 49 percent of all income in 1996, while those in the bottom one-fifth received 3.7 percent....Average income for the top quintile rose 2.2 percent between 1995 and 1996. It rose 1.5 percent for the middle quintile. It fell 1.8 percent for the lowest quintile." (p2)

"Income Is Rising. So Is Poverty." Forecast v17 n11 Nov 1997. p1-2. article-level access: <http://www.demographics.com/publications/fc/97_fc/9711_fc/fc97111.htm> (ISSN0732-1597).

"A 1995 O.E.C.D. study that compared the distribution of post-tax and transfer income in sixteen industrialized countries found that the United States had the largest spread between the top and bottom decile of workers of any of the economies studied. The 90-10 ratio, showing the earnings of a worker in the top decile relative to someone in the poorest decile, was 4.45 for men in 1996, up from 3.67 in 1979. For women, the rise was from 2.71 in 1979 to 4.02 in 1996, according to the Economic Policy Institute's 'The State of Working America 1996-1997.'...Federal Reserve figures indicate that not only do the richest 10 percent of U.S. citizens hold more than two-thirds of total wealth, but over the period from 1983 to 1995 this group received 70 percent of the total gain. E.P.I. research shows that between 1983 and 1992, the top 1 percent of the population had a 28 percent increase in wealth, while the bottom 40 percent saw theirs drop by nearly half." (p30)

Chase, Edward T. "Books & the Arts: Market Value-Free." Nation v265 n11 13 Oct 1997. p30-31. (ISSN0027-8378).

"Between 1947 and the mid-seventies the ratio of the income of the top 5 percent of [U.S.] families to the lower 20 percent dropped from a ratio of 14-1 to 11-1. Since then the ratio has risen to 19-1. Newly released census data also show that incomes fell on average for the bottom 60 percent of households over the past seven years. In 1974, the average C.E.O. of a major company was paid thirty-four times the earnings of the average worker. Today he is making about 180 times the worker's pay." (p20)

Faux, Jeff. "The 'American Model' Exposed." Nation v265 n13 27 Oct 1997. p18,20-22. (ISSN0027-8378).

The U.S. has "more than 36 million people living below the poverty line--and millions more living in poverty above it. The latest poverty thresholds are $7,995 for a single person and $12,516 for a family of three. According to the Census Bureau, the top 5 percent of households (with incomes above $119,540) increased their share of national income from 15.6 percent in 1981 to 21.4 percent last year; the bottom 80 percent lost ground to those above. The top 5 percent has an even larger share of national wealth, holding about 60 percent of all net worth, according to economist Edward Wolff." (p7)

Sklar, Holly/Collins, Chuck. "Editorials: Forbes 400 World Series." Nation v265 n12 20 Oct 1997. p6-7. (ISSN0027-8378).

INCOME DISTRIBUTION--UNITED STATES--MEN

A University of Michigan "study of more than 1,300 [U.S.] men (58 percent white, 42 percent African American) between the ages of 25 and 35...found that boys raised in poor families earn 41 percent-63 percent less per year and 29 percent less per hour than boys raised in middle-income households....A depressed labor market is strongly linked to lower earnings, smaller wages and fewer work hours for African American men, but not for white men. Each increase of 1 percentage point in the male unemployment rate is associated with a 6.6 percent loss in annual earnings, a 3.5 percent loss in hourly wages and a 3.1 percent loss in yearly work hours for Black men....White men raised in communities where more than 30 percent of the residents are poor earn 54 percent less money per year, 36 percent less per hour and work 3 percent fewer hours than white men who grew up in non-poor neighborhoods." (p1-2)

University of Michigan. News and Information Services. "Men Raised in Poor Families Earn Less Money Than Those From Middle-Class Backgrounds, Says U-M Study." University of Michigan News Release 24 Jul 1997. p1-2.

INCOME TAX--UNITED STATES

In the U.S., "according to the IRS, the top 1 percent of taxpayers, those with incomes above $209,105, paid more than 30 percent of all individual income taxes in 1995. In 1994, this group paid 28.7 percent. On average, the top 1 percent of taxpayers forked over 28.5 percent of their income to the federal government in 1995, up from 27.9 percent a year earlier....The top 5 percent of taxpayers, those with incomes above $96,104, paid almost 49 percent of income taxes. The top 10 percent of taxpayers paid more than 60 percent of income taxes, and the top 25 percent paid slightly more than 80 percent. The top 50 percent of taxpayers, everyone with an income above $22,361, paid more than 95 percent of income taxes. This means that the bottom 50 percent paid less than 5 percent....The trend toward higher tax payments by the wealthy was going on well before 1993 and even during periods when tax rates were being cut. In 1981, the top 1 percent of taxpayers paid just 17.6 percent of income taxes, rising to 27.4 percent by the end of the Bush administration in 1992." (p10 secA)

Bartlett, Bruce. "Bartlett's Notations: Wealthy Pay More Taxes, Despite Claims to Contrary." Detroit News 22 Sep 1997. p10 secA.

INDEBTEDNESS

see DEBT

INDEMNITY--UNITED STATES (v26)

INDIA--ECONOMIC CONDITIONS (v26)

INDIA--ECONOMIC CONDITIONS--SOCIAL CONDITIONS

"India's annual per-capita income is a mere $1,910, trailing even neighboring Bangladesh and well behind China's $4,050 (Canada's is $30,660). Almost half the population is illiterate, and a quarter lack safe drinking water. Most of the new foreign investment--$3.7 billion last year alone--has been spent on making and marketing upscale retail items." (p28)

Morris, Nomi. "World: Special Report: India's Passage." Maclean's v110 n33 18 Aug 1997. p26-30. (ISSN0024-9262).

INDIA--EMPLOYMENT

In India, bonded labor "is a traditional worker-employer relationship that dates back more than 1,500 years, and continues today with more than sixty-five million people in its grip. It is closely linked to caste; an estimated 80 percent of India's bonded laborers are 'Dalits' (previously, the 'untouchables') or are indigenous tribal people, the 'adivasi.' In some industries, including carpet weaving, 98 percent of the bonded child laborers are members of these castes and tribes." (p575)

Tucker, Lee. "Child Slaves in Modern India: The Bonded Labor Problem." Human Rights Quarterly v19 n3 Aug 1997. p572-629. (ISSN0275-0392).

INDIA--HEALTH AND HYGIENE

"With 950 million people, India is the world's second most populous nation after China....The country has established an impressive network of more than 2,300 community health centers; 21,000 primary health centers; and 131,000 village-level sub-centers to provide primary health care, including maternal and child health care and family planning at the grassroots level. According to India's Ministry of Health and Family Welfare (MFHW), more than 40 percent of eligible couples are using contraception. MFHW's figures also show that over 60 percent of mothers had received tetanus-toxoid immunizations during their most recent pregnancy, over 50 percent of mothers had received iron-folate tablets to combat anemia, and over 60 percent of infants had received at least one immunization."

World Bank. "India Reproductive and Child Health Project Signals Policy Change for Family Welfare Program: About...Program." Press Release 29 May 1997. document-level access: <http://www.worldbank.org/html/extdr/extme/1368.htm>

Infant mortality rates in India "fell from 146 deaths per thousand births in the 1950s to 80 at the start of this decade. Yet the Indian rate is still one of the highest in the world. Maternal mortality (437 per 100,000) remains high and accounts for a quarter of maternal deaths worldwide. Life expectancy at birth--60 years--remains well below that of China--69 years."

World Bank. "India Shows Mixed Progress in the War against Poverty." Press Release 26 Aug 1997. document-level access: <http://www.worldbank.org/html/extdr/extme/1449.htm>

INDIA--POPULATION

"India--the world's second most populous country with nearly 970 million people--adds more people each year than any other country, according to a recent report by the U.S. Bureau of the Census....With its population growing at a rate of 1.7 percent annually--about 70 percent higher than that of China--and projected to continue to grow faster than China for many years to come, India will most likely surpass China in population size by the middle of next century. Thirty-five percent of India's population is under 15 years of age...." (p3)

"25 Million Births in India Each Year." Popline v19 Jul-Aug 1997. p3.

INDIA--SOCIAL CONDITIONS (v26)

"Since India achieved independence in 1947, life expectancy has approximately doubled from about 32-33 years to 62 years in 1997. Over that same time frame, the infant mortality rate has declined from 220-225 infant deaths per 1,000 births to 66--lower than its immediate neighbors Pakistan (91) and Bangladesh (77) but much higher than China (31), Sri Lanka (17) and various other Southeast Asian countries. Among India's major states, infant mortality ranges from 15 to 109 per 1,000 births. Uttar Pradesh, the largest state with more than 140 million people, has one of the highest rates (93)." (p3)

"25 Million Births in India Each Year." Popline v19 Jul-Aug 1997. p3.

"Close to 600 million Indians are illiterate...." (p18) "Twelve million blind people--a quarter of the world's sightless--live in India....Up to six million people live in the slums of Bombay in cardboard boxes, ragged tents, or simply on the pavement...." (p19)

Abramsky, Sasha. "TF Reports: Asia: Handicapped by History." Toward Freedom v46 n5 Sep-Oct 1997. p18-20. (ISSN0048-9898).

INDIAN RESERVATIONS--ENVIRONMENTAL ASPECTS --UNITED STATES

The National Tribal Environmental Council's 1994 "national environmental review" survey of 149 federally recognized U.S. Indian Tribes found that "53 percent of the Tribes had no environmental programs. Only 23 percent regulated discharges to surface water. Although half had underground storage tanks, only 21 percent regulated them. Seventy-three percent had no hazardous substance emergency response program." (p36)

Dubrowski, Fran. "Cover Story: Crossing the Finish Line." Environmental Forum v14 n4 Jul-Aug 1997. p28-37. (ISSN0731-5732).

INDIAN ROADS (v26)

INDIAN UNIVERSITIES AND COLLEGES (v26)

INDIAN UNIVERSITIES AND COLLEGES--UNITED STATES--APPROPRIATIONS AND EXPENDITURES (v26)

INDIANA--ECONOMIC CONDITIONS

"The primary economic sectors for Indiana are durable goods manufacturing (22.6 percent of earnings), services (20.5 percent), and state and local government (10.7 percent)....The state ranked eleventh in the nation in 1993 in sales of agricultural products. The state's 1992 population was 5,544,000. In this same year, the state had a labor force of 2,849,000, total employment of 2,663,000, an unemployment rate of 6.5 percent, and per capita income of $18,366." (p381)

Rubin, Barry M./Gailmard, Sean/Marsh, Duncan/Septoff, Alan. "Assessing the State-Level Consequences of Global Warming: Socioeconomic and Energy Demand Impacts." World Resource Review v9 n3 Sep 1997. p379-398. (ISSN1042-8011).

INDIANS--EMPLOYMENT--MICHIGAN--DETROIT

"Indians, on average, are in the top 5 percent of Metro Detroit's wage-earning population, said Atmaram Varavadaker, chairman of the Indian American Forum for Political Education. Engineers make up 12.73 percent of Indian immigrants, and 3.14 percent are physicians, according to 1994 U.S. Census Bureau statistics." (p1 secC)

Sekhar, Anjali J./Lynch, Arana. "Metro: Indians Shedding Image of Isolation." Detroit News 28 Jul 1997. p1-2 secC.

INDIANS OF NORTH AMERICA

see also NAVAJO INDIANS

INDIANS OF NORTH AMERICA--EDUCATION

"In terms of educational attainment, half of all American Indians in the fourth grade--in both BIA [Bureau of Indian Affairs] and public schools--read below the expected proficiency level, compared to 42 percent of all students who are below this level. American Indian students have the highest dropout level of any racial ethnic group at 36 percent. They also have the lowest high school completion rate and the lowest rate of college attendance. Only 66 percent of all American Indians are high school graduates compared to 78 percent in the general population." (pS5877)

Domenici, Pete V. (Sen.-N.Mex.). "Senate Resolution 100--Relative to the Education of American Indians and Alaska Natives." Congressional Record. Daily ed. v143 n84 17 Jun 1997. pS5876-5878. section/page-level access: <http://thomas.loc.gov/cgi-bin/query/R?r105:FLD001:S05877:> (ISSN0363-7239). (X1.1A.105/1).

INDIANS OF NORTH AMERICA--GAMBLING

"Since the enactment of the Indian Gaming Regulatory Act in 1988, there has been a dramatic increase in the amount of gaming activity among the Indian tribes [in the U.S.]. Indian gaming is now estimated to yield gross revenues of about $6 billion per year and net revenues are estimated at $750 million. There are about 160 class II bingo and card games in operation and over 145 tribal/State compacts governing class III gaming in 2 States. Indian gaming comprises about 3 percent of all gaming in the United States. Gaming activities operated by State governments comprise about 36 percent of all gaming, and the private sector accounts for the balance of the gaming activity in the Nation....Annual revenues derived from Indian agricultural resources have been estimated at $550 million and have historically been the leading source of income for Indian tribes and individuals. Annual revenues from oil, gas, and minerals are about $230 million and Indian forestry revenue are estimated at $61 million. Gaming revenues now equal or exceed all of the revenues derived from Indian natural resources. In addition, Indian gaming has generated tens of thousands of new jobs for Indians and non-Indians. On many reservations, gaming has meant the end of unemployment rates of 90 to 100 percent and the beginning of an era of full employment." (pS8191)

McCain, John (Sen.-Ariz.). "Statements on Introduced Bills and Joint Resolutions." Congressional Record. Daily ed. v143 n108 28 Jul 1997. pS8186-8202. section/page-level access: <http://thomas.loc.gov/cgi-bin/query/R?r105:FLD001:S08191:> (ISSN0363-7239). (X1.1A.105/1).

In the U.S., "Native American tribes have opened casinos in nearly half the states, most of them since 1990. As of March [1997], 183 of the nation's 557 federally registered tribes ran 274 separate gaming operations, according to the National Indian Gaming Commission, a federal regulatory body. An estimated five to 10 percent of all commercial casinos are owned by Indian tribes. In 1995, tribally owned bingo and casino operations earned about $4 billion out of a U.S. total of $44 billion in legal gambling proceeds, according to an annual survey published in INTERNATIONAL GAMING AND WAGERING BUSINESS." (p4)

McCormick, Kathleen. "In the Clutch of the Casinos." Planning v63 n6 Jun 1997. p4-9. (ISSN0001-2610).

INDIANS OF NORTH AMERICA--GAMBLING --CALIFORNIA

Of California's 104 Native American tribes, "about 45 operate or are planning some kind of gambling casino. Together, these casinos take in an estimated $2 billion....In 1986, when [Daniel Tucker's Sycuan tribe, near San Diego,] was operating bingo games, each tribe member received about $3,600 a year. Then in 1990 they introduced video slot machines. Today, each tribe member earns about $48,000 a year....Tucker estimates that some tribes earn 90 percent of their revenue from the electronic games....Between 1994 and 1996, the number of slot machines on reservations tripled, going from 4,780 to 12,100, according to the California Department of Justice." (p8-9)

Ainsworth, Bill. "Betting on Politics." California Journal v28 n8 Aug 1997. p6-10. (ISSN0008-1205).

INDIANS OF NORTH AMERICA--GAMBLING--TAXATION --MICHIGAN (v26)

INDIANS OF NORTH AMERICA--HEALTH AND HYGIENE

For American Indians, "since 1973, infant mortality has decreased by 54 percent, maternal mortality by 65 percent. From 1940 to 1990, the life expectancy gap between American Indians and whites narrowed from 13.2 years to 2.9 years." (p15) "In 1996, the IHS [Indian Health Service] spent $1,578 on health care for each American Indian, compared to $3,920 per person in the general population, according to a report to Congress by IHS director Dr. Michael Trujillo. The physician ratio for Indian communities is 89.9 per 100,000 population, while for non-Indian communities it's 229 per 100,000 population....According to the IHS publication REGIONAL DIFFERENCES IN INDIAN HEALTH, in comparison to the general population, American Indians have a 703 percent greater alcoholism rate, 282 percent greater accident rate, 248 percent greater diabetes mellitus rate, 89 percent greater suicide rate and 68 percent greater homicide rate." (p16)

Humphrey, Dana. "You Say You Want a Revolution." New Physician v46 n6 Sep 1997. p14-20. (ISSN0028-6451).

Since 1973, American Indian "infant mortality has decreased by 54 percent, maternal mortality by 65 percent. From 1940 to 1990, the life-expectancy gap between American Indians and whites narrowed from 13.2 years to 2.9 years." (p15)

Humphrey, Dana. "When Worlds Collide." New Physician v46 n8 Nov 1997. p15-21. (ISSN0028-6451).

INDIANS OF NORTH AMERICA--LAND TENURE

"The Native Americans in this land are the poorest of the poor in the United States. Why? Because...[the government] took their land and their life-style. By 1887, they had about 138 million acres, a minute fraction of the land that they used to live on, and then over the next 47 years we took 90 million acres back from them. Since 1934, the Department of the Interior has restored 10 percent of that land, about 9 million acres...." (pH5226)

Moran, Jerry (Rep.-Kans.). "Department of the Interior and Related Agencies Appropriations Act, 1998." Congressional Record. Daily ed. v143 n100 15 Jul 1997. pH5214-5245. section/page-level access: <http://thomas.loc.gov/cgi-bin/query/R?r105:FLD001:H05226:> (ISSN0363-7239). (X1.1A.105/1).

INDIANS OF NORTH AMERICA--LANGUAGES

"There are about 2 million native Americans in the US. Of those, 281,990 who are five years old or older live in households where a tribal language is spoken. The survey by the US Bureau of the Census did not include Eskimo and Aleut languages. In 1492, there were more than 300 native languages spoken in North America. Today, 155 of these are still spoken in the US. Of these 155, only 12 or 13 percent are fully vital--that is, spoken by people of all ages." (p11)

"Volley 1: The Readers Ask." The Christian Science Monitor v89 n191 27 Aug 1997. p10-11. The Christian Science Monitor search engine: <http://www.csmonitor.com/plweb-cgi/iops1.pl> To retrieve this article, enter the following search: ED=19970827 AND ask. In the "retrieved list," click the title that matches this record. (ISSN0882-7729).

INDIANS OF NORTH AMERICA--MICHIGAN (v26)

INDIANS OF NORTH AMERICA--MORTALITY

"In 1993-95 the age-adjusted death rates for American Indian males and American Indian females under 55 years of age were about 40 percent higher than the corresponding rates for white males and white females. The death rate for American Indian children 1-4 years of age was almost double that for white children."

U.S. Dept. of Health and Human Services. "Report on Nation's Health Documents Toll of Injuries in U.S.: Firearm Mortality Down 11%, Traffic Fatality...Up...." Press Release 24 Jul 1997. document-level access: <http://www.cdc.gov/nchswww/releases/97news/97news/hus96rel.htm>

INDIANS OF NORTH AMERICA--POPULATION (v26)

INDIANS OF NORTH AMERICA--SOCIAL CONDITIONS (v26)

Fifty-six "percent of the American Indian population in our Nation is age 24 or younger. There is, demographically, a huge number of people of college age and younger; 90 percent of tribal college students qualify for need-based financial aid; 85 percent live in poverty; more than 50 percent are parents; 70 percent of these young people attending tribal colleges are female." (pS9190)

Johnson, Tim (Sen.-S.Dak.). "Department of the Interior and Related Agencies Appropriations Act, 1998." Congressional Record. Daily ed. v143 n120 11 Sep 1997. pS9167-9192. section/page-level access: <http://thomas.loc.gov/cgi-bin/query/R?r105:FLD001:S09190:> (ISSN0363-7239). (X1.1A.105/1).

U.S. Indian reservations have "unemployment averaging 57 percent. We pride ourselves with our low unemployment rate in our Nation of 5.2....Some unemployment rates [on reservations] are as high as 92 percent....The suicide rate among the young people in Indian country is eight times our national norm. Some 50 percent of the young ladies in Indian country have considered suicide." (pS9557)

Inouye, Daniel K. (Sen.-Hawaii). "Department of the Interior and Related Agencies Appropriations Act, 1998." Congressional Record. Daily ed. v143 n125 18 Sep 1997. pS9553-9574. section/page-level access: <http://thomas.loc.gov/cgi-bin/query/R?r105:FLD001:S09556:> (ISSN0363-7239). (X1.1A.105/1).

"Nearly one in three Indians lives in poverty, the highest rate of any ethnic group in America. In 1991, unemployment among Indians was 45 percent, and only 28 percent of those with jobs earned more than $7,000 annually." (p4)

McCormick, Kathleen. "In the Clutch of the Casinos." Planning v63 n6 Jun 1997. p4-9. (ISSN0001-2610).

INDIANS OF NORTH AMERICA--WARFARE

"One survey of 157 western North American Indian tribes found only 20 of these groups (13 percent) 'never or rarely' raided other tribes. Another sample of 90 groups concluded that only 12 (13 percent) 'rarely or never' engaged in warfare. In addition, the frequency of primitive warfare is very high. The survey revealed that 86 percent of these nonstate societies were raiding or resisting the raids of their neighbors more than once a year." (p675)

Bryjak, George J. "Book Reviews: Lawrence H. Keely, WAR BEFORE CIVILIZATION: THE MYTH OF THE PEACEFUL SAVAGE." Armed Forces & Society v23 n4 Sum 1997. p675-677. (ISSN0095-327X).

INDIANS OF SOUTH AMERICA

see MAPUCHE INDIANS; PANARA INDIANS

INDICTMENTS--CANADA--YOUTH (v26)

INDIGENOUS PEOPLES

see also ECONOMIC ASSISTANCE--CARIBBEAN AREA--INDIGENOUS PEOPLES; HOUSEHOLDS--UNITED STATES--INDIGENOUS PEOPLES; LATIN AMERICANS; POPULATION GEOGRAPHY--UNITED STATES--INDIGENOUS PEOPLES; UNEMPLOYMENT--CANADA--INDIGENOUS PEOPLES

"Today there are an estimated 300 million indigenous people, more than 5 percent of the world's population (some have placed the number as high as 600 million). The term 'indigenous' is more a rough description than a precise category. An indigenous nation (there are some 6,000 in the world) usually has a unique language and culture and strong, often spiritual, ties to an ancestral homeland." (p389)

Watson, Douglas. "Indigenous Peoples and the Global Economy." Current History v96 n613 Nov 1997. p389-391. (ISSN0011-3530).

INDIGENOUS PEOPLES--ALASKA

"Across Alaska's vast wilderness lie America's most traditional tribal societies--more than 220 Eskimo, Aleut, Athabascan, Tlingit, and Haida village communities spread over an enormous land mass encompassing one-sixth of the United States....They own or control but 5 percent of the state, mostly through native-controlled corporations." (p19)

Echohawk, John E. "Opinion/Essays: A Fight for Sovereignty in Alaska's Native Villages." The Christian Science Monitor v89 n148 26 Jun 1997. p19. The Christian Science Monitor search engine: <http://www.csmonitor.com/plweb-cgi/iops1.pl> To retrieve this article, enter the following search: ED=19970626 AND villages. In the "retrieved list," click the title that matches this record. (ISSN0882-7729).

INDIGENOUS PEOPLES--AUSTRALIA--SUBSTANCE USE (v26)

INDIGENOUS PEOPLES--BRAZIL

"In 1990, there were some 235,000 Indians in Brazil, while today there are 270,000....Today, Indigenous peoples have constitutionally guaranteed rights to some 11% of Brazil's territory, although only part of this area has been fully officially documented." (p38)

Schwartzman, Stephan. "Self Determination and Territory: Success Story in Brazil: The Return of the Panara." Abya Yala News v10 n3 Sum 1997. p22-25,38. (ISSN1056-5876).

INDIGENOUS PEOPLES--CANADA (v26)

INDIGENOUS PEOPLES--CANADA--SOCIAL CONDITIONS (v26)

INDIGENOUS PEOPLES--EMPLOYMENT--AUSTRALIA (v26)

INDIGENOUS PEOPLES--HEALTH AND HYGIENE --AUSTRALIA (v26)

According to the report, "Demography SA, 1995," by the Australian Bureau of Statistics, in South Australia, "births to Indigenous mothers have fallen by 17.5 per cent since 1990, although the fertility rate for Indigenous females is still higher than that of the total population (2.346 compared to 1.750). In 1995, the Indigenous males experienced a death rate three times greater than the rate for all South Australian males, while the death rate of Indigenous females was two and a half times greater than the South Australian rate for females."

Australian Bureau of Statistics. "South Australians--Living Longer." Media Release 11 Jun 1997. document-level access: <http://www.abs.gov.au/websitedbs/d3110125.nsf/4a255eef008309e44a255eef00061e57/6d35166d881934c74a2564b30004f29d?OpenDocument>

INDIGENOUS PEOPLES--HONG KONG

About 300,000 indigenous Chinese live in the large rural area and collection of offshore islands that the British leased in 1898, "the New Territories, although today they make up only about 10 percent of the region's population....Here people live in walled villages where the names of their ancestors, going back 15 generations or more, are still inscribed in ancestral halls. 'More than 100 places in Hong Kong have the word 'wai' in their name, and it denotes a walled village,' explains British colonialist and local historian Dan Waters....There are still 26 walled villages in Hong Kong, many of them well preserved." (p4)

Crowell, Todd. "Walled Off from Hong Kong's Neon." The Christian Science Monitor v89 n151 1 Jul 1997. p4. The Christian Science Monitor search engine: <http://www.csmonitor.com/plweb-cgi/iops1.pl> To retrieve this article, enter the following search: ED=19970701 AND neon. In the "retrieved list," click the title that matches this record. (ISSN0882-7729).

INDIGENOUS PEOPLES--HOUSING--AUSTRALIA (v26)

INDIGENOUS PEOPLES--MEXICO--MEXICO CITY

Mexico City "is home to one out of every twenty Indians in Mexico, most of them living in conditions of extreme poverty....Together they are 446,243 Indians trying to eek out a living under...harsh circumstances, working for pennies in the Metropolitan heart of Mexico City to stave off starvation. And together they make up 5.32 percent of the total Indigenous population of Mexico....The Indigenous people have divided the metropolitan area into five municipalities or delegations; Iztapalapa, the largest delegation, contains 22,242 Indigenous, mainly Nahuas from the state of Mexico and Otomies from Queretaro; the municipality of Naucalpan, numbering 18,890, mostly Triquis from Chicahuaxtla in Oaxaca; the third largest municipality, Nezahualcoyotl, numbering some 17,582 Mixtecos and Zapotecos from Oaxaca; Ecatepec, with 16,112 Indigenous people; [and] La Gustavo A. Madero with 13,743 Indigenous people representing 1.25 percent of the entire population within this demarcation." (p17) "The last report of INEGI [Instituto Nacional de Estadistica, Geografia e Informatica] established that 1.36 percent of the Indigenous population lived in Mexico City in 1930 and by 1990 the percentage had risen to 1.5." (p18)

"Indian City: Unseen and Forgotten in Mexico City." Abya Yala News v10 n3 Sum 1997. p17-19. (ISSN1056-5876).

INDIGENOUS PEOPLES--RUSSIA

"Two thirds of Russia's vast northern and eastern territories are inhabited by about 30 'small' indigenous peoples which number from only 200 (Enets) up to 50,000 (Nenets) people....The life expectancy of indigenous people is 10-20 years below the Russian average which after the breakup of the Soviet Union has fallen to the lowest level of all industrialised countries." (p6)

"International News: News from the Net: Land and Indigenous Peoples: Siberia: UN Committee on Economic...Peoples." Freedom (Anarchist Fortnightly) v58 n16 16 Aug 1997. p6. (ISSN0016-0504).

INDIGENOUS PEOPLES--UNITED STATES --POPULATION

"On August 1, 1997, the American Indian, Eskimo and Aleut population in the United States stood at 2.3 million, or 0.9 percent of the total population. Since July 1, 1990, this racial group has grown 12 percent, while the non-Hispanic White population increased 3 percent. The nation's American Indian, Eskimo and Aleut population is projected to grow steadily, to 2.4 million in 2000, 3.1 million in 2020, and 4.4 million in 2050. The proportion of the U.S. population that is American Indian, Eskimo or Aleut would rise to 1.1 percent in 2050. Regionally speaking, nearly half of the projected increase in American Indians, Eskimos, and Aleuts between 1995 and 2025 would be added in the West....The nation's American Indian, Eskimo and Aleut population is young, with about half under 27.2 years old on August 1, 1997. By comparison, non-Hispanic Whites were about a decade older, with a median age of 37.4 years."

U.S. Dept. of Commerce. Economic & Statistics Administration. "Census Facts for Native American Month." Census Bureau Fact Sheet 31 Oct 1997. document-level access: <http://www.census.gov/Press-Release/fs97-11.html>

INDIGENOUS PEOPLES--VENEZUELA

"The indigenous population in Venezuela numbers roughly 400,000, comprised of twenty-five culturally and linguistically distinct groups in the states of Anzoategui, Amazonas, Apure, Bolivar, Delta Amacuro, Monagas, Sucre, and Zulia. Over 50 percent of this population occupy traditional lands and approximately 42 percent reside in urban areas....Some 83 percent of the urban indigenous population are Wayuu people living in 48 indigenous neighborhoods in Maracaibo, the second most important city in the country. The other 17 percent are Pemon, Yecuana, Guahibo, Piaroa, Anu, Panare, Warao, Bare, etc." (p20) "According to the 1992 [Venezuelan] government economic census of the indigenous population, 48 percent of the people exist at a subsistence level only, 31 percent are partially employed, and only 21 percent have regular incomes." (p21)

Gonzalez, Jesus Manuel. "Indian City: To Be Urban and Indian in Venezuela: Assimilation or Cultural Reaffirmation?" Abya Yala News v10 n3 Sum 1997. p20-21. (ISSN1056-5876).

INDONESIA--ECONOMIC CONDITIONS (v26)

INDONESIA--POPULATION (v26)
INDONESIA--SOCIAL CONDITIONS (v26)
INDUCED ABORTION
see ABORTION
INDUSTRIAL ACCIDENTS--GREAT BRITAIN--COSTS
"The Health and Safety Executive estimate that the total cost to the British economy of work accidents (including preventable damage-only accidents) and work-related ill health was between 6 billion [pounds sterling] and 12 billion [pounds sterling] in 1990....The estimate in the draft reply of 6 billion [pounds sterling]-12 billion [pounds sterling] (1990 prices) is about 1-2 per cent of national output....An estimate of the total cost to society, which includes an allowance for the human costs of pain, grief and suffering, is 11 billion [pounds sterling]-16 billion." (c337)
Eagle, Angela (H.C.-Wallasey). "Written Answers to Questions: Occupational Injury and Ill Health." Great Britain. Parliament. House of Commons. Debates. 7 Jul 1997. c337. section-level access: <http://www.parliament.the-stationery-office.co.uk/pa/cm199798/cmhansrd/cm970707/debtext/70707w09.htm#70707w09.html_sbhd2>
INDUSTRIAL ACCIDENTS--MEXICO
In Mexico, "in 1988, the number of work accidents in manufacturing industry was 97,000. In 1991 it rose to 266,000, then slowly descended to a level of 200,000 accidents annually in 1995, that is, an accident rate of 7 per 100 workers. Over the last five years, an average of 2000 workers were killed in work accidents, ground down by the interminable chain of 'industrial competitiveness.'" (p104)
Roman, Richard/Arregui, Edur Velasco. "Zapatismo and the Workers Movement in Mexico at the End of the Century." Monthly Review v49 n3 Jul-Aug 1997. p98-116. (ISSN0027-0520).
INDUSTRIAL ACCIDENTS--MICHIGAN
"Forty-six people--all men--died in on-the-job accidents last year in Michigan, state labor officials say. Nearly half of the fatalities were in Wayne, Oakland and Macomb counties....Through May of this year, 27 Michigan residents had died on the job. At that rate, Michigan could end 1997 with 65 job-related fatalities....Another 350,000 Michigan workers sustain injuries and job-induced illnesses each year that force some of them to miss work." (p1 secA) "Today, benefits to workers hurt or killed on the job total $1.4 billion a year in Michigan, according to the Bureau of Workers' Disability Compensation." (p6 secA)
Cole, Kenneth. "Precautions Offer Safety Net for Those in Dangerous Jobs." Detroit News 25 Jul 1997. p1,6 secA.
INDUSTRIAL ACCIDENTS--UNITED STATES (v26)
"Using official reports, a research team led by J. Paul Leigh of San Jose State University found that, on average, 18 U.S. workers are killed and another 36,000 suffered significant injuries in job-related mishaps every day in 1992....The economic burden, in direct treatment, administrative shuffling, and lost wages, was about $171 billion in 1992. Exclude certain administrative costs and the number drops to $155 billion--still over 50% more than the cost of AIDS and Alzheimer's Disease combined (in 1992, these expenses were $30 billion and $67 billion, respectively)." (p4)
"The Short Run: Work Environment 1: The Deaths and Injuries Mount." Dollars and Sense n214 Nov-Dec 1997. p4. (ISSN0012-5245).
According to J. Paul Leigh, a member of San Jose State's economics department and head of a research team that released a report about job-related injuries and illnesses, "some 6,500 American workers died and over 13 million other workers were injured from work-related causes during...[1992]. In addition, the researchers reported that there were 60,300 deaths and that over 862,000 workers got sick from lung diseases, lead poisoning and other such occupational diseases during 1992....According to the researchers, the 'direct costs' of this carnage and misery visited upon thousands of workers in 1992 was $65 billion; the 'indirect costs,' $106 billion, making the total cost $171 billion--greater than the costs of cancer ($170.7 billion), heart and blood vessel diseases ($164.3 billion), arthritis, osteoporosis and other musculoskeletal diseases ($149 billion)." (p3)
Karp, Nathan. "13 Million Workers Injured in Single Year, Study Finds." The People v107 n6 Sep 1997. p3. (ISSN0199-350X).
INDUSTRIAL ACCIDENTS--UNITED STATES --MORTALITY
"In 1995, 6,210 workers died on the job due to traumatic accidents, an estimated 50,000 workers died from occupational diseases and more than 6.6 million injuries and illnesses were reported in private-sector workplaces, according to 'Death on the Job: The Toll of Neglect,' the AFL-CIO's sixth annual report on safety and health protections for American workers....Transportation incidents were the leading cause of workplace deaths in 1995, with 2,560 fatalities. Violence was the second leading cause of on-the-job deaths, claiming the lives of 1,262 workers...." (p22)
"Shoptalk: Deadly Jobs." America@Work v2 n6 Jul 1997. p22. (ISSN1091-594X).
INDUSTRIAL DISPUTES
see LABOR DISPUTES
INDUSTRIAL EFFLUENT
see SEWAGE
INDUSTRIAL HYGIENE--GREAT BRITAIN
"A 1994 report of the Health and Safety Commission of the United Kingdom showed that during the financial year 1993-94, there were at least 107,000 people in the UK alone suffering from musculoskeletal symptoms brought on as a direct result of poor workplace design. Half of these symptoms caused an absence of three or more days off work. The cost of these to British industry, including lost output, medical treatment and individual suffering, exceeded UK90 million [pounds sterling] (US$ 144 million). The total cost of musculoskeletal symptoms to British industry is conservatively estimated at UK25 billion [pounds sterling] (US$ 40 billion) a year." (p7)
Rosskam, Ellen. "Listening to Our Pain: Preventing Workplace Injuries and Illnesses through Ergonomics." World of Work n21 Sep-Oct 1997. p5-8. (ISSN1020-0029).
INDUSTRIAL HYGIENE--SWEDEN
"Outlined in the 1994 issue of Euro Review on Research in Health and Safety at Work, research has shown that in Sweden...one out of every four workplace accidents and more than 50 per cent of the reported cases of occupational disease involve the musculoskeletal system. Two thirds, or around 19,000 of the cases involve symptoms of the neck, arm/shoulder, or hand. On average, musculoskeletal injuries lead to more than 100 sick leave days per case....The risk of musculoskeletal disease among women who perform assembly work in the Swedish electronics industry has been reported to be 20 times higher than in the country's working population as a whole....Another startling statistic from Sweden reveals that across the board, injuries of the lower back are estimated to make up almost 40% of all musculoskeletal injuries on the job, in any country, with some cases resulting in permanent disability." (p6)
Rosskam, Ellen. "Listening to Our Pain: Preventing Workplace Injuries and Illnesses through Ergonomics." World of Work n21 Sep-Oct 1997. p5-8. (ISSN1020-0029).

INDUSTRIAL HYGIENE--THAILAND (v26)

INDUSTRIAL HYGIENE--UNITED STATES

"In the United States, back disorders caused more than 27 per cent of all non-fatal occupational injuries and illnesses involving days away from work in 1993. Government studies have put total costs of low back pain to society at between US$ 50 billion and US$ 100 billion annually. Moreover, up to 30 per cent of US workers routinely perform activities that may increase their risk of developing low back disorders, and it is estimated that half of the workers in the US hold jobs which have the potential for causing them cumulative trauma disorders." (p5)

Rosskam, Ellen. "Listening to Our Pain: Preventing Workplace Injuries and Illnesses through Ergonomics." World of Work n21 Sep-Oct 1997. p5-8. (ISSN1020-0029).

INDUSTRIAL HYGIENE--UNITED STATES--MORTALITY

In 1993, the U.S. spent $291 million on the Occupational Safety and Health Administration, "and, unfortunately, that year we had 6,331 deaths [in the workplace]....In 1994 we increased our spending in OSHA and we spent $297.2 million, but what happened? The death rate went up in the workplace, to 6,588. Then we go to 1995 and we funded OSHA at $312 million, and we had 6,210 deaths. But then we lowered our spending in 1996 to $305 million and the death rate came down....[Of] the 6,588 occupational fatalities reported by the BLS [Bureau of Labor Statistics] in 1992, 42 percent were caused by transportation accidents, and another 20 percent were caused by acts of violence, suicide, and homicide." (pH6987)

Norwood, Charlie (Rep.-Ga.). "Departments of Labor, Health and Human Services, And Education...Appropriations Act, 1998." Congressional Record. Daily ed. v143 n117 8 Sep 1997. pH6977-6999. section/page-level access: <http://thomas.loc.gov/cgi-bin/query/R?r105:FLD001:H06986:> (ISSN0363-7239). (X1.1A.105/1).

INDUSTRIAL POLICY--CHINA (v26)

INDUSTRIAL PRODUCTIVITY--CHINA

"The value of China's industrial output increased by 15 percent in 1996, down 5 percentage points from the growth rate of 1995, the lowest since 1992. The national industrial value-added figure reached $344.3 billion in 1996, an increase of 12.7 percent in real terms from the previous year. While one-third of industrial output is still from state-owned enterprises, growth of state-owned enterprises' production was much slower than those of the other types of firms. Growth of output from state-owned enterprises was 6.7 percent, whereas output from collectively owned enterprises increased by 23.6 percent, and increased by 18.6 percent for other types of firms...." (p4)

Diao, Xinshen/U.S. Dept. of Agriculture. Economic Research Service. "China Controlled Inflation in 1996." China: International Agriculture and Trade Reports Situation and Outlook Series Jun 1997. p3-5.

INDUSTRIAL PRODUCTIVITY--CZECH REPUBLIC (v26)

INDUSTRIAL PRODUCTIVITY--HONG KONG

In Hong Kong, "the index of industrial production for the second quarter of 1997 decreased slightly by 0.8% over the same quarter in 1996, according to the results of a survey released...by the Census and Statistics Department. Analysed by industry group, output of the wearing apparel (except footwear) industry and the basic metals and fabricated metal products industry decreased by 5.2% and 3.6% respectively. A decrease of 3.9% was registered in the output of the industry group of electrical and electronic products, machinery, professional equipment and optical goods. Within this group, output of the consumer electrical and electronic products industry decreased by 13.6%, whereas output of the machinery, equipment, apparatus, parts and components industry increased by 5.9%. However, output of the food, beverages and tobacco industry and the paper products and printing industry increased moderately by 5.6% and 4.3% respectively."

Hong Kong. Census and Statistics Department. "Quarterly Index of Industrial Production for 2nd Quarter of 1997." Press Release 16 Oct 1997. document-level access: <http://www.info.gov.hk/censtatd/hkstat/press/pro22q97.htm>

INDUSTRIAL PRODUCTIVITY--IRELAND

In Ireland, "Industrial Local Units with three or more persons engaged had a gross output of 35,566m [million] [pounds sterling] in 1995 and a net output of 17,444m [pounds sterling], the detailed 'Census of Industrial Production 1995' released by the Central Statistic Office...reveals. The gross output was up 20% on the 1994 figure and the net output increased by 21%. Employment in industrial local units increased by 14,200 to 238,900. A total of 3,740m [pounds sterling] was paid in wages and salaries in the year."

Ireland. Central Statistics Office. "Census of Industrial Production 1995." Press Release 18 Nov 1997. document-level access: <http://www.cso.ie/pressreleases/prelcip95.html>

INDUSTRIAL PRODUCTIVITY--UNITED STATES

For U.S. productivity growth rates from 1970 to 1994, "the above-average performers include railroad transportation, where productivity grew at an average of 6.3 percent annually between 1970 and 1992; the telephone communication industry, where productivity growth averaged 5.7 percent annually between 1970 and 1994; and the steel industry, which averaged 4.2 percent annually over the same period....The below-average-productivity growth sectors...include crude petroleum and natural gas (-1.7 percent annually), gas utilities (-1.4 percent annually), laundry, cleaning, and garment services (no growth over the period), and automotive repair shops (0.1 percent annually).....Automotive repair shops recorded a 24.4 percent average annual growth rate of investment in IT [information technology] but only a 0.1 percent annual growth in productivity." (p16)

Allen, Donald S. "Where's the Productivity Growth (From the Information Technology Revolution)?" Review v79 n2 Mar-Apr 1997. p15-25. (ISSN0147-9032).

In the U.S., "the productivity of the durables sector of manufacturing grew at an average annual rate of 4.9 percent from first quarter 1991 to first quarter 1996. This compares with an average annual growth rate of 2.9 percent the previous five years from first quarter 1986 to first quarter 1991." (p23)

Allen, Donald S. "Where's the Productivity Growth (From the Information Technology Revolution)?" Review v79 n2 Mar-Apr 1997. p15-25. (ISSN0147-9032).

In the U.S., "in the four-plus years since President Clinton took office,...[productivity] rose a mere 2.5 percent. One possible sign of a productivity revival is this year's first-quarter output, up at a faster than expected 2.6 percent annual rate. At that rate, productivity will rise more in 1997 than in the past 17 quarters....In 1996, business put so much money into new or modernized plant and equipment that the investment amounted to 10.4 percent of gross domestic product (GDP), the nation's output of goods and services. That ratio will notch up to 10.7 percent in the next few years, up from 8.9 percent of GDP in 1989, says Mr. Lasky, of DRI/McGraw-Hill in Lexington, Mass....Lasky expects more than a 1.2 percent growth in productivity this year and for several years to come, an important advance over 0.7 percent in 1996." (p8)

Francis, David R. "Business & Money: Economic Scene: More Widgets--Is PC Finally Affecting GDP?" The Christian Science Monitor v89 n147 25 Jun 1997. p8. The Christian Science Monitor search engine: <http://www.csmonitor.com/plweb-cgi/iops1.pl> To retrieve this article, enter the following search: ED=19970625 AND widgets. In the "retrieved list," click the title that matches this record. (ISSN0882-7729).

INDUSTRIAL SAFETY--UNITED STATES

"A recent comprehensive study of occupational injury and illness found that workplace illnesses and injuries cost...[the U.S.] at least $171 billion a year. Yet, OSHA [Occupational Safety and Health Administration] has only enough inspectors to inspect each workplace for which it is responsible once every 167 years. Six thousand five hundred workers die every year as a result of occupational injuries. Sixty thousand more workers are killed every year as a result of occupational illnesses. The cost of AIDS, Alzheimer's and cardiovascular diseases are less than the cost of occupational death and illness....Since 1970 the job fatality rate in this country has been cut in half; since passage of OSHA, at least 140,000 lives have been saved." (pH6981)

Clay, William (Rep.-Mo.). "Departments of Labor, Health and Human Services, And Education...Appropriations Act, 1998." Congressional Record. Daily ed. v143 n117 8 Sep 1997. pH6977-6999. section/page-level access: <http://thomas.loc.gov/cgi-bin/query/R?r105:FLD001:H06980:> (ISSN0363-7239). (X1.1A.105/1).

INDUSTRIALIZATION--VIETNAM--HO CHI MINH CITY

In Vietnam, Ho Chi Minh City's "regional economy is growing by 15 percent a year, and the city's population (which has doubled since 1975) is set to double by 2010. Streets are clogged with 1.2 million motorcycles and scooters, 200,000 cars and buses and 125,000 people per square mile....While 20 new office highrises have been built (with 80 more on the way), one-third of the city still lacks running water, and garbage is piling up 10 times faster than it's trucked away." (p16)

"The Global Marketplace: Taiwan Takover in Vietnam." Earth Island Journal v12 n3 Sum 1997. p16. (ISSN1041-0406).

INEQUALITY OF INCOME

see INCOME DISTRIBUTION

INFANTS

see also AIR--POLLUTION--UNITED STATES--INFANTS; LIFE EXPECTANCY--UNITED STATES--INFANTS; WOMEN, INFANTS, AND CHILDREN PROGRAM

INFANTS--ALABAMA--MORTALITY

"Alabama had an infant mortality rate of 10.5 deaths per thousand live births in 1996, an increase from the 9.8 rate of 1995....Overall, Alabama had 634 infant deaths in 1996, up from 592 in 1995....Tuscaloosa County infant deaths decreased from 31 in 1995 to 20 in 1996. Baldwin County experienced the second greatest decrease from 20 to 10 for the year....[In Jefferson County,] the number of deaths decreased from 108 in 1995 to 102,...[its] lowest total ever....The 1996 rate of 11.3 was down from 11.6 in 1995 and was the second lowest infant mortality rate ever in the county, only surpassed by the 11.0 rate in 1992. Deaths to Montgomery County infants increased from 33 to 45 over the year, the largest increase among counties."

Alabama. Dept. of Public Health. "1996 County Infant Mortality: Good News and Bad News." News Release 25 Jun 1997. document-level access: <http://www.alapubhealth.org/Press/pr062597.htm>

Data from the Alabama Department of Public Health on 1996 infant mortality show that "while there has been a slight improvement in the rate of infant mortality among black and other races from 15.0 to 14.9, there was an increase in the white rate last year from 7.1 to 8.2. In 1996, 634 infants died, 42 more than in 1995. There were seven fewer black and other race infant deaths in 1996 than in 1995....Of the 49 additional white infant deaths from 1995 to 1996, there was an increase of 33 deaths from babies of multiple births. Infants of white teenage mothers who smoked had an infant mortality rate of 25.4 per 1,000 live births compared to infants of those who did not smoke who had a rate of 11.2."

Alabama. Dept. of Public Health. "Infant Mortality Rate Increase Attributed to Multiple Births." News Release 18 Jun 1997. document-level access: <http://www.alapubhealth.org/Press/pr061897l.htm>

INFANTS--BANGLADESH--MORTALITY

In Bangladesh, "the infant mortality rate is more than twice as high for the households of landless people (90 to 95 per 1000 births) as it is for those of landowners (40 per 1000 births). The disparity between slum-dwellers and other communities within the urban area is similar (129 per 1000 compared to 63 per 1000), while the overall rural-urban disparity is also revealing (103 per 1000 compared to 81 per 1000)." (p28)

Sen, Binayak/Acharya, Shambhu. "Health and Poverty in Bangladesh." World Health v50 n5 Sep-Oct 1997. p28-29. (ISSN0043-8502).

INFANTS--BURKINA FASO--INDONESIA--PERU --MORTALITY

"In Burkina Faso, the infant mortality rate was 111 deaths per 1,000 births for women with no education, compared with 90 infant deaths per 1,000 for women who had completed primary school, and 53 deaths per 1,000 for children of mothers with secondary or higher education....In Indonesia, the death rate for children under age five drops from 131 per 1,000 births for mothers with no formal education to 51 for the most educated mothers. In Peru, the infant mortality rate sinks from 100 to 34, and the under-five mortality rate from 150 to 45, as the mother's education increases from none to secondary or higher." (p20)

Riley, Nancy E. "Gender, Power, And Population Change." Population Bulletin v52 n1 May 1997. p2-46. (ISSN0032-468X).

INFANTS--DEVELOPING COUNTRIES--MORTALITY (v26)

INFANTS--HEALTH AND HYGIENE--UNITED STATES

In the U.S., "according to Minkler and Roe (1993), estimates of the drug-exposure rate for infants range from 2% (Besharov, 1989) to 11% (Chasnoff, 1988); the figure approaches 15%-20% in large urban hospitals (Lewis, Bennett, & Schmeder, 1989). Michaels and Levine (1993) project that by the year 2000, 72,000 to 125,000 of children and adolescents nationwide will be left motherless as a result of AIDS. The Centers for Disease Control offers an estimate of 125,000 to 150,000 children." (p491)

Burnette, Denise. "Article: Grandparents Raising Grandchildren in the Inner City." Families in Society v78 n5 Sep-Oct 1997. p489-499. (ISSN1044-3894).

INFANTS--IRAQ--UNITED STATES--MORTALITY

"An unpublished World Health Organization report indicates that infant mortality in Iraq has shot up to 92.7 per 1,000 live births. In the U.S., by way of contrast, the figure is about 8.4 per 1,000 live births." (p940)

"News: Iraq's Health System Devastated by Sanctions." Christian Century v114 n29 22 Oct 1997. p939-940. (ISSN0009-5281).

INFANTS--MARYLAND--MORTALITY

"The report, 'Infant Mortality in Maryland 1996,' shows the death rate dropped by 3.4 percent last year from 8.7 deaths per 1,000 live births in 1995 to 8.4 deaths per 1,000 live births in 1996....The white infant mortality rate fell 1.7 percent from 6.0 per 1,000 live births in 1995 to 5.9 per 1,000 births in 1996. The infant mortality rate for African Americans fell 5.2 percent from 15.3 in 1995 to 14.5 in 1996."

Maryland. Dept. of Health and Mental Hygiene. "Governor Glendening Issues Call to Reduce Maryland's High Infant Mortality Rate." News Release 11 Jul 1997. document-level access: <http://www.charm.net/~epi9/news34.htm>

INFANTS--MICHIGAN--MORTALITY (v26)

The second "Critical Health Indicators" report was compiled by the Michigan Department of Community Health in July 1997. It found that "for the sixth year in a row, the death rate among babies less than a year old declined. There were 1,110 infant deaths in Michigan in 1995, the last year for which records were available. The death rate is now 8.3 deaths per 1,000 live births, down from 12.8 deaths per 1,000 live births in the early 1980s." (p2 secC)

Cain, Charlie. "Metro: Special Report: Health Snapshot: Michigan Gaining Ground in the Fight against Diseases." Detroit News 17 Jul 1997. p1-2 secC.

INFANTS--MICHIGAN--WASHTENAW COUNTY --MORTALITY

In Michigan, infant mortality "remained stable for Washtenaw County in 1995. The rate was 7.0 deaths per 1,000 births in 1994 and 1995, up from 5.8 per 1,000 in 1993 but down from 9.5 per 1,000 in 1992. The county infant mortality rate is still better than Michigan's rate of 8.6 per 1,000 and the national rate of 10.6 per 1,000." (p14 secA)

Wahlberg, David. "Births to Teen-Age Mothers Plunge." Ypsilanti Press 6 Jun 1997. p1,14 secA.

INFANTS--MORTALITY (v26)

"Among world regions, infant mortality is highest in sub-Saharan Africa, at 93 deaths per 1,000 live births. Fertility is also highest, at 6 births per woman. Conversely, infant mortality is lowest in North America and Europe, with 10 or fewer deaths per 1,000 live births. These two regions also have the lowest levels of fertility, 1.9 and 1.4, respectively." (p4)

Gelbard, Alene. "A Primer: Population 101." Population Today v25 n9 Sep 1997. p4-5. (ISSN0749-2448).

"Every year more than 8 million infants die before their first birthday. More than half survive for less than a month--while they are still classed as newborn. Almost all the 5.1 million deaths in the neonatal period (the 28 days after birth) take place in developing countries. Nearly two-thirds (3.3 million) of them occur within a few days of birth." (p28) "WHO estimates that 85% of...[infant deaths] are due to infections, birth asphyxia, birth injury and problems linked with preterm (or premature) birth....Nearly half of all stillborn babies die as a result of complications during labour and delivery." (p29)

"WHO Advises...: Most Deaths of Newborn Infants Can Be Avoided." World Health v50 n2 Mar-Apr 1997. p28-30. (ISSN0043-8502).

INFANTS--UNITED STATES--MORTALITY (v26)

In the U.S., "between 2,300 and 2,500 babies under age 1 died each month between January and June 1996. The rate fluctuated between 6.8 and 7.6 per 1,000 live births. In the 12 months ending June 1996, 28,500 children under age 1 died, or 7.4 per 1,000 live births." (p20)

Miller, Berna. "Current Conditions: Population Update for June." American Demographics v19 n6 Jun 1997. p20. article-level access: <http://www.demographics.com/publications/ad/97_ad/9706_ad/ad97066.htm> (ISSN0163-4089).

"The U.S. infant mortality rate, which is the rate at which babies die before their first birthday, is at an historic low of 7.2 deaths per 1,000 live births in 1996, and the proportion of mothers getting early prenatal care is at a record high of 82 percent. The infant mortality rate has dropped 5 percent since 1994 and 17 percent since 1990."

U.S. Dept. of Health and Human Services. "HHS Invests in America's Children." Fact Sheet 23 Jul 1997. document-level access: <http://www.hhs.gov/news/press/1997pres/970917.html>

In the U.S., "the 1995 infant mortality rate of 7.6 deaths per 1,000 live births was a record low, continuing the long downward trend. The death rate from sudden infant death syndrome (SIDS) was down 15 percent between 1994 and 1995. Since 1989 SIDS deaths have been on the decline."

U.S. National Center for Health Statistics. "1995 Final Mortality Statistics Released." Fact Sheet 12 Jun 1997. document-level access: <http://www.cdc.gov/nchswww/releases/97facts/97sheets/95morrel.htm>

According to the CDC's 1996 Vital Statistic Report, in the U.S., "infant mortality reached another new low of 7.2 deaths per 1,000 live births. The white infant mortality rate declined 5 percent (from 6.3 to 6.0), while the black rate declined 6 percent (from 15.1 to 14.2). An estimated 15 percent decline in mortality rates from Sudden Infant Death Syndrome (SIDS) explains approximately a third of the 1995-96 decline in total infant mortality."

U.S. Dept. of Health and Human Services. "Vital Statistics Report Shows Significant Gains in Health." Press Release 11 Sep 1997. document-level access: <http://www.hhs.gov/news/press/1997pres/970911a.html>

In the U.S., "during 1996 the estimated death rate in the first year of life fell substantially to 7.2 per 1,000 live births. This is another record low and represents the 34th consecutive annual decline. In 1995 the infant death rate was 7.6 per 1,000 and in 1994 it was 8.0 per 1,000." (p3)

Kranczer, Stanley. "Record High U.S. Life Expectancy." Statistical Bulletin v78 n4 Oct-Dec 1997. p2-8. (ISSN0790-8334).

INFECTIOUS DISEASES

see COMMUNICABLE DISEASES

INFECTIOUS HEPATITIS

see HEPATITIS A

INFIDELITY, MARRIAGE

see ADULTERY

INFLATABLE RESTRAINT SYSTEMS

see AIR BAG RESTRAINT SYSTEMS

INFLATION (FINANCE)

"While the OECD nations have an average inflation rate of less than 2 percent, inflation is roaring at full tilt in many poorer countries. Prices have increased in the last year by 77 percent in Turkey, 74 percent in Venezuela, 24 percent in Mexico, 11 percent in India, 10 percent in South Africa, and 8 percent in Brazil." (p70)

Clark, Gregory. "Riding the Wave." Reason v29 n4 Aug-Sep 1997. p68-71. (ISSN0048-6906).

INFLATION (FINANCE)--ARGENTINA

In Argentina, "inflation, which had stubbornly refused to yield to the government's stabilization efforts throughout the second half of 1990 (totalling over 90% for the semester) and which reached as high as 27% in February 1991, suddenly plummeted to 2.8% in May 1991 and was down to just 0.4% in November of that same year; inflation for the second half of 1991 averaged only 8.3% for that entire period (Republica Argentina, 1995...)." (p92)

Starr, Pamela K. "Government Coalitions and the Viability of Currency Boards: Argentina under the Cavallo Plan." Journal of Interamerican Studies & World Affairs v39 n2 Sum 1997. p83-133. (ISSN0022-1937).

INFLATION (FINANCE)--BRAZIL (v26)

INFLATION (FINANCE)--EUROPE (v26)

INFLATION (FINANCE)--UNITED STATES

In the U.S., inflation "is lower now than it has been in more than 30 years. If retail prices continue rising as slowly as they have for the first six months of the year, the government said..., they would only grow by 1.4 percent for all of 1997. That would be the smallest annual increase since the Consumer

Price Index rose 1.3 percent in 1964 and 1.6 percent in 1965...." (p1 secA)

Fix, Janet L. "A Golden Age for Making Money Rolls On: Prices: Whatever Happened to Inflation?: Not since the Mid-1960s...This Low." Detroit Free Press 17 Jul 1997. p1,6 secA.

In the U.S., inflation "has averaged 5.2 percent during the 1990s. One hundred dollars in 1990 is worth about $83 in 1997. That's a loss of one-sixth in seven years." (p8)

Parry, Bruce E. "What's the Story with Inflation?" People's Tribune v24 n11 Nov 1997. p8. (ISSN1081-4787).

INFLUENZA--UNITED STATES (v26)

"Each year in the United States, the flu attacks 35 million to 50 million people. More than 20,000 people, mostly the elderly but also those with other chronic illnesses, die from the disease. Not counting the cost of lost work days, an estimated $4.6 billion is spent each year on health care costs related to the flu." (p1 secE)

Moss, J. Jennings. "Discovery: A 'Flu Shot' That Doesn't Hurt." Detroit News 3 Nov 1997. p1 secE.

"Each year, between 35 and 50 million Americans contract influenza, and more than 20,000 people die. In addition to work days lost, an estimated $4.6 billion is spent annually on direct medical costs related to influenza....The attack rate in children is two to ten times that seen in adults....More than 90 percent of influenza-associated deaths occur in people age 65 or older...."

U.S. National Institutes of Health. "Nasal Spray Flu Vaccine Proves Effective in Children." News Release 14 Jul 1997. document-level access: <http://www.nih.gov/news/pr/jul97/niaid-14.htm>

INFLUENZA--UNITED STATES--COSTS

"Each year, between 35 and 50 million Americans contract influenza, and more than 20,000 of them die. In addition to lost work days, an estimated $4.6 billion is spent annually on direct medical costs related to influenza. A severe influenza epidemic including more than 172,000 hospitalizations would cost at least $12 billion in medical costs and lost productivity." (p9)

U.S. National Institute of Allergy and Infectious Diseases. "Infectious Disease: Nasal Spray Flu Vaccine Proves Effective in Children." Healthline v16 n10 Oct 1997. p8-9. (ISSN0736-7929).

INFLUENZA--UNITED STATES--MORTALITY (v26)

INFLUENZA VACCINES--UNITED STATES (v26)

Hunein F. Maassab, a professor of epidemiology at the University of Michigan School of Public Health, has developed an influenza vaccine that uses a living virus rather than a dead one. "The studies done on Maassab's vaccine have shown that it is a more effective tool to prevent the flu than the vaccine now on the market. In a study involving 1,070 children in 10 research sites across...[the U.S.], only one person who received the vaccine rather than a placebo came down with the flu. Of the 532 children who took the placebo, 18 percent got sick. This means that the Maassab vaccine provided 93 percent protection from the flu compared with about a 70-percent protection rate using the conventional vaccine, according to U-M and NIH [National Institutes of Health] releases." (p1 secE)

Moss, J. Jennings. "Discovery: A 'Flu Shot' That Doesn't Hurt." Detroit News 3 Nov 1997. p1 secE.

In the U.S., "a new type of influenza vaccine administered in a nasal spray is very effective at preventing the flu in healthy young children, according to results from a large multicenter study supported by the National Institute of Allergy and Infectious Diseases (NIAID) and the biopharmaceutical company Aviron. Overall, the weakened-live-virus vaccine provided 93 percent protection against influenza in this population. Only 1 percent of 1,070 children who received the vaccine developed culture-confirmed influenza during last year's flu season, versus 18 percent of 532 children the same age who received a placebo." (p8) "The currently licensed flu shot is between 70 and 90 percent effective at preventing disease in people under age 65." (p9)

U.S. National Institute of Allergy and Infectious Diseases. "Infectious Disease: Nasal Spray Flu Vaccine Proves Effective in Children." Healthline v16 n10 Oct 1997. p8-9. (ISSN0736-7929).

The U.S. "Centers for Disease Control and Prevention reports...that 58 percent of Americans aged 65 and older received the flu shot in 1995, an 8 percent increase since 1993, when Medicare began paying for the shots. However, among older African-Americans, only 39 percent got their shots in 1995, and among older Hispanics, just 50 percent did....In the United States each winter, a flu epidemic sweeps the country killing, in a typical year, 20,000 Americans, most of them over age 65....The vaccine takes about 10-14 days to begin its full protection."

U.S. Dept. of Health and Human Services. "Time to Get This Year's Flu Shot, Secretary Shalala Advises Older Americans." Press Release 2 Oct 1997. document-level access: <http://www.hhs.gov/news/press/1997pres/971002.html>

INFLUENZA VACCINES--UNITED STATES--AGED

"In 1995, 58 percent of the nation's elderly--nearly all of them Medicare beneficiaries--received their annual flu shots, an 8 percent jump from 1993, according to a survey released...by the [U.S.] Department of Health and Human Services....Despite the availability of preventive vaccines, flu and pneumonia remain the fifth leading cause of death among the elderly, taking as many as 70,000 lives each year. It is estimated that up to 80 percent of deaths from the flu could be prevented with a flu shot....The states with the highest percentage of residents 65 and older getting the flu vaccine in 1995 were Utah at 70 percent and Oregon at 67 percent. Tennessee had the largest percentage gain in flu shots for the elderly, recording a 17 percentage-point rise, 46 percent to 63 percent, from 1993 to 1995."

U.S. Dept. of Health and Human Services. "HHS Reports 58% of Elderly Received Flu Shots in 1995, 8% Higher Than in 1993." Press Release 16 May 1997. document-level access: <http://www.hhs.gov/news/press/1997pres/970516.html>

INFORMATION TECHNOLOGY

see HIGH TECHNOLOGY INDUSTRIES

INFORMATION TECHNOLOGY--AUSTRALIA (v26)

INFORMATION TECHNOLOGY--JAPAN--UNITED STATES (v26)

INFRASTRUCTURE (ECONOMICS)--CANADA (v26)

INFRASTRUCTURE (ECONOMICS)--EAST ASIA

"Private flows to East Asian infrastucture projects--from both international and domestic concerns--increased to $13-16 billion, accounting for 12-18 percent of all infrastructure investments, 1996 data show. This is a noticeable improvement over the 10 percent share of recent years but well short of what is necessary for the region to sustain long term economic growth and competitiveness, improve quality of life, and continue the momentum toward a greater role in the global economy."

World Bank. "Infrastructure in East Asia: How to Increase Private Investment." Press Release 20 Sep 1997. document-level access: <http://www.worldbank.org/html/extdr/extme/ampr_003.htm>

INFRASTRUCTURE (ECONOMICS)--PHILIPPINES (v26)

INFRINGEMENT OF COPYRIGHT

see COPYRIGHT INFRINGEMENT

INHERITANCE AND TRANSFER TAX--UNITED STATES (v26)

In the U.S., "the estate tax not only places a burden on assets that have already been taxed but it does not discriminate between cash funds and the nonliquid assets and property that make daily activities possible for a family business or farm. These asset-rich, cash-poor businesses can have their livelihood eliminated in order to pay a tax of up to 55 percent...of market value of the property left to them. Ironically, the estate tax raises only 1 percent of the Federal Government's revenue but helps to prevent up to 75 percent of family businesses from being passed to a second generation....Repeal of the estate tax would benefit the economy. George Mason University Professor Richard Wagner has stated that the elimination of the estate tax would enhance the output of the country by $79.2 billion...and would create up to 228,000 jobs." (pS5900)

Allard, Wayne (Sen.-Colo.). "Estate Tax Reform." Congressional Record. Daily ed. v143 n85 18 Jun 1997. pS5900. section/page-level access: <http://thomas.loc.gov/cgi-bin/query/R?r105:FLD001:S05900:> (ISSN0363-7239). (X1.1A.105/1).

In the U.S., in 1992, "stocks and bonds made up about one-half of the assets of estates worth more than $600,000. Real estate made up another one-fifth. The remaining 30% of assets were divided among several categories including noncorporate business assets. But noncorporate business assets--mostly of small businesses and farms--are just 3.6% of the total....After deductions, small businesses and family farms do make up a somewhat larger share of estates' taxable assets, but they were still a small portion--10.3% in 1995." (p27)

Miller, John. "More Wealth for the Wealthy: The Estate Tax Giveaway and What to Do about It." Dollars and Sense n214 Nov-Dec 1997. p26-28,33. (ISSN0012-5245).

INJURIES

see ACCIDENTS

INLAND NAVIGATION--UNITED STATES--FINANCE (v26)

INOCULATION

see VACCINATION

INSECTS

see also FIRE ANTS; GRASSHOPPERS; HELICOVERPA ARMIGERA; MONARCH BUTTERFLY; TERMITES

INSECTS--FEEDING AND FEEDS

Geocoris punctipes (big-eyed bugs) and Chrysoperla carnea (lacewings) are insects that feed on plant-destroying insects in the U.S. "A lacewing that is mass-marketed requires a diet of insect eggs that costs more than $300 per pound to produce....[A new artificial] diet can be made for about $2.50 per pound. And each pound of the new diet can produce about 30,000 big-eyed bug adults or up to 10,000 lacewing adults that will yield about 3 million eggs during their lifespan." (p5) "A big-eyed bug punctures another insect with a sharp, stingerlike structure that comes out of its mouth. Then it squirts a digestive enzyme that dissolves or breaks down the prey's insides. The big-eyed bug can then use the hollow stinger as a straw to suck up its meal. This is not unique among such insects; about 80 percent of all predatory insects and their relatives eat this way, including spiders, mites, scorpions, and centipedes....[Allen C. Cohen, the Agricultural Research Service entomologist who invented the artificial diet says,] 'and eat they do--up to 25 to 50 percent of their own body weight in prey each day...'." (p6) Insects that eat the artificial "diets produce more offspring, often mature faster, and are up to 1-1/2 times larger than those feeding in the wild....Cohen has so far reared 16 successive generations of 'C. carnea,' 130 of 'G. punctipes', 3 of 'Serangium parcesetosum' (a lady beetle), and 3 of 'Orius insidiosus' (a minute pirate bug)." (p7)

Senft, Dennis/U.S. Dept. of Agriculture. Agricultural Research Service. "Mass-Reared Insects Get Fast-Food." Agricultural Research v45 n6 Jun 1997. p4-7. (ISSN0002-161X).

INSOLVENCY

see BANKRUPTCY

INSTITUTES, RESEARCH

see RESEARCH INSTITUTES

INSTITUTIONAL CARE

see HANDICAPPED--INSTITUTIONAL CARE

INSTRUCTION

see EDUCATION

INSTRUCTIONAL TECHNOLOGY

see EDUCATIONAL TECHNOLOGY

INSULIN-DEPENDENT DIABETES

see DIABETES

INSURANCE--CHILE (v26)

INSURANCE--EUROPE (v26)

INSURANCE--UNITED STATES--WOMEN--ATTITUDES

"Half of Americans agree that unless they file a claim, the companies that provide them with automobile and homeowners' insurance are the only ones who benefit. At the same time, 84 percent admit that the premiums they pay are worthwhile for the security they provide....Eighty-six percent [of women] agree that when it comes to homeowners' insurance, 'in addition to the actual protection provided by the policy, I also receive a sense of satisfaction and security,' according to a survey conducted by Roper Starch Worldwide Inc. for the Insurance Research Council Inc. The share of women who feel this way about auto insurance is 82 percent." (p35)

Crispell, Diane. "Kaleidoscope: No Worries with Insurance." American Demographics v19 n6 Jun 1997. p35. article-level access: <http://www.demographics.com/publications/ad/97_ad/9706_ad/ad970617.htm> (ISSN0163-4089).

INSURANCE, ACCIDENT

see also WORKERS' COMPENSATION

INSURANCE, ACCIDENT--UNITED STATES--TRADE-UNIONS

In the U.S., "nearly three-quarters of all union members, or 72 percent, were eligible for sickness and accident insurance through their place of employment. Nonunion members received this benefit at half that rate, or 36 percent." (p4)

"Economic: Pension and Health Benefits." Maritime Newsletter v29 n11 Nov 1997. p4. (ISSN0161-9373).

INSURANCE, AUTOMOBILE--UNITED STATES (v26)

INSURANCE, CROP

see CROP INSURANCE

INSURANCE, DISABILITY--GREAT BRITAIN (v26)

According to a recent report, "The Real Level of Unemployment," released in Great Britain, "the number of people claiming benefit for sickness or invalidity for more than six months has seen a startling rise in the last sixteen years. In April 1981, 574,000 people fell into this category, a figure which, by April 1995, had risen to 1,809,000. Once those on severe disablement allowance and those incapacitated for work due to sickness for less than six months have been added, the total number of people of working age who are claiming sickness-related benefits, based on Department of Social Security statistics for August 1996, rises to 2.48 million." (p7)

Hunt, Duncan. "Features & Letters: Labour Market Flexibility." Freedom (Anarchist Fortnightly) v58 n21 1 Nov 1997. p7. (ISSN0016-0504).

INSURANCE, DISABILITY--UNITED STATES (v26)

In the U.S., "over the period beginning in 1989 and ending in 1994, the number of DI [Disability Insurance]-disabled worker beneficiaries grew from about 2.8 million to nearly 4 million, a 40-percent increase. Benefit payments for the DI total program grew from about $23 billion in calendar year 1989 to nearly $38 billion in 1994, an increase of 65 percent." (p3)

Schechter, Evan S. "Work While Receiving Disability Insurance Benefits: Additional Findings from the New Beneficiary Followup Survey." Social Security Bulletin v60 n1 1997. p3-17. (ISSN0037-7910).

INSURANCE, DISABILITY--UNITED STATES --CHILDREN (v26)

INSURANCE, DISABILITY--UNITED STATES --VETERANS (v26)

INSURANCE, EARTHQUAKE--CALIFORNIA

In California, in July 1996, "the state Department of Insurance logged 2,800 complaints from people who said they couldn't find any company willing to write them a homeowner's policy. In February, two months after the privately-funded, publicly-managed CEA [California Earthquake Authority] opened for business, the department says it fielded only 70 complaints--a 40-fold decrease." (p38) "The CEA policies carry a 15 percent deductible, as compared with 5 to 10 percent deductibles available prior to [the] Northridge [earthquake]....Prior to Northridge, earthquake premiums averaged $2 per thousand dollars of insured property. Now, the average CEA premium across the state is $3.29 per thousand....The CEA...issued 396,000 policies to homeowners, renters and condominium owners in its first seven months. That's one-third of the CEA's goal....Farmer's [Insurance], which had sold 91,452 CEA policies by July 1 [1997], reported that it has already offered renewals to most of its policyholders with pre-CEA quake policies and only 41 percent have agreed to renew their policies on the CEA's terms." (p40) "The insurers participating in the earthquake authority write a combined 71 percent of homeowner's insurance in California." (p41) "Of an estimated three million households in Los Angeles County, only about 130,000, or 4 percent, have bought CEA policies....Only about 25 percent of California homeowners have taken out earthquake policies even though recent studies suggest that up to 75 percent of the states population lives in areas with the potential for earthquake damage within the next 50 years." (p42)

Blumberg, Peter. "A Rocky Beginning." California Journal v28 n9 Sep 1997. p38-43. (ISSN0008-1205).

INSURANCE, FLOOD--UNITED STATES (v26)

INSURANCE, HEALTH

see also HEALTH MAINTENANCE ORGANIZATIONS; MEDICAID; MEDICALLY UNINSURED PERSONS; MEDICARE; WORKERS' COMPENSATION

INSURANCE, HEALTH--CALIFORNIA--NEW YORK (STATE)--TEXAS (v26)

INSURANCE, HEALTH--EMPLOYMENT--UNITED STATES

In the U.S., "of persons aged 20 or older, the percentage insured for benefits has steadily increased over time. The percent permanently insured (those with enough covered work experience to qualify for retired-worker benefits at retirement age) rose from 50% in 1970 to 67% in 1997. The percent fully insured increased from 77% to 87%." (p10)

U.S. Social Security Administration. Office of Research, Evaluation, And Statistics. "OASDI Program: Workers and Insured Status." Fast Facts & Figures about Social Security 1997. p10.

INSURANCE, HEALTH--FLORIDA--CHILDREN

In Florida, a public/private health insurance "partnership called Healthy Kids Corporation is billed as a model for other states. About 35 percent of the cost is paid for by parents; the rest is covered by county and state and by charitable donations from businesses....There are only about 45,000 children enrolled out of about 500,000 uninsured children in Florida. State officials say they're likely to use their portion of the federal $24 billion to expand the program to as many as 100,000 new school-aged children." (p20)

"The Monitor's View: Kids' Health Coverage." The Christian Science Monitor v89 n199 9 Sep 1997. p20. The Christian Science Monitor search engine: <http://www.csmonitor.com/plweb-cgi/iops1.pl> To retrieve this article, enter the following search: ED=19970909 AND coverage. In the "retrieved list," click the title that matches this record. (ISSN0882-7729).

INSURANCE, HEALTH--GREAT BRITAIN (v26)

In Great Britain, "5.7 million people now have private medical insurance--about 10 per cent of the population....Only about 5 per cent of people over 60 have medical insurance--a proportion significantly lower than that in the population in general....In 1989, there were about 400,000 individuals over 60 with private medical insurance. Today, there are 600,000....[Between 1990 and 1997,] the total number of individuals covered by medical insurance dropped by 7 per cent in the early 1990s and rose over the following seven years to broadly the 1990 level....There was no overall increase in the number of people covered by medical insurance between 1990 and 1997, yet there was a 50 per cent increase in the number of people over 60 who were covered. The over-60s now account for one third of all individuals with medical insurance, compared with only one quarter when the relief was introduced." (c426)

Gibb, Nick (H.C.-Bognor Regis and Littlehampton). "Orders of the Day: Finance Bill." Great Britain. Parliament. House of Commons. Debates. 16 Jul 1997. c426. section-level access: <http://www.parliament.the-stationery-office.co.uk/pa/cm199798/cmhansrd/cm970716/debtext/70716-27.htm#70716-27_spnew10>

INSURANCE, HEALTH--MICHIGAN

In Michigan's "two most heavily unionized sectors, manufacturing and government, only 6.4 percent and 8.9 percent of workers lack [health] insurance, compared with self-employed workers (30.4 percent) and agriculture workers (18.6 percent). Three-quarters of Michigan's workforce has employer-provided health insurance, compared with 64 percent nationally." (p12 secA)

Mishra, Raja. "Children First: A Free Press Campaign: Health: A $400 Million Infusion: Federal Cash to Help State's Uninsured Kids." Detroit Free Press 8 Aug 1997. p1,12 secA.

INSURANCE, HEALTH--MICHIGAN--CHILDREN (v26)

INSURANCE, HEALTH--NETHERLANDS--UNITED STATES (v26)

INSURANCE, HEALTH--NEW YORK (N.Y.) (v26)

INSURANCE, HEALTH--NEW YORK (STATE) --CHILDREN

A Children's Defense Fund "study estimates that there are 10 million children nationally and half-a-million children in New York State who lack health insurance. These children are from working families who are ineligible for Medicaid but cannot afford private insurance coverage. Statistically, 88% of uninsured children have parents who work and nearly 64% have parents who work full time during the entire year. Approximately, two-thirds live in families with incomes above the poverty level. Typically, these children go without insurance because their parents work for employers who offer little or no health insurance." (p12)

"Around the Nation: Uninsured Children in New York City." Health Advocate n188 Spr 1997. p12.

INSURANCE, HEALTH--OREGON

Oregon's mandated point-of-service law "permits nonprofit health plans to limit out-of-network care to 5 percent of revenues or 5 percent of total business (MCW 1995...)....Oregon's mandated POS law requires HMOs to provide a POS option to employer groups with more than twenty-five workers who request it (but the HMO need not offer the option)." (p1143)

Marsteller, Jill A./Bovbjerg, Randall R./Nichols, Len M./ Verrilli, Diana K. "The Resurgence of Selective Contracting Restrictions." Journal of Health Politics, Policy and Law v22 n5 Oct 1997. p1133-1189. (ISSN0361-6878).

INSURANCE, HEALTH--SWEDEN (v26)

INSURANCE, HEALTH--UNITED STATES (v26)

In the U.S., "we have 41 million [people] without [health] insurance, 90 percent of whom are working or are members of working families. Seven million of these are in California alone....On Feb. 24, THE NEW YORK TIMES reported that one quarter of New York City residents under the age of 65 now have no health insurance." (p9) "In 1997 we are spending over a trillion dollars on health care, and over 40 million of our fellow citizens remain uninsured...." (p10)

Dukakis, Michael S. "Health Care Reform--Not a Dead Issue." America v176 n16 10 May 1997. p8-10. (ISSN0002-7049).

"In 1988, 71 percent of insured non-elderly Americans were in traditional fee-for-service insurance plans. They visited a doctor when they felt they needed to, and their insurance companies picked up the tab for covered services. By the end of last year 75 percent were in some form of managed care plan instead." (p16) "Today, of approximately 150 health care purchasing coalitions, at least 20 are union-based. Most have 15 to 20 member funds, and most include construction, retail and service industry unions." (p17)

"Health Care Clout." America@Work v2 n10 Nov 1997. p16-18. (ISSN1091-594X).

In the U.S., "about 13% of midlife women have no health insurance....According to a 1995 study from the Agency for Health Care Policy and Research in Rockville, MD, about 29 million Americans have health insurance that leaves them with annual out-of-pocket expenses of more than 10% of their incomes." (p62)

Harris, Marlys. "Timeless Health: Can You Afford to Get Old?" American Health v16 n6 Jul-Aug 1997. p60-63,108. (ISSN0730-7004).

In the U.S., "in 1996, the percentage of persons without health insurance by income ranged from 7.6 percent (among those in households with incomes of $75,000 or more) to 24.3 percent (among those in households with incomes less than $25,000). In 1996, most people (70.2 percent) were covered by a private insurance plan; 25.9 percent had government coverage, i.e. Medicare (13.2 percent), Medicaid (11.8 percent), and military health care (3.3 percent). Many people had coverage by more than one plan during the year. About 30.8 percent of the nation's poor (11.3 million) had no health insurance of any kind in 1996."

U.S. Dept. of Commerce. Economic & Statistics Administration. "Income Improves, Poverty Levels Stabilize, Health Insurance Coverage Slips, Census Bureau Reports." Census Bureau Press Release 29 Sep 1997. document-level access: <http://www.census.gov/Press-Release/cb97-162.html>

"In 1980, 54 percent of employees at medium and large companies [in the U.S.] had employers who paid the full cost of family coverage. By 1993 more than 79 percent of these employees were required to pay for their insurance. And the average employee now pays over $1,600 a year for family coverage, and employees of small businesses are paying an average $1,900 a year." (pH2660)

Pallone, Frank, Jr. (Rep.-N.J.). "Health Insurance for the Nation's Children." Congressional Record. Daily ed. v143 n63 14 May 1997. pH2657-2662. section/page-level access: <http://thomas.loc.gov/cgi-bin/query/R?r105:FLD001:H02660:> (ISSN0363-7239). (X1.1A.105/1).

"There are over 23 million self-employed in the United States today. Unfortunately, over 5 million of these people have no health insurance. The rate is higher for self-employed people than the rate for salaried and waged workers. On the average, salaried and waged workers have only 16.8 percent of their membership uninsured, as against 25 percent of the self-employed that are uninsured. The simple fact of the matter is there is a 50 percent higher likelihood that a person is uninsured--without health insurance--if they are self-employed, as opposed to being a salaried employee. Not only are the self-employed less likely to have health insurance, but those that do pay on the average 30 percent more for their health insurance premiums." (pS6348-6349)

Durbin, Richard J. (Sen.-Ill.). "Revenue Reconciliation Act of 1997." Congressional Record. Daily ed. v143 n91 25 Jun 1997. pS6344-6356. section/page-level access: <http://thomas.loc.gov/cgi-bin/query/R?r105:FLD001:S06348:> (ISSN0363-7239). (X1.1A.105/1).

In the U.S., "between 1993 and 1995 the age-adjusted proportion of the population under 65 years of age with private health insurance has remained stable at 70-71 percent after declining from 77 to 71 percent between 1989 and 1993. Changes in eligibility rules in the Medicaid program resulted in an increase in the proportion of the population with Medicaid coverage from 6 percent in 1989 to 10-11 percent during 1993 to 1995. The age-adjusted proportion of the population under 65 years of age without any health care coverage has stayed around 17 percent from 1989 to 1995. Hispanic persons were more than twice as likely to have no coverage as non-Hispanic white persons in 1995 (32 percent and 13 percent). In 1995 the age-adjusted percent of persons under 65 years of age with no health care coverage declined steadily with increasing income from 34 percent among those with family incomes of less than $14,000 to 5 percent among those with family incomes of $50,000 or more."

U.S. Dept. of Health and Human Services. "Report on Nation's Health Documents Toll of Injuries in U.S.: Firearm Mortality Down 11%, Traffic Fatality...Up...." Press Release 24 Jul 1997. document-level access: <http://www.cdc.gov/nchswww/releases/97news/97news/hus96rel.htm>

In the U.S., in 1995, of all ambulatory care visits to various health care settings, "private insurance was the most frequently expected source of payment, accounting for over 44 percent of the visits. Medicare accounted for one-fifth of the visits and Medicaid accounted for 13 percent of the visits. Roughly 1 in 10 visits had an expected source of payment of self-pay. Medicaid as a payment source ranged from 11 percent of visits in physician offices to a high of 29 percent on hospital outpatient departments."

U.S. National Center for Health Statistics. "Monitoring Health Care in America: Spotlight on: Ambulatory Care in the U.S." Quarterly Fact Sheet Jun 1997. document-level access: <http://www.cdc.gov/nchswww/releases/97facts/97sheets/mhc0697.htm>

INSURANCE, HEALTH--UNITED STATES--AGED (v26)

INSURANCE, HEALTH--UNITED STATES--CHILDREN (v26)

"Of the 71 million children in the United States, more than 86 percent are covered by some type of health insurance; two-thirds are covered by insurance through the private sector; 23 percent of all children in the United States under age 18 are covered by Medicaid, and another 3 percent are covered by other public insurance progams. Of the 9.8 million children who are not insured, 2.9 million children live in families with incomes above 200 percent of the Federal poverty level. Half of these children live in families with incomes of about 300 percent of the Federal poverty level....300 percent of the poverty level is over $48,000 for a family of four." (pS6068)

Roth, William V., Jr. (Sen.-Del.). "Balanced Budget Act of 1997." Congressional Record. Daily ed. v143 n88-89 23 Jun 1997. pS6058-6072. section/page-level access: <http://thomas.loc.gov/cgi-bin/query/R?r105:FLD001:S06067:> (ISSN0363-7239). (X1.1A.105/1).

In the U.S., "each year 600,000 sick children do not receive any medical care, because they are uninsured. Each year, 400,000 children go without the medicine their doctors have prescribed because they have no insurance. Each year, 1 1/2 million children go without the dental care they need, because they have no insurance. Each year, 600,000 uninsured children suffer from asthma and less than half see a physician even once. Each month, 1 million uninsured children suffer from sore throats with high fever....Each year, 300,000 uninsured children have chronic, untreated ear infections. Uninsured children are 50 percent more likely to die in the hospital than other children because their parents couldn't afford the health insurance they needed." (pS4785)

Kennedy, Edward M. (Sen.-Mass.). "Concurrent Resolution on the Budget." Congressional Record. Daily ed. v143 n68 21 May 1997. p4782-4849. section/page-level access: <http://thomas.loc.gov/cgi-bin/query/R?r105:FLD001:S04785:> (ISSN0363-7239). (X1.1A.105/1).

In the U.S., children without health insurance "are 73 percent as likely to have injuries treated by a medical provider. Uninsured white children are 1.46 times as likely to die in the hospital as insured white children. The rate for uninsured black children compared with their insured peers is 1.88. Uninsured children are twice as likely to be inadequately immunized." (p12 secA)

Mishra, Raja. "Children First: A Free Press Campaign: Health: A $400 Million Infusion: Federal Cash to Help State's Uninsured Kids." Detroit Free Press 8 Aug 1997. p1,12 secA.

INSURANCE, HEALTH--UNITED STATES--CHILDREN --FINANCE

In the U.S., "the Children's Health Insurance Program, which President Clinton signed into law...provides $24 billion in federal matching funds over five years to help states expand health care coverage to the nation's estimated 10 million uninsured children. Nearly $4.3 billion is available in fiscal year 1998 to help states provide coverage to uninsured low-income children....A state that now gets $1 from the federal government for every $2 spent on its Medicaid program will get $1.30 for every $2 spent on its children's health insurance plan."

U.S. Dept. of Health and Human Services. "HCFA Announces State Allotments for Children's Health Insurance Program." Press Release 10 Sep 1997. document-level access: <http://www.hhs.gov/news/press/1997pres/970910b.html>

INSURANCE, HEALTH--UNITED STATES--COSTS (v26)

INSURANCE, HEALTH--UNITED STATES--EXECUTIVES --ATTITUDES (v26)

INSURANCE, HEALTH--UNITED STATES--FARMERS (v26)

INSURANCE, HEALTH--UNITED STATES--MINORITIES (v26)

INSURANCE, HEALTH--UNITED STATES--OFFICIALS AND EMPLOYEES (v26)

INSURANCE, HEALTH--UNITED STATES--PUBLIC OPINION

In the U.S., "a November 1996 ballot initiative to make provider choice a constitutional right was proposed by Floridians for Health Care Choice....A local poll showed 72 percent of respondents would vote for such an amendment (NJ 1996)....A survey by the American Association of Health Plans found that HMOs and PPOs [preferred provider organizations] were still very concerned about AWP [any willing provider] legislation. AWP was ranked as a 'very' or 'moderately important' state legislative issue by 97.6 percent of responding HMOs and by 86.2 percent of PPOs (D'Andrea 1996)." (p1138)

Marsteller, Jill A./Bovbjerg, Randall R./Nichols, Len M./Verrilli, Diana K. "The Resurgence of Selective Contracting Restrictions." Journal of Health Politics, Policy and Law v22 n5 Oct 1997. p1133-1189. (ISSN0361-6878).

INSURANCE, HEALTH--UNITED STATES--RETIREES

"In 1992, employer-related retiree health plans paid for only 6 percent of health expenditures for persons over age 65 [in the U.S.]....Many employers are now reducing or canceling retiree health coverage for both early retirees and Medicare-eligible retirees. According to one study, in 1988, 62 percent of firms offered retiree coverage to those under age 65, and 55 percent offered benefits to those eligible for Medicare. In just 4 years, by 1992, the numbers of firms offering retiree health coverage had dropped nearly 10 percent in both categories--to 52 and 46 percent, respectively." (pS6092)

Kennedy, Edward M. (Sen.-Mass.). "Balanced Budget Act of 1997." Congressional Record. Daily ed. v143 n88-89 23 Jun 1997. pS6084-6093. section/page-level access: <http://thomas.loc.gov/cgi-bin/query/R?r105:FLD001:S06092:> (ISSN0363-7239). (X1.1A.105/1).

INSURANCE, HEALTH--UNITED STATES--TRADE-UNIONS

In the U.S., "in 1993, at companies with more than 100 employees, 90 percent of all union members were covered by health insurance through their jobs. Only 79 percent of nonunion workers could make the same claim." (p4)

"Economic: Pension and Health Benefits." Maritime Newsletter v29 n11 Nov 1997. p4. (ISSN0161-9373).

INSURANCE, HEALTH--UNITED STATES--WOMEN

In the U.S., "women spend 68 percent more in out-of-pocket costs for health care than men. Reproductive health care services account for much of this difference. According to a study done by the Alan Guttmacher Institute, 49 percent of all large-group health care plans do not routinely cover any contraceptive method at all, and only 15 percent cover all five of the most common contraceptive methods. Women are forced to use disposable income to pay for family planning services not covered by their health insurance--the pill--one of the most common birth control methods, can cost over $300 a year." (pS4488)

Reid, Harry (Sen.-Nev.). "Statements on Introduced Bills and Joint Resolutions." Congressional Record. Daily ed. v143 n63 14 May 1997. pS4479-4489. section/page-level access: <http://thomas.loc.gov/cgi-bin/query/R?r105:FLD001:S04488:> (ISSN0363-7239). (X1.1A.105/1).

INSURANCE, LONG-TERM CARE--UNITED STATES

In the U.S., "only between 4 percent and 5 percent of older persons now have any type of private long-term care coverage. A quality insurance policy from a leading insurance company costs about $2,607 a year if purchased at age 65; the cost skyrockets to $8,492 by age 79. Thus, a married couple purchasing a policy at retirement would pay about $5,200 annually....The cost for a 50-year-old policyholder would be about $1,160....As of December 1995, the total number of long-term care insurance policies sold since 1987 grew to 4.35 million, according to the Health Insurance Association of America (HIAA), Washington, DC. During that year, 517,000 policies were sold, the largest number in a single year since 1987. Between 1987 and 1995, the average annual growth rate for all long-term care insurance policies was 23 percent. The total premium volume for individual and group association policies sold in 1995 was $616.5 million." (p8)

Wright, Anne Pavuk/Eades-Goudy, Dianne. "Current Issues:

Financing Long-Term Care: Who Will Pay?" Perspectives in Health and Aging v12 n1 1997. p7-8.

INSURANCE, STATE AND COMPULSORY

see SOCIAL SECURITY

INSURANCE, UNEMPLOYMENT--CANADA (v26)

INSURANCE, UNEMPLOYMENT--DENMARK (v26)

INSURANCE, UNEMPLOYMENT--EUROPE--NORTH AMERICA

"Between 1961 and 1991, 6 of 12 European Community countries increased the maximum period for which unemployment benefits are available....A composite index of overall unemployment benefit generosity--taking account of both benefit levels and accessibility--provides an even crisper comparison. In 1961, the simple average of this generosity index in the European Community countries was 17.4; by 1991, it had climbed to 31.5--an 80 percent increase. In the Scandinavian countries (plus Austria and Switzerland), this same index increased more than four-fold, from 8.3 to 34.5. In contrast, the simple average indicator for North America stood at 19.5 in both 1961 and 1991, while for the United States alone, it fell from 17 to 11." (p4)

Haveman, Robert H. "New Democracy Forum: Equity with Employment." Boston Review v22 n3-4 Sum 1997. p3-8. (ISSN0734-2306).

INSURANCE, UNEMPLOYMENT--MASSACHUSETTS

In Massachusetts, "for the entire 1988-96 period, construction firms drew a net subsidy of over $25 per $1,000 of payroll, while employers as a whole were making a net contribution of $1.40 per $1,000. Over the nine-year period, the construction sector received 22 percent of all UI [Unemployment Insurance] benefits and made only 9 percent of all contributions, while accounting for 5 percent of total wages paid to covered employees." (p17)

Tannenwald, Robert/O'Leary, Christopher J. "Unemployment Insurance Policy in New England: Background and Issues." Federal Reserve Bank of Boston New England Economic Review May-Jun 1997. p3-22. (ISSN0028-4726).

INSURANCE, WORKERS' COMPENSATION

see WORKERS' COMPENSATION

INTEREST RATES--CANADA (v26)

INTERNAL MIGRATION

see MIGRATION, INTERNAL

INTERNATIONAL AGENCIES (v26)

see NON-GOVERNMENTAL ORGANIZATIONS

INTERNATIONAL AGENCIES--UNITED STATES --APPROPRIATIONS AND EXPENDITURES (v26)

INTERNATIONAL AWARD

see ARBITRATION, INTERNATIONAL

INTERNATIONAL BUSINESS ENTERPRISES (v26)

"As of the early 1990s, an estimated 40,000 companies owned or controlled 171,000 foreign affiliates. The nonfinancial MNEs [multi-national enterprises] employed seventy million workers in 1992, 20 percent of the nonfarm OECD labor force....According to Edward M. Graham, writing in GLOBAL CORPORATIONS AND NATIONAL GOVERNMENTS, intrafirm trade by MNEs accounted for almost 50 percent of U.S. exports and well over 50 percent of U.S. imports of merchandise in 1991." (p58)

Brand, H. "Global Capitalism and the Decay of Employment Policy." Dissent v44 n4 Fall 1997. p56-62. (ISSN0012-3846).

"The scale of the operations of the world's 40,000 multinational corporations is staggering. The top 500 multinationals, 95 per cent of which are located in OECD countries, account for 80 per cent of foreign investment and 70 per cent of world trade. Annual sales of the eight largest multinationals exceed the GDP of the 50 poorest countries, which contain more than half the world's population." (c867)

Chaytor, David (H.C.-Bury, North). "Investment (OECD Multilateral Agreement)." Great Britain. Parliament. House of Commons. Debates. 23 Jul 1997. c866. section-level access: <http://www.parliament.the-stationery-office.co.uk/pa/cm199798/cmhansrd/cm970723/debtext/70723-01.htm#70723-01_head0>

"The ratio of exports to GDP roughly doubled from 1960 to 1990 among the OECD countries (the richest 24 nations) from under 10 percent to over 20 percent. The stock of international bank lending rose from 4 percent of OECD GDP in 1980 to 44 percent in 1990...." (p20-21) "Production by TNCs [transnational corporations] outside their country of origin is important, yet 85 percent of industrial output is produced by domestic corporations in a single geographic location. The multinationals account for about 15 percent of the world's industrial output." (p22)

Tabb, William K. "Globalization Is an Issue, The Power of Capital Is the Issue." Monthly Review v49 n2 Jun 1997. p20-30. (ISSN0027-0520).

"Multinational companies are those that do more than half of their business abroad. In 1970, there were 7,000 of them. Today there are 40,000 and they control 206,000 subsidiaries while employing only 3% of the world's population (about 73 million people). The budget of these corporations in 1991 was greater than all of the world's exports of goods and services ($4.8 trillion); they control either directly or indirectly a good third of the world's revenue and the top 200 of these companies monopolize a quarter of the world's revenue and the top 200 of these companies monopolize a quarter of the world's economic activity. Nearly 33% of world trade now takes place among the subsidiaries of the same corporations, not between different corporations....The budget of General Motors ($132 billion) is greater than the GNP of Indonesia; Ford's ($100.3 billion), greater than the GNP of Turkey; Toyota's greater than the GNP of Portugal; Unilever's greater than the GNP of Pakistan; Nestle's greater than the GNP of Egypt, etc." (p121-122)

Benoist, Alain de. "Confronting Globalization." Telos n108 Sum 1996. p117-137.

INTERNATIONAL BUSINESS ENTERPRISES --CALIFORNIA

"California, with 12 percent of the US population, accounts for a quarter of the nation's merchandise trade. One of every 7 jobs in California is linked to foreign trade and investment, says Philip Romero, chief economist for...[California Governor] Pete Wilson (R)." (p18)

Sneider, Daniel. "Mile-High Economic Summit: The G-7: In New West, Disk Drives Replace the Cattle Drives." The Christian Science Monitor v89 n142 18 Jun 1997. p1,18. The Christian Science Monitor search engine: <http://www.csmonitor.com/plweb-cgi/iops1.pl> To retrieve this article, enter the following search: ED=19970618 AND drives. In the "retrieved list," click the title that matches this record. (ISSN0882-7729).

INTERNATIONAL BUSINESS ENTERPRISES--CORRUPT PRACTICES

There have been "disturbing news reports of the extent of corruption and illegal practices which are adversely affecting U.S. businesses abroad. A NEW YORK TIMES article of May 24, 1997, cited a Commerce Department finding that U.S. companies lost approximately $11 billion in contracts since mid-1994 because of bribery by their foreign competitors of foreign officials. And, this staggering loss is attributed only to those high-profile cases which were identified. Another report cited in the June 2, 1997, Economist Intelligence Unit, cited a loss of $45 billion to American companies because of

corruption." (pS9727)
Campbell, Ben Nighthorse (Sen.-Colo.). "Statements on Introduced Bills and Joint Resolutions." Congressional Record. Daily ed. v143 n126 19 Sep 1997. pS9726-9729. section/page-level access: <http://thomas.loc.gov/cgi-bin/query/R?r105:FLD001:S09727:> (ISSN0363-7239). (X1.1A.105/1).

INTERNATIONAL DEBTS
see DEBTS, EXTERNAL

INTERNATIONAL EXCHANGE
see FOREIGN EXCHANGE

INTERNATIONAL GRANTS-IN-AID
see ECONOMIC ASSISTANCE

INTERNATIONAL INVESTMENT
see INVESTMENTS, FOREIGN

INTERNATIONAL MIGRATION
see EMIGRATION AND IMMIGRATION

INTERNATIONAL POLICE--HEALTH AND HYGIENE --CANADA (v26)

INTERNATIONAL RELATIONS (v26)
see also ARBITRATION, INTERNATIONAL

INTERNATIONAL RELATIONS--COSTS (v26)

INTERNATIONAL RELATIONS--UNITED STATES --PUBLIC OPINION

In a November 1995 Program on International Policy Attitudes "poll, 71% said 'the US is playing the role of world policeman more than it should be.'...In a June 1995 poll by the Americans Talk Issues Foundation, when asked who should be 'the policeman of the world,' only 19% said United States, while 76% said the United Nations....In a January 1994 ABC/WASHINGTON POST poll, only 27% endorsed the statement: 'Because the United States is the world's strongest and richest country, it has the responsibility to take the leading role in world affairs,' while 67% preferred the statement, 'Because the United States has limited resources and its own problems at home, it needs to reduce its involvement in world affairs.'" (p2)
Kull, Steven. "Americans Have Not Turned Isolationist." Public Perspective v8 n5 Aug-Sep 1997. p1-4. (ISSN1050-5067).

INTERNATIONAL TRADE (v26)
see also ARMS TRANSFERS; BALANCE OF TRADE; EXPORTS; IMPORTS

"International trade is now worth around $5 trillion a year, which adds up to about 20 percent of global output. For individual Western economies, the ratio of trade to GDP regained gold-standard levels by the early 1970s and has now surpassed them, reaching from 30 to 40 percent of output, and in some cases much higher....Whereas previously there was almost negligible trade in services, it now constitutes around 20 percent of international trade...." (p273)
Goldblatt, David/Held, David/McGrew, Anthony/Perraton, Jonathan. "Economic Globalization and the Nation-State: Shifting Balances of Power." Alternatives: Social Transformation and Human Governance v22 n3 Jul-Sep 1997. p269-285. (ISSN0304-3754).

"In 1990 international exchange was already 15% of world business. In only five years, from 1985 to 1990, exports increased by 13.9%....The annual rate of growth has gone from 15% between 1970 and 1985 to 28% from 1985 to 1990, during which time direct investments quadrupled in volume, going from $43 billion in 1985 to $167 billion in 1990." (p117-118)
Benoist, Alain de. "Confronting Globalization." Telos n108 Sum 1996. p117-137.

INTERNET (COMPUTER NETWORK) (v26)

"From the four linked sites of its 1969 precursor, the Internet has developed into an advanced telecommunications network that was unimagined only a decade ago. Today, over 15,000,000 households are currently connected to the Internet, and some industry analysts expect this number to rise to 43,000,000 by the year 2000....According the the WALL STREET JOURNAL, online commerce was estimated at $518 million in 1996 and is expected to reach $1.14 billion in 1997. Not surprisingly though, the surge of Internet use has led to some unexpected difficulties. Industry studies indicate that Internet usage is growing at up to 42 percent per year, and some Local Exchange Carrier's (LEC) contend this increasing traffic could exceed the current phone system's capacity." (pS4612)
Abraham, Spencer (Sen.-Mich.). "Senate Resolution 86--Relative to Telephone Access Charges for Use of the Internet." Congressional Record. Daily ed. v143 n64 15 May 1997. pS4611-4613. section/page-level access: <http://thomas.loc.gov/cgi-bin/query/R?r105:FLD001:S04612:> (ISSN0363-7239). (X1.1A.105/1).

"The original design of the Internet was intended for 256 computer networks in the United States. Today, the Internet is a constellation of more than 135,000 networks throughout the world and growing. It is estimated that one-fifth of the American population is already connected to the Internet. The number of worldwide Internet users tripled between 1993 and 1995, to somewhere between 40 and 60 million users. There will be a quarter billion regular users by the year 2000. About 100 countries have Internet access, with 22 joining in 1995. There were fewer than 30,000 Internet-linked computer networks 2 years ago. Today, there are more than 90,000." (pH7297)
Jackson-Lee, Sheila (Rep.-Tex.). "Computer Security Enhancement Act of 1997." Congressional Record. Daily ed. v143 n123 16 Sep 1997. pH7293-7298. section/page-level access: <http://thomas.loc.gov/cgi-bin/query/R?r105:FLD001:H07297:> (ISSN0363-7239). (X1.1A.105/1).

"Between 1997 and 2001, according to the IDC [International Data Corporation], the number of users of the Internet's World Wide Web will increase sixfold in the US to 180 million, fourfold in Western Europe to 43 million, and nearly six times in the Asia-Pacific region (including Japan) to 49 million....Nearly 8 million Japanese are estimated to be using either an online service or receiving direct Internet access." (p7)
Belsie, Laurent. "Japan and Other Nations Try to Match US on Internet Business." The Christian Science Monitor v90 n21 24 Dec 1997. p7. The Christian Science Monitor search engine: <http://www.csmonitor.com/plweb-cgi/iops1.pl> To retrieve this article, enter the following search: ED=19971224 AND business. In the "retrieved list," click the title that matches this record. (ISSN0882-7729).

"In less than three years, more than a quarter of Internet users have purchased an item or service online. Nearly a third of commercial Web sites today are profitable, according to market researcher ActivMedia, and an additional quarter expect to make money within the coming year. The optimistic forecasters, like Jupiter Communications, say that Internet shopping, which now stands at $2.6 billion, could increase to $37.5 billion in the next five years, approaching the size of today's $46 billion mail-order business." (p86)
Cohen, Warren. "1998 Tech Guide: Online Malls Move Closer to Home." U.S. News & World Report v123 n21 1 Dec 1997. p86. article-level access: <http://www.usnews.com/usnews/issue/971201/1COMM.HTM> (ISSN0041-5537).

INTERNET (COMPUTER NETWORK)--CANADA--UNITED STATES

"About 23 percent of people aged 16 and older in the U.S. and Canada have used the Internet in the last month and have access today, according to the January 1997 wave of an ongoing survey by CommerceNet and Nielsen Media Research. In the fall of 1995, only 10 percent had used the Internet in the three months prior to the survey....About 58 percent of current Internet users are men, compared with 66 percent in fall 1995. About 39 percent of users hold professional or managerial jobs, down from 50 percent in 1995." (p10)

Edmondson, Brad. "Statmeister: The Wired Bunch." American Demographics v19 n6 Jun 1997. p10,12-15. article-level access: <http://www.demographics.com/publications/ad/97_ad/9706_ad/ad97063.htm> (ISSN0163-4089).

INTERNET (COMPUTER NETWORK)--COMMERCE --UNITED STATES (v26)

INTERNET (COMPUTER NETWORK)--GAMBLING (v26)

"By the year 2000, according to conservative estimates, online gambling will be an $8-$10 billion business. About 20 sites already offer live, online betting on casino games, sporting events, and lotteries." (p42)

Rosenzweig, Sandra. "Easy Money: World Wide Wagering." Mother Jones v22 n4 Jul-Aug 1997. p42-43. article-level access: <http://www.motherjones.com/coinop_congress/easymoney/rosenzweig.html> (ISSN0362-8841).

"There are some 30 gambling locations in cyberspace today--twice the number operating in January [1997]. By year's end, their number is expected to double again, and by 2000 worldwide casino gambling online could reach $8.6 billion, according to one estimate." (p1)

Belsie, Laurent. "Growing Number of States Say 'No Dice' to Gambling on Internet." The Christian Science Monitor v89 n143 19 Jun 1997. p1,7. The Christian Science Monitor search engine: <http://www.csmonitor.com/plweb-cgi/iops1.pl> To retrieve this article, enter the following search: ED=19970619 AND internet. In the "retrieved list," click the title that matches this record. (ISSN0882-7729).

INTERNET (COMPUTER NETWORK)--GERMANY

"At the end of 1996, half of all Internet users in Germany were still students. This group has now been overtaken by employees....Approximately 35% of all enterprises with more than ten employees now have access to the information superhighway, and around 13% would no longer be able to do business without the Internet. According to a survey carried out by Business Online, more than 40% of German companies will be investing in a presence on the Internet over the next twelve months. The total volume of investment planned amounts to some 3.75 billion marks, an average of approximately 30,000 marks per business....Almost 60% of Internet users read an online newspaper or magazine at least once a week....Shopping via the Internet is still not particularly highly developed, but in a recent survey more than two thirds of the netsurfers questioned said they would definitely or perhaps shop through the Internet in the future....The number of users will double in Germany by the year 2000." (p39)

"Internet: The Advance of the Internet Now Seems Unstoppable." Deutschland n6 Dec 1997. p39. (ISSN0945-6791).

INTERNET (COMPUTER NETWORK)--GERMANY --EMPLOYEES (v26)

INTERNET (COMPUTER NETWORK)--GERMANY--HIGH SCHOOLS

"Currently, one in five German high schools has its own home page on the Internet. According to the statistics, in North Rhine-Westphalia, for example, 123 out of 623 high schools have a home page. The figure in Saxony is 39 out of 194, in Bavaria 79 out of 369, and in Hesse 42 out of 278." (p47)

Behler, Bettina. "Websurfer: Schools on the Net." Deutschland n6 Dec 1997. p46-49. article-level access: <http://www.government.de/ausland/index_e.html> (ISSN0945-6791).

INTERNET (COMPUTER NETWORK)--PUBLIC OPINION

"Recently, 60 percent of respondents to an online survey stated that privacy concerns created a significant barrier to their acceptance of electronic commerce. In another survey, 2 out of 3 said they would leave a Web site if they were asked to provide personal information--or worse, that they would provide information that was false." (p18)

Dionne, Joseph L. "Opinion/Essays: Making Room for Privacy in the Global Village." The Christian Science Monitor v89 n175 5 Aug 1997. p18. The Christian Science Monitor search engine: <http://www.csmonitor.com/plweb-cgi/iops1.pl> To retrieve this article, enter the following search: ED=19970805 AND village. In the "retrieved list," click the title that matches this record. (ISSN0882-7729).

"When International Data Corporation (IDC) surveyed 11,000 information-technology executives worldwide, it found 52 percent of the executives in the Asia-Pacific region (excluding Japan) thought an Internet strategy was important or very important. Japanese executives were on par with Americans at 30 percent, while Western Europeans trailed at 16 percent." (p7)

Belsie, Laurent. "Japan and Other Nations Try to Match US on Internet Business." The Christian Science Monitor v90 n21 24 Dec 1997. p7. The Christian Science Monitor search engine: <http://www.csmonitor.com/plweb-cgi/iops1.pl> To retrieve this article, enter the following search: ED=19971224 AND business. In the "retrieved list," click the title that matches this record. (ISSN0882-7729).

INTERNET (COMPUTER NETWORK)--TRAVEL--UNITED STATES

"Despite the increasing abundance of travel information and booking services online, three in four [U.S.] adults say they have no definite plans to book their next trip using the Internet or an online service provider, according to the Travel Industry Association of America. Three reasons top the list. Respondents either don't have a computer (40 percent); don't want to use a computer (21 percent); or prefer talking to a travel agent (9 percent)....One-third of frequent pleasure travelers and nearly half of frequent business travelers have online access, compared with 16 percent of the total population." (p37)

Heubusch, Kevin. "Kaleidoscope: Few 'Click Here' for Takeoff." American Demographics v19 n6 Jun 1997. p37. article-level access: <http://www.demographics.com/publications/ad/97_ad/9706_ad/ad970623.htm> (ISSN0163-4089).

INTERNET (COMPUTER NETWORK)--UNITED STATES (v26)

In the U.S., "thirty-six percent of 18-to-34-year-old online users participate in chat sessions, compared with less than 20 percent of those aged 35 to 54....Nine in ten online users aged 45 to 64 had sent e-mail within the previous six months, compared with 80 percent of 25-to-34-year-olds and 75 percent of 18-to-24-year-olds....Over half of online users aged 45 to 54 visit bulletin boards, compared with 28 percent of those aged 18 to 24." (p34-35)

Heubusch, Kevin. "Kaleidoscope: Cyber Chats." American Demographics v19 n7 Jul 1997. p34-35. article-level access: <http://www.demographics.com/publications/ad/97_ad/9707_ad/ad970730.htm> (ISSN0163-4089).

"Of the 162 million U.S. adults who do not use the Internet, two-thirds (106 million) say they either are not aware of it or have no need for it, according to a survey conducted in July 1997 by FIND/SVP. About one in eight non-users (21 million adults) says he or she plans to go online in the next 12 months. The remaining 22 percent of non-users (35 million adults) say they want to 'learn more' about the Internet. America's current Internet users are mostly well-educated, middle-aged, male, and affluent. Of the 31 million adults who now go online, 42 percent are college graduates, 50 percent are aged 30 to 49, and 64 percent are men, with a median household income of $47,600." (p1)

"Who's in Line to Log On." Forecast v17 n10 Oct 1997. p1-2. article-level access: <http://www.demographics.com/publications/fc/97_fc/9710_fc/fc97101.htm> (ISSN0732-1597).

In the U.S., "nearly two-thirds of the 602 planners who responded to a PLANNING survey last November [1996] reported that they had access to the Internet, America Online, CompuServe, Prodigy, or a similar online computer network, and nearly half said they regularly logged on during the workday....Of those who don't now have network access, two-thirds expect to have it within a year." (p20)

O'Mara, W. Paul. "Planning Practice: Catching Up With the Net." Planning v63 n7 Jul 1997. p20-22. (ISSN0001-2610).

INTERNET (COMPUTER NETWORK)--UNITED STATES --AGED

"The 55-and-over age group is the fastest-growing demographic group for computer sales and Internet use, says Glen Gilbert, director of public relations for SeniorNet, based in San Francisco. Approximately 15 percent of them are regular Internet users, accounting for 8 million of the 50 million users....The number of overall e-mail accounts has risen to 93 million, up from 62 million a year ago....SeniorNet, an Internet pioneer, runs learning centers nationwide offering peer-to-peer computer instruction to people 55 and older. Five years ago there were about 40 learning centers; today there are 110. By the end of this year there will be 22 more." (p10)

Conover, Kirsten A. "Lifestyle: The New Generation of Net Surfers: Seniors." The Christian Science Monitor v90 n1 25 Nov 1997. p10-11. The Christian Science Monitor search engine: <http://www.csmonitor.com/plweb-cgi/iops1.pl> To retrieve this article, enter the following search: ED=19971125 AND seniors. In the "retrieved list," click the title that matches this record. (ISSN0882-7729).

INTERNET (COMPUTER NETWORK)--UNITED STATES --EMPLOYEES (v26)

In the U.S., "more than 50 percent of FORTUNE 500 companies have given employees Internet access, with more to follow.... Webster [Network Strategies of Naples, Fla.,] studies...show that at some companies, employees average as much as 90 minutes per day fooling around with Internet sites that couldn't conceivably have anything to do with the firm's business." (p18)

Stuller, Jay. "Games Workers Play." Across the Board v34 n7 Jul-Aug 1997. p16-22. (ISSN0147-1554).

INTERNET (COMPUTER NETWORK)--UNITED STATES --PUBLIC OPINION (v26)

In the U.S., "among adults who plan to go online between July 1997 and July 1998, one-third are college graduates and 53 percent are women. In the 'like to learn more' group, 20 percent are college graduates and 49 percent are women. Among adults who know about the Internet but see no need for it, 14 percent are college graduates and 56 percent are women. In the 'unaware' group, 12 percent are college graduates and 56 percent are women." (p1) "A majority of the 'plan to begin using' group is aged 30 to 49, two-thirds are married, and 57 percent have children living at home. In fact, the survey finds that the presence of young children is perhaps the strongest predictor that a household will be interested in going online. Two-thirds of non-user parents who want their children to use the Internet say that the main reason is to help the child with homework. Half say the Internet would enhance their child's career prospects, and one-third say it is a better form of entertainment than TV....Among non-user parents, 59 percent of women want their children to go online, compared with 41 percent of men. Nearly two-thirds of non-user parents aged 30 to 49 want their kids online." (p2)

"Who's in Line to Log On." Forecast v17 n10 Oct 1997. p1-2. article-level access: <http://www.demographics.com/publications/fc/97_fc/9710_fc/fc97101.htm> (ISSN0732-1597).

INTERNET (COMPUTER NETWORK)--UNITED STATES --SCHOOLS (v26)

While over half of U.S. "public schools have access to the Internet, only 13 percent of teachers, computer coordinators, and school librarians believe that it helps students' performance in school, according to a new survey by Market Data Retrieval and Education Market Research....Three-fourths say it is useful as a research tool. However, 81 percent believe that the Internet needs to be more closely connected with curriculum and textbooks....Those with a favorite web site were more likely to use the Internet frequently: 43 percent use it daily and 33 percent weekly." (p38-39)

Kate, Nancy Ten. "Kaleidoscope: Surfin' at School." American Demographics v19 n11 Nov 1997. p38-39. article-level access: <http://www.demographics.com/publications/ad/97_ad/9711_ad/ad971116.htm> (ISSN0163-4089).

INTERNET (COMPUTER NETWORK)--UNITED STATES --STUDENTS

In the U.S., "the share of public schools with access to the Internet is expected to increase from 65 percent in the fall of 1996 to 95 percent in 2000, according to the National Center for Education Statistics (NCES)....Only 25 percent of private schools had Internet access in the fall of 1995, according to the NCES, and 45 percent of private schools in that survey had no plans for future access....More than half of parents with online access say their kids surf or browse the Internet, and 46 percent say their kids use it for informal learning." (p5)

"The Internet Goes to School." Forecast v17 n9 Sep 1997. p5. article-level access: <http://www.demographics.com/Publications/FC/97_fc/9709_fc/FC97094.htm> (ISSN0732-1597).

INTERNET (COMPUTER NETWORK)--UNITED STATES --SURVEYS

"About 17 percent of marketers surveyed who work in some of the 2,000 largest U.S. companies have used data from online surveys, according to an October 1996 study by the Council of American Survey Research Organizations (CASRO). Most of those who have used online surveys expect to use more of them in the future, and 42 percent of marketers who have not conducted research online expect to try it within five years....The quiet crisis in market research is that most Americans now refuse to be surveyed. About two-thirds of households have a telephone answering machine, and about half of householders sometimes use their answering machine to screen their calls, according to a 1995 study by CASRO. When they are contacted by telephone, about six in ten Americans refuse to answer survey questions." (p10)

Edmondson, Brad. "Statmeister: The Wired Bunch." American Demographics v19 n6 Jun 1997. p10,12-15. article-level access: <http://www.demographics.com/publications/ad/97_ad/9706_ad/ad97063.htm> (ISSN0163-4089).

INTERNET (COMPUTER NETWORK)--UNITED STATES --TEACHERS--ATTITUDES (v26)

INTERNET (COMPUTER NETWORK)--UNITED STATES --VOTING (v26)

INTERNSHIP PROGRAMS--UNITED STATES

"Nine out of 10 four-year colleges now offer some sort of structured work experience connected to a student's major or career interest, according to the American Council on

Education....Many schools now boast that well over 50 percent of their grads land jobs through their internship programs. The numbers are so convincing that nearly 1 in 5 institutions--including small schools...now requires that students take internships as a condition of graduation." (p76)

Tooley, Jo Ann. "U.S. News: News You Can Use: Colleges: Working for Credit." U.S. News & World Report v123 n19 17 Nov 1997. p76-78. article-level access: <http://www.usnews.com/usnews/issue/971117/17INTE.HTM> (ISSN0041-5537).

INTERRACIAL ADOPTION--CALIFORNIA (v26)

INTERRACIAL ADOPTION--MEXICAN AMERICANS --ATTITUDES (v26)

INTERRACIAL DATING--UNITED STATES

"According to a recent Gallup poll, 57 percent of US teens who date say they have gone out with a person from another race or ethnic group. That compares with 17 percent in 1980 (but that poll did not specifically include Hispanics.)...Interracial marriage is on the rise, with the number of couples quadrupling since the 1970s. Today, nearly two-thirds of whites say they approve of interracial marriage." (p1) "Nearly two-thirds of parents of teens nationwide say they have no problem with cross-racial and ethnic dating, according to a Gallup poll." (p18)

Tyson, Ann Scott. "It's a Date: Young Love Bridges Race Divide." The Christian Science Monitor v90 n6 3 Dec 1997. p1,18. The Christian Science Monitor search engine: <http://www.csmonitor.com/plweb-cgi/iops1.pl> To retrieve this article, enter the following search: ED=19971203 AND divide. In the "retrieved list," click the title that matches this record. (ISSN0882-7729).

INTERRACIAL MARRIAGE--HISPANIC AMERICANS

In the U.S., "one-sixth (18 percent) of Hispanic wives were married to a non-Hispanic husband in 1996. One-seventh of the Hispanic married men had a non-Hispanic wife....[Non-Mexican] Hispanics were most likely to marry a non-Hispanic (34 percent of women and 32 percent of men)." (p28)

del Pinal, Jorge/Singer, Audrey. "Generations of Diversity: Latinos in the United States." Population Bulletin v52 n3 Oct 1997. p2-47. (ISSN0032-468X).

INTERRACIAL MARRIAGE--UNITED STATES

"Black-white unions are still relatively rare among the 51 million married couples in the United States, and marriages of white women to black men are the more common combination--more than 200,000 were in existence in 1995 compared with 122,000 of the reverse mix. But from 1990 to 1995, the number of black women married to white men doubled, rising from 61,000, according to the U.S. Census Bureau. Since 1970, the increase has been five-fold." (p1 secF) "About one in ten black men now marries outside his race." (p4 secF)

Oguntoyinbo, Lekan. "The Way We Live: Black Women White Men: More African-American Women Are Marrying outside Their Race." Detroit Free Press 14 Sep 1997. p1,4 secF.

In the U.S., the "Jewish community has an intermarriage rate of 50 per cent or more....Asians and Hispanics, although most relatively recent immigrants, already have intermarriage rates of about 30 per cent. According to the 1980 census,...98.7 per cent of black native-born women married other blacks. Conversely, in-marriage among women of Puerto Rican descent was 78.7 per cent, and among Mexican American women, 76 per cent." (p6)

O'Neill, William L. "A Wise and Temperate Book." New Leader v80 n9 19 May 1997. p5-6. (ISSN0028-6044).

INTERSCHOLASTIC ATHLETICS

see SCHOOL SPORTS

INTESTINES--DISEASES

"The Global Burden of Disease project estimated that more than 4 billion cases of diarrheal diseases occur every year. At any one time, there are about 72 million cases worldwide." (p9)

Olshansky, S. Jay/Carnes, Bruce/Rogers, Richard G./Smith, Len. "Infectious Diseases--New and Ancient Threats to World Health." Population Bulletin v52 n2 Jul 1997. p2-46. (ISSN0032-468X).

INTOXICANTS

see ALCOHOLIC BEVERAGES

INTOXICATION

see ALCOHOLISM

INTRAFAMILY VIOLENCE

see FAMILY VIOLENCE

INVASIVE PLANTS--UNITED STATES

"Jointed goatgrass has become a serious pest of winter wheat in the Great Plains and western U.S. It infests an estimated 5,000,000 acres and is spreading at a rate of at least 50,000 acres per year....Direct costs to wheat growers from jointed goatgrass are estimated at $35,000,000 in yield losses and $10,000,000 in penalties for grain quality." (p87)

U.S. Dept. of Agriculture. "Agriculture, Rural Development, Food and Drug Administration...Approp. for 1998 (Part 4)." Hearing. U.S. House. Committee on Appropriations. Washington, D.C. : GPO, 1997. (ISBN0160551560). (Y4.Ap6/1:Ag8/997/pt.4).

Our food supply is "being increasingly threatened by new and emerging plant diseases and pests that affect the approximately 150 crops grown in the United States....Karnal bunt disease of wheat has seriously disrupted the export market for wheat growers in the southwestern U.S. Head scab of wheat and barley has caused an estimated $2 billion in losses since 1993....And noxious and invasive exotic weeds which already infest 17 million acres of public lands are expected to double in five years." (p551)

Knipling, Edward B. (Acting Administrator, U.S. Agricultural Research Service). "Agriculture, Rural Development, Food and Drug Administration...Approp. for 1998 (Part 4)." Hearing. U.S. House. Committee on Appropriations. Washington, D.C. : GPO, 1997. (ISBN0160551560). (Y4.Ap6/1:Ag8/997/pt.4).

INVESTMENT AND SAVING

see SAVING AND INVESTMENT

INVESTMENT TRUSTS

see MUTUAL FUNDS

INVESTMENTS

see also MUTUAL FUNDS; SAVING AND INVESTMENT; STOCK EXCHANGES; VENTURE CAPITAL

"The Citizens Index Portfolio is up 20.3 percent so far this year through June 23, ahead of the Standard & Poor's 500 stock index at 18.6 percent. The Domini Social Equity Index Fund, up 20.9 percent this year, recently ranked as the top growth-and-income fund over five years, according to Morningstar, the Chicago firm that tracks mutual-fund performance....The stocks in these funds are weighted by company size. So in the Domini fund, 42 percent of investors' money goes into 20 big companies such as Coca-Cola, Intel, Microsoft, and Merck, even though the Domini index includes 400 corporations....Both Citizens and Domini use complex 'social audits' to screen companies. Domini, for example, asks 140 questions." (p8)

Trumbull, Mark. "Business & Money: Mutual Funds: Socially Screened Index Funds Top S&P 500." The Christian Science Monitor v89 n148 26 Jun 1997. p8. The Christian Science Monitor search engine: <http://www.csmonitor.com/plweb-cgi/iops1.pl> To retrieve this article, enter the following search: ED=19970626 AND index. In the "retrieved list," click the title that matches this record. (ISSN0882-7729).

Equity-income funds are a little less conservative than growth-and-income funds. "They look for stocks that pay high dividends. Balanced funds are more conservative, typically 60 percent stocks, 40 percent bonds." (p9)

Halverson, Guy. "Business & Money: Mutual Funds: And the Winner Is: Mr. Slowpoke." The Christian Science Monitor v89 n138 12 Jun 1997. p9. The Christian Science Monitor search engine: <http://www.csmonitor.com/plweb-cgi/iops1.pl> To retrieve this article, enter the following search: ED=19970612 AND slowpoke. In the "retrieved list," click the title that matches this record. (ISSN0882-7729).

Growth-and-income funds "gained more than 14 percent a year for the past five years, according to the Value Line Mutual Fund Survey....Since 1984, the growth-and-income category has consistently ranked No. 1 or No. 2 at the equity-fund box office, in terms of new investor dollars....Many G&I funds now invest heavily in bonds,...[Sheldon Jacobs of the No-Load Fund Investor in New York] says. The average allocation: 87 percent equity (stocks) and 13 percent bonds. By contrast, growth funds, which stress increasing share price without regard to income, are about 97 percent equity; and aggressive-growth funds, (which often invest in small companies), are about 99 percent equity." (p9)

Halverson, Guy. "Business & Money: Mutual Funds: And the Winner Is: Mr. Slowpoke." The Christian Science Monitor v89 n138 12 Jun 1997. p9. The Christian Science Monitor search engine: <http://www.csmonitor.com/plweb-cgi/iops1.pl> To retrieve this article, enter the following search: ED=19970612 AND slowpoke. In the "retrieved list," click the title that matches this record. (ISSN0882-7729).

INVESTMENTS--AFRICA

Despite "dependence of many African countries on development aid, net official flows to Africa plunged by 48 per cent in 1996 to $3.2 bn [billion], the lowest level for a decade, the International Monetary Fund (IMF) reports in its latest 'World Economic Outlook.'" (p1) "There was also a 43 per cent fall in the IMF's soft loan approvals to Africa through its enhanced structural adjustment facility (ESAF)....Sub-Saharan Africa saw a 38 per cent drop in its primary source of World Bank lending--soft loans from the International Development Association (IDA)....The total decline in net capital flows to Africa was...17 per cent (to $13.9 bn) in 1996....Net private flows...rose by $0.1 bn to $10.7 bn....Within the private flows, net direct investment rose by over 78 per cent to $5 bn, the highest for at least a decade, and more than offset a 68 per cent plunge in volatile portfolio investment from $1.9 bn to $0.6 bn. As the IMF publication does not provide a breakdown of the distribution of these flows, it is unclear whether there has been any change since the 1985-95 period when Africa's nine oil-exporting countries took 73 per cent of foreign direct investment (FDI). IMF loan approvals to sub-Saharan Africa fell substantially, with ESAF loans--the main vehicle for IMF lending to the region--down by 43 per cent to $672 mn [million] from $1.19 bn in 1995/96. Total ESAF approvals in turn fell from $1.47 bn to $911 mn. New loan commitments by the World Bank to sub-Saharan Africa for the fiscal year to June 1997 in turn dropped 36 per cent to $1.73 bn--their lowest levels this decade, and well below the average annual $3.2 bn of the 1987-91 period--while disbursements fell by 17 per cent to $2.47 bn." (p4)

Katsouris, Christina. "Special Report: Agriculture in Africa: Sharp Fall in Resource Flows to Africa." Africa Recovery v11 n2 Oct 1997. p1,4.

INVESTMENTS--CANADA (v26)

In Canada, "investors poured $30 billion into mutual funds during the first six months of 1997, boosting industry assets to $258.4 billion. Investors in Canadian equity funds were rewarded with an average 9.3-percent return, slightly worse than the 9.6-per-cent rise in the benchmark Toronto Stock Exchange 300 index over the same period." (p42)

Schofield, John. "Personal Finance: Mid-Year Mutual Fund Rankings." Maclean's v110 n31 4 Aug 1997. p42. (ISSN0024-9262).

INVESTMENTS--DEVELOPING COUNTRIES (v26)

INVESTMENTS--EUROPE (v26)

INVESTMENTS--GREAT BRITAIN (v26)

INVESTMENTS--HONG KONG--UNITED STATES (v26)

INVESTMENTS--SINGAPORE

In Singapore, "investment commitments in the manufacturing sector amounted to $2.2 billion in the third quarter of 1997. These are estimated to generate about $2.4 billion of value added and 6,200 jobs when the projects are fully implemented. Projects were committed mainly in the electronics, chemicals and transport equipment industries. Foreign commitments accounted for $1.6 billion....Local investors committed $575 million."

Singapore. Ministry of Trade and Industry. "Third Quarter 1997 Economic Survey of Singapore." Press Release 1997. document-level access: <http://www.singstat.gov.sg/PRESS/97qes3.htm>

INVESTMENTS--SOUTH ASIA

"Private capital flows to South Asia increased sharply in the 1990s, but by 1996 its share of net private flows to developing countries was 4.3 percent, down from 7.6 percent in the 1980s. Foreign direct investment was about 0.5 percent of the region's GNP in 1996, compared with 4.2 percent for East Asia and 1.9 percent for other developing regions."

World Bank. "South Asia Can Reap Further Gains from Global Integration." Press Release 17 Sep 1997. document-level access: <http://www.worldbank.org/html/extdr/extme/1487.htm>

INVESTMENTS--UNITED STATES

In the U.S., "the portion of computers in total non-residential fixed investment increased from less than one-tenth of 1 percent of total PNFI [private nonresidential fixed investment] in 1970 to 12.8 percent by 1995. During this period, information processing equipment increased from 7.2 percent of PDE [Producers' Durable Equipment] in 1970 to 37.6 percent by the end of 1995. Expressed another way, investment in information processing equipment increased more than 1800 percent, while total PNFI increased about 250 percent." (p15-16)

Allen, Donald S. "Where's the Productivity Growth (From the Information Technology Revolution)?" Review v79 n2 Mar-Apr 1997. p15-25. (ISSN0147-9032).

INVESTMENTS--UNITED STATES--DATA PROCESSING

In the U.S., "among online-investing households, 2.7 million have active, serious investors and a high degree of familiarity with computers and online services. Another 3.8 million are heavy investors with low computer skills, and 2.6 million are technophiles with moderate investment needs. All these households tend to be affluent. High-need, high-skills households have a median net worth of $448,000. Technophile households with moderate investment needs are worth a median of $236,000. Online households that invest heavily but have low computer skills are the best off of all, with median net worth of $500,000." (p32)

Klein, Matthew. "Kaleidoscope: Web-Shy Investors." American Demographics v19 n5 May 1997. p32. article-level access: <http://www.demographics.com/Publications/AD/97_ad/9705_ad/AD970520.htm> (ISSN0163-4089).

INVESTMENTS--UNIVERSITY OF MICHIGAN (v26)

INVESTMENTS--WALES (v26)

INVESTMENTS, AMERICAN--BRAZIL (v26)

INVESTMENTS, AMERICAN--EUROPE (v26)

INVESTMENTS, EUROPEAN (v26)

INVESTMENTS, FOREIGN (v26)

see also DEBTS, EXTERNAL

"Annual issues of international bonds now comprise more than 70 percent of the international capital markets and the cumulative value of the stock of bonds now exceeds $2.4 trillion. Annual issues have risen from less than $20 billion in the early 1970s to more than $300 billion in the 1990s....The percentage of government bonds held by foreigners has risen across the West in the 1980s and early 1990s. In the cases of Britain and Germany the rise is from around 10 percent to 20 percent. In France, it has risen dramatically, from less than 1 percent to 45 percent." (p276)

Goldblatt, David/Held, David/McGrew, Anthony/Perraton, Jonathan. "Economic Globalization and the Nation-State: Shifting Balances of Power." Alternatives: Social Transformation and Human Governance v22 n3 Jul-Sep 1997. p269-285. (ISSN0304-3754).

"Cross-border transactions in equities and bonds in major advanced economies...jumped from less than 10 percent of GDP in 1980 to well over 100 percent in 1995. Relative to world GDP, total foreign direct investment (FDI) flows doubled between 1980 and 1994. The most explosive growth has occurred in the foreign exchange market, where the average daily turnover surged from about $200 billion in the mid-1980s to around $1.2 trillion in 1995--approximately 85 percent of total world reserves." (p384)

Heredia, Blanca. "Prosper or Perish?: Development in the Age of Global Capital." Current History v96 n613 Nov 1997. p383-388. (ISSN0011-3530).

"Foreign investment increased by 800 per cent between 1983 and 1990, and in a single year, 1994-95, by a staggering 46 per cent....Most of that investment is concentrated in the three major economic powers--Europe, Japan and North America. Over the past 10 years, 70 per cent of all foreign direct investment has gone to just 10 countries. By contrast, the 48 least well-developed countries, with a combined population of 570 million, have received a mere 3 per cent of global investment in the past two decades. Of the $100 billion invested in developing countries, two thirds goes to south-east Asia, with China being the principal beneficiary. In recent years, investment in sub-Saharan Africa amounted to less than 1 per cent of its gross domestic product." (c866)

Chaytor, David (H.C.-Bury, North). "Investment (OECD Multilateral Agreement)." Great Britain. Parliament. House of Commons. Debates. 23 Jul 1997. c866. section-level access: <http://www.parliament.the-stationery-office.co.uk/pa/cm199798/cmhansrd/cm970723/debtext/70723-01.htm#70723-01_head0>

"In the 1980s, the Triad [North America, Europe, and Japan] accounted for 94 percent of all foreign direct investment (FDI) outflows, and only 22 percent of those outflows went to developing countries. In 1993-95, the Triad share of FDI outflows (now exceeding $315 billion per year) fell to 84 percent, and 38 percent of all outflows went to developing countries. Most impressive may be the increase in outward FDI from developing countries themselves--from 0.3 percent of all FDI in the 1970s to 15 percent in 1993-95, with half the FDI flows from Asian developing countries invested in the same region." (p30)

Du Boff, Richard B./Herman, Edward S. "A Critique of Tabb on Globalization." Monthly Review v49 n6 Nov 1997. p27-35. (ISSN0027-0520).

Global foreign direct investment "outflows have been steadily increasing, and in 1995, reached a record $339 billion, up 35 percent from 1994 (all data are in nominal terms). FDI outflows grew a further 2 percent in 1996. During 1973-96, the estimated value of annual FDI outflows multiplied more than thirteen times (from $25 billion to $339 billion), while the value of merchandise exports multiplied about ten and one half times (from $575 billion to $6.1 trillion)." (p1)

U.S. Dept. of Agriculture. Economic Research Service. "Spotlight on Foreign Direct Investment (FDI)." Newly Independent States & Baltics Update: Agriculture and Trade Report 20 Oct 1997. p1-10.

"American investors are pouring $3 billion a month into foreign stock mutual funds, hoping to spread their risks beyond a dauntingly high market in the United States. But the 25 percent surge in net money flows from last year has left many investors poorer, if better diversified. World stock funds are up 12 percent on average for the year to date, and were flat in the July-September quarter. US stock funds, by comparison, are up 26 percent for the year, and almost 12 percent for the quarter, according to Lipper Analytical Services in New York....European-stock funds took the lead last quarter with a 6.4 percent gain (18 percent for the year). Latin America funds were up 5.5 percent after a stunning first-half performance, for a year-to-date return of 42.6 percent. Asia funds took a drubbing, with a weak Japanese economy and currency turmoil that spread from Thailand throughout Southeast Asia. Pacific funds are down 6 percent for the year, after slumping 12 percent in the third quarter." (p6 secB)

Francis, David R. "Mutual Funds: Global Markets: Europe Hums as Asia Dips." The Christian Science Monitor v89 n221 9 Oct 1997. p6 secB. The Christian Science Monitor search engine: <http://www.csmonitor.com/plweb-cgi/iops1.pl> To retrieve this article, enter the following search: ED=19971009 AND dips. In the "retrieved list," click the title that matches this record. (ISSN0882-7729).

INVESTMENTS, FOREIGN--AFRICA (v26)

"Although the barriers to investment in Africa remain imposing, hints of change are in the air....Foreign direct investment in Africa reached $4.5 billion in 1996, triple the average annual levels for 1990 to 1993. Americans were the biggest spenders, with U.S. companies pouring a record $1.2 billion into the region last year. In the big picture, investment in Africa is tiny--just 1.5 percent of the world's $349 billion total foreign investments in developing countries in 1996....Investment by U.S. firms in general manufacturing in sub-Saharan Africa--excluding South Africa and Nigeria--grew from an almost nonexistent $18 million in 1990 to $235 million in 1996. Sub-Saharan economies grew at an average of 4.9 percent in 1996...." (p37)

Lovgren, Stefan/Whitelaw, Kevin. "World Report: Instead of Aid, Trade." U.S. News & World Report v123 n14 13 Oct 1997. p37-38. article-level access: <http://www.usnews.com/usnews/issue/971013/13INVE.HTM> (ISSN0041-5537).

INVESTMENTS, FOREIGN--CHINA

"In 1993, China was the largest single recipient of FDI [foreign direct investment] among low-income countries, absorbing $27.5 billion, which was 14 percent of global FDI, and 68 percent of FDI flows to Asian developing countries. FDI (actually used) in China reached $33.9 billion in 1994, $37.8 billion in 1995, and $42.3 billion in 1996, making China the second largest FDI recipient country in the world after the United States (DRC [Development Research Center], 1996). However, less than 2 percent of those funds went to agricultural sectors." (p14)

Wang, Zhi/U.S. Dept. of Agriculture. Economic Research Service. "China's Agricultural Trade in 1996: Commodity Structure, Geographical Distribution, And Its Role in U.S...Trade." China: International Agriculture and Trade Reports Situation and Outlook Series Jun 1997. p6-15.

"Between 1991 and 1994, 192,728 foreign direct investment

contracts with a total agreed foreign contribution of U.S. $264.2 billion were signed in China. In comparison, China signed only 29,049 foreign direct investment contracts with a total agreed foreign contribution of U.S. $40.4 billion between 1979 and 1990." (p105)

Ho, Samuel P. S. "Technology Transfer to China during the 1980s--How Effective?: Some Evidence from Jiangsu." Pacific Affairs v70 n1 Spr 1997. p85-106. (ISSN0030-851X).

INVESTMENTS, FOREIGN--CHINA--HONG KONG

"Mainland Chinese companies are now the second-largest foreign investor in Hong Kong after Britain. Their total investment is estimated to exceed USD [U.S. dollars] 25 billion. In addition, there are almost two thousand Mainland Chinese-controlled enterprises with combined assets of more than USD 42.5 billion in Hong Kong. They are dominant in travel and tourist services, controlling about 60% of the total. Next come cargo transportation and handling, making up 25% of the total. With assets accounting for 12% of the total in Hong Kong, The Bank of China Group has become the second-largest banking group after HSBC Holdings, a British giant. In terms of bank deposits, China controlled about 25% of the total in the territory. China-owned interests are estimated to hold 5-10% of the territory's property. The number of Mainland Chinese enterprises listed on the Hong Kong stock exchange has doubled in two years, representing 8.2% of the total market capitalization." (p235)

Kuan, Hsin-Chi. "Does Hong Kong Have a Future?" Security Dialogue v28 n2 Jun 1997. p233-236. (ISSN0967-0106).

INVESTMENTS, FOREIGN--CUBA

"Companies from Spain, Canada, Mexico, France, Israel, and many other countries have formed joint ventures and signed economic association agreements with the Cuban government, with a typical participation of up to 49 percent. In late 1996, Cuban ministers reported 260 registered joint ventures from 43 countries, present in 34 economic sectors (28 in mining, 25 in petroleum, 56 in the general industrial sector, and 34 in tourism)." (p52)

Werlau, Maria C. "Foreign Investment in Cuba: The Limits of Commercial Engagement." World Affairs v160 n2 Fall 1997. p51-69. (ISSN0043-8200).

INVESTMENTS, FOREIGN--DEVELOPING COUNTRIES (v26)

The share of world foreign direct investment "going to developing countries jumped from an average of 24 percent between 1983 and 1987 to 32 percent in 1995. Equity and bond flows grew even faster, rising from 0.5 percent of GDP in 1983 to 1989 to between 2 and 4 percent from 1994 to 1996....Between 1989 and 1992...72 percent of total FDI flows to developing countries went to only 10 countries (China, Mexico, Malaysia, Argentina, Thailand, Indonesia, Brazil, Nigeria, Venezuela, and South Korea)....Between 1989 and 1993, only 10 countries received 90 percent of the total gross portfolio investments flowing to the developing world (Mexico, Brazil, Argentina, Hungary, South Korea, Greece, Turkey, China, Venezuela, and Thailand)." (p385)

Heredia, Blanca. "Prosper or Perish?: Development in the Age of Global Capital." Current History v96 n613 Nov 1997. p383-388. (ISSN0011-3530).

INVESTMENTS, FOREIGN--EGYPT (v26)

INVESTMENTS, FOREIGN--EUROPE (v26)

INVESTMENTS, FOREIGN--HONG KONG

"At the end of 1995, the stock of inward direct investments in the non-manufacturing sectors of Hong Kong totalled $487.3 billion, 6% higher than the amount at the end of 1994, according to the results of the latest round of a survey on external investments in non-manufacturing sectors released...by the Census and Statistics Department. Analysed by individual investor country/territory, the United Kingdom was the largest investor country, accounting for 29% ($143.1 billion) of the total at the end of 1995. This was followed by China and Japan, which accounted for 21% ($104.6 billion) and 14% ($69.9 billion) of the total respectively. The United States of America was the fourth largest investor country and accounted for 12% ($58.8 billion) of the total. Taken together, these four investor countries accounted for around 77% of the total value of the stock of inward direct investments in the non-manufacturing sectors of Hong Kong....Analysed by business sector, banks and deposit-taking companies attracted the largest share (40% or $193.6 billion) of the total value of the stock of inward direct investments in the non-manufacturing sectors at the end of 1995."

Hong Kong. Census and Statistics Department. "External Investments in HK's Non-Manufacturing Sectors." Press Release 27 Mar 1997. document-level access: <http://www.info.gov.hk/censtatd/hkstat/press/exinv95.htm>

INVESTMENTS, FOREIGN--JAPAN--UNITED STATES

"Japan is the world's biggest donor country in volume, but it is second to last among major donors in terms of ODA [official development assistance] as a proportion of gross national product (GNP). Its ratio of ODA to GNP fell from 0.28 per cent in 1995 to 0.20 in 1996, the biggest decline among major donors. But this was still ahead of the US, which stayed in last place with a ratio of 0.12 per cent, up from 0.10 per cent in 1995. In US dollar terms, Japanese ODA fell some 35 per cent in 1996 to $9.6 bn [billion]...." (p26)

"Africa in Brief: Japan's Aid Cuts to Hit Africa and Some UN Agencies Also." Africa Recovery v11 n2 Oct 1997. p26.

INVESTMENTS, FOREIGN--MOLDOVA--RUSSIA --UKRAINE

In Russia, foreign direct investment "in the food sector has increased over the last 3 years, from less than 5 percent of total FDI in 1994 to around one-third in 1996 (as a share of total foreign investment, the food sector accounts for around 12 percent). In Ukraine, the share of total FDI in the food sector is around 10 percent, while in Moldova, it reportedly accounts for more than a quarter of total FDI." (p3)

U.S. Dept. of Agriculture. Economic Research Service. "Spotlight on Foreign Direct Investment (FDI)." Newly Independent States & Baltics Update: Agriculture and Trade Report 20 Oct 1997. p1-10.

INVESTMENTS, FOREIGN--RUSSIA

"In 1996 foreign investors put as little as $2 billion into Russian operations....Proctor and Gamble, General Electric, Mars, Polaroid, Kodak, Otis Elevator (a division of United Technology), Coca-Cola, Pepsi-Cola, McDonald's, and all the tobacco companies have sales to Russia that often exceed $100 million a year....In the case of Mars, for example, after sales increased from $200,000 in 1990 to $300 million in 1993, the company decided that to guarantee itself enough product to sell within Russia, it had to invest $150 million in the construction of two factories not far from Moscow. Once built the factories became a target for all forms of government extortion, including 18 different taxes totaling $60 million in 1996." (p317)

Goldman, Marshall I. "Russia's Reform Effort: Is There Growth at the End of the Tunnel?" Current History v96 n612 Oct 1997. p313-318. (ISSN0011-3530).

INVESTMENTS, FOREIGN--UNITED STATES (v26)

Product sales from affiliates of U.S.-owned companies in the Asia-Pacific Economic Cooperation "region totaled $40 billion in 1996, 67 percent higher than in 1990, and one-third of all U.S. food industry affiliate sales abroad. Affiliate sales are supported by the U.S. cumulative foreign direct investment of $10 billion in the APEC food processing industries. FDI is defined as the book value of APEC food processing establishments in which U.S. firms have at least a 10-percent equity share. More than 50 of the United States' largest food processing companies have affiliates in the APEC region...." (p26)

Bolling, Chris/Handy, Charles/Neff, Steve/U.S. Dept. of Agriculture. Economic Research Service. "Trade Environment in APEC: U.S. Direct Investment in the APEC Food Processing Sector." APEC: International Agriculture and Trade Reports Situation and Outlook Series Aug 1997. p26-28.

U.S. "foreign direct investment (FDI) represents the largest component of private capital going to developing countries--around 50 percent, or $80 billion, in 1994....Countries in sub-Saharan Africa attracted only $3 billion in 1994. In fact, seven countries--Brazil, Argentina, Malaysia, Mexico, Indonesia, Thailand, and especially China--receive more than half of all FDI to the developing world." (p17-18)

U.S. Congressional Budget Office. "The Flow of Foreign Aid and Private Capital to Developing Countries." The Role of Foreign Aid in Development May 1997. p7-19.

INVESTMENTS, JAPANESE--CHINA (v26)

IODINE DEFICIENCY DISEASES (v26)

IODINE DEFICIENCY DISEASES--INDONESIA --CHILDREN (v26)

IODINE DEFICIENCY DISEASES--PAKISTAN

"Prior to a 1990-92 study, Pakistani officials believed IDD [iodine deficiency disorder] was a problem only in the mountainous Northwest Territories, where more than 80 percent of the people are at risk. The study, however, revealed a troubling truth: 64 percent are at risk of IDD in Quetta, 76 percent in Peshawar, even 76 percent in the capital city of Islamabad....But progress has been made. In 1994, only 2 percent of Pakistan's households had access to iodized salt. In 1996, 23 percent could obtain it." (p9)

"Intercom: Pakistan Seeks to Protect Its Population." Kiwanis v82 n8 Sep 1997. p9. (ISSN0162-5276).

IRAN--POPULATION

"Iran's 1996 census found the nation's population totaled 60 million--about 6 million to 7 million lower than estimates used by the UN and other international organizations....The percent of Iran's population under age 5 dropped from 18 percent in 1986 to 10 percent in 1996." (p4)

Roudi, Farzaneh. "Surprising Decline in Iran's Growth Rates." Population Today v25 n11 Nov 1997. p4-5. (ISSN0749-2448).

IRAQ--ECONOMIC CONDITIONS--SOCIAL CONDITIONS (v26)

IRAQ--HEALTH AND HYGIENE (v26)

IRAQ--SOCIAL CONDITIONS (v26)

IRAQ-KUWAIT CRISIS, 1990-1991

see PERSIAN GULF WAR, 1991

IRAQ-KUWAIT CRISIS, 1990-1991--UNITED STATES --VETERANS--HEALTH AND HYGIENE (v26)

IRELAND--COMMERCE

In Ireland, "exports of goods and services rose at a significantly lower level in volume (10.0%) compared with the average of the previous two years (16.9%). However, imports also rose at a lower rate (11.4%) in 1996 compared with the average for the previous two years (15.3%). The gap between exports and imports at constant 1990 prices continued to widen (by 215m [million] [pounds sterling] in 1996) but at a slower rate than in the previous two years when it increased on average by 980m [pounds sterling]. The biggest impact on the trade balance has been a sharp increase in service imports (including royalties). Service imports in 1996 exceeded those of 1995 by 1.154bl [billion] [pounds sterling] or 19%."

Ireland. Central Statistics Office. "National Income and Expenditure 1996 and Regional Accounts 1993." Press Release 19 Jun 1997. document-level access: <http://www.cso.ie/pressreleases/prelnie96.html>

IRELAND--ECONOMIC CONDITIONS

In Ireland, "Gross National Product (GNP) increased by 6.9% at constant prices in 1996, according to National Income and Expenditure results for 1996, released by the Central Statistics Office....The corresponding increase in Gross Domestic Product (GDP) was 7.8%. The preliminary estimates also show that the strong growth in the volume of GDP and GNP have maintained the trends over the previous two years where the average increase in GDP was 8.3%, and 7.8% in GNP. Contributing to the rise in the 1996 aggregates was boutant consumer spending which increased by 6.3% in volume over 1995. There was also a sizeable increase in investment in capital goods (15.9% in volume terms)."

Ireland. Central Statistics Office. "National Income and Expenditure 1996 and Regional Accounts 1993." Press Release 19 Jun 1997. document-level access: <http://www.cso.ie/pressreleases/prelnie96.html>

In Ireland, "the weekly expenditure of the average household was 312 [pounds sterling] in 1994-95, compared with 223 [pounds sterling] in 1987--an increase of 40%, a survey released...by the Central Statistics Office reveals....The survey shows that households in the top income group spent 664 [pounds sterling] a week in 1994-95 while those at the other end of the scale spent 87 [pounds sterling] a week. This compares with 1987's weekly expenditure of 465 [pounds sterling] in the high income homes and 70 [pounds sterling] a week in the low income ones. The weekly expenditure of 87 [pounds sterling] in the poorest households in 1994-95 can be viewed against as average household expenditure of 312 [pounds sterling]. However, it should be noted that the lowest income households were smaller, having only 1.2 people, compared with the highest income households which had 4.3 people. Basic items like food, and fuel and light accounted for 43% of the expenditures in the poorest households...."

Ireland. Central Statistics Office. "Household Budget Survey 1994-95 Volume 1." Press Release 31 Jul 1997. document-level access: <http://www.cso.ie/pressreleases/prelhbsv1.html>

IRELAND--EMPLOYMENT

In Ireland, "there was an increase of 41,000 in the number at work and a drop of 12,000 in unemployment in [the] year to April 1997, the annual 'Labour Force Survey' from the Central Statistics Office (CSO) revealed....The 1997 results compare with a rise of 49,000 in the number at work and a drop of 1,000 in unemployment in the previous year. The report shows that the increase of 41,000 in the numbers at work in the year to April 1997 was comprised of 22,000 men and 19,000 women. However, the fall of 8,000 in male unemployment was greater than that of just over 4,000 for females....The four-year period since 1993 has been one of exceptional employment growth with a total increase in employment of 186,000, the CSO publication shows."

Ireland. Central Statistics Office. "1997 Labour Force Survey Report." Press Release 29 Oct 1997. document-level access: <http://www.cso.ie/pressreleases/prellfs97.html>

IRELAND--MANUFACTURES

In 1995, "almost 36% of the output of Irish owned manufacturing firms was exported compared to 89% for foreign owned firms, 23% of the value of materials purchased by Irish owned firms was imported compared to 67% for foreign owned firms; The gross output of Irish owned manufacturing firms increased to 11,686m [million] [pounds sterling]. However, this value as a percentage of the total gross output (35%), represents a drop of nearly four percentage points since 1994. The numbers employed in the Irish owned manufacturing firms increased by 7,000 to 116,700...."

Ireland. Central Statistics Office. "Census of Industrial Production 1995." Press Release 18 Nov 1997. document-level access: <http://www.cso.ie/pressreleases/prelcip95.html>

IRELAND--SOCIAL CONDITIONS (v26)

IRRIGATION (v26)

IRRIGATION--CALIFORNIA (v26)

IRRIGATION--CHINA

"In China today, the largest share of water for irrigation and drainage comes from diesel and electric powered pumps. Currently, there are over 9 million pumps being used in China to pump water. Diesel engines provide power for about 48 percent of the water pumped. Electric motors account for the remaining 52 percent. In 1996, rural electric power consumption totaled 183.4 billion kWh [kilowatt hours], presumably a good portion of this electrical energy is used by farmers to irrigate and drain their fields." (p17)

Crook, Frederick W./U.S. Dept. of Agriculture. Economic Research Service. "Input Supplies Adequate for 1997." China: International Agriculture and Trade Reports Situation and Outlook Series Jun 1997. p16-18.

IRRIGATION FARMING

"Between 1950 and 1990, the amount of irrigated land in the world increased from 94 million to 240 million hectares, or 2.4 percent per year. Between 1990 and 1994, however, the official data show irrigated area increasing by only another 9 million hectares, or 0.9 percent per year." (p11) "Japan, which has the highest yield among the major rice producers, irrigates 99 percent of its riceland...--as does South Korea, which ranks second. In Bangladesh, where the irrigated share falls to 24 percent, farmers harvest less than half as much rice per hectare as the Japanese or Koreans do." (p13)

Brown, Lester R. "Can We Raise Grain Yields Fast Enough?" World Watch v10 n4 Jul-Aug 1997. p8-17. (ISSN0896-0615).

IRRIGATION FARMING--AFRICA

"The Food and Agriculture Organization estimates that in 1990, only 2 per cent of sub-Saharan Africa's arable land was irrigated. With an annual rate of population growth at nearly 3 per cent, crop yields must be increased significantly if countries are to advance towards food self-sufficiency....But only 4 per cent of the approximately 4 trillion cubic metres of renewable water available is currently being used, due to lack of appropriate infrastructure and technical and financial means." (p22)

Novicki, Margaret A. "UN System-Wide Special Initiative on Africa: Improving Africa's Water Supply." Africa Recovery v11 n2 Oct 1997. p22-24.

IRRITABLE COLON--UNITED STATES

In the U.S., "many patients who complain of irritable bowel syndrome (IBS) were young victims of sexual assault, according to Sherry Falsetti, PhD. She, together with R. Bruce Lydiard, MD, PhD, conducted what they call the first nationally representative survey of men and women with IBS....Preliminary data from 87 persons with IBS revealed that 43% had been sexually assaulted before age 13, and more than 48% had been physically assaulted. Findings also indicate that 12% of the patients who were seeking treatment for IBS had experienced post-traumatic stress disorder in the previous 6 months, and that 13% suffered from panic disorder." (p26)

"Clinical News: Irritable Bowel Syndrome Is Often Linked to Sexual Assault; Stress Reduction Can Be Beneficial." Modern Medicine v65 n7 Jul 1997. p26. (ISSN0026-8070).

ISLAMIC RELIGIOUS EDUCATION--UNITED STATES

In the U.S., "about 200 Islamic schools educate an estimated 20,000 students, said the Department of Education and the North American Council for Islamic Education. The number of schools is a 182-percent increase since 1993....Just one of every 100 private schools nationwide is Islamic." (p6 secA)

Shepardson, David. "News Special: Education: Faith, Values Drive Growth of Islamic Schools: New Academy Opens as Local Enrollment Booms." Detroit News 15 Sep 1997. p1,6 secA.

ISRAEL--COMMERCE--UNITED STATES (v26)

ISRAEL--ECONOMIC CONDITIONS (v26)

"Firms of US and British stockbrokers bought up more than $600m [million] of Israeli shares in 1995, a symptom of financial stability. Growth was at 6% per annum between 1992 and 1996 and growth in exports was at 11%. The drop in military expenditure, following the peace negotiations, was from 30% of the budget in 1982 to 7% in 1995 which also contributed to the expansion of the Israeli economy." (p6)

"International News: Israel: Bad Politics." Freedom (Anarchist Fortnightly) v58 n22 15 Nov 1997. p6. (ISSN0016-0504).

In Israel, "inflation continues to run at 10 percent annually--high by Western standards, but low for Israel....Until recently, the jobless rate was about 6 percent, low on a European scale. Now it appears to be climbing. Israel's foreign currency reserves have risen to an unprecedented $16 billion, enough to cover all of the country's foreign currency needs for six months....European countries draw tens of millions of foreign tourists a year; Israel barely gets 2 million." (p55)

Caspi, Arie. "Viewpoint: The Lightweight." Jerusalem Report v8 n4 26 Jun 1997. p55. (ISSN0792-6049).

"Israel now has one of the highest GDP growth rates among Western economies. Its per capita GDP today exceeds $15,000, compared to $3,400 twenty years ago, placing it 20th among 200 countries in the world. Israel now spends less than 10% of its GDP on defense as compared to 30% in the 1970s." (p274)

Aruri, Naseer H. "Netanyahu's Real Peace." Peace Review v9 n2 Jun 1997. p273-278. (ISSN1040-2659).

ISRAEL--JORDAN--MOROCCO--TUNISIA--ECONOMIC CONDITIONS (v26)

ISRAEL--PALESTINIAN ARABS--PUBLIC OPINION (v26)

ISRAEL--POLITICS AND GOVERNMENT--PUBLIC OPINION (v26)

ISRAEL--PUBLIC OPINION

"On the occasion of Israel's 49th birthday, the YEDIOT AHARONOT newspaper commissioned a comprehensive poll of the country's populace. Asked where in all the world they'd live, given the choice, 79 percent answered Israel. Fully 88 percent were satisfied with their families, 87 percent with their jobs, and 91 percent with their lives in general. Only 30 percent said they smoked, and an impressive 57 percent of the Jews said they observe kashrut. One question that elicited an intriguing range of responses was, 'What about Israel annoys you the most?' One percent said Arabs. Another 1 percent, corruption. Two percent each complained about the hot weather and the deep divisions in society. Four percent said road safety, 8 percent the government, and in first place, with 13 percent: 'The Israeli mentality.'" (p50)

Schoffman, Stuart. "From the Mezzanine: The Best Country on Earth." Jerusalem Report v8 n4 26 Jun 1997. p50. (ISSN0792-6049).

ISRAEL--SOCIAL CONDITIONS (v26)

ITALY--COMMERCE--JAPAN (v26)

ITALY--ECONOMIC CONDITIONS (v26)

ITALY--EMIGRATION AND IMMIGRATION (v26)

IVORY INDUSTRY--AFRICA (v26)

Last year, Mr. Mike Faye, director of the Congo program of the Wildlife Conservation Society, "and a US television crew came across 200 [elephant] carcasses, faces hacked away, in a clearing in a northern Congo forest....Ten elephants have been killed in the past 15 months on the Kenya-Tanzania border....Today poachers with AK-47s take out entire elephant families, including nursing mothers. Data from...[an Amboseli

Reserve field study of elephant behavior] show that no infant calves survive a mother's death; only 30 percent orphaned at ages 2 to 5 and 50 percent orphaned at ages 5 to 10 make it." (p18)

Spence, Betty. "Opinion/Essays: Elephants and the Ivory Trade." The Christian Science Monitor v89 n139 13 Jun 1997. p18. The Christian Science Monitor search engine: <http://www.csmonitor.com/plweb-cgi/iops1.pl> To retrieve this article, enter the following search: ED=19970613 AND trade. In the "retrieved list," click the title that matches this record. (ISSN0882-7729).

IVORY INDUSTRY--SOUTH AFRICA

"Delegates of 140 countries have agreed to allow three countries to resume limited trade in ivory and other elephant products....Those three countries, unlike other countries farther north, demonstrated in their proposals that they have large, increasing elephant populations (80,000 in Botswana, over 60,000 in Zimbabwe, and 7,000 in Namibia), and that those populations were both outstripping the carrying capacity of their land and coming into growing conflict with their human populations....An experimental quota will be allocated for each country: 25.3 tons for Botswana, 20 tons for Zimbabwe, and 13.8 tons for Namibia." (p9)

Sugal, Cheri. "Environmental Intelligence: Elephants of Southern Africa Must Now 'Pay Their Way.'" World Watch v10 n5 Sep-Oct 1997. p9. (ISSN0896-0615).

JAILS--UNITED STATES

In the U.S., "those awaiting trial constitute 51% of the national jail population; posttrial inmates make up the other 49%....Of the 3,304 jails in the United States in 1993, 74% were run by counties, 22% by cities, and 4% were administered jointly. A 1994 mid-year census revealed a total national jail population of 479,757 persons (Bureau of Justice Statistics, 1994). The average length of stay in jails in 1993 was 63 days for pretrial detainees and 129 days for sentenced inmates (Criminal Justice Institute, 1994). Most convicted criminals (67%-75%) serve their sentences in jails." (p421)

Walsh, Joseph/Bricout, John. "Article: Services for Persons with Mental Illness in Jail: Implications for Family Involvement." Families in Society v78 n4 Jul-Aug 1997. p420-428. (ISSN1044-3894).

JAMAICA--ECONOMIC CONDITIONS

When inflation in Jamaica "reached 80 percent in 1991, the government began a stabilization program that cut price rises in half the subsequent year. Inflation now stands at 15 percent....A rise in the demand for Jamaican bank deposits helped finance a domestic lending boom, which in turn supported an expansion of domestic spending that brought the current account deficit to nearly 8 percent of GDP in 1996." (p9)

Drosdoff, Daniel. "The Region: Reform: Same Tune, Different Steps." IDB v24 n9-10 Sep-Oct 1997. p8-9. (ISSN0145-2274).

JAPAN--ARMED FORCES--APPROPRIATIONS AND EXPENDITURES (v26)

JAPAN--COMMERCE (v26)

JAPAN--ECONOMIC CONDITIONS (v26)

"The Japanese economy recorded a growth rate of 3.7 percent in 1996....The yen fell more than 30 percent against the dollar from 80 yen per dollar in mid-1995 to 127 in March 1996. Since then the yen has remained relatively weak and is currently around 120 per dollar." (p6)

Jerardo, Alberto/Huang, Sophia Wu/U.S. Dept. of Agriculture. Economic Research Service. "Regional Overviews: APEC to Resume Healthy Growth." APEC: International Agriculture and Trade Reports Situation and Outlook Series Aug 1997. p6-8.

In 1992, "the current account surplus for Japan--essentially Japan's net foreign investment--totaled $121 billion, compared with $70 billion for all other surplus countries combined....In Japan, the expected retirement period for men nearly doubled between 1975 and 1990--from 4.4 to 8.7 years." (p4)

Mason, Andrew. "Population and the Asian Economic Miracle." Asia-Pacific Population & Policy n43 Oct 1997. p1-4. (ISSN0891-6683).

"No major nation suffers from deflation, but Japan comes close. For the past six years, Japanese consumer prices have risen an average of 1 percent annually, the stock market has plunged 50 percent, and economic growth has been minimal. Retail sales are down 4.5 percent in 1997, and, in the second quarter, gross domestic product fell at an 11.4 percent annual rate." (p65)

Glassman, James K. "Commentary: If Prices Fall Too Far, Duck." U.S. News & World Report v123 n16 27 Oct 1997. p65. article-level access: <http://www.usnews.com/usnews/issue/971027/27GLAS.HTM> (ISSN0041-5537).

JAPAN--EMPLOYMENT

"Construction currently employs about 7 million workers, more than 10 percent of Japan's labor force, while the financial industry accounts for 2.5 million....Japan's jobless rate is already near its all-time high of 3.5 percent. US unemployment in October was 4.7 percent." (p7)

Nomura, Takehiko. "International: Bankruptcies Jolt Japan toward Freer Markets." The Christian Science Monitor v90 n2 26 Nov 1997. p7. The Christian Science Monitor search engine: <http://www.csmonitor.com/plweb-cgi/iops1.pl> To retrieve this article, enter the following search: ED=19971126 AND markets. In the "retrieved list," click the title that matches this record. (ISSN0882-7729).

JAPAN--FOREIGN RELATIONS--UNITED STATES --PUBLIC OPINION (v26)

JAPAN--MANUFACTURES (v26)

JAPAN--SOCIAL CONDITIONS (v26)

JERUSALEM (ISRAEL)--POLITICS AND GOVERNMENT --PUBLIC OPINION

In Jerusalem, a poll in the Hebrew daily MA'ARIV, in which readers were asked to compare the two governments of Benjamin Netanyahu and Yitzhak Rabin, "showed that 52 percent believed the Rabin-Peres administration was 'better'; 29 percent chose the current administration. Asked to rank ministers' performance, the public in the MA'ARIV poll placed Yitzhak Mordechai far ahead--with a mark of 7.96 out of 10--followed by Communications Minister Limor Livnat on 6.64 and Internal Security Minister Avigdor Kahalani on 6.58. Netanyahu placed 15th, with a score of 5.17. Last, with 4.23, was Justice Minister Tsachi Hanegbi." (p18)

Hirschberg, Peter/Shaviv, Miriam/Eichler, Jeremy. "The Government's First-Year Report Card." Jerusalem Report v8 n4 26 Jun 1997. p18. (ISSN0792-6049).

JET SKIS

see PERSONAL WATERCRAFT

JEWELRY--UNITED STATES (v26)

JEWELRY STORES--UNITED STATES (v26)

JEWISH DAY SCHOOLS--MICHIGAN

"Enrollment at six southeastern Michigan Jewish day schools this year tops 2,200, an increase of about 1,000 over the last decade." (p1 secC) Hillel Day School in Farmington Hills, "Metro Detroit's only non-Orthodox Jewish day school, has undergone a nearly 40-percent growth spurt in the last decade, from 519 students to 712. This year alone, its enrollment is up by 28 students. That is comparable to the largest Metro Detroit Orthodox day school, Yeshiva Beth Yehudah in Southfield, which has grown from 476 to 755, and is up by 27 students this year....Enrollment has fluctuated more from year to year at Akiva Hebrew Day School in Lathrup Village, which now has 296 students in K-12." (p4 secC)

Heinlein, Gary. "Metro: News Special: Education: Culture Drives Jewish School Growth." Detroit News 28 Nov 1997. p1,4 secC.

JEWISH DAY SCHOOLS--UNITED STATES

In the U.S., "Jewish day school enrollment has grown from about 130,000 to 190,000....The increase actually has been steady for more than 30 years, mostly at traditional Orthodox Jewish schools, said David Shluker of the Jewish Education Service of North America....Orthodox Jews...now have more than 500 day schools in the United States...." (p1 secC) "'Over a dozen new Reform Jewish day schools have opened in the U.S.,' said [Mark] Smiley, immediate past president of a national association of Conservative Jewish day schools." (p4 secC)

Heinlein, Gary. "Metro: News Special: Education: Culture Drives Jewish School Growth." Detroit News 28 Nov 1997. p1,4 secC.

JEWISH SECTS--ISRAEL

In Israel, ultraorthodox Jews, or the "haredim," "constitute perhaps 8 percent of the population but make up a fifth of the country's poor. In all, 47 percent of them live in poverty. They also have Israel's highest birthrates. Half of all first graders in Jerusalem are 'haredi.'" (p38) "According to a study just released by Hebrew University, no developed nation between 1970 and 1993 had a smaller share of 25-to-54-year-old males in the work force than did Israel. The study found nearly 15 percent of Israeli children living in homes where prime-aged males did not work. Meanwhile, yeshiva attendance for males has nearly doubled since 1980." (p39)

Makovsky, David. "World Report: Religion on Welfare." U.S. News & World Report v123 n4 28 Jul 1997. p37-39. article-level access: <http://www.usnews.com/usnews/issue/970728/28UNDE.HTM> (ISSN0041-5537).

JEWISH THEOLOGICAL SEMINARIES

see RABBINICAL SEMINARIES

JEWS--EMIGRATION AND IMMIGRATION

Ex-Union of Soviet Socialist Republic Jewish emigration for August "1997 compared with 1996 data: In...[August] 1996, the total was 7,112, of whom 5,090 went to Israel and 2,022 to the USA. In...[August] 1997, the total fell to 5,910, of whom 4,371 went to Israel and 1,539 to the USA." (p47)

Katz, Lyber. "Around the World: Abroad." Jewish Currents v51 n10 Nov 1997. p46-47. (ISSN0021-0639).

JEWS--EMIGRATION AND IMMIGRATION--FORMER SOVIET REPUBLICS (v26)

JEWS--FORMER SOVIET REPUBLICS (v26)

JEWS--HONG KONG (v26)

JEWS--ISRAEL--ATTITUDES (v26)

JEWS--PALESTINIAN ARABS--ISRAEL--JERUSALEM --POPULATION

The Jewish population in Jerusalem "in 1967 was around 198,000, but it increased to 393,000 by 1993. The Palestinian population...doubled from 69,000 in 1967, to 152,000 in 1993....By 1990, 135,000, roughly one-third of the Israeli Jewish population of Jerusalem, lived on estates and in neighborhoods within the annexed areas." (p63)

Talhami, Ghada Hashem. "Palestinians in Jerusalem: The Denationalization of a Community." Middle East Policy v5 n3 Sep 1997. p57-68. (ISSN1061-1924).

JEWS--PENNSYLVANIA--PHILADELPHIA--POPULATION

A study of the distribution of Jewish population in the Philadelphia region, conducted by Ukeles Associates Inc. was reported in the June 19, 1997 JEWISH EXPONENT. It found that "while in 1983 54% of the Jewish population lived in the city, in 1996 only 40% still lived there. There has also been a significant drop of 16.7% in these 13 years in the total Jewish population in the region, from 240,000 to 200,000, although the number of households dropped only by 6.7%, because the average household decreased from 2.33 persons to 2.06." (p45-46)

Katz, Lyber. "Around the World: At Home." Jewish Currents v51 n8 Sep 1997. p45-46. (ISSN0021-0639).

JEWS--POLITICS AND GOVERNMENT--UNITED STATES (v26)

JEWS--POPULATION

"World Jewish population was estimated in 1995 (latest available data) in the AMERICAN JEWISH YEAR BOOK, 1997 at 13,059,000, an increase of 57,300 over 1994. Of these, 96.3% are in the following 10 countries: 1. United States, 5,900,000--2.2% of the U.S. population/45.2% of world Jewry; 2. Israel, 4,549,500--81%/34.8%; 3. France, 525,000--0.9%/4%; 4. Canada, 362,000--1.2%/2.8%; 5. Russia, 360,000--0.2%/2.8%; 6. England, 292,000--0.5%/2.2%; 7. Argentina, 206,000--0.6%/1.6%; 8. Ukraine, 180,000--0.4%/1.4%; 9. Brazil, 100,000--0.1%/0.8%; 10. South Africa, 95,000--0.2%/0.7%." (p46)

Katz, Lyber. "Around the World: Abroad." Jewish Currents v51 n10 Nov 1997. p46-47. (ISSN0021-0639).

JEWS--UNITED STATES (v26)

JEWS--UNITED STATES--ATTITUDES

"The '1997 Annual Survey of American Jewish Opinion' interviewed a 'representative sample of 1,160 adult Jewish respondents' by telephone Feb. 3-11; 39% thought anti-Semitism will increase over the next few years while 48% thought it will remain the same. The Religious Right and Muslims were viewed as the most anti-Semitic with Fundamentalist Protestants with 30% and Blacks following with 27%; 60% thought abortion should be 'legal under any circumstances' and 80% favor the death penalty; 61% expressed support for the Netanyahu government, but this was before the Har Homa controversy." (p31)

Dimow, Joseph. "Inside the Jewish Community: Surveys--Good or Bad." Jewish Currents v51 n8 Sep 1997. p31. (ISSN0021-0639).

JEWS--UNITED STATES--CHARITIES (v26)

JEWS--UNITED STATES--POPULATION (v26)

"The 1996 Jewish population in the USA is estimated at 5,900,000 (2.2% of the approximate total population of 262,755,000), according to data compiled by Jeffrey Scheckner for the AMERICAN JEWISH YEAR BOOK 1997, Vol. 97, published by the American Jewish Committee....The states with a Jewish population of over 100,000, their percentage in the state's total population, and changes from 1995, are, in order of magnitude: 1. NY, 1,652,000, 9.1%, up 7,000; 2. CA, 921,000, 2.9%, down 1,000; 3. FL, 644,000, 4.5%, up 3,000; 4. NJ, 435,000, 5.5%, down 1,000; 5. PA, 325,000, 2.7%, down 5,000....The metropolitan areas with major Jewish concentrations and their percentage of the USA Jewish populations are: 1. Greater N.Y. Metro area--1,937,000, 32.9%....L.A. Metro area--590,000, 10%; 3. Southeast Florida--533,000, 12.6%; 4. Philadelphia Metro area--280,000, 4.8%; 5. Chicago Metro area--263,000, 4.5%...." (p45-46)

Katz, Lyber. "Around the World: At Home." Jewish Currents v51 n10 Nov 1997. p45-46. (ISSN0021-0639).

JEWS--UNITED STATES--SOCIAL CONDITIONS

In the U.S., "almost 90 percent of college-age Jews are enrolled in higher education. Per-capita Jewish income is almost double that of non-Jews. But one-third of blacks live in poverty. One-third of young black men are in jail or on parole. Half the black men between ages 24 and 35 lack full time jobs." (p31)

Beiser, Vince. "Jewish World: Cover Story: Farrakhan Talks to the Jews." Jerusalem Report v8 n4 26 Jun 1997. p26-27,30-32. (ISSN0792-6049).

JEWS, AMERICAN--ISRAEL--POLITICS AND GOVERNMENT--ATTITUDES

"According to a new poll, about 80 percent of American Jews agree with a U.S. call for Israel to at least temporarily stop building additional homes for Jews in the West Bank. The poll, released September 29 [1997] by the New York-based Israel Policy Forum, found 57 percent of American Jews also have a favorable opinion of Israeli Prime Minister Benjamin Netanyahu, despite his vow to continue constructing new West Bank housing...." (p969) "Eighty-nine percent said they either strongly or somewhat support the [peace] process....Fifty-six percent said they believe the Oslo accords, the basis for the Israeli-Palestinian peace process, are 'failing but salvageable,' while 18 percent said the accords are 'completely dead.'" (p970)

"News: U.S. Jews: 'Timeout' on New Settlements." Christian Century v114 n30 29 Oct 1997. p969-970. (ISSN0009-5281).

In mid-September 1997 "the Israel Policy Forum polled 1,198 American Jews right after...[U.S. Secretary of State Madeleine] Albright's first effort to bring together both sides in Israel. Asking each person polled a list of 53 questions, the professional pollsters issued their findings, of which an extensive excerpt covered a half-page in the FORWARD of Oct. 17....[A sample of the replies were as follows:] 1) 83%--Israel cannot have 'real security without peace with its neighbors'; 13% thought it could. 2) 68% 'strongly support...the Israeli-Palestinian peace process,' 2% 'somewhat support' it; only 8% oppose it. 3) Has Netanyahu 'done enough to promote the cause of peace?'--only 18% thought he had; 71% said 'he could do more.' 4) About U.S. government policy on Arafat: 81% said 'it is important to influence Arafat to take steps towards peace,' but 16% said it was 'wrong for the U.S. to push Arafat.'" (p3)

"Editorial: Working to Break Mideast Impasse." Jewish Currents v51 n11 Dec 1997. p3. (ISSN0021-0639).

JOB ACTIONS

see LABOR DISPUTES

JOB CREATION--CANADA

"In the last four years under this Prime Minister the Canadian public has created over 970,000 new jobs. This year under this Prime Minister the Canadian public has created over 260,000 new jobs, the vast majority of those in the private sector." (p24)

Martin, Paul (MP-PQ). "Oral Question Period: Employment." Canada. Parliament. House of Commons. Debates. v135 n3 24 Sep 1997. p23-25. section-level access: <http://www.parl.gc.ca/36/1/parlbus/chambus/house/debates/003_1997-09-24/han003-e.htm#LINK47> (ISSN0704-5603). (X3-361E).

JOB CREATION--SINGAPORE (v26)

JOB CREATION--UNITED STATES (v26)

JOB DISCRIMINATION

see DISCRIMINATION IN EMPLOYMENT

JOB HUNTING--AUSTRALIA (v26)

JOB PROMOTIONS

see PROMOTIONS

JOB SAFETY

see INDUSTRIAL SAFETY

JOB STRESS--COSTS (v26)

JORDAN--PALESTINIAN ARABS (v26)

JORDAN RIVER--PALESTINE

"One of the three principal sources of the Jordan River (the other two being the Dan River in Israel proper and the Hasbani River originating in Lebanon), [is] the Banias spring [which] lies at the base of the northwestern Golan escarpment....The average annual volume of water provided by the Banias to the Jordan River is 120 million cubic meters (MCM), or about 20 percent of the Jordan's flow as it enters Lake Tiberias." (p130)

Hof, Frederic C. "The Water Dimension of Golan Heights Negotiations." Middle East Policy v5 n2 May 1997. p129-141. (ISSN1061-1924).

JOURNALISM

see BROADCAST JOURNALISM; NEWS AGENCIES

JOURNALISM--UNITED STATES--PUBLIC OPINION (v26)

JOURNALISTS

see also COOKERY--UNITED STATES--NEWSPAPER EDITORS; FOOD HANDLING--UNITED STATES--NEWSPAPER EDITORS

JOURNALISTS--CRIMES AGAINST

"Since 1988, 173 journalists have been killed in Latin America, according to the Washington-based Interamerican Press Society. That's almost one-third of the 600 journalists that the Paris-based Reporters sans Frontieres says have been killed worldwide in the last 10 years....'Of those 600 killings, 95 percent were never punished, and most simply went uninvestigated,' says Robert Menard, secretary-general of Reporters sans Frontieres." (p7)

LaFranchi, Howard. "International: Risky Business: Press Perils Mar Latin America Freedom." The Christian Science Monitor v89 n187 21 Aug 1997. p1,7. The Christian Science Monitor search engine: <http://www.csmonitor.com/plweb-cgi/iops1.pl> To retrieve this article, enter the following search: ED=19970821 AND freedom. In the "retrieved list," click the title that matches this record. (ISSN0882-7729).

JOURNALISTS--DISTRICT OF COLUMBIA--SOCIAL CONDITIONS

"A recent survey of 320 men and women journalists working in Washington, D.C., conducted by the Northwestern University Survey Laboratory, found that nearly half the women--45 percent--had never been married, compared to just 22 percent of the men. It also found that 64 percent of the women reporters have never had a child, compared with 40 percent of the males. The average age of the reporters surveyed was 42." (p5)

Walsh, Catherine. "Perspectives." America v176 n18 24 May 1997. p5. (ISSN0002-7049).

JOURNALISTS--MORTALITY (v26)

"According to a recent study by the International Federation of Journalists (IFJ), 47 journalists and media workers were killed in the course of their work in 1996. This is a decrease from 1994, when 120 were killed, many while reporting on the Rwandan genocide." (p12)

Rodwan, John G., Jr. "Censorship by Capitalism: Silencing the Messengers." People's Tribune v24 n9 Sep 1997. p12. (ISSN1081-4787).

JOURNALISTS--TURKEY--SOCIAL CONDITIONS

"Half of all the world's imprisoned journalists reside in Turkey, say two international press organizations, the US-based Committee to Protect Journalists (CPJ), and the Paris-based Reporters Sans Frontieres (RSF). The RSF's 1997 report states that 154 Turkish journalists were victims of police abuse in 1996. One journalist died, 31 were tortured in custody, 53 were beaten up, and 69 were threatened." (p19)

Snow, Nancy E. "MediaReports: Press Freedom: Occupational Hazards." Toward Freedom v46 n7 Dec 1997-Jan 1998. p19-20. (ISSN0048-9898).

JOURNALISTS--UNITED STATES--COLLEGE STUDENTS

According to the Student Press Law Center, in the U.S., "requests for legal help from college student media were down slightly, from 806 in 1995 to 771 last year. Questions regarding public access to records and meetings (31 percent), censorship (30 percent) and libel/privacy law (18 percent) were most on the mind of the college media." (p3)

"Roundup: Legal Requests from High Schools Reach Record High at SPLC in '96." Student Press Law Center Report v18 n3 Fall 1997. p3. (ISSN0160-3825).

JOURNALISTS--UNITED STATES--HIGH SCHOOL STUDENTS

In the U.S., according to the Student Press Law Center, "605 high school student journalists or their advisers contacted them in 1996 for legal help. The previous high was 542, recorded during 1995....Questions about censorship topped the list of high school concerns (37 percent), followed by questions about libel/privacy law (30 percent) and copyright law (18 percent)." (p3)

"Roundup: Legal Requests from High Schools Reach Record High at SPLC in '96." Student Press Law Center Report v18 n3 Fall 1997. p3. (ISSN0160-3825).

JUDAISM--FORMER SOVIET REPUBLICS

Rachel Blustain, the Moscow correspondent of the FORWARD, "reported that 'Today, foreign organizations openly pump some $40 million into Jewish programs in the FSU (Former Soviet Union) every year. More than 100 Jewish charity centers have opened throughout the FSU, serving not only the Jewish elderly and needy, but also Jewish activists. In Russia, approximately 2,500 students study in Jewish day schools. An estimated 4,000 more receive Jewish education in supplementary schools.' It appears that no more than 5% of the Russian Jews are religious, and only a third of those listing their nationality as 'Jewish' claim to practice the Jewish faith." (p47)

Katz, Lyber. "Around the World: Abroad." Jewish Currents v51 n6 Jun 1997. p46-47. (ISSN0021-0639).

JUDGES--UNITED STATES--ATTITUDES

In the U.S., a "survey of federal judges revealed: 'While one-fourth of the judges thought rehabilitation was an extremely important goal of sentencing, 19 percent thought it was no more than 'slightly' important; conversely, about 25 percent thought 'just deserts' was a very important or extremely important purpose of sentencing, while 45 percent thought it was only slightly important or not important at all.'" (p6)

Robinson, Paul H. "One Perspective on Sentencing Reform in the United States." Criminal Law Forum v8 n1 1997. p1-41. (ISSN1046-8374).

JUDICIARY

see COURTS

JUICE INDUSTRY

see FRUIT JUICE INDUSTRY; GRAPE JUICE INDUSTRY; GRAPEFRUIT JUICE INDUSTRY; ORANGE JUICE INDUSTRY

JUNIOR COLLEGES

see COMMUNITY COLLEGES

JUNK BONDS--UNITED STATES (v26)

JUNK MAIL

see ADVERTISING, DIRECT-MAIL

JURY--UNITED STATES (v26)

JUSTICE, ADMINISTRATION OF--CANADA--PUBLIC OPINION (v26)

JUSTICE, ADMINISTRATION OF--GREAT BRITAIN (v26)

JUSTICE, ADMINISTRATION OF--UNITED STATES --COSTS (v26)

JUVENILE DELINQUENCY--MICHIGAN--WAYNE COUNTY (v26)

JUVENILE DELINQUENTS

see also GANGS; SCHOOL VIOLENCE

JUVENILE DELINQUENTS--TEXAS

The Texas Youth Commission "handles the most seriously disturbed and delinquent 2 to 3 percent of the youth who are arrested. In 1995, 133,866 youth were referred to juvenile court and 2,387 youth were committed to TYC. Last year, 1996, 36 percent of the youth were committed to the TYC for violent offenses, a 356 percent increase since 1988. The following characteristics provide a profile of the types of youth for whom the agency is responsible: 41 percent known gang members; 23 percent diagnosed as having severe mental illness; 77 percent known drug or alcohol users; 35 percent classified as special education, with median reading and math levels at 5th grade; 77 percent minority youth; 43 percent considered dangerous to others; 16 percent considered dangerous to self; 7 percent history of setting fires; 64 percent history of cocaine/crack abuse; 73 percent history of marijuana abuse; vast majority have history of abuse and neglect; vast majority have family members with history of violence, substance abuse, criminal behavior, and/or mental impairments; 58 percent come from poverty; 71 percent come from chaotic environments; 80 percent of families lack discipline skills." (p10)

Briscoe, Judy. "Breaking the Cycle of Violence: A Rational Approach to At-Risk Youth." Federal Probation v61 n3 Sep 1997. p3-13. (ISSN0014-9128).

JUVENILE DELINQUENTS--UNITED STATES

"During 1995, law enforcement agencies in the United States reported: there were an estimated 2.7 million arrests of persons under the age of 18, or 18 percent of all arrests; juvenile arrests for Violent Crime Index Offenses (murder, forcible rape, robbery, and aggravated assault) declined 3 percent; the number of juvenile crime arrests was 12 percent greater than in 1991; and the number of juvenile crime arrests was 67 percent above the 1986 level....Juveniles were involved in 13 percent of all drug arrests in 1995, a 138 percent increase since 1991." (p3)
"One in four juvenile arrests in 1995 were arrests of females." (p4)

Briscoe, Judy. "Breaking the Cycle of Violence: A Rational Approach to At-Risk Youth." Federal Probation v61 n3 Sep 1997. p3-13. (ISSN0014-9128).

"John Scalia, Bureau of Justice statistician, reports that during 1995, U.S. attorneys filed cases against 240 persons for alleged acts of juvenile delinquency. Of these, 122 cases were adjudicated in federal court, representing 0.2 percent of the 56,243 cases (both adult and juvenile) adjudicated during 1995. Almost one-half of the juvenile cases involved a violent offense (32 percent) or a drug offense (15 percent). Federal prosecutors declined further action against 228 other juveniles referred to them. Many (61 percent) of the juveniles adjudicated in the federal courts are Native Americans." (p72-73)

Cohn, Alvin W. "Juvenile Focus." Federal Probation v61 n3 Sep 1997. p71-73. (ISSN0014-9128).

JUVENILE DETENTION HOMES--UNITED STATES

In the U.S., "juveniles in private facilities increased 9.6 percent from 1991 to 1995, according to a Joseph Moone report prepared for the Office of Juvenile Justice and Delinquency Prevention (OJJDP). Private juvenile residential facilities held 39,671 juveniles in early 1995 while there were only 35,626 in 1993 and 36,190 in 1991....Since 1991, private facilities have seen a decline in the proportion and number of...non-offenders--a drop of 1.9 percent from 1991 to 1995. Within this same period, private facilities experienced a substantial increase in the number of juveniles held for delinquent offenses, with such a population growth at 24.4 percent, from 14,433 in 1991 to 17,781 in 1995. Moreover, 74 percent of juveniles in private facilities in 1995 were committed by the juvenile justice system. Also, the study reports, there are slight increases in the numbers of males, minority youths, and youths over the age of 16 in these facilities when 1991 figures are compared to 1995 data." (p71)

Cohn, Alvin W. "Juvenile Focus." Federal Probation v61 n3 Sep 1997. p71-73. (ISSN0014-9128).

JUVENILE JUSTICE, ADMINISTRATION OF--CANADA (v26)

JUVENILE JUSTICE, ADMINISTRATION OF --MICHIGAN (v26)

JUVENILE JUSTICE, ADMINISTRATION OF--UNITED STATES (v26)

"U.S. courts with juvenile jurisdiction handled 1,471,200 cases of delinquency in 1992, with a disproportionate increase in violent offenses (e.g., 80 percent more aggravated assaults than in 1991, 86 percent more charges involving weapons)....The largest increase among the four major status offenses was for petitioned truancy cases: an increase of 22 percent between 1987 and 1991 (U.S. Department of Justice 1994)....Florida...ranked second highest in the nation for juvenile crime in 1992, with 751 violent criminal arrests per thousand. The national average was 483 per thousand." (p323)

"Habitual Truancy Leads to Juvenile Crime." Clearing House v70 n6 Jul-Aug 1997. p323. (ISSN0009-8655).

KALA-AZAR (v26)

KANE COUNTY (UTAH) (v26)

KARNSTAKA (INDIA)--SOCIAL CONDITIONS

In Karnataka, India, "adult literacy is 56 percent compared with the national figure of 52 percent, and infant mortality stands at about 65 deaths per 1,000 live births, compared with the all-India average of 78 deaths. In terms of health and family planning services, the state is also progressive. According to the 1992-93 National Family Health Survey, 38 percent of deliveries in Karnataka are institutional, compared with 26 percent for the entire country. Similarly, contraceptive practice among married couples is relatively high at 49 percent, compared with an all-India estimate of 41 percent." (p101)

Bhatia, Jagdish C./Cleland, John/Bhagavan, Leela/Rao, N. S. N. "Levels and Determinants of Gynecological Morbidity in a District of South India." Studies in Family Planning v28 n2 Jun 1997. p95-103. (ISSN0039-3665).

KASHMIR (INDIA)--RELIGION (v26)

KASHMIR, VALE OF (INDIA)--ECONOMIC CONDITIONS (v26)

KASHMIR, VALE OF (INDIA)--POPULATION (v26)

KELP BED ECOLOGY--CALIFORNIA

In California, "Point Loma's forest, which covers 8 square kilometers (3 square miles), is dominated by the giant 'Macrocystis pyrifera,' a kelp that anchors itself on the sea floor at depths of from 4-1/2 to 18 meters (15 to 60 feet), then rises until its stalk-like stipes reach the surface....Currently valued at $75 million a year, sea urchin harvesting surged in the late 1980s to become California's largest fishery, according to industry figures." (p15)

Spotts, Peter N. "Habitat: Marine Scientists Seek Help for Shrinking Undersea Kelp." The Christian Science Monitor v89 n175 5 Aug 1997. p15. The Christian Science Monitor search engine: <http://www.csmonitor.com/plweb-cgi/iops1.pl> To retrieve this article, enter the following search: ED=19970805 AND kelp. In the "retrieved list," click the title that matches this record. (ISSN0882-7729).

KENYA--ECONOMIC CONDITIONS

In Kenya, "exchange and price controls have been removed, and stringent fiscal policies have brought inflation down from more than 40 percent in 1993 to 9 percent in 1996. The deficit has been slashed from 9.2 percent in 1993 to an estimated 1.8 percent in 1996. Privatization has been a driving force, with 140 of 207 state companies slated for sale in 1991 already sold." (p7)

Santoro, Lara. "International: African Company's Use of Merit Pay, Other Reforms Shows Way to Success." The Christian Science Monitor v89 n167 24 Jul 1997. p7. The Christian Science Monitor search engine: <http://www.csmonitor.com/plweb-cgi/iops1.pl> To retrieve this article, enter the following search: ED=19970724 AND success. In the "retrieved list," click the title that matches this record. (ISSN0882-7729).

"A government economic survey released in June [1997] disclosed that 47 percent of rural Kenyans couldn't afford the minimum food requirement of 2500 calories a day, costing $12.70 per month....Only seven percent of Kenya's population controls the nation's wealth." (p20)

Onyango, William. "TF Reports: Africa: Losing Ground." Toward Freedom v46 n5 Sep-Oct 1997. p20-21. (ISSN0048-9898).

KENYA--NETHERLANDS--POPULATION (v26)

KENYA--SOCIAL CONDITIONS

"Roughly one in four Kenyans lives in a city. Almost one in three is illiterate. Nevertheless, this African nation continues to show steady economic growth and a positive international debt balance. It has 1 radio set for every 33 people, and 1 TV for every 109. Newspaper circulation is slightly more than 1 million for a population of 25 million." (p58-59)

Cassino, Kip D. "A World of Advertising." American Demographics v19 n11 Nov 1997. p57-60. article-level access: <http://www.demographics.com/publications/ad/97_ad/9711_ad/ad971131.htm> (ISSN0163-4089).

KERALA (INDIA)--SOCIAL CONDITIONS (v26)

KIBBUTZIM--UNITED STATES (v26)

KILLING, MERCY

see EUTHANASIA

KITCHENS--UNITED STATES--REMODELING--COSTS --PUBLIC OPINION

"REMODELING magazine pegged the cost of an average kitchen tune-up at $8,507 in its 1996-1997 Cost vs. Value Report. A major kitchen remodel averaged $21,262....According to the new...[American Express] home improvement survey,...the majority of homeowners...opt to do the job themselves. Two-thirds of consumers (78 percent of men, 54 percent of women) plan on swinging a hammer or wielding a paint brush....(65 percent)...admit that if price were no object, they would prefer to hire it done....69 percent of shoppers listed price as the most important characteristic they look for in a home improvement store. Quality was only a consideration for 49 percent....(46 percent of women, 55 percent of men)...think the job will be done quickly (in less than a month) and relatively cheap. The average home improvement budget was $2,660, according to the...[American Express] Retail Index...." (p33 secD)

Haege, Glenn. "Homestyle: The Handyman: Realize Quality Doesn't Come Cheap in Any Remodeling Project." Detroit News 21 Jun 1997. p33 secD.

KIWIFRUIT INDUSTRY--UNITED STATES

"As a net importer of kiwifruit, the United States imported 88.0 million pounds in 1996, and exported 12.7 million pounds....Imports originated mainly from Chile (79 percent), New Zealand (11 percent), and Italy (9 percent)....Among the three major U.S. suppliers, imports from Italy in 1996 more than doubled from a year earlier, shipments from New Zealand were up 33 percent, while the volume coming from Chile declined 6 percent....Exports fell 27 percent from a year earlier, with smaller shipments to key markets such as Canada (down 12 percent), Korea (down 36 percent), and Taiwan (down 66 percent), Korea (down 36 percent), and Taiwan (down 66 percent). These markets account for more than 85 percent of total U.S. fresh kiwifruit exports." (p22-23)

U.S. Dept. of Agriculture. Economic Research Service. "Noncitrus Fruit Outlook." Fruit and Tree Nuts Situation and Outlook Report Aug 1997. p7-26.

"U.S. fresh kiwifruit imports rose 5 percent from a year earlier in 1996, but the smaller California crop pushed domestic supplies down 22 percent. Consequently, the season-average grower price for fresh-market kiwifruit increased from 23.7 cents a pound ($473 per ton) in 1995 to 25.1 cents ($502 per ton) in 1996....The large decline in domestic production more than offset the rise in grower prices, causing the value of the 1996 crop to drop about $1.7 million from a year earlier to $13.4 million." (p22)

U.S. Dept. of Agriculture. Economic Research Service. "Noncitrus Fruit Outlook." Fruit and Tree Nuts Situation and Outlook Report Aug 1997. p7-26.

KOPECK--RUSSIA

"The kopeck was last sighted in Russia in early 1992, disappearing in a blizzard of hyperinflation that made the national currency literally worth less than the paper it was printed on....A box of matches that used to cost one kopeck today costs 100 rubles--10,000 times as much. The five-kopeck Moscow subway ride of Soviet urban folklore is now a fairy tale: The same ride nowadays costs 40,000 times more: 2,000 rubles, or the equivalent of 35 cents." (p6)

Ford, Peter. "International: Russians Return to Small Change: Kopeck Is Back." The Christian Science Monitor v89 n175 5 Aug 1997. p6. The Christian Science Monitor search engine: <http://www.csmonitor.com/plweb-cgi/iops1.pl> To retrieve this article, enter the following search: ED=19970805 AND back. In the "retrieved list," click the title that matches this record. (ISSN0882-7729).

KOREA (NORTH)--ARMED FORCES (v26)

KOREA (SOUTH)--ECONOMIC CONDITIONS

"South Korea's GDP growth slowed to 7.1 percent in 1996 from 9 percent in the previous year, and South Korea's current account deficit swelled to a record $23.7 billion (4.7 percent of GDP), second only to the United States....The Korean Composite Stock Price Index fell below the psychological barrier of 700 points in December 1996...." (p6)

Jerardo, Alberto/Huang, Sophia Wu/U.S. Dept. of Agriculture. Economic Research Service. "Regional Overviews: APEC to Resume Healthy Growth." APEC: International Agriculture and Trade Reports Situation and Outlook Series Aug 1997. p6-8.

KOREA (SOUTH)--ECONOMIC CONDITIONS--SOCIAL CONDITIONS (v26)

KOREA (SOUTH)--POLITICS AND GOVERNMENT --PUBLIC OPINION

According to public opinion surveys in South Korea, in 1993, 17 percent "agreed with the statement, 'Dictatorship is more successful than a democratic government in solving the nation's serious problems.' In 1994, however, more than three times as many (61 percent) at least 'somewhat agreed' with the statement, 'Dictatorial rule led by a strong leader like Park Chung Hee is much better than a democracy to tackle the various problems facing the country.' And in 1996, a majority (53 percent) agreed with the statement, 'For our country these days, strong leadership is needed more than democracy.'" (p116-117)

Shin, Doh Chull/Shyu, Huoyan. "Public Opinion in New Democracies: Political Ambivalence in South Korea and Taiwan." Journal of Democracy v8 n3 Jul 1997. p109-124. (ISSN1045-5736).

KOREANS--CALIFORNIA

"Koreans are becoming a major economic force in southern California. The 500,000-strong community owns 40 percent of the dry-cleaning industry in Los Angeles and more than half of its small groceries, reports THE ECONOMIST. L.A.'s 'Koreatown' has become a communications force, with three TV stations and three radio stations." (p5)

Poe, Randall/Courter, Carol Lee. "Fast Forward: Korea-fornia." Across the Board v34 n7 Jul-Aug 1997. p5. (ISSN0147-1554).

KURDS--MIDDLE EAST--RUSSIA--SOUTH ASIA --POPULATION

"The Kurds are estimated to number some 20-25 million living largely in four Middle East countries: Turkey, with 10-12 million; Iran, with 5-6 million; Iraq, with 3.5 million and Syria, with 1 million. Some 70,000-80,000 Kurds also live in Armenia and in Azerbaijan. Recent reports suggest there are 300,000-1 million Kurds living within the Russian Federation." (p168)

Olson, Robert. "Turkey-Syria Relations since the Gulf War: Kurds and Water." Middle East Policy v5 n2 May 1997. p168-193. (ISSN1061-1924).

KURDS--TURKEY--ECONOMIC CONDITIONS--SOCIAL CONDITIONS

In Turkey, "unemployment among Kurds rose by 150 percent between 1967 and 1977. By the early 1990s, less than 10 percent of adults in the Kurdish southeast had industrial jobs, and those tended to be in low-skilled industries. On the large landowners' estates, peasants would work eleven hours a day for $2. Children--the fortunate survivors of a 30 percent mortality rate--would work alongside their parents. Less than a third of the population received any formal education and less than one in five women attended school." (p23)

Tirman, John. "Essay: Ataturk's Children." Boston Review v22 n6 Dec 1997-Jan 1998. p22-25. (ISSN0734-2306).

KURUMPATTI (INDIA)--SOCIAL CONDITIONS

In Kurumpatti, India, in 1993-1994, "there were 259 households in the entire village (including Kurumpatti village and four hamlets) with an average of 5.64 persons per household. The majority of them belonged to marginal (50.1 per cent) and medium (23 per cent) landowning categories, while only 1.9 per cent were large farmers....The remaining 25 per cent of the people were landless. For 71 per cent of the village population, the main economic activity was agriculture, and in the case of the remaining 29 per cent it was sericulture (rearing) and agriculture....95 per cent of the male population engaged in farming....Sericulturists (farmers) had about 83 per cent of their cultivated land under irrigation. Non-sericulturists on the other hand had only about 24 per cent of their land under irrigation." (p43-44) "51 per cent of the males and 35 per cent of the females were literate." (p45)

Inbanathan, Anand/Vijayalakshmi, V. "Women, Sericulture and Development: A Case in South India." Journal of Third World Studies v14 n1 Spr 1997. p37-63. (ISSN8755-3449).

KUWAIT--ECONOMIC CONDITIONS

"In 1992 alone, Kuwait not only paid Washington [D.C.] $16 billion as part of a deal to cover all the costs of Operation Desert Storm, it also authorized $11.7 billion of new arms imports--largely from the US. To cover these outlays, the Kuwaiti government has had to liquidate many of its hard currency assets, including much more than half of the $100 billion it had invested abroad through the Kuwait Investment Office (KIO). This liquidation has continued to affect the country long after wartime damages were repaired. The Kuwaiti government budget consumed 50 percent of GDP....Even before the Iraqi invasion, oil exports had covered only about 40 percent of this bill; income from foreign investments had contributed another 35 percent....In the 1990s, the [budget] deficit averaged around $5 billion each year...." (7-8)

Sadowski, Yahya. "The End of the Counterrevolution? The Politics of Economic Adjustment in Kuwait." Middle East Report v27 n3 Jul-Sep 1997. p7-11. (ISSN0899-2851).

LA ESPERANZA (ECUADOR)

"La Esperanza is situated roughly 7 km to the southeast of Ibarra, capital of Imbabura province in the north of Ecuador. There are 18 Quichua speaking communities in the region, each with a population ranging from 200 to 800 people or 50 to 200 families. The average land holding per family is about 1 to 2 hectares, mostly on slopes ranging from 2200 m to 3600 m above

sea level in the Andean highlands (Sierra)." (p130)
Indigena, Fundacion Sabiduria/Kothari, Brij. "Rights to the Benefits of Research: Compensating Indigenous Peoples for Their Intellectual Contribution." Human Organization v56 n2 Sum 1997. p127-137. (ISSN0018-7259).

LABELS--EUROPE

"The number of products awarded the...[EU's ecolabel is] rising to more than 160, representing 6 out of 12 product groups for which criteria have been drawn up....The label has been awarded in 9 out of the 15 EU member states: Denmark, Finland, France, Ireland, The Netherlands, Portugal, Spain, Sweden, and the UK." (p2)
"The EU Scheme: Need to Keep Momentum Going." Environment Watch: Western Europe v6 n16 1997. p2-3. (ISSN1066-6001).

LABELS--GERMANY

"As of 1 January 1997, the most recent date for which figures are available,...[Germany's Blue Angel ecolabel] covered 76 product categories and had been awarded to 3,723 products." (p5) "In a 1996 survey, 51% of consumers in the western states of Germany and 30% of consumers in the eastern states said they took the Blue Angel into account when shopping. Twenty-nine percent and 26%, respectively, paid no attention to the label, while 20% and 44%, respectively, were unfamiliar with it." (p6)
"Germany: Adding Criteria." Environment Watch: Western Europe v6 n16 1997. p5-6. (ISSN1066-6001).

LABELS--NORWAY

As of 29 July 1997, Jan Erik Stokke at Stiftelsen Nordisk Miljomerking had "licensed 330 companies to use the [Nordic] Swan [ecolabel] on some 1,000 products. The scheme currently covers 44 product groups 'including almost everything but foodstuffs,' according to Stokke. Four new sets of criteria--for plastic folders, windows, lubricating oil, and wood--are due to be issued this year. An additional 20 are under development, but release dates for them have yet to be set." (p4)
"The Nordic Swan: Looking beyond the Region." Environment Watch: Western Europe v6 n16 1997. p3-5. (ISSN1066-6001).

LABELS--SPAIN

"Spain's national ecolabeling scheme, AENOR Medio Ambiente, has issued criteria for just two product groups--paints and varnishes and polyethylene bags--since its creation in late 1994. It has awarded labels to 17 brands of paints and varnishes." (p9)
"Spain: Few Official Labels." Environment Watch: Western Europe v6 n16 1997. p9-10. (ISSN1066-6001).

LABOR

see also AGRICULTURAL LABORERS; AUTOMOBILE INDUSTRY AND TRADE--LABOR PRODUCTIVITY; BLUE COLLAR WORKERS; CONVICT LABOR; EMPLOYEES; HOME LABOR; HOURS OF LABOR; MIGRANT LABOR; SEXUAL DIVISION OF LABOR; WAGES

LABOR--UNITED STATES--RURAL CONDITIONS

According to the "1996 Current Population Survey" by the U.S. Bureau of Labor Statistics, "about one in five rural workers employed in farming, forestry, and fishing held more than one job in 1996....Among rural workers who held more than one job, the largest percentage of second jobs was in farming, forestry, and fishing occupations (19 percent). Farming was the most common second job for moonlighters in blue-collar occupations including protective service (20 percent), precision production and craft (42 percent), machine operation and assembly (23 percent), and transportation (37 percent), and among handlers, cleaners, helpers, and laborers (33 percent)." (p22)
Parker, Timothy S. "Farm & Rural Communities: Multiple Jobholding among Rural Workers." Agricultural Outlook Nov 1997. p22-24.

LABOR, MIGRANT

see MIGRANT LABOR

LABOR, ORGANIZED

see TRADE-UNIONS

LABOR, PREMATURE--HEALTH ASPECTS--UNITED STATES (v26)

LABOR (OBSTETRICS)--UNITED STATES

"Of the 3,899,589 births recorded in the United States in 1995, 16 percent (622,497) involved stimulation and another 16 percent (618,497) involved induction of labor. Two percent, or 74,167 births, were both stimulated and induced." (p20) "The rates of both stimulation and induction of labor in the United States rose steadily from 1989 to 1995....During this seven-year period the stimulation rate rose by 48 percent (from 109 to 161 per 1,000 live births). The rate for induction of labor increased by 77 percent (from 90 to 160 per 1,000 live births). Rates of stimulation decline with advancing maternal age. In 1995 the rate was 168 per 1,000 for teenagers as compared with 139 per 1,000 for women in their 40s...." (p21)
Mathews, T. J. "Trends in Stimulation and Induction of Labor 1989-1995." Statistical Bulletin v78 n4 Oct-Dec 1997. p20-26. (ISSN0790-8334).

LABOR AND LABORING CLASS

see WORKING CLASS

LABOR DISPUTES--AUSTRALIA

"The number of working days lost from industrial disputes increased from 547,600 to 928,500 between 1995 and 1996, according to data released...by the Australian Bureau of Statistics....New South Wales recorded the highest increase, recording 377,900 working days lost, a rise of 264,300 from 1995, and accounted for 41 per cent of the total for Australia in 1996. In Western Australia, working days lost decreased from 101,600 in 1995 to 47,300 in 1996. The Construction industry reported 334,800 working days lost or 36 per cent of the all industries total. Other industries to experience high levels of working days lost included Education, Health and Community Services with 239,800 working days lost and Coal Mining with 160,800 working days lost. Within Education, Health and Community Services, disputation in Education was most significant with 233,900 working days lost reported compared to 5,900 recorded for the Health and Community services industry."
Australian Bureau of Statistics. "More Working Days Lost through Industrial Disputes in 1996." Media Release 22 Jul 1997. document-level access: <http://www.abs.gov.au/websitedbs/d3110125.nsf/4a255eef008309e44a255eef00061e57/48ac06d560a453994a2564db007e03c7?OpenDocument>

LABOR DISPUTES--EUROPE

In Europe, the number of labor disputes over the last twenty years "was high in four large countries: France, Italy, Spain and the United Kingdom. There was a marked decrease in Italy (some 80 per cent between 1970 and 1990) and in the United Kingdom (about 90 per cent). On the other hand, the number of strikes fell less sharply in France (50 to 60 per cent between 1970 and 1980 or 1990), and still less in Spain (40 per cent between 1975 and 1990)....As regards smaller countries, Finland, for example, registered an average of over 1,200 disputes per year during the 20-year period in question." (p78)
Aligisakis, Maximos. "Labour Disputes in Western Europe: Typology and Tendencies." International Labour Review v136 n1 Spr 1997. p73-94. (ISSN0020-7780).

LABOR PRODUCTIVITY--EUROPE--UNITED STATES (v26)

LABOR PRODUCTIVITY--GERMANY (v26)

LABOR PRODUCTIVITY--JAPAN--UNITED STATES

A worldwide survey released in October 1997 "on auto plant productivity says Honda Motor Co.'s Suzuka plant in Japan ranked head and shoulders above other car assembly plants. The Suzuka plant turned out 118.6 Civics per employee in 1996, making it the world's most productive vehicle assembly plant and placing it far ahead of the most efficient Big Three plant in the United States. Ford Motor Co.'s Taurus and Sable assembly plant in Chicago was this country's most efficient assembly plant, making 77.4 cars per employee in 1996. Right behind it: the Atlanta Taurus-Sable plant at 76.8 vehicles per employee. The survey, based on 1996 production numbers, was done by the business information firm Economist Intelligence Unit of London and was released at the Tokyo Motor Show." (p2 secE)

Evanoff, Ted. "Business: Japanese Auto Plants Lead World in Efficiency." Detroit Free Press 22 Oct 1997. p2 secE.

LABOR SUPPLY

see also UNEMPLOYMENT

LABOR SUPPLY--FRANCE

"A study conducted in France showed that, in the private sector, middle managers were less frequently replaced (42 per cent) than low-skilled workers (59 per cent), though the reverse was found to be the case in the public service, with 86 and 65 per cent, respectively." (p123)

"Perspectives." International Labour Review v136 n1 Spr 1997. p109-128. (ISSN0020-7780).

LABOR SUPPLY--GERMANY (v26)

LABOR SUPPLY--SOUTHERN STATES

In the U.S., "data collected by the EEOC [Equal Employment Opportunity Commission] indicate a shift of 10 percent of the South's jobs from blue-collar work to white-collar work. Blue-collar jobs, which dropped from 57 to 47 percent of all jobs in the South, remained the largest job category for southern workers in 1994, while the number of white-collar jobs grew from 29 percent of all the workforce in 1975 to 39.2 percent in 1994....The South's best blue-collar jobs--skilled craft and semi-skilled operative positions--dropped in number from 40.3 percent to 28.2 percent of the job market from 1975 to 1994, while the number of lowest paying blue-collar jobs--low-skilled laborer and service positions--increased from 16.7 percent to 19 percent of the job market in that same period....The only decline in white-collar work has taken place in official/ managerial positions, which went from 11.2 percent of the jobs in 1985 and to 10.1 percent in 1994, after having grown during the previous decade." (p8)

Eckman, Anne/Green, Jordan/Braasch, Peter/Schulman, David. "Job Equity in the Downsized South: A Special Report on Work in the 1990s." Southern Exposure v25 n3-4 Fall-Win 1997. p7-11. (ISSN0146-809X).

LABOR SUPPLY--SWEDEN (v26)

LABOR SUPPLY--UNITED STATES (v26)

In the U.S., "the labor force participation rate of men aged 55 to 64 declined from 85 percent in 1965 to 68 percent in 1985 and 66 percent in 1994, according to the BLS [Bureau of Labor Statistics]. For women that age, the rate was steady at about 42 percent until 1985, then rose to reach 49 percent in 1994....If the participation rates of men and women remain at their current levels, the number of workers aged 55 to 64 may increase from 11.7 million in 1994 to 22 million in 2025." (p9)

"If Aging Boomers Work Smart." Forecast v17 n6 Jun 1997. p9. article-level access: <http://www.demographics.com/Publications/FC/97_fc/9706_fc/FC97068.htm> (ISSN0732-1597).

LABORATORY SCHOOLS--UNITED STATES--TEACHERS --ATTITUDES (v26)

LAKE HURON

see FISHERIES--HURON, LAKE (MICH. AND ONT.)

LAKE MICHIGAN

see BOATING ACCIDENTS--MICHIGAN, LAKE; FISHERIES--MICHIGAN, LAKE; FISHES--DISEASES--MICHIGAN, LAKE; SALMON FISHING--MICHIGAN, LAKE

LAKE POWELL

see WATER--POLLUTION--UTAH--LAKE POWELL

LAMAISM

see BUDDHISM

LAND, BURNING OF

see BURNING OF LAND

LAND DEGRADATION (v26)

"Use of pesticides and poor farming methods have taken a heavy toll: 300 million hectares of farmland worldwide are now severely degraded and farming abandoned. Another 1.2 billion hectares show moderate fertility loss. Desertification (degradation of drylands) affects one quarter of the Earth's land area--3.6 billion hectares." (p28)

"Desertification and Drinking Water: If the Land Is Barren, How Are You Going to Halve Hunger?" UN Chronicle v34 n3 1997. p28. (ISSN0251-7329).

LAND DEGRADATION--UNITED STATES (v26)

LAND REFORM

The People's Participation Programme, created by the United Nations Food and Agriculture Organization in 1983, "aims to improve living conditions by increasing access to rural services, encouraging group savings, and fostering self-reliance, with a special emphasis on the needs of women....By 1995, the program had created 230 small groups in Zambia's Western Province. Of the 2,550 people directly affected, 73 percent were women, 32 percent of whom represented female-headed households. As a result of the PPP, access to agricultural extension services increased for 67 percent of the groups engaged in farming....Research showed that from 1983 to 1994, the average land under cultivation in three districts participating in the program had increased between 30 and 90 percent....Today, the Zambian PPP encompasses 386 groups serving 4,402 members (indirectly reaching about 22,500 household members), and similar PPPs reach out to poor and rural men and women in other parts of Africa, Asia, and Central America." (p44)

"Women in Poverty: A New Global Underclass: Planting Seeds of Hope." Foreign Policy n108 Fall 1997. p44. (ISSN0015-7228).

LAND REFORM--BRAZIL

The Landless Rural Workers' Movement (MST) in Brazil, has "organized over 139,000 families into productive cooperatives, some of whom are engaged in export agriculture. They have 'expropriated' a total of 7.2 million hectares of land, and have organized 55 rural cooperatives in 12 states. They have established 880 schools with 38,000 pupils....The MST Congress in July 1995 drew over 5,000 delegates representing several hundred thousand peasants....In 1995 the MST led 92 land occupations. By June 1996, 120 land occupations had taken place and there were a total of 168 'campamentos' (land site occupations) with 40,000 families awaiting government expropriation." (p24)

Petras, James. "Latin America: The Resurgence of the Left." New Left Review n223 May-Jun 1997. p17-47. (ISSN0028-6060).

LAND SETTLEMENT--ISRAEL

Mosi Raz, director of the left-wing Israeli group, Peace Now, "says that natural growth in Israel is around 3 percent a year, but the [land] settlements have been growing at a rate of 9 to 10 percent this year and last. Of the 13,000 new settlers last year, 8,500 were newcomers." (p6)

Prusher, Ilene R. "International: While Talks Drag On, Israel Builds." The Christian Science Monitor v89 n240 6 Nov 1997. p1,6. The Christian Science Monitor search engine: <http://www.csmonitor.com/plweb-cgi/iops1.pl> To retrieve this article, enter the following search: ED=19971106 AND builds. In the "retrieved list," click the title that matches this record. (ISSN0882-7729).

LAND SETTLEMENT--ISRAEL--JERUSALEM

The Oslo II agreement divided the city of Jerusalem into what became known as "A", "B" and "C" areas. Control of these areas were divided among the Palestinians and the Israelis. In the "West Bank area, about 60% of the territory, remained...under full Israeli control as part of the 'C' areas. The 'C' areas included all the Israeli settlements in the West Bank and Gaza Strip, including about 140,000 inhabitants (excluding East Jerusalem). Some 30,000 of these settlers actually moved to the West Bank during the Rabin administration, when all settlement activity was supposed to have ceased." (p418)

Newman, David. "Conflicting Israeli Peace Discourses." Péace Review v9 n3 Sep 1997. p417-424. (ISSN1040-2659).

LAND SETTLEMENT--NICARAGUA

"At the end of Nicaragua's civil war in 1990, agricultural colonists began streaming into lands traditionally occupied by indigenous Mayangna and Miskito. Thousands of newcomers have cleared chunks of the forest--74,132 acres in four years--for cattle and farming, thereby fragmenting the largest intact rain forest north of the Amazon....'The Miskito and Mayangna are the original conservationists,' according to Brady Watson, the [Nature] Conservancy's Nicaraguan program director. 'Ninety-two percent of their land is primary forest....'" (p6-7)

Green, Martha Hodgkins/Kinch, John A. "Sightings: This Land Is Our Land." Nature Conservancy v47 n4 Jul-Aug 1997. p6-7. (ISSN0028-5200).

LAND TENURE (v26)

see also FARM OWNERSHIP

LAND TENURE--BRAZIL

"According to Brazil's new Super Ministry of Land Policy, created immediately after the Eldorado dos Carajas massacre, small family farmers with 10 hectares of land or less comprise 30.4 percent of all Brazilian farmers, but together hold only 1.5 percent of all agricultural lands. Since 1985 the number of small farms has sharply decreased from just over 3 million to under 1 million. In contrast the country's largest farms, of 1,000 hectares or more, comprise only 1.6 percent of all farms, but hold 53.2 percent of all agricultural land. The largest 75 farms, with 100,000 hectares or more, control over five times the combined total area of all small farms." (p2)

Langevin, Mark S./Rosset, Peter. "Land Reform from Below: The Landless Workers Movement in Brazil." Food First Backgrounder v4 n3 Fall 1997. p1-3.

"The annual CONFLICTS IN RURAL AREAS: 1996 report issued by the Land Pastoral Commission...in Brasilia once again confirms that violence and impunity still prevail in land conflicts in rural areas in Brazil. According to the report, conflicts grew by 26% in relation to 1995, from 554 to 750, the highest figure recorded by the commission in the eleven years it has been documenting them....Altogether, 54 rural workers were killed in 1996, thirteen more than in 1995. Last year, 653 land conflicts, nineteen cases of slave labour, and 78 incidents involving labor issues, unions, the agricultural policy and miners were registered, averaging two conflicts a day. Most cases, 256, were reported in the Northeast, but the state of Para was the one where violence prevailed more than in any other, with 72 deaths, including the massacre in Eldorado de Carajas. In 1996, more land areas (398) were occupied by landless workers than in the last eleven years, and the number of families involved (63,080) was almost twice the figure registered in 1995....976 persons were murdered in rural areas in the last eleven years, and there were 891 attempts on people's lives and 2,500 death threats. In average, 81.3 murders were registered, one each 4.5 days. Of these, only 56 cases were brought before the courts and only fourteen persons behind the crimes were judged, of whom only seven were convicted, five are in prison and two fled." (p6)

"International News: News from the Net: Land and Indigenous Peoples: Land Pastoral Commission Denounces More...Areas." Freedom (Anarchist Fortnightly) v58 n16 16 Aug 1997. p6. (ISSN0016-0504).

In Northeastern Brazil, "large land holdings (more than 10,000 hectares) comprise less than 0.01% of rural holdings, while controlling more than 8.9% of the total area. By contrast, small holdings (less than 10 hectares) comprise more than 70% of all holdings but account for only 5.4% of the total area." (p138)

Costa, Alberto C. G./Kottak, Conrad P./Prado, Rosane M. "The Sociopolitical Context of Participatory Development in Northeastern Brazil." Human Organization v56 n2 Sum 1997. p138-146. (ISSN0018-7259).

"In Brazil, the richest 20 percent of the population owns 88 percent of land, while the poorest 40 percent holds only 1 percent. According to the MST [Landless Rural Workers' Movement], Brazil has 195 million acres of fallow land, or some 62 percent of its arable territory, which is often used for speculation and tax write-offs. This skewed distribution of land, MST leaders argue, is the major reason for migration of millions to urban slums and the chronic rural violence that has resulted in the deaths of nearly 1,000 people since 1985, according to the Roman Catholic Church's Pastoral Land Commission. In the last two years, 95 peasants were killed in 1,304 conflicts, and 17 more died in 1997, according to the commission." (p6)

Epstein, Jack. "International: Brazil Makes Land Grabs by Peasants Tougher." The Christian Science Monitor v89 n157 10 Jul 1997. p6. The Christian Science Monitor search engine: <http://www.csmonitor.com/plweb-cgi/iops1.pl> To retrieve this article, enter the following search: ED=19970710 AND tougher. In the "retrieved list," click the title that matches this record. (ISSN0882-7729).

LAND TENURE--BRAZIL--GUATEMALA--UNITED STATES (v26)

LAND TENURE--CENTRAL AMERICA (v26)

LAND TENURE--GAZA STRIP--WEST BANK

For the entire interim accords "period, Isreal was able to maintain complete control over the 144 Jewish settlements in the West Bank and Gaza Strip as well as the vast areas of land and huge quantities of water that had been illegally appropriated for establishment of the settlements." (p14) "The Palestinian Authority, set up by the [interim] accords, controls less than 7 percent of the West Bank and barely 60 percent of the tiny Gaza Strip." (p15)

Khalidi, Rashid. "Middle East: A Flawed Peace." In These Times v21 n16 30 Jun 1997. p14-16. (ISSN0160-5992).

LAND TENURE--GUATEMALA (v26)

LAND TENURE--MEXICO--CHIAPAS HIGHLANDS (v26)

LAND TENURE--PHILIPPINES (v26)

LAND TENURE--UNITED STATES (v26)

"Foreign ownership of U.S. agricultural land has remained relatively stable from 1981 through 1995, varying slightly above or below 1 percent of the privately owned agricultural land in the United States. Foreign persons reported owning 15.1 million acres, or slightly more than 1 percent of the 1.3 billion acres of privately owned U.S. agricultural land--farm and forest property--as of December 31, 1995. This represents a 899,744 acre decrease from the comparable 1994 period....Foreign holdings in 1995 by major land use were distributed as follows: forest land, 50 percent of total foreign holdings; grassland, pasture, and range, 31 percent; cropland, 16 percent; and non-agricultural land, 3 percent." (p468)

U.S. Dept. of Agriculture. "Agriculture, Rural Development, Food and Drug Administration...Approp. for 1998 (Part 4)." Hearing. U.S. House. Committee on Appropriations. Washington, D.C. : GPO, 1997. (ISBN0160551560). (Y4.Ap6/1:Ag8/997/pt.4).

"Since 1872 the U.S. Government...has given away 3.244 million acres of land. We have given it away for $2.50 an acre. Sometimes we got as much as $5 an acre. There are 330,000 claims still pending in this country. And the Mineral Policy Center estimates that since 1872 we have patented land containing $243 billion worth of minerals--land that used to belong to the taxpayers of this country. We now have a moratorium on all but 235 patent applications." (pS9579)

Bumpers, Dale (Sen.-Ariz.). "Department of the Interior and Related Agencies Appropriations Act, 1998." Congressional Record. Daily ed. v143 n125 18 Sep 1997. pS9575-9600. section/page-level access: <http://thomas.loc.gov/cgi-bin/query/R?r105:FLD001:S09579:> (ISSN0363-7239). (X1.1A.105/1).

LAND USE (v26)

see also INDIAN RESERVATION; REAL ESTATE BUSINESS

LAND USE--BRAZIL

In Brazil, "42.6 percent of agricultural land is not cultivated, and among Brazil's largest landholdings of 1,000 hectares or more 88.7 percent of arable land is permanently idle." (p3)

Langevin, Mark S./Rosset, Peter. "Land Reform from Below: The Landless Workers Movement in Brazil." Food First Backgrounder v4 n3 Fall 1997. p1-3.

LAND USE--CHINA (v26)

LAND USE--ENVIRONMENTAL ASPECTS--AFRICA

In Africa, "topsoil losses have been reported to range from 25 tonnes to 250 tonnes per hectare, across the region. One study has estimated that soil degradation and erosion in Africa reduces the productivity of land about 1 per cent a year....The Soil Reference and Information Centre in the Netherlands estimates that 321 mn [million] hectares of African land are moderately to extremely degraded....Only 7 per cent of sub-Saharan Africa's total land area, or about 150 mn hectares, is devoted to crops....Only another 30 mn hectares of unused land can easily be brought under cultivation without further jeopardizing the environment....Only about 2 per cent of sub-Saharan Africa's arable land benefits from irrigation, compared with one-third in South Asia....Only an average of 11 kilograms (kgs) of fertilizer are applied per hectare of farmland in sub-Saharan Africa, compared with 69 kgs in South Asia, 71 kgs in Latin America and well over 100 kgs in the developed countries." (p8) "According to the FAO [UN Food and Agriculture Organization], while export crop farmers in Africa use an average of 30 kgs of chemical fertilizer per hectare, for food farmers the average falls to just 5 kgs." (p9)

Harsch, Ernest. "Agriculture in Africa: Africa Strives to Revitalize Agriculture." Africa Recovery v11 n2 Oct 1997. p6-9.

LAND USE--EUROPE--UNITED STATES (v26)

LAND USE--GREAT BRITAIN

"Britain has 100,000 acres of nature reserve but half a million acres of domestic gardens....In 1995 in England the owners of 544,900 hectares of farmland were being paid for growing nothing on them under the terms of the European Union's agricultural policy and...this was,...[according to an urban geographer,] 'three times the amount of land needed to accommodate all forecast urban development over the coming quarter century.'" (p4)

Ward, Colin. "Features: Anarchist Notebook: Re-Settling Rural England." Freedom (Anarchist Fortnightly) v58 n17 6 Sep 1997. p4. (ISSN0016-0504).

LAND USE--GREAT LAKES REGION (v26)

LAND USE--HIMALAYA MOUNTAINS (v26)

LAND USE--ISRAEL--JERUSALEM

In Jerusalem, private land "dealers have turned about a dozen residential units in Silwan over to Jews, as well as some 60-odd in the Old City. On the other hand, in expanding Jerusalem after 1967, Israel extended its rule over 70.5 square kilometers of land, the ownership of which was 'overwhelmingly Palestinian,' says...[Daniel Seidemann, an Israeli lawyer who has represented many Arab petitioners in cases over property rights]. Of that, a third was expropriated as state land for new Jewish neighborhoods, and 40,000 housing units were erected for Israelis. Jerusalem Palestinians, who are permanent residents rather than citizens, 'are not entitled to acquire rights to any land in Israel,' says Seidemann." (p22) "Of the remaining two-thirds, some 60 percent remains 'unplanned,' meaning that it is not zoned for building; of that, over 40 percent has been defined as 'green space' in which it is actually forbidden to build. That leaves a total of less than 10 percent available for construction of any kind whatsoever." (p23)

Kershner, Isabel. "Palestinian Affairs: The Killing Season." Jerusalem Report v8 n4 26 Jun 1997. p22-23. (ISSN0792-6049).

LAND USE--MEXICO (v26)

LAND USE--MICHIGAN

"Michigan converted 8 percent of its farmland to nonagricultural uses between 1982 and 1992, an average of 133 square miles per year....Housing demand has increased while the number of dwelling units per acre of land has declined 75 percent since World War II. Michigan also has the largest number of second homes and the second-largest number of golf courses in the United States." (p1 sec C) "Gov. John Engler has said that in the last 10 years Michigan lost farmland equal to the state of Rhode Island. But [former State representitive Margaret] O'Conner points out that Rhode Island is equal to only 1.8 percent of the land of Michigan....If the current trend continues, between 63 percent and 87 percent more land will be urbanized in Michigan over the next 25 years...." (p3 secC)

Waldsmith, Lynn. "Business: Special Report: Suburban Sprawl: Development Invades Rural Life: Washtenaw...Tax to Preserve Farmland." Detroit News 13 Jul 1997. p1,3 secC.

LAND USE--MICHIGAN--WASHTENAW COUNTY

"The issue of farmland preservation has touched a raw nerve in Washtenaw County, which lost 16 percent of its farmland between 1982 and 1992. The county loses 4,000 acres of farmland every year, according to the Citizens Task Force for Farmland and Open Space Preservation in Washtenaw County." (p1 secC)

Waldsmith, Lynn. "Business: Special Report: Suburban Sprawl: Development Invades Rural Life: Washtenaw...Tax to Preserve Farmland." Detroit News 13 Jul 1997. p1,3 secC.

LAND USE--MICHIGAN--WASHTENAW COUNTY --PUBLIC OPINION (v26)

LAND USE--NEVADA

"According to the Nevada Division of State Lands, there are 70 million acres of land in the state....The total amount of urbanized land in the state covers approximately 227,000 acres, or 0.32% of the state's land area. Private croplands, primarily pasture and alfalfa production for livestock, are 9.2 million acres or 13% of the land. Some 87% of the state is under federal government management, primarily the BLM [Bureau of Land Management] and Forest Service." (p59)

Wuerthner, George. "Conservation Strategy: Subdivisions and Extractive Industries." Wild Earth v7 n3 Fall 1997. p57-62. (ISSN1055-1166).

LAND USE--PHILIPPINES--CASIGURAN (v26)

LAND USE--UKRAINE

"While private household plots in Ukraine occupied only about 12 percent of agricultural land in 1996, they produced over 47 percent of total agricultural output....Private farms occupy only 2 percent of agricultural land...." (p32) "Some estimates show that over 64 percent of land is currently in some form of non-state ownership. As of August 1, 1996, land was distributed to over 9,500 collectives and other forms of non-state ownership. Approximately 21.9 million hectares, or 60 percent of agricultural farm land, were transferred from state to collective ownership, and about 0.8 million hectares are located in private farms...." (p33)

Bjornlund, Britta S./U.S. Dept. of Agriculture. Economic Research Service. "Ukrainian Land Reform and Farm Privatization: Still a Long Road Ahead." Newly Independent States and the Baltics: International Agriculture and Trade Reports Situation and Outlook Series May 1997. p32-34.

LAND USE--UNITED STATES (v26)

"Of the roughly 3 billion acres in the United States, 1 billion acres are farm and ranch land. Excluding Alaska, some 64% of non-federal lands are devoted to agriculture (including livestock grazing), and the majority of federal lands as well--with 90% of BLM [Bureau of Land Management] lands and 69% of US Forest Service lands leased for livestock grazing. By comparison, only 5% of US non-federal (and none of the federal) lands are urbanized." (p58) "In the Pacific Northwest, farming occupies 25 million acres, or 16% of the land. Add the private lands used for livestock production, and nearly 40% of the land in the Northwest is devoted to agricultural production--and this figure doesn't include public lands committed to livestock production." (p59)

Wuerthner, George. "Conservation Strategy: Subdivisions and Extractive Industries." Wild Earth v7 n3 Fall 1997. p57-62. (ISSN1055-1166).

LAND USE, RURAL--MICHIGAN (v26)

LAND USE, RURAL--UNITED STATES (v26)

LAND USE, URBAN--INDONESIA (v26)

LANGUAGE AND EDUCATION--BRITISH COLUMBIA (v26)

LANGUAGE AND EDUCATION--UNITED STATES (v26)

LANGUAGE AND LANGUAGES (v26)

see also CHINESE LANGUAGE; EDUCATION, BILINGUAL; ENGLISH LANGUAGE; FRENCH LANGUAGE; INDIANS OF NORTH AMERICA--LANGUAGES; MASS MEDIA--SPANISH LANGUAGE; SIGN LANGUAGE; STUDENTS--CALIFORNIA--LOS ANGELES--LANGUAGES; UNITED STATES--LANGUAGES

LANGUAGE AND LANGUAGES--STUDY AND TEACHING

"Nearly a third of the [U.S.'s] public and private elementary schools offer foreign-language classes, up 10 percent since 1987." (p1) "The average American student starts learning a foreign language at age 14, six years after the average student in Austria, France, or Russia....Only 12 percent of the world [speaks English]....Nearly 27 percent of all high schoolers study Spanish, 9.3 percent study French, and Latin barely makes the list, with 1.6 percent....French children...study English for nine years on average, starting at age 10. Italian students study English for 11 years and start at age 8." (p10)

Baldauf, Scott. "Children Say 'Oui' to Foreign Languages." The Christian Science Monitor v89 n139 13 Jun 1997. p1,10. The Christian Science Monitor search engine: <http://www.csmonitor.com/plweb-cgi/iops1.pl> To retrieve this article, enter the following search: ED=19970613 AND languages. In the "retrieved list," click the title that matches this record. (ISSN0882-7729).

LATIN AMERICA--COMMERCE (v26)

In Latin America, "total exports among Mercosur countries went from $4 billion in 1990 to $14.5 billion in 1995. Combined GDP has grown by an annual average of 3.5 percent since 1990, while the rise in people's purchasing power within Mercosur has exceeded Latin America's average by about 30 percent. Mercosur today represents more than half of the Latin American market and the fourth largest integrated market, after NAFTA, the European Union (EU), and Japan. Its two hundred million consumers boast an average of $3,500 (U.S.) per capita income, with a $750 billion GDP (1993), and $65 billion worth of imports." (p235)

Tussie, Diana/Vasquez, Patricia I. "The FTAA, Mercosur, and the Environment." International Environmental Affairs v9 n3 Sum 1997. p232-248. (ISSN1041-4665).

LATIN AMERICA--ECONOMIC CONDITIONS (v26)

In Latin America, "in 1995, 15 of the region's 17 countries had levels of income inequality exceeding those normally associated with their level of development....Between 1990 and 1995 Latin America's average annual GDP grew 3.2 percent; in South Asia and East Asia the corresponding figures were 4.6 percent and 10.3 percent, respectively." (p386) "In 1995,...the share in total exports of the top 25 exporting firms--many of them transnationals--was 44 percent in Argentina, 26 percent in Brazil, and 56 percent in Mexico....Between 1990 and 1995, market capitalization as a percentage of GDP jumped from 2.3 to 13.5 in Argentina, from 3.4 to 21.8 in Brazil, and from 13.2 to 36.3 in Mexico....In Mexico, 10 firms received over 50 percent of total foreign investment in equities in 1993." (p387)

Heredia, Blanca. "Prosper or Perish?: Development in the Age of Global Capital." Current History v96 n613 Nov 1997. p383-388. (ISSN0011-3530).

"Two in five Latin Americans--210 million people--are poor. That's an increase of 60 million in one decade, giving Latin America the dubious distinction of having the world's most unequal distribution of wealth....Five countries now have unemployment rates of more than 15 percent." (p6)

Chepesiuk, Ron. "Legacy of a Hero." Toward Freedom v46 n6 Nov 1997. p5-6. (ISSN0048-9898).

LATIN AMERICA--ECONOMIC CONDITIONS--PUBLIC OPINION

"According to a 1995 poll conducted in 16 of the region's countries, the average person in Latin America does not perceive his condition to be improving. Despite the fact that the number of people below the poverty line has stabilized at around 150 million since the early 1990s, some 75 percent of Latin Americans think that poverty has increased in the past few years." (p8)

Silva, Samuel. "Figuratively Speaking: Reforms: Economic Perceptions versus Reality." IDB v24 n5 May 1997. p8-9. (ISSN0145-2274).

LATIN AMERICANS--UNITED STATES (v26)

LAUNDERING OF MONEY

see MONEY LAUNDERING

LAW

see also ACTIONS AND DEFENSES; AUTOMOBILES--UNITED STATES--FUEL CONSUMPTION--LAW AND LEGISLATION; CHILDREN--EMPLOYMENT--LAW AND LEGISLATION; COMPENSATION (LAW); COURTS; DRUG ABUSE--LAW AND LEGISLATION; DRUG TRAFFIC--LAW AND LEGISLATION; DRUGS--LAW AND LEGISLATION; FIREARMS--LAW AND LEGISLATION; GLOBAL WARMING--LAW AND LEGISLATION; JUSTICE, ADMINISTRATION OF; MENTALLY ILL--EMPLOYMENT--LAW AND LEGISLATION; PRISONERS--SUFFRAGE--LAW AND LEGISLATION; PRODUCT SAFETY--LAW AND LEGISLATION; TOBACCO INDUSTRY--LAW AND LEGISLATION; TOYS--LABELING--LAW AND LEGISLATION; TRUCKING--LAW AND LEGISLATION

LAW--EUROPE (v26)

LAW, POVERTY

see LEGAL ASSISTANCE TO THE POOR

LAW ENFORCEMENT--UNITED STATES--COSTS (v26)

LAW ENFORCEMENT OFFICERS

see POLICE

LAW FIRMS--UNITED STATES--SOFTWARE

In the U.S., "at least 50 percent of all malpractice claims lodged against lawyers arise from calendaring mistakes, according to Polk Communications and Research, which does marketing for CompuLaw. In a 1991 survey the company found that about two-thirds of the surveyed insurance companies offered premium reductions for firms with automatic calendaring programs. The reductions ranged from about 2 percent to 10 percent. Three companies said they wouldn't insure a law firm without docketing software." (p47)

Davis, Susan E. "Tech: Docket Science." California Lawyer v17 n9 Sep 1997. p47,52-53. (ISSN0279-4063).

LAW SCHOOLS--UNITED STATES--MINORITIES --ADMISSION

In the U.S., "as recently as the late 1960s, the combined proportion of black and Hispanic students nationwide in medical and law school stood at 4 percent and 5 percent, respectively. By the early 1990s, these numbers had more than doubled to 12 and 10 percent....At Berkeley's Boalt Hall School of Law, black and Latino admissions have plummeted by 81 percent and 50 percent....Once the nation's leading producer of minority lawyers, UT [University of Texas]-Austin expects only about a dozen Hispanics--and not a single black--in an entering class of 500....The law school at UCLA [University of California at Los Angeles]...[had] a decline in the numbers of blacks and Latinos of 80 percent and 32 percent, respectively." (p18)

Karabel, Jerome. "Opinion/Essays: Time for the President to Defend Affirmative Action." The Christian Science Monitor v89 n139 13 Jun 1997. p18. The Christian Science Monitor search engine: <http://www.csmonitor.com/plweb-cgi/iops1.pl> To retrieve this article, enter the following search: ED=19970613 AND action. In the "retrieved list," click the title that matches this record. (ISSN0882-7729).

LAW STUDENTS

see also AFRO-AMERICAN LAW STUDENTS; CANADA--LAW STUDENTS; MINORITY LAW STUDENTS

LAW STUDENTS--CANADA

"The 6,400 students at Canada's 16 common-law schools can count themselves among the favored few. At some schools, four out of five who apply to take an LLB degree are turned away. Many institutions require a solid A average and a score in the top 20 per cent of those who write the Law School Admission Test (LSAT)....At the University of Victoria, market pressure has pushed up average entering grades 6.5 per cent and LSAT scores by almost 15 per cent in just 10 years." (p17)

Dwyer, Victor. "Cover: Privilege and Pressure." Maclean's v110 n40 6 Oct 1997. p16-20. (ISSN0024-9262).

LAW STUDENTS--HARVARD UNIVERSITY

"Ronald Fox, the former director of the Public Interest Counseling Center at Harvard Law School, reports that 'about 40 percent of the first-year class express some interest in public sector law. That figure drops to 12 percent after the second year and to about six percent following the last year of law school' (Rubin, 1990)." (p155) A study of Harvard University Law students conducted by Robert Granfield and Thomas Koenig found that "most of the 21 percent of the third-year students who envisioned a future in public interest or government work ended up joining large commercial law firms....While 77 percent of first-year working class students report being interested in family law, only 43 percent of their second- and third-year counterparts find this area of practice rewarding....While nearly 79 percent of first-year working class students consider litigation fulfilling, only 58 percent of the second- and third-year students report similar evaluations....While 58 percent of the first-year students rate personal injury law as rewarding, less than 35 percent of the second- and third-year students feel this way....While fewer than six percent of the first-year working class students sampled believe tax law to be stimulating, nearly 40 percent of their second-and third-year counterparts offer this evaluation." (p158-159) "Today, more than 90 percent of all Harvard Law School graduates enter commercial law firms." (p171)

Granfield, Robert/Koenig, Thomas. "Can Law School Idealism Survive? Implications for Progressive Lawyers." Guild Practitioner v54 n3 Sum 1997. p155-172. (ISSN0017-5390).

A study of Harvard University Law students conducted by Robert Granfield and Thomas Koenig found that "more than half of the first-year working class students report being under high levels of stress as compared to 32 percent of those students from more privileged backgrounds....Nearly 62 percent of the first-year working class students report experiencing excessive grade pressure as compared to 35 percent of the more advantaged students." (p160)

Granfield, Robert/Koenig, Thomas. "Can Law School Idealism Survive? Implications for Progressive Lawyers." Guild Practitioner v54 n3 Sum 1997. p155-172. (ISSN0017-5390).

LAW STUDENTS--UNITED STATES

In the U.S., "since 1991, legal education has lost a third of its applicant pool, declining in size nationally from 100,000 to 70,900....A legal education now typically costs more than $60,000; the median indebtedness for 1995 graduates was $40,300." (p11 secA)

Doctoroff, Andrew S. "Other Voices: More Doesn't Mean Better When It Comes to New Lawyers." Detroit Free Press 18 Jul 1997. p11 secA.

LAWNS--UNITED STATES--COSTS

"The Lawn Institute estimates there are at least 54 million homeowners in...[the U.S.] sweating over their yards on any given weekend. In comparison, there are fewer than 2 million farmers." (p1) "In 1994, consumers spent $25.9 billion on do-it-yourself lawn and garden activities, according to a national Gallup poll. They spent an additional $13.4 billion on professional lawn and landscape activities that same year, which was an increase of $900 million from the previous year." (p12)

DeVore, Brian. "The American Lawn Just Isn't Cutting It." Land Stewardship Letter v15 n2 Apr-May 1997. p1,10-12.

LAWNS--WEED CONTROL--UNITED STATES

"In an average year, American lawn lovers...apply between 70 and 75 million pounds of chemicals that kill weeds, insects and fungi. Today the typical lawn owner annually applies on a per-acre basis 2.38 pounds of pesticides, 4.28 pounds of herbicides and 1.69 pounds of fungicides, according to the EPA. In comparison, corn farmers on average apply less than a pound of herbicides or insecticides per acre." (p10)

DeVore, Brian. "The American Lawn Just Isn't Cutting It." Land Stewardship Letter v15 n2 Apr-May 1997. p1,10-12.

LAWSUITS

see ACTIONS AND DEFENSES

LAWYERS

see also LAW FIRMS; WOMEN LAWYERS

LAWYERS--CANADA

"A recent survey by the Law Society of Upper Canada found that civil litigators now earn an average of $131,000 a year. For labor lawyers, the figure is $140,000; for patent lawyers, $167,000--a figure that is only a fraction of what senior partners in major firms can take home annually. Even immigration attorneys, many of whom work with less affluent clients, pocket a respectable $62,000 on average." (p17) "In Ontario alone, the number of lawyers has risen to 24,800 this year from 10,500 in 1976, at a time when the population has grown only 30 per cent. Canada as a whole has 60,000. Each year, roughly 2,000 more common-law lawyers hit the market." (p18)

Dwyer, Victor. "Cover: Privilege and Pressure." Maclean's v110 n40 6 Oct 1997. p16-20. (ISSN0024-9262).

LAWYERS--EMPLOYMENT--UNITED STATES

In the U.S., "today, only two-thirds of law school graduates find full-time legal positions; in 1988, 85 percent did. The incomes of those fortunate enough to secure employment have declined; between 1990 and 1995, the average starting salary at private firms, adjusted for inflation, fell by 15 percent. Because well paying jobs are so difficult to find, nearly 20 percent of all private loans to law school graduates are in default (this, an all-time high, compares to a 3.2 percent rate in June 1993)." (p11 secA)

Doctoroff, Andrew S. "Other Voices: More Doesn't Mean Better When It Comes to New Lawyers." Detroit Free Press 18 Jul 1997. p11 secA.

LAWYERS--HEALTH AND HYGIENE--UNITED STATES

A U.S. study "that tracked 584 female law graduates found those who worked more than 45 hours a week were three times more likely to have a miscarriage than those who worked less than 35 hours. Another study of men's suicide cases found that male lawyers were two times as likely to commit suicide as the general population....Nearly half of the women lawyers surveyed said they feel high stress. Of the women who worked 45 hours or more a week, 63 percent indicated they were tense much, most or all of the time." (p28)

Gatland, Laura. "News: Dangerous Dedication." ABA Journal v83 Dec 1997. p28-30. (ISSN0747-0088).

LAWYERS--ISRAEL (v26)

LAWYERS--MICHIGAN--PUBLIC OPINION (v26)

LAWYERS--SALARIES, ETC.--MICHIGAN (v26)

LAWYERS--SALARIES, ETC.--UNITED STATES

"Starting salaries at large New York firms appear to be hovering around $87,000 annually, although some are as high as $91,000. In contrast, Los Angeles-based Latham & Watkins pays $80,000 annually to start, plus bonuses that average $14,500. Even in St. Louis starting pay has reached $60,000. Those figures don't include the stipend paid to individuals who are studying for the bar, which can be as much as $7,000 in New York and $3,000 in St. Louis. Bonuses also can be hefty; one firm reportedly gave associates a bonus of 50 percent of their base salary at year end." (p35-36)

Samborn, Hope Viner. "News: Business Is Booming." ABA Journal v83 Oct 1997. p34-36. (ISSN0747-0088).

LAWYERS--UNITED STATES

In 1996-1997, the American Bar Association "membership increased, for the second year in a row, to 392,418 members, up 1.9 percent from the prior year....Membership across all sections, divisions and forums at the end of association year 1996-97 totaled 393,080--an increase of 0.8 percent over the prior year." (p102)

Stein, Robert A. "Your ABA/Executive Director's Report: Our Numbers Keep Growing." ABA Journal v83 Nov 1997. p102-103. (ISSN0747-0088).

LAWYERS--UNITED STATES--ACCOUNTING

In the U.S., "one survey of more than 400 law firms, recently released by Altman Weil Pensa, based in Newtown Square, Pa., reported that gross revenue per lawyer rose more than $25,000, from the 1993 total of $239,677 to $264,689 in 1996....The legal consulting firm's survey reports that billables for partners with 25 to 29 years of experience and associates with five years experience averaged 1,614 and 1,842 respectively in 1993 while in 1996 they averaged 1,646 and 1,847 respectively. For many firms, required billables exceed 2,000, according to most experts. Billing rates also have been climbing steadily, according to the Altman survey. They stood at an average of $184 an hour in 1993 for lawyers with 25 to 29 years of experience and $200 in 1996." (p34)

Samborn, Hope Viner. "News: Business Is Booming." ABA Journal v83 Oct 1997. p34-36. (ISSN0747-0088).

LAWYERS--UNITED STATES--ETHICS--ATTITUDES

"Nearly 100 lawyers attending the ABA [American Bar Association] Annual Meeting participated in an on-the-fly survey on ethics issues related to litigation....When the question was asked, 'Is it ethically permissible to engage in settlement "puffery" that involves some misrepresentation?' 61 percent of the lawyers responding to the query said, 'Yes.'...The number of respondents who engaged in puffery themselves was even higher, 73 percent....82 percent of the respondents agreed it would be improper to threaten to file a disciplinary complaint against an adversary to increase settlement leverage....Of the respondents, 54 percent reported they had been asked by another lawyer to do something unethical, and 56 percent said they had been asked by a client to do something the client knew was unethical....59 percent of the litigators said a client has knowingly asked them to commit an ethics violation, while 54 percent of business, tax and real estate lawyers have been asked by a client to do something unethical. And criminal lawyers? All 20 who responded said clients have asked them to do something unethical." (p97)

Carter, Terry. "Your ABA/Annual Meeting Report: Ethics by the Numbers." ABA Journal v83 Oct 1997. p97. (ISSN0747-0088).

LEAD--TOXICOLOGY--NEW JERSEY

"The U.S. Centers for Disease Control and Prevention has set the acceptable blood level of lead at below 10 micrograms per deciliter (ug/dl)....[The National Institute of Environmental Health Sciences in New Jersey] recruited 100 Jersey City families whose children had blood lead levels of 10-20 ug/dl for the Children's Lead Assessment and Reduction Study (CLEARS). Half the families got detailed instructions in cleaning their homes to lower lead levels and a cleaning crew visited these homes every 2 weeks for 1 year to vacuum thoroughly, dust, and wash down the walls with detergent and water....'At the end of the year, the children in the cleaning group had lowered their lead values by a little more than 15%, and for the children of moms who had really cooperated with us, the leads had gone down about 30%,'...[NIEHS Core IV co-director George Rhoads] says." (p793)

Young, Patrick/U.S. National Institute of Environmental Health Sciences. "NIEHS News: Environmental Health Gold Mine in New Jersey." Environmental Health Perspectives v105 n8 Aug 1997. p792-793.

LEAD--TOXICOLOGY--UNITED STATES

The U.S. Occupational Safety and Health Administration "estimated that nearly a million people work on construction projects involving lead each year....Approximately 57,000 workers, primarily painters, laborers and ironworkers, are annually exposed to lead in highway and railroad bridge and water and petroleum tank repainting and rehabilitation projects. The Federal Highway Administration estimates that 90 percent of steel bridges in the U.S. are coated with lead-based paint....Although workers on structural steel projects constitute only 6 percent of the total construction work force exposed to lead, they are exposed to the highest and most persistent levels experienced in the industry." (p66) "A study of the causes of U.S. workers' death at age 65 or younger found that construction workers are much more likely to die of lung diseases, several cancers, and liver disease as compared to other workers." (p67)

Roelofs, Cora. "Does Health Pay?: Economic Incentives for the Protection of Construction Workers from Lead." New Solutions v7 n4 Sum 1997. p66-73. (ISSN1048-2911).

LEAD--TOXICOLOGY--UNITED STATES--CHILDREN (v26)

LEAD IN THE BODY--UNITED STATES (v26)

LEAD POISONING IN AFRO-AMERICAN CHILDREN

In the U.S., "lead poisoning in children, an environmental hazard of major proportions, is estimated to affect three to four million children under the age of six. One out [of] every six children in the United States has a blood lead level higher than the trigger levels established by the Centers for Disease Control, but African-American children consistently have higher levels than whites, and among low-income African-American children, the rate approaches an astounding 70 percent." (p74)

Field, Rodger C. "Environmental Justice: Risk and Justice: Capitalist Production and the Environment." Capitalism, Nature, Socialism v8 n2 Jun 1997. p69-94. (ISSN1045-5752).

LEAD POISONING IN CHILDREN--MASSACHUSETTS

"The Massachusetts Department of Public Health (DPH) reports 323 cases (25mcg/dl) [of lead poisoned children] in fiscal year 1996, down 33% from a reported 487 cases in FY 1995. Lead poisoning is defined as having 25 micrograms or greater of lead per deciliter of whole blood....The report showed a continuing decline in the lead poisoning rate (cases per 1000 population) from 5.5 in 1987 to 3.0 in 1991 and down to 1.2 in 1996. In Boston, the number of new cases of lead poisoned children declined from 100 in FY 1995 to 64 in FY 1996....In 1995, there were 722 children with elevated blood lead levels across the state, while 1996 numbers dropped to 566, a 22% decline."

Massachusetts. Dept. of Public Health. "'Child Lead Poisoning Rates Down.'" Press Release 25 Feb 1997. document-level access: <http://www.magnet.state.ma.us/dph/lead97.htm>

LEAD POISONING IN CHILDREN--UNITED STATES

"Nearly nine percent of US preschoolers, 1.7 million, have lead poisoning. Federal agencies spend nearly $200 million each year to prevent lead poisoning, test young children, and research solutions." (p70)

Dunkiel, Brian S. "Conservation Strategy: How Government Tax Subsidies Destroy Habitat." Wild Earth v7 n2 Sum 1997. p69-71. (ISSN1055-1166).

LEADERSHIP

In the U.S, "in a forthcoming Conference Board Report on leadership in the private sector, only 54 percent of survey respondents believed their companies had the leaders needed to respond effectively to change, while 91 percent said leadership--not management--was essential to growth and performance. In December 1996, the NAPA [National Academy of Public Administration] Center for Human Resources Management surveyed federal agencies and other public sector organizations and...56 percent of respondents believed that they, too, did not have sufficient leaders to meet emerging changes in government....The Conference Board found that 61 percent of private corporations have a formal company succession program; 32 percent have a more informal approach that they are changing to formal. Half link succession planning to their strategic business plan, and 64 percent link it to their leadership development program....28 percent of NAPA governmental respondents had or planned to have a succession management program, only 44 percent had any sort of leadership development program, only 11 percent link succession/leader development efforts to the agency's strategic plan, and...15 percent protect such efforts as a budget priority." (p41-42)

Blunt, Ray/Clark, Hugh. "Series: HRM Developing Issues: Growing Public Service Leaders." Public Manager v26 n2 Sum 1997. p41-45. (ISSN1061-7639).

LEARNING DISABILITIES--WALES (v26)

LEARNING DISABLED--UNITED STATES (v26)

LEARNING DISABLED CHILDREN--EDUCATION --UNITED STATES (v26)

LEAVE, PARENTAL

see PARENTAL LEAVE

LEAVE OF ABSENCE--AUSTRALIA

According to the report, "Career Experience, Australia, November 1996," by the Australian Bureau of Statistics, "an estimated 227,700 employees who had worked with their current employer for more than six months had taken a break from their current employment of six months or more. Females made up the majority (67 per cent) of these persons. Females also made up 98 per cent of all persons who took a break from work for family reasons. Of those employees with children under six years of age, 685,500 employees had taken leave or left the labour force when their youngest child was born. Females made up 95 per cent of 83,400 employees who had left the labour force when their youngest child was born. Males made up 90 per cent of persons who took paid leave only and females made up 74 per cent of persons who took unpaid leave only."

Australian Bureau of Statistics. "Australia's Employment Experience--ABS." Media Release 27 Jun 1997. document-level access: <http://www.abs.gov.au/websitedbs/d3110125.nsf/4a255eef008309e44a255eef00061e57/aa9c2c6faed989664a2564c200798129?OpenDocument>

LEBANON--ECONOMIC CONDITIONS

In Lebanon, "debt service stands at more than 40 percent of the 1997 budget....Economic growth has been estimated at nine and 6.5 percent in 1994 and 1995 respectively, and at four percent in 1996...." (p17)

Perthes, Volker. "Myths and Money: Four Years of Hariri and Lebanon's Preparation for a New Middle East." Middle East Report v27 n2 Spr 1997. p16-21. (ISSN0899-2851).

LEBANON--RELIGION (v26)

LEGAL ASSISTANCE TO THE POOR--MICHIGAN (v26)

LEGAL ASSISTANCE TO THE POOR--UNITED STATES

Doreen D. Dodson of St. Louis, a member of the ABA Standing Committee on Legal Aid and Indigent Defendants, noted that between 1995 and 1996, "cases handled by legal services programs nationwide dropped almost 15 percent, from 1.6 million to 1.4 million; yet more than 40 million Americans live in households with incomes below the poverty level. Another 11 million just above the poverty level also may qualify for legal services....Opponents of the LSC [Legal Services Corp.] prevailed on a House appropriations subcommittee vote that approved only $141 million for the program, less than half its current level of $283 million....The Senate Appropriations Committee, which in the past has provided stronger support for the LSC, voted to increase program funding to $300 million....All these resources together still are meeting only about 20 percent of the legal needs of the poor." (p96)

McMillion, Rhonda. "Your ABA/Washington Report: No Reprieve for LSC." ABA Journal v83 Sep 1997. p96. (ISSN0747-0088).

LEGAL HOLIDAYS

see HOLIDAYS

LEGAL PROFESSION

see LAWYERS

LEGAL SERVICES--AUSTRALIA

"At the end of June last year, Australia's 9,796 legal practices had an operating profit margin of almost 32 per cent, according to information released...by the Australian Bureau of Statistics

(ABS)....The 9,796 legal practices represented an 11 per cent increase in the number of practices since June 1993. In this period the number of solicitor practices increased by 15 per cent to 6,403 and the number of barrister practices by 5 per cent to 3,350. In terms of total employment, 95 per cent of these practices were small (employing less than 20 people). These practices generated $5,591 million in income in 1995-96 with commercial, finance and business services legal work ($1,785 million) and property conveyancing ($683 million) being the major sources of this income. The industry recorded an operating profit before tax of $1,750 million, which represented an operating profit margin of 31.5 per cent, a small decrease on the 32.6 per cent recorded in 1992-93."

Australian Bureau of Statistics. "Legal Profits Steady, Accounting Industry Grows." Media Release 10 Nov 1997. document-level access: <http://www.abs.gov.au/websitedbs/d3110125.nsf/4a255eef008309e44a255eef00061e57/4870c6ee56dae103ca25654b0004d5e2?OpenDocument>

LEGAL SERVICES--EMPLOYMENT--AUSTRALIA

According to the Australian Bureau of Statistics, "there were 67,494 people employed in the [legal services] industry at the end of June 1996, of which 27,000 were qualified barristers or solicitors. Eighty-one percent of employment was on a full-time basis with females accounting for 83 per cent of part-time employment. Labour costs of $1,906 million represented about half of practice expenses."

Australian Bureau of Statistics. "Legal Profits Steady, Accounting Industry Grows." Media Release 10 Nov 1997. document-level access: <http://www.abs.gov.au/websitedbs/d3110125.nsf/4a255eef008309e44a255eef00061e57/4870c6ee56dae103ca25654b0004d5e2?OpenDocument>

LEGAL SERVICES--UNITED STATES

In the U.S., approximately 97 percent of the Legal Services "Corporation's budget goes directly to local programs that provide legal services to the poor, with only three percent going to the Corporation's centralized oversight, management and disbursement functions....Local programs build upon their grants from the LSC with funding from additional sources. In 1995 grantees reported having received $254 million from state and local governments, the private bar, other private contributors and other federal agencies....Basic field programs are required to devote an amount equal to one-eighth of their LSC grants to private attorney involvement. More than 130,000 lawyers are registered as volunteer attorneys in organized 'pro bono' programs. In recent years they have been handling approximately a quarter of a million cases per year." (p9-10)

Eakeley, Douglas S. (Chair, Legal Services Corporation)/ Erlenborn, John N. (Vice Chair, Legal Services Corporation)/ Bergmark, Martha (President, Legal Services Corporation). "Departments of Commerce, Justice, And State, The Judiciary...Approp. for 1998 (Part 8)." Hearing. U.S. House. Committee on Appropriations. Washington, D.C. : GPO, 1997. (ISBN0160551641). (Y4.Ap6/1:C73/2/997/pt.8).

In the U.S., of almost 1.7 million Legal Services Corporation "cases closed by local programs in 1995, the vast majority were resolved through advice, brief services, administrative proceedings, or negotiated settlements. Only 8 percent were resolved through a court decision. Of these, over two-thirds (68 percent) were family law cases in which court intervention was required under state law, such as divorces, protective orders, and child custody and support decisions. An additional 24 percent were housing, consumer finance, and juvenile cases." (p91)

Legal Services Corporation. "Departments of Commerce, Justice, And State, The Judiciary...Approp. for 1998 (Part 8)." Hearing. U.S. House. Committee on Appropriations. Washington, D.C. : GPO, 1997. (ISBN0160551641). (Y4.Ap6/1:C73/2/997/pt.8).

LEGAL SERVICES--UNITED STATES--FINANCE (v26)

LEGISLATORS--UNITED STATES

In the U.S., "today, only eight out of 49 house speakers and nine out of 50 senate presiding officers held that office just seven years ago. Eighty-six percent of legislative leaders have left their leadership positions since 1990. In 1996, 920 of the nation's legislators decided not to seek reelection. In 1994, the numbers were even higher--1,154 sat out the election." (p50)

Hansen, Karen. "Term Limits for Better or Worse." State Legislatures v23 n7 Jul-Aug 1997. p50-51,53,55,57. (ISSN0147-6041).

LEGITIMACY (LAW)

see ILLEGITIMACY

LEISURE--CHILDREN

"When asked to name their favorite activity, 55 percent of children surveyed in the U.S., Germany, the U.K., Japan, China, and France say the same thing: 'being with friends.' Watching TV is an extremely popular activity, with over 90 percent of children in the six countries watching television at least three days a week....Kids in the U.S. are the busiest shoppers: 55 percent report shopping as a favorite activity. Forty-seven percent of Japanese children and 46 percent of Chinese like to shop, followed by 37 percent of British, French, and German kids." (p35)

Kate, Nancy Ten. "Kaleidoscope: Are All Children the Same?" American Demographics v19 n6 Jun 1997. p35-36. article-level access: <http://www.demographics.com/publications/ad/97_ad/9706_ad/ad970619.htm> (ISSN0163-4089).

LENDING

see LOANS

LEPROSY (v26)

The total of newly detected cases of leprosy "regarded as skin-smear positive--that is, where samples from the skin of suspects are shown by tests to have very high numbers of bacilli--has fallen sharply from a peak of close to 1 million ten years ago to only an estimated 70,000 worldwide in 1996....WHO's Action Programme for the Elimination of Leprosy has reported that well over 97 per cent of known cases are being treated with MDT [multidrug therapy]. The number of countries showing prevalence rates above 1 case per 10,000 population has fallen from 122 in 1985 to 55 at the beginning of 1997. Most of those countries have comparatively few cases, since 16 major endemic countries account for 91 per cent of the global leprosy burden. Besides the 8.4 million patients who have been cured, more than 1 million individuals have been saved by multidrug therapy from becoming disabled." (p76)

"Healthwatch: Simplified Treatment for Leprosy." UN Chronicle v34 n3 1997. p76. (ISSN0251-7329).

There has "been an astonishing 84% decrease in the global leprosy burden since 1985. The total of registered cases in 1997 stands at around 888,000. Leprosy is still a public health problem in 55...[countries] or areas. Of these, only 16 are rated as 'the most endemic countries,' and they account for 91% of all cases....By the beginning of 1997, some 8.4 million patients had been cured with MDT [multidrug therapy], which had also prevented the development of physical disabilities in well over one million individuals. The global coverage of known cases with MDT currently stands at over 97%." (p2)

World Health Organization. "Leprosy." WHO Fact Sheet n101 Jun 1997. p1-3. document-level access: <http://www.who.ch/programmes/inf/facts/fact101.htm>

"In spite of the remarkable progress that has been made in curing more than 8.5 million people [of leprosy], about two million cases still remain to be detected and treated before the

WHO goal of eliminating the disease by the year 2000 is attained. In the mid-1980s, there were an estimated 12 million cases in the world. Today that estimate has been revised to only around one million, while the number of registered cases receiving MDT [multidrug therapy] stands at less than 890,000. Where there were 122 countries with prevalence rates above one case per 10,000 population in 1985, there are now only 55." (p2)

World Health Organization. "Secretary-General Inaugurates Leprosy Exhibition at UN HQ." WHO Press n77 30 Oct 1997. p1-2. document-level access: <http://www.who.ch/press/1997/pr97-77.html>

LEPTOSPIROSIS--HAWAII

"A total of 22 cases of leptospirosis have been reported to the [Hawaii] Department of Health (DOH) through July 21, 1997. This compares with seven reported during the same period in 1996....Of the 22 cases reported this year, eight have been from Kaua'i, seven from Hawai'i, and five from O'ahu. Two of the cases were individuals exposed to the germ in Micronesia. Of the 16 persons who could provide information on where they could have become infected, possible exposures (including multiple exposures) include contact with animals (8), taro farming (5), swimming in fresh water streams (5), use of water catchment systems (5), and other kinds of farming (3). In addition, six of the cases had predisposing skin wounds at the time of exposure."

Hawaii. Dept. of Health. "DOH Warns about Rise in Leptospirosis Cases." Press Release 1997. document-level access: <http://www.hawaii.gov/health/press/prleptos.htm>

LETTER WRITING--UNITED STATES (v26)

LETTUCE INDUSTRY--UNITED STATES

Of all vegetable sales in the U.S. in 1996, "lettuce suffered the largest decline in value, $563 million or 28 percent, compared with 1995. In 1995, cash receipts from lettuce had soared to 56 percent above those of 1994....In 1996, the lettuce harvest rebounded and prices retreated. Although lettuce growers brought only about 6 percent more product to the market than in 1995, these additional market offerings were enough to cause head lettuce prices to drop by almost 37 percent (nearly back to their 1994 level). California and Arizona accounted for 97 percent of 1996 lettuce receipts." (p8)

U.S. Dept. of Agriculture. Economic Research Service. "1996 Farm Income Estimates: Net Value-Added and Net Farm Income Attain New Highs in 1996." Agricultural Income and Finance Situation and Outlook Report Sep 1997. p4-13.

In the U.S., "in 1996, romaine accounted for 13 percent of lettuce area, compared with 7 percent in 1992. The share of lettuce area devoted to leaf varieties has risen from 14 to 15 percent since 1992. Lettuce area overall has increased 2 percent since 1992, but head lettuce has lost market share." (p4)

U.S. Dept. of Agriculture. Economic Research Service. "Summary." Vegetables and Specialties Situation and Outlook Yearbook Jul 1997. p3-5.

LEVEES--CALIFORNIA

"California has over 6,000 miles of flood control levees....In 1986, four levees failed, three in the delta, one in Yuba County. In 1995, 25 levees failed. In 1997, there were 62 significant levee breaks, according to the Corps of Engineers. Of these, 40 were federally maintained levees, and the rest were non-Federal. On January 2, the Feather River broke through the levee at Star Bend, flooding 15 square miles of farmland and the community of Olivehurst. The breach was 1,500 feet long....On January 4, a Sutter bypass levee failed at Meridian, flooding a 35,000 acre basin with more than 60 homes and businesses. The breach at Meridian was 1,100 feet long. On January 4, the San Joaquin River plunged through levees in 14 places near the town of Mendota, flooding about 10,000 acres of farmland on both sides of the river in Madera and Fresno Counties. The biggest levee break, at Firebaugh, was 2,500 feet long. On January 5, more levees broke along the Stanislaus, Tuolomne, and San Joaquin Rivers, causing flooding near Modesto." (pS4177)

Feinstein, Dianne (Sen.-Calif.). "Supplemental Appropriations and Rescissions Act of 1997." Congressional Record. Daily ed. v143 n59 8 May 1997. pS4137-4205. section/page-level access: <http://thomas.loc.gov/cgi-bin/query/R?r105:FLD001:S04177:> (ISSN0363-7239). (X1.1A.105/1).

LIBERTY (v26)

"The president of Freedom House, an American organization that keeps careful score of gains and losses in freedom around the world, reported recently that in 1995 he classified 76 of the existing 191 sovereign states and related territories as free democracies--this as compared with 53 of 167 in 1985. That gain of 23 democracies in ten years, however, must be weighed against a sharp decline in the percentage of the world's people included in the free states over the same decade--a decline of 15 percent from 35 percent in 1985 to only 20 percent in 1995. The remaining 80 percent were divided about equally between the partly free and the decidedly unfree states." (p354-355)

Woodward, C. Vann. "The Aging of Democracies." American Scholar v66 n3 Sum 1997. p349-358. (ISSN0003-0937).

LIBERTY--AFRICA--AMERICA (v26)

LIBERTY--ASIA--MIDDLE EAST (v26)

LIBERTY--FORMER SOVIET REPUBLICS (v26)

LIBRARIES

see LIBRARY OF CONGRESS THOMAS JEFFERSON BUILDING (WASHINGTON, D.C.)

LIBRARIES--UNITED STATES (v26)

LIBRARY OF CONGRESS THOMAS JEFFERSON BUILDING (WASHINGTON, D.C.) (v26)

"The statistics are mind-boggling: more than 111 million items--books, recordings, photographs, maps and manuscripts--in the [U.S.] Library of Congress, the world's largest library. This treasure trove covers 532 miles of bookshelves--or as Dr. Billington once said, 'Imagine the distance from Washington D.C., to Detroit, every inch of the drive lined with books.'... In fiscal 1996, more than 23,000 pieces were received by the Library each working day." (p292)

Urschel, Donna. "The Desire to Acquire: Detailing the Library's Selective Acquisition Process." Library of Congress Information Bulletin v56 n14 Sep 1997. p292-295. (ISSN0041-7904).

LICENSE SYSTEM--MICHIGAN--DETROIT

"With a population of just over 1 million in Detroit, according to the 1990 Census, and a quota of one license for every 1,500 residents, Detroit is allowed 685 liquor licenses for bars and restaurants. Detroit has 809 current licenses because those who had them before the 1990 Census didn't lose their permits with the population drop." (p1 secC)

Josar, David. "The Metro: Liquor License Prices Likely to Soar." Detroit News 30 Jun 1997. p1 secC.

LICENSES (PATENTS)

see PATENT LICENSES

LIFE, QUALITY OF

see QUALITY OF LIFE

LIFE EXPECTANCY (v26)

"Half a century ago, the great majority of the global population died before the age of 50. Today, most survive well beyond that age. Average life expectancy at birth globally reached 65 years in 1996. In many countries, it is now well over 70 years, and is approaching 80 years in a few others. There are today an estimated 380 million people aged 65 years or more. By 2020,

that number is expected to rise to more than 690 million." (p2-3)
World Health Organization. "World Health Report 1997." Press Release 5 May 1997. p1-7. document-level access: <http://www.who.ch/whr/1997/presse.htm>

"Among the 25 largest countries, the gap in life expectancy between women and men is largest in the Russian Federation (13.6 years), Ukraine (10.2) and France (8.2). That gap is smallest in Iran (0.9 years) and India (0.4 years). In Bangladesh, life expectancy for men is longer than for women by almost one year." (p77)
"The Chronicle Library Shelf: Demographic Yearbook 1995." UN Chronicle v34 n3 1997. p77. (ISSN0251-7329).

"Calculations of life expectancy at birth and at 65 years show almost everywhere a divergence in favour of women. Worldwide in 1995, the average figure at birth was 67 years for women and 63 years for men. At one extreme is Japan, where women at birth can expect to live on average for over 83 years and men for nearly 77 years; at the other extreme is sub-Saharan Africa where the average figures are 52 years for women and 49 years for men." (p9)
Stuckelberger, Astrid. "Men and Women Age Differently." World Health n4 Jul-Aug 1997. p8-9. (ISSN0043-8502).

LIFE EXPECTANCY--AFRICA, EASTERN--EUROPE

"Life expectancy for 1990 to 1995 in eastern Africa is estimated at 46.7 years, which is 3.9 years lower than projected in the previous Revision [of the official United Nations population estimates and projections report]....In Eastern Europe,...life expectancy declined from 70 to 68 years from 1990 to 1995. In Western Europe, life expectancy increased slightly faster than previously expected, reaching 76.7 years." (p72)
"Population 2050: 9.4 Billion." UN Chronicle v34 n3 1997. p72. (ISSN0251-7329).

LIFE EXPECTANCY--AUSTRALIA

"In 1994-96 the life expectancy for Australian males was 75.2 years while that for females was 81.1 years. Females born in the period 1994-96 can expect to live almost six years longer than males....Experimental life tables indicate that life expectancy for Aboriginal and Torres Strait Islander people born in the period 1991-1996 is around 57 years for males and 66 years for females, 15-18 years less than the non-Indigenous population."
Australian Bureau of Statistics. "Death Rates Lower for Married Australians--ABS." Media Release 31 Oct 1997. document-level access: <http://www.abs.gov.au/websitedbs/d3110125.nsf/4a255eef008309e44a255eef00061e57/ae9c580551bbf55bca2565400075e403?OpenDocument>

LIFE EXPECTANCY--CZECH REPUBLIC (v26)

LIFE EXPECTANCY--EUROPE

"Highest EU life expectancy in 1996 was of French baby girls at 81.9 years. Two-thirds of Member States had female life expectancy of 80+. Lowest rate was of Portuguese baby boys at 71, nearly two years below next lowest Denmark (72.8). However, the Portuguese--and EU males in general (74)--are far better off than baby boys in India (61.3) and China (68.3), and those born in the Russian Federation can anticipate 15 years less than their EU cousins. Japanese boys come in at 77, approached only in the EU by the Swedes (76.5). 'World champions' are Japanese baby girls at 83.3. US life expectancy is not as high as the EU's: 72.7 (boys) and 79.4 (girls). The report adds that average annual rise in EU life expectancy in the '90s was around two months with three months in Austria, Finland and Sweden (boys only)."
Eurostat. "EU Women Average 1.44 Babies." Press Release 1 Aug 1997. document-level access: <http://europa.eu.int/en/comm/eurostat/compres/en/5697/6305697a.htm>

LIFE EXPECTANCY--LATIN AMERICA (v26)

LIFE EXPECTANCY--RUSSIA (v26)

LIFE EXPECTANCY--UGANDA (v26)

LIFE EXPECTANCY--UNITED STATES (v26)

In the U.S., "in 1995 life expectancy at birth was 75.8 years, equal to the record high in 1992. Women currently are expected to outlive men by an average of 6.4 years, and the difference between life expectancy for the white population (76.5 years) and the black population (69.6) remains at about 7 years."
U.S. National Center for Health Statistics. "1995 Final Mortality Statistics Released." Fact Sheet 12 Jun 1997. document-level access: <http://www.cdc.gov/nchswww/releases/97facts/97sheets/95morrel.htm>

According to the CDC's 1996 Vital Statistic Report, in the U.S., "life expectancy reached an all-time high of 76.1 years in 1996, up from 75.8 in 1995. Record high life expectancies were reached for white and black males (73.8 and 66.1 years, respectively), and for black females (74.2). The gender gap in life expectancy narrowed from 6.4 years in 1995 to 6.0 years in 1996, while the race differential between the white and black populations narrowed from 6.9 years to 6.5 years."
U.S. Dept. of Health and Human Services. "Vital Statistics Report Shows Significant Gains in Health." Press Release 11 Sep 1997. document-level access: <http://www.hhs.gov/news/press/1997pres/970911a.html>

In the U.S., "at age 25, average remaining lifetime for men was 49.5 years compared with 49.2 years in 1995 and 49.1 years in 1994 and 1992. Male average future lifetime at ages 45 and 65 in 1996 was 31.5 years and 15.7 years, respectively. For women, the average number of remaining years increased slightly at ages 15-45. Nonetheless, their 1996 life expectancies still are below their longevity peaks recorded in 1992....Between 1989-91 and 1995, expectation of life for infant white boys increased by 0.7 years, while the comparable gain among girls was 0.1 year. For newborns of all other races, the rise among boys was 0.9 years and for girls 0.3 years. African-American infant boys gained 0.7 years of additional life in the period, while the increase among girls was 0.2 years." (p3)
Kranczer, Stanley. "Record High U.S. Life Expectancy." Statistical Bulletin v78 n4 Oct-Dec 1997. p2-8. (ISSN0790-8334).

In the U.S., "while white male life expectancy is 73.1 years, black male life expectancy is only 64.6 years. For white women, the figure is 79.5 years; for black women, it's 73.7 years." (p19)
Rueter, Ted. "Opinion/Essays: Senior Citizen Discounts Are Affirmative Action for the Wealthy." The Christian Science Monitor v89 n194 2 Sep 1997. p19. The Christian Science Monitor search engine: <http://www.csmonitor.com/plweb-cgi/iops1.pl> To retrieve this article, enter the following search: ED=19970902 AND wealthy. In the "retrieved list," click the title that matches this record. (ISSN0882-7729).

LIFE EXPECTANCY--UNITED STATES--AGED (v26)

LIFE EXPECTANCY--UNITED STATES--INFANTS

"According to preliminary life tables prepared by MetLife statisticians, average future lifetime for all babies [in the U.S.] reached 75.9 years or 0.1 year higher than the previous peak established in 1992 and matched in 1995....For infant boys, average future lifetime rose to 72.8 years in 1996, 0.3 years more than the 1995 high of 72.5 years. Among newborn females, life expectancy at birth rose from 78.9 years in 1995 to 79.0 years in 1996. However, this expectancy is still below the peak of 79.1 years reached in 1992....During 1996 baby girls could expect to live, on the average, 6.2 years more than baby boys; in 1992 their longevity advantage was 6.8 years and in 1990 and 1986 it was 7.0 years." (p2)

Kranczer, Stanley. "Record High U.S. Life Expectancy." Statistical Bulletin v78 n4 Oct-Dec 1997. p2-8. (ISSN0790-8334).

LIFE EXPECTANCY--UNITED STATES--MEN

In the U.S., "in 1940, a 65-year-old man could expect to live another 12 years. Today, he can expect to live another 15 years, and by 2040, this will rise to 17 years." (p15 secA)

Bartlett, Bruce. "Comment: There's No 'Free Lunch' with Social Security." Detroit News 3 Dec 1997. p15 secA.

LIFE ON OTHER PLANETS--MICHIGAN--PUBLIC OPINION (v26)

LIGHTNING

"The heat from lightning exceeds 50,000 degrees F. [Fahrenheit], which makes it three times hotter than the surface of the sun. Its speed is 1,000 feet per millionth of a second, and the thickness of an actual bolt is one to two inches. The average flash of lightning contains enough electricity to light a 100 watt bulb for more than three months....More than 2,000 thunderstorms are in process at any one time around the globe, says...[Richard Kithil, Director of the National Lightning Safety Institute, Boulder, Colorado]. Kithil estimates that lightning costs the...[U.S.] more than $2 million a year.... Flash to Bang is the time that elapses from when you see the lightning to when you hear the thunder. The rule is, for every five second count, lightning is one mile away. Therefore 25 seconds equals five miles away; 20 seconds equals four miles away." (p12-13)

Dashiell, Judy. "Learning Lightning Safety." ChemEcology v26 n7 Oct 1997. p12-14. (ISSN0738-7776).

LIMA (OHIO)--ECONOMIC CONDITIONS

Lima, Ohio is "a declining industry city of 45,000....Lima has lost several thousand jobs in the past few years, and now British Petroleum has announced the closing of its refinery, which employs 470 workers....The county's Metropolitan Housing Authority (an agency funded by the Department of Housing and Urban Development) has announced plans to build 28 new housing units throughout Lima's dwindling middle- and working-class neighborhoods." (p37)

Greenhut, Steven. "Correspondence: Letter from Lima: HUD Strikes Again." Chronicles v21 n8 Aug 1997. p37-38. (ISSN0887-5731).

LIMOUSINES--MICHIGAN

"There is no active enforcement of the 1,102 limousines registered in Michigan, transportation officials concede. More than half of those vehicles are in Metro Detroit....Secretary of State spokeswoman Elizabeth Boyd noted that her office in April 1991 started a subscription service that automatically notifies businesses if a driver has received a ticket or suspension. Some 504 agencies use the service in Michigan, including 133 government agencies and businesses covering 64,925 drivers." (p6 secA)

Shepardson, David. "Red Wings: A Shattered Celebration: State Lawmaker Wants Crackdown on Limo Industry." Detroit News 17 Jun 1997. p6 secA.

LION ATTACKS--UNITED STATES

"In the United States far more people die each year from bees (40), dogs (18-20), rattlesnakes (12) and black widow spiders (3) than from cougars (Weiss, 1990). Nevertheless, the number of reported lion sightings rose rapidly after 1990 (Gibbons, 1995), and there have been more attacks against humans in the last 20 years than there have been in the 80 years prior (Beier,1991). Within the past 10 years there have been a dozen non-fatal cougar attacks on humans in the United States, 7 of which occurred in California....There also have been 4 fatal attacks, 2 occurring in California." (p97-98)

Wolch, Jennifer R./Gullo, Andrea/Lassiter, Unna. "Changing Attitudes toward California's Cougars." Society & Animals v5 n2 1997. p95-116. (ISSN1063-1119).

LIONS--COLORADO

"Lions have killed fewer than a dozen people in the United States this century, including two in the last seven years in Colorado, where the lion population is estimated at around 3,000. The last fatal attack in Colorado took the life of an Idaho Springs jogger in 1991....Last year, hunters took 319 mountain lions, double the annual average 10 years ago." (p3)

Murray, Jamie/Chilson, Peter. "A Colorado Reality Check: Lions Roam and Kill." High Country News v29 n14 4 Aug 1997. p3. (ISSN0191-5657).

LIQUOR LICENSE SYSTEM

see LICENSE SYSTEM

LIQUOR PROBLEM

see ALCOHOLISM

LITERACY (v26)

LITERACY--AFGHANISTAN (v26)

LITERACY--AUSTRALIA

"Almost half of Australians aged 15-74 (6.2 million people) have 'poor' or 'very poor' prose literacy skills. Another 35 per cent (4.7 million) could be expected to cope with many of the demands of daily life, but not always at a high level of proficiency. Some 17 per cent (2.3 million) could be considered to have prose literacy skills of a high order....On all three literacy scales, some 2.6 million people aged 15 to 74 are at Level 1 (very poor literacy skills), and could be expected to face considerable difficulties in using many printed materials that are encountered in everyday life. About 3.6 million people are at Level 2 and could be expected to experience some difficulties. Level 3 is the largest category--the skills of the 4.7 million people at this level would enable them to cope with many printed materials, but not always at a high level. Some 2.3 million people are at Level 4/5, representing good to very good skills and the ability to manage the literacy demands of everyday life....High levels of formal education are not necessarily reflected in high literacy abilities--less than half (48 per cent) of people with a degree or postgraduate qualification are at Level 4/5. Twelve per cent of employed people have Level 1 skills and 22 per cent have Level 4/5 skills. For unemployed people the corresponding figures are 30 per cent and 11 per cent."

Australian Bureau of Statistics. "Australians' Literacy Skills Put to the Test." Media Release 8 Sep 1997. document-level access: <http://www.abs.gov.au/websitedbs/d3110125.nsf/4a255eef008309e44a255eef00061e57/0b3aaf7d5903d8254a25650b00813f85?OpenDocument>

LITERACY--AUSTRALIA--PUBLIC OPINION (v26)

LITERACY--BANGLADESH--CHINA

In 1990, "55 percent of men in Bangladesh ages 15 to 24 were illiterate, 73 percent of women in the same age group were. In China, illiteracy has decreased greatly across all population groups, but a large gap remains between women and men. Among those over age 25, 23 percent of men and 54 percent of women were illiterate; among Chinese 15 to 25 years old, 4 percent of men but 13 percent of women were illiterate." (p7)

Riley, Nancy E. "Gender, Power, And Population Change." Population Bulletin v52 n1 May 1997. p2-46. (ISSN0032-468X).

LITERACY--EUROPE (v26)

LITERACY--INDIA

In India, "currently, less than half of India's children are in school, and the overall literacy rate for the country is 41 percent. Among agricultural workers the rate of literacy is far lower. In one village of 1,540 adult and child bonded agricultural laborers, a researcher found only one person who

was able to read and write." (p576)
Tucker, Lee. "Child Slaves in Modern India: The Bonded Labor Problem." Human Rights Quarterly v19 n3 Aug 1997. p572-629. (ISSN0275-0392).

LITERACY--MEXICO

"In Mexico, a recent survey revealed that more than 1 in 5 homes don't have a single book. (At the same time, nearly 9 in 10 have a color TV)....About 10 percent of those over age 15 are unable to read and write, according to INEGI, the country's national statistics institute. But that figure hides the much higher levels of illiteracy in poor states with high indigenous populations. For example, in Chiapas nearly 1 in 5 men and 1 in 3 women can't read. Oaxaca and Guerrero States have similar numbers. Chalco's heavily immigrant population includes members of 40 of Mexico's 56 indigenous groups, many coming from states with the highest illiteracy, says municipal historian Alejandro Lopez." (p6)
LaFranchi, Howard. "In Land of TVs, A Fair Tries to Boost Literacy." The Christian Science Monitor v89 n139 13 Jun 1997. p6. The Christian Science Monitor search engine: <http://www.csmonitor.com/plweb-cgi/iops1.pl> To retrieve this article, enter the following search: ED=19970613 AND literacy. In the "retrieved list," click the title that matches this record. (ISSN0882-7729).

LITERACY--NEPAL

In Nepal, "female literacy jumped from 3.7 percent in 1971 to 25.6 percent in 1991, but remains low compared to male rates (54 percent). The total combined literacy rate in 1991 was 40 percent." (p7)
Rauniyar, Durga S. "Spotlight: Nepal." Population Today v25 n6 Jun 1997. p7. (ISSN0749-2448).

LITERACY--UNITED STATES (v26)

LITERACY--UNITED STATES--CHILDREN

"In studying approximately 10 thousand [American] children over the past 15 years, we have learned the following: (1) At least 20%, and in some states 50 to 60%, of children in the elementary grades can not read at basic levels. They can not read fluently and they do not understand what they read. (2) However, the majority of these children--at least 90 to 95%--can be brought up to average reading skills IF: (A) children at-risk for reading failure are identified during the kindergarten and first grade years and, (B) early intervention programs that combine instruction in phonological awareness, phonics, and reading comprehension are provided by well trained teachers. If we delay intervention until nine-years-of-age (the time that most children are currently identified), approximately 75% of the children will continue to have reading difficulties through high school." (pS6003)
Alexander, Duane. "Statements on Introduced Bills and Joint Resolutions." Congressional Record. Daily ed. v143 n86 19 Jun 1997. p6000-6005. section/page-level access: <http://thomas.loc.gov/cgi-bin/query/R?r105:FLD001:S06003:> (ISSN0363-7239). (X1.1A.105/1).

LITIGATION

see ACTIONS AND DEFENSES

LITTLE PIKED WHALE

see BALAENOPTERA ACUTOROSTRATA

LIVER--CANCER

Liver cancer is "a major problem in developing countries, with China alone accounting for 55% of all cases. The risk is twice as high in men as in women everywhere; 83% of all cases are attributable to infection with hepatitis B virus. Most other cases are linked to excessive alcohol consumption. Only about 6% of patients survive more than five years." (p5)
World Health Organization. "World Health Report 1997." Press Release 5 May 1997. p1-7. document-level access: <http://www.who.ch/whr/1997/presse.htm>

LIVER--INFLAMMATION

see HEPATITIS

LIVER--TRANSPLANTATION--UNITED STATES (v26)

LIVERMORE (CALIF.) (v26)

LIVESTOCK

see also CATTLE TRADE; POULTRY INDUSTRY; SWINE; TURKEY INDUSTRY

LIVESTOCK--BRAZIL (v26)

LIVESTOCK--FEEDING AND FEEDS

see FEEDS

LIVESTOCK--KOREA (SOUTH)--TAIWAN

In the late 1970s, livestock sector output was "30 percent of agricultural output in Taiwan and South Korea. The livestock sectors of these countries expanded steadily under their government's protectionist umbrella to more than 50 percent of agricultural output in 1995 (Food and Agriculture Organization, 1997). Consequently, South Korea and Taiwan became very dependent upon imported feedstuffs. In total, they produced only 6 percent of their coarse grain use for 1995-96." (p20)
Vocke, Gary/U.S. Dept. of Agriculture. Economic Research Service. "Special Article: Emerging Import Markets in Asia." APEC: International Agriculture and Trade Reports Situation and Outlook Series Aug 1997. p13-25.

LIVESTOCK--RUSSIA (v26)

LIVESTOCK--UNITED STATES

In the U.S., "total livestock and poultry purchases fell $1.2 billion (9.6 percent) in 1996 to $11.1 billion. The value of interstate sales of cattle and calves, which constitutes 75 percent of all livestock and poultry purchases, fell $1.4 billion (14.4 percent). This is the third straight year that interstate sales of cattle and calves have fallen more than $1 billion." (p9)
U.S. Dept. of Agriculture. Economic Research Service. "1996 Farm Income Estimates: Net Value-Added and Net Farm Income Attain New Highs in 1996." Agricultural Income and Finance Situation and Outlook Report Sep 1997. p4-13.

The U.S. Bureau of Land Management "manages approximately 177 million acres of land in the eleven western states. In 1991 BLM authorized 19,482 livestock grazers to use 13.5 million Animal Unit Months (AUM) of forage on about 167 million acres of BLM land. Based on these data, an average BLM permittee is authorized to use approximately 8500 acres of public land (about 13 square miles) and his livestock can consume approximately 690 AUMs of forage annually, which is enough to support 115 cows for 6 months....Over twelve acres are required to feed one cow for one month....Only twenty-seven percent of BLM's permittees are authorized to use eighty-seven percent of BLM's 'active use' AUMs of forage....Forage consumed by beef cattle on federal lands represents seven percent of all beef cattle forage consumed, and only two percent of the total feed consumed by beef cattle in the contiguous states....In the West, federally permitted use comprises only twenty-five percent of the total forage consumed by beef cattle, and only a third of beef cattle actually graze federal ranges....Only twenty-two percent of western beef cattle producers have federal grazing permits.... Nineteen percent of western sheep producers hold federal grazing permits....In the West only about one in five livestock producers holds a federal grazing permit." (p522-523)
Pendery, Bruce M. "Reforming Livestock Grazing on the Public Domain: Ecosystem Management-Based Standards and Guidelines...Management." Environmental Law v27 n2 Sum 1997. p513-609. (ISSN0046-2276).

In the U.S., "in 1997, the four largest beef packers accounted for 25 percent of the industry's output. By 1992, the four largest firms accounted for 71 percent of output....Over the same period, the four largest hog slaughtering firms increased their share of industry output from 36 to 54 percent.... According to the most recent 1992 Census Bureau data, large plants (those with more than 400 employees) accounted for nearly 90 percent of all hog slaughter and 72 percent of cattle slaughter. Large plants were far less prevalent 20 years earlier, accounting for a little more than half of hog slaughter and only a third of beef slaughter....Plants that slaughtered more than half a million cattle a year handled only 12 percent of cattle slaughter in 1977 (the earliest year for which we have data), but 61 percent of all cattle slaughter in 1992." (p22)

MacDonald, James M./Ollinger, Michael/U.S. Dept. of Agriculture. Economic Research Service. "Market Trends: U.S. Meat Slaughter Consolidating Rapidly." Food Review v20 n2 May-Aug 1997. p22-27. (ISSN1056-327X).

LIVESTOCK INDUSTRY

see ANIMAL INDUSTRY

LIVING, COST OF

see COST AND STANDARD OF LIVING

LIVING ALONE--EUROPE (v26)

LIVING ALONE--IRELAND--AGED

According to Ireland's 1996 Census, "one in four people aged 65 years and over lived alone in 1996. However, in Leitrim 31% of those in that age category lived alone. South Dublin had the lowest percentage of 65+ people living alone at 20%. For those aged 70 and over, 28% lived alone. Again Leitrim had the highest percentage at 33%."

Ireland. Central Statistics Office. "1996 Census--Volume 3, Household Composition and Family Unit." Press Release 27 Nov 1997. document-level access: <http://www.cso.ie/pressreleases/prelcen96v3.html>

LIVING TOGETHER

see UNMARRIED COUPLES

LOAN FUNDS, STUDENT

see STUDENT LOAN FUNDS

LOAN SERVICING--UNITED STATES (v26)

LOANS (v26)

see also BANK LOANS, SAVINGS AND LOAN ASSOCIATION FAILURES; STUDENT LOAN FUNDS

LOANS--CANADA (v26)

LOANS--JAPAN--MALAYSIA

In Malaysia, "bank loans equal 100 percent of GDP. In Japan, they equal 150 percent." (p9)

Grier, Peter. "US Capitalism Is New 'Tiger.'" The Christian Science Monitor v90 n13 12 Dec 1997. p1,9. The Christian Science Monitor search engine: <http://www.csmonitor.com/plweb-cgi/iops1.pl> To retrieve this article, enter the following search: ED=19971212 AND tiger. In the "retrieved list," click the title that matches this record. (ISSN0882-7729).

LOANS--UNITED STATES (v26)

"Most Americans have relationships with banks, but a growing number do not. And they pay a high price for it: as much as 20% interest on mortgages, 240% on pawn-shop loans, 36% on finance-company loans, 100% to 300% to buy televisions on the installment plan from rent-to-own stores, and 2,000%...to get a quick 'payday loan' from a check-cashing outlet." (p15)

Hudson, Michael. "The New Loan Sharks." Dollars and Sense n212 Jul-Aug 1997. p14-17. (ISSN0012-5245).

In the U.S., "between 1991 and 1995, while conventional home-purchase loans to whites increased by two-thirds, loans to blacks tripled (from 45,000 to 138,000 a year) and those to Hispanics more than doubled. During the same period, loans in predominantly minority neighborhoods rose by 137%, while loans in areas where the population was almost all white grew by just 37%." (p36)

Campen, Jim. "The Community Reinvestment Act: A Law that Works." Dollars and Sense n214 Nov-Dec 1997. p34-38. (ISSN0012-5245).

LOANS, PERSONAL--UNITED STATES

In the U.S., "the market for auto loans to 'high risk' borrowers has become crowded with Wall Street companies. Stock analysts estimate it is now a $70 billion a year market. Analysts estimate that the market for high-rate mortgages to consumers with low incomes or flawed credit records may soon exceed $120 billion a year....Consumer finance loans--smaller, higher interest loans not secured by real estate--exceed $100 billion a year." (p15)

"The New Loan Sharks: The Poverty Industry." Dollars and Sense n212 Jul-Aug 1997. p15. (ISSN0012-5245).

LOBBYING

see POLITICAL ACTION COMMITTEES

LOCAL GOVERNMENT--UNITED STATES

"Revenues of the nation's local governments reached $720 billion in 1994, according to tabulations on government revenues, expenditures, debts and assets released on the Internet...by the [U.S.] Commerce Department's Census Bureau. The major share of local revenue dollars was collected from taxes ($252 billion), state aid ($218 billion), user charges ($100 billion) and government operated utility sales ($63 billion)....Expenditures for local governments were primarily for services such as education ($258 billion), hospitals ($37 billion), police ($33 billion), public welfare ($31 billion) and highways ($28 billion). Local governments also had outstanding debt totaling $664 billion, interest payments on debt of nearly $40 billion and cash and security holdings of $640 billion."

U.S. Census Bureau. Economic and Statistics Administration. "Local Government Revenues Surpass $720 Billion, Census Bureau Says." Press Release 29 May 1997. document-level access: <http://www.census.gov/Press-Release/cb97-90.html>

LOCAL TRANSIT

see also BUS LINES; TAXICABS

LOCAL TRANSIT--ENVIRONMENTAL ASPECTS --UNITED STATES

In the U.S., mass "transit produces real environmental benefits. On average, riding transit instead of driving cuts hydrocarbon emissions that produce smog by 90 percent and carbon monoxide by more than 75 percent. One person using mass transit for a year instead of driving to work saves our environment 9 pounds of hydrocarbons, 62 pounds of carbon monoxide, and 5 pounds of nitrogen oxides....Over the past 30 years, the U.S. transit industry and its riders have prevented the emission of 1.6 million tons of hydrocarbons, 10 million tons of carbon monoxide, and 275,000 tons of nitrogen oxides into the air; the importation of 20 billion gallons of gasoline; and the construction and maintenance of the 20,000 lane-miles of freeways and arterial roads and 5 million parking places to meet demands, saving at least $220 billion a year." (pS10533)

Lautenberg, Frank R. (Sen.-N.J.). "Intermodal Surface Transportation Efficiency Act of 1997--Motion to Proceed." Congressional Record. Daily ed. v143 n139 8 Oct 1997. pS10522-10536. section/page-level access: <http://thomas.loc.gov/cgi-bin/query/R?r105:FLD001:S10531:> (ISSN0363-7239). (X1.1A.105/1).

LOCAL TRANSIT--UNITED STATES--COST OF OPERATION (v26)

LOCAL TRANSIT--UNITED STATES--FINANCE (v26)

LOGGING--INDONESIA (v26)

LOGGING--ONTARIO--ALGONQUIN PROVINCIAL PARK

In Canada, "logging is still allowed in much of Algonquin Provincial Park, and 90% of the park has been logged to some degree during the past 120 years. Some of the remaining 10% is protected in designated areas." (p19)

Davis, Mary Byrd. "Eastern Old Growth: More Threatened Eastern Old Growth: Part 1." Wild Earth v7 n2 Sum 1997. p19-21. (ISSN1055-1166).

LOGGING, AERIAL--ACCIDENTS--BRITISH COLUMBIA--COSTS

"According to Workers' Compensation Board estimates, heli-logging [transporting timber by helicopter] in B.C. [British Columbia] in 1992 accounted for 103 disability claims totalling $471,656 in benefits and 3,110 lost working days. Consistent with the growth of the industry, by 1996 the number of claims had more than doubled, benefits paid had risen to $2.9 million and lost days had ballooned to 9,424. (Overall, B.C.'s logging industry accounted for $73.5 million in injury costs in 1996, making it easily the most dangerous sector in the provincial work force.)" (p74)

Pynn, Larry. "Flying Timber." Canadian Geographic v117 n6 Nov-Dec 1997. p66-76. (ISSN0008-3658).

LOGGING, AERIAL--BRITISH COLUMBIA

"Helicopter logging is the fastest growing sector in...[British Columbia's] $14.6-billion-a-year forest industry....At $3 million for a 20-year-old, American-built Sikorsky helicopter that sucks up 700 litres of fuel an hour and requires two $150-an-hour pilots plus a full-time maintenance crew, heli-logging is affordable only where cheaper, conventional logging methods are impractical." (p68) "In the Vancouver forest region, encompassing most of the B.C. coast, heli-logging operators in 1996 were charged an average stumpage fee of $10.64 per cubic metre compared with an industry-wide average of $26.93." (p73)

Pynn, Larry. "Flying Timber." Canadian Geographic v117 n6 Nov-Dec 1997. p66-76. (ISSN0008-3658).

LONDON (ENGLAND) (v26)

LONDON (ENGLAND)--ECONOMIC CONDITIONS

"The size of London's economy, estimated as 75 billion [pounds sterling] ($115 billion) by the British government is close to Russia's and larger than that of Greece or Portugal. Economic activity in London accounts for 15 percent of the United Kingdom's gross domestic product. More than 100 of Europe's 500 largest companies have their headquarters in London, which has more miles of subway track per head than either Paris or Berlin." (p8)

MacLeod, Alexander. "International: London Will Finally Get to Elect Its Own Mayor." The Christian Science Monitor v89 n177 7 Aug 1997. p8. The Christian Science Monitor search engine: <http://www.csmonitor.com/plweb-cgi/iops1.pl> To retrieve this article, enter the following search: ED=19970807 AND mayor. In the "retrieved list," click the title that matches this record. (ISSN0882-7729).

LONG-TERM CAPITAL GAINS

see CAPITAL GAINS

LONG-TERM CARE FACILITIES--UNITED STATES

"About 5.8 million persons age 65 and older, 5.3 million adults between the ages of 18 and 64, and 400,000 children currently need long-term care services, or services and support for anyone with physical or mental impairments that hinder independent functioning, according to the U.S. Department of Health and Human Services (HHS)." (p1) "Seventy-three percent of informal caregivers are women, and 12 percent are over age 65, according to data from a recent AARP [American Association of Retired Persons] survey." (p2) "A 1996 research study found that about 23 percent of nursing home residents could have been provided a lower level of care than that found in a nursing home...." (p4)

Wright, Anne Pavuk/Eades-Goudy, Dianne. "Ensuring a Responsive Long-Term Care System: New Challenge for a New Century." Perspectives in Health and Aging v12 n1 1997. p1-6.

LONG-TERM CARE FACILITIES--UNITED STATES --COSTS

In the U.S., "nursing home care...typically costs as much as $46,000 annually, while the cost of an assisted living facility could range anywhere between $12,000 and $36,000 a year...." (p2) "The average national cost of home care in 1996 was $78 per visit for nursing or physical therapy." (p4) Assisted living "facilities charge between $1,000 and $3,000 monthly.... [In board and care homes,] monthly costs range from $350 to more than $3,000, and half of all board and care home residents rely on public funding to pay for their care." (p5)

Wright, Anne Pavuk/Eades-Goudy, Dianne. "Ensuring a Responsive Long-Term Care System: New Challenge for a New Century." Perspectives in Health and Aging v12 n1 1997. p1-6.

LONG-TERM CARE FACILITIES--UNITED STATES --FINANCE

In 1992, half of all U.S. "states spent 12 percent or less of their total long-term care expenditures on HCBS [home and community based services]--15 of these states spent less than 10 percent, and only six states spent more than 22 percent of their long-term care dollars on HCBS. Oregon was the most invested in these services at 50 percent; Mississippi the least at 4 percent." (p7)

Kane, Robert L. "Current Issues: Robert Kane Says: States Face Barriers to Home and Community Based Services Spending." Perspectives in Health and Aging v12 n1 1997. p7.

In the U.S., "in 1995, national aggregate long-term care expenditures exceeded $100 billion annually, of which 37.8 percent was financed by Medicaid, 32.5 percent by individuals and their families, 17.8 percent by Medicare, 5.5 percent by private insurance and 7.3 percent from other private and public sources, according to the US Health and Human Services Department's Health Care Financing Administration (HCFA).... Last year, Medicaid spent $51.5 billion on long-term care, with 77.3 percent, or $40.8 billion, covering institutional care....In addition to Medicare and Medicaid, the US Department of Veterans Affairs (VA) spends about $2.5 billion annually on long-term care for eligible veterans." (p7)

Wright, Anne Pavuk/Eades-Goudy, Dianne. "Current Issues: Financing Long-Term Care: Who Will Pay?" Perspectives in Health and Aging v12 n1 1997. p7-8.

LONG-TERM CARE INSURANCE

see INSURANCE, LONG-TERM CARE

LONGER-TERM SKILLED NURSING FACILITIES

see NURSING HOMES

LONGLEAF PINE--FLORIDA

Elgin Air Force Base in the Florida Panhandle "is probably the world's best remnant of longleaf pine forest, an increasingly rare ecosystem that once stretched over 90 million acres from Virginia to Texas. Longleaf pine woodlands, called sandhills, cover three-fourths of the base and include 10,000 acres of what is believed to be the largest remaining stand of old-growth longleaf pine in the world." (p14) "Through growing-season burns, the planting of more than three million longleaf pine seedlings, the mechanical removal of slash and sand pines and other activities, more than 200,000 acres have been restored to longleaf pine dominance in the past five years." (p16)

Biondo, Brenda. "In Defense of the Longleaf Pine." Nature Conservancy v47 n4 Sep-Oct 1997. p10-17. (ISSN0028-5200).

LONGLEAF PINE--UNITED STATES

"Today, longleaf pine ecosystems cover only about three percent of their former area, now limited primarily to the coastal plains of the Carolinas, Georgia, Florida, Alabama, Mississippi, Louisiana and Texas....More than 30 species of plants and animals associated with longleaf pine ecosystems are threatened or endangered." (p14)

Biondo, Brenda. "In Defense of the Longleaf Pine." Nature Conservancy v47 n4 Sep-Oct 1997. p10-17. (ISSN0028-5200).

LOOMIS STATE FOREST (WASH.)

The Loomis Forest in Washington "comprises about 134,000 acres adjacent to the Pasayten Wilderness in Okanogan County....The Loomis Landscape Plan, approved in June of last year, calls for construction of up to 350 miles of new logging roads, and the logging of over 108,000 acres of this remote forest....Over 30,000 acres of the Loomis are wild and roadless." (p21)

Friedman, Mitch. "NWEA Sues for 'Gods Country': State Plan for Loomis Forest Would Threaten Water, Wildlife." Northwest Conservation Sum 1997. p21.

LOONS--HEALTH--KEJIMKUJIK NATIONAL PARK (N.S.) (v26)

LOONS--MICHIGAN (v26)

LOS ANGELES (CALIF.)--ECONOMIC CONDITIONS

Los Angeles "is home to more than nine million people--three out of every 10 Californians. Its financial heft, expressed in terms of gross product, is estimated to be $282 billion in 1997--nearly 30 percent of the California economy. More significant, Los Angeles, which suffered 70 percent of the state's job loss during the early 1990's, was the engine that drove the recent recession....Its school system is crowded with 1.5 million students--a third of whom are regarded as English-limited and who speak one of more than 100 languages as a mother tongue." (p7)

Block, A. G. "Commentary: Two Cents: Los Angeles." California Journal v28 n7 Jul 1997. p7. (ISSN0008-1205).

LOS ANGELES (CALIF.)--POPULATION (v26)

LOS ANGELES COUNTY (CALIF.)--ECONOMIC CONDITIONS

Since the 1992 riots, "the desertion of many finance jobs from the central city caused office vacancy rates to climb above 20 percent in downtown L.A. [Los Angeles]....'Seventy-one percent of the total job loss in the state happened in Los Angeles County,' said Jack Kyser, chief economist for the Economic Development Corporation of Los Angeles County." (p16)

Scott, Steve. "The Morphing Economy." California Journal v28 n7 Jul 1997. p14-19. (ISSN0008-1205).

LOST PROFITS DAMAGES--CANADA (v26)

LOTTERIES--ALABAMA (v26)

LOTTERIES--EMPLOYMENT--UNITED STATES --PUBLIC OPINION

According to a Gallup Poll, "while winning the lottery is the dream of millions of Americans who participate each week, six in ten workers say that even if they won 10 million dollars they would still continue to work. However, just 35% of workers overall would continue at the same job, while another 24% would find some other endeavor. Four in ten American workers say they would simply quit. Among those who say they are satisfied with their jobs, 39% say they would continue with it even after winning the lottery; just 4% of the dissatisfied group would continue."

Moore, David W./Gallup Organization. "One of Four Workers Would Fire the Boss." Press Release 2 Sep 1996. document-level access: <http://www.gallup.com/poll/news/970902b.html>

LOTTERIES--GREAT BRITAIN

In Great Britain, "nine out of 10 adults play [the lottery] at least occasionally. There have been 180 million winning tickets: 360 of them for more than 1 million [pounds sterling]. The lottery has already raised more than 3.5 billion [pounds sterling] for good causes. By the time the current licence ends, we expect that it will have raised 10 billion [pounds sterling]. Thanks to the initiative and hard work of those who have been involved in developing projects, and the lottery distribution bodies, funds have already been committed to more than 24,000 projects throughout the United Kingdom." (c685)

Smith, Chris (H.C.-Islington, South and Finsbury). "National Lottery." Great Britain. Parliament. House of Commons. Debates. 21 Jul 1997. c685. section-level access: <http://www.parliament.the-stationery-office.co.uk/pa/cm199798/cmhansrd/cm970721/debtext/70721-05.htm#70721-05_head0>

In Britain, "the National Lottery is widely judged to be a great success. Camelot [the consortium that has run the lottery for the past three years,] was awarded the lottery franchise by the former Conservative government. Last year, out of profits of 4.7 billion [pounds sterling], it donated 1.8 billion [pounds sterling] for a wide range of charities. The company claims that in terms of profit the lottery is three times more successful than originally had been expected. Camelot has placed 36,000 lottery terminals around Britain, and surveys show that up to two-thirds of adult Britons are purchasing tickets for the twice-weekly draw." (p7)

MacLeod, Alexander. "Big Business in Britain Asks if Labour Is Friend or Foe." The Christian Science Monitor v89 n137 11 Jun 1997. p7. The Christian Science Monitor search engine: <http://www.csmonitor.com/plweb-cgi/iops1.pl> To retrieve this article, enter the following search: ED=19970611 AND foe. In the "retrieved list," click the title that matches this record. (ISSN0882-7729).

LOTTERIES--MICHIGAN (v26)

In Michigan, "79 percent of last week's survey respondents say they play one or more lottery games per week. Thirteen percent say they play once or twice a month, while 8 percent say they play a few times a year. If the jackpot were $5 million, 50 percent say they'd bet $5 or $10. Thirty-five percent say they'd bet $1 or $2, 12 percent say they would invest $25, and 3 percent say a jackpot that size would entice them to spend more than $50." (p1 secE)

Pipp, Tracy L. "Accent: Survey of the Week: We Take Lottery Fun and Games Seriously." Detroit News 1 Oct 1997. p1 secE.

LOTTERIES--UNITED STATES (v26)

LOUISIANA--EMPLOYMENT (v26)

LOW BIRTH WEIGHT

see BIRTH WEIGHT, LOW

LOW INCOME HOUSING

see PUBLIC HOUSING

LOW INCOME PEOPLE

see POOR

LUMBER TRADE

see also TIMBER

"Only six countries (Malaysia, Singapore, Indonesia, the Philippines, Cameroon, and Liberia) account for more than 95 percent of the world's legal trade of tropical timber. In Malaysia, cutting down forests (for export mainly to Japan) earned that nation more than $1.5 billion per year." (p30)

Artaza-Regan, Maria Paz. "In the Name of Economic Well-Being." Christian Social Action v10 n6 Jun 1997. p29-32. (ISSN0897-0459).

LUMBER TRADE--EMPLOYMENT--UNITED STATES (v26)

LUMBER TRADE--UNITED STATES

"Fuel and pulp are the two largest uses for wood resources in the United States. Only 28 percent of all the wood harvested is used for lumber. But of all the hardwood that is harvested for lumber, the largest share--38 percent--goes to the production of pallets. (Pallets account for 6 percent of softwood harvested for lumber). A large portion of pallets are recovered and reused each year. Even so, in 1995, the United States manufactured 411 million new pallets, says Bob Bush, director of the Center for Forest Products Marketing and Management at Virginia Tech. Each pallet uses 12 to 16 board feet of lumber. If that timber had not been cut at all, about 3 million acres of logged-over forest would still be standing, according to estimates from David McKeever of the Forest Products Laboratory." (p10)

Lavendel, Brian. "A Growing Demand: A Hard Look at a Hard Business: Wood Recycling." Inner Voice v9 n6 Nov-Dec 1997. p8-11.

LUNGS--CANCER

"Lung cancer is now the commonest cause of death from cancer in women in the US. In the European Union countries, a 33% increase in female lung cancer cases is predicted by 2005. Worldwide, about 85% of lung cancers in men and 46% in women are tobacco-related. The ratios in developed countries are 91% and 62%. There is no effective treatment for lung cancer. Only 7%-12% of patients are alive five years after diagnosis." (p5)

World Health Organization. "World Health Report 1997." Press Release 5 May 1997. p1-7. document-level access: <http://www.who.ch/whr/1997/presse.htm>

LUNGS--CANCER--UNITED STATES (v26)

LUNGS--CANCER--UNITED STATES--TOBACCO USE (v26)

LUNGS--CANCER--UNITED STATES--WOMEN

"Smoking-related diseases kill more than 140,000 women annually, according to the federal Centers for Disease Control and Prevention in Atlanta....Lung cancer is overwhelmingly tobacco-related: About 85 percent of all cases in the United States are linked to smoking. Indeed, lung cancer, which accounted for just 3 percent of cancer deaths among women in 1950, passed breast cancer as the leading cause of cancer death in 1987 and now accounts for more than 25 percent of the total, according to the American Cancer Society. The society estimates that 66,000 women will die this year from lung cancer." (p8 secF)

Mishra, Raja/Arnett, Elsa C. "Body & Mind: Cover Story: Boredom Stress Image Addiction: Four Big Reasons Explain Smoking's Hold on People." Detroit Free Press 18 Nov 1997. p6-8 secF.

LUNGS--DISEASES--MORTALITY (v26)

LUNGS--DISEASES--UNITED STATES--MORTALITY (v26)

LUPUS--UNITED STATES (v26)

LUTHERAN CHURCH--UNITED STATES--LITURGY

"Pastoral compassion is leading more and more ELCA [Evangelical Lutheran Church in America] congregations--almost 60%--now to offer a non-alcoholic alternative to wine, despite specific recommendations against this in previous ELCA statements. According to recent statistics compiled by the ELCA Office of the Secretary, the number of congregations reporting that they offer 'wine only' at communion has declined (in 1995) to 40.84%. The percentage of congregations reporting that they offer a non-alcoholic alternative has increased from 48% in 1993 to 57% in 1995." (p271-272)

Rossing, Barbara. "'Are You Able to Drink the Cup?': Grape Juice at Holy Communion." Currents v24 n3 Jun 1997. p267-272.

LUTHERANS (v26)

LUTHERANS--AFRICA (v26)

LYME DISEASE--CALIFORNIA

In California, "more than half of Lyme disease cases are contracted during the spring and summer months which is when the tick, in its very small nymphal stage, is most commonly found. The western black-legged tick (Ixodes pacificus) is the only tick of the 48 species found in California that is known to transmit Lyme disease. The nymphal tick is roughly the size of a poppy seed and the adult is about 1/4 inch in length....The western black-legged tick has been found in 55 of the 58 California counties but is most common in the humid northwestern coastal areas and the western slope of the northern Sierra Nevada range....Symptoms and signs of the early state of Lyme disease can include: fatigue, chills and fever, headache, muscle and joint pain, and a skin rash called erethema migrans. Erethema migrans (EM) is a red, blotchy, expanding rash that may grow to several inches in diameter and commonly clears in the center producing a ring-like appearance. EM usually occurs 3 to 30 days after the bite of an infected tick in 60 to 80 percent of patients. One or more EM lesions may occur and not necessarily at the tick bite site."

California. Dept. of Health Services. "State Health Director Reminds Californians of Lyme Disease Threat." News Release Jun 1997. document-level access: <http://www.dhs.cahwnet.gov/opahome/prssrels/31-97.htm>

LYME DISEASE--UNITED STATES

In the U.S., "as of 1995, cases of Lyme disease had been reported in 48 of the 50 states and appear to be increasing, both in numbers of people affected and in geographic distribution." (p338) "Since 1990, between 9,000 and 14,000 cases of Lyme disease have been reported annually to federal health officials, although the true number of cases is unknown." (p339) "The vast majority of larval ticks--well over 99 percent--hatch from eggs free of the Lyme-disease bacterium....In Lyme-disease-endemic areas, approximately 25 to 35 percent of nymphs and 50 to 70 percent of adult ticks are infected with 'Borrelia burgdorferi' [the agent of Lyme disease]." (p341) "In Lyme-disease-endemic counties in the northeastern and north-central states, the number of cases remains about 10 to 30 per 100,000 individuals, and in the rest of the United States, cases per 100,000 are well below 10." (p346)

Ostfeld, Richard S. "The Ecology of Lyme-Disease Risk." American Scientist v85 n4 Jul-Aug 1997. p338-346. (ISSN0003-0996).

LYMPHATICS--DISEASES (v26)

LYMPHOMAS--UNITED STATES

Non-Hodgkin's lymphoma "is a cancer of the lymphatic system, part of the body's immune defense system. In 1997 an estimated 53,600 new NHL cases will be diagnosed in the United States, and 23,800 people will die of the disease. Treatment most commonly involves chemotherapy with or without radiation therapy. The five-year survival rate for NHL patients is just over 50 percent."

U.S. National Cancer Institute. "Study Finds PCBs May Increase Risk for Non-Hodgkin's Lymphoma." Press Release 24 Jul 1997. document-level access: <http://rex.nci.nih.gov/massmedia/pressreleases/pcbs.html>

LYNX

"The lynx is a brownish-grey wild member of the cat family, usually weighing less than thirty pounds....[The lynx] glides about on massive paws that can spread 30 percent larger for traveling on snow....Research in the North Cascades indicates that 90 percent of the lynx' diet is snowshoe hare." (p17)

"Lynx: Ghost Cat of the Mountains." Northwest Conservation n32 Nov 1997. p17.

MACADAMIA NUT INDUSTRY--HAWAII (v26)

"Although the 1996 acreage of Hawaii macadamia nuts slipped to 19,200 acres, production increased to a record 56.5 million pounds, in-shell basis....Grower prices improved in 1996, averaging 78 cents per pound, compared with 74 cents in 1995 and 69 cents in 1994." (p33)

U.S. Dept. of Agriculture. Economic Research Service. "Tree Nut Outlook." Fruit and Tree Nuts Situation and Outlook Report Aug 1997. p32-33.

MACEDONIA (GREECE) (v26)

MACEDONIA--ECONOMIC CONDITIONS

In Macedonia, "between 1990 and 1995, recorded statistics show that real GDP fell nearly 30 percent, the volume of trade flows dropped about 40 percent, and the volume of investment in 1995 was less than half its 1990 level. The rate of registered unemployment increased from 17 percent in 1990 to 24 percent in 1995, and a large share of the working-age population dropped out of the labor force."

World Bank. "World Bank and IDA Support Economic Reforms in Former Yugoslav Republic of Macedonia." Press Release 6 May 1997. document-level access: <http://www.worldbank.org/html/extdr/extme/1334.htm>

"Estimates suggested that because of the Greek embargo Macedonia lost approximately $700 million. Inflation was between 20 and 30 percent a month during 1993. The average annual income dropped from over US$3,000 to about US$350 in three years, ranking with some of the poorest countries in the developing world." (p96) "Because of the embargoes, production has dropped every year since 1990. GNP has fallen from $2,559 million in 1990 to $1,500 million in 1994....GNP shrank by 14 percent in 1992 and 14.1 percent in 1993. The real GNP growth was down only 7.2 percent in 1994....1995 and 1996 saw growth at -2 percent and 2 percent respectively. For 1997, growth is predicted to be about 4 percent." (p98)

Dion, Richard Read. "Macedonia: Coming In from the Cold." World Affairs v160 n2 Fall 1997. p96-103. (ISSN0043-8200).

MACKINAC BRIDGE (MICH.)

In Michigan, the Mackinac Bridge spans "8,614 feet from one suspension anchorage to the other...." (p1 secD) "The two main towers each hold two huge pins that allow the span to rotate up to 1 1/2 degrees in a hard wind. That means that within the 3,800-foot center span, the roadway flexes out as much as 35 feet...." (p2 secD)

"Connection: Span for All Seasons: For 40 Years the Mackinac Bridge Has Withstood Wind and Waves;...Will Last Forever." Ann Arbor News 4 Nov 1997. p1-2 secD.

MACOMB COUNTY (MICH.)--OAKLAND COUNTY (MICH.)--POPULATION (v26)

MADNESS

see MENTAL ILLNESS

MAIL

see POSTAL SERVICE

MAKEUP (COSMETICS)

see COSMETICS INDUSTRY

MALARIA (v26)

MALARIA--AFRICA, SUB-SAHARAN--COSTS (v26)

MALARIA--EUROPE (v26)

MALARIA--MEXICO

"Approximately 60% of the Mexican territory, representing an area inhabited by close to 45 million people, provides an environment suitable for malaria transmission. According to Cristina Cortinas de Nava, coordinator of the Union of Chemical Substances and Environmental Evaluation at the Mexican National Institute of Ecology in Mexico City, the NARAP [North American Regional Action Plan] for DDT [Dichlorodiphenyltrichloroethane] will build upon the country's existing malaria control program--which has successfully reduced the annual incidence of the disease from 2.4 million cases in the 1940s and 1950s to approximately 5,000 cases today--while simultaneously reducing annual domestic DDT production and use from 25,000 tons to a production rate of approximately 600 tons." (p790)

U.S. National Institute of Environmental Health Sciences. "Environews: Forum: Mexico Moves to Phase Out DDT and Chlordane." Environmental Health Perspectives v105 n8 Aug 1997. p790-791.

MALARIA--UNITED STATES (v26)

MALES

see MEN

MALIBU (CALIF.)--ECONOMIC CONDITIONS

Since 1991, Malibu, California "has suffered four major natural disasters--including a 1993 brush fire that destroyed 270 houses. Coping with all this has cost Malibu nearly $15 million, says City Manager Harry Peacock, pushing its reserves below the 5 percent of annual budget considered a minimum emergency cushion for California cities....While much of the money the city fronted for disaster recovery has been reimbursed by the state and federal governments, Malibu is still owed some $3.1 million--and given changing federal policies, city officials aren't expecting, realistically, much more than $2.5 million....Competing with the need to bolster the city's emergency reserve are equally pressing needs such as maintaining and upgrading roads and storm drains--a bill may eventually reach $20 million." (p3)

Blair, James. "United States: A Letter from Malibu, Calif.: Malibu May Wake Rudely from Its California Dream." The Christian Science Monitor v89 n180 12 Aug 1997. p3. The Christian Science Monitor search engine: <http://www.csmonitor.com/plweb-cgi/iops1.pl> To retrieve this article, enter the following search: ED=19970812 AND dream. In the "retrieved list," click the title that matches this record. (ISSN0882-7729).

MALICIOUS PROSECUTION--UNITED STATES (v26)

MALIGNANT TUMORS

see CANCER

MALNUTRITION (v26)

MALNUTRITION--AFRICA, SUB-SAHARAN (v26)

In sub-Saharan Africa, "some 40 per cent of the population remains chronically undernourished and 17 countries, as of August, were confronting serious food emergencies, mainly due to drought and civil conflict." (p6) "According to a major study by the UN Food and Agriculture Organization (FAO), 'World Agriculture: Towards 2010,' the amount of food available per person in sub-Saharan Africa, measured in daily calories, declined from 2,140 in 1969-71 to 2,100 in 1988-90, increasing the number of undernourished people from 94 million to 175 million over the same period." (p7)

Harsch, Ernest. "Agriculture in Africa: Africa Strives to Revitalize Agriculture." Africa Recovery v11 n2 Oct 1997. p6-9.

MALNUTRITION--DEVELOPING COUNTRIES (v26)

MALNUTRITION--KOREA (NORTH)

By mid-August 1997, the United Nations Children's Fund "estimated that at least 80,000 children under the age of six [in North Korea] were suffering from 'severe malnutrition,' and the North Korean government confirmed more than a hundred child deaths due to the famine....During the worst stretches of the famine, the official ration has fallen to 100 grams of rice per day, or about 350 calories. This is about a sixth of what is normally distributed in refugee centers." (p4)

Moon, Orson. "North Korea: Country with Few Remaining Allies, And the Wrong Enemies." Peacework n280 Dec 1997. p4-5. (ISSN0748-0725).

MALNUTRITION IN CHILDREN

Each year, "12 million children under the age of five perish because of malnutrition....Nearly 800 million people in today's developing countries face chronic undernutrition, and almost 200 million children suffer from protein or energy deficiencies." (p20)

Sedge, Michael H. "International: Feeding the World, Forever." Kiwanis v82 n10 Nov-Dec 1997. p20-23,39. (ISSN0162-5276).

MALNUTRITION IN CHILDREN--DEVELOPING COUNTRIES (v26)

MALNUTRITION IN CHILDREN--IRAQ

"According to a Nutrition Status Report released at the end of May [1997], over 750,000 Iraqi children, or 27.5 per cent, of children surveyed in the 15 central and southern governorates are malnourished to some extent....The report confirms the serious nutritional status of young children in the three northern governorates, noting that nearly 1 in 5 children (19 per cent) is underweight and that 1 in 4 (26 per cent) under five years of age is chronically malnourished." (p52)

"Peacewatch: Iraq." UN Chronicle v34 n3 1997. p51-52. (ISSN0251-7329).

MALNUTRITION IN CHILDREN--MALI

According to the second Demographic and Health survey carried out in Mali, "twenty-three percent of Malian children under three years of age are 'wasted,' too thin for their height--the result of a recent failure to receive adequate nutrition that may be affected by acute illness, especially diarrhea.... According to the survey, only 12 percent of children under four months are exclusively breastfed as recommended by the World Health Organization (WHO). WHO also recommends that solid foods be introduced at around six months because breast milk alone is no longer sufficient to maintain a child's optimal growth. But nearly 42 percent of children age 7-9 months in Mali are still not receiving solid foods--most of them being breastfed or receiving water--and at 12-13 months, 15 percent of Malian children are still not properly fed." (p2)

"23% of Children in Mali Too Thin." Popline v19 Sep-Oct 1997. p2.

MALNUTRITION IN CHILDREN--MALI--MORTALITY

According to the second Demographic and Health survey carried out in Mali, "improvements in childhood mortality in Mali have been limited by the worsening nutritional status of young children. Since 1987, infant mortality has declined by 22 percent to 123 deaths per 1,000 and under-five mortality has declined by 30 percent to 238 deaths per 1,000. But the proportion of children who are alive and malnourished has increased. An estimated 57 percent of deaths that occur before the age of five are related to malnutrition--136 per 1,000." (p2)

"23% of Children in Mali Too Thin." Popline v19 Sep-Oct 1997. p2.

MALNUTRITION IN CHILDREN--RUSSIA (v26)

MALTA FEVER

see BRUCELLOSIS

MALTREATED AGED

see ABUSED AGED

MALTREATED CHILDREN

see ABUSED CHILDREN

MALTREATED WOMEN

see ABUSED WOMEN

MALTREATMENT OF CHILDREN

see CHILD ABUSE

MAMMALS

"Between the 1983 and 1993 editions of MAMMAL SPECIES OF THE WORLD, 459 entries were added. In the last four years, biologists have discovered dozens more....Currently, about 4,600 mammal species are recognized." (p59)

Tangley, Laura. "Culture & Ideas: New Mammals in Town." U.S. News & World Report v122 n22 9 Jun 1997. p59-60. article-level access: <http://www.usnews.com/usnews/issue/970609/9MAMM.HTM> (ISSN0041-5537).

MAMMAPLASTY--UNITED STATES (v26)

MAMMOGRAPHY

see BREAST--RADIOGRAPHY

MAN-HOURS

see HOURS OF LABOR

MAN-WOMAN RELATIONSHIPS--CANADA (v26)

MANAGED CARE PLANS (MEDICAL CARE)

see also HEALTH MAINTENANCE ORGANIZATIONS

MANAGED CARE PLANS (MEDICAL CARE)--UNITED STATES (v26)

"Managed care now provides coverage for 77 percent of Americans and their dependents who are insured through their employers, according to Mercer/Foster Higgins employer survey data. In addition, 80,000 elderly Americans each month are switching to Medicare HMOs, largely because of the cost savings they offer....Health care premiums have been reined in--they rose just 2.5 percent last year, compared with as much as 18.6 percent a year in the last half of the 1980s." (p60)

Brink, Susan/Shute, Nancy. "America's Top HMOs: Are HMOs the Right Prescription?" U.S. News & World Report v123 n14 13 Oct 1997. p60-64. article-level access: <http://www.usnews.com/usnews/issue/971013/13HMOS.HTM> (ISSN0041-5537).

MANAGED CARE PLANS (MEDICAL CARE)--UNITED STATES--PHYSICIANS (v26)

MANAGEMENT OF CONFLICT

see CONFLICT MANAGEMENT

MANAGERS

see EXECUTIVES

MANGO INDUSTRY--FLORIDA

"Florida's mango production declined one-third from a year earlier to 5.5 million pounds....Decreased production contributed to a 30-percent higher grower price, at $15.00 per ton in 1996. Despite higher prices, the lower production caused a decline in the value of the 1996 crop to $1.5 million, down 13 percent from 1995." (p24)

U.S. Dept. of Agriculture. Economic Research Service. "Noncitrus Fruit Outlook." Fruit and Tree Nuts Situation and Outlook Report Aug 1997. p7-26.

MANGO INDUSTRY--UNITED STATES

"U.S. mango consumption has been growing rapidly in recent years, increasing about 19 percent annually since 1993. In 1996, per capita mango consumption reached a record 1.36 pounds....To meet growing domestic demand and offset lower Florida production, mango imports rose 21 percent in 1996....Mexico is the principal source for the U.S. market, accounting for 81 percent of mango imports in 1996, totaling 311.7 million pounds, 22 percent above 1995. Haiti, Guatemala, and Brazil were the next major sources, each providing over 1 million pounds." (p24)

U.S. Dept. of Agriculture. Economic Research Service. "Noncitrus Fruit Outlook." Fruit and Tree Nuts Situation and Outlook Report Aug 1997. p7-26.

MANHOLE COVERS--MICHIGAN--DETROIT (v26)

MANILA (PHILIPPINES)--SOCIAL CONDITIONS (v26)

MANITOBA--ECONOMIC CONDITIONS (v26)

MANITOBA--EMPLOYMENT (v26)

MANNERS AND CUSTOMS

see also BATHING CUSTOMS; CLOTHING AND DRESS; DATING (SOCIAL CUSTOMS)

MANNERS AND CUSTOMS--UNITED STATES--PUBLIC OPINION

"Sixty-one percent of the general public agrees Americans are rude, according to a 1995 survey by Princeton Survey Research Associates for NEWSWEEK. While a majority of all demographic groups think Americans are rude, women are somewhat more likely than men to think so (62 versus 56 percent) and blacks more than whites (73 versus 57 percent). Sixty-five percent of people aged 30 to 44 and 61 percent of those under age 30 think

Americans are rude, versus a smaller 53 percent of people aged 45 and older....Eight in ten think we're less civil now than we were ten years ago. Sixty-seven percent think Americans are more likely to use vulgar language than they were ten years ago, and 75 percent think parents are less civil about keeping their children under control. Seventy-one percent also think drivers are less civil. When asked whether they themselves have ever shouted, cursed, or made gestures to other drivers, 61 percent of Americans admit to doing so." (p12)

Russell, Cheryl. "Trend Cop: The Favor of Your Reply Is Requested." American Demographics v19 n5 May 1997. p12,15. article-level access: <http://www.demographics.com/Publications/AD/97_ad/9705_ad/AD97053.htm> (ISSN0163-4089).

MANSLAUGHTER

see HOMICIDE; MURDER

MANUFACTURES (v26)

see also IRELAND--MANUFACTURES; MIDDLE WEST--MANUFACTURES; UNITED STATES--MANUFACTURES

"The share of manufactures in total OECD imports has nearly doubled over the past 30 years to exceed 75 percent, with the importance of machinery (including cars) growing strongly....Manufacturing only constituted 18 percent of OECD employment in 1994 (ranging from 16 percent in the United States to 26 percent in Germany); for the OECD this represents a decline of one third as compared to 1974." (p6)

Glyn, Andrew. "New Democracy Forum: Egalitarianism in a Global Economy." Boston Review v22 n6 Dec 1997-Jan 1998. p4-8. (ISSN0734-2306).

MANUFACTURES--ENVIRONMENTAL ASPECTS (v26)

MAPLE SYRUP INDUSTRY--CANADA (v26)

MAPUCHE INDIANS--CHILE--SANTIAGO--POPULATION

Chilean population and housing "census results showed that around 400,000 Mapuches (44% of the 930,000 persons 14 years old or older who identified themselves as Mapuche) live in Santiago." (p12) "The census figures showed that 54% of the roughly 400,000 Mapuche population that resides in Santiago represents persons 15-34 years of age." (p13)

Jara, Jose Ancan. "Indian City: Urban Mapuches: Reflections on a Modern Reality in Chile." Abya Yala News v10 n3 Sum 1997. p12-13. (ISSN1056-5876).

MAQUILADORA INDUSTRY

see OFFSHORE ASSEMBLY INDUSTRY

MARIJUANA--MEXICO

"There are about 200 drug trafficking organizations in Mexico....The US State Department estimated that total marijuana cultivation in Mexico in 1994 was 19,045 hectares and net marijuana production was 5,540 metric tons, almost all of which was bound for the US market. The DEA estimates that this represents 60 to 80 per cent of the foreign-grown marijuana available in the US in 1994, or between 50 and 60 per cent of the total amount of the drug consumed." (p473-474)

Van de Velde, James R. "Issues of Law Intensity Conflict and Law Enforcement: The Growth of Criminal...Drug Trafficking." Low Intensity Conflict & Law Enforcement v5 n3 Win 1996. p466-483. (ISSN0966-2847).

MARIJUANA--UNITED STATES (v26)

"An estimated 150 million Americans (nearly 60 percent) have tried marijuana. (Scientific American Medicine). An estimated 20 million Americans smoke pot regularly. (Substance Abuse and Mental Health Administration)....Twenty five years ago, an ounce of marijuana cost $15. Today, a quarter-ounce costs $40." (p33)

Cason, Steve. "34 Curious Facts about Marijuana." Liberty v11 n3 Jan 1998. p33,35. (ISSN0894-1408).

"Americans themselves now grow indigenously 20 to 50 per cent of the marijuana they consume and of particularly high potency too. Marijuana harvests now exceed $41 billion a year wholesale in the US. Over 67 million Americans are reported to have [at] least tried marijuana. Over 17 million are reported to have used marijuana in 1995." (p470)

Van de Velde, James R. "Issues of Law Intensity Conflict and Law Enforcement: The Growth of Criminal...Drug Trafficking." Low Intensity Conflict & Law Enforcement v5 n3 Win 1996. p466-483. (ISSN0966-2847).

"In 1996, an estimated 10.1 million Americans were current (past month) marijuana or hashish users. This represents 4.7 percent of the population aged 12 and older. Marijuana is by far the most prevalent drug used by illicit drug users. Approximately three-quarters (77 percent) of current illicit drug users were marijuana or hashish users in 1996."

U.S. Dept. of Health and Human Services. "National Drug Survey Results Released: Overall Drug Use Levels Stay the Same; Possible Decrease in Youth Drug Use." Press Release 6 Aug 1997. document-level access: <http://www.hhs.gov/news/press/1997pres/970806.html>

MARIJUANA--UNITED STATES--YOUTH (v26)

"Marijuana use by eighth-graders...[in the U.S.] tripled from 6 percent in 1991 to 18 percent in 1996, according to the study conducted by the U-M [University of Michigan] Research Center. More than 49,000 students in 435 public and private schools were surveyed in the 1996 study. Among 10th graders, marijuana use doubled from 15 percent in 1992 to 34 percent in 1996. Use among 12th graders increased from 22 percent in 1992 to 36 percent in 1996." (p5 secC)

Ilka, Douglas. "Suburban News: In Wayne County: Program Helps Teens Kick Pot." Detroit News 3 Oct 1997. p5 secC.

In the U.S., "in 1996, 23.1 percent of eighth graders had tried marijuana at least once in their lifetime and 11.3 percent were current users, increases from 1995 rates of 19.9 percent and 9.1 percent respectively. (MTFS [Monitoring the Future Study], 1996) Among eighth graders, past year use of marijuana nearly tripled, from 6.2 percent in 1991 to 18.3 percent in 1996. Among tenth graders, past year use has almost doubled from 16.5 percent in 1991 to 33.6 percent in 1996. (MTFS, 1996)"

U.S. Dept. of Health and Human Services. "Substance Abuse--A National Challenge." Fact Sheet 20 May 1997. document-level access: <http://www.hhs.gov/news/press/1997pres/970520c.html>

MARINE DRILLING PLATFORMS

see DRILLING PLATFORMS

MARITAL INFIDELITY

see ADULTERY

MARKETING--UNITED STATES (v26)

MARKING (STUDENTS)

see GRADING AND MARKING (STUDENTS)

MARLIN--PACIFIC OCEAN

An observer-based study, run by Commonwealth Scientific and Industrial Research Organisation's Dr. Robert Campbell, indicated that "about 1450 black marlin were caught as bycatch by longliners targeting bigeye and yellowfin in Area E [a region in the waters of North Queensland] from August 1995 to September 1996. These marlin were all returned to the sea, with more than 70% alive at the time of release....Conservative estimates of the annual number of black-marlin mortalities in the Western and Central Pacific alone are between 20,000 and 30,000. The number of black marlin dying as a result of longlining in Area E therefore represent about 2% of the number taken in this vast region." (p7)

Johnson, Katherine. "Fishing for Clues: Can We Help the Marlin Slip the Hook?" Ecos Win 1997. p6-9.

MARMOTS--BRITISH COLUMBIA--VANCOUVER ISLAND

"Recent surveys indicate that fewer than 150 of the [Vancouver

Island Marmots]...remain....About the size of a large house cat, the Vancouver Island marmot is one of 14 marmot species worldwide....An adult Vancouver Island marmot weighs about 3.5 kilograms in May when it emerges from its hibernation burrow but will pack on an additional two kilograms by late August....If the [captive breeding] program succeeds and a facility is ready by the year 2000,...[biologist Andrew Bryant, scientific advisor to the Vancouver Island Marmot Recovery Team,] predicts it will take 10 to 20 years to rebuild the wild population to 400 to 600 animals." (p18)

Goldberg, Kim. "Geo Watch: Dwindling Marmots." Canadian Geographic v117 n5 Sep-Oct 1997. p18. (ISSN0008-3658).

MARRIAGE

see also DIVORCE; INTERRACIAL MARRIAGE

"Among the 25 largest countries in the world, the highest average age [at first marriage] is reported in Germany (males 30.3, females 27.5). The lowest rate is in the Russian Federation (males 24.4, females 21.8) and Indonesia (males 25.2, females 21.6)." (p77)

"The Chronicle Library Shelf: Demographic Yearbook 1995." UN Chronicle v34 n3 1997. p77. (ISSN0251-7329).

MARRIAGE--AFRO-AMERICAN WOMEN

In the U.S., according to Linda "Waite (1995) the percentage of black women 15 years old and older who had never married rose from roughly 21% in 1950 to 37% in 1990. During the same period the percentage not currently married climbed from less than 40% to nearly 60%." (p1217)

Tolnay, Stewart E. "The Great Migration and Changes in the Northern Black Family, 1940 to 1990." Social Forces v75 n4 Jun 1997. p1213-1238. (ISSN0037-7732).

MARRIAGE--AFRO-AMERICANS (v26)

MARRIAGE--ANNULMENT

The annual statistical yearbook of the Holy See reports that in 1994, "the number of marriages declared null and void through ordinary process in the first instance as 50,950." (p11) In 1994, "within the same category, 36,460 annulments were granted in the United States: they amount to about 71 percent of the world-wide numbers....In the year 1992, for which we have documentation, 262,683 Catholics in the United States were granted a civil divorce. Of these only about 19 percent applied for an annulment....In 1992 the divorce rate in France was only about one third of that in the United States, and it is estimated that a mere 4 percent or less of the French Catholic divorcees petitioned for an annulment." (p12)

Orsy, Ladislas. "Marriage Annulments: An Interview with Ladislas Orsy." America v177 n10 4 Oct 1997. p10-12, 14,16,18. (ISSN0002-7049).

MARRIAGE--AUSTRALIA

According to the report, "Demography SA, 1995," by the Australian Bureau of Statistics, "the crude marriage rate of 5.8 per 1,000 population continued the downward trend which commenced in 1972, with 8,547 marriages registered South Australia in 1995. The median age at divorce was 39.9 years for men and 37.2 years for women, similar to the Australian median ages. In South Australia in 1995 there were 4,199 divorces granted."

Australian Bureau of Statistics. "South Australians--Living Longer." Media Release 11 Jun 1997. document-level access: <http://www.abs.gov.au/websitedbs/d3110125.nsf/4a255eef008309e44a255eef00061e57/6d35166d881934c74a2564b30004f29d?OpenDocument>

The publication "Marriages and Divorces, Australia," by the Australian Bureau of Statistics, "says that of the population aged over 15 years 4,458,600 or 31 percent had never married, compared with 25 percent in 1976, and 942,000 or 7 percent were divorced, compared with 2 percent in 1976. Over this period, percentage decreases were recorded for currently married (falling from 65 percent to 56 percent) and widowed (falling from 7 percent to 6 percent)....In 1996, 106,100 marriages were registered in Australia, a fall of nearly 8 percent on 1986 registrations (114,900) and the lowest number since 1979 (104,400). The crude marriage rate of 5.8 per 1,000 population was the lowest recorded in Australia this century. The median age at first marriage for all men was 29.6 years and 27.2 years for all women, which is an increase of 2.3 years for both bridegrooms and brides. The peak age group at first marriage for both men and women remained the age group 25-29 years. Remarriage rates, per 1,000 widowed and divorced men or women, decreased in all but one female age group between 1986 and 1996. The peak age groups at remarriage in 1996 were 30-34 years for men (98.8) and 25-29 years for women (104.7)."

Australian Bureau of Statistics. "Australians Marry Less and Later but Divorce More." Media Release 30 Jul 1997. document-level access: <http://www.abs.gov.au/websitedbs/d3110125.nsf/4a255eef008309e44a255eef00061e57/4b6e63a715002b084a2564e3007937fe?OpenDocument>

MARRIAGE--DEVELOPING COUNTRIES--UNITED STATES

"The average age at first marriage in the United States in 1994 was 24.5 for women and 26.7 for men....The gap tends to be much wider in many less industrialized countries, especially in Asia and Africa. In Niger, Africa, the average marriage age is 16 for women and 24 for men. In Bangladesh, it is 18 for women and 26 for men." (p12)

Riley, Nancy E. "Gender, Power, And Population Change." Population Bulletin v52 n1 May 1997. p2-46. (ISSN0032-468X).

MARRIAGE--EDUCATION--BRAZIL

In Brazil, in 1994, "more than half of the women ages 15 to 49 with no formal education married before age 20; over 40 percent became mothers while still in their teens. In contrast, only 14 percent of women who stayed in school beyond the primary level married before age 20, and less than 10 percent became teenage mothers." (p22)

Riley, Nancy E. "Gender, Power, And Population Change." Population Bulletin v52 n1 May 1997. p2-46. (ISSN0032-468X).

MARRIAGE--EDUCATION--THAILAND

In 1994, in Thailand, "where about a third of women were still in school at age 15, age at marriage is strongly associated with women's educational attainment. The average age at marriage for women with no education is just under 21, while it is over age 25 for those with a secondary or higher education." (p22)

Riley, Nancy E. "Gender, Power, And Population Change." Population Bulletin v52 n1 May 1997. p2-46. (ISSN0032-468X).

MARRIAGE--EUROPE (v26)

MARRIAGE--FRANCE--PUBLIC OPINION

"More than 90 percent of French adults think it is morally acceptable to have a baby outside of marriage, a Gallup poll found this year. In the US, the figure was 50 percent....France's divorce rate has tripled since 1973, to 1 in 3 marriages, lower than the US rate of nearly 1 in 2. But an October poll by the French magazine PARIS MATCH found that 72 percent of those surveyed think a divorce is too easy to get....The number of unmarried couples here has increased ninefold since 1960, and the number of single-parent families has steadily climbed from 9.3 percent in 1968 to 13 percent today, according to the National Institute of Statistics....Though France is a mainly Catholic country, just 12 percent of the French regularly fill the Sunday pews. And last year, 65 percent of Catholics told French pollster CSA they disapproved of the pope's attitudes on personal morality and sexuality, a 30 percent rise from seven years ago." (p8)

Gaouette, Nicole. "France Asks 'What Is a Family?'" The Christian Science Monitor v90 n3 28 Nov 1997. p1,8. The Christian Science Monitor search engine: <http://www.csmonitor.com/plweb-cgi/iops1.pl> To retrieve this article, enter the following search: ED=19971128 AND family. In the "retrieved list," click the title that matches this record. (ISSN0882-7729).

MARRIAGE--IRELAND

According to Ireland's 1996 Census, "in the State as a whole 41% of the population aged 15 and over were single and 49% were married (excluding those separated). The remaining 10% were either widow or separated. However, in the university towns of Maynooth and Galway County Borough the opposite was true. Singles make up 53% of the population in Maynooth with married people accounting for 42%,...[and] in Galway County Borough singles were also in the majority with a 52% to 40% divide. The number of single people grew by nearly 150,000 (15%) between 1986 and 1996 compared with an increase in married people of just over 50,000 (4%) over the same period. The CSO report also reveals that Dublin County Borough has the highest proportion of separated people (expressed as a percentage of those ever-married excluding widows) at 9%. This was followed by Limerick County Borough (8%). At the other end of the scale the counties of Roscommon and Cavan had the lowest proportions at 3% of those who ever married."

Ireland. Central Statistics Office. "1996 Census--Volume 2, Ages and Marital Status." Press Release 30 Oct 1997. document-level access: <http://www.cso.ie/pressreleases/prelcen96v2.html>

According to Ireland's Central Statistics Office, "the number of marriages declined fairly steadily from 21,800 in 1980 to 15,600 in 1995. There was an increase of just over 600 to 16,300 in 1996."

Ireland. Central Statistics Office. "Births, Marriages and Deaths in 1996." Press Release 22 May 1997. document-level access: <http://www.cso.ie/pressreleases/vstats1996.html>

MARRIAGE--KOREA (SOUTH)

In South Korea, in July 1997, "the Constitutional Court overturned the law enforcing the centuries-old taboo [of 'same-name/same-place' marriages]....In a country that shares just a handful of last names--Kim, Park, Lee, etc.--finding a spouse who has a different last name can be quite difficult. There are 2,379,000 Lees from Chonju, 3,767,000 Kims from Kimhae, and 2,704,000 Parks from Maryang....The court's July 13 decision has allowed about 200,000 'nonregistered' couples to register their unsanctioned marriages and receive benefits, says Kwak Pae-hee, an advocate at Seoul-based Korea Legal Aid Center on Family Relations....Couples were temporarily exempted from the law in 1978, '88, and '96. During these small victories, 60,000 couples registered their marriages, according to Kwak [Pae-hee]." (p6)

Baker, Michael. "International: South Korea Ends a Taboo, Strikes Blow for True Love." The Christian Science Monitor v89 n174 4 Aug 1997. p6. The Christian Science Monitor search engine: <http://www.csmonitor.com/plweb-cgi/iops1.pl> To retrieve this article, enter the following search: ED=19970804 AND love. In the "retrieved list," click the title that matches this record. (ISSN0882-7729).

MARRIAGE--NEPAL

"According to the most recent Nepal Family Health Survey, the median age at marriage has risen from 15.5 years among Nepalese women now age 45-49 to 17.1 years among women age 20-24....The median age at first marriage for women with no formal education is 16 years, compared with 19.8 years for women with some secondary education." (p4)

"Fertility Is Declining in Nepal." Popline v19 Sep-Oct 1997. p4.

MARRIAGE--PHILIPPINES

According to the Young Adult Fertility and Sexuality Study conducted in 1994 in the Philippines, "altogether, 24 percent of the women and 10 percent of the men interviewed during the survey described themselves as married. Among all the women who said they were married, only 47 percent had been married in a church. Another 26 percent had been married before a judge in a civil ceremony. The remaining 27 percent reported that they were currently living with a partner....Among currently married men, 47 percent had been married in church, 21 percent in a civil ceremony, and 32 percent were living with a partner." (p3)

"Survey Sheds New Light on Marriage and Sexuality in the Philippines." Asia-Pacific Population & Policy n42 Jul 1997. p1-4. (ISSN0891-6683).

MARRIAGE--THAILAND (v26)

MARRIAGE--UNITED STATES (v26)

According to the U.S. Census Bureau and National Center for Health Statistics, "in 1970, there was one unmarried couple for every 100 married couples. By 1995, that had risen to seven unmarried couples for every 100 married couples. In 1970 and 1980, the rate stayed constant: 10.6 out of every 1,000 got married. But in 1990, the rate per thousand had shrunk to 9.8, statistics show. Back in 1940, 12 of every 1,000 people married. In Metro Detroit, the percentage of males and females over 15 who never married ranged from a low 17 percent in Livingston County to a high 32 percent in Washtenaw, according to 1990 Census figures." (p1 secE)

Lewis, Shawn D. "The Metro: Special Report: Declining Marriage Rate: More Prefer the Single Life." Detroit News 4 Jun 1997. p1,6 secE.

In the U.S., "the likelihood that a couple married in 1995 will remain together for 50 years is more than 3 times greater than it was in 1900, according to a new analysis by the Metropolitan Life Insurance Company....In 1995, the median age for marrying couples was 26.9 for men and 24.5 for women. The average bride and groom's chances of both living for another 50 years were 333 in 1,000, compared with 79 in 1,000 at the beginning of the century....Today, a 30-year-old man and a 28-year-old woman can can expect to stay together 39.9 years before death does them part....A 30-year-old man and a 30-year-old woman wed in 1989-91 could expect 39.2 years together. If the woman was 32, the expectation decreases to 38.5 years....Two 65-year-olds who married in 1989-91 can expect 11.8 years of wedded life." (p5)

"Longer Lives Mean Longer Marriages." Forecast v17 n11 Nov 1997. p5. article-level access: <http://www.demographics.com/publications/fc/97_fc/9711_fc/fc97114.htm> (ISSN0732-1597).

In the U.S., "in 1970, 72 percent of Hispanics ages 18 years and older were married, almost the same as the figure for all whites (which included Hispanics). About 64 percent of African Americans were married. But marriage declined among all three groups over the ensuing decades. By 1995, the percentage of those ages 18 and older who were currently married was down to 59 percent for Hispanics, 63 percent for whites, and 43 percent for African Americans." (p29)

del Pinal, Jorge/Singer, Audrey. "Generations of Diversity: Latinos in the United States." Population Bulletin v52 n3 Oct 1997. p2-47. (ISSN0032-468X).

"Even though the proportion of [U.S.] marriages that end in divorce has climbed over the past few decades, from less than one in ten to nearly one in every two, the likelihood that today's newlyweds will remain married for the next 50 years is 3 1/4 times higher than the chances in 1900-02. In 1995 median age at first marriage for a man was 26.9 and 24.5 for a woman. This represents a 2.6-year increase in age for the bride while only a 1-year increase for the groom since the beginning of the century. Based on the United States 1989-91 general population life tables, the chances for both surviving for an additional 50 years are 333 in 1,000 compared with only 79 in 1,000 in 1900-02. At the beginning of the century the median age at first marriage for a groom was 26 and for a bride 22, and the likelihood that both would live an additional half century was 105 in 1,000." (p28-29)

Kranczer, Stanley. "Enhanced Likelihood of a Golden Wedding Anniversary." Statistical Bulletin v78 n3 Jul-Sep 1997. p28-32. (ISSN0790-8334).

MARRIAGE--UNITED STATES--ARMED FORCES (v26)

MARRIAGE--UNITED STATES--MORTALITY (v26)

MARRIAGE--UNITED STATES--PUBLIC OPINION (v26)

MARRIAGE--UNITED STATES--RELIGIOUS ASPECTS

In the U.S., "more than half of Buddhist and Jewish adherents who marry do so outside the faith. Some 40 percent of Muslims do; the Roman Catholic marriage rate to non-Catholics is between 30 and 40 percent." (p9)

Marquand, Robert. "Parental Divide: Kids' Choice of Religion in Divorce." The Christian Science Monitor v90 n13 12 Dec 1997. p1,9. The Christian Science Monitor search engine: <http://www.csmonitor.com/plweb-cgi/iops1.pl> To retrieve this article, enter the following search: ED=19971212 AND divorce. In the "retrieved list," click the title that matches this record. (ISSN0882-7729).

MARRIAGE--UNITED STATES--WOMEN (v26)

MARRIAGE AGE--UNITED STATES--WOMEN (v26)

MARSHALL ISLANDS--HEALTH AND HYGIENE

"Between the years 1946 and 1958...[the U.S.] tested approximately 66 atomic and hydrogen nuclear bombs at Bikini and Enewetak Atolls in the Marshall Islands....The legacy of the United States nuclear testing program has resulted in a nightmare of health problems for the Marshallese people, including the elevated rates of thyroid cancer. Cervical cancer mortality rates are 60 times the U.S. rate; breast cancer mortality rates, 5 times greater than in the United States, and reproductive complications involving high rates of miscarriage and deformed stillborn babies." (pH4335)

Faleomavaega, Eni F. H. (Del.-Amer. Samoa). "In Honor of the President of the Republic of the Marshall Islands, His Excellency Imata Kabua, And...Phillip Muller." Congressional Record. Daily ed. v143 n90 24 Jun 1997. pH4334-4336. section/page-level access: <http://thomas.loc.gov/cgi-bin/query/R?r105:FLD001:H04335:> (ISSN0363-7239). (X1.1A.105/1).

MASS COMMUNICATION

see COMMUNICATION AND TRAFFIC

MASS CULTURE

see POPULAR CULTURE

MASS MEDIA

see also MURDER IN MASS MEDIA; NEWS AGENCIES; PERSIAN GULF WAR, 1991--UNITED STATES--MASS MEDIA AND THE WAR; VIOLENCE IN MASS MEDIA

MASS MEDIA--CANADA (v26)

MASS MEDIA--CANADA--FINANCE (v26)

MASS MEDIA--GREAT BRITAIN (v26)

MASS MEDIA--RUSSIA

"Only one in three Russians has access to a television or radio. On the other hand, Russians are better-educated than people in less-developed nations, and a healthy 26 million newspapers circulate each day through a vast nation spanning six time zones. Furthermore, every form of media reaches beyond the most wealthy 20 percent of the nation's population, and outdoor ads are potentially seen by everyone." (p59)

Cassino, Kip D. "A World of Advertising." American Demographics v19 n11 Nov 1997. p57-60. article-level access: <http://www.demographics.com/publications/ad/97_ad/9711_ad/ad971131.htm> (ISSN0163-4089).

MASS MEDIA--SPANISH LANGUAGE

According to Octavio Nuiry, one of the editors of THE 1997 NATIONAL HISPANIC MEDIA DIRECTORY, "'the circulation of Hispanic newspapers, 76 percent published exclusively in Spanish, has jumped a phenomenal 1,225 percent since 1970, growing from 420,000 to more than 24.1 million today.'...[THE NATIONAL HISPANIC DIRECTORY] lists 1,085 Hispanic publications in the U.S. and Puerto Rico, with a combined circulation of 28 million. Those titles include 450 newspapers and 222 magazines. Among Hispanic broadcasters, there are more than 625 Spanish-language radio stations and 200 TV stations. In all, the directory lists and describes more than 2,500 Hispanic media outlets." (p3)

Swift, Paul. "Reviews: 45 Percent Larger than Last Year's." Public Relations Quarterly v42 n3 Fall 1997. p3-4. (ISSN0033-3700).

MASS MEDIA--UNITED STATES (v26)

In the U.S., "eighty percent of the daily newspapers...were independently owned at the end of World War II....Today, 80 percent of daily newspapers are owned by corporate chains. Just 11 companies control more than half of the dailies, half of the Nation's daily newspaper circulation....In fact, 98 percent of the daily newspapers in America have a monopoly as the only paper in town....Although there are more than 11,000 magazines published in the United States, today just two corporations control more than half of all magazine revenues....Although there are 11,000 local cable television systems, only 7 companies have a majority of the 60 million cable TV subscribers. Three companies own more than half the television business, four companies own more than half of the movie business, five companies rake in more than half of all book revenues." (pH3264)

Sanders, Bernard (Rep.-Vt.). "Destroying Organized Labor and Making Workers Powerless in this Country." Congressional Record. Daily ed. v143 n74 3 Jun 1997. pH3263-3269. section/page-level access: <http://thomas.loc.gov/cgi-bin/query/R?r105:FLD001:H03264:> (ISSN0363-7239). (X1.1A.105/1).

"The U.S. commercial media system is currently dominated by a few conglomerates--Disney, the News Corporation G.E., cable giant T.C.I., Universal, Sony, Time Warner and Viacom--with annual media sales ranging from $7 billion to $23 billion....The [media] system has a second tier of another fifteen or so companies, like Gannett, Cox Communications, Dow Jones, The New York Times Co. and Newhouse's Advance Communications, with annual sales ranging from $1 billion to $5 billion." (p11)

McChesney, Robert W. "The Communications Ripoff." Human Quest v211 n4 Jul-Aug 1997. p11. (ISSN0897-8786).

MASS MEDIA--UNITED STATES--POLITICS AND GOVERNMENT

According to the Information Access's NATIONAL NEWSPAPER INDEX, "the total number of print stories in which Democratic congressional candidates were mentioned was 5.92 times more than the number of print stories in which Republican congressional candidates were mentioned (529 mentions of Democratic candidates and 89 mentions of Republican candidates). With respect to network television news, a similar comparison [by Vanderbilt's TELEVISION NEWS INDEX AND ABSTRACT (1992)] yielded 3.68 times as much time devoted to women Democratic candidates as Republicans (129 Democratic mentions and 35 Republican mentions)." (p103)

Havick, John. "Determinants of National Media Attention." Journal of Communication v47 n2 Spr 1997. p97-111. (ISSN0021-9916).

MASS MEDIA--UNITED STATES--PUBLIC OPINION (v26)

"In 1997, 56 percent of [American] adults responding to a question posed by The Pew Research Center For The People & The Press said that news organizations are often inaccurate, up from 24 percent in 1985. The share of whites with this view rose from 36 percent to 56 percent, but the share of nonwhites in agreement grew even faster, from 27 to 58 percent." (p33)

Crispell, Diane. "Kaleidoscope: Hot Topics: Unfair Reporting Practices." American Demographics v19 n6 Jun 1997. p33. article-level access: <http://www.demographics.com/publications/ad/97_ad/9706_ad/ad970626.htm> (ISSN0163-4089).

"In 1989, 34 percent of Americans thought the press dealt fairly with all sides in political and social issues. Today, the number is down to 27 percent, with 67 percent believing the media tend to favor one side or the other, according to the Pew Research Center, a nonprofit media research group in Washington....In 1985, 55 percent of Americans believed the media got their facts straight most of the time. Today, that's down to 37 percent." (p3)

Marks, Alexandra. "United States: News Media Seek Credibility." The Christian Science Monitor v89 n191 27 Aug 1997. p3. The Christian Science Monitor search engine: <http://www.csmonitor.com/plweb-cgi/iops1.pl> To retrieve this article, enter the following search: ED=19970827 AND credibility. In the "retrieved list," click the title that matches this record. (ISSN0882-7729).

MASS MEDIA--UNITED STATES--WOMEN (v26)

MASS MEDIA AND THE POOR--AFRO-AMERICANS

A U.S. "study confirms that media outlets keep applying blackface to this nation's afflictions. Only 29 percent of the poor in the US are Black--but when Yale University scholar Martin Gilens examined coverage of poverty in national news magazines like TIME and NEWSWEEK, he found that 62 percent of the pictures were of Blacks. On network TV evening newscasts, the figure was 65 percent." (p14)

Solomon, Norman. "Image Distortion." Toward Freedom v46 n7 Dec 1997-Jan 1998. p14. (ISSN0048-9898).

MASS MEDIA AND TRIALS--UNITED STATES

At the time of the O.J. "Simpson case, 35 states permitted cameras in criminal trials, according to the [U.S.] National Center for State Courts. Immediately after the trial, only three states--California, Georgia, and Oklahoma--considered restricting cameras in criminal trials. Only one state--New York--has not renewed a program for cameras in trial court." (p34-35)

Canlen, Brae. "I'm O.J.--You're O.J.: How the O.J. Simpson Case Has Affected the Legal System." California Lawyer v17 n10 Oct 1997. p28-35,77. (ISSN0279-4063).

MASS TRANSIT

see LOCAL TRANSIT

MATHEMATICAL ABILITY (v26)

MATHEMATICAL ABILITY--UNITED STATES--HIGH SCHOOL STUDENTS (v26)

MATHEMATICAL ABILITY--UNITED STATES--STUDENT TESTING

In the U.S., according to the National Assessment of Educational Progress Math Report Card, "the national average score for fourth graders in 1996 was 224, 11 points over the national average for 1990; for eighth graders in 1996, the national average was 272, a nine point increase over 1990; and the average score for 12th graders was 304, an increase of ten points; for fourth graders, the percentage performing at or above the 'basic' level was 64 percent in 1996, as compared to only 50 percent in 1990; for eighth graders, 62 percent as compared to 52 percent; and for 12th graders, 69 percent compared to 58 percent...."

U.S. National Center for Education Statistics. "Riley Encouraged by Student Progress in Math Achievement; Urges Stronger Efforts to Reach International Standards." News Release 27 Feb 1997. document-level access: <http://www.ed.gov/PressReleases/02-1997/math96.html>

MATHEMATICS--STUDY AND TEACHING--GERMANY--JAPAN--UNITED STATES (v26)

MATHEMATICS--STUDY AND TEACHING--UNITED STATES

According to "Pursuing Excellence," a report by the U.S. National Center for Education Statistics, "in math, 9 percent of U.S. fourth-graders are among the top 10 percent of students in the world, according to the study....But our percentage of top scorers is well below that of Singapore (39 percent), Korea (26 percent), and Japan (23 percent)....U.S. fourth-grade teachers devote about 4.2 hours per week to teaching math, compared to an international average of 3.9 hours....About 71 percent of fourth-grade teachers here assign math homework three to five times a week, compared to an international average of 66 percent." (pA22)

"Education Vital Signs: Common Measures." American School Board Journal v184 n12 Dec 1997. pA18-A23. (ISSN0003-0953).

MATRIMONY

see MARRIAGE

MAYAS--GUATEMALA (v26)

In 1997, "the estimated Mayan population is 4 to 5 million, making it the 'largest indigenous group in North and Central America,' says Robert Sitler, a Spanish teacher and authority on Mayan culture at Stetson University in DeLand, Fla. The Guatemalan government says 40 percent of the population is Mayan....[Gaspar Pedro Gonzalez, a Mayan author and scholar living in Guatemala City,] claims the figure is probably closer to 60 percent." (p12)

Press, Robert M. "Mayan Culture Struggles in a TV World." The Christian Science Monitor v89 n137 11 Jun 1997. p12. The Christian Science Monitor search engine: <http://www.csmonitor.com/plweb-cgi/iops1.pl> To retrieve this article, enter the following search: ED=19970611 AND world. In the "retrieved list," click the title that matches this record. (ISSN0882-7729).

MAYAS--GUATEMALA--SOCIAL CONDITIONS

In Guatemala, "Mayans comprise 60 percent of the country's population, but control only a tiny fraction of its wealth. Seventy percent live in poverty, 80 percent are illiterate in Spanish, and 90 percent illiterate in their native language." (p11)

Woodard, Colin. "Reports: Guatemala: After the Killing." Bulletin of the Atomic Scientists v53 n4 Jul-Aug 1997. p9-11. (ISSN0096-3402).

MEASLES--DEVELOPING COUNTRIES

"In the mid-1990s, an estimated three-fourths of one-year-old children in developing countries were fully immunized against measles. Coverage ranged from 51 percent in sub-Saharan Africa and 79 percent in the Middle-Eastern Arab states, to 94 percent in East Asia (excluding China). Measles still infects 43 million people and kills 1 million children annually." (p6)

Olshansky, S. Jay/Carnes, Bruce/Rogers, Richard G./Smith, Len. "Infectious Diseases--New and Ancient Threats to World Health." Population Bulletin v52 n2 Jul 1997. p2-46. (ISSN0032-468X).

MEAT INDUSTRY AND TRADE (v26)

see also BEEF INDUSTRY; CATTLE TRADE; PORK INDUSTRY AND TRADE; POULTRY INDUSTRY; SWINE; TURKEY INDUSTRY

MEAT INDUSTRY AND TRADE--AUSTRALIA (v26)

MEAT INDUSTRY AND TRADE--FORMER SOVIET REPUBLICS

In 1996 extra Newly Independent States of the Soviet Union and the Baltics "meat imports to the region reached 2 million tons, roughly half of them poultry. Russia accounts for about 95 percent of extra-NIS/B meat imports. Extra-NIS/B meat imports have risen about five times from 1992 imports, while intra-NIS/B meat trade has decreased, as producers are less able to compete with foreign suppliers....In 1996, aggregate NIS/B animal inventories and meat production were both down for the seventh straight year. Since 1991, total NIS/B cattle inventories have decreased 34 percent (with cows down 16 percent), hogs 47 percent, and poultry 45 percent....Since 1991, total meat (beef, pork, and poultry) output has dropped almost 45 percent....Poultry meat production has declined the most at 60 percent, followed by pork at almost 50 percent, and beef at nearly 40 percent." (p12)

Foster, Christian J./Liefert, Olga/Mitchell, Jay K./Hoskin, Roger L./U.S. Dept. of Agriculture. Economic Research Service. "NIS/B Farm Sector Continues Adjustment to Market Forces; U.S. Agricultural Exports to Region Post Recovery." Newly Independent States and the Baltics: International Agriculture and Trade Reports Situation and Outlook Series May 1997. p10,12-15,18,20,22-24.

Since 1991, aggregate Newly Independent States of the Soviet Union and the Baltics "output of processed meat products has fallen nearly 75 percent....In the Caucasus countries, the industry has almost ceased operations, with output down nearly 95 percent. The smallest decline in processed meat output in the region has been in Russia and Belarus (around 65 percent)....In Kazakstan, Krygyzstan, Moldova, Armenia, Georgia, and Azerbaijan, the share of meat either sold in farmers' markets or bartered now exceeds 70 percent of total marketed production. In Russia, the share rose from 30 percent in 1994 to 44 percent in 1996, while the share in Belarus in 1996 was 38 percent, the lowest among the NIS/B countries....Since 1992, Russian imports of beef and pork, used mainly for processing, have increased by roughly 150 percent." (p11)

U.S. Dept. of Agriculture. Economic Research Service. "NIS/B Farm Sector Continues Adjustment to Market Forces...: Meat Producers Bypass Processors." Newly Independent States and the Baltics: International Agriculture and Trade Reports Situation and Outlook Series May 1997. p11.

MEAT INDUSTRY AND TRADE--GABON

"In Gabon, a country of about 1.2 million people, some 8 million pounds of bushmeat are consumed annually, half of it in urban areas. Primates are a large component of this total--in neighboring Equatorial Guinea they constitute up to 25 percent of the bushmeat marketed." (p16)

Tuxill, John. "Death in the Family Tree." World Watch v10 n5 Sep-Oct 1997. p12-21. (ISSN0896-0615).

MEAT INDUSTRY AND TRADE--NORTH CAROLINA

"According to the 1996 North Carolina Department of Agriculture report, North Carolina was first in the nation in turkey production with 59.5 million heads; our State was number two in hog production, exceeded by Iowa, at 9.8 million heads; and in commercial broilers North Carolina was fourth with 681 million heads, exceeded by Arkansas, Georgia, and Alabama. While we slightly dropped off in turkey production in 1996, we increased hog production by 1.5 million head and increased commercial broiler production by 37 million heads over the last statistical reporting period." (pS8604)

Helms, Jesse (Sen.-N.C.). "Workplace Religious Freedom Act." Congressional Record. Daily ed. v143 n111 31 Jul 1997. pS8590-8607. section/page-level access: <http://thomas.loc.gov/cgi-bin/query/R?r105:FLD001:S08604:> (ISSN0363-7239). (X1.1A.105/1).

MEAT INDUSTRY AND TRADE--RUSSIA (v26)

"From 1992 to 1996, total Russian meat imports have more than tripled, while their share in domestic meat consumption is estimated to have increased from about 8 to 35 percent (reaching more than 50 percent for poultry)...." (p14) "The EU dominates Russian extra-NIS/B [Newly Independent States of the Soviet Union and the Baltics] imports of beef (more than 80 percent in 1995 and 1996), while China's share rose to about 10 percent in 1996. China is the primary pork exporter to Russia, accounting for nearly half of extra-NIS/B supplies, with Eastern Europe in second place with about a quarter of the market. During the Soviet period, about 40 percent of Russia's meat imports came from other parts of the USSR--that is, from what are now other NIS/B countries. However, by 1996 these nations were supplying only 15 percent of Russia's meat imports. In 1996, meat exports by both Kazakstan and Belarus to Russia fell 45 percent from the previous year, while those of Ukraine stayed flat." (p15)

Foster, Christian J./Liefert, Olga/Mitchell, Jay K./Hoskin, Roger L./U.S. Dept. of Agriculture. Economic Research Service. "NIS/B Farm Sector Continues Adjustment to Market Forces; U.S. Agricultural Exports to Region Post Recovery." Newly Independent States and the Baltics: International Agriculture and Trade Reports Situation and Outlook Series May 1997. p10,12-15,18,20,22-24.

MEAT INDUSTRY AND TRADE--RUSSIA--UNITED STATES (v26)

MEAT INDUSTRY AND TRADE--UNITED STATES (v26)

U.S. exports of consumer-ready food products to the Asia-Pacific Economic Cooperation "region in fiscal 1996 reached a record $14 billion or 71 percent of total U.S. consumer-ready food exports....Red meats, mainly beef and pork, have been historically the most important consumer-ready products imported by the region, which received 92 percent of total U.S. red meat exports in fiscal 1996. Total U.S. red meat exports to the APEC region increased 8 percent from fiscal 1995 to a record $4 billion. Beef was the largest component ($2.5 billion versus $1.5 billion for non-beef red meats), but pork rose at a faster rate (30 percent versus 3.9 percent for non-pork red meats)." (p9)

Huang, Sophia Wu/U.S. Dept. of Agriculture. Economic Research Service. "U.S. Agricultural Exports to APEC Region at Another Record." APEC: International Agriculture and Trade Reports Situation and Outlook Series Aug 1997. p9-12.

U.S. "meat packing exports jumped 21 percent to $6.1 billion in 1995, but fell $100 million last year....Meat packing product exports to Japan, the largest U.S. market, fell 3 percent to $2.9 billion. Sales to South Korea fell 17 percent to $860 million, due primarily to economic sluggishness in South Korea and the strength of the dollar against the South Korean won. Mexico was a bright spot for U.S. meat packing product exports, as exports jumped more than 50 percent to $470 million in 1996, after plunging 50 percent in 1995 after peso devaluation." (p11)

Ruppel, Fred J./Handy, Charles R./Malanoski, Margaret A./U.S. Dept. of Agriculture. Economic Research Service. "World Agriculture & Trade: U.S. Processed Food Trade Continues to Expand." Agricultural Outlook Jul 1997. p11-13.

In the U.S., "meat-packing wages have dropped 31.4 percent since 1982. In 1982, the $9 average meat-packing plant wage was 51 cents above the average wage for all manufacturing workers. Now, the average industry wage of $9.82 is almost $3 below the average manufacturing wage." (p20)

Seymour, Chris. "Corporate America: Low-Wage Innovations." In These Times v21 n19 11 Aug 1997. p18-20. (ISSN0160-5992).

U.S. May 1997 "beef and veal shipments were $206 million, down 11 percent from 1996. October-May beef exports were $1.5 billion, down from $1.9 billion a year earlier." (p1)

U.S. Dept. of Agriculture. Economic Research Service. "Exports." U.S. Agricultural Trade Update 23 Jul 1997. p1.

MEDAL OF HONOR

"The Medal of Honor, often called the Congressional Medal of Honor, is still the highest award for bravery given in the U.S. Armed Forces. Since 1961, about 3,425 medals have been issued, according to the Congressional Medal of Honor Society. There are about 169 living recipients." (p11 secA)

Joseph, Karen. "Grave Markers to Honor Civil War Heroes." Ypsilanti Press 25 May 1997. p1,11 secA.

MEDALS--CANADA (v26)

MEDIATION--UNITED STATES

"The ranks of attorney-mediators continue to swell. The Southern California Mediation Association (SCMA) increased its membership by 25 percent last year alone. Some 70 percent of the 1,200 mediators on the American Arbitration Association's (AAA) national panel are lawyers; 5 percent of the arbitrators and mediators are retired judges, and the remainder are business and industry professionals. Although AAA requires 10 to 15 years of experience in a particular field (construction, for instance), mediators in California, as in most states, need no special credentials or accreditation." (p17)

Newsome, Melba. "California, ESQ.: Mediation Madness: Dissatisfied Lawyers Are Rushing into the ADR Business." California Lawyer v17 n7 Jul 1997. p17-18. (ISSN0279-4063).

In the U.S., "a recent study conducted by Cornell University found that of the 88 percent of the nation's largest corporations that had used mediation within the past three years, 81 percent considered it more satisfactory than litigation, and approximately 90 percent found it less costly. Despite this, nearly half of the Cornell survey respondents said they lacked confidence in the arbitrators and mediators they hired, and almost 30 percent questioned their qualifications." (p17)

Newsome, Melba. "California, ESQ.: Mediation Madness: Dissatisfied Lawyers Are Rushing into the ADR Business." California Lawyer v17 n7 Jul 1997. p17-18. (ISSN0279-4063).

MEDICAID (v26)

In the U.S., "since 1992, enrollment in Medicaid managed care plans has increased by more than 170 percent, including a 33 percent increase from 1995 to 1996. As of June 30, 1996, 13.3 million Medicaid beneficiaries were enrolled in managed care plans, representing 40 percent of all beneficiaries."

U.S. Dept. of Health and Human Services. "Managed Care in Medicare and Medicaid." Fact Sheet 20 Nov 1997. document-level access: <http://www.hhs.gov/news/press/1997pres/971120b.html>

Since 1992, enrollment in "Medicaid managed care plans has increased by more than 170 percent, including a 33 percent increase from 1995 to 1996. As of June 30, 1996, 13.3 million Medicaid beneficiaries were enrolled in managed care plans, representing 40 percent of all beneficiaries. Currently, 48 states offer some form of managed care....Since January 1, 1993, comprehensive health care reform demonstration waivers have been approved for 16 states and nine have already been implemented. When all 16 are implemented, nearly 2.6 million previously uninsured individuals are expected to receive health coverage."

U.S. Dept. of Health and Human Services. "Managed Care in Medicare and Medicaid." Fact Sheet 15 Jul 1997. document-level access: <http://www.hhs.gov/news/press/1997pres/970715b.html>

In the U.S., "in 1995, 36.3 million people received Medicaid-funded services. Of these recipients, about 4.4 million were over age sixty-five, 5.6 million were blind or disabled, 17.2 million were children under age twenty-one, and 7.6 million were AFDC-receiving adults. Although the elderly and disabled constitute a minority of Medicaid recipients (27 percent), the services they receive account for 72 percent of Medicaid payments. Except for the costs of administration, all Medicaid spending goes to providers. In 1995, these payments totaled $120.1 billion--about $29 billion for hospital care, $20 billion for physician services and services in outpatient settings, $49 billion for nursing home care and home care services, $10 billion for prescription drugs, and $12 billion for dental services, family planning, lab services, and other types of care." (p842)

Kronebusch, Karl. "Medicaid and the Politics of Groups: Recipients, Providers, And Policy Making." Journal of Health Politics, Policy and Law v22 n3 Jun 1997. p839-878. (ISSN0361-6878).

In the U.S., "the number of dependent children under age twenty-one who received Medicaid-funded services rose 76 percent from 1985 to 1994, while the number of adults in families with dependent children who received Medicaid services increased only 37 percent. The result of this differential growth is that the share of Medicaid recipients who are children rose from about 45 percent to 49 percent over that period, while the share of Medicaid recipients who are adults receiving AFDC fell from 25 percent to 22 percent (...[author's] calculations, based on data from U.S. House of Representatives 1996...)." (p872)

Kronebusch, Karl. "Medicaid and the Politics of Groups: Recipients, Providers, And Policy Making." Journal of Health Politics, Policy and Law v22 n3 Jun 1997. p839-878. (ISSN0361-6878).

Medicaid already serves as the U.S.'s "No. 1 insurance plan for low-income children, covering nearly 40 percent of American births and more than 18 million children at any given time. The State Children's Health Insurance Program allows states to expand Medicaid to cover children in families with incomes up to 200 percent of federal poverty guidelines (or 50 percentage points higher than their existing eligibility ceiling when it exceeds 150 percent of poverty)....Wyoming currently covers children age 6 through 14 who live in families with incomes up to 133 percent of the poverty line, the federal minimum. Wyoming could raise its ceiling to 200 percent of poverty ($26,660 for a family of three) under the new law. Wisconsin covers the same age group with family income up to 185 percent of poverty, so would be allowed to increase its income ceiling to 235 percent of poverty." (p22) "'Between 40 percent and 50 percent of Wyoming families have income at or below 200 percent of the federal poverty rate and could potentially qualify for assistance under the new federal program,'...[Wyoming Senator Charles Scott] says." (p26)

King, Martha P. "Year of the Child in Health Care." State Legislatures v23 n10 Dec 1997. p22-26. (ISSN0147-6041).

In the U.S., "the amount of federal outlays for grants to state and local government has grown by more than 60 percent since 1967....Medicaid grants amounted to 2 percent of state and local aid in 1967. By 1977, Medicaid was 7 percent of the total. In 1987, it reached 21 percent. In 1997, outlays to states and localities for Medicaid are estimated to be 45 percent of all grant-in-aid dollars." (p2)

"Federal Tax and Budget Report." States' Advocate Dec 1997. p2.

MEDICAID--AGED--COSTS (v26)

MEDICAID--CHILDREN (v26)

MEDICAID--CHILDREN--COSTS (v26)
MEDICAID--COSTS (v26)
MEDICAID--FLORIDA

"An extremely successful Florida Medicaid antifraud program requires providers of durable medical equipment, home health, and transportation services to post a $50,000 surety bond to participate in the Medicare Program....Durable medical equipment suppliers have dropped by 62 percent, from 4,146 to 1,565; home health agencies have decreased by 41 percent, from 738 to 441; providers of transportation services have disenrolled from the State's Medicaid Programs in droves--from 1,759 to 742, a drop of 58 percent. Fewer providers bilking the State's Medicaid Program is projected to save over $192 million over the next 2 years in Florida." (pS5455)

Graham, Bob (Sen.-Fla.). "Statements on Introduced Bills and Joint Resolutions." Congressional Record. Daily ed. v143 n80 10 Jun 1997. pS5444-5464. section/page-level access: <http://thomas.loc.gov/cgi-bin/query/R?r105:FLD001:S05455:> (ISSN0363-7239). (X1.1A.105/1).

MEDICAID--HANDICAPPED (v26)
MEDICAID--MEDICARE (v26)
MEDICAID--MEDICARE--PHYSICIANS--ATTITUDES (v26)
MEDICAID--MICHIGAN (v26)
MEDICAID--MICHIGAN--COSTS (v26)
MEDICAID--WEST VIRGINIA--CHILDREN (v26)
MEDICAL CARE

see also AGED--MEDICAL CARE; AMBULATORY MEDICAL CARE; CHILDREN--MEDICAL CARE; MANAGED CARE PLANS (MEDICAL CARE); MEDICAID; MEDICARE; PRISONERS--MEDICAL CARE; TERMINAL CARE

MEDICAL CARE--AUSTRALIA (v26)
MEDICAL CARE--CANADA--FINANCE (v26)
MEDICAL CARE--CANADA--PUBLIC OPINION (v26)
MEDICAL CARE--CANADA--UNITED STATES (v26)
MEDICAL CARE--CANADA--UNITED STATES --PUBLIC OPINION (v26)
MEDICAL CARE--CUBA

"A country with merely 11 million people, Cuba has become a powerhouse of medical innovation. In this small country there are 284 hospitals, 440 clinics, 11 research institutes, and 15 medical colleges, while with some 60,000 doctors and more than 5000 researchers the 'national average ratio of physicians to total population is one doctor for every 180 people, and this does not count...nurses, physical therapists, medical technicians and medical researchers.'" (p17) "Each urban neighborhood has a community clinic that serves 30,000-40,000 people and offers treatment for minor ailments." (p18) "Using both the clinics and medical practitioners 98 percent of all children have been vaccinated against twelve major diseases including meningitis-B and hepatitis-B." (p19)

Schwab, Peter. "Cuban Health Care and the U.S. Embargo." Monthly Review v49 n6 Nov 1997. p15-26. (ISSN0027-0520).

MEDICAL CARE--EUROPE--FINANCE (v26)
MEDICAL CARE--FORMER SOVIET REPUBLICS --FINANCE

In the Central Asian Republics of the former Soviet Union "health spending has decreased from about 6% to only 3% of GNP and per capita spending has declined by almost half....The inefficient hospital sector has led to a fundamental imbalance in health sector financing with hospitals consuming over 70% of health spending compared with 30% for public health and primary care." (p16)

Borowitz, Michael/O'Dougherty, Sheila. "Inverting the Pyramid." World Health v50 n5 Sep-Oct 1997. p16-17. (ISSN0043-8502).

MEDICAL CARE--FRANCE (v26)
MEDICAL CARE--GREAT BRITAIN (v26)
MEDICAL CARE--GREAT BRITAIN--FINANCE (v26)
MEDICAL CARE--HAWAII

"Health costs in Hawaii are 30 percent less than in California....Hawaiians spend 40 percent less time in the hospital, thanks to universal primary care. About 60 percent of them are covered by Blue Cross & Blue Shield, about 22 percent by Kaiser Permanente." (p10)

Dukakis, Michael S. "Health Care Reform--Not a Dead Issue." America v176 n16 10 May 1997. p8-10. (ISSN0002-7049).

MEDICAL CARE--MICHIGAN--WASHTENAW COUNTY

In Michigan, "Washtenaw County's inpatient hospitalization program for the indigent is undergoing a major change, increasing the number of patients served from 300 a year to 3,000, with the same $500,000 budget....Each contractor will be reimbursed $144 per year per patient (or $12 per month). Individuals and families with annual income below 185 percent of national poverty guidelines will be eligible to enroll, said Ellen Rabinowitz, county health planner. A single person would qualify with income of $14,597 or less; a family of four, $29,693, she said." (p4 secC)

Pyen, Chong W. "Local: Clinics to Serve More Uninsured." Ann Arbor News 6 Jun 1997. p4 secC.

MEDICAL CARE--PUBLIC OPINION (v26)
MEDICAL CARE--TURKEY--FINANCE

"The financing of health care in Turkey, which amounts to about 4 percent of GNP is complex because of the large number of agencies involved in providing and/or financing health care services. Approximately, one-third is financed by taxation, 17 percent by social insurance funds, and the remaining 50 percent by direct out-of-pocket payments. 67 percent of the population currently has coverage under existing social insurance system, leaving approximately 21 million people without coverage."

World Bank. "World Bank Improves Primary Health Care in Turkey: Reforming Health Care in Turkey." Press Release 24 Jun 1997. document-level access: <http://www.worldbank.org/html/extdr/extme/1396.htm>

MEDICAL CARE--UNITED STATES (v26)

"Nearly 13 million of the roughly 110 million families in the United States--11.6 percent of all families--experienced difficulty or delays in obtaining medical care or did not get the care they needed during 1996, according to new estimates from the federal Agency for Health Care Policy and Research (AHCPR). The most common barrier, experienced by 7.6 million families or roughly 60 percent of all those reporting difficulty with access, was not being able to afford care they needed....Uninsured families were more likely than the average family to experience problems obtaining needed health care. More than 27 percent of them, or 3.3 million uninsured families, experienced barriers, including the inability to afford care. Hispanic families were more likely than white or black families to encounter problems. Roughly 1.4 million Hispanic families (15 percent of all Hispanic families) reported barriers. For almost seven in 10 of these Hispanic families, the problem was the cost of health care."

U.S. Dept. of Health and Human Services. "Millions Face Barriers to Obtaining Medical Care." Press Release 26 Nov 1997. document-level access: <http://www.hhs.gov/news/press/1997pres/971126b.html>

In the U.S., "an estimated 860.9 million visits were made to physician offices, hospital outpatient departments, and hospital emergency departments in 1995, a rate of 3.3 visits per person. Visits to office-based physicians accounted for 81 percent of ambulatory care utilization, followed by emergency departments (11 percent) and outpatient departments (nearly 8 percent)....Less than two-thirds of the ambulatory care visits by black persons were to physician offices....'General medical exam' was the most frequently listed reason for visit as stated in the patient's own listed reason for visit as stated in the patient's own words, occurring in 6 percent of the visits. 'Cough' was the leading reason related to illness or injury, occurring in over 3 percent of visits."

U.S. National Center for Health Statistics. "Monitoring Health Care in America: Spotlight on: Ambulatory Care in the U.S." Quarterly Fact Sheet Jun 1997. document-level access: <http://www.cdc.gov/nchswww/releases/97facts/97sheets/mhc0697.htm>

MEDICAL CARE--UNITED STATES--FINANCE (v26)

MEDICAL CARE--UNITED STATES--PUBLIC OPINION (v26)

"The latest data from the independent congressional advisory panel--the Physician Payment Assessment Commission--shows that only 4 percent of all Medicare beneficiaries [in the U.S.] reported having trouble getting health care in the last year. About 11 percent had a medical problem, but failed to see a physician, while 12 percent did not have a physician's office as a usual source of care. Roughly 10 percent of Medicare beneficiaries delayed care due to cost. Considering all four access measures, about 26 percent of Medicare beneficiaries cited experiencing at least one of these problems. PhysPRC reports that from their surveys of those who failed to see a physician for their serious medical problem, 43 cited cost as the reason. About 8 percent of those who failed to see a physician could not get an appointment or find an available physician. For another 8 percent, transportation was the problem, 13 percent felt there was nothing a doctor could do, and 11 percent were afraid of finding out what was wrong." (pE1820)

Stark, Fortney Pete (Rep.-Calif.). "People Have Trouble Seeing Doctors Because They Don't Have Enough Money...." Congressional Record. Daily ed. v143 n128 23 Sep 1997. pE1820. section/page-level access: <http://thomas.loc.gov/cgi-bin/query/R?r105:FLD001:E01820:> (ISSN0363-7239). (X1.1A.105/1).

MEDICAL CARE--VENEZUELA--FINANCE

"Currently Venezuela devotes only 2.5 percent of its GNP to health, compared to six percent in 1991 and to the 10 percent recommended by the World Health Organization. Of these funds, 80 percent goes to salaries of health workers, leaving only 17 cents per patient in public hospitals." (p4)

Rodriguez, Lisa. "In Venezuela Everything Is Not 'Chevere.'" NewsNotes v22 n6 Nov-Dec 1997. p3-4. (ISSN1064-1556).

MEDICAL CARE, AMBULATORY

see AMBULATORY MEDICAL CARE

MEDICAL CARE, COST OF

"Data from France and the Netherlands shows that the aging population only increases health care costs by 0.3 per cent per year and the British projection is even lower (Abel-Smith 1996). It is estimated that some 20 per cent of health care costs are used for treating people in their last year of life and that these costs are heavily concentrated in the last two months (Fuchs 1984). People who die over the age of 80 use only 80 per cent of the resources of those who die aged 65-79 (Scitovsky 1988), which suggests that if death could be postponed to after the age of 80 health care costs could be reduced. These data, however, might just be a reflection of age discrimination against older people (75% of whom are women) receiving complex (and high cost) medical technologies." (p197)

Bond, John. "Health Care Reform in the UK: Unrealistic or Broken Promises to Older Citizens?" Journal of Aging Studies v11 n3 Fall 1997. p195-210. (ISSN0890-4065).

In the U.S., "the $51 billion increase in national health expenditures in 1995 represented 16 percent of the dollar increase in GDP. The incremental change is expected to amount to about 17 percent of the gain in the economy for 1997 and be in the vicinity of one-fifth by the year 2000....In 1995 per capita national health expenditures amounted to over $3,620....This per capita figure represents a gain of 35 percent from 1990, compared with a 42 percent gain for total health expenditures, an indication of the isolated impact of population growth. Adjusting per capita data for inflation provides insight into actual changes in utilization. Between 1990 and 1995 with this adjustment, there was actually a slight decline in expenditures. This contrasts to an almost 8 percent gain during the previous five years." (p14) "Medical care inflation as measured in the Consumer Price Index (CPI) rose just 3.5 percent in 1996, thereby continuing the deceleration begun in 1991....The increase was just 0.5 percentage points above the overall CPI--substantially lower than the gap experienced in recent years." (p15)

Vincenzino, Joseph V. "Trends in Medical Care Costs--Revisited." Statistical Bulletin v78 n3 Jul-Sep 1997. p10-16. (ISSN0790-8334).

MEDICAL CARE, COST OF--GREAT BRITAIN (v26)

"In the UK the cost of health care increased annually at a rate of four per cent between 1960-1992. As a proportion of Gross Domestic Product (GDP) health care expenditure increased in the UK from 3.9% in 1960, 4.5% in 1970, 5.8% in 1980 to 7.1% in 1992 (OECD 1992; Abel-Smith 1996). Expenditure on older people in 1990 was estimated to be 47% of all health expenditure or 3.1% of GDP (Bond and Buck 1994; Pacolet et al. 1994)." (p196-197)

Bond, John. "Health Care Reform in the UK: Unrealistic or Broken Promises to Older Citizens?" Journal of Aging Studies v11 n3 Fall 1997. p195-210. (ISSN0890-4065).

MEDICAL CARE, COST OF--MASSACHUSETTS --BOSTON (v26)

MEDICAL CARE, COST OF--NEW YORK (N.Y.) (v26)

MEDICAL CARE, COST OF--UNITED STATES (v26)

"More Americans are concerned about financing long-term care (69 percent) than about paying for retirement (56 percent), according to a 1996 survey sponsored by the National Council on the Aging and John Hancock Mutual Life Insurance Company. Eighty-seven percent of respondents feel that providing long-term care is a very or fairly big problem in the U.S. Sixty percent worry they or their spouse will some day need long-term care. Adults aged 35 to 44 are more worried about needing long-term care than younger or older adults." (p34)

Miller, Berna. "Kaleidoscope: Worries about Long-Term Care." American Demographics v19 n6 Jun 1997. p34-35. article-level access: <http://www.demographics.com/publications/ad/97_ad/9706_ad/ad970616.htm> (ISSN0163-4089).

In the U.S., "increased research will reduce health care costs. Let me give some examples of annual economic costs. Cancer, $104 billion annually; heart disease, $128 billion; Alzheimer's, $100 billion; diabetes, $138 billion; mental disorders, $148 billion; stroke, $30 billion....For every $1 spent on measles/mumps/rubella vaccine, $21 is saved. For diphtheria/tetanus/pertussis vaccine, $29 is saved....Hip fractures, common among the elderly, are a leading cause of nursing home admissions. They account for one in every 5 admissions. NIH [National Institutes of Health] research found that estrogen therapy reduces osteoporosis and hip fractures. In 1991, 1 year alone, the reduction in fractures in women taking estrogen replacement saved $333 million in these nursing home admission costs. Medicaid and Medicare: 56 percent of nursing home costs are paid by these programs. They total over $44 billion annually....By delaying the onset of chronic aging-related illnesses, spending for nursing home care could be cut by $35 billion." (pS4864-4865)

Feinstein, Dianne (Sen.-Calif.). "Concurrent Resolution on the Budget." Congressional Record. Daily ed. v143 n68 21 May 1997. pS4851-4876. section/page-level access: <http://thomas.loc.gov/cgi-bin/query/R?r105:FLD001:S04864:> (ISSN0363-7239). (X1.1A.105/1).

The U.S. "spends far more per capita on health care than many industrialized countries such as Canada, Germany, France, Sweden, Japan, and the United Kingdom. This excess spending varies from 50 percent more per capita than Canada to 175 percent more per capita than the United Kingdom....In 1991, the United States spent $838 billion or over $3,000 per person for health care....About 17 percent of Americans do not have any form of payment scheme to cover the costs of health care." (p19)

Carter, Michael A. "The Promise of Nurse Practitioners." Nursing Administration Quarterly v21 n4 Sum 1997. p19-24. (ISSN0363-9568).

In the U.S., "the Office of the Actuary in the Health Care Financing Administration (HCFA) prepares annual estimates of health and medical care expenditures from both public and private sources. These are based on the National Health Accounts....In 1994, total spending for health amounted to $949.4 billion or 13.7 percent of GDP...; the private-sector share amounted to $528.6 billion, 55.7 percent. Private health payments have grown from 4.5 percent of GDP in 1972 to 7.6 percent in 1994. The relative shares of private and public expenditures for health remained fairly constant from 1972 to 1990....[From 1990 to 1994], the Federal share of national health spending rose from 28.1 to 30.0 percent, while the private-sector share dropped from 59.2 to 55.7 percent. State and local governments (the other contributors to the public spending category) paid about 12.3 percent in both 1990 and 1994." (p54,56)

"Private Social Welfare Expenditures, 1972-94." Social Security Bulletin v60 n1 1997. p54-60. (ISSN0037-7910).

"The latest official data from the Health Care Financing Administration (HCFA) show that national health expenditures in the United States rose to $988.5 billion in 1995, for an increase of 5.5 percent from the previous year....The rate of growth was slightly higher than the 5.1 percent increase recorded in 1994....According to the latest HCFA data, spending on personal health care totaled almost $879 billion in 1995, up 6.1 percent from the previous year. The annual growth rate for personal health care averaged 5.9 percent during the three-year period ending in 1995, compared to 10.4 percent for the previous three years." (p11) "Expenditures for health care goods and services amounted to 13.6 percent of gross domestic product (GDP) in 1995, the same ratio as in 1993...." (p12)

Vincenzino, Joseph V. "Trends in Medical Care Costs--Revisited." Statistical Bulletin v78 n3 Jul-Sep 1997. p10-16. (ISSN0790-8334).

"In 1980, Americans spent $247 billion on health care, or 8.9 percent of the gross domestic product. Ten years later, that figure was $697 billion, or 12.1 percent of the GDP. Since 1993, though, spending has stabilized at about 13.5 percent." (p26)

Jenkins, Kent, Jr./Walsh, Kenneth T./Brink, Susan. "U.S. News: Health Care Politics: The Sequel." U.S. News & World Report v123 n21 1 Dec 1997. p24-27. article-level access: <http://www.usnews.com/usnews/issue/971201/1HEAL.HTM> (ISSN0041-5537).

MEDICAL CARE, COST OF--UNITED STATES --MORTALITY

"U.S. health care costs could plummet by as much as $80 billion a year as more Americans die at home surrounded by friends, rather than in a hospital surrounded by machines. The savings may reach $2.8 billion a year in Michigan alone....Of the about $1 trillion Americans spend on health care each year, about 10 percent--or $100 billion--is spent on care for people in the last year of life. Of that, about $40 billion is spent in the final month, according to government reports and university studies." (p1 secA)

French, Ron. "Dying at Home Saves Billions." Detroit News 29 Sep 1997. p1,4 secA.

MEDICAL CARE, PREPAID

see INSURANCE, HEALTH

MEDICAL COLLEGE GRADUATES--UNITED STATES (v26)

MEDICAL COLLEGES--CALIFORNIA--MINORITIES (v26)

MEDICAL COLLEGES--MICHIGAN--MINORITIES

In the U.S., minority enrollments in first-year medical school classes are "down 7 percent nationally and a whopping 38 percent at Michigan State [University]. Most of MSU's drop came in the number of African Americans enrolled: seven this year compared with 15 last year. Overall, MSU's medical schools have 16 minority students--down from 26 a year earlier." (p1 secD) At the University of Michigan medical school, "minority applications fell 17 percent, while...Wayne State's minority applications dropped 19 percent this year. MSU experienced a 2-percent decline in applications overall, but a 12.7-percent drop among under-represented minorities....Wayne State...medical school ranks fourth nationally in the number of minority students enrolled. Michigan ranks fifth nationally, and MSU is 31st." (p2 secD)

Hoover, Rusty/Cohen, Jodi S. "Metro: Med School Minorities Plunge." Detroit News 17 Nov 1997. p1-2 secD.

MEDICAL COLLEGES--UNITED STATES--COSTS (v26)

MEDICAL COLLEGES--UNITED STATES--MINORITIES (v26)

MEDICAL DOCTORS

see PHYSICIANS

MEDICAL EDUCATION--UNITED STATES--FINANCE (v26)

MEDICAL ERRORS--UNITED STATES

"A recent study in THE LANCET found that 17.7 percent of patients admitted to the ICU [intensive care unit] or surgical floor of a particular U.S. teaching hospital suffered a 'serious adverse event'--i.e., an error occurred at the hospital that hurt or killed the patient....More than one in six patients [were] hurt or killed by the system that was supposed to help them. There are other studies that support these findings. In one of them, 31 percent of the internal medicine residents who responded said that their worst error had killed someone." (p13)

Stahlhut, Rick. "InfoMed: To Err Is Human." New Physician v46 n8 Nov 1997. p13-14. (ISSN0028-6451).

MEDICAL OFFICES--UNITED STATES--PUBLIC OPINION (v26)

MEDICAL PERSONNEL

see also EMERGENCY MEDICAL TECHNICIANS; MENTAL HEALTH PERSONNEL; NURSES; PHYSICIANS

MEDICAL PERSONNEL--UNITED STATES

In the U.S., "the median annual income of a PA [physician assistant] in general practice is about half that of a doctor ($60,000 compared with $110,000). Students...pay about $21,000 on average to earn a PA degree, significantly less than the $80,000 required for a physician's degree....About 85 percent [of PAs] were employed in their field within a year of graduation, according to the American Academy of Physician Assistants in Alexandria, Va. The Bureau of Labor Statistics predicts a growth rate of 50 percent above the norm through 2005....In the past two years alone, the number of schools offering PA programs leaped 33 percent from 64 to 85....The annual number of graduates from PA programs has nearly doubled to 2,500 in the past 10 years." (p3 secF)

Corcoran, Megan E. "Strategies: Careers: Medicine Appeals to

Many Entering a 2nd Career." Detroit News 17 Nov 1997. p3 secF.

MEDICAL STUDENTS--UNITED STATES

"Currently, the total number of U.S. residency slots is 140 percent of the number of medical school graduates....With an oversupply of physicians looming; with the number of IMGs [international medical graduates] training in U.S. residencies at an all-time high--almost 27,000 last year, up from 11,500 in 1989...." (p5)

Humphrey, Dana/Durso, Christopher. "Monitor: COGME Says: Cut IMGs." New Physician v46 n6 Sep 1997. p5-6. (ISSN0028-6451).

MEDICAL STUDENTS--UNITED STATES--ATTITUDES

According to the Association of American Medical Colleges's most recent survey of entering students, the opportunity to make a difference in people's lives "was cited as 'very important' in their career choice by 87 percent of medical students....Prestige, authority and high income ranked low in motivating medical students, with more than 90 percent of respondents identifying those elements as 'only somewhat important.'" (p6)

Humphrey, Dana. "Monitor: A Classy Calling." New Physician v46 n8 Nov 1997. p6. (ISSN0028-6451).

MEDICAL TECHNOLOGY

An article in the January 1997 issue of MEDICAL ECONOMICS "talks about the enormous explosion of the various devices, talking of the demand for devices to treat arteriosclerosis, enlarged prostates, infertility and many others creates a worldwide market of $120 billion, including about $50 billion in the United States. That's growing by 8 percent annually. Feeding this demand are technologies that offer new ways to treat disease, allow doctors to treat illness more quickly, effectively and safely. The coronary stint, for example, created a submarket that exploded from $220 million globally to more than $1 billion in 1996. Sales of this device are growing 30 to 40 percent." (pS9774)

Kennedy, Edward M. (Sen.-Mass.). "Food and Drug Administration Modernization and Accountability Act of 1997." Congressional Record. Daily ed. v143 n128 23 Sep 1997. pS9772-9775. section/page-level access: <http://thomas.loc.gov/cgi-bin/query/R?r105:FLD001:S09772:> (ISSN0363-7239). (X1.1A.105/1).

MEDICAL TECHNOLOGY--CALIFORNIA

"California is the Nation's premier medical technology base, public and private. Many of the Nation's leading drug, biotech, and device companies collaborate with the State's nine academic medical centers and conduct some of the world's leading health research. The UC [University of California] system has spawned 30 Nobel laureates. Forty percent of California's biotech companies were started by UC scientists. The Nation's largest concentration of health care technology companies [who employ 165,000 people] is in California....California's 900 health care technology companies are producing leading edge products....California produces 19 percent of all U.S. medical instruments, 20 percent of all diagnostic materials, and 13 percent of all biologics. There are 915 drugs, biologics, and devices under development in...[California]." (pS9843)

Feinstein, Dianne (Sen.-Calif.). "Food and Drug Administration Modernization and Accountability Act of 1997." Congressional Record. Daily ed. v143 n129 24 Sep 1997. pS9811-9847. section/page-level access: <http://thomas.loc.gov/cqi-bin/query/R?r105:FLD001:S09843:> (ISSN0363-7239). (X1.1A.105/1).

MEDICAL TECHNOLOGY--UNITED STATES (v26)

"A new report from the National Center for Health Statistics examines the use of assistive technology devices for vision, hearing, mobility, and orthopedic impairments....An estimated 7.4 million persons in the U.S. household population use assistive technology devices for mobility impairments, the most frequent reason for using an assistive device. Almost 5 million people use canes, the single most utilized assistive device. Another 4.6 million use assistive devices such as back braces and artificial limbs to compensate for orthopedic impairments. 4.5 million use hearing aids, amplified telephones, closed caption television, and other assistive devices for hearing impairments. 500,000 use these devices for vision impairments."

U.S. National Center for Health Statistics. "New Report on Disability Available from NCHS." Press Release 13 Nov 1997. document-level access: <http://www.cdc.gov/nchswww/releases/97facts/97sheets/disable.htm>

MEDICAL TRANSPLANTATION

see TRANSPLANTATION OF ORGANS, TISSUES, ETC.

MEDICAL WASTES--UNITED STATES

A report "released by a coalition called Health Care Without Harm, hospitals, nursing homes and other health care facilities...[in the U.S.] produce a mountain of medical waste totaling 2 million tons annually....According to the report, hospitals and other medical facilities are among the top two or three sources of dioxin, an extremely potent carcinogen that has also been linked to reproductive, immune, and developmental diseases....More than 5.6 million American children under the age of 16 live within two miles of a permitted medical waste incinerator. More than 7 million people of color--15 percent of the minority population--live within two miles of a permitted medical waste incinerator. By comparison, nine percent of white Americans live within two miles of such facilities. One American in seven who is living below the poverty level also lives within two miles of a medical waste incinerator." (p5)

"Southern News: Roundup: First, Do No Harm." Southern Exposure v25 n1-2 Spr-Sum 1997. p5. (ISSN0146-809X).

MEDICALLY UNINSURED PERSONS--HAWAII

"Results from the 1996 Hawai'i Health Survey reveal that an estimated nine percent of Hawai'i residents do not have any health insurance coverage. This represents an increase over previous surveys that showed a rate between four and six percent. The survey also reveals that an estimated 88.9 percent of residents are covered by one of the health insurance plans in the state and 1.2 percent are not sure whether they are covered. The highest uninsured rates are on Kaua'i where 14.7 percent of residents are estimated to be uninsured. The lowest rate is on Lana'i where only 1.2 percent of the population is estimated to have no health insurance. O'ahu, at 8.2 percent, has the lowest rate of the major islands. Younger people--those under 35 years--are more likely to be uninsured than those 35 years and over. 10.3 percent of residents in the younger age group are estimated to be uninsured, while only 7.6 percent of the older age group have no coverage."

Hawaii. Dept. of Health. "Hawai'i Health Survey Reveals Jump in Number of Residents without Health Insurance." Press Release 1997. document-level access: <http://www.hawaii.gov/health/press/pruninsu.htm>

MEDICALLY UNINSURED PERSONS--UNITED STATES (v26)

In the U.S., "the number of uninsured children under 18 grew to 10.6 million (14.8 percent) in 1996; both the number and percentage were statistically higher than the 1995 figures of 9.8 million and 13.8 percent, respectively. Overall, an estimated 41.7 million, or 15.6 percent, of Americans had no health insurance during all of 1996. This number was up 1.1 million from the previous year, but the percentage was not statistically different."

U.S. Dept. of Commerce. Economic & Statistics Administration. "Income Improves, Poverty Levels Stabilize,

Health Insurance Coverage Slips, Census Bureau Reports." Census Bureau Press Release 29 Sep 1997. document-level access: <http://www.census.gov/Press-Release/cb97-162.html>

By 1992, when U.S. President Bill Clinton "was elected, the number of...uninsured working poor had increased to 9.6 million, or 48 percent of the working poor....[In 1995,] the total of working poor living below the poverty line who had no health insurance was 9.4 million, still representing 48 percent of the working poor." (p3)

"Millions of Poor Workers Can't Afford to Get Sick." The People v107 n6 Sep 1997. p3. (ISSN0199-350X).

MEDICARE (v26)

"Medicare is the $176-billion [U.S.] federal program that provides health insurance for citizens 65 and older. It insures 36 million people, 1.5 million of them in Michigan. Medicare is paid for through a 2.9-percent payroll tax split by workers and companies." (p2 secA)

Mishra, Raja. "Hospitals Sweat as Medicare Cuts Loom." Detroit Free Press 12 Aug 1997. p1-2 secA.

In the U.S., "Medicare, which covers 33 million seniors and 5 million disabled, now costs more than $200 billion annually and has been growing at an annual rate of 7.2 percent a year. In terms of federal spending, Medicare's girth ranks behind only Social Security, national defense and interest on the national debt." (p13 secA)

Ryan, Richard A. "Medicare Reform to Cost Seniors." Detroit News 10 Jul 1997. p1,13 secA.

In the U.S., "as of July, 1997, 5.5 million Medicare beneficiaries were enrolled in a total of 391 managed care plans, accounting for 14 percent of the total Medicare population. That represents a 132 percent increase in managed care enrollment since 1992. Currently, about 80,000 Medicare beneficiaries are voluntarily enrolling in risk-bearing HMOs [health maintenance organizations] each month....Currently, 88 percent of Medicare beneficiaries in managed care are in risk plans. As of July 1, 1997, risk plans made up 287 of the 391 managed care plans participating in Medicare."

U.S. Dept. of Health and Human Services. "Managed Care in Medicare and Medicaid." Fact Sheet 15 Jul 1997. document-level access: <http://www.hhs.gov/news/press/1997pres/970715b.html>

In the U.S., "as of October 1997, more than 5.73 million Medicare beneficiaries were enrolled in a total of 415 managed care plans, accounting for 15 percent of the total Medicare population. That represents a 147 percent increase in managed care enrollment since 1992. Currently, about 80,000 Medicare beneficiaries are voluntarily enrolling in risk-bearing HMOs each month."

U.S. Dept. of Health and Human Services. "Managed Care in Medicare and Medicaid." Fact Sheet 20 Nov 1997. document-level access: <http://www.hhs.gov/news/press/1997pres/971120b.html>

MEDICARE--AGED

A recent study at Duke University "shows that the most important factor driving Medicare costs [in the U.S.] is not how many seniors are in the program, but how sick they are....In 1995, the average disabled senior citizen cost the program seven times as much as a nondisabled beneficiary. Saving just one senior citizen from disability saves Medicare an incredible $18,000 a year in costs on the average. Over the last 12 years, the rate of disability dropped by an average of 1.3 percent per year." (pS5961)

Kennedy, Edward M. (Sen.-Mass.). "Our Goal Is to Save Medicare, Not Destroy It." Congressional Record. Daily ed. v143 n86 19 Jun 1997. pS5960-5962. section/page-level access: <http://thomas.loc.gov/cgi-bin/query/R?r105:FLD001:S05960:> (ISSN0363-7239). (X1.1A.105/1).

MEDICARE--APPROPRIATIONS AND EXPENDITURES (v26)

The U.S. "General Accounting Office estimates that up to 10 percent of Medicare payments could be lost to fraud, waste, and abuse. That adds up to about $18 billion a year....[An] analysis of Medicare payments for a sample of medical supplies and equipment from saline solution to hospital beds reveals that Medicare is paying up to six times more for these items than other Government or private-sector entities. For just 18 items reviewed, Medicare could save over 50 percent, or up to $236 million this year....If Medicare were just to pay wholesale rates offered to others around the country, it could save $218 million this year....We found that if Medicare just went down to the local drugstore and paid retail taxes, it could save $371 million over the next 7 years....We found that Medicare pays up to $182.80 to rent an air mattress, more than six times the wholesale price of $29.95, three times the price of $53.88. Medicare is paying $99.35 for a simple commode chair that the VA [Veterans Administration] is able to buy for $24.12. Medicare is paying $7.90 for a bottle of sterile saline solution; the VA buys it for $2.38." (pS6076)

Harkin, Tom (Sen.-Iowa). "Balanced Budget Act of 1997." Congressional Record. Daily ed. v143 n88-89 23 Jun 1997. pS6075-6084. section/page-level access: <http://thomas.loc.gov/cgi-bin/query/R?r105:FLD001:S06075:> (ISSN0363-7239). (X1.1A.105/1).

MEDICARE--PUBLIC OPINION

"Most Americans--61%--believe that senior citizens with higher incomes should pay more for Medicare than those with lower incomes. Given a choice, only about a third support the current practice, where all recipients essentially pay the same amount regardless of income. Support for the principle of higher costs for higher incomes is highest among those most directly affected--senior citizens themselves--who favor it by a margin of 69% to 26%, compared with more modest support from the youngest Americans, who favor it by a margin of 56% to 40%."

Moore, David W./Gallup Organization. "Public Supports Higher Medicare Costs for Wealthier Senior Citizens." Press Release 4 Jul 1997. document-level access: <http://www.gallup.com/poll/news/970704.htm>

MEDICARE--UNITED STATES--PUBLIC OPINION (v26)

MEDICARE FRAUD

U.S. medicare "claims paid in 1996 from all 10 regions of the country and for a range of services. It found that 1 out of every 3 claims contained a mispayment; the average error was $670. The errors were not all simple mistakes by health-care providers. Forty-six percent of the bad claims were improperly documented; 36 percent involved services that were not medically necessary; and 8 percent were caused by providers using the wrong billing code." (p3)

Goodrich, Lawrence J. "United States: Medicare Fraud Puts 'Waste Patrols' on Alert." The Christian Science Monitor v89 n163 18 Jul 1997. p3. The Christian Science Monitor search engine: <http://www.csmonitor.com/plweb-cgi/iops1.pl> To retrieve this article, enter the following search: ED=19970718 AND alert. In the "retrieved list," click the title that matches this record. (ISSN0882-7729).

In the U.S., "nearly 40 percent of all the money distributed by Medicare for home health care services does not meet the program's reimbursement requirements. One in four home health agencies receiving funds from Medicare has abused or defrauded the program, or misappropriated Medicare funds. Investigators found several agencies that serve as money laundering fronts for drug dealers. The cost of Medicare's home care program has risen nearly sevenfold--from $2.6 billion in 1989 to $17.7 billion in 1996. On its current course, spending will top $26 billion by the turn of the century." (p19)

Longman, Phillip J./Pasternak, Douglas. "U.S. News: Who Is the Victim?" U.S. News & World Report v123 n6 11 Aug 1997. p18-20. article-level access: <http://www.usnews.com/usnews/issue/970811/11MEDI.HTM> (ISSN0041-5537).

MEDICATION ERRORS--UNITED STATES (v26)

MEDICINE (v26)

see also ALTERNATIVE MEDICINE; DISEASES; GYNECOLOGY; HEALTH

MEDICINE--RESEARCH (v26)

MEDICINE--SPECIALTIES AND SPECIALISTS --EMPLOYMENT--UNITED STATES (v26)

MEDICINE--STUDY AND TEACHING--UNITED STATES (v26)

MEDICINE--UNITED STATES (v26)

In the U.S., "there is a 30% to 50% chance that people will not take prescription drugs as directed by their physicians, according to the National Council on Patient Information and Education in Washington. At least 7% of patients never fill their prescriptions in the first place....Thirty-two percent fail to purchase refills....In 1993 a task force made up of government and industry representatives estimated that...[medication noncompliance] costs the U.S. $100 billion annually in reduced productivity, absence from work, hospital admissions and added treatment costs. According to Jon C. Schommer, Ph.D., an assistant professor at Ohio State University College of Pharmacy in Columbus, noncompliance results in as many as 2.5 million medical emergencies and 125,000 deaths every year." (p67)

Hochman, Gloria. "Family Health: Prescription for Disaster." American Health v16 n6 Jul-Aug 1997. p66-67,106,108. (ISSN0730-7004).

"In a joint survey by PREVENTION magazine and the American Pharmaceutical Association, 33 percent of U.S. adults say they have exceeded the recommended dosage of an over-the-counter drug because they felt their symptoms demanded it. This occurs even though a similar share (35 percent) say it is very or somewhat likely that their self-treatment may hide serious symptoms that require a doctor's attention....The majority of Americans (58 percent) say they used over-the-counter medications in at least four of eight major categories in the last year. Pain-relief medication is by far the most widely used, with 44 percent of consumers reporting ten or more uses in a year. The next most common are antacids or heartburn medication (24 percent); allergy, asthma, or sinus congestion (22 percent); cold or cough (16 percent); fever (12 percent); diarrhea (8 percent); menstrual cramps (14 percent of women); and yeast infection (3 percent of women)." (p6)

"The Over-Medicated American." Forecast v17 n12 Dec 1997. p6. article-level access: <http://www.demographics.com/publications/fc/97_fc/9712_fc/f971206.htm> (ISSN0732-1597).

In the U.S., "there are currently about 100,000 OTC [over-the-counter] drug products available nationwide. Consumers self-treat four times as many health conditions as they seek treatment for with their doctors. And 60 to 95 percent of all illnesses are initially treated at home, often including the use of OTC drugs....Older people...use almost 30 percent of the OTC drugs sold....According to the American Pharmaceutical Association's HANDBOOK OF NONPRESCRIPTION DRUGS, OTC drug purchases currently account for less than 2 percent of the U.S. health care dollar." (p6)

"Useful OTC Drug Labels." People's Medical Society Newsletter v16 n4 Aug 1997. p6. (ISSN0736-4873).

In studies comparing the health-economic impact of different antimanic agents in the U.S., "Frye and colleagues...reported that hospital stay was 40 percent shorter for patients treated with valproate monotherapy than for those treated with lithium monotherapy and carbamazepine monotherapy. Keck and associates...reported that the initial hospital stay was 14.3 days for patients on valproate monotherapy, 18.4 days for those on lithium monotherapy, and 24.5 days for those on lithium plus valproate therapy." (p1037-1038)

Sajatovic, Martha/Gerhart, Connie/Semple, William. "Association between Mood-Stabilizing Medication and Mental Health Resource Use in the Management of Acute Mania." Psychiatric Services v48 n8 Aug 1997. p1037-1041. (ISSN1075-2730).

In the U.S., "medication therapy was reported at 6 of every 10 ambulatory visits in 1995, and at 7 of every 10 emergency department visits. There were 1.2 billion drugs mentioned at ambulatory care visits, which includes drugs either prescribed or provided at the visit (an average of 1.4 drugs mentioned per visit). Drugs for pain relief, antimicrobials and cardiovascular-renal drugs were the leading therapeutic classes of the medications prescribed (each accounting for about 14 percent of the drug mentions)."

U.S. National Center for Health Statistics. "Monitoring Health Care in America: Spotlight on: Ambulatory Care in the U.S." Quarterly Fact Sheet Jun 1997. document-level access: <http://www.cdc.gov/nchswww/releases/97facts/97sheets/mhc0697.htm>

"About 25% of the US drugs market comprises compounds whose active ingredients are based on or extracted from plants (Brown, 1985; Joffe and Thomas, 1989; Reid, 1994). The sales of these drugs amounted to $15.5 billion in 1990." (p163)

Zamora, Carlos/Thomas, Sandra M. "User/Supplier Relationship: Ownership of Plant Genetic Resources: Screening and Industrial Utilisation." Science and Public Policy v24 n3 Jun 1997. p161-172. (ISSN0302-3427).

MEDICINE--UNITED STATES--RELIGIOUS ASPECTS --PUBLIC OPINION (v26)

MEDICINE, ALTERNATIVE

see ALTERNATIVE MEDICINE

MEDITATION, TRANSCENDAL

see TRANSCENDAL MEDITATION

MEKONG RIVER

"The Mekong River is the twelfth longest river in the world, running 2,600 miles in a generally southward direction from the high plateau of Tibet to its mouths at the South China Sea in southern Vietnam. Measured by volume of flow, it is the tenth greatest world river. The Mekong and its tributaries form a drainage basin of more than 300,000 square miles, an area larger than France or Texas. Three-quarters of that extent is in the lower basin below Myanmar. More than 50 million people live along the main stream and 240 million people populate the basin....The Mekong is the central artery of continental Southeast Asia, although for nearly half its length it runs through Chinese territory. Its source in Tibet, located in 1994, is more than 16,000 feet above sea level. The upper Mekong drops precipitously through the gorges and mountain valleys of Tibet and China's Yunnan Province. Yunnan is the source of 30 percent of the river's flow." (p168)

Weatherbee, Donald E. "Cooperation and Conflict in the Mekong River Basin." Studies in Conflict & Terrorism v20 n2 Apr-Jun 1997. p167-184. (ISSN1057-610X).

MEKONG RIVER DELTA (VIETNAM AND CAMBODIA) --SOCIAL CONDITIONS (v26)

MELILLA--POPULATION

Melilla's "population of 65,000 includes 10,000 soldiers...." (p9) "Every month the border police turn away some 15,000 people and expel an average of 900." (p10)

Cembalest, Robin. "Spain's African Enclave: Letter from

Melilla." New Leader v80 n13 11 Aug 1997. p9-10. (ISSN0028-6044).

MELON INDUSTRY--CHINA

In China, "watermelons accounted for 77 percent, and muskmelon (tiangua) accounted for 15 percent of total melon area....Urban per capita consumption of melons increased from 20 kilograms in 1985 to 23 kilos in 1994....Rural residents consumed an average of 4 kilograms [of watermelons] during 1994...." (p49)

Crook, Frederick W./U.S. Dept. of Agriculture. Economic Research Service. "Introduction to China's Horticultural Economy." China: International Agriculture and Trade Reports Situation and Outlook Series Jun 1997. p47-51.

MELON INDUSTRY--UNITED STATES (v26)

MEMBERSHIP, CHURCH

see CHURCH MEMBERSHIP

MEN

see also AFRO-AMERICAN MEN; BALDNESS--UNITED STATES--MEN; DEPRESSION, MENTAL--UNITED STATES--MEN; FATHERS; INCOME DISTRIBUTION--UNITED STATES--MEN; LIFE EXPECTANCY--UNITED STATES--MEN; UNEMPLOYMENT--UNITED STATES--MEN; WAGES--UNITED STATES--MEN

MEN--EMPLOYMENT--AUSTRALIA

According to the publication, "Labour Force Experience, Australia, February 1997," by the Australian Bureau of Statistics, "85 per cent of males aged between 15 and 69 were either working or looking for work during the 12 months to February 1997....Males were more likely to work the full 52 weeks, with 71 per cent of males working for the whole year compared to 61 per cent of females....About 96 per cent of males with children under 15 participated in the labour force at some time during the year, compared with 81 per cent for males without children under 15."

Australian Bureau of Statistics. "Female Labour Force Participation Continues to Rise." Media Release 1 Aug 1997. document-level access: <http://www.abs.gov.au/websitedbs/d3110125.nsf/4a255eef008309e44a255eef00061e57/654318539623b1e54a2564e5007fa39d?OpenDocument>

MEN--EMPLOYMENT--SOUTHERN STATES

In U.S. Southern States, "in 1994, close to 30 percent of white men worked in the two highest-paying categories of white-collar jobs--officials/managers and professionals. Meanwhile, only 13 percent of employed white men worked in more poorly compensated laborer and service positions. By contrast, in 1994 over 40 percent of all black men worked in laborer and service positions, and only 8 percent of all black men worked as officials/managers, or professionals." (p11)

Eckman, Anne/Green, Jordan. "Dislocation & Workforce Equity: The South at Work in the 1990s: But Segregation Continues...." Southern Exposure: Institute for Southern Studies Report 1997. p11-12.

MEN--HEALTH AND HYGIENE--RUSSIA

"The odds of a Russian male being murdered are 20 times greater than those faced by a Western European. His chances of dying by accidental poisoning are 20 times higher than an American's. Percentage of draftees found unfit for military service because of poor health: 33. Percentage rejected in 1985 for similar reasons: five." (p14)

"Opening Notes: Death at an Earlier Age." Maclean's v110 n22 2 Jun 1997. p14. (ISSN0024-9262).

MENINGITIS--AFRICA (v26)

"Epidemic meningitis is a recurrent problem in the 'meningitis belt' of Africa; this stretches from Senegal to Ethiopia and includes all or part of at least 15 countries, with an estimated total population of approximately 300 million. The meningitis season runs approximately from November to April. While the 1995-96 season was particularly severe, epidemics in the 1996-97 season were also significant, with 59,461 cases of meningitis reported as of 1 June, of which 6,055 were fatal." (p2)

World Health Organization. "Meningitis Control in Africa in 1997: A Successful International Effort." WHO Press n49 24 Jun 1997. p1-2. document-level access: <http://www.who.ch/press/1997/pr97-49.html>

MENINGITIS, CEREBROSPINAL--AFRICA (v26)

MENOPAUSE--CANADA (v26)

MENTAL DEPRESSION

see DEPRESSION, MENTAL

MENTAL HEALTH

see CHILD MENTAL HEALTH; DEPRESSION, MENTAL; GIRLS--MENTAL HEALTH; VETERANS--MENTAL HEALTH

MENTAL HEALTH PERSONNEL--INDIANA--ILLINOIS --OREGON

According to a report based on samples of case managers for persons with severe mental illness in the state of Oregon and representative samples in Indiana and Illinois, "nearly half (49.5%) of CMs were bachelor's prepared and another 39.5% had a master's degree....Sixty percent of Oregon CMs were master's prepared, in contrast with 12.1% and 15.3% of Indiana and Illinois CMs, respectively." (p417) "Responses to CM reports of actual activities performed were aggregated across all CMs....The aggregate suggests that CMs allocate 36% time to administrative tasks such as meetings and paperwork, 23% to case coordination efforts such as housing acquisition and crisis management, 20% to skills training, 13% to therapy, 6% providing education or consultation, and 1% to alcohol and drug interventions." (p421)

Hromco, Joseph G./Lyons, John S./Nikkel, Robert E. "Styles of Case Management: The Philosophy and Practice of Case Managers." Community Mental Health Journal v33 n5 Oct 1997. p415-428. (ISSN0010-3853).

MENTAL HEALTH PERSONNEL--UNITED STATES --SOCIAL WORKERS

Studies conducted in the U.S. "between 1988 and 1995 show that mental health is the primary practice area of the largest proportion of members of the National Association of Social Workers (NASW), and that the proportion in primary mental health practice increased from 34.4 percent in 1988 to 38.8 percent in 1995....In 1995 NASW members totaled 153,814, of whom 113,352 were employed and met the requirements of regular membership....The vast majority of social workers in mental health (93.5 percent) have a master's degree. Most (88.6 percent) are licensed by the state in which they practice. Like the overall NASW membership, more than 77 percent are female, a proportion that has risen consistently since 1988.

Approximately 22 percent of social workers in mental health are employed part time. The largest proportion of social workers in mental health, 39 percent, work in not-for-profit agencies. Thirty-two percent work in government agencies (including federal, local, and state governments and the military), and 29 percent work in for-profit agencies." (p1509)

Gibelman, Margaret/Schervish, Philip. "Datapoints: Areas of Practice of Social Workers in Mental Health." Psychiatric Services v48 n12 Dec 1997. p1509. (ISSN1075-2730).

MENTAL HEALTH SERVICES--UNITED STATES

"Approximately 168.5 million Americans, or 75 percent of those with health insurance, are enrolled in some type of managed behavioral health program, according to a survey conducted last January by OPEN MINDS newsletter....Of that number, 149 million are enrolled in specialty managed behavioral health programs, and 19.5 million receive behavioral health benefits through internally managed programs in health maintenance organizations (HMOs). The 1997 enrollment reflects a 19 percent increase from

1996, when the figure was 141.6 million. Value Behavioral Health had the highest enrollment among behavioral health companies, 24.4 million, representing almost 11 percent of the insured population and 14.5 percent of the total managed behavioral health market share....The survey indicates that of the 168.5 million Americans in managed behavioral health programs, 39.2 million are in utilization review programs, 38.9 million are in risk-based network programs, 32 million are in non-risk-based network programs, 28.3 million are in employee assistance programs, 19.5 million are in programs managed internally by HMOs, and 10.7 million are in integrated employee assistance-managed behavioral programs....Value Behavioral Health had the largest enrollment in utilization review programs (6.8 million) and non-risk-based network programs (9.7 million)." (p1094)

"News & Notes: 75 Percent of Insured Americans Now Enrolled in Managed Behavioral Health Care Programs." Psychiatric Services v48 n8 Aug 1997. p1094-1095. (ISSN1075-2730).

MENTAL ILLNESS

see also DEPRESSION, MENTAL

"Dementia, particularly Alzheimers disease, are likely to become one of the leading causes of disability in the elderly worldwide. Already an estimated 29 million people suffer from dementia, and the risk of developing the condition rises steeply with age in people over 60 years. By the year 2025, Africa, Asia and Latin America between them could have more than 80 million sufferers. At least 400 million people suffer from other mental disorders, ranging from mood and personality disorders to neurological conditions such as epilepsy, which alone is estimated to affect 40 million people." (p7)

World Health Organization. "World Health Report 1997." Press Release 5 May 1997. p1-7. document-level access: <http://www.who.ch/whr/1997/presse.htm>

MENTAL ILLNESS--CANADA (v26)

MENTAL ILLNESS--TREATMENT--UNITED STATES (v26)

In the U.S., "for mental health and substance abuse services, managed care is often provided by specialty firms, so-called managed behavioral health care organizations. About 111 million people have at least some of their care managed by a managed behavioral health care firm. Of these, 53 million people, in both the public and the private sectors, are enrolled in some type of carve-out program....Approximately 21.8 million people are enrolled in what has become known at risk-based carve-out contracts....Umland reported that 35 percent of employers with 5,000 or more employees had contracts with a managed behavioral health care vendor, whereas only 3 percent of firms with fewer than 500 employees did so. Fourteen state employee health plans have adopted managed behavioral health carve-out arrangements....By the end of 1995, a total of 12 states had adopted some form of managed behavioral health carve-out program for their Medicaid program." (p1147)

Frank, Richard G./McGuire, Thomas G. "Savings from a Medicaid Carve-Out for Mental Health and Substance Abuse Services in Massachusetts." Psychiatric Services v48 n9 Sep 1997. p1147-1152. (ISSN1075-2730).

MENTAL ILLNESS--TREATMENT--UNITED STATES --COSTS (v26)

MENTAL ILLNESS--UNITED STATES (v26)

"The prevalence of serious mental illness among Americans age 18 and over during a 12-month period is estimated to be 5.4 percent, or 10 million people, according to the proposed methodology developed by the federal Center for Mental Health Services (CMHS). Of that group, 2.6 percent, or 4.8 million persons, are estimated to have severe and persistent mental illness. When adults with any DSM-III-R [Diagnostic and Statistical Manual of Mental Disorders] diagnosis within a 12-month period are included, the national prevalence rate for mental disorders is 23.9 percent, or 44.2 million people." (p1216)

"News & Notes: New Methodology for Estimating Prevalence of Mental Illness Finds 10 Million Adults Affected." Psychiatric Services v48 n9 Sep 1997. p1216. (ISSN1075-2730).

MENTAL ILLNESS--UNITED STATES--COSTS

In the U.S., "on average, it costs about $269 a day to keep someone in a state [mental] hospital. It costs about $74 a day to keep a mentally ill person in group or adult foster care homes." (p8 secA)

"A Step Outside." Detroit Free Press 18 Jul 1997. p1,8-9 secA.

MENTAL ILLNESS--UNITED STATES--MORTALITY (v26)

MENTAL ILLNESS--UNITED STATES--MOTHERS

In a study funded by the National Institute of Mental Health, University of Michigan "researchers Carol Mowbray and Daphna Oyserman found that only 17 percent of mothers [in the U.S.] with a mental illness said they could receive support and advice on parenting from their mental health care providers....According to Mowbray, most of the 379 mothers in the study--all of whom cared for at least one child under age 17--were satisfied with the services offered by their mental health care providers." (p1) "Such moms have more children (the median is three) than the population average, are often single parents (about 70 percent do not live with a husband, boyfriend, or partner) and have severe economic problems (monthly median family income is $923). In fact, 78 percent of the mothers reported some difficulty in paying monthly bills, 62 percent have faced a financial crisis in the last year, and 57 percent are not happy with their overall financial status....Women in the sample have custody of nearly 86 percent of the total number of their minor children....Roughly 70 percent of the moms were minorities." (p2)

University of Michigan. News and Information Services. "Mothers with Mental Illnesses Need Better Parenting Support from Mental Health Services, Says U-M Study." University of Michigan News Release 24 Jun 1997. p1-2.

MENTAL ILLNESS--UNITED STATES--SUBSTANCE USE--COSTS (v26)

MENTAL ILLNESS--UNITED STATES--YOUTH

"Approximately 14 to 20 percent (8 to 13 million) of all American children experience mental and emotional disturbances. Included in this group are 3.5 million youth--5 percent of the American child and adolescent population--who have serious emotional disturbances."

U.S. Dept. of Health and Human Services. "HHS Invests in America's Children." Fact Sheet 23 Jul 1997. document-level access: <http://www.hhs.gov/news/press/1997pres/970917.html>

MENTAL TESTS

see EDUCATIONAL TESTS AND MEASUREMENTS

MENTALLY ILL--EMPLOYMENT--LAW AND LEGISLATION --UNITED STATES

The Equal Employment Opportunity Commission released guidelines in March 1997 to clarify and strengthen the workplace rights of the mentally ill in the U.S. "Since the guidelines were released, judges have sided with employers in the vast majority of cases where workers claimed discrimination based on mental disability. Employers prevailed in 32 of 37 mental disability decisions published from April through August, research by the ABA JOURNAL has found. Employers won 26 of 30 motions for dismissal at the trial level, and six of seven appellate decisions." (p24)

Higgins, Michael. "News: No Sudden Impact." ABA Journal v83

Nov 1997. p24,26. (ISSN0747-0088).

MENTALLY ILL--UNITED STATES (v26)

In the U.S., "in 1991, approximately 8.6% of the total jail population had a diagnosable serious mental illness (Torrey et al., 1992). Five percent of that number were estimated to be actively psychotic....Torrey and colleagues' (1992) nationwide survey of 1,391 jails, which hold 62% of the nation's inmates, found that the average daily population of persons with mental illness within jails nationwide was 30,700. Smaller jails tended to have smaller percentages of detainees with mental illness, with a range of 3.3% for jails holding fewer than 50 persons to 8.7% in those housing more than 1,000 persons. At least 39% of jails held persons with mental illness without formal charges for short periods; smaller jails were more likely to do so than were large facilities (5% compared with 36.7%, respectively)....[A survey by] Solomon and Draine (1995) found that 42% to 52% of all persons with mental illness are arrested at least once. In their study, 23% of charges involved family members, most often with restraining orders....In Torrey and colleagues' (1992) survey, the five most commonly reported crimes leading to arrest were assault and battery, theft of property, disorderly conduct, alcohol- or drug-related charges, and trespassing." (421-422)

Walsh, Joseph/Bricout, John. "Article: Services for Persons with Mental Illness in Jail: Implications for Family Involvement." Families in Society v78 n4 Jul-Aug 1997. p420-428. (ISSN1044-3894).

MENTALLY ILL--UNITED STATES--FAMILY RELATIONSHIPS (v26)

MENTALLY ILL--UNITED STATES--SEXUAL BEHAVIOR (v26)

MERCHANT MARINE--GREAT BRITAIN (v26)

MERCHANT MARINE--GREAT BRITAIN--MORTALITY (v26)

MERCY KILLING

see EUTHANASIA

MESOTHELIOMA--GREAT BRITAIN (v26)

METAL TRADE

see LEAD

METHAMPHETAMINE--MISSOURI--INDEPENDENCE

In 1996, "authorities busted 75 methamphetamine labs...[in Independence, Missouri]--the largest number per capita in the nation. This year, local law-enforcement officials have already added 94 more....Almost half of all meth labs seized last year were in the Midwest, and seizures in Missouri have increased by 535 percent in the past two years alone." (p1,18)

Stewart, Phil/Sitaramiah, Gita. "America's Heartland Grapples with Rise of Dangerous Drug." The Christian Science Monitor v89 n244 13 Nov 1997. p1,18. The Christian Science Monitor search engine: <http://www.csmonitor.com/plweb-cgi/iops1.pl> To retrieve this article, enter the following search: ED=19971113 AND drug. In the "retrieved list," click the title that matches this record. (ISSN0882-7729).

METHAMPHETAMINE--UNITED STATES (v26)

"According to the '1995 National Household Survey on Drug Abuse,' 4.7 million persons have tried methamphetamine in their lifetime or 2.2 percent of the [U.S.] population in 1995. In 1994, the estimate had been 3.8 million. In the West, the statistics are more alarming. The latest Drug Abuse Warning Network figures indicate that methamphetamine related episodes tripled in Phoenix [Ariz.] between 1992 and 1994, and the number of deaths related to this drug increased five fold. Los Angeles has had a 71 percent increase in emergency room visits related to methamphetamine abuse, and a 222 percent increase in meth-related deaths." (p1388)

U.S. Dept. of Justice. "Departments of Commerce, Justice, And State, The Judiciary...Approp. for 1998 (Part 2)." Hearing. U.S. House. Committee on Appropriations. Washington, D.C. : GPO, 1997. (ISBN0160549094). (Y4.Ap6/1:C73/2/997/pt.2).

METHANE

see also BROMOMETHANE

METHANE--SIBERIA

"Lakes in Siberia may have a large effect on seasonal changes in atmospheric methane in the Northern Hemisphere, according to a report in the 8 Aug [1997] issue of SCIENCE....[S. A. Zimov, of the Russian Academy of Sciences, and researchers] estimate that the lakes release about 2 million metric tons of methane to the atmosphere each year, of which 75% is emitted during the winter....The researchers point out that these winter methane emissions represent some 25% of the high-latitude accumulation of methane in the atmosphere during the winter." (p6)

"Science Update: Siberian Lakes Major Methane Source." Global Environmental Change Report v9 n15 8 Aug 1997. p6. (ISSN1049-9083).

METHANE--UNITED STATES (v26)

METHYL BROMIDE

see BROMOMETHANE

METHYLPHENIDATE HYDROCHLORIDE--UNITED STATES (v26)

"Attention deficit disorder afflicts about 3.5 million children in the United States, or as high as 5 percent of children up to the age of 18. More than a million children take Ritalin [or methylphenidate hydrochloride] regularly, and sales of the drug topped $350 million in 1995....Among teens, Ritalin-related visits to the emergency room have jumped more than 700 percent, according to the Drug Enforcement Agency (DEA)....The DEA reports that Ritalin is among the top 10 drugs in pharmaceutical theft and has found growing abuse and illegal trafficking." (p11 secA)

Atkins, Larry. "Comment: Ritalin Abuse Rises among Teens, Adults." Detroit News 15 Aug 1997. p11 secA.

METHYLPHENIDATE HYDROCHLORIDE--UNITED STATES --CHILDREN (v26)

METHYLPHENIDATE HYDROCHLORIDE--UNITED STATES --YOUTH (v26)

MEXICAN AMERICANS

"Latinos of Mexican descent make up 64 percent of the Hispanic population. In 1996, more than 18 million Hispanics of Mexican descent lived in the United States....In 1996, more than 70 percent of U.S. Hispanics of Mexican descent were immigrants or the children of immigrants. Less than 30 percent were third generation or higher. Despite the continuous, high migration flow from Mexico, the post-1980 immigrants make up about one-fifth of the large Mexican-American population." (p8-9)

del Pinal, Jorge/Singer, Audrey. "Generations of Diversity: Latinos in the United States." Population Bulletin v52 n3 Oct 1997. p2-47. (ISSN0032-468X).

MEXICAN AMERICANS--EMPLOYMENT

"More than half of Mexican American males work in either precision production, craft and repair jobs (20%) or as operators, fabricators and laborers (29%). Only 9% hold managerial or professional positions....More Mexican American females work in technical, sales or administrative support jobs (39%) than work in service occupations (25%). Like the males, many (16%) of females also work as operators, fabricators or laborers. More females (14%) than males work in managerial or professional positions." (p26)

"Targeting Minority Publics: Employment of Hispanic Americans by Country of Origin." Public Relations Quarterly v42 n2 Sum 1997. p26. (ISSN0033-3700).

MEXICANS--UNITED STATES (v26)

MEXICO--COMMERCE--UNITED STATES (v26)

"Before NAFTA, the United States had a trade surplus of nearly

$2 billion with Mexico. After NAFTA, the surplus has deteriorated to the point where we have a $16 billion trade deficit." (pH8030) "Revolving door exports have surged 230 percent since NAFTA, rising from 18 billion in 1993 to 42 billion last year. These exports accounted for 40 percent of our total exports to Mexico in 1993, but that share grew up to 62 percent last year." (pH8031)

Bonior, David E. (Rep.-Mich.). "Fast-Track Trade Negotiations." Congressional Record. Daily ed. v143 n131 26 Sep 1997. pH8029-8036. section/page-level access: <http://thomas.loc.gov/cgi-bin/query/R?r105:FLD001:H08029:> (ISSN0363-7239). (X1.1A.105/1).

"Since the passage of NAFTA, Mexican imports to the United States are up 82 percent and nearly 70 percent of these imports come across the United States border by trucks....12,000 trucks per day...[cross] from Mexico into the United States, carrying fruits and vegetables and meat. So that is a total of 3.3 million trucks coming into this country carrying poultry and vegetables and meat into the United States, and only 1 percent...are actually being inspected....Besides the increased flow of traffic of foods, there is evidence that Mexican fruit have high levels of illegal pesticides. On studies performed by the environmental working group using data before and after NAFTA, 42 different fruits and vegetables, which comprise 96 to 83 percent of all the fruits and vegetables coming into this country, they found that the imported crops from Mexico have very high rates of illegal pesticides, including strawberries. This is a violation rate of...18.4 percent. Lettuce from Mexico is at 15.6 percent violation, and carrots are at 12.3 percent." (pH7114)

Stupak, Bart (Rep.-Mich.). "Fast Track Trade Authority." Congressional Record. Daily ed. v143 n118 9 Sep 1997. pH7112-7116. section/page-level access: <http://thomas.loc.gov/cgi-bin/query/R?r105:FLD001:H07113:> (ISSN0363-7239). (X1.1A.105/1).

The U.S. "had about a $2 billion surplus with Mexico prior to NAFTA, which is only 3 1/2 years ago. We have a $16 billion deficit today....That means they are sending us here a lot more than we are sending them there. We are sending them a few more things, but listen to what is happening to those things that we send them....[Professor Harley Shaiken, of the University of California at Berkeley,] analyzing trade data, shows that the vast majority of export growth has been in what he calls the revolving door exports. And what do we mean by revolving door? Those are goods that are shipped to Mexico as components, therefore counted as exports, but then they are assembled right on that maquiladora border. They get over the line, they are assembled and they come right back here, shipped right back to the United States. The revolving door exports have surged 230 percent since NAFTA, rising from $18 billion in 1993 to $42 billion last year. These exports accounted for 40 percent of our total exports to Mexico in 1993, but that share grew [to] 62 percent last year. So 62 percent of our exports to Mexico are shipped right back here." (pH4905)

Bonior, David E. (Rep.-Mich.). "On Trade." Congressional Record. Daily ed. v143 n95 8 Jul 1997. pH4903-4907. section/page-level access: <http://thomas.loc.gov/cgi-bin/query/R?r105:FLD001:H04904:> (ISSN0363-7239). (X1.1A.105/1).

MEXICO--ECONOMIC CONDITIONS (v26)

"Twenty-eight thousand small businesses have failed in Mexico since NAFTA. The number of unemployed in Mexico doubled in 2 years. Our own embassy in Mexico estimated in late 1995 that 35 percent of Mexicans were either unemployed or underemployed. Real wages in Mexico are 27 percent lower than in 1994 and 37 percent lower than they were in 1980....And 19 percent of workers made less than the minimum wage, which is only $3.30 a day....And 66 percent of workers lack any benefits at all, any pension or health benefits....Since NAFTA, eight million people in Mexico have fallen from middle class status into poverty." (pH4904)

Bonior, David E. (Rep.-Mich.). "On Trade." Congressional Record. Daily ed. v143 n95 8 Jul 1997. pH4903-4907. section/page-level access: <http://thomas.loc.gov/cgi-bin/query/R?r105:FLD001:H04903:> (ISSN0363-7239). (X1.1A.105/1).

In Mexico, by 1994, the year of the devaluation of the peso, "the purchasing power of the 7-10 percent of Mexican workers who earned the minimum wage (less than $5 a day at that point) had already fallen by about 30 percent in the comparatively prosperous period from 1987 to 1994....From 1994 to the first half of 1997, Mexicans' real wages lost 26 percent of their purchasing power, according to the Mexican Senate's Commission on Distribution and Management of Consumer Goods; the Mexican Association of Studies for the Defense of the Consumer (AMEDEC) reports that consumption of meat, milk, and chicken fell between 26 and 30 percent during the same period. The formal economy lost 751,041 jobs in the first eight months of 1995, almost exclusively from production for the domestic market, according to Banco de Mexico (Banxico), the national bank." (p30)

Wilson, David L. "Do Maquiladoras Matter?" Monthly Review v49 n5 Oct 1997. p28-34. (ISSN0027-0520).

MEXICO--SOCIAL CONDITIONS (v26)

"Mexico is often still seen as a rural country, though 75 percent of the population lives in urban areas and 50 percent of those in rural areas live through the sale of their labor power. Real unemployment is around 20 percent in urban areas and 50 percent in rural areas." (p98)

Roman, Richard/Arregui, Edur Velasco. "Zapatismo and the Workers Movement in Mexico at the End of the Century." Monthly Review v49 n3 Jul-Aug 1997. p98-116. (ISSN0027-0520).

MEXICO CITY (MEXICO)--ECONOMIC CONDITIONS

"Mexico City generates more than 25 percent of Mexico's wealth. But it was severely hit by the 1994 peso devaluation and ensuing recession. More than 22,000 small businesses closed. Today more than 3.5 million Chilangos live on less than $7 a day....10 percent of the city's families hold 70 percent of its wealth, with 3 percent living in extreme wealth. (Mexico ranks fourth worldwide in the number of billionaires)." (p6)

LaFranchi, Howard. "International: Mexico City: A Pinata Full of Big Troubles--And Many Delights." The Christian Science Monitor v89 n50 30 Jun 1997. p6. The Christian Science Monitor search engine: <http://www.csmonitor.com/plweb-cgi/iops1.pl> To retrieve this article, enter the following search: ED=19970630 AND delights. In the "retrieved list," click the title that matches this record. (ISSN0882-7729).

MEXICO CITY (MEXICO)--POPULATION

"With its 9 million people in the city proper and 18 million in the metropolitan area, Mexico City is bigger than many developing countries....80 percent of the current population is under 44 years of age....Officials estimate the city lacks 800,000 housing units to satisfy the current population...." (p6)

LaFranchi, Howard. "International: Mexico City: A Pinata Full of Big Troubles--And Many Delights." The Christian Science Monitor v89 n50 30 Jun 1997. p6. The Christian Science Monitor search engine: <http://www.csmonitor.com/plweb-cgi/iops1.pl> To retrieve this article, enter the following search: ED=19970630 AND delights. In the "retrieved list," click the title that matches this record. (ISSN0882-7729).

MEXICO CITY (MEXICO)--SOCIAL CONDITIONS

In Mexico City, "more than 114,000 teachers teach 2.5 million schoolchildren. A graduate takes an average of one year to 18 months to find a job. At the same time, the capital boasts the country's lowest illiteracy rate, at 3 percent of the population....With 120 bookstores, Mexico City accounts for almost half of all the bookstores in Mexico. It also has 161 museums, four pre-Colombian archaeological sites, and two sites on UNESCO's [UN's Educational, Scientific and Cultural Organization's] list of mankind's universal heritage....Chilangos consume more than 100 million tortillas every day." (p6)

LaFranchi, Howard. "International: Mexico City: A Pinata Full of Big Troubles--And Many Delights." The Christian Science Monitor v89 n50 30 Jun 1997. p6. The Christian Science Monitor search engine: <http://www.csmonitor.com/plweb-cgi/iops1.pl> To retrieve this article, enter the following search: ED=19970630 AND delights. In the "retrieved list," click the title that matches this record. (ISSN0882-7729).

In Mexico City, Mexico, "pollution is so bad that the city's air rates 'satisfactory' just 35 days a year. Police are so inefficient that it takes 60 officers to make the same number of arrests that New York City does with one. Corruption is so endemic that the city's 250,000 sidewalk vendors pay inspectors an estimated $5 million in bribes a week." (p44)

Robinson, Linda/Conger, Lucy. "World Report: The Monster of Mexico." U.S. News & World Report v123 n3 21 Jul 1997. p44-45. article-level access: <http://www.usnews.com/usnews/issue/970721/21MEXI.HTM> (ISSN0041-5537).

MICHIGAN--ARMED FORCES--RECRUITING, ENLISTMENT, ETC.

"Army recruitment is down about 25 percent in Michigan. The Air Force is down more than 10 percent, while the Navy was down 50 percent over its July [1997] goal of 125 recruits for Michigan and has only met its goals two of the first seven months. Marine recruitment in Michigan also has declined more than 10 percent....The decline follows a nationwide trend. The Army, which has dropped to 495,000 soldiers from 775,000 in 1990, has only recruited 87 percent of its goal. Of the four branches, only the Marine Corps has met national recruiting goals in the last two years." (p1 secA)

Shepardson, David. "News Special: Military Recruiting: State Enlistments Plummet." Detroit News 22 Jul 1997. p1,4 secA.

MICHIGAN--ECONOMIC CONDITIONS

"Michigan is one of only five states in which the number of people living in poverty declined last year. According to federal data..., the state's poverty rate declined from 13.2 percent in 1995 to 11.7 percent in 1996....[Margarete Gravina, a spokeswoman for the Family Independence Agency,] noted that the state social service agency has closed 126,276 welfare cases since it began implementing welfare reform in 1992. That amounts to roughly 400,000 people who have gotten off assistance, she said. The unemployment rate has fallen steadily over the past three years and stands at 3.7 percent, compared with 5.9 percent in 1994, said Jim Tobin, spokesman for the Michigan Jobs Commission. Tobin said the commission has found 100,000 jobs for welfare clients in the past three years." (p1 secC) "In Michigan, median income rose to $38,364 from $37,429, a 2.5 percent gain. The percent of Michiganians without health insurance dropped to 9.3 from 10.3." (p4 secC)

Bivins, Larry. "Metro: Michigan Sees Drop in Annual Poverty Rate." Detroit News 30 Sep 1997. p1,4 secC.

MICHIGAN--EDUCATION (v26)

MICHIGAN--EMPLOYMENT (v26)

In Michigan, since 1991, "total employment has grown to 4.6 million people, a record high in just six years. "Over the same period the state unemployment rate was cut in half from a high of nearly 10%...to a low of 4% in May of this year." (p904)

Schmidt, Werner (MP-BC). "Government Orders: Supply." Canada. Parliament. House of Commons. Debates. v135 n17 21 Oct 1997. p879-911. section-level access: <http://www.parl.gc.ca/36/1/parlbus/chambus/house/debates/017_1997-10-21/han017-e.htm#LINK59> (ISSN0704-5603). (X3-361E).

"In 1996, seven of every 10 jobs in Michigan were in the service sector, compared with about five out of 10 in 1960....Employment in Michigan's auto industry dropped from 331,000 in 1960 to 274,000 in 1996, a decline of 17 percent....Manufacturers employ 967,000 people statewide, down only slightly from 976,000 in 1960." (p2 secA)

Craig, Charlotte W. "State's Jobless Rate Drops to All-Time Low." Detroit Free Press 14 Aug 1997. p1-2 secA.

MICHIGAN--INDUSTRIAL PRODUCTIVITY

"Michigan agriculture generates $4 billion in direct economic activity from more than 46,000 farms in our state. That balloons to $40 billion in related economic activity each year. It is our state's second leading industry, yet we continue to let it disappear because of development at the rate of 10 acres every hour. Michigan tourism provides direct employment to about 130,000 people and generates about $8 billion annually. Michigan forests yield jobs and income through lumber and wood products, through wood furniture and fixtures, through pulp and paper manufacturing. The totals are astounding: 70,000 jobs and more than $3 billion annually. Michigan annually generates more than $3 billion in non-fuel mining and oil and gas production. Twenty-one minerals are mined here, making this one of the most diverse mineral-producing states in the nation." (p11 secA)

Milliken, William. "Other Voices: Michigan's Soul Is in Its Land." Detroit Free Press 12 Nov 1997. p11 secA.

MICHIGAN--MANUFACTURES (v26)

MICHIGAN--OFFICIALS AND EMPLOYEES--SALARIES, ETC. (v26)

MICHIGAN--POLITICS AND GOVERNMENT

Michigan "State representatives were in session 32 weeks this year; state senators, 31 weeks....[As of 10 Dec 1997,] lawmakers in both chambers had introduced 2,264 bills. That's 100 fewer than their predecessors in the previous Legislature unveiled in their first year....Only about 150 of the bills introduced by legislators this year have been signed into law by Republican Gov. John Engler, compared to nearly 300 at the midway point for the previous Legislature." (p1 secC) "One of the first things lawmakers did this year was accept a 2.5 percent pay raise, which will jack up their annual salary to $53,192 next year." (p6 secC)

Cole, Kenneth. "Metro: News Special: Public Accountability: Legislature Had Easy 1st Half." Detroit News 11 Dec 1997. p1,6 secC.

MICHIGAN--POPULATION (v26)

MICHIGAN--SOCIAL CONDITIONS--PUBLIC OPINION (v26)

MICHIGAN. DEPT. OF TRANSPORTATION --APPROPRIATIONS AND EXPENDITURES (v26)

MICHIGAN STATE UNIVERSITY

see FOREIGN STUDY--MICHIGAN STATE UNIVERSITY

MIDDLE CLASS--UNITED STATES (v26)

MIDDLE EAST--POPULATION (v26)

MIDDLE EAST--UNITED STATES--PUBLIC OPINION

In a recent Gallup poll, "when asked if there will ever come a time when 'Israel and the Arab nations will be able to settle their differences and live in peace,' only 36% of those polled on August 12 and 13 said yes, while 56% said no. Older Americans who have lived through more years of Middle Eastern wars and aborted peace settlements are considerably more pessimistic than younger Americans: only 25% of Americans 65 and older say that Middle East peace will ever be possible, compared with 44% of those 18-29....In the most recent poll in August, 38% of those polled say their sympathies lie with the Israelis, compared to only 8% whose sympathies lie with the Palestinians. The rest--over half--say either that they don't have an opinion, or that their sympathies lie with neither or both sides."

Newport, Frank/Gallup Organization. "Public Skeptical Lasting Peace Will Ever Come to Mideast." Press Release 5 Sep 1997. document-level access: <http://www.gallup.com/poll/news/970905.HTML>

MIDDLE WEST--EMPLOYMENT

According to the Kansas City Fed's Second Quarter 1997 REGIONAL ECONOMIC DIGEST, "the number of jobs in the [Middle West] region rose 0.9 percent in the first quarter and was 2.8 percent higher than a year ago....National employment was up 0.6 percent in the first quarter and was 2.3 percent higher than a year ago. Kansas led the district in job growth in the first quarter--up 3.7 percent from last year. Oklahoma and Colorado employment grew 3.5 percent, while Nebraska employment grew 2.6 percent, slightly below the district average of 2.8 percent. In the...[U.S.], employment growth averaged 2.3 percent." (unpaginated)

"Regional Economy Enjoys Solid Growth in First Quarter." Federal Reserve Bank of Kansas City Fed Letter Aug 1997.

According to the Kansas City Fed's Third Quarter 1997 REGIONAL ECONOMIC DIGEST, the number of jobs in the Tenth Federal District, which includes Colorado, Kansas, Missouri, Nebraska, New Mexico, Oklahoma and Wyoming, "slipped 0.1 percent in the second quarter and was 2.0 percent higher than a year ago....In comparison, national employment was up 0.6 percent in the second quarter and was 2.2 percent higher than a year ago....Oklahoma employment grew 2.5 percent over the previous year. Colorado employment growth equaled the district average at 2.0 percent over a year ago....In the nation, employment growth averaged 2.2 percent." (unpaginated)

"Regional Economy Continued to Expand in Second Quarter of '97." Federal Reserve Bank of Kansas City Fed Letter Oct 1997.

MIDDLE WEST--MANUFACTURES

According to the Kansas City Fed's Second Quarter 1997 REGIONAL ECONOMIC DIGEST, in the Middle West, "manufacturing jobs grew 0.5 percent in the first quarter, led by continued strength in durable goods. Compared with last year, manufacturing employment in the district was up 0.9 percent. In the...[U.S.], factory employment was up 0.2 percent in the first quarter but was unchanged from the previous year." (unpaginated)

"Regional Economy Enjoys Solid Growth in First Quarter." Federal Reserve Bank of Kansas City Fed Letter Aug 1997.

MIDWIVES--UNITED STATES (v26)

MIGRAINE--CANADA (v26)

MIGRAINE--UNITED STATES

In the U.S., "26 million Americans--two-thirds of whom are women--...suffer from migraines....The pain results from blood vessels in the brain tightening, then relaxing, distorting the vessels and resulting in the throbbing characteristic of a migraine. Other symptoms include nausea (experienced by 87 percent of patients); vomiting (56 percent); sensitivity to light, sound and smells; malaise; and diarrhea. Peak prevalence is between the ages of 20 and 45." (p1 secE)

Pipp, Tracy L. "Accent: Health: Program Shows How to 'Take Charge' of Migraine Headaches." Detroit News 23 Sep 1997. p1 secE.

MIGRANT LABOR (v26)

see also MIGRATION, INTERNAL

MIGRANT LABOR--ASIA (v26)

MIGRANT LABOR--CANADA (v26)

MIGRANT LABOR--MEXICO--UNITED STATES

"In 1996, Mexico's Colegio de la Frontera Norte estimated that 5 million Mexicans worked in the United States without documents, earning about $30 billion a year, of which they sent $3.6 billion back to family members in Mexico. The Mexican group claimed that these payments were the third largest source of hard currency for Mexico, after $8.423 billion from petroleum exports and $4.924 billion from the maquiladora sector. The number of undocumented Mexican workers in the United States seemed to be growing by about 150,000 a year. If these figures are roughly accurate, about 10 percent of the total Mexican work force of 50 million has been transformed into some 3 percent of the U.S. work force, now at about 135 million; these 'illegals' average a little more than $100 a week, far below minimum wage." (p31-32)

Wilson, David L. "Do Maquiladoras Matter?" Monthly Review v49 n5 Oct 1997. p28-34. (ISSN0027-0520).

MIGRANT LABOR--PHILIPPINES (v26)

"In 1994, over 300,000 Filipina women left the Philippines to seek work in other countries. Today, the nation constitutes the world's largest 'exporter' of female labor. Filipina migrant laborers, now half of the migrant labor population, contribute--along with their male counterparts--$6 billion in remittances to the Philippines per year, $1.8 billion of which helps finance the interest on the national debt." (p411) "Both male and female contract workers often find themselves forced to turn over up to 25% of the earnings just to pay for costly contracts and recruiters." (p413)

Fernandez, Mary Rose. "Commodified Women." Peace Review v9 n3 Sep 1997. p411-416. (ISSN1040-2659).

MIGRANT LABOR--UNITED STATES (v26)

MIGRANT LABOR--WASHINGTON (STATE)--SOCIAL CONDITIONS

The average annual income for migrant farmworkers in central Washington "is only $7,000, far below the official poverty level....According to the Washington State Health Department, 'More than half of the migrant workers--37,700 of the 62,300 who pick cherries, apples and other crops on about 1,000 farms--are without suitable shelter." (p8)

Turner, Charles. "Immigrants Risk Injury, Death at U.S. Border." The People v107 n7 Oct 1997. p8. (ISSN0199-350X).

MIGRATION, INTERNAL

see also RURAL-URBAN MIGRATION

MIGRATION, INTERNAL--AFGHANISTAN

In Afghanistan, "an estimated one million [internally displaced persons] have been displaced in the last five years alone. An additional 300,000 people abandoned their homes between October 1996 and July 1997." (p7)

"The Biggest Caseload in the World: The Dilemma of the Internally Displaced." Refugees v2 n108 1997. p7. (ISSN0252-791X).

MIGRATION, INTERNAL--AUSTRALIA (v26)

MIGRATION, INTERNAL--MICHIGAN (v26)

MIGRATION, INTERNAL--NEW JERSEY (v26)

MIGRATION, INTERNAL--NORTH CAROLINA--SOUTH CAROLINA--AGED (v26)

MIGRATION, INTERNAL--SOUTH CAROLINA--AGED (v26)

MIGRATION, INTERNAL--UNITED STATES

In the U.S., "about 320,000 more people move out of the Northeast than move in every year, according to 1984-94 data from the Census Bureau. In the Midwest, the net migration loss is about 30,000 a year. Meanwhile, the South is seeing a net gain of about 250,000 people a year from internal migration, and the West gains about 100,000 a year....Between 1990 and 1995, 61 of the nation's 272 metropolitan areas had population increases that exceeded 10 percent. Twelve of these were in Florida, 9 were in Texas, and 6 were elsewhere in the South. Thirty were in the West. But none of the hot 61 were in the Northeast, and the only Midwesterners on the list were 2 small Missouri metros and Sioux Falls, SD (pop. 153,300 in 1995, up 10.1 percent since 1990). Only 18 of the nation's 61 fastest-growing metros... experience what the Federal Emergency Management Agency defines as 'extreme cold'....Only 8 of the hot 61 experience moderate snowfall, and another 8 experience heavy snowfall. At the other end of the scale are 21 metro areas that lost population between 1990 and 1995....Among the 21 losers, 15 had heavy or moderate snowfall and extreme cold." (p19)

Edmondson, Brad. "New Frontiers: Cold Comfort." American Demographics v19 n11 Nov 1997. p18-19. article-level access: <http://www.demographics.com/publications/ad/97_ad/9711_ad/ad97115.htm> (ISSN0163-4089).

"A quarter of a million more people left...[U.S.] metropolitan areas than moved into them during a 12-month period that ended in March 1996 the second time since the mid-1980s that metropolitan areas lost population due to migration, according to a report released...by the Commerce Department's Census Bureau....Between 1995 and 1996, the central cities lost 2.4 million while the suburbs gained 2.2 million as the result of migration."

U.S. Dept. of Commerce. Economic & Statistics Administration. "More People Left than Moved Into Metro Areas in 1995-96, Census Bureau Reports." Census Bureau Press Release 3 Dec 1997. document-level access: <http://www.census.gov/Press-Release/cb97-194.html>

MIGRATION, INTERNAL--UNITED STATES--AGED (v26)

MIGRATION, INTERNATIONAL

see EMIGRATION AND IMMIGRATION

MIGRATION, RURAL-URBAN

see RURAL-URBAN MIGRATION

MILITARY ASSISTANCE, AMERICAN--ISRAEL

"According to U.S. Government Accounting Office figures, the United States directly provided $125.5 million out of a total of $156.9 million for Phase I of the [Arrow Continuation Experiments Series, or ACES] program [in Israel], representing 80 percent of the funding. However, this does not include $7.9 million in U.S. Foreign Military Financing (FMF) grants provided to Tel Aviv. Adding FMF funds to the stated U.S. contribution increases the U.S. financial stake in Phase I to 85 percent. An examination of costs associated with ACES reveals that the United States is directly providing $238.1 million out of a total of $330.7 million, 72 percent of the funding. However, this again does not include $90 million in FMF grants provided to Tel Aviv. Adding these FMF funds to the direct U.S. contribution increases the U.S. financial stake in ACES to over 99 percent." (p84)

DelGenis, Tony. "Israel's Gulf War Experience: A Brief Synopsis." Middle East Policy v5 n2 May 1997. p79-92. (ISSN1061-1924).

"US military aid to Israel since 1948 has totaled $40 billion, about twice as much as the amount provided for any other country. For FY 1996, the $1.8 billion in grants to Israel accounted for 56 percent of all US military aid." (p15)

Gilbert, David. "TF Reports: Middle East: Facts of Death." Toward Freedom v46 n5 Sep-Oct 1997. p4,15. (ISSN0048-9898).

MILITARY BASE CONVERSION--UNITED STATES

In the U.S., a new law aimed at creating more jobs and taxable businesses on former military facilities "promises to speed the replacement of some of the nearly 82,000 civilian jobs lost during the military downsizing that has shut down 50 bases since 1989. Another 47 bases are slated to close on or before the year 2001, Pentagon officials say....The Fort Harrison Reuse Authority (FHRA), headed by [J. Lynn] Boese, started work in mid-1995 and less than a year later purchased 550 acres and some 400 buildings from the Army for $6.9 million. The money is repayable over nine years. In only a few months, the FHRA has sold three sections of land for more than $6 million for residential development....The FHRA deals have led to the creation of 555 new jobs, or more than 12 percent of the 4,240 civilian jobs lost when the base closed." (p3)

Tyson, Ann Scott. "United States: Military Fights Cutbacks with Midwestern Charm." The Christian Science Monitor v89 n185 19 Aug 1997. p3. The Christian Science Monitor search engine: <http://www.csmonitor.com/plweb-cgi/iops1.pl> To retrieve this article, enter the following search: ED=19970819 AND charm. In the "retrieved list," click the title that matches this record. (ISSN0882-7729).

MILITARY BASES

see also AIR BASES

MILITARY BASES, AMERICAN (v26)

Nearly 100 American military "bases have been closed or are scheduled to be closed as a result of the four 'BRAC' (Base Closure and Realignment) rounds in 1989, 1991, 1993, and 1995. But the resulting 21% decrease in base infrastructure ultimately will be overmatched by a 32% cut in active-duty people, let alone a 60% cut in procurement spending power since 1985...." (p92)

Truver, Scott C. "Tomorrow's Fleet." Proceedings v123 n9 Sep 1997. p90-96. (ISSN0041-798X).

MILITARY BASES, AMERICAN--ASIA (v26)

MILITARY BASES, AMERICAN--ENVIRONMENTAL ASPECTS--UNITED STATES

In the U.S., "more than 100 federally listed threatened or endangered species are known to inhabit the 25 million-plus acres of land controlled by the Department of Defense (DoD)....Under a cooperative agreement signed with the DoD in 1988 and updated in 1995, the [Nature] Conservancy and state Natural Heritage Programs have worked with the military on more than 200 conservation projects at 170 bases in 41 states...." (p12)

Biondo, Brenda. "In Defense of the Longleaf Pine." Nature Conservancy v47 n4 Sep-Oct 1997. p10-17. (ISSN0028-5200).

MILITARY BASES, AMERICAN--GEORGIA

In Georgia, Warner Robins Air Force Base "is 16 miles south of Macon...and covers 8,722 acres. Almost 16,000 people work at the base. More than 40 units are based there...." (p6)

Lambert, Verdelle. "Air Force Megabase Grows, Savannah District Builds." Engineer Update v21 n8 Aug 1997. p6-7. (ISSN0733-8163).

MILITARY BASES, AMERICAN--GERMANY (v26)

MILITARY BASES, AMERICAN--GERMANY--JAPAN --SOUTH KOREA--COSTS (v26)

MILITARY BASES, AMERICAN--JAPAN--OKINAWA (v26)

"Okinawa makes up 0.6 percent of the total of the country's land mass but is home to 75 percent of the US military forces in Japan. In a 1996 referendum, nearly 90 percent of voters in Okinawa favored downsizing the US military presence. The vote was not legally binding....Since 1972, when the US ceded control of Okinawa back to Japan, Tokyo has poured in nearly 5 billion yen (about $40 million at current exchange rates) to develop Okinawa." (p6)

Nomura, Takehiko. "International: US Military's Plan for Ocean Heliport Sends Okinawa Spinning." The Christian Science Monitor v90 n5 2 Dec 1997. p6. The Christian Science Monitor search engine: <http://www.csmonitor.com/plweb-cgi/iops1.pl> To retrieve this article, enter the following search: ED=19971202 AND spinning. In the "retrieved list," click the title that matches this record. (ISSN0882-7729).

MILITARY BASES, AMERICAN--JAPAN--OKINAWA --PUBLIC OPINION (v26)

MILITARY BASES, AMERICAN--UNITED STATES

"According to Congressman [Joel] Hefley, the chairman of the House National Security Committee's Subcommittee on Military Installation and Facilities, if you measure by plant replacement the value of bases in the United States and around the world, base infrastructure has fallen by 27 percent, very close to the one-third or 33 percent reduction in force structure. Other estimates of reduction in base structure are either not calculating the plant replacement value or they are calculating values of only bases in the Continental United States, which ignores the 43 percent reduction in U.S. bases overseas. In addition to that, the military's operational bases--that is, the bases that host the combat units--are already closing down in proportion to the defense drawdown. For example, when all the...[base realignment closings] are done, the Air Force will have closed 22 of 74 major air bases, 30 percent; the Navy will have closed 10 of 17 naval stations, nearly 60 percent, and 12 of 29 naval air stations, 40 percent; the Army will have closed 10 major combat and training facilities, about one-third of those Army bases." (pS7068)

Dorgan, Byron L. (Sen.-N.Dak.). "Chinese Military Expansion and United States National Security." Congressional Record. Daily ed. v143 n96 9 Jul 1997. pS7052-7091. section/page-level access: <http://thomas.loc.gov/cgi-bin/query/R?r105:FLD001:S07067:> (ISSN0363-7239). (X1.1A.105/1).

MILITARY BASES, AMERICAN--UNITED STATES --COSTS

A U.S. Congressional Budget Office's "analysis shows that the Pentagon has consistently overestimated the savings that will accrue from a given round of base closures. In the first round, the Pentagon estimated that we would achieve $844 million in savings for the period 1990 to 1995. Subsequently, it turned out that instead of saving money, the round actually lost $517 million. For the second round of base closures, the Pentagon initially estimated that we would save $2.916 billion from 1992 to 1997....We did not save $2.9 billion. We will be fortunate to save about one-third of that amount, roughly $972 million. For the third round, the Pentagon estimated that we would lose $715 million for the period 1994 to 1999. It now estimates we will not lose quite as much, about $553 million." (pS7081)

Daschle, Thomas A. (Sen.-S.Dak.). "Chinese Military Expansion and United States National Security." Congressional Record. Daily ed. v143 n96 9 Jul 1997. pS7052-7091. section/page-level access: <http://thomas.loc.gov/cgi-bin/query/R?r105:FLD001:S07080:> (ISSN0363-7239). (X1.1A.105/1).

MILITARY CADETS

see WAR--UNITED STATES--MILITARY CADETS

MILITARY HELICOPTERS--UNITED STATES

The Helicopter Mine Countermeasures Squadron, HM-14 at Naval Air Station, Norfolk, Virginia, "operated six MH-53Es [minesweeping helicopters] in the Persian Gulf from October 1990 to July 1991; HM-15 [Helicopter Mine Countermeasures Squadron at NAS Corpus Christi, Texas] flew logistics missions. The minesweeping helicopters cleared 768 square miles of sea lanes--nearly 8,000 linear miles--with 93% effectiveness against moored mines. They cut loose 30 moored mines with mechanical sweep gear, located 7 bottom mines with sonar, and detonated 2 influence mines with magnetic sweep sleds." (p64)

Colucci, Frank. "Professional Notes: Don't Forget the Sea Dragons." Proceedings v123 n11 Nov 1997. p64-67. (ISSN0041-798X).

MILITARY SALES

see ARMS TRANSFERS; DEFENSE INDUSTRIES

MILITARY WEAPONS

see also CHEMICAL WEAPONS; NUCLEAR WEAPONS

MILITARY WEAPONS--MEXICO

"The US government sells Mexico $40 million per year in military equipment and has trained over 700 of their officers over the last ten years. Through military credits and drug enforcement and eradication grants, the Mexican armed forces, which now number over 200,000 troops, have acquired over 80 Huey, Bell and Blackhawk helicopters and 75 Swiss-made P-7 jet trainers and 250 French tanks." (p28)

Miller, Brad. "Self Determination and Territory: Mexico's Hired Guns." Abya Yala News v10 n3 Sum 1997. p26-29. (ISSN1056-5876).

MILITARY WEAPONS--UNITED STATES

Annually the U.S. spends "millions of dollars on the production of new munitions of all types. At the other end of the pipeline however is the vexing problem of disposing of outdated munitions of all types....The stocks managed by the Army, DOD's [Department of Defense's] Manager for Conventional Ammunition (MCA), currently stored in 26 States totals approximately 449,308 tons of material and costs over $12 million annually to store according to a DOD 1995 Joint Demilitarization Study. More serious however is the fact that the study predicts an additional 730,420 tons will be generated into that stockpile by the end of fiscal year 2001....Through the end of fiscal year 2001, over 1.2 million tons of material will pass through or reside in the military conventional ammunition account. This is enough ammunition to exceed 2800 earth covered magazines and will cost over $1.2 billion to destroy if we assume that it costs approximately $120 million to destroy 107,000 tons of material using fiscal year 1995 projections." (pS7267)

Sessions, Jeff (Sen.-Ala.). "Gulf War Veterans' Health." Congressional Record. Daily ed. v143 n98 11 Jul 1997. pS7253-7284. section/page-level access: <http://thomas.loc.gov/cgi-bin/query/R?r105:FLD001:S07267:> (ISSN0363-7239). (X1.1A.105/1).

MILITARY WEAPONS INDUSTRY

see WEAPONS INDUSTRY

MILITIA--UNITED STATES (v26)

MILK CONSUMPTION--HEALTH ASPECTS

"Scandinavian countries devour enormous amounts of milk, yet they have the worst bone fracture rates on the planet. Americans consume more milk than many other populations do, yet our bone fracture rates are high as well. On the other hand, Asian countries generally avoid milk, yet they have very low fracture rates. In Singapore, the average calcium intake is less than 300 milligrams per day, but they have only one-fifth of our bone fracture rate....In a study of 78,000 women, aged 34 to 59, those who drank three or more glasses of milk per day had no reduction in the risk of hip or arm fractures over a 12-year period, compared with those who drank little or no milk, even after adjustment for weight, menopausal status, smoking, and alcohol use." (p10 secA)

Barnard, Neal D. "Special Letter: Get Calcium from Vegetables, Not Milk." Detroit News 11 Nov 1997. p10 secA.

MILK CONSUMPTION--UNITED STATES (v26)

MILK PRODUCTION--CANADA--UNITED STATES (v26)

MILK PRODUCTION--UNITED STATES (v26)

MILLIONAIRES

see also BILLIONAIRES; WEALTH

"The new annual survey by FORBES MAGAZINE shows that the Sultan of Brunei, [is] the richest man in the world, with an estimated wealth of $38bn [billion]....The US magazine estimates that Saddam Hussein, the President of Iraq, is now worth considerably more than he was before the Gulf War, with $5,000m [million]." (p19)

McWhirter, Norris. "News and Comment: Lest We Forget...: Cuban Economic Magic." Freedom Today v22 n4 Aug 1997. p19.

"The number of billionaires in the world increased from 145 to 358 during the seven-year period from 1987 to 1994. 'Together they control a capital of $761.9 billion, about the equivalent to the annual per-capita income of 45 percent of the world's population,' says [POWER LINES author Alejandro Bendana]." (p20)

Ney, Chris. "Activist Reviews: Lines of Inequality." Nonviolent Activist v14 n4 Jul-Aug 1997. p20. (ISSN8755-7428).

MILLIONAIRES--GREAT BRITAIN (v26)

MILLIONAIRES--UNITED STATES (v26)

US millionaires "are far more likely to have earned their pile than to be drawing on ancestral trust funds. Some 3.5 million households in the US now have wealth exceeding $1 million, according to Thomas Stanley and William Danko, writing in their book, THE MILLIONAIRE NEXT DOOR. Yet fewer than 20 percent of surveyed millionaires inherited more than one-tenth of their wealth, they found. More than half never got $1 of inheritance." (p3)

Francis, David R. "United States: More Go from Rags to Riches--And Reverse--As Class Barriers Fall." The Christian Science Monitor v89 n132 4 Jun 1997. p3. The Christian Science Monitor search engine: <http://www.csmonitor.com/plweb-cgi/iops1.pl> To retrieve this article, enter the following search: ED=19970604 AND fall. In the "retrieved list," click the title that matches this record. (ISSN0882-7729).

NEWSWEEK "said there are about 70,000 millionaires and billionaires in the...[U.S.] today, up from only 13,500 in 1979....That's an increase of 419 percent!...70,000 is just a hair's breadth above zero percent of the country's 267 million people." (p1)

"Support THE PEOPLE: Capitalism's 'Prosperity' Machine." The People v107 n6 Sep 1997. p1. (ISSN0199-350X).

MILWAUKEE (WIS.)--ECONOMIC CONDITIONS

"For almost three years, Wisconsin's unemployment rate has stayed below 4%, and metropolitan Milwaukee has fared even better, scoring an unemployment rate of 3% in 1995....The official unemployment rate...[in Milwaukee's central city] rages at 21.5%--more than seven times the rate for the metropolitan region....The overall poverty rate in central city Milwaukee is 50%, and some 70% of children live below the official poverty line." (p31)

Fung, Archon/Rogers, Joel. "Grassroots Report: 'High Road' Job Creation: The New Party's Urban Agenda." Dollars and Sense n214 Nov-Dec 1997. p30-33. (ISSN0012-5245).

MINERAL INDUSTRIES--AUSTRALIA (v26)

MINERAL INDUSTRIES--EMPLOYMENT--AUSTRALIA (v26)

MINES (MILITARY EXPLOSIVES) (v26)

"No less than 25 percent of land mine victims are children....[According to Mary Wareham, coordinator of the U.S. Campaign to Ban Land Mines,] 'Now we are faced with a situation involving over 100 million anti-personnel land mines laid in over 65 countries, killing or maiming a person every 20 minutes. The three countries worst affected are Afghanistan, Angola and Cambodia.' An estimated 26,000 people are killed or wounded each year by mines....The NEW YORK TIMES on March 17, 1996, reported that an official of the U.S. Arms Control and Disarmament Agency had stated the previous week that the number of mines worldwide is increasing by two million a year. According to the United Nations, more than 50 countries, including the United States, are believed to produce each year between 500,000 and one million mines." (p14-15) "The International Committee of the Red Cross has documented that only 24.6 percent of land mine victims reach medical assistance within six hours, and 16 percent must travel more than three days to reach a facility....As many as 54 percent of land mine victims may die before they reach medical help....The United Nations estimates that the cost to remove the current stock of planted mines approaches $33 billion. It reported that 100,000 land mines were cleared in 1995." (p16)

Griffin, Regina. "The Land Mine Menace." America v177 n2 19 Jul 1997. p14-17. (ISSN0002-7049).

Land mines "kill or injure 25,000 people a year....[People lose their limbs, their sight and their lives from land mines] 25,000 times a year; 2,000 times a month, 70 times a day. Most of the victims live in the third world (one out of every 236 Cambodians is a land-mine amputee)....[According to Kevin Cahill, M.D., of New York,] 'while cheap mines are sold for as little as $3 each, it is estimated that it costs almost $1,000 to detect and defuse one.'" (p4)

Golway, Terry. "Life in the 90's." America v177 n10 4 Oct 1997. p4. (ISSN0002-7049).

"According to the International Red Cross, landmines kill or maim someone, often children, every 22 minutes. There are an estimated 100 million mines scattered throughout 68 nations....Thus far, in Bosnia, landmines have injured more than 250 soldiers under United Nations or NATO command, and they have killed 29 peacekeepers. In fact, landmines are responsible for every single death of American troops in the Balkans." (pS5721)

Collins, Susan M. (Sen.-Maine). "Chinese Companies Exporting Dangerous Weapon." Congressional Record. Daily ed. v143 n84 17 Jun 1997. pS5719-5722. section/page-level access: <http://thomas.loc.gov/cgi-bin/query/R?r105:FLD001:S05721:> (ISSN0363-7239). (X1.1A.105/1).

"Every 22 minutes someone is killed or maimed by a landmine, more than 26,000 men, women, and children, mainly civilians, each year and every year. In at least 68 countries there are over 110 million unexploded landmines lying in fields, deserts, roads, along rivers and streams, in forests, and on footpaths....The average lifespan of an antipersonnel landmine is 50 to 100 years." (pH3806)

McGovern, James P. (Rep.-Mass.). "Ban Landmines Now." Congressional Record. Daily ed. v143 n84 17 Jun 1997. pH3806-3807. section/page-level access: <http://thomas.loc.gov/cgi-bin/query/R?r105:FLD001:H03806:> (ISSN0363-7239). (X1.1A.105/1).

"One hundred ten million active landmines are hidden in as many as 64 countries. And while 100,000 landmines a year are identified, deactivated and removed, another 2 million to 5 million are planted. These landmines claim about 2,000 victims a month." (pS5721)

Reed, Jack (Sen.-R.I.). "Chinese Companies Exporting Dangerous Weapon." Congressional Record. Daily ed. v143 n84 17 Jun 1997. pS5719-5722. section/page-level access: <http://thomas.loc.gov/cgi-bin/query/R?r105:FLD001:S05721:> (ISSN0363-7239). (X1.1A.105/1).

According to the U.S. "Department of State, a limb or a life is lost every 22 minutes as a result of land mines. Over 5 million land mines are produced annually. Over 50 percent of them are deployed. With only 100,000 land mines being removed each year, villages, fields and paths are turned into death traps. Ninety percent of the victims are civilians. In 70 countries around the world, more than 100 million land mines continue to fight battles that ended months, years and even decades ago." (pH2776)

McGovern, James P. (Rep.-Mass.). "Stop the Scourge of Landmines." Congressional Record. Daily ed. v143 n64 15 May 1997. pH2776-2778. section/page-level access: <http://thomas.loc.gov/cgi-bin/query/R?r105:FLD001:H02776:>

(ISSN0363-7239). (X1.1A.105/1).

"An estimated 100 million land mines remain in 68 countries, killing and injuring hundreds of civilians every month. Bosnia has become a devil's garden of land mines, where they have injured 200 UN peacekeepers and killed 20. In Vietnam, children, farmers, and other innocents continue to be killed by mines, two decades after the end of the war." (p12 secA)

"In Our Opinion: Land Mines." Detroit Free Press 27 Jun 1997. p12 secA.

"Up to 110 million active mines are deployed in more than 60 countries, according to the International Campaign to Ban Land Mines. The U.S. State Department says someone is injured or killed by a land mine every 22 minutes. Land mines can cost as little as $3. The search for and removal of mines is estimated to cost as much as $1,000 per mine, including equipment and personnel. The International Red Cross says land mines kill or wound 26,000 people each year, 87 percent of them civilians." (p4 secG)

"The Way We Live: The Legacy of Land Mines: Land Mine Facts." Detroit Free Press 30 Nov 1997. p4 secG.

"According to estimates by the experts, a total of more than 100 million...[land mines] have been buried in some sixty countries around the world--an estimated 23 million landmines remain hidden in grass and sand in Angola alone. More than 20,000 people in the African country have had arms or legs amputated following a mine injury; Cambodia is able to count one mine victim for every 234 inhabitants. Every twenty minutes a mine explodes somewhere around the world. A total of more than 26,000 people are injured, severely maimed, or killed by mines every year. One third of those killed are children." (p16)

Moniac, Rudiger. "Nobel Peace Prize for the International Campaign to Ban Landmines." Deutschland n6 Dec 1997. p14-17. (ISSN0945-6791).

"The populations of more than 60 nations are still endangered by concealed land mines. According to a Department of Defense report, there are approximately 90 to 100 million uncleared mines worldwide; thousands of people are killed or injured by them annually. A team of five universities, led by the University of Missouri-Rolla, has received a $5-million grant from the Department of Defense for a five-year study to develop new methods to detect and neutralize the mines." (p14)

Wexler, Devra. "News Notes: New Methods for Detecting Land Mines." Geotimes v42 n10 Oct 1997. p14. (ISSN0016-8556).

"There are an estimated 100 million land mines planted around the world, with the highest concentrations in such war-torn countries as Angola, Bosnia, Cambodia and Mozambique. Each year, some 26,000 people--many of them children--are killed or maimed by stepping on weapons of this type." (p3)

"Editorials: Beyond Land Mines." Nation v265 n14 3 Nov 1997. p3. (ISSN0027-8378).

"There are more than 100 million uncleared landmines in fields and along roads and footpaths around the world, and they claim over 500 victims a week, according to the U.S. Campaign to Ban Landmines....In Cambodia alone there are more than 35,000 amputees who have lost limbs to landmine explosions....The campaign says, 'it costs about 100 times more to remove one mine than to produce it.'...The U.N. estimates that it costs as much as $1,000 to clear a single mine. The campaign says that more than 50 countries have produced about 200 million anti-personnel land mines in the last 25 years--there are more than 350 different types in existence....The campaign reports that the 'U.S. Army (has) estimated that 90 percent of landmines and booby traps used against U.S. troops in Vietnam were either U.S.-made or included U.S.-made components in them.'...Between 1985 and 1996, 47 U.S. firms produced more than 10 million new anti-personnel mines." (p26)

"Nation/World: From Vatican to Diocese, Church Works to Ban Landmines." Observer v62 n17 1 Aug 1997. p26-27. (ISSN0029-7712).

"According to the best available estimates, 26,000 people now fall victim to landmines every year, and many of these die. A recent survey establishes that 59% of mine casualties in Afghanistan are fatal. The same survey identifies 4% of the victims as soldiers, and 18% of the casualties as having occurred during fighting....The United Nations estimates that one mine, which costs USD [U.S. dollars] 3 to deploy, costs USD300-1,000 to remove." (p278)

Harpviken, Kristian Berg/Fixdal, Mona. "Anti-Personnel Landmines: A Just Means of War?" Security Dialogue v28 n3 Sep 1997. p271-285. (ISSN0967-0106).

"There are currently an estimated 110 million land mines planted in ditches, homes, fields, and roads in 64 countries, the worst affected of which are among the world's poorest countries. The devices claim some 26,000 casualties a year--8,000 of them children--and wreak billions of dollars of economic damage by blocking reconstruction, agricultural development, trade, and transportation. The UN estimates that it would take decades and at least $33 billion--about $1,000 per mine--to eliminate the existing problem....Treating and rehabilitating the tens of thousands of people who lose limbs to explosions is now put at some $750 million and rising." (p6)

Landay, Jonathan S. "International: The Next Job: 110 Million Mines Already in the Ground." The Christian Science Monitor v89 n207 19 Sep 1997. p6. The Christian Science Monitor search engine: <http://www.csmonitor.com/plweb-cgi/iops1.pl> To retrieve this article, enter the following search: ED=19970919 AND ground. In the "retrieved list," click the title that matches this record. (ISSN0882-7729).

"There are more than 100 million antipersonnel mines scattered around the world with another 100 million in military inventories worldwide. Approximately 26,000 people a year are killed or maimed by mines....That works out to a death or injury about every 22 minutes....In Vietnam, the US Army estimated that 90 percent of the mines and booby traps used against its troops were either US-made or made with US parts." (p19)

Isenberg, David. "Opinion/Essays: US Lauds, But Thwarts, Diana's Call for Mine Ban." The Christian Science Monitor v89 n200 10 Sep 1997. p19. The Christian Science Monitor search engine: <http://www.csmonitor.com/plweb-cgi/iops1.pl> To retrieve this article, enter the following search: ED=19970910 AND ban. In the "retrieved list," click the title that matches this record. (ISSN0882-7729).

"Experience suggests that it takes 100 times as long to detect, remove, and disarm a mine as to plant it. A mine is extremely cheap to manufacture (typically $3-$20), but expensive to remove ($300-$1,000). The estimated costs of clearing all mines worldwide are astronomical, ranging from $33 to $85 billion....Accidents happen at a rate of one per 1,000-2,000 mines lifted....With the present global demining capacity it would take almost 1,100 years to get rid of all those mines already scattered." (p30)

Renner, Michael. "Small Arms, Big Impact: The Next Challenge of Disarmament." Worldwatch Paper n137 Oct 1997. p5-77.

"More than 250 million landmines have been produced since the early 1970s: appproximately 60 million anti-tank mines and 190 million anti-personnel mines....Production may run as high as 10 to 30 million each year....Some 100 companies in 50 countries have been producing more than 360 different types of mines. At least 35 countries have exported mines in a trade worth about $100 million per year. An estimated 120 million anti-personnel landmines are currently scattered in 71 countries, most of them poor developing countries." (p27-28)

Renner, Michael. "Small Arms, Big Impact: The Next Challenge of Disarmament." Worldwatch Paper n137 Oct 1997. p5-77.

MINES (MILITARY EXPLOSIVES)--ANGOLA

"Angola is twice the size of Texas, yet within its 481,000 square miles are an estimated 15 million-plus land mines, about 1.5 mines for each person. Even half that in the US would be seen as a crisis of staggering size....[Angola's mines] were laid during the decades of superpower-supported civil war that followed Angola's independence from Portugal. Nearly 77,000 of Angola's citizens are 'mutilados' [persons maimed by the mines], 20 years later." (p19)

Taylor, Clarice. "Opinion/Essays: Post-Oslo: Can We Face the Land-Mine Victims?" The Christian Science Monitor v89 n208 22 Sep 1997. p19. The Christian Science Monitor search engine: <http://www.csmonitor.com/plweb-cgi/iops1.pl> To retrieve this article, enter the following search: ED=19970922 AND victims. In the "retrieved list," click the title that matches this record. (ISSN0882-7729).

MINES (MILITARY EXPLOSIVES)--UNITED STATES

Andrew Cooper, land mines researcher for the Human Rights Watch Arms Project in Washington, D.C., "observed that although the U.S. Department of Defense estimates that land mines have killed or wounded 100,000 Americans since World War I, a forthcoming Arms Project report will identify 48 companies located in 23 states throughout the country that are present or past producers of anti-personnel mines or mine components....A total of 4.4 million anti-personnel mines, he commented, were exported by the United States from 1969 to 1992 to countries in Asia, the Middle East and South America....He said the United States currently has ten million...inexpensive mines (costing between $3 and $15 to make) in stock. The Government, he noted, is already in the process of destroying all but a million of them, which will be reserved to support operations in the demilitarized zone in Korea....He said that the United States currently has a stockpile of one million of these smart mines and has no intention of destroying this supply. Mr. Cooper informed me, however, that the Arms Project, using the Government's own statistics and reports, calculates the current number of stockpiled mines to be 18 million." (p15)

Griffin, Regina. "The Land Mine Menace." America v177 n2 19 Jul 1997. p14-17. (ISSN0002-7049).

MINES (MILITARY EXPLOSIVES)--VIETNAM (v26)

MINES AND MINERAL RESOURCES

see also COAL MINES AND MINING; DIAMOND MINES AND MINING; GOLD MINES AND MINING

The Metals Economics Group estimates that mineral "exploration budgets for 1996 totaled $4.6 billion--31 percent higher than for 1995....The MEG total includes planned spending of $3.5 billion reported by 223 surveyed companies (about 76 percent of the estimated amount). Budgets in Latin America, the area with the largest increase ($178 million), account for $963 million or 27.3 percent of the reported budgets....MEG's breakdown of exploration budgets by commodity shows 61 percent of expenditures directed to gold, 19 percent to copper, 12 percent to other base metals, 6 percent to diamonds, and 2 percent to other commodities." (p28)

Newell, Roger A. "Industry Watch: Mining." Geotimes v42 n9 Sep 1997. p28. (ISSN0016-8556).

MINES AND MINERAL RESOURCES--ALBERTA (v26)

MINES AND MINERAL RESOURCES--BRITISH COLUMBIA (v26)

MINES AND MINERAL RESOURCES--CANADA (v26)

MINES AND MINERAL RESOURCES--EMPLOYMENT --BRITISH COLUMBIA (v26)

MINES AND MINERAL RESOURCES--EMPLOYMENT --CANADA (v26)

MINES AND MINERAL RESOURCES--EMPLOYMENT --NEVADA

"The most recent information from the State of Nevada indicates that direct mining employment in Nevada exceeds 13,000 jobs. The average annual pay for these jobs, the highest of any sector in the state, is about $46,000, compared to the average salary in Nevada of about $26,000 per year. In addition to the direct employment in mining, there are an estimated 36,000 jobs in the state related to providing goods and services needed by the industry." (pS8563)

Bryan, Richard H. (Sen.-Nev.). "Statements on Introduced Bills and Joint Resolutions." Congressional Record. Daily ed. v143 n111 31 Jul 1997. pS8533-8571. section/page-level access: <http://thomas.loc.gov/cgi-bin/query/R?r105:FLD001:S08563:> (ISSN0363-7239). (X1.1A.105/1).

MINES AND MINERAL RESOURCES--MANITOBA (v26)

MINES AND MINERAL RESOURCES--NEW BRUNSWICK (v26)

MINES AND MINERAL RESOURCES--NEWFOUNDLAND (v26)

MINES AND MINERAL RESOURCES--NORTHWEST TERRITORIES (v26)

MINES AND MINERAL RESOURCES--NOVA SCOTIA (v26)

MINES AND MINERAL RESOURCES--ONTARIO (v26)

MINES AND MINERAL RESOURCES--QUEBEC (PROVINCE) (v26)

MINES AND MINERAL RESOURCES--SASKATCHEWAN (v26)

MINES AND MINERAL RESOURCES--SWEDEN (v26)

MINES AND MINERAL RESOURCES--TAXATION --NEVADA

"Nevada mining companies must pay taxes like any other business, and they also pay an additional Nevada tax called the 'Net Proceeds of Mines Tax.' The total Net Proceeds tax paid to the State in 1995 was approximately $33 million. With the addition of sales and property tax, the industry paid approximately $141 million in State and local taxes in 1995. In addition, the Nevada mining industry paid approximately $95 million in Federal taxes in 1995." (pS8563)

Bryan, Richard H. (Sen.-Nev.). "Statements on Introduced Bills and Joint Resolutions." Congressional Record. Daily ed. v143 n111 31 Jul 1997. pS8533-8571. section/page-level access: <http://thomas.loc.gov/cgi-bin/query/R?r105:FLD001:S08563:> (ISSN0363-7239). (X1.1A.105/1).

MINES AND MINERAL RESOURCES--TAXATION --UNITED STATES

"According to the National Mining Association, the industry, coal and hard rock, paid more than $600 million in [U.S.] Federal taxes in 1995. The General Accounting Office issued a report recently...that indicates the average tax rate for the mining industry from 1987 to 1992 was 35 percent. Now, that is compared with 23 percent for the automobile industry, 19 percent for the chemical industry, and 33 percent for the transportation industry. In Nevada alone, the gold mining industry paid more than $141 million in State and local taxes in 1995, including $32.7 million in property taxes." (pS6344)

Bryan, Richard H. (Sen.-Nev.). "Revenue Reconciliation Act of 1997." Congressional Record. Daily ed. v143 n91 25 Jun 1997. pS6332-6344. section/page-level access: <http://thomas.loc.gov/cgi-bin/query/R?r105:FLD001:S06343:> (ISSN0363-7239). (X1.1A.105/1).

MINES AND MINERAL RESOURCES--UNITED STATES

"More than 90% of the total impact of mining on the economy of the United States in 1995 was in the form of indirect personal, business, and government income generated by the circulation and recirculation through the nation's economy of the mining industry's direct payments to persons, other businesses, and governments. Those direct payments, while making up only 9% of the total impact, were themselves substantial, particularly in those states where mining activity took place....Direct payments to mining firms to individuals, other businesses, and governments in the United States in 1995 totalled more than $48 billion. Of that total, the industry paid over $14.5 billion (30%) as personal income to employees, former employees, and stockholders. More than 85% of that amount went to pay the wages and salaries of current employees, while nearly all of the remaining 15% went to pay pensions to former employees and dividends to investors. The biggest share (56%) of the mining industry's direct contributions to the national economy...went to other businesses....Those direct payments to suppliers of materials, equipment, energy, and services used in mining amounted to over $27 billion....The amount of...direct payments by mining firms to state and local governments in 1995 approached $3.4 billion....Direct payments by mining firms to the United States Government in payroll taxes, income taxes, and other taxes and fees surpassed $3.5 billion in 1995. That represented more than 7% of the industry's total direct contribution to the American economy last year." (pS8560)

Leaming, George F. "Statements on Introduced Bills and Joint Resolutions." Congressional Record. Daily ed. v143 n111 31 Jul 1997. pS8533-8571. section/page-level access: <http://thomas.loc.gov/cgi-bin/query/R?r105:FLD001:S08559:> (ISSN0363-7239). (X1.1A.105/1).

"The direct contributions of the mining industry to the economies of the various [U.S.] states in 1995 tended to be the greatest in those states in which the most mining activity was conducted and which had the most suppliers providing goods and services to mining firms in other states. Thus, California, with major metal mining, construction minerals, and industrial minerals mining industries,...led the list with a direct impact from mining of almost $2.9 billion. West Virginia, with the country's biggest coal mining industry (in terms of value), was second with a direct impact in 1995 of more than $2.8 billion. Kentucky, with the nation's second largest coal mining industry, is third in impact with a direct impact on its economy of nearly $2.7 billion. Texas, with major metals, construction minerals, industrial minerals, and coal mining output, was fourth...with over $2.5 billion. Pennsylvania, the nation's fifth most important source of mined coal and third biggest producer of construction minerals, was fifth...with more than $2.3 billion. Arizona, with the nation's largest copper mining industry was sixth, receiving a direct impact of nearly $2.3 billion, while Nevada, with the nation's largest gold mining industry, was seventh with a direct economic gain of more than $1.7 billion. Illinois was eighth, also with an impact of over $1.7 billion." (pS8560)

Leaming, George F. "Statements on Introduced Bills and Joint Resolutions." Congressional Record. Daily ed. v143 n111 31 Jul 1997. pS8533-8571. section/page-level access: <http://thomas.loc.gov/cgi-bin/query/R?r105:FLD001:S08559:> (ISSN0363-7239). (X1.1A.105/1).

The "clean-up cost of all the abandoned mining sites in the United States...[is] somewhere between $32.7 and $71.5 billion....The Mineral Policy Center says there are 557,000 abandoned mines in the United States....59 of those are on the Superfund National Priority List. Mining has also produced 12,000 miles of polluted streams....2,000 of those 557,000 sites are in our national parks." (pS9577)

Bumpers, Dale (Sen.-Ariz.). "Department of the Interior and Related Agencies Appropriations Act, 1998." Congressional Record. Daily ed. v143 n125 18 Sep 1997. pS9575-9600. section/page-level access: <http://thomas.loc.gov/cgi-bin/query/R?r105:FLD001:S09577:> (ISSN0363-7239). (X1.1A.105/1).

In the U.S., "the extent of the destruction wrought by mining is indicated by the more than 550,000 abandoned mines spread over 32 states....[A] tax break permits mining companies to automatically deduct a certain percentage from their gross income to reflect a mine's reduced value over time....The fixed percentages range from 5% to 22% and are based on the type of substance mined....Government estimates show that this loophole has subsidized mining activities costing taxpayers $2.8 billion over five years." (p70)

Dunkiel, Brian S. "Conservation Strategy: How Government Tax Subsidies Destroy Habitat." Wild Earth v7 n2 Sum 1997. p69-71. (ISSN1055-1166).

MINES AND MINERAL RESOURCES--WEST VIRGINIA

A 1994 survey by the West Virginia "Department of Water Resources found that all but 24 percent of the state's streams and rivers are polluted. Much of this--no one knows exactly how much--is caused by surface mining....Mountaintop [coal] removal accounts for only 4,317 workers in the state--less than 1 percent of its job force. Overall, mining employment in the state has fallen from 130,000 in the 1940s and 1950s to just 22,000 last year." (p29) "The amount of coal extracted from West Virginia increased from 131 million tons in 1986 to a record 174 million tons last year. And the value of this coal last year--$4.4 billion--was greater than that of coal mined in any other state." (p32)

Loeb, Penny. "Special Report: Shear Madness." U.S. News & World Report v123 n6 11 Aug 1997. p26-29,32-36. article-level access: <http://www.usnews.com/usnews/issue/970811/11COAL.HTM> (ISSN0041-5537).

MINES AND MINERAL RESOURCES--YUKON TERRITORY (v26)

MINIMUM WAGE--CANADA (v26)

MINIMUM WAGE--MEXICO

"In Mexico today, the average minimum daily salary equals 24.50 pesos, which is the equivalent of approximately $3.00 (about 40 cents per hour); seventeen million of the thirty-three million gainfully employed persons earn an income around the minimum wage. 75 percent of the rural population have incomes equivalent to the minimum wage and 54 percent of the population in urban areas have incomes that are in a narrow range just above and below the minimum wage. Fifty million people, half of the Mexican population, in turn, depend on the income of these seventeen million minimum wage workers. These fifty million inhabitants live on a wage mass of only $36 billion. To put this into perspective, the OECD estimated that the Mexican GNP in 1994 was $371 billion....Whereas 10 percent of all families have annual incomes of at least $100,000 (utilizing the technique of 'purchasing power parities' of the OECD), 50 percent of the population finds itself immersed in profound misery, subsisting on a salary mass equal to 10 percent of the GNP....The buying power of the minimum wage has fallen by 75 percent, while that of contractual salaries has diminished by 60 percent." (p101-102)

Roman, Richard/Arregui, Edur Velasco. "Zapatismo and the Workers Movement in Mexico at the End of the Century." Monthly Review v49 n3 Jul-Aug 1997. p98-116. (ISSN0027-0520).

MINIMUM WAGE--NORTHERN MARIANA ISLANDS

"According to US Interior Department statistics, the CNMI [Commonwealth of the Northern Mariana Islands] set the minimun wage at $2.90 for construction and garment industry workers and $3.05 for workers in other industries. Domestics and agricultural workers reportedly are legally working for less than $1.00 an hour." (p22)

"Word from Washington: President Clinton Wants US Law Extended to Islands." Christian Social Action v10 n7 Jul-Aug 1997. p22. (ISSN0897-0459).

MINIMUM WAGE--UNITED STATES--PUBLIC OPINION (v26)

MINIMUM WAGE--VENEZUELA (v26)

MINISTERS
see CLERGY

MINISTRY
see CHURCH WORK

MINKE WHALE
see BALAENOPTERA ACUTOROSTRATA

MINNESOTA--EMPLOYMENT

Unemployment in Minnesota "stands at a scant 3 percent and in Minneapolis is the lowest in the nation." (p1) "For every 10,000 jobs that go unfilled, economists estimate, the state loses as much as $500 million in economic activity....In Minneapolis, where unemployment is just 2.3 percent--the lowest tally for any US metropolitan area--the STAR TRIBUNE is running about 5,500 'help wanted' ads in its Sunday editions....At present, demographers estimate that 18,000 people move to Minnesota each year for jobs....According to...[Minnesota state economist Tom Stinson,] about 88 percent of all people here between the ages of 16 and 65 are currently working." (p9)

Walker, Sam. "Business & Money: Harbinger of 'Help Wanted' Economy." The Christian Science Monitor v89 n207 19 Sep 1997. p1,9. The Christian Science Monitor search engine: <http://www.csmonitor.com/plweb-cgi/iops1.pl> To retrieve this article, enter the following search: ED=19970919 AND economy. In the "retrieved list," click the title that matches this record. (ISSN0882-7729).

MINOR PLANETS
see ASTEROIDS

MINORITIES
see also EDUCATIONAL TESTS AND MEASUREMENTS--CALIFORNIA--LOS ANGELES--MINORITIES; HIGH TECHNOLOGY INDUSTRIES--CALIFORNIA--SILICON VALLEY--MINORITIES; INCOME--UNITED STATES--MINORITIES; LAW SCHOOLS--UNITED STATES--MINORITIES; MEDICAL COLLEGES--MICHIGAN--MINORITIES; POOR CHILDREN--UNITED STATES--MINORITIES; POPULATION FORECASTING--UNITED STATES--MINORITIES; SCHOOL BOARD MEMBERS--UNITED STATES--MINORITIES; SEGREGATION; SMALL BUSINESS--UNITED STATES--MINORITIES; TEENAGE PREGNANCY--UNITED STATES--MINORITIES; UNITED STATES--CENSUS--MINORITIES; UNIVERSITY OF CALIFORNIA--MINORITIES; UNIVERSITY OF MICHIGAN--MINORITIES; UNIVERSITY OF TEXAS--ADMISSION--MINORITIES

MINORITIES--CALIFORNIA--SAN FRANCISCO BAY AREA--POPULATION (v26)

MINORITIES--DELAWARE--WILMINGTON--POPULATION

"Between 1970 and 1990, the proportion of...[Wilmington, Delaware's] total population that was minority grew substantially. In 1970, 44% of the city's population was minority. This percentage increased to 56% in 1980 and rose to 59% by 1990. Almost all of Wilmington's minority population has been and continues to be African-American. Hispanics grew from 2.2% of the city's population in 1970 to 4.9% in 1980 and 7.1% in 1990." (p212)

Curtis, Karen A. "Urban Poverty and the Social Consequences of Privatized Food Assistance." Journal of Urban Affairs v19 n2 1997. p207-226. (ISSN0735-2166).

MINORITIES--EDUCATION--CHINA

In China, "94 percent of the population is classified as 'Han,' while the other 6 percent is divided among 55 minority nationalities." (p3) In 1988, "the illiteracy rate for Li [a minority group] between twelve and forty years old was 50-60 percent, and 90 percent for people over forty. In 1992 ethnographers and Hainan residents said that most Li youths could write their names and count, but remained functionally illiterate. While Li children generally enter primary school,...[it is] estimated that only about 20 percent reach junior middle school, 10 percent senior middle school, and 5 percent postsecondary education." (p10)

Netting, Nancy S. "The Deer Turned Her Head: Ethnic Options for the Hainan Li." Bulletin of Concerned Asian Scholars v29 n2 Apr-Jun 1997. p3-17. (ISSN0007-4810).

MINORITIES--EDUCATION (HIGHER)--MICHIGAN

Figures from the Michigan Department of Education show "that minority enrollments at the Ann Arbor campus of the University of Michigan...declined from 12.93 percent in 1993 to 12.76 percent in 1995. The gain at Michigan State University...has been a modest 0.39 percent. Yet the number of 'underrepresented' minorities in Michigan's public universities has gone up: It was 11.41 percent in 1993 and 11.81 in 1995--the latest year for which figures are available. Eastern Michigan University has shown an impressive gain of 2.34 percentage points for the same period." (p14 secA)

"Is Academia Resegregating?" Detroit News 5 Jun 1997. p14 secA.

MINORITIES--EMPLOYMENT--SOUTHERN STATES

In the U.S., "in 1994, close to 30 percent of white men [in the South] worked in the two highest-paying categories of white-collar jobs--officials/managers and professionals. Meanwhile, only 13 percent of employed white men worked in the more poorly compensated laborer and service positions. By contrast, in 1994 over 40 percent of all black men worked in laborer and service positions, and only 8 percent of all black men worked as officials/managers or professionals." (p9)

Eckman, Anne/Green, Jordan/Braasch, Peter/Schulman, David. "Job Equity in the Downsized South: A Special Report on Work in the 1990s." Southern Exposure v25 n3-4 Fall-Win 1997. p7-11. (ISSN0146-809X).

In the U.S. Southern States, "the representation of Latinos and Native Americans in white-collar jobs remains virtually unchanged since 1975, at parity levels of 0.71 and 0.81 respectively. The gains made by African Americans in the white-collar workplace have slowed, with their increases in parity from 1985 to 1994 half of what they were during the prior decade. African Americans' parity ratio for all white-collar work reached only 0.58 by 1994....Blacks and Latinos are still more than twice as likely as whites to work jobs as low-skilled laborers. And, although they made up only 30 percent of the workforce, in 1994 people of color held almost exactly half of all service jobs, with a parity ratio of 1.65 compared to 0.72 for whites." (p11)

Eckman, Anne/Green, Jordan. "Dislocation & Workforce Equity: The South at Work in the 1990s: But Segregation Continues...." Southern Exposure: Institute for Southern Studies Report 1997. p11-12.

MINORITIES--EMPLOYMENT--UNITED STATES

In the U.S., "97 percent of senior-level male managers are white, while .6 percent are African-American, .3 percent Asian, and .4 percent Hispanic. African-American men with professional degrees earn only 79 percent of the amount of their white male counterparts, while African-American women with professional degrees earn only 60 percent." (p92)

Goldfield, Michael. "Race and Labor Organization in the United States." Monthly Review v49 n3 Jul-Aug 1997. p80-97. (ISSN0027-0520).

MINORITIES--FRANCE--PUBLIC OPINION (v26)

MINORITIES--HONG KONG (v26)

MINORITIES--MASSACHUSETTS--BOSTON --POPULATION (v26)

MINORITIES--NEW JERSEY--JERSEY CITY (v26)

MINORITIES--UNITED STATES--CURRICULA (v26)

MINORITIES--UNITED STATES--MORTALITY

"Overall mortality for black Americans continues to be about 60 percent higher than for white Americans....In 1995 the age-adjusted homicide rate for black Americans was 6 times the rate for white Americans and the AIDS death rate was nearly 5 times that for white Americans....In 1995 the death rate for Hispanic males 15-24 years of age was 53 percent higher than for non-Hispanic white males."

U.S. Dept. of Health and Human Services. "Report on Nation's Health Documents Toll of Injuries in U.S.: Firearm Mortality Down 11%, Traffic Fatality...Up...." Press Release 24 Jul 1997. document-level access: <http://www.cdc.gov/nchswww/releases/97news/97news/hus96rel.htm>

MINORITIES--UNITED STATES--POPULATION (v26)

The U.S. Census Bureau's annual "report shows black people now make up 12.8 percent of the population. This means the black population has grown since 1990, when the figure was 12.3 percent, but not as quickly as other ethnic groups....The Asian/Pacific Islander population grew from 3 percent to 3.7 percent from 1990 to 1996, and the Latino population grew from 9 percent to 10.9 percent during those years." (p5 secA)

Eversley, Melanie. "Nation & World: Study Finds Drop in Black Families Led by Married Couples." Detroit Free Press 27 Jun 1997. p5 secA.

MINORITIES--UNITED STATES--SOCIAL CONDITIONS (v26)

MINORITY BUSINESS ENTERPRISES--EMPLOYMENT --UNITED STATES (v26)

MINORITY BUSINESS ENTERPRISES--UNITED STATES

"The number of businesses owned by American Indians and Alaska Natives in the United States increased 93 percent between 1987 and 1992, from 52,980 to 102,271. The rate of increase for all U.S. firms was 26 percent, 13.7 million in 1987 to 17.3 million in 1992. In 1992, the United States had 95,040 American Indian-owned, 2,738 Aleut-owned and 4,493 Eskimo-owned firms. Receipts for the nation's American Indian- and Alaska Native-owned businesses increased 115 percent from 1987 to 1992, from $3.7 billion to $8.1 billion. Receipts for all U.S. firms during the same period grew by 67 percent, from $2 trillion to $3.3 trillion."

U.S. Dept. of Commerce. Economic & Statistics Administration. "Census Facts for Native American Month." Census Bureau Fact Sheet 31 Oct 1997. document-level access: <http://www.census.gov/Press-Release/fs97-11.html>

"The number of minority women-owned businesses increased by 153 percent, which is three times the rate of overall business growth in the United States, the rate of employment by minority firms grew by 276 percent, and revenues rose by 318 percent. Between 1987 and 1996, the number of Hispanic women-owned firms grew 206 percent, the number of Asian, American Indian and Alaska native women-owned firms increased by 138 percent, and the number of African-American women-owned firms increased by 135 percent." (pH7819)

Millender-McDonald, Juanita (Rep.-Calif.). "Women Owned Businesses in America." Congressional Record. Daily ed. v143 n129 24 Sep 1997. pH7819. section/page-level access: <http://thomas.loc.gov/cgi-bin/query/R?r105:FLD001:H07819:> (ISSN0363-7239). (X1.1A.105/1).

MINORITY BUSINESS ENTERPRISES--UNITED STATES --WOMEN

In the U.S., women of color "now own 13 percent of all women-owned businesses. They employ 1.7 million workers and generate more than $184 billion in annual sales, according to research funded by IBM and conducted by the National Foundation for Women Business Owners, NAWBO's [National Association of Women Business Owners] research arm. Between 1987 and 1996, the number of minority women-owned firms increased by 153 percent, and employment grew by 276 percent. The number of firms owned by Hispanic women more than tripled, while the number of companies owned by black, Asian and American Indian women doubled. The study, based on U.S. Census Bureau information, estimates that in 1996, black women owned 405,200 firms, Hispanic women owned 382,200, and 305,700 were owned by women of Asian, American Indian or Alaska Native heritage." (p11 secF)

Applegate, Jane. "Business Monday: Small Business: Women's Group Aims to Recruit Minorities." Detroit Free Press 18 Aug 1997. p11 secF.

MINORITY COLLEGE STUDENTS--CALIFORNIA (v26)

MINORITY COLLEGE STUDENTS--MICHIGAN (v26)

MINORITY COLLEGE STUDENTS--UNITED STATES (v26)

MINORITY FARMERS--UNITED STATES (v26)

MINORITY FARMERS--UNITED STATES--ECONOMIC CONDITIONS (v26)

MINORITY JUDGES--UNITED STATES (v26)

MINORITY LAW STUDENTS--UNITED STATES

At the University of Texas "there are only 10 African-Americans among the 944 law school admittees this year, according to a report [being prepared for the American Bar Association Commission on Opportunities for Minorities in the Profession]....The percentage of minorities enrolled in ABA approved law schools increased from 8.4 percent of all enrollees in 1976 to 20 percent in 1995, or 25,553 students, according to the report. At so-called elite law schools, minorities made up 23.9 percent of all students in 1995." (p100)

Gibeaut, John. "Your ABA/Annual Meeting Report: Marking a Decade of Struggle." ABA Journal v83 Oct 1997. p100. (ISSN0747-0088).

MINORITY PRISONERS--CALIFORNIA

"African Americans in California are imprisoned at nine times the rate of whites. No fewer than 1,951 per 100,000 African Americans are in California's prisons, dwarfing the white rate of 215 per 100,000. Although African Americans constitute under seven percent of the state's total population, they make up 32% of prison inmates. Similarly, Latinos occupy California's state prisons at a rate of 543 per 100,000. Although they account for 24% of the state's total population, they make up 34% of the CDC's [California Dept. of Corrections] population. If these two groups were imprisoned at the rate of whites, the CDC's total population would be 57,700 inmates, less than half its current number." (p40-41)

Koetting, Mark G./Schiraldi, Vincent. "Singapore West: The Incarceration of 200,000 Californians." Social Justice v24 n1 Spr 1997. p40-53. (ISSN0094-7571).

MINORITY SCIENTISTS--EMPLOYMENT--UNITED STATES (v26)

MINORITY SCIENTISTS--UNITED STATES (v26)

MINORITY STUDENTS--UNITED STATES

"The dropout rate of African-American students--ages 16 to 24--declined from 22.9 percent in 1975 to 12.1 percent in 1995. Total minority enrollment at colleges and universities increased 63.4 percent in the past decade. Since 1990, the number of Latino and Hispanic students enrolled in higher education increased by 35 percent, the number of African-American students increased by 16 percent and the number of American-Indian students increased by 24 percent." (pH7379)

Jackson-Lee, Sheila (Rep.-Tex.). "Departments of Labor, Health and Human Services, And Education...Appropriations Act, 1998." Congressional Record. Daily ed. v143 n124 17 Sep 1997. pH7372-7380. section/page-level access: <http://thomas.loc.gov/cgi-bin/query/R?r105:FLD001:H07379:> (ISSN0363-7239). (X1.1A.105/1).

MINORITY TEACHERS--UNITED STATES

"In 1993-94, only 7.4 percent of the nation's teachers were African American, while 15.8 percent of the students were black. Hispanics made up 12.7 percent of the U.S. student body, but Hispanic teachers accounted for only 4.2 percent of the profession. In fact, less than 10 percent of students seeking teaching certificates in this country are members of any non-European ethnic group." (p42)

Simpson, Grant W. "Teaching: To Grow a Teacher." American School Board Journal v184 n9 Sep 1997. p42-43. (ISSN0003-0953).

"Although 33 percent of the...[U.S.'s] public-school students are minorities, only 13 percent of teachers are from minority groups. In Georgia, according to the most-recent census figures, 15 percent of those working as teachers are from minority groups, while minorities are 29 percent of the population." (p3)

Little, Jane Braxton. "United States: Janitors, Bus Drivers Go to Front of Class." The Christian Science Monitor v89 n244 13 Nov 1997. p3. The Christian Science Monitor search engine: <http://www.csmonitor.com/plweb-cgi/iops1.pl> To retrieve this article, enter the following search: ED=19971113 AND class. In the "retrieved list," click the title that matches this record. (ISSN0882-7729).

MINORITY WOMEN

see also AIDS (DISEASE)--UNITED STATES--MINORITY WOMEN

MINORITY WOMEN--EMPLOYMENT--MASSACHUSETTS --BOSTON (v26)

MINORITY WOMEN--EMPLOYMENT--SOUTHERN STATES

U.S. Equal Employment Opportunity Commission "numbers show that women's participation in the southern workforce has increased by one fifth since 1975, and they now account for 46 percent of the workforce....Latinos have nearly doubled their share of all southern jobs, from 3.9 percent to 7.1 percent, while the number of Asian American workers in the South has increased five-fold in the past twenty years, from 0.3 percent in 1975 to 1.7 percent of the total workforce in 1994. Native Americans' participation in the southern workforce has increased slightly since 1975, although they remain the smallest group tracked by the EEOC, making up 0.4 percent of the workforce." (p9)

Eckman, Anne/Green, Jordan. "Dislocation & Workforce Equity: The South at Work in the 1990s: Diversity and Continued Segregation." Southern Exposure: Institute for Southern Studies Report 1997. p9.

MINORITY WOMEN--EMPLOYMENT--UNITED STATES (v26)

In 1995, "64.1 percent of American women participated in the labor force...up from about 33 percent in 1950....Despite some improvement, women workers continue to earn less than male workers (70 percent)....African-Americans...[represent] slightly more than 11 percent of the total population of the country, and slightly less than 11 percent of the workforce....Hispanics now form over 9 percent of the civilian labor force. To this can be added growing numbers of Asian Americans, so that, by some estimates, non-whites now comprise almost 25 percent of the labor force." (p32-33)

Meiksins, Peter. "Same as It Ever Was?: The Structure of the Working Class." Monthly Review v49 n3 Jul-Aug 1997. p31-45. (ISSN0027-0520).

MINORITY WOMEN--MEDICAL CARE--UNITED STATES (v26)

MINORITY YOUTH

see AIDS (DISEASE)--UNITED STATES--MINORITY YOUTH

MISDEMEANORS

see CRIME

MISSILES, BALLISTIC

see BALLISTIC MISSILES

MISSISSIPI--EMPLOYMENT--MANUFACTURES (v26)

MISTREATMENT OF ANIMALS

see ANIMAL WELFARE

MITRAL VALVE--UNITED STATES--DISPLACEMENT (v26)

MOBILE HOMES--UNITED STATES (v26)

MOBILE TELEPHONE

see CELLULAR RADIO

MOHAMMEDANS

see MUSLIMS

MOJAVE DESERT (CALIF.)

The Mojave Desert "occupies some 25,000 square miles in southern Nevada and southeastern California....The highest recorded temperature in US history was in the Mojave (134 degrees F. [Fahrenheit] in the shade in Death Valley). Average annual precipitation in the Mojave is four inches, chiefly in the form of winter and late summer rains....Although the Mojave Desert has the simplest vegetation patterns and low species diversity, nearly 25% of all the Mojave Desert plants are endemics." (p43)

Cooperrider, Allen Y./Johnston, David W. "Biodiversity Reports: Change in the Desert--Geological and Human." Wild Earth v7 n3 Fall 1997. p42-45. (ISSN1055-1166).

MOLESTING OF CHILDREN

see CHILD SEXUAL ABUSE

MONARCH BUTTERFLY--NORTHERN MARIANAS ISLANDS --TINIAN

"A total of 116 Tinian monarch nests were located during the 1994 and 1995 field seasons. Over 60 percent of the nests were found in native tree species....There are more monarchs in the 5 percent of Tinian that is native forest than there are in the 19 percent that is secondary forest, and almost as many as in the 38 percent that is tangantangan forest." (p11)

Balis-Larsen, Martha/Sutterfield, Tim/U.S. Dept. of the Interior. Fish and Wildlife Service. "Navy Protects Island Monarch." Endangered Species Bulletin v22 n3 May-Jun 1997. p10-11.

MONEY

see also BANKS AND BANKING; COUNTERFEITS AND COUNTERFEITING; DOLLAR, AMERICAN; INFLATION (FINANCE); KOPECK

MONEY--UNITED STATES (v26)

In Berkeley, California, "a group of residents has introduced a new local currency to take the place of U.S. dollars....One BREAD (Berkeley Region Exchange and Development) hour has a value of $12, which is redeemable for that amount of labor or an equivalent value in goods. Since BREAD was introduced in May [1997], organizers have signed up 77 people offering goods and services ranging from carpentry and catering to desktop publishing and pet care. So far $1,848 worth of BREAD has entered circulation....BREAD is only the newest of 40 local currency projects nationwide. The granddaddy of them all is in Ithaca, N.Y., where a local currency was launched in 1991. $63,000 worth of Ithaca HOURS are now in circulation." (p8)

McFadyen, Deidre. "Currency: Berkeley's Funny Money." In These Times 19 Oct 1997. p8. (ISSN0160-5992).

MONEY--VALUATION--EUROPE (v26)

MONEY--VALUATION--EUROPE--JAPAN--UNITED STATES (v26)

MONEY--VALUATION--JAPAN--MEXICO--UNITED STATES (v26)

MONEY LAUNDERING (v26)

"A European Parliament study estimated that over $100 billion in profits from drug activity was successfully laundered throughout the world in 1995 from illegal drug trafficking. The same study estimated that in the decade of the 1980s laundered drug money throughout the world earned $820 billion in interest. Most of this money came from the US." (p479)

Van de Velde, James R. "Issues of Law Intensity Conflict and Law Enforcement: The Growth of Criminal...Drug Trafficking." Low Intensity Conflict & Law Enforcement v5 n3 Win 1996. p466-483. (ISSN0966-2847).

MONEY LAUNDERING--COLOMBIA--UNITED STATES

A recent New York undercover operation known as "El Dorado" "used a Treasury Department tool known as a GTO-Geographic Targeting Order. Under the GTO, designated money remitters were required to report detailed information about all cash transfers to Colombia over $750. The results of Operation 'El Dorado' were phenomenal: cash transfers by three major remitters plummeted from $67 million to $2 million; the overall number of transactions by those same remitters dropped 95 percent and the dollar amount dropped 97 percent; there has been $30 million in currency seizures, three arrests and one conviction." (pS7214)

D'Amato, Alfonse M. (Sen.-N.Y.). "Statements on Introduced Bills and Joint Resolutions." Congressional Record. Daily ed. v143 n97 10 Jun 1997. pS7210-7217. section/page-level access: <http://thomas.loc.gov/cgi-bin/query/R?r105:FLD001:S07214:> (ISSN0363-7239). (X1.1A.105/1).

MONEY LAUNDERING--ECUADOR

"In Ecuador $700 million of foreign currency was exchanged in 1990, up from $317 million in 1989. Yet according to an Ecuadorian commission's investigations, only $250-300 million of the $700 million could be attributed to legal activities such as tourism and money sent by Ecuadorians from abroad." (p479)

Van de Velde, James R. "Issues of Law Intensity Conflict and Law Enforcement: The Growth of Criminal...Drug Trafficking." Low Intensity Conflict & Law Enforcement v5 n3 Win 1996. p466-483. (ISSN0966-2847).

MONGOLISM (DISEASE)

see DOWN'S SYNDROME

MONKEYPOX--ZAIRE (v26)

MONTGOMERY GI BILL (v26)

MOON

"According to University of Michigan astronomer Richard Teske, the moon is 15 billion inches from Earth--give or take an inch....Mirrors were placed on the moon's Earth-facing hemisphere by three teams of Apollo astronauts and by one of the unmanned Soviet Lunakhod missions....In the experiment, laser radiation launched toward the moon from one of the telescopes on Earth bounces off one of the lunar mirrors and returns to the same telescope about 2.6 seconds later. Scientists determine the moon's distance by measuring as precisely as possible the time it takes laser pulses to make the round trip." (p1)

University of Michigan. News and Information Services. "How Far Is the Moon? 15 Billion Inches, Says U-M Astronomer." University of Michigan News Release 16 Dec 1997. p1-2.

MORMON CHURCH

"With 10 million members worldwide, Mormonism is one of the world's fastest growing faiths. The church is now the seventh-largest organized religion in the United States, gaining an average 1,000 members a day, according to the church....With 23,200 congregations in 160 countries, the church predicts in its literature that its global reach could soon make it the first 'world religion.'...[According to Armand Mauss, professor of sociology and religious studies at Washington State University] 'Eighty-five percent of the church's members are in the Western Hemisphere.'...[Mormon] missionaries now number 55,000, with half working in the US and half in the rest of the world....Women, who make up 53 percent of members, are not allowed into the priesthood." (p1,12)

Smillie, Dirk. "Mormon Trek Now Has a Global Reach." The Christian Science Monitor v89 n166 23 Jul 1997. p1,12. The Christian Science Monitor search engine: <http://www.csmonitor.com/plweb-cgi/iops1.pl> To retrieve this article, enter the following search: ED=19970723 AND reach. In the "retrieved list," click the title that matches this record. (ISSN0882-7729).

MOROCCO--ECONOMIC CONDITIONS (v26)

MORTALITY (v26)

see also MORTALITY, under specific topic, e.g., CANCER--MORTALITY

THE WORLD HEALTH REPORT 1997 "says the number of cancer cases is expected to at least double in most countries during the next 25 years. There will be a 33% rise in lung cancers in women and a 40% increase in prostate cancers in men in European Union countries alone by 2005." (p1) "Circulatory diseases such as heart attacks and stroke together kill 15.3 million people a year. Cancer in all its forms kills 6.3 million people a year. Chronic obstructive pulmonary disease kills 2.9 million people a year. These add up to 24.5 million deaths, or 47% of the annual global total of deaths from all causes. Of the remainder, infectious and parasitic diseases account for 17.3 million, or 33%; deaths from perinatal and neonatal causes account for 3.5 million; there are 585,000 maternal deaths; and 6 million deaths from other and unknown causes, including accidents, violence, homicide and suicide." (p2)

World Health Organization. "World Health Report 1997." Press Release 5 May 1997. p1-7. document-level access: <http://www.who.ch/whr/1997/presse.htm>

MORTALITY--AUSTRALIA

According to the Australian Bureau of Statistics, in Australia, "deaths from diabetes mellitus numbered 2,991 in 1996 and was the sixth leading cause of death, up from 7th in 1995. The 2,755 deaths from senile and presenile organic conditions, lifted this from 10th leading cause in 1995 to the eighth leading cause in 1996. The ABS, in its publication 'Causes of Death Australia'..., reports that there were 128,711 deaths registered in Australia in 1996, up 2.9 per cent on the 1995 figure. Half of these deaths were due to cancer (27 per cent of total) and Ischaemic heart disease (23 per cent of total)."

Australian Bureau of Statistics. "Deaths from Diabetes and Senile Dementia Increase." Media Release 31 Oct 1997. document-level access: <http://www.abs.gov.au/websitedbs/d3110125.nsf/4a255eef008309e44a255eef00061e57/b963d1a23d007204ca25654000761a86?OpenDocument>

According to the report, "Demography SA, 1995," by the Australian Bureau of Statistics, in South Australia, "deaths in 1995 increased by 6.9 per cent to 11,218, although the crude death rate fell from 7.7 per 1,000 population to 7.6. The leading causes of death were heart disease (31.1 per cent) and cancer (26.4 per cent)."

Australian Bureau of Statistics. "South Australians--Living Longer." Media Release 11 Jun 1997. document-level access: <http://www.abs.gov.au/websitedbs/d3110125.nsf/4a255eef008309e44a255eef00061e57/6d35166d881934c74a2564b30004f29d?OpenDocument>

The publication "Deaths, Australia," by the Australian Bureau of Statistics, says that death rate "differences are more pronounced for men. Males aged 20-69 years who had never married, experienced death rates two to four times higher than those who were married, and while the pattern is similar for women, the differences are less marked. In 1996, 128,700 deaths were registered in Australia, the highest number ever recorded. This represents an increase of 12 per cent on the number of deaths registered in 1986 (115,000) and a 14 per cent increase on those registered in 1976 (112,700)."

Australian Bureau of Statistics. "Death Rates Lower for Married Australians--ABS." Media Release 31 Oct 1997. document-level access: <http://www.abs.gov.au/websitedbs/d3110125.nsf/4a255eef008309e44a255eef00061e57/

ae9c580551bbf55bca2565400075e403?OpenDocument>

MORTALITY--GREAT BRITAIN

In Great Britain, "in 1995, stillbirth rates for all registrations where manual or non-manual status could be assigned were 5.9 per 1,000 total births among manual groups and 4.5 per 1,000 total births among non-manual groups. Rates were thus more than 30 per cent higher in manual groups....Over the period 1991 to 1993, death rates among men aged 20 to 64 were 524 per 100,000 in manual groups and 325 per 100,000 in non-manual groups. Rates were thus more than one and a half times higher in manual groups." (c749-750)

Boateng, Paul (H.C.-Brightside). "Stillbirth and Mortality Rates." Great Britain. Parliament. House of Commons. Debates. 22 Jul 1997. c749-750. section-level access: <http://www.parliament.the-stationery-office.co.uk/pa/cm199798/cmhansrd/cm970722/debtext/70722-04.htm#70722-04_sbhd3>

"According to the Office for National Statistics, during 1994, 32,143 people in England and Wales died from lung cancer. Heart disease dispatched 135,440. Chronic liver disease killed 3,244. There were 508 deaths from AIDS. Deaths caused by falling down the stairs came to 481 (plus two from escalators). There were 373 people murdered. Excessive heat or cold killed 301. Thirty-eight died from salmonella. Thirty people drowned in the bath. Eighteen people fell from cliffs. Eleven died from Listeria poisoning." (p43)

Green, Emily. "Food: Bacteria Aren't All Bad, But Try Telling That to Sainsbury's." New Statesman 23 May 1997. p43. (ISSN0028-6842).

MORTALITY--IRELAND

According to Ireland's Central Statistics Office, "there were 31,500 deaths in 1996 (16,500 males and 15,000 females) including 278 deaths of infants under one year of age. The infant mortality rate of 5.5 per cent per 1,000 births is in line with the European average of 5.7....13,900 deaths were due to diseases of the circulatory system and some 7,600 of these were due to heart disease (including almost 5,100 due to heart attacks); 7,300 deaths were due to various types of cancer; 4,800 deaths were caused by diseases of the respiratory system; and 1,300 deaths were caused by injuries and poisonings."

Ireland. Central Statistics Office. "Births, Marriages and Deaths in 1996." Press Release 22 May 1997. document-level access: <http://www.cso.ie/pressreleases/vstats1996.html>

MORTALITY--NEW YORK (N.Y.) (v26)

MORTALITY--POLITICS AND GOVERNMENT

"A study to be released by George W. Scully, 'Murder by the State,' to be published by the...[National] Center for Policy Analysis, Dallas, states that at least four-times more people have been killed this century by their own...[governments] than by war....In this century an estimated 42M [million] combatants have died in wars. Yet at least 170M persons and possibly as many as 360M have been killed by...[government] action. Communist...[governments] have been the biggest slaughterers: the Soviet Union and China have killed millions." (unpaginated)

"The Biggest Killer of All: Rogue Governments." Security Letter v27 n15 2 Sep 1997. (ISSN0363-4922).

MORTALITY--UNITED STATES (v26)

"In 1995, 2.3 million people died in the U.S., the greatest one-year total ever recorded....The age-adjusted death rate (which takes into account the age structure of the population) hit an all-time low in 1995, at 503.9 per 100,000 population. Life expectancy at birth continued to increase, reaching 75.8 in 1995. The infant death rate also dipped to an all-time low of 7.6 per 1,000 live births." (p40)

Miller, Berna. "Kaleidoscope: For Whom the Bell Tolls." American Demographics v19 n11 Nov 1997. p40. article-level access: <http://www.demographics.com/publications/ad/97_ad/9711_ad/ad971120.htm> (ISSN0163-4089).

"In 1995 a record 2,312,132 deaths were registered in the United States, 33,138 more than the previous high recorded in 1994. The crude death rate for 1995 was 880 deaths per 100,000 population, slightly higher than the year before. However, the 1995 age-adjusted death rate for the total population decreased to an all-time low of 503.9 per 100,000....Heart disease, cancer, and stroke continue as the three leading causes of death. Chronic obstructive pulmonary disease and accidents round out the top five causes. The only change in the ranking from 1994 to 1995 was a drop in homicide from 11th to 12th in the ranking. The death rate for homicide dropped 8.7 percent from 1994 to 1995, the largest decline in more than a decade."

U.S. National Center for Health Statistics. "1995 Final Mortality Statistics Released." Fact Sheet 12 Jun 1997. document-level access: <http://www.cdc.gov/nchswww/releases/97facts/97sheets/95morrel.htm>

According to the CDC's 1996 Vital Statistic Report, in the U.S., "the age-adjusted homicide rate dropped an estimated 11 percent in 1996, from 9.4 homicides per 100,000 population in 1995 to 8.4 in 1996. The age-adjusted suicide rate dropped an estimated 4 percent in 1996, from 11.2 to 10.8....Although they have declined for the total population, homicide and suicide remain the second and third leading cause of death respectively among young persons ages 15-24."

U.S. Dept. of Health and Human Services. "Vital Statistics Report Shows Significant Gains in Health." Press Release 11 Sep 1997. document-level access: <http://www.hhs.gov/news/press/1997pres/970911a.html>

"According to provisional data there were 2,311,000 deaths last year [in the U.S.] compared with a final total of 2,312,132 in 1995 and 2,278,994 in 1994. The corresponding death rates were 8.7 per 1,000 in 1996 and 8.8 per 1,000 during the two previous years." (p2)

Kranczer, Stanley. "Record High U.S. Life Expectancy." Statistical Bulletin v78 n4 Oct-Dec 1997. p2-8. (ISSN0790-8334).

MORTGAGE GUARANTEE INSURANCE--UNITED STATES --COSTS (v26)

MORTGAGE LOANS, REVERSE--UNITED STATES --AGED (v26)

MORTGAGES--MICHIGAN--DETROIT (v26)

MOSCOW (RUSSIA)--ECONOMIC CONDITIONS

"Moscow--a city of more than 2,000 banks--hoards more than three-quarters of Russia's financial resources. Its businesses generate nearly 20 percent of the national wealth. Its residents have more money to spend than any other Russians....Moscow is now the third-most-expensive city in the world, according to international surveys." (p7)

Ford, Peter. "International: Moscow at 850: Dowdy and Drab Gets High Gloss." The Christian Science Monitor v89 n196 4 Sep 1997. p1,7. The Christian Science Monitor search engine: <http://www.csmonitor.com/plweb-cgi/iops1.pl> To retrieve this article, enter the following search: ED=19970904 AND gloss. In the "retrieved list," click the title that matches this record. (ISSN0882-7729).

MOTHERS

see MENTAL ILLNESS--UNITED STATES--MOTHERS; TEENAGE MOTHERS

MOTHERS--DEVELOPING COUNTRIES--MORTALITY (v26)

MOTHERS--HEALTH AND HYGIENE (v26)

MOTHERS--MORTALITY (v26)

MOTHERS--UNITED STATES (v26)

MOTHERS--UNITED STATES--IMMIGRANTS (v26)

MOTHERS--ZIMBABWE--MORTALITY (v26)

MOTION PICTURE INDUSTRY--EUROPE (v26)

MOTION PICTURE INDUSTRY--QUEBEC (PROVINCE) --MONTREAL

In Montreal, Quebec, "in the past five years, foreign shooting--mostly American, and mostly TV movies of the week and feature films--has steadily increased, reaching $86 million in 1996. Domestic production, particularly for TV (which accounts for 70 per cent of Montreal's activity overall), is booming as well, especially with the proliferation of specialty channels. Last year, both foreign and domestic producers spent a record-breaking $405 million on entertainment programming and commercials in Montreal, placing the city third behind Toronto and Vancouver." (p88)

Branswell, Brenda. "Films: Montreal, Movie Capital." Maclean's v110 n42 20 Oct 1997. p88-89. (ISSN0024-9262).

MOTION PICTURE THEATERS--SWEDEN (v26)

MOTION PICTURES

see also SMOKING IN MOTION PICTURES

MOTION PICTURES--RATING OF--UNITED STATES --PUBLIC OPINION

According to an annual public-opinion survey conducted for the Motion Picture Association of America, "in 1996, 80 percent of parents said they found the current [movie] rating system either fairly useful or very useful....The National Institute on Media and the Family (NIMF) surveyed parents in 1996 and found that 61 percent think the current movie-rating system does not provide enough information for them to make 'good decisions.' And 89 percent say they'd like more detailed information." (p3)

Marks, Alexandra. "United States: One Mom's Crusade to Make Cinema Safe for Young Tots." The Christian Science Monitor v90 n11 10 Dec 1997. p3. The Christian Science Monitor search engine: <http://www.csmonitor.com/plweb-cgi/iops1.pl> To retrieve this article, enter the following search: ED=19971210 AND tots. In the "retrieved list," click the title that matches this record. (ISSN0882-7729).

MOTOR VEHICLES

see AUTOMOBILES; LIMOUSINES; RECREATIONAL VEHICLES; SCHOOL BUSES; SNOWMOBILES; SPORT UTILITY VEHICLES

MOTORCYCLING ACCIDENTS--CALIFORNIA (v26)

MOTORS--BRAZIL (v26)

MOUNTAINS--CHINA (v26)

MOVING, HOUSEHOLD--MICHIGAN--DETROIT

"Between 1985 and 1990, Metro Detroiters moved from city-to-city within the tricounty area 950,000 times, according to the Census--an average of 522 moves between cities per day....71 percent of suburban residents have lived in at least one other Metro Detroit city...; 38 percent of Detroiters have lived elsewhere in the region." (p7 secA)

French, Ron/Daugherty, Jane/Kiska, Tim. "Archer Landslide: THE DETROIT NEWS WWJ 950 Exit Poll: Suburbs Back Archer and Rebirth of Detroit." Detroit News 5 Nov 1997. p1,7 secA.

MOVING, HOUSEHOLD--UNITED STATES (v26)

According to the U.S. Census Bureau, "about 43 million Americans, 16 percent of the population, moved during the March 1995-March 1996 time frame. Most of the moves during the 1995-96 period were local: About two-thirds of movers (26.7 million) stayed in the same county, 8 million moved between counties within the same state, 6.5 million changed states and 1.4 million moved to the U.S. from abroad....Persons aged 20-29 years were the most likely movers (33 percent) during the survey period while those ages 55 and over were the least likely to be movers (less than 10 percent in each age group)....Whites had lower overall rates of moving (16 percent) than either African Americans or Asian and Pacific Islanders (about 20 percent each). Persons of Hispanic origin had the highest move rate (23 percent). Renters were about four times more likely than homeowners to have moved during the period of the survey (34 percent versus 8 percent)."

U.S. Dept. of Commerce. Economic & Statistics Administration. "More People Left than Moved into Metro Areas in 1995-96, Census Bureau Reports." Census Bureau Press Release 3 Dec 1997. document-level access: <http://www.census.gov/Press-Release/cb97-194.html>

In the U.S., "of the 42 million people, or 16.5 million households, who moved in 1994, most were headed by people ages 20-24. People between 25 and 29 were the next most mobile, and 30-35 were next, with the likelihood of moving decreasing with each year, according to the U.S. Census Bureau." (p1 secE) "Fewer than 16 percent of those moving in any year change states; far fewer move thousands of miles...." (p2 secE)

Dickson, Barbara S. "Accent: Starting Over." Detroit News 24 Jul 1997. p1-2 secE.

"Almost half of the 43 million Americans who are changing addresses this year will do so between May and Labor Day, industry specialists say. The average American, the US Census Bureau adds, makes 12 moves during a lifetime....The average shipment of household goods now weighs in at a record 7,100 pounds, according to Mayflower Transit." (p9)

Gardner, Marilyn. "Making Connections: Getting a Move On--A New Address, A New Perspective." The Christian Science Monitor v89 n157 10 Jul 1997. p9. The Christian Science Monitor search engine: <http://www.csmonitor.com/plweb-cgi/iops1.pl> To retrieve this article, enter the following search: ED=19970710 AND perspective. In the "retrieved list," click the title that matches this record. (ISSN0882-7729).

MOVING, HOUSEHOLD--UNITED STATES--RETIREES

In the U.S., "every year, 5 percent of retirees--about 400,000 people, according to the 1990 Census--move out of state. Another 5 percent change residences within their own state....Already, as the first baby boomers turn 50, 18 percent say they expect to move out of state when they retire, according to a 1997 study by the Del Webb Corp. in Phoenix." (p10)

Gardner, Marilyn. "New Outlooks on Retirement: Mobile Retirees Have More than Florida on Their Minds." The Christian Science Monitor v89 n241 7 Nov 1997. p10-11. The Christian Science Monitor search engine: <http://www.csmonitor.com/plweb-cgi/iops1.pl> To retrieve this article, enter the following search: ED=19971107 AND minds. In the "retrieved list," click the title that matches this record. (ISSN0882-7729).

MOVING, HOUSEHOLD--UNITED STATES--WHITES (v26)

MOVING PICTURE INDUSTRY

see MOTION PICTURE INDUSTRY

MOZAMBIQUE--ECONOMIC CONDITIONS

The World Bank lists Mozambique's "annual GNP at US$80 per person--the lowest of any country in the world....About 75 percent of all public investment in health care, schools, and family planning is paid for by international aid....Mozambique's economy is beginning to grow again--at about 6 percent per year in the 1990s." (p7)

Weber, Elizabeth. "Spotlight: Mozambique." Population Today v25 n9 Sep 1997. p7. (ISSN0749-2448).

MOZAMBIQUE--SOCIAL CONDITIONS (v26)

In Mozambique, "illiteracy has fallen to about 67 percent from more than 90 percent in 1975....The average age of the Mozambican population is 17 years, and at current growth rates, the population will double within 25 years....About 80 percent of the labor force in Mozambique is involved in agriculture, much of it at the subsistence level....The UN's most recent estimate of the number of remaining land mines is 100,000, down from 2 million." (p7)

Weber, Elizabeth. "Spotlight: Mozambique." Population Today v25 n9 Sep 1997. p7. (ISSN0749-2448).

MUDFLOWS--IDAHO

"After heavy rains triggered 905 massive mudslides during the winter of 1995-96 on the Clearwater National Forest in central Idaho, agency officials ordered an investigation of the causes and extent of damage to streams from 400,000 cubic yards of debris....Preliminary results released by Deputy Northern Regional Forester Kathy McAllister showed that 58 percent of the slides were related to logging roads....The agency's preliminary results showed that 29 percent of the mudslides were natural, and 12 percent came from logged slopes, according to McAllister." (p5)

Lenderman, Jason. "Hotline: Idaho: Activists Wade through Mudslides." High Country News v29 n20 27 Oct 1997. p5. (ISSN0191-5657).

MULTICULTURALISM--CANADA (v26)

MULTICULTURALISM--CANADA--PUBLIC OPINION (v26)

MULTICULTURALISM--UNITED STATES

"The U.S. Census Bureau reports that the number of interracial marriages in 1990 was about 1.1 million, up from 150,000 20 years earlier. Mixed-race children rose from 4 percent of all children nationwide in 1980 to 6 percent in 1990." (p1 secB)

Oguntoyinbo, Lekan. "Local News: Racial Categories Stir Discord." Detroit Free Press 9 Jul 1997. p1,3 secB.

MULTICULTURALISM--UNITED STATES--PUBLIC OPINION

In a July 1994 U.S. survey, published in the September 21 edition of the GLOBE AND MAIL, "a majority of whites (51%) believed that equal rights for racial minorities have been pushed too far, up from 42% two years earlier. 82% of US residents believe that people moving to the US to live should be subjected to more restrictions and controls....A record 65% of US whites approved of cross-racial dating--up from 47% in 1987. 60% denied school boards the right to fire teachers who are known homosexuals, up from 42% in 1987." (p35)

Adam, Heribert. "Anti-Semitism and Anti-Black Racism: Nazi Germany and Apartheid South Africa." Telos n108 Sum 1996. p25-46.

MULTINATIONAL CORPORATIONS

see INTERNATIONAL BUSINESS ENTERPRISES

MULTIPHASIC HEALTH SCREENING--UNITED STATES

"The US-based Environmental Defense Fund (EDF) has requested commitments from the CEOs of the 100 top chemical manufacturers in the US to complete--and publicly disclose the results of--preliminary health screening tests on each company's top-selling chemicals before the year 2000....EDF...released a study, 'Toxic Ignorance,' that documents the absence of health-effects screening tests for 71% of the 3,000 highest-volume chemicals in the US economy (excluding pesticides, food additives, and drugs and cosmetics)....EDF says the total cost of the health screening tests would be 1/10 of a cent to 2/3 of a cent per dollar of profit for the top 100 US companies, which made profits of US $29.4 billion last year on $230.5 billion of chemical sales." (p12)

"Regulatory and Policy Trends: Chemical Reporting in the Spotlight in North America." Business and the Environment v8 n9 Sep 1997. p12-13. (ISSN1052-7206).

MULTIPLE BIRTH

see also TWINS

"Some 20 to 25 percent of IVF [in vitro fertilization] pregnancies result in multiple births, including triplets and higher-order multiple births in 2 to 3 percent of cases (American Society for Reproductive Medicine 1995)....Twins naturally occur in only about seven deliveries per one thousand, and triplets, quadruplets, and quintuplets occur in 1 in 9,520, 1 in 600,000, and 1 in 15,000,000 births, respectively (Kelly 1986; Petrikovsky and Vintzileos 1989). One recent study reported that assisted reproductive technology contributed to 22 percent of U.S. triplet and higher-order multiple births during 1990 and 1991 (Wilcox et al. 1996)." (p1229)

Neumann, Peter J. "Should Health Insurance Cover IVF?: Issues and Options." Journal of Health Politics, Policy and Law v22 n5 Oct 1997. p1215-1239. (ISSN0361-6878).

MULTIPLE BIRTH--ALABAMA

"In 1975, 1.9 percent of births in Alabama resulted from multiple deliveries, but by 1995 this had grown to 2.5 percent, a 32 percent increase. The increase in multiple births has been especially great for Alabama pregnancies with more than two fetuses. In 1975 there were only 15 babies born in pregnancies with more than two fetuses. In 1995 there were 76, a staggering 400 percent increase in these births."

Alabama. Dept. of Public Health. "Multiple Deliveries Increase Risks." News Release 13 Jun 1997. document-level access: <http://www.alapubhealth.org/Press/pr061397b.htm>

MULTIPLE BIRTH--HEALTH ASPECTS--UNITED STATES

In the U.S., "the 1995 infant mortality rate for infants in multiple deliveries (50.5 deaths per 1,000 live births) was almost six times as high as the rate for babies in single deliveries (8.8 per 1,000 live births)....In 1995, 61.8 percent of babies in multiple deliveries were of low birth weight. This was eight times as high as the percent for infants in single deliveries. Babies born in multiple deliveries are even more likely to be of very low birth weight (less than 1,500 grams). In 1995, 14.8 percent of multiple birth babies were of very low birth weight, compared to 1.5 percent of singleton infants. Thus, these babies were 10 times as likely to be born at very low birth weights as were their singleton counterparts."

Alabama. Dept. of Public Health. "Multiple Deliveries Increase Risks." News Release 13 Jun 1997. document-level access: <http://www.alapubhealth.org/Press/pr061397b.htm>

In the U.S., "triplet births are at much greater risk than single births. Infant mortality rates are 12 times higher for these births than for single births. The average birth weight of a triplet newborn is only half that of a single birth and the period of gestation is, on average, 7 weeks shorter. For 1995, 92 percent of triplets were born preterm compared with just over 10 percent of births in single deliveries. Moreover, triplets are 12 times more likely to die within the first year of life."

U.S. National Center for Health Statistics. "Multiple Births Multiply during Past Two Decades." Press Release 13 Nov 1997. document-level access: <http://www.cdc.gov/nchswww/releases/97facts/97sheets/triple2.htm>

MULTIPLE BIRTH--UNITED STATES (v26)

In the U.S., "the number of triplet and other higher order multiple births continues to increase, up 8 percent from 1994 to 1995. The number of twin births declined slightly, but the overall multiple birth ratio rose to 26.1 per 1,000 births."

U.S. National Center for Health Statistics. "1995 Birth Statistics Released." Fact Sheet 10 Jun 1997. document-level access: <http://www.cdc.gov/nchswww/releases/97facts/97sheets/95natrel.htm>

In the U.S., "up from 1,034 births in 1971 to 4,973 for 1995, the increase in higher order multiple births (triplets, quadruplets, and quintuplets) reflect the rising number of births to women in their thirties, who are more likely to have a multiple birth, and the use of fertility-enhancing drugs and techniques....Over the last decade, increases in the number of triplet births averaged 11 percent a year. The ratio of triplet births per 100,000 births rose 272 percent between 1980 and 1995. In 1995 the 4,973 triplet and other higher order multiple births included 4,551 triplets, 365 quadruplets, and 57 quintuplets and greater births....Massachusetts reported the highest triplet birth ratio for combined years 1992-94, more than twice as high as the Nation as a whole. Other States reporting ratios at least 50 percent higher than the U.S. as a whole were New Hampshire, New Jersey and Iowa."

U.S. National Center for Health Statistics. "Multiple Births Multiply during Past Two Decades." Press Release 13 Nov 1997. document-level access: <http://www.cdc.gov/nchswww/releases/97facts/97sheets/triple2.htm>

MUNICIPAL BUDGETS--UNITED STATES (v26)

MUNICIPAL TRANSIT

see LOCAL TRANSIT

MUNICIPALITIES

see CITIES AND TOWNS

MUNITIONS

see ARMS TRANSFERS; DEFENSE INDUSTRIES; MILITARY WEAPONS; WEAPONS INDUSTRY

MURDER

see also HOMICIDE

MURDER--MICHIGAN--DETROIT (v26)

MURDER IN MASS MEDIA--UNITED STATES

"Between 1993 and 1996, the homicide rate...[in the U.S.] dropped by 20 percent. Yet, since 1993, coverage of murders on the ABC, CBS, and NBC evening news increased by an astonishing 721 percent." (p15)

Ziedenberg, Jason. "MediaReports: Justice: Cashing In on Crime." Toward Freedom v46 n7 Dec 1997-Jan 1998. p15. (ISSN0048-9898).

MUSEUM STORES--UNITED STATES

The Detroit Institute of Arts, "having expanded from one on-site gift shop to two additional shops in suburban malls,...saw its annual retail sales grow from around $350,000 10 years ago to nearly $3 million today....In the mid-1980s, the Museum Store Association, a nonprofit trade group, counted around 700 institutional members. Today, the number has grown to 1,800....Store sales are up 10 percent this year at Delaware's Winterthur Museum and up 25 percent at the Newark Museum.... The Metropolitan Museum [of Art], with 14 satellite shops in the United States and 20 franchises abroad, pulled in nearly $83 million in gross sales in 1996. The Museum of Modern Art (MoMA), with its two stores, reaped more than $21 million in total retail sales last year....At MoMA, the most successful exhibition-related product sales were generated by its 1993 Matisse retrospective ($7.5 million out of total annual shop sales of $25 million). The Philadelphia Museum of Art had both blockbuster attendance and sales at its critically acclaimed Cezanne retrospective last year. Museum sales zoomed up 169 percent to $7.2 million. Among items that flew out of the gift shop were 8,750 baseballs, emblazoned with Cezanne's signature in eye-popping orange or blue letters." (p10)

Strickland, Carol. "Arts: More Registers Ring in Museum Shops." The Christian Science Monitor v89 n143 19 Jun 1997. p10-11. The Christian Science Monitor search engine: <http://www.csmonitor.com/plweb-cgi/iops1.pl> To retrieve this article, enter the following search: ED=19970619 AND shops. In the "retrieved list," click the title that matches this record. (ISSN0882-7729).

MUSEUMS--CANADA (v26)

MUSEUMS--SWEDEN (v26)

MUSEUMS--UNITED STATES (v26)

MUSHROOM INDUSTRY--UNITED STATES

U.S. "mushroom output declined fractionally in 1995/96, and average grower prices for Agaricus (white button) mushrooms declined fractionally to 93.5 cents per pound. While fresh-market volume rose 1 percent, processing volume fell 4 percent. Prices for fresh-market sales rose 4 percent from the previous season to $1.09 per pound, while processing prices fell 15 percent to $0.579 per pound....For Shiitake mushrooms, increased output led to 9 percent lower grower prices. Specialty mushroom sales totaled $30 million, compared with $728 million for Agaricus mushrooms. Within the Agaricus category, brown mushrooms (including the portobello and crimini) were valued at $39 million. Per capita use of all mushrooms has been creeping upward and now totals 4 pounds, with fresh use accounting for 53 percent." (p5)

U.S. Dept. of Agriculture. Economic Research Service. "Summary." Vegetables and Specialties Situation and Outlook Yearbook Jul 1997. p3-5.

MUSHROOMS (v26)

MUSHROOMS--UNITED STATES (v26)

MUSIC

see also COUNTRY MUSIC

MUSIC--SWEDEN (v26)

MUSIC--UNITED STATES (v26)

In the U.S., "in 1990, fifty-two commercial radio stations nationwide programmed classical music; by last year, the number had dropped to forty-one, which represents .004 percent of the country's 10,237 commercial radio outlets. In 1960, classical music accounted for 15.5 percent of all record sales; today, despite the arrival of tapes and CDs, the figure is 3 percent and falling." (p38)

Pollak, Richard. "Articles: Can Disney Save Classical Music from a Mickey Mouse World?: Pop Invades Classical Space." Nation v265 n6 25 Aug 1997. p36,38-39. (ISSN0027-8378).

MUSIC TRADE

More musicians are bypassing records stores and releasing their singles or albums on the Internet first. There are a few reasons why artists are doing this, says a pop/rock singer Todd Rundgren "spokeswoman: It gives the artist and consumer a more direct relationship, and artists are able to keep up to 80 percent of the royalties (as compared with 10 percent if distributed from record stores)....'Something like 40 percent of the people who like a song online will go out the next day and buy the band's album,'...[Robin Bechtel, senior director of New Media at Capitol Records] says." (p13)

Parney, Lisa Leigh. "Music: Musicians Check Out the Internet for Releasing Albums." The Christian Science Monitor v89 n146 24 Jun 1997. p13. The Christian Science Monitor search engine: <http://www.csmonitor.com/plweb-cgi/iops1.pl> To retrieve this article, enter the following search: ED=19970624 AND albums. In the "retrieved list," click the title that matches this record. (ISSN0882-7729).

MUSIC TRADE--AUSTRALIA

According to the Australian Bureau of Statistics, in 1995-1996, "total income for the music business was $1,064 million. This was shared between 541 businesses comprising record companies, distributors, manufacturers of recorded music, music publishers and sound recording studios. Some 3,886 people (including working proprietors) were employed, with 60 per cent employed by record companies and distributors, 21 per cent by sound recording studios and the remainder by music publishers and manufacturers....Total sales of goods and services were valued at $897 million with record companies and distributors generating $726 million (81 per cent) and manufacturers of recorded music generating $94 m [million] (11 per cent). Publishing and sound recording royalties accounted for $136 million (13 per cent) of total income. Of these royalties, $94 million was earned by music publishers and $42 million by record companies and distributors."

Australian Bureau of Statistics. "Music Makes a Billion Dollar Sound: ABS Survey." Media Release 3 Oct 1997. document-level access: <http://www.abs.gov.au/websitedbs/d3110125.nsf/4a255eef008309e44a255eef00061e57/dc872be7bb99f9774a25652500011856?OpenDocument>

MUSIC TRADE--UNITED STATES

In the U.S. music industry, "sales of rock have been going down--from 46 percent of the total U.S. market in 1987 to 33 percent last year--and pop has also slipped (from 14 to 10 percent). R&B [rhythm and blues] and country have each jumped a bit (to 11 and 16 percent, respectively), and rap has jumped three points (to 9 percent)." (p12)

Miller, Mark Crispin. "Articles: The National Entertainment State III: Who Controls the Music?" Nation v265 n6 25 Aug 1997. p11-12,15-16. (ISSN0027-8378).

MUSLIM RELIGIOUS EDUCATION

see ISLAMIC RELIGIOUS EDUCATION

MUSLIMS

"Worldwide, Sunnis make up 90 percent of Islam, so Shiites are a minority overall. Iran is the one major country in which Shiites comprise 90 percent of the population. While there has never been a precise census of the Islamic community in the Detroit area, there are probably 50,000 Muslims, evenly divided between the Sunni and Shiite traditions." (p9 secA)

Crumm, David. "Conference Brings Muslim Groups Closer." Detroit Free Press 8 Dec 1997. p1,9 secA.

MUSLIMS--POLITICS AND GOVERNMENT

"Over 700 million Muslims live in democratic or semidemocratic states--Pakistan (140 million), Bangladesh (110 million), Turkey (60 million), Iran (65 million), Malaysia (20 million), Indonesia (200 million) and India (135 million). In three Islamic states, women have been elected as the top government leader: Tansu Ciller in Turkey, Begum Khalida Zia in Bangladesh and Benazir Bhutto in Pakistan." (p148)

Khan, M. A. Muqtedar. "Policy Entrepreneurs: The Third Dimension in American Foreign-Policy Culture." Middle East Policy v5 n3 Sep 1997. p140-154. (ISSN1061-1924).

MUTILATION

see GENERATIVE ORGANS, FEMALE--MUTILATION

MUTUAL FUNDS

International mutual "funds now post $239 billion in assets, compared with $7 billion in 1987, according to the Investment Company Institute, a fund industry trade group....Some studies show that a portfolio with 30 percent in foreign stocks and 70 percent in American stocks would have delivered higher returns at lower risk than an all-US portfolio during the past 20 years. But another study, by Birinyi Associates in Greenwich, Conn., finds that foreign markets, on average, move in the same direction as America's 77 percent of the time....International funds have gained only about 10 percent annually since 1987, compared with 16 percent for the typical domestic equity fund, according to Lipper Analytical Services." (p8)

Willis, Clint. "Business & Money: Mutual Funds: Cross Oceans to Soften Risks." The Christian Science Monitor v89 n225 16 Oct 1997. p8. The Christian Science Monitor search engine: <http://www.csmonitor.com/plweb-cgi/iops1.pl> To retrieve this article, enter the following search: ED=19971016 AND risks. In the "retrieved list," click the title that matches this record. (ISSN0882-7729).

MUTUAL FUNDS--CANADA (v26)

MYCOTOXINS--QUEBEC (PROVINCE)

"One consultant on indoor air contamination, Marie-France Pinard, of the Montreal firm Laboratoire Vital/Air, presented the results of microbial testing in more than 300 houses in Quebec's Saguenay region....The highly toxigenic fungus 'S. [Stachybotrys] atra' (now renamed 'Stachybotrys chatarum') was found growing on surfaces in 15% of the inspected homes. 'Stachybotrys'...does not grow readily in dust, where it turned up in only 1% of the homes." (p9)

Schoen, Deborah. "Research Updates: From the Annual Meeting in Montreal, Quebec, Of the American Institute...Sciences: Fungal Sleuths." BioScience v48 n1 Jan 1998. p9-10. (ISSN0006-3568).

MYOCARDIAL INFARCTION--UNITED STATES (v26)

MYOCARDIAL INFARCTION--UNITED STATES--AGED (v26)

MYOCARDIAL INFARCTION--UNITED STATES--WOMEN --ATTITUDES

"PREVENTION magazine conducted a survey of [American] women and their perceived health risks in September 1996. Only one-third of women surveyed realize that they are at far greater risk of dying from a heart attack than from breast cancer. In fact, women are five times more likely to die of a heart attack than breast cancer....When asked how likely women thought they were to have a heart attack at some point in their lives, only 14 percent of respondents think it is very likely and 32 percent think it is somewhat likely." (p27)

Kate, Nancy Ten. "Kaleidoscope: Taking It to Heart." American Demographics v19 n5 May 1997. p26-27. article-level access: <http://www.demographics.com/Publications/AD/97_ad/9705_ad/AD970510.htm> (ISSN0163-4089).

MYOCARDIUM--DISEASES--UNITED STATES (v26)

MYSTICISM--ISRAELIS--ATTITUDES

"A recent survey by 'the mass circulation daily YEDIOT AHRONOT...showed...that 11% of Israelis believe that crystals can heal, 22% believe in seances, 27% believe that a person's future can be foreseen by reading his hands, 39% believe in astrology, 40% believe in reincarnation and 41% believe in the power of blessings or curses of rabbis thought to have supernatural powers. Moreover, among religious Israelis, this last figure rose 82%.'" (p11)

Foner, Henry. "It Happened in Israel." Jewish Currents v51 n7 Jul-Aug 1997. p10-11. (ISSN0021-0639).

NAMES, GEOGRAPHICAL--UNITED STATES

"According to the U.S. Geological Survey, more than 1,000 sites nationwide have 'squaw' in their name, including 189 in Oregon alone. Native American activists are calling for a national solution. Last year they submitted a request to the Federal Board on Geographic Names to ban the word 'squaw.' A similar ban was enacted in 1963, changing the name at 143 sites from 'Nigger' to 'Negro.' Minnesota, which has a large Native American population, already banned the word 'squaw' in 1996....[Minnesota] mandated that all geographical features named 'squaw' be renamed. So far, 8 of 23 sites have been changed." (p11)

Tomas, Lois. "Native America: What's in a Name." In These Times 19 Oct 1997. p11. (ISSN0160-5992).

NANNIES--UNITED STATES (v26)

NARCOTIC TRADE

see DRUG TRAFFIC

NARCOTICS

see also COCAINE; HEROIN; MARIJUANA

NARCOTICS--DEVELOPING COUNTRIES

"It is estimated that in the late 1980s Latin America produced between 500 and 700 metric tons of cocaine base. In 1996, that jumped to between 800 and 1,200 tons. In 1988, Burma and Afghanistan were producing an estimated 1,600 to 2,000 metric tons of opium. In 1996, production had jumped to 4,500 tons." (p4)

Marks, Alexandra. "United States: 'Mom and Pop' Drug Runners Replace Cartels." The Christian Science Monitor v89 n212 26 Sep 1997. p4. The Christian Science Monitor search engine: <http://www.csmonitor.com/plweb-cgi/iops1.pl> To retrieve this article, enter the following search: ED=19970926 AND cartels. In the "retrieved list," click the title that matches this record. (ISSN0882-7729).

NARCOTICS--ECONOMIC ASPECTS--COLOMBIA

"Most experts put the estimate of incomes from the [Colombian] drug trade within a range of $1.5-3 billion per year. This sum is equal to twice the income produced by the sale of other cash crops and represents about 4% of the GDP (El Espectador, 1995). The size of the social sector that is directly involved with the production and/or trade in illicit drugs (coca, poppies, marijuana) is approximately equal to the number of coffee growers, i.e., from 250-300,000 persons." (p58)

Richani, Nazih. "The Political Economy of Violence: The War-System in Colombia." Journal of Interamerican Studies & World Affairs v39 n2 Sum 1997. p37-81. (ISSN0022-1937).

NARCOTICS--UNITED STATES

"According to the 1994 Clinton 'National Drug Control Strategy Report,' since only 1988 $52 billion have been spent on counterdrug efforts by the US. Yet there are now 2.7 million hardcore drug users, according to the same source. The White House report, 'Reducing the Impact of Drugs on American Society, 1995,' notes that $49 billion are spent by Americans annually on illicit drugs: $30.8 billion on cocaine, $7.1 billion on heroin, $9.0 billion on marijuana, [and] $1.8 billion on all other illegal drugs. (As comparisons, $19 billion are spent on all books per year in the US, $28 billion on all sporting equipment and toys combined. Over $44 billion are spent on alcohol per year by Americans, $37 billion on tobacco; federal, state and local expenditures on criminal justice total $46 billion.) The wholesale value alone of illicit drugs smuggled into the US each year is $25 billion. The White House claims that drugs cost the nation's taxpayers $67 billion a year." (p466-467)

Van de Velde, James R. "Issues of Law Intensity Conflict and Law Enforcement: The Growth of Criminal...Drug Trafficking." Low Intensity Conflict & Law Enforcement v5 n3 Win 1996. p466-483. (ISSN0966-2847).

In the U.S., "the number of occasional cocaine users (people who used in the past year but on fewer than 12 days) was 2.6 million in 1996, similar to what it was in 1995....The rate of current use of hallucinogens among youth age 12-17 has nearly doubled in two years (1.1 percent in 1994, 1.7 percent in 1995, and 2.0 percent in 1996)....There were an estimated 141,000 new heroin users in 1995, and there has been an increasing trend in new heroin use since 1992."

U.S. Dept. of Health and Human Services. "National Drug Survey Results Released: Overall Drug Use Levels Stay the Same; Possible Decrease in Youth Drug Use." Press Release 6 Aug 1997. document-level access: <http://www.hhs.gov/news/press/1997pres/970806.html>

NARCOTICS--UNITED STATES--YOUTH--ATTITUDES (v26)

NARCOTICS, CONTROL OF--GREAT BRITAIN (v26)

NARCOTICS, CONTROL OF--MEXICO (v26)

NARCOTICS, CONTROL OF--MICHIGAN

LAWNET, the Livingston and Washtenaw Narcotics Enforcement Team, "is one of 24 task forces in 80 of the 83 counties in Michigan....In 1996, LAWNET executed 88 search warrants and seized drugs with an estimated street value of $2,885,546. Other seizures were used to fund the operation: $202,282 in confiscated cash, $59,452 in real estate and $32,864 worth of personal property, such as cars....But the $294,000 in 1996 forfeitures left the unit about $99,000 in the hole for operating costs." (p1 secC)

Oppat, Susan L. "Local: Drug Fighters Going Broke: Wised-Up Dealers Have Cut Off Funding Source." Ann Arbor News 19 Oct 1997. p1,4 secC.

"The 20 'multi-jurisdictional task forces' that cover most of Michigan received $6 million in federal grants in 1996, a year when they arrested 3,800 suspected drug violators, confiscated nearly 1,000 firearms and took $69 million in illegal drugs off the street....Annual reports submitted to State Police for 1996 indicate 80 percent of the drug-team arrests were classified as either users or the lowest level drug dealers. Among the common street drugs, the teams reported 115 charges involving heroin; 567 involving crack; 1,147 involving cocaine; and 3,307 involving marijuana." (p1,9 secA)

Hoogterp, Edward/Oppat, Susan. "Pairing Police." Ypsilanti Press 3 Aug 1997. p1,9 secA.

NARCOTICS, CONTROL OF--UNITED STATES (v26)

NARCOTICS, CONTROL OF--UNITED STATES --FINANCE (v26)

NARCOTICS, CONTROL OF--UNITED STATES. NATIONAL GUARD (v26)

NARCOTICS AND CRIME--MEXICO--TIJUANA (v26)

NASAL ALLERGY

see HAY FEVER

NATIONAL DEBTS

see DEBTS, PUBLIC

NATIONAL HOLIDAYS

see HOLIDAYS

NATIONAL PARKS AND RESERVES

see also AMERICAN BISON--YELLOWSTONE NATIONAL PARK; UNITED STATES. NATIONAL PARK SERVICE; WOLVES--IDAHO--YELLOWSTONE NATIONAL PARK; YELLOWSTONE NATIONAL PARK

NATIONAL PARKS AND RESERVES--ARGENTINA

"Argentina has an extensive and well-developed national park system that does not equitably represent the country's 18 ecoregions. The country has a total land area of 2.7 million square kilometers, or about two percent of the world's land surface, which accounts for 12.3 percent of the world's mushroom species, 12.2 percent of the world's gymnosperm species, 10.9 percent of birds, and 8.7 percent of mammals."

World Bank. "Global Environment Facility Helps Protect Argentine Biodiversity." Press Release 22 Oct 1997. document-level access: <http://www.worldbank.org/html/extdr/extme/1510.htm>

NATIONAL PARKS AND RESERVES--CALIFORNIA --ORANGE COUNTY

In California, "in July 1996, the 38,000-acre Orange County Nature Reserve officially opened. This permanent reserve was created by combining 21,000 acres of land set aside by The Irvine Company, the county's largest landowner and developer, with 17,000 acres held by other local entities, including county and state parks. Private landowners and public agencies, including the Orange County Transportation Corridor Agencies, are slated to contribute a $10.6 million permanent endowment to manage the reserve system over time....Among the reserve's wildlife residents are 40 imperiled species, including the tiny arboreal salamander, a lizard called the orange-throated whiptail, a flower known as the Laguna Beach dudleya and many endangered birds: least Bell's vireo, peregrine falcon, southwestern willow flycatcher and...the California gnatcatcher." (p21)

Holing, Dwight. "The Coastal Sage Scrub Solution." Nature Conservancy v47 n4 Jul-Aug 1997. p16-24. (ISSN0028-5200).

NATIONAL PARKS AND RESERVES--ENVIRONMENTAL ASPECTS--OREGON

"The World Wildlife Fund, a Washington, D.C. environmental organization, this year gave a group of biologists from around the world free access to scientific databases, and asked them to assess 200 of the world's most diverse 'eco-regions.' The biologists working on North America ranked the Klamath-Siskiyou area [in Oregon] third among temperate, coniferous forests for richness of plant and wildlife species, says Dominick DellaSala, director of the fund's U.S. Forest Conservation Program. But logging and mining have also made the area the world's 'second most endangered' ecologically sensitive region....Under [U.S. President Bill] Clinton's Forest Plan, 93 percent of the Siskiyou National Forest, is 'fairly' restricted to logging and mining. This means the agency manages 7 percent of the forest for timber, while the rest is in reserve where only treatment logging is done." (p3)

Chilson, Peter. "Western Roundup: In Oregon, Tension over Coho and Trees." High Country News v29 n13 7 Jul 1997. p3. (ISSN0191-5657).

NATIONAL PARKS AND RESERVES--MICHIGAN

In the June 1997 issue of CONSUMERS REPORT, Sleeping Bear Dunes National Lakeshore in Empire, Michigan "was rated second in a poll of the magazine's readers--scoring 86 out of a possible 100. Point Reyes National Seashore in California was No. 1, with a score of 87....Sleeping Bear is among 100 federal sites charging vehicle entrance fees for the first time, under a pilot program. The cost is $7 a vehicle, which is good for a week, or $15 for the entire year. [Superintendent, Ivan] Miller [of Sleeping Bear] estimates the fees will provide an additional $300,000 for operations. About 1.2 million people visit the park annually to hike the unspoiled sand hills, walk along the Lake Michigan beaches and canoe the Platte River." (p3 secB)

Bevier, Thomas. "Michigan: Sleeping Bear Dunes Fights a Shrinking Federal Budget." Detroit News 22 Jun 1997. p3 secB.

NATIONAL PARKS AND RESERVES--UNITED STATES (v26)

"Less than 5 percent of America's native and ancient forests remain standing....In 1995,...nearly 4 billion board feet of timber was produced from taxpayer-supported raids of national forests....Less than 5 percent of the 100 billion board feet of wood consumed annually in the US comes from national forests....Well over $1 billion was spent in 1996 alone to log our national forests." (p8)

Orr, David. "Earth Island in Action: John Muir Project: Zero Cut on Public Lands." Earth Island Journal v12 n3 Sum 1997. p8. (ISSN1041-0406).

"The number of recreation visits to National Park Service (NPS) facilities in Ohio increased 133 percent between 1991 and 1996, more than in any other state. Other growth states for National Parks include Alaska (up 51 percent), West Virginia (37 percent), Texas (25 percent), Idaho (22 percent), and Wyoming (17 percent). In the U.S. as a whole, however, the number of recreation visits to NPS facilities is down. It increased from 268 million in 1991 to 273 million in 1993, but has since declined to 269 million in 1995 and 266 million in 1996....In 1993,...Gulf Islands National Seashore in Florida had 5.5 million visitors. In October 1995, Hurricane Opal visited. In 1996, only 2.6 million people came....In Ohio,...expansions to the Cuyahoga Valley National Recreation Area brought 3.5 million visitors in 1996, compared with 1.4 million in 1991....California NPS sites have the most visitors of any state, but they may be full: visits there declined from 36.3 million in 1991 to 34.6 million in 1996." (p1-2)

"Hot Markets for Outdoor Vacations." Forecast v17 n7 Jul 1997. p1-2. article-level access: <http://www.demographics.com/Publications/FC/97_fc/9707_fc/FC97071.htm> (ISSN0732-1597).

"In 1996, the nation's park system logged 265.7 million visitors, the result of a precipitous climb since about 1950 when only 25 million or so people set foot in the parks. Arches [in Utah], basically a drive-through park of only 73,000 acres, counted 856,000 visitors last year, up from only 290,000 in 1980." (p18)

Biele, Katharine. "Smaller Parks Fight Big-Park Problems." The Christian Science Monitor v89 n142 18 Jun 1997. p1,18. The Christian Science Monitor search engine: <http://www.csmonitor.com/plweb-cgi/iops1.pl> To retrieve this article, enter the following search: ED=19970618 AND problems. In the "retrieved list," click the title that matches this record. (ISSN0882-7729).

NATIONAL PARKS AND RESERVES--UNITED STATES --PUBLIC OPINION

"In a recent CONSUMER REPORTS reader survey, 93 percent of those polled said their trip to...[U.S. national parks] 'mostly' or 'completely' lived up to expectations, and 95 percent rated park personnel as 'good' or 'excellent.' But tourists may not feel that way for long if park service projections are any indication. In 1963, there were 100 million visits to national parks. By 1976, that figure had doubled. Officials expect visits to total 271 million this year, and the millennium is expected to draw 340 million tourists. In 2010...the park service expects a half-billion visitors." (p28)

Satchell, Michael. "U.S. News: Parks in Peril." U.S. News & World Report v123 n3 21 Jul 1997. p22-28. article-level access: <http://www.usnews.com/usnews/issue/970721/21PARK.HTM> (ISSN0041-5537).

NATIONAL RIFLE ASSOCIATION (v26)

NATIONAL SCHOOL LUNCH PROGRAM (v26)

In the U.S., "the second-largest food-assistance program behind food stamps, the National School Lunch Program had outlays of $5.3 billion in fiscal 1996, or an increase of almost 4 percent over fiscal 1995. The program served a total of 4.3 billion lunches in fiscal 1996, an increase of 1 percent from the previous year....The program...is available in 99 percent of all public schools and 83 percent of all schools public or private....Each school day, about 26 million children, representing about 58 percent of all children in the nearly 94,000 participating schools and residential childcare institutions, participated in the program. About 49 percent of these children received a free lunch, while another 8 percent received a reduced-price lunch...." (p51)

Oliveira, Victor/U.S. Dept. of Agriculture. Economic Research Service. "Food Assistance: Food-Assistance Spending Held Steady in 1996." Food Review v20 n1 Jan-Apr 1997. p49-56. (ISSN1056-327X).

NATIONAL SCHOOL LUNCH PROGRAM--NUTRITIONAL ASPECTS

In the U.S., in 1995, "the calcium density in school meals was 672 mg [milligrams] per 1,000 calories--42 percent higher than the calcium density in home foods eaten by children. The fiber density in school meals was 7.2 grams per 1,000 calories--4 percent higher than that in home foods eaten by children...." (p37-38)

Lin, Biing-Hwan/Frazao, Elizabeth/U.S. Dept. of Agriculture. Economic Research Service. "Nutrition: Nutritional Quality of Foods at and away from Home." Food Review v20 n2 May-Aug 1997. p33-40. (ISSN1056-327X).

In the U.S., school lunch "is the only 'complete' meal many of the 92 million children participating in the school lunch program will get all day....While...[USDA] guidelines specify that no more than 30 percent of each day's calories should come from fat (a figure that many health experts believe is too high), the average school meal derives 35 to 40 percent of calories from fat, and much of this is artery-clogging saturated fat." (p16)

Raymond, Jennifer. "Teaching Kids and Food Service about Plant-Based Foods: Helping School Lunches Make the Grade." Vegetarian Voice v22 n3 Aut 1997. p16-17,37.

(ISSN0271-1591).

NATIONAL SECURITY

see also CIVILIAN-BASED DEFENSE

NATIONAL SECURITY--ISRAEL

The Oslo agreements divided the occupied territories in Israel "into three zones. Only in Zone A, 3% of the total land area, is the Palestinian Authority responsible for security. Israel investigators found that the perpetrators of the most recent bombing came from the 97% under Israel security control." (p3)

"Editorial: Back to the Talks." Jewish Currents v51 n10 Nov 1997. p3. (ISSN0021-0639).

NATIONAL SECURITY--NEW ZEALAND--PUBLIC OPINION

In New Zealand, "according to a nationwide poll conducted late...[in May 1997], nearly three-quarters of those under 30--a category that once constituted the legislation's most popular support--say that effective security arrangements are very important for the country. The figure is up from 56 percent less than a year ago." (p7)

Cohen, David. "International: No Nukes Is Good Nukes? Ten Years after, Kiwis Soften Stance." The Christian Science Monitor v89 n141 17 Jun 1997. p7. The Christian Science Monitor search engine: <http://www.csmonitor.com/plweb-cgi/iops1.pl> To retrieve this article, enter the following search: ED=19970617 AND stance. In the "retrieved list," click the title that matches this record. (ISSN0882-7729).

NATIONAL SECURITY--UNITED STATES

In the U.S., "only 22 percent of F.B.I. internal security and terrorism cases disposed of by federal prosecutors from 1992 to 1996--forty of a total of 182--resulted in a conviction. In other words, more than three-quarters were declined by the prosecutors, dismissed by the judges or ended with a not-guilty verdict. Among the vast majority of cases that the Justice Department declined to prosecute, 65 percent were tossed out because the evidence was weak or they were otherwise legally flawed. The principal charges brought against the forty convicted people involved a wide range of crimes. Eight of those convicted had been charged with gathering defense information or delivering it to a foreign government. In seven cases the lead violation was the sale or receipt of stolen goods, in four it was counterfeiting or forgery and in two it was money laundering. There was one conviction under a law prohibiting the harboring or concealing of a person wanted in a national security case, one against the importation of obscene materials, one for the use of a fictitious name and one for the use of a counterfeit access device....The lead charge in two of the forty convictions was malicious mischief." (p21-22)

Burnham, David. "Articles: The FBI." Nation v265 n5 11 Aug 1997. p11-12,14-16,18-24. (ISSN0027-8378).

NATIVE RACES

see INDIGENOUS PEOPLES

NATURAL COMMUNITIES

see BIOTIC COMMUNITIES

NATURAL DISASTERS

see also EARTHQUAKES; ENVIRONMENTAL DEGRADATION; FLOODS; FOREST FIRES

"Economic damage from weather-related disasters reached $60 billion in 1996, the worst year on record. The damage total between 1990 and 1996 is more than $200 billion worldwide, more than four times as much damage as there was in 1980--89....Insurance company losses from weather disasters came to $9 billion in 1996, including $1.6 billion from flooding associated with Hurricane Fran and another $1.6 billion from floods in California. But this was well below the $22 billion in losses in 1992, the year of Hurricane Andrew....In July 1996, floods in China killed 2,700 people, drove 2 million from their homes, and caused economic losses of $26 billion. Just 1.5 percent of those losses were insured." (p8)

"Big Storms Flatten Insurance Profits." Forecast v17 n7 Jul 1997. p8. article-level access: <http://www.demographics.com/Publications/FC/97_fc/9707_fc/FC97077.htm> (ISSN0732-1597).

NATURAL DISASTERS--COSTS (v26)

NATURAL FOODS--PRICES--UNITED STATES (v26)

NATURAL FOODS--UNITED STATES--NUTRITIONAL ASPECTS (v26)

NATURAL FOODS--UNITED STATES--PUBLIC OPINION (v26)

NATURAL FOODS INDUSTRY--EUROPE

The European Union "where the principles of organic production originated, is the largest market for organic food outside the United States--valued at approximately $1.7 billion in 1990. Organic food sales grew by 25 percent per year in the early 1990's in France and Germany--the two largest EU member states in terms of organic sales. In 1994, these two countries alone had organic retail food sales of approximately $2 billion, equal in size to the entire U.S. organic food market." (p30)

Vandeman, Ann M./Hayden, Beth/U.S. Dept. of Agriculture. Economic Research Service. "Market Trends: New Law Paves Way for Expanding Organic Market." Food Review v20 n2 May-Aug 1997. p28-32. (ISSN1056-327X).

NATURAL FOODS INDUSTRY--NETHERLANDS

The organic agriculture "sector grew 12 percent in 1996, accounting for about 1 percent of arable land in the Netherlands. The market share of organic foodstuffs has risen slightly to 3 percent. Organic foodstuffs produced in the Netherlands bear the EKO label and sell at a price premium of about 50-100 percent....The market share for organic potatoes for fresh consumption was 4 percent in 1995." (p6)

Proost, Jet/Matteson, Patricia. "Reducing Pesticide Use in the Netherlands: With Stick and Carrot." Journal of Pesticide Reform v17 n3 Fall 1997. p2-8. (ISSN0893-357X).

NATURAL FOODS INDUSTRY--UNITED STATES

In the U.S., "sales of organic grocery and dairy products, (meaning products grown and manufactured without the use of added hormones, pesticides or synthetic fertilizers) grew by 26.3 percent to $3.5 billion in 1996. 1995 sales were $2.8 billion. This is according to NATURAL FOODS MERCHANDISER, an industry publication, in its 16th annual 'Market Overview,' published in its June, 1997 issue....Organic dairy sales increased by about 50 percent in the year, with 1996 sales reaching $120 million." (p4)

"Eco-Update: News from around the World: Organic Dairy Sales Boom in 1996." Acres, U.S.A. v27 n8 Aug 1997. p4. (ISSN1076-4968).

In the U.S., "sales of organic grocery and dairy products increased by 26 percent in 1996 to a total of $3.5 billion in sales, an increase from $2.8 billion in sales in 1995, according to NATURAL FOODS MERCHANDISER (June, 1997). Last year marked the seventh consecutive year organic sales increased by at least 20 percent; exports and direct sales increased from $714 million in 1995 to $872 million in 1996....Sales of 'natural products,' which include organic foods and beverages, dietary supplements, and all-natural personal care products, increased by more than 25 percent in 1996 to $11.5 billion; 1995 sales were $9.17 billion. Last year was the fourth consecutive year the natural products industry reported double-digit growth." (unpaginated)

"Organic Sales Increase by 26 Percent in 1996." Alternative Agriculture News v15 n7 Jul 1997. (ISSN8755-4941).

A study conducted by the Rodale Institute Research Center in Pennsylvania found that "cash expenditures (seed, fertilizer, lime, pesticides, machinery costs, hired labor, and land rental)

required by the organic rotations averaged roughly $160/A [dollars per acre], about 18% lower than the $195/A required by the conventional system in 1991-1995. Revenue was 12% lower for the organic rotation although the organic yield of corn was only 3% less than conventional. The reason was that corn was grown much less frequently in the organic rotation (33% of the time in the organic rotation compared with 60% in the conventional one during 1991-1995)." (p6-7)

Hanson, James C./Lichtenberg, Erik/Peters, Steven E. "Organic versus Conventional Grain Production in the Mid-Atlantic: An Economic and Farming System Overview." American Journal of Alternative Agriculture v12 n1 1997. p2-9. (ISSN0889-1893).

In the U.S., "since 1990, organic food sales have jumped 20 percent annually, reaching $3.3 billion in 1996, and are projected to grow to $6.5 billion by the year 2000. Organic cropland has more than doubled since 1991, and organic dairy sales are increasing by more than 100 percent a year." (p18)

Cummins, Ronnie. "World News: US Plans to Define Bio-Engineered Foods as 'Organic.'" Earth Island Journal v12 n4 Fall 1997. p18. (ISSN1041-0406).

NATURAL GAS--CHINA (v26)

NATURAL GAS--UNITED STATES

"Consumption of natural and supplemental gas in July 1997 [in the U.S.] was forecast as 1.5 trillion cubic feet, 5 percent above the level in July 1996. Consumption of natural gas and supplemental gas during the first 7 months of 1997 was an estimated 13.2 trillion cubic feet, 1 percent lower than consumption during the first 7 months of 1996." (p71)

U.S. Dept. of Energy. Energy Information Administration. "Natural Gas." Monthly Energy Review Aug 1997. p71-79. (ISSN0095-7356).

In the U.S., "the estimated average wellhead price of natural gas for January 1997 was $3.58 per thousand cubic feet, 72 percent above the January 1996 price. The average price of natural gas delivered to electric utility plants was $3.98 per thousand cubic feet in December 1996 (latest date for which data are available) 54 percent above the December 1995 price. The average price of natural gas used by residential consumers in January 1997 was $6.69 per thousand cubic feet, 19 percent higher than the January 1996 price. The average price of natural gas used by commercial consumers in January 1997 was $6.06 per thousand cubic feet, 15 percent more than the January 1996 price. The average price of natural gas used by industrial consumers in January 1997 was $4.58 per thousand cubic feet, 36 percent above the January 1996 price." (p109)

U.S. Dept. of Energy. Energy Information Administration. "Energy Prices." Monthly Energy Review May 1997. p109-128. (ISSN0095-7356).

NATURAL GAS--UNITED STATES--COSTS (v26)

NATURAL GAS INDUSTRY

see GAS INDUSTRY

NATURAL RESOURCES

see also CONSERVATION OF NATURAL RESOURCES; FISHERIES; FORESTS AND FORESTRY; MINES AND MINERAL RESOURCES; WATER RESOURCES DEVELOPMENT

NATURAL RESOURCES--GERMANY--JAPAN --NETHERLANDS--UNITED STATES

According to the report "Resource Flows: The Material Basis of Industrial Economies," "individuals in the United States, Germany, Japan, and the Netherlands consume an average of 45 to 85 metric tons of natural resources per year....That is roughly equal to 300 shopping bags full of natural resources per person per week....Germany's use of coal for power requires extracting and removing 29 metric tons of earth per person per year. And in the United States, agricultural production causes 15 metric tons of topsoil erosion per person per year....Measuring the total resource requirements of the four countries studied reveals that hidden flows make up a striking 55 to 75 percent of the total resources utilized....Countries such as Japan or the Netherlands import 50 to 70 percent of their material flow...." (p10)

Runyan, Curtis. "Environmental Intelligence: New Measures of Material Consumption." World Watch v10 n5 Sep-Oct 1997. p10-11. (ISSN0896-0615).

NATURAL RESOURCES--UNITED STATES (v26)

NATURALIZATION--HISPANIC AMERICANS

"Despite their low naturalization rates, Latin Americans made up more than one-third of the nearly one-half million immigrants who became citizens in 1995. Mexico represented 15 percent of all naturalizations, more than twice any other group. Cuba, Colombia, El Salvador, and the Dominican Republic were the other top countries of origin for these new Americans. Nevertheless, nearly one-third of U.S. Hispanics are not citizens...." (p41)

del Pinal, Jorge/Singer, Audrey. "Generations of Diversity: Latinos in the United States." Population Bulletin v52 n3 Oct 1997. p2-47. (ISSN0032-468X).

NATURALIZATION--UNITED STATES (v26)

"Of the nearly half a million immigrants admitted to the U.S. in 1982, just 41.5 percent had become American citizens by 1995....The naturalization rate for 1982 immigrants from Taiwan reached 71 percent in 1995, according to the Immigration and Naturalization Service. For Vietnamese and Filipinos, it was 63 percent. But only 11 percent of 1982 immigrants from Germany have become citizens....Immediate relatives of U.S. citizens have low rates of naturalization, with only 31.4 percent of 1982 immigrants in this category becoming citizens." (p8)

"Asians Lead the Citizenship Boom." Forecast v17 n12 Dec 1997. p8. article-level access: <http://www.demographics.com/publications/fc/97_fc/9712_fc/f971208.htm> (ISSN0732-1597).

In the U.S., "nearly 45 percent of those immigrants admitted from the 15 leading countries of origin during the 1970s were naturalized by 1995. Of the four Latin American countries on the list, three (Mexico, Cuba, and the Dominican Republic) had naturalization rates well below the average. The rate for Colombia, the fourth Latin American country, was just above the average--51 percent of the 1970s immigrants from Colombia had naturalized by 1995....More than 96 percent of the Vietnamese who entered during the 1970s--primarily as refugees--had become citizens by 1995....In 1996, 1.3 million permanent residents were naturalized, more than four times the number in 1993, the previous high point." (p40)

del Pinal, Jorge/Singer, Audrey. "Generations of Diversity: Latinos in the United States." Population Bulletin v52 n3 Oct 1997. p2-47. (ISSN0032-468X).

Under the Immigration Reform and Control Act of 1986, undocumented foreigners who had lived in the U.S. before 1982 could apply for legal status under special amnesty provisions. "As of 1996, nearly 2.7 million IRCA legalizations were approved, of which nearly 2.5 million appear as new admissions in immigration statistics between 1989 and 1991. About 59 percent (1.6 million) of the immigrants gained legal residency under the amnesty provision. Another 41 percent (1.1 million) were admitted under the Special Agricultural Worker (SAW) provisions that granted legal status to undocumented migrants who had worked in agriculture at least 90 days." (p20)

del Pinal, Jorge/Singer, Audrey. "Generations of Diversity: Latinos in the United States." Population Bulletin v52 n3 Oct 1997. p2-47. (ISSN0032-468X).

NAVAJO INDIANS

"The Navajo Nation is the second largest tribe in the United

States, with close to 220,000 people reporting affiliation, according to the 1990 U.S. Census....According to the U.S. Census Bureau, the Navajo people are the poorest of the 10 largest tribes, with a poverty level approaching 50 percent." (p18)

Humphrey, Dana. "You Say You Want a Revolution." New Physician v46 n6 Sep 1997. p14-20. (ISSN0028-6451).

NAVAJO INDIANS--ECONOMIC CONDITIONS

"Unemployment hovers around 35 percent on the Navajo Reservation, but it is less severe than on many other reservations--on some, it can reach 90 percent--and energy development is a large part of the reason. Some 70 percent of the work forces of the mines and power plants are Navajo, and they provide about half of the tribe's revenues." (p11)

Asmus, Peter. "News and Comment: Landscapes of Power: Can Renewable Energy Help Native Americans...Resources?" Amicus Journal v19 n4 Win 1998. p11-13. (ISSN0276-7201).

NAVAL AIR BASES

see AIR BASES

NEAR-DEATH EXPERIENCES--UNITED STATES (v26)

NEAR EAST

see MIDDLE EAST

NEBRASKA--ECONOMIC CONDITIONS

According to George Kahn, vice president and economist at the Federal Reserve Bank of Kansas City, "employment grew at a 2 percent annual rate in...[Nebraska] through 1996 and the first half of 1997....The strong employment growth during the current recovery has pushed the unemployment rate in Nebraska to 2.3 percent as of July, the lowest rate of any state in the nation....Personal income in the state shot up almost 6 percent in 1996 and has risen about 4 percent during the first half of this year....Service sector employment in Nebraska has grown between 4 and 5 percent per year on average throughout the current recovery...." (unpaginated)

"Nebraska Economic Forums Discuss National Economy, State Banking." Federal Reserve Bank of Kansas City Fed Letter Nov 1997.

"While the national jobless rate has sunk to its lowest level in a quarter of a century, workers in Nebraska are reveling in an unemployment rate that's half as much: 2.3 percent, the lowest in the US." (p1) "Workers in the Omaha-area made an average of $12.67 an hour last year, nearly $1.50 more than the national median pay....A recent chamber study showed that 65 percent of local companies had trouble finding qualified workers....Workers with computer skills or even blue-collar talents, such as plumbing and carpentry, can command up to 25 percent more in salary here,...[Terri Miller at the Greater Omaha Chamber of Commerce] says. 'If you've got a few years experience in a computer-related field, you can start anywhere from $22,000 to $35,000 a year in Omaha,' she says. 'If you're already making that much in another city, you could probably move here and get a $10,000 raise.'" (p18)

Tucker, Randy. "Life in a State Where Jobs Sprout Like Rows of Corn." The Christian Science Monitor v89 n152 2 Jul 1997. p1,18. The Christian Science Monitor search engine: <http://www.csmonitor.com/plweb-cgi/iops1.pl> To retrieve this article, enter the following search: ED=19970702 AND corn. In the "retrieved list," click the title that matches this record. (ISSN0882-7729).

NEGLECT OF ANIMALS

see ANIMAL WELFARE

NEGRITOS--ASIA, SOUTHEASTERN (v26)

NEIGHBORHOOD HEALTH CENTERS

see COMMUNITY HEALTH SERVICES

NEPAL--ECONOMIC CONDITIONS

"Nepal remains one of the poorest countries in the world, with a per capita income of US$200, compared to $460 in Pakistan and $340 in India. An estimated 9 million people, or almost half the population, were absolutely poor in 1994....About 82 percent of workers are employed in the agricultural sector, which generates 43 percent of the gross domestic product....About half of the economically active population is employed for only part of each year, more than 70 percent of whom work in agriculture." (p7)

Rauniyar, Durga S. "Spotlight: Nepal." Population Today v25 n6 Jun 1997. p7. (ISSN0749-2448).

NEPAL--MORTALITY

In Nepal, "the crude death rate declined from 30 per 1,000 in 1954 to 15 per 1,000 in 1988. Infant mortality rates declined from 98 per 1,000 in 1991 to 79 per 1,000 in 1996, according to the 1996 Nepal Family Health Survey (NFHS). Two-thirds of deaths among children under age five occur during the first year of life. The under-five mortality rate is 118 per 1,000 births....Maternal mortality remains high at 515 per 100,000 live births, according to the 1991 Nepal Fertility, Family Planning, and Health Status Survey, in part because of lack of medical services, poor nutrition, and frequent childbirths." (p7)

Rauniyar, Durga S. "Spotlight: Nepal." Population Today v25 n6 Jun 1997. p7. (ISSN0749-2448).

NERVOUS SYSTEM--DISEASES--GREAT BRITAIN (v26)

NERVOUS SYSTEM, CENTRAL

see CENTRAL NERVOUS SYSTEM

NETHERLANDS--ECONOMIC CONDITIONS (v26)

NEUROLOGIC MANIFESTATIONS OF GENERAL DISEASES (v26)

NEUROLOGISTS--GREAT BRITAIN (v26)

NEUTRALITY--UNITED STATES--PUBLIC OPINION

"Back in 1947, as the cold war was getting under way, 68 per cent of Americans said that the United States should play an active international role, while 25 per cent said it should not play much of an international role. Last year, the figures were almost identical, with 67 per cent saying yes to an active international role and 28 per cent saying no. These figures, from the archives of the National Opinion Research Center, reveal a highly durable consensus. The proportion of those calling for an active role has never fallen below 65 per cent (in 1986) nor risen above 73 per cent (in 1991). The proportion wanting to stay out of world affairs has never risen above 32 per cent (in 1976 and 1986) nor dropped below 24 per cent (in 1991)." (p395-396)

Walker, Martin. "A New American Isolationism?" International Journal v52 n3 Sum 1997. p391-410. (ISSN0020-7020).

NEW AGE MOVEMENT--UNITED STATES (v26)

NEW YORK (N.Y.)--PUBLIC OPINION

In 1993, when Mayor Rudolph Giuliani "assumed office, 4% of city residents thought the previous year had been better for New York compared to 61% who thought the city had gotten worse. A February Marist Poll found that 46% think the city has improved in the past year and only 14% think it has worsened. Similarly, by 55% to 32% they feel New York City is headed in the right direction; a reversal from 34% to 54% two years ago." (p48) "More than one-third of New Yorkers still believe there is an economic recession, and more than two-thirds say they always or sometimes worry that their income won't meet their monthly expenses." (p49)

Miringoff, Lee M./Carvalho, Barbara L. "Republican Giuliani Forges His Own Identity in Democratic New York." Public Perspective v8 n5 Aug-Sep 1997. p48-49. (ISSN1050-5067).

NEW ZEALAND (v26)

"New Zealand is similar in size to Great Britain (270,500 square kilometers; NEW ZEALAND OFFICIAL YEARBOOK, 1994) and consists mainly of two islands--North Island and South Island. It has a population of 3.5 million and is bicultural: 9.5% are Maori or of Maori descent, with the majority being mainly of European descent." (p925)

Drummond, Wilhelmina J. "Adolescents at Risk: Causes of Youth Suicide in New Zealand." Adolescence v32 n128 Win 1997. p925-934. (ISSN0001-8449).

NEW ZEALAND--ECONOMIC CONDITIONS

In New Zealand, "the constant price increase of 2.4 per cent, reported earlier for 1996/97, was below the 3.1 per cent increase for the previous year, but above the annual average growth experienced over the previous decade of 1.8 per cent. In current dollars, the increase in Gross Domestic Product in 1997 was 4.4 per cent, down from the 6.0 per cent increase in the previous March year....Compensation of employees, which is the largest income component, was up by 5.5 per cent following a 6.6 per cent rise in the previous year. Over this two-year period, employment, as measured by the Household Labour Force Survey, increased by 6.5 per cent."

Statistics New Zealand. "National Accounts Production, Income and Expenditure--Year Ended March 1997." Press Release 12 Nov 1997. document-level access: <http://www.stats.govt.nz/statsweb.nsf/52518ce3e01f62f4cc256388000c48c0/cfd664903b1f92714c25654c00814a59?OpenDocument>

NEW ZEALAND--EMIGRATION AND IMMIGRATION

"During the September 1997 quarter there was a net gain to New Zealand of 2,360 permanent and long-term migrants, compared to a net gain of 6,230 for the same period last year. While there were 4,820 permanent and long-term arrivals from Asia in the quarter, departures totalled 1,660 with a resulting net gain of 3,160. This compares to a net gain of 5,090 migrants from Asia in the September 1996 quarter. There was a net loss of 3,230 migrants from New Zealand to Australia and a net inflow of 470 migrants from Europe."

Statistics New Zealand. "External Migration--September 1997 Quarter." Press Release 12 Nov 1997. document-level access: <http://www.stats.govt.nz/statsweb.nsf/52518ce3e01f62f4cc256388000c48c0/ae8760ddd0ec300f4c25654c0083ac25?OpenDocument>

NEW ZEALAND--EMPLOYMENT

In New Zealand, "on a seasonally adjusted basis, there were some 1,691,000 people employed in the September 1997 quarter, comprising 939,000 males and 752,000 females. The latest quarter shows a fall of 2,000 (0.1 per cent) from the June quarter. The number of people in seasonally adjusted full-time employment was estimated at 1,304,000 compared with 389,000 people in part-time employment."

Statistics New Zealand. "Household Labour Force Survey--September 1997 Quarter." Press Release 5 Nov 1997. document-level access: <http://www.stats.govt.nz/statsweb.nsf/52518ce3e01f62f4cc256388000c48c0/9baf462b0ec25b954c256545006da738?OpenDocument>

In New Zealand, "total filled jobs have increased by 33,100 or 2.2 per cent in the year to August 1997. The increase of 13,000 in full-time jobs is the lowest annual increase since 1993. Part-time jobs...increased by 20,100, an increase of 4.6 per cent which is the same as the increase in the year to May 1997."

Statistics New Zealand. "Quarterly Employment Survey--August 1997 Quarter." Press Release 19 Nov 1997. document-level access: <http://www.stats.govt.nz/statsweb.nsf/52518ce3e01f62f4cc256388000c48c0/643ce4a7904078754c25655300718c6c?OpenDocument>

NEW ZEALAND--POPULATION (v26)

"New Zealand's usually resident population at 30 September 1997 was provisionally estimated to have been 3,770,000, according to the Deputy Government Statistician Dianne Macaskill. This represents an increase of 42,700 or 1.1 per cent over the 30 September 1996 figure. During the 1991-96 intercensal period, the growth rate averaged 1.4 per cent per annum. During the 1997 September quarter, there was an estimated increase in population of 9,200 or 0.25 percent. This resulted from a natural increase (excess of births over deaths) of 6,900 and a net permanent and long-term migration gain of 2,300. In the 1996 September quarter, the estimated increase was significantly higher at 13,200. The smaller growth in the 1997 September quarter compared with the same quarter in 1996 was due mainly to smaller net permanent and long-term migration gain--2,300 as against 6,700."

Statistics New Zealand. "National Population Estimates--September 1997 Quarter." Press Release 10 Nov 1997. document-level access: <http://www.stats.govt.nz/statsweb.nsf/52518ce3e01f62f4cc256388000c48c0/4a6cc4d5a48ac4c25654b00096f8c?OpenDocument>

NEWS AGENCIES--UNITED STATES--PUBLIC OPINION

In the U.S., a news survey that surveyed over 3,000 people conducted by Clark, Martire and Bartolomeo, Inc., for the Newspaper Association of America found that "84 percent of respondents thought local news coverage was of great importance, but only 64 percent rated local newspapers' coverage as a strong point in comparison to local television stations, and only 38 percent described newspapers as their primary source of local news....Only 45 percent of weekday newspaper readers would miss the paper 'a great deal' if it were not available, compared with 62 percent of Sunday newspaper readers (56 percent of viewers of local television news programs would miss them a great deal)....Newspapers came off better than local television in believability (57 percent of respondents rate newspapers very good or excellent, compared with 47 percent for television), accuracy (56 percent to 50 percent) and fairness (47 percent to 41 percent)....Weekday papers still reach about six out of 10 adults (local television news reaches seven out of 10, and seven out of 10 adults on Sunday)." (p52)

Morton, John. "The Business of Journalism: Well, At Least They Like the Ads." American Journalism Review v19 n5 Jun 1997. p52. (ISSN1067-8654).

NEWS BROADCASTING

see BROADCAST JOURNALISM

NICARAGUA--ECONOMIC CONDITIONS (v26)

NIGERIA--SOCIAL CONDITIONS (v26)

NILE RIVER--EGYPT

"Today, nearly 90 percent of Egypt's 62 million people live on and work the land in the Nile River Delta, which totals only four percent of Egypt's entire area....Legal agreements with Sudan and Ethiopia, who control the headwaters of the Nile, entitle Egypt to 55.5 billion cubic meters of water each year. Currently, the country uses every drop and more (recycling programs produce an extra 7.5 billion cubic meters per year). This leaves a paltry 300 million cubic meters to flow into the Mediterranean Sea annually--a fraction of the river's natural flow." (p5)

Gladman, Aaron. "Africa: Massive Nile River Diversions Planned." World Rivers Review v12 n3 Jun 1997. p5. (ISSN0890-6211).

NISKA INDIANS--TREATIES--PUBLIC OPINION (v26)

NITROGEN (v26)

NITROGEN IN AGRICULTURE--UNITED STATES (v26)

"Soil microbes and lightning fix just 90 to 140 million tons of nitrogen per year. But humans are now adding at least 140 million tons annually by manufacturing industrial fertilizer, burning fossil fuels, and cultivating legumes, which support nitrogen-fixing bacteria. Industrial fertilizer--distinct from manure and other organic fertilizers that merely transfer already-fixed nitrogen from one place to another--contributes the most newly-fixed nitrogen, 80 million tons." (p11)

O'Meara, Molly. "Environmental Intelligence: The Nitrogen Cycle Is out of Balance." World Watch v10 n5 Sep-Oct 1997. p11. (ISSN0896-0615).

NITROGEN IN ANIMAL NUTRITION

"Normally, only 25 percent of the nitrogen fed to an animal is recovered as milk protein. The rest is excreted, with as much as half escaping into the air as ammonia gas and other odorous compounds. Less than 35 percent of the nitrogen is left to recycle as a nutrient for crops." (p12)

Lee, Jill/U.S. Dept. of Agriculture. Agricultural Research Service. "Making the Most of Manure." Agricultural Research v45 n6 Jun 1997. p12-13. (ISSN0002-161X).

NOGALES (MEXICO)--COMMERCE--UNITED STATES

"Bite into a fresh, juicy tomato this winter and more than likely you are tasting fruit grown in Mexico and imported through [Nogales]....Nearly two thirds of all winter produce eaten in the United States--about 600 million servings per day--comes into the country through the Nogales checkpoint....The sheer volume of trade means that about 70 percent of the trucks sail through the Nogales entry gates without anyone from any agency inspecting the cargo at all. Since 1989, trucks carrying Mexican produce through Nogales have increased by 62 percent, to 150,744 annually; in the same period, fresh produce passing through has nearly doubled, from 1.9 billion to 3.7 billion pounds per year." (p84)

McGraw, Dan. "Culture & Ideas: Imported Bugs: Maybe Jell-O Wasn't So Bad." U.S. News & World Report v123 n20 24 Nov 1997. p84. article-level access: <http://www.usnews.com/usnews/issue/971124/24FOOB.HTM> (ISSN0041-5537).

NON-COMMERCIAL TELEVISION

see PUBLIC TELEVISION

NON-GOVERNMENTAL ORGANIZATIONS--BOLIVIA

"In 1990 foreign aid [to non-governmental organizations in Bolivia] totalled $738 million....Prior to 1980 there were 100 NGOs; by 1992 there were 530 and growing....Of the tens of millions allocated to the NGOs, only 15 to 20 percent reached the poor." (p19)

Petras, James. "Imperialism and NGOs in Latin America." Monthly Review v49 n7 Dec 1997. p10-27. (ISSN0027-0520).

NON-GOVERNMENTAL ORGANIZATIONS--JAPAN (v26)

NON-GOVERNMENTAL ORGANIZATIONS--PERSIAN GULF REGION

In the Persian Gulf, the number of non-political organizations and institutions "exceeds 80, with 32,000 active members of both sexes. There are eighteen such organizations in Bahrain, with 5,430 members: professional societies form 38.9 percent, charity 33.3 percent, and women's associations 27.8 percent....In Kuwait the number of cooperative societies has reached 42, with more than 170,000 members, who control more than 80 percent of the retail food market." (p169)

Fakhro, Munira A. "Gender, Politics and the State: What Do Middle Eastern Women Want?: Gender, Politics and the State in the Gulf Region." Middle East Policy v5 n3 Sep 1997. p166-170. (ISSN1061-1924).

NONCONSENSUAL SEXUAL INTERCOURSE

see RAPE

NONPROFIT ORGANIZATIONS--UNITED STATES (v26)

NONPROFIT ORGANIZATIONS--UNITED STATES --FINANCE (v26)

NONVIOLENT DEFENSE

see CIVILIAN-BASED DEFENSE

NORDIC SKIING

see CROSS-COUNTRY SKIING

NORGESTREL--UNITED STATES (v26)

NORTH AMERICAN FREE TRADE AGREEMENT (v26)

"In NAFTA's first three years, trade deficits with Canada and Mexico have cost...[the U.S.] 420,000 lost jobs. Under NAFTA, our trade deficit with Mexico and Canada has more than quadrupled--from $9 billion to a staggering $39 billion--almost one quarter of our total global deficit....Since 1993, the average hourly compensation for a Mexican manufacturing worker has fallen 36 percent, from $2.40 to only $1.51, including benefits. That's about one-eleventh what a comparable U.S. worker earns."

Trumka, Richard/American Federation of Labor and Congress of Industrial Organizations. "Statement by Richard Trumka, Secretary-Treasurer, AFL-CIO on NAFTA and President Clinton's Trip to Mexico." Press Release 5 May 1997. document-level access: <http://www.aflcio.org/publ/press97/pr05053.htm>

Since NAFTA took effect on 1 January 1994, "US exports to Mexico have grown 37 percent, reaching a high of $57 billion. By the end of 1997, that 'third world' country will buy more American products than any country except Canada, surpassing second-place Japan, which has an economy 15 times larger. US exports to Canada since NAFTA was implemented have risen 33 percent, also reaching record levels....During NAFTA's first three years, 39 of the 50 states increased their exports to Mexico." (p18)

Kengor, Paul. "Opinion/Essays: From Deep in the 'Rust Belt,' A Shining View of NAFTA." The Christian Science Monitor v89 n155 8 Jul 1997. p18. The Christian Science Monitor search engine: <http://www.csmonitor.com/plweb-cgi/iops1.pl> To retrieve this article, enter the following search: ED=19970708 AND shining. In the "retrieved list," click the title that matches this record. (ISSN0882-7729).

NORTH AMERICAN FREE TRADE AGREEMENT--CANADA --UNITED STATES

"U.S. beef exports to Canada were about 100 percent higher in 1996 because of NAFTA, while U.S. imports of beef from Canada were about 50 percent higher. Bilateral trade between the United States and Canada in wheat and wheat products and vegetable oils were 5 to 10 percent higher in 1996 than they would have been without the agreement." (p5)

U.S. Dept. of Agriculture. Economic Research Service. "Executive Summary." NAFTA: International Agriculture and Trade Reports Situation and Outlook Series Sep 1997. p3-6.

NORTH AMERICAN FREE TRADE AGREEMENT --EMPLOYMENT (v26)

"According to a study recently released by the NAALC [North American Agreement on Labor Cooperation], U.S. workers experienced the largest overall drop in real wages, with 1995 levels 8.5% lower than in 1984, and Canadian earnings down 0.4%. In Mexico, real wages in the private sector fell between 1984 and 1988, but by 1994 were above their levels 10 years earlier....By August 1995, Mexican earnings had fallen 12% from the year before and remained about five percent below 1984 levels." (p150)

Connolly, Catherine/Tennant-Burt, Julie. "The NAFTA Labor Agreement and U.S. Employment-Discrimination Law." Social Justice v24 n1 Spr 1997. p148-162. (ISSN0094-7571).

NORTH AMERICAN FREE TRADE AGREEMENT --EMPLOYMENT--UNITED STATES

"In 1993, NAFTA boosters said that as many as 200,000 jobs would accrue in the United States based on the substantial trade surplus we would have with Mexico. Initial trade surpluses quickly changed to a trade deficit of $16.2 billion in 1996. Most of that deficit is concentrated in manufacturing industries. Although the Office of the United States Trade Representative claims that some 311,000 new jobs have been created because of trade with NAFTA countries, one estimate is that 420,000 jobs were lost because of trade deficits....Since the passage of NAFTA, many firms have also used the threat of moving to Mexico as a way to stifle demands for wage increases and union organization. Cornell University Prof. Kate Bronfenbrenner found that half of the firms used threats to shut down during union organizing drives, and 15 percent actually closed part or all of a plant, a rate that tripled after NAFTA." (p9 secA)

Malveaux, Julianne. "Other Voices: After 3 Years, NAFTA's Fruits Aren't Sweet, Safe, Or Profitable." Detroit Free Press 1 Jul 1997. p9 secA.

NORTH AMERICAN FREE TRADE AGREEMENT--MEXICO

"NAFTA hasn't made life better for the Mexican people. The portion of Mexican citizens who are 'extremely poor' has risen from 32 percent to 51 percent in the three years of NAFTA. Eight million people have fallen from the middle class into poverty. As many as 10 million children work in Mexico, in violation of that country's child-labor laws, and wages have dropped by 27 percent." (p9 secA)

Malveaux, Julianne. "Other Voices: After 3 Years, NAFTA's Fruits Aren't Sweet, Safe, Or Profitable." Detroit Free Press 1 Jul 1997. p9 secA.

In Mexico, "close to 300 companies, almost all of them transnationals, are responsible for 70 percent of the exports [to the U.S.]. Excluding the products from the 'maquiladoras,' there are only 17 types of products that make possible 60 percent of these exports. In the area of agriculture, granulated coffee, tomato and vegetables compose 73 percent of the agricultural exports in the first two years of NAFTA. Almost half of the exports are produced in 'maquiladoras,' but the Mexican makeup of this merchandise, including the labor, is approximately 22 percent. In 1996, the 'maquiladoras' only consumed 1.83 percent of the raw materials and employed 803,060 workers....Of total Mexican exports in 1987, 87 percent were of national content and in 1994 it had dropped to 42.24 percent. In the first year of NAFTA, it dropped four more percentage points....In 1994, only $3 billion more were exported than in 1983." (p9)

"Who Has NAFTA Benefited?" People's Tribune v24 n7 Jul 1997. p9. (ISSN1081-4787).

NORTH AMERICAN FREE TRADE AGREEMENT--MEXICO --UNITED STATES (v26)

"The US Department of Labor recently reported that NAFTA has cost the US 600,000 jobs. Global Trade Watch reports that since NAFTA went into effect, the US' $1.7 billion trade surplus with Mexico has become a $16.3 billion deficit. More than 2 million Mexican workers have lost their jobs, while real wages have plunged by 50 percent." (p17)

"The Global Marketplace: Fix NAFTA? Nix NAFTA!" Earth Island Journal v12 n3 Sum 1997. p17. (ISSN1041-0406).

"The official White House line is that 90,000 to 160,000 new jobs have been created [in the U.S.] as a result of NAFTA, while maybe 32,000 to 100,000 have been lost. The net, then, is anywhere from--10,000 to 128,000....The Labor Department program set up to help those who allegedly lost their jobs because of NAFTA counts 125,000 eligible people....The U.S. trade deficit with Mexico has grown to $16 billion, despite 36 percent export growth, because imports from Mexico increased almost twice as much....Total merchandise trade with Mexico adds up to just 0.8 percent of the U.S. gross domestic product." (p10)

Doherty, Brian. "Editorials: Swap Meat." Reason v29 n5 Oct 1997. p10-11. (ISSN0048-6906).

NORTH AMERICAN FREE TRADE AGREEMENT --MICHIGAN (v26)

NORTH AMERICAN FREE TRADE AGREEMENT --PENNSYLVANIA

"In Pennsylvania, statistics indicate that 21 of 30 industries enjoyed increases in exports to Mexico since NAFTA, and 29 of 32 saw rises in exports to Canada. Of the 21 industries with gains to Mexico, 12 had double-digit growth and six had triple-digit rises. Of the 29 industries that saw gains to Canada, 26 had double- or triple-digit increases in exports. NAFTA's tariff-cutting provisions have made Pennsylvania and Pittsburgh-area products cheaper than the products of non-NAFTA nations competing in those two markets....The tariffs on Heinz's products have gone from 20 percent to 4 percent on their way to zero in 1998. Prior to NAFTA, Heinz had no sales in Mexico. In 1996, Heinz sold $3 million to $5 million in products in Mexico....Likewise with Harrisburg-based AMP Inc., which makes electrical parts, and numerous other Pennsylvania firms. From 1993 to '96, AMP's exports increased by 66 percent to Canada and by 98 percent to Mexico....On the negative side, 69 Pennsylvania companies, comprising 10,150 workers, have been certified as hurt by either NAFTA or 'foreign competition,' and are thus eligible for unemployment compensation and trade adjustment assistance (TAA). Of the 10,150 eligible workers, 587 are receiving NAFTA-related TAA unemployment benefits....Even Pennsylvania industries that include companies who claim they've been hurt by NAFTA have seen significant increases in exports. The clothing/apparel industry has had a 506 percent rise in business with Mexico and a 124 percent jump with Canada. Electrical component manufacturers had rises of 27 percent for Mexico and 38 percent for Canada." (p18)

Kengor, Paul. "Opinion/Essays: From Deep in the 'Rust Belt,' A Shining View of NAFTA." The Christian Science Monitor v89 n155 8 Jul 1997. p18. The Christian Science Monitor search engine: <http://www.csmonitor.com/plweb-cgi/iops1.pl> To retrieve this article, enter the following search: ED=19970708 AND shining. In the "retrieved list," click the title that matches this record. (ISSN0882-7729).

"Pennsylvania is one of the nation's top 10 trading states, a leader in agricultural exports, and one of Canada's most significant trading partners. It exported $5.3 billion in products to Canada in 1996....Pennsylvania exports to Mexico from 1993 to '96 increased 27 percent, hitting a record $827 million....Pennsylvania's exports to Canada are up 34 percent since the start of NAFTA, twice the rate of increase during the four years before the trade pact. The Pittsburgh region has witnessed gains in total exports to both Mexico and Canada since NAFTA's implementation. The region's exports to Canada increased 13 percent. Regional exports to Mexico in 1995 (a recession year) were 4 percent higher than pre-NAFTA levels; they jumped 24 percent in the first year of NAFTA." (p18)

Kengor, Paul. "Opinion/Essays: From Deep in the 'Rust Belt,' A Shining View of NAFTA." The Christian Science Monitor v89 n155 8 Jul 1997. p18. The Christian Science Monitor search engine: <http://www.csmonitor.com/plweb-cgi/iops1.pl> To retrieve this article, enter the following search: ED=19970708 AND shining. In the "retrieved list," click the title that matches this record. (ISSN0882-7729).

NORTH AMERICAN FREE TRADE AGREEMENT--UNITED STATES

"Since NAFTA went into effect,...[the U.S.'s] $10 billion deficit with Canada turned into a larger $23 billion deficit. Our $1.7 billion surplus with Mexico slid into a $16 billion deficit....Four years ago, in 1993, we all heard the mantra of 200,000 jobs over and over again....It is now 1997 and we have lost an estimated 400,000 jobs." (pH3649)

Lipinski, William O. (Rep.-Ill.). "NAFTA Is a Failure." Congressional Record. Daily ed. v143 n80 10 Jun 1997. pH3649-

3653. section/page-level access: <http://thomas.loc.gov/cgi-bin/query/R?r105:FLD001:H03649:> (ISSN0363-7239). (X1.1A.105/1).

"United States auto imports from Mexico are more than 10 times the value of United States exports to Mexico. The United States auto trade deficit has grown since NAFTA by about 400 percent, $14.6 billion from $3.6 billion....The Department of Labor's own figures of [U.S.] jobs lost due to NAFTA estimate over 120,000 jobs lost. Respectable academic estimates of jobs lost due to NAFTA put the number of jobs lost at about 420,000." (pH5925)

Kucinich, Dennis J. (Rep.-Ohio). "NAFTA Is Costing America Too Much." Congressional Record. Daily ed. v143 n109 29 Jul 1997. pH5925-5926. section/page-level access: <http://thomas.loc.gov/cgi-bin/query/R?r105:FLD001:H05925:> (ISSN0363-7239). (X1.1A.105/1).

"Investment in U.S. agriculture and rural areas was about 0.19 percent higher in 1996 than it would have been without NAFTA. Employment in U.S. agriculture and related industries was about 0.07 percent higher in 1996 than it would have been without NAFTA." (p6)

U.S. Dept. of Agriculture. Economic Research Service. "Executive Summary." NAFTA: International Agriculture and Trade Reports Situation and Outlook Series Sep 1997. p3-6.

"According to one report, the U.S. Department of Labor has certified over 41,000 American workers for assistance because of lost jobs as a result of trade with Mexico or Canada, and more claims are pending (Cannon, 1995)....According to Mexican labor economist Alejandro Alvarez Bejac (1994...), American industry saved $25,000 per worker in 1990 by using Mexican labor, resulting in a $10 billion loss to U.S. workers in jobs and wages." (p151)

Connolly, Catherine/Tennant-Burt, Julie. "The NAFTA Labor Agreement and U.S. Employment-Discrimination Law." Social Justice v24 n1 Spr 1997. p148-162. (ISSN0094-7571).

U.S. "agricultural exports to Canada and Mexico were worth $11.6 billion last year....Indeed, the US Department of Agriculture (USDA) says beef exports to Mexico rose 81 percent during the first six months of this year....Since NAFTA went into effect, Canadian consumption of American pork has doubled, according to the USDA. Exports to Mexico during the first six months of 1997 are up 36 percent and climbing." (p4)

Bryce, Robert. "United States: Under NAFTA, Pigs Are Big on Border." The Christian Science Monitor v89 n223 14 Oct 1997. p4. The Christian Science Monitor search engine: <http://www.csmonitor.com/plweb-cgi/iops1.pl> To retrieve this article, enter the following search: ED=19971014 AND border. In the "retrieved list," click the title that matches this record. (ISSN0882-7729).

NORTH AMERICAN FREE TRADE AGREEMENT--UNITED STATES--PUBLIC OPINION (v26)

NORTH ATLANTIC TREATY ORGANIZATION--ARMED FORCES (v26)

"Ground forces committed by nations to the [NATO] Alliance...have been cut by 35 per cent, major naval combatants by over 30 per cent and air force combat squadrons by some 40 per cent....US forces in Europe...have been cut by about two-thirds and the majority of allied forces once stationed in Germany have now left. Nuclear forces committed to NATO have been greatly reduced, with sub-strategic weapons based in Europe cut by 80 per cent." (p32-33)

Cragg, Anthony. "Internal Adaptation: Reshaping NATO for the Challenges of Tomorrow." NATO Review v45 n4 Jul-Aug 1997. p30-35. (ISSN0255-3813).

NORTH ATLANTIC TREATY ORGANIZATION--FINLAND--PUBLIC OPINION (v26)

NORTH ATLANTIC TREATY ORGANIZATION--GERMANY--PUBLIC OPINION (v26)

NORTH ATLANTIC TREATY ORGANIZATION--UKRAINE--PUBLIC OPINION

"Opinion polls differ with regard to the Ukrainian population's attitudes towards NATO. In a May 1997 poll, 37% of respondents said they were in favour of Ukraine's joining NATO, and 28% said they were against. However, in a December 1996 poll, only 36% of the respondents approved of Ukrainian participation in NATO's PfP [Partnership for Peace] programme. In this poll 41% of the respondents reported that they did not know what to answer, were not interested in the issue or did not care....According to a June 1996 survey, only 12% of Ukrainian officers support the cooperation with NATO policy." (p369)

Bukkvoll, Tor. "Ukraine and NATO: The Politics of Soft Cooperation." Security Dialogue v28 n3 Sep 1997. p363-374. (ISSN0967-0106).

NORTH ATLANTIC TREATY ORGANIZATION--UNITED STATES--PUBLIC OPINION (v26)

"A survey conducted by the Pew Research Center for the People and the Press earlier this year found that [in the U.S.] only a narrow plurality--40 percent to 45 percent--favored the admission of new members [to NATO]. But only 20 percent of Americans had followed the issue of NATO expansion....A majority--62 percent--is ready to bless NATO expansion as long as the US does not bear an inordinate share of the responsibilities and acts in concert with its partners, according to a survey conducted by the University of Maryland's Program on International Policy Attitudes." (p8)

Landay, Jonathan S. "Are Americans Ready to Go to War for Prague?" The Christian Science Monitor v89 n155 8 Jul 1997. p1,8. The Christian Science Monitor search engine: <http://www.csmonitor.com/plweb-cgi/iops1.pl> To retrieve this article, enter the following search: ED=19970708 AND prague. In the "retrieved list," click the title that matches this record. (ISSN0882-7729).

NORTHEASTERN STATES--POPULATION (v26)

NORTHERN FOREST

"From western New York to the tip of Maine, 26 million acres of timberland make up the Northern Forest--the largest contiguous forest east of the Mississippi. More than 35 conservation groups have banded together since 1990 to protect the most wild and vulnerable areas in the region as well as foster sustainable logging practices and economic development....Eighty-five percent of the 26 million-acre forest is privately owned." (p4)

Marks, Alexandra. "United States: Old Northeast Forests Face Deep-Rooted Problems." The Christian Science Monitor v89 n204 16 Sep 1997. p4. The Christian Science Monitor search engine: <http://www.csmonitor.com/plweb-cgi/iops1.pl> To retrieve this article, enter the following search: ED=19970916 AND problems. In the "retrieved list," click the title that matches this record. (ISSN0882-7729).

NORTHERN IRELAND--MANUFACTURES (v26)

NORTHERN MARIANA ISLANDS--ECONOMIC CONDITIONS (v26)

NORTHWEST TERRITORIES--ECONOMIC CONDITIONS (v26)

NOVI (MICH.) (v26)

NUCLEAR ENERGY

"About 487 large nuclear reactor plants currently produce electricity worldwide. The US leads with 126, followed by France with 54, Japan with 51, Britain with 35, and Germany with 20. The former USSR [Union of Soviet Socialist Republics], India, and Far East have 90 altogether. Canada has 20, and Latin America has 10 in Brazil, Argentina, Cuba, and Mexico. At least 39 more are being built elsewhere....The decline in support for nuclear power is reflected in the number of plants built in each of the past three decades: from 60 in the 1970s to 46 a decade later, and three in the 90s....The International Atomic Energy Agency, a branch of the UN based in Vienna, estimates that more than 300 facilities around the world will have to be decommissioned by 2010. In the US, 15 small plants have been taken out of service prematurely after operating for an average of only 12.7 years....According to the US Council of Energy Awareness, 431 operating reactors in 34 countries have a maximum dependable capacity of 341,000 mw [megawatts]. A 1000-mw facility can produce enough electricity for a city of 700,000. In France, the nuclear portion of its domestic electricity is about 76 percent; in the US it's only 19 percent, but countries such as Sweden (51 percent), Germany (29), the former USSR (41) and Japan (28) are more dependent." (p7)

Rubin, Hal. "The Cost of Closing Pandora's Box." Toward Freedom v46 n4 Aug 1997. p7-8. (ISSN0048-9898).

NUCLEAR ENERGY--UNITED STATES

"In February 1997, U.S. nuclear generating units produced a total of 51 net terawatthours (billion kilowatthours) of electricity, 9 percent lower than in February 1996. Nuclear units generated at an average capacity factor of 67.6 percent, 12.3 percentage points lower than in February 1996. Nuclear power supplied 21.6 percent of the total electric utility-generated electricity in February 1997, compared with 22.8 percent of February 1996." (p103)

U.S. Dept. of Energy. Energy Information Administration. "Nuclear Energy." Monthly Energy Review May 1997. p103-108. (ISSN0095-7356).

"In May 1997, U.S. nuclear generating units produced a total of 47 net terawatthours (billion kilowatthours) of electricity, 15 percent lower than in May 1996. Nuclear units generated at an average capacity factor of 63.0 percent, 11 percentage points lower than in May 1996. Nuclear power supplied 19.3 percent of the total electric utility-generated electricity in May 1997, compared with 22.1 percent in May 1996." (p103)

U.S. Dept. of Energy. Energy Information Administration. "Nuclear Energy." Monthly Energy Review Aug 1997. p103-108. (ISSN0095-7356).

NUCLEAR INDUSTRY (v26)

NUCLEAR MATTER SMUGGLING--EUROPE--FORMER SOVIET REPUBLICS (v26)

NUCLEAR POWER PLANTS

see also CHERNOBYL NUCLEAR ACCIDENT, CHERNOBYL', UKRAINE, 1986

NUCLEAR POWER PLANTS--ENVIRONMENTAL ASPECTS --UNITED STATES (v26)

NUCLEAR POWER PLANTS--UNITED STATES (v26)

"On February 28, 1997, there were 110 operable nuclear generating units in the United States, with a collective net summer capability of 100.7 million kilowatts of electricity. Of the 110 operable units, 23 units generated at less than 25 percent of capacity because of maintenance, refueling, or repair outage, and 20 of the 23 units generated no electricity during the month. The aggregate net design capacity of the 110 operable units was 102.3 million kilowatts....There were 6 other units with construction permits, although construction for all 6 units was canceled or halted." (p103)

U.S. Dept. of Energy. Energy Information Administration. "Nuclear Energy." Monthly Energy Review May 1997. p103-108. (ISSN0095-7356).

"On May 31, 1997, there were 110 operable nuclear generating units in the United States, with a collective net summer capability of 100.7 million kilowatts of electricity. Of the 110 operable units, 35 units generated at less than 25 percent of capacity because of maintenance, refueling, or repair outage, and 30 of the 35 units generated no electricity during the month. The aggregate net design capacity of the 110 operable units was 102.3 million kilowatts." (p103)

U.S. Dept. of Energy. Energy Information Administration. "Nuclear Energy." Monthly Energy Review Aug 1997. p103-108. (ISSN0095-7356).

"The US nuclear-power sector is the largest in the world, with 110 reactors providing about 20 percent of the nation's electricity. But no new plants are planned; the last to go on line began operating in February 1996. The DOE [Department of Energy] forecasts that by 2015, US nuclear capacity will have declined by 36 percent over 1995, due to the retirement of aging reactors and the absence of new orders." (p6)

Landay, Jonathan S. "US-China Ties: US Nuclear Industry Banks on China's Demand." The Christian Science Monitor v89 n233 28 Oct 1997. p6-7. The Christian Science Monitor search engine: <http://www.csmonitor.com/plweb-cgi/iops1.pl> To retrieve this article, enter the following search: ED=19971028 AND demand. In the "retrieved list," click the title that matches this record. (ISSN0882-7729).

NUCLEAR REACTORS (v26)

"Almost all of the world's 400-plus [nuclear] power reactors rely on uranium fuel rather than thorium. Natural uranium is 99.3 percent uranium 238, which cannot sustain a chain reaction. But it also contains 0.7 percent uranium 235, a fissile isotope that can sustain a chain reaction. Most power reactors operate with slightly enriched uranium--typically, about 4 percent uranium 235." (p19)

Friedman, John S. "Perspectives: More Power to Thorium?" Bulletin of the Atomic Scientists v53 n5 Sep-Oct 1997. p19-20. (ISSN0096-3402).

NUCLEAR REACTORS--CANADA--UNITED STATES

"Canada's 21 nuclear reactors supply 17 percent of the nation's power needs. Nuclear energy supplies about 22 percent of US power needs." (p6)

Clayton, Mark. "Canada Pays Price for Taking Nuclear Safety for Granted." The Christian Science Monitor v89 n183 15 Aug 1997. p1,6. The Christian Science Monitor search engine: <http://www.csmonitor.com/plweb-cgi/iops1.pl> To retrieve this article, enter the following search: ED=19970815 AND granted. In the "retrieved list," click the title that matches this record. (ISSN0882-7729).

NUCLEAR WASTES

see RADIOACTIVE WASTES

NUCLEAR WEAPONS (v26)

The Nunn-Lugar program, sometimes called the cooperative threat reduction, "has helped deactivate 4,500 nuclear warheads, put over 200 ICBM [intercontinental ballistic missile] silos out of operation, destroyed 20 heavy bombers, eliminated 64 submarine-launched ballistic missiles and sealed 58 nuclear testing tunnels. Nunn-Lugar has helped the three former nations of the Soviet Union, Ukraine, Belarus, and Kazakhstan totally denuclearize." (pH4199)

Spratt, John M., Jr. (Rep.-S.C.). "National Defense Authorization Act for Fiscal Year 1998." Congressional Record. Daily ed. v143 n88-89 23 Jun 1997. pH4167-4212. section/page-level access: <http://thomas.loc.gov/cgi-bin/query/R?r105:FLD001:H04199:> (ISSN0363-7239). (X1.1A.105/1).

NUCLEAR WEAPONS--CHINA--TIBET

In Tibet, "at least 17 secret radar stations and 14 military airfields are established, as well as at least five bases for ICBMs [intercontinental ballistic missiles] and intermediate range nuclear missiles. About 300,000 troops and a quarter of China's 350 nuclear missiles are based in Tibet." (p18)

Ma, Natasha. "TF Reports: Asia: Endangered Rooftop." Toward Freedom v46 n6 Nov 1997. p18-19. (ISSN0048-9898).

NUCLEAR WEAPONS--HEALTH ASPECTS--NEVADA --TESTING

"Based on the average doses calculated by county for different age groups, NCI [U.S. National Cancer Institute] estimates that between 10,000 and 75,000 exposed persons might develop [nuclear] fallout-associated thyroid cancer during their lifetime [as a result of exposure to fallout from nuclear bomb tests in the 1950s and 1960s in Nevada]. Nearly all of these persons were under 15 years of age at the time of exposure, and about 75 percent were under age 5. It is estimated that about 30 percent of fallout-related thyroid cancers have been diagnosed already. (About 95 million Americans were under age 20 at some time during 1951 to 1962, the period of above-ground tests at the Nevada Test Site. According to current cancer rates, about 420,000 thyroid cancers would be expected to occur in a population of that size during their lifetimes.)"

U.S. National Institutes of Health. "NCI Releases Results of Nationwide Study of Radioactive Fallout from Nuclear Tests." News Release 1 Aug 1997. document-level access: <http://www.nih.gov/news/pr/aug97/nci-01.htm>

NUCLEAR WEAPONS--RUSSIA (v26)

NUCLEAR WEAPONS--RUSSIA--UNITED STATES

"The US spends roughly $400 million per year on the Nunn-Lugar program, also known as the Cooperative Threat Reduction program....Russia willingly accepts roughly $400 million each year in Nunn-Lugar denuclearization funds for a total of $1.6 billion since 1992....Despite administration opposition, [the U.S.] Congress cut Nunn-Lugar funds from $400 million to $377 million--a 6 percent reduction." (p18)

Martel, William C. "Opinion/Essays: Russia's 'Loose Nukes'--A Myth that Distorts US Policy." The Christian Science Monitor v89 n140 16 Jun 1997. p18. The Christian Science Monitor search engine: <http://www.csmonitor.com/plweb-cgi/iops1.pl> To retrieve this article, enter the following search: ED=19970616 AND policy. In the "retrieved list," click the title that matches this record. (ISSN0882-7729).

"The United States has 2,000 land-based warheads aimed at Russia, while Russia has 3,500 aimed at American targets. Together with submarine-based missiles, more than 5,000 nuclear weapons could be launched over the North Pole in less time than it takes for a trip to the grocery store." (p5)

Bills, Robert A. "Nuclear Arms More Menacing than Ever." The People v107 n10 Jan 1998. p5. (ISSN0199-350X).

NUCLEAR WEAPONS--UNITED STATES (v26)

"U.S. nuclear weapons are currently stored at some 26 locations in 15 states and seven foreign countries....Since 1992 nuclear weapons have been withdrawn from 10 states: Alaska, Arkansas, Florida, Hawaii, Kansas, Maine, Michigan, New Jersey, New York, and South Carolina....From a recent peak in the 1980s of some 24,000 warheads, the number of U.S. nuclear weapons in all categories (operational, hedge, reserve, and retired warheads awaiting dismantlement) currently stands at 12,500. Of these, some 1,750 warheads are scheduled for disassembly over the next three years. This will leave a stockpile in the 10,500-warhead range for operational forces, the hedge, and reserve....Of the 15 states that host nuclear weapons, New Mexico ranks number one by virtue of the many warheads stored at the Kirtland Underground Munitions Storage Complex (KUMSC), a modern $43 million, 300,000-square-foot facility opened in 1992....Georgia and Washington rank second and third. Each has a naval base for Trident ballistic missile submarines (SSBNs). Kings Bay has 10 SSBNs, Bangor eight....Nevada ranks fourth, with the second major air force storage site at Nellis AFB [Air Force Base]." (p62)

Norris, Robert S./Arkin, William M. "NRDC Nuclear Notebook: Where the Bombs Are, 1997." Bulletin of the Atomic Scientists v53 n5 Sep-Oct 1997. p62. (ISSN0096-3402).

NUCLEAR WEAPONS--UNITED STATES--COSTS

The U.S. is "spending about $30 billion a year now to maintain our nuclear stockpile....It turns out that from right after the end of World War II until now, the United States has spent more than $300 billion...about a third of a trillion dollars, for nuclear weapons and nuclear weapons materials." (pS5435)

Harkin, Tom (Sen.-Iowa). "The Comprehensive Test Ban Treaty and the 34th Anniversary of President Kennedy's Call for the...Pursuit of Peace." Congressional Record. Daily ed. v143 n80 10 Jun 1997. pS5433-5437. section/page-level access: <http://thomas.loc.gov/cgi-bin/query/R?r105:FLD001:S05435:> (ISSN0363-7239). (X1.1A.105/1).

NUPTIALITY

see MARRIAGE

NURSES--EDUCATION--UNITED STATES

In the U.S., "at the close of 1994, nearly 32 percent of registered nurses had earned the BSN [Bachelor of Science in Nursing] as their highest academic degree, according to the latest federal estimate." (p15) "Of the more than 2 million registered nurses nationwide, 119,636 (5.3%) have a masters degree in nursing, and 48,314 (2.2%) have a masters degree in related fields." (p16)

McGriff, Erline P. "Graduate Education in Nursing: An Update." Imprint v44 n1 Jan 1997. p15-16,18. (ISSN0019-3038).

NURSES--EDUCATION (HIGHER)--UNITED STATES (v26)

NURSES--UNITED STATES (v26)

NURSING HOME CARE

see also HANDICAPPED--INSTITUTIONAL CARE

NURSING HOME CARE--UNITED STATES (v26)

NURSING HOME CARE--UNITED STATES--COSTS

"Nursing home costs in New York City can reach $70,000 per year or approximately $200 a day. Some rural areas [in the U.S.] offer care as low as $30,000 per year or approximately $80 a day (Wilke, 1996)....A home health care agency on average charges $74 for a four-hour visit. The cost of home health care agency range from $38 to $121 per visit (Wilke, 1996). Ninety percent of those staying in a nursing home will deplete their wealth within the first two years (Chassen, 1994; Geer, 1991)....Medicaid pays benefits to 66% of the elderly in nursing homes, but only 12% of the elderly are living in poverty (Merline, 1996)." (p20-21)

Fuller, Phillip/Zietz, Emily Norman/Calcote, Roger. "The Role of Financial Counselors in Long-Term Health Care Planning." Financial Counseling and Planning v8 n1 1997. p19-24. (ISSN1052-3073).

NURSING HOME PATIENTS--ABUSE OF--UNITED STATES

In the U.S., "according to a random-sample survey of nursing home staff, 10 percent admitted committing at least one act of physical abuse in the preceding year, and 40 percent committed psychological abuse. Thirty-six percent of the sample had seen at least one incident of physical abuse in the preceding year by other staff members....In fact, the Office of Inspector General at the Department of Health and Human Services has reported that 46 percent of respondents questioned believed abuse is only sometimes or rarely reported." (pS8586)

Kohl, Herb (Sen.-Wis.). "The Ronald H. Brown Federal Building Designation Act of 1997." Congressional Record. Daily ed. v143 n111 31 Jul 1997. pS8571-8590. section/page-level access: <http://thomas.loc.gov/cgi-bin/query/R?r105:FLD001:S08586:> (ISSN0363-7239). (X1.1A.105/1).

NURSING HOMES--AFRO-AMERICAN AGED WOMEN --ATTITUDES (v26)

NURSING HOMES--UNITED STATES (v26)

In the U.S., "almost nine in ten nursing-home residents are aged 65 and older. The U.S. population that age increased 18 percent between 1985 and 1995....The number of people in nursing homes increased only 4 percent between 1985 and 1995....More than 1.5 million Americans lived in nursing homes in 1995. Fifty-three percent were aged 65 to 84, 11 percent under 65, and the balance are older. Because women have a longer life expectancy than men, nearly three quarters of residents are women." (p28)

Heubusch, Kevin. "Kaleidoscope: Boom Gone Bust." American Demographics v19 n5 May 1997. p28-29. article-level access: <http://www.demographics.com/Publications/AD/97_ad/9705_ad/AD970513.htm> (ISSN0163-4089).

"Over two million Americans reside in nursing facilities. Approximately half of the population over 85 years of age need nursing assistance. Of the 2.2 million people who turned 65 in 1990, studies show that 43% will spend some time in a nursing home (Geer, 1991). From 1993 to 2018 elderly use of nursing homes are projected to increase from 2.2 million to 3.6 million; use of home care will increase from 5.2 million to 7.4 million (Wiener & Illston, 1994)." (p20)

Fuller, Phillip/Zietz, Emily Norman/Calcote, Roger. "The Role of Financial Counselors in Long-Term Health Care Planning." Financial Counseling and Planning v8 n1 1997. p19-24. (ISSN1052-3073).

In the U.S., "nursing homes, while largely privately owned, get about 80 percent of their revenue from Medicare and Medicaid reimbursements....Eighty-five percent of the workers are women, and 28 percent are non-white....A 1994 SEIU [Service Employees International Union] survey found that certified nurse's aides earned $6.03 per hour on average, while dietary and laundry aides earned $5.75 per hour....Seventeen percent of nursing-home workers suffer occupational illnesses or injuries each year, chiefly back injuries incurred lifting residents--double the rate a decade ago." (p20)

Gustafson, Fred. "Labor: Broken Homes." In These Times v21 n17 14 Jul 1997. p20-22. (ISSN0160-5992).

A University of Michigan study "analyzed 1990 data from a sample of 2,128 residents of 268 nursing homes in 10 [U.S.] states, then obtained 1993 data from 2,088 patients in 254 of the same homes. Among the major findings: The prevalence of dehydration and stasis ulcer declined significantly from 1990 to 1993. While almost 5 percent of residents had ulcers in 1990, only 3 percent had the condition in 1993. For dehydration, the prevalence dropped from 2 percent to 1 percent." (p2) "The prevalence of daily pain rose from about 13 percent in 1990 to 17 percent in 1993." (p3)

University of Michigan. News and Information Services. "The Condition of U.S. Nursing Home Patients Improves, But Pain Is More Common than Ever." University of Michigan News Release 21 Jul 1997. p1-3.

NURSING HOMES--UNITED STATES--HANDICAPPED

In the U.S., "in 1994, there were an estimated 1.7 million elderly people in institutions. If the 1982 chronic disability rates had prevailed (adjusted for an older elderly population), 2.1 million persons would have been institutionalized. The net difference of 400,000 persons in part represents actual improvements in rates of chronic disability. At an annual per capita nursing home cost in 1994 of $43,300, the difference suggests savings of up to $17.3 billion in nursing home expenses that year." (p3)

"Chronic Disability Declines Dramatically among U.S. Elderly." Population Today v25 n9 Sep 1997. p3. (ISSN0749-2448).

NUT INDUSTRY

see also ALMOND INDUSTRY; FILBERT INDUSTRY; MACADAMIA NUT INDUSTRY; PEANUT INDUSTRY; PECAN INDUSTRY; PISTACHIO INDUSTRY; SUNFLOWER SEED INDUSTRY; WALNUT INDUSTRY

"Turkey, the world's second-largest tree nut producer, leads the world in output of hazelnuts and also produces significant quantities of walnuts, almonds, and other tree nuts. The United States ranks second behind China in walnut production and Iran in production of pistachios, but it produces the most almonds and pecans....The United States will remain the leading almond producer, typically accounting for 65-70 percent of the world total and four times as much as Spain, the second-largest almond producing country. The United States commands about 80 percent of total world almond exports." (p35)

Johnson, Doyle C./U.S. Dept. of Agriculture. Economic Research Service. "Special Article: United States Is World Leader in Tree Nut Production and Trade." Fruit and Tree Nuts Situation and Outlook Report Aug 1997. p35-39.

NUT INDUSTRY--UNITED STATES

"The quantity of China's tree nut exports has remained stable for the past decade at about 75,000 tons per year. But the export value of these nuts increased from $130 million in the mid-1980s to $170 million in the mid-1990s....In 1994, China's tree nut exports totaled $182 million: shelled walnuts ($27 million); chestnuts ($80 million); Gingko ($29 million); and pine nuts ($27 million)....China's imports of tree nuts increased from 10,000 tons ($12 million) in the mid-1980s to 27,000 tons ($24 million) in the mid-1990s. In 1994, major nut suppliers included: $11.5 million of cashews from Vietnam; $2.7 million of chestnuts from North Korea; and $3.6 million of pistachios from the United States...." (p49)

Crook, Frederick W./U.S. Dept. of Agriculture. Economic Research Service. "Introduction to China's Horticultural Economy." China: International Agriculture and Trade Reports Situation and Outlook Series Jun 1997. p47-51.

"The United States exported $1.4 billion of all tree nuts or about 424,000 metric tons in 1996. More than one-half of all U.S. tree nut exports go to the European Union, where primary markets include Germany, Spain, the Netherlands, United Kingdom, France, and Italy. Other significant European markets are Belgium, Sweden, Denmark, and Switzerland, Latin America buys about 5 to 10 percent of all U.S. tree nut exports, with Mexico representing one-half of the export value to Latin America. Canada generates 10 to 15 percent of total purchases while Asia consumes about 25 percent of all U.S. tree nut exports." (p35)

Johnson, Doyle C./U.S. Dept. of Agriculture. Economic Research Service. "Special Article: United States Is World Leader in Tree Nut Production and Trade." Fruit and Tree Nuts Situation and Outlook Report Aug 1997. p35-39.

"The United States produces more than one-third of the total world output of tree nuts, followed by Turkey with about 25 percent (mostly hazelnuts), China 12 percent (mostly walnuts), and Iran with about 5 percent (mostly pistachios). The United States also commands about 40 percent of world tree nut exports....In 1997, the United States will produce about 2.4 billion pounds of all tree nuts (in-shell basis) including the following and their approximate share of the total: almonds (57 percent), walnuts (19), pecans (13), pistachios (6), hazelnuts (3), and macadamia nuts (2)." (p35)

Johnson, Doyle C./U.S. Dept. of Agriculture. Economic Research Service. "Special Article: United States Is World Leader in Tree Nut Production and Trade." Fruit and Tree Nuts Situation and Outlook Report Aug 1997. p35-39.

In the U.S., "the production value for all tree nuts fell 4 percent in 1996 from a year earlier to $1.7 billion because of reduced grower prices. Despite reduced grower prices for almonds, higher production increased the crop's value to $1 billion, the highest on record. The 1996 U.S. almond crop accounted for 60 percent of tree nut production....Higher production and lower prices resulted in total domestic use rising to 590 million pounds (shelled basis), equal to 2.1 pounds per person. Domestic consumption was also boosted by a 9-percent increase in imported nuts, including Brazil nuts, pine nuts, chestnuts, cashews, and mixed nuts." (p3)

U.S. Dept. of Agriculture. Economic Research Service. "Summary." Fruit and Tree Nuts Situation and Outlook Report Oct 1997. p2-3.

In 1997, U.S. "nut exports were 376,000 tons, down 25 percent from 1996. The value of nut shipments were $1 billion, nearly the same as a year ago as export prices were higher." (p1)

U.S. Dept. of Agriculture. Economic Research Service. "Exports." U.S. Agricultural Trade Update 23 Jul 1997. p1.

NUTRITION

see also AGED--UNITED STATES--NUTRITION; CALCIUM IN HUMAN NUTRITION; FOLIC ACID IN HUMAN NUTRITION; FOOD; MALNUTRITION; NATIONAL SCHOOL LUNCH PROGRAM--NUTRITIONAL ASPECTS; NITROGEN IN ANIMAL NUTRITION

NUTRITION--UNITED STATES

In the U.S., "the average daily calorie intake recorded by NHANES [National Health and Nutrition Examination Survey] III for adults aged 20 to 74 was 2,200 in 1988-91, up from 1,969 for NHANES II in 1976-80. The average total number of fat grams consumed each day also increased, from 81 to 85.6. There was little change in the average percent of daily calories attributed to fat, at 34 percent in 1988-91." (p41)

Dortch, Shannon. "America Weighs In." American Demographics v19 n6 Jun 1997. p38-43,45. article-level access: <http://www.demographics.com/publications/ad/97_ad/9706_ad/ad970629.htm> (ISSN0163-4089).

NUTRITION--UNITED STATES--PUBLIC OPINION

Americans "appear to have at least a rudimentary understanding of the link between diet and health. More than nine in ten women who are the main meal preparers in their households know that there are health problems related to being overweight, according to the USDA's 1989-91 Diet and Health Knowledge Survey. Almost 80 percent know that high fat intake may lead to health problems, 86 percent are aware that cholesterol can mean trouble, and 88 percent know that sodium may have negative effects on health." (p42)

Dortch, Shannon. "America Weighs In." American Demographics v19 n6 Jun 1997. p38-43,45. article-level access: <http://www.demographics.com/publications/ad/97_ad/9706_ad/ad970629.htm> (ISSN0163-4089).

NUTRITION LABELING--UNITED STATES (v26)

NUTRITIONALLY INDUCED DISEASES--UNITED STATES

"At least five of the top 10 causes of death in the United States are linked to diet....Research conducted over the past two decades at the Harvard School of Public Health suggests that cancer deaths in the United States could be cut by as much as 40 percent by a change in diet." (p19) "The Framingham Heart Study that was published in the JOURNAL OF THE AMERICAN DIETETIC ASSOCIATION determined that if Americans reduced saturated fat intake to 9 percent of total energy, roughly 100,000 first-time coronary events could be averted by 2005, with associated cost savings of approximately $13 billion." (p20)

Milani, Laura. "The Edible Physician." New Physician v46 n5 Jul-Aug 1997. p18-22. (ISSN0028-6451).

OAHU (HAWAII)--POPULATION (v26)

OAKLAND COUNTY (MICH.)--EMPLOYMENT (v26)

OAKLAND COUNTY (MICH.)--EMPLOYMENT --MANUFACTURES (v26)

OAKLAND COUNTY (MICH.)--POPULATION (v26)

OATS INDUSTRY--UNITED STATES (v26)

OBESITY

"The prevalence of obesity in adults is 10% to 25% in most countries of western Europe and 20% to 25% in some countries in the Americas. This figure increases up to 40% for women in eastern European and Mediterranean countries, and black women in the USA." (p1-2)

World Health Organization. "Obesity Epidemic Puts Millions at Risk from Related Diseases." WHO Press n46 12 Jun 1997. p1-2. document-level access: <http://www.who.ch/press/1997/pr97-46.html>

OBESITY--ARIZONA

"The 1995 Behavioral Risk Factor Survey, an annual telephone survey of adult Arizonans, showed that 24.5% of all respondents reported being overweight, compared to 23.1% in 1994. In 1995, 59.8% of all respondents said they led a sedentary lifestyle, compared to 58.1% the previous year and 53% in 1993....According to the 1995 survey, the groups at highest risk for being overweight were those in the 45-54 year age group (34%) and those in the 35-44 year age group (31%). Those same groups were also at highest risk for a sedentary lifestyle, with 67.4% in the 45-54 year age group and 65.6% in the 35-44 year age group reporting no physical activity or physical activity done for 20 minutes or less, fewer than three times a week. Respondents in the $15,000-$19,999 income group reported the highest incidence of obesity (32.4%) and sedentary lifestyles (69.1%)."

Arizona. Dept. of Health Services. "Obesity, Sedentary Lifestyle Rates Up, Health Survey Says." News Release 2 Apr 1997. document-level access: <http://www.hs.state.az.us/news/obesity.htm>

OBESITY--DEVELOPING COUNTRIES (v26)

OBESITY--UNITED STATES (v26)

In the U.S., "the percent of adults aged 20 to 74 who are obese based on their body mass index increased from 24 percent in the 1960s to 33 percent in 1988-91. By 1994, the share of all adults aged 20 and older who are overweight climbed further, to 35 percent. Applying that rate to the adult population yields a total of 65 million U.S. adults aged 20 or older who were overweight in 1988-94....The share of children aged 6 to 11 who are overweight increased from 11 percent in the late 1970s to 14 percent in 1994. For children aged 12 to 17, the share doubled to 12 percent in 1994." (p39)

Dortch, Shannon. "America Weighs In." American Demographics v19 n6 Jun 1997. p38-43,45. article-level access: <http://www.demographics.com/publications/ad/97_ad/9706_ad/ad970629.htm> (ISSN0163-4089).

"An estimated 31 percent of Michigan adults are overweight, the fifth-highest percentage among the states. And a new report from the Michigan Department of Community Health predicts if the trend continues, 38 percent of all adults will be chubby by 2000....The state with with the heaviest folks is Indiana, where 35 percent are overweight....Only 22 percent of Hawaiian adults are considered overweight." (p1 secC)

Cain, Charlie. "Metro: Special Report: Health Snapshot: State Residents Tipping the Scales as Fifth-Heaviest in the Nation." Detroit News 17 Jul 1997. p1 secC.

"According to a recent report from the Centers for Disease Control and Prevention, 35 percent of adult Americans are overweight and a significant minority are seriously obese. At any given time, tens of millions of people are dieting, even if they aren't overweight. A quarter of all adult men and nearly half of all adult women are currently trying to lose weight....It has been estimated that 25 to 45 percent of those who seek treatment for obesity and 5 to 8 percent of obese people in the general community are binge eaters." (p6)

Nash, Joyce D. "Eating Disorders: Binge Eating." Healthline v16 n9 Sep 1997. p6-7. (ISSN0736-7929).

"Statistics show that in 1980, 25 percent of the [U.S.] population was overweight. By 1990 that number had risen to 33 percent, or one out of every three Americans....These statistics are true for children as well as for adults." (p10)

Raymond, Jennifer. "Another Fad Diet Crumbles Upon Examination: Caution: Approaching the Zone." Vegetarian Voice v22 n3 Aut 1997. p10-13. (ISSN0271-1591).

OBESITY--UNITED STATES--ADOLESCENTS

In the U.S., "in a study of 16-year-olds, physicians rated 15.2% of the females as obese, compared with 8.9% identified as obese by using relative weight; 7.8% were classified as obese using both methods (Moynihan et al., 1986). Only 6.4% of the males were rated as obese by the physicians, compared with 7.2% using relative weight, and 4.6% by both methods." (p876-877)

Pritchard, Mary E./King, Sondra L./Czajka-Narins, Dorice M. "Adolescent Body Mass Indices and Self-Perception." Adolescence v32 n128 Win 1997. p863-880. (ISSN0001-8449).

OBESITY--UNITED STATES--YOUTH

In the U.S., "many more children and teens are more seriously overweight than they were in 1980, which is the result of eating more calories and not exercising enough, according to Cynthia Ogden with the National Center for Health Statistics....About 14 percent of children age 6 to 11 are overweight, as are 12 percent of adolescents age 12 to 17. That is up from 8 percent of children and 6 percent of adolescents in 1980." (p72)

Cohn, Alvin W. "Juvenile Focus." Federal Probation v61 n3 Sep 1997. p71-73. (ISSN0014-9128).

OBESITY IN CHILDREN--CANADA--UNITED STATES

"American kids top the childhood heavyweight list: One in four who are ages five to twelve is 20 percent or more over his or her proper weight, according to the Centers for Disease Control in Atlanta, Georgia....'In a single decade, body weights of kids under six in the US increased 6 percent,'...[Lynn McIntyre, MD, dean of faculty of health professions at Dalhousie University in Halifax, Nova Scotia] says....Health professionals who monitor the eating habits of young children have found that with a daily fat intake of 30 percent of calories, one cheeseburger with fries can equal the total amount of fat a child should consume in two days. 'Current studies show that most US and Canadian kids have a diet that is about 40 to 45 percent fat,' McIntyre adds....According to the National Institute of Nutrition in Ottawa, Ontario, if both parents tip the scales at a normal weight, the probability of a child becoming obese is about 10 percent. But if one parent is overweight, the child's odds of matching that physical trait rise to 49 percent. If both the mother and father are overweight, a child stands an 80 percent chance of becoming obese...." (p40-41) Fourteen "percent of four- and five-year-old American children are overweight." (p42)

Downey, Charles. "Children: The Weight of Childhood Obesity." Kiwanis v82 n7 Aug 1997. p40-43. (ISSN0162-5276).

OBESITY IN CHILDREN--UNITED STATES (v26)

OCCUPATIONAL HEALTH AND SAFETY

see INDUSTRIAL HYGIENE; INDUSTRIAL SAFETY

OCCUPATIONAL INJURIES

see INDUSTRIAL ACCIDENTS

OCCUPATIONAL MORTALITY--UNITED STATES (v26)

OCCUPATIONS--UNITED STATES (v26)

OCCUPATIONS--UNITED STATES--PUBLIC OPINION (v26)

OCEAN DRILLING PLATFORMS

see DRILLING PLATFORMS

OCEAN TRAVEL--NORTH AMERICA (v26)

In 1996, there were over 6.2 million ocean cruise "passengers worldwide--and 75 percent were Americans....Cruises are the fastest growing segment of the tourism industry. They bring in over $7.5 billion in revenues. And 113 vessels currently operate in the North American market--1 American. Of the 30 companies operating in the North American market, 3 companies--foreign companies...command over 70 percent of the market." (pS9953)

Inouye, Daniel K. (Sen.-Hawaii). "Department of Defense Appropriations Act, 1998--Conference Report." Congressional Record. Daily ed. v143 n130 25 Sep 1997. pS9940-9956. section/page-level access: <http://thomas.loc.gov/cgi-bin/query/R?r105:FLD001:S09953:> (ISSN0363-7239). (X1.1A.105/1).

ODOMETERS--UNITED STATES (v26)

OFFENDERS

see CRIMINALS

OFFENDERS, FEMALE

see FEMALE OFFENDERS

OFFENDERS, JUVENILE

see JUVENILE DELINQUENTS

OFFENSES, REPEAT

see RECIDIVISM

OFFICE BUILDINGS--UNITED STATES (v26)

"The United States had 4.6 million commercial buildings in 1995, averaging 12,840 square feet in size. Total U.S. commercial floorspace--nearly 59 billion square feet--exceeded the area of the State of Delaware. Two-thirds of commercial buildings were used as retail stores, offices, warehouses, or places of education; six percent were vacant....Ninety-seven percent of commercial floorspace used electricity and 66 percent used natural gas. Seventy percent of commercial buildings counted water heating, lighting, space heating, and cooling as dominant energy uses. At least one method of energy conservation was used in 89 percent of commercial buildings, and conservation efforts increased since 1989." (unpaginated)

U.S. Dept. of Energy. Energy Information Administration. "Energy Plug: Commercial Buildings Characteristics 1995." Monthly Energy Review Jul 1997. (ISSN0095-7356).

OFFICE SURGERY

see AMBULATORY SURGERY

OFFSHORE ASSEMBLY INDUSTRY--EMPLOYMENT --MEXICO

"Between January and October of 1995--the period in which Mexico's economy lost three quarters of a million jobs--employment in the country's maquiladora sector rose by 20 percent to 648,000, according to the WEFA Group consulting firm. The Mexican National Institute of Statistics (INEGI) reports that the number had risen to 873,748 by April 1997. In 1995 WEFA predicted that the total would reach 943,000 by 2000; that figure now seems conservative. In other words, the Mexican maquiladora sector is expected to have grown by 400,000 jobs--75 percent--between 1995 and 2000." (p32)

Wilson, David L. "Do Maquiladoras Matter?" Monthly Review v49 n5 Oct 1997. p28-34. (ISSN0027-0520).

OFFSHORE ASSEMBLY INDUSTRY--HEALTH ASPECTS --MEXICO (v26)

OFFSHORE ASSEMBLY INDUSTRY--HOUSING--MEXICO

In Nogales, Sonora, Mexico, "the first 500 single-family, worker-owned homes were built last year, and another 250 will be finished by this summer." (p21) "Many, if not most, of the more than 800,000 maquiladora workers in Mexico live in crowded squatters' camps surrounding the factories....Maquiladoras...pay a 5 percent housing tax to the Mexican government...." (p22) "At least one worker at each of the 41 companies that belong to the Nogales Maquiladora Association--employers of some 90 percent of the 25,000 maquiladora workers in town--received a house." (p23)

Davidson, Miriam. "Maquiladora Workers Get Homes of Their

Own." APF Reporter v18 n3 1997. p21-26. (ISSN0913-4562).

OFFSHORE ASSEMBLY INDUSTRY--JAPAN (v26)

OFFSHORE ASSEMBLY INDUSTRY--MEXICO--JUAREZ (v26)

OFFSHORE ASSEMBLY INDUSTRY--MEXICO--TIJUANA (v26)

OFFSHORE INVESTMENTS

see INVESTMENTS, FOREIGN

OIL DRILLING PLATFORMS

see DRILLING PLATFORMS

OIL INDUSTRIES (v26)

"China's annual demand for transport fuel is set to increase from 47 million tonnes to 120 million tonnes by the year 2010....Exxon believes that only one trillion barrels of oil equivalent has been used out of a total available 4.7 trillion. The US Geological Survey estimates that up to 2.1 trillion barrels of oil could ultimately be produced economically worldwide, which could sustain the current rate of consumption for another 95 years." (p99)

Rowell, Andrew. "Crude Operators: The Future of the Oil Industry." Ecologist v27 n3 May-Jun 1997. p99-100,102,105-106. (ISSN0261-3131).

"International trade in oilseeds increased in 1996/97 by 2.2 million metric tons to 46.7 million, principally due to increased soybean exports. Global soybean import demand grew 13 percent in 1996/97...." (p7) "The EU imported 15.1 million tons of soybeans in 1996/97, up 6 percent from the previous year." (p8)

U.S. Dept. of Agriculture. Economic Research Service. "World Oilseed Situation." Oil Crops Situation and Outlook Series Oct 1997. p7-8.

"World oilseed production in 1996/97, at 257.2 million metric tons, remained nearly unchanged from 1995/96....World soybean production increased 6 percent, but was nearly offset by reductions in the output of rapeseed (down 12 percent), sunflowerseed (8 percent), and cottonseed (4 percent). The overall increase in the production of soybeans was fueled mostly by a 10-percent increase in the United States and a 13-percent increase in Brazil....Soybeans' share of world oilseed production increased from 49 percent to 51 percent and accounted for more than 77 percent of global oilseed trade." (p7)

U.S. Dept. of Agriculture. Economic Research Service. "World Oilseed Situation." Oil Crops Situation and Outlook Series Oct 1997. p7-8.

In 1996-1997, "international trade of oilseeds increased 5 percent to 46.7 million tons, resulting in a substantial 24-percent decrease in global ending stocks. These very low world oilseed stocks (16.2 million tons) are expected to trigger a substantial supply response in 1997/98 in several countries." (p7)

U.S. Dept. of Agriculture. Economic Research Service. "World Oilseed Situation." Oil Crops Situation and Outlook Series Oct 1997. p7-8.

OIL INDUSTRIES--CHINA

"A drop in production of the three major oilseeds (cottonseed, rapeseed and peanuts) reduced China's total oilseeds production by 5.3 percent in 1996....Total vegetable oil production will decline by 48,000 tons in 1996/97 because of the large drop in oilseed production in 1996....Production and planted area of the four major oilseeds (soybeans, peanuts, rapeseed, and cottonseed) account for more than 95 percent of China's total oilseed area and production. In 1995, the share of each oilseed in total oilseed output was: soybeans, 31.3 percent; peanuts, 23.6 percent; rapeseed, 22.6 percent; and cottonseed, 19.5 percent. In the last 2 years, soybean output fell from 16 million tons in 1994 to 13.5 million tons in 1995 and 1996. For peanuts, rapeseeds, and cottonseeds, production in 1996 fell by 0.06, 0.61 and 0.88 million tons, respectively, from the previous year, compared with production increases in 1994 and 1995." (p36)

Diao, Xinshen/U.S. Dept. of Agriculture. Economic Research Service. "China Becoming a Net Importer of Oilseeds, Oil, And Meal." China: International Agriculture and Trade Reports Situation and Outlook Series Jun 1997. p36-40.

"China's switch from being a net oilseed exporter to a net oilseed importer occurred in 1996/97. Total 1996/97 exports of the top five oilseeds dropped to 0.65 million tons while imports reached 2.1 million tons. In the space of 3 years, China went from net exports of 1.6 million tons in 1993/94 to estimated net imports of 1.5 million tons in 1996/97. Soybean imports account for 99 percent of total oilseed imports." (p37)

Diao, Xinshen/U.S. Dept. of Agriculture. Economic Research Service. "China Becoming a Net Importer of Oilseeds, Oil, And Meal." China: International Agriculture and Trade Reports Situation and Outlook Series Jun 1997. p36-40.

OIL INDUSTRIES--ECUADOR

"In Ecuador, pollution combined with loss of land and infestation of new diseases by colonists have devastated the local indigenous peoples since oil companies began exploring and producing oil in the rainforest two decades ago. The population of the Cofan peoples has been reduced from 70,000 to 3,000 in just 30 years....Since 1972, oil companies have dumped over 19 billion gallons of untreated toxic production wastes in the Ecuadorean rainforest....In Ecuador, 53 million cubic feet of gas is flared every day. Gas flaring causes local pollution as well as global warming." (p101)

"Crude Operators: The Future of the Oil Industry: The Ecological Impacts of the Oil Industry." Ecologist v27 n3 May-Jun 1997. p101. (ISSN0261-3131).

OIL INDUSTRIES--ENVIRONMENTAL ASPECTS

Roads are built on previously inaccessible areas before drilling for oil can begin. These roads "invariably lead to settlement, logging and mining. The World Bank estimates that for each mile of new road built by the oil industry, 400 to 2,400 hectares of land are colonized....As a result of drilling for oil, some 55,000 tonnes of oil are released each year into drill cuttings and muds, contaminating them with potentially toxic metals such as arsenic, cadmium and mercury....Worldwide there are approximately 700 oil refineries, which also cause spillages and create air and water pollution." (p101)

"Crude Operators: The Future of the Oil Industry: The Ecological Impacts of the Oil Industry." Ecologist v27 n3 May-Jun 1997. p101. (ISSN0261-3131).

OIL INDUSTRIES--IRAQ

"On the eve of the invasion of Kuwait, Iraq was pumping just over three million b/d [barrels/day of oil]. After the Gulf War, its output fell to around 600,000 b/d....Since December 1996, Iraq increased its exports under UN Security Council Resolution 986, which makes provisions for Iraq to sell $2 billion worth of oil to pay for food and medicine imports after deducting reparations and other payments....International oil prices fell some $4 to $5 per barrel when Iraqi supplies returned to the market." (p4)

Mohamedi, Fareed. "Oil, Gas and the Future of Arab Gulf Countries." Middle East Report v27 n3 Jul-Sep 1997. p2-6. (ISSN0899-2851).

OIL INDUSTRIES--KAZAKHSTAN

The Tengiz oil field in Kazakhstan, "is now considered one of the 10 largest oil fields in the world and...its oil output is expected to reach 750 thousand barrels per day by 2010." (p16) "As of 1993,...[Western Kazakstan] had produced 1 billion barrels of oil. Its identified reserves were calculated at 16 billion barrels of oil and 100 trillion cubic feet of gas and its speculative reserves at about 45 billion barrels of oil/ condensate and 260 trillion cubic feet of gas." (p17)

Cook, Harry E./Zempolich, William G./Zhemchuzhnikov, Viacheslav G./Corboy, James J. "Inside Kazakstan: Cooperative Oil and Gas Research." Geotimes v42 n11 Nov 1997. p16-20. (ISSN0016-8556).

OIL INDUSTRIES--MIDDLE EAST

"Proven oil reserves in the Arab countries at the beginning of 1997 were 346.0 billion barrels, representing 62 percent of world reserves, while at the same time oil production of all Arab states was 18.7 million barrels a day (b/d). In addition, Arab states are producing less than their current capacity of 21.0 million b/d. In the natural gas sector, Arab countries have estimated reserves of 23.0 trillion cubic meters, or about 22 percent of the world's gas reserves. Potential new discoveries in this part of the world are estimated at around 185.0 billion barrels of oil and around 20 trillion cubic meters of gas." (p32)

Horn, M. K. "Industry Watch: Oil and Gas Geology." Geotimes v42 n12 Dec 1997. p32. (ISSN0016-8556).

"Saudi Arabia is projected to increase its [oil] production from about 8.5 million barrels a day to 14.9 mbd by the year 2010....The Department of Energy projects that Iraq will be an oil producer that will pump 4.4 mbd in the year 2000 and 5.7 mbd in the year 2010. Iran not only maintains its current rate of oil production but somehow raises it to 5.5 mbd." (p8)

Cordesman, Anthony H. "Symposium--The Challenge in the Gulf: Building a Bridge from Containment to Stability." Middle East Policy v5 n2 May 1997. p1-21. (ISSN1061-1924).

OIL INDUSTRIES--NIGERIA (v26)

Shell Oil's "figures indicate that since 1989 there have been 190 oil spills a year in Nigeria....Up to 76 percent of gas extracted in Nigeria is flared (compared to 4.3 per cent in the UK); much of the flaring takes place close to villages." (p101)

"Crude Operators: The Future of the Oil Industry: The Ecological Impacts of the Oil Industry." Ecologist v27 n3 May-Jun 1997. p101. (ISSN0261-3131).

OIL INDUSTRIES--NORTH DAKOTA

In North Dakota, in 1996, the oil industry "brought the state $52.6 million from extraction and production taxes, a $9.4 million increase over 1995. [The oil industry] turned over $1.6 million to the state's Lands and Minerals Trust and more than $8.4 million to the Board of University and School Lands Trust. [The industry] increased oil sector jobs by about 500 over 1995 figures to 2,525. [It] produced crude oil valued at over $624 million in 1996. [The oil industry] used horizontal drilling techniques to drill 104 wells. [The industry] averaged 18 oil rigs a day, up from an average of 11 in 1995." (p8)

Cobb, Kathy. "State Roundups: North Dakota: Oil Continues to Boost Western North Dakota Economy." Federal Reserve Bank of Minneapolis Fedgazette v9 n3 Jul 1997. p8.

OIL INDUSTRIES--PERSIAN GULF REGION

"It was Iraq's invasion of Kuwait in August 1990, when both countries' [oil] exports, estimated between 4-4 1/2 mb/d [million barrels/day], were shut down completely that prices went up from $17/b to $41/b in a very short period." (p28) "In 1990-94 when, despite more than 11 percent rise in crude exports, oil revenues fell from more than $147 billion to about $120 billion." (p29)

Amuzegar, Jahangir. "OPEC's Seventh Life." Middle East Policy v5 n3 Sep 1997. p25-39. (ISSN1061-1924).

"In 1990, the international embargo on Iraq after it invaded Kuwait led to a decline of nearly three million b/d [barrels/ day] in crude oil on world markets....Saudi Arabia was able to make up for part of the reserve loss by raising its output by three million b/d. Kuwaiti output, also knocked out by the UN embargo and later by Iraqi sabotage, rebounded to two million b/ d in the early 1990s, nearly 700,000 b/d higher than pre-invasion levels. Adding small increases by the UAE [United Arab Emirates], Qatar and Oman, the Gulf has hiked its output by 4.8 million b/d since 1988. The region, therefore, only took one-third of the incremental demand increases of 12.1 million b/d between 1988 and 1996." (p3)

Mohamedi, Fareed. "Oil, Gas and the Future of Arab Gulf Countries." Middle East Report v27 n3 Jul-Sep 1997. p2-6. (ISSN0899-2851).

OIL INDUSTRIES--RUSSIA

"More than 70 per cent of Russia's crude oil comes from Western Siberia, even though the region's oil and gas industry is only 20 years old....Annual production dropped 44 per cent between 1988 and 1993 from 420 million tons to 235 million tons and is still falling....According to a 1995 Russian parliamentary commission, some five million tons of oil and gas, worth 72 billion rubles and 'enough to cover Russia's budget deficit', escape into the environment every year through leaky, antiquated pipelines or as the result of negligence." (p21)

Schmidt, Ellen. "The World Bank and Russian Oil." Ecologist v27 n1 Jan-Feb 1997. p21-27. (ISSN0261-3131).

OIL INDUSTRIES--TAXATION--UNITED STATES

In the U.S., a "tax break allows large oil and gas producers to immediately deduct 70% of their 'intangible' drilling and development costs--the costs of wages, fuel, repairs, hauling, supplies, and site preparation. The remaining 30% of these costs may be deducted over five years....It is estimated that this tax break provides a $2.5 billion subsidy for oil and gas exploration over five years." (p70)

Dunkiel, Brian S. "Conservation Strategy: How Government Tax Subsidies Destroy Habitat." Wild Earth v7 n2 Sum 1997. p69-71. (ISSN1055-1166).

OIL INDUSTRIES--UNITED ARAB EMIRATES

The United Arab Emirates "produces more than two million barrels of petroleum per day....It has nearly 100 billion barrels of recoverable reserves (more than four times that of the United States), enough to allow current production to continue for over 100 years." (p15)

Rugh, William A. "The United Arab Emirates: What Are the Sources of Its Stability?" Middle East Policy v5 n3 Sep 1997. p14-24. (ISSN1061-1924).

OIL INDUSTRIES--UNITED STATES

In the U.S., "the average price of domestic crude oil purchased at the wellhead was $19.41 per barrel in February 1997, 25 percent higher than the level in February 1996. The refiner acquisition cost of imported crude oil in February 1997 was $20.58 per barrel, 16 percent higher than the February 1996 level. The average cost of domestic crude oil in February 1997 was $22.49, 24 percent higher than the February 1996 average." (p109)

U.S. Dept. of Energy. Energy Information Administration. "Energy Prices." Monthly Energy Review May 1997. p109-128. (ISSN0095-7356).

In the U.S., "the estimated number of exploratory and development oil and gas wells drilled during April 1997 was 1,613, 15 percent lower than the previous month but 20 percent higher than the number drilled in April 1996. The estimated number of oil wells drilled was 842, and the estimated number of gas wells drilled was 771, 23 percent higher and 18 percent higher, respectively, than their April 1996 levels. The estimated number of dry holes drilled in April 1997 was 523, up 3 percent from March 1997 and up 23 percent from April 1996." (p81)

U.S. Dept. of Energy. Energy Information Administration.

"Oil and Gas Resource Development." Monthly Energy Review May 1997. p81-84. (ISSN0095-7356).

OIL RESERVES

see PETROLEUM RESERVES

OIL SPILLS--UNITED STATES (v26)

OIL WELL DRILLING--UNITED STATES (v26)

OIL WELL DRILLING RIGS--GULF OF MEXICO

"The number of drilling rigs in the Gulf of Mexico has grown to more than 1,000--double what it was five years ago. Oil production in the area is expected to rise from 1.1 billion barrels a day to nearly 2 billion within three years." (p1)

Baldauf, Scott. "Deep Drilling, Big Cars Drive Oil Boom." The Christian Science Monitor v89 n189 25 Aug 1997. p1,18. The Christian Science Monitor search engine: <http://www.csmonitor.com/plweb-cgi/iops1.pl> To retrieve this article, enter the following search: ED=19970825 AND boom. In the "retrieved list," click the title that matches this record. (ISSN0882-7729).

OIL WELL DRILLING RIGS--MIDDLE WEST

According to the Kansas City Fed's Second Quarter 1997 REGIONAL ECONOMIC DIGEST, "despite lower crude oil and natural gas prices, the average number of drilling rigs operating in the [Middle West] district was up 4.2 percent over the previous quarter and was 22.7 percent above last year's levels. The national rig count rose 1.3 percent in the first quarter and was 20.9 percent higher than a year ago." (unpaginated)

"Regional Economy Enjoys Solid Growth in First Quarter." Federal Reserve Bank of Kansas City Fed Letter Aug 1997.

OIL WELL DRILLING RIGS--UNITED STATES (v26)

In the U.S., "the April 1997 rotary rig count of 901 was less than 1 percent higher than the count in March and 22 percent higher than the count in April 1996. Of the total number of rigs in operation in April 1997, 775 were onshore and 126 were offshore. For April 1997, the number of onshore rigs was up 23 percent and the number of offshore rigs rose 12 percent from their April 1996 values." (p81)

U.S. Dept. of Energy. Energy Information Administration. "Oil and Gas Resource Development." Monthly Energy Review May 1997. p81-84. (ISSN0095-7356).

The July 1997 rotary oil well drilling "rig count of 969 [in the U.S.] was 1 percent lower than the count in June but 24 percent higher than the count in July 1996. Of the total number of rigs in operation in July 1997, 844 were onshore and 125 were offshore. For July 1997, the number of onshore rigs was up 25 percent and the number of offshore rigs rose 17 percent from their July 1996 values." (p81)

U.S. Dept. of Energy. Energy Information Administration. "Oil and Gas Resource Development." Monthly Energy Review Aug 1997. p81-84. (ISSN0095-7356).

OIL WELL DRILLING RIGS--WEST (U.S.)

"Employment in the 'oil patch' of North Dakota stands at its highest level in six years, and twice as many drill rigs are now probing the state's western plains as three years ago. Drilling activity in a six-state area of the West is up 12 percent over a year ago--particularly in Wyoming and New Mexico." (p1)

Baldauf, Scott. "Deep Drilling, Big Cars Drive Oil Boom." The Christian Science Monitor v89 n189 25 Aug 1997. p1,18. The Christian Science Monitor search engine: <http://www.csmonitor.com/plweb-cgi/iops1.pl> To retrieve this article, enter the following search: ED=19970825 AND boom. In the "retrieved list," click the title that matches this record. (ISSN0882-7729).

OIL WELLS--ABANDONMENT--UNITED STATES (v26)

OILS AND FATS (v26)

OILS AND FATS--UNITED STATES (v26)

OILS AND FATS, EDIBLE (v26)

OKINAWA (JAPAN)--ECONOMIC CONDITIONS (v26)

OKLAHOMA CITY FEDERAL BUILDING BOMBING, OKLAHOMA CITY, OKLA., 1995

"The bombing of the Alfred P. Murrah federal building in Oklahoma City on April 19, 1995, constituted the worst terrorist act in U.S. history. The event resulted in 168 deaths and more than 800 injuries. More than 16,000 persons were in the downtown area at the time, where they felt and heard the blast and witnessed death and destruction. An additional 12,000 were involved in rescue efforts, including body handling and caring for the injured....In the first six months, almost 9,000 persons received services from Project Heartland [a special program for persons reporting distress from exposure to the blast]." (p1191)

Tucker, Phebe/Dickson, Warren/Pfefferbaum, Betty/McDonald, Nicholas B./Allen, Gwen. "Traumatic Reactions as Predictors of Posttraumatic Stress Six Months after the Oklahoma City Bombing." Psychiatric Services v48 n9 Sep 1997. p1191-1194. (ISSN1075-2730).

OLD AGE, SURVIVORS AND DISABILITY INSURANCE

see INSURANCE, DISABILITY; SOCIAL SECURITY

OLDER PERSONS

see AGED

OMAN--SOCIAL CONDITIONS (v26)

ONCHOCERCIASIS (v26)

ONCHOCERCIASIS--LATIN AMERICA

"The Onchocerciasis Elimination Program for the Americas (OEPA) recently reported that teams in Brazil, Colombia, Ecuador, Guatemala, Mexico and Venezuela distributed...[a drug that could prevent onchocerciasis, one of the leading causes of blindness in Latin America] to about 200,000 people in 1996, 60 percent of their goal. In all, coverage was 98 percent in the high risk areas of Latin America where the effects of the disease are most severe. According to the OEPA officials, there have been no new cases of the disease in coastal Ecuador for more than a year and none in Oaxaca State, Mexico, for more than two years." (p12) "Head offices for the Onchocerciasis Elimination Program in the Americas were established in Guatemala, which has 31 percent of all cases of river blindness disease in Latin America....'Education is one of the main reasons Ecuador has nearly 100 percent coverage in its endemic areas,' says Dr. Guillermo Zea, OEPA's deputy director...." (p13)

"The Bank in Action: Region: River Blindness in Retreat." IDB v24 n7 Jul 1997. p12-13. (ISSN0145-2274).

ONCHOCERCIASIS--WEST AFRICA (v26)

ONE-PARENT FAMILY

see SINGLE-PARENT FAMILY

OPERATION DESERT STORM, 1991

see PERSIAN GULF WAR, 1991

OPIUM TRADE--AFGHANISTAN (v26)

ORAL CONTRACEPTIVES--MICHIGAN--NORTH CAROLINA

"Despite the seeming simplicity of birth control pills, 27 percent of women in a contraceptive use study [in the U.S.] didn't take the pill for two or more consecutive days and used no backup contraceptives in the following week, so they were at increased risk of pregnancy....The study of 103 women in Michigan and North Carolina was conducted by researchers at the University of Michigan School of Nursing and Family Health International, a research firm in Research Triangle Park, N.C....About 18 million U.S. women take the pill. According to electronic devices that recorded the time and date that each pill was removed from the blister pack, 52 percent of the women took each pill or never missed more than one pill at a time after the first week of the initial cycle. Eighteen percent of the women missed two or more consecutive pills but modified their risk by avoiding intercourse for the next seven days, while another 3 percent who missed pills protected themselves by using backup contraception such as condoms for the next seven days." (p1)

University of Michigan. News and Information Services. "'Pregnant? How Could I Be? I'm on the "Pill."' Twenty-Seven Percent of Women in...Study Missed Two Pills...." University of Michigan News Release 8 Dec 1997. p1-2.

ORANGE COUNTY (CALIF.)--POPULATION

In Orange County, California, "over the past 30 years the population has skyrocketed from 700,000 people to more than 2.5 million. Another 600,000 are expected by 2010." (p18)

Holing, Dwight. "The Coastal Sage Scrub Solution." Nature Conservancy v47 n4 Jul-Aug 1997. p16-24. (ISSN0028-5200).

ORANGE RIVER (v26)

ORANGE INDUSTRY--FLORIDA (v26)

For 1996-1997, "Florida harvested 225.7 million 90-pound boxes, 134.2 million boxes of early and midseason oranges and an estimated 91.5 million boxes of Valencias....Because of the large crop, prices received by growers fell this year, averaging $3.69 during December-June, 29 percent lower than a year earlier and 18 percent below the previous 2-year average...." (p28-29)

U.S. Dept. of Agriculture. Economic Research Service. "Citrus Fruit Outlook." Fruit and Tree Nuts Situation and Outlook Report Aug 1997. p27-31.

ORANGE INDUSTRY--UNITED STATES (v26)

ORANGE JUICE INDUSTRY--BRAZIL--MEXICO --UNITED STATES (v26)

ORANGE JUICE INDUSTRY--UNITED STATES

In the U.S., "along with record fruit production, [orange] juice yield estimates are...up this year at 1.58 gallons per box, 4 percent higher than last year. The increased production and yields raise frozen concentrated orange juice (FCOJ) production estimates to 1.456 billion single-strength gallons, 13 percent above last year and the third year of production increases. While FCOJ consumption is projected to rise 3 percent this year to 1.442 billion single-strength gallons, it is not growing fast enough to keep up with production. Therefore, stocks at the end of the year are expected to reach 382 million gallons, more than a year's supply. The large FCOJ production has brought down futures prices, which ranged from $0.751 to $0.887 per pound solids between December and June, 36 percent below last year....While both futures and growers' prices have been down throughout the 1996/97 marketing year, orange juice retail prices have remained about 6 percent above a year ago, ranging from $1.727 to $1.768 for 16 fluid ounces." (p29)

U.S. Dept. of Agriculture. Economic Research Service. "Citrus Fruit Outlook." Fruit and Tree Nuts Situation and Outlook Report Aug 1997. p27-31.

U.S. "orange juice exports during December 1996 to May 1997 rose 40 percent from the previous year. Exports to the European Union, which accounted for 36 percent of the U.S. orange juice export market, rose 53 percent. Exports to Japan, which accounted for 9 percent of exports, fell 8 percent. The large supply of orange juice on the world market due to large crops in the United States and Brazil, have lowered the world price, and the value of U.S. exports in 1996/97 rose 12 percent from a year ago." (p29)

U.S. Dept. of Agriculture. Economic Research Service. "Citrus Fruit Outlook." Fruit and Tree Nuts Situation and Outlook Report Aug 1997. p27-31.

OREGON--SOCIAL CONDITIONS (v26)

ORES--SWEDEN (v26)

ORGAN DONATION

see DONATION OF ORGANS, TISSUES, ETC.

ORGAN TRANSPLANTS

see TRANSPLANTATION OF ORGANS, TISSUES, ETC.

ORGANIC FARMING--UNITED STATES (v26)

ORGANIC FOODS INDUSTRY

see NATURAL FOODS INDUSTRY

ORGANIZATION OF PETROLEUM EXPORTING COUNTRIES --ECONOMIC CONDITIONS

"The 11 countries comprising the Organization of Petroleum Exporting Countries wrapped up their annual meeting in Austria...after pledging to rein in excess production. 'We can hope if our members restrain their output, it will help the market go up,' said Rilwanu Lukman of Nigeria, OPEC's secretary-general. Crude oil now sells for about $17 a barrel on average, down from about $23 late last year." (p3 secB)

Raphael, Steve. "Inside Business: OPEC Leaders Say They Will Cut Excess Production." Detroit News 27 Jun 1997. p3 secB.

The Organization of Petroleum Exporting Countries "basket price of $18.28 in April 1995 was the highest monthly average since April 1993, and remained below that level for the whole year. Most of the 2 mb/d [million barrels/day] increase in demand for oil during 1993-95 went to non-OPEC producers, while OPEC's output remained only about half a million barrels on average over its official ceiling of 24.52 mb/d. While the situation subsequently improved, and out of the 1.8 mb/d increase in the global demand for oil during 1997, some 600,000 barrels are expected to be supplied by OPEC...." (p33)

Amuzegar, Jahangir. "OPEC's Seventh Life." Middle East Policy v5 n3 Sep 1997. p25-39. (ISSN1061-1924).

ORGANIZATIONAL DOWNSIZING

see DOWNSIZING OF ORGANIZATIONS

ORGANIZATIONS, BUSINESS

see BUSINESS ENTERPRISES

ORGANIZATIONS, NON-GOVERNMENTAL

see NON-GOVERNMENTAL ORGANIZATIONS

ORGANIZED CRIME--CANADA--COSTS (v26)

ORGANOPHOSPHORUS COMPOUNDS--GREAT BRITAIN (v26)

ORNAMENTAL FISH TRADE--UNITED STATES

"U.S. exports of ornamental fish were valued at $8.4 million in first-half 1997, up 1 percent from the same period in 1996....Exports remain 17 percent below the $10.1 million recorded in first-half 1994....Imports of ornamental fish during the first 6 months of 1997 fell 8 percent to $25.9 million, well below those of the last 2 years." (unpaginated)

Harvey, Dave/U.S. Dept. of Agriculture. Economic Research Service. "Ornamental Fish Exports Rise, Imports Fall." Aquaculture Outlook 3 Oct 1997.

OSTEOPATHIC PHYSICIANS--UNITED STATES (v26)

OSTEOPATHIC SCHOOLS--UNITED STATES (v26)

OSTEOPOROSIS--UNITED STATES (v26)

OSTEOPOROSIS--UNITED STATES--COSTS (v26)

OSTEOPOROSIS--UNITED STATES--PREVENTION

"Osteoporosis, a progressive bone disease, affects some 25 million Americans, 80 percent of them women. It causes hip, spinal and wrist fractures, shortened stature and stooped posture....Last year, the American College of Rheumatology issued guidelines to prevent drug-issued osteoporosis. Among them: Daily calcium intake of 1,500 milligrams. (An 8-ounce glass of 1-percent milk has 800 milligrams.) 800 international units a day of vitamin D, or 50,000 international units three times a week. Bone density measurements at the onset of steroid therapy and six to 12 months later." (p5 secA)

Anstett, Patricia. "Steroid Users Risk Bone Disease: Calcium, Vitamin D Are Important for Prevention." Detroit Free Press 13 Nov 1997. p5 secA.

OSTEOPOROSIS--UNITED STATES--WOMEN (v26)

"Severe-bone loss, osteoporosis, is a disease which affects 20 million American women and millions of older men....A woman's risk for hip fracture alone is equal to the combined risk of developing breast, uterine and ovarian cancer....Studies have shown that up to half of persons who have had a hip fracture lose their ability to walk independently, up to a third become totally dependent, and up to 20 percent die from conditions related to the fracture or to surgery....For women over age 50, there is almost a 50 percent chance of having a bone broken due to osteoporosis. Experts have suggested that one-half of the fractures from osteoporosis could be prevented by the practice of good nutrition along with healthy lifestyles."

Alabama. Dept. of Public Health. "As Hip Fractures Increase in the Southeast, Osteoporosis Prevention and Treatment Encouraged." News Release 10 May 1997. document-level access: <http://www.alapubhealth.org/Press/pr051097b.html>

OSTRICH FARMING--UNITED STATES

"Ostriches are becoming popularly raised in the United States and elsewhere for their plumes and eggs. Fertilized eggs sell for as much as $1500, while young hens go for around $3,000 or more. A pair of fertile, productive adults can sell for $30,000 to $75,000....Durable ostrich leather can be made into expensive wallets and other leather goods, with boots selling for over $600 a pair....At about $20 per pound, there are a wealth of cuts to be had from an average 400 pound bird. Ostrich meat has half the calories of beef, one-seventh the amount of fat and considerably less cholesterol, tasting similar to beef tenderloin. Far more profitable than cattle, as of 1992 there were about 20,000 birds on 2,000 ostrich farms in the United States, even as far north as Oklahoma." (p16)

Saunders, Melvin D. "Finding Opportunity in Diversity...: Raising Exotic Livestock." Acres, U.S.A. v27 n9 Sep 1997. p16-17. (ISSN1076-4968).

OUTDOOR RECREATION

see also CAMPING

OUTDOOR RECREATION--MICHIGAN--YPSILANTI

In Ypsilanti, Michigan, "more than 5,000 people use Rutherford Municipal Pool each summer, more than 2,000 take part in the city's sports camps. An average of 40 senior citizens use the Senior Center each day. The city's playground program has a summer enrollment of about 400 kids." (p1 secD)

Stewart, Will. "Local: Making a Difference: Recreation Director Has Brought Life to Programs." Ann Arbor News 17 Aug 1997. p1 secD.

OUTDOOR RECREATION--UNITED STATES

"The average U.S. adult participated in 3.7 different outdoor activities in 1997, according to a Roper poll conducted in April for the Recreation Roundtable. That is down from 5.2 activities in 1994....Walking for fitness or recreation is always the most popular pastime on the list, and 42 percent of respondents said they walked for fun in 1997. Following in popularity were driving for pleasure, at 34 percent; swimming, 31 percent; picnicking, 26 percent; and fishing, 20 percent....About half the respondents in both years said that they participate in outdoor recreation at least once a month." (p4)

"Fewer Outings in 1997." Forecast v17 n11 Nov 1997. p4. article-level access: <http://www.demographics.com/publications/fc/97_fc/9711_fc/fc97113.htm> (ISSN0732-1597).

"Wildlife watchers are people who participate in wildlife observation, feeding, or photography as a primary activity. Their numbers declined 17 percent in the U.S. between 1991 and 1996, according to the National Survey of Fishing, Hunting, and Wildlife-Associated Recreation by the U.S. Fish and Wildlife Service....Consumer expenditures on wildlife watching increased 10 percent in inflation-adjusted dollars, to $27 billion. Within that total, spending on wildlife-watching trips declined 5 percent, to $9.4 billion. Spending on magazines, dues, and contributions was unchanged at $1.9 billion. But wildlife watchers' spending on equipment increased 24 percent, to $15.7 billion." (p4)

"The Wildlife Bunch." Forecast v17 n8 Aug 1997. p4. article-level access: <http://www.demographics.com/Publications/FC/97_fc/9708_fc/FC97082.htm> (ISSN0732-1597).

OUTDOOR RECREATION--UNITED STATES. ARMY CORPS OF ENGINEERS

Today, 4,331 U.S. Army Corps of Engineers-developed "recreation areas on 463 lakes and waterways are available to the public. The Corps itself operates and maintains 57 percent of these sites....Of those operated by the Corps, 746 areas, with a total of 46,000 campsites, charge a fee for use. Only about 28 percent are reserveable." (p17)

Moore, Chris. "Reservation Systems." Grist v41 n2 Spr 1997. p17-18.

OUTPATIENT MEDICAL CARE

see AMBULATORY MEDICAL CARE

OUTPATIENT SURGERY

see AMBULATORY SURGERY

OVARIES--CANCER--UNITED STATES (v26)

In the U.S., women with ovarian cancer have "a five-year survival rate of less than 40 percent....Ovarian cancer is the leading cause of death from gynecologic malignancies in the United States, where 1 in 70 women ultimately develop the cancer. The median age of women at diagnosis ranges between 60 and 65 years, and over 85 percent are postmenopausal. While there are several kinds of ovarian cancer (since there are several kinds of cells composing an ovary), epithelial ovarian carcinoma (EOC) is the most common (80 to 90 percent) variety." (p6) "Up to 40 percent of women with a family history of EOC (and about 15 percent without such a history) carry a mutant cancer-suppressing gene (BRCA). Hereditary ovarian cancer syndromes (three are currently identified) account for less than 10 percent of all cases but should be considered in women with family histories of breast, ovary, uterus, pancreas, or colon cancers." (p7)

Scannell, Kate A. "Cancer: Ovarian Cancer." Healthline v16 n7 Jul 1997. p6-7. (ISSN0736-7929).

OVERTIME--UNITED STATES

According to the following U.S. "Department of Labor statistics: one-fourth of workers who depend on overtime earn under $12,000 per year. Sixty-one percent earn $20,000, or less. More than 80 percent of overtime recipients earn less than $28,000 a year....Employers violate current overtime provisions at an alarming rate. One-third, or 13,687, of the investigations by the Department of Labor in 1996 disclosed overtime violations. The Department ordered over $100 million in back pay for 170,000 workers who were victims of those overtime violations. In addition, there was a backlog of 16,000 unexamined complaints pending at the Department of Labor at the end of 1996. That backlog accounts for about 40 percent of the annual number of complaints." (pS4343)

Harkin, Tom (Sen.-Iowa). "Family Friendly Workplace Act." Congressional Record. Daily ed. v143 n62 13 May 1997. pS4327-4354. section/page-level access: <http://thomas.loc.gov/cgi-bin/query/R?r105:FLD001:S04342:> (ISSN0363-7239). (X1.1A.105/1).

OVERUSE INJURIES--UNITED STATES (v26)

OVERWEIGHT

see OBESITY

OWNERSHIP

see PROPERTY

OWNERSHIP BY EMPLOYEES

see EMPLOYEE OWNERSHIP

OWNERSHIP OF FARMS
see FARM OWNERSHIP
OWNERSHIP OF HOMES
see HOME OWNERSHIP
OWNERSHIP OF STOCK
see STOCK OWNERSHIP
OZONE LAYER (v26)
OZONE LAYER--ARCTIC REGIONS (v26)
OZONE LAYER--HUDSON BAY (v26)
OZONE LAYER DEPLETION
see also ATMOSPHERIC OZONE

A report released by Environment Canada on 15 September 1997, "Global Benefits and Costs of the Montreal Protocol on Substances that Deplete the Ozone Layer," estimates that the global phaseout of ozone-depleting substances "will cost US $235 billion....Of this cost, 40% will be incurred by the refrigeration and air-conditioning sectors. On the other hand, the study estimates that global economic benefits will total some $459 billion--$238 billion from reduced damage to fisheries, $191 billion from reduced damage to agriculture, and $30 billion from reduced damage to materials....The report estimates that 19 million cases of nonmelanoma skin cancer and 1.5 million cases of melanoma skin cancer will be prevented, more than 129 million cases of cataracts will be prevented, and 333,500 skin cancer fatalities will be prevented by compliance with the Montreal Protocol." (p4)

"Policy and Economics: Benefits of Montreal Protocol Outweigh Costs." Global Environmental Change Report v9 n18 26 Sep 1997. p4. (ISSN1049-9083).

OZONE LAYER DEPLETION--ANTARCTIC

According to bulletins from the British Antarctic Survey and the World Meteorological Organization (WMO), ozone depletion in the Antarctic during August 1997, "was 'comparable' to the average ozone deficit observed during August over the past six years, ranging from 22% below normal at Syowa to 29% below normal at Halley. Levels above Halley had fallen to 35% below normal as of 5 September. During August, ozone levels over the mid-latitudes (35-60 [degrees]) of the Southern Hemisphere also reached their second-lowest average since the early 1980s...." (p3)

"Focus Report: Methyl Bromide, HCFCs to Dominate Montreal Meeting." Global Environmental Change Report v9 n17 12 Sep 1997. p1-3. (ISSN1049-9083).

OZONE LAYER DEPLETION--CANADA

"Environment Canada released a report on 8 September [1997] stating that the greatest ozone depletion over Canada to date occurred this spring, when ozone levels in the high Arctic dropped to 45% below normal. The previous spring, levels dropped to 30% below normal." (p2-3)

"Focus Report: Methyl Bromide, HCFCs to Dominate Montreal Meeting." Global Environmental Change Report v9 n17 12 Sep 1997. p1-3. (ISSN1049-9083).

PACs
see POLITICAL ACTION COMMITTEES
PAGERS (BEEPERS)
see BEEPERS (PAGERS)
PAIN--AFRO-AMERICANS

According to an EPIC/MRA survey, in the U.S., "black people complain less about pain than white people and wait longer to get help....They have much higher rates of depression than whites--68 percent, compared to 46 percent for whites. More than half of blacks--56 percent--also say pain has made their lives terrible, compared to 20 percent of whites who take it to that level....Blacks missed work slightly more than whites did, (32 percent to 27 percent) because of pain." (p6 secA)

Anstett, Patricia. "The State of Pain: Gender, Race and Age Affect Who Seeks Relief, Poll Shows." Detroit Free Press 14 Oct 1997. p1,6 secA.

PAIN--MICHIGAN

"For about 1.2 million people in Michigan, every day is a pain. More than one in five adults in the state report being in chronic pain, which can last for years and is often so severe that it rules their days and overwhelms their spirits. Many of them say doctors and medicine have been no help. Those are among the findings of a major study...[released on October 13, 1997]. 'The State of Pain in Michigan' is the largest study of chronic pain ever conducted in Michigan, and one of the most extensive undertakings of its kind in the nation....The telephone poll of 1,500 Michigan adults was conducted...[in October 1997] by EPIC/MRA, a Lansing polling firm." (p1 secA)

Anstett, Patricia. "The State of Pain: Search for Relief Sometimes Leads to More Suffering." Detroit Free Press 13 Oct 1997. p1,8 secA.

PAIN--UNITED STATES

According to an EPIC/MRA survey, in the U.S., "women are more likely to report pain than men--23 percent of women say they have recurring pain, compared to 17 percent of men. But men are more likely to have lasting, unrelieved pain. About 81 percent of men who said they were in pain reported that it has gone on for more than a year; 75 percent of women in pain said it had been ongoing that long....Men and women attribute their pain to different causes. Among men, 47 percent blame pain on injuries or accidents, compared to 20 percent of women, who more often associate pain with ongoing health problems." (p6 secA)

Anstett, Patricia. "The State of Pain: Gender, Race and Age Affect Who Seeks Relief, Poll Shows." Detroit Free Press 14 Oct 1997. p1,6 secA.

PAIN--UNITED STATES--COSTS (v26)
PAIN--UNITED STATES--PUBLIC OPINION

According to an EPIC/MRA survey, in the U.S., "young men are most vulnerable to thoughts of suicide over chronic pain. About 17 percent of men under 50 have contemplated suicide, the highest of any group. Young people--both men and women--are more likely to grow depressed about pain than are older adults, although depression is a major problem among all people with chronic pain. Under age 50, 56 percent of women and 54 percent of men say they have been depressed about living with pain. Above age 50, 42 percent of women and 41 percent of men experienced depression." (p6 secA)

Anstett, Patricia. "The State of Pain: Gender, Race and Age Affect Who Seeks Relief, Poll Shows." Detroit Free Press 14 Oct 1997. p1,6 secA.

PAKISTAN--ECONOMIC CONDITIONS (v26)
PAKISTAN--POPULATION

"Pakistan, with some 139 million people, is the world's sixth most populous country. But, at its present 2.7 percent annual growth rate, it will double its population in only 25 years and exceed the current population of the United States, the world's third most populous country after China and India....[According to Pakistan's Minister of Population Welfare, H.E. Syeda Abida Hussain, Pakistan's government] "has made a commitment to reduce the growth rate to 1.7 percent in only five years....She pointed out that to lower the growth rate by a full percentage point will require raising contraceptive prevalence from the current 24.8 percent of married women to 51 percent. But she noted that only six years ago the rate was a mere 12.1 percent....The average Pakistani woman, she said, now has 5.8 children during her reproductive lifetime." (p3)

"Pakistan's Future Hinges on Stabilizing Population." Popline v19 Jul-Aug 1997. p3.

PALESTINE--ECONOMIC CONDITIONS (v26)

PALESTINIAN ARABS
see also HOUSING--JERUSALEM--PALESTINIAN ARABS; JEWS--PALESTINIAN ARABS
PALESTINIAN ARABS--EMPLOYMENT (v26)
PALESTINIAN ARABS--ISRAEL--JERUSALEM
"Residency permits of more than 1,000 East Jerusalem Arabs and their relatives have been revoked in the last year and a half....The non-Jewish population in Jerusalem is now 180,000 in a city of 600,000, or 30 percent." (p7)
"Dateline Migration: International: Israel Says Arabs Born in Jerusalem Are Aliens." Migration World v25 n4 1997. p7. (ISSN1058-5095).
PALESTINIAN ARABS--ISRAEL--SOCIAL CONDITIONS
In Israel, "there were 17 blockades in the Occupied Territories between the onset of the Intifada in December 1987 and September 1993, totaling 145 days. During these periods, people and goods were prevented from moving from the West Bank and Gaza to Jerusalem and Israel....There were eight...super-blockades in 1994 alone, covering 77 days. Since the Palestinian economy relies on its workers inside Jerusalem and Israel, this restriction on Palestinian labor has been disastrous--up to $6 million a day. The Israeli military has destroyed 31 agricultural dirt roads in an attempt to stop residents from using them to commute to and from West Bank towns. Soldiers have...invaded 45 villages." (p16) "Thus far in 1997, the Israeli government has imposed four sieges on the West Bank. One covered all Palestinian-controlled areas; the others were partial sieges closing the towns of Hebron, Nablus, and nearby villages for 38 days. In all, there have been an estimated 48 Israeli super-blockades or sieges on the Occupied Territories for a combined period of 436 days." (p17)
"Punishing the Innocent." Toward Freedom v46 n5 Sep-Oct 1997. p16-17. (ISSN0048-9898).
PALESTINIAN ARABS--JORDAN (v26)
PALM PRODUCTS--AFRICA--UNITED STATES (v26)
PANARA INDIANS--BRAZIL
In Brazil, the Panara Indians "now number about 160, with at least 60% of the population under 20 years old, and more than half under 14." (p24) "In December 1994, the president of FUNAI [National Indian Foundation] published the decree (portaria) recognizing the Panara's rights to an area of 488,000 hectares in northern Mato Grosso and southern Para states in the Diario Oficial." (p25)
Schwartzman, Stephan. "Self Determination and Territory: Success Story in Brazil: The Return of the Panara." Abya Yala News v10 n3 Sum 1997. p22-25,38. (ISSN1056-5876).
PANIC DISORDERS--UNITED STATES (v26)
PAP TEST--UNITED STATES (v26)
PAPAYA INDUSTRY--UNITED STATES
In the U.S., "in 1996, fresh papaya imports increased 72 percent from 1995, boosting domestic consumption to more than half a pound per person annually. Papaya consumption has been growing steadily since 1991 when it was 0.17 pound per person versus 0.55 pound in 1996, a 224-percent increase....In 1996, imports rose to 126 million pounds, 72 percent over 1995 imports....Mexico is the principal source for U.S. papayas, with 88 percent of the import market. Other major suppliers include Belize, Jamaica, Dominican Republic, and Costa Rica; each providing over 2 million pounds during the year." (p24)
U.S. Dept. of Agriculture. Economic Research Service. "Noncitrus Fruit Outlook." Fruit and Tree Nuts Situation and Outlook Report Aug 1997. p7-26.
PAPER INDUSTRY (v26)
PAPER INDUSTRY--CHINA (v26)
PAPER INDUSTRY--RECYCLING--EUROPE
"The Confederation of European Paper Industries (CEPI) said the 1996 recycling rate reached 49.8%, 3.5 percentage points higher than in 1995 and up from 39% five years earlier. CEPI said last year's level was well above the world average of 37% and the 45% rate achieved in the US and Canada, though slightly below Japan's rate of 51.3%....National recycling rates in Western Europe ranged from 71.1% in Germany down to 12.2% in Ireland....Almost 20% of the waste paper recycled in Europe has to cross a border before it arrives at the pulp plant." (p4-5)
"In Brief...: European Paper Recycling Rate Advances." Environment Watch: Western Europe v6 n17 5 Sep 1997. p4-5. (ISSN1066-6001).
PAPER INDUSTRY--UNITED STATES (v26)
"Each American on average consumes more than 730 pounds of paper each year, and collectively the US produces and consumes more than 80 million tons annually. Less than a third is from recycled (post and pre-consumer) sources. The rest is from virgin fiber sources. In the US, 99% of the virgin fiber used in paper making comes from trees." (p4)
Rosemarin, Heather. "Cover Story: The Paper Challenge." Positive Alternatives v7 n4 Sum 1997. p4-5. (ISSN1065-0075).
PAPERWORK (OFFICE PRACTICE)--UNITED STATES (v26)
PARACHUTING--UNITED STATES
"The U.S. Parachute Association reports that its membership, which stands at 33,500, has been growing 10 percent annually for the last two years. 'Probably somewhere between 130,000 and 150,000 people skydive every year,' says USPA executive director Chris Needels....'By far the fastest-growing segment of our membership is coming from people in the 40-plus group,' says Needels. The largest portion of members, 36 percent, are in their 30s, and 28 percent are 29 or younger. But 22 percent are in their 40s, 7 percent are in their 50s, and 7 percent of skydiving association members are aged 60 and older." (p47)
Heath, Rebecca Piirto. "You Can Buy a Thrill: Chasing the Ultimate Rush." American Demographics v19 n6 Jun 1997. p47-51. article-level access: <http://www.demographics.com/publications/ad/97_ad/9706_ad/ad970631.htm> (ISSN0163-4089).
PARAMEDICS, EMERGENCY
see EMERGENCY MEDICAL TECHNICIANS
PARENT AND CHILD
see also ADOPTION; CHILD ABUSE; SEX OF CHILDREN, PARENTAL PREFERENCES FOR; SINGLE-PARENT FAMILY
PARENT AND CHILD--UNITED STATES--ATTITUDES (v26)
PARENT AND CHILD--UNITED STATES--PUBLIC OPINION
"Only 37 percent of Americans now believe that today's children, once grown, will make the country a better place, according to a new report....Only one in five adults says it is very common for parents to be good role models and teach their children right from wrong....Half of white parents, 58 percent of black parents, and 49 percent of Hispanic parents say that parents who fail to discipline their children are very common. Although four in five Americans agree that it is much harder to be a parent these days, most Americans also feel that parents are not rising to meet the challenge....More than two-thirds say that improving the quality of public schools would be a 'very effective' way to help kids, and a majority think the same of after-school programs in community centers, more flexible work schedules, nighttime curfews for kids, and more involvement by volunteer organizations like the YMCA [Young Men's Christian Association]. Yet only 10 percent say that increasing government funding for welfare programs like food stamps would be 'very effective.'" (p9)
"What's with Parents These Days?" Forecast v17 n8 Aug 1997. p9. article-level access: <http://www.demographics.com/

Publications/FC/97_fc/9708_fc/FC97086.htm>
(ISSN0732-1597).

PARENTAL LEAVE--EUROPE

"According to the OECD, under 5 per cent of eligible fathers take parental leave in Denmark, Finland, Germany and Norway. In Sweden, however, the proportion was 25 per cent in 1987 (up from 20 per cent in 1978), though Swedish fathers take such leave only for short periods and often on a part-time basis. In terms of the number of days of paid parental leave taken in Sweden, the proporition taken by men falls to 7 per cent in 1988 (4 per cent in 1978). Elsewhere this proportion is around 1 per cent." (p125)

"Perspectives." International Labour Review v136 n1 Spr 1997. p109-128. (ISSN0020-7780).

PARENTAL LEAVE--SWEDEN (v26)

PARENTAL LEAVE--UNITED STATES

"In the United States, a study conducted three years after the entry into force of the Family and Medical Leave Act...by the Commission on Family and Medical Leave (set up to monitor the application of the legislation) found that parental leave accounted for about 13 per cent of all the forms of leave taken under the new Act. Leave taken for other reasons was distributed between: health of the eligible employee (60 per cent), health of a daughter or son (8 per cent), health of a spouse, parent or other relative (15.5 per cent), and maternity (4 per cent). Considering all these forms of leave, the Commission also found that: 66 per cent of workers were employed by companies meeting the criteria fixed by the Act, but only 55 per cent met the length-of-service requirements; over half of the parents eligible for leave did not know they were, while 86 per cent of employers did...." (p119) "16.5 per cent of employees had taken one form of leave, while 3.5 per cent had given up the idea because of the loss of income it entailed; leave was taken for an average of ten days, but parental leave tended to be taken for longer; parental leave (13 per cent of the total) was more or less equally distributed between women (12.5 per cent) and men (14.5 per cent)." (p120)

"Perspectives." International Labour Review v136 n1 Spr 1997. p109-128. (ISSN0020-7780).

In the U.S., the Commission on Family and Medical Leave, set up to monitor the application of the Family and Medical Leave "Act (i.e. all forms of leave covered), found that only 2.5 per cent of the employers surveyed in 1996 reported savings thanks to a slow-down in staff turnover and higher job commitment. In general, the application of the Act was regarded as having no particular impact on the various indicators concerning company and employee performance (in 80 to 95 per cent of the companies surveyed). Reported positive effects outweighed reported negative effects on employee performance, especially as regards productivity (12.5 against 5 per cent); while reported negative effects outweighed reported positive effects on company performance." (p124)

"Perspectives." International Labour Review v136 n1 Spr 1997. p109-128. (ISSN0020-7780).

PARENTAL LEAVE--UNITED STATES--COSTS

A "cost study was conducted in the United States on the basis of data supplied by a high technology corporation with a liberal parental leave policy....The authors concluded that it was much more cost-effective to evolve a well-planned parental leave policy than to lose the worker concerned and have to replace him/her permanently. The average cost of leave was 32 per cent of annual salary: it was 28 per cent for non-management and 39 per cent for management staff, whereas the cost of replacing an employee permanently ranged from 75 per cent of annual salary for the former to 150 per cent for the latter." (p123-124)

"Perspectives." International Labour Review v136 n1 Spr 1997. p109-128. (ISSN0020-7780).

PARENTAL PREFERENCES FOR SEX OF CHILDREN

see SEX OF CHILDREN, PARENTAL PREFERENCES FOR

PARENTS

see FATHERS; GRANDPARENTS AS PARENTS; MOTHERS; SINGLE FATHERS; SINGLE MOTHERS; SINGLE-PARENT FAMILY; SINGLE PARENTS; TEENAGE MOTHERS

PARKING, AUTOMOBILE

see AUTOMOBILE PARKING

PARKINSONISM (v26)

PARKS

see also AMERICAN BISON--YELLOWSTONE NATIONAL PARK; LOGGING--ONTARIO--ALGONQUIN PROVINCIAL PARK; NATIONAL PARKS AND RESERVES; UNITED STATES. NATIONAL PARK SERVICE; WOLVES--IDAHO--YELLOWSTONE NATIONAL PARK; YELLOWSTONE NATIONAL PARK

PARKS--CALIFORNIA (v26)

PARKS--NEW YORK (N.Y.)

"Private donations to New York City parks have increased almost four-fold since 1987, at the same time as public spending has been slashed by 31 percent in real dollars." (p25) "The city did rent out...[Central Park's] Great Lawn to Disney for the premiere of its movie POCAHONTAS (for $1 million, 20 percent of which went to pay police overtime for the event) in June 1995." (p26) "Over the last 10 years, city parks funding has been slashed to the bone. The city now spends less than 0.5 percent of its budget on parks, the lowest rate of any major U.S. city. (That the parks haven't fallen apart completely can be credited to the city's workfare program, which has funneled 5,000 welfare participants into unpaid part-time park-cleaning jobs, even as the parks department has laid off over half that many permanent employees.) In Manhattan, which recieves two-thirds of all private parks donations (more than three-quarters of which goes to the Central Park Conservancy alone), total park spending, public and private combined, has dropped by 21 percent since 1987. In the Bronx, combined parks funding has plummeted 46 percent over the same period, and the other outer boroughs have fared nearly as poorly." (p28)

deMause, Neil. "Parks: It Isn't Easy Staying Green." In These Times v21 n16 30 Jun 1997. p25-28. (ISSN0160-5992).

PARKS, NATIONAL

see NATIONAL PARKS AND RESERVES

PAROCHIAL SCHOOLS

see CHURCH SCHOOLS

PAROLE--MICHIGAN (v26)

PAROLE--UNITED STATES

In the U.S., "704,709 adults at year-end 1996 were on parole, which is conditional, supervised release following a prison term. Parolees are subject to re-incarceration for rule violations. Almost all of the offenders on parole (96 percent) had served a felony sentence. Fewer than half of all those entering parole in 1996 had received their release as a result of a parole board decision; 48 percent had received a mandatory release because of a sentencing statute or a good-time provision that released them from prison."

U.S. Dept. of Justice. "Nation's Probation and Parole Population Reached Almost 3.9 Million Last Year." Press Release 14 Aug 1997. document-level access: <http:// www.ojp.usdoj.gov/pub/bjs/press/papp96.pr>

PAROXYSMAL TACHYCARDIA--UNITED STATES (v26)

PART-TIME EMPLOYMENT--AUSTRALIA--PUBLIC OPINION (v26)

PART-TIME EMPLOYMENT--CALIFORNIA

The California Employment Development Department "estimates that the number of people employed on a part-time basis increased from 1,639,000 in 1975 to 2,494,000 in 1993, with little change in the proportion of the part-time to total employment. In 1993, the EDD estimated that regular part-time work accounted for 16.3 per cent of total employment, up from 14.9 per cent in 1990, but down from a high of 18.4 per cent in 1983...." (p35)

Carnoy, Martin/Castells, Manuel/Benner, Chris. "Labour Markets and Employment Practices in the Age of Flexibility: A Case Study of Silicon Valley." International Labour Review v136 n1 Spr 1997. p27-48. (ISSN0020-7780).

PART-TIME EMPLOYMENT--EUROPE

"According to a Eurostat study, 16 per cent of workers in the European Union have part-time jobs. Some 81 per cent of all part-time workers are women. The Dutch lead the way here, with 38 per cent of workers holding down part-time positions, whereas Germany's 16.3 per cent is just above the European Union average. Only 3.6 per cent of men in Germany have part-time jobs." (p13)

"Nachrichten News: Social Policy." Deutschland n6 Dec 1997. p13. (ISSN0945-6791).

"For the EU as a whole, some 33.8 per cent of all service workers have part-time jobs, whereas only 4.6 per cent of production workers and 5.6 per cent of managerial employees work part time. On average, about 20 per cent of the people employed in the sales and clerical groups have part-time jobs. In the Netherlands and the United Kingdom more than half the number of service workers have part-time jobs, as do almost half the number of service workers in Denmark. These three countries also show the highest proportions of sales workers and clerical workers with part-time jobs. Fifty-six per cent of all part-time employment in the EU occurs in low-skill occupational groups (service workers, agricultural workers, production workers and sales workers)." (p53-54)

DeGrip, Andries/Hoevenberg, Jeroen/Willems, Ed. "Atypical Employment in the European Union." International Labour Review v136 n1 Spr 1997. p49-71. (ISSN0020-7780).

"In 1991 an average of 15 per cent of the EU's total working population worked on a part-time basis....However, there are wide variations between member States. The Netherlands has by far the largest proportion of part-time employment (32.4 per cent)." (p53) In the EU, "the average proportion of part-time to total employment increased by 1.4 percentage points in the period 1983-91....The share of part-time employment decreased by 1-1.5 percentage points in Denmark, Greece and Spain, whereas it increased in the other member States. The Netherlands, Ireland and Belgium had the greatest increases in the incidence of part-time employment, with rises of 12, 5.6 and 5 percentage points, respectively....In more recent years the increase of part-time employment in the EU has accelerated, with an average increase of 2.2 percentage points in the period 1991-95. Again the Netherlands had the greatest increase with 4.7 percentage points. Ireland, France and Spain also recorded above-average increases in part-time employment, with rises of 3.7, 3.5, and 2.3 percentage points, respectively." (p55)

DeGrip, Andries/Hoevenberg, Jeroen/Willems, Ed. "Atypical Employment in the European Union." International Labour Review v136 n1 Spr 1997. p49-71. (ISSN0020-7780).

"When asked if working part-time, 16% of all employed people in the EU say 'yes', Eurostat--Statistical Office of the European Communities in Luxembourg--reveals....And 63% of part-timers aged 25 and over say they don't want a full-time job. Part-time work is most prevalent in the Netherlands (38%); least so in Greece (5%)....Part-time work varies from lows in Greece (5%), Italy (7%), Luxembourg (8%), Spain (8%) and Portugal (9%) to highs in Denmark (21%) Sweden (23%), the UK (24%) and particularly the Netherlands (38%). EU-wide, 63% of part-timers aged 25 and over say they don't want a full-time job. This is highest in the Netherlands (88%) and the UK (84%). For 18% of part-timers aged 25 and over, it's not what they prefer but they can't find full-time work. Highs are in Finland (46%), France and Greece (both 37%). In Denmark, Sweden, Finland and the Netherlands 40-57% of 15 to 24-year-olds have a part-time job. EU-wide, half combine it with education and training."

Eurostat. "16% of EU Workers Are Part-Time." Press Release 18 Sep 1997. document-level access: <http://europa.eu.int/en/comm/eurostat/compres/en/6597/6306597a.htm>

PART-TIME EMPLOYMENT--EUROPE--WOMEN

"Part-time work is more frequent among women [in Europe]: 32% of total female employment compared with 5% for men. The Netherlands is way ahead with 69% of the female workforce part-time. In Belgium, Germany and Luxembourg, part-time employment of women is some 10 times that of men."

Eurostat. "16% of EU Workers Are Part-Time." Press Release 18 Sep 1997. document-level access: <http://europa.eu.int/en/comm/eurostat/compres/en/6597/6306597a.htm>

PART-TIME EMPLOYMENT--IRELAND

In Ireland, "there has been an increase of 42,000 in the numbers working part-time (from 128,000 to 170,000) since 1993. Almost 9 out of every 10 persons working part-time are not looking for full-time work. Almost three-quarters of those working part-time are women."

Ireland. Central Statistics Office. "1997 Labour Force Survey Report." Press Release 29 Oct 1997. document-level access: <http://www.cso.ie/pressreleases/prellfs97.html>

PART-TIME EMPLOYMENT--UNITED STATES

"According to government statistics, 18 percent of U.S. workers--some 20 million people--are part-time....The U.S. Department of Labor says the use of temporary workers has shot up 400 percent since 1982....A consulting firm's survey, released this year, found that, among the 428 fastest-growing companies in the country, 83 percent now outsource jobs, up from 64 percent three years ago. Employee 'leasing' is the ultimate form of outsourcing; this is where a company essentially fires all its workers, who then become employees of another company that leases them back to their original employer. The worker leasing industry predicts it will employ 37 million people by 2007, up from 2.5 million in 1995." (p2)

"The UPS Strike: Contingent Workers and the Fight for a New Society." People's Tribune v24 n9 Sep 1997. p2. (ISSN1081-4787).

In the U.S., "more than 80 percent of part-time employees say they want part-time work, according to the Bureau of Labor Statistics....Government statistics lump anyone who works from one to 34 hours a week into the part-time category....Some 4.5 million of the nation's 30 million part-time employees are over age 55...." (p4)

Nifong, Christina. "United States: How Part-Timers Fare in US Economy." The Christian Science Monitor v89 n182 14 Aug 1997. p4. The Christian Science Monitor search engine: <http://www.csmonitor.com/plweb-cgi/iops1.pl> To retrieve this article, enter the following search: ED=19970814 AND economy. In the "retrieved list," click the title that matches this record. (ISSN0882-7729).

In the U.S., "some 17 percent of employed people today work part time. In 1979, another period of relatively low employment, the figure was 18 percent, according to Robert Lerman, an economist with the Urban Institute in Washington....Some experts estimate that 75 percent of people who hold part-time jobs today prefer shorter hours." (p20)

"The Monitor's View: Part-Time vs. Full-Time." The Christian Science Monitor v89 n177 7 Aug 1997. p20. The Christian Science Monitor search engine: <http://www.csmonitor.com/plweb-cgi/iops1.pl> To retrieve this article, enter the following search: ED=19970807 AND time. In the "retrieved list," click the title that matches this record. (ISSN0882-7729).

PARTICLES

"Total anthropogenic global emissions of particles less than 10 micrometers in diameter are approximately 1 million metric tons (Mt) annually. Approximately 35% of these particles are airborne sulfates from oxidation of sulfur dioxide emissions...." (p7)

"Science Update: Aerosols Could Double by 2040." Global Environmental Change Report v9 n12 27 Jun 1997. p7. (ISSN1049-9083).

PARTIES, POLITICAL

see POLITICAL PARTIES

PARTY AFFILIATION--AUSTRIA

In Austria, the Green party "are least numerous in rural areas, where they never averaged even five per cent, not even in 1994 (4.3 per cent in 1996). In small and medium-sized towns, their share was somewhat higher (6.4 per cent in 1996). It reached its highest point in the five biggest cities: 6.2 per cent in 1995 and 10.1 per cent in 1996." (p191-192)

Lauber, Volkmar. "The Mixed Fortunes of the Austrian Greens in the Mid-1990s." Environmental Politics v6 n1 Spr 1997. p185-192. (ISSN0964-4016).

PARTY AFFILIATION--UNITED STATES (v26)

PASSIVE SMOKING

"Studies have found that nonsmokers exposed to environmental tobacco smoke increase their risk of coronary heart disease by 20-30%...." (p788) According to a study published in CIRCULATION, "compared to women who reported no exposure to secondhand smoke, women occasionally exposed had a 58% greater chance of developing coronary heart disease, and women regularly exposed to smoke had a 91% greater chance of developing the disease." (p789)

U.S. National Institute of Environmental Health Sciences. "Environews: Forum: Secondhand Smoke and Heart Disease." Environmental Health Perspectives v105 n8 Aug 1997. p788-789.

PASSIVE SMOKING--HEALTH ASPECTS--CHINA --UNITED STATES--CHILDREN (v26)

PASSIVE SMOKING--UNITED STATES--PUBLIC OPINION

"The Gallup Poll first asked Americans about the effects of second-hand smoke in 1994. At that time only 36% felt it was very harmful to adults while another 42% said it was somewhat harmful. Even then...only 18% felt second-hand smoke was not too harmful or not harmful at all. Since then, there has been a rapid and substantial increase in public concern about the dangers inherent in exposure to other people's smoking, with the percent rating it very harmful rising from 36% in 1994 to 48% in 1996 and 55% in 1997....Today, only 49% of men but 61% of women think second-hand smoke is very harmful to adults. In 1994 only 27% of men and 45% of women felt this way....Today 64% of non-smokers, but only 30% of smokers, consider it very harmful. In 1994 the figures were 45% for non-smokers and 14% for smokers."

Saad, Lydia/Gallup Organization. "More Americans Fear Risk of Second-Hand Smoke." Press Release 18 Jul 1997. document-level access: <http://www.gallup.com/poll/news/970718~1.htm>

PASSIVE SMOKING--UNITED STATES--WOMEN (v26)

In a Nurses Health Study, "the authors studied 32,046 women, aged 36 to 61 [in the U.S.], who had never smoked and who did not have CHD [coronary heart disease], stroke, or cancer. Of these, 81% reported that they had regular or occasional exposure to passive smoke at home or at work. During 10 years of follow-up, 152 of these women died of CHD or had had a non-fatal myocardial infarction. Compared with the women who were not exposed to second-hand smoke, those who were had a significantly higher relative risk (RR) of total CHD (1.71), after adjustments were made for age and for other risk factors, including behavior and diet." (p55)

"Abstracts: Cardiovascular Disease: More Evidence that Second-Hand Smoke Raises Heart Disease Risk in Non-Smokers." Modern Medicine v65 n8 Aug 1997. p55. (ISSN0026-8070).

PASTORS

see CLERGY

PATENT LICENSES--UNITED STATES

A study conducted by CHI Research Incorporated for the National Science Foundation, found that "papers produced by publicly financed scientists accounted for 73.3 percent of the main citations in 2,841 patents issued to U.S. industrial firms in 1993-94. Institutions based in the United States accounted for 43.9 percent and foreign sources for 29.4 percent....The results of this...study suggest that publicly funded research serves as the foundation for most commercial innovation in the United States. Only 20.4 percent of the citations in the patents referred to papers produced by U.S. firms. Papers produced by researchers from foreign companies comprised 6.3 percent." (p22)

"Spectrum: In Praise of Public Research." Environment v39 n6 Jul-Aug 1997. p22-23. (ISSN0013-9157).

PATERNITY--UNITED STATES (v26)

PATIENTS, UNINSURED

see MEDICALLY UNINSURED PERSONS

PAWNBROKING--VIRGINIA

Virginia's pawnbroking legal limits are "5% a month for loans over $100, which works out to an annual percentage rate of 60%....[Out of] 31 pawnshops around the state...just four...seemed to consistently follow the law. Of the rest, 18 appeared to be charging around twice the legal rate; nine appeared to be charging three to four times the legal rate, with annual percentage rates as high as 240%." (p16)

"The New Loan Sharks: Loan Sharks Ignored." Dollars and Sense n212 Jul-Aug 1997. p16. (ISSN0012-5245).

PAYROLL TAX--UNITED STATES

In the U.S., "there are two main payroll taxes, split equally between bosses and workers. The first, at 12.4 percent, funds Social Security. A second, at 2.9 percent, pays for the hospital portion of Medicare. Since 1950, these taxes have quietly crept up 3 percent per decade, from a combined 3 percent in 1950 to 15.3 percent today. The wage on which these taxes apply has skyrocketed over the same period, from the first $3,000 earned to the first $65,400 (the smaller Medicare tax has applied to all earnings since 1993). As a result, taxes that raised just 11 percent of federal revenue in 1950 account for 36 percent today. Payroll taxes now bring in nearly as much money ($535 billion) as the income tax ($670 billion). And counting the employer portion, which economists agree is indirectly paid by employees in the form of lower wages or benefits, three in four workers now 'pay' more in payroll taxes than income tax." (p7 secA)

Miller, Matthew. "Comment: Payroll Tax Sting Hurts More Than Ever." Detroit News 4 Aug 1997. p7 secA.

PAYROLL TAXES (SOCIAL SECURITY)

see SOCIAL SECURITY TAXES

PEACE TREATIES

see also ARBITRATION, INTERNATIONAL

PEACE TREATIES--AFRICA--ASIA--MIDDLE EAST

In the period of 1989-1996, "10 of the 17 terminated conflicts in Africa--close to 60%--ended in a peace agreement....The Middle East and Asia, which together account for about 40% of the world's conflicts, only had two peace agreements, or 10%." (p342)

Wallensteen, Peter/Sollenberg, Margareta. "Armed Conflicts,

Conflict Termination and Peace Agreements, 1989-96." Journal of Peace Research v34 n3 Aug 1997. p339-358. (ISSN0022-3433).

PEACEFUL COEXISTENCE

see INTERNATIONAL RELATIONS

PEACH INDUSTRY--CALIFORNIA--GEORGIA--SOUTH CAROLINA (v26)

PEACH INDUSTRY--UNITED STATES (v26)

"U.S. exports of fresh-market peaches and nectarines gained about 13 percent in 1996/97 (May-April) over 1995/96 exports, reaching 166.4 million pounds. Exports to Canada and Taiwan rose 4 percent and 65 percent, respectively, while exports to Mexico dropped 25 percent. Combined, these three countries made up 89 percent of the total export volume....U.S. imports of fresh-market peaches and nectarines rose 2 percent to 92.1 million pounds in 1996/97, with shipments from Chile making up 99 percent of the volume and shipments from Canada the remainder. Imports from both countries rose 1 percent and 96 percent, respectively from the previous season." (p15)

U.S. Dept. of Agriculture. Economic Research Service. "Noncitrus Fruit Outlook." Fruit and Tree Nuts Situation and Outlook Report Aug 1997. p7-26.

In the U.S., "grower prices for fresh-market peaches in May-July 1997 averaged 24 percent or about 7 cents a pound lower than prices during the same period last year....Grower prices for fresh-market peaches in July averaged 19.8 cents a pound, down from 30.4 cents in May. The California Canning Peach Association reported a three-tiered price scale negotiated with canners for the 1997 clingstone peach crop. The price scale ranged from a minimum of $214 per ton to a high of $224 per ton. The established price in 1996 was $200 per paid ton." (p15)

U.S. Dept. of Agriculture. Economic Research Service. "Noncitrus Fruit Outlook." Fruit and Tree Nuts Situation and Outlook Report Aug 1997. p7-26.

PEANUT INDUSTRY--GEORGIA (v26)

PEANUT INDUSTRY--UNITED STATES

In the U.S., "area planted to peanuts continued falling--down 8 percent from 1995 to 1.4 million acres in 1996. Production was up 5 percent from 1995 levels at 3.6 billion pounds, but still below 1994 levels. Although the quota price was unchanged at $678 per ton for the 1995 and 1996 crops, the average harvest month price fell from 29 cents per pound in 1995 to 26 cents per pound in 1996. On average, yields rose 13 percent to 2,443 pounds per planted acre, and returns rose as well." (p24-25)

U.S. Dept. of Agriculture. Economic Research Service. "1996 Cost of Production for Crops and Livestock: Although Input Expenses Rose in 1996,...Led to Higher Net Returns." Agricultural Income and Finance Situation and Outlook Report Sep 1997. p23-27.

"Despite a drop in 1996 planted peanut area of 136,000 acres to 1.402 million, the lowest since the 1982 season, U.S. peanut production rose 5.8 percent to 3.661 billion pounds, in-shell basis. The increase was due to a 16-percent rise in average yields to 2,653 pounds per harvested acre....USDA announced a national peanut poundage quota for the 1996 marketing year of 1.1 million short tons (2.2 billion pounds), in-shell basis, well below the 1.35 million short tons for the 1995 season. With a lower quota support rate in the 1996 season, $610 per short ton versus $678.36 the previous season, the average price received by farmers for peanuts averaged lower at 28.5 cents per pound, down from 29.3 cents in the 1995 season." (p3)

U.S. Dept. of Agriculture. Economic Research Service. "Summary." Oil Crops Situation and Outlook Series Oct 1997. p3.

PEAR INDUSTRY--CALIFORNIA--OREGON --WASHINGTON (STATE) (v26)

PEAR INDUSTRY--MEXICO--UNITED STATES (v26)

PEAR INDUSTRY--UNITED STATES (v26)

"During the previous season, exports of U.S. fresh pears between July 1996 and May 1997 totaled 257.4 million pounds, down 17 percent from the same period a year earlier, reflecting low U.S. supplies and the sharply higher domestic prices. In the same time, Canada received 33 percent of the exports and was the leading destination for U.S. fresh pears, although the volume declined 11 percent. Other major markets were Mexico (26 percent), Brazil (15 percent), Taiwan (4 percent), and the European Union (6 percent). Exports to these other major markets declined except to Mexico where U.S. pear shipments rose 10 percent....U.S. imports of fresh pears between July 1996 and May 1997 totaled 163.8 million pounds, up 37 percent from the same period a year earlier. Chile and Argentina were the major suppliers, accounting for 46 percent and 42 percent of the total imports. Pear shipments from these two countries rose 9 percent and 106 percent, respectively. Combined shipments from New Zealand, Republic of South Africa, and South Korea made up 11 percent of total U.S. fresh pear imports." (p13)

U.S. Dept. of Agriculture. Economic Research Service. "Noncitrus Fruit Outlook." Fruit and Tree Nuts Situation and Outlook Report Aug 1997. p7-26.

"The season-average grower price for all [U.S.] pears in 1996 was record high, up 38 percent from the prior year, as utilized production declined 13 percent to 1.64 billion pounds. Fresh use, including exports, fell 16 percent and amounted to 56 percent of the utilized pear crop in 1996. Consequently, last season's grower prices for all fresh-market pears averaged 24.7 cents per pound ($494 per ton), 44 percent above the prior year and almost the highest on record. Grower prices for Bartlett fresh pears averaged 39 percent higher, while grower prices for non-Barlett fresh-market pears averaged 49 percent higher. Processing accounted for 44 percent of the 1996 utilized pear output and the quantity processed fell 11 percent from a year earlier. Barlett pears represented 84 percent of all processed pears. Low processing supplies pushed grower prices for all processing pears up 26 percent from a year earlier in 1996, and Bartlett processing pear prices were up 30 percent." (p12-13)

U.S. Dept. of Agriculture. Economic Research Service. "Noncitrus Fruit Outlook." Fruit and Tree Nuts Situation and Outlook Report Aug 1997. p7-26.

PECAN INDUSTRY--MEXICO--UNITED STATES (v26)

In the U.S., typically pecan imports from Mexico "account for 10-20 percent of the total supply....Recent estimates are that Mexico planted 107,570 acres of irrigated pecans in various stages of maturity. Mexico's production in 1996/97 is estimated at 44,600 metric tons, in-shell basis, compared with 41,569 tons in 1995/96 and 31,750 in 1994/95, according to figures from the International Tree Nut Council." (p33)

U.S. Dept. of Agriculture. Economic Research Service. "Tree Nut Outlook." Fruit and Tree Nuts Situation and Outlook Report Aug 1997. p32-33.

PECAN INDUSTRY--UNITED STATES (v26)

In the U.S., 1996 pecan "production totaled 222 million pounds (in-shell basis), compared with an average crop of 268 million in 1995, and a small crop of 199 million pounds in 1994. The second-largest crop on record of 365 million pounds was produced in 1993....The U.S. grower price for all pecans was very weak last year, averaging 63.7 cents per pound for the entire season, compared with $1.01 for the 1995 crop and $1.04 in 1994." (p33)

U.S. Dept. of Agriculture. Economic Research Service. "Tree Nut Outlook." Fruit and Tree Nuts Situation and Outlook Report Aug 1997. p32-33.

PEDESTRIAN ACCIDENTS--MICHIGAN (v26)

PEDESTRIAN ACCIDENTS--UNITED STATES (v26)

PEDESTRIAN ACCIDENTS--UNITED STATES --MORTALITY

In the U.S., "according to a report called 'Mean Streets: Pedestrian Safety and Reform of the Nation's Transportation Laws,' more than 6,100 pedestrians were killed in traffic accidents each year between 1986 and 1995--the equivalent of a commercial airline crash every 11 days....While pedestrians account for 14 percent of all traffic fatalities, just 1 percent of federal highway funds go to pedestrian safety....Three of the five most dangerous [cities] are in Florida, home to a large number of seniors, who account for 23 percent of all pedestrian fatalities but only 13 percent of the population....In 1990, 364 pedestrians were killed in New York City. Last year the total fell to 250." (p3)

Thompson, Neal. "United States: Urban Pedestrians Tire of Walking on the Wild Side." The Christian Science Monitor v89 n169 28 Jul 1997. p3. The Christian Science Monitor search engine: <http://www.csmonitor.com/plweb-cgi/iops1.pl> To retrieve this article, enter the following search: ED=19970728 AND side. In the "retrieved list," click the title that matches this record. (ISSN0882-7729).

PEDIATRIC AIDS

see AIDS (DISEASE) IN CHILDREN

PEDIATRIC ASTHMA

see ASTHMA IN CHILDREN

PEDIATRIC BURNS

see BURNS AND SCALDS IN CHILDREN

PEDIATRIC LEAD POISONING

see LEAD POISONING IN CHILDREN

PEDIATRIC MALNUTRITION

see MALNUTRITION IN CHILDREN

PEDIATRIC MENTAL HEALTH

see CHILD MENTAL HEALTH

PEDIATRIC OBESITY

see OBESITY IN CHILDREN

PEDIATRIC TOXICOLOGY--UNITED STATES (v26)

PEDIATRIC VISION DISORDERS

see VISION DISORDERS IN CHILDREN

PEDIATRICIANS--UNITED STATES--WOMEN

In the U.S., "42 percent of all pediatricians and 58 percent of those under age 45 are women, according to the 1996 Pediatric Specialty Survey. The share will continue to grow; in 1995, 63 percent of pediatric interns were women....Among those under age 45, 16 percent of female and 6 percent of male pediatricians are single. Of pediatricians under age 45, 28 percent of women are childless, compared with 10 percent of men....Female pediatricians who are mothers also have fewer children than their male counterparts. Fifty-six percent of male pediatricians have three or more children, nearly twice the 32 percent of women doctors with big families." (p29)

Kate, Nancy Ten. "Kaleidoscope: Dr. Mom--Not!" American Demographics v19 n7 Jul 1997. p29. article-level access: <http://www.demographics.com/publications/ad/97_ad/9707_ad/ad970720.htm> (ISSN0163-4089).

PELL GRANTS--UNITED STATES

"Since its creation, over 60 million Pell grants have been awarded, providing over $75 billion in aid to students across the...[U.S.]. In the first year of the program, 1973-74 over 176,000 students received the Pell grants. By 1980-81, this total had grown to 2.7 million recipients. Today, over 3.6 million American students receive Pell grants....This investment clearly assists our neediest students. In 1995-96, 54 percent of Pell grant recipients had income levels of less than $10,000. Only 9 percent of recipients had incomes over $30,000.... This year the appropriated maximum Pell grant was only $2,700...." (pS4977)

Reed, Jack (Sen.-R.I.). "Concurrent Resolution on the Budget." Congressional Record. Daily ed. v143 n69 22 May 1997. pS4944-4994. section/page-level access: <http://thomas.loc.gov/cgi-bin/query/R?r105:FLD001:S04977:> (ISSN0363-7239). (X1.1A.105/1).

PELVIC INFLAMMATORY DISEASE--UNITED STATES

"Each year more than 1 million U.S. women experience an episode of PID [pelvic inflammatory disease]. At least one-quarter of women with acute PID experience serious long-term sequelae, the most common and important of which are ectopic pregnancy (the development of a fetus outside the uterus) and tubal-factor infertility (infertility resulting from blockage or damage to the fallopian tubes)....At least 15 percent of all infertile American women are infertile because of tubal damage caused by PID." (p5)

The Committee on Prevention and Control of STDs. Institute of Medicine. "The Hidden Epidemic: Confronting Sexually Transmitted Diseases." SIECUS Report v25 n3 Feb-Mar 1997. p4-14. (ISSN0091-3995).

PENAL INSTITUTIONS

see PRISONS

PENNY--UNITED STATES (v26)

PENSIONS

see also SOCIAL SECURITY; TRADE-UNIONS--PENSIONS

PENSIONS--AGED (v26)

PENSIONS--AUSTRALIA (v26)

PENSIONS--CANADA

"Today in Canada there are approximately five million Canadians who in one way or another are receiving payments from the Canada pension plan. We have approximately 3.7 million plus another 1.2 million under the Quebec pension plan. Of that group some 2.4 million Canadians and 800,000 under the Quebec plan are receiving retirement benefits. In the disability portion of the plan we have some 300,000 Canadians in other provinces along with another 50,000 people in the province of Quebec." (p636)

Hubbard, Charles (MP-NB). "Government Orders: Canada Pension Plan Investment Board Act." Canada. Parliament. House of Commons. Debates. v135 n12 7 Oct 1997. p619-646. section-level access: <http://www.parl.gc.ca/36/1/parlbus/chambus/house/debates/012_1997-10-07/han012-e.htm#LINK228> (ISSN0704-5603). (X3-361E).

"In 1996, an estimated 540,000 Canadians--10.5 per cent of those who were covered by employer pensions--belonged to defined-contribution plans, compared with 325,320, or seven per cent, a decade earlier. An overwhelming 88 per cent of Canadians in company pensions enjoy the security of traditional defined-benefit plans--still the pensions of choice for unionized workforces in the public sector and Canada's biggest companies. (Those Statistics Canada figures do not count employees who have no company pension plan--more than half of the country's paid workers.)...[Defined contribution plans] represent the fastest-growing portion of the $500-billion company pension market. A 1996 survey of more than 100 mid-size and large companies by the Financial Executives Institute Canada showed that 15 per cent had introduced defined-contribution plans in the previous five years, while another 20 per cent were thinking about it." (p47)

Scott, Sarah. "Cover: More Risk, Higher Rewards?" Maclean's v110 n39 29 Sep 1997. p46-48. (ISSN0024-9262).

PENSIONS--CHILE (v26)

The essential feature of the Chilean pension system "is that the future pensions of Chilean workers will be financed out of a fixed part (10 per cent) of their gross pay, to be individually deposited in investment funds. These funds are managed by private companies known as Pension Fund Associations (Asociaciones de Fondos de Pensiones--or AFPs), which were specially created for this purpose and are strictly regulated by the State." (p90) The AFP system has helped the savings rate in Chile to climb to approximately 30 per cent of GDP, one of the highest levels in the world. The funds accumulated in AFPs presently amount to just under $30 billion, almost half of the country's GDP....On the Chilean stock exchange, the AFPs keep their investments a little below the permitted upper limit of 30 percent of the total pension fund....The Chilean AFPs' stake of a little over $8 billion--roughly a sixth of the listed total value--makes them by far the largest investor in the national stock market....The rest of the funds are invested in government bonds (42 per cent), in securities issued by Chilean finance institutions and companies (28 per cent), and in foreign holdings (0.5 per cent)." (p91-92) Provida, the largest AFP, "was handling a sum of $5,326 million, or 19.7 per cent of the total accumulated within the system." (p93)

Fazio, Hugo/Riesco, Manuel. "The Chilean Pension Fund Associations." New Left Review n223 May-Jun 1997. p90-100. (ISSN0028-6060).

PENSIONS--DENMARK (v26)

PENSIONS--FRANCE--WOMEN (v26)

PENSIONS--GERMANY--WOMEN (v26)

PENSIONS--GREAT BRITAIN (v26)

PENSIONS--HISPANIC AMERICANS

Dr. Fernando Torres-Gil, director of the center on aging at the University of California-Los Angeles and a former assistant secretary for aging in the U.S. Department of Health and Human Services, said that "in the last 10 years...the number of Hispanics covered by company pension plans has declined to 32 percent from 39 percent." (p20 secA)

Ryan, Richard A. "Preparing for the Golden Years: Minorities: Many Blacks and Hispanics Will Face Post-Work Years with Fewer Funds." Detroit News and Free Press 16 Nov 1997. p20 secA.

PENSIONS--NETHERLANDS--WOMEN (v26)

PENSIONS--SWEDEN--WOMEN (v26)

PENSIONS--UNITED STATES (v26)

"As the average age of Americans is rising at a steady rate, we all have become more aware of the importance of retirement programs and retirement security. At the same time, only about half of all workers are covered by a retirement program--and of those, many who are covered, work for a Federal, State, or local government entity. An incredible 87 percent of workers employed by small businesses, those with fewer than 20 employees, have no private retirement or pension coverage. Less than 40 percent of the 33 million Americans aged 65 and older collect a pension, other than Social Security." (pS6362)

Jeffords, James M. (Sen.-Vt.). "Statements on Introduced Bills and Joint Resolutions." Congressional Record. Daily ed. v143 n91 25 Jun 1997. pS6359-6372. section/page-level access: <http://thomas.loc.gov/cgi-bin/query/R?r105:FLD001:S06362:> (ISSN0363-7239). (X1.1A.105/1).

"Half of all older Americans have incomes of less than $11,300. This is because their incomes are drawn primarily from Social Security, which, on average, pays $8,460 to retired workers. That is less than today's minimum wage. Very little of their income comes from individual savings....A very disturbing image forms when we begin to think about the retirement security of low-wage workers, particularly women and minorities. Many of these workers will never receive a pension. We know that less than half of all working women are covered by a pension. Those who are fortunate enough to be covered by a plan can expect to receive lower benefits in retirement because their wages were lower while they were working. A recent study noted an alarming trend in private pension coverage among African-Americans and Latino-Americans....The report shows that the percentage of blacks covered by private pensions of all types plummeted from 45.1 percent in 1979 to 33.8 percent in 1993, while coverage of Latinos fell from 37.7 to 24.6 percent during the same period." (pH3084)

Payne, Donald M. (Rep.-N.J.). "Savings Are Vital to Everyone's Retirement Act of 1997." Congressional Record. Daily ed. v143 n68 21 May 1997. pH3082-3088. section/page-level access: <http://thomas.loc.gov/cgi-bin/query/R?r105:FLD001:H03084:> (ISSN0363-7239). (X1.1A.105/1).

"The typical retired American today receives retirement income from a variety of sources. On average, 41.7 percent comes from Social Security, 20.5 percent from asset income, 20.1 percent from pensions, 14.8 percent is annually earned, and the remaining 3 percent comes from a variety of other sources, including welfare programs such as SSI [Supplemental Security Income] and unemployment compensation....This is only an average picture. The reality varies greatly from American to American. We need to look at the oldest of Americans to see the future of an aging nation. Americans currently 80 and older receive 52.6 percent of their income from Social Security, whereas their pensions provide proportionally less--down to 15.3 percent. And, of course, they are less able to earn money at this age, thus earnings make up only 3.9 percent of their income." (pS5528)

Gregg, Judd (Sen.-N.H.). "Statements on Introduced Bills and Joint Resolutions." Congressional Record. Daily ed. v143 n81 11 Jun 1997. pS5508-5541. section/page-level access: <http://thomas.loc.gov/cgi-bin/query/R?r105:FLD001:S05528:> (ISSN0363-7239). (X1.1A.105/1).

In the U.S., "in 1980, the Employment Retirement Income Security Act allowed 57.9 million people to participate in private pension programs sponsored by employers and employees, and by 1992 the number had grown to 81.9 million participants. The total amount of contributions into private pension programs has grown from $66.2 billion in 1980 to $128.8 billion in 1992. Although these numbers are encouraging they are still far from what they should be with a total national work force of 124 million according to the Statistical Abstract of the United States." (pH3087)

Jackson-Lee, Sheila (Rep.-Tex.). "Savings Are Vital to Everyone's Retirement Act of 1997." Congressional Record. Daily ed. v143 n68 21 May 1997. pH3082-3088. section/page-level access: <http://thomas.loc.gov/cgi-bin/query/R?r105:FLD001:H03087:> (ISSN0363-7239). (X1.1A.105/1).

According to research conducted by KPMG Peat Marwick of Washington, DC, the widening gap between the participation of the highest-paid and the lower-paid in 401(k) pension plans, in the U.S., "has increased from 14 percentage points in 1995 to 26 points in 1996. That means 90% of those earning over $66,000 participated as opposed to 64% of those who earned less than that." (p4)

"The Short Run: Savings: 401(k)'s Are Great--If You Can Afford One." Dollars and Sense n214 Nov-Dec 1997. p4. (ISSN0012-5245).

PENSIONS--UNITED STATES--WOMEN (v26)

PEREGRINE FALCON--CALIFORNIA (v26)

PERFORMING ARTS SPONSORSHIP--CANADA (v26)

PERFUMES INDUSTRY--UNITED STATES

In the U.S., "perfumes and fragrances are a $5 billion retail industry. The lion's share of this market should really be called the lioness's share, because women's perfumes are two-thirds of the business, according to The Fragrance Foundation in New York City. Households purchase women's colognes or perfumes once every 83 days, according to ACNielsen." (p32)

Mogelonsky, Marcia. "Kaleidoscope: Checkout Line: Dollars and Scents." American Demographics v19 n6 Jun 1997. p32.

article-level access: <http://www.demographics.com/publications/ad/97_ad/9706_ad/ad970625.htm> (ISSN0163-4089).

PERIDURAL ANESTHESIA--UNITED STATES

"In the United States today, 80 percent of women in childbirth receive some form of pain medication; 33 percent of those use epidurals, or twice the percentage of women who used that kind of analgesic 15 years ago. In some big hospitals, 80 percent of obstetric patients get epidurals. Epidurals have also become the anesthetic of choice for Caesarean sections: 23 percent of deliveries in the United States are through C-section." (p94)

Shute, Nancy. "1997 Health Guide: No More Hard Labor." U.S. News & World Report v123 n18 10 Nov 1997. p92-95. article-level access: <http://www.usnews.com/usnews/issue/971110/10BIRT.HTM> (ISSN0041-5537).

PERIODICALS--SWEDEN (v26)

PERSIAN GULF REGION--ARMED FORCES

The Gulf Cooperation Council's "10,000-man joint force consists of units from all six countries [Bahrain, Kuwait, Oman, Qatar, Saudi Arabia and the United Arab Emirates] and is stationed at Hafr al-Batin, a settlement near the Saudi Arabian border with Kuwait. The force is being expanded to 25,000." (p38)

Anthony, John Duke. "The U.S.-GCC Relationship: A Glass Half-Empty or Half-Full?" Middle East Policy v5 n2 May 1997. p22-41. (ISSN1061-1924).

PERSIAN GULF REGION--COMMERCE--UNITED STATES

Total U.S. Gulf Corporation Council "trade grew 16 percent in 1996 to reach almost $25 billion, about equally divided between exports and imports in both directions....Exports from the United States to the GCC grew 22 percent last year to reach $12.4 billion. GCC exports to the United States were $12.5 billion in 1996, an increase of 10 percent over the previous year. In 1995, U.S. companies had invested an estimated $9.4 billion in the GCC, an increase of 26 percent over 1994." (p74)

Kalicki, Jan H. "A Vision for the U.S.-Saudi and U.S.-Gulf Commercial Relationship." Middle East Policy v5 n2 May 1997. p73-78. (ISSN1061-1924).

PERSIAN GULF REGION--POPULATION

"It takes only about 60 percent of the time to double the population in the [Persian] Gulf that it does in the developing world as a whole." (p8) "More than 40 percent of the population of the Gulf is under 14 years of age." (p9)

Cordesman, Anthony H. "Symposium--The Challenge in the Gulf: Building a Bridge from Containment to Stability." Middle East Policy v5 n2 May 1997. p1-21. (ISSN1061-1924).

PERSIAN GULF WAR, 1991

"During the 1990-91 Desert Shield/Desert Storm war, the Iraqi people were surrounded by an estimated 700 nuclear warheads, and Saddam Hussein was repeatedly threatened with their use. Tens of thousands of 'depleted uranium' shells were used to destroy Iraqi artillery--apparently resulting in radiation poisoning and cancer for Iraqi civilians and contributing to the 'Gulf War Syndrome' suffered by many returning US warriors." (p3)

Gerson, Joseph. "Questioning the Obvious: Why Preparations for Nuclear War Remain the 'Cornerstone' of US Strategy." Peacework n278 Oct 1997. p3-4. (ISSN0748-0725).

PERSIAN GULF WAR, 1991--COSTS

"When the Iraqis invaded Kuwait in August 1990, oil prices more than doubled overnight--from $19 per barrel to $42. In the first year after the invasion, it is estimated that the U.S. economy lost $60 billion in exports and $200 billion in lost productivity. That figure worldwide was about $1 trillion." (p7)

Hanlon, Edward J., Jr. "Naval Expeditionary Warfare: Opening the Door." Surface Warfare v22 n4 Jul-Aug 1997. p6-9. (ISSN0145-1073).

PERSIAN GULF WAR, 1991--ENVIRONMENTAL ASPECTS

During the Persian Gulf War, "the United States shot more than a million shells encased in depleted uranium throughout Iraq and Kuwait. Deployed as tank armor, and as armor-penetrating ammunition by M1A1 Abrams tanks and A-10 attack planes, DU, which is 16 times denser than lead, proved so effective that not a single U.S. tank was destroyed by Iraqi fire. In addition, 'artillery pieces, armored personnel carriers and other equipment destroyed by DU rounds number in the thousands. By the war's end, roughly 300 tons of uranium from spent rounds lay scattered in various sizes and states of decay across the battlefields of Iraq and Kuwait.'...The Pentagon says DU is relatively harmless, emitting 'only' 60 percent of the radiation of non-depleted uranium....According to independent scientists, 'a DU antitank round outside its metal casing can emit as much radiation in one hour as fifty chest X-rays.'...As much as 70 percent of...[DU] is released as a radioactive and highly toxic dust that can be inhaled or ingested and then trapped in the lungs or kidneys. One researcher found that a single molecular particle of depleted uranium will subject an individual to radiation at a level 800 times what is permitted by federal regulations for external exposure....Leaving more than 600,000 pounds of depleted uranium scattered throughout the region, by war's end the U.S. turned the Gulf area into a deadly radioactive grid, affecting not only U.S. soldiers but hundreds of thousands, perhaps millions of people who live in the Gulf." (p30)

Cohen, Mitchel. "Glowing in the Gulf: Drugged Soldiers & Radiation." Fifth Estate v32 n2 Fall 1997. p1,30.

PERSIAN GULF WAR, 1991--IRAQ--UNITED STATES --MORTALITY

During the Persian Gulf War, "250,000 people (mostly civilians) were killed outright by the U.S. bombardment and another 750,000 have died as a result of the U.N. international embargo spearheaded by the U.S." (p1) "'Only' 376 U.S. troops were killed in the Gulf, almost all of them by other U.S. soldiers--so-called 'friendly fire.' While 3,700 Iraqi tanks were obliterated, only 14 U.S. M1A1 Abrams tanks were destroyed--again by 'friendly fire' from other M1A1s." (p30)

Cohen, Mitchel. "Glowing in the Gulf: Drugged Soldiers & Radiation." Fifth Estate v32 n2 Fall 1997. p1,30.

PERSIAN GULF WAR, 1991--KUWAIT

At the end of the Persian Gulf War, "the departing Iraqi army detonated and set aflame more than 700 oil wells [in Kuwait,] an unprecedented assault on the atmosphere and on an economic resource. As much as five million barrels of oil remains in the desert sand." (p52)

Futrell, J. William. "ELI Report: Closing Statement: Addressing the Environmental Consequences of War." Environmental Forum v14 n6 Nov-Dec 1997. p52. (ISSN0731-5732).

PERSIAN GULF WAR, 1991--LOGISTICS

"Desert Shield/Desert Storm involved one of the largest logistical operations in modern history. By the time it was over, 3.8 million tons of cargo and 503,000 troops had been moved into theater. Of these totals, 95% of the cargo was moved by sea on board approximately 500 ships...." (p59)

Connaughton, Sean T. "Reinventing Sealift." Proceedings v123 n12 Dec 1997. p59-61. (ISSN0041-798X).

PERSIAN GULF WAR, 1991--UNITED STATES--MASS MEDIA AND THE WAR

At the time of the Gulf War, "eighty-nine percent of Americans used television as [a] main source for information about war news. Only 51 percent read a daily newspaper. During the Gulf

War this increased, but 67 percent of those who read newspapers during the war reported that they offered the same news as did television." (p4)

Smith, Andrew F. "International Conflict and the Media." Issues in Global Education n143 Oct 1997. p1-11.

PERSIAN GULF WAR, 1991--UNITED STATES. AIR FORCE RESERVE

"Before the Gulf War, more than 181,000 [U.S. Air Force] reservists had been mobilized to support the country in time of national emergency. After Iraq's invasion of Kuwait, President George Bush recalled 200,000 reservists to active duty....Within 15 days, more than 5,700 [Air Force Reservists] volunteered for duty." (p10)

MacMackin, Margaret. "Volunteerism and Accessibility: Reservists Represent Best of Citizen-Soldier Tradition." Citizen Airman v49 n5 Oct 1997. p10-11. (ISSN0887-9680).

PERSIAN GULF WAR, 1991--VETERANS--HEALTH ASPECTS (v26)

PERSIAN GULF WAR, 1991--VETERANS--UNITED STATES--HEALTH ASPECTS (v26)

PERSONAL ACTIONS

see ACTIONS AND DEFENSES

PERSONAL HEALTH SERVICES

see MEDICAL CARE

PERSONAL INCOME

see INCOME

PERSONAL INCOME TAX

see INCOME TAX

PERSONAL WATERCRAFT--ACCIDENTS--MICHIGAN

Registrations for personal "watercraft in Michigan doubled between 1994 and 1996 to about 80,000. But as their popularity has grown, so have the number of accidents. Personal watercraft make up about 5 percent to 7 percent of the registered boats in Michigan, but are involved in about 40 percent of the accidents, said Lt. Lyle Belknap, boating law administrator for the state Department of Natural Resources. In Oakland County--which has the largest number of registered watercraft in the state--about half of the 59 reported boating accidents in 1996 involved personal watercraft. Most accidents involve 19-to-29-year-olds. About 75 percent of those involved in the accidents have not taken boating-safety courses; 95 percent of accidents involve people with little or no boating experience, Belknap said." (p3 secA)

Conner, Rick/McDiarmid, Hugh, Jr. "Outcry in Wake of Crash." Detroit Free Press 1 Jul 1997. p1,3 secA.

PERSONAL WATERCRAFT--ENVIRONMENTAL ASPECTS --UNITED STATES

"According to the EPA, two-stroke engines [found in jet skis] are the main source of toxic water pollution in the US. Two-strokes run on a mix of motor oil and gasoline, discharging as much as one-third of their fuel--unburned--into the water and air. This means an average 2-hour ride dumps 2.5 gallons of unburned gas and oil into the water." (p9)

Morgan, Kathryn. "Earth Island in Action: Bluewater Network: Jet Skis Hit Bumpy Water." Earth Island Journal v12 n4 Fall 1997. p9. (ISSN1041-0406).

PERSONAL WATERCRAFT--MICHIGAN

"Michigan has the most registered watercraft of any state: 945,817 were licensed in 1996, up 18 percent from 1995. While registrations have increased steadily for years, the number of watercraft under 16 feet doubled from 1994 to 1996--to about 80,000....In 1996, personal watercraft accounted for less than 8 percent of boat registrations yet were involved in more than half of all accidents,...[Michigan Association of Insurance Agents spokesman Gary Mitchell] said." (p1 secB)

Laitner, Bill. "Local News: Local Dateline: Metro Area: Boat Mishaps Fall across State." Detroit Free Press 20 Jun 1997. p1 secB.

PERSONAL WATERCRAFT--UNITED STATES

Jet skis, "the fastest-growing segment of the boating industry, now account for one-third of all boat sales in the US. The $1.4 billion-a-year jet ski industry sells about 200,000 units per year. Worldwide, the number of jet skis sold tops 1.2 million. According to the US Coast Guard, 10 percent of all boats on US waters are jet skis, but jet skis account for 36 percent of all boating accidents. Jet skis are involved in 40 percent of all boating-related injuries and 8 percent of all boating deaths." (p9)

Morgan, Kathryn. "Earth Island in Action: Bluewater Network: Jet Skis Hit Bumpy Water." Earth Island Journal v12 n4 Fall 1997. p9. (ISSN1041-0406).

PERSONS WITHOUT HEALTH INSURANCE

see MEDICALLY UNINSURED PERSONS

PERU

"Peru has a population of 24 million (45 percent of its people are indigenous; 37 percent are mestizo), and more than half live in poverty....Total direct foreign investment in Peru increased from $1.7 billion in 1993 to $4.5 billion in 1995....The International Press Service reports that 750,000 acres of Peru's Amazon rainforest is clearcut each year. The Peruvian highlands are deforested at a rate of 250,000 acres per year....Experts estimate that oil companies have co-opted at least 17 million acres of native lands in the Peruvian Amazon." (p41)

Oakley, Charmaine. "Other Voices: The Media Missed the Mark in Peru." Earth Island Journal v12 n3 Sum 1997. p41. (ISSN1041-0406).

PESTICIDE RESIDUES IN FOOD--UNITED STATES (v26)

PESTICIDES (v26)

"Some 2.5 million metric tons of pesticides are applied annually worldwide to protect crops, yet still about 35 percent of all crops are lost to pests and a further 20 percent to other pests after harvest. Over 500 species of insects, 270 species of weeds, and 150 species of plant pathogens are now resistant to pesticides. And, according to the World Health Organization, one million people are poisoned and 20,000 killed by pesticides each year." (p29)

Fox, Michael W. "Ruminations of a Radical Veterinarian: Breaking the Circle of Poverty & Famine." Acres, U.S.A. v27 n10 Oct 1997. p28-29. (ISSN1076-4968).

"In 1993, approximately 4.5 billion pounds of 'conventional pesticide active ingredients' used for agricultural purposes were applied throughout the world; 24% of those pesticides or over 1 billion pounds used in the US alone--equivalent to 4.1 pounds per person. In 1995, California applied over 210 million pounds of active ingredient, (almost five percent of global use) or...6.6 pounds per person." (p4)

Bourque, Martin/Bekkers, Ingrid. "Silent Spring II?: Recent Discoveries Reveal New Threats of Pesticides to Our Health." Backgrounder v4 n2 Sum 1997. p1-5,7-8.

PESTICIDES--DENMARK

"Danish Environment Minister Svend Auken has announced bans on 40 pesticides considered by Denmark's environment agency to be particularly hazardous to human health and the environment....Last year the government imposed a ban on 150 pesticides, most of them presenting a risk to groundwater. Together with the 40 banned now, they account for more than 1,200 tons of the 5,500 tons of active substances sold for agricultural uses in Denmark in 1995." (p6)

"Chemicals and Substances: Denmark to Ban Range of Pesticides." Environment Watch: Western Europe v6 n13 4 Jul 1997. p6. (ISSN1066-6001).

PESTICIDES--DEVELOPING COUNTRIES

"The technology used to spray pesticides in most developing countries reflects technical standards of 40 years ago, resulting in environmental damage and pesticides waste, according to [a] recent report by the U.N. Food and Agriculture Organization (FAO) transmitted via the Pesticide Action Network....In Colombia, flowers are sprayed weekly with up to 6,000 liters per hectare (l/ha) and in Brazil, application volumes of 10,000 l/ha in orchard crops have been reported. Application volumes at this rate cause run off and lead to soil and groundwater contamination....[The FAO] stated that, for efficient pest control with appropriate technologies, less than 10 percent of these volumes would be more than enough." (p4)

"Eco-Update: Unsafe Pesticide Use Rampant in Developing Countries." Acres, U.S.A. v27 n9 Sep 1997. p4. (ISSN1076-4968).

PESTICIDES--HEALTH ASPECTS--AGRICULTURAL LABORERS

According to the International Labour Organization representative, Ali Taqi, "exposure to pesticides and agrochemicals constitutes one of the major risks faced by farm workers, accounting in some countries for as much as 14% of all occupational injuries in the agricultural sector and 10% of all fatal injuries. Despite deficiencies in national reporting systems which make data on pesticide poisonings notoriously under-estimated, according to Mr. Taqi, developing countries consume more than 20% of the world production of agrochemicals, which are responsible for approximately 70% of the total cases of acute poisoning in the working population, i.e. more than 1.1 million cases. The World Health Organization, another UN agency, estimates the total cases of pesticide poisoning worldwide at between 2 and 5 million workers each year, of which 40,000 are fatal."

International Labour Organization. "ILO Warns on Farm Safety: Agriculture Mortality Rates Remain High: Pesticides Pose Major Health Risks to...Workforce." Press Release 22 Oct 1997. document-level access: <http://www.unicc.org/ilo/public/english/235press/pr/1997/23.htm>

PESTICIDES--HEALTH ASPECTS--MINNESOTA (v26)

PESTICIDES--HEALTH ASPECTS--THAILAND (v26)

PESTICIDES--ILLINOIS--MINNESOTA--WISCONSIN (v26)

PESTICIDES--NETHERLANDS

In the Netherlands, according to the coordinating body of the 1991 Multi-Year Crop Protection Plan, "pesticide use reduction is the program's biggest success. Mostly due to a 77 percent reduction in soil sterilant use and a 14 percent reduction in herbicide use, an overall reduction of 41 percent had been achieved by 1995....Annual sales of active ingredients sank from an average of 21.3 million tons in 1984-1988 to 12.6 million tons in 1995." (p6)

Proost, Jet/Matteson, Patricia. "Reducing Pesticide Use in the Netherlands: With Stick and Carrot." Journal of Pesticide Reform v17 n3 Fall 1997. p2-8. (ISSN0893-357X).

PESTICIDES--SOUTH AMERICA

"The most commonly used pesticides in South America, representing 40% of use, are organophosphates and carbamates." (p795) "Pesticide poisoning is a major risk for the estimated 40 million-plus agricultural workers in Latin America and the Caribbean. It is estimated that 1,000-2,000 pesticide poisonings occur annually in each of the small countries, and proportionately more in larger countries." (p796) "Pesticide poisonings among minors are growing: 1994 PAHO [Pan American Health Organization] figures for Latin America showed that 10-20% of cases involved children under 18....Considering untreated wastewater in 60% of rural communities, runoff from pesticides and fertilizers, industrial effluents, and urban waste, South America pollutes almost 11 times more fresh water per capita than Europe." (p797)

Joyce, Stephanie/U.S. National Institute of Environmental Health Sciences. "Focus: Growing Pains in South America." Environmental Health Perspectives v105 n8 Aug 1997. p794-799.

PESTICIDES--UNITED STATES (v26)

"Methyl parathion, commonly known as 'cotton poison,' is a synthetic pesticide related to nerve gas that by law can be used only in open fields [in the U.S.]....As of mid-July 1997, approximately 4,500 premises have been reported sprayed with methyl parathion; 18,000 people have been affected, including 10,000 children; and 2,300 people have been relocated until their homes can be cleaned up. The US Environmental Protection Agency (EPA) estimates that the cost of this problem as of July 1997 is $200 million." (p4)

"ATSDR: Agencies Are Sharing Strategies for More Effective Response to Methyl Parathion Health Threat." Hazardous Substances & Public Health v7 n3 Fall 1997. p4-5.

In the U.S., "as of March 1997, 380 of the 604 active ingredients requiring reregistration were still being supported by pesticide manufacturers. (Supported pesticides are those for which the manufacturer pays registration fees and submits reregistration data to EPA.) Of these 380, only 148 had completed the reregistration process....EPA now estimates that the reregistration process will take until 2002." (p3) "Since 1984, an average of over 16 new products (ranging between 8 and 40 per year) have come on the market annually." (p4)

Cox, Caroline. "Pesticide Registration: No Guarantee of Safety." Journal of Pesticide Reform v17 n2 Sum 1997. p2-9. (ISSN0893-357X).

In the U.S., "the herbicide metolachlor was reregistered in 1995. It is the second most widely used herbicide in U.S. agriculture....It is persistent and mobile in soil, has been found in the groundwater in 20 states, and is among the top five pesticides detected in surface and drinking water in the Midwest. Chlorpropham, reregistered in 1996, is a sprout inhibitor used on about 60 percent of the potatoes eaten in the U.S....Children every day are consuming between 85 and 231 percent (depending on what assumptions are made) of what EPA believes is an acceptable amount of chlorpropham." (p4)

Cox, Caroline. "Pesticide Registration: No Guarantee of Safety." Journal of Pesticide Reform v17 n2 Sum 1997. p2-9. (ISSN0893-357X).

PESTICIDES--VIETNAM (v26)

PESTICIDES INDUSTRY--CALIFORNIA--CANADA (v26)

PET FISH TRADE

see ORNAMENTAL FISH TRADE

PET OWNERS--UNITED STATES (v26)

"An estimated 27 million households [in the U.S.] give Christmas presents to their dogs, according to Gallup, and 6 million give birthday presents to their cats. More than 6 million householders even say they like to dress their dog up in a little costume. Most U.S. households (57 percent) owned at least one dog or cat in 1996, an increase from 54 percent in 1990. Twenty-six percent of households only have dogs, 14 percent only have cats, and 17 percent have both. The total number of pet dogs and cats in the U.S. is estimated at 128 million in 1996, up from 107 million in 1990. In other words, the pet population of the U.S. increased 20 percent between 1990 and 1996, while the human population increased about 7 percent....9 million dog owners and 6 million cat owners still admit to...[leaving their radio, TV, or stereo on for the pet when they aren't home]. Perhaps this is because 36 percent of dog owners and 48 percent of cat owners say their pet occasionally 'seems to be watching TV.'" (p6)

"Give Your Love a Rawhide Chew." Forecast v17 n9 Sep 1997. p6. article-level access: <http://www.demographics.com/Publications/FC/97_fc/9709_fc/FC97095.htm> (ISSN0732-1597).

PETROL

see GASOLINE

PETROLEUM--WELL BORING

see OIL WELL DRILLING RIGS

PETROLEUM AS FUEL--UNITED STATES

"Kerosene-type jet fuel supplied in July 1997 averaged 1.6 million barrels per day [in the U.S.], 3 percent higher than both the previous month's rate and the July 1996 rate. Kerosene-type jet fuel stocks measured 43 million barrels at the end of July 1997, the same as the stock level in the previous month but 5 million barrels higher than the stock level 1 year earlier." (p41)

U.S. Dept. of Energy. Energy Information Administration. "Petroleum." Monthly Energy Review Aug 1997. p41-70. (ISSN0095-7356).

In the U.S., "the February 1997 national average price, excluding taxes, of heating oil sold to residential customers was $1.05 per gallon, 3 percent lower than the previous month's price but 10 percent higher than the price 1 year earlier. The average price of No. 2 fuel oil sold to all end users was 70 cents per gallon in January 1997, 7 percent lower than the February 1997 price but 10 percent higher than the February 1996 price." (p109)

U.S. Dept. of Energy. Energy Information Administration. "Energy Prices." Monthly Energy Review May 1997. p109-128. (ISSN0095-7356).

In the U.S., "the average price, excluding taxes, of residual fuel oil sold to end users in February 1997 was 44 cents per gallon, 10 percent lower than the previous month's price and 2 percent lower than the February 1996 average. The average resale price, excluding taxes, of residual fuel oil in February 1997 was 40 cents per gallon, 7 percent lower than the previous month's average and 1 percent lower than the price 1 year earlier." (p109)

U.S. Dept. of Energy. Energy Information Administration. "Energy Prices." Monthly Energy Review May 1997. p109-128. (ISSN0095-7356).

U.S. "distillate fuel oil supplied during April 1997 averaged 3.5 million barrels per day, 2 percent lower than the previous month's rate but 2 percent higher than the April 1996 rate. Distillate fuel oil ending stocks for April 1997 were 96 million barrels, 6 million barrels below the stock level in the previous month but 6 million barrels above the level 1 year earlier." (p41)

U.S. Dept. of Energy. Energy Information Administration. "Petroleum." Monthly Energy Review May 1997. p41-70. (ISSN0095-7356).

U.S. "distillate fuel oil supplied during July 1997 averaged 3.3 million barrels per day, 2 percent higher than the previous month's rate and 9 percent higher than the July 1996 rate. Distillate fuel oil ending stocks for July 1997 were 123 million barrels, 5 million barrels above the stock level in the previous month and 16 million barrels above the level 1 year earlier." (p41)

U.S. Dept. of Energy. Energy Information Administration. "Petroleum." Monthly Energy Review Aug 1997. p41-70. (ISSN0095-7356).

U.S. "residual fuel oil supplied in April 1997 averaged 0.7 million barrels per day, 3 percent lower than both the previous month's rate and the April 1996 rate. Residual fuel oil stocks measured 42 million barrels at the end of April 1997, 1 million barrels higher than the stock level in the previous month...." (p41)

U.S. Dept. of Energy. Energy Information Administration. "Petroleum." Monthly Energy Review May 1997. p41-70. (ISSN0095-7356).

PETROLEUM INDUSTRY AND TRADE (v26)

see also OIL INDUSTRIES; OIL WELL DRILLING RIGS; ORGANIZATION OF PETROLEUM EXPORTING COUNTRIES

"For all OECD countries, petroleum stocks at the end of December 1996 totaled 3.6 billion barrels, less than 1 percent lower than the ending stock level in December 1995. Stocks were higher in Japan (+3 percent) and the United Kingdom (+1 percent). Stock levels were lower in Italy and Canada (both -5 percent), the United States (-3 percent), Germany (-2 percent), and France (-1 percent), compared with levels 1 year earlier." (p129)

U.S. Dept. of Energy. Energy Information Administration. "International Energy." Monthly Energy Review May 1997. p129-144. (ISSN0095-7356).

"World crude oil production during April 1997 was 67 million barrels per day, up 0.5 million barrels per day from the level in the previous month. Organization of Petroleum Exporting Countries (OPEC) production during April 1997 averaged 29 million barrels per day, up 0.2 million barrels per day from the level during the previous month. During April 1997, production increased in Iraq by 120 thousand barrels per day, Nigeria by 70 thousand barrels per day, Saudi Arabia by 53 thousand barrels per day, and Venezuela by 20 thousand barrels per day." (p129)

U.S. Dept. of Energy. Energy Information Administration. "International Energy." Monthly Energy Review Jul 1997. p129-144. (ISSN0095-7356).

In December 1996, consumption of petroleum "in all Organization for Economic Cooperation and Development (OECD) countries was 42.2 million barrels per day, 2 percent lower than the December 1995 rate. The consumption rate was higher than it was 1 year ago in the United Kingdom (+3 percent) and Germany (+2 percent). Consumption rates were lower in Canada (-8 percent), Italy (-7 percent), Japan (-5 percent), and the United States and France (both less than -1 percent), compared with the rate 1 year earlier." (p129)

U.S. Dept. of Energy. Energy Information Administration. "International Energy." Monthly Energy Review May 1997. p129-144. (ISSN0095-7356).

PETROLEUM INDUSTRY AND TRADE--AUSTRALIA (v26)

PETROLEUM INDUSTRY AND TRADE--AZERBAIJAN (v26)

PETROLEUM INDUSTRY AND TRADE--CALIFORNIA

"Located about 35 miles west of Bakersfield, Calif., the Elk Hills [Naval Petroleum Reserve] field produces nearly 60,000 barrels of oil and more than 350 million cubic feet of natural gas per day. The federal government owns or controls about 80 percent of the field, which was set aside in the early 1990s to guarantee the U.S. Navy a secure source of crude oil." (p8)

Childress, Janice O. "News Notes: Going Once, Going Twice...." Geotimes v42 n7 Jul 1997. p8. (ISSN0016-8556).

PETROLEUM INDUSTRY AND TRADE--CANADA (v26)

PETROLEUM INDUSTRY AND TRADE--COSTA RICA (v26)

PETROLEUM INDUSTRY AND TRADE--ENVIRONMENTAL ASPECTS--UNITED STATES

According to a 1995 American Petroleum Institute "report, the amount of chemicals released from petroleum refineries has declined by 26 percent since 1988; during this period, carcinogen levels have declined by 46 percent....API member companies claim that more than 90 percent of their underground storage tanks already meet the 1998 federal standards for preventing groundwater contamination...." (p9)

Wexler, Devra. "News Notes: Environmental Record Improving, Says API." Geotimes v42 n8 Aug 1997. p9. (ISSN0016-8556).

PETROLEUM INDUSTRY AND TRADE--MICHIGAN (v26)
PETROLEUM INDUSTRY AND TRADE--PERSIAN GULF REGION (v26)
PETROLEUM INDUSTRY AND TRADE--TEXAS (v26)
PETROLEUM INDUSTRY AND TRADE--UNITED STATES (v26)

"Energy consumption in January 1997 in the United States totaled 8.697x10 [to the fifteenth power] British thermal units. According to the Energy Department's Energy Information Administration, petroleum accounted for 3.079x10 [to the fifteenth power] Btu (35.40 percent)....Domestic field production of petroleum in January 1997 was estimated at 8,487 thousand barrels a day (crude oil--6,387; natural gas plant liquids--1,815), according to the Energy Information Administration....U.S. imports of crude oil and petroleum products in March 1997 averaged an estimated 9,664 thousand barrels a day, an increase of 7.8 percent from March 1996." (p7)

Childress, Janice O. "News Notes: Energy in Brief." Geotimes v42 n7 Jul 1997. p7. (ISSN0016-8556).

Total U.S. "petroleum imports averaged 10.1 million barrels per day in April 1997, 4 percent higher than the previous month's rate and 8 percent higher than the April 1996 rate. In April 1997, 18.4 million barrels per day of petroleum products were supplied for domestic use, 3 percent higher than the April 1996 rate. Motor gasoline accounted for 43 percent of the total; distillate fuel oil, 19 percent; and residual fuel oil, 4 percent." (p41)

U.S. Dept. of Energy. Energy Information Administration. "Petroleum." Monthly Energy Review May 1997. p41-70. (ISSN0095-7356).

Total U.S. "petroleum imports averaged 9.9 million barrels per day in July 1997, 4 percent lower than the previous month's rate but 1 percent higher than the July 1996 rate. In July 1997, 18.9 million barrels per day of petroleum products were supplied for domestic use, 4 percent higher than the July 1996 rate. Motor gasoline accounted for 45 percent of the total; distillate fuel oil, 17 percent; and kerosene-type jet fuel, 9 percent." (p41)

U.S. Dept. of Energy. Energy Information Administration. "Petroleum." Monthly Energy Review Aug 1997. p41-70. (ISSN0095-7356).

PETROLEUM PRODUCTS
see GASOLINE

PETROLEUM PRODUCTS--PRICES--UNITED STATES (v26)
PETROLEUM RESERVES--CHINA (v26)
PETROLEUM RESERVES--MIDDLE EAST (v26)
PETROLEUM RESERVES--UNITED STATES

"According to the Energy Information Administration, U.S. dependence on oil imports will rise from the current level of 50 percent to 60 percent in the year 2010. As oil imports increase, the strategic petroleum reserve will provide less and less energy security. The logical response should be to stockpile more oil. Yet, exactly the opposite is occurring. Some $315 million in revenue from the Operation Desert Storm drawdown was diverted to pay operating expenses rather than purchase replacement oil. Annual purchases of crude for the SPR [Strategic Petroleum Reserve] have been halted, and we have begun to sell oil from the reserve as a deficit reduction measure. During fiscal years 1996 and 1997, the Department of Energy sold $450 million barrels of oil for this purpose....With its current inventory, the SPR has more than 100 million barrels of available, but unused storage." (pS3999)

Akaka, Daniel K. (Sen.-Hawaii). "Statements on Introduced Bills and Joint Resolutions." Congressional Record. Daily ed. v143 n57 6 May 1997. pS3998-4010. section/page-level access: <http://thomas.loc.gov/cgi-bin/query/R?r105:FLD001:S03998:> (ISSN0363-7239). (X1.1A.105/1).

PETS
see also CATS; DOGS; ORNAMENTAL FISH TRADE; PIT BULL TERRIERS

PETS--GREAT BRITAIN (v26)
PETS--UNITED STATES (v26)

"An estimated 4.5 million Americans are bitten [by pets] each year. Children, particularly those under 10 years of age, are the unfortunate recipients of nearly 10 percent of these bites, according to a report just released by Jeffrey Sacks, a medical epidemiologist with the Centers for Disease Control (CDC) in Atlanta....According to the CDC report, the majority of victims in the 25 fatal dog attacks reported in 1995 and 1996 were children ages 6 to 10, making them the most high-risk group." (p30)

Marder, Amy. "Pets & Children: Safety First." Animals v130 n4 Jul-Aug 1997. p30-33. (ISSN0030-6835).

PHARMACEUTICAL INDUSTRY--LAW AND LEGISLATION --UNITED STATES (v26)
PHARMACEUTICAL INDUSTRY--UNITED STATES

"U.S. retail sales of nonprescription pain management drugs totaled $3.2 billion in 1995, up from $2.7 billion in 1990, according to Find/SVP. Prescription pain killer sales were $8.6 billion in 1995. The combined prescription-non-prescription total of $11.8 billion in 1995 is expected to grow to $17.7 billion by 2000." (p6)

"The Over-Medicated American." Forecast v17 n12 Dec 1997. p6. article-level access: <http://www.demographics.com/publications/fc/97_fc/9712_fc/f971206.htm> (ISSN0732-1597).

PHARMACEUTICALS
see DRUGS

PHD DEGREE
see DOCTOR OF PHILOSOPHY DEGREE

PHILADELPHIA (PA.)--ECONOMIC CONDITIONS

"Between 1950 and 1990 Philadelphia lost 25% of its population and 27% (250,000) of its jobs. Between 1970 and 1990 median household income dropped by 22% (adjusted for inflation), from $31,600 to $24,600....Between 1981 and 1991 the City raised taxes 19 times. This included the City's wage tax, at 5% a large and highly regressive levy on workers. By 1994 the average state and local taxes paid by a family of four in Philadelphia, with a gross income of $50,000, was $5,927 a year--one of the highest rates among the nation's large cities." (p18-19) According to the Pennsylvania Intergovernmental Cooperation Authority, "'during the first half of the 1990s the city lost another 5.5% of its population, more than any other major city in the nation. The poverty rate was 20% in 1989, but by 1993 has risen to between 23% and 31%. And among children the rate rose from 29% to somewhere above 40%. From 1992 through 1996 the number of housing units provided for the homeless doubled from 3,100 to 6,300, reflecting worsening economic conditions....'" (p20)

Breslow, Marc. "'Miracle' in Philidelphia: Can Fiscal Management Really Save the Cities?" Dollars and Sense n212 Jul-Aug 1997. p18-21. (ISSN0012-5245).

PHILANTHROPY
see CHARITIES; SOCIAL SERVICE

PHILIPPINES--ECONOMIC CONDITIONS (v26)
PHILIPPINES--POPULATION (v26)
PHILIPPINES--SEXUAL BEHAVIOR

According to the Young Adult Fertility and Sexuality Study conducted in 1994 in the Philippines, "reports of premarital conceptions by married women...suggest that at least 52 percent of married women had sex before marriage, rather than the 35 percent who reported premarital sex when questioned directly....This figure for married women closely approximates the level of premarital sexual experience (59 percent) reported by married men....Among married respondents, 57 percent of men and 51 percent of women reported having had sex with their spouse before they were married. Of these, very few of the women (3 percent) reported having had any additional partners, whereas 37 percent of the men reported additional premarital partners." (p2) "63 percent of the same married men reported that their first sexual experience was not with their spouse.... Of all married men in the sample, about 21 percent had premarital sexual relations with multiple partners including their future spouses." (p3)

"Survey Sheds New Light on Marriage and Sexuality in the Philippines." Asia-Pacific Population & Policy n42 Jul 1997. p1-4. (ISSN0891-6683).

PHILIPPINES--THAILAND--SOCIAL CONDITIONS (v26)

PHLEBOTOMY--UNITED STATES (v26)

PHOSPHORUS--MICHIGAN--ANN ARBOR (v26)

PHOTOGRAPHIC INDUSTRY--UNITED STATES

In the U.S., "sales of photography equipment, film, and processing were essentially flat between 1994 and 1995, at $12.6 billion. Photo processing is the single largest component of photography-related sales, accounting for 43 percent of total revenue in 1995, or $5.4 billion. Americans processed more rolls of film in 1995 than in 1990 (710 million, compared with 698 million), a 1.7 percent increase. The number of exposures developed increased at a slightly slower rate of 1.2 percent over the same period, reaching 17 billion exposures in 1995....Despite increases in the number of rolls of film and exposures developed, the $5.4 billion in photo-processing sales in 1995 represented a 2 percent decline from 1990, in unadjusted dollars." (p4)

Heubusch, Kevin. "Tomorrow's Markets: Look at the Birdie." American Demographics v19 n7 Jul 1997. p4,6-10. article-level access: <http://www.demographics.com/publications/ad/97_ad/9707_ad/ad97072.htm> (ISSN0163-4089).

PHOTOGRAPHY--UNITED STATES--FILMS

In the U.S., "film sales, the second largest component of industry revenue, accounted for 20 percent of total sales in 1995, at $2.6 billion. Between 1990 and 1995, moderately increasing sales of popular films, such as 35mm [millimeter], were offset by rapidly declining sales of 110 and disc film. That resulted in slow sales growth of 2.2 percent over the period. In contrast, sales of 35mm film increased 17 percent, to 704 million rolls, partly due to the popularity of single-use cameras." (p4,6)

Heubusch, Kevin. "Tomorrow's Markets: Look at the Birdie." American Demographics v19 n7 Jul 1997. p4,6-10. article-level access: <http://www.demographics.com/publications/ad/97_ad/9707_ad/ad97072.htm> (ISSN0163-4089).

PHOTOGRAPHY--UNITED STATES--PROCESSING (v26)

PHOTOVOLTAIC POWER GENERATION (v26)

"The global photovoltaic industry is expected to grow by a record-breaking 15-30% again in 1997 and residential rooftop solar energy systems are part of the fastest-growing segment of the solar energy industry. An estimated 400,000 families around the world have installed solar home systems in the last decade, and approximately 80,000 systems are being added annually." (p22)

Biondo, Brenda. "Cover Story: Pushing Solar Energy through the Roof." Solar Industry Journal v8 n2 1997. p21-24,26-30,33.

"Existing passive solar designs reduce home energy use by about 40 percent. Advanced technologies...have the potential to slash residential heating bills by as much as 95 percent and lighting bills by 80 percent." (p23)

"Renew the Parks: Exemplary Living at the Grand Canyon." Solar Today v11 n4 Jul-Aug 1997. p23. (ISSN1042-0630).

PHOTOVOLTAIC POWER GENERATION--ARIZONA

At the Yuma Proving Ground in Arizona, the U.S. Army Corps of Engineers uses photovoltaic power to save on energy costs. "The system uses 8,184 individual 55-watt solar modules. There are 11 series-connected solar modules per panel; two panels make a series string or sub-circuit. Overall, there are 372 sub-circuits connected in parallel. The entire photovoltaic system is rated at 400 kilowatts (kW) direct current which, after conversion to alternating current, yields 375 kW--enough to supply more than 100 average homes. With the battery storage added, the system can provide up to 900 kW during peak demand periods, more than enough to operate YPG's water treatment plant during an emergency power outage. Before the power station came on-line, YPG received 93 percent of its electrical needs from Western Area Power Administration....[The power station] is expected to save at least $400,000 per year in energy costs." (p8)

Goss, Mona Lee. "Sun Power: Photovoltaic Array Generates Electricity in Arizona." Engineer Update v21 n6 Jun 1997. p8. (ISSN0733-8163).

PHOTOVOLTAIC POWER GENERATION--CALIFORNIA --SACRAMENTO

"The Sacramento Municipal Utility District (SMUD) Solarport--a photovoltaic array and electric vehicle charging station at Sacramento...[California] International Airport--went on-line in May. The $1.08 million Solarport project, with costs shared by the Department of Energy, Utility PhotoVoltaic Group and SMUD, has an expected design life of 30 years....The Solarport...includes electric vehicle charging stations for four electric vehicles and has an output rating of 128 kW [kilowatts], enough electricity to power more than 50 homes. The cantilevered structure consists of three rows that utilize 2,772 PV modules from Siemens Solar [Industries]. The structure measures 3903 feet long, 30 feet wide and 14 feet in height and provides shaded parking for 75 cars....SMUD estimates that during its 30-year design life, the Solarport will produce the equivalent amount of energy of 825,000 gallons of oil, 1.1 billion cubic feet of natural gas or 10 million pounds of coal." (p3)

"SMUD Opens PV-Powered Electric Vehicle Charging Station at Airport." Photovoltaic Insider's Report v16 n6 Jun 1997. p3. (ISSN0731-4671).

PHOTOVOLTAIC POWER GENERATION--CANADA (v26)

PHOTOVOLTAIC POWER GENERATION--JAPAN (v26)

"Japan's national budget for promoting PV [photovoltaic power] has increased at least 15% every year since 1992. Japan's 1996 budget for PV surpassed US$120 million and included $33 million for the country's Residential PV Rooftop Program. For 1997, the government approved spending US$196 million for PV, including $109 million for a rooftop program through its Ministry of International Trade and Industry (MITI) and the New Energy and Industrial Technology Development Organization (NEDO), Japan also is shifting more of its spending on PV from research and development to market development. From 1994 to 1996, R&D received 54% of the budget, with the remaining 46% allocated to market development....In a recent poll, 85% of Japanese citizens said they would spend up to $10,000 on a residential PV system." (p23)

Biondo, Brenda. "Cover Story: Pushing Solar Energy through the Roof." Solar Industry Journal v8 n2 1997. p21-24,26-30,33.

PHOTOVOLTAIC POWER GENERATION--SWITZERLAND

"The Swiss government has launched a new photovoltaic technology support program which, in effect, subsidizes about 25% of current on-grid PV market prices. Launched in February, the new program supports all PV on- and off-grid installations from 1 to 100 kW [kilowatts] at the rate of 3,000 CHF per kW/p [kilowatt power] (approximately US $2,000). 'This is approximately 25% of today's on-grid market prices,' according to Thomas Nordmann, president of the Swiss Solar Industry Association....This is a follow-up to the successful Swiss PV school initiative in which, between 1992-1996, a total capacity of 800 kW of PV systems were installed on 170 public school buildings....Switzerland now runs and operates more than 8.2 MW/p [megawatt power] of PV capacity, equal to approximately 1.2 W [watts] per capita." (p4)

"Report from Switzerland: New Swiss Initiative Subsidizes 25% of On-Grid PV Installations." Photovoltaic Insider's Report v16 n6 Jun 1997. p4. (ISSN0731-4671).

PHOTOVOLTAIC POWER GENERATION--UNITED STATES (v26)

According to Douglas DeNio, a U.S. park service engineer who spearheads the Renew the Parks program, "the average installed cost of photovoltaic systems has been about $16,000 to $17,000 per kilowatt....Energy costs for photovoltaics currently average about 25 [cents] per kilowatt-hour....Monetary values are an attempt to quantify the hidden costs of energy production and use such as acid-rain damage to forests. Carbon dioxide emissions are valued at $8.00 per ton, with sulfur dioxide emissions valued at $0.75 per pound and nitrous oxides at $3.40 per pound....More than 270 million visitors visit the park system every year, and the cost of the proposed energy projects totals about $28 million." (p22)

Brown, Linda R. "Renew the Parks." Solar Today v11 n4 Jul-Aug 1997. p20-23. (ISSN1042-0630).

In 1994, the National Park Service "teamed up with the U.S. Department of Energy's (DOE's) Sandia National Laboratory to conduct a survey of existing photovoltaic systems and assess the potential for future projects. The survey had some surprising results--as many as 600 photovoltaic systems were already in use in the national park system, primarily for small applications such as powering outdoor lights, restroom ventilation and communication devices. Park personnel reported that about 97 percent of these systems were operating in a satisfactory manner. When asked for suggestions for future projects, park staff responded with...643 proposals totaling $28 million. Three of the proposed projects...carry price tags of more than $1.7 million apiece." (p21)

Brown, Linda R. "Renew the Parks." Solar Today v11 n4 Jul-Aug 1997. p20-23. (ISSN1042-0630).

PHYSICAL EDUCATION FOR CHILDREN--UNITED STATES (v26)

PHYSICAL FITNESS--MICHIGAN (v26)

PHYSICAL FITNESS--UNITED STATES (v26)

In the U.S., according to the CDC, "the highest percentages [of adults who report no leisure-time physical activity] (up around 45 percent) were in Alabama, Kentucky, North Carolina, West Virginia and the District of Columbia....Among adults who reported being overweight, Indiana reported the most (34.6 percent), followed by Missouri, Michigan and Mississippi; the lowest percentage of rotund respondents was Hawaii's (21.8), followed by Colorado, Massachusetts and New Mexico." (p11)

"Stateline: Unhealthy Habits (CDC)." State Legislatures v23 n9 Oct-Nov 1997. p11. (ISSN0147-6041).

PHYSICAL FITNESS CENTERS--UNITED STATES --WOMEN

"Only 5 percent of the more than 13,000 exercise clubs in the United States are single-sex gyms....In 1996 women were 57 percent of health club patrons, almost triple the amount 15 years ago,...[said Meredith Swain, spokeswoman for the International Health, Raquet and Sports Club Association]." (p5 secC)

Jackson, Lisa. "MetroLife: All-Female Health Clubs a Big Hit." Detroit News 5 Nov 1997. p5 secC.

PHYSICAL THERAPISTS--STUDY AND TEACHING --UNITED STATES (v26)

PHYSICAL THERAPISTS--UNITED STATES --IMMIGRANTS (v26)

PHYSICIAN-ASSISTED SUICIDE

see ASSISTED SUICIDE

PHYSICIANS

see also PEDIATRICIANS; PSYCHIATRISTS

PHYSICIANS--EMPLOYMENT--UNITED STATES

"According to the American Medical Association (AMA), more and more physicians are working as employees. In 1995, 45 percent of patient-care physicians were employees, compared to 24 percent in 1983. The numbers are even higher among young physicians: 64 percent of physicians with zero to five years of practice experience were employees in 1995, up from 47 percent in 1983. During this same period, the percentage of physicians in self-employed solo practices dropped from 35 percent to 28 percent." (p24) "Search firms estimate that 70 percent to 80 percent of new physicians leave their first position within three years." (p25)

Tschida, Molly. "Where the Jobs Are." New Physician v46 n8 Nov 1997. p22-27. (ISSN0028-6451).

PHYSICIANS--EUROPE (v26)

PHYSICIANS--MALPRACTICE--UNITED STATES (v26)

PHYSICIANS--MICHIGAN--DISCIPLINE

"More than 30,500 doctors are licensed to practice in Michigan; last year, the state took action against 83 of them. That puts the state's discipline rate at three actions per 1,000 doctors....At least 27 states had a higher rate of discipline last year, according to Public Citizen [Health Research Group, a nonprofit group in Washington, D.C.]. Mississippi topped the list, with about 11 actions taken per 1,000 doctors. North Dakota and Iowa followed, with 9.16 and 8.57 serious actions per 1,000 doctors. Michigan has been improving, moving toward the national average of four actions per 1,000 doctors since 1993, when the state Board of Medicine took action against 49 doctors, according to state records." (p10 secE)

Schulz, Karen. "State: State Lags in Doctor Discipline." Ann Arbor News 14 Sep 1997. p10 secE.

In Michigan, "of the 58 medical doctors disciplined between Oct. 1, 1996, and Aug. 22, 1997, three had their licenses revoked....Twenty-six doctors had their licenses suspended, records show. Substance abuse, including illegal or inappropriate use of prescription drugs, was the cause for discipline against at least 15 doctors during the 10-month period. A handful of other doctors were disciplined for fraud or sexual misconduct....In 17 of the cases involving doctors since October 1996, the Board of Medicine fined doctors a total of $56,750." (p10 secE)

Schulz, Karen. "State: State Lags in Doctor Discipline." Ann Arbor News 14 Sep 1997. p10 secE.

PHYSICIANS--SALARIES, ETC.--MICHIGAN (v26)

PHYSICIANS--SALARIES, ETC.--UNITED STATES (v26)

PHYSICIANS--UNITED STATES (v26)

"With 189 generalist physicians per 100,000 population and 342 specialists per 100,000, no state has anything close to the concentration of doctors found in...[Washington, D.C.]....[Hawaii] has 86 generalists per 100,000 population, according to a new report from the American Association of Retired Persons....Massachusetts has the second largest number of both generalists and specialists per 100,000 population, with 121 and 202, respectively." (p28)

Stoneman, Bill. "Kaleidoscope: Is There a Doctor in the State?" American Demographics v19 n7 Jul 1997. p28-29. article-level access: <http://www.demographics.com/

publications/ad/97_ad/9707_ad/ad970719.htm> (ISSN0163-4089).

"Approximately 22 percent of the nation's current physician workforce is foreign-trained (U.S. Department of Health and Human Services 1992...)....27 percent of the nation's first-year medical residents are also foreign-trained (Physician Payment Review Commission 1995...)....In 1970,...the nation had approximately 327,000 physicians, or about 157 physicians for every 100,000 citizens; by 1991 there were over 620,000 physicians, or about 244 for every 100,000 citizens (U.S. Department of Health and Human Services 1992...)." (p793) "Approximately 50 percent of the provider workforce of most health maintenance organizations (HMOs) are generalists....By 1992 less than 20 percent of the nation's first-year medical residents were choosing generalist careers (Association of American Medical Colleges 1992...)." (p794)

Sparer, Michael S. "Laboratories and the Health Care Marketplace: The Limits of State Workforce Policy." Journal of Health Politics, Policy and Law v22 n3 Jun 1997. p789-814. (ISSN0361-6878).

"A 1994 study in the JOURNAL OF THE AMERICAN MEDICAL ASSOCIATION (JAMA) predicted 'given 40 percent to 65 percent of Americans are in managed care plans, there will be a surplus of 165,000 physicians by the year 2000, with an adequate supply of primary care physicians and 60 percent excess of specialists.' MEDICAL ECONOMICS reported in 1995 that by the year 2000, there could be a surplus of 125,000 specialists, along with a 'modest' shortage of 20,000 generalists....The ratio of physicians per 100,000 has risen dramatically, from 198 in 1980, to 233 in 1990, to projections of 276 by 2000 and 298 by 2020, according to a 1992 COUNCIL ON GRADUATE MEDICAL EDUCATION REPORT." (p11)

Buterakos, James. "Perspectives: Dawn of a New Era." New Physician v46 n6 Sep 1997. p11-12. (ISSN0028-6451).

"Of the nearly 700,000 practicing physicians in the United States, 809 are on staff at the Indian Health Service (IHS), the government organization that provides health-care services to American Indians in 34 states around the country." (p15) "Starting annual salaries [are] about $45,000 less than what can be made 'outside'....Physician vacancy rate hovers around 12 percent to 15 percent within the organization....Of all the facilities in the IHS,...[Ray Bayles, physician recruiter for the Navajo Area IHS,] says he's got 13 of the 15 easiest to fill. And 90 percent of his doctors were in the top 15 percent of their class....The vacancy rate [for the Aberdeen Area, which covers the Dakotas, Nebraska and Iowa,] remains at 28 percent, according to estimates by IHS recruiter Patricia Yee-Spencer." (p20)

Humphrey, Dana. "When Worlds Collide." New Physician v46 n8 Nov 1997. p15-21. (ISSN0028-6451).

"A recent study from Johns Hopkins University, published in the JOURNAL OF THE AMERICAN MEDICAL ASSOCIATION, looked at the different communication styles of practitioners and polled both doctors and patients about their communication preferences. The researchers listened in on office visits between 127 physicians and 527 patients, then analyzed the conversations. They found that in 32 percent of visits, doctors asked simple yes-or-no questions and primarily used medical jargon to communicate. In 33 percent of visits, this communication style was combined with slightly more personal communication. Twenty percent of visits involved equal amounts of medical talk and personal conversation. Eight percent of conversations were dominated by personal exchanges...." (p1,8)

"Hey Doc, Let's Talk!" People's Medical Society Newsletter v16 n4 Aug 1997. p1,8. (ISSN0736-4873).

"A survey undertaken by researchers at the University of Kansas School of Medicine, Kansas City, asked both patients and physicians about the time they spent in the hospital talking about instructions for after discharge....Doctors...believed that 89 percent of their patients understood the side effects of their prescribed medications, but ony 57 percent of patients said they understood. Doctors believed that 95 percent of patients understood when they could resume normal activities. In actuality, only 58 percent of patients understood (ARCHIVES OF INTERNAL MEDICINE, May 12, 1997)." (p8)

"Hey Doc, Let's Talk!" People's Medical Society Newsletter v16 n4 Aug 1997. p1,8. (ISSN0736-4873).

In the U.S., "compliance with universal infection control precautions varies significantly, according to a study that appeared in the March 1997 JOURNAL OF OCCUPATIONAL AND ENVIRONMENTAL MEDICINE. The study, which looked at the procedures followed by 307 hospital-based physicians, found that while 94 percent follow glove use guidelines and 92 percent follow CDC guidelines for needle disposal, only 54 percent wear protective clothing and only 56 percent follow proper needle recapping procedures. Only 30 percent complied with all the universal precautions." (p7)

"Consumer Alert: Antibiotic Resistance Is Growing!" People's Medical Society Newsletter v16 n4 Aug 1997. p1,7. (ISSN0736-4873).

PHYSICIANS--UNITED STATES--ATTITUDES

"If they had to do it all over again, 83 percent of specialist physicians [in the U.S.] would still go into medicine....Generalists and specialists are equally satisfied with their jobs today, at about 75 percent. But when asked to look ahead three years, an entirely different picture emerges. Nearly half--46 percent--of specialists think their job satisfaction will decrease, compared with 32 percent of family practitioners. Increased satisfaction is anticipated by 23 percent of family practitioners and only 13 percent of the specialists." (p28)

Stoneman, Bill. "Kaleidoscope: This May Hurt." American Demographics v19 n7 Jul 1997. p28. article-level access: <http://www.demographics.com/publications/ad/97_ad/9707_ad/ad970718.htm> (ISSN0163-4089).

PHYSICIANS--UNITED STATES--POPULATION

In the U.S., "in 1993, the national average number of active physicians per 100,000 residents was 189, according to the DARTMOUTH ATLAS OF HEALTH CARE. But there were 317 and 303 active physicians per 100,000 residents in San Francisco and White Plains, New York, respectively. In stark contrast, there were only 155 and 154 active physicians per 100,000 residents in Lexington, Kentucky, and Birmingham, Alabama, respectively." (p25)

Tschida, Molly. "Where the Jobs Are." New Physician v46 n8 Nov 1997. p22-27. (ISSN0028-6451).

PHYSICIANS--UNITED STATES--RELIGION --ATTITUDES (v26)

PID

see PELVIC INFLAMMATORY DISEASE

PIGS

see SWINE

PILL, THE

see ORAL CONTRACEPTIVES

PINEAPPLE INDUSTRY--HAWAII

"Hawaii's pineapple production rose to 694 million pounds in 1996, up 1 percent from 1995. This was the first increase in 4 years. Most of the increase went to processed production; fresh use fell 8 percent. With fresh production at its lowest level in at least 5 years, shipments out of Hawaii fell to 190.1 million pounds." (p26)

U.S. Dept. of Agriculture. Economic Research Service. "Noncitrus Fruit Outlook." Fruit and Tree Nuts Situation and

Outlook Report Aug 1997. p7-26.

PINEAPPLE INDUSTRY--UNITED STATES

"U.S. consumption of fresh pineapple fell slightly in 1996 as it has for the previous 2 years. While imports set a record at 298.2 million pounds, they were not sufficient to offset declining domestic production and increasing exports. Costa Rica supplies about 63 percent of imported fresh pineapples to the United States....Hawaiian pineapples going to processing increased 5 percent from 1995. Imports of pineapple juice, however, declined about 1 percent and canned increased less than 1 percent from a year earlier, contributing to the level consumption. Imports represented about 80 percent of the supply of pineapple juice and 88 percent of canned in 1996. The Philippines, Thailand, and Indonesia continue to be the major suppliers of both juice and canned pineapple to the U.S. market....These countries contributed 86 percent of canned imports and 89 percent of juice imports. The Philippines alone accounted for 42 percent of canned pineapple imports and 44 percent of pineapple juice imports in 1996." (p25)

U.S. Dept. of Agriculture. Economic Research Service. "Noncitrus Fruit Outlook." Fruit and Tree Nuts Situation and Outlook Report Aug 1997. p7-26.

PING PONG

see TABLE TENNIS

PINUS RADIATA--CALIFORNIA--MONTEREY COUNTY (v26)

PIRATES

The International Maritime Bureau "estimates that losses from piracy reach $200 million a year. That is still substantially less than the toll taken by other forms of maritime theft. One increasingly popular scam involves so-called phantom ships. A syndicate will buy an old freighter, set up a network of dummy offices, and forge documents. When an unwitting shipper consigns a cargo to the fake company, the ship sails off, changes its name, and unloads the goods on the black market. The IMB informally estimates that these and other scams cost at least $1 billion a year. Yet over the past two years, piracy incidents counted by the IMB have more than doubled, to 224 last year, and experts believe that half or more of attacks go unreported because shipowners worry that the costs of disclosure outweigh the benefits." (p34)

Moulier, Philippe B./Casey, Ethan. "World Report: Pirates? What Pirates?" U.S. News & World Report v122 n24 23 Jun 1997. p33-34. article-level access: <http://www.usnews.com/usnews/issue/970623/23PIRA.HTM> (ISSN0041-5537).

PISTACHIO INDUSTRY--CALIFORNIA (v26)

For 1997, "the California pistachio industry is anticipating a record crop of 170 million pounds, in-shell basis, compared with the existing record of 152 million pounds harvested in 1993....In 1996, California pistachio production dropped to 105 million pounds, in-shell basis. This performance compares with 148 million pounds in 1995 and 129 million in 1994. Bearing acreage was 64,300 in 1996 compared with 60,300 in 1995 and 57,500 acres in 1994....The grower price last season averaged $1.16 per pound, in-shell basis, compared to $1.09 per pound in 1995 and 92.1 cents in 1994. The in-shell pistachio inventory was 22.8 million pounds on June 30, 1997, nearly the same as on June 30, 1996. Shelling stock this June stood at 2.0 million pounds, compared with 6.2 million a year ago. Domestic in-shell shipments totaled 51.4 million pounds (September 1-June 30) this year compared with 59.9 million a year earlier." (p33)

U.S. Dept. of Agriculture. Economic Research Service. "Tree Nut Outlook." Fruit and Tree Nuts Situation and Outlook Report Aug 1997. p32-33.

PIT BULL TERRIERS--OHIO--LUCAS COUNTY

In 1987, Ohio legislators restricted ownership of pit bulls and other fighting dogs. In 1988, "Lucas County officials took 337 pit bulls. In 1989, it took fewer than 200. In following years, about 50 dogs were confiscated annually, [chief dog warden Thomas] Skeldon said. But in 1996, Lucas County dog wardens took in more than 200 pit bulls. The 1997 number has reached 100 already, and officials expect it to continue rising." (p4 secD)

Pearce, Jeremy. "Metro: Special Report: Dogfighting: 'More We Charge, More We Find'." Detroit News 7 Jul 1997. p1,4 secD.

PITTSFIELD TOWNSHIP (MICH.) (v26)

PLACE-NAMES

see NAMES, GEOGRAPHICAL

PLANNED PARENTHOOD

see BIRTH CONTROL

PLANT GERMPLASM RESOURCES

see GERMPLASM RESOURCES, PLANT

PLANT POPULATIONS--SIERRA NEVADA (CALIF. AND NEV.)

According to the Sierra Nevada Ecosystem Project report, "of California's 7,000 vascular plant species, about 50 percent occur in the Sierra Nevada. Of these, more than 400 species--of which half are rare--are found only in the Sierra Nevada. The southern Sierra is richest in species, and the sequoias grow in the most fertile land in that region. The 15- and 20-foot diameters of the older trees make it clear that they've been here for millennia." (p34)

Solnit, Rebecca. "Among the Giants." Sierra v82 n4 Jul-Aug 1997. p30-37,63. (ISSN0161-7362).

PLANTOIDS

see ASTEROIDS

PLANTS

see also INVASIVE PLANTS

PLANTS--CHINA

In China, "there are about 2000 species of bryophyte, 2600 sinopteris species, 25000 species of angiosperm, which totally amount to 30000 species. Its fauna and flora make up 10% respectively out of the world's total." (p129) "Currently, there are 61 national nature reserves, 302 provincial ones, 275 municipal and country level ones, of which the Qingzang Nature Reserve is the largest, with an area of 24 million hectares, ranking first in Asia....Most of the endangered wild plants under vital state protection are included in nature reserves, with only 40 exceptions, which take up 11.6% of the total of plants under vital protection. More than 10 species have been domesticated to fine varieties." (p130)

Jianming, Jin. "The Construction and Management of Nature Reserves in China." Journal of Environmental Sciences v9 n2 Jun 1997. p129-140. (ISSN1001-0742).

PLANTS--SOUTH AFRICA

"Although South Africa occupies less than 1 percent of the world's land mass, it contains 10 percent of all the Earth's species of plants. In an area smaller than Vermont, the so-called Cape Floral Kingdom hosts more than 8,600 plant species, 5,800 of which are unique to the area. South Africa has a third of the world's succulent plant species, over 2,000 'Mesembryanthemaceae' species, and more than 100 'Pelargonium' (geranium) species." (p9) Thomas S. Elias, director of the U.S. National Arboretum says, "'about 1,700 of the 8,600 flowering plants indigenous to the Cape are listed as being critically rare, endangered, or vulnerable....29 of these are known to have already become extinct.'...The Fynbos [Cape Floral Kingdom] comprises about 17,000 square miles of the southern and southwestern Cape....The Cape Floral Kingdom is both the smallest and richest floral kingdom, with the highest known concentration of plant species--about 1,300 per 4,000 square miles. Its nearest rival, the South American rain forest, has a concentration of only 400 plants per 4,000 square miles." (p10) "South Africa has the richest geophyte flora in the world. It is home to over 2,000 flowering bulb species, of which more than 1,400 are found in the Cape Floral Kingdom....Elias says that South Africa has 96 of the 160 'Gladiolus' species found throughout the world. 'The country also boasts 88 recorded species of the lily 'Lachenalia,' out of an estimated world total of 110....'" (p11)

Becker, Hank/U.S. Dept. of Agriculture. Agricultural Research Service. "Floral Gems: Binational Cooperation Yields a Wealth of New Blooms for America's Markets." Agricultural Research v45 n9 Sep 1997. p8-13. (ISSN0002-161X).

PLANTS, INVASIVE

see INVASIVE PLANTS

PLASTICS--RECYCLING--UNITED STATES (v26)

In the U.S., "a full-size, heavy-duty [recycled plastic warehouse] pallet costs about $35, which is more than the initial cost of the traditional wood pallet....It takes about 60-70 pounds of recycled plastic to make one pallet, or about 100 recycled two-gallon jugs....Every 25 pallets saves one mature tree." (p8) "The demand for plastic lumber in the U.S. has been growing at a rate of 40% a year for the past three years. In 1995, 16 million board feet (40 million pounds) of plastic lumber were sold. Given a $5 billion annual market for pallets, even a small market share for plastic pallets will lead to big sales." (p9)

Davis, Trey. "Spotlight: The Environment Goes to Work." Positive Alternatives v8 n1 Fall 1997. p8-9. (ISSN1065-0075).

PLUM INDUSTRY--CALIFORNIA (v26)

PLUTONIUM--CANADA (v26)

PLUTONIUM--EUROPE--JAPAN--RUSSIA (v26)

PLUTONIUM--UNITED STATES (v26)

PNEUMOCOCCAL VACCINE--UNITED STATES (v26)

PNEUMONIA--TREATMENT--CANADA--UNITED STATES (v26)

POISONING, FOOD

see FOOD POISONING

POISONOUS WASTES

see HAZARDOUS WASTES

POLAND--ECONOMIC CONDITIONS

In Poland, "trade and price liberalization, tax reforms, and fiscal decentralization have fueled growth: it averaged at 6.1 percent in 1994-96. Fiscal deficit averaged 2.65 percent in 1994-96, while inflation declined to 18.5 percent by 1996. By the same year, the share of the private sector in the economy reached 63 percent. The share of trade in the GDP (Gross Domestic Product) has risen sharply (over 50 percent in 1996), signaling Poland's integration into the international trade system. Confidence of foreign investors has been reflected in growing foreign direct and portfolio investments which totaled more than US$5 billion in 1996."

World Bank. "More Reforms for Poland on the Road to Europe: Poland's Bold Economic Transformation." Press Release 6 Aug 1997. document-level access: <http://www.worldbank.org/html/extdr/extme/1433.htm>

"With a population of 40 million, located between Russia and Germany, Poland offers by far the largest market in the region. Privatization through National Investment Funds has been relatively successful (over 26 million people have bought in--90 percent of the eligible population), though the process remains incomplete. The country's private sector is vibrant and accounts for over two-thirds of both the economy and employment. Over 1 million new enterprises have been created in the last five years and private-sector profits are surging. Despite a general lack of working capital and the slow emergence of a consumer class, Poland leads the region in economic growth with 7 percent in 1995, 6 percent last year, and 5.7 percent predicted for this year. Investment from the US, already the largest from any Western country, was up nearly 50 percent in 1996." (p18)

Randolph, R. Sean. "Opinion/Essays: Hungarians, Czechs, Poles Race to Join EU." The Christian Science Monitor v89 n180 12 Aug 1997. p18. The Christian Science Monitor search engine: <http://www.csmonitor.com/plweb-cgi/iops1.pl> To retrieve this article, enter the following search: ED=19970812 AND hungarians. In the "retrieved list," click the title that matches this record. (ISSN0882-7729).

POLES--UNITED STATES (v26)

POLICE

see also BORDER PATROLS; HOUSING--UNITED STATES--POLICE; TRAFFIC ACCIDENTS--UNITED STATES--POLICE

POLICE--ACCIDENTS--UNITED STATES (v26)

POLICE--CANADA

"Since 1992, the number of RCMP [Royal Canadian Mounted Police] officers has declined 4.2 per cent, to 14,997 from 15,661, while the population has grown 6.3 per cent. And over the same period, far from seeing an increase in their annual budget--$1.8 billion this year--the Mounties have had to absorb cutbacks of $173 million. Wages have been frozen for five years, with the result that RCMP officers now earn barely half as much as their counterparts in U.S. federal police agencies....In 1994, the force reported that it had seized assets--such as boats and homes--valued at $48.5 million, but when these assets were sold they produced only $7.2 million for the treasury. In 1995, the Mounties valued their take at $43.7 million, but they realized only $14 million." (p14)

Palango, Paul. "Cover: Canada: Mountie Misery." Maclean's v110 n30 28 Jul 1997. p10-15. (ISSN0024-9262).

POLICE--CANADA--MORTALITY (v26)

POLICE--CANADA--UNITED STATES

"The United States has about 100 specialized federal law enforcement agencies whose officers have the power of arrest--from the FBI and the Secret Service to the Bureau of Alcohol, Tobacco and Firearms, the National Parks Service, the Drug Enforcement Administration and the Immigration and Naturalization Service. But since the amalgamation of the old Royal North West Mounted Police and the Dominion Police in 1920, Canada has had one federal police force--the RCMP [Royal Canadian Mounted Police], an extraordinary hybrid whose 15,000 officers try to do everything that the 100 U.S. police agencies do--and much more....In addition to being the federal force, the Mounties are the provincial police in eight provinces (all except Ontario and Quebec), the territorial police in Yukon and Northwest Territories and the municipal police in 200 towns across Canada." (p13-14)

Palango, Paul. "Cover: Canada: Mountie Misery." Maclean's v110 n30 28 Jul 1997. p10-15. (ISSN0024-9262).

POLICE--COMPLAINTS AGAINST--MICHIGAN --DETROIT

A 1997 "EPIC/MRA telephone poll found that 61 percent of Detroiters surveyed said cops treat people worse because of their race or where they live....In 1994, the latest year for which statistics were available, of the 98,672 people arrested, 85,438 were non-white and 13,234 were white. The number of citizens' complaints against police officers for harassment, offensive demeanor, use of force, improper arrest and other violations has risen steadily from 693 in 1992 to 901 in 1995, according to the latest statistics available from the Board of Police Commissioners....The Detroit Police Department is now 58 percent black, up from 56 percent in 1993. If Latinos and

Asians are included, minorites make up 61 percent of the force." (p6 secA)

Siegel, Suzanne. "City Issues '97: Detroiters Say Cops Still Aren't Fair." Detroit Free Press 28 May 1997. p6 secA.

POLICE--GREAT BRITAIN (v26)

POLICE--GREAT BRITAIN--APPROPRIATIONS AND EXPENDITURES (v26)

POLICE--MICHIGAN--ANN ARBOR--PUBLIC OPINION (v26)

POLICE--UNITED STATES (v26)

In the U.S., "a recent poll conducted for LAW AND ORDER magazine determined that 74 percent of police departments of various sizes operate bicycle patrols. Of the 26 percent that do not, more than one-half say they plan to introduce them in the near future." (p42)

Sharp, Arthur G. "'Surprise! You're Busted, Mr. Crook.'" Kiwanis v82 n9 Oct 1997. p40-42. (ISSN0162-5276).

"An estimated 45 million United States residents--one in five--have some sort of face-to-face contact with law enforcement officers annually, according to a new Justice Department study. Among those with such contacts, a third seek police help or offer assistance. Another third witness a crime or report a crime to law enforcement officers. A little less than a third said the police initiated the contact. About 1 percent of those who came in contact say police used force or threatened to use force against them, although a majority of those respondents say their own actions may have provoked the police....The Police-Public Contact Survey found about 23 percent of males, 19 percent of females, 22 percent of whites, 16 percent of blacks and 15 percent of Hispanic residents had some sort of contact with law enforcement officers during a 12-month period ending in mid 1996."

U.S. Dept. of Justice. Bureau of Justice Statistics. "One in Five U.S. Residents in Contact with Police during Year." Press Release 22 Nov 1997. document-level access: <http://www.ojp.usdoj.gov/pub/bjs/press/puof.pr>

POLIOMYELITIS--SOUTH ASIA (v26)

POLIOMYELITIS--VACCINATIONS--ASIA (v26)

POLIOMYELITIS--VACCINATIONS--GREAT BRITAIN (v26)

POLITICAL ACTION COMMITTEES--UNITED STATES (v26)

In Michigan, "political action committees run by 10 of the state's 15 public universities spent $174,861 in the 1996 election cycle. That's more than any other state, save Texas. According to the [U.S.] Chronicle of Higher Education, only 24 universities nationwide have PACs." (p12 secA)

Luke, Peter. "Colleges Turn to PACs for Lansing Clout." Ann Arbor News 19 May 1997. p1,12 secA.

"As of July 1997, there were 3,875 political action committees, or PACs, registered with the FEC [Federal Election Commission]. That figure represents a drop of 204 PACs since the last survey was taken in December 1996." (p3)

"Statistics: Semiannual PAC Count Shows Decrease." Federal Election Commission Record v23 n9 Sep 1997. p3.

For the U.S. congressional elections in 1996, political action committees posted "a 12 percent increase in money raised and an 11 percent increase in expenditures compared with the 1994 election cycle. PACs raised $437.4 million and spent $429.4 million....Incumbents were able to attract far more PAC money than their challengers--$146.4 million to $31.6 million....In federal elections where there was an open seat, PACs contributed $39.8 million to candidates. In addition to those contributions, PACs made $10.6 million in independent expenditures, almost double what they spent in the last election cycle." (p9-10)

"Statistics: Congressional, PAC Fundraising and Expenditures Continue Strong Showings in 1996 Election Cycle." Federal Election Commission Record v23 n6 Jun 1997. p9-10.

POLITICAL ACTION COMMITTEES--UNITED STATES --WOMEN

EMILY'S List--EMILY stands for Early Money is Like Yeast--is "the first partisan organization set up to fund women candidates in the United States....EMILY'S List received a major boost in 1992, when the all-male Senate Judiciary Committee confirmed Clarence Thomas to the U.S. Supreme Court despite law professor Anita Hill's accusations of sexual harassment. A torrent of female outrage turned into a record flood of financial support for female candidates in that year's elections. EMILY'S List grew from 3,000 to 23,000 members and raised $6 million....According to Rutgers University's Center for the American Woman and Politics, 11 national and 47 state or local PACs [political action committees] and donor networks now either give money predominantly to women or receive most of their contributions from women." (p30)

"Women in Power: From Tokenism to Critical Mass: The Old Girls Network." Foreign Policy n108 Fall 1997. p30. (ISSN0015-7228).

POLITICAL AFFILIATION

see PARTY AFFILIATION

POLITICAL CORRUPTION--CHINA

"A national domestic survey revealed that ordinary Chinese regard corruption as the most serious problem after inflation, though 52% expressed doubt that the government could do anything about it....In Beijing alone, 1,085 cases of corruption were uncovered in 1995, and in 1996 corruption cases reached 2,262....In 504 cases, the amount of money involved exceeded one million yuan (approximately 76,000 [pounds sterling]). According to official statistics for the whole of China, the number of prosecutions for corruption, bribery and misappropriation of public funds in the four year period from 1991-1995 was 460,000. The number of defendants holding the post of county leader and above was 6,200: of these, 291 were prefecture leaders or other equivalent heads, and five were provincial leaders, ministers or other equivalent heads. Over this period, the relatively modest sum of 8 billion (approx. 608,000 [pounds sterling]) of direct economic losses was retrieved through criminal proceedings." (p4)

Levi, Michael. "Law and Economics: Stealing from the People." China Review n8 Aut-Win 1997. p4-9. (ISSN1359-5091).

POLITICAL PARTICIPATION--UNITED STATES (v26)

POLITICAL PARTIES

see also PARTY AFFILIATION

POLITICAL PARTIES--AFRICA

"Nigeria once had about 120 presidential candidates during its zig-zag march to the now-defunct third republic. Algeria had, at one point, about 112 political parties and organizations on the political scene. Guinea had 46 opposition parties by early 1995; Mauritania has 20 political parties; and Mali has 57 opposition parties....The 1994 election in Ethiopia generated a 90% turnout of the registered voters, but they were confused by having to make 534 choices from a total of 1,471 candidates, representing 39 different parties and 937 independents." (p376)

Ihonvbere, Julius O. "Democratization in Africa." Peace Review v9 n3 Sep 1997. p371-378. (ISSN1040-2659).

POLITICAL PARTIES--BANGLADESH (v26)

POLITICAL PARTIES--EMPLOYMENT--GREAT BRITAIN

In Great Britain, "in 1992 (and the 1997 landslide barely altered the social makeup of the two parties) 62 per cent of Tory MPs [Members of Parliament] were private-school educated, against 15 per cent of Labour MPs. More than a third of Tories were former or serving company executives, against a paltry 3.7

per cent of Labour MPs. As for the professions, the law and accountancy claimed one in four Tory MPs but fewer than one in ten on the Labour side. Nearly a third of Labour MPs were former teachers, against one in 15 on the Tory side. Taking all MPs together, a solid three-quarters of Tories count as private-sector professional, facing a solid three-quarters of Labour MPs who are either public-sector professional or have a trade union, local government, clerical or manual worker backgrounds and have come as MPs to adopt a broadly 'public professional' mentality....Teachers are the largest single occupational group in both parties. But the second largest group among Tories is financial service workers, including accountants, underwriters, brokers and tax specialists, while two-thirds of Labour members are in public-sector work, the great majority unionised." (p25)

Adonis, Andrew. "Argument: Our Classless Self-Delusion: The Old Hierarchy May Have Gone but a New One Has Taken Its Place." New Statesman 3 Oct 1997. p25. (ISSN0028-6842).

POLITICAL PARTIES--ENVIRONMENTAL ASPECTS --MEXICO

"The six-year-old Green Ecologist Party of Mexico will go from no seats in the lower house of Congress to nine (out of 500 total seats)." (p1) "The success of the Greens--about 1 million votes nationwide, or about 4 percent of the vote and almost 8 percent of the vote in Mexico City--reflects a growing awareness of environmental issues among Mexicans." (p6)

LaFranchi, Howard. "Sprouting of Young Party May Yield Earth-Friendlier Mexico." The Christian Science Monitor v89 n158 11 Jul 1997. p1,6. The Christian Science Monitor search engine: <http://www.csmonitor.com/plweb-cgi/iops1.pl> To retrieve this article, enter the following search: ED=19970711 AND mexico. In the "retrieved list," click the title that matches this record. (ISSN0882-7729).

POLITICAL PARTIES--GREAT BRITAIN

In Britain, "since 1992, some 100,000 members have left the [Labour] Party and some 200,000 joined--leaving the Party with a current claimed membership of about 400,000. According to Labour's own surveys, about half of current members are in social classes A and B (professional and managerial), and only 10 per cent are manual workers." (p131)

Marqusee, Mike. "Scanner: New Labour and Its Discontents." New Left Review n224 Jul-Aug 1997. p127-142. (ISSN0028-6060).

POLITICAL PARTIES--RUSSIA

In Russia, "in 1993, 13 parties competed for seats on the proportional representation list; in 1995, 43 parties made the ballot. The 1995 parliamentary vote may have induced consolidation, since only 4 of these 43 parties received 5 percent of the vote, the minimum needed to win seats through proportional representation." (p322)

McFaul, Michael. "Democracy Unfolds in Russia." Current History v96 n612 Oct 1997. p319-325. (ISSN0011-3530).

POLITICAL PARTIES--UNITED STATES--PUBLIC OPINION

"In 1994, the Gallup Poll surveyed Americans regarding their political views....Gallup labeled the largest group (30%) 'conservative'--people who want the government to have less control over the economy but more control over our social lives. The smallest group (16%) was 'liberal'--those who want more government control of the economy but less of our social lives. The third largest group (20%) was considered 'populist'--those who want more government control in both areas....Gallup labeled...[the second largest group] 'libertarian' (22%)--people who want less government control in any area." (p16)

Browne, Harry. "Strategy: Debate: The 22% Solution." Liberty v11 n1 Sep 1997. p16. (ISSN0894-1408).

POLITICAL REFUGEES

see REFUGEES, POLITICAL

POLITICAL SCIENCE (v26)

see AFRO-AMERICAN POLITICIANS; AUTONOMY; CALIFORNIA--POLITICS AND GOVERNMENT; CHINA--POLITICS AND GOVERNMENT; DEMOCRACY; ELECTIONS; HISPANIC AMERICAN POLITICIANS; JERUSALEM (ISRAEL)--POLITICS AND GOVERNMENT; JEWS, AMERICAN--ISRAEL--POLITICS AND GOVERNMENT; KOREA (SOUTH)--POLITICS AND GOVERNMENT; LIBERTY; LOCAL GOVERNMENT; MASS MEDIA--TAIWAN--POLITICS AND GOVERNMENT; MICHIGAN--POLITICS AND GOVERNMENT; MORTALITY--POLITICS AND GOVERNMENT; MUSLIMS--POLITICS AND GOVERNMENT; REFUGEES, POLITICAL; RELIGION AND POLITICS; STATE GOVERNMENTS; UNITED STATES--POLITICS AND GOVERNMENT; WESTERN SAHARA--POLITICS AND GOVERNMENT; WOMEN IN POLITICS

POLITICAL SCIENCE--COMMUNIST COUNTRIES --PUBLIC OPINION (v26)

POLITICIANS

see AFRO-AMERICAN POLITICIANS; HISPANIC AMERICAN POLITICIANS; WOMEN IN POLITICS

POLITICIANS--MAINE--NEW JERSEY--PUBLIC OPINION (v26)

POLITICIANS--UNITED STATES--ATTITUDES (v26)

POLITICIANS--UNITED STATES--PUBLIC OPINION (v26)

POLITICIANS, AFRO-AMERICAN

see AFRO-AMERICAN POLITICIANS

POLITICS AND RELIGION

see RELIGION AND POLITICS

POLLS

see ELECTIONS

POLLUTANTS, AIR

see AIR--POLLUTION

POLLUTION (v26)

see also AIR--POLLUTION; HAZARDOUS WASTES; WATER--POLLUTION

POLLUTiON--CHINA

In China, "an estimated 178,000 people in major cities suffer premature deaths each year because of pollution. Indoor air pollution--primarily from burning coal and biomass for cooking and heating--causes 111,000 premature deaths each year, mainly in rural areas. Each year some 7.4 million work-years are lost to health damages related to air pollution. Acid rain in the high-sulfur coal regions of southern and southwestern China threatens to damage 10 percent of the land area, and may already have reduced crop and forestry productivity by 3 percent. Children in Shenyang, Shanghai, and other major cities have blood-lead levels averaging 80 percent higher than levels considered dangerous to mental development. The costs of water pollution are at least US$4 billion a year."

World Bank. "Clear Water, Blue Skies within China's Reach: The Costs of Excessive Pollution." Press Release 19 Sep 1997. document-level access: <http://www.worldbank.org/html/extdr/extme/ampr_002.htm>

POLLUTION--INDIA (v26)

"Nearly 40 percent of India's population of 960 million live in the Gangetic basin, most of them without access to sewer and sanitation facilities. Dozens of cities spew millions of gallons of untreated human and industrial waste into its sluggish waters every day....According to the World Health Organization, virtually all of India's surface water is polluted....The state of India's skies is not much better. India has become the world's sixth-largest and second-fastest growing producer of greenhouse gases. The level of air pollution in at least 20 cities is classified as dangerous.

Vehicles, which have risen in number from 300,000 in 1951 to 30 million in 1991, contribute the most to the black haze hanging over cities like New Delhi, followed by power plants and industrial units. The private Tata Energy Research Institute (TERI) estimates air pollution will contribute to 2.5 million early deaths across the country this year." (p5)

Zubrzycki, John. "International: Pollution of Rivers in India Reaches a Crisis." The Christian Science Monitor v89 n234 29 Oct 1997. p5. The Christian Science Monitor search engine: <http://www.csmonitor.com/plweb-cgi/iops1.pl> To retrieve this article, enter the following search: ED=19971029 AND crisis. In the "retrieved list," click the title that matches this record. (ISSN0882-7729).

POLLUTION--UNITED STATES (v26)

"In 1972, only about one third of American lakes and rivers were safe for fishing and swimming; today, almost two thirds are safe, a stunning improvement that occurred even during sustained economic growth. Since 1970, smog in the U.S. has diminished by nearly a third; the number of cars has almost doubled. Most studies suggest the health benefits of declining smog exceed the price of controls by a clear margin--as much as $40 in health-care costs saved for every $1 in anti-smog investment, according to a recent Environmental Protection Agency analysis." (p58)

"Between 1970 and 1995, U.S. energy consumption per dollar of gross domestic product went down 32 percent, which means the economy saved up to $200 billion yearly in fuel costs that it would have spent if old energy inefficiencies had remained." (p59)

Easterbrook, Gregg/Palmer, Brian. "Culture & Ideas: Greenhouse Common Sense." U.S. News & World Report v123 n21 1 Dec 1997. p58-62. article-level access: <http://www.usnews.com/usnews/issue/971201/1GLOB.HTM> (ISSN0041-5537).

POLYVINYL CHLORIDE--FIRES AND FIRE PREVENTION--UNITED STATES

"The National Fire Protection Association (NFPA) estimates that the number of U.S. residential fires with PVC [polyvinyl chloride] as the first material ignited grew from 6,600 in 1980 (with $23 million in damages) to 10,700 in 1992 (with $56 million in damages). In the same period, non-residential fires involving PVC as the ignition material grew from 2,600 in 1980 to 4,600 in 1992....The total number of fires is much larger (almost 700,000 in 1992, according to NFPA)." (p18)

Cray, Charlie. "Phase Out PVC: Opportunities to Phase Out PVC." New Solutions v7 n4 Sum 1997. p17-29. (ISSN1048-2911).

POOR (v26)

see also ELECTRIC UTILITIES--NEW HAMPSHIRE--POOR; LEGAL ASSISTANCE TO THE POOR; MASS MEDIA AND THE POOR; POPULATION GEOGRAPHY--UNITED STATES--POOR

"An estimated 1.3 billion people on the planet--about one in four--subsist on less than US$1 a day. Perhaps more meaningful is the fact that nearly a billion people are illiterate. Some 840 million go hungry. And nearly a third of the people in least developed countries, most of which are in sub-Saharan Africa, are not expected to survive to age 40....[In] Eastern Europe and the former Soviet Union,...the number of people living below the poverty line has surged from four million to 120 million." (p10)

Speth, James Gustave. "Commentary: Even in the Land of Plenty." Choices v6 n3 Jul 1997. p10.

"The UN Human Development Report shows that more than three billion people, over half of the world's population, exist on incomes of less than $2 a day. This report also demonstrates that 70 percent of the world's poor are the most defenseless: women and children." (p6)

Mattern, Douglas. "Globalized Corporate Capitalism: 'It's the Economy, Stupid!'" Human Quest v211 n5 Sep-Oct 1997. p6-7. (ISSN0897-8786).

"Of the 6 billion persons on this planet, 3.5 billion already are in poverty. Eighty million of them live in the United States. As for wealth, 447 individuals now control more wealth than the poorest 2.75 billion." (p2)

"July 4, 1997: Today's Revolution Is for a New America." People's Tribune v24 n7 Jul 1997. p1-2. (ISSN1081-4787).

The World Bank estimates "that 18% of the Third World is 'extremely poor' and 33% is 'poor.' The World Bank's poverty line is set at a per capita income of one dollar a day. Population groups with incomes in excess of one dollar a day are arbitrarily identified as 'non-poor.' Thus, the World Bank estimate for Latin America and the Caribbean is that only 19% of the population is 'poor.'...Statistics indicate...that over half of the Latin American population live in intolerable poverty and upwards of two-thirds of the population of some countries live in 'abject poverty.' In addition, the U.S. Census Bureau estimates that 20% of Americans live below the poverty line." (p112)

Felice, William. "International Initiatives: The Copenhagen Summit: A Victory for the World Bank?" Social Justice v24 n1 Spr 1997. p107-118. (ISSN0094-7571).

In the U.S., Germany, Great Britain, Belgium, the Netherlands, and Australia, "one in four children and three out of five single-parent households are poor, reports the UN. Worldwide, 1.3 billion people barely survive on a dollar a day or less; in the West, 100 million people live in poverty." (p12)

"Notebook: Seven away from Ending Poverty." Toward Freedom v46 n4 Aug 1997. p12. (ISSN0048-9898).

POOR--ASIA

"As many as 900 million Asians, from Mongolia to South India, live in dire poverty despite the fact that Asia's surging growth has brought the region unprecedented prosperity, according to two new World Bank reports....Poverty has fallen dramatically in East Asia (down 27 percent from 1975-85, and a further 35 percent from 1985-95)....The reports note that two-thirds of the world's poor still live in these same regions, struggling to live on less than a dollar a day, with little access to skilled jobs, education, medical treatment, and adequate nutrition....[According to Gautam Kaji, World Bank Managing Director for Operations,] 'in 1975, six out of ten East Asians lived in poverty, now only two out of ten do.'"

World Bank. "Poverty and Inequality--The Other Face of the Asia Miracle." Press Release 26 Aug 1997. document-level access: <http://www.worldbank.org/html/extdr/extme/1450.htm>

POOR--BANGLADESH

In Bangladesh, "about 52% of the rural population lived in absolute poverty in 1994, and they could be divided into two distinct groups: moderately poor (29%) and extremely poor (23%)....The incidence of rural poverty is about 12% higher in female-headed households than in male-headed households....The extremely poor households in Bangladesh currently spend between 7% and 10% of their income on health, which is a sizeable burden by any reckoning." (p29)

Sen, Binayak/Acharya, Shambhu. "Health and Poverty in Bangladesh." World Health v50 n5 Sep-Oct 1997. p28-29. (ISSN0043-8502).

POOR--CANADA (v26)

POOR--CARIBBEAN AREA--LATIN AMERICA

"A new Human Poverty Index (HPI), produced by the United Nations Development Programme and published in the UNDP's 'Human Development Report 1997,' shows that eight Latin American and Caribbean nations rank among the top 10 in a survey of the 78 developing nations for which there is sufficient information. Trinidad and Tobago, Cuba, Chile and Costa Rica are among the top five in the list....Haiti ranks higher than 17 other countries, and conditions in Guatemala are better than in 32 other developing countries....The poverty-stricken Northeast region [of Brazil] has an HPI of 46 percent, the same as Guatemala. But the Southeast, with an HPI of 14 percent, ranks Brazil among the top 15 in the list." (p9)

"Figuratively Speaking: Rankings: Money Isn't Everything." IDB v24 n7 Jul 1997. p9. (ISSN0145-2274).

POOR--CHINA

"More than one-quarter of all Chinese--about 350 million people--subsist on less than $1 a day; most are concentrated in the peripheral but strategically important areas of Tibet, Xinjiang, and Inner Mongolia. Moreover, for the first time a significant number of urban dwellers--15 million or more--are falling below the poverty line without a state welfare net to catch them. Some 100 million rural Chinese are part of a floating population that drifts from city to city, and hundreds of thousands of Chinese are escaping their homeland in search of better economic opportunities in foreign countries." (p247)

Kim, Samuel S. "China as a Great Power." Current History v96 n611 Sep 1997. p246-251. (ISSN0011-3530).

POOR--EAST ASIA

The number of poor people in East Asia "fell by 27 percent during 1975-85, and 34 percent in 1985-95--the fastest pace of poverty reduction in all of the developing world. In 1975, 6 out of 10 East Asians lived in poverty; 2 out of 10 do now. The region's most populous countries, China and Indonesia, alone held 92 percent of the region's poor in 1975. China's poverty incidence dropped by 63 percent, while Indonesia's poverty incidence fell by 82 percent. Other countries had similarly impressive achievements--Thailand's poverty incidence fell by 90 percent (from 8.1 to less than 1 percent), and Malaysia's fall was of 95 percent (from 17.4 to less than 1 percent)."

World Bank. "Everyone's Miracle?: Revisiting Poverty and Inequality in East Asia." Press Release 26 Aug 1997. document-level access: <http://www.worldbank.org/html/extdr/extme/1448.htm>

POOR--EDUCATION--UNITED STATES

In the U.S., in 1995, "among those in the labor force half a year or longer, the rate of poverty for those workers with less than a high school diploma (17.2 percent) was almost triple that of high school graduates (6.1 percent). Poverty rates were 3.3 percent for workers with an associate degree, and 1.5 percent for those with a 4-year college degree. Poverty rates were generally higher for black workers than for white workers, at both higher and lower education levels."

Hale, Thomas W./U.S. Dept. of Labor. Bureau of Labor Statistics. "A Profile of the Working Poor, 1995." Press Release Aug 1997. document-level access: <http://stats.bls.gov/cpswp96.htm>

POOR--EMPLOYMENT--UNITED STATES

In the U.S., "in 1995, seven and a half million persons were classified as the 'working poor,' nearly 200,000 fewer than in 1994. The working poor are individuals who spent at least 27 weeks in the labor force (working or looking for work), but whose incomes fell below the official poverty level. The ratio of the working poor to all persons in the labor force for at least 27 weeks--the poverty rate--declined for the second year in a row, to 5.9 percent; previous rates were 6.7 percent in 1993, and 6.2 percent in 1994....Overall, 36.4 million people were living below the official poverty level in 1995--1.6 million fewer than in 1994. Although the vast majority of the Nation's poor were not in the labor force in 1995, about 1 in 5 were labor force participants for more than half the year. About 60 percent of these working poor usually worked full time, although full-time work greatly reduces a person's likelihood of being poor. In fact, among persons in the labor force for 27 weeks or more, the poverty rate among those who usually worked full time was 4.3 percent."

Hale, Thomas W./U.S. Dept. of Labor. Bureau of Labor Statistics. "A Profile of the Working Poor, 1995." Press Release Aug 1997. document-level access: <http://stats.bls.gov/cpswp96.htm>

POOR--EUROPE, WESTERN--UNITED STATES

"Poverty rates in the United States, despite the recent economic expansion, are two to three times those of Western Europe. The poverty rate for children under 6 in France is 6 percent. In the United States it is 22 percent." (p20)

Faux, Jeff. "The 'American Model' Exposed." Nation v265 n13 27 Oct 1997. p18,20-22. (ISSN0027-8378).

POOR--GREAT BRITAIN (v26)

In Great Britain, "in the early 1990s, 11 million of our citizens were living in poverty, 3.5 million more than in 1983. A fifth of the total population were in poverty, measured by those generally accepted standards: 10 million of our citizens lived in inadequate housing as the living areas of their homes were damp, unheated or overcrowded; 7 million people were without essential clothing, such as a warm waterproof overcoat; 2.5 million children were forced to go without at least one of the things that they needed, such as three meals a day, toys or out-of-school activities; 5 million were not properly fed by today's standards; and 6.5 million people could not afford essential household goods such as a fridge, a telephone or carpets for living areas." (c828)

Pond, Chris (H.C.-Gravesham). "Orders of the Day: Social Security Bill." Great Britain. Parliament. House of Commons. Debates. 22 Jul 1997. c828. section-level access: <http://www.parliament.the-stationery-office.co.uk/pa/cm199798/cmhansrd/cm970722/debtext/70722-23.htm#70722-23_spnew1>

POOR--HEALTH AND HYGIENE--DEVELOPING COUNTRIES

"The number of urban poor is growing rapidly and it is estimated that in the year 2000 at least 1000 million people in urban areas will be counted among the poor. On the average, 50% of the urban population in developing countries live in conditions of extreme deprivation and the figure may be higher in some cities. Among the major contributory factors of ill health are lack of sanitation, poor water supply, poor food safety, air pollution (particularly indoor air quality in developing countries), and poor housing. For example, 2,900 million people were without adequate sanitation in 1994 and 1,100 million did not have access to safe water supplies. The coverage of sanitation in rural areas in 1994 was 18% whereas in urban areas it was 63%; in the case of access to water, the coverage in rural areas was 70% while in urban areas it was 82%. As many as 1000 million people, mostly women and children in developing countries, are exposed to high levels of indoor air pollution. An estimated 3 million premature deaths, mainly in acute and chronic respiratory infections, are now being attributed to exposure to air pollution on a world-wide basis; 2.8 million of these deaths are due to indoor air pollution exposures and 90% of these occur in developing countries." (p1-2)

World Health Organization. "Health and Environment in Sustainable Development." WHO Fact Sheet n170 Jun 1997. p1-4. document-level access: <http://www.who.ch/programmes/inf/facts/fact170.htm>

POOR--HISPANIC AMERICANS

In the U.S., "about one-sixth of Hispanic families received less than $10,000 in 1995, three times the percentage of white families. About one-fourth of Puerto Rican families fell into the lowest income category, compared with only one-tenth of Cuban families. Interestingly, the proportion of very low-income families maintained by Latino householders born in the United States (15 percent) was similar to that for householders born abroad (17 percent)....In 1995, more than one-quarter (27 percent) of Hispanic families had incomes below the poverty level, about the same level as for black families, and more than four times the rate for non-Hispanic white families. Nearly half of Hispanic families headed by women were poor, compared with 45 percent of black, and 22 percent of white female-headed families." (p38-39)

del Pinal, Jorge/Singer, Audrey. "Generations of Diversity: Latinos in the United States." Population Bulletin v52 n3 Oct 1997. p2-47. (ISSN0032-468X).

POOR--HOUSING--TEXAS--HOUSTON

In Houston, Texas, the Committee on Housing and Urban Development "cites that there are 27,170 individuals on the waiting list for privately owned assisted housing. Between 1978 and 1993, the number of families with worst-case needs grew by 1.5 to 5.3 million families with incomes below 50 percent of median who pay more than half of their incomes for rent and utilities or live in severely substandard housing. Between 1985 and 1993, the supply of rental housing affordable to very low-low income families decreased. In 1993 there were only 6.9 million units affordable for the 8.6 million extremely low-income renter families. More than half of these units were occupied by families with higher incomes, thus making even fewer affordable units available for extremely low-income families. Among working poor families with children--those with incomes below 30 percent of median, which is roughly the equivalent of the poverty level--67 percent of those not receiving housing assistance--675,000 households--have worst-case housing needs. Usually this means they are paying over half their income for rent; sometimes they are also living in severely substandard housing." (pH5327)

Jackson-Lee, Sheila (Rep.-Tex.). "Departments of Veterans Affairs and Housing and Urban Development...Appropriations Act, 1998." Congressional Record. Daily ed. v143 n101 16 Jul 1997. pH5309-5371. section/page-level access: <http://thomas.loc.gov/cgi-bin/query/R?r105:FLD001:H05326:> (ISSN0363-7239). (X1.1A.105/1).

POOR--HOUSING--UNITED STATES (v26)

POOR--ILLINOIS (v26)

POOR--INDIA

"In the early 1950s, nearly half of India's population was living in poverty....Today, roughly one-third of the population is poor by the same standards as the early 1950s. However, because of rapid population growth, even these modest rates of poverty reduction have not been sufficient to reduce the numbers of poor people, which have risen from about 164 million in 1951 to 312 million in 1993-94....Almost three out of four Indians and 77 percent of the Indian poor live [in rural areas]."

World Bank. "India Shows Mixed Progress in the War against Poverty." Press Release 26 Aug 1997. document-level access: <http://www.worldbank.org/html/extdr/extme/1449.htm>

"There has been a marked but slow decline in poverty since India became independent in 1947. At that time nearly half its population was living below the poverty line. Today, 50 years later, roughly a third of India's people are poor....In 1951, 164 million Indians were living in poverty, compared with 312 million in 1993-94....If the Indian economy, which has grown by an average of 6-7 percent over the past three years, can maintain its present course and income distribution stays at its current levels, the country's incidence of poverty could plummet from its current rate of approximately 35 percent to a mere 6.3 percent by 2005."

World Bank. "Poverty and Inequality--The Other Face of the Asia Miracle." Press Release 26 Aug 1997. document-level access: <http://www.worldbank.org/html/extdr/extme/1450.htm>

POOR--LATIN AMERICA (v26)

POOR--LEGAL STATUS, LAWS, ETC.

see LEGAL ASSISTANCE TO THE POOR

POOR--MASSACHUSETTS--BOSTON (v26)

POOR--MINNESOTA (v26)

POOR--PENNSYLVANIA--ALLEGHENY COUNTY

In Pennsylvania's Allegheny County, "200,000 working-age adults, or 25 percent of the total population, and 111,000 children, or 39 percent, were in...[the] lowest income bracket....For Allegheny County as a whole, 104,000, or nearly 52 percent of the low-income adults, were employed, while 96,000, or 48 percent, were unemployed." (p1)

"Pittsburgh, PA.: Poverty Persists Despite 'Prosperity.'" The People v107 n10 Jan 1998. p1. (ISSN0199-350X).

POOR--ROMANIA

"Poverty in Romania has increased sharply to five times that recorded in 1989....About 22 percent of Romania's population (approximately 5 million individuals and 1.6 million households) live below the poverty line."

World Bank. "World Bank Helps Romania Fight Poverty and Expand Economic Reforms." Press Release 3 Jun 1997. document-level access: <http://www.worldbank.org/html/extdr/extme/1373.htm>

POOR--RUSSIA (v26)

POOR--TEXAS (v26)

POOR--UNITED STATES (v26)

"At the beginning of the 1970s, the rate of poverty defined by the United States government stood at about 11 percent; by 1992, over 14.5 percent of the nation's population lived in poverty. Between 1973 and 1992, the number of people officially classified as poor increased from 23 million to 37 million persons." (p5) "Low minimum wages and weak social protection, among other factors, have led to a more than 30 percent jump in the US poverty rate since the 1970s, and a more than 60 percent increase in the number of poor people." (p6)

Haveman, Robert H. "New Democracy Forum: Equity with Employment." Boston Review v22 n3-4 Sum 1997. p3-8. (ISSN0734-2306).

In the U.S., "before 1994, the South had the highest regional poverty rate. Since that year the West has experienced a poverty rate not significantly different from that of the South--15.4 percent for the West and 15.1 percent for the South in 1996. Neither the overall poverty rate for all children (20.5 percent), nor that for those aged 65 and over (10.8 percent), were statistically different between 1995 and 1996. In 1996, 14.4 million people had incomes of less than half of their poverty threshold, up from 13.9 million in 1995."

U.S. Dept. of Commerce. Economic & Statistics Administration. "Income Improves, Poverty Levels Stabilize, Health Insurance Coverage Slips, Census Bureau Reports." Census Bureau Press Release 29 Sep 1997. document-level access: <http://www.census.gov/Press-Release/cb97-162.html>

In the U.S., "the share of people living below the poverty line has grown from 16 per cent in 1974 to around 19 per cent in 1994....In New York City alone, nearly a quarter of a million people have had to rely on public shelters at some time during the last five years....Today, one in four children under the age of 18 and one in five senior citizens in the United States live in poverty, the worst record among OECD countries. Three out of five single-parent households now fall below the poverty line." (p10)

Speth, James Gustave. "Commentary: Even in the Land of

Plenty." Choices v6 n3 Jul 1997. p10.

"The latest numbers from the Bureau of Census (for 1995) show 35 million poor people in America. The number includes 14 million children below the age of 18, give or take a few hundred thousand hungry children." (p31)

Wogaman, Phil. "Breaking the Silence about Poverty." Christian Social Action v10 n11 Dec 1997. p31. (ISSN0897-0459).

In the U.S., "in 1996, the poorest fifth saw yet another decline in average income, losing $210. But the top five percent saw their income grow another $6443....The percentage of people below the poverty line failed to drop, remaining at 13.7 percent in 1996 (or 36.5 million people). The rate is still higher than it was before the last recession (13.1 percent in 1989). The number of 'very poor' Americans--those making less than half the poverty line--increased by a half million in 1996, up to 14.4 million people. The poverty line for a family of four was $16,036 in 1996." (p8)

"Growing Inequality: One Consequence of Low Wages." Community Change n19 Fall 1997. p8.

"The Census Bureau released data for 1996 on the incomes and poverty status of Americans....Those with low incomes were worse off in 1996, with the lowest 20 percent of families seeing a 1.8 percent decline in their average income from $11,598 in 1995 to $11,388 in 1996....Although the percentage of people living in poverty fell, the actual number of people in poverty rose by 100,000. The poverty rate fell significantly only in the South. It rose in the West and Northeast and was basically unchanged in the Midwest." (p8 secA)

Bartlett, Bruce. "Bartlett's Notations: New 'Prosperity' Data Actually Cause for Alarm." Detroit News 6 Oct 1997. p8 secA.

In October 1997, the U.S. Census Bureau "reported that 13.7 percent of Americans remained in poverty....The agency also found that just 5.6 percent of married families are poor. Among married families where at least one partner worked full time, year-round, no matter how menial the job, poverty has almost disappeared: Just 1.8 percent of those families--less than one in 50--are poor. In stark contrast, nearly one-third of families headed by a single woman were poor; so was almost one in seven families headed by a single man....The poverty rate for families today is about 17 percent higher than in 1976." (p5 secB)

Brownstein, Ronald. "Outlook: Battle to Eliminate Poverty Must Focus on Fatherless Families." Detroit News 12 Oct 1997. p5 secB.

In the U.S., "the share of households with incomes below the poverty line was 13.7 percent in 1996, unchanged from 1995. The number of impoverished Americans was also steady from 1995, at 36.5 million, although that number is 5 million greater than in 1989." (p2)

"Income Is Rising. So Is Poverty." Forecast v17 n11 Nov 1997. p1-2. article-level access: <http://www.demographics.com/publications/fc/97_fc/9711_fc/fc97111.htm> (ISSN0732-1597).

In the U.S., "more than 35 million people live below the official poverty line. (That's one out of every seven people.) More than 20 percent of all children live in poverty....In 1994, 15 percent of households with children and a person working full-time were poor....Roughly 30 percent of both African Americans and Hispanics were below the poverty line in 1995. Close to 45 percent of households headed by women were classifed as poor in that year. Women as a group still make only 71 cents for each dollar a man is paid." (p8)

Rodwan, John G., Jr. "Guess Who Is Losing the Numbers Game?: Guess Who Can Win It?: The Resurgence of the Working Class." People's Tribune v24 n9 Sep 1997. p8. (ISSN1081-4787).

POOR--UNITED STATES--SOCIAL CONDITIONS (v26)

POOR AGED--UNITED STATES (v26)

According to the publication "A Profile of Older Americans, 1997," "about 3.4 million elderly persons lived below the poverty level in 1996. Another 2.4 or 7.6% of the elderly were classified as 'near poor' (income between the poverty level and 125% of this level). In total, almost one fifth (18.4%) of the older population was poor or 'near poor' in 1996."

U.S. Administration on Aging. "AoA Announces Availability of 'A Profile of Older Americans, 1997.'" Press Release 3 Oct 1997. document-level access: <http://www.aoa.dhhs.gov/pr/profile97.html>

In the U.S., "in 1990, 12.2 percent of people aged 65 or older fell below the official poverty threshold (which was $8,233 for an elderly couple). This was below the rate of 13.7 percent for people younger than age 65....Women older than age 65 living alone had a poverty rate of 23.6 percent in 1990. People aged 85 or older had a poverty rate of 20.2 percent, and nearly 40 percent had incomes below 150 percent of the poverty line." (p49)

Steuerle, C. Eugene/Bakija, Jon M. "Retooling Social Security for the 21st Century." Social Security Bulletin v60 n2 1997. p37-60. (ISSN0037-7910).

POOR AGED WOMEN--UNITED STATES

A study of female poverty in the U.S., conducted by Sharmila Choudhury and Michael V. Leonesio, found that "for the poor/near-poor group of women aged 62 or older, Social Security and other government cash transfers constituted 80 percent of family income on average, while composing only 33 percent of total income for all other women....Private transfers (alimony, child support, other family members' income), while vastly different in magnitude, constitute about 12 percent of total income for both the aged poor/near-poor and all others." (p23-24)

Choudhury, Sharmila/Leonesio, Michael V. "Life-Cycle Aspects of Poverty among Older Women." Social Security Bulletin v60 n2 1997. p17-36. (ISSN0037-7910).

POOR CHILDREN (v26)

"The Maryland-based humanitarian agency Bread for the World reports more than 21 percent of all U.S. children--an estimated 13.6 million--are living below or on the verge of the accepted poverty level. Australia has the next highest figure, at 14.1 percent, with Canada third at 13.5 percent....Denmark, Sweden, and Switzerland...[have] child poverty levels near 3 percent. Finland has the lowest rate, estimated at 2.5 percent." (p19)

"U.S. Tops List for Child Poverty." Human Quest v211 n5 Sep-Oct 1997. p19. (ISSN0897-8786).

POOR CHILDREN--CANADA (v26)

In Canada, "the incidence of child poverty was 14.5% in 1989....At the present time, the figure is 20.5%, a rise of 4.5%...." (p926)

Loubier, Yvan (MP-PQ). "Government Orders: Supply." Canada. Parliament. House of Commons. Debates. v135 n17 21 Oct 1997. p925-953. section-level access: <http://www.parl.gc.ca/36/1/parlbus/chambus/house/debates/017_1997-10-21/han017-e.htm#LINKT66> (ISSN0704-5603). (X3-361E).

POOR CHILDREN--ILLINOIS (v26)

POOR CHILDREN--MICHIGAN

"According to the 1990 Census, 12.5 percent of Michigan's population is below the poverty level of $18,438 for a family of four." (p1 secD) In Michigan, "15.9 percent of all children are below the poverty level, and for those children in families headed by single mothers, the figure jumps to 48 percent." (p6 secD)

Lewis, Shawn D. "Metro: News Special: Food Banks Find Growing Ranks of Hungry." Detroit News 9 Dec

1997. p1,6 secD.

POOR CHILDREN--UNITED STATES (v26)

In the U.S., "about 46% of black children and 40% of Hispanic children lived in poverty in 1991 as compared with 16% of their white peers. The percentage of all poor children living in female-headed households has risen...from 24% in 1960 to 59% in 1991, and from 29% to 83% for black children (United States Department of Education, 1993)." (p885)

Dondero, Grace M. "Mentors: Beacons of Hope." Adolescence v32 n128 Win 1997. p881-886. (ISSN0001-8449).

In the U.S., "poverty seriously impairs young children's language development, math skills, IQ scores, and their later school completion. Poor young children also are at heightened risk of infant mortality, anemia, and stunted growth. Of the 12 million children under the age of 3 in the United States today, 3 million--25 percent--live in poverty....Three out of five mothers with children younger than 3 work, but one study found that 40 percent of the facilities at child care centers serving infants provided care of such poor quality as to actually jeopardize children's health, safety, or development....In more than half of the States, one out of every four children between 19 months and 3 years of age is not fully immunized against common childhood diseases....Children younger than 3 make up 27 percent of the 1 million children who are determined to be abused or neglected each year. Of the 1,200 children who died from abuse and neglect in 1995, 85 percent were younger than 5 and 45 percent were younger than 1." (pS10957)

Kerry, John F. (Sen.-Mass.). "Statements on Introduced Bills and Joint Resolutions." Congressional Record. Daily ed. v143 n143 22 Oct 1997. pS10950-10961. section/page-level access: <http://thomas.loc.gov/cgi-bin/query/R?r105:FLD001:S10957:> (ISSN0363-7239). (X1.1A.105/1).

In the U.S., "in families with heads under age 30...median income declined in real terms by almost a third between 1973 and 1990, while child poverty in those families soared from 20% to 40% (Johnson, Sum & Weill 1992). Since 1985, overall poverty rates for children under 18 have ranged between 19% and 22%, and it is the youngest children who are at greatest risk--24% of children under age 6 in 1992 versus 21% of all children (U.S. Bureau of the Census 1994...)....From the late 1960s into the 1990s, poverty rates in single-parent homes hovered around 50%. But whereas in 1965 only 10% of (own) children under 18 lived in single-parent households, by 1994 it was 25% overall and 60% among African Americans (U.S. Dept. of Education 1996...). In 1994, female-headed households accounted for 54% of all children in poverty, up from 24% in 1960. The figures for African Americans are more astounding still: 82% in 1994 versus approximately 30% in 1960 (U.S. Dept. of Education 1996...)." (p4)

Alexander, Karl L. "Public Schools and the Public Good." Social Forces v76 n1 Sep 1997. p1-30. (ISSN0037-7732).

POOR CHILDREN--UNITED STATES--MINORITIES

In the U.S., "seventy percent of children in communities of color live in extreme poverty, and children in these communities are more likely to live in poverty than their Caucasian counterparts. In fact, the Poverty Rates for Youth (PRYs) between 16 and 17 years old is 41.9 percent in the African-American population and 35.2 percent in the Latino population. In stark contrast, the PRY for Caucasian youth this age is 14 percent." (p15)

"Fact Sheet: Sexuality and Underserved Youth in Communities of Color." SIECUS Report v25 n5 Jun-Jul 1997. p15-16. (ISSN0091-3995).

POOR RELIEF

see CHARITIES; PUBLIC WELFARE

POOR WOMEN--UNITED STATES

A study of female poverty in the U.S., conducted by Sharmila Choudhury and Michael V. Leonesio, found that "almost 13 percent of the sample were poor and 7 percent near-poor in 1991-92. The economic histories of these women strongly predict their financial circumstances at age 62 or older. Seventy-five percent of women who were poor in 1991-92 had earlier documented poverty spells. Only 4 percent of women who had never experienced poverty were poor in 1991-92, while 60 percent of women who had been Predominantly Poor were still poor in 1991-92." (p27)

Choudhury, Sharmila/Leonesio, Michael V. "Life-Cycle Aspects of Poverty among Older Women." Social Security Bulletin v60 n2 1997. p17-36. (ISSN0037-7910).

POPULAR CULTURE--UNITED STATES

"A Pew Research Center survey conducted in May found that 80 percent of Americans can identify Dennis Rodman, the basketball star who found fame in hair dye and cross-dressing, and 62 percent are familiar with Ellen DeGeneres, lesbian sitcom phenom. On the other hand, only 15 percent of Americans have any idea that Trent Lott is the Senate Majority Leader...." (p10)

Bleifuss, Joel. "In Short: American Exceptionalism." In These Times v21 n16 30 Jun 1997. p10. (ISSN0160-5992).

POPULATION (v26)

see also AGE-STRUCTURED POPULATIONS; GENERATION X; HOUSEHOLDS; RURAL POPULATION; the term POPULATION under specific subjects, e.g., AFRICA--POPULATION

"The world's population in mid-1997 is 5.85 billion. Annual growth averages 1.8 percent in less-developed regions, where 80 percent of the world's people live, and 0.4 percent elsewhere. The global annual growth rate of 1.48 percent for 1990-95 is significantly lower than the 1.57 percent projected by the United Nations in 1994." (p3)

"Fertility Declines Reported." Popline v19 May-Jun 1997. p3.

"In mid-1997, the world population totaled 5.84 billion, with 86 million people added each year....Nearly 1 billion people are added to the world's population approximately every 11 years. It took all of human history until the early 1800s for the world's population to reach the first billion, 130 years to reach the second, 30 years to add the third, 15 years to add the fourth, and 12 years to add the fifth." (p4)

Gelbard, Alene. "A Primer: Population 101." Population Today v25 n9 Sep 1997. p4-5. (ISSN0749-2448).

"According to United Nations statistics, the annual rate of world population growth peaked at about 2% in the early 1960s and has since been gradually slowing. The latest population figures indicate that the world's population is now growing by about 81 million people per year and the annual rate of growth has slowed to just under 1.5%."

Gallup Organization. "Global Study of Family Values: An International Gallup Poll: Family Values Differ Sharply around the World." Press Release 7 Nov 1997. document-level access: <http://www.gallup.com/poll/special/family.html>

The U.S. Census Bureau reported that "in 1994, 86.8 million persons were added to the world population--contrary to its World Population Profile: 1991 prediction that 95 million persons would be added every year and by '2015 to 2020, about 100 million will be added annually.'...For 1996 the US Census Bureau indicates that the world population increase will be something over 79 million, partly due to a rise in the death rate....In little more than two year's time the annual population growth rate of the world, by US Census Bureau figures, fell from well over 90 million to below 80 million." (p6)

Lamont, Mary. "Coming Population Implosion?" ProLife News

v22 n7 Jul-Aug 1997. p6.

"In its biennial count, the UN estimated last year that the world population stood at 5.77 billion, 29 million less than predicted in 1994. The reason was a drop in fertility to a world average of 2.96 children per woman instead of the anticipated 3.1. Lower fertility in populous China, Indonesia, and Brazil was especially significant....The world's annual population growth rate peaked at a rapid 2.04 percent in the late 1960s. In 1990-95, it fell to 1.48 percent a year. A third peak in the number of people added to the world population arrived in 1985-1990 at 87 million annually. Last year, 'only' 81 million were added--roughly the population of Germany....The UN projection used most often sees the fertility rate declining to 2.1 in 2050 when the world's population would reach 9.4 billion. That's nearly half a billion below the estimate two years ago. Population would stabilize at 10.7 billion in 2120." (p9)

Francis, David R. "Business & Money: Economic Scene: Global Crowd Control Starts to Take Effect." The Christian Science Monitor v89 n229 22 Oct 1997. p1,9. The Christian Science Monitor search engine: <http://www.csmonitor.com/plweb-cgi/iops1.pl> To retrieve this article, enter the following search: ED=19971022 AND effect. In the "retrieved list," click the title that matches this record. (ISSN0882-7729).

"Women in the former East Germany are having on average less than one child, a fertility rate of 0.7. In Italy, the fertility rate is 1.2. In Western Europe as a whole, it is 1.4--well below the 2.1 needed to stabilize a population....In developing countries, fertility rates are expected to fall below replacement levels around 2010 to 2030, according to the UN projection....The ratio of population between the third world and developed world, now 4:1, would be 7:1 by 2050. By 2050, Africans will outnumber Europeans more than 3:1. The ratio is about 1:1 now. Nigeria will edge out the US as the fourth most populous country in about 2050....A median of 42 by 2050. It is 25 now." (p9)

Francis, David R. "Business & Money: Economic Scene: An Erosion of the Ties that Bind." The Christian Science Monitor v89 n229 22 Oct 1997. p9. The Christian Science Monitor search engine: <http://www.csmonitor.com/plweb-cgi/iops1.pl> To retrieve this article, enter the following search: ED=19971022 AND bind. In the "retrieved list," click the title that matches this record. (ISSN0882-7729).

The 1996 Revision of the official United Nations population estimates and projections "report indicates that currently 4.59 billion persons--80 per cent of the world's population--live in the less developed regions and 1.18 billion live in the more developed regions. The average annual growth rate is about 1.8 per cent in the less developed and 0.4 per cent in the other regions....According to the United Nations, the countries with the largest population after China are India (945 million), the United States (269 million) and Indonesia (200 million). Six other countries have populations of more than 100 million: Brazil (161 million); the Russian Federation (148 million); Pakistan (140 million); Japan (125 million); Bangladesh (120 million); and Nigeria (115 million). Those nations are the only ones whose populations have currently exceeded the 100 million mark." (p72)

"Population 2050: 9.4 Billion." UN Chronicle v34 n3 1997. p72. (ISSN0251-7329).

"Although global population growth has slowed somewhat during the 1990s, dropping to 1.4 percent in 1996, the world is continuing to add 80 million people a year because the population base is expanding. Providing for population growth alone now requires an expansion in the world grain harvest of 26 million tons a year." (p10)

Brown, Lester R. "The Agricultural Link: How Environmental Deterioration Could Disrupt Economic Progress." Worldwatch Paper n136 Aug 1997. p5-73.

POPULATION CONTROL

see BIRTH CONTROL

POPULATION FORECASTING (v26)

"Worldwide, urban residents were 46 percent of the globe in mid-1996....[According to the U.N.'s 'World Urbanization Prospects,'] developed nations may see their urban populations grow from 75 percent in mid-1996 to 84 percent in 2030. Less-developed nations could see an increase from 38 percent to 57 percent. Specifically, Asia's urban dwellers may increase from 35 percent to 55 percent, while Africa's may increase from 36 percent to 54 percent....Tokyo should hold on to its current status as the world's largest city, with a projected 28.9 million inhabitants in 2015, but Japan may be the only industrial nation represented among the world's five largest cities. After Tokyo, the largest cities in 2015 could be Bombay (26.2 million); Lagos, Nigeria (24.6 million); Sao Paulo, Brazil (20.3 million); and Dhaka, Bangladesh (19.5 million)." (p8)

"The World's Biggest Markets." Forecast v17 n11 Nov 1997. p8. article-level access: <http://www.demographics.com/publications/fc/97_fc/9711_fc/fc97117.htm> (ISSN0732-1597).

"In 1997, the world's developing countries accounted for 98 percent of world population increase....World population now stands at 5.8 billion, 4.7 of whom live in the developing countries. By the century's end, world population will likely total 6.1 billion. And, by 2025, today's developing countries are projected to total about 6.8 billion while the developed countries remain at 1.2, the same as today....United Nations projections [of world population] for the year 2050 range from 7.7 to 11.2 billion by 2050. Similar projections from the International Institute for Applied Systems Analysis (IIASA) in Europe carry the scenarios further, to the year 2100. IIASA projections show an even wider range, from 4 to 23 billion for the more distant year 2100....India's population size by mid-century may rise to 1.2 billion and then slowly decline or it may be almost 2 billion and still growing."

Population Reference Bureau. "Developing Nations Account for 98 Percent of World Population Growth." Press Release 1997. document-level access: <http://www.prb.org/media/pressrel.htm>

POPULATION FORECASTING--AFRICA (v26)

POPULATION FORECASTING--AFRO-AMERICANS (v26)

POPULATION FORECASTING--AGED

"By 2020, the world will have more than 1 billion people age 60 and over, and 710 million of these will live in developing countries. Today there are an estimated 540 million people in the world age 60 and over, 330 million of whom live in developing countries. The proportion of older people in the world's population will also continue to rise: Europe will retain the distinction of being the 'oldest' region, with the proportion of people 60 and over rising to 24% in 2020 from 19% today, while, for instance, North America's proportion of people 60 and over will rise to 23% and East Asia's to 17%. The 'oldest' country by 2020 will be Japan (with 31% of its population age 60 and over), followed by Germany, Greece, Italy and Switzerland, which will all have proportions of older people above 27%. Today, the country with the highest proportion of older people is Greece (22%)." (p1)

World Health Organization. "Rio De Janeiro & Geneva to Launch Global Movement for Healthy Ageing." WHO Press n69 26 Sep 1997. p1-2. document-level access: <http://www.who.ch/press/1997/pr97-69.html>

POPULATION FORECASTING--ALABAMA (v26)
POPULATION FORECASTING--ALABAMA--AGED (v26)
POPULATION FORECASTING--ALABAMA--MINORITIES --WOMEN (v26)
POPULATION FORECASTING--ASIA (v26)
POPULATION FORECASTING--ASIAN AMERICANS

"The Census Bureau, in its middle series projections, [which assume that by the year 2050 total fertility will average 2.25 children, life expectancy will be 82.0 years and net immigration will be 820,000 annually,] shows 34.4 million Asian Americans by the year 2050....At that date, nearly one in 11 Americans (almost 9 percent) is expected to be of Asian or Pacific Islander origin. These projections assume that net immigration through the year 2050 will include 235,000 Asians per year. Even if immigration were to stop today, the API population would continue to grow to 14.2 million in 2050--a 46 percent increase from 1996--due to the number of young Asians who will be reaching childbearing age in the next century." (p3)

Pollard, Kelvin M./De Vita, Carol J. "A Portrait of Asians and Pacific Islanders in the United States." Statistical Bulletin v78 n3 Jul-Sep 1997. p2-9. (ISSN0790-8334).

POPULATION FORECASTING--CALIFORNIA (v26)
POPULATION FORECASTING--CANADA--MINORITIES (v26)
POPULATION FORECASTING--CHINA (v26)
POPULATION FORECASTING--DEVELOPING COUNTRIES (v26)

"Developing countries now account for 98 percent of world population growth, according to the Population Reference Bureau, a Washington, D.C. based demographic research group. PRB's recently published 1997 World Population Data Sheet shows that 4.7 billion of the world's current 5.8 billion people live in developing countries. By the year 2025, today's developing countries are projected to total about 6.8 billion while developed countries remain at 1.2 billion--the same as today." (p6)

"98% of Growth in Developing Countries." Popline v19 May-Jun 1997. p6.

"During the 1990-2025 period, almost all of the world's urban growth--some 90 percent--will take place outside of the developed world. Every day, the urban population in the developing world increases by 150,000 people. During the past five decades, the developing world's urban population has increased 500 percent to 1.5 billion. By 2025, according to United Nations estimates, this urban population will have tripled again, to 4.4 billion. Today, nearly 40 percent of the developing world's residents are city dwellers; by 2025, two-thirds of them will be." (p373)

Rosenau, William G. "'Every Room Is a New Battle': The Lessons of Modern Urban Warfare." Studies in Conflict & Terrorism v20 n4 Oct-Dec 1997. p371-394. (ISSN1057-610X).

POPULATION FORECASTING--EUROPE (v26)
POPULATION FORECASTING--GERMANY (v26)
POPULATION FORECASTING--HISPANIC AMERICANS

"The Hispanic population is expected to contribute 35 percent of the...[U.S.'s] population growth from 1995 to 2000, 44 percent from 2000 to 2020, and 62 percent from 2020 to 2050. By the middle of the next century, the nation's Hispanic population is expected to reach 96.5 million (24.5 percent of the total population). Each year from now to 2050, the Hispanic population is projected to add more people to the United States than the non-Hispanic White population (or any other single race/ethnic group)....By 2025, Hispanics would be the largest race or ethnic group in California, comprising 43 percent of the population."

U.S. Dept. of Commerce. Economic and Statistics Administration. "Census Facts for Hispanic Heritage Month." Census Bureau Fact Sheet 11 Sep 1997. document-level access: <http://www.census.gov/Press-Release/fs97-10.html>

In the U.S., "the Hispanic, or Latino, population is projected to swell from 28 million in 1996 to about 100 million in 2050, and is projected to outnumber African Americans by 2005. Latinos already compose about 40 percent of the school-age population in California, and are projected to form a majority of the state's public school enrollment by 2006." (p2)

del Pinal, Jorge/Singer, Audrey. "Generations of Diversity: Latinos in the United States." Population Bulletin v52 n3 Oct 1997. p2-47. (ISSN0032-468X).

The number of Hispanics in the U.S. "is projected to surpass 52 million in 2020, and reach 97 million by 2050, assuming moderate levels of fertility and immigration....If immigration and fertility run at slightly higher levels, Hispanics will number 62 million in 2020 and 133 million in 2050. Under the lowest fertility and immigration levels projected by the Census Bureau, Latinos will number 43 million in 2020 and 62 million in 2050....About 40 percent of the population growth between 1995 and 2050 will come from Hispanics, 30 percent from Asians, 20 percent from non-Hispanic whites, and 10 percent from non-Hispanic blacks." (p15)

del Pinal, Jorge/Singer, Audrey. "Generations of Diversity: Latinos in the United States." Population Bulletin v52 n3 Oct 1997. p2-47. (ISSN0032-468X).

"Early in the 21st century, Hispanic Americans will become the country's largest ethnic minority. By 2050, the Hispanic, or Latino, population is projected to number around 100 million and constitute 25 percent of U.S. population, up from 11 percent in 1996. Hispanic Americans are expected to outnumber African Americans by 2005. Latinos already compose about 40 percent of the school-age population in California, and are expected to form a majority of that state's public school enrollment by 2006."

Population Reference Bureau. "Diverse Hispanic Population to Become Largest U.S. Minority." Press Release 1997. document-level access: <http://www.prb.org/media/pressrel.htm>

POPULATION FORECASTING--HONG KONG

"The population of Hong Kong is projected to increase at an average annual rate of 1.3 per cent, from 6.29 million in mid-1996 to 7.38 million in mid-2006 and 8.21 million in mid-2016....In 1996, 19 per cent of the population aged under 15. This proportion is projected to decrease to 16 per cent in 2006 and 15 per cent in 2016. The proportion of those aged 65 and over is projected to rise from 10 per cent in 1996 to 11 per cent in 2006 and further to 13 per cent in 2016.

Correspondingly, the median age of the population is projected to rise from 34 in 1996 to 39 in 2006 and further to 41 in 2016."

Hong Kong. Census and Statistics Department. "Hong Kong Population Projections 1997-2016." Press Release 5 May 1997. document-level access: <http://www.info.gov.hk/censtatd/hkstat/press/proj2016.htm>

POPULATION FORECASTING--JAPAN--AGED (v26)
POPULATION FORECASTING--LATIN AMERICA (v26)
POPULATION FORECASTING--MICHIGAN (v26)
POPULATION FORECASTING--MIDDLE EAST (v26)
POPULATION FORECASTING--UNITED STATES

"The 10-year group of 25-to-34-year-olds in the U.S. rivals that of the 20-year group aged 55 to 74, at 40 million. By 2010, however, the number of 55-to-64-year-olds will be nearly as large as the number of young adults, at 35 million compared with 38 million. Altogether, the 55-to-74 contingent will outnumber 25-to-34s by 18 million." (p15)

Russell, Cheryl. "Trend Cop: The Ungraying of America." American Demographics v19 n7 Jul 1997. p12,14-15. article-level access: <http://www.demographics.com/publications/ad/

97_ad/9707_ad/ad97073.htm> (ISSN0163-4089).

"Today we have 133 million Americans who are working; they are supporting about 39 million beneficiaries in the Social Security program. In 2030, when a baby born today will be 33 years of age, there will be 163 million workers, a 20-percent increase, but there will be more than a doubling of number of people who will then be beneficiaries, 80 million....In 1996, 29 percent of our population is under the age of 20. In 2030, 24 percent of our population will be under the age of 20. So again, in 33 years, a relatively short period of time, we are going to go from 79 million people under the age of 20 to 83 million people under the age of age 20. But in the over 65 category we will go from 13 percent to 20, from 34 million to 68 million, a doubling of that population." (pS4831)

Kerrey, J. Robert (Sen.-Nebr.). "Concurrent Resolution on the Budget." Congressional Record. Daily ed. v143 n68 21 May 1997. pS4782-4849. section/page-level access: <http://thomas.loc.gov/cgi-bin/query/R?r105:FLD001:S04831:> (ISSN0363-7239). (X1.1A.105/1).

In the U.S., "Hispanic children are expected to outnumber black children by 1998, and to make up 31 percent of all children by 2050. Non-Hispanic whites, a projected 53 percent of the 2050 population, may make up 43 percent of children, while African Americans are expected to account for 16 percent....The Census Bureau projects that the population 65 years and older will expand from 39 million in 2010 to 69 million in 2030, as the baby boom generation (born between 1946 and 1964) reaches retirement age....By 2050, non-Hispanic whites are projected to form two-thirds of the elderly (ages 65 and older), while Hispanics are likely to make up less than one-sixth of the elderly." (p16)

del Pinal, Jorge/Singer, Audrey. "Generations of Diversity: Latinos in the United States." Population Bulletin v52 n3 Oct 1997. p2-47. (ISSN0032-468X).

POPULATION FORECASTING--UNITED STATES--AGED (v26)

"The number of Americans aged 65 and older is projected to increase 135 percent between 1995 and 2050, according to the Census Bureau. In the same period, the population as a whole may grow by a considerably slower 50 percent." (p35)

Klein, Matthew. "Kaleidoscope: Site to See: Old News." American Demographics v19 n11 Nov 1997. p35. article-level access: <http://www.demographics.com/publications/ad/97_ad/9711_ad/ad971122.htm> (ISSN0163-4089).

According to the publication "A Profile of Older Americans, 1997," "by the year 2030, there will be about 70 million older persons, more than twice their number in 1996. The 85+ population is projected to increase from 3.8 million in 1996 to 8.5 million in 2030. Minority populations are projected to represent 25% of the elderly population in 2030, up from 13% in 1990."

U.S. Administration on Aging. "AoA Announces Availability of 'A Profile of Older Americans, 1997.'" Press Release 3 Oct 1997. document-level access: <http://www.aoa.dhhs.gov/pr/profile97.html>

POPULATION FORECASTING--UNITED STATES --IMMIGRANTS

"The U.S. Immigration and Naturalization Service predicts that in the 1990s the U.S. will receive the largest number of immigrants of any decade in our nation's history: 10 million people, almost twice the population of Indiana. This surpasses the previous record decade for immigration, 1901-1910, which had less than 9 million immigrants. However, because our population has grown greatly since the early 1900s, the percentage of foreign-born people is actually far less than earlier in this century. Foreign-born people currently represent 9% of the American population, which is half the proportion they made up in 1910. Indiana ranks among states with fewest immigrants. Legal and illegal immigrants are only about 1% of the state's population, with a smaller percentage in Southern Indiana." (pE1337)

Hamilton, Lee H. (Rep.-Ind.). "Immigration." Congressional Record. Daily ed. v143 n93 27 Jun 1997. pE1337. section/page-level access: <http://thomas.loc.gov/cgi-bin/query/R?r105:FLD001:E01337:> (ISSN0363-7239). (X1.1A.105/1).

"If today's immigration totals hold steady, it will account for about two-thirds of U.S. population growth over the next 50 years....Population projections in the report show that with no immigration, the U.S. population would increase 47 million between 1995 and 2040, to 310 million....If immigration continues at present levels of 820,000 a year, the population in 2040 could be 370 million and growing at a rate of about 1 percent every two years. If immigration should double, to 1.64 million new arrivals a year, the population in 2040 could be 429 million, or 119 million more than in the zero immigrant scenario....With high rates of immigration, there could be 27 older people for every 100 working-age people in the year 2030. With low immigration, there could be 30 older people per 100 workers." (p7)

"U.S. Minus Immigration Equals ZPG." Forecast v17 n7 Jul 1997. p7. article-level access: <http://www.demographics.com/Publications/FC/97_fc/9707_fc/FC97076.htm> (ISSN0732-1597).

POPULATION FORECASTING--UNITED STATES --MINORITIES (v26)

"America's elementary and secondary schools will become more diverse in the next 10 years. Between 1995 and 2005, for example, Hispanic Americans between the ages of 5 and 17 will increase by 2.4 million. African American students in this same age group will increase by another 1.1 million. Asian Americans and other minorities will number an additional 1.1 million." (pH7327)

Hinojosa, Ruben (Rep.-Tex.). "Departments of Labor, Health and Human Services, And Education...Appropriations Act, 1998." Congressional Record. Daily ed. v143 n123 16 Sep 1997. pH7324-7350. section/page-level access: <http://thomas.loc.gov/cgi-bin/query/R?r105:FLD001:H07326:> (ISSN0363-7239). (X1.1A.105/1).

POPULATION GEOGRAPHY--ASIAN AMERICANS (v26)

"Most Asian Americans (56 percent) live in three states--California, New York and Hawaii....California alone is home to 39 percent of Asian Americans....In Hawaii, Asian Americans form the majority (64 percent) of the state population, up from 62 percent in 1990. In California, this group comprises 12 percent of the state population--more than twice the proportion in Washington, the state with the third largest concentration of Asian Americans....[In 1996,] one in four Asian Indians...lived in New York or New Jersey; one in nine Vietnamese called Texas home; one in 10 Cambodians lived in Massachusetts; and more than one in three Hmong resided in either Minnesota or Wisconsin." (p5)

Pollard, Kelvin M./De Vita, Carol J. "A Portrait of Asians and Pacific Islanders in the United States." Statistical Bulletin v78 n3 Jul-Sep 1997. p2-9. (ISSN0790-8334).

POPULATION GEOGRAPHY--HISPANIC AMERICANS

In the U.S., "Hispanics live in every state, but historically their population is concentrated in nine states: California, Texas, New York, Florida, Illinois, New Jersey, Arizona, New Mexico, and Colorado. About 85 percent of Hispanics lived in these states in the mid-1990s. The largest population of Latinos is in California, where approximately 9 million, or one-third of all Latinos, resided in 1996. About 5 million Hispanics lived in Texas, 2.5 million in New York, 2 million in

Florida, and 1 million in Illinois....New Mexico has the highest proportion of Hispanics, with more than one in three (39 percent) of the state's 1.7 million residents claiming Hispanic origin. Latinos make up 28 percent of California's 31 million residents, and 27 percent of Texas's 18 million population. About one-fifth of Arizona's 4 million residents are of Hispanic origin." (p10)

del Pinal, Jorge/Singer, Audrey. "Generations of Diversity: Latinos in the United States." Population Bulletin v52 n3 Oct 1997. p2-47. (ISSN0032-468X).

POPULATION GEOGRAPHY--TENNESSEE (v26)

POPULATION GEOGRAPHY--UNITED STATES (v26)

POPULATION GEOGRAPHY--UNITED STATES --ILLEGAL ALIENS

In the U.S., "more than 2 million undocumented immigrants, or 40 percent of the total, lived in California in 1996. Another 43 percent lived in the states of Texas, New York, Florida, Illinois, New Jersey, and Arizona." (p20)

del Pinal, Jorge/Singer, Audrey. "Generations of Diversity: Latinos in the United States." Population Bulletin v52 n3 Oct 1997. p2-47. (ISSN0032-468X).

POPULATION GEOGRAPHY--UNITED STATES --INDIGENOUS PEOPLES

"In 1995, more of the nation's American Indians, Eskimos and Aleuts lived in Oklahoma than in any other state [in the U.S.] (257,000, or 13 percent). Arizona, California, New Mexico, and Alaska were the next most popular states of residence. By 2025, Oklahoma and Arizona are projected to continue to rank first and second, respectively, in American Indian, Eskimo and Aleut population, while New Mexico would move ahead of California and Washington would move up to fifth place. Combined, these five states would be home to about 45 percent of the nation's American Indian, Eskimo and Aleut population."

U.S. Dept. of Commerce. Economic & Statistics Administration. "Census Facts for Native American Month." Census Bureau Fact Sheet 31 Oct 1997. document-level access: <http://www.census.gov/Press-Release/fs97-11.html>

POPULATION GEOGRAPHY--UNITED STATES--POOR

In the U.S., "between 1970 and 1990 in the country's 100 largest cities, the population living in census tracts with poverty rates of 40% or greater (Wilson's 1987, cutoff for extreme poverty tracts) more than doubled, increasing from 5.2% to 10.7% (Kasarda 1993). For the poverty population specifically, the corresponding figures are 16.5% and 28.2%, which increase to 55.1% and 68.8% when Wilson's 20% threshold for identifying high poverty census tracts is used....In 1990, a fourth of all blacks (versus 15.5% in 1970) and 41.6% of poor blacks (up from 28.1% in 1970) resided in extreme poverty tracts in these 100 cities, while over 80% of poor blacks resided in high-poverty tracts (Kasarda 1993)." (p6)

Alexander, Karl L. "Public Schools and the Public Good." Social Forces v76 n1 Sep 1997. p1-30. (ISSN0037-7732).

PORK INDUSTRY AND TRADE--CANADA--JAPAN --UNITED STATES (v26)

PORK INDUSTRY AND TRADE--CHINA (v26)

PORK INDUSTRY AND TRADE--JAPAN--UNITED STATES (v26)

PORK INDUSTRY AND TRADE--PRICES--UNITED STATES

In the U.S., "retail pork prices rose 10 percent in 1996, the first significant increase since 1990. The increase was most significant for bacon, with prices up 20 percent or more throughout 1996. A reduction in pork output (down 4 percent), along with a strong export market (up 280 percent in 1996) and high domestic demand by the fast-food industry for bacon on burgers, meant less pork on supermarket shelves, boosting retail prices." (p3)

Clauson, Annette/U.S. Dept. of Agriculture. Economic Research Service. "Food Prices: Economic Factors Holding Down Food Price Increases." Food Review v20 n2 May-Aug 1997. p2-4. (ISSN1056-327X).

PORK INDUSTRY AND TRADE--RUSSIA (v26)

PORK INDUSTRY AND TRADE--UNITED STATES (v26)

In the U.S., "just 10 years ago, a third of all hogs were found on farms that had more than 1,000 hogs. Today, more than two-thirds of all hogs are produced on farms with more than 1,000 pigs....In 1970, 2 percent of hogs slaughtered were obtained through contracts and integrated operations. By 1993, this percentage had increased to 11 percent, and packers expect 29 percent of hogs will be obtained through contracts and integrated operations in 1998." (p17)

Martinez, Steve/Smith, Kevin/Zering, Kelly/U.S. Dept. of Agriculture. Economic Research Service. "Food Prices: Changing Pork Business Affects Pork Prices and Quality." Food Review v20 n2 May-Aug 1997. p17-21. (ISSN1056-327X).

PORNOGRAPHY--CANADA (v26)

PORNOGRAPHY--UNITED STATES (v26)

PORNOGRAPHY--UNITED STATES--WOMEN--ATTITUDES (v26)

PORT DISTRICTS--NEW YORK (N.Y.)--SAFETY MEASURES--PUBLIC OPINION (v26)

PORTUGAL--ECONOMIC CONDITIONS

In Portugal, "GDP over the 1986-1990 period grew at an average rate of 4.5 percent. The unemployment rate decreased by half in 1990, falling to 6 percent. The inflation rate fell to an average level of 12 percent in 1990, compared with 32 percent in 1983." (p68)

Nunes, Joao/Montanheiro, Luiz. "Privatisation in Portugal: An Insight into the Effects of a New Political Strategy." Competitiveness Review v7 n2 1997. p59-78. (ISSN1059-5422).

POST-TRAUMATIC STRESS DISORDER--UNITED STATES--CHILDREN

In the U.S., "many children whose mothers are emotionally or physically abused develop symptoms of post-traumatic stress disorder, according to a University of Michigan study....More than half of the 64 children studied suffered from unwanted, intrusive memories or 'flashbacks' of the violence, and 42 percent had sleep problems, difficulty concentrating or other symptoms of traumatic arousal, such as extreme vigilance. About 3.3 million children each year are estimated to witness the domestic abuse of their mothers." (p1)

University of Michigan. News and Information Services. "Damage to Children of Abused Mothers Starts Early, Is Often Severe, U-M Studies Find." University of Michigan News Release 18 Nov 1997. p1-2.

POSTAL SERVICE--CANADA--UNITED STATES

"The U.S. postal service handles 40% of the world's mail while its postmaster general Marvin Runyon earns a salary of $205,000 Canadian per year. The Canadian post office handles 3% of the world's mail while its president Georges Clermont just had his contract renegotiated for another two years for $380,000 Canadian per year." (p763)

Stoffer, Peter (MP-NS). "Adjournment Proceedings: Canada Post." Canada. Parliament. House of Commons. Debates. v135 n14 9 Oct 1997. p763-764. section-level access: <http://www.parl.gc.ca/36/1/parlbus/chambus/house/debates/014_1997-10-09/han014-e.htm#LINK257> (ISSN0704-5603). (X3-361E).

POSTAL SERVICE--UNITED STATES (v26)

POSTAL SERVICE--UNITED STATES. CONGRESS

The U.S. "Congress has done an excellent job cutting back the taxpayer funding of franked mail. Fiscal year 1997's level of funding was 40 percent lower than 1996's level of funding....Furthermore, Members are prohibited from sending mailings 90 days within the general election....In 1995, the House sent out four times more mail than it received. If the House had responded only to letters it received, franked mail costs would have been only $12.4 million, saving $18.6 mililon or 60 percent from actual mail costs. In addition, use of the frank increases cyclically during every election year. During the 103rd Congress, the House spent $24 million in 1993, and $42 million in 1994." (pE1699)

Castle, Michael N. (Rep.-Del.). "Introduction of a Bill to Provide for the Establishment of an Official Mass Mailing...." Congressional Record. Daily ed. v143 n118 9 Sep 1997. pE1699-1700. section/page-level access: <http://thomas.loc.gov/cgi-bin/query/R?r105:FLD001:E01699:> (ISSN0363-7239). (X1.1A.105/1).

POSTEMPLOYMENT BENEFITS--UNITED STATES --PUBLIC OPINION (v26)

POSTPARTUM DEPRESSION--UNITED STATES (v26)

POTABLE WATER

see DRINKING WATER

POTASH INDUSTRY AND TRADE--NEW BRUNSWICK (v26)

POTATO INDUSTRY

see also SWEET POTATO INDUSTRY

POTATO INDUSTRY--CANADA--UNITED STATES (v26)

POTATO INDUSTRY--UNITED STATES (v26)

"In 1996, favorable weather in most areas led to a national record-high potato yield, and U.S. potato production jumped 12 percent to a record 497 million hundredweight (cwt). Despite weather-delayed planting and frost damage in some areas, the fall-season potato crop totaled 452 million cwt--up 12 percent from 1995's output and 6 percent above the previous record high in 1994. With increased demand for processed potato products, the percentage of the U.S. potato crop coming from the fall storage crop has risen from 84 percent in the early 1970's to 91 percent today. Because of the small 1995 crop, domestic shipments of fresh (tablestock) potatoes were flat in calendar year 1996, while movement of chip stock declined 9 percent....With a record-large fall crop, the 1996/97 season-average price for fresh-market potatoes was estimated at $5.62 per cwt, down 37 percent from 1995/96. The average grower price for processing potatoes was estimated at $4.77 per cwt--down 8 percent--with the decline blunted by contracts with processors." (p3)

U.S. Dept. of Agriculture. Economic Research Service. "Summary." Vegetables and Specialties Situation and Outlook Yearbook Jul 1997. p3-5.

In the U.S., in 1996, "the net value of potato trade (export value minus import value) fell to $370 million, down 15 percent from the previous year. The value of potato and potato-product imports increased 34 percent to $242 million due to increased fresh and frozen imports from Canada. On the export side, the value of 1996 potato and potato-product exports declined 1 percent to $612 million. On a fresh-weight-equivalent basis, the volume of all potato exports totaled 34.4 million cwt [hundredweight], down 7 percent from 1995. Frozen products accounted for 17.2 million cwt (up 3 percent) while dried and dehydrated products accounted for about 6.3 million cwt (down 35 percent)." (p4)

U.S. Dept. of Agriculture. Economic Research Service. "Summary." Vegetables and Specialties Situation and Outlook Yearbook Jul 1997. p3-5.

The U.S. Department of Agriculture's November 1997 "estimate of U.S. fall-season potato production is 418 million hundredweight (cwt), down 8 percent from last year's record crop, but 4 percent above fall 1995. Decreased harvested area (down 7 percent from last fall) and lower yields (down 1 percent to 360 cwt per acre) contributed to the reduced output....Despite the reductions from a year ago, 1997 fall production was still 2 percent above the average of the five previous fall seasons." (p11)

U.S. Dept. of Agriculture. Economic Research Service. "Potatoes." Vegetables and Specialties Situation and Outlook Report Nov 1997. p11-13.

POTHOLES (ROADS)--MICHIGAN (v26)

POTHOLES (ROADS)--MICHIGAN--OAKLAND COUNTY (v26)

POULTRY

see also BROILERS (POULTRY); TURKEYS

POULTRY INDUSTRY (v26)

see also CHICKEN INDUSTRY; EGG AS FOOD; TURKEY INDUSTRY

POULTRY INDUSTRY--EGYPT (v26)

POULTRY INDUSTRY--POTOMAC RIVER

"The poultry industry has dramatically expanded in the Potomac Headwaters, from production at approximately 46.6 million birds in 1992 to 90 million birds in 1996. Recognizing the potential growth of the industry, as early as 1990, a cooperative program between Federal and State agencies was launched to design and implement the best soil and water conservation management practices." (pS5392) "To date, 80 percent of the eligible farmers in the Potomac Headwaters...have electively enrolled in the Potomac Headwaters Land Treatment Watershed Project, the recommended action plan to protect the Potomac from possible agricultural pollution....Implementing...measures will cost the average farmer in the program $12,000 over 5 years. The average farmer in the Potomac Headwaters has a net annual income of $15,000 from poultry production." (pS5393)

Byrd, Robert C. (Sen.-W.Va.). "West Virginia Poultry Farmers Committed to Stewardship." Congressional Record. Daily ed. v143 n79 9 Jun 1997. pS5392-5393. section/page-level access: <http://thomas.loc.gov/cgi-bin/query/R?r105:FLD001:S05392:> (ISSN0363-7239). (X1.1A.105/1).

POULTRY INDUSTRY--RUSSIA (v26)

POULTRY INDUSTRY--UNITED STATES (v26)

U.S. "poultry exports have averaged 31-percent annual growth for the past 3 years, and in 1996 jumped 23 percent to a record $2.6 billion. More than 60 percent of the 1996 increase was due to soaring exports to Russia. Russian purchases of U.S. poultry rose from $84 million in 1993 to $914 million in 1996 (AO [AGRICULTURAL OUTLOOK] January-February 1997)." (p11)

Ruppel, Fred J./Handy, Charles R./Malanoski, Margaret A./ U.S. Dept. of Agriculture. Economic Research Service. "World Agriculture & Trade: U.S. Processed Food Trade Continues to Expand." Agricultural Outlook Jul 1997. p11-13.

In the U.S., in 1996, "poultry meat exports jumped 23 percent to a record $2.5 billion. Export volume rose 17 percent to nearly 2.4 million tons. Shipments to Russia were a record 937,000 tons, and value rose 50 percent to $913 million. Exports to all the former Soviet republics exceeded $1 billion, and accounted for 42 percent of the value of U.S. poultry meat exports. Shipments to Hong Kong gained 4 percent to $419 million, and Mexico's shipments jumped 27 percent to $208 million. Exports to Japan and Canada were unchanged from 1995 at $171 million and $169 million, respectively. One of the most rapidly expanding markets for poultry meat in 1996 was China, where exports jumped 77 percent to $60 million." (p2)

Greene, Joel/U.S. Dept. of Agriculture. Economic Research Service. "Agricultural Exports Surpass $60 Billion." Foreign Agricultural Trade of the United States Jan-Mar 1997. p2-3.

U.S. poultry meat exports in May 1997, "totaled $207 million, 15 percent greater than a year ago. Cumulative poultry meat exports reached $1.7 billion, an 8-percent increase

over 1996." (p1)
U.S. Dept. of Agriculture. Economic Research Service. "Exports." U.S. Agricultural Trade Update 23 Jul 1997. p1.

POWER PLANTS, ELECTRIC
see ELECTRIC POWER PLANTS

POWER PLANTS, NUCLEAR
see NUCLEAR POWER PLANTS

POWER RESOURCES
see ELECTRIC LIGHTING; ELECTRIC POWER; ELECTRIC UTILITIES; ENERGY CONSERVATION; ENERGY CONSUMPTION; ENERGY DEVELOPMENT; ENERGY INDUSTRIES; NUCLEAR POWER; NUCLEAR POWER PLANTS; PHOTOVOLTAIC POWER GENERATION; WIND POWER

POWER RESOURCES--HAWAII (v26)

POWER RESOURCES--SWEDEN (v26)

POWER RESOURCES DEVELOPMENT
see ENERGY DEVELOPMENT

POWER SUPPLY, ELECTRIC
see ELECTRIC POWER

PRAIRIES--UNITED STATES--RURAL CONDITIONS (v26)

PREFABRICATED HOUSES--UNITED STATES (v26)

PREGNANCY
see also ECTOPIC PREGNANCY; LABOR (OBSTETRICS); SUBSTANCE ABUSE IN PREGNANCY; TEENAGE PREGNANCY

PREGNANCY--DEVELOPING COUNTRIES (v26)

PREGNANCY--MORTALITY (v26)

PREGNANCY--PREVENTION
see BIRTH CONTROL

PREGNANCY--SIGNS AND DIAGNOSIS--UNITED STATES

In the U.S., "childfree couples under age 35 are 435 percent more likely than their share of the population suggests to buy...[home pregnancy] kits, according to ACNielsen. Those hoping to increase their brood, couples with children under age 6, are 341 percent more likely than expected....Only 15 percent of households buy more than one a year....Sales in supermarkets alone topped $578 million in 1995." (p28)
Mogelonsky, Marcia. "Kaleidoscope: Checkout Line: Oh, Baby." American Demographics v19 n5 May 1997. p28. article-level access: <http://www.demographics.com/Publications/AD/97_ad/9705_ad/AD970524.htm> (ISSN0163-4089).

PREGNANCY--UNITED STATES (v26)

In the U.S., "the infant mortality rate has dropped from 20 deaths per 1,000 live births in 1970 to 7.2 deaths per 1,000 live births in 1996....In 1996, 82 percent of mothers began prenatal care within the first trimester of pregnancy, the seventh consecutive year of increase from 75.5 percent in 1989....Teen births dropped for the fifth straight year in 1996 and smoking among pregnant women has been decreasing in recent years."
U.S. Dept. of Health and Human Services. "Improving Women's Health." Fact Sheet 25 Oct 1997. document-level access: <http://www.hhs.gov/news/press/1997pres/971025c.html>

"Nearly 60 percent of the six million pregnancies that occur annually in the United States are unintended, including eight in 10 pregnancies among teenagers, according to a new report by the Alan Guttmacher Institute. About 1.6 million abortions result annually from unintended pregnancies, as well as 1.5 million births that the women either did not want until later or did not want at all. Each year, one in 10 young women aged 15-19 becomes pregnant. Slightly more than half gives birth....Nine in 10 women in the United States who are sexually active, fertile, and do not wish to become pregnant use a contraceptive method. Free or low-cost contraceptive services are available in all 50 states and in 85 percent of U.S. counties. The Guttmacher report notes that although most birth control methods, when used consistently and correctly, are extremely effective in preventing pregnancy, more than three million American couples conceive unintentionally each year, leading to high rates of abortion and unwanted births. The report concludes that in almost half of these pregnancies--particularly when the woman is unmarried, poor or young--the contraceptive method the couple used simply did not work as it should have, or they used it inconsistently or incorrectly. In the rest, however, the couple used no contraceptive method. Consequently, slightly more than half of all unintended pregnancies occur among the 10 percent of American women who report that they do not use birth control." (p1)
"60% of U.S. Pregnancies Unintended." Popline v19 Jul-Aug 1997. p1.

PREGNANCY, TEENAGE
see TEENAGE PREGNANCY

PREGNANCY TERMINATION
see ABORTION

PREGNANT WOMEN
see also AIDS (DISEASE)--UNITED STATES--PREGNANT WOMEN

PREGNANT WOMEN--FINLAND--SUICIDAL BEHAVIOR (v26)

PREGNANT WOMEN--MORTALITY (v26)

Five hundred eighty-five thousand "women--one every minute--die each year from pregnancy-related causes, nearly all in developing countries....About 200,000 maternal deaths per year result from the lack or failure of contraceptive services." (p1)
"UNFPA Stresses Gender Equality, Maternal Health." Popline v19 May-Jun 1997. p1.

PREGNANT WOMEN--UNITED STATES--SUBSTANCE USE (v26)

PREGNANT WOMEN--UNITED STATES--TOBACCO USE

In the U.S., "the overall smoking rate for pregnant women is slowly declining, the smoking rate for pregnant teens is increasing....For black teenagers specifically, the rate rose 6 percent, the first increase since this information first became available in 1989. And even with this increase, smoking rates for white teenagers are still four to five times the rate for black teenagers. Furthermore, the smoking rate for those between the ages of 15 and 24 is 23 percent higher than the smoking rate among all pregnant women. In...Missouri, this public health program is even more dramatic: 20 percent of all pregnant women in Missouri admit to smoking. This is 44 percent higher than the national average. This, unfortunately, may be connected to the fact that our incidence of birth defects and infant mortality is 50 percent higher than the national average....Increases in maternal and fetal risk causes 20 to 30 percent of fetal and infant deaths in the United States. Smoking triples the risk of sudden infant death syndrome....Smoking may impede the growth of a fetus and increase the likelihood of mental retardation by 50 percent, and smoking increases the risk of respiratory illness in infants and children. Adding to this devastating problem, the proportion of women who quit smoking during pregnancy but then relapse at 6 months postpartum is nearly 63 percent, thereby exposing their infants to passive smoke and increasing their risk for SIDS [sudden infant death syndrome] and other health-related problems." (pS6001)
Bond, Christopher S. (Sen.-Mo.). "Statements on Introduced Bills and Joint Resolutions." Congressional Record. Daily ed. v143 n86 19 Jun 1997. pS6000-6005. section/page-level access: <http://thomas.loc.gov/cgi-bin/query/R?r105:FLD001:S06000:> (ISSN0363-7239). (X1.1A.105/1).

"Smoking may be responsible for 20 to 30 percent of all low birth weight babies in the United States. Studies indicate about 20 percent of pregnant women in the U.S. smoke, and one in four Medicaid-supported obstetrical care patients smokes. In the populations receiving Medicaid, white pregnant smoker rates (30 percent) are higher than black smoker rates (10 percent)....In a 1994 paper co-authored by Dr. [Richard] Windsor and published in PREVENTIVE MEDICINE, Dr. Windsor estimates that smoking cessation education nationally could prevent 1,500 to 6,000 low birth-weight infants annually; with health care savings of $22 million to $59 million. Maternal smoking may result in more than 46,000 low birth weight infants every year in this country."

Alabama. Dept. of Public Health. "Project Will Address Smoking among Pregnant Women." News Release 5 May 1997. document-level access: <http://www.alapubhealth.org/Press/pr050597.html>

PREMARITAL SEX--PHILIPPINES (v26)

PREMARITAL SEX--PHILIPPINES--HUSBANDS (v26)

PREMARITAL SEX--UNITED STATES--PUBLIC OPINION (v26)

PREMENSTRUAL SYNDROME--UNITED STATES (v26)

PRENATAL CARE--UNITED STATES

In the U.S., "the percent of mothers who began prenatal care within the first trimester improved to 81.3 percent for 1995, the highest level ever recorded....Tobacco use during pregnancy has declined steadily since 1989. In 1995, 14 percent of pregnant women smoked....Women who smoke are almost twice as likely to have a low birthweight infant as nonsmokers."

U.S. National Center for Health Statistics. "1995 Birth Statistics Released." Fact Sheet 10 Jun 1997. document-level access: <http://www.cdc.gov/nchswww/releases/97facts/97sheets/95natrel.htm>

PRENATAL SUBSTANCE ABUSE

see SUBSTANCE ABUSE IN PREGNANCY

PREPAID HEALTH PLANS

see HEALTH MAINTENANCE ORGANIZATIONS

PRESCHOOL CHILDREN--UNITED STATES

About 4.4 million of the children in the U.S. "were enrolled in nursery school in October 1995. This translates to nearly half (45 percent) of 3- and 4-year-olds, considerably higher than the one-tenth enrolled in 1968. More than half of nursery school enrollment (54 percent) was in private school. Nursery school enrollment rates for children aged 3 and 4 were highest for those in families with incomes of $40,000 or more (59 percent). Public programs such as Head Start enabled 34 percent of those in low-income families (under $20,000) to attend, as 27 percent attended public schools and 7 percent private."

U.S. Dept. of Commerce. Economic and Statistics Administration. "Census Back to School Facts." Census Bureau Fact Sheet 18 Aug 1997. document-level access: <http://www.census.gov/Press-Release/fs97-08.html>

PRESCHOOL EDUCATION

see EDUCATION, PRESCHOOL

PRESCRIBING OF DRUGS

see DRUGS--PRESCRIBING

PRESCRIPTION WRITING--UNITED STATES (v26)

PRESIDENTIAL CANDIDATES--UNITED STATES --PUBLIC OPINION (v26)

PRESIDENTS--ELECTION (v26)

PRESIDENTS--UNITED STATES--ELECTION (v26)

PREVENTION OF CRIME

see CRIME PREVENTION

PREVENTION OF INDUSTRIAL ACCIDENTS

see INDUSTRIAL SAFETY

PRICE LABELS

see LABELS

PRIESTS--UNITED STATES (v26)

"The absolute number of priests in the United States peaked in 1966 (at just under 60,000, compared to about 48,100 in 1996)....In 1966 there were about 780 Catholics per priest, as compared to 1,272 Catholics per priest today." (p18) "The priest today performs a few more baptisms (20.34 then, 24.28 now), witnesses about the same number of marriages each year (6.29 then, 6.17 now), but presides over about three more funerals (6.58 then, 9.46 now)." (p19-20)

Kennedy, Robert G. "Will We Ever Have Enough Priests?" America v177 n6 13 Sep 1997. p18-22. (ISSN0002-7049).

PRIMATES (v26)

"The 233 non-human species of primates, including chimpanzees and other apes as well as monkeys, are collectively the most imperiled group of mammals on our planet. Almost half already face extinction, and nearly 20 percent more may soon reach threatened status, reports the Worldwatch Institute in 'Death in the Family Tree', an article in the September/October 1997 issue of WORLD WATCH magazine." (p1) "In south and east Asia, decades of commercial logging, colonization, and other intensive human uses of forests have left 90 percent of primate species threatened or near-threatened with extinction. Orangutans, the great apes of Southeast Asia, have lost over 80 percent of their forests in just 20 years. In Madagascar, where all non-human primates are lemurs--the most ancient primate lineage alive today--some 80 percent of the island's old-growth forests have been lost since the arrival of humans about 1,000 years ago. That loss helped drive some 15 species to extinction before Europeans arrived, and of the 30 remaining, 20 are imperiled....Of the roughly 50,000 macaques remaining in Japan about 5,000 are captured or killed each year in what some researchers call a 'civil war' between monkeys and farmers. Worldwide, one in three threatened primate species faces excessive hunting for food, with hunters often working closely with logging companies operating in the region." (p2)

Worldwatch Institute. "Half of All Primate Species Face Extinction." News Release 28 Aug 1997. p1-4.

As the human "population has soared to nearly 6 billion, other primate populations have dropped sharply, and the continued survival of many species is now in doubt. According to the World Conservation Union (IUCN), primates are now the most imperiled major order of mammals. Nearly half of all primates are already threatened with extinction, and the IUCN considers another one-fifth 'near-threatened.'...Forest loss and other forms of habitat degradation are a factor in the decline of nearly 90 percent of threatened primate species, making this the single biggest problem they face." (p14)

Tuxill, John. "Death in the Family Tree." World Watch v10 n5 Sep-Oct 1997. p12-21. (ISSN0896-0615).

PRIMATES--ASIA, SOUTHEASTERN

"In south and east Asia, the IUCN [World Conservation Union] has classified a full 90 percent of all primate species as threatened or near-threatened. In Indonesia and Malaysia, orangutans...have lost over 80 percent of their forests in just 20 years....Vietnam's Tonkin snub-nosed monkey may now be the rarest primate in the world. Hunting and the loss of nearly 90 percent of its lowland rainforest habitat since 1950 have reduced it to a handful of populations totaling fewer than 200 individuals, all of them living in forest patches outside the country's national parks and nature reserves." (p14)

Tuxill, John. "Death in the Family Tree." World Watch v10 n5 Sep-Oct 1997. p12-21. (ISSN0896-0615).

PRIMATES--BRAZIL--ATLANTIC FOREST

"Centuries of colonization and agriculture have reduced Brazil's unique Atlantic forest to little more than a few tattered patches; only 1 to 5 percent of the original forest still stands. Collectively, the Atlantic forest monkeys form the world's most endangered primate assemblage: 11 of the forest's

12 endemic species are right on the edge of extinction....The 12- to 15-kilogram muriqui, the largest of all New World primates, has an estimated population of only around 500. The Atlantic forest is also home to the tiny lion tamarins...; their populations range from 250 to 2,500." (p15)

Tuxill, John. "Death in the Family Tree." World Watch v10 n5 Sep-Oct 1997. p12-21. (ISSN0896-0615).

PRIMATES--MADAGASCAR

"All of Madagascar's primates are endemic to Madagascar and to the nearby Comoros Islands....Since the arrival of humans roughly 1,000 years ago, Madagascar has lost at least 80 percent of its old growth forest....Of the surviving 30 or so [primate] species, fully two-thirds are threatened with extinction, primarily because of forest loss." (p15)

Tuxill, John. "Death in the Family Tree." World Watch v10 n5 Sep-Oct 1997. p12-21. (ISSN0896-0615).

PRINTERS--UNITED STATES

"Pollution prevention is becoming standard business practice for printers in the Great Lakes region as a result of the Great Printers Project, a four-year partnership initiated by EDF's [Environmental Defense Fund's] Pollution Prevention Alliance....Four Great Lakes states have created programs to register Great Printers, who pledge to take steps such as using alternative materials that pollute less. Already 275 printers have signed up: 65 in Illinois, 70 in Michigan, 23 in Minnesota, and 117 in Wisconsin." (p3)

"Project Makes Printing Cleaner and Greener." EDF Letter v28 n4 Sep 1997. p3. (ISSN0163-2566).

PRINTING INDUSTRY--EMPLOYMENT--CANADA (v26)

PRISON SENTENCES--MICHIGAN

In Michigan, "the number of inmates who have served longer than their court-imposed minimum sentence has gone from less than 6,000 in December 1991 to nearly 12,000 last July." (p1 secA) According to a Department of Corrections "report, between 1991 and 1997, the Parole Board...reduced grants of parole from 66.1 percent of all applications to 55.7 percent. [They] nearly doubled the number of inmates who serve their maximum sentences. [They] increased the number of inmates returned to prison for parole violations from about 1,400 a year to about 2,300 a year." (p2 secA)

Bell, Dawson. "Inmates Do More of Their Time." Detroit Free Press 22 Sep 1997. p1-2 secA.

PRISON SENTENCES--UNITED STATES. FEDERAL BUREAU OF INVESTIGATION

In the U.S., "in 1996 the median prison sentence imposed on all 11,855 people convicted on the basis of F.B.I. referrals was twenty-four months. But in the Maryland (Baltimore) district the median sentence was forty-eight months. This compared with thirty-three months for F.B.I. defendants in California Central (Los Angeles), twenty-seven months in Pennsylvania East (Philadelphia), twenty-four months in Florida South (Miami), fourteen months in Massachusetts (Boston) and thirteen months in New York South (Manhattan and several counties to the north) and six months in California North (San Francisco)." (p14)

Burnham, David. "Articles: The FBI." Nation v265 n5 11 Aug 1997. p11-12,14-16,18-24. (ISSN0027-8378).

PRISON VIOLENCE--UNITED STATES

In the U.S., "corrections officials reported more than 14,000 assaults on prison employees in 1995--up 32 percent from 1990 but the number of assaults per 1,000 employees remained unchanged at 15. Almost 26,000 inmates were assaulted during 1995--up 20 percent since 1990. However, the number per 1,000 inmates dropped from 31 assaults in 1990 to 27 in 1995."

U.S. Dept. of Justice. "Prison Construction Keeping Pace with Population Growth." Press Release 7 Aug 1997. document-level access: <http://www.ojp.usdoj.gov/pub/bjs/pres/csfcf95.pr>

PRISONERS

see also ABUSED WOMEN PRISONERS; AFRO-AMERICAN PRISONERS; CHILDREN OF PRISONERS; CONVICT LABOR; DRUG ABUSE--TREATMENT--UNITED STATES--PRISONERS; MINORITY PRISONERS; WOMEN PRISONERS

PRISONERS--ARIZONA--HISPANICS

Arizona's "prison population hovers around 23,150, with about 10 percent of the inmates being Mexican nationals serving sentences for mostly drug-related crimes. The state currently spends more than $16,600 a year to house each inmate, but officials figure they could shave 30 to 50 percent off operational costs with a Mexico-based prison. 'Then there's the savings on the capital cost of building the prison,' says Arizona Department of Corrections Director Terry Stewart. With the average prison costing $34,000 a bed to build in Arizona, another 50 percent savings in this area is possible, he says." (p8)

LaFranchi, Howard. "Arizona Plans to Export Mexican Inmates." The Christian Science Monitor v89 n141 17 Jun 1997. p8. The Christian Science Monitor search engine: <http://www.csmonitor.com/plweb-cgi/iops1.pl> To retrieve this article, enter the following search: ED=19970617 AND inmates. In the "retrieved list," click the title that matches this record. (ISSN0882-7729).

PRISONERS--ASIA--CALIFORNIA

"Japan incarcerates its citizens at one-eighteenth the rate of California, yet California's violent crime rate is nearly 56 times that of Japan. Whereas Indonesia's incarceration rate is nearly negligible compared to California's, Indonesia's homicide rate is a mere seven percent of California's. Finally, even though California's general population is 27 times smaller than India's, California keeps about 3,000 more people behind bars." (p46)

Koetting, Mark G./Schiraldi, Vincent. "Singapore West: The Incarceration of 200,000 Californians." Social Justice v24 n1 Spr 1997. p40-53. (ISSN0094-7571).

PRISONERS--CALIFORNIA (v26)

"California currently holds approximately 200,000 adults behind bars and the number is growing steadily. The state incarcerates adult offenders at a rate of 626 per 100,000 people in the general population, based on total state institution and local jail statistics. In the last 23 years, this rate increased 175%; in 1970 it was at 228 per 100,000. Yet, in that same period, the violent crime rate climbed 125%....The state's Department of Corrections (CDC) witnessed its inmate population exceed 126,000 in August 1994, while the department predicts a total of 171,000 inmates by 1999. On the local level, city and county jails confined 67,576 people in 1993, and the Board of Corrections expects an additional 31,000 in the next half decade." (p40) "California currently confines approximately 75,000 people in its prison system for nonviolent drug and property offenses." (p44) "California maintains over twice the number of Latinos in prison than the total number of prisoners in Peru, a nation of over 20 million." (p45)

Koetting, Mark G./Schiraldi, Vincent. "Singapore West: The Incarceration of 200,000 Californians." Social Justice v24 n1 Spr 1997. p40-53. (ISSN0094-7571).

"In 1990, the United States had the highest incarceration rate in the world, five times higher than France and Germany and over four times greater than Britain's rate (Foote, 1993). California has the dubious distinction of having the largest prison system in the country and the second largest in the world following China (Ibid). One out of every eight U.S. prisoners is incarcerated in the Golden State. In less than 20 years, California's prison population has exploded by 631%, from 19,000 in 1977 to 139,000 in 1996; over 97,000 persons are presently on parole. An additional 71,000 Californians were local jail inmates as of April 1996 and 400,000 former California jail inmates were on probation in 1995 (Criminal Justice Institute, 1994)." (p153)

Reed, Diane F./Reed, Edward L. "Children of Incarcerated Parents." Social Justice v24 n3 Fall 1997. p152-169. (ISSN0094-7571).

PRISONERS--CALIFORNIA--EUROPE, WESTERN

"Whereas California's general population equals approximately nine percent of Western Europe's total population, the former's incarcerated population equals no less than 74% of Western Europe's total incarcerated population. Furthermore, California currently locks up more offenders than France, the United Kingdom, Spain, Italy, Switzerland, Sweden, and Finland combined....These countries are inhabited by approximately 240 million people, compared to California's 32 million." (p44)

Koetting, Mark G./Schiraldi, Vincent. "Singapore West: The Incarceration of 200,000 Californians." Social Justice v24 n1 Spr 1997. p40-53. (ISSN0094-7571).

PRISONERS--CALIFORNIA--GREAT BRITAIN

"If California were to lock up offenders at the rate of the United Kingdom, it would need to reduce its incarcerated population by over 170,000." (p44) "The last time California experienced a violent crime rate as low as the U.K.'s--which averages 316 per 100,000--was in 1970. In addition, it has been 40 years since California's homicide rate was as low as England's 2.3 per 100,000. England nevertheless has an incarceration rate that is one-sixth that of California." (p45)

Koetting, Mark G./Schiraldi, Vincent. "Singapore West: The Incarceration of 200,000 Californians." Social Justice v24 n1 Spr 1997. p40-53. (ISSN0094-7571).

PRISONERS--CALIFORNIA--SPAIN

"California incarcerates offenders at a rate seven times that of Spain. Even though Spain's general population exceeds California's by several million, the latter keeps about 164,000 more offenders behind bars. Indeed, California's local jail population alone is almost double Spain's entire incarcerated population....California's total crime rate is 24% higher than Spain's. Additionally, approximately 220,000 more violent crimes were committed in California than in Spain, including 3,000 more homicides. Even if California's prison system displayed...racial and ethnic parity...and reduced its prison population to about 57,000 inmates, it would still have more people behind bars than Spain. Indeed, Spain confines fewer offenders (35,246) than California does Latinos (42,000 in prisons alone). This disparity is highlighted by the fact that there are more people in Spain (39 million) than the total population of California (32 million)." (p45)

Koetting, Mark G./Schiraldi, Vincent. "Singapore West: The Incarceration of 200,000 Californians." Social Justice v24 n1 Spr 1997. p40-53. (ISSN0094-7571).

PRISONERS--CALIFORNIA--YOUTH

"In California, the total juvenile arrests in 1994 were 257,389 young folks. Of those arrested, only 22,053 or 8 percent were violent offenders. That leaves 235,336 nonviolent juvenile arrests." (pH2431)

Millender-McDonald, Juanita (Rep.-Calif.). "In Support of Increased Funding for Crime Prevention." Congressional Record. Daily ed. v143 n59 8 May 1997. pH2431. section/page-level access: <http://thomas.loc.gov/cgi-bin/query/R?r105:FLD001:H02431:> (ISSN0363-7239). (X1.1A.105/1).

PRISONERS--CANADA--YOUTH

Canada incarcerates "10 times as many young people as Europe, 15 times as many as Australia and New Zealand....[Canada incarcerates] twice as many young people as the United States." (p10141)

Telegdi, Andrew (MP-ON). "Routine Proceedings: Committees of the House: Justice and Legal Affairs." Canada. Parliament. House of Commons. Debates. v134 n163 24 Apr 1997. p10141-10142. page-level access: <http://www.parl.gc.ca/hansard/163_97-04-24/163RP1E.html#10141> section-level access: <http://www.parl.gc.ca/hansard/163_97-04-24/163RP1E.html#JUSTICEANDLEGALAFFAIRS> (ISSN0704-5603). (X3-352E).

PRISONERS--CHINA--RUSSIA--UNITED STATES

"Nearly 1.6 million Americans are currently living behind bars. China, with its large population, ranks second, at 1.2 million prisoners. Russia weighs in at just over 1 million. The numbers are contained in a report by the Washington-based Sentencing Project, a sentencing-reform advocacy group....The US prisoner population is at its highest point in history, with federal and state prisons operating beyond their designated capacities by 16 percent to 25 percent, according to a recent Justice Department report....The Sentencing Project calculates that the incarceration rate for the US is 600 prisoners for every 100,000 people. It ranks second in the world to Russia's rate of 690. China and most of the countries of Western Europe have rates near 100." (p3)

Richey, Warren. "United States: Bulging US Prisons Prompt Cross-Cultural Comparisons." The Christian Science Monitor v89 n148 26 Jun 1997. p3. The Christian Science Monitor search engine: <http://www.csmonitor.com/plweb-cgi/iops1.pl> To retrieve this article, enter the following search: ED=19970626 AND comparisons. In the "retrieved list," click the title that matches this record. (ISSN0882-7729).

PRISONERS--EDUCATION--MICHIGAN (v26)

PRISONERS--EDUCATION--UNITED STATES (v26)

In the U.S., "the Center on Crime, Communities and Culture, based in New York City, has collected...studies from around the country, examined them and come out with a new report. It concludes that prison-based education programs dramatically reduce recidivism rates. That's the rate at which ex-offenders offend again and get arrested and jailed again. Nationally, about 60 percent of released convicts are arrested again and about 40 percent are reincarcerated, according to the federal Bureau of Criminal Justice Statistics. But, for inmates involved in prison-based education programs, the center found recidivism drops to 15.5 percent and, in some states, as low as 1 percent. Overall, inmates with at least two years of college education have only a 10 percent rearrest rate, compared with a national rate of 60 percent. For juveniles, who have a rearrest rate of almost 80 percent, the rearrest rate is reduced by 20 percent or more when they are involved in high-quality reading instruction programs, according to a congressional study the center cites." (p9 secB)

Page, Clarence. "Comment: Helms' Heavy Hand Chops Prison Frills." Detroit News 2 Nov 1997. p9 secB.

PRISONERS--EMPLOYMENT--UNITED STATES

The U.S. Federal Prison Industries "is the Federal corporation charged by Congress with the mission of training and employing Federal prison inmates....The average Federal inmate is 37 years old, has only an 8th grade education, and has never held a steady legal job....On jobs there is substantial evidence that FPI actually creates a substantial number of private sector jobs. In fiscal year 1996, some 14,000 vendors nationwide registered with FPI, and supplied over $276 million in sales to FPI. Every dollar FPI receives in revenue is recycled into the private sector. Out of each dollar, 56 cents go to the purchase of raw materials from the private sector; 19 cents go to salaries of FPI staff; 17 cents go to equipment, services, and overhead, all supplied by the private sector; 7 cents go to inmate pay, which in turn is passed along to pay victim restitution, child support, alimony, and fines. FPI inmates are required to apply 50 percent of their earnings to these costs. One cent goes to activating new FPI factories--again, with equipment purchased from the private sector." (pS7111-7112)

Hatch, Orrin G. (Sen.-Utah). "Balancing the Budget." Congressional Record. Daily ed. v143 n96 9 Jul 1997. pS7092-7113. section/page-level access: <http://thomas.loc.gov/cgi-bin/query/R?r105:FLD001:S07111:> (ISSN0363-7239). (X1.1A.105/1).

PRISONERS--GREAT BRITAIN (v26)

PRISONERS--GREAT BRITAIN--DRUG USE (v26)

PRISONERS--GREAT BRITAIN--DRUG USE--COSTS (v26)

PRISONERS--GREAT BRITAIN--SOUTH AFRICA

Britain has a "prison population of 61,000....[South Africa,] with only 70 per cent of Britain's population,...has many more than twice as many prisoners--140,000 in all." (p18)

"Lest We Forget...: City of Gold Decays." Freedom Today v22 n6 Dec 1997. p18.

PRISONERS--GREAT BRITAIN--SUBSTANCE USE --TREATMENT (v26)

PRISONERS--MEDICAL CARE--MICHIGAN--OAKLAND COUNTY

In Michigan, "hospitalizations have nearly tripled and health care costs have soared 86 percent under a 2-year-old plan to save tax dollars by privatizing medical care for Oakland County Jail inmates....Before 1995, doctors visited the jail's clinic and sent about six inmates a month to local hospitals." (p1 secA) Between 1994 and 1995, "inmate hospitalizations leaped 83 percent--from 76 to 139....In 1996, the most recent year for which figures were available, 212 inmates were hospitalized. The jump in hospitalizations--along with an increase in outside doctor appointments...--boosted health care costs from $1.5 million to $2.7 million....The hospitalizations have driven up the sheriff's department's overtime by more than $1 million....[In 1994,] deputies spent 7,651 hours guarding hospitalized inmates. By 1996, that number had jumped to 25,795." (p16 secA)

Brasier, L. L. "Health Costs at Oakland Jail Soar: Hospital Is Giving Inmates Tip-Top Care." Detroit Free Press 11 Dec 1997. p1,16 secA.

PRISONERS--MEXICO

"In 1994, Mexico was a country with almost 90 million inhabitants and a prison population of 91,788. Men comprised 96.4 percent of the total, with women accounting for the remaining 3.6 percent. In Mexico City, which boasts a population of more than 10 million inhabitants, the inmate population totaled 7,855 of which 95.3 percent were men and 4.7 percent women." (p331)

Azaola, Elena. "Women Serving Time for Homicide in Mexico City." International Journal of Comparative and Applied Criminal Justice v21 n2 Fall 1997. p331-340.

PRISONERS--MICHIGAN (v26)

PRISONERS--RWANDA (v26)

PRISONERS--SUFFRAGE--LAW AND LEGISLATION --UNITED STATES (v26)

PRISONERS--SUFFRAGE--NEW YORK (STATE) (v26)

PRISONERS--UNITED STATES (v26)

"Over 1.5 million Americans are locked behind the bars of our jails and prisons on any given day....Over 40 percent of state prison inmates have not completed high school or obtained a G.E.D. [general equivalency diploma]...." (p3)

"Editorial: Bishops on Prisons." America v177 n10 4 Oct 1997. p3. (ISSN0002-7049).

In the U.S., "since 1980 our national inmate population has been increasing by a staggering 65,208 prisoners per year....Over-crowding forces judges and parole boards to discharge prisoners early. On the national level they have to trim the population down far enough to make room for the 1,254 new prisoners they receive each week....Recent figures indicate that the average cost of housing one inmate varies from $35-40 thousand per year. That means the cost of housing the nation's inmates may be increasing by as much as $843,942 per week." (p8)

Warburton, Robert. "'Lock 'Em Up and Leave 'Em There!" Christian Social Action v10 n9 Oct 1997. p8-10. (ISSN0897-0459).

From the early 1940s through the early 1980s, the inmate population in the U.S. federal Bureau of Prison's "25 to 30 facilities fluctuated within a narrow range of 17,000 to 25,000....Today, the BOP has a staff of approximately 30,000 and a total inmate population of more than 106,000. About 96,000 of those inmates are held in the Bureau's 86 institutions. The remaining 10,000 are held in Community Corrections Centers or other contract facilities....The U.S. Marshals Service has primary responsibility for handling pretrial detainees and other prisoners waiting to appear in federal courts and has contracts with state, local, and private facilities to house approximately 70 percent of them. The remaining 30 percent are held in BOP facilities." (p54)

Roberts, John W. "The Federal Bureau of Prisons: Its Mission, Its History, and Its Partnership with Probation and Pretrial Services." Federal Probation v61 n1 Mar 1997. p53-57. (ISSN0014-9128).

In the U.S., "more than 20 percent of the offenders currently in federal prison are described by Bureau of Prison officials as first-time, nonviolent offenders (CRIMINAL JUSTICE NEWSLETTER, 1994...)....A high percentage of offenders supervised in the community are returned to prison for technical violations of supervision. According to the SAN MATEO TIMES, in 1989 less than 20 percent of first-year California Department of Corrections parolees successfully completed their supervision....According to the Administrative Office of the U.S. Courts, between 1986 and 1994 the system maintained, on average, a success rate of 77 percent--that is, 77 percent of all offenders successfully completed their term of supervision....The State of California's success rate for offenders on parole over the same period is 26.8 percent." (p5)

Buddress, Loren A. N. "Federal Probation and Pretrial Services--A Cost-Effective and Successful Community Corrections System." Federal Probation v61 n1 Mar 1997. p5-12. (ISSN0014-9128).

The American prison population "increased more than 180 percent between 1980 and 1993. Federal and state prisons hold over 1.3 million people. The incarceration rate--455 out of every 100,000 Americans--is the highest in the world. By contrast, Venezuela had a rate of 177 per 100,000: in Canada, the rate was 111 per 100,000, and in England, it was 97 per 100,000 (Rothman 1994...Christie 1994)....The overall incarceration rate (455 per 100,000 people) rises to a stunning 1,860 for African Americans (Rothman 1994...Miller 1992)." (p1000)

Morone, James M. "Enemies of the People: The Moral Dimension to Public Health." Journal of Health Politics, Policy and Law v22 n4 Aug 1997. p993-1020. (ISSN0361-6878).

In the U.S., "approximately 4 percent of state inmates and 21 percent of federal inmates were known to be citizens of other countries. Between 1990 and 1995 their number doubled from 25,250 to 51,500. About one-half of 1 percent of all state and federal prisoners were less than 18 years old in 1995, unchanged from 1990. As of June 30, 1995, state prisons held 5,309 inmates younger than 18. Federal prisons did not hold people younger than 18. However, 64 offenders less than 18 years old were held in other facilities under federal contracts."

U.S. Dept. of Justice. "Prison Construction Keeping Pace with Population Growth." Press Release 7 Aug 1997. document-level access: <http://www.ojp.usdoj.gov/pub/bjs/press/csfcf95.pr>

In the U.S., the "adult prison population grew by 55,876 inmates last year, bringing the total to a new record of 1,182,169 federal and state prisoners as of last December 31, the Justice Department reported today. Overall, the number of inmates increased by 5 percent, which was less than the average annual growth rate of 7.3 percent recorded since 1990. The 1996 increase was the equivalent of adding more than 1,075 more inmates each week. The report, by the Department's Bureau of Justice Statistics (BJS), said the number of federal and state prisoners more than doubled between 1985 and 1996--growing from 502,507 to 1,182,169."

U.S. Dept. of Justice. "Nation's Prison Population Increased 5 Percent Last Year." Press Release 22 Jun 1997. document-level access: <http://www.ojp.usdoj.gov/pub/bjs/press/p96.pr>

"A U.S. Department of Justice jail study (1992) found that 44% of women and 34.5% of males reported having a close family member who served time in jail or prison. Bloom et al. (1994) found that nearly 75% of women incarcerated in California prisons had family members who had been arrested and 63% reported having close relatives who had been incarcerated. The American Correctional Association (1990) reported that up to 50% of incarcerated juveniles have a parent who has been incarcerated." (p160)

Reed, Diane F./Reed, Edward L. "Children of Incarcerated Parents." Social Justice v24 n3 Fall 1997. p152-169. (ISSN0094-7571).

PRISONERS--UNITED STATES--VOTING (v26)

PRISONERS--UNITED STATES--YOUTH

"According to the American Psychological Association, children confined in adult institutions are five times more likely to be sexually assaulted, twice as likely to be beaten by staff, and 50 percent more likely to be attacked with a weapon than children detained in juvenile facilities." (pH2369) "Although African-American juveniles age 10 to 17 constitute 15 percent of the total population of the United States, they constitute 26 percent of juvenile arrests, 32 percent of delinquency referrals to juvenile court, 41 percent of the juveniles detained in delinquency cases, 46 percent of the juveniles in correctional institutions, and 52 percent of the juveniles transferred to adult criminal court after judicial hearings." (pH2370)

Cummings, Elijah E. (Rep.-Md.). "Juvenile Crime Control Act of 1997." Congressional Record. Daily ed. v143 n59 8 May 1997. pH2356-2398. section/page-level access: <http://thomas.loc.gov/cgi-bin/query/R?r105:FLD001:H02369:> (ISSN0363-7239). (X1.1A.105/1).

In the U.S., "juveniles in adult institutions are five times as likely to be assaulted or beaten by staff and 50 percent more likely to be attacked with a weapon than youths in a juvenile facility....The National Council for Crime and Delinquency says only 10 percent of all juvenile offenders need to be incarcerated." (p11)

Bilezikian, Sara. "From Cradle to College: Juvenile Injustice." Nonviolent Activist v14 n6 Nov-Dec 1997. p11. (ISSN8755-7428).

PRISONS

see also JAILS

PRISONS--CALIFORNIA (v26)

PRISONS--CONNECTICUT--COSTS

"In 1980, Connecticut incarcerated an average of 3,800 people on any given day. Today, that number has more than quadrupled to 16,000. The cost of incarceration has skyrocketed from $55 million in 1980 to more than $400 million today. Compare that with the state's spending on education: It was $400 million in 1980, and it remains $400 million today." (p9)

Marks, Alexandra. "Connecticut Tries 'Gentler' Approach to Curb Drug Use." The Christian Science Monitor v89 n250 21 Nov 1997. p1,9. The Christian Science Monitor search engine: <http://www.csmonitor.com/plweb-cgi/iops1.pl> To retrieve this article, enter the following search: ED=19971121 AND use. In the "retrieved list," click the title that matches this record. (ISSN0882-7729).

PRISONS--EMPLOYMENT--UNITED STATES

The U.S. Federal Prison Industries "produces more than 85 different products and services and in 1994 sold approximately $392 million worth of goods and services to the federal government, causing it to be ranked 54th among the 'Top 100 Federal Contractors.'" (pS7112)

Josten, R. Bruce. "Balancing the Budget." Congressional Record. Daily ed. v143 n96 9 Jul 1997. pS7092-7113. section/page-level access: <http://thomas.loc.gov/cgi-bin/query/R?r105:FLD001:S07112:> (ISSN0363-7239). (X1.1A.105/1).

In the U.S., "between 1990 and 1995 the number of state and federal correctional employees grew 31 percent to 347,320. Correctional officers accounted for 64 percent of all prison staff members, while professional, technical and educational employees comprised 16 percent. The remaining 20 percent were administrative, clerical, maintenance or food service personnel."

U.S. Dept. of Justice. "Prison Construction Keeping Pace with Population Growth." Press Release 7 Aug 1997. document-level access: <http://www.ojp.usdoj.gov/pub/bjs/press/csfcf95.pr>

PRISONS--GREAT BRITAIN

In Great Britain, at the end of 1992, "the inmate population stood at 40,600. By end of 1996 it had climbed to 58,500--an increase of 44 percent over four years...." (p115)

O'Donnell, Ian. "Prisons and Penal Purpose: Measuring 'Performance' in English Jails." Criminal Law Forum v8 n1 1997. p111-123. (ISSN1046-8374).

In Great Britain, "the Director-General of the Prison Service, Richard Tilt, has begun reviewing military bases as secure compounds for category C--low-risk--prisoners, to cope with the fact that England and Wales' 135 jails have reached their full capacity of 62,628....The cost of keeping prisoners in police cells is said to have risen to 2,000 [pounds sterling] per week per prisoner. This is more than seven times as expensive as sending a child to Eton College." (p6)

"Europe/Politics: The Hunt Is On for More Jail Space." Freedom Today v22 n4 Aug 1997. p6.

PRISONS--MICHIGAN--COSTS (v26)

PRISONS--NEW YORK (STATE)--COSTS (v26)

PRISONS--OVERCROWDING--UNITED STATES

In the U.S., "during 1995 state prisons on average were operating at 3 percent above their rated capacities. Federal prisons were about 24 percent above capacity. As of the 1995 census approximately one in four state correctional facilities was under a court order or consent decree to limit population or to address specific confinement conditions. However, the number of facilities ordered by courts to limit their populations declined from 183 in 1990 to 174."

U.S. Dept. of Justice. "Prison Construction Keeping Pace with Population Growth." Press Release 7 Aug 1997. document-level access: <http://www.ojp.usdoj.gov/pub/bjs/press/csfcf95.pr>

PRISONS--UNITED STATES (v26)

In the U.S., "the nine top-performing private-prison stocks have soared in value an average of 36.89 percent since January 1

[1997]. Private companies now guard upward of 85,000 inmates around the country; industry insiders are confident of 250,000 within five years." (p5)

Shapiro, Bruce. "Editorials: Law and Order: Portfolio Prisons." Nation v265 n12 20 Oct 1997. p4-5. (ISSN0027-8378).

"More than 94 percent of all [U.S.] prisons operated inmate work programs in 1995. About 63 percent of all state inmates and 90 percent of all federal inmates participated in some type of work program. Eighty percent of all prisons offered a General Equivalency Diploma or other secondary educational program, and almost one-quarter of all prisoners were enrolled. About 70 percent of all facilities offered psychological or psychiatric inmate counseling."

U.S. Dept. of Justice. "Prison Construction Keeping Pace with Population Growth." Press Release 7 Aug 1997. document-level access: <http://www.ojp.usdoj.gov/pub/bjs/press/csfcf95.pr>

"State and federal officials built 213 new prisons--168 state and 45 federal facilities--with more than 280,000 beds between 1990 and 1995 to keep pace with the growing prison population, the [U.S.] Justice Department announced....As of mid-year 1995, there were 1,500 state and federal prisons with a capacity of 976,000 beds--up 41 percent in the five-year period, according to the 'Census of State and Federal Correctional Facilities, 1995,' published by the Department's Bureau of Justice Statistics (BJS)."

U.S. Dept. of Justice. "Prison Construction Keeping Pace with Population Growth." Press Release 7 Aug 1997. document-level access: <http://www.ojp.usdoj.gov/pub/bjs/press/csfcf95.pr>

The U.S. has gone "on a prison-building binge that shows no sign of slowing. Space for some 1 million more beds has been constructed since 1985, at an estimated cost of $50 billion. (The nation's inmate population is now roughly 1.7 million.) An additional 700,000 prison beds at a cost of $35 billion are expected to be needed over the next five years." (p54)

Vogelstein, Fred. "Business & Technology: Cons, Don't Leave Home without It." U.S. News & World Report v123 n3 21 Jul 1997. p53-54. article-level access: <http://www.usnews.com/usnews/issue/970721/21PRIS.HTM> (ISSN0041-5537).

PRIVACY--UNITED STATES--PUBLIC OPINION

In the U.S., "a 1995 Louis Harris poll found that 82 percent of respondents were concerned about their personal privacy, up from 64 percent in 1978. Over the same period, the proportion of those who were 'very concerned' about privacy increased almost 50 percent." (p11)

Shapiro, Andrew L. "Articles: Privacy for Sale: Peddling Data on the Internet." Nation v264 n24 23 Jun 1997. p11-12,15-16. (ISSN0027-8378).

PRIVATE FOUNDATIONS

see CHARITABLE USES, TRUSTS, AND FOUNDATIONS

PRIVATE SCHOOLS

see also CHURCH SCHOOLS

PRIVATE SCHOOLS--UNITED STATES--FINANCE

Currently, notes Gerald A. Reynolds, president of the Center for New Black Leadership, "some 32 privately funded school-choice scholarship programs, enrolling 12,500 students, have sprung up around the...[U.S.], with another 40,000 on waiting lists. In New York City this past April, the School Choice Scholarships Foundation lined up $6 million in private donations to fund private school scholarships--$1,400 per year for three years--for the city's most needy public school students in grades one through five. As a measure of the dissatisfaction with the public schools, the parents of nearly 20,000 of the city's most at-risk public school children applied for the first 1,300 scholarships....85 percent of the scholarships will go to students now enrolled in the city's public elementary schools with the lowest reading scores." (p6)

Reiland, Ralph R. "Of Other Things: School Choice: Threat or Solution?" America v177 n8 27 Sep 1997. p6-7. (ISSN0002-7049).

PRIVATE SCHOOLS--UNITED STATES--FINANCE --PUBLIC OPINION

According to a Gallup survey released Aug. 26, 1997, in the U.S., "in 1993, less than one-fourth (24 percent) of respondents favored public funding of private education while 74 percent opposed it. This year, 44 percent of respondents favored the idea while 52 percent opposed it. A slight majority (49 percent to 48 percent) favored a 'proposal that would allow parents to send their school-age children to any public, private or church-related school they choose,' with the government paying for all or part of the tuition at private and church-related schools. Last year, 54 percent opposed this proposal while 43 percent favored it. The 1997 survey also found that 78 percent of respondents think nonpublic schools that receive public funds should be 'required to accept students from a wider range of backgrounds and academic ability than is now generally the case.' Sixty-five percent of those surveyed indicated it would be 'higher-achieving' students who would take the opportunity to attend private schools." (p2)

"News & Comment...: Opposition to Vouchers Softening, Survey Shows." Report from the Capital v52 n17 9 Sep 1997. p2. (ISSN0346-0661).

PRIVATE SECURITY SERVICES--COLOMBIA

In Colombia, "today there are approximately 385 private security agencies, with 104 branches spread throughout 627 departments; there are 7 agencies that specialize in the protection of securities (such as banks), with 49 branches. At last count, the total number of people employed by these agencies numbered 89,159 operatives, plus 5,210 administrative personnel....Assuming that the average family consists of at least four people, then some 396,396 persons must benefit from this...security. It has been estimated that private groups (both businesses and individuals) spend about $150 million (0.3% of the GNP) to protect their properties and ensure their personal safety (Rubio, 1995...)." (p56)

Richani, Nazih. "The Political Economy of Violence: The War-System in Colombia." Journal of Interamerican Studies & World Affairs v39 n2 Sum 1997. p37-81. (ISSN0022-1937).

PRIVATE SECURITY SERVICES--EMPLOYMENT --UNITED STATES (v26)

PRIVATE SECURITY SERVICES--UNITED STATES

"In the United States, there are now roughly three times as many private security guards as there are police officers. Only 280,000 in 1950, they were estimated at about 1.5 million in 1990; industry executives expect the number of private guards to surge to 2 million by the year 2000, although some experts say that level may already have been reached." (p17) "In 1990, annual spending for private security in the United States reached $52 billion, compared with a $30 billion budget for the country's police forces." (p18)

Renner, Michael. "Small Arms, Big Impact: The Next Challenge of Disarmament." Worldwatch Paper n137 Oct 1997. p5-77.

PRIVATIZATION

"Brazil's government expects to generate $56 billion in revenues from selling publicly-owned assets, such as its telephone and electricity companies, between 1997 and 1999....Since 1980, privatization sales in Western Europe alone run to some $200 billion, and the global total exceeds $600 billion. With telecommunications opening up, sales may pass $1 trillion by the year 2000." (p10) "Banker fees in privatization sales have ranged from 1.5% to 7% of gross revenue....With global privatization sales of perhaps $100 billion annually in recent years, an average 3% fee means $3 billion a year to the bankers. In Britain from 1981 through 1988, bankers, brokers, accountants and management consultants earned 730 million [pounds sterling] (roughly $1.1 billion) in fees." (p11)

Herman, Edward S. "Economy in Review: Privatization, Part II: The Global Attack on Democracy, Labor, & Public Values." Dollars and Sense n213 Sep-Oct 1997. p10-15. (ISSN0012-5245).

PRIVATIZATION--NEW ZEALAND (v26)

PRIVATIZATION--UNITED STATES (v26)

PROBATION--UNITED STATES

In the U.S., "almost three-quarters of all probationers had had some type of contact with their probation officers during the month before being surveyed, the Justice Department's Bureau of Justice Statistics (BJS) said....Sixty-one percent had a face-to-face meeting in a probation office, at home, at work or elsewhere. More than a quarter had been contacted by mail or telephone. In addition, for more than a quarter of all probationers, probation officers had made contacts with other persons, such as employers, teachers, counselors, relatives, and police officers to gather information....The data are from the first national survey of probationers, which revealed that in 1995 about 58 percent of the offenders were serving sentences of probation for a felony offense, 39 percent for a misdemeanor and 3 percent for other infractions."

U.S. Dept. of Justice. Bureau of Justice Statistics. "Nearly Three-Quarters of All Probationers Had Some Recent Contact with Their Probation Officers." Press Release 3 Dec 1997. document-level access: <http://www.ojp.usdoj.gov/pub/bjs/press/cap95.pr>

In the U.S., at the end of 1996, "3,180,363 adult offenders were on probation. More than half (55 percent) had been convicted of a felony, 26 percent had been convicted of a misdemeanor, 17 percent for driving while intoxicated or under the influence of alcohol and 2 percent for other offenses."

U.S. Dept. of Justice. "Nation's Probation and Parole Population Reached Almost 3.9 Million Last Year." Press Release 14 Aug 1997. document-level access: <http://www.ojp.usdoj.gov/pub/bjs/press/papp96.pr>

PRODUCE TRADE

see FOOD PRICES; FOOD SUPPLY; FRUIT TRADE; GRAIN TRADE; VEGETABLE TRADE

PRODUCE TRADE--UNITED STATES (v26)

PRODUCER PRICE INDEXES

see WHOLESALE PRICE INDEXES

PRODUCT SAFETY--LAW AND LEGISLATION--UNITED STATES

In the U.S., "products that were supposed to take the FDA 90 days to approve often took up to 200 days, and those that had 180 days by statute took as long as 800 days....The FDA has cut that response time in half in the last couple years." (p3 secB)

Zagaroli, Lisa. "Business: Bill Proposed to Hasten FDA Approvals." Detroit News 16 Jul 1997. p3 secB.

PRODUCTIVITY, INDUSTRIAL

see INDUSTRIAL PRODUCTIVITY

PRODUCTIVITY, LABOR

see LABOR PRODUCTIVITY

PRODUCTIVITY OF LABOR

see LABOR PRODUCTIVITY

PRODUCTS

see BRAND NAME PRODUCTS; DAIRY PRODUCTS INDUSTRY

PROFESSIONAL SPORTS--AFRO-AMERICANS (v26)

PROFESSIONAL SPORTS--AFRO-AMERICANS --ATTITUDES (v26)

PROFESSIONAL SPORTS--SALARIES, ETC.--UNITED STATES (v26)

PROFESSIONAL SPORTS--UNITED STATES --MINORITIES (v26)

PROFESSIONAL SPORTS--UNITED STATES--YOUTH --ATTITUDES (v26)

PROFESSORS

see COLLEGE TEACHERS

PROFIT (v26)

see CAPITAL GAINS

PROMISE KEEPERS--CANADA--UNITED STATES

In 1991, in the U.S., the Promise Keepers "drew just 4,200 men to rallies. That swelled to 727,000 in 1995 and 1.1 million last year. This year, says spokesman Mark DeMoss, it has 368 staff members and expects revenues of $120 million from selling $83 tickets to events, as well as from books, videos and souvenirs....In Canada, a separate and smaller Promise Keepers group has operated since 1995 out of headquarters in Burlington, Ont., as well as offices in Kitchener, Ont., Winnipeg and Langley, B.C. It has a mailing list of 70,000 and has held rallies across the country, drawing as many as 11,500 men in Vancouver and Hamilton." (p52)

Phillips, Andrew. "World: Christian Men on the March." Maclean's v110 n40 6 Oct 1997. p52-53. (ISSN0024-9262).

PROMOTIONS--AUSTRALIA

According to the report, "Career Experience, Australia, November 1996," by the Australian Bureau of Statistics, "full-time employees were more likely to be promoted or transferred (8 per cent promoted and 9 per cent transferred) than part-time employees (3 per cent promoted and 4 per cent transferred)....An estimated 12 per cent of employees aged 20-29 years had been promoted and 11 per cent had been transferred. Some 7 per cent of employees aged 30-54 years had been promoted and 7 per cent had been transferred. People employed as managers and administrators had the highest rate of promotion (11 per cent) and associate professionals had the highest rate of transfer between jobs (12 per cent) than other occupations. Intermediate clerical, sales and service workers also had a high rate of promotion or transfer (11 per cent promoted and 11 per cent transferred)."

Australian Bureau of Statistics. "Australia's Employment Experience--ABS." Media Release 27 Jun 1997. document-level access: <http://www.abs.gov.au/websitedbs/d3110125.nsf/4a255eef008309e44a255eef00061e57/aa9c2c6faed989664a2564c200798129?OpenDocument>

PROPERTY

see also REAL PROPERTY; STOCK OWNERSHIP

PROPERTY--CHINA

According to the Gallup Organization, "half (50%) of all urban homes [in China] now have a telephone, 69% have refrigerators, 81% have clothes washing machines, 22% have VCRs, and 4% even a computer (nationwide levels: 25%, 35%, 49%, 12%, and 2%, respectively). Nationwide, 21% of all Chinese households plan to purchase a color TV within the next two years, and only slightly fewer plan to buy refrigerators and washing machines (16% each). Motorcycles, air conditioners, video compact disk players and microwave ovens are on the 'will buy' list for significant numbers of Chinese families (9%, 8%, 8%, 4%)."

Gallup Organization. "1997 Survey: The People's Republic of China: Consumer Attitudes & Lifestyle Trends." Press Release 27 Oct 1997. document-level access: <http://www.gallup.com/poll/special/china/chinarel.html>

PROPERTY--CRIMES AGAINST--MICHIGAN--DETROIT (v26)

PROPERTY--VALUATION

see VALUATION

PROPERTY TAX--MASSACHUSETTS--BOSTON (v26)
PROPHYLACTICS (BIRTH CONTROL)
see CONDOMS
PROSPECTING--CANADA--COSTS (v26)
PROSTATE--CANCER--AUSTRALIA--MORTALITY
According to the Australian Bureau of Statistics, "between 1982 and 1996 the number of deaths from prostate cancer has nearly doubled, from 1,356 in 1982 to 2,660 in 1996. The increase in the age standardised death rate (deaths per 100,000 of population) during this period was 19 per cent."
Australian Bureau of Statistics. "Deaths from Diabetes and Senile Dementia Increase." Media Release 31 Oct 1997. document-level access: <http://www.abs.gov.au/websitedbs/d3110125.nsf/4a255eef008309e44a255eef00061e57/b963d1a23d007204ca25654000761a86?OpenDocument>
PROSTATE--CANCER--CANADA
"Prostate cancer is the most frequently diagnosed cancer among Canadian men, with an estimated 80 men being diagnosed every working day. Its incidence is 40...[per] cent greater than that of breast cancer and only lung cancer kills more men than does prostate cancer. "Prostate cancer, because it strikes one man in eight, is, like breast cancer, a serious disease which affects huge numbers of Canadian families. Yet prostate cancer, which kills 4,000 men each year, was ignored in the government's throne speech. It continues to receive just one-ninth of the funding of breast cancer research and one-fiftieth of the research money given to AIDS." (p93)
White, Ted (MP-BC). "Statements by Members: Prostate Cancer." Canada. Parliament. House of Commons. Debates. v135 n4 25 Sep 1997. p93. section-level access: <http://www.parl.gc.ca/36/1/parlbus/chambus/house/debates/004_1997-09-25/han004-e.htm#LINK107> (ISSN0704-5603). (X3-361E).
PROSTATE--CANCER--MICHIGAN
According to a Michigan state health report, "prostate cancer was the leading type of cancer in 1995. About 14 percent of Michigan men will be diagnosed [with] it; about 3 percent of them will die of the disease. From 1993 to 1995, 22,611 cases of prostate cancer were among the 129,491 cases of cancer statewide. In Washtenaw County, there were 404 cases of prostate cancer among the 2,726 cases of cancer reported between 1993 and 1995. Of the 1,129 cases of cancer reported in Livingston County during that same period, 170 were prostate cancer cases." (p13 secA)
Schulz, Karen. "Cancer Diagnoses Fall; Cancer Deaths Up Slightly." Ypsilanti Press 22 Nov 1997. p1,13 secA.
PROSTATE--CANCER--TREATMENT--UNITED STATES (v26)
PROSTATE--CANCER--UNITED STATES (v26)
A study from the Washington University School of Medicine looked at men in the U.S. with normal digital rectal examination tests and prostate-specific antigen "levels of between 2.6 and 4.0 ng/ml [nanograms per milliliter]--levels that are not necessarily high enough to warrant further testing. Yet when biopsies were done, cancer was detected in 22 percent of the men....A new study from the Johns Hopkins University School of Medicine suggests that some men should have the [PSA] test done every other year....While this could result in great cost savings for men between 50 and 70 years of age, there is a slight risk that a cancer could be missed or could grow beyond a 'curable' range in the two-year interval. The authors estimate the latter risk at 4 percent...." (p4)
"New Studies Cloud Prostate Issues." People's Medical Society Newsletter v16 n4 Aug 1997. p4-5. (ISSN0736-4873).
PROSTITUTION
"Each year 2 million girls between ages 5 and 15 are introduced to commercial sex....It is estimated that 300,000 Nepalese women have been sent or sold to brothels in India....An estimated 500,000 women, largely from Eastern Europe, have been forced into commercial sex....In several EU member states, commercial sex workers are predominantly foreign: in Germany, an estimated three quarters of prostitutes are foreign born; in Milan, 80 percent of street prostitutes, in Vienna, 80 percent of women working as dancers and hostesses in sex clubs....In some studies up to 80 percent [of sex workers] have been found to be HIV-positive." (p7)
"'A Slave Trade in Women.'" Popline v19 May-Jun 1997. p7.
PROSTITUTION--BURMA--THAILAND (v26)
PROSTITUTION--PHILIPPINES (v26)
According to the Young Adult Fertility and Sexuality Study conducted in 1994 in the Philipines, among single men age 15-24, "the proportion who had ever paid for sex rose steadily with age, from 0 percent among 15-year-olds to 22 percent by age 24. Among married men the pattern was different: the proportion who reported having ever paid for sex peaked at age 21 (at 18 percent) and then declined with age, to 10 percent by age 24." (p2)
"Survey Sheds New Light on Marriage and Sexuality in the Philippines." Asia-Pacific Population & Policy n42 Jul 1997. p1-4. (ISSN0891-6683).
In the Philippines "today, a million women work in the sex trade, and 85% of tourists to the Philippines are men." (p415) "Between 30,000 and 50,000 Filipinos are HIV positive, not counting Filipinas engaged in the overseas sex industry." (p416)
Fernandez, Mary Rose. "Commodified Women." Peace Review v9 n3 Sep 1997. p411-416. (ISSN1040-2659).
PROTECTION OF ANIMALS
see ANIMAL WELFARE
PROTECTION OF ENVIRONMENT
see ENVIRONMENTAL PROTECTION
PROTECTION OF WILDLIFE
see WILDLIFE CONSERVATION
PROTECTIVE CLOTHING--UNITED STATES
"The U.S. military and law enforcement agencies account for the bulk of the $200 million-a-year domestic market for bulletproof gear (up from $150 million five years ago). Today, 64 percent of the nation's 700,000 local, state, and federal law enforcement officers don bulletproof vests, compared with 23 percent a decade ago. But sales of body armor to civilians have jumped from practically nothing to roughly $10 million a year....Nationwide, the number of stores (including gun shops) selling bulletproof gear has increased to roughly 2,000, compared with just a handful 10 years ago." (p46)
Chappell, Kevin. "Business & Technology: A Death-Defying Business." U.S. News & World Report v123 n6 11 Aug 1997. p46-47. article-level access: <http://www.usnews.com/usnews/issue/970811/11PROO.HTM> (ISSN0041-5537).
PROTESTANTS--CUBA
"Hector A. Hunter, general superintendent of the Pentecostal Church in Cuba, told us that while his denomination--one of 54 Protestant groups in Cuba--has been here since the 1930s, it is only in the past five years that it has achieved rapid growth. It now has 34 churches with over 50,000 members--up from 7,000 members in 1992." (p579)
Wall, James M. "Cuba's Religion Factor: Diplomatic Dance." Christian Century v114 n19 18 Jun 1997. p579-580. (ISSN0009-5281).
PROTESTANTS--UNITED STATES (v26)
PROVINCIAL GOVERNMENTS
see STATE GOVERNMENTS
PSYCHIATRIC PERSONNEL
see MENTAL HEALTH PERSONNEL
PSYCHIATRISTS--IOWA (v26)

PSYCHIATRISTS--SOUTH AFRICA (v26)

PSYCHIATRISTS--UNITED STATES (v26)

In the U.S., "demand-based estimates, in which managed care organizations decide what services are reimbursed (thereby determining the 'demand'), suggest that less than four psychiatrists per 100,000 population will be necessary to provide services to 'consumers.' Richard Kronick and colleagues...predicted a large surplus of psychiatrists, citing a current ratio of 14.6 per 100,000 population and an estimated requirement of only 3.8 per 100,000 population under capitation. These figures suggest a current 74 percent surplus of psychiatrists." (p1012)

Smith, Douglas A. "Economic Grand Rounds: Past Is Prologue: Moving Forward from Psychiatric Training." Psychiatric Services v48 n8 Aug 1997. p1011-1012,1016. (ISSN1075-2730).

In the U.S., "the percentage of female psychiatrists increased from 14 percent in 1982 to 25 percent in 1996..., and the trend is likely to continue, given that 44 percent of psychiatric residents in 1995-1996 were female....Male psychiatrists reported spending a greater percentage of patient-care time in solo office practice (42 percent) and in group office practice (10 percent) than did female psychiatrists (37 percent and 7 percent, respectively)....Female psychiatrists spent a greater percentage of time in public and private clinics and outpatient facilities (21 percent compared with 15 percent). When asked to indicate the setting where they spend the most hours in outpatient care, a greater percentage of male psychiatrists reported individual practice (53 percent) compared with female psychiatrists (41 percent). A greater percentage of female psychiatrists spent most of their outpatient care hours in group practice (51 percent) compared with male psychiatrists (43 percent)....Seventy-nine percent of female psychiatrists were under the age of 55, or in the early or mid stages of their careers..., compared with only 54 percent of male psychiatrists." (p1387)

Zarin, Deborah A./Peterson, Brennan D./Suarez, Ana/Pincus, Harold Alan. "Datapoints: Sources of Patient-Care Income, Work Settings, And Age of Male and Female Psychiatrists." Psychiatric Services v48 n11 Nov 1997. p1387. (ISSN1075-2730).

PSYCHIC READINGS--UNITED STATES

In the U.S., "the Psychic Friends Network generates about $100 million a year, according to the Associated Press....The second-largest group is the Psychic Readers Network, which brings in about $50 million a year. Also profiting: AT&T, which controls about 60 percent of the 1-900 industry, and MCI, which controls about 20 percent." (p5)

Poe, Randall/Courter, Carol Lee. "Fast Forward: 1-900-Psychic." Across the Board v34 n7 Jul-Aug 1997. p5. (ISSN0147-1554).

PSYCHOLOGISTS--SALARIES, ETC.--UNITED STATES (v26)

PUBLIC CONTRACTS--UNITED STATES--FINANCE (v26)

PUBLIC DEBTS

see DEBTS, PUBLIC

PUBLIC EMPLOYEES

see CIVIL SERVICE

PUBLIC HOUSING--ILLINOIS--CHICAGO

In Chicago, public housing "is home to 86,000 of the city's poorest people, with a median household income of just $4,000. Nearly 90 percent of public-housing residents are black and 70 percent of the 15,000 voucher holders are concentrated in the poorer areas of the city's south suburbs. In the next 10 years, CHA [Chicago Housing Authority] must tear down 17,500 of its worst high-rise apartments and help families find rent-subsidized alternatives." (p3)

Walker, Sam. "United States: US Eyes Public Housing--And Begins to Remodel." The Christian Science Monitor v89 n199 9 Sep 1997. p3. The Christian Science Monitor search engine: <http://www.csmonitor.com/plweb-cgi/iops1.pl> To retrieve this article, enter the following search: ED=19970909 AND remodel. In the "retrieved list," click the title that matches this record. (ISSN0882-7729).

PUBLIC HOUSING--MASSACHUSETTS--BOSTON --MINORITIES (v26)

PUBLIC HOUSING--MICHIGAN--DETROIT--RENT

U.S. President Bill "Clinton has signed legislation allowing the U.S. Department of Housing and Urban Development to adjust rents in subsidized units if officials determine they're too high. By adjusting the rates, taxpayers could save $1.6 billion by 2002, said HUD spokesman Victor Lambert....In Detroit, monthly rent at eight subsidized housing developments...averages $716 per unit. The fair market for those units, according to HUD, is $499. Over 12 months, that costs taxpayers $217,217 above the fair market rate for the Detroit rents. Tenants pay 30 percent of their income toward rent; taxpayers pick up the rest." (p1,4 secD)

Esparza, Santiago. "Metro: News Special: New Law May Boost Public Housing Amenities." Detroit News 11 Nov 1997. p1,4 secD.

PUBLIC HOUSING--UNITED STATES (v26)

"Under a program known as HOPE VI, authorized by [the U.S.] Congress in 1993, the Clinton administration has started to tear down 100,000 of the nation's 1.3 million public-housing units and spend nearly $1 billion fixing up existing projects and building new units....HUD [Housing and Urban Development] has spent $440 billion in the last 30 years on public housing." (p3)

Walker, Sam. "United States: US Eyes Public Housing--And Begins to Remodel." The Christian Science Monitor v89 n199 9 Sep 1997. p3. The Christian Science Monitor search engine: <http://www.csmonitor.com/plweb-cgi/iops1.pl> To retrieve this article, enter the following search: ED=19970909 AND remodel. In the "retrieved list," click the title that matches this record. (ISSN0882-7729).

PUBLIC PROSECUTORS--UNITED STATES (v26)

PUBLIC SCHOOLS

see also HIGH SCHOOLS; VOLUNTARISM--UNITED STATES--PUBLIC SCHOOLS

PUBLIC SCHOOLS--MASSACHUSETTS--BOSTON (v26)

PUBLIC SCHOOLS--MICHIGAN--PUBLIC OPINION (v26)

PUBLIC SCHOOLS--UNITED STATES--PUBLIC OPINION

"Americans consistently rank drug abuse, lack of discipline and fighting, violence and gangs as the top three problems facing public schools, according to a Gallup Poll conducted annually for PHI DELTA KAPPAN, a magazine for educators, and released two months before the 1996 [presidential] elections....The 1996 poll found that 81 percent would favor security guards [in schools], 75 percent the use of drug-sniffing dogs, 63 percent random drug testing of students, and 53 percent mandatory uniforms. Politicians and school administrators also find strong support, with 73 percent of those surveyed saying they believe school boards are committed to improving schools and 70 percent expressing the same confidence in school superintendents. Teachers came out on top, with an 80 percent rating." (p62)

Gibeaut, John. "Juvenile Justice: Who's Raising the Kids?" ABA Journal v83 Aug 1997. p62-67. (ISSN0747-0088).

PUBLIC SCHOOLS--UNITED STATES--TEACHERS --ATTITUDES

According to the Public Agenda report, "Different Drummers: How Teachers of Teachers View Public Education," "more than six in

10 [teacher educators] (64 percent) say schools should avoid competitions such as honor rolls, and 78 percent want less reliance on multiple-choice exams....Too many public school systems are top-heavy with bureaucracy and administration, say 77 percent of the professors. Parents should be allowed to choose among public schools, say 52 percent, and another 35 percent agree--but 'only under certain conditions.' Many criticisms of public schools are politically motivated and 'come from right-wing groups who want to undermind public education,' say 54 percent." (p10)

"Before the Board: Teacher Educators Stress Process over Content." American School Board Journal v184 n12 Dec 1997. p10. (ISSN0003-0953).

PUBLIC SHELTERS--PENNSYLVANIA--PHILADELPHIA (v26)

PUBLIC SPENDING POLICY

see GOVERNMENT SPENDING POLICY

PUBLIC TELEVISION--UNITED STATES

"Public television reaches 90 percent of American households....Four out of five teachers in this country used television in their classroom during the 1990 and 1991 school year, serving close to 24 million students. Three of the five most used programs cited by teachers and 6 of the top 10 were initially broadcast by public television. Public television stations air nearly 1,900 hours of children's programming every single year. Almost 50 percent of the television programs for children which are aired each year is funded by CPB [Corporation for Public Broadcasting], quality, noncommercial, non-violent television." (pH7208)

DeLauro, Rosa L. (Rep.-Conn.). "Departments of Labor, Health and Human Services, And Education...Appropriations Act, 1998." Congressional Record. Daily ed. v143 n120 11 Sep 1997. pH7206-7247. section/page-level access: <http://thomas.loc.gov/cgi-bin/query/R?r105:FLD001:H07207:> (ISSN0363-7239). (X1.1A.105/1).

According to a U.S. "Department of Education study, 71.5% of preschool children from households earning $25,000 or less watch public broadcasting educational programming (Sesame Street, Barney, Mr. Rogers, or Reading Rainbow) at least once a week. 75% of Americans ranked children's programming aired on public television higher than children's programs available from other sources, such as broadcast networks and cable. Access to Public TV is free. Many households cannot afford to pay $300-$600 per year for cable TV. 69% of teachers report using PBS programming for educational purposes in the classroom at least once a month--more than double the next most frequently used source. GED [General Equivalency Diploma] on TV enables 88,000 adults per year to obtain a GED certificate. Over 2 million adults have received a GED certificate through this program since its inception. Public television stations broadcast an average of 5 1/2 hours per day of Instructional television (ITV) used by 1.8 million teachers to reach 29.5 million students in 70,000 schools. Public television's Adult Learning Service (ALS) is used by 2/3 of the nation's colleges. Over the past 15 years, over 4 million adults have participated in ALS with 400,000 working adults using the service each semester." (pH7211)

Engle, Eliot L. (Rep.-N.Y.). "Departments of Labor, Health and Human Services, And Education...Appropriations Act, 1998." Congressional Record. Daily ed. v143 n120 11 Sep 1997. pH7206-7247. section/page-level access: <http://thomas.loc.gov/cgi-bin/query/R?r105:FLD001:H07210:> (ISSN0363-7239). (X1.1A.105/1).

PUBLIC TRANSPORTATION

see TRANSPORTATION

PUBLIC UTILITIES

see ELECTRIC UTILITIES; RAILROADS

PUBLIC WELFARE

see also AID TO FAMILIES WITH DEPENDENT CHILDREN PROGRAMS; CHILD WELFARE; FOOD RELIEF; LEGAL ASSISTANCE TO THE POOR; SOCIAL WORKERS; SUPPLEMENTAL SECURITY INCOME PROGRAM

PUBLIC WELFARE--CALIFORNIA (v26)

PUBLIC WELFARE--CALIFORNIA--ILLEGAL ALIENS

"The Citizenship Reform Act of 1997 amends the Immigration and Naturalization Act to deny automatic citizenship to children born in the United States who were not born by parents who are legal resident aliens or permanent residents, or U.S. citizens....In California alone, we have addressed this issue and seen this issue grow. Over 250,000 children of illegal aliens are now qualified in the county...of Los Angeles, over 250,000 qualify for benefits such as Medicare, AFDC, WIC [Women, Infants and Children program], and SSI [Supplemental Security Income]. In fact, two-thirds of the births...in the public hospitals of Los Angeles County, are to parents who are illegal aliens. The fact is that the cost to the State of California alone is $500 million for providing welfare and health benefits to the children of illegal aliens. Forty percent of all births in the State of California are children of illegal aliens." (pH8984)

Bilbray, Brian P. (Rep.-Calif.). "The Citizenship Reform Act of 1997." Congressional Record. Daily ed. v143 n143 22 Oct 1997. pH8984-8985. section/page-level access: <http://thomas.loc.gov/cgi-bin/query/R?r105:FLD001:H08984:> (ISSN0363-7239). (X1.1A.105/1).

PUBLIC WELFARE--EMPLOYMENT--UNITED STATES

In the U.S., "with welfare reform, researchers at the Economic Policy Institute estimate that the bottom 30% of earners will fall on average by 11.9% to absorb the nearly one million new low-wage workers it will produce....In New York City alone, Chris Tilly found in a study for the Russell Sage Foundation that 30,000 workfare placements would displace 20,000 other workers and reduce wages for the bottom third of the labor force by 9%. In Minnesota, 31 workers would compete for every job that required little training and paid a livable wage (set at $10.96 after taxes)." (p35)

McCrate, Elaine. "Hitting Bottom: Welfare 'Reform' and Labor Markets." Dollars and Sense n213 Sep-Oct 1997. p34-35. (ISSN0012-5245).

PUBLIC WELFARE--MARYLAND--BALTIMORE

"According to the Welfare Rights Union, at least 300 'workfare' workers work at the Johns Hopkins University Hospital [in Baltimore, Maryland] (as well as at many other locations throughout the city)....Workfare workers make $1.50 an hour or less. Next year, 13,000 local workers are due to be cut off welfare altogether, and forced into the Baltimore labor market." (p3)

"Campaign for Jobs Amendment Comes to Baltimore." People's Tribune v24 n7 Jul 1997. p3. (ISSN1081-4787).

PUBLIC WELFARE--MASSACHUSETTS (v26)

PUBLIC WELFARE--MICHIGAN (v26)

"Nearly two-thirds of all Michigan welfare recipients...have lost some benefits under a stricter policy about reporting deadbeat parents [who] live in Wayne and Oakland counties....In September [1997], 1,534 Michigan families were sanctioned--366 live in Oakland County, 547 are in Wayne County, 37 in Macomb County and 39 in Washtenaw County. The total number of families on welfare in the state is about 143,500. Oakland County has only about 5 percent of the state's welfare cases but 24 percent of September's sanctions...." (p1,5 secA)

Wendland, Wendy. "Welfare Rule Seeks Absent Parents' Cash: Clients Must Help or Face Cutoff." Detroit News and Free Press 1 Nov 1997. p1,5 secA.

"Under Michigan policy, welfare parents must go to work, and the state will pay for child care during work hours....The state keeps county-by-county statistics on delays in approving families for state-paid day care. Any case that takes longer than 45 days is considered overdue. Generally, around 13 percent of cases are overdue, but in June [1997] it was 19 percent. That spiked to 22 percent in July, the month after many state employees took advantage of early retirement. It then dropped to 17 percent in August and 13 percent in September. Washtenaw County was one of the 10 counties with the slowest rate of child-care reimbursements, with 13 percent of the cases overdue out of 267 cases....Livingston County had no overdue cases, according to state statistics....In September, 86,000 children were in state-paid day care; last year the state spent $184 million in state and federal dollars on child care....In September, Muskegon County was the slowest in opening new cases, with overdue cases at 32 percent. Kent County was next, followed by Ingham, Genesee, Wayne and Kalamazoo." (p1,10 secA)

Putnam, Judy. "Late Day-Care Payments Threaten Welfare Reform." Ypsilanti Press 3 Nov 1997. p1,10 secA.

PUBLIC WELFARE--MICHIGAN--APPROPRIATIONS AND EXPENDITURES

"Michigan's AFDC expenditures have fallen by $275 million since 1994, or about one-quarter. Over the same period, Lansing has boosted what it previously spent on job-training programs by an extra $61 million in creating Work First. The budget will grow by $18 million this coming year. Net savings to the treasury? About $214 million." (p18 secA)

Hodges, Michael H. "From Welfare to Work: At Issue: Kids vs. Career: Caseloads Drop, But Does That Mean Success?" Detroit News 21 Sep 1997. p18 secA.

PUBLIC WELFARE--MICHIGAN--IMMIGRANTS (v26)

PUBLIC WELFARE--NEW YORK (N.Y.) (v26)

"Long Island's NEWSDAY (3/16/97) reported that from 1994 to early 1997, as New York City Mayor Rudolph Giuliani reduced the city's welfare rolls by 245,000 people, the number of meals served by city soup kitchens and food pantries rose by 70 percent." (p26) "One recent survey of people queued up at New York City food pantries (Community Food Research Center, 4/97) found that more than 10 percent had seen their benefits cut off in the previous 12 months, many for reasons never explained to them, a termination notice simply arriving one day in the mail. Of 96 welfare recipients who said they had left the welfare rolls, only three reported that it was because they had found a job." (p27)

deMause, Neil. "Out of Sight, Out of Mind: 1.4 Million Welfare Recipients Get Disappeared." Extra! v10 n6 Nov-Dec 1997. p25-27.

PUBLIC WELFARE--PENNSYLVANIA--PHILADELPHIA (v26)

PUBLIC WELFARE--UNITED STATES (v26)

"Welfare rolls have indeed fallen dramatically--down 3.4 million during [U.S. President Bill] Clinton's presidency, perhaps as much as 1.3 million in the year since the federally guaranteed Aid to Families with Dependent Children program was replaced by block grants to the states. That's...[a] 24 percent decline." (p5) "States now pick up roughly 40 percent of the welfare bill....Only 20 percent of welfare clients will remain exempt from being cut off come 2002." (p6)

"Commonweal: Miles to Go." Commonweal v124 n16 26 Sep 1997. p5-6. (ISSN0010-3330).

In the U.S., "in 1993 a single parent with two children receiving average benefits from AFDC, food stamps, Medicaid, housing assistance, WIC [Women, Infants and Children program], and school meals received about $17,209 in direct payments or benefits. If the parent had four children, that amount was $25,000." (pH2247)

Goodling, William F. (Rep.-Pa.). "A Successful Educational Program." Congressional Record. Daily ed. v143 n57 6 May 1997. pH2247-2248. section/page-level access: <http://thomas.loc.gov/cgi-bin/query/R?r105:FLD001:H02247:> (ISSN0363-7239). (X1.1A.105/1).

In the U.S., "the welfare caseload fell by 3.4 million recipients, from 14.1 million in January 1993 to 10.7 million in May 1997, a drop of 24 percent since President Clinton took office. Forty-eight out of fifty states have seen their caseloads decline, with ten states reducing their rolls by 40 percent or more in the last four years. This is the largest welfare caseload decline in history and the lowest percentage of the population on welfare since 1970."

U.S. Dept. of Health and Human Services. "Clinton Administration Moving Forward on the Promise of Welfare Reform." Fact Sheet 22 Aug 1997. document-level access: <http://www.hhs.gov/news/press/1997pres/970822.html>

"The only national study to date, released by the federal Council of Economic Advisers in May [1997], chalked up 44 percent of the [U.S. welfare] caseload drop to an improved economy, and 31 percent to the effects of workfare and other new restrictions. The other 25 percent were marked simply 'other factors.'" (p28)

deMause, Neil. "Move 'Em Out." In These Times v22 n1 14 Dec 1997. p27-29. (ISSN0160-5992).

"In 1994, 26.4 million elderly Americans were receiving Social Security retirement benefits (U.S. Bureau of the Census 1996...). On the other hand, the number of AFDC recipients in December 1994 was 14 million (of which 9.5 million were children), while the number of SSI [Supplemental Security Income] recipients was 6.3 million--4.8 million persons with disabilities and 1.5 million poor elderly persons (U.S. Bureau of the Census 1996...)." (p847)

Kronebusch, Karl. "Medicaid and the Politics of Groups: Recipients, Providers, And Policy Making." Journal of Health Politics, Policy and Law v22 n3 Jun 1997. p839-878. (ISSN0361-6878).

In the U.S., welfare "caseloads declined by 20 percent from January 1993 to January 1997. This is the largest decline in over 50 years. In 17 states, caseloads declined by more than 30 percent. In 17 others, they declined between 21 percent and 30 percent, so that two-thirds of all the states have had declines of more than 20 percent. In only four states have caseloads increased during this time." (p18)

Tweedie, Jack. "A Good Time for Welfare Reform." State Legislatures v23 n7 Jul-Aug 1997. p18-19. (ISSN0147-6041).

U.S. President Bill Clinton "boasted recently that the welfare rolls have shrunk by 1.2 million people since August [1996]....So far, more than 200 companies have joined Clinton's Welfare to Work Partnership. The goal is to have 1,000 companies signed on within the next six months....At least 20 states are imposing shorter time limits than five years on all or part of their caseload....As many as 100,000 to 150,000 former welfare recipients per year could be competing for a less-rapidly growing number of jobs, the Urban Institute calculates." (p4)

Francis, David R. "United States: How Welfare Reform Helps Ada Cardoza." The Christian Science Monitor v89 n169 28 Jul 1997. p4. The Christian Science Monitor search engine: <http://www.csmonitor.com/plweb-cgi/iops1.pl> To retrieve this article, enter the following search: ED=19970728 AND cardoza. In the "retrieved list," click the title that matches this record. (ISSN0882-7729).

U.S. President Bill Clinton "has proclaimed welfare reform a success, citing a 24 percent decline in caseloads since he took office. The president also lauded a 1.4 million person shrinkage in welfare rolls since his signing last year of a landmark reform law." (p20)

"The Monitor's View: Declining Welfare Rolls." The Christian Science Monitor v89 n185 19 Aug 1997. p20. The Christian Science Monitor search engine: <http://www.csmonitor.com/plweb-cgi/iops1.pl> To retrieve this article, enter the following search: ED=19970819 AND rolls. In the "retrieved list," click the title that matches this record. (ISSN0882-7729).

PUBLIC WELFARE--UNITED STATES --APPROPRIATIONS AND EXPENDITURES

In the U.S., "viewed as a gross domestic product (GDP), private-sector social welfare has gradually...increased from 7.7 percent in 1972 to 13.3 percent in 1994....In the latter year, total expenditures were $921,465 billion, compared with $873,871 billion in 1993 (an increase of 5.4 percent). By comparison, public expenditures for social welfare programs increased from 16.6 percent of GDP in fiscal year 1972 to 21.1 percent in 1993. Total spending for social welfare programs, both public and private, increased from 23.5 percent of GDP in 1972 to a 33.0 percent share in 1993." (p54)

"Private Social Welfare Expenditures, 1972-94." Social Security Bulletin v60 n1 1997. p54-60. (ISSN0037-7910).

PUBLIC WELFARE--UNITED STATES--CHILDREN (v26)

PUBLIC WELFARE--UNITED STATES--PUBLIC OPINION (v26)

PUBLISHERS AND PUBLISHING--CANADA (v26)

PUBLISHERS AND PUBLISHING--SWEDEN--FINANCE (v26)

PUBLISHERS AND PUBLISHING--UKRAINE (v26)

PUERTO RICAN AGED--CARE--MASSACHUSETTS --SPRINGFIELD (v26)

PUERTO RICANS--EMPLOYMENT--UNITED STATES

"Puerto Rican American males divide quite equally among four areas of employment: operators, fabricators and laborers (24%), precision production, craft and repair (18%), service (22%)..., and technicians, sales and administrative support (23%). Only 11% hold managerial and professional positions. The largest percentage (48%) of Puerto Rican American females work in technical, sales or administrative support. Another 21% hold managerial and professional positions, 18% work in service occupations, and 11% work as operators, fabricators, and laborers." (p26)

"Targeting Minority Publics: Employment of Hispanic Americans by Country of Origin." Public Relations Quarterly v42 n2 Sum 1997. p26. (ISSN0033-3700).

PUERTO RICANS--UNITED STATES--POPULATION

In the U.S., "Puerto Ricans are the largest single Hispanic group, after Mexicans. In 1996, an estimated 3.1 million Puerto Ricans lived in the United States, about 11 percent, of Hispanics. An additional 3.8 million people (primarily Hispanics) live in Puerto Rico." (p9-10)

del Pinal, Jorge/Singer, Audrey. "Generations of Diversity: Latinos in the United States." Population Bulletin v52 n3 Oct 1997. p2-47. (ISSN0032-468X).

PUERTO RICO--SOCIAL CONDITIONS

"In 1993, there were 24 homicides in Puerto Rico per 100,000 inhabitants, compared with 9 in the United States, 4 in Costa Rica, and 1 in the United Kingdom. In 1991 Puerto Rico had 1,972 drug addicts per 100,000 inhabitants, compared with 1,176 in the United States and 179 in the United Kingdom....Forty-seven percent of the island's labor force has some post-secondary education; 25 percent of those working are professionals and managers." (p110-111)

Martinez, Ruben Berrios. "Puerto Rico's Decolonization." Foreign Affairs v76 n6 Nov-Dec 1997. p100-114. (ISSN0015-7120).

PUNISHMENT, CAPITAL

see CAPITAL PUNISHMENT

PUPILS

see STUDENTS

PURCHASE TAX

see SALES TAX

PURDUE UNIVERSITY

see ENGINEERING STUDENTS--PURDUE UNIVERSITY

PVC

see POLYVINYL CHLORIDE

PYROTECHNICS

see FIREWORKS

QUAKES (EARTHQUAKES)

see EARTHQUAKES

QUALITY OF LIFE

see also COST AND STANDARD OF LIVING

QUALITY OF LIFE--AFRO-AMERICANS

"According to a recent Gallup poll, 74 percent of American blacks are satisfied with their personal lives and standards of living, even as many continue to endure prejudice. They are enjoying an employment boom. For married black men, the unemployment rate is 5.3 percent; for married black women, it is 4.3 percent." (p82)

Zuckerman, Mortimer B. "Editorial: The Route to Racial Healing." U.S. News & World Report v123 n1 7 Jul 1997. p82. article-level access: <http://www.usnews.com/usnews/issue/970707/7EDIT.HTM> (ISSN0041-5537).

QUALITY OF LIFE--CANADA

"Canada's well-being is obvious. Almost none of its 28 million people live in what would qualify in the United States as a slum dwelling. The population is homogeneous: almost 90 percent of European origin. Polls consistently indicate that about 90 percent of both English- and French-speaking Canadians believe they live in the world's most pleasantly habitable country, and the United Nations has recognized Canada's quality of life as the highest of any country in the world for the last two years." (p99)

Black, Conrad. "Canada's Continuing Identity Crisis." Foreign Affairs v74 n2 Mar-Apr 1995. p99-115. (ISSN0015-7120).

QUALITY OF LIFE--CHINA

According to a nationwide survey in China, conducted by the Gallup Organization, "adults rate the quality of their life as being nearly a third better than it was five years ago (29%)--and expect its quality to improve by a further 32% over the next five years. While the homes of just 2% of all Chinese nationwide have hot running water, virtually all are electrified, nine in ten have televisions, and over half now have color televisions. Increasing affluence, access to new products, and changing fashions have made the possessions and habits of this generation unlike any before: most families in Guangzhou now own an electronic pager, and nearly three-quarters of urban women under age thirty wear lipstick or lip gloss....Scarcely 1% of Chinese adults say their family owns an automobile--but 10% have flown in an airplane, as have over a third of those living in the country's largest cities. 98% of those in China's largest cities agree with the notion that more should be done to try to improve the quality of the air and water where they live."

Gallup Organization. "1997 Survey: The People's Republic of China: Consumer Attitudes & Lifestyle Trends." Press Release 27 Oct 1997. document-level access: <http://www.gallup.com/poll/special/china/chinarel.html>

QUALITY OF LIFE--CHINA--PUBLIC OPINION

In China, "the average rating given to describe the overall

quality of one's personal life was near the mid-point--5.09 on a ten point scale where 10 represented 'the best possible life you can imagine', and one 'the worst possible life you can imagine' one-to-ten scale. Residents of urban areas tended to give slightly higher ratings of their life than did those living in the countryside, but the difference was not dramatic (urban Chinese: 5.33, rural Chinese: 4.93). When asked where they stood five years ago, the average rating given nationwide was only 3.94--some 1.15 points lower than the average current rating. In other words, across China there has been an average improvement of fully 29% in the self-described quality of one's personal life over the past five years. Urban Chinese gave their personal condition five years ago an average score of 4.49, while rural Chinese gave a rating of 3.58. Compared with current scores, the average rural resident thus feels a greater improvement in his or her life quality over the past five years (up 40%) than does the typical urbanite (up 19%), though admittedly from a lower initial base."

Gallup Organization. "1997 Survey: The People's Republic of China: Consumer Attitudes & Lifestyle Trends." Press Release 27 Oct 1997. document-level access: <http://www.gallup.com/poll/special/china/chinarel.html>

QUALITY OF LIFE--UNITED STATES

In the U.S., "some 55 percent of those between age 18 and 24 said they were willing to make only 'some' sacrifices in their personal or family life for their career or education, according to a 1993 survey by the Families and Work Institute in New York....In a survey of executives at top US companies, 36 percent said business must improve quality-of-life issues to attract [Generation-] Xers." (p9)

Coolidge, Shelley Donald. "X-ers at Work: 'I'm New; When's Vacation?'" The Christian Science Monitor v89 n155 8 Jul 1997. p1,9. The Christian Science Monitor search engine: <http://www.csmonitor.com/plweb-cgi/iops1.pl> To retrieve this article, enter the following search: ED=19970708 AND vacation. In the "retrieved list," click the title that matches this record. (ISSN0882-7729).

QUALITY OF WATER

see WATER QUALITY MANAGEMENT

QUEBEC (PROVINCE)--CIVILIZATION--FRENCH INFLUENCES--PUBLIC OPINION (v26)

QUEBEC (PROVINCE)--ECONOMIC CONDITIONS (v26)

QUEBEC (PROVINCE)--EMIGRATION AND IMMIGRATION (v26)

RNs

see NURSES

RVs

see RECREATIONAL VEHICLES

RABBINICAL SEMINARIES--ISRAEL--STUDENTS

Figures show "'that the number of yeshiva students in Israel has grown by 25% in the last year, to nearly 200,000, while state funding for yeshivas has increased by 40% to almost $250 million.'...'The students' failure to enter the workforce costs the country about $1 billion in lost production each year, according to Treasury estimates.'" (p11)

Foner, Henry. "It Happened in Israel." Jewish Currents v51 n10 Nov 1997. p10-11. (ISSN0021-0639).

RABIES--UNITED STATES (v26)

RACE DISCRIMINATION (v26)

RACE DISCRIMINATION--UNITED STATES (v26)

RACE DISCRIMINATION--UNITED STATES--PUBLIC OPINION

According to a survey released by the Joint Center for Political and Economic Studies, in the U.S., "more than 92 percent of blacks, nearly 87 percent of Hispanics and 76 percent of whites said they think discrimination is common. By comparison, in the Gallup poll [of southeast Michigan by DETROIT FREE PRESS] only 45 percent of blacks said blacks were treated badly or not as well as whites in their communities: 17 percent of whites agreed. The Joint Center surveyed 1,702 adults--half black, half white, including 100 Hispanics--during the end of March and beginning of April [1997]." (p8 secA)

Eversley, Melanie. "Bias View Worsens with Age." Detroit Free Press 18 Jun 1997. p1,8 secA.

RACE DISCRIMINATION IN EDUCATION

see DISCRIMINATION IN EDUCATION

RACE DISCRIMINATION IN EMPLOYMENT

see DISCRIMINATION IN EMPLOYMENT

RACE RELATIONS

see also INTERRACIAL DATING; INTERRACIAL MARRIAGE

RACE RELATIONS--MICHIGAN--PUBLIC OPINION

"Unlike their elders, most young whites in Michigan believe the U.S. government should apologize to blacks for slavery, according to a poll...[by EPIC/MRA of Lansing]. Among white voters ages 18-29, 52 percent said they approve of legislation pending in Congress that calls for the government to say it is sorry for the enslavement of black Americans during the two centuries before the Civil War. A dozen white lawmakers in Washington have called for the apology, similar to the one issued nearly a decade ago for the internment of Japanese Americans during World War II. Overall, about six of 10 whites statewide said they oppose an apology. Almost seven of 10 black voters favored it in the June 23-36 telephone poll of 600 registered voters." (p1 secB)

McGraw, Bill. "Local News: Poll Says Views on Race Differ with Age." Detroit Free Press 2 Jul 1997. p1-2 secB.

RACE RELATIONS--UNITED STATES

"A good two-thirds of [U.S.] respondents in a recent Knight-Ridder survey indicated that they were 'not at all worried' by the surge of Asians and Hispanics in the country or by the forecast that whites of European ancestry will become a minority by the middle of the next century. Findings of a Gallup poll...showed racial tolerance and acceptance among whites to be at an all-time high: About 93 percent of whites polled noted that they were willing to vote for a black president. And 61 percent approve of interracial marriages now, versus 25 percent in 1972." (p8 secA)

"Comment: Preaching about Diversity." Detroit News 17 Jun 1997. p8 secA.

In the U.S., "thirty years ago, two-parent black families earned only two-thirds as much as similar white families; today they earn 87 percent as much. In 1958, only 4 percent of whites said they approved of interracial marriage; today the figure is 61 percent, according to the Gallup Poll." (p7 secA)

Brownstein, Ronald. "Comment: To Deal with Race, We Must Go beyond Race." Detroit News 22 Jul 1997. p7 secA.

"The CHICAGO TRIBUNE (June 11, 1997) quotes a Gallup Poll on changes in 'racial' attitudes of whites between 40 years ago and now. Today, 93 percent of white Americans could put a qualified black person in the White House as opposed to 35 percent in 1958. Sixty-one percent approve of mixed marriages as opposed to 4 percent 40 years ago, and 18 percent today say they would leave a neighborhood if 'a large number of blacks moved in' as opposed to 80 percent in 1958." (p2)

"Society Is Responding to the Political Attacks." People's Tribune v24 n7 Jul 1997. p2. (ISSN1081-4787).

RACE RELATIONS--UNITED STATES--PUBLIC OPINION (v26)

In the U.S., according to a survey released by the Joint Center for Political and Economic Studies, "of more than 1,700 Americans...nearly 60 percent of whites describe race relations in their communities as good; only 40 percent of blacks agree. Among retirement-age people, just over 27 percent of blacks thought race relations were good, compared with 75 percent of whites. But among 18-to-25-year-olds, just over 48 percent of blacks said race relations in their communities were excellent or good, compared with just over 37 percent of whites. The national survey results are similar to the findings of an April [1997] FREE PRESS poll of southeast Michigan that showed 18-to-24-year-olds are about twice as likely as any older age group to believe that race relations have improved in the past decade." (p8 secA)

Eversley, Melanie. "Bias View Worsens with Age." Detroit Free Press 18 Jun 1997. p1,8 secA.

RACE RELATIONS--UNITED STATES--TEENAGERS --ATTITUDES

According to a recent Gallup Youth Survey, only 10 percent of U.S. "teens are satisfied and 24 percent are somewhat satisfied [with race relations], leaving 56 percent thoroughly dissatisfied with race relations and 10 percent with no opinion....Black teens are especially inclined to believe relations will deteriorate over the next ten years, at 42 percent, compared with 28 percent of white teens. Thirty-four percent of black teens and 48 percent of white teens believe race relations will improve in the next decade." (p36-37)

Kate, Nancy Ten. "Kaleidoscope: Teens and Race." American Demographics v19 n6 Jun 1997. p36-37. article-level access: <http://www.demographics.com/publications/ad/97_ad/9706_ad/ad970622.htm> (ISSN0163-4089).

RACES OF MAN

see ETHNOLOGY

RACETRACKS (AUTOMOBILE RACING)--MICHIGAN

The Michigan Speedway's "30th season comes with more than $4 million in off-season upgrading and a modified track name: No longer is it known as Michigan International Speedway. Nearly 5.5 infield acres have been paved to provide more and bigger motor home parking spaces for team members. In the middle of the 162-space luxury lot is a playground for their families. Two sets of temporary grandstands in turn 4 have been replaced by permanent structural steel and aluminum ones, with a third set of grandstands added between turns 3 and 4. The speedway's new total of reserved seats...is 106,775. Also new this year, the 150-acre infield has been sectioned off into about 2,600 reserved sites, about 15-by-40-feet each." (p11 secD)

Crowe, Steve. "Sports: Auto Racing: Earnhardt's Rare Winless Streak Has People Talking." Detroit Free Press 12 Jun 1997. p11 secD.

RADIATION

"NASA has acknowledged that in the case of an atomspheric disaster 'approximately 5 billion of the 7 to 8 billion people on earth in 1999 could receive 99% or more of the radiation exposure.' Dr. Ernest Sternglass, professor emeritus of radiological physics of the University of Pittsburgh, estimates that the death toll could be as high as 30 to 40 million people." (p14)

Parry, Renee-Marie Croose. "More Profiles in Civic Courage: Medea Benjamin and Bruce Gagnon Deserve Recognition." Human Quest v211 n5 Sep-Oct 1997. p13-14. (ISSN0897-8786).

RADIO--CANADA--ECONOMIC CONDITIONS (v26)

RADIO IN PROPAGANDA--CANADA (v26)

RADIOACTIVE WASTES--UNITED STATES (v26)

In the U.S., "there are now more than 35 thousand metric tons of radioactive waste from nuclear reactors, a toxic stockpile that is increasing by 5 tons a day. Scientists estimate that this glowing mountain of waste will take about 4 billion years to decay to a 'harmless' condition." (p8)

St. Clair, Jeffrey. "Nuclear Waste: Gambling on 'Mobile Chernobyl.'" In These Times v22 n1 14 Dec 1997. p9. (ISSN0160-5992).

RADON--UNITED STATES (v26)

RAFTING (SPORTS)--UNITED STATES (v26)

RAILROAD ACCIDENTS--CANADA (v26)

RAILROAD ACCIDENTS--UNITED STATES (v26)

RAILROAD STATIONS--MICHIGAN--ANN ARBOR (v26)

RAILROAD TRAVEL--UNITED STATES--PUBLIC OPINION (v26)

RAILROADS--GREAT BRITAIN--FINANCE (v26)

RAILROADS--NEW YORK (STATE)--COMMUTING

"New York is home to the two largest commuter railroads in the Nation--the Long Island Rail Road (LIRR) and the Metro North railroad. Each day, approximately 235,000 commuters depend on these two railroads to get to work and back home again. Almost half of these commuters--108,000 or 46 percent--transfer to subways and buses once they arrive in New York City." (pS8311)

D'Amato, Alfonse M. (Sen.-N.Y.). "Department of Transportation and Related Agencies Appropriations Act, 1998." Congressional Record. Daily ed. v143 n110 30 Jul 1997. pS8311-8312. section/page-level access: <http://thomas.loc.gov/cgi-bin/query/R?r105:FLD001:S08311:> (ISSN0363-7239). (X1.1A.105/1).

RAILROADS--UNITED STATES

Since 1980, "the number of railroads in the United States has doubled to around 550....Special charges of $1.2 billion dropped the industrywide rate of return on investments from 9 percent to 7 percent in 1995 (the last year for which official figures are available), operating revenues that year rose 4.8 percent on a record 1.3 trillion revenue-ton miles." (p1)

Page, Dave. "From Small to Big, And Back Again." Federal Reserve Bank of Minneapolis Fedgazette v9 n4 Oct 1997. p1.

RAILROADS--UNITED STATES--COSTS (v26)

RAILROADS--UNITED STATES--FINANCE (v26)

RAIN FORESTS (v26)

RAINBOW BRIDGE (UTAH)

In Utah, "Rainbow Bridge, at 290 feet tall and 275 feet long, is the world's largest natural stone arch....Today, as many as 1,000 boaters from Lake Powell swarm the bridge daily." (p1)

Smith, Chris/Manning, Elizabeth. "The Sacred and the Profane Collide in the West." High Country News v29 n10 26 May 1997. p1,8-12. (ISSN0191-5657).

RAISIN INDUSTRY--UNITED STATES

"The United States is one of the world's major raisin exporters, second only to Turkey. U.S. raisin exports rose 2 percent from a year earlier in 1996 to 272 million pounds....The United Kingdom has been the major market for U.S. raisins, followed closely by Japan. Exports to Japan, however, exceeded those to the United Kingdom where shipments declined by a fraction. Each of the two countries accounted for about 23 percent of all U.S. raisin exports last year, while Canada, the Federal Republic of Germany, Denmark, and Sweden combined, made up the next 23 percent. U.S. raisin imports generally average only about 3 percent of domestic supplies, and in 1996 totaled 25.2 million pounds, down 4 percent from the prior year." (p11)

U.S. Dept. of Agriculture. Economic Research Service. "Noncitrus Fruit Outlook." Fruit and Tree Nuts Situation and Outlook Report Aug 1997. p7-26.

RAPE--MICHIGAN--MACOMB COUNTY

In Michigan, "reported rapes skyrocketed 138 percent in Macomb County's two largest communities in the first six months of 1997....In Warren, with a population of 144,000, reported rapes jumped from 16 to 41, according to FBI statistics. Sterling Heights, with 120,737 residents, reported nine rapes, five more than a year ago." (p5 secC)

Pardo, Steve. "Macomb: Rapes Up in Sterling Hts., Warren: Experts Attribute Increase to Victims' Willingness to Report Crime." Detroit News 15 Dec 1997. p5 secC.

RAPE--RWANDA (v26)
RAPE--RWANDA--YUGOSLAVIA (v26)
RAPE--UNITED STATES (v26)

In the U.S., "many women in uniform argue that the Army is more comfortable for females--who now represent 14 percent of the Army's 495,000 soldiers--than recent sex scandals suggest....In a 1995 Defense Department survey, 8 percent of Army women said they had been subjected to a rape or attempted rape. Although direct comparisons between the military and civilian worlds are hard to make, separate studies of universities have found that between 10 percent and 28 percent of college women say they have been victims of rape." (p50)

Newman, Richard J. "Culture & Ideas: Army Sex Ed 101." U.S. News & World Report v123 n6 11 Aug 1997. p50-52. article-level access: <http://www.usnews.com/usnews/issue/970811/11ARMY.HTM> (ISSN0041-5537).

RAPESEED INDUSTRY

"World production of rapeseed in 1996/97 fell 12 percent from the previous season to 30.6 million metric tons....Rapeseed production in the EU fell 14 percent to 7.1 million tons, and by 5 percent in China to 9.2 million tons. Timely January rains helped produce record yields in India, raising production to a record 6.3 million tons." (p7)

U.S. Dept. of Agriculture. Economic Research Service. "World Oilseed Situation." Oil Crops Situation and Outlook Series Oct 1997. p7-8.

RARE FISHES--UNITED STATES (v26)
RATE OF INFLATION

see INFLATION (FINANCE)

REACTORS, NUCLEAR

see NUCLEAR REACTORS

READING--CANADA--YOUTH (v26)
READING AND BOOKS

see BOOKS AND READING

READINGS, PSYCHIC

see PSYCHIC READINGS

REAL ESTATE BUSINESS

see also RENTAL HOUSING

REAL ESTATE BUSINESS--AUSTRALIA

Data released "by the Australian Bureau of Statistics showed that, at the end of June 1996, there were 8,082 businesses in Australia's real estate agents industry, an 11 per cent rise since June 1993. These businesses generated $3,370 million in income. Most of this was from sales and leasing commissions from residential properties which accounted for 43 per cent ($1,463 million) of total income. The other major source of income was property management fees which accounted 26 per cent ($868 million) of total income. The industry's operating profit before tax was $275 million. This represents an operating profit margin of 8.3 per cent."

Australian Bureau of Statistics. "Real Estate Agents Industry Grows." Media Release 10 Sep 1997. document-level access: <http://www.abs.gov.au/websitedbs/d3110125.nsf/4a255eef008309e44a255eef00061e57/740317403180f1594a25650e000391f9?OpenDocument>

REAL ESTATE BUSINESS--EMPLOYMENT--AUSTRALIA

According to the Austalian Bureau of Statistics, "a total of 55,785 people were working in the [real estate agents] industry at the end of June 1996. This consisted of 45,956 employed and 9,830 working on a commission only basis. Compared to June 1993, employment in the industry rose by 12 per cent while people working on a commission only basis fell by 10 per cent. During the same period full-time and part-time employment in the industry rose by 13 per cent and seven per cent respectively. At the end of June 1996, 97 per cent of businesses in the industry employed less than 20 people. These businesses accounted for 82 per cent (45,753) of people working in the industry and generated 76 per cent ($2,560 million) of total income."

Australian Bureau of Statistics. "Real Estate Agents Industry Grows." Media Release 10 Sep 1997. document-level access: <http://www.abs.gov.au/websitedbs/d3110125.nsf/4a255eef008309e44a255eef00061e57/740317403180f1594a25650e000391f9?OpenDocument>

REAL ESTATE BUSINESS--ISRAEL (v26)
REAL PROPERTY--MICHIGAN--DETROIT (v26)
REAL PROPERTY--VALUATION--MICHIGAN

"Comparing the price of previously owned homes in September 1997 to the same time last year, the typical U.S. house price rose 5 percent, compared with a 2.2 percent rise in overall consumer prices. But many areas in the South and Midwest saw prices climb more than 10 percent. And several cities in Michigan were among those experiencing the biggest increases. Kalamazoo registered the second-biggest increase in home prices in the country. The median price of an existing house went up 14.5 percent in the past year, to $100,900. Only Waterloo, Iowa, climbed faster, with prices jumping 17.2 percent, to $68,200. Saginaw-Bay City also saw a big jump--10.3 percent, to $72,800. Metro Detroit, meanwhile, saw house prices jump by 8.1 percent, to a median of $122,500....Among 136 metropolitan areas surveyed, Grand Rapids registered a 6.8 percent increase in home prices, to $93,800, and Lansing saw home prices rise 7.5 percent to $94,700." (p1-2 secE)

Rose, Judy. "Business: Detroit-Area Home Values Soar." Detroit Free Press 11 Nov 1997. p1-2 secE.

REAL PROPERTY--VALUATION--UNITED STATES

In the U.S., "in addition to Kalamazoo, Saginaw [Michigan] and Waterloo [Iowa], other towns where house prices increased more than 10 percent the past year were: New Orleans, La., and Fort Lauderdale, Fla., both 11.3 percent; Memphis, Tenn., 11.2 percent; Austin, Texas, 10.9 percent; Bradenton, Fla., 10.2 percent; and San Francisco, 10.1 percent....Norfolk, Va., had the sharpest decline of 11.9 percent. It was followed by Honolulu, Hawaii, 6 percent; Beaumont, Texas, 4.4 percent; El Paso, Texas, and Hartford, Conn., both 3.8 percent. The five metro areas with the highest median prices in the July-September quarter were: Honolulu, at $315,000; San Francisco, $300,600; Orange County, Calif., $233,000; New York, $212,500, and Boston, $204,400. The five with the lowest prices were: Ocala, Fla., $65,700; Beaumont, Texas, $67,100; Waterloo, Iowa, $68,200; Davenport, Iowa, $71,700, and Daytona Beach, Fla., $73,600." (p2 secE)

Rose, Judy. "Business: Detroit-Area Home Values Soar." Detroit Free Press 11 Nov 1997. p1-2 secE.

RECIDIVISM--CALIFORNIA (v26)
RECIDIVISM--CANADA (v26)
RECIDIVISM--GREAT BRITAIN (v26)
RECIDIVISM--UNITED STATES (v26)

In South Carolina, "for those prisoners who have worked in prison industry, the probability that when they get out they are going to commit a crime again and end up back in prison is 2 percent. For those who have not worked in prison industry it is 35 percent. In the State of Florida the recidivism rate, people coming back to prison who have worked in prison industries, is 11 percent; it is 26.7 percent for people who have not worked in prison, not acquired a work ethic, not acquired any skills. In Wisconsin it is 11 percent for people that worked in prison industries, it is 22 percent for those who did not. In Kentucky 36 percent come back to prison versus 65 percent who do not work in Federal Prison Industries." (pS7150)

Gramm, Phil (Sen.-Tex.). "National Defense Authorization Act for Fiscal Year 1998." Congressional Record. Daily ed. v143 n97 10 Jul 1997. pS7145-7205. section/page-level access: <http://thomas.loc.gov/cgi-bin/query/R?r105:FLD001:S07149:> (ISSN0363-7239). (X1.1A.105/1).

RECIDIVISM--UNITED STATES--SEX OFFENDERS

In the U.S., "a National Institute of Justice study published in June [1997] indicates that, after 25 years, the repeat rate [for sex offenders] is 52 percent. Researchers in Canada reported in August 1996 that 8.2 percent of sex offenders were arrested for another sex crime within two years, though in that group, the rate for pedophiles was higher than that of rapists or those who committed incest. In May, the Washington State Institute for Public Policy noted that 12 percent of sex offenders in that state were arrested on similar charges within seven years; a 15-year study in California found a 20 percent rearrest rate, and a University of California at Berkeley expert wrote in the LOS ANGELES TIMES that recidivism among sex offenders is about that of drunk drivers--26 percent are convicted again within two years." (p40)

Sheppard, Judith. "Double Punishment." American Journalism Review v19 n9 Nov 1997. p36-41. (ISSN1067-8654).

RECREATION--UNITED STATES (v26)

RECREATION, OUTDOOR

see OUTDOOR RECREATION

RECREATION AREAS--UNITED STATES (v26)

RECREATIONAL VEHICLES--UNITED STATES

"Americans now own some 9 million RVs [recreational vehicles]. And that number is increasing by 100,000 each year, according to RV industry statistics. Michiganders alone own about 300,000 RVs....On average, each one travels 23 days a year, covering 5,900 miles." (p4 secF)

Volgenau, Gerry. "Travel: Parked in Heaven." Detroit Free Press 29 Jun 1997. p1,4 secF.

RECYCLING (WASTE, ETC.)

see also ALUMINUM--RECYCLING; AUTOMOBILES--RECYCLING; PAPER INDUSTRY--RECYCLING; PLASTICS--RECYCLING

"Nutrients in the garbage and yard wastes of states belonging to the Organisation for Economic Cooperation and Development (OECD) equal some 7 percent of the nutrients in fertilizer applied in those countries....Nutrients in discarded human waste in OECD countries equal another 8 percent of applied fertilizer." (p7)

Gardner, Gary. "Recycling Organic Waste: From Urban Pollutant to Farm Resource." Worldwatch Paper n135 Aug 1997. p5-59.

RECYCLING (WASTE, ETC.)--AUSTRALIA (v26)

RECYCLING (WASTE, ETC.)--CHINA (v26)

RECYCLING (WASTE, ETC.)--DENMARK

"A new tax on hazardous waste, tougher permitting requirements for heavy polluters, and a waste exchange are among the measures being proposed by the Danish environment agency (Miljostyrelsen) to reduce the growing amount of waste produced by trade and industry....On average, industry recycles 56% of its waste. The highest rate, 85%, is achieved by the construction sector. For the trade sector, offices, and institutions, the average is 38%." (p5)

"In Brief...: Danish Agency Starts Nonhousehold Waste Debate." Environment Watch: Western Europe v6 n17 5 Sep 1997. p5. (ISSN1066-6001).

RECYCLING (WASTE, ETC.)--EUROPE (v26)

In the EU, "some 75% of a car's weight is already recycled since it is made of metal. The ['end-of-life vehicles'] proposal is aimed at ensuring that a greater proportion of the 25% left over is recycled or reused instead of the current practices of landfill or incineration....Shredder waste totals around 2 million metric tons per year in the EU, representing up to 10% of the hazardous waste generated annually." (p2) "The current cost of recycling a car more or less completely ranges between 20 and 200 Ecu [European currency units] (US $22.40 and $224), according to the [European] Commission." (p3)

"Negotiated Agreements Dropped from EU Car Recycling Initiative." Environment Watch: Western Europe v6 n14 18 Jul 1997. p1-4. (ISSN1066-6001).

In the EU, the typical recovery rates of recycling waste electrical and electronic equipment "achieved in trial schemes to date are only 30%-40% for large items and 10% for small ones....WEEE accounts for less than 1% by weight of the total solid waste stream in the EU, although it makes up about 4% of municipal solid waste arisings. WEEE is, however, expected to grow at an average of 3%-5% per year." (p4-5)

"EU Commission Set to Draft Electronics Waste Law." Environment Watch: Western Europe v6 n14 18 Jul 1997. p4-5. (ISSN1066-6001).

RECYCLING (WASTE, ETC.)--GERMANY (v26)

RECYCLING (WASTE, ETC.)--JAPAN

"Japanese researchers have developed a way to turn 'sewer sludge' into hydrogen using the hydrogen to power a 200-kilowatt fuel cell....Gases produced from the sludge are comprised of 65% methane--a chief component of natural gas--and 35% carbon dioxide. The gases are then fed through a system that produces hydrogen, which is then run through a fuel cell to generate enough electricity to power 100 average households." (p15)

"Hydrogen Progress in Fuel Cells." Hydrogen Today v8 n2 1997. p15.

RECYCLING (WASTE, ETC.)--UNITED STATES

"According to Paul Gardner, a general contractor in Palo Alto, California, 60 to 65 percent of a building that's dilapidated beyond repair is reusable. And since a good chunk of the cost of demolition is in the fees the contractor pays to unload at a landfill, reusing even one-quarter of a house can save thousands of dollars." (p20-21)

Holmes, Hannah. "Hearth & Home: Bringing Down the House." Sierra v82 n5 Sep-Oct 1997. p20-21. (ISSN0161-7362).

REDUCING DIETS--UNITED STATES

"According to a recent report by the Centers for Disease Control, 40 percent of women and 25 percent of men in the United States are trying to lose weight at any one time. Most utilize some form of dieting to achieve their weight loss. In a weight loss study conducted at the USDA/ARS [Agricultural Research Service] Western Human Nutrition Research Center in San Francisco, California, scientists found that about half of the women developed borderline anemia and also displayed poor cognitive performance on a sustained attention test." (p65)

U.S. Dept. of Agriculture. "Agriculture, Rural Development, Food and Drug Administration...Approp. for 1998 (Part 4)." Hearing. U.S. House. Committee on Appropriations. Washington, D.C. : GPO, 1997. (ISBN0160551560). (Y4.Ap6/1:Ag8/997/pt.4).

REDUCTION OF OZONE LAYER

see OZONE LAYER DEPLETION

REEFS, CORAL

see CORAL REEFS AND ISLANDS

REFUGEE CHILDREN (v26)

REFUGEE CHILDREN--RWANDA (v26)

REFUGEES (v26)

"Worldwide there are an estimated 14.6 million refugees who have fled their homeland fearing persecution for reasons of race, religion, nationality or for their social or political opinions. For some 99 percent of those refugees, resettlement occurs in neighboring countries; repatriation may even be possible after time passes. But for the remaining fraction, third-country resettlement, such as in the U.S., is the most viable option. In 1995 about 70,000 people sought refuge in one of the ten nations that accept third-country resettlement. Among those ten the U.S. ranks fifth in the per capita number of refugees it admits--behind Sweden, Canada, Australia and Denmark." (p967)

"News: Churches Assist Refugees." Christian Century v114 n30 29 Oct 1997. p967-968. (ISSN0009-5281).

"Worldwide, in 1995 the number of refugees was estimated at about 15 million, five times their number in 1976....Another estimated 3 million people have fled their home countries but are not formally recognized by governments as refugees (but are included in this category in this report). These include an estimated 700,000 Palestinians in Jordan and 350,000 Burmese in Thailand." (p5)

Gardner, Robert/Blackburn, Richard. "People Who Move: New Reproductive Health Focus." Population Reports v24 n3 Nov 1996. p1-27.

"A recent released World Refugee Survey says the worldwide total of refugees and asylum seekers is at the lowest level since 1988, estimated at 14.5 million people....The group representing the largest reduction in the worldwide refugee total in 1996 was the 1.3 million Rwandans who returned home." (p18)

Frelick, Bill. "Opinion/Essays: Changing the Way We Think of Refugees." The Christian Science Monitor v89 n136 10 Jun 1997. p18. The Christian Science Monitor search engine: <http://www.csmonitor.com/plweb-cgi/iops1.pl> To retrieve this article, enter the following search: ED=19970610 AND refugees. In the "retrieved list," click the title that matches this record. (ISSN0882-7729).

In 1996, "the number of international refugees reached a seven-year low of 15 million, according to the '1997 World Refugee Survey,' published by the U.S. Committee for Refugees. But during the last decade, the number of internally displaced people has doubled to an estimated 25 to 30 million--a trend increasingly driven by the international community's growing reluctance to grant asylum to those who need it....Developed countries, according to...[an Amnesty International] report, host only 15 percent of all refugees and employ numerous legal and bureaucratic measures to prevent that fraction from growing." (p6)

Runyan, Curtis. "Environmental Intelligence: No Asylum for Refugees." World Watch v10 n6 Nov-Dec 1997. p6. (ISSN0896-0615).

REFUGEES--AFGHANISTAN (v26)

REFUGEES--AFRICA (v26)

REFUGEES--AFRICA, SUB-SAHARAN (v26)

REFUGEES--ASIA

"Pakistan has an estimated 870,000 refugees, mostly from Afghanistan. Of the estimated 320,000 refugees in India, over one-third are from China. Most of the 100,000 refugees in Nepal are from Bhutan." (p7)

Gardner, Robert/Blackburn, Richard. "People Who Move: New Reproductive Health Focus." Population Reports v24 n3 Nov 1996. p1-27.

REFUGEES--BOSNIA

"About 250,000 Bosnians who fled the country during the war came back to Bosnia last year....This year some 200,000, including many of the 320,000 Bosnians who took refuge in Germany and are now being deported from there, are expected to arrive." (p8)

"Dateline Migration: International: Bosnian Refugees as Political Pawns." Migration World v25 n4 1997. p8. (ISSN1058-5095).

REFUGEES--CAMBODIA--THAILAND

In Cambodia, "more than 30,000 displaced people have fled far from their homes, traveling up to 330 miles to live in makeshift shelters along the road and in the mine-riddled forest....With the help of nongovernmental organizations and the United Nations High Commissioner for Refugees (UNHCR), Thailand has allowed 120 tons of rice and other supplies into Cambodia....[On] Aug. 1,...some 3,000 refugees, including 2,640 women and elderly people and 350 disarmed royalist soldiers, were allowed to cross into Thailand and settled in areas north of Aranyaprathet....At another area near the border is an overcrowded 30-bed hospital in Kap Choeng, Thailand, where royalist soldiers wounded in battle and more than 70 civilian Cambodians have been treated." (p6)

Stanmeyer, Anastasia. "International: Cambodian Ruler's Troops Pin Refugees at Thai Border." The Christian Science Monitor v89 n180 12 Aug 1997. p6. The Christian Science Monitor search engine: <http://www.csmonitor.com/plweb-cgi/iops1.pl> To retrieve this article, enter the following search: ED=19970812 AND border. In the "retrieved list," click the title that matches this record. (ISSN0882-7729).

REFUGEES--CUBA--HAITI--UNITED STATES

"During the whole of 1993, around 2,000 Haitians put to sea in search of asylum in the United States; in June 1994 alone, the number jumped to 5,603; and then the floodgates really opened as close to 6,000 decamped in the first four days of July." (p378) "For the whole of 1993, only 3,656 Cubans were intercepted by the U.S. Coast Guard en route to Florida; between the beginning of August and early September the number surged to 30,000." (p379-380)

Morley, Morris/McGillion, Chris. "'Disobedient' Generals and the Politics of Redemocratization: The Clinton Administration and Haiti." Political Science Quarterly v112 n3 Fall 1997. p363-384. (ISSN0032-3195).

REFUGEES--DEVELOPING COUNTRIES

"At least three-fourths of the world's refugees are in developing countries (235,290). Africa and the Near East each contain over 30% of the total--more than 5 million in each region....In 1995, 15,000 refugees from Mauritania lived in Mali, while 35,000 from Mali lived in Mauritania....In 1995 Iran had about 2 million refugees, more than any other country. Two-thirds of them were Afghanis...." (p5,7)

Gardner, Robert/Blackburn, Richard. "People Who Move: New Reproductive Health Focus." Population Reports v24 n3 Nov 1996. p1-27.

REFUGEES--GERMANY--NETHERLANDS--PUBLIC OPINION

"An August 1993 survey in the Netherlands indicates that an overwhelming 77 percent of the respondents felt that their nation should undertake measures to limit the growing influx of refugees and asylum-seekers." (p87) "In September 1991, 69 percent of West Germans responding and 64 percent of East Germans responding [to surveys] favored changing the political asylum laws to prevent so many refugees from entering the country...." (p88)

Mandel, Robert. "Perceived Security Threat and the Global Refugee Crisis." Armed Forces & Society v24 n1 Fall 1997. p77-103. (ISSN0095-327X).

REFUGEES--IRAN

"In the 1990s, Iran sheltered a staggering 4.5 million exiles from Afghanistan and Iraq, the largest refugee caseload any single country has handled in modern times. The numbers have shrunk in the last few years to slightly more than two million people, but that figure is still twice as high as anywhere else." (p14)

Wilkinson, Ray. "An Iranian Surprise." Refugees v2 n108 1997. p14-15. (ISSN0252-791X).

REFUGEES--MACEDONIA

"Near the end of 1994, Macedonia had received only about 15,000 refugees from the war [in Yugoslavia]. By October 1995, that number had dropped to 6,500, about .2 percent of the refugees from the war." (p98)

Dion, Richard Read. "Macedonia: Coming In from the Cold." World Affairs v160 n2 Fall 1997. p96-103. (ISSN0043-8200).

REFUGEES--MALI

As of May 1997, "102,429 Malian refugees had been repatriated, 40,960 of them from Mauritania. Still due to return were 15,000 from Mauritania, 24,000 from Burkina Faso, 4,000 from Algeria, and 20,000 from Niger, according to Fidda ag Mohamed Ousmane, an official at the United Nations refugee agency in Tombouctou." (p7)

Matloff, Judith. "International: Nomadic 'Blue Men' of the Desert Try to Go Roam Again." The Christian Science Monitor v89 n199 9 Sep 1997. p7. The Christian Science Monitor search engine: <http://www.csmonitor.com/plweb-cgi/iops1.pl> To retrieve this article, enter the following search: ED=19970909 AND roam. In the "retrieved list," click the title that matches this record. (ISSN0882-7729).

REFUGEES--NEW YORK (N.Y.) (v26)

REFUGEES--ONTARIO--QUEBEC (PROVINCE) (v26)

REFUGEES--TANZANIA (v26)

REFUGEES--UNITED STATES

"On August 29 the State Department released a report showing that the number of refugees admitted to the U.S. had dropped some 40 percent since 1992, when 132,000 refugees were admitted....In the fiscal year ending September 30, the number of refugees admitted to the U.S. totaled no more than 78,000--the lowest number in a decade." (p967)

"News: Churches Assist Refugees." Christian Century v114 n30 29 Oct 1997. p967-968. (ISSN0009-5281).

REFUGEES--WOMEN

"The UN High Commissioner for Refugees (UNHCR) estimates that women make up a large proportion of the estimated 14 million people around the world who have left their homelands to escape political or economic strife. There are an estimated 91 female refugees for every 100 male refugees worldwide. In Africa--which contains about half of the world's refugees--women constitute the majority of refugees." (p34)

Riley, Nancy E. "Gender, Power, And Population Change: Forced Migration: Special Dangers for Women." Population Bulletin v52 n1 May 1997. p2-46. (ISSN0032-468X).

REFUGEES, AFGHAN--IRAN--PAKISTAN

From 1985 to 1990, when they "peaked at a staggering 6.2 million in Iran and Pakistan alone, Afghan refugees consistently supplied just under half the world's total refugee population. In 1997, with 2.7 million remaining in Iran, Pakistan and other countries in the region, Afghans have the unhappy distinction of remaining UNHCR's [United Nations High Council for Refugees] biggest single refugee caseload in the world for the 17th year in succession. Since October 1979, UNHCR alone has spent well over one billion dollars on Afghan refugees in Pakistan, and another $150 million in Iran. The World Food Program spent nearly $1.4 billion for Afghan refugees in Pakistan alone...." (p4) When the communist government fell in April 1992, there were "no fewer than 1.2 million Afghans returning from Pakistan within six months--all of them assisted by an extremely stretched UNHCR. Another 300,000 returned spontaneously from Iran during the same period." (p6) The scale of the return is "a total of 3.9 million people by 1997....During the 20 months leading up to the Taliban capture of the western Afghan city of Herat in September 1995, some 200,000 refugees had returned from Iran with UNHCR assistance. According to the Iranian government another 200,000 returned spontaneously. Over the following 20 months, fewer than 10,000 have gone back." (p8)

Colville, Rupert. "The Biggest Caseload in the World." Refugees v2 n108 1997. p3-9. (ISSN0252-791X).

REFUGEES, POLITICAL

Sudan "contains more internally displaced persons than any other country, an estimated 4 million people, or about one-seventh of its total population. Other countries that are estimated to have at least 1 million internally displaced persons are Angola, Iraq, Liberia, Sierra Leone, Turkey, and Bosnia and Herzegovina, where an estimated one-quarter of the population are either refugees or internally displaced persons....In 1993 an estimated 12% of Rwanda's people were displaced within the country...." (p7)

Gardner, Robert/Blackburn, Richard. "People Who Move: New Reproductive Health Focus." Population Reports v24 n3 Nov 1996. p1-27.

REFUGEES, POLITICAL--EUROPE

"The number of asylum-seekers in Ireland has grown from 39 in 1992 to 1,179 last year....In 1992, just 2.7 percent of the Irish population were noncitizens. This compared with 3.5 percent in Britain, 6.3 percent in France, and 8.5 percent in Germany." (p6)

Rafter, Kevin. "International: Irish, Great Emigrants, Not Keen on Outsiders." The Christian Science Monitor v89 n173 1 Aug 1997. p6. The Christian Science Monitor search engine: <http://www.csmonitor.com/plweb-cgi/iops1.pl> To retrieve this article, enter the following search: ED=19970801 AND outsiders. In the "retrieved list," click the title that matches this record. (ISSN0882-7729).

REFUGEES, RWANDAN (v26)

REFUGEES, RWANDAN--ZAIRE (v26)

REFUGEES, VIETNAMESE

"Today, more than 1 million of those of Vietnamese descent live in the US, mainly in California and Texas. About 500,000 others have resettled in Australia, Canada, France, and other countries in Europe. Since 1990, more than 800,000 'Viet kieu,' or overseas Vietnamese living mainly in the US and France, have returned home, sending or bringing back with them $600 million or $700 million annually to help friends and families start small businesses." (p7)

Dizon, Lily. "Special Report: US Ends Era of Welcome for Vietnam's Refugees." The Christian Science Monitor v89 n223 14 Oct 1997. p1,7. The Christian Science Monitor search engine: <http://www.csmonitor.com/plweb-cgi/iops1.pl> To retrieve this article, enter the following search: ED=19971014 AND refugees. In the "retrieved list," click the title that matches this record. (ISSN0882-7729).

REFUGEES, WOMEN

see WOMEN REFUGEES

REFUSE AND REFUSE DISPOSAL (v26)

see also HAZARDOUS WASTES; RECYCLING (WASTE, ETC.)

REFUSE AND REFUSE DISPOSAL--BRAZIL--SAO PAULO (v26)

REFUSE AND REFUSE DISPOSAL--ENVIRONMENTAL ASPECTS--UNITED STATES--INDIAN RESERVATIONS

"In a 1995 survey, the Indian Health Service identified more than 650...dump sites on Indian reservations around the...[United States]. The study, required under the 1993 federal Indian Lands Open Dump Cleanup Act, classified 97 sites as a 'high threat' to the environment." (p3)

Donovan, Bill. "Western Roundup: Navajo Tribe Embarks on a Long-Term Cleanup." High Country News v29 n15 18 Aug 1997. p3. (ISSN0191-5657).

REFUSE AND REFUSE DISPOSAL--GERMANY (v26)

REFUSE AND REFUSE DISPOSAL--GREAT BRITAIN (v26)

"According to the latest waste statistics,...England and Wales produced just under 24 million tons of municipal waste in 1995-1996. Of this total, 83% went to landfills, 5% was incinerated without energy recovery, and the remainder was recycled, composted, or went to incineration with energy recovery." (p19)

"News Briefs: New UK Minister Announces Packaging Review."

Environment Watch: Western Europe v6 n12 20 Jun 1997. p19. (ISSN1066-6001).

REFUSE AND REFUSE DISPOSAL--MICHIGAN

"Nearly 15 of every 100 pounds of trash buried in Michigan, 5.5 million cubic yards, was trucked in from out of state last year, according to state estimates....The state has 15-20 years of landfill capacity." (p7 secF)

Luke, Peter. "Opinion: It's Michigan, My Michigan, But It's Their Dumping Ground." Ann Arbor News 22 Jun 1997. p7 secF.

REFUSE AND REFUSE DISPOSAL--UNITED STATES (v26)

In the U.S., "the Clean Water Act set aside 0.5 percent of sewage funds for Tribal planning and sewage treatment plant construction. In fiscal year 1997, this provided roughly $7 million to Tribes....In 1990, the most recent year reported, EPA calculated Tribes needed $633 million for wastewater treatment and collection alone. Seventy-four percent of this total (or $468 million) was for Alaska....The Navaho and Oklahoma City areas each needed $30 million, according to EPA." (p35-36)

Dubrowski, Fran. "Cover Story: Crossing the Finish Line." Environmental Forum v14 n4 Jul-Aug 1997. p28-37. (ISSN0731-5732).

REFUSE AND REFUSE DISPOSAL--VIETNAM (v26)

REGIONAL DEVELOPMENT

see COMMUNITY DEVELOPMENT

REHABILITATION ECOLOGY

see RESTORATION ECOLOGY

REHABILITATION VOCATIONAL

see VOCATIONAL REHABILITATION

RELIEF (AID)

see CHARITIES

RELIGION

see also ALBANIA--RELIGION; BUDDHISM; CATHOLIC CHURCH; CHINA--RELIGION; CHRISTIANS; CHURCH BUILDINGS; CHURCH MEMBERSHIP; CHURCH SCHOOLS; CHURCH WORK; CUBA--RELIGION; CULTS; EPISCOPALIANS; FRANCE--RELIGION; GREAT BRITAIN--RELIGION; MARRIAGE--UNITED STATES--RELIGIOUS ASPECTS; PROTESTANTS; UNITED STATES--RELIGION

"Globally there are 1.9 billion Christians, 1.2 billion Muslims and only 14 million Jews. For comparison, consider that the Southern Baptist Convention has over 15 million members in the U.S. alone. The 2.3 percent of Americans who identify with Judaism make up a cohort one-tenth the size of each of the following three groups: Catholics, mainstream Protestants and evangelical Protestants." (p643)

Marty, Martin E. "Religious Rifts: Trauma in Judaism." Christian Century v114 n21 16 Jul 1997. p643-644. (ISSN0009-5281).

RELIGION AND POLITICS--SOUTH CAROLINA --PUBLIC OPINION

"According to a POST AND COURIER/News 2 survey of 801 South Carolina voters, 49 percent disagree with the drive to display the Ten Commandments in public buildings while 36 percent support it. In addition, only 28 percent consider themselves supporters of the Christian Coalition while 72 percent do not. (However, 81 percent of Christian Coalition allies think the Ten Commandments belong in public buildings.) Sixty percent of respondents do not agree with the Southern Baptist Convention's decision to boycott the Disney Corporation while only 19 percent agree with the boycott. A minuscule 2 percent of those polled consider abortion the top issue facing South Carolina." (p21)

"AU Bulletin: Poll Shows Support for Separation in South Carolina." Church & State v50 n9 Oct 1997. p21. (ISSN0009-6334).

RELIGION AND POLITICS--UNITED STATES (v26)

Michael Barkun, a premiere scholar on the radical right, "estimates 100,000-200,000 members of the racist right in the United States." (p327) "Among those belonging to the racist right, Barkun further estimates that 20,000-30,000 adhere to the basic precepts of Christian Identity, an umbrella term which refers to the common religious ideology of those who affiliate with the racist right." (p328)

Nessan, Craig L. "From Waco to Oklahoma City to Your Backyard: Religious Rationale and the Racist Right." Currents v24 n4 Aug 1997. p326-335.

In the 1996 U.S. presidential election, "Catholics constituted 29% of the total votes cast, while those who identified themselves as part of the conservative Religious Right were only 17%. [Presidential candidate Robert] Dole won 65% of the vote of the Religious Right, but just 37% of the Catholic vote. And while the Religious Right made up 27% of Dole's vote, the Catholic vote was 32% of [President] Clinton's winning total." (p48)

White, John Kenneth/D'Antonio, William. "The Catholic Vote in Election '96." Public Perspective v8 n4 Jun-Jul 1997. p45-48. (ISSN1050-5067).

RELIGION IN THE PUBLIC SCHOOLS--UNITED STATES--SCHOOL BOARD MEMBERS--ATTITUDES (v26)

RELIGIOUS BROADCASTING--UNITED STATES (v26)

RELIGIOUS COMMUNITIES--UNITED STATES

"The Center for Applied Research in the Apostolate (CARA) conducted an annual survey of U.S. religious communities from 1989 to 1993 (King, 1993). Each year CARA mailed questionnaires to the major superiors of all Catholic religious communities in the United States, receiving a response of 70 percent or higher each year. The 531 women religious communities responding to the 1993 survey reported a total of 2,136 women in formation programs. This total is similar to the figures from the 1990-1992 CARA surveys, but represents a steep drop when compared with earlier surveys: 28,627 in formation programs in 1966 and 3,923 in 1981 (Neal, 1984...). Not only was the number small for 1993, but the distribution of recruits varied widely--with 22 percent of all communities having no members in a formation program." (p419)

Finke, Roger. "The Rewards of a Costly Religious Community." Review for Religious v56 n4 Jul-Aug 1997. p412-427. (ISSN0034-639X).

RELIGIOUSNESS

According to a worldwide study based at the University of Michigan, "fully 44 percent of Americans attend church once a week, not counting funerals, christenings and baptisms, compared with 27 percent of people in Great Britain, 21 percent of the French, 4 percent of Swedes and 3 percent of Japanese. Moreover, 53 percent of Americans say that religion is very important in their lives, compared with 16 percent, 14 percent, and 13 percent, respectively, of the British, French and Germans." (p1)

University of Michigan. News and Information Services. "In U.S., Religious Spirit Isn't Just a Sign of the Season, According to U-M Study...Religiosity, Church Attendance." University of Michigan News Release 17 Dec 1997. p1-3.

RELIGIOUSNESS--UNITED STATES

A "random survey by Yankelovich Partners found that Americans report they spend about 16 hours on Christmas shopping and the same amount on worship....The survey, taken in October [1997] among 1,027 adults picked at random, also showed that most believed the holidays are far too commercial, the Lutheran Brotherhood reported. It showed that people with incomes below $20,000 and people in rural areas spend more time in holiday worship than do those with incomes over $50,000 and in urban areas--22 or 23 hours compared with 12 hours." (p5 secC)

Heinlein, Gary. "Suburban News: In Metro Detroit: Worship

Increases during Holidays." Detroit News 2 Dec 1997. p5 secC.

RELOCATION (HOUSEHOLD MOVING)
see MOVING, HOUSEHOLD

REMODELING OF DWELLINGS
see DWELLINGS--UNITED STATES--REMODELING

RENEWABLE ENERGY SOURCES (v26)
see also WIND POWER

"The global wind power industry is a $2-billion-a-year business, growing at 25 percent a year....The world market for solar cells has gone from $350 million in 1988 to roughly $1 billion in 1997. Some 400,000 homes worldwide now rely on solar power." (p18)

Flavin, Christopher/Dunn, Seth. "Opinion/Essays: Global Warming Treaty: Economic Boom or Bust?: Boom--Huge New Energy Markets." The Christian Science Monitor v90 n13 12 Dec 1997. p18. The Christian Science Monitor search engine: <http://www.csmonitor.com/plweb-cgi/iops1.pl> To retrieve this article, enter the following search: ED=19971212 AND markets. In the "retrieved list," click the title that matches this record. (ISSN0882-7729).

RENEWABLE ENERGY SOURCES--CHINA--JAPAN

"Japan has already installed 9,400 homes under its ambitious solar rooftop program, which allowed it to claim one third of the world solar cell market in 1996....Cogeneration accounts for 12 percent of energy use in China...." (p3)

Worldwatch Institute. "Kyoto Agreement Could Be Boon to Global Climate and World Economy." News Release 22 Nov 1997. p1-4.

RENEWABLE ENERGY SOURCES--NETHERLANDS

"Power utilities in the Netherlands announced in February that they will boost renewable power fourfold by the year 2000, according to Reuters news agency. The Dutch utility association EnergieNed said the companies aim to collectively cut emissions of carbon dioxide by 2.7 million tons per year from present levels....The Dutch government has previously called for renewables to provide 10 percent of the country's energy by the year 2020." (p13)

"News Briefs: Alternatives: Netherlands." World Rivers Review v12 n3 Jun 1997. p13. (ISSN0890-6211).

RENEWABLE ENERGY SOURCES--UNITED STATES (v26)

"In six pilot projects around the U.S., 20% of electricity customers voluntarily paid more for power generated from renewable resources. If 20% of customers in newly competitive markets chose renewable power for half their electricity, it would be the same as closing eight mid-sized coal-fired power plants...." (p1)

"Many Americans Soon Can Choose 'Green' Electricity." EDF Letter v28 n4 Sep 1997. p1,5. (ISSN0163-2566).

"Barbara Farhar, of the National Renewable Energy Laboratory in Golden, Colorado, culled data from 700 surveys conducted in the United States over the past 18 years and found that a strong majority prefer renewable electricity over their current sources. An estimated 10 to 20 percent...were willing to pay a premium price for renewable electricity....24 utilities in the U.S. are conducting 'green' market research, and 12 of these...have begun to offer renewables through 'green pricing' programs that allow customers to pay a premium to support existing or planned projects." (p32)

Dunn, Seth. "Power of Choice." World Watch v10 n5 Sep-Oct 1997. p30-35. (ISSN0896-0615).

RENEWABLE ENERGY SOURCES--UNITED STATES --FINANCE

In the U.S., "the Budget Resolution as approved by the House and Senate allocates $3.1 billion in budget authority for all energy programs in fiscal year 1998, with an increase to $3.5 billion for 1999, and decreases to $3.2 billion for 2000, and $2.9 billion for 2001. The Energy and Water bill allocates funding to renewable energy programs along with water and other environmental projects....[President Bill Clinton's] request included $343.9 million for renewable energy programs, which would represent a roughly 28 percent increase over the $269.2 million level for 1997." (p9)

Hochanadel, Joel R. "The View from Washington: Renewables and the Budget Battle." Solar Today v11 n4 Jul-Aug 1997. p9. (ISSN1042-0630).

RENT CHARGES--GREAT BRITAIN

"The average weekly rent for local authority tenants in England increased from 6.49 [pounds sterling] to 40.05 [pounds sterling] between 1979-80 and 1996-97, which represents a 135 per cent increase in real terms after adjusting for inflation as measured by the GDP market price deflator. The closest comparison that can be made for average private sector rents is between 1978 and 1996-97 when rents rose from 6.70 [pounds sterling] to 76.49 [pounds sterling], a 263 per cent increase in real terms." (c549)

Raynsford, Nick (H.C.-Greenwich). "Written Answers to Questions: Rent Rises." Great Britain. Parliament. House of Commons. Debates. 31 Jul 1997. c549. section-level access: <http://www.parliament.the-stationery-office.co.uk/pa/cm199798/cmhansrd/cm970731/debtext/70731w37.htm#70731w37.html_sbhd5>

RENT CHARGES--NEW YORK (N.Y.) (v26)

RENT CONTROL--NEW YORK (N.Y.)

"According to detailed census bureau studies conducted this year, half the families living under rent regulations [in New York City] earn less than $25,000 a year....More than half of the city's 1.1 million rent-stabilized tenants are immigrants, and 56 percent are non-white." (p23)

Neuwirth, Robert. "Renting and Raving: The Press vs. Affordable Housing." Extra! v10 n6 Nov-Dec 1997. p23-24.

"Apartments represent two-thirds of New York City's 3 million housing units. Only about 70,000 units are still under the old rent-control system, which covers apartments built before 1947 in which the same tenants (or immediate family members) have lived since 1971. These units tend to have the lowest rents (averaging $428 a month) and poorest tenants (average income: $13,428). About 1 million apartments fall under the city's rent-stabilization system, which covers apartments built before 1947 in which tenants vacated rent-controlled units, those built between 1947 and 1969, and a few recent buildings with special tax breaks. (There are another 60,000 rent-stabilized apartments in the Nassau, Westchester and Rockland County suburbs.) Rents in stabilized apartments average $600, about $80 below rents in unregulated units, although the size of the 'discount' varies widely." (p17)

Dreier, Peter. "The Landlords Stage a Rent Strike." Nation v264 n24 23 Jun 1997. p17-18,20-22. (ISSN0027-8378).

"Contrary to landlord propaganda, only about 5 percent of rent-stabilized households (and fewer than 1 percent of rent-controlled households) [in New York City] have incomes above $100,000. In fact, according to the 1996 New York City housing and vacancy survey, about one-quarter of the approximately 1.1 million households in rent-stabilized apartments are poor. About 48 percent have annual household incomes below $25,000, and 68 percent earn below $40,000. Even in rent-stabilized apartments, the typical tenant spends one-third of household income on rent. Twenty-nine percent spend at least half their income on rent." (p20)

Dreier, Peter. "The Landlords Stage a Rent Strike." Nation v264 n24 23 Jun 1997. p17-18,20-22. (ISSN0027-8378).

RENT CONTROL--UNITED STATES (v26)

RENTAL HOUSING--NEW YORK (N.Y.) (v26)

RENTAL HOUSING--UNITED STATES (v26)

In the U.S., "housing credits are the primary Federal-State tool for producing affordable rental housing across the country. Since 1987, State agencies have allocated more than $3 billion in housing credits to help finance nearly 900,000 apartments for low-income families, including 75,000 apartments in 1996. In...New York, the credit is responsible for helping finance 44,000 apartments for low-income New Yorkers, including 4,450 apartments in 1996. Earlier this year, the General Accounting Office issued a comprehensive report giving the housing credit a clean bill of health....Though the law allows housing credit apartment renters to earn up to 60 percent of the area median income, GAO documented the average tenant's income at just 37 percent, and found that more than three out of four renters have incomes under 50 percent of the area median income. GAO also found that rents in housing credit apartments are well below market rents, up to 23 percent less than the maximum permitted, and 25 percent below HUD's [Dept. of Housing and Urban Development's] national fair market rent." (pS10322)

D'Amato, Alfonse M. (Sen.-N.Y.). "Statements on Introduced Bills and Joint Resolutions." Congressional Record. Daily ed. v143 n136 3 Oct 1997. pS10319-10332. section/page-level access: <http://thomas.loc.gov/cgi-bin/query/R?r105:FLD001:S10322:> (ISSN0363-7239). (X1.1A.105/1).

In the U.S., "the average monthly rent paid by all public housing residents is $185, far less than operating costs or most market rents, and 75 percent of all current residents have annual incomes that are less than $10,000." (pH2234)

Gonzalez, Henry B. (Rep.-Tex.). "Housing Opportunity and Responsibility Act of 1997." Congressional Record. Daily ed. v143 n57 6 May 1997. pH2188-2243. section/page-level access: <http://thomas.loc.gov/cgi-bin/query/R?r105:FLD001:H02233:> (ISSN0363-7239). (X1.1A.105/1).

RENTAL HOUSING--UNITED STATES--COSTS (v26)

REPARATION--AFRO-AMERICANS (v26)

REPEAT OFFENSES

see RECIDIVISM

REPTILES--INFECTIONS--UNITED STATES (v26)

REPTILES AS PETS--UNITED STATES (v26)

RESEARCH (v26)

see also AGRICULTURE--RESEARCH; BIOTECHNOLOGY--RESEARCH; GEOLOGY--RESEARCH; UNIVERSITY OF MICHIGAN--RESEARCH

RESEARCH--CANADA (v26)

RESEARCH--CHINA

"By 1992, 44 percent of China's 4,871 state-owned R & D [research & development] units had established linkages with enterprises. Of those with linkages, 21.8 percent had either merged with a medium/large enterprise or joined an industrial group, 14.8 percent had either combined with or had contracted the operation of a small/medium enterprise, 28.1 percent had joined one of the many 'technology development centers' that do contract work for enterprises, and 35.3 percent had contractual arrangements with enterprises for the development of technology." (p105-106)

Ho, Samuel P. S. "Technology Transfer to China during the 1980s--How Effective?: Some Evidence from Jiangsu." Pacific Affairs v70 n1 Spr 1997. p85-106. (ISSN0030-851X).

RESEARCH--CROATIA (v26)

RESEARCH--CROATIA--FINANCE (v26)

RESEARCH--EMPLOYMENT--CROATIA (v26)

RESEARCH--EMPLOYMENT--UKRAINE (v26)

RESEARCH--FRANCE (v26)

RESEARCH--GREAT BRITAIN--FINANCE (v26)

RESEARCH--QUEBEC (PROVINCE)--FINANCE (v26)

RESEARCH--UKRAINE--FINANCE (v26)

RESEARCH--UNITED STATES (v26)

In the U.S., "President Clinton's budget request for fiscal year (FY) 1998 includes $75 billion for scientific R&D [research and development]. This amount represents a 1.8-percent increase over current funding levels, but fails to keep up with an inflation rate projected to reach 2.6 percent." (p12)

Childress, Janice O. "News Notes: Just Say 'Yes' to R&D." Geotimes v42 n7 Jul 1997. p12. (ISSN0016-8556).

RESEARCH--UNITED STATES--FINANCE (v26)

RESEARCH AND DEVELOPMENT CONTRACTS--FRANCE (v26)

RESEARCH AND DEVELOPMENT CONTRACTS--GREAT BRITAIN

"In 1996, the ratio of research and development spending to sales in the UK was lower than in any other major industrialised country. Among the top 300 companies in the world that spend on research and development, the average ratio of research and development spending to sales was about 4.3 per cent; for British companies in that 300, it was about half that average, at 2.3 per cent, and the trend was downwards....In the early 1990s, Britain's average dividend yield was 40 per cent higher than in the United States of America, 150 per cent higher than in Germany and 10 times the level in Japan." (c1105)

Beard, Nigel (H.C.-Bexleyheath and Crayford). "Orders of the Day: Finance Bill." Great Britain. Parliament. House of Commons. Debates. 10 Jul 1997. c1105. section-level access: <http://www.parliament.the-stationery-office.co.uk/pa/cm199798/cmhansrd/cm970710/debtext/70710-15.htm#70710-15_spnew2>

RESEARCH INSTITUTES

"Major news media continued to give greater prominence to conservative think tanks in 1996, according to a survey of major paper and broadcast media citations in the Nexis computer database. Of the ten most-media-cited think tanks, six are conservative or right-leaning, three are centrist and one is left-leaning. More than half of the total citations of think tanks were to conservative or right-leaning institutions; only 13 percent cited progressive or left-leaning institutions." (p24)

Dolny, Michael. "New Survey on Think Tanks." Extra! v10 n4 Jul-Aug 1997. p24.

RESERVATIONS, INDIAN

see INDIAN RESERVATIONS

RESERVES, NATIONAL

see NATIONAL PARKS AND RESERVES

RESIDENCES

see DWELLINGS

RESOURCE RECOVERY

see RECYCLING (WASTES, ETC.)

RESOURCES, NATURAL

see NATURAL RESOURCES

RESPIRATORY INFECTIONS

see INFLUENZA

RESPIRATORY ORGANS

see LUNGS

RESTAURANTS

see also FAST FOOD RESTAURANTS

RESTAURANTS--CANADA--UNITED STATES--ECONOMIC CONDITIONS (v26)

RESTAURANTS--HONG KONG

According to Hong Kong's Census and Statistics Department, "the value of total receipts for the restaurants sector in the second quarter of 1997, estimated at $14.4 billion, increased by 11% when compared with the same quarter in 1996. The value of total purchases of restaurants increased by 9% to $5.1 billion....After discounting the effect of price changes over the period, total restaurant receipts increased by 6% in volume. Compared with a year ago, the total receipts of bars had the most rapid growth, showing an increase of 14% in value and 9% in volume. Likewise, the total receipts of fast food shops and Chinese restaurants also went up, by 12% and 11% in value respectively. In volume terms, they both rose by 7%. The total receipts of non-Chinese restaurants increased by 8% in value and 4% in volume....Comparing the first half of 1997 with the same period of 1996, total restaurant receipts rose by 10% in value and 6% in volume."

Hong Kong. Census and Statistics Department. "Provisional Statistics of Restaurant Receipts and Purchases for 2nd Quarter 1997." Press Release 26 Sep 1997. document-level access: <http://www.info.gov.hk/censtatd/hkstat/press/d32q97.htm>

RESTAURANTS--UNITED STATES (v26)

"More than half of Americans who eat at restaurants dine out on their natal day, according to the National Restaurant Association....Forty-one percent of married men who ever go to a restaurant went out to dinner on their wife's big day, compared with just 29 percent of married women who went out on their husband's birthday." (p29-30)

Edmondson, Brad. "Kaleidoscope: It's My Birthday; We'll Go Out If I Want To." American Demographics v19 n5 May 1997. p29-30. article-level access: <http://www.demographics.com/Publications/AD/97_ad/9705_ad/AD970515.htm> (ISSN0163-4089).

"On any given day, about 46 percent of American adults depend on meals prepared at a restaurant or fast-food place. The typical American eats 4.1 commercially prepared meals a week. That's 213 meals a year--and the number keeps growing." (p1 secF)

"Food: So Many Restaurants, So Little Time." Detroit Free Press 17 Sep 1997. p1 secF.

In the U.S., "food eaten away from home accounted for over 47 percent of total food dollars in 1995, up from 34 percent in 1970 and 44 percent in 1990....According to U.S. Retail Trade Census data, food sales by restaurants and fast-food establishments increased 32 percent from 1987 to 1992 (the most recent census year), although the number of these eating establishments increased only 14 percent....Only about a third of the food-away-from-home dollar...[goes] toward the actual cost of the food, and another third...[goes] toward salaries and benefits....According to Bureau of the Census data for 1992, payroll expenses accounted for nearly 30 percent of sales in the restaurant and fast-food industry." (p4)

Clauson, Annette/U.S. Dept. of Agriculture. Economic Research Service. "Food Prices: Economic Factors Holding Down Food Price Increases." Food Review v20 n2 May-Aug 1997. p2-4. (ISSN1056-327X).

RESTAURANTS--UNITED STATES--CHILDREN (v26)

RESTORATION ECOLOGY--FLORIDA--FLORIDA KEYS

The EPA awarded the Florida Audubon Society "$400,000 in special restoration funds for four restoration pilot projects in the [Florida] Keys." (p16) "Since 1981, the [Florida Keys Environmental Restoration] Trust Fund has successfully completed 18 restoration projects from Key Largo to Key West....The EPA funds will be supplemented by other governmental funds and community involvement. The projects will receive an additional $100,000 from the U.S. Fish and Wildlife Service, Florida Department of Environmental Protection, city of Key West, and Florida Keys Environmental Mitigation Fund." (p17)

Kruer, Curtis. "America's Tropics: FAS Restoration: Florida Audubon Spearheading Restoration in the Florida Keys." Florida Naturalist v70 n2 Sum 1997. p16-17. (ISSN0015-4172).

RESTRAINT SYSTEMS, AIR BAG

see AIR BAG RESTRAINT SYSTEMS

RETAIL ADVERTISING

see ADVERTISING

RETAIL SALES TAX

see SALES TAX

RETAIL TRADE

see also ADVERTISING; FRANCHISES (RETAIL TRADE); SHOPPING; WHOLESALE TRADE

RETAIL TRADE--ALABAMA (v26)

RETAIL TRADE--BRAZIL--RIO DE JANEIRO (v26)

RETAIL TRADE--CANADA (v26)

RETAIL TRADE--EMPLOYMENT--BRAZIL--RIO DE JANEIRO (v26)

RETAIL TRADE--SWEDEN (v26)

RETAIL TRADE--UNITED STATES (v26)

"Retail employment in the U.S. stood at 21 million in 1995, 18 percent of all nonfarm wage and salary employees, according to the Bureau of Labor Statistics." (p4) "The average weekly earnings of all U.S. retail workers in 1995 were $222, according to the Bureau of Labor Statistics, compared with $244 in 1986 (in 1995 dollars). Retail earnings per worker fell in all but nine metros between 1986 and 1996, after adjusting for inflation. San Francisco topped the per-worker-earnings ranking in 1996, at $23,200, but this was down from $25,100 in 1986." (p6-7) "Nationwide, the number of retail jobs grew 18 percent between 1986 and 1995, according to the Bureau of Labor Statistics." (p8)

Crispell, Diane. "Tomorrow's Markets: Retailing's Next Decade." American Demographics v19 n5 May 1997. p4,6-10. article-level access: <http://www.demographics.com/Publications/AD/97_ad/9705_ad/AD97052.htm> (ISSN0163-4089).

According to the National Retail Federation and the Center for Retailing Education and Research at the University of Florida, unexplained losses in the U.S. "differ widely according to the type of retailer--from a low of 0.33% at consumer electronic stores to 5.5% within camera/photo stores. A total of $43.8B [billion] was estimated lost by retailers in the most recent years. Supermarkets/grocery stores ranked first in loss with $6.9B (16%) followed by dept. stores with $4.9B (11%), and discount stores at $3.0B (7%)....Employee theft is slightly greater than shoplifting (38% v. 36%) in the estimation of retail security practitioners....Shoplifters are regarded as responsible for almost two-thirds of all losses to recorded music/video stores. The lowest loss from shoplifters (12% of total shrink) occurs in furniture stores." (unpaginated)

"Retail: Shrinkage Varies Ten-Fold According to Type of Business." Security Letter v27 n14 4 Aug 1997. (ISSN0363-4922).

RETIREES

see also INSURANCE, HEALTH--UNITED STATES--RETIREES; MOVING, HOUSEHOLD--UNITED STATES--RETIREES

RETIREES--UNITED STATES

The American Association of Retired Persons's "members range in age from 50 to well over 100, and more than half are under 65. More than one-third of the membership still work; 55% of the members are women and 45% are men. In addition, the Association currently has more than 50,000 members in 152 other countries, and most of these are not Americans." (p24-25)

Deets, Horace B. "'To Serve, Not to Be Served.'" World Health n4 Jul-Aug 1997. p24-25. (ISSN0043-8502).

RETIREES--UNITED STATES--WOMEN

"Women now make up 60 percent of the 65-and-over population in the United States. By 2010, almost half of adult women will be at least 50....Almost three-quarters of those over 65 who are living below the poverty line are women. Women average 14.7 years out of the labor force, compared with 1.6 years for men, according to...[Deborah Briceland-Betts, executive director of the Older Women's League in Washington]. Those years are averaged into Social Security records as zeroes. Payments are based on a worker's 35 highest-earning years." (p10,11)

Gardner, Marilyn. "New Outlooks on Retirement: Women Seek New Models for Later Years." The Christian Science Monitor v89 n244 13 Nov 1997. p10-11. The Christian Science Monitor search engine: <http://www.csmonitor.com/plweb-cgi/iops1.pl> To retrieve this article, enter the following search: ED=19971113 AND years. In the "retrieved list," click the title that matches this record. (ISSN0882-7729).

RETIREMENT--CANADA

In Canada, "today, for every person of retirement age there are five persons of working age. In 20 years, there will be one person of retirement age for every four persons of working age. When today's youth retire 40 years from now, that ratio will be just one to three." (p635)

Wayne, Elsie (MP-NB). "Government Orders: Canada Pension Plan Investment Board Act." Canada. Parliament. House of Commons. Debates. v135 n12 7 Oct 1997. p619-646. section-level access: <http://www.parl.gc.ca/36/1/parlbus/chambus/house/debates/012_1997-10-07/han012-e.htm#LINK227> (ISSN0704-5603). (X3-361E).

RETIREMENT--LATIN AMERICA (v26)

RETIREMENT--UNITED STATES (v26)

In the U.S., "the elderly are expected to rise from 12 percent of the population to 20 percent by 2050. The number of retirees will rise from 34 million to 80 million....There were more than five workers for each retiree in 1960. Today, there are 3.3. And by 2030, there will be just two workers to pay all the taxes required to pay the benefits of each retiree." (p15 secA)

Bartlett, Bruce. "Comment: There's No 'Free Lunch' with Social Security." Detroit News 3 Dec 1997. p15 secA.

RETIREMENT--UNITED STATES--PUBLIC OPINION

According to a 1997 survey conducted by the Employee Benefit Research Institute, in the U.S., "66 percent of those polled want to retire before 65. Thirty-three percent want to retire by 55....Of those polled age 53 and older, 47 percent expected Social Security and employer funded pension plans to make up the bulk of their retirement income. But of those 33 and younger, 61 percent said they expect their personal savings to be the most important source of retirement income." (p21 secA)

Ryan, Richard A./Hunter, George. "Preparing for the Golden Years: Retirement Shock: Millions Learn Their Savings Are Short." Detroit News and Free Press 16 Nov 1997. p1,21 secA.

RETIREMENT INCOME--CANADA

According to Kevin Moriarty, a principal at Toronto-based William M. Mercer Ltd., Canada's largest pension consulting firm, "by the time they leave the workforce, people need to have at least $100,000 stashed away for every $10,000 a year they hope to generate in retirement income from annuities; in other words, a $50,000 income would require $500,000 in savings. To reach that level, a 35-year-old investor would have to save $5,000 a year in constant dollars inside an RRSP [Registered Retirement Savings Plan] for 30 years and earn an annual return on investments of eight per cent. If the same person waited until age 45 to begin saving, he or she would need to put away $14,000 a year for 20 years. The figure jumps to a staggering $35,000 a year if the saving begins at age 55 and there are only 10 years left until retirement." (p39-40) "Even among households in which the main income earner is between 55 and 64, fully 48 per cent have less than $50,000 in investments (excluding the equity in their homes), according to Marketing Solutions. Only 17 per cent are sitting on a nest egg worth more than $250,000, while 35 per cent have accumulated between $50,000 and $250,000." (p41)

Fennell, Tom/Cazzin, Julie/Janigan, Mary. "Cover: Getting Ready for Retirement." Maclean's v110 n39 29 Sep 1997. p38-41. (ISSN0024-9262).

RETIREMENT INCOME--UNITED STATES

"Sixty-nine percent of [U.S.] workers said they now save regularly, up from 61 percent from a year ago. But only 27 percent of working Americans have any idea of how much money they will need to retire when they want and with the standard of living they desire....Financial planners generally advise clients they will need at least 70 percent of current net pay in retirement to maintain the same standard of living they enjoy now. That goes up to 80 percent if they still have a mortgage and a little higher if they own multiple homes, said Marilyn Gunther, a certified financial planner at the Center for Financial Planning in Southfield....Gunther estimates that it will take more than $1 million in savings for a 25-year-old worker today to enjoy a comfortable retirement." (p21 secA)

Ryan, Richard A./Hunter, George. "Preparing for the Golden Years: Retirement Shock: Millions Learn Their Savings Are Short." Detroit News and Free Press 16 Nov 1997. p1,21 secA.

RETIREMENT INCOME--UNITED STATES--BABY BOOM GENERATION--ATTITUDES (v26)

RETIREMENT INCOME--UNITED STATES--PUBLIC OPINION

In the U.S., "workers' confidence in their retirement income prospects dropped sharply during the past year, according to the 1996 Retirement Confidence Survey (Yakoboski & Schiffenbauer, 1997). In 1996, 19% of workers were very confident that they would have enough money to live comfortably throughout retirement compared with 22% in 1995. An additional 43% were somewhat confident in 1996 regarding retirement income compared to 52% in 1995. Although workers believe that their retirement income prospects will depend heavily on their personal savings decisions, only 62% report saving regularly and more than one-third have nothing saved for retirement." (p25)

Todd, Kelly J./DeVaney, Sharon A. "Financial Planning for Retirement by Parents of College Students." Financial Counseling and Planning v8 n1 1997. p25-32. (ISSN1052-3073).

RETIREMENT PENSIONS

see PENSIONS

RETURN MIGRATION--AFRICA (v26)

RETURN MIGRATION--ANGOLA (v26)

RHEUMATIC FEVER--UNITED STATES (v26)

RHINOSCEROSES--TIGERS (v26)

RICE--VARIETIES--ASIA (v26)

RICE TRADE (v26)

Rice trade under state trading enterprises in the Asia-Pacific Economic Cooperation region "was valued at $1.2 billion during 1990-95. Importing state traders such as the JFA [Japan Food Agency], China's COFCO [National Cereal, Oils, and Foodstuffs Import/Export Corporation], Indonesia's BULOG [National Logistics Authority], and the Philippines' STE imported an average of more than $755 million of rice annually during 1990-95. In terms of market share, they held 14 percent of the world market, with Indonesia BULOG holding nearly 8 percent during the period....Japan and Indonesia imported 100 percent of their countries' rice imports...." (p31)

Langley, Suchada/U.S. Dept. of Agriculture. Economic Research Service. "State Trading Enterprises in the APEC Region: Grain Markets." APEC: International Agriculture and Trade Reports Situation and Outlook Series Aug 1997. p29-32.

World rice "trade increased to a record 21 million tons in 1995 and has remained at an elevated level since then. From 1980/81 through 1990/91, world rice trade had accounted for under 4 percent of total use and never reached 14 million tons. Since 1995, trade has accounted for almost 5 percent of total use." (p12)

Childs, Nathan/U.S. Dept. of Agriculture. Economic Research Service. "Commodity Spotlight: High Prices Pull Up U.S. Rice Acreage." Agricultural Outlook Sep 1997. p10-12.

RICE TRADE--ARKANSAS (v26)

RICE TRADE--ASIA

"Japan, which has the highest yield among the major rice producers..., irrigates 99 percent of its riceland--as does South Korea, which ranks a close second. In Bangladesh, where farmers harvest less than half as much rice per hectare as the Japanese or Koreans do, the irrigated share falls to 24 percent. Three fourths of the riceland in Bangladesh is subject to the whims of the monsoon." (p41)

Brown, Lester R. "The Agricultural Link: How Environmental Deterioration Could Disrupt Economic Progress." Worldwatch Paper n136 Aug 1997. p5-73.

RICE TRADE--CALIFORNIA

California rice "producers achieve average yields 40 percent higher than in the South....California, which grows primarily medium grain rice and accounts for the bulk of the U.S. medium grain crop, reported rice plantings of 515,000 acres, up 13,000 from 1996, including a 7,000-acre increase for medium grain. An additional 5,000 acres of the increase was in short grain plantings, accounting for the entire 25-percent increase in U.S. short grain acreage....California short grain acreage has increased steadily over the past 2 years--from 10,000 acres in 1995 to 13,000 in 1996 and 18,000 for 1997." (p11)

Childs, Nathan/U.S. Dept. of Agriculture. Economic Research Service. "Commodity Spotlight: High Prices Pull Up U.S. Rice Acreage." Agricultural Outlook Sep 1997. p10-12.

RICE TRADE--CHINA

"China's rice exports are projected to increase slowly from around 300,000 tons in 1995/96 to 400,000 tons in 2005/06....Rice imports are projected to increase from 850,000 tons in 1995/96 to 1.5 million tons in 2005/06....Rice output for 1996 was 195 million tons (paddy basis), up 5.3 percent from the 185-million-ton 1995 crop....The primary reason for the increase stemmed from a 2-percent increase in area and a 3.2-percent increase in yields." (p28) "The japonica crop accounts for about 27 percent of China's total rice crop, while indica crops account for about 73 percent. Urban retail prices for japonica rice fell from 3,480 RMB [renminbi] per ton in January to 3,210 RMB in December. Urban retail prices for indica rice fell slightly from 3,040 RMB in January to 2,970 RMB in December 1996....China's rice imports soared from 700,000 tons in 1993/94 to 2.0 million tons in 1994/95 but fell to 850,000 tons in 1995/96....China's rice exports dropped sharply from 1.5 million in 1993/94 to 32,000 tons in 1994/95, but rebounded to 300,000 tons in 1995/96." (p29)

Crook, Frederick W./U.S. Dept. of Agriculture. Economic Research Service. "Good Grain Crop Projected for 1997." China: International Agriculture and Trade Reports Situation and Outlook Series Jun 1997. p26-31.

RICE TRADE--LOUISIANA (v26)

RICE TRADE--MISSISSIPPI (v26)

RICE TRADE--UNITED STATES (v26)

"About 40 percent of Texas [rice] producers typically harvest a ratoon crop, accounting for about 10 percent of the state's total output....Arkansas, which produces over 40 percent of the U.S. crop, accounts for 69 percent of the net gain in U.S. rice area this year....Mississippi and Missouri expanded long grain plantings 29 and 8 percent....Texas is the only state to report declining rice area for 1997. Long grain area--which accounts for over 95 percent of the the state's crop--is down 35,000 acres, a 12-percent decline, while medium grain area fell 5,000 acres, a 50-percent decline....Texas rice acreage...had been declining steadily in recent years and is down nearly 100,000 acres from the early 1990's and nearly 300,000 since 1980/81." (p10)

Childs, Nathan/U.S. Dept. of Agriculture. Economic Research Service. "Commodity Spotlight: High Prices Pull Up U.S. Rice Acreage." Agricultural Outlook Sep 1997. p10-12.

"For long grain rice--which accounts for nearly 70 percent of U.S. rice production--ending stocks in 1996/97 were only 9.1 million cwt [hundredweight], yielding a stocks-to-use ratio of 7.4 percent....The medium grain situation in 1996/97 was less tight, with ending stocks estimated at 14.2 million cwt and the stocks-to-use ratio at 24 percent, although both were down from a year earlier. An 11-percent increase in production in 1996, with only a very small increase in exports in 1996/97, account for the relatively abundant medium grain supply situation." (p11)

Childs, Nathan/U.S. Dept. of Agriculture. Economic Research Service. "Commodity Spotlight: High Prices Pull Up U.S. Rice Acreage." Agricultural Outlook Sep 1997. p10-12.

In the U.S., in August 1997, "rice heading advanced to 65% complete, 12 percentage points behind last year but only 2 points behind the average....Overall, 4% of the [rice] acreage was harvested, behind the average of 9%." (p14)

U.S. Dept. of Commerce. Dept. of Agriculture. "National Agricultural Summary: August 4-10, 1997: Highlights." Weekly Weather and Crop Bulletin v84 n32 12 Aug 1997. p14. (ISSN0043-1974).

RICHES

see WEALTH

RIFLES, ASSAULT

see ASSAULT RIFLES

RIGHT OF ASYLUM

see ASYLUM, RIGHT OF

RIGHT TO DIE

see EUTHANASIA

RIGHT TO DIE--UNITED STATES (v26)

RIGHTS, HUMAN

see HUMAN RIGHTS

RIGS, OIL

see OIL WELL DRILLING RIGS

RIOTS--CALIFORNIA--LOS ANGELES, 1992 (v26)

In Los Angeles, California, "in the violence of April 29th through May 2nd [1992], 52 people were killed: 25 African-Americans, 15 Latinos, 2 Asians, 7 Whites, and 3 unknown (information from Los Angeles Coroners' Office). Another 2,664 persons suffered injuries, 227 critical (L.A. County Department of Health Services). The L.A. fire department reported more than 8,000 structural fires, at least 517 of which were residential dwellings....In addition, an estimated 20,000 individuals lost their jobs as a result of the fires and looting that destroyed or closed down businesses and stores; at least 5,000 of these jobs were permanently eradicated (Sahagun & Rivera, 1992)." (p236)

Stuber, Margaret L./Nader, Kathleen O./Pynoos, Robert S. "The Violence of Despair: Consultation to a HeadStart Program Following the Los Angeles Uprising of 1992." Community Mental Health Journal v33 n3 Jun 1997. p235-241. (ISSN0010-3853).

RITALIN (REGISTERED TRADEMARK)

see METHYLPHENIDATE HYDROCHLORIDE

RIVER BLINDNESS
see ONCHOCERIASIS
RIVERS--BANGLADESH--INDIA
The Ganga, Brahmaputra, and Barak (Meghna) system "has an annual discharge of a little less than 1,000 million acre-feet (maf) of water of which some 100 maf is generated within Bangladesh. For the rest, the Barak contributes 50 maf, the Brahmaputra some 430 maf, and the Ganga the balance. The Ganga has to sustain a population (1991) of 356 million people and a cultivated area of more than 60 million hectares (ha) in India and 34 million people and 3.14 million ha in Bangladesh. The corresponding figures for the Brahmaputra basin are 29 million people and 12.15 million ha in India and 81.40 million people and 3.75 million ha in Bangladesh. These basin-dependent populations will double over the next half century by which time demographic stability may be attained. As much as 30 percent of the total annual discharge of all rivers in India is contributed by the Brahmaputra, which constitutes the vast bulk of the surplus waters available in what is otherwise rapidly becoming a water-short subcontinent." (p186-187)
Verghese, B. G. "Water Conflicts in South Asia." Studies in Conflict & Terrorism v20 n2 Apr-Jun 1997. p185-194. (ISSN1057-610X).
RIVERS--ENVIRONMENTAL ASPECTS--GERMANY (v26)
RIVERS--ENVIRONMENTAL ASPECTS--ILLINOIS
"The Mackinaw River wends for 130 miles through farm fields and towns, draining a 1,100-square-mile watershed in central Illinois....Although much of the Mackinaw remains in good shape, it has been degraded from siltation and nutrient pollution, leading to disappearing aquatic life. In fact, fish and mussel species have disappeared by about 25 percent, according to Jim McMahon, the [Nature] Conservancy's central Illinois area director." (p28)
Kinch, John A. "Landmarks: Pulling Together." Nature Conservancy v47 n4 Jul-Aug 1997. p28. (ISSN0028-5200).
RIVERS--HAWAII (v26)
ROADS
see also COMMERCIAL STRIPS; FOREST ROADS; RACETRACKS (AUTOMOBILE RACING); TRAILS
ROADS--CANADA
In Canada, "the 1992 federal-provincial study revealed that 30% of the 24,449 kilometres National Highway System was deficient in minimum geometric design, service ability, structural strength or riding comfort standards. Of the 3,534 bridges on the system, 790 would require major strengthening or rehabilitation within the next five years." (p12)
"Association News: Federation of Canadian Municipalities: National Transportation and Communications." Municipal World v107 n8 Aug 1997. p11-12. (ISSN0027-3589).
ROADS--CHINA
In China, "in 1996, all but one county (in a remote part of Tibet) is linked by a road network. More than 97 percent of towns and townships and 79 percent of administrative villages can be reached by car and truck....Improvements can be made in the road system, as currently only 23 percent of China's roads are paved with asphalt or concrete." (p18)
Crook, Frederick W./U.S. Dept. of Agriculture. Economic Research Service. "Input Supplies Adequate for 1997." China: International Agriculture and Trade Reports Situation and Outlook Series Jun 1997. p16-18.
ROADS--ENVIRONMENTAL ASPECTS--UNITED STATES
"Studies by the Forest Service and other fire scientists have found that more than 90 percent of all wildfires in the United States are human-caused, and 75 percent of these start within 265 feet of a road....There are currently 378,000 miles of roads throughout the national forest system, which is eight times the mileage of the U.S. interstate highway system. That's enough to circle the earth nearly 15 times....The General Accounting Office has found that 70 percent of the Nation's subsidized logging roads are used almost exclusively by private timber companies and their contractors....While the environment suffers and the timber industry enriches itself, the taxpayer picks up the tab. In fact, the taxpayer pays toward the costs of each road three times: first to build the road, second to maintain it, and third to fix the environmental damage caused by road-induced fires and flood." (pS9456)
Kerry, John F. (Sen.-Mass.). "Department of the Interior and Related Agencies Appropriations Act, 1998." Congressional Record. Daily ed. v143 n124 17 Sep 1997. pS9450-9485. section/page-level access: <http://thomas.loc.gov/cgi-bin/query/R?r105:FLD001:S09455:> (ISSN0363-7239). (X1.1A.105/1).
ROADS--FINANCE
The U.S. annually hands "out $55 billion in direct subsidies and another $66 billion for parking and other road-related services. Its support of road transport outweighs that of public transit by at least seven to one. In Japan, supports for road use have been estimated at $16 billion, with up to another $50 billion for road-related services and parking. Because of higher fuel taxes, such subsidies are far lower in Europe and in some cases negative, ranging from a road subsidy of some $13 billion per year in Germany to an annual net tax on road users of about $5 billion in both France and the Netherlands." (p28-29)
Flavin, Christopher/Dunn, Seth. "Rising Sun, Gathering Winds: Policies to Stabilize the Climate and Strengthen Economies." Worldwatch Paper n138 Nov 1997. p5-84.
ROADS--ILLINOIS--MAINTENANCE AND REPAIR (v26)
ROADS--INDIA--ANDHRA PRADESH
"The state of Andhra Pradesh, with a population of 70 million, is the fifth largest state in India. Of the state's 164,000 kilometer road network, sixty percent of the traffic is carried on about 40,000 kilometers of State Highways and Major District Roads, many of which are single lane. With trucks or buses accounting for 65 to 90 percent of motorized vehicles, many of the road links are already congested. Meanwhile, vehicle registration has increased by approximately 16 percent a year during the last five years, and traffic is projected to grow at least seven to eight percent a year."
World Bank. "India State Highway Project to Overhaul Andhra Pradesh's Road Network: AP's Road Network." Press Release 18 Jun 1997. document-level access: <http://www.worldbank.org/html/extdr/extme/1392.htm>
ROADS--LATIN AMERICA--UNITED STATES (v26)
ROADS--MICHIGAN (v26)
"Trucks are responsible for about 40 percent of road costs, but historically have paid only 20 percent or so of Michigan's road fees and taxes. The Michigan Department of Transportation (MDOT) confirms this figure--but the 40-percent cost share applies only to the roads that trucks actually travel, not the entire road system, which includes smaller streets trucks do not use....The 20-percent share of taxes and fees doesn't include a recent hike in the motor carrier taxes that truckers pay." (p6 secA)
"Weighting on Trucks." Detroit News 24 Jun 1997. p6 secA.
ROADS--MICHIGAN--FINANCE (v26)
ROADS--MICHIGAN--MAINTENANCE AND REPAIR (v26)
A federal "study estimates that 60 percent--or 435 miles--of the 720 miles of highways in Michigan's urban areas are in poor to just fair condition....Drivers in Grand Rapids pay $10.9 million a year and Flint motorists pay $9.1 million. People in Ann Arbor pay $5 million even though just 9 percent of their roads are deemed in poor or mediocre condition, compared to 34 percent of the roads falling into that federal category in Metro

Detroit." (p4 secA)

Stertz, Bradley A./Shepardson, David. "Road to Repair: Bad Roads Cost Drivers $150 Million." Detroit News 16 Sep 1997. p1,4 secA.

ROADS--MICHIGAN--MAINTENANCE AND REPAIR --TAXATION--PUBLIC OPINION (v26)

ROADS--MICHIGAN--WASHTENAW COUNTY --MAINTENANCE AND REPAIR (v26)

ROADS--NEW MEXICO--MAINTENANCE AND REPAIR (v26)

ROADS--QUEBEC (PROVINCE)--MAINTENANCE AND REPAIR (v26)

ROADS--QUEBEC (PROVINCE)--MAINTENANCE AND REPAIR--FINANCE (v26)

ROADS--SWEDEN (v26)

ROADS--UNITED STATES (v26)

"Across America, our infrastructure is crumbling. Thirty percent of our interstate system needs to be rebuilt; 25 percent of our bridges are structurally deficient. There are 41,000 people killed on our highways every year. And we are told that 30 percent of those deaths are caused by inadequate construction of the highways....Congestion in our 50 largest cities costs $51 billion a year." (pH2991)

Shuster, Bud (Rep.-Pa.). "Concurrent Resolution on the Budget, Fiscal Year 1998." Congressional Record. Daily ed. v143 n67 20 May 1997. pH2960-3065. section/page-level access: <http://thomas.loc.gov/cgi-bin/query/R?r105:FLD001:H02991:> (ISSN0363-7239). (X1.1A.105/1).

In the U.S., "over the last 15 years, direct Government expenditures for construction and reconstruction of forest roads may total $3.2 billion. It is estimated that for the national forest road system alone, over the years, this has resulted in the construction of 380,000 miles in forest roads....There is enough mileage through our national forests to circle the globe 15 times....We have built 8 miles of road through pristine national forests for every 1 mile that has been constructed in the National Interstate Highway System. The result of all these years of construction is that now we face $440 million worth of backlog of road maintenance." (pS9460)

Torricelli, Robert G. (Sen.-N.J.). "Department of the Interior and Related Agencies Appropriations Act, 1998." Congressional Record. Daily ed. v143 n124 17 Sep 1997. pS9450-9485. section/page-level access: <http://thomas.loc.gov/cgi-bin/query/R?r105:FLD001:S09459:> (ISSN0363-7239). (X1.1A.105/1).

In the U.S., "the primary use of the national forest road system is recreation. All told, about 97 percent of the road system in any given national forest is open to recreational use. Ten years ago, recreation use on the national forests was less than 250 million visits. Today, recreation use is approaching 350 million visits, an increase of 40 percent." (pS9458)

Burns, Conrad R. (Sen.-Mont.). "Department of the Interior and Related Agencies Appropriations Act, 1998." Congressional Record. Daily ed. v143 n124 17 Sep 1997. pS9450-9485. section/page-level access: <http://thomas.loc.gov/cgi-bin/query/R?r105:FLD001:S09457:> (ISSN0363-7239). (X1.1A.105/1).

ROADS--UNITED STATES--FINANCE

The U.S. "transportation department spent $77 per Michigan resident in the 1996 fiscal year, for a total of $743 million, according to...[a] study by the Northeast Midwest Institute, a non-profit policy organization....Michigan's per-capita share of U.S. transportation dollars compares to $879 per capita in...Alaska, $296 in Wyoming and $252 in Montana....Connecticut, a small state with a third of Michigan's 9.6 million population, got $179 per person. New Jersey, which has 8 million residents, got $148 per person from the federal agency that funds roads, bridges and other transportation projects." (p1 secC)

Zagaroli, Lisa. "Metro: State Last in U.S. Road Money." Detroit News 11 Jul 1997. p1 secC.

The U.S. House of Representatives "opted to support a substitute amendment by Rep. Norm Dicks (D-WA) that...reduced the road construction and reconstruction budget from $160 million to $154 million and cut purchaser road credits from $50 to $25 million....According to the General Accounting Office road construction costs from 1992-94 were nearly $245 million. Road building is also a major contributor to below cost timber sales which cost taxpayers $1 billion between FY92-94." (p20)

Vincent, Brian. "House Votes for Roads, More Roads: Rep. Dicks Proposal Undercuts Conservation Efforts." Northwest Conservation Sum 1997. p20.

ROADS--UNITED STATES--MAINTENANCE AND REPAIR (v26)

In the U.S., "maintenance is keeping any forest road, timber, recreation, or general purpose, in good repair. The average cost of maintaining a mile of road is about $543. The average cost of reconstructing a mile of road is more than $12,000 a mile....According to the Forest Service, logging roads are built at a lower standard and cost less than recreation and general purpose roads. Logging roads are usually unpaved dirt and are often usable only by high-clearance vehicles, while recreation and general purpose roads generally are either paved or gravel and are usable by all passenger cars. On average, purchaser credit logging roads cost $15,000 per mile in 1996, while recreation roads cost $63,000, and general purpose roads cost $65,000 per mile." (pS9452)

Bryan, Richard H. (Sen.-Nev.). "Department of the Interior and Related Agencies Appropriations Act, 1998." Congressional Record. Daily ed. v143 n124 17 Sep 1997. pS9450-9485. section/page-level access: <http://thomas.loc.gov/cgi-bin/query/R?r105:FLD001:S09450:> (ISSN0363-7239). (X1.1A.105/1).

According to a federal study, "49 percent of American voters prefer fixing bad roads over new road construction....Consumers nationwide are paying an estimated $4.8 billion to fix their cars because of damage from bad highways. The cost calculations are based on federal formulas that show tire wear on good highways runs 1 penny a mile, but costs 1.5 cents on a poor road. Likewise, maintenance costs from poor roads jump to 6.47 cents for every mile driven from 4.2 cents a mile on a good freeway." (p4 secA)

Stertz, Bradley A./Shepardson, David. "Road to Repair: Bad Roads Cost Drivers $150 Million." Detroit News 16 Sep 1997. p1,4 secA.

"A study by the American Petroleum Institute focused on what percentage of motor-related taxes and fees actually goes to pay for roads and bridges....The states spending the smallest percentage of their motor-related tax money on roads were Indiana, 33 percent; Connecticut, 33.2 percent; and South Carolina, 35.4 percent. The national average was 58 percent in 1994, the most recent year with complete information." (p8)

"Stateline: Road Fees Don't Pay for Roads." State Legislatures v23 n8 Sep 1997. p8. (ISSN0147-6041).

ROADS--UNITED STATES. FOREST SERVICE

The U.S. "Forest Service is continuing its efforts to reduce the number of roads. In recent years, the Forest Service has annually reduced more than three times as much road mileage as compared to new construction. In 1996, the Forest Service reduced 1,400 miles of roads. For the past 6 years combined, the Forest Service has reduced over 18,000 miles of roads." (pS9459)

Smith, Gordon (Sen.-Oreg.). "Department of the Interior and Related Agencies Appropriations Act, 1998." Congressional

Record. Daily ed. v143 n124 17 Sep 1997. pS9450-9485. section/page-level access: <http://thomas.loc.gov/cgi-bin/query/R?r105:FLD001:S09458:> (ISSN0363-7239). (X1.1A.105/1).

According to the U.S. "General Accounting Office, Forest Service road construction costs from 1992-94 were nearly $245 million....According to the Forest Service, nearly 1,000 communities get their drinking water from national forest streams that are frequently impacted by logging road construction....There are nearly 380,000 miles of roads in national forests....The [Forest] Service says it has a backlog of $440 million of road maintenance needs." (p8)

Vincent, Brian. "Roads Reform Rejected." Northwest Conservation n32 Nov 1997. p8.

ROADS--VISIBILITY

"European research, especially that conducted by the Swedish National Road Administration, has examined the effect of UV [ultraviolet] headlights on highway visibility. UV headlights--with emission spectra between 320 nanometers and 400 nanometers--and fluorescent road markings were used to create a full-light effect in conditions of poor visibility without blinding the oncoming traffic." (p2) Tests in the U.S. found that "the UV headlights provided a very noticeable increase in delineation visibility. In dynamic testing, the mean subjective rating of the roadway delineation with the UV headlights was 19 percent higher than with regular low beams. In the static testing, with the UV headlights and UV-activated pavement markings, subjects were able to see an average of 25 percent farther along the edge line and 29 percent more of the center skip lines. In the static testing, the subjective rating of visibility increased 47 percent with the UV headlights." (p6)

Mahach, Karen R./Knoblauch, Richard L./Simmons, Carole J./Nitzburg, Marsha/Arens, John B./Tignor, Samuel C./U.S. Dept. of Transportation. Federal Highway Administration. "A Preliminary Field Evaluation of Ultraviolet-Activated Fluorescent Roadway Delineation." Public Roads v61 n1 Jul-Aug 1997. p2-7. (ISSN0033-3735).

ROADS--WASHINGTON (STATE)

"If all of Washington's highways and logging roads were laid end to end, the result would be a stretch of asphalt and dirt 95,000 miles long. A person driving the entire length of that road would circumnavigate the earth nearly four times." (p12)

Friedman, Greg. "The End of the Road?: The Bad, The Ugly and the Awful Reasons We Don't Need Any More Roads." Northwest Conservation Sum 1997. p12-13.

ROADSIDE BUSINESS DISTRICTS

see COMMERCIAL STRIPS

ROBBERIES, BANK

see BANK ROBBERIES

ROBBERY--ONTARIO--TORONTO

In 1995, the city of Toronto "reported 5,938 incidents [of robbery], and 5,833 last year....So far this year, Toronto...has had 267 bank/financial...[institution] robberies and 672 'swarmings' involving three or more robbers, usually youths. And 1,011 retail businesses have been robbed." (unpaginated)

"Intl. Security Briefs." Security Letter v27 n18 16 Oct 1997. (ISSN0363-4922).

ROBBERY--UNITED STATES

In the U.S., "robbery declined 7% over the previous year to 202 robberies per 100K [thousand] population. Monetary loss from robbery is about $500M [million] with bank robberies averaging the highest of categories at $4,207 and gas station robberies the lowest at $487." (unpaginated)

"Serious Crime in the US Declines for the Fifth Consecutive Year." Security Letter v27 n18 16 Oct 1997. (ISSN0363-4922).

ROCK FEVER

see BRUCELLOSIS

ROMANIA--ECONOMIC CONDITIONS (v26)

ROSACEA--UNITED STATES (v26)

ROSES--UNITED STATES

"The rose is still the best selling individual flower [in the U.S.], with more than 1.1 billion stems sold last year, about 4 stems per capita. Retail florists report that roses accounted for 17 percent of floral item sales in 1996. Imports supplied 800 million stems, 73 percent of the total. According to the National Promoflor Council, floral arrangements lead in annual sales of fresh cut flowers, with 55 percent, followed by bouquets/bunches (23 percent), single stems (16 percent), loose boxed (3 percent), and corsages, boutonnieres, and unspecified (3 percent)." (p10)

Johnson, Doyle. "Commodity Spotlight: 'Green' Industry Grower Receipts to Exceed $11 Billion." Agricultural Outlook Jul 1997. p9-10.

ROTARY DRILLING--UNITED STATES (v26)

RUBBER INDUSTRY AND TRADE (v26)

RUBBER INDUSTRY AND TRADE--SRI LANKA

"Sri Lankan rubber commands 15 percent of the world market for industrial tires....In 1994, after the private management companies improved plantation operating conditions, productivity reached an average of 960 kg per hectare. However, this was much lower than its neighboring producers--who averaged over 1,400 kg per hectare....World rubber consumption has increased substantially in the last three decades from 8.8 million tons in 1960 to 15.1 million tons in 1990."

World Bank. "Sri Lankan Rubber Industry Ready to Take Off in Global Market." Press Release 20 Aug 1997. document-level access: <http://www.worldbank.org/html/extdr/extme/1445.htm>

RUBBISH

see REFUSE AND REFUSE DISPOSAL

RUBELLA--UNITED STATES (v26)

RUG AND CARPET INDUSTRY--EMPLOYMENT--INDIA--CHILDREN

"There are 300,000 children working to produce India's handwoven wool carpets. Ninety percent of these children, or about 270,000, are bonded laborers....A skilled child carpet knotter will earn at most ten rupees a day, far below minimum wage....Carpet exports totalled more than half a billion dollars in 1994 and $650 million in 1995. There are currently more than 2,000 carpet exporters in India, representing a one hundred-fold increase in about two decades....Between 75 and 80 percent of India's handwoven wool carpets are produced in the 'carpet belt' of Uttar Pradesh." (p608) "Seventy-five percent of the carpet-makers in this region are children....Of the 300,000 children producing carpets in India, as many as 50 percent were trafficked from one region or state to another by carpet agents." (p609) "One study of child weavers found that 71 percent reported being beaten for mistakes in weaving...." (p612)

Tucker, Lee. "Child Slaves in Modern India: The Bonded Labor Problem." Human Rights Quarterly v19 n3 Aug 1997. p572-629. (ISSN0275-0392).

RUG AND CARPET INDUSTRY--EMPLOYMENT--SOUTH ASIA--CHILDREN

Rugmark, a two-year-old carpet label, was "founded by a coalition of German and Indian groups whose inspectors ensure that participating carpet producers use neither enslaved nor 'free' child workers....Over 200 carpet makers in India, Nepal and Pakistan pay the label a small fee to participate. More than 250,000 of their rugs have been exported with child-free labor, and their fees have funded education and rehabilitation programs for released children....In South Asia, 90% of child carpet workers are slaves, says UNICEF [United Nations Children's Fund]. In India alone, the carpet industry is a $700 million business, so it is not surprising that government officials and local police overlook or even cover up the practice." (p10)

Barry, Skip. "Taking Aim at Child Slavery." Dollars and Sense n212 Jul-Aug 1997. p10. (ISSN0012-5245).

RUHR (GERMANY : REGION) (v26)

RUNAWAY CHILDREN--UNITED STATES (v26)

RURAL CONDITIONS

see LABOR--UNITED STATES--RURAL CONDITIONS; UNITED STATES--EMPLOYMENT--RURAL CONDITIONS

RURAL DEVELOPMENT--COLORADO--STEAMBOAT SPRINGS (v26)

RURAL DEVELOPMENT--UNITED STATES (v26)

RURAL POPULATION--AFRO-AMERICAN AGED (v26)

RURAL POPULATION--UNITED STATES (v26)

RURAL-URBAN MIGRATION--CHINA

"The total floating population in China in 1992 was about 60 million, among which 35.75 million were from rural areas, and of this group, 28.74 million actively searched for employment. The average stay of employed rural workers in cities was 259 days (Du, 1994). In the recent past, the floating population has continued to increase. Lin (1993) reported that in the first two months of 1993, the period around the Chinese New Year, a total of 50 million farmers moved into cities to search for employment opportunities....From 1977 to 1992, the number of workers in rural areas increased by 135.7 million, while 80.5 million found employment in local industries, such as construction, transportation, commerce, and trade." (p103)

Yang, Dennis Tao. "China's Land Arrangements and Rural Labor Mobility." China Economic Review v8 n2 Fall 1997. p101-115. (ISSN1043-951X).

RURAL-URBAN MIGRATION--UNITED STATES

In the U.S., "the share of nonmetropolitan counties with more births than deaths declined from 90 percent in the 1980s to 73 percent in 1990-96, while the share with a population increase due to net migration jumped from 27 percent to 67 percent....The population of counties classified as nonmetropolitan in 1993 increased nearly 3 million between 1990 and 1996, compared with a gain of fewer than 1.3 million between 1980 and 1989. Nonmetro counties have seen a net gain of 1.8 million migrants from 1990 to 1996, compared with a loss of 1.4 million in the 1980s....Three-quarters of the nation's 2,304 nonmetro counties have grown in the 1990s, compared with 45 percent in the 1980s. In half of nonmetro counties, jobs are based on retirement, recreation, federal lands, or commuting to metro areas; more than 90 percent have grown in the 1990s." (p5)

"The Rural Rebound Keeps Rolling." Forecast v17 n6 Jun 1997. p5. article-level access: <http://www.demographics.com/Publications/FC/97_fc/9706_fc/FC97064.htm> (ISSN0732-1597).

RUSSIA--ARMED FORCES (v26)

"More than 75 percent of eligible Russian youths now routinely evade the draft. Desertion is also rampant, with as many as 120 cases reported each week. Partly this stems from an abusive initiation practice called 'dedovshchina', or the bullying of new conscripts by second-year servicemen. In 1993, 169 Russian conscripts reportedly died in hazing incidents....The proportion of noncommissioned manning in the air and air defense forces has dropped to 50 percent or below in many units; the Soviet high command had stipulated that units at 70 percent or below were incapable of military operations." (p90)

Lambeth, Benjamin S. "Russia's Wounded Military." Foreign Affairs v74 n2 Mar-Apr 1995. p86-98. (ISSN0015-7120).

RUSSIA--ARMED FORCES--EDUCATION

"By the end of next year, the Russian armed forces must shed half a million troops, slimming to an overall strength of 1.2 million, according to President Boris Yeltsin's latest decrees. Those cuts come on top of the 1.1 million men and women who have been discharged since 1992....The government...has done little to smooth the path into civilian life for officers obliged to take early retirement, often without a pension. 'We have an annual budget of 30 billion rubles (about $5 million),' says Capt. Valeri Barannovsky, the Defense Ministry official in charge of retraining programs to help former servicemen find new jobs....Germany paid approximately $74 million to retrain Soviet officers as part of a deal to have them withdraw quickly from the former East Germany....Basic courses [launched by the British Ministry of Defense], run by a college in Shcholkovo, where the military makes up 20 percent of the population, are offered in marketing, labor law, accounting, computers, and tax regulations, among other topics, packed into a four-month diploma....[Squadron Leader Max Jardim, the Royal Air Force officer overseeing the British project], whose program funds new courses at colleges only if he sees that their graduates find work, says that between 60 percent and 80 percent of the men and women going through his courses have found a job within four months of earning their diploma." (p1,7)

Ford, Peter. "International: Troops Retrain: Downsized and Out in Russia." The Christian Science Monitor v89 n219 7 Oct 1997. p1,7. The Christian Science Monitor search engine: <http://www.csmonitor.com/plweb-cgi/iops1.pl> To retrieve this article, enter the following search: ED=19971007 AND russia. In the "retrieved list," click the title that matches this record. (ISSN0882-7729).

RUSSIA--COMMERCE

"Russia has a trade surplus exceeding $20 billion; according to some estimates the surplus may be as high as $40 billion....Foreign products still make up as much as 60 percent of all the consumer goods sold in the country." (p316) "In 1995 and 1996,...the United States imported almost $1 billion annually of Russian aluminum." (p317)

Goldman, Marshall I. "Russia's Reform Effort: Is There Growth at the End of the Tunnel?" Current History v96 n612 Oct 1997. p313-318. (ISSN0011-3530).

RUSSIA--ECONOMIC CONDITIONS (v26)

"While Russian spokesmen point with pride to the fact that inflation in 1996 had been reduced to 22 percent and 80 percent of the state sector had been privatized, what they usually neglect to mention is that to stop inflation the government had to institute a tight money policy that pushed real interest rates up above 200 percent a year....Factories are lucky if they receive 10 percent of their bills in rubles rather than in barter or no payment at all. Workers go on average without their wages for three to four months at a time, and federal tax collection frequently reaches only 9 percent of the GDP, a significantly low rate of collection." (p317)

Goldman, Marshall I. "Russia's Reform Effort: Is There Growth at the End of the Tunnel?" Current History v96 n612 Oct 1997. p313-318. (ISSN0011-3530).

"Boris Berezovsky, head of one of Russia's biggest financial-industrial empires, bragged to the FINANCIAL TIMES that just seven tycoons control half of Russia's gross domestic product....Russia's government currency commission conservatively estimates that $150 billion has left the country over the past six years--$2 billion per month--or nearly three times the total of incoming foreign loans, aid and investment....According to Harvard University's Davis Center for Russian Studies, the number of small businesses in Russia plunged by 50,000, or about 7 percent, between 1995 and

1997." (p22)

Weir, Fred. "Robbing Russia Blind." In These Times v22 n3 11 Jan 1998. p21-23. (ISSN0160-5992).

In Russia, "the fall in production, down nearly 50 percent since 1991, continues, and unemployment is expected to exceed at least 10 percent by next year. Capital investment dropped 18 percent last year and 8 percent in the first quarter of this year....According to official statistics, 25 to 30 percent of Russians now live in poverty....Tens of millions of citizens, among them workers, teachers, doctors and soldiers, still have not received months of salaries....In a recent survey, 60 percent of Russian experts on military affairs responded that a coup, mutiny or complete disintegration of the army is likely within eighteen months." (p25)

Heuvel, Katrina Vanden/Cohen, Stephen F. "Moscow 97: The Other Russia." Nation v265 n5 11 Aug 1997. p24-26. (ISSN0027-8378).

In Russia, "after five years of reforms, more than 70 percent of domestic production now originates in the private sector; [and] inflation has dropped to a manageable 15-16 percent....Output has fallen by 40 percent since 1992....Poverty, now affecting one in four Russians, has risen dramatically."

World Bank. "World Bank Optimistic about Russia's Growth." Press Release 26 Sep 1997. document-level access: <http://www.worldbank.org/html/extdr/extme/1492.htm>

In Russia, "as a result of falling output and high inflation, real wages in 1996 averaged less than half of their level in 1991. Emerging open unemployment, along with the prevailing hidden unemployment and underemployment, is estimated to have reached 15 percent by 1997....In 1996 only about 40 percent of the work force was paid fully and on time....25-35 percent of Russia's population--primarily families with children, the unemployed, and the elderly living on minimum pension--is living in poverty today."

World Bank. "World Bank Loan Supports Russia's Social Reforms." Press Release 26 Jun 1997. document-level access: <http://www.worldbank.org/html/extdr/extme/1408.htm>

"In 1996 alone, gross domestic product (GDP) of the Russian Federation decreased by 6 per cent and industrial production by 5 per cent." (p26) "In 1996 profits earned amounted to slightly more than half--or 55 per cent--of profit levels recorded during the previous year. The proportion of loss-making enterprises in the main branches of the economy rose as high as 43 per cent....The number of persons employed was still declining, although at a slower rate--in 1996 employment decreased by 1 per cent compared with a 2 per cent decrease logged in 1995." (p27)

"News Section: National Conference on Enterprise Development and Job Creation in Russia." World of Work n21 Sep-Oct 1997. p26-28. (ISSN1020-0029).

RUSSIA--HISTORY--CIVIL WAR

"On 31 December 1994 Russian armor columns moved into central Grozny....Although Russian military leaders claimed to have highly restrictive rules of engagement (ROE) in place, artillery, rockets, and close air support killed 25,000 of Grozny's 400,000 inhabitants during the first month of the battle and destroyed half of the city's buildings....Russian forces...[numbered] some 6,000 men....Some 70 percent of the Russian tanks involved in the attack were wiped out....[There was a] 5:1 Russian advantage in troops (60,000 Army and Interior Ministry troops versus 12,000 Chechens in and around Grozny)...." (p382-383)

Rosenau, William G. "'Every Room Is a New Battle': The Lessons of Modern Urban Warfare." Studies in Conflict & Terrorism v20 n4 Oct-Dec 1997. p371-394. (ISSN1057-610X).

RUSSIA--POPULATION (v26)

RUSSIA. NAVY--OFFICERS (v26)

RWANDA--ECONOMIC CONDITIONS (v26)

RWANDA--POPULATION (v26)

SACRAMENTO-SAN JOAQUIN ESTUARY (CALIF.) (v26)

SAFETY, INDUSTRIAL

see INDUSTRIAL SAFETY

SAFETY CLOTHING

see PROTECTIVE CLOTHING

ST. PAUL (MINN.)--ECONOMIC CONDITIONS

"With a third of the city's land mass and a third of its population of 272,000, the East Side [of St. Paul, Minnesota] became a concern as it slid into poverty. Two-fifths of Ramsey County's welfare recipients live on the East Side, and nearly two-fifths of the neighborhood's workers are unemployed, according to the city's planning department. The percentage of residents in poverty jumped from 13.6 percent in 1980 to 29.5 percent in 1990." (p18)

Jossi, Frank. "Planning Practice: St. Paul Overhaul." Planning v63 n11 Nov 1997. p18-19. (ISSN0001-2610).

SALE OF MILITARY EQUIPMENT

see DEFENSE INDUSTRIES

SALES TAX--CANADA (v26)

SALES TAX--CANADA--PUBLIC OPINION (v26)

SALES TAX--MICHIGAN

"Michigan shoppers have skipped out on an estimated $500 million in sales taxes they should have paid on items from mail-order catalogues and the Internet during the past five years....A recent Michigan auditor general's report estimated the tax loss from out-of-state purchases at $134 million during 1995. That $134 million in unpaid sales taxes could have financed the construction of four minimum-security prisons, built seven miles of new rural freeway or paid the state's cost of running the judicial system for a year." (p1 secA)

Cain, Charlie. "Mail-Order Shoppers Cost State Millions." Detroit News 17 Nov 1997. p1,4 secA.

SALES TAX--QUEBEC (PROVINCE) (v26)

SALINE WATER CONVERSION--MIDDLE EAST (v26)

SALMON

see also CHINOOK SALMON

SALMON--BRITISH COLUMBIA (v26)

SALMON--COLUMBIA RIVER (v26)

SALMON--FRANCE--ALLIER RIVER

In France, "in 1996, only 67 salmon were counted on the upper Allier River....Located near the sources of the Allier River, [the] Saint-Etienne-du-Vigan [dam] sterilized 70 acres of the basin's best salmon spawning grounds. Before this 44-foot-high dam was built, the surrounding villages produced approximately 10 tons of salmon per year, which contributed heavily to the local economy." (p11)

Arnould, Marie. "Loire Dams to Be Dismantled for Salmon." World Rivers Review v12 n4 Aug 1997. p11. (ISSN0890-6211).

SALMON--SACRAMENTO RIVER (CALIF.) (v26)

SALMON FISHING--MICHIGAN, LAKE

On Lake Michigan in 1997, "anglers enjoyed their best catch rates since 1986--considered the peak of the fishery--according to Department of Natural Resources statistics. 'Overall, the catch rates for salmonoids for 1997 was 13.3 fish per 100 angler hours,' said Jerry Rakoczy, of the Great Lakes Research Station in Charlevoix. 'It's the second best year in the 13-year data series. And it was 19 percent greater than '85-'96 average.' Anglers caught 14.7 trout and salmon per 100 hours in 1986. The DNR only has reliable data back to 1985." (p2 secC)

"Venture Outdoors: Lake Michigan Has One of Its Best Fishing Seasons Ever in '97." Ann Arbor News 29 Nov 1997. p2 secC.

SALMON INDUSTRY--BRITISH COLUMBIA (v26)

SALMON INDUSTRY--UNITED STATES (v26)

"During first-half 1997, the United States imported 76 million pounds of Atlantic salmon, 12 percent more than in first-half 1996. The value of imports rose 19 percent to almost $180 million....Imported Atlantic salmon averaged $2.38 a pound in first-half 1997, up about 14 cents from a year earlier. Imports of filleted salmon continue to gain market share, increasing 30 percent in first-half 1997. Atlantic salmon fillets (fresh and frozen) accounted for 29 percent of all Atlantic salmon imports, compared with 16 percent in first-half 1996....U.S. fresh salmon imports rose 6 percent and their average price went up 14 percent to $2.42. The chief beneficiary of this increase was Canada, whose fresh salmon exports to the U.S. market rose 40 percent....After accounting for less than 200,000 pounds or only 1 percent of the imports of filleted Atlantic salmon in first-half 1996, Canada's shipments rose to 2.3 million in first-half 1997, or 11 percent of first-half imports." (unpaginated)

Harvey, Dave/U.S. Dept. of Agriculture. Economic Research Service. "Salmon Imports Rise 12 Percent." Aquaculture Outlook 3 Oct 1997.

SALMONELLOSIS--EUROPE--NORTH AMERICA --COSTS (v26)

SALMONELLOSIS--UNITED STATES

"Microbial pathogens of the genus Salmonella are among the leading causes of foodborne illness in the United States. Between 696,000 and 3,840,000 cases of foodborne salmonellosis occur each year, causing mild to acute gastrointestinal symptoms, such as abdominal pain, frequent diarrhea, vomiting, fever, and chills....These human illness cases and deaths cost society between $600 million and $3.5 billion each year in medical treatment, lost productivity, and loss of life....According to the CDC, the proportion of cases of salmonellosis due to Salmonella enteritidis increased from 5 percent in 1976 to 26 percent in 1994 when compared to all reported cases of salmonellosis reported to CDC. The CDC also reported that, between 1985 and 1995, there were 582 Salmonella enteritidis outbreaks (two or more people became ill from eating the same food), which accounted for 24,058 cases of illness, 2,290 hospitalizations, and 70 deaths....Raw or undercooked eggs and foods containing them have been implicated in about 80 percent of those Salmonella enteritidis outbreaks in which a food source was identified. And, 87 percent of the outbreaks between 1990 and 1994 were associated with eggs prepared in foodservice and in institutions, such as nursing homes and hospitals." (p27)

Lin, C. -T. Jordan/Morales, Roberta A./Ralston, Katherine/ U.S. Dept. of Agriculture. Economic Research Service. "Food Safety: Raw and Undercooked Eggs: A Danger of Salmonellosis." Food Review v20 n1 Jan-Apr 1997. p27-32. (ISSN1056-327X).

"The CDC estimates that 800,000 to 4 million cases of salmonellosis occur each year in the United States. Illness from the bacterium Salmonella usually appears 6 to 72 hours after eating contaminated food and lasts for a day or two. Common symptoms are nausea, diarrhea, stomach pain, and sometimes vomiting....USDA estimates that 3 percent of the annual cases of salmonellosis (24,000 to 120,000 cases) are attributed to consumption of insufficiently cooked ground beef. ERS [USDA Economic Research Service] calculates that the annual medical costs and productivity losses for these cases range between $30 million and $111 million, respectively." (p35)

Morrison, Rosanna Mentzer/Buzby, Jean C./Lin, C. -T. Jordan/ U.S. Dept. of Agriculture. Economic Research Service. "Food Safety: Irradiating Ground Beef to Enhance Food Safety." Food Review v20 n1 Jan-Apr 1997. p33-37. (ISSN1056-327X).

SALT LAKES--SASKATCHEWAN

"Waters in Saskatchewan vary in salinity, reaching highs of 400 grams per litre at Patience Lake, southeast of Saskatoon. This is more than 10 times saltier than the ocean." (p64) "Some 500 Saskatchewan lakes greater than four square kilometres are saline, about 0.5 percent of the province's total number of lakes. The largest body, at 180 square kilometres, is Big Quill Lake near Wynyard." (p65) "The Saskatchewan Minerals plant at Chaplin Lake produces some 100,000 tons...of sodium sulphate a year. A sister plant at nearby Ingebrigt Lake turns out 190,000 tons annually. The 64 square kilometres of Chaplin Lake...is a giant evaporation pan. To keep salt in solution for harvesting, the water level in the lake is maintained by Saskatchewan Minerals at about 30 centimetres....The Chaplin Lake deposit is a rich resource; Saskatchewan Minerals estimates its reserves at more than three million tons. Marketing its salt at approximately $130 a ton, the Chaplin plant has pumped many millions of dollars into the local economy since it started producing in 1946. The mine employs 42 people year-round, providing an alternate source of employment to the region's dominant industry, agriculture." (p67)

Marty, Sid. "The Brine of Life." Canadian Geographic v117 n5 Sep-Oct 1997. p62-72. (ISSN0008-3658).

SAN FRANCISCO (CALIF.)--ECONOMIC CONDITIONS --SOCIAL CONDITIONS

Due to the decline of traditional blue-collar, semiskilled jobs and the early 1990s recession, San Francisco has lost "more than 40,000 jobs....[Will Lightbourne, executive director of the Department of Human Services for the city and county of San Francisco,] indicated that about 15 percent of the population in San Francisco 'stood on the outside of prosperity.'" (p5) "An estimated 6,000 homeless people live in the Bay Area....Lightbourne says that 70 to 80 percent of the homeless come from outside San Francisco County....With one of the highest housing costs in the nation, the average monthly rent is $675 for a studio apartment and approximately $1265 for a two-bedroom apartment in San Francisco. However, only $345 is the average monthly payment for a person living on General Assistance." (p6) "Some 25,000-33,700 San Franciscans are HIV postive...." (p7)

Bryant, Shanta M. "'Real Pain' in Urban America." Christian Social Action v10 n10 Nov 1997. p4-7. (ISSN0897-0459).

SANCTIONS (INTERNATIONAL LAW)--UNITED STATES (v26)

SANCTUARY (LAW)

see ASYLUM, RIGHT OF

SAT (EDUCATIONAL TEST)

see SCHOLASTIC ASSESSMENT TEST

SAUDI ARABIA--COMMERCE--UNITED STATES

"The United States supplies over 20 percent of Saudi Arabia's import market and purchases about 15 percent of its exports. In 1996, our total bilateral trade reached $16.7 billion, an increase of almost 12 percent over 1995. By the end of that year, U.S. companies had invested over $6.7 billion in Saudi Arabia, at 46.2 percent the largest share of the total foreign investment in this country." (p73)

Kalicki, Jan H. "A Vision for the U.S.-Saudi and U.S.-Gulf Commercial Relationship." Middle East Policy v5 n2 May 1997. p73-78. (ISSN1061-1924).

SAUDI ARABIA--ECONOMIC CONDITIONS (v26)

SAVANNAH RIVER SITE (S.C.) (v26)

SAVING AND INVESTMENT--GREAT BRITAIN (v26)

SAVING AND INVESTMENT--NEW ZEALAND

In New Zealand, "with the marked increase in business income paid to the rest of the world, national savings fell by $1,296 million. Although total investment on fixed assets and stocks increased by only $309 million in the latest year, the large falls in domestic savings and migrant capital transfers resulted in investment increasingly funded by overseas borrowing. Net borrowing from the rest of the world has risen by $1,991 million and is now 4.9 per cent of Gross Domestic Product."

Statistics New Zealand. "National Accounts Production, Income and Expenditure--Year Ended March 1997." Press Release 12 Nov 1997. document-level access: <http://www.stats.govt.nz/statsweb.nsf/52518ce3e01f62f4cc256388000c48c0/cfd664903b1f92714c25654c00814a59?OpenDocument>

SAVING AND INVESTMENT--UNITED STATES (v26)

In the U.S., "national net savings fell from 7.1 to 1.8 percent from the 1970's to the 1990's....In a 1994 survey by the Employee Benefits Research Institute (EBRI): 14 percent of workers who were saving for their retirement did not know [how] much they had saved, and 13 percent saved less than $1,000. In another survey by Merrill Lynch of workers in their forties and early fifties, savings levels had dropped by 6 percent from 1988 to 1994. According to the 1996 Retirement Confidence Survey released earlier this year by the EBRI: Only one-third of American workers have calculated how much money they will need to have saved by retirement in order to live comfortably; of the workers that have tried to determine how much money they should be saving, only one-third felt very confident that they had determined an accurate figure; when asked how much they calculated that they would need to save, 42 percent could not give an amount; and less than 20 percent had a specific number with which to work." (pS4658)

Grassley, Charles E. (Sen.-Iowa). "Statements on Introduced Bills and Joint Resolutions." Congressional Record. Daily ed. v143 n65 16 May 1997. pS4658-4660. section/page-level access: <http://thomas.loc.gov/cgi-bin/query/R?r105:FLD001:S04658:> (ISSN0363-7239). (X1.1A.105/1).

In the U.S., "the 1995 Survey of Consumer Finances revealed that the proportion of all families who indicated retirement was an important reason for saving increased from 18 to 24% between 1989 and 1995 (Kennickell, Starr-McCluer & Sunden, 1997). Liquidity was the only savings motive considered more important than saving for retirement. Saving for liquidity was identified as important by one-third of all families in each of 1989 and 1995. Comparable figures for education were 8 and 11%, respectively." (p25)

Todd, Kelly J./DeVaney, Sharon A. "Financial Planning for Retirement by Parents of College Students." Financial Counseling and Planning v8 n1 1997. p25-32. (ISSN1052-3073).

In the U.S., "in 1996 saving amounted to 4.9 percent of disposable personal income, with the latter representing income, less taxes. This compares to 4.6 percent the year before and equals the rate averaged during the 1990s. However, the accumulation of financial wealth rose by 10.1 percent in 1996..., on top of a 13.3 percent gain in 1995. For the three prior years, the gains averaged just 5.0 percent." (p31)

Vincenzino, Joseph V. "Personal Income and Finances: Regional Comparisons." Statistical Bulletin v78 n4 Oct-Dec 1997. p27-32. (ISSN0790-8334).

"Americans have kicked almost $900 billion into 401(k) plans, the type offered by private-sector companies....29 million Americans feel comfortable enough about their 401(k) plans to sign up....KPMG will release a new survey of benefit plan participants....Preliminary figures, says...[Martha Priddy Patterson, a Washington-based benefits consultant at KPMG Peat Marwick], show that at firms with 200 or more employees, 66 percent of eligible workers are signed up. But that figure is up only 5 percent from a 1993 survey....The participation rate is even lower with nonprofit firms, whose voluntary plans are called 403(b)s: The rate is slightly less than 50 percent for large non-profits, she says....Some 41 percent of participants in big-company plans are now enrolled in their equity mutual fund option. That is up from 30 percent in 1994. Employees participating in company stock plans have dropped from 45 percent in 1994 to about 35 percent now." (p9)

Halverson, Guy. "Business & Money: Mutual Funds: Declare Financial Independence." The Christian Science Monitor v89 n153 3 Jul 1997. p9. The Christian Science Monitor search engine: <http://www.csmonitor.com/plweb-cgi/iops1.pl> To retrieve this article, enter the following search: ED=19970703 AND independence. In the "retrieved list," click the title that matches this record. (ISSN0882-7729).

SAVINGS AND LOAN ASSOCIATION FAILURES --UNITED STATES

The Resolution Trust Corporation managed the closure or the assets of almost 750 different Savings & Loans in the U.S. "During the 6 years of the RTC 747 failed thrifts transferred to it were resolved. In the process, the RTC protected 25 million federally insured deposit accounts. The RTC disposed of $458 billion in assets through December 21, 1995, recovering $397 billion with a rate in excess of 86 percent of book value. The RTC disposed of more than 98 percent of the assets that came under its supervision. Roughly $7.7 billion--book value--in assets were placed under FDIC [Federal Deposit Insurance Corporation] management when the RTC closed....The Affordable Housing Program disposed of 24,000 properties with a book value of $2.5 billion and also provided more than 109,000 housing units for low- and moderate-income families through the single-family program and the multifamily buildings." (pH7617)

Vento, Bruce F. (Rep.-Minn.). "Thrift Depositor Protection Oversight Board Abolishment Act." Congressional Record. Daily ed. v143 n128 23 Sep 1997. pH7614-7617. section/page-level access: <http://thomas.loc.gov/cgi-bin/query/R?r105:FLD001:H07616:> (ISSN0363-7239). (X1.1A.105/1).

SAWDUST

see WOOD WASTE

SCALDS

see BURNS AND SCALDS

SCHEDULES, SCHOOL--UNITED STATES--STUDENTS --ATTITUDES (v26)

SCHISTOSOMIASIS

"Many parasitic diseases rarely cause death directly but degrade the health of millions of people. Schistosomiasis is one of the most prevalent--with more than 200 million people infected....More than 200,000 people who currently live with the disease (also known as bilharziasis) experience chronic ill health as eggs from the flatworm parasite travel through their bloodstream to the intestines and bladder." (p8-9)

Olshansky, S. Jay/Carnes, Bruce/Rogers, Richard G./Smith, Len. "Infectious Diseases--New and Ancient Threats to World Health." Population Bulletin v52 n2 Jul 1997. p2-46. (ISSN0032-468X).

"Schistosomiasis (sometimes-called bilharziasis or bilhartzia) ranks second behind malaria in terms of socio-economic and public health importance in tropical and subtropical areas. The disease is endemic in 74 developing countries, infecting more than 200 million people in rural agricultural and peri-urban areas. Of these, 20 million suffer severe consequences from the disease and 120 million are symptomatic. It is estimated that 80% of the transmission takes place in sub-Saharan Africa." (p1)

World Health Organization. "Schistosomiasis." WHO Fact Sheet n115 Nov 1997. p1-3. document-level access: <http://www.who.ch/programmes/inf/facts/fact115.htm>

SCHIZOPHRENIA--TREATMENT--UNITED STATES (v26)

SCHIZOPHRENIA--UNITED STATES--COSTS

"The Epidemiologic Catchment Area (ECA) study reported that 13.7 percent of persons with schizophrenic disorders received Supplemental Security Income (SSI). Another 22.9 percent received other welfare payments....Among another sample of 143 'psychiatrically impaired' males, 32 of the 55 subjects with schizophrenia (58 percent) were receiving disability payments from the Social Security Administration or from the Department of Veterans Affairs. The estimated total economic cost of schizophrenia in the United States in 1991 was $65 billion. A total of 371,040 individuals with schizophrenia received disability benefits through SSI in December 1993, accounting for 9.7 percent of the SSI caseload." (p948)

Ho, Beng-Choon/Andreasen, Nancy/Flaum, Michael. "Dependence on Public Financial Support Early in the Course of Schizophrenia." Psychiatric Services v48 n7 Jul 1997. p948-950. (ISSN1075-2730).

SCHIZOPHRENIA--UNITED STATES--SEXUAL BEHAVIOR (v26)

SCHOLASTIC ACHIEVEMENT TESTS

see ACHIEVEMENT TESTS

SCHOLASTIC ASSESSMENT TEST--UNITED STATES

In the U.S., on the Scholastic Assessment Test, "the average mathematics score increased by 3 points to 511 this year; but the average verbal score remained unchanged from last year's 505. More minority students than ever before (32 percent of testtakers) took the SAT....Black students who took the SAT are entering college with an average of 17.5 yearlong courses of academic study, up from 16.8 in 1987. Among those students, 59 percent hope to go on to earn a master's or a doctorate--an increase of 11 percentage points from a decade ago." (pA19)

"Education Vital Signs: Common Measures." American School Board Journal v184 n12 Dec 1997. pA18-A23. (ISSN0003-0953).

SCHOOL ATTENDANCE--CALIFORNIA--BELLFLOWER

In California, in the Bellflower School District, the Citizens' Task Force "was one of the community-based notions that helped the schools deal with truancy, now a non-problem with a 98 percent attendance rate. 'Out of 900,000 cumulative days of school, we only had 90 days of truancy,'...[Dr. Rebecca Turrentine, Superintendent] says." (p33)

Fitzgerald, Michael J. "A Tale of Districts." California Journal v28 n6 Jun 1997. p28-35. (ISSN0008-1205).

SCHOOL ATTENDANCE--COLLEGE

see COLLEGE ATTENDANCE

SCHOOL ATTENDANCE--UNITED STATES

In the U.S., "according to one 1992 study, 27.5 percent of Hispanics in the 18 to 24 age group had dropped out of school. This compares to 16 percent for African-Americans and 10 percent for whites." (p47)

Rodriguez, Steve. "Leadership: Marine Corps Observance of National Hispanic Heritage Month: More Substance, Less Fiesta Is Required." Marine Corps Gazette v81 n8 Aug 1997. p46-47. (ISSN0025-3170).

An analysis of data taken from the National Educational Longitudinal Study, which is comprised of U.S. eighth graders surveyed in 1988 with follow-ups in 1990 and 1992, indicates that "the odds of leaving school are reduced substantially (about 57%) for children who attend a Catholic school. Compared to families with two natural parents, the odds of dropping out of school are consistently and substantially greater for stepparent families (96%), families headed by never-married women (69%), father-only families (200%) and other-parent families (88%)." (p1352)

Teachman, Jay D./Paasch, Kathleen/Carver, Karen. "Social Capital and the Generation of Human Capital." Social Forces v75 n4 Jun 1997. p1343-1359. (ISSN0037-7732).

SCHOOL BOARD MEMBERS--UNITED STATES --ATTITUDES (v26)

According to a survey by THE AMERICAN SCHOOL BOARD JOURNAL and Virginia Tech University, in the U.S., "nearly half (46 percent) of the...[school] board members have graduate degrees, and 29 percent have four-year college degrees but no advanced degrees. The higher levels of education clearly pay off: About 60 percent of board members earn $50,000 or more per year, the survey found. About 44 percent are employed in professional and managerial positions, and 13 percent own their own business....About 43 percent of board members do not have children currently attending public schools, according to the survey." (pA15)

"Education Vital Signs: Leadership." American School Board Journal v184 n12 Dec 1997. pA15. (ISSN0003-0953).

SCHOOL BOARD MEMBERS--UNITED STATES --MINORITIES

According to a survey by THE AMERICAN SCHOOL BOARD JOURNAL and Virginia Tech University, in the U.S., "although the number of women on school boards is increasing (44 percent--up 7 percentage points from 10 years ago), minorities remain generally underrepresented in school board service. Seventeen percent of American students are black, but only 5 percent of board members are black. And, only 2 percent of board members are Hispanic, even though 14 percent of public school students are Hispanic. About 87 percent of school board members, and 65 percent of students are white." (pA15)

"Education Vital Signs: Leadership." American School Board Journal v184 n12 Dec 1997. pA15. (ISSN0003-0953).

SCHOOL BREAKFAST PROGRAMS--UNITED STATES

In the U.S., "outlays for the School Breakfast Program rose almost 7 percent in fiscal 1996 to $1.1 billion. The number of meals served under the program totaled 1.1 billion in fiscal 1996, an increase of 4 percent over fiscal 1995. About 80 percent of all school breakfasts were served free, and another 6 percent were served at reduced prices in fiscal 1996....Some 20 percent of the students in the over 67,000 participating schools and residential childcare institutions participated in the program in fiscal 1996." (p51)

Oliveira, Victor/U.S. Dept. of Agriculture. Economic Research Service. "Food Assistance: Food-Assistance Spending Held Steady in 1996." Food Review v20 n1 Jan-Apr 1997. p49-56. (ISSN1056-327X).

SCHOOL BUILDINGS--IOWA--MAINTENANCE AND REPAIR

"In 1995, Iowa State University conducted a comprehensive survey about the condition of school buildings in the state and estimated that $3.4 billion is needed to repair and rebuild these facilities. This survey was updated a few months ago and the tab has risen to $4 billion." (pS4931)

Harkin, Tom (Sen.-Iowa). "Concurrent Resolution on the Budget." Congressional Record. Daily ed. v143 n69 22 May 1997. pS4925-4943. section/page-level access: <http://thomas.loc.gov/cgi-bin/query/R?r105:FLD001:S04931:> (ISSN0363-7239). (X1.1A.105/1).

SCHOOL BUILDINGS--LOUISIANA--MAINTENANCE AND REPAIR (v26)

SCHOOL BUILDINGS--UNITED STATES--MAINTENANCE AND REPAIR (v26)

"The nationwide school facilities problem was publicized in a series of 1996 reports by the U.S. General Accounting Office, which said that one-third of the schools serving about 14 million students nationwide needed extensive repair or at least partial replacement. Updating these and other buildings to comply with federal mandates would cost a whopping $111 billion over three years." (p20) "Although schools spent nearly $11 billion on new construction and renovation in 1996, according to AMERICAN SCHOOL & UNIVERSITY's annual construction report, observers such as Northern Illinois University's Thomas E. Glass say that isn't nearly enough. With construction costs increasing by about 7 percent a year and with maintenance on existing problems continuing to be deferred--which often leads to more serious structural problems--the $111 billion GAO estimate is bound to grow, Glass says." (p21)

Hardy, Lawrence. "School Facilities Report: Covering Construction Costs." American School Board Journal v184 n10 Oct 1997. p20-23. (ISSN0003-0953).

In Illinois, "with an improved bond rating, Chicago has financed almost 1.5 billion dollars' worth of school improvements in the last 2 years. Chicago schools, however, need 3 billion dollars' worth of improvements. The problem is not confined to big cities like Chicago. The GAO [General Accounting Office] found that in urban areas [around the U.S.], 38 percent of schools are crumbling, while in rural areas the figure is 30 percent, and in the suburbs, it's 29 percent." (pS9085)

Moseley-Braun, Carol (Sen.-Ill.). "The Educational Facilities Improvement Act." Congressional Record. Daily ed. v143 n119 10 Sep 1997. pS9081-9085. section/page-level access: <http://thomas.loc.gov/cgi-bin/query/R?r105:FLD001:S09085:> (ISSN0363-7239). (X1.1A.105/1).

"A U.S. General Accounting Office (GAO) study released in 1996 revealed that one-third of schools nationwide need extensive repair or replacement. Further, 60 percent of schools surveyed reported at least 'one major building feature' in disrepair such as the roof, exterior walls, windows, plumbing, heating and air conditioning or electrical power. Forty-six percent lack the basic electrical wiring to support computers, modems and modern communications. More than 14 million students attend the schools surveyed by the GAO....While 38 percent of schools in urban areas reported at least one inadequate building, 30 percent of rural schools and 29 percent of suburban schools documented similar concerns." (p15)

Dahlkemper, Lesley. "Rundown Schools: Whose Responsibility?" State Legislatures v23 n8 Sep 1997. p14-19. (ISSN0147-6041).

SCHOOL BUS ACCIDENTS--UNITED STATES --MORTALITY

Sgt. Sharon VanCampen of the Michigan State Police said that "school buses are 11 times safer than any other vehicle on the road....According to the National Transportation Highway Safety Administration, about 10 students die each year as a result of injuries suffered in school bus crashes. From 1985-95, 156 students and drivers were killed in school bus accidents." (p2 secC)

Lopez, Manny. "The Metro: Special Report: School Bus Safety: Parents, Advocates Urge Districts to Add Seat Belts." Detroit News 12 Jun 1997. p1,2 secC.

SCHOOL BUSES--SAFETY MEASURES--MICHIGAN (v26)

SCHOOL BUSES--SAFETY REGULATIONS--MICHIGAN

"More than 700 Metro Detroit school buses had defects so serious in recent inspections that the Michigan State Police ordered them off the road." (p1 secA) Preliminary results of the 1997 Michigan State Police bus report indicate that "the fleets of 15 public school districts in Metro Detroit were ranked poor. Fourteen fleets of parochial and private schools in Wayne, Oakland and Macomb counties were ranked poor. Statewide, state police examined 14,788 buses; inspectors 'red-tagged' 2,128--14.5 percent--and 'yellow-tagged' 949--6.5 percent....Overall, the state's school buses, which carry about 850,000 school children and cover 320 million miles a year, were rated 'good,' the same as last year....Of 18 parochial schools inspected by state police in Metro Detroit, 14--78 percent--had bus fleets rated 'poor.' Of the 57 buses used by the schools, 54 percent were red-tagged and ordered off the road. Of the 31 downriver and western Wayne school districts, 19--61 percent--rated 'poor.' Of 872 buses, 29 percent were red-tagged." (p8 secA)

Cole, Kenneth. "School Buses Found Unsafe." Detroit News 22 Sep 1997. p1,8 secA.

SCHOOL BUSES--MICHIGAN--SAFETY MEASURES (v26)

SCHOOL CHILDREN--FOOD

see NATIONAL SCHOOL LUNCH PROGRAM

SCHOOL CHILDREN--INDIA (v26)

SCHOOL CHILDREN--PENNSYLVANIA --TRANSPORTATION (v26)

SCHOOL CHILDREN--UNITED STATES

In the U.S., "about 32 million children were enrolled in elementary school (grades 1-8) in October 1995--not significantly different from 1994 but nearly 5 million more than a decade earlier. Eleven percent of elementary students attended a private school, down from 15 percent in 1963."

U.S. Dept. of Commerce. Economic and Statistics Administration. "Census Back to School Facts." Census Bureau Fact Sheet 18 Aug 1997. document-level access: <http://www.census.gov/Press-Release/fs97-08.html>

SCHOOL CHOICE--UNITED STATES--PUBLIC OPINION

In the U.S., "almost seven in ten favor school choice, that is, 'allowing students and their parents to choose which public schools in this community the students attend regardless of where they live'....Although Republicans are the most supportive of school choice (74%), substantial majorities of Democrats (69%) and ticket-splitters (64%) also favor it." (p51)

Ferguson, Gary A. "Consensus in Education Reform?: Searching for Consensus in Education Reform." Public Perspective v8 n4 Jun-Jul 1997. p49-52. (ISSN1050-5067).

SCHOOL DISCIPLINE--UNITED STATES--PUBLIC OPINION

Surveys conducted by Public Agenda, a New York-based nonprofit organization, "suggest that 'nearly 9 in 10 [U.S.] teachers (88 percent) favor removing persistent troublemakers from class; and roughly the same percentage favor emphasizing work habits such as being on time, dependability and discipline.'...About 70 percent of pupils thought disruptive students and cheating are 'serious' problems in their classes, and most worried about tardiness and slacking on class work, too. A majority of the general public said schools didn't enforce good discipline and work habits. But education professors were less likely to put the onus of good behavior on the student than on the school. Just 37 percent thought it 'absolutely essential to develop teachers trained to maintain discipline and order in the classroom.' And although another 38 percent of the education school professors found this training important, 61 percent said that when a public school teacher faces 'a disruptive class,' it's a sign 'the teacher has failed to make lessons engaging enough.'" (p14 secA)

"Outmoded and Mistaken?" Detroit News 5 Nov 1997. p14 secA.

SCHOOL DROPOUTS

see DROPOUTS

SCHOOL ENROLLMENT

"According to an article in the February 1997 issue of UNICEF's EDUCATION NEWS, worldwide primary school enrollment has risen by an estimated 50 million since the World Conference on Education for All in 1990 focused worldwide attention on the issue of providing education for all the world's people....Today there are 20 million fewer children out of school than at the start of the decade." (p7)

"Fact and Fiction." Reading Today v15 n3 Dec 1997-Jan 1998.

p7. (ISSN0737-4208).

SCHOOL ENROLLMENT--CALIFORNIA--MINORITIES

African Americans represent 7.4 percent of California's "population in 1990 and 6.6 percent of the state's post-secondary enrollment. Hispanics represent 25.8 percent of the state's population and 12.9 percent of the post-secondary enrollment....African Americans represent less than 6 percent of enrollment in four-year colleges and universities; Hispanics less than 11 percent." (p16)

Conrad, Cecilia A./Sharpe, Rhonda V. "The Impact of the California Civil Rights Initiative (CCRI) on...Admissions and...California Economy." Review of Black Political Economy v25 n1 Sum 1996. p13-59. (ISSN0034-6446).

SCHOOL ENROLLMENT--MICHIGAN--DETROIT

"Enrollment in Metro Detroit schools is up slightly this fall, but the trend during the 1990s is an overall decline of students, anchored by a sharp drop in Wayne County. A DETROIT NEWS review of public school enrollment patterns show that Oakland and Macomb schools had modest pupil gains this fall over last year and for the decade as well. Among the three counties, Macomb led the way with a 3.2-percent increase in students this year, followed by Oakland with 1.4-percent growth. The number of students is critical to districts because their state aid is directly linked to pupil head counts. The average per-pupil state grant is nearly $5,900." (p1 secA) "Wayne County fell by less than a percent from last year, but the number of public school students is down nearly 9 percent since 1991....Oakland County, where student population has risen nearly 4 percent in the '90s, had eight of the region's top 10 growth districts this decade....Meanwhile, six of the 10 districts that had the steepest declines in the '90s were in Wayne County. Detroit, the state's largest school district with 166,000 students, stayed about even with last year's count; but this year's enrollment is off nearly 9 percent from the start of the decade." (p6 secA)

Hornbeck, Mark/Cain, Charlie. "'90s See Major Shift in Student Population." Detroit News 11 Nov 1997. p1,6 secA.

In the Detroit area, no school "district has experienced a higher growth rate in the '90s than Walled Lake, where enrollment has increased by 31 percent to 13,132....Oxford had the region's second-highest pupil growth. The district's student population is up 30.5 percent this decade....Warren Woods' enrollment was 9,000 in the early 1970s, plummeted to about 2,000 by the late '80s and now stands at 3,000....The biggest student decline in the '90s occurred in Ferndale, where the student enrollment fell by half....The district's student count of 4,766 is down only slightly from 1991 if adult education students are factored out. Madison School District lost about 45 percent of its enrollment this decade....In the last year, Madison schools lost 1.6 percent of students....Rich Witkowski, executive director of business services in the 4,859-student Garden City School District, said the 30-percent drop this decade is evidence of an aging population....[In Mt. Clemens schools,] though the head count is down 21 percent in this decade, it's up 31 percent this year over last year." (p6 secA)

Hornbeck, Mark/Cain, Charlie. "'90s See Major Shift in Student Population." Detroit News 11 Nov 1997. p1,6 secA.

SCHOOL ENROLLMENT--MICHIGAN--WASHTENAW COUNTY (v26)

SCHOOL ENROLLMENT--UNITED STATES

In the U.S., "in 1997, a record 51.7 million students were enrolled in public and private schools, 400,000 more than the previous high in 1971 at the close of the baby boom....The public schools are expected to add about 800,000 students during the next several years, reaching 54.6 million by 2006." (pA7)

Hardy, Lawrence. "Education Vital Signs: Main Events." American School Board Journal v184 n12 Dec 1997. pA4-A8. (ISSN0003-0953).

In the U.S., "this fall, 52.2 million kids were enrolled in the nation's public and private schools--nearly a million more than last year's all-time high. The ascent will continue until 2007, peaking at about 54.3 million kids, the Education Department says in a recent report on enrollment....[Education Secretary Richard Riley] foresees the need in the next decade to build about 6,000 additional schools and to hire about 2 million more teachers--260,000 to 300,000 in California alone. California is among those states that will be feeling the enrollment surge most. Over the next decade, its student population is expected to grow by 35 percent. In addition, North Carolina's enrollment will grow by 27 percent; Arizona's by 25 percent; Nevada's by 24 percent; Massachusetts' by 23 percent; and Rhode Island's by 21 percent, according to the report." (p13)

"Before the Board: The Kids Keep Coming." American School Board Journal v184 n11 Nov 1997. p13. (ISSN0003-0953).

In the U.S., "forty-one percent of...families, or nearly 30 million, had at least one child aged 5 to 17 enrolled in kindergarten, elementary school or high school in October 1995. About 4 million children attended kindergarten in October 1995."

U.S. Dept. of Commerce. Economic and Statistics Administration. "Census Back to School Facts." Census Bureau Fact Sheet 18 Aug 1997. document-level access: <http://www.census.gov/Press-Release/fs97-08.html>

"School enrollment in the United States is breaking all previous records. A new Department of Education report found that more than 52 million children just enrolled in schools this last fall. The fastest growing group is high school students, with high school enrollment expected to grow by 13 percent over the next 10 years. In Massachusetts, that growth is projected to be 23 percent." (pH7489)

McGovern, James P. (Rep.-Mass.). "Education Should Be America's Number One Priority." Congressional Record. Daily ed. v143 n124 17 Sep 1997. pH7488-7494. section/page-level access: <http://thomas.loc.gov/cgi-bin/query/R?r105:FLD001:H07488:> (ISSN0363-7239). (X1.1A.105/1).

"The vast majority of U.S. children ages 5 to 15 are in school, regardless of racial or ethnic group, but the enrollment gap widens at age 16 when students can leave school legally in most states. In 1995, about 88 percent of Latino 16- and 17-year-olds were enrolled, compared with 94 percent and 93 percent of whites and blacks, respectively. By ages 18 and 19, the proportion in school falls to 46 percent for Hispanics, compared with 62 percent for whites and 58 percent for blacks." (p34)

del Pinal, Jorge/Singer, Audrey. "Generations of Diversity: Latinos in the United States." Population Bulletin v52 n3 Oct 1997. p2-47. (ISSN0032-468X).

SCHOOL INTEGRATION--MICHIGAN--SOUTHFIELD (v26)

SCHOOL LUNCH PROGRAM (UNITED STATES)

see NATIONAL SCHOOL LUNCH PROGRAM

SCHOOL LUNCHROOMS, CAFETERIAS, ETC.--RHODE ISLAND (v26)

SCHOOL LUNCHROOMS, CAFETERIAS, ETC.--UNITED STATES (v26)

SCHOOL SPORTS--ECONOMIC ASPECTS--UNITED STATES

In the U.S., "when the National Federation of State High School Associations surveyed its members in 1994, it found that about 25 percent charged athletic fees. Of those that didn't assess athletic fees, 17 percent said they were considering them in the future. The median fee per sport was $30, but individual districts varied widely. Almost 80 percent of participating schools waived fees for parents who couldn't afford them, the survey said....The money the fees generated was usually not much, the survey said--less than $10,000 per year for 48 percent of the districts, from $10,000 to $20,000 for 24 percent, and more than $20,000 for 28 percent." (p26)

Hardy, Lawrence. "Pay to Play." American School Board Journal v184 n8 Aug 1997. p25-27. (ISSN0003-0953).

SCHOOL VIOLENCE--ARIZONA--TUCSON

In Tucson, Arizona, "schools using the PeaceBuilders program [for the prevention of youth violence] show a 15 percent drop in visits to the school nurse for injuries and a 50 percent drop in referrals for misconduct to the principal's office; and teachers happily report a 10-30 percent increase in the time students can spend on learning....PeaceBuilders is now used in over 200 schools nationwide." (p15)

Stoker, Genie. "PeaceBuilding: Preventing Youth Violence." Christian Social Action v10 n7 Jul-Aug 1997. p15-16,25. (ISSN0897-0459).

SCHOOL VIOLENCE--NORTH CAROLINA

"According to the North Carolina Center for the Prevention of School Violence, over 8,100 incidents of school violence were reported in North Carolina during the last full school year. Possession of a controlled substance, possession of a weapon other than a firearm, and assault on a school employee together accounted for 85 percent of those incidents." (pS4678)

Helms, Jesse (Sen.-N.C.). "Statements on Introduced Bills and Joint Resolutions." Congressional Record. Daily ed. v143 n66 19 May 1997. pS4677-4682. section/page-level access: <http://thomas.loc.gov/cgi-bin/query/R?r105:FLD001:S04678:> (ISSN0363-7239). (X1.1A.105/1).

SCHOOL VIOLENCE--UNITED STATES (v26)

"The most recent national Parents' Resource Institute for Drug Education (PRIDE) survey found that students [in the U.S.] who carried guns to school were 20 times more likely to use cocaine than those who did not bring a gun to school. Gang members were 12 times more likely to use cocaine, and students who threaten others were 6 times more likely to be coke users. The findings of a recent Department of Education report prepared by the Research Triangle Institute, in...North Carolina, confirmed the findings of the PRIDE study. The Research Triangle Institute, found...'[t]he use of drugs was related to violent behavior in schools. A much larger percentage of current users of alcohol and/or other drugs (32 percent of them) reported being involved in school fights as the aggressors than did current nonusers (14 percent of those students) or students who had never tried drugs (6 percent)'....That report went on to say that 37 percent of the students reported that they are afraid of attacks at school while 29 percent said they feared attacks when traveling to and from school." (pS4678)

Helms, Jesse (Sen.-N.C.). "Statements on Introduced Bills and Joint Resolutions." Congressional Record. Daily ed. v143 n66 19 May 1997. pS4677-4682. section/page-level access: <http://thomas.loc.gov/cgi-bin/query/R?r105:FLD001:S04678:> (ISSN0363-7239). (X1.1A.105/1).

"In the late 1980s and early '90s, youth crime [in the U.S.] was so bad that it was spilling into the schoolyards. Some 3 million crimes a year were taking place on or near school property. Four of 5 school districts nationwide cited an increased concern about school violence. Between 1987 and 1991, juvenile arrests for murder soared 85 percent, according to data collected by the National School Board Association in Arlington, Va." (p3)

Nifong, Christina. "United States: Kentucky Shooting Spree Is Exception Amid Safer Schools." The Christian Science Monitor v90 n8 5 Dec 1997. p3. The Christian Science Monitor search engine: <http://www.csmonitor.com/plweb-cgi/iops1.pl> To retrieve this article, enter the following search: ED=19971205 AND schools. In the "retrieved list," click the title that matches this record. (ISSN0882-7729).

SCHOOLS

see also BUSINESS SCHOOLS; CATHOLIC SCHOOLS; CHARTER SCHOOLS; CHURCH SCHOOLS; CLASSROOMS; COMPUTERS--UNITED STATES--SCHOOLS; DRUG TRAFFIC--UNITED STATES--SCHOOLS; HIGH SCHOOLS; INTERNET (COMPUTER NETWORK)--UNITED STATES--SCHOOLS; JEWISH DAY SCHOOLS; LAW SCHOOLS; NATIONAL SCHOOL LUNCH PROGRAM; PRIVATE SCHOOLS; PUBLIC SCHOOLS; UNIVERSITIES AND COLLEGES

SCHOOLS--AUSTRALIA (v26)

SCHOOLS--CALIFORNIA--LOS ANGELES

"Total enrollment in the Los Angeles Unified School District in 1996-97: 667,624 and climbing." (p32) "As of fall 1996, according to district figures, fully 68 percent of the student body in Los Angeles Unified was Hispanic, with African Americans a distant second at 14 percent, non-Hispanic whites 11 percent, Asians 4.4 percent and Filipinos 1.9 percent. Only .7 percent were classified as Pacific Islander/American Indian/Alaska Native." (p33)

Bathen, Sigrid. "Los Angeles Unified School District." California Journal v29 n1 Jan 1998. p32-38. (ISSN0008-1205).

SCHOOLS--COLORADO

"In the last decade, Colorado's school enrollment has grown by 100,000, says Phil Fox, associate director of the Colorado Association of School Executives. Of 176 districts, 140 are growing....Colorado provides an average of only $105 per student in capital money, so districts must rely heavily on local property taxes....In Sanford, a small district in South Central Colorado, the assessed value per pupil is $9,000. In Aspen, it is about $750,000." (p21-22)

Hardy, Lawrence. "School Facilities Report: Covering Construction Costs." American School Board Journal v184 n10 Oct 1997. p20-23. (ISSN0003-0953).

SCHOOLS--CURRICULA (v26)

SCHOOLS--FLORIDA--DADE COUNTY

"With almost 300 schools already built and another 29 under construction, Dade County's public school system [in Florida] is the fourth largest in the nation....Enrollment in the county's elementary and high schools increased by almost 40 percent between 1984 and 1995. Kindergarten enrollment rose by over 70 percent during the same period." (p17)

Malizia, Emil/Norton, Richard/Richardson, Craig. "Reading, Writing, And Impact Fees." Planning v63 n9 Sep 1997. p17-19. (ISSN0001-2610).

SCHOOLS--GREAT BRITAIN (v26)

In Great Britain, a report from the Office for Standards in Education published in 1995, "found that the higher the attainment level of a school intake (as judged by the inspectors), the higher the average class size. Only 14 per cent of classes where inspectors judged the intake attainment to be 'low' had more than 30 children, against 28 per cent overall....Though the pupil-teacher ratio in schools deteriorated in the first half of the 1990s, the pupil-adult ratio actually improved (from 18.6:1 to 18.4:1)." (p20)

"Adding and Taking Away in Class." New Statesman 3 Oct 1997. p20-21. (ISSN0028-6842).

SCHOOLS--MICHIGAN (v26)

"When it comes to desirable class size--teachers in elementary classrooms with fewer than 25 students--Michigan ranks near the bottom at 47th in the country. Overall, the state's elementary school students attend classes that average 27.6 pupils per room, fifth-highest in the nation, according to the U.S. Department of Education." (p1 secA) "Teachers...[in Michigan] are the fifth-highest paid in the nation, first when the state's relatively modest cost of living is factored in....Research has shown class size works best when there are about 15 to 17 students per class." (p6 secA)

Naylor, Janet. "News Special: Education: State Class Sizes among Worst in U.S." Detroit News 26 Sep 1997. p1,6 secA.

SCHOOLS--MICHIGAN--DETROIT (v26)

SCHOOLS--MICHIGAN--DETROIT--PUBLIC OPINION (v26)

SCHOOLS--MICHIGAN--GAY YOUTH (v26)

SCHOOLS--MICHIGAN--MINORITIES (v26)

SCHOOLS--NEW MEXICO

"As of 1994, 94 percent of...[New Mexico's] schools needed to upgrade or repair onsite buildings, and 29 percent had crumbling roofs. In 1996, 44 percent of districts in New Mexico had at least one building in need of serious repair or replacement--much higher than the 33-percent average nationwide. Over 70 percent of high school students in...[New Mexico] attend schools of 900 or more students, a size that is too large to be an effective learning environment, some studies say. There is a $475 million backlog in school construction and repair for BIA [Bureau of Indian Affairs] schools, of which there are 45 in New Mexico. Meeting the demand to repair and build schools is difficult because New Mexico is one of the fastest growing States in the Nation, and 47 percent of its student population attends school in rural areas....Over the last 10 years, student enrollment in New Mexico has jumped by 57,000 students, 23.7 percent. In just 3 years, enrollment will grow by another 20,000 students--the same number of students as are in Las Cruces, the State's second largest district." (pS4937)

Bingaman, Jeff (Sen.-N.Mex.). "Concurrent Resolution on the Budget." Congressional Record. Daily ed. v143 n69 22 May 1997. pS4925-4943. section/page-level access: <http://thomas.loc.gov/cgi-bin/query/R?r105:FLD001:S04937:> (ISSN0363-7239). (X1.1A.105/1).

SCHOOLS--NEW YORK (N.Y.)

"Public and Catholic schools in New York City now enroll about the same proportion of students with multiple risk factors, states Mayor Rudolph W. Giuliani; yet the Catholic schools have a dropout rate of 0.1 percent compared with 18 percent for the public schools. And contrary to popular belief, the city's Catholic schools have an expulsion rate of only 2 percent." (p6)

Reiland, Ralph R. "Of Other Things: School Choice: Threat or Solution?" America v177 n8 27 Sep 1997. p6-7. (ISSN0002-7049).

SCHOOLS--UNITED STATES (v26)

SCHOOLS--UNITED STATES--MAINTENANCE AND REPAIR (v26)

SCHOOLS--UNITED STATES--SECURITY MEASURES

"A study by the American School Board revealed that 50% of school districts conduct locker searches, 36% conduct search and seizure activities, 36% maintain security personnel in schools, 31% have gun-free school zones, and 15% have metal detectors (Natale, 1994). Approximately one-fourth of large urban school districts in the United States use metal detectors to help reduce weapon-carrying in schools (Centers for Disease Control, 1993)....Students who attended schools with metal detector programs were as likely as those attending schools without metal detectors to carry weapons elsewhere, but were less likely to have carried a weapon inside the school building (7.8% versus 13.6%) or going to and from school (7.7% versus 15.2%)." (p510-511)

Page, Randy M./Hammermeister, Jon. "Weapon-Carrying and Youth Violence." Adolescence v32 n127 Fall 1997. p505-513. (ISSN0001-8449).

SCHOOLS--UNITED STATES--STUDENTS--ATTITUDES

In a U.S., study of nearly 1,000 8- to 17-year-olds, conducted by the polling group Roper Starch Worldwide, "when asked to prioritize a list of 10 ways to make schools better, 44 percent of respondents told Roper they would keep troublemakers out of class, 41 percent said they would hire better teachers, and 33 percent said they would make classes smaller. New computers and better school facilities in general also gained favorable mention, with 28 percent and 25 percent, respectively." (p18)

Baldauf, Scott. "How Children Would Run Public Schools." The Christian Science Monitor v89 n203 15 Sep 1997. p1,18. The Christian Science Monitor search engine: <http://www.csmonitor.com/plweb-cgi/iops1.pl> To retrieve this article, enter the following search: ED=19970915 AND schools. In the "retrieved list," click the title that matches this record. (ISSN0882-7729).

SCHOOLS--WISCONSIN--MILWAUKEE

"In Milwaukee, after four years of the nation's first tax-funded school choice program, the average reading and math scores of choice students, 70 percent of whom are African-American, were 5 and 12 percentile points higher, respectively, than those of comparable low-income public school students, according to a recent study by Paul E. Peterson of Harvard University's Program in Education Policy and Governance." (p6) "The graduation rate in Milwaukee's urban public high schools...is below 50 percent, while private schools in the same neighborhoods have graduation rates of nearly 90 percent." (p7)

Reiland, Ralph R. "Of Other Things: School Choice: Threat or Solution?" America v177 n8 27 Sep 1997. p6-7. (ISSN0002-7049).

SCHOOLS, BUSINESS

see BUSINESS SCHOOLS

SCHOOLS, CATHOLIC

see CATHOLIC SCHOOLS

SCHOOLS, CHURCH

see CHURCH SCHOOLS

SCHOOLS, JEWISH DAY

see JEWISH DAY SCHOOLS

SCHOOLS, LAW

see LAW SCHOOLS

SCHOOLS, OSTEOPATHIC

see OSTEOPATHIC SCHOOLS

SCHOOLS, PAROCHIAL

see PAROCHIAL SCHOOLS

SCHOOLS, PRIVATE

see PRIVATE SCHOOLS

SCIENCE

see also EARTH SCIENCES

SCIENCE--RESEARCH

see RESEARCH

SCIENCE--STUDY AND TEACHING--GERMANY--JAPAN--UNITED STATES (v26)

SCIENCE--STUDY AND TEACHING--UNITED STATES (v26)

According to "Pursuing Excellence," a report by the U.S. National Center for Education Statistics, "in science,...16 percent of U.S. fourth-graders are among the top 10 percent in the world, compared to 17 percent in Korea, 14 percent in Australia, and 13 percent in England, Singapore and Japan have 11 percent each....[U.S. fourth-grade teachers devote about] 2.7 hours per week teaching science, compared to an international average of 1.9 hours." (pA22)

"Education Vital Signs: Common Measures." American School Board Journal v184 n12 Dec 1997. pA18-A23. (ISSN0003-0953).

In the U.S., "four out of 10 high school seniors don't know basic science that should be taught at their grade level, according to the 1996 National Assessment of Educational Progress (NAEP) science assessment....Only 3 percent of the youngsters in all three grades scored at an advanced level. A third or more of the students, depending on the grade, showed partial mastery, defined as basic knowledge. Less than a third were ranked as proficient, or having the competency to deal with challenging subject matter....43 percent of the 12th graders scored below basic, and only 21 percent reached the proficient level." (p10) "Nearly 40 percent of eighth-graders scored below basic, while 29 percent were at or above proficient. A third of fourth-graders were below basic, while 29 percent were at or above proficient." (p11)

"Before the Board: NAEP: Science Fades in High School." American School Board Journal v184 n12 Dec 1997. p10-11. (ISSN0003-0953).

SCIENCE--STUDY AND TEACHING--UNITED STATES --COLLEGE STUDENTS--ATTITUDES (v26)

SCIENCE--STUDY AND TEACHING--UNITED STATES --FINANCE

"As part of the Department of Energy's commitment to improve science education, the Office of Nuclear Energy, Science and Technology recently awarded grants to 30 U.S. universities under the DOE/Industry Matching Grants and Reactor Sharing Programs....Under the cost-shared program, a private company, usually an electric utility with one or more nuclear power plants, provides a grant of up to $50,000 annually to a university nuclear engineering program. Contributions are matched dollar-for-dollar by DOE. In fiscal year 1997, awards totalling $1.38 million went to 15 universities....There are 30 universities in 23 states participating in the sharing program. In fiscal year 1997, $421,500 in grants, ranging from $3,000 to $50,000 each, were awarded." (p13)

U.S. Dept. of Energy. "Education Notes: DOE Grants Improve Nuclear Science Education." DOE This Month v20 n10 Oct 1997. p13. (ISSN1057-5782).

SCIENCE--STUDY AND TEACHING--UNITED STATES --GERMANY--JAPAN (v26)

SCIENCE--UNITED STATES (v26)

SCIENCE--UNITED STATES--MINORITIES--WOMEN (v26)

SCIENCE--UNITED STATES--PUBLIC OPINION

Last spring in the U.S., the CHRISTIAN SCIENCE MONITOR "reported the results of an opinion survey in which half of the 10- to 17-year-olds ranked science at or near the top of their list of favorite subjects. But only half said their teacher challenged them to discuss planation for things. Forty-seven percent said their teacher 'does most of the talking' or 'calls on us to see who knows the right answer.' Give us more experiments to do in the lab, these students said (88 percent). Let us use science to solve problems in our neighborhoods, they suggested (85 percent)." (p20)

"The Monitor's View: Science Needs and Nerds." The Christian Science Monitor v89 n231 24 Oct 1997. p20. The Christian Science Monitor search engine: <http://www.csmonitor.com/ plweb-cgi/iops1.pl> To retrieve this article, enter the following search: ED=19971024 AND nerds. In the "retrieved list," click the title that matches this record. (ISSN0882-7729).

SCIENCE--UNITED STATES--STUDENTS--ATTITUDES (v26)

SCIENTISTS--UNITED STATES (v26)

SCOTLAND--ECONOMIC CONDITIONS (v26)

SCOTLAND--EMPLOYMENT (v26)

SEA LEVEL (v26)

SEA OTTER (v26)

SEA OTTER--CALFORNIA--MORTALITY (v26)

SEA OTTER--NORTH PACIFIC OCEAN (v26)

SEA OTTER--UNITED STATES (v26)

SEA TRAVEL

see OCEAN TRAVEL

SEAFOOD INDUSTRY

see BLUEFIN TUNA FISHERIES; CATFISH FISHERIES; CHINOOK SALMON; CRAYFISH INDUSTRY; SALMON FISHING; SHELLFISH TRADE; SHRIMP FISHERIES; SWORDFISH

SEALING--CANADA (v26)

SEALING (TECHNOLOGY)--UNITED STATES (v26)

SEALS (ANIMALS)--GREAT BRITAIN (v26)

SEASONAL AFFECTIVE DISORDER--UNITED STATES

"It's estimated that 6 percent of Americans have severe problems with Seasonal Affective Disorder, or SAD, a form of depression linked to dwindling daylight....Another 14 percent of the population, however, experience SAD in a milder form, estimates Dr. Norman Rosenthal, a leading SAD researcher and author of 'Winter Blues.'" (p1 secD)

Rueter, Anne. "Connection: Got the Winter Blues?: These Tips Can Help You Chase Them Away." Ann Arbor News 4 Nov 1997. p1-2 secD.

SEAT BELTS, AUTOMOBILE

see AUTOMOBILES--SEAT BELTS

SECONDARY SCHOOLS

see HIGH SCHOOLS

SECONDHAND SMOKING

see PASSIVE SMOKING

SECRETARIES--UNITED STATES (v26)

SECRETARIES--WISCONSIN--WHITEWATER --TERMINOLOGY (v26)

SECURITIES INDUSTRY

see also BONDS

SECURITIES INDUSTRY--UNITED STATES

"Foreign issuer offerings of securities in U.S. markets have almost quintupled, from about $30 billion in 1990 to approximately $144 billion in 1996. Since January 1, 1996, over 160 foreign companies from 35 countries have entered...[the Securities and Exchange Commission's] reporting system, including companies from Chile, China, France, Indonesia, Italy, Russia, and the United Kingdom. As of December 31, 1996, 843 foreign reporting companies representing 47 countries were registered with the Commission." (p120)

Levitt, Arthur (Chair, U.S. Securities and Exchange Commission). "Departments of Commerce, Justice, And State, The Judiciary...Approp. for 1998 (Part 8)." Hearing. U.S. House. Committee on Appropriations. Washington, D.C. : GPO, 1997. (ISBN0160551641). (Y4.Ap6/1:C73/2/997/pt.8).

In the U.S., "market researchers from the Leading Edge Group (LEG) of Business Trend Analysts have published a new report, 'Security Industry Markets: Products and Services.' It estimates the US security industry at $39.4B [billion] as of 1996, and is expected to continue to grow at a compound rate of almost 8%....The average annual GDP during this time was 4.2%....The percentage of security revenues grew from 0.46% in 1992, to 0.52% last year. It is predicted to grow further to 0.60% by 2000 and still more to 0.69% by 2004....Security services including alarm monitoring services, guarding, and investigations, grew 31.8% from 1992-96, while electronic security equip. [equipment] sales rose 52.0%....Guard services achieved revs. [revenues] of $13.3B in 1996, reflecting a 23.1% rise since '92....Central station services grew from $9.3B to $13.2B last year, an increase of 41.9%." (unpaginated)

"US Security Industry Projected to Grow 8% to Year 2000." Security Letter v27 n17 1 Oct 1997. (ISSN0363-4922).

SECURITY CLASSIFICATION (GOVERNMENT DOCUMENTS)--UNITED STATES--COSTS

The U.S. "Information Security Oversight Office report to Congress last week estimated the direct costs of secrecy at $5.2 billion in 1996 alone. The same Office reports that in 1995 we had 21,871 original new top secret designations and another

374,244 derivative top secret designations. Meaning that, in a single year, roughly 400,000 new secrets were created at the Top Secret level alone--the disclosure of any one of which would cause exceptionally grave damage to the national security." (pS4110)

Moynihan, Daniel Patrick (Sen.-N.Y.). "Statements on Introduced Bills and Joint Resolutions." Congressional Record. Daily ed. v143 n58 7 May 1997. pS4106-4115. section/ page-level access: <http://thomas.loc.gov/cgi-bin/query/ R?r105:FLD001:S04110:> (ISSN0363-7239). (X1.1A.105/1).

SECURITY CONSULTANTS

see UNIVERSITIES AND COLLEGES--SECURITY CONSULTANTS

SECURITY SERVICES, PRIVATE

see PRIVATE SECURITY SERVICES

SECURITY SYSTEMS--UNITED STATES (v26)

SEGREGATION--MICHIGAN--DETROIT

"In 1990 blacks made up 76% of...[Detroit's] population of 1,028,000. Ninety-two percent of Detroit's three-county metropolitan area's white population lived in the suburban ring, while only 8% lived in the city of Detroit (only 222,000 whites remained in the city)....The metropolitan area's index of dissimilarity is 88, and the indices of segregation are uniform across both educational attainment and family income categories. The Detroit metropolitan area is also the only US locality with a population over 500,000 where segregation increased in the 1980s (Farley, Steeh, & Krysan, 1994)." (p125)

Turner, Susan C. "Barriers to a Better Break: Employer Discrimination and Spatial Mismatch in Metropolitan Detroit." Journal of Urban Affairs v19 n2 1997. p123-141. (ISSN0735-2166).

SEGREGATION--UNITED STATES (v26)

SELENIUM--PHYSIOLOGICAL EFFECT (v26)

SELF-EMPLOYED--CALIFORNIA--SANTA CLARA COUNTY

According to the 1990 U.S. Census, "52,000 people in Santa Clara County [California] were self-employed, accounting for approximately 6.5 per cent of the county's employment, up from 5.9 per cent in the 1980 census. According to projections made by Joint Venture Silicon Valley, the proportion of self-employment to total employment was over 7 per cent in 1995....In the four largest towns in Silicon Valley, the number of single-employee business licenses increased by 44 per cent between 1989 and 1995, from 19,600 to 28,400." (p36)

Carnoy, Martin/Castells, Manuel/Benner, Chris. "Labour Markets and Employment Practices in the Age of Flexibility: A Case Study of Silicon Valley." International Labour Review v136 n1 Spr 1997. p27-48. (ISSN0020-7780).

SELF-EMPLOYED--GERMANY

"According to figures from the Bonn-based Institute for Research into Small and Medium-sized Enterprises, the proportion of self-employed among the [German] workforce rose from 7.3% to 8.9% between 1991 and 1996. In Germany, 3.4 million people were self-employed in 1996--400,000 more than in 1991." (p23)

"Wirtschaft Business: Employment." Deutschland n6 Dec 1997. p23. (ISSN0945-6791).

SELF-EMPLOYED--QUEBEC (PROVINCE)

"The 'Analysis of Independent Work' states that at the time of the 1991 census, 304,955 workers in Quebec were self-employed, i.e., roughly 12 per cent of the labour force. Between 1990 and 1995, 55 per cent of all new jobs created in Quebec were created by the self-employed. In 1991, mainly men (75 per cent) and baby-boomers (57 per cent are aged between 35 and 54) dominated this form of work. The majority are highly dedicated to their work (putting in an average of 43 hours per week as opposed to 37 for wage earners) and earn relatively little. A self-employed worker with no employees, working a 42-hour week, earned Canadian $24,740 as opposed to Canadian $25,820 for a wage earner putting in 37 hours. The highest concentrations of self-employed workers can be found in entertainment, leisure activities and services for private individuals (16.2 per cent), agriculture (15.74 per cent), the retail trade (13.9 per cent), services for enterprises (11.93 per cent) and construction (10.37 per cent)." (p13)

Marsan, Jean-Sebastien. "Self-Employed Workers Call for the Same Social Protection as Wage Earners." World of Work n21 Sep-Oct 1997. p13-14. (ISSN1020-0029).

SELF-EMPLOYED--UNITED STATES--ECONOMIC CONDITIONS (v26)

SELF GOVERNMENT

see DEMOCRACY

SEMICONDUCTOR INDUSTRY--JAPAN--UNITED STATES (v26)

SEMINARIANS--UNITED STATES

"In 1966 there were about 45,400 seminarians in the United States in about 575 seminaries, while there are only about 4,600 today in 200 seminaries." (p18) "The majority of the 45,000...were high school or college-level students, but the 4,600 counted today are principally collegiate and post-collegiate students....The dropout rate for high school and college seminarians was enormous; some have suggested as high as 80 to 90 percent, while the dropout rate today for collegiate and post-collegiate seminarians is smaller." (p19)

Kennedy, Robert G. "Will We Ever Have Enough Priests?" America v177 n6 13 Sep 1997. p18-22. (ISSN0002-7049).

SEMINARIES, RABBINICAL

see RABBINICAL SEMINARIES

SENILE DEMENTIA

see ALZHEIMER'S DISEASE

SENIOR CITIZENS

see AGED

SENTENCES (CRIMINAL PROCEDURE)--UNITED STATES (v26)

The U.S. "criminal justice system is currently failing to hold criminals accountable for their crimes. Of the 10.3 million violent crimes committed in 1992,...only 3.3 million were reported to the police. About 641,000 led to arrests, 165,000 to convictions, and only 100,000 violent criminals received a prison sentence. About 76 percent of those prisoners will be back on the streets in 4 years or less." (pH3841)

McCollum, Bill (Rep.-Fla.). "Juvenile Crime." Congressional Record. Daily ed. v143 n84 17 Jun 1997. pH3840-3846. section/ page-level access: <http://thomas.loc.gov/cgi-bin/query/ R?r105:FLD001:H03840:> (ISSN0363-7239). (X1.1A.105/1).

In the U.S., in 1995, "almost all probationers had conditions attached to their sentences, and 82 percent had three or more. The most common (84 percent) was one or more monetary requirements--61 percent were ordered to pay supervision fees, 56 percent to pay a fine and 55 percent to pay court costs....Almost one-third were ordered to pay restitution to the victim or victims of their crimes. One in ten probationers were restricted from contacting any victim. One in four were required to perform some type of community service. Two in five were formally directed to maintain employment or to enroll in some type of educational or training program. Ten percent had limitations placed on their movements, including directives to stay away from certain places, such as bars or certain businesses, house arrest, curfew or electronic monitoring. An estimated 29 percent were required to get treatment for alcohol abuse or dependency and 23 percent for drug abuse. Almost one-third of all probationers were required to undergo drug testing. Almost one in five were required to participate in other treatment programs, such as special psychiatric or psychological counseling or domestic violence counseling."

U.S. Dept. of Justice. Bureau of Justice Statistics. "Nearly Three-Quarters of All Probationers Had Some Recent Contact with Their Probation Officers." Press Release 3 Dec 1997. document-level access: <http://www.ojp.usdoj.gov/pub/bjs/press/cap95.pr>

SENTENCES, PRISON
see PRISON SENTENCES

SERVICE INDUSTRIES
see also FINANCIAL SERVICES INDUSTRY; HOSPITALITY INDUSTRY; TOURIST TRADE

SERVICE INDUSTRIES--EMPLOYMENT--FLORIDA (v26)

SERVICE INDUSTRIES--EMPLOYMENT--GEORGIA (v26)

SERVICE INDUSTRIES--EMPLOYMENT--GERMANY --SWEDEN--UNITED STATES

"In 1994, the United States employed altogether 41 percent of its working-age population in domestic services, and Sweden was not far behind at 38 percent. Germany, by contrast, was only able to provide employment for 28 percent of its potential workforce in the sheltered service sectors....Public-sector employment dominates domestic services in Sweden, amounting to 24 percent of the working-age population, as compared to only 10 percent in the United States as well as in Germany. By contrast, in the United States service employment in the private sector amounts to an employment ratio of almost 31 percent, as compared to 19 percent in Germany and only 15 percent in Sweden." (p10)

Scharpf, Fritz W. "New Democracy Forum: Can a 'Third Way' Work?: European Distinctions." Boston Review v22 n3-4 Sum 1997. p9-11. (ISSN0734-2306).

SERVICE INDUSTRIES--EMPLOYMENT--LOUISIANA (v26)

SERVICE INDUSTRIES--EMPLOYMENT--MICHIGAN --OAKLAND COUNTY (v26)

SERVICE INDUSTRIES--EMPLOYMENT--MISSISSIPPI (v26)

SERVICE INDUSTRIES--EMPLOYMENT--TENNESSEE (v26)

SERVICE INDUSTRIES--HONG KONG

According to Hong Kong's Census and Statistics Department, "comparing the second quarter of 1997 with the same quarter a year earlier, the value of business receipts in the financing (except banking) industry registered the fastest growth, by 62%. This was followed by those in the real estate and the communications industries, which grew by 27% and 18% respectively....Within the financing (except banking) industry, the financial market and fund management sector recorded triple-digit growth of 110% in business receipts....Considerable increases in business receipts were also registered in the banking (+13%), insurance (+12%), business services (+11%) and restaurants (+11%) industries."

Hong Kong. Census and Statistics Department. "Quarterly Business Receipts Indices for Service Industries 2nd Quarter 1997." Press Release 14 Oct 1997. document-level access: <http://www.info.gov.hk/censtatd/hkstat/press/d22q97.htm>

SERVICE INDUSTRIES--KANSAS--LAWRENCE (v26)

SERVICE INDUSTRIES--UNITED STATES (v26)

SERVICE STATIONS--MICHIGAN--DETROIT--WOMEN (v26)

SERVITUDES--IDAHO--BLAINE COUNTY

In the Silver Creek Valley in Blaine County, Idaho, "a handful of landowners have protected more than 9,600 acres of private land, permanently." (p19) "Some 8,700 acres of ranchland and farmland, and 25 miles of stream, are now under easement--more than 10 times what the [Nature] Conservancy owns in the valley." (p21)

Green, Martha Hodgkins. "How Green Is My Valley?" Nature Conservancy v47 n4 Sep-Oct 1997. p18-23. (ISSN0028-5200).

SETTLEMENT OF LAND
see LAND SETTLEMENT

SEWAGE (v26)

SEWAGE--CZECH REPUBLIC (v26)

SEWAGE--HEALTH ASPECTS--DEVELOPING COUNTRIES

"The United Nations Children's Fund estimates that 3 billion people worldwide live without essential sanitation services. Diarrhea, linked to poor sewage management, kills approximately 2.2 million children annually." (p12)

Oakley, Charmaine. "Around the World: The Means for Latrines." Earth Island Journal v12 n4 Fall 1997. p12. (ISSN1041-0406).

SEWAGE--PURIFICATION--UNITED STATES (v26)

SEWAGE DISPOSAL--UNITED STATES (v26)

SEWAGE DISPOSAL--UNITED STATES--COSTS (v26)

SEWAGE DISPOSAL PLANTS--CHINA (v26)

SEWAGE SLUDGE PRECIPITANTS--UNITED STATES (v26)

SEX CRIMES
see ADULTERY; CHILD SEXUAL ABUSE; RAPE

SEX CRIMES--AUSTRALIA (v26)

SEX CRIMES--UNITED STATES (v26)

SEX CUSTOMS--UNITED STATES--PUBLIC OPINION (v26)

SEX IN TELEVISION--UNITED STATES (v26)

"Studies show Americans spending up to one-third of their free time in front of the tube; the average teenager spends more time watching TV than sleeping....The average daytime drama contains more than three sexual acts per hour, and research from 1994 showed that out of 50 hours of programming (containing 156 acts of intercourse), only five references were made to contraception or safe sex. The one time HIV/AIDS was mentioned, it was contracted through IV drug use." (p23)

Rysavy, Tracy. "The Soap Summit." Yes! A Journal of Positive Futures n4 Win 1997-1998. p23-26. (ISSN1089-6651).

SEX IN TELEVISION--UNITED STATES--PUBLIC OPINION (v26)

SEX INSTRUCTION--UNITED STATES

"Data shows that only 11 percent of US teens get most STD [sexually transmitted disease] information from their parents or other family members. Eighty-nine percent get it from peers and the media." (p31)

Britton, Mariah. "Breaking Silence." Yes! A Journal of Positive Futures n4 Win 1997-1998. p30-31. (ISSN1089-6651).

SEX INSTRUCTION--UNITED STATES--SCHOOL BOARD MEMBERS--ATTITUDES (v26)

SEX INSTRUCTION--UNITED STATES--YOUTH (v26)

SEX OF CHILDREN, PARENTAL PREFERENCES FOR --INDIA--THAILAND--UNITED STATES

According to an international Gallup poll, on the question of child gender preferences, "in Thailand, 44% would want a boy, 27% a girl--yielding a 17% preference for boys, with only 29% expressing no preference. In India there is a 13 percentage point preference for a boy, 40% to 27%. In the U.S. 42% of those surveyed have no preference, but among those who do, boys are favored by a 12 point margin, 35% to 23%."

Gallup Organization. "Global Study of Family Values: An International Gallup Poll: Family Values Differ Sharply around the World." Press Release 7 Nov 1997. document-level access: <http://www.gallup.com/poll/special/family.html>

SEX OF CHILDREN, PARENTAL PREFERENCES FOR --UNITED STATES (v26)

SEX OFFENDERS
see RECIDIVISM--UNITED STATES--SEX OFFENDERS

SEX OFFENDERS--REHABILITATION--QUEBEC (PROVINCE)--COSTS (v26)

SEX OFFENDERS--UNITED STATES (v26)

SEX ORGANS

see GENERATIVE ORGANS

SEX RATIO--CHINA--KOREA

"In every society, about 105 boys are born for every 100 girls....The sex ratio was 112.5 in Korea, and 113.8 in China in 1990. In China alone, these skewed sex ratios suggest that 550,000 infant girls per year were unaccounted for during the 1980s." (p16)

Riley, Nancy E. "Gender, Power, And Population Change." Population Bulletin v52 n1 May 1997. p2-46. (ISSN0032-468X).

SEX ROLE--PUBLIC OPINION (v26)

SEXUAL ABSTINENCE--UNITED STATES

In the U.S., "fewer than 7 percent of men and 20 percent of women aged 18 to 59 were virgins when they were married. Only 10 percent of adult men and 22 percent of adult women report that their first sexual experience was with their spouse, many of whom had their first intercourse when they were engaged prior to marriage." (p11)

Haffner, Debra W. "What's Wrong with Abstinence-Only Sexuality Education Programs?" SIECUS Report v25 n4 Apr-May 1997. p9-13. (ISSN0091-3995).

SEXUAL ABUSE OF CHILDREN

see CHILD SEXUAL ABUSE

SEXUAL ABUSE VICTIMS--UNITED STATES

"Sexual coercion (the act of forcing, pressuring, or tricking persons into a sexual act against their will) is now known to be a common occurrence. An estimated 40% of girls [in the U.S.] are sexually coerced during childhood, almost half of women in college and in the workplace experience sexual harassment, and 25% of women are rape victims (Benson, Charlton, & Goddhart, 1992; Davis, Peck, & Storment, 1993; Tanzman, 1992)." (p419) "For male adolescents, the percentage of boys reporting unwanted sexual activity range from 11 to 15% (Davis, Peck, & Storment, 1993; Erickson & Rapkin, 1991). College age men report higher rates of experience with sexual coercion (34%) possibly as a function of having had more time in which to be subjected to unwanted sexual activity (Struckman & Struckman, 1994)....A recently completed national survey...[found that] men and women who had been sexually touched as children by an adult were more likely to have in excess of 10 sex partners, to engage in group sex, to identify themselves as gay or bisexual, and to express difficulties in sexuality (Michael, 1994)." (p420)

Anderson, Virginia/Reis, Janet/Stephens, Yvonne. "Male and Female Adolescents' Perceived Interpersonal Communication Skills According to History of Sexual Coercion." Adolescence v32 n126 Sum 1997. p419-427. (ISSN0001-8449).

SEXUAL BEHAVIOR

see AGED--ISRAEL--SEXUAL BEHAVIOR; CHILD SEXUAL ABUSE; GIRLS--NIGERIA--SEXUAL BEHAVIOR; HOMOSEXUALITY; PHILIPPINES--SEXUAL BEHAVIOR; TEENAGERS--UNITED STATES--SEXUAL BEHAVIOR; UNITED STATES. ARMY--SEXUAL BEHAVIOR; YOUNG ADULTS--PHILIPPINES--SEXUAL BEHAVIOR; YOUTH--CALIFORNIA--SEXUAL BEHAVIOR; YOUTH--NEW YORK (N.Y.)--SEXUAL BEHAVIOR; YOUTH--NIGERIA--SEXUAL BEHAVIOR; YOUTH--RUSSIA--DRUG USE--SEXUAL BEHAVIOR; YOUTH--RUSSIA--SEXUAL BEHAVIOR; YOUTH--UNITED STATES--SEXUAL BEHAVIOR

SEXUAL DIVISION OF LABOR--INDIA--KURUMPATTI

A study conducted in Kurumpatti, India, in 1993-1994 found that "in a day, on an average, men worked for about 7 hours and 10 minutes, while women worked for 10 hours and forty minutes which included both economic and household work....The time input of women in activities related to sericulture was about 64 per cent, and 36 per cent by men. In agricultural activities, it was the reverse, with 68 per cent of the labor requirement provided by men and 32 per cent by women. Further, women contributed about 57 per cent of the total time required for beedi rolling." (p52)

Inbanathan, Anand/Vijayalakshmi, V. "Women, Sericulture and Development: A Case in South India." Journal of Third World Studies v14 n1 Spr 1997. p37-63. (ISSN8755-3449).

SEXUAL HARASSMENT--UNITED STATES (v26)

In the U.S., "new sexual harassment complaints filed with the federal Equal Employment Opportunity Commission jumped 150 percent from 1990 to 1996--from 6,127 to 15,342, with 90 percent to 92 percent of the complaints filed by women each of those years. In the Detroit EEOC office alone, sex harassment complaints increased from 54 in 1990 to 113 this year....The EEOC alone filed 68 class-action suits in 1996, more than double the number it filed in 1991....The total damages paid for the 15,342 EEOC cases filed in 1996...totaled $27.8 million; $7.7 million was paid on 6,127 cases in 1990. In Detroit, the number of cases filed increased from 60 in 1990 to 91 in 1996; separate payment figures for Detroit were not available. Nationally, more than 33 percent of sex harassment complaints received by the EEOC were found to be groundless; 40 percent of the employees filing complaints dropped them. In 20 percent of the complaints, employees received some form of compensation for suffering harassment." (p6 secC)

Daugherty, Jane. "Metro: Harassment Complaints Up Sharply." Detroit News 22 Oct 1997. p6 secC.

SEXUAL HARASSMENT--UNITED STATES--ARMED FORCES

The U.S. "Army released its report on the extent of sexual harassment in its ranks....According to the findings of the review, 78 percent of women in the Army have experienced crude or offensive behavior, 47 percent have received unwanted sexual attention, and 15 percent have experienced actual sexual coercion....It is important to note that while the spotlight of harassment has focused on women, and certainly that is a tremendous problem, the review also shows that men have also been subject to unevenhanded treatment. Seventy-six percent of men questioned said they had experienced crude or offensive behavior, 30 percent have received unwanted sexual attention, and 8 percent have been subject to coercion." (pH7488)

DeLauro, Rosa L. (Rep.-Conn.). "Sexual Harassment in the Army." Congressional Record. Daily ed. v143 n124 17 Sep 1997. pH7488. section/page-level access: <http://thomas.loc.gov/cgi-bin/query/R?r105:FLD001:H07488:> (ISSN0363-7239). (X1.1A.105/1).

SEXUAL HARASSMENT--UNITED STATES--YOUTH (v26)

SEXUAL HARASSMENT--UNITED STATES--YOUTH --ATTITUDES (v26)

SEXUAL HARASSMENT OF WOMEN--UNITED STATES --ARMED FORCES (v26)

In the U.S., "the Pentagon conducted large-scale studies in 1988 and 1995 of sexual harassment of female GIs. The second involved responses by 50,000 women--from all service branches--to a confidential questionnaire....56 percent of the women reported that they had experienced at least one episode of sexual harassment (ranging from cat-calls to rape) during the previous 12 months, a rate representing only a slight decline from the 64 percent harassment rate reported in the 1988 survey. The category that registered the largest decline--a drop of 15 percent--from the first to the second study was whistling and cat-calls....Rape/assault went down only one point, from five percent to four percent over the seven-year span between the two studies." (p6)

Ensign, Tod. "The Military's War on Women: The Wrong Stuff."

Nonviolent Activist v14 n4 Jul-Aug 1997. p6-7. (ISSN8755-7428).

A 1995 U.S. Defense Department survey "found that 47 percent of Army women had experienced unwanted sexual attention. A 1994 article by a team including staffers from the Army Research Institute, the service's social-science arm, found that about 13 percent of high-quality female officers who decided to leave the Army cited sexual harassment as a reason. Almost four times as many--nearly half of those surveyed--cited discrimination. In a 1995 ARI study, 42 percent of drill sergeants--many of whom come from all-male combat units--said their training prepared them slightly or not at all for working in mixed-sex units." (p29)

Newman, Richard J. "U.S. News: 'Human Relations' Offensive." U.S. News & World Report v123 n11 22 Sep 1997. p29. article-level access: <http://www.usnews.com/usnews/issue/970922/22ABER.HTM> (ISSN0041-5537).

SEXUAL HARASSMENT OF WOMEN--UNITED STATES --TEENAGERS

"According to a survey by Louis Harris & Associates for the American Association of University Women Foundation published in 1993, more than three-quarters of the teenage girls reported that they had been the target of unwanted sexual advances (Costello & Stone, 1994). Further, 43% of the girls surveyed said that this type of behavior made them have less confidence in themselves." (p717)

Kaplan, Elaine Bell. "Women's Perceptions of the Adolescent Experience." Adolescence v32 n127 Fall 1997. p715-734. (ISSN0001-8449).

SEXUALLY TRANSMITTED DISEASES

see also CHLAMYDIA INFECTIONS

The World Bank estimates that sexually transmitted diseases, "excluding AIDS, are the second leading cause of loss of healthy life among women between the ages of 15 and 44 in the developing world. The World Health Organization (WHO) recently estimated that there were 333 million new cases of the four curable STDs (gonorrhea, chlamydial infection, syphilis, and trichomoniasis) worldwide in 1995 among adults 15 to 49 years of age." (p5)

The Committee on Prevention and Control of STDs. Institute of Medicine. "The Hidden Epidemic: Confronting Sexually Transmitted Diseases." SIECUS Report v25 n3 Feb-Mar 1997. p4-14. (ISSN0091-3995).

SEXUALLY TRANSMITTED DISEASES--MASSACHUSETTS

"The Massachusetts Department of Public Health has released annual data on sexually transmitted disease (STD) for 1996....Gonorrhea cases decreased 19% (2,658 to 2,163--lowest since 1959). Chlamydia cases decreased 8% (7,402 to 6,791). Infectious syphilis cases increased 23% (69 to 85)."

Massachusetts. Dept. of Public Health. "1996 Sexually Transmitted Disease Data Released." Press Release 27 Mar 1997. document-level access: <http://www.magnet.state.ma.us/dph/std97.htm>

SEXUALLY TRANSMITTED DISEASES--MICHIGAN

"Six years ago, more than 1,300 Michigan residents were treated for syphilis, a bacterial infection that is passed during sexual relations and has the potential to kill or blind. Last year, 183 cases were reported....[The level for HIV infection] has remained relatively stable, with an estimated 1,000 new cases recorded each year." (p1 secA) "Michigan's most recent health figures show a 16-percent decline in gonorrhea and a 7-percent decline in chlamydia....At least 35,000 Michigan residents were treated last year for one of the three major sexually transmitted illnesses, 4,800 fewer people than in 1995. Another 11,500 are believed to have HIV." (p3 secA)

Pearce, Jeremy. "Venereal Disease Plummets in Michigan." Detroit News 5 Aug 1997. p1,3 secA.

SEXUALLY TRANSMITTED DISEASES--UNITED STATES (v26)

"HIV frequently leads to AIDS, which killed 30,700 Americans during the first nine months of 1996, according to the latest federal records. Gonorrhea and chlamydia are rarely fatal, but infected more than 850,000 Americans in 1995, the same records show." (p1 secA)

Pearce, Jeremy. "Venereal Disease Plummets in Michigan." Detroit News 5 Aug 1997. p1,3 secA.

"Of the top ten most frequently reported diseases in 1995 in the United States, five are sexually transmitted diseases (STDs). With approximately 12 million new cases of STDs occurring annually, rates of curable STDs in the United States are the highest in the developed world. In 1995, STDs accounted for 87 percent of all cases reported that year among the top ten most frequently reported diseases in the United States." (p4) "Every year, approximately 3 million American teenagers acquire an STD." (p5)

The Committee on Prevention and Control of STDs. Institute of Medicine. "The Hidden Epidemic: Confronting Sexually Transmitted Diseases." SIECUS Report v25 n3 Feb-Mar 1997. p4-14. (ISSN0091-3995).

In the U.S., "at least 1 person in 4 will contract an STD [sexually transmitted disease] at some point in his or her life. More than 12 million Americans, 3 million of whom are teenagers, are infected with an STD each year. As many as 56 million American adults and adolescents may have an incurable viral STD other than HIV....More than 4 million cases [of chlamydial infection] occur each year. Just 23 percent of American adults under 65 cite chlamydia when asked to name any STDs. About 200,000 to 500,000 new cases of genital herpes occur each year, and 31 million Americans are already infected with the genital herpes virus (herpes simplex virus, or HSV). At least 24 million people are infected with human papillomavirus (HPV) or genital warts, and as many as 1 million new infections occur each year....Between 1987 and 1991, the number of annually reported cases of syphilis--over 100,000--was at its highest level in 40 years. At least 800,000 cases of gonorrhea occur each year." (p22)

"Fact Sheet: Sexually Transmitted Diseases in the United States." SIECUS Report v25 n3 Feb-Mar 1997. p22-24. (ISSN0091-3995).

"More than 25 infectious organisms are sexually transmitted. Untreated, they can cause infertility, cancer, chronic pain, complications for infants of infected mothers and death. They include HIV, syphilis, chlamydia, herpes and hepatitis B....Five of the top 10 frequently reported diseases in...[the U.S.] in 1995 were sexually transmitted. Nationally, some 12 million new cases are reported each year." (p8)

"On First Reading: Sexually Transmitted Diseases: When Silence Is Deadly." State Legislatures v23 n6 Jun 1997. p8. (ISSN0147-6041).

SEXUALLY TRANSMITTED DISEASES--UNITED STATES --COSTS

Partly based on updated estimates of the economic burden of sexually transmitted diseases by K. Siegel, the Committee on Prevention and Control of Sexually Transmitted Diseases in the U.S. "estimates that the total costs for a selected group of major STDs and related syndromes, excluding HIV infection, were approximately $10 billion in 1994....The estimated annual cost of sexually transmitted HIV infection in 1994 was approximately $6.7 billion. Including these costs raises the overall cost of STDs in the United States to nearly $17 billion in 1994." (p7)

The Committee on Prevention and Control of STDs. Institute of Medicine. "The Hidden Epidemic: Confronting Sexually Transmitted Diseases." SIECUS Report v25 n3 Feb-Mar 1997. p4-14. (ISSN0091-3995).

SEXUALLY TRANSMITTED DISEASES--UNITED STATES --WOMEN--ATTITUDES

In a 1993 national survey of 1,000 women from 18 through 60 years of age in the U.S., "almost two-thirds knew nothing or very little about STDs [sexually transmitted diseases] other than HIV/AIDS and only 11 percent were aware that STDs can be more harmful to women than to men. The lack of knowledge among women in high-risk groups was dramatic: 65 percent of young women reported 'almost none' or 'very little' knowledge regarding STDs....84 percent of women surveyed were not concerned about acquiring an STD, including 72 percent of young women (age 18 to 24) and 78 percent of women who reported having had 'many' sexual partners." (p10)

The Committee on Prevention and Control of STDs. Institute of Medicine. "The Hidden Epidemic: Confronting Sexually Transmitted Diseases." SIECUS Report v25 n3 Feb-Mar 1997. p4-14. (ISSN0091-3995).

SEXUALLY TRANSMITTED DISEASES--UNITED STATES --YOUTH (v26)

"An estimated 12 million cases of STD [sexually transmitted disease] occur each year in the United States, including 3 million teenagers (American Association of World Health, 1994). Adolescents are particularly vulnerable because they are more likely to have multiple partners and less likely to prevent or recognize STDs (Biro & Rosenthal, 1992). Among heterosexual adolescents, STD rates are higher for females than males, possibly because females are more likely to acquire an STD following a single act of unprotected intercourse with an infected partner: an estimated 50% of women will contract gonorrhea (Potterat, Dukes, & Rothenberg, 1987) and 30% to 40% will contract chancroid, chlamydia, herpes, or syphilis (Harlap et al., 1991)." (p772)

Grimley, Diane M./Lee, Patricia A. "Condom and Other Contraceptive Use among a Random Sample of Female Adolescents: A Snapshot in Time." Adolescence v32 n128 Win 1997. p771-779. (ISSN0001-8449).

In the U.S., "one in four STDs [sexually transmitted diseases] occurs among adolescents. Chlamydia, an STD that can cause pelvic inflammatory disease and infertility, now occurs in 1 in 10 teens." (p7 secF)

Anstett, Patricia. "Body & Mind: Cover Story: An Unkind World for Girls." Detroit Free Press 16 Dec 1997. p6-8 secF.

In the U.S., "over 3 million adolescents are infected yearly with an STD [sexually transmitted disease]. Young people aged 15 to 19 have the highest rates of gonorrhea infection in the United States....In 1995, African-American women in this age group had 4,433 cases per 100,000 population and African-American teenage men had 3,267 cases per 100,000 population. These rates are 27 percent higher than those of Caucasian adolescents." (p15)

"Fact Sheet: Sexuality and Underserved Youth in Communities of Color." SIECUS Report v25 n5 Jun-Jul 1997. p15-16. (ISSN0091-3995).

In the U.S., "three million teenagers--about 1 in 4 sexually experienced teenagers--acquire an STD [sexually transmitted disease] every year. By the end of 1995, there were more than 2,300 teenagers diagnosed with AIDS....Chlamydia is more common among teenagers than among adult men and women; in some studies, up to 30 percent of sexually active teenage women and 10 percent of sexually active teenage men tested for STDs were infected with chlamydia." (p23)

"Fact Sheet: Sexually Transmitted Diseases in the United States." SIECUS Report v25 n3 Feb-Mar 1997. p22-24. (ISSN0091-3995).

SHARKS (v26)

"Atlantic sharks have declined dramatically during the past decade, with numbers of some species down from 75 to 80 percent....A quota of 2570 metric tons was put on sharks in 1993 as part of a fishery management plan covering 39 shark species....Commercial landings stood at 3000 metric tons in 1986 but at only 750 metric tons in 1995....According to the Ocean Wildlife Campaign, 40,000 blue sharks were unintentionally snagged and killed by US commercial fishing vessels in 1995 in the Atlantic and the Gulf of Mexico." (p663)

Baker, Beth. "Washington Watch: New Regulations Protect Sharks." BioScience v47 n10 Nov 1997. p663. (ISSN0006-3568).

"The National Marine Fisheries Service issued important regulations for shark fishing that include a 50 percent cut in the commercial quota for large coastal sharks....Large coastal sharks have declined in the Atlantic and Gulf of Mexico by 50 percent to 80 percent since the 1970s....At its peak, worldwide kills soon reached 30 to 70 million sharks per year....'As far-ranging as these measures may be, the reduction in the large coastal quota provides only a 50 percent chance that these sharks will start to recover by the end of this century,' [says Dr. Merry Camhi, a scientist in the National Audubon Living Oceans Program]...." (p24)

"State News: Sharks off the Hook: New Regulations Will Help Declining Shark Populations." Florida Naturalist v70 n2 Sum 1997. p24. (ISSN0015-4172).

SHEEP INDUSTRY--UNITED STATES (v26)

SHEEP RANCHES--MICHIGAN--WASHTENAW COUNTY (v26)

SHELLFISH FISHERIES--UNITED STATES (v26)

SHELLFISH TRADE

see also CRAYFISH INDUSTRY; SHRIMP FISHERIES

SHELLFISH TRADE--UNITED STATES

In the U.S., in first-half 1997, "the quantity of oyster and clam exports rose 45 and 9 percent, respectively, but exports of mussels plummeted 64 percent." (unpaginated) "Mussel exports fell to only $330,000 in first-half 1997. During the first 6 months of 1997, U.S. imports of mollusks (oysters, clams, and mussels) totaled 21.6 million pounds valued at $29.3 million....Most of the volume increase came from higher imports of mussels, up 15 percent....Over this period the value of imports has risen from just less than $4 million in first-half 1992 to $12.3 million in 1997....Oyster imports, while slightly higher in first-half 1997, have been trending downward. Over the last 4 years they have fallen 38 percent." (unpaginated)

Harvey, Dave/U.S. Dept. of Agriculture. Economic Research Service. "U.S. Oyster and Clam Exports Higher, Mussel and Oyster Imports Up." Aquaculture Outlook 3 Oct 1997.

SHELTERS, ANIMAL

see ANIMAL SHELTERS

SHELTERS FOR THE HOMELESS--NEW YORK (N.Y.) (v26)

SHELTERS FOR THE HOMELESS--UNITED STATES

"Eighty-four percent of New York City soup kitchens and food pantries report increased demand for services; they turn away 2,400 people daily, nearly double the figure from five years ago. In Milwaukee, which accounts for 60 percent of Wisconsin's welfare caseload, the number of families in homeless shelters last winter was up about 25 percent over the previous winter." (p29)

deMause, Neil. "Move 'Em Out." In These Times v22 n1 14 Dec 1997. p27-29. (ISSN0160-5992).

SHIITES--BAHRAIN--POPULATION

"The population of Bahrain in the early 1950s was about equally divided between Shia and Sunni, with a slight Shia majority....Since that time,...the number of Shia has steadily increased, and today they constitute some 70 percent of the population. Of these a slight majority are native Baharna; about 8 percent are Persian speakers." (p50)

Bahry, Louay. "The Opposition in Bahrain: A Bellwether for the Gulf?" Middle East Policy v5 n2 May 1997. p42-57. (ISSN1061-1924).

SHIITES--EMPLOYMENT--BAHRAIN

In Bahrain, there "is a high unemployment rate among the Shia--over 30 percent for Shia between the ages of 18 and 50, while among the population as a whole it is half that rate. At the same time, 63 percent of Bahrain's work force is foreign." (p50) "In some government ministries (health, works and transportation, education, and electricity) the Shia comprise about 80 percent of the labor force." (p51)

Bahry, Louay. "The Opposition in Bahrain: A Bellwether for the Gulf?" Middle East Policy v5 n2 May 1997. p42-57. (ISSN1061-1924).

SHIPMENT OF GOODS--UNITED STATES (v26)

SHIPPING (v26)

SHIPPING--CANADA (v26)

SHIPPING--EMPLOYMENT--UNITED STATES (v26)

SHIPPING--HONG KONG

"In the second quarter of 1997, 11,138 ocean vessels with a total capacity of 50.5 million net registered tons entered Hong Kong, according to the figures released...by the Census and Statistics Department. Compared with the second quarter of 1996, the number of vessels increased by 12% and capacity increased by 11%....In the second quarter of 1997, the total tonnage of seaborne inward cargo, comprising seaborne imports and seaborne inward transhipment, was estimated at 23.7 million tonnes, representing an increase of 10% over the same quarter in 1996. The respective increases in the total tonnage of seaborne imports and seaborne inward transhipment were 9% and 16%....In the second quarter of 1997, the top five countries/territories of loading for seaborne inward cargo were Singapore (accounted for 16% in tonnage terms), Japan (13%), Taiwan (11%), mainland of China (10%) and the Republic of Korea (9%). The top five countries/territories of discharge for seaborne outward cargo were mainland of China (26%), the USA (20%), Taiwan (7%), Japan (5%) and Federal Republic of Germany (4%)."

Hong Kong. Census and Statistics Department. "Shipping Statistics for Second Quarter of 1997." Press Release 24 Oct 1997. document-level access: <http://www.info.gov.hk/censtatd/hkstat/press/sh12q97.htm>

SHIPPING--QUEBEC--MONTREAL (v26)

SHIPPING--UNITED STATES (v26)

SHIPS (v26)

SHIPS--SCRAPPING (v26)

SHOE INDUSTRY (v26)

SHOES--UNITED STATES--WOMEN--ATTITUDES

In 1996, half of American "women surveyed by Porter/Novelli of Chicago said they wear heels on a daily basis, down from 60 percent in 1986. Twenty-one percent never wear them, but another 25 percent wear them sometimes....Among those who don't wear heels every day, 55 percent say it's because the shoes hurt....Forty-three percent of women say they've gotten blisters from high heels, 39 percent report pain in the balls of their feet, 23 percent each report corns and calluses, and 22 percent have experienced back pain." (p30)

Crispell, Diane. "Kaleidoscope: Have High Heels, Will Limp." American Demographics v19 n5 May 1997. p30-31. article-level access: <http://www.demographics.com/Publications/AD/97_ad/9705_ad/AD970516.htm> (ISSN0163-4089).

In the U.S., "a 1996 survey by The Data Group for Dr. Scholl's and the American Podiatric Association shows an increase in women who say they don't wear high heels. In their first study, conducted in 1986, 39% of women reported they didn't wear high heels daily. Ten years later, that number had spiked to 46%....Eighty percent of the women in the survey say they would wear high heels more often if they were more comfortable....Today, 31% of women in the Dr. Scholl's/APA survey consider a shoe with a one-inch heel to be high, whereas only 10 years ago, 18% said a one-inch heel was high. The leveling impulse is clearly being driven by the young. Among 18 to 24-year-old women, a plurality, 42%, considered a one-inch heel high. A Roper Starch survey for Rockport shoes finds that over six-in-ten women say that shoes are their favorite item of clothing to buy....58% of women told Roper Starch/Rockport that one can never have too many pairs of shoes." (p58,60)

Bowman, Karlyn H. "American Fashion Embraces the Casual and Comfortable." Public Perspective v8 n5 Aug-Sep 1997. p58-60. (ISSN1050-5067).

SHOPLIFTING--MICHIGAN--WASHTENAW COUNTY

In the U.S., "national estimates put the loss at $25 million a day from about 23 million shoplifters, despite high-tech surveillance techniques, ubiquitous store detectives and stiff penalties for those who get caught. In Michigan, shoplifting cases are prosecuted under retail fraud statutes. First-degree retail fraud, a felony, is the theft of more than $100 worth of goods and carries a maximum sentence of two years in prison. Second-degree retail fraud, a misdemeanor, involves less than $100 worth of property and carries a maximum sentence of 93 days in jail. Sentences can go higher for repeat offenders. In Washtenaw County, the prosecutor's office authorized 723 retail fraud warrants in 1996, and 131 involved felony charges, said Chief Assistant Prosecutor Joseph Burke." (p2 secB)

Barton, John. "Local: Searching for Shoplifters: Addicted to Steal: New Support Group Aims to Help Shoplifters." Ann Arbor News 10 Dec 1997. p1-2 secB.

SHOPPING--UNITED STATES

"Americans expect to spend an average of $816 this holiday season, totaling more than $160 billion in overall purchases, according to a November survey conducted by Quicken and the Roper Starch survey group....Surveys conducted by the national Foundation for Consumer Credit last season showed nearly one-third of Americans overspent by $322. Men admitted going over their budgets an average $339, while women claim to have exceeded their budgets by $305. Ten percent exceeded their budgets by as much as $999 and 1 percent overspent by more than $1,000. Almost 20 percent reported they would continue making holiday bill payments into the summer...." (p7 secF)

Seebacher, Noreen. "Strategies: Draw Up Plan to Avoid Overspending on Gifts." Detroit News 1 Dec 1997. p7 secF.

SHOPPING CARTS--WOUNDS AND INJURIES--UNITED STATES--CHILDREN

In the U.S., "an average of 21,600 kids age 5 and under were treated each year from 1985 to 1996 for injuries from falling from, tipping, or running into shopping carts. Moreover, the number of injuries has increased from 16,900 in 1985 to 22,200 in 1996....Industry officials estimate that about half of the nation's carts are currently equipped with safety straps." (p3)

Bowers, Faye. "United States: Child Safety Goes Shopping." The Christian Science Monitor v89 n154 7 Jul 1997. p3. The Christian Science Monitor search engine: <http://www.csmonitor.com/plweb-cgi/iops1.pl> To retrieve this article, enter the following search: ED=19970707 AND shopping. In the "retrieved list," click the title that matches this record. (ISSN0882-7729).

SHOPPING CENTER PARKING FACILITIES--UNITED STATES

In the U.S., "from 1965 to 1981, shopping mall parking lots were designed for use at the 10th busiest hour of the year--with almost six spaces per 1,000 square feet of retail space. A 1981 study by ULI [Urban Land Institute] and the International Council of Shopping Centers shaved the standard to four spaces per 1,000 square feet in shopping centers of 25,000 to 40,000 square feet; four to five spaces for centers with 400,000 to 600,000 square feet, and five spaces for the largest malls....'The design hour has been pulled back from the 10th to the 20th busiest hour of parking, but most highways are designed for the 30th busiest hour of driving,'...[Donald Shoup, American Institute of Certified Planners, director of the Institute of Transportation Studies at the University of California Los Angeles] says. Shoup points out that designing for the 20th busiest hour of use leaves at least half of a shopping center's parking spaces vacant a minimum of 40 percent of the time." (p12)

Wormser, Lisa. "Planning Practice: Don't Even Think of Parking Here." Planning v63 n6 Jun 1997. p10-15. (ISSN0001-2610).

SHOPPING MALLS--UNITED STATES--PUBLIC OPINION (v26)

SHRIMP FISHERIES--MEXICO, GULF OF

The Gulf of Mexico Council's amended shrimp plan, backed by the National Coalition for Marine Conservation, "was approved on July 30 [1997]. The escape devices in Gulf trawls, according to the council, will reduce by at least 50 percent of the incidental capture of severely overfished red snapper. Shrimping with unmodified nets kills an estimated 35 million young snapper every year, or more than 80% of each new generation. Unmodified shrimp nets also kill billions of other juvenile fish, including croaker and mackerel...." (p6)

"A Good Summer for BRDs: NMFS Backs Councils to Reduce Bycatch." NCMC Marine Bulletin n79 Spr-Sum 1997. p6.

SHRIMP INDUSTRY--UNITED STATES (v26)

In the U.S., "after falling in first-half 1996, the quantity and value of shrimp imports rose 3 and 12 percent, respectively, in first-half 1997 compared to a year earlier." (unpaginated) "Frozen shrimp imports were only slightly higher and fresh shrimp imports fell more than 50 percent....In first-half 1997,...[Ecuador, Thailand, and Indonesia] accounted for 57 percent of the total quantity of imported shrimp and 64 percent of the total value." (unpaginated)

Harvey, Dave/U.S. Dept. of Agriculture. Economic Research Service. "Quantity and Value of Shrimp Imports Up in 1997." Aquaculture Outlook 3 Oct 1997.

SHUTTLES, SPACE

see SPACE SHUTTLES

SICK LEAVE--SWEDEN (v26)

SICKLE CELL ANEMIA--AFRO-AMERICANS

Eighty thousand African Americans live "with sickle-cell anemia, the inherited blood disorder found primarily among black people." (p7 secF) "About one in 12 blacks have the sickle-cell trait, which means they carry the gene to pass on the disease but don't have the symptoms. If two such people have a child there is: a one-in-four chance their child will have sickle-cell anemia; a two-in-four chance their child will have the sickle-cell trait; a one-in-four chance their child will have neither. About 150 in every 100,000 black children are born with sickle-cell anemia." (p8 secF)

Mishra, Raja. "Body & Mind: Cover Story: Living with Sickle-Cell." Detroit Free Press 30 Sep 1997. p6-8 secF.

SICKNESS

see DISEASES

SICKNESS INSURANCE

see INSURANCE, HEALTH

SIDS

see SUDDEN INFANT DEATH SYNDROME

SIGN LANGUAGE--UNITED STATES

In the U.S., "hundreds of post-secondary schools offer ASL [American Sign Language] instruction. According to one count, more than 70 universities and colleges accept ASL to fulfill a foreign-language requirement....At least 200 different forms [of sign language] exist around the world." (p12)

Conover, Kirsten A. "Learning: In Gesture toward Change, Schools Sign On to 'Signing.'" The Christian Science Monitor v90 n17 18 Dec 1997. p12. The Christian Science Monitor search engine: <http://www.csmonitor.com/plweb-cgi/iops1.pl> To retrieve this article, enter the following search: ED=19971218 AND signing. In the "retrieved list," click the title that matches this record. (ISSN0882-7729).

SILICON VALLEY (CALIF.)--ECONOMIC CONDITIONS --SOCIAL CONDITIONS (v26)

SILICOSIS--UNITED STATES (v26)

SILK INDUSTRY--EMPLOYMENT--INDIA--CHILDREN

In India, "bonded child labor" refers to the phenomenon of children working in conditions of servitude in order to pay off a debt. "The rate of bondage for...child workers [in the silk industry] is 100 percent....Ninety percent of India's silk thread is produced in the southern state of Karnataka, where approximately 400,000 people make their living on the cultivation of silkworms or the production of silk thread. An estimated 100,000 of these workers are children." (p599) "More than 80 percent of silk reelers are under twenty years of age, with most of them between ten and fifteen years old....In one 'taluk' (subdivision of a district) alone, there are about one hundred [silk] twining factories, employing more than 8,000 children, all of them believed to be bonded....Advances from twining factory owners range from 2,000 to 10,000 rupees. During the first six months of their employment, children earn just two or three rupees a day, enough for a snack, or, for those living far away, enough for bus fare to the factory. After this initial 'training' period ends, children earn between fifty paise and two rupees an hour, depending on their age and skill. The typical work day is from 7:00 a.m. until 8:00 p.m...." (p600-601) "In Kanchipuram, 40,000 to 50,000 children work in bondage on the silk handlooms, while in Varanasi the number of bonded child laborers working on the handlooms is approximately 85,000....In Varanasi, advances reportedly range from 2,000 to 5,000 rupees, while in Kanchipuram the advances are the highest of any industry, with children as young as six bringing in advances of 10,000 rupees and older children being traded for advances of up to 15,000 rupees." (p604)

Tucker, Lee. "Child Slaves in Modern India: The Bonded Labor Problem." Human Rights Quarterly v19 n3 Aug 1997. p572-629. (ISSN0275-0392).

SILVER INDUSTRY--EMPLOYMENT--INDIA--CHILDREN

In India, "an estimated 10,000 children work in the silver smithies of Salem district [in Tamil Nadu]. In one town, there were five hundred occupants, two hundred of whom were children under the age of fifteen. One hundred and thirty-five of these children were laboring in the production of silver." (p593) "The average advance for a six-year-old is 5,000 rupees. Although interest is not added to the principal amount owed, the extremely low rate of wages paid makes for effective annual interest rates in the range of 300 percent....Depending on the employer, children work six days a week, six and a half days a week, or twenty-eight days a month, with the days of the new and full moon off. The typical work day is twelve hours long, from 8:00 a.m. to 8:00 p.m." (p594)

Tucker, Lee. "Child Slaves in Modern India: The Bonded Labor Problem." Human Rights Quarterly v19 n3 Aug 1997. p572-629. (ISSN0275-0392).

SINGAPORE--COMMERCE (v26)

In Singapore, "total trade grew strongly in the third quarter of 1997. The volume of total trade increased by 13%. In value terms, total trade increased by 12% to reach a record high of

$99.3 billion. Total exports increased by 8.8% to reach $47.8 billion. Domestic exports increased by 7.6% while re-exports increased by 10%. With the recovery in global electronics demand, in particular from the major markets such as the US and the EU, non-oil domestic exports increased by 9.4% to $23.6 billion in the third quarter of 1997, up from the moderate increase of 4.4% in the last quarter. Non-oil domestic exports increased in all but one of the top 5 markets. Growth to the US, EU, Malaysia, and Hong Kong rose by 11%, 13%, 4.8% and 20% respectively. However, growth to Japan continued to shrink, falling by 8%."

Singapore. Ministry of Trade and Industry. "Third Quarter 1997 Economic Survey of Singapore." Press Release 1997. document-level access: <http://www.singstat.gov.sg/PRESS/97qes3.htm>

SINGAPORE--ECONOMIC CONDITIONS (v26)

"With electronics making up 44 percent of manufacturing output and 60 percent of its non-oil exports, Singapore was especially hurt by the weakness of the world electronics market in 1996. Singapore's GDP growth dropped 2.2 points to 6.7 percent." (p6)

Jerardo, Alberto/Huang, Sophia Wu/U.S. Dept. of Agriculture. Economic Research Service. "Regional Overviews: APEC to Resume Healthy Growth." APEC: International Agriculture and Trade Reports Situation and Outlook Series Aug 1997. p6-8.

In Singapore, "economic growth continued to pick up in the third quarter of 1997. On a year-on-year basis, the economy expanded by...10.1%, up from 8.2% in the second quarter....Manufacturing output continued to recover in the third quarter, growing by...9.5%, substantially stronger than the 3.5% a quarter earlier. Growth was higher in almost all segments, led by chemicals (34%), petroleum (16%) and electronics (9.8%)....The construction sector expanded by 13%, due to higher public and private-sector residential activity and public civil engineering works, helped by dry weather during the quarter. The commerce sector grew by 8.6% in the third quarter, up from 8% a quarter earlier....Overall, the financial and business services sector rose by 12% in the third quarter, largely unchanged from the 11% growth a quarter earlier."

Singapore. Ministry of Trade and Industry. "Third Quarter 1997 Economic Survey of Singapore." Press Release 1997. document-level access: <http://www.singstat.gov.sg/PRESS/97qes3.htm>

SINGAPORE--EMPLOYMENT (v26)

In Singapore, "the seasonally adjusted unemployment rate in September 1997 was 1.8%, slightly higher than the 1.7% in June 1997. There was a net increase of 28,200 jobs, higher than the 22,100 jobs created in the same period last year....Most of the employment gains continued to come from the construction sector (16,100). In line with its recovery, the manufacturing sector saw an increase of 2,100 jobs after five consecutive quarters of falling employment. Employment rose by 3,500 in the financial and business services sector and 900 in the transport and communications sector. The commerce sector saw a drop in employment of 1,600, after a hefty increase of 5,000 jobs in the previous quarter. The remaining sectors contributed a total of 7,200 jobs."

Singapore. Ministry of Trade and Industry. "Third Quarter 1997 Economic Survey of Singapore." Press Release 1997. document-level access: <http://www.singstat.gov.sg/PRESS/97qes3.htm>

SINGLE FATHERS--AFRO-AMERICANS

In the U.S., "the number of African American children being raised by their fathers has increased from 2% in 1970 to 3% in 1993 (Bennett, 1995)....The U.S. Bureau of the Census (Bennett, 1995) reports that the majority of African American fathers raising children alone have never been married (54%) or are divorced (23%)." (p343)

Cochran, Donna L. "Article: African American Fathers: A Decade Review of the Literature." Families in Society v78 n4 Jul-Aug 1997. p340-350. (ISSN1044-3894).

SINGLE FATHERS--UNITED STATES (v26)

In the U.S., "in 1995, 2.5 million children (4 percent) lived with their father, but not their mother. Among these children's fathers, 48 percent were divorced, 28 percent had never been married, 18 percent were married but not living with their wife and 5 percent were widowed."

U.S. Dept. of Commerce. Economic and Statistics Administration. "Census Facts for Father's Day." Census Bureau Fact Sheet 9 Jun 1997. document-level access: <http://www.census.gov/Press-Release/fs97-06.html>

In the U.S., "the number of single fathers with children under 18 grew from 400,000 in 1970 to 1.7 million in 1995. As a proportion of all family groups with children, they increased fivefold over the same period: from 1 percent to 5 percent....For children living with their father only: 1994 median family income was $23,155. Twenty-six percent were poor. Six out of 10 lived with at least one sibling. Seventy-six percent of their fathers had a high school diploma; 12 percent had a bachelor's degree or more. Seventy-nine percent had a father who was working. Five out of 10 lived in rental housing."

U.S. Dept. of Commerce. Economic and Statistics Administration. "Census Facts for Father's Day." Census Bureau Fact Sheet 9 Jun 1997. document-level access: <http://www.census.gov/Press-Release/fs97-06.html>

SINGLE MOTHERS--AFRO-AMERICANS

"The percentage of all African American babies who were born to unmarried women climbed from about 25% in 1960 to 65% in 1990 (Smith et al. 1996)." (p1217) "Since 1960, the percentage of mothers who had never been married has risen sharply from only 3% to more than 35%." (p1228) "By 1990, nonmarital motherhood accounted for fully 50% of African American children in central cities residing separately from their fathers." (p1230)

Tolnay, Stewart E. "The Great Migration and Changes in the Northern Black Family, 1940 to 1990." Social Forces v75 n4 Jun 1997. p1213-1238. (ISSN0037-7732).

SINGLE MOTHERS--TEXAS

In the U.S., "displaced homemakers and single parent programs specialize in individually targeted pre-employment training and counseling services....In...Texas, 52 percent of displaced women rated the displaced homemaker or single parent program as much better than any other government program in which they have participated....There are 1.2 million displaced homemakers in Texas: 47 percent of displaced homemakers are under 50 years old; and 39 percent of displaced homemakers are African-American, Asian, and Hispanic. There are 561,342 single mothers in Texas: 61 percent of Texan single mothers are between the ages of 25-44; 47 percent of single mothers are African-American and Hispanic; and 53 percent are nonminority." (pH5440)

Johnson, Eddie Bernice (Rep.-Tex.). "Carl D. Perkins Vocational-Technical Education Act Amendments of 1997." Congressional Record. Daily ed. v143 n102 17 Jul 1997. pH5413-5440. section/page-level access: <http://thomas.loc.gov/cgi-bin/query/R?r105:FLD001:H05440:> (ISSN0363-7239). (X1.1A.105/1).

SINGLE-PARENT FAMILY (v26)

SINGLE-PARENT FAMILY--AUSTRALIA

According to the report, "Labour Force Status and Other Characteristics of Families," by the Australian Bureau of Statistics, "the number of one parent families continued to grow to 721,100 in June 1997 compared with 672,000 in June 1996. Women headed 84 per cent of one parent families. For one parent families with dependants: 47 per cent of parents were employed, 9 per cent were unemployed and 44 per cent were not in the labour force; half of unemployed parents had been looking for work for 29 weeks or longer; the parent was not employed in 272,000 of these families, with over 400,000 children aged 0-14 (11 per cent of all children aged 0-14)."

Australian Bureau of Statistics. "Australia's Families and the Workforce--ABS." Media Release 30 Sep 1997. document-level access: <http://www.abs.gov.au/websitedbs/d3110125.nsf/4a255eef008309e44a255eef00061e57/ed1997d7b1f812a84a25652100810827?OpenDocument>

SINGLE-PARENT FAMILY--GERMANY

"The number of single parents raising children in Germany has risen sharply in the last couple of years. There were 1.7 million one-parent families in 1995, of which 1.5 million were headed by mothers. Three out of five single parents raising children are divorced or separated from their partners, one out of five are widowed, and the remaining fifth are unmarried." (p13)

"Nachrichten News: Social Policy." Deutschland n6 Dec 1997. p13. (ISSN0945-6791).

SINGLE-PARENT FAMILY--WISCONSIN (v26)

SINGLE PARENTS--IRELAND

In Ireland, "Census 96 Volume 3--Household Composition and Family Units" "shows that there has been a 15% increase in the number of lone-parent households with children in the State, from 109,600 in 1991 to 125,500 in 1996. Almost 72% of lone-parent households were in urban areas."

Ireland. Central Statistics Office. "1996 Census--Volume 3, Household Composition and Family Unit." Press Release 27 Nov 1997. document-level access: <http://www.cso.ie/pressreleases/prelcen96v3.html>

SINGLE PEOPLE

see INCOME--AUSTRALIA--SINGLE PEOPLE; UNMARRIED COUPLES

SINGLE PEOPLE--AUSTRALIA

According to the report, "Labour Force Status and Other Characteristics of Families," by the Australian Bureau of Statistics, "there were 2,377,300 persons in June 1997 who were not members of a family. The majority (64 per cent) of these people lived alone. Of those living alone, only 43 per cent were employed (57 per cent of men but only 31 per cent of women), reflecting the older age profile of this group. In contrast, 72 per cent of people not living alone (but not members of a family) were employed."

Australian Bureau of Statistics. "Australia's Families and the Workforce--ABS." Media Release 30 Sep 1997. document-level access: <http://www.abs.gov.au/websitedbs/d3110125.nsf/4a255eef008309e44a255eef00061e57/ed1997d7b1f812a84a25652100810827?OpenDocument>

SINGLE PEOPLE--FRANCE

"Singles number 26.5 million of France's 58 million population, according to European Union statistics. Popular magazines trumpet the fact that Paris not only claims more singles than any other European capital, but that more than 50 percent of Parisians live alone." (p10)

Gaouette, Nicole. "Global Report: Matchmakers: Giving Cupid a Nudge: Paris." The Christian Science Monitor v89 n224 15 Oct 1997. p1,10-12. The Christian Science Monitor search engine: <http://www.csmonitor.com/plweb-cgi/iops1.pl> To retrieve this article, enter the following search: ED=19971015 AND paris. In the "retrieved list," click the title that matches this record. (ISSN0882-7729).

SINGLE PEOPLE--TRAVEL

"Nearly 40 percent of adult Americans are single--unmarried, divorced, or widowed, according to the US Census Bureau....When Paul Spillar of Ross, Calif., publisher of THE SINGLE TRAVELER newsletter, surveyed singles in four English-speaking countries, nearly 90 percent admitted being 'rankled' by the travel industry's 'discrimination and unfair treatment.'" (p12)

Gardner, Marilyn. "Travel: Going Solo Is Easy and Adventurous for Today's Travelers." The Christian Science Monitor v89 n152 2 Jul 1997. p12. The Christian Science Monitor search engine: <http://www.csmonitor.com/plweb-cgi/iops1.pl> To retrieve this article, enter the following search: ED=19970702 AND travelers. In the "retrieved list," click the title that matches this record. (ISSN0882-7729).

SINGLE PEOPLE--UNITED STATES

In the U.S., "the percentage of Hispanic adults who had never married grew from 19 percent to 29 percent between 1970 and 1995, while the percentage of whites remaining single rose from 16 percent to 21 percent. The delay or avoidance of marriage was most pronounced among African Americans--the percentage who had not married rose from 21 percent to 38 percent over the same period." (p29-30)

del Pinal, Jorge/Singer, Audrey. "Generations of Diversity: Latinos in the United States." Population Bulletin v52 n3 Oct 1997. p2-47. (ISSN0032-468X).

SINGLE WOMEN--UNITED STATES (v26)

SKI RESORTS--VERMONT (v26)

SKI TOURING

see CROSS-COUNTRY SKIING

SKIN--CANCER--UNITED STATES (v26)

Melanoma is "a potentially deadly form of skin cancer that is diagnosed in about 40,000 Americans each year....An estimated one out of every 10 Americans has at least one abnormal mole, or dysplastic nevus (plural: dysplastic nevi)....Several small studies have suggested that dysplastic nevi could account for 29 percent to 49 percent of nonfamilial melanoma."

U.S. National Cancer Institute. "Abnormal Moles Found to Increase Risk for Melanoma." Press Release 13 May 1997. document-level access: <http://rex.nci.nih.gov/massmedia/pressreleases/melanoma.html>

SKIRTS--UNITED STATES--WOMEN--ATTITUDES

In the U.S., "a third of women have a floor-length dress or skirt for evening wear, but only 4% wear it repeatedly. Moving from long to short, 22% of women own a miniskirt but fewer than 10% usually wear it. A 1994 Harris survey showed that only 1% of women usually wear skirts or dresses at miniskirt length, and just 3% put their hems considerably above their knees. About 18% say the right length for them is just above the knee and 14% place the perfect hem at the knee. The largest number in the survey, 34%, say their skirts and dresses fall just below the knee while 22% say their skirts are considerably longer." (p58)

Bowman, Karlyn H. "American Fashion Embraces the Casual and Comfortable." Public Perspective v8 n5 Aug-Sep 1997. p58-60. (ISSN1050-5067).

SLAVE-TRADE--RUSSIA--WOMEN (v26)

SLAVERY--UNITED STATES--PUBLIC OPINION

"Two Gallup polls conducted in June [1997] asked respondents if the U.S. government should pass legislation which 'officially apologizes to American blacks for the fact that slavery was practiced before the Civil War in this country.' Whites opposed the idea by a 67% to 26% margin. Blacks favored the idea by almost the same margin, 65% to 28%....White Southerners are solidly opposed to an official apology, by a fifty-one point margin: 22% favor an apology while 73% oppose it. Outside the South the margin is not quite as wide, with 28% in favor and only 64% opposed. The greatest degree of support among whites for an official apology comes from young adults, with 36% of those aged 18-29 in favor, compared to 24% of those aged 30 and older. Women are slightly more likely than men to favor the

idea of an apology: 30% of women vs. 22% of men."
Newport, Frank/Gallup Organization. "Whites Oppose Formal Apology for Slavery." Press Release 25 Jul 1997. document-level access: <http://www.gallup.com/poll/news/970725b.htm>

SLEEP DISORDERS--FRANCE--AGED (v26)

SLEEP DISORDERS--UNITED STATES (v26)

SLEEPING CUSTOMS--JAPAN--MARRIED PEOPLE (v26)

SLOT MACHINES--UNITED STATES

In the U.S., slot machines "accounted for $10.8 billion in gross casino revenue in 1995--twice that of table games (not including revenues from non-casino venues and Indian casinos). Las Vegas alone houses nearly 165,000 slot machines. That's enough for almost one in nine Nevadans....Casinos increased slots 10 percent in 1995 and realized a 17 percent slot profit, according to Christiansen/Cummings." (p39)
Heubusch, Kevin. "Taking Chances on Casinos." American Demographics v19 n5 May 1997. p34-40. article-level access: <http://www.demographics.com/Publications/AD/97_ad/9705_ad/AD970530.htm> (ISSN0163-4089).

SMALL BUSINESS--CANADA (v26)

"There are nearly one million businesses with paid employees in Canada, of which 97 percent have less than 50 workers, and 1.1 million Canadians who describe themselves as self-employed.... "Consider that 75 percent of all businesses in Canada have less than five employees." (p264)
Ritz, Gerry (MP-SK). "Government Orders: Supply." Canada. Parliament. House of Commons. Debates. v135 n7 30 Sep 1997. p247-281. section-level access: <http://www.parl.gc.ca/36/1/parlbus/chambus/house/debates/007_1997-09-30/han007-e.htm#LINKT26> (ISSN0704-5603). (X3-361E).

"Today about 52% of all Canadians employed in the private sector are in small business with fewer than 100 employees per business. "At least 85% of all new jobs created in Canada are created by small business." (p912)
Schmidt, Werner (MP-BC). "Statements by Members: Small Business Week." Canada. Parliament. House of Commons. Debates. v135 n17 21 Oct 1997. p912. section-level access: <http://www.parl.gc.ca/36/1/parlbus/chambus/house/debates/017_1997-10-21/han017-e.htm#LINK80> (ISSN0704-5603). (X3-361E).

SMALL BUSINESS--CHINA (v26)

SMALL BUSINESS--ENVIRONMENTAL ASPECTS --CHINA (v26)

SMALL BUSINESS--MARYLAND

"More than 97.8 percent of Maryland's full-time firms have fewer than 500 employees, and there are an additional 131,000 individuals who are self-employed. The significance of these businesses to Maryland's economy is evident in study after study, such as the Small Business Administration's recent report that Maryland firms with fewer than 20 employees increased employment by 10.4 percent between 1991 and 1995. Minority-owned businesses also have made great strides in recent years. Between 1987 and 1992, Maryland's number of women-owned businesses rose by 48.7 percent, its number of African-American owned firms rose 65 percent and its number of Hispanic-owned firms rose 148.7 percent." (pS5374)
Sarbanes, Paul S. (Sen.-Md.). "Small Business Week 1997." Congressional Record. Daily ed. v143 n76 5 Jun 1997. pS5374. section/page-level access: <http://thomas.loc.gov/cgi-bin/query/R?r105:FLD001:S05374:> (ISSN0363-7239). (X1.1A.105/1).

SMALL BUSINESS--MICHIGAN (v26)

SMALL BUSINESS--QUEBEC (PROVINCE)

In Quebec, "in 1995, there were 177,000 businesses with fewer than five employees. If we add to that the 436,000 self-employed workers, we have some idea of the changes the work force is currently undergoing. "Moreover, between 1978 and 1995, the proportion of total jobs which were in businesses with 50 employees or less rose from 28% to 38%, while the proportion for large businesses dropped from 46% to 37%." (p1039)
Lalonde, Francine (MP-PQ). "Statements by Members: Small Business Week." Canada. Parliament. House of Commons. Debates. v135 n19 23 Oct 1997. p1039. section-level access: <http://www.parl.gc.ca/36/1/parlbus/chambus/house/debates/019_1997-10-23/han019-e.htm#LINK80> (ISSN0704-5603). (X3-361E).

SMALL BUSINESS--TENNESSEE

Since its creation in 1984, the Tennessee Small Business Development Center "has counseled over 2,800 small-business owners and would-be entrepreneurs. About two-thirds of its work...is spent on two functions: advising on start-ups (sometimes advising against them) and assisting with financing." (p11) "One study of its operations compared the growth rate in gross sales of TSBDC clients with that of all businesses. The results: 7.3 percent sales growth for all businesses, 21.6 percent for TSBDC clients. A similar study of employment growth rates yielded the following results: 4.2 percent employment growth for all businesses, 32.9 percent growth for TSBDC clients. The analysts concluded that every dollar from state and federal funds spent on the TSBDC counseling program (excluding costs of other functions like research) returned $8.91 in new, incremental state and federal tax revenues during the base year considered." (p12)
Baldwin, Fred D. "Small Is Big Business in Eastern Tennessee." Appalachia v30 n2 May-Aug 1997. p6-13. (ISSN0003-6595).

SMALL BUSINESS--UNITED STATES

From 1991 through 1995, "the American economy added a net total of 7.7 million new jobs. Virtually all of those jobs were generated by firms with fewer than 500 employees, the definition of 'small' used by the SBA [Small Business Administration] for most statistical purposes....35 percent of the jobs were generated by firms the SBA calls 'microbusinesses'--businesses with fewer than 5 employees--and another 32 percent were generated by firms with 5 to 19 employees." (p6) "The SBA reports that the number of all small businesses, nationally, has increased 49 percent since 1982....The number of woman-owned businesses more than doubled during that same period--up by 225 percent....Small businesses provide about 67 percent of initial job opportunities....A 1982 survey showed that small firms produced 55 percent of all innovations; by 1991 small firms accounted for 25 percent of the jobs in high-technology sectors, according to the SBA....93 percent of high-technology firms fit the SBA definition of 'small,' and 70 percent have fewer than 20 employees." (p8)
Baldwin, Fred D. "Small Is Big Business in Eastern Tennessee." Appalachia v30 n2 May-Aug 1997. p6-13. (ISSN0003-6595).

"Nearly half of the 17 million small businesses in the United States were home-based, according to a new report released...by the Commerce Department's Census Bureau. 'Only 2 percent of these home-based businesses had $250,000 or more in receipts while 74 percent brought in less than $25,000,' said Mary Frauenfelder, author of the report, '1992 Characteristics of Business Owners'....More than 14 million of the 17 million small businesses in the United States (82 percent) were owner-operated and had no paid employees....Thirty-five percent of the owners had at least a bachelor's degree and 42 percent of the owners of service businesses had bachelor's and/or professional degrees....Fifty-seven percent of the owners started or acquired their businesses with less than $5,000 in capital and 25 percent required no capital. Only 19 percent used capital based on a personal loan."

U.S. Dept. of Commerce. Economic & Statistics Administration. "Almost Half of All U.S. Small Businesses Home-Based, Census Bureau Reports." Census Bureau Press Release 5 Nov 1997. document-level access: <http://www.census.gov/Press-Release/cb97-182.html>

In the U.S., "small businesses have carried an often unbearable load from unwarranted and unjustified lawsuits. Data from San Diego's superior court published by the Washington Legal Foundation revealed that punitive damages were requested in 41 percent of suits against small businesses....The National Federation of Independent Business has reported that 34 percent of Texas small business owners have been sued or threatened with court action seeking punitive damages." (pS5347)

Abraham, Spencer (Sen.-Mich.). "Statements on Introduced Bills and Joint Resolutions." Congressional Record. Daily ed. v143 n76 5 Jun 1997. pH5342-5368. section/page-level access: <http://thomas.loc.gov/cgi-bin/query/R?r105:FLD001:H05346:> (ISSN0363-7239). (X1.1A.105/1).

"Small firms continue to be the primary source of total jobs in the [Tenth District, which includes Colorado, Kansas, Missouri, Oklahoma, Nebraska, New Mexico, and Wyoming], accounting for 60 percent of all jobs in 1994....Small firms in 1994 accounted for less than a third of all manufacturing jobs in the district....Small firms provided at least 60 percent of all jobs in all district states except in Nebraska and Missouri, where they accounted for 58 and 54 percent, respectively. In Wyoming, small firms provided 75 percent of jobs in 1994, the largest share among district states." (p9) "Small firms provided 77.9 percent of all jobs in the retail trade sector in 1994." (p10) "Small firms were the largest provider of service sector jobs in 1994." (p11) "In construction, small firms accounted for 82 percent of jobs. In wholesale trade, small firms provided over three fourths of all jobs. In finance, insurance, and real estate, small firms provided nearly two thirds of all jobs." (p12)

Henderson, Jason. "How Important Are Small Businesses in the Tenth District?" Federal Reserve Bank of Kansas City Regional Economic Digest v8 n3 Fall 1997. p9-12. (ISSN1049-5339).

SMALL BUSINESS--UNITED STATES--FINANCE (v26)

SMALL BUSINESS--UNITED STATES--MINORITIES --WOMEN

In the U.S., "minorities received only 3.2 percent of all federal small business contracts in fiscal 1996, according to the Urban Institute, a liberal think tank based in Washington, D.C. That's down from 1987-92 when minority firms won 6.4 percent of federal contracts. Women-owned businesses fared even worse. Although women own more than 32 percent of all small businesses in the United States, they receive only 1.5 percent of government contracts." (p10 secF)

Hunter, George. "Strategies: Small Business: Minorities Get Shortchanged, Critics Say." Detroit News 21 Jul 1997. p10 secF.

SMOKING (v26)

see also CIGAR HABIT; CIGARETTE HABIT; PASSIVE SMOKING

"According to the World Health Organization, tobacco is estimated to kill more than 3 million people per year and if current trends continue, the death toll will rise to 10 million deaths per year between 2020 and 2030....A study by a World Bank economist has estimated that tobacco use results in a global net loss of $200 billion per year, which includes direct medical care for tobacco-related illnesses, absenteeism from work, fire losses, reduced productivity and forgone income due to early death."

Alabama. Dept. of Public Health. "Tobacco Use: A Public Health Disaster." News Release 29 May 1997. document-level access: <http://www.alapubhealth.org/Press/pr052997a.htm>

"Today, more American cigarettes are smoked abroad than at home. One-third of the cigarettes smoked worldwide are smoked in China, most of them of Chinese manufacture....American exports of tobacco products have tripled in the past 20 years since the dangers of smoking became an issue in America. In the next 40 years, the World Health Organization estimates 10 million tobacco-related deaths worldwide, 70 percent of them in developing countries." (p19)

Schorr, Daniel. "Opinion/Essays: Watch Out, World, Here Comes the Marlboro Man." The Christian Science Monitor v89 n149 27 Jun 1997. p19. The Christian Science Monitor search engine: <http://www.csmonitor.com/plweb-cgi/iops1.pl> To retrieve this article, enter the following search: ED=19970627 AND man. In the "retrieved list," click the title that matches this record. (ISSN0882-7729).

In the U.S., "ever since the tobacco companies agreed to get rid of the advertising camels and cowboys, as well as fork over $368 billion over the next 25 years, other countries have begun to ask, 'Can it happen here too?'" (p1) "By August, Israel plans to hit tobacco giants with a lawsuit asking for $7.8 billion to pay for smoking-related medical costs and an antismoking campaign....The world's largest tobacco company, Philip Morris, has increased over-seas sales 80 percent over the last five years....A preliminary hearing was held in London July 1 on whether British tobacco companies were negligent because they didn't reduce tar levels in cigarettes. The case, the first of its kind in Britain, has been brought by 47 lung-cancer patients against Imperial Tobacco PLC and Gallaher Group PLC." (p6)

Scherer, Ron. "Global Report: US Fires Up World: A Second Wind in Tobacco Fight." The Christian Science Monitor v89 n152 2 Jul 1997. p1,6-7. The Christian Science Monitor search engine: <http://www.csmonitor.com/plweb-cgi/iops1.pl> To retrieve this article, enter the following search: ED=19970702 AND fight. In the "retrieved list," click the title that matches this record. (ISSN0882-7729).

"It is estimated that globally, approximately 12% of women and 47% of men smoke. In developed countries, around one fourth of women smoke, compared to around 7% of women in developing countries. For men, the rates are 42% and 48%, respectively." (p1)

World Health Organization. "Smoking and Women: The Next Wave of the Tobacco Epidemic." WHO Fact Sheet n176 Aug 1997. p1-4. document-level access: <http://www.who.ch/programmes/inf/facts/fact176.htm>

In the Western Pacific region of the World Health Organization, "an estimated 60% of men and 8% of women smoke. 'This percentage translates into some 340 million men and 45 million women who smoke,' stated Dr Sang Tae Han, Regional Director of the WHO Regional Office for the Western Pacific region." (p3)

World Health Organization. "The Smoking Epidemic--'A Fire in the Global Village.'" WHO Press n61 25 Aug 1997. p1-3. document-level access: <http://www.who.ch/press/1997/pr97-61.html>

SMOKING--AFRO-AMERICANS

According to the University of Michigan's Monitoring the Future Study, "the percentage of African-American high school seniors who reported smoking one cigarette or more a day during the previous 30 days fell from 26.8 percent in 1976 to just 7.0 percent in 1996. This contrasts starkly with a small drop from 28.8 percent to 26.1 percent in smoking by white students and with evidence that African-American adults are slightly more likely to smoke than white adults." (p18 secA)

"Ifs, Ands and Butts." Detroit News 12 Dec 1997. p18 secA.

SMOKING--ASIA

"There is no doubt the entry of American tobacco overseas has dramatically increased consumption worldwide. In Taiwan, smoking rates of high school students jumped from 22 to 32 percent in the 2 years after American cigarettes were introduced. In Korea, the rate for male teens grew from 18 to 30 percent in just 1 year. In Japan, 26 percent of high school senior girls were smoking in 1990 after U.S. cigarettes were introduced." (pH8010)

DeGette, Diana (Rep.-Colo.). "Departments of Commerce, Justice, And State, The Judiciary...Appropriations Act, 1998." Congressional Record. Daily ed. v143 n131 26 Sep 1997. pH8003-8023. section/page-level access: <http://thomas.loc.gov/cqi-bin/query/R?r105:FLD001:H08010:> (ISSN0363-7239). (X1.1A.105/1).

SMOKING--ASIA, SOUTHEASTERN (v26)

SMOKING--AUSTRALIA--CANADA--COSTS

In Canada and Australia, "tobacco losses rank on the order of 1.4 percent of GDP. Tobacco's toll--in death, illness, and lost productivity--accounts for about one-fourth of all public health expenditures in both of those countries." (p25)

McGinn, Anne Platt. "The Nicotine Cartel." World Watch v10 n4 Jul-Aug 1997. p18-27. (ISSN0896-0615).

SMOKING--CALIFORNIA

"According to a report by John P. Pierce of the University of California, San Diego, in California, more than 102,000 kids per year become regular smokers. One-third of them will die prematurely of cancer, emphysema, heart disease, or other diseases caused by smoking....The California Chronic and Sentinel Diseases Surveillance Program has estimated that more than 42,000 deaths annually in California were attributed to smoking in 1988. That makes smoking the number one preventable cause of death in California, killing more people each year than alcohol, cocaine, crack, heroin, homicide, suicide, car accidents, fires, and AIDS combined."

California. Dept. of Health Services. "California Launches Aggressive New Anit-Tobacco Advertising Campaign." News Release Mar 1997. document-level access: <http://www.dhs.cahwnet.gov/opahome/prssrels/16-97.htm>

"After two years of increases, the rate of youth smoking in California flattened out last year at 11.6 percent....Youth smoking measured 10.9 percent in 1994, and 11.9 percent in 1995. Adult smoking increased from 16.7 percent in 1995 to 18.6 percent in 1996....While the national average for adult smokers was 25.5 percent in 1994, California's average in 1996 was 18.6 percent."

California. Dept. of Health Services. "California Announces New Rates of Smoking for Adults and Youth." News Release Mar 1997. document-level access: <http://www.dhs.cahwnet.gov/opahome/prssrels/15-97.htm>

"An estimated 3,000 teenagers pick up the smoking habit every day, swelling the ranks of the 45 million smokers in the United States, according to national health groups....Over the past decade, California has spent large sums on campaigns to reduce smoking among its citizens--particularly youngsters. And it has cut adult cigarette use by some 40 percent....Today, 18 percent of Californians smoke, compared with a 25 percent nationwide average. But despite the effort, since 1993 the rate among teens has climbed from 9 percent to 11.6 percent." (p3)

Katz, Nancie L. "United States: Wind Shift in California's Battle against Teen Smoking." The Christian Science Monitor v90 n3 28 Nov 1997. p3. The Christian Science Monitor search engine: <http://www.csmonitor.com/plweb-cgi/iops1.pl> To retrieve this article, enter the following search: ED=19971128 AND smoking. In the "retrieved list," click the title that matches this record. (ISSN0882-7729).

"Of the 400,000 smoking-related deaths in the United States each year, one-tenth occur in California. In part because of cultural norms in their home countries, some ethnic groups have a higher incidence of smoking than does the general population--and rates have been rising, statistics show. Since 1993, smoking use and addiction have doubled among teen and preteen Asian-Americans in California. About 280 California children per day become addicted, according to the Centers for Disease Control in Atlanta." (p4)

Wood, Daniel B. "United States: California Airs Antismoking Ads with Ethnic Appeal." The Christian Science Monitor v89 n163 18 Jul 1997. p4. The Christian Science Monitor search engine: <http://www.csmonitor.com/plweb-cgi/iops1.pl> To retrieve this article, enter the following search: ED=19970718 AND appeal. In the "retrieved list," click the title that matches this record. (ISSN0882-7729).

SMOKING--CANADA (v26)

SMOKING--CANADA--MORTALITY (v26)

SMOKING--CHINA

In China, "there are currently about 300 million smokers, or about the same number as in all developed countries combined. China is the world's leading consumer of cigarettes--one in three cigarettes smoked in the world today are smoked in China. The Chinese consume four times as many cigarettes as the next largest consumer, the United States of America....From 1985 to 1992, cigarette consumption per adult dropped by 13% in highly developed countries, but at the same time increased by 20% in China....According to a 1996 national survey, 63% of Chinese men smoked, compared to only 4% of Chinese women." (p1) "In 1996, the median starting age for men was 20 years, while women tended to start smoking, on average, at the age of 25....In China, public awareness of the health hazards of smoking is still low, and the majority (83%) of smokers do not indicate an interest in quitting." (p2)

World Health Organization. "Smoking in China: A Time Bomb for the 21st Century." WHO Fact Sheet n177 Aug 1997. p1-4. document-level access: <http://www.who.ch/programmes/inf/facts/fact177.htm>

SMOKING--CHINA--MORTALITY (v26)

"There are currently around three-quarters of a million deaths each year in China caused by tobacco. Based on current trends, these figures will only get worse, and by 2020, around 2 million annual deaths are projected in China due to tobacco. Based on current trends, of all the children and young people under the age of 20 years alive today in China, 200 million will become smokers, and at least 50 million of these will eventually die prematurely because of tobacco use." (p2)

World Health Organization. "Smoking in China: A Time Bomb for the 21st Century." WHO Fact Sheet n177 Aug 1997. p1-4. document-level access: <http://www.who.ch/programmes/inf/facts/fact177.htm>

SMOKING--COSTS

"According to a rough global estimate developed by the World Bank, feeding one smoker's habit typically takes from 1 to 5 percent of a family's income....In China,...tobacco sometimes absorbs up to 17 percent of household income and 60 percent of personal income. And in many developing countries--from Jamaica to Ghana--households with just one smoker commonly spend more on cigarettes than they do on all of their health care." (p25)

McGinn, Anne Platt. "The Nicotine Cartel." World Watch v10 n4 Jul-Aug 1997. p18-27. (ISSN0896-0615).

SMOKING--EUROPE--MORTALITY

"In 1995, tobacco was responsible for 1.2 million deaths, or 14% of all deaths in the European region of WHO....WHO estimates that in 1995, there were about 700,000 deaths in FSE [Former Socialist Economies of Europe] countries caused by tobacco, or about 25% of the world total....70% to 75% of these deaths were in middle age....In FSE countries, it is estimated that in 1995, 41% of all deaths among men aged 35-69 years were caused by tobacco. In FSE countries, around 14% of all deaths in 1990 were due to tobacco use....In middle-aged men, nearly 60% of cancers and over 40% of deaths from CVD [Cardiovascular Disease] and as much as 85% of chronic obstructive lung disease (COLD) are a result of smoking." (p1-2)

World Health Organization. "The Tobacco Epidemic Rages On in Eastern and Central Europe." WHO Fact Sheet v6 n156 May 1997. p1-2. document-level access: <http://www.who.ch/programmes/inf/facts/fact156.htm>

SMOKING--FORMER SOVIET REPUBLICS--MORTALITY (v26)

SMOKING--GREAT BRITAIN (v26)

SMOKING--HEALTH ASPECTS

"On average, lifetime smokers have a 50% chance of dying from tobacco. And half of these will die in middle age (age 35-69), losing more than 20 years of normal life expectancy. Tobacco is a known or probable cause of about 25 diseases." (p1)

World Health Organization. "Tobacco Epidemic in the Western Pacific: Deaths from Smoking Will Increase Dramatically in the Next Quarter-Century." WHO Fact Sheet n175 Aug 1997. p1-4. document-level access: <http://www.who.ch/programmes/inf/facts/fact175.htm>

SMOKING--HEALTH ASPECTS--UNITED STATES (v26)

"Smoking kills 420,000 Americans a year (one in five deaths) and costs the country $50 billion annually in medical expenses. Tobacco affects not only the heart, lungs, circulation, and skin of smokers, but, according to the Environmental Protection Agency, actually contributes to the death of 15,000 nonsmokers yearly. While the number of smokers has declined slightly, some 61 million Americans will light up this month. That number will include thousands of new teen-age smokers, a group in which smoking is on the rise and a critical component in big tobacco's long-term profits: 90 percent of new smokers come from that group, and 70 percent of them, according to the American Cancer Society, will be hooked long-term." (p5)

"Slow Burn." Commonweal v124 n10 23 May 1997. p5-6. (ISSN0010-3330).

In the U.S., "each year about 3,000 nonsmoking adults die of lung cancer as a result of breathing the smoke of others' cigarettes. The risk of dying of lung cancer is 30 percent higher for a nonsmoker living with a smoker....The National Health Interview Study data show that cigarette smoking among adults aged 18 and over declined from 42 to 25 percent between 1965 and 1990. If they had it to do over, 81 percent of current smokers state they would not start smoking again. Approximately 89 percent of adults who have smoked started smoking by age 18, an age which by Food and Drug Administration regulation and all state laws is illegal to sell tobacco to youth."

Alabama. Dept. of Public Health. "Tobacco Use: A Public Health Disaster." News Release 29 May 1997. document-level access: <http://www.alapubhealth.org/Press/pr052997a.htm>

"Harvard University researchers have found that heavy smokers [in the U.S.] double their risk of developing macular degeneration, an untreatable disease that has caused vision impairment in about 1.7 million Americans. Advanced cases of macular degeneration affect one in 14 people age 75 or older....In studies published in the JOURNAL OF THE AMERICAN MEDICAL ASSOCIATION, those who smoked a pack a day or more were 2.5 times as likely to get the disease as those who had never smoked." (p15)

"Info: Health News & Notes: Blind to Your Smoking Habit?" Your Health and Fitness v19 n3 Sum 1997. p15.

SMOKING--HEALTH ASPECTS--UNITED STATES --COSTS (v26)

SMOKING--HEALTH ASPECTS--UNITED STATES --PUBLIC OPINION (v26)

SMOKING--JAPAN (v26)

SMOKING--LATIN AMERICA (v26)

SMOKING--LATIN AMERICA--MORTALITY (v26)

SMOKING--MICHIGAN

"Michigan ranks 7th nationally in smoking with about 1.7 million or 25.7 percent of state residents who smoke, according to a 1996 Centers for Disease Control and Prevention report. The national average is 22.9 percent. State officials estimate 15,000 Michigan residents die each year of tobacco-related causes." (p15 secA)

Kellogg, Sarah. "State Expects $1 Billion a Year to Treat Smokers." Ann Arbor News 21 Jun 1997. p15 secA.

SMOKING--MICHIGAN--MORTALITY

The second "Critical Health Indicators" report was compiled by the Michigan Department of Community Health in July 1997. It found that "Michigan residents continue to smoke more than the nation at large: 25.9 percent of adults...[in Michigan] still smoke (down from one-third in 1982), compared with 22.4 percent nationwide. Officials estimate that 15,000 Michigan smokers die each year from tobacco-related illness and another 2,000 people die from exposure to secondhand smoke." (p1-2 secC)

Cain, Charlie. "Metro: Special Report: Health Snapshot: Michigan Gaining Ground in the Fight against Diseases." Detroit News 17 Jul 1997. p1-2 secC.

SMOKING--MICHIGAN--PUBLIC OPINION

"Seventy-one percent of Michigan voters are very concerned about tobacco use among kids, and most favor raising the price of cigarettes by $1.50 a pack if youth smoking isn't significantly reduced, according to a poll released [in December 1997]....The poll of 821 Michigan voters was commissioned by the Campaign for Tobacco-Free Kids, a national antismoking group....82 percent of Michigan voters strongly favor prohibiting smoking in public places and most work places, or restrict it to separately ventilated locations. 61 percent favor enlarging warnings on cigarette packs and ads." (p6 secB)

Wendland, Wendy. "Local News: Smoking Poll Basis of New Campaign." Detroit Free Press 12 Dec 1997. p6 secB.

SMOKING--MICHIGAN--YOUTH

"In Michigan, 38.8 percent of all high school students have smoked cigarettes in the past month and over 21 percent of all the high school boys have used smokeless tobacco, according to a recent study by the Centers for Disease Control and Prevention. About 15,000 Michiganders die each year from smoking-related disease, according to the CDC." (p6 secB)

Wendland, Wendy. "Local News: Smoking Poll Basis of New Campaign." Detroit Free Press 12 Dec 1997. p6 secB.

SMOKING--MORTALITY

"Within a few decades, the World Health Organization estimates that 10 million people will die annually from tobacco-related disease, up from 3 million per year. An astonishing 70 percent of those deaths will be in developing countries....For comparison, in America, today, approximately 400,000 die a year from tobacco. While smoking has declined 10 percent since 1990 in developed countries, the WHO concludes it has risen an alarming 67 percent in developing countries during that same period. American tobacco exports have increased by almost 340 percent since the mid-1970's, and these exports now account for more than half of our tobacco companies' sales." (pS7959)

Lautenberg, Frank R. (Sen.-N.J.). "Statements on Introduced Bills and Joint Resolutions." Congressional Record. Daily ed. v143 n105 23 Jul 1997. pS7950-7965. section/page-level access: <http://thomas.loc.gov/cgi-bin/query/R?r105:FLD001:S07959:> (ISSN0363-7239). (X1.1A.105/1).

"Worldwide, smoking kills 3 million people a year. Unless

current trends are reversed, by the year 2025 this figure will rise to 10 million. The developing world will account for 7 million of these deaths, with 2 million in China alone." (p2)

World Health Organization. "Tobacco Epidemic in the Western Pacific: Deaths from Smoking Will Increase Dramatically in the Next Quarter-Century." WHO Fact Sheet n175 Aug 1997. p1-4. document-level access: <http://www.who.ch/programmes/inf/facts/fact175.htm>

SMOKING--PACIFIC AREA

In the Western Pacific Region "as a whole, an estimated 60% of men and 8% of women smoke. In absolute figures, there are at present some 340 million men and 45 million women who smoke." (p1) "In these countries and areas, per capita consumption of cigarettes has nearly doubled from the early 1970s to the early 1990s from 1100 cigarettes to 2010 cigarettes per adult per year." (p2)

World Health Organization. "Tobacco Epidemic in the Western Pacific: Deaths from Smoking Will Increase Dramatically in the Next Quarter-Century." WHO Fact Sheet n175 Aug 1997. p1-4. document-level access: <http://www.who.ch/programmes/inf/facts/fact175.htm>

SMOKING--POLAND--MORTALITY (v26)

SMOKING--QUEBEC (PROVINCE) (v26)

SMOKING--RUSSIA--MORTALITY

"Today, 55% of all deaths in Russia are due to heart diseases, which are followed by cancers accounting for another 20%. Between 25% and 30% of both groups of diseases are caused by smoking. Tobacco causes about 280,000 deaths per year in the Russian Federation alone, 32% of all male deaths and 5% of all female deaths." (p2)

World Health Organization. "Tobacco Epidemic in the Russian Federation Kills 750 People Every Single Day." WHO Fact Sheet v6 n157 May 1997. p1-3. document-level access: <http://www.who.ch/programmes/inf/facts/fact157.htm>

SMOKING--UNITED STATES (v26)

"There are about 48 million Americans who smoke. About 2 million Americans use other tobacco products like chewing tobacco. There are 3 million kids who smoke....One out of five cancers is caused by smoking; four out of five lung cancers are caused by smoking; 3,000 kids are starting to smoke every day; 50 percent of all smokers begin before age 15, 90 percent before the age 18; 419,000 American smokers die annually....Cigarettes are a major cause of fire fatalities in the United States. In 1990, cigarettes were responsible for about one-quarter of all deaths associated with residential fires. This represented over 1,000 deaths in our society....About 8 in 10 smokers begin to use tobacco before age 18 and about one-half of all smokers started at age 14 or earlier. According to a 1994 CDC report, tobacco costs our society $100 billion annually--$50 billion in direct medical costs. Of 24 billion cigarette packs sold in 1993, $2.06 per pack in medical care costs. Of this, 89 cents was paid by public sources; $10 billion Medicare, $5 billion Medicaid, $4.75 billion other Federal, and $16.75 billion higher insurance premiums." (pS4784)

Hatch, Orrin G. (Sen.-Utah). "Concurrent Resolution on the Budget." Congressional Record. Daily ed. v143 n68 21 May 1997. pS4782-4849. section/page-level access: <http://thomas.loc.gov/cgi-bin/query/R?r105:FLD001:S04783:> (ISSN0363-7239). (X1.1A.105/1).

"Tobacco accounts for an estimated 419,000 American deaths annually. In 1993, cigarettes killed more of our fellow citizens than AIDS, alcohol, car accidents, fire cocaine, heroin, murders, and suicides combined. About 50 million Americans smoke. About 1 in 5 deaths are smoking related. 4 of 5 smokers begin by age 18. About half by age 14. Each day 3000 young Americans begin to smoke. Experts believe that tobacco costs society $100 billion annually, including $50 billion in direct health care costs. Of this $50 billion, there are $10 billion in annual costs to Medicare; $5 billion in Medicaid; $4.75 billion to other federal programs; and, $17 billion in increased insurance premiums." (pS6160)

Hatch, Orrin G. (Sen.-Utah). "Balanced Budget Act of 1997." Congressional Record. Daily ed. v143 n90 24 Jun 1997. pS6120-6163. section/page-level access: <http://thomas.loc.gov/cgi-bin/query/R?r105:FLD001:S06157:> (ISSN0363-7239). (X1.1A.105/1).

"Tobacco companies continue to produce cigarettes at the rate of 5.5 trillion a year. That is nearly 1,000 cigarettes for every person on the planet, including our young children. Every day, over 3,000 [American] kids become regular smokers, despite laws in every State that prohibit tobacco use by minors. Every year, 1 million young children start using tobacco, with the average teenage smoker starting at 13 and becoming a daily smoker by 14 1/2. An estimated 419,000 Americans die each year from diseases caused by smoking. That number is more than [those who] die from AIDS, alcohol, illegal drugs, fires, car crashes, suicides, and murder combined....Ninety percent of all adult smokers begin smoking before the age of 18." (pH5498)

McGovern, James P. (Rep.-Mass.). "A Fresh Look at the Anti-Tobacco Campaign." Congressional Record. Daily ed. v143 n104 22 Jul 1997. pH5498-5499. section/page-level access: <http://thomas.loc.gov/cgi-bin/query/R?r105:FLD001:H05498:> (ISSN0363-7239). (X1.1A.105/1).

"The percentage of Americans who say they have smoked a cigarette within the past week is currently 26%. This represents a significant decline from the 1940s through the middle of the 1970s when Gallup found more than 40% of Americans saying they smoked. Cigarette smoking fell to about one-third of adults in the 1980s and has been steady at about 27% during the 1990s."

Saad, Lydia/Gallup Organization. "More Americans Fear Risk of Second-Hand Smoke." Press Release 18 Jul 1997. document-level access: <http://www.gallup.com/poll/news/970718~1.htm>

In the U.S., "between 1990 and 1994 the age-adjusted prevalence of current cigarette smoking among persons 18 years of age or over has remained stable at 25-26 percent. In 1994 the age-adjusted prevalence of current cigarette smoking among persons 25 years of age and over ranged from 12 percent for college graduates to 38 percent for persons with less than a high school education."

U.S. Dept. of Health and Human Services. "Report on Nation's Health Documents Toll of Injuries in U.S.: Firearm Mortality Down 11%, Traffic Fatality...Up...." Press Release 24 Jul 1997. document-level access: <http://www.cdc.gov/nchswww/releases/97news/97news/hus96rel.htm>

A 1994 study conducted by Cynthia S. Pomerleau, a researcher with the University of Michigan Substance Abuse Research Center and the Nicotine Research Laboratory in the U-M Department of Psychiatry "found that 42 percent of men and 38 percent of women diagnosed with ADHD [Attention Deficit Hyperactivity Disorder] were current smokers--nearly twice the rate of the standard population. Also the 'quit ratio' was 29 percent for the ADHD patients who had ever smoked compared with 48 percent in the general population." (p2)

University of Michigan. News and Information Services. "More Studies Show That Hard Core Smokers May Be Using Nicotine to Manage Depression, ADHD, Anxiety or Bulimia." University of Michigan News Release 6 Aug 1997. p1-3.

SMOKING--UNITED STATES--COSTS (v26)

A 1994 study by the U.S. Centers for Disease Control and Prevention "reported that 48 million American smokers buy 24 billion packs of cigarettes a year. Given an estimated $50 billion in smoking-related hospital charges, doctor fees, drugs, and nursing home bills, says CDC, each pack carries with it just over $2 in hidden health costs. Meanwhile, the economy sees an additional $47 billion go up in smoke, as tobacco-related illnesses mean time off the job and smoking-related deaths rob the economy of up to 400,000 workers yearly." (p52)

Miller, Matthew. "Business & Technology: Clean Lungs at a Price." U.S. News & World Report v123 n1 7 Jul 1997. p52-53. article-level access: <http://www.usnews.com/usnews/issue/970707/7SMOK.HTM> (ISSN0041-5537).

"Today, the United States spends $50 billion in medical expenses directly attributable to smoking--or $2.06 for every pack of cigarettes sold in the country....(Smoking is very expensive for employers in the United States, who pay out, on average, $960 per year in lost work time and health expenses for every smoker on their payroll.) If these indirect costs are included in the bill, the total cost of smoking in the United States swells to nearly $100 billion, or 1.8 percent of the GDP in 1993." (p25)

McGinn, Anne Platt. "The Nicotine Cartel." World Watch v10 n4 Jul-Aug 1997. p18-27. (ISSN0896-0615).

SMOKING--UNITED STATES--GIRLS

In the U.S., "ninety percent of women who smoke started in adolescence, says Dr. Vicki Seltzer, a gynecologist at New York's Albert Einstein College of Medicine...." (p6 secF)

"Twenty percent of girls smoke by eighth grade, and 30 percent do by 10th grade, she says." (p7 secF)

Anstett, Patricia. "Body & Mind: Cover Story: An Unkind World for Girls." Detroit Free Press 16 Dec 1997. p6-8 secF.

SMOKING--UNITED STATES--MORTALITY

"Each day, almost 3,000 young people in the United States become regular smokers, and nearly 1,000 of them will die prematurely from diseases related to tobacco use. Each year, more than 400,000 Americans die from smoking-related diseases, more Americans than are killed each year by AIDS, alcohol, car accidents, murders, suicides, illegal drugs, and fires combined."

U.S. Dept. of Health and Human Services. "HHS Invests in America's Children." Fact Sheet 23 Jul 1997. document-level access: <http://www.hhs.gov/news/press/1997pres/970917.html>

SMOKING--UNITED STATES--PUBLIC OPINION

"In 1991, two in three Americans said that warning notices on cigarette packs excused the industry from legal responsibility to families of people who die from smoking-related causes, according to the GALLUP POLL MONTHLY. By 1996, just over half (51 percent) thought these warnings let tobacco companies off the hook....Nearly six in ten of those with incomes in the $20,000 to $49,999 range agree that warning labels are sufficient. The least affluent and the most affluent are the least accepting. Current smokers are more likely than average to accept labels as solid legal protection for tobacco companies, at 62 percent. Those who've never smoked or have kicked the habit are less likely to agree, at 46 percent and 52 percent, respectively." (p31)

Klein, Matthew. "Kaleidoscope: Hot Topics: Holes in the Smoke Screen." American Demographics v19 n7 Jul 1997. p31. article-level access: <http://www.demographics.com/publications/ad/97_ad/9707_ad/ad970734.htm> (ISSN0163-4089).

SMOKING--UNITED STATES--TEENAGERS

"From 1975 to 1995, according to the University of Michigan's...Monitoring the Future Study, cigarette use by [U.S.] high school seniors fluctuated and decreased overall, despite a recent rise. The net decline in the percentage of 12th graders who reported smoking cigarettes at least once was almost 13 percent; it was nearly 20 percent for those who smoked daily." (p18 secA)

"Ifs, Ands and Butts." Detroit News 12 Dec 1997. p18 secA.

SMOKING--UNITED STATES--YOUTH (v26)

In the U.S., "each and every day another 3,000 young people become regular smokers and 1,000 of them will die before their time because of their smoking....Illegal sales to minors is a serious part of the problem of children and adolescents becoming regular smokers--studies show that about 70 percent of the time minors try to buy cigarettes from retailers they succeed in doing so....There are an estimated 400,000 to 500,000 retailers in this country who sell tobacco." (p475)

U.S. Food and Drug Administration. "Agriculture, Rural Development, Food and Drug Administration...Approp. for 1998 (Part 2)." Hearing. U.S. House. Committee on Appropriations. Washington, D.C. : GPO, 1997. (Y4.Ap6/1:Ag8/997/pt.2).

In the U.S., "eighty-two percent of adults with any history of smoking had their first cigarette before the age of 18, and more than half of them had already become regular smokers by that age. Each year, one million youngsters in this country become regular smokers--and one-third of them will die prematurely of lung cancer, emphysema, and similar diseases linked to their addiction. About three million of our adolescents smoke, and another one million boys use smokeless tobacco....Despite the fact that it is against the law in all 50 states to sell cigarettes and smokeless tobacco to minors, our young people purchase an estimated 1.26 billion dollars' worth of tobacco products each year." (p503-504)

Friedman, Michael A. (Deputy Commissioner for Operations, U.S. Food and Drug Administration). "Agriculture, Rural Development, Food and Drug Administration...Approp. for 1998 (Part 2)." Hearing. U.S. House. Committee on Appropriations. Washington, D.C. : GPO, 1997. (Y4.Ap6/1:Ag8/997/pt.2).

"According to a spring 1996 survey conducted by the University of Michigan Institute for Social Research, the prevalence of youth tobacco use in America has been on the increase over the last 5 years. It rose by nearly 50 percent among 8th and 10th graders, and by nearly 20 percent among high school seniors between 1991 and 1996....Ninety percent of current adult smokers began to smoke before they reached the age of 18. Ninety-five percent of teenage smokers say they intend to quit in the near future--but only a quarter of them will actually do so within the first 8 years of beginning to smoke....In addition, the Center on Addiction and Substance Abuse at Columbia University has found that smoking is a gateway to the use of illegal drugs. Children between the ages of 12 and 17 who smoke are 12 times more likely to use heroin and 19 times more likely to use cocaine than nonsmokers." (pS7916)

Kennedy, Edward M. (Sen.-Mass.). "Agriculture, Rural Development, Food and Drug Administration...Appropriations Act, 1998." Congressional Record. Daily ed. v143 n105 23 Jul 1997. pS7912-7919. section/page-level access: <http://thomas.loc.gov/cgi-bin/query/R?r105:FLD001:S07916:> (ISSN0363-7239). (X1.1A.105/1).

In the U.S., "4.5 million kids aged 12 to 17 are smokers today. Almost 90 percent of adult smokers began at or before the age of 18. The average youth smoker begins at age 13 and becomes a daily smoker by the age of 14 1/2....Every day, 3,000 young Americans will begin smoking and 1,000 of them will die from it. At current rates, 5 million American kids under 18 who are alive today will be killed by smoking-related disease....The statistics on smoking among young women and girls are just as shocking. Smoking among eighth grade girls...jumped over 60 percent from 1991 to 1996, with rates of smoking now higher for 8th- and 10th-grade girls than for boys. And smoking among black children of this age nearly doubled during this time period." (pS7913)

Harkin, Tom (Sen.-Iowa). "Agriculture, Rural Development, Food and Drug Administration...Appropriations Act, 1998." Congressional Record. Daily ed. v143 n105 23 Jul 1997. pS7912-7919. section/page-level access: <http://thomas.loc.gov/cgi-bin/query/R?r105:FLD001:S07912:> (ISSN0363-7239). (X1.1A.105/1).

"Though smoking by adults in the United States has declined steadily in the past 40 years, smoking among 10th-graders jumped 30 percent between 1991 and 1995, and 40 percent for ninth-graders during that period. The latest reports show that 4.1 million youths ages 12 to 17 years smoke, or 18 percent of that age group....In 1995, 10th-grade girls for the first time passed 10th-grade boys in percentage of those who said they had smoked in the last 30 days, according to the annual 'Monitoring the Future' survey carried out by the University of Michigan. The percentage of eighth-grade girls who said they smoked jumped from 13 percent in 1991 to 21 percent in 1996; among 12th-graders, 32 percent reported smoking in the last month, up from 27 percent in 1991." (p7-8 secF)

Mishra, Raja/Arnett, Elsa C. "Body & Mind: Cover Story: Boredom Stress Image Addiction: Four Big Reasons Explain Smoking's Hold on People." Detroit Free Press 18 Nov 1997. p6-8 secF.

In the U.S., "each day, 3,000 children become smokers--more than 1 million kids a year. One-third will eventually die from a tobacco-related disease. Advertising is a major influence on kids--86 percent of those who smoke prefer the three most heavily advertised brands: Marlboro, Camel and Newport." (p29)

Addis, Ilana. "AMSA Focus: News of the American Medical Student Association: Eye on the National Project--Kids and Smoking." New Physician v46 n8 Nov 1997. p29. (ISSN0028-6451).

"University of Michigan social psychologists Lloyd Johnston, Jerald Bachman, and Patrick O'Malley, senior research scientists at the U-M Institute for Social Research, are releasing the results of their 23rd national survey of high school seniors and seventh national survey of eighth- and 10-grade students." (p1) "During the period 1992 to 1996, the proportion of eighth-graders (most of whom are 13- or 14-years-old) who reported smoking daily in the 30-day period preceding the survey increased by half--from 7.0 percent in 1992 to 10.4 percent in 1996. In 1997 this rate fell to 9.0 percent. Among 10th-graders, daily smoking also rose by half, from 12.3 percent in 1992 to 18.3 percent in 1996, and remained virtually unchanged in 1997 (at 18.0 percent). At the 12th-grade level, daily smoking rose less in proportional terms between 1992 and 1996--from 17.2 percent to 22.2 percent--but in 1997 it continued to rise significantly to 24.6 percent. This represents a 43 percent increase in the daily smoking rate for 12th-graders in the last five years....Additionally, another 12 percent of the seniors smoke occasionally but not yet daily...." (p2-3)

University of Michigan. News and Information Services. "Cigarette Smoking Rates May Have Peaked among Younger Teens." University of Michigan News Release 18 Dec 1997. p1-4.

SMOKING IN MOTION PICTURES--UNITED STATES

"A recent study by the University of California at San Francisco indicates that half the movies released [in the U.S.] between 1990 and 1995 included a major character who smoked, up from 29 percent during the 1970s. The American Lung Association of Sacramento examined last year's major film releases and found that 77 percent showed tobacco use." (p8 secF)

Mishra, Raja/Arnett, Elsa C. "Body & Mind: Cover Story: Boredom Stress Image Addiction: Four Big Reasons Explain Smoking's Hold on People." Detroit Free Press 18 Nov 1997. p6-8 secF.

SMUGGLING OF DRUGS

see DRUG TRAFFIC

SNACK FOOD INDUSTRY--UNITED STATES

"Data from the 1996 Snack Food Association's 'Consumer Snacking Behavior Report' shows total per capita U.S. snack consumption at 21.7 pounds and snack nuts at 1.6 pounds. Snack nuts account for 9 percent of the total snack market volume (5.69 billion pounds) or 7 percent of the total retail dollar sales ($15.05 billion)....In 1994 estimated snack consumption in Germany reached 5.1 pounds per capita, while consumption in other EU countries ranged from a low of 2.2 pounds in Italy to a high of 11.5 pounds per capita in United Kingdom. U.S. snack exports are increasing rapidly, rising almost 50 percent from $592 million in 1991 to $885 million in 1994....This snack category increased 20 percent in 1994 from the previous year and is the fastest growing segment of the snack food industry." (p39)

Johnson, Doyle C./U.S. Dept. of Agriculture. Economic Research Service. "Special Article: United States Is World Leader in Tree Nut Production and Trade." Fruit and Tree Nuts Situation and Outlook Report Aug 1997. p35-39.

SNACK FOODS--UNITED STATES--CHILDREN (v26)

SNOW REMOVAL--HEALTH ASPECTS

Health experts at William Beaumont Hospital in Royal Oak, Michigan, "analyzed the cardiac and energy demands of heavy snow shoveling in apparently healthy but inactive men....Each subject cleared a 4-inch-high tract of wet snow in the cold for 10 minutes using a lightweight plastic shovel. The men were asked to repetitively lift and throw snow at a rate used to remove snow at home. Among the findings: After only two minutes of shoveling, the heart rate response of most subjects exceeded the upper limit commonly recommended for aerobic exercise, that is, 85 percent of the maximal heart rate. Energy expenditure during shoveling was nearly six times that at rest, equivalent to the energy cost of playing singles tennis....During the relatively brief bout of shoveling, the average subject lifted and threw nearly a ton of snow (12 lifts per minute at 16 pounds per lift times 10 minutes equals 1,920 pounds)." (p6 secA)

Franklin, Barry. "Read before Shoveling; A Lot Is at Stake." Detroit Free Press 11 Dec 1997. p6 secA.

SNOWBOARDING--UNITED STATES (v26)

Snowboarding is "the fastest growing segment of the [U.S.] snowsports industry....Snowboard participants...have nearly tripled their numbers since 1990. There were about 1.5 million snowboarders at the beginning of the decade. This year, more than 4 million people are expected to try the sport....[Teens] are still the largest segment of the snowboard market (38 percent), but that's slowly changing." (p2 secC)

Terrell, Mike. "Venture Outdoors: 'Boarding Is Big: 'Outlaw' Sport Catches On Here and in Olympics." Ann Arbor News 6 Dec 1997. p1-2 secC.

SNOWMOBILE ACCIDENTS--MICHIGAN--MORTALITY

In Michigan, "last season, 44 people died in snowmobile accidents across the state--nearly double the number who died five years before. Three of the deaths occurred around Metro Detroit." (p1 secC) "Profiles of fatal snowmobile accidents show that more than 90 percent of victims are males, generally between 20 and 40 years old. Typical accidents involve single snowmobiles wrecking on the shoulder of a trail or a road. More than half the deaths involve alcohol." (p2 secC)

Pearce, Jeremy. "Metro: News Special: Leisure: Snowmobilers See Races As Way to Keep Trails Safe." Detroit News 8 Dec 1997. p1-2 secC.

SNOWMOBILES--MONTANA

"Advocates claim snowmobile use in Montana went up 73 percent in the last decade, and U.S. sales doubled between 1992 and

1996....In a 1994 University of Montana survey, 91 percent of trail hikers said walking is incompatable with motorcycles, and three quarters of cross-country skiers couldn't stomach the presence of snowmobiles. Yet the state of Montana spends nearly $1 million a year promoting ATV [all-terrain vehicle] and snowmobile use, and...58 percent of national forest trails in Montana are open to some type of motorized vehicle." (p20)

Adams, John. "The West from a Snowmobile: A 50 Million-Acre Theme Park." High Country News v29 n24 22 Dec 1997. p20. (ISSN0191-5657).

SNOWMOBILING--MICHIGAN--MORTALITY (v26)

SNOWMOBILING ACCIDENTS--MAINE (v26)

SNOWSHOES AND SNOWSHOEING--UNITED STATES (v26)

SOCCER--ECONOMIC ASPECTS--ITALY

In Italy, "20 out of 58 million people tuned in for the World Cup [soccer tournament] final against Brazil in 1994, a team of...[Internazionale's] caliber can safely expect to earn slightly more than $230 million in the next nine years, with $75 million coming directly from fans expected to invest in season passes. Hugely popular state-sanctioned betting on match results also provides an extra $2 billion yearly." (p8)

Santoro, Lara. "Ronaldo-Mania: Italy Drools over Dribbler from Brazil." The Christian Science Monitor v89 n185 19 Aug 1997. p1,8. The Christian Science Monitor search engine: <http://www.csmonitor.com/plweb-cgi/iops1.pl> To retrieve this article, enter the following search: ED=19970819 AND brazil. In the "retrieved list," click the title that matches this record. (ISSN0882-7729).

SOCCER--UNITED STATES

Attendance at the 1996 U.S. inaugural soccer season "swelled to an average of 17,416 per game....The [soccer] league attracted $70 million in corporate sponsorships over four years and showed a $19 million loss--$3 million less than anticipated." (p78)

Goldin, Greg. "A League of His Own." California Lawyer v17 n9 Sep 1997. p42-45,76-79,82. (ISSN0279-4063).

As the U.S. Major League Soccer hits its 1 1/2-year mark, "it finds a 17 percent decline in attendance from last year's inaugural season....MLS drew an average of 17,416 fans a game last year--31 percent more than forecast....In the 1970s and '80s, the Tampa Bay Rowdies of the now-defunct North American Soccer League (NASL) drew more than 30,000 fans to their games. Now, average attendance for the MLS's Mutiny is wavering at about 11,000....In Kansas City things are worse. Last year, a mediocre team drew a paltry 12,901 fans. This year, the team is in first place, and attendance has slipped to about 8,600....Wary of paying big bucks for players who might not attract enough fans to recoup the cost, MLS executives have kept a tight rein on expenses--no team can spend more than $1.3 million on yearly player salaries. In a world where the best soccer players are paid more than $4 million a year, many say that big crowds won't go watch the second-rate players who can fit under the $1.3 million cap." (p10-11)

Sappenfield, Mark. "Sports: After an Initial Bounce, Soccer Zeal Dribbles Off." The Christian Science Monitor v89 n155 8 Jul 1997. p10-11. The Christian Science Monitor search engine: <http://www.csmonitor.com/plweb-cgi/iops1.pl> To retrieve this article, enter the following search: ED=19970708 AND off. In the "retrieved list," click the title that matches this record. (ISSN0882-7729).

In 1996, "more than 3 million American children played organized soccer, according to the Soccer Industry Council of America. That's a 350 percent increase since 1980....[According to the US Soccer Foundation,] there are $40 million worth of soccer facilities under construction nationwide." (p5)

Walker, Sam. "United States: Values Clash: Defending the Sabbath from Soccer." The Christian Science Monitor v89 n225 16 Oct 1997. p1,5. The Christian Science Monitor search engine: <http://www.csmonitor.com/plweb-cgi/iops1.pl> To retrieve this article, enter the following search: ED=19971016 AND soccer. In the "retrieved list," click the title that matches this record. (ISSN0882-7729).

SOCIAL ANTHROPOLOGY

see ETHNOLOGY

SOCIAL CAPITAL

see INFRASTRUCTURE (ECONOMICS)

SOCIAL CUSTOMS

see MANNERS AND CUSTOMS

SOCIAL DEFENSE

see CIVILIAN-BASED DEFENSE

SOCIAL GROUPS--CUBA--AGED

In Cuba, "a decade ago the 'circulos de abuelos' (grandparents' groups) began as a neighbourhood social support network. Today some 20% of elders in Cuba belong to such a group, where older people can go to find companionship and feel at home....In 1991 a group of 200 elderly people were interviewed when they first joined a 'circulo' and a second time after a year of participation. At the start of the programme, 85% were suffering from a chronic disease such as arthritis, hypertension, diabetes, asthma or emphysema. At that time 72.6% of men and 85.2% of women had never participated in an exercise programme before, and 82% were taking at least one form of medication on a daily basis. A year later the study showed that the members of this group were managing their chronic illness better and were taking less medication than a year earlier. In fact 35% of the members no longer needed medication and 22% were using a lower dose. In addition, 89% of those who at the beginning of the year had seen loneliness and depression as an important problem in their lives now saw this as less of a problem." (p28)

Vega, Enrique. "Cuba's 'Circulos de Abuelos.'" World Health n4 Jul-Aug 1997. p28. (ISSN0043-8502).

SOCIAL HISTORY (v26)

SOCIAL SECURITY

see also INSURANCE, DISABILITY; SUPPLEMENTAL SECURITY INCOME PROGRAM

"Between 1974 and 1993, the simple average of replacement rates in European Community disability benefit programs increased slightly, from the mid-40s to the upper 40s. For the Scandinavian countries plus Austria and Switzerland, the 1981 rate was a very high 66 percent; by 1993, it had fallen slightly to 61 percent. For North America, the replacement rate increased from the mid-20s in 1974 to about 30 percent in 1993." (p4)

Haveman, Robert H. "New Democracy Forum: Equity with Employment." Boston Review v22 n3-4 Sum 1997. p3-8. (ISSN0734-2306).

SOCIAL SECURITY--EUROPE (v26)

SOCIAL SECURITY--GERMANY--WOMEN (v26)

SOCIAL SECURITY--GREAT BRITAIN (v26)

SOCIAL SECURITY--GREAT BRITAIN--WIDOWS (v26)

SOCIAL SECURITY--JAPAN (v26)

SOCIAL SECURITY--NEVADA (v26)

SOCIAL SECURITY--UNITED STATES (v26)

"Today, 200,000 Americans turn 65 every year. By 2011, 1.5 million Americans will turn 65 every year, a trend that will continue for 20 years. As the elderly population inceases, our younger working population will shrink. Today, there are 4.9 workers paying for every retiree's benefits in programs like Social Security and Medicare. In 2030, when we will have many more retirees to support, there will only be 2.8 workers to support each beneficiary." (pS5045)

Frist, Bill (Sen.-Tenn.). "Concurrent Resolution on the

Budget." Congressional Record. Daily ed. v143 n70 23 May 1997. pS5023-5066. section/page-level access: <http://thomas.loc.gov/cgi-bin/query/R?r105:FLD001:S05045:> (ISSN0363-7239). (X1.1A.105/1).

According to the U.S. "Department of Labor, the average worker will need about 70 percent of his preretirement income to maintain his standard of living after retirement, but Social Security will not provide that level of retirement income. Social Security pays the average worker only about 40 percent of preretirement income and only about 27 percent for workers that earn over $60,000 or more." (pH3085)

Kolbe, Jim (Rep.-Ariz.). "Savings Are Vital to Everyone's Retirement Act of 1997." Congressional Record. Daily ed. v143 n68 21 May 1997. pH3082-3088. section/page-level access: <http://thomas.loc.gov/cgi-bin/query/R?r105:FLD001:H03085:> (ISSN0363-7239). (X1.1A.105/1).

In the U.S., "in 1950, 16 workers supported each Social Security recipient. Today, there are three workers per beneficiary. By 2030, when all the baby boomers have retired, the ratio will be two workers for each retiree. When the Social Security Act was passed in 1935, the average life expectancy was age 63. Today, it is 76 and growing." (p20 secA)

Ryan, Richard A. "Preparing for the Golden Years: Safety Net: Social Security Nears Bankruptcy." Detroit News and Free Press 16 Nov 1997. p20 secA.

The U.S. Social Security program "is solvent enough to pay 100 percent of benefits for the next 32 years and 75 percent of benefits for at least 100 years....In 1983, the age at which a person can draw full benefits was raised to 67 from 65." (p21 secA)

Ryan, Richard A./Hunter, George. "Preparing for the Golden Years: Retirement Shock: Millions Learn Their Savings Are Short." Detroit News and Free Press 16 Nov 1997. p1,21 secA.

In the U.S., "in 1996, 144 million workers had earnings in employment covered by the Social Security program. Of these workers, 6% had earnings that equaled or exceeded the maximum amount subject to Social Security taxes...." (p9)

U.S. Social Security Administration. Office of Research, Evaluation, And Statistics. "OASDI Program: Workers and Insured Status." Fast Facts & Figures about Social Security 1997. p9.

In the U.S., Social Security "benefits were awarded to 3.8 million persons in 1996. Forty-two percent were retired workers and 16% were disabled workers." (p12)

U.S. Social Security Administration. Office of Research, Evaluation, And Statistics. "OASDI Program: Benefit Awards." Fast Facts & Figures about Social Security 1997. p12.

In the U.S., among Old-Age, Survivors, and Disability Insurance "beneficiaries, 92% are 62 or older. Among DI beneficiaries--disabled workers and their spouses and children--most are under age 62." (p17)

U.S. Social Security Administration. Office of Research, Evaluation, And Statistics. "OASDI Program: Beneficiaries by Age." Fast Facts & Figures about Social Security 1997. p17.

In the U.S., in 1996, "about one-fifth of the SSI [Supplemental Security Income] recipients were eligible on the basis of age; over three-fourths were eligible on the basis of disability....Among SSI recipients aged 65 or older, 31% were disabled." (p26)

U.S. Social Security Administration. Office of Research, Evaluation, And Statistics. "SSI Program: Basis for Eligibility." Fast Facts & Figures about Social Security 1997. p26.

The U.S. Social Security Administration's "Web service--SSA Online--began modestly in early 1994 with a range of publications and downloadable forms, and has expanded to include over 10,000 pages of information important to citizens and taxpayers....SSA's Web services have also proven increasingly popular, with growth since 1994 averaging more than 20 percent a month. Through June 1997, more than 1.6 million customers have visited SSA Online and have downloaded more than 24 million files. In June 1997, more than 119,000 visitors have accessed more than 3 million files. Our visitors also give us a lot of feedback--almost 50,000 comments, complaints, praise, and suggestions for improvement." (p55)

Sabo, John T. "Series: Managing for Outcomes: Lessons Learned: Providing Government Internet Services with Public Trust." Public Manager v26 n3 Fall 1997. p55-58. (ISSN1061-7639).

In the U.S., "up to 85 percent of [Social Security] benefits can be subject to tax for people whose incomes exceed certain thresholds....Only 25 percent of recipients pay any taxes on their benefits, and the net reduction in benefits is only 3.5 percent....Legislation passed by Congress in 1993 increases the portion of benefits subject to tax for those with incomes above a second set of thresholds ($34,000 for singles and $44,000 for joint returns), and raises the maximum taxable portion to 85 percent." (p55)

Steuerle, C. Eugene/Bakija, Jon M. "Retooling Social Security for the 21st Century." Social Security Bulletin v60 n2 1997. p37-60. (ISSN0037-7910).

SOCIAL SECURITY--UNITED STATES--AGED (v26)

In the U.S., "Social Security provides more than 80 percent of income to the lowest-income 40 percent of the elderly and disabled and more than half of income to all but the richest 20 percent of the elderly....Social Security lifts 6 percent of the US population out of poverty, twice the achievement of all other cash and in-kind assistance combined." (p11)

Aaron, Henry J. "Mini-Forum: Social Security Reform: Social Insurance Works: Fix It, Don't Scrap It." Public Manager v26 n2 Sum 1997. p11-16. (ISSN1061-7639).

In the U.S., "if you retire at the 'normal' retirement age (65), you receive 100 percent of the basic [Social Security] benefit amount, also known as the 'primary insurance amount' (PIA)....If you retire fully at age 62, you receive a benefit equal to only 80 percent of the PIA for the rest of your life. If...you delay retirement until after age 65, you receive a 'delayed retirement credit' (DRC). For workers turning age 65 in 1995, the DRC increases benefits permanently by 4.5 percent for every year retirement is delayed;...if you retire at 67, you receive a benefit equal to 109 percent of your PIA. This DRC is scheduled to increase gradually for future generations of retirees until it reaches 8 percent per year for those reaching age 65 in 2008. If you want to continue working yet still receive Social Security benefits, you are subject to an 'earnings test.' In 1993, the earnings test reduces Social Security benefits by 50 cents for every dollar earned over a basic exempt amount of $7,680 for those younger than age 65, and 33 cents for every dollar earned above $10,560 for people between ages 65-70. In 1996, legislation gradually raised the earnings thresholds for beneficiaries who have attained age 65 to $30,000 by 2002....An average-wage worker choosing between continuing to work until age 70 and retiring in full at age 65 faces an implicit tax rate (extra taxes plus loss in benefits) from Social Security of 18.4 percent on future earnings. The corresponding tax rate for a high-wage worker is 20.3 percent....As of 1991, only 11.6 percent of the population worked past age 65 at all...." (p51-52)

Steuerle, C. Eugene/Bakija, Jon M. "Retooling Social Security for the 21st Century." Social Security Bulletin v60 n2 1997. p37-60. (ISSN0037-7910).

SOCIAL SECURITY--UNITED STATES--CHILDREN

In the U.S., "over 3 million children received OASDI [Old-Age, Survivors, and Disability Insurance] benefits in December 1996, about half of them as children of deceased workers....Overall, the average monthly benefit amount was $335." (p33)

U.S. Social Security Administration. Office of Research, Evaluation, And Statistics. "Children and Social Security: Children and OASDI." Fast Facts & Figures about Social Security 1997. p33.

In the U.S., "tens of thousands of children are losing their federal disability benefits....The average monthly payment [of Supplemental Security Income] per child is $410....Of the total national caseload, about one-quarter were slated for possible cutoff, and most assessments are completed. Mississippi has the highest cutoff rate--82 percent of reviewed cases. The lowest rate is in Washington, D.C., at 36 percent. The national average is nearly 60 percent. As of Oct. 4 [1997], the date for which the most recent data are available, 135,841 children had been removed from SSI. According to SSA [the Social Security Administration], between 70 and 80 percent were receiving SSI for 'mental disorders,' such as retardation, psychotic disorders, learning disabilities, and attention-deficit disorder." (p4)

Feldmann, Linda. "United States: Fraud-Busters Cut Benefits for Disabled Children." The Christian Science Monitor v89 n231 24 Oct 1997. p4. The Christian Science Monitor search engine: <http://www.csmonitor.com/plweb-cgi/iops1.pl> To retrieve this article, enter the following search: ED=19971024 AND children. In the "retrieved list," click the title that matches this record. (ISSN0882-7729).

SOCIAL SECURITY--UNITED STATES--HANDICAPPED CHILDREN

In the U.S., "150,000 disabled children are having their Supplemental Security Income cut because their disabilities are not considered sufficiently severe. The $800 million a year saved by cutting those kids from S.S.I. amounts to less than one-third the cost of building and maintaining a single B-2 [bomber]." (p6)

Scheer, Robert. "Editorials: Our Rained-Out Bomber." Nation v265 n8 22 Sep 1997. p6-7. (ISSN0027-8378).

SOCIAL SECURITY TAXES--UNITED STATES

In the U.S., "the population growth of seniors is going up at the rate of 73 percent. The population rate of workers is increasing at 14 percent. That means that there is fewer workers paying in their taxes to cover the benefits....In 1950, we had 17 people working paying in their taxes for each Social Security recipient. Today there are only three people working. By 2029, there is going to be two people working....We have increased taxes 36 times since 1971. So today most of the American workers pay more in the Social Security tax than they pay in the payroll tax; 78 percent of American workers now pay more in the Social Security tax than they do in the income tax." (pH8447)

Smith, Nick (Rep.-Mich.). "Cure for Social Security Dilemma." Congressional Record. Daily ed. v143 n138 7 Oct 1997. pH8447-8448. section/page-level access: <http://thomas.loc.gov/cgi-bin/query/R?r105:FLD001:H08447:> (ISSN0363-7239). (X1.1A.105/1).

In the U.S., "in the last 50 years, the Social Security payroll tax has jumped to 12.4 percent from 2 percent. As recently as 1971, the tax applied to only the first $7,800 of income. Now workers and employers must pay the higher tax on all income up to $65,400. For 75 percent of Americans, Social Security and Medicare taxes are the heaviest tax burden they bear." (p20 secA)

Ryan, Richard A. "Preparing for the Golden Years: Safety Net: Social Security Nears Bankruptcy." Detroit News and Free Press 16 Nov 1997. p20 secA.

SOCIAL SERVICE--UNITED STATES

A 1994 study of American social workers found that "of the 52 diagnostic categories or descriptive problem areas identified in...[the] study, nine were frequently (half the time to almost always) encountered by at least half of the 2,640 respondents: anxiety disorders (73 percent), intrapsychic issues of self (73 percent), mood disorders (71 percent), couple relationship problems (67 percent), parent-child relationships (61 percent), single adult relationships (59 percent), personality disorders (57 percent), behavior dysfunctions (54 percent), and adult or adult parent relationships (51 percent). From 30 percent to 47 percent of respondents frequently served clients with problems associated with reconstituted family relationships (47 percent), adolescent psychosocial functioning (38 percent), employment (36 percent), child abuse and neglect (36 percent), child psychosocial functioning (31 percent), body issues (31 percent), and physical health issues (30 percent). About one-fourth frequently treated clients with problems associated with chemical dependency (28 percent), being victims of violence (27 percent), self-sufficiency (26 percent), and education (25 percent)." (p377)

Timberlake, Elizabeth M./Sabatino, Christine A./Martin, James A. "Advanced Practitioners in Clinical Social Work: A Profile." Social Work v42 n4 Jul 1997. p374-385. (ISSN0037-8046).

SOCIAL WELFARE

see PUBLIC WELFARE

SOCIAL WORKERS

see also CHILD WELFARE WORKERS; GAYS--UNITED STATES--SOCIAL WORKERS; MENTAL HEALTH PERSONNEL--UNITED STATES--SOCIAL WORKERS

SOCIAL WORKERS--MICHIGAN--ATTITUDES (v26)

SOCIAL WORKERS--UNITED STATES

A 1994 survey of American social workers found that "the 2,640 respondents used an average of eight theories in their clinical social work practice. Four-fifths (84 percent) frequently used a psychosocial theoretical perspective. Two-thirds frequently used family systems (70 percent) and cognitive (65 percent) theories. One half to three-fifths frequently used ego psychology (61 percent), life span development (59 percent), object relations (59 percent), stress (57 percent), and self-psychology (51 percent). Fewer than half of the respondents frequently used psychoanalytic (49 percent), crisis (47 percent), behavioral (43 percent), and role (39 percent) theories." (p377-378)

Timberlake, Elizabeth M./Sabatino, Christine A./Martin, James A. "Advanced Practitioners in Clinical Social Work: A Profile." Social Work v42 n4 Jul 1997. p374-385. (ISSN0037-8046).

A 1994 survey of American social workers found that "three-fifths or more of the 2,640 respondents frequently used 17 of the 45 clinical techniques in moderate, time-limited practice models (about 20 appointments). The techniques frequently used by three-fourths of the respondents included providing emotional support (74 percent) and developing confidence and self-worth (74 percent). Two-thirds usually used eight techniques: clarifying interpersonal issues (72 percent), empowering clients (71 percent), facilitating decision making (71 percent), problem solving (70 percent), building interpersonal skills (70 percent), reducing stress levels (70 percent), providing clarifying information (67 percent), and handling ambivalence (67 percent). The remainder included handling resistance to change (65 percent); developing insight (65 percent); supporting defenses (63 percent); clarifying or modifying defenses or repetitive themes (63 percent); providing feedback or instruction (60 percent); interpreting (60 percent); and role modeling, teaching, or coaching (60 percent)." (p381)

Timberlake, Elizabeth M./Sabatino, Christine A./Martin, James A. "Advanced Practitioners in Clinical Social Work: A Profile." Social Work v42 n4 Jul 1997. p374-385. (ISSN0037-8046).

A 1994 survey of American social workers found that "three-fifths or more of the 2,640 respondents frequently used 23 of the 45 clinical techniques in a longer-term practice model. The techniques most often used included developing confidence and self-worth (80 percent), providing emotional support (80 percent), developing insight (79 percent), clarifying interpersonal issues (78 percent), working through resistance (77 percent), clarifying or modifying defenses or repetitive themes (76 percent), handling ambivalence (76 percent), handling resistance to change (76 percent), handling separation or termination issues (76 percent), clarifying intrapsychic themes and issues (75 percent), engaging in reflective discussion of the past (75 percent), empowering clients (75 percent), building interpersonal skills (74 percent), handling transference issues (73 percent), and facilitating decision making (70 percent). The remainder included interpreting (67 percent), reducing stress levels (67 percent), problem solving (66 percent), providing clarifying information (66 percent), providing corrective relationship (65 percent), facilitating recovery of repressed material (64 percent), lessening internal threat (61 percent), and using confrontation (60 percent)." (p383)

Timberlake, Elizabeth M./Sabatino, Christine A./Martin, James A. "Advanced Practitioners in Clinical Social Work: A Profile." Social Work v42 n4 Jul 1997. p374-385. (ISSN0037-8046).

SOCIALIZED MEDICINE

see INSURANCE, HEALTH

SOFTWARE INDUSTRY, COMPUTER

see COMPUTER SOFTWARE INDUSTRY

SOFTWARE PROTECTION (v26)

SOIL CONSERVATION--UNITED STATES (v26)

SOIL EROSION (v26)

"In 1990, three scientists from the Agricultural University in Wageningen, the Netherlands, published a global scale study of the extent and severity of soil-degradation induced losses of productivity. Roel Oldeman, Hakkeling, and Wim Sombroeck based their calculations on a survey of more than 200 soil specialists around the world....To obtain global values, Oldeman and his coauthors used 1990 data from the United Nations Food and Agriculture Organization (FAO) indicating that 8,735 million hectares of land worldwide were being used for permanent and annual crops and permanent pasture or maintained as forest and woodland. With this information and the responses to the survey, they calculated that 1,965 million hectares (22 percent) were degraded to some extent: 33 percent lightly, 46 percent moderately, 20 percent strongly, and 1 percent extremely. Wind and water erosion accounted for 85 percent of the degradation and a combination of chemical degradation (primarily the loss of soil nutrients and salinization) and physical degradation (compaction of the soil by heavy farm machinery or cattle) for the remaining 15 percent. Significantly, 6,770 million of the 8,735 million hectares (77 percent) were judged not to be degraded at all and presumably to be suffering no degradation-induced losses of productivity as a result." (p8)

Crosson, Pierre. "Will Erosion Threaten Agricultural Productivity?" Environment v39 n8 Oct 1997. p4-9,29-31. (ISSN0013-9157).

SOIL EROSION--CHINA

"A nationwide survey conducted on almost half of China's farmland identified various degrees of excessive soil erosion on 31 percent of the land....In Sichuan, the country's most populous province with a population of more than 110 million, 44 percent of fields were eroding beyond a sustainable level during the late 1980s. This figure represented a fourfold increase in erosion compared to the early 1950s. Annual erosion losses on two million hectares of cultivated slopeland (nearly one-third of Sichuan's total) averaged 110 tons per hectare." (p34)

Smil, Vaclav. "China Shoulders the Cost of Environmental Change." Environment v39 n6 Jul-Aug 1997. p6-9,33-37. (ISSN0013-9157).

SOIL EROSION--EUROPE--UNITED STATES (v26)

SOIL EROSION--HAITI--SOUTH AFRICA (v26)

SOIL EROSION--UNITED STATES (v26)

In the U.S., much of the Palouse area of eastern Washington and Oregon and western Idaho "receives only enough moisture to support a crop every other year. So on nearly 4.5 million acres of the Palouse, farmers...grow winter wheat one year and leave the land fallow the next, to collect water....Annual soil losses freqently reach 50 tons per acre and have been as high as 150." (p20)

Stelljes, Kathryn Barry/U.S. Dept. of Agriculture. Agricultural Research Service. "Chilly Research Thwarts Soil Erosion." Agricultural Research v45 n6 Jun 1997. p20-21. (ISSN0002-161X).

SOIL FUNGI

"Fungi account for 70% of the microbial activity in soil. Fungi are incredibly diverse, encompassing an estimated 1.5 million species globally." (p546)

Rossman, Amy Y. "Books: Looking Belowground for Aboveground Change." BioScience v47 n8 Sep 1997. p546-547. (ISSN0006-3568).

SOIL SALINIZATION (v26)

SOLAR ENERGY (v26)

see also PHOTOVOLTAIC POWER GENERATION

"The worldwide manufacture of solar photovoltaic (PV) cells surged by an estimated 25 percent in 1997, reaching more than 110 megawatts (MW)--compared to just 47 megawatts in 1990. The cost of solar cells has fallen from more than $70,000 per kilowatt in the 1970s to $4,000 today and is expected to drop to as low as $1,000 per kilowatt in the next decade. An estimated 400,000 homes, most of them in remote areas not connected to power lines, already have solar power." (p20)

Flavin, Christopher/Dunn, Seth. "Rising Sun, Gathering Winds: Policies to Stabilize the Climate and Strengthen Economies." Worldwatch Paper n138 Nov 1997. p5-84.

SOLAR ENERGY--CHINA (v26)

SOLAR ENERGY--UNITED STATES--PUBLIC OPINION (v26)

SOLAR WATER HEATERS--AUSTRALIA--UNITED STATES

"More than 300,000 people in the U.S. have decided to have a commercially-made solar pool heater installed." (p23) "Research has shown that swimming pools themselves are actually effective solar collectors, absorbing more than 75 percent of the solar energy hitting the pool surface and keeping that heat in the pool....In Australia...more than half of all the new swimming pools are currently being installed with solar heaters, and about 20 percent of existing domestic pools in the country already use active solar heaters....While typical systems around the...[U.S.] cost about $3500 to $4000, depending on location, length of swimming season desired and other factors, the cost savings over using fossil fuels usually means a payback of just a couple of years." (p24)

Sheinkopf, Ken. "Solar Pool Heaters: The Simplest Use of Active Solar Energy." Solar Today v11 n6 Nov-Dec 1997. p22-24. (ISSN1042-0630).

SOLDIERS
see UNITED NATIONS--ARMED FORCES--SOLDIERS
SOLDIERS, AFRO-AMERICAN
see AFRO-AMERICAN SOLDIERS
SOLICITORS
see LAWYERS
SOLID WASTE MANAGEMENT
see REFUSE AND REFUSE DISPOSAL
SOLOMON ISLANDS--SOCIAL CONDITIONS (v26)
SONGBIRDS--UNITED STATES
"Since 1980, the number of Baltimore orioles has declined between 25 and 30 percent, according to the US Breeding Bird Survey. The population of wood thrushes has dropped more than 40 percent and the number of golden-winged warblers have been cut almost in half." (p3)
Marks, Alexandra. "United States: Environmentalists Target Java-Drinkers to Save Birds." The Christian Science Monitor v89 n157 10 Jul 1997. p3. The Christian Science Monitor search engine: <http://www.csmonitor.com/plweb-cgi/iops1.pl> To retrieve this article, enter the following search: ED=19970710 AND birds. In the "retrieved list," click the title that matches this record. (ISSN0882-7729).
SORGHUM INDUSTRY--UNITED STATES (v26)
In the U.S., "area planted to sorghum rose almost 40 percent, or 13 million acres, from 1995 to 1996. Production rose 75 percent to just over 800 million bushels....As a result of higher production, the average harvest month price fell from $2.75 to $2.70 per bushel from 1995 to 1996. On average yields rose about 23 percent, and both gross value and returns rose as well." (p24)
U.S. Dept. of Agriculture. Economic Research Service. "1996 Cost of Production for Crops and Livestock: Although Input Expenses Rose in 1996,...Led to Higher Net Returns." Agricultural Income and Finance Situation and Outlook Report Sep 1997. p23-27.
SORORITIES
see GREEK LETTER SOCIETIES
SOUND RECORDING INDUSTRY--UNITED STATES (v26)
SOUTH AFRICA--ECONOMIC CONDITIONS (v26)
The economies of the Southern African Development Community "members grew by an average 6.5 percent last year--well above the 2.4 percent of the United States. For most SADC members, the budget deficit is less than 6 percent. And in all 12 countries, inflation is coming down....[In Angola,] fighting continues between the government and rebels in the diamond area, where $500-million in revenue is siphoned off by insurgents yearly....Diamonds are Botswana's best friend and accounted for last year's GDP growth of a whopping 7 percent....[Mozambique] has posted some extraordinary economic growth--a hefty 6.4 percent last year--but is still the most aid-dependent country on earth....[South Africa's] dominant economy has a GDP of some $125 billion. South Africa accounts for 76.8 percent of SADC market share." (p6)
Matloff, Judith. "International: Southern Africa's Other Story: Economies Roar." The Christian Science Monitor v89 n177 7 Aug 1997. p6. The Christian Science Monitor search engine: <http://www.csmonitor.com/plweb-cgi/iops1.pl> To retrieve this article, enter the following search: ED=19970807 AND roar. In the "retrieved list," click the title that matches this record. (ISSN0882-7729).
SOUTH AFRICA--ECONOMIC CONDITIONS--SOCIAL CONDITIONS (v26)
"Murders have declined marginally in South Africa in recent years to an average of 65 per day--seven times the rate in America....Poor blacks...make up 70 percent of South Africa's 38 million citizens....Employment outside the farm sector fell by 1 percent in 1996 to more than 20 percent....Since 1994, electricity has been extended to 1.2 million houses; another 1.7 million South Africans have ready access to clean water." (p8)
Dunn, Kate. "International: S. Africans Head toward Life without Mandela." The Christian Science Monitor v90 n17 18 Dec 1997. p1,8. The Christian Science Monitor search engine: <http://www.csmonitor.com/plweb-cgi/iops1.pl> To retrieve this article, enter the following search: ED=19971218 AND mandela. In the "retrieved list," click the title that matches this record. (ISSN0882-7729).
SOUTH AFRICA--SOCIAL CONDITIONS (v26)
SOUTH AMERICA--ECONOMIC CONDITIONS (v26)
SOUTH AMERICA--SOCIAL CONDITIONS
In South America, "infant mortality and deaths in children under age 5 have declined by about 50% over the last 15 years; life expectancy has risen by an average of 8 years....Seventy-four percent rural in the 1940s, the region is now 74% urban. Some 40% of the population, or 115 million people, are poor....Health care expenditures in the region were 3-6% of the gross domestic product, as compared to 12.7% in the United States." (p794)
Joyce, Stephanie/U.S. National Institute of Environmental Health Sciences. "Focus: Growing Pains in South America." Environmental Health Perspectives v105 n8 Aug 1997. p794-799.
SOUTH AMERICAN TRYPANOSOMIASIS
see CHAGAS' DISEASE
SOUTH AMERICANS--EMPLOYMENT--UNITED STATES
In the U.S., "the largest percentage (27%) of Central South Americans work as operators, fabricators, and laborers. The remaining majority are divided among four areas of employment: service (22%), precision production, craft and repair (18%), and technicians, sales and administrative support (17%). Only 14% work as managers or professionals. The largest percentage (35%) of Central South American females work in service occupations. Another 30% work in technical, sales or administrative support; 16% work as operators, fabricators, and laborers, and 15% hold managerial and professional positions." (p26)
"Targeting Minority Publics: Employment of Hispanic Americans by Country of Origin." Public Relations Quarterly v42 n2 Sum 1997. p26. (ISSN0033-3700).
SOUTH ASIA--ARMED FORCES
South Asia, "the poorest, most illiterate region in the world is spending $14 billion a year on arms....India has the fourth-largest army in the world and Pakistan's is ranked eighth....South Asia could finance primary education for 110 million children, safe drinking water for 600 million people and family planning services for an additional 55 million--if it only stopped arms-shopping." (p12)
Oakley, Charmaine. "Around the World: Let Them Eat Bullets." Earth Island Journal v12 n4 Fall 1997. p12. (ISSN1041-0406).
SOUTH ASIA--COMMERCE
In South Asia, "real exports grew at 11 percent a year in the 1990s, faster than in any other region except East Asia....Per capita exports are five times lower than in other developing countries, and South Asia's share in world trade is just 1 percent, compared with 4 percent for China. Intra-regional trade is still minuscule, accounting for 4 percent of total trade."
World Bank. "South Asia Can Reap Further Gains from Global Integration." Press Release 17 Sep 1997. document-level access: <http://www.worldbank.org/html/extdr/extme/1487.htm>
SOUTH ASIA--ECONOMIC CONDITIONS--SOCIAL CONDITIONS
"South Asia's average per capita income at US$309 a year is

nearly half that of sub-Saharan Africa as a whole, and much less than the $825 of East Asia (including China). The adult literacy rate at 48 per cent is lower than that of sub-Saharan Africa and neighbouring Southeast Asian countries such as Thailand (94 per cent). Two-thirds of the children in South Asia are malnourished compared to one-third in Africa." (p25)

"Notebook: Guns, Or Better?" Choices v6 n4 Oct 1997. p25.

SOUTHERN STATES--EMPLOYMENT

"Blue-collar jobs, which dropped from 57.0 to 47.02 percent of all jobs in the [U.S.] South, remained the largest job category for southern workers in 1994, while the number of white-collar jobs grew from 29.0 percent of all the workforce in 1975 to 39.2 percent in 1994....At the same time, the South's best blue-collar jobs--skilled craft and semi-skilled operative positions--dropped in number from 40.3 percent to 28.2 percent of the job market from 1975 to 1994, while the number of lowest paying blue-collar jobs--low-skilled laborer and service positions--increased from 16.7 percent to 19.0 percent of the job market in that same period....The only decline in white-collar work has taken place in official/managerial positions which went from 11.2 percent of the jobs in 1985 and to 10.1 percent in 1994, after having grown during the previous decade." (p7)

Eckman, Anne/Green, Jordan. "Dislocation & Workforce Equity: The South at Work in the 1990s: A Growing Divide." Southern Exposure: Institute for Southern Studies Report 1997. p7.

SOUTHERN STATES--POPULATION (v26)

SOYBEAN CURD

see TOFU

SOYBEAN CYST NEMATODE--UNITED STATES

In the U.S., the soybean cyst nematode, Heterodera glycine, "is the No. 1 disease pest of soybeans, contributing to annual losses estimated at 64 million bushels nationwide....Soybean growers may lose 10 to 15 percent of their yield to this pest...." (p7)

Lyons-Johnson, Dawn/U.S. Dept. of Agriculture. Agricultural Research Service. "Soybean Cyst Nematodes, Look Out!" Agricultural Research v45 n9 Sep 1997. p7. (ISSN0002-161X).

SOYBEAN INDUSTRY (v26)

"Together, the U.S. and Brazil accounted for 70 percent of global soybean output in 1996/97, with shares of 51 and 19 percent. A larger crop is also projected for the world's third-largest producer, Argentina (9-percent world share in 1996/97)...." (p7)

Ash, Mark/U.S. Dept. of Agriculture. Economic Research Service. "Commodity Spotlight: Market Braces for Record U.S. Soybean Crop." Agricultural Outlook Sep 1997. p6-9.

"World soybean production in 1996/97 increased to 131.4 million tons, but was still short of the record 137.7 million tons in 1994/95. Foreign soybean production increased 2 percent overall to 66.5 million tons." (p7)

U.S. Dept. of Agriculture. Economic Research Service. "World Oilseed Situation." Oil Crops Situation and Outlook Series Oct 1997. p7-8.

"From 1950 to 1996, the world's harvest of soybeans--which dominates oilseed production--climbed from 17 million to 133 million tons as demand for protein supplements for livestock and poultry feed and for cooking oil soared. With farmers unable to raise rapidly the yield per hectare of this crop, the land in soybeans increased from 14 million hectares in 1950 to 62 million hectares in 1995, with growth coming largely at the expense of grain, especially during the last two decades." (p21)

Brown, Lester R. "The Agricultural Link: How Environmental Deterioration Could Disrupt Economic Progress." Worldwatch Paper n136 Aug 1997. p5-73.

SOYBEAN INDUSTRY--ARGENTINA--BRAZIL (v26)

SOYBEAN INDUSTRY--BRAZIL

"Stronger prices and better farm finances raised Brazilian soybean area 8 percent in 1996/97....The 1996/97 Brazilian soybean crop increased 12 percent to 26.5 million tons, a new record." (p7)

U.S. Dept. of Agriculture. Economic Research Service. "World Oilseed Situation." Oil Crops Situation and Outlook Series Oct 1997. p7-8.

SOYBEAN INDUSTRY--CHINA (v26)

"In the 1993/94 marketing year, China exported 1.1 million metric tons of soybeans and 1.05 million tons of soybean meal....Only 200,000 tons of soybeans and 30,000 tons of soybean meal are projected to be exported from China in 1997/98. With greater harvested area projected for 1997/98, China's soybean output is forecast up 7 percent." (p8)

Ash, Mark/U.S. Dept. of Agriculture. Economic Research Service. "Commodity Spotlight: Market Braces for Record U.S. Soybean Crop." Agricultural Outlook Sep 1997. p6-9.

"China, the third largest producer of soybeans, was exporting as much as 1.1 million tons in 1993/94 to nearby Asian markets. In 1996/97, China was a net importer, taking as much as 2.2 million tons, up 175 percent from 1995/96." (p8)

U.S. Dept. of Agriculture. Economic Research Service. "World Oilseed Situation." Oil Crops Situation and Outlook Series Oct 1997. p7-8.

SOYBEAN INDUSTRY--EUROPE--UNITED STATES

"In 1995/96, U.S. soybean exports to the EU were 7.8 million metric tons (valued at $2.1 billion), about one-third of total U.S. soybean trade. U.S. soybean meal exports to the EU totaled 0.9 million tons (nearly $200 million), about 15 percent of total U.S. soybean meal trade." (p7)

Ash, Mark/U.S. Dept. of Agriculture. Economic Research Service. "Commodity Spotlight: Market Braces for Record U.S. Soybean Crop." Agricultural Outlook Sep 1997. p6-9.

SOYBEAN INDUSTRY--MISSISSIPPI (v26)

SOYBEAN INDUSTRY--TURKEY--UNITED STATES (v26)

SOYBEAN INDUSTRY--UNITED STATES (v26)

In the U.S., "both prices and yields of soybeans moved higher in 1996, resulting in record returns. Soybean prices rose above $8 per bushel in 1996 and settled near $7 at harvest, up about 10 percent from 1995....Higher prices and yields sent the value of soybeans at harvest above $250 per acre, a record high. Likewise, average returns above cash costs, at $130 per acre, were the highest reported since 1975." (p23)

U.S. Dept. of Agriculture. Economic Research Service. "1996 Cost of Production for Crops and Livestock: Although Input Expenses Rose in 1996,...Led to Higher Net Returns." Agricultural Income and Finance Situation and Outlook Report Sep 1997. p23-27.

"U.S. farmers are forecast to harvest a record soybean crop in 1997, with production up 14 percent from last year. Extremely high soybean prices during the spring months triggered a 10-percent increase in seedings, resulting in the largest planted area of soybeans since 1982 and the third highest on record....The U.S. season-average farm price is forecast down sharply to $5.75-$6.85 per bushel, from $7.38 in 1996/97." (p2)

Simone, Mark/U.S. Dept. of Agriculture. Economic Research Service. "Briefs: Field Crops: Overview: Major U.S. Field Crops." Agricultural Outlook Nov 1997. p2-3.

"U.S. soybean acreage planted in 1997 is the largest in 15 years and the third highest on record, according to USDA's ACREAGE report released June 30....The estimate for 1997 soybean plantings is 70.9 million acres, 10 percent above last year. Farmers are expected to harvest 69.8 million acres of soybeans and produce a record 2.69 billion bushels....Iowa expanded soybean plantings by an estimated 1 million acres, while Minnesota followed closely with an 850,000-acre year-to-year increase." (p2)

Simone, Mark/U.S. Dept. of Agriculture. Economic Research Service. "Commodity Briefs: Field Crops: Sharp Rise in U.S. Soybean Acreage Planted for 1997." Agricultural Outlook Aug 1997. p2-4.

"U.S. soybean farmers responded to this spring's strong prices by planting an estimated 70.9 million acres, up 10 percent and the highest in 15 years, according to USDA's June ACREAGE report. This would be the third-largest soybean area planted on record and the first time in history that U.S. planted acreage for soybeans has exceeded wheat area. The bumper crop is expected to pressure 1997/98 U.S. farm prices into the range of $5.40-$6.60 per bushel, down sharply from 1996/97's estimated season average of $7.38." (p6)

Ash, Mark/U.S. Dept. of Agriculture. Economic Research Service. "Commodity Spotlight: Market Braces for Record U.S. Soybean Crop." Agricultural Outlook Sep 1997. p6-9.

In the U.S., "soybean volume rose 12 percent to a record 25.6 million tons in 1996....Exports to China soared to a record 1.5 million tons, compared with 199,000 in 1995. Shipments to Mexico jumped 31 percent to 2.6 million tons, and exports to Indonesia soared 171 percent to 735,000 tons. At $286 per ton, soybean export prices were nearly 21 percent higher than in 1995, boosting total value of soybean shipments 36 percent to a record $7.3 billion." (p2)

Greene, Joel/U.S. Dept. of Agriculture. Economic Research Service. "Agricultural Exports Surpass $60 Billion." Foreign Agricultural Trade of the United States Jan-Mar 1997. p2-3.

In the U.S., in 1996, "sharply higher prices for soybean meal boosted the value of exports 45 percent to $1.4 billion, the highest export value since 1988. Higher prices accounted for much of the gain as volume only increased 6 percent to 5.2 million tons....The United States shipped a record 418,000 tons to China...." (p2)

Greene, Joel/U.S. Dept. of Agriculture. Economic Research Service. "Agricultural Exports Surpass $60 Billion." Foreign Agricultural Trade of the United States Jan-Mar 1997. p2-3.

In 1996-1997, "U.S. soybean meal exports increased from 6.0 million short tons in 1995/96 to 6.9 million....Domestic meal disappearance rose 2 percent to 27.2 million short tons. Already high-priced soybean meal became even more costly, rising to an average $270 per ton, versus $236 in 1995/96. Lower soybean oil prices, averaging 23.5 cents per pound, encouraged a robust 6-percent increase in domestic disappearance to 14,215 million pounds. U.S. exports of soybean oil also rebounded, more than doubling from 1995/96 to 2,050 million pounds." (p3)

U.S. Dept. of Agriculture. Economic Research Service. "Summary." Oil Crops Situation and Outlook Series Oct 1997. p3.

On 4 April 1996, U.S. "President Clinton signed the Federal Agricultural Improvement and Reform Act, which establishes farm policy through 2001/02....Producers' payments are now made on 85 percent of a farm's contract acreage and program yield....Loan rates for oilseeds were set at 85 percent of the average price for the preceding 5 years (excluding the high and low years)....The rates cannot fall below $4.92 per bushel for soybeans or exceed $5.26. Under the new formula, the 1996 rate was $4.97 per bushel and with high prices again in 1996, the loan rate was $5.26 by 1997. The loan rate for 1995 was $4.92....The minimum and maximum loan rates are $8.90 and $9.30 per hundredweight, respectively, for sunflowerseed, canola, rapeseed, safflowerseed, flaxseed, and mustard seed....The act capped CRP [Conservation Reserve Program] enrollment at 36.4 million acres." (p4)

U.S. Dept. of Agriculture. Economic Research Service. "U.S. Soybean Situation." Oil Crops Situation and Outlook Series Oct 1997. p4-6.

U.S. "cumulative 1996/97 soybean imports were 9 million bushels, but accounted for only 0.4 percent of total supplies....Ample supplies permitted 1996/97 domestic crush to reach a record 1,436 million bushels and soybean exports to reach 882 million bushels. U.S. soybean exports in November were 152 million bushels...." (p5)

U.S. Dept. of Agriculture. Economic Research Service. "U.S. Soybean Situation." Oil Crops Situation and Outlook Series Oct 1997. p4-6.

"U.S. soybean exports dropped to 632,000 tons in July [1997] from 878,000 in June. Nevertheless, at $6.3 billion, soybean export value for the year continues 14 percent above 1996....U.S. exports of soybean oil in July more than tripled, reaching 65,000 tons, up from 20,000 tons in June....Year-to-year soybean oil exports have risen 70 percent to $422 million." (unpaginated)

Whitton, Carol/U.S. Dept. of Agriculture. Economic Research Service. "Exports." U.S. Agricultural Trade Update 23 Sep 1997.

U.S. soybean exports in May 1997 "were 1.1 million tons, 3 percent less than May 1996. October-May exports reached 20.3 million tons, a 19-percent increase over 1996. October to May soybean shipments to the European Union-15 were 7.8 million tons, up 9 percent from a year ago. Exports to Japan, the second largest importer of soybeans, were up 7 percent reaching a cumulative total of 2.9 million tons. The $5.8 billion year-to-date export value was up 23 percent from a year ago as higher volume and export prices boosted value....Cumulative soybean meal exports were 4.7 million tons, up from 3.3 million tons in 1996. In May, soybean meal shipments were 288,000 tons, down 20 percent from 1996. The fiscal year-to-date value of soybean meal exports reached $1.3 billion, up 65 percent from a year ago due to stronger prices. May exports of soybean oil were 13,000 tons, down from 29,000 tons in 1996. The 1997 cumulative soybean oil export value remained 57 percent above 1996 at $371 million." (p1)

U.S. Dept. of Agriculture. Economic Research Service. "Exports." U.S. Agricultural Trade Update 23 Jul 1997. p1.

In the U.S., in August 1997, soybean "pods were setting on 96% of the acreage, ahead of both 90% in 1996 and the average of 92%. Leaves were dropping on 2% of the national acreage, behind 3% for both 1996 and the average." (p10)

U.S. Dept. of Commerce. Dept. of Agriculture. "National Agricultural Summary: August 25-31, 1997: Highlights." Weekly Weather and Crop Bulletin v84 n35 3 Sep 1997. p10. (ISSN0043-1974).

SPACE SHUTTLES--UNITED STATES

"In 1991, the probability of catastrophic loss on ascent for...[a U.S. Space] Shuttle was one in 78. Today it is one in 248. NASA has achieved a 50% reduction in the number of in-flight anomalies per flight since FY 1993, from 14.3 to 6.8. The Agency also has reduced the number of monthly mishaps during Shuttle processing at the Kennedy Space Center almost 50%, from 0.9 in FY 1993 to 0.5 in FY 1996. At the same time, the Agency has worked diligently to reduce Shuttle operating costs. In FY 1993, it had been $4.1 billion dollars. Today it is $3.1 billion. The number of people required to operate the Shuttle--contractors and civil servants--has been reduced nearly 22% since FY 1993, the amount of overtime has been reduced 37%." (p98)

Goldin, Daniel S. (Administrator, National Aeronautics and Space Administration). "Departments of Veterans Affairs and Housing and Urban Development...Approp. for 1998 (Part 1)."

Hearing. U.S. House. Committee on Appropriations. Washington, D.C. : GPO, 1997. (ISBN0160549884). (Y4.Ap6/1:V64/4/997/pt.1).

SPACE SURVEILLANCE--UNITED STATES--FINANCE (v26)

SPACE VEHICLES--UNITED STATES--COSTS

"From 1990-1994, the average cost per [U.S.] spacecraft launched was $590 million. For 1995-1999, it will be $190 million. Our goal beyond the year 2000 is $77 million. At the same time we are achieving reduction in average development time per spacecraft. For 1990-1994 it was 8.3 years. For 1995-1999, it will be 4.6 years. For 2000 and beyond, our goal is 3.1 years. Because we are reducing the cost and time for development, we can launch more missions. For FY 1990-1994, NASA averaged 2 flights per year. For 1995-1999 it will be 9 flights per year. For 2000 and beyond, our goal is 16 flights a year." (p97)

Goldin, Daniel S. (Administrator, National Aeronautics and Space Administration). "Departments of Veterans Affairs and Housing and Urban Development...Approp. for 1998 (Part 1)." Hearing. U.S. House. Committee on Appropriations. Washington, D.C. : GPO, 1997. (ISBN0160549884). (Y4.Ap6/1:V64/4/997/pt.1).

SPAS

see PHYSICAL FITNESS CENTERS

SPASTIC COLON

see IRRITABLE COLON

SPECIAL EDUCATION--MASSACHUSETTS--BOSTON (v26)

SPECIAL EDUCATION--MICHIGAN

"Ypsilanti and Ann Arbor were two of 84 Michigan school districts to sue the state 17 years ago for what they believed to be the under-funding of special education programs and transportation. With interest accumulated, the latest compensation figures come to almost $17 million for Ann Arbor and more than $13 million for Ypsilanti, according to attorney Dennis Pollard, whose Bloomfield Hills firm of Pollard & Albertson represents the districts....In the years after the 84 districts filed the suit, about 300 additional districts--including the WISD [Washtenaw Intermediate School District] and several of its individual districts--filed complaints as well." (p1 secC) "Currently the state gives area school districts 7 percent above the regular foundation allowance for special education students and the county, through a WISD special millage, pays for 37 percent of the balance. In Ypsilanti, it costs $28,000 per year to educate a special education student, compared to $5,000 for general elementary students,...[Alan Dowdy, the Ypsilanti school district's executive director for business and finance] said." (p6 secC)

Hollander, Sarah. "Local: Schools Hope Court Ruling Leads to Funds." Ann Arbor News 12 Jun 1997. p1,6 secC.

SPECIAL EDUCATION--NEW YORK (N.Y.)--COSTS (v26)

SPECIAL EDUCATION--NEW YORK (STATE)--COSTS (v26)

SPECIAL EDUCATION--UNITED STATES (v26)

SPECIAL EDUCATION TEACHERS--UNITED STATES

"In the 1992-93 school year, 69,919 of U.S. special education teachers were employed in cross-categorical programs [in which they taught students with learning disabilities of all types] (U.S. Department of Education, 1994). That is almost one fourth of the total number of special education teachers." (p440)

Reynolds, Maynard C./Heistad, David. "20/20 Analysis: Estimating School Effectiveness in Serving Students at the Margins." Exceptional Children v63 n4 Sum 1997. p439-449. (ISSN0014-4029).

SPECIES (v26)

SPECIES--UNITED STATES (v26)

SPECIES, ENDANGERED

see ENDANGERED SPECIES

SPECIES, EXOTIC

see EXOTIC SPECIES

SPEED (DRUG)

see METHAMPHETAMINE

SPEED LIMITS--COLORADO--MONTANA--SOUTH DAKOTA--TEXAS (v26)

SPEED LIMITS--UNITED STATES

"In California, where interstate speed limits are set at 70 m.p.h. [miles per hour], the fatality rate declined 4 percent between 1995 and 1996--the best record since 1961. In Mississippi, the fatality rate dropped an impressive 21 percent after the highway limit was raised from 55 to 70 m.p.h. On the much disparaged 'Montanabahn'--where there are no specific daytime speed limits (the 'reasonable and prudent' standard applies), fatalities dropped 5 percent between 1995 and 1996....On the typical American interstate, measured 85th-percentile speeds are between 70-80 m.p.h." (p13 secA)

Peters, Eric. "Other Voices: 70-M.P.H. Limits: Raising Highway Speeds Hasn't Resulted in More Deaths." Detroit Free Press 13 Aug 1997. p13 secA.

SPEED LIMITS--UNITED STATES--MORTALITY

In the U.S., "in 1987, states were allowed to raise their [speed] limits on rural interstates and 40 adopted 65 mph [miles per hour] limits....After 1987, the higher speed limit reduced statewide fatality rates by 3.4 percent to 5.1 percent, compared with the rates in states that did not raise limits. True, the actual number of fatalities continued to increase after 1987, but the volume of traffic increased even faster....When in November 1995 Congress empowered states to set such limits as they chose, fatalities did not increase the 10 percent to 14 percent predicted by the Cassandras who foresaw 4,400-6,000 extra deaths per year. Neither did fatalities increase even the 2 percent to 3 percent that would have been expected, extrapolating from recent trends. Instead,...fatalities have declined slightly (0.14 percent) even as total vehicle miles increased 2 percent." (p8 secA)

Will, George. "Column: A Cautionary Tale about Puzzling Statistics: Speed May Not Kill." Detroit News 10 Nov 1997. p8 secA.

In the U.S., "over the past two years, a dozen states have increased their speed limits on rural interstates and urban freeways. Five states have raised their speed limits to 75 mph....12 states with a speed limit increase have already showed considerable variance from those which have not raised their limit. IIHS [Insurance Institute for Highway Safety] says that these states have shown a 12% increase in fatalities on interstates and freeways and a 6% increase on all roads associated with the raised speed limits. This change has accounted for 500 additional fatalities in a five month period." (unpaginated)

"Transportation: Higher Speed Limits Increases Corporate, Personal Risks." Security Letter v27 n19 1 Nov 1997. (ISSN0363-4922).

SPEEDWAYS (AUTOMOBILE RACING)

see RACETRACKS (AUTOMOBILE RACING)

SPERMATOZOA (v26)

SPERMATOZOA--EUROPE--UNITED STATES

A report from the California Department of Health shows that "sperm counts in the United States and Europe have dropped enormously in the last 60 years. The report found that U.S. sperm counts have fallen an average of 1.5 percent per year since the 1930s, a far sharper decline than earlier studies indicated. The drop in Europe is twice as steep....In 1992,...a group of European scientists looked at 61 studies and asserted that from 1938 to 1990 sperm counts worldwide dropped from 113 million sperm per milliliter of semen--about 18 droplets from an eyedropper--to 66 million sperm per milliliter, a decline of about 1 percent per year." (p5 secA)

Schulte, Brigid. "Nation & World: Sperm Counts Drop Sharply, Study Says." Detroit Free Press 24 Nov 1997. p5 secA.

SPICE TRADE--CHINA

"China produces a small amount of coffee, a little over 3,000 tons in 1995....Also in 1995, China produced 23,000 tons of cinnamon; 21,000 tons of anise; 12,000 tons of hops; 10,000 tons of pepper; and 400 tons of vanilla." (p48)

Crook, Frederick W./U.S. Dept. of Agriculture. Economic Research Service. "Introduction to China's Horticultural Economy." China: International Agriculture and Trade Reports Situation and Outlook Series Jun 1997. p47-51.

SPINA BIFIDA--UNITED STATES (v26)

SPINAL CORD--WOUNDS AND INJURIES--CALIFORNIA

"Of those injured from 1980 through 1993 and rehabilitated for firearm associated spinal cord injuries within the Southern California Spinal Cord Injury Model System, 94.2 percent have been from ethnic minority groups, predominately Latino (54.1 percent) or African American (36.3 percent)....Of all Latinos...rehabilitated within the Southern California System during the same period, 49.2 percent have sustained their injuries by firearms. For African Americans,...of those treated within the system, 61.0 percent have sustained their injuries by firearms....8.5 percent of all non-Latino white patients treated within the system had firearm associated spinal cord injury." (p11)

Waters, Robert L./Cressy, Jeffrey/Adkins, Rodney H. "Spinal Cord Injuries Due to Violence." American Rehabilitation v22 n3 Aut 1996. p10-15. (ISSN0362-4048).

SPINAL CORD--WOUNDS AND INJURIES--EMPLOYMENT --UNITED STATES

"At the time of injury 14.3 percent of persons [in the U.S.] with spinal cord injury were unemployed. This rate is almost twice the average unemployment rate for the U.S. general population over the past 20 years....By the time of the first anniversary year after injury, only 16 percent of those working at the time of injury have returned to work. Eight percent of those initially working have entered school for more education....Employment rates gradually increased to reach a peak of 32 percent at about 10 years after injury for males and 33 percent at 11 years for females. The educational level of persons with spinal cord injury 5 years after injury is somewhat less than that of the U.S. population as a whole." (p30)

Stover, Samuel L. "Facts, Figures, And Trends on Spinal Cord Injury." American Rehabilitation v22 n3 Aut 1996. p25-32. (ISSN0362-4048).

According to the U.S. Spinal Cord Injury National Model Systems database, "by the first year post-injury, 16 percent of those who at the time of injury were working have returned to work, and 8 percent have entered school; more than 70 percent consider themselves to be unemployed. Employment following SCI increases steadily, until at 10 to 11 years postinjury one-third of those in the database were working." (p12)

Gordon, Wayne A./Brown, Margaret. "Community Integration of Individuals with Spinal Cord Injuries." American Rehabilitation v23 n1 Spr 1997. p11-14. (ISSN0362-4048).

SPINAL CORD--WOUNDS AND INJURIES--UNITED STATES

"A survey by the Breaking New Ground Resource Center revealed that more than 30 percent of [U.S.] farmers and ranchers with SCI [spinal cord injuries] purchased and obtained service on their wheelchairs and other mobility aids more than 100 miles away from their homes....34 percent lived more than 51 miles from rehabilitation services." (p2)

Hagglund, Kristofer/Clay, Daniel L. "Rural Healthcare Initiatives in Spinal Cord Injury." American Rehabilitation v23 n1 Spr 1997. p2-6. (ISSN0362-4048).

"Although only 2.7 percent of persons in the [U.S. National Spinal Cord Injury Model Systems Database]...are less than 15 years of age at the time of injury, 12.4 percent have education levels of eighth grade or below....With a median age of this SCI population of 26 years, 59.3 percent have at least completed high school. Of those between the ages of 18 and 21 years, 66 percent are at least high school graduates; however, the comparable figure for the U.S. general population is 86 percent." (p30)

Stover, Samuel L. "Facts, Figures, And Trends on Spinal Cord Injury." American Rehabilitation v22 n3 Aut 1996. p25-32. (ISSN0362-4048).

"Persons with spinal cord injury also frequently have associated injuries which are caused by the traumatic event leading to the injury....More than half (55.2 percent) of persons [in the U.S.] with spinal cord injury have what is considered a significant associated injury. Fractures of the long bones are most freqent (29.3 percent) and traumatic pneumothorax or hemothorax occurs in 17.8 percent. Loss of consciousness occurred in 28.2 percent, with 18.4 percent diagnosed as having a definite traumatic brain injury." (p29-30)

Stover, Samuel L. "Facts, Figures, And Trends on Spinal Cord Injury." American Rehabilitation v22 n3 Aut 1996. p25-32. (ISSN0362-4048).

Because the median age of persons in the U.S. with spinal cord injury is young, "most persons are single (53.5 percent) at the time of injury. Almost one-third (30.6 percent) are married, and the others are divorced, separated, or widowed. In 8 years of postinjury followup, marriages are more likely to end in divorce than expected compared to age and specific rates for the general U.S. population (44 percent vs. 23 percent). Of those persons married at the time of initial hospital discharge, 81.2 percent were still married 5 years after injury, compared with an expected value of 88.7 percent in the absence of spinal cord injury. Of those marriages which took place after injury, 21.7 percent terminated in separation or divorce, which is significantly higher than the 15 percent for preinjury marriages." (p30)

Stover, Samuel L. "Facts, Figures, And Trends on Spinal Cord Injury." American Rehabilitation v22 n3 Aut 1996. p25-32. (ISSN0362-4048).

In the U.S., "as many as 10 percent of all patients admitted for SCI [spinal cord injury] rehabilitation have been found to be delayed in their discharge due to a lack of appropriate settings for discharge. The average costs associated with these delays was $29,280." (p3)

Hagglund, Kristofer/Clay, Daniel L. "Rural Healthcare Initiatives in Spinal Cord Injury." American Rehabilitation v23 n1 Spr 1997. p2-6. (ISSN0362-4048).

In the U.S., "during the period 1973-78, violence accounted for 13.3 percent of cases entered into the...[Spinal Cord Injury Model System Database maintained at the National Spinal Cord Injury Statistical Center in Birmingham, Alabama]; in 1979-82 it accounted for 15.1 percent; 1983-86, 17.2 percent; 1987-90, 20.8 percent; and 1991-94, 30.4 percent (National Spinal Cord Injury Statistical Center [NSCISC], 1994). While this percentage shift may be partially due to a decrease in injuries due to motor vehicle crashes, an increase in injuries caused by firearms that has accounted for 88 percent of the violence related spinal cord injuries is also evident (Stover, DeLisa, & Whiteneck, 1995). Violence is more prominent in facilties drawing from urban versus rural catchment areas. In the urban facilities the percentages of injuries due to violence ranged from 21.1 to 50.0 percent; in the rural facilities the range was 6.6 to 21.2

percent (NSCISC, 1994)." (p11)

Waters, Robert L./Cressy, Jeffrey/Adkins, Rodney H. "Spinal Cord Injuries Due to Violence." American Rehabilitation v22 n3 Aut 1996. p10-15. (ISSN0362-4048).

In the U.S., "from 1973 through 1977, 76.9 percent of persons enrolled in the National SCI [Spinal Cord Injury] Database were white, 14.0 percent were African-American, 6.2 percent Hispanic, 2.1 percent American Indians, and 0.8 percent Asians....From 1990 to 1992 only 56.3 percent of persons were white, 29.9 percent were African-American, 11.2 percent Hispanic, 1.6 percent Asian, and 0.4 percent American Indians." (p27)

Stover, Samuel L. "Facts, Figures, And Trends on Spinal Cord Injury." American Rehabilitation v22 n3 Aut 1996. p25-32. (ISSN0362-4048).

In the U.S., "prior to 1979, motor vehicular crashes caused 46.9 percent of spinal cord injuries, whereas from 1991 to 1994 they caused only 35.9 percent. Sports injuries have decreased from 14.4 percent to 7.4 percent during this same time period....Acts of violence have more than doubled, increasing from 13.2 percent to 29.8 percent." (p27)

Stover, Samuel L. "Facts, Figures, And Trends on Spinal Cord Injury." American Rehabilitation v22 n3 Aut 1996. p25-32. (ISSN0362-4048).

In the U.S., "spinal cord injury occurs most frequently in teenagers and young adults. The most common age at injury is 19, with 32.8 percent of all injuries occurring between the ages of 17 and 23. Almost 80 percent of injuries occur between the ages of 16 to 45....The average (mean) age of injury is 30.7 years, with a median age at injury of 26 years. The mean age of injury is only slightly higher for females--32.2 years--than for males--30.3 years. There has been an increase of 4.9 years in the mean age at time of injury since 1973. Those who were at least 61 years of age at the time of injury increased from 4.5 percent for the period 1973-1977 to 8.5 percent since 1990." (p26-27)

Stover, Samuel L. "Facts, Figures, And Trends on Spinal Cord Injury." American Rehabilitation v22 n3 Aut 1996. p25-32. (ISSN0362-4048).

In the U.S., "while spinal cord injury happens to males predominately (82.2 percent), for injuries associated with violence the gender gap is somewhat larger. Of the 2,169 cases recorded in the local database of the Southern California [Spinal Cord Injury] System, 91.5 percent of those injured by violence are male." (p11)

Waters, Robert L./Cressy, Jeffrey/Adkins, Rodney H. "Spinal Cord Injuries Due to Violence." American Rehabilitation v22 n3 Aut 1996. p10-15. (ISSN0362-4048).

In the U.S., "while violence appears to result in spinal cord injury in all age groups, the Model Spinal Cord Injury Systems reports that 21.1 percent of those under 15 years of age, 18.1 percent of those between 16 and 30, 17.5 percent of those between 31 and 45, 11.1 percent of those aged 46 to 60, 4.8 percent of those 61 to 75, and 2.7 percent of those over 76 have been injured as a result of violence." (p11)

Waters, Robert L./Cressy, Jeffrey/Adkins, Rodney H. "Spinal Cord Injuries Due to Violence." American Rehabilitation v22 n3 Aut 1996. p10-15. (ISSN0362-4048).

In the U.S., incomplete injuries to the nerve fibers within the spinal cord have "increased from 44.5 percent between 1973 and 1978 to as high as 56.4 percent between 1987 and 1990....Between 1991 and 1995, there was a decline in the number of incomplete injuries to 51.3 percent." (p29)

Stover, Samuel L. "Facts, Figures, And Trends on Spinal Cord Injury." American Rehabilitation v22 n3 Aut 1996. p25-32. (ISSN0362-4048).

In the U.S., of all persons entered into the Spinal Cord Injury "database, 52.9 percent are classified as tetraplegia (cervical injuries), 46.2 percent as paraplegia (thoracolumbosacral injuries), and the remaining 0.9 percent experienced complete neurologic recovery by the time of hospital discharge. From 1979 to 1982, the number of persons with tetraplegia (or quadriplegia) peaked at 55.1 percent....From 1991 to 1995, there has been a gradual decline in the number of persons with tetraplegia to 47.2 percent, so that paraplegia is more common than tetraplegia at the present time....89.7 percent of all sports injuries result in tetraplegia, while 70.3 percent of all acts of violence result in paraplegia." (p28) "Acts of violence more frequently cause complete paraplegia (42.1 percent) and incomplete paraplegia (27.5 percent)....Sports accidents most often result in complete tetraplegia (42.5 percent) and incomplete tetraplegia (48.0 percent). Incomplete tetraplegia is the most common type of injury following a fall (35.1 percent)." (p29)

Stover, Samuel L. "Facts, Figures, And Trends on Spinal Cord Injury." American Rehabilitation v22 n3 Aut 1996. p25-32. (ISSN0362-4048).

In the U.S., the majority of cases in the National Spinal Cord Injury Model Systems Data Base "(54.2 percent) were single at the time of rehabilitation discharge....30.1 percent were married, 9.0 percent divorced, 4.4 percent separated, and 2.1 percent widowed. During the first 6 years, from 1 year to the next, on average 2-2.5 percent of those who were single (never married) become married. From 10-30 percent of all those in a not married category at injury have married by the 15th anniversary. Of those who are married, in any year a small percentage gets separated or divorced. The separation rate declines from 4.2 percent in the first year after injury to close to 0 percent in year 15. The divorce rate varies between 2.0 and 3.1 percent in years 1 through 8, and thereafter quickly declines to almost 0 percent." (p20-21)

Dijkers, Marcel. "Quality of Life after Spinal Cord Injury." American Rehabilitation v22 n3 Aut 1996. p18-24. (ISSN0362-4048).

Recently published data from the U.S. National Spinal Cord Injury "Model Systems database (Dijkers, Abela, Gans, & Gordon, 1995) indicate that, following initial rehabilitation, most individuals with SCI (92 percent) are discharged to private residences in the community. Nursing home discharge was associated with three variables: Age: Close to 30 percent of those 70 or older, compared to about 2 percent of those younger than 20, were discharged into nursing homes. Marital status: Higher rates of being discharged into nursing homes were seen amongst divorced (9 percent), separated (11 percent) and widowed persons (24 percent), compared to those who were single or married (4 percent). Severity of injury: Tetraplegics were more than twice as likely to be discharged to a nursing home than paraplegics (8 percent vs. 3 percent)." (p12)

Gordon, Wayne A./Brown, Margaret. "Community Integration of Individuals with Spinal Cord Injuries." American Rehabilitation v23 n1 Spr 1997. p11-14. (ISSN0362-4048).

The data in the National Spinal Cord Injury "Model Systems Data Base show that upon completing initial rehabilitation, the vast majority of persons with spinal cord injury [in the U.S.] (92.3 percent) are discharged to a private residence in the community. Very small numbers go to hospitals (1.4 percent), or nursing homes (4.0 percent). Some go to group living facilities (e.g. correctional institutions), usually for reasons other than medical or personal care needs (1.9 percent)." (p19)

Dijkers, Marcel. "Quality of Life after Spinal Cord Injury." American Rehabilitation v22 n3 Aut 1996. p18-24. (ISSN0362-4048).

The data in the National Spinal Cord Injury Model Systems Data

Base indicate "that whereas over 60 percent of persons with spinal cord injury [in the U.S.] were working preinjury, at 1 year postinjury the most frequently reported status is unemployed (61.9 percent). By the first anniversary of injury, only 16.1 percent of those working at the time of injury have returned to work. About 8 percent of them have entered school and more than 70 percent consider themselves unemployed....Almost half of those who were homemakers at the time of injury have revived that role (49.1 percent), and almost 71 percent of those who were students have resumed their education." (p20)

Dijkers, Marcel. "Quality of Life after Spinal Cord Injury." American Rehabilitation v22 n3 Aut 1996. p18-24. (ISSN0362-4048).

The data in the National Spinal Cord Injury Model Systems Data Base show that at the time of their latest follow up, 15.1 percent of persons with spinal cord injuries in the U.S. "had improved their education level from the time of injury....The change is most pronounced for those under 17 at the time of injury (49.3 percent). Of those who were 17 through 25 years old at injury, 19.3 percent have improved their grade level, as have 6.2 percent of those who were at least 26 at the time they incurred their spinal cord injury." (p20)

Dijkers, Marcel. "Quality of Life after Spinal Cord Injury." American Rehabilitation v22 n3 Aut 1996. p18-24. (ISSN0362-4048).

SPINAL CORD--WOUNDS AND INJURIES--UNITED STATES--COSTS

In the U.S., "the majority of the costs associated with the first year of [spinal cord] injury are a result of hospitalization, including acute care and rehabilitation. With all charges adjusted to 1992 dollars using the medical care component of the U.S. CONSUMER INDEX, the mean first year charges for all persons with spinal cord injury is $198,335 and the median charge is $161,110....Of these charges, approximately 34.6 percent are for emergency and acute hospital care, 48.3 percent for inpatient rehabilitation, and 17.1 percent for equipment, environmental modifications, attendant care, outpatient services, and other charges." (p31)

Stover, Samuel L. "Facts, Figures, And Trends on Spinal Cord Injury." American Rehabilitation v22 n3 Aut 1996. p25-32. (ISSN0362-4048).

SPINAL NERVES--TREATMENT--UNITED STATES (v26)

SPIRITUAL HEALING--UNITED STATES--PUBLIC OPINION (v26)

SPOILAGE OF FOOD

see FOOD SPOILAGE

SPORT UTILITY VEHICLES--NORTH AMERICA (v26)

SPORT UTILITY VEHICLES--UNITED STATES

In the U.S., "a recent study by the National Highway Transportation Safety Administration (NHTSA) found that fatalities due to rollovers are nearly three times higher for SUVs [sport-utility vehicles] than for other passenger vehicles. Earlier this year, another NHTSA study revealed that 5,447 Americans died in collisions involving a light truck and a car in 1996. Of those killed, 80 percent were riding in cars.... Surveys show that fewer than 10 percent of all SUV owners ever take their vehicles offroad." (p18)

Walker, Sam. "SUV Backlash: Not a Ride, But a Daily Expedition." The Christian Science Monitor v90 n17 18 Dec 1997. p1,18. The Christian Science Monitor search engine: <http://www.csmonitor.com/plweb-cgi/iops1.pl> To retrieve this article, enter the following search: ED=19971218 AND expedition. In the "retrieved list," click the title that matches this record. (ISSN0882-7729).

SPORTS

see also BASKETBALL; BOWLING; COLLEGE SPORTS; GOLF; SCHOOL SPORTS; SNOWBOARDING; SNOWMOBILES; SOCCER; SURFING; WINTER SPORTS; WOMEN IN SPORTS

SPORTS--AUSTRALIA

According to the report, "Participation in Sport and Physical Activities, Australia," by the Australian Bureau of Statistics, "nearly 6 million people (one third of the population) participated in an organised sport or physical activity in the year ended June 1996, according to data released by the Australian Bureau of Statistics....Thirty-one per cent of people aged 15 and over participated in organised sport or physical activities. The most popular activities were aerobics, golf, tennis and netball. Males had a higher participation rate (34 per cent compared to 27 per cent)....In the 15-24 age group the most popular activities were aerobics, netball and basketball, while for those people 45 years and over the most popular activities were lawn bowls and golf."

Australian Bureau of Statistics. "One Third into Organised Physical Activities." Media Release 10 Jun 1997. document-level access: <http://www.abs.gov.au/websitedbs/d3110125.nsf/4a255eef008309e44a255eef00061e57/19d5a5ad59c15bc44a2564b20007flbd?OpenDocument>

The Australian Bureau of Statistics "publication 'Involvement in Sport, Australia, March 1995,' states there were 4.7 million people, or 32.4 per cent of people aged 15 years and over, involved in sport in the year ended March 1997. This is 165,000 more people than 1993. Of this number, there were an additional 151,600 players. The number of people involved in sport who received payment increased by more than 50 per cent over this four year period. In 1997, seven per cent (328,500) of those involved in sport received some payment, compared with 4.7 per cent (213,300) people in 1993. Out of the 4.1 million people who played sport in 1997, 142,600 received some payment. Over 1.1 million players had additional non-playing commitments, including activities such as coaching, umpiring, as a committee member or administrator, or other non-playing involvement such as timekeeping or providing medical support. This is a 25.3 per cent increase in the number of players prepared to take on non-playing responsibilities since 1993."

Australian Bureau of Statistics. "Sport: More Play and More Get Paid." Media Release 13 Nov 1997. document-level access: <http://www.abs.gov.au/websitedbs/d3110125.nsf/4a255eef008309e44a255eef00061e57/876c47f263c852acca25654d007fedbc?OpenDocument>

SPORTS--AUSTRALIA--COSTS

According to the report, "Participation in Sport and Physical Activities, Australia," by the Australian Bureau of Statistics, "for each participant aged 15 and over it cost an average of $652 to be engaged in organised sport or physical activity. Costs for the most popular activities were aerobics ($371), golf ($822), tennis ($307) and netball ($233). These costs included membership fees, transport and weekly fees, clothing and equipment and other miscellaneous expenses. The most expensive organised sport or physical activities for people aged 15 and over were horse riding ($1833), motor sports ($1653), air sports eg. hang gliding, gliding ($1301), ice/snow sports ($959) and scuba diving ($958). In total, participants spent $2.8 billion on sport and physical activities in 1995-96."

Australian Bureau of Statistics. "One Third into Organised Physical Activities." Media Release 10 Jun 1997. document-level access: <http://www.abs.gov.au/websitedbs/d3110125.nsf/4a255eef008309e44a255eef00061e57/19d5a5ad59c15bc44a2564b20007flbd?OpenDocument>

SPORTS--AUSTRALIA--YOUTH

According to the report, "Participation in Sport and Physical

Activities, Australia," by the Australian Bureau of Statistics, "sixty-two per cent of children aged between 5 and 14 participated in either school organised or club organised sport or physical activities, the most popular activities being swimming, basketball, netball and soccer. Boys were more likely to be involved than girls (65 per cent compared to 58 per cent)."

Australian Bureau of Statistics. "One Third into Organised Physical Activities." Media Release 10 Jun 1997. document-level access: <http://www.abs.gov.au/websitedbs/d3110125.nsf/4a255eef008309e44a255eef00061e57/19d5a5ad59c15bc44a2564b20007flbd?OpenDocument>

SPORTS--GREAT BRITAIN

In Great Britain, "the general household survey estimates that about 29 million adults--almost 60 per cent of the entire population--regularly take part in sport or some form of physical recreation....Some 31 million people were attracted through the turnstiles to watch football [soccer] last season....Sport directly produces employment for nearly half a million people and sport and leisure account for some 10 billion [pounds sterling] in consumer expenditure, generating 3.5 billion [pounds sterling] for the Treasury...." (c1084)

Hawkins, Nick (H.C.-Surrey Heath). "Sport for All." Great Britain. Parliament. House of Commons. Debates. 27 Jun 1997. c1084. section-level access: <http://www.parliament.the-stationery-office.co.uk/pa/cm199798/cmhansrd/cm970627/debtext/70627-06.htm#70627-06_spnew2>

SPORTS--GREAT BRITAIN--YOUTH

In Great Britain, "in 1993, a shoe company undertook some research, which showed that three out of five teenage girls played no sport at all outside school. For young women, the only sporting activities being undertaken twice a week are cycling, walking, keep fit and weight training. Further research shows that 66 per cent of girls dislike the kind of sport on offer in schools and particularly object to competitive sports where there are winners and losers. It is different for boys: only 38 per cent said that they disliked sports with a competitive element....Only 30 per cent of 14 to 16-year-old girls undertook sport to be with their friends, which compares with 52 per cent of boys....Of all the television sports coverage in this country, only 6 per cent is devoted to women's sport, and the figure for newspaper coverage is only 13 per cent." (c1091-1092)

Spelman, Caroline (H.C.-Meriden). "Sport for All." Great Britain. Parliament. House of Commons. Debates. 27 Jun 1997. c1091-1092. section-level access: <http://www.parliament.the-stationery-office.co.uk/pa/cm199798/cmhansrd/cm970627/debtext/70627-08.htm#70627-08_spnew0>

SPORTS--SWEDEN (v26)

SPORTS--SWEDEN--FINANCE (v26)

SPORTS--UNITED STATES

The Amateur Athletic Union "conducts over 2,000 sporting events throughout the...[U.S.]. Fifty eight AAU Associations are chartered to operate within defined geographic territories. Their brochure lists opportunities in 33 different sports; annually, they sponsor the Junior Olympics where 10,000 athletes from 50 states participate in 23 different sports." (p34)

"She Mentioned a Solution?" Home Education Magazine v14 n4 Jul-Aug 1997. p34. (ISSN088-4633).

"Heart-racing activities such as downhill mountain biking, backcountry snowboarding, and sky diving are capturing an ever growing chunk of the $40 billion plus that America spends on sporting goods annually....Rock climbing has moved from the fringe to the mainstream over the past few years; according to one estimate, a half-million Americans now find joy in dangling from cliffs, up from 50,000 in 1989. Wakeboarding, a snowboarding-waterskiing hybrid that allows participants to flip, spin, and carom off buoys at high speeds, had 100,000 adherents in 1991; four years later, that figure had jumped to three quarters of a million." (p52)

Koerner, Brendan I. "Culture & Ideas: Extreeeme." U.S. News & World Report v122 n25 30 Jun 1997. p50-53,56-60. article-level access: <http://www.usnews.com/usnews/issue/970630/30EXTR.HTM> (ISSN0041-5537).

SPORTS ADMINISTRATION--SWEDEN--WOMEN (v26)

SPORTS AND TOURIST TRADE--NORTH AMERICA

Lisa Delpy, of "George Washington University, argued that 25% of tourism receipts in North America are related to sports tourism. This amounts to $350 billion annually in the United States, with an industry growth rate between 8% to 10%." (p76)

DiPersio, Cindy/Hayden, Gin/Goeldner, C. R./Frechtling, Douglas. "Research Notes & Communications: Highlights of the 28th Annual TTRA Conference Norfolk/Virginia Beach, June 15-18." Journal of Travel Research v36 n1 Sum 1997. p73-84. (ISSN0047-2875).

SPORTS FACILITIES--UNITED STATES--COSTS (v26)

SPOTTED OWL--SIERRA NEVADA (CALIF. AND NEV.)

Underway since 1990, a study of the California Spotted Owl "covers an area of 250 square miles in the Sierra National Forest and 130 square miles in Sequoia/Kings Canyon National Parks....Preliminary estimates of population trends calculated from 1988 through 1996 indicate statistically significant declines of 7% in the Sierra National Forest and 5% in Sequoia/Kings Canyon National Parks....Pellet contents were examined to identify the species of prey taken by the owls. In oak woodland and riparian deciduous habitats, 20 prey species were identified. The dusky-footed woodrat comprised about 80% of the prey biomass taken by the owls in these lower-elevation habitats. Pocket gophers made up 11% of the biomass....In higher-elevation conifer sites, 35 prey species were identified from owl pellets. Flying squirrels were predominant, accounting for 51% of the biomass...." (p17-18)

Kings River Team./Gill, Connie/U.S. Dept. of Agriculture. Forest Service. "Kings River Sustainable Forest Ecosystem Project." Forestry Research West Sep 1997. p15-22. (ISSN0195-5861).

SPOTTED OWL--WEST (U.S.)

Since 1990, when the northern spotted owl "was listed as a threatened species, the federal government has approved eight HCPs [Habitat Conservation Plans] covering nearly 2.4 million acres of state and private lands in Washington, Oregon and California. Thirty-seven more, covering an additional 5.8 million acres, are in the works....Simpson Timber Co. pioneered the [HCP] process with a 1992 owl plan that covered 380,000 acres of redwoods in northern California....[A 1995 plan covering Weyerhaeuser Co.'s 209,000-acre Millicoma tree farm in the Oregon Coast Range] offers minimal protection for the 79 owls on or near the land, allowing the company to cut nearly all the owl habitat during the first 20 years of the plan." (p16)

Durbin, Kathie. "Habitat Plans Are in Full Flood." High Country News v29 n14 4 Aug 1997. p16-17. (ISSN0191-5657).

SPY SATELLITES

see SPACE SURVEILLANCE

SQUASH INDUSTRY--UNITED STATES (v26)

SRI LANKA--HISTORY--CIVIL WAR--MORTALITY

In Sri Lanka, "about 70,000 people have committed suicide since the beginning of the Tamil civil war. This compares with 50,000 deaths directly because of the war." (p11)

"Comment: Reflections by Yorick: Death by Attitude." Freedom Today v22 n4 Aug 1997. p11.

SRI LANKA--SOCIAL CONDITIONS (v26)

STANDARD OF LIVING
see COST AND STANDARD OF LIVING
STATE AND ENVIRONMENT
see ENVIRONMENTAL POLICY
STATE GOVERNMENTS--UNITED STATES (v26)
"There are 7,424 state legislators in the United States; 2,615, or 35 percent, serve under term limits....Turnover in state legislatures is, on average, 20 percent every two years. In 10 years, theoretically, everybody is new. A study of turnover in state legislatures between 1987 and 1997 showed actual turnover to be 72 percent for the nation's state senates and 84 percent for houses. The statistics for leadership turnover are even more impressive: From 1990 to 1997, 86 percent of senate presidents, house speakers and majority and minority leaders changed." (p16) "Today, the terms of legislators in 20 states are limited." (p18)
Hansen, Karen. "Living within the Limits." State Legislatures v23 n6 Jun 1997. p12-13,15-16,18-19. (ISSN0147-6041).
STATE GOVERNMENTS--UNITED STATES --APPROPRIATIONS AND EXPENDITURES (v26)
In the U.S., "nearly one-third (31 percent) of 1996 state expenditures went to education and 23 percent were spent on public welfare,...data on revenue and expenditures for the 50 states and the nation show....Nationwide, state revenues and expenditures totaled $967 billion and $860 billion respectively....Vermont had the lowest revenues of any state at $2.1 billion and one of the lowest expenditure levels at $2.1 billion."
U.S. Dept. of Commerce. Economic and Statistics Administration. "Nearly One-Third of 1996 State Expenditures Spent on Education, According to Census Bureau Data for 50 States." Census Bureau Press Release 15 Sep 1997. document-level access: <http://www.census.gov/Press-Release/cb97-146.html>
STATE GOVERNMENTS--UNITED STATES--ECONOMIC CONDITIONS
New Mexico "received $3,262 more per capita in federal spending last year than it paid in taxes, while...[New Jersey] paid $1,915 more in taxes per capita than it received in spending. As in 1977, New York last year was still in a net negative position, paying $773 more in taxes per capita than it got in spending. And Michigan pays almost $1,400 a person more in taxes than it receives in federal spending....Residents of high-income states like New Jersey tend to pay more taxes than residents of low-income states like New Mexico. According to the Census Bureau, in 1996, New Jersey had a median household income of $46,345--second highest in the United States--and New Mexico had an income of just $25,922--second lowest." (p8 secA)
Bartlett, Bruce. "Bartlett's Notations: Does Michigan Truly Get Its Money's Worth?" Detroit News 10 Nov 1997. p8 secA.
STATE PARKS
see PARKS
STATE SUCCESSION--INDIA--KASHMIR, VALE OF (v26)
STATURE--NETHERLANDS--SCANDINAVIA--UNITED STATES (v26)
STDs (DISEASES)
see SEXUALLY TRANSMITTED DISEASES
STEEL INDUSTRY AND TRADE
According to an International Labour Organization study, per capita consumption of steel "ranges from an average of 17 kilograms per year in Africa to 625 kilograms in Japan....'Strong growth is...expected in Asia (40% over the...[next decade]), notably in China (150%) and, to a lesser extent, in Latin America (18%)'. Steel is currently produced in about 100 countries, says the report pointing out that 'in the 15 years between 1981 and 1996 the share of world steel production held by industrialized market economy countries has fallen slightly from 54.5% to 51.2%. Production in the CIS [Commonwealth of Independent States] and Eastern Europe, however, has halved from 29% of the total to 14.3%, whereas production in China and other Asian countries (excluding Japan) has almost trebled from 9.6% to 25.5%'. With nearly 3.2 million steelworkers, China has, by far, the largest workforce. 'China, the CIS and India together account for about 70% of the industry's total labour force, but only about 30% of steel production'."
International Labour Organization. "Meeting at ILO Examines Future of Steel Industry Workforce." Press Release 23 Oct 1997. document-level access: <http://www.unicc.org/ilo/public/english/235press/pr/1997/24.htm>
STEEL INDUSTRY AND TRADE--EMPLOYMENT
According to a recent International Labour Organization study, "'in the European Union, the total number of steel jobs dropped by over 65% (from 991,000 to 326,000) in 1975-95. In France and the United Kingdom steel employment fell by 75% and 80%, while production fell by 16% and 14% respectively. In the United States and Japan 51% and 48% of steel jobs were lost compared with falls in production of, respectively, 10% and 1%'....In the Russian Federation, approximately 10% of steel industry jobs have been eliminated over the last five years."
International Labour Organization. "Meeting at ILO Examines Future of Steel Industry Workforce." Press Release 23 Oct 1997. document-level access: <http://www.unicc.org/ilo/public/english/235press/pr/1997/24.htm>
STEEL INDUSTRY AND TRADE--ENVIRONMENTAL ASPECTS
According to a recent International Labour Organization report, "the steel industry is second only to the cement industry in the weight and volume of material processed. Worldwide, the 750 million tonnes of steel currently produced each year generate some 30 million tonnes of solid waste. 'But the environmental impact of iron- and steelmaking has been dramatically reduced over the last 20 years', says the report, 'half as much solid waste is produced per tonne of steel than in the 1970s' as a result of both new technologies and the introduction of stricter environmental legislation. Steel itself is routinely recycled. Today, 'over 300 million tonnes of used scrap steel (40% of production) is used in making new steel products'."
International Labour Organization. "Meeting at ILO Examines Future of Steel Industry Workforce." Press Release 23 Oct 1997. document-level access: <http://www.unicc.org/ilo/public/english/235press/pr/1997/24.htm>
STEEL INDUSTRY AND TRADE--SWEDEN (v26)
STINGS AND BITES
see BITES AND STINGS
STOCK (ANIMALS)
see LIVESTOCK
STOCK EXCHANGES (v26)
The U.S. stock "market is up 27 percent this year, measured by the Standard & Poor's 500 index....London's main market index is up 17 percent this year, outpaced by France (21 percent), Germany (33 percent), Italy (43 percent), the Netherlands (34 percent), Spain (29 percent), and Switzerland (41 percent). Compare that to Japan, down 18 percent, or Singapore and South Korea, down about 24 percent....About 80 percent of all European economic activity takes place in the four largest markets: Germany, Britain, France, and Italy." (p7 secB)
Halverson, Guy. "Work & Money:...Should US Investors Follow?" The Christian Science Monitor v89 n251 24 Nov 1997. p7 secB. The Christian Science Monitor search engine: <http://www.csmonitor.com/plweb-cgi/iops1.pl> To

retrieve this article, enter the following search: ED=19971124 AND follow. In the "retrieved list," click the title that matches this record. (ISSN0882-7729).

STOCK EXCHANGES--DEVELOPING COUNTRIES (v26)

STOCK EXCHANGES--UNITED STATES (v26)

STOCK OWNERSHIP

see also EMPLOYEE OWNERSHIP

STOCK OWNERSHIP--UNITED STATES (v26)

Attributing its information to the Nasdaq Stock Exchange, THE NEW YORK TIMES "asserted that '43 percent of American adults now own stock, and most of them have bought in since 1980, thanks to accessible vehicles like 401(k) benefit plans and mutual funds and to convenient technologies like computer modems and electronic telephone menus. One in three households owns stock today, compared with one in 17 in 1980, according to the North American Securities Administrator's Association.'...[In its 1 September 1997 issue, BUSINESS WEEK said] 'some 71 percent of households own no shares at all or hold less than $2,000 worth in any form, including mutual funds, 401(k)s and traditional pensions, according to a 1996 study by Massachusetts Institute of Technology economist James M. Poterba and Dartmouth College economist Andrew A. Samwick. So juicy market returns do little for the average person. Instead, they fatten the wallets of the top quarter of households, which own 82 percent of all stock, they found.'" (p3)

"Stock Market Crash Exposed Fatal Flaw of Capitalism." The People v107 n9 Dec 1997. p3,8. (ISSN0199-350X).

STOCK OWNERSHIP--UNITED STATES--EMPLOYEES

According to the U.S. "National Center for Employee Ownership, 8.7 million employees participate in ESOPs [employee stock ownership plans] and similar plans. The number of ESOP companies has swelled almost 700% since 1975. Today employees own stock through ESOPs at 10,000 companies, holding majority stakes in about 2,000." (p4)

Scharf, Adria/Marens, Richard. "ESOPs: The Revolution Hasn't Arrived Yet." Left Business Observer n80 17 Nov 1997. p4-5. (ISSN1042-0134).

STOCK REPURCHASING--UNITED STATES (v26)

STOCKHOLDERS--CANADA (v26)

STOCKHOLDERS--CANADA--ATTITUDES (v26)

STOCKHOLDERS--UNITED STATES (v26)

"The wealthiest 10 percent of households owned virtually all the...[U.S.] corporate stock in 1995, $2.3 trillion of the total of $2.74 trillion....In the 1992-95 period, the stock market blessed the top 0.5 percent of households. The $865 billion of stocks held by this group, 15 percent of their total assets, was up 78 percent from 1992. In 1995, 40 percent of this group's wealth consisted of businesses, their value up 40 percent from 1992. Investment in real estate represented 15 percent of wealth, or $728 billion, down 25 percent from 1992. The entry 'fee' for the top 0.5 percent in 1995 was $4.7 million. Owning a medium-sized business would qualify you for that category. The minimum needed for the 99 to 99.5 percent category was $2.5 million. For the 90-99 percent bracket it was $368,300." (p8)

Francis, David R. "Business & Money: Economic Scene: Where Did All the Money Go? Not Far." The Christian Science Monitor v89 n161 16 Jul 1997. p8. The Christian Science Monitor search engine: <http://www.csmonitor.com/plweb-cgi/iops1.pl> To retrieve this article, enter the following search: ED=19970716 AND far. In the "retrieved list," click the title that matches this record. (ISSN0882-7729).

STORES, MUSEUM

see MUSEUM STORES

STOVES, BIOMASS

see BIOMASS STOVES

STRATOSPHERIC OZONE

see OZONE LAYER DEPLETION

STRAWBERRY INDUSTRY

see also WAGES--STRAWBERRY INDUSTRY

STRAWBERRY INDUSTRY--CALIFORNIA (v26)

STRAWBERRY INDUSTRY--EMPLOYMENT--UNITED STATES (v26)

STRAWBERRY INDUSTRY--UNITED STATES (v26)

"U.S. fresh strawberry exports are shipped mainly to Canada, Japan, Mexico, and the United Kingdom. During 1996, fresh exports totaled 116.0 million pounds, up 4 percent from the year before. The four major U.S. export markets accounted for 76 percent, 12 percent, 4 percent, and 4 percent, respectively of the total volume....Fresh exports during January-March 1997 were down 2 percent from the same period last year, with reduced exports to Canada and the United Kingdom. U.S. exports of frozen strawberries totaled 46.9 million pounds in 1996, down 12 percent from a year earlier, reflecting lower U.S. supplies of frozen strawberries (including imports and carryover inventories) and strong domestic demand. Most of these shipments went to Japan (71 percent), Canada (19 percent), Mexico (4 percent), and Australia (3 percent)." (p20)

U.S. Dept. of Agriculture. Economic Research Service. "Noncitrus Fruit Outlook." Fruit and Tree Nuts Situation and Outlook Report Aug 1997. p7-26.

In the U.S., "monthly grower prices [for strawberries] from January through July 1997 averaged 67 cents per pound, compared with 62 cents the year before. At the same time, grower prices declined seasonally from $1.02 per pound in January to 52.7 cents in July....Retail prices from February through June 1997 followed the seasonal movement in grower prices, and averaged $1.26 per pound, compared with $1.20 in 1996. Expected higher fresh strawberry prices in 1997, lower prices for other fresh fruits, and likely lower imports could lead to reduced domestic consumption in 1997. Last year, increased fresh-market supplies and lower prices helped boost domestic demand, with U.S. consumption estimated at 4.39 pounds per person, up from 4.15 pounds in 1995." (p19)

U.S. Dept. of Agriculture. Economic Research Service. "Noncitrus Fruit Outlook." Fruit and Tree Nuts Situation and Outlook Report Aug 1997. p7-26.

STREAMS

see RIVERS

STREET GANGS

see GANGS

STREET LIGHTING--MICHIGAN--DETROIT (v26)

STREET PEOPLE

see HOMELESS PERSONS

STREPTOCOCCUS PNEUMONIAE--UNITED STATES (v26)

STREPTOCOCCUS PNEUMONIAE--UNITED STATES --MINORITIES (v26)

STRESS DISORDER, POST-TRAUMATIC

see POST-TRAUMATIC STRESS DISORDER

STRIKES AND LOCKOUTS--EUROPE

Italy had "an average of over 7 million workers on strike per year for the entire period (1970-93), which represents 55 per cent of the west European workforce involved in industrial action....At an annual average of 2 million strikers, the number of workers involved was considerable in Spain....In the United Kingdom and France,...there were sizeable numbers of workers on strike: over a million each year in the period under consideration (1970-93), but a marked and fairly steady decline set in, especially as from the 1980s. On the other hand, Germany seems to have been only slightly affected, with an annual average of fewer than 200,000 strikers and with a degree of stability during the period under review." (p78-79)

Aligisakis, Maximos. "Labour Disputes in Western Europe: Typology and Tendencies." International Labour Review v136 n1 Spr 1997. p73-94. (ISSN0020-7780).

STRIKES AND LOCKOUTS--UNITED STATES (v26)

"After dropping for a decade to an all-time low in 1995, [U.S.] strike statistics rose in 1996. The number of 'major' strikes (one thousand or more workers) that started in 1996 rose to thirty-seven from thirty-one in 1995. The number of workers involved grew from 192,000 in 1995 to 273,000 in 1996. Only the total number of days spent on strike by all workers dropped." (p68)

Moody, Kim. "American Labor: A Movement Again?" Monthly Review v49 n3 Jul-Aug 1997. p63-79. (ISSN0027-0520).

STRIKES AND LOCKOUTS--VENEZUELA (v26)

STRIPS, COMMERCIAL

see COMMERCIAL STRIPS

STRIPTEASE--UNITED STATES (v26)

STROKE

see CEREBROVASCULAR DISEASE

STUDENT ATTENDANCE

see SCHOOL ATTENDANCE

STUDENT LOAN FUNDS--UNITED STATES (v26)

In the U.S., "the student loan default rate has declined 50 percent--falling from a high of 22.4 percent in 1990 to 10.7 percent in 1994, according to the Education Department. In Michigan, the rate also appears to be falling: Between 1992 and 1994, the default rate for students whose loans were guaranteed by the state-designated Michigan Guaranty Agency dropped from 17.6 percent to 13.3 percent....Between 1995 and 1996, the agency made about 94,000 loans totaling about $300 million." (p1 secD)

Beaupre, Becky. "Metro: Special Report: Student Borrowers: Defaults on College Loans Are Dropping." Detroit News 24 Jul 1997. p1,4 secD.

STUDENT VIOLENCE

see SCHOOL VIOLENCE

STUDENTS

see also AFRO-AMERICAN COLLEGE STUDENTS; AFRO-AMERICAN HIGH SCHOOL STUDENTS; AFRO-AMERICAN LAW STUDENTS; COLLEGE COSTS--CANADA--LAW STUDENTS; COLLEGE STUDENTS; COLLEGE STUDENTS, FOREIGN; DROPOUTS; ENGINEERING STUDENTS; GRADING AND MARKING (STUDENTS); HIGH SCHOOL STUDENTS; INTERNET (COMPUTER NETWORK)--UNITED STATES--STUDENTS; LAW STUDENTS; MATHEMATICAL ABILITY--UNITED STATES--HIGH SCHOOL STUDENTS; MEDICAL STUDENTS; MINORITY LAW STUDENTS; MINORITY STUDENTS; RABBINICAL SEMINARIES--ISRAEL--STUDENTS; SCHOOL CHILDREN; SCHOOLS--UNITED STATES--STUDENTS; SCIENCE--UNITED STATES--STUDENTS; SEMINARIANS

STUDENTS--CALIFORNIA--LOS ANGELES--LANGUAGES

"Primary languages spoken by 'limited English proficient' (LEP) students [in the Los Angeles Unified School District]: more than 80, most of them Spanish speaking (286,983), but also 4,923 Armenian, 3,916 Korean, 3,044 Chinese, 2,511 Filipino, 1,568 Vietnamese, 1,484 Russian, 899 Farsi, 730 Khmer, 471 Thai. Down the list in this dizzying linguistic melting pot to the double and finally the single digits: nine Finnish, six Nepali, five Swedish, five Yoruba, two each Afrikaans, Fijian, Javanese, Khmu, Marshallese, Melanesian, Norwegian and Mongolian. A sole Swahili speaker, an Albanian, a Cherokee, a Dane, a Guamanian and a Kurd....The percentage of students whose primary language is English was 35 percent. In 1981-82, LEP students accounted for 22 percent of total enrollment; by 1996-97, that figure had jumped to 47 percent." (p32-33)

Bathen, Sigrid. "Los Angeles Unified School District." California Journal v29 n1 Jan 1998. p32-38. (ISSN0008-1205).

STUDENTS--GRADING AND MARKING

see GRADING AND MARKING (STUDENTS)

STUDENTS--GREAT BRITAIN (v26)

STUDENTS--TEXAS

In Texas, "every year, 80,000 more students come into the state; 70 percent of them are Hispanic or African American. Of the 46,000 new Hispanic students each year, 75 percent will qualify for Limited English Proficiency status." (p42)

Simpson, Grant W. "Teaching: To Grow a Teacher." American School Board Journal v184 n9 Sep 1997. p42-43. (ISSN0003-0953).

STUDENTS--TRANSPORTATION--IRELAND

According to Ireland's Central Statistics Office, "walking is the most popular way to get to college with almost one third (28.8%) of students striding out in 1991. This was followed by the bus (24.9%), and then cycling (17.9%). Nearly four out of ten primary school children went to school on foot in 1991, over a quarter were driven by car and one in five travelled by bus."

Ireland. Central Statistics Office. "Census 1991--Volume 11: Travel to Work, School and College." Press Release 10 Jul 1997. document-level access: <http://www.cso.ie/pressreleases/prelcentrav.html>

STUDENTS--UNITED STATES

In the U.S., in 1996, "51.7 million students were enrolled in public and private schools, breaking the record of 51.3 million set in 1971. Over the next 10 years, enrollment is expected to continue rising in 33 states, with the West and Southwest leading the way." (p21)

Hardy, Lawrence. "School Facilities Report: Covering Construction Costs." American School Board Journal v184 n10 Oct 1997. p20-23. (ISSN0003-0953).

Eighty "percent of Americans do not have children in school....40 percent of students are in 4 percent of the schools. 23 percent of our students are in 1 percent of the poorest schools." (p2)

Vasquez, JoAnne. "Board News & Views: A Look Back, And Thanks!" NSTA Reports! v8 n6 May-Jun 1997. p2-3.

STUDENTS--UNITED STATES--ATTITUDES (v26)

STUDENTS, FOREIGN (v26)

STUDENTS, FOREIGN--CANADA (v26)

STUDENTS, FOREIGN--UNITED STATES (v26)

"According to the Institute of International Education's (1995) annual census conducted in the 1993-94 academic year, the number of international students in higher education on U.S. campuses rose 2.5% over the same period a year earlier, to a total of 449,749. During the 1992-93 academic year, the number had increased 4.5% over the previous year, to 438,618. The Institute of International Education also estimated that cost-of-living expenditures by international students in the 1994-95 academic year were approximately $4 trillion." (p59)

Hsu, Cathy H. C./Sung, Shihlin. "Travel Behaviors of International Students at a Midwestern University." Journal of Travel Research v36 n1 Sum 1997. p59-65. (ISSN0047-2875).

The number of American students "getting college credit for overseas study leapt 10 percent in the 1994-1995 school year. This increase has brought the number of students studying abroad to 84,000, compared with 48,500 nine years ago....A semester is still the top choice. But 30 percent of college students are choosing a summer term sojourn." (p12)

Lipscomb, Laura. "Learning: Overseas Study Choices Send Students Packing." The Christian Science Monitor v89 n159 14 Jul 1997. p12. The Christian Science Monitor search engine: <http://www.csmonitor.com/plweb-cgi/iops1.pl> To retrieve this article, enter the following search: ED=19970714 AND packing. In the "retrieved list," click the title that matches this record. (ISSN0882-7729).

STUDENTS, TRANSFER OF--MICHIGAN

In Michigan, the schools-of-choice "program expanded from 7,781 students in 1996, the first year, to 10,882 this year. The state's public schools serve 1.6 million students. Under the schools of choice law, parents can transfer their children to other districts within the county. The home district cannot veto the move, but the district to which the students wants to move can refuse to accept them. Students cannot transfer across county lines." (p2 secA)

Hornbeck, Mark. "Few Choose Schools of Choice Option." Detroit News 11 Dec 1997. p1-2 secA.

STUDENTS, TRANSFER OF--MICHIGAN--DETROIT

"Michigan's schools-of-choice law...is being used by less than 1 percent of Metro Detroit's public school students....Of the 3,151 transfers within Wayne, Oakland and Macomb counties, nearly half moved from Detroit and Pontiac to suburban schools, according to a state Education Department report." (p1 secA) "Dearborn Heights has attracted 285 schools-of-choice students--mostly from Detroit and Westwood--adding about $1.5 million to its district budget....Highland Park received the highest number of schools-of-choice transfers--700--with more than 500 of them going to the [Career and Technical] Academy." (p2 secA)

Hornbeck, Mark. "Few Choose Schools of Choice Option." Detroit News 11 Dec 1997. p1-2 secA.

STUDY ABROAD

see FOREIGN STUDY

STURGEONS--CASPIAN SEA

"The Caspian Sea is the source of more than 90 percent of the world's caviar--the jam-like mass of tiny, greenish-black eggs of the sturgeon, recently declared endangered....The Beluga sturgeon can weigh up to a ton-and-a-half, matures at about 18 years, and can occasionally live to be 150." (p10) The sturgeon "numbers are one-tenth what they were 20 years ago, according to...[Dr. Vladimir Ivanov, director of the Caspian Fisheries Research Institute, in Aatrkhan]." (p11)

Ingwerson, Marshall. "Caspian Journey: Ancient Fish of the Caviar Trade Now Face Smugglers, Oil Drills." The Christian Science Monitor v89 n185 19 Aug 1997. p10-11. The Christian Science Monitor search engine: <http://www.csmonitor.com/plweb-cgi/iops1.pl> To retrieve this article, enter the following search: ED=19970819 AND drills. In the "retrieved list," click the title that matches this record. (ISSN0882-7729).

SUBSIDIES, AGRICULTURAL

see AGRICULTURAL SUBSIDIES

SUBSTANCE ABUSE

see also ALCOHOLISM; ATTENTION-DEFICIT HYPERACTIVITY DISORDER--UNITED STATES--SUBSTANCE ABUSE; CIGARETTE HABIT; COCAINE HABIT; DRUG ABUSE; GIRLS--UNITED STATES--SUBSTANCE USE; HEROIN HABIT; TEENAGERS--MICHIGAN--ANN ARBOR--SUBSTANCE USE; TOBACCO HABIT; WOMEN--UNITED STATES--SUBSTANCE USE; YOUTH--UNITED STATES--SUBSTANCE USE

SUBSTANCE ABUSE--AUSTRALIA (v26)

According to the 1995 Australian National Health survey, "overall, 24 per cent of adults were smokers, with the highest proportion in younger age groups (31 per cent of those aged less than 35). Over half (55 per cent) of adults reported having an alcoholic drink in the previous week, but 85 per cent of these reported drinking at levels considered to be a low health risk."

Australian Bureau of Statistics. "ABS Health Report on Australia." Media Release 28 Aug 1997. document-level access: <http://www.abs.gov.au/websitedbs/d3110125.nsf/4a255eef008309e44a255eef00061e57/7ad11af58d37387a4a25650100031cfd?OpenDocument>

SUBSTANCE ABUSE--CALIFORNIA--SAN FRANCISCO --COSTS (v26)

SUBSTANCE ABUSE--GREAT BRITAIN (v26)

SUBSTANCE ABUSE--ITALY

"It is estimated that currently 300,000 persons (0.5% of the total population) regularly use heroin in Italy. In 1994, 73,335 persons had contacts with some public addiction treatment services and 3,917 were admitted to therapeutic communities (Il medico d'Italia, 1995). Up to 90.45% of all patients referred to drug addiction centres in 1993 were abusers of opiates, 4.95% of cannabis, 1.66% of cocaine (Margaron, 1994)." (p431-432)

Fioritti, Angelo/Ferri, Stefano/Galassi, Lorella/Warner, Richard. "Substance Use among the Mentally Ill: A Comparison of Italian and American Samples." Community Mental Health Journal v33 n5 Oct 1997. p429-442. (ISSN0010-3853).

SUBSTANCE ABUSE--MICHIGAN (v26)

SUBSTANCE ABUSE--MICHIGAN--MORTALITY (v26)

SUBSTANCE ABUSE--MORTALITY (v26)

SUBSTANCE ABUSE--TAXATION--UNITED STATES (v26)

SUBSTANCE ABUSE--TREATMENT--MICHIGAN (v26)

SUBSTANCE ABUSE--TREATMENT--UNITED STATES

According to a report by the U.S. Substance Abuse and Mental Health Services Administration, "about 30 percent of females compared to 35 percent of males who needed drug treatment received it in the past year. Among adult women who needed but did not receive treatment, 40 percent were age 18-25, 41 percent were alcohol dependent, 28 percent had some college, 55 percent worked full or part time, and 32 percent lived with two or more children under age 18 and 71 percent had initiated alcohol or drug use before the age of 15."

U.S. Dept. of Health and Human Services. "New National Study on Substance Use among Women in the United States Released." Press Release 22 Sep 1997. document-level access: <http://www.hhs.gov/news/press/1997pres/970922.html>

SUBSTANCE ABUSE--UNITED STATES (v26)

"An estimated 30 million Americans suffer from drug and alcohol addiction. Alarmingly, of the 59 million women of child bearing age, nearly 5 million are using illicit drugs such as marijuana, cocaine, and heroin. Economically, drug and alcohol abuse cost this country more than $1600 billion annually." (pS6329)

Balster, Robert L. (Public Policy Officer, College on Problems of Drug Dependence, Inc.). "Balanced Budget Act of 1997." Congressional Record. Daily ed. v143 n91 25 Jun 1997. pS6301-6332. section/page-level access: <http://thomas.loc.gov/cgi-bin/query/R?r105:FLD001:S06329:> (ISSN0363-7239). (X1.1A.105/1).

"Data from the 1996 National Household Survey on Drug Abuse, which is conducted by the Substance Abuse and Mental Health Services Administration, provide the following estimates of substance use in the United States: There were about 9 million current alcohol, including beer, wine, and distilled spirits, drinkers under age 21 in 1996. Of these, 4.4 million were binge drinkers, including 1.9 million heavy drinkers. In 1996, an estimated 10.1 million Americans were current, past month, marijuana or hashish users. This represents 4.7 percent of the population aged 12 and older. Marijuana is by far the most prevalent drug used by illicit drug users. Approximately three-quarters, 77 percent of current illicit drug users were marijuana or hashish users in 1996. The number of occasional cocaine users...was 2.6 million in 1996, similar to what it was in 1995. The number of users was down significantly from 1985, when it was 7.1 million. The rate of current use of hallucinogens among youth age 12-17 has nearly doubled in 2 years, 1.1 percent in 1994, 1.7 percent in 1995, and 2.0 percent in 1996. There were an estimated 141,000 new heroin users in 1995, and there has been an increasing trend in new heroin use since 1992." (pS8824)

Wellstone, Paul D. (Sen.-Minn.). "Statements on Introduced Bills and Joint Resolutions." Congressional Record. Daily ed. v143 n115 4 Sep 1997. pS8823-8831. section/page-level access: <http://thomas.loc.gov/cgi-bin/query/R?r105:FLD001:S08823:> (ISSN0363-7239). (X1.1A.105/1).

SUBSTANCE ABUSE IN PREGNANCY--CANADA (v26)

SUBSTANCE ABUSE IN PREGNANCY--UNITED STATES

According to a report by the U.S. Substance Abuse and Mental Health Services Administration, "an estimated 62,000 or 2.3 percent of all pregnant [women] under age 44 reported using any illicit drug in the past month. About a fifth (21.2%) of pregnant women under age 44 had used alcohol in the past month. Of this pregnant, alcohol-using group, nearly a third reported having three or more drinks on the days they drank. About a fifth (21.5%) of pregnant women under age 44 said they had smoked cigarettes in the past month. And more than a quarter of these pregnant smokers reported heavy smoking in the past month--i.e., one or more packs of cigarettes each day."

U.S. Dept. of Health and Human Services. "New National Study on Substance Use among Women in the United States Released." Press Release 22 Sep 1997. document-level access: <http://www.hhs.gov/news/press/1997pres/970922.html>

SUBSTITUTE TEACHERS--MICHIGAN--DETROIT

"On a typical school day in Detroit, one out of every seven teachers is a substitute who lacks state certification to lead a classroom, the FREE PRESS found in a review of district personnel records. About 616 substitutes are filling in for absent teachers. Another 624 are long-term substitutes in regular positions in areas where the district lacks certified teachers, such as math and science. Also, none of the 624 long-term substitutes has a state-issued permit allowing them to be in a classroom on a regular basis. About a third do not even have a basic substitute permit that allows them to teach for a maximum of 150 days a year, according to an analysis done by the Michigan Department of Education for the FREE PRESS." (p1 secA)

Cha, Ariana E./Robles, Jennifer Juarez. "Schools Relying on Subs: Permits Lacking in Detroit." Detroit Free Press 5 Jun 1997. p1,4 secA.

SUBURBS--NORTHWEST, PACIFIC (v26)

SUBURBS--UNITED STATES (v26)

In the U.S., "for every middle- or high-income person that moves into a major city, three to four move out. In 1970, suburbs housed 25 percent more families than cities; today, suburbs house 75 percent more families than cities. From 1990-93, 97 percent of new businesses were created in the suburbs. In that same time period, 87 percent of all new lower-paying jobs were created in the suburbs (so cities aren't creating the jobs they need as residents move from welfare to work)." (p20)

"The Monitor's View: Help for the Cities." The Christian Science Monitor v89 n151 1 Jul 1997. p20. The Christian Science Monitor search engine: <http://www.csmonitor.com/plweb-cgi/iops1.pl> To retrieve this article, enter the following search: ED=19970701 AND cities. In the "retrieved list," click the title that matches this record. (ISSN0882-7729).

SUBWAYS--NEW YORK (N.Y.) (v26)

SUDDEN INFANT DEATH SYNDROME--UNITED STATES

Sudden Infant Death Syndrome, "sometimes known as crib death, is the sudden and unexplained death of an infant under one year of age that strikes nearly 4,000 babies in the United States every year....Prior to the 1992 recommendation by the American Academy of Pediatrics (AAP) to place babies on their backs [which reduces the risk of SIDS] and the initiation of the 'Back to Sleep' campaign in 1994, nearly 70% of babies were sleeping on their stomachs. Today, only about 25% of babies are stomach sleeping."

U.S. National Institutes of Health. "New Sudden Infant Death Syndrome (SIDS) Fact Sheet, AAP Statement on Bed Sharing Now Available." News Release 16 Sep 1997. document-level access: <http://www.nih.gov/news/pr/sept97/nichd-16.htm>

Sudden Infant Death Syndrome, "which strikes nearly 3,000 babies [in the U.S.] each year, is the sudden, unexplained death of an infant in the first year of life....Prior to the start of the public-private 'Back to Sleep' campaign by the U.S. Department of Health and Human Services in 1994, nearly 70 percent of babies were stomach sleeping. Today...about 21 percent of babies are stomach sleeping. The result has been a 38 percent drop in the SIDS death rate between 1992 and 1996."

U.S. Dept. of Health and Human Services. "Tipper Gore Alerts Parents about Increased SIDS Incidence during Cold Winter Weather." Press Release 30 Oct 1997. document-level access: <http://www.hhs.gov/news/press/1997pres/971030c.html>

SUGAR BEET INDUSTRY--GREAT PLAINS

Sugarbeet "acreage planted for the 1997/98 crop is up 14 percent over last year in the Great Plains States, which consist of Montana, Wyoming, Nebraska, Colorado, Texas, and New Mexico. About 275,000 acres were planted....Acreage harvested in Colorado is up 31 percent from last year and is the highest since 1981....In Colorado, as of September 7, 84 percent of sugarbeets were in good or excellent condition...." (p4-5)

U.S. Dept. of Agriculture. Economic Research Service. "U.S. Sugar." Sugar and Sweetener Situation and Outlook Series Sep 1997. p4-11.

SUGAR BEET INDUSTRY--IDAHO--OREGON

Sugarbeet "area harvested in Idaho is forecast up 6.5 percent to 196,000 acres [for 1997-1998]....Area harvested in Oregon is up 5 percent to 17,100 acres." (p5)

U.S. Dept. of Agriculture. Economic Research Service. "U.S. Sugar." Sugar and Sweetener Situation and Outlook Series Sep 1997. p4-11.

SUGAR BEET INDUSTRY--UNITED STATES

"U.S. farmers planted beets on about 1.37 million acres and produced 26.57 million tons in 1996, 5.3 percent below 1995's production....Rising input prices resulted in a 2.3-percent rise in total variable cash costs. Hired labor, chemicals, and fertilizers were the major cash expenses, accounting for about 60 percent of total variable costs. In 1996, expenses for these three inputs rose an average 3.5 percent over 1995. Costs of processing the 1996 beet crop rose 2-3 percent from 1995. Total processing costs are estimated at 12.498 cents per pound, an increase of about 0.3 cent over the previous year." (p24)

U.S. Dept. of Agriculture. Economic Research Service. "1996 Cost of Production for Crops and Livestock: Although Input Expenses Rose in 1996,...Led to Higher Net Returns." Agricultural Income and Finance Situation and Outlook Report Sep 1997. p23-27.

U.S. "beet sugar production for the first 10 months of 1996/97 (October-April) totaled 3.7 million tons, accounting for 91.6 percent of the forecast for the year. For the previous 3 years, beet sugar production in the first 10 months averaged 90.4 percent of the year's total." (p6)

U.S. Dept. of Agriculture. Economic Research Service. "U.S. Sugar." Sugar and Sweetener Situation and Outlook Series Sep 1997. p4-11.

SUGAR FACTORIES--ENVIRONMENTAL ASPECTS --CHINA--GUANGXI PROVINCE (v26)

SUGAR TRADE--AUSTRALIA (v26)

SUGAR TRADE--FLORIDA (v26)

"The Florida Sugarcane League estimates that the sugar industry provides $2 billion in revenue for the state and directly employs 11,200 people....Florida ranks first in the nation as a sugar producer, providing 24 percent of the sugar produced in the United States." (p9)

Lee, Jill/U.S. Dept. of Agriculture. Agricultural Research Service. "To Aid the Everglades Ecosystem, Scientists Are...Changing Sugarcane." Agricultural Research v45 n12 Dec 1997. p8-10. (ISSN0002-161X).

SUGAR TRADE--HAWAII (v26)

"Sugar production in Hawaii has declined from over 1 million tons in the mid-1980's to a projected 340,000 tons in 1997/98. Three mills closed in 1996, and sugar production has now ceased entirely on the islands of Hawaii and Oahu. Three mills remain on Maui and three on Kauai." (p7)

Lord, Ron/U.S. Dept. of Agriculture. Economic Research Service. "Commodity Briefs: Specialty Crops: Sugar Beet Crop to Outpace 96/97 despite Flooding." Agricultural Outlook Jul 1997. p7-8.

SUGAR TRADE--LOUISIANA (v26)

"Louisiana sugar production in 1997/98 is forecast at 975,000 tons, down 7 percent from the near-record 1996/97 crop....A new growing area of about 6,000 acres in western Louisiana will be harvested this fall for seed cane to expand plantings; the new plantings will be harvested in fall of 1998. This new area may expand to 30,000 or more acres within a few years. Nineteen mills will be processing in Louisiana this fall, after which one mill is scheduled to close." (p7)

Lord, Ron/U.S. Dept. of Agriculture. Economic Research Service. "Commodity Briefs: Specialty Crops: Sugar Beet Crop to Outpace 96/97 despite Flooding." Agricultural Outlook Jul 1997. p7-8.

"Louisiana sugarcane area for sugar and seed is up in 1997/98 to 410,000 acres, above the record 400,000 acres of 1995/96....As of September 6, 77 percent of sugarcane was in good or excellent condition, while 2 percent was in poor condition....By September 6, 55 percent of cane plantings were done, compared with 18 percent last year and an average of 36 percent." (p6)

U.S. Dept. of Agriculture. Economic Research Service. "U.S. Sugar." Sugar and Sweetener Situation and Outlook Series Sep 1997. p4-11.

SUGAR TRADE--PUERTO RICO--TEXAS (v26)

SUGAR TRADE--RUSSIA--UKRAINE

"Russia and Ukraine together account for 90 percent of NIS/B [Newly Independent States of the Soviet Union and the Baltics] sugar production and more than 75 percent of NIS/B sugar consumption....Since 1991/92, the last year before reform, Russia's total sugar imports have declined from 3.9 million tons to a projected 3.0 million in 1997/98, which still represents 60 percent of total consumption....The 1997/98 sugar consumption projections for Russia and Ukraine are 5 million and 2.1 million tons, respectively, both down nearly 1 million tons from 1991/92, but virtually unchanged from last year. Total NIS/B sugar consumption for 1997/98 is projected at 9.5 million tons, down from 12.6 million in pre-reform 1991/92." (p24)

Foster, Christian J./Liefert, Olga/Mitchell, Jay K./Hoskin, Roger L./U.S. Dept. of Agriculture. Economic Research Service. "NIS/B Farm Sector Continues Adjustment to Market Forces; U.S. Agricultural Exports to Region Post Recovery." Newly Independent States and the Baltics: International Agriculture and Trade Reports Situation and Outlook Series May 1997. p10,12-15,18,20,22-24.

SUGAR TRADE--UNITED STATES (v26)

In the U.S., "total cash expenses for growing an acre of sugarcane in 1996 fell by 1.1 percent....Lower 1996 sugar recovery rates were responsible for a 3-percent rise in variable cash growing expenses at the cents-per-pound-of-sugar level. Processing the 1996 crop cost about 2 percent more per pound of sugar than in 1995." (p24)

U.S. Dept. of Agriculture. Economic Research Service. "1996 Cost of Production for Crops and Livestock: Although Input Expenses Rose in 1996,...Led to Higher Net Returns." Agricultural Income and Finance Situation and Outlook Report Sep 1997. p23-27.

"Total U.S. processed sugar production for 1997/98 (October-September) is projected at 7.5 million short tons, raw value, up over 3 percent from 1996/97. Beet sugar production is projected at 4.3 million tons, up 6 percent from this year, while cane sugar production is projected at 3.2 million tons, unchanged from 1996/97. Planting intentions released in March indicated 1997/98 U.S. sugar beet planted acreage would be 1.45 million acres, up over 6 percent from the current year....The share of national acreage in the non-irrigated, eastern growing region--Minnesota, North Dakota, Michigan, and Ohio--was less than 25 percent in the early 1970's, reached 30 percent in 1975 and 50 percent by 1986, and is now approaching 60 percent." (p7)

Lord, Ron/U.S. Dept. of Agriculture. Economic Research Service. "Commodity Briefs: Specialty Crops: Sugar Beet Crop to Outpace 96/97 despite Flooding." Agricultural Outlook Jul 1997. p7-8.

"U.S. sugar production in 1997/98 (October 1997-September 1998), is projected at 7.635 million short tons, raw value, up 5.3 percent from 1996/97. Beet sugar production is forecast at 4.3 million tons, up 250,000 tons. Cane sugar is up 130,000 tons to 3.34 million tons. Sugar production for 1996/97 is estimated at 7.25 million tons, 4.05 million tons of beet sugar and 3.2 million tons of cane sugar." (p3)

U.S. Dept. of Agriculture. Economic Research Service. "Summary." Sugar and Sweetener Situation and Outlook Series Sep 1997. p3.

According to USDA's Sweetener Market Data, compiled and published by the Farm Service Agency, U.S. "sugar stocks on August 1, 1997, totaled 2.3 million tons, up 400,000 tons from a year earlier. Beet processors held 1.08 million tons, 47 percent of the total, up 389,000 tons from a year earlier....The remaining stocks were held by cane mills, 591,000 (26 percent), and cane sugar refiners, 625,000 tons (27 percent)." (p10)

U.S. Dept. of Agriculture. Economic Research Service. "U.S. Sugar." Sugar and Sweetener Situation and Outlook Series Sep 1997. p4-11.

In the U.S., "the initial raw cane sugar import tariff-rate quota (TRQ) for 1997/98 was set on September 17, 1997, at 1.8 million metric tons, raw value (1.984 million short tons). The raw sugar TRQ is allocated to 40 countries....Under an administrative plan similar to that of fiscal 1996/97, three tranches of 200,000 metric tons each are reserved until January, March, and May 1998. In each of those months, if the ending stocks-to-use ratio published in the monthly World Agricultural Supply and Demand Estimates (WASDE) report is at 15.5 percent or lower (rounded to one tenth of a percent), then that month's 200,000-metric-ton tranche will be made available for allocation by the United States Trade Representative (USTR), otherwise it will be canceled....Brazil, the Dominican Republic, and the Philippines will be allowed to ship up to 25 percent of their initial allocation during each quarter of fiscal 1997/98. Argentina, Australia, Colombia, El Salvador, Guatemala, Nicaragua, Panama, Peru, and South Africa will be allowed to ship up to 50 percent of their initial allocations in the first 6 months of fiscal year 1998....Though there is an allocation of 25,000 metric tons, raw value, to Mexico under NAFTA provisions in both the raw cane sugar TRQ and the refined sugar TRQ, Mexico is limited to a combined total of 25,000 metric tons under both categories. Thus, total allowable entries in fiscal 1997/98 under the combined raw and refined TRQs is equal to 1.825 million metric tons (2.01 million short tons), which is the sum of the raw TRQ (1.8 million metric tons) plus the refined sugar TRQ (50,000 metric tons) minus 25,000 tons (to avoid double counting with regard to Mexico)." (p9-10)

U.S. Dept. of Agriculture. Economic Research Service. "U.S. Sugar." Sugar and Sweetener Situation and Outlook Series Sep 1997. p4-11.

Through the first 10 months of the 1997 fiscal year, October-July, U.S. sugar "deliveries were 7.95 million short tons, raw value, or about 81.5 percent of the forecast level. The latest 5-year average October-July deliveries as a share of the fiscal year total is 81.2 percent." (p8)

U.S. Dept. of Agriculture. Economic Research Service. "U.S. Sugar." Sugar and Sweetener Situation and Outlook Series Sep 1997. p4-11.

The U.S. "National Audubon Society is proposing an auction system to raise as much as $100 million a year from foreign sugar growers seeking to sell their product in the United States. Audubon President John Flicker says the US government could auction the right to some 40 countries to sell their sugar in the highly regulated American market. US sugar prices are generally 10 cents per pound higher than world prices, so foreign producers realize a windfall when granted access to the American market." (p3-4)

Richey, Warren. "United States: Saving Everglades: Who Should Pay?" The Christian Science Monitor v89 n181 13 Aug 1997. p3-4. The Christian Science Monitor search engine: <http://www.csmonitor.com/plweb-cgi/iops1.pl> To retrieve this article, enter the following search: ED=19970813 AND pay. In the "retrieved list," click the title that matches this record. (ISSN0882-7729).

SUGARCANE INDUSTRY--FLORIDA (v26)

SUICIDE (v26)

see also AGED--ARIZONA--SUICIDAL BEHAVIOR; AGED--UNITED STATES--SUICIDAL BEHAVIOR; ASSISTED SUICIDE; TEENAGERS--UNITED STATES--SUICIDAL BEHAVIOR; YOUTH--NEW ZEALAND--SUICIDAL BEHAVIOR; YOUTH--UNITED STATES--SUICIDAL BEHAVIOR

SUICIDE--UNITED STATES (v26)

"Currently there are nearly 31,000 suicides annually in the United States--83 suicides per day; or 1 suicide every 17 minutes--with 12 of every 100,000 Americans taking their own lives....More people die from suicide than from homicide in the United States. On an average day in this country, an estimated 1,900 adults attempt suicide....In 1994, the latest year for which we have statistical data, the 10 highest suicide rates, averaging twice those of the mid-Atlantic region, were found in States within the intermountain region of the west....Nevada leads the Nation in this public health tragedy....Suicide is the eighth leading cause of death in the United States. Males commit suicide at rates and numbers of suicides three to four times those of females. Firearms are currently the most often utilized method of suicide by essentially all groups--that is males, females, young, old, white, nonwhite--and the rates are increasing....Rates of suicide are highest among the older adult population above 65....Elderly adults have rates of suicide more than 50 percent higher than the Nation as a whole and the young--15 to 24....For young people 15 to 24 years old, suicide is the third leading cause of death, behind unintentional injury and homicide." (pS4012)

Reid, Harry (Sen.-Nev.). "Senate Resolution 83--Recognizing Suicide as a National Problem." Congressional Record. Daily ed. v143 n57 6 May 1997. pS4012-4013. section/page-level access: <http://thomas.loc.gov/cgi-bin/query/R?r105:FLD001:S04012:> (ISSN0363-7239). (X1.1A.105/1).

In the U.S., "it is estimated that there are 750,000 suicide attempts annually....Although there are no official statistics on attempted suicide, it is generally estimated that there are at least 8 to 20 attempts for each death by suicide. Risk of attempted suicide is greatest among females and the young. Females have generally been found to make 3 to 4 times as many attempts as males. Estimate of the ratio of young attempted suicides to suicidal deaths have generally ranged between 100 to 1 and 200 to 1." (pS4012)

Reid, Harry (Sen.-Nev.). "Senate Resolution 83--Recognizing Suicide as a National Problem." Congressional Record. Daily ed. v143 n57 6 May 1997. pS4012-4013. section/page-level access: <http://thomas.loc.gov/cgi-bin/query/R?r105:FLD001:S04012:> (ISSN0363-7239). (X1.1A.105/1).

In the U.S., "since the 1950s, suicide rates among youth have nearly tripled. Between 1980 and 1990, the suicide rate increased by 30% in the 10 to 19 year-old age group. For older Americans over 65, the suicide rate increased nine percent between 1980 and 1992. Elderly Americans make up about 13 percent of the country's population, but account for about 20 percent of all suicides." (pS3996)

Fowler, Raymond D. (Exec. Vice President and CEO, American Psychological Association). "Suicide in America." Congressional Record. Daily ed. v143 n57 6 May 1997. pS3995-3997. section/page-level access: <http://thomas.loc.gov/cgi-bin/query/R?r105:FLD001:S03996:> (ISSN0363-7239). (X1.1A.105/1).

SUITS (LAW)

see ACTIONS AND DEFENSES

SULPHUR DIOXIDE--UNITED STATES (v26)

SUNFLOWER SEED INDUSTRY

"Foreign sunflowerseed production fell 8 percent in 1996/97 to 22.1 million tons. The decline was mostly due to a large reduction in Russia (down 33 percent to 2.8 million tons), and in Argentina, where the crop declined 7 percent to 5.2 million tons." (p7)

U.S. Dept. of Agriculture. Economic Research Service. "World Oilseed Situation." Oil Crops Situation and Outlook Series Oct 1997. p7-8.

SUNFLOWER SEED INDUSTRY--RUSSIA

"As prices approached world levels, Russian sunflowerseed exports nearly doubled from 1992/93 to 1994/95. By 1995 production reached a near-record 4.2 million tons....Exports for 1996/97 will decline to an estimated 1 million tons from 1.2 million last year....The Russian government's 1997 production target for sunflowerseed is 4.3 million tons...." (p22)

Foster, Christian J./Liefert, Olga/Mitchell, Jay K./Hoskin, Roger L./U.S. Dept. of Agriculture. Economic Research Service. "NIS/B Farm Sector Continues Adjustment to Market Forces; U.S. Agricultural Exports to Region Post Recovery." Newly Independent States and the Baltics: International Agriculture and Trade Reports Situation and Outlook Series May 1997. p10,12-15,18,20,22-24.

SUNFLOWER SEED INDUSTRY--UNITED STATES

"U.S. sunflower plantings were 2.6 million acres, down 26 percent from the previous year. All the decline was in oil-type sunflowers, as non-oil type acreage was unchanged at 568,000 acres. Although acreage dropped, national average sunflowerseed yield improved to 1,435 pounds per acre, 21 percent above the 1995 average. Given this yield and 2.5 million acres harvested, sunflowerseed production fell to 3,587 million pounds in 1996. Despite ample seed supplies, crushings totaled 1,861 million pounds, down 8 percent from 1995/96. U.S. sunflowerseed oil production dropped to 849 million pounds, the lowest in 3 years. Sunflowerseed prices increased slightly to $11.80 per hundredweight from $11.50 in 1995/96. U.S. export shipments of

sunflowerseed oil slipped to 739 million pounds." (p3)
U.S. Dept. of Agriculture. Economic Research Service. "Summary." Oil Crops Situation and Outlook Series Oct 1997. p3.

SUNRIVER (OREGON)

"The community of Sunriver is located in Central Oregon, 15 miles south of Bend....It draws approximately 1.5 million visitors a year....Sunriver averages about 300 days a year of sunshine, with average daytime temperatures of 85 degrees F. [fahrenheit] in summer and 30 in winter. The winter months bring about 70 inches of snowfall....The community is surrounded by the Deschutes National Forest, and homes have been built in this heavily timbered area. More than 80 percent of these are wood-sided with shake roofs." (p24)
Horton, Era. "Profile: Sunriver (OR) Fire Department." American Fire Journal v49 n6 Jun 1997. p24. (ISSN0739-3709).

SUPPLEMENTAL SECURITY INCOME PROGRAM --CALIFORNIA (v26)

SUPPLEMENTAL SECURITY INCOME PROGRAM --HOUSING--UNITED STATES

In the U.S., most Supplemental Security Income "recipients (92 percent) resided in a household setting...." (p19) "About 14 percent of the 6.3 million SSI recipients had ownership interest in their home; 46 percent had rental liability. Approximately 32 percent lived in shared households where they were neither owners nor renters. These households included situations where SSI recipients shared expenses either for food, shelter, or for both; lived in rent-free shelters; lived in another person's household where one-third reduction was applied; or were children who lived in their parents' households. A small proportion (2 percent) of the recipients were in noninstitutional care situations....About 5 percent of all SSI recipients were institutionalized." (p20)
Kochhar, Satya/Scott, Charles G. "Living Arrangements of SSI Recipients." Social Security Bulletin v60 n1 p18-28. (ISSN0037-7910).

SUPPLEMENTAL SECURITY INCOME PROGRAM--MIDDLE WEST--SOUTHERN STATES

In the U.S., the South has a larger proportion of Supplemental Security Income recipients "than any other area. Of the total SSI population (6.3 million recipients), about 40 percent live in the South. Among all U.S. residents, 35 percent are in the South. Nearly 44 percent of all aged SSI recipients live in the South, compared with 35 percent of the Nation's total aged population....Almost 19 percent of the SSI recipient population live in the Midwest, compared with 24 percent of the total population. Among the aged, SSI recipients represent only 10 percent of the Midwest population; those aged 65 or older represent about 24 percent of the population in that area." (p19)
Kochhar, Satya/Scott, Charles G. "Living Arrangements of SSI Recipients." Social Security Bulletin v60 n1 1997. p18-28. (ISSN0037-7910).

SUPPLEMENTAL SECURITY INCOME PROGRAM--UNITED STATES--AGED WOMEN (v26)

SUPPLEMENTAL SECURITY INCOME PROGRAM--UNITED STATES--CHILDREN (v26)

SUPPLEMENTAL SECURITY INCOME PROGRAM--UNITED STATES--IMMIGRANTS (v26)

SUPPORT OF CHILDREN

see CHILD SUPPORT

SURFING--UNITED STATES

"America's surfing community has grown steadily in the 1990s, reaching 1.7 million last year, with a 15 percent jump in women surfers....In 1976, when the first world [surfing] championship was held, [Ian] Carins was the top-earning surfer with annual winnings of $8,000. Kelly Slater...earns close to $1 million in prize money and sponsorship each year." (p3)
Gaouette, Nicole. "United States: A Letter from Huntington Beach, Calif.: Surfers Ride 'Rad' Money Wave." The Christian Science Monitor v89 n181 13 Aug 1997. p3. The Christian Science Monitor search engine: <http://www.csmonitor.com/plweb-cgi/iops1.pl> To retrieve this article, enter the following search: ED=19970813 AND wave. In the "retrieved list," click the title that matches this record. (ISSN0882-7729).

SURGERY, OUTPATIENT

see AMBULATORY SURGERY

SURGICAL CLINICS--UNITED STATES

"In addition to the ambulatory surgery offered by hospitals, the number of freestanding ambulatory surgery centers [in the U.S.] grew from 239 in 1983 to more than 1,800 in 1993." (p18) National Survey of Ambulatory Surgey "data indicate that 27.7 million surgical and nonsurgical procedures were performed in 1994 during 18.4 million visits to U.S. ambulatory surgery settings....According to the NHDS [National Hospital Discharge Survey], 40.7 million procedures were performed on 19.6 million hospital inpatients during 1994. Thus, ambulatory procedures made up 40 percent of the total procedures estimated in the two surveys. Eighty-five percent of the ambulatory procedures (23.4 million) were performed in hospital-based settings and 15 percent (4.3 million) were in freestanding settings...." (p19)
Hall, Margaret Jean/Kozak, Lola Jean/Gillum, Brenda S. "National Survey of Ambulatory Surgery: 1994." Statistical Bulletin v78 n3 Jul-Sep 1997. p18-27. (ISSN0790-8334).

SURPLUSES, TRADE

see BALANCE OF TRADE

SURVIVORS' BENEFITS--CHILE (v26)

SUSPENDED SENTENCE

see PROBATION

SWEATSHOPS--UNITED STATES (v26)

"The U.S. General Accounting Office (GAO) estimates that more than one-third of New York's 6,500 garment manufacturing and production workplaces are sweatshops....As many as 4,500 of the 5,000 garment production operations in Los Angeles are sweatshops, as are 80 percent in Miami and many others in Portland (Ore.), New Orleans, Chicago, San Antonio and Philadelphia, according to the GAO. In Orange County's Little Saigon near Los Angeles, $1 an hour is a common wage, while the wage floor in New York's Chinatown is near $2." (p11) "U.S. consumers spend $184 billion on apparel each year, 60 percent of which goes for imports By roaming the world seeking the lowest wages, the fewest labor protections and the fewest environmental regulations, companies have dragged workers into a 'race to the bottom,' paying workers as little as 12 cents an hour in Haiti and 31 cents in Honduras....In public opinion polls, 79 percent of Americans say they would avoid a retailer they knew dealt in sweatshop goods, and 72 percent want all trade agreements to include strict rules covering human rights and environmental protection, according to the National Labor Committee (NLC), the campaign's organizer." (p12)
Parks, James B. "This Holiday Season: No Sweat." America@Work v2 n10 Nov 1997. p11-12. (ISSN1091-594X).

SWEATSHOPS--UNITED STATES--PUBLIC OPINION (v26)

SWEDEN (v26)

SWEDEN--ARMED FORCES--WOMEN

"In Sweden, similar in size to California but with a population of only 8.8 million, women have been accepted into the military since 1979, but few choose to join. Of 33,000 noncommissioned soldiers in active service in the Army, Navy, and Air Force, only 150 are women; 321 female officers serve out of a corp of

15,000." (p11)

Andersson, Martha. "Global Report: Europe's Quiet Approach: Sex Issues in US Military Puzzle, Fascinate the World: Sweden." The Christian Science Monitor v89 n142 18 Jun 1997. p11. The Christian Science Monitor search engine: <http://www.csmonitor.com/plweb-cgi/iops1.pl> To retrieve this article, enter the following search: ED=19970618 AND sweden. In the "retrieved list," click the title that matches this record. (ISSN0882-7729).

SWEDEN--ECONOMIC CONDITIONS (v26)

SWEDEN--EMPLOYMENT (v26)

SWEDEN--EMPLOYMENT--MANUFACTURES (v26)

SWEDEN--LANGUAGES (v26)

SWEDEN--NEWSPAPERS (v26)

SWEDEN--POPULATION (v26)

SWEDEN--RELIGION (v26)

SWEDEN--SOCIAL CONDITIONS (v26)

SWEET POTATO INDUSTRY--UNITED STATES (v26)

In the U.S., "the 1996 sweet potato crop was estimated at 13.5 million cwt [hundredweight], up 4 percent from the previous year. The season-average price was estimated at $14.40 per cwt, compared with $15.90 in 1995. U.S. yields rose 3 percent to 159 cwt per acre--3 cwt less than the record set in 1994. North Carolina's output declined 10 percent to 4.3 million cwt, with the State's share of U.S. production falling from 37 percent to 32 percent. Mississippi's crop increased 57 percent to 1.3 million cwt as acreage and yields both increased." (p4)

U.S. Dept. of Agriculture. Economic Research Service. "Summary." Vegetables and Specialties Situation and Outlook Yearbook Jul 1997. p3-5.

SWINE--CANADA--UNITED STATES (v26)

SWINE--ENVIRONMENTAL ASPECTS--UNITED STATES

According to an article in U.S. NEWS & WORLD REPORT (July 28, 1997), "'hundreds of millions of gallons of untreated, nutrient-rich hog feces and urine produced at...loosely regulated factory [hog] farms are stored in earthen lagoons that sometimes leak or collapse. In 1995...25 million gallons of liquid swine manure--more than twice the volume of the Exxon Valdez oil spill in Prince William Sound--flowed into the New River after a lagoon was breached.'" (unpaginaged)

"Hog Farms Contribute to Spread of Toxic Algae, Reports Magazine." Alternative Agriculture News v15 n8 Aug 1997. (ISSN8755-4941).

SWINE--MISSOURI (v26)

SWINE--OKLAHOMA

"In the past two years, Oklahoma has tripled its swine breeding herd numbers which resulted in an increased market share of 359%. In 1997, Oklahoma's hog population totals more than 1.3 million (Hinton, 1997). NATIONAL HOG FARMER...reported that within the next few years there will be enough production capacity within a 100-mile radius of Guymon, OK, to produce 10% of the U.S. hog marketings...(Vansickle, 1997)." (p8)

Stephens, Michelle. "Controversy over Corporate Hog Farming Was a Major Impetus of New Legislation in Oklahoma." Kerr Center Newsletter v23 n4 1997. p8-9.

SWINE--TAIWAN

"In 1960, about 94 percent of Taiwan's farms raised hogs, but with an average of only four head per farm. By 1995, only 3 percent of Taiwanese farms raised hogs, but the per-farm average had increased to 402 head. Although about two-thirds of Taiwan's hog operations had less than 200 head, larger farms with herds of over 1,000 head accounted for 57 percent of the total inventory--close to the 61 percent of inventory held in the U.S. by operations of that size." (p3)

Southard, Leland/Riley, Pete/U.S. Dept. of Agriculture. Economic Research Service. "Commodity Briefs: Livestock, Dairy & Poultry: Hog Disease in Taiwan Affects U.S. Pork & Corn Exports." Agricultural Outlook Jun 1997. p3-5.

SWINE--UNITED STATES (v26)

In the U.S., "market hog prices varied in the $50-$60 per cwt [hundredweight] range during much of 1996, up from $40 to $50 in 1995. Feeder pig prices were also up sharply from 1995, mostly in the $70-$80 range....Feed costs rose about 30 percent among all producer types." (p25)

U.S. Dept. of Agriculture. Economic Research Service. "1996 Cost of Production for Crops and Livestock: Although Input Expenses Rose in 1996,...Led to Higher Net Returns." Agricultural Income and Finance Situation and Outlook Report Sep 1997. p23-27.

An Iowa State University "study found that smaller hog operations [in the U.S.] purchased 69 percent of their feed within 10 miles, while larger operations purchased 42 percent of their feed that close to home....Larger operations made 35 percent of their equipment purchases and 12 percent of their building supply purchases over 50 miles away from the operation, while smaller operations made only 3 percent of their purchases in both categories that far away." (p3)

Thompson, Nancy. "Are Large Hog Operations Good for Rural Communities?" Center for Rural Affairs Newsletter Nov 1997. p3-4.

In the U.S., the 1 June 1997 "hogs and pigs inventory totaled 58.2 million head, up 2 percent from a year ago and up 4 percent from March 1. Breeding hog numbers, at 6.95 million head, were up 1 percent from a year ago and up 2 percent from March 1." (p1)

U.S. Dept. of Agriculture. Economic Research Service. "Hog Inventory Increases." Livestock, Dairy and Poultry Situation and Outlook Series 17 Jul 1997. p1.

SWORDFISH--ATLANTIC OCEAN--MEXICO, GULF OF

Along the Atlantic and Gulf of Mexico coasts, "the average size of swordfish landed has declined from over 266 pounds prior to 1963--an eight year old fish that could have spawned several times--to 90 pounds in 1995--a fish three years old that would not spawn for two years. In 1995, 88 percent of the swordfish landed by the domestic commercial fishing industry were juvenile fish that had never spawned once....In 1994, 40 percent of the swordfish caught on longlines were discarded; 25 percent of the total catch were discarded dead....This mortality is contrary to the objectives of the ICCAT [International Commission for the Conservation of Atlantic Tunas] swordfish management program, which is intended to protect young fish in order to restore the adult spawning stock, currently only 58% of the population size needed to support the optimum yield." (p4)

"Bad Medicine: NCMC Opposes Swordfish Limited Entry." NCMC Marine Bulletin n79 Spr-Sum 1997. p4.

SWORDFISH FISHING (v26)

SYCAMORE--UNITED STATES (v26)

SYPHILIS--UNITED STATES (v26)

SYRIA--ECONOMIC CONDITIONS

In Syria, "domestic oil production crested at around 600,000 barrels per day in the early 1990s, generating between $1.6 and $2 billion a year. Syrian agriculture was booming, with bumper crops of wheat, cotton and citrus, contributing to a seven percent increase in Syria's GDP in 1992. Aleppo, fast becoming the Syrian center for private sector development, currently boasts over 27,000 industrial firms. Despite these growth rates, signs of stagnation began to appear in 1994. The trade deficit that year was estimated at $1 billion, and oil revenues and exploration activities had begun to recede....Without... reforms, the economy will be overtaken by a population growth rate of more than 3.4 percent, one of the highest in the world." (p3)

Melhem, Hisham. "Syria between Two Transitions." Middle East Report v27 n2 Spr 1997. p2-7. (ISSN0899-2851).

TABLE TENNIS

"Table tennis balls have been clocked at nearly 100 mph [miles per hour]....A very strong loop--an arcing shot that drives an opponent far, far back--has been measured at nearly 7,000 revolutions per minute...[says U.S. Open director Bob Allshouse]." (p3 secE)

Wolff, Carlo. "Accent: Table Tennis Takes Off: Pingpong Tourney Draws World's Best Players to Cobo." Detroit News 28 Nov 1997. p1,3 secE.

TABLE TENNIS--UNITED STATES

"About 40 million Americans play table tennis, says [U.S. Open director Bob Allshouse], the vast majority basement hobby players. Just 8,000 to 9,000 are members of the U.S. Association of Table Tennis, the rating organization based in Colorado Springs." (p1,3 secE)

Wolff, Carlo. "Accent: Table Tennis Takes Off: Pingpong Tourney Draws World's Best Players to Cobo." Detroit News 28 Nov 1997. p1,3 secE.

TAHUAYO RIVER (PERU)

In Peru, "average annual rainfall and monthly temperature for the...[Tahuayo River Valley] is high, between 2000 to 3000 mm [millimeters] and 25.9 [degrees Celsius] respectively. Despite the heavy rainfall, the rise and fall of the Tahuayo River follows the flood cycle of the Amazon river, and is connected to precipitation patterns in the Andes mountains (Moran 1993). The river level rises from December to May, then drops to low water during August-October. Typically, the water levels for the Tahuayo River vary by 6 to 8m [meters], more or less half that of the Amazon River (Coomes 1993)." (p148)

McDaniel, Josh. "Communal Fisheries Management in the Peruvian Amazon." Human Organization v56 n2 Sum 1997. p147-152. (ISSN0018-7259).

TAIGAS--ENVIRONMENTAL ASPECTS (v26)

TAILINGS (METALLURGY)--ENVIRONMENTAL ASPECTS --CANADA (v26)

TAIWAN--ECONOMIC CONDITIONS

In 1976, Taiwan's "total trade volume was $15.6 billion US dollars; last year, 1996, our export import trade volume reached $217.2 billion US dollars, with a surplus $14.7 billion US dollars. The Republic of China has been fortunate and had a 6% annual growth for the past ten years, bringing our per capita gross national product to $12,000. Exports have made our economy. Today the Republic of China [in Taiwan] is a leading producer of electronics, computers and other industrial products....Last year, we had $11.6 billion in computer-hardware production. We are the largest computer manufacturer in the world after the United States, Japan and Germany. Our trade with the European Union has grown rapidly in a very encouraging way in the past three years. The volume grew from $23 billion in 1994 to $29.5 billion in 1995 and $31.3 billion in 1996. Of our European trading partners, Germany enjoys the highest volume of $8.6 billion, followed by the Netherlands with $5.2 billion, UK $4.6 billion, France $4.2 billion and Italy $2.6 billion. And Belgium is our 7th trading partner with a volume of $1.32 billion, after Switzerland of $1.75 billion, ahead of Sweden of $1.13 billion....In less than 50 years, Taiwan ranks as the world's 20th largest economy with a gross national product of $275 billion. We are the 13th largest trading nation in the world and have accumulated [the] world's third largest reserves of foreign exchange." (pS5397)

Chang, John (Minister of Foreign Affairs, Republic of China on Taiwan). "Historic Address by Taiwan Minister of Foreign Affairs to the European Parliament." Congressional Record. Daily ed. v143 n79 9 Jun 1997. pS5396-5398. section/ page-level access: <http://thomas.loc.gov/cgi-bin/query/R?r105:FLD001:S05396:> (ISSN0363-7239). (X1.1A.105/1).

TAIWAN--POLITICS AND GOVERNMENT--PUBLIC OPINION

In Taiwan, when a "1993 survey asked its respondents how strongly they agreed with the statement, 'We can leave all things to morally upright leaders,' nearly two-thirds (63 percent) refused to disagree with it. More notably, only 2 percent 'disagreed strongly' with this statement, indicating that nearly all Taiwanese have not yet fully dissociated themselves from the undemocratic tradition of rule by the morally superior....The 1993 survey asked respondents how strongly they agreed with the statement, 'If a government is often restrained by a legislative assembly, it will be unable to achieve great accomplishments.' Only one in three (32 percent) people disagreed with the statement, while only about one in 33 (3 percent) 'strongly disagreed' with it." (p117)

Shin, Doh Chull/Shyu, Huoyan. "Public Opinion in New Democracies: Political Ambivalence in South Korea and Taiwan." Journal of Democracy v8 n3 Jul 1997. p109-124. (ISSN1045-5736).

"According to the UNITED DAILY, Taiwan's largest newspaper and one that has conducted over twenty such surveys since 1978, Taiwanese support for unification with China dropped from its peak of 69 percent in 1989 to a record low level of 36 percent in 1994 while support for Taiwan's independence had surged from a negligible 4 percent to 33 percent after the slaughter of Taiwanese tourists visiting the Thousand Island Lake during the same period of time. Support for independence has remained above 20 percent since that event. Another public opinion poll showed that Taiwanese support for a 'speedy declaration of independence' increased from 14 percent to 19.1 percent and that support for 'speedy unification' declined substantially from 34.7 percent in 1993 to 17.7 percent in 1994. Those in favor of maintaining the status quo and adopting a wait-and-see attitude increased from 32.1 percent to 48.7 percent." (p9)

Yu, Taifa. "Taiwanese Democracy under Threat: Impact and Limit of Chinese Military Coercion." Pacific Affairs v70 n1 Spr 1997. p7-36. (ISSN0030-851X).

TAJIKISTAN--ECONOMIC CONDITIONS (v26)

TAJIKISTAN--POPULATION

"When the breakup of the Soviet Union made it independent at the end of 1991, Tajikistan had a population of slightly more than 5 million people, more than 60 percent of whom were Tajiks. The Tajiks are Persian-speaking, and are descended from the earliest known inhabitants of Central Asia. Almost all Tajiks (more than 4 million as of the 1989 census) lived in Tajikistan or neighboring Uzbekistan, and a roughly equal number lived in Afghanistan....Uzbeks made up almost 25 percent of the population (more than 1 million people); the presence of some 14 million more Uzbeks across the border in Uzbekistan added to the importance of Tajikistan's Uzbek minority. Russians were far fewer in number (under 8 percent) but occupied important positions in industry, the professions, the political police (the KGB and its successors), and the military." (p336)

Atkin, Muriel. "Tajikistan's Civil War." Current History v96 n612 Oct 1997. p336-340. (ISSN0011-3530).

TAJIKISTAN--SOCIAL CONDITIONS

As a result of the war between Tajikistan and Afghanistan "more than 60,000 private citizens [of Tajikistan] have...perished. About a million residents of the republic have been forced to leave. Fewer than 100,000 Russian-speaking people now reside in Tajikistan, 80 per cent of whom live in the North, where there has never been any combat....In the South where there is fighting, no Russians remain, except for two to three thousand primarily elderly people who are in mixed marriages." (p118)

Slipchenko, V. I. "Russia's Political and Military Problems in Central Asia." European Security v6 n1 Spr 1997. p114-124. (ISSN0966-2839).

TAMARINS (v26)

TANGERINE INDUSTRY--UNITED STATES (v26)

TANKS (MILITARY SCIENCE)--UNITED STATES --ARMED FORCES

The U.S. "Pentagon has been dumping old tanks....Last year, the Pentagon gave 45 tanks to Bosnia and another 50 to Jordan. It shipped 91 tanks to Brazil under a no-cost, five-year lease and 60 to Bahrain on the same terms. Another 160 tanks were sold to Taiwan for $130,000 each, priced at 10 cents on the dollar of their original price. Egypt got 700 for free by picking up transportation costs. One way or another, the Army has disposed of nearly 6,000 older tanks and armored personnel carriers during the last six years." (p64)

Greider, William. "National Affairs: Fortress America." Rolling Stone n764-765 10 Jul 1997. p61-66,68,70,72-73,136-138. (ISSN0035-791X).

TANZANIA--ECONOMIC CONDITIONS (v26)

"Tanzania's tourist hotels produced $205 million in revenue in 1995. But that's only 6.7 percent of the country's gross domestic product. This compared to the 6 percent of the GDP produced by Tanzania's 'transport and communication sector.'" (p104)

O'Rourke, P. J. "Inside Tanzania: Part Two." Rolling Stone n764-765 10 Jul 1997. p101-102,104,106,108,110,114. (ISSN0035-791X).

TAP WATER

see DRINKING WATER

TAX AUDITING--UNITED STATES (v26)

TAX REFUNDS--MICHIGAN (v26)

TAXABLE INCOME

see INCOME TAX

TAXATION (v26)

see also ALCOHOL FUEL INDUSTRY--TAXATION; CASINOS--TAXATION; CIGARETTE TAX; GASOLINE--TAXATION; INCOME TAX; INHERITANCE AND TRANSFER TAX; MINES AND MINERAL RESOURCES--TAXATION; OIL INDUSTRIES--TAXATION; PROPERTY TAX; SALES TAX; SOCIAL SECURITY TAXES

In an international comparison of personal income, capital gains, and corporate profit tax rates, in the 86 countries studied "80 percent of corporate income tax codes are flat (at an average rate of 30.5 percent) and that about half of capital gains codes are flat (with an average rate of 28.2 percent)....Only 12 out of 86 countries charged flat taxes on wages and personal income; half apply 'steeply progressive codes,' with effective top rates of 50 percent to 90 percent. The average top personal income rate for all countries was 42.8 percent....On average and in constant dollars per capita, GDP in countries with 'flat personal income tax(es)' grew at 2.1 percent annually over the past 15 years, versus 1.1 percent for all countries. Developing nations with flat personal income taxes averaged 2.7 percent annual growth over the same period, compared with 0.7 percent for developing nations as a whole." (p16)

Gillespie, Nick. "Citings: Flat-Tax Societies." Reason v29 n4 Aug-Sep 1997. p15-16. (ISSN0048-6906).

TAXATION--CANADA (v26)

Since 1993, the Canadian "government has increased taxes no less than 40 times: 12 hikes in the 1994 budget, 11 hikes in the 1995 budget, 10 in the 1996 budget and more in the budget of this year.... "Taxes in Canada now account for almost 40 percent of GDP." (p190)

Jones, Jim (MP-ON). "Government Orders: Speech from the Throne." Canada. Parliament. House of Commons. Debates. v135 n6 29 Sep 1997. p177-202. section-level access: <http://www.parl.gc.ca/36/1/parlbus/chambus/house/debates/006_1997-09-29/han006-e.htm#LINKT20> (ISSN0704-5603). (X3-361E).

TAXATION--CANADA--PUBLIC OPINION

A recent poll published in the FINANCIAL POST "states that 28 percent of Canadians would like to see a personal income tax cut, 3 percent want to see a business tax cut, and another 20 percent want to see both personal income taxes and corporate taxes reduced. That is a plurality of people who want to see tax relief, at least 51 percent. The people who want to see personal income tax cuts compared to the people who want to see taxes rise are outnumbered by a margin of 28:1." (p248)

Solberg, Monte (MP-AB). "Government Orders: Supply." Canada. Parliament. House of Commons. Debates. v135 n7 30 Sep 1997. p247-281. section-level access: <http://www.parl.gc.ca/36/1/parlbus/chambus/house/debates/007_1997-09-30/han007-e.htm#LINKT5> (ISSN0704-5603). (X3-361E).

TAXATION--CANADA--UNITED STATES (v26)

TAXATION--DENMARK--GERMANY--UNITED STATES (v26)

TAXATION--EUROPE (v26)

British taxpayers "will have to pay another 2bn [billion pounds sterling] to Brussels next year. Gross contributions will then be 8.3bn [billion pounds sterling]. This penalty has been incurred because of Britain's better economic performance and an increase in EU spending of 3 per cent, to 59bn [billion pounds sterling]....Britain's share of the tax bill rises from 11 per cent to 14 per cent." (p4)

"Europe: EU Fact: Euro Taxes Up another 2bn." Freedom Today v22 n4 Aug 1997. p4.

"A report from Eurostat, Statistical Office of the European Communities in Luxembourg, places Sweden on top of EU Member States, with 55.2% of GDP taken last year by taxes and social contributions (TSC). Denmark is next with 52.0%. Ireland is lowest with 34.5% and Spain next (35.2%). EU average is 42.4%....In 1996 the EU average TSC ratio passed its previous peak of 42.0% in 1995....The tax ratio in 1996 was 27.2% of GDP, up slightly on 27.0% in 1995. This is just below the 1989 peak of 27.3%, but the highest since then. In the '90s it has fluctuated around a margin of 0.5 percentage points. Ratio of social contributions last year was a new high of 15.3% of GDP after last year's previous record 15.0%. The 1980 figure was 13.2%."

Eurostat. "New High for EU Taxes & Social Contributions." Press Release 2 Sep 1997. document-level access: <http://europa.eu.int/en/comm/eurostat/compres/en/6097/6206097a.htm>

In 1995, in the EU15, taxes on employed labour as a percentage of compensation of employees (called implicit tax rate) totaled "42.1%. The 1970 EU6 share was 28.7%. In 1995 EU15 raised 51.4% of total tax receipts on employed labour; 25 years earlier the figure for EU6 was 43.2%. As a share of GDP, EU15 taxes on employed labour stood at 21.4% in 1995. The 1970 EU6 equivalent was 14.5%....[In terms of implicit tax rate, the] highest 1995 values were in Sweden (56.2%) and Finland (53.7%). Lowest was the UK's 27%....Steepest rises from 1985 to 1995 were in Germany (from 39.5% to 44.1%), Spain (from 32.3% to 38%), Italy (36.6% to 44%), Portugal (21.4% to 36.7% (1993)) and Finland (42.9% to 53.7%)....[As a percentage of total taxes,] Sweden (62.8%) and Finland (59.5%) again led in 1995. Share was relatively high in Germany (56.2%), the Netherlands (55.5%) and Austria (55.2%). It was lowest in Luxembourg (37.4%), Ireland (39.5%) and the UK (42%)."

Eurostat. "Employment Taxes Keep Rising." Press Release 14 Nov 1997. document-level access: <http://europa.eu.int/en/comm/eurostat/compres/en/7697/6207697a.htm>

TAXATION--EUROPE--UNITED STATES

"According to a White Paper by the European Commission, 'statutory charges on labor'--the sum of income taxes and social security contributions (which include unemployment tax) in the European Union rose from 34 percent of GDP in 1970 to 40 percent in 1991; in the United States they increased from 29 to 30 percent. One-tenth of these charges go to the support of the unemployed." (p60)

Brand, H. "Global Capitalism and the Decay of Employment Policy." Dissent v44 n4 Fall 1997. p56-62. (ISSN0012-3846).

TAXATION--GREAT BRITAIN (v26)

TAXATION--IRELAND

In Ireland, a Central Statistics Office "survey shows that in the Dublin area 89 [pounds sterling] a week is spent on tax out of direct income of 357 [pounds sterling], but this falls to 33 [pounds sterling] from an income of 176 [pounds sterling] in small towns (those with a population under 1,500). In large towns (those with 10,000+ populations) the amount spent on tax is 69 [pounds sterling] from an income of 305 [pounds sterling], it falls to 55 [pounds sterling] from an income of 252 [pounds sterling] in towns with a population between 1,500 and 10,000 and it is 43 [pounds sterling] in rural areas from an income of 249 [pounds sterling]."

Ireland. Central Statistics Office. "Household Budget Survey 1994-95--Volume 2: Detailed Results for Urban and Rural Households." Press Release 1 Dec 1997. document-level access: <http://www.cso.ie/pressreleases/prelhbsv2.html>

TAXATION--JAPAN (v26)

TAXATION--JAPAN--KOREA (SOUTH)--UNITED STATES

"In 1972, taxes amounted to just 12.6 percent of gross domestic product in Korea and 20.7 percent in Japan, well below the 26.6 percent figure in the United States. But by 1995, taxes in Korea had virtually doubled to 22.3 percent and risen to 28.5 percent in Japan, putting Japan's taxes above those here." (p10 secA)

Bartlett, Bruce. "Bartlett's Notations: Industrial Policy Fails to Fuel Asia's Economies." Detroit News 15 Dec 1997. p10 secA.

TAXATION--MICHIGAN

"Michigan got back 78 cents in federal money for every $1 it sent to Washington in 1996--a nickel less than it got the previous year. Michiganians paid an average of $5,629 in federal taxes in 1996; the amount returned was just $4,095, or just 78 cents on the dollar. That's 48th among the states....All federal spending in Michigan last year totaled $39 billion, compared to the $54 billion that taxpayers here sent to Washington." (p1 secC)

Bivins, Larry. "Metro: Feds Cut Funding to State." Detroit News 12 Dec 1997. p1 secC.

TAXATION--QUEBEC (PROVINCE) (v26)

TAXATION--SWEDEN (v26)

TAXATION--TANZANIA

"In a Feb. 10, 1997, story about a Tanzanian crackdown on illegal tour operators, THE EAST AFRICAN newspaper mentioned these taxes just in passing: 'a hotel levy (20 percent), sales tax on food (15 percent), sales tax on fresh juices and cakes (30 percent), stamp duty (1 percent of turnover), withholding tax on goods and services (2 percent), training levy (10 percent on expatriate-employees' taxable income), payroll levy (4 percent on gross taxable income of all employees), vocational-education training-agency tax (2 percent on gross taxable income of all employees).'" (p104,106)

O'Rourke, P. J. "Inside Tanzania: Part Two." Rolling Stone n764-765 10 Jul 1997. p101-102,104,106,108,110,114. (ISSN0035-791X).

TAXATION--UNITED STATES (v26)

Over the last 20 years in the U.S., "federal taxes as a percentage of national income declined from 22 percent to 21.6 percent....Between 1953 and 1993, corporate income taxes as a share of the nation's tax revenues took a nosedive--from 31 percent to only 9 percent. Along came the Reagan administration's tax cuts, and families whose annual earnings were $560,000 or more saw their taxes go down--by an average of $15,674--between 1977 and 1995. For the average family earning $48,000, taxes increased by an average $287 during the same period." (p11)

Kameras, David. "The Top 10 Myths about the Economy." America@Work v2 n5 May-Jun 1997. p10-12. (ISSN1091-594X).

"According to the Americans for Tax Reform Foundation, the cost of this Government this year equals $3.5 trillion, or 36.2 percent of our country's net national product. Now, that amounts to $13,500 for every man, woman, and child in America, $13,500 a year per individual to run this Government....That means that the average American will work 183 days this year to pay for the government's insatiable spending appetite and the thousands of regulations that emanate from this town every year. In the last 14 months, over 4,700 new regulations have been issued by Federal agencies of the Clinton administration....Over 50 percent of a family's hard-earned income goes to the country...." (pH4147)

DeLay, Tom (Rep.-Tex.). "Regarding Cost of Government Day." Congressional Record. Daily ed. v143 n88-89 23 Jun 1997. pH4147-4149. section/page-level access: <http://thomas.loc.gov/cgi-bin/query/R?r105:FLD001:H04147:> (ISSN0363-7239). (X1.1A.105/1).

"On average, Americans will spend 2 hours and 49 minutes each day laboring to pay taxes....A bottle of beer is 43 percent taxes; an airplane ticket, 40 percent taxes; a bottle of liquor, 72 percent taxes; the electric bill, 25 percent taxes; a loaf of bread, 31 percent taxes; a car, 45 percent taxes; a hotel bill, 43 percent taxes; restaurant meal, 27 percent taxes; a package of cigarettes, 75 percent taxes; the telephone bill, 50 percent taxes; a pizza, 38 percent taxes; a can of Coca Cola, 35 percent taxes; and a gallon of gas, approximately 54 percent taxes." (pH8569)

Kingston, Jack (Rep.-Ga.). "Congress Must Continue the Path toward Tax Relief." Congressional Record. Daily ed. v143 n138 7 Oct 1997. pH8569-8570. section/page-level access: <http://thomas.loc.gov/cgi-bin/query/R?r105:FLD001:H08569:> (ISSN0363-7239). (X1.1A.105/1).

In the U.S., "the wealthiest taxpayers--$200,000 and up--currently pay 30 percent of all federal income taxes....Families that make less than $20,000 a year...pay only 3.3 percent of all federal income taxes." (p10 secA)

"The 'Fairness' Doctrine." Detroit News 18 Jun 1997. p10 secA.

In the U.S., "nineteen states and the District of Columbia provide a tax credit for child and dependent care, in addition to the federal benefit....The federal benefit ranges from 20 percent to 30 percent of qualified expenses, depending on a taxpayer's adjusted gross income (AGI). For claimants whose adjusted gross income is $10,000 or less, the credit may be as much as 30 percent....It decreases as the combined income of a husband and wife exceeds $10,000. Once the adjusted gross income of a taxpayer tops $28,000, the credit percentage levels off at 20 percent....If a claimant's employer helps with dependent-care costs, those amounts must be deducted from expenses eligible for the tax break. After this reduction, the maximum amount that taxpayers can take into account for the credit is $2,400 for one qualifying dependent and $4,800 for two or more." (p5)

"Statestats: Giving Tax Credits for Child and Dependent Care." State Legislatures v23 n10 Dec 1997. p5. (ISSN0147-6041).

In the U.S., the Taxpayer Relief Act of 1997 "taxes profits at a maximum 20 percent, down from 28 percent. For investors in the lowest tax bracket (15 percent), the rate falls from 15 to 10 percent....But to get the lower rate, you must own investments longer, 18 months instead of the previous 12. Beginning Jan. 1, 2001, assets held at least five years will be taxed no more than 18 percent. Investors in the 15 percent bracket will pay a paltry 8 percent. The simplest benefit goes to parents, a tax credit of $400 per child, $500 in 1999. That means $400 off your tax bill. The credit fades as family income reaches $110,000. It disappears at $120,000. Taxpayers with a hankering for parenthood also get a $5,000 credit for adoption expenses, $6,000 for children 'with special needs.'...Beginning next year, a taxpayer may underpay estimated tax by $1,000 without penalty." (p7 secB)

Tyson, James L. "Work & Money: Start Now on 1998 Tax Moves." The Christian Science Monitor v90 n14 11 Dec 1997. p7 secB. The Christian Science Monitor search engine: <http://www.csmonitor.com/plweb-cgi/iops1.pl> To retrieve this article, enter the following search: ED=19971211 AND moves. In the "retrieved list," click the title that matches this record. (ISSN0882-7729).

TAXATION--UNITED STATES--PUBLIC OPINION (v26)

In 1995, "a READERS DIGEST poll asked Americans: 'What is the highest percentage of income that is fair for a family of four making $200,000 to pay in all taxes?' The median response, regardless of whether the respondent was rich or poor, black or white, was 25 percent. A similar Grassroots Research poll last March discovered that a majority of Americans would favor a constitutional amendment that would prohibit Federal, State, and local taxes from taking 'a combined total of more than 25 percent of anyone's income in taxes.' Yet, the Tax Foundation tells us that a dual-income family today pays an average 38.4 percent of their income in taxes to State, local, and Federal Governments." (pS5031)

Abraham, Spencer (Sen.-Mich.). "Concurrent Resolution on the Budget." Congressional Record. Daily ed. v143 n70 23 May 1997. pS5023-5066. section/page-level access: <http://thomas.loc.gov/cgi-bin/query/R?r105:FLD001:S05030:> (ISSN0363-7239). (X1.1A.105/1).

In the U.S., "as Congress and the White House prepare to battle over the most significant tax cut in 16 years, most Americans from California to Colorado, Vermont to Florida are responding with a yawn and a nod of skepticism. The booming economy--not the prospect of extra money back from next year's Form 1040--is the predominant money matter on US citizens' minds....Among the crucial details still to be settled are whether children of low-income parents who don't pay taxes will be able to qualify as a $500 tax credit on their parents' return, and how deep a capital-gains cut the president will accept." (p1) "A survey by Peter Hart Associates, a Democratic polling firm in Washington, found that only 14 percent of citizens believe the budget pact will produce the promised deficit reduction and tax relief within the allotted five years." (p18)

Marks, Alexandra. "How Tax Plans Play in Peoria." The Christian Science Monitor v89 n152 2 Jul 1997. p1,18. The Christian Science Monitor search engine: <http://www.csmonitor.com/plweb-cgi/iops1.pl> To retrieve this article, enter the following search: ED=19970702 AND peoria. In the "retrieved list," click the title that matches this record. (ISSN0882-7729).

TAXATION--WASHINGTON (D.C.)

"As stated in the recent Brookings Institution study on [Washington,] D.C. entitled 'The Orphan Capital' taxing metropolitan area residents where they live instead of where they work creates a revenue boon for Maryland and Virginia and a revenue disaster for the District. D.C. is the only city in a multi-State configuration in the country that has an income tax but is not able to tax its non-resident workers....The result is that $20 billion in wages leaves the District each year without being taxed, resulting in hundreds of millions of dollars flowing each year to the treasuries of Maryland and Virginia. Only 1 percent of this amount goes in the other direction--from D.C. residents working in the suburbs back in to D.C." (pS8155)

Jeffords, James M. (Sen.-Vt.). "Statements on Introduced Bills and Joint Resolutions." Congressional Record. Daily ed. v143 n107 25 Jul 1997. pS8153-8156. section/page-level access: <http://thomas.loc.gov/cgi-bin/query/R?r105:FLD001:S08155:> (ISSN0363-7239). (X1.1A.105/1).

TAXATION--WYOMING

In Wyoming in 1997, "mineral severance taxes contribute about $65 million a year to the...[general fund, which pays for general government services]....The mineral companies,...pay taxes--6 percent of the production value in state severance tax, about the same percentage in local property taxes, and 12.5 percent or more in federal revenues, half of which is returned to Wyoming....According to a recent study from University of Wyoming economist Shelby Gerking, a family of four living on an income of $15,000...pay up to $1,000 or $1,200, 7 or 8 percent, respectively, of their income in state and local taxes....Gerking's study found that a family with a $40,000 income pays a little more than 5 percent of their income in state and local taxes. But a family with a $70,000 income pays a little over 4 percent, half the amount that poorer families pay....While Wyoming's mineral companies might contribute 18 or 20 percent of their gross income to the state and local government revenue stream, and the state's poorest families contribute 7 or 8 percent of their income, the railroads might pay only three-tenths of 1 percent." (p15)

Jackson, Hugh. "Taxing the Wrong Side of the Tracks." High Country News v29 n13 7 Jul 1997. p15. (ISSN0191-5657).

TAXICAB DRIVERS--UNITED STATES--MORTALITY (v26)

TAXICABS--UNITED STATES--COST OF OPERATION

The Detroit "City Council is considering revisiting an ordinance, based on a Consumer Affairs Department recommendation, to increase biannual taxicab inspection fees from 50 cents to $140....Detroit's current inspection costs and $800 taxicab licenses or medallions aren't the highest or the lowest in the industry. Boston charges $80,000 per vehicle for a lifetime medallion, which covers two vehicle inspections a year. Philadelphia, by contrast, charges $875 per year per vehicle, inspections included. New York cabs are inspected every three months at $50 a crack. Medallions in Chicago cost $500 per year with required inspections every three months included." (p10 secA)

"Cab Fair." Detroit News 9 Dec 1997. p10 secA.

TEA--CHINA

In China, "area in tea orchards expanded rapidly from 486,000 hectares in 1970 to 1 million hectares in 1977. Since then, area increased slightly to 1.1 million hectares in 1995....Yield increases supported output growth in the late 1970s, 1980s, and early 1990s so that production reached 593,000 tons in 1996....China produces several different kinds of tea. Output as a percentage of total follows: red tea (13.5%); green tea (69.3%); Oolong tea (7.1%); Jinya tea (9%); and other tea (1.1%).... Of the 560,000 tons of tea produced in 1992, the State Commerce and Cooperatives purchased 300,000 tons (53 percent of production,...State Commerce and Cooperatives retailed 177,800 tons (32 percent of production)....The Ministry of Internal Trade entities processed 162,269 tons of tea in 1993, up 13 percent from 1992....Urban per capita tea consumption has remained fairly constant at around 0.24 kilograms per capita from 1985 to 1995....Rural per capita tea consumption was 0.33 kilograms, 38 percent higher than urban areas....China's tea exports have remained fairly constant from the mid-1980s, with 174,000 tons to 179,000 tons in 1994. On average, China exported $350 million worth of tea a year." (p47-48)

Crook, Frederick W./U.S. Dept. of Agriculture. Economic Research Service. "Introduction to China's Horticultural Economy." China: International Agriculture and Trade Reports Situation and Outlook Series Jun 1997. p47-51.

TEA--UNITED STATES

"As a region, the South consumes more than 40 percent of the...[U.S.'s] tea in pounds, and nearly 35 percent of the population drinks tea--more than in any other area of the country....Numbers show that at least 80 percent of the population is drinking it cold and much of that cold tea is sweetened." (p70)

Kerr, Mary Lee. "Still the South: The Southern Character: The Tea Belt." Southern Exposure v25 n3-4 Fall-Win 1997. p70. (ISSN0146-809X).

TEA TRADE--SRI LANKA

"A 67 percent decrease in the world prices for tea from 1970 to 1995, and tight state control in the industry, took a heavy toll on...[Sri Lanka's] export earnings and the tea industry as a whole....Between 1986 and 1995, Kenya's tea production increased 44 percent and Tanzania's by 58 percent. In comparison, Sri Lanka's production increased by only 10 percent--its global market share dropped 50 percent from 1970 to 1990."

World Bank. "Sri Lanka Poised to Regain the Global Tea Market." Press Release 18 Aug 1997. document-level access: <http://www.worldbank.org/html/extdr/extme/1441.htm>

TEACHERS

see also AFRO-AMERICAN TEACHERS; COLLEGE TEACHERS; HOURS OF LABOR--TEACHERS; HOURS OF LABOR--UNITED STATES--TEACHERS; MINORITY TEACHERS; PUBLIC SCHOOLS--UNITED STATES--TEACHERS; SPECIAL EDUCATION TEACHERS; SUBSTITUTE TEACHERS

TEACHERS--CERTIFICATION--UNITED STATES (v26)

TEACHERS--CRIMES AGAINST--UNITED STATES (v26)

TEACHERS--EDUCATION--UNITED STATES (v26)

TEACHERS--MICHIGAN

A DETROIT NEWS review of the Michigan state teacher profile shows that "six of every 10 teachers in the state is a white female. In elementary schools, white women make up 77 percent of the teaching force. Black women comprise 8 percent of the Michigan teaching ranks in elementary and junior and senior high schools. White males make up 29 percent of all teachers, but only 12 percent of elementary staffs. The average age of a teacher in the state is 45, slightly higher than five years ago. Teachers earn about $46,000 a year, a salary that ranks in the top five nationally. Annual teachers' salaries have grown by 12 percent over the past five years. Michigan's teaching force is well-educated--48 percent have master's degrees, while 47 percent have bachelor's degrees....Teachers with a master's degree earn an average salary of $52,600, about $12,000 a year more than those with a bachelor's degree." (p11 secA)

Hornbeck, Mark. "News Special: Education: Only 2 Percent of Teachers in Michigan Are Black Males: Educators: Students...Role Models." Detroit News 14 Aug 1997. p1,11 secA.

TEACHERS--SALARIES, ETC.--UNITED STATES

"The average teacher salary in the United States is $38,509, according to the National Education Association. That represents a 2 percent increase over last year's $37,846. Average teacher salaries fluctuate widely from state to state, however, ranging from a low of $26,764 in South Dakota to a high of $50,647 in Alaska." (pA25)

"Education Vital Signs: State of the States." American School Board Journal v184 n12 Dec 1997. pA24-A25. (ISSN0003-0953).

TEACHERS--SALARIES, ETC.--UNITED STATES --ATTITUDES (v26)

TEACHERS--UNITED STATES (v26)

In 1996, a "report by the National Commission on Teaching and America's Future entitled, 'What Matters Most: Teaching for America's Future', sheds light on the disheartening state of the teaching profession in the United States: more than 12 percent of all newly hired teachers have no training whatsoever in educational technique and pedagogy; more than 14 percent enter the teaching profession without meeting State standards; 23 percent of all secondary teachers do not have even a minor in the main teaching field which they have been hired to perform, including more than 30 percent of mathematics teachers; and, in schools with the highest minority enrollments, students have less than a 50-percent chance of getting a science or mathematics teacher who holds a license and degree in the field which they are teaching....As a USA TODAY article from earlier this year points out, 17 percent of new teachers leave the classroom after 1 year, and a 1987 study by Grissmer and Kirby estimated that 30 to 50 percent of new teachers leave the profession within 3 to 5 years. Add to this defection from the ranks of the profession the increased student enrollment due to the continuing Baby Boom Echo which will reach a record 52.2 million in 1997...." (pS9213)

Reed, Jack (Sen.-R.I.). "Statements on Introduced Bills and Joint Resolutions." Congressional Record. Daily ed. v143 n120 11 Sep 1997. pS9198-9218. section/page-level access: <http://thomas.loc.gov/cgi-bin/query/R?r105:FLD001: S09213:> (ISSN0363-7239). (X1.1A.105/1).

In the U.S., "annually, more than 50,000 underprepared teachers enter the classroom. One in four new teachers do not fully meet State certification requirements, and 12 percent of new hires have had no teacher training at all. Students in inner-city schools have only a 50-percent chance of being taught by a qualified science or math teacher. In Massachusetts, 30 percent of teachers in high-poverty schools do not even have a minor degree in their field." (pS9795)

Kennedy, Edward M. (Sen.-Mass.). "The Property Owners Access to Justice Act of 1997." Congressional Record. Daily ed. v143 n128 23 Sep 1997. pS9789-9800. section/page-level access: <http://thomas.loc.gov/cgi-bin/query/R?r105: FLD001:S09795:> (ISSN0363-7239). (X1.1A.105/1).

In the U.S., "fifty-four percent of current teachers have received a master's degree or completed comparable college work, a rate twice as high as it was in 1971. They also constitute a 'veteran' group, in that they average 16 years of experience compared with 10 years two decades ago. The typical American teacher today is a 43-year-old married woman who earns an average of $35,549 a year. The average age of teachers has risen steadily the past 20 years according to the study, from 36 years old in 1976 to 43 currently. The study also found that about 83 percent of teachers have classroom jobs that match their college majors, which is up from about 70 percent in the early 1960s....For males, the number entering the profession is declining, dropping from 34 percent in 1971 to 25 percent today." (p71)

Cohn, Alvin W. "Juvenile Focus." Federal Probation v61 n3 Sep 1997. p71-73. (ISSN0014-9128).

During the 1993-1994 school year, according to the U.S. Department of Education's National Center for Education Statistics, "nearly seven [teachers] out of eight (87 percent) are white; 7 percent are black; and 4 percent are Hispanic. Nearly two thirds (65 percent) have 10 or more years of full-time teaching experience....Public school teachers earned an average salary of US$37,846 in 1995-1996." (p7)

"A Look at Teachers." Reading Today v15 n2 Oct-Nov 1997. p7. (ISSN0737-4208).

In the U.S., "at present, fewer than 4% of all new teachers come from culturally different backgrounds--different in the sense of being nonwhite, non-Euro-American, and non-middle-class (Cannella and Reiff, 1994)....It is estimated that for now and the near future, around 96% of new teachers are and will be white, and most will be middle-class and female (Cannella and Reiff, 1994; Sleeter, 1994)....When one looks at the demographics of those students now enrolled in institutional teacher preparation programs, most (81%) are female and white (92%); fewer than 3% speak another language, and very few (9%) would choose to teach in an urban school (1991 'ATE Report,' cited in Cannella and Reiff, 1994)." (p130)

Yeo, Frederick. "Teacher Preparation and Inner-City Schools: Sustaining Educational Failure." Urban Review v29 n2 Jun 1997. p127-143. (ISSN0042-0972).

TEACHERS--UNITED STATES--PUBLIC OPINION (v26)

TEACHING HOSPITALS--UNITED STATES (v26)

TECHNOLOGY

see also BIOTECHNOLOGY INDUSTRIES; BUS LINES--TECHNOLOGICAL INNOVATIONS; HIGH TECHNOLOGY INDUSTRIES; MEDICAL TECHNOLOGY

TECHNOLOGY--CANADA--PUBLIC OPINION (v26)

TECHNOLOGY--CHINA

"More than one billion Chinese have access to television. An estimated seven million have cellular telephones. There are 150,000 Internet accounts, a number expected to grow tenfold in the next two years." (p8 secA)

Slevin, Peter. "Nation & World: New China Open for Business but Little Else, Jiang Confirms." Detroit Free Press 31 Oct 1997. p5,8 secA.

TECHNOLOGY--EMPLOYMENT--GERMANY

"In Germany today one in two employees is...working in...[the information and communication industry]." (p18) "The hopes of creating new jobs through innovation have been fulfilled. In 1995, the federal government, the unions, and employers' representatives agreed that in [the] future the reform of an existing occupation should not take longer than 12 months, and the creation of a new occupation no longer than 24 months. In 1996 three new media occupations were approved, and 19 existing occupations updated in line with today's requirements. This year, approximately 800,000 school-leavers will be able to choose from 14 new training courses, 35 of the 370 occupational training courses on offer were reformed at the beginning of the year." (p20-21)

Behler, Bettina. "New Work." Deutschland n5 Oct 1997. p18-21. (ISSN0945-6791).

TECHNOLOGY--EMPLOYMENT--UNITED STATES

In the U.S., "from 1986 to 1994, the number of graduates receiving bachelor's degrees in computer science dropped 43 percent to 24,200 persons....The shortage means pay is rising sharply. It jumped nearly 20 percent from 1995 to 1996. Software engineers typically pulled down salaries of $47,000 in 1991. Today, the positions pay $60,000 or more." (p90)

Hannon, Kerry. "1998 Career Guide: Wanted: The Wired and Well-Spoken Techies." U.S. News & World Report v123 n16 27 Oct 1997. p90. article-level access: <http://www.usnews.com/usnews/issue/971027/27INFO.HTM> (ISSN0041-5537).

TECHNOLOGY--UNITED STATES--FINANCE (v26)

TECHNOLOGY--UNITED STATES--TEENAGERS --ATTITUDES

In 1997, a NEWSWEEK poll of American teenagers found that "92 percent think computers will improve their educational opportunities. Almost as many think technology will create better jobs in the future and help people live longer, healthier lives. 28 percent believe technology is not helping, and may actually be harming, the environment....98 [percent] credit technology for making a positive difference in their lives." (p6)

"News of the Profession: Parents & Reading: Teens and Technology." Reading Today v15 n1 Aug-Sep 1997. p6. (ISSN0737-4208).

TECHNOLOGY--UNITED STATES--WOMEN--ATTITUDES (v26)

TECHNOLOGY--UNIVERSITY OF MICHIGAN (v26)

TECHNOLOGY--VIRGINIA

In the U.S., "there is a shortage of nearly 200,000 workers....Virginia, with its growing high-tech industry, is particularly hard hit--it is currently estimated that 18,000 jobs are currently unfilled. Technology-based businesses in Virginia number over 2,450, employ more than 290,000 workers, and contribute more than $13.8 billion in wages to the State's economy. At current rates of growth, by 2002 these numbers are expected to jump to over 4,000 companies, employing about 330,000, with $22 billion in wages. The average technology sector worker in Virginia earned $45,288 in 1996, compared to an average wage of $26,608 in the Virginia economy as a whole. By 2002, the average technology sector wage could grow to over $63,000....Education is a key component of the solution to this problem. However, schools are not graduating enough qualified individuals to meet the need. From 1986 to 1994, the number of bachelor degrees in computer science, for example, fell 43 percent from 42,195 to 24,200." (pS5014)

Warner, John W. (Sen.-Va.). "The Gun Kingpin Death Penalty Act of 1997." Congressional Record. Daily ed. v143 n69 22 May 1997. pS5013-5014. section/page-level access: <http://thomas.loc.gov/cgi-bin/query/R?r105:FLD001:S05014:> (ISSN0363-7239). (X1.1A.105/1).

TECHNOLOGY, EDUCATIONAL

see EDUCATIONAL TECHNOLOGY

TEENAGE AUTOMOBILE DRIVERS--MICHIGAN (v26)

TEENAGE AUTOMOBILE DRIVERS--MICHIGAN --MORTALITY (v26)

TEENAGE GANGS

see GANGS

TEENAGE GIRLS--UNITED STATES--SEXUAL BEHAVIOR (v26)

TEENAGE MARRIAGE--UNITED STATES (v26)

TEENAGE MOTHERS--CRIMES AGAINST--UNITED STATES

In the U.S., "62 percent of school-age mothers are victims of sexual abuse before becoming pregnant--at least two and more likely five times larger than among the general population of teenage girls....43 percent of school-age mothers are rape victims; 5 percent of them conceived their first child by rape. Physical abuse is also rampant: 59 percent have been hit with a belt or strap, 31 percent have been hit with a stick, 26 percent have been thrown against a wall, 5 percent have been intentionally burned or scalded, and 22 percent have been beaten up by a man to the point of requiring medical treatment." (p19)

Durning, Alan Thein/Crowther, Chris. "Sex, Lies, & Child Abuse." Yes! A Journal of Positive Futures n4 Win 1997-1998. p18-20. (ISSN1089-6651).

TEENAGE MOTHERS--MICHIGAN (v26)

In Michigan, "births to teen-age mothers in Washtenaw County plummeted 35 percent in 1995....No other Michigan county with a sizable population saw such a dramatic decrease. The closest was Wayne County, where births to teens went down 10 percent. Livingston County saw an increase of 15 percent. Statewide, the figure dropped 3.6 percent. From 1989 to 1994, the average annual number of babies born to teen-age mothers in the Washtenaw County was 340, with 349 in 1994. In 1995, it dipped to 228....The total number of births in the county was down 3 percent in 1995, and the number of abortions among teens shot up 8 percent, but those factors account for only a small part of the 35-percent drop in births to teens. Statewide, total births went down 2.6 percent." (p1 secA)

Wahlberg, David. "Births to Teen-Age Mothers Plunge." Ypsilanti Press 6 Jun 1997. p1,14 secA.

TEENAGE MOTHERS--UNITED STATES

"The number of teenage pregnancies in the United States continues to reach alarming levels. According to data compiled by the Alan Guttmacher Institute, in 1992, the most recent year for which statistics are available, approximately 931,000 women aged 15 to 19 became pregnant. Further, the National Center for Health Statistics reports that there were 500,744 births to women aged 15 to 19 in 1995, and an additional 12,318 births to women under 15 years of age. By comparison, the United Nations Population Division reports that the United States teenage birth rate, 64 births per 1,000 females aged 15 to 19 for the period 1990-95, is the highest in the industrialized world. France and Japan report some of the lowest teenage birth rates, at 9 and 4 births per 1,000 females, respectively....According to Child Trends, Inc., the percentage of births to mothers under age 20 that occurred outside of marriage rose from 48 percent in 1980 to 76 percent in 1994." (pS5933)

Specter, Arlen (Sen.-Pa.). "Statements on Introduced Bills and Joint Resolutions." Congressional Record. Daily ed. v143 n85 18 Jun 1997. pS5927-5935. section/page-level access: <http://thomas.loc.gov/cgi-bin/query/R?r105:FLD001:S05932:> (ISSN0363-7239). (X1.1A.105/1).

TEENAGE MOTHERS--UNITED STATES--COSTS

In the U.S., "teenage mothers face more complications in childbirth, and their children are 50 percent more likely to be born premature. These children also have a greater risk of dying in the first year of life, suffering developmental problems, and becoming teen parents themselves. Further, the Office of Population Affairs of the U.S. Department of Health and Human Services reports that 80 percent of children born to unwed teenage mothers who have not completed high school live in poverty. By contrast, of those children born to 20-year-old married parents who are high school graduates, only 8 percent live in poverty. In addition, more than three-fourths of unmarried teen mothers began receiving Aid to Families with Dependent Children (AFDC) within 5 years after the birth of their first child. A report released in 1996 by the Robin Hood Foundation estimated that adolescent childbearing costs the taxpayers $6.9 billion each year in welfare and food stamp benefits, medical care expenses, lost tax revenue, incarceration expenses, and foster care." (pS5933)

Specter, Arlen (Sen.-Pa.). "Statements on Introduced Bills and Joint Resolutions." Congressional Record. Daily ed. v143 n85 18 Jun 1997. pS5927-5935. section/page-level access: <http://thomas.loc.gov/cgi-bin/query/R?105:FLD001:S05932:> (ISSN0363-7239). (X1.1A.105/1).

TEENAGE MURDERERS--UNITED STATES (v26)

TEENAGE PREGNANCY

"Of all the babies born in the world, one in ten is born to an adolescent. That's 15 million births to teenagers every year....The percent of teen births that are unplanned ranges from 20 percent in some Asian countries to 75 percent in the United States." (p36)

Miller, Berna. "Kaleidoscope: Young Mothers." American Demographics v19 n6 Jun 1997. p36. article-level access: <http://www.demographics.com/publications/ad/97_ad/9706_ad/ad970621.htm> (ISSN0163-4089).

TEENAGE PREGNANCY--ALABAMA

"According to statistics from the Alabama Department of Public Health, 16,490 Alabama teenagers between the ages of 10-19 became pregnant in 1996; of these 558 pregnancies were to teens ages 10-14 (preliminary data as of April 30). In 1995, one of every five births was to a teenager; on average every day 46 teenagers became pregnant. There were 11,175 births to Alabama teens, of which 7,887 or 70.6 percent were to unmarried mothers....Infant mortality rates (13.6 per 1,000 live births compared to 9.8 per 1,000 live births for all mothers) are highest among teenage mothers."

Alabama. Dept. of Public Health. "May Is Teen Pregnancy Prevention Awareness Month." News Release 12 May 1997. document-level access: <http://www.alapubhealth.org/Press/pr051297c.html>

TEENAGE PREGNANCY--CALIFORNIA--LOS ANGELES COUNTY

"The state of California has the highest incidence of teenage pregnancy in the...[U.S.], in 1992, 70,996 teenagers gave birth. In Los Angeles county alone, during the same year, 13,000 teenagers became mothers (Child Trends, 1995)." (p813)

Medora, Nilufer P./von der Hellen, Cheryl. "Romanticism and Self-Esteem among Teen Mothers." Adolescence v32 n128 Win 1997. p811-824. (ISSN0001-8449).

TEENAGE PREGNANCY--CANADA (v26)

TEENAGE PREGNANCY--DEVELOPING COUNTRIES (v26)

TEENAGE PREGNANCY--INDIANA--INDIANAPOLIS

Indianapolis, Indiana's "teen birth rate of 82 births per 1,000 girls aged 15 to 19--or 2,100 births in 1993--is significantly higher than the national average. The city since 1995 has prosecuted nearly 60 men for sexual misconduct with a minor, obtaining dozens of convictions and sentences averaging 4.6 years in jail." (p9)

Tyson, Ann Scott. "Latest Watchword in Preventing Teen Pregnancy: 'No.'" The Christian Science Monitor v89 n190 26 Aug 1997. p1,9. The Christian Science Monitor search engine: <http://www.csmonitor.com/plweb-cgi/iops1.pl> To retrieve this article, enter the following search: ED=19970826 AND teen. In the "retrieved list," click the title that matches this record. (ISSN0882-7729).

TEENAGE PREGNANCY--MICHIGAN

"Michigan's birth rate among 15- to 19-year-old girls fell from 59 per thousand in 1991 to 49 per thousand in 1995, the latest year for which complete figures are available from the U.S. Centers for Disease Control and Prevention." (p1 secA) "That's a drop of nearly 17 percent--higher than any other urban, industrial state....In Detroit, the decline was even more dramatic--25 percent from 1991 to 1995, a DETROIT NEWS analysis of state health statistics shows. That compares with a 14-percent drop in Oakland County; a 4-percent drop in out-county Wayne; and a 4-percent increase in births to teens in Macomb County....In Detroit...3,668 infants were born to 15- to 19-year-olds in 1995." (p8 secA)

Tobin, James. "Teen Pregnancy Rate Falls." Detroit News 23 Sep 1997. p1,8 secA.

TEENAGE PREGNANCY--NETHERLANDS (v26)

TEENAGE PREGNANCY--NIGERIA

In Nigeria, "two out of every 5 secondary school girls interviewed admitted to at least one previous pregnancy. Over 900,000 births to adolescents occur annually and 150 out of every 1,000 women who give birth in Nigeria are 19 years old and under....Pregnant girls who are 15 years old and under have a maternal mortality rate of 7 times higher than that of women 20 to 24 years old." (p7)

"Facts about Adolescent Reproductive Health in Nigeria." SIECUS Report v25 n2 Dec 1996-Jan 1997. p7. (ISSN0091-3995).

TEENAGE PREGNANCY--TENNESSEE

In Tennessee, "the pregnancy rate for 10 to 17 year-olds was 22.8 pregnancies per 1,000 females in 1995 and in 1994, down from 23.3 in 1993 and 23.8 in 1992. When 18- and 19-year olds were included in the rate, there was actually a decrease this year from 46.3 in 1994 to 46.0 in 1995. Pregnancies include live births, fetal deaths and abortions reported to the Department of Health. Pregnancy rates dropped in the past year for black adolescents from 45.1 pregnancies per 1,000 females in 1994 to 44.8 in 1995, while the rate for white adolescents rose slightly from 17.0 to 17.1. The rate for 10 to 14 year olds fell to 2.6 from 3.1 in 1994, while the rate for 15 to 17 year old girls rose from 54.7 to 55.8."

Tennessee. Dept. of Health. "1995 Adolescent Pregnancy Rate Remains Stable." News Release 9 Sep 1996. document-level access: <http://170.142.16.205/cgi-bin/health/news2.pl?filename=/www/wwwroot/health/news/items/preg.txt>

TEENAGE PREGNANCY--UNITED STATES (v26)

"The number of sexually active adolescents has steadily increased in the United States over the past two decades (Creatsas, 1993). More than half of all females aged 15 to 19 have had sexual intercourse (Harlap, Kost, & Darroch Forrest, 1991). As a result, both pregnancy and sexually transmitted diseases (STDs) are at epidemic proportions among this population. For example, 40% of females in the U.S. become pregnant prior to age 17, with approximately 75% of these pregnancies labeled as 'unplanned' (Creatsas, 1993). In New York State, nearly 9% of all females aged 15 to 19 give birth each year (Brown, 1991). Among this age group, pregnancy ends in spontaneous or induced abortion nearly as often as it ends in birth (Harlap et al., 1991)." (p771)

Grimley, Diane M./Lee, Patricia A. "Condom and Other Contraceptive Use among a Random Sample of Female Adolescents: A Snapshot in Time." Adolescence v32 n128 Win 1997. p771-779. (ISSN0001-8449).

"The rate of teenage pregnancy in the U.S. is more than twice as high as the rates in England, France, and Canada, almost three times as high as in Sweden, and seven times as high as in the Netherlands (Alan Guttmacher Institute, 1990). Approximately 46% of these pregnancies result in live births, 41% are aborted, and the remainder end in miscarriage or stillbirth (Baber, 1994). Among sexually experienced youth, about 9% of 14-year-olds, 18% of 15- to 17-year-olds, and 22% of 18- to 19-year-olds become pregnant each year (Alan Guttmacher Institute, 1994). More teenage females become mothers than teenage males become fathers. For example, in 1988, 489,000 teenage females became mothers, but only 195,000 adolescent males became fathers. This is because the majority of the males who impregnate teenagers are not teenagers themselves; they are older men (Alan Guttmacher Institute, 1994; Males, 1993)." (p812)

Medora, Nilufer P./von der Hellen, Cheryl. "Romanticism and Self-Esteem among Teen Mothers." Adolescence v32 n128 Win 1997. p811-824. (ISSN0001-8449).

"U.S. teenagers have the highest rate of pregnancy of any industrialized democracy--twice as high as that of England, France, and Canada, and nine times as high as the Netherlands and Japan (Miller & Moore, 1990; Alan Guttmacher Institute, 1994). The rate of births to unmarried teenagers has increased annually from 15.3 per 1,000 females in 1960 to 44.8 in 1991. Each year over one million adolescents become pregnant in the U.S. (Alan Guttmacher Institute, 1994)." (p991)

Bailey, C. Everett/Piercy, Fred P. "Enhancing Ethical Decision Making in Sexuality and AIDS Education." Adolescence v32 n128 Win 1997. p989-998. (ISSN0001-8449).

"Every year approximately 1 million teenagers in...[the U.S.] become pregnant and 90 percent of those pregnancies are unintended. The teen pregnancy rate for women under 20 has increased by more than 20 percent since the early 1970's. Of the 1 million teens who become pregnant, about half give birth, about 40 percent choose abortion, and the remaining 10 percent miscarry. There are significant social and economic costs associated with premature parenthood for the child, the parent, and for society at large. Fewer than 60 percent of teen mothers graduate from high school by age 25--compared to 90 percent of those who postpone childbearing. According to one study, early childbearing reduced schooling by 1 to 3 years....In addition to the personal and societal costs of teen pregnancy the economic costs are terrific, totalling more than $20 billion each year. This amount could be halved if childbearing were postponed until the mother was age 20." (pH7037)

Jackson-Lee, Sheila (Sen.-Tex.). "Departments of Labor, Health and Human Services, And Education...Appropriations Act, 1998." Congressional Record. Daily ed. v143 n118 9 Sep 1997. pH7023-7084. section/page-level access: <http://thomas.loc.gov/cgi-bin/query/R?r105:FLD001:H07036:> (ISSN0363-7239). (X1.1A.105/1).

In the U.S., "surveys show 85 percent of teen pregnancies are unintended....Thirty percent of girls under age 15 have babies fathered by males at least 6 years older than they are." (p7 secF)

Anstett, Patricia. "Body & Mind: Cover Story: An Unkind World for Girls." Detroit Free Press 16 Dec 1997. p6-8 secF.

"Each year, approximately one million pregnancies occur among American teenagers aged 15-19. And about 200,000 teens aged 17 and younger have children....About 80 percent of the children born to unmarried teenagers who dropped out of high school are poor. In contrast, just 8 percent of children born to married high school graduates aged 20 or older are poor....After rising steadily from 1986 to 1991, the birth rate for teens aged 15-19 declined for the fourth straight year in 1995, from a high of 62.1 per 1,000 teens aged 15-19 in 1991 to 56.8 in 1995. The decline was nine percent between 1991 and 1995 and four percent from 1994 to 1995. Thirty-seven states had a sustained decline in their teen birth rates between 1991 and 1994, and 10 of these states had declines of more than 10 percent over this period. In addition, from 1991 to 1992, the pregnancy rate for 15-19 year-olds fell three percent."

U.S. Dept. of Health and Human Services. "Preventing Teenage Pregnancy." Fact Sheet 12 Jun 1997. document-level access: <http://www.hhs.gov/news/press/1997pres/970612b.html>

In the U.S., "the birth rate for teenagers declined 4 percent from 1994 to 1995. The decline in birth rates was noted for young teenagers 15-17 years and was slightly more pronounced than for those teenagers 18-19 years. Although declines were observed for all racial and Hispanic origin groups, the largest decline--8 percent overall--was reported for black teenagers. Teenage birth rates are highest for Mexican American, Puerto Rican, and black women."

U.S. National Center for Health Statistics. "1995 Birth Statistics Released." Fact Sheet 10 Jun 1997. document-level access: <http://www.cdc.gov/nchswww/releases/97facts/97sheets/95natrel.htm>

According to the CDC's 1996 Vital Statistic Report, in the U.S., "the teen birth rate for 15-19 year-olds dropped 4 percent in 1996, from 56.8 to 54.7. The teen birth rate has declined by 12 percent since 1991. In 1996, the birth rate for teens ages 15-

17 dropped 6 percent while the rate for 18-19 year-olds dropped 3 percent. Among black teens 15-17 years of age, the rate fell 7 percent between 1995 and 1996 and 23 percent between 1991 and 1996."

U.S. Dept. of Health and Human Services. "Vital Statistics Report Shows Significant Gains in Health." Press Release 11 Sep 1997. document-level access: <http://www.hhs.gov/news/press/1997pres/970911a.html>

"About one in eight births in the United States in 1994, or about 505,000 out of 4 million, was to a teenager 15 to 19, according to AMERICAN DEMOGRAPHICS. The teen birth rate in 1994 was 58.9 per 1,000, and preliminary data indicate that it declined to 56.9 in 1995...." (p13)

"Stateline: Birthrate Down for Teenage Mothers." State Legislatures v23 n7 Jul-Aug 1997. p13. (ISSN0147-6041).

One million U.S. teens become "pregnant every year, and 13 percent of all American babies [are] born to teens...." (p1)

"80 percent of teens who have a child become pregnant again, and 25 percent have a second child within two years...." (p9)

Tyson, Ann Scott. "Latest Watchword in Preventing Teen Pregnancy: 'No.'" The Christian Science Monitor v89 n190 26 Aug 1997. p1,9. The Christian Science Monitor search engine: <http://www.csmonitor.com/plweb-cgi/iops1.pl> To retrieve this article, enter the following search: ED=19970826 AND teen. In the "retrieved list," click the title that matches this record. (ISSN0882-7729).

TEENAGE PREGNANCY--UNITED STATES--COSTS

A "report by the Alan Guttmacher Institute (1994) noted that 60% of [U.S.] teenagers who became mothers were living in poverty at the time they gave birth. It was also reported that in 1988, low-income females accounted for 83% of those aged 15-19 who gave birth. This report stated that 60% of adolescents who gave birth for the first time had their delivery fees paid by public funds, usually Medicaid (in California, MediCal)....The Centers for Disease Control and Prevention (1995) reported that from 1985 to 1990, public costs for families started by teen mothers was $120.3 billion. This amount accounted only for Aid to Families with Dependent Children (AFDC), Medicaid/MediCal, and food stamps. It did not include government expenditures on WIC [Women, Infants, and Children supplemental food program], job training, housing subsidies, subsidized school meals, special educational programs, or day-care and foster-care programs for teen mothers and their children." (p812)

Medora, Nilufer P./von der Hellen, Cheryl. "Romanticism and Self-Esteem among Teen Mothers." Adolescence v32 n128 Win 1997. p811-824. (ISSN0001-8449).

Senator Arlen Spector noted in 1995 "that 'society spends an estimated $34 billion on behalf of [U.S.] families in which the first birth occurred when the mother was a teenager....'...A finding stated in PRWORA [Personal Responsibility and Work Opportunity Reconciliation Act of 1996] is, 'Between 1985 and 1990, the public cost of births to teenage mothers under the aid to families with dependent children program, the food stamp program and the medicaid program has been estimated at $120,000,000,000.'...[A summary report released at a White House Press Conference by the Robin Hood Foundation] claimed enormous social costs resulting from teenage childbearing (ranging from 6.9 to 29 billion dollars per year)." (p416-417)

Geronimus, Arline T. "Teenage Childbearing and Personal Responsibility: An Alternative View." Political Science Quarterly v112 n3 Fall 1997. p405-430. (ISSN0032-3195).

TEENAGE PREGNANCY--UNITED STATES--MINORITIES

"One in five African-American teenagers and one in six Latina teenagers become pregnant each year....Over 46 percent of sexually active [Native-American] males, and 42 percent of sexually active [Native-American] females worry about pregnancy. Among Native-American mothers, 41 percent had their first child before the age of 20 as compared to 23 percent of all mothers in the United States." (p16)

"Fact Sheet: Sexuality and Underserved Youth in Communities of Color." SIECUS Report v25 n5 Jun-Jul 1997. p15-16. (ISSN0091-3995).

TEENAGERS

see also BRAND NAME PRODUCTS--UNITED STATES--TEENAGERS; COMPUTERS--UNITED STATES--TEENAGERS; RACE RELATIONS--UNITED STATES--TEENAGERS; SEXUAL HARASSMENT OF WOMEN--UNITED STATES--TEENAGERS; TECHNOLOGY--UNITED STATES--TEENAGERS; TELEVISION AND TEENAGERS; TRAFFIC ACCIDENTS--MICHIGAN--TEENAGERS; TRAFFIC ACCIDENTS--UNITED STATES--TEENAGERS

TEENAGERS--MICHIGAN--ANN ARBOR--DRUG USE

In Michigan, statistics for Ann Arbor teen-age drug use are higher than the national average "in some areas, according to a survey of local high schools done in 1995 by the Kercher Center for Social Research at Western Michigan University. About 6.3 percent of Ann Arbor 12th-graders said they used marijuana on a daily basis, compared to 3.6 percent of the national sample. Local seniors who said they have had five or more drinks in a row--considered binge drinking--in the past two weeks totaled 32 percent, compared to 28 percent nationally. And about 55 percent of Ann Arbor seniors said they had used an illicit drug, compared with 36 percent nationally." (p1,10 secA)

Rzepka, Marianne. "Teens & Drugs: Easy Access, Rising Use: Marijuana, Alcohol, Cigarettes Drugs of Choice for Local Teens." Ypsilanti Press 19 Oct 1997. p1,10 secA.

TEENAGERS--MICHIGAN--ANN ARBOR--SUBSTANCE USE

In the U.S., "daily use of marijuana among high school seniors jumped from a low of 1.9 percent in 1992 to the current 4.9 percent, according to...'Monitoring the Future,' a national study ongoing since 1975....Statistics for Ann Arbor [Michigan] teenagers are even higher in some areas, according to a survey of local high schools done by the Kercher Center for Social Research at Western Michigan University. About 6.3 percent of Ann Arbor 12th-graders said they used marijuana on a daily basis, compared to 3.6 of the national sample. Seniors who said they had five or more drinks in a row--considered binge drinking--in the past two weeks totaled 32 percent, compared to 28 percent nationally." (p1 secC)

Rzepka, Marianne. "Local: Teens & Drugs: Groups Take Aim at Teens' Drug, Alcohol Abuse." Ann Arbor News 12 Oct 1997. p1,4 secC.

TEENAGERS--UNITED STATES--ALCOHOL USE (v26)

TEENAGERS--UNITED STATES--DRUG USE

In the U.S., in 1997, the National Center on Addiction and Substance Abuse at Columbia University found that "among teens who report no other problem behaviors, those who drank and smoked cigarettes at least once in the past month are 30 times more likely to smoke marijuana than those who didn't. Among teens with no ther problem behaviors, those who used cigarettes, alcohol and marijuana at least once in the past month are almost 17 times likelier to use another drug like cocaine, heroin or acid." (p9 secC)

Califano, Joseph A. "Other Voices: Sharp Edges of Smoking Pot Undermine 'Soft-Drug' Status." Ann Arbor News 19 Oct 1997. p9 secC.

In the U.S., in 1996, teen-age drug use declined "nationwide for the first time in five years. The rate of illicit drug use among teens ages 12-17 declined to 9 percent in 1996 from 10.9 percent the previous year. The use of marijuana, the most popular drug among that age group, declined to 7.1 percent from

8.2 percent." (p8 secA)
"Election '97: Detroit's Future:...Voter Priorities: THE DETROIT NEWS WWJ 950 Exit Poll:...Issues for City...: Drugs." Detroit News 5 Nov 1997. p8 secA.

In the U.S., "the Monitoring the Future survey, run by University of Michigan social psychologist Lloyd Johnston, has looked at national teen-age drug abuse every year since 1975. Its most recent results show: In some age groups, the percentage of students who reported smoking during the previous month increased 10 percent in one year. Daily use of marijuana among high school seniors jumped from a low of 1.9 percent in 1992 to the current 4.9 percent. Binge drinking is up among eighth-, 10th-, and 12th-graders." (p1 secA)
Rzepka, Marianne. "Teens & Drugs: Easy Access, Rising Use: Marijuana, Alcohol, Cigarettes Drugs of Choice for Local Teens." Ypsilanti Press 19 Oct 1997. p1,10 secA.

TEENAGERS--UNITED STATES--MORTALITY

According to the 1997 KIDS COUNT DATA BOOK, issued by the Annie E. Casey Foundation, "the rate of teen deaths by accident, homicide, and suicide [in the U.S.] rose 10 percent between 1985 and 1994. There were 69 deaths per 100,000 teens ages 15 to 19 in 1994, compared to 63 in 1985. Between 1985 and 1994, a decline in teen deaths due to accidents was offset by a doubling in the number of homicides. The number of teen deaths caused by accidents went from 8,202 in 1985 to 6,565 in 1994, while the number of teen homicides went from 1,602 to 3,569 during the same period. The number of teen suicides increased slightly during the period, from 1,849 to 1,948." (p3)
"Report Gauges U.S. Child Welfare." Population Today v25 n6 Jun 1997. p3. (ISSN0749-2448).

TEENAGERS--UNITED STATES--SEXUAL BEHAVIOR

In 1997, a study of U.S. teenagers found that "over half the sample (52%; 121 of 235) had 'ever' engaged in vaginal intercourse, 80% (97) of whom reported having vaginal sex within the last 6 months. Over a third (36%) reported three or more sex partners since becoming sexually active (mean=2). Average age at onset of sexual activity was 15 years. Six percent had been pregnant--all pregnancies were reported as being 'unintended.'" (p774) "Only 15% (15) of the sexually active females reported having intercourse with someone other than a primary partner...." (p776)
Grimley, Diane M./Lee, Patricia A. "Condom and Other Contraceptive Use among a Random Sample of Female Adolescents: A Snapshot in Time." Adolescence v32 n128 Win 1997. p771-779. (ISSN0001-8449).

"A majority of American teenagers date, over 85 percent have had a boyfriend or girlfriend and have kissed someone romantically, and nearly 80 percent have engaged in deep kissing....More than 50 percent engage in 'petting behaviors.' By the age of 14, more than 50 percent of all boys have touched a girl's breasts, and 25 percent have touched a girl's vulva. By the age of 18, more than 75 percent have engaged in heavy petting. From 25 to 50 percent of teens report that they have experienced fellatio and/or cunnilingus." (p10-11)
Haffner, Debra W. "What's Wrong with Abstinence-Only Sexuality Education Programs?" SIECUS Report v25 n4 Apr-May 1997. p9-13. (ISSN0091-3995).

"More than half of American teenagers in schools have had sexual intercourse. The latest data from the Youth Risk Behavior Surveillance System of the U.S. Centers for Disease Control and Prevention found that 54 percent of high school students had sexual intercourse, a rate virtually unchanged since the study began in 1990. By the time they reach the age of 20, 80 percent of boys and 76 percent of girls have had sexual intercourse." (p11)
Haffner, Debra W. "What's Wrong with Abstinence-Only Sexuality Education Programs?" SIECUS Report v25 n4 Apr-May 1997. p9-13. (ISSN0091-3995).

TEENAGERS--UNITED STATES--SEXUAL BEHAVIOR --ATTITUDES

In 1997, a study of 235 U.S. teenagers found that "of the 114 adolescents who had never engaged in intercourse, almost 18% (20) said they were 'seriously' thinking about having vaginal intercourse within the next 6 months. Level of concern regarding STDs [sexually transmitted diseases] was high--87% of sexually active adolescents (and 86% of those who had never engaged in sexual intercourse) reported that they were 'very' to 'extremely' concerned that they could contract an STD from heterosexual intercourse." (p774)
Grimley, Diane M./Lee, Patricia A. "Condom and Other Contraceptive Use among a Random Sample of Female Adolescents: A Snapshot in Time." Adolescence v32 n128 Win 1997. p771-779. (ISSN0001-8449).

TEENAGERS--UNITED STATES--SOCIAL CONDITIONS (v26)

According to the 1997 KIDS COUNT DATA BOOK, issued by the Annie E. Casey Foundation, "the rate of births to young women ages 15 to 17 climbed 23 percent nationwide between 1985 and 1994. Only eight states improved on this measure....The nation experienced a 70 percent increase in the juvenile violent crime arrest rate between 1985 and 1994....The proportion of 16- to 19-year-olds who are high school dropouts fell from 11 percent in 1985 to 9 percent in 1994. However, the share of dropouts actually rose in eight states between 1985 and 1994, and it was unchanged in eight other states." (p3)
"Report Gauges U.S. Child Welfare." Population Today v25 n6 Jun 1997. p3. (ISSN0749-2448).

TEENAGERS--UNITED STATES--SUBSTANCE USE (v26)

TEENAGERS--UNITED STATES--SUICIDAL BEHAVIOR

"Clinical psychologist Michael Abramsky, whose practice in Birmingham [Michigan] includes treatment of adolescents, said national increases in teen suicides, from 1,849 in 1985 to more than 2,000 last year, don't tell the whole story. For every teen suicide, experts estimate there are 300-350 attempts." (p2 secC)
Daugherty, Jane. "The Metro: Suicide Attempts Shock Roeper." Detroit News 12 Jun 1997. p1,2 secC.

TEETH--CARE AND HYGIENE--UNITED STATES

The November 1993 issue of the JOURNAL OF PUBLIC HEALTH DENTISTRY claims there is "a tooth decay epidemic in the United States even after 50 years of fluoridation in which 60 percent of the population is drinking artificially fluoridated water. Forty-two percent of the average 65-year-olds have no natural teeth at all, 40-year-olds have an average of 30 decays, and 17-year-olds average 11 decays. Fluoride changes the decay rate from .35 per tooth per year to .70 [per] tooth per year according to the large multi-thousand Japanese, Indian and Tucson studies carried out by chemists, and United States studies carried out by the National Institute of Dental Research." (p37)
"Health & Healing: One Doctor's Nutritional Formula...: Prescription for Perfect Teeth." Acres, U.S.A. v27 n11 Nov 1997. p37. (ISSN1076-4968).

TELECOMMUNICATION (v26)

see TELEVISION

TELECOMMUNICATION--FRANCE (v26)

TELECOMMUNICATION--GREAT BRITAIN (v26)

TELECOMMUNICATION--SWEDEN (v26)

TELECOMMUNICATION IN MEDICINE--UNITED STATES --RURAL CONDITIONS (v26)

TELECOMMUTING--UNITED STATES

"About 11 million Americans telecommute, estimates New York-based research group FIND/SVP Inc. That compares with 4 million who worked from home for an outside company in 1990....[According to Robert Moskowitz, president of the American Telecommuting Association,] most telecommuters spend one to three days a week at home. Typical hours: 18 to 19 a week, according to the FIND/SVP survey....Telecommuting isn't meant to last forever, either. Most workers do it for nine to 18 months, until a promotion or change in duties brings them back to the office, says Gildon Gordon, who runs a telecommuting consulting firm in New Jersey....About two-thirds of Fortune 500 firms have employees who telecommute, consultant Gordon estimates." (p1,9)

Coolidge, Shelley Donald. "Business & Money: Workplace: Home Work: Tele-Work Still a Slow Commute." The Christian Science Monitor v89 n223 14 Oct 1997. p1,9. The Christian Science Monitor search engine: <http://www.csmonitor.com/plweb-cgi/iops1.pl> To retrieve this article, enter the following search: ED=19971014 AND commute. In the "retrieved list," click the title that matches this record. (ISSN0882-7729).

TELEMARKETING--UNITED STATES

"One survey, done by Walker Research in 1990, showed that 70 percent of Americans consider telemarketing an invasion of their privacy. To make matters worse, telephone scam artists reap an estimated $40 billion a year from unwary consumers, especially the elderly and the poor, according to the Federal Trade Commission....Telemarketing now employs more than 400,000 people, yielding $435 billion a year in sales. Some analysts predict an annual growth rate of as much as 300 percent....Politicians...rely on telemarketing campaigns to raise money, sway voters, and conduct public opinion polls during elections. During the 1996 presidential campaign, for example, Bill Clinton and Bob Dole each paid nearly $1 million to large commercial telemarketing firms." (p18)

Barney, James R. "Opinion/Essays: It's Dinnertime, And the Phone Starts Ringing." The Christian Science Monitor v89 n219 7 Oct 1997. p18. The Christian Science Monitor search engine: <http://www.csmonitor.com/plweb-cgi/iops1.pl> To retrieve this article, enter the following search: ED=19971007 AND ringing. In the "retrieved list," click the title that matches this record. (ISSN0882-7729).

TELEPHONE (v26)

see also CELLULAR RADIO

"The number of telephone lines in the 48 least-developed countries...is just over 1.5 million. That's about one per cent of the number of lines in the United States, which has less than half the population of those 48 countries. The US has 600 telephone lines for every 1,000 people; Bangladesh has two per 1,000." (p11)

Anderson, Walter Truett. "Cyber-Realities of the Information Age." Choices v6 n3 Jul 1997. p11-15.

TELEPHONE--AFRICA (v26)

TELEPHONE--FRANCE--UNITED STATES (v26)

TELEPHONE--MARYLAND--EMERGENCY REPORTING SYSTEMS

In Maryland, "in October 1996, the Baltimore City Police Department, aided by a $350,000 award from the COPS office, established a new telephone line for non-emergency calls. This 311 line is staffed by limited duty officers specifically trained to handle both emergency and non-emergency calls, and citizen understanding of the differences between the 311 and 911 lines has been heightened by an intensive public awareness campaign....As a result of the implementation of the new 311 number, emergency calls to 911 have decreased by 25 percent, leaving Baltimore's police with more time to address in an expeditious manner true emergencies. In fact, statistics show that 911 operators now answer the phone on an average of 2 seconds, as compared to 6.5 seconds before the 311 line was set up, and that 80 percent fewer callers to 911 receive a message asking them not to hang up....Moreover, the reduction in 911 calls has allowed Baltimore's police to spend more time patrolling their beats, a consequence of which has been a declining crime rate in the city of 15 percent in fiscal year 1997, as opposed to an 11 percent decline in fiscal year 1996. These and other statistics appear in an October 2 NEW YORK TIMES article entitled 'Baltimore Cites Success with Alternative to 911.'..." (pS10442)

Sarbanes, Paul S. (Sen.-Md.). "Baltimore's 311 Initiative." Congressional Record. Daily ed. v143 n137 6 Oct 1997. pS10442-10443. section/page-level access: <http://thomas.loc.gov/cgi-bin/query/R?r105:FLD001:S10442:> (ISSN0363-7239). (X1.1A.105/1).

TELEPHONE--MICHIGAN--DETROIT--EMERGENCY REPORTING SYSTEMS

Detroit, Michigan "911 operators handle twice as many calls as others across the nation...City Councilwoman Kay Everett says....The city has 57 operators and nine civilian supervisors. The operators handle about 1.8 million calls a year, averaging more than 10 calls an hour. In contrast, Boston uses 130 operators to field 800,000 calls, and Chicago uses 444 to handle about 3.4 million....The 911 operators accounted for $700,000 in overtime last year, but police officials decided not to expand staffing....About 60 percent of all 911 calls are for matters such as a cat stuck in a tree, weather questions and medical situations not warranting an ambulance." (p3 secC)

Esparza, Santiago. "City & Suburban News: In Detroit: Everett: 911 in State of Emergency." Detroit News 22 Sep 1997. p3 secC.

TELEPHONE--MICHIGAN--EMERGENCY REPORTING SYSTEMS

In Michigan, "an audit showing more than 190,000 errors in the state's 911 emergency phone number database has confirmed serious shortcomings in the Ameritech-managed system, critics say. The audit showed that 2.7 percent of the 7.1 million numbers in the 911 database were faulty, according to a report Ameritech filed...with the state's Public Service Commission. Ameritech had estimated that only 0.2 percent of the data was erroneous." (p3 secA)

McDiarmid, Hugh, Jr. "Second Front Page: 911 Audit Finds Logs Flawed: Ameritech Reports 190,000 Errors." Detroit Free Press 13 Dec 1997. p3 secA.

TELEPHONE--UNITED STATES (v26)

TELEPHONE--UNITED STATES--LONG DISTANCE --COSTS

"Americans are spending roughly $2 billion more annually than they should for long-distance phone calls, mainly because about 56 million households have never bothered to secure a discounted calling plan, according to a study just released by the United Homeowners' Association....Admittedly, the vast majority of people who pay basic rates--about 50.5 million of the 56 million basic rate payers--are low-volume users--people who spend less than $25 per month on long-distance. Nonetheless, by simply making a phone call, each of these families could save anywhere from $30 to $75 per year." (p1 secB)

Kristof, Kathy. "Business: Consumers Throw $2 Billion down Drain on Too-Pricey Long-Distance Calls." Detroit News 15 Jul 1997. p1 secB.

TELEPHONE--UNIVERSITY OF MICHIGAN (v26)

TELEPHONE--WALES (v26)

TELEPHONE, CELLULAR

see CELLULAR RADIO

TELEPHONE COMPANIES--UNITED STATES

Slamming is "the practice of changing a telephone customer's long-distance carrier without the customer's knowledge or consent. Slamming is the [U.S.] Federal Communications Commission's largest source of consumer complaints. In 1995, more than a third of the consumer complaints filed with the FCC's Common Carrier Bureau involved slamming. Last year, 16,000 long-distance telephone consumers filed slamming complaints with the FCC. Since 1994, the number of slamming complaints has tripled....THE LOS ANGELES TIMES reports that more than 1 million American telephone consumers have been slammed in the last 2 years." (pS8602-8603)

Durbin, Richard J. (Sen.-Ill.). "Workplace Religious Freedom Act." Congressional Record. Daily ed. v143 n111 31 Jul 1997. pS8590-8607. section/page-level access: <http://thomas.loc.gov/cgi-bin/query/R?r105:FLD001:S08602:> (ISSN0363-7239). (X1.1A.105/1).

TELEPHONE SEX--UNITED STATES (v26)

TELESCOPES--BRITISH COLUMBIA--VICTORIA

Developed by National Research Council observatory scientists in Victoria, "the Adaptive Optics Bonnette (AOB) system uses computer technology and a flexible mirror to correct--at an amazing 1,000 times per second--the distortion created as light passes through the earth's atmosphere. It would allow a telescope viewer to clearly see a car's headlights from some 4,000 kilometres away compared to 800 kilometres without the AOB." (p18)

Lamont, Colin. "Geo Watch: Twinkle Twinkle Littler Star." Canadian Geographic v117 n5 Sep-Oct 1997. p18. (ISSN0008-3658).

TELEVISION

see also PUBLIC TELEVISION; SEX IN TELEVISION

TELEVISION--CHINA

According to a Gallup survey, "some 89% of Chinese homes now have television sets, and for the first time, color television sets are now more widely owned than black and white sets (56% vs. 46%). Even in rural China, a television set has become a standard household possession (83%)."

Gallup Organization. "1997 Survey: The People's Republic of China: Consumer Attitudes & Lifestyle Trends." Press Release 27 Oct 1997. document-level access: <http://www.gallup.com/poll/special/china/chinarel.html>

TELEVISION--EUROPE (v26)

TELEVISION--GREAT BRITAIN--COSTS (v26)

TELEVISION--HISPANIC AMERICANS--ATTITUDES (v26)

TELEVISION--ISRAEL

In Israel, "virtually every home (94%) has a television set, and the modal viewing time is 2 to 3 hours....[In 1990,] one third of the leisure time of adult Israelis was spent viewing television. Of the 5 hours of leisure time on working days, an average of 1.7 hours went to viewing television; of the 14.1 hours of leisure time on the two days of the weekend, 4.3 hours went to viewing television." (p6) In 1990, among television offerings "viewers ranked information highest (43%), tied for first place with entertainment (43%)." (p7)

Katz, Elihu/Haas, Hadassah/Gurevitch, Michael. "20 Years of Television in Israel: Are There Long-Run Effects on Values, Social Connectedness, And Cultural Practices?" Journal of Communication v47 n2 Spr 1997. p3-20. (ISSN0021-9916).

TELEVISION--UNITED STATES

In the U.S., "the people who use the Internet most heavily are not the biggest TV watchers. Those with at least a year of online experience watch about 11.5 hours of TV a week, compared with 14.5 hours for the general public, according to Crestwood Associates of Kirkland, Washington....Interest in a TV that also acts as a computer is reasonably high; 45 percent of a random sample of adults say they might buy one, finds Aragon Consulting Group of St. Louis. On the other hand, 45 percent say it's not likely. (The remaining 10 percent are neutral, undecided, or refused to answer the question.)" (p32-33)

Crispell, Diane. "Kaleidoscope: The Internet on TV." American Demographics v19 n5 May 1997. p32-33. article-level access: <http://www.demographics.com/Publications/AD/97_ad/9705_ad/AD970522.htm> (ISSN0163-4089).

In the U.S., television "viewership, which draws advertising dollars, has been in a free fall at CBS, NBC, and ABC. Fifteen years ago, they snared 80 percent of the prime-time audience. By the 1996-1997 season, that figure had fallen to 49 percent, the first time networks captured less than half the total viewers." (p4)

Gaouette, Nicole. "United States: Behind Networks' Concern over TV Ratings: Ad Dollars." The Christian Science Monitor v89 n149 27 Jun 1997. p1,4. The Christian Science Monitor search engine: <http://www.csmonitor.com/plweb-cgi/iops1.pl> To retrieve this article, enter the following search: ED=19970627 AND dollars. In the "retrieved list," click the title that matches this record. (ISSN0882-7729).

TELEVISION--UNITED STATES--PUBLIC OPINION (v26)

TELEVISION, PUBLIC

see PUBLIC TELEVISION

TELEVISION ADVERTISING--CENSORSHIP--UNITED STATES

In a survey of U.S. members of Investigative Reporters and Editors employed at commercial television stations, "two questions addressed the issue of self-censorship. Asked whether there had been 'pressure from within your stations to not produce news stories that advertisers might find objectionable,' 59 percent of respondents said there had been." (p12) "As for whether there had 'been pressure from within your station to produce news stories to please advertisers,' 56 percent of respondents reported that there was....As for the sources of internal pressure, 35 reporters specifically mentioned the sales manager or sales department as being the source of pressure, 23 mentioned the general manager or 'management,' and nine mentioned the news director." (p13)

Soley, Lawrence. "Special Section: 'The Power of the Press Has a Price.'" Extra! v10 n4 Jul-Aug 1997. p11-13.

TELEVISION ADVERTISING--UNITED STATES

In the U.S., of 241 questionnaires about advertiser pressures sent to members of Investigative Reporters and Editors employed at commercial television stations, "just under 50 percent of the questionnaires sent out were completed and returned. Nearly three-quarters of the respondents reported that advertisers had 'tried to influence the content' of news at their stations." (p11) "More than two-thirds reported that advertisers threatened to withdraw their advertising because of the content of news stories. Forty-four percent of the respondents reported that advertisers had 'actually withdrawn advertising because of the content of a news report.' The responses of reporters at large and small market stations did not differ. For example, 75 percent of the respondents at large market stations reported that advertisers had 'tried to influence the content' of news stories, compared to 74 percent of respondents at small market stations. As for whether advertisers had actually 'withdrawn advertising because of the content of a news report,' 44 percent of reporters at stations in both large and small markets responded affirmatively....Questioned whether advertisers 'succeeded in influencing a news report at your station,' nearly as many said their stations had capitulated (40 percent) as had withstood the pressure (43 percent)." (p12)

Soley, Lawrence. "Special Section: 'The Power of the Press Has a Price.'" Extra! v10 n4 Jul-Aug 1997. p11-13.

TELEVISION ADVERTISING--UNITED STATES --COSTS (v26)

TELEVISION AND SEX
see SEX IN TELEVISION
TELEVISION AND TEENAGERS--UNITED STATES
In the U.S., "teens watch an average of four to six hours of TV a day, [Harvard Medical School specialist in adolescent gynecology, Dr. Anne] Davis says, citing one survey. That exposes them to 14,000 instances of sexual behavior, of which only 165 showed any negative consequence, she says." (p6 secF)
Anstett, Patricia. "Body & Mind: Cover Story: An Unkind World for Girls." Detroit Free Press 16 Dec 1997. p6-8 secF.
TELEVISION BROADCASTING
see PUBLIC TELEVISION
TELEVISION BROADCASTING--UNITED STATES (v26)
TELEVISION BROADCASTING OF NEWS--UNITED STATES (v26)
TELEVISION IN EDUCATION--UNITED STATES (v26)
TELEVISION IN POLITICS--UNITED STATES (v26)
TELEVISION SUPPLIES INDUSTRY--MEXICO --TIJUANA (v26)
TELEVISION VIEWERS--FRANCE
In France, "in the first four months of 1997, more than 1 million people here stopped watching television....Most of the 1.28 million TV deserters are urbanites, according to Mediametrie....These rebels represent a small portion of France's 59 million potential viewers...." (p1,8)
Gaouette, Nicole. "International: Sets Go Dark: French Turn Off the Tube." The Christian Science Monitor v89 n238 4 Nov 1997. p1,8. The Christian Science Monitor search engine: <http://www.csmonitor.com/plweb-cgi/iops1.pl> To retrieve this article, enter the following search: ED=19971104 AND tube. In the "retrieved list," click the title that matches this record. (ISSN0882-7729).
TELEVISION VIEWERS--UNITED STATES (v26)
TELLERS, AUTOMATED
see AUTOMATED TELLERS
TEMPERATURE CHANGES, GLOBAL
see GLOBAL TEMPERATURE CHANGES
TEMPORARY EMPLOYMENT--CALIFORNIA--SANTA CLARA COUNTY
"According to data developed by Michael Neidle at Optimal Management, a management consulting firm in San Mateo, manufacturing companies and service sector companies account for 61.2 per cent of all billable hours of THS [temporary help services] in Santa Clara County [California]. Manufacturing alone accounts for 30.2 per cent of the THS market in Santa Clara County, a rate that is nearly twice the California-wide average...." (p41-42)
Carnoy, Martin/Castells, Manuel/Benner, Chris. "Labour Markets and Employment Practices in the Age of Flexibility: A Case Study of Silicon Valley." International Labour Review v136 n1 Spr 1997. p27-48. (ISSN0020-7780).
In Santa Clara County, California, "since 1984, employment in THS [temporary help services] agencies has grown from a yearly average of 12,340 to 28,060, i.e. from 1.6 to 3.4 per cent of the county's total employment....This rate is roughly three times the national average. In the past 11 years, employment with THS agencies in the county has grown 127 per cent while total employment has only grown 7.5 per cent. Between 1990 and 1995 employment in THS agencies grew by 70 per cent while overall employment was stagnant." (p34)
Carnoy, Martin/Castells, Manuel/Benner, Chris. "Labour Markets and Employment Practices in the Age of Flexibility: A Case Study of Silicon Valley." International Labour Review v136 n1 Spr 1997. p27-48. (ISSN0020-7780).
TEMPORARY EMPLOYMENT--EUROPE (v26)
"In the EU, 9.3 per cent of total employment is under temporary contract. This means that temporary jobs are a substantially less widespread phenomenon than is part-time work, which accounts for 15 per cent of total employment....Belgium has the smallest proportion of workers on temporary contracts (4 per cent), and Spain has the largest (24.1 per cent). Portugal, which has the second highest proportion, has just 11.9 per cent....The majority of temporary employment (63 per cent) is low-skilled occupations." (p55) In the EU, "in the period 1983-91, the average proportion of workers on a temporary contract increased by 5.4 percentage points....In Spain the proportion of temporary employment increased by 13.2 percentage points due to the relaxation of restrictions on fixed-term contracts in that country (Meulders, Plasman and Plasman, 1994)....In more recent years the incidence of temporary employment continued to increase...with only 1.1 percentage point gained in the period 1991-95....There are also strongly opposing tendencies between various member States, with large increases in the Netherlands, Spain and France (3.7, 2.8, and 2.1 percentage points, respectively) and sharp decreases in Portugal and Greece (6.4 and 4.5 percentage points, respectively)." (p57)
DeGrip, Andries/Hoevenberg, Jeroen/Willems, Ed. "Atypical Employment in the European Union." International Labour Review v136 n1 Spr 1997. p49-71. (ISSN0020-7780).
"The total number of Europeans out of work remains above 18 million, or around 11 percent, more than double the American rate of 4.7 percent. And yet, without state aid, Europe is creating jobs: temporary jobs. As many as 1.2 million people in the European Union countries now earn a living through a temporary agency. And the figure is expected to double in the next seven years." (p1) "In the Netherlands...more than 3 percent of the working population are temps, about twice the American rate. Dutch unemployment is among Europe's lowest--about 6 percent....At first, most temps were women, employed mainly as secretaries. Not anymore. Two thirds of temps today are men....More than 10 percent of temps are university graduates, says Jean-Claude Daoust, president of the European Federation of Temporary Work." (p8)
Echikson, William. "International: Rule-Heavy Europe Goes Temp." The Christian Science Monitor v90 n1 25 Nov 1997. p1,8. The Christian Science Monitor search engine: <http://www.csmonitor.com/plweb-cgi/iops1.pl> To retrieve this article, enter the following search: ED=19971125 AND temp. In the "retrieved list," click the title that matches this record. (ISSN0882-7729).
TEMPORARY EMPLOYMENT--MICHIGAN (v26)
TEMPORARY EMPLOYMENT--UNITED STATES (v26)
In the U.S., "more than 2.3 million temporary workers were employed on an average day in the first quarter of 1997, an increase of 10 percent over the first quarter of 1996, according to the National Association of Temporary and Staffing Services....Total wages paid to temps in professional fields such as accounting, law, and management leapt 60 percent between the first quarters of 1996 and 1997....Office and clerical workers remain the largest share of the temp payroll, but just barely. Their share of wages stood at 35 percent in the first quarter of 1997, down from 48 percent in 1991. Workers in industrial occupations have drawn nearly even with office temps, claiming 34 percent of total wages." (p36)
Heubusch, Kevin. "Kaleidoscope: Temporary Liaisons." American Demographics v19 n11 Nov 1997. p36-37. article-level access: <http://www.demographics.com/publications/ad/97_ad/9711_ad/ad971113.htm> (ISSN0163-4089).
"Some 90 percent of U.S. businesses use temps or contract workers in every industry imaginable, according to temporary agencies. There are some 15,000 staffing firms nationwide and dozens in the Detroit area." (p8 secF) "About 25 percent of

America's temporary workers have been on the same job for a year or more, and 48 percent have not changed jobs in six months, according to the National Association of Temporary and Staffing Services in Washington D.C....According to the national temporary association, an estimated 6 million workers moved from temporary to permanent positions in 1996, more than five million of which were full-time jobs." (p9 secF)

Teegardin, Carol/Rohan, Barry. "Business Monday: Cover Story: One Job at a Time." Detroit Free Press 3 Nov 1997. p8-9 secF.

In the U.S., "in 1989, white-collar jobs accounted for 58 per cent of THS [temporary help services] employment, and blue-collar jobs for 30 per cent. By 1994, white-collar employment had dropped to 49 per cent of the THS total, while blue-collar employment had risen to 40 per cent." (p41)

Carnoy, Martin/Castells, Manuel/Benner, Chris. "Labour Markets and Employment Practices in the Age of Flexibility: A Case Study of Silicon Valley." International Labour Review v136 n1 Spr 1997. p27-48. (ISSN0020-7780).

In the U.S., employment in temporary help services agencies "has grown by 48 per cent since 1989, as compared to growth of approximately 5 per cent in total non-farm employment in the same period (Bureau of Labor Statistics, 1995). Since 1982, employment in THS agencies has tripled, while total employment has grown by only 20 per cent. The Bureau of Labor Statistics (BLS) estimates that between 1975 and 1987, the number of THS companies in the United States grew from 3,133 to 10,611, an increase of 239 per cent. In February 1995, there was a nationwide total of 1,181,000 workers in THS agencies, out of a total employment of 123.2 million. At any given time, THS employment thus accounts for approximately 1 per cent of total employment in the United States." (p34)

Carnoy, Martin/Castells, Manuel/Benner, Chris. "Labour Markets and Employment Practices in the Age of Flexibility: A Case Study of Silicon Valley." International Labour Review v136 n1 Spr 1997. p27-48. (ISSN0020-7780).

In the U.S., temporary jobs "account for just 10 percent of the total growth in jobs since 1992, and just over 2 percent of total employment. All-in-all, according to a BLS [Bureau of Labor Statistics] survey, workers classified as 'contingent'--temp and contract workers with explicitly limited job tenure--accounted for under 5 percent of total employment in 1995." (p25)

Henwood, Doug. "Talking about Work." Monthly Review v49 n3 Jul-Aug 1997. p18-30. (ISSN0027-0520).

TENNESSEE--ECONOMIC CONDITIONS

"Economic losses due to labor shortages totaled only $3.7 million in 1995, or less than 0.2% of Tennessee's gross farm marketings. Eighty-six percent of the economic losses were suffered by operations specializing in one of three commodity groups. The nursery industry accounted for 60% of the reported economic losses, while dairy and tobacco operations each accounted for 13% of the economic losses caused by labor shortages." (p9)

Pompelli, Greg/Danekas, Gene/Allen, Fred. "Ag Laborers--Who's Working Where and for What Wages?" Tennessee Agri Science n182 Spr 1997. p6-10.

TENNESSEE--EMPLOYMENT--MANUFACTURES (v26)

TENNESSEE--HEALTH AND HYGIENE

According to the results of the 1995 Behavioral Risk Factor Surveillance Survey conducted by the Tennessee Department of Health, "almost three-quarters of those surveyed had visited the doctor for a routine checkup within the past year, and more than 90 percent had their blood pressure checked....About 15 percent said they changed their sexual behavior in the past year because of what they knew about HIV....Despite being more health conscious in some areas, the number of Tennesseans who reported being obese surged to the highest level ever, rising from 31.9 percent in 1994 to 35.4 percent in 1995. Ten years ago, the rate was only 22 percent. The percentage of smokers remained stable at 26.5 percent....Although 55 percent of the men had smoked at some time in their lives compared to 38 percent of women, almost half the men had stopped while about two-thirds of the women continued to smoke....Only one percent of respondents reported drinking and driving, 1.5 percent reported chronic drinking (more than 60 drinks a month), and 5.2 percent engaged in binge drinking (five or more drinks on one occasion at least once in the past month)."

Tennessee. Dept. of Health. "Tennesseans Becoming More Health Conscious?" News Release 19 Aug 1996. document-level access: <http://170.142.16.205/cgi-bin/health/news2.pl?filename=/www/wwwroot/health/news/items/brfss.txt>

TENNESSEE VALLEY AUTHORITY (v26)

TENURE OF COLLEGE TEACHERS

see COLLEGE TEACHERS--TENURE

TENURE OF LAND

see LAND TENURE

TERMINAL CARE--UNITED STATES--PUBLIC OPINION (v26)

TERMINATION OF PREGNANCY

see ABORTION

TERMITES--ONTARIO--TORONTO

Toronto's "Housing Department, which took over the termite control program in 1990, estimates that by then a total of 515 city blocks were infested with termites. But lack of funds...meant that of the 27,000 houses at risk of infestation, only about 6,500 were known to be affected and treated....The infestation spread...by an extra 21 blocks over the following year. By 1992, the number of afflicted blocks had increased to 543--18 percent of the city's blocks." (p48-49)

Grady, Wayne. "Toronto's War on Termites." Canadian Geographic v117 n5 Sep-Oct 1997. p46-52. (ISSN0008-3658).

TERRORISM--UNITED STATES

"Bombing attacks have soared in the US in recent years....[Bureau of Alcohol, Tobacco and Firearms] statistics show that criminal explosions and attempted explosions almost tripled in one decade--from 1,103 in 1985 to 3,163 in 1994. The number of pipe-bomb attacks has doubled in the past 10 years." (p3)

Nifong, Christina. "United States: Atlanta's Unsolved Mysteries: Solution May Lie with the Public." The Christian Science Monitor v89 n249 20 Nov 1997. p3. The Christian Science Monitor search engine: <http://www.csmonitor.com/plweb-cgi/iops1.pl> To retrieve this article, enter the following search: ED=19971120 AND public. In the "retrieved list," click the title that matches this record. (ISSN0882-7729).

TEST TUBE BABIES

see FERTILIZATION IN VITRO, HUMAN

TESTS AND MEASUREMENTS IN EDUCATION

see EDUCATIONAL TESTS AND MEASUREMENTS

TESTS OF ACHIEVEMENT AND PROFICIENCY

see also ACHIEVEMENT TESTS

TESTS OF ACHIEVEMENT AND PROFICIENCY--UNITED STATES

"On a recent report card of science and achievement, American fourth, eighth, and 12th graders scored dismally. At each grade level tested for the National Assessment of Educational Progress report, a federal survey, fewer than 30 percent of all students reached the 'proficient' level of understanding. More than 40 percent of the high school seniors who took the test could not meet the minimum academic expectations set." (p20)

"The Monitor's View: Science Needs and Nerds." The Christian Science Monitor v89 n231 24 Oct 1997. p20. The Christian Science Monitor search engine: <http://www.csmonitor.com/plweb-cgi/iops1.pl> To retrieve this article, enter the following search: ED=19971024 AND nerds. In the "retrieved list," click the title that matches this record. (ISSN0882-7729).

TETRACHLORODIBENZODIOXIN--UNITED STATES

In the U.S., "EPA documents show that daily doses of dioxin in the general population are 300-600 times higher than the 'safe' threshold for cancer set by EPA, while breastfeeding children are getting 50 times more than adults. That translates into 15,000-30,000 times the 'safe' threshold. The World Health Organization recently classified dioxin as a Class I known human carcinogen." (p8)

Cohen, Gary. "Comments & Controversies: Why Organized Labor Needs a Coherent Strategy on Chlorinated Chemicals." New Solutions v7 n4 Sum 1997. p6-9. (ISSN1048-2911).

TEXAS--EMPLOYMENT

"According to the Statistical Abstract of the United States for 1996, there were 605,000 unemployed residents in the State of Texas. In the 18th Congressional District in March of this year there were 3,936 people receiving unemployment insurance benefits. During that same month the Texas Workforce Commission recorded 13,167 applicants for jobs and only 1,031 job openings with a total of 304 job placements. In the city of Houston 986,939 people are listed as members of the labor force. The employment totals are 921,636 with an unemployment rate of 65,303. The highest concentration of unemployment are African-American at 29,974, followed by Hispanic unemployment at 17,958, and white unemployment at 15,216. Statewide the Texas Workforce Commission identified 127,295 people receiving unemployment insurance benefits in the month of March. During this same month 442,251 job applicants were received and 38,112 job openings were registered with only 17,037 placements [taking]...place." (pH2808)

Jackson-Lee, Sheila (Rep.-Tex.). "Employment, Training, And Literacy Enhancement Act of 1997." Congressional Record. Daily ed. v143 n65 16 May 1997. pH2797-2851. section/page-level access: <http://thomas.loc.gov/cgi-bin/query/R?r105:FLD001:H02807:> (ISSN0363-7239). (X1.1A.105/1).

TEXAS--SOCIAL CONDITIONS

The 11-county region that Southwest Texas Community College "serves is among the poorest in the country. In 1996 the median family income in the area was $11,550, compared to the statewide average of $21,992. The median income for Hispanics, who make up the majority of the population, was even lower: $9,237. The unemployment rate in Uvalde hovers near 12 percent and is as high as 27 percent in some of the counties along the U.S.-Mexico border. Illiteracy is widespread and the high school dropout rate is almost 50 percent. Over the years, Southwest Texas has experienced a major demographic shift, with low-income Hispanics now making up more than 75 percent of its student body....According to Gloria Rivera, dean of the college's instructional services, more than 50 percent of its entering students need remedial instruction in core subjects like English and mathematics." (p20)

Higuera, Jonathan J. "Going Home, Staying Home." Ford Foundation Report v28 n2 Spr 1997. p19-22. (ISSN1063-7281).

TEXTBOOKS--CALIFORNIA (v26)

TEXTBOOKS--CANADA--COSTS (v26)

TEXTBOOKS--UNITED STATES (v26)

In August 1997, "New York became the fifth of the five largest textbook markets to increase its text budget for the 1997-98 school year. New York, Texas, Florida, Illinois, and California allocated a combined $817.2 million to K-12 textbook purchases for the school year, up 12.2 percent from the previous year. These five states account for at least 40 percent of U.S. instructional materials sales." (p6)

"Two Factors Predict Textbook Sales." Forecast v17 n11 Nov 1997. p6. article-level access: <http://www.demographics.com/publications/fc/97_fc/9711_fc/fc97115.htm> (ISSN0732-1597).

"In 1960, over 100 companies produced the vision of society and history taught in U.S. schools. In 1995, almost 90% of high-school textbook production was subsumed under just seven major media companies, each owned by larger corporations. In 1995, the 'el-hi' (elementary to high school) market generated almost $2 billion in sales. These textbooks comprised 30% of the entire market for books in the U.S." (p69) "The production of a single full-sized textbook may take 5 years and cost up to $2 million." (p70)

Perlmutter, David D. "Manufacturing Visions of Society and History in Textbooks." Journal of Communication v47 n3 Sum 1997. p68-81. (ISSN0021-9916).

TEXTILE INDUSTRY (v26)

see also CLOTHING TRADE; COTTON TRADE; RUG AND CARPET INDUSTRY; SILK INDUSTRY

TEXTILE INDUSTRY--CHINA

"China's total textile exports rose to US$8.7 billion in the first quarter of 1997, an increase of nearly 36 percent over the same period in 1996. The 1.0 percent increase in consumption in 1996/97 and the rise in export value in early 1997 may be attributable in part to the government finally beginning to make good on at least a portion of the 3 years of accumulated export tax rebates (9 percent in 1996) owed to textile exporters." (p43)

Colby, Hunter/U.S. Dept. of Agriculture. Economic Research Service. "China's Cotton Imports Rise despite High Stocks." China: International Agriculture and Trade Reports Situation and Outlook Series Jun 1997. p41-43.

TEXTILE INDUSTRY--TURKEY--UNITED STATES (v26)

THAILAND--ECONOMIC CONDITIONS (v26)

"Thailand's economy weakened to 6.5 percent in 1996 after a decade of more than 8 percent annual GDP growth." (p6) "Thai inflation in 1996 reached 5.9 percent, while the current account deficit fell only slightly to 8 percent of GDP....The Thai stock market lost more than 35 percent of its value between January and December 1996, and fell to a 3-year low." (p7)

Jerardo, Alberto/Huang, Sophia Wu/U.S. Dept. of Agriculture. Economic Research Service. "Regional Overviews: APEC to Resume Healthy Growth." APEC: International Agriculture and Trade Reports Situation and Outlook Series Aug 1997. p6-8.

THEFT, AUTOMOBILE

see AUTOMOBILE THEFT

THEFT, FIREARMS

see FIREARMS THEFT

THEFT FROM MOTOR VEHICLES--MICHIGAN--TROY

Theft from automobiles is a chronic problem in Troy, Michigan, "where 40 percent of the crimes happen in the victims' driveways. Another 36 percent happen while victims are shopping or out dining, and 24 percent occur in workplace parking lots, police Sgt. Michael Kerr said....In 1996, the department investigated 1,181 larcencies from vehicles. Thieves specialized in the following items: tools and sporting goods, 32 percent; cellular phones, 25 percent; radio, CD [compact disc] player, radar detector or tapes, 13 percent; wheel covers and tires, 12 percent; wallets and purses, 11 percent; and air bags, 7 percent....Kerr said 38 percent of people arrested and accused of larceny from a vehicle are caught because of a citizen's call to police about a suspicious person. 'Twenty-five percent of our arrests are by officers on routine patrol who see someone cruising a parking lot...'....'Another 21 percent are caught by our plainclothes officers who target particular areas, and the remaining 16 percent are arrested after police investigations.'...'Last year, Michigan auto insurance companies paid $22.5 million in claims for theft from vehicles....'" (p5 secC)

Ilka, Douglas. "Suburban News: HALT Calls on Public to Help Stop Auto Theft." Detroit News 1 Jul 1997. p5 secA.

THEOLOGICAL STUDENTS

see SEMINARIANS

THEOLOGY, MYSTICAL

see MYSTICISM

THERAPEUTIC SYSTEMS

see ALTERNATIVE MEDICINE

THREATENED ANIMAL SPECIES

see ENDANGERED SPECIES

THREE GORGES DAM (CHINA) (v26)

THYROID GLAND--CANCER--UNITED STATES

"In 1997, an estimated 16,100 Americans will be diagnosed with thyroid cancer and 1,230 will die from the disease. The incidence rate for women is more than twice as high as that for men. Thyroid cancer is highly curable: The 5-year survival rate is about 95 percent....Thyroid cancer is relatively uncommon compared with other forms of cancer, accounting for about 1 percent of all cancers diagnosed in the United States....The number of new cases is about 10 times higher than the number of deaths, estimated at 1,230 in the United States in 1997....Incidence rates for 1994--the most recent year available--were 7.6 per 100,000 U.S. women of all ages combined, and 2.8 per 100,000 U.S. men. Thyroid cancer mortality rates for that year were 0.3 per 100,000 for both men and women. Lifetime risk for thyroid cancer is estimated at 0.66 percent for women (about 1 in 152) and 0.27 percent for men (about 1 in 370)."

U.S. National Institutes of Health. "NCI Releases Results of Nationwide Study of Radioactive Fallout from Nuclear Tests." News Release 1 Aug 1997. document-level access: <http://www.nih.gov/news/pr/aug97/nci-01.htm>

THYROID GLAND--DISEASES--UNITED STATES

"Malfunction of the thyroid gland is quite common, affecting an estimated 13 million Americans. Women are hit by thyroid disease about five times as often as men, and the incidence of thyroid disease increases with increasing age. The two most common forms of thyroid dysfunction, Hashimoto's disease and Graves' disease, are referred to as autoimmune disorders." (p10)

Kemp, Nancy. "Endocrinology: Should You Get Tested for Thyroid Disease?" Healthline v16 n7 Jul 1997. p10-11. (ISSN0736-7929).

TIBET (CHINA) (v26)

TIGERS

"Of the eight tiger subspecies that were recognized as endangered in 1969 by the IUCN [International Union for Conservation of Nature and Natural Resources]-World Conservation Union, three ('Panthera tigris vigata,' 'P. t. sondaica,' and 'P. t. balica') are now extinct, and one ('P. t. amoyensis,' the South China tiger) is critically endangered, with fewer than 80 individuals remaining in the wild (...Jackson 1993)....Fewer than 400 Siberian tigers ('P. t. altaica') exist in isolated pockets of eastern Russia, northeast China, and North Korea (Jackson 1993). Fewer than 500 wild Sumatran tigers ('P. t. sumatrae') live on Sumatra, largely in five fragmented protected areas (Tilson and Brady 1992). Approximately 250 tigers are needed in a population to sustain adequate genetic diversity, which is defined as 90% of the current gene variation for the next 100 years (Foose 1987). But achieving this target for tigers in nature would require a habitat free of human disruption that is at least 25,000-50,000 km2 [kilometers squared] (Foose 1987), or approximately the combined areas of Maryland and New Jersey." (p689)

Wildt, David E./Rall, William F./Critser, John K./Monfort, Steven L./Seal, Ulysses S. "Genome Resource Banks." BioScience v47 n10 Nov 1997. p689-698. (ISSN0006-3568).

TIGERS--INDIA

"Sixty percent of the world's tigers are found in India. The Indian government estimates that fewer than 3,750 Royal Bengal tigers remain. The IUCN [International Union for Conservation of Nature and Natural Resources] Cat Specialist Group (CSG) places the number at 3,000. The Tiger Trust fears that only 2,500 Royal Bengal tigers survive. The CSG believes that poachers kill 300-400 tigers annually...." (p15)

"World News: A World without Tigers?" Earth Island Journal v12 n4 Fall 1997. p15. (ISSN1041-0406).

TILAPIA--UNITED STATES (v26)

In the U.S., "in first-half 1997, tilapia imports increased 34 percent from first-half 1996....The value of tilapia imports rose only 21 percent to $24.6 million, as average prices fell a dime to 99 cents a pound. Average prices vary considerably among the three product categories: Whole frozen fish averaged only 64 cents a pound, while fresh fillets were $2.21, and frozen fillets were $2.05 a pound. On a liveweight equivalent basis, the United States now uses approximately 90 to 100 million pounds of tilapia per year. In first-half 1997, U.S. tilapia imports on a liveweight basis were just over 38 million pounds, up 10 million from the same period in 1996." (unpaginated)

Harvey, Dave/U.S. Dept. of Agriculture. Economic Research Service. "Tilapia Imports Increase 34 Percent." Aquaculture Outlook 3 Oct 1997.

TIMBER--UNITED STATES (v26)

In the U.S., "Federal timber sales have declined precipitously, primarily from limitations placed on the Forest Service by environmental considerations and species protection efforts for spotted owls, marbled murrelets, and various species of salmon. In 1987, the timber sales program provided nearly 12 billion board feet of timber. Ten years later, less than 4 billion board feet were sold....Small businesses account for two-thirds of all timber harvested in national forests." (pS9457)

Burns, Conrad R. (Sen.-Mont.). "Department of the Interior and Related Agencies Appropriations Act, 1998." Congressional Record. Daily ed. v143 n124 17 Sep 1997. pS9450-9485. section/page-level access: <http://thomas.loc.gov/cgi-bin/query/R?r105:FLD001:S09457:> (ISSN0363-7239). (X1.1A.105/1).

TINIAN (NORTHERN MARIANA ISLANDS)

"Tinian is one of the 15 islands in the Marianas Islands Archipelago. The northern 14 islands form the Commonwealth of the Northern Mariana Islands (CNMI), which is politically affiliated with the United States, while Guam, the southernmost island, is a U.S. territory. Tinian is a small island, only 20 kilometers (12 miles) long and 8 km (5 miles) at maximum, but it is the second largest island in the CNMI. Nearly the entire population of Tinian, or approximately 2,000 people, live in San Jose Village on the southwest coast. The northern two-thirds is leased to the U.S. Navy from the CNMI government." (p10)

Balis-Larsen, Martha/Sutterfield, Tim/U.S. Dept. of the Interior. Fish and Wildlife Service. "Navy Protects Island Monarch." Endangered Species Bulletin v22 n3 May-Jun 1997. p10-11.

TIPPING--UNITED STATES--PUBLIC OPINION (v26)

TIREDNESS

see FATIGUE

TIRES, RUBBER--UNITED STATES (v26)

TIRES, RUBBER--WASTE DISPOSAL--UNITED STATES (v26)

TISSUE DONATION

see DONATION OF ORGANS, TISSUES, ETC.

TISSUE TRANSPLANTATION

see TRANSPLANTATION OF ORGANS, TISSUES, ETC.

TOADSTOOLS

see MUSHROOM INDUSTRY

TOBACCO--DISEASES AND PESTS--CONTROL --UNITED STATES (v26)

TOBACCO--TOXICOLOGY--UNITED STATES (v26)

TOBACCO HABIT

see also CHILDREN--TOBACCO USE; CIGAR HABIT; CIGARETTE HABIT; PREGNANT WOMEN--UNITED STATES--TOBACCO USE; UNITED STATES--ARMED FORCES--TOBACCO USE; WOMEN--TOBACCO USE; YOUTH--COLORADO--TOBACCO USE; YOUTH--HAWAII--TOBACCO USE; YOUTH--MICHIGAN--OAKLAND COUNTY--TOBACCO USE; YOUTH--UNITED STATES--TOBACCO USE

TOBACCO HABIT--CANADA (v26)

TOBACCO HABIT--COSTS (v26)

"For every 1,000 tons of tobacco produced, nearly 1,000 people will eventually die from tobacco-related illnesses. Worldwide, these illnesses are estimated to cost nearly $200 billion a year in direct health care expenses and lost productivity. One third of this cost--$66 billion--is already borne by developing countries, a total that is expected to skyrocket as smoking in those countries continues to grow." (p19)

McGinn, Anne Platt. "The Nicotine Cartel." World Watch v10 n4 Jul-Aug 1997. p18-27. (ISSN0896-0615).

TOBACCO HABIT--HEALTH ASPECTS (v26)

TOBACCO HABIT--HEALTH ASPECTS--ALABAMA

"More than 7,000 people in Alabama die from tobacco-related illnesses every year. 'These illnesses burden our state with close to $1 billion every year in total health costs,' said Dr. Donald E. Williamson, state health officer....Due to second hand smoke, 4,900 Alabama children may develop lung problems each year. As many as 244 children may be hospitalized each year in Alabama from complications related to secondhand smoke."

Alabama. Dept. of Public Health. "Health Department Opposes Tobacco Use." News Release 15 Apr 1997. document-level access: <http://www.alapubhealth.org/Press/pr041597a.html>

TOBACCO HABIT--HEALTH ASPECTS--COSTS (v26)

TOBACCO HABIT--HEALTH ASPECTS--UNITED STATES

According to Donald E. Williamson, Alabama state health officer, in the U.S., "'children and teenagers nationwide constitute 90 percent of all new smokers, and one-third of new smokers will eventually die of tobacco-related diseases.' Each year the tobacco industry spends an estimated $4 billion on advertising campaigns to recruit new smokers--90 percent of them are children with the average teenage smoker starting smoking at age 13. Tobacco-related diseases are the nation's largest public health problem costing $50 billion in excess health care expenditures. Tobacco usage is the single most preventable cause of death in the U.S. One in six deaths is the direct effect of tobacco. In excess of 87 percent of lung cancer is directly attributable to smoking and 21 percent of all coronary heart disease deaths are smoking-related....Smoking is responsible for 20 to 30 percent of all low weight babies in the U.S., is the principal cause of infant respiratory diseases, and is linked with Sudden Infant Death Syndrome....Workers exposed to second hand smoke are 34 percent more likely to get lung cancer than workers in smoke-free environments."

Alabama. Dept. of Public Health. "Health Department Opposes Tobacco Use." News Release 15 Apr 1997. document-level access: <http://www.alapubhealth.org/Press/pr041597a.html>

TOBACCO HABIT--MORTALITY (v26)

According to the WORLD HEALTH REPORT 1997, "tobacco-related deaths, primarily from lung cancer and circulatory disease, already amount to 3 million a year, or 6% of total deaths. Smoking accounts for one in 7 cancer cases worldwide." (p2)

World Health Organization. "World Health Report 1997." Press Release 5 May 1997. p1-7. document-level access: <http://www.who.ch/whr/1997/presse.htm>

"Each year, tobacco causes about 3.5 million deaths throughout the world and this will increase to 10 million annual deaths during the 2020s, with seven million of these deaths occurring in developing countries. Fifty per cent of these unnecessary deaths are occurring in middle age (35-69), robbing those killed of around 22 years of normal life expectancy....According to WHO's Director-General, the situation is especially worrisome in less developed countries--the home of 80% of the world's population...." (p1)

World Health Organization. "The Smoking Epidemic--'A Fire in the Global Village.'" WHO Press n61 25 Aug 1997. p1-3. document-level access: <http://www.who.ch/press/1997/pr97-61.html>

"Tobacco-caused cancers killed 1.1 million people worldwide in 1993, accounting for one out of every seven cancer deaths....Worldwide, tobacco is expected to more than double the incidence of lung cancer alone by 2020, from 945,000 deaths in 1990 to 2.4 million....Some 90 percent of all smokers have their first cigarette by age 20....On average, smokers who light their first cigarette at age 25 lose about 4 years of life; those who start at age 15 lose 8 years....Richard Peto, an epidemiologist at Oxford University's Imperial Cancer Research Fund, calculated that tobacco killed 3 million people in 1995, 1 million of whom lived in developing countries. By 2025, Peto estimates, tobacco's annual death toll will reach at least 10 million. More than 7 million of the victims will die in developing countries--a 700-percent increase in just one generation. If present trends continue, according to the World Bank's '1993 World Development Report,' tobacco-related deaths will in 30 years' time exceed the death toll from AIDS, tuberculosis, and complications in childbirth combined." (p20-21)

McGinn, Anne Platt. "The Nicotine Cartel." World Watch v10 n4 Jul-Aug 1997. p18-27. (ISSN0896-0615).

TOBACCO HABIT--OREGON (v26)

TOBACCO HABIT--UNITED STATES

"The rate of smokeless tobacco [use by 12- to 17-year-olds in the U.S.] has declined significantly from 2.8 percent in 1995 to 1.9 percent in 1996....An estimated 62 million Americans were current smokers, including 4.1 million adolescents aged 12-17. This represents a national smoking rate of 29 percent. Youths age 12-17 who currently smoked cigarettes were about nine times as likely to use illicit drugs and 16 times as likely to drink heavily as non-smoking youths."

U.S. Dept. of Health and Human Services. "National Drug Survey Results Released: Overall Drug Use Levels Stay the Same; Possible Decrease in Youth Drug Use." Press Release 6 Aug 1997. document-level access: <http://www.hhs.gov/news/press/1997pres/970806.html>

TOBACCO HABIT--UNITED STATES--COSTS (v26)

TOBACCO HABIT--UNITED STATES--MORTALITY (v26)

"Of the roughly 420,000 tobacco-related deaths every year in the United States...nearly half of these are from heart disease and stroke....In 1993, lung cancer accounted for about one quarter of all tobacco-related deaths in the United States." (p20) "40 times as many U.S. citizens die from tobacco use as from the use of all illegal drugs combined." (p23)

McGinn, Anne Platt. "The Nicotine Cartel." World Watch v10 n4 Jul-Aug 1997. p18-27. (ISSN0896-0615).

TOBACCO INDUSTRY

see also CIGAR INDUSTRY; CIGARETTE INDUSTRY

"Tobacco companies are cranking out cigarettes at the rate of 5.5 trillion a year--that's nearly 1,000 cigarettes for every man, woman, and child on the planet. Already, one person out of every five is a smoker....The industry is dominated by seven multinational companies, which in 1995 accounted for almost 45 percent of global cigarette sales....(The largest cigarette producer of all, the China National Tobacco Corporation, accounts for 32 percent of global sales, but because it sells only within China, it has little influence on the international market.)" (p19)

McGinn, Anne Platt. "The Nicotine Cartel." World Watch v10 n4 Jul-Aug 1997. p18-27. (ISSN0896-0615).

TOBACCO INDUSTRY--CALIFORNIA (v26)

TOBACCO INDUSTRY--CHINA

"China is the largest producer of tobacco in the world, producing four times as much tobacco as the next largest producer, the USA. The government monopoly,...[the China National Tobacco Corporation,] employs 10 million farmers growing tobacco leaf, over half a million workers in industry, and 3 million retailers. In 1993, CNTC sold 1700 billion cigarettes which amounts to 31% of the global market, or about the same market share as the three largest multinational tobacco companies combined....In 1995, [tobacco] export revenue was US$600 million....In 1996, China collected more than US$10 billion in tobacco taxes, and tobacco is the largest industrial tax source." (p2-3)

World Health Organization. "Smoking in China: A Time Bomb for the 21st Century." WHO Fact Sheet n177 Aug 1997. p1-4. document-level access: <http://www.who.ch/programmes/inf/facts/fact177.htm>

"In 1995, China reported that it took in a total of $8.6 billion in tobacco revenues, which made that industry the country's single largest domestic source of tax revenue. But a study by China's Academy of Preventive Medicine showed that the national costs of smoking (both direct and indirect) amounted to $11.3 billion in 1993, and the bill in 1995 was presumably even higher." (p26)

McGinn, Anne Platt. "The Nicotine Cartel." World Watch v10 n4 Jul-Aug 1997. p18-27. (ISSN0896-0615).

TOBACCO INDUSTRY--EMPLOYMENT--CANADA (v26)

TOBACCO INDUSTRY--EMPLOYMENT--INDIA --CHILDREN

In India, "with more than 500 billion beedi cigarettes produced and smoked each year, beedi is one of India's most significant domestic products. More than 325,000 children labor in the beedi industry, most in the southern state of Tamil Nadu." (p587) "Most of the older children--those over 10--roll 1,500 to 2,000 beedies each day....Children working under bondage [to pay off a debt] in the beedi industry work between ten and fourteen hours a day, with short breaks for lunch and dinner. They work six and a half days a week year-round, but are only paid for six--the half day on Sunday is a designated 'catching up' day....Bonded beedi rollers are paid between 20 and 30 percent of the wages they would be entitled to on the open market. The remaining 70 to 80 percent of the value of their wages is kept by the agents, presumably as interest. This system results in effective annual interest rates ranging from 300 to 500 percent." (p588-589)

Tucker, Lee. "Child Slaves in Modern India: The Bonded Labor Problem." Human Rights Quarterly v19 n3 Aug 1997. p572-629. (ISSN0275-0392).

TOBACCO INDUSTRY--FLORIDA

"Florida is about to become the first of 40 states to go to trial to recover billions of dollars in state health-care funds spent treating smoking-related illnesses." (p1) "The industry is also defending a $5 billion class-action suit in Miami filed by flight attendants who say they got sick from secondhand smoke....Estimates are that any settlement of the Florida case would be in the $15 billion to $20 billion range." (p8)

Richey, Warren. "Florida Tackles Big Tobacco for Big Money by Blocking 'Smoker's Responsibility' Strategy." The Christian Science Monitor v89 n175 5 Aug 1997. p1,8. The Christian Science Monitor search engine: <http://www.csmonitor.com/plweb-cgi/iops1.pl> To retrieve this article, enter the following search: ED=19970805 AND strategy. In the "retrieved list," click the title that matches this record. (ISSN0882-7729).

TOBACCO INDUSTRY--KENTUCKY

"Kentucky produced about 420 million pounds [of tobacco] last year. Last year the average price per pound was about $1.90 per pound....The American Economics Group, Inc. (AEG) estimates that 78,280 Kentucky residents have jobs in sectors linked to the production, distribution, and retailing of tobacco products....Nearly $130 million of Kentucky's tax revenue relates to tobacco production, and local governments receive approximately $5.5 million in property taxes from the value of the quota system alone." (pS4792) "Twenty-three counties, all in eastern Kentucky, rely on tobacco for more than one-half of their farm income. Owsley County--88 percent of farm income is from tobacco. Wolfe County--80 percent of farm income is from tobacco. Morgan County--75 percent of farm income is from tobacco." (pS4793)

McConnell, Mitch (Sen.-Ky.). "Concurrent Resolution on the Budget." Congressional Record. Daily ed. v143 n68 21 May 1997. pS4782-4849. section/page-level access: <http://thomas.loc.gov/cgi-bin/query/R?r105:FLD001:S04791:> (ISSN0363-7239). (X1.1A.105/1).

TOBACCO INDUSTRY--KENTUCKY--NORTH CAROLINA (v26)

TOBACCO INDUSTRY--KENTUCKY--TENNESSEE --VIRGINIA (v26)

TOBACCO INDUSTRY--LAW AND LEGISLATION --UNITED STATES (v26)

TOBACCO INDUSTRY--MARYLAND--PENNSYLVANIA (v26)

TOBACCO INDUSTRY--TAXATION (v26)

TOBACCO INDUSTRY--UNITED STATES (v26)

In the U.S., "variable costs of producing an acre of flue-cured tobacco in 1996 averaged $2,026, up almost 7 percent from 1995....Burley tobacco production was 29 percent above 1995. The variable costs of producing and selling burley tobacco increased from $1,249 per acre in 1995 to $1,343 in 1996. Total fixed costs decreased from 1995 to 1996 by almost $61 per acre." (p25)

U.S. Dept. of Agriculture. Economic Research Service. "1996 Cost of Production for Crops and Livestock: Although Input Expenses Rose in 1996,...Led to Higher Net Returns." Agricultural Income and Finance Situation and Outlook Report Sep 1997. p23-27.

"U.S. exports of unmanufactured tobacco leaf in 1996 advanced 5 percent over a year earlier to 486 million pounds declared weight, the highest since 1992....In 1996, exports to Asia and Africa declined, while shipments to Europe advanced 21 percent as a result of increased European cigarette production....Cigarette exports have continued to rise, pushing U.S. cigarette output to a record 755 billion pieces in 1996." (p4)

Capehart, Thomas, Jr./U.S. Dept. of Agriculture. Economic Research Service. "Commodity Briefs: Specialty Crops: New

Markets Boost U.S. Tobacco Prospects." Agricultural Outlook Sep 1997. p3-5.

Tobacco "leaf imports for consumption to the U.S. surged 59 percent in 1996 after declining the previous year. Stocks of imported leaf were being replenished after a tariff-rate quota replaced a 25-percent limit on foreign tobacco content in U.S.-produced cigarettes in 1996. Imports in 1996 reached 668 million pounds, a gain of 59 percent." (p4)

Capehart, Thomas, Jr./U.S. Dept. of Agriculture. Economic Research Service. "Commodity Briefs: Specialty Crops: New Markets Boost U.S. Tobacco Prospects." Agricultural Outlook Sep 1997. p3-5.

U.S. "tobacco acreage expanded by about 8.5 percent in response to higher production quotas for flue-cured and burley tobacco. Flue-cured and burley are the two major types of tobacco grown in the U.S., accounting for 95 percent of the crop....The 1997 effective quota for flue-cured tobacco--the amount growers can sell, adjusted for over- and undermarketings of the previous year--is up 8 percent to 1,019.4 million pounds, and the burley effective quota is up 22 percent to 880 million pounds." (p3)

Capehart, Thomas, Jr./U.S. Dept. of Agriculture. Economic Research Service. "Commodity Briefs: Specialty Crops: New Markets Boost U.S. Tobacco Prospects." Agricultural Outlook Sep 1997. p3-5.

U.S. tobacco import "volume was up 59 percent at 302,000 tons....The value of tobacco imports in 1996 was up sharply, reaching $923 million, a 68-percent increase from 1995. In October, tobacco imports soared to 65,000 tons with Turkey supplying nearly 50 percent. For the remainder of the year, tobacco imports dropped to less than 20,000 tons per month." (p6)

Gehlhar, Mark/U.S. Dept. of Agriculture. Economic Research Service. "Imports Advance 12 Percent in 1996." Foreign Agricultural Trade of the United States Jan-Mar 1997. p6-7.

"In 1995, U.S. consumers spent an estimated $48.7 billion on tobacco products. The farm value of U.S.-grown tobacco leaf was less than $2.6 billion, and a large share of that was exported as either raw leaf or manufactured products. Tobacco is grown on about 124,000 farms in about 20 States....Many persons receive payments for rental or lease of tobacco quota. Grise estimates that about 236,000 tobacco quota holders do not grow tobacco, but receive income from renting their farm (with its assigned tobacco quota) or leasing their quota to others." (p37)

Gale, Fred/U.S. Dept. of Agriculture. Economic Research Service. "Special Article: Tobacco Dollars and Jobs." Tobacco Situation and Outlook Report Sep 1997. p37-43.

"U.S. cigarette manufacturers purchased 603 million pounds (farm sales weight) of flue-cured tobacco during the July 1996-June 1997 marketing year, 15 million pounds less than the previous year. Actual purchases were 127 percent of manufacturers purchase intentions of 475.5 million pounds....Manufacturers purchased 617.5 million pounds of flue-cured tobacco in 1995." (p12)

U.S. Dept. of Agriculture. Economic Research Service. "U.S. Tobacco Leaf Situation and Outlook." Tobacco Situation and Outlook Report Sep 1997. p12-13.

"U.S. exports of unmanufactured tobacco during 1996/97 (July-June) increased to 534.7 million pounds, (687.8 million pounds farm sales weight)....Export value for all unmanufactured tobacco reached $1.57 billion, 16 percent greater than 1995/96....The value of U.S. tobacco leaf and product exports in 1996/97 (July-June) was $6.7 billion, $66 million higher than the previous year." (p9)

U.S. Dept. of Agriculture. Economic Research Service. "U.S. Exports and Imports." Tobacco Situation and Outlook Report Sep 1997. p9-11.

In the U.S., "arrivals or general imports of unmanufactured tobacco increased by 22 percent from 1995/96 to 1996/97 (July-June)....U.S. leaf imports for consumption had climbed from 413 million pounds in 1990 to more than 1 billion pounds in 1993." (p33)

Capehart, Tom/U.S. Dept. of Agriculture. Economic Research Service. "Special Article: U.S. Tobacco Import Update." Tobacco Situation and Outlook Report Sep 1997. p33-36.

In the U.S., "convenience stores that sell food and/or gasoline (some are classified as food stores, some as gasoline service stations) account for 32.5 percent of retail [tobacco] sales, about the same as the share sold by supermarkets. The remaining third of tobacco sales is split among gas stations, general merchandise stores, drug stores, liquor, and other stores. Food stores and gas stations have increased their share of tobacco sales from about half of sales in the 1960's to nearly three-fourths in 1992." (p38)

Gale, Fred/U.S. Dept. of Agriculture. Economic Research Service. "Special Article: Tobacco Dollars and Jobs." Tobacco Situation and Outlook Report Sep 1997. p37-43.

In the U.S., "in the marketing year ending September 30, 1997, about 74 percent of the [burley tobacco] crop will be used for cigarettes, 25 percent exported, and the remainder used for other products, primarily smoking tobacco....For the first 9 months of 1996/97, burley exports totaled 198.2 million pounds, farm sales weight, about 29 percent above a year earlier....The 1996 crop sold for an average of $1.922 per pound, 6.7 cents above the previous marketing year." (p18)

U.S. Dept. of Agriculture. Economic Research Service. "Burley." Tobacco Situation and Outlook Report Sep 1997. p18-19.

In the U.S., "output of smoking tobacco, used in pipes and roll-your-own cigarettes, fell by 642,000 pounds in 1996/97 (July-June), continuing a decade-long decline in 1997. Output for the 1996/97 period fell to 11.7 million pounds from 11.8 million pounds the previous year. On a July-June basis, 1996/97 smoking tobacco consumption declined by 5 percent." (p6)

U.S. Dept. of Agriculture. Economic Research Service. "Tobacco Products." Tobacco Situation and Outlook Report Sep 1997. p4-8.

In the U.S., "exports accounted for 33 percent of total cigarette production in 1996--up from 8 percent in 1984. In 1996, the United States had a $5.3 billion trade surplus in tobacco." (p23) "In Chicago, a study based on data from the 1990 U.S. census found three times as much tobacco billboard advertising in poorer neighborhoods, where most residents are Black or Hispanic, as it did in White areas--a ratio nearly one-third higher than would have been expected strictly in terms of population." (p24)

McGinn, Anne Platt. "The Nicotine Cartel." World Watch v10 n4 Jul-Aug 1997. p18-27. (ISSN0896-0615).

In the U.S., "in 1957, farmers earned 16 cents for every retail dollar of tobacco sales; by 1993, farmers' share of that dollar was 3 cents. That year, manufacturers and wholesalers made 63 cents on every dollar, and 29 cents went for excise taxes. Even the retail share--5 cents--was 40 percent more than what the farmers made....A 1995 survey of 529 U.S. tobacco farmers showed that 73 percent favored a 5-cent increase in the federal excise tax on tobacco...." (p26)

McGinn, Anne Platt. "The Nicotine Cartel." World Watch v10 n4 Jul-Aug 1997. p18-27. (ISSN0896-0615).

TOBACCO INDUSTRY--UNITED STATES--CIGARETTE SMOKERS--ATTITUDES (v26)

TOBACCO INDUSTRY--UNITED STATES--COSTS

In the U.S., "considerable value is added to tobacco leaf as it is funneled from thousands of small labor-intensive farms through a handful of capital-intensive tobacco manufacturers and distributed to consumers by several thousand wholesale establishments and more than 280,000 retail stores. Value added in manufacturing accounts for the biggest share of the retail tobacco dollar (about 38 cents) while nontobacco materials represent about 5 cents. A further 27 cents is added by wholesale and retail marketing. Finally, about 26 cents of the tobacco dollar is collected by State, Federal, and local Governments as excise tax revenue." (p37)

Gale, Fred/U.S. Dept. of Agriculture. Economic Research Service. "Special Article: Tobacco Dollars and Jobs." Tobacco Situation and Outlook Report Sep 1997. p37-43.

TOBACCO INDUSTRY--UNITED STATES--PUBLIC OPINION (v26)

TOBACCO INDUSTRY--ZIMBABWE (v26)

"The growth of Zimbabwe's tobacco export industry has pulled some 3 percent of the country's arable land, or 72,000 hectares, into tobacco production. Yet Zimbabwe still relies on international food aid. Overall, about 0.3 percent of the world's arable land is in tobacco. If converted to food crops, that land might feed as many as 17.5 million people a year." (p26)

McGinn, Anne Platt. "The Nicotine Cartel." World Watch v10 n4 Jul-Aug 1997. p18-27. (ISSN0896-0615).

TOFU--UNITED STATES

"There are about 100 U.S. tofu processors, and their product represents $130-$150 million in retail value. All the tofu consumed in this country is made from American-grown soybeans, but less than 1 percent of U.S. soybean crop is used for tofu. U.S. shoppers are doubling their consumption of tofu about every 3 to 4 years, according to the Soyfoods Center of Lafayette, California, which monitors such trends." (p13)

Lee, Jill/U.S. Dept. of Agriculture. Agricultural Research Service. "New Soybeans Fill Tofu Niche." Agricultural Research v45 n11 Nov 1997. p13. (ISSN0002-161X).

TOILET TRAINING--UNITED STATES (v26)

TOILETS--UNITED STATES (v26)

TOLL BRIDGES--NEW YORK (STATE)

"On New York's Tappan Zee Bridge over the Hudson River...350 to 400 vehicles per hour get through the lanes where tolls are collected manually. But up to 1,000 vehicles per hour move through the electronic toll lanes, according to the Spring 1997 issue of ITS QUARTERLY." (p26)

Koklanaris, Maria/U.S. Dept. of Transportation. Federal Highway Administration. "Intelligent Transportation Systems: ITS Is Already Paying Dividends." Public Roads v61 n2 Sep-Oct 1997. p26-29. (ISSN0033-3735).

TOMATO INDUSTRY--CANADA--MEXICO--UNITED STATES

In the U.S. "fresh tomato export volume increased 20 percent during the first 8 months of 1997....U.S. shippers sold 26 million pounds of fresh market tomatoes in Mexico through August compared with 3 million a year ago. Exports to Canada, which accounted for 85 percent of volume shipped, were up 6 percent." (p7)

U.S. Dept. of Agriculture. Economic Research Service. "Fresh-Market Vegetables." Vegetables and Specialties Situation and Outlook Report Nov 1997. p5-8.

TOMATO INDUSTRY--MEXICO--UNITED STATES (v26)

"U.S. imports of fresh market tomatoes are up 2 percent through the first 8 months of 1997 compared with a year ago. Imports from Mexico actually declined 2 percent during this time, partly due to the impact of bad weather on output. Mexico's share of the U.S. tomato import market declined to just under 90 percent during the first 8 months of 1997 compared with 93 percent a year ago." (p7)

U.S. Dept. of Agriculture. Economic Research Service. "Fresh-Market Vegetables." Vegetables and Specialties Situation and Outlook Report Nov 1997. p5-8.

TOMATO INDUSTRY--UNITED STATES (v26)

In the U.S., "during the first 5 months of 1997, fresh-market tomato import volume was 2 percent higher than a year earlier....At the same time, imports (mostly greenhouse and hydroponic product) from countries such as Canada, the Netherlands, Israel, and Spain jumped 53 percent as U.S. consumers embraced higher quality (and higher priced) hothouse tomatoes. The average import value for tomatoes (largely field-grown) from Mexico was $0.36 per pound, but hothouse product from countries like Canada ($0.82 per pound) and the Netherlands ($0.87 per pound) averaged considerably more." (p4)

U.S. Dept. of Agriculture. Economic Research Service. "Summary." Vegetables and Specialties Situation and Outlook Yearbook Jul 1997. p3-5.

TONGASS NATIONAL FOREST (ALASKA)

In Alaska, "the Tongass National Forest, comprised of almost 17 million acres, is the nation's largest national forest. Within its borders are mountain peaks, narrow fjords, old-growth forests, over a thousand islands, and nearly eleven thousand miles of shoreline. With approximately 5.7 million acres designated as wilderness and another 4.7 million acres with wilderness characteristics, the Tongass is mostly wild and undeveloped. Roughly 65,000 people live in southeast Alaska, almost all of whom live in thirty-three communities along the island and mainland coasts. Most of these communities are either surrounded by or are next to Tongass forest land....Of the Tongass's 17 million acres, roughly only ten million acres are forested. The Forest Service considers only 5.7 million acres of this land to be 'productive forest.' Only 5.05 million acres of the productive forest is productive old-growth and only 600,000 acres of this is high-volume old-growth....Intensive harvesting between 1954 and 1990 has reduced the stands of high-volume old-growth by thirty-nine percent." (p615-616)

Cheyette, Dan. "Comments: Breaking the Trail of Broken Promises: 'Necessary' in Section 810 of Anilca Carries Substantive Obligations." Environmental Law v27 n2 Sum 1997. p611-639. (ISSN0046-2276).

TONGASS NATIONAL FOREST (ALASKA) --ENVIRONMENTAL ASPECTS

"The Tongass National Forest in Alaska is one of the Nation's largest National Forests at 17 million acres." (p3) "About 16 percent of the high-volume old growth outside of legislative withdrawals in the Tongass National Forest has already been harvested." (p4) "Some of the most highly developed karst and cave terrain, the most fragile and sensitive to management disturbance, is concentrated in the alpine and subalpine zones and on slopes greater than 70 percent. At lower elevations within the forest zone, about 30 to 50 percent of the karst terrain in the Ketchikan Area and 10 to 20 percent in the Chatham and Stikine Areas are believed to be highly sensitive to human disturbance." (p6)

Richardson, Sherri/U.S. Dept. of Agriculture. Forest Service. "Tongass Management Plan: Research Played a Key Role." Forestry Research West Sep 1997. p3-7. (ISSN0195-5861).

TOOLS--FIRES AND FIRE PREVENTION--UNITED STATES (v26)

TOURIST INDUSTRY--CHINA--HONG KONG--TAIWAN (v26)

TOURIST TRADE (v26)

see also TRAVEL AGENTS

"In the 1990s, tourism is becoming one of the world's largest industries, employing one out of every fifteen workers around the planet. More importantly, nearly 430 million people, or about eight percent of the world's population travelled from one country to another as tourists, spending billions in the process....In 1991, 450 million international travellers provided $3 trillion in revenues for the tourism industry, and nearly 68 million of them, or 15 percent of all tourists, took some sort of nature-related trip." (p49-50)

Luke, Timothy W. "The World Wildlife Fund: Ecocolonialism as Funding the Worldwide 'Wise Use' of Nature." Capitalism, Nature, Socialism v8 n2 Jun 1997. p31-61. (ISSN1045-5752).

"In purely financial terms the United States is the world's biggest generator and beneficiary of tourism, accounting for around 15 percent of total spending; but the United States would not go broke if tourists stopped coming. Countries like the Bahamas, where tourism makes up more than half of G.N.P. and an estimated 35 percent of employment, probably would....In some Caribbean countries, up to 80 percent of the nominal inflows of foreign currency [from tourism] flow straight out again, into the hands of airlines, tour operators and travel agents. Figures of 70 percent leakage have been estimated for a beach holiday in Kenya, 77 percent for charter operations in Gambia and 60 percent for Thailand. The World Bank has reported that in some countries as little as 10 cents out of every dollar spent goes to local people. In Bali, where 200 people--an entire village--perform the Kechak dance for visitors, one study found that a group of tourists paid $250 in entrance fees to operators but the village received only $20--10 cents per performer." (p14)

Nicholson-Lord, David. "Articles: The Politics of Travel." Nation v265 n10 6 Oct 1997. p11-12,14,16-18. (ISSN0027-8378).

TOURIST TRADE--ALGERIA--EUROPE (v26)

TOURIST TRADE--AUSTRALIA

"During June 1997, 303,700 visitors arrived in Australia, which brought the total number of overseas visitors during 1996-97 to a record 4,248,100, according to data released...by the Australian Bureau of Statistics (ABS). This was an increase of 7 percent (281,900) over the 3,966,200 overseas visitors in 1995-96. The ABS publication, 'Overseas Arrivals and Departures--Australia..., June 1997,' also showed that during 1996-97, the main source countries of these visitor arrivals to Australia were Japan at 19 per cent (801,800), New Zealand at 16 per cent (676,700), the United Kingdom at 9 per cent (384,900), the United States of America at 8 per cent (321,400) and Korea at 6 per cent (250,000)."

Australian Bureau of Statistics. "Record Number of Overseas Visitors." Media Release 21 Jul 1997. document-level access: <http://www.abs.gov.au/websitedbs/d3110125.nsf/4a255eef008309e44a255eef00061e57/3cb378d86d380d684a2564db000a85d2?OpenDocument>

TOURIST TRADE--CALIFORNIA--LOS ANGELES

"In 1994, 22.2 million tourists spent $9.5 billion [in L.A.], which translates into a total economic impact of $22 billion in revenue generated by the tourism industry in L.A. County (LOS ANGELES TIMES, 1995). The tourism industry is a large job generator, including 50,000 hotel workers, 227,000 in restaurants and bars, plus an additional 50,000 workers at amusement parks, recreation, and race tracks (many of these workers cater directly to tourists). This is a grand total of 337,000 employees in the L.A. hotel and tourism industry. In the entire tourism industry, fewer than 10% are unionized workers." (p87)

Geron, Kim. "The Local/Global Context of the Los Angeles Hotel-Tourism Industry." Social Justice v24 n2 Sum 1997. p84-102. (ISSN0094-7571).

TOURIST TRADE--CANADA (v26)

"The number of American visitors to Canada rose 2.1 per cent in the first five months of the year over the same period a year earlier....Since 1994, Canada has moved from 12th place to 10th among the world's most popular tourist destinations, placing it just behind Poland. Almost half the record $12.1 billion that tourists spent in Canada last year came from countries other than the United States." (p32) Prince Edward Island "is attracting an estimated 25-per-cent more visitors, most of them day-trippers from New Brunswick and Nova Scotia....[Vancouver] expects a record eight million tourists this year, up from 7.6 million in 1996....[July's] 10-day Calgary Stampede beat all attendance records, herding 1.7 million visitors through the turnstiles....Fully a third of all overseas trips to Canada last year included a stop in Toronto. About 23 million visitors are expected this year, making the city Canada's most popular destination....The country's tourism deficit--the shortfall between the amount spent by Canadians outside the country and the amount spent here by foreigners--fell to $4 billion last year from about $8 billion in 1992." (p33)

Schofield, John/Wood, Chris/Eisler, Dale/DeMont, John/Branswell, Brenda/McKenna, Barbara. "Business: Passport to Profit." Maclean's v110 n30 28 Jul 1997. p32-33. (ISSN0024-9262).

TOURIST TRADE--CANADA--UNITED STATES (v26)

TOURIST TRADE--CHINA (v26)

TOURIST TRADE--COLORADO--PUBLIC OPINION (v26)

TOURIST TRADE--CUBA (v26)

In Cuba, "in recent years, tourism has surpassed sugar as the regime's principal source of revenue, growing by more than 20 percent annually since 1990. The government is counting on more than 1 million tourists, mainly from Europe and Canada, to spend perhaps $1.8 billion this year." (p6)

LaFranchi, Howard. "International: In Cuba, Revolt Cuts Two Ways." The Christian Science Monitor v89 n199 9 Sep 1997. p6. The Christian Science Monitor search engine: <http://www.csmonitor.com/plweb-cgi/iops1.pl> To retrieve this article, enter the following search: ED=19970909 AND ways. In the "retrieved list," click the title that matches this record. (ISSN0882-7729).

TOURIST TRADE--CUBA--HAVANA

In Cuba, "80 percent of the tourists--both men and women--who come to Havana from Europe and North America are looking for sex." (p12) "20 percent of visitors to Cuba stay in private homes." (p13)

Bleifuss, Joel. "The First Stone: 90 Miles Away." In These Times v21 n19 11 Aug 1997. p12-13. (ISSN0160-5992).

TOURIST TRADE--CYPRUS--EUROPE (v26)

TOURIST TRADE--EGYPT

"Three million tourists visited Egypt last year, spending a record three billion dollars, making tourism the nation's biggest growth industry. The minister of tourism says he expects these numbers to double by the end of the century. With Egypt's population expected to rise from 64 million to 100 million in the next fifty years, the government is counting on a growing tourist industry to meet the country's rapidly expanding needs." (p40) "The cost of a ten-minute visit to the tomb [of Queen Nefertari in Luxor] is 100 Egyptian pounds (about $34 U.S. dollars) per person, which is the same as the monthly salary of a trained archeologist or a museum guard working for the Supreme Council of Egyptian Antiquities....Despite the extremely high cost, as many as 150 tourists have been lining up each day to see the tomb...." (p43-44)

Stille, Alexander. "Is Modern Egypt Obliterating Its Past?" APF Reporter v18 n3 1997. p39-44. (ISSN0913-4562).

TOURIST TRADE--EGYPT--EUROPE (v26)

TOURIST TRADE--EUROPE (v26)

TOURIST TRADE--EUROPE--ISRAEL (v26)

TOURIST TRADE--EUROPE--JORDAN (v26)

TOURIST TRADE--EUROPE--MALTA (v26)

TOURIST TRADE--EUROPE--MOROCCO (v26)

TOURIST TRADE--EUROPE--SYRIA (v26)

TOURIST TRADE--EUROPE--TUNISIA (v26)

TOURIST TRADE--EUROPE--TURKEY (v26)

TOURIST TRADE--FLORIDA (v26)

"In Florida, an outbreak of crimes against tourists in 1993, caused a decline of 11% in the number of overseas tourists and a 16% decline in the number of Canadian tourists, in the first seven months of 1994. The number of European visitors declined nearly 20%--from 1.3 million to 1.05 million. Tourism from Great Britain and Germany, the top European markets for Florida and the two countries that had a number of their citizens who visited Florida attacked or murdered, declined by 22%. Altogether, Florida's total share of foreign visitors to the USA declined from 23% to 20% in the first seven months of 1994. (Pizam and Mansfeld 1996...)" (p23)

Pizam, Abraham/Tarlow, Peter E./Bloom, Jonathan. "Making Tourists Feel Safe: Whose Responsibility Is It?" Journal of Travel Research v36 n1 Sum 1997. p23-28. (ISSN0047-2875).

TOURIST TRADE--FLORIDA--ORLANDO

"Metropolitan Orlando is the leading tourism destination in the United States. In 1994, Orlando received a total of 15 million out-of-state tourists, of which 2.3 million were international visitors. The majority of the domestic tourists (81%) came for leisure purposes and stayed an average of 5.7 nights, while international tourists stayed an average of 7.2 nights. The top four origin markets for Orlando's international tourism, which together generated more than 50% of the total, are the United Kingdom, Brazil, Germany, and Venezuela. The Orlando/Orange County Convention and Visitors Bureau estimates the direct economic impact to be U.S.$10.67 billion for domestic tourism and U.S.$3.73 billion for international tourism (Orlando/Orange County Convention and Visitors Bureau 1995)." (p25)

Pizam, Abraham/Tarlow, Peter E./Bloom, Jonathan. "Making Tourists Feel Safe: Whose Responsibility Is It?" Journal of Travel Research v36 n1 Sum 1997. p23-28. (ISSN0047-2875).

TOURIST TRADE--FRANCE

"Projections show that by the end of 1997, some 65 million people will have visited France, 8 million more than actually live there and a notable increase over 1996 (62 million). France is yet again the No. 1 tourism destination in the world. Some 2.8 million Americans are expected this year, up 7 percent from 1996. The British are coming in even greater droves (up 20 percent to 10 million, largely due to a strong pound and the opening of three-hour direct train service via the channel tunnel between London and Paris)....Eastern European tourists still account for only a little under 2 million visitors to France annually. But that figure climbed by 17 percent from last year." (p1,8)

Moutet, Anne-Elisabeth. "Tourist Shock: Bargains, English...In France?" The Christian Science Monitor v89 n189 25 Aug 1997. p1,8. The Christian Science Monitor search engine: <http://www.csmonitor.com/plweb-cgi/iops1.pl> To retrieve this article, enter the following search: ED=19970825 AND france. In the "retrieved list," click the title that matches this record. (ISSN0882-7729).

TOURIST TRADE--GREAT BRITAIN (v26)

TOURIST TRADE--HAWAII--OAHU (v26)

TOURIST TRADE--HONG KONG (v26)

TOURIST TRADE--IRELAND (v26)

TOURIST TRADE--ISRAEL

In Israel, "tourism dropped by 7 percent in 1996 compared to 1995, with 2.3 million visitors arriving in Israel in a year when the predicted increase had been 10 percent....'In the past five years, tourism to Israel and the Middle East grew by 7 percent annually, and that's a big increase,'...[Avi Rosental, chairman of the Israel Hotel Association] notes....'We're expecting about 25 million tourists and $16 billion in tourism income in the region--Israel, Jordan, Turkey, Egypt and Cyprus--in 10 years' time, up from 15 million last year who spent $8 billion in foreign currency.'" (p40)

Sugarman, Margo Lipschitz. "Special Report: Tourism: Chain Reaction." Jerusalem Report v8 n5 10 Jul 1997. p40,42. (ISSN0792-6049).

TOURIST TRADE--LOUISIANA--NEW ORLEANS

"In 1994 a total of 9.6 million domestic trips were made to New Orleans, and the average length of stay was 4.0 nights. That same year 570,000 international tourists visited the city and stayed an average of 6.6 nights (Chacko 1996)." (p25)

Pizam, Abraham/Tarlow, Peter E./Bloom, Jonathan. "Making Tourists Feel Safe: Whose Responsibility Is It?" Journal of Travel Research v36 n1 Sum 1997. p23-28. (ISSN0047-2875).

TOURIST TRADE--MEXICO

"Between 1980 and 1990, air transportation was the primary mode of travel for tourists to...[Mexico]; 63.4% of tourists traveling to Mexico did so by air. In that decade, air traffic increased 5.7% annually. The number of tourists arriving in Mexico by land also increased 2.3% annually during this period....The number of domestic passengers carried by air reached the 14.4 million mark in 1990....In...1989-91, the number of tourists arriving in Mexico by land increased markedly, showing growth of 11% annually....[By the end of 1990,] the number of tourists who arrived...at the eight Mexican ports offering cruise-ship docking service was 1.2 million, a 0.1% increase compared with the total for 1989. Cozumel was the most active port, registering 34% of the total dockings." (p47)

Casado, Matt A. "Mexico's 1989-94 Tourism Plan: Implications of Internal Political and Economic Instability." Journal of Travel Research v36 n1 Sum 1997. p44-51. (ISSN0047-2875).

"In 1990, Texas and California were the two main generators of tourists to Mexico, with 54% of the total; Canada generated just 4.6%....The number of tourists traveling to Mexico from Europe and Latin America decreased in the 1980-90 period: European tourism fell from 11.6% to 5.8%, while the Latin America market decreased from 7.1% to 5.1%." (p48)

Casado, Matt A. "Mexico's 1989-94 Tourism Plan: Implications of Internal Political and Economic Instability." Journal of Travel Research v36 n1 Sum 1997. p44-51. (ISSN0047-2875).

"The number of Mexican tourists visiting foreign countries grew by an average of 2.6% annually....The number of Mexican tourists going abroad rose from 3.4 million in 1988 to 4.3 million in 1990, an increase of 11.9%....In 1990, Mexican tourists made 36.5 million leisure trips...." (p48)

Casado, Matt A. "Mexico's 1989-94 Tourism Plan: Implications of Internal Political and Economic Instability." Journal of Travel Research v36 n1 Sum 1997. p44-51. (ISSN0047-2875).

TOURIST TRADE--MICHIGAN

"In-state travel boosted Michigan to the No. 6 ranking among the nation's trip destinations this year, and No. 1 in the Midwest, according to the American Travel Survey conducted by the U.S. Department of Transportation....Nearly two-thirds of the 34 million trips projected for 1997 originated from inside state borders." (p1 secC) "Michigan ranks fourth in the nation for in-state travel and 17th for attracting out-of-state

visitors...." (p6 secC)
Hornbeck, Mark. "Metro: News Special: Leisure: More Tourists See Michigan As Travel Spot." Detroit News 10 Dec 1997. p1,6 secC.

TOURIST TRADE--MICHIGAN--DETROIT (v26)

"Between 1994 and 1996, the number of international overnight visitors to the Detroit area surged 40 percent, from 996,600 to about 1.4 million....Despite the surge, Detroit doesn't rank among the nation's top 10 cities for international overnighters." (p1 secE) "In 1992, about a million foreign visitors spent one or more nights in the Detroit area. But their numbers fell to 606,000 in 1993." (p2 secE)
Fricker, Daniel G. "Business: Detroit Has Become Foreigners' Stopover." Detroit Free Press 8 Aug 1997. p1-2 secE.

TOURIST TRADE--MONTANA (v26)

TOURIST TRADE--NEW JERSEY--ATLANTIC CITY

"An amazing number of tour buses (10,197,884 in 1996) filled with eager gamblers speed down the Garden State Parkway [towards Atlantic City]....[There are] 37 million annual visitors to Atlantic City who, in 1996, dropped $39,963,075,000 in casino hotel activity....In 1996 Atlantic City's hotel occupancy rate was 89.5 percent, with 3,368,871 room-nights filled." (p6)
Graham, William C. "Of Other Things: The Sadness of a City." America v177 n1 5 Jul 1997. p6-7. (ISSN0002-7049).

TOURIST TRADE--NEW ZEALAND

"Visitor arrivals to New Zealand in the September 1997 quarter declined by 4,000 compared to the previous September quarter, due largely to a decrease of 8 per cent in visitors from the Asian region, said Deputy Government Statistician Dianne Macaskill. Visitor increases from Australia (up 3 per cent), Europe (up 5 per cent) and North America (up 4 per cent) partly offset this decline. There were 303,700 visitor arrivals in the September 1997 quarter. Visitor numbers from Australia totalled 106,300, an increase of 3,100 on the previous September quarter. There were 96,900 visitors from Asia, a decrease of 8,500. Visitors from Europe totalled 36,700, an increase of 1,800, with more than half of them coming from the UK."
Statistics New Zealand. "External Migration--September 1997 Quarter." Press Release 12 Nov 1997. document-level access: <http://www.stats.govt.nz/statsweb.nsf/52518ce3e01f62f4cc256388000c48c0/ae8760ddd0ec300f4c25654c0083ac25?OpenDocument>

TOURIST TRADE--NORTH AMERICA (v26)

TOURIST TRADE--NORTH DAKOTA (v26)

TOURIST TRADE--NORTHERN IRELAND (v26)

TOURIST TRADE--PALAU (v26)

TOURIST TRADE--SOUTH AFRICA--CAPE TOWN

"It is estimated that in 1995 a total of 504,000 international tourists visited the Cape Town metropolitan area (out of a total of 4.2 million international tourists who visited South Africa) and stayed an average of 8.8 nights. Of those tourists, 87% came for leisure purposes and the remaining 13% visited for business purposes (South African Tourism Board 1995). The size of the 1995 domestic market was estimated to be 1.56 million trips or 3.12 million tourists. The South African Tourist Board estimates total domestic expenditures to be R1.69 billion, which is equivalent to U.S.$365 million (South African Tourism Board 1995)." (p25)
Pizam, Abraham/Tarlow, Peter E./Bloom, Jonathan. "Making Tourists Feel Safe: Whose Responsibility Is It?" Journal of Travel Research v36 n1 Sum 1997. p23-28. (ISSN0047-2875).

TOURIST TRADE--SWEDEN (v26)

TOURIST TRADE--SWITZERLAND (v26)

TOURIST TRADE--TUNISIA (v26)

TOURIST TRADE--UNITED STATES (v26)

"Americans are traveling more for pleasure, and they most often choose to go by car. Leisure trips grew 25 percent between 1990 and 1995...according to the Travel Industry Association of America in Washington, D.C. The automobile was the preferred mode of transportation, accounting for 84 percent of all pleasure trips taken 100 or more miles one-way away from home in 1995, up from 82 percent in 1990. Air travel made up only 13 percent of pleasure trips in 1995, while bus, train, and other modes of transportation accounted for 3 percent. Leisure travel by car grew 28 percent from 1990 to 1995, while leisure travel by plane increased 15 percent." (p48)
Fisher, Christy. "Cars and Kids Go Together Like Peanut Butter and Jelly." American Demographics v19 n5 May 1997. p48. article-level access: <http://www.demographics.com/Publications/AD/97_ad/9705_ad/AD970532.htm> (ISSN0163-4089).

"This year, the average American's vacation budget is $1,806. But people aged 65 and older plan to spend the most ($2,146), according to a MasterCard International survey." (p32) "Travelers pay for their vacation expenses most frequently with a credit card (35 percent) or cash (32 percent). Seventeen percent use travelers checks, and 4 percent use personal checks. Only 5 percent say they will use a debit/ATM [automated teller machine] card on their next vacation, but one-third of travelers obtained cash at an ATM machine on their last trip." (p33)
Kate, Nancy Ten. "Kaleidoscope: Have Credit, Will Travel." American Demographics v19 n6 Jun 1997. p32-33. article-level access: <http://www.demographics.com/publications/ad/97_ad/9706_ad/ad970614.htm> (ISSN0163-4089).

"Commercial and recreational fishing provides 1.5 million jobs and an estimated $111 billion annually to the...[U.S.] economy, and more than 30 percent of the United States GNP is produced in coastal counties. Americans love the ocean and beaches: they are our leading tourist destination, with 85 percent of tourist revenues being spent in coastal States. In 1993 more than 180 million Americans visited coastal waters nationwide, and in California alone the revenue generated by tourism is approximately $38 billion annually. The beautiful coasts and ocean in...[California] are key to the areas's $1.5 billion travel and tourism industry." (pE1866)
Farr, Sam (Rep.-Calif.). "The Oceans Act of 1997." Congressional Record. Daily ed. v143 n130 25 Sep 1997. pE1866-1867. section/page-level access: <http://thomas.loc.gov/cgi-bin/query/R?r105:FLD001:E01866:> (ISSN0363-7239). (X1.1A.105/1).

"France is now the sixth-largest source of foreign tourists to the U.S., and Italy is number ten. By 1999, they should be eighth and eleventh, respectively, as Brazil, South Korea, Taiwan, and Switzerland move up in the rankings. The total number of non-North American visitors in 1996 was 22.1 million; in 1999, it may be 26.1 million, or more than Mexico and Canada combined." (p7)
"Asians Lead Tourism Growth." Forecast v17 n9 Sep 1997. p7. article-level access: <http://www.demographics.com/Publications/FC/97_fc/9709_fc/FC97096.htm> (ISSN0732-1597).

"Over one-fourth of U.S. adults (54 million) took at least one trip in the last year that included a visit to an historic site or museum, according to the Travel Industry Association. One in six (33 million) took a trip that included a visit to a cultural event or festival, and one in ten adults did both....[History-oriented travelers] spend an average of $688 per trip, compared with $425 for all U.S. travelers. Travelers to cultural events and festivals are more likely to be on a day trip or short trip, but they still manage to spend an average of $557." (p5)
"Will Boomers Buy History?" Forecast v17 n10 Oct 1997. p5. article-level access: <http://www.demographics.com/

publications/fc/97_fc/9710_fc/fc97104.htm>
(ISSN0732-1597).

TOURIST TRADE--WASHINGTON (D.C.) (v26)

TOURIST TRADE--WISCONSIN (v26)

TOWNS
see CITIES AND TOWNS

TOWNSHIP GOVERNMENT
see LOCAL GOVERNMENT

TOXIC WASTES
see HAZARDOUS WASTES

TOXICOLOGY
see LEAD--TOXICOLOGY; WATER BIRDS--TOXICOLOGY

TOXICS, AIR
see AIR--POLLUTION

TOYS--LABELING--LAW AND LEGISLATION --UNITED STATES

In the U.S., "since passage of the 1994 Child Safety Protection Act, toy manufacturers are required to include choke hazard warnings on small parts, balls, marbles and balloons. The law also increased the size of small balls banned for sale to children under 3 to 1.75 inches from 1.25 inches." (p1 secB) According to a report by the Public Interest Research Group of Michigan, "more than 140,000 children were treated in hospital emergency rooms for toy-related injuries in 1996, down from 150,800 the year before....Nearly half of the injuries occurred among children under 5. Choking continues to be the leading cause of toy-related deaths, killing about 15 children each year. 'Balloons are the No. 1 toy choking killer, year after year,'...[said Public Interest Research Group spokeswoman Caroline Schwarz]." (p2 secB)

Waldsmith, Lynn. "Business: Group Warns of Toy Hazards." Detroit News 26 Nov 1997. p1-2 secB.

TRACHOMA (v26)

TRACKS (AUTOMOBILE RACING)
see RACETRACKS (AUTOMOBILE RACING)

TRADE
see BUSINESS; COMMERCE

TRADE, BALANCE OF
see BALANCE OF TRADE

TRADE, INTERNATIONAL
see INTERNATIONAL TRADE

TRADE-UNIONS

Union "densities between 60 percent and 80 percent exist in the Scandinavian nations, while in the other advanced capitalist states, they range between 10 percent in France to 40 percent in Great Britain and 33 percent in Germany. In Canada, with many similar economic features, density is around 30 percent. Even in New Zealand, which has experienced a profoundly anti-labor legal restructuring, 23 percent of employees are union members." (p46)

Gapasin, Fernando/Yates, Michael. "Organizing the Unorganized: Will Promises Become Practices?" Monthly Review v49 n3 Jul-Aug 1997. p46-62. (ISSN0027-0520).

TRADE-UNIONS--AUSTRALIA (v26)

"In less than two decades, mergers have reduced the total number of Australian unions by two-thirds. As recently as 1981, 316 Australian unions represented about 2.7 million workers. Eighty percent had fewer than 50,000 members. But the recession in the early 1980s brought double-digit unemployment and a continuing loss of union membership--just as it did in the United States. Australian unions were able to organize only seven of every 100 new workers added to the labor force, and from 1982 to 1994, the unionized percentage of the workforce fell from 50 percent to 35 percent, according to author Gary N. Chaison in UNION MERGERS IN HARD TIMES: A VIEW FROM FIVE COUNTRIES." (p19)

"Marriage for Muscle: In Australia, Consolidation for Survival." America@Work v2 n6 Jul 1997. p19. (ISSN1091-594X).

TRADE-UNIONS--CANADA (v26)

TRADE-UNIONS--PENSIONS--UNITED STATES

In the U.S., "eighty-one percent of union members had contributions made by their employers to defined-benefit pensions. Less than half, or 48 percent, of nonunion workers were covered." (p4)

"Economic: Pension and Health Benefits." Maritime Newsletter v29 n11 Nov 1997. p4. (ISSN0161-9373).

TRADE-UNIONS--UNITED STATES (v26)

"The numbers show fewer Americans belonging to unions than in the 1950s (14.5 percent now vs. 35 percent then)....Labor is investing $20 million a year on organizing. In the early 1990s, unions spent $2.5 million a year." (p12)

Budd, John F., Jr. "Soundings: What the Teamsters Knew." Across the Board v34 n10 Nov-Dec 1997. p12. (ISSN0147-1554).

In the U.S., "in the last five years alone, there have been 18 mergers among affiliated unions, involving more than 5 million members, up from 10 mergers in the previous five-year period." (p16) "Only 22 of the 78 affiliated unions have 100,000 or more members, according to the '1995 Executive Council Report to the Convention.'...UFCW [United Food and Commercial Workers International Union] has gained over 70,000 new members through four mergers in the last five years. USWA [United Steelworkers of America] has gained 116,000 members through two mergers over the same period, and SEIU [Service Employees International Union] has grown by 40,000." (p17)

Parks, James B. "Marriage for Muscle." America@Work v2 n6 Jul 1997. p16-19. (ISSN1091-594X).

In the U.S., "the number of union government jobs nationwide has stayed relatively constant for the past 15 years at about 38 percent, according to the Bureau of Labor Statistics. Meanwhile, unionized manufacturing jobs have declined steadily to about 19 percent of those working in factories from almost 30 percent in 1983." (p13 secA)

Knox, Noelle. "The Shrinking UAW: Public Payrolls: Union Hopes to Take Advantage of Workers' Fears of Downsizing." Detroit News and Free Press 13 Jul 1997. p13 secA.

In the U.S., the United Auto Workers Union's "membership dropped to 742,454 last year from 1.5 million members in 1979. Dues have remained relatively constant the past 16 years--despite the membership slide--thanks to wage increases won at the bargaining table, records show. But when adjusted for inflation, the union's financial clout has declined nearly 42 percent since 1980." (p1 secA)

Howes, Daniel/Phillips, Dave. "Special Report: UAW Looks South for Renewed Clout." Detroit News and Free Press 13 Jul 1997. p1 secA.

In the U.S., "between 1990 and 1991, public sector unions added 147,000 members, but between 1991 and 1992, they added only 21,000 members....The percentage of workers represented in the 1990-91 year remained unchanged at 43.3%, while between 1991 and 1992, the percentage represented actually dropped slightly to 43.2%." (p29) Between 1994 and 1995 "membership fell by 164,000....The largest decrease in membership took place at the State level (65,000), second largest at the Federal level (50,000), followed by Local Government (35,000), and then Postal Service (14,000) (Hirsch, Barry T., and Macpherson, David A., UNION MEMBERSHIP AND EARNINGS DATA BOOK: 1996)." (p30)

Troy, Leo. "Has Public Sector Labor Topped Out?" Government Union Review v17 n2 Spr 1996. p1-40. (ISSN0270-2487).

In the U.S., "while the average penetration rate of the New Unionism is currently 38% (compared to just over 10% in the private sector), in key public employment occupations, the rate is not far from double the average--teaching, about 65%; police, 67%; and fire, 70%. The U.S. Postal Service tops them all, with just under 75% (Hirsch and Macpherson, 1996)....In the public sector, the National Education Association and the American Federation of Teachers have a combined membership exceeding three million; and that accounts for nearly 40% of all public sector membership." (p38)

Troy, Leo. "Has Public Sector Labor Topped Out?" Government Union Review v17 n2 Spr 1996. p1-40. (ISSN0270-2487).

In the U.S., between 1994 and 1995, union "memberships dropped off by 168,000 (just over 2%), and market share decreased from 38.7% to 37.8%." (p1) "Just about thirty years ago, public sector unionism accounted for approximately 6% of total membership; now it is 42% of the entire union population. Since peaking in 1970, private sector unions have shed about 7 million members; currently government unions enroll almost 7 million adherents. Moreover, government unions' penetration rate of Federal, State and local employment (38%) is a penetration rate never achieved by their counterpart in business. Private sector unions peaked at 36% of non-farm, private employment; and that occurred more than forty years ago, in 1953." (p2)

Troy, Leo. "Has Public Sector Labor Topped Out?" Government Union Review v17 n2 Spr 1996. p1-40. (ISSN0270-2487).

In the U.S., today union density "is a mere 14.9 percent. What is more, the current figure masks the fact that density in the private sector of the economy is now a paltry 10.3 percent....Union density in the public sector is 37.7 percent....In private sector manufacturing, once the bedrock of the labor movement, union membership has also fallen by half since 1973, from 38.9 percent to 17.6 percent in 1996....In 1983 union membership was approximately 17.7 million, but it was only 16.4 million in 1995....Here are some representative numbers, showing the decrease in paid membership from the peak membership year to 1995: United Auto Workers (UAW)-509,000; Carpenters-372,000; Communication Workers (CWA)-46,000; Electrical Workers (IBEW)-177,000; Laborers (LIUNA)-123,000; Machinists (IAM)-179,000; Musicians-215,000; Oil and Chemical (OCAW)-77,000; Steelworkers (USW)-659,000....The Service Employees (SEIU) has shown a dramatic increase in membership, from 480,000 in 1975 to 688,000 in 1985 to more than one million in 1995." (p47)

Gapasin, Fernando/Yates, Michael. "Organizing the Unorganized: Will Promises Become Practices?" Monthly Review v49 n3 Jul-Aug 1997. p46-62. (ISSN0027-0520).

TRADE-UNIONS--UNITED STATES--ELECTIONS

In the U.S., a study on union certification elections that Bronfenbrenner and Juravich (B&J) did for the AFL-CIO "found that unions won with commanding margins, winning an average 85% of representation elections and 83% of votes cast....Professional groups accounted for nearly 20% of all State and local elections; another 9% of elections occurred in supervisory and managerial units. In all of these, the unions averaged higher than an 80% win rate (BNA, Inc., Government Employee Relations Report, March 20, 1995)." (p22-23) "When an election was stipulated or ordered, the union win rate dropped from the average of 85% to 60%....B&J report that in the private sector, less than half of the elections are consent elections, with win rates at about 50%. In NLRB [National Labor Relations Board] ordered elections, the win rate drops to 17%." (p26)

Troy, Leo. "Has Public Sector Labor Topped Out?" Government Union Review v17 n2 Spr 1996. p1-40. (ISSN0270-2487).

TRADE-UNIONS--UNITED STATES--POLITICAL ACTIVITY--PUBLIC OPINION (v26)

TRADE-UNIONS--UNITED STATES--PUBLIC OPINION

A "Gallup poll shows that by a margin of 64% to 34%, the [U.S.] public feels that unions mostly help rather than hurt the workers, but is about evenly divided over the effect unions may have on the economy: 48% think unions have a positive effect; 45% say it is negative....The poll shows that by a margin of 65% to 29%, Americans believe workers have not received their fair share of the benefits created over the past few years by the improved economy. Similarly, 65% of Americans say businesses are only concerned with profits and not with the economic interests of their workers; less than half that number--32%--believe that businesses do take their workers' interests into account while trying to make 'reasonable' profits."

Moore, David W./Gallup Organization. "Public: Labor Unions Beneficial for Workers; Not That Good for Economy." Press Release 2 Sep 1997. document-level access: <http://www.gallup.com/poll/news/970902.html>

TRADE-UNIONS--UNITED STATES--WOMEN

"Karen Nussbaum, the director of the AFL-CIO's new Women's Department, points out that...women make up 40% of [U.S.] union membership....[Statistics published by the AFL-CIO show that] in 1996, women earned 75 cents for every dollar earned by men. But union women earned 84 cents for every dollar earned by union men, and 38% more than their nonunion counterparts....Only 13.2% of the AFL-CIO executive council members are women....Even in unions with vast majorities of women members, such as UNITE, the garment workers' union, leadership is less than 5% female." (p6)

Patterson, Cara. "Active Culture: What Women Want." Dollars and Sense n213 Sep-Oct 1997. p6. (ISSN0012-5245).

In the U.S., "by 1996, women accounted for 39 percent of all union members, and the majority of new ones....A 1996 poll by Peter Hart and the Mellman Group, oft cited by the A.F.L.-C.I.O., found that women are much more supportive of collective action--workers joining together to achieve goals--than of self-reliance. Seven percent more women than men said they would definitely or probably vote for a union, a gender gap that has shown up in surveys for twelve years. Women are an even larger proportion--46.2 percent, according to the Bureau of Labor Statistics--of the civilian labor force as a whole." (p12) "The A.F.L.-C.I.O. represents 5.6 million working women--which makes it the largest working women's organization in the country....Unionized women earned 38 percent more than nonunion women in 1996--and their median weekly wages were 5.5 percent more than nonunion men." (p14)

Waldman, Amy. "Articles: Labor's New Face: Women Renegotiate Their Role." Nation v265 n8 22 Sep 1997. p11-12,14,16. (ISSN0027-8378).

TRADITIONS

see MANNERS AND CUSTOMS

TRAFFIC

see COMMUNICATION AND TRAFFIC

TRAFFIC ACCIDENTS

see also BOATING ACCIDENTS; DRINKING AND TRAFFIC ACCIDENTS; PEDESTRIAN ACCIDENTS; SCHOOL BUS ACCIDENTS; SNOWMOBILE ACCIDENTS; TRUCK ACCIDENTS

TRAFFIC ACCIDENTS--ARIZONA--MORTALITY

In Arizona, in 1996, "nearly 90% of the 135 deaths from motor vehicle crashes were deemed preventable. Only two of the child passengers or drivers who died in motor vehicle crashes were reported to have been wearing safety restraints. In 30 of the deaths, alcohol and/or other drugs were known to be a factor. Eleven children died in bicycle-related incidents with motor vehicles, and of the five for whom helmet use or non-use was recorded, none wore a helmet."

Arizona. Dept. of Health Services. "Hundreds of Child Deaths Preventable, Report Finds." Press Release 13 Nov 1997. document-level access: <http://www.hs.state.az.us/news/news81.htm>

TRAFFIC ACCIDENTS--AUSTRALIA--MORTALITY

According to "Motor Vehicles in Australia, 1997," by the

Australian Bureau of Statistics, "in 1995, there were 2,017 fatalities on Australian roads, 1,413 of which were men and 604 women, at a rate of 11.2 per 100,000 persons. The 17-25 years age group, which comprised 13.9 per cent of the population in 1995, accounted for almost 30 per cent of these fatalities. Males comprised about 78 per cent of fatalities. When fatality rates are adjusted for distance driven, the gender imbalance almost disappears, with 1.68 driver fatalities per 100 million kilometres travelled for males under 25 and 1.43 for females in the same age category."

Australian Bureau of Statistics. "Motor Vehicle Related Statistics--New ABS Compendium." Media Release 27 Jun 1997. document-level access: <http://www.abs.gov.au/websitedbs/d3110125.nsf/4a255eef008309e44a255eef00061e57/abae37bef5c8b3874a2564c200793fda?OpenDocument>

TRAFFIC ACCIDENTS--CALIFORNIA

In 1987, when the U.S. raised "rural interstate speed limits to 65 mph, a 15-20 percent increase in deaths on interstate highways resulted, amounting to an increase of 500 deaths per year. Now, after the States were allowed, at their option, to raise speed limits in 1995, we see once again the result of high speed limits. Every time we raise the speed limit more people die....For example in California on roads where speed limits were increased to 70 or 75 miles per hour there has been a 12 percent increase in fatalities. On roads where there was an increase to 65 miles per hour there has been a 22 percent increase in fatalities. However, sometimes the numbers can be misleading. In California they have a reduction in traffic fatalities....The reason for the overall reduction in deaths is the result of an 8 percent reduction in death on roads that remained at the 55 miles per hour speed limit." (pE1486)

Rahall, Nick J., II (Rep.-W.Va.). "Increased Highway Fatalities Due to Faster Speed Limits." Congressional Record. Daily ed. v143 n105 23 Jul 1997. pE1486. section/page-level access: <http://thomas.loc.gov/cgi-bin/query/R?r105:FLD001:E01486:> (ISSN0363-7239). (X1.1A.105/1).

TRAFFIC ACCIDENTS--CALIFORNIA--MONTANA --MORTALITY

"In California, traffic fatalities rose 18.8 percent--from 495 to 588--last year on freeways enforcing increased speed limits, according to a study conducted by the state's transportation department. Meanwhile, the total death count on California roads dropped by nearly 5 percent, 4,192 to 3,989. In Montana, where the highways do not have a fixed daytime speed limit, the amount of highway deaths nearly doubled, from 12 to 22 during the first nine months of 1996, while the sum of fatalities on all of the state's roads decreased." (p8 secA)

Harmon, Brian. "News Special: Speed Doesn't Kill, Road Report Finds." Detroit News 23 Jul 1997. p1,8 secA.

TRAFFIC ACCIDENTS--CALIFORNIA--YOUTH

In nine counties surrounding the San Francisco Bay Area, in California, "teen drivers age 15 to 19, who represent 4 to 5 percent of licensed drivers, became involved in 10 percent of all fatal and/or serious bodily injury crashes, a rate approaching 2.5 times their licensed driving population. Only 16.3 percent of all teenagers killed in motor vehicle crashes wore seat belts. One in 4,000 teens involved in fatal accidents as drivers or occupants used alcohol, the highest among any driving population. Nearly half of teens killed in vehicle crashes were in the company of other teens...." (p6)

Murdo, Larry/U.S. Dept. of Justice. Federal Bureau of Investigation. "Focus on Youth: The Chief Operator Teen Driver Program." FBI Law Enforcement Bulletin v66 n12 Dec 1997. p6-7. (ISSN0014-5688).

TRAFFIC ACCIDENTS--GERMANY (v26)

TRAFFIC ACCIDENTS--MICHIGAN (v26)

Six people "died in Michigan last year when they hit deer or attempted to avoid them. More than 2,200 others were injured in the record 68,233 vehicle-deer crashes; property damage topped $100 million....[The Michigan Deer Crash Coalition] reported that deer-vehicle crashes now account for better than one of every seven accidents in Michigan. The average repair cost per vehicle is $1,600, usually to fix front-end damage. And such claims have gone up by 25 percent in the last four years. More than half the vehicle-deer crashes occur in southern Michigan, near population centers on heavily traveled arteries: In Wayne County, the number of accidents increased by 13.2 percent over 1995. In Oakland County, it was up 12.7 percent. In Macomb County, the number grew by 3.3 percent." (p9 secA)

Cain, Charlie. "Deer Hunting in Michigan: Safety: Michigan Drivers May See More Deer-Car Crashes." Detroit News 1 Oct 1997. p9 secA.

TRAFFIC ACCIDENTS--MICHIGAN--MORTALITY (v26)

The U.S. "National Highway Traffic Safety Administration said 1,505 people died on Michigan roads in 1996--a 1.6-percent drop from the 1,530 that perished in car wrecks in 1995. Through July 20 this year there have been 683 traffic deaths, compared with 791 at the same time last year. Among the 27 states that raised speed limits in 1996, there was a 0.4 percent decrease in road fatalities." (p1 secA)

Harmon, Brian. "News Special: Speed Doesn't Kill, Road Report Finds." Detroit News 23 Jul 1997. p1,8 secA.

TRAFFIC ACCIDENTS--MICHIGAN--TEENAGERS

"In Michigan alone last year, 308 teen drivers were involved in fatal crashes." (p1 secA) "In Michigan in 1996, teens had 15,726 collisions resulting in injury. Studies say teen drivers are almost four times more likely to be involved in a crash with injuries than drivers aged 25 to 34." (p12 secA)

Keenan, Marney Rich. "Dying to Drive: Part One: The Crash: Fatal Mistake at Wheel Shatters Teen-agers' Lives and Hopes." Detroit News and Free Press 26 Oct 1997. p1,12 secA.

TRAFFIC ACCIDENTS--MICHIGAN--YOUTH

In traffic crashes involving young drivers, "'in 93 percent of the cases, the driver was at fault,' [said] Gerald Basch of AAA [Automobile Association of America] Michigan....'For kids between the ages of 15 and 20, their No.1 killer is an automobile,' said Basch, manager of Community Safety Services for AAA. While 7 percent of Michigan drivers are teenagers, they account for 20 percent of all crashes with injuries and 14 percent of the state's crash fatalities." (p1 secC)

Keenan, Marney Rich. "Metro: More Training Key to Safe Teen Drivers, Expert Says." Detroit News 31 Oct 1997. p1-2 secC.

TRAFFIC ACCIDENTS--MORTALITY (v26)

TRAFFIC ACCIDENTS--NEW YORK (N.Y.) --MORTALITY (v26)

TRAFFIC ACCIDENTS--UNITED STATES (v26)

In the U.S., death and injuries related to driving are "responsible for the loss of 1.2 million pre-retirement years of life a year; more than is lost to cancer or heart disease. It is the leading cause of death for Americans between the ages of 15 and 24. Last year, more than 41,900 Americans died from this epidemic and more than 3 million suffered serious injury. In Nebraska alone, the epidemic claimed 293 lives in 1996 up from 254 the year before....About $14 billion a year in health care costs are attributable to traffic accidents. Taxpayers bear $11.4 billion of that cost. In terms of lost productivity, property damage and health care costs, these accidents extracted $150 billion out of the economy for the last year that statistics are available." (pS9018)

Kerrey, J. Robert (Sen.-Nebr.). "Statements on Introduced Bills and Joint Resolutions." Congressional Record. Daily ed. v143 n118 9 Sep 1997. pS9018-9019. section/page-level access: <http://thomas.loc.gov/cgi-bin/query/R?r105:FLD001:S09018:> (ISSN0363-7239). (X1.1A.105/1).

In the U.S., "according to one study, 60 percent of crashes at intersections and about 30 percent of head-on collisions could be avoided if drivers had an additional half-second to react. Nearly 75 percent of vehicular crashes are caused by inattentive drivers." (p19)

Little, Cheryl/U.S. Dept. of Transportation. Federal Highway Administration. "Intelligent Transportation Systems: The Intelligent Vehicle Initiative: Advancing 'Human-Centered' Smart Vehicles." Public Roads v61 n2 Sep-Oct 1997. p18-25. (ISSN0033-3735).

TRAFFIC ACCIDENTS--UNITED STATES--CHILDREN --MORTALITY

"Motor vehicle crashes are the leading cause of unintentional injury-related death for children ages 14 and under. In 1995 in Alabama, 74 children age 14 and under died as a result of vehicle crashes. Each year in the U.S. approximately 2,800 children ages 14 and under are killed and an estimated 330,000 are injured as passengers in motor vehicles....The correct use of child safety seats is extremely effective, reducing the risk of death by 69 percent for infants, and by 47 percent for toddlers (ages 1 to 4)."

Alabama. Dept. of Public Health. "Child Vehicle Safety Is the Goal of National Child Passenger Safety Awareness Week." News Release 17 Jan 1997. document-level access: <http://www.alapubhealth.org/Press/pr011797a.htm>

TRAFFIC ACCIDENTS--UNITED STATES--MORTALITY (v26)

The National Highway Traffic Safety Administration "reports that every year over 41,000 Americans are killed on our Nation's highways--that is an average of 114 lives every day. In just the past 5 years alone, over 160,000 Americans have lost their lives, and more than 12 million have suffered serious injuries due to traffic accidents and road hazards--at a cost [of] over $700 billion dollars....Almost 25 percent of these traffic fatalities involve children. In 1995, over 9,000 kids were killed in auto accidents....Most accidents are due to reckless behavior, such as drunk driving. According to NHTSA, alcohol-related accidents are responsible for over 40 percent of traffic fatalities." (pS10153)

Hollings, Ernest F. (Sen.-S.C.). "Statements on Introduced Bills and Joint Resolutions." Congressional Record. Daily ed. v143 n132 29 Sep 1997. pS10153-10176. section/page-level access: <http://thomas.loc.gov/cgi-bin/query/R?r105:FLD001:S10153:> (ISSN0363-7239). (X1.1A.105/1).

TRAFFIC ACCIDENTS--UNITED STATES--POLICE

In the U.S., "1995 statistics show that 40 percent of all high-speed [police] pursuits end in accidents....According to the U.S. Department of Transportation, there were 377 deaths nationwide in 1996, and 27 percent of these deaths were police officers or innocent bystanders that died as a result of high-speed chases....An alarming 60 percent of all police pursuits originate from minor traffic violations....73 percent of all police officers reporting that they have been involved in a high-speed pursuit in the last 12 months...." (pS10175)

Dorgan, Byron L. (Sen.-N.Dak.). "Statements on Introduced Bills and Joint Resolutions." Congressional Record. Daily ed. v143 n132 29 Sep 1997. pS10153-10176. section/page-level-access: <http://thomas.loc.gov/cgi-bin/query/R?r105:FLD001:S10175:> (ISSN0363-7239). (X1.1A.105/1).

TRAFFIC ACCIDENTS--UNITED STATES--TEENAGERS --MORTALITY

In the U.S., "every year more than 6,500 teens nationwide die as a result of traffic crashes, according to the National Highway Traffic Safety Administration. While teens make up about 7 percent of the nation's driving population, they account for about 14 percent of motor vehicle deaths." (p1 secA)

Keenan, Marney Rich. "Dying to Drive: Part Two: The Tragedy Unfolds: Sounds of Grief Pierce Tiny Community." Detroit News 27 Oct 1997. p1,8 secA.

"Traffic crashes are the No. 1 cause of death for teen-agers 15 and older, according to the National Highway Traffic Safety Administration. Forty percent of all deaths in that age group are the result of car crashes. That's more than die by disease, homicide or suicide." (p1 secA)

Keenan, Marney Rich. "Dying to Drive: Part One: The Crash: Fatal Mistake at Wheel Shatters Teen-agers' Lives and Hopes." Detroit News and Free Press 26 Oct 1997. p1,12 secA.

TRAFFIC ACCIDENTS--UNITED STATES--YOUTH (v26)

TRAFFIC ACCIDENTS--UNITED STATES--YOUTH --MORTALITY (v26)

TRAFFIC ACCIDENTS AND DRINKING

see DRINKING AND TRAFFIC ACCIDENTS

TRAFFIC CONGESTION--GREAT BRITAIN (v26)

TRAFFIC CONGESTION--ILLINOIS--CHICAGO (v26)

TRAFFIC CONGESTION--MICHIGAN

In Michigan, "about 251,530 more cars, trucks, vans and other vehicles are on the road this year in Wayne, Oakland and Macomb counties as compared with five years ago, state figures show. Tens of thousands of cars cruise the intersections near major malls: The exit to Twelve Oaks Mall from Interstate 96 in Novi handles about 30,000 vehicles a day. The stretch of the Southfield Freeway that runs along Fairlane Town Center in Dearborn--from Michigan Avenue to Ford Road--handles 98,300 vehicles a day. A total of 42,400 vehicles drive along a stretch of Hall Road that runs along Lakeside Mall in Sterling Heights." (p1 secA)

Martindale, Mike/Garrett, Craig/Pardo, Steve. "Malls Fight Traffic Congestion, Crime: Security Measures Range from Videos to Cops on Horseback." Detroit News 9 Dec 1997. p1-2 secA.

TRAFFIC CONGESTION--MICHIGAN--DETROIT

"Clogged highways are costing Metro Detroit motorists $2 billion a year in spent fuel and wasted hours stuck in traffic, according to a new national study. 'Most cities, including Detroit, are losing the battle against traffic gridlock,' said David Schrank, a traffic researcher at the Texas Transportation Institute, part of Texas A&M University. His team conducted a 12-year study of traffic in the 50 largest metropolitan areas and found that congestion increased an average of 22 percent during that time....On average, congestion costs each Detroit commuter $820 a year, behind only three other cities....[In 1994, the Texas researchers] calculated that 89 miles of new lanes were needed and only 24 miles were added." (p1 secC)

"Gary Naeyaert, a Michigan Department of Transportation (MDOT) spokesman, said traffic headaches also can be viewed as good news: The number of miles driven in Michigan is up 30 percent in the last 10 years, which he said reflects more employed commuters, more state tourism and a stronger economy....The Texas researchers say congestion delays now tie up the average Metro Detroit commuter for 57 hours a year--ninth-highest in the nation." (p4 secC)

Shepardson, David/Garrett, Craig. "Metro: News Special: Urban Development: Motorists in Metro Detroit Lose Billions to Traffic Gridlock." Detroit News 5 Nov 1997. p1,4 secC.

TRAFFIC ENGINEERING--EMPLOYMENT--UNITED STATES--ATTITUDES

"According to a survey conducted by the Institute of Traffic Engineers (ITE) [in the U.S.], 44 percent of the respondents working within local agencies judged their ability to operate and maintain advanced traffic management systems as fair or poor, and 35 percent of those same respondents stated that the lack of qualified technical and maintenance personnel was a severe or major problem. For state agencies, 50 percent of the respondents rated their ability to operate advanced systems as fair or poor, and 66 percent rated their ability to maintain such systems as fair or poor. Of these respondents, 71 percent felt that improved training would increase their ability to operate their systems, and 100 percent said improved training would increase their ability to maintain such systems." (p37)

Humphrey, Thomas F./U.S. Dept. of Transportation. Federal Highway Administration. "Intelligent Transportation Systems: The ITS Professional Capacity Building Program." Public Roads v61 n2 Sep-Oct 1997. p36-38. (ISSN0033-3735).

TRAFFIC ENGINEERING--OREGON--HELLS CANYON (v26)

TRAFFIC ENGINEERING--TEXAS--SAN ANTONIO

San Antonio, Texas, "is operating an advanced traffic management system, called TransGuide. The first phase of TransGuide--42 kilometers of highway in a proposed system of 307 kilometers--went online two years ago at a cost of about $33 million. TransGuide...uses a digital communications network to warn drivers about conditions ahead of them and to transmit information about accidents and other incidents to police and rescue workers as quickly as possible....The Texas Transportation Institute and the Texas Department of Transportation teamed up to evaluate the accident rate and response time before TransGuide and after TransGuide. The transportation officials compared the time periods from Aug. 1 to Dec. 31 in 1992, 1993, and 1994--when TransGuide was not online--with the time period from Aug. 1 to Dec. 31, 1995, the first five months of TransGuide deployment. They found that accidents decreased 15 percent, and the response time for major and minor traffic incidents decreased by an average of 20 percent, according to ITS QUARTERLY, Spring 1997. ITS QUARTERLY further reports that the savings associated with these reductions amounts to $4.95 million and would total $67 million over 20 years." (p28)

Koklanaris, Maria/U.S. Dept. of Transportation. Federal Highway Administration. "Intelligent Transportation Systems: ITS Is Already Paying Dividends." Public Roads v61 n2 Sep-Oct 1997. p26-29. (ISSN0033-3735).

TRAFFIC VIOLATIONS

see DRINKING AND TRAFFIC ACCIDENTS; DRUNK DRIVING

TRAFFIC VIOLATIONS--DIPLOMATS--NEW YORK (N.Y.) (v26)

TRAILS--MONTANA

"A 1994 study by the Montana Department of Fish, Wildlife and Parks showed that non-motorized activities such as hiking, backpacking, horseback riding and mountain biking accounted for 90% of Montana resident trail use while offroad vehicle riding, only 10%....When it comes to 1997 national forest summer trail use funding under the Symms Rider [National Recreation Trails Funding Act], 89% goes to motorized uses and only 11% to nonmotorized uses. Ninety-two percent of Montana trails are located on national forests. Winter trail use funding is...unbalanced with 92% going to snowmobile trails and only 8% cross-country skiing." (p10)

"Report from Capitol Hill: Symms 'Trails' Rider Up for Reauthorization." Networker v9 n2 Sum 1997. p10.

TRANSCENDENTAL MEDITATION--HEALTH ASPECTS --UNITED STATES

According to a U.S. study reported in the August 28, 1996 issue of HYPERTENSION, "men who practiced transcendental meditation twice daily for 20 minutes per session saw their systolic blood pressure (the higher number in a blood pressure reading) drop by 12.7 mm Hg [millimeters of mercury] compared with those who made lifestyle modifications and 6.6 mm Hg compared with those who practiced muscle relaxation techniques. Their diastolic pressure (the lower number in a blood pressure reading) dropped by 8.1 mm Hg and 1.9 mm Hg, respectively....Those [women] in the transcendental meditation group saw their systolic blood pressure drop by 10.4 mm Hg and their diastolic pressure drop by 5.9 mm Hg compared with those who made lifestyle modifications." (p7)

"Medicate and Meditate?" People's Medical Society Newsletter v16 n3 Jun 1997. p7. (ISSN0736-4873).

TRANSFER OF STUDENTS

see STUDENTS, TRANSFER OF

TRANSFER PAYMENTS--QUEBEC (PROVINCE) (v26)

TRANSIENT LABOR

see MIGRANT LABOR

TRANSPLANTATION OF ORGANS, TISSUES, ETC.

see also HEART--TRANSPLANTATION

TRANSPLANTATION OF ORGANS, TISSUES, ETC. --GREAT BRITAIN (v26)

TRANSPLANTATION OF ORGANS, TISSUES, ETC. --MICHIGAN (v26)

"Only 47 Michigan patients received hearts last year, while 18 died waiting for a transplant, according to the Ann Arbor-based Transplantation Society of Michigan. There are 74 Michigan heart patients waiting on a national list....It costs an average of $150,000 for the transplant surgery, and the cost of care rises to $316,000 for the first five years following surgery." (p7 secA)

Putnam, Judy. "The Heart of the Matter." Ypsilanti Press 17 Aug 1997. p1,7 secA.

TRANSPLANTATION OF ORGANS, TISSUES, ETC. --UNITED STATES (v26)

TRANSPORTATION

see also AUTOMOBILE TRAVEL; BRIDGES; BUS LINES; COMMUTING; HONG KONG--COMMERCE--TRANSPORTATION; LOCAL TRANSIT; OCEAN TRAVEL; RAILROADS; ROADS; SHIPPING; STUDENTS--TRANSPORTATION--IRELAND; VEHICLES

TRANSPORTATION--AUSTRALIA

According to the Australian Bureau of Statistics, "use of road and air transport increased markedly between 1973-74 and 1995-96 (road up 91 per cent, air up 71 per cent), and the total number of urban passenger-kilometres travelled increased by 72 per cent between 1974 and 1993. Most of this was due to an 80 per cent increase in the use of cars for urban journeys....At February 1997, the transport industry, including services to transport, employed a total of over 382,000. The biggest employer in the industry was road transport, which employed 51 per cent of employees in February 1997, followed by services to transport (19 per cent). The transport industry contributed $25.46 billion to GDP in 1995-96, amounting to 6 per cent of total GDP."

Australian Bureau of Statistics. "Transport Uses a Quarter of National Energy." Media Release 4 Jun 1997. document-level access: <http://www.abs.gov.au/websitedbs/d3110125.nsf/4a255eef008309e44a255eef00061e57/be793bae9859b1e64a2564ac000247d9?OpenDocument>

TRANSPORTATION--AUSTRALIA--PUBLIC OPINION (v26)

TRANSPORTATION--CHINA

In China, "annual sales of motorcycles in rural areas are 3 to 4 million. The number of motorcycles per hundred rural households increased sharply from 1 in 1990 to 8 in 1996. Small tractors powered with 10 to 15 horsepower diesel engines have become the prime beasts of burden in rural China. A large portion of the more than 8 million of these small tractors participate in some transportation service during each calendar year....The number of agricultural use trucks rose from 624,000 in 1990 to 790,000 in 1995." (p17)

Crook, Frederick W./U.S. Dept. of Agriculture. Economic Research Service. "Input Supplies Adequate for 1997." China: International Agriculture and Trade Reports Situation and Outlook Series Jun 1997. p16-18.

TRANSPORTATION--ENERGY CONSUMPTION --AUSTRALIA

"The Australian transport industry consumed a quarter of our national energy in 1995-96, according to 'Australian Transport and the Environment' released...by the Australian Bureau of Statistics. Of the total energy used by all transport, 72 per cent was consumed by road transport while 15 per cent was consumed by air transport. Cars accounted for 66 per cent of the energy used by road transport....Since 1988, the consumption of unleaded petrol as a proportion of total petrol has increased from 21 per cent to 38 per cent in 1991, and 57 per cent in 1995."

Australian Bureau of Statistics. "Transport Uses a Quarter of National Energy." Media Release 4 Jun 1997. document-level access: <http://www.abs.gov.au/websitedbs/d3110125.nsf/4a255eef008309e44a255eef00061e57/be793bae9859b1e64a2564ac000247d9?OpenDocument>

TRANSPORTATION--ENERGY CONSUMPTION--CHINA (v26)

TRANSPORTATION--ENVIRONMENTAL ASPECTS --EUROPE

In the EU, carbon dioxide emissions "from road transport rose by 1.2% between '94 and '95. Emissions from air transport--domestic plus international flights--were up by 4% on 1994. There were big rises in the Netherlands (14.9%), Spain (8.2%), Italy (5.9%), France (3.7%) and the UK (4%). These countries produced over 63% of EU air transport emissions."

Eurostat. "EU CO2 Emissions Rise by 1.7% in 1995." Press Release 27 Nov 1997. document-level access: <http://europa.eu.int/en/comm/eurostat/compres/en/8097/6808097a.htm>

TRANSPORTATION--EUROPE (v26)

TRANSPORTATION--EUROPE--FINANCE

"The European Commission, which runs the [Cohesion] Fund, decided in 1995 that a 50-50 balance should be achieved between environment and transport projects over the life of the Fund....The Commission's report on the Fund's operations for 1996 says 49.9% of last year's financing commitments were for environment projects and 50.1% for transport. The average for 1993-1996 shows environmental spending still behind at 47.3%, however....Roads and highways took 78.4% of spending commitments for transport, with rail, at just 18.1%, receiving an even smaller proportion than in previous years. The Fund is worth a total of 15.15 billion Ecu [European currency units] (US $17.0 billion) between 1993 and 1999." (p15)

"General Policy: In Brief...: Road/Rail Spending Imbalance of EU Fund Widens." Environment Watch: Western Europe v6 n14 18 Jul 1997. p15. (ISSN1066-6001).

TRANSPORTATION--GREAT BRITAIN (v26)

TRANSPORTATION--ISRAEL (v26)

TRANSPORTATION--MICHIGAN (v26)

TRANSPORTATION--MICHIGAN--ANN ARBOR

In mid-May 1997, "the Ann Arbor, Michigan, transit authority unveiled 'The Ride,' its version of a smart intermodal system." (p12) "The cost of the project: $2.5 million, with five percent coming from local funds, 85 percent from federal sources, and 10 percent from the state....Last year, usage rose eight percent on Ann Arbor's 27 bus routes in part because of improved service." (p13)

McGuckin, Timothy. "Going Smart." Planning v63 n7 Jul 1997. p12-14. (ISSN0001-2610).

TRANSPORTATION--MISSOURI

"According to the Federal Highway Administration, Missouri has the country's sixth largest highway system. According to the Road Information Program, vehicle travel in Missouri grew by 51 percent between 1985 and 1995, compared to a national average of 37 percent. It is the home of the second and third largest rail hubs, the second fastest-growing airport in the world, and the second largest inland port in the United States." (pS11030)

Bond, Christopher S. (Sen.-Mo.). "ISTEA." Congressional Record. Daily ed. v143 n144 23 Oct 1997. pS11029-11032. section/page-level access: <http://thomas.loc.gov/cgi-bin/query/R?r105:FLD001:S11029:> (ISSN0363-7239). (X1.1A.105/1).

TRANSPORTATION--TEXAS--SAN ANTONIO

"San Antonio's TransGuide Operations Center, which is run by the Texas Department of Transportation, won $7.1 million in federal funds to equip 100,000 cars and vans with 'intelligent vehicle tags,' which are used to monitor speed....According to the Texas Transportation Institute at Texas A&M [Agricultural & Mechanical] University, the two-year-old TransGuide system has already led to a 15 percent reduction in accidents and a 20 percent reduction in emergency response time." (p14)

McGuckin, Timothy. "Going Smart." Planning v63 n7 Jul 1997. p12-14. (ISSN0001-2610).

TRANSPORTATION--UNITED STATES (v26)

Currently, about 10 different in-vehicle navigation systems "are available in the U.S., with a median price of about $2,500. General Motors reported that in 1995 it sold more than 1,000 cars fitted with the GuideStar Navigation system. The company forecasts that by 2001, every GM car can be so equipped--at the buyer's option. Car rental agencies are already a big market. Hertz has equipped 8,000 of its Florida rental cars, and Avis--catching up--has 1,000 in 14 cities nationwide." (p13)

McGuckin, Timothy. "Going Smart." Planning v63 n7 Jul 1997. p12-14. (ISSN0001-2610).

According to U.S. Bureau of Transportation Statistics Director Dr. T. R. Lakshmanan, "'Americans spend an average of 19 percent of their income on transportation-related expenditures. Transportation represents nearly 11 percent of our gross domestic product, moves more than 12 billion tons of goods annually, and supports 17,200 passenger miles per person per year."

U.S. Dept. of Transportation. "DOT Releases Overview of Transportation in the U.S." Press Release 4 Apr 1997. document-level access: <http://www.dot.gov:80/affairs/dot4297.htm>

In the U.S., "cars, light trucks and vans were by far the dominant means of transportation for long distance trips in 1995, accounting for more than 80 percent of person trips, which is about the same as in 1977. Air travel was the second most popular means of transportation, accounting for 16 percent of trips, growing from 12 percent in 1977....Between 1977 and 1995, the number of bus trips increased 37 percent and train trips, 22 percent. In 1995, there were 20 million bus trips and 5 million train trips....Nearly 9 out of 10 air travelers used a car to get to the airport, and one out of every 10 intercity bus travelers walked to the bus station; 181 million long-distance trips, or about one of every five trips, involved the use of more than one mode. People in households with less than $25,000 annual income are half of all intercity bus riders; about 25 percent of train riders have less than $25,000 annual income."

U.S. Dept. of Transportation. "Transportation Secretary Slater Says New American Travel Survey Results Underscore Need for Investment...." Press Release 10 Nov 1997. document-level access: <http://www.dot.gov/affairs/dot18597.htm>

In New Haven, Connecticut, the 1991 Intermodal Surface Transportation Efficiency Act "is funding a door-to-door 'dial a ride' transit service for disabled people in 19 towns with a total population of over 500,000. In 1996 the program provided more than 110,000 rides for disabled passengers....In San Jose, Calif., ISTEA has made possible a new state-of-the-art child-care facility at one of the city's major transportation hubs, providing convenient child care to commuters and saving an estimated 700,000 miles of commuter trips a year....New York State, with one-third of the nation's transit riders (and the largest percentage of people who walk to work), has among the lowest per capita gasoline consumption in the...[U.S.]: 358 gallons per year versus a national average of more than 550 gallons per year." (p18)

Pataki, George E. "Opinion/Essays: A Transportation Act That's Good for the Environment." The Christian Science Monitor v89 n143 19 Jun 1997. p18. The Christian Science Monitor search engine: <http://www.csmonitor.com/plweb-cgi/iops1.pl> To retrieve this article, enter the following search: ED=19970619 AND environment. In the "retrieved list," click the title that matches this record. (ISSN0882-7729).

TRANSPORTATION--UNITED STATES--COSTS (v26)

TRANSPORTATION--UNITED STATES--FINANCE (v26)

In 1996, the U.S. "spent $20 billion for highways, while capital investment for Amtrak was less than $450 million. In relative terms, between fiscal year 1980 and fiscal year 1994, transportation outlays for highways increased 73 percent, aviation increased 170 percent, and transportation outlays for rail went down by 62 percent. In terms of growth, between 1982 and 1992 highway spending grew by 5 percent, aviation by 10 percent, while rail decreased by 9 percent." (pS8477)

Roth, William V., Jr. (Sen.-Del.). "Railroad Deficit Reduction Fuel Taxes." Congressional Record. Daily ed. v143 n111 31 Jul 1997. pS8465-8480. section/page-level access: <http://thomas.loc.gov/cgi-bin/query/R?r105:FLD001:S08477:> (ISSN0363-7239). (X1.1A.105/1).

According to a U.S. Dept. of Transportation report, "Transportation Receipts and Outlays in the Federal Budget: Fiscal Years 1977-94," transportation "receipts totaled more than $25 billion in 1994....Transportation outlays constituted only 2.67 percent of total federal outlays in 1994: $39 billion versus $1.5 trillion. This proportion ranged from a high of 4.08 percent in 1977 to a low of 2.43 percent in 1990. Highway and aviation taxes accounted for nearly 90 percent of all federal transportation receipts collected from 1977 to 1994; highway and aviation accounted for 70 percent of all federal transportation outlays during the same period."

U.S. Dept. of Transportation. "Federal Transportation Financial Report Released by DOT." Press Release 18 Jun 1997. document-level access: <http://www.dot.gov/affairs/dot8697.htm>

"Since 1991, about 30 percent of ITS [Intelligent Transportation Systems] Program funding has supported research and development efforts [in the U.S.] to improve the state of the art of enabling technologies, advanced metropolitan travel management systems, rural ITS applications, CVO [commercial vehicle operations], collision-avoidance systems, and AHS [automated highway systems]....About 57 percent of obligated funds has supported field testing and demonstration projects as part of operational tests or the ITS Priority Corridors Program, and 73 percent of this amount was directed by Congress....The ITS Program has spent roughly 13 percent of its funding to facilitate understanding, acceptance, and deployment of ITS services." (p8)

Johnson, Christine M./U.S. Dept. of Transportation. Federal Highway Administration. "Intelligent Transportation Systems: The National ITS Program: Where We've Been and Where We're Going." Public Roads v61 n2 Sep-Oct 1997. p6-14. (ISSN0033-3735).

TRASH

see REFUSE AND REFUSE DISPOSAL

TRAVEL (v26)

see also AUTOMOBILE TRAVEL; INTERNET (COMPUTER NETWORK)--TRAVEL; OCEAN TRAVEL; SINGLE PEOPLE--TRAVEL

TRAVEL--NEW ZEALAND

"The number of New Zealand residents making short visits overseas in the [September 1997] quarter rose 2 per cent when compared to the September 1996 quarter. This compares with an increase of 17 per cent between the September 1995 and 1996 quarters. There were 176,600 short-term departures to Australia, slightly down on the 179,800 who took short trips in the previous September quarter. There were fewer visits to Fiji, down 2 per cent to 23,100. New Zealand residents visiting Europe and those visiting Asia both increased by 13 per cent. Visits to the USA increased 8 per cent compared with the previous September quarter and over the same period, short-term visits to Canada by New Zealand residents increased by 12 per cent."

Statistics New Zealand. "External Migration--September 1997 Quarter." Press Release 12 Nov 1997. document-level access: <http://www.stats.govt.nz/statsweb.nsf/52518ce3e01f62f4cc256388000c48c0/ae8760ddd0ec300f4c25654c0083ac25?OpenDocument>

TRAVEL--UNITED STATES

"Americans took about 1 billion long distance trips during 1995, which accounts for about 25 percent of all travel in the United States....Americans traveled nearly 827 billion miles in 1995--enough distance for each person in the United States to go from Portland, Maine, to Portland, Ore. The average American traveled more than 3,100 miles on long distance trips in 1995, up from 1,800 miles in 1977 on trips longer than 100 miles....Minority groups increased their trip-making, but white Americans still travel about twice as much as African-Americans and Hispanic-Americans....Seventy-four percent of trips longer than 1,000 miles are by plane, and nearly 25 percent of trips longer than 1,000 miles are by car. Nearly all travel that is less than 500 miles round trip, is by car. About four percent is by bus or train and only two percent is by plane."

U.S. Dept. of Transportation. "Transportation Secretary Slater Says New American Travel Survey Results Underscore Need for Investment...." Press Release 10 Nov 1997. document-level access: <http://www.dot.gov/affairs/dot18597.htm>

TRAVEL, AUTOMOBILE

see AUTOMOBILE TRAVEL

TRAVEL, OCEAN

see OCEAN TRAVEL

TRAVEL AGENTS--UNITED STATES

"An estimated 34,000 travel agents book about 80 percent of the flights in the US annually. For their services, they're paid more than $6 billion in commissions from the airlines. Agents used to earn an average of 10 percent on any tickets they sold. Over the past two years, however, the airlines have dropped that to 8 percent and capped commissions at $50 a ticket." (p3)

Marks, Alexandra. "United States: Travel Agents: Always Putting Clients First?" The Christian Science Monitor v90 n24 30 Dec 1997. p3. The Christian Science Monitor search engine: <http://www.csmonitor.com/plweb-cgi/iops1.pl> To retrieve this article, enter the following search: ED=19971230 AND first. In the "retrieved list," click the title that matches this record. (ISSN0882-7729).

TRAVEL COSTS--UNITED STATES (v26)

TREATIES OF PEACE

see PEACE TREATIES

TREATMENT
see ATTENTION-DEFICIT HYPERACTIVITY DISORDER--TREATMENT; BREAST--CANCER--TREATMENT; DRUG ABUSE--TREATMENT; EPILEPSY--TREATMENT; MENTAL ILLNESS--TREATMENT; SUBSTANCE ABUSE--TREATMENT

TREE PLANTERS (PERSONS)--CANADA (v26)

TREVISO (ITALY)--EMPLOYMENT (v26)

TRIAL-DOCKETS
see COURT CALENDARS

TRIALS AND MASS MEDIA
see MASS MEDIA AND TRIALS

TRINIDAD AND TOBAGO--SOCIAL CONDITIONS (v26)

TRITIUM (v26)

TROPIC-BIRDS--LATIN AMERICA (v26)

TROPICAL FISH TRADE
see ORNAMENTAL FISH TRADE

TROUT INDUSTRY--UNITED STATES

The U.S. Dept. of Agriculture's "September trout report showed 1997 (September 1, 1996 to August 31, 1997) sales of trout products at $78 million, up $6 million from the previous year." (unpaginated) "A 6-percent increase in the quantity of the foodsize trout sold was the sole reason behind the over $3 million increase in the value of foodsize fish sales, as the average price remained at $1.06 a pound, the same as in 1996....Idaho's volume was up 5 percent in 1997, but the price of foodsize fish fell a nickel from 1996 to only $0.75 a pound....Following a 15-percent jump in 1996, sales of stockers rose 48 percent in 1997 to $11 million. Much of the increase resulted from higher prices, as the volume of sales rose 20 percent....Egg exports fell 20 percent, as lower sales to Canada were not fully offset by increased sales to Asia. Total exports of trout products (fresh or frozen) declined to $1.2 million, down about $400,000...." (unpaginated)

Harvey, Dave/U.S. Dept. of Agriculture. Economic Research Service. "Trout Sales Reach $78 Million." Aquaculture Outlook 3 Oct 1997.

TRUCK ACCIDENTS--UNITED STATES

In the U.S., "according to PARADE magazine, in '1995, while large trucks made up 3 percent of all registered vehicles they accounted for 21 percent of all deaths in crashes involving two or more vehicles.'...The blind spots on the right side of a truck account for about 50 percent of what drivers cannot see, and on the left side about 25 percent." (p8)

"Longer Big Rigs Threaten Jobs, Safety on Highways." The People v107 n7 Oct 1997. p8. (ISSN0199-350X).

"Crashes involving large trucks on U.S. roads declined in 1995 (the most recent year with complete crash data), says a University of Michigan researcher. About 129,000 single-unit commercial trucks and single and multiple semi-trailer trucks were involved in fatal, injury or tow-away crashes in 1995--down from 151,000 the year before and the fewest total since 1991. The figures are from the...1995 edition of the TRUCK AND BUS CRASH FACTBOOK, an annual publication produced by the U-M Center for National Truck Statistics for the Federal Highway Administration's Office of Motor Carriers. The Center, directed by Kenneth L. Campbell, is part of the U-M Transportation Research Institute." (p1) "Less than 1 percent of truck drivers involved in all crashes had been using alcohol, compared with more than 5 percent of passenger car drivers involved in crashes. About 61 percent of truck drivers killed in crashes used no safety belts....About 4 percent of trucks involved in fatal collisions were carrying hazardous materials. More than 70 percent of all truck crashes occurred on dry roads. About one-fourth of fatal truck crashes occurred at night." (p2)

University of Michigan. News and Information Services. "Large Truck Crashes Declined in 1995, Says a U-M Study." Univeristy of Michigan News Release 25 Sep 1997. p1-2.

TRUCK ACCIDENTS--UNITED STATES--MORTALITY

According to a report released by the University of Michigan, in the U.S., "4,631 trucks were involved in fatal crashes (resulting in nearly 5,100 deaths) in 1995, compared with more than 5,300 deaths in nearly 4,800 fatal collisions the year before....[Daniel F. Blower, author of the study, says,] 'There was one truck for every 28 passenger cars involved in a crash, but one truck for every seven cars involved in a fatal crash. Differences in mass, obviously, help explain this disparity.' Blower says that of the nearly 5,100 deaths resulting from truck crashes, 78 percent were occupants of other non-truck vehicles involved. About 13 percent of the fatalities were the drivers or passengers in the trucks, and about 9 percent were non-motorists, such as pedestrians and bicyclists. About two-thirds of the fatal truck collisions, Blower says, involved just one other vehicle, and in these crashes, driver-related factors contributing to the crash were attributed to less than 30 percent of the truck drivers. On the other hand, nearly 80 percent of the drivers in the other vehicle in these crashes were coded for driving errors, such as speeding, improper turns, failure to yield and failure to obey traffic controls....The study shows that in fatal rear-end collisions, trucks are struck about twice as often by other cars as they are the striking vehicles. In addition, head-on crashes accounted for about 23 percent of fatal truck involvements....Nearly 70 percent of the truck driver fatalities occured in single-vehicle crashes (i.e., no other vehicles were involved)." (p1-2)

University of Michigan. News and Information Services. "Large Truck Crashes Declined in 1995, Says a U-M Study." University of Michigan News Release 25 Sep 1997. p1-2.

TRUCKING--LAW AND LEGISLATION--MICHIGAN

In Michigan, senators "defeated efforts to make trucks weighing upward of 160,000 pounds pay more in licensing fees than trucks weighing half that....The Senate approved $66 million in new, permanent road funding. Charging heavy trucks more would have increased that pot by $12 million....The action starts work on [Governor John] Engler's plan to boost road funding by more than $560 million annually....The Senate voted, 20-17, to increase big truck fees by 30 percent, which will raise an estimated $36 million in new road revenue....Michigan and Louisiana are the only states that allow trucks as heavy as 160,000 pounds on state roads. Thirty-five other states, including Michigan's neighbors, have weight limits of 80,000 pounds." (p6 secC)

Luke, Peter. "Local: Process Under Way to Raise Road Funds." Ann Arbor News 13 Jun 1997. p6 secC.

TRUCKING--MICHIGAN

"Michigan and Louisiana are the only states that permit truck weights of as much as 160,000 pounds. The national standard is 80,000 pounds....Annual mileage driven by trucks in Michigan jumped by a third between 1990 and 1995, from 3.2 billion to 4.3 billion miles a year....[There are] nearly 1,000 trucking companies in...[Michigan]." (p2 secB)

Magner, Mike/Barton, John. "Local: Truck Traffic Shifts into High Gear." Ann Arbor News 16 Nov 1997. p1-2 secB.

TRUCKING--UNITED STATES (v26)

In the U.S., "overall, truck traffic has increased 25 percent since 1990. Measured by vehicle miles traveled, the trucking industry fatality rate decreased 40 percent during the past decade. But, while trucks represent only 7 percent of total miles driven in the United States, they're involved in 12 percent of fatal accidents." (p18)

Kolstad, James L. "Opinion/Essays: What If Bigger Trucks Were to Barrel down the Interstate?" The Christian Science Monitor v89 n202 12 Sep 1997. p18. The Christian Science Monitor search engine: <http://www.csmonitor.com/plweb-cgi/

iops1.pl> To retrieve this article, enter the following search: ED=19970912 AND interstate. In the "retrieved list," click the title that matches this record. (ISSN0882-7729).

TRUCKS--MICHIGAN--WAYNE COUNTY--WEIGHT

In Michigan, "a 13-month pilot program to crack down on dangerously overweight trucks in western Wayne County by increasing patrols has been such a success that it will be expanded soon, Wayne County Sheriff Robert Ficano said. Sheriff's deputies have written 8,489 citations totaling about $1 million in fines since the program began 13 months ago in Melvindale, Inkster, Highland Park, Allen Park, Sumpter Township, Grosse Ile and Gibraltar, Ficano said....So far, about $250,000 has been given to the Sheriff's Department and another $250,000 has gone to participating cities." (p3 secC)

Schabath, Gene. "Wayne: In Western Wayne County: Cops Nab Overweight Trucks." Detroit News 11 Dec 1997. p3 secC.

TRUST (PSYCHOLOGY)--CANADA--LATIN AMERICA --SWEDEN

According to a 1996 Latinobarometro survey of 17 Latin American countries, "in Uruguay, one out of three citizens trusts others most of the time; the rest of the region shows still lower proportions of such trust, ranging from barely one in four (Argentina, Paraguay, and Colombia) to only one in ten (Brazil and Venezuela). The contrast with established democracies such as Sweden is huge. There, according to the 1990 World Values Survey, six out of ten people trust others. In Canada, the comparable figure is five out of ten." (p128)

Lagos, Marta. "Public Opinion in New Democracies: Latin America's Smiling Mask." Journal of Democracy v8 n3 Jul 1997. p125-138. (ISSN1045-5736).

TUBERCULOSIS (v26)

TUBERCULOSIS--ASIA (v26)

TUBERCULOSIS--MARYLAND

According to the Maryland Department of Health and Mental Hygiene, in 1995, "there were 370 cases of TB [tuberculosis] in Maryland, compared to 362 cases in 1994. The rate of cases per 100,000 people remained at 7.3 for both years....In 1995, for the first time, Montgomery County's case count of 102 exceeded that of Baltimore City, which had 97 cases. Other Maryland counties with a significant number of cases include Prince George's County with 62 cases, Baltimore County with 32 cases, Anne Arundel County with 19 and Howard County with 12 cases."

Maryland. Dept. of Health and Mental Hygiene. "Maryland to Observe World Tuberculosis Day; Releases 1995 State TB Figures." News Release 22 Mar 1996. document-level access: <http://www.charm.net/~epi9/news5.htm>

TUBERCULOSIS--MORTALITY (v26)

TUBERCULOSIS--TEXAS

"The Texas Department of Health (TDH) has announced a decline in tuberculosis (TB) cases in Texas for the second consecutive year. There were 2,103 cases of TB reported in 1996, a decrease of 11 percent from the 2,369 cases reported in 1995, and a 17 percent decrease from the 2,542 cases reported in 1994....Among the 77 counties where TB increased, Travis County reported 89 cases of TB in 1996, an increase of 10 percent over the 81 cases reported in 1995....Nine of Texas' 254 counties (Bexar, Cameron, Dallas, El Paso, Harris, Hidalgo, Nueces, Tarrant and Travis) reported 70 percent of the 1996 cases. Minority racial and ethnic populations accounted for 77 percent of the 1996 cases, with Hispanics (42 percent) and African Americans (26 percent) representing the majority of cases in Texas. Nine percent of the cases were reported in Asian/Pacific Islanders."

Texas. Dept. of Health. "Texas Sees Second Year of Declining Tuberculosis Rates." News Release 24 Mar 1997. document-level access: <http://www.tdh.texas.gov/news/b_new127.htm>

TUBERCULOSIS--UNITED STATES (v26)

"A drug-resistant strain of tuberculosis is spreading across the United States....So far, 196 cases of tuberculosis have been reported across...[Michigan]....Nationally, 42 states have recorded cases of the drug-resistant strain, which is up from 13 states in 1991....From 1993 through 1996 there were about 66,000 cases of some sort of TB reported across the nation. Of those cases, 1,457 were of the multidrug resistant strain." (p1 secC)

Lopez, Manny. "Metro: Testing Checks Spread of TB." Detroit News 11 Sep 1997. p1 secC.

TUBERCULOSIS--UNITED STATES--IMMIGRANTS (v26)

TUITION

see COLLEGE COSTS

TUNA--PACIFIC OCEAN

"Somewhere around 6 million dolphin (the mammals) are estimated to have been killed in tuna nets in the eastern tropical Pacific since the 1960s. Through a combination of factors, this number has been reduced to about 5,000-10,000 dolphins a year...." (p7)

"Tuna-Safe Tuna Bill." NCMC Marine Bulletin n79 Spr-Sum 1997. p7.

TUNA FISHERIES, BLUEFIN

see BLUEFIN TUNA FISHERIES

TURKEY--ECONOMIC CONDITIONS (v26)

"Turkey's GDP growth rate, averaging around 6 percent a year from 1963 to 1992, is one of the most robust among the members of the Organization for Economic Cooperation and Development (OECD), and it has led to a more than twofold increase in per-capita GDP....Industrial production's share of GDP rose from 17.1 percent in 1963 to 26.5 percent by 1992. The share of agricultural production, on the other hand, declined from 34.6 percent in 1963 to 15.8 percent by 1992." (p174)

Erdogan, Meftun/Dahl, Carol. "Energy Demand in Turkey." Journal of Energy and Development v21 n2 Spr 1996. p173-188. (ISSN0361-4476).

In Turkey, "in 1994, inflation reached 149.6 percent, while gross domestic product (GDP) fell by 6 percent and unemployment rose by a comparable figure. By early 1996, the national debt, largely accumulated during the time when Ozal was premier and used to fund economic modernization programs, stood at U.S. $67.8 billion." (p199)

Lombardi, Ben. "Turkey--The Return of the Reluctant Generals?" Political Science Quarterly v112 n2 Sum 1997. p191-215. (ISSN0032-3195).

TURKEY INDUSTRY

see also CHICKEN INDUSTRY; POULTRY INDUSTRY

TURKEY INDUSTRY--RUSSIA--UNITED STATES (v26)

TURKEY INDUSTRY--UNITED STATES (v26)

In the U.S., "more than 279 million turkeys were sold by farmers in 1992. In 1992, North Carolina and Minnesota sold nearly 99 million turkeys, which was 35 percent of the turkeys sold in the United States. Duplin County, NC, was the top county in turkeys sold, with 12 million. Rockingham County, VA, and Union County, NC, were second and third, respectively. Kandiyohi County, MN, with 7.8 million sold, was fourth."

U.S. Dept. of Commerce. Economic & Statistics Administration. "Census Facts for Thanksgiving: Thanksgiving Feast--An American Tradition." Census Bureau Fact Sheet 20 Nov 1997. document-level access: <http://www.census.gov/Press-Release/fs97-12.html>

TURKEYS--REPRODUCTION (v26)

TURKMENISTAN (v26)

TUSCALOOSA COUNTY (ALA.) (v26)

TWINS--UNITED STATES

"Michigan has one of the 10 highest rates of twin births in the country, according to a recent article in the JOURNAL OF THE AMERICAN MEDICAL ASSOCIATION....In general, twin births are increasing across the country. From 1980 to 1994, twin births jumped 42 percent, according to the JAMA article." (p16 secD)

Bondi, Nicole. "MetroLife: Child Birth: Older Mothers Make State a Leading Producer of Twins." Detroit News 24 Jul 1997. p16 secD.

TWO-YEAR COLLEGES

see COMMUNITY COLLEGES

TYPE I DIABETES

see DIABETES

TYPHOID VACCINE

"The old typhoid vaccine, developed in 1917, hurt like the blazes, was 70 percent effective for up to three years and the side effects felt like the worst flu bout of your life. In 1990, a new live-bacteria pill was developed. You take it every other day for eight days....[Dr. Jeffrey Band, director of the Beaumont Interhealth Service in Royal Oak, Michigan] says it has 'one one-thousandth of the side effects' and is good for up to five years....Then in 1995, a new polysaccharide was introduced. This shot gives all the protection of the four-dose oral drug, but you just need one dose, which is effective for three years." (p1 secH)

Volgenau, Gerry. "Travel: New Vaccines Fight Hepatitis, Typhoid." Detroit Free Press 7 Dec 1997. p1 secH.

UGANDA--ECONOMIC CONDITIONS (v26)

UGANDA--POPULATION (v26)

UKRAINE--COMMERCE

"Ukrainian-Polish trade accounted for USD [U.S. dollars] 280 million in 1993 and USD 550 million in 1994. The same year, the Ukrainian-Slovak trade volume stood at USD 430 million, and that of Ukraine and Hungary barely reached USD 400 million. The trade between Ukraine and Romania and the Czech Republic was even smaller: USD 290 million and USD 280 million respectively." (p353) "Economically, Ukraine remains oriented toward Russia, which accounts for 41% of Ukraine's total trade volume." (p355)

Pavliuk, Oleksandr. "Ukraine and Regional Cooperation in Central and Eastern Europe." Security Dialogue v28 n3 Sep 1997. p347-361. (ISSN0967-0106).

UKRAINE--ECONOMIC CONDITIONS (v26)

ULTRAVIOLET RADIATION--UNITED STATES (v26)

UNDERGRADUATES

see COLLEGE STUDENTS

UNDOCUMENTED ALIENS

see ILLEGAL ALIENS

UNDULANT FEVER

see BRUCELLOSIS

UNEMPLOYMENT (v26)

Finland "has gone from 3.4% unemployment in 1989 to 17.1% in 1995, according to figures in THE STATE OF WORKING AMERICA, a book from the Economic Policy Institute. In 1995, unemployment was 11.6% in France, 12.2% in Italy and 22.7% in Spain, compared to 5.5% in the U.S." (p6) "The Netherlands...saw its unemployment rate decline rom 8.3% in 1989 to 6.5% in 1995. Between 1989 and 1994, it produced jobs at a rate more than three times faster than that in the U.S. (measured as a percentage of 1989 jobs). The average unemployment rate of the seven largest developed countries (which includes Japan and Canada) was 6.8% in 1995, a little more than a percent higher than the rate in the U.S...." (p7)

"An Economic Miracle...Or Misery?" Community Change n19 Fall 1997. p6-7.

UNEMPLOYMENT--AFRO-AMERICANS (v26)

"The unemployment rate among African American males has averaged 39.7 percent this year; 33.1 percent of African American teens are unemployed in Georgia....African American applicants received unfavorable treatment in 20 percent of job searches, according to a 1990 study by the Urban Institute which used pairs of identically qualified black and white male college students in Washington and Chicago." (p5)

Slaughter, Gloria. "National Education Association Convenes in Atlanta: Teachers Can Help Rally the Nation to Save Our Children." People's Tribune v24 n7 Jul 1997. p5. (ISSN1081-4787).

In the U.S., "the unemployment rate for black workers fell to 9.3 percent in August, the lowest monthly figure in more than 23 years. This year, a smaller part of the black labor force is without work than in any year since 1973, according to the Bureau of Labor Statistics....A decline in black joblessness could help reduce corrosive income disparities with whites, whose unemployment rate last month was just 4.2 percent.... Unemployment among black teens age 16 to 19 remains extremely high--over 33.6 percent, last year, compared with 14.2 percent for white teenagers, according to bureau data." (p8)

Tyson, James L. "Business & Money: Workplace: Jobless Rate for Blacks Falls to 23-Year Low." The Christian Science Monitor v89 n214 30 Sep 1997. p8. The Christian Science Monitor search engine: <http://www.csmonitor.com/plweb-cgi/iops1.pl> To retrieve this article, enter the following search: ED=19970930 AND low. In the "retrieved list," click the title that matches this record. (ISSN0882-7729).

In the U.S., "while the official national unemployment rate for all workers is said to be at its lowest rate in almost a quarter of a century, hovering between 4 and 5 percent, there is no getting around the continuing wage gaps between African American and white workers. In fact, even in this period of economic 'upturn,' joblessness for Blacks remains double that of whites, at 10.4 percent." (p11)

"Trendwatch: The Gaps Widen." Third Force v5 n5 Nov-Dec 1997. p11. (ISSN1067-3237).

UNEMPLOYMENT--AUSTRALIA (v26)

UNEMPLOYMENT--AUSTRALIA--IMMIGRANTS

In November 1996, "the unemployment rate for migrants who had arrived, as adults, in Australia after 1970, and had obtained permanent resident status, was 9.7 per cent. This compared with 7.7 per cent for those born in Australia, and 9.2 per cent for all migrants to Australia, according to figures published...by the Australian Bureau of Statistics in the publication 'Labour Force Status and Other Characteristics of Migrants.'...The unemployment rates for males and female migrants were 9.1 per cent and 10.5 per cent respectively."

Australian Bureau of Statistics. "Migrants Have Higher Unemployment Rate." Media Release 11 Jun 1997. document-level access: <http://www.abs.gov.au/websitedbs/d3110125.nsf/4a255eef008309e44a255eef00061e57/67dbd33c47ca98f04a2564b3000526f7?OpenDocument>

UNEMPLOYMENT--AUSTRALIA--QUEENSLAND --TASMANIA (v26)

UNEMPLOYMENT--BRAZIL (v26)

UNEMPLOYMENT--CALIFORNIA

In California, "the May [1997] jobless rate of 6.3 percent was still a point above the national average....According to figures [by Jean Ross of the California Budget Project,] the ratio of job seekers to jobs is more than 15-to-one in 11 California counties and between 14 and 10-to-one in another 12 counties. In 23 counties, including San Diego, Riverside, San Bernardino, Los Angeles, San Francisco, Contra Costa, Alameda, Sacramento and Yolo, the ratio is five to nine job seekers per job. The counties with the closest match--one to four job seekers per job-include Orange, Ventura, Santa Clara, San Mateo and Marin." (p25)

Rasky, Susan. "The Bottom Line: Commentary." California Journal v28 n8 Aug 1997. p25. (ISSN0008-1205).

UNEMPLOYMENT--CANADA (v26)

"Right now we have 1.4 million unemployed Canadians, almost exactly what it was when the government came to power. There is 20 per cent plus unemployment in Cape Breton and Newfoundland. The national youth unemployment figure is 17 per cent. The real unemployment rate when we count all the people who have dropped out of the workforce is approaching 11 per cent." (p10229)

Solberg, Monte (MP-AB). "Oral Question Period: Liberal Party of Canada." Canada. Parliament. House of Commons. Debates. v134 n164 25 Apr 1997. p10229. page-level access: <http://www.parl.gc.ca/hansard/164_97-04-25/164OQ1E.html#10229> section-level access: <http://www.parl.gc.ca/hansard/164_97-04-25/164OQ1E.html#LIBERALPARTYOFCANADA> (ISSN0704-5603). (X3-352E).

Canada now has "1.4 million Canadians who are unemployed, 1.6 million Canadians who are underemployed or who have just dropped out of the workforce and millions more on welfare across this country. Officially 9% of the Canadian population is unemployed." (p882)

Nystrom, Lorne (MP-SK). "Government Orders: Supply." Canada. Parliament. House of Commons. Debates. v135 n17 21 Oct 1997. p879-911. section-level access: <http://www.parl.gc.ca/36/1/parlbus/chambus/house/debates/017_1997-10-21/han017-e.htm#LINK38> (ISSN0704-5603). (X3-361E).

In Canada, in October 1993, "144,000 Atlantic Canadians were unemployed. "At the end of last month, three and a half years...[later], 173,000 Atlantic Canadians were unemployed according to Statistics Canada, an increase of 29,000 unemployed, or 20 per cent." (p10188)

Ablonczy, Diane (MP-AB). "Oral Question Period: Employment." Canada. Parliament. House of Commons. Debates. v134 n163 24 Apr 1997. p10188. page-level access: <http://www.parl.gc.ca/hansard/163_97-04-24/163OQ1E.html#10188> section-level access: <http://www.parl.gc.ca/hansard/163_97-04-24/163OQ1E.html#EMPLOYMENT> (ISSN0704-5603). (X3-352E).

UNEMPLOYMENT--CANADA--EUROPE--UNITED STATES (v26)

UNEMPLOYMENT--CANADA--INDIGENOUS PEOPLES

"The royal commission report states aboriginal unemployment in the [Canadian] labour force rose from 15.4% in 1981 to 24.6% in 1991 despite advances in education. Aboriginal participation in the labour force is 57%, below that of all Canadians at 68%. The cost to the economy in foregone income, $5.8 billion, plus the remedial expenditures lead to a loss of $7.5 billion annually. Some 300,000 new jobs will have to be created for aboriginal people in the next 20 years just to reach that...9% to 10% unemployment level." (p897)

Desjarlais, Bev (MP-MB). "Government Orders: Supply." Canada. Parliament. House of Commons. Debates. v135 n17 21 Oct 1997. p879-911. section-level access: <http://www.parl.gc.ca/36/1/parlbus/chambus/house/debates/017_1997-10-21/han017-e.htm#LINKT27> (ISSN0704-5603). (X3-361E).

UNEMPLOYMENT--CANADA--YOUTH

In Canada, "youth unemployment is double the national average. At this time almost 500,000 young people are unemployed. Since the Liberals took office in 1993, 40,000 more young people have ended up on the unemployment roles." (p936)

Davies, Libby (MP-BC). "Government Orders: Supply." Canada. Parliament. House of Commons. Debates. v135 n17 21 Oct 1997. p925-953. section-level access: <http://www.parl.gc.ca/36/1/parlbus/chambus/house/debates/017_1997-10-21/han017-e.htm#LINKT80> (ISSN0704-5603). (X3-361E).

UNEMPLOYMENT--CHINA

China's "State Statistical Bureau reported that those who registered as unemployed amounted to 3 percent of the labor force in the state sector, but actual unemployment is believed to be much higher....Real unemployment and underemployment in Shanghai, the largest city of China, was estimated at between 15 and 20 percent. The World Bank acknowledges that its estimate that redundant workers (who are still registered with the state enterprise) account for more than 10 percent of the workforce at most state enterprises is conservative....In addition, more than 120 million transient laborers from rural areas have rushed into the country's cities in the past 10 years. This accounts for nearly 10 percent of the country's population, and will further increase the supply of workers in the urban areas of China." (p5)

Diao, Xinshen/U.S. Dept. of Agriculture. Economic Research Service. "China Controlled Inflation in 1996." China: International Agriculture and Trade Reports Situation and Outlook Series Jun 1997. p3-5.

UNEMPLOYMENT--EUROPE (v26)

According to Eurostat, the Statistical Office of the European Communities in Luxembourg, "eighteen million people--almost half of them women--had no job but were available and looking for work. Nearly five million of these were under 25....The EU [had] a jobless rate of 10.7% in the week in question. Lowest was Luxembourg's 3.3%, highest Spain's 22.2% with Finland next at 15.6%. 48.3% of jobless had been looking for work for over a year. 49.6% of jobless had not completed upper secondary education. 20.5% of the unemployed were looking for their first job--53.7% in Italy."

Eurostat. "149.3 Million in the EU with a Job." Press Release 22 Jul 1997. document-level access: <http://europa.eu.int/en/comm/eurostat/compres/en/5397/6305397a.htm>

In April 1990, "all but two of Europe's governments were conservative, and unemployment stood at 7.9 percent. Now all but two of Europe's governments are left or center-left. Conservatives are governing only in Germany and Spain, and unemployment across Europe has topped 11.4 percent, representing some 18 million Europeans out of work." (p8)

Chaddock, Gail Russell. "France Sets Fire under Euro-Unity." The Christian Science Monitor v89 n137 11 Jun 1997. p1,8. The Christian Science Monitor search engine: <http://www.csmonitor.com/plweb-cgi/iops1.pl> To retrieve this article, enter the following search: ED=19970611 AND unity. In the "retrieved list," click the title that matches this record. (ISSN0882-7729).

UNEMPLOYMENT--EUROPE--NORTH AMERICA

"In North America, the standardized unemployment rate from 1990-93 was 6.9 percent, which is about 110 percent of its 1960-90 level. In the European Community, the 1990-93 unemployment rate of 9.2 percent was equal to its value in the 1980s, but more than 300 percent of its level during the 1960s and 1970s....From the 1970s to the 1990s, the jobless rate in...[the group of males aged 25-54] in the United States increased by about one-third--from about 9 percent to about 12 percent. In the European Community, that rate has doubled over the same period, increasing from about 7 percent to 14 percent." (p4)

Haveman, Robert H. "New Democracy Forum: Equity with Employment." Boston Review v22 n3-4 Sum 1997. p3-8. (ISSN0734-2306).

UNEMPLOYMENT--FORMER SOVIET REPUBLICS (v26)

UNEMPLOYMENT--FRANCE (v26)

UNEMPLOYMENT--GREAT BRITAIN

According to a recent report, "The Real Level of Unemployment," released in Great Britain, there is "an estimated real level of unemployment for January 1997 of 3.9 million, or 14.4% of the workforce. This is compared to the 1.7 million unemployed according to the official claimant count. In comparing these figures for unemployment levels estimated for April 1991 the authors note that while the claimant count has fallen by

250,000, the 'real employment' level has risen by 500,000." (p7)
Hunt, Duncan. "Features & Letters: Labour Market Flexibility." Freedom (Anarchist Fortnightly) v58 n21 1 Nov 1997. p7. (ISSN0016-0504).

UNEMPLOYMENT--HUNGARY

"Starting from a negligable level at the start of the transition, unemployment in Hungary developed rapidly in 1991, and reached a maximum of 13.6 percent in 1993. Although the unemployment rate has subsided slightly since then, it remains high: 475,000 people are currently unemployed--10.2 percent of the labor force....Unemployment rates are highest for workers aged 16-19 (38.5 percent), and decline progressively with age. Most of the unemployed are young; 50.8 percent are 35 years or less."
World Bank. "World Bank Loan Helps Reduce Youth Unemployment in Hungary: Unemployment in Hungary." Press Release 11 Sep 1997. document-level access: <http://www.worldbank.org/html/extdr/extme/1470.htm>

UNEMPLOYMENT--IRELAND

In Ireland, the International Labor Organization "measure of unemployment shows a one year fall of 20,000 (down to 159,000) bringing the total fall since 1993 to 61,000. Under this approach, the number of persons looking for full-time work is 137,000 with a further 22,000 looking for part-time work....The number unemployed (ILO approach) for one year or more was 86,000 in 1997, down 17,000 the previous year and down 39,000 since 1993. This means that just under two thirds of the fall in unemployment since 1993 has been due to a fall in long-term unemployment."
Ireland. Central Statistics Office. "1997 Labour Force Survey Report." Press Release 29 Oct 1997. document-level access: <http://www.cso.ie/pressreleases/prellfs97.html>

UNEMPLOYMENT--LATIN AMERICA (v26)

UNEMPLOYMENT--MANITOBA--SASKATCHEWAN (v26)

UNEMPLOYMENT--MASSACHUSETTS--BOSTON --MINORITIES (v26)

UNEMPLOYMENT--MICHIGAN (v26)

"Michigan has three to five unemployed people for every low-skill job opening, according to a report by Northern Illinois University. In Detroit, the range is even higher, six to 15 for every job....The report found that just 17.1 percent of the available entry-level jobs in Michigan pay at least poverty wages, $12,278 a year for a family of three. Michigan has 150,000 families on welfare, about 90 percent of which are headed by a single mother. About 40 percent of adults receiving welfare assistance haven't graduated from high school and 55 percent, according to the study, haven't worked for at least a year." (p1 secB)
Wendland, Wendy. "Local News: Few Jobs for Welfare Recipients, Study Says." Detroit Free Press 23 Jul 1997. p1,6 secB.

"The unemployment rate in Michigan is under 5 percent and is the lowest in 30 years. Since 1991, there have been more than 400,000 jobs created in Michigan." (p1 secC)
Hunter, George/King, R. J. "Business: Area Homes Sell at Rapid Pace: Builders, Sellers Enjoy Strong Real Estate Market." Detroit News 15 Jun 1997. p1,3 secC.

In Michigan, "in Metro Detroit, Washtenaw County tops the list with only 2.3 percent of its workforce unemployed. It ranks 84th nationwide. Oakland and Livingston tie at 400th with 3.2-percent unemployed. Macomb is 939th with 4.2 percent unemployed. Even Wayne County is almost halfway up the national list at 1,684 with 5.5 percent unemployed. Nationally, Detroit still has among the highest unemployment rates of any of America's 10 largest city's. With 9.1 percent out of work, Detroit has more unemployment than any city except Los Angeles....Since 1992, when unemployment in Detroit peaked at 17 percent, the level has dropped steadily but surely--a trend that continues today,...[Bruce Weaver, a labor analyst with the Michigan Consumer and Industry Department] said....Overall, the Flint metropolitan area--including surrounding towns, has an unemployment rate of 6.3 percent. That compares to 4.5 percent for Metro Detroit and 2.9 percent for metro Ann Arbor." (p4 secC)
Linsalata, Phil. "The Metro: Special Report: Job Boom: Metro Detroit Facing Surplus of Work." Detroit News 18 Jun 1997. p1,4 secC.

UNEMPLOYMENT--MICHIGAN--DETROIT (v26)

"Unemployment rates reached record lows in October [1997] in Metro Detroit and four other Michigan labor markets, according to the Michigan Jobs Commission. The jobless rate in the Detroit metropolitan market fell to 3.2 percent--its lowest level in 27 years, according to David Littmann, senior economist at Comerica Bank. About 70,000 workers were considered unemployed out of a total workforce of 2.2 million in the metro market, which includes Wayne, Oakland, Macomb, Monroe, Lapeer and St. Clair counties. That's down from 78,000 in September [1997] and 85,000 in October 1996." (p3 secB)
"Inside Business: Area Jobless Rate Hits 27-Year Low." Detroit News 2 Dec 1997. p3 secB.

UNEMPLOYMENT--MIDDLE WEST

According to the Kansas City Fed's Second Quarter 1997 REGIONAL ECONOMIC DIGEST, the Middle West "district's unemployment rate fell to 4.0 percent from 4.6 percent in the fourth quarter of 1996....The national unemployment rate was unchanged at 5.3 percent." (unpaginated)
"Regional Economy Enjoys Solid Growth in First Quarter." Federal Reserve Bank of Kansas City Fed Letter Aug 1997.

According to the Kansas City Fed's Third Quarter 1997 REGIONAL ECONOMIC DIGEST, in the Tenth Federal Reserve District, which includes Colorado, Kansas, Missouri, Nebraska, New Mexico, Oklahoma and Wyoming, "unemployment edged down in the second quarter to 3.9 percent. In comparison, the national unemployment rate fell to 4.9 percent." (unpaginated)
"Regional Economy Continued to Expand in Second Quarter of '97." Federal Reserve Bank of Kansas City Fed Letter Oct 1997.

UNEMPLOYMENT--MIDWEST STATES (v26)

UNEMPLOYMENT--NEW ZEALAND

In New Zealand, "the seasonally adjusted unemployment rate was 6.8 per cent in the September 1997 quarter, up on the 6.7 per cent in the June 1997 quarter. This is the highest quarterly unemployment rate since December 1994, when 7.4 per cent was recorded....Seasonally adjusted figures show that 67,000 males and 57,000 females, totalling 124,000 were unemployed in the September 1997 quarter. This compares with 122,000 unemployed in the June quarter and 117,000 in the March quarter. Since the September 1996 quarter, the seasonally adjusted number of unemployed has grown by 10,000 (8.8 per cent)."
Statistics New Zealand. "Household Labour Force Survey--September 1997 Quarter." Press Release 5 Nov 1997. document-level access: <http://www.stats.govt.nz/statsweb.nsf/52518ce3e01f62f4cc256388000c48c0/9baf462b0ec25b954c256545006da738?OpenDocument>

UNEMPLOYMENT--OHIO--CLEVELAND

In Cleveland, Ohio, "between 1989 and 1996, downtown employment rose 4.8 percent to 137,979 jobs....[The citywide unemployment rate] hovered around 10 percent for most of the 1990s--hitting a 13.7 percent average in 1992 and falling slightly after the recession. For the first five months of 1997, unemployment averaged 10.6 percent. The national unemployment rate for the same period averaged 5.1 percent." (p14 secA)

Beaupre, Becky. "Renaissance: Taking Detroit into the 21st Century: Is Cleveland's Rebirth for Real?" Detroit News and Free Press 27 Jul 1997. p1,14 secA.

UNEMPLOYMENT--PENNSYLVANIA--PHILADELPHIA

"While the New York and Los Angeles suburbs...had 6.4% unemployment rates in February of 1997, New York City's own joblessness was 10.1% and Los Angeles' was 8.4%. In Philadelphia the rate was 6.2%...,but the average for the entire metropolitan area was 4.9%, and in Montgomery County, the affluent suburbs to the west, it was only 3.7%." (p20)

Breslow, Marc. "'Miracle' in Philadelphia: Can Fiscal Management Really Save the Cities?" Dollars and Sense n212 Jul-Aug 1997. p18-21. (ISSN0012-5245).

UNEMPLOYMENT--SWEDEN (v26)

UNEMPLOYMENT--UNITED STATES (v26)

"The United States recently completed its sixth year of economic recovery. The upturn added more than 13 million new jobs, helping to push the unemployment rate down to 5 percent and lower, the lowest levels in more than two decades.... In June,...6.8 million workers were listed as officially unemployed, resulting in a relatively low rate of 5 percent. That total didn't include the marginally attached, discouraged and involuntary part-time workers....When these folks are counted, the unemployment rate is actually 9.2 percent, or 12.7 million workers....The 1997 Economic Report of the President states that the 2 percent drop in the unemployment rate since 1992...produced a 4 percent increase in annual output. That works out to roughly $300 billion, or $3,000 for every American household--which means a lot more demand for products." (p8)

Kameras, David. "Like It Is: Is Unemployment Really Too Low for Our Own Good?" America@Work v2 n7 Aug 1997. p8. (ISSN1091-594X).

In the U.S., "unemployment averaged 5.4 percent last year and is dropping lower this year." (p1 secC) "During 1996, 21 states averaged unemployment rates under 5 percent, 24 metropolitan areas were below 3 percent and 33 counties were below 2 percent....Among the nation's 315 metropolitan areas, 172 had unemployment that averaged under 5 percent last year.... Metropolitan Boston, Atlanta, Denver and San Jose had average unemployment under 4 percent." (p4 secC)

Linsalata, Phil. "The Metro: Special Report: Job Boom: Metro Detroit Facing Surplus of Work." Detroit News 18 Jun 1997. p1,4 secC.

The U.S. unemployment figure has "hit 4.7 percent, the lowest rate since 1973. With 13.5 million jobs added to the economy since 1993, more Americans are working with hourly earnings that continue to rise. Even in California, where recession hit harder and later than in the US as a whole, the unemployment drop has been steady--from 9.7 percent statewide in 1992 and 1993 to 7.1 a year ago to 6.3 percent in September....According to Jared Bernstein, research economist at the Economic Policy Institute, the 2.5 percent rise in real wages (from $6.52 on average to $6.68) for these workers is a much larger increase than anytime since 1982." (p4)

Wood, Daniel B. "United States: Stores Seek More Help for the Holidays." The Christian Science Monitor v89 n245 14 Nov 1997. p4. The Christian Science Monitor search engine: <http://www.csmonitor.com/plweb-cgi/iops1.pl> To retrieve this article, enter the following search: ED=19971114 AND holidays. In the "retrieved list," click the title that matches this record. (ISSN0882-7729).

On November 7, 1997, the U.S. "Department of Labor reported that the rate of unemployment had dropped to 4.7 percent....[THE WALL STREET JOURNAL said] unemployed workers were taking less time to find a job, a mere 7.6 weeks compared to 8.3 weeks a year ago." (p1) The chief economist at the Harris Bank/Bank of Montreal "noted that the current average wage was 4.2 percent higher in October 1997 than in October 1996. That 4.2 percent rise, he added, is the largest for any 12-month period since July 1989." (p8)

Karp, Nathan. "Unemployment Remains a Grim Social Problem." The People v107 n9 Dec 1997. p1,8. (ISSN0199-350X).

UNEMPLOYMENT--UNITED STATES--MEN

In the U.S., "the overall unemployment rate for men 16 years of age and older in 1994 was 7.1% compared with 18.9% for men 16 to 19 years of age....For White men between 16 and 19 years of age, the rate was 19.1%, for African American men it was 40.3%, and for Hispanic men it was 25.4 % (Bureau of Labor Statistics, 1994)." (p371)

Kost, Kathleen A. "Article: The Effects of Support on the Economic Well-Being of Young Fathers." Families in Society v78 n4 Jul-Aug 1997. p370-382. (ISSN1044-3894).

UNEMPLOYMENT--UNITED STATES--SCIENTISTS (v26)

UNEMPLOYMENT--UNITED STATES--YOUTH

The U.S. "Department of Labor's Bureau of Labor Statistics reported that 32.7 percent of all black teenagers were out of work compared to 14.5 percent of...white teens....Teenage Hispanic females--with an unemployment rate of about 23 percent--are also finding it difficult to get jobs." (p5)

Scherer, Ron. "Whose Boat the Economy Isn't Floating." The Christian Science Monitor v89 n173 1 Aug 1997. p1,5. The Christian Science Monitor search engine: <http://www.csmonitor.com/plweb-cgi/iops1.pl> To retrieve this article, enter the following search: ED=19970801 AND floating. In the "retrieved list," click the title that matches this record. (ISSN0882-7729).

UNEMPLOYMENT--VENEZUELA--YOUTH

In Venezuela, "the high unemployment rate of 20 percent nationwide is even higher among youth, reaching 35 percent. Over one million youth between the ages of 15 and 25 neither work nor study." (p4)

Rodriguez, Lisa. "In Venezuela Everything Is Not 'Chevere.'" NewsNotes v22 n6 Nov-Dec 1997. p3-4. (ISSN1064-1556).

UNEMPLOYMENT--WALES (v26)

UNEMPLOYMENT INSURANCE

see INSURANCE, UNEMPLOYMENT

UNFUNDED MANDATES--UNITED STATES (v26)

UNINSURED PERSONS (HEALTH INSURANCE)

see MEDICALLY UNINSURED PERSONS

UNIONS

see TRADE-UNIONS

UNIPOLAR DEPRESSION

see DEPRESSION, MENTAL

UNITED ARAB EMIRATES--ECONOMIC CONDITIONS (v26)

UNITED NATIONS (v26)

UNITED NATIONS--ARMED FORCES (v26)

"Between 1988 and 1996, seventeen new UN peacekeeping operations were conducted, employing 70,000 personnel. That is more than the number of UN operations in the preceding four decades, and it does not count operations conducted under other auspices. As for costs, between 1990 and 1994, these increased twofold to $3.3 billion. In sharp contrast with many expectations in the 1980s, about seventy percent of UN peacekeeping expenditure has been spent on operations within Europe--in Cyprus, Georgia, and the former Yugoslavia." (p328)

Dandeker, Christopher/Gow, James. "The Future of Peace Support Operations: Strategic Peacekeeping and Success." Armed Forces & Society v23 n3 Spr 1997. p327-347. (ISSN0095-327X).

"United Nations peacekeeping personnel and equipment cost $2.8 billion in 1995, reflecting the expense of UN peacekeeping in the former Yugoslavia. Peacekeeping costs fell in 1996, to $1.4

billion--and assessments for 1997 are expected to total $1.2 billion....As of March 1997, Member States owed the United Nations $1.9 billion in current and back peacekeeping dues. Of the five permanent members of the Council, all but France and the United Kingdom owe varying amounts of past years' peacekeeping dues, including $1 billion, as of March 1997, by the United States. In 1995, UN procurement of goods and services for peacekeeping totalled $399 million. The single largest share of those contracts--48 per cent--went to businesses in the United States....As of February 1997, the top five contributors of troops to current missions were: Pakistan (1,725 soldiers); India (1,211); Bangladesh (1,145); the Russian Federation (1,125); Jordan (1,101); Poland (1,095); and Canada (1,084). The small-island nation of Fiji has taken part in virtually every UN peacekeeping operation, as has Canada....For every dollar that all Governments spent on military activities in 1995, less than half a cent went to UN peacekeeping." (p65)

"Peacewatch: UN Peacekeeping: Some Questions and Answers." UN Chronicle v34 n2 1997. p64-65. (ISSN0251-7329).

UNITED NATIONS--ARMED FORCES--SOLDIERS --ATTITUDES

In 1994, American soldiers who participated in Operation Able Sentry in Macedonia were surveyed about their views concerning peacekeeping missions. "The majority of respondents believed that soldiers were a better choice than civilians for peacekeeping operations....Of those who approved of the mission, only 4 percent thought civilians were a better choice; 17 percent of those soldiers unsure about the mission thought that civilians might be better; and 25 percent of soldiers who disapproved of the mission would have preferred to see civilians perform the mission. When all soldiers were combined (to compensate for the greater number of mission approvers than disapprovers), only 12 percent agreed with the civilian option, while 74 percent disagreed." (p425-426)

Miller, Laura L. "Do Soldiers Hate Peacekeeping?: The Case of Preventive Diplomacy Operations in Macedonia." Armed Forces & Society v23 n3 Spr 1997. p415-449. (ISSN0095-327X).

UNITED NATIONS--CHINA

"As one of the permanent members of the Security Council, China should be contributing a significant percentage of the peacekeeping budget, certainly more than 0.978 percent. The United Kingdom, with the second-lowest assessment rate (6.372 percent) among the five permanent members, contributes nearly seven times as much as China. At the regular budget assessment rate of 0.72 percent, China's contributions to the UN regular budget are surpassed by other third world member states such as Brazil (1.62 percent), South Korea (0.80 percent), Saudi Arabia (0.80 percent), and Mexico (0.78 percent)." (p250)

Kim, Samuel S. "China as a Great Power." Current History v96 n611 Sep 1997. p246-251. (ISSN0011-3530).

UNITED NATIONS--FINANCE (v26)

"As of 31 August 1997, the UN owed approximately $1.2 billion to over 70 troop contributing countries. At that time, over $50 million was owed to Pakistan, $40 million to India, and some $21 million to Bangladesh....(The US currently contributes only about 4 percent of troops). Several US allies are also owed significant amounts with $148 million owed to France, almost $71 million to Great Britain, and over $46 million to Canada." (p5-6)

Caldwell, Zarrin T. "Special Issue: The Year in Review: US Legislation and the UN System." Washington Weekly Report v23 n36 12 Dec 1997. p1-6.

"Karl Theodor Paschke, Under Secretary General for the UN's Office of Internal Oversight Services (OIOS), reported that $29.3 million in cost savings had been identified and $17.8 million of this amount had been recovered during the period 1 July 1996 to 30 June 1997....The figures released for this reporting period represent an increase over the $18.7 million in savings identified and $15.8 million recovered from 1 July 1995 to 30 June 1996....Since the creation of OIOS in the summer of 1994 through 30 June 1996, UN documents specify that approximately 70 percent of over 4,000 recommendations have been implemented." (p4-5)

"Annual UN Inspector General's Report Indicates Progress and Pitfalls." Washington Weekly Report v23 n34 10 Nov 1997. p4-6.

As of 30 September 1997, UN "member states' unpaid assessments for the international tribunals and the UN's regular budget and peacekeeping accounts totaled $2.4 billion; of this amount, $1.45 billion, or approximately 60 percent, is owed by the United States. The next largest debtors include Ukraine, at $246 million, and the Russian Federation at $198 million. About 98 percent of the Russian Federation's debt is to peacekeeping....According to [Joseph] Connor, 89 of 185 member states have paid their contributions in full to the regular budget." (p5)

"UN General Assembly Informed of Organization's Dire Financial Situation." Washington Weekly Report v23 n31 13 Oct 1997. p4-5.

UNITED NATIONS--GERMANY--COSTS (v26)

UNITED NATIONS--NEW YORK (N.Y.) (v26)

UNITED NATIONS--UNITED STATES --APPROPRIATIONS AND EXPENDITURES (v26)

UNITED NATIONS--UNITED STATES--FINANCE (v26)

In mid-May 1997, the U.S. State Department "submitted certifications to Congress that would allow a remaining US contribution of $62.694 million to be made to the UN regular budget. This action would bring total payment to $313.5 million, the amount appropriated for the US contribution in FY1997....Congress also appropriated $282.4 million for US assessed contributions to peacekeeping activities in FY1997, and State Department officials confirmed that payments of $113.642 million have been made over the past several months for 'regular, planned needs' of UN peacekeeping. Because only a portion of these bills have yet been received, a balance of $169 million remains to be paid." (p3-4)

"State Department Certifies Remaining FY1997 Funds to UN; Some Payments Made to Peacekeeping." Washington Weekly Report v23 n17 27 May 1997. p3-4.

UNITED NATIONS--UNITED STATES--PUBLIC OPINION (v26)

In the U.S., "a June 1995 Times Mirror poll found that 81% felt 'strengthening the United Nations' should be a 'priority' (45%) or a 'top priority' (36%) as a US foreign policy goal. An October 1994 poll by the Chicago Council on Foreign Relations found 84% support for strengthening the UN....Polls conducted by Times Mirror in June 1995 and by PIPA [Program on International Policy Attitudes] in January and April 1995 and June 1996 have found that 60% feel the US pays more than its fair share for 'UN activities,' 50% for UN dues, 60% for troops to UN peacekeeping, and 81% for development aid." (p2-3)

Kull, Steven. "Americans Have Not Turned Isolationist." Public Perspective v8 n5 Aug-Sep 1997. p1-4. (ISSN1050-5067).

UNITED STATES--APPROPRIATIONS AND EXPENDITURES

In 1995, the U.S. government had "annual outlays in excess of 1.5 trillion dollars (U.S. Bureau of the Census 1995...)....Spending as a proportion of gross domestic product (GDP) first exceeded 20 percent in 1972, reached as high as 24.4 percent in 1983, hovered between 22 and 24 percent until the early 1990s, and is now moving down. Indeed, federal spending as a proportion of GDP was lower (21.9 percent) in 1995 than it had been for the previous fifteen years." (p694)

Anton, Thomas J. "New Federalism and Intergovernmental Fiscal Relationships: The Implications for Health Policy." Journal of Health Politics, Policy and Law v22 n3 Jun 1997. p691-720. (ISSN0361-6878).

UNITED STATES--ARMED FORCES (v26)

"The U.S. deploys soldiers to the Sinai Peninsula on six-month rotations to support the Camp David Accord signed in 1979. Since its implementation in 1982, there have been 28 rotations. The 28th rotation initiated deployment in January, 1995, and comprised a battalion of 80% reserve and 20% active component soldiers. This is the first time that the U.S. deployed a battalion of this type (mixed active and reserve personnel) as part of the MFO [Multinational Force and Observers]. Soldiers for the U.S. battalion were drawn from 35 states." (p392)

Lakhani, Hyder/Abod, Elissa T. "The Effectiveness of Economic Incentives for Career Commitment of Peacekeepers in the Sinai." Armed Forces & Society v23 n3 Spr 1997. p391-414. (ISSN0095-327X).

"According to the General Accounting Office, 63 percent of active duty [U.S.] Army troops are deployable at any given time. So out of the 495,000 total, 312,000 troops are available for operations. At the end of 1996, the Army says, 35,800 troops were deployed in operations, mainly in Bosnia....Multiply 35,800 by 4 and the number of troops affected by deployments is 143,200, which is 46 percent of the deployable force. The other 54 percent of the force, of course, is supposed to be training hard to be ready for two major regional wars." (pH2479)

Skelton, Ike (Rep.-Mo.). "Special Orders: The Future of the U.S. Military." Congressional Record. Daily ed. v143 n61 12 May 1997. pH2477-2481. section/page-level access: <http://thomas.loc.gov/cgi-bin/query/R?r105:FLD001:H02478:> (ISSN0363-7239). (X1.1A.105/1).

"From 1950 to 1989, almost 40 years, the United States of America used its military 10 times. Since 1989, we have used our military 25 times, a 15-fold increase. Let's quickly review some of the major recent actions in which the U.S. Army played a critical role: in 1991, Operation Desert Storm in Southwest Asia and Provide Comfort in Turkey and Iraq; in 1992, relief efforts after Hurricane Andrew; in 1993, Restore Hope in Somalia; in 1994, fighting fires in the Western United States, Uphold Democracy in Haiti, and Support Hope in Rwanda; and in 1995 and 1996, Joint, Joint Endeavor and Joint Guard in Bosnia....During the past 7 years, the Army has done 70 to 80 percent of the heavy lifting, and they have done it for less than 24 percent of the budget given to the Department of Defense." (pE1175)

McHugh, John M. (Rep.-N.Y.). "Army Birthday Tribute." Congressional Record. Daily ed. v143 n80 10 Jun 1997. pE1174-1176. section/page-level access: <http://thomas.loc.gov/cgi-bin/query/R?r105:FLD001:E01174:> (ISSN0363-7239). (X1.1A.105/1).

The U.S. has "gone from 18 Army divisions in 1991 to 10. We have cut the Army almost in half. We have gone from 24 fighter airwings to 13. So we have cut our air power almost in half. And we have gone from 546 Navy ships to 346 so we have cut the Navy by about 40 percent in terms of structure." (pH3899)

Hunter, Duncan (Rep.-Calif.). "National Security." Congressional Record. Daily ed. v143 n85 18 Jun 1997. p3898-3904. section/page-level access: <http://thomas.loc.gov/cgi-bin/query/R?r105:FLD001:H03898:> (ISSN0363-7239). (X1.1A.105/1).

In the U.S., "in the last decade military personnel strength has been reduced by approximately 600,000....There are 97 US military bases already closed or slated for closure...." (p7)

"Getting the Military out of Humanitarian Relief." Defense Monitor v26 n6 Oct 1997. p1-7. (ISSN0195-6450).

The U.S. "Navy active-duty and reserve end strength will be reduced by 18,000 and 4,100 people, and the civilian job force will be cut by 8,400 people. Of all the services, the [U.S.] Marine Corps will enjoy the smallest number of personnel reductions, losing only 1,800 active-duty personnel, 4,200 reservists, and 400 civilians. The [U.S.] Air Force took the biggest hits: 26,900 active-duty personnel, 700 reservists, and 18,300 civilians are on the block." (p93)

Truver, Scott C. "Tomorrow's Fleet." Proceedings v123 n9 Sep 1997. p90-96. (ISSN0041-798X).

"After four rounds of base closings, the number of the...[U.S.'s] military forces has been trimmed by 30 percent, while the civilian support staff has been cut by only 25 percent....The Pentagon's Quadrennial Defense Review, a projection of the military's long-term needs, suggested trimming 61,000 military jobs--including reducing the military's civilian force by another 20 percent." (p9)

Nifong, Christina. "Next Big Defense-Cut Target: Civilians." The Christian Science Monitor v89 n180 12 Aug 1997. p1,9. The Christian Science Monitor search engine: <http://www.csmonitor.com/plweb-cgi/iops1.pl> To retrieve this article, enter the following search: ED=19970812 AND civilians. In the "retrieved list," click the title that matches this record. (ISSN0882-7729).

UNITED STATES--ARMED FORCES--APPROPRIATIONS AND EXPENDITURES (v26)

Every active military person costs the American "taxpayer an average of $160,000 per year. By comparison the average cost per Coast Guard position is only $100,000 per year....Because the Coast Guard performs only non-combat roles, it costs only 60% as much." (p3)

"Getting the Military out of Humanitarian Relief." Defense Monitor v26 n6 Oct 1997. p1-7. (ISSN0195-6450).

The drop in U.S. Military "procurement spending since the Persian Gulf War has been dramatic, amounting to a real decline of 60% between fiscal years 1990 and 1997....The fiscal year 1996 budget completed the reduction of the Army to 10 divisions with 495,000 troops, down from 18 divisions with 750,000 troops in 1990." (p61)

Hawkins, William R. "Must We Repeat History?" Proceedings v123 n11 Nov 1997. p58-61. (ISSN0041-798X).

UNITED STATES--ARMED FORCES--HOUSING (v26)

UNITED STATES--ARMED FORCES--MEDICAL CARE (v26)

UNITED STATES--ARMED FORCES--PANAMA (v26)

UNITED STATES--ARMED FORCES--PAY, ALLOWANCES, ETC.

In the U.S., "military and federal civilian pay raises..., by law, are set at .5% behind nationwide wage growth as measured by the Bureau of Labor Statistics' Employment Cost Index (ECI).... The most recent ECI data show paychecks of U.S. workers rose 3.3% in the last year. Consequently, the military, and, on average, federal civilians will get a 2.8% pay raise on 1 January 1998....The gap between military and private sector pay levels...[is] now estimated at 13%." (p90)

Philpott, Tom. "Points of Interest: 'Our People Are Not Bad Off.'" Proceedings v123 n11 Nov 1997. p90. (ISSN0041-798X).

UNITED STATES--ARMED FORCES--RECRUITING, ENLISTMENT, ETC.

According to the U.S. Pentagon's latest Youth Attitude Tracking Survey of 1996, in the fall of 1991, after the Gulf War, the propensity of males to enlist in the U.S. military "was strong, with 26.2% responding positively....The latest survey hits a record low. Only 20.7% of young males expect to enter active service....In 1991, 41.4% [of black males] expected to enter service. The figure fell the next year to 34%. It has leveled off the past two years at 27.5%. Interest in the military among Hispanic males actually has climbed, from 37.7% in 1991 to 39.3% in 1996. But the propensity to enlist among white males fell significantly over the period, from 21.3% to 15.2%. Even as white and black males grow less inclined to serve, interest in the military among young females is rising. Their propensity to enlist fell initially after the Gulf War, but rose from 8.5% in 1993 to 10.6% in 1996." (p122)

Philpott, Tom. "Points of Interest: Interest in Military Service Wanes." Proceedings v123 n9 Sep 1997. p122. (ISSN0041-798X).

Colonel Dan Rose, deputy chief of staff for U.S. Marine Corps recruiting says, "'only about 10 percent of our recruits actually walk in. We actually do most of our work over the telephone and getting into the high schools.'...[The Army] has also decided that only 90 percent of its annual recruitment target must be high school graduates. The previous number was 95 percent. The remaining 10 percent comprises enlistees who have high school equivalency diplomas and score in the upper percentiles of the Armed Services Aptitude Test." (p3)

Landay, Jonathan S. "United States: Army Recruiting Shortfall May Presage Problems." The Christian Science Monitor v89 n153 3 Jul 1997. p3. The Christian Science Monitor search engine: <http://www.csmonitor.com/plweb-cgi/iops1.pl> To retrieve this article, enter the following search: ED=19970703 AND problems. In the "retrieved list," click the title that matches this record. (ISSN0882-7729).

UNITED STATES--ARMED FORCES--REGULATIONS --PUBLIC OPINION

According to a recent Gallup poll, "overall, only 16% of Americans take the hard line on adultery in the military, saying it should lead to dismissal in all cases. Twenty-nine percent think there should be rules against it but with exceptions for affairs that took place in the past, while 49% think there should be no rules against adultery in the armed forces....More than half of Americans, 55%, believe that an affair between a military officer and someone of lesser rank is grounds for dismissal from the military, while only 37% say it is not.... Only 29% of Americans think that an affair between a military officer and someone outside of the military should be grounds for dismissal."

Saad, Lydia/Gallup Organization. "Most Americans Would Soften U.S. Military's Rules against Adultery." Press Release 13 Jun 1997. document-level access: <http://www.gallup.com/poll/news/970613.htm>

UNITED STATES--ARMED FORCES--SOCIAL CONDITIONS (v26)

UNITED STATES--ARMED FORCES--TOBACCO USE

"The need to attack tobacco addiction in the military was crystallized in a report by the Inspector General of the [U.S.] Department of Defense last December. The DOD IG's analysis concluded that between health care and lost productivity attributed to tobacco use, tobacco addiction costs the Defense Department, and American taxpayers, about $930 million a year. Roughly $453 million of this is in hospitalization costs alone.... Tobacco use among military personnel has continued at higher levels than that of the civilian population. Nearly 36 percent of civilian males aged 18 to 25 smoke cigarettes. However, for the same age group in the Army, 41 percent smoke tobacco products as do 39 percent in the Navy and 44.7 percent in the Marine Corps." (pS7127)

Lautenberg, Frank R. (Sen.-N.J.). "Tobacco in the Military." Congressional Record. Daily ed. v143 n96 9 Jul 1997. pS7127. section/page-level access: <http://thomas.loc.gov/cgi-bin/query/R?r105:FLD001:S07127:> (ISSN0363-7239). (X1.1A.105/1).

UNITED STATES--ARMED FORCES--WOMEN

It was not until 1948 that women were integrated into the regulars in the American military, "and then they were limited by law to 2 percent of the total force. What makes the present situation different is the relatively large percentage of women in the ranks (overall about 11 percent with the Air Force the highest at 14 percent and the Marines the lowest at 5 percent)...." (p60)

Trainor, Bernard E. "Focus on Women in the Corps: Women in the Military." Marine Corps Gazette v81 n11 Nov 1997. p60-63. (ISSN0025-3170).

"With some 195,000 female personnel, the US military is the nation's biggest employer of women and has the largest percentage of women--13.5 percent--among NATO forces." (p1) "In a 1996 Pentagon survey...55 percent of women questioned reported encountering offensive conduct by male personnel." (p10)

Landay, Jonathan S. "Global Report: Europe's Quiet Approach: Sex Issues in US Military Puzzle, Fascinate the World." The Christian Science Monitor v89 n142 18 Jun 1997. p1,10-11. The Christian Science Monitor search engine: <http://www.csmonitor.com/plweb-cgi/iops1.pl> To retrieve this article, enter the following search: ED=19970618 AND world. In the "retrieved list," click the title that matches this record. (ISSN0882-7729).

UNITED STATES--CENSUS (v26)

UNITED STATES--CENSUS--MINORITIES

"All evidence reviewed from the 1990 [U.S.] census clearly demonstrates the inaccuracy of a persistent undercount. The Census Bureau acknowledges that this last decennial count failed to include more than 4 million residents--the highest undercount ever recorded. These included a disproportionate number of racial and ethnic minorities in this country. Hundreds of thousands of Asian-Pacific-Americans were not counted by census, at an estimated rate of 2.3 percent. For Hispanics this rate was 5.0 percent and for African-Americans, 4.4 percent. It is inexcusable that these rates were two times, five times and four times greater than the undercount for white Americans." (pH3543)

Mink, Patsy T. (Rep.-Hawaii). "Conference Report on H.R. 1469, 1997 Emergency Supplemental Appropriations Act...Recovery from Natural Disasters...." Congressional Record. Daily ed. v143 n76 5 Jun 1997. pH3520-3544. section/page-level access: <http://thomas.loc.gov/cgi-bin/query/R?r105:FLD001:H03543:> (ISSN0363-7239). (X1.1A.105/1).

"Statistical work in the 1940's demonstrated that we can estimate how many people the [U.S.] census misses. The estimate for 1940 was 5.4 percent of the population. After decreasing steadily to 1.2 percent in 1980, the 1990 undercount increased to 1.8 percent, or more than 4 million people. More significantly, the undercount is not distributed evenly. The differential undercount, as it is known, of minorities was 4.4 percent for blacks, 5.0 percent for Hispanics, 2.3 percent for Asian-Pacific Islanders, and 4.5 percent for Native Americans, compared with 1.2 percent for non-Hispanic whites. The difference between the black and nonblack undercount was the largest since 1940....The Census Bureau estimates that the total undercount will reach 1.9 percent in 2000 if the 1990 methods are used instead of sampling." (pS4195)

Moynihan, Daniel Patrick (Sen.-N.Y.). "Supplemental Appropriations and Rescissions Act of 1997." Congressional Record. Daily ed. v143 n59 8 May 1997. pS4137-4205. section/page-level access: <http://thomas.loc.gov/cgi-bin/query/R?r105:FLD001:S04194:> (ISSN0363-7239). (X1.1A.105/1).

UNITED STATES--CENSUS, 1990

The net Census undercount for the U.S. "in 1990 was 1.6 percent, or about 4 million people. That's the difference between the 10 million people who were missed and the 6 million who were counted twice....By contrast, the undercount of rural renters in 1990 was 5.9 percent. Owner/renter status is a proxy for income, so the proportion of poor rural people who were missed was far greater than the Nation as a whole. Ninety percent of the rural renters missed were not minorities....In the South, in 1990, the undercount of white renters was 6.23 percent, representing more than 10 percent of the total national undercount. For American Indians living on reservations, the 1990 undercount was more than 12 percent." (pH8231)

Clayton, Eva M. (Rep.-N.C.). "Departments of Commerce, Justice, And State, The Judiciary...Appropriations Act, 1998." Congressional Record. Daily ed. v143 n133 30 Sep 1997. pH8229-8244. section/page-level access: <http://thomas.loc.gov/cgi-bin/query/R?r105:FLD001:H08231:> (ISSN0363-7239). (X1.1A.105/1).

UNITED STATES--COMMERCE (v26)

"From 1990 to 1995, U.S. exports to Asian APEC [Asia-Pacific Economic Cooperation] expanded 63 percent, while U.S. imports from the region rose 58 percent....U.S. exports to and imports from the rest of the world increased 41 percent." (p8)

Jerardo, Alberto/Huang, Sophia Wu/U.S. Dept. of Agriculture. Economic Research Service. "Regional Overviews: APEC to Resume Healthy Growth." APEC: International Agriculture and Trade Reports Situation and Outlook Series Aug 1997. p6-8.

The U.S.'s "trade balance with Mexico has deteriorated from a surplus of $1.7 billion in 1993 to a deficit of $17 billion last year. Trade foes say that's cost us 420,000 jobs. By White House math, however, the same deal has instead created 122,000 jobs....American tariffs...[average] just 3 percent, and most other countries'...[range] from 10 percent to 30 percent...." (p9 secA)

Miller, Matthew. "Comment: 'Fast-Track' Debate Clouds Trade Picture." Detroit News 15 Sep 1997. p9 secA.

"In 1996, the United States' overall trade with Asia stood at $570 billion, compared to $270 billion with Europe....Exports today make up 30 percent of the United States' GDP, up from 13 percent in 1970 and 25 percent in 1992....Between 1992 and 1996 the value of American exports to Japan grew 47 percent and exports to the rest of East Asia, excluding China, by the same figure....Altogether 11.5 million high-paying American jobs rely on exports to the world." (p151)

Mahbubani, Kishore. "An Asia-Pacific Consensus." Foreign Affairs v76 n5 Sep-Oct 1997. p149-158. (ISSN0015-7120).

"Over the past 15 years, imports as a share of America's gross domestic product rose to 4 percent, a gain of only 1.5 percentage point....Nineteen states...saw exports to Canada and Mexico grow more than 25 percent in the 1993-95 period. Three states--Kentucky, Louisiana, and Mississippi--enjoyed more than 75 percent growth in that period....US imports from Mexico rose 82.7 percent and from Canada 41.1 percent from 1993 to 1996. As a result, a US trade surplus with Mexico of $1.7 billion in 1993 became a deficit of $16.2 billion in 1996. America's deficit with Canada in 1996 rose to $22.8 billion. Critics say those growing deficits cost the US 420,208 jobs, the report says." (p8)

Francis, David R. "Business & Money: Economic Scene: NAFTA Set to Head South, Beyond Mexico." The Christian Science Monitor v89 n156 9 Jul 1997. p8. The Christian Science Monitor search engine: <http://www.csmonitor.com/plweb-cgi/iops1.pl> To retrieve this article, enter the following search: ED=19970709 AND mexico. In the "retrieved list," click the title that matches this record. (ISSN0882-7729).

"Since 1988, nearly 70 percent of US economic growth has come from the export of goods and services. Nearly 1 in 5 jobs in today's work force is supported by trade....In 1996, US exports to Chile were worth more than $4.1 billion, and our trade surplus with the country was $1.6 billion." (p18)

Graham, Bob/DeWine, Mike. "Opinion/Essays: Fast-Track to Freer Trade Promises Bumpy Ride: Speed Up...Or We'll Derail...." The Christian Science Monitor v89 n207 19 Sep 1997. p18. The Christian Science Monitor search engine: <http://www.csmonitor.com/plweb-cgi/iops1.pl> To retrieve this article, enter the following search: ED=19970919 AND derail. In the "retrieved list," click the title that matches this record. (ISSN0882-7729).

U.S. "exports and imports of goods and services accounted for a record 28.4 percent of gross domestic product (GDP) in the second quarter of 1997, according to US Commerce Department figures. Five years ago, the comparable figure was less than 21 percent....Exports of US goods have increased 24 percent since last fall. It's a surge that accounts for almost half of the overall growth in the US economy over that time period, say economists. Exports alone still account for a relatively small slice of the overall GDP, about 12 percent." (p9)

Grier, Peter/Bachus, Richard C. "National Report: Selling Sandpaper 'Sticks' to India: Exports: Rocket Fuel of US Economy." The Christian Science Monitor v89 n215 1 Oct 1997. p1,9. The Christian Science Monitor search engine: <http://www.csmonitor.com/plweb-cgi/iops1.pl> To retrieve this article, enter the following search: ED=19971001 AND economy. In the "retrieved list," click the title that matches this record. (ISSN0882-7729).

UNITED STATES--COMMERCE--PUBLIC OPINION (v26)

In the U.S., a nationwide poll released by a Lansing, Michigan "firm has found that public backing for trade agreements has reached a new high of 61 percent. It's particularly appealing to people in the Midwest (65 percent approval), where lowering barriers once was considered a major threat to our jobs. It's also...strong with union workers (64 percent approval)....[Ed Sarpolus, vice-president of EPIC/MRA, which conducted the poll writes,] 'labor unions and politicians lag far behind when Americans are asked who they "trust the most to talk about trade issues." Topping the list are economists (30 percent), American business (18 percent) and educators (13 percent.)'...Nine out of 10 Americans told EPIC/MRA that they believe 'America's economic strength in the future depends on our ability to compete in the global marketplace,'...." (p1 secB)

Pepper, Jon. "Business: Public Knows Value of Free Trade and Accepts the Challenge to Compete Worldwide." Detroit News 25 Jun 1997. p1 secB.

UNITED STATES--CONSTITUTION--PUBLIC OPINION

"A recently released poll reveals some astonishing facts about how the [American] public perceives [the U.S. Constitution]....The survey reports that 91 percent consider the Constitution important and 89 percent are proud of it....How many U.S. senators are there? Only one out of two Americans knew the answer is 100. How many branches are there in the federal government? Only 40 percent knew the answer to that difficult question. The Associated Press reported that fewer than one-fifth of those surveyed could correctly answer eight of ten basic questions....Sixteen percent think the Constitution declares Christianity the official religion of the United States. And 24 percent cannot name any of the First Amendment rights--freedom of speech, press, religion and assembly. Only 41 percent specifically recalled freedom of religion." (p3)

Walker, J. Brent. "Church-State Intersection." Report from the Capital v52 n18 23 Sep 1997. p3. (ISSN0346-0661).

UNITED STATES--CONSTITUTIONAL LAW --AMENDMENTS

A "Roper/Newseum survey indicates that 29 per cent of Americans could not name any of the five freedoms...[the First Amendment] explicitly guarantees. While 64 per cent identified free speech, only 15 per cent named freedom of the press. Even after being reminded of this liberty, 65 per cent--two-thirds--agreed with the statement, 'There are times when the press should not be allowed to publish or broadcast certain things.'" (p21)

Frank, Reuven. "On Television: Do Americans Deserve a Free Press?" New Leader v80 n10 2 Jun 1997. p20-21. (ISSN0028-6044).

UNITED STATES--DESCRIPTION AND TRAVEL

According to the Travel Industry Association of America, "the share of summer vacationers who plan to camp or climb increased from 40 percent to 45 percent between 1996 and 1997....Fully 84 percent in this group plan to take a summer vacation trip, compared with 78 percent of all adult travelers. Also, 43 percent of young adults say they are more likely to travel in the summer of 1997 than they were a year ago, compared with just 25 percent of all adults....Adults aged 18 to 24 plan to spend an average of $828 on their longest 1997 summer trip, compared with a national average of $1,112. The biggest spenders on summer travel are adults aged 55 to 64, who plan to spend an average of $1,344. The oldest baby boomers are now aged 51." (p2)

"Hot Markets for Outdoor Vacations." Forecast v17 n7 Jul 1997. p1-2. article-level access: <http://www.demographics.com/Publications/FC/97_fc/9707_fc/FC97071.htm> (ISSN0732-1597).

UNITED STATES--ECONOMIC CONDITIONS (v26)

"In the past 12 months alone, the U.S. securities markets have experienced exponential growth: the Dow Jones Industrial Average has broken the 5,000, 6,000, and 7,000 point levels; the New York Stock Exchange and the Nasdaq Stock Market have each seen stock trading volume hit all-time highs; and assets in mutual funds have reached record levels of $3.5 trillion--a figure that surpasses the more than $2.6 trillion Americans have on deposit at commercial banks--and continue to grow monthly. This growth builds on 1996, a year when: total dollar volume traded on the exchanges and the Nasdaq Stock Market exceeded 1995 volume by 31 percent; registered public offerings grew to $1.045 trillion, an increase of 36 percent from 1995 offerings; and initial public offerings rose to $50 billion, up from $30 billion in 1995, a 67 percent increase." (p106)

Levitt, Arthur (Chair, U.S. Securities and Exchange Commission). "Departments of Commerce, Justice, And State, The Judiciary...Approp. for 1998 (Part 8)." Hearing. U.S. House. Committee on Appropriations. Washington, D.C. : GPO, 1997. (ISBN0160551641). (Y4.Ap6/1:C73/2/997/pt.8).

"The U.S. economic performance in 1996 was relatively strong, completing its fifth year of expansion with 2.4 percent GDP growth....The unemployment rate, 5.4 percent in 1996, was in its fourth straight year of decline. Inflation was 2 percent as measured by the GDP deflator and 2.9 percent according to the consumer price index....The U.S. current account deficit climbed to $164.1 billion in 1996 (2 percent of GDP)...." (p6)

Jerardo, Alberto/Huang, Sophia Wu/U.S. Dept. of Agriculture. Economic Research Service. "Regional Overviews: APEC to Resume Healthy Growth." APEC: International Agriculture and Trade Reports Situation and Outlook Series Aug 1997. p6-8.

"U.S. GDP in 1996 grew by 2.8 percent, somewhat faster than in 1995. Job growth was rapid--payroll employment rose almost 2.0 percent as about 2.3 million jobs were added to the economy.... For 1996, the average 3-month T-bill yield fell from 5.5 percent in 1995 to 5.0 percent in 1996." (p28)

U.S. Dept. of Agriculture. Economic Research Service. "Farm Business Outlook: General Economy Strong in 1997, Speedup from Moderate 1996." Agricultural Income and Finance Situation and Outlook Report Sep 1997. p28-29.

"U.S. gross domestic product (GDP) grew at...[an] annual rate of 5.8 percent in the first quarter of 1997. The only major component of GDP that fell was net exports as the real trade deficit widened by almost $18 billion. Exports rose at an 11-percent annual rate, $18 billion, while imports rose 23 percent, or $36 billion. A risk to continued economic growth prospects evaporated as crude oil prices, which had peaked at over $23 per barrel in late 1996, fell below $20 per barrel this spring." (p15)

U.S. Dept. of Agriculture. Economic Research Service. "Ecomonic Growth to Moderate for Rest of 1997." Agricultural Income and Finance Situation and Outlook Series Jun 1997. p15-16.

In the U.S., "despite robust GDP growth and a tightening labor market, inflation has been modest. The producer price index fell 5 months in a row for the first time in over 40 years. May's consumer prices were only 2.2 percent higher than a year ago. GDP deflator inflation was 2.2 percent in the first quarter of 1997, the same as a year earlier." (p15)

U.S. Dept. of Agriculture. Economic Research Service. "Economic Growth to Moderate for Rest of 1997." Agricultural Income and Finance Situation and Outlook Series Jun 1997. p15-16.

In the U.S., "over 2 million jobs have been added in the last year. More than half the jobs added in 1996 were in categories with above average compensation. The wage increases in 1996 beat inflation for the first time since the recovery began in 1991. May's 4.8-percent unemployment rate is as low as it has been in almost 20 years." (p15)

U.S. Dept. of Agriculture. Economic Research Service. "Economic Growth to Moderate for Rest of 1997." Agricultural Income and Finance Situation and Outlook Series Jun 1997. p15-16.

"Daniel Weinberg, chief of the Census Bureau's Housing and Household Economic Statistics Division, said the number of poor Americans in 1996 totaled 36.5 million, representing 13.7 percent of the nation's total population. Weinberg said, neither figure was significantly different from the previous year's estimate. In 1996, the average poverty threshold for a family of four was $16,036. 'During this same period,' Weinberg said, 'the real median income of households rose by 1.2 percent, increasing from $35,082 to $35,492. In addition, this was the third consecutive year in which there was no year-to-year change in overall income inequality.'"

U.S. Dept. of Commerce. Economic & Statistics Administration. "Income Improves, Poverty Levels Stabilize, Health Insurance Coverage Slips, Census Bureau Reports." Census Bureau Press Release 29 Sep 1997. document-level access: <http://www.census.gov/Press-Release/cb97-162.html>

In the U.S., "in 1995, family median net worth was $56,400....In 1995, the average family spent $1,775 or 5.5 percent of its total expenditures on entertainment or reading. In 1995, 8 million households received food stamps, 9 million received free or reduced-priced school lunches, 5 million received public or subsidized housing and 14 million received Medicaid....In 1995, about 16 million families received Social Security or railroad retirement income, representing about 24 percent of all families."

U.S. Dept. of Commerce. Economic & Statistics Administration. "New Statistical Abstract Highlights Household Lifestyles." Census Bureau Press Release 4 Dec 1997. document-level access: <http://www.census.gov/Press-Release/cb97-199.html>

In the U.S., "the employment picture, with 12 million new jobs, is the best employment situation our country has faced in its history....Consumer confidence has increased 14 percent in the last 4 years....Deficit reduction has been reduced to under 1 percent of gross domestic product in 1997....Home ownership has increased from 63 percent to 65 percent, the best ever....The stock market has gone from 3,500 to more than 8,000, a growth record that has been matched only once, and that was during World War II. Median family income is up $1,600 since 1993...." (pS8330)

Daschle, Thomas A. (Sen.-S.Dak.). "Balanced Budget Act of 1997--Conference Report." Congressional Record. Daily ed. v143 n110 30 Jul 1997. pS8314-8355. section/page-level access: <http://thomas.loc.gov/cgi-bin/query/R?r105:FLD001:S08330:> (ISSN0363-7239). (X1.1A.105/1).

Since 1992, the U.S. "economy has grown from $6.5 to $8 trillion dollars. Inflation has fallen to 2 percent. We have added a net gain of more than 12 million jobs. And while from 1986 to 1993 real wages fell every year, since 1994 real wages have risen every year....Deficit reduction from $290 billion in 1992 to $36 billion before the recent budget agreement....[There] has been a nearly 50 percent jump in exports, from just over $600 billion in 1992 to nearly $900 billion this year." (pS9732)

Baucus, Max (Sen.-Mont.). "Trade Negotiating Authority." Congressional Record. Daily ed. v143 n126 19 Sep 1997. pS9732-9733. section/page-level access: <http://thomas.loc.gov/cgi-bin/query/R?r105:FLD001:S09732:> (ISSN0363-7239). (X1.1A.105/1).

The U.S. Congressional Budget Office "projects that the deficit will be $67 billion for fiscal year 1997, far below original estimates. Inflation was just two-tenths of 1 percent in May--equivalent to an annual inflation rate of only 2 percent. The unemployment rate stands at 4.8 percent, its lowest in more than a quarter century, and the WALL STREET JOURNAL reported... that the measurement of consumer confidence in the economy is at a 28-year high." (pS6335)

Moynihan, Daniel Patrick (Sen.-N.Y.). "Revenue Reconciliation Act of 1997." Congressional Record. Daily ed. v143 n91 25 Jun 1997. pS6332-6344. section/page-level access: <http://thomas.loc.gov/cgi-bin/query/R?r105:FLD001:S06335:> (ISSN0363-7239). (X1.1A.105/1).

"Nearly 14 percent of all Americans--36.5 million--were living below the poverty threshold last year, down from 1995. Real median household income rose 1.2 percent, to $35,492 from $35,082....[In 1996,] the average income for the 5 percent of people at the bottom rung of the ladder fell 1.8 percent; the income for the richest 5 percent rose 2.2 percent....The poverty rate for people living in the inner cities declined to 19.6 percent from 20.6 percent. The overall poverty rate for children, 20.5 percent, and Americans aged 65 and over, 10.8 percent, remained virtually unchanged. The number of children without health care insurance grew to 10.6 million, or 14.8 percent." (p4 secC)

Bivins, Larry. "Metro: Michigan Sees Drop in Annual Poverty Rate." Detroit News 30 Sep 1997. p1,4 secC.

In the U.S., when President "Bill Clinton took office, federal revenues consumed 19 percent of the gross domestic product (GDP)-not far above the postwar average until that time of 18.5 percent. But since then, revenues have risen steadily. By the second quarter of last year, they broke the previous record, reaching 20.9 percent of GDP. In the fourth quarter of 1996 and the first quarter of 1997, revenues hit another all-time high of 21 percent of GDP. Prior to the Clinton administration, the highest percentage ever achieved was 20.7 percent, in the first part of 1969 and again in early 1981....This country would need a tax cut of $160 billion this year alone and more every subsequent year just to get federal taxes back down to where they were when Clinton took office. That is 22 times more than taxpayers would receive next year under...[House Ways & Means Committee Chairman Bill Archer's] tax cut, which only reduces taxes $85 billion over five years." (p10 secA)

Bartlett, Bruce. "Bartlett's Notations: Tax Cut No Problem in Time of Record Tax Bite." Detroit News 16 Jun 1997. p10 secA.

According to George Kahn, vice president and economist, and Russel Lamb, economist at the Federal Reserve Bank of Kansas City, since the beginning of the economic "expansion in 1991, real economic growth [in the U.S.] has averaged a solid 2.8 percent annually. In the first half of this year, the economy has growth at an even stronger pace of 4.1 percent...." (unpaginated)

"Nebraska Economic Forums Discuss National Economy, State Banking." Federal Reserve Bank of Kansas City Fed Letter Nov 1997.

In the Tenth District, which includes Colorado, Kansas, Missouri, Oklahoma, Nebraska, New Mexico, and Wyoming, employment "slipped 0.1 percent in the second quarter [of 1997]....Compared with the previous year, district employment was 2.0 percent higher....The Tenth District's unemployment rate edged lower to 3.9 percent from 4.0 percent in the first quarter of 1996....Kansas continues to set the pace in the district [in employment] and was closely followed by Oklahoma with growth of 2.5 percent over the previous year. Colorado employment growth equaled the district average at 2.0 percent over the previous year....Real personal income grew 1.2 percent in the first quarter, the most recent quarter for which data are available. Compared with a year ago, income rose 3.8 percent.... Manufacturing employment declined slightly, 0.1 percent below the previous quarter....Compared with a year ago, manufacturing employment was up 0.6 percent....The total value of construction contracts rose 16.3 percent above the prior quarter but was 9.6 percent below the previous year....Contract growth failed to lift employment as levels slipped 1.8 percent in the second quarter, 2.7 percent above a year ago." (p2)

Henderson, Jason. "Regional Economic Update." Federal Reserve Bank of Kansas City Regional Economic Digest v8 n3 Fall 1997. p2. (ISSN1049-5339).

In the U.S., "employment rose 0.6 percent in the second quarter to a level 2.2 percent above a year ago....The...unemployment rate fell to 4.9 percent....Employment growth averaged 2.2 percent....Income grew 1.3 percent in the quarter and 4.0 percent over the previous year....Manufacturing employment edged up 0.1 percent, 0.2 percent over the previous year....The total value of construction contracts advanced 26.5 percent in the quarter but was 1.7 percent below year-ago levels." (p2)

Henderson, Jason. "Regional Economic Update." Federal Reserve Bank of Kansas City Regional Economic Digest v8 n3 Fall 1997. p2. (ISSN1049-5339).

By 1997, the U.S.'s "net foreign debt was more than $1 trillion and was increasing at an annual rate of 15 to 20 percent, with Japan owning almost $300 billion and China more than $50 billion in U.S. treasury bonds. Between 1963 and 1967, the outflow of foreign direct investment from the United States was more than ten times the inflow to the United States ($24.5 billion versus $2.1 billion). During the late 1970s and 1980s,...the inflow increased dramatically and by the early 1990s exceeded the outflow ($198.3 billion in versus $168.9 billion out for 1989-93.) In the early 1960s, the number of Americans going abroad far exceeded the number of foreigners coming to the United States, an average of 6.1 million foreigners arriving each year between 1960 and 1964. By 1990-1994 the inflows and outflows were equal, an average of 44.2 million Americans going abroad each year versus 44.1 million foreigners coming to the United States." (p45)

Huntington, Samuel P. "The Erosion of American National

Interests." Foreign Affairs v76 n5 Sep-Oct 1997. p28-49. (ISSN0015-7120).

"In 1993 27 percent of all U.S. workers were in jobs that didn't pay them enough to live above the poverty level, and only a little over a third of all workers had wholly employer financed medical insurance....Twenty percent of all full time workers have no retirement or medical coverage....Welfare benefits to families with children which were 71 percent of the poverty line for a family of three in 1970 were 40 percent of the poverty line by 1992, and are less today....The top one percent of American households have more wealth than the bottom 90 percent." (p27)

Tabb, William K. "Globalization Is an Issue, The Power of Capital Is the Issue." Monthly Review v49 n2 Jun 1997. p20-30. (ISSN0027-0520).

In the U.S., in 1993 real compensation (wages plus benefits) "fell by 0.4 percent; in 1994, fell by 0.9 percent; in 1995, fell by 0.3 percent; and in 1996, rose by 0.3 percent. By the end of 1996 a family of four in the median bracket had income 3 percent below that of a similar family in 1989, and just 1.6 percent above that of such a family in 1973....About one-third of the U.S. labor force makes $15,000 or less....Between 1992 and 1995, 15 percent of people holding jobs for more than a year lost those jobs; their new jobs, if they found one, paid 14 percent less on average....This great boom is the slowest in the postwar period, bumping along at an average of 2.6 percent growth in gross domestic product between 1992 and 1996." (p9)

Cockburn, Alexander. "Beat the Devil: The Witch Hunt and the Crash." Nation v265 n16 17 Nov 1997. p9. (ISSN0027-8378).

"Between 1989 and 1993, the median family income of U.S. workers fell every year; by 1993, it was down by $2,700, or 7 percent, compared to 1989....It's been estimated that, of the 126 million jobs in this country, 90 to 95 million of them will be automated during the next two decades." (p2)

"Editorial: Cooperation vs. Competition." People's Tribune v24 n11 Nov 1997. p2. (ISSN1081-4787).

In the U.S., "the median income of households for 1995 was estimated at $34,076, representing a gain of 5.6 percent above 1994. The personal saving rate--saving as a percentage of personal disposable income--rose to 4.9 percent in 1996, but is still low by historic standards. The household sector's debt outstanding in 1996 is at an all-time high, amounting to over $5.4 trillion or 84 percent of personal income." (p27)

Vincenzino, Joseph V. "Personal Income and Finances: Regional Comparisons." Statistical Bulletin v78 n4 Oct-Dec 1997. p27-32. (ISSN0790-8334).

"California's mammoth economy has just surpassed a $1 trillion output and created 1.3 million jobs, reversing the state's worst recession this century. Revenue surpluses last year returned $680 million to education; this year another $1 billion will go to a middle-class tax cut. Michigan has just announced a jobless rate of 3.7 percent, the lowest in recorded history. The state is boasting the hottest real estate market in the country and a $1 billion rainy-day fund. Texas voters just passed the largest tax cut in state history--$1 billion--amid that state's dramatic return from the cellar of oil-business depression. Wisconsin has created 600,000 new jobs in five years, the biggest increase of manufacturing jobs in the US. Unemployment is at a 30-year low (3.4 percent)." (p5)

Wood, Daniel B. "United States: GOP Looks to Future, Sees Governors." The Christian Science Monitor v89 n209 23 Sep 1997. p1,5. The Christian Science Monitor search engine: <http://www.csmonitor.com/plweb-cgi/iops1.pl> To retrieve this article, enter the following search: ED=19970923 AND governors. In the "retrieved list," click the title that matches this record. (ISSN0882-7729).

In New Bedford, Massachussetts, in 1991, "the jobless rate was 14 percent....[In 1997,] the unemployment rate has shrunk to 9.2 percent for the city and 7.6 percent for the greater New Bedford metro area....New Bedford is not alone. Around the country, regions long considered economic wastelands are reviving...." (p1) In 1995, "the difference in economic growth between the top areas of the country and the laggards was five to six percentage points. Today, that spread is down to two to three percentage points. All but three of the top 100 metropolitan statistical areas are now reporting positive job growth." (p18)

Scherer, Ron. "Ironman Economy: The Laggards: Small Economies Ride High." The Christian Science Monitor v89 n130 2 Jun 1997. p1,18. The Christian Science Monitor search engine: <http://www.csmonitor.com/plweb-cgi/iops1.pl> To retrieve this article, enter the following search: ED=19970602 AND high. In the "retrieved list," click the title that matches this record. (ISSN0882-7729).

In the U.S., "according to popular economic theory, inflation should pick up when unemployment falls below 5 or 6 percent. But the jobless rate seems stuck near 4.8 percent, and inflation is still stable--a modest 0.2 percent in July and 2.2 percent in the last 12 months....Economist Mickey Levy of NationsBanc Capital Markets in New York says the US economy is able to grow at a 3 percent real rate--a bit higher than many economists believe possible. With the Fed keeping growth in current dollars to 5 percent, there is only room left for 2 percent inflation (5 percent nominal growth minus 3 percent real growth)." (p8)

Francis, David R. "Global Report: Falling Prices: Cheap Labor Ripples through Global Economy." The Christian Science Monitor v89 n186 20 Aug 1997. p1,8. The Christian Science Monitor search engine: <http://www.csmonitor.com/plweb-cgi/iops1.pl> To retrieve this article, enter the following search: ED=19970820 AND economy. In the "retrieved list," click the title that matches this record. (ISSN0882-7729).

In the U.S., "over the past decade, 401(k) money in mutual funds swelled 1,300 percent to $261 billion, according to the Investment Company Institute (ICI), a mutual-fund trade group in Washington. At the same time, savings at commercial banks and savings institutions in the US rose just 19 percent, from $3 trillion to $3.6 trillion, according to the Federal Reserve....The stock market has lured record numbers of US investors--between 75 million and 80 million people, according to David Hale at Zurich Kemper Investments Inc. in Chicago. Total stock mutual-fund assets have exploded from $242 billion in September 1987 to $2.2 trillion in August 1997, according to the ICI. Stocks now exceed 30 percent of household net worth, compared with roughly 14 percent last decade." (p11)

Tyson, James L. "America's Consuming Love Affair with Stocks." The Christian Science Monitor v89 n226 17 Oct 1997. p11. The Christian Science Monitor search engine: <http://www.csmonitor.com/plweb-cgi/iops1.pl> To retrieve this article, enter the following search: ED=19971017 AND stocks. In the "retrieved list," click the title that matches this record. (ISSN0882-7729).

In the U.S., "the consumer price index (CPI), the most common inflation gauge, has risen at only a 1.4 percent annual rate this year, versus 3.3 percent for all of 1996....Low unemployment (5 percent in June) and rapid economic growth (a 5.9 percent annual rate in the first quarter) are commonly regarded as two ingredients in the recipe for accelerating inflation....The percentage of men age 25 to 54 in the labor force has risen. Men age 55 to 64 have been postponing retirement. Overall, 67 percent of adults are participating in the labor force, an all-time record." (p18)

Francis, David R. "Could Inflation Really Be Gone for Good?"

The Christian Science Monitor v89 n154 7 Jul 1997. p1,18. The Christian Science Monitor search engine: <http://www.csmonitor.com/plweb-cgi/iops1.pl> To retrieve this article, enter the following search: ED=19970707 AND good. In the "retrieved list," click the title that matches this record. (ISSN0882-7729).

In the U.S., "unemployment in May [1997] dropped to 4.8 percent, the lowest in 24 years....This year producer prices have been declining at an annual rate of 3.9 percent....Some 12.2 percent of those unemployed in May left their work voluntarily. A year earlier, only 9.4 percent of the jobless had quit for their own reasons." (p1,15)

Francis, David R. "Good-Times US Economy Shows Little Sign of Abating." The Christian Science Monitor v89 n140 16 Jun 1997. p1,15. The Christian Science Monitor search engine: <http://www.csmonitor.com/plweb-cgi/iops1.pl> To retrieve this article, enter the following search: ED=19970616 AND abating. In the "retrieved list," click the title that matches this record. (ISSN0882-7729).

The U.S. "federal government deficit shrank to $22.6 billion in the just-ended fiscal year 1997. But a surplus in local and state governments close to or exceeding $30 billion has meant that government as a whole enjoys a budget surplus in the nation....As a result of...combined developments, the federal government itself has shrunk. It consumes about 20 percent of all goods and services produced in the nation, down from 22.5 percent in 1991 in the midst of a recession. Contrariwise, federal revenues have risen from around 17 to 18 percent of gross domestic product several years back to 20 percent now....Overall, fiscal 1997 revenues were up nearly 9 percent and spending rose only about 2.5 percent." (p3)

Francis, David R. "United States: Federal Deficit Fading into Economic Sunset." The Christian Science Monitor v89 n233 28 Oct 1997. p3. The Christian Science Monitor search engine: <http://www.csmonitor.com/plweb-cgi/iops1.pl> To retrieve this article, enter the following search: ED=19971028 AND sunset. In the "retrieved list," click the title that matches this record. (ISSN0882-7729).

According to figures released by the U.S. Department of Labor, "the unemployment rate in May [1997] dropped to 4.8 percent....Timothy Taylor, managing editor of the JOURNAL OF ECONOMIC PERSPECTIVES, noted recently that a report by the president's Council of Economic Advisers indicated 'that households in the bottom fifth of the income distribution saw their incomes rise at an annual rate of 3.4 percent from 1993 to 1995, while the top fifth saw an annual increase of only 1.2 percent.' (SAN JOSE MERCURY NEWS, June 11.)" (p1) "Despite the offical 4.8 percent unemployment rate, the official jobless rate for African-American workers is over 10 percent; for Hispanics almost 7.5 percent; for teenagers 15.6 percent and for black teenagers...32.6 percent." (p6)

Karp, Nathan. "Economic 'Boom' Doing Little for Worker Majority." The People v107 n4 Jul 1997. p1,6. (ISSN0199-350X).

"More than 70 million new jobs have been created in America since 1980, a stunning 60 percent of the work force, while some 40 million were lost by attrition. The net job creation has been 32.3 million--about eight times the number of new jobs created in Europe despite Europe's larger population and economy....The high-tech sector makes up, by far, the largest component of our economic growth, accounting for some 40 percent of the total....Exports grew to 12 percent of gross domestic product from 7 percent, while U.S. goods made abroad have sales at three times our exports. A stunning 40 percent of our growing exports are in sophisticated capital goods." (p80)

Zuckerman, Mortimer B. "Editorial: Boom from the Bottom Up." U.S. News & World Report v123 n14 13 Oct 1997. p80. article-level access: <http://www.usnews.com/usnews/issue/971013/13EDIT.HTM> (ISSN0041-5537).

In the U.S., "from the end of World War II until 1973, economic growth averaged around 3.5 percent. But during the 1980s, growth averaged just 2.7 percent and since 1989 only about 2 percent....The dramatic increase in the percentage of working women during this period was another prime reason why the postwar economy expanded. In 1963, just 38 percent of the U.S. population was in the labor force; today, more than 50 percent is....The size of the labor force, which grew by as much as 3.2 percent a year in the 1970s, will grow by only about 0.9 percent in the next decade." (p38) "The portion of American workers employed in manufacturing declined from 31 percent in 1960 to just 15.8 percent in 1995." (p39)

Longman, Phillip J. "Business & Technology: Is Prosperity Permanent?" U.S. News & World Report v123 n18 10 Nov 1997. p36,38-39. article-level access: <http://www.usnews.com/usnews/issue/971110/10LONG.HTM> (ISSN0041-5537).

In the U.S., "only five years ago, the annual deficit was a record $290 billion. For the year that ends...[in September 1997], it will be a mere $34 billion, the smallest since 1974....[The Congressional Budget Office] notes that total tax receipts are up an incredible 9.2 percent over last year. Since 1992, revenues have been rising by 7.3 percent annually, even though inflation has averaged less than 3 percent." (p49)

Glassman, James K. "Commentary: Time to Pay Off the Debt?" U.S. News & World Report v123 n9 8 Sep 1997. p49. article-level access: <http://www.usnews.com/usnews/issue/970908/8GLAS.HTM> (ISSN0041-5537).

UNITED STATES--ECONOMIC CONDITIONS--PUBLIC OPINION

In the U.S., "the University of Michigan's Index of Consumer Sentiment averaged 102.9 in 1997 surveys, the highest level since it averaged 103.4 in 1965, said Richard Curtin, director of the university's Surveys of Consumers....42 percent of families surveyed said they expected their financial situation to improve in 1998. Only 8 percent expected their finances to worsen." (p1 secE)

Brennan, Mike. "Business: Confidence in Economy Is Soaring: U-M Survey Index Highest in 32 Years." Detroit Free Press 21 Nov 1997. p1,8 secE.

"A question on a WALL STREET JOURNAL poll from late June [1997] as to whether globalization of the [U.S.] economy was a good or bad development--by a margin of 48 percent to 42 percent, people thought it bad--revealed a fairly extreme, if predictable, class polarization. College graduates thought it good by 58 percent to 30 percent; respondents with no more than a high school diploma judged it bad by 59 percent to 33 percent. The professional/managerial class supported globalization 55 percent to 35 percent; blue-collar workers opposed it 57 percent to 36 percent." (p28)

Meyerson, Harold. "Can Liberalism Survive Clinton?" Dissent v44 n4 Fall 1997. p27-32. (ISSN0012-3846).

UNITED STATES--EDUCATION (v26)

UNITED STATES--EMIGRATION AND IMMIGRATION

"The number of legal immigrants admitted to the United States from Mexico was 90,000 in 1995, or 12 percent of all legal immigrants. That is the lowest total since 1987. Because the Immigration and Reform Act of 1986 (IRCA) offered amnesty to many Mexicans who were here illegally, the number officially admitted rose from 72,000 in 1987 to 95,000 in 1988, 405,000 in 1989, 679,000 in 1990, and 946,000 in 1991. The number dropped to 214,000 in 1992 and has been declining since....The U.S. admitted more than 720,000 legal immigrants in 1995, two-thirds from the 20 countries contributing the most immigrants; in 1985, the share was three-fourths." (p32-33)

Miller, Berna. "Kaleidoscope: Mexican Immigrants Retreat." American Demographics v19 n7 Jul 1997. p32-33. article-level access: <http://www.demographics.com/publications/ad/97_ad/9707_ad/ad970726.htm> (ISSN0163-4089).

"Experts estimate that roughly 250,000 to 300,000 Americans move overseas each year....Currently 3.2 million Americans are living abroad, up by more than 1 million in the 1990s alone, U.S. State Department estimates show." (p10) "There are an estimated 627,000 Americans living in Canada and 550,000 Americans in Mexico." (p11)

"Dateline Migration: National: Many Seek American Dream--Outside America." Migration World v25 n4 1997. p10-11. (ISSN1058-5095).

UNITED STATES--EMIGRATION AND IMMIGRATION --PUBLIC OPINION

Results of a U.S. poll on immigration for the Knight-Ridder newspapers show "forty-five percent said immigration benefits the nation, 42 percent said it hurts, and 10 percent said its effects are mixed. But the poll conducted...by Princeton Survey Research Associates clearly shows a drop in anti-immigrant feeling since 1993, when three out of five Americans told pollsters for NEWSWEEK magazine that the influx of foreigners was bad." (p1 secA)

Dewar, Heather. "More in U.S. Open to New Arrivals." Detroit Free Press 16 Jun 1997. p1,8 secA.

UNITED STATES--EMPLOYMENT (v26)

In the U.S., "twenty-five percent of today's jobs are managerial and professional, requiring a college degree, according to Louis Glazer, executive director of Michigan Future Inc., an Ann Arbor-based, nonprofit citizens organization that gathers information on the economy. Technical jobs make up 20 percent of the job market, and the rest are lower-skilled." (p2 secE)

Clotman, Louis S. "Business: Good Technical Skills Land Well-Paid Jobs, Execs Say." Detroit Free Press 20 Jun 1997. p2 secE.

"Employment in the manufacture, programming, sale, and deployment of computer and communications equipment accounts for just 5% of U.S. job growth since 1992. That pales next to the 20% accounted for by retail trade (which includes bars and restaurants as well as stores), 10% by state and local government, and the 9% each by health services and temp firms." (p8)

"Miscellany: Computer Jobs." Left Business Observer n78 17 Jul 1997. p8. (ISSN1042-0134).

In the U.S., "over 1.4 million new jobs were created in 1992, and the total since the recession trough is over 12 million new jobs....Between the February 1992 trough in employment (which came eleven months after the official end to the 1990-91 recession) and April 1997, part-time employment grew by 1.4 million....Nearly twice as many people hold down multiple jobs as are involuntarily limited to part-time work (7.9 million vs. 4.1 million)--and well over half the multiply employed hold at least one full-time job....As a recent BLS [Bureau of Labor Statistics] study has shown, the total number of annual hours put in by the average employed male increased by one hundred hours between 1976 and 1993, or two-and-a-half full work weeks--and, more eye-poppingly, the number clocked by the average working woman increased by 223 hours, or nearly six full workweeks." (p24-25)

Henwood, Doug. "Talking about Work." Monthly Review v49 n3 Jul-Aug 1997. p18-30. (ISSN0027-0520).

U.S. Bureau of Labor statistics "surveys show that in 1996 the average (median) worker had been at his or her job for 3.8 years, little changed from 1983's 3.5 years....Tenure for men in every age group fell, with 55-64 year olds falling the most, from 15.3 to 10.5; 35-44 year olds, from 7.3 to 6.1. But since workers are, on average, getting older, and tenure rises with age, the average for all men fell only slightly, from 4.1 to 4.0. Tenure for women rose on average from 3.1 to 3.5 years, and in half the age groups." (p25)

Henwood, Doug. "Talking about Work." Monthly Review v49 n3 Jul-Aug 1997. p18-30. (ISSN0027-0520).

"According to the American Management Association's 1996 survey of the U.S. work force, 49 percent of large and mid-sized firms reported job eliminations in the 12 months ending in June 1996. Another 1996 poll, this one reported in BUSINESS NEWS (Oct. '96), asked people how they felt about their own job security. Only 40 percent of the respondents described their jobs as 'very secure;' 49 percent of the affluent report a high confidence in their job security vs. 33 percent of their lowest income counterparts." (p24)

"The U.S. Bishops Statement for Labor Day 1997: 'Economic Progess: Looking beyond the Numbers.'" Observer v62 n19 5 Sep 1997. p24-25,30. (ISSN0029-7712).

The Federal Reserve Bank of San Francisco has discovered that "a record share of the working-age population [in the U.S.]--67.25 percent--is either employed or looking for work." (p16) "Since August of last year, when the welfare bill went into effect, the annual labor force growth rate for single women with families has jumped from 2.4 percent between July 1995 and July 1996 to an annual rate of 6.5 percent in the succeeding months....The report ['Labor Force Developments and Welfare Reform in the United States and the Twelfth District']...notes that 'black women, Hispanics, and white teenagers, all of whom have higher than average unemployment rates, accounted for about 60 percent of the total growth in the labor force over the past twelve months'...." (p17)

Plummer, James/Henderson, Rick. "Citings: Rolling off the Rolls." Reason v29 n6 Nov 1997. p16-17. (ISSN0048-6906).

"There are now 121.8 million jobs in America--more than ever before....The national unemployment rate is 4.8 percent, the lowest in 23 years....Some 57 metropolitan regions around the country have jobless rates below 3 percent." (p50) "While 43 million jobs were lost since 1980, 71 million new ones were created." (p53)

Saltzman, Amy/Lord, Mary/McMurray, Scott/Sieder, Jill Jordan. "Special Report: Making It in a Sizzling Economy." U.S. News & World Report v122 n24 23 Jun 1997. p50-53,56-58. article-level access: <http://www.usnews.com/usnews/issue/970623/23JOBS.HTM> (ISSN0041-5537).

UNITED STATES--EMPLOYMENT--MANUFACTURES (v26)

UNITED STATES--EMPLOYMENT--PUBLIC OPINION (v26)

"A new Gallup poll finds that one in four [U.S.] workers--24%--say that if they could do so, they would fire their boss. Overall, the vast majority of Americans--86%--say they are satisfied with their jobs, but among those who are not satisfied, more than half say they would fire their boss. Even among those who are satisfied with their jobs, 20% would still give their boss the ax."

Moore, David W./Gallup Organization. "One of Four Workers Would Fire the Boss." Press Release 2 Sep 1996. document-level access: <http://www.gallup.com/poll/news/970902b.html>

UNITED STATES--EMPLOYMENT--RURAL CONDITIONS

According to the "1996 Current Population Survey" by the U.S. Bureau of Labor Statistics, "professional specialty occupations accounted for 13 percent of second jobs held by rural workers, and rural workers whose primary occupations were in professional specialty fields were the most likely to hold more than one job....Rural elementary and secondary school teachers were the most likely to hold a second job, with a rate of 12 percent.

Teachers also accounted for the largest absolute number of rural multiple jobholders. Other professional specialty occupations such as health assessment and treatment (9 percent), technicians (11 percent), and college and university teachers (10 percent) had high multiple jobholding rates, as did rural workers in administrative support (8 percent), technicians (11 percent), and police and firefighters (10 percent)." (p22)

Parker, Timothy S. "Farm & Rural Communities: Multiple Jobholding among Rural Workers." Agricultural Outlook Nov 1997. p22-24.

UNITED STATES--ENVIRONMENTAL ASPECTS (v26)

UNITED STATES--ENVIRONMENTAL ASPECTS --PUBLIC OPINION

"By better than three to one, the American people believe either that our environmental laws do not go far enough (forty-five percent) or that they strike the right balance in protecting the environment (twenty-eight percent), as opposed to those who say they go too far (nineteen percent)." (p332) "Two-thirds of Americans oppose oil drilling in Alaska. Almost eighty percent want to know about toxics in our air and water, even when the cost of compiling this data is passed on to the consumer." (p333)

Schiffer, Lois J./Dowling, Timothy J. "Remarks: Reflections on the Role of the Courts in Environmental Law." Environmental Law v27 n2 Sum 1997. p327-342. (ISSN0046-2276).

UNITED STATES--FOREIGN ECONOMIC RELATIONS

According to a study of the U.S. Congressional Research Service, "foreign policy spending is now at its lowest level in 20 years. Stated in fiscal 1998 dollars, the budget in the current fiscal year is $18.77 billion, which is 25 percent below the annual average of $25 billion over the past two decades, and 30 percent below the level of 10 years ago, near the end of the Reagan administration....Spending dropped by 3.8 percent in fiscal 1994, by 5.6 percent in fiscal 1995, by 10.2 percent in fiscal 1996, and finally by 3.7 percent in fiscal 1997....For the past two decades, international affairs spending, as measured against the rest of the discretionary budget, held reasonably steady. The average was 4.1 percent, but it rarely deviated much from that average. In fact, the trend, from 1987 to 1995, was virtually a straight line. But then the line started to take a dive in 1996, dropping to 3.7 percent; and in 1997, it fell still further to 3.6 percent....Over the past two decades, international affairs funding comprised, on average, 1.7 percent of the entire Federal budget. In fiscal 1997, such funding was just 1.1 percent of the Federal budget, the lowest level in the past 20 years and about one-third below the historical average." (pS4912)

Biden, Joseph R., Jr. (Sen.-Del.). "Enhancing Our Diplomatic Readiness--A Critical Test of American Leadership." Congressional Record. Daily ed. v143 n68 21 May 1997. pS4911-4913. section/page-level access: <http://thomas.loc.gov/cgi-bin/query/R?r105:FLD001:S04911:> (ISSN0363-7239). (X1.1A.105/1).

UNITED STATES--FOREIGN RELATIONS --APPROPRIATIONS AND EXPENDITURES (v26)

UNITED STATES--FOREIGN RELATIONS--PUBLIC OPINION (v26)

UNITED STATES--HEALTH AND HYGIENE (v26)

UNITED STATES--HEALTH AND HYGIENE--PUBLIC OPINION (v26)

UNITED STATES--LANGUAGES (v26)

In the U.S., "in the 1990 census, 15 million Hispanics ages 5 and older reported they speak a language other than English at home. This group constitutes nearly eight out of every 10 Hispanics ages 5 or older. Spanish is the second most common language spoken at home in the United States. French, the next most common language, runs a distant third. Less than 2 million people reported speaking French at home in the 1990 census." (p34)

del Pinal, Jorge/Singer, Audrey. "Generations of Diversity: Latinos in the United States." Population Bulletin v52 n3 Oct 1997. p2-47. (ISSN0032-468X).

UNITED STATES--MANUFACTURES (v26)

"The United States shipped more than one-third of all domestically manufactured exports in 1996 to two countries Canada (25 percent) and Mexico (10 percent), according to a study released...by the Commerce Department's Census Bureau. Manufactured products comprised 78 percent of all goods exported in 1996 and are growing on pace to exceed $500 billion in 1997, said a Census Brief titled 'Manufactured Exports Approach $500 Billion a Year'....In 1996, one-quarter of all manufactured exports came from just two states California ($78 billion) and Texas ($59 billion). Every state had export shipments of at least $125 million."

U.S. Dept. of Commerce. Economic & Statistics Administration. "More than One-Third of U.S. Manufactured Exports Go to Canada and Mexico, Census Bureau Reports." Census Bureau Press Release 13 Nov 1997. document-level access: <http://www.census.gov/Press-Release/cb97-184.html>

In the U.S. manufacturing sector, "productivity rose at an average annual rate of 2.8 percent between 1960 and 1979, while employment grew at a rate of 1.2 percent. Between 1979 and 1995, however, while productivity rose at a rate of 3.1 percent per year, employment declined by close to 1 percent annually." (p61)

Brand, H. "Global Capitalism and the Decay of Employment Policy." Dissent v44 n4 Fall 1997. p56-62. (ISSN0012-3846).

The U.S. Census Bureau defines a manufacturing establishment, or plant, as a single physical location where manufacturing is performed. "The Bureau recently reported that in 1992 more than 82,000 such establishments exported their products from the United States, and that 77 percent of them were small, with fewer than 100 employees....71 percent of the large establishments (500 employees or more) engaged in exporting, while only 19 percent of the small ones did." (p25)

Fieleke, Norman S. "Popular Myths about the World Economy." Federal Reserve Bank of Boston New England Economic Review Jul-Aug 1997. p17-26. (ISSN0028-4726).

UNITED STATES--MANUFACTURES--EDUCATION --EMPLOYMENT

In the U.S., "today, 25 percent of the nation's 19 million factory workers have finished a year or two of college, up from 17 percent in 1985, according to the Bureau of Labor Statistics. Another 19 percent have college diplomas today, versus 16 percent a decade ago." (p8)

Challenger, John A. "Business & Money: The New Boss in the New Workplace--It's You." The Christian Science Monitor v89 n156 9 Jul 1997. p8. The Christian Science Monitor search engine: <http://www.csmonitor.com/plweb-cgi/iops1.pl> To retrieve this article, enter the following search: ED=19970709 AND boss. In the "retrieved list," click the title that matches this record. (ISSN0882-7729).

UNITED STATES--NEWSPAPERS (v26)

UNITED STATES--OFFICIALS AND EMPLOYEES (v26)

"With just under 3 million civilian employees in 1994, of whom 1.6 million were in only two agencies, the Department of Defense and the U.S. Postal Service, the national government can hardly be called small....Since 1970, when the national government employed 2.997 million civilian workers, national employment has been essentially flat, decreasing slightly during the seventies, rising slightly during the later years of the Reagan administration, reaching a high of 3.233 million workers in 1990 under President Bush, and declining again to an estimated 2.971 million workers in 1994 under President Clinton (U.S. Bureau of the Census 1995...)." (p693) "Federal employees constituted 27.5 percent of all public employees in 1960 but only 13.5 percent in 1995....As a percentage of the total population, federal employment has dropped from 1.3 percent in 1960 to .99 percent in 1995, while state and local employment has jumped from 3.5 to 6.3 percent during the same period. Or, as a percentage of the civilian labor population, federal workers comprised 3.5 percent in 1960 but only 2.2 percent in 1995." (p694)

Anton, Thomas J. "New Federalism and Intergovernmental Fiscal Relationships: The Implications for Health Policy." Journal of Health Politics, Policy and Law v22 n3 Jun 1997. p691-720. (ISSN0361-6878).

As of January 1997, the U.S. "federal workforce had been reduced by about 308,000 positions since this administration took office. That's more than a 14 percent reduction, in real people....Only about 10 percent of the 308,000 who have left government so far were RIFed [reduced in force]." (p21)

King, James B. "Mini-Forum: Status of Human Resource Management: The Government of the Future: A Personnel Perspective." Public Manager v26 n2 Sum 1997. p21-22. (ISSN1061-7639).

Between 1993 and 1996 the U.S. "government has reduced its supervisory staff by 20 percent, its headquarters staff by 14 percent, and employees in 'control positions' (e.g., procurement, budget, personnel) by 9 percent. Of the 'control positions,' the greatest decrease was in personnel or HRM [human resources management] staff with a reduction of over 19 percent to date. In a governmentwide MSPB [Merit Systems Protection Board] survey last year (1996), to which over 9,700 employees responded....Over half (57 percent) of managers in responding to that 1996 survey confirmed that the personnel office providing service to them had been downsized....Almost one-third of the respondents think that there are serious problems in the way their agencies promote people in that they believe promotions are not based solely on the relative ability, knowledge, and skills of the candidates. Better than two-thirds of all respondents do not think their organizations consistently hire well-qualified individuals when selecting new employees from outside their agency. Approximately half of all respondents (51 percent) said their agencies do not take corrective action regarding poorly performing employees who cannot or will not improve that performance. One-fifth of the survey respondents believe that their organizations regularly fail to promote--within the workforce--high standards of integrity, conduct, and concern for the public interest." (p19)

Erdreich, Ben L. "Mini-Forum: Human Resource Management Futures: The Future of Merit in the Personnel System." Public Manager v26 n2 Sum 1997. p17-20. (ISSN1061-7639).

The results of the U.S. Office of Personnel Management's Career Transition Program show that of the employees affected by the reductions in force "occuring in 1994, 88 percent were placed in jobs or 'settled' to their satisfaction within six months of the first RIF. (By November 1994, 344, or 78 percent were working, and 36, or 7 percent, had retired....21 persons, nearly 5 percent, declined assistance and did not participate in the program). Additional RIFs in 1994 and 1995 increased the total number of RIFs in OPM to 1,130. OPM's successful experience with each group was sustained at or above the 88 percent level." (p30)

Cronin, Michael. "Article: OPM's Experience with Career Transition Programs." Public Manager v26 n2 Sum 1997. p27-30. (ISSN1061-7639).

In 1997, the U.S. "federal government is about 300,000 people smaller than it was in 1993 when President Clinton took office--a total reduction of 14 percent....The US Office of Personnel Management (OPM), is 48 percent smaller than it was in early 1993....The total federal civilian work force is...about 1.5 percent...of the total number of jobs in existence across the nation." (p19)

King, James B. "Opinion/Essays: Welfare Work: How to Hire: Welfare Recipients into a Dwindling Work Force." The Christian Science Monitor v89 n130 2 Jun 1997. p19. The Christian Science Monitor search engine: <http://www.csmonitor.com/plweb-cgi/iops1.pl> To retrieve this article, enter the following search: ED=19970602 AND force. In the "retrieved list," click the title that matches this record. (ISSN0882-7729).

UNITED STATES--OFFICIALS AND EMPLOYEES --ATTITUDES

"The annual membership survey of the Federal Executive Institute Alumni Association (FEIAA) was conducted in the Fall of 1996 [in the U.S.]....Eight hundred and ninety six (896) members participated in the survey. This represents a response rate of 50 percent of the FEIAA membership....Forty-seven percent of executives rated morale low in 1995. For 1996, 58 percent of executives noted that morale was low....The majority of federal executives and managers expressed higher satisfaction with their agencies (60 percent) in 1996 than with the federal government (52 percent)....54 percent expressed satisfaction with working for their agencies in the 1995 annual survey." (p25) "One out of every two executives (50 percent) said there were no opportunities for mobility within their own federal agencies. Sixty-nine percent noted the absence of opportunities for mobility between federal agencies. Forty-seven percent of current executives and managers would not encourage young people to consider a career with the federal government. Forty-six percent of respondents believed neither the Office of Management and Budget (OMB) nor the General Services Administration (GSA) were effective in their oversight activities, while 58 percent expressed concerns with oversight practices of the Office of Personnel Managment (OPM)....Fifty-three percent of respondents indicated that the quality of clerical staff had changed for the worse compared to five years ago. Thirty-nine percent of respondents said that executive-level staff had changed for the worse compared with five years ago." (p26)

Brown, David Y./Manderscheid, Ronald W. "Article: Federal Executives Assess Current Situation." Public Manager v26 n2 Sum 1997. p25-26. (ISSN1061-7639).

UNITED STATES--OFFICIALS AND EMPLOYEES --CORRUPT PRACTICES

"During FY 1996, the United States Attorneys' offices filed 470 criminal cases charging 646 defendants with official corruption. These prosecutions included official corruption in federal procurement, federal programs, federal law enforcement and other federal activities, as well as corruption by state, local and other officials. During FY 1996, the United States Attorneys also terminated 448 cases against 603 official corruption defendants. This represents an increase of 7.4 percent in cases terminated and an 8.3 percent increase in defendants terminated. Eighty-seven percent of the defendants terminated were convicted and 44.6 percent sentenced to prison. Increases are also observed in the number of cases and defendants pending. At the end of FY 1996, there were 472 official corruption cases pending. Official corruption cases are among the most hotly contested and highly sensitive of all criminal cases prosecuted by the United States Attorneys. During FY 1996, 13.6 percent of the official corruption defendants whose cases were terminated were terminated by trial." (p725-726)

U.S. Dept. of Justice. "Departments of Commerce, Justice, And State, The Judiciary...Approp. for 1998 (Part 2)." Hearing. U.S. House. Committee on Appropriations. Washington, D.C. : GPO, 1997. (ISBN0160549094). (Y4.Ap6/1:C73/2/997/pt.2).

UNITED STATES--PENSIONS--OFFICIALS AND EMPLOYEES (v26)

UNITED STATES--POLITICS AND GOVERNMENT

In the U.S., "on April 26, 1996, President Clinton signed legislation which ended a 7 month budget stalemate. That stalemate involved no fewer than 15 continuing resolutions, 2 full-fledged Government shutdowns--one lasting a record 27 days--and numerous Presidential vetoes. By President Clinton's own account, it cost the taxpayers $1.5 billion. But the costs of this shutdown went beyond this $1.5 billion. Thousands upon thousands of Federal employees were furloughed. Thousands of small businesses, particularly those near national parks closed during the Government shutdown, suffered crippling loss of business. And American citizens suffered innumerable inconveniences, many of them quite serious....10,000 new Medicare applications, 212,000 Social Security card requests, 360,000 individual office visits and 800,000 toll-free calls for information and assistance were turned away each day. Hundreds of thousands of ordinary Americans were inconvenienced, or had to temporarily forego benefits for which the Government requires things like Social Security cards, because we could not reach a budget agreement....Some of our most vulnerable people suffered from the Government shutdown: 13 million AFDC recipients, 273,000 foster care children, over 100,000 children receiving adoption assistance services and over 100,000 Head Start children had their services delayed. And I have not even mentioned the 9 million Americans whose vacations and outings were ruined because they were turned away from our national parks and museums." (pS4103-4104)

Abraham, Spencer (Sen.-Mich.). "Supplemental Appropriations and Rescissions Act of 1997." Congressional Record. Daily ed. v143 n58 7 May 1997. pS4082-4104. section/page-level access: <http://thomas.loc.gov/cgi-bin/query/R?r105:FLD001:S04103:> (ISSN0363-7239). (X1.1A.105/1).

UNITED STATES--POLITICS AND GOVERNMENT --APPROPRIATIONS AND EXPENDITURES

Between 1986 and 1991, the U.S. "State Department requested a total of $54 million for the TSWG [Technical Support Working Group] projects, yet Congress only approved $25 million. In 1991 only thirteen of fifty proposed projects were funded. The distribution of funding for 1991 among the six TSWG subcommittees was heavily biased toward Intrusion Detection (48 percent). Chemical/Biological Incident Response received less than 20 percent of the funds, and Nuclear Incident Response received no funding. Threat Analysis and Explosive Detection each received about 15 percent, and the remaining funds went to Conventional Incident Response (less than 4 percent)." (p302)

Medd, Roger/Goldstein, Frank. "International Terrorism on the Eve of a New Millennium." Studies in Conflict & Terrorism v20 n3 Jul-Sep 1997. p281-316. (ISSN1057-610X).

"U.S. spending on foreign aid reached its lowest level in the post-World War II era in 1997, falling to less than 1 percent....That share compares...with almost 16 percent for defense, almost 21 percent for Social Security, and 15 percent for interest on the national debt....Foreign aid outlays fell by 32 percent between 1985 and 1995. Overall federal spending rose by almost 15 percent during that period." (p10)

U.S. Congressional Budget Office. "The Flow of Foreign Aid and Private Capital to Developing Countries." The Role of Foreign Aid in Development May 1997. p7-19.

UNITED STATES--POLITICS AND GOVERNMENT --PUBLIC OPINION (v26)

A U.S. poll about the government found that "eighty-one percent say government is wasteful and inefficient, and 79 percent say it spends too much money on the wrong things. Only half that number say that it is interfering too much in people's lives or that the problems that it is trying to solve cannot be solved by the federal government....Some complaints about poor performance may also be criticisms of scope, and...40 percent feel that the scope of government is too broad...." (p101)

Nye, Joseph S., Jr. "In Government We Don't Trust." Foreign Policy n108 Fall 1997. p99-111. (ISSN0015-7228).

In the U.S., "in 1994, Luntz Research found that 73% believe 'the federal government is much too large and has too much power'; Roper found that 67% believe 'big government is the biggest threat to the country in the future'; the Times Mirror Center found that 63% think 'government regulation of business usually does more harm than good'; and the New York Times found that only 22% 'trust the government in Washington to do what is right most of the time." (p16)

Browne, Harry. "Strategy: Debate: The 22% Solution." Liberty v11 n1 Sep 1997. p16. (ISSN0894-1408).

UNITED STATES--POPULATION (v26)

"In 1991, when today's kindergartners were born, the average life expectancy at birth for Americans was 79 years for a woman and 71 years for a man. That's almost double what it was in 1900. Over the past decade, the over-65 age group grew by a third, while the general population rose only 11 percent. By the year 2030, there will be twice as many U.S. citizens over the age of 65 as there are today." (p2)

"Health Advances Extend Life." ChemEcology v26 n5 Jun-Jul 1997. p2-4. (ISSN0738-7776).

"In 1996, natural increase added 1,558,000 people to the U.S. population. Only 14 percent of U.S. natural increase happened in northeastern states, although the Northeast has 20 percent of the U.S. population. Only 20 percent came to the Midwest, which has 24 percent of the U.S. population. One-third of natural increase happened in the South, home to 35 percent of Americans. The one place where babies still boom is the West, which has 33 percent of natural increase but just 22 percent of population." (p2)

"No More Baby Booms." Forecast v17 n9 Sep 1997. p1-2. article-level access: <http://www.demographics.com/Publications/FC/97_fc/9709_fc/FC97091.htm> (ISSN0732-1597).

UNITED STATES--POPULATION--ENVIRONMENTAL ASPECTS (v26)

UNITED STATES--PUBLIC OPINION (v26)

In 1996, the Gallup Organization asked a nationally representative sample of U.S. adults to name up to three things they were most thankful for. "Family tops the list, with six in ten adults naming it among the three things for which they are most thankful....Two in ten say they are especially thankful for their children, while 12 percent say the same of their spouse. Half of U.S. adults don't take their health for granted when they consider good fortune....One-fourth of 18-to-29-year-olds are thankful for their jobs, as are 27 percent of adults aged 30 to 49. But the share declines sharply for those aged 50 to 64 and 65 and older, to 17 percent and 2 percent, respectively." (p37)

Dortch, Shannon. "Kaleidoscope: Hot Topics: Thanksgiving Thoughts." American Demographics v19 n11 Nov 1997. p37. article-level access: <http://www.demographics.com/publications/ad/97_ad/9711_ad/ad971124.htm> (ISSN0163-4089).

UNITED STATES--PUBLIC OPINION

In April 1996, the Gallup Organization released a poll measuring public opinion on a variety of public policy issues. While both African Americans and whites "opposed the legalization of marijuana, one group was slightly more adamant about it--75 percent to 21 percent, in one case; 73 percent to 24 percent, in the other. Both groups strongly supported making English the nation's official language. But, again, one group was more gung-ho--84 percent to 15 percent versus 82 percent to 16 percent. One group favored a constitutional amendment permitting school prayer by 80 percent to 17 percent. The other favored it by 71 percent to 26 percent. Neither group supported legalizing same-sex marriages. One group disapproved by a margin of 71 percent to 23 percent; the other by a margin of 66 percent to 29 percent. While both favored government-funded school choice programs, including public, private, and parochial schools, the margin varied. One group supported them by 73 percent to 24 percent, while the other supported them by 57 percent to 39 percent. One group was even more supportive of a flat tax than the other--51 percent to 41 percent versus 49 percent to 38 percent. By 51 percent to 49 percent, one group supported reducing federal spending on health, education, and welfare, while the other group opposed it by 52 percent to 44 percent....In each case, the more 'conservative' group was not the white one, but the black...." (p18)

Ervin, Clark Kent. "Opinion/Essays: Guess Who's at the Heart of the Silent Majority." The Christian Science Monitor v89 n183 15 Aug 1997. p18. The Christian Science Monitor search engine: <http://www.csmonitor.com/plweb-cgi/iops1.pl> To retrieve this article, enter the following search: ED=19970815 AND majority. In the "retrieved list," click the title that matches this record. (ISSN0882-7729).

UNITED STATES--RELIGION (v26)

UNITED STATES--RELIGION--JEWS--ATTITUDES

An American Jewish Committee "survey reported in JEWISH WEEK July 4 [1997] found that 63% of American Jews 'definitely' believe in God and 22% 'probably' do. The rest either definitely or probably don't believe or are not sure; 63% believe there is a 'special relationship' of God and Jews and 70% believe God dictated the Torah to Moses." (p31)

Dimow, Joseph. "Inside the Jewish Community: Surveys--Good or Bad." Jewish Currents v51 n8 Sep 1997. p31. (ISSN0021-0639).

UNITED STATES--RELIGION--PUBLIC OPINION

A recent survey by the Princeton Religion Research Center shows "in 1947, 90 percent of Americans said they pray regularly. In 1997, 90 percent say the same thing. Fifty years ago, 41 percent of Americans said they attend church 'frequently.' Today 41 percent say they attend church 'frequently.' In 1947, 95 percent said they believe in God. Today, 95 percent say they believe in God." (p23)

Lynn, Barry W. "Perspective: Fit and Fifty: AU's First Five Decades." Church & State v50 n10 Nov 1997. p23. (ISSN0009-6334).

UNITED STATES--SOCIAL CONDITIONS (v26)

"In 1995, the incidence of AIDS in the United States was 27 persons per 100,000 population. In 1993, the incidence rate for AIDS was 40.2 persons per 100,000 population. In fiscal year 1995, the U.S. immigration rate was 2.7 legal immigrants for every 1,000 residents. During the peak immigration years between 1901 and 1910, U.S. immigration averaged 10.4 immigrants per 1,000 residents....In 1996, 29 percent of families with children were headed by single parents. Of those families, 82 percent were headed by women. In African-American families with children, 60 percent were headed by single parents in 1996. If its 1995 growth rate were to continue, the United States would double its population in about 78 years."

Population Reference Bureau. "Today's U.S. Population: Details and Definitions." Press Release 1997. document-level access: <http://www.prb.org/media/pressrel.htm>

"The news on US class barriers isn't all good. In recent decades economic growth has been slower and, thus, a less reliable class-busting force....In the early 1970s, 13 percent of US adults were downwardly mobile--they lived in a lower class than their parents, according to Michael Hout, a sociologist at the University of California, Berkeley. Today that figure has increased to 23 percent." (p3)

Francis, David R. "United States: More Go from Rags to Riches--And Reverse--As Class Barriers Fall." The Christian Science Monitor v89 n132 4 Jun 1997. p3. The Christian Science Monitor search engine: <http://www.csmonitor.com/plweb-cgi/iops1.pl> To retrieve this article, enter the following search: ED=19970604 AND fall. In the "retrieved list," click the title that matches this record. (ISSN0882-7729).

UNITED STATES. AIR FORCE (v26)

UNITED STATES. AIR FORCE--APPROPRIATIONS AND EXPENDITURES

In the U.S., "six business process teams of representatives from the five air logistics centers, Air Force Materiel Command headquarters and the major commands were chartered. Their goals are to reduce process flow times by 50 percent, reduce the cost of doing business by 30 percent by fiscal 1997, improve quality and schedule performance by 10 percent, and improve linkage/responsiveness to customer requirements." (p14) "In testing at two Air Force bases, the...[Standard Transportation Industry Information Processor] cut express shipment processing times by nearly 50 percent....The Air Force has established over 80 restoration advisory boards at its installations to allow local community stakeholders to participate in cleanup of their bases....The result [of the advisory boards] has been a reduction of violation notices from over 200 in 1991 to 70 in 1996." (p15)

"National Performance Review: A Force for Positive Change: Air Force." Defense 97 n3 1997. p4-15.

UNITED STATES. AIR FORCE RESERVE (v26)

see also PERSIAN GULF WAR, 1991--UNITED STATES. AIR FORCE RESERVE

On average the U.S. Air Force "Reserve deploys 700 people (unit reservists as well as individual mobilization augmentees) each month in support of overseas contingency and real-world operations. This has ranged from a high of 1,700 people in June 1997 to a low of 508 in November 1995. Of the total Air Force combat capability, the Reserve supplies 20 percent." (p10) "Aircrew members spend an average of about 110 days a year fulfilling Reserve training and active-duty support requirements, while support people spend an average of 60 days. Before 1990, the Reserve had been involved in 12 real-world operations. Since then, it has participated in 44 real-world operations--relying entirely on volunteers." (p11)

MacMackin, Margaret. "Volunteerism and Accessibility: Reservists Represent Best of Citizen-Soldier Tradition." Citizen Airman v49 n5 Oct 1997. p10-11. (ISSN0887-9680).

UNITED STATES. AIR FORCE RESERVE--ATTITUDES

"A total of 4,422 people--654 officers and 3,768 enlisted members--took part in...[a wide-ranging U.S. Air Force Reserve Command quality of life survey], which was developed by the Air Force Personnel Center at Randolph Air Force Base, Texas, in conjunction with the Reserve Career Management and Policy Board." (p10) "In the area of career intent, 91 percent of the officers and 83 percent of the enlisted members indicated they plan on staying in the Reserve until they reach retirement age.

When asked if they would accept an extended active-duty tour if the occasion arises, 56 percent of the officers and 67 percent of enlisted members said yes....95 percent of all respondents said reservists supporting active-duty contingency operations should be guaranteed the same benefits and entitlements as their active-duty counterparts, regardless of tour length....90 percent of the people responding to the survey said reservists performing any type of active duty who are billeted in government quarters should be entitled to basic allowance for quarters." (p11) "On the enlisted side, 38 percent reported that it has been five years or more since they received their last performance report. Fifty-eight percent couldn't remember when they received their last evaluation....An even number of officers and enlisted members--38 percent--said being away due to military duties has an adverse financial impact on their families. Thirty-nine percent of officers and 28 percent of enlisted members reported that their families have problems with child care when they are away due to military duties." (p12)

Tyler, Cliff. "Quality of Life." Citizen Airman v49 n6 Dec 1997. p10-12. (ISSN0887-9680).

"The results of a 1995 employer support survey back up...[Commander of the 514th Air Mobility Wing at McGuire Air Force Base, N.J., Colonel Bruce Carskadon's,] contention that the shorter the [deployment] mission, the more likely reservists are to volunteer. More than 90 percent of the reservists who responded to the survey indicated they would be willing to volunteer for an extra two weeks of duty for overseas humanitarian missions, domestic disaster relief or military training....The number of positive responses plummeted to between 16 percent and 20 percent when reservists were asked about volunteering for more than six months of active duty....Aircrew members average about 110 days of military duty a year, and about 37 percent who responded to the employer support survey said they were being asked to spend too much time flying for the Reserve." (p8)

Snyder, Annette. "Volunteerism and Accessibility: Commander Impressed with Troops' Willingness to Serve." Citizen Airman v49 n5 Oct 1997. p6-8. (ISSN0887-9680).

UNITED STATES. AIR FORCE RESERVE--WOMEN

"Today, 14,219 women comprise 20.27 percent of the total [U.S. Air Force] Reserve force. That breaks down to 3,800 officers, or 24.38 percent, and 10,419 enlisted members, 19.09 percent." (p14) "Women reservists supported the Gulf War in 1991....Of the 22,000 reservists mobilized, 5,390, or 24.5 percent, were women. Of the 7,209 reservists who deployed, 2,148 (29.8 percent) were women." (p15)

MacMackin, Margaret. "The History of the Air Force Reserve." Citizen Airman v49 n6 Dec 1997. p14-15. (ISSN0887-9680).

UNITED STATES. ARMY (v26)

see also FAMILY VIOLENCE--UNITED STATES. ARMY

In the U.S., "since 1989, the active Army has reduced from 18 to 10 divisions, with the Army Guard decreasing from 10 to eight divisions. The Guard has also transformed 23 brigade equivalents into 15 enhanced separate brigades and three strategic reserve brigades." (p3)

Grange, David L./Telander, Phillip D./U.S. Army. "Reserve Components, Active Partners." Soldiers v52 n6 Jun 1997. p2-3. (ISSN0093-8440).

In the U.S., "the Army has deployed for major operations 25 times in the past seven years, and on any given day in 1996 averaged more than 35,000 deployed soldiers in over 70 countries....At home, mission requirements range from 11,500 soldiers supporting the 1996 Olympic games in Atlanta to about 4,000 soldiers supporting America's counterdrug efforts. Abroad, more than 30,000 soldiers have deployed on peacekeeping and humanitarian missions in places such as Haiti, Rwanda and Somalia....In 1996, active component forces were deployed away from their home stations an average of 138 days each." (p2)

Grange, David L./Telander, Phillip D./U.S. Army. "Reserve Components, Active Partners." Soldiers v52 n6 Jun 1997. p2-3. (ISSN0093-8440).

In 1980, U.S. Army "male recruits were required to do 35 sit-ups, females 22. Today, those numbers are 42 for men and 40 for women....Between 1980 and 1997, the number of hours recruits spent on tasks ranging from weapons instruction to field training increased from just over 300 to almost 500." (p4)

Moniz, Dave. "United States: Despite What Old-Timers Think, Training Is Tougher Today." The Christian Science Monitor v89 n233 28 Oct 1997. p4. The Christian Science Monitor search engine: <http://www.csmonitor.com/plweb-cgi/iops1.pl> To retrieve this article, enter the following search: ED=19971028 AND today. In the "retrieved list," click the title that matches this record. (ISSN0882-7729).

The U.S. "Army's recruiting goal jumped this year by nearly 20,000 to a total of 90,000. But the service has had difficulty meeting monthly quotas and recently scaled back its goal to 85,000." (p18)

Moniz, Dave. "The New Drill for Sergeants at Boot Camp." The Christian Science Monitor v89 n174 4 Aug 1997. p1,18. The Christian Science Monitor search engine: <http://www.csmonitor.com/plweb-cgi/iops1.pl> To retrieve this article, enter the following search: ED=19970804 AND camp. In the "retrieved list," click the title that matches this record. (ISSN0882-7729).

UNITED STATES. ARMY--ACCIDENTS

Throughout the whole U.S. Army, "571 soldiers were injured in ground field training exercises in fiscal year 1996, according to SFC [Sergeant First Class] William Gunter, chief of the combat support section at the Army Safety Center at Fort Rucker, Ala. Eleven of the accidents are Class As, those that either killed the soldier or left him permanently and totally disabled and/or resulted in property damages of $1 million or more. The most frequent field training accident--accounting for 48 injuries and two deaths in fiscal year 1996--involved improper parachute landing falls....Individual misjudgment is also the reason for the second highest injury category--accidents while entering and exiting vehicles, Gunter said. 'Soldiers often jump off the back of vehicles and twist ankles or, because they use their hands to break a fall, they break fingers and wrists instead.' The practice injured 44 soldiers in FY 96....Four soldiers died in tactical vehicle accidents in FY 96, according to Army Safety Center reports. Two of the four died in tank-related accidents." (p24)

Hasenauer, Heike/U.S. Army. "Staying Alive in the Field." Soldiers v52 n6 Jun 1997. p22-25. (ISSN0093-8440).

UNITED STATES. ARMY--AFRO-AMERICANS

In the U.S. Army, "blacks are overrepresented, accounting for 27 percent of the total Army personnel. This figure breaks down to 30 percent of the enlisted force and 11 percent of the officer corps. Additionally, blacks reenlist at a rate that is 50 percent higher than that of whites, insuring a larger selection pool for advancement to the higher ranks." (p670)

Stanley, Jay. "Book Reviews: Charles C. Moskos and John Sibley Butler, ALL THAT WE CAN BE: BLACK LEADERSHIP...INTEGRATION...ARMY WAY." Armed Forces & Society v23 n4 Sum 1997. p669-672. (ISSN0095-327X).

UNITED STATES. ARMY--EDUCATION

The U.S. National Science Center "and the Army's Recruiting Support Command at Fort Knox, Ky., co-sponsor Mobile Discovery, a mobile math and science education program. Two tractor-trailers and two van-sized vehicles with exhibits and soldier-demonstrators travel the nation to visit with more than 60,000 middle school and high school students each year. To date, more than 163,000 students have visited Mobile Discovery vans nationwide....Seven math and science summer camps started in 1993 provided hands-on experiences to some 3,800 students in five Junior Reserve Officers Training Corps summer camp programs. In 1996, 17,000 JROTC campers learned more about math and science through NSC-TF [Task Force]." (p6)

U.S. Army. "What's New: Science News: Innovative Fort Discovery Science Center Opens." Soldiers v52 n6 Jun 1997. p6. (ISSN0093-8440).

UNITED STATES. ARMY--PROMOTIONS

"About 26,000 qualified specialists Armywide will pin on sergeant's stripes in the months ahead, said SGM [Sergeant Major] William T. Hursh, enlisted promotion proponent in the [U.S.] Office of the Deputy Chief of Staff for Personnel in the Pentagon....In April 1996, Hursh said, approximately 35,000 specialists were on the recommended list for promotion to sergeant. This April about 14,700 specialists will be on the sergeants' promotion list." (p9)

U.S. Army. "What's New: Career News: Sergeants' Promotion Forecast." Soldiers v52 n6 Jun 1997. p9. (ISSN0093-8440).

UNITED STATES. ARMY--RESERVES

In the U.S. Army, "100 percent of railway units, 97 percent of civil affairs units and 83 percent of psychological operations units are in the Reserve....A 1994 action by Congress extended the limits of the Presidential Selected Reserve Call-up for individuals and units from 90 days to 270 days with no extensions. Under PSRC authority, the president can involuntarily mobilize up to 200,000 Selected Reserve soldiers." (p2) "To date, more than 340 units and 12,000 Guard and Reserve soldiers have been mobilized....The Army Reserve...has restructured from 23 Army Reserve Commands to three ARCs and 10 Regional Support Commands. The reserve components' cumulative end strength at the end of 1996 was 603,000.... The reserve components now constitute nearly 55 percent of the aggregate Army force." (p3)

Grange, David L./Telander, Phillip D./U.S. Army. "Reserve Components, Active Partners." Soldiers v52 n6 Jun 1997. p2-3. (ISSN0093-8440).

UNITED STATES. ARMY--SEXUAL BEHAVIOR --ATTITUDES

According to a recent survey of U.S. Army soldiers, "78 percent of the women and 76 percent of the men experienced 'crude or offensive behavior.' 72 percent of the women and 63 percent of the men had experienced 'sexist behavior;' 47 percent of the women and 30 percent of the men received 'unwanted sexual attention.' 15 percent of the women and 8 percent of the men had experienced 'sexual coercion;' 7 percent of the women and 6 percent of the men had experienced 'sexual assault.'" (p1 secA)

"Army Vows to End Sexual Harassment." Detroit News 12 Sep 1997. p1 secA.

UNITED STATES. ARMY CORPS OF ENGINEERS (v26)

see OUTDOOR RECREATION--UNITED STATES. ARMY CORPS OF ENGINEERS

UNITED STATES. ARMY CORPS OF ENGINEERS --ACCIDENTS (v26)

UNITED STATES. ARMY CORPS OF ENGINEERS --MORTALITY (v26)

UNITED STATES. CENSUS BUREAU --APPROPRIATIONS AND EXPENDITURES (v26)

UNITED STATES. COAST GUARD (v26)

UNITED STATES. CONGRESS (v26)

see also CAMPAIGN FUNDS--UNITED STATES. CONGRESS

UNITED STATES. CONGRESS--HISPANIC AMERICANS

"While there were only 10 members of Hispanic origin in the U.S. Congress in 1989, there were 17 voting members and two nonvoting members of Hispanic origin in June 1997. Six were from Texas, four from California, two each from Florida and New York, and one each from Arizona, Illinois, and New Jersey. Puerto Rico and Guam each send a nonvoting Hispanic delegate to the U.S. Congress. Despite the increase in Hispanic Congressional members, the number falls well short of the 57 to 58 representatives that would represent the Latino population's 11 percent share of the U.S. population." (p43)

del Pinal, Jorge/Singer, Audrey. "Generations of Diversity: Latinos in the United States." Population Bulletin v52 n3 Oct 1997. p2-47. (ISSN0032-468X).

UNITED STATES. CONGRESS--MINORITIES (v26)

UNITED STATES. CONGRESS--RELIGION (v26)

UNITED STATES. CONGRESS. HOUSE (v26)

In the U.S. House of Representatives elections in 1996, "votes were almost perfectly divided between the two parties' House candidates--48.9 percent for the Republicans versus 48.6 percent for Democrats. It was the closest balance in modern history and the first time neither side reached 50 percent....An almost identical number of members from each party (49 Republicans and 45 Democrats) won their seats by less than 55 percent of the vote." (p3)

Feldmann, Linda. "United States: After Budget Deal, Party Focus Shifts to 1998 Vote." The Christian Science Monitor v89 n173 1 Aug 1997. p3. The Christian Science Monitor search engine: <http://www.csmonitor.com/plweb-cgi/iops1.pl> To retrieve this article, enter the following search: ED=19970801 AND vote. In the "retrieved list," click the title that matches this record. (ISSN0882-7729).

UNITED STATES. CONGRESS. HOUSE --APPROPRIATIONS AND EXPENDITURES

"During the first six months of 1997 and more than a year before the 1998 general election, [U.S.] House incumbents reported $52.9 million in receipts, up $7.4 million from the comparable period for incumbents in 1995. Republicans outpaced their Democratic counterparts in fundraising by nearly $9 million--$30.8 million to $22.1 million. The tallies are based on reports filed by 227 Republican incumbents and 207 Democrats. The typical Republican incumbent reported receipts of $105,987, but if that Republican incumbent was a freshman, mid-year receipts increased to $146,833. The same figure for Democratic incumbents was $72,726 and, for Democratic freshmen, $115,228. Thirty-two Republican freshmen and 42 Democratic freshmen were included in these median figures." (p1)

"Statistics: Congressional Financing Heats Up." Federal Election Commission Record v23 n12 Dec 1997. p1-2.

UNITED STATES. CONGRESS. HOUSE--RECYCLING (v26)

UNITED STATES. CONGRESS. SENATE --APPROPRIATIONS AND EXPENDITURES

"Candidates vying for 34 [U.S.] Senate seats in 1998 raised $42.6 million, according to the mid-year reports....In 1991, with the same 34 contested seats plus two special elections, 55 candidates reported raising $33.3 million in mid-year reports. In 1993, 50 Senate campaigns reported collecting nearly $25 million in the same report. And, in 1995, 49 candidates vying for Senate seats raised $24 million during the first six months of the year." (p2)

"Statistics: Congressional Financing Heats Up." Federal Election Commission Record v23 n12 Dec 1997. p1-2.

UNITED STATES. CONSUMER PRODUCT SAFETY COMMISSION (v26)

UNITED STATES. DEFENSE LOGISTICS AGENCY (v26)

UNITED STATES. DEPT. OF DEFENSE (v26)

The U.S. Dept. of Defense "is in the process of consolidating its accounting offices, moving from 333 offices to only 21 in less than 5 years. DOD had closed 230 accounting offices through fiscal year 1996 and is scheduled to close an additional 103 in fiscal year 1997 and fiscal year 1998. As a result, DOD has been able to reduce employment at the Defense Finance and Accounting Service (DFAS) from more than 31,000 in fiscal year 1993 to 24,000 today. DFAS operating costs have dropped 24 percent in 4 years, from $1.6 billion in fiscal year 1993 to $1.2 billion in fiscal year 1997, in constant fiscal year 1993 dollars. DOD has consolidated its civilian pay systems from 25 systems in fiscal year 1991 to 2 systems today and hopes to be down to a single system next year. The system that DOD has designated to take over all civilian pay accounts has gone from handling 15 percent of DOD accounts in fiscal year 1992 to a projected 73 percent in fiscal year 1996 and 83 percent in fiscal year 1997. DOD has consolidated its military pay systems from 24 systems in fiscal year 1991 to 4 systems today and hopes to be down to 2 systems next year, with only the Marine Corps maintaining a separate system. The system that DOD has designated to take over all military pay accounts has gone from handling 15 percent of DOD accounts, other than Marine Corps accounts, in fiscal year 1991 to a projected 65 percent in fiscal year 1996 and 90 percent in fiscal year 1997." (pS8110)

Grassley, Charles E. (Sen.-Iowa). "Executive Calendar." Congressional Record. Daily ed. v143 n106 24 Jul 1997. pS8107-8111. section/page-level access: <http:// thomas.loc.gov/cgi-bin/query/R?r105:FLD001:S08110:> (ISSN0363-7239). (X1.1A.105/1).

"Since 1985, America has...[reduced] its defense budget by some 38 percent, its force structure by 33 percent, and its procurement programs by 63 percent. Today, the budget of the Department of Defense is $250 billion, 15 percent of our national budget, and an estimated 3.2 percent of our Gross National Product. We now have 1.45 million men and women under arms, 200,000 overseas, 900,000 in the Reserves, and 800,000 civilians employed by the Department. Today, $44 billion is devoted to the acquisition of weaponry from a smaller defense industrial base employing 2.2 million workers." (p22)

Cohen, William S. "Quadrennial Defense Review: The Secretary's Message." DISAM Journal v19 n4 Sum 1997. p21-29.

The U.S. "Defense Logistics Agency's Prime Vendor contracts allow the government to use its purchasing power to negotiate lower prices and long-term distribution arrangements with commercial distributors of market-ready or commercial products....We now buy pharmaceuticals this way. Our lead time has gone from 27 days to 24 hours. We have been able to reduce our inventory for over 170,000 pharmaceutical items. We are buying auto parts this way now, and the lead time for parts has gone from 36 days to seven days. For helicopter parts, the lead time has gone from 270 days to eight days with a 70 percent cost savings." (p68)

Kaminski, Paul G. "Fielding Equipment Second to None." DISAM Journal v19 n4 Sum 1997. p58-85.

From 1989 to 1997, the U.S. Dept. of Defense "reduced total active duty military end strength by 32 percent, a figure that will grow to 36 percent by 2003....Even after the completion of four rounds of base realignment and closure, the worldwide base structure will have been reduced only 26 percent. The reduction in domestic-only facilities has been 21 percent....Personnel employed in infrastructure activities have been reduced only 28 percent since 1989--plans developed before the Quadrennial Defense Review were projected to yield a 33 percent reduction by 2003...." (p38) "The 24 defense agencies and about 80 defensewide programs provide services ranging from intelligence to commissaries to health care to research and development. In fiscal 1997, they accounted for 22 percent of the department's total infrastructure funding and employed 117,000 civilian and 128,000 military personnel." (p39)

"QDR: Achieving the Right Infrastructure." Defense 97 n4 1997. p38-41.

UNITED STATES. DEPT. OF DEFENSE --APPROPRIATIONS AND EXPENDITURES (v26)

U.S. Dept. of Defense "contract overpayments have dropped from $592 million in fiscal year 1993 to $184 million in fiscal year 1996. The two most significant categories of problem disbursements--unmatched disbursements and negative unliquidated obligations (NULO)--have dropped from $34.3 billion in June 1993 to $7.9 billion in January 1997. Unmatched disbursements are cases in which a payment has been made, but cannot be matched to its obligation authority; NULO's are cases in which too much money is disbursed, for example, contractor overpayments, or the wrong obligation has been charged. The third category of problem disbursements--in-transit disbursements--has increased recently, but is still down substantially over the long run, from $16.8 billion in June 1993 to $11.1 billion in January 1997. In-transit disbursements are cases in which a payment has been made, but the obligation has not yet been matched to its obligation authority, and more than 180 days have passed." (pS8110-8111)

Grassley, Charles E. (Sen.-Iowa). "Executive Calendar." Congressional Record. Daily ed. v143 n106 24 Jul 1997. pS8107-8111. section/page-level access: <http:// thomas.loc.gov/cgi-bin/query/R?r105:FLD001:S08110:> (ISSN0363-7239). (X1.1A.105/1).

In 1985, during the Cold War era, the U.S. "Defense Department budget in 1997 dollars was $400 billion, which was about 28 percent of our national budget. But the global environment has changed, and we have reduced our defense budget by 38 percent, our force structure by 33 percent, and our procurement programs by 63 percent. Today, the budget is $250 billion or 15 percent of our national budget and an estimated 3.2 percent of our Gross Domestic Product." (p22)

Hoeper, Paul J. "International Armaments Cooperation for the New Millennium." DISAM Journal v20 n1 Fall 1997. p22-25.

The U.S. Federal Acquisition Streamlining Act of 1994 "established a Simplified Acquisition Threshold (SAT) of $100,000; authorized the use of simplified acquisition procedures up to $50,000...; and created a micropurchase authority up to $2,500. These provisions allow DoD [Dept. of Defense] to reduce the administrative cost of doing business for almost 99 percent of DoD contracting actions." (p75)

Kaminski, Paul G. "Fielding Equipment Second to None." DISAM Journal v19 n4 Sum 1997. p58-85.

From the end of fiscal 1993 through fiscal 1995, the U.S. Department of Defense "reduced the civilian work force by about 153,000. DoD plans to reduce its infrastructure by another 100,000 civilians by fiscal 1999." (p4) "The consolidation of DoD finance systems is nearly complete--the 38 in use by the end of fiscal 1997, down from 94 in 1991, will save $98 million annually. The long-term goal is to cut those systems to eight. DoD continues consolidating general fund and other accounting systems from 103 in 1991 to 63 by the end of fiscal 1997 to, ultimately, no more than nine....Since 1990, the department reduced its inventory from $104 billion to approximately $76 billion through fiscal 1994 in constant fiscal 1995 dollars. Further reductions will leave an inventory of $55 billion by 2001 in constant fiscal 1995 dollars." (p5) "In the past three years, changes to the women assignment policy have resulted in some 260,000 additional positions [at the Department of Defense]. More than 90 percent of all career fields can now be filled by either men or women." (p7)

"National Performance Review: A Force for Positive Change." Defense 97 n3 1997. p4-15.

In the U.S., the Pentagon's Quadrennial Defense Review's "1997 defense budget dropped to $14.5 billion. Defense procurement fell 39 percent between 1995-1996 and is still at historically low levels. The decline for key weapons was even greater: 59 percent in shipbuilding, 42 percent in aircraft and in rocket/ space sector, and 41 percent in ammunition and special chemicals." (p6)

"The QDR: Dead on Arrival or Deja Vu: Weapons Program." Defense Monitor v26 n5 Aug 1997. p6. (ISSN0195-6450).

Between the peak of the Reagan administration program in 1985 and today, the U.S. "defense budget in real terms has dropped by one-third. The largest cut has been in procurement of new equipment and weapons, where the drop has been 63%....Between 1992 and 1996, annual defense outlays declined by $32.6 billion in a budget that increased overall by $306.2 billion. Since the Gulf War, the Army has declined from 18 divisions to 10, the Navy from 569 ships to 357, and the Air Force from 25 active fighter wings to 13." (p31)

Hunter, Duncan. "QDR Misses the Point." Proceedings v123 n10 Oct 1997. p30-32. (ISSN0041-798X).

UNITED STATES. DEPT. OF DEFENSE--EMPLOYMENT

By FY 1995, the U.S. Dept. of Defense "acquisition work force was 35 percent below the 1989 peak level of employment. It was 18 percent below the 1980 level and continuing to fall....By the end of FY 1996, these organizations were over 36 percent smaller than in 1989, and there were approximately 200,000 fewer people. We forecast that by the end of FY 2000, these same organizations will effectively be 48 percent smaller, or down by more than 288,000 people." (p82)

Kaminski, Paul G. "Fielding Equipment Second to None." DISAM Journal v19 n4 Sum 1997. p58-85.

UNITED STATES. DEPT. OF JUSTICE

see also HUMAN RIGHTS--UNITED STATES. DEPT. OF JUSTICE

Within the Dept. of Justice, "the Commercial Litigation Branch represents the United States in litigation arising from billions of dollars of buying, selling, lending and other transactions. In 1996, the majority of these cases, 83 percent, were defensive. The affirmative caseload involved actions to recoup for the government billions of dollars lost through fraud, bankruptcies and loan defaults. The total caseload during 1996 was 11,851 cases, a 20 percent increase over 1995. Over $45 billion was at issue in the 1996 caseload. In 1996, Commercial Litigation Branch attorneys spent over 90 percent of their time litigating cases. On average, each attorney handled 54 cases and reported 45 days of unpaid overtime during 1996. The total overtime hours reported translate into 38 additional workyears for 1996." (p399) "In defensive litigation, the target is to defeat at least 75 percent of the amount sought in 70 percent of the cases resolved. In 1996, the Branch achieved this target while defeating $6.2 billion in claims. Although the majority of this amount was defeated in two cases, the Hughes appeal and Boeing, over $1.1 billion was defeated in other cases--nearly a threefold increase over the 1995 total. In affirmative cases, the Branch won $695 million in 1996....More than $318 million in fraud recoveries--including $22 million for relators--was secured in 1996 by the Branch working in conjunction with U.S. Attorneys....Over $120 million was recovered in health care fraud cases in 1996, including $11 million for relators....Nearly $420 million was secured in corporate/ financial litigation in 1996...." (p403) "Foreign litigation recoveries totaled $8.5 million in 1996." (p404)

U.S. Dept. of Justice. "Departments of Commerce, Justice, And State, The Judiciary...Approp. for 1998 (Part 2)." Hearing. U.S. House. Committee on Appropriations. Washington, D.C. : GPO, 1997. (ISBN0160549094). (Y4.Ap6/1:C73/2/997/pt.2).

Within the Dept. of Justice, "the Federal Programs Branch defends the officers and agencies of the United States Government in a wide variety of suits challenging the constitutionality and legality of federal statutes, programs and initiatives....In 1996, 85 percent of the Branch's 883 cases were defensive. Attorneys spent the majority of their time, nearly 89 percent, litigating cases in 1996. The remainder of the attorneys' time was spent advising client agencies and the U.S. Attorneys Offices. On average, each attorney reported 31 days of unpaid overtime in 1996. The total overtime hours reported translate into more than 13 additional workyears for 1996." (p407) "The Branch measures its success by tracking the number of closed trial cases in which federal programs and policies were successfully defended, or remedies for statutory violations of federal programs were enforced. The viability of numerous congressional enactments and federal programs was preserved in 89 percent of closed trial cases in 1996, exceeding the Branch's target under the Government Performance and Results Act (GPRA)." (p408)

U.S. Dept. of Justice. "Departments of Commerce, Justice, And State, The Judiciary...Approp. for 1998 (Part 2)." Hearing. U.S. House. Committee on Appropriations. Washington, D.C. : GPO, 1997. (ISBN0160549094). (Y4.Ap6/1:C73/2/997/pt.2).

Within the U.S. Dept. of Justice, "the Office of Consumer Litigation safeguards the public by enforcing federal consumer protection laws, such as the Food, Drug and Cosmetic Act, the Consumer Product Safety Act and the Federal Trade Commission Act." (p411) "The Consumer Litigation caseload totaled 641 cases in 1996, an average of 21 cases per attorney. Attorneys spent the majority [of] their time, about 84 percent, litigating cases in 1996. Most of the remaining time was spent advising state and federal agencies and the U.S. Attorneys Offices. Attorneys reported an average of 49 days of unpaid overtime. The total overtime hours reported translate into six additional workyears for 1996. To measure its performance, the Office tracks the number of affirmative cases in which injunctive or monetary relief was obtained and the number of defensive cases in which an agency's policies or programs were defended. In 1996, the Office was successful in 96 percent of cases closed. In addition, $19.4 million in criminal fines and civil penalties was obtained." (p412)

U.S. Dept. of Justice. "Departments of Commerce, Justice, And State, The Judiciary...Approp. for 1998 (Part 2)." Hearing. U.S. House. Committee on Appropriations. Washington, D.C. : GPO, 1997. (ISBN0160549094). (Y4.Ap6/1:C73/2/997/pt.2).

UNITED STATES. DEPT. OF JUSTICE--EMIGRATION AND IMMIGRATION

Within the U.S. Dept. of Justice, "the Office of Immigration Litigation is the last line of defense along an immigration enforcement continuum that involves the Immigration and Naturalization Service (INS), the immigration courts, the Board of Immigration Appeals and the federal courts....Nearly 90 percent of the caseload involves petitions to the courts of appeals by individual aliens seeking to challenge determinations by immigration officers, immigration judges, and the Board of Immigration Appeals." (p414) "Attorneys spent most of their time, about 79 percent, litigating cases in 1996. The remainder of attorneys' time was mostly spent advising client agencies and the U.S. Attorneys Offices. On average, each attorney handled 31 cases and reported 37 days of unpaid overtime in 1996. The total overtime hours reported translate into 11 additional workyears for 1996. The Office measures its success in preserving federal immigration policies by tracking the number of cases it wins. In 1996, the Office won 97 percent of the personally and jointly handled cases decided or dismissed by the courts, exceeding its 90 percent target under the Government Performance and Results Act (GPRA)." (p415)

U.S. Dept. of Justice. "Departments of Commerce, Justice, And State, The Judiciary...Approp. for 1998 (Part 2)." Hearing. U.S. House. Committee on Appropriations. Washington, D.C. : GPO, 1997. (ISBN0160549094). (Y4.Ap6/1:C73/2/997/pt.2).

UNITED STATES. DEPT. OF VETERANS AFFAIRS --SUBSTANCE USE--TREATMENT (v26)

UNITED STATES. DRUG ENFORCEMENT AGENCY

see ACTIONS AND DEFENSES--UNITED STATES. DRUG ENFORCEMENT AGENCY

UNITED STATES. FEDERAL BUREAU OF INVESTIGATION

see also ACTIONS AND DEFENSES--UNITED STATES. DRUG ENFORCEMENT AGENCY--UNITED STATES. FEDERAL BUREAU OF INVESTIGATION; ACTIONS AND DEFENSES--UNITED STATES. FEDERAL BUREAU OF INVESTIGATION; FINGER PRINTS--UNITED STATES. FEDERAL BUREAU OF INVESTIGATION; PRISON SENTENCES--UNITED STATES. FEDERAL BUREAU OF INVESTIGATION; WIRETAPPING--UNITED STATES. FEDERAL BUREAU OF INVESTIGATION

"In 1996, Justice Department records show, F.B.I. investigations resulted in 11,855 convictions in federal court--45 for every million persons in the United States. The largest identifiable chunk of the 1996 cases--about a quarter of the total--involved 2,919 people found guilty on a variety of drug charges. The next largest grouping, involving 1,898 persons, concerned fraud and embezzlement situations where banks, savings and loan associations and credit unions were the victims, often through the misuse of credit cards. Old-fashioned bank robberies--with 1,341 convictions--made up the third-largest category of cases." (p12)

Burnham, David. "Articles: The FBI." Nation v265 n5 11 Aug 1997. p11-12,14-16,18-24. (ISSN0027-8378).

In the U.S., "in 1993, according to a secret document sent by the F.B.I. to the White House's Office of Management and Budget, the...[FBI's Surreptitious Entry Team] conducted 300 break-ins, six times as many as it did in 1985....In 1996, according to a report by the Administrative Office of U.S. Courts, federal investigative agencies obtained warrants to install 581 taps and bugs in connection with criminal cases--more than twice the number they planted only ten years before. During a recent year federal agents listened to some 1.3 million conversations, only 15 percent of which were said to include incriminating material....[In national security investigations,] the government reportedly obtained 839 warrants for taps, bugs and break-ins in 1996, 20 percent more than in 1995 and more than three times the number reported in the first year of the program....A third kind of F.B.I. surveillance uses equipment designed to record all numbers dialed from a particular telephone and the numbers of the telephones that are calling a person under surveillance. Between 1987 and 1993, the government reports that warrants for these 'pen registers' and 'trap and trace' devices more than doubled, growing to 3,423 in 1993." (p16)

Burnham, David. "Articles: The FBI." Nation v265 n5 11 Aug 1997. p11-12,14-16,18-24. (ISSN0027-8378).

UNITED STATES. FOREST SERVICE

see ROADS--UNITED STATES. FOREST SERVICE

UNITED STATES. GOVERNMENT PRINTING OFFICE --APPROPRIATIONS AND EXPENDITURES

Everytime the U.S. Government Printing Office prints a document it costs "roughly 2 times what it would cost us to do if we did it in the private sector. In 1991, the Government Printing Office lost $1.2 million; in 1992 it lost $5 million; in 1993 it lost $14 million; in 1994 it lost $21 million....In 1995 the loss was $3 million, but...this year it ballooned up to $16.9 million, nearly $17 million. This year through June of 1997 we are losing an additional $4 million." (pH5889)

Klug, Scott L. (Rep.-Wis.). "Legislative Branch Appropriations Act, 1998." Congressional Record. Daily ed. v143 n108 28 Jul 1997. pH5868-5895. section/page-level access: <http://thomas.loc.gov/cgi-bin/query/R?r105:FLD001:H05889:> (ISSN0363-7239). (X1.1A.105/1).

UNITED STATES. INTERNAL REVENUE SERVICE (v26)

"When the income tax was first enacted 84 years ago [in the U.S.], there was one page of instructions coupled with a one-page form. Today, there are 480 IRS tax forms and 17,000 pages of IRS laws and regulations. Even the instructions alone for the 1040 EZ form are 28 pages long, and 293,760 trees must be cut down each year just to supply the 8 billion pages of paper needed for filing the country's income taxes. The complexity of the system requires 136,000 employees at the IRS and elsewhere in the Government to administer the laws, costing the American taxpayers $13.7 billion to enforce and oversee the Code....In a recent survey, American taxpayers rated the IRS last in customer satisfaction among 200 private companies, [and] local government agencies....The GAO [Government Accounting Office] reports that the IRS has been unable to accurately balance its own books for the last 4 years, reporting that in 1992 the IRS could not even account for 64 percent of its own budget." (pH8165)

Stearns, Cliff (Rep.-Fla.). "Overhaul the IRS." Congressional Record. Daily ed. v143 n133 30 Sep 1997. pH8165. section/page-level access: <http://thomas.loc.gov/cqi-bin/query/R?r105:FLD001:H08165:> (ISSN0363-7239). (X1.1A.105/1).

UNITED STATES. INTERNAL REVENUE SERVICE --PUBLIC OPINION

In a recent Gallup poll, in the U.S., "seventy-three percent of those polled agree that 'the IRS has been given more power than it needs to do the job it is charged with carrying out', and 69% say that the IRS 'frequently abuses its powers'. These findings are similar to those in a Gallup poll conducted in 1995, at which time 63% of Americans said that the IRS had too much power, thus putting it at the top of the 'too much power' list based on 20 American institutions....The Gallup poll...asked Americans if they had personally ever had any direct contact with the IRS, other than the routine filing of taxes and receiving refunds. Only 43% responded affirmatively. Of that group, when asked how they were treated, the majority said they felt that the IRS was just doing the job it was required to do by law. Overall, only 15% of the population said that they had ever been treated unfairly by the IRS."

Newport, Frank/Gallup Organization. "Public by 3 to 1 Margin Believes IRS Abuses Its Powers." Press Release 3 Oct 1997. document-level access: <http://www.gallup.com/poll/news/971003.html>

UNITED STATES. MARINE CORPS--AFRO-AMERICANS

According to the U.S. "Marine Corps statistics from fiscal years 1991-93 (FY91-93), blacks accounted for 6.5 percent, 6.7 percent, and 6.6 percent of officer accession goals, yet accounted for 27.1 percent, 32.4 percent, and 33.5 percent of the mental aptitude waivers assigned. Quality indicators for the OCC [Officer Candidates Class] program from FY90-96 show that, on average, black applicants scored 31 points lower on their Scholastic Aptitude Test and 4.6 points lower on their Armed Services Vocational Aptitude Battery EL score than their white counterparts." (p38)

Kehrmeyer, Randall J. "Focus: The Officer Candidates Class: A Myopic Approach to 12-12-5." Marine Corps Gazette v81 n9

Sep 1997. p38-40. (ISSN0025-3170).

In the U.S. Marine Corps, the Officer Candidates Class "program is a 10-week program that is attended by college graduates. Upon graduation, candidates are commissioned as second lieutenants and immediately assigned to active duty at TBS [The Basic School]....Over 37 percent of black candidates who reported for the OCC program from FY92-96 failed to graduate, compared with an overall attrition rate of slightly more than 21 percent for black candidates reporting to OCS [Officer Candidates School] from all other commissioning programs. More recently, there was a 13 percent increase in black OCC candidates at OCS in FY96 over FY95, yet because the attrition rate increased proportionately, the same number of black candidates graduated from the OCC program in both years. During this same period, nearly half of the accessions of black officers came from the OCC program, versus 37 percent and 20 percent overall accessions (all ethnic categories) for fiscal years 1995 and 1996, respectively. At the same time only 15 percent of white officer accessions have been through the OCC program over the past two fiscal years." (p39)

Kehrmeyer, Randall J. "Focus: The Officer Candidates Class: A Myopic Approach to 12-12-5." Marine Corps Gazette v81 n9 Sep 1997. p38-40. (ISSN0025-3170).

UNITED STATES. MARINE CORPS--DISEASES (v26)

UNITED STATES. MARINE CORPS--RECRUITING, ENLISTMENT, ETC.

Currently all U.S. "Marine Corps recruiters (military occupational specialty 8411/8412), except those pending relief, receive a monthly special allowance for being on recruiting duty. This allowance is paid regardless of a recruiter's performance during the previous month. The Marine Corps could save almost $2.5 million per year by paying recruiters this special duty allowance based on the number of people they enlist into the Marine Corps each month." (p28) Special duty assignment "pay is presently set at $375 per month for 8411s/8412s. During...[1994-95], the district director...said that each month every recruiter would need to enlist a net of two applicants into the DEP [Delayed Entry Program] for the district to attain its shipping mission. Therefore, each recruiter could be paid up to $190 for every applicant that he or she enlists into the DEP and ships to boot camp." (p29) "In fiscal year 1994, the Marine Corps enlisted 48,447 applicants into the DEP. Of these, 9,162 were discharged from the DEP before they shipped to boot camp. Nationwide, an average of 2,588 recruiters were on production per month. The Marine Corps paid approximately $7.98 million in recruiter SDA....In 1994, the Marine Corps wasted $2.48 million on unproductive recruiters." (p30)

Barrett, Michael R. "Focus on Recruiting: An Incentive to Recruit." Marine Corps Gazette v81 n9 Sep 1997. p28-30. (ISSN0025-3170).

The U.S. "Marine Corps Recruiting Command recently released statistics regarding the number of officers commissioned in the Marine Corps in 1995 from the top 229 national universities in the United States, as identified by U.S. NEWS AND WORLD REPORT. The Marine Corps recruited 740 of its 1,257 officers from these highly regarded schools. Adding the 124 service academy commissions (not included in the study) and 64 officers commissioned from Virginia Military Institute and the Citadel, the total rises to 928. With approximately 4,300 accredited degree-granting institutions in the United States, this means that 73.8% of our college-graduated officers commissioned during 1995 came from the top 5.4% of U.S. colleges and universities." (p108)

Anderson, David. "Nobody Asked Me, But...: Recruit Leaders, Not Scholars." Proceedings v123 n9 Sep 1997. p108. (ISSN0041-798X).

UNITED STATES. MARINE CORPS--SEXUAL BEHAVIOR (v26)

UNITED STATES. MARINE CORPS--WOMEN

Currently, women in the U.S. Marine Corps are not eligible for both the Platoon Leader Class Junior and Senior programs. A woman must wait to join PLC until her junior year of college, whereas a man can join as a freshman or sophomore. "Candidates who complete any session of OCS [Officer Candidates School] are eligible for $150 of financial assistance per month during the school year--a total of $1,350 per year. Candidates who enroll as freshmen and complete both 6-week sessions of OCS, following their freshman and junior years, can earn a total of $4,050. Those who wait to enroll as sophomores can earn up to $2,700. Male candidates who wait to enroll as juniors and women who must wait until they are juniors to enroll can only earn a total of $1,350. Therefore, a woman who would like to enroll as [a] freshman, but cannot, loses $2,700 in potential financial assistance." (p32)

Florian, Timothy A. "Focus: Women Should Have the Same PLC Options as Men." Marine Corps Gazette v81 n9 Sep 1997. p31-33. (ISSN0025-3170).

UNITED STATES. NATIONAL AERONAUTICS AND SPACE ADMINISTRATION--EMPLOYEES

In the U.S., "in 1993, we had 24,900 civil service employees at NASA. At the end of FY 1996, we had a workforce totaling 21,000. Today, we are under 20,000. By FY 2000 we will have 17,979." (p97)

Goldin, Daniel S. (Administrator, National Aeronautics and Space Administration). "Departments of Veterans Affairs and Housing and Urban Development...Approp. for 1998 (Part 1)." Hearing. U.S. House. Committee on Appropriations. Washington, D.C. : GPO, 1997. (ISBN0160549884). (Y4.Ap6/1:V64/4/997/pt.1).

UNITED STATES. NATIONAL PARK SERVICE

The U.S. National Park Service "employs only 40 geologists. Compare that to the agency's 900 biologists....Fully one quarter of the 374 units in the national park system--which includes national parks, monuments, seashores, historical parks, recreation areas, and other sites--were created solely for their geologic qualities, and 140 of the units contain significant geologic features." (p15)

Applegate, David. "Political Scene: National Parks: Geology Matters." Geotimes v42 n8 Aug 1997. p15. (ISSN0016-8556).

UNITED STATES. NAVY (v26)

In the U.S. Navy, "four hundred junior officers entered the submarine nuclear power program in fiscal year 1990; 370 junior officers remained in the submarine force in fiscal year 1993; and 125 junior officers remained in the submarine force at the end of fiscal year 1997. The retention rate for year group 1990 would be calculated as 125/370, or 34%." (p27)

Kennedy, Silas Ray. "Retaining the JOs: Looking Up or Going Down?" Proceedings v123 n6 Jun 1997. p26-29. (ISSN0041-798X).

Surface warships in the U.S. Naval active force "will be reduced from 128 in 1997 to 116....The nuclear-powered attack submarine force will be reduced from 73 SSNs [ship, submersible (nuclear-powered)] in 1997 to 50 in 2003 (the BUR [Bottom-Up Review] called for 45-50 SSNs). And some combat logistics support ships will be transferred from the active fleet to the Military Sealift Command. The resulting fleet size will be closer to no more than 330 ships compared to the 1993 force objective of 346." (p92-93)

Truver, Scott C. "Tomorrow's Fleet." Proceedings v123 n9 Sep 1997. p90-96. (ISSN0041-798X).

UNITED STATES. POSTAL SERVICE (v26)

"In a 1995 speech, Postmaster General Marvin Runyon said that the legislative framework governing the USPS [United States Postal Service] is no longer in tune with the Nation's long-term postal needs. A major reason cited by the Postmaster General was the competition the USPS is facing from e-mail, electronic financial transfers, and fax machines. He went on to point out that the USPS had already lost 35 percent of its financial mail in the previous 5 years and 33 percent of its business mail to alternative forms of communication and transmission....By the end of 1999, the U.S. Department of the Treasury plans to collect $1 trillion in tax payments via computers. Already, the Treasury Department says that 55 percent of all payments made by the Federal Government are now sent electronically....The savings to the taxpayers from these electronic transfers become apparent when you consider that it costs the Government 43 cents to send a payment by check versus 2 cents per payment to send funds electronically." (pE1051)

Crane, Philip M. (Rep.-Ill.). "Privatize the U.S. Postal Service." Congressional Record. Daily ed. v143 n70 23 May 1997. pE1051. section/page-level access: <http://thomas.loc.gov/cgi-bin/query/R?r105:FLD001:E01051:> (ISSN0363-7239). (X1.1A.105/1).

The U.S. "Postal Service has installed 232 parcel and bundle sorters since 1988 and has just approved 46 more sorters, which should save in excess of $25 million a year when fully operational in 2000....The sorters can only make out about 2 percent of...[handwritten addresses] and shoot the rest of the letters to a human operator. The operator reads the address and types in the bar code, but it's 10 times more expensive to do it this way. The Postal Service has been eager to automate the process since 15 to 20 percent of the mail is still handwritten. Using software developed at the State University of New York at Buffalo, the machines now read about a quarter of the handwritten addresses, saving hundreds of thousands of dollars. A new software version should boost accuracy up to 30 percent." (p13)

Belsie, Laurent. "Science & Technology: Tech Trends: UPS Strike Puts Competitors' Systems in the Spotlight." The Christian Science Monitor v89 n180 12 Aug 1997. p13. The Christian Science Monitor search engine: <http://www.csmonitor.com/plweb-cgi/iops1.pl> To retrieve this article, enter the following search: ED=19970812 AND spotlight. In the "retrieved list," click the title that matches this record. (ISSN0882-7729).

UNITED STATES. RURAL UTILITIES SERVICE --APPROPRIATIONS AND EXPENDITURES (v26)

UNITED STATES. STATE DEPARTMENT --APPROPRIATIONS AND EXPENDITURES (v26)

UNIVERSITIES AND COLLEGES

see also COLLEGE APPLICATIONS--UNIVERSITY OF TEXAS; COLLEGE SPORTS; CRIME--UNITED STATES--UNIVERSITIES AND COLLEGES; ENGINEERING STUDENTS--PURDUE UNIVERSITY; ENGLISH LANGUAGE--STUDY AND TEACHING--CITY UNIVERSITY OF NEW YORK COLLEGES; FOREIGN STUDY--MICHIGAN STATE UNIVERSITY; LAW SCHOOLS; LAW STUDENTS--HARVARD UNIVERSITY

UNIVERSITIES AND COLLEGES--APPLICATIONS

see COLLEGE APPLICATIONS

UNIVERSITIES AND COLLEGES--CALIFORNIA --MINORITIES--ADMISSIONS (v26)

UNIVERSITIES AND COLLEGES--EUROPE (v26)

UNIVERSITIES AND COLLEGES--FINANCE

see COLLEGE COSTS

UNIVERSITIES AND COLLEGES--GERMANY

"Germany's 600-year-old university system has become a haven for slackers, according to the government. On average, students take 14 semesters--some seven years--to finish programs designed to take four to five years. In western Germany, the on-time completion rate is only 40 percent....More than 17 percent of university students in western Germany, and 5.9 percent of students in eastern Germany, hail from working-class families, according to a government-funded survey." (p8)

Sacirbey, Omar. "International: German Universities May Soon Hand Out Bills with Report Cards." The Christian Science Monitor v89 n246 17 Nov 1997. p8. The Christian Science Monitor search engine: <http://www.csmonitor.com/plweb-cgi/iops1.pl> To retrieve this article, enter the following search: ED=19971117 AND cards. In the "retrieved list," click the title that matches this record. (ISSN0882-7729).

UNIVERSITIES AND COLLEGES--MICHIGAN --FINANCE

Glen Stevens, executive director of the Presidents Council, State Universities of Michigan, explained that, in Michigan, "in 1972-73, state funding accounted for 75.1 percent of university budgets, with tuition and fees making up the remaining 24.9 percent....But a downturn in Michigan's cyclical economy led to a decrease in state funding--and that led to an increase in tuition. In 1994-95, tuition peaked at an average of 44.5 percent of university budgets....In 1995-96, a 5-percent increase in state funding pushed the state's share of university budgets up to 57 percent and tuition's share down slightly to 43 percent." (p7 secA)

Walsh-Sarnecki, Peggy. "Michigan Low on College Grad List." Detroit Free Press 4 Aug 1997. p1,7 secA.

UNIVERSITIES AND COLLEGES--MISSISSIPPI --ADMISSION (v26)

UNIVERSITIES AND COLLEGES--SECURITY CONSULTANTS--SALARIES, ETC.

According to a report from the College & University Personnel Association, "the median pay at all institutions for security-related positions has inched up 2% in the past year. The...[director] of environmental health & safety (incl. security) earns $53,282. Doctoral-granting universities, average pay $66,652. For...[director] of campus security specifically, the...[average] pay is $44,335 for the 1996-97 academic year for all institutions." (unpaginated)

"Compensation Average Campus Security & Safety Dirs. Have 2% Pay Raise in Past Year." Security Letter v27 n15 2 Sep 1997. (ISSN0363-4922).

UNIVERSITIES AND COLLEGES--TEACHERS

see COLLEGE TEACHERS

UNIVERSITIES AND COLLEGES--UNITED STATES

In the U.S., "examples of a large university serving as an anchor in a small metropolitan area with very low unemployment are numerous: the University of Florida's flagship campus in Gainesville (2.8 percent); the Bloomington campus of Indiana University (2.7 percent); the State College home of Penn State (2.9 percent); and Iowa City's University of Iowa (2.9 percent)....Madison, Wis.,...ties for first place in the low-unemployment race. With only 1.7 percent unemployed, Madison is the state capital and home to the University of Wisconsin....Its annual unemployment rate has been less than 5 percent since 1985." (p4 secC)

Linsalata, Phil. "City & Suburban News: Steady Workforce at U-M Is Shot in the Arm for Ann Arbor." Detroit News 18 Jun 1997. p4 secC.

In the U.S., "Ivy League schools enroll only 0.5% of all undergraduates; the top 26 universities and colleges represent only 1% of these students. These universities house many graduates from the nation's most prestigious prep schools, whose students hail from families that earn 400% more than the median American family (Kingston & Lewis 1991)." (p1433)

Davies, Scott/Guppy, Neil. "Fields of Study, College

Selectivity, And Student Inequalities in Higher Education." Social Forces v75 n4 Jun 1997. p1417-1438. (ISSN0037-7732).

UNIVERSITIES AND COLLEGES--UNITED STATES --EMPLOYEES (v26)

UNIVERSITIES AND COLLEGES--UNITED STATES --SECURITY MEASURES

"According to a Department of Education study released in February, just over 10 percent of schools are in violation of the [Campus Security] Act. The study...found that the schools in violation were not compiling mandatory reports, and the biggest violators of the act tended to be trade schools and colleges with less than 200 students....A 1995 study conducted by Bonnie Fisher, a University of Cincinnati political science professor, reported that more than 50 percent of schools did not make security information available to students who requested it, a violation of the act. About 36 percent of schools were fully complying with the mandates of the Campus Security Act." (p14)

"Campus Crime: A Matter of Interpretation." Student Press Law Center Report v18 n3 Fall 1997. p13-14. (ISSN0160-3825).

UNIVERSITIES AND COLLEGES, AFRO-AMERICAN

see AFRO-AMERICAN UNIVERSITIES AND COLLEGES

UNIVERSITY ATTENDANCE

see COLLEGE ATTENDANCE

UNIVERSITY GRADUATES

see COLLEGE GRADUATES

UNIVERSITY OF ALABAMA--EMPLOYMENT (v26)

UNIVERSITY OF ALABAMA--TUSCALOOSA COUNTY --ECONOMIC CONDITIONS (v26)

UNIVERSITY OF CALIFORNIA--ADMISSION

In July 1997, the the University of California "Board of Regents decided to vastly expand...minority outreach programs, doubling current spending to $120 million yearly. In addition to existing efforts focused on aiding individual students, the nine university campuses will also forge partnerships with entire school systems, targeting 50 of the state's worst-performing high schools, all with overwhelmingly minority student bodies. The aim is to at least double the number of UC-eligible students in five years by narrowing the still-large gap between the academic performance of white and Asian students and African-Americans and Latinos....Under California state guidelines, the UC system aims to admit the top 12.5 percent of all of the state's high school graduates, but state Sen. Teresa Hughes proposes to take the top 12.5 percent from each school instead....According to the UC task-force report, the top quintile of California's almost 800 high schools, as measured by average SAT [Scholastic Assessment Test] scores, has only 17 percent minority enrollment. In contrast, the bottom fifth is 79 percent minority. Nationwide, more than two-thirds of African-American and Latino students attend predominately minority schools, reports the Washington-based Education Trust....The top public schools, located in largely white and Asian-populated suburban neighborhoods, send as many as 40 percent of their graduates to UC. In contrast, inner-city schools send as little as 1 percent to UC universities." (p4)

Sneider, Daniel. "Seeking Diversity, Shunning Preferences." The Christian Science Monitor v89 n175 5 Aug 1997. p4. The Christian Science Monitor search engine: <http://www.csmonitor.com/plweb-cgi/iops1.pl> To retrieve this article, enter the following search: ED=19970805 AND preferences. In the "retrieved list," click the title that matches this record. (ISSN0882-7729).

UNIVERSITY OF CALIFORNIA-BERKELEY--ADMISSION

"For the past five years there has been an average of 23 black students at Berkeley's Boalt Hall, the University of California's premier law school. This year, in the class of 2000, there is one....Only 14 black students were accepted, compared with 75 the previous year--an 80 percent decline. Latino admissions dropped nearly 50 percent." (p22)

Chaplin, Heather. "California, ESQ.: Affirmative Reaction." California Lawyer v17 n9 Sep 1997. p22-23. (ISSN0279-4063).

UNIVERSITY OF CALIFORNIA LAW SCHOOL --ADMISSION--MINORITIES

In 1997 "offers of admission to African-Americans at Boalt Hall, U.C. [University of California at] Berkeley's law school, are down 81 percent; to Hispanics, down 50 percent; and to Native Americans, down 78 percent. At U.C.L.A.'s law school, offers to African-Americans are down 80 percent, to Hispanics 32 percent." (p5)

Jackson, Jesse L. "Editorials: Civil Rights Gone Wrong." Nation v264 n22 9 Jun 1997. p5. (ISSN0027-8378).

UNIVERSITY OF MICHIGAN--ADMISSION

A DETROIT NEWS computer analysis of University of Michigan "law school admissions data for 1995 reveals disparities in the percentages of students admitted: None of the nine Asian applicants and just 4.76 percent of Caucasian students with grade point averages between 3.0 and 3.24, and test scores from 161 to 163 (a 180-point scale), were admitted (2 of 42). Meanwhile, all African Americans (7 of 7) and all Mexican Americans (3 of 3) who had those numbers were accepted." (p1 secD)

Hoover, Rusty. "Metro: U-M Law Students Step Up to Defend Policy." Detroit News 9 Dec 1997. p1 secD.

UNIVERSITY OF MICHIGAN--ADMISSION --MINORITIES (v26)

UNIVERSITY OF MICHIGAN--ALUMNI AND ALUMNAE

The University of Michigan's "roster of about 401,700 living alumni is among the largest in the nation. Outside of Michigan, California has the largest U-M alumni contingent with 28,777. New York City has 17,044 U-M alums and Ohio has 12,760, the Michigan Alumni Association said." (p2 secC)

Halls, Bill. "Metro: Go Blue Monday: U-M Fans Show Blue, Spend Green." Detroit News 8 Dec 1997. p1-2 secC.

UNIVERSITY OF MICHIGAN--EMPLOYMENT

"With the lowest jobless rate in Michigan and one of the lowest in the nation, Ann Arbor's 2.9-percent unemployment shows that America's university cities benefit from strong, stable economies. About 28,000 employees work at the University of Michigan, including its medical center workforce of 8,000. That translates to an annual payroll of $1.2 billion for the last fiscal year, said...Cindy Kabza, campus director of employment and executive services." (p4 secC)

Linsalata, Phil. "City & Suburban News: Steady Workforce at U-M Is Shot in the Arm for Ann Arbor." Detroit News 18 Jun 1997. p4 secC.

UNIVERSITY OF MICHIGAN--ENDOWMENTS (v26)

UNIVERSITY OF MICHIGAN--MINORITIES

"The University of Michigan enrolled the largest freshman class in its history with 5,534 students this fall. But for the first time in 11 years, minority enrollment has leveled off at 25.4 percent, according to figures released...[in October 1997]. The increase of 207 freshmen this year helped to boost total enrollment by 470 students. Total enrollment at the Ann Arbor campus is 36,995. Black enrollment dipped slightly to 8.6 percent. Most of the decline was at the graduate and professional level, according to U-M figures." (p1 secB)

"Minority enrollment has increased from 12.7 percent in 1986 to 25.4 percent in 1996. Because of the larger number of students enrolled this year, the number of minority students actually rose from 8,209 last year to 8,314, but the percentage remained at 25.4." (p3 secB)

George, Maryanne. "Local News: Minority Enrollment Stays Constant for U-M, MSU." Detroit Free Press 29 Oct 1997. p1,3 secB.

UNIVERSITY OF MICHIGAN--MINORITY EMPLOYEES (v26)

UNIVERSITY OF MICHIGAN--RESEARCH--FINANCE

"The University of Michigan's research expenditures increased by 3.9 percent in 1996-97, reaching another record total of $458,478,301....[Frederick C. Neidhardt, interim vice president for research,] noted that the University's total research expenditures have increased by 95.4 percent over the past decade, from $234.6 million in 1987-88 to $458.5 million in 1996-97. Real purchasing power of these expenditures (discounted for inflation) has also continued to increase, rising by 42.8 percent in constant (fiscal year 1988) dollars. Of the U-M's 1996-97 total research expenditures, $300,447,504--or 65.5 percent of the U-M total--came from federal agencies. Major funding agencies included the Department of Health and Human Services, $173,318,378; National Science Foundation, $43,456,477; Department of Defense, $32,758,026; NASA, $11,342,385; and the Department of Energy, $9,536,764. Research support from non-federal sources accounted for $108,400,252, or 23.7 percent of the U-M total, and included $31,571,189 from industry and $76,829,063 from others....U-M funds accounted for 10.8 percent of the University's total research expenditures." (p1-2)

University of Michigan. News and Information Services. "U-M's Research Expenditures Totaled $458.5 Million in 1996-97, Another All-Time High." University of Michigan News Release 18 Dec 1997. p1-2.

UNIVERSITY OF TEXAS

see COLLEGE APPLICATIONS--UNIVERSITY OF TEXAS

UNIVERSITY OF TEXAS--ADMISSION

The number of minorities applying to Universiy of Texas's "law school fell last year, as did the number of admitted minorities who decided to attend....In years past, as many as 60 blacks have earned spots in first-year classes....[In May 1997, Texas] legislators passed a new law requiring public colleges to offer admission to the top 10 percent high school students." (p4)

Walker, Sam. "United States: Texas Hunts for Ways to Foster Diversity." The Christian Science Monitor v89 n138 12 Jun 1997. p4. The Christian Science Monitor search engine: <http://www.csmonitor.com/plweb-cgi/iops1.pl> To retrieve this article, enter the following search: ED=19970612 AND diversity. In the "retrieved list," click the title that matches this record. (ISSN0882-7729).

UNIVERSITY OF TEXAS--ADMISSION--MINORITIES

In 1997, on the Austin campus of the University of Texas, "minority enrollment dropped 2 percent despite a 20-percent rise in the number of freshmen. On the top six campuses, the percentage of blacks and Hispanics in the freshman class dropped 1.4 percent, though enrollment rose 4 percent." (p1 secA) "Graduate school enrollment dropped 19 percent for blacks and 6 percent for Hispanics. Law school enrollments declined 23 percent for blacks and 19 percent for Hispanics. And medical school admissions plunged 38 percent for blacks and 22 percent for Hispanics....This fall, 60 percent of minority freshmen on the Austin campus received scholarships, compared with almost 100 percent a year ago." (p3 secA)

Walsh-Sarnecki, Peggy. "If It Loses Suit, U-M Could See Fewer Minorities." Detroit Free Press 31 Oct 1997. p1,3 secA.

UNIVERSITY OF WISCONSIN-MILWAUKEE

"The University of Wisconsin-Milwaukee is located in a metropolitan area of approximately 1.5 million: 83% are White Americans, 14% are African Americans, and 4% are Latinos (Metropolitan Milwaukee Association of Commerce, 1992)." (p114) "Of the nearly 24,000 students, African Americans constitute 7.3%, and Latinos represent 3%." (p115)

Tiezzi, Linda J./Cross, Beverly E. "Utilizing Research on Prospective Teachers' Beliefs to Inform Urban Field Experiences." Urban Review v29 n2 Jun 1997. p113-125. (ISSN0042-0972).

UNIVERSITY STUDENTS

see COLLEGE STUDENTS

UNMARRIED COUPLES

see also SINGLE PARENTS

UNMARRIED COUPLES--CANADA (v26)

UNMARRIED COUPLES--PHILIPPINES

According to the Young Adult Fertility and Sexuality Study conducted in 1994 in the Philippines, "seventy percent of respondents who had lived with a partner before a church or civil marriage had lived together for three months or less. Only six percent reported living together for two years or longer. Among men who reported having lived with a partner but who were not formally married at the time of the survey, the time spent living together averaged 23 months; for women in this category the average time spent living together was 29 months." (p4)

"Survey Sheds New Light on Marriage and Sexuality in the Philippines." Asia-Pacific Population & Policy n42 Jul 1997. p1-4. (ISSN0891-6683).

UNMARRIED COUPLES--UNITED STATES

In the U.S., "more than four in ten women aged 15 to 44 in 1995 have been in an unmarried domestic partnership at some point in their lives, according to the National Survey of Family Growth....Slightly more than half of women aged 25 to 39 have cohabited, and boomers were aged 31 to 49 in 1995. Seven percent of all U.S. women aged 15 to 44 were cohabiting in 1995, up from 6.4 percent in 1982....Only 10 percent of women aged 15 to 44 reported that their first cohabitation was still intact in 1995, and only 37 percent said that their first partner was their current husband. One-third had dissolved the cohabitation, and 21 percent married their partner and then divorced....21 percent of cohabiting women were formerly married....More than 1 million women aged 35 and older were cohabiting in 1995...." (p7)

"New Lifestage: Trial Marriage." Forecast v17 n10 Oct 1997. p7. article-level access: <http://www.demographics.com/publications/fc/97_fc/9710_fc/fc97106.htm> (ISSN0732-1597).

UNMARRIED PEOPLE

see SINGLE PEOPLE

URABA (COLOMBIA)--HISTORY--CIVIL WAR

As a result of Colombia's civil war, in Uraba, "more than 90 percent of the casualties are civilian--the armed groups execute those they suspect of collaboration with the other side. There were well over 1,000 so-called 'political killings' in Uraba last year. Of the 15,000 indigenous Colombians in Antioquia, says...[Guzman Caizamo, vice president of the Indigenous Organization of Antioquia], some 12,000 live in the Uraba region....There have been two killings of indigenous men in Uraba this year. Last year, 10 were killed....'We were 10 million indigenous in Colombia when the Spanish arrived. Today, we are 800,000,' says Caizamo." (p6)

Lawrence, David Aquila. "International: In Colombia's Civil War, Neutrality Can Pay Off." The Christian Science Monitor v89 n149 27 Jun 1997. p6. The Christian Science Monitor search engine: <http://www.csmonitor.com/plweb-cgi/iops1.pl> To retrieve this article, enter the following search: ED=19970627 AND off. In the "retrieved list," click the title that matches this record. (ISSN0882-7729).

URANIUM MILL TAILINGS--RUSSIA (v26)

URBAN AGRICULTURE (v26)

"In 1970, 20 percent of families in Moscow were involved in some kind of agricultural activity, while today about 65 percent of Muscovites practice urban agriculture, according to UNDP [United Nations Development Program]....In Kenya and Tanzania, 3 out of 5 families in towns and cities are farming. And in the United States, more than one-third of the dollar value of agricultural products is produced in urban regions....At last count, Cairo had 80,000 head of livestock in the city, according to UNDP. Or take Dar es Salaam, Tanzania. Between 1968 and 1992, the number of urban farmers grew from 18 percent to 68 percent. Today, 90 percent of leafy green vegetables sold in the city's markets are grown in the city." (p9)

Prince, Cathryn J. "Global Report: City Farms: All Built Up, Places to Grow." The Christian Science Monitor v89 n205 17 Sep 1997. p1,9. The Christian Science Monitor search engine: <http://www.csmonitor.com/plweb-cgi/iops1.pl> To retrieve this article, enter the following search: ED=19970917 AND grow. In the "retrieved list," click the title that matches this record. (ISSN0882-7729).

URBAN AREAS

see CITIES AND TOWNS

URBAN CRIME

see CRIME

URBAN RENEWAL--UNITED STATES

In the U.S., the first business improvement districts "started about 20 years ago, but since the late '80s the concept has really taken off. Now the number of BIDs is estimated to range from 450 to 1,200. New York City alone now has about 40 of them....Des Moines is starting a BID. So is Spencer, Iowa, population 20,000." (p18)

Feldmann, Linda. "Cities Seek Disney-Style Cleanliness and Safety." The Christian Science Monitor v89 n187 21 Aug 1997. p1,18. The Christian Science Monitor search engine: <http://www.csmonitor.com/plweb-cgi/iops1.pl> To retrieve this article, enter the following search: ED=19970821 AND safety. In the "retrieved list," click the title that matches this record. (ISSN0882-7729).

URBAN-RURAL MIGRATION--CALIFORNIA (v26)

URBAN-RURAL MIGRATION--UNITED STATES (v26)

URBANIZATION

"A century ago, just 15% of the world's population lived in urban areas. Today that figure is over 50% and climbing. Of the expected increase of 2.7 billion in the world's population between now and 2025, some 2.4 billion or about 90%, will occur in urban areas." (p15)

"Association News: Federation of Canadian Municipalities: Making Our Cities Sustainable." Municipal World v107 n8 Aug 1997. p15. (ISSN0027-3589).

Habitat II, the second U.N.-sponsored conference on global urban collapse, was held in Istanbul, Turkey last year. The "conference estimated that 1 billion of the earth's 5.8 billion people are inadequately housed, and that an additional 100 million people have no shelter at all. The conference noted that over the past 50 years 100 of the world's largest cities have tripled in size. Since 1975, when one-third of all people lived in cities, global population has increased from 4.2 billion to 5.8 billion people. By 2005 this ratio of urban to rural population is expected to grow to one-half, and by 2025 two-thirds of the population will be festering in megalopolitan squalor." (p5)

"'NGOs' Can't End the Crisis of the Cities." The People v107 n6 Sep 1997. p5. (ISSN0199-350X).

"Mexico City became the second largest [urban] agglomeration in the world, with 16.9 million inhabitants in 1996. It is followed by Sao Paulo (16.8 million), New York (16.4 million) and Bombay (15.7 million). The remaining 16 mega-cities--defined as urban agglomerations with 10 million or more--are: Shanghai (13.7 million), Los Angeles (12.6 million), Calcutta (12.1 million), Buenos Aires (11.9 million), Seoul (11.8 million), Beijing (11.4 million), Lagos (10.9 million), Osaka (10.6 million), Delhi (10.3 million), Rio de Janeiro (10.3 million) and Karachi (10.1 million). According to the report, Tokyo will remain the world's largest city, with a population of 28.9 million persons by 2015." (p77)

"And Other News of Interest...: Tokyo, Mexico City 'Largest Urban Agglomerations.'" UN Chronicle v34 n2 1997. p77. (ISSN0251-7329).

"Some 46 per cent of the world's people are now urban dwellers, a figure expected to rise to half the population by the year 2006, according to the recently released '1996 Revision of World Urbanization Prospects.'...As of mid-1996, 75 per cent of the population in the more developed regions lived in urban areas, while only 38 per cent in the less developed regions were urban dwellers. In 1996, 2.6 billion persons lived in urban areas, including 1.8 billion in the less developed regions. The world urban population grew at a rate of 2.4 per cent per annum between 1990 and 1995, more than three times that of rural populations (0.7 per cent per annum). As a result, urban areas absorbed 59 million additional persons each year, compared with 22 million for the rural areas....While almost 3 of every 4 persons were urban dwellers in Europe, North America and Latin America and the Caribbean in 1996, only about 1 in 3 lived in urban areas in Africa and Asia, respectively. In Oceania, 7 of every 10 people lived in cities in 1996." (p75)

"Systemwatch: Revitalizing Habitat: Half of World Population Expected to Live In Cities by 2006." UN Chronicle v34 n3 1997. p75. (ISSN0251-7329).

URBANIZATION--ARGENTINA--BUENOS AIRES

"Argentina is one of the most urbanized countries in Latin America. More than 12.4 million persons live in the metropolitan area of Buenos Aires, where 2.5 million cars circulate daily. Car ownership in the city is increasing at a rate of 150,000 a year--producing congestion, rising air pollution, and more accidents....Suburban passenger volumes [in Buenos Aires] have increased and in 1996 are 95 percent above the level of 1993, and subway passengers have increased by 37 percent...."

World Bank. "World Bank Finances Improvements to the Urban Transport System in Greater Buenos Aires." Press Release 15 May 1997. document-level access: <http://www.worldbank.org/html/extdr/extme/1350.htm>

URBANIZATION--CHINA (v26)

URBANIZATION--DEVELOPING COUNTRIES

"Just over 25% urban in 1975, developing countries were nearly 40% urban by 1995....The number of people in urban areas of developing countries has risen from about 800 million in 1975 to about 1.7 billion today....In Latin America and the Caribbean seven countries are at least three-fourths urban--Venezuela (92%), Uruguay (90%), Argentina (88%), Chile (84%), Brazil (78%), Cuba (76%), and Mexico (75%). In North Africa and the Near East, Libya is about 85% urban, and Saudi Arabia, about 80% urban....By 2015 over half of people in developing countries will live in urban areas (145,289)....By then the estimated urban population of the developing world will exceed 3 billion. Of these, over 1.2 billion will be living in 'million-plus' cities." (p5)

Gardner, Robert/Blackburn, Richard. "People Who Move: New Reproductive Health Focus." Population Reports v24 n3 Nov 1996. p1-27.

URBANIZATION--FLORIDA--FLORIDA KEYS

"The existing law allows 255 units to be built each year in the [Florida] Keys, based on a 20-year capacity build-out....Out of the 255 yearly residential permits allowed for all the Keys, Big Pine Key [which has more buildable endangered species habitat (primarily for Key deer) than any other Florida Key,] will be allowed to use only eight, down from 119 under existing law....When US 1 traffic reached its capacity on Big Pine Key in 1994, the Department of Community Affairs (DCA) exempted 20 units of new development per year, provided that the county enter a Habitat Conservation Plan (HCP) with the U.S. Fish and Wildlife Service....Based on county computer records, an estimated 100 new Big Pine Key units have been given permits or permit allocations since mid-1994...." (p18)

Morgenstern, Henry Lee. "America's Tropics: Managing Monroe County's Unbridled Growth." Florida Naturalist v70 n2 Sum 1997. p18. (ISSN0015-4172).

URBANIZATION--MICHIGAN (v26)

URBANIZATION--OREGON--PORTLAND

In Portland, Oregon, "the average lot size of new single-family houses has dropped from about 10,000 square feet in 1979 to about 7,000 last year. Metro officials are planning for 600,000 new residents in the next forty years but plan to add as much as 18,600 acres of new land to the Urban Growth Boundary--a 40 percent increase in population being accommodated with only 8 percent growth in area. (By contrast, the Detroit metropolitan region has increased 0.3 percent in population over the past two decades but expanded in size by 18 percent.)...John Fregonese, Metro's director of growth-management services, notes that the municipality of Portland granted permits for 2,600 new units of housing last year...." (p12)

Walljasper, Jay. "What Works?: Portland's Green Peace: At Play in the Fields of Urban Planning." Nation v265 n11 13 Oct 1997. p11-15. (ISSN0027-8378).

URINARY INCONTINENCE--UNITED STATES--WOMEN (v26)

USE OF LAND

see LAND USE

UTERINE CERVIX

see CERVIX UTERI

UTERUS--CANCER--UNITED STATES

In the U.S., "cancer of the uterus is the fourth most common cancer in women. This year, an estimated 34,900 women will learn they have the disease. However, most uterine cancers are detected before the tumor has spread outside the uterus, and the five-year survival rate for these early stage patients is over 90 percent."

U.S. National Cancer Institute. "Estrogen for Survivors of Uterine Cancer? A New Study Will Resolve Debate." Press Release 29 Apr 1997. document-level access: <http://rex.nci.nih.gov/massmedia/pressreleases/estrogenuterine.HTM>

UTILIZATION OF LAND

see LAND USE

UZBEKISTAN--COMMERCE

In Uzbekistan, trade with Commonwealth of Independent States "partners fell by 27 percent in the first half of last year from the same period in 1995, while trade with non-CIS countries grew by 80 percent. Only 8 percent of Uzbekistan's exports are sold to Russia now; five years ago that figure was close to 100 percent." (p9)

Ford, Peter. "The Comeback Empire? Russia Five Years after the Fall: Ex-Russian Satellite Enjoys Setting Its Own Agenda." The Christian Science Monitor v89 n131 3 Jun 1997. p9,11. The Christian Science Monitor search engine: <http://www.csmonitor.com/plweb-cgi/iops1.pl> To retrieve this article, enter the following search: ED=19970603 AND agenda. In the "retrieved list," click the title that matches this record. (ISSN0882-7729).

VACATIONS--UNITED STATES (v26)

VACCINATION

see also INFLUENZA VACCINES; HEPATITIS A--VACCINATION; TYPHOID VACCINE

VACCINATION--AFRICA--ASIA

"A vigorous immunization program in Southeast Asia between 1988 and 1994 led to declines of 77 percent to 83 percent in reported cases of polio, neonatal tetanus, diphtheria, and pertussis. In Africa, multidrug treatments for leprosy reduced the prevalence of this disease from 483,000 in 1990 to 159,000 in 1993. Improved surveillance and immunization of women of childbearing ages has almost eliminated neonatal tetanus in 12 to 46 nations on the African continent." (p16-17)

Olshansky, S. Jay/Carnes, Bruce/Rogers, Richard G./Smith, Len. "Infectious Diseases--New and Ancient Threats to World Health." Population Bulletin v52 n2 Jul 1997. p2-46. (ISSN0032-468X).

VACCINATION OF CHILDREN--MICHIGAN

For 1996, "Michigan immunization levels have increased to 76 percent....In 1994, the CDC reported that Michigan ranked last in the nation in childhood immunizations, with only 61% of Michigan 2-year-olds fully immunized....Michigan currently ranks higher than 12 other states in immunization levels....A 1994 retrospective study by the Department showed immunizations among two-year-olds in 1991 were 42% statewide. An earlier CDC study showed the immunization level among two-year-olds in Detroit during the same year was 29%. The new CDC study ranks the City of Detroit at 65%."

Michigan. Dept. of Community Health. "Michigan Makes Greatest Gain in Immunization Levels in Nation." News Release 23 Jul 1997. document-level access: <http://www.mdch.state.mi.us/DCH/NewsRels/immun723.htm>

VACCINATION OF CHILDREN--UNITED STATES

"According to CDC's most recent National Immunization Survey, which surveys parents of preschoolers nationwide, a record high 78 percent of two-year-olds in the United States received their full series of shots as recommended. In addition, President Clinton announced on July 23, 1997 that the nation had exceeded its childhood vaccination goals for 1996, with 90 percent or more on America's toddlers receiving the most critical doses of most of the routinely recommended vaccines for children by age 2. Also in 1996, reported levels of disease were at or near record lows and 3 diseases reached the elimination targets (tetanus under age 15, polio and mumps)."

U.S. Dept. of Health and Human Services. "HHS Invests in America's Children." Fact Sheet 23 Jul 1997. document-level access: <http://www.hhs.gov/news/press/1997pres/970917.html>

"The U.S. Department of Health and Human Services announced...that the nation exceeded its childhood vaccination goals for 1996, with 90 percent or more of America's toddlers receiving the most critical doses of most of the routinely recommended vaccines for children by age 2....According to CDC's National Immunization Survey, 95 percent of 2-year-olds received three doses of diphtheria, tetanus, pertussis vaccine (DTP); 91 percent received three doses of polio vaccine; 92 percent received three doses of 'Haemophilus influenzae' type b (causes a form of meningitis) vaccine; and 91 percent received a measles-containing vaccine. In 1993, the goal set for the newly recommended hepatitis B vaccine was 70 percent by 1996; hepatitis B vaccination reached 82 percent in 1996. The overall national immunization coverage level for the most commonly used combined series, which includes 4 doses of DTP, 3 doses of polio and a measles-containing vaccine, increased to 78 percent in 1996, the highest national level ever reported in the United

States for preschool children."

U.S. Dept. of Health and Human Services. "Nation Reaches 1996 Immunization Goals with Highest-Ever Coverage Levels." Press Release 23 Jul 1997. document-level access: <http://www.hhs.gov/news/press/1997pres/970723a.html>

VALENTINES--UNITED STATES (v26)

VALUATION--CALIFORNIA--LOS ANGELES COUNTY

In the Long Beach-Los Angeles, Calif. Metropolitan Area, "the median value of homeowners' residences in 1995 was $192,800, down 26 percent from a 1995 constant dollar figure of $261,600 for 1989. Of the 19,400 owner-occupied homes built or purchased during the last four years, 94 percent cost $100,000 or more; 70 percent of the owners of new homes used savings or cash-on-hand for their down payment."

U.S. Dept. of Commerce./U.S. Dept. of Housing and Urban Development. "Twenty-Two Percent of the Los Angeles-Long Beach Metropolitan Area's Households Give High Marks to...Neighborhood...." Census Bureau Press Release 22 Oct 1997. document-level access: <http://www.census.gov/Press-Release/cb97h11.html>

VALUATION--COLORADO--DENVER

In the Denver, Colo. Metropolitan Area, "the median value of homeowners' residences in 1995 was $119,700, up 17 percent from a 1995 constant dollar figure of $102,600 for 1990. Of the 37,700 owner-occupied homes built and purchased during the last four years, 92 percent cost $100,000 or more; 36 percent of the owners of new homes used savings or cash-on-hand for their down payment."

U.S. Dept. of Commerce./U.S. Dept. of Housing and Urban Development. "Twenty-Nine Percent of the Denver Metropolitan Area's Households Give High Marks to Their Neighborhood...." Census Bureau Press Release 28 Oct 1997. document-level access: <http://www.census.gov/Press-Release/cb97h15.html>

VALUATION--FLORIDA

In the Miami-Fort Lauderdale Fla. Metropolitan Area, "the median value of homeowners' residences in 1995 was $97,100. This value was not significantly different from the 1995 constant dollar value of $94,700 for 1990. Of the 56,900 owner-occupied homes built or purchased during the last four years, 72 percent cost $100,000 or more; 54 percent of the owners of new homes used savings or cash-on-hand for their down payment."

U.S. Dept. of Commerce./U.S. Dept. of Housing and Urban Development. "Thirty-One Percent of the Miami-Fort Lauderdale Metropolitan Area's Households Give High Marks to...Neighborhood...." Census Bureau Press Release 20 Oct 1997. document-level access: <http://www.census.gov/Press-Release/cb97h01.html>

VALUATION--ILLINOIS--CHICAGO

In the Chicago, Ill. Metropolitan Area, "the median value of homeowners' residences in 1995 was $136,000, up 5 percent from a 1995 constant dollar figure of $130,000 for 1991. Of the 104,000 owner-occupied homes built or purchased during the last four years, 95 percent cost $100,000 or more; 29 percent of the owners of new homes used savings or cash-on-hand for their down payment."

U.S. Dept. of Commerce./U.S. Dept. of Housing and Urban Development. "Thirty-One Percent of the Chicago Metropolitan Area's Households Give High Marks to Their Neighborhood...." Census Bureau Press Release 20 Oct 1997. document-level access: <http://www.census.gov/Press-Release/cb97h02.html>

VALUATION--LOUISIANA--NEW ORLEANS

In the New Orleans, La. Metropolitan Area, "the median value of homeowners' residences in 1995 was $75,800, down 4 percent from a 1995 constant dollar figure of $78,800 for 1990. Of the 8,600 owner-occupied homes built or purchased during the last four years, 47 percent cost $100,000 or more; 56 percent of the owners of new homes used savings or cash-on-hand for their down payment."

U.S. Dept. of Commerce./U.S. Dept. of Housing and Urban Development. "Thirty-Four Percent of the New Orleans Metropolitan Area's Households Give High Marks to Their Neighborhood...." Census Bureau Press Release 22 Oct 1997. document-level access: <http://www.census.gov/Press-Release/cb97h07.html>

VALUATION--MASSACHUSETTS--BOSTON (v26)

VALUATION--MICHIGAN (v26)

"Last year, property values in Michigan increased 9.3 percent--the highest in the United States, according to the Office of Federal Housing Enterprise Oversight in Washington D.C. The average property value increase nationwide was 3.4 percent. In Wayne County, the number of homes sold through the first five months of 1997 is 6.7 percent off the torid pace of 1996--but the median sales price of homes in the county is up 4.8 percent to $92,900. Oakland County has seen an even bigger jump in home values. Although sales are down 5.7 percent from 1996, the median sales price through the end of April is up to $138,900--a 6.5 percent increase....In 1996, 4.1 million existing homes and 758,000 new homes were sold....[William Wilson, Comerica bank economist] credits Proposal A, the 1994 bill that reduced Michigan property taxes, as another reason for the strong market. 'Prop A reduced housing property taxes in Michigan an average of about 50 percent,' said Wilson." (p1 secC)

Hunter, George/King, R. J. "Business: Area Homes Sell at Rapid Pace: Builders, Sellers Enjoy Strong Real Estate Market." Detroit News 15 Jun 1997. p1,3 secC.

VALUATION--MICHIGAN--DETROIT (v26)

In the Detroit, Mich. Metropolitan Area, "the median value of homeowners' residences in 1995 was $89,600, up 8 percent from a 1995 constant dollar figure of $83,000 for 1993. Of the 53,700 owner-occupied homes built or purchased during the last four years, 84 percent cost $100,000 or more; 24 percent of the owners of new homes used savings or cash-on-hand for their down payment."

U.S. Dept. of Commerce./U.S. Dept. of Housing and Urban Development. "Thirty-Seven Percent of the Detroit Metropolitan Area's Households Give High Marks to Their Neighborhood...." Census Bureau Press Release 22 Oct 1997. document-level access: <http://www.census.gov/Press-Release/cb97h10.html>

VALUATION--MICHIGAN--LIVINGSTON COUNTY (v26)

VALUATION--MICHIGAN--WASHTENAW COUNTY (v26)

VALUATION--MISSOURI--KANSAS CITY

In the Kansas City, Mo.-Kan. Metropolitan Area, "the median value of homeowners' residences in 1995 was $78,500. This value was not statistically different from the 1995 constant dollar value of $77,800 for 1990. Of the 34,000 owner-occupied homes built or purchased during the last four years, 66 percent cost $100,000 or more; 3.8 percent of the owners of new homes used savings or cash-on-hand for their down payment."

U.S. Dept. of Commerce./U.S. Dept. of Housing and Urban Development. "Thirty-Two Percent of the Kansas City Metropolitan Area's Households Give High Marks to Their Neighborhood...." Census Bureau Press Release 28 Oct 1997. document-level access: <http://www.census.gov/Press-Release/cb97h13.html>

VALUATION--NEW JERSEY

In the Northern New Jersey Metropolitan Area, "the median value of homeowners' residences in 1995 was $176,700, down 7 percent from a 1995 constant dollar figure of $190,000 for 1991. Of the 54,000 owner-occupied homes built or purchased during the last four years, 84 percent cost $100,000 or more; 36 percent of the owners of new homes used savings or cash-on-hand for their down payment."

U.S. Dept. of Commerce./U.S. Dept. of Housing and Urban Development. "Thirty-Two Percent of the Northern New Jersey Metropolitan Area's Households Give High Marks to Their Neighborhood...." Census Bureau Press Release 20 Oct 1997. document-level access: <http://www.census.gov/Press-Release/cb97h04.html>

VALUATION--NEW YORK (N.Y.)

In the New York-Nassau-Suffolk-Orange, N.Y. Metropolitan Area, "the median value of homeowners' residences in 1995 was $172,700, down 11 percent from a 1995 constant dollar figure of $195,100 for 1991. Of the 22,500 owner-occupied homes built or purchased during the last four years, about 100 percent cost $100,000 or more; 69 percent of the owners of new homes used savings or cash-on-hand for their down payment."

U.S. Dept. of Commerce./U.S. Dept. of Housing and Urban Development. "Twenty-One Percent of the New York-Nassau-Suffolk-Orange Metropolitan...Households Give High Marks...Neighborhood...." Census Bureau Press Release 20 Oct 1997. document-level access: <http://www.census.gov/Press-Release/cb97h03.html>

VALUATION--NORTH CAROLINA--CHARLOTTE

In the Charlotte, N.C.-S.C. Metropolitan Area, "the median value of homeowners' residences in 1995 was $86,800. Of the 38,000 owner-occupied homes built or purchased during the last four years, 55 percent cost $100,000 or more; 53 percent of the owners of new homes used savings or cash-on-hand for their down payment."

U.S. Dept. of Commerce./U.S. Dept. of Housing and Urban Development. "Forty Percent of the Charlotte Metropolitan Area's Households Give High Marks to Their Neighborhood, Census...Says." Census Bureau Press Release 20 Oct 1997. document-level access: <http://www.census.gov/Press-Release/cb97h05.html>

VALUATION--OHIO--COLUMBUS

In the Columbus, Ohio Metropolitan Area, "the median value of homeowners' residences in 1995 was $93,000, up about 8 percent from a 1995 constant dollar figure of $86,000 for 1991. Of the 34,400 owner-occupied homes built or purchased during the last four years, 70 percent cost $100,000 or more; 40 percent of the owners of new homes used savings or cash-on-hand for their down payment."

U.S. Dept. of Commerce./U.S. Dept. of Housing and Urban Development. "Thirty-Two Percent of the Columbus Metropolitan Area's Households Give High Marks to Their Neighborhood...." Census Bureau Press Release 20 Oct 1997. document-level access: <http://www.census.gov/Press-Release/cb97h06.html>

VALUATION--OREGON--PORTLAND

In the Portland, Ore. Metropolitan Area, "the median value of homeowners' residences in 1995 was $127,700, up 43 percent from a 1995 constant dollar figure of $89,500 for 1990. Of the 36,100 owner-occupied homes built or purchased during the last four years, 87 percent cost $100,000 or more; 27 percent of the owners of new homes used savings or cash-on-hand for their down payment."

U.S. Dept. of Commerce./U.S. Dept. of Housing and Urban Development. "Twenty-Nine Percent of the Portland Metropolitan Area's Households Give High Marks to Their Neighborhood...." Census Bureau Press Release 22 Oct 1997. document-level access: <http://www.census.gov/Press-Release/cb97h09.html>

VALUATION--PENNSYLVANIA--PHILADELPHIA

In the Philadelphia, Pennsylvania Metropolitan Area, "the median value of homeowners' residences in 1995 was $112,800, down 11 percent from a 1995 constant dollar figure of $127,400 for 1989. Of the 37,200 owner-occupied homes built or purchased during the last four years, 84 percent cost $100,000 or more; 63 percent of the owners of new homes used savings or cash-on-hand for their down payment."

U.S. Dept. of Commerce./U.S. Dept. of Housing and Urban Development. "Thirty-Four Percent of the Philadelphia Metropolitan Area's Households Give High Marks to Their Neighborhood...." Census Bureau Press Release 28 Oct 1997. document-level access: <http://www.census.gov/Press-Release/cb97h14.html>

VALUATION--PENNSYLVANIA--PITTSBURGH

In the Pittsburgh, Pa. Metropolitan Area, "the median value of homeowners' residences in 1995 was $73,400, up 11 percent from a 1995 constant dollar figure of $66,300 for 1990. Of the 22,100 owner-occupied homes built or purchased during the last four years, 67 percent cost $100,000 or more; 36 percent of the owners of new homes used savings or cash-on-hand for their down payment."

U.S. Dept. of Commerce./U.S. Dept. of Housing and Urban Development. "Forty Percent of the Pittsburgh Metropolitan Area's Households Give High Marks to Their Neighborhood...." Census Bureau Press Release 22 Oct 1997. document-level access: <http://www.census.gov/Press-Release/cb97h08.html>

VALUATION--TEXAS--SAN ANTONIO

In the San Antonio, Texas Metropolitan Area, "the median value of homeowners' residences in 1995 was $62,600, which is not statistically different than the 1995 constant dollar figure of $59,900 for 1990. Of the 19,100 owner-occupied homes built or purchased during the last four years, 49 percent cost $100,000 or more; 51 percent of the owners of new homes used savings or cash-on-hand for their down payment."

U.S. Dept. of Commerce./U.S. Dept. of Housing and Urban Development. "Thirty-Five Percent of the San Antonio Metropolitan Area's Households Give High Marks to Their Neighborhood...." Census Bureau Press Release 28 Oct 1997. document-level access: <http://www.census.gov/Press-Release/cb97h12.html>

VASCULAR SYSTEM

see CARDIOVASCULAR SYSTEM

VD (DISEASE)

see SEXUALLY TRANSMITTED DISEASES

VEGETABLE OIL INDUSTRY--CHINA (v26)

VEGETABLE TRADE

see also ASPARAGUS; BEAN INDUSTRY; CANNED VEGETABLES INDUSTRY; CARROT INDUSTRY; CHILE PEPPER INDUSTRY; LETTUCE INDUSTRY; MUSHROOM INDUSTRY; POTATO INDUSTRY; RAPESEED INDUSTRY; SOYBEAN INDUSTRY; SWEET POTATO INDUSTRY; TOMATO INDUSTRY

VEGETABLE TRADE--CANADA--MICHIGAN (v26)

VEGETABLE TRADE--CHINA

"China is a major exporter of fresh and preserved vegetables....Exports rose from 2.2 million tons ($721 million) in 1986 to 3.1 million tons ($2.4 billion) in 1995. According [to] China's Custom Bureau, the top ten vegetable export markets in 1996 include: Japan ($809 million); Hong Kong ($160 million); Republic of Korea ($82 million); the United States ($44); Germany ($39 million); Italy ($35 million); Indonesia ($34 million); Brazil ($28 million); Singapore ($25 million); and Russia ($25 million)....Imports in 1995 totaled $71 million--mostly dried legumes and dried cassava." (p47)

Crook, Frederick W./U.S. Dept. of Agriculture. Economic Research Service. "Introduction to China's Horticultural Economy." China: International Agriculture and Trade Reports Situation and Outlook Series Jun 1997. p47-51.

In China, "area sown to vegetables (including melons used as vegetables) more than tripled from 3.2 million hectares in 1980 to 10.5 million in 1996....Ministry of Agriculture statisticians are in the process of refining their vegetable output series. Their most recent estimate is that farmers produced 431 million tons in 1995; 257 million tons of fresh vegetables; 163 million tons of potatoes; an estimated 10 million tons of dry peas and beans; and 1 million tons of mushrooms..., which makes China the largest vegetable producer in the world. In 1995, the United States produced 56 million tons of vegetables (including vegetables, potatoes, dry peas and beans, and mushrooms)...." (p47)

Crook, Frederick W./U.S. Dept. of Agriculture. Economic Research Service. "Introduction to China's Horticultural Economy." China: International Agriculture and Trade Reports Situation and Outlook Series Jun 1997. p47-51.

VEGETABLE TRADE--CHINA--UNITED STATES

"U.S. vegetable imports from China in 1996 totaled $141 million, of which major items were dried and fresh mushrooms, water chestnuts, peas, and beans. U.S. vegetable exports to China totaled $12.2 million in 1996, but some products were transshipped into China from Hong Kong. Major items included canned vegetables, frozen potatoes, and hops." (p47)

Crook, Frederick W./U.S. Dept. of Agriculture. Economic Research Service. "Introduction to China's Horticultural Economy." China: International Agriculture and Trade Reports Situation and Outlook Series Jun 1997. p47-51.

VEGETABLE TRADE--FLORIDA--MEXICO (v26)

VEGETABLE TRADE--HONG KONG--UNITED STATES

"The value of U.S. vegetable exports to Hong Kong (including potatoes, melons, pulses, mushrooms, and vegetable seed) totaled $101 million in 1996, up 14 percent from a year earlier. Six commodities accounted for two-thirds of the vegetables exported to Hong Kong. The major items exported to Hong Kong were canned sweet corn ($17 million), frozen french fries ($16 million), lettuce ($12 million), celery ($6 million), potato chips ($5 million), and tomato ketchup ($4 million)." (p5)

U.S. Dept. of Agriculture. Economic Research Service. "Summary." Vegetables and Specialties Situation and Outlook Yearbook Jul 1997. p3-5.

VEGETABLE TRADE--JAPAN--UNITED STATES (v26)

VEGETABLE TRADE--MEXICO (v26)

VEGETABLE TRADE--UNITED STATES (v26)

In the U.S., in 1996, "more than 47 percent of U.S. cash receipts from vegetables come from California and Florida. Cash receipts from vegetables represent about 32 percent of California's cash receipts from all crops and 26 percent of Florida's....Potatoes were Idaho's leading commodity in cash receipts, generating more than 21 percent of the State's total cash receipts from all commodities." (p8)

U.S. Dept. of Agriculture. Economic Research Service. "1996 Farm Income Estimates: Net Value-Added and Net Farm Income Attain New Highs in 1996." Agricultural Income and Finance Situation and Outlook Report Sep 1997. p4-13.

U.S. "fresh and frozen vegetable imports continued at a strong pace in 1996, rising 18 percent to reach $2 billion.... Cucumbers, onions, peppers, cauliflower, and broccoli accounted for $624 million, an increase of 22 percent over the previous year. Tight domestic supplies drew greater tomato imports, mainly from Mexico, reaching a record $672 million, an increase of 49 percent." (p6)

Gehlhar, Mark/U.S. Dept. of Agriculture. Economic Research Service. "Imports Advance 12 Percent in 1996." Foreign Agricultural Trade of the United States Jan-Mar 1997. p6-7.

"In 1996, the United States exported nearly 8 percent of its fresh-market vegetable supplies (production plus imports), down fractionally from 1995. On the other side of the ledger, the United States imported about 12 percent of its fresh vegetable supplies, up from 11 percent a year earlier. About 6 percent of canned vegetable supplies were exported in 1996, while 2 percent were imported. In 1996, 7 percent of vegetables for freezing (excluding potatoes) were exported. Imports accounted for 10 percent of freezing supply, and broccoli accounted for half of all frozen vegetable imports." (p4)

U.S. Dept. of Agriculture. Economic Research Service. "Summary." Vegetables and Specialties Situation and Outlook Yearbook Jul 1997. p3-5.

"U.S. vegetable production (including potatoes, sweet potatoes, and pulses) in 1996 increased 5 percent from the previous year to 1.3 billion cwt [hundredweight]. Production was stronger for fresh-market vegetables and melons (up 4 percent) and sweet potatoes (up 4 percent) but was smaller for processing vegetables (down fractionally), dry edible beans (down 11 percent), and dry peas and lentils (down 48 percent)....Fresh vegetable output totaled 405 million cwt in 1996. Stronger yields resulted in higher production for honeydew melons (23 percent), cantaloups (15 percent), bell peppers (14 percent), and watermelons (9 percent). Reduced area limited output of snap beans (16 percent) and tomatoes (11 percent). Larger acreage brought 15 percent gains in output for romaine lettuce and carrots. Continued strong domestic demand prompted California garlic growers to increase area 11 percent, which contributed to a 17-percent surge in output. Reduced acreage in the summer crop cut onion production 4 percent to 62 million cwt in 1996. New York onion output fell 32 percent due to adverse weather which caused increased acreage abandonment at harvest and a 25-percent cut in yield." (p3)

U.S. Dept. of Agriculture. Economic Research Service. "Summary." Vegetables and Specialties Situation and Outlook Yearbook Jul 1997. p3-5.

In the U.S., "per capita use of 56 selected vegetable and melon categories rose 3 percent in 1996 to 443 pounds (farm-weight basis)....Fresh vegetable and melon use (excluding potatoes) increased 5 percent to 154 pounds per person--the highest since the mid-1940's....Watermelon use totaled 17.4 pounds in 1996....In 1996, fresh carrot use rose 13 percent to 10.2 pounds, compared with an average of 7.5 pounds in the 1980's. Per capita use of vegetables for processing (excluding potatoes and mushrooms) fell slightly to 129 pounds per person as use of canning vegetables fell 1 percent. Per capita use of vegetables for freezing (excluding potatoes) rose 3 percent to 23.5 pounds. Per capita use of frozen vegetables has increased 43 percent since 1978, mirroring a 39-percent surge in fresh use. Canning vegetables increased 14 percent during this time due to rising use of processed tomato products. Excluding tomato products, canning vegetable use has declined about 17 percent since 1978." (p5)

U.S. Dept. of Agriculture. Economic Research Service. "Summary." Vegetables and Specialties Situation and Outlook Yearbook Jul 1997. p3-5.

VEGETARIANS--UNITED STATES--ATTITUDES (v26)

VEHICLES

see also AUTOMOBILES; ELECTRIC VEHICLES; LIMOUSINES; RECREATIONAL VEHICLES; SCHOOL BUSES; SNOWMOBILES; SPACE SHUTTLES; SPACE VEHICLES; SPORT UTILITY VEHICLES; TAXICABS

VEHICLES--ACCIDENTS

see TRAFFIC ACCIDENTS

VEHICLES--UNITED STATES (v26)

In the U.S., sales of full-size sport-utility vehicles "are up 337 percent since 1992, according to Ward's Automotive Reports, a trade journal. In the...1997 model year, 523,000 of these full-size...[vehicles] were sold, up from 119,800 in 1992. An

AutoPacific survey of 25,900 new car buyers...[in October 1997] found that close to half of them want larger vehicles....The highest percentage of buyers (56 percent) in the AutoPacific survey who said they wanted bigger vehicles were buyers younger than 30....Big sport-utility vehicles, with profit margins of around $10,000 per vehicle, are fueling record profits for Big Three automakers, analysts say." (p1-2 secE)

Haglund, Rick. "Business: From Vehicles to Burgers, To Homes and Furniture, Americans Are Living Large." Ann Arbor News 16 Nov 1997. p1-2 secE.

VENEREAL DISEASES

see SEXUALLY TRANSMITTED DISEASES

VENEZUELA--ECONOMIC CONDITIONS

"Food consumption in Venezuela...dropped another seven percent in 1997, [according to] an announcement made by CAVIDEA (Venezuelan Chamber of Food Industry)....In 1996, 73 percent of Venezuelans fell into poverty; this figure grew to 81 percent in 1997....Venezuelans today have one-third the capacity to buy food as they did in 1968. More than 48 percent of Venezuelans fall into the category of 'extreme poverty' meaning that they do not earn enough even to cover the costs of the basic food items deemed indispensable by the World Health Organization." (p3)

Rodriguez, Lisa. "In Venezuela Everything Is Not 'Chevere.'" NewsNotes v22 n6 Nov-Dec 1997. p3-4. (ISSN1064-1556).

VENTURA COUNTY (CALIF.)--POPULATION (v26)

VENTURA COUNTY (CALIF.)--SOCIAL CONDITIONS (v26)

VENTURE CAPITAL--UNITED STATES

In the U.S., "the term 'angel' was coined on Broadway to flatter wealthy people who invested in theatrical productions. These days it extends to private investors in businesses that have outgrown credit cards and loans from friends and family as a source of new capital but are still too small to attract professional venture capital. The U.S. Small Business Administration estimates that 250,000 angels are active in the country, funneling capital into 30,000 small companies a year, for a total investment of $20 billion. That's twice what the professional venture-capital industry invested in its record year of 1996. The informal angel market plugs a gap caused by the very success of professionals. The total amount of money managed by venture-capital funds has grown dramatically, from $2.3 billion in 1980 to over $43 billion today. Yet it takes as much time to properly research a small investment as it does a larger one. As a result, the average investment of a venture fund has grown from $2.3 million per company in 1987 to $6.6 million last year...." (p44)

Sherrid, Pamela. "Business & Technology: Angels of Capitalism." U.S. News & World Report v123 n14 13 Oct 1997. p43-45. article-level access: <http://www.usnews.com/usnews/issue/971013/13ANGE.HTM> (ISSN0041-5537).

VETERANS--HEALTH ASPECTS--UNITED STATES

"As of April 1, 1996, out of the hundreds of thousands of atomic veterans there have been a total of 18,515 radiation claim cases [in the U.S.], with service-connection granted in 1,886 cases. According to VA [Veterans Administration] statistics current as of December 1, 1995, only 463 involve the granting of presumptive service-connection. Thus, if we were to exclude the 463 veterans who were granted presumptive service-connection, atomic veterans had an incredibly low claims approval rate of less than 8 percent." (pS7828)

Wellstone, Paul D. (Sen.-Minn.). "Departments of Veterans Affairs and Housing and Urban Development...Appropriations Act, 1998." Congressional Record. Daily ed. v143 n104 22 Jul 1997. pS7824-7857. section/page-level access: <http://thomas.loc.gov/cgi-bin/query/R?r105:FLD001:S07828:> (ISSN0363-7239). (X1.1A.105/1).

VETERANS--MEDICAL CARE--UNITED STATES (v26)

VETERANS--MENTAL HEALTH--UNITED STATES (v26)

Data were collected as part of a national study to determine service patterns in U.S. Veterans Administration mental health clinics between October 15 and October 26, 1990. "After age standardization, 3.95 percent of mental health outpatients in this sample were women....Of the total sample of 70,979 outpatients, 57,304 patients (80.7 percent) had a primary psychiatric diagnosis, and 13,675 patients (19.3 percent) had a primary substance abuse diagnosis. Women made up 4.5 percent of those with a primary psychiatric diagnosis and 1.7 percent of those with a primary substance abuse diagnosis." (p1410) "Altogether, 70.3 percent of those with a substance-related diagnosis received specialized outpatient substance abuse services. However, only 16.3 percent of the women with a substance-related diagnosis received such care, compared with 71.2 percent of the men." (p1411)

Hoff, Rani A./Rosenheck, Robert A. "Utilization of Mental Health Services by Women in a Male-Dominated Environment: The VA Experience." Psychiatric Services v48 n11 Nov 1997. p1408-1414. (ISSN1075-2730).

VETERANS--NURSING HOME CARE--UNITED STATES (v26)

VETERANS--UNITED STATES (v26)

VICTIMS OF ABUSE

see ABUSED CHILDREN

VICTIMS OF CRIMES

see also ABORTION SERVICES--CRIMES AGAINST; ABUSED AGED; ABUSED CHILDREN; ABUSED WOMEN; ABUSED WOMEN PRISONERS; JOURNALISTS--CRIMES AGAINST; REPARATION; TEENAGE MOTHERS--CRIMES AGAINST; VICTIMS OF FAMILY VIOLENCE; YOUTH--CRIMES AGAINST

VICTIMS OF CRIMES--UNITED STATES (v26)

From the time of the O.J. Simpson "murders to the February 1997 civil verdict, there was a 66 percent rise in wrongful death appeals, according to the [U.S.] National Victim Center in Arlington, Virginia....Five months into Simpson's criminal trial, the National Institute of Justice published a survey of prosecutors in which 91 percent of the respondents cited domestic violence as a 'workload problem.'" (p34)

Canlen, Brae. "I'm O.J.--You're O.J.: How the O.J. Simpson Case Has Affected the Legal System." California Lawyer v17 n10 Oct 1997. p28-35,77. (ISSN0279-4063).

VICTIMS OF DROWNING

see DROWNING VICTIMS

VICTIMS OF FAMILY VIOLENCE--UNITED STATES (v26)

VICTIMS OF FAMINE--KOREA (NORTH)

"World Vision, the evangelical international relief agency, says a survey it has taken along the North Korea-China border suggests that somewhere between 500,000 and 1 million Koreans have died as a result of the devastating combined impact of floods, drought and famine....The survey, taken in the northern region of the country, reported that an average of 15 percent of the people have died in certain villages." (p867)

"News: Toll from Famine Grows in North Korea." Christian Century v114 n27 8 Oct 1997. p867. (ISSN0009-5281).

VICTIMS OF SEX CRIMES

see SEXUAL ABUSE VICTIMS

VIDEO RENTAL SERVICES--NORTH AMERICA (v26)

VIDEO TAPE INDUSTRY--EUROPE (v26)

VIDEO TAPE RECORDERS--SWEDEN (v26)

VIETNAM--ECONOMIC CONDITIONS (v26)

VIETNAM--SOCIAL CONDITIONS (v26)

VIETNAMESE REFUGEES

see REFUGEES, VIETNAMESE

VIOLENCE

see also CONJUGAL VIOLENCE; FAMILY VIOLENCE;

PRISON VIOLENCE; SCHOOL VIOLENCE

VIOLENCE--ALBANIA

In Albania, "roughly 1 million firearms are said to be in circulation in a Balkan nation of only 3.2 million. Official reports state some 1,600 people have died since January, but...[Arden Rakipi, a lawyer and former judge who is chairman of the nonprofit Albanian Foundation for Reconciliation of Disputes,] says the number may be closer to 5,000....Rakipi says he and his team of lawyers, sociologists, and psychologists are working to reconcile an estimated 200 to 500 new blood feuds spawned in the past three months....[Ndrek Pjetri, who travels to reconcile feuding families,] says he has prevented 288 murders in Albania since 1991, plus another 20 abroad." (p8)

Jordan, Michael J. "International: Feud Culture: In Albania, A Return to 'Eye for Eye'." The Christian Science Monitor v89 n177 7 Aug 1997. p1,8. The Christian Science Monitor search engine: <http://www.csmonitor.com/plweb-cgi/iops1.pl> To retrieve this article, enter the following search: ED=19970807 AND eye. In the "retrieved list," click the title that matches this record. (ISSN0882-7729).

VIOLENCE--AUSTRALIA--WOMEN (v26)

VIOLENCE--COLOMBIA (v26)

VIOLENCE--ISRAEL

"According to B'Tselem, the Israeli human rights group, 144 Palestinian civilians have been killed by Israeli security forces since the Cairo Agreement was signed in 1994; 19 Palestinian police officers have also been killed by Israeli forces. During the same time period, 104 Israeli civilians have been killed by Palestinians, with another 60 Israeli soldiers and police being killed." (p4)

"Action Alert: Remember All the Victims of Violence." EXTRA! Update Oct 1997. p4.

VIOLENCE--ISRAEL--MORTALITY

Figures compiled by B'Tselem, a non-governmental Israeli human rights group, say that "from the beginning of the Intifada (Palestinian uprising) in December 1987 through April 1997, the total number of Israeli civilians killed in Israel and the Occupied Territories was 234. Over the same time and space, Palestinian civilians killed by Israelis (security forces as well as civilians) totaled 1468--including 200 after the Oslo 'Peace Agreement.' Of those, 69 were children under the age of 13....Human Rights Watch (HRW) provides an in-depth assessment [for the Israel-Lebanon border area] in its May 1996 report, 'Civilian Pawns.' During Israel's July 1993 attack in Lebanon, two civilians in northern Israel were killed as a result of across-the-border shelling by the Islamic militant group, Hizballah. In the same period, however, the invading Israeli Defense Forces (IDF) and its South Lebanese Army (SLA) killed 118 Lebanese and refugee Palestinian civilians there. The respective numbers of civilians wounded were 24 to about 500. During Israel's April 1996 assault, the approximately 150 civilian deaths were all on the Lebanese-Palestinian side, including 102 people killed when the IDF shelled the UN refugee compound in Qana." (p4)

Gilbert, David. "TF Reports: Middle East: Facts of Death." Toward Freedom v46 n5 Sep-Oct 1997. p4,15. (ISSN0048-9898).

VIOLENCE--LATIN AMERICA (v26)

VIOLENCE--MORTALITY (v26)

VIOLENCE--UNITED STATES

According to a hospital study by the U.S. Dept. of Justice on cases of non-fatal injuries from violence or suspected violence, "among injuries for which the place of occurrence was reported, almost half (48 percent) were sustained in someone's home. Twenty-nine percent were in or near a store, an office or a factory. Bruises and contusions accounted for just over one-third of the injuries, and cuts, stab wounds or internal injuries comprised 31 percent. Fractures, sprains, dislocations, dental injuries or other muscular/skeletal injuries made up 17 percent. Head injuries accounted for 4 percent. Gunshot injuries were 5 percent."

U.S. Dept. of Justice. "1.4 Million People Treated in Hospital Emergency Rooms for Violence-Related Injuries." Press Release 24 Aug 1997. document-level access: <http://www.ojp.usdoj.gov/pub/bjs/press/vrithed.pr>

In the U.S., "hospital emergency departments treated approximately 1.4 million people for non-fatal injuries from confirmed or suspected violence during 1994, the Justice Department announced....Of these injuries, 1.3 million were confirmed to have been caused by violent attacks. An additional 82,000 people were injured in incidents of suspected violence. The Department's Bureau of Justice Statistics (BJS) said 94 percent had been injured during assaults, 5 percent had been injured during rapes or sexual assaults and 2 percent during robberies. Sixty percent were males. Almost half of the victims were injured by someone they knew, and 23 percent were injured by strangers. In almost 30 percent of the incidents, the relationship between the person inflicting the injury and the patient was not recorded."

U.S. Dept. of Justice. "1.4 Million People Treated in Hospital Emergency Rooms for Violence-Related Injuries." Press Release 24 Aug 1997. document-level access: <http://www.ojp.usdoj.gov/pub/bjs/press/vrithed.pr>

VIOLENCE--UNITED STATES--YOUTH

In the U.S., "recent studies indicate that 80 percent to 90 percent of children living in urban settings are direct victims of or witnesses to significant acts of violence in their neighborhoods, schools, or communities (Fitzpatrick & Boldizar, 1993; Jenkins & Bell, 1997; Osofsky, Wewers, Hamn, & Fick, 1993; Richters & Martinez, 1993). Fatal violence from handguns alone has claimed the lives of more American children and youths over the past decade and a half than the total number of American soldiers killed in the Vietnam War (Metzenbaum, 1994). Especially profoundly affected are African American youths, who have a fourfold greater risk of being murdered than white children (Snyder & Sickmund, 1995)." (p495) "Between 1984 and 1993 the number of handgun murders against children and youths rose by 500 percent (Snyder & Sickmund, 1995) before slightly decreasing in 1994 and 1995." (p496)

Guterman, Neil B./Cameron, Mark. "Assessing the Impact of Community Violence on Children and Youths." Social Work v42 n5 Sep 1997. p495-505. (ISSN0037-8046).

VIOLENCE IN HOSPITALS--UNITED STATES (v26)

VIOLENCE IN MASS MEDIA--UNITED STATES

In the U.S., "since 1993, the homicide rate nationwide dropped by 20 percent. Yet since 1993, coverage of murders on the ABC, CBS, and NBC evening news increased by 721 percent. In 1993 the number of Americans ranking crime as the No. 1 problem increased six-fold....Sixty-five percent of Americans report that most of what they know about violent crime they get from the media, compared to 21 percent whose primary source of information is personal experience. So, while 19 percent of those arrested in 1994 for violent crime were juveniles, national polls show Americans believe that juveniles commit 43 percent of all violent crime....The majority of times teenagers are depicted on the evening news, it is in connection with some form of violence, even though fewer than one half of 1 percent of America's juveniles were arrested for a violent crime in 1996....Attorney General Janet Reno reported that violent juvenile crime had dropped a combined 11.9 percent over the past two years...." (p19)

Schiraldi, Vincent. "Opinion/Essays: Hyping Juvenile Crime--

A Media Staple." The Christian Science Monitor v89 n240 6 Nov 1997. p19. The Christian Science Monitor search engine: <http://www.csmonitor.com/plweb-cgi/iops1.pl> To retrieve this article, enter the following search: ED=19971106 AND staple. In the "retrieved list," click the title that matches this record. (ISSN0882-7729).

VIOLENCE IN PRISON
see PRISON VIOLENCE

VIOLENCE IN SCHOOLS
see SCHOOL VIOLENCE

VIOLENCE IN TELEVISION--UNITED STATES (v26)

VIOLENCE IN THE WORKPLACE--UNITED STATES

"Statistics show that one of every four American workers will be attacked, threatened, or harassed at work in his or her lifetime. In an average week, 20,000 workers are assaulted on the job--and 18 are murdered. In fact, homicide is the leading cause of death on the job for women and the second-leading cause of job-related death for all workers." (p22)

O'Neill, Colleen M. "Shoptalk: Violence in the Workplace." America@Work v2 n5 May-Jun 1997. p22. (ISSN1091-594X).

Homicides in the workplace declined last year in the U.S., "falling 15.5% in two years to 912 incidents....Workplace suicides dropped to under 200 for the first time in a decade. Robbery and other crimes accounted for 80% of the workplace fatalities....But the next highest source of death, 8%, resulted from conflicts among coworkers or former coworkers. And 6% of the perpetrators were customers or clients." (unpaginated)

"Workplace Deaths at Five Year Low According to a Bureau of Labor Statistics (BLS) Study." Security Letter v27 n16 15 Sep 1997. (ISSN0363-4922).

VIOLENT CRIMES--CANADA (v26)

VIOLENT CRIMES--CANADA--YOUTH (v26)

VIOLENT CRIMES--EL SALVADOR (v26)

VIOLENT CRIMES--GREAT BRITAIN (v26)

VIOLENT CRIMES--MICHIGAN (v26)

VIOLENT CRIMES--MICHIGAN--DETROIT (v26)

VIOLENT CRIMES--NORTHERN IRELAND (v26)

VIOLENT CRIMES--OHIO--COLUMBUS (v26)

VIOLENT CRIMES--UNITED STATES (v26)

According to U.S. "Bureau of Justice statistics, violent criminals--those who commit murder, rape, assault, or armed robbery--serve only an average of 48 percent of their sentences, and one out of every three offenders admitted to State prisons were either on probation or parole for a previous offense at the time. According to the committee report accompanying this bill, on any given day there are three convicted offenders on probation or parole for every one convicted felon in prison." (pH5864)

Levin, Sander M. (Rep.-Mich.). "Expressing Sense of Congress that States Should Work More...To Attack Problem of Repeat Criminals." Congressional Record. Daily ed. v143 n108 28 Jul 1997. pH5860-5864. section/page-level access: <http://thomas.loc.gov/cgi-bin/query/R?r105:FLD001:H05864:> (ISSN0363-7239). (X1.1A.105/1).

"The nation's violent crime rate fell 10 percent last year and was 16 percent lower than in 1993, the [U.S. Justice] Department's Bureau of Justice Statistics (BJS) announced....There were an estimated 2.7 million completed violent crimes in 1996 (a rate of 12.4 per 1,000 U.S. residents 12 years old and older), compared to 3 million such crimes in 1995 (a rate of 13.8 per 1,000 residents 12 and older)....Forty-eight percent of all victims of violence in 1996 knew the offender....About 43 percent of the violent crimes and 35 percent of the property crimes were reported to law enforcement agencies during 1996."

U.S. Dept. of Justice. Bureau of Justice Statistics. "Violent Victimizations Fell 10 Percent Last Year: Property Crimes Declined 8 Percent." Press Release 15 Nov 1997. document-level access: <http://www.ojp.usdoj.gov/pub/bjs/press/cv96.pr>

In the U.S., "violent crimes fell 3% last year in absolute terms, led by a 9% decline in murders, according to the FBI's annual release....The murder rate for '96 was 7.4 offenses per 100K [thousand] inhabitants, down 17% from four years earlier....Weapons used in the commission of violent crime included firearms (29%). But hands and feet accounted for even more mayhem (30%)." (unpaginated)

"Serious Crime in the US Declines for the Fifth Consecutive Year." Security Letter v27 n18 16 Oct 1997. (ISSN0363-4922).

In the U.S., "on an average day, more than 65 people die from homicide, another 18,000 are violently victimized and more than 6,000 of these victims suffer physical injuries (Dobrin, Wiersema, Loftin, & McDowal, 1996)....The biggest increase in violent crime arrests has been among persons aged 30 to 49, up 245% since 1980." (p183)

Arluke, Arnold/Lockwood, Randall. "Guest Editors' Introduction: Understanding Cruelty to Animals." Society & Animals v5 n3 1997. p183-193. (ISSN1063-1119).

VIOLENT CRIMES--UNITED STATES--YOUTH (v26)

"According to the Annie E. Casey Foundation, young people [in the U.S.] are committing violent crimes at a rate similar to 10 years ago--however, the violence has intensified and is causing more deaths. In fact, between 1991 and 1995, the number of juveniles arrested for violent crimes increased by 12 percent, yet violent crime arrests for all ages increased by 2.5 percent. And, between 1985 and 1994, the number of juveniles arrested for weapon violations, specifically related to increases in firearm usage in violent crimes, rose by 113 percent. Equally disturbing is the fact while African-Americans represent 12 percent of the United States' population, African-American youth are nearly 28 percent of all juvenile arrests." (pE1448)

Stokes, Louis (Rep.-Ohio). "Juvenile Crime Control and Delinquency Prevention Act of 1997." Congressional Record. Daily ed. v143 n102 17 Jul 1997. pE1448-1449. section/page-level access: <http://thomas.loc.gov/cgi-bin/query/R?r105:FLD001:E01448:> (ISSN0363-7239). (X1.1A.105/1).

"Offenders under the age of 18 commit more than one out of every five violent crimes in America; that is one-fifth of all murders, rapes, robberies, and assaults. In 1995, they committed nearly 2 million crimes; 18-year-olds committed more murders than any other age group and 17-year-olds, more rapes. Juveniles 15 and younger were responsible for 64 percent of the violent offenses handled by the juvenile courts in 1994....If these trends continue, juvenile arrests for violent crimes will more than double by the year 2010. The FBI predicts juveniles arrested for murder will increase 145 percent, forcible rape arrests will increase 66 percent, and aggravated assault arrests by 129 percent. Why? In the remaining years of this decade and throughout the next, America will experience a 31-percent increase in teenagers as the children of baby boomers come of age." (pH2324)

McCollum, Bill (Rep.-Fla.). "Providing for Consideration of H.R. 3, Juvenile Crime Control Act of 1997." Congressional Record. Daily ed. v143 n58 7 May 1997. pH2313-2333. section/page-level access: <http://thomas.loc.gov/cgi-bin/query/R?r105:FLD001:H02323:> (ISSN0363-7239). (X1.1A.105/1).

In the U.S., "between 1965 and 1992, the number of 12-year-olds arrested for violent crime rose 211 percent; the number of 13- and 14-year-olds rose 301 percent; and the number of 15-year-olds arrested for violent crime rose 297 percent....Older teenagers, ages 17, 18, and 19, are the most violent in America. More murder and robbery are committed by 18-year-old males than any other group." (pH2392)

Buyer, Stephen E. (Rep.-Ind.). "Juvenile Crime Control Act of 1997." Congressional Record. Daily ed. v143 n59 8 May 1997. pH2356-2398. section/page-level access: <http://thomas.loc.gov/cgi-bin/query/R?r105:FLD001:H02392:> (ISSN0363-7239). (X1.1A.105/1).

In the U.S., "only 10 percent of violent juvenile offenders that commit murder and rape and robbery and assault receive any kind of jail time at all. Many juveniles receive no punishment at all. Almost 40 percent of violent juvenile offenders who come into contact with the justice system have their cases dismissed....In many cases, by the time the courts finally lock up an older teenager on a violent crime charge, that offender has a long list of violations with arrests starting way back in the early years. According to the Justice Department numbers, 43 percent of juveniles in State institutions had more than 5 prior arrests and 20 percent had been arrested more than 10 times. Approximately 80 percent of those offenders had previously been on probation." (pH2314)

Solomon, Gerald B. H. (Rep.-N.Y.). "Providing for Consideration of H.R. 3, Juvenile Crime Control Act of 1997." Congressional Record. Daily ed. v143 n58 7 May 1997. pH2313-2333. section/page-level access: <http://thomas.loc.gov/cgi-bin/query/R?r105:FLD001:H02314:> (ISSN0363-7239). (X1.1A.105/1).

In the U.S., from 1983 to 1992, "juvenile arrests for violent crimes increased 57 percent. Specifically, juvenile arrests for aggravated assaults increased 95 percent while juvenile arrests for murder rose 128 percent. To put it in more concrete terms, over 2 million juveniles are arrested each year, many for violent crimes. In 1995 alone, teenagers committed almost 4,000 murders." (pS5662)

Sessions, Jeff (Sen.-Ala.). "Fighting Juvenile Crime." Congressional Record. Daily ed. v143 n83 16 Jun 1997. pS5662-5664. section/page-level access: <http://thomas.loc.gov/cgi-bin/query/R?r105:FLD001:S05662:> (ISSN0363-7239). (X1.1A.105/1).

In the U.S., "juveniles were involved in 32 percent of all robbery arrests, 23 percent of weapon arrests, and 15 percent of murder and aggravated assault arrests in 1995. Juveniles under age 15 were responsible for 30 percent of juvenile violent crime arrests in 1995, but they accounted for more than one-half (55 percent) of the decline in these arrests between 1994 and 1995. Juvenile murder arrests declined 14 percent between 1994 and 1995....Arrests of juveniles accounted for 14 percent of all violent crimes cleared by arrest in 1995--9 percent of murders, 15 percent of forcible rapes, 20 percent of robberies, and 13 percent of aggravated assaults cleared by arrest." (p3)

Briscoe, Judy. "Breaking the Cycle of Violence: A Rational Approach to At-Risk Youth." Federal Probation v61 n3 Sep 1997. p3-13. (ISSN0014-9128).

In the U.S., "violent juvenile crime dropped 9 percent this year, and...all forms of juvenile arrest are declining....82 percent of all counties in the US experienced no juvenile murders in 1994....Violent crimes by kids--including murder--dropped 12 percent since 1994....While kids accounted for about 19 percent of all violent crime arrests in 1994 (down from 23 percent in 1973), people responding to national polls believe they're responsible for almost half." (p15)

Ziedenberg, Jason. "MediaReports: Justice: Cashing In on Crime." Toward Freedom v46 n7 Dec 1997-Jan 1998. p15. (ISSN0048-9898).

VISION DISORDERS

"Currently, close to 150 million people worldwide suffer from significant visual disability, 38 million of whom are blind. WHO experts say that more than two thirds of this blindness and visual disability could be avoided through adequate and timely prevention or treatment. At present, approximately 7 million people become blind each year. Over 70 per cent of these people receive treatment and their vision is restored. Thus, the number of blind persons worldwide is currently increasing by up to 2 million per year. Eighty per cent of these new cases are related to aging....Major age-related avoidable causes of blindness and visual disability include cataract (which accounts for around 16 million blind people), glaucoma (5.2 million), and diabetic retinopathy (around 2 million)." (p81)

"Healthwatch: 300 Million Will Have Impaired Vision in 2020." UN Chronicle v34 n2 1997. p81. (ISSN0251-7329).

VISION DISORDERS IN CHILDREN--UNITED STATES

"Current estimated figures for the United States show that more than 4,000 premature babies weighing 3.3 pounds or less develop eye damage or vision loss from ROP [retinopathy of prematurity] each year. If cryotherapy were not available, 750 of the babies with the severe form of the disease would become legally blind each year, according to researchers' predictions. With widespread use of cryotherapy, a smaller number of babies, 400, become blind from the disease annually, researchers estimate."

U.S. National Eye Institute. "Study Confirms Value of Treatment to Prevent Blindness in Premature Babies." Press Release 14 Apr 1996. document-level access: <http://www.nei.nih.gov/news/4-15%20press%20release.htm>

VITAMIN A DEFICIENCY IN CHILDREN--DEVELOPING COUNTRIES (v26)

VOCATIONAL EDUCATION--EUROPE

In the European Union, "unemployment of 20 to 29-year-olds with additional vocational education and training is less than half that of those with only basic education--11.5% compared with 23.5%....An analysis of 20 to 29-year-olds who were employed in 1994 showed that 5.2% of those with only compulsory education lost their jobs in 1995, whereas only 3.1% of those with additional vocational education did. Almost one-third (29%) of young Europeans between 15 and 19 years of age are engaged in initial vocational training. This percentage is particularly high in Austria (55%), Belgium (45%) and Germany (40%). In Austria and Sweden nearly all trainees in initial vocational education are under 20. But Finland and, to a lesser degree, Denmark, Ireland and the Netherlands have a lot over 20 (over 40%) and even over 25 (10%). In the UK, participation of those 25 to 29 is over double the average--12% of all trainees. In Finland 15% are 30+. Latest data show that some 60% of EU enterprises with 10 or more employees offer some form of continuing vocational training (CVT). Highest proportions are in Denmark (86.8%), Germany (85.3%), the UK (81.6%) and Ireland (76.8%); lowest recorded are in Portugal (13.1%). Larger firms are more likely to offer CVT--98% of those with 1,000 or more employees compared to 52% of those with 10-49 employees."

Eurostat. "Vocational Training Key to Finding & Keeping a Job." Press Release 6 Oct 1997. document-level access: <http://europa.eu.int/en/comm/eurostat/compres/en/6897/6306897a.htm>

VOCATIONAL EDUCATION--NEW YORK (STATE) (v26)

VOCATIONAL REHABILITATION--NEW HAMPSHIRE

The New Hampshire vocational rehabilitation program "rehabilitated 1,150 people in 1993, 1,217 in 1994, 1,275 in 1995, and 1,401 in 1996; this represents an incease of 27 percent in the number of rehabilitations since 1992. The number of severely disabled individuals placed has increased by 40 percent." (p17)

Langton, Maryanne S. "Streamlining in Vermont and New Hampshire." American Rehabilitation v23 n2 Sum 1997.

p12-17. (ISSN0362-4048).

VOCATIONAL REHABILITATION--NEW YORK (STATE)

In New York state, total vocational rehabilitation "placements have increased 77.6 percent since 1991. In this same period, competitive placements have increased 91.8 percent and supported employment placements have increased 324.5 percent, while sheltered employment placements have decreased 22.4 percent....The total first year earnings of the 16,041 people with disabilities who were successfully placed in state fiscal year (SFY) 1996 was $171 million. Using the approximately 9,000 per year as a base, more than $75 million of this total can be attributed to reform efforts in SFY 1996....In federal fiscal year (FFY) 1990, only 56 percent of all applicants were found to be eligible for VESID [Vocational and Educational Services for Individuals with Disabilities] services, while 69.8 percent of all applicants were found to be eligible for services in FFY 1996. In FFY 1996, an average of 4,108 individuals were referred to VESID each month, a 34 percent increase in monthly referrals since FFY 1990. The number of people applying for services has grown by 53 percent, from 2,610 per month in FFY 1990 to 3,994 per month in FFY 1996." (p30-31)

Gloeckler, Lawrence C. "Redesigning the State Rehabilitation Program in New York State." American Rehabilitation v23 n2 Sum 1997. p27-32. (ISSN0362-4048).

VOCATIONAL REHABILITATION--OREGON

The Oregon Vocational Rehabilitation Division's "job placements have increased 17 percent (from 2,145 to 2,509) during 1995-96....Results reported for January-March 1997 indicate a client satisfaction rate of 81.1 percent; employer satisfaction, 77 percent; staff satisfaction, 79.5 percent; average wage at closure, $7.69 per hour (this is 79 percent of the average job order registered with the Employment Department); and 66 percent of our successfully closed clients are employed 18 months following closure." (p22)

Ruttledge, Lynnae M. "Organizational Transformation: A Bold Journey, Not a Guided Tour." American Rehabilitation v23 n2 Sum 1997. p18-22. (ISSN0362-4048).

VOCATIONAL REHABILITATION--VERMONT

In 1993, the Vermont vocational rehabilitation program "had achieved 546 rehabilitations. That changed to 581 rehabilitations in the second year and 664 in the third year. In FY 1996, they rehabilitated 683 people....The state agency reports that they have doubled the annual earnings of rehabilitated consumers. In 1995, they conducted a 5-year survey on duration of employment, and they found that 78 percent of consumers remained on the job 5 years after placement." (p15)

Langton, Maryanne S. "Streamlining in Vermont and New Hampshire." American Rehabilitation v23 n2 Sum 1997. p12-17. (ISSN0362-4048).

VOLUNTARISM--CANADA (v26)

VOLUNTARISM--JAPAN

"A spokeswoman for Japan's National Welfare Council says that while the exact figure of Japanese volunteers is unavailable, the number of volunteers they surveyed in 1995 increased from 4.1 million in 1991 to 5.3 million....In a survey conducted by the council, the percentage of Japanese who wanted to volunteer doubled from 40 percent in 1994, to more than 80 percent in 1995. The number of nongovernmental organizations has also grown from 186 in 1991 to 351 in 1995, says the Japanese NGO Center for International Cooperation in Tokyo." (p8)

Nomura, Takehiko. "International: Culture Shift: Good Works Get a Boost in Japan." The Christian Science Monitor v89 n208 22 Sep 1997. p1,8. The Christian Science Monitor search engine: <http://www.csmonitor.com/plweb-cgi/iops1.pl> To retrieve this article, enter the following search: ED=19970922 AND japan. In the "retrieved list," click the title that matches this record. (ISSN0882-7729).

VOLUNTARISM--MICHIGAN

"About 39,000 of the 180,000 4-H members across the state are in southeastern Michigan. Of the 30,000 teenagers and adults who volunteer their time to help in 4-H programs, 3,000 are in Wayne, Oakland, Macomb and Washtenaw counties. Michigan 4-H Clubs are run through the county offices of the Michigan State University Extension Service, which has a budget of $46.7 million for all its programs." (p1 secC)

Lopez, Manny. "Metro: News Special: Education: 4-H Club Hoping to Boost Image, Membership." Detroit News 1 Oct 1997. p1-2 secC.

VOLUNTARISM--MICHIGAN--DETROIT

"Focus:HOPE was started in the wake of Detroit's devastating 1967 riot in which 43 people were killed. The organization now trains hundreds of African-American Detroiters each year to be skilled machinists and automotive engineers. It also feeds more than 50,000 people each month and operates a model child care center for its students and 850 employees." (p1 secD)

Daugherty, Jane. "The Metro: Fr. Cunningham: 'He Was One of the Saints.'" Detroit News 30 May 1997. p1-2 secD.

VOLUNTARISM--UNITED STATES (v26)

VOLUNTARISM--UNITED STATES--COLLEGE STUDENTS (v26)

VOLUNTARISM--UNITED STATES--HIGH SCHOOL STUDENTS

"A 1997 statistical analysis from the U.S. Department of Education reports that 86 percent of all students in sixth through 12th grades attend schools that encourage community service, either through requiring participation or by arranging or offering community service. And 49 percent of these students say they have participated in community service at some time during the 1995-96 school year....Some $3 million in scholarship awards has been set aside, as part of the federally funded National Service Scholars Program, for students recognized by their home districts for performing community service." (p27-28)

Black, Susan. "Research: Helping Hands." American School Board Journal v184 n7 Jul 1997. p27-29. (ISSN0003-0953).

"The second National Education Longitudinal Study of 1988...follow-up survey, administered to [U.S.] high school students (and dropouts) in 1992, provides estimates of secondary school students' participation in service. About 44 percent of twelfth graders had done some type of unpaid service (school or community-based) during the previous two years and, of these volunteers, nearly 18 percent had done the work because a school class required it. Although NELS data do not provide a direct estimate of participation rates in service learning (classroom-based programs that link student activity with academic work), these numbers indicate that only about 8 percent of students worked in a school-based service program in the last two years of secondary school. Among all high school seniors, 28 percent were currently doing some type of community service, but only 11 percent did this work at least once a week." (p8)

Alt, Martha Naomi. "Service Learning: How Effective an Educational Tool Is Student Community Service?" NASSP Bulletin v81 n591 Oct 1997. p8-16. (ISSN0192-6365).

VOLUNTARISM--UNITED STATES--PUBLIC SCHOOLS

A 1997 Phi Delta Kappa/Gallup poll "showed that 69 percent of the [American] public would be willing to work as an unpaid volunteer in a community public school. This represented a significant increase from the 59 percent who said they would be willing to volunteer in 1992. More than three out of four parents (78 percent) who have children in the public schools said they would be willing to volunteer (up from 72 percent in 1992)." (p7)

"Fact and Fiction." Reading Today v15 n3 Dec 1997-Jan 1998.

p7. (ISSN0737-4208).

VOTING--AFRO-AMERICAN PRISONERS (v26)

VOTING--AUSTRIA

In Austria's parliamentary elections, "more than half (52 per cent) of the...[voters for the green party] in 1995 were between 18 and 29 years old. Another 34 per cent were aged 30-44, whereas only 3 per cent were 60 or older. Concerning the active electorate as a whole (i.e. those who actually went to vote), the share of the greens was ten per cent in the youngest age group (18-29), only half that amount in the next (30-44) and almost negligible beyond that age. In 1996, these figures had increased to 12 per cent (18-29), 8 per cent (30-44) and 5 per cent (45-59) respectively....In 1995, 58 per cent of the green voters had either university education or at least a 'Matura' (a diploma from an upper-track secondary school); only five per cent just had compulsory education. According to a telephone poll, the share of the greens among those with either 'Matura' or university education was about 15 per cent in the age group 18-45, and about seven per cent above that age (mostly women; only one per cent of the men over 45 with the higher educational standard voted Green). Among voters without this formal education, the share of the Greens dropped to about five per cent in the younger and to 1.5 per cent in the older age group." (p191)

Lauber, Volkmar. "The Mixed Fortunes of the Austrian Greens in the Mid-1990s." Environmental Politics v6 n1 Spr 1997. p185-192. (ISSN0964-4016).

In Austria's parliamentary elections, the Green party "in 1995 achieved their highest share among those who, after the age of 18, were still in education or training. Among the voters of this group, they scored...19 per cent, compared to 25 per cent for the Social Democrats, 22 per cent for the Conservatives, 15 per cent for the Freedom Party and 18 per cent for the Liberal Forum. They also made a respectable showing in the liberal professions, among civil servants and white collar workers (about seven per cent)." (p191)

Lauber, Volkmar. "The Mixed Fortunes of the Austrian Greens in the Mid-1990s." Environmental Politics v6 n1 Spr 1997. p185-192. (ISSN0964-4016).

VOTING--BANGLADESH (v26)

VOTING--CALIFORNIA

"In 1994, California voters passed Proposition 187, which banned all state spending on illegal immigrants. The measure proved popular, winning 59% support at the polls. But whereas whites gave it 64% backing, 69% of Hispanics disapproved." (p46)

White, John Kenneth/D'Antonio, William. "The Catholic Vote in Election '96." Public Perspective v8 n4 Jun-Jul 1997. p45-48. (ISSN1050-5067).

VOTING--CALIFORNIA--AGED (v26)

VOTING--CALIFORNIA--LOS ANGELES

African-American turnout in the April 1997 Los Angeles mayoral "election amounted to 13 percent of all voters; that is reflective of the percentage of African-Americans in the city's population. Latinos comprise nearly 40 percent of L.A.'s residents but have historically voted in much smaller numbers--about eight percent to 10 percent of the voters in a typical municipal election. This year, however, things changed. Latinos accounted for 15 percent of the vote in the April mayoral race--an historic high....Anglos constitute about 40 percent of the population, but this past April they were 65 percent of the electorate. Blacks and Latinos make up over a majority of the city's residents, but they accounted for less than a third of the electorate in April." (p30-31)

Jeffe, Sherry Bebitch. "Tug of War." California Journal v28 n7 Jul 1997. p28-32. (ISSN0008-1205).

VOTING--GREAT BRITAIN--YOUTH (v26)

VOTING--HISPANIC AMERICANS

In the U.S., "about 31 percent of Hispanics 18 years and over reported they were registered to vote in the November 1994 Congressional elections, but only 20 percent reported voting. In contrast, 65 percent of whites registered and 47 percent voted; among blacks, 59 percent registered and 37 percent voted. The percentage of Hispanics who voted rises to 34 when only those eligible to vote are included in the calculation." (p42)

del Pinal, Jorge/Singer, Audrey. "Generations of Diversity: Latinos in the United States." Population Bulletin v52 n3 Oct 1997. p2-47. (ISSN0032-468X).

In the U.S., "more than one-fifth (22 percent) of all Latinos of voting age are 18 to 24, the ages least likely to vote, while 14 percent of the total population are in these ages. Furthermore, more than one-third of the Latino population are less than 18 years of age--too young to vote, while just over one-fourth of all Americans are under age 18. Only 16 percent of the Latino population are in the age group that votes the most, ages 55 and older, compared with 28 percent of the total population. Many Latinos of voting age are not naturalized citizens, which diminishes the pool of potential voters. In 1996, about 42 percent of Latinos ages 18 and over were not naturalized U.S. citizens. In contrast, only 12 percent of Hispanics under age 18 were not citizens." (p42)

del Pinal, Jorge/Singer, Audrey. "Generations of Diversity: Latinos in the United States." Population Bulletin v52 n3 Oct 1997. p2-47. (ISSN0032-468X).

"Latinos now represent 11 percent of the US population, or about 30 million, of which some 10 million are eligible to vote. Of those, 6.5 million are registered and 5.2 million vote. The number of Latino voters jumped 28 percent from 1992 to 1996--the largest four-year leap in history." (p8)

Wood, Daniel B. "Latino Voter Influence Reaching New Levels." The Christian Science Monitor v90 n10 9 Dec 1997. p1,8. The Christian Science Monitor search engine: <http://www.csmonitor.com/plweb-cgi/iops1.pl> To retrieve this article, enter the following search: ED=19971209 AND levels. In the "retrieved list," click the title that matches this record. (ISSN0882-7729).

VOTING--ISRAEL

"Only 25% of the Arab Israeli electorate in the past decade have voted for exclusively Arab parties....10% chose not to vote altogether for ideological reasons (Frisch, 1995)." (p260)

Frisch, Hillel. "Ethnicity, Territorial Integrity, And Regional Order: Palestinian Identity in Jordan and Israel." Journal of Peace Research v34 n3 Aug 1997. p257-269. (ISSN0022-3433).

VOTING--MICHIGAN

In Michigan, in the 1997 Ann Arbor "school board election, 95.6 percent of registered voters stayed home--the lowest turnout in at least 20 years....In Ypsilanti, only 140 of the district's 26,386 voters trickled into area voting precincts, 120 of them to re-elect incumbent Diane Kerr, who ran unopposed....Only 11 percent of the district's voters turned out to narrowly pass a $59.5 million bond last September. Lincoln Consolidated Schools are spread out over five different townships including, Augusta, Sumpter, Van Buren, Washtenaw, Wayne, and York, and yet only 3.5 percent of the voters turned out for the recent school election....Mike Furlong, director of business services for Lincoln schools [said]..., 'The last election, there was 1,143 who voted on a registered pool of 12,512. This time, approximately a third of the voters came out compared to a year ago." (p1 secA) "Local elections historically have much lower turnouts than national elections like the 1996 presidential election in which 57 percent of Washtenaw County's registered voters went to the polls." (p12 secA)

Rioux, Paul/Abercrombie, Shena. "Apathy a Landslide School Winner." Ann Arbor News 16 Jun 1997. p1,12 secA.

VOTING--NICARAGUA (v26)

VOTING--OREGON (v26)

VOTING--SOUTH AMERICA (v26)

VOTING--UNITED STATES (v26)

In the Federal Election Commission's second report on the implementation of the U.S. National Voter Registration Act, "the FEC's Office of Election Administration reported that, while the number of people registering to vote in the nation surged by more than 9 million from 1992 to 1996, the number of people who actually went to the polls last November declined by 5 percent. Just 49 percent of registered voters went to the polls during the last presidential election. The report covers election data from 44 states and the District of Columbia....The report found that there were nearly 143 million people registered to vote in the United States in 1996, or 72.8 percent of the voting-age population. The increase in the number of registered voters between 1992 and 1996 was 1.8 percent. The report also found that the most popular place for people to register to vote in 1995 and 1996 was at their local motor vehicle offices, with 33.1 percent of voter registration applications being filled out in DMV [Department of Motor Vehicle] offices. Post card registrations accounted for 29.7 percent of new registrants, and registrars' offices and voter registration drives accounted for 26.1 percent of those registering to vote." (p10)

"Election Administration: 'Motor Voter' Report Sent to President and Congress." Federal Election Commission Record v23 n8 Aug 1997. p10.

In the U.S., "the turnout for eligible white voters in the 1994 election was 50 percent, and 39 percent for eligible African American and Asian voters....Twenty-five percent of Latinos, 24 percent of African Americans, and 29 percent of whites ages 18 to 24 and enrolled in college reported voting in 1994. Among young adults who were not in college, voter participation dropped to 6 percent for Hispanics, 16 percent for blacks, and 18 percent for whites." (p42-43)

del Pinal, Jorge/Singer, Audrey. "Generations of Diversity: Latinos in the United States." Population Bulletin v52 n3 Oct 1997. p2-47. (ISSN0032-468X).

VOTING--UNITED STATES--CATHOLIC WOMEN

In the 1996 U.S. presidential election, Catholic women were heavily Democratic--backing President "Clinton by an extraordinary 27 percentage point margin....Working Catholic women were strong Clinton backers: 60% to just 32% for [presidential candidate Robert] Dole. But Catholic women not in the paid labor force were less Democratic, going for Clinton by 50% to 40%." (p48)

White, John Kenneth/D'Antonio, William. "The Catholic Vote in Election '96." Public Perspective v8 n4 Jun-Jul 1997. p45-48. (ISSN1050-5067).

VOTING--UNITED STATES--CATHOLICS

In the U.S. 1996 presidential election, when all Catholics are considered, President Clinton's margin over presidential candidate Robert Dole "increased to a decisive 15 percentage points. This support proved crucial in such important states as Pennsylvania, where Clinton received 53% of the Catholic vote; Illinois, 54%; and California, 54%....Clinton's support among...[the Hispanic] Catholic population rose 11% from his 1992 posting. Even staunchly pro-Republican Cubans cast aside their hatred of Communism and Fidel Castro to give Clinton 40% of their vote, support that proved crucial in Clinton's capture of Florida....Of Catholics who said taxes were most important, Dole won 73% of the vote; likewise of those who mentioned the deficit, 54% backed Dole. Interestingly, just 4% named foreign policy as an important factor in their voting decision and of this minuscule number, 48% backed Dole and 45% supported Clinton." (p46)

White, John Kenneth/D'Antonio, William. "The Catholic Vote in Election '96." Public Perspective v8 n4 Jun-Jul 1997. p45-48. (ISSN1050-5067).

In the U.S., in 1996, "fifty-five percent of all Catholics cast a Democratic ballot in the House contests while just 41% voted Republican--a big shift from the two-point Catholic GOP majority in 1994. Even white Catholics voted 51% Democratic. Still, they continued their Republican shift. In 1992, white Catholics went 14 points more Democratic than Republican in House races; in 1996 they were just six points more so...." (p46)

White, John Kenneth/D'Antonio, William. "The Catholic Vote in Election '96." Public Perspective v8 n4 Jun-Jul 1997. p45-48. (ISSN1050-5067).

In the U.S., the 1996 Voter News Service exit poll shows that President "Clinton won a majority of Catholic voters in all age categories, but he was particularly strong with ages 18-29 (57% to 30% for [presidential candidate Robert] Dole) and those 65 and older (53% to 39%). Even more striking was how well Clinton did with first time Catholic voters, whipping Dole 65% to 32%. Clinton ran well ahead of Dole among Catholics earning under $50,000 a year, and among those with less than a college degree....The data reveal a significant 'marriage gap' existed among Catholics. Among those married (64%), the race was relatively close: 48% for Clinton; 42% for Dole. But among Catholic singles (36%) it was no contest: 59% backed Clinton; just 30% voted for Dole." (p48)

White, John Kenneth/D'Antonio, William. "The Catholic Vote in Election '96." Public Perspective v8 n4 Jun-Jul 1997. p45-48. (ISSN1050-5067).

VOTING--UNITED STATES--MINORITIES (v26)

VOUCHERS, EDUCATIONAL

see EDUCATIONAL VOUCHERS

WAGE DIFFERENTIALS--SINGAPORE (v26)

WAGE DIFFERENTIALS--UNITED STATES (v26)

"In 1991, median weekly earnings for [American] men who were employed full-time were $573 (in 1996 dollars), or 35 percent higher than women's earnings ($424). By 1996, the gap closed by 2 percentage points, as men's earnings ($557) were 33 percent higher than women's ($418) median weekly earnings....In 1991, half of all male psychological therapists earned more than $703 a week (in 1996 dollars), an amount 14 percent higher than women's median earnings of $619. Today, female therapists' median earnings ($678) are 3 percent higher than male therapists' median earnings ($658). Between 1991 and 1996, male therapists saw a decline of 6 percent in their median earnings, while female therapists saw a 10 percent rise." (p31)

Miller, Berna. "Kaleidoscope: Where Women Out-Earn Men." American Demographics v19 n6 Jun 1997. p31. article-level access: <http://www.demographics.com/publications/ad/97_ad/9706_ad/ad970611.htm> (ISSN0163-4089).

WAGES (v26)

see also EQUAL PAY FOR EQUAL WORK; MINIMUM WAGE; OVERTIME

"In the early-1990s the minimum wage in the Netherlands and France stood at over 50 percent of the average wage, while in the North American countries it was roughly 35 percent of the average wage." (p4) "Since 1970, the 10 percent real wage growth of the United States contrasts with real wage growth of nearly 60 percent in the European Community; conversely, over the same period the nearly 60 percent employment increase in the United States compares with a small 10-15 percent increase in the European Community....In North America, Australia, Japan, and the United Kingdom, the relative wage of low-skilled workers fell by 10-25 percent during the 1980s...." (p6)

Haveman, Robert H. "New Democracy Forum: Equity with Employment." Boston Review v22 n3-4 Sum 1997. p3-8. (ISSN0734-2306).

WAGES--ALABAMA (v26)

WAGES--AUSTRALIA (v26)

WAGES--BRAZIL (v26)

WAGES--CALIFORNIA (v26)

WAGES--CHILDREN (v26)

WAGES--CIVIL SERVICE--MARYLAND--BALTIMORE (v26)

WAGES--CLOTHING TRADE (v26)

WAGES--EFFECT OF EDUCATION ON--CALIFORNIA

In California, "for an African American male, a college degree increases the present discounted value of lifetime earnings by $360,630; for a female, by $303,563. For a Hispanic male, a college degree increases earnings by $379,561; for a female, by $311,204." (p31)

Conrad, Cecilia A./Sharpe, Rhonda V. "The Impact of the California Civil Rights Initiative (CCRI) on...Admissions and...California Economy." Review of Black Political Economy v25 n1 Sum 1996. p13-59. (ISSN0034-6446).

WAGES--EFFECT OF EDUCATION ON--UNITED STATES

"According to the US Census Bureau, the earnings premium among male workers for completing college was 19 percent in 1980--meaning that a male worker with a college degree earned 19 percent more, on average, than a male worker without a degree. By 1993, the earnings premium increased to 57 percent. Among female workers during the same time period, the earnings premium for completing a college degree increased from 52 percent to 99 percent." (p18)

Tregarthen, Suzanne. "Opinion/Essays: Think College Is out of Reach? Think Again." The Christian Science Monitor v89 n178 8 Aug 1997. p18. The Christian Science Monitor search engine: <http://www.csmonitor.com/plweb-cgi/iops1.pl> To retrieve this article, enter the following search: ED=19970808 AND college. In the "retrieved list," click the title that matches this record. (ISSN0882-7729).

WAGES--EUROPE, EASTERN--WOMEN

"In Russia, women's wages slipped from 70 percent of men's in 1989 to 40 percent in 1995, and in most sectors women are the last hired and first fired. In Slovakia, between 1989 and 1993 women earned just over half what men did--although more women were university graduates. In Belarus, where the majority of specialists are female, women search for a job three times longer than their male counterparts....In Ukraine,...women constitute 70 percent of the unemployed, and the trend is sharply worsening." (p3)

Hunt, Swanee. "Women's Vital Voices: The Costs of Exclusion in Eastern Europe." Foreign Affairs v76 n4 Jul-Aug 1997. p2-7. (ISSN0015-7120).

WAGES--FIRE FIGHTERS--INDIANS OF NORTH AMERICA

"Firefighters from Montana's Blackfeet tribe brought home about $3 million last year and nearly $7 million in 1994, according to fire management officer Calvin Herrera....Indian firefighters who are organized under the Bureau of Indian Affairs earn more than $10,000 in a good year and also qualify for unemployment benefits over the winter. Firefighting wages range from $7.15 an hour for rookie ground-pounders to $14.85 for a smokejumper foreman. Add 50 percent an hour for overtime, and 25 percent hazard pay when on a fire...." (p3)

Matthews, Mark. "Western Roundup: Wet Summer a Bust for Firefighters." High Country News v29 n17 15 Sep 1997. p3. (ISSN0191-5657).

WAGES--FOOD INDUSTRY AND TRADE--UNITED STATES

In the U.S., "hourly earnings of food manufacturing and food store employees rose almost 3 percent in 1996, similar to 1995....Average hourly earnings of wholesaling employees rose over 2 percent, compared with 2.5 percent in 1995. The average hourly wage for employees in the foodservice sector, one of the highest contributors to U.S. job growth in 1996, advanced about 3.5 percent, compared with 2 percent in 1995. This higher rate of growth reflects brisk sales in the away-from-home market over the last decade, when sales increased an average of 5 percent per year. Wage supplements, about 20 percent of total labor costs, increased because of rising health insurance premiums and pension costs." (p15)

Elitzak, Howard/U.S. Dept. of Agriculture. Economic Research Service. "Food & Marketing: Marketing Costs for Food Rose Slightly in 1996." Agricultural Outlook Aug 1997. p15-16.

WAGES--GERMANY

In Germany, "the average gross monthly earnings in 1995 amounted to DM [deutschmark] 4,962 in the former territory of the Federal Republic, while they totalled DM 3,537 in the new Lander. Consequently, the gross monthly earnings covered by the survey of wages and salaries were up 21.8% in the western part and 35.4% in the eastern part of Germany compared with the results of previous surveys....Net earnings were up 14.9% from DM 2,812 to DM 3230 in the western part and up 26.0% from DM 1,866 to DM 2,353 in the eastern part of the country....The group of employees with gross monthly earnings between DM 4,000 and DM 5,000 was the largest in western Germany (29.2%) in 1995. In 1990, the largest group consisted of employees earning between DM 3,000 and DM 4,000. A total of 36.5% of all full-time employees were included in the above income bracket at that time. Almost four tenths of the employees in the new Lander (37.7%) received earnings between DM 3,000 and DM 4,000 in October 1995. In 1992, nearly half of all employees in the new Lander (45.8%) earned less than DM 2,400 per month."

Germany. Federal Statistical Office. "1996 Survey of the Wage and Salary Structure in 1995: Detailed Results Showing the Situation of Earnings." Press Release 8 Oct 1997. document-level access: <http://www.statistik-bund.de/presse/englisch/pm/p7293043.htm>

WAGES--HAITI

In Haiti, "in 1995 the legal minimum wage was raised from 15 gourdes ($1) a day to 36 gourdes ($2.40) a day....If a company does pay the minimum wage, workers earn $14.40 a week, working eight hours a day, six days a week. A full-time minimum wage salary provides less than 60% of a family's basic needs. A wage of $1 a day, common in apparel plants producing for US companies, provides less than 25% of a family's basic needs. In order to satisfy the minimum needs for food, shelter and education a family in Port-au-Prince must spend at the very least 363 gourde ($24.40) per week." (p6)

"Garment Production in Haitian Export Processing Zones." Freedom (Anarchist Fortnightly) v58 n15 2 Aug 1997. p6. (ISSN0016-0504).

WAGES--HONG KONG

According to statistics by Hong Kong's "Census and Statistics Department, average labour earnings in all major sectors of the economy, as measured by payroll per person engaged, recorded an increase of 10.1% in nominal terms in the second quarter of 1997 over a year earlier. After discounting changes in consumer prices, there was a notable increase of 4.4% in real terms. Analysed by industry sector, average payroll per person engaged in the manufacturing sector increased by 8.5% in nominal terms or 2.9% in real terms. For the wholesale, retail and import/

export trades, restaurants and hotels sector, average payroll per person engaged increased by 6.5% in nominal terms or 1.0% in real terms. Average payroll per person engaged in the transport, storage and communications sector showed an increase of 6.8% in nominal terms or 1.3% in real terms. Average payroll per person engaged in the financing, insurance, real estate and business services sector recorded a large increase of 12.3% in nominal terms or 6.5% in real terms....As for the community, social and personal services sector, average payroll per person engaged also recorded a marked increase of 12.2% in nominal terms or 6.4% in real terms."

Hong Kong. Census and Statistics Department. "Payroll and Wage Statistics." Press Release 17 Oct 1997. document-level access: <http://www.info.gov.hk/censtatd/hkstat/press/1b32q97.htm>

WAGES--ISRAEL--WOMEN

In Israel, a mid-May 1997 Finance Ministry report indicated that, "calculating salaried and independent income, on the average, Israeli men earned 1.9 times more than women per month in 1996....The bombshell report...showed men's gross monthly income at $1,946 and women at only $1,027....In 1995, 63.4 percent of all working women in Israel worked 15 or fewer hours per week. Tsipi Galyam, head of the revenue administration and research at the ministry, estimates that when hourly wages are taken into consideration, the [income] gap is much smaller--around 30 percent." (p37)

Sugarman, Margo Lipschitz. "Business: Shortchanged." Jerusalem Report v8 n4 26 Jun 1997. p37-38. (ISSN0792-6049).

WAGES--MANUFACTURES--SWEDEN (v26)

WAGES--MASSACHUSETTS--SUFFOLK COUNTY (v26)

WAGES--MEXICO

According to the U.S. "Labor Department, the wage gap between United States and Mexico workers is widening, rather than narrowing. In 1993, Mexican wages were 15 percent of those in the United States. Today, they are 8 percent. This decline in wages is not solely the effect of the Mexican peso crisis. In 1994--before the peso collapse--real hourly wages in Mexico had already dropped to nearly 30 percent below their 1980 level...[according to the University of California at] Berkeley sociologist Harley Shaiken. Mexico's financial problems only exacerbated the trend. Since 1994, real wages in Mexico have dropped another 25 percent to roughly half their 1980 level." (pS10462)

Feinstein, Dianne (Sen.-Calif.). "Bosnia and NATO Enlargement." Congressional Record. Daily ed. v143 n138 7 Oct 1997. pS10456-10462. section/page-level access: <http://thomas.loc.gov/cgi-bin/query/R?r105:FLD001:S10462:> (ISSN0363-7239). (X1.1A.105/1).

WAGES--MICHIGAN (v26)

WAGES--MINIMUM WAGE

,see MINIMUM WAGE

WAGES--MINNESOTA

"Only half the jobs in Minnesota pay a 'livable' wage ($20,000 a year for a family of four), according to the JOBS NOW coalition. There were an average of 2.7 people seeking each new job, while six people pursued each new livable wage job. An average of 31 people competed for each livable wage job that didn't require extensive training." (p2)

"From Where Will All the (Decent) Jobs Come?" Community Change n19 Fall 1997. p1-3,5.

WAGES--NEW ZEALAND

In New Zealand, "average weekly earnings, excluding overtime earnings, have increased by 3.4 per cent to $624.92 in the 12 months to August 1997. This is the lowest annual increase since the year to May 1996, when there was an increase of 3.1 per cent. Average hourly earnings rose by 4.4 per cent in the Auckland region during the year to August....The annual increase in average hourly earnings in the Wellington region was 1.9 per cent, the lowest level of increase since May 1994."

Statistics New Zealand. "Quarterly Employment Survey--August 1997 Quarter." Press Release 19 Nov 1997. document-level access: <http://www.stats.govt.nz/statsweb.nsf/52518ce3e01f62f4cc256388000c48c0/643ce4a7904078754c25655300718c6c?OpenDocument>

WAGES--RUSSIA (v26)

"According to a recent report, prepared by the ILO [International Labour Organization] Bureau for Workers' Activities, in cooperation with the Federation of Independent Trade Unions of Russia (FNPR), wage arrears of companies in Russia at the beginning of 1997 amounted to 39 trillion roubles--more than double the figure for February of last year. Meanwhile, the total amount of wage arrears, including wages paid by both companies and governments, totalled 50 trillion roubles, representing more than a month of the total wage bill of all workers in Russia. Arrears as a percentage of GDP have increased more rapidly since the beginning of 1996, and at the end of the year, arrears by companies, excluding those to banks, accounted for 23 percent of the GDP of the last 12 months." (p27)

"News Section: Russian Wage Arrears Reach Astronomical Proportions." World of Work n21 Sep-Oct 1997. p27. (ISSN1020-0029).

WAGES--SCHOOL EMPLOYEES--GREAT BRITAIN (v26)

WAGES--STRAWBERRY INDUSTRY--CALIFORNIA

While California's strawberry "industry is booming with annual sales of $650 million, workers pick berries for up to 12 hours a day and earn only about $8,500 a season--the second-lowest rate among 19 categories of California agriculture workers tracked by the state." (p16) "A new study by the California Policy Seminar found that while strawberry wages account for just 6 percent of all California farm wages, berry farms accounted for 24 percent of warnings issued from 1992 to 1994 by state and federal agencies enforcing safety, health and labor laws....As little as five cents per pint of strawberries would raise wages by as much as 50 percent." (p17)

"Springtime in the Strawberry Fields." America@Work v2 n5 May-Jun 1997. p14-17. (ISSN1091-594X).

WAGES--STRAWBERRY INDUSTRY--UNITED STATES (v26)

WAGES--UNITED STATES (v26)

In the U.S., "only 2% of the 107M [million] workers earn $4.25 or close to it. Additionally, 9% more earn from $4.35 and $5.15 and should be directly affected by the proposal [to raise the minimum wage by 90 cents over the next two years to $5.15]." (unpaginated)

"Wages: The Battle to Increase the Hourly Minimum: Little Effect for Security Personnel." Security Letter v27 n18 16 Oct 1997. (ISSN0363-4922).

In the U.S., "from 1973 to 1993, wages of laborers went down 15%. Wages of production workers went down 20%. Wages of college grads went down 24%. Wages of high school grads went down 30%. And total wages of those earning $1 million/year went up 243% per year--an increase of 5000%!" (p3)

Bowman, Robert M. "How Can We Make a Difference?" Space and Security News v14 n2 Aug 1997. p2-5. (ISSN1071-2569).

The "Bureau of Labor Statistics in Washington reports that wages and salaries were up 3.3 percent in the year ending in June. Total compensation, which includes such benefits as health and pension costs as well as wages, was up 2.9 percent. Both increases beat the rise in the consumer price index of 2.5 percent in the same time." (p1,4)

Francis, David R. "Working Class Gets First Raise in Years."

The Christian Science Monitor v89 n176 6 Aug 1997. p1,4. The Christian Science Monitor search engine: <http://www.csmonitor.com/plweb-cgi/iops1.pl> To retrieve this article, enter the following search: ED=19970806 AND years. In the "retrieved list," click the title that matches this record. (ISSN0882-7729).

In the U.S., "in 1979, 24 percent of workers were union members. Today, with 14.5 percent, unions have less clout to insist on higher pay packages. Adjusted for inflation, median weekly wages have dropped from the equivalent of $519 back then to $490 now....White-collar workers, meanwhile, are increasingly being paid on a variable scale, with bonuses, stock options, and profit-sharing packages tied to company success. About one third of the 3,000 companies surveyed by the Conference Board, a business-research group, have instituted variable pay plans, says analyst Charles Peck." (p78)

Smith, Anne Kates/Brindley, David. "1998 Personal Finance Guide: Bye-Bye Inflation." U.S. News & World Report v123 n22 8 Dec 1997. p74-76,78. article-level access: <http://www.usnews.com/usnews/issue/971208/8PRIC.HTM> (ISSN0041-5537).

WAGES--UNITED STATES--MEN

In the U.S., "the average wage for a young male high school graduate fell 28.1% between 1973 and 1995, plummeting 21.8% between 1979 and 1989 alone (adjusted for inflation). This means that he earned $2.96 less an hour. In contrast, wages for men with a high school diploma and 31 to 35 years experience fell 'only' 14.8%." (p50)

Garnett, Stacie. "Economy in Numbers: It's Tough to Be Young Today." Dollars and Sense n213 Sep-Oct 1997. p50. (ISSN0012-5245).

WAGES--UNITED STATES--WOMEN (v26)

In the U.S., "in nearly a quarter of dual-income marriages--22 percent, says the Bureau of Labor Statistics--women are bringing home most of the bacon. According to the bureau, women in 1996 earned 75 cents for every dollar men earned, compared with 1986, when women earned 52 cents for every dollar. Total earnings of women rose from $202 billion in 1975 to more than $930 billion in 1990, according to the U.S. Department of Commerce." (p1 secE)

Swoyer, Megan. "Accent: Check Mates." Detroit News 22 Jul 1997. p1,5 secE.

In the U.S., wages for women in entry level positions dropped "19% between 1973 and 1995. Older women, however, fared better--they lost only 1.1%....Even though their wages did not fall as fast as those of men, women still earned less--$9.92 for a female high school grad with 31 to 35 years experience versus $14.41 for the equivalent male in 1995." (p50)

Garnett, Stacie. "Economy in Numbers: It's Tough to Be Young Today." Dollars and Sense n213 Sep-Oct 1997. p50. (ISSN0012-5245).

WAGES--WISCONSIN--MILWAUKEE (v26)

WAITING LISTS FOR HOSPITALS

see HOSPITALS--GREAT BRITAIN--WAITING LISTS

WALES--ECONOMIC CONDITIONS (v26)

WALES--EMPLOYMENT (v26)

WALKING PATIENT CARE

see AMBULATORY MEDICAL CARE

WALLEYE (FISH)--DETROIT RIVER (MICH. AND ONT.) (v26)

WALNUT INDUSTRY--CALIFORNIA (v26)

"California walnut production is forecast at 230,000 tons, in-shell basis, 11 percent higher than the 1996 crop, but slightly below 1995. Bearing acreage in 1997 is estimated at 170,000 acres, up slightly from last year....In-shell shipments between August 1, 1996, and June 30, 1997, reached 139 million pounds, up 2 percent from a year earlier. Shelled shipments totaled 122 million pounds through June 30, 1997, compared with 140 million pounds the previous year. Total domestic shipments through June 30 exceeded 120,000 tons (in-shell equivalent), down 17 percent from last season, while export shipments totaled more than 93,000 tons, up 4 percent." (p32)

U.S. Dept. of Agriculture. Economic Research Service. "Tree Nut Outlook." Fruit and Tree Nuts Situation and Outlook Report Aug 1997. p32-33.

WAR (v26)

see also ARMS CONTROL; PERSIAN GULF WAR, 1991; RUSSIA--HISTORY--CIVIL WAR; RWANDA--WARS; SRI LANKA--HISTORY--CIVIL WAR; URABA (COLOMBIA)--HISTORY--CIVIL WAR

"The number of conflicts active in any given year worldwide rose steadily from 1945 to 1992. According to the Wars, Armaments, and Development Research Unit at the University of Hamburg, that number peaked at 51 in 1992....The number of armed conflicts declined to 37 in 1995....According to a detailed analysis by researchers at the University of Uppsala in Sweden, only 6 out of 101 conflicts in the period 1989-96 were international, involving the forces or territory of more than one state. The 101 armed conflicts had as many as 254 separate conflict parties." (p12)

Renner, Michael. "Small Arms, Big Impact: The Next Challenge of Disarmament." Worldwatch Paper n137 Oct 1997. p5-77.

WAR--AFRICA--CHILDREN (v26)

WAR--CASUALTIES (STATISTICS, ETC.)--ALGERIA

In August 1997, "300 civilians were slaughtered or seriously injured in a village about 30 miles south of Algiers. They were casualties in a five-year war between the military-backed authorities in Algeria and militant Muslim opponents. The 5-yr. war has killed about 60K [thousand]." (unpaginated)

"The Biggest Killer of All: Rogue Governments." Security Letter v27 n15 2 Sep 1997. (ISSN0363-4922).

WAR--CHILDREN (v26)

WAR--MORTALITY

"During the first half of the 1990s, at least 3.2 million people died of war-related causes, bringing the cumulative toll since 1945 to at least 25 million....Civilians have accounted for a large share of the victims: perhaps 70 percent of all war casualties since World War II, but more than 90 percent in the 1990s." (p13)

Renner, Michael. "Small Arms, Big Impact: The Next Challenge of Disarmament." Worldwatch Paper n137 Oct 1997. p5-77.

WAR--SIERRA LEONE (v26)

WAR--UNITED STATES--MILITARY CADETS --ATTITUDES

According to a survey of cadets in all four classes at the United States Military Academy at West Point, "almost all cadets agreed that 'sometimes war is necessary to protect the national interest,' and more than three-quarters thought that war was an inevitable part of human nature. Whereas almost three-quarters of...[freshmen] agreed that the military's 'most important role' (70 percent) and its 'primary focus' (73 percent) were preparation for and conduct of combat operations, nine out of ten seniors viewed war to be the military's main purpose (92 percent and 90 percent respectively)." (p44)

Franke, Volker C. "Warriors for Peace: The Next Generation of U.S. Military Leaders." Armed Forces & Society v24 n1 Fall 1997. p33-57. (ISSN0095-327X).

WAR AND CHILDREN

see CHILDREN AND WAR

WAREHOUSES--UNITED STATES (v26)

WARMING, GLOBAL

see GLOBAL WARMING

WASHINGTON (D.C.)--SOCIAL CONDITIONS (v26)
WASTE DISPOSAL
see REFUSE AND REFUSE DISPOSAL
WASTE DISPOSAL SITES--UNITED STATES --MINORITIES (v26)
WASTE RECYCLING
see RECYCLING (WASTES, ETC.)
WASTE WATERS
see SEWAGE
WASTES, HAZARDOUS
see HAZARDOUS WASTES
WASTES, MEDICAL
see MEDICAL WASTES
WASTES, RADIOACTIVE
see RADIOACTIVE WASTES
WATER (v26)
see also DRINKING WATER; FLOODS; RIVERS
WATER--DISEASES (v26)
WATER--NEVADA

"Urban and rural domestic use accounts for only 4% of all water consumption in...[Nevada]. Industry accounts for another 6%. And agriculture--in a state that is mostly sagebrush, not crops--takes fully 90% of all water consumed in Nevada." (p59)

Wuerthner, George. "Conservation Strategy: Subdivisions and Extractive Industries." Wild Earth v7 n3 Fall 1997. p57-62. (ISSN1055-1166).

WATER--PERU

In Peru, "available water has decreased from about 4,800 cubic meters per person in 1955 to about 2,100 in 1990, and is expected to fall to about 1,050 cubic meters by the year 2025....Only an estimated 78 percent of...[Arequipa's] population has access to safe water, and only 69 percent have sewerage services." (p4)

Hamilton, Roger. "The Region: Resources: New Currents in Water Resources Management." IDB Aug 1997. p4-5. (ISSN0145-2274).

WATER--POLLUTION

"A third of the world's population lives in countries facing moderate to severe water stress; by 2025 that figure may reach two thirds unless action is taken. One fifth of humanity lacks access to safe water and half lack adequate sanitation." (p28)

"Desertification and Drinking Water: If the Land Is Barren, How Are You Going to Halve Hunger?" UN Chronicle v34 n3 1997. p28. (ISSN0251-7329).

"Marine pollution--about 80 per cent of which is caused by land-based activities--impacts the health and livelihoods of two-thirds of humanity living in coastal areas. Some 60 per cent of global fish stocks are overfished or fully fished." (p27)

"Oceans and Marine Resources: Agreements We Have, Full Implementation We Don't." UN Chronicle v34 n3 1997. p27. (ISSN0251-7329).

WATER--POLLUTION--CANADA--SWEDEN--UNITED STATES (v26)
WATER--POLLUTION--CHINA

"Several years ago, a survey of nearly 900 of...[China's] major rivers found that more than four-fifths of them were polluted to some degree, more than 20 percent so badly that their water could not be used for irrigation. Drinking water meets official quality standards in only 6 out of the 27 largest cities that draw on surface sources and in just 4 out of those 27 that use underground sources." (p9) "The frequency of ascariasis, ancylostomiasis, and trichuriasis among China's vegetable farmers exceeds 90 percent in some regions." (p33)

Smil, Vaclav. "China Shoulders the Cost of Environmental Change." Environment v39 n6 Jul-Aug 1997. p6-9,33-37. (ISSN0013-9157).

WATER--POLLUTION--CHINA--COSTS

Vaclav Smil, a professor in the department of geography at the University of Manitoba, Winnepeg, Manitoba, Canada, calculated "the total cost of China's air and water pollution at roughly 30 billion to 45 billion 1990 yuan....[A] Chinese study came up with a total close to 100 billion 1992 yuan. Even if the more conservative estimate were increased by about 20 percent to account for China's high rate of inflation during the early 1990s, the estimates of the Chinese study are still considerably higher....The Chinese study uses average treatment costs of 2,100 and 12,700 yuan, respectively....[Smil] estimated the same costs on the basis of a different set of Chinese figures as 800 and 5,000 yuan, respectively." (p33)

Smil, Vaclav. "China Shoulders the Cost of Environmental Change." Environment v39 n6 Jul-Aug 1997. p6-9,33-37. (ISSN0013-9157).

WATER--POLLUTION--CZECH REPUBLIC (v26)
WATER--POLLUTION--GREAT BRITAIN (v26)
WATER--POLLUTION--MICHIGAN (v26)

In Michigan, "water in 20 wells of 1,493 tested (1.3 percent) in Oakland [County] since 1983 contained dangerous levels of arsenic, a heavy metal that builds up in body tissue. No wells tested in Macomb or Wayne counties had levels exceeding 50 parts per billion, the dangerous level set by the EPA....[County commission Vice-Chairperson Ruth Johnson] said that if 1.3 percent of the wells have dangerous levels of arsenic, that means nearly 3,000 homes are affected." (p1 secC)

Harmon, Brian. "Metro: News Special: Health: Oakland Arsenic Fears Resurface." Detroit News 3 Dec 1997. p1,4 secC.

WATER--POLLUTION--UNITED STATES (v26)

"The first cycle of the U.S. Geological Survey's National Water Quality Assessment has found widespread pesticides in streams and groundwater, with most of the 84 pesticide compounds investigated detected in those waters at least once, according to a preliminary summary of the assessment's first results. The assessment was conducted on 5,000 samples of groundwater and surface water in 20 major hydrologic basins from 1991 to 1995, predominantly in agricultural and urban settings....The 84 pesticides investigated account for approximately 75% of the agricultural uses and a substantial portion of urban and suburban uses in the United States....At least one pesticide was found in every stream and in half the wells sampled. There was an average of seven to eight pesticides in each stream sample." (unpaginated)

"U.S. Geological Survey Finds Widespread Pesticides in Water." Alternative Agriculture News v15 n10 Oct 1997. (ISSN8755-4941).

"Since 1970, discharges of untreated sewage into the...[U.S.'s] rivers have decreased by 90 percent. Wetland losses in the past decade have averaged about 200,000 acres a year less than in the mid-1970s through mid-1980s....Only 36 percent of rivers, lakes, and estuaries were safe for swimming or fishing in 1970; today, that figure has risen to about two-thirds....Millions of pounds of toxics are still going into surface waters. A full third of lakes, rivers, and estuaries are so polluted that they are unsafe for human use....Roughly 100,000 acres of wetlands are still being lost every year, far too many in a country that has already destroyed more than half of its original wetlands. The Environmental Protection Agency considers only 15 percent of watersheds across the country to be blessed with 'better' health. Of the rest, 24 percent are missing in action, with too little data available to be assessed; 37 percent are ailing; and 24 percent have still more serious problems." (p14)

"Editorial: Happy 25th Birthday, Clean Water Act--And Many More." Amicus Journal v19 n3 Fall 1997. p14-15. (ISSN0276-7201).

In the U.S., "agriculture is the leading source of impairment in rivers and lakes, affecting 60 percent of impaired river miles and 50 percent of impaired lake acres. In estuaries,...agriculture...interferes with 34 percent of impaired waters, but other nonpoint sources take up the slack. For example, urban runoff and storm sewers interfere with public use of 46 percent of impaired estuarine waters." (p33) "Arizona reports that nonpoint sources play a role in degrading 96 percent of impaired river miles and 93 percent of impaired lake acres." (p34)

Dubrowski, Fran. "Cover Story: Crossing the Finish Line." Environmental Forum v14 n4 Jul-Aug 1997. p28-37. (ISSN0731-5732).

WATER--POLLUTION--UTAH--LAKE POWELL

At Lake Powell in Utah, "last year when the lake level was low, some 2.6 million tourists and their canine companions occasionally used the lakeshore for a toilet. This summer, as the lake rises to its 'full pool' of 3,700 feet above sea level, the fecal bacteria that tourists left behind will spread out, leading to possible disease and beach quarantines." (p15)

Marston, Betsy. "Heard around the West." High Country News v29 n10 26 May 1997. p15. (ISSN0191-5657).

WATER, DRINKING

see DRINKING WATER

WATER BIRDS--TOXICOLOGY--NORTH AMERICA

"In North America, alone, the death from lead shot poisoning has been estimated at 1.5-4.0 million waterfowl annually (Feierabend 1983)....A single ingestion of 0.2-2.0 grams of lead shot may prove acutely fatal to most waterfowl (Pain and Rattner 1988; Rattner et al. 1989). Yet each year about 6,000 tonnes of lead shot are deposited in the wetlands of Europe and about 3,000 tonnes in North American wetlands by waterfowl hunters, alone." (p185-186)

Thomas, Vernon G. "Attitudes and Issues Preventing Bans on Toxic Lead Shot and Sinkers in North America and Europe." Environmental Values v6 n2 May 1997. p185-199. (ISSN0963-2719).

WATER CONSUMPTION (v26)

WATER CONSUMPTION--UNITED STATES (v26)

WATER HEATERS, SOLAR

see SOLAR WATER HEATERS

WATER-PIPES (v26)

WATER-PIPES--CANADA

"The Canadian National Research Council, a quasi-governmental think tank, surveyed municipalities throughout Canada about their water main break rates....Responses showed that ductile iron mains averaged 9.5 breaks per 60 miles of pipe, a big improvement over cast iron pipes, which broke at a rate of 36 breaks per 60 miles of pipe in the ground. The winner, PVC [polyvinyl chloride], had .7 breaks per 60 miles of pipe. NRC estimates that breaks cost between $2,500 - $10,000 each to fix, adding up to about $750 million in revenue loss for wasted water throughout the nation." (p12)

Lyon, Betsey. "PVC Pipes Replace Cast Iron." ChemEcology v26 n6 Aug 1997. p11-12. (ISSN0738-7776).

WATER-POWER--CHINA (v26)

WATER-POWER--UNITED STATES (v26)

WATER QUALITY (v26)

WATER QUALITY--CARIBBEAN AREA--LATIN AMERICA (v26)

WATER QUALITY--EUROPE

The European Commission's annual report on bathing water quality across the EU for 1996 shows that "the compliance rate for coastal bathing waters progressed to 91.4% from 85.3% in 1995. The much tougher 'guide' values were met in 81.9% of cases. For inland waters, compliance also improved significantly, from 51.7% to 68.9%. However, the proportion of inland bathing areas insufficiently sampled was 'still relatively high' at 20.8%, while 9.8% did not meet the quality standards." (p13)

"Water Management: Bjerregaard Urges More Effort to Clean Up Inland Bathing Sites." Environment Watch: Western Europe v6 n11 6 Jun 1997. p13-14. (ISSN1066-6001).

WATER QUALITY--HEALTH ASPECTS--THAILAND (v26)

WATER QUALITY--UNITED STATES (v26)

WATER QUALITY--VIETNAM (v26)

WATER QUALITY MANAGEMENT--NEW JERSEY

"The 'polluter pay' amendment to New Jersey's constitution, [was] supported by 69 percent of voters on last fall's Question 2 ballot initiative....The measure...dedicates 4 percent of state corporate taxes for the environment. Initial annual revenues for water quality protection and monitoring, toxic waste and leaking underground storage tank cleanups will total $52 million." (p9)

"State File: New from the Grassroots: New Jersey (NJ Environmental Federation)." Clean Water Action News v24 n1 1997. p8-9.

WATER QUALITY MANAGEMENT--SPAIN

The OECD's newly published peer review of Spain's environmental performance found that although "irrigation accounts for 80% of total water consumption, the efficiency of water use in agriculture is only 47%. Losses from urban water systems range from 25% to 50%....Less than 60% of the population was connected to a [wastewater] treatment system in the early 1990s, and a number of large cities had no wastewater treatment at all. In the area of waste management, the review notes that over the last 15 years, the share of urban solid waste dumped in unregulated landfills has dropped from 60% to 25%, though in some regions it still amounts to more than half." (p12)

"General Policy: Spain Must Match Economic with Environmental Performance, OECD Says." Environment Watch: Western Europe v6 n14 18 Jul 1997. p12-13. (ISSN1066-6001).

WATER QUALITY MANAGEMENT--UNITED STATES --FINANCE (v26)

WATER RESOURCES DEVELOPMENT--EGYPT

"The Egyptian government has broken ground on what will become the world's largest water pumping station, able to move 22,712 cubic meters (6 billion gallons) of Nile River water per day....The project's cost is to be more than US$2 billion. The massive pumping station, which will lift water 55 meters from Lake Nasser, will cost $810 million. The rest of the money will provide for construction of a three-mile tunnel and a canal, which may become the world's longest, at 150 miles (240 kilometers). This channel will provide irrigation for over 500,000 acres and link the oases of El Kharga and Farafra. Nearly 10 percent of all the water collected each year in Lake Nasser would be pumped along this ditch into the Western Desert." (p5)

Gladman, Aaron. "Africa: Massive Nile River Diversions Planned." World Rivers Review v12 n3 Jun 1997. p5. (ISSN0890-6211).

WATER RESOURCES DEVELOPMENT--INDIA

"The Indian northeast has a hydroelectric potential of 50,000 megawatts (MW), which, fed into a grid, could feed Bangladesh and the power-hungry Indian heartland....Many Himalayan storage sites lie in Bhutan and Nepal, which have an assessed potential of 20,000 MW and 83,000 MW, respectively." (p190)

Verghese, B. G. "Water Conflicts in South Asia." Studies in Conflict & Terrorism v20 n2 Apr-Jun 1997. p185-194. (ISSN1057-610X).

WATER RESOURCES DEVELOPMENT--LAOS

"Laos, which has little else to offer in terms of factors of production, is abundantly endowed with hydro capacity. It is estimated that more than half of the potential hydropower capacity of the Mekong Basin is in the rivers, streams, and lakes of Laos. A study by the Swedish International Development Authority estimates that Laos' total potential could be as high as 18,000 MW [megawatts]....The export of 200 MW of electricity to Thailand through the two existing World Bank-financed Ngam Ngum and Xeset dams is Laos' single most important source of revenue. In June 1993, a memorandum of understanding was signed in which Thailand agreed to buy an additional 1,500 MW from Laos by the year 2000. A third dam, at Houay Ho, with a 150-MW capacity, is expected to be on line in 1998. It is constructed on a 'build-operate-transfer' basis in which 60 percent of the equity is held by South Korea's Daewoo group." (p174-175)

Weatherbee, Donald E. "Cooperation and Conflict in the Mekong River Basin." Studies in Conflict & Terrorism v20 n2 Apr-Jun 1997. p167-184. (ISSN1057-610X).

WATER-SUPPLY (v26)

"Currently, over 270 million hectares of cultivated land are irrigated worldwide, accounting for one-sixth of the world's cropland and one-third of the world's harvests....By 2020, 35 countries are expected to be classified as 'water-scarce'--up from 20 in the mid-1990s."

Population Reference Bureau. "Can We Feed the Future World Population?" Press Release 1997. document-level access: <http://www.prb.org/media/pressrel.htm>

WATER-SUPPLY--AFRICA, NORTH--MIDDLE EAST (v26)

WATER-SUPPLY--CALIFORNIA

"California, predominantly an arid state, is home to the largest agricultural industry in the country. To produce 45 percent of the nation's fruits and vegetables, California farms drink up more than 80 percent of the state's developed water supplies....Today, state and federal water projects divert and deliver 10 million acre-feet of water each year using twenty dams and 500 miles of canals." (p50)

"NRDC: On the Agenda: Searching for Solutions: NRDC's Work to Protect California's Water Resources." Amicus Journal v19 n2 Sum 1997. p50-51. (ISSN0276-7201).

"California has a long-term average annual precipitation of some 200 million acre-feet (maf), of which some 70 maf could be available for diversion, storage, and use. Only 34 maf has been so developed." (p140) "According to a 1991 economic study, agriculture uses about 80 percent of the developed water of the state, yet directly accounts for less than 3 percent of its economy; 1000 acre-feet of water used on a farm supports on average 9 jobs, while the same amount in industry supports about 2600 jobs; an acre-foot of water used in San Joaquin Valley farming accounts on average for a product valued at $350, whereas an acre-foot used in major industry accounts on average for a product valued at over $300,000." (p143)

Boronkay, Carl/Abbott, Warren J. "Water Conflicts in the Western United States." Studies in Conflict & Terrorism v20 n2 Apr-Jun 1997. p137-166. (ISSN1057-610X).

WATER-SUPPLY--CALIFORNIA--SAN DIEGO (v26)

WATER-SUPPLY--GAZA STRIP--WEST BANK (v26)

WATER-SUPPLY--ISRAEL (v26)

WATER-SUPPLY--MIDDLE EAST (v26)

WATER-SUPPLY--UNITED STATES (v26)

WATER-SUPPLY--UTAH

"Utah has recently expanded the water-storage capacity of its major reservoir by 200 percent....The reservoir, buttressed by 730 35-foot columns, is intended to help satisfy the water needs of 500,000 customers, says David Ovard of the Salt Lake County Water Conservancy District." (p3)

Carlile, William H. "United States: Underground Aquifiers Are 'Banks' for Southwestern Gold." The Christian Science Monitor v89 n155 8 Jul 1997. p3. The Christian Science Monitor search engine: <http://www.csmonitor.com/plweb-cgi/iops1.pl> To retrieve this article, enter the following search: ED=19970708 AND gold. In the "retrieved list," click the title that matches this record. (ISSN0882-7729).

WATER USE (v26)

WATER USE--IRELAND (v26)

WATER USE--UNITED STATES (v26)

WATERCRAFT, PERSONAL

see PERSONAL WATERCRAFT

WATERFOWL

see also CANADA GOOSE

WATERFOWL--MICHIGAN

According to Department of Natural Resources "biologist Earl Flegler, the population of breeding Canada geese [in Michigan] is 192,000, up 20 percent from 159,000 last year and a 23 percent increase from the previous five-year average. The index for mallards is 446,000, up 32 percent from last year (339,000) and up 11 percent from the long-term average. The state's breeding wood duck population is 186,000, up 31 percent from 142,000 last year and up 27 percent from the average....Neither mallards nor Canada geese set records. The mallard population peaked in 1995 at 515,000. The Canada goose population peaked at 224,000 in 1994." (p4 secC)

Gwizdz, Bob. "Venture Outdoors: Waterfowl Survey Shows Populations on the Rise." Ann Arbor News 5 Jul 1997. p4 secC.

WATERWAYS--GREAT BRITAIN (v26)

WAYNE COUNTY (MICH.)--POPULATION (v26)

WEALTH (v26)

see also BILLIONAIRES; COST AND STANDARD OF LIVING; INCOME; MILLIONAIRES; PROFIT; SAVING AND INVESTMENT

"United Nations data reveal that only 20 percent of the world's people now own 83 percent of the world's wealth. The same rich 20 percent consume 80 percent of the world's resources. The bottom 20 percent own a total of 1 percent of the world's wealth. The 1996 United Nations Human Development Report shows that only 358 people, all of them billionaires, have as much collective wealth as 45 percent of humanity." (p6)

Mattern, Douglas. "Globalized Corporate Capitalism: 'It's the Economy, Stupid!'" Human Quest v211 n5 Sep-Oct 1997. p6-7. (ISSN0897-8786).

According to Institute for Policy Studies "calculations (based on information collected by FORBES and the U.N.), the 358 billionaires around the globe in 1995 possessed a collective wealth of $762 billion, and that equaled the income of the poorest 45 percent of all people on the planet. In 1996 the mega-rich did even better. That year, the world's 447 billionaires (a growing class) were worth a total of $1.1 trillion, which was equivalent to the income of the globe's bottom 52 percent." (p7)

"In Fact...: Richie Rich." Nation v265 n11 13 Oct 1997. p7. (ISSN0027-8378).

"The real GNP per person in the Southern hemisphere today is only 17% of that in its Northern counterpart. The industrial world, which represents only a quarter of humanity, possesses 85% of the world's wealth. The G7 [Group of Seven] nations constitute 11% of the world population but two thirds of the planet's GNP. New York City alone uses more electricity than all of sub-Saharan Africa. Between 1975 and 1995, American wealth increased by 60%, but this increase was monopolized by 1% of the population....The holdings of the 358 billionaires on the planet today is more than the cumulative annual revenue of the 2.3 billion poorest individuals, or the equivalent of nearly half of humanity." (p127)

Benoist, Alain de. "Confronting Globalization." Telos n108 Sum 1996. p117-137.

"The world's seven richest men could wipe out global poverty, according to the UN's 1997 HUMAN DEVELOPMENT REPORT. Access to basic social services and income transfers to the poverty-stricken would cost just $80 billion, less than the net wealth of these seven billionaires. In fact, the ten wealthiest people have 1.5 times as much money as the combined incomes of the 48 poorest countries." (p12)

"Notebook: Seven away from Ending Poverty." Toward Freedom v46 n4 Aug 1997. p12. (ISSN0048-9898).

WEALTH--EMPLOYMENT--UNITED STATES (v26)

WEALTH--GREAT BRITAIN (v26)

WEALTH--UNITED STATES (v26)

"Over 46 percent of the corporate stock held in...[the U.S.] is held by the richest one percent--families with net worth in excess of $2.35 million....The share of the nation's wealth held by the top 1 percent of families has grown from 22 percent in 1976 to 42 percent in 1992, nearly double in just 16 years." (p1)

"Why the Estate Tax Should Not Be Repealed." Center for Rural Affairs Newsletter Jun 1997. p1.

"The wealthiest 1 percent of U.S. households own about one-third of total household net worth, while the top 1 percent of the income distribution receives about 10 percent of total income. At the other end, a few percent of households have negative net worth, and the poorest 20 percent have no net worth as a whole....Households in the poorest 20 percent are generally young; about two-thirds are single individuals; more than one-third have not finished high school. Only about half are white...." (p25)

Weicher, John C. "The Rich and the Poor: Demographics of the U.S. Wealth Distribution." Federal Reserve Bank of St. Louis Review v79 n4 Jul-Aug 1997. p25-37.

In the U.S., "the richest 0.5% of the population claimed 8% of income in 1995--but 28% of net worth, almost as much as the bottom 90% of the population (32%). (Other, earlier studies show that the wealth of the bottom 90% is almost entirely accounted for by its upper third; the bottom 40% of the population has just 1% of total wealth.)...The richest 10% of the population--about 10 million households--owned 84% of the stock and 90% of the bonds held by individuals (including that held indirectly in mutual funds)." (p3)

"Measuring Privilege." Left Business Observer n78 17 Jul 1997. p3. (ISSN1042-0134).

In the U.S., between 1992 and 1995, "incomes of the bottom 90% rose 0.9% after inflation (total, not per year)--but those of the top 0.5% were up 44%. Nonresidential net worth was up 1.5% for the bottom 90%--but 26% for the very richest." (p3)

"Measuring Privilege." Left Business Observer n78 17 Jul 1997. p3. (ISSN1042-0134).

"The net assets of the 400 richest Americans are $300 billion. (1994 figures....) The net assets of the bottom 60% of us--150 million Americans--are zero!" (p3)

Bowman, Robert M. "How Can We Make a Difference?" Space and Security News v14 n2 Aug 1997. p2-5. (ISSN1071-2569).

"Between 1992 and 1995, the wealthiest 500,000 American households added $1.6 trillion to their assets....In 1992, the really rich 0.5 percent of households owned 22.7 percent, or $4 trillion, of the country's personal net worth of $17.77 trillion. By 1995, their share had risen to 27.5 percent of $20.52 trillion. By contrast, the share of the 90 to 99 percent bracket declined 3.7 percentage points to 33.2 percent in that period....Median wealth in 1995 was $55,100, up from $52,800 in 1992. The median is the amount at which half of households have more wealth, half have less." (p8)

Francis, David R. "Business & Money: Economic Scene: Where Did All the Money Go? Not Far." The Christian Science Monitor v89 n161 16 Jul 1997. p8. The Christian Science Monitor search engine: <http://www.csmonitor.com/plweb-cgi/iops1.pl> To retrieve this article, enter the following search: ED=19970716 AND far. In the "retrieved list," click the title that matches this record. (ISSN0882-7729).

WEAPONS

see also AK-47 RIFLE; ASSAULT RIFLES; CHEMICAL WEAPONS; FIREARMS; MILITARY WEAPONS; NUCLEAR WEAPONS

"More than 500 million military style hand-held weapons exist now--enough to arm every 12th human on earth--and millions more are produced each year, reports a new Worldwatch study....These small arms are the tools for as much as 90 percent of the killings in today's wars, and are the fuel of criminal violence." (p1)

Worldwatch Institute. "Small Arms Proliferation--The Next Disarmament Challenge." News Release 25 Oct 1997. p1-4.

WEAPONS--GREAT BRITAIN (v26)

WEAPONS--WASHINGTON (D.C.)--YOUTH

"In a study of two public inner-city junior high schools in Washington, D.C., 47% of males reported having ever carried knives, and 25% reported having ever carried guns for protection or to use in case they got into a fight; 37% of females reported having carried a knife for these purposes. Both schools are located in high-crime areas (Webster, Gainer, & Champion, 1993)." (p506)

Page, Randy M./Hammermeister, Jon. "Weapon-Carrying and Youth Violence." Adolescence v32 n127 Fall 1997. p505-513. (ISSN0001-8449).

WEAPONS, NUCLEAR

see NUCLEAR WEAPONS

WEAPONS INDUSTRY (v26)

"The United Nations Institute for Disarmament Research (UNIDIR) in Geneva has identified close to 300 companies in 52 countries that were manufacturing small arms and related equipment in 1994--a 25 percent increase in the number of such countries since the mid-1980s. Licensed production is taking place in at least 22 developing countries, 16 of which are also exporting these kinds of weapons." (p31)

Renner, Michael. "Small Arms, Big Impact: The Next Challenge of Disarmament." Worldwatch Paper n137 Oct 1997. p5-77.

WEAPONS INDUSTRY--DEVELOPING COUNTRIES (v26)

WEAPONS INDUSTRY--DEVELOPING COUNTRIES --UNITED STATES

"Despite government assurances that exports are carefully vetted, over the last four years 84 percent of U.S. arms transfers to the developing world have gone to countries the State Department considers undemocratic. In addition, U.S. weapons are involved in 45 of the world's 50 largest ethnic and territorial conflicts....Turkey, for instance, has a weak economy and a bloated military, and gets many weapons from the United States--either as giveaways or purchases made with U.S. taxpayer-backed loan guarantees. It has turned those weapons against the Kurdish population of southeastern Turkey, where 3,000 villages have been bombed." (p41)

Washburn, Jennifer. "When Money Talks, Congress Listens." Bulletin of the Atomic Scientists v53 n4 Jul-Aug 1997. p38-41. (ISSN0096-3402).

WEAPONS INDUSTRY--GREAT BRITAIN

"Currently, Indonesia buys 60 percent of its arms imports from Britain....Defense writer Michael Evans notes that close to half of Britain's 5 billion [pounds sterling] ($8.3 billion) in annual arms exports last year went to Saudi Arabia, whose government is often criticized for human rights infringements.

Also, according to arms-industry statistics, some 90,000 British jobs are dependent on military exports." (p6)

MacLeod, Alexander. "International: Arms to Rough Customers: Big Exports for Britain Clashes with New Ethic." The Christian Science Monitor v89 n180 12 Aug 1997. p6. The Christian Science Monitor search engine: <http://www.csmonitor.com/plweb-cgi/iops1.pl> To retrieve this article, enter the following search: ED=19970812 AND ethic. In the "retrieved list," click the title that matches this record. (ISSN0882-7729).

WEAPONS INDUSTRY--IRAN

"Iran was importing over $3 billion worth of arms a year during the Iran-Iraq War, with a far weaker economy than it has today. Its recent imports have been about $400 to $500 million a year." (p18)

Cordesman, Anthony H. "Symposium--The Challenge in the Gulf: Building a Bridge from Containment to Stability." Middle East Policy v5 n2 May 1997. p1-21. (ISSN1061-1924).

WEAPONS INDUSTRY--IRAQ

"Iraq was importing $4 billion worth of arms a year on average between 1980 and 1990. Its imports now, mostly on the black market, are probably around $60 million to $80 million a year." (p18)

Cordesman, Anthony H. "Symposium--The Challenge in the Gulf: Building a Bridge from Containment to Stability." Middle East Policy v5 n2 May 1997. p1-21. (ISSN1061-1924).

WEAPONS INDUSTRY--LATIN AMERICA--UNITED STATES

"Between 1992-1995 the United States was the single largest supplier of weapons to Latin America, capturing more than 25 percent of that market. According to the Congressional Research Service during fiscal years 1993-1996, U.S. arms sales to Latin American nations averaged nearly $200 million annually." (pS6753)

Dodd, Christopher J. (Sen.-Conn.). "Title II--Protection for Ancient Forests, Roadless Areas, Watershed Protection Areas, Special Areas, And Federal...." Congressional Record. Daily ed. v143 n93 27 Jun 1997. pS6735-6761. section/page-level access: <http://thomas.loc.gov/cgi-bin/query/R?r105:FLD001:S06752:> (ISSN0363-7239). (X1.1A.105/1).

WEAPONS INDUSTRY--UNITED STATES

In the 1995-1996 election cycle, according to a study by "William Hartung of the World Policy Institute, the top 25 U.S. weapons-exporting firms doled out a record $10.8 million in political action committee (PAC) and soft money contributions--a 56 percent increase over the industry's previous high in 1991-92....The industry's lobbying efforts seem to have paid off. With budgets remaining at average Cold War levels, in 1995 Congress added an additional $7 billion to the Pentagon's already bloated request, and last year it added $9 billion more." (p38) "In 1995, the arms industry scored big, winning two major victories that were at the top of their lobbying wish list: a $15 billion arms export loan program, guaranteed by the U.S. government, and a $200 million annual tax break....The break allows the president to waive the 'recoupment fees' normally attached to foreign arms sales. The fees, which had generated anywhere from $200 to $500 million in taxes each year, were designed to partially reimburse the government for its investment in research and development on weapon systems that were later sold for profit." (p39) "Since 1990, the United States has written off nearly $10 billion in arms-related loans." (p40)

Washburn, Jennifer. "When Money Talks, Congress Listens." Bulletin of the Atomic Scientists v53 n4 Jul-Aug 1997. p38-41. (ISSN0096-3402).

"U.S. arms dealers currently sell $10 billion in weapons to non-democratic governments each year, according to Caleb Rossiter, director of the Demilitarization for Democracy project....During 1993,...U.S. foreign military contracts soared to $36 billion....By 1995, U.S. government-negotiated sales had leveled off at between $9 billion and $13 billion a year. The United States, Britain, Russia, France and China dominate today's $32 billion global arms trade....Washington's share of the business jumped from 16 percent in 1988 to 50 percent between 1992 and 1994....According to a 1995 Pentagon forecast, the United States accounts for 63 percent of worldwide arms deals already signed for the period between 1994 and 2000." (p14) "Since 1985, participants in 45 ongoing conflicts received over $42 billion worth of U.S. weapons, according to a 1995 World Policy Institute report. Among the major conflicts in 1993 and 1994, 90 percent involved one or more parties that had received U.S. weapons or military technology prior to the outbreak of fighting." (p15)

Honey, Martha. "Weapons: Guns 'R' Us." In These Times v21 n19 11 Aug 1997. p14-17. (ISSN0160-5992).

WEARINESS

see FATIGUE

WEATHER (v26)

see also CLOUDINESS; LIGHTNING

According to the National Climatic Data Center, "so far this century, extreme weather events have increased by 20 percent. Annual precipitation is up 6 percent since 1900, and total winter precipitation is up 8 percent....Last winter, a couple of major blizzards buried California's Sierra Nevada, but a New Year's warm spell melted much of it, resulting in massive flooding in the Central Valley, causing 36 deaths and billions of dollars in damage....A Japanese government study predicts a 60 percent increase in the number of hurricanes hitting the eastern United States." (p40)

Rauber, Paul. "Heat Wave: Extreme Weather." Sierra v82 n5 Sep-Oct 1997. p40-41. (ISSN0161-7362).

WEATHER--CALIFORNIA--SONORA (v26)

WEATHER--ECONOMIC ASPECTS (v26)

WEDLOCK

see MARRIAGE

WEEDS--CONTROL--UNITED STATES (v26)

WEIGHT LIFTING--UNITED STATES

In the U.S., "weightlifting is still dominated by males--26 million men lifted at least once last year, according to the latest in a series of annual surveys by the Fitness Products Council, a manufacturers' association. But in another survey by the same group, the number of women who use free weights more than doubled between 1987 and 1996, from 7.4 million to 16.8 million....A study by Brigham Young University researchers, published last year in the JOURNAL OF THE AMERICAN DIETETIC ASSOCIATION, found that women who lifted weights three times a week for three months reduced their fat intake to 30 percent of total calories--perhaps because they became more health conscious, the researchers suggested." (p61)

Marcus, Mary Brophy. "News You Can Use: Health & Fitness: Women Hit the Weight Room." U.S. News & World Report v123 n5 4 Aug 1997. p61-62. article-level access: <http://www.usnews.com/usnews/issue/970804/4IRON.HTM> (ISSN0041-5537).

WEIGHT LOSS

see also BODY WEIGHT; REDUCING DIETS

WEIGHT LOSS--UNITED STATES (v26)

"The failure of weight-loss dieting to yield lasting results may be wearing on many Americans. The percent of both men and women who say they've been on a weight-loss diet in the past six months declined between 1986 and 1996. The share for men dropped to 8 percent from 10 percent in 1986. The decline was more significant for women, dropping to 16 percent in 1996 from 20 percent ten years earlier, according to Mediamark Research of New York City....In 1996, 14 percent of women aged 18 to 24 were on a weight-loss diet, compared with 21 percent ten years earlier. The share also declined for 25-to-34-year-olds, to 18 percent from 25 percent in 1986." (p43)

Dortch, Shannon. "America Weighs In." American Demographics v19 n6 Jun 1997. p38-43,45. article-level access: <http://www.demographics.com/publications/ad/97_ad/9706_ad/ad970629.htm> (ISSN0163-4089).

WELFARE, ANIMAL

see ANIMAL WELFARE

WELFARE, PUBLIC

see PUBLIC WELFARE

WELFARE RECIPIENTS--EMPLOYMENT--UNITED STATES (v26)

WELFARE RECIPIENTS--GREAT BRITAIN (v26)

WELFARE RECIPIENTS--MICHIGAN

A "state-conducted study looked at Michigan's early welfare reforms that cut monthly cash assistance by 25 percent for a year, then completely removed the welfare check if families failed to cooperate with work requirements....Sanctioned families had a 50 percent higher incidence of child abuse and neglect than the general welfare population....About half of the 67 families who consented to in-depth interviews were employed two months after welfare ended....Twenty-seven percent had insufficient food; 18 percent were facing utility cutoffs. Two families were homeless, and eight had received eviction notices a month after being cut from welfare....The report found that 30 percent of children in sanctioned families were in families where abuse or neglect had occured in the past." (p6 secC)

Putnam, Judy. "State: Families Cope with Loss of Welfare, State Says." Ann Arbor News 10 Jun 1997. p6 secC.

WELFARE RECIPIENTS--NEW YORK (N.Y.) (v26)

WELFARE RECIPIENTS--UNITED STATES (v26)

WELFARE RECIPIENTS--UNITED STATES --IMMIGRANTS (v26)

WELFARE RECIPIENTS--UNITED STATES--SOCIAL CONDITIONS

In the U.S., about one third of women "on public assistance are depressed. Some 55 percent of welfare families have the television on seven hours or longer each day. Only half have 10 or more books in the house, and reading to kids is not routine....More than a third of welfare recipients test at the 'least proficient' literacy level....One study in Washington State showed that 55 percent of welfare mothers had been victimized by violent boyfriends or spouses." (p37)

Ackerman, Elise. "U.S. News: Workfare Mary Poppins." U.S. News & World Report v123 n17 3 Nov 1997. p36-37. article-level access: <http://www.usnews.com/usnews/issue/971103/3CARE.HTM> (ISSN0041-5537).

WELFARE RECIPIENTS--UNITED STATES--SUBSTANCE USE (v26)

WEST (U.S.)--POPULATION (v26)

WESTERN AND COUNTRY MUSIC

see COUNTRY MUSIC

WESTERN SAHARA--POLITICS AND GOVERNMENT

"The Algerian-backed Polisario rebels are seeking independence for the largely Moroccan-controlled Western Sahara, which is approximately the size of Colorado and stretches along the Atlantic coast for 1,100 kilometers between Morocco and Mauritania. The population of the phosphate-rich territory is estimated at 150,000-220,000." (p13) "UN officials said in 1995 that they had already spent over $250 million on the peacekeeping mission and voter registration drive. The UN force has been reduced to about 230 military personnel stationed at 10 observation sites along the boundaries of the territory and a small civilian component." (p17)

"Western Sahara: Crocker Helps Seek Settlement of Conflict." Peace Watch v3 n4 Jun 1997. p13,16-17. (ISSN1080-9864).

WETLANDS (v26)

WETLANDS--ALASKA (v26)

WETLANDS--CHINA

"China has 60 million hectares of wetlands. Twenty five million hectares of natural wetlands include peatland, coastal wetlands and riverine and laucstrine areas. Artificial wetlands include thirty-four million hectares of paddy fields and over two million hectares of aquaculture areas. For agriculture and fisheries, drinking water and raw materials for industry and shelter, and for controlling floods they are of vast importance for China's 1.2 billion people. China's wetlands support biodiversity of domestic and international importance, including 500 species of freshwater fish and 31 of the 57 endangered waterbird species in Asia." (p34)

Claridge, Gordon. "Environment: Wetlands Conservation." China Review n7 Sum 1997. p34-37. (ISSN1359-5091).

WETLANDS--ECONOMIC ASPECTS--CALIFORNIA

"A 1992 study on the economic value of wetlands to the State of California showed that the State's 450,000 acres of wetlands provided over $22 billion in flood control benefits. These wetlands saved us over $3 billion in water quality treatment and a similar amount in water supply, annually. Over $160 million in recreational dollars are generated annually by these few wetlands and about $100 million in fisheries." (p7)

Feinstein, Arthur. "Feature: Habitat Restoration on Bases." Positive Alternatives v8 n1 Fall 1997. p6-7. (ISSN1065-0075).

WETLANDS--NORTH AMERICA (v26)

WHALES

see also WHITE WHALE

"Biologists have identified three stocks of Northern Right Whales, two of which are poorly known, probably because the populations contain so few whales. In the Pacific, scientists speculate that there are 100-300 individuals (NMFS [National Marine Fisheries Service] 1991); however, only a few sightings have been reported in the last 25 years (Scarff 1991, Carretta et al. 1994). Likewise, in the eastern Atlantic, there is evidence of a few individuals surviving (Brown 1986)....At this time of year, the location of the...western Atlantic population (80 to 85% of the individuals) is unknown....Scientists estimate there are less than 300 Northern Right Whales, of which only about 65 are known to breed (Knowlton, Kraus and Kenney 1994)." (p29) "Published estimates of birth and death rates for the population yield a yearly growth rate of about 2.5%, which is one-half to one-third of values for Southern Right Whale populations. On average, 12 calves were born each year between 1987 and 1992, but there were also at least 6 deaths per year of which at least 2 on average are attributable to human causes (Knowlton et al. 1994)....Birth rates of Northern Right Whales are low--only about one-third those of the closely related Southern Right Whale." (p30)

Stevenson, Robert. "Biodiversity Reports: Humans Threaten the Extinction of the Northern Right Whale." Wild Earth v7 n3 Fall 1997. p28-33. (ISSN1055-1166).

WHALES--MORTALITY

"Of the 41 Northern Right Whale necropsies performed from 1970 to 1996, 15 deaths have been attributed directly to collisions with ships. Two were the result of entanglement with fishing gear. The remaining 24 animals died from unknown or natural causes. Thus, at a minimum, 41% of recent whale deaths are human-related, and the percentage is likely to be higher because some of the unknown deaths are very likely related to human activities. The impact of human activities on whales is further indicated by the scars on living whales: 57% show marks of having been entangled with fishing gear, especially lobster pots, while 12% of the population bear scars indicating that they were injured by collisions with boat hulls or propellers (Kraus 1990)....In the last six years 2 of the approximately 50 whales (4%) known to have died were killed by Coast Guard boats." (p30-31)

Stevenson, Robert. "Biodiversity Reports: Humans Threaten the Extinction of the Northern Right Whale." Wild Earth v7 n3 Fall 1997. p28-33. (ISSN1055-1166).

WHEAT TRADE (v26)

"Thirteen of the eighteen member countries of the Asia-Pacific Economic Cooperation (APEC) forum use STEs [state trading enterprises]. Commodities traded under APEC's STEs are diverse, but wheat dominates with at least 34 percent of world wheat exports and 21 percent of world wheat imports during 1990-95, based on the Food and Agriculture Organization database." (p29) "Total trade value of wheat exports and imports of five major STE countries averaged $8 billion annually during 1990-95, and accounted for nearly 28 percent of world wheat trade. The AWB [Australian Wheat Board] and the CWB [Canadian Wheat Board] accounted for 34 percent of world wheat exports, in quantity terms, with each holding 22.3 and 11.4 percent, respectively, of world wheat exports during the period. The AWB controls 100 percent of the country's wheat exports, while the CWB handles 96-99 percent of Canada's wheat exports....About 21 percent of world wheat imports was bought by China, Japan, and Indonesia, with an import value of more than $3.6 billion during 1990-95." (p30) The Japan Food Agency "bought about 67 percent of Japan's wheat imports in 1995. China alone accounted for nearly 12 percent of world wheat imports and Japan captured about 7 percent of the share, in quantity terms, during 1990-95." (p31)

Langley, Suchada/U.S. Dept. of Agriculture. Economic Research Service. "State Trading Enterprises in the APEC Region: Grain Markets." APEC: International Agriculture and Trade Reports Situation and Outlook Series Aug 1997. p29-32.

Kazakhstan, the largest wheat producer "among the central Asian republics, produced only 0.6 tons per hectare in 1995...; France, the largest producer in Europe, produced more than 10 times as much that year--6.8 tons per hectare....In France, wheat yields have nearly quadrupled since mid-century, climbing from 1.8 tons per hectare in 1950 to 7.0 tons in 1996....By 1995, India had nearly tripled its yield, to 2.5 tons. Australia has increased to only 1.7 tons." (p38)

Brown, Lester R. "The Agricultural Link: How Environmental Deterioration Could Disrupt Economic Progress." Worldwatch Paper n136 Aug 1997. p5-73.

WHEAT TRADE--AUSTRALIA

"Average wheat yields in Australia have increased by about 0.5 metric tons per hectare since 1952--an increase of about 45%. Over the same time period, mean annual maximum temperatures averaged across the country increased by 0.58 [degrees Celsius]..., mean annual minimum temperatures increased by 1.02 [degrees Celsius]..., and annual average rainfall increased by 39 millimeters....[An analysis by Neville Nicholls of the Bureau of Meteorology Research Centre (Melbourne)] suggests that between 30% and 50% of the observed increase in wheat yields can be attributed to climate trends...." (p6)

"Science Update: Climate Change Has Increased Wheat Yields." Global Environmental Change Report v9 n11 13 Jun 1997. p5-6. (ISSN1049-9083).

WHEAT TRADE--AUSTRALIA--UNITED STATES

"Prior to deregulation, the United States had a 100 percent share of the milling wheat market. Now, the U.S. share is 70 percent, and Australia has a 28 percent share." (p19)

Vocke, Gary/U.S. Dept. of Agriculture. Economic Research Service. "Special Article: Emerging Import Markets in Asia." APEC: International Agriculture and Trade Reports Situation and Outlook Series Aug 1997. p13-25.

WHEAT TRADE--CANADA (v26)

WHEAT TRADE--CHINA

China's "wheat output for 1997 is projected at a record 114 million tons, 3.7 million tons more than the record 1996 crop....Urban retail standard wheat flour prices rose about 10 percent in calendar year 1996, rising from 2,690 RMB [renminbi] per ton in January to 2,960 RMB in December. Wheat imports for the July/June 1997/98 year are projected to increase by 0.5 million tons to 3.5 million. Imports are projected at a low level compared with 12 million tons in 1995/96 because of large domestic stocks and a record crop in 1996 and another record crop in 1997." (p26) Wheat "area increased by more than 700,000 hectares to 29.6 million, and yields increased 5.4 percent to 3.73 tons per hectare in 1996....Wheat production was up 8 percent in 1996/97...and imports fell by 75 percent." (p27)

Crook, Frederick W./U.S. Dept. of Agriculture. Economic Research Service. "Good Grain Crop Projected for 1997." China: International Agriculture and Trade Reports Situation and Outlook Series Jun 1997. p26-31.

WHEAT TRADE--FORMER SOVIET REPUBLICS (v26)

WHEAT TRADE--PHILIPPINES--UNITED STATES (v26)

WHEAT TRADE--UNITED STATES (v26)

"U.S. farmers planted wheat on 75.6 million acres and produced about 2,282 million bushels, up 4.5 percent from 1995....Total cash costs of producing wheat rose 2.3 percent in 1996, while economic costs rose 6.2 percent. Total economic costs averaged $5.94 on a per-bushel basis, up 11.6 percent from 1995, primarily due to higher production costs and lower yields." (p23)

U.S. Dept. of Agriculture. Economic Research Service. "1996 Cost of Production for Crops and Livestock: Although Input Expenses Rose in 1996,...Led to Higher Net Returns." Agricultural Income and Finance Situation and Outlook Report Sep 1997. p23-27.

"Total U.S. wheat production is forecast a 2.43 billion bushels [for 1997], up 7 percent from 1996 and 8 percent above the first forecast in May....The average price received by farmers for wheat in 1997/98 is forecast between $3.10 and $3.70 per bushel, down from $4.35 in 1996/97 and $4.55 in 1995/96. This would be the largest year-over-year drop since the $1.11-per-bushel decline in 1990/91 when bumper yields followed a 1989 drought in the Southern Plains." (p8)

Shields, Dennis A./Barnes, James N./U.S. Dept. of Agriculture. Economic Research Service. "Commodity Spotlight: Seasonal Rise Ahead for Wheat Prices." Agricultural Outlook Aug 1997. p8-10.

"Total U.S. wheat production is forecast at 2.26 billion bushels in 1997, down 1 percent from last year. With larger beginning stocks and steady year-over-year imports, the U.S. wheat supply in 1997/98 is forecast to rise almost 3 percent....The season-average farm price of wheat is forecast at $3.60-$4.20 per bushel in 1997/98, down from $4.35 in 1996/97 and $4.55 in 1995/96." (p2)

Shields, Dennis A./Barnes, James N./U.S. Dept. of Agriculture. Economic Research Service. "Commodity Briefs: Field Crops: Mother Nature Stirs Up Wheat Market." Agricultural Outlook Jun 1997. p2-3.

In the U.S., "Soft Red Winter (SRW) wheat production is forecast at 455 million bushels in 1997, up 33 million from last year....White Winter (WW) wheat production is forecast at 264 million bushels, down 10 percent from 1996 due to planting problems in both the Pacific Northwest and Michigan....WW harvested area is forecast down 6 percent, and yields are expected down from last year's high levels in Washington, Oregon, and Idaho, which together account for about 90 percent of WW production. WW wheat, typically used for noodles, cakes, and cereal, normally accounts for about 11 percent of the U.S. crop." (p9)

Shields, Dennis A./Barnes, James N./U.S. Dept. of Agriculture. Economic Research Service. "Commodity Spotlight: Seasonal Rise Ahead for Wheat Prices." Agricultural Outlook Aug 1997. p8-10.

In the U.S., "only 1.5 million tons of wheat was exported in March [1997], about the same as in February 1997, but a sharp decrease from a year ago. Cumulative 1997 U.S. wheat export value declined 44 percent from 1996 to $1.8 billion." (unpaginated)

Whitton, Carol/U.S. Dept. of Agriculture. Economic Research Service. "Exports." U.S. Agricultural Trade Update 23 May 1997.

In the U.S., "wheat exports reached 2.5 million tons in July [1997], up from 1.8 million tons shipped in June. But at $3.1 billion, cumulative wheat exports for 1997 are still 43 percent below 1996, despite recent monthly gains." (unpaginated)

Whitton, Carol/U.S. Dept. of Agriculture. Economic Research Service. "Exports." U.S. Agricultural Trade Update 23 Sep 1997.

U.S. wheat exports in May 1997 "were down 1.3 million tons, down from 2.1 million tons a year ago. Cumulative wheat exports were 13.8 million tons, down 36 percent from 1996. The year-to-date value of wheat was $2.4 billion, a 44-percent decrease from a year ago. Exports to Egypt fell from 3.2 million tons in 1996 to 680,000 tons in 1997." (p1)

U.S. Dept. of Agriculture. Economic Research Service. "Exports." U.S. Agricultural Trade Update 23 Jul 1997. p1.

WHISKEY INDUSTRY--SCOTLAND

"Some 71,300 people in the United Kingdom depend on the Scotch whisky industry, according to a prestigious report produced by the Fraser of Allander Institute. That is three times the number of jobs dependent on computer manufacturing and four times the number dependent on the pharmaceutical industry. In Scotland, 14,000 direct Scotch whisky jobs support 47,460 jobs in our nation." (c45)

Ewing, Margaret (H.C.-Moray). "Orders of the Day: Finance Bill." Great Britain. Parliament. House of Commons. Debates. 28 Jul 1997. c45. section-level access: <http://www.parliament.the-stationery-office.co.uk/pa/cm199798/cmhansrd/cm970728/debtext/70728-13.htm#70728-13_spnew3>

WHISTLE BLOWING--LAW AND LEGISLATION --UNITED STATES (v26)

WHITE COLLAR CRIMES--CANADA

"The annual loss from all varieties of fraud in Canada is estimated to exceed 1.5 per cent of the country's $800-billion gross domestic product--or more than $12 billion a year stolen from individuals, corporations and governments." (p10) "This year, the Mounties will spend just $36.7 million investigating commercial crime of all types in all parts of the country. That is barely two per cent of the RCMP's [Royal Canadian Mounted Police] overall budget and less than half of the amount--$83 million--that Canadian businesses lost last year to just one form of commercial crime: credit-card fraud." (p15)

Palango, Paul. "Cover: Canada: Mountie Misery." Maclean's v110 n30 28 Jul 1997. p10-15. (ISSN0024-9262).

WHITE HOUSE (WASHINGTON, D.C.)--ENERGY CONSERVATION (v26)

WHITE WHALE

The Beluga whale's "skin is from 11 to 13 mm [millimeters] thick, and the blubber is from 37 to 66 mm thick, depending on the age and condition of the animal (Doidge, 1990). Body blubber accounts for 90% of the fat on a beluga. Another 4% is in the head and tail, while the bones contain only 1.7% of the total fat." (p250)

Morseth, C. Michele. "Twentieth-Century Changes in Beluga Whale Hunting and Butchering by the Kanigmiut of Buckland, Alaska." Arctic v50 n3 Sep 1997. p241-255. (ISSN0004-0843).

WHITE WOMEN--EMPLOYMENT--SOUTHERN STATES

In the U.S. Southern States, "between 1975 and 1994, white women experienced the most dramatic gains in parity in white-collar jobs. White women have gone from under-representation to slight over-representation in professional and technician positions--with their parity ratio jumping from 0.85 to 1.32 in professional jobs and from 0.92 to 1.09 in technician jobs. They remain over-represented in the traditionally white female position of sales work, and are now over-represented in all categories of white-collar work with the notable exception of official/manager positions, where white women's parity ratio is still only 0.77." (p10)

Eckman, Anne/Green, Jordan. "Dislocation & Workforce Equity: The South at Work in the 1990s: Women Make Inroads into White-Collar Work." Southern Exposure: Institute for Southern Studies Report 1997. p10.

WHITES

see AFRO-AMERICAN POLITICIANS--WHITES--ATTITUDES

WHITEVILLE (N.C.)

Whiteville, North Carolina, "is a small southern city located in Columbus County in the southeastern section of the state. Its 5,600 residents are 65.5 percent white, 33.1 percent African American, 1.1 percent Native American, and .5 percent Hispanic....Personal incomes vary widely, and approximately 26.5 percent of the population lives in poverty....Whiteville hosts nearly 10,000 to 20,000 people per day, who come to shop or obtain services....The Whiteville Police Department consists of 26 sworn officers, 10 auxiliary officers, and 4 civilians." (p9)

Aragon, Randall/Adams, Richard E./U.S. Dept. of Justice. Federal Bureau of Investigation. "Community-Oriented Policing: Success Insurance Strategies." FBI Law Enforcement Bulletin v66 n12 Dec 1997. p8-17. (ISSN0014-5688).

WHOLESALE PRICE INDEXES--UNITED STATES

In the U.S., wholesale prices fell in May 1997 "for the fifth consecutive month--an event unmatched since 1952. The Labor Department reported...that prices paid to producers ranging from farms to factories fell 0.3 percent in May from the month before....The seasonally adjusted drop in May's Producer Price Index followed a 0.6-percent decrease in April from March." (p11 secB) "Although wholesale prices this May were 0.3-percent lower than in April, they still were 0.3 percent higher than in May 1996." (p12 secB)

Craig, Charlotte W. "Business: Wholesale Prices Drop." Detroit Free Press 14 Jun 1997. p11-12 secB.

WHOLESALE TRADE--NEW ZEALAND

In New Zealand, "wholesale sales in the September 1997 quarter were $12,326.5 million, an increase of 1.6 per cent on the September 1996 quarter sales, said Deputy Government Statistician Ian Ewing when releasing the results of the latest Wholesale Trade Survey. Eight of the 13 storetypes recorded increases in sales when compared with the September 1996 quarter with the food and grocery storetype recording the largest percentage increase. Other large percentage increases over the period were recorded by the metals storetype, up 13.4 per cent and pharmaceuticals and chemicals which went up by 8.6 per cent. Over the same period a decrease in sales was recorded by the storetypes of household appliances, furniture and floor coverings (down 13.7 per cent), motor vehicles (down 12.9 per

cent) and machinery and equipment (down 12.1 per cent)."
Statistics New Zealand. "Wholesale Trade Survey September 1997 Quarter." Press Release 28 Nov 1997. document-level access: <http://www.stats.govt.nz/statsweb.nsf/52518ce3e01f62f4cc256388000c48c0/b73e3ff4eccc874c25655d000f34e1?OpenDocument>

WIDOWS--JAPAN (v26)

WILD TURKEYS--MICHIGAN (v26)

WILDLIFE

see also AMERICAN BISON; BEARS; BIRDS; CANADA GOOSE; CROCODILES; DEER; ELEPHANTS; ELK; GRIZZLY BEAR; LIONS; LYNX; RHINOCEROSES; WOLVES

WILDLIFE CONSERVATION

As World Wildlife Fund-US President Kathryn S. Fuller indicates, "the WWF has helped 'establish, fund or manage nearly 450 parks and reserves world wide, from the Wolong Panda Reserve in China to Peru's spectacular Manu National Park. The protected areas WWF-US has supported cover more than 260 million acres of wildlife habitat--an area twice the size of California.'" (p36)
Luke, Timothy W. "The World Wildlife Fund: Ecocolonialism as Funding the Worldwide 'Wise Use' of Nature." Capitalism, Nature, Socialism v8 n2 Jun 1997. p31-61. (ISSN1045-5752).

WILDLIFE CONSERVATION--FINANCE

In 1993, the World Wildlife Fund-US "received 60 percent of its revenues from individuals as personal contributions through its system of annual membership dues. Sixteen percent came from government grants, nine percent from miscellaneous sources (like nature products, licensing deal, etc.), seven percent from foundation grants, six percent from investment earnings, and two percent from corporate donations. In 1994, however, these numbers shifted considerably. Operating with a budget of nearly $80 million in 1994, the WWF-US received a majority of its funds from government grants and contracts, or $32 million, while individual contributions were a hefty $29.4 million. During 1994, most government funds came from US-AID [Agency for International Development] (85 percent) and the EPA (98 percent), while 60 percent of corporate support from 281 corporations came from five foundations....Two hundred eighty-one companies gave generously, but many donations were at the small $1,000-10,000 range....Under the presidencies of Russel E. Train, Bill Reilly and Kathryn Fuller, the WWF grew from 25,000 members with an annual budget of about $2 million in 1978 to a membership of 1.2 million and an annual budget of $79 million in the mid-1990s by pushing...[an] ecocolonialist agenda." (p36-38)
Luke, Timothy W. "The World Wildlife Fund: Ecocolonialism as Funding the Worldwide 'Wise Use' of Nature." Capitalism, Nature, Socialism v8 n2 Jun 1997. p31-61. (ISSN1045-5752).

WILDLIFE REFUGES--UNITED STATES (v26)

WIND POWER (v26)

"Global wind energy capacity soared 32 percent from 1994 to '95....Wind power has been called the world's fastest growing energy source, increasing at an average rate of 20 percent annually, 150 percent since 1990." (p3)
Dabi, Chris. "Business Discovers Profit in Alternative Energy Investments: Natural Gas Firm Commits Capital to Wind Energy." Climate Alert v10 n3 Jul-Aug 1997. p1,3-4.

Windmills "generate up to 1.65 Megawatts of electric power each....Wind is the fastest growing energy source, producing 26% of electricity worldwide. From Amsterdam northeast to Lelystad there has been an array of 35-300 KW [kilowatt] turbines quietly producing grid electricity for the last six years. These are now being replaced with 18-750 KW units." (p22)
Jennings, Richard. "The First, World Sustainable Energy Trade Fair." Hydrogen Today v8 n2 1997. p22,26.

"Worldwide, with 6,190 megawatts of capacity installed and 8.5 billion invested, wind employs about 40,000 people. Growing 25 percent in 1996, by 2000 it's expected to generate some $3 billion in annual global revenues. The World Energy Council predicts wind will account for anywhere from 180,000 to 474,000 installed megawatts by the year 2020, depending on how seriously energy planners take global warming and how many nuclear reactors go offline....It costs about half as much to build a new field of wind turbines as it does to install a nuclear plant with comparable capacity....And the electricity can arrive reliably at one-half to one-third the price, or less." (p12)
Wasserman, Harvey. "Articles: Inherit the Wind." Nation v264 n23 16 Jun 1997. p11-15. (ISSN0027-8378).

"Between 1994 and 1996, more than 3,200 MW [megawatts] of wind power capacity was installed worldwide. The last two years were record-setters for the wind industry, which racked up $1.5 billion in international sales during 1995 and again in 1996. The world's total wind power capacity is now approaching 7,000 MW, according to Kevin Rackstraw, AWEA's [American Wind Energy Association] director of international programs, and total investment in wind power projects exceeds $8.5 billion....The wind industry's expected growth rate over the next 20 years--about 3.6% annually--exceeds that of any other energy industry." (p1) "AWEA...has projected large additions of wind power around the world by 2006: 14,310 MW in Europe; 5,970 MW in Asia; 6,950 MW in North and South America; and 2,495 MW throughout the rest of the world." (p2)
"Wind Market Expected to Surge as Major Energy Players Join In." Windletter v24 n8 Aug 1997. p1-2. (ISSN0747-5500).

"Over the past year more wind power generating capacity was manufactured and sold by the Danish wind industry than ever before over a 12 month period. Much of the reason for this new record--959 MW [megawatts] sold in 12 months representing a 67% increase over the previous period--can be attributed to the opening up of relatively new markets, China and Spain in particular, reports the Danish Association of Wind Turbine Manufacturers....Orders for 234 MW of wind turbines were placed between April and June this year, providing the industry with its second best quarterly sales ever. During the period, Denmark continued as the single largest market with purchases of 67 MW, followed by China (54 MW), Germany (37 MW), Spain (30 MW) and Britain (20 MW). Argentina, the US and the Netherlands took around 6 MW apiece, with the remaining 6 MW shared between a selection of European companies, except for three turbines which went to Australia. The best quarter ever was at the end of last year when Danish companies sold 336 MW." (p20)
Harrison, Lyn. "Wind Latest: Sales Boom as New Markets Open Up." Windpower Monthly v13 n9 Sep 1997. p20-21. (ISSN0109-7318).

"The global wind power industry, which now provides less than 1 percent of world electricity, has become a $2 billion-a-year business, and is expanding at a rate of 25 percent per year....Since 1990, thousands of wind turbines have been installed in a dozen European nations--providing 5 to 10 percent of the electricity in some regions....According to our estimates, wind power could provide 20 percent or more of the world's electricity by the middle of the next century, displacing at least one third of today's fossil-fuel-fired power plants." (p19-20)
Flavin, Christopher/Dunn, Seth. "Rising Sun, Gathering Winds: Policies to Stabilize the Climate and Strengthen Economies." Worldwatch Paper n138 Nov 1997. p5-84.

WIND POWER--AUSTRALIA (v26)

WIND POWER--CALIFORNIA (v26)

WIND POWER--CHINA (v26)

"China is beginning to exploit the estimated 800 billion KWH [kilowatt-hour] wind resource in the Xinjian Region which is in the Northwest area of China. The Xinjian Region which is now responsible for producing 44 percent of China's power now has about 25,000 kilowatts of installed wind turbine capacity." (p20)

McAlister, Kathy. "Wind Advances." Hydrogen Today v8 n2 1997. p20.

WIND POWER--DENMARK

Danish domestic wind power "sales of over 300 MW [megawatts] between June 1996 and June 1997--resulting in the erection of a record breaking 537 turbines during the period--have brought the average installation rate for the past decade to just under 90 MW a year. 'Six per cent of Danish electricity consumption is now covered by wind, a figure which was only 4% a year ago,' says...[Soren Krohn, of the Danish Association of Wind Turbine Manufacturers]. The average size of turbines now being sold by Danish firms is over 600 kW [kilowatts]. 'The latest 537 turbines in Denmark produce as much electricity as the 3000 wind turbines erected during the decade from 1980 to 1990,' says Krohn. There are about 4400 turbines turning in Denmark today amounting to 992 MW installed capacity with every indication that the national target of 1500 MW by 2000 will be reached ahead of time." (p20)

Harrison, Lyn. "Wind Latest: Sales Boom as New Markets Open Up." Windpower Monthly v13 n9 Sep 1997. p20-21. (ISSN0109-7318).

WIND POWER--DENMARK--GERMANY

"Germany's 'electricity-feed law' has spurred the addition of 2,000 megawatts of wind since 1991 and created some 10,000 new jobs in the wind industry....Wind power already provides 6 percent of Denmark's electricity, while cogeneration comprises another 40 percent." (p3)

Worldwatch Institute. "Kyoto Agreement Could Be Boon to Global Climate and World Economy." News Release 22 Nov 1997. p1-4.

WIND POWER--GERMANY (v26)

In 1996, "Germany's 4,500 wind-powered generators produced 2.7 billion kilowatts--50 percent more energy than in the previous year. In 1996, the number of German wind generators increased 26 percent." (p17)

"The Global Marketplace: No Longer Number One." Earth Island Journal v12 n4 Fall 1997. p17. (ISSN1041-0406).

"A record amount of new capacity was installed in Germany in the first six months of the year, with 216 MW [megawatts] of wind turbines representing a 5.8% increase over the same period in 1995, hitherto the record year. Compared with last year, 30% more wind capacity went in the ground between January and June, reports the Deutsche Windenergie-Institut (DEWI), bringing total capacity in Germany to 1764 MW. The new capacity is provided by 360 turbines, a 12.2% increase in the number of units erected compared with installations during the first six months of 1996. The average size of turbines being installed in Germany is now 600 kW [kilowatts]. Total investment in new wind plant was DEM 480 million, the institute reports. Over 4700 wind turbines have now been installed in Germany." (p4)

"Wind Wire: The Month in Brief: New Market Record: Germany." Windpower Monthly v13 n8 Aug 1997. p4. (ISSN0109-7318).

WIND POWER--GERMANY--PUBLIC OPINION (v26)

WIND POWER--GREAT BRITAIN (v26)

"Wind capacity in the UK has been increasing at a rate of about 34% each year over the last four years. It has increased five-fold since 1992, while the electricity generated has increased by a factor of 14." (p12)

"Wind Wire: Britain: Room for Optimism." Windpower Monthly v13 n9 Sep 1997. p12,14. (ISSN0109-7318).

WIND POWER--GREAT BRITAIN--CORNWALL ISLAND (N.W.T.)--PUBLIC OPINION (v26)

WIND POWER--GREAT BRITAIN--PUBLIC OPINION

In August 1997, "more than 2000 people visited the site of a wind plant in England....A questionnaire completed by over 300 people showed that after seeing the turbine more were in favour of wind energy than when they arrived. Before the open day 80% approved and 17% were neutral, while at the end of the day, 93% approved--a swing of 13%." (p23)

Massy, Janice. "Wind Latest: Open Day Success: Seeing Is Believing." Windpower Monthly v13 n9 Sep 1997. p23. (ISSN0109-7318).

WIND POWER--INDIA (v26)

WIND POWER--SWEDEN (v26)

"Winds were poor in Sweden last year, reaching only 84% of a normal year's energy content, reported Kenneth Averstad from state utility Vattenfall at Vind 97....The number of wind turbines in Sweden increased from 220 to 303 and the installed capacity from 67 MW [megawatts] to 105 MW, an increase of 57%. The technical availability of the turbines was 97.7%." (p48)

Wizelius, Tore. "Conference Report: Progress So Far." Windpower Monthly v13 n9 Sep 1997. p48. (ISSN0109-7318).

WIND POWER--UNITED STATES (v26)

"The US share of the world wind energy market, which was 90 percent in 1988, has shrunk to 30 percent....Wind power on less than one percent of the land in the 48 contiguous states could provide 20 percent of current US power needs." (p4)

Dabi, Chris. "Business Discovers Profit in Alternative Energy Investments: Natural Gas Firm Commits Capital to Wind Energy." Climate Alert v10 n3 Jul-Aug 1997. p1,3-4.

WIND POWER--UNITED STATES--APPROPRIATIONS AND EXPENDITURES

For fiscal year 1998, the U.S. Department of Energy's wind energy program "received $32.4 million in House-approved energy appropriations legislation and $34.6 million in the appropriations bill approved by the Senate. (DOE's wind program budget is $29 million for Fiscal Year 1997.)" (p3)

"Legislative Update." Windletter v24 n8 Aug 1997. p3. (ISSN0747-5500).

WIND POWER INDUSTRY (v26)

WIND POWER INDUSTRY--DENMARK (v26)

WIND POWER INDUSTRY--DENMARK--GERMANY --GREAT BRITAIN (v26)

WIND POWER INDUSTRY--GERMANY (v26)

WINE INDUSTRY--AUSTRALIA (v26)

WINE INDUSTRY--CALIFORNIA (v26)

"California is expected to harvest 45 percent of its entire 1997 grape crop to wine grape varieties, up 21 percent from a year ago and the largest on record....Bearing acreage for wine grape varieties totaled 311,000 acres in 1996, up 3 percent from a year earlier and up about 6 percent from the 1990-91 average. Bearing acreage increased 2 percent from 1995 for white wine-type varieties and 5 percent for red wine-type varieties." (p9)

U.S. Dept. of Agriculture. Economic Research Service. "Noncitrus Fruit Outlook." Fruit and Tree Nuts Situation and Outlook Report Aug 1997. p7-26.

WINE INDUSTRY--EUROPE--UNITED STATES (v26)

"In 1996, 50 percent of U.S. wine exports went to Western Europe, mainly to the United Kingdom (U.K.), Germany, Switzerland, and the Netherlands. Canada accounted for 20 percent, Japan 10 percent, and Caribbean countries most of the remainder of 1996 exports....U.S. exports [to the U.K.] have increased 23 percent annually over the last 10 years, reaching 375,500 hectoliters in 1996. Switzerland, importing nearly 60 percent of its wine consumption, is another growing market for the U.S. During the last decade, U.S. wine exports to Switzerland increased 36 percent per year on average to reach 85,932 hectoliters in 1996....Although combined wine production for 1996 in Italy, France, Spain, Germany, Switzerland, the U.S., Argentina, Chile, and South Africa--representing more than 80 percent of the world total--increased over the preceding 2 years, worldwide wine supplies are not sufficient to meet demand." (p13-14)

Love, John/U.S. Dept. of Agriculture. Economic Research Service. "Commodity Spotlight: The U.S. Wine Market Uncorked." Agricultural Outlook Aug 1997. p12-14.

WINE INDUSTRY--GERMANY--NETHERLANDS --UNITED STATES (v26)

WINE INDUSTRY--SWITZERLAND (v26)

WINE INDUSTRY--UNITED STATES (v26)

"A total of 2.45 million metric tons of U.S. grapes was used for wine in 1994, 8 percent less than the previous 5-year average....While wine-type grape supplies are limited, U.S. consumption of wine increased from 16.3 million hectoliters in 1992 to 21.8 million in 1995. (One hectoliter--100 liters--is slightly more than 11 cases of wine.) Wine consumption dipped 6 percent in 1996, but is likely to increase slightly in 1997. Per capita consumption in the U.S. remains less than 1 case per person annually....USDA's Economic Research Service (ERS) forecasts wine inventories at 22 million hectoliters entering 1998, about equal to the 1990-95 average and 15 percent above 1997." (p13)

Love, John/U.S. Dept. of Agriculture. Economic Research Service. "Commodity Spotlight: The U.S. Wine Market Uncorked." Agricultural Outlook Aug 1997. p12-14.

"Nearly 55 percent of the 1996 U.S. grape crop was used for wine, and farm value was estimated at $1.25 billion, compared with $547 million in 1986. Winemaking and distribution added another $12 billion in value to 1996 retail sales of food and beverages, according to industry sources....U.S. wine exports will likely reach a record $400 million in 1997, up 25 percent from 1996. During 1985-95, the value of U.S. wine exports increased 22 percent annually, far outstripping the 6.5-percent trend for the rest of U.S. agriculture....With limited domestic supplies in 1996, U.S. producers and distributors boosted wine imports 25 percent to a record $1.4 billion, the first sharp increase since 1992. Through May 1997, import growth reached 23 percent above the same period last year." (p12)

Love, John/U.S. Dept. of Agriculture. Economic Research Service. "Commodity Spotlight: The U.S. Wine Market Uncorked." Agricultural Outlook Aug 1997. p12-14.

In 1996, "market promotion funds for the American wine industry totaled approximately $5 million, whereas the heavily subsidized European wine industries received $1 1/2 billion. The money we spend to increase the markets for American agricultural products is money well spent. Because of assistance from the market access program, U.S. wine exports had their 12th consecutive record-breaking year in 1996, reaching $320 million. This level is an $85 million increase in 1 year, which means that each Market Access Program dollar being spent generated a $17 increase in exports. In the last 10 years, an additional 7,500 full-time jobs and 5,000 part-time jobs have been created by exporting wine." (pH5721)

Woolsey, Lynn C. (Rep.-Calif.). "Agriculture, Rural Development, Food and Drug Administration...Appropriations Act, 1998." Congressional Record. Daily ed. v143 n106 24 Jul 1997. pH5672-5732. section/page-level access: <http:// thomas.loc.gov/cgi-bin/query/R?r105:FLD001:H05721:> (ISSN0363-7239). (X1.1A.105/1).

"The United States remains a net importer of wine, with imports amounting to 3.57 million hectoliters during 1996 and exports at 1.63 million hectoliters. U.S. wine imports and exports both rose from a year ago, up 28 percent and 23 percent, respectively. Wine shipments from Italy, France, Chile, and Spain made up 82 percent of all U.S. wine imports last year, up 13 percent, 31 percent, 117 percent, and 4 percent from a year earlier, respectively. More than half of total U.S. wine exports are shipped to the United Kingdom, Canada, and Japan. U.S. shipments to these three major markets in 1996 rose 15 percent, 21 percent, and 5 percent, respectively, from the prior year." (p11)

U.S. Dept. of Agriculture. Economic Research Service. "Noncitrus Fruit Outlook." Fruit and Tree Nuts Situation and Outlook Report Aug 1997. p7-26.

WINERIES--UNITED STATES (v26)

WINTER SPORTS--UNITED STATES

John Packer, of "SnowSports Industries America, estimates total snow sports recreation at 53.9 million visits in 1996, 52.7 million in 1995, 54.6 million in 1994, 54 million in 1993, and 50.8 million in 1992. Snow sports had a $12.4 billion economic impact in the 1996-97 period. Snow activities are planned in a shorter time period than most travel; 14.5% of the participants make no reservations, 10.7% make a reservation within one week of the trip, and 14.3% make a reservation less than one month before. Over half of snow vacationers are interested in dining and 36.2% in shopping, in addition to their main sporting event." (p76)

DiPersio, Cindy/Hayden, Gin/Goeldner, C. R./Frechtling, Douglas. "Research Notes & Communications: Highlights of the 28th Annual TTRA Conference Norfolk/Virginia Beach, June 15-18." Journal of Travel Research v36 n1 Sum 1997. p73-84. (ISSN0047-2875).

WIRE SERVICES

see NEWS AGENCIES

WIRELESS COMMUNICATION SYSTEMS

see CELLULAR RADIO

WIRELESS COMMUNICATION SYSTEMS--UNITED STATES (v26)

WIRETAPPING--CANADA

"Jukeboxes" are "computerized surveillance recording systems--the latest thing in wiretapping technology--and just one example of an array of sophisticated devices whose use has been pioneered by Canada's national police. The RCMP [Royal Canadian Mounted Police]--which is perhaps the world's most technologically advanced police force when it comes to tapping telephones--has pairs of jukeboxes in operation in 27 locations across the country. In small centres, the Mounties have the ability to monitor 20 telephone lines at a time. In busier places, such as Montreal, Toronto and Vancouver, the system will handle 100 lines simultaneously and can be expanded to 640 lines....While most of the conversations are transcribed live by operators--in Toronto, for example, the listening room has 50 workstations--all conversations are stored on high-density optical diskettes." (p16)

Palango, Paul. "Cover: Police Secrets." Maclean's v110 n30 28 Jul 1997. p16. (ISSN0024-9262).

WIRETAPPING--UNITED STATES

In the U.S., "in 1996 there were only about 1,500 legal wiretaps used in investigations, but more than 33,000 federal prosecutions and a larger number of state ones....As for kidnapping cases, between 1968-93, wiretapping was used in only two or three cases a year." (p19)

Landau, Susan/Diffie, Whitfield. "Opinion/Essays: Cryptography Control: FBI Wants It, But Why?" The Christian Science Monitor v89 n218 6 Oct 1997. p19. The Christian Science Monitor search engine: <http://www.csmonitor.com/ plweb-cgi/iops1.pl> To retrieve this article, enter the following search: ED=19971006 AND cryptography. In the "retrieved list," click the title that matches this record. (ISSN0882-7729).

WIRETAPPING--UNITED STATES. FEDERAL BUREAU OF INVESTIGATION

In the U.S., "when the FBI announced plans in October 1995 to expand its wiretapping ability in digital communications and to increase the number of taps from 5 percent to 8 percent each year, it encountered widespread opposition. Last January the bureau scaled back its plans, requesting that telephone companies set aside the capacity for as many as 60,000 simultaneous law enforcement wiretaps and other electronic intercepts--a figure roughly 60 times the number of wiretaps conducted by law enforcement in 1995." (p39)

Littman, Jonathan. "The Hacker's Secrets." California Lawyer v17 n6 Jun 1997. p38-41,80. (ISSN0279-4063).

WOLVES--ADIRONDACK PARK (N.Y.)--PUBLIC OPINION (v26)

WOLVES--ARIZONA

In Arizona, "since bottoming out at a population of 7 in 1960, the Mexican gray [wolf] has been bred in zoos, and currently numbers around 150. The Arizona Game and Fish Department now expects three families (up to 15 animals) to be moved to acclimation pens in Apache-Sitgreaves National Forest by year's end." (p27)

Bergman, B. J. "Lay of the Land: Rekindling the Fierce Green Fire." Sierra v82 n5 Sep-Oct 1997. p26-27. (ISSN0161-7362).

WOLVES--IDAHO--YELLOWSTONE NATIONAL PARK

Since the U.S. Department of Interior's wolf "reintroduction program began in 1995, the Yellowstone [National Park] wolf population has grown from 41 to about 90. The central Idaho group has grown from 25 to approximately 73." (p4)

Larmer, Paul. "Western Roundup: Hotline: Yellowstone: Judge Says Wolf Reintroduction Was Illegal." High Country News v29 n24 22 Dec 1997. p4. (ISSN0191-5657).

WOLVES--MICHIGAN (v26)

"With numbers up 315 percent from five years ago, Michigan's wolves have reached a critical point....A DNR [Dept. of Natural Resources] survey finished three months ago counted 136 wolves on the Upper Peninsula and Isle Royale in Lake Superior, but biologists say the total could be as high as 160." (p13 secA)

Pearce, Jeremy. "Wolves Rebound to Cries of Joy and Alarm." Detroit News and Free Press 29 Jun 1997. p1,13 secA.

WOLVES--MICHIGAN--UPPER PENINSULA (v26)

WOLVES--YELLOWSTONE NATIONAL PARK (v26)

WOMB

see UTERUS

WOMEN

see also ABUSED WOMEN; ABUSED WOMEN PRISONERS; AFRO-AMERICAN WOMEN; AGED WOMEN; AMBULATORY SURGERY--UNITED STATES--WOMEN; BODY WEIGHT--UNITED STATES--WOMEN; CANADA--ARMED FORCES--WOMEN; CHLAMYDIA INFECTIONS--UNITED STATES--WOMEN; CIVIL SERVICE--EUROPE, EASTERN--WOMEN; COLLEGE SPORTS--WOMEN; COMMUTING--IRELAND--WOMEN; EARTH SCIENCE--STUDY AND TEACHING--UNITED STATES--WOMEN; ENGINEERING STUDENTS--PURDUE UNIVERSITY--WOMEN; FAMILY VIOLENCE--MEXICO--WOMEN; FOLIC ACID IN HUMAN NUTRITION--UNITED STATES--WOMEN; FRANCE--ARMED FORCES--WOMEN; HOUSEHOLDS--CARIBBEAN AREA--LATIN AMERICA--WOMEN; HUMAN REPRODUCTION--HEALTH ASPECTS--DEVELOPING COUNTRIES--WOMEN; INCOME--UNITED STATES--WOMEN; INSURANCE--UNITED STATES--WOMEN; INSURANCE, HEALTH--UNITED STATES--WOMEN; LUNGS--CANCER--UNITED STATES--WOMEN; MINORITY BUSINESS ENTERPRISES--UNITED STATES--WOMEN; MINORITY WOMEN; MOTHERS; MYOCARDIAL INFARCTION--UNITED STATES--WOMEN; OSTEOPOROSIS--UNITED STATES--WOMEN; PART-TIME EMPLOYMENT--EUROPE--WOMEN; PASSIVE SMOKING--UNITED STATES--WOMEN; PHYSICAL FITNESS CENTERS--UNITED STATES--WOMEN; POLITICAL ACTION COMMITTEES--UNITED STATES--WOMEN; POOR AGED WOMEN; POOR WOMEN; PREGNANT WOMEN; REFUGEES--WOMEN; RETIREES--UNITED STATES--WOMEN; SEXUAL HARASSMENT OF WOMEN; SEXUALLY TRANSMITTED DISEASES--UNITED STATES--WOMEN; SHOES--UNITED STATES--WOMEN; SKIRTS--UNITED STATES--WOMEN; SMALL BUSINESS--UNITED STATES--MINORITIES--WOMEN; SWEDEN--ARMED FORCES--WOMEN; TRADE-UNIONS--UNITED STATES--WOMEN; UNITED STATES--ARMED FORCES--WOMEN; UNITED STATES. AIR FORCE RESERVE--WOMEN; UNITED STATES. MARINE CORPS--WOMEN; WAGES--EUROPE, EASTERN--WOMEN; WAGES--ISRAEL--WOMEN; WAGES--UNITED STATES--WOMEN; WHITE WOMEN

WOMEN--AFRICA--SOCIAL CONDITIONS

"According to official labour force statistics issued by the World Bank and other institutions, 42 per cent of the economically active population involved in agriculture in Africa is female....The FAO [UN Food and Agriculture Organization] found, in a survey of nine African countries in 1996, that women's contribution to the production of food crops ranges from 30 per cent in Sudan to 80 per cent in the Republic of Congo....The FAO estimates that in sub-Saharan Africa as a whole, 31 per cent of rural households are headed by women...; in Latin America and the Caribbean only 17 per cent of rural households are headed by women, and in Asia, 14 per cent....Only 5 per cent of the resources provided through extension services in Africa are available to women, notes Ms. Marie Randriamamonjy, Director of the FAO's Women in Development Service, 'although, in some cases, particularly in food production, African women handled 80 per cent of the work. Of total extension agents at work in Africa today, only 17 per cent are women.'...In Benin,...only 8 per cent of rural women belong to formal cooperatives, but an estimated 90 per cent participate in traditional women's savings and credit groups." (p11)

"Agriculture in Africa: Women Farmers, The 'Invisible' Producers." Africa Recovery v11 n2 Oct 1997. p11.

WOMEN--BANGLADESH--SOCIAL CONDITIONS

A survey of the changing status of women in rural Bangladesh shows that "nearly one-fourth [of women] seldom or never travel outside their village....Three-fourths of the women surveyed have little or no say in deciding whether to see a doctor when they become ill or whether to buy medicine for a sick child....One-third...report that they have little say in allocating the money that they earn themselves....One-half report that they are allowed to leave their homes to visit a family planning clinic. Still smaller proportions feel that they may leave their homes to attend a film or festival (23 percent) or to earn money (17 percent). Nearly two-thirds report that they may take a sick child to a hospital outside their village 'only in an emergency' or 'almost never.'...28 percent feel that women should be allowed to travel outside their villages on their own, but only 7 percent may do so. Sixty-five percent feel that women should be able to decide whether to see a doctor when they are ill or to buy medicine for a sick child, but only 7 percent actually make these decisions on their own. The majority approve of women working outside their homes, but only 11 percent do so." (p1-2)

Balk, Deborah. "Change Comes Slowly for Women in Rural Bangladesh." Asia-Pacific Population & Policy n41 Apr 1997. p1-4. (ISSN0891-6683).

WOMEN--DEVELOPING COUNTRIES--ECONOMIC CONDITIONS

"The number of rural women living in poverty in the developing world has increased by almost 50 per cent over the past 20 years, to more than 500 million....In Brazil,...the chances of a child's survival increase by about 20 per cent when income is in the hands of the mother rather than the father....In Latin America and the Caribbean,...women constitute only seven to 11 per cent of the beneficiaries of credit programmes." (p19)

Speth, James Gustave. "Commentary: Tend to Those Who Tend to the Future." Choices v6 n4 Oct 1997. p19.

WOMEN--EDUCATION

Demographic and Health Surveys data show "in Bolivia over 60% of nonmigrant women have a secondary education compared with under 25% of migrant women. In Morocco the comparable statistics are about 40% for nonmigrants versus about 10% for migrants; in the Philippines, 80% compared with 60%; and in Kenya, about 50% compared with 40%." (p15-16)

Gardner, Robert/Blackburn, Richard. "People Who Move: New Reproductive Health Focus." Population Reports v24 n3 Nov 1996. p1-27.

WOMEN--EDUCATION--EUROPE (v26)

WOMEN--EDUCATION--SOCIAL CONDITIONS

"Of the 143 million children in the developing world not attending school, 56 percent are girls. Of the world's 900 million illiterate adults, nearly two thirds are women. World Bank studies have estimated that each additional year of education for a young girl results in a 10-percent decrease in birth rates and child death rates, and a 10 to 20 percent increase in wages earned." (pS7867)

Murray, Patty (Sen.-Wash.). "Statements on Introduced Bills and Joint Resolutions." Congressional Record. Daily ed. v143 n104 22 Jul 1997. pS7863-7869. section/page-level access: <http://thomas.loc.gov/cgi-bin/query/R?r105:FLD001:S07866:> (ISSN0363-7239). (X1.1A.105/1).

WOMEN--EDUCATION--UNITED STATES (v26)

WOMEN--EDUCATION (HIGHER)--UNITED STATES (v26)

WOMEN--EMPLOYMENT (v26)

"One in 3 small- or medium-sized companies in the United States is run by a woman; 1 out of 3 Finnish entrepreneurs is a woman, says the [report by the Geneva-based International Labor Organization]....Women hold on average 20 percent of the management positions worldwide....In the US, where women make up 46 percent of the managerial work force, the weekly median earnings of women are just 68 percent that of men, says the ILO....In the Philippines, women hold 29 percent of the upper level public service posts, says [Linda Wirth, an ILO expert and main author of the report]....In Colombia, the proportion of women managers swelled from 14 percent in 1980 to 37 percent last year." (p6)

Tyson, James L. "International: Women Head for the Top." The Christian Science Monitor v90 n13 12 Dec 1997. p6. The Christian Science Monitor search engine: <http://www.csmonitor.com/plweb-cgi/iops1.pl> To retrieve this article, enter the following search: ED=19971212 AND top. In the "retrieved list," click the title that matches this record. (ISSN0882-7729).

An International Labor Organization's report "shows women in America now holding more than 40 percent of 'administrative and managerial jobs.'...Worldwide, about 20 percent of administrative/managerial positions are occupied by women." (p16)

"The Monitor's View: Women-trepreneurs." The Christian Science Monitor v90 n14 15 Dec 1997. p16. The Christian Science Monitor search engine: <http://www.csmonitor.com/plweb-cgi/iops1.pl> To retrieve this article, enter the following search: ED=19971215 AND women. In the "retrieved list," click the title that matches this record. (ISSN0882-7729).

WOMEN--EMPLOYMENT--AUSTRALIA

According to the publication, "Labour Force Experience, Australia, February 1997," by the Australian Bureau of Statistics, "labour force participation of females aged 15 to 69 has steadily increased from 63 per cent in 1987 to 70 per cent in 1997....39 per cent of females with children under 15 participated in the labour force for the full 52 weeks, compared with 48 per cent of females without children under 15."

Australian Bureau of Statistics. "Female Labour Force Participation Continues to Rise." Media Release 1 Aug 1997. document-level access: <http://www.abs.gov.au/websitedbs/d3110125.nsf/4a255eef008309e44a255eef00061e57/654318539623b1e54a2564e5007fa39d?OpenDocument>

WOMEN--EMPLOYMENT--CANADA (v26)

WOMEN--EMPLOYMENT--EUROPE (v26)

A study conducted for the Commission of the European Communities on the characteristics of women's working lives in the 12-nation European Union "showed an inverse relationship between female labour force participation and women's career continuity. In countries where the participation rate is high (over 90 per cent), the percentage of women who take a career break is under 60 per cent (Denmark, Germany, United Kingdom). Conversely, when female labour force participation is low (between 60 and 70 per cent), the percentage of women who continue their careers without a break is higher, between 70 and 80 per cent (Greece, Italy and Spain)." (p125)

"Perspectives." International Labour Review v136 n1 Spr 1997. p109-128. (ISSN0020-7780).

WOMEN--EMPLOYMENT--JAPAN (v26)

WOMEN--EMPLOYMENT--KUWAIT

"In Kuwait, 93 percent of the Kuwaiti labor force (148,766 people), are employees of the state. Women comprise nearly 33 percent of the total. However, in higher administrative positions, women hold only 5 percent of all administrative positions. This percentage increases to 11 percent in middle management." (p167)

Fakhro, Munira A. "Gender, Politics and the State: What Do Middle Eastern Women Want?: Gender, Politics and the State in the Gulf Region." Middle East Policy v5 n3 Sep 1997. p166-170. (ISSN1061-1924).

WOMEN--EMPLOYMENT--LATIN AMERICA (v26)

In Latin America, "women hold an average of 25 percent of administrative and managerial positions in the region, and the figure goes as high as 37 percent in some countries....Regionwide, women account for only 6 percent of cabinet ministers and 10 percent of national legislators....A full 28 percent of the members of the Argentine House of Representatives are female." (p4)

Htun, Mala. "The Region: Equity: The Unfinished Revolution." IDB v24 n5 May 1997. p4-5. (ISSN0145-2274).

WOMEN--EMPLOYMENT--MASSACHUSETTS--BOSTON (v26)

WOMEN--EMPLOYMENT--SOUTHERN STATES

In U.S. Southern States, "in 1994, fully 41 percent of employed white women worked pink-collar or sales jobs--a concentration little changed from the 1975 rate of 43 percent. The majority of black women, the EEOC [Equal Employment Opportunity Commission] data show, still work in the least secure, poorest paid occupations: pink-collar, service, and laborer jobs. In 1994, 50.8 percent of black women were employed in these jobs, a proportion virtually unchanged from the 51.4 percent in 1975....Where 5.5 percent of all black women's work in 1975 was in sales, as of 1994 sales work made up more than 12 percent of jobs held by black women." (p11-12)

Eckman, Anne/Green, Jordan. "Dislocation & Workforce Equity: The South at Work in the 1990s: But Segregation Continues...." Southern Exposure: Institute for Southern

Studies Report 1997. p11-12.

WOMEN--EMPLOYMENT--TAIWAN (v26)

WOMEN--EMPLOYMENT--UNITED STATES (v26)

"Women's share of the total U.S. work force rose 2 percentage points between 1985 and 1995, from 44 percent to 46 percent....They grew from 59 percent to 80 percent of medicine and health managers; from 57 to 65 percent of personnel, training, and labor-relations specialists; from 68 to 75 percent of recreation workers; and from 75 to 84 percent of statistical clerks....They accounted for nearly twice the share of clergy in 1995 as in 1985, but remained a small 11 percent of the total. Their share of sheriffs, bailiffs, and other law-enforcement officers doubled, but just from 8 percent to 16 percent." (p37)

Crispell, Diane. "Kaleidoscope: Women's Work." American Demographics v19 n11 Nov 1997. p37-38. article-level access: <http://www.demographics.com/publications/ad/97_ad/9711_ad/ad971114.htm> (ISSN0163-4089).

In the U.S., "the proportion of women aged 16 and older in the civilian work force rose in 1996, reaching 59.5 percent." (p31) "The labor force rate for women with children under age 7 now exceeds the average, at 62 percent in 1996. Women with children under age 1 are nearly on a par with all women, at 57 percent in 1995, up from 50 percent in 1990." (p32)

Heubusch, Kevin. "Kaleidoscope: Enlightened and Still Working." American Demographics v19 n6 Jun 1997. p31-32. article-level access: <http://www.demographics.com/publications/ad/97_ad/9706_ad/ad970612.htm> (ISSN0163-4089).

"The U.S. Department of Labor reported there were nearly 62 million women in the civilian labor force in 1996--about 46 percent of the total. That's up from 24 percent in 1940. Female journalists also have made inroads, although more modest. They accounted for nearly 34 percent of the work force at daily newspapers in 1992, up from about 22 percent in 1971, according to a study conducted by Indiana University professors David Weaver and G. Cleveland Wilhoit." (p28)

Harvey, Chris. "Family Values." American Journalism Review v19 n5 Jun 1997. p26-31. (ISSN1067-8654).

In the U.S., vocational education programs "give women the skills they need to get jobs that pay a livable wage....The Department of Labor in Florida showed that over 70 percent of the women who participated in their programs in 1992 and 1993 doubled their income after completing the program. A study of the participants in Oregon's program showed that the graduates had expanded employment opportunities, increased salaries, and reduced dependency on public assistance. In 1992, less than 7 percent of all working women were employed in non-traditional occupations. Yet those women earned 20 to 30 percent more than women in more traditional jobs...." (pH5435)

Woolsey, Lynn C. (Rep.-Calif.). "Carl D. Perkins Vocational-Technical Education Act Amendments of 1997." Congressional Record. Daily ed. v143 n102 17 Jul 1997. pH5413-5440. section/page-level access: <http://thomas.loc.gov/cgi-bin/query/R?r105:FLD001:H05435:> (ISSN0363-7239). (X1.1A.105/1).

In the U.S., "women who work full-time now earn 74 percent as much as working men do....In 1980, 43 percent of women said they worked to bring in extra money, while 19 percent worked to support their families. Now the numbers have nearly reversed: only 23 percent of women work to bring in extra money, and 44 percent work to support a family." (p7)

"Women Move In with Money." Forecast v17 n12 Dec 1997. p7. article-level access: <http://www.demographics.com/publications/fc/97_fc/9712_fc/f971207.htm> (ISSN0732-1597).

WOMEN--ERITREA--SOCIAL CONDITIONS

In Eritrea, "most women have six to seven children over the course of their reproductive lives." (p17) "In some rural regions, up to 1,000 women die for every 100,000 live births, one of the highest rates in the world....[According to a family planning educator,] 'close to 70 percent of the women in this country suffer from chronic anemia due to heavy work loads and too many births, spaced too close together.'...Nearly 90 percent of all Eritrean women are illiterate...." (p18)

Hinrichsen, Don. "International Notebook: Building (and Greening) from Scratch." Amicus Journal v19 n3 Fall 1997. p16-19. (ISSN0276-7201).

WOMEN--EUROPE--ECONOMIC CONDITIONS

In Ukraine, "80 percent of the jobless are women. In Russia, 75 percent." (p10) "In Russia, women's wages were 70 percent of men's in 1989; two years ago they'd slipped to only 40 percent." (p11)

von Kreisler, Kristin. "E. European Women Battle for a Better Workplace." The Christian Science Monitor v89 n178 8 Aug 1997. p10-11. The Christian Science Monitor search engine: <http://www.csmonitor.com/plweb-cgi/iops1.pl> To retrieve this article, enter the following search: ED=19970808 AND workplace. In the "retrieved list," click the title that matches this record. (ISSN0882-7729).

WOMEN--HEALTH AND HYGIENE

see also CLOTHING AND DRESS

WOMEN--HEALTH AND HYGIENE--DEVELOPING COUNTRIES

"In the less developed countries, more than 100 million women of reproductive age do no want to get pregnant, but they are not practicing contraception. As a result, about one in every five births in these countries is unwanted, and about 25 million abortions take place in the developing world annually." (p41)

Bongaarts, John/O'Neill, Brian C./Gaffin, Stuart R. "Commentary: Global Warming Policy: Population Left Out in the Cold." Environment v39 n9 Nov 1997. p40-41. (ISSN0013-9157).

WOMEN--HEALTH AND HYGIENE--GAZA STRIP

"A 1992 survey found more than 30 percent of pregnant women [in the Gaza Strip] lacked access to adequate prenatal care. More than half the deliveries were not attended by trained midwives, according to the Israeli Ministry of Health. Only 17 to 30 percent of women received post-natal care. Screening for breast and cervical cancer was almost nonexistent." (p3)

"Services Improving in Gaza Strip." Popline v19 May-Jun 1997. p3.

WOMEN--INDIA--SOCIAL CONDITIONS

In India, "although 18 is the legal minimum age of marriage, child marriages are still quite common in rural areas. Early childbearing and a high rate of unsafe abortion contribute to the high maternal mortality, estimated at 570 deaths per 100,000 live births. Dowry giving, although illegal, remains customary....Some 5,000 dowry-related deaths were reported in 1993, and many cases go unreported or are attributed to accidents." (p2)

"India Implementing Cairo, Beijing Goals." Popline v19 May-Jun 1997. p2.

WOMEN--MASSACHUSETTS--BOSTON (v26)

WOMEN--METABOLISM

"The bulk of our caloric output--60% to 75% daily--goes to our basal metabolic rate (BMR), the energy the body uses for basic functions....A woman's BMR decreases 4% to 5% per decade after age 48; by 65 she needs only 1,600 calories a day to maintain her weight. Menopause appears to have an independent effect, resulting in a 100-calorie-a-day decrease in BMR." (p37)

Reichman, Judith. "Office Visit: Fighting Fat after 40." American Health v16 n6 Jul-Aug 1997. p37. (ISSN0730-7004).

WOMEN--PAKISTAN--SOCIAL CONDITIONS

"The Human Rights Commission of Pakistan said in its annual report that one woman is raped every three hours in Pakistan and one in two rape victims is a juvenile. According to Women's Action Forum, a woman's rights organization, 72% of all women in police custody in Pakistan are physically and sexually abused. Furthermore, 75% of all women in jail are there under charges of 'zina' [illegal sexual intercourse]....Pakistan is one of only four countries in the world where female life expectancy (51 years) is lower than the male (52 years); the average female life expectancy for all poor countries is 61 years. A large number of Pakistani women die in pregnancy or childbirth, six for every 1,000 live births....The average fertility rate per woman in Pakistan is 6.9. Pakistan is also among the world's bottom ten countries for female attendance at primary schools. Some people put female literacy in the rural areas as low as 2% (ECONOMIST, March 5, 1994)." (p36)

Warraq, Ibn. "Islam and Women's Rights: Islam's Shame: Lifting the Veil of Tears." Free Inquiry v17 n4 Fall 1997. p30-34,36. (ISSN0272-0701).

WOMEN--PENSIONS--UNITED STATES (v26)

WOMEN--RWANDA--ECONOMIC CONDITIONS--SOCIAL CONDITIONS (v26)

WOMEN--SAUDI ARABIA--SOCIAL CONDITIONS

"The number of Saudi working women is less than 5 percent, most of them in the health and education sectors." (p167) "Nearly a million Saudi women are now enrolled at various levels [of the educational system] and constitute about 45 percent of the national student population. By 1987, more than 80,000 Saudi women were employed in the government and the education and health sectors." (p168)

Fakhro, Munira A. "Gender, Politics and the State: What Do Middle Eastern Women Want?: Gender, Politics and the State in the Gulf Region." Middle East Policy v5 n3 Sep 1997. p166-170. (ISSN1061-1924).

WOMEN--SOCIAL CONDITIONS

"Out of an estimated 13.5 million refugees in the world today, three-quarters are women and children. Even in the field of education, glaring inequalities still exist: two-thirds of the world's illiterates are women." (p22)

Aulagnon, Michele. "What Women Want." Choices v6 n4 Oct 1997. p22.

"Global literacy statistics show that in 1990 there were only 74 literate women for every 100 literate men. Schooling statistics reveal a similar trend. Worldwide, 77 million girls of primary school age (6-11 years) are out of school, compared with 52 million boys...." (p40) "Economist and philosopher Amartya Sen of Harvard University has estimated that more than 100 million females are 'missing' globally--a stark figure that he attributes to the comparative neglect of female health and nutrition, especially, but not exclusively, during childhood." (p41) "In some countries in sub-Saharan Africa, approximately one woman in 50 dies during childbirth--a grim contrast to Scandinavia where the rate is one per 20,000." (p42)

Buvinic, Mayra. "Women in Poverty: A New Global Underclass." Foreign Policy n108 Fall 1997. p38-53. (ISSN0015-7228).

WOMEN--TOBACCO USE

Today, according to World Health Organization estimates, "there are about 200 million female smokers in the world....Smoking among women is most prevalent in the Former Socialist Economies (FSE) and Eastern Europe (28%), countries with established market economies (23%) and Latin America and Caribbean countries (21%). In all other regions less than 10% of women smoke...." (p1) "The country with the highest percentage of women (15 years of age and over) who smoke is Denmark--37% (1993). It is followed by Norway--35.5% (1994), the Czech Republic--31% (1994)....The Russian Federation (1993) with 30% of female smokers rank fifth in this list....Followed by Canada (1991), Netherlands (1994) and Poland (1993) with 29%. Greece (1994), Iceland (1994), Ireland (1993) and Papua New Guinea (1990) close the list of the top 10 with 28% of women who smoke." (p2)

World Health Organization. "Smoking and Women: The Next Wave of the Tobacco Epidemic." WHO Fact Sheet n176 Aug 1997. p1-4. document-level access: <http://www.who.ch/programmes/inf/facts/fact176.htm>

"'More than half a million smoking deaths occur in women,' said Dr Judith Mackay from Hong Kong, a member of the WHO Expert Advisory Panel on Tobacco or Health....'Globally, approximately 12% of women smoke as compared to 47% of men....'" (p3)

World Health Organization. "The Smoking Epidemic--'A Fire in the Global Village.'" WHO Press n61 25 Aug 1997. p1-3. document-level access: <http://www.who.ch/press/1997/pr97-61.html>

WOMEN--TOBACCO USE--MORTALITY

"At present, the widespread use of tobacco is responsible for three million deaths worldwide--or about 6% of all deaths--per year. More than half a million of these deaths occur in women....Already by the early 1990s, the death rate from lung cancer among women in highly industrialized countries was more than 300% higher than the level prevailing in the early 1950s." (p2)

World Health Organization. "Smoking and Women: The Next Wave of the Tobacco Epidemic." WHO Fact Sheet n176 Aug 1997. p1-4. document-level access: <http://www.who.ch/programmes/inf/facts/fact176.htm>

WOMEN--UGANDA--SOCIAL CONDITIONS (v26)

WOMEN--UNITED STATES--ATTITUDES (v26)

WOMEN--UNITED STATES--ECONOMIC CONDITIONS (v26)

A report released by the Economic Policy Institute says that in the U.S., "'while overall unemployment has averaged 5.2 percent over the past year, unemployment among young African-American women (ages 15 to 25) with a high school diploma was 19.7 percent.' Fifty percent of the women who have been on welfare for an extended period of time do not even have high school diplomas....Women make up 58.2 percent of the low-wage sector." (p11 secA)

Herbert, Bob. "Other Voices: Greenspan's Economy Is Good, But It Can't Be Good for Everyone." Detroit Free Press 24 Nov 1997. p11 secA.

In the U.S., "the share of women who say they feel 'quite confident' about financial matters is rising quickly, according to Roper Starch Worldwide....37 percent said they felt confident about deciding how to save money in Roper's December 1996 survey, up from 29 percent in December 1994. Women's confidence about buying home, auto, or liability insurance is up 11 percentage points; about planning for their family's financial future, up 8 points; about retirement planning, up 7 points; and about buying life insurance or financing their home, up 6 points....70 percent of women view self-directed retirement plans like IRAs [individual retirement accounts] and 401(k)s as 'good' or 'excellent' values, up 18 points from 1994. And 43 percent of women have similar confidence in common stocks (up 19 points). The share of women with self-directed retirement plans is 33 percent for all women and 43 percent of working women." (p7)

"Women Move In with Money." Forecast v17 n12 Dec 1997. p7. article-level access: <http://www.demographics.com/publications/fc/97_fc/9712_fc/f971207.htm> (ISSN0732-1597).

In the U.S., "50 percent of working women and 80 percent of retired women today have no pensions. Women 65 and older are the fastest-growing group of people in poverty, and 75 percent of the elderly poor are women....Despite progress, women still earn an average of 76 cents for every $1 a man makes." (p9)

Call, Toni. "Business & Money: Personal Finance: Investing Hurdles: Women Must Jump Higher." The Christian Science Monitor v89 n208 22 Sep 1997. p9. The Christian Science Monitor search engine: <http://www.csmonitor.com/plweb-cgi/iops1.pl> To retrieve this article, enter the following search: ED=19970922 AND higher. In the "retrieved list," click the title that matches this record. (ISSN0882-7729).

WOMEN--UNITED STATES--ECONOMIC CONDITIONS --ATTITUDES (v26)

WOMEN--UNITED STATES--MORTALITY (v26)

WOMEN--UNITED STATES--PUBLIC OPINION (v26)

WOMEN--UNITED STATES--SEXUAL BEHAVIOR (v26)

WOMEN--UNITED STATES--SOCIAL CONDITIONS (v26)

WOMEN--UNITED STATES--SUBSTANCE USE (v26)

In the U.S., "the National Institute of Drug Abuse estimates that five million women of childbearing age used illegal substances in 1988 (U.S. General Accounting Office, 1990). Further, the Centers for Disease Control (1994) reported that intravenous drug use was implicated in 68% of AIDS cases among women and that women of childbearing ages represented nearly 12% of the 401,749 AIDS cases reported in the United States as of June 1994." (p491)

Burnette, Denise. "Article: Grandparents Raising Grandchildren in the Inner City." Families in Society v78 n5 Sep-Oct 1997. p489-499. (ISSN1044-3894).

WOMEN, ABUSED

see ABUSED WOMEN

WOMEN, AFRO-AMERICAN

see AFRO-AMERICAN WOMEN

WOMEN, AGED

see AGED WOMEN

WOMEN, INFANTS, AND CHILDREN PROGRAM

In the U.S., "in fiscal 1996, the number of participants [in the Women, Infants, and Children program] increased 4 percent up to an average 7.2 million people per month....Participants, of whom over three-quarters were infants or children, received an average of $31.19 per month in food benefits. WIC program costs totaled $3.7 billion in fiscal 1996, almost 8 percent greater than the previous year." (p52)

Oliveira, Victor/U.S. Dept. of Agriculture. Economic Research Service. "Food Assistance: Food-Assistance Spending Held Steady in 1996." Food Review v20 n1 Jan-Apr 1997. p49-56. (ISSN1056-327X).

WOMEN, INFANTS, AND CHILDREN PROGRAM--UNITED STATES (v26)

In the U.S., the Cooperative State Research, Education, and Extension Service and the Women, Infants, and Children "Nutrition Education Initiative was designed to change behavior and promote the nutritional well-being of the neediest Women, Infants, and Children--WIC--participants....Over 260 WIC Clinics nationwide collaborated with the Cooperative Extension System to serve over 141,650 participants....In Washington, 92 percent of participants reported increased knowledge about planning nutritionally balanced meals: in Nebraska, 90 percent of program graduates reported improvements in their ability to plan meals; in Hawaii, 84 percent of the program graduates showed increased knowledge in their ability to interpret food labels, select, buy, and/or prepare appropriate foods to meet nutritional needs for themselves and their families; in New Jersey, more than 70 percent of the participants could identify missing food groups from planned meals or could use food models to develop a well balanced menu, and 85 percent of the participants demonstrated proper handling procedures during food preparation; in Arizona, 81 percent of the participants demonstrated increased knowledge or skill related to diets of lactating women and their infants; and in Iowa, 46 percent of participants scored 100 on the Lactation Inventory which measured the knowledge of breast feeding." (p289)

U.S. Dept. of Agriculture. "Agriculture, Rural Development, Food and Drug Administration...Approp. for 1998 (Part 4)." Hearing. U.S. House. Committee on Appropriations. Washington, D.C. : GPO, 1997. (ISBN0160551560). (Y4.Ap6/1:Ag8/997/pt.4).

WOMEN AND RELIGION--UNITED STATES--ATTITUDES (v26)

WOMEN ANTHROPOLOGISTS--UNITED STATES (v26)

WOMEN ATHLETES--UNITED STATES

"The 1994 men's World Cup [Soccer tournament] held...[in the U.S.] drew an average 68,600 spectators per game. The [U.S.] women's [soccer] team played before 76,489 fans in the final Olympic game against China. Outside the Olympics, the largest crowd for a US women's game has been 17,000. Officials are hoping for crowds averaging 25,000 for the WWC [Women's World Cup]....[The WWC] budget is $20 million; they hope to raise $8 to $10 million through corporate sponsorship." (p13)

Siegel, Laura A. "US Women's Soccer Goal: Draw Cash and Crowds." The Christian Science Monitor v89 n174 4 Aug 1997. p13. The Christian Science Monitor search engine: <http://www.csmonitor.com/plweb-cgi/iops1.pl> To retrieve this article, enter the following search: ED=19970804 AND crowds. In the "retrieved list," click the title that matches this record. (ISSN0882-7729).

At Brooklyn College, "57 percent of the student body are women and 57 percent of the school's collegiate athletes are women....At the University of Michigan, Ann Arbor, women comprise 49 percent of the student body and 45 percent of athletes. The University of Washington in Seattle--the target of a 1979 sports discrimination lawsuit--has a female enrollment of 47 percent and a female sports participation rate of 46 percent....According to the NCAA [National Collegiate Athletic Association], the number of [U.S.] schools with women's crew teams has increased from 12 in 1991, to 83 in 1996, and the number of schools with women's soccer teams increased from 318 to 581 during the same period. Despite continuing enforcement problems with Title IX, the [women's rights] law is helping to transform sports throughout the US. Before passage of the law in 1972, roughly 32,000 collegiate women participated in athletics in the US. By 1995 that number jumped to 110,540, according to the NCAA. Increased opportunities are causing changes at the high school level as well. In the past 25 years the number of high school girls in competitive sports rose from 300,000 to 2.37 million, according to a recent survey....In addition, women representing the US won 19 Olympic medals in the 1996 Summer Games." (p3)

Richey, Warren. "United States: How Some Colleges Score Parity for Women's Athletics." The Christian Science Monitor v89 n133 5 Jun 1997. p3. The Christian Science Monitor search engine: <http://www.csmonitor.com/plweb-cgi/iops1.pl> To retrieve this article, enter the following search: ED=19970605 AND athletics. In the "retrieved list," click the title that matches this record. (ISSN0882-7729).

WOMEN CLERGY--MICHIGAN--EPISCOPAL CHURCH (v26)

WOMEN COACHES--MICHIGAN (v26)

WOMEN COLLEGE GRADUATES--UNITED STATES (v26)

WOMEN EXECUTIVES--CANADA--UNITED STATES

"Canada now has women running 10 of the top 500 revenue-churning, publicly traded companies in the land....According to Catalyst, a New York City research firm that assesses and promotes the advancement of women, just 57 women held positions of executive vice-president or higher in Fortune 500 companies in 1995. Catalyst totted up the top five earners in each of the

Fortune 500 companies. Of the group of 2,500, just 47 were women. Sixteen had made chief financial officer and one...woman had made CEO...." (p60) "An earlier Catalyst study on women's career advancement found that 60 per cent of American women sampled held staff positions--HR [human resources], administration and so on. In Canada, the number of women managers and administrators, outside of government, rose to more than 410,000 in 1991 from 257,000 in 1986." (p61)

Wells, Jennifer. "Cover: Stuck on the Ladder." Maclean's v110 n42 20 Oct 1997. p60-62,64. (ISSN0024-9262).

WOMEN EXECUTIVES--UNITED STATES--PUBLIC OPINION

"In the United States last year, Catalyst surveyed more than 450 executive women (vice-presidents and up) as well as more than 300 CEOs of Fortune 1000 companies. Three-quarters of the women surveyed said one of the keys to career success lies in consistently exceeding performance expectations, that to be considered to be equal, women have to be better. Ninety-six per cent said that developing a style with which male managers were comfortable was an essential career-enhancing strategy." (p60-61)

Wells, Jennifer. "Cover: Stuck on the Ladder." Maclean's v110 n42 20 Oct 1997. p60-62,64. (ISSN0024-9262).

WOMEN HEADS OF HOUSEHOLDS--MASSACHUSETTS --BOSTON--ECONOMIC CONDITIONS (v26)

WOMEN IMMIGRANTS--CALIFORNIA--SAN FRANCISCO --ECONOMIC CONDITIONS--SOCIAL CONDITIONS (v26)

WOMEN IMMIGRANTS--EMPLOYMENT--UNITED STATES

In the U.S., "of all working-age female immigrants, 25 percent reported having no work experience at any time in the last 5 years." (p21) In 1990, immigrant women "accounted for 9.8 percent of all working women, up 3.2 percentage points from the 1980 figure....In 1990, labor force participation among immigrant women (62.5%) was over 7 percentage points lower than that of native women (69.7%). The unemployment rate for immigrant women (8.4%) was almost 3 points higher than that of native women (5.7%)....In 1990, only 58 percent of recent immigrant women were in the labor force, compared to 65 percent of immigrant women who had been in the United States for more than 10 years....The labor force participation of immigrant women is 24 percentage points below the labor force participation of immigrant men...." (p22)

Enchautegui, Maria E./Malone, Nolan J. "Female Immigrants: A Socio-Economic Portrait." Migration World v25 n4 1997. p18-23. (ISSN1058-5095).

WOMEN IMMIGRANTS--UNITED STATES

In the U.S., "in 1990, roughly 50 percent of all immigrants, ages 18 to 64, were women....In 1980, 50 percent of the working age immigrants that entered the United States between 1970 and 1980 were women. As of 1990, 46 percent of the working age immigrants that came between 1980 and 1990 were women." (p19) "By early 1994, the immigration flow since 1990 was 49 percent female." (p20)

Enchautegui, Maria E./Malone, Nolan J. "Female Immigrants: A Socio-Economic Portrait." Migration World v25 n4 1997. p18-23. (ISSN1058-5095).

WOMEN IMMIGRANTS--UNITED STATES--SOCIAL CONDITIONS

"Tabulations from the 1994 March Current Population Survey show that 55 percent of the women that entered the United States between 1992 and 1994 are married, while only 37 percent of the men are married....Roughly 60 percent of immigrant women have at least completed high school, and 17 percent have a Bachelor's degree, Master's degree or a Ph.D....Over 53 percent of immigrant women reported that they speak English exclusively or 'very well.'" (p21)

Enchautegui, Maria E./Malone, Nolan J. "Female Immigrants: A Socio-Economic Portrait." Migration World v25 n4 1997. p18-23. (ISSN1058-5095).

WOMEN IN BUSINESS--CANADA (v26)

WOMEN IN BUSINESS--CANADA--PUBLIC OPINION

In Canada, "Environics Communications recently surveyed more than 650 'affluent women'--defined as those in households with more than $137,000 in annual income. Three-quarters of the women surveyed, the majority of whom have careers, said the Old Boys network still makes it difficult for women to succeed in corporations. Sixty-nine per cent said the opportunities offered to women are more limited than those offered to men, and 68 per cent said that taking a maternity leave can be an impediment to corporate promotions." (p60)

Wells, Jennifer. "Cover: Stuck on the Ladder." Maclean's v110 n42 20 Oct 1997. p60-62,64. (ISSN0024-9262).

WOMEN IN BUSINESS--MICHIGAN (v26)

WOMEN IN BUSINESS--UNITED STATES (v26)

"As of 1996, there were nearly 8 million women-owned businesses...[in the U.S.], employing more than 18.5 million people and generating close to $2.3 trillion in sales. According to the National Foundation for Women Business Owners, women-owned businesses are growing faster than the overall economy in each of the top 50 metropolitan areas in the United States, including Philadelphia and Pittsburgh. In a study released in March 1997, the foundation reported that as of 1996, Philadelphia's 127,100 women-owned enterprises employed 448,500 people and generated over $56 billion in sales, and Pittsburgh's 54,800 women-owned enterprises employed 141,800 people and generated over $17 billion in sales." (pS5600)

Specter, Arlen (Sen.-Pa.). "Statements on Introduced Bills and Joint Resolutions." Congressional Record. Daily ed. v143 n82 12 Jun 1997. pS5596-5622. section/page-level access: <http://thomas.loc.gov/cgi-bin/query/R?r105:FLD001: S05600:> (ISSN0363-7239). (X1.1A.105/1).

"In America today, there are over 22 million small businesses compared with only 14,000 big businesses. We see more women than ever exploring the entrepreneurial frontier. Women-owned businesses represent one-third of all U.S. companies, contribute more than $1.5 trillion in sales to the U.S. economy, and employ more people than the Fortune 500. Women-owned sole proprietorships have a start-up rate twice that of male-owned businesses." (pS6359-6360)

Kerry, John F. (Sen.-Mass.). "Statements on Introduced Bills and Joint Resolutions." Congressional Record. Daily ed. v143 n91 25 Jun 1997. pS6359-6372. section/page-level access: <http://thomas.loc.gov/cgi-bin/query/R?r105:FLD001: S06359:> (ISSN0363-7239). (X1.1A.105/1).

Within the U.S. Small Business Administration's "7(a) and 504 loan programs, the agency reports that it has tripled its number of loans to women borrowers from 3,588 in 1992 to 11,452 in 1996. That represents an increase in the dollar amount from $634 million in 1992 to $1.6 billion in 1996....[However,] these figures mean that women recipients constitute approximately one-fifth of the total loan clientele and receive approximately one-seventh of the loan guarantee funds. This is at a time when the SBA reports that over the last decade, 'new women-owned firms--one-third of all firms--have grown at twice the rate of men-owned businesses." (pS5597)

Domenici, Pete V. (Sen.-N.Mex.). "Statements on Introduced Bills and Joint Resolutions." Congressional Record. Daily ed. v143 n82 12 Jun 1997. pS5596-5622. section/page-level access: <http://thomas.loc.gov/cgi-bin/query/R?r105: FLD001:S05596:> (ISSN0363-7239). (X1.1A.105/1).

WOMEN IN POLITICS (v26)

"From 1975 to 1995, the number of women legislators doubled in the developed West; the global average rose from 7.4 percent to nearly 11 percent....Of the 32 women who have served as presidents or prime ministers during the twentieth century, 24 were in power in the 1990s. In the United States, women now make up 11.2 percent of Congress, about one-third the proportion in Nordic countries, but substantially higher than the 5 percent in 1987. And although only 23 women won seats in the Diet in Japan's 1996 elections, an unprecedented 153 women ran for office. In 1997, the Inter-Parliamentary Union reported only nine countries with no women in their legislatures. From 1987 to 1995, the number of countries without any women ministers dropped from 93 to 47, and 10 countries reported that women held more than 20 percent of all ministerial-level positions, although generally in 'female' portfolios like health, education, and environment rather than the 'power ministries' like finance and defense....[In the New Independent States of the former Soviet Union and the former members of the Eastern bloc,] representation has dropped from earlier highs under communist rule of 25 to 35 percent women...to around 8 to 15 percent today, and numbers are lower in the largely Muslim states of Central Asia. Where women's representation is still under Communist Party control, as in China, North Korea, and Vietnam, women still account for about 20 percent of the national legislators." (p26-27)

Jaquette, Jane S. "Women in Power: From Tokenism to Critical Mass." Foreign Policy n108 Fall 1997. p23-37. (ISSN0015-7228).

"Quotas account for the high levels of female representation in the Nordic countries and for the recent doubling (to 18 percent) of the number of women in the House of Commons in Britain when the Labour Party swept the election. A quota law in Argentina increased the women in its house of representatives from 4 percent in 1991 to over 16 percent in 1993 and 28 percent in 1995. In Brazil, when quotas were used in the 1997 congressional elections, the number of women legislators increased by nearly 40 percent since the last elections." (p32)

Jaquette, Jane S. "Women in Power: From Tokenism to Critical Mass." Foreign Policy n108 Fall 1997. p23-37. (ISSN0015-7228).

WOMEN IN POLITICS--ARGENTINA (v26)

WOMEN IN POLITICS--CANADA (v26)

WOMEN IN POLITICS--SOUTHERN STATES

In the U.S., "most Southern states have no women representatives in Congress, and minuscule numbers of women hold statewide offices. Of the 10 states with the fewest women elected to state legislatures, eight are below the Mason-Dixon Line. Alabama is last, with just 4.3 percent of women in legislative seats." (p15)

Spaid, Elizabeth Levitan. "Dixie Politics: Boys Clubs Still Prevail." The Christian Science Monitor v89 n136 10 Jun 1997. p1,15. The Christian Science Monitor search engine: <http://www.csmonitor.com/plweb-cgi/iops1.pl> To retrieve this article, enter the following search: ED=19970610 AND prevail. In the "retrieved list," click the title that matches this record. (ISSN0882-7729).

WOMEN IN SCIENCE--UNITED STATES (v26)

WOMEN IN SPORTS--UNITED STATES (v26)

In the U.S., "since 1972, the number of college women participating in competitive athletics has gone from fewer than 32,000 to over 110,000 in 1994-95. Before title IX, fewer than 300,000 high school girls played competitive sports. By 1996, that number had climbed to almost 2.4 million....According to a recent NCAA [National Collegiate Athletic Association] study, only 23 percent of all current college athletic budgets are allocated to women, and women receive only 38 percent of athletic scholarship dollars. Only 27 percent of funding spent to recruit new athletes target women. In high-school athletic competitions, there are two boys to every one girl participating." (pS6380-6381)

Snowe, Olympia J. (Sen.-Maine). "Fair Play Act." Congressional Record. Daily ed. v143 n91 25 Jun 1997. pS6380-6381. section/page-level access: <http://thomas.loc.gov/cgi-bin/query/R?r105:FLD001:S06380:> (ISSN0363-7239). (X1.1A.105/1).

In the U.S., according to a 1996 survey of 35,000 households by the National Sporting Goods Association, "among team sports, female participation has increased most dramatically in soccer and basketball--57 and 56 percent, respectively, since 1991. 'This far exceeds the growth for those two sports (39 and 27 percent) in the same five years,' said Thomas Doyle, NSGA vice president of information and research....[In the outdoors category,] 'growth was most significant for kayaking and rafting, where female participation increased 116 percent.'...In 1996, women represented 50 percent or more in 12 activities: step aerobics, aerobic exercising, gymnastics, roller skating, walking, ice skating, horseback riding, exercising with equipment, badminton, volleyball, swimming and calisthenics." (p5 secF)

"Body & Mind: Your Play: Rec Notes: More Women Turn to Vigorous Sports." Detroit Free Press 12 Aug 1997. p5 secF.

In the U.S., "girls' participation in high school sports has spiked from about 300,000 in 1971 to 2.4 million in 1996. At the college level, where competition is tougher, the number of female athletes has increased to 123,832 from 80,040 in 1982, says the National Collegiate Athletic Association." (p88)

Marcus, Mary Brophy. "1998 Career Guide: If You Let Me Play...." U.S. News & World Report v123 n16 27 Oct 1997. p88,90. article-level access: <http://www.usnews.com/usnews/issue/971027/27TEAM.HTM> (ISSN0041-5537).

WOMEN IN THE CIVIL SERVICE--CANADA (v26)

WOMEN LAWYERS--CANADA

"A 1996 report by the Law Society of Upper Canada, entitled 'Women in a Changing Legal Profession,' found that women were making only 60 percent of men's salaries in some areas of law. And the wage ghetto comes with its own glass ceiling: only 13.5 per cent of women had been awarded partnership status in their firms; the figure for men was 30 per cent." (p19)

Dwyer, Victor. "Cover: Privilege and Pressure." Maclean's v110 n40 6 Oct 1997. p16-20. (ISSN0024-9262).

WOMEN LEGISLATORS (v26)

WOMEN LEGISLATORS--UNITED STATES (v26)

WOMEN OFFENDERS

see FEMALE OFFENDERS

WOMEN-OWNED BUSINESS ENTERPRISES--CALIFORNIA

"In California, from 1987 to 1996 the number of women-owned firms has grown by 78 percent, employment has increased by 255 percent and sales have grown by 313 percent. Women-owned businesses now account for more than one-third of all firms in California. As a result, California ranks first out of the 50 States in the number of women-owned firms, first in employment and first in sales." (pH7819)

Millender-McDonald, Juanita (Rep.-Calif.). "Women Owned Businesses in America." Congressional Record. Daily ed. v143 n129 24 Sep 1997. pH7819. section/page-level access: <http://thomas.loc.gov/cqi-bin/query/R?r105:FLD001:H07819:> (ISSN0363-7239). (X1.1A.105/1).

WOMEN-OWNED BUSINESS ENTERPRISES--CANADA (v26)

"At the recent Women Leaders' Network for APEC [Asian Pacific Economic Cooperation] Economies held in Ottawa, it was noted that 700,000 companies in Canada are owned by women and that they employ 1.7 million people, which is greater than the CANADIAN BUSINESS top 100 companies. They are also creating jobs at a rate four times the national average." (p14)

Bulte, Sarmite (MP-ON). "Speech from the Throne." Canada. Parliament. House of Commons. Debates. v135 n2 23 Sep 1997. p13-18. section-level access: <http://www.parl.gc.ca/36/1/parlbus/chambus/house/debates/002_1997-09-23/han002-e.htm#LINKT6> (ISSN0704-5603). (X3-361E).

WOMEN-OWNED BUSINESS ENTERPRISES--EMPLOYMENT --CANADA (v26)

WOMEN-OWNED BUSINESS ENTERPRISES--UNITED STATES (v26)

"Between 1987 and 1996, the number of firms owned by women grew by 78 percent, which is almost twice the rate of increase in the number of all U.S. firms, which is 47 percent. Sales increased by 236 percent, nearly $2.3 trillion, and employment increased by 183 percent....There are...approximately 8 million women-owned firms, providing jobs for 15.5 million people and generating nearly $1.4 trillion in sales. Women-owned businesses...employ 35 percent more people in the United States than the Fortune 500 companies employ worldwide....Women-owned firms grew by 171 percent in construction, by 157 percent in wholesale trade, by 140 percent in transportation--communications, by 130 percent in agriculture, and by 112 percent in manufacturing." (pH7819)

Millender-McDonald, Juanita (Rep.-Calif.). "Women Owned Businesses in America." Congressional Record. Daily ed. v143 n129 24 Sep 1997. pH7819. section/page-level access: <http://thomas.loc.gov/cqi-bin/query/R?r105:FLD001:H07819:> (ISSN0363-7239). (X1.1A.105/1).

In the U.S., "in 1996, women-owned businesses employed 1 out of every 4 workers, totaling 18.5 million employees. Last year, these businesses accounted for an estimated $2.3 trillion in sales. Increasingly, women are becoming small business owners and according to the National Foundation of Women Business Owners, the growth of these women-owned small businesses outpaced overall business growth nearly 2 to 1. In Georgia alone, there are 143,045 women-owned businesses, both full and part-time." (pS8974)

Coverdell, Paul (Sen.-Ga.). "Small Business Reauthorization Act of 1997." Congressional Record. Daily ed. v143 n118 9 Sep 1997. pS8971-8989. section/page-level access: <http://thomas.loc.gov/cgi-bin/query/R?r105:FLD001:S08974:> (ISSN0363-7239). (X1.1A.105/1).

WOMEN PHYSICIANS--UNITED STATES (v26)

WOMEN PRISONERS

see also ABUSED WOMEN PRISONERS

WOMEN PRISONERS--CALIFORNIA

"The number of women incarcerated in California prisons increased nearly eightfold from 1,100 in 1980 to 8,500 in 1995 (CDC, 1995). Nationally, incarcerated women are more likely than men to be serving time for a drug offense and less likely to have been sentenced for a violent crime. About 60% of incarcerated women grew up in a single-parent household, and over 40% reported prior physical or sexual abuse (USDJ [United States Department of Justice], 1994). Over half the women in California prisons are African American (35%) and Latina (17%) (Bloom et al., 1994). Seven out of ten women incarcerated in California are serving time for nonviolent drug and property crimes; in 1993, one-third were reimprisoned due to parole violations (Bloom, 1995)." (p154)

Reed, Diane F./Reed, Edward L. "Children of Incarcerated Parents." Social Justice v24 n3 Fall 1997. p152-169. (ISSN0094-7571).

WOMEN PRISONERS--UNITED STATES (v26)

In the U.S., "the number of women in Federal prisons has grown astronomically. There was 75 percent growth in the last decade. The annual growth rate is considerably greater than for State prisons. There is twice the growth rate for these women as for men. The rate of infection for HIV and AIDS exceeds the rate of infection for men in prison. Five percent of these women enter prison pregnant....Forty percent have been sexually abused. Half committed the offense under the influence of alcohol or drugs. More than half used drugs the month before committing the offense. Forty percent use drugs daily. Fifty-eight percent use alcohol, 20 percent every day. Who are the children of these inmates? They are five times as likely to be imprisoned as other children. Half of the children in the juvenile justice system have a parent in prison....Blacks, regardless of sex, are six times more likely to go to prison than whites. Black women have nearly the same chance as white men of going to prison." (pH7815)

Norton, Eleanor Holmes (Del.-D.C.). "Departments of Commerce, Justice, And State, The Judiciary...Appropriations Act, 1998." Congressional Record. Daily ed. v143 n129 24 Sep 1997. pH7786-7818. section/page-level access: <http://thomas.loc.gov/cqi-bin/query/R?r105:FLD001:H07815:> (ISSN0363-7239). (X1.1A.105/1).

"Approximately 75% of the 90,000 women incarcerated in U.S. prisons and jails in 1991 were mothers: 37,000 mothers were in federal and state prisons and 30,000 were in jails (U.S. Department of Justice, 1993). Approximately 53% of the children of incarcerated mothers live with their grandparent(s), typically a grandmother--meaning that approximately 32,000 older women are caring for their grandchildren for an extended period as a result of an adult daughter's incarceration (Dressel & Barnhill, 1994)." (p491)

Burnette, Denise. "Article: Grandparents Raising Grandchildren in the Inner City." Families in Society v78 n5 Sep-Oct 1997. p489-499. (ISSN1044-3894).

In a survey of 2094 inmates conducted under the auspices of the American Correctional Association, "almost half of the women had other family members incarcerated (48.4 percent) and almost half had run away from home while growing up (46.5 percent). Thirty percent of those sampled said they took drugs to make themselves feel better, and almost 28 percent had attempted suicide (Crawford, 1988)....Crawford (1988) found that women [in prison] continue to be disproportionately black (36 percent) and Hispanic (15 percent); and they continue to be in their late twenties and early thirties. The women surveyed had the following marital status: married (36.5 percent), divorced or separated (33.8 percent), and single (21.6 percent). Most had completed some years of high school, although only 39 percent had graduated or attained an equivalence degree. More than one-third of the women who had quit high school stated that they quit because they were pregnant. Eighty percent of the women had at least one child. Almost one-third of these women had their first child before they were seventeen years old (Crawford, 1988)." (p190)

Janeksela, Galan M. "Female Criminality: An Overview." International Journal of Comparative and Applied Criminal Justice v21 n2 Fall 1997. p181-205.

In the U.S., in 1996, "the number of female prisoners grew 9.1 percent during the year, almost double the 4.7 percent increase in male inmates. At the end of the year, 6.3 percent (74,730 inmates) were women."

U.S. Dept. of Justice. "Nation's Prison Population Increased 5 Percent Last Year." Press Release 22 Jun 1997. document-level access: <http://www.ojp.usdoj.gov/pub/bjs/press/p96.pr>

"A record number of American women--75,000--were serving prison sentences last year, the Justice Department reported recently. The number of women in jail or awaiting mandatory sentences increased 9.1 percent over 1995, the study said." (p20)

"The Monitor's View: Women in Prison." The Christian Science Monitor v89 n167 24 Jul 1997. p20. The Christian Science Monitor search engine: <http://www.csmonitor.com/plweb-cgi/iops1.pl> To retrieve this article, enter the following search: ED=19970724 AND prison. In the "retrieved list," click the title that matches this record. (ISSN0882-7729).

WOMEN SCIENTISTS--EMPLOYMENT--UNITED STATES (v26)

WOMEN VETERANS--HEALTH AND HYGIENE--UNITED STATES (v26)

WOMEN'S CLOTHING

see CLOTHING AND DRESS

WOOD PRODUCTS--UNITED STATES (v26)

WOOD PRODUCTS--UNITED STATES--PUBLIC OPINION (v26)

WOOD WASTE--UNITED STATES

In the U.S., "one half of all wood used is wasted by outdated technologies and the lack of reuse or recycling. At least one quarter of the wood cut from public lands ends up pulped for paper, despite the existence of ecologically preferable tree-free and recycled alternatives. Nearly half of all hardwood lumber is used for shipping pallets, and half of those are used once and discarded in landfills." (p8)

Orr, David. "Earth Island in Action: John Muir Project: Zero Cut on Public Lands." Earth Island Journal v12 n3 Sum 1997. p8. (ISSN1041-0406).

"The United States consumed 350 million metric tons of wood in 1994 and tossed about one-tenth of that. The wood we dispose of makes up one-fifth of municipal solid waste....Last year, Americans produced a total of 39.2 million metric tons of wood waste....David McKeever of the Forest Products Laboratory in Madison, Wis., a Forest Service research center, estimates that 4.5 million metric tons were recovered while another 15.2 million metric tons were potentially recoverable." (p8)

Lavendel, Brian. "A Growing Demand: A Hard Look at a Hard Business: Wood Recycling." Inner Voice v9 n6 Nov-Dec 1997. p8-11.

In the U.S., "according to industry estimates, if builders cut the amount of waste produced in residential construction by half, they would free up enough material to build one additional house for every 20 built. Researchers at Cornell University found that construction of a single four-bedroom house produced 1,338 pounds of wood waste, including 46 pounds of sawdust." (p16-17)

Rasmussen, Matt. "A Growing Demand: The Straw Alternative." Inner Voice v9 n6 Nov-Dec 1997. p16-18.

WOODS (FORESTS)

see FORESTS AND FORESTRY

WOOL INDUSTRY--AUSTRALIA (v26)

WORK AND FAMILY--CANADA (v26)

WORK AND FAMILY--CANADA--PUBLIC OPINION (v26)

WORK CLOTHES--UNITED STATES

According to Roper Starch Worldwide data, in the U.S., "in 1994, 48% described a 'casual day at work' as 'in' and only two years later that number grew to 65%. A 1997 study by Bruskin-Goldring Research finds that slightly over half of those surveyed--52%--can dress casually at their workplace any day of the week. Only a quarter--27%--say they can't dress down at all....Only 30% of those who work in an office say they can't dress casually at their workplace." (p58)

Bowman, Karlyn H. "American Fashion Embraces the Casual and Comfortable." Public Perspective v8 n5 Aug-Sep 1997. p58-60. (ISSN1050-5067).

WORK ENVIRONMENT--HEALTH ASPECTS

see INDUSTRIAL HYGIENE

WORK ETHIC--UNITED STATES

"A majority of American workers (56 percent) say they face pressures at work to act unethically or illegally. Nearly half of this group say they've actually engaged in unethical or illegal activities, according to a national study by the American Society of Chartered Life Underwriters & Chartered Financial Consultants and the Ethics Officer Association." (p5)

Poe, Randall/Courter, Carol Lee. "Fast Forward: The Company Made Me Do It." Across the Board v34 n7 Jul-Aug 1997. p5. (ISSN0147-1554).

WORK GROUPS--UNITED STATES (v26)

WORK HOURS

see HOURS OF LABOR

WORKERS, CHILD CARE

see CHILD CARE WORKERS

WORKERS' COMPENSATION--NEW YORK (STATE)

"The New York State workers' compensation system covers nearly 7.9 million workers. Of the more than 450,000 accidents reported in 1996 to the Workers' Compensation Board which administers the system, about 180,000 resulted in claims filed....In 1992-93, 38 percent of the covered employers--primarily small businesses--were insured by the public State Insurance fund while 41 percent purchased policies from private insurance companies....Annual workers' compensation premiums paid by New York employers total approximately $5 billion a year, of which about $2 billion go to private carriers." (p35) "Wage-replacement benefits are capped at $400 per week, which currently represents less than 60 percent of New York's average weekly wage....In 1994,...[private carriers] collected $2 billion in workers' comp premiums and paid out only $1 billion in wage replacement and medical benefits. This loss ratio of 50.4 percent was among the lowest in the nation." (p36) "Between 1987 and 1993, workers' compensation premiums paid by New York employers to private carriers rose 106 percent...while benefits paid to workers increased only 45 percent." (p40)

Tarpinian, Greg/Tuminaro, Dom/Shufro, Joel. "The Politics of Workers' Compensation in New York State: Developing... Strategy to Defeat...'Reform'...for Workers." New Solutions v7 n4 Sum 1997. p35-45. (ISSN1048-2911).

WORKING CLASS--UNITED STATES

In the U.S., "a poll conducted in the winter of 1995-96 found that 61 percent of people in the United States considered themselves to belong to the working class. The remaining 39 percent divided themselves among the middle and upper classes. In a similar poll in 1983, 48 percent of respondents classified themselves as working class." (p8)

Rodwan, John G., Jr. "Guess Who Is Losing the Numbers Game?: Guess Who Can Win It?: The Resurgence of the Working Class." People's Tribune v24 n9 Sep 1997. p8. (ISSN1081-4787).

WORKING MOTHERS--CANADA (v26)

WORKING MOTHERS--UNITED STATES (v26)

WORKOUTS (EXERCISE)

see EXERCISE

WORKPLACE VIOLENCE

see VIOLENCE IN THE WORKPLACE

WORLD HEALTH (v26)

WORLD ORDER

see INTERNATIONAL RELATIONS

WORLD TEMPERATURE CHANGES

see GLOBAL TEMPERATURE CHANGES

WORLD TRADE

see INTERNATIONAL TRADE

WORLD WAR, 1939-1945--UNITED STATES--ARMED FORCES (v26)

WORLD WIDE WEB (INFORMATION RETRIEVAL SYSTEM) (v26)

see ADVERTISING--WORLD WIDE WEB (INFORMATION RETRIEVAL SYSTEM)

WORMS--UNITED STATES

In the U.S., "vermiculture ventures, the biggest of which involve 50 million worms chowing down on almost 90 tons of waste per week, have boomed over the past few years....Many outfits are prospering thanks in part to the growing popularity of organic foods, which are expected to become a $6.5 billion-a-year business by 2000, up from $3.5 billion last year. With the U.S. Department of Agriculture estimating that 25 percent of Americans purchase organically grown foods at least once a week, organic farmers' demand for worm feces far outstrips supply." (p53)

Koerner, Brendan I. "Business & Technology: It's All Business for Worms." U.S. News & World Report v123 n11 22 Sep 1997. p53. article-level access: <http://www.usnews.com/usnews/issue/970922/22WORM.HTM> (ISSN0041-5537).

WRITING--CANADA--YOUTH (v26)

WYOMING--ECONOMIC CONDITIONS

"All of agriculture--cows, sheep, wheat, sugar beets and other crops--accounts for only about 2 percent of...[Wyoming's] economy. By comparison, tourism, concentrated mostly in and around Yellowstone [National Park], contributes 14 percent." (p8) "Everything in Wyoming starts with the state's tax structure, under which minerals account for about 50 percent of all revenue." (p9) "Idaho, Montana and Colorado boomed in the 1990s with 6 percent-plus job growth; Wyoming sputtered with 1.3 percent growth in jobs....In 1996,...1,000 people left Wyoming. State statisticians said they failed to find good-paying jobs, while those who stayed accepted an average weekly paycheck in 1995 of $350, compared to $435 nationally....In 1994, less than 5 percent of the state's jobs were in manufacturing, compared to about 16 percent nationwide." (p10)

Krza, Paul. "While the New West Booms, Wyoming Mines, Drills...And Languishes." High Country News v29 n13 7 Jul 1997. p1,8-10,12-13. (ISSN0191-5657).

X GENERATION

see GENERATION X

YELLOWSTONE NATIONAL PARK

"Yellowstone is the world's oldest national park, founded on March 1, 1872. Of its 2.2 million acres, only 1 percent is developed for human use, even though 3 million visitors came in 1996. Ninety-one percent of the park is in northwestern Wyoming, with slight overlaps into southwestern Montana and southeastern Idaho. Lodgepole pine and other conifers head 1,050 species of native plants. Grizzly and black bears, bison, moose, elk, wolves, and coyotes are among 56 species of mammals. Aso present are fish, reptiles, amphibians and 290 species of birds." (p6 secH)

Volgenau, Gerry. "Travel: If You Go to Yellowstone National Park." Detroit Free Press 17 Aug 1997. p6 secH.

"Three million people visit Yellowstone [National Park] each year....With the park at the ecosystem's core, the surrounding buffer zone spreads over 20 counties and includes Grand Teton National Park, seven national forests, three national wildlife refuges, and more than 3 million acres of private land, where the heaviest development is occurring. The region's population has increased by over 12 percent since 1990, to more than 322,000 people...." (p24) "Yellowstone's annual operating budget of around $20 million was cut by $2.2 million in 1996 and by $3 million this year." (p25)

Satchell, Michael. "U.S. News: Parks in Peril." U.S. News & World Report v123 n3 21 Jul 1997. p22-28. article-level access: <http://www.usnews.com/usnews/issue/970721/21PARK.HTM> (ISSN0041-5537).

YEN, JAPANESE--VALUATION (v26)

YOUNG ADULTS

see also AIDS (DISEASE)--UNITED STATES--YOUNG ADULTS

YOUNG ADULTS--CANADA--ATTITUDES

"One of Canada's chartered banks has recently undertaken a comprehensive national study of the attitudes of Canada's nexus generation who are young people between the ages of 18 and 35. This study reveals that this group is much more entrepreneurial and positive than usually depicted. One-third of nexus respondents stated that their most desirable profession was entrepreneur, suggesting that young Canadians are determined to turn their innovative ideas into business realities." (p14)

Bulte, Sarmite (MP-ON). "Speech from the Throne." Canada. Parliament. House of Commons. Debates. v135 n2 23 Sep 1997. p13-18. section-level access: <http://www.parl.gc.ca/36/1/parlbus/chambus/house/debates/002_1997-09-23/han002-e.htm#LINKT5> (ISSN0704-5603). (X3-361E).

YOUNG ADULTS--EMPLOYMENT--UNITED STATES --ATTITUDES

In the U.S., four in ten young adults "say they had a difficult time finding a decent job, according to a 1996 survey by Massachusetts Mutual Life Insurance. Almost seven in ten of the young adults surveyed by MassMutual think it is better to stay at one job than move around to get ahead. However, almost half expect to be at their current job for less than two years, and one-third expect to be there for less than one year. Fifty-one percent of teenagers aged 15 to 19 planned to stay at their current job for less than one year...." (p31-32)

Miller, Berna. "Kaleidoscope: Movers and Slackers." American Demographics v19 n7 Jul 1997. p31-32. article-level access: <http://www.demographics.com/publications/ad/97_ad/9707_ad/ad970724.htm> (ISSN0163-4089).

YOUNG ADULTS--PHILIPPINES--SEXUAL BEHAVIOR

According to a study of young adult fertility and sexuality in the Philippines, "of the 10,879 young men and women interviewed, 59 percent of the married men and 25 percent of the married women reported sexual experience before marriage, and 22 percent of the single men compared with only 2 percent of single women reported sexual experience....Twenty-five percent of the 24-year-old men who 'never had a girlfriend' reported sexual experience, and 22 percent of those still single at age 24 reported that they had visited a commercial sex worker." (p2)

"Philippines Break from Past Policies." Popline v19 Sep-Oct 1997. p2.

YOUNG MEN--PHILIPPINES--SEXUAL BEHAVIOR (v26)

YOUNG WOMEN

see ANOREXIA NERVOSA--UNITED STATES--YOUNG WOMEN

YOUNG WOMEN--PHILIPPINES--SEXUAL BEHAVIOR (v26)

YOUTH

see also AIDS (DISEASE)--UNITED STATES--MINORITY YOUTH; AIDS (DISEASE)--UNITED STATES--YOUTH; ARSON--UNITED STATES--YOUTH; CIGAR HABIT--MASSACHUSETTS--YOUTH; CIGAR HABIT--UNITED STATES--YOUTH; CLERGY--UNITED STATES--YOUTH; CONDOMS--UNITED STATES--YOUTH; CONTRACEPTION--UNITED STATES--YOUTH; CRIME--MICHIGAN--YOUTH; CRIME--UNITED STATES--YOUTH; CURFEW--UNITED STATES--YOUTH; DROPOUTS; FIREARMS--AFRO-AMERICAN YOUTH; FIREARMS--UNITED STATES--YOUTH; FOOD HABITS--UNITED STATES--YOUTH; HOSPITALS--UNITED STATES--EMERGENCY SERVICE--YOUTH; MARIJUANA--UNITED STATES--YOUTH; MENTAL ILLNESS--UNITED STATES--YOUTH; OBESITY--UNITED STATES--YOUTH; PRISONERS--CALIFORNIA--YOUTH; PRISONERS--CANADA--YOUTH; PRISONERS--UNITED STATES--YOUTH; SEXUALLY TRANSMITTED DISEASES--UNITED STATES--YOUTH; SMOKING--MICHIGAN--YOUTH; SMOKING--UNITED STATES--YOUTH; SPORTS--AUSTRALIA--YOUTH; SPORTS--GREAT BRITAIN--YOUTH; TRAFFIC ACCIDENTS--

CALIFORNIA--YOUTH; TRAFFIC ACCIDENTS--MICHIGAN--YOUTH; UNEMPLOYMENT--CANADA--YOUTH; UNEMPLOYMENT--UNITED STATES--YOUTH; VIOLENCE--UNITED STATES--YOUTH; VIOLENT CRIMES--UNITED STATES--YOUTH; WEAPONS--WASHINGTON (D.C.)--YOUTH

YOUTH--ASIA--EUROPE--LATIN AMERICA--ECONOMIC CONDITIONS

"Two-thirds of Asia's population is under 30, with 652 million consumers in their 20s possessing $1.2 trillion in annual purchasing power. In Latin America, about 87 million people in their 20s control $203 billion in annual spending. Within Europe, 118 million people ages 20 to 29 have $684 billion a year in buying power." (p10)

Smillie, Dirk. "Global Report: Marketing Bonanza: Tuning in First Global TV Generation." The Christian Science Monitor v89 n132 4 Jun 1997. p1,10-12. The Christian Science Monitor search engine: <http://www.csmonitor.com/plweb-cgi/iops1.pl> To retrieve this article, enter the following search: ED=19970604 AND generation. In the "retrieved list," click the title that matches this record. (ISSN0882-7729).

YOUTH--ASIA--TOBACCO USE (v26)

YOUTH--CALIFORNIA--SEXUAL BEHAVIOR--PUBLIC OPINION

"A study of 7,326 seventh and eighth graders in California who participated in an abstinence-only program found that the program did not have a measurable impact upon either sexual or contraceptive behaviors. Nearly two-thirds of teenagers think teaching 'Just Say No' is an ineffective deterrent to teenage sexual activity." (p21)

"Fact Sheet: Adolescence and Abstinence." SIECUS Report v26 n1 Oct-Nov 1997. p21-22. (ISSN0091-3995).

YOUTH--CANADA--TOBACCO USE (v26)

YOUTH--CHINA--KOREA (SOUTH)--TOBACCO USE (v26)

YOUTH--COLORADO--TOBACCO USE

"In Colorado, the state health department reports than 71 percent of youths have smoked by age 13. In Denver high schools, that percentage runs even higher: A 1995 study reveals that more than 75 percent of 13-year-olds have tried smoking at least once--translating to one of the highest youth-smoking figures in the country." (p18)

Lloyd, Jillian. "Views on Teen Smoking from Denver Schoolyard." The Christian Science Monitor v89 n208 22 Sep 1997. p1,18. The Christian Science Monitor search engine: <http://www.csmonitor.com/plweb-cgi/iops1.pl> To retrieve this article, enter the following search: ED=19970922 AND schoolyard. In the "retrieved list," click the title that matches this record. (ISSN0882-7729).

YOUTH--CRIMES AGAINST--UNITED STATES (v26)

YOUTH--EDUCATION

see EDUCATION

YOUTH--EMPLOYMENT--CANADA (v26)

YOUTH--FLORIDA--TOBACCO USE (v26)

YOUTH--GREAT BRITAIN--ALCOHOL USE (v26)

"In a British survey, 7 out of 10 police officers who work combating teen drinking said alcopops are the favorite alcoholic drink of under 18-year-olds. Earlier this year, a study of 2,500 young people by Britain's Health Education Authority found that more than 1 in 5 girls aged 13 to 16 who drink alcohol at least once a month said alcopops were their favorite drink. A survey in June by a school health-education unit in Exeter, England, found that half of 12- and 13-year-olds regularly drank alcohol, and one quarter of that age group 'drink to get drunk.'" (p14)

MacLeod, Alexander. "Global Report: Countries Put Cork in Marketing to Teens: Sweet Drinks that Lure Kids Pack a Surprise--Alcohol." The Christian Science Monitor v89 n181 13 Aug 1997. p1,14. The Christian Science Monitor search engine: <http://www.csmonitor.com/plweb-cgi/iops1.pl> To retrieve this article, enter the following search: ED19970813 AND alcohol. In the "retrieved list," click the title that matches this record. (ISSN0882-7729).

YOUTH--GREAT BRITAIN--DRUG USE (v26)

YOUTH--HAWAII--TOBACCO USE

In Hawaii, in 1996, "inspections of tobacco sales to minors conducted on a random sample of stores thoughout the state found 44 percent to be illegally selling tobacco to young people. In the spring of 1997, the Department of Health, in collaboration with the University of Hawai'i Cancer Research Center and the Honolulu Police Department, began a series of tobacco 'stings.'...The 'stings' were followed up by random, unannounced inspections carried out in June and July. In these inspections, which did not include any citations, seventy-nine--or 22.8 percent--of 343 stores sold tobacco to minors....The DOH 1996 Hawai'i Student Alcohol and Drug Use Survey revealed that 37 percent of Hawai'i's sixth graders, 63 percent of eighth graders, 81 percent of tenth graders and 89 percent of twelfth graders purchase their cigarettes from stores."

Hawaii. Dept. of Health. "DOH Winning the Fight against Sales of Tobacco to Minors." Press Release 1997. document-level access: <http://www.hawaii.gov/health/press/prtobsal.htm>

YOUTH--HUNGARY--TOBACCO USE (v26)

YOUTH--MICHIGAN

A study by the U.S. National Institutes of Health revealed that teen-age birth rates "increased 23 percent in Michigan and the rest of the country. Low birth rates--babies weighing 5.5 pounds or less--also increased by 15 percent statewide and 7 percent nationwide....The report showed improvement in some areas, such as a decreasing number of children living in poverty. In the past 10 years, the rate of Michigan children living in poverty fell 9 percent, though it hasn't changed nationwide. Child and infant mortality rates improved 19 percent and 25 percent respectively in Michigan. The percentage of teens who were not attending school and not working dropped 27 percent." (p5 secA)

Potts, Laura A. "Nation World: Teens March toward Wild Side." Detroit News 1 Jul 1997. p5 secA.

YOUTH--MICHIGAN--ANN ARBOR--DRUG USE (v26)

YOUTH--MICHIGAN--DETROIT--MORTALITY

"During the first five months of this year, shootings claimed the lives of nine boys aged 16 and younger in Detroit. Twenty in that age group died in the city from gunshots in 1996, down from 31 the year before, according to records kept by THE DETROIT NEWS." (p8 secA)

Woolley, Wayne. "Detroit Cop Gives At-Risk Youth a Dose of Reality." Detroit News 16 Jul 1997. p1,8 secA.

YOUTH--MICHIGAN--OAKLAND COUNTY--TOBACCO USE (v26)

"According to a survey of 3,000 high school seniors in Oakland County [Michigan] in 1994-95 and 1995-96, more than 40 percent had smoked in the past 30 days. The national average was about 31 percent. Close to 27 percent of the Oakland County group smoked a pack of cigarettes a day, compared with 19 percent nationally. The survey was conducted by Western Michigan University." (p4 secB)

Abraham, Molly/Mishra, Raja. "Local News: City Hastens Its Pace to Snuff Out Teenage Smoking." Detroit Free Press 11 Aug 1997. p1,4 secB.

YOUTH--MICHIGAN--SOCIAL CONDITIONS (v26)

YOUTH--MONTREAL ISLAND (QUEBEC)--RELIGION (v26)

YOUTH--NEW YORK (N.Y.)--SEXUAL BEHAVIOR

"In New York City, of all adolescents between the ages of 15 and

19, 50% of females and 60% of males had engaged in sexual intercourse. With a high percentage of sexual activity (80%), a high number of pregnancies per year (13,000), and the highest rate of venereal diseases (one in seven), New York City teens had yet to use contraceptives (Britton, de Mauro, Alan, and Gambrell, 1992)." (p155)

Elbaz, Gilbert. "Adolescent Activism for Postmodern HIV/AIDS Education: A New Social Movement." Urban Review v29 n3 Sep 1997. p145-174. (ISSN0042-0972).

YOUTH--NEW ZEALAND--SUICIDAL BEHAVIOR

In New Zealand, "suicide in the 15-19 age group has increased over the last twenty years, from 5.8 per 100,000 in 1970 to 15.7 in 1991. In 1991, the suicide rate for the 20-24 age group was 31.3 per 100,000, with the increase much higher among males than females (Aldridge, 1994). Thus the peak suicide rate occurs in the twenties, not in the teenage years (Joyce & associates, 1994). Nevertheless, for the joint 15-24 age group, the suicide rate is highest. Suicide is very rare under age 15 (Townsend, 1993; Joyce & associates, 1994)....Suicide is the second most common cause of death for young people, the first being motor vehicle accidents (Joyce & associates, 1994). Of the leading causes of death in the total population, youth suicide was ranked tenth in 1989 (Townsend, 1993)....Males aged 15-19 commit suicide at the rate of 26.9 per 100,000, while the rate for teenage girls is only 3.6 (Aldridge, 1994)." (p926)

Drummond, Wilhelmina J. "Adolescents at Risk: Causes of Youth Suicide in New Zealand." Adolescence v32 n128 Win 1997. p925-934. (ISSN0001-8449).

YOUTH--NIGERIA--SEXUAL BEHAVIOR

In Nigeria, "7 out of 10 Nigerian boys and 5 out of every 10 Nigerian girls attending secondary school are sexually experienced before the age of 20....Young people account for more than 50 percent of those contracting STDs [sexually transmitted diseases] and HIV/AIDS annually in Nigeria." (p5)

"Providing Nigerian Youth with a Better Life, Future." SIECUS Report v25 n2 Dec 1996-Jan 1997. p5. (ISSN0091-3995).

YOUTH--RUSSIA--DRUG USE--SEXUAL BEHAVIOR

A 1995 survey in Russia, compiled by the Transnational Family Research Institute, found that "boys and girls who do not smoke are more than two times less likely to have had sexual intercourse. On the other hand, 80 percent of regular smokers--boys and girls equally--were more likely to have had sexual intercourse. More than 30 percent of the females and more than 50 percent of the males had had their first sexual relationship after drinking alcohol. The same correlation was made with drugs: 25 percent of the females and 30 percent of the males had had their first sexual relationship after using other drugs." (p9)

Chervyakov, Valeriy. "Survey Supports Arguments to Start Sexuality Education in Russia." SIECUS Report v25 n2 Dec 1996-Jan 1997. p8-9. (ISSN0091-3995).

YOUTH--RUSSIA--SEXUAL BEHAVIOR

"Comparisons between 1993 and 1995 surveys conducted by the Transnational Family Research Institute in Moscow show that the number of sexually active 14- and 15-year-olds [in Russia] increased by more than 30 percent. The 1993 survey itself showed that half of the surveyed young men and a third of the young women were having sexual relationships before they were 16 years old and that one in eight school-age males and one in 16 school-age females had sexual intercourse by their fourteenth birthday....Twenty percent of all 14-year-old boys in vocational schools had experienced at least one sexual relationship." (p8)

Chervyakov, Valeriy. "Survey Supports Arguments to Start Sexuality Education in Russia." SIECUS Report v25 n2 Dec 1996-Jan 1997. p8-9. (ISSN0091-3995).

YOUTH--TOBACCO USE (v26)

YOUTH--UNITED STATES--ALCOHOL USE (v26)

In the U.S., "two out of every three teenagers who drink report that they can buy their own alcoholic beverages....Junior and senior high school students drink 35 percent of all wine coolers and consume 1.1 billion cans of beer a year....Alcohol is a factor in the three leading causes of death for 15- to 24-year-olds: accidents, homicides, and suicides. In approximately 50 to 60 percent of youth suicides, alcohol is a factor....In 1995, there were 1,666 alcohol-related fatalities of children between the ages of 15 and 19....According to a WASHINGTON POST article from July 17, 1997, entitled, 'The Corner Store,' the District outranks every State with regard to deaths and diseases related to alcohol. In addition, according to Joye M. Carter, chief D.C. medical examiner, in 1993, 50 percent of the homicide victims had consumed alcohol." (pS10215)

Byrd, Robert C. (Sen.-W.Va.). "District of Columbia Appropriations Act, 1998." Congressional Record. Daily ed. v143 n133 30 Sep 1997. pS10211-10216. section/page-level access: <http://thomas.loc.gov/cgi-bin/query/R?r105:FLD001:S10215:> (ISSN0363-7239). (X1.1A.105/1).

In the U.S., "between 1995 and 1996, daily alcohol use increased among eighth graders from 0.7 to 1.0 percent. In addition, more eighth graders reported having 'been drunk' in the past month during 1996 (9.6 percent) than during 1995 (8.3 percent). (MTFS [Monitoring the Future Study], 1996) In 1995, 111 million Americans age 12 and older had used alcohol in the past month (52 percent of the population). Of the 10 million current drinkers under age 21 in 1995, 4.4 million were binge drinkers, including 1.7 million heavy drinkers. (NHSDA [National Household Survey of Drug Abuse], 1995)"

U.S. Dept. of Health and Human Services. "Substance Abuse--A National Challenge." Fact Sheet 20 May 1997. document-level access: <http://www.hhs.gov/news/press/1997pres/970520c.html>

"Alcohol use among 12- to 17-year-olds [in the U.S.] declined significantly from 21.1 percent in 1995 to 18.8 percent in 1996....There were about 9 million current alcohol (including beer, wine, and distilled spirits) drinkers under age 21 in 1996. Of these, 4.4 million were binge drinkers, including 1.9 million heavy drinkers."

U.S. Dept. of Health and Human Services. "National Drug Survey Results Released: Overall Drug Use Levels Stay the Same; Possible Decrease in Youth Drug Use." Press Release 6 Aug 1997. document-level access: <http://www.hhs.gov/news/press/1997pres/970806.html>

Lloyd "Johnston and his colleagues, Jerald G. Bachman and Patrick M. O'Malley, senior research scientists at the U-M [University of Michigan] Institute for Social Research, are reporting the results of the 1997 survey they conducted of 51,000 eighth-, 10th-, and 12th-grade students located in 429 secondary schools...[in the U.S.]." (p1-2) According to Johnston, alcohol use "'has been in the form of a very gradual upward drift in the very low proportions who say that they have been drunk frequently (20 or more times in the prior 30 days)--these rates are 0.2 percent, 0.6 percent, and 2.0 percent in 1997 in grades 8, 10, and 12, respectively--or in the much larger proportions who indicated recent binge drinking.' (Binge drinking is defined as having five or more drinks in a row on at least one occasion in the prior two weeks.) In 1997 some 15 percent, 25 percent, and 31 percent of eighth-, 10th-, and 12th-graders, respectively, indicated such binge drinking and these rates are slightly higher than they were in the early 1990s...." (p5)

University of Michigan. News and Information Services. "Drug Use among American Teens Shows Some Signs of Leveling after a Long Rise." University of Michigan News Release 18 Dec 1997. p1-7.

YOUTH--UNITED STATES--DRUG USE (v26)

"Research conducted by the National Parents' Resource Institute for Drug Education (PRIDE) shows that 7 out of 10 American parents are not talking to their children about the dangers of drug use. These numbers are especially alarming in light of the fact that PRIDE's research indicates that mobilizing parents is one of our most effective ways of fighting this rising epidemic. For example, among students who said they never hear from their parents on the subject of drugs, 35.5% reported using illicit drugs in the last year. Yet this number falls to 26.6%--a relative decrease of 25% for students whose parent often discuss this issue with them. In response to the rise of teenage drug use in the 1980's, parents across the country became active in the anti-drug movement. Their efforts played a key role in reducing drug use by teenagers from the all-time high of 54 percent in 1979 to just 27 percent by 1992." (pS4873)

Coverdell, Paul (Sen.-Ga.). "Concurrent Resolution on the Budget." Congressional Record. Daily ed. v143 n68 21 May 1997. pS4851-4876. section/page-level access: <http://thomas.loc.gov/cgi-bin/query/R?r105:FLD001:S04873:> (ISSN0363-7239). (X1.1A.105/1).

A "study by the U.S. Department of Justice's National Institute of Justice found that the percentage of 18- to 20-year-olds in Detroit who were arrested and tested positive for recent cocaine use dropped to 5 percent last year from 45 percent in 1987. In Manhattan and Philadelphia, the percentage dropped to 21 percent from 70 percent in the nine-year period." (p4 secB)

Bivins, Larry. "Outlook: A Revolution in Handling Drug Offenders: Washington Clashes on Different Sentences for Crack, Powder Cocaine." Detroit News 10 Aug 1997. p4 secB.

In the U.S., "the rate of illicit drug use among teens ages 12-17 declined to 9 percent in 1996 from 10.9 percent the previous year. The use of marijuana, the most popular drug among that age group, declined slightly to 7.1 percent from 8.2 percent.... The new survey, conducted by the Substance Abuse and Mental Health Services Administration, was based on interviews with more than 18,000 people at home." (p5 secA)

Bivins, Larry. "Nation World: Teen Drug Use Dips Slightly." Detroit News 7 Aug 1997. p5 secA.

In the U.S., a survey released in August 1997 "by the National Center on Addiction and Substance Abuse at Columbia University found that 23.5 percent of 12-year-olds knew a peer who had tried drugs like cocaine or heroin, up from 10.6 percent a year earlier....The percentage of eighth-graders saying they used marijuana before seventh grade rose to 12.7 percent in 1996 from 7.7 percent in 1992. The number of 9 to 12-year-olds who tried pot doubled to 4 percent in the past year. Binge drinking--having five or more alcoholic beverages at a sitting--rose to 15.6 percent of eighth-graders from 12.9 percent. Trying 'gateway drugs'--cigarettes, alcohol or marijuana--made it 17 times more likely a 12 to 17-year-old without other 'problem behaviors' would try harder drugs." (p1 secA)

Stertz, Bradley A. "'Hard' Drug Use among Preteens More than Doubles." Detroit News 14 Aug 1997. p1 secA.

In the U.S., "juvenile drug offenses in 1994 were up 82 percent from 1991, according to Jeffrey A. Butts with the National Juvenile Court Data Archive....Juvenile courts in 1994 handled an estimated 120,200 delinquency cases involving drug law violations. Drug offenses accounted for 8 percent of all delinquency cases in 1994. The number of drug offense cases processed during 1994 was 35 percent greater than in 1993 and 82 percent more than in 1991. Between 1991 and 1994, the number of drug cases involving white juveniles increased sharply by 118 percent. The proportion that involved black youth grew from 18 percent in 1985 to 44 percent in 1990, then declined to 37 percent in 1994. Males were involved in 86 percent of drug offenses in 1994, compared with 82 percent in 1985. In 1994, 58 percent of drug offense cases involved juveniles age 16 or older, which is the same percentage as found in 1985. More than a quarter (28 percent) of the drug offense cases that juvenile courts disposed in 1994 involved the use of secure detention at some point between referral and disposition, which was down compared with 1990 (37 percent), but greater than in 1985 (21 percent)." (p72)

Cohn, Alvin W. "Juvenile Focus." Federal Probation v61 n3 Sep 1997. p71-73. (ISSN0014-9128).

The National Household Survey on Drug Abuse "found a slight decline in use of illegal drugs among [U.S.] teenagers 12 to 17 in 1996, from 10.9 percent in 1995 to 9 percent by July 1996. Marijuana use declined slightly, from 8.2 percent to 7.1 percent of all teenagers. However, from 1990 to 1995, rates of first use of heroin rose for all teenagers, up from 1.8 percent to 2.5 percent for ages 18-25. The survey also reported that over one-half of Americans aged 26-34 have sampled illegal drugs." (p73)

Cohn, Alvin W. "Juvenile Focus." Federal Probation v61 n3 Sep 1997. p71-73. (ISSN0014-9128).

In the U.S., "the rate of teenage use for all illicit drugs declined from 10.9 percent in 1995 to 9.0 percent in 1996. While the rate of marijuana use by teens remained statistically unchanged from last year's survey, falling very slightly from 8.2 percent to 7.1 percent, the decline indicates a possible shift in the trend that has seen marijuana use by teens double from 1992 to 1995....The percent of youths 12-17 reporting great risk in using cocaine once a month decreased from 63 percent in 1994 to 54 percent in 1996. More than half of youths age 12-17 reported that marijuana was easy to obtain in 1996, and about one-quarter reported that heroin was easy to obtain. Fifteen percent of youths reported being approached by someone selling drugs in the month prior to the interview."

U.S. Dept. of Health and Human Services. "National Drug Survey Results Released: Overall Drug Use Levels Stay the Same; Possible Decrease in Youth Drug Use." Press Release 6 Aug 1997. document-level access: <http://www.hhs.gov/news/press/1997pres/970806.html>

Lloyd "Johnston and his colleagues, Jerald G. Bachman and Patrick M. O'Malley, senior research scientists at the U-M [University of Michigan] Institute for Social Research, are reporting the results of the 1997 survey they conducted of 51,000 eighth-, 10th-, and 12th-grade students located in 429 secondary schools...[in the U.S.]." (p1-2) "The proportion of 1997 students reporting any use of LSD [lysergic acid diethylamide] in the 12 months prior to the survey was 3.2 percent, 6.7 percent, and 8.4 percent for grades 8, 10, and 12, respectively. For other hallucinogens the rates were 1.8 percent, 3.3 percent, and 4.6 percent....The proportion of 1997 12th-graders reporting any use of ice [also called crystal methamphetamine, and which, like crack, is often smoked or burned in rock form,] in the prior 12 months was 2.3 percent, or nearly one in every 40 students." (p3) "In 1997 the proportions of students reporting any use of ecstasy in the prior 12 months were 2.3 percent, 3.9 percent, and 4.0 percent among eighth-, 10th-, and 12th-graders....The proportions of students in 1997 reporting any use of stimulants in the prior 12 months are 8 percent, 12 percent, and 10 percent for grades 8, 10, and 12....The proportions of 1997 students reporting any use of cocaine powder in the prior 12 months are 2.2 percent, 4.1 percent, and 5.0 percent in grades 8, 10, and 12, respectively....In 1997 the annual prevalence rates for crack were 1.7 percent, 2.2 percent, and 2.4 percent among eighth-, 10th-, and 12th-graders." (p4)

University of Michigan. News and Information Services. "Drug Use among American Teens Shows Some Signs of Leveling after a Long Rise." University of Michigan News Release 18 Dec 1997. p1-7.

YOUTH--UNITED STATES--MORTALITY (v26)

YOUTH--UNITED STATES--RELIGION--ATTITUDES (v26)

YOUTH--UNITED STATES--SEXUAL BEHAVIOR (v26)

In the U.S., "more children are sexually active today. The numbers grow, from 40 percent in ninth grade to 66 percent of high school seniors. Some 15 percent of girls report having had four or more sexual partners. But only 40 percent of teenagers seek contraceptive help in the first year of sexual activity, says Dr. Anita Nelson, medical director of the Women's Health Care Clinic at Harbor University of California Medical Center, in Torrance." (p7 secF)

Anstett, Patricia. "Body & Mind: Cover Story: An Unkind World for Girls." Detroit Free Press 16 Dec 1997. p6-8 secF.

"According to researchers, more than 85 percent of teenagers [in the U.S.] report having a girlfriend or boyfriend and having kissed someone romantically. By age 14, more than 50 percent of all boys have touched a girl's breast and 25 percent have touched a girl's vulva....Seventy-three percent of young men and 56 percent of young women have experienced intercourse's onset by their 18th birthday....RAND analyst and U.C.L.A. [University of California Los Angeles] pediatrician Mark Schuster and colleagues reported in the AMERICAN JOURNAL OF PUBLIC HEALTH that among 2,026 urban high school students surveyed, 47 percent were virgins. Yet about 30 percent of the high school virgins had masturbated a partner, 9 percent had engaged in heterosexual fellatio including ejaculation and 10 percent had engaged in cunnilingus....More than a quarter of teenage girls have had intercourse by age 15. More than 1 million U.S. teenagers become pregnant and 3 million acquire sexually transmitted diseases each year." (p20)

Stryker, Jeff. "Abstinence or Else!" Nation v264 n23 16 Jun 1997. p19-21. (ISSN0027-8378).

"Wendy Lowe, director of the Calgary Pregnancy Care Centre, says that sexual activity among American girls under 19 has dropped from 55% in 1990 to 50% in 1995; and for boys, from 60% to 55%....A recent survey of 1500 adolescents aged 12 to 18 shows that 32% of girls and 36% of boys agreed that movies and television suggest that it is normal for teenagers to 'have sex.'" (p4)

Lamont, Mary. "In Loving Them Both, We Need to Start Early." ProLife News v22 n8 Sep 1997. p4.

In the U.S., "more than half of teenagers are virgins until they are at least 17 years of age. By the time they reach the age of 20, 20 percent of boys and 24 percent of girls have not had sexual intercourse. The largest study of adult sexual behavior found that only 6.9 percent of men and 21 percent of women aged 18 to 59 had their first intercourse on their wedding night." (p21)

"Fact Sheet: Adolescence and Abstinence." SIECUS Report v26 n1 Oct-Nov 1997. p21-22. (ISSN0091-3995).

In the U.S., "seventy percent of high school seniors have engaged in sexual intercourse by the time they graduate. Among males aged 15 to 19, 81 percent of African-Americans, 60 percent of Latinos, and 57 percent of Caucasians have had sexual intercourse. Among females aged 15 to 19, 59 percent of African-Americans, 45 percent of Latinas, and 48 percent of Caucasians have had sexual intercourse. Sixty-five percent of male and 56.6 percent of female Native-Americans have had sexual intercourse by the 12th grade." (p15)

"Fact Sheet: Sexuality and Underserved Youth in Communities of Color." SIECUS Report v25 n5 Jun-Jul 1997. p15-16. (ISSN0091-3995).

In the U.S., a longitudinal study begun in 1987 found that "about three-quarters of the teenage boys [surveyed] (72.2 percent) and almost half of the girls (46.7 percent) reported onset of sexual activity at age 15 or younger....Less than one-fifth (17.5 percent) of the boys initiated intercourse at age 16 or older, and 10.3 percent remained sexually inexperienced. Of the girls, 29.7 percent became sexually active after age 16, and 23.6 percent were still inactive during the study." (p338)

Smith, Carolyn A. "Factors Associated with Early Sexual Activity among Urban Adolescents." Social Work v42 n4 Jul 1997. p334-346. (ISSN0037-8046).

In the U.S., "57% of adolescents were sexually active as early as age 17; in some neighborhoods, teens' first intercourse occurred between the ages of 11 and 12. Annually, 1 out of 10 women aged 15 to 19 became pregnant, totaling over a million pregnancies (Henshaw and Van Vort, 1989)." (p155)

Elbaz, Gilbert. "Adolescent Activism for Postmodern HIV/AIDS Education: A New Social Movement." Urban Review v29 n3 Sep 1997. p145-174. (ISSN0042-0972).

YOUTH--UNITED STATES--SOCIAL CONDITIONS (v26)

In the U.S., "one in four adolescents have some form of serious, long-term problems (Carnegie Council on Adolescent development, 1989). For example, approximately 1 million teenage girls become pregnant each year, and half of them give birth (Carnegie Council on Adolescent development, 1989). Approximately 500,000 young people drop out of school each year (Kaufman & Frase, 1990)." (p430)

Chung, Woo Sik/Pardeck, John T. "Explorations in a Proposed National Policy for Children and Families." Adolescence v32 n126 Sum 1997. p429-436. (ISSN0001-8449).

"According to the Youth Risk Behavior Surveillance System, a nationwide study conducted by the [U.S.] Centers for Disease Control and Prevention (CDC), more than half of today's high school students use alcohol (one-third engage in what CDC terms 'episodic heavy drinking'), and about one-quarter use marijuana and inhalants. One million teens get pregnant each year, CDC says, and countless more contract sexually transmitted diseases." (p42)

Black, Susan. "Research: Picture of Health." American School Board Journal v184 n10 Oct 1997. p42-44. (ISSN0003-0953).

According to two books on the 13th Generation, 13TH GENERATION: ABORT, RETRY, IGNORE, FAIL? and MARKETING TO GENERATION X, teenagers "represent 9.4 percent of the...[U.S.'s] population. More than 24 million strong, over half are females, 80 percent are white, 15 percent African American, 12 percent Hispanic, and 4 percent from other ethnic origins....These are the latchkey kids where 12 percent of the elementary, 30 percent of the middle school, and 38 percent of the high schoolers spend time home alone in the afternoon. Every day among American children 2,500 see their parents divorce, 90 are taken from their parents' care and placed in foster homes, 13 commit suicide, and 16 are murdered." (p43)

Selvage, Donald R. "Focus: Recruiting the Corps of the 21st Century." Marine Corps Gazette v81 n9 Sep 1997. p41-44. (ISSN0025-3170).

In the U.S., "an estimated 300,000 homeless runaways engaged in prostitution each year, increasing their risk of HIV infection (Bruce, 1992). Equally unequivocal were research findings on drug use and alcohol consumption among adolescents: 44% of high-school seniors had used illicit drugs at some time in their lives, more than a third used marijuana, 1% used heroin, and 1% used crack. Additionally, about 40% of young people between the ages of 12 and 17 had used alcohol, potentially hampering their ability to make rational decisions (Johnston, 1992)." (p158)

Elbaz, Gilbert. "Adolescent Activism for Postmodern HIV/AIDS Education: A New Social Movement." Urban Review v29 n3 Sep

1997. p145-174. (ISSN0042-0972).

YOUTH--UNITED STATES--SUBSTANCE USE (v26)

According to the U.S. National Center for Education Statistics, "sixteen percent of kids in grades six to eight say alcohol is easily available at school, and about 43 percent of high school kids say alcohol is easily available. Twelve percent of students in grades six to eight say marijuana is easily available at school, and about 44 percent of high school students say marijuana is easy to get on school grounds....About 21 percent of students from schools with 300 students or fewer say alcohol is easily available, while roughly 38 percent from schools with 1,000 or more students say the same thing. The percentage saying marijuana is readily available doubles from 14 percent for small schools to 29 percent for large schools." (pA23)

"Education Vital Signs: Common Measures." American School Board Journal v184 n12 Dec 1997. pA18-A23. (ISSN0003-0953).

YOUTH--UNITED STATES--SUICIDAL BEHAVIOR (v26)

In the U.S., "in 1990, 67.3% of all suicides among teenagers aged 15-19 were the result of firearms. Since 1985 the overall rate of suicide for teenagers by firearms increased from 6.0 to 7.5 per 100,000. The group of teenagers with the largest percent increase was African-American males; however, white male teenagers (13.5 per 100,000) had a higher firearm suicide rate in 1990 compared with African-American males (8.8 per 100,000)." (p509)

Page, Randy M./Hammermeister, Jon. "Weapon-Carrying and Youth Violence." Adolescence v32 n127 Fall 1997. p505-513. (ISSN0001-8449).

YOUTH--UNITED STATES--TOBACCO USE (v26)

"Spit tobacco leads to nicotine addiction, gum disease, and tooth loss, as well as mouth and throat cancer. Oral cancer is diagnosed in 30,000 people annually and kills approximately 8,000 people annually [in the U.S.]. While spit tobacco used to be used primarily by older men, boys and young men are now the primary consumers of this deadly product. In Illinois, 10 percent of junior high and high school boys have used smokeless tobacco in the past month. Across the country, nearly 20 percent of high school boys are current users of spit tobacco, and the average age at which children first try the product is under age 10....According to a study by the Illinois Department of Public Health, 70 percent of children who report regular use of smokeless tobacco are members of organized sports teams....Every year, the tobacco companies lose 2 million American customers. Four hundred thousand die of tobacco-related diseases and the rest quit smoking or die of other causes." (pS4035)

Durbin, Richard J. (Sen.-Ill.). "Major League Baseball Players Say 'No' to Spit Tobacco." Congressional Record. Daily ed. v143 n57 6 May 1997. pS4035. section/page-level access: <http://thomas.loc.gov/cgi-bin/query/R?r105:FLD001:S04035:> (ISSN0363-7239). (X1.1A.105/1).

In the U.S., "cigarette smoking among high school seniors is at a 17-year high. Smoking among 8th and 10th graders has increased by over 50 percent since 1991....Almost 90 percent of today's adult smokers started using tobacco before age 18. The average youth smoker begins at age 13 and becomes a daily smoker by age 14 1/2....Studies of over-the-counter sales have found that children and adolescents were able to successfully buy tobacco products 67 percent of the time. Despite the fact that it is illegal in all 50 States to sell cigarettes and smokeless tobacco to minors, our young people purchase an estimated 1.26 billion dollars' worth of tobacco products each year." (pH5678)

Hansen, James V. (Rep.-Vt.). "Agriculture, Rural Development, Food and Drug Administration...Appropriations Act, 1998." Congressional Record. Daily ed. v143 n106 24 Jul 1997. pH5672-5732. section/page-level access: <http://thomas.loc.gov/cgi-bin/query/R?r105:FLD001:H05677:> (ISSN0363-7239). (X1.1A.105/1).

In the U.S., "between 1995 and 1996, past month use of cigarettes increased from 19.1 to 21.0 percent among eighth graders and from 27.9 to 30.4 percent among tenth graders. (MTFS [Monitoring the Future Study], 1996) Since 1991, current smoking has increased from 14.3 to 21.0 percent for eighth graders; 20.8 to 30.4 percent for tenth graders, and 28.3 to 34.0 percent for twelfth graders. (MTFS, 1996) An estimated 62 million Americans were current smokers in 1996, including an estimated 4.1 million adolescents aged 12-17. (NHSDA [National Household Survey on Drug Abuse], 1996) This represents a national smoking rate of 29 percent."

U.S. Dept. of Health and Human Services. "Substance Abuse--A National Challenge: Prevention, Treatment and Research at HHS." Fact Sheet 6 Aug 1996. document-level access: <http://www.hhs.gov/news/press/1997pres/970806d.html>

"More than 3 million American adolescents currently smoke cigarettes, and a million more youths take up smoking every year. Indeed, a 1996 University of Michigan study indicates that this number is rising. The study asked students if they had smoked during the past month, and 50 percent more high school students said yes in 1996 than in 1991." (p18)

Lloyd, Jillian. "Views on Teen Smoking from Denver Schoolyard." The Christian Science Monitor v89 n208 22 Sep 1997. p1,18. The Christian Science Monitor search engine: <http://www.csmonitor.com/plweb-cgi/iops1.pl> To retrieve this article, enter the following search: ED=19970922 AND schoolyard. In the "retrieved list," click the title that matches this record. (ISSN0882-7729).

In the U.S., "90 percent of adult smokers begin before they turn 19....Smoking among high-school seniors has reached a 17-year high....3,000 young people...[become] regular smokers every day....Well over 400,000 Americans a year will die from tobacco-related diseases." (p19)

Novelli, William D. "Opinion/Essays: Tobacco Deal Is about Kids, Not Lawyer Fees or Revenge." The Christian Science Monitor v89 n167 24 Jul 1997. p19. The Christian Science Monitor search engine: <http://www.csmonitor.com/plweb-cgi/iops1.pl> To retrieve this article, enter the following search: ED=19970724 AND revenge. In the "retrieved list," click the title that matches this record. (ISSN0882-7729).

YOUTH--WEST VIRGINIA--SOCIAL CONDITIONS (v26)

ZAIRE--ECONOMIC CONDITIONS (v26)

In Zaire, "copper production, 440,000 tons in 1989, dropped to 33,600 tons in 1994. The hyperinflation of the early 1990s made the currency all but worthless, and in 1993 the foreign debt was $11.3 billion. Per-capita GDP seems to be about $220 a year, among the world's lowest." (p82)

Schatzberg, Michael G. "Beyond Mobutu: Kabila and the Congo." Journal of Democracy v8 n4 Oct 1997. p70-84. (ISSN1045-5736).

ZAMBIA--ECONOMIC CONDITIONS

"In Zambia, where a wide-ranging privatization program began in 1991, about 60 percent of monthly household expenditures go for food....Over half of all households consider themselves poor. According to a survey by the Central Statistical Office, 550,000 children have lost at least one parent, in most cases the father." (p20)

Onyango, William. "TF Reports: Africa: Losing Ground." Toward Freedom v46 n5 Sep-Oct 1997. p20-21. (ISSN0048-9898).